S0-BYL-791

DICTIONARY OF DEITIES AND DEMONS IN THE BIBLE

DICTIONARY OF DEITIES AND DEMONS IN THE BIBLE

(DDD)

Karel van der Toorn
Bob Becking
Pieter W. van der Horst

Editors

E.J. BRILL
LEIDEN · NEW YORK · KÖLN
1995

Published under the auspices of
the Faculty of Theology
of Utrecht University.

The paper in this book meets the guidelines for permanence and durabilit Committee on Production Guidelines for Book Longevity of the Council on Library Resources.

Library of Congress Cataloging-in-Publication Data

Dictionary of deities and demons in the Bible (DDD) / Karel van der Toorn, Bob Becking, Pieter W. van der Horst, editors.
p. cm.
Includes bibliographical references and index.
ISBN 9004103139 (cloth : alk. paper)
1. Gods in the Bible—Dictionaries. 2. Demonology in the Bible--Dictionaries. I. Toorn, K. van der. II. Becking, Bob. III. Horst, Pieter Willem van der.
BSB80.G57053 1995
220.3—dc20 95-11503
CIP

Die Deutsche Bibliothek – CIP-Einheitsaufnahme

Dictionary of deities and demons in the Bible : (DDD) / Karel van der Toorn ... ed. – Leiden ; New York ; Köln : Brill, 1995
ISBN 90-04-10313-9
NE: Toorn, Karel van der [Hrsg.]; (DDD)

ISBN 90 04 10313 9

PRINTED IN THE NETHERLANDS

CONTENTS

CONSULTANTS

LIST OF CONTRIBUTORS

Tzvi ABUSCH, Waltham
(Eṭemmu, Ishtar, Marduk)

Larry J. ALDERINK, Moorhead
(Demeter, Nike, Stoicheia)

Bendt ALSTER, Copenhagen
(Tammuz, Tiamat, Tigris)

Jan ASSMANN, Heidelberg
(Amun, Isis, Neith, Re)

David E. AUNE, Chicago
(Archai, Archon, Hera, Heracles)

Tjitze BAARDA, Amsterdam
(Sabbath)

Michael L. BARRÉ, Baltimore
(Lightning, Night, Rabiṣu)

Hans M. BARSTAD, Oslo
(Dod, Sheol, Way)

Bernard F. BATTO, Greencastle
(Behemoth, Curse, Zedeq)

Bob BECKING, Utrecht
(Abel, Amalek, Ancient of Days, Breasts-and-womb, Cain, Day, El-rophe, Ends of the earth, Exalted ones, Girl, Hubal, Ishḫara, Jaghut, Jalam, Japheth, Jordan, Kenan, Lagamar, Protectors, Qatar, Rapha, Raven, Sarah, Sasam, Sha, Shalman, Shelah, Shem, Shunama, Sisera, Thillakhuha, Thukamuna, Vanities, Varuna,Virgin, Yaʿûq, Yehud, Zamzummim)

Hans-Dieter BETZ, Chicago
(Authorities, Dynamis, Legion)

Jan den Boeft, Utrecht
(Saviour)

Jan N. Bremmer, Groningen
(Ares, Hades, Hymenaios, Linos, Narcissus, Nereus, Nymph)

Cilliers Breytenbach, Berlin
(Hypsistos, Nomos, Satan)

Roelof van den Broek, Utrecht
(Apollo, Phoenix)

Mordechai Cogan, Jerusalem
(Ashima, Shulman, Shulmanitu, Sukkoth-benoth, Tartak)

John J. Collins, Chicago
(Daniel, Gabriel, Liers-in-wait, Prince, Saints of the Most High, Watcher)

Peter W. Coxon, St. Andrews
(Gibborim, Nephilim, Noah)

Peggy L. Day, Winnipeg
(Anat, Jephtah's daughter, Satan)

Meindert Dijkstra, Utrecht
(Abraham, Adat, Aliyan, Clay, Esau, Ishmael, Jacob, Joseph, Leah, Mother, Rachel)

Ken Dowden, Birmingham
(Aeneas, Daphne, Dioskouroi, Jason, Makedon, Menelaos, Patroklos, Perseus,Quirinus, Silvanus, Skythes, Thessalos)

Han J. W. Drijvers, Groningen
(Aion, Atargatis, Mithras)

Eric E. Elnes, Princeton
(Elyon, Olden Gods)

Reinhard Feldmeier, Koblenz
(Almighty, Mediator II, World rulers)

Jarl E. Fossum, Ann Arbor
(Dove, Glory, Simon Magus, Son of God)

Hannes D. GALTER, Graz
(Aya, Bashtu, Hubur)

Richard L. GORDON, Ilmmünster
(Anthropos, Helios, Poseidon, Pronoia)

Fritz GRAF, Basel
(Aphrodite, Athena, Bacchus, Dionysus, Heros, Zeus)

Jonas C. GREENFIELD, Jerusalem
(Apkallu, Hadad)

Mayer I. GRUBER, Beer-Sheva
(Abomination, Azabbim, Gillulim, Lies, One)

John F. HEALEY, Manchester
(Dagon, Dew, Ilib, Mot, Tirash)

Matthieu S. H. G. HEERMA VAN VOSS, Amsterdam
(Hathor, Horus, Osiris, Ptah)

George C. HEIDER, Seward
(Lahmu, Molech, Tannin)

Ronald S. HENDEL, Dallas
(Nehushtan, Serpent, Vampire)

Jan Willem VAN HENTEN, Amsterdam
(Angel II, Archangel, Dragon, Mastemah, Python, Roma, Ruler cult, Typhon)

Wolfgang HERRMANN, Stuttgart
(Baal, Baal-zebub, El, Rider-upon-the-clouds)

Pieter W. VAN DER HORST, Utrecht
(Ananke, Chaos, Dike, Dominion, Father of the lights, God II, Hosios kai dikaios, Hyle, Lamb, Mammon, Thanatos, Themis, Unknown God)

Cornelis HOUTMAN, Kampen
(Elijah, Moses, Queen of Heaven)

Herbert B. HUFFMON, Madison
(Brother, Father, Name, Shalem)

Manfred HUTTER, Graz
(Abaddon, Asmodeus, Earth, Heaven, Heaven-and-earth, Lilith, Shaushka)

Bernd JANOWSKI, Tübingen
(Azazel, Jackals, Satyrs, Wild Beasts)

Ab F. DE JONG, Utrecht
(Khvarenah, Mithras, Wrath)

Marinus DE JONGE, Leiden
(Christ, Emmanuel, Heaven, Sin, Thrones)

Jean KELLENS, Liège
(Arta, Baga, Haoma)

Ernst Axel KNAUF, Geneva
(Edom, Qôs, Shadday)

Matthias KÖCKERT, Berlin
(Fear of Isaac, Mighty One of Jacob, Shield of Abraham)

Marjo C. A. KORPEL, Utrecht
(Rock, Stone, Thornbush)

Bernard LANG, Paderborn
(Wisdom)

Fabrizio LELLI, Florence
(Stars)

Theodore J. LEWIS, Athens (USA)
(Dead, First-born of death, Teraphim)

Bert Jan LIETAERT PEERBOLTE, Leiden
(Antichrist)

Edouard LIPIŃSKI, Louvain
(Lamp, Light, Shemesh)

Alasdair LIVINGSTONE, Birmingham
(Assur, Image, Nergal)

Johan LUST, Louvain
(Gog, Magog)

Michael MACH, Tel Aviv
(Jeremiel, Michael, Raphael, Uriel)

P. Kyle McCARTER, Baltimore
(Evil spirit of God, Id, Zion)

Meir MALUL, Haifa
(Strong Drink, Taboo, Terror of the Night)

Luther H. MARTIN, Burlington
(Fortuna, Hermes, Tyche)

Samuel A. MEIER, Columbus
(Angel I, Angel of Yahweh, Destroyer, Mediator I)

Tryggve N. D. METTINGER, Lund
(Cherubim, Seraphim, Yahweh zebaoth)

A. R. MILLARD, Liverpool
(Adrammelech, Anammelech, Nabû, Nibhaz)

Patrick D. MILLER, Princeton
(Elyon, Olden Gods)

Hans-Peter MÜLLER, Münster
(Chemosh, Falsehood, Malik)

Martin J. MULDER†, Leiden
(Baal-berith, Carmel, God of fortresses)

E. Theodore MULLEN, Indianapolis
(Baalat, Go'el, Witness)

Gerard MUSSIES, Utrecht
(Amaltheia, Artemis, Giants, Jezebel, Olympus, Tabor, Titans)

Nadav NA'AMAN, Tel Aviv
(Baal toponyms, Baal-gad, Baal-hamon, Baal-hazor, Baal-hermon, Baal-judah, Baal-meon, Baal-perazim, Baal-shalisha, Baal-tamar)

George W. E. NICKELSBURG, Iowa City
(Son of Man)

Herbert NIEHR, Tübingen
(Baal-zaphon, God of heaven, He-of-the-Sinai, Host of heaven, Zaphon)

Kirsten NIELSEN, Århus
(Oak, Sycomore, Terebinth)

Gregorio DEL OLMO LETE, Barcelona
(Bashan, Deber, Og)

Dennis PARDEE, Chicago
(Asham, Eloah, Gepen, Gether, Koshar, Kosharoth)

Simon B. PARKER, Boston
(Council, Saints, Shahar, Sons of (the) God(s))

Martin F. G. PARMENTIER, Utrecht
(Mary)

Emile PUECH, Jerusalem
(Lel, Lioness, Milcom)

Albert DE PURY, Geneva
(El-olam, El-roi, Lahai-roi)

Jannes REILING, Utrecht
(Elders, Holy Spirit, Melchizedek, Unclean Spirits)

Sergio RIBICHINI, Rome
(Adonis, Baetyl, Eshmun, Gad, Melqart)

Greg J. RILEY, Fairfax
(Demon, Devil, Midday demon)

Wolfgang RÖLLIG, Tübingen
(Baal-shamem, Bethel, El-creator-of-the-earth, Hermon, Lebanon, Sirion)

Hedwige ROUILLARD-BONRAISIN, Paris
(Rephaim)

Christopher ROWLAND, Oxford
(Enoch)

David T. RUNIA, Leiden
(Logos)

Udo RÜTERSWÖRDEN, Kiel
(Horeph, Horon, King of terrors)

Brian SCHMIDT, Ann Arbor
(Al, Moon)

Choon-Leong SEOW, Princeton
(Am, Face, Lim, Torah)

S. David SPERLING, New York
(Belial, Meni, Sheben)

Klaas SPRONK, Kampen
(Baal of Peor, Dedan, Lord, Noble ones, Rahab, Travellers)

Marten STOL, Amsterdam
(Kaiwan, Mulissu, Nanea, Sakkuth, Sîn)

Fritz STOLZ, Zürich
(River, Sea, Source)

Karel VAN DER TOORN, Leiden
(Amurru, Arvad, Avenger, Beltu, Boaz, Cybele, Euphrates, Gabnunnim, God I, Gush, Ham, Haran, Hayin, Hebat, Humbaba, Jael, Kelti, Laban, Meriri, Min, Mouth, Nahor, Qatar, Rakib-El, Ram, Serug, Seth, Shahan, Sheger, Shepherd, Shimige, Sidon, Terah, Yahweh)

Joseph TROPPER, Berlin
(Spirit of the dead, Wizard)

Christoph UEHLINGER, Fribourg
(Leviathan, Nimrod, Nisroch)

Herman TE VELDE, Groningen
(Bastet, Bes, Khonsu, Nile)

Richard L. VOS, Capelle aan de IJssel
(Apis, Atum, Ibis, Thoth)

Wilfred G. E. WATSON, Newcastle upon Tyne
(Fire, Flame, Helel, Lah, Misharu)

Nicholas WYATT, Edinburgh
(Asherah, Astarte, Calf, Eve, Kinnaru, Oil, Qeteb)

Paolo XELLA, Rome
(Barad, Haby, Mountains-and-valleys, Resheph)

Larry ZALCMAN, Tel Aviv
(Orion, Pleiades)

Ida ZATELLI, Florence
(Aldebaran, Constellations, Libra)

Dieter ZELLER, Mainz
(Jesus, Kyrios)

INTRODUCTION

The *Dictionary of Deities and Demons in the Bible* (henceforth *DDD*) is in some ways unlike any other dictionary in the field of biblical studies. This is the first catalogue of its kind, one which discusses all the gods and demons whose names are found in the Bible. Complementing the usual surveys and histories of Mesopotamian, Egyptian, Ugaritic, Syro-Palestinian, Persian, Greek, and Roman religion, *DDD* assesses the impact of contemporary religions on Israel and the Early Church by focusing on those gods that actually left traces in the Bible.

The deities and demons dealt with in this dictionary are not all of one kind. Even though the distinction between major and minor gods is a delicate one, some of the gods here discussed are more representative of their culture than others; Marduk's place in Babylonian religion is more central than that of the god Euphrates. If both have nevertheless found their way into *DDD*, it is because the two of them are mentioned in the Bible. Other gods, however, despite their importance, have no separate entry in *DDD* because there is not a single mention of them in the biblical books: Enlil is an example of this. The imbalance produced by a selection based on the occurrence of a god's name in the Bible is redressed, to some degree, by a system of cross-references throughout *DDD* and an index at the end. Thus Anu, the Mesopotamian god of heaven, does not have a separate entry, but is discussed under 'Heaven', and in various other articles indicated in the index. The inevitable disproportion caused by the criterion on which *DDD* has been conceived is often more optical than real.

The criterion by which *DDD* has selected its gods has just been summarized as mention of the god's name in the Bible. Yet things are not as straightforward as this rule of thumb measurement might suggest. The boundaries of the Bible, to begin with, change from the one religious community to the other. In order to make the selection of deities as representative as possible, the editors have chosen to base it on the most comprehensive canon currently used, viz. that of the Orthodox Churches, which consists of the complete canon of the Septuagint version (including 3 and 4 Maccabees) plus the Greek New Testament. The term Bible as used in the title of *DDD* covers in fact the Masoretic text of the Hebrew Bible; the complete Septuagint (including the so-called Apocrypha); and the twenty-seven books of the New Testament. Though many articles pay attention to the subsequent development of notions and concepts in the Pseudepigrapha, the latter have not been used as an independent quarry of theonyms.

Many gods discussed in *DDD* are mentioned by name in the Bible. They constitute what one might call the first group. Obvious examples are Asherah, Baal, El, Hermes, Zeus and others. These gods were still recognized or recognizable as such by the author of the relevant passage and by the audience. In some instances the names are found only in the Septuagint and not in the corresponding section of the Masoretic text. An interesting example is Apis: at Jer 46:15 the Greek Old Testament has ἔφυγεν ὁ Ἆπις,

"(Why) has Apis fled?", where the Masoretic text reads נסחף, "(Why) was it swept away?" Should the Greek be a misunderstanding of the Hebrew text (which is not certain), it is valuable as a reflection of the religious milieu surrounding the—Jewish—community in which the translator was at home.

A second group of deities listed in *DDD* are mentioned in the Bible, not independently, but as an element in personal names or place names. Such theophoric anthroponyms and toponyms are a rich source of information on the religious milieu of the Israelites and the Early Christians. It need hardly be said that the occurrence of a deity in a place name, such as Anat in Anathoth, or Shemesh in Beth-shemesh, does not automatically imply that the deity in question was in fact worshipped by the people who lived there; nor need someone called Artemas or Tychicus (Tit 3:12) have been a devotee of Artemis or Tyche. Yet such names reflect a certain familiarity with the deities in question, if not of the inhabitants of the town or the bearer of the name, then at least of their ancestors or their surroundings. The deities in question may therefore be said to have been part of the religious milieu of the Bible.

A third group of deities consists of gods mentioned in the Bible, but not in their capacity as gods. They are the so-called demythologized deities. Examples abound. One of the Hebrew words for moon used in the Bible is *yārēaḥ*; this is the etymological equivalent of Yarikh, the moon-god known from the Ugaritic texts. Although the moon may have retained faint traces of divinity in the Bible, it has basically been divested of its divine status. The same holds true of the sun (*šemeš*): the Hebrew word corresponds with the god Shamash in Akkadian, and the goddess Shapshu in Ugaritic. There are many other, more trivial instances, such as *tîrōš*, the Hebrew word for new wine, etymologically the equivalent of the Mesopotamian deity Sirish and the Canaanite god Tirash. Although the Hebrew words (and there are also Greek examples) no longer stand for deities, the very fact that the corresponding terms in other Semitic languages do, is revealing. We have included many examples of such dethroned deities, not only to draw attention to the mythological overtones still occasionally perceptible, but also to demonstrate how Israelites, Jews, and Early Christians were part of a religious culture from which they are to be distinguished at the same time.

The fourth group consists of gods whose presence and/or divinity is often questionable. In the course of biblical scholarship, a wealth of alleged deities has been discovered whose very presence in the texts it not immediately evident. A famous example is that of Belti and Osiris. By slightly revocalizing Isa 10:4, and altering the division of the words, Paul de Lagarde obtained a reference to Belti and Osiris where generations of scholars before him had read a negation (*biltî*) and the collective designation of prisoners (*ʾassîr*). Such emendations sometimes conjure up gods hitherto unknown; in many cases they are phantom deities, in the sense that they are unattested elsewhere in the Bible or in ancient Near Eastern texts, or that the textual proposal is simply unwarranted. In the category of speculated deities fall also the suggestions concerning the appellative use of certain epithets, such as Shepherd or Stone. The reinterpretation of good Hebrew words (such as *raʿ*, 'evil') as theonyms (such as Re, the Egyptian sun-god) is another case in point. In a limited number of cases, the supposed deity is established as the hidden reality behind a human figure;

thus Jephthah's daughter has allegedly been modelled after a goddess. The inclusion of such deities often is more a tribute to the scholarly ingenuity of colleagues, present and past, than an accurate picture of the religious situation in biblical times. Also, it has proved impossible to be exhaustive in this domain. Some suggestions have no doubt escaped our notice, or simply been judged too far-fetched to qualify for inclusion in *DDD*.

The fifth and final category of gods is constituted by human figures who rose to attain divine or semi-divine status in a later tradition. Jesus and Mary belong to this group, but also Enoch, Moses and Elijah. At times the process of glorification, or more precisely divinization, started during the biblical period; before the closing of the first century CE divinity was ascribed to Jesus. In most cases, however, the development leading to divine status has been postbiblical. It tells more about the *Wirkungsgeschichte* than about the perception of such exceptional humans by their contemporaries. Yet the borderlines between human and divine are not always crystal clear; neither is the precise point at which the divinization began. What is found in its full-blown form in postbiblical writings is often contained *in nuce* in the Bible.

The aims of *DDD*, in short, cannot be reduced to a single object. It is meant primarily as an up-to-date source-book on the deities and demons found in the Bible. Its various attendant aims are hardly less important, though. It is meant as a scholarly introduction to the religious universe which the Israelites and the Early Christians were part of; it is meant as a tool to enable readers to assess the distinctiveness of Israelite, Jewish and Early Christian religions; it is meant as a survey of biblical scholarship with respect to the mythological background of various biblical notions and concepts; and it is meant, finally, as a means to discover that the Bible has not only dethroned many deities, but has also produces new ones.

Most articles of DDD consist of four sections, each marked by a Roman numeral. Section I discusses the name of the god, including its etymology, as well as its occurrence in the various ancient civilisations surrounding Israel and Judah. The biblical evidence is briefly surveyed, and a general indication as to the capacity in which the name occurs is given. Section II deals with the identity, character and role of the deity or demon in the culture of origin. When an originally non-Israelite deity is discussed, such as Amun, Marduk or Zeus, the section focuses on the cult of the god outside the Bible. If the god is primarily attested in the Bible, section II is devoted to a discussion of the extra-biblical references and parallels. Section III deals with the role and nature of the deity in the books of the Bible. Section IV consists of the relevant bibliography. An asterisk prefixed to the name of the *author marks a publication as particularly important for the subject. Studies containing further bibliographical information are followed by the observation '& lit' between brackets after the title. A supplementary section is sometimes added to discuss the post-Biblical attestations and developments.

Many people have collaborated over the past four years to carry *DDD* to completion. It is a pleasure to mention some of those who have been involved with the project. The initial impetus came from Michael Stone (Jerusalem). His idea of creating a dictionary of ancient Near Eastern religions found favour with Brill; one of its publishers, Elisabeth Erdman, began to look for an editor. The three editors she eventually found decided to curtail Stone's ambitious project to far more modest dimensions; and even as modest a project as *DDD* has proved more time-consuming than any of us expected.

During the first year a list of entries was prepared, sample articles were written, and over a hundred authors were solicited. Several of the latter suggested entries previously overlooked by the editors. The major part of the job began at the end of the second year when articles started coming in. Though the scholarly work on the manuscripts (or rather hard copy) was done by the editorial team, if need be after consulting with the advisors, the bulk of the articles were processed and made ready for publication by various assistants. Mrs Gerda Bergsma, Ms Kim de Berg, Mr Joost van Meggelen, Mr Hans Baart, and Mr Theo Bakker have assisted us with the preparation of the manuscript, for different amounts of time. We owe a special debt of gratitude to Ms Meta Baauw who saw most of the articles through the final stage of preparation. Mr Hans van de Berg (Utrecht University) was invaluable for his assistance with all matters pertaining to computers and software. Dr Peter Staples (Utrecht University) and Mrs Helen Richardson have polished the language of the articles, often written by scholars for whom English is not their primary—nor, for many, their secondary—tongue. Dr Gerard Mussies (Utrecht University) joined us in reading the proofs. The collaboration with all of them, and—though less immediately—with the international group of respected colleagues who have written the various contributions, has been one of the rewards of editing *DDD*.

K. van der Toorn
B. Becking
P. W. van der Horst

November, 1994

GENERAL ABBREVIATIONS

Akk	Akkadian	MB	Middle Babylonian
Ar	Arabic	ms(s)	manuscript(s)
Aram	Aramaic	MT	Masoretic Text
bk.	book	n(n).	note(s)
c.	century	no(s).	number(s)
ca.	circa	NT	New Testament
chap(s).	chapter(s)	obv.	obverse
col(s).	column(s)	OG	Old Greek
Copt	Coptic	OL	Old Latin
D	Deuteronomist	OSA	Old South Arabic
DN	divine name	OT	Old Testament
Dtr	Deuteronomistic redactor(s)	P	Priestly Document
E	Elohist	p(p).	page(s)
Eg	Egyptian	Pers	Persian
Eng	English	Phoen	Phoenician
Eth	Ethiopic	pl(s).	plate(s)
fig(s).	figure(s)	PN	personal name
FS	Festschrift	QL	Qumran Literature
G	Greek (versions)	r.	reverse
Gk	Greek	sec.	section
Heb	Hebrew	Sum	Sumerian
Hit	Hittite	Syr	Syriac
IE	Indo-European	Ug	Ugaritic
J	Yahwist	v(v)	verse(s)
Lat	Latin	Vg	Vulgate
LXX	Septuagint	VL	Vetus Latina

ABBREVIATIONS OF BIBLICAL BOOKS (INCLUDING THE APOCRYPHA)

Gen	Hab	Bar
Exod	Zeph	Bel
Lev	Hag	1-2 Esdr
Num	Zech	4 Ezra
Deut	Mal	Jdt
Josh	Ps (*pl.*: Pss)	Ep Jer
Judg	Job	1-2-3-4 Macc
1-2 Sam	Prov	Pr Azar
1-2 Kgs	Ruth	Pr Man
Isa	Cant	Sir
Jer	Eccl (*or* Qoh)	Sus
Ezek	Lam	Tob
Hos	Esth	Wis
Joel	Dan	Matt
Obad	Ezra	Mark
Amos	Neh	Luke
Jonah	1-2 Chr	John
Mic	1-2-3-4 Kgdms	Acts
Nah	Add Esth	Rom

1-2 Cor	1-2 Thess	Jas
Gal	1-2 Tim	1-2 Pet
Eph	Titus	1-2-3 John
Phil	Phlm	Jude
Col	Heb	Rev

ABBREVIATIONS OF PSEUDEPIGRAPHICAL AND EARLY PATRISTIC WORKS

Adam and Eve	Books of Adam and Eve
2-3 Apoc. Bar	Syriac, Greek Apocalypse of Baruch
Apoc. Mos.	Apocalypse of Moses
Ass. Mos.	Assumption of Moses
1-2-3 Enoch	Ethiopic, Slavonic, Hebrew Enoch
Ep. Arist.	Epistle of Aristeas
Jub.	Jubilees
Mart. Isa.	Martyrdom of Isaiah
Odes Sol.	Odes of Solomon
Or.Jo.	Prayer of Joseph
Pss. Sol.	Psalms of Solomon
Sib. Or.	Sibylline Oracles
T. 12 Patr.	Testaments of the Twelve Patriarchs
T. Levi	Testament of Levi
T. Benj.	Testament of Benjamin, etc.
Acts Pil.	Acts of Pilate
Apoc. Pet.	Apocalypse of Peter
Gos. Eb.	Gospel of the Ebionites
Gos. Eg.	Gospel of the Egyptians
Gos. Heb.	Gospel of the Hebrews
Gos. Naas.	Gospel of the Naassenes
Gos. Pet.	Gospel of Peter
Gos. Thom.	Gospel of Thomas
Prot. Jas.	Protevangelium of James
Barn.	Barnabas
1-2 Clem.	1-2 Clement
Did.	Didache
Diogn.	Diognetus
Herm. *Man.*	Hermas, Mandate
Sim.	Similitude
Vis.	Vision
Ign. *Eph.*	Ignatius, Letter to the Ephesians
Magn.	Letter to the Magnesians
Phld.	Letter to the Philadelphians
Pol.	Letter to Polycarp
Rom.	Letter to the Romans
Smyrn.	Letter to the Smyrnaeans
Trall.	Letter to the Trallians
Mart. Pol.	Martyrdom of Polycarp
Pol. *Phil.*	Polycarp to the Philippians

ABBREVIATIONS OF DEAD SEA SCROLLS AND RELATED TEXTS

CD	Cairo (Geniza text of) Damascus (Document)
Ḥev	Naḥal Ḥever texts
Mas	Masada texts
Mird	Khirbet Mird texts
Mur	Wadi Murabbaʿat
p	Pesher (commentary)
Q	Qumran
1Q, 2Q, 3Q, etc.	Numbered caves of Qumran, yielding written material; followed by abbreviation of biblical or apocryphal book
1QapGen	*Genesis Apocryphon* of Qumran Cave 1
1QH	*Hôdāyôt (Thanksgiving Hymns)* from Qumran Cave 1
1QIsa[a,b]	First or second copy of Isaiah from Qumran Cave 1
1QpHab	*Pesher on Habakkuk* from Qumran Cave 1
1QM	*Milḥāmâ (War scroll)*
1QS	*Serek Hayyaḥad (Rule of the Community, Manual of Discipline)*
1QSa	Appendix A *(Rule of the Congregation)* to 1QS
1QSb	Appendix B *(Blessings)* to 1QS
3Q*15*	Copper Scroll from Qumran Cave 3
4QFlor	*Florilegium* (or *Eschatological Midrashim*) from Qumran Cave 4
4Q Mess ar	Aramaic "Messianic" text from Qumran Cave 4
4QPrNab	Prayer of Nabonidus from Qumran Cave 4
4QTestim	*Testimonia* text from Qumran Cave 4
4QTLevi	*Testament of Levi* from Qumran Cave 4
4QPhyl	Phylacteries from Qumran Cave 4
11QMelch	*Melchizedek* text from Qumran Cave 4
11QTgJob	*Targum of Job* from Qumran Cave 11

ABBREVIATIONS OF TARGUMIC MATERIAL

Frg. Tg.	*Fragmentary Targum*
Pal. Tgs.	*Palestinian Targums*
Sam. Tg.	*Samaritan Targum*
Tg. Esth I 'and' *II*	*First* 'and' *Second Targum of Esther*
Tg. Isa.	*Targum of Isaiah*
Tg. Ket.	*Targum of the Writings*
Tg. Neb.	*Targum of the Prophets*
Tg. Neof.	*Targum Neofiti I*
Tg. Onq.	*Targum Onqelos*
Tg. Ps.-J.	*Targum Pseudo-Jonathan*
Tg. Yer. I	*Targum Yerušalmi I*
Tg. Yer. II	*Targum Yerušalmi II*
Yem. Tg.	*Yemenite Targum*

ABBREVIATIONS OF PERIODICALS, REFERENCE WORKS, AND SERIES

AAA *Annals of Archaeology and Anthropology*
AAAS *Annales archéologiques arabes syriennes*
AASF Annales Academiae Scientiarum Fennicae
AASOR Annual of the American Schools of Oriental Research
AB Anchor Bible
AbB Altbabylonische Briefe in Umschrift und Übersetzung
ABD *Anchor Bible Dictionary*
ABL R. F. HARPER, *Assyrian and Babylonian Letters*
ABRT J. A. CRAIG, *Assyrian and Babylonian Religious Texts*
AC *Antiquité classique*
AcOr *Acta Orientalia*
ADAJ *Annual of the Department of Antiquities of Jordan*
ADD C. H. W. JOHNS, *Assyrian Deeds and Documents*
ADPV Abhandlungen des Deutschen Palästinavereins
ÄA Ägyptologische Abhandlungen
ÄAT Ägypten und Altes Testament
ÄF Ägyptologische Forschungen
AEO A. H. GARDINER, *Ancient Egyptian Onomastica*
Aeg *Aegyptus*
AfO *Archiv für Orientforschung*
AfO Beih. *AfO* Beiheft
AGH E. EBELING, *Die akkadische Gebetsserie "Handerhebung"*
AGJU Arbeiten zur Geschichte des antiken Judentums und des Urchristentums
AHAW Abhandlungen der Heidelberger Akademie der Wissenschaften
AHW W. VON SODEN, *Akkadisches Handwörterbuch*
AION *Annali dell'Istituto orientale di Napoli*
AIPHOS *Annuaire de l'Institut de philologie et d'histoire orientales et slaves*
AJA *American Journal of Archaeology*
AJBA *Australian Journal of Biblical Archaeology*
AJP *American Journal of Philology*
AJSL *American Journal of Semitic Languages and Literature*
AkkGE K. TALLQVIST, *Akkadische Götter-epitheta* (= StOr 7)
AKM Abhandlungen für die Kunde des Morgenlandes
AKT *Ankara Kültepe Tabletleri* (1990)
ALASP Abhandlungen zur Literatur Alt-Syriens-Palästinas
ALBO Analecta Lovaniensa Biblica et Orientalia
ALGHJ Arbeiten zur Literatur und Geschichte des Hellenistischen Judentums
ALGRM *Ausführliches Lexikon der griechischen und römischen Mythologie*, ed. W. H. Roscher (= LGRM)
AlT D. J. WISEMAN, *Alalaḫ Texts*
ALUOS *Annual of the Leeds University Oriental Society*
AMI *Archäologische Mitteilungen aus Iran*
AnBib Analecta Biblica
AncSoc *Ancient Society*
ANEP *Ancient Near East in Pictures*, ed. J. B. Pritchard
ANET *Ancient Near Eastern Texts*, ed. J. B. Pritchard
AnOr Analecta Orientalia
ANQ *Andover Newton Quarterly*
ANRW *Aufstieg und Niedergang der Römischen Welt*
AnSt *Anatolian Studies*
AntAfr *Antiquités Africaines*
ANTF Arbeiten zur Neutestamentliche Textforschung
Anton *Antonianum*
AOAT Alter Orient und Altes Testament
AoF *Altorientalische Forschungen*
APAW Abhandlungen der Preussischen Akademie der Wissenschaften, Berlin
APOT *Apocrypha and Pseudepigrapha of the Old Testament*, ed. R. H. Charles
ARAB D. D. LUCKENBILL, *Ancient Records of Assyria and Babylonia*
Arch *Archaeology*
ARE *Ancient Records of Egypt*, ed. J. H. Breasted
ARES Archivi reali di Ebla, studi
ARET Archivi reali di Ebla, testi
ARI A. K. GRAYSON, *Assyrian Royal Inscriptions*
ARM Archives royales de Mari
ArOr *Archiv Orientální*
ARTU J. C. DE MOOR, *An Anthology of Religious Texts from Ugarit*

ARW *Archiv für Religionswissenschaft*
AS Assyriological Studies (Chicago)
ASAE *Annales du service des antiquités de l'Egypte*
ASAW Abhandlungen der Sächsischen Akademie der Wissenschaften, Phil.-hist. Kl., Berlin
ASNU Acta Seminarii Neotestamentici Upsaliensis
ASOR American Schools of Oriental Research
ASSR *Archives des sciences sociales des religions*
ASTI *Annual of the Swedish Theological Institute*
ATANT Abhandlungen zur Theologie des Alten und Neuen Testaments
Atr. W. G. LAMBERT & A. R. MILLARD, *Atra-ḫasīs: The Babylonian Story of the Flood*
AuA *Antike und Abendland*
Aug *Augustinianum*
AulOr *Aula Orientalis*
AUSS *Andrews University Seminary Studies*
BA *Biblical Archaeologist*
Bab. *Babyloniaca*
BAe Bibliotheca Aegyptica
BAGB *Bulletin de l'Association Guillaume Budé*
BAGD W. BAUER, W. F. ARNDT, F. W. GINGRICH & F. W. DANKER, *Greek-English Lexicon of the New Testament*
BagM *Baghdader Mitteilungen*
BAM F. KÖCHER, *Die babylonisch-assyrische Medizin in Texten und Untersuchungen*
BAR *Biblical Archaeologist Reader*
BARev *Biblical Archaeology Review*
BASOR *Bulletin of the American Schools of Oriental Research*
BASP *Bulletin of the American Society of Papyrologists*
BBB Bonner Biblische Beiträge
BBR H. ZIMMERN, *Beiträge zur Kenntnis der babylonischen Religion*
BBVO Berliner Beiträge zum vorderen Orient
BCH *Bulletin de correspondance hellénique*
BD Book of the Dead
BDB F. BROWN, S. R. DRIVER & C. A. BRIGGS, *Hebrew and English Lexicon of the Old Testament*
BdE Bibliothèque d'étude, Institut français d'archéologie orientale
BDR F. BLASS, A. DEBRUNNER & F. REHKOPF, *Grammatik des neutestamentlichen Griechisch*
BE Babylonian Expedition of the University of Pennsylvania, Series A: Cuneiform Texts
BeO *Bibbia e oriente*
BETL Bibliotheca Ephemeridum Theologicarum Lovaniensium
BHH *Biblisch-Historisches Handwörterbuch*, ed. B. Reicke & L. Rost
BHK *Biblia Hebraica*, ed. R. Kittel
BHS *Biblia Hebraica Stuttgartensia*
Bib *Biblica*
BibOr Biblica et Orientalia
BICS *Bulletin of the Institute of Classical Studies*
BIES *Bulletin of the Israel Exploration Society (= Yediot)*
BIFAO *Bulletin de l'Institut français d'archéologie orientale*
BiMes Bibliotheca Mesopotamica
BIN Babylonian Inscriptions in the Collection of J. B. Nies
BiOr *Bibliotheca Orientalis*
BIOSCS *Bulletin of the International Organisation for Septuagint and Cognate Studies*
BJR(U)L *Bulletin of the John Rylands (University) Library*
BJS Brown Judaic Studies
BKAT Biblischer Kommentar: Altes Testament
BM tablets in the collections of the British Museum
BMC British Museum Coin Catalogues
BMS L. W. KING, *Babylonian Magic and Sorcery*
BN *Biblische Notizen*
Bo. field numbers of tablets excavated at Boghazköy
BoSt Boghazköi-Studien
BR *Biblical Research*
BRA Beiträge zur Religionsgeschichte des Altertums
BRL² *Biblisches Reallexikon,* ed. K. Galling
BRM Babylonian Records in the Library of J. Pierpont Morgan
BSFE *Bulletin de la Société française d'égyptologie*
BSOAS *Bulletin of the School of Oriental and African Studies*
BullEpigr *Bulletin épigraphique*
BWANT Beiträge zur Wissenschaft vom Alten und Neuen Testament

BWL	W. G. Lambert, *Babylonian Wisdom Literature*
BZ	*Biblische Zeitschrift*
BZAW	Beihefte zur *ZAW*
BZNW	Beihefte zur *ZNW*
BZRGG	Beihefte zur *ZRGG*
CAD	*The Assyrian Dictionary of the Oriental Institute of the University of Chicago*
CAH	*Cambridge Ancient History*
CBQ	*Catholic Biblical Quarterly*
CBQMS	*CBQ* Monograph Series
CCDS	Corpus Cultus Deae Syriae
CCSL	Corpus Christianorum Series Latina
CCT	Cuneiform Texts from Cappadocian Tablets
CdE	*Chronique d'Egypte*
CIG	*Corpus Inscriptionum Graecorum*
CIJ	*Corpus Inscriptionum Judaicarum*
CIL	*Corpus Inscriptionum Latinorum*
CIMRM	Corpus Inscriptionum et Monumentorum Religionis Mithriacae
CIS	*Corpus Inscriptionum Semiticarum*
CJ	*Classical Journal*
CML	J. C. L. Gibson, *Canaanite Myths and Legends*
ConB	Coniectanea Biblica
CP	*Classical Philology*
CPJ	*Corpus Papyrorum Judaicarum*
CPSI	*Corpus of Proto-Sinaitic Inscriptions*, ed. J. Biggs & M. Dijkstra
CQ	*Classical Quarterly*
CRAIBL	*Comptes rendues de l'Académie des inscriptions et belles lettres*
CRB	Cahiers de la Revue biblique
CRINT	Compendia Rerum Iudaicarum ad Novum Testamentum
CRRA	Compte rendu, Rencontre assyriologique internationale
CT	Cuneiform Texts from Babylonian Tablets
CT	*Coffin Texts*
CTA	A. Herdner, *Corpus des tablettes alphabétiques*
CTH	E. Laroche, *Catalogue des textes hittites*
CTM	Calwer Theologische Monographien
DAGR	*Dictionnaire des antiquités grecques et romaines*, ed. C. V. Daremberg & E. Saglio
DBAT	*Dielheimer Blätter zum Alten Testament*
DBATBeih	Dielheimer Blätter zum Alten Testament, Beiheft
DBSup	*Dictionaire de la Bible, Supplément*
Dendara	E. Chassinat & F. Daumas, *Le temple de Dendara*
DISO	C.-F. Jean & J. Hoftijzer, *Dictionnaire des inscriptions sémitiques de l'ouest*
DJD	Discoveries in the Judaean Desert
DOTT	*Documents from Old Testament Times*, ed. D. W. Thomas
EA	J. A. Knudtzon, *Die El-Amarna-Tafeln* (= VAB 2); *EA* 359-379: A. Rainey, *El Amarna Tablets 359-379* (= AOAT 8)
EdF	Erträge der Forschung
Edfou	M. de Rochemonteix & E. Chassinat, *Le temple d'Edfou*
Ee	*Enuma Elish*
EKK	Evangelisch-Katholischer Kommentar
Emar	D. Arnaud, *Recherches au pays d'Aštata. Emar VI.1-4*
EncBibl	*Encyclopedia Biblica,* London
EncIsl	*Encyclopedia of Islam*
EncJud	*Encyclopedia Judaica*
EncMiqr	*Entsiqlopēdiā Miqrā'īt,* Jerusalem
EPRO	Etudes préliminaires aux religions orientales dans l'empire romain
ER	*Encyclopedia of Religion*
ERE	*Encyclopedia of Religion and Ethics*
ErIsr	*Eretz Israel*
ErJb	*Eranos Jahrbuch*
ESE	Ephemeris für Semitische Epigraphik
Esna	S. Sauneron, *Le temple d'Esna*
ETL	*Ephemerides Theologicae Lovanienses*
EWNT	*Exegetisches Wörterbuch zum Neuen Testament*
ExpTim	*Expository Times*
FAOS	Freiburger Altorientalische Studien
FF	*Forschungen und Fortschritte*
FGH	*Fragmente der griechischen Historiker*, ed. F. Jacoby
FRLANT	Forschungen zur Religion und Literatur des Alten und Neuen Testaments
FS	Festschrift
FzB	Forschungen zur Bibel
GAG	W. von Soden, *Grundriss der akkadischen Grammatik*
Ges.[17]	W. Gesenius, *Hebräisches und aramäisches Handwörterbuch*, (17th. ed.)
Ges.[18]	W. Gesenius, *Hebräisches und aramäisches Handwörterbuch*, (18th. ed.)
GGA	*Göttingische Gelehrte Anzeigen*
Gilg.	Gilgāmeš epic

GK	*Gesenius' Hebräische Grammatik*, 28th ed., ed. E. Kautzsch
GLAJJ	M. Stern, *Greek and Latin Authors on Jews and Judaism*
GM	*Göttinger Miszellen*
GNT	Grundrisse zum Neuen Testament
GOF	Göttinger Orientforschungen
GRBS	*Greek, Roman and Byzantine Studies*
GTA	Göttinger Theologische Arbeiten
HAB	Hamburger Ägyptologische Beiträge
HALAT	W. Baumgartner *et al.*, *Hebräisches und Aramäisches Lexikon zum Alten Testament*
HAR	*Hebrew Annual Review*
HAT	Handbuch zum Alten Testament
HAW	*Handbuch der Altertums-wissenschaften*
HdO	Handbuch der Orientalistik
Hey	*Heythrop Journal*
HIsl	*Handwörterbuch der Islam* (Leiden 1941)
HNT	Handbuch zum Neuen Testament
HR	*History of Religion*
HSCP	*Harvard Studies in Classical Philology*
HSM	Harvard Semitic Monographs
HSS	Harvard Semitic Studies
HTKNT	Herders Theologischer Kommentar zum Neuen Testament
HTR	*Harvard Theological Review*
HTS	Harvard Theological Studies
HUCA	*Hebrew Union College Annual*
IBHS	B. K. Waltke & M. O'Connor, *An Introduction to Biblical Hebrew Syntax*
IBS	*Irish Biblical Studies*
ICC	International Critical Commentary
IDB	*The Interpreter's Dictionary of the Bible*
IDBS	*The Interpreter's Dictionary of the Bible, Supplementary Volume*
IDélos	Inscriptions de Délos
IEJ	*Israel Exploration Journal*
IFAO	Institut français d'archéologie orientale
IG	Inscriptiones Graecae
IGLS	*Inscriptions grecques et latines de la Syrie*
IGR	Inscriptiones Graecae ad res Romanas pertinentes
IJT	*Indian Journal of Theology*
IKyme	*Inschriften von Kyme*
IM	tablets in the collections of the Iraq Museum, Baghdad
Int	*Interpretation*
IOS	*Israel Oriental Society*
IPN	M. Noth, *Die israelitischen Personennamen*
IrAnt	*Iranica Antiqua*
JA	*Journal asiatique*
JAAR	*Journal of the American Academy of Religion*
JAC	*Jahrbuch für Antike und Christentum*
JANES	*Journal of the Ancient Near Eastern Society of Columbia University*
JAOS	*Journal of the American Oriental Society*
JARCE	*Journal of the American Research Center in Egypt*
JAS	*Journal of Asian Studies*
JB	Jerusalem Bible
JBL	*Journal of Biblical Literature*
JCS	*Journal of Cuneiform Studies*
JDS	Judaean Desert Studies
JEA	*Journal of Egyptian Archaeology*
JEOL	*Jaarbericht ... Ex Oriente Lux*
JEN	Joint Expedition with the Iraq Museum at Nuzi
JESHO	*Journal of the Economic and Social History of the Orient*
JETS	*Journal of the Evangelical Theological Society*
JHNES	Johns Hopkins Near Eastern Studies
JHS	*Journal of Hellenic Studies*
JJS	*Journal of Jewish Studies*
JNES	*Journal of Near Eastern Studies*
JNSL	*Journal of Northwest Semitic Languages*
JPOS	*Journal of the Palestine Oriental Society*
JPSV	*Jewish Publication Society Translation of the Bible*
JQR	*Jewish Quarterly Review*
JR	*Journal of Religion*
JRAS	*Journal of the Royal Asiatic Society*
JRelS	*Journal of Religious Studies*
JRH	*Journal of Religious History*
JRS	*Journal of Roman Studies*
JSHRZ	Jüdische Schriften aus Hellenistisch-Römischer Zeit
JSJ	*Journal for the Study of Judaism in the Persian, Hellenistic and Roman Periods*
JSNT	*Journal for the Study of the New Testament*
JSOT	*Journal for the Study of the Old Testament*
JSOTSup	Journal for the Study of the Old Testament, Supplement Series
JSP	*Journal for the Study of the Pseudepigrapha*

JSS — *Journal of Semitic Studies*
JSSEA — *Journal of the Society for the Study of Egyptian Antiquities*
JSSR — *Journal for the Scientific Study of Religion*
JTS — *Journal of Theological Studies*
K. — tablets in the Kouyunjik collections of the British Museum
KAI — H. DONNER & W. RÖLLIG, *Kanaanäische und aramäische Inschriften*
KAR — E. EBELING, *Keilschrifttexte aus Assur religiösen Inhalts*
KAT — Kommentar zum Alten Testament
KAV — E. EBELING, *Keilschrifttexte aus Assur verschiedenen Inhalts*
KB — L. KOEHLER & W. BAUMGARTNER, *Lexicon in Veteris Testamenti libros*
KBo — Keilschrifttexte aus Boghazköi
KEK — Kritisch-exegetischer Kommentar
KHAT — Kurzer Handkommentar zum Alten Testament
KJV — King James Version
KlF — Kleinasiatische Forschungen
KP — *Kleine Pauly*
KS — *Kleine Schriften*
KTU — M. DIETRICH, O. LORETZ & J. SANMARTÍN, *Die keil-alphabetische Texte aus Ugarit* (AOAT 24)
KUB — Keilschrifturkunden aus Boghazköi
LÄS — Leipziger Ägyptologische Studien
LAB — *Liber Antiquitatum Biblicarum*
LAPO — Littératures anciennes du Proche-Orient
LAS — S. PARPOLA, *Letters of Assyrian Scholars* (AOAT 5)
LAW — *Lexikon der Alten Welt*
LCL — Loeb Classical Library
LdÄ — *Lexikon der Ägyptologie*
Legends — L. GINZBERG, *The Legends of the Jews*
Leš — *Lešonēnu*
LfgrE — *Lexikon des frühgriechischen Epos*
LIMC — *Lexicon Iconographicum Mythologiae Classicae*
LKA — E. EBELING, *Literarische Keilschrifttexte aus Assur*
LKU — A. FALKENSTEIN, *Literarische Keilschrifttexte aus Uruk*
LSAM — *Lois sacrées de l'Asie Mineure*, ed. F. Sokolowski
LSCG — *Lois sacrées des cités grecques*, ed. F. Sokolowski
LSJ — LIDDELL-SCOTT-JONES, *Greek-English Lexicon*
LSS — Leipziger semitische Studien
LTK — *Lexikon für Theologie und Kirche*
LUÅ — Lunds Universitets Årsskrift
MAD — Materials for the Assyrian Dictionary
MAIS — *Missione archeologica italiana in Siria*
MÄS — Münchener Ägyptologische Studien
MAMA — Monumenta Asiae Minoris Antiqua
Maqlu — G. MEIER, *Maqlu* (= *AfO* Beiheft 2)
MARI — *MARI Annales de recherches interdisciplinaires*
MDAIK — *Mitteilungen des Deutschen Archäologischen Instituts, Abteilung Kairo*
MDOG — *Mitteilungen der Deutschen Orient-Gesellschaft*
MDP — Mémoires de la délégation en Perse
MEE — Materiali epigrafici di Ebla
MEFR(A) — *Mélanges d'archéologie et d'histoire de l'École française (antiquité)*
MGWJ — *Monatsschrift für Geschichte und Wissenschaft des Judentums*
MIO — *Mitteilungen des Instituts für Orientforschung*
MM — J.H. MOULTON & G. MILLIGAN, *The Vocabulary of the Greek Testament*
Mnem — *Mnemosyne*
MRS — Mission de Ras Shamra
MSL — Materials for the Sumerian Lexicon
Mus — *Le Muséon*
MusHelv — *Museum Helveticum*
MUSJ — *Mélanges de l'Université Saint-Joseph*
MVAÄG — Mitteilungen der Vorder-Asiatisch-Ägyptischen Gesellschaft
NABU — *Nouvelles assyriologiques brèves et utilitaires*
NAWG — Nachrichten von der Akademie der Wissenschaften zu Göttingen
NBL — *Neues Bibel-Lexikon*, ed. M. Görg & B. Lang
NCB — New Century Bible
NEB — New English Bible
NedTTs — *Nederlands Theologisch Tijdschrift*
Neot — *Neotestamentica*
NESE — Neue Ephemeris für Semitische Epigraphik
NewDocs — *New Documents Illustrating Early Christianity*, ed. G. H. R. Horsley
NHC — *Nag Hammadi Codex*
NHS — Nag Hammadi Studies
NorTT — *Norsk Teologisk Tidsskrift*
NovT — *Novum Testamentum*
NovTSup — Novum Testamentum Supplements
NRSV — New Revised Standard Version

NTOA Novum Testamentum et Orbis Antiquus
NTS *New Testament Studies*
NTStud *Nieuwe Theologische Studiën*
NTTS New Testament Tools and Studies
Numen *Numen: International Review for the History of Religions*
OBO Orbis Biblicus et Orientalis
OBTR S. DALLEY, C. B. F. WALKER & J. D. HAWKINS, *Old Babylonian Texts from Tell Rimah*
OCD *Oxford Classical Dictionary*
OECT Oxford Editions of Cuneiform Texts
OGIS *Orientis Graeci Inscriptiones Selectae*, ed. W. Dittenberger
OIP Oriental Institute Publications
OLA Orientalia Lovaniensia Analecta
OLD *Oxford Latin Dictionary*
OLP Orientalia Lovaniensia Periodica
OLZ *Orientalistische Literaturzeitung*
OMRO *Oudheidkundige Mededelingen uit het Rijksmuseum van Oudheden te Leiden*
Or *Orientalia*
OrAnt *Oriens Antiquus*
OrChr *Oriens Christianus*
OrSu *Orientalia Suecana*
OrSyr *l'Orient syrien*
OTL Old Testament Library
OTP *The Old Testament Pseudepigrapha*, ed. J. H. Charlesworth
OTS Oudtestamentische Studiën
PAAJR *Proceedings of the American Academy of Jewish Research*
PAPS Proceedings of the American Philosophical Society
PBS Publications of the Babylonian Section, University Museum, University of Pennsylvania
PEFQS *Palestine Exploration Fund, Quarterly Statement*
PEQ *Palestine Exploration Quarterly*
PG Patrologia Graeca, ed. J. Migne
PGM *Papyri Graecae Magicae*, ed. K. Preisendanz
Philol *Philologus*
PhilQuart *Philosophical Quarterly*
PIFAO Publications de l'Institut français d'archéologie orientale du Caire
PJ *Palästina-Jahrbuch*
PL Patrologia Latina, ed. J. Migne
PLRE *Prosopography of the Later Roman Empire*
PMG *Poetae Melici Graeci*
POS Pretoria Oriental Series
POxy Oxyrhynchus Papyri
PRU *Palais royal d'Ugarit*
PSBA *Proceedings of the Society of Biblical Archaeology*
PVTG Pseudepigrapha Veteris Testamenti Graeca
PW PAULY-WISSOWA, *Realencyclopädie der klassischen Altertums-wissenschaft*
PWSup Supplement to PW
Pyr. K. SETHE, *Die altägyptischen Pyramidentexte*
Qad *Qadmoniot*
QD Questiones Disputatae
QDAP *Quarterly of the Department of Antiquities in Palestine*
R H. C. RAWLINSON, *The Cuneiform Inscriptions of Western Asia*
RA *Revue d'Assyriologie et d'archéologie orientale*
RAAM H. GESE, M. HÖFNER & K. RUDOLPH, *Die Religionen Altsyriens, Altarabiens und der Mandäer*
RAC *Reallexikon für Antike und Christentum*
RAcc F. THUREAU-DANGIN, *Rituels accadiens*
RÄRG H. BONNET, *Reallexikon der ägyptischen Religionsgeschichte*
RANE Records of the Ancient Near East
RArch *Revue Archéologique*
RB *Revue Biblique*
RdM Die Religionen der Menschheit
RE *Realencyclopädie für protestantische Theologie und Kirche*
REA *Revue des études anciennes*
REB Revised English Bible
RECAM *Regional Epigraphic Catalogue of Asia Minor*
REg *Revue d'égyptologie*
REG *Revue des études grecques*
REJ *Revue des études juives*
REL *Revue des études latines*
RES *Répertoire d'épigraphie sémitique*
RevQ *Revue de Qumran*
RevScRel *Revue des sciences religieuses*
RevSem *Revue sémitique*
RGG *Die Religion in Geschichte und Gegenwart* (^{3}1957-1965)
RGRW Religions in the Graeco-Roman World
RGTC Répertoire géographique des textes cunéiformes
RGVV Religionsgeschichtliche Versuche und Vorarbeiten
RHA *Revue hittite et asianique*
RhMus *Rheinisches Museum für Philologie*

RHPR	*Revue d'histoire et de philosophie religieuses*
RHR	*Revue de l'histoire des religions*
RIH	field numbers of tablets excavated at Ras Ibn-Hani
RIMA	The Royal Inscriptions of Mesopotamia Assyrian Periods
RivBib	*Rivista Biblica Italiana*
RivStorAnt	*Rivista di storia antica*
RLA	*Reallexikon der Assyriologie*
RQ	*Römisches Quartalschrift für christliche Altertumskunde und Kirchengeschichte*
RR	*Review of Religion*
RS	field numbers of tablets excavated at Ras Shamra
RSF	*Rivista di studi fenici*
RSO	*Rivista degli studi orientali*
RSOu	Ras Shamra - Ougarit
RSP	*Ras Shamra Parallels*, ed. S. Rummel (*AnOr* 51; Rome 1981)
RSR	*Recherches de science religieuse*
RSV	Revised Standard Version
RT	*Recueil de travaux relatifs à la philologie et à l'archéologie égyptiennes et assyriennes*
RTL	*Revue théologique de Louvain*
SAA	State Archives of Assyria
SAAB	*State Archives of Assyria Bulletin*
SAK	Studien zur Altägyptischen Kultur
SANE	Sources from the Ancient Near East
SB	*Sammelbuch griechischer Urkunden aus Aegypten*
SBAW	Sitzungsberichte der bayerischen Akademie der Wissenschaften
SBB	Stuttgarter Biblische Beiträge
SBH	G. A. REISNER, *Sumerisch-babylonischen Hymnen nach Thontafeln griechischer Zeit*
SBL DS	Society of Biblical Literature Dissertation Series
SBLMS	SBL Monograph Series
SBLSBS	SBL Sources for Biblical Studies
SBLTT	SBL Texts and Translations
SBLWAW	SBL Writings of the Ancient World
SBS	Stuttgarter Bibelstudien
SBT	Studies in Biblical Theology
SBTU	*Spätbabylonische Texte aus Uruk*
SCHNT	Studia ad Corpus Hellenisticum Novi Testamenti
SCR	*Studies in Comparative Religion*
ScrHier	Scripta Hierosolymitana
SDAW	Sitzungsberichte der Deutschen Akademie der Wissenschaften
SEÅ	*Svensk Exegetisk Årsbok*
Sef	*Sefarad*
SEG	*Supplementum Epigraphicum Graecum*
SEL	*Studi epigrafici e linguistici*
Sem	*Semitica*
SGL	A. FALKENSTEIN & J. VAN DIJK, *Sumerische Götterlieder*
SHANE	Studies in the History of the Ancient Near East
SHT	Studies in Historical Theology
SIG	*Sylloge Inscriptionum Graecarum*, ed. W. Dittenberger
SIRIS	*Sylloge inscriptionum religionis Isiacae et Sarapiacae*, ed. L. Vidman
SJLA	Studies in Judaism in Late Antiquity
SJOT	*Scandinavian Journal of the Old Testament*
ŠL	A. DEIMEL, *Šumerisches Lexikon*
SMS	*Syro-Mesopotamian Studies*
SMSR	*Studi e Materiali di Storia delle Religioni*
SNTSMS	Society for New Testament Studies Monograph Series
SO	Sources orientales
SOTSMS	Society for Old Testament Studies Monograph Series
SPAW	Sitzungsberichte der Preussischen Akademie der Wissenschaften, Phil.-hist. Kl., Berlin
SPhA	*Studia Philonica Annual*
SR	*Studies in Religion*
SRT	E. CHIERA, *Sumerian Religious Texts*
SSEAJ	*Society for the Study of Egyptian Antiquities Journal*
SSS	Semitic Studies Series
ST	*Studia Theologica*
StAeg	Studia Aegyptiaca
STBoT	Studien zu den Boğazköy-Texten
STDJ	Studies in the Texts of the Desert of Judah
StEb	*Studi Eblaiti*
StOr	Studia Orientalia
StPsm	Studia Pohl Series Maior
STT	O. R. GURNEY, J. J. FINKELSTEIN & P. HULIN, *The Sultantepe Tablets*
Str-B	[H. STRACK &] P. BILLERBECK, *Kommentar zum Neuen Testament aus Talmud und Midrasch*
StSem	Studi Semitici
StudNeot	Studia Neotestamentica
SUNT	Studien zur Umwelt des Neuen Testaments
Šurpu	E. REINER, *Šurpu* (= *AfO* Beiheft 11)
SVF	Stoicorum Veterum Fragmenta

SVTP Studia in Veteris Testamenti Pseudepigrapha
Syll. *Sylloge Inscriptionum Graecarum*, ed. W. Dittenberger
Tākultu R. Frankena, *Tākultu, De sacrale maaltijd in het assyrische ritueel*
TAM *Tituli Asiae Minoris*
TCGNT B. M. Metzger, *A Textual Commentary on the Greek New Testament*
TCL Textes cunéiformes du Louvre
TCS Texts from Cuneiform Sources
TDNT *Theological Dictionary of the New Testament*, ed. R. Kittel & G. Friedrich
TDOT *Theological Dictionary of the Old Testament*
TDP R. Labat, *Traité akkadien de diagnostics et pronostics médicaux*
TGF Tragicorum Graecorum Fragmenta
THAT *Theologisches Handwörterbuch zum Alten Testament*, ed. E. Jenni & C. W. Westermann
ThStud Theologische Studien
ThZ *Theologische Zeitschrift*
TIM Texts in the Iraq Museum
TLZ *Theologische Literatur Zeitung*
TM Tell Mardikh, tablets from Ebla
TRE *Theologische Realenzyklopädie*
TRev *Theologische Revue*
TRu *Theologische Rundschau*
TSAJ Texte und Studien zum antiken Judentum
TSK *Theologische Studien und Kritiken*
TSSI J. C. L. Gibson, *Textbook of Syrian Semitic Inscriptions*
TUAT *Texte aus der Umwelt des Alten Testaments*, ed. O. Kaiser
TWAT *Theologisches Wörterbuch zum Alten Testament*, ed. G. J. Botterweck & H. Ringgren
TWNT *Theologisches Wörterbuch zum Neuen Testament*, ed. R. Kittel & G. Friedrich
TZ *Theologisches Zeitschrift*
UBL Ugaritisch-Biblische Literatur
UCOP University of Cambridge Oriental Publications
UET Ur Excavation Texts
UF *Ugarit-Forschungen*
UFBG W. Mayer, *Untersuchungen zur Formensprache der babylonischen "Gebetsbeschwörungen"* (= StPsm 5)
Ug *Ugaritica*
UM C.H. Gordon, *Ugaritic Manual*
UNT Untersuchungen zum Neuen Testament
UPZ *Urkunden der Ptolemäerzeit*, ed. U. Wilcken
Urk. II K. Sethe, *Hieroglyphische Urkunden der griechisch-römischen Zeit*
Urk. IV K. Sethe, *Urkunden der 18. Dynastie*
Urk. V H. Grapow, *Religiöse Urkunden*
USQR *Union Seminary Quarterly Review*
UT C. H. Gordon, *Ugaritic Textbook*
UVB Vorläufiger Bericht über die ... Ausgrabungen in Uruk-Warka (Berlin, 1930)
VAB Vorderasiatische Bibliothek
VAS Vorderasiatische Schriftdenkmäler
VAT tablets in the collections of the Staatliche Museen, Berlin
VC *Vigiliae Christianae*
VO *Vicino Oriente*
VP *Vivre et Penser* (= *RB* 1941-1944)
VT *Vetus Testamentum*
VTSup Vetus Testamentum, Supplements
W. field numbers of tablets excavated at Warka
Wb. *Wörterbuch der Aegyptischen Sprache*
WBC Word Biblical Commentary
WbMyth *Wörterbuch der Mythologie*, ed. H. W. Haussig
WHJP World History of the Jewish People
WMANT Wissenschaftliche Monographien zum Alten und Neuen Testament
WO *Welt des Orient*
WS *Wiener Studien*
WTJ *Westminster Theological Journal*
WUNT Wissenschaftliche Untersuchungen zum Neuen Testament
WUS J. Aistleitner, *Wörterbuch der ugaritischen Sprache*
WVDOG Wissenschaftliche Veröffentlichungen der Deutschen Orientgesellschaft
WZ *Wissenschaftliche Zeitschrift*
WZKM *Wiener Zeitschrift für die Kunde des Morgenlandes*
YBC tablets in the Babylonian Collection, Yale University Library
YOS Yale Oriental Series, Babylonian Texts
ZA *Zeitschrift für Assyriologie*
ZÄS *Zeitschrift für ägyptische Sprache*
ZAH *Zeitschrift für Althebraistik*
ZAW *Zeitschrift für die Alttestamentliche Wissenschaft*

ZDMG *Zeitschrift der Deutschen Morgenländischen Gesellschaft*
ZDPV *Zeitschrift des Deutschen Palästinavereins*
ZNW *Zeitschrift für die Neutestamentliche Wissenschaft*
ZPE *Zeitschrift für Papyrologie und Epigraphik*
ZRGG *Zeitschrift für Religions- und Geistesgeschichte*
ZTK *Zeitschrift für Theologie und Kirche*

ENTRIES

AB → FATHER

ABADDON

I. The noun *ʾăbaddôn* is derived from the Heb root אבד, which is common Semitic (cf. Ug and Aram *ʾbd*, Akk *abātu*) and means 'to destroy'. The Hebrew noun has the meaning 'place of destruction' which basically fits all occurrences in the Bible; only in the NT is Ἀβαδδών (Rev 9:11) construed as a proper name.

II. Though the religions of the ancient Near East know a considerable number of deities and demons relating to the netherworld, there occurs no divine name of such a being which can be derived from the root *ʾbd*. In the OT *ʾăbaddôn* occurs six times in Wisdom literature mostly meaning 'place of destruction'. Thus in Prov 15:11; 27:20 and Job 26:6 we find it in parallelism to *šĕʾōl* ('underworld'; →Sheol), while in Ps 88:12 *ʾăbaddôn* occurs in parallelism with *qeber* ('grave'). When *ʾăbaddôn* occurs without a parallel noun, as in Job 31:12, its reference is topographical. It is this locative aspect which can also be seen in the writings from Qumran (e.g. 1QH 3:16.19.32), partly again in parallel with *šĕʾōl*. In the Babylonian Talmud (*Er* 19a) it is given as the second of the seven names of Gehenna.

The mythological implications of Abaddon come to the fore in Job 28:22: *ʾabaddôn* and *māwet* ('death', →Mot) are both referred to as personified beings who can speak and hear. This is the biblical starting point for speculations about *ʾăbaddôn* as a separate entity, as the realm of an angel of death and the netherworld. We can mention, from *Apoc. Zeph.* 10:3, the angel Eremiel who resides in the underworld where all the souls are locked in; also *1 Enoch* 20:2 is comparable to this idea of a personified angel of the *ʾăbaddôn*. This is also the background of the use of Ἀβαδδών in Rev 9:11 as a proper name. After the fifth angel has blown his trumpet, the depth of the underworld is opened and smoke and huge locusts come up from it; their king is called "in Hebrew Abaddon, and in Greek he is called →Apollyon". This Greek expression is not only derived from the verb ἀπόλλυμι, but there is also an allusion to the Greek god →Apollo who is a god of pestilence and destruction; Aeschylus already (*Agam.* 1028. 1081; cf. Plato, *Krat.* 404e.405e) connects the god's name with this verb. Thus Ἀβαδδών or Ἀπολλύων can be seen as a demon who brings destruction and whose realm is the underworld.

The explicit use of *ʾăbaddôn* for a demonic being is rare, as it is used mainly as the name of a place. Maybe two occurrences of the word are secondarily open to personification: Prov 27:20 tells us that Abaddon cannot be satiated; this anthropomorphous diction may be a slight hint of Abaddon's demonic character. Also Job 26:5-6 is to be mentioned once more: In Job's speech, the shades in the underworld tremble before God and there is no shelter to cover Abaddon. Thus it is perhaps not too speculative to assume that Abaddon is not only a place of destruction but also a demon of destruction. But on the whole Abaddon's role as a demon certainly does not figure prominently in the Bible—though the OT is aware of such underworldly beings.

III. *Bibliography*

J. Jeremias, Ἀβαδδών, *TWNT* 1 (1933) 4; A. Oepke, Ἀπολλύων, *TWNT* 1 (1933) 396; B. Otzen, אבד ʾāḇaḏ, *TWAT* 1 (1970-1973) 20-24.

M. Hutter

ABBA → FATHER

ABEL הבל

I. Abel is a novelistic figure in Gen 4. His name is etymologically related to *hebel* 'breath; nullity; vapor' (→Vanities). He has been related to the personal name *é-bil* // *ʾà-bil* in texts from Ebla. Within the paradigm that the antediluvian patriarchs were demigods or at least heroes, GORDON seems to suggest, that Abel was a deity in Ebla (1988:154). In a later Jewish Hellenistic speculation Abel is seen as a judging →angel.

II. The texts referred to by Gordon point to a person called **Ebil* and not to a deity. The names *é-bil* (MEE II 12 Rev ii:6; II 7 Rev i:6) and *é-bí-lum* (MEE I 1044) are not preceded by the determinative for a deity. So the antediluvian Abel cannot be interpreted as a deity.

III. In the OT Abel occurs only in Gen 4:2.4.8-9.25. His name is derived from the noun *hebel* 'breath' (SEYBOLD 1974:337; HESS 1993) indicating that he is a person with a transient character. A connection with Akk *ibilu* and Arab *ʾibil* 'camel' (*HALAT* 227) is less probable.

In the Epistle to the Hebrews, Abel is seen as one of the 'heroes of faith' (Heb 11:4): "By faith Abel offered unto God a more excellent sacrifice than →Cain". The author of this letter refers to the unanswerable question why Cain's sacrifice was rejected and Abel's accepted. This problem is discussed in some Hellenistic-Jewish and Rabbinic sources too: Josephus, *Ant.* 1, 53-54 (God had more pleasure in animals linked with nature than in fruits as the product of culture); Philo, *De sacrificiis Abelis et Caini*; *Tg. Ps.-J.* Gen 4:8; T. *Sota* 4,19 (here Cain is listed among the ungodly). The Greek translation of Theodotion offers an independent interpretation according to which fire came down from heaven to consume Abel's sacrifice but not Cain's. Another passage from the Epistle to the Hebrews interprets the blood of Abel in christological terms (Heb 12:24).

In a throne vision in the longer recension of the *Testament of Abraham*, Abel is depicted as the "sun-like angel, who holds the balance" (ὁ ἄγγελος ὁ ἡλιόμορφος ὁ τὸν ζύγον κατέχων). As son of the first born in history, Abel is sitting as judge in heaven and he will judge the entire creation (*T. Abr. B* XIII:1-3; cf. FOSSUM 1985:276-277; MACH 1992:198, who wrongly quotes the passage as TAbr B 10,8f). In the shorter recension of the *Testament of Abraham*, Abel is seen only as an angel (*T. Abr. A.* XI:2). A relation with the angel *Hibil* known as a demiurg in Mandaic sources cannot be excluded (FOSSUM 1985:262-263).

IV. *Bibliography*

J. E. FOSSUM, *The Name of God and the Angel of the Lord. Samaritan and Jewish Concepts of Intermediation and the Origin of Gnosticism* (WUNT 36; Tübingen 1985); C. H. GORDON, Notes on Proper Names in the Ebla Tablets, in: *Eblaite Personal Names and Semitic Name-giving* (A. Archi ed.; ARES 1; Roma 1988) 153-158; R. S. HESS, *Studies in the Personal Names of Genesis 1-11* (AOAT 234; Neukirchen-Vluyn 1993) 27-28.223-225; M. MACH, *Entwicklungsstadien des jüdischen Engelglaubens in vorrabbinischer Zeit* (TSAJ 34; Tübingen 1992); K. SEYBOLD, הֶבֶל *hæbæl*, *TWAT* 2 (1974) 334-343.

B. BECKING

ABOMINATION שִׁקּוּץ

I. The singular noun *šiqqûṣ* 'abomination' as a dysphemism meaning 'god, goddess' appears seven times in the Massoretic text of Hebrew Scripture. This term refers respectively to (a) →Milcom, the chief god of the Ammonites (1 Kgs 11:5, 7); (b) →Chemosh, the chief god of Moab (1Kgs 11:5; 23:18); (c) Ashtoreth (→Astarte), the chief goddess of the Sidonians (2 Kgs 11:5, 7); and (d) the abomination of desolation (*šiqqûṣ mĕšōmēm*, Gk βδέλυγμα ἐρημώσεως, Dan 11:31; 12:1), which most modern interpreters identify with the statue of →Zeus Olympios which Antiochus IV Epiphanes set up in the Temple of the LORD (→Yahweh) at Jerusalem on December 6th in the year 167 BCE. It is generally agreed that the reading *siqqûṣîm mĕšōmēm* is the result of dittography and that the original and correct reading should be here also *siqqûṣ mĕšōmēm*, i.e., 'abomination (singular) of desolation'.

It is likewise generally agreed that the latter designation of Zeus Olympios is a play upon →Baal shamem, 'Lord of heaven', which is the Phoenician title of both Canaanite →Hadad and Greek Zeus, who were perceived to be the same deity under different names just as, *mutatis mutandis,* modern Muslims, Christians and Jews perceive Allah, Jehovah, and Adonai as different names for the same deity.

The plural *šiqqûṣîm*, 'abominations', refers to unspecified deities other than the LORD and their respective cult statues in Deut 29:16; Jer 7:30;16:18; 32:34; Ezek 5:11; 7:20; 11:21; 20:7, 8, 30; 37:23. Only in Zech 9:7 and Isa 66:3 is the plural *šiqqûṣîm* employed in the sense of *šĕqāṣîm,* 'non-kosher foods'. In Hos 9:10 the term means 'disgusting people', and it refers to the Israelites who were enticed by way of licentious behaviour with the Midianite women into worship of the Midianite deity, →Baal of Peor (cf. Num 25:3-5). In Nah 3:6 the noun *šiqqûṣîm* refers to disgusting objects (possibly excrement) which God promises to throw at personified Nineveh in order to bespatter the city which had until now attracted the admiration of all the world with her charms.

Unquestionably, referring to deities and their cult objects as *šiqqûṣîm*, whose primary meaning is 'disgusting objects', was meant to repel Israelites, who might otherwise be tempted to worship prohibited deities. In the same way, Lev 18 asserts that various types of sexual relations, which some persons might perceive to be alternative lifestyles, are so repulsive that they make even the personified land of Israel vomit.

II. *Bibliography*

R. GALATZER-LEVY & M. I. GRUBER, What an Affect Means: A Quasi-Experiment about Disgust, *The Annual of Psychoanalysis* 20 (1992) 69-92; L. F. HARTMAN & A. A. DILELLA *Daniel* (AB 23; Garden City 1978); J. MILGROM, Two Priestly Terms: šeqeṣ and ṭāmē', *Tarbiz* 60 (1991) 423-428.

M. I. GRUBER

ABRAHAM אברהם

I. The 'original' name of the patriarch *'abrām* belongs to the common stock of West Semitic names known since the beginning of the second millennium BCE. It is a contracted form of *'ăbîrām* (*HALAT* 9; DE VAUX 1968:11; 1 Kgs 16:32; Num 16:1; 26:9; Ps 106:17), written *abrm* in Ugarit (*KTU* 4.352:2,4 = [I]*A-bi-ra-mu/i*; *PRU* 3,20; 5,85:10; 107:8, cf. also Mari, H. B. HUFFMON, *Amorite Personal Names in the Mari Texts* [Baltimore 1965] 5), *'brm* in Elephantine (E. SACHAU, *Aramäische Papyrus und Ostraka aus einer Militär-Kolonie zu Elephantine* [Leipzig 1911] no. 75/1 II.8). It occurs perhaps also in the toponym *pȝ ḥqr ȝbrm* 'the fortress of Abram' mentioned in the Sheshonq-list (J. SIMONS, *Handbook of Egyptian Topographical Lists* [Leiden 1973] XXXIV:71-72; MEYER 1906:266; Y. AHARONI, *The Land of the Bible* [London 1979^2] 328; *pace* M. NOTH, Die Schoschenkliste, *ZDPV* 61 [1938] 291-292 = *Aufsätze zur biblischen Landes- und Altertumskunde* 2 [ed. H. W. Wolff; Neukirchen Vluyn 1971] 83-84), but identification with biblical Abraham remains extremely uncertain. *'Abrāhām* is an extended form of *'abrām*. The extension is rather due to reverence and distinction than dialectic variance. In historical times, tradition—confirmed by folkloristic etymology (Gen 17:5; Neh 9:7)—knew the patriach only by his name *'abrāhām* (Mic 7:20; Ps 47:10 etc.).

II. At one time the patriarchs were interpreted as local Canaanite deities (LUTHER 1901; MEYER 1906, cf. WEIDMANN 1968: 89-94) or in terms of astral myth (GOLDZIHER 1876:109-110, 122, 182-183; JEREMIAS 1906), particularly Abraham, since he was associated with centres of the Mesopotamian →moon cult (Ur and →Haran). →Sarah was equated with the moon-goddess and Abraham's father →Terah with the moon (= Yerah). Though in biblical tradition, there are allusions to the ancient cults of Abraham's place of origin (Josh 24:2), mythological interpretation of the Abraham-cycle plays no role in recent discussion. Still, the religio-historical role of father Abraham as the most venerated ancestor and saint of Judaism, Christianity and Islam (Matt 3:9; 8:6, Luke 16:22-23; John 8:39 etc.; Str-B I 116-121; III 186-201; JEREMIAS 1958; BUSSE 1988:81-92) and his mythic image as →Rock, i.e. begetter, (Isa 51:1) is of interest. This latter veneration of 'Father Abraham' may derive from an early Israelite, viz. Canaanite ancestral cult of Abraham at Machpelah (→Cybele) (WEIDMANN 1968: 27-30; LORETZ 1978:192).

Recent scholarship became sceptical about the historicity of Abraham and the patriarchal era (THOMPSON 1974; VAN SETERS 1975; BLUM 1984:491-506; KÖCKERT 1988:300-323). Tracing the origins of Abraham within the complicated traditions of the Pentateuch is extremely difficult. Pentateuchal traditions picture him as the founder of a number of cult-places (Shechem →Thukamuna, Gen 12:6-7; →Bethel, Gen 12:8; 13:3-4; Mamre, Gen 13:18; Beersheba, Gen 21:23; Moriah / Jerusalem?, Gen 22:2; 1 Chron 3:1); he came either from Ur or from Haran in Mesopotamia (Gen 11:27-32; 15:7); his pastoral and sedentary life is mainly concentrated in the environment of the Negev (Beersheba, E) and/or Hebron (Mamre, JP) and he was buried in the cave of Machpelah (Gen 23:1-20, JP; 25:1-7, P). Traditio-historical research basically agrees that his connections with Haran, Shechem and Bethel are of a secondary character and originated when tradition identified Abraham as the father of Isaac and ancestor of the Northern tribes (→Jacob; NOTH 1948: 112-127). The traditions of Mamre and the ancestral tomb of Machpelah near Hebron possess, however, a certain credibility. The traditions about Abraham, the Hebrew, who lived near the →Terebinths of the Amorite Mamre (Gen 14:13 with parallel accounts in Gen 13:18; 14:18; 18:1; 23:1.19) show that the cult of Abraham was originally at home around Hebron (ALT, *KS* 1, 54-55; JEPSEN 1953-54:144, 149).

III. Pre-Judaean traditions about Abraham were kept and fostered by the clan of Caleb, the Kenizite, who settled and lived at Hebron (Josh 14:6.13-15; 15:13-19 = Judg 1:10-15.20) before they merged with the Judaean confederation. At the sanctuary in Mamre-Hebron, Abraham was 'a father of many nations' as early as the emergence of the monarchy. At the end of the second millennium BCE at least two tribal federations, the Judaean Israelites and the Ishmaelites claimed Abraham as one of their ancestors. It is not until the end of the monarchic period, however, that in Judaean-Israelite tradition 'our father' Abraham emerges out of the shadow of Jacob (Isa 29:23; Mic 7:20), probably because of his more 'ecumenical' character (Jer 33:26; Ezek 33:24; Isa 41:8; 51:2; 63:16; VAN DER MERWE 1956:90-101, 121-124). Pleas based on the election of Abraham as friend and servant of God (resp. Isa 41:8; 2 Chr 20:7; Jas 2:23; cf. Gen 26:24; Exod 32:13; Ps 105:42; also Koranic *al-ḫalîl*, Surah 4:125) and his fathership of Israel may reflect a growing reverence for him as an ancestral saint and intercessor (Gen 18:22-33; 20:17; 23:6 [?]; cf. Isa 63:15-16; Str-B I 116-121). Abraham's image as a rock-begetter parallel to Sarah as a childbearing rock-cleft (Isa 51:1) may even refer to the ancient cult-legend of Machpelah (VAN UCHELEN 1968; *pace* FABRY, *TWAT* 4 1982-84:982). If so, it would be the oldest reference to Machpelah outside the Pentateuch. From Gen 23:1-20; 25:7-11 (P) it might be inferred that at the least in early post-exilic times the motif of the patriarchal tomb had become established in Israelite-Ishmaelite tradition. In this period Hebron was no Judaean territory (Neh 11:25), but part of the hyparchy Idumea (1 Macc 6:65; ALT, *KS* 2, 327-329; AHARONI 1979:416). Already at this stage the existence of Jewish and Idumaean pilgrimages seems to be implied and *Jub.* 22:3-4 and Josephus (*Bell.* IV 532) may confirm this. The present edifice which houses the epitaphs of the patriarchs and their wives, the Haram el-Khalîl, is a work of Herodian architecture (JEREMIAS 1956; WEIPPERT, *BRL*^{2}, 145 [& lit]). It was presumably built over a more modest shrine, called *byt ʾbrhm* (Heb *Jub.* 22:24; 23:6; DJD III 269; lat *baris Abraham*) also known as *byt hbrk* 'house of the Blessed' (*3Q*15 XII,8; Mur 43:2; LIPIŃSKI 1974:50-51). This 'house of Abraham/the Blessed' is most probably not identical with the cult-place of Mamre, which at present is located at Ramat al-Khalil, 3 km. north of Hebron (*Bell.* IV 533; 1QapGen XXI,19). Though Mamre is nowhere mentioned explicitly outside Genesis, it was an ancient sanctuary and a centre of pilgrimage (2 Sam 2:4; 5:3). According to Josephus the ancient terebinth, called Ogyges was still shown there (*Bell.* IV 533; *Ant.* I 186). The place was destroyed by Hadrian after the Bar Kochba revolt and turned into a marketplace. Constantine built a basilica inside the Herodian wall (Sozomenus, *Hist. Eccl.* II 4; JEREMIAS 1958; WEIPPERT, BRL^2, 145; MAGEN 1991). The still impressive remains of both places and the unbroken tradition testify to Abraham's religious significance as the father of all who are of the faith of Abraham (Rom 4:16), and to his ancestral cult, in the Haram el-Khalîl still observed by Jews, Christians and Muslims (JEREMIAS 1958).

IV. *Bibliography*

E. BLUM, *Die Komposition der Vätergeschichte* (WMANT 57; Stuttgart 1984); H. BUSSE, *Die theologischen Beziehungen des Islams zu Judentum und Christentum* (Grundzüge 72; Darmstadt 1988); I. GOLDZIHER, *Der Mythos bei den Hebräern und seine geschichtliche Entwicklung* (Leipzig 1876; repr. 1987); A. JEPSEN, Zur Überlieferungsgeschichte der Vätergestalten, *WZ-Leipzig* 2/3 (1953-54) 267-281 = FS ALT (Leipzig 1953-54) 139-155; A. JEREMIAS, *Das Alte Testament im Lichte des alten Orients* (Leipzig 1906); J. JEREMIAS, *Heiligengräber in Jesu Umwelt* (Göttingen 1958) 90-100; M. KÖCKERT, *Vätergott und Väterverheissungen* (FRLANT 142; Göttingen 1988); E. LIPIŃSKI, 'Anaq-Kiryat ʾArbaʿ-Hébron et ses sanctuaires tribaux, *VT* 24 (1974) 41-55; O. LORETZ, Vom kanaanäischen Totenkult zur jüdischen Patriarchen- und Elternehrung, *Jahrbuch für Anthropologie und Religionsgeschichte* 3 (1978) 149-203; B. LUTHER, Die israelitischen Stämme, *ZAW* 21 (1901) 1-76; Y. MAGEN, Elonei Mamre. A Herodian Cult Site, *Qadmoniot* 24 (1991) 46-55 [Hebr]; E. MEYER, *Die Israeliten und ihre Nachbarstämmme* (Halle 1906); B. J. VAN DER MERWE, *Pentateuchtradisies in die Prediking van Deuterojesaja* (Groningen 1956); T. L. THOMPSON, *The Historicity of the Patriarchal Narratives* (Berlin 1974); N. A. VAN UCHELEN, Abraham als Felsen (Jes 51,1), *ZAW* 80 (1968) 183-191; J. VAN SETERS, *Abraham in History and Tradition* (New Haven and London 1975); R. DE VAUX, *Die Patriarchenzählungen und die Geschichte* (Stuttgart 1968); DE VAUX, *Histoire ancienne d'Israel. Des origines à l'installation en Canaan* (Paris 1971); H. WEIDMANN, *Die Patriarchen und ihre Religion im Licht der Forschung seit Julius Wellhausen* (FRLANT 94; Göttingen 1968); M. WEIPPERT, Abraham der Hebräer? Bemerkungen zu W. F. Albrights Deutung der Väter Israels, *Bib* 52 (1971) 407-432; C. WESTERMANN, *Genesis 12-36*, BKAT I/2 (Neukirchen 1981).

M. DIJKSTRA

ADAT אדת

I. The Ugaritic male title *adn* (→Lord) for god and men has a female counterpart: *adt* (< **adattu* < **adāntu*). EISSFELDT (1939) proposed to read in the lament Jer 22:18 *wĕhôy ʾādāt*, 'oh, Mistress', implying that a female deity is invoked.

II. At Ugarit, *adt* occurs as the female counterpart to *adn*. *adt* is not only used to indicate the Ugaritic queen-mother, but also the mother-goddess as can be inferred from names like *bn adty* = DUMU *a-da-ta-ya* (*PRU* VI, 83 iv:11); ^{f}*A-da-ti-ya* (*PRU* III, p.114:29); *ʿbdadt* = ⌈ÌR-*a-da-te* (F. GRÖNDAHL, *Die Personennamen der Texte aus Ugarit* [StP 1; Roma 1967] 45.90; *KTU* 3.3:12; *PRU* VI, 79:19, 185:2'); *hyadt* (*PRU* II, 47:22); ^{f}*Šùm-a-da-te* (*PRU* VI, 107:6); [^{f}]*Um-mi-a-da-te* (*PRU* V, 107:7). The title *ʾdt*, 'mistress', is attested in Phoenicia for Baʿalat of Byblos (*KAI* 6:2; 7:4) and for →Astarte (*KAI* 29:2). In a proto-sinaitic inscription from Serabit el-Khadim →Baalat (= →Hathor) is given this epitheton (*CPSI* No. 37). It also occurs in Palmyra (J. CANTINEAU, *Syria* 17 [1936] 334-335; NOTH 1937:345). Finally, the Egyptian-Asiatic female personal name *ʾdwtw* (Papyrus Brooklyn 35.1446 vs 15a; SCHNEIDER 1987:264) must be noted. In Aramaic inscriptions the title *mr(ʾ)t/mārât* (= →Atargatis?) is used next to *mārāʾ*, 'lord', more than once (*DISO* 166-167; *KAI* 242).

III. It is not settled whether or not the female title 'mistress' for the divine occurs in the Old Testament. EISSFELDT (1938:489; cf. *HALAT* 12. 231) proposed to read in the lament Jer 22:18 *wěhôy ʾādāt*, 'oh, Mistress', (parallel to *ʾāḥôt* in the preceding colon), though the masoretic text, *wěhôy hōdô*, 'oh, his majesty', is rather clear (but see W. L. HOLLADAY, *Jeremiah 1* [Philadelphia 1986] 592, 597). The only indication that the title was known in an Israelite context is found in a Judaean seal belonging to a woman: *ʾdtʾ ʾšt pšḥr* (TIGAY 1986:65). Ugaritic and Palmyrene parallels suggest her name (and perhaps the woman) to be of foreign origin. If she was Israelite, her name reflects either the existence of the cult of a female deity like →Asherah in Judah or it was used despite its original non-Israelite character like e.g. Aramaic Martha who is attested in Jewish contexts (*DISO* 166; TIGAY 1986:71).

IV. *Bibliography*

O. EISSFELDT, Neue Belege für אדת "Herrin", *OLZ* 40 (1947) 345-346; M. NOTH, Zum phönizischen אדת, *OLZ* 31 (1938) 553-558; T. SCHNEIDER, Die semitischen und ägyptischen Namen der syrischen Sklaven des Papyrus Brooklyn 35.1446 Verso, *UF* 19 (1987) 255-282; J. H. TIGAY, *You Shall Have No Other Gods* (HSS 31; Atlanta 1986).

M. DIJKSTRA

ADDIRIM → NOBLE ONES

ADON → LORD

ADONAY → LORD; YAHWEH

ADONIS Ἄδωνις

I. Adonis (originally 'Lord', see Hesychius s.v.) is a hero of classical mythology, beloved by →Aphrodite and Persephone. He has been identified with a Phoenician god in Byblos who is referred to as ᵈDA.MU in the Amarna letters. The divine name *Adonis* occurs in Vulg Version of Ezek 8:14 instead of VL and LXX *Thammuz*. As *ḥemdat nāšîm*, 'Darling of women', Adonis occurs possibly in Dan 11:37. References to his cult are perhaps also to be found in some chapters of Isaiah.

II. According to classical tradition (e.g. Anton. Liber. 34; Apollod. III 14, 3-4; Ovid, *Metam.* X 298-739; Hygin., *Fab.* 58), Adonis was born from an incestuous union between the heroine Myrrha, who had incurred the displeasure of Aphrodite, and her own father Kinyras (or Theias), king of Cyprus (or of Assyria/Syria). He divides his time between the realm of the living and the underworld. Central themes in the myths about Adonis are Aphrodite's love for him, and his premature and shameful death; he was killed by a wild boar while hunting. His love and death are the subject of the Adonia festivals celebrated in classical Athens, in Ptolemaic Alexandria and in the Roman world. In addition to a ritual mourning, there were other rites varying with each locality and period. The Athenian celebrations (5th-4th century BCE) were a private festival; they were characterized by the high numbers of women participating, their atmosphere of frolic and licentiousness, and their ritual mourning. One of the chief items on the agenda was the preparation of the 'Adonis gardens', i.e. small earthenware pots in which seeds of cereals and vegetables had been planted; these began to sprout within a week, and were then left on the roofs under the summer sun. The miniature 'gardens', with seeds blooming in the dog-days and wilting as soon as they sprouted, were regarded as a symbol of an unfruitful agriculture; they were thought to represent the opposite of the normal cycle of seasons (e.g., Plato, *Phaedrus* 276 B; Simplicius, *in Phys*. VII 4). Likewise Adonis, beautiful and young but inefficient as a hunter, was deemed a paragon of anti-heroic behaviour. A young lover of deities who reigned over opposite realms, Aphrodite over the earth and Persephone over the underworld, Adonis was in many ways the opposite of the positive sides of matrimony and manliness. The private Athenian worship of Adonis by concubines and prostitutes contrasts with the public worship of →Demeter by wives and mothers. On account of the intrusion of such idiosyncratic values, the cult of the Greek Adonis marks a crisis in the city ideology. It is to be viewed as such rather than as a cosmic drama involving the death of a god (DETIENNE 1989).

A 4th century BCE inscription from Athens (IG II^2 1261) allows Cypriots in the city to celebrate the Adonis festival 'according to the customs of their homeland'—which shows that the rites varied locally. According to the account of Cyril of Alexandria (*in Isa* 18:1-2; 4th-5th century CE), the Adonis festival was a show performed in the sanctuaries by a chorus and by singers commemorating Aphrodite's journey to the nether world in search of her lover. According to Theocritus, however (*Idyll.* 15; 4th-3rd century BCE), the Alexandrinian Adonis festival was celebrated in the royal palace. The first day the participants celebrated the union between the two lovers, represented in the course of a banquet under a kiosk of dill stems and surrounded by fruits, delightful gardens, pots of perfumes and a big variety of cakes. On the second day the epithalamium gave way to a lament as the worshippers gathered for a funeral procession to carry the image of Adonis to the seashore. The Adonis celebrations at Byblos, on the Phoenician coast, described in pseudo-Lucian's *De Syria Dea* 6-9 (2nd century CE) were performed in the great temple of Aphrodite (→Astarte). Legend has it that the beginning of the rites was signalled by the arrival of a message sent by the women of Alexandria and carried by the waves to the harbour of the Poenician town, to the effect that Aphrodite had found Adonis. Occurring at about the same time of year, the reddening of the Adonis river which sprung from Mt. →Lebanon, was interpreted as a token of Adonis' death (*De Syria Dea* 6-7; cf. Cyril, *in Isa* 18:1-2.). The festival consisted of a period of general mourning, followed by the joyful proclamation that 'Adonis continues to live' beyond death. There is no reference to 'Adonis gardens'. The hero received sacrifices 'as if he were dead', women offered up some of their hair or engaged in sacral prostitution, and the celebrations ended on a note of cheerfulness.

According to local exegesis (quoted by the author of *De Syria Dea*, cit.), the Adonis of Byblos was a model of the Egyptian →Osiris, i.e. a great dying god of cosmic significance. Moreover, since Strabo (XVI 2,18) attests that Byblos was dedicated to Adonis he must indeed have been a god of high rank. It is probable that the cult of Adonis in Byblos continued the worship of a Phoenician →'Baal', conceived as a dying and rising god. This god was not merely a spring deity or a vegetation spirit, as Frazer believed, but an important city god comparable to →Melqart in Tyre and →Eshmun in Sidon. Honoured as king of his city, and heir of the ancient Syrian cult of royal ancestors, he was worshipped by the periodical celebration of his death and access to divine life. In fact, the classical tradition about the hero Adonis may well go back, ultimately, to a Syro-Palestinian model. The latter was often designated by a title (Baal, Adon) instead of a proper name. Finally, we must remember that in the 2nd century CE a temple was built for Adonis in Dura Europos, on the →Euphrates, where he was worshipped, perhaps together with the goddess →Atargatis (RIBICHINI 1981:166-167).

III. In the Vulgate version of Ezek 8:14 the name of Adonis is used to render Heb *Tammûz* and Gk Θαμμούζ (→Tammuz), for whom women were weeping in the temple of Jerusalem. It is possible that the reference is indeed to the Mesopotamian Tammuz whose cult was accepted by exiled Judaeans

(EISSFELDT 1970:21; DELCOR 1978:378). The Alexandrian translators of LXX did not bother to identify the god with Adonis, whose name and cult must have been known in Egypt, but are satisfied to transcribe Tammuz's name from Hebrew to Greek. Only in the 3th century CE is the identification of Greek Adonis with the Hebrew and Syriac Tammuz explicitly made (see Origen, *Sel. in Ezek* 8:13-14). The cult of the Mesopotamian god was considered to resemble that of Canaanaite Baal/Adon (RIBICHINI 1981:181-192; LORETZ, in *Adonis. Relazioni* ..., 32). The similarity was also noted by other exegetes (Jerome, *in Ezek* 8:14 and *Ep.* 58:3 [about mourning rites for Tammuz/Adonis in Bethlehem]; Cyril of Alex., *in Isa* 18:1-2 and *in Hos* 4:15; Theodoret, *in Ezek* 8:14; Procopius Gaz., *in Isa* 18:1-7; *Chronicon Paschale* 130 [PG 92, 329]; see also W. BAUDISSIN, *Adonis und Eshmun* [Leipzig 1911], 94-97, 352-54). There was some confusion between the Greek Adonis and the oriental Tammuz, also in later Syriac sources (see esp. Isaac Antioch., XXV 125-126; Theodore Bar Koni, *Lib. schol.* I [ed. Scher; Paris 1910] 204-205, 312-31; Melit., *Or. ad Anton. Caes.*, 5 ; Ishodad of Merv, Bar Bahlul, Bar Hebraeus, etc.).

Some commentators have taken the mention of the "one desired by women" in Dan 11:37 (combated by Antiochus Epiphanes) as an allusion to the cult of Adonis, 'thrice-beloved', according to Theocritus (XV 86) and Hippolytus (*Ref. haer.* 5:9). Yet there is not the slightest evidence in the historical records that Antiochus ever opposed the cult of Adonis. The expression *ḥemdat nāšîm* could mean simply 'the love of women' or, better, 'the desire of women'; then perhaps it merely points to the cruelty Antiochus showed toward all women he was sexually involved with.

Echoes of an Adonis ritual have also been found in the oracle against Moab in Isa 15 (BONNET 1987); some scholars believe that Isa 17:10-11 denounces the tending of miniature gardens for Adonis; the Hebrew expression *niṭʿê naʿămānîm* ('pleasant plants') could be understood as 'plants for the Pleasant One', the 'Pleasant One' being Adonis. In a similar way Isa 1:29-30; 65:3 and 66:17 have been said to contain references to sacrifices and other rites 'in the gardens' for Adonis (EISSFELDT 1970:19-20; DELCOR 1978). These interpretations are based on the hypothesis that the Adonis gardens, well-known in the Greco-Roman world, continued an oriental (esp. Syro-Palestinian) tradition (cf. the Egyptian 'beds of Osiris', or the Syro-Palestinian cultic practices in the gardens). This would mean that gardens were regarded as suitable places for ritual mournings for Baal, symbolizing fertility and revival (see XELLA, in *Adonis. Relazioni...*, 110-111, for the analogies between the Greek and biblical polemics about this cult).

IV. In the 3rd century CE, Origen (*Sel. in Ez* 8:14) sums up the exegesis of Adonis that was current in his days (see DE VAUX 1971): "The god whom the Greeks called Adonis is called Tammuz by the Jews and the Syrians, as they say. It seems that certain sacred ceremonies are practised each year; first, they weep for him as if he had ceased to live; then they rejoice for him as if he had risen from the dead. But those who claim to be specialists in the interpretation of Greek mythology and so-called mythical theology affirm that Adonis symbolizes the fruits of the earth: men weep when they sow the seeds, but the seeds grow and, by their growth, give joy to those who work the land". In fact, a 'resurrection' of Adonis, in the cults celebrated in Near East, is clearly testified not only by Origen, but also by Procopius, Cyril and Jerome. In several other literary sources, moreover, Adonis is said to be a symbol of the ripe and cut grain and contrasts with Attis as a symbol of spring flowers (Porphyry, *Imag.* 7 in Eus., *P. E.* III 11,12;13,14; Ammianus Marc. XIX 1,11; XXII 9,15). Note, finally, that the syncretism with other heroic or divine figures, by Greek and Latin authors, includes the identification of Adonis with Attis, Osiris, Pygmaion, →Dionysos, etc.; he is also termed Gingras, Aoios, Gauas, Kirris, Itaios, Pherekles, and lends his name to a river (Nahr Ibrahim), a kind of flower (anemone), fish, bird, song, and a metric verse.

V. *Bibliography*
**Adonis. Relazioni del Colloquio in Roma (22-23 maggio 1981)* (ed. S. Ribichini; Roma 1984); W. ATALLAH, *Adonis dans la littérature et l'art grecs* (Paris 1966); G. J. BAUDY, *Adonisgärten. Studien zur antiken Samensymbolik* (Beiträge zur klassischen Philologie 176; Frankfurt 1986); P.L. VAN BERG, *Corpus cultus Deae Syriae*, 2 vols. (Leiden 1972); C. BONNET, Échos d'un rituel de type adonidien dans l'oracle contre Moab d'Isaïe (*Isaïe*, 15), *SEL* 4 (1987) 101-119; M. DELCOR, Le problème des jardins d'Adonis dans Isaïe 17,9-11 à la lumière de la civilisation syro-phénicienne, *Syria* 55 (1978) 371-394; *M. DETIENNE, *Les jardins d'Adonis*, 2nd ed. (Paris 1989); R. DE VAUX, *The Bible and the Ancient Near East* (Garden City, NY, 1971) 210-237; *O. EISSFELDT, *Adonis und Adonaj* (Berlin 1970); O. LORETZ, Vom Baal-Epitheton *adn* zu Adonis und Adonaj, *UF* 12 (1980) 287-292; G. PICCALUGA, Adonis, i cacciatori falliti e l'avvento dell'agricoltura, *Il mito greco* (ed. B. Gentili & G. Paione; Roma 1977) 33-48; S. RIBICHINI, *Adonis. Aspetti 'orientali' di un mito greco* (StSem 55; Roma 1981); N. ROBERTSON, The Ritual Background of the Dying God in Cyprus and Syro-Palestine, *HTR* 75 (1982) 313-359; B. SOYEZ, *Byblos et la fête des Adonies* (Leiden 1977); B. SOYEZ, Adonis, *LIMC* I, 222-229; R. TURCAN, *Les cultes orientaux dans le monde romain* (Paris 1989) 142-146; P. WELTEN, Bethlehem und die Klage um Adonis, *ZDPV* 99 (1983) 189-203.

S. RIBICHINI

ADRAMMELECH אדרמלך

I. Adrammelech is a god worshipped by the people of Sepharvaim whom the Assyrians settled in Samaria, coupled with →Anammelech, 2 Kgs 17:31.

II. No attempt to identify Sepharvaim or its deities has yet commanded general acceptance. An interesting proposal has been produced by ZADOK (1976). Building on a study by DRIVER (1958) he argued that the place was Assyrian Saparrê, Babylonian Sipirani, from a putative Siprayn, situated in Chaldaea, south of Nippur. Its inhabitants could have revered gods with West Semitic names. Yet a location in Syria also deserves serious consideration, in view of the fact that Sepharvaim is mentioned after Hamath and Arpad in both 2 Kgs 18:34 and 19:13 (DAY 1989:46).

Since P. JENSEN proposed the minor emendation from *ʾdr* to *ʾdd* (*ZA* 13 [1898] 333 n.1), many scholars have accepted Adadmelech as a form of Hadad-melech, →'Hadad is king', encouraged by the reading of Adad-milki in cuneiform sources (so J. A. MONTGOMERY & H. S. GEHMAN, *Kings* [Edinburgh 1951] 476; DRIVER 1958; M. COGAN & H. TADMOR, *II Kings* [New York 1988] 212). Now the support has disappeared since O. PEDERSÉN has shown that the signs read Adad-milki are simply to be read Dada or Dadda, caritative forms of Adad (*OrSu* 33-35 [1984-1986] 313-316). Moreover, the divine name would appear in West Semitic as Hadad, *hdd*. If the Sepharvites were of Aramean or Phoenician origin, it is very unlikely that the name of their god would have lost its initial *h*, unless the Hebrew authors of Kings copied the information from a cuneiform text in Babylonian, which would not express it.

The Hebrew Text's reading is a perfectly acceptable West Semitic form, best reconstructed as *ʾaddîr-melek* 'the glorious one is king'. The adjective occurs in Ugaritic and in Phoenician. It is a title of →Baal in a 6th century BCE inscription from Byblos (*KAI* 9 B5). On fourth century coins of Byblos a local king is named *ʾdrmlk* (PECKHAM 1968:47-50). However, the root is absent from Aramaic, indicating a Canaanite or Phoenician origin for this deity. The movement of peoples and their cults by natural processes of migration and trade, as well as Assyrian deportations, could have brought a group of worshippers to Babylonia, only for their descendants to be transplanted to Samaria (see in general B. ODED, *Mass Deportations and Deportees in the Neo-Assyrian Empire* [Wiesbaden 1979]).

III. The Sepharvites honoured Adrammelech and his companion Anammelech by burning their children (2 Kgs 17:31). The expression *śārap* (*bāʾēš*), 'to burn (in/with fire)', has been interpreted as reflecting the deuteronomistic polemics against foreign deities (e.g. WEINFELD 1972). This view, however, has been seriously challenged (e.g. by KAISER 1976). Both Adrammelech and Anammelech may be seen as aspects of →Molech whose worship involved similar action. So long as no information about these gods or their home is available from other ancient Near Eastern sources, it is impossible to clarify the biblical references further.

The deity Adrammelech should not be confused with the character Adrammelech, the murderer of Sennacherib (2 Kgs 19:37; Isa 37:38; →Mulissu).

IV. *Bibliography*

B. BECKING, *The Fall of Samaria. An Historical and Archaeological Study* (SHANE 2; Leiden 1992) 99-102; J. DAY, *Molech: A God of Human Sacifice in the Old Testament* (Cambridge 1989) 41-46; G. R. DRIVER, Geographical Problems, *ErIsr* 5 (1958) 16-20; O. KAISER, Der Erstgeborene deiner Söhne sollst du mir geben, *Denkender Glaube* (FS C. H. Ratschow; ed. O. Kaiser; Berlin/New York 1976) 24-48; B. PECKHAM, *The Development of the Late Phoenician Scripts* (HSS 20; Cambridge, Mass. 1968); M. WEINFELD, The Worship of Molech and the Queen of Heaven and its Background, *UF* 4 (1972) 133-154; R. ZADOK, Geographical and Onomastic Notes, *JANES* 8 (1976) 114-126.

A. R. MILLARD

AENEAS Αἰνέας/Αἰνείας

I. Aeneas, already a prominent Trojan hero in Homer's *Iliad*, is best known to us as the central figure of Virgil's *Aeneid*, whose task it is to create the Roman identity and destiny. His name occurs as that of the paralysed man cured by Peter at Acts 9:33-34. The name appears to be Greek, based on the root for 'praise' (αἰν-). The form Aineas (as at Acts 9:33), as opposed to Aineias, is originally the Doric dialect form according to PAPE-BENSELER 1884 s.v.; the Latin is in either case Aeneas.

II. Aeneas, the son of lame Anchises and the Goddess →Aphrodite (Venus), is presented as a member of a cadet branch of the Trojan royal family and the most distinguished Trojan warrior other than Hektor. He is specially favoured and protected in the *Iliad*, by →Apollo, →Poseidon and of course Aphrodite. Poseidon is made to base this protection (*Iliad* 20:306-8) on a prophecy that Aeneas and his descendants will rule the Trojans after the destruction of the line of Priam. This leads to a legend of his travels to account for the existence of Aineia in the Chalkidike, whose coins depicted him as early as the late 6th century BCE (MALTEN 1931:35; GALINKSY 1969:111-112) and several other places and peoples in Greece (MALTEN 1931:56-57).

A special role in European cultural history is played by the development of the myth that Aeneas' arrival in Italy led to the foundation of Rome. Though elements may go back to Stesichoros in the 6th century BCE (GALINSKY 1969:106-13; OGILVIE 1965: 33, but cf. PERRET 1942:849), by the 5th century it was accepted (GALINSKY 1969: 77.103) that Trojans had reached Sicily (Thucydides 6, 2, 3) and that Aeneas had founded Rome (Hellanikos, *FGH* 4F84). This migration of the myth may be traceable to the western interests and westward movements of Phokaians in the 7th and 6th centuries BCE and, in particular, their association with the Etruscans (BÖMER 1951: 36-9). The theme was certainly securely established in Roman literary tradition long before Virgil's definitive presentation in his *Aeneid*. His epic depicts Aeneas as a man of exemplary piety towards the gods (as in his emblematic rescue of the holies from Troy), towards his family (as in his emblematic rescue of Anchises from Troy, carried on his shoulders) and towards his people. The character of Aeneas is instrumental in Virgil's presentation of a Roman mission to rule the world with civilised imperialism, reflecting the régime of Augustus and its claim to moral authority after the collapse of the Roman state into civil war (49-31 BCE).

III. It may seem curious that so elevated a name should be assigned to the cripple in

Acts 9:33-34, but Greek culture—to which the author of Acts belonged—was unlikely to have taken cognisance of a Latin text such as Virgil's. It is best regarded as a solid, traditional name dignified by its bearer in Homeric epic (→Jason). Examples occur, if not overly frequently, throughout Greek history—for instance, a Corinthian representative in Thucydides (4:119; 423 BCE), or an Arcadian general (367 BCE) mentioned by Xenophon who is the probable author of an extant work on military strategy ('Aeneas Tacticus'). FRASER-MATTHEWS list 35 instances (but 183 for Jason), several in the last century BCE, but very few after Christ, probably a sampling error. One Aeneas is an emissary sent by the high priest (late 2nd century BCE Pergamene decree in Jos. *Ant.* 14, 10, 22), the son of 'Antipatros', perhaps grandson of 'Jason' son of Eleazar, and the whole embassy is stocked with Jews bearing good Greek names.

IV. *Bibliography*

A. ALFÖLDI, *Die trojanischen Urahnen der Römer* (Basel 1957); F. BÖMER, *Rom und Troja: Untersuchungen zur Frühgeschichte Roms* (Baden-Baden 1951); P. M. FRASER & E. MATTHEWS (eds.), *A Lexicon of Greek Personal Names*, vol. I, 'The Aegean Islands, Cyprus, Cyrenaica' (Oxford 1987); G. K. GALINSKY, *Aeneas, Sicily, and Rome* (Princeton 1969); W. HOFFMANN, Rom und die griechische Welt im 4. Jahrhundert, *Philol.* Suppl. 27,1 (1935) 1-144 esp. 107-28; N. M. HORSFALL, The Aeneas-Legend from Homer to Virgil, *Roman Myth and Mythography* (ed. J. N. Bremmer & N. M. Horsfall; BICS 52; London, 1987) 12-24; L. MALTEN, Aeneas, *ARW* 29 (1931) 33-59; R. M. OGILVIE, *A Commentary on Livy Books 1-5* (Oxford 1965) 33-34; W. PAPE, revised by G. E. BENSELER, *Wörterbuch der griechischen Eigennamen* (Braunschweig 1884); J. PERRET, *Les Origines de la légende troyenne de Rome (281-31)* (Paris 1942) [but cf. A. Momigliano's review in *JRS* 35 (1945) 99-104].

K. DOWDEN

AH → BROTHER

AION αἰών

I. Aion does not occur as a divine name or concept in the Bible, although REITZENSTEIN (1921) followed by others (BAGD, *s.v.*) considered Aion in Eph 2:2, 7; 3:9 and Col 1:26 a deity, the evil ruler of the cosmos. Aion in Greek has a wide range of meanings, 'lifetime, life, age, generation, period, eternity' (LSJ, *s.v.*; *TWNT* I, 197-204), and can even be identical with cosmos.

II. REITZENSTEIN (1921) identified Aion with Persian *zervan akarana*, 'the endless time', and believed it a deity with a real cult. He based his opinion on a passage in Epiphanius, *Pan.* 52.22.8-10, describing a feast of Kore in Alexandria in celebration of her giving birth to Aion on the night of January 5-6. Aion is represented by a naked figure of wood on a bier which is carried seven times round the inner part of the temple. The same Ptolemaic Aion would be reflected in an Eleusinian dedication of a statue of Aion (IG II.4705) and in *Ps.Call.* 1.33, 2 (cf. Lydus, *De mens.* iv.1). Later research makes it highly unlikely that Aion in these contexts reflects either a Ptolemaic divine concept or deity or Persian *zervan* (NOCK 1934:79-99; FRASER 1972:336-338). The attribution of a festival to Aion was a late innovation, perhaps originating in Alexandrian coins of Antoninus Pius of 138/139 with the legend Aion and a representation of a →phoenix celebrating the beginning of a new era (VAN DEN BROEK 1972:417, 429-430). Aion often is an attribute of the sun god →Helios, who represents the course of time, and as such Aion occurs in the magical papyri (e.g. *PGM* I, 200; IV, 1169; FESTUGIÈRE 1954:176-199). Aion as a philosopical concept is frequently found in the Chaldaean oracles, where it represents the second god, a middle figure between the highest deity and the world (LEWY 1978:99-105). The philosophical sense going back to Plato, *Tim.* 37d, also appears in *Corpus Hermeticum* XI (FESTUGIÈRE 1954:152-175) and in Philo of Byblos, *Phoenician History*, in Eusebius,

Praep. Ev. I 10,7 (BAUMGARTEN 1981:146-148).

In particular during the second century of the common era, when nearly all these texts were written, there was a certain fascination with Aion and with all aspects linked with it, but Aion never was a well-defined divine concept, and certainly not a personal deity.

III. In the Bible *aiōn* is a very common word which usually has the meaning 'eternity' or 'world' (cf. Heb *'ôlām*). It never occurs as a divine concept or a deity *pace* Reitzenstein and his followers.

IV. *Bibliography*

A. I. BAUMGARTEN, *The Phoenician History of Philo of Byblos* (EPRO 89; Leiden 1981) 146-148; R. VAN DEN BROEK, *The Myth of the Phoenix according to Classical and Early Christian Traditions* (EPRO 80; Leiden 1972) 128, 429-430; A. J. FESTUGIÈRE, *La rélévation d'Hermès Trismégiste* IV. *Le dieu inconnu et la gnose* (Paris 1954) 141-199; P. M. FRASER, *Ptolemaic Alexandria* II (Oxford 1972) 336-338; H. LEWY, *Chaldaean Oracles and Theurgy* (sec. ed. M. Tardieu; Paris 1978) 99-105; M. P. NILSSON, *Geschichte der griechischen Religion* II (München 1950) 478-484; A. D. NOCK, A Vision of Mandulis Aion, *HTR* 27 (1934) 53-104 = *Essays on Religion and the Ancient World* I (Oxford 1972) 357-400; R. PETTAZONI, Aion-(Kronos) Chronos in Egypt, *Essays on the History of Religions* (Leiden 1954) 171-207; R. REITZENSTEIN, Das iranische Erlösungsmysterium, *Religionsgeschichtliche Untersuchungen* (Bonn 1921) 171-207; H. SASSE, αἰών, *TWNT* I, 197-208; O. WEINRICH, Aion in Eleusis, *ARW* 19 (1918/19) 174-190.

H. J. W. DRIJVERS

AL

I. Heb Ali or Eli (< *'ly*) and Alu or Elu (< *'lw*) have been identified as the shorter and more ancient forms of the term →Elyon (*'lywn*), 'Most High', mentioned in the Hebrew Bible. Elyon is a well documented divine name or epithet in biblical traditions and poetic passages like 2 Sam 22:14 = Ps 18:14 and Ps 21:8 unequivocally associate Elyon with the divine name YHWH (→Yahweh). Nevertheless, modern scholarship has identified Elyon as originally the name of an ancient Canaanite deity or as a divine epithet, that only with the passage of time made its way into early Yahwistic religious traditions. In support of this reconstruction, interpreters have cited the Ugaritic texts, the Hebrew onomastica, Philo of Byblos' treatment of the history of Kronos where Elyon is apparently mentioned, as well as the biblical form *'ly*.

II. A passage from one of the Ugaritic texts describes the deity →Baal as 'the Most High' and in this instance the short form *'ly*, not *'lyn*, is employed: *b'l 'ly* (*KTU* 1.16 iii:5-9). Another Ugaritic text written in syllabic transcription mentions "the fields of *'aliyu*" A.ŠÀ$^{hi.a}$ ^{d}*al-i-yi* (RS 18.22:3'-4 = *PRU* 6 [1970] 55, ll.3'-4'). It has been suggested that on the analogy of the phrase A.ŠA$^{hi.a}$ ^{d}IŠTAR, "the fields of →Ishtar", which appears elsewhere in the same text (1.6'-11'), Aliyu in 11.3'-4' might likewise function as the name of a god or as a divine epithet: "the fields of the Ascendant". Although the god →El at Ugarit is closely associated with the epithet 'Most High' in *KTU* 1.111:17-18: *'ly[n]//'il*, "Elyon... // El... ", the proposed reading and relationship of the two forms remains a matter of debate (cf. *KTU*, *pace* DE MOOR 1979:652-653 and note Old South Arabic *'l t 'ly*, "El the Most High", in *RES* 3882:4-5, 3962: 5-6, 3965:4, 4335:2-3 following U. OLDENBURG, *ZAW* 82 [1970] 189-190, 195 n.42).

In support of the existence of an ancient divine name or epithet *'ly[n]* it should be mentioned for the sake of completeness that a deity or divine epithet *ḫal-* (= *'al-*?) apparently shows up at Ebla and later at Mari. Whether or not this form is to be related to Heb *'ly[wn]*, 'Most High', however, is difficult to assess (it might be related to Semitic *ḫal*, 'maternal uncle'). In any case, Elyon's Canaanite origins as well as the distinct identities of Elyon and El appear again a millennium and a half later in Philo of Byblos' *Phoenician History*. In the fragments that have come down to us via Eusebius' *Praep. Ev.* (1.10:15-30), Philo depicts Kronos as the offspring of one Elioun (= Elyon). Moreover, Eusebius' Philo attributes to Elioun the status of Most High or *hypsistos* (→Hypsistos) and describes him as the object of ancient Phoenician worship following his death at the hands of wild beasts. Kronos on the other hand is equated with Elos (= El).

Ancient Hebrew onomastics might preserve the divine name or epithet *ʿly* in preexilic and exilic Israelite society. Hebrew inscriptional personal names preserved on bullae dating from the 6th cent. BCE attest to the function of the *ʿly* element as an epithet of YHWH or *yhw(h)*: *yhwʿly*, "Yahu is Most High", *ywʿly*, "Yaw is Most High", *ʿlyhw*, "Most High is Yahu" and *ʿlyw*, "Most High is Yaw" (N. AVIGAD, *Bullae and Seals from a Post Exilic Judaean Archive* [Qedem Monographs 4; Jerusalem 1976]). Moreover, the *ʿly* element in the personal name *yḥwʿly* inscribed on an 8th cent. BCE ostracon from Samaria might function as a divine name "May the Most High give life" (no. 55:2).

III. Scholars have cited several biblical texts where they conjecture that the short form of the epithet 'Most High', *ʿly* occurs. While most of the proposed passages have been rejected by scholars owing to the lack of textual or contextual support, there are a handful of biblical passages that might document the possible use of *ʿly* as a divine epithet or name associated with YHWH. Such passages include Deut 33:12; 1 Sam 2:10; 2 Sam 23:1 and Hos 11:7 and provide some ancient testimony or contextual indicators that lends support to the reading and interpretation of *ʿly* as 'Most High' (for a lengthy list of additional but less likely passages from Hosea, Isaiah, Jeremiah, the Psalms and Job, see VIGANÒ 1976).

Such criteria as the assumed antiquity of the poem preserved in Deut 33, exclusive reliance on its consonantal text (with the goal to reconstruct an original) and the assumed pervasiveness of the poem's synonymous parallelism have led to the identification of *ʿly* in v 12 (in its first ocurrence) as the divine name or epithet 'Most High' (cf. also NRSV). While on the one hand the text reflected in the medieval Hebrew codices of Deut 33:12a reads "may the beloved of YHWH rest securely beside Him" (cf. also *JPSV*) in which a Hebrew form corresponding to the 'Most High' is lacking, the ancient Greek manuscripts read on the other hand "the beloved of the LORD shall dwell in confidence, God (*ho theos*) overshadows him always ...". In other words, the *ʿlyw* of v 12a was apparently read by the Greek translators as some form of a divine name or epithet (perhaps *ʿly* 'Most High'). Although this could plausibly explain the Greek reading *ho theos* and the verse's restructured syntax, one would have expected the Greek equivalent *hypsistos* here. In any case, several of the versions omit the first *ʿlyw* of the medieval Hebrew manuscripts (Samaritan, Syriac, Vulgate) suggesting that synonymous parallelism was not inherent to the context. Thus the presence of the divine name or epithet *ʿly* here is doubtful.

The assumed antiquity of a given verse as well as the presence of synonymous parallelism has similarly infomed the reconstruction *ʿly* as 'Most High' in 1 Sam 2:10: "YHWH, his enemies will be shattered, the Most High will thunder in heaven, YHWH will judge the ends of the earth" (cf. NRSV). The medieval Hebrew manuscripts read however, "YHWH, his enemies will be shattered, He will thunder against them in heaven, YHWH will judge the ends of the earth" (cf. *JPSV*; →Ends of the earth) and there appears some ancient versional support for the reading of *ʿl(y)w* here as the preposition *ʿal-* with pronominal suffix (cf. the Syriac *wʿlyhwn*, Targum *ʿlyhwn*, Vulgate *et super ipsos*). In any case, the scribes of the ancient Greek manuscripts read *ʿl(y)w* not as the divine epithet or name 'Most High', but as a form of the verb ʿLH, 'to ascend', "the LORD has ascended to the heavens and has thundered".

In a passage from still another supposed ancient poem, 2 Sam 23:1, the form *ʿal* has been rendered as the divine name or epithet, "the man whom the Most High raised up". But in this instance the form could be the occasionally attested noun *ʿāl* 'height' (cf. also *JPSV* and Gen 27:39, 49:25, 50:4; Exod 20:4; Hos 7:16, 11:7). In any case, the Qumran manuscript of 2 Sam reads *ʾēl* at 23:1, that is 'El' or →'God' for *ʿāl* (4QSam[a]) "the oracle of the man (whom) El/God exalted" which is in essential agreement with the ancient Greek manuscripts "... the man whom God (*ho theos*) raised up".

The identification of *ʿly*,'Most High', in Hos 11:7 is based on the assumption that *ʿl* in the book of Hosea denotes the divine name or epithet associated with Baal that we earlier noted appears at Ugarit (cf. also Hos 7:16 and 10:5). According to this view, the prevalence of Baal polemic throughout the book justifies such a conjecture "to the Most High (*ʿal*) they call, but He does not raise them up at all". The reading of the ancient medieval Hebrew manuscripts is "when it (the people) is summoned upward (*ʿal*), it does not rise at all" while the Greek manuscripts preserve an independent reading "God shall be angry with his precious things". In the final analysis, the unlikelihood of the occurrence of the short form *ʿly* 'Most High' in the previously treated passages and the ancient versional witnesses in favour of the reading of *ʿal* as anything other than the divine name or epithet lessens the plausibility of reading *ʿal* as 'Most High' in Hos 11:7 (cf. the LXX on Hos 7:16 *eis outhen/ouden* "as nothing" = Heb *ʿal*; LXX Hos 10:5 *epi* = the third occurrence of Heb *ʿal* 'over, for').

The name of the priest at Shiloh, Eli, has been cited as further evidence for the presence of the divine name or epithet *ʿly* 'Most High' in biblical tradition. Whether the name indicates that the priest so designated once served a Canaanite deity *ʿly* (like Baal, cf. Ugarit) other than and prior to the appearance of YHWH, or that the hypocoristicon alludes to a title already appropriated by YHWH is impossible to decide on historical grounds. Although 1 Sam 3:1 states that "the word of YHWH was rare in those days", this might be taken to refer to the non-existence of the YHWH cult rather than to the neglect of YHWH's commandments.

In conclusion, while the epithet 'Most High' is attested in ancient Levantine cultures both in the form *ʿlywn* of biblical traditions and in the form *ʿly* of extra-biblical sources, the short form of the divine name or epithet *ʿly* does not appear in the Hebrew Bible.

IV. *Bibliography*

G. W. AHLSTRÖM, *The History of Ancient Palestine from the Paleolithic Period to Alexander's Conquest* (Sheffield 1993) 368-369, 390; M. DAHOOD, The Divine Name ʿEli in the Psalms, *Theological Studies* 14 (1953) 452-457; G. R. DRIVER, Hebrew *ʿal* ('high one') as a Divine Title, *ExpTim* 50 (1938-39) 92-93; J. HUEHNERGARD, *Ugaritic Vocabulary in Syllabic Transcription* (Atlanta 1987) 160; R. LACK, Les origines de Elyon, le Très-Haut, dans la tradition culturelle d'Israel, *CBQ* 24 (1962) 44-64; J. C. DE MOOR, Contributions to the Ugaritic Lexicon, *UF* 11 (1979) 652-653; H. NYBERG, *Studien zum Hoseabuch* (Uppsala 1935) 57-60, 74, 89; NYBERG, Studien zum Religionskampf im Alten Testament, *ARW* 35 (1938) 329-387; L. VIGANÒ, Nomi e titoli di YHWH alla luce del semitico del Nord-ovest, *BeO* 31 (1976) 34-62 [& lit, esp. p. 34 n. 4].

B. SCHMIDT

ALAY → AL

ALDEBARAN עיש

I. The noun עיש occurs in the Bible in Job 38:32, vocalized *ʿayiš*. The term *ʿāš*, which appears in Job 9:9, is generally considered a variant reading or a less correct form of *ʿayiš*; it has also been considered a dittography of *ʿśh*, which immediately precedes it (B. DUHM, *Das Buch Hiob erklärt* [KHAT; Tübingen 1897] *ad loc.*). The context of both occurrences in Job clearly shows that *ʿayiš* is the name of a →star or →constellation. Its etymological parallels Jewish Aramaic *yûtāʾ* and Syr *ʿyûtoʾ* and *ʿiyûtoʾ* always denote a star or constellation. Some scholars have deduced from these late occurrences that the correct Hebrew vocalisation should be *ʿayūš* or *ʿiyūš* (DRIVER & GRAY 1977:335). The Hebrew form is more likely to be of the type *qaṭl*, then extended in Aramaic to the *qaṭūl* type, reinterpreting the noun. Among the most noteworthy derivations are Ar *ʿay(y)ūṯ*, 'lion', 'ravager' (KB, 702 and *HALAT*, 778) and Ar *gaiṯu(n)*, 'rain'. The latter derivation is widely accepted (MOWINCKEL 1928:62-63; DRIVER 1956:2; HORST 1974[3]:146).

II. It is difficult to identify the star named *ʿayiš*. Valid reasons have been given for refuting the suggestion, above all based on an unsound etymology, of identifying it as the constellation of Leo. Indeed it is not easy to explain the entire expression in Job 38:32 *ʿayiš ʿal-bānêhā*, 'above' or 'with her children'. It has been supposed (KB, 702) that it may be the large constellation of Leo according to the ancient Arabic conception that does not recognize Cancer and includes the stars of the latter in Leo; furthermore the 'children' are the stars β, γ, δ, η of Virgo, that the Arabs call 'the dogs barking after the Lion'.

The most widely accepted opinion goes back to Ibn Ezra (SCHIAPARELLI 1903: 70-71; MOWINCKEL 1928:55) according to whom it is the constellation of the Great Bear (*Ursa Major*): *db*, *ʿglh*, *šbʿh kwkbym*. Most of the dictionaries preceding KB, and translations of the book of Job offer this interpretation. Some ancient authors (W. GESENIUS, *Thesaurus* II [Leipzig 1839] 894-896) associate this term with the Arabic root NʿŠ, from which derives the noun 'bier' or 'litter', which the Arabs use to denote the Great Bear. They call the stars ε, ζ, η that form the tail of the Great Bear or the shaft of the Plough *banāt naʿš*, daughters of *naʿš* ('the mourning women'), an expression that is reminiscent of the one in Job 38:32.

The Biblical context does not seem to confirm this interpretation. The verbs 'lead' and 'come out' (at a definite time), do not fit in well with the Bears, which are entirely circumpolar constellations for the latitude of Israel, and do not have periodical appearances but are present at night throughout the year. Supposing that the identification of the heavenly bodies mentioned in Job 38:31 *kymh* and *ksyl* with the →Pleiades and →Orion is correct, the identification of *ʿyš ʿl bnyh* of v 32 with Aldebaran and the Hyades emerges as the most plausible answer (SCHIAPARELLI 1903:72-76; MOWINCKEL 1928:62-64; DRIVER 1956:1-2; HORST 1974[3]:146; A. DE WILDE 1981:366-368), also in view of the many references to winter found throughout the text. In Job 9:9 *ʿš* is named along with *ksyl* and *kymh* too; the Pleiades, the Hyades and Orion are winter constellations grouped in the same portion of the sky, while the Great Bear is distant from them. Aldebaran, the giant red star which represents the eye of the Bull, seems to guide and overlook the Hyades arranged in a V formation behind it (the Assyrians called them *is lê*, 'jaw of the Bull'). The heliacal rising of Aldebaran and the Hyades in autumn coincides with the arrival of bad weather and rain. These stars are therefore believed to bring rain, and this would justify a derivation of the term *ʿayiš* from the Ar *gaiṯu(n)*.

III. In the book of Job there are undoubtedly traces of an ancient divine conception of the stars: see Job 15:15; 25:5 and particularly 38:7 where the expression *kôkĕbê bōqer*, morning stars, appears in perfect parallelism with *bĕnê ʾĕlōhîm* →sons of God. However in the passage under examination the constellations are mentioned to show the creative power and the organizing wisdom of the God of Israel.

Some scholars see in the expression *ʿayiš ʿal-bānêhā tanḥēm*, "can you guide Ayiš with her children?" (Job 38:32) a veiled reference to a myth (MOWINCKEL 1928:52-54) referring to a divine portent (for example bringing the lost children back to their mother). However, MOWINCKEL himself (1928:63-64) is sceptical about the existence of a saga relating to *ʿayiš*, and thinks that the image of a mother with her children is an immediate reflexion of the particular heavenly configuration of the constellation, and 'leading' in his opinion refers to its periodical and punctual appearances in autumn-winter season.

The LXX and the Vg evidently have

great difficulty in understanding *'ayiš/'āš*. The LXX renders the occurrence in Job 9:9 with 'Pleiades', and that in Job 38:32 with 'Vesper'; on one occasion the Vg translates it 'Arcturus' (and renders the Pleiades in the same verse with 'Hyades'), and on the other 'Vesper'. For the ancients they were all very important stars and were often named together. There is an enlightening passage in the Talmud, b.*Berakot* 58b-59a: it debates whether this constellation is the tail of Aries (the Pleiades) or the head of the Bull (the Hyades), and it narrates a cosmic legend according to which in order to stop a flood on the earth the Lord God took two stars from *'ayiš*. But one day He will return them to her and reinterpreting *tnḥm* as deriving from the verb NḤM, 'to comfort', the Talmud quotes Job thus: "and *'ayiš* will be comforted for her children".

IV. *Bibliography*

G. R. DRIVER, Two Astronomical Passages in the Old Testament, *JTS* 7 (1956) 1-11; S. R. DRIVER & G. B. GRAY, *The Book of Job* (Edinburgh 1977) 86, 335; F. HORST, *Hiob* (Neukirchen-Vluyn 1974³) 137, 146; A. KOHUT, *Aruch Completum ... auctore Nathane filio Jechielis* (Vienna 1878, New York 1892) I 332; IV 121; VI 277; S. MOWINCKEL, *Die Sternnamen im Alten Testament* (Oslo 1928) 52-64; G. SCHIAPARELLI, *L'astronomia nell'Antico Testamento* (Milano 1903) 69-76; G. SHARPE, *Syntagma Dissertationum quas olim auctor doctissimus Thomas Hyde S.T.P. separatim edidit* (Oxford 1767) I 27-29, 90-91; A. DE WILDE, *Das Buch Hiob* [OTS 22; Leiden 1981] 366-368.

I. ZATELLI

ALIYAN

I. The negation *lō'* revocalized as *lē'* has been interpreted as a divine epithet 'Victor' (e.g. M. DAHOOD, *Psalms I 1-50* [AB 16; New York 1966] 46; VIGANÒ 1976; COOPER 1981) derived from the root L'Y. The same root is at the basis of the →Baal epithets *aliyn* and *aliy qrdm* and the element *l'y/l't* in a number of West Semitic names, ancient titles of Baal and his consort (SZNYCER 1963). The name of →Jacob's wife →Leah (לֵאָה, Gen 29:16; Ruth 4:11) has been connected with the same root (*HALAT* 487).

II. Aliyan, usually translated as 'almighty, victorious, puissant', is a frequently used epithet in the mythology of the Ugaritic Baal. It is often seconded by other epithets like *rkb 'rpt* "→Rider-upon-the-Clouds", also twice in *KTU* 1.92, *zbl b'l arṣ* "the Prince, the Lord of the Earth, Baal" and *aliy qrdm* "the mightiest of heroes". Whenever used, *aliyn* always precedes the name of Baal, as is usual in epithets of gods; compare e.g. *ṯr il ab* (→El), *rbt aṯrt ym* (→Asherah), *btlt 'nt* (→Anat) and →*'ădōnay Yahweh* (→Yahweh). Aliyan never occurs as an independent divine name. From a stylistic point of view the epithet *aliyn* describes an aspect of Baal which distinguishes him from other gods. Outside Ugarit the epithet is possibly attested on the so-called Job-stela from Sheikh Sa'd dating from the reign of Ramses II (R. STADELMANN, *Syrisch-Palästinensische Gottheiten in Ägypten* [Leiden 1967] 45-46, but see also J. C. DE MOOR, *Rise of Yahwism* [Louvain 1990] 126).

In *KTU* 1.5 ii:17-18 one finds the singular phrase *aliyn bn b'l*, but this is most probably a scribal error (see *CTA*, p. 33 n. 1; GESE 1970:122, different *ARTU* 73). On the basis of this and other—scanty—evidence Dussaud assumed the existence of an originally independent Canaanite god Aliyan, a god of →sources and perennial →rivers whose realms are the depths of the →earth. This lord of the earth (*b'l arṣ*) was first adopted as Baal's son and finally identified with the Northern Baal in the double name Aliyan-Baal (DUSSAUD 1941). Neither the religio-historical evidence, nor the literary patterns of the Baal-myth are in favour of this hypothesis (SZNYCER 1963:26-27; GESE 1970:123-124; VAN ZIJL 1972:341-345). R. DUSSAUD (La mythologie phénicienne d'après les tablettes de Ras Schamra, *RHR* 104 [1931] 387), H. BAUER (Die Gottheiten von Ras Schamra, *ZAW* 51 [1933] 97) and EISSFELDT (1939) may be right in their assumption that the Greek word αἴλινος, either understood as a wailing cry or as a noun meaning 'dirge', goes back to the phrase *iy aliyn bʿl iy.zbl.bʿl.arṣ* as in *KTU* 1.6 iv:15-16 (cf. →Jezebel). Whether this implies a connection between Aliyan and the Greek hero →Linos is less certain. In all probability the Ugaritic epithet *aliyn* did not originate as the name of an older god of vegetation.

The epithet *aliy qrdm* appears only in the fixed formula that introduces Baal's messages: *tḥm aliyn bʿl ḥwt aliy qrdm* (*KTU* 1.3 iii:13-14 passim); the parallelism with *aliyn* suggests that the latter was the shortened form of this epithet. *aliy* is usually understood as an adjective on the pattern of **aqṭalu*, perhaps with superlative force. A translation of both *aliyn* and *aliy* 'most vigorous', indicating Baal's vigour and youthfulness as distinctive aspects of his divinity, is more appropriate than 'victorious'. *qrdm* is most probably a plural noun to be connected with Akk *qarrādu* or *qurādu*, also an epithet of the weather-god Adad (→Hadad). For a similar expression cf. *li-ʾ-um qar-du* 'heroic warrior' (*BWL* 86: 263). DIETRICH & LORETZ (1980), however, mention the possibility of a chthonic aspect, relating *qrdm* to Mandaic *qardum* 'spirit, demon'. This would tally with Baal's connection to the *rpum* in *KTU* 1.6 vi and *KTU* 1.22 i (→Rephaim).

III. The verbal root Lʾ Y ('to be strong, vigorous') is attested in Ugarit (*KTU* 1.14 i:33; 1.16 vi:2.14; 1.100:68) together with a number of derivations other than *aliyn* or *aliy* like *tliyt* 'victory' or 'power' (*KTU* 1.19 ii:35-36 *//nṣḥy*), *lan* 'strength' (*KTU* 1.108:24-25) and perhaps also in the female divine epithet or name *alit (KTU* 1.90:19; J. C. DE MOOR, The Semitic Pantheon of Ugarit, *UF* 2 [1970] 187-228 no.27). Nevertheless, the root Lʾ Y with the opposite meaning 'to be weak' also occurs (*KTU* 1.3 v:18 and parallels). The same semantic polarity was probably developed in Akkadian, followed by a phonetic distinction *laʾû(m)* 'weak, infant' and *leʾû* 'to be strong, able' (*AHW* 540; *CAD* L 151-156; 160-161). It exists in Aramaic, in which language also a phonetic variant Lʿ Y/Lʿʾ occurs (*DISO* 133 s.v. לאי, 138 s.v. לעי; JASTROW, *Dictionary*, 714 s.v. לעי), and most probably in Hebrew too (RINGGREN 1982-84:409; SZNYCER 1963). In Hebrew, however, contrary to Ugaritic, the meaning 'to be weak, exhausted' prevails. Compare, for instance, *tĕlāʾâ*, 'hardship, trouble' versus Ugaritic *tliyt* 'victory' or 'power'. In Hebrew the verb sometimes implies strong efforts and exertion, usually in vain (Gen 19:11; Isa 47:13; Jer 20:9). There is no proof whatsoever that it should still have the meaning 'to be victorious, vanquish' in Ps 68:10 (*pace* e.g. M. DAHOOD, Hebrew-Ugaritic Lexicography IV, *Bib* 47 [1966] 403-419, esp. 408 s.v. לאה; E. LIPIŃSKI, Les conceptions et couches merveilleuses de ʿAnath, *Syria* 42 [1965] 45-73, esp. 68 n. 3; DE MOOR, *Rise of Yahwism*, 120 n. 93). In the light of the inner-Hebrew semantic development of the root Lʾ Y, the existence of a divine epithet *lōʾ* or *lēʾ*, 'victor' in Hebrew is most improbable (cf. M. Pope apud COOPER 1981:428-431).

IV. *Bibliography*

A. COOPER, Divine names and Epithets in the Ugaritic texts, *RSP* III (Rome 1981) 333-469; M. DIETRICH & O. LORETZ, Die Baʿal-Titel *bʿl arṣ* und *aliy qrdm*, *UF* 12 (1980) 391-392; R. DUSSAUD, *Les découvertes de Ras Shamra (Ugarit) et l'ancien Testament* (Paris 1941) 101-102; O. EISSFELDT, Linos und Alijan, *Mélanges Syriens offerts à Monsieur René Dussaud* (F. Cumont et al.; Paris 1939) Vol. 1:161-170 = *KS* 3 150-159; H. GESE, *RAAM* (Stuttgart 1970) 121-122; O. LORETZ, Die Titelsucht Jahwes im Panugaritischen Aberglauben, *UF* 10 (1978) 350-352; H. RINGGREN, לאה *lāʾāh*, *TWAT* 4 (1982-84) 409-411; M. SZNYCER, A propos du nom propre punique *ʿbdlʾy*, *Sem* 13 (1963) 21-30; L. VIGANÒ, *Nomi e titoli di YHWH alla luce del semitico del Nord-ovest* (Rome 1976) 34-118; P. VAN ZIJL, *Baal. A Study of Texts in Canaan with Baal in the Ugaritic Epics* (AOAT 10; Neukirchen-Vluyn 1972) 341-345.

M. DIJKSTRA

ALLON → OAK

ALMAH → VIRGIN

ALMIGHTY παντοκράτωρ

I. *pantokratōr*, 'almighty', 'all-sovereign', 'controlling all things', as a divine designation, occurs both as an adjective and as a noun. Found relatively rarely in pagan literature, it is used frequently for God in the LXX and in early Jewish writings. In the NT this is continued in the Revelation of John, which calls God *pantokratōr* 9 times. Otherwise, the word can be found once more in Paul (2 Cor 6:18), and there it is a quotation from the OT.

II. In the pagan sphere, *pantokratōr* occurs from time to time as an attribute of deities such as →Hermes (Epigr. Graeca 815, 11; *PGM* 7,668), Eriunios Hermes (*CIG* 2569,12), Isis (IG V 2,472) and the Egyptian sun-god Mandulis (*SB* 4127,19). In addition there are paraphrases of the term, as for example in this (Egyptian) inscription: *Dii tōi pantōn kratounti kai Mētri megalēi tēi pantōn kratousēi* (*SIG* 3,1138,2-4). This could be at least partially due to Jewish influence (see KRUSE 1949).

III. Bearing in mind the sparseness of the pagan references, there is a remarkable frequency in the LXX's use of *pantokratōr* as a divine designation (ca. 180 times). For the most part (ca. 120 times) it is a rendering of *ṣĕbāʾôt* (→Yahweh zebaoth), a feminine plural of *ṣābāʾ* = armies. This is usually interpreted as an intensive abstract-plural, i.e. as an expression of divine might. There are an additional 60 or so uses of the term *pantokratōr* in the LXX, 16 of them in the Book of Job, as a translation of *šadday* (→Shadday). If the rendering of *ṣĕbāʾôt* as *pantokratōr* is not necessarily conclusive, then this translation of *šadday*, whose etymology can no longer be definitely clarified, is at least dubious. What is more, the LXX has some dozen of occurrences of *pantokratōr* which do not appear in the Hebrew text. This shows that the concept of God's power was reinforced by the translators of the LXX, and sometimes even introduced (as is the case, by the way, with *kyrios* as the translation of the tetragram). This should probably be understood as a Jewish reaction to the idea of a comprehensive global power, introduced by Alexander the Great and adopted by the Hellenistic monarchies and, finally, by the Roman Empire, an idea which, after all, is also given a religious basis (cf. the religious epithets of the rulers, such as *sōtēr*, *epiphanēs*, *deus et dominus*, etc. →ruler cult). The Hellenistic and Roman sense of mission and superiority thus expressed, resulted not only in the continued political and increasing economic dependence of Palestine, but also in greater pressure on Jewish belief, and on the way of life it conditioned in Israel and the diaspora, to assimilate to Hellenistic culture (cf. 1 Macc 1:11-15). In what was probably a conscious move to keep at a distance from this concept, the translators of the LXX emphasised the (already current) concept of the power of their God over the whole of his created reality.

The early Jewish apocryphal and pseudepigraphical literature confirms this interpretation. Presumably written between 150 and 100 BCE, the Book of Judith mentions *kyrios pantokratōr* five times, always in the context of inimical threat either still existing or having been repelled (Jdt 4:13; 8:13; 15:10; 16:5.17). Significantly, the final song of Judith ends with the prospect of the ultimate victory of *kyrios pantokratōr* against all the enemies of God's People: "Woe to the nations that rise up against my people. The Lord Almighty will punish them on the Day of Judgement" (Jdt 16:17). Similarly, also in the context of inimical threat and inimical repulsion, 2 Macc speaks of God as the Almighty (cf. 2 Macc 1:25; 3:22.30; 8:24; 15:8). A characteristic example of the polemical edge to this divine designation is the speech of Judas Maccabeus, who rouses his people to attack with the words: "They ... trust both to weapons and audacity, but we rely on the God Almighty, who is able to overthrow our assailants and the whole world with a nod of His head" (2 Macc 8:18). It is therefore appropriate that this

'Almighty' is presented in 2 Macc as the judge of human deeds and misdeeds (6:26; 7:35.38; 8:11 cf 15:32). Also significant is the use of this divine name in 3 Macc, the work of an Alexandrian Jew of the 1st century BCE. In the face of Ptolemy IV Philopator's intention to enter the temple (3 Macc 1), the high priest Simon appeals to God against this arrogant ruler: "LORD, LORD (*kyrios*), king (*basileus*) of heaven, ruler (*despotēs*) of all creation, holy among holy ones, sole ruler (*monarchos*), all-sovereign (*pantokratōr*), pay heed to us who are sorely vexed by a wicked and corrupt man, reckless in his effrontery and might. For you who created all things and govern (*epikratōn*) the whole world are a just ruler (*dynastēs*) ..." (3 Macc 2:2-3). With unique intensity, this *invocatio* heaps upon God almost all the available titles for rulers in order to identify him as the true ruler of this world in the face of pressing political pressure. Correspondingly, the first part of the ensuing *pars epica* recapitulates the salvation history in the context of God's resistance to the arrogant ruler. It closes with the praising of God as ruler (*dynasteuōn*) of all creation and as all-sovereign (*pantokratōr*). The ensuing reminder to God of his promises (vv 9-12) is in turn introduced with the invocation to God as king (*basileus*), an address that then finally also introduces the *prex ipsa* (vv 13-20) (*hagios basileus*). A similar structure can be found in the prayer of Eleazar in 3 Macc 6. Like the threatened people (3 Macc 5:7), he too invokes God as *pantokratōr*, and the God who then comes to the aid of the Jews against their persecutors is thus named (3 Macc 6:18) and recognised (3 Macc 6:28).

Philo—presumably due to the Stoic doctrine of the *hēgemonikon*—prefers the designation *panhēgemōn* for God; he uses the term *pantokratōr* only twice, more or less as a formula (*Sacr AC* 63; *Gig* 64). *Pantokratōr* is used in a similarly formulaic way in a few pseudepigraphical writings, as a form of divine address by mortals (*3 Bar* 1:3; *4 Bar* 1:5; 9:5; Pr Man 1) or angels (*T. Abr.* 8:3; 15:12), and in a blessing (*Ep. Arist.* 185). But what is noticeable here is that the address is almost always linked with God's creation, often with his day of judgement, and sometimes also explicitly with his sovereignty and his kingdom (cf. Philo *Gig* 64; *T. Abr.* 8:3; 15:12). Furthermore, *3 Bar* 1:3; *4 Bar* 1:5; 9:5 and probably also *Pr Man* 1 (cf. 2 Chr 33:1-20) are in the context of enemy repulsion and the request for God's help and power. Perhaps it is because of these political implications that *pantokratōr* does not occur in Josephus. The all-sovereignty of God in *Ant* 10,263 is paraphrased (by the Persian Great King Darius) as *to pantōn kratos echōn*.

Surveying all this, it is noticeable that in early Judaism the addressing or designation of God as *pantokratōr* can be found with amazing frequency in the context of enemy threat. The emphasis on 'all-sovereignty' seems mainly directed against the claim for power (also religiously based) by the Hellenistic and Roman rulers. The Jews counter this claim for power with the declaration of belief in the global sovereignty of their God as Creator and Judge. Finally, the divine designation *pantokratōr* must presumably be understood as a Hellenistic-Jewish equivalent to the concept of the Kingdom of God (*basileia tou theou*), also very important for the preaching of Jesus.

IV. A look at the NT reveals two contrasting tendencies. Outside the Revelation of St John the word occurs only once in 2 Cor 6:18 at the end of a combination of Old Testament quotations. The Pauline origin of the whole section 2 Cor 6:14-7:1 is disputed. However that may be, it is remarkable that the divine predicate occurs in a passage where the community is urged to make a radical break away from the 'unbelievers' with a harshness of tone that is without parallel in the whole of the Corpus Paulinum.

For most of early Christianity, then, the divine name *pantokratōr* does not seem to have been of major importance although, as the example of 2 Cor 6:18 shows, it was not consciously avoided. The Revelation of St John offers a picture that deviates completely from this, with *pantokratōr* occurring nine times as God's epithet (1:8; 4:8; 11:17; 15:3; 16:7.14; 19:6.15; 21:22). This is no accident and confirms again the 'political' character of this divine attribute. The Revelation of John, written in a desperate situation regarded by the seer as a prelude to a satanic attempt to exterminate the Christians, opposes the Roman Empire and its claim to power with a harshness that is unique in the NT. In opposition to this world power, which, as the 'whore of Babylon', is →Satan's henchman, John the seer announces God's new world, which will reverse all present injustices and bring about final salvation. The prerequisite of this hope, however, is the certainty that God is already the lord of the whole world and has checked the apparently triumphant forces of evil, has indeed even defeated them (cf. Rev 12:7-12). The shortened expression *ho theos ho pantokratōr* occurs twice in connection with God's, or his Messiah's, battle against the godless people and their kings (16:14; 19:15). The more detailed expression *kyrios ho theos ho pantokratōr* is used seven times. This is the case five times in hymnic passages; in the initial vision of the throne it is the four beasts who sing his praises night and day with the Trishagion (Rev 4:8, with the *sabaōth* from Isa 6:3 LXX being transformed into *pantokratōr*). Another three times God is praised for the judgement he has carried out—by the 24 elders (11:17), by those who had been rescued (15:3), and by the altar (16:7). And finally a great multitude acclaims him because he has begun reigning his kingdom (19:6). The expression occurs again at the beginning and the end of the book. At the beginning God presents himself as he who is, who was, and who is to come (1:8). The core of this statement is 'to come', i.e. that God as the lord of history also has the future of this world in his hands (cf. also 4:8 and 11:17). God is called Almighty for the last time in 21:22, in the description of the celestial city that needs no temple since God himself has his throne in it (cf. 22:3). This latter point again suggests the motif of God's reign over his kingdom, a motif which occurs astonishingly often in the Revelation of St John in connection with the designation of God as *pantokratōr*. It is directly mentioned in 11:17 (*ebasileusas*), 15:3 (*ho basileus tōn ethnōn*), 19:6 (*ebasileusen*) and 19:16 (*basileus basileōn*). The divine attribute *pantokratōr* therefore stresses, in opposition to the Roman Empire's claim for world power, God's royal power, which embraces the whole cosmos. However, this power is—typically apocalyptic—still hidden; God must first bring it to light in the battle against the anti-divine forces.

In the early Christian literature, *pantokratōr* is occasionally used for God (cf. *Did* 10,3; *1 Clem.* 2,3; 32,4; 60,4; 62,2), sometimes explicitly setting off God the Father against the Son (cf. Pol., *2 Phil*, prol.; Justin, *dial.* 16,4). But even Clement of Alexandrina calls Christ, the Father's →Logos, *pantokratōr* (*Paed.* 1,9; cf. also Irenaeus, *Adv.Haer.* 5,18,2), and Origen makes parallel use of the predicate for both Father and Son (*Sel. in Ps.* 23:10). Under the pressure of the anti-Arian controversy, Athanasius then emphatically called Christ *pantokratōr* (cf. *Or. 2 c. Arian* 23).

In summary, the following points can be emphasized: *pantokratōr* as a divine designation intends to express something similar to the more dynamic concept of the kingdom of God, namely that God is the Lord of his Creation and that in it he has realised or shall realise his will. Seen in this way, this divine designation is a declaration of faith by means of which the believers adhere to their God against a reality in which this God is painfully hidden and in which completely different beings conduct themselves as lords and saviours of the world. It is sensible to recall this original '*Sitz im Leben*' because the common idea of the Pantocrator as the inapproachable celestial ruler is too strongly influenced by the Byzantine image of →Christ, used by a now Christian empire to create a divine ideal in order to legitimise its own claim to world power.

V. *Bibliography*

P. BIARD, *La puissance de Dieu* (Paris

1960); T. BLATTER, *Macht und Herrschaft Gottes* (Fribourg 1962); A. GRILLMEIER, *Jesus der Christus im Glauben der Kirche*, Vol. 1 (Freiburg, Basel, Vienna 1979) 94-95; A. DE HALLEUX, Dieu le Père tout-puissant, *RTL* 8 (1977) 401-422; D. L. HOLLAND, Παντοκράτωρ in NT and Creed, *Studia Evangelica* VI (1973) 265-266; H. HOMMEL, Pantokrator, *Theologia Viatorum* 5 (1953/1954) 322-378; H. HOMMEL, *Schöpfer und Erhalter* (Berlin 1956); G. KRUSE, Παντοκράτωρ, *PW* 18,3 (1949) 829-830; H. LANGKAMMER, Παντοκράτωρ, *EWNT* 3 (1982) 25-27; W. MICHAELIS, κρατέω κτλ., *TWNT* 3 (1938) 913-914; R. ZOBEL, צְבָאוֹת ṣᵉbā'ôt, *TWAT* 6 (1989) 876-892.

R. FELDMEIER

ALÛ → AL

ALUQQAH → VAMPIRE

AM עם

I. *ʿAm(m)* occurs widely as a theophoric element in Semitic proper names, although in the cuneiform texts it is not ordinarily marked by the determinative indicating divinity. Among the names that are commonly classified as "Amorite", there are over two hundred with *ʿAmm* as an element. This represents by far the largest group; but *ʿAm(m)*-names are also attested in epigraphic Arabic (Qatabanian, Safaitic, and Thamudic), Hebrew, Ugaritic, Old Aramaic, Phoenician, Punic, Ammonite, Moabite, and, perhaps, Eblaite. Occurrences of the deity ʿAm(m) in the Hebrew Bible are limited to personal names and place names.

II. On the one hand, *ʿAm(m)* occurs frequently in the position normally taken by a divine name, as in Amorite *Ì-lí-ḫa-mu = ʾIlī-ʿammu* "My God is *ʿAmm*" (*RA* 57 [1963] 178), Heb *ʾlyʿm* "My God is *ʿAm(m)*" (2 Sam 11:3; cf. Ammonite *ʾlyʿm* [HERR 1978:35], Phoen *ʾlʿm* [*CIS* 147.6]; Safaitic *ʿmʾl* [see RYCKMANS 1934:244]) and *ʾdnʿm* "My Lord is *ʿAm(m)*" attested in a Samaria Ostracon (LAWTON 1984). This suggests that *ʿAm(m)* was perceived to be a divine name or a substitute for one. On the other hand, *ʿAm(m)* also appears as an appellation in some cases. This is suggested by the occurrence of the element with the pronominal suffix (e.g. Amorite *A-a-ḫa-mu-ú= ʾayya-ʿammu-hū*, *BASOR* 95 [1945] 23) and/or with obvious divine names, as in the Akkadian names *Amma-Suʾen* (*A-ma-*ᵈ*EN.ZU* in MDP II, A 5:3), Amorite names analyzed as *ʿAmmī-ʾIl*, *ʿAmmī-Hadad*, *ʿAmmī-Dagan*, and *ʿAmmī-ʿAnat* (see GELB 1980), Hebrew *ʿmyʾl* (Num 13:12), or Moabite *kmšʿm* (HERR 1974:156). In each case, the meaning of the personal name is "(the god) so-and-so is (my) *ʿAm(m)*". In a few instances, *ʿm* appears to be hypocoristic, as in Phoenician *ʿm*, *ʿmy*, *ʿmʾ* (see BENZ 1972). Several Eblaite names, too, may be so analyzed (KREBERNIK 1988). The names in such cases probably stood for fuller, presumably theophoric, names.

The element *ʿAm(m)* is most commonly connected with Arabic *ʿamm* "paternal uncle", a term contrasted with *ḫāl* "maternal uncle". Thus, Amorite *Ḫammurapi* has correctly been compared with *Ḫālurapi* (HUFFMON 1964). Levy's explanation of the theophoric element in names like *Ḫammurapi* as coming from ḤMM "to be hot" (hence designating a solar deity) is belied by the spelling of the name at Ugarit as *Am-mu-ra-pi* (*PRU* IV, Pl. LVII, 17.355, 12, 16) and *ʿmrpi* (*KTU* 2.39:2; LEVY 1944). The theophoric element is *ʿAmm*, which was understood as "Paternal Uncle" in old South Arabic (so *RES* 2775.1-2). On the other hand, in a Kassite king-list, Amorite *ḫammu* is interpreted as *kimtum* "family, kin". Thus, *Ḫammurapi* is interpreted as *Kimtum-Rapaštum* "Extensive Family" (i.e. *ʿAmmu-rabi*; cf. Heb *rḥbʿm*?), and the name *Ḫammiṣaduqa* is interpreted as *Kimtum-Kittum* "Legitimate Family" (5 R 44 i 21-22). It is possible, then, that *ʿAm(m)* had a wider range of meaning than "paternal uncle". The word originally probably meant "kin". Hence the name *ʿAmmī-Anat* means "(the goddess) Anat is my Kin".

ʿAm(m) is the patron deity of the ancient

Qatabanians of South Arabia, who were known as *bnw ʿm* "the children of *ʿAmm*". It is clear from the inscriptions that *ʿAmm* was a lunar deity in Qataban. Among his epithets are *ryʿn w-śhrm* "He who waxes and revolves", *ḏ-šqr* "The bright shining one", and *ḏ-ysrm* "The little one", the latter two referring respectively to the →moon in full phase and the new moon (BEESTON 1951). The worship of *ʿAmm* in South Arabia is corroborated by an Arabic tradition about an idol called *ʿAmm-ʾanas* ("the Paternal Uncle of Humanity") that was worshipped in the pre-Islamic period (FAHD 1968).

Since the Qatabanians were called "children of *ʿAmm*", it has been suggested that the name of the eponymous ancestor of the Ammonites in Gen 19:38, *bn ʿmy*, may indicate that the Ammonites also venerated that lunar deity (HOMMEL 1900). But whereas *ʿAmm* was the national deity of the Qatabanians, there is no evidence that he played such a prominent role in the Ammonite cult. Apart from the name *ʿmndb* and the single occurrence of the name *ʾlyʿm* (HERR 1978:35), there are no *ʿAm(m)*-names among the Ammonites (HÜBNER 1992:256-258). The name *bn ʿmy* is unique as an allusion to the Ammonites; the most common designation for them in the Bible is *bn(y) ʿm(w)n*. And that is, indeed, their own designation for themselves, as is attested in the Tell Siran Bottle (ll. 2-3; *BASOR* 212 [1973] 5-11). The etymology of Ammon remains uncertain. It appears, then, that apart from the Qatabanian moon-god, there are no references to *ʿAm(m)* as the name of a particular deity. It is more likely that *ʿAm(m)* in most Semitic proper names was originally an appellation, which may have been understood as referring to various deities. In the case of the Qatabanians, *ʿAmm* was the standard designation for their national god.

III. It has been suggested that *ʿAm(m)* appears in the Bible in Hos 4:4 and Isa 2:6 (NYBERG 1935). In both cases, however, *ʿm* appears with a pronominal suffix. Indeed, apart from the personal names and a few toponymns (notably *yqnʿm*), there is no reference in the Bible to the deity known as *ʿAm(m)*.

IV. *Bibliography*

A. F. L. BEESTON, On Old South Arabian Lexicography III, *Muséon* 64 (1951) 130-131; F. L. BENZ, *Personal Names in the Phoenician and Punic Inscriptions* (StPsm 8; Rome 1972) 172.379; *T. FAHD, *Le panthéon de l'Arabie centrale à la veille de l'Hégire* (Paris 1968) 44-46; I. J. GELB, *Computer-Aided Analysis of Amorite* (AS 21; Chicago 1980) 260-264; *R. M. GOOD, *The Sheep of His Pasture* (HSM 29; Chico 1983) 10-12.30-31; L. HERR, *The Scripts of Ancient Northwest Semitic Seals* (HSM 18; Missoula, Montana 1978); *M. HÖFNER, ʿAmm (ʿM, ʿAMM, ʿMN), *WbMyth* I/1 (Stuttgart 1965) 494-495; F. HOMMEL, *Aufsätze und Abhandlungen* (München 1900) 149-165; U. HÜBNER, *Die Ammoniter* (ADPV 16; Wiesbaden 1992) 256-258; H. B. HUFFMON, *Amorite Personal Names in the Mari Texts* (Baltimore 1964) 196-198; A. JAMME, Le panthéon sud-arabe préislamique, *Le Muséon* 60 (1967) 57-147; M. KREBERNIK, *Die Personennamen der Ebla-Texte* (Berlin 1988) 72.125-126; R. B. LAWTON, Israelite Personal Names on Pre-exilic Hebrew Inscriptions, *Bib* 65 (1984) 333; J. LEWY, The Old West Semitic Sun-God Ḥammu, *HUCA* 19 (1944) 429-488; H. S. NYBERG, *Studien zum Hoseabuch* (Uppsala 1935) 27; G. RYCKMANS, *Les noms propres sud-sémitiques* (Louvain 1934) I, 26-27; II, 107.

C. L. SEOW

AMALEK עמלק

I. In the Old Testament, the tribe of Amalek is one of Israel's enemies of old (Ex 17:8-16; Num 13:29 etc.). Their ancestor is seen as a grandson of →Esau (Gen 36:12-16). Amalek can also designate a topographical area as in the expression *har hāʿămālēqî* 'the mountain of the Amalekites' (Judg 12:15). An etymological explanation of the name Amalek has been impossible until now (WEIPPERT 1974:252). The suggestion has been made to relate the name Amalek to a mountain deity *ḥmrq* known from an Egyptian source (GÖRG 1987:14-15).

II. The Egyptian Leiden Magical Papyrus I 343 + I 345* (ed. MASSART 1954) mentions in the context of deities venerated in the Canaanite area a mountain deity *ḥmrq* (III 9; XXIII 3). This deity seems to be related to a mountainous area probably in the Eastern Sinai. The identity of the deity is further unknown. GÖRG (1987) suggested the identity of *ḥmrq* with Amalek and the interchangeability of the tribal name with the divine name. His surmise is based on an assumed phonetic similarity between Egyptian *ḥmrq* and Hebrew *ʿmlq*. Egyptian /r/ can easily be equated with Hebrew /l/. Egyptian /ḥ/ is more problematical. It generally stands for Hebrew /ḥ/, while Hebrew /ʿ/ is rendered in Egyptian with /ʿ/ (as in *ʿynw* עיון Ijjon); /q/ (as in *qḏt* עזה Gaza) or /g/ (as in *gḏt* עזה Gaza). Therefore, Görg's surmise is not convincing.

In the OT there are otherwise no traces of a divine background of the topographic designation or the tribal name.

III. *Bibliography*

*M. GÖRG, Ein Gott Amalek?, *BN* 40 (1987) 14-15; A. MASSART, *The Leiden Magical Papyrus I 343 + I 345* (Leiden 1954); M. WEIPPERT, Semitische Nomaden des zweiten Jahrtausends. Über die *Š3św* der ägyptischen Quellen, *Bib* 55 (1974) 265-280, 427-433.

B. BECKING

AMALTHEIA Ἀμάλθεια

I. Amaltheia is the name of the goat that suckled baby →Zeus right after his birth (so Callimachus, Apollodorus, Diodorus Siculus), or of the nymph who nursed and fed him on goat's milk (so Ovid and Hyginus). The 'Horn of Amaltheia' (Ἀμαλθείας Κέρας) was one of the horns of this goat or, according to others, a horn possessed by the nymph, which provided in abundance whatever one wished, and became the well-known image of the 'horn of plenty' or cornucopia. This occurs in the LXX of Job 42:14 and in *T. Job* 1, 3 as the name of one of Job's second set of three daughters. Etymologically, ἀ-μάλθε-ια is probably a substantive formed from a privative adjective *ἀ-μαλθής, -ές meaning 'not softening', said of the goat's udder, that is, always tightly full of milk (cf. μαλθακός etc., and for the formation: ἀ-λήθε-ια from ἀ-ληθής 'not escaping notice, not hiding; true').

II. After Zeus had been born in Crete, or in Arcadia according to Callimachus, *Hymn on Zeus* 244, he had to be hidden there in a cave, either in Mt Dicte or in Mt Ida, in which Amaltheia nursed or suckled him, because his father Kronos devoured all his children. He did so in order to thwart the oracle which had predicted that a child of his would dethrone him as the ruler of the universe. One of the horns of the goat, says Ovid (*Fasti* 5, 111-128), broke off, was filled with fruits by the nymph Amaltheia, and offered to Zeus. Much earlier, however, Pherecydes (*frg.* 42) told the story that the nymph was in possession of a bull's horn, which, according to desire, supplied any food or drink in abundance.

A third version has been preserved by Zenobius, who assigned to the 'Horn of Amaltheia' a place in his collection of proverbial expressions, and stated that it was equivalent with another saying, namely 'Heavenly Goat'. The explanation he gives is that Zeus, when fully grown, turned the goat, in gratitude, into a →constellation, but gave one of its horns to the two nymphs Adrasteia and Ida, who had been his nurses (cf. Apollodorus 1, 1, 6). On that occasion, he endowed the horn with its famous miraculous power (2,48; cf. 1,26).

III. According to the MT of Job 42:14 the later three daughters bore the names respectively of Yĕmîmâ 'dovelet' (?), Qĕsîʿâ 'cassia' (an aromatic), and Qeren-happûk 'horn of antimony' or 'stibium' (used as an eye-liner). In the LXX these names are represented by Ἡμέρα →'day' (evidently deriving Yĕmîmâ from *yôm*), Κασία and Ἀμαλθείας Κέρας. We have the explicit statement of Pliny the Elder (*Nat. Hist.* preface 24) that the Latin equivalent of the last name was 'copiae cornu'. It is interesting, therefore, to see that the Vulgate version has retained the former two as 'Dies' and 'Cassia', but that the third name is now the more correct counterpart of the Hebrew name as in the MT: 'Cornu Stibii'. This certainly indicates that Jerome was not content here with the LXX, and also that the Hebrew original underlying it must have been different from the Hebrew text which he could use when revising the Vetus Latina. What the LXX-translator read was in all probability *qeren tāpûṣ* ('a horn will overflow'), the graphical confusion of hê and taw, and of kaph and ṣâdê being quite possible in handwriting of the 3rd and 2nd centuries BCE. In this case the rendering Ἀμαλθείας Κέρας would be quite understandable.

IV. According to Lactantius, Amaltheia was also the name of the Sibyl of Cumae who sold a collection of Sibylline Oracles to Tarquinius Priscus, the fifth king of Rome (*Div. Inst.* 1,6,10-11).

V. *Bibliography*

H. VON GEISAU, Amaltheia, *KP* 1 (1975) 287; P. GRIMAL (A. R. Maxwell-Hyslop transl.), Amaltheia, *The Dictionary of Classical Mythology* (Oxford [UK] - New York 1986) 35-36; J. NAVEH, *Early History of the Alphabet. An Introduction to West Semitic Epigraphyand Palaeography* (Leiden 1982), see fig. 100 p. 113, line 3 for kaph/ṣâdê and line 5 for hê/taw; J. B. BAUER, H. BRAKMANN, D. KOROL, G. SCHWARZ, Horn (I), *RAC* 16 (1992) 524-574 (especially 'Füllhorn' 539-547, and 'Horn der Amaltheia' 560-561).

G. MUSSIES

AMUN אמון

I. Amun, *ỉmn*, from JMN 'to hide': the "Hidden one". The Greeks identified Amun with →Zeus because of his function as chief of the Egyptian pantheon. Amun occurs as divine name in Jer 46:25 (*ʾāmôn minnōʾ* Amon of No: Amon of Thebes) and Nah 3:8 (*nōʾ ʾāmôn* No-Amon: the city of Amon).

II. The original nature of Amun is determined by two factors: 1. the close relationship with →Min of Koptos, the god of kingship, fertility and virility; 2. the role of Amun as one of the personifications of preexistence (cf. *Pyr.* 466: Amun and Amaunet as feminine counterpart, alongside *Njw* and Naunet [water], →Atum and Ruti [creator] and Shu and Tefnut [air], see SETHE 1929:§61). Two further aspects develop since the 11th dynasty with the equation of Amun with the sun god →Re and his establishment as the city god of Thebes and the state god of a reunified Egypt, which implies his status as chief of the pantheon ('king of the gods', Eg. *Jmn-Rʿw-nsw-nṯrw,* Gk *Ammonrasonther*, and other titles of royal character, see SETHE 1929:§11). In this function of state god, Amun is venerated in the temple of Karnak. The most important theriomorphic aspect and sacred animal of Amun is the ram (ovis platyura aeg.) whose characteristic horns appear in the iconography of Alexander the Great after his ritual 'divinization' (initiation as Egyptian king) in the temple of Luxor. This latter temple (built by Amenophis III) is specifically devoted to the god-king relationship and the Luxor festival celebrates the annual renewal of divine kingship (L. BELL, *JNES* 44 [1985] 251-294). A third Theban temple of Amun, built by Hatshepsut and Thutmosis III on the west bank at Medinet Habu, is devoted to his primordial aspect as Kematef, Gk *Kneph* "who has accomplished his time" (SETHE 1929: §§103-110). In Ptolemaic times, the three Theban forms of Amun are organized as three generations: Kematef (grandfather), Amun-Re (father) and Amun-of-Luxor (son) (SETHE 1929:§115 goes a little too far in distinguishing even four generations).

The theology of Amun as formulated in a multitude of hymns (see ASSMANN 1975; 1983) develops in two stages: 1. from the Middle Kingdom until Amarna; 2. from post-Amarna until the Graeco-Roman period. In the first stage (see ASSMANN 1983:145-188; 1984:221-232), the nature of Amun is unfolded in 5 aspects: (1) primordial god, (2) creator god, (3) ruler (city god, state god and king of the gods), (4) preserver, "life god", sun god and (5) judge and saviour (ethical authority, the god of the individual). The second stage reacts to the monotheistic revolt of Akhenaten and must be interpreted as an attempt to combine both the monotheistic idea of the uniqueness or 'oneness' of god and the polytheistic worship of the different deities whose ongoing cooperation and antagonism forms cosmic reality (ASSMANN 1983:189-286). The result is the pantheistic idea of a god who is both hidden and cosmic, both transcendent and immanent, the "One-and-All", eg. "the One who made himself into millions" (ASSMANN 1983:208-218; ZANDEE 1992:168-176). Amun is the god both of preexistence and of creation. This means that he did not create the world out of chaos, but that he transformed himself into the world. The world in its tripartite form as heaven-earth-underworld develops as the realm for the god in his tripartite existence as 'Ba' (sun), 'image' (cult statue at Thebes) and 'corpse' (ASSMANN 1983:241-246). But in his function as life-god, Amun is immanent in a triad of life-giving elements viz. light, air and water (ASSMANN 1983:250-263). The most important concept in this theology is 'Ba', a kind of soul, which leaves the body at the moment of death and is able to pass into a celestial or underworld abode and to come back to visit the mummy in the tomb. This anthropological concept has been extended already in the Coffin Texts to the divine world in order to explain the relationship of a deity and his/her cosmic manifestation: the wind as "the ba of Shu", the light as "the ba of Re" etc. In the Ramesside theology of Amun, the Ba concept is used to work in two different directions: to designate the many gods as the Ba-'manifestation' of the hidden 'One', but also the hidden 'One' as the 'soul' whose body is the cosmos (ASSMANN 1983:189-218). In this aspect, the name 'Amun' is avoided in the hymns and the god is called "the mysterious Ba" (ASSMANN 1983:203-207). The cosmic body of god comprises →heaven and →earth as head and feet, sun and →moon as the two eyes, the air as the breath and the water as the sweat of the god, but there are many other elaborations of the idea of the "cosmic god". (ASSMANN 1979; H. STERNBERG-EL HOTABI, *Der Propylon des Month-Tempels in Karnak-Nord* [Wiesbaden 1993] 23-26).

The most elaborated conception of this Ba-theology appears in temples of the Late Period (7th and 6th centuries BCE) and distinguishes ten 'Bas' of Amun as modes of his intramundane manifestion (J. C. GOYON, *The Edifice of Taharqa* [eds. R. A. Parker, J. Leclant & J. C. Goyon; Providence 1979] 69-79, 40-41, pl.27.): the first two Bas are sun and moon, the eyes of the cosmic gods, they stand for 'time' as one of the life-giving elements; the next two are the Bas of Shu and Osiris for 'air' and 'water'. 'Light', in this theology, is represented by the Ba of Tefnut. Then come five 'Bas' standing for five classes of living beings: mankind, quadrupeds (living on earth), birds (living in the sky), fishes (living in the water) and snakes, scarabs and the dead (living in the earth). Most important is the Ba responsible for mankind: he is identified with the "king's ka", i.e. the divine institution of pharaonic kingship.

Among the Theban festivals, four are most important: the festivals of Luxor, of the valley, of Min and of Sokar. The first two are closely linked with the Egyptian concept of kingship. During the Luxor festival (*LdÄ* 4:574-579; L. BELL, *JNES* 44 [1985] 251-294), the barks of the Karnak triad (Amun, Mut and →Khonsu) and the bark of the king visit the temple of Luxor. The king, during this visit, undergoes a spiritual rebirth as son of Amun. The festival thus performs an annual renewal of kingship. During the valley festival (*LdÄ* 6:187-189), the divine barks cross the →Nile and visit the mortuary temples of the kings. Whereas the Luxor festival confirms the divine descent of the king, the festival of the valley confirms his genealogical legitimation; it performs an annual renewal of the community with the →dead. Around the festival of the valley originates a new form of god-man-relationship which later comes to be known as "Personal Piety" (ASSMANN 1989:68-82 [& lit]). In the form of a procession the god, who is usually hidden in his temple and is strictly unapproachable to everybody except the priests on service, appears to his people and can be approached by everyone who wants to appeal to the god for healing from a sickness or protection against a danger or persecution etc. Some of the prayers to the god from the time of Amenophis II have been preserved on ostraca; they seem to have been presented to the god in this form during his procession (G. POSENER, *REg* 27 [1975] 195-210). These texts seem to be first instances of "Personal Piety", a movement which was suppressed during the Amarna period and which after the failure of this monotheistic revolution expanded all over Egypt. Amun remained the exponent of this new religiosity. His aspect as judge and saviour of the poor became central and a model for the theology of other deities as well. The traditional 'theology of maintenace' concentrating on cosmic life and its cyclical renewal now changed into a 'theology of will' concentrating on historical and biographical fate and significance. Catastrophical events, as well as miraculous salvations, are now interpretated as divine interventions, a traditional conception in the Near East (B. ALBREKTSON, *History and the Gods* [Lund 1967]) but quite new in the Egyptian context (see ASSMANN 1989).

Around the festival of Luxor originated a new form of oracular intervention, which during the 18th dynasty is restricted to Amun and to questions of the royal succession but which after Amarna expanded to other deities and to all kinds of human problems (*LdÄ* 4:600-606). This development culminated in the establishment of a regular theocracy during the 21st dynasty (end of 11th century), when Amun assumed the role of supreme ruler and exerted this rule by means of oracular decisions (*LdÄ* 2:822-823). Even after this rather revolutionary period the Theban region and its neighbouring nomes continued to form a "divine state" within the state, ruled by Amun, his clergy and above all by the "god's wife of Amun", a royal princess (*LdÄ* 2:792-812).

The temple and the festival of Luxor are devoted to Amun as the god of divine kingship. This aspect of Amun finds its most explicit expression in the "myth of the royal birth", a cycle of pictures and accompanying texts represented in the funerary temple of Hatshepsut at Deir el Bahari, the temple of Luxor and the Ramesseum (BRUNNER 1964; ASSMANN 1982). It tells and shows how Amun decides to create a new king, falls in love with a beautiful woman who turns out to be the queen of the reigning king, visits her in the shape of her husband, begets the future king, orders →Thoth to announce to her the approaching events and Khnum to form the child in the mother's womb, vivifies the child and supports the pregnant woman by his breath. The birth and suckling of the child are shown, then follow scenes where Amun recognizes the new-born child as his son and presents him as the future king to the ennead. The cycle ends with scenes of circumcision and purification. In all extant versions, this cycle of birth scenes is complemented by a cycle of coronation scenes. Both cycles belong together. The meaning of the birth cycle is the adoption of the king by Amun as the first step of the coronation ceremony. Together with kingship the king enters a new filiation and acquires a new biography. In Graeco-Roman times this cycle was transposed entirely into the divine sphere and the role of the king was now played by the child-god of the divine triad. The festival called *mswt nṯr* "divine birth" was performed in a special building called (in Coptic) "mammisi" (birth-place). The myth shows close parallels not only to the Greek myth of Amphitryon but also to the birth of →Christ as told by Luke.

The much debated character of Amun as 'pneuma' (SETHE 1929:§§231-235), however, seems to be based on a misunderstanding. The aspect of Amun as a god of 'wind' (SETHE 1929:§§187-230) has to be seen in context of his other cosmic manifestations: light and water. The air is just one of his forms of live-giving intramundane manifestations, but not the original nature of the god. If there are correspondences between Amun and →Yahweh (SETHE 1929:§§255-260), they have to be seen in the political, ethical and social character of Amun, acting both as god of the state and as judge and saviour of the poor (see also J. DE MOOR, *The Rise of Jahwism* [Leuven 1990]).

Another typical trait of Amun that might bring him into a certain proximity to Yahweh is his comparatively non-mythical and 'non-constellative' character. There are no myths which have Amun for a protagonist. Amun has a female counterpart (Amaunet, also Mut), but is otherwise unrelated. The association of Khonsu as his son is a local construction.

III. The deity Amun is referred to in an oracle against Egypt (Jer 46:25). Within this context, Amun is the only Egyptian deity mentioned by name. Therefore, it can be inferred that he was seen as a or the major deity of Egypt by the sixth century BCE Judahites. In Nah 3:8 the city No-Amon is mentioned in comparison. The fate of the city should be an indication to the Assyrians that their rule will not remain unchallenged. The identity of name of the Egyptian deity Amun with the Judahite king Amon (2 Kgs 21:19-26; 2 Chron 33:21-25) rests on homonymy.

IV. *Bibliography*

J. Assmann, *Ägyptische Hymnen und Gebete* (Zürich 1975); Assmann, Primat und Transzendenz, Struktur und Genese der ägyptischen Vorstellung eines 'Höchsten Wesens', *Aspekte der spätägyptischen Religion* (ed. W. Westendorf; GOF IV.9; Wiesbaden 1979) 7-40; Assmann, Die Zeugung des Sohnes. Bild, Spiel, Erzählung und das Problem des ägyptischen Mythos, *Funktionen und Leistungen des Mythos* (J. Assman, W. Burkert & F. Stolz; OBO 48; Fribourg 1982) 13-61; Assmann, *Sonnenhymnen in thebanischen Gräbern (Theben I)* (Mainz 1983); Assmann, *Ägypten - Theologie und Frömmigkeit einer frühen Hochkultur* (Stuttgart 1984); Assmann, State and Religion in the New Kingdom, *Religion and Philosophy in Ancient Egypt* (ed. W. K. Simpson; Yale Egyptological Studies 3; New Haven 1989) 55-88; J. F. Borghouts, Divine Intervention in Ancient Egypt and its Manifestation, *Gleanings from Deir el-Medina*, (R. J. Demarée & J. J. Janssen; Leiden 1982) 1-70; Brunner, Der freie Wille Gottes in der ägyptischen Weisheit, *Sagesses du Proche Orient ancien* (Paris 1963) 103-117; Brunner, *Die Geburt des Gottkönigs* (ÄA 10; Wiesbaden 1964); Brunner, Persönliche Frömmigkeit, *LdÄ* 4 (1982) 951-963; E. Otto, *Osiris und Amun* (München 1966); Otto, Amun, *LdÄ* 1 (1975) 237-248; S. Sauneron & J. Yoyotte, *La naissance du monde selon l'Egypte ancienne* (SO I; Paris 1959) 17-91; K. Sethe, *Amun und die acht Urgötter von Hermopolis* (APAW; Berlin 1929); J. Zandee, *De hymnen aan Amon van Papyrus Leiden I 350* (OMRO 28; Leiden, 1947); Zandee, *Der Amunhymnus des Papyrus Leiden I 344, Verso*, 3 Vols. (Leiden 1992).

J. Assmann

AMURRU

I. Amurru is the eponymous god of the nomadic peoples of the western desert that began to manifest themselves in Mesopotamia from the late third millennium BCE onward. These peoples are known in cuneiform sources as 'Amorites' (*Amurru*, Sum MAR-TU). Their god, known as Amurru (Akkadian) or Martu (Sumerian), is best characterized as a storm god, comparable in type with →Hadad or →Yahweh. References to Amurru in the Hebrew Bible are either indirect or debated. As the god is eponymous, his name can be heard in the ethnic designation *ʾĕmōrî*, 'Amorite'. The name Amraphel (Gen 14:1.9) may contain Amurru as a theophoric element, assuming it should be interpreted as 'Amurru-has-answered' (*Amurru-īpul*). A number of scholars believe the name →Shadday, usually found as El-shadday, reflects the epithet *bēl šadê*, 'Lord of the Mountain', currently carried by Amurru.

II. The Sumerian name of the god Amurru is still a matter of debate. The pronunciation 'Martu' is conventional, since the writing dMAR-TU would also permit the pronunciation 'Mardu' or 'Ĝardu'. It is evident from Old Assyrian theophoric personal names that Sum Martu is equated at an early stage with Akk Amurru (H. Hirsch, *Untersuchungen zur altassyrischen Religion* [AfO Beih. 13/14; Vienna 1961] 5). Though there is no proof of a phonetic correspondence between the two, some such correspondence must be assumed as the basis for the equation (cf. the unclarified relationship between Kiengir and Šumeru, the Sumerian resp. Akkadian designation for 'Sumer'). Sum 'Martu' and Akk 'Amurru' were presumably both attempts to render the unknown vocable by which the Amorite peoples designated themselves. Alongside the writing dMAR-TU there is an alternative orthography AN-AN-MAR-TU, perhaps to be read as dIl-Amurrim, 'god of Amurrum' (see EDZARD 1989:437 for a full discussion). The name underscores the fact that the god must be seen as the personification of the Amorites.

Amurru was introduced into the Mesopotamian pantheon at a rather late stage, since he was not included in the family of Enlil. A son of An, the god of heaven and perhaps a form of →El in this connection, Martu appears to be a West-Semitic storm god similar to Hadad. According to a Sumerian hymn, Amurru is a warrior god, strong as a lion, equipped with bow and arrows, and using storm and thunder as his weapons (A. FALKENSTEIN, *Sumerische Götterlieder*, Vol. 1 [Heidelberg 1959] 120-140). His role as a storm god explains why one of the younger god lists identifies Amurru as 'Adad of the inundation' (dIŠKUR *šá a-bu-be*, CT 24 pl. 40:48). In addition, Amurru is known as the 'exorcist' (*muššipu*) of the gods; his curved staff (*gamlu*) frees from punishment (*paṭār ennetti*, *Šurpu* VIII 41-47, cf. W. G. LAMBERT, Gàm šen not a weapon of war, *NABU* 1987/3 no. 92). A similar combination is extant in the theology of →Marduk. According to the Myth of Martu (also known as the *Marriage of Martu*), Amurru had Suḫinun as his mother and acquired Adgarudu (others read Adnigkidu) as his wife (for the *Marriage of Martu* see J. BOTTÉRO & S. N. KRAMER, *Lorsque les dieux faisaient l'homme* [Pars 1989] 430-437; J. KLEIN, Additional Notes to 'the Marriage of Martu', *Memorial Volume Kutscher* [ed. A. F. Rainey; Tel Aviv 1993] 93-106). Both goddesses are little known. More common than with Adgarudu, however, is the pairing of Amurru with the West Semitic goddess Ashratu (→Asherah; cf. KUPPER 1961:59).

According to his mythology, Amurru inhabits the PA.DÙN = **ḫur-sag**, literally "the mountain", actually a designation of the steppe (CAVIGNEAUX 1987); Amurru is indeed the *bēl šadê*, 'Lord of the mountain' (*AkkGE* 54), as well as the *bēl ṣēri*, 'Lord of the steppe' (C. B. F. WALKER, apud D. COLLON, *Catalogue of the Western Asiatic Seals in the British Museum. Cylinder Seals III, Isin/Larsa and the Old Babylonian Periods* [London 1986] 96:140). He bears the epithet "the →Shepherd who treads on the mountains (i.e. the steppe)" (L. LEGRAIN, *The Culture of the Babylonians from their Seals in the Collections of the Museum* [PBS 14; Philadelphia 1925] no. 342). The correspondence between the god Amurru and the Amorites is evident: since the latter have the steppe as their original habitat, their god is believed to dwell there as well. His behaviour typically reflects the characteristics of Amorite nomads as perceived by civilized Mesopotamians. According to a passage in the *Marriage of Martu*, the god "dresses in sheepskins [...], lives in a tent, at the mercy of wind and rain, [...] does not offer sacrifice [...]. He digs up truffles in the steppe, but does not know how to bow his knee [i.e. he is not accustomed to sit down for a meal (?)]. He eats raw meat. In life he has no house, in death he lies not buried in a grave" (E. CHIERA, *Sumerian Epics and Myths* [OIP 15; Chicago 1934] no. 58 iv 23-29).

The earliest attestation to the cult of Amurru dates from the late Sargonic Period. His name is a frequent theophoric element in personal names under the Third Dynasty of Ur (H. LIMET, *L'anthroponymie sumérienne dans les documents de la 3e dynastie d'Ur* [Paris 1968] 158). The god gained prominence in the popular religion of the Old and Middle Babylonian periods, as witnessed by his frequent mention (often alongside Ashratu) in legends of cylinder seals (KUPPER 1961:57-60). In his capacity as family god ('god of the father'), Amurru did on occasion receive letter prayers (AbB 12 no. 99). The cult of Amurru was not limited to Mesopotamia proper. Also in such 'peripheral' places as Emar and Alalakh, the god Amurru was known (note the *ḫarranu ša* ^{d}*[A]murri*, *Emar* no. 169:6', cf. J.-M. DURAND, *RA* 84 [1990] 66 for the correct reading; a cylinder seal from Alalakh depicts Amurru as a naked yong man, D. COLLON, *The Seal Impressions from Tell Atchanah/Alalakh* [AOAT 27; Neukirchen-Vluyn 1975] 73 no. 135).

III. Though the Amorites are known in the Hebrew Bible (as *hāʾĕmōrî*), the god Amurru as such is not unambiguously attested. The personal name Amraphel (אמרפל, Gen 14:1.9) might possibly be analyzed as *Amurru-īpul, but other etymologies have been proposed as well (note especially Amar-pî-El, see *Ges.*[18] 78; cf. also the suggestion by M. C. ASTOUR, Amraphel, *ABD* 1 (1992) 217-218).

In spite of the absence of the theonym Amurru in the Bible, the god nevertheless plays a significant role in OT scholarship. The reason for this is the interpretation of Shadday (often occurring in the combination El-shadday) as 'Mountaineer' or 'the Mountain One' (first proposed by W. F. ALBRIGHT, The Names *Shaddai* and *Abram*, *JBL* 54 [1935] 173-204, esp. 184). Various authors consider this the Canaanite equivalent of Amurru's epithet *bēl šadê*, 'Lord of the Mountain'; they draw the conclusion that Shadday (or El-shadday) is to be identified with Amurru (e.g. E. BURROWS, The Meaning of El Šaddai, *JTS* 41 [1940] 152-161; L. R. BAILEY, Israelite *ʾĒl šadday* and Amorite *Bêl šadê*, *JBL* 87 [1968] 434-438; J. OUELLETTE, More on ʾĒl šadday and Bêl šadê, *JBL* 88 [1969] 470-471; R. DE VAUX, *Histoire ancienne d'Israël des origines à l'installation en Canaan* [Paris 1971] 264; CROSS 1973:57; T. N. D. METTINGER, *In Search of God* [Philadelphia 1988] 71). CROSS explains the combination El-shadday by assuming that Amurru is the Amorite name (or form) of El. He argues that El as the divine warrior of important western tribes or leagues was reintroduced into Mesopotamia under the name Amurru (1973:59). This speculative theory is unlikely. There is little in the biography of Amurru that might identify him as El: he is a warrior and a storm god, resembling →Baal and Yahweh more than El; if there is a connection, Amurru is the son of El (or An in Mesopotamian mythology). The interpretation of *šadday* as 'the Mountain One', moreover, is far from certain. On the basis of Ug *šd(y)* and Heb *śādeh*, a meaning 'of the field' is much more plausible. The equation of (El-)Shadday with Amurru must therefore be rejected as unfounded.

IV. *Bibliography*

A. CAVIGNEAUX, PA.DÙN = hursag et le dieu Amurru, *NABU* 1987/2 no. 26; F. M. CROSS, *Canaanite Myth and Hebrew Epic* [Cambridge, Mass. 1973] 56-59; *D. O. EDZARD, Martu, *RLA* 7/5-6 (1989) 433-438; J.-R. KUPPER, *Les nomades en Mésopotamie au temps des rois de Mari* (Paris 1957) 245-247; KUPPER, *L'iconographie du dieu Amurru dans la glyptique de la I*[re] *dynastie babylonienne* (Paris 1961).

K. VAN DER TOORN

ANAKIM → REPHAIM

ANAMMELECH ענמלך

I. Anammelech is a god whom the people of Sepharvaim settled in Samaria by the Assyrians worshipped beside →Adrammelech, 2 Kgs 17:31. On Sepharvaim as a West Semitic settlement in Babylonia, see Adrammelech.

II. Many explain the divine name as a combination of Babylonian Anu with West Semitic *melek*, 'Anu is king' (GRAY 1977: 596; cf. J. A. MONTGOMERY & H. S. GEHMAN, *Kings* [ICC; Edinburgh 1951] 476; M. COGAN & H. TADMOR, *II Kings* [AB 11; New York 1988] 212). However, the ancient Sumerian sky-god's name is never written in cuneiform with any hint of an initial guttural, and where it occurs in Semitic transcription it is written *ʾn* (J. A. FITZMYER & S. A. KAUFMAN, *An Aramaic Bibliography, Part I: Old, Official and Biblical Aramaic*

[Baltimore 1992] 170 seal no. 24, 52 Uruk Bricks), so it is mistaken to seek it here (so already A. ŠANDA, *Die Bücher der Könige* [Münster 1912] 231-232). Thus there is no evidence for syncretism of Babylonian Anu with West Semitic Melek (= Athtar) here, as GRAY (1977) argued. Rather, the initial element of the name is the male counterpart of the well-known West Semitic goddess →Anat (*ʿnt*), written *ʿn* (so DRIVER 1958:19; ZADOK 1976:117). Personal names from the early second millennium BCE onwards incorporate the form (H. B. HUFFMON, *Amorite Personal Names in the Mari Texts* [Baltimore 1965] 199; R. ZADOK, *On West Semites in Babylonia during the Chaldean and Achaemenian Periods* [Jerusalem 1977] 39), yet the deity remains "an obscure figure, known only from personal names" (S. RIBICHINI & P. XELLA, *SEL* 8 (1991) 149-170, esp. 166). Alternatively, it is possible that Anammelech is an assimilation of *Anat-Melech, a form comparable to Anat-Yahu known from the Elephantine papyri. The suggestion of VAN DER TOORN (Anat-Yahu and the Jews of Elephantine, *Numen* 39 [1992] 93) that *ʿnmlk* should be read as **ʿgmlk* (→Og) is less preferable.

III. No light can be shed on the cult of this god and his fellow apart from the biblical narrator's remark that the people "burned their children in fire" to them. The expression *śārap* (*bāʾēš*), 'to burn (in/with fire)', has been interpreted as reflecting the deuteronomistic polemics against foreign deities (e.g. WEINFELD 1972). This view, however, has been seriously challenged (e.g. by KAISER 1976). The action then suggests a relationship with the god →Molech.

III. *Bibliography*

B. BECKING, *The Fall of Samaria. An Historical and Archaeological Study* (SHANE 2; Leiden 1992) 99-102; G. R. DRIVER, Geographical Problems, *ErIsr* 5 (1958) 16-20; J. GRAY, *I and II Kings* (OTL; London 1977[3]); O. KAISER, Der Erstgeborene deiner Söhne sollst du mir geben, *Denkender Glaube* (FS C. H. Ratschow; ed. O. Kaiser; Berlin & New York 1976) 24-48; M. WEINFELD, The Worship of Molech and the Queen of Heaven and its Background, *UF* 4 (1972) 133-154; R. ZADOK, Geographical and Onomastic Notes, *JANES* 8 (1976) 114-126.

A. R. MILLARD

ANANKE Ἀνάγκη

I. Anankē, 'necessity, constraint', presented as the personification of the inevitable and inescapable, hence of the inexorable Fate, plays an important role in Greek religious and philosophical literature (SCHRECKENBERG 1964). The word occurs 43 times in the LXX and 18 times in the NT with the meanings 'necessity, compulsion, obligation; distress, suffering, calamity; inevitability' (STROBEL 1980) but never as a personification of Fate.

II. Anankē is mentioned by Plato in the myth of Er (*Resp.* 616c-617c) as the enthroned governor of the kosmos and as the mother of the Moirai, the goddesses of Fate, and he presents her as more powerful even than the gods (*Leg.* 818e; SCHRECKENBERG 1964:81-101). The great tragedians, too, testify to her unrivalled power over all other beings and her inexorable character (Aeschylus, *Prom.* 515-520; Euripides, *Or.* 1330, *Alc.* 965, *Hel.* 514; cf. Sophocles, *Ant.* 944-954 and the scholion *ad loc.*), as did already the Presocratic philosophers, especially Parmenides, in whose writings she plays a role of paramount importance together with →Dikē and Moira (→Fortuna). She figures in (late?) Orphic mythology, e.g. as the mother of Heimarmene and of the triad Aither, →Chaos and Erebos (FAUTH 1975; but see SCHRECKENBERG 1964:131-134 against the theory of her Orphic origin); and Proclus indicates that she played an important role in the beliefs of several mystery religions in late antiquity (*Comm. in Remp.* II 344-5 KROLL). In two Hermetic excerpts in Stobaeus the author discusses the mutual demarcation of the roles of →Pronoia, Heimarmene and Anankē (fr. XII in *Anth.* I 5, 20, and fr. XIV in *Anth.* I 5, 16, with the comments of A.-J. FESTUGIÈRE & A. D. NOCK, *Corpus Hermeticum* III [Paris

1954] lxxix-lxxx). Her role in the magical papyri as a 'Zaubergottheit' (SCHRECKENBERG 1964:139-145) still needs further investigation; cf. also her function in the *Oracula Chaldaica* and in Gnostic sources (F. SIEGERT, *Nag-Hammadi-Register* [Tübingen 1982] 211). The growing 'popularity' of Anankē in late antiquity is certainly connected with the increasing influence of astrology and its accompanying fatalism. People often felt themselves "dominated and crushed by blind forces that dragged them on as irresistably as they kept the celestial spheres in motion" (F. CUMONT, *Oriental Religions in Roman Paganism* [New York 1911] 181; for the astrological setting also NILSSON 1961: 506). Pausanias mentions a sanctuary of Anankē and Bia (Force) in Corinth, "into which it is not customary to enter" (*Descriptio Graeciae* II 4,6; note the same combination of deities in the Gnostic NHC VII 61).

III. Although the personified Anankē occurs neither in the Greek Bible nor in the Jewish pseudepigrapha, there is an interesting Jewish prayer in a Berlin magical papyrus (PGM I 197-222, with a parallel in PGM IV 1167-1226) in which Adam prays to be saved from the ὥρα ἀνάγκης (221). As PETERSON (1959:124) has demonstrated, this must be interpreted in the light of an earlier petition in the same prayer in which Adam asks to be protected from the power of the δαίμων ἀέριος and of εἱμαρμένη (for the connection of ἀήρ and Anankē see Proclus, *Comm. in Remp.* II 109 KROLL). This rather syncretistic prayer depicts the situation of Adam (= Man?) as one who is helplessly at the mercy of Fate, over which only the God of Israel can exercise power, a motif also adumbrated in other magical papyri.

IV. *Bibliography*

W. FAUTH, Anankē, *KP* I (München 1975) 332; *W. GUNDEL, *Beiträge zur Entwicklungsgeschichte der Begriffe Anankē und Heimarmene* (Giessen 1914); M. P. NILSSON, *Geschichte der griechischen Religion* II (München 1961²); E. PETERSON, Die Befreiung Adams aus der ἀνάγκη, *Frühkirche, Judentum und Gnosis* (Rome 1959) 107-128; *H. SCHRECKENBERG, *Anankē. Untersuchungen zur Geschichte des Wortgebrauchs* (München 1964); A. STROBEL, ἀνάγκη etc., *EWNT* I (Stuttgart 1980) 185-190.

P. W. VAN DER HORST

ANAT ענת

I. The MT makes no direct reference to the goddess Anat, though several scholars have proposed interpretations and conjectural emendations that would create references or allusions to her in the biblical text. As the MT stands, however, her name appears unequivocally only as a component of one personal and one place name, Shamgar ben Anat (Judg 3:31) and Beth Anat (Josh 19:38 and Judg 1:33) respectively. Her name might also be evidenced in the place names Anathoth and Beth Anot and the personal name Anathoth.

In Ugaritic Anat's name is written *ʿnt,* and in Akkadian (which cannot represent ʿ) it is written *Ḫanat, Anat,* and (once) *Kanat.* Given the Hebrew spelling with *ʿayin,* and given that the Ugaritic alphabet included the consonants *ǵ* and *ḫ*, it seems clear that the first radical of her name goes back to proto-Semitic *ʿ. In texts from Emar the name of the goddess may be hidden behind the Sumerogram ᵈNIN.URTA (NAʾAMAN 1990: 254).

There has been a great deal of speculation concerning the etymology of the name Anat, with no conclusive results. For collections of the various suggestions, which typically are based on scholars' perceptions of Anat's character, see GRAY (1979:321 and n. 42), DEEM (1978:25-27 and notes), PARDEE (1990:464-466) and SMITH (forthcoming). Of these, Kapelrud's proposal to understand Anat's name in connection with the verb *ʿānâ* "to sing" (1969:28: KB's *ʿnh* IV) can be dismissed on the grounds that the first radical of the Arabic cognate is *ǵ*, and DEEM's suggestion of a hypothetical root **ʿnh* "to make love" lacks evidence. The most attractive proposal is GRAY's suggestion to compare Anat's name with Arabic

ʿanwat "force, violence" (KB's *ʿnh* II, **ʿnw*). This accords well with a primary feature of Anat's character, and dovetails with W. G. LAMBERT's (VTSup 40 [1986] 132) proposal to see an etymological connection between Anat's name and the Hanaeans (*Ḫa-nu-ú*; see KUPPER 1957:1 n. 1). The Hanaeans were an Amorite/northwest Semitic group who are referred to numerous times in the eighteenth century BCE Mari archives. Also mentioned numerous times in the archives is *dḫa-na-at*, and a place called *dḫa-na-at*ki or *bīt dḫa-na-at*ki, which was located about 125 kilometers downstream from Mari. While no text explicitly calls the goddess Hanat goddess of the Hanaeans, Lambert's proposal seems nevertheless attractive. However, it should be noted that the city of Hanat was not located in primarily Hanaean territory (M. ANBAR, *Les tribus amurrites de Mari* [OBO 108; Göttingen 1991]).

II. The available evidence indicates that Anat was originally a north-west Semitic goddess. The main source of information about her in this context is the Ugaritic corpus of texts. The predominant view among scholars is that the Ugaritic texts present Anat as a "fertility goddess" who is the consort of the god →Baal. It is also often stated that she is the mother of Baal's offspring. Some scholars further allege that the texts present her as acting like a prostitute, either to entice Baal specifically, or in her general conduct. Even when she is described in what seems to be more respectful terms as Baal's sacred bride, this carries overtones of illegitimate sexuality because it implies cultic enactments of the so-called sacred marriage, which is also referred to by many scholars as ritual prostitution. For a critique of the widely held scholarly assumption that all ancient Near Eastern goddesses are sexually active "fertility" goddesses, see HACKETT (1989:65-76) and WALLS (1992:13-75; for Anat in particular, cf. AMICO 1989:457-492). For a review and evaluation of the evidence for the alleged practice of ritual prostitution in north-west Semitic religion, see ODEN (*The Bible Without Theology* [San Francisco 1987] 131-153).

The view that Anat is depicted in the Ugaritic texts as a sexually active and possibly reproductive deity has been recently challenged by DAY (1991 and 1992) and WALLS (1992), who argue that there is no clear reference in the Ugaritic texts to Anat engaging in sexual intercourse. Rather, Anat's alleged sexual activity has, in some cases, been entirely reconstructed in available lacunae, and *hapax legomena* and other cryptic words and episodes have been invested with appropriately supportive meanings. The argument based on identifying Anat with cows that Baal has sex with is demonstrably erroneous. In *KTU* 1.10 ii:26-29 Anat is clearly distinguishable from a cow that Baal presumably mates with, as 1.10 iii:33-36 clearly announces the birth of his bovine children. The heifer that Baal mates with in *KTU* 1.5 v:18-22 is also clearly not Anat, for Anat subsequently does not know where Baal is, and her search leads her to the place where he and the heifer mated (1.5 vi:26-31). The fact that Anat is both described and depicted as horned is surely not a feature to be literally understood and physically attributed to *female* bovines, but rather is a symbol of royal or divine authority. Anat's frequent designation as the sister (*aḫt*) of Baal is not conclusive evidence of a sexual liason. Her epithet *ybmt limm* has thus far defied confident translation and hence can not be used as a basis for arguing that she is procreative. *KTU* 1.3 iii:4-8 is most plausibly interpreted as Anat singing about the mutual attraction between Baal and Pidray, Tallay and Arṣay (N. WALLS 1992:116-122). The description of Anat as a wetnurse (*KTU* 1.15 ii:26-28) denotes her special associations with warriors and with royalty (WALLS 1992:152-154; cf. Isa 49:23; 60:16) and does not necessitate viewing her as procreative (DAY 1992:190 n. 63). Arguments for Anat's alleged procreativity that are based on theophoric personal names evidenced at Ugarit and elsewhere (e.g. EATON 1964:14), such as *a-na-ti-um-mì* ("Anat is my mother") and *bin-anat* ("son of Anat" [both names cited by GRÖNDAHL 1967:321]) can be challenged by interpreting such kinship names as metaphorically denoting status relationships, and by viewing these names alongside other names such as *adanu-ummu* ("the Lord is mother"), *ʿṯtr-um* ("Ashtar is mother" [both names cited by GRÖNDAHL 1967:46]) and *ḫa-mi-dḪa-na-at* ("Anat is my paternal uncle [?]" [H. HUFFMON, *Amorite Personal Names in the Mari Texts* (Baltimore 1965) 201] cf. →Am). Finally, *KTU* 1.96 does not mention Anat, and even if her name should be read in place of *ʿnh*, the first word of the text, what seems clear from the opening lines is cannibalistic, not sexual (cf. SMITH, forthcoming).

Anat is depicted in the Ugaritic mythological texts as a volatile, independent, adolescent warrior and hunter. Her epithet *btlt* indicates that she is (as defined by her culture) a marriageable adolescent female, but it is precisely because she "refuses to grow up" and take her place in the adult, female sphere of marriage and reproductivity that she can remain active in the male spheres of combat and hunting. As a warrior she vanquishes both human (*KTU* 1.3 ii) and supernatural (*KTU* 1.3 iii:38-46) foes, employing typical weapons of combat such as the bow (*KTU* 1.3 ii:16) and sword (*KTU* 1.6 ii:31). Her bloodthirsty nature is shockingly explicit in one well-known text (*KTU* 1.3 ii:3-30) in which she is described as joyously wading thigh-deep in the blood of slain warriors. She claims (*KTU* 1.3 iii:38-42; cf. 1.83 8-10) to have defeated Yamm/the twisting →serpent (→Sea, →Leviathan), a conquest elsewhere attributed to Baal (*KTU* 1.2 iv; 1.5 i:1-3) and a necessary step towards Baal's aquisition of kingship. Though supportive of Baal's quest for a palace and kingship in the Baal Cycle (*KTU* 1.3 v), her interests and actions run contrary to Baal's in the Aqhat Epic. In the Aqhat Epic, Aqhat's existence is attributed to Baal's petitioning →El on Danel's behalf for a royal heir. Yet Anat resolves to murder Aqhat in order to obtain his hunting bow, which he has denied her partially on the grounds that bows and hunting belong in the male domain (*KTU* 1.17 vi:39-40; 1.18 iv; DAY 1992:181-182). Vowing revenge for Aqhat's refusal to give her his bow, Anat storms off and threatens El with violence in order to secure his support for her retaliation. She then feigns reconciliation with Aqhat, and possibly offers to teach him how to hunt (*KTU* 1.18 i:24, 29; DAY 1992:181-182). When it becomes clear that Anat intends to murder Aqhat in order to obtain his bow and arrows, the method she is described as employing to achieve her purpose clearly befits a huntress: she uses her accomplice Yatpan like an eagle (*nšr*), a bird of prey used by hunters in the ancient Near East, to attack and kill Aqhat, her quarry (1.18 iv; cf. BARNETT 1978:29* n.10). Two other texts also portray Anat as a huntress. In *KTU* 1.22 i:11 birds are her prey, and in *KTU* 1.114 22-23 she leaves El's banquet to go hunting. In addition to being a huntress, *KTU* 1.10 and 1.13 possibly portray Anat as a benefactress of animals (DAY 1992:183-188).

Extrabiblically, and in addition to the Ugaritic texts, the following evidence for Anat on Syro-Palestinian soil has been adduced. In a document from Hazor that W. Hallo and H. Tadmor date to the 18th-16th centuries BCE, the personal names *mDUMU-ḫa-nu-ta* and *mSu-um-ḫa-nu-ta* are explained by HALLO & TADMOR as Anat names (A Lawsuit From Hazor, *IEJ* 27 [1977] 1-11). *EA* 170:43 mentions a person from Byblos named Anati, and a Syrian ship captain named *bn ʿnt* is mentioned in the time of Ramesses II (compare EATON 1964:28 with BOWMAN 1978:225). Several campaign records from Egypt mention a Levantine Beth Anat (BOWMAN 1978:210-212) and a place named *qrt-ʿnt* also might be Levantine (EATON 1964:31). A 13th c. BCE Egyptian ostracon mentions a festival of Anat at Gaza (B. GRDSELOFF, *Les Débuts du Culte de Rechef en Égypte* [Cairo 1942] 35-39), and a stele depicting Anat was found in a temple built by Ramesses III at Beth Shan. Both Gaza and Beth Shan were important Egyptian military posts of the time. The Beth Shan stele refers to Anat (spelled *ʿntt*, but the final *t* is simply a graphic marker of feminine gender [personal communications, T. O. LAMBDIN and J. F. BORGHOUTS]) as "the →queen of heaven, the mistress of all the gods" (A. ROWE, *The Four Canaanite Temples of Beth-Shan* [Philadelphia 1940] 33) which echoes *KTU* 1.108 6-7, where she is called "the mistress of kingship, the mistress of dominion, the mistress of the high heavens" (*bʿlt mlk bʿlt drkt bʿlt šmm rmm)* and which is also consistent with 19th Dynasty evidence from Egypt (see below). An arrowhead that F. M. CROSS (1980:4 and 6-7) thinks belonged to the El-Khaḍr hoard and dates ca. 1100 BCE is inscribed with the personal name *ʿbdlbʾt bn ʿnt*. Commenting on this arrowhead in light of other onomastic evidence, including the Biqaʿ Dart, which he reconstructs as containing the reading *bn bn ʿn[t]*, Cross notes that the surname *Bin ʿAnāt* is associated with military families, and that in this context "names bearing—as an element—the epithet or proper name of the war goddess were no doubt deemed fitting if not phylactic" (CROSS 1980:7). The surname *bn ʿnt* is also found on an Hebrew seal of unknown provenance that N. AVIGAD (Two Seals of Women and Other Hebrew Seals, *ErIsr* 20 [1989] 95 [Hebrew], 197*) dates to the 8th-7th centuries BCE. Two 7th c. BCE Esarhaddon treaties can be confidently reconstructed in light of each other to refer to a West Semitic deity *dA-na-ti-Ba-a-a-ti-DINGiR.MEŠ,* though scholars are divided over whether the component *A-na-ti* should be understood as the name Anat or as a common noun (e.g. compare VAN DER TOORN 1992:80-85 and nn. with OLYAN 1987:170). BOWMAN (1978:247-248) attributes to Gaza an inscribed situla of Prince Psammetichus upon which there is a representation of a goddess identified by the inscription as Anat, "Lady of Heaven". HVIDBERG-HANSEN (1979:86) asserts that the situla dates from the time of Psammetichus I, following GRDSELOFF (*op. cit.*, 28), who originally published the situla. Yet there seems to be no evidence linking this situla to Gaza, nor any confirmation that the Psammetichus in question is Psammetichus I. Indeed, J. LECLANT (1973:257 n. 37) expresses doubts about the authenticity of this situla (as well as about the uninscribed frontispiece of U. Cassuto's *The Goddess Anath* which, some scholars have argued, depicts Anat as pregnant), based upon repeated documentational irregularities regarding pieces in the Michaelides collection (personal communication). Finally, numerous scholars still follow W. F. ALBRIGHT (1925:88-90) in understanding the divine name Atta as the Aramaean equivalent of Anat, and in understanding the divine name →Atargatis as evidence that Anat and →Astarte merged to become this single deity. However, due to the general tendency among many scholars of the Hebrew Bible and the ancient Near East to presume that goddesses are not clearly distinguishable from one another in terms of their roles and functions (HACKETT 1989:65-76), the validity of proposals to equate goddesses or to see in a single divine name the blending of goddesses needs critical reassessment on a case by case basis. For Atta personal names in Syria, see BOWMAN 1978:218-219.

Four Phoenician inscriptions from Idalion, Cyprus, three of which were found in the vicinity of the Athena/Anat temple, mention Anat. Her name is written on an equestrian blinder and on a spearhead (*RES* 1209a and 1210), thus attesting to her continued martial associations. O. MASSON & M. SZNYCER (*Recherches sur les Phéniciens à Chypre* [Paris 1972] 110) date the blinder to the 7th century BCE, and É. PUECH (Remarques sur quelques inscriptions phéniciennes de Chypre, *Sem* 29 [1979] 29) dates the spearhead late fifth/early fourth c. BCE. Both publications interpret these items as votive. *RES* 453, found in the church of St. George, reads *lʿnt* in a broken context and her name is written on a piece of bronze (M. OHNEFALSCH-RICHTER, *Kypros, the Bible and Homer* [1893] pl. CXLI, no. 4). Also on Cyprus, Anat is named in the Phoenician portion of a bilingual text from Larnaka that names →Athena in the corresponding place in the Greek portion of the inscription (*CIS* 95). Given Athena's well-known martial associations as well as her characterization as a non-sexually active, non-reproductive goddess, once again the Cypriot evidence is consistent with the Ugaritic and other mainland evidence. For Anat as a component of Punic personal names, see F. L. BENZ (*Personal Names in the Phoenician and Punic Inscriptions* [Rome 1972] 382) and HVIDBERG-HANSEN (1979:143 n. 328). Contra OLYAN (1987:169) and ACKERMAN (1992:19), the relative paucity of Phoenicio-Punic Anat names should not be considered an accurate indicator of Anat's waned popularity or lack of importance in mythology in the Phoenicio-Punic world. At Ugarit, where she clearly plays a central role in the mythology, her name seldom appears as a component of personal names (GRØNDAHL 1967:83). Note also that Olyan and Ackerman neglect to cite the evidence from Idalion mentioned above as well as much of the first millennium Egyptian evidence cited by Leclant and Bowman (see below) in their discussions of first millennium data relevant to Anat.

As stated in section one, Hanat/Anat is mentioned numerous times in the 18th c. BCE Mari archives, as is a place called ^{d}*Ḫa-na-at*^{ki} or *Bīt* ^{d}*Ḫa-na-at*^{ki}, an important city in the extreme south-east of the territory controlled by Mari. For example, ARM 26 1/1 no. 196 makes reference to an oracle of ^{d}*Ḫanat* concerning troops from Eshnunna advancing towards her city (J.-M. DURAND, ARM 26 1/1, 423 note e) and ARM 26 1/2 no. 507 mentions her temple, presumably in the city of Hanat. ARM 21 no. 110 lists offerings that Zimri-Lim took to Hanat for the goddess. The city is mentioned several times in Assyrian and Babylonian campaign annals (B. K. ISMRIL [*sic*, Ismail] et al., ʿAna in the Cuneform [*sic*] Sources, *Sumer* 39 [1983] 191-194). A recently published text (CAVIGNEAUX & ISMAIL 1990, text no. 17) indicates that Hanat/Anat continued to be an important deity in this city into the 8th c. BCE. Indeed, in this eighth century text she is called "the most exalted of the goddesses, the strongest of the goddesses, the greatest of the Igigi...whose valour among the goddesses has no counterpart" (*šá-qa-a-at i-la-a-ti gaš-rat* ^{d}EŠ$_4$.DAR^{meš} GAL-*at* ^{d}*i-gi*$_4$*-gi*$_4$*-e* ... *ša i-na* ^{d}EŠ$_4$.DAR^{meš} *la iš-šá-an-na-nu qur-di-šu*). For Anat and Atta personal names in Mesopotamia, see EATON (1964:20) and BOWMAN (1978:205-208). D. ARNAUD (*Emar* VI.3 no. 216) finds the PN *A-nat-um-mi* at Emar.

Evidence for Anat in Egypt has been collected by J. LECLANT (1973:253-258; add the Memphite bowl published by D. B. REDFORD in the same year [1973:36-49]), whose article is a necessary corrective to BOWMAN's (1978:223-259) generally well-informed discussion. The available evidence indicates that Anat made her debut in Egypt in conjunction with the Hyksos (for Sinai, see M. DIJKSTRA & I. BRIGGS, Proto-Sinaitic Sinai 527- A Rejoinder, *BN* 40 [1987] 7-10), and she continued to be worshipped in Egypt into the Greek and Roman eras.

What follows is a selective rather than comprehensive presentation of the Egyptian evidence. The inscriptions, stelae and statuary of Ramesses II provide the earliest sustained body of evidence for Anat in Egypt (LECLANT 1973:253-254 and nn. 5-15; BOWMAN 1978:225-234). Ramesses regularly calls her the Mistress or Lady of (the) Heaven(s) in the context of claiming Anat's support in battle and legitimation of his right to 'universal' rule. It is in this context that he claims a mother/son relationship with her (cf. the royal ideology of Pss 2:7-9; 89:10-11.21-28; 110:3). Also in the context of an assertion of Ramesses' prowess in battle he is called *mhr* of Anat, most likely to be translated "suckling" on the basis of an Egyptian etymology rather than "soldier" on the basis of an Ugaritic etymology. He had a hunting dog named "Anat is Protection" and a sword inscribed "Anat is Victorious". In short, the picture that emerges is remarkably consistent with what we know of Anat from the Ugaritic texts. With regard to Anat's alleged sexual activity and procreativity, papyrus Chester Beatty VII can no longer be rallied as evidence. Prior to its collation with an unnumbered Turin papyrus (A. ROCCATI, Une légende égyptienne d'Anat, *REg* 24 [1972] 154-159) Anat's name was read into the lacuna that named →Seth's sexual partner. The Turin papyrus demonstrates that it is The Seed, not Anat, who copulates with Seth. Two other texts (Chester Beatty I = *The Contendings of Horus and Seth* and Harris Magical Papyrus III) which are typically cited as evidence of Anat's sexual activity and procreativity are amenable to other interpretations (WALLS 1992:145-146, 149-152). Even if it should be undoubtedly established, however, that Anat is portrayed as sexually active/reproductive in Egyptian mythology, the Egyptian evidence should not automatically be used as a basis for reconstructing Anat's persona in northwest Semitic mythology (WALLS 1992:144-145). With regard to the contention that Anat and Astarte are not always distinguished from one another, Anat and Astarte are indeed sometimes paired in Egyptian sources but perhaps this is because both were originally foreign goddesses from an Egyptian point of view, and so they could both, under certain circumstances, signify similar things. For example, in magical texts both are invoked as protection against wild animals and to ward off demons, 'logical' functions for goddesses who are at the same time both familiar/assimilated into Egyptian mythology and strange/of foreign origin. This is not to say, however, that their identities had been completely merged. To my knowledge, for pre-Hellenistic times, only the Winchester relief, which depicts a single goddess but names three (Qudshu, Astarte and Anat) provides possible evidence for the actual merging of northwest Semitic goddesses in Egypt. According to I. E. S. EDWARDS (A Relief of Qudshu-Astarte-Anath in the Winchester College Collection, *JNES* 14 [1955] 49-51 and pl.III), who originally published the relief, it is of unknown provenance and peculiar in a number of ways. His overall evaluation is that the piece departs from strict convention both representationally and textually, which he interprets as an indication that "the piece was the work of an artist who did not belong to the orthodox school and who was not completely familiar with the Egyptian script" (*ibid.*, 51). The present whereabouts of the relief is, according to collection's curator, apparently unknown (S. WIGGINS, The Myth of Asherah: Lion Lady and Serpent Goddess, *UF* 23 [1991] 387). Finally, mention should be made of evidence from Aramaic texts in Egypt. The DN Anat may be a component in two DNs at Elephantine, *ʿntyhw* and *ʿntbytʾl*. Again, scholars are divided over whether to understand the component *ʿnt* as Anat or as a common noun. If it is indeed correct to read Anat as the initial component of these names, it does not inevitably follow that the names should be interpreted to mean "Anat (consort of) →Bethel" and "Anat (consort of) Yahu". Indeed, it would be most odd to find a single goddess sexually paired with two gods on a standard basis at the same time in the same location. Dupont-Sommer's decision to read "Baal, spouse of Anat" in the last line of a stele of unknown provenance (Une stèle araméenne d'un prêtre de Baʿal trouvée en Égypte, *Syria* 33 [1956] 79-87) is largely based on his understanding that Anat is represented as Baal's wife at Ugarit and thus proceeds from a debatable reading of the Ugaritic evidence with which I do not agree. S. ACKERMAN (1992:17-18) raises doubts about the authenticity of an Aramaic inscription that names a certain *mšhʾl* as a priest of Anat. The piece was in the Michaelides collection (see above).

III. The MT makes no direct reference to the goddess Anat. However, proposals to conjecturally emend two texts to include mention of Anat have attracted serious scholarly attention, two additional texts have been interpreted as referring to her by epithet, and two more texts have been understood to allude to her. In addition, one text may make a veiled reference to the Anat temple at Beth Shan.

Several scholars have maintained that MT's *ʿannôt* in Exod 32:18 either should be conjecturally emended to read Anat or makes an allusion to Anat. When explanations for the appropriateness of such proposals are offered, one is that the golden calf constructed by the Israelites was a representation of Anat in bovine form, and another (not necessarily separate) explanation is that the licentious behaviour that the Israelites were allegedly engaging in as part of their celebration is consistent with Anat's 'nature'. In response to the former, it has been demonstrated above that there is no text that portrays Anat in bovine form, and in any event the calf in Exod 32 is *ʿgl*, "a young bull", and not a heifer (*ʿglh*). In response to the latter, while there is ample evidence in the Hebrew Bible of both the metaphorical equation of non-Yahwistic worship and illicit sexual behaviour as well as the characterization of non-Yahwistic worship as including extraconjugal intercourse, there is no evidence that licentious behaviour should be associated with celebrations in honour of Anat. Hence the plausibility of understanding *ʿannôt* to mean "revelling" or the like does not entail positing an allusion to Anat.

A number of scholars have recently put forward arguments in support of emending Hos 14:9b (English 14:8b) to refer to Anat and →Asherah (or an *ʾăšērâ*). The plausibility of the emendation is seen to be enhanced by the discovery at Kuntillet Ajrud of an inscription referring to Yahweh of Samaria and his *ʾăšērâ* /Asherah. (For discussion of the interpretation of the inscription, see S. OLYAN, *Asherah and the Cult of Yahweh in Israel* [Atlanta 1988] 23-34.) While this inscription certainly advances our understanding of biblical references to Asherah's/her cult symbol's relationship to Yahweh, it does not shed light on the alleged pairing of Anat and Asherah in Hos 14, nor does it clarify in what sense Yahweh allegedly affirms that he *is* Ephraim's Anat and Asherah. It is not a sufficient explanation to say, as M. WEINFELD (1984:122) does, that Anat and Asherah are similar in character and that both are responsible for 'fertility', hence Hosea's alleged point is that Yahweh is claiming the goddesses' powers of fertility. In short, no convincing argument has been made to support the proposed emendation, and MT as it stands makes good sense.

In his detailed discussion of Job 31:1, A. CERESKO (1980:105-108) proposed understanding MT's *bĕtûlâ* as a reference to Anat by the Hebrew equivalent of *btlt*, the epithet frequently applied to Anat in the Ugaritic texts (cf. M. POPE, *Job* [Garden City [3]1973] 229). The form-critical and other issues involved in determining the plausibility of Ceresko's suggestion within the broader context of Job 29-31 are too complex to present here: the interested reader should consult the standard commentaries for discussion and bibliography. Broader issues aside, the more conventional interpretation, which draws attention to Sir 9:5, makes plausible sense, while following Ceresko's line of reasoning it is unclear why Job's author would choose a veiled reference to Anat to make the general point that Job has not worshipped other gods.

Largely on the basis of Ugaritic and Egyptian evidence that Anat was referred to as the Mistress of the Heavens and like titles (see above), several scholars have suggested that the →Queen of Heaven referred to in Jer 7:18 and 44:17 is Anat. The issue of the Queen of Heaven's identity has been treated recently and in depth by S. OLYAN (1988:161-174) and S. ACKERMAN (1992:5-35). Although they do not reach the same conclusion, their arguments militate against seeing Anat as Jeremiah's Queen of Heaven.

Two proposals to see allusions to Anat in the biblical text can be mentioned briefly. P. G. CRAIGIE (Deborah and Anat: A Study of Poetic Imagery (Judges 5), *ZAW* 90 [1978] 374-381) argued that five specific features are shared by Anat and the biblical judge Deborah. The features elicited are unconvincing. A similarly unconvincing argument to see an allusion to Anat in Cant 7 has been made by M. POPE (*Song of Songs* [Garden City 1977] 606). In light of the discovery of an Anat temple at Beth Shan (see section two, above) A. ROWE (*The Four Canaanite Temples of Beth-Shan* [Philadelphia 1940] 31) suggested that the Beth Shan temple mentioned in 1 Sam 31:10 as the place where the Philistines took the slain Saul's armour was the Anat temple. Though Rowe arrived at this conclusion based in part on the erroneous presupposition that Anat and Ashtoreth were names of a single goddess, the proposition differently argued is a plausible one. The MT refers to the place where Saul's armour was deposited as the *bêt*, "temple", of the *'ăštārôt*, and other references to *'ăštārôt* in the Deuteronomistic history (Judg 2:13; 10:6; 1 Sam 7:3; 12:10) make it clear that this plural form had the generic meaning "goddesses" (cf. the contemporaneous Akkadian plural *ištarātu*, "goddesses"). Thus MT does not identify the temple as belonging to Ashtoreth/ Astarte, but rather altogether avoids naming any particular goddess by using the vague, dismissive, and possibly inaccurate plural. Given Anat's clear portrayal as a warrior and a patron or guardian of warriors and royalty in extrabiblical sources, and given that we know she had a temple in Beth Shan, it makes good sense to suggest that the armour of a vanquished warrior-king would be brought to her temple by the grateful victors.

Aside from the possibility that Anat is mentioned or alluded to in one or more of the above texts, her name appears in the Hebrew Bible as a component of the name Shamgar ben Anat, a warrior reputed to have slain with a mere oxgoad six hundred Philistines (Judg 3:31; cf. Shupak 1989 and see also the El Khaḍr arrowhead and Hebrew seal discussed in section two) and in the place name Beth Anat (Josh 19:38; Judg 1:33). It has also been argued that a dialect variant of her name is found in the place name vocalized in the MT as *bêt 'ănôt*. A. G. Auld 1977:85-86 can be consulted for references and a counter argument. For a discussion of whether the place name Anathoth (e.g. Jer 1:1) and the personal name Anathoth (Neh 10:20; 1 Chr 7:8) should be derived from the name Anat, see Bowman 1978:209-210 and Eaton 1964: 33.

IV. *Bibliography*

S. Ackerman, *Under Every Green Tree. Popular Religion in Sixth-Century Judah* (Atlanta 1992) esp. 5-35; E. B. Amico, *The Status of Women at Ugarit* (unpublished Ph.D. dissertation University of Wisconsin 1989) esp. 457-492; A. G. Auld, A Judean Sanctuary of 'Anat (Josh. 15:59)?, *Tel Aviv* 4 (1977) 85-86; R. D. Barnett, The Earliest Representation of 'Anath, *ErIsr* 14 (1978) 28*-31*; C. H. Bowman, *The Goddess 'Anatu in the Ancient Near East* (unpublished Ph.D. Dissertation; Berkeley 1978) [& lit]; A. Cavigneaux & B. K. Ismail, Die Statthalter von Suḫu und Mari im 8. Jh. v. Chr., *BagM* 21 (1990) 321-456; A. R. Ceresko, *Job 29-31 in the Light of Northwest Semitic* (Rome 1980); I. Cornelius, Anat and Qudshu as the «Mistress of Animals». Aspects of the Iconography of the Canaanite Goddesses, *SEL* 10 (1993) 21-45; F. M. Cross, Newly Found Inscriptions in Old Canaanite and Early Phoenician Scripts, *BASOR* 238 (1980) 1-20; J. Crowley, *The Aegean and the East* (Copenhagen 1989); P. L. Day, Why is Anat a Warrior and Hunter?, *The Bible and the Politics of Exegesis* (eds. D. Jobling *et al.*; Cleveland 1991) [& lit.]; Day, Anat: Ugarit's "Mistress of Animals", *JNES* 51 (1992) 181-190 [& lit]; A. Deem, The Goddess Anath and Some Biblical Hebrew Cruces, *JSS* 23 (1978) 25-30; M. Delcor, Une allusion à 'Anath, déesse guerrière en Ex 32:18?, *JJS* 33 (1982) 145-160; A. W. Eaton, *The Goddess Anat: The History of Her Cult, Her Mythology and Her Iconography* (unpublished Ph.D. dissertation; Yale 1964); R. M. Good, Exodus 32:18, *Love and Death in the Ancient Near East* (eds. J. H. Marks & R. M. Good; Guilford 1987) 137-142 [& lit]; J. Gray, The Blood Bath of the Goddess Anat in the Ras Shamra Texts, *UF* 11 (1979) 315-324; F. Gröndahl, *Die Personennamen der Texte aus Ugarit* (Rome 1967); *J. Hackett, Can a Sexist Model Liberate Us? Ancient Near Eastern 'Fertility' Goddesses, *Journal of Feminist Studies in Religion* 5 (1989) 65-76; J.-G. Heintz, Une tradition occultée? La déesse cananéenne 'Anat et son *'ašērâh* [*sic*] dans le livre du prophète Osée (chap. 14, v. 9b), *Ktema* 11 (1986) 3-13; F. O. Hvidberg-Hansen, *La déesse TNT* (Copenhagen 1979); A. S. Kapelrud, *The Violent God-*

dess: Anat in the Ras Shamra Texts (Oslo 1969); J.-R. KUPPER, *Les nomades en Mésopotamie au temps des rois de Mari* (Paris 1957); J. LECLANT, Anat, *LdÄ* I (1973) 253-258 [& lit]; O. LORETZ, ʿAnat-Aschera (Hos 14:9) und die Inschriften von Kuntillet ʿAjrud, *SEL* 6 (1989) 57-65; N. NA'AMAN, On Gods and Scribal Traditions in the Amarna Letters, *UF* 22 (1990) 247-255; W. L. MICHEL, "BTWLH, "Virgin" or "Virgin (Anat)" in Job 31:1?", *Hebrew Studies* 23 (1982) 59-66; S. M. OLYAN, Some Observations Concerning the Identity of the Queen of Heaven, *UF* 19 (1987) 161-174; D. PARDEE, Ugaritic Proper Names, *AfO* 37 (1990) 390-513 (esp. 464-466) [& lit]; D. B. REDFORD, New Light on the Asiatic Campaigning of Ḥoremheb, *BASOR* 211 (1973) 36-49; N. SHUPAK, New Light on Shamgar ben ʿAnath, *Bibl* 70 (1989) 517-525; M. S. SMITH, Anat's Warfare Cannibalism and the West Semitic Ban, *Whoever Loves Discipline Loves Knowledge, But One Who Hates Reproof is Stupid: Memorial Essays in History and Historiography in Honor of Gösta W. Ahlström* (eds. S. W. Holladay & L. K. Handy; forthcoming); K. VAN DER TOORN, Anat-Yahu, Some Other Deities, and the Jews of Elephantine, *Numen* 39 (1992) 80-101; A. VAN SELMS, Judge Shamgar, *VT* 14 (1964) 294-309; *N. H. WALLS, *The Goddess Anat in Ugaritic Myth* (Atlanta 1992) [& lit]; M. WEINFELD, Kuntillet ʿAjrud Inscriptions and their Significance, *SEL* 1 (1984) 121-130.

P. L. DAY

ANCIENT OF DAYS

I. In a throne vision with mythological traits, God is depicted as the *ʿattîq yômîn/yômayyāʾ*, traditionally rendered as 'the Ancient of Days' (Dan 7:9.13.22). The expression is to be interpreted as a construct chain expressing a genetivus partitivus. The basic meaning of the common semitic root ʿTQ is 'to be advanced'. The expression then can be rendered as 'advanced in days' implying that the deity was seen as one 'far gone in years' or 'ancient of days'. The background of the imagery in Dan 7 has been looked for in Canaanite mythology (EMERTON 1958; COLLINS 1977; 1993); in a Mesopotamian text (KVANVIG 1988); and in contemporary Hellenistic/Egyptian mythological patterns (VAN HENTEN 1993). The imagery of the Ancient of Days has influenced the throne visions in *1 Enoch*.

II. The struggle between Antiochus IV Epiphanes//'the →Sea' and the 'one like a →Son of Man' in Dan 7 has been interpreted as a late rewriting of the mythic themes in the Ugaritic Baal-cycle in which the younger god →Baal enpowered by the older →El defeats the inimical Yammu (Sea; e.g. EMERTON 1958; COLLINS 1993). Although this view does not go unchallenged (FERCH 1980) and although it provokes problems on the level of interpretation, it must be conceded that in the Ugaritic texts El has some traits in common with the imagery of the 'Ancient of Days'. El is depicted as venerably aged; the grey hair of his beard (*šbt dqn*) is referred to (*KTU* 1.3 v:2. 25; 1.4 v:4; 1.18 i:12 [restored]). Moreover, he receives the epithet *ab šnm*, 'father of the years', by which he is portrayed as the oldest among the gods.

However, the rendition 'father of the years' for *ab šnm* read as **abu šanima* has not remained unchallenged. This challenge is provoked by two different features. 1) The plural of the Ugaritic noun for 'years' is normally construed in the feminine *šnt* and not the masculine *šnm*. Therefore, scholars have been arguing for different interpretations of the noun *šnm*. J. REIDER (Etymological Studies in Biblical Hebrew, *VT* 4 [1954] 283-284) and A. A. WIEDER (Three Philological Notes, *Bulletin of the Institute of Jewish Studies* 2 [1974] 108-109) proposed a translation '→Exalted Ones'. M. POPE (*El in the Ugaritic Texts* [VTSup 2; Leiden 1955] 34-36) suggested 'Father of the Eldest' which would indicate both the high age and the consequent weakness of El. 2) *šnm* occurs as the second element in the binomial deity *Ṯkmn-w-Šnm*, →Thukamuna-wa-→Shunama. H. GESE (*RAAM* 97-98. 193-104), A. JIRKU (*Šnm* (Schunama), der

Sohn des Gottes ʾIl, *ZAW* 82 [1970] 278-279) and C. H. GORDON (El, Father of Šnm, *JNES* 35 [1976] 261-262; FERCH 1980:82-83) read the expression *ab šnm* as an epithet for El: 'the father of Shunama'. Besides, J. AISTLEITNER (*WUS* Nr. 312) interprets *šnm* as "Die Bezeichnung der hochgelegenen himmlischen Wohnung Els". These alternative interpretations, however, are not convincing: 1) The epithet *ab šnm* occurs only in a formulaic sentence: "She/He/They appeared in the encampment of El and entered the camp of the King, the Father of Years" (Baal-epic: *KTU* 1.1 iii:23-34; 1.2 v:6; 1.3 v:7-8; 1.4 iv:23-24; 1.5 vi:1-2; 1.6 i:35-36; Aqhat: *KTU* 1.17 vi:48-49). 2) Although *šnm* is the regular plural for the feminine noun 'year', it should be noted that other nouns have variant plural-forms; e.g. *riš*, 'head' is attested in the plural as *rišt* as well as *rišm* (COLLINS 1993:127n. 25). 3) The deity Shunama occurs in Ugaritic texts only together with Thukamuna (D. PARDEE, *Ṯukamuna wa Šunama*, *UF* 20 [1988] 195-199). Although Shunama, together with Thukamuna, is presented as a son of El in the Ugaritic texts (*KTU* 1.65:1-4; 1.114) and the deity Thukamuna-wa-Shanuma holds a relatively prominent position in the Ugaritic pantheon-lists (J. C. DE MOOR, The Semitic Pantheon of Ugarit, *UF* 2 [1970] 215-216) it is not quite clear why the formulaic epithet *ab šnm* should refer to a deity not attested on its own in the mythological texts.

KVANVIG (1988) has tried to relate elements of the throne vision in Dan 7 with a seventh century BCE Assyrian text: 'The Underworld Vision of an Assyrian Prince' (SAA III, No. 32) in which 15 deities are portrayed in hybrid forms. Although this might give some religio-historical background to the vision of the four beasts, the depiction of God as 'ancient of days' is not elucidated by it, since in the Assyrian text an expression or epithet parallel to *ʿattîq yômîn/yômayyāʾ* cannot be found (COLLINS 1993:128-131).

VAN HENTEN (1993) has related the imagery of Dan 7 with contemporary Hellenistic-Egyptian material. He interprets the 'eleventh horn' as referring to Antiochus IV Epiphanes and as a character framed on the model of →Seth-→Typhon. As regards the designation 'Ancient of Days', VAN HENTEN (1993:227-228) refers to the fact that →Zeus has been regarded as the "author of days and years" and that →Thot was venerated as "lord of time" and "lord of old age".

III. In the designation 'Ancient of Days' two traits of Gods are interwoven. The concept of God's eternal existence (e.g. Ps 9:8; 29:10; 90:2; see also →El-olam) expressed in epithets as *ʾăbî ʿād*, 'everlasting father' (Isa 9:5) and *melek ʿôlām*, 'eternal king' (Jer 10:10). The notion of God as an old man popular in Hellenistic times (HARTMAN & DI LELLA 1978:217-218) may have traces in the OT (e.g. Job 36:26).

In the throne vision of Dan 7 the Ancient of Days appears sitting at the head of the divine →Council. From the continuation of the vision it becomes clear that the Ancient of Days is identical with Yahweh, the God of Israel. He takes away the power from the fourth beast and enpowers the one like a →Son of Man with 'dominion, glory and kingdom' in order to rule righteously over the →Saints of the Most High.

The designation 'Ancient of Days' has influenced the imagery in the Similitudes of *1 Enoch*. In various throne visions, God is depicted as *rēʾša mawāʿēl*, 'Head/Sum of Days' (*1 Enoch* 46:1. 2; 47:3; 55:1; 60:2; 71:10-14) who likewise will enpower the forthcoming Son of Man with everlasting rule.

IV. *Bibliography*

J. J. COLLINS, *The Apocalyptic Vision of the Book of Daniel* (HSM 16; Missoula 1977); COLLINS, Stirring up the Sea. The religio-historical Background of Daniel 7, *The Book of Daniel in the Light of New Findings* (A. S. van der Woude, ed.; BETL 106; Leuven 1993) 121-136; J. A. EMERTON, The Origin of the Son of Man Imagery, *JTS* 9 (1958) 225-242; A. J. FERCH, Daniel 7 and Ugarit: a Reconsideration, *JBL* 99 (1980) 75-86; L. F. HARTMAN & A. A. DI LELLA, *The Book of Daniel* (AB 23; Garden City 1978); J. W. VAN HENTEN, Antiochus IV as a Typhonic

Figure in Daniel 7, *The Book of Daniel in the Light of New Findings* (A. S. van der Woude, ed.; BETL 106; Leuven 1993) 223-243; H. KVANVIG, *Roots of Apocalyptic* (WMANT 61; Neukirchen-Vluyn 1988); H. SCHMOLDT, *'tq*, *TWAT* 6 (1987) 487-489.

B. BECKING

ANGEL I מלאך

I. The consonants L'K in the Semitic languages signify 'send', with a more focused nuance in certain languages of specifically 'send with a commission/message' (CUNCHILLOS 1982). The *mēm-* prefix and *a*-vowels of Heb *mal'āk* conform generally to what is expected for an instrumental noun *(maqtal)* identifying the vehicle or tool by which the action of the verb is accomplished (in this case, the means by which a message is sent, hence 'messenger'). Because the verb is not attested in Hebrew, some suspect that this noun is a loan word from another language. However, since the root is widely attested in the Semitic languages, and since even the verb is attested in north-west Semitic (Ugaritic), it is best to see the Hebrew noun as a relic of a once more generative root that otherwise disappeared in Hebrew because of a semantic overlap with a preferred and less specific term ŠLḤ 'send'.

The Bible characteristically uses *mal'āk* to designate a human messenger (e.g. 1 Sam 11:4; 1 Kgs 19:2). A smaller number of the over 200 occurrences of the word in the OT refer to God's supernatural emissaries. As God's envoys, they represent extensions of God's authority and activity, beings "mighty in strength, who perform His word" (Ps 103:20).

Supernatural messengers in other ancient Near Eastern cultures typically are identified by the lexical item in that language also used to identify human messengers or subordinates sent on missions (Sum **kin-gi$_4$-a**, **sukkal**; Akk *mār šipri*; Eg *wpwty*; Ug *ǵlm, ml'ak*; Eth *mal'ak*). There is therefore no specially reserved term to distinguish a class of such gods from other gods on the one hand or from human messengers on the other. This is in contrast to the English 'angel', which is just such a specialized term qualitatively distinguishing God from his assistants, and a term which cannot be used of humans apart from metaphor (cf. the Vulgate's consistent use of *angelus* for divine messengers in contrast to human messengers identified by the noun *nuntius*). It is possible that the proper name of one Mesopotamian messenger deity (Malak, CT XXIV 33.24-31) preserves the West Semitic noun as a loan word in Akkadian.

II. The gods of the ancient Near East, like humans, communicated with each other over great distances by means of messengers. They were neither omniscient nor capable of immediately transporting themselves from one location to another. Although the gods were privy to knowledge largely unavailable to humans (cf. 2 Sam 14:20), they communicated and learned information about events and the cosmos in the same way humans did. Although many aspects of human communication find their counterpart in the divine realm, there are nevertheless several discontinuities (for data on generalizations below with respect to human messenger activity see MEIER 1988).

Those gods who cluster near the upper echelons of the pantheon typically dispatch as their envoys a single messenger who is a high official, often the **sukkal** in Mesopotamia (a Sumerian term that early on could designate a position of intimacy and authority second only to one's lord or mistress). Just as human messengers normally travelled alone unless there were special circumstances, so in the Mesopotamian god lists, there is a tendency to identify one specific messenger (*mār šipri*) in the employ of a god who needs such a figure. This reflects the general pattern found in mythological texts as well, where a god typically sends a single, specific, lower-ranking messenger god. Nuska and Kakka are messenger gods who appear frequently in Mesopotamian sources, serving different masters. One does find exceptions where larger numbers of messenger gods are in the employ of high ranking gods (e.g. seven and even eighteen messenger deities are attested for a single god [CT XXIV 33.24-31]). The war or storm god is unusual in typically dispatching more than one messenger god on errands (cf. GINZBERG 1944), perhaps safety or strength in numbers being a concomitant of his more belligerent profile.

The story of →Nergal and Ereshkigal suggests that a messenger deity might have abilities or privileges unparalleled among the other gods. In that account, the boundary between the underworld and the upper realm of the gods could be described as safely bridged only by a messenger deity, as the gods articulate: "We can not descend to you nor can you ascend to us" (Amarna version lines 4-5; in the Sultantepe version, the messengers bridge the distance by employing a stairway connecting the two realms; cf. the rainbow as the path along which the Greek divine female messenger Iris travels). The perception of the privileged status of a messenger god in bridging the gap is comparable to that of the Greek divine herald, →Hermes, who as the god of communication across boundaries is specifically associated with the boundary between the living and the →dead.

Some features of human messenger activity are not duplicated in the divine realm. The provision of escorts for human messengers was a common courtesy, if not a necessity, for safe or trouble-free communication. Passports and the circumvention of bureaucratic hurdles was a persistent feature of human communication. Provision for lodging and meals along an extended route was a necessity. None of these aspects of human communication reappears in depictions of divine messenger activity.

III. The translation of *mal'āk* by 'angel' in English Bibles obscures the ancient Israelite perception of the divine realm. Where English 'angel' is the undifferentiating term for all of God's supernatural assistants, *mal'āk* originally could be applied only to those assistants whom God dispatched on missions as messengers. Thus, an early Israelite from the period of the monarchy would probably not have identified the theriomorphic →cherubim and →seraphim as *mal'ākîm* 'messengers', for the frightful appearance of these creatures made them unlikely candidates to serve as →mediators of God's message to humans (and indeed, there is no record of their ever having done so in the Old Testament). Even the Greek word *angelos* meant at first simply 'messenger' (→Angel II). It is only in later texts in the Old Testament, and everywhere in Apocryphal and NT texts, that the words *mal'āk* and *angelos* become generic terms for any of God's supernatural assistants, whether they functioned as messengers or not. When English borrowed the term "angel" from Greek, it was not in its earlier sense 'messenger' but in its later significance of any supernatural being under God's authority.

Not all sections of the Bible describe divine messengers. In the D and P sections of the Pentateuch they are never mentioned, nor do they appear in most of the pre-exilic prophetic literature where prophets receive their messages directly from God. In texts where God speaks frequently and directly to humans, there is of course less need for a messenger to mediate God's message to humans. A tension is evident in the Bible between an earlier worldview evident in some texts where God speaks freely and comfortably with humans, while in other later passages God prefers to send subordinate emissaries to deal with humankind.

When God's messengers are portrayed in narratives as primary actors interacting with other characters, they typically are presented as individuals who work alone. The most obvious example of this is the →angel of Yahweh. Only occasionally are supernatural messengers (*mal'ākîm*) identified in groups of two or more in the OT. God is assumed to have a numerous pool—at one place described as a "camp" (Gen 32:2-3[1-2])—of these figures at his behest who bless and praise him (Pss 103:20; 148:2), employ a ladder to travel between heaven and earth (Gen 28:12), protect from physical harm the traveller who trusts in God (Ps 91:11-12), and are as swift and inscrutable in the performance of their task as the wind (Ps 104:4; both the masculine *rwḥy* and feminine *rwḥwt* plural construct of this word for 'wind, spirit' become one of the most common designations for angels at Qumran). More than one messenger may appear where Yahweh's envoys enter hostile territory or confront inimical humans (Gen 19:1-22; Ps 78:49).

A frequent role played by a messenger in the ancient Near East was to act as an escort to individuals who were travelling under the protection of the sender. Similarly, a divine messenger despatched by God accompanies humans on their travels to protect them *en route* in order to bring them safely to journey's end and the accomplishment of their tasks (Gen 24:7.40; Exod 14:19; 23:20-23; 32:34; 33:2; Tob 5:21), even providing food and drink for the traveller (1 Kgs 19:5-6). The later angelic protection of God's people in any context can be perceived as an extension of this original messenger task (Dan 3:28; 6:23[22]; Bar 6:6 [= Ep Jer 6]).

It is important to distinguish this protection *en route* from the custom of dispatching messengers in advance of distinguished travellers in order to inform their future hosts of their soon arrival. The Mari archives in particular point to an elaborate system of advance notification of arrivals and departures of significant travellers within a kingdom's territory. This aspect of messenger activity is not reproduced frequently in the divine realm, but it is found in a highly charged eschatological context that becomes the object of frequent attention in Judaism and Christianity: God sends his messenger in advance "to prepare a way before me" (Mal 3:1; cf. David b. Kimchi).

The primary burden of the messenger in the ancient Near East was not the verbatim delivery of a memorized message but the diplomatically nuanced explication of the sender's intent. It is appropriate, then, for a supernatural messenger from God not only to give messages from God to humans (1 Kgs 13:18; Zech 1:14), and even to other divine messengers (Zech 2:7-8[1:3-4]), but also to entertain questions from humans and explain perplexing features of messages from God (Zech 1:9; 2:2[1:19]; 4:1-6; 5:5-11; 6:4-5). This interpretative and hermeneutical role (the latter adjective derived from Hermes, the Greek divine herald who played a similar role) also accounts for the mediatorial function that divine messengers fulfilled in representing humans before God (Job 33:23-24, Tob 12:15): in the same way that human messengers completed their task by bringing the response of the addressee back to the sender, so God's messengers were responsible for bringing back and explicating the response of the humans to whom they were dispatched.

Human messengers were often responsible for the collection of debts and fines, and in general the satisfaction of outstanding obligations owed to their senders. When an obligation was not satisfied, appropriate measures were taken to enforce payment and punish the offender. God's supernatural messengers can function in a similar capacity, appearing in a combative and bellicose role *vis-à-vis* those who resist or rebel against God (Gen 32:25-29[24-28]; Hos 12:4; Ps 78:49; see →Destroyer).

Messengers were typically given provisions by the hosts to whom they were sent, and indeed Genesis 18 depicts God's messengers eating and drinking with humans. But other traditions insist that this is only apparent and not real (*Pal. Tgs.* Gen 18:8, "It seemed to him as if they were eating"), for divine messengers do not eat or drink terrestrial fare ("I did not eat or drink, but you saw a vision", Tob 12:19; cf. Judg 13:16; *b. Yoma* 75b). It is unconscionable for a messenger to refuse a friendly host's offer of food among humans, but the seemingly brusk behaviour of God's messengers in this regard may be tolerated in consideration of the fact that the food they are accustomed to is of a higher quality, more like manna (Ps 78:25; Wis 16:20; 4 Ezra 1:19 see F. SIEGERT, Können Engel essen?, in his *Drei hellenistisch-jüdische Predigten* II [Tübingen 1992] 253-255).

A divine messenger dispatched by God

has considerable authority and is to be obeyed as the representative of God that he is (Exod 23:20-22). This should not be taken, however, to imply that God's messengers were cast of the same moral rectitude and deserved the same trust as God himself. As humans invariably had problems with the veracity of their messengers, so divine messengers could not always be trusted to tell the truth or to reveal the entire purpose of their errands. God does not trust his own messengers (Job 4:18), and there are accounts of prevaricating and misleading messengers sent by God (1 Kgs 22:19-23; 2 Kgs 19:7; cf. 1 Kgs 13:18). Even Paul anticipates this possibility (Gal 1:8).

Divine messengers are usually depicted as indistinguishable from human beings (Heb 13:2; Gen 19:1-22; 32:25-31[24-30]; Dan 8:15; Tob 5:8.16; Luke 24:4; cf. Judg 13:3-23), while it is in the later books of the OT that they are depicted in overwhelmingly supernatural terms (Dan 10:6). Therefore, since humans could also be perceived as messengers sent from God—notably prophets (Hag 1:13), priests (Mal 2:7), and kings (1 Sam 29:9; 2 Sam 14:17.20; 19:28[27])—the use of the same term *malʾāk* to identify both human and supernatural messengers results in some passages where it is unclear which of the two is intended if no further details are provided (Judg 2:1-5; 5:23; Mal 3:1; Eccl. 5:5).

It is frequently asserted that messengers, when delivering their messages, often did not distinguish between themselves and the one who sent them. It is true that messengers do speak in the first person as if they were the sender of the message, but it is crucial to note that such speech, in unequivocal messenger contexts, is always preceded by a prefatory comment along the lines of "PN [the sender] said to you" after which the message is provided; thus, a messenger always clearly identifies the words of the one who sent the message. A messenger would subvert the communication process were he or she to fail to identify the one who sent the messenger on his or her mission. In texts that are sufficiently well preserved, there is never a question as to who is speaking, whether it be the messenger or the one who sent the messenger (MEIER 1992).

There is therefore no evidence for the frequently made assertion that messengers need not make any distinction between themselves and the ones who sent them. In its extreme form, this argument will even claim that messengers could be called by the names of the ones who sent them (cf. David b. Kimchi on Zech 3:2). The only contexts in biblical and ancient Near Eastern literature where no distinction seems to be made between sender and messenger occur in the case of the "angel (literally "messenger") of Yahweh" (*malʾak YHWH*). It is precisely the lack of differentiation that occurs with this figure, and this figure alone among messengers, that raises the question as to whether this is even a messenger of God at all. Some see it as originally Yahweh himself, modified through the insertion of the word *malʾāk* into the text in order to distance God from interacting with humans (possible motivations including a reticence to associate God with certain activities, or a developing tendency toward God's transcendence). It must be underscored that the angel of YHWH in these perplexing biblical narratives does not behave like any other messenger known in the divine or human realm. Although the term 'messenger' is present, the narrative itself omits the indispensable features of messenger activity and presents instead the activities which one associates with Yahweh or the other gods of the ancient Near East. "We can, omitting the word *malʾāk*, find in the J and E messenger stories exactly the same motifs and the same literary patterns as are common in all ancient Near Eastern literature" pertaining to the gods themselves, not their messengers (IRVIN 1978:103).

Some features of divine messenger activity elsewhere in the ancient Near East are not duplicated in Israel's religion by the very nature of Israel's monotheism. Enlil, for example, sends his envoy Nuska to negotiate a marriage for Enlil in the story of

Enlil and Sud, a task in which human messengers are frequently attested (cf. Genesis 24). Since God has no spouse (apart from his metaphorical bride Israel), he needs no messengers to arrange his nuptials. The angel who assists Tobit in overcoming the dangers of his marriage is a completely different matter, a function of the envoy who assists God's people in their endeavours (Tob 6:15-17).

IV. In literature written after the Old Testament, including the Apocrypha and New Testament, the functions typical of messengers continue to apply to what are now better termed in English as "angels". Thus, angels continue to serve as protectors to those who travel (*T. Jud.* 3:10), to relay and interpret God's messages to humans (2 *Bar* 55:3-56:56), or to requite disobedience to God (Acts 12:23). However, in this later literature, which continues to use the same messenger vocabulary (*mal'āk*, *angelos*), the role of messenger *per se* becomes less significant than the exalted, supernatural status of the marvelous being who now communicates God's message to humans. As a result, there is usually no problem in the later literature in distinguishing an angel from a human being, for the former's appearance is often quite awe-inspiring and frightening (e.g. Matt 28:3), and these later angels are carefully categorized according to an intricately complex hierarchy hardly detectable in the Old Testament. The reticence in the Old Testament to provide divine messengers with personal names is also abandoned in post-biblical literature, which even returns to the laconic biblical texts and supplies them with the names they originally lacked (e.g. Zagnugael in *Tg. Ps.-J.* Exod 3:2; see OLYAN 1993).

In Semitic texts, the word *mal'āk*, therefore, broadens its original significance of "messenger" and tends to become the word of choice to designate all supernatural beings who do God's work. If it applies to supernatural creatures opposed to God, it usually is qualified by an adjective such as "evil". Mandaean gnostic texts are a noteworthy exception, employing the word *mal'āk* not to describe good angelic-type beings (for which they instead employ the term *'uthra*) but instead the genii of sorcery or →evil spirits.

V. *Bibliography*

P. BONESCHI, Is *malak* an Arabic Word?, *JAOS* 65 (1945) 107-111; J.-L. CUNCHILLOS, La'ika, mal'āk et Mᵉlā'kāh en sémitique nord-occidental, *RSF*10 (1982) 153-160; H. L. GINZBERG, Baal's Two Messengers, *BASOR* 95 (1944) 25-30; D. IRVIN, *Mytharion. The Comparison of Tales from the Old Testament and the Ancient Near East* (Neukirchen-Vluyn 1978); S. MEIER, *The Messenger in the Ancient Semitic World* (HSM 45; Atlanta 1988); S. MEIER, *Speaking of Speaking. Marking Direct Discourse in the Hebrew Bible* (Leiden 1992) 277-291; S. M. OLYAN, *A Thousand Thousands served Him. Exegesis and the Naming of Angels in Ancient Judaism* (Tübingen 1993); P. SCHÄFER, *Rivalität zwischen Engeln und Menschen. Untersuchungen zur rabbinischen Engelvorstellung* (Studia Judaica 8; Berlin 1975).

S. A. MEIER

ANGEL II ἄγγελος

I. *Angelos* ("messenger"; Vg and VL *angelus*) is in Greek, Early Jewish and Christian literature the most common designation of an otherworldly being who mediates between →God and humans. In LXX the word is usually the translation of *mal'ak*. It occurs 175 times in NT (according to the editions of Nestle-Aland[26] and the Greek New Testament[3], including Luke 22:43, which is often considered as a later addition). It is used sometimes of human messengers (e.g. Jdt 1:11; in the NT Luke 7:24; 9:52; Jas 2:25, and the OT quotation referring to John the Baptist in Mark 1:2-3 and parallels). The most detailed 'angelology' in the NT is found in Rev (67 occurrences of *angelos*).

II. Angels are self-evident figures in Early Jewish and Christian literature, although not all Jewish groups accepted their existence (see Acts 23:8 concerning the Sadducees). OT conceptions of the *Mal'ak Yhwh* (→Angel of Yahweh) and the divine →council underlie the early Jewish and Christian ideas (MACH 1992), but pagan influences should be taken into account too. The etymology of *angelos* is not clear. The word originated somehow from the East (cf. ἄγγαρος "mounted courier" in Persia). The connection with Sanskrit *ángiras* is based on the assumption that this name refers to →mediators between gods and men and is not certain (H. FRISK, *Griechisches Etymologisches Wörterbuch* 1 [Heidelberg 1960] 7-8). To a certain extent angels could correspond to the →demons in Greek religion (cf. Philo, *Gigant.* 6; 16; →Demon). The Greeks were familiar with messengers from the gods since the archaic period, as appears from the *Iliad* and *Odyssey* where birds bring divine messages to humans (*Il.* 24:292, 315) and →Hermes acts as the *angelos* of the gods (*Od.* 5:29). For most of the appearances and functions of angels pagan parallels can be found, and in some cases the absorption of pagan conceptions is quite probable. This does apply already to older ideas like the heavenly army of YHWH (Josh 5:14, →Yahweh zebaoth) and the →sons of the gods (*Bĕnê ʾēlîm/ʾĕlōhîm*), which have parallels in North West Semitic mythology (MULLEN 1980); it is certainly also true for the Hellenistic period with its intensive cultural exchange. The traditions concerning (mounted) angels in 2 Maccabees are connected with the common motif of the *epiphaneia* of the patron god of the temple (2 Macc 2:21; 3:24), who protects his temple by causing natural phenomena or by sending his messengers. In the description of the rescue of the sanctuary of Delphi from the Gauls in 279 BCE by Pausanias the heroes Hyperochus, Laodocus, Pyrrhus and Phylacus appear in this role (10.23.1-2). The angels who assist the Jews on the battlefield (e.g. 2 Macc 10:29-31) correspond to pagan supernatural helpers like the →*Dioskouroi*. Compare also the guardian angels with certain Mesopotamian gods (A. FINET 1989:37-52), the fiery appearance of angels and divine messengers in North West Semitic texts (M. S. SMITH, Biblical and Canaanite Notes to the *Songs of the Sabbath Sacrifice* From Qumran, *RQ* 12 [1985-1987] 585-588), and angels as companions of the soul (*psychopompos*) after death (e.g. *T. Job* 52; cf. Luke 16:22; see →Demon, and →Hermes).

From the third century BCE onward the appearances of angels increase, their manifestations are described more extensively and their functions diverge more and more (see for instance *1 Enoch*, Tob, Dan, *Jub.*, 2 Macc). This development should not be explained by the coming into being of apocalyptic literature only (cf. MICHL 1962: 64: "Dabei ist es die mit dem Buche Daniel aufkommende Apokalyptik, die den fruchtbarsten Boden für diese Entwicklung bietet"; also MACH 1992:115), but also by the assimilation of popular ideas (see e.g. Tob) and the absorption of pagan conceptions (e.g. *Jos. and As.* and 2 Macc, MACH 1992: 242-249 and 265-278). In LXX ἄγγελος/-οι can be an interpretative translation of Hebrew or Aramaic expressions concerning sons of God or members of the divine council (e.g. LXX Job 2:1 for *Bĕnê ʾĕlōhîm*; LXX Dan 3:92 ὁμοίωμα ἀγγέλου θεοῦ for 3:25 MT דמה לבר־אלהין; Theodotion differently); LXX Dan 4:13.23 for עיר וקדיש Dan 4:10.20 MT (→Watcher). According to MACH (1992:65-113) the translators tried to avoid references to a (polytheistic) conception of several figures acting as gods/sons of God and to relate certain actions which were ascribed to God in MT rather to angels, because it did not become God to do these things (esp. LXX Job).

III. In Early Jewish and Christian literature the angelic messenger of the Lord is very common (*angelos kyriou/theou*). He appears on earth (e.g. →Gabriel in Luke 1-2) or manifests himself in a dream (Matt 1:20; 2:13.19) to bring a message from God or to help people (e.g. Acts 5:19). →Raphael accompanies Tobias (Tob 5:4-12:22) and helps him to get rid of the demon who caused the death of the earlier husbands of his bride Sarah (8:2-3). As a consequence of the fusion of the conceptions of the messenger of the Lord and the divine council, angels usually reside in heaven, i.e. near the throne of God (Rev 5:2.11), where they worship and praise him. The saying of →Jesus that the risen will live like angels in heaven (Mark 12:25 and parallels) can be connected to sources which refer to a coming community of humans and angels or a transformation to angels or →stars (e.g. *1 Enoch* 39:4-5; 71:11; 104:6; 4 Ezra 7:85. 95; in Qumran texts a common worship by humans and angels can be realized also in the present). Angels move forward in the air, but are rarely represented with wings (*1 Enoch* 61:1 according to some manuscripts). The angel of the Lord transports Habakkuk in one day from Judah to Babylon and back by carrying him by his hair to bring Daniel a meal in the lion-pit (Bel 33-39; cf. Ezek 8:3). Angels often resemble humans (Dan 8:15; 10:18; *Jos. As.* 14:3) and can have a shining or fiery appearance (Dan 10:5-6).

Angels engage in a variety of activities. They act as intermediaries for the revelation of the →Torah (Acts 7:53; Gal 3:19), reveal divine knowledge and explain revelations (Zech 1:9; 4:5-6; Dan 8:16; *4QSerekh Shirot ʿOlat ha-Shabbat* [NEWSOM 1985]; →Uriel in *4 Ezra*). The angel of the Lord gives the spirit of understanding to →Daniel (LXX Sus 44-45). The angel of Jesus reveals to John's hearers his testimony for the churches (Rev 22:16). The heavenly visitor (→Michael) mentions the angel *Metanoia* as his sister to Aseneth after her confession (*Jos. As.* 15:7-8). Metanoia is a daughter of the Most High (STROTMANN 1991) and will intercede for Aseneth and all who repent in the name of the Most High (cf. Phanuel as angel of repentance in *1 Enoch* 40:9, and the anonymous angel of repentance in Hermas, *Vis.* 5:8; Clemens Alexandrinus, *Quis dives* 42:18; *Test. Gad* 5:7-8 and the personification of *metanoia* in pagan texts, e.g. *Tabula Cebetis* 10-11). Angels bring death to the enemy and godless people (→Angel of Yahweh) according to 2 Kgdms 19:35 (parallels Isa 37:36 and 2 Chr 32:21; reminiscences in 1 Macc 7:41; 2 Macc 15:22-23; Sir 48:21; Josephus, *Bell.* 5:388; cf. Exod 12:23; 2 Sam 24:16; 1 Chr 21:12.15; Sus 55; 59 and LXX Sus 62; Acts 12:23 and LXX Job 33:23 *aggeloi thanatēphoroi* [GAMMIE 1985]). Similar functions are mentioned in an eschatological context: angels are witnesses of the events on earth and write down the acts of men in the heavenly books (*1 Enoch* 89:62-64). They take part in the final judgement, intercede on behalf of the faithful, bring charges against the godless and execute the sentence (cf. the seven angels with the final plagues in Rev 15-17; 21:9 and the angel of the abyss →*Apollyōn* or →*Abaddōn* in Rev 9:11; 20:1).

As far as names of angels are concerned in biblical literature only, the names of Gabriel (Dan 8:16; 9:21; Luke 1:26), Michael (Dan 10:13, 21; 12:1; Rev 12:7), *Abaddōn/ Apollyōn* and Beliar (2 Cor 6:15; →Belial) occur. In Tob 5-12 Raphael/ Azarias already appears. Several Jewish and Christian extra-canonical writings contain numerous names of angels (e.g. *1 Enoch* and *Jub.*; see further →Enoch for Metatron, →Melchizedek and the overview by MICHL 1962:200-254; OLYAN 1993). Several categories of angels are (later) connected with the heavenly court; some of them guard the heavenly throne of God: →Seraphim, →Cherubim, Ophannim, Zebaoth, Běnê ʾělōhîm, →Saints and Watchers. Further groups of four, six or seven higher angels (→Archangel) occur. The angels of the nations appear e.g. in 4QDeut 32:8-9 and LXX Deut 32:8-9, *Jub.* 15:31-32, *1 Enoch* 89:59; 90:22.25 and Dan 10:20-21; 12:1 (Michael). Other groups of angels performing the same duty are the angels of death and those who accompany the Son of Man at his second coming (e.g. Matt 13:41; 16:27; 24:31 and 25:31 (cf. 2 Thess 1:7; →Son of Man). →Satan has his own angels (cf. 2 Cor 12:7) waging war with Michael and his angels (Rev 12:7). The fall from heaven of Satan (→Dragon) and his angels in Rev 12:7-9 (cf. John 12:31), which causes the suffering of the people of God in the final period of history might be an adaptation of the idea of the fall of certain angels (→Giants) in primaeval time (Gen 6; *1 Enoch* 6-11).

IV. *Bibliography*
J. H. CHARLESWORTH, The Portrayal of the Righteous as an Angel, *Ideal Figures in Ancient Judaism. Profiles and Paradigms* (SBLSCS 12; eds. J. J. Collins & G. W. E. Nickelsburg; Chico 1980) 135-151; F. CUMONT, Les anges du paganisme, *RHR* 72 (1915) 159-182; M. J. DAVIDSON, *Angels at Qumran. A Comparative Study of 1 Enoch 1-36, 72-108 and Sectarian Writings from Qumran* (JSP SS 11; Sheffield 1992) [& lit]; J. DILLON & D. WINSTON, Philo's Doctrine of Angels, *Two Treatises of Philo of Alexandria. A Commentary on De Gigantibus and Quod Deus Sit Immutabilis* (BJS 25; Chico 1983) 197-205; A. FINET, *Anges et démons.* Actes du Colloque de Liège et de Louvain-La-Neuve 25-26 novembre 1987 (ed. J. Ries; Louvain-La-Neuve 1989) 37-52; J. G. GAMMIE, The Angelology and Demonology in the Septuagint of the Book of Job, *HUCA* 56 (1985) 1-19; *M. MACH, *Entwicklungsstadien des jüdischen Engelglaubens in vorrabbinischer Zeit* (TSAJ 34; Tübingen 1992) [& lit]; *J. MICHL, Engel (I-IX), *RAC* 5 (Stuttgart 1962) 53-258; E. T. MULLEN, *The Divine Council in Canaanite and Early Hebrew Literature* (HSM 24; Chico 1980); C. NEWSOM, *Songs of the Sabbath Sacrifice: A Critical Edition* (HSS 27; Atlanta 1985), esp. 23-38 and 77-78; NEWSOM, He Has Established for Himself Priests, Human and Angelic Priesthood in the Qumran Sabbath Shirot, *Archaeology and History in the Dead Sea Scrolls* (JSP SS 8; ed. L. H. Schiffman; Sheffield 1990) 101-120; S. M. OLYAN, *A Thousand Thousands Served Him. Exegesis and the Naming of Angels in Ancient Judaism* (Tübingen 1993); A. ROFÉ, *The Belief in Angels in Israel in the First Temple Period in the Light of the Biblical Traditions* (Jerusalem 1969) [Hebrew]; C. ROWLAND, *The Open Heaven. A Study of Apocalyptic in Judaism and Early Christianity* (London 1982) 78-123; C. ROWLAND, A Man Clothed in Linen. Daniel 10.6ff. and Jewish Angelology, *JSNT* 24 (1985) 99-110; P. SCHÄFER, *Rivalität zwischen Engeln und Menschen. Untersuchungen zur rabbinischen Engelvorstellung* (SJLA 8; Berlin/New York 1975); E. SCHICK, *Die Botschaft der Engel im Neuen Testament* (Stuttgart 1940; Basel[3] 1946); A. R. R. SHEPPARD, Pagan Cults of Angels in Roman Asia Minor, *Talanta* 12-13 (1980-1981) 77-101; A. SHINAN, The Angelology of the "Palestinian" Targums on the Pentateuch, *Sefarad* 43 (1983) 181-198; A. STROTMANN, *"Mein Vater bist Du!" (Sir 51,10). Zur Bedeutung der Vaterschaft Gottes in kanonischen und nichtkanonischen frühjüdischen Schriften* (Frankfurt 1991) 271-276; G. A. G. STROUMSA, *Another Seed: Studies in Gnostic Mythology* (NHS 24; Leiden 1984); D. W. SUTER, Fallen Angel, Fallen Priest: The Problem of Family Purity in 1 Enoch 6-16, *HUCA* 50 (1979) 115-135; M. ZIEGLER, *Engel und Dämon im Lichte der Bibel mit Einschluß des ausserkanonischen Schrifttums* (Zürich 1957).

J. W. VAN HENTEN

ANGEL OF DEATH → ANGEL

ANGEL OF YAHWEH מלאך יהוה

I. The word →'angel' in this phrase is literally 'messenger'. The juxtaposition of the common noun "messenger" with a following divine name in a genitive construction signifying a relationship of subordination is attested elsewhere in the ancient Near East (e.g. *mlak ym*, *KTU* 1.2; *mār šipri ša DN*, cf. *CAD* M/1 265). However, most of the appearances in the Bible of the phrase *mal'ak YHWH* are not easily explicable by recourse to near eastern paradigms, for the *mal'ak YHWH* in the Bible presents a number of unique problems.

II. It is typical for gods in the ancient Near East to have at their disposal specific, lower-ranking deities who do their bidding in running errands and relaying messages. These messenger deities function primarily as links between gods and not between gods and humans; when a major god wishes to communicate with a human, he or she can be expected to make a personal appearance. When supernatural messengers are named at Ugarit, those of →Baal are characteristically

Gapnu (→Vine) and Ugaru, while Qadish and Amrar serve Athirat (→Asherah). Papsukkal is a typical envoy of the high gods in Sumerian texts, and in Akkadian texts Kakka or Nuska is the messenger of their choice. In Greece, →Hermes is the messenger and herald *par excellence*, with a female counterpart in Iris. These deities all behave in a fashion similar to their human counterparts who function as messengers on earth for all humans, from royalty to commoners.

It is precisely these features of ancient Near Eastern messenger gods that make analysis of the *mal'ak YHWH* so vexing, for these features do not always characterize the latter. In contrast to the messenger deities of the ancient Near East, the *mal'ak YHWH* is never given a name in the OT, and he does not always behave like a human messenger. Because the OT is reluctant to provide names for God's angels (angels are given proper names only in Daniel 8-12; cf. Gen 32:29; Judg 13:17-18), there is no onomastic evidence from within the Bible to determine if →Yahweh, like other deities in the ancient Near East, prefers dispatching a particular supernatural being on missions. Furthermore, although in many early narratives Yahweh himself appears to humans (just like other ancient near eastern deities), in later texts there is a marked preference for Yahweh to send a messenger in his place.

III. The phrase *mal'ak YHWH* (where *mal'āk* is singular) is not uniformly distributed in the Bible. It can refer to a human messenger sent by →God (priest and prophet respectively in Mal 2:7 and Hag 1:13; cf. what may be a personal name "Malachi" meaning "my messenger" in Mal 1:1; cf. however, LXX Μαλαχίας 'Messenger of Yahweh'). Elsewhere, the phrase is either unclear or certainly supernatural in its orientation. The single book with the most appearances of the phrase is Judges (2:1.4; 5:23; 6:11-22; 13:3-21). It appears in only two psalms which are contiguous (34:8; 35:5.6), four contexts in the Pentateuch (Gen 16:7-11; 22:11.15; Exod 3:2; Num 22:22-35), one passage in the books of Samuel and Chronicles (2 Sam 24:16 // 1 Chr 21:12-30), and three contexts in the books of Kings (1 Kgs 19:7; 2 Kgs 1:3.15; 19:35). In the prophets the single occurrence in Isaiah (37:36) is a passage parallel to one already mentioned in 2 Kings (19:35), and apart from a single reference in Hosea (12:5) it is confined to Zechariah (Zech 1:11 *bis;* 3:1-6; 12:8).

Since the Hebrew definite article cannot be employed in the construct when the *nomen rectum* is a proper name, and since not all construct phrases with a proper name are to be construed as definite (*IBHS* 13.4c; Hirth 1975:25-26), a problem of specificity arises that can be seen by contrasting two recent Bible translations: the New Jewish Publication Society typically translates *mal'ak YHWH* when it first appears in a narrative as "*an* angel of the Lord" where the New Revised Standard Version translates "*the* angel of the Lord". If the latter translation is more accurate, then another problem arises: is this figure a unique envoy who is always sent by God, or can a number of different supernatural beings be dispatched as "the angel of Yahweh"? In other words, is the phrase "angel of Yahweh" a description of an office held by different creatures, or is the phrase a title borne by only one unique figure?

Because Greek, like English, usually must distinguish definite from indefinite in genitive constructions (unlike Hebrew and Latin), early evidence from Greek is invaluable in discerning how the Bible's earliest accessible interpreters understood the phrase. The NT knows of no single "The angel of the Lord/God", for the definite article never appears when a figure identified by this phrase makes its first appearance—it is always "an angel of the Lord" (Matt 1:20; 2:13.19; 28:2; Luke 1:11; 2:9; John 5:4; Acts 5:19; 8:26; 10:3 ["of God"]; 12:7.23; Gal 4:14). The Septuagint generally follows suit in translating *mal'ak YHWH* in the OT, although there are a few exceptional cases where the definite article appears when the figure first appears in a narrative (Num 22:23; Jud 5:23 [LXX cod. A]; 2 Sam

24:16; contrast the far more numerous cases where LXX presents the figure as indefinite: Gen 16:7; 22:11.15; Exod 3:2; 4:24 [LXX]; Judg 2:1; 5:23 [LXX cod. B]; 6:11.12 [LXX Cod. A].22a.22b [LXX Cod. B]; 13:3.6.16b. 21b; 2 Kgs 1:3.15; 19:35 [// Isa 37:36]; 1 Chr 21:12; Zech 3:1; 12:8).

Parallel passages within the MT support the early perception of a figure which was not definite: 2 Chr 32:21 rephrases the "angel of Yahweh" of 2 Kgs 19:35 to read simply "an angel". Even within a single passage, "an angel" (indefinite) will first be introduced only later to be reidentified as *mal'ak YHWH* (1 Kgs 19:5-7; 1 Chr 21:15-16); this sequence confirms that the latter phrase in these contexts means no more than simply an angel of no particular significance sent from Yahweh. Extra-biblical Jewish literature presents the "angel of Yahweh" as a designation applicable to any number of different angels (STIER 1934:42-48). Other early witnesses who are forced to make a choice in this regard will be noted below, and their overwhelming consensus is that the phrase is to be translated as indefinite.

When one scrutinizes the OT itself, a major obstacle for analysis lies in the many passages that are textually problematic. Few generalizations can be made about all the passages, and each must be discussed on its own terms. If one can trust the evidence of early translations such as the LXX, Vulgate, and Syriac, these translations presume a *Vorlage* that is often at variance with the Hebrew text in its description of this figure. This obstacle seems to be related to a further problem that resists an easy solution, namely, the figure of the *mal'ak YHWH* is often perplexingly and inconsistently identified with Yahweh himself. One or both of these difficulties can be found in the following ten passages: the phrase "messenger of Yahweh" appears six times in Judg 6:11-23 to identify a figure who is also described as a "messenger of God" (v 20) and as Yahweh (vv 14.16). The LXX levels all descriptions so that everywhere he is called "messenger of Yahweh" (even in vv 14.16. 20). Josephus recounts this event about "a spectre (*phantasmatos*) in the form of a young man" (*Ant.* V.213-14). The figure speaks but never claims to have been sent from Yahweh nor to be speaking words that another gave him. At only one point does he possibly refer to Yahweh as distinct from himself, but as a greeting the statement may be purely conventional ("Yahweh is with you", v 12). He seems to have sufficient authority in his own right, never claiming it is grounded in another: "Have not I sent you?" (v 14) and "I will be with you" (v 16) are most comfortable as statements coming from God's mouth, but the *mal'āk* speaks these himself. He works wonders in touching meat with his staff, causing it to be consumed with fire, after which he vanishes (v 21). The final reference to Yahweh who verbally comforts Gideon after the disappearance of the *mal'āk* is disorienting, for it raises the question why the *mal'āk* was ever sent at all if Yahweh can speak this easily to Gideon (v 23).

In Judg 13:3-23, the figure in question is identified in the MT by a number of different designations in the first part of the story where he is "the man" (vv 10-11), "the man of God" who seemed to be a *mal'āk* of God (v 6) sent by YHWH (v 8), and who actually was a *mal'āk* of God (v 9). In the second part of the story (as well as the very first reference in the story) he is identified as *mal'ak YHWH* (vv 13.15.16 *bis*.17.18.20. 21*bis*), until the final allusion where he is called *'ĕlōhîm* (v 22). The LXX once inserts an additional reference to simply "the messenger" (v 11). Josephus' summary of this account (*Ant.* V.277-84) speaks of "a spectre (*phantasma*), an angel of God in the likeness of a comely and tall youth." The *mal'āk* refuses an hospitable offer of food, recommending instead that an offering be made to Yahweh (v 16). This *mal'āk* talks about God as someone distinct from himself (v 5), but never refers to the fact that he has been sent from God, nor that the words he speaks come from God. Indeed, it is not God's word that is to be heeded, but "Let her take heed to all that I said" (v 13), and "Take heed to all that I commanded her" (v

14). He is reluctant to identify himself by name, describing his name as "full of wonder" (v 18). It is not clear if it is Yahweh or the *mal'āk* who performed wonders in v 19 while Manoah and his wife looked on. The *mal'āk* ascends to heaven with the flame from the sacrifice (v 20).

In Numbers 22:22-35, Yahweh himself is active (opening a donkey's mouth and Balaam's eyes) in the midst of an extended description of the *mal'ak YHWH*'s activity. The versions are not in agreement as to how to identify this figure: the Hebrew text presents the *mal'ak YHWH* at work everywhere (except of course for Yahweh's activity in vv 28.31a); the LXX generally identifies this figure as the messenger of "God" and not Yahweh (with some exceptions and even variations within the manuscript tradition); the Vulgate mentions the "angel of the Lord" only in v 22 and everywhere else simply calls the figure an *angelus* or omits reference to it entirely (vv 25.34). Josephus' summary of the account (*Ant.* IV.108-111) refers to it as "an angel of God" and a "divine spirit" (*theiou pneumatos*) in contrast to the LXX "the messenger of God" (v 23). The narrative describes this *mal'ak YHWH* as an adversary (*śāṭān,* vv 22.32), standing in roads and vineyards (vv 22.23.24.26.31) with drawn sword in hand (vv 23.31), receiving homage from a human (v 31). Balaam treats this *mal'āk*—and not God—as the ultimate court of appeal ("If it is displeasing in your eyes", v 34). The *mal'āk* does not indicate that he has been sent by God, for he speaks of himself as an independent authority ("I came out as an adversary because your way was contrary to me", v 32; "I would have killed you", v 33; "Only the word I speak to you shall you speak", v 35).

In Gen 16:7-13, all texts agree that a figure identified as "messenger of Yahweh" (vv 7.9.10.11) speaks (LXX adds a further reference to this figure in v 8, while Vg deletes its mention in vv 10-11). When it first appears in Josephus (*Ant.* I.189), it is simply called "a messenger of Yahweh" (cf. *Jub.* 17:11, "an angel of the Lord, one of the holy ones"). Only once does the *mal'āk* seem to speak of Yahweh as someone distinct from himself (v 11), but he never intimates that Yahweh sent him or that the words he speaks come from Yahweh. Instead, the *mal'āk* speaks as if he were God: "I will greatly multiply your descendants" (v 10). Even the narrator closes by noting that it was Yahweh who spoke to Hagar, prompting her to be surprised that she still remained alive (v 13).

In Judg 2:1-4, where MT clearly has a lacuna in the introduction, the phrase *mal'ak YHWH* appears twice (vv 1.4). The words spoken by the *mal'āk* in the MT are entirely in the first person as if God were speaking ("the land which I swore to your fathers"). But LXX Cod. B prefaces these words with a citation formula ("*Thus says the Lord,* '...the land which I swore...'"), while LXX[A] modifies the person in the first half of the speech without the citation formula ("the land which he [i.e., Yahweh] swore..."). The Targum interpreted this messenger as a human prophet (for a similar interchange, cf. apocryphal Ps 151:4 "his prophet" in 11QPs[a] which appears as "his *aggelos*" in Greek).

God's revelation to →Moses at the burning bush (Exod 3:2-4:17) encompasses 38 verses in which Yahweh is explicitly and repeatedly described as speaking with Moses. But the entire account is made problematic when it is prefaced with the phrase, "*mal'ak YHWH* appeared to him in a blazing fire" (Exod 3:2), which is quoted in the NT as an indefinite "an angel" with no reference to "the Lord" (Acts 7:30; cf. vv 35.38). On the other hand, the Vulgate simply reads, "Yahweh appeared...," preserving no reference to a *mal'āk* (Josephus refers only to a "voice" that speaks from the bush before God is identified in *Ant.* II.264-2).

Although most versions present Yahweh as the one who intends to kill Moses in Exod 4:24 over the issue of circumcision, the LXX identifies "an angel of the Lord" as the aggressor (the Targums also insert the word *mal'āk,* cf. *b. Ned.* 32a; *Jub.* 48:2-4 sees it as the wicked angel →Mastemah; see →Destroyer).

Although God himself had earlier commanded →Abraham to sacrifice Isaac (Gen 22:1-2), in Gen 22:11-18 it is only a *mal'ak YHWH* that speaks "from heaven" with Abraham when the sacrifice is in progress (vv 11.15). *Jubilees* calls it the "angel of the presence" (*mal'ak happānîm*; 18:9-11; cf. 2:1), but Josephus depicts only God speaking (*Ant.* I.233-236). With the exception of a reference to God in the third person (v 12), the speech of the *mal'āk* sounds like God talking: "You have not withheld your son from me" (v 12), "I will greatly bless you" (v 17), "you obeyed my voice" (v 17). Nowhere does this *mal'āk* indicate that he was sent from God or that he speaks these words at God's command. Although the phrase "says (*nĕ'ûm*) the Lord" is inserted in the midst of the *mal'āk*'s speech at one point (v 16), this phrase is found only here in Genesis, and no other biblical *mal'āk YHWH* ever employs it.

As →Elijah flees from →Jezebel in 1 Kings 19, he is twice provided in the MT by a *mal'āk* with food and drink for his long journey (vv 5.7). This *mal'āk* is called a *mal'ak YHWH* only when it is mentioned on the second occasion (some Vulgate MSS also call the first appearance a *mal'ak YHWH*). In the LXX the first mention of the *mal'āk* does not identify it as such, simply saying "someone", while the second appearance appears with the definite article. Josephus never mentions a *mal'āk* in his account (*Ant.* VIII.349), simply saying "someone".

The phrase *mal'ak YHWH* appears three times in Zechariah's vision of the High Priest Joshua in Zechariah 3. Joshua stands before this angel (vv 1.5; cf. v 3) who admonishes him with words prefaced by, "Thus says Yahweh" (v 6), and who orders bystanders to remove Joshua's filthy garments (vv 5-6). Because Yahweh speaks awkwardly in v 2, one should take seriously the Syriac rendition of v 2 which includes instead another reference to the figure: "and the angel of the Lord said...."

In contrast to the ten preceding passages, the following two passages present neither textual problems nor internal conflicts in identifying who is speaking: the words and actions of the *mal'ak YHWH* present no conceptual difficulties. Nevertheless, the texts evince certain peculiarities that require attention.

In 2 Kings 1, a *mal'ak YHWH* (vv 3.15) appears and twice gives orders to Elijah as to what he is to say and do. Thus, Elijah himself is to function as God's *mal'āk* "messenger" in relaying a message from God ("Thus says the Lord", vv 4.6), but Elijah does not receive the commission directly from God. This fact is striking since God elsewhere in the Elijah stories typically speaks directly to this prophet (or the phrase appears "the word of Yahweh came to Elijah"). Josephus summarizes this account without mentioning a *mal'āk*: it is God who speaks (*Ant.* IX.20-21.26).

In the Song of Deborah, the sentence appears, "'Curse, Meroz,' said the angel of the Lord, 'utterly curse its inhabitants'" (Judg 5:23). The sudden, unmotivated, and unclear significance of a reference to *mal'ak YHWH* at this point prompts many to be uncomfortable with the originality of the phrase "said the angel of the Lord."

The following four passages pose no problems in analysing the *mal'ak YHWH*, for there is nothing inconsistent with this being's function as a supernatural envoy sent by Yahweh, and any textual variants are not problematic. 2 Kgs 19:35 (= Isa 37:36; cf. 2 Chr 32:21) narrates tersely how a *mal'ak YHWH* (LXX indefinite) "went out" and destroyed Sennacherib's army as it besieged Jerusalem (→Destroyer). When 2 Macc 15:22-23 records a later request by second century BCE Jews to re-enact this miracle for them, it is simply "an angel" (indefinite) that they anticipate from God.

An "angel of Yahweh", clearly distinct from Yahweh, does not speak but does act in accord with Yahweh's commands regarding the devastation of David's kingdom (2 Sam 24:16; cf. 1 Chr 21:12.15.16.18.30). This creature is also described as "the destroying angel", the "smiting angel" and a "destroying angel of Yahweh".

In the only two psalms to mention *mal'ak YHWH*, one of the benefits accruing to God-fearers is that a *mal'ak YHWH* camps (ḤNH participle) around them and delivers them (Ps 34:8[7]). The phrase appears twice in imprecations in Ps 35:5-6 summoning a *mal'ak YHWH* to pursue relentlessly (DḤH, RDP) the enemies of the psalmist. LXX treats all three as indefinite.

The last group of texts confirms that Yahweh can, indeed, send out a supernatural envoy to do his bidding, much like the messengers sent out by other gods of the ancient Near East. Unlike the other cultures, however, there is no firm evidence that Yahweh had a particular subordinate who fulfilled this role.

The first group of ten texts, however, presents a different picture with their textual variants and vacillating identifications of the "angel of Yahweh" (distinct from Yahweh? identical to Yahweh?). Among proposals offered to explain the evidence, one finds the angel of Yahweh in these passages interpreted as Yahweh in a theophany, the preincarnate →Christ, a means of crystallizing into one figure the many revelatory forms of an early polytheism, a hypostatization, a supernatural envoy of Yahweh where the confusion in identity results from messenger activity that merges the personality or speech of the messenger with the sender, or an interpolation of the word *mal'āk* into the text where originally it was simply Yahweh speaking and at work.

The notion that the identity of messenger and sender could be merged in the ancient Near East is incorrect: any messenger who failed to identify the one who sent him subverted the entire communication process (see →Angel). On the other hand, those who posit an identity (whether by theophany or hypostatization) between Yahweh and the *mal'ak YHWH* apart from this theory do not do justice to the full significance of the term *mal'ak* which must mean a subordinate (in contrast to other later terms such as →Logos, Memra, Shekinah, Kabod, see →Glory). The biblical poetic parallelism Yahweh // *mal'āk* (Isa 63:9; Hos 12:4-5[3-4]; Mal 3:1) does not justify the necessary equation of the two terms any more than the parallelism of Saul // David (1 Sam 18:7) or →heaven // →earth (Deut 32:1) identifies the respective elements. The identification of the *mal'ak YHWH* with the preincarnate Christ violates the original intent of the texts' authors. Instead, the remarkable textual instability in identifying the figure is best resolved by the interpolation theory, especially since there are passages where the interpolation is undeniable when it is not found in all witnesses (e.g. Exod 4:24). According to this theory, the figure is identified with Yahweh in some texts because it was, in fact, Yahweh before the interpolation of the word *mal'āk*. The behaviour of the *mal'ak YHWH* in many of these disputed passages is precisely that of a deity and not a deity's messenger (IRVIN 1978). The word *mal'āk* was inserted in certain contexts because of theological discomfort with Yahweh appearing as a *śāṭān* adversary (Numbers 22), or in visible form or with the actions of a man (Gen 16:13; Judges 6; 13; cf. Gen 22:14), or in contexts where the actual presence of God was otherwise theologically troublesome (Exod 4:24). In many passages, inadequate data hinder confidence in determining if the *mal'āk YHWH* is in fact an envoy or an interpolation.

In the Apocrypha, Susanna provides further evidence that there was a time when a choice between either the activity of God or an "angel of Yahweh" was a live option for writers. The Theodotian text indicates that "an angel of the Lord" gave a spirit of →wisdom to →Daniel in contrast to the LXX that specifies God as the source (v 45). LXX texts picture Daniel twice referring to "the angel of the Lord" who with his sword will slay the wicked (vv 55.59); Theodotian texts here preserve instead "an angel of God" and "the angel of God" respectively. Finally, LXX (not Theodotion) describes "the angel of the Lord" casting fire upon the two wicked men (v 62).

Elsewhere in the Apocrypha, there is never any question of identifying the "angel of Yahweh" with God, for the figure consistently conforms to the pattern of a messenger despatched by God (usually without the definite article). Each time the figure is mentioned in Bel and the Dragon (LXX and Theodotion vv 34.36.39[LXX "of God"]), he is transporting Habakkuk by his hair to and from Babylon (no definite article when first mentioned), and when the angel speaks to Habakkuk, Theod prefaces its words with "Thus says the Lord", omitted by the LXX. In a prose interlude in the Song of the Three Children, "an angel of the Lord" (LXX; Theod "the angel of the Lord") descends to join the youths in the furnace and to dissipate the flames.

In the book of Tobit, no reference appears to an "angel of the Lord" until the close of the book. In 12:22 →Raphael, who has been active throughout the book and referred to elsewhere by the narrator simply as "an angel" (5:4) and by other characters as merely a "man" (5:8.16), ascends to God, at which time the onlookers in 12:22 refer to him as "the angel of the Lord" (LXX^{BA}; LXX^{S} "an angel of God"). Before he does so, he identifies himself as one of the seven holy angels who bring the prayers of God's people into God's presence (12:15).

In conclusion, there is in the Bible no single "*The* angel of Yahweh". The phrase *mal'ak YHWH* is better translated as "an angel (or messenger) of Yahweh" when it first appears in a narrative, for it represents the appearance of an unspecified supernatural envoy sent from Yahweh. In cases where a simultaneous identity and discontinuity is uncomfortably present between Yahweh and his messenger, the term *mal'āk* is probably a secondary addition to the text in response to changing theological perspectives.

IV. The phrase *mal'ak YHWH* is not yet attested in published, non-biblical materials from Qumran, despite a sophisticated and extensive angelology in these texts. This omission correlates with the non-specificity of the figure in early witnesses, for in spite of the proliferation of details about angels in extra- and post-biblical texts, the "angel of Yahweh" receives in general no special attention in Judaism. It is true that one may trace in Jewish apocalyptic the development of a single exalted angel that some have tried to derive from the earlier *mal'ak YHWH* (ROWLAND 1982:94-113), but the connection between the two remains undemonstrated and the terminology is different. Quite the contrary, a vigorous element in early Judaism resisted sectarians who believed that a certain principal angel was a special →mediator between God and man (SEGAL 1977:70). Developing descriptions about the highest-ranking angels tend to avoid the phrase "angel of the Lord" in favour of more elaborate titles. Extensive gnostic speculations about demiurges and the cosmic hierarchy likewise tend to bypass the nomenclature of the "angel of the Lord", although the "Messenger" is a significant divine emanation in some gnostic traditions such as Manichaeism (cf. Samaritan gnosticism [FOSSUM 1985]).

V. *Bibliography*

J. E. FOSSUM, *The Name of God and the Angel of the Lord - Samaritan and Jewish Concepts of Intermediation and the Origin of Gnosticism* (WUNT 36; Tübingen 1985); F. GUGGISBERG, *Die Gestalt des Mal'ak Jahwe im Alten Testament* (Dach 1979); V. HIRTH, *Gottes Boten im Alten Testament* (Theologische Arbeiten 32; Berlin 1975); D. IRVIN, *Mytharion. The Comparison of Tales from the Old Testament and the Ancient Near East* (Neukirchen-Vluyn 1978); H. RÖTTGER, *Mal'ak Jahwe - Bote von Gott. Die Vorstellung von Gottes Boten im hebräischen Alten Testament* (Frankfurt 1978); C. ROWLAND, *The Open Heaven - A Study of Apocalyptic in Judaism and Early Christianity* (London 1982); A. F. SEGAL, *Two Powers in Heaven - Early Rabbinic Reports About Christianity and Gnosticism* (Leiden 1977); F. STIER, *Gott und sein Engel im Alten Testament* (Alttestamentliche Abhandlungen 12,2; Münster 1934).

S. A. MEIER

ANTHROPOS Ἄνθρωπος

I. One designation, with or without qualification, of the highest being in many gnostic systems: *quae est super omnia virtus, et continet omnia, Anthropos vocatur* (Irenaeus, *Adv. haer.* 1.12.4). The name draws attention to the direct or indirect link between supreme divinity and humanity, esp. the 'unwavering race', thanks to which redemption from the world created by the →Archons is possible. The name Anthropos signifies that →God is the prototype of Man (*anthropos*), because man is made, directly or indirectly, in his image. The *Religionsgeschichtliche Schule* and others claimed that an oriental *Urmensch*-myth lay behind the gnostic doctrine. This account has been invoked to explain the Pauline passages (1 Cor 15:21-2, 45-49; Rom 5: 12-21) in which →Christ is compared and contrasted with the first man, Adam. Neither of these views has worn well.

II. There are two related types of gnostic anthropological myth, both of which draw upon a motif, an image reflected in water, that goes back to Satornil and thus 'Samaritan' gnosis (Irenaeus, *Adv. haer.* 1.24.1) (SCHENKE 1962:64-68). They share the basic premise that (human) man is at least potentially a higher being than the demiurge of the world, who enviously withheld this knowledge (the forbidden fruit of Gen 2:16-17) from Adam. The simpler is best exemplified by the long recension of the *Apocryphon of John* (NHC II.1, 14:13-21:16). This envisages Adam's 'choic' or material body as modelled by the Archons of the demiurge directly upon a glimpsed reflection of the image of the Perfect Man (the highest god) (14:24-15:12). His *psyche* is likewise created by the Archons; but his divine *pneuma* derives from Sophia. Coming directly from the world of light, it in fact pre-exists choic and psychic bodies. The second type, exemplified by the Naassene exegesis (in the distorted and lacunate account of Hippolytus *Ref. haer.* 5.7.3-9.9), protects the transcendence of the highest divinity by interpolating a hypostasis between Anthropos and Man: the hypostasis or →image (*eikōn*) supplies both the model for physical man and the divine particle of light. The Perfect Man, the Father of All, Adam, produces a son 'of the same substance'. The physical body of human Adam made by the Archons of the demiurge Esaldaios is (indirectly) modelled upon this son. When the son, probably in the form of divine light, descends to vivify the creature, he is trapped; over the generations descending from Adam, the light is split up into innumerable fragments, each of which may return to the Light World (FRICKEL 1984: 263). This principle could be indefinitely extended: any emanation from the Perfect Man may be named Anthropos, even the female Barbelo in *Apocryphon of John*, because she is 'the image of the Father' (14: 23; cf. 5:7; 6:4). In *Eugnostos*, a series of emanations from the First-Father, also called Anthropos (NHC III.3, 77:14), is named in turn First Man, Immortal Man, →Son of Man, →Saviour (78:3; 85:10-14).

As a key gnostic motif, Anthropos has figured in all accounts of the genesis or proto-history of gnosticism. Older accounts may be briefly summarized. W. BOUSSET claimed that an ancient oriental myth, the creation of the world from the parts of a sacrificial victim, the prototypical man, must underlie the narratives of *Poimandres* 12-15 and several Christian accounts of gnostic systems (*Hauptprobleme der Gnosis* [Göttingen 1907, repr. 1973] 160-223). The best-known of these myths, that of the Iranian *Gayōmart*, stimulated R. REITZENSTEIN in turn to propose the existence of an Iranian popular cult of a redeemed redeemer, which ultimately inspired the gnostic myth as a whole (e.g. *Das iranische Erlösungsmysterium*, Bonn 1921). C. H. KRAELING attempted to link Bousset's view to Jewish Messianism (*Anthropos and the Son of Man*, New York 1927), G. WIDENGREN to find the redeemed redeemer in early Iranian texts (*The great Vohu Manah,* Uppsala 1945). None of these views survived the criticisms of COLPE (1961:140-70; cf. 1969:411) and SCHENKE (1962:69-114), though it was still possible for RUDOLPH in 1964 to stress the supposed Iranian antecedents of gnosticism. The decisive considerations, as SCHENKE showed, were the new texts from Nag Hammadi, which provided far more reliable accounts of gnostic Anthropos than had been available, and an appreciation of the character of post-Biblical Jewish techniques of exegesis (cf. TRÖGER 1980:155-168). There is simply no evidence for the redeemed redeemer in gnosis until Manicheism. The key texts that inspire all gnostic anthropology are Gen 1:26-27; 2:7 & 2:21-24, together with the post-Biblical Jewish exegeses of these passages (cf. QUISPEL 1953:215-217, 226; PEARSON 1973:51-81; 1990). Certainly, gnostic 'systems' are syncretic, but no precise antecedent of the basic macro-/microcosmic scheme is required; and syncretism is only one of the processes involved in the elaboration of the complex gnostic scenarios. TARDIEU (1974) has provided a convincing account of the varied sources of inspiration, and the narrative logic, of one such anthropology, in the *Origin of the World* (NHC II.5). Iran, to say nothing of ancient oriental myths, has disappeared totally from RUDOLPH's most recent summary (1990:99-130).

III. Within NT studies, the authority of R. BULTMANN, who tended to accept the 'oriental' origins of gnosis as a fact (e.g. 1964; 1984), caused it to be widely canvassed, and not only among his pupils (see e.g. J. JEREMIAS, s.v. Adam, *TWNT* 1 [1933] 142-143; H. SCHLIER, *RAC* 3 [1956] 437-53), that the Christology of Pauline Christianity was significantly influenced by "Urmensch und Erlöser", however they came to be combined into an eschatological Adam. But the objections to any direct relation between gnostic myth and Pauline Christology are decisive (SCHENKE 1973). Thus COLPE showed that 'Son of Man' has no genetic link with Gnostic ideas (1969:414-418). The basic premises of W. SCHMITHALS' *Die Gnosis in Korinth* 3 (1969) were undermined by SCHENKE & FISCHER, *Einleitung in die Schriften des NT* (Berlin 1978-1979) 1:103-5. The contrast between *pneumatikos* and *psychikos* in 1 Cor 14:44-46 derives from Hellenistic-Jewish wisdom speculation, and was thus freely available both to Gnostics and to early Christians (PEARSON 1973). The differences in the structure and meaning of gnostic anthropology by contrast with the Pauline scheme have been noted by FISCHER 1980:289-294.

Although the inverse assumption viz., that the Pauline Adam-Christ inverted parallelism has Judaic sources, can also not be conclusively demonstrated, there have been adequate treatments of the Pauline Adam-Christ typology which do not concede even the limited gnostic influence allowed by BRANDENBURGER (1962) or SCHOTTROFF (1970). COLPE (1969:475-477) showed that 1 Cor 15:45-49 is an elaboration through reduplicated antithesis of 15:21, and that no prior schema underlies the passage. In Rom 5:12-21, which is derivative from the Cor passage, an apocalyptic notion, →Jesus as the Son of Man, has been recast into the prototype Man of the resurrection, contrasted with the death brought about by Adam. BARRETT (1985) analysed the role of exegesis of Gen 1-2 in 1 Cor 15, stressing the probable allusion to the representative Man of Dan 7:13 and the implied rejection of Philo's Platonism in *Leg Alleg.* 1:31 (cf. LIETZMANN ad 1 Cor 15:45-49). FISCHER has urged that 1 Cor 15:45-49 is a unique melding of strands of belief derived both from Jewish Apocalyptic (4 Ezra, *2 Apoc. Bar.*) and from gnostic myth (1980:294-298), but that no coherent gnostic doctrine inspired Paul negatively or positively. Even this version probably concedes too much to the old view.

IV. *Bibliography*

F. ALTERMATH, *Du corps psychique au corps spirituel* (Beitr. Gesch. bibl. Exeg. 18; Tübingen 1977); C. K. BARRETT, The Significance of the Adam-Christ Typology for the Resurrection of the Dead, *Résurrection du Christ et des chrétiens* (ed. L. de Lorenzi; Sér. monogr. Bénédict., sect. bibl.-oec. 8; Rome 1985) 99-122; E. BRANDENBURGER, *Adam und Christus* (WMANT 7; Neukirchen 1962); R. BULTMANN, Adam und Christus nach Römer 5, *Der alte und der neue Mensch in der Theologie des Paulus* (Darmstadt 1964) 41-66, repr. from

ZNW 50 (1959) 145-65; BULTMANN, *Theologie des NT*, (Tübingen 1984[9]) 166-186; C. COLPE, *Die religionsgeschichtliche Schule* (Göttingen 1961); COLPE, *ὁ υἱὸς τοῦ ἀνθρώπου*, *TWNT* 8 (1969) 403-481; K. M. FISCHER, Adam und Christus, *Altes Testament - Frühjudentum - Gnosis* (ed. K. Tröger; Berlin 1980) 283-98; J. FRICKEL, *Hellenistische Erlösung in christlicher Deutung: der gnostische Naassenerschrift* (NHS 19; Leiden 1984) 259-269; B. A. PEARSON, *The Pneumatikos-Psychikos Terminology in 1 Corinthians* (SBLDS 12; Missoula 1973); PEARSON, *Gnosticism, Judaism and Egyptian Christianity* (Minneapolis 1990) 29-38; G. QUISPEL, Der gnostische Anthropos und die jüdische Tradition, *ErJb* 22 (1953) 195-234; K. RUDOLPH, Stand und Aufgabe in der Erforschung des Gnostizismus (1964), repr. in *Gnosis und Gnostizismus* (ed. K. Rudolph; Darmstadt 1975) 510-553; RUDOLPH, *Die Gnosis* (Göttingen 1990[3]); H-M. SCHENKE, *Der Gott 'Mensch' in der Gnosis* (Göttingen 1962); M. SCHENKE, Die neutestamentliche Christologie und der gnostische Erlöser, *Gnosis und Neues Testament* (ed. K. Tröger; Berlin 1973) 205-229; L. SCHOTTROFF, *Der Glaubende und die feindliche Welt* (WMANT 37; Neukirchen 1970); M. TARDIEU, *Trois mythes gnostiques* (Paris 1974) 86-139.

R. L. GORDON

ANTICHRIST ἀντίχριστος

I. The word *antichristos* is found only in 1 John 2:18.22; 4:3; 2 John 7, and in post-biblical Christian literature. Morphologically the closest analogy is *antitheos* which was in use since Homer (*Od.* 11:117; 13:378; 14:18). In Homer *antitheos* means 'godlike'. In later times it comes to mean 'contrary to God' (for instance Philo, *Poster.* 37:3; 123:4; *Congr.* 118:1; *Fug.* 140:3). The term *antichristos* is ambiguous ('opponent of →Christ' or 'false Christ') owing to the twofold meaning of *anti* in composita: it can mean 'against' (*antistratēgos*: 'the enemy's general', Thucydides 7:86) or 'instead of' (*antipsychos*: 'something offered instead of one's life', Dio Cassius 59:8; neuter in 4 Macc 6:29; 17:21).

In the Epistles of John *antichristos* is used as a designation for the ultimate eschatological opponent of →Jesus Christ. The appearance of the *antichristos* is expected to precede the *parousia* of Christ. The author of 1 and 2 John refers to this expectation as an existing tradition (1 John 2:18: 'as you have heard ...'), although the tradition of Antichrist is not attested in its full form before Irenaeus (*Adv. Haer.* 5:25-30). After having referred to the tradition the author uses the word *antichristos* to characterize his opponents who as *antichristoi* deny Christ (1 John 2:18—plural; 1 John 2:22; 2 John 7—singular). Their teaching is inspired by the spirit of Antichrist, and presented by the author as proof that Antichrist has already come (1 John 4:3). By interpreting the conflict with those who deny Christ (1 John 2:22) by means of the expectation of Antichrist, the author of the Epistles of John argues the nearness of the end (1 John 2:18!).

II. Neither the word *antichristos* nor a Hebrew or other equivalent is used in any of the versions of the OT or in extra-biblical literature of the period. But although the word is not used before the Epistles of John, the concept of eschatological opposition reaching its climax in the appearance and activity of a single person is already found in some OT passages: Ezek 38-39 mentions →Gog of →Magog as Israel's final enemy (cf. Rev 20:8); Dan 7-8.11 describes the appearance of an evil tyrant who will act as the final enemy of God and Israel. The tradition of an evil tyrant as the climax of eschatological evil should be understood as a specification of the tradition of the eschatological enmity of the pagan peoples and Israel (cf. Isa 5:25-30; 8:18-20; 10:5-7; 37:16-20; Nah 3:1-7; Joel 4; Zech 14). This expectation of eschatological hostility between Israel and the peoples is also expressed in extra-biblical sources. Sometimes the hostility is thought to reach a climax in the rise of an eschatological tyrant (*1*

En. 90:9-16; *Ass. Mos.* 8; *2 Apoc. Bar.* 36-40; 70; *4 Ezra* 5:1-13; 12:29-33; 13:25-38). Among the various passages of the Qumran literature containing forms of eschatological dualism, the account of Melchizedek and Melchiresha in 4Q280-282 and 4QAmram takes a special place as an analogy: as in the case of Christ and Antichrist the typology of agent (= prototype) and opponent (= antitype) appears to have been constitutive.

There are a number of passages in the NT that predict or record the appearance of eschatological opponents without using the word *antichristos*. In Mark 13:22 false Christs (*pseudochristoi*) and false prophets (*pseudoprophētai*) are described as appearing before the end (cf. v 6). They will deceive people by doing signs and wonders (cf. Matt 7:15; 24:11.23-24). Obviously, the evangelist is referring here to people of his own time. Some interpreters wrongly regard the 'desolating sacrilege' of Mark 13:14 as referring to Antichrist (see for instance J. GNILKA, *Das Evangelium nach Markus* [EKK II/2; Neukirchen 1979] 195-196). As there is no hint whatsoever in this direction, the masculine participle *hestēkota* should be explained in a different way (for instance as a reference to 'the Roman').

In 2 Thess 2:3-12 the coming of the 'Lawless One' is described as preceding the *parousia* of Christ. This Lawless One will act haughtily, and proclaim himself as a god. He will act with the power of →Satan, and deceive people by doing signs and wonders. Ultimately, he will be vanquished by Christ (v 8). Although the word *antichristos* is not used, the Lawless One is often regarded as the earliest description of Antichrist. This interpretation is attested at least since Irenaeus (*Adv. Haer.* III:8.7). Still it should be noted that the Lawless One is rather a future, eschatological 'anti-God' than an Antichrist (v 4).

In Revelation there are a number of eschatological opponents. The most prominent of these are the →Dragon and the two Beasts mentioned in chaps. 12-13; 16:13; 20:10. The Dragon is presented as "the Old →Serpent", "Satan" (20:2). The second Beast, the Beast from the Land (13:11-18), is identified as "the false prophet" (16:13; 20:10). The first Beast is only spoken of as "the Beast" (*to thērion*), and is also described without the Dragon and the second Beast (11:7; chap. 17). This adversary is often wrongly spoken of as Antichrist. With the images of the Beasts the author of Revelation is referring to the dangers of his own time.

At least three different traditions form the background of the tradition of Antichrist, which is attested in its full form from Irenaeus onward: that of Satan / →Belial, that of the coming of eschatological false prophets (cf. MEEKS 1967), and that of the final eschatological tyrant as described in Daniel. Possibly, also the myth of Nero-redivivus played a part. The old view of an esoteric, pre-Christian tradition of Antichrist (GUNKEL 1895; BOUSSET 1895; CHARLES 1920) was successfully refuted by ERNST 1967 and JENKS 1991. They rightly argued that the concept of Antichrist is a Christian idea and that it was not fully developed until the late 2nd century CE. As a result, the various passages before Irenaeus that describe eschatological opponents should be regarded as witnesses of separate traditions, not of one continuous tradition. The agreement between these passages lies in the fact that they all reflect upon events that were thought to precede the *parousia* of Christ. Yet the ways in which these events are described differ widely: in the Epistles of John the tradition of Antichrist is used for the interpretation of the conflict with the deniers of Christ. Thus the nearness of the end is argued. In 2 Thess the coming of the Lawless One is predicted in order to justify that the end will *not* come shortly. The images of the Beasts in Rev describe the contemporary situation of persecution and argue that Christ will overcome this situation of distress. And Mark 13:22 (and par.) speaks about false prophets and false Christs as a standard feature of the last days, but assuming that those last days had already begun.

III. Of post- and extra-biblical literature *Did.* 16 and *Asc. Isa.* 4 contain the earliest and most extensive descriptions of an eschatological opponent of Christ. The word 'Antichrist' is used in neither of these descriptions, however. It is mentioned for the first time in post-biblical literature in Polycarpus' *Phil.* 7:1, a reference to 1 John 4:2-3. Extensive speculations on the rise, character, outlooks, etc., of Antichrist are found in Christian literature from the latter part of the second century onward: one could mention Tertullian, *Res. Car.* XXIV: 60,24; XXVII: 64,26; 65,10; *Adv. Marcionem* I:22,1; III:8,2; V:16,4; Hippolytus, *De Antichristo*, passim; *Comm. Dan.* IV:24,7-8 and numerous other passages (see JENKS 1991:27-116).

IV. *Bibliography*

O. BÖCHER, Antichrist II, *TRE* 3 (Berlin, New York 1978) 21-24; *W. BOUSSET, *Der Antichrist in der Überlieferung des Judentums, des Neuen Testaments und der frühen Kirche* (Göttingen 1895); R. E. BROWN, *The Epistles of John* (AB 30; Garden City, New York 1982); *R. H. CHARLES, *The Revelation of St. John* (Edinburgh 1920) II, 76-87; *J. ERNST, *Die eschatologischen Gegenspieler in den Schriften des Neuen Testaments* (Regensburg 1967); M. FRIEDLÄNDER, *Der Antichrist in den vorchristlichen jüdischen Quellen* (Göttingen 1901); K. GRAYSTON, *The Johannine Epistles*, (NCB; Grand Rapids / Basingstoke 1984) 76-82; H. GUNKEL, *Schöpfung und Chaos in Urzeit und Endzeit* (Göttingen 1895); *G. C. JENKS, *The Origins and Early Development of the Antichrist-Myth* (BZNW 59; Berlin & New York 1991); L. J. LIETAERT PEERBOLTE, *The Earliest Christian Views on Eschatological Opponents. A Traditio-Historical Study* (f.c.); E. LOHMEYER, 'Antichrist', *RAC* 1 (1941), 450-457; W. A. MEEKS, *The Prophet-King. Moses Traditions and the Johannine Christology* (Leiden 1967) 47-55; B. RIGAUX, *L'Antéchrist et l'opposition au royaume messianique dans l'Ancien et le Nouveau Testament* (Gembloux 1932); G. STRECKER, *Die Johannesbriefe* (KEK 14; Göttingen 1989) 337-343; STRECKER, Der Antichrist. Zum religionsgeschichtlichen Hintergrund von 1 Joh 2:18.22; 4:3 und 2 Joh 7, *Text and Testimony* (eds. T. Baarda, A. Hilhorst, G. P. Luttikhuizen & A. S. van der Woude; Kampen 1988) 247-254; R. SCHNACKENBURG, *Die Johannesbriefe* (HTKNT XIII/3; Freiburg 1979) 145-149.

L. J. LIETAERT PEERBOLTE

ANU → **HEAVEN**

APHRODITE Ἀφροδίτη

I. Aphrodite was the Greek goddess of love whose sacred animal is the →dove (PIRENNE-DELFORGE 1994). The Greeks derived her name from ἀφρός "foam", and explained it from her birth myth (Hesiod *Theog.* 191). Modern etymologies found no general consent, be it the rare Indo-European ones or those deriving her name from a Semitic language (BURKERT 1977:240 n.18). The goddess was identified with several Oriental goddesses, from Egyptian Nephthys to Phoenician →Astarte, Assyrian →Ishtar and Arabian Alilat (Herodot. 3,8. 131; M. HÖFNER, *WbMyth* I/1, 423; MORA 1985:86-90). The Romans identified her with the Italian Venus (from **venus*, "beauty, grace"; SCHILLING 1954), the Etruscans with Turan (PFIFFIG 1975:260-263). In the Bible, Aphrodite occurs only as a theophoric element in the anthroponym Epaphroditus (and its shortened form Epaphras), e.g. Phil 2:25; Col 1:7.

II. Already in Homer, Aphrodite is the goddess of sexual pleasure. In *Iliad* 5,429 Zeus assigns her the *erga gamoio*; while *gamos* stresses her social functions as the divinity responsible for the sexual functioning of marriage, this does not exclude extramarital relationships, exemplified in her patronship over Helen (*Iliad* 3, 383-388) or her relationship to Hephaestos her husband and →Ares her lover (*Od.* 8, 266-269); in archaic poetry, she protects Sappho and her girls (e.g. Sappho frg.1 L.-P.) and the lovemaking of youth in general. This differentiates her from →Hera, who protects marriage as a social institution but who, though the legitimate wife of →Zeus, needs the assistance of Aphrodite in order to seduce him (Homer *Iliad* 14, 187-196). Several divinities who symbolize her powers consort with her. Eros, "Love" as sexual passion, and Himeros "Longing" accompany her after her birth, when she enters the assembly of the gods (Hesiod *Theog.* 201); later, Eros and Himeros - or his equivalent Pothos, "Desire", Aeschylus, *Suppl.* 1040 - are her children (SHAPIRO 1993:110-124). The Charites ("Graces") accompany her (Hom. *Od.*8, 364, see 18, 194 *Charites himeroentes*), or the Horai, "Seasons, Youths, Beauties" (Hom. *hymn.* 6, 5); other followers are Harmonia (SHAPIRO 1993:95-109) and Peitho, "Persuasion" (BUXTON 1983; SHAPIRO 1993:186-207), who is also said to be her daughter (Aeschylus *Suppl.* 1040). Together, these personifications add up to a picture of erotic seduction around the goddess of love; the negative consequences are expressed in a fragment from an Orphic poem, where she is escorted by Zelos, "Rivalry" and Apate, "Deceit" (Orph. frg. 127 Kern; hellenistic?).

Since her main field of influence and action is private rather than public, Aphrodite lacks important public festivals. The Aphrodisia were mostly festivals of *hetairai*, as in Athens (DEUBNER 1932:216) or in Corinth, where *hetairai* and free women celebrated the festival separately (Alexis ap. Athenaeus 13,33, who attests drinking and reveling [*kōmos*] of the *hetairai*).

Besides, Aphrodite is involved in the prenuptial and nuptial rituals of the young girls. Plutarch (*Quaest. Rom.* 2) lists her among the divinities necessary for the marrying couple, Zeus Teleios and Hera Teleia, →Artemis, Aphrodite and Peitho. In some places, she receives sacrifices from marrying girls or remarrying widows (Hermione Pausanias 2,34,12; Sparta ibid.3,12,8-9, see also Naupactus ibid. 10,38,12); in the Hellenistic age, Aphrodite Laodikeia, the divine form of queen Laodike, received the sacrifices from marrying couples (*Annuario della Scuola Archeologica di Atene* 45/46 (1969) 445 no. 2). Sometimes, the ritual background of girls' initiation rites is still visible, as in Athens, where the Arrhephoroi descend to the sanctuary of Aphrodite in the Gardens, at the end of their year of service on the Acropolis and before returning to a life closer to adulthood (BRULÉ 1987:83-98). The same background lies behind the cultic association of Aphrodite and →Hermes which has been analyzed especially for Locri in Southern Italy (SOURVINOU-INWOOD 1991:177-178) and the well documented sanctuary of Hermes and Aphrodite in Cretan Kato Syme (LEBESSI 1985).

As early as Sappho (frg. 140. 168 Lobel-Page, see also Hes. frg. 139), the Adonia attest another form of women's festival connected with Aphrodite and her sphere. The Athenian festival (DEUBNER 1932:220-222) included the exposition of →Adonis' body and his burial (Plutarch *Alcib.*18,5), but also drinking and dancing (Aristophanes *Lys.* 392-398); to the classical vase painters, its most conspicuous ritual was the "Gardens of Adonis", sherds planted with seeds which were exposed on the roof-tops in order to grow and wither rapidly (see also Plato *Phaedr.* 276 B; BURKERT 1979:105-111); the cult in Alexandria (well attested in Theocritus, *Id.* 15), began with a *hieros gamos* and banquet of Aphrodite and Adonis, followed by the laments for Adonis and his burial in the sea. The Semitic origin of Adonis is evident already from his name which probably derives from *'ādôn*, "(My) Lord". Frazerian interpretations had concentrated on Adonis the Dying God; social and structural analysis rather underlines the release from intensive every-day pressure which the festival with its blend of exotism, sensual seduction and high emotions offered to Greek women (DETIENNE 1972, who emphasizes the structural opposition to →Demeter, the other main goddess of women). The ritual exposure of short-lived gardens is not necessarily an original part of the festival: it has parallels in many parts of the Ancient and Modern East. Rather than stressing the short life of the plants, recent analysis focuses on the quick growth and proposes to see in it a ritual testing of seeds

(BAUDY 1986:9-13) which leads away from Aphrodite's central concerns.

From the 4th cent. BCE onwards, Aphrodite's sexual aspects appear as two polar oppositions, Aphrodite Urania and Aphrodite Pandemos. Plato, *Symp.*180 E (see also Xenophon *Symp.*8,9) contrasts them as ideal, spiritual love among males versus ordinary heterosexual love and prostitution. He connects this dichotomy with her double genealogy, the Hesiodean one which makes Aphrodite the motherless result of Uranus' castration (*Theog.* 188-195), and the Homeric one where she is the offspring of Zeus and Dione (*Iliad* 5,370). Though very popular afterwards, this dichotomy radically modifies the significance of the epithets involved. Urania, an epithet already at the root of the Hesiodic genealogy, continues a Near Eastern epithet (see below), whereas Pandemos, "She of the Entire Demos", declares Aphrodite as responsible for political harmony. She had an ancient sanctuary in Athens and a state festival celebrated with a procession (*LSCG* no. 39, from 287/286 BCE; it prescribes also a cathartic sacrifice of a dove). Several epigraphical documents attest also sacrifices by magistrates to Aphrodite (SOKOLOWSKI 1964; CROISSANT & SALVIAT 1966). In some instances, they are the officials responsible for the women (*gynaikonomoi*), and Aphrodite receives cult as their helper. In other cases, the sacrifice is offered at the end of service, to mark the return from duty to the pleasures of private life.

A special problem is presented by the statues of an armed Aphrodite which are attested for Laconia (Aphrodite Areia, Pausanias 3,17,5; Enoplios *IG* 5:1 no. 602, Kythera Paus.3,23,1) and Corinth (Paus.2,5,1) (FLEMBERG 1991). Like the armed →Athena, the iconography must derive from the Near East (see below). In a more functionalist view, such statues are equivalent to stories about fighting women; both point to an unusual ritual in the cult of Aphrodite (GRAF 1984).

Besides sexuality (especially female sexuality) and the state, Aphrodite is associated with the →sea. As patron goddess of seafaring, she bears the epithets Euploia ("Giving good sailing"), Pontia and Limenia; as such, she receives sacrifices and votive gifts from sailors and fishermen (*Anth. Pal.*9, 143).

Aphrodite is among the few Greek divinities not attested in the Linear B texts; this makes it likely that she came to Greece only after the fall of the Mycenaean civilization. Her Near Eastern associations point to an Oriental origin (BURKERT 1977:238-240), even when etymologies (e.g. from →Astarte) may seem dubious. Sumerian Innana, Akkadian Ishtar, Phoenician Astarte (already Herodotus 1,105) all share significant characteristics with Aphrodite: bisexuality (Aphroditos on Cyprus Paion FGH 757 F 1; Macrobius, *Sat.*3,8), temple prostitution (in Corinth, Pindar frg. 122; not in Locri, SOURVINOU 1991: 179), the epithet Urania (Assyrian according to Pausanias 1,14,7), the association with the sea and with the garden (Aphrodite In the Gardens in Athens), the iconography of a frontally naked goddess (BÖHM 1990, AMMERMAN 1991) and of an armed goddess (COLBOW 1991), the symbol of the ladder (SERVAIS-SOYEZ 1983).

One of Aphrodite's main cult centres was Cyprus. Already in Homer (*Od.* 8,363), Hesiod (*Theog.* 193) and the Homeric *Hymn. Ven.* 58, Cyprus houses her main sanctuary; *Kypria* (Cypria) is her standard epithet throughout antiquity. In 333/332 BCE, the Athenians granted a lease of land for the building of a sanctuary to Aphrodite in Piraeus "on the same terms as for →Isis to the Egyptians" (SOKOLOWSKI 1969, no. 37) to the merchants from Kition living in Piraeus: Aphrodite was their national divinity. Her main Cypriot sanctuaries were at Amathous and at Paphos. Both antedate the advent of the Phoenicians in the 9th cent.; Paphos goes back to the 12th cent. and preserves a typically Mycenaean tripartite façade until late antiquity, according to local coins. Paphos also included an oracle still consulted by the young Titus in 79 CE (Tacitus, *Hist.* 2,1; Suetonius, *Tit.* 5,1). Perhaps, the goddess even had the Mycenaean royal title Vanassa, "Queen". These clear signs of a Mycenaean past complicate the history of Greek Aphrodite (there still is no solution) without, however, radically jeopardizing the theory of an Oriental origin.

Apart from this mainstream Oriental model, Greek Aphrodite was associated with the Anatolian Great Goddess, Cybele (→Ma-Cybele). Charon of Lampsacus, a local writer of the 5th cent. BCE, identifies Aphrodite and Kubebe (*FGH* 262 F 5); the description of the goddess' appearance in the Homeric *Hymn. Ven.* 68-72 as a mistress of wild animals follows a pattern belonging to the Great Goddess. The main myth of the same hymn, however, the seduction of Anchises which resulted both in the birth of →Aeneas and the lameness of Anchises, follows a mythical theme attested both for Cybele and for Innana-Ishtar, the love of the goddess which destroys her mortal lover (PICCALUGA 1974): the Anatolian Aphrodite seems to combine features of different origin. The same holds true for the main polis cult of Aphrodite in Asia Minor, the cult of Aphrodisias in Caria (LAUMONIER 1958: 478-504, esp. 480-481).

Other cult centres were Cnidus on the Anatolian West coast, the island of Kythera off the south coast of the Peleponessus, and Corinth. Cythera came second in importance after Cyprus, Cytherea became a common epithet. The sanctuary and its cult must have retained oriental features, since Herodotus called it a Phoenician foundation (1,105); the statue was that of an armed goddess (Pausanias 3,23,1). Cnidus had three sanctuaries, of Aphrodite Doritis, Akraia, and Euploia, according to Pausanias (1,1,3); the main sanctuary, of Aphrodite Euploia, housed the famous statue by Praxiteles. The sanctuary at Corinth ("Aphrodite's town", Euripides, frg. 1084 Nauck) contained another statue of an armed Aphrodite (Pausanias 2,5,1); it was famous for its sacred prostitution (Pindar frg. 122). The sanctuary on Mt. Eryx in Sicily, finally, started as a purely Phoenician one, until its Romanization after the First Punic War. The Platonic transformation of Aphrodite Pandemos and Urania into opposing principles of love was continued by the Neoplatonist philosophers and enthusiastically received in Florentine Neo-Platonism (WIND 1967:141-151). The overtly sexual mythology of Aphrodite on the other hand lent itself to heavy Christian polemics, from her birth from Uranus' genitals over her different affairs with gods and men (Ares, Kinyras, Adonis, Anchises) to the Pygmalion myth.

III. The Bible does not mention Aphrodite, not even Acts, although Paul visited Paphus (Acts 13:6) and Corinth (Acts 18:1-17), two of her main cult places. Adonia are attested for Antiochia in Syria, Byblus and Alexandria, though without the gardens (BAUDY 1986:20); the expansion of his cult in the ancient Near East might have included Jerusalem and its womenfolk.

IV. *Bibliography*

R. M. AMMERMAN, The Naked Standing Goddess. A Group of Archaic Terracotta Figurines from Paestum, *AJA* 95 (1991) 203-230; G. J. BAUDY, *Adonisgärten. Studien zur antiken Samensymbolik* (Frankfurt 1986); S. BÖHM, *Die "Nackte Göttin". Zur Ikonographie und Deutung unbekleideter weiblicher Figuren in der frühgriechischen Kunst* (Mainz 1990); P. BRULÉ, *La fille d'Athènes. La religion des filles à Athènes à l'époque classique. Mythes, cultes et société* (Paris 1987); W. BURKERT, *Griechische Religion der archaischen und klassischen Epoche* (RdM 15; Stuttgart 1977); BURKERT, *Structure and History in Greek Mythology and Ritual* (Sather Classical Lectures 47; Berkeley 1979); R. G. A. BUXTON, *Persuasion in Greek Tragedy. A Study of Peitho* (Cambridge 1983); G. COLBOW, *Die kriegerische Ištar. Zu den Erscheinungsformen bewaffneter Gottheiten zwischen der Mitte des 3. und der Mitte des 2. Jahrtausends* (Münchener Vorderasiatische Studien 12; Munich 1991); F. CROISSANT & F. SALVIAT, Aphrodite gardienne des magistrats, *BCH* 90 (1966) 460-471; M. DETIENNE, *Les jardins d'Adonis. La mythologie des aromates en Grèce* (Paris 1972); L. DEUBNER, *Attische Feste* (Berlin 1932); L. R. FARNELL, *The Cults of the Greek States*, vol. 2 (Oxford 1896) 618-761; J. FLEMBERG, *Venus Armata. Studien zur bewaffneten Aphrodite in der griechisch-römischen Kunst* (Stockholm-

Göteborg 1991); F. GRAF, Women, War, and Warlike Divinities, *ZPE* 55 (1984) 245-254; A. LAUMONIER, *Les cultes indigènes en Carie* (Paris 1958); A. LEBESSI, *To iero tou Ermi kai tis Aphroditis sti Symi Viannou*, vol. 1 (Athens 1985); F. MORA, *Religione e religioni nelle storie di Erodoto* (Milan 1985); V. PIRENNE-DELFORGE, *L'Aphrodite grecque. Contribution à l'étude de ses cultes et de sa personnalité dans le panthéon archaïque et classique* (Liège 1994); A. J. PFIFFIG, *Religio Etrusca* (Graz 1975); G. PICCALUGA, La ventura di amare una divinità, *Minutal* (Rome 1974) 9-35; R. SCHILLING, *La religion romaine de Vénus* (Paris 1954, repr. 1982); B. SERVAIS-SOYEZ, Aphrodite Ouranie et le symbolisme de l'échelle. Un message venu d'Orient, *Le mythe, son langage et son message. Actes du colloque de Liège et Louvain-la-Neuve 1981* (ed. H. Limet & J. Ries; Louvain-la-Neuve 1983) 191-208; H. A. SHAPIRO, *Personifications in Greek Art. The Representation of Abstract Concepts 600-400 B.C.* (Kilchberg 1993); F. SOKOLOWSKI, Aphrodite as Guardian of Greek Magistrates, *HTR* 57 (1964) 1-8; C. SOURVINOU-INWOOD, *'Reading' Greek Culture* (Oxford 1991); M. L. WEST, *The Orphic Poems* (Oxford 1983); E. WIND, *Pagan Mysteries in the Renaissance* (Harmondsworth 1967).

F. GRAF

APIS חף

I. Apis, the sacred bull of Memphis, occurs in the LXX version of Jer 46:15 as the most prominent of Egypt's gods whose flight is mocked by the prophet as a signal of the destruction about to befall Egypt by the hand of God. Most commentators and translators reconstruct Apis in the Hebrew text by a redivision and revocalisation of the MT *nisḥap* 'is prostrated' as *nās ḥap* 'Apis has fled'. The LXX version would then be the correct rendering of a corrupt MT rather than Jewish polemics (cf. the →Ibis in the LXX versions of Lev 11:17 and Deut 14:16) against the cult of Apis (S. MORENZ, Ägyptische Spuren in den Septuaginta, *Mullus* [FS Theodor Klauser; eds. A. Stuiber & A. Hermann = *JAC* Ergänzungsband 1; Münster 1964] 250-258; MUSSIES 1978:831-832). A dubious instance is the name Eliaph (→Horeph) (Gk *Eliaph*), 'my-god-is-Apis', found in the LXX version of 1 Kgs 4:3 (R. DE VAUX, Mélange, *RB* 48 [1939] 399).

Spelled *ḥap* or *ḥapî*, Apis appears as a theophoric element in names found in Aramaic, Phoenician and Neobabylonian texts (*KAI* 269, 272; cf. 268; MUSSIES 1978:831; E. LIPIŃSKI, La stèle égypto-araméenne de Tumma', *CdE* 50 [1975] 93-104; H. RANKE, *Die ägyptischen Personennamen* I: *Verzeichnis der Namen* [Glückstadt 1935]). The Greek spelling Ἆπις, instead of the expected Ἅπις, has been understood as a case of psilosis, characteristic of the Ionian dialect (MUSSIES 1978:830-831). Semitic and Greek spellings reflect Eg *ḥp*, Copt *hape*, *hapi* 'Apis', which has been tentatively explained as *ḥp*, 'the Runner', referring to Apis's cultic running to fertilize the fields (OTTO 1964:11; cf. MARTIN 1984:786).

II. Apis is the most famous of the sacred bulls of the Egyptians, kept at Memphis in a stall and worshipped there from the time of king Aha at the beginning of the First Dynasty (K. SIMPSON, A Running of the Apis in the Reign of 'Aḥa and Passages in Manetho and Aelian, *Or* 26 [1957] 139-142) until the late 4th century CE. Throughout its history, the Apis cult has been a royal cult (MALAISE 1972:212, with references). As far back as the Old Kingdom queens were linked to the cult of Apis (VANDIER 1949:234). The popularity of Apis during the Late Period is a secondary development.

The divine nature of Apis is closely linked to fertility and regeneration. Since the processes of renewed life can be observed in numerous phenomena in the cosmos as well as on earth, Apis is associated with gods of rebirth and resurrection whose hidden creative forces are revealed on earth by Apis as their visible manifestation. This relationship between Apis and these gods is expressed by the Egyptian term Ba (L. V. ŽABKAR, Ba, *LdÄ* 1 [1975] 588-590).

Apis represents →Ptah, creator god of Memphis, who as a god of vegetation is sometimes called 'Bull of the Earth' and

'Great →Nile'. Apis's title *wḥm Ptḥ*, 'who repeats Ptah', 'Herald of Ptah', has been explained by OTTO (1964:24-26) and others as referring to the bull's well-known role as an oracle god. The title, however, seems to point to the fact that Apis reveals the power of Ptah's creative word (Eg *ḥw*) by bringing food (Eg *ḥw*) and life into this world (J. ZANDEE, Das Schöpferwort im alten Ägypten, *Verbum. Essays on Some Aspects of the Religious Function of Words Dedicated to Dr. H. W. Obbink* [Utrecht 1964] 33-66). Indeed Apis is addressed as the noble Ba of Ptah. It should be noted that Apis's stall is situated to the south of the temple of Ptah and that the embalming place of the bull is in the south-west corner of that vast temple complex. The obsequies of Apis are carried out by the priests of Ptah, not by the bull's own priests.

Since the 18th Dynasty (from 1550 BCE), the period in which the sun doctrine was elaborated by Egyptian theologians, Apis had been associated with →Atum, the evening appearance of the sun god, who rises from the earth in the form of a scarab beetle (= khepri), image of the rejuvenated sun god, to create light, life and vegetation in a cyclic process. Up to Roman times, Apis is depicted (KATER-SIBBES & VERMASEREN 1975: I nos. 78, 82-84) with a sun disc and uraeus between the horns and on his back a hawk and a winged scarab beetle as symbols of the sun. The white triangle on Apis's brow is perhaps a solar symbol (M. J. VERMASEREN & C. C. VAN ESSEN, *The Excavations in the Mithraeum of the Church of Santa Prisca* [Leiden 1965] 344-346). The fact that Apis is called many-coloured (Gk *poikilos*: Lucian, *Deorum Concil.* 10; cf. Macrobius, *Saturn.* 1.21) also points to the god's solar nature (J. ASSMANN, *Liturgische Lieder an den Sonnengott* [MÄS 19; Berlin 1969] 171). According to Classical writers Apis has a wart (= scarab beetle) under his tongue (Herodotus, *Hist.* 3.28; Pliny, *Nat. hist.* 8.184). During the funeral of Apis solar rites play a major role (Vos 1993:40).

Apis is also dedicated to the →moon which was conceived of as a large bull (*CT* VII.25h.35a and P. DERCHAIN, Mythes et dieux lunaires en Egypte, *La lune, mythes et rites* [SO 5; Paris 1962] 17-68, 50). It is uncertain whether the relationship between Apis and →Thoth, god of the moon, can be traced back to the beginning of Egyptian history as has been stated by HERMANN (1960:39 n. 46; cf. MARTIN 1984:786, with n. 52; W. HELCK, Zu den "Talbezirken" in Abydos, *MDAIK* 28 [1972] 95-99). In fact, Apis's lunar aspects became especially prominent in the Roman period. From the 18th Dynasty onwards the moon was venerated in the Memphite necropolis (ZIEGLER 1988:441-449) and a famous temple of Thoth is adjacent to that of Apis (M. GUILMOT, Le Sarapieion de Memphis - Etude topographique, *CdE* 37 [1962] 359-381, 370-371, 379, 381). The so-called Apis-period of 25 years, which is said to be the lifespan of Apis, is of an obvious lunar nature, since at the end of that period the moonphases return on the same day (VERCOUTTER 1975:346). In Roman times Apis is depicted with the moon between the horns and a mark in the shape of the waxing moon on his right or, in rare cases, his left side (GRIMM 1968:20-24; KATER-SIBBES & VERMASEREN 1975: II nos. 272, 283, 290, 350). The waxing moon was considered to bring the inundation and fertility to the land (P. DERCHAIN, Mythes et dieux lunaires en Egypte, *La lune, mythes et rites* [SO 5; Paris 1962] 34). Apis's cultic running to fertilize the fields seems to be related to the phases of the moon and the annual flooding of the Nile (MARTIN 1984:784). Shortly after his birth, when the moon was waxing, Apis visited the House of the Inundation of the Nile (Nilopolis; OTTO 1964:16), and at his death priests of that same House were involved in the obsequies as a sign of the god's rejuvenation (Vos 1993:164). Apis was enthroned at full moon and he played a part in the king's accession rites which took place at full moon (M.-T. DERCHAIN-URTEL, Thronbesteigung, *LdÄ* 6 [1986] 529-532).

Because of his lunar nature and his relation to the inundation, Apis was easily associated with →Osiris Lunatus (ZIEGLER 1988:447-449), who is called *kꜣ rnpy*, 'Bull rejuvenating (in the sky)' (QUAEGEBEUR 1983:31). Osiris played an important role in Memphis (VANDIER 1961:112-113). As a god of vegetation Osiris was identified with the Nile and the life-giving inundation (VANDIER 1949:59). Apis is sometimes associated with the Canopic jars containing the holy water of the Nile emanating from Osiris (KATER-SIBBES & VERMASEREN 1975: II nos. 296-297, 536).

Best known is Apis's association with Osiris in his capacity of the funeral god. Apis is basically black in colour and Osiris is sometimes called 'Bull of the West' or 'Big black Bull'. Apis is identified with →Horus, son of Osiris (VANDIER 1949:235). A few bronzes show Apis with a bird behind the horns, which could point to the falcon →Horus (KATER-SIBBES & VERMASEREN 1975: II nos. 303, 568; cf. 489, 535, 562). The bull is sometimes represented as the young Horus, fed by →Isis to obtain eternal youth (QUAEGEBEUR 1983:31; KATER-SIBBES & VERMASEREN 1975: I nos. 101, 112, 117). In the Memphite Serapeum Isis is often the Mother of Apis (H. S. SMITH & D. G. JEFFREYS, The Sacred Animal Necropolis, North Saqqâra: 1975/76, *JEA* 63 [1977] 20-28, 23). This relationship between Isis and Apis became a prominent feature of the Hellenized Isis cult and was often depicted on coins. As a manifestation of Horus (or Anubis) Apis assists Isis in collecting and transporting the limbs of the deceased (= Osiris) from the West to the East, the place of resurrection, in a ritual running which can be parallelled with the life-giving running of Apis to fertilize the fields (M. SAMI GABRA, Un sarcophage de Touna, *ASAE* 28 [1928] 77; VANDIER 1961: 117-120). During this ritual running the bull is sometimes depicted wearing the *menat*, a beaded necklace sacred to →Hathor, which brings new life and wards off any evil that might endanger it (QUAEGEBEUR 1983:17-39). Apis is associated with →Bes, dwarf-god of fertility, who protects women and babies (KATER-SIBBES & VERMASEREN 1975: I nos. 65, 91, 99-100).

Upon his death Apis becomes Osiris-Apis and he is embalmed after the example of Osiris in a 70-day process. He is buried in an underground vault of the Serapeum, the burial place of the Apis bulls west of Memphis. The Vienna Apis Embalming Ritual (2nd century BCE) describes burial rites in which, according to theological conceptions of the Late Period, solar and Osirian rites of resurrection are interwoven. This fits in with Apis's complex nature which is closely connected with vegetative and cosmic phenomena of renewed life. The Egyptians express Apis's comprehensive being by assimilating him in a syncretistic way to composite divinities like Osiris-Atum-Horus, Ptah-Rēᶜ-Horsiesis and Ptah-Osiris-Sokaris.

In the Late Period Apis worship took on the form of a national cult. It has been suggested that during this period of foreign rule the Egyptians tried to maintain their cultural identity by turning to their animal gods, the worship of which was repugnant to foreigners (SMELIK & HEMELRIJK 1984:1863-1864). For political reasons the Ptolemaic Kings favoured the popular cult of Apis. Ptolemy I Soter tried to reconcile Egyptian and Greek religions by introducing the god Sarapis (Osiris-Apis) but the cult was so heavily Hellenized that up to the Roman period it failed to arouse much interest among native Egyptians. A few rare examples show Apis with the sun disc between the horns and instead of the uraeus a modius, emblem of fertility of Sarapis (KATER-SIBBES & VERMASEREN 1975: I nos. 43, 120).

Generally speaking, Roman religious policy was less favourably inclined towards Apis, although a number of Alexandrian coins, from Nero to Commodus, bear a figure of Apis represented as a bull (HERMANN 1960:38). From Delos, Apis was imported in →Rome, not as a separate deity but as part of the rapidly growing cults of Isis and Sarapis (GRIMM 1968: 25-26; SMELIK & HEMELRIJK 1984:1920, n. 424). Numerous statuettes of Apis, including a few rare ones representing Apis in human form, but with a bull's head and clothed as a Roman emperor (*Apis imperator*), have been found all over Europe. The Apis imperator was perhaps a symbol of divine power rather than a defender of Osiris against the crimes of →Seth (S. MORENZ, *Die Begegnung Europas mit Ägypten* [Zürich/Stuttgart 1969] 200-201, n. 81 and 82). In Greek texts from Brahlia in Syria (1st-2nd centuries CE) Apis was associated with →Zeus-El-Kronos and perhaps incorporated in the cults of the Dea Roma and the Emperor (Y. HAJJAR, Dieux et cultes non Héliopolitains de la Béqaʿ, *ANRW* II 18,4 [1990] 2554-2555, 2579).

III. Apis frequently appears in the works of Christian writers. In their polemics against the most popular representative of Egyptian animal worship these writers reflect the OT rejection of animal cult (Exod 8:26; cf. *Exod Rabbah* 16.3). It is not surprising then that the Christian writers associate Apis with the Golden →Calf (SMELIK & HEMELRIJK 1984:1918 n. 412; 1995 n. 929) whose cult is called the Egyptian disease (Basilius Seleucensis, *Orat.* 6.3). Jerome, *in Oseam* 10.4 (cf. Cyrillus Alexandrinus, *in Oseam* 5.8.9 and F. M. ABEL, La géographie sacrée chez S. Cyrille d'Alexandrie, *RB* 31 [1922] 408-409), identifies the two golden calves of 1 Kgs 12:25, one of which Jeroboam placed in Bethel and the other in Dan, with Apis, the bull of Ptah in Memphis, and Mnevis, the bull of →Re in Heliopolis (P. GALPAZ, The Reign of Jeroboam and the Extent of Egyptian Influences, *BN* 60 [1991] 13-19, 18). Also according to Egyptian sources of the Ptolemaic period, these bull-gods were closely connected and they regularly visited each other. Although the equation of Apis and the Golden Calf cannot be accepted, the Christian writers often gave important factual information concerning Apis for which they drew heavily on what they had learned from Graeco-Roman literature. The role of Apis as a god of fertility has not been forgotten (Rufinus, *Hist. mon.* 7; cf. Diodorus Siculus 1.85; Ammianus Marcellinus 22.14). Augustine, *Civ. Dei* 18.4 rightly differentiates between Apis and Sarapis and he knows of the relationship between Isis and Apis, her godly companion (*Confess.* 8.2; cf. P. COURCELLE, Sur un passage énigmatique des Confessions de Saint Augustin, *REL* 29 [1951] 295-307). The Church-father (*Civ. Dei* 18.5), however, fancifully explained the name of Sarapis as meaning 'coffin of Apis', thus following a tradition according to which Apis was a king of the Argives (cf. *Bibliothèque Augustinienne* 36 [1960] 747-748, with many references).

The physical features of Apis are mentioned by several authors: his black colour, the inverted white triangle on his forehead and the white markings on his skin (Augustine, *Civ. Dei* 18.3.5; Cyrillus Alexandrinus, *in Oseam* 3.56; Eudocia, *Violar.* 8.15; Rufinus, *Hist. eccles.* 2.23; cf. the numerous passages in Classical writers cited by HOPFNER 1913:78).

The lunar aspects of Apis are often referred to. Apis was miraculously generated by the light of the moon (Cosmas Hierosol., *Comment. ad Greg. Nazianz.* 270; Theodoretus, *Curatio* 3.46; Eudocia, *Violar* 8.15; cf. Plutarch, *de Isid.* 43, 368C; Suda s.v. Ἆπις). There seems to be no genuine Egyptian evidence for the procreation of Apis by the moon (BONNET 1952:50), although FAULKNER strongly believed to have found it in *CT* II.209a (R. O. FAULKNER, The pregnancy of Isis, *JEA* 54 [1968] 40-44; FAULKNER, "The pregnancy of Isis", a Rejoinder, *JEA* 59 [1973] 218-219). According to Cyrillus Alexandrinus, *in Oseam* 3.56; 10.3 (cf. Eusebius, *Praep. Evang.* 3.13; Ammianus Marcellinus 22.14), the cosmic parents of Apis are the sun and the moon.

The birth of an Apis occurs at intervals and is attended by great public joy (Eudocia, *Violar.* 8.15; cf. Herodotus 3.27; J. VERCOUTTER, Une Epitaphe Royale Inédite du Sérapéum, *MDAIK* 16 [1958] 333-345, 344). The obsequies entailed lavish expense (Gregory of Nazianzus, *Oratio* 39; cf. Diodorus Siculus 1.84) and led to the diligent searching up and down the country for his successor (Augustine, *Civ. Dei* 18.5).

Some Christian writers seemingly make an exception to the rule that Apis is not positively assessed (SMELIK & HEMELRIJK 1984:1982). Clemens Alexandrinus (*Coh.* 2.34; *Protrept.* 2.39) is of the opinion that

Apis is to be preferred to the adulterous gods of the Greeks, and Tertullian (*Monog.* 18; *Exhort. cast.* 13; *Ieiunio* 9.2) makes the priests of Apis an example of chastity (P. COURCELLE, L'oracle d'Apis et l'oracle du jardin de Milan (Augustin, "Conf.", VIII, 11, 29), *RHR* 139 [1951] 216-231, 227). It is also remarkable that Christian writers often sharply disapprove of the murder of Apis by Cambyses (SMELIK & HEMELRIJK 1984:1865, 1868). The story is contrary to Egyptian evidence, although the king did make drastic reductions in the state contributions to the temples.

In 391 CE the pious emperor Theodosius abruptly closed all pagan temples and ordered the destruction of the Alexandrian Serapeum, which must have deeply affected Christians and pagans alike (Augustine, *De Divin. Daemon.* 1.1; cf. A. D. NOCK, Augustine and the prophecy of the destruction of the Serapeum, *VC* 3 [1949] 56). Theodosius' actions almost certainly put an end to the cult of Apis as well. Perhaps the last bull of this kind is mentioned by Ammianus Marcellinus 22.14 and praised by Claudian, pagan poet at the Christian court of Ravenna (HERMANN 1960:44-46).

IV. *Bibliography*

H. BONNET, Apis, *RÄRG* (Berlin/New York 1971²) 46-51; G. GRIMM, Eine verschollene Apisstatuette aus Mainz, *ZÄS* 95 (1968) 17-36; J. HANI, *La religion égyptienne dans la pensée de Plutarque* (Paris 1976) 622-632, 837-838; A. HERMANN, Der letzte Apisstier, *JAC* 3 (1960) 34-50; T. HOPFNER, *Der Tierkult der alten Ägypter* (Vienna 1913); G. J. F. KATER-SIBBES & M. J. VERMASEREN, *Apis* I-III (EPRO 48/I-III; Leiden 1975-1977); K. MARTIN, Sedfest, *LdÄ* 5 (1984) 782-790; M. MALAISE, *Les conditions de pénétration et de diffusion des cultes égyptiens en Italie* (EPRO 22; Leiden 1972); G. MUSSIES, Some Notes on the Name of Sarapis, *Hommage à Maarten J. Vermaseren* (eds. M. den Boer *et al.*; EPRO 68/II; Leiden 1978) 831-832; E. OTTO, *Beiträge zur Geschichte der Stierkulte in Ägypten* (Hildesheim 1964); J. QUAEGEBEUR, Apis et la menat, *BSFE* 98 (1983) 17-39; K. A. D. SMELIK & E. A. HEMELRIJK, "Who Knows Not What Monsters Demented Egypt Worships?", Opinions on Egyptian Animal Worship in Antiquity as Part of the Ancient Conception of Egypt, *ANRW* II 17,4 (Berlin/New York 1984) 1852-2000; J. VANDIER, Memphis et le taureau Apis dans le papyrus Jumilhac, *Mélanges Mariette* (IFAO 32; Cairo 1961) 105-123; VANDIER, *La religion égyptienne*, MANA 1/I (Paris 1949) 233-237; J. VERCOUTTER, Apis, *LdÄ* 1 (1975) 338-350; R. L. VOS, *The Apis Embalming Ritual. P. Vindob. 3873* (OLA 50; Leuven 1993); C. ZIEGLER, Les Osiris-lunes du Sérapéum de Memphis, *Akten des Vierten Internationalen Ägyptologen-Kongresses München 1985*, III: *Linguistik - Philologie - Religion* (ed. S. Schoske; SAK Beihefte 3; Hamburg 1989) 441-451.

R. L. VOS

APKALLU

I. In Mesopotamian religion, the term *apkallu* (Sum **abgal**) is used for the legendary creatures endowed with extraordinary →wisdom. Seven in number, they are the culture →heroes from before the Flood. Some of the mythological speculations in which they figure have exerted influence on certain biblical and post-biblical traditions. Examples are the figure of →Enoch and the tale of the →Nephilim (Gen 6:1-4).

II. Akk *apkallu* is derived from Sum **abgal**, a term used in the 3rd millennium for a high official. In the Sumerian incantations of the Old Babylonian period **abgal** refers to a sage at the court of Enki. Based on a tradition that goes back to the 3rd millennium, the term *apkallu* is used for legendary creatures endowed with wisdom, seven in number, who existed before the flood. In the myth of the 'Twenty-one Poultices' the 'seven *apkallū* of Eridu', who are also called the 'seven *apkallū* of the Apsu', are at the service of Ea (Enki). Ea is called the 'sage among the gods' (*apkallu ilī*) and the title was also used of his son →Marduk. A variety of wisdom traditions from the antediluvian period were supposedly passed on by the *apkallū*. We learn from the 'Etiological Myth of the Seven Sages' that the *apkallū* were "of human descent, whom the lord Ea has endowed with wisdom". The tradition of the *apkallū* is preserved in the *bīt-mēseri* ritual series and also by Berossus. The seven sages were created in the river and served as "those who insured the correct functioning of the plans of heaven and earth" (*muštēširū uṣurāt šamê u erṣeti*). Following the example of Ea, they taught mankind wisdom, social forms and craftsmanship. The authorship of texts dealing with omens, magic and other categories of 'wisdom' such as medicine is attributed to the seven *apkallū*. Gilgamesh, "who saw everything" (*ša naqba īmuru*), is credited with having brought back knowledge whose origin was before the flood (*ša lām abūbi*) and on a cylinder seal he is called "master of the *apkallū*". In the course of the development of the traditions concerning them, the seven *apkallū* became associated with laying the foundations of the seven ancient cities: Eridu, Ur, Nippur, Kullab, Kesh, Lagash and Shuruppak. In the epic of Gilgamesh they are called 'counsellors' (*muntalkī*) and all of the seven sages were considered responsible for laying the foundations of Uruk (Gilg. I 9; XI 305). According to the Erra epic, the *apkallū* returned to the Apsu, the great abyss which was the home of Ea, and were never again within reach.

Uanna of Eridu, the first of the seven *apkallū* who served the early kings, was considered the master of a great store of knowledge. In some texts Adapa, a human sage who lived at that time and who bears the epithet *apkallu,* is assimilated to him. Adapa is at times called the son of Ea, but this refers to his being wise, rather than to his parentage. In turn the name Adapa became synonymous with wisdom. Oannes, in the late tradition transmitted by Berossus, "emerged daily from the Erythrean Sea in the time of the first king of history to teach mankind the arts of civilization". He is credited with giving man knowledge of letters and science and all types of crafts. Not only were highly qualified diviners given the title *apkallu,* but it was also popular among the late Assyrian kings. Sennacherib brags of having been given knowledge equal to that of the *apkallu* Adapa (D. D. LUCKENBILL, *The Annals of Sennacherib* [OIP 2; Chicago 1924] 117:4). Ashurbanipal, proud of his mastery of the skills of the scribe, boasted of having grasped "the craft of the *apkallu* Adapa, the esoteric secret of the entire scribal tradition" (M. STRECK, *Assurbanipal und die letzten Assyrischen Könige* [VAB 7; Leipzig 1916] 254:13; 367: 13). He is called the offspring of both an *apkallu* (Sennacherib) and Adapa (Esarhaddon) by one of his haruspices (*ABL* 923; *LAS* 117). It was probably in the neo-Assyrian period that the title *apkallu* spread to the Arameans and also to the Arabian tribes. In the Nabatean, Palmyrean and Hatrene inscriptions it is a sort of priest. Apkallatu occurs as the personal name of a queen of the Arabs in an inscription of Esarhaddon. In the Early South Arabian inscriptions *ʾfkl* is also a priest (cf. J. TEIXIDOR, Notes hatréennes 3: Le titre d' "aphkala", *Syria* 43 [1966] 91-93, and J. RYCKMANS, *JSS* 25 [1980] 199 n. 3).

The postdiluvian sages were called *ummânu*, a term which indicates mastery of a difficult subject, or being highly trained in a craft. Various literary works are attributed to specific *ummânū* and in the late period the *ummânu* functioned as the counsellors of the realm. The *apkallū* were also the keepers of esoteric lore which then became the prized possession of the *ummânū* In a tablet from the Seleucid period found during the excavations at Uruk the antediluvian *apkallū* and the postdiluvian *ummânū* are listed in conjunction with the king whom they served. Thus Uanna (Oannes) is the *apkallu* of Aialu (elsewhere Alulu) the first king, and the list ends with Abaʾenlildari, whom the Arameans call Ahiqar, the *ummânu* of king Esarhaddon.

In a variety of rituals, clay figurines of the seven *apkallū* were used with an apotropaic function. There were three types of *apkallū*, the seven anthropomorphic *ūmu-apkallū*, placed at the head of the bed of the sick person, the seven bird-*apkallū* buried against the wall, but in an adjoining room, and the seven fish-*apkallū*, who guard the threshold of the bedroom, with two further groups of fish-*apkallū*, buried in front and behind the chair kept in the room. The *ūmu-apkallū* were made of wood, but the bird- and fish-*apkallū* were made of →clay. The fish-*apkallū* are the best known since the fish-garbed men have been found in excavations in groups of seven (e.g. Nimrud). Their use is detailed in a variety of rituals. The fish-*apkallū* must be distinguished from the *kulullû*, a centaur-like fish-man. These *apkallū* are also found on wall-panels in Assyrian palaces or with apotropaic function flanking the doorways of temples and palaces. Berossus described Oannes as having the body of a fish, a human head below the fish head and human feet below the tail.

III. The tradition of the seven sages spread during the 2nd and 1st millennium to the West, reaching as far as Greece. It has been proposed that the tale of the →Nephilim, alluded to in Gen 6:1-4, is based on some of the negative aspects of the *apkallū* tradition. An echo of the role of the seven *apkallū* may be found in Prov 9:1 which should in all likelihood be rendered "→Wisdom built her house, the Seven set its pillars" instead of the traditional translation "Wisdom built her house, she set out its seven pillars". →Enoch, who was the "first among the children of men who had learned writing, science and wisdom" (*Jub.* 4:17), and taught knowledge to mankind was the seventh starting with Adam (*Jub.* 7:39). His ascension to →heaven is in all likelihood based on the tale of the seventh antediluvian *apkallu* Utuabzu who ascended to heaven according to the third tablet of the *bīt mēseri* series. The later tradition, preserved by pseudo-Philo, of Enoch building seven cities, may hark back to the seven antediluvian cities noted above. The images of the seven patriarchs found on the throne of Solomon, the embodiment of Wisdom, may also have its origin in the myth of the seven sages.

IV. *Bibliography*

J. BLACK & A. GREEN, *Gods, Demons and Symbols of Ancient Mesopotamia* (London 1992) 82-83; 100-101, 163-164; R. BORGER, Die Beschwörungsserie *bīt mēseri* und die Himmelfahrt Henochs, *JNES* 33 (1974) 183-196; S. M. BURSTEIN, *The Babyloniaca of Berossus* (Malibu 1978) 13-14; J. J. A. VAN DIJK, *La sagesse suméro-accadienne* (Leiden 1953) 20 n. 56; A. GREEN, Neo-Assyrian Apotropaic Figures, *Iraq* 45 (1983) 87-96; J. C. GREENFIELD, The Seven Pillars of Wisdom (Prov 9:1)—a Mistranslation, *JQR* 86 (1985) 13-20; A. D. KILMER, The Mesopotamian Counterparts of the Biblical Nepilim, *Perspectives on Language and Text, Essays and Poems in Honor of F. I. Andersen* (Winona Lake 1987) 39-43; W. G. LAMBERT, The Twenty-One "Poultices", *AnSt* 30 (1980) 77-83; S. PARPOLA, *Letters from Assyrian and Babylonian Scholars* (SAA 10; Helsinki 1993) xvii-xxiv; S. A. PICCHIONI, *Il poemetto di Adapa* (Budapest 1981); E. REINER, The Etiological Myth of the 'Seven Sages', *Or*NS 30 (1961) 1-11; F. A. M. WIGGERMANN, *Mesopotamian Protective Spirits, The Ritual Texts* (Groningen 1992) 73-79.

J. C. GREENFIELD

APOLLO Ἀπόλλων

I. Apollo is a Greek god whose name occurs as a theophoric element in the names Ἀπόλλως (Acts 18:24, var. lect.: Ἀπελλῆς, Ἀπολλώνιος [of which Apollos is a diminutive]; 19:1, var. lect.: Ἀπελλῆς, 1 Cor 1:12; 3:4, 5, 6, 22; 4:6; 16:12 and Titus 3:13), Ἀπελλῆς (Rom 16:10), Ἀπολλωνία (Acts 17:1, var. lect. Ἀπολλωνίς), and Ἀπολλύων (Rev 9:11).

II. Apollo is the most typical divine representative of classical Greek culture, the Greek god *par excellence*, though there is no doubt that he was of non-Greek origin. The two cult centres of Apollo, Delos and Delphi, date from the eighth century BCE. The Delos sanctuary was primarily devoted to →Artemis, Apollo's twin sister according to the myth (BURKERT 1977:226). At Delphi

Apollo was considered an intruder by the Greeks themselves: there is was that he killed the snake →Python, the son of →'Earth' and the Lord of that place (*Hom. Hymn* 3:182-387; see FONTENROSE 1950:13-27 for five different versions of this myth) and had to leave Delphi again in search of purification (*int. al.* Pausanias 2:7.7). The attempts to locate his origin in a specific region, especially the North-East of Europe or Asia Minor (GUTHRIE 1950:73-87), proved unsuccessful because of the lack of conclusive evidence; (the once promising alleged Hittite god Apulunas disappeared thanks to a better decipherment of the Hittite hieroglyphs [BURKERT 1975:2-4]). Of the many etymological explanations which have been proposed for the name Apollo (WERNICKE 1896:2-3; NILSSON 1955:555-559; FAUTH 1975:441-442) none has found general acceptance. However, following a suggestion by HARRISON (1927), BURKERT has again pointed out that there is a close connection with the name of the month *Apellaios* and the institution of the *apellai* (BURKERT 1975). In epic literature and at Delos and Delphi the god's name is always spelled *Apollōn*. In the Doric dialect we find *Apellōn* and on Cyprus Apeilōn, in Thessaly *Aploun*. At the beginning of the present era the form *Apollōn* had almost completely superseded the Doric form *Apellōn*, but the latter was certainly the older one: the spelling with *o* has to be taken as a secondary vocal assimilation to the ending *-ōn*. The month *Apellaios* and the *apellai* are also found in the whole Doric region. In Delphi *Apellaios* was the first month of the year, in which the *apellai* were held. The *apellai* were annual meetings in which tribal associations or communities purified themselves from ritual and spiritual contaminations, and in which the new members of the community, the Ephebi, were initiated. The god *Apellōn/Apollōn* may have derived his name from the *apellai*. He was 'the arch-ephebos' (HARRISON 1927:441), the true *kouros*.

Apollo was considered the author of evil and its averter as well (a), the god of purification, law and order (b) and the god of prophecy (c). These three aspects deserve a brief discussion.

(a) The beginning of the *Iliad* introduces Apollo as the frightening god who sends a deadly pestilence into the cattle and the army of the Achaeans. One of the oldest etymologies of Apollo's name is its derivation from *apollymi/apollyō* (Aeschylus, *Agam.* 1081; Euripides, frg. 781, 11; see WERNICKE 1896:2). But the author of the disease is also the one who can stop it; to that end one has to propitiate Apollo by means of sacrifices, hymns and prayers (NILSSON 1955:538-544), as was in fact done by the Achaeans (*Iliad* I:48-52, 450-456). In the second and third centuries CE, this way of propitiating the god to avert a plague was still advised by Apollo himself in several oracles given at Clarus and Didyma (R. LANE FOX, *Pagans and Christians* [New York 1987] 231-235). Similarly ambivalent gods, said to be both the cause of evil and of its disappearance, are found all over the world; in India, it is the god Rudra who shows a remarkable similarity to Apollo (LORENZ 1988:4, 8).

(b) Apollo was generally held to be the giver and interpreter of laws and city constitutions (GUTHRIE 1950:182-204; NILSSON 1955:625-653). In cities like Athens and Sparta there were official interpreters of civil and religious law who were closely related to the Delphic oracle, which enabled Apollo (and Delphi) to exercise a considerable influence on the internal affairs of the Greek city states. A special duty of the *exegetai* concerned advise on the rules of purification in cases of homicide (e.g. Plato, *Laws* 11, 916c; [Demosthenes], *Orat.* 47, 68). Murder inevitably brings pollution (*miasma*) on the killer, even if the latter has acted in self-defence, and therefore he is in need of purification (*katharsis*). Apollo, who according to the myth had to be purified himself after the killing of Python, remained the Greek god of purification (R. PARKER, *Miasma* [Oxford 1983] 275-276, 378, 393), although in the course of the centuries he changed his views from prescribing a vendetta to regulating legal jurisdiction over homicide (Orestes on the Areopagus underwent "the first trial for bloodshed," according to Aeschylus, *Eumen.* 683). It was probably his character as god of law and order which caused Apollo's identification with the sun, that "sees and hears all things" (Homer, *Iliad*:3, 277). His name *Phoibos*, from which the name Phoebe derives (Rom 16:3), has often been interpreted as 'Shining'; its precise meaning, however, is unknown (FAUTH 1975:442; BURKERT 1975:14 n. 56). The legal aspect of Helios Apollo is clearly brought out in a number of inscriptions concerning 'manumissions' of children and confessions of guilt from the temple of Apollo at Lairbenos in Phrygia, near Heliopolis, dating from the 2nd and 3rd centuries CE (MAMA IV, 275-278; MILLER 1985).

(c) Apollo was an oracle-speaking god from the beginning. His sanctuary at Delphi became the most influential political and religious centre of the Greek world (NILSSON 1955:I, 544-547, 625-653; for its history PARKE & WORMELL 1956:I). Apollo responded to questions on regulations of communal life, of which religion was an integral part, on wars and their outcome, the founding of colonies, etc. Also individuals came to Delphi with personal and sometimes rather trivial questions, though the evidence for this kind of oracle is quite scarce (614 responses in PARKE & WORMELL 1956:II; a critical classification in FONTENROSE 1978:240-416). The oracles were given by a woman, the Pythia, who was seated on the tripod. What exactly happened during the mantic sessions is almost completely unknown. The traditional picture holds that the tripod was placed above a chasm from which vapours ascended which brought the Pythia into a state of frenzy or trance, in which she uttered wild shouts which had to be interpreted by the *prophētēs*. But the evidence to support this view is too scanty (FONTENROSE 1978:196-232). After a short period of revived oracular activity in the second century CE Apollo almost completely relapsed into silence (see, however, the response to Amelius' question as to where Plotinus' soul had gone [ca. 260], Porphyry, *Vita Plotini* 22; PARKE & WORMELL 1956:II 92-193 [nr. 473]; FONTENROSE 1978:264-265 [H. 69], who conjectures that Amelius only sought Apollo's approval of his own poem on his beloved master).

In Asia Minor, there were two other great oracular sanctuaries of Apollo, at Didyma and Clarus (see R. LANE FOX, *Pagans and Christians* [New York 1987] 168-261, 711-727). The method of consultation at both sanctuaries is for the greater part unknown (Iamblichus' report on the mantic procedures at both sites, *De myst.* 3.11, reflects the final stage of Apollo's oracular practice, and possibly also the author's own interests). Clarus had a prophet and Didyma a prophetess who uttered Apollo's responses after drinking from an underground spring (Clarus) or inhaling the vapors which came from a surface spring in the sanctuary (Didyma) The oracles were put into neat metrical verse by the thespode, the 'singer of oracles' (Clarus) or a prophet (Didyma). The consultations of Apollo, by cities and individuals alike, did not substantially differ from those at Delphi or those of →Zeus at Dodona (VAN DEN BROEK 1981:4-7). Of the known oracular responses, 39 have been ascribed to Clarus and 93 to Didyma (ROBINSON 1981; see also FONTENROSE 1978:417-429 [50 responses from Didyma]), but in many cases the place of origin remains uncertain. An interesting group of the oracles from Clarus and Didyma in the 2nd and 3rd centuries is formed by the so-called 'theological oracles', which express the view that there is only one highest god whose servants or manifestations are the gods of the traditional religions. Of these oracles that found at Oenoanda has received most attention (ROBERT 1971; VAN DEN BROEK 1981:9-17; LANE FOX 1987:168-171), but a thorough study of the theology of all of them remains a desideratum. In the 3rd century Apollo fell silent. Julian the Apostate (359-361) tried to revive the Delphic oracle but the attempt failed (PARKE & WORMELL 1956:I 289-290; II 194-195, no. 476).

III. The popularity of Apollo is reflected in the frequency of theophoric personal names and toponyms: Apollodorus, Apollonia, Apollonius, Apollonides, Apollophanes, Apollos, etc.. Apart from the NT passages mentioned above (sub I), we find such names also in the books of the Maccabees and in early Christian literature (see e.g. the Christian presbyter Apollonius in Ignatius, *Magn.* 2:1). Christian polemic against Apollo directed itself especially at his oracular sites (D. DETSCHEW, *RAC* 1 [1950] 528-529), but nonetheless in some places his cult survived as late as the sixth century CE.

IV. *Bibliography*

R. VAN DEN BROEK, *Apollo in Asia. De Orakels van Clarus en Didyma in de tweede en derde eeuw na Chr.* (Leiden 1981); W. BURKERT, *Griechische Religion der archaischen und klassischen Epoche* (Stuttgart 1977) 225-233; BURKERT, Apellai und Apollon, *RhMus* 118 (1975) 1-21; W. FAUTH, Apollon, *KP* I (München 1975) 441-448; J. FONTENROSE, *Python. A Study of Delphic Myth and its origins* (Berkeley, Los Angeles, London 1950); FONTENROSE, *The Delphic Oracle: Its Responses and Operations, with a Catalogue of Responses* (Berkeley, Los Angeles, London 1978); W. K. C. GUTHRIE, *The Greeks and their Gods*, (London 1950; reprinted, with corrections, Boston 1954); J. E. HARRISON, *Themis. A Study of the Social Origins of Greek Religion*, (Cambridge 1927, 2nd ed.) 439-444; G. LORENZ, Apollon—Asklepios—Hygieia. Drei Typen von Heilgöttern in der Sicht der Vergleichende Religionsgeschichte, *Saeculum* 39 (1988) 1-11; K. M. MILLER, Apollo Lairbenos, *Numen* 32 (1985) 47-70; M. P. NILSSON, *Geschichte der griechischen Religion*, I (München 1955); H. W. PARKE & D. E. W. WORMELL, *The Delphic Oracle*, I: *The History*, II: *The Oracular Responses* (Oxford 1956); L. ROBERT, Un oracle gravé à Oinoanda, *CRAIBL* 1971 (Paris 1972) 597-619; T. L. ROBINSON, *Theological Oracles and the Sanctuaries of Claros and Didyma* (Thesis Harvard University 1981); K. WERNICKE, Apollon, PW 2 (1896) 1-111.

R. VAN DEN BROEK

APOLLYON → ABADDON; APOLLO

APSU → ENDS OF THE EARTH

AQAN → YAʿÛQ

ARCHAI Ἀρχαί

I. The Gk term *archē*, and its equivalent Lat translation *principium*, carries the basic meaning of primacy in time or rank. It is an abstract term for power often used with the meaning 'sphere of authority', i.e. power which is wielded by someone in a position of political, social or economic authority, such as a public official (Luke 20:20; *Sib. Or.* 5,20, 153). In the singular or plural *archē* is sometimes paired with *exousia* with the meaning 'office and authority' (Plato *Alcibiades* 135a; Philo *Leg.* 71; Luke 12:11; Titus 3:1; *Mart. Pol.* 10:2). It is also paired with *basileis*, 'kings' (*Pss. Sol.* 2:30; Philo *Somn.* 1.290), and also linked with 'kings and rulers', *hēgoumenoi* (*1 Clem* 32:2). It also is used in a more concrete sense referring to those who rule or govern, i.e. 'magistrate', 'ruler', 'governor' (Luke 12:11). When used with the latter meaning, *archē* belongs to the same semantic subdomain as *archōn*; in the Greek version of *1 Enoch* 6:7-8, e.g. *archē* and *archōn* are used interchangeably. By extension, *archē* can be used as a title for a supernatural force or power, whether good or evil, which has some control over the activities and destiny of human beings (Eph 6:12). Since the phrase *archai kai exousiai* is a stock expression used of 'magistrates and →authorities' (Luke 12:11; Titus 3:1; *Mart. Pol.* 10:2), it is likely that this political terminology was simply applied by figurative extension to supernatural beings who were thought to occupy vague positions of authority over other supernatural beings or over human beings.

II. The term *archai* (and its Lat equivalent *principia*), when used of supernatural beings, appears to have been used exclusively in early Christianity, and perhaps antecedently in early Judaism and early Christianity until it was eventually adopted by Christian

Gnostics and appropriated by Neoplatonic philosophers. Though it is generally presumed that early Christianity borrowed the language for various classes of angelic beings (→Angels) including *archai* from Judaism, the evidence is problematic. One supposed Jewish apocalyptic antecedent to Paul's use of the term 'principalities' (*archai*) in Rom 8:38-39 (where it is linked with 'angels' in one of the earliest occurrences of the term as an angelic category) is found in *1 Enoch* 61:10: "And he will call all the host of the heavens, and all the holy ones above, and the host of the LORD, and the →Cherubim, and the →Seraphim and the Ophannim, and all the angels of power, and all the angels of the principalities (presumably *archai*)." Yet the dating of *1 Enoch* 37-71 (the so-called Similitudes of Enoch in which this statement is found), is problematic; there is no persuasive evidence requiring a date prior to the middle of the first century CE. Further, it is possible that the Ethiopic phrase for 'angels of principalities' may be translating the Greek phrase *angeloi kuriotētōn* (→Dominions) rather than *angeloi archōn* (BLACK 1982). Similarly, the Theodotianic version of Dan 10:20 speaks of the 'prince of Persia' and the 'prince of Greece', certainly angelic beings in charge of particular nations (→Prince). In *1 Enoch* 6:8 (preserved in Gk and Aram in addition to Eth), *archai* is used of twenty named angels or →watchers, each of whom commands ten angels of lesser status. This angelic organization appears to have a military origin, for the Israelite army was arranged under leaders of thousands, hundreds, fifties and tens (Exod 18:21, 25; Deut 1:15; 1 Macc 3:55; 1QM 3.16-17; 4.1-5, 15-17). Josephus refers to the organization of the Maccabean army in 1 Macc 3:55 as "the old traditional manner" (*Ant.* 12.301). In the LXX Exod 18:21, 25 and 1 Macc 3:55 the term *dekadarchai* is used for commanders of the lowest level of military organization, which was also common in the Hellenistic world (Xenophon *Cyr.* 8.1.14; Polybius 6.25.2; Josephus *War* 2.578; Arrian *Anab.* 7.23.3). There are several other places in *1 Enoch*, where the term *archai* or *archontes* very probably lies behind the Ethiopic *1 Enoch* 71:5 speaks of "the leaders of the heads of thousands who are in charge of the whole creation" and *1 Enoch* 80:6 mentions that "many heads of the →stars in command will go astray" (see also *1 Enoch* 82:11-20). In *Jub.* 10:8, →Mastemah is called "the chief of the spirits". In 4Q Shir Shab the term *nĕśî'îm*, 'princes', is used of angels several times (4Q403 1 i 1, 10, 21; 4Q400 3 ii 2; 4Q405 13 2-3, 7; NEWSOM 1985:26-27), as is the term *rā'šîm*, 'chiefs' (4Q403 1 ii 11; 4Q405 23 ii 10; NEWSOM 1985:27), and these are combined in the title 'chief princes' (4Q403 1 ii 20, 21; 4Q405 8-9 5-6). In the LXX, the term *rō'š*, is occasionally translated with *archōn* (Deut 33:5; Job 29:25; Ezek 38:2-3) or *archē*, meaning 'chief', 'master', 'sovereign', 'prince', i.e. a term for leadership in the military, political and priestly ranks. Another use of the term *archai* for a category of angelic beings in Judaism occurs in the Theod. Dan 7:27 (Theodotion, the reviser of an earlier 'Ur-Theodotianic' version of the Gk OT, was active toward the end of the second century CE): "Then kingship and authority and the greatness of the kingdoms under the entire heaven were given to the holy ones (*hagioi*) of the Most High, and his kingship is an eternal kingship and all rulers (*hai archai*) shall serve and obey him." Here *archai*, 'rulers' (the LXX has *exousiai*, 'authorities') is parallel to *hagioi* ('the holy ones'), a Gk translation of the Heb term *qĕdôšîm*, a designation often used of angels (→saints, Ps 89:6; Job 5:1; 15:15; Zech 14:5; Dan 4:14; 8:13; see also Tob 12:15; *T. Levi* 12:15; *Pss. Sol.* 17:49). The Aram phrase underlying *hagioi* in Theod. Dan 7:27 is actually *'am qaddîšîm*, 'the people of the saints', i.e. Israel is the people of the holy ones [angels] (COLLINS 1977).

III. There are several problems in interpreting the term *archai* in the NT. One problem is that of determining whether or not the *archai* refer to human rulers or supernatural rulers. Another is that of determining whether, when supernatural beings are in view, they are good or evil. A third problem is that of determining whether supernatural categories of beings such as *archai* are distinct from other categories, such as *exousiai* and *dynameis*, or whether such designations are largely interchangeable. Paul includes angels, principalities (*archai*) and powers in in a list of obstacles which might separate the believer from the love of God in Rom 8:38. Clement of Alexandria interprets these as evil supernatural powers (*Strom.* 4.14). He may be correct, for since angels and *archai* appear to be antithetical in Rom 8:38, it is possible that the former are good while the latter are evil. In 1 Cor 15:24 it is clear that the *archai*, along with every authority and power, are considered hostile, since they are subject to destruction and are parallel to the term 'enemies' in 1 Cor 15:25, though here these categories may (but probably do not) refer to human rulers. There can be little doubt that the powers mentioned in Eph 1:21 and 6:12, and specifically the *archai* must be understood as evil supernatural powers.

In general it must be concluded that the lists of supernatural beings including the *archai* in Pauline and Deutero-Pauline literature are hostile supernatural beings. Further, it appears that the various categories are largely interchangeable, though it is possible that both authors and readers shared certain understandings about such beings which they did not find necessary to make more explicit.

Lists of Angelic Beings. The terms *archai* and *exousiai*, or their Lat equivalents *principia* and *potestates* were frequently paired in a formulaic way to refer to supernatural beings (Eph 3:10; Col 1:16; 2:10, 15; Justin *1 Apol.* 41.1; Irenaeus *Adv. haer.* 1.21.5; *Act. Phil.* 132, 144; Methodius *Symp.* 6; Epiphanius *Pan.* 31.5.2 [a Valentinian source]). When the three terms *archai*, *exousiai* and *dynameis* are used together (almost always in that order), supernatural beings are usually in view (1 Cor 15:24; Justin *Dial.* 120.6; *T. Sol.* 20.15; *Act. John* 98 [here the order is *dynameis*, *exousiai*, and *archai*, the reverse of the normal order, and the list goes on to include 'demons', activities {*energeiai*}, threatenings {*apeilai*}, passions {*thymoi*}, calumnies, →Satan and the inferior root]). Short lists of angelic beings occur in early Christian magical procedures such as *PGM* 13.15: *archai kai exousiai kai kosmokratores*, 'rulers and authorities and cosmic rulers' (the same brief list found in Origen *De principiis* 1.6.3), and *PGM* 21.2-3: *pasēs archēs kai exousias kai kuriotētos*, 'every ruler and authority and ruling power'. These lists seem to imply that *archai* are one among several classes of angelic beings, though the hierarchization of such beings appears to be a later step.

Angelic Classes and Hierarchies. In Judaism, Christianity and Gnosticism, there were numerous attempts to classify or systematize the various traditional terms for angelic beings. Despite frequent claims to the contrary, these speculations are not attested earlier than the first century CE. In *T. Levi* 3:1-8 (part of a more extensive Jewish interpolation in 2:3-6:2), a variety of angelic beings are correlated with some of the seven heavens, though *archai* are not mentioned. The third heaven (3:3) contains the 'powers of the hosts' (*hai dynameis tōn parembolōn)*, in the fourth heaven (3:8) are '→thrones and authorities' (*thronoi*, *exousiai*), in the fifth heaven (3:7) are angels, and in the sixth heaven (3:5) are the 'angels of the presence of the Lord'. While the Grundschrift of the *T. 12 Patr* may be as early as 200 BCE, this Jewish interpolation is probably much later, i.e. the first century CE. *Archai* are apparently mentioned in a classification of ten angelic orders in Slavonic *2 Enoch* 20:1 found in the longer recension which cannot with any assurance be dated earlier than the second century CE: (1) archangels, (2) incorporeal forces (*dynameis*?), (3) dominions (*kuriotētes*), (4) origins (*archai*?), (5) authorities (*exousiai*?), (6) cherubim, (7) seraphim, (8) many-eyed thrones (*thronoi*?), (9) regiments and (10) shining '*otanim*'(?) stations. In one of the eight Syriac manuscripts of the *T. Adam,* there is a list of heavenly powers placing them in a hierarchical arrangement beginning from the lowest and proceeding to the highest order: angels, archangels, archons (*archai*) authorities, powers, dominions, and finally at the highest level, thrones, seraphim and cherubim are grouped together (4:1-8). In *De caelesti hierarchia*, Ps.-Dionysius Areopagita, strongly influenced by Neoplatonic angelology, presents a hierarchy of angelic beings in three orders consisting of three types of angels in each order: (1) the highest order consists of seraphim, cherubim and thrones, 7.1-4, (2) the middle order consists of Dominions (*kuriotētes*), Authorities, (*exousiai*), and Powers, (*dynameis*), 8:1, and (3) the lowest order consists of principalities (*archai*), archangels (*archangeloi*), and angels, (*angeloi*), 9:1-2. This author also uses the terms angels and heavenly powers, *dynameis ouranias*, as generic terms for heavenly beings (4.1; 11.1-2). Iamblichus lists supernatural beings which reveal a god, such as an angel, archangel, demon, archon or a soul (*De myst.* 2.3). In an inscription written over the heads of angels in a Mosaic in the Koimesis Church, the terms *archai, dynameis, kuriotētes*, and *exousiai* appear (SAHIN, I:497).

IV. *Bibliography*

C. E. ARNOLD, *Ephesians: Power and Magic* (Cambridge 1989); H. BIETENHARD, *Die himmlische Welt im Urchristentum und Spätjudentum* (Tübingen 1951) 104-108; M. BLACK, Pasai exousiai autōi hypotagesontai, *Paul and Paulinism: Essays in Honour of C. K. Barrett* (London 1982) 73-82; G. B. CAIRD, *Principalities and Powers* (Oxford 1956); F. CUMONT, Les anges du paganisme, *RHR* 72 (1915) 159-182; W. CARR, *Angels and Principalities* (Cambridge 1983); J. J. COLLINS, *The Apocalyptic Vision of the Book of Daniel* (Missoula 1977) 141-144; M. DIBELIUS, *Geisterwelt im Glauben des Paulus* (Göttingen 1909); O. EVERLING, *Die paulinische Angelologie und Dämonologie* (Göttingen 1888); W. GRUNDMANN, *Der Begriff der Kraft in der neutestamentlichen Gedankenwelt* (Stuttgart 1932) 39-55; J. Y. LEE, Interpreting the Demonic Powers in Pauline Thought, *NovT* 12 (1970) 54-69; G. H. C. MACGREGOR, Principalities and Powers: The Cosmic Background of Paul's Thought, *NTS* 1 (1954-55) 17-28; C. MORRISON, *The Powers That Be: Earthly Rulers and Demonic Powers in Romans 13:1-7* (London 1960); C. NEWSOM, *Songs of the Sabbath Sacrifice* (HSS 27; Atlanta 1985); M. PESCE, *Paolo e gli Archonti a Corinto* (Brescia 1977) 261-336; S. E. ROBINSON, *The Testament of Adam* (Chico 1982) 142-44, 146-48; S. SAHIN, *Inschriften des Museums von Iznik (Nikaia)* (Bonn 1979-82); H. SCHLIER, *Principalities and Powers in the New Testament* (Freiburg 1961); W. WINK, *Naming the Powers* (Philadelphia 1984) 13-15, 151-156.

D. E. AUNE

ARCHANGEL ἀρχάγγελος

I. The figure of the archangel already appears in the Hebrew Bible, but the Greek term *archangelos* (Latin *archangelus*) does not occur in the Greek versions of the OT. The word appears in (early) Greek passages in the OT Pseudepigrapha (e.g. Greek text of *1 Enoch*) and there are two occurrences in NT (1 Thess 4:16; Jude 9).

II. In Jewish literature from the Second Temple period a tendency can be observed to differentiate between groups and categories of angels (cf. *1 Enoch* 61:10; *2 Enoch* 19:1-5; →Angel) and to bring a hierarchy in the angelic world. Some scholars assume influence here from pagan conceptions. FONTINOY (1989:124), for instance, thinks of Persian influence and notes the similarity between the seven angels of the face (cf. Tob. 12:15) with Persian angelology. BOUSSET & GRESSMANN 1926:325-326 assume Babylonian influence. In any case, several angels act in Jewish and Early Christian texts as individuals with a specific function and were assigned the status of the highest angels in the hierarchy (especially →Michael and →Gabriel). In magical texts, which are often influenced by Jewish and Christian ideas, archangels also appear (e.g. *PGM* IV 3051; MICHL 1962:56).

III. A forerunner of the archangel appears already in Josh 5:13-15. Joshua sees a man who reveals himself as the captain of the heavenly army (→Angel). LXX reads *archistratēgos*, which word is sometimes used as a synonym for *archangelos* (e.g. *T. Abr.* rec. long. 1:4 and 14:10; *3 Apoc. Bar.* 11:8; cf. Dan 8:11; ROWLAND 1985:101). In Daniel and the Qumran writings the →Prince of the heavenly host might still be an independant figure, who came to be identified with Michael or another archangel only from the first century C.E. onwards (G. BAMPFYLDE, The Prince of the Host in the Book of Daniel and the Dead Sea Scrolls, *JSJ* 14 [1983] 129-134).

In Daniel there are already two exalted angels: Michael as one of the chief princes and protector of Israel in the context of the battle of the angels of the nations (10:13, 21; 12:1) and Gabriel, the *angelus interpres* for the seer (8:15-26). Also in Jude 9 and Rev 12:7 Michael acts as contestant (→Dragon; →Satan) and in Jude *archangelos* is used in this connection. Gabriel too is superior to other angels. According to *1 Enoch* 40:9 he is set over all the powers and given the function of divine annunciator (cf. Luke 1). According to 1 Thess 4:16 an anonymous archangel heralds the descent of the Lord and the resurrection of the →dead. In *Apoc. Mos.* 22 Michael appears in a similar role before God's punishment of Adam and →Eve.

Besides the elevation of individual angels appear groups of (usually four or seven) special angels, to which Michael, →Raphael and Gabriel usually belong if the angels are given names. Seven angels appear as executers of divine punishment in Ezek 9. The same number is mentioned in Tob 12:15, where Raphael presents himself as one of the seven angels who transmit the prayers of the holy ones (see mss B and A; ms S: "who stand in attendance [on the Lord]") and enter the glorious presence of the Lord (see also *T. Levi* 8:2; *1 Enoch* 20). *1 Enoch* 20 gives a list of seven angels. In the Gizeh Papyrus only six names are mentioned, but in both of the extant Greek papyri the list ends with a reference to the names of seven *archangeloi* (20:7). The names of these angels "who keep watch" (so Eth; Greek: "angels of the powers") are: →Uriel, Raphael, Raguel, Michael, Sariel, Gabriel and Remiel.

1 Enoch 9 has a list of four archangels: Michael, Sariel (uncertain; Greek: Uriel; many Eth mss Suryal), Raphael and Gabriel. Usually Uriel (in the Book of Parables in *1 Enoch* 37-71 Phanuel) figures in the lists of four archangels instead of Sariel (e.g. *Sib. Or.* 2:215; *Apoc. Mos.* 40:2; *Pirke de-Rabbi Eliezer* 4), but Sariel belongs to the oldest tradition of the four archangels according to BLACK 1985:129, 162-163, referring to the Aramaic fragments and to 1QM 9:14-16 (cf. DAVIDSON 1992:50, 325-326). The name of Uriel is replaced by that of Phanuel in *1 Enoch* 40:9; 54:6 and 71:8-9. The group of four archangels probably developed from the four living creatures from Ezek 1. They are standing on the four sides of the divine throne (cf. the 'Angels of Presence', e.g. 1QH 6:12-13; 1QSb 4:25-26; 4Q400 col. 1 lines 4 and 8) and say praises before the Lord of Glory (*1 Enoch* 40), pray on behalf of the righteous on earth (*1 Enoch* 40:6; Tob 12:15) and act as intercessors for the souls of righteous ones who have died (*1 Enoch* 9; *T. Abr.* 14). They play an important part at the final judgement. Thus they lead among other things the souls of men to the tribunal of the Lord (*Sib. Or.* 2:214-219) and will cast kings and potentates in the burning furnace on the great day of judgement (*1 Enoch* 54:6; on the groups of archangels and their functions see further MICHL 1962:77-78, 89-91, 169-174, 182-186).

Sometimes, archangels are mentioned who do not belong to one of the lists of four or seven of the principal angels (e.g. →Jeremiel, 4 Ezra 4:36; Dokiel, *T. Abr.* 13:10 rec. long.). Phanael acts as angelic messenger during Baruch's heavenly journey and is described as archangel and interpretor of revelations (*3 Apoc. Bar.* 10:1; 11:7). In *1 Enoch* 87-88 three archangels put →Enoch in positions to observe carefully what is being revealed to him. Philo identifies the *archangelos* with the divine →*Logos* (DECHARNEUX 1989).

IV. *Bibliography*

M. BLACK, *The Book of Enoch or I Enoch. A New English Edition with Commentary and Textual Notes* (SVTP 7; Leiden 1985); W. BOUSSET & H. GRESSMANN, *Die Religion des Judentums im späthellenistischen Zeitalter* (HNT 27; Tübingen 1926) 325-329; I. BROER, ἄγγελος, *EWNT* I (Stuttgart 1980) 36-37; *M. J. DAVIDSON, *Angels at Qumran. A Comparative Study of 1 Enoch 1-36, 72-108 and Sectarian Writings from Qumran* (JSP Supplement Series 11; Sheffield 1992) 49-53, 75-78, 97-98, 104-105, 157, 194-196, 228, 301, 325-326 [& lit]; B. DECHARNEUX, Anges, démons et Logos dans l'oeuvre de Philon d'Alexandrie, *Anges et démons. Actes du Colloque de Liège et de Louvain-La-Neuve 25-26 novembre 1987* (ed. J. Ries; Louvain-La-Neuve 1989) 147-175; C. FONTINOY, Les anges et les démons de l'Ancien Testament, *Anges et démons* (see above) 117-134; W. LUEKEN, *Michael. Eine Darstellung und Vergleichung der jüdischen und der morgenländisch-christlichen Tradition vom Erzengel Michael* (Göttingen 1898); *M. MACH, *Entwicklungsstadien des jüdischen Engelglaubens in vorrabbinischer Zeit* (TSAJ 34; Tübingen 1992) [& lit]; J. MICHL, Engel (I-IX), *RAC* 5 (Stuttgart 1962) 53-258.

J. W. VAN HENTEN

ARCHON Ἄρχων

I. The term *archōn*, a participial form of the verb *archein* used as a substantive, carries the root meaning of primacy in time or rank. After the overthrow of the monarchies in the Greek city-states (ca. 650 BCE), the term *archōn*, meaning 'high official' or 'chief magistrate', became widely used for a variety of high public officials. Originally it was primarily limited as a designation for the highest officials (Thucydides 1.126; Aristotle *Ath. Pol.* 13, 10-12). A typical Greek polis had two or more magistrates (*archontes*), a council (*boulē*) and an assembly of the people (*dēmos*); see Josephus *Ant.* 14.190; 16.172. Public and private leadership terms formulated with the prefix *arch-* were extremely common in the Hellenistic period. During the late Hellenistic and early Roman period the term *archōn*, in both singular and plural forms, began to be used in early Judaism and early Christianity and then in Neoplatonism and Gnosticism as designation for supernatural beings such as →angels, →demons and →Satan and planetary deities who were thought to occupy a particular rank in a hierarchy of supernatural beings analogous to a political or military structure.

II. There was a widespread notion in the ancient world that the planets either were deities or were presided over by deities, a view which probably originated in Babylonia and involved astral fatalism. Philo refers to the popular conception that the →sun, →moon and →stars were gods, but he argues that →Moses regarded the heavenly bodies as *archontes*, governing those beings which exist below the moon, in the air or on the →earth (*De spec. leg.* 1.13-14). The term *kosmokratores* was also used of the planets, personified as rulers of the heavenly spheres (a term used with some frequency later in the Greek magical papyri). While these supernatural beings were not unambiguously regarded as either good or evil, there was a strong tendency to regard them as hostile if not evil.

The Neoplatonist Iamblichus (ca. 250-325 CE), dependent on Babylonian-Chaldaean astrology, perhaps as mediated by a lost work called *Hyphegetica* by Julian the Theurgist, posited a hierarchy of supernatural beings between God and the soul: →archangels, angels, demons, two kinds of archons, heroes and souls. The two types of archons, which function only in the sublunar region, included cosmic archons, *kosmokratores*, and hylic archons, *tēs hylēs parestēkotes* (Iamblichus, *De myst.* 2.3.71). It is significant that the *archontes* of Iamblichus are much lower on the hierarchy of being than archangels and angels.

III. In the LXX, the term *archōn* is used to translate thirty-six different Hebrew terms with such meanings as 'chief', 'head', 'leader' or 'ruler'. Two of the more significant of these Hebrew words include *rō'š*, which is occasionally translated with *archōn* (Deut 33:5; Job 29:25; Ezek 38:2.3), and *nāśî'*, meaning 'chief', 'master', 'sovereign', 'prince', i.e. a term for leadership in the military, political and priestly ranks. Judaism used the term *archōn* of synagogue leaders, and *archōn* was sometimes interchangeable with *archisynagōgos* (both are used of Jairus in Luke 8:41.49), but at other times they were apparently distinguished (Acts 14:2 var.lect.).

In early Judaism and early Christianity, *archōn* was one of the designations used to refer to the evil spiritual ruler of human beings and the cosmos, known by a variety of aliases including Satan, →Devil, →Belial, and →Mastemah. The synoptic gospels occasionally refer to Satan as the *archōn tōn daimoniōn*, 'prince of demons' (Matt 9:34; 12:24; Mark 3:22; Luke 11:15), because demons (like angels), were thought to be organized like an army or a political hierarchy. The notion that a large host of celestial beings was commanded by →Yahweh is an ancient conception in Israel (1 Sam 1:3.11; 1 Kgs 22:19; 2 Chr 18:18). This is reflected in the divine name *yhwh ṣĕbā'ôt*, →'Yahweh Zebaoth', a title which occurs some 267 times in the OT (e.g., 1 Sam 4:4; 2 Sam 6:2; Isa 31:4). However, the mirror conception of Satan leading a host of evil angels or demons does not appear to be older than the second century BCE. Similarly in *Jub.*, Mastemah (a designation of Satan) is called the "chief of spirits" (10:8). Porphyry claimed that Sarapis and Hekate were the *archontes* of evil demons (Eusebius *Praep. evang.* 4.22.174a), but this use of the term in a pagan context is so rare that it perhaps can be explained as a borrowing from early Judaism or early Christianity. Somewhat surprisingly, the term *archōn* is not applied to supernatural beings, whether good or evil, in the non-Christian Greek magical papyri, though the related term *kosmokratōr* is. Another use of the term *archōn* for Satan focuses on his domination of the present world or age (the Heb word *'ôlām* can mean either). In John 12:31, for example, he is called *ho archōn tou kosmou toutou*, 'the prince of this world', but (in accordance with Johannine theology) his imminent expulsion is emphasized. In John 14:30, the Johannine →Jesus says that though the prince of this world is coming, he has no power over Jesus, and in John 16:11 Jesus is made to say that the prince of this world has been judged. The same title occurs in a number of other texts where there is no indication that Satan's sovereignty is in imminent jeopardy (*T. Sol.* 2:9; 3:5-6; 6:1; *Asc. Isa.* 1:3; 2:4; 10:29). In *Barn.* 18:2 (part of the Two-Ways tradition also found in *Did.* 1-6 and 1QS 3.13-4.26), he is called "the prince of the present time of iniquity" who controls the way of darkness, a title which has a clear precedent in Judaism in the title *śr mmšlt rš'h*, 'prince of the →dominion of ungodliness' (1QM 17.5-6). The context for the conception of Satan as ruler of this world or age is the apocalyptic world view which consisted in a temporal or eschatological dualism in which the present age (*hā'ôlām hazzeh*, 'this world or age') is dominated by wickedness through the influence of Satan, while the imminent future age (*hā'ôlām habbā'*, literally 'the coming world or age') will be inaugurated by the victory of →God over all evil (Matt 12:32; Luke 16:8; Gal 1:4). The introduction of the future era will be accomplished by the climactic intervention of God (either directly or through a human agent, i.e. a Messiah), and will be preceded by the destruction of the wicked and the final deliverance of the righteous. In Eph 2:2, Satan is called "the prince of the power of the air", i.e. the prince whose domain is the air. This title is clearly a designation for Satan, for he is also described as "the →spirit (*pneuma*) now at work in the sons of disobedience" (Eph 2:2). The air was regarded as the dwelling place of →evil spirits in the ancient world (Philo *De gig.* 6; *2 Enoch* 29:4; *Asc. Isa.* 7:9). Ignatius, who uses the name 'Satan' once (*Eph.* 13:1), and the term 'Devil' four times (*Eph.* 10:3; *Trall.* 8:1; *Rom.* 5:3; *Smyrn.* 9:1), tends to prefer the more descriptive designation 'prince of this age', *archōn tou aiōnos toutou,* emphasizing the temporal rule of Satan (*Eph.* 17:1; 19:1; *Magn.* 1:2; *Trall.* 4:2; *Rom.* 7:1; *Philad.* 6:2). Satan is called "the wicked prince" in *Barn.* 4:13, a title which corresponds to "the prince of error" in *T. Simeon* 2:7 and *T. Judah* 19:4.

The term *archontes* used as a designation for angelic beings first occurs in the LXX Dan 10:13, and seven times in Theod. Dan 10:13, 20-21; 12:1, where the LXX has *stratēgos*, 'commander', 'magistrate', all translations of the Aram *śar*, 'prince'. Dan 10:10-21 contains the first references to the conception of angelic beings who are the patrons of specific nations on earth. The late merkavah work entitled *3 Enoch* refers to the seventy or seventy-two *śarê malkuyyôt,* 'princes of kingdoms' continuing the similar conception found in Dan 10:20-21 (*3 Enoch* 17:8; 18:2; 30:2); the angelic princes of Rome and Persia are mentioned specifically in *3 Enoch* 26:12, an allusion to Dan 10:33. In the Greek version of *1 Enoch* 6 by Syncellus, the term *archōn* is used of Semyaza, the leader of the fallen angels or →watchers, but also for various angelic leaders subordinate to Semyaza, reflecting traditional Near Eastern military models. After Dan, the earliest reference to *archontes* as angelic beings is found in Ignatius of Antioch. In *Smyrn.* 6:1, Ignatius mentions "the glory of angels and princes (*archontes*) visible and invisible", referring to two categories of angels, as the parallel in *Trall.* 5:1 suggests, where he refers to "the places of angels and the gatherings of rulers (*archontikas*)". Since these lists are so short, it is unclear whether the angels are superior to archons or the reverse. Similarly in the *Epistle to Diognetus* 7:2, the author argues that God did not send an angel or a prince [*archōn*] into the world, but Christ the agent of all creation. In rabbinic and merkavah texts, the *śar hā'ôlām*, 'prince of the world' is mentioned, but (unlike John 12:31 and parallels) is never an evil figure (*b.Yeb.* 16b; *b.Ḥull.* 60a; *b.Sanh.* 94a; *Exod Rabbah* 17:4; *3 Enoch* 30:2; 38:3).

In 1 Cor 2:6.8, a much disputed passage (see PESCE 1977), Paul speaks of 'the rulers (*archontes*) of this world'. Here the *archontes* can refer to political authorities (SCHNIEWIND 1952), but more probably to demons (Origen *De princ.* 3.2; Tertullian *Adv. Marc.* 5.6; SCHLIER 1961:45-46). Justin (*Dial.* 36.6) speaks of the 'princes in heaven' (*hoi en ouranōi archontes*) who did not recognize →Christ when he descended into the world (though he does not specify whether these were good or evil), and it was these same princes who were commanded to open the gates of heaven when Christ ascended (36.5; here Justin is interpreting the term *hoi archontes* found in the LXX version of Ps 23:7.9, a possible but unlikely translation of the Hebrew). A similar view is reflected in *Asc. Isa.* 11:23-29, and it is specifically claimed in *Asc. Isa.* 11:6 that the birth of Jesus was hidden from all the heavens, all the princes and every god of this world. Ignatius similarly claims that the virginity of Mary as well as the birth and death of Jesus were hidden from the "prince of this world" (*Eph.* 19:1).

IV. The *archontes* play an important mythological role in some Gnostic cosmologies. The seven spheres (the sun, moon, and the five planets Mercury, Venus, Mars, Jupiter and Saturn, bounded by the region of the fixed stars) are controlled by supernatural beings designated by various terms including *archontes.* Seven *archontes* are usually presided over by a chief *archōn*, who is also the demiurge who created the world, and resides in the Ogdoad, the eighth region above the seven planetary spheres. Since the attainment of salvation is linked with attaining to the sphere of the →unknown God, passage through the concentric ranks of hostile archons is necessary. One specific form of this myth is presented in the Coptic Gnostic treatise *The Hypostasis of the Archons*, where the *archontes* are said to guard the gates of the seven planetary spheres, impeding the upward movement of souls. Irenaeus is the earliest author to mention the names of the seven archons, which are so strikingly Hebraic that their Jewish origin appears highly likely (*Adv. haer.* 1.30): Ialdabaoth (the chief *archōn*), Iao, Sabaoth, Adoneus, Eloeus, Oreus and Astanphaeus. Origen later provided a list of the seven archons in Ophite mythology (*Contra Celsum* 6.31): Ialdabaoth, Iao, Sabaoth, Adonaios, Astaphaios, Eloaios and Horaios, together with the specific formulas which must be used in order to get past each archon. A Gnostic sect named the Archontici took its name from the archons of the seven planetary spheres (the Gk term *archontikoi*, transliterated as *archontici* or *archontiaci* in Lat, is an adjective used as a substantive formed from *archōn*; see Epiphanius *Pan.* 40.2). In the *Apocryphon of John* 48.10-17, the words of Gen 1:26, "Let us make man in our image and likeness" are attributed to the seven archons who created Adam. This reflects the Jewish tradition that man was made by the angels (Irenaeus *Adv. haer.* 1.24.1-2).

V. *Bibliography*

W. CARR, *Angels and Principalities* (Cambridge 1981); CARR, The Rulers of This Age—1 Corinthians 2.6-8, *NTS* 23 (1976-77) 20-35; F. W. CREMER, *Die chaldäischen Orakel und Jamblich de mysteriis* (Meisenheim am Glan 1969) 86-91; G. DELLING, archōn, *TDNT* 1, 488-489; M. DIBELIUS, *Die Geisterwelt im Glauben des Paulus* (Göttingen 1909), 88-99; S. EITREM, *Some Notes on the Demonology in the New Testament*, (Oslo 1966[2]); W. GRUNDMANN, *Der Begriff der Kraft in der Neutestamentlichen Gedankenwelt* (Stuttgart 1932) 39-55, G. MILLER, ARCHONTON TOU AIONOS TOUTOU—A New Look at 1 Corinthians 2: 6-8, *JBL* 91 (1972) 522-528; M. PESCE, *Paolo e gli Arconti a Corinto: Storia della ricerca (1888-1975) ed esegesi di 1 Cor. 2,6.8* (Brescia 1977); H. SCHLIER, *Principalities and Powers in the New Testament* (New York 1961); J. SCHNIEWIND, Die Archonten dieses Äons, 1. Kor. 2,6-8; *Nachgelassene Reden und Aufsätze* (Berlin 1952) 104-109.

D. E. AUNE

ARES Ἄρης

I. Ares is the god of war of the Greek pantheon, who also represents the warrior side of other gods, such as →Zeus Areios, →Athena Areia, →Aphrodite Areia and, apparently already in Mycenean times, →Hermaas Areias (BURKERT 1985:169). In the Bible he perhaps appears as a theophoric element in the name Areopagus in Acts 17. The name already occurs in Linear-B as *Are* (KN Fp 14), but its etymology is debated. Perhaps it was an ancient abstract noun meaning 'throng of battle, war' (BURKERT 1985:169, but see also PETERS 1986: 371-375). Ares' name in Greek literature often indiscriminately alternates with that of Enyalios, another old war god, but in cult both gods are clearly separated, as was already the case in Mycenean times (GRAF 1985:266-267). Ares was identified in Scythia (Herodotus 4.59-62), Asia Minor (ROBERT, *Hellenica* VII.69-70; X.72-78, 214 note 5; XIII.44; 1966, 91-100), Arabia and Syria (SEYRIG 1970; AUGÉ 1984) with indigenous war gods and the Romans identified him with Mars.

II. Ares is the warrior *par excellence*, especially in his more fierce and destructive shape and the only god to fight like a human on the Trojan battlefield. Homer depicts him as young, strong, big and fast; in short, he possesses all the desirable qualities of the archaic warriors, who are characterised as 'members of his retinue' (*therapontes*, *ozoi*: MAADER 1979:1254-1255). But he is also 'ruinous to men' (*Il.* 5.31) and the embodiment of the 'Unvernunft des Nur-Kriegers' (MAADER 1979:1251). As Zeus puts it: "You are the most hateful to me of all the gods who hold →Olympus, since forever strife is dear to you and wars and battles" (*Il.* 5.890-1). Typically, when Sisyphus has managed to fetter →Thanatos and thus stopped people dying, it is Ares who liberates the god of death, as Aeschylus narrated in his *Sisyphus Drapetes* (see S. RADT, *Tragicorum Graecorum fragmenta* [vol. 3 Aeschylus; Göttingen 1985] 337). It is this role as raging, ravaging warrior which may explain why magic-healers ascribed possession to Ares (Hippocrates, *Sacred Disease* 4) and Sophocles (*Oedipus Rex* 190) could identify Ares with the plague. Ares is an indispensable god but at the same time his murderous character makes him undesirable. It is especially the latter quality which comes to the fore in myth and ritual.

Myth located the birth of Ares in Thrace (*Il.* 13.301; *Od.*8.361), the country which was considered, if wrongly, as wild and barbarous; here was also his grave (Ps-Clement, *Recogn.* 10.24). The parallel with →Dionysos, who was also born in Thrace, shows that the Greeks liked to situate negative figures outside their own culture not that these gods were originally aliens. His father was Zeus and his mother →Hera (*Il.* 5.892-893), who in various Greek cities was worshipped with a martial aspect (M. L. WEST, *Hesiod: Theogony* [Oxford 1966] *ad* 922). His sister and companion was Eris, or 'Strife' (*Il.* 4. 440-1) and his daughters were the fierce Amazons (Pherecydes, *FGH* 3 F 15a); in the Cyclic *Aethiopis* (fr. 1) he is already the father of Penthesileia. Among his sons he counted Phobos 'Rout' and Deimos, 'Terror' (WEST, *Hesiod: Theogony,* comm. *ad* 934; add Artemidorus 2.34), the brutal Lapith Phlegyas (R. JANKO, *The Iliad: A commentary* IV [Cambridge 1992], comm. on *Il.* 13.301-303), Askalaphos, or the nightly, predatory 'owl' (JANKO, comm. on *Il.* 13.478-480), and the great hunter Meleagros (Hesiod fr. 25)—genealogy being a typical Greek way of connecting related figures.

As the god of war, who represents the brutal aspects of war not matters of defence, Ares is indispensable but he is often coupled with →Athena, the embodiment of responsibility and cleverness in battle. Thus on the shield of Achilles Homer (*Il.* 18.516) represents Ares and Athena as leading the warriors; Odysseus pretends that Ares and Athena had given him courage (*Od.* 14.216), and on the vases the two gods often battle together; in archaic imagery Ares is even sometimes represented as helping with the birth of Athena (BRUNEAU 1984: 491).

In the *Iliad* we can observe various strategies of dealing with the negative sides of Ares. First, when Ares confronts Athena in battle, he is always the loser, as when the goddess helped Diomedes against Ares (5.824), disarmed him in order to prevent him avenging his son Askalaphos (15.121-141) and knocked him down with a stone (21.391-415). Similarly, when in Ps-Hesiods's *Shield* →Heracles battles against Ares' son Cycnus, who wanted to build a temple from human skulls, he wins due to the help of Athena despite Ares' support of his son: it is always the goddess of cleverness and responsibility who wins. It fits in with Ares being a 'loser' that on the frieze of the treasure house of Siphnos and on archaic vases he is mostly positioned at the very margin of the representation (BRUNEAU 1984:491).

The complicated relationship between Ares and Athena is also well brought out in the foundation myth of Thebes as related by 'Apollodorus' (3.4.1-2). When Cadmus had reached Thebes, he killed a dragon, an offspring of Ares, who guarded a fountain. On the advice of Athena he sowed the teeth of the monster which grew into armed men, the Spartoi. These, in turn, started to fight with one another and only five survived this fratricidal strife. Subsequently, Cadmus had to serve Ares for a whole year in order to atone for his share in their death. After his servitude he became king of Thebes through Athena and married the daughter of Ares and →Aphrodite, Harmonia: 'murderous war ends in harmonious order' (BURKERT 1985:170). Here as well, it is in the end Athena who helps Cadmus to defeat the influence of Ares.

A more drastic approach is mentioned in *Iliad* 5:385-391 (see also Nonnus, *Dion.* 302-304), one of the very few real Ares myths. Here Homer tells how the sons of Aloeus, Otos and Ephialtes, tied the god down and locked him up in a bronze barrel for thirteen months. He only survived because the stepmother of his captors passed word to →Hermes, who managed to liberate him; variants of the story are also recorded in much later sources (FARAONE 1992:86-87). The myth seems to be the reflection of a cult in which the statue of Ares was normally fettered but untied only once a year (so already FARNELL 1909:407). Similar cults all point to gods which are perceived as dangerous for the social order (GRAF 1985:81-96). The dangerous nature of these gods is sometimes stressed by the small size and uncanny appearance of their statues and the tradition that the statue of Ares which Pausanias (3.19.7) saw on the road from Sparta to Therapnai was fetched from faraway Colchi by the Dioscures (→Dioskouroi) points in the same direction.

Cults of Ares were few and far between; not even Thebes seems to have known a temple dedicated to Ares, unlike Athens and various cites on the Peloponnesus and Crete (GRAF 1985:265). The marginality of Ares is underscored by the fact that he received a dog for sacrifice, just like spooky Hecate and messy Eileithyia: Ares' cult did not lead to eating peacefully together as would have been the case with edible sacrifice (GRAF 1985:422). It fits in with this asocial character of Ares' cult that some, untrustworthy traditions mention a human sacrifice to Ares among the Spartans (Apollodorus *FGH* 244 F 125) and on Lemnos (Fulgentius *Ant. serm.* 5, cf. Jacoby on Sosicrates *FGH* 461 F 1).

In some cities the macho nature of Ares was stressed by excluding women from his worship (Pausanias 2.22.4-5, 3.22.6), just as women were forbidden entry into the temples of Enyalios (Teles 24.11). This is the more natural ritual, yet the reverse also took place. It was told in Tegea that the women had once rescued the town by attacking the Spartans. After their victory the women performed the victory rites for Ares and the males did not even receive part of the sacrificial meat. In memory to this feat a stele to Ares Gynaikothoinas, 'Feaster of Woman' or 'One whom the women feast', was erected in the Tegean agora. Apparently, our source, Pausanias (8.48.4-5), no longer found a ritual, but the myth strongly suggests that at one time the Tegean women performed sacrifices in the Tegean agora from which the men were excluded. This uncommon female cult of the masculine god points to a ritual in which the normal social order was temporarily subverted (GRAF 1984).

Ares was regularly connected with Aphrodite in literature, as witnessed by the delightful story of their liaison (*Od.* 8.266-369); in art, where he seems to be represented as even assisting with the birth of the goddess, as he did with Athena (BRUNEAU 1984:491), and in cult, as their communal temples and altars show (GRAF 1985:264). The connection rests on a twofold association. On the one hand, there is the warrior aspect of Aphrodite. On the other, there is the strong contrast between the two gods as expressed in the *Homeric Hymn to Aphrodite*, which says of Athena that she took no pleasure 'in the works of the golden Aphrodite but liked wars and the work of Ares' (9-10). The contrast also appears clearly in Thebes where the polemarchs celebrated the Aphrodisia at the end of their term of office. Here the cult of Aphrodite eases the transition from warlike activities to peaceful private life by a festival of dissolution (GRAF 1984:253-254), just as on Aegina an uncanny festival to masculine →Poseidon was terminated with the Aphrodisia (Plutarch, *Mor.* 301). Despite the opposition, the gods do belong together: as the foundation myth of Thebes shows, it is only the pairing of Ares and Aphrodite which produces Harmonia (BREMMER 1994:45-46).

At the end of the fifth century the importance of Ares seems to diminish. Admittedly, comedy could still nick-name the tough Athenian general Phormio (d. ca. 429/8) 'Ares' (Eupolis fr. 268.15) and a bold man a 'young of Ares' (Plato fr. 112), but on the Athenian vases the god is becoming only rarely recognizable. In the Hellenistic period Ares is only little mentioned (ROBERT, *Hellenica* X 77), but in the second century CE one could still dream of being sexually taken by Ares (Artemidorus 5.87).

III. In the Bible the name of Ares is commonly taken as occurring in the names of the Areopagus and Dionysius Areopagites (Acts 17). And indeed, folk etymology connected the 'hill of Ares' with the god by way of various myths. Yet there was no cult of the god on the hill and the most recent explanations tend to connect the first element of the name with a homonym *areios*, 'solid', and explain the name as 'solid rock' (WALLACE 1989:213-214).

IV. *Bibliography*

C. AUGÉ, Ares (in peripheria orientali), *LIMC* II.1 (1984) 493-495; I. BECK, *Ares in Vasenmalerei, Relief und Rundplastik* (Mainz 1983); J. N. BREMMER, *Greek Religions* (Oxford 1994); P. BRUNEAU, Ares, *LIMC* II.1 (1984) 478-492; W. BURKERT, *Greek Religion* (Oxford 1985); C. A. FARAONE, *Talismans & Trojan Horses. Guardian Statues in Ancient Greek Myth and Ritual* (New York & Oxford 1992); L. R. FARNELL, *The Cults of the Greek States* V (Oxford 1909) 396-414; F. GRAF, Women, War, and Warlike Divinities, *ZPE* 55 (1984) 245-254; GRAF, *Nordionische Kulte* (Rome 1985); A. HEUBECK, Amphiaraos, *Die Sprache* 17 (1971) 8-22; F. JOUAN, Le dieu Arès: figure rituelle et image littéraire, *Le point théologique* 52 (1989) 125-140; B. MAADER, Ares, *LfgrE* I (Göttingen 1979) 1246-1265; M. PETERS, Probleme mit anlautenden Laryngalen, *Die Sprache* 32 (1986) 365-383; L. ROBERT, *Hellenica* I-XIII (Paris 1940-1965); ROBERT, *Documents de l'Asie Mineure méridionale* (Paris & Geneva 1966); H. SEYRIG, Les dieux armés et les Arabes en Syrie, *Syria* 47 (1970) 77-112; R. W. WALLACE, *The Areopagos Council to 307 B.C.* (Baltimore & London 1989); P. WATHELET, Arès le mal aimé, *Les Etudes Classiques* 60 (1992) 113-128.

J. N. BREMMER

ARTA

I. The word *arta*, as theophoric element in the first part of the name Artaxerxes (e.g. Ezra 4:7), translates "the decisive confessional concept of Zoroastrianism (or Mazdaism)", as LOMMEL wrote (1930:48). The written form *arta* in the name of the Achaemenid king represents both the specifically Old-Persian form of the word and the undifferentiated pan-Iranian form which was probably still in use at the time. In the Avesta, the sacred book of Mazdaism, the word became *aša* as a result of phonetic changes due to oral transmission, *š* probably representing a dorsal spirant that could be noted phonetically as [*hl*].

aša corresponds to Vedic Sanskrit *ṛtá* and represents therefore a notion inherited from a common Indo-Iranian tradition. Its meaning has been interpreted in three different ways:

1. The meaning of 'truth'—the ancient meaning according to Plutarch (*De Iside et Osiride* 47), who translates *aša* as ἀλήθεια—has been strongly championed by LÜDERS (1959 passim), who believes it can cover every instance of the word. See also, more recently, SCHLERATH 1987:694-696.

2. Since the very beginning of Indo-Iranian philology, a large number of specialists have shared the opinion that such a fundamental notion as *aša/ṛtá* "cannot be precisely rendered by some single word in another tongue" (see BOYCE 1975:27) and that the word often occurs with what may be the original meaning of 'order', understood as cosmic, social, liturgical and moral order.

3. More recently, the present author has defended the hypothesis that, at least in the oldest texts, *aša/ṛtá* had kept the etymological sense of 'organization' or 'lay-out' (Indo-European **H2rtó* -) and expressed, first and foremost, the principle of cohesion of the universe, the creator of which is the great god Ahura Mazda, metaphorically represented in the cosmogonic pattern showing the organization of the universe as the putting up of a tent (KELLENS 1991:41-47).

II. The concept represented by *aša* was personified. In the ancient Avesta, Aša is the most frequently mentioned among an undetermined number of entities composing a kind of secundary pantheon around Ahura Mazda, so that the allegory of truth or of the cosmic organization is second in rank among the ancient Mazdaean deities. In the recent Avesta and in the Pahlavi books, Aša ranks second in the canonical group of the six *ameša spenta*, or "Beneficient Immortals" co-existing with the traditional Indo-Iranian pantheon. Its patronage of the element →fire, which appears clearly in Sassanid Mazdaism, probably derives from the older conception that fire and light, pervading as they do the world of day, enable man to see the organization of the universe, while at the same time being its essential components (Lommel, in SCHLERATH 1976: 266-269; NARTEN 1982:121-123).

The concept of *aṣ̌a* concentrates all the elements of Mazdaean dualism. Its systematic opposition to the concept of *druj*, or 'deceit' (and not simply to its negative *ánṛta* as in Vedic Sanskrit) creates a fundamental split among deities and among men, who are defined as *aṣ̌auuan*, 'followers of Aṣ̌a', or as *dreguuant*, 'deceivers', according to whether they support one or the other principle.

The enthronement name *artaxšaça*, 'Artaxerxes', may well be a 'Zitatname', reproducing a common clausula in the ancient Avesta by associating, without any necessary logical link, the names of the two entities *aṣ̌a* and *xsaϑra* ('power') (KELLENS & PIRART 1988:40).

III. *Bibliography*

M. BOYCE, *A History of Zoroastrianism*, Vol 1 (Leiden 1975) 27; J. KELLENS, *Zoroastre et l'Avesta ancien* (Paris 1991) 41-47; J. KELLENS & E. PIRART, *Les textes vieil-avestiques*, Vol 1 (Wiesbaden 1988) 40; H. LOMMEL, *Die Religion Zarathustras* (Tübingen 1930) 48; H. LÜDERS, *Varuṇa II* (Göttingen 1959); J. NARTEN, *Die Ameṣ̌a Spəṇtas im Avesta* (Wiesbaden 1982) 121-123; SCHLERATH (ed.), *Zarathustra* (Darmstadt 1976) 266-269; SCHLERATH, Aša, *Encyclopaedia Iranica*, Vol 2 (London/New York 1987) 694-696.

J. KELLENS

ARTEMIS Ἄρτεμις

I. Artemis is the Greek virgin goddess originally of hunting and animal fertility. It occurs as a divine name in Acts 19 (in Jewish literature only *Sib. Or.* 5,293-295); moreover one of Paul's companions had the theophoric name Ἀρτεμᾶς, a hypocoristic derived from Ἀρτεμίδωρος 'gift of Artemis' (Titus 3:12). Being the divine huntress, her name, especially its Doric-Aeolian form Ἄρταμις, has been connected etymologically with Attic ἄρταμος 'butcher; slaughterer', or else with ἄρκ(τ)ος 'bear', because the bear was one of the animals sacrificed to her, and her young priestesses were sometimes called 'she-bears'. Both explanations fail, however, to account for the phonetic difference in Attic between her name and the adduced appellatives from that same dialect, unless one supposes that Ἄρτεμις itself is not originally Attic but stems from yet another dialect. It has even been suggested, therefore, that the form Ἄρταμις, the other way round, owes its existence to popular etymology on the basis of ἄρταμος. In the Linear-B tablets from Pylos her name occurs twice, as A-te-mi-to (gen. sg), and as A-ti-mi-te (dat. sg.). The alternative explanation, now generally adopted, is that her name is not Indo-European at all, but of pre-Greek origin, like those of so many other Greek gods and heroes. In Lydian she was called Artimus, in Etruscan Artumes (nom. sg.), Aritimi (dat. sg.), in Imperial Aramaic she appears as ארתמו (*KAI* 260B7) or ארתמוש (*Fouilles de Xanthos* VI, p. 137 line 24). Unlike that of her brother →Apollo, the Romans and Latins did not take over her Greek name, but identified her, instead, with the indigenous Diana.

II. General Survey. In Greece Artemis is attested since 1200 BCE, and in Greek literature from Homer onward. According to the most current version of her myth she was the elder twin-sister of Apollo, the two of them being the offspring of →Zeus and his first cousin Leto, a daughter of the →Titans Coeus and →Phoebe. As the pregnant Leto had to roam in flight from →Hera, the jealous spouse of Zeus, she gave birth to Artemis in Ortygia or 'quails' land', which some located near Ephesus. Subsequently she bore Apollo in the island of Delos, at this second birth being assisted according to some authors by her new-born daughter Artemis. Originally the realm of Artemis was the world of wild animals and natural vegetation. Homer summarizes her character as "Mistress of the Animals (πότνια θηρῶν), Artemis the Huntress" who uses "to kill the animals in the mountains" (*Iliad* 21,470-471;485).

Positively, therefore, she is the one who rules over fertility in general, in particular the fertility of women, over animals hunted by man such as the deer and the boar, and wild trees. She is also the one who keeps under control animals that are dangerous to mankind, such as the bear and the wolf. To a lesser extent cultivated trees, cereals and domesticated animals seem to have fallen under her sway as well. With the other gods she was entitled to the first fruits of the annual crops. At Patrae, in archaic times, the human sacrifices made to her wore on their heads garlands of corn ears (Pausanias 7,20,1). In Thasos she was venerated under the epithet of Πωλώ or 'Protectress of Foals', in other places as Δαφν(α)ία or 'Goddess of the Laurel'. Normally, however, it was →Demeter who made the corn grow, →Poseidon who was the horse-god, and Apollo to whom the laurel was especially sacred. Moreover, she never competed with →Dionysus or →Athena as far as the vine or the olive tree were concerned.

Negatively, she could show her power by killing women in childbirth, by sending monsters by way of punishment, such as the 'Calydonian' Boar to Calydon in order to devastate the arable land and kill the cattle, because its inhabitants had forgotten to include her name in the invocations at the annual sacrifice. She changed her hunting companion Callisto into a she-bear, because she was found to be pregnant. When her temple at Patrae had been desecrated she caused the earth to yield no harvest and sent diseases as well (Pausanias 7,19,3). Being generally of a rather vindictive character, she had the hunter Actaeon killed by his own hounds for having seen her naked when bathing, and →Orion by a scorpion because he had tried to rape her; together with her brother she shot down six of the seven daughters and six of the seven sons of Niobe, who had insulted her mother Leto for having only two children.

Only seldom in myth does she help a human, one of the rare instances being little Atalanta who had been exposed on Mt. Parthenion by her father, because he only wanted sons. Her life was saved by a she-bear who suckled her. After that she grew up to be a swift-footed virgin huntress, who would only marry the man that could beat her in running. The bear, being one of Artemis' sacred animals, had, of course, been sent by the goddess (Apollodorus, *Libr.* 3,9,2). For the rest her myths are concerned with killing, and, unlike the mythology of other goddesses, not at all with love.

Being a huntress, she is often depicted carrying bow and arrows. So is her brother Apollo, but in his case because his original function probably was to protect the herds from the attacks of wolves, hence in all likelihood his epithet Λυκεῖος. This is explained as 'wolf-killing' by Sophocles (*Electra* 6-7), but secondarily interpreted as 'Lycian' because his mother Leto was in reality a Lycian goddess. His Homeric epithet Λυκηγενής would then be the equivalent of Λητογενής. In Troezen, to match her brother in this respect, Artemis was venerated as Λυκεῖα, while Apollo in his turn was sometimes invoked as 'the Hunter' (Ἀγρεύς, Ἀγραῖος).

As Artemis had a special relation to women, presiding over their fertility and being called upon during the hours of labour (epithets: Λεχώ and Λοχεῖα, 'protectress of the child-bed', Σωωδίνα, 'who saves from travail'), she was naturally in course of time also connected via the menstrual cycle with the →moon. As a counterpart to this development, but for other reasons, her brother became the god of the sun. Here a third etymology of Λυκεῖος has played its part, the one which derived it from λύκη 'morning twilight' (cf. Macrobius, *Sat.* 1,17,36-41). In both cases the connections with the celestial bodies are clearly secondary; they are still unknown to Homer. For Hesiod, too, Selene and her brother →Helios are still the children of the Titans Hyperiōn and Theia

(*Theog.* 371), but in later times Philo of Alexandria could simply say that some of mankind (i. e. the Greeks) "call the moon Artemis" (*De decal.* 54). A further parallelism between Artemis and Apollo is the unmarried status of both, Artemis being emphatically venerated as a virgin. This latter characteristic may be in accordance with the fact that the wild animals with whom she is often associated, the deer, the boar and the bear, do not live in pairs, the bear normally living solitary outside the mating season. The sacrifices made to her were the wild animals mentioned, also wolves, even a fox at Ephesus, goats, edible birds and the fruits of trees. There are several testimonies to earlier human sacrifices having been replaced by other rites. The most widely known reminiscence of the former practice is, of course, the story of king Agamemnon's daughter Iphigeneia, who was sacrificed but in the last moment replaced by a hind or a she-bear. In spite of the OT instances of Isaac and →Jephtha's daughter, pagan gods were readily criticized by Christian church fathers on the point of human sacrifices; Artemis, e.g., by Tatian (*Or.* 29,2).

Artemis was depicted as wearing a short hunting tunic or a long robe (Ἄρτεμις κατεσταλμένη). In iconography she is often accompanied by a hind and carries bow and quiver, sometimes a torch. The latter attribute she assumed from the goddess Hecate, with whom she was often identified because the two shared a number of characteristics (such as her lunar associations). Her appearance in dreams of hunters or pregnant women was considered a propitious sign, but when she appeared naked it was an ill omen (Artemidorus, *Onirocr.* 2,35).

She was widely venerated in Greece and more particularly in Asia Minor, sometimes together with Apollo (so e. g. at Mantinea, Daphne near Antioch, Syracuse). Pausanias, who describes many local varieties of the different deities, each with a distinctive surname, lists no less than 64 of such epithets for Artemis, many of which are, of course, only geographical, such as 'Ephesia'. In this respect she was only marginally surpassed by Zeus (67 epithets); but she herself surpassed Athena (59), Apollo (58), →Aphrodite and Dionysus (both 27), and Demeter (26). Her great popularity was undoubtedly due to the fact that she was one of the rare goddesses who presided over the exclusively female aspects of life like pregnancy, childbirth and the rearing of infants. When boys and girls came of age they sacrificed a hairlock to the goddess on the third and last day of the Apatouria or clan festival. A boy did so when his epheby ended and he was enlisted in his father's phratry or clan, and became a full-fledged citizen himself; girls made this sacrifice before their marriage was solemnized, probably in the phratry of the future husband.

In various places the local calendar included a month named after Artemis: e.g. Artamitios at Sparta, Artemisiaon at Erythrae, and Artemisios in the Macedonian calendar used in the Hellenistic kingdoms. In Athens the month was called Elaphēbolīōn after her epithet Elaphēbolos ('deer huntress'); her festival, the Elaphēbolia, was celebrated in this month.

In Greece Artemis was at times conflated with other goddesses, mainly with Hecate, to whom she owed her association with magical practices. Abroad she was often identified with others, with several mother goddesses in Asia Minor, with the Near Eastern →Nanaia (so 2 Macc 1,13, but Josephus' version in *Ant.* 12,354 has "Artemis"), with the Persian Anaitis, one of the three imperial deities of the later Achaemenids, with the Thracian Bendis, with the Italian Diana, and in Egypt with (Bu)bastis, i. e. →Bastet, the cat-goddess.

III. As there is no way of knowing which Artemis the parents of Artemas (Titus 3,12) had in mind when they gave a name to their son, the further NT references to the goddess are only to the Artemis of Ephesus. All the same it was this man who unwittingly retained the name of the goddess in Christian times, for in later tradition he was considered to have belonged to the seventy apostles, and to have become bishop of

Lystra. As a consequence a festive day was devoted to him in the calendar on the 21st of June.

Artemis Ephesia was an early identification with one of the various Anatolian fertility and mother goddesses, an identification which may well go back to the very first Greek immigrants in the 11th century BCE. The name of the indigenous goddess was probably Upis (Callimachus, *Hymn to Artemis* 240) or Ôpis (Macrobius, *Sat.* 5,22,4-6). It was this particular cult of Artemis, which in the course of the ages, became more important than all her other local cults and was world famous by the time of Paul. Her temple, built by Chersiphron and his son Metagenes, was so imposing that it was the only one, so Solinus, that was spared by king Xerxes when he was setting fire to all the other Greek sanctuaries in Asia (Solinus 40,2-4). In 356 BCE it nevertheless succumbed to the torch in the hand of Herostratus, whose sole purpose it was to become in this way as famous as the building itself; as a result his name is now better known than those of the architects. After it had been rebuilt by Dinocrates it was traditionally reckoned among the Seven Wonders of the World, and functioned not only as a sanctuary, but also as a place of asylum and as a bank of deposit. In the last mentioned capacity it had already been used by Xenophon in the period between his military expedition to Persia and the Spartan war against Boeotia, in which he also took part. Paul's younger contemporary, Dio Chrysostom of Prusa, describes it as a place where people from all over the Roman empire, private persons, allied kings and townships, had deposited large sums of money (*Or.* 31,54). Although Dio denies it, there are others who say that this money was also lent out (Nicolaus of Damascus *frg* 65). The area of the asylum had had different extents in the course of time, but was finally reduced by Augustus, because it attracted too many criminals (Strabo 14,1,23). The new area was probably marked by boundary stones like the one which carries this bilingual inscription: "Imp. Caesar Augustus fines Dianae restituit. Αὐτοκράτωρ Καῖσαρ Σεβαστὸς ὅρους Ἀρτέμιδι ἀποκατέστησεν" (*IGLS* 3239). The goddess, however, was also the owner of estates in the neighbourhood, marked by similar stones.

The regular cult as well as the festivals attracted many visitors from abroad for whom lodging and nutrition had to be provided. In addition to this there was a whole industry of miniature Artemis temples, which may have been both dedicatory gifts and souvenirs, and although they are known only from the 7th century, the silver pins carrying a bee, the sacred animal of Artemis Ephesia, were in all likelihood still fabricated in the Roman period as well. Altogether this means that the temple of 'the Goddess' was one of the major sources of wealth and prosperity for Ephesus, of which the economical importance can hardly be overestimated.

Although 'Ephesia' may have been in origin an Anatolian mother goddess, like the Phrygian Matar Kubileya (→Cybele), the identification with Artemis was carried through to the very point of virginity, so that the poet Antipater of Sidon around 125 BCE could call her temple a 'Parthenōn', like that of her virgin half-sister Athena. She was also a huntress, for hunting weapons were carried by those who formed her festive procession, in which horses and hounds paraded as well. The Ephesians maintained, however, that both Artemis and Apollo had been born on Asian soil. Another difference was that she always wore a long robe and a kind of apron covered with what were and are usually considered to be female breasts, a token of fertility. This interpretation as πολύμαστος goes back to Antiquity (e. g. Minucius Felix, *Oct.* 22,5), but is certainly secondary, for a similar apron is worn by the male Zeus Labraundenus of Tegea. And as it is stated in so many words of yet another goddess, Berecynthia, that she was covered with testicles, what Ephesia was wearing were in all likelihood the testicles of the bulls sacrificed to her. The bee was her sacred animal, and as it does not itself procreate, it may have been a symbol of her chastity. It appears on the coins of Ephesus from the 7th to the 3rd centuries BCE, after that the image of the goddess herself begins to replace her emblem. The virgins, who served in her cult as priestesses, were also called μέλισσαι 'bees', and because the queen-bee, whose function was not understood in Antiquity, was mostly thought to be male and called 'the king', one of the titles of her priests was ἐσσήν, an indigenous word for 'ruler'. According to Strabo those priests had to be eunuchs (14,1,23), but Pausanias states that they only had to abstain from sexual intercourse for a period of one year (8,1,3). The change may be due to the intervening edict of Hadrian, who forbade castration even if consent was given (*Digestae* 48,8,4,2). Both priests and priestesses had to sacrifice their fertility to the goddess in their own way.

Without the slightest doubt it was Artemis who was the most important deity of the city. An inscription calls her "the goddess who rules (προεστῶσα) our city" (*SIG* 867,29). Other epithets, like Μεγίστη, as well as Μεγάλη (Acts 19:26; cf. Achilles Tatius 8,9,13) and Πρωτοθρονία, emphasize that she was first in rank, but certainly not the only deity venerated. No less than about twenty-five other gods were worshipped in Ephesus, among whom there were several Egyptian deities. This latter point is of some importance for the interpretation of Acts 19, because it underlines that the opposition described was hardly against the introduction of a foreign god as such.

As the bilingual boundary stone of Augustus shows, the Romans also referred to Artemis Ephesia as 'Diana'. In fact the cult statue in her temple on the Aventine Hill in Rome was supposed to be the copy of the statue in Marseille, which, in turn, was a replica of the Ephesian statue (Strabo 4,1,5). Consequently, the Vulgate version also has 'Diana' in Acts 19, and this was then taken over by Luther's version, the King James Version, etc.

The Ephesian goddess had filial sanctuaries all over the world, not only in nearby Greece (Alea; Scillus, founded by Xenophon), but also in Massalia (Marseille), and even as far away as Hemeroscopion in Spain (Denia). According to inscriptions the goddess communicated with her adherents and worked through oracles and epiphanies, and is reported to have effected healings. It is often stated by modern scholars that she was particularly connected with magic. This was indeed the case, but not particularly so, and she owed this connection mostly to her being identified with Hecate, the goddess of magic *par excellence*. That may explain why the Christian Tatian can say rather curtly: "Artemis is a magos" (*Or. ad. Gr.* 8,2). The emphasis, therefore, which is laid on this aspect is hardly justified, and has probably been brought about by the simple fact that in Acts 19 the story of the burning of magic books at Ephesus is immediately followed by one about the riot of the silversmiths in favour of Artemis, but such a burning could easily have happened elsewhere, too. A second factor has undoubtedly been the fact that magical words and formulae were often called 'ephesia grammata' in Antiquity. Yet it is not at all certain that this means 'Ephesian' and a derivation from ἔφεσις (from ἐφίημι 'send against; put on') is quite possible. That such words were inscribed on the statue of Artemis Ephesia is stated only by Pausanias the Lexicographer (2nd cent. CE), but is not corroborated by others or by iconographical data. It is also true that the name of Artemis, or characteristic epithets of hers like Ἰοχέαιρα or Λυκώ are found in the magical papyri, in the hymns and prayers that form part of them, but here again, nearly always together with the name of Hecate or epithets of hers like Τρικάρανος, Τριοδῖτις, Κυνώ, etc. Only once does she occur here with her epithet Λύκαινα, and without Hecate, in a spell for procuring knowledge of future events in which now also →Isis, →Osiris, →Amun, →Moses, Iaō, and →Helios →Mithras play a part (*PGM* III 434). Finally, the collection of magical papyri contains a love charm which does not mention Artemis, but only her or Selene's epithet Phōsphoros. The verso of this papyrus makes it clear, however, who this particular Phōsphoros is, as it carries a drawing which unmistakably depicts the 'many-breasted' Artemis Ephesia. Moreover, it makes mention of Phnun, here rather "the Abyss" than the Egyptian god Nun, and ends with a triple invocation of Iaō (*PGM* LXXVIII). The latter two instances may show how syncretistic magic could be: a situation in which the distinctive character of each individual deity is hardly highlighted.

In Ephesus the whole month Artemisiōn was sacred to her and all its days were holy days, which implied *int. al.* that all juridical activity had ceased. The main festival was the Artemisia during which sacrifices, banquets, processions and games took place. There were also mysteries and mystic sacrifices, but no further details are known about their character, except that they were performed by the college of six or more 'curetes', in the sacred grove 'Ortygia', or on Mt. Solmissos above it (Strabo 14,1,20). They were named after those ancient curetes or armed dancers who, at the birth of Artemis, had made such a terrible noise that they frightened away the jealous →Hera. This motif has undoubtedly been taken over from the story of the birth of Zeus in Crete, in which the curetes play a comparable role. The original function of these priests may have been to represent the Artemis temple and its estates in the city council of Ephesus.

IV. The presence of Jews in Asia goes back at least to about 345 BCE when the philosopher Aristotle met there with a Jew who had come from Coele-Syria and who could converse with him in Greek (Josephus, *Apion* 1,176-182). King Seleucus I started to grant to the Jews who lived there civic rights in specific places, and so probably did his grandson Antiochus II (Josephus *Ant.* 12,119;125). These rights amounted at least to *isonomia* (*ibid.* 16,160), which implied that Jews were allowed to live there in accordance with their own laws and customs, so that Jewish and Greek legislation were both treated as equally valid by the king. Such a construction harbours, of course, the seeds of conflicts, and these arose on several occasions during the first century BCE. The pagans asked whether Jews were not obliged to venerate their gods, too, and whether it was permissible for them to collect their own temple-tax and send it to Jerusalem. Both questions reveal that the Jewish practice was considered detrimental to the local economy, all citizens having to contribute to Artemis, for instance, instead of transferring large sums abroad. The Jews on their part objected against having to appear in law-courts on the →sabbath, and also against military service. The Roman officials, however, repeatedly reinforced the principle of isonomy, so that the Jews could not be forced to transgress their own laws. It should be noted in this connection that, in general, Jews were not averse to bearing pagan theophoric names. As far as Artemis is concerned, this is confirmed by an Egyptian papyrus from the 2nd cent. BCE which mentions a "Dositheos, son of Artemidoros, Jew" (*CPJ* 30,18); Dio Cassius, too, makes mention of an Artemiōn, who was the leader of the Jewish revolt in Cyprus around 117 CE (*Roman Hist.* 68,32).

This unstable equilibrium was endangered when Paul, outside the synagogue, started to preach that man-made idols were not gods at all (Acts 19,9-10; 26; cf. 17,29). Apparently, this idea had thusfar never been propagated by Jews except within their own congregation. Earlier, persons who had insulted and violated the filial cult of the goddess in Sardis had even been sentenced to death (*I. Eph.* Ia,2; IV BCE). Quite understandably, since Paul was naturally to be considered as one of its members, the other Jews wanted to put things right by distancing themselves from him or even declaring him to be an apostate (Acts 19:33-34). This, however, did not help much. The motley crowd that flocked together in the theatre apparently knew quite well that the Jews, although they did not directly endanger the manufacture and sale of the silver Artemis temples, were not venerators of the goddess either. The core of Paul's preaching against her, viz. that her statue was man-made and not divine, was dismissed by the 'secretary' of the city as incorrect by the use of one single word only. He simply reminded his audience of the fact that the statue was διοπετές, "fallen down from Zeus" or "from heaven" (Acts 19,35), and therefore of divine origin. In some cases this could imply that an image had been made out of a meteorite, but it is known for a fact that the statue of Artemis Ephesia was a rather dark wooden image (Pliny, *Nat. Hist.* 16,213-214). Centuries earlier the Athenian audience of Euripides found nothing contradictory in the assertion that a wooden image of Artemis had as such fallen down from heaven (*Iph. Taur.* 87-88; 977; 1044-1045). In the 2nd century, Athenagoras wrote an apology for the Christian religion to Marcus Aurelius and his son Commodus. It devotes a whole chapter to famous cult statues of the time and mentions the various sculptors who had carved them so as to show that they were man-made and not divine. It is certainly no coincidence that the statue of Artemis of Ephesus opens the enumeration because of its role in the NT. Athenagoras ascribes it to Endoeus, a pupil of the well-known Daedalus who was the architect of the Cretan labyrinth (*Supp.* 17,4).

In the Letter to the Church of Ephesus in the Book of Revelation, the congregation is praised for not having yielded to the doctrine of the Nicolaitans (2:6), which held that Christians were allowed to eat meat sacrificed to idols (2:14-15). At Ephesus this would certainly have involved the Artemis-cult. Some forty years earlier Paul, likewise, had forbidden this practice as long as it more or less implied one's partaking of a sacred pagan meal (1 Cor 8; 10:28). But if such meat had found its way from a temple to a market it was, according to Paul, sufficiently secularized for Christians to eat it (1 Cor 10:25-27).

The Jewish attitude towards the Artemis-cult can hardly ever have been much more positive than that of the Christians, and must have been comparable to some kind of armistice. The 5th book of the Sibylline Oracles, written under Marcus Aurelius, openly predicts her downfall, saying that her temple "by yawnings and quakes of the earth" will fall into the sea (293-297). Ironically, the temple survived vandalization by the Goths in 263 CE and ended up as a Christian church; it was rather the *retreating* sea, which, through the silting up of the estuary of the river Cayster, ultimately caused Ephesus to become desolate with temple and all.

V. *Bibliography*

H. J. ROSE, *A Handbook of Greek Mythology* (London [6th ed. 1958] 1965) 112-119; K. HOENN, *Artemis. Gestaltwandel einer Göttin* (Zürich 1946); M. P. NILSSON, *Geschichte der griechischen Religion,* vol. I (München 1955) 483-500; vol. II (München 1961) 368-369 (= Artemis Ephesia); H. WALTER, *Griechische Götter. Ihre Gestaltwandel aus den Bewusstseinsstufen des Menschen dargestellt an den Bildwerken* (München 1971) 203-216; R. FLEISCHER, *Artemis von Ephesos und verwandte Kultstatuen aus Anatolien und Syrien* (EPRO 35; Leiden 1973); *NewDocs* 4 (1987) nrs 19 and 28; 5 (1989) nr 5 (pp. 104-107); 6 (1992) nrs 29 and 30 (Artemis Ephesia).

G. MUSSIES

ARVAD ארוד

I. The city of Arvad (modern Ruad) is the most northern of Phoenician cities, situated on an island two miles off-shore. Less illustrious than Tyre and Sidon, Arvad and its inhabitants are mentioned only a few times in the Bible (Gen 10:18//1 Chr 1:16; Ezek 27:8.11). It has been said that the city is homonymous with an Assyrian deity (LEWY 1934).

II. In Neo-Assyrian annals, the city of Arvad is sometimes referred to as *Ar-ma-da* (S. PARPOLA, *Neo-Assyrian Toponyms* [AOAT 6; Neukirchen-Vluyn 1970] 37). This spelling corresponds exactly to that of the god Armada whose name has been read in a dedicatory brick inscription of Shalmaneser III (858-824 BCE). The text in question (O. SCHROEDER, *Keilschrifttexte aus Assur historischen Inhalts*, Vol. 2 [WVDOG 37;

Leipzig 1922] no. 103) quotes the king as saying "a golden (statue of) Armada of the temple of Assur my lord, which did not exist before, I made upon my own intuition" (lines 4-6: ^{d}*Ar-ma-da ša* É *Aš+šur* EN-*ia, šá ina pa-na la ib-šu, ina ḫi-sa-at* ŠÀ-*ia ša* KÙ.GI *e-pu-šu*; for a translation of the text see also *ARAB* 1, no. 709). SCHROEDER concluded that "^{d}Ar-ma-da was presumably the principal god of the homonymous city and territory of Arvad" (1922:168); LEWY adopted the same conclusion (1934). Except for this one text, however, a deity Armada is never mentioned in the cuneiform sources. There is the distinct possibility that the reading is based on an error (of either the ancient scribe or the modern copyist). Even if there ever was a god Armada, we cannot be sure of the connection with the city of Arvad, as the toponym is spelled in quite different ways; the writing *A-ru-ad-da* for instance is far more frequent (PARPOLA, AOAT 6, 37).

III. In the few instances in which Arvad is mentioned in the Bible, there is no hint of a divine nature of the city or a god by that name.

IV. *Bibliography*

J. LEWY, Les textes paléo-assyriens et l'Ancien Testament, *RHR* 110 (1934) 49; O. SCHROEDER, Zur Rezipierung des ^{d}*Ar-ma-da* unter Salmanassar III., *ZA* 34 (1922) 168-169; E. UNGER, Arwad, *RLA* 1 (1932) 160-161.

K. VAN DER TOORN

ASHAM אשׁם

I. The divine name *iṯm* is attested as the second element of the divine binomial *šgr w iṯm* in the sacrificial list recorded on RS 24.643 *verso* (*KTU* 1.148:31) and has been interpreted as related to the Hebrew word *ʾāšām*, 'guilt' and 'guilt-offering' (ASTOUR 1966:281-282).

II. A new syllabically written 'pantheon' text from Ras Shamra now lays to rest the identification of *iṯm* with Hebrew *ʾāšām*. In 1992.2004:14 (reading and interpretation courtesy D. Arnaud) the entry corresponding to *šgr w iṯm* is ^{d}**ḫar** *ù* ^{d}**gir**$_{3}$, indicating that *iṯm* is the Ugaritic equivalent of the Mesopotamian deity Išum (on this deity see EDZARD 1965; ROBERTS 1972; cf. →Fire).

The identification of Shaggar with a →moon deity is explicit in Hieroglyphic Hittite correspondences to syllabically written personal names (^{d}30 = sà-ga+ra/i; E. LAROCHE, *Akkadica* 22 [1981] 11; H. GONNET, *apud* D. ARNAUD, *Textes syriens de l'âge du Bronze Récent* [AulOr Suppl 1; Barcelona 1991] 199, 207), while in an Emar ritual the fifteenth day of the month is ascribed to Shaggar (D. ARNAUD, *Annuaire de l'Ecole Pratique des Hautes Etudes, Section des Sciences Religieuses* 92 [1983-84] 234; idem, *Emar* VI/3 [1986] 350-66, text 373 = Msk 74292a + 74290d + 74304a + 74290c). It appears thus that this deity not only had a connection with small cattle (cf. COOPER 1981:415-416; cf. →Sheger) but also with the moon, and the pair *šgr w iṯm* thereby shows a certain similarity to the *ad hoc* pair *yrḫ w ršp* (*KTU* 1.107:15 = line 40' in the re-edition of PARDEE 1988). Given the fact that Yarihu is the primary lunar deity at Ugarit and Rashap the primary underworld deity, Shaggar and Yarihu would bear a functional resemblance to each other (Shaggar being perhaps the deity of the full moon), while ʾIṯum would be related to Rashap as Išum is related to →Nergal in Mesopotamian religion (cf. EDZARD 1965; ROBERTS 1972).

Finally, the connection between the certain divine name *iṯm* and the form *iṯmh* in *KTU* 1.108:14 cannot be elucidated because *iṯmh* occurs in a badly broken context (cf. PARDEE 1988 chap. II).

III. In the absence of a Ugaritic example, there is no evidence for the existence of a Semitic or biblical deity whose name is based on the root denoting 'guilt'. ASTOUR's tentative identification (1966) must therefore be rejected (see also COOPER 1981:344-345; WANSBROUGH 1987).

IV. *Bibliography*

M. C. ASTOUR, Some New Divine Names from Ugarit, *JAOS* 86 (1966) 277-284; A. COOPER, Divine Names and Epithets in the Ugaritic Texts, *RSP* III (1981) 333-469; D.

O. EDZARD, *WbMyth* I (1965) 90-91; D. PARDEE, *Les textes para-mythologiques de la 24e campagne (1961)* (RSO IV; Paris 1988) 227-256; PARDEE, *Les textes rituels* (RSO; Paris, f.c.) chap. 66; J. J. M. ROBERTS, *The Earliest Semitic Pantheon. A Study of the Semitic Deities Attested in Mesopotamia before Ur III* [Baltimore 1972] 40-41; J. WANSBROUGH, Antonomasia: the Case for Semitic *'TM*, *Figurative Language in the Ancient Near East* (eds. M. Mindlin, *et al.*; London 1987) 103-116.

D. PARDEE

ASHERAH אשרה

I. The Hebrew term *'ăšērâ*, *'ăšērâ*, seems to be used in two senses in the Bible, as a cultic object (asherah) and as a divine name (Asherah).

It is the presence of possibly cognate words in other Semitic languages, where goddesses are frequently understood to be denoted, that has raised interesting questions for the interpretation of the OT references, and the linguistic problems are now compounded by the inscriptions of Khirbet el Qom and Kuntillet Ajrud. The etymological possibilities are considerable. Thus South Arabic *aṯr* means 'shining'; Hebrew *'āšēr* means 'happy' (cf. the tribal name Asher, which may be a divine name in origin), or 'upright' (which is consonant with the probable pole-structure of the cultic object, the asherah); Hebrew *'āšar*, Ugaritic *'aṯr*, may mean 'to advance, walk' (exploited in explanations of the goddess as 'walker', or 'trampler', but denied in this sense by MARGALIT 1990:268); the common noun *aṯr* (*'ašr*), meaning '(sacred) place' is most widely attested in the Semitic languages (ALBRIGHT, *AJSL* 41 [1925] 99-100; DAY 1986:388), and perhaps offers the least difficulties, as being able to stand on its own, and may represent the original sense, though MARGALIT's suggestion (1990, passim), of a wife 'following' her husband (Ugaritic *aṯr* = 'after'), and therefore as a denominative, 'wife', 'consort', is attractive. A new proposal by WATSON (1993) is suggested by the title 'Mistress of fates' (*be-le-e[t] ši-ma-tim*) which occurs in a hymn to →Amurru in parallel with *daš-ra-t[um ši?]-ma-tim*. On the basis of this he suggests that *aṯrt ym* may be construed as 'She who organises the day'. In any event a West Semitic origin for the goddess is most likely (DAY 1986:386; WIGGINS 1993:278)—even though the earliest evidence is in Akkadian—so that a West Semitic etymology should be sought. We may be sure that all possible wordplays were entertained by the ancients, however, in exploring her theology, so that ruling an etymology out of account on philological grounds does not rule out possible mythological and theological developments, or cult-titles as suggested above. This 'symbolic extension' of divine names is often not sufficiently recognised by scholars.

II. Ugarit. Ugaritic literature provides our primary source concerning the goddess. The name is spelt *aṯrt*, usually vocalised as 'Athirat(u)', or, following Hebrew convention, 'Asherah'. She appears in the following contexts. In the 'Baal cycle' of myths, *KTU* 1.1-6, she is a great goddess, mother of the minor gods of the pantheon, referred to as 'the seventy sons of Athirat' (*šbʿm bn aṯrt*, *KTU* 1.4 vi:46), who intercedes for →Baal and →Anat before →El (*KTU* 1.4 iv), and who supplies a son to reign following the descent of Baal into the netherworld (*KTU* 1.6 i:45-55). In one obscure episode (cf. *KTU* 1.4 ii:1-11 with 4 iii:15-22) it is possible that she attempts to seduce Baal, or is thought by him to have done so (HOFFNER 1990:69). It may also be that Baal kills large numbers of her children (*KTU* 1.4 ii:23-26 with 1.6 v:1-4; HOFFNER 1990:69). She appears to be the consort of El (*il*), though this is nowhere stated. In the Keret story, *KTU* 1.14-16, the king, while travelling to claim his bride, makes a vow to "Athirat of the Tyrians, and the goddess of the Sidonians" (*KTU* 1.14:38-39), indicating that the poet regards her as a goddess of Tyre and →Sidon. When the vow is broken, her vengeance entails the complete undoing of all El's plans to redeem Keret. Further, the heir to Keret's throne is described as one "who will drink the milk of Athirat, draining the breast of the Virgin [ ]" (*KTU* 1.15 ii:27 —the completion of the lacuna by →'Anat' is gratuitous: WYATT, *UF* 15 [1983] 273-274 and n. 13). This has an important bearing on the goddess' ideological role, suggesting that kings are made quasi-divine by divine suckling. Apart from mention in sacrificial and pantheon lists, the goddess also appears in two theogonic texts, *KTU* 1.12 i and 1.23, the former describing the birth of 'the Devourers' to the handmaids of Athirat and Yarihu, the latter describing two wives of El (seemingly Athirat and perhaps Shapsh) who consummate their marriage with him, and give birth to →Shahar and →Shalem, the →Dioskouroi. These texts have a bearing on several biblical traditions, such as Gen 16, 19:30-38, Ps 8 etc. (WYATT 1993). The goddess' name appears in the longer title *rbt aṯrt ym*, meaning perhaps 'the Great Lady who walks on the Sea' (the name therefore apparently understood as 'Walker'), but this should not be understood to point to the true etymology (above), and is not falsified by an appeal to etymology, being perhaps an example of 'popular' (rather 'hieratic') etymologising. Likewise, WATSON's proposal (1993) has at least this status, and would also be consonant with occasional hints that she has solar connections (such as the pairing with Shapsh in *KTU* 1.23).

Under West Semitic evidence we should also note the personal name *Abdi-Aširta*, occurring in various transcriptions as a ruler of Amurru, Ugarit's neighbour to the south, mentioned some 92 times in the Amarna letters (*EA*). In the hymn cited by Watson (1993), Ashratum is the consort of the god Amurru. In addition, she appears in a letter from Taanach dating to the 15th century (ALBRIGHT, *BASOR* 94 [1944] 18, Taanach letter 1, l. 21) and in one Aramaic inscription (*KAI* 228) as a goddess of Tema. This last is of interest in view of →Yahweh's possible associations with Tema (cf. Hab 3:3 - LXX renders both *têmā'* and *têmān* of MT by Thaiman). The reading is however questioned by CROSS (*CBQ* 48 [1986] 387-394) and DAY (1992:485).

Egypt. Athirat has been identified as 'Qudshu' ('the Holy One') appearing in *KTU* 1.2 i:21 etc. (the phrase *bn qdš* being misconstrued as 'the sons of Qudshu'), and thus a link is made between her and the so-called Qudshu stelae from Thebes (so most recently DAY 1986:388-389, 399). However, on the stelae the name reads *qdšt* (feminine), and there is in any case no justification for identifying the goddess of the stelae with Athirat. Furthermore, the *qdš* of the Ugaritic texts should be construed as denoting El, or less probably as the abstract 'holiness'. If this term referred to Athirat, it would require a final *t* to denote the feminine. Reiteration of elementary errors of this sort by subsequent generations of scholars only compounds the error! (See WIGGINS 1991 for a sober view on these matters.)

Mesopotamia. The forms *Ašratu(m)*, *Aširatu*, *Aširtu* (here 'Ashratu') appear infrequently in Akkadian and Hittite documents, and give only the sketchiest information concerning the goddess. The fact that she appears as the consort of Amurru (above) is evidence of Ashratu(m)'s Amorite (thus, West Semitic) origin. The earliest reference is in a votive inscription in Sumerian from Hammurabi's time (18th century), BM 22454. In this her epithets include 'daughter-in-law of An', 'Lady of voluptuousness and happiness' and 'Lady with patient mercy'. She also appears in a number of god-lists, the list K. 3089 indicating that she had a temple in Babylon, and on a number of cylinder-seals and impressions. Ashratum also appears in one personal name from the time of Hammurabi: *Ašratum-Ummi*. Finally, she is mentioned in three ritual texts from the Seleucid period. The Sumero-Akkadian evidence has been recently summarised and evaluated by WIGGINS (1993:190-217).

A Hittite text contains the myth of Elkunirsha (→El-creator-of-the-earth) and Ashertu, which appears to be derived by Hurrian mediation from a Canaanite prototype. *Elkurnirša* is generally accepted as a transcription of **il qny arṣ* (cf. Gen 14:19), and *Ašertu* as one of *aṯrt*. This narrates how the goddess tries to seduce the storm-god (Tešub = Baal →Hadad). When he reports this to Elkunirsha, he is told to humiliate the goddess. But he does this, both sexually, apparently (see HOFFNER's translation: cf. *ANET* 519), and by telling her how he killed her children. She and Elkunirsha then plot against the storm-god, but Anat-Ashtart reveals their plotting to him. The storm-god is then apparently injured (through witchcraft?), but is subsequently exorcised. (HOFFNER 1990:69-70)

Arabia. A goddess Athirat has been discerned in the epigraphic South Arabian inscriptions, dating from the mid-first millennium BCE. The term *aṯrt* occurs in various inscriptions in the dialects of the region, and can mean 'sanctuary', in addition to being a divine name in some instances. Unfortunately, very little information can be gleaned for our purposes from the texts. *RES* 3534B and 3550 mention a temple of Wadd and Athirat, while *RES* 3689 alludes to offerings to ʿAmm and Athirat. Wadd is the Qatabanian moon-god, and ʿAmm the national god, who may be lunar, and thus another name for Wadd. Whether or not Athirat is the consort of the god in each case, and is therefore solar in South Arabia, cannot be decided on the basis of the evidence available.

III. The term (*hā-ʾăšērâ*, var. *ʾăsērâ*), appears some 40 times in MT, usually with the article. When the plural is used, the forms *ʾăšērîm* and *ʾăšērôt* both occur. A cultic object appears most commonly to be denoted, which can be 'made' (*ʿāśâ*), 'cut down' (KRT) and 'burnt' (ŚRP). Probably a stylised tree, or a lopped trunk, is intended—see Deut 16:21, which prohibits the 'planting' of any tree (or: wood) as an asherah, and Judg 6:25-26, where it can become sacrificial fuel—and is frequently singled out for opprobrium by the Deuteronomist. However, not only is the attitude of the biblical writers not entirely consistent, but neither is the usage, the article being absent, or not presupposed by suffixes, in 8 cases. The term also appears in both singular and plural, and in the latter can apparently be masculine or feminine (the latter is however dubious—see below). Furthermore, the matter of the reference of a given passage, to cultic object or goddess, is independent of the use of the article. This is clear from the fact that in every instance where 'Baal' is mentioned in the Hebrew Bible, the article is used (allowed for in this instance by GK §126d, on the ground that it is specifying a generic term), as it is with a number of the 'Ashtoreth' (→Astarte) references. Since in both these cases there is no question of it not being a deity of some kind that is referred to, whether specific or generic, it follows that the same rule may at least in principle apply in the case of 'the asherah'. The presence or absence of the article is therefore not, in the present writer's view, a determinant in our analysis; what it probably does is to remove the proper name status of the noun, making it into a general term for a deity, though the use of the article with *ʾĕlōhîm* in its designation of the god of Israel suggests that the mechanical application of grammatical rules may be premature (see above: GK §126d). The first problem with the biblical allusions is therefore where a goddess is to be discerned behind the references and where the cult object. It is general contextual considerations which are to be taken into account. Thus references to constructing, erecting, removing or burning the asherah are in principle to be understood as referring to the cult object. LXX apparently understood its arboreal nature by its commonest translation as *alsos*, 'grove'. The Mishnah (*ʿAbodah Zarah* 3:7) regards the Asherah as a tree. We shall consider below the relationship between object and deity.

The most important single source is the Deuteronomistic History, which contains 24 of the 40 references. One of its chief concerns is cultic purity, a strictly monolatrous Yahwism, and it therefore regards the presence of the asherah as evidence of apostasy. The Deuteronomistic historians have done their work so well that scholars are prone to talk of the asherah and other cultic elements as evidence of syncretism, or of (extraneous) 'Canaanite' elements in the Israelite and Judahite cults. In view of the epigraphic evidence to be discussed below, it is safer to begin from the supposition that the religion of both kingdoms only gradually moved towards monolatry and then monotheism, through prophetic and deuteronom(ist)ic influence, and was otherwise, at both popular and official levels, basically polytheistic in nature. Furthermore, there is no justification for ideas of 'foreignness' about the Canaanite elements in religion in Palestine. Israel and Judah are to be seen as wholly within that cultural tradition. Historically speaking, it is their emergence from it which is striking (though often overstated) rather than its inherently alien nature. If we set aside those passages which treat the asherah specifically as an object to which certain things could be done, we are left with the following passages which may reasonably be understood to denote the goddess.

Judg 3:7 is a general statement on apostasy, and states that the Israelites served the Baals and the 'Asheroth'. This would be a generic use of the term, but should be corrected in accordance with Judg 2:13, where the goddess(es) are called Ashtaroth (*ʿAštārôt*). 1 Kgs 15:13 (= 2 Chr 15:16) says that Maacah made an "obscene thing for (the) asherah" (*mipleṣet lāʾăšērâ*) and that Asa cut it (sc. the 'obscene thing', not the asherah) down. The Kgs text has the article, the Chr text omits it. The principle of the article with divine names noted above applies, and there is no need to see a shift in understanding between the two versions. The Kgs passage undoubtedly has the goddess in mind, (and apparently has her left standing!) though the article reduces her name to a generality. 1 Kgs 18:19 mentions 400 prophets of Asherah: the article is used, but the deity must be intended, unless the text be rejected as a gloss, as by some commentators. LXX repeats the phrase at v 22, and there is no objective reason for omitting it here. In the accompanying reference to the 450 prophets of Baal, the article is of course used, so both divine names must, on retention of the text, be interpreted consistently. 2 Kgs 13:6 appears to be an attempt to incorporate the asherah among the sins of Jeroboam (though this is originally singular, as in 1 Kgs 16:19, and refers to the calf-images of 1 Kgs 12:28-29). REB translates *hāʾăšērâ* here as the divine name, but the sacred pole is probably intended. 2 Kgs 21:7 states that Manasseh 'set up an image of the asherah', which again appears to refer to the goddess (so REB). But the verse should perhaps be harmonised with v 3, which simply alludes to the sacred pole. Finally within the Deuteronomistic History, 2 Kgs 23:4-7, in the account of Josiah's reform, v 4 refers to items made *labbaʿal wĕlāʾăšērâ*, 'for (the) Baal and for (the) Asherah', while v 7 speaks of the 'clothes' (*bottîm*: perhaps 'shrines'?, WIGGINS 1993:165) the women wove for the asherah. The first of these verses can only refer to the goddess, while the second is ambiguous, since it may be a matter of hangings for the sacred pole.

Among the other 16 references to the asherah, 15 are in the plural, and thus clearly do not denote the goddess. They range from Exod 34:13 (thoroughly deuteronomistic in style), through 11 references in 2 Chr (of which only 15:16 [1 Kgs 15:13] is singular), most of which parallel the same data in Kgs, two references in Isaiah (17:8 and 27:9) and one each in Jeremiah (17:2) and Micah (5:13). The paucity of prophetic references is striking, and raises the possibility that the violent objection to goddess and cult object belongs to one particular theological school (viz. the deuteronomistic) in Judah. Above all, the absence of any reference in Hosea is cause for surprise. (WELLHAUSEN's proposal for 14:9 [*Die kleine Propheten* (Berlin 1898[3]) 20] remains conjectural.) The few prophetic allusions noted are all best explained as later additions to the text. All the plural forms are in the masculine, with the exception of 2 Chr 33:3, which has the feminine plural. Since the parallel in 2 Kgs 21:3 has the singular, there is a case for emendation here. All the plural occurrences in the Deuteronomistic History are also masculine, and since we have already discounted Judg 3:7, it means that the only genuine plural form is masculine. (There may be a case for a further instance of the masculine plural use: 1 Sam 7:3 has in MT *wĕhāʿaštārôt*, but LXX reads *...kai ta alsē*, presupposing *hāʾăšērîm*.

Why is the masculine form used in the plural usage? WIGGINS (1993:169-170, 186) suggests that in the Deuteronomistic History the usage is in accordance with the double redaction principle: the feminine singular references are by and large preexilic, the masculine plural ones exilic. This then becomes normative, among later editors and writers who may have only the vaguest idea, if any, what the singular term actually denoted. The plural term is a code-word for something cultically deviant.

The usage of *ʾăšērâ*, in the singular denoting the goddess or the cult object, and in the plural meaning the latter, and developing the vaguer sense just noted, is an excellent basis for discussion of the whole Israelite and Judahite attitude to image-worship ('idolatry' is a pejorative term). The first principle in the understanding of this is the deliberate perversity of the biblical view (e.g. at Isa 17:8; 44:9-20; Jer 2:27-28) which recognises the inherently 'incarnational' thought of image-worship, that man-made objects can, through cultic use, become the media for hierophanies, and yet turns this argument in on itself as a parody of true religion. The real significance of Isa 17:8, with its reference to 'the work of his hands, and what his fingers have made', is however to be determined by Isa 2:8, where the identical formula, with singular suffixes in a context of plural verbs, can only indicate that it is Yahweh's hands and fingers that have made the objects. And this is no simple statement of creatureliness, but a metaphor of theogony. The asherah is indeed the work of Yahweh's hands and fingers, but in a mythological sense (see WYATT 1994). The Isaianic reference to the asherah is thus fully aware of the dangerous power of the goddess. Her reality is not in question, and the distinction between deity and cult object is ultimately not an ancient, but a modern one.

This brings us to the intriguing question of the supposed 'Yahweh's Asherah', turning up as the only extra-biblical evidence for the goddess, if to be so construed, in two sites, Khirbet el Qom and Kuntillet Ajrud. On walls at the former, and on pithoi at the latter, inscriptions have been found, giving rise to a lively debate. For a thorough survey see HADLEY (1989). Space precludes lengthy discussion here. The inscriptions refer to *yhwh wʾšrth*, *yhwh šmrn wʾšrth* and *yhwh tmn wʾšrth*, "Yahweh (Yahweh of Samaria, Yahweh of Teman [probably = K. Ajrud]) and his *ʾăšērâ*". In all cases the deity and his *ʾăšērâ* are invoked for blessing and protection. The status of the *ʾăšērâ* is problematic. It cannot be the divine name according to the grammatical rule which precludes a proper noun taking a suffix; but we have seen that the use of the article in MT is not determinative in the debate. If it is the cult object, it may nevertheless have been viewed as noted above, that is with no practical distinction drawn between object and the deity symbolised. Some kind of divine reference is supported by two iconographical features found in context. Inscription 3 at Khirbet el Qom is written above an engraved hand. This has a widely attested apotropaic significance (SCHROER 1983), but may also be tentatively linked with the hand symbol of Tanit of Carthage, the prototype of which appeared on a stela at Hazor. A link between Tanit and Asherah is possible, though unproven (see discussion in HVIDBERG-HANSON 1979:115-119). One of the K. Ajrud pithoi has three figures drawn below the inscription. To the right a seated figure plays a stringed instrument. To the left two figures are flanked by a diminutive bull. Attempts to identify these figures with Bes are quite unwarranted. MARGALIT's explanation of them as "Yahweh and his consort" (1990:277, see above etymology) is cogent, and consistent with details of the drawings. But perhaps judgment should be reserved.

The conclusion many scholars have drawn that Asherah was the consort of Yahweh may be approached from another angle. If Yahweh developed out of local Palestinian forms of El, then we might expect a simple continuity of the old El-Asherah (Ilu-Athirat) relationship which appears to obtain at Ugarit. But it has been increasingly argued in recent years that Yahweh has 'baalistic' characteristics, or is even a form of Baal himself. It has been argued that Baal effectively usurps El's role at Ugarit, and takes El's consort at the same time. There is no evidence from Ugarit to support this, and the hypothesis is based on a reading back of the Hurro-Hittite Elkunirsha myth to its putative Canaanite prototype (which need not have been the pattern at Ugarit). Within the biblical context, it has been supposed that Yahweh-Baal is thus the consort of Asherah, since Baal and Asherah were the local 'Canaanite' deities evidenced at Judg 3:7 MT. But we have seen that MT's reading here is to be rejected. The hypothesis has nothing to commend it.

The theology of the goddess remains obscure in spite of the complex evidence noted above. We cannot be certain that every Ugaritic trait was preserved in the later environment, and even there much remains unknown. The firmest evidence, i.e. that cited from the Keret story above, and the goddess' role in choosing Athtar as king in the Baal cycle, points to her role in kingship rituals, as 'incarnate' in the chief queen, who in Ugarit appears to have borne the title *rabitu*, 'Great Lady', (GORDON 1988) which is used of Asherah herself as well as of Shapsh, and which would correspond to the office of *Gĕbîrâ*, also something like 'Great Lady' in Israelite and Judahite royal ideology. Maacah, a *Gĕbîrâ*, is noted for her particular devotion to Asherah in 1 Kgs 15:13, and Bathsheba is undoubtedly to be seen fulfilling the role in 1 Kgs 2:13-19 (WYATT, *ST* 39 [1985] 46; *UF* 19 [1987] 399-404). AHLSTRÖM very appositely calls the Judahite queen "the ideological replica of the mother of the gods..." (1976:76; cf. ACKERMANN 1993). It is this inseparable tie with the royal cultus which may explain the goddess' apparently complete disappearance from the post-exilic world, though echoes of her are discernible in the figure of →Wisdom (LANG 1986:60-81).

IV. *Bibliography*

S. ACKERMAN, The Queen Mother and the Cult in Ancient Israel, *JBL* 112 (1993) 385-401; G. W. AHLSTRÖM, *Aspects of Syncretism in Israelite Religion* (Horae Soederblomianae V, Lund 1963); K-H. BERNHARDT, Aschera in Ugarit und im Alten Testament, *MIO* 13 (1967) 163-174; J. DAY, Asherah in the Hebrew Bible and Northwest Semitic Literature, *JBL* 105 (1986) 385-408; DAY, Asherah, *ABD* I (1992) 483-487; M. DIETRICH & O. LORETZ, *Yahwe und seine Aschera* (UBL 9; Münster 1992); C. H. GORDON, Ugaritic *rbt/rabitu*, *Ascribe to the Lord* (ed. F. S. Craigie, JSOTSup 67; Sheffield 1988) 127-132; J. M. HADLEY, *Yahweh's Asherah in the Light of Recent Discoveries* (diss. Oxford 1989); HADLEY, Yahweh and "His Asherah": Archaeological and Textual Evidence for the Cult of the Goddess, *Ein Gott Allein* (eds. W. Dietrich & M. A. Klopfenstein; Freiburg/Göttingen 1994) 235-268; H. A. HOFFNER, *Hittite Myths* (Atlanta 1990) 69-70; F. O. HVIDBERG-HANSON, *La déesse TNT* (Copenhagen 1979) i 71-81, 115-119, ii 69-100; A. JAMME, Le panthéon sud-arabe préislamique d'après les sources épigraphiques, *Mus* 60 (1947) 57-147; O. KEEL & C. UEHLINGER, *Göttinnen, Götter und Gottessymbole* (Freiburg 1992) 199-321; B. LANG, *Wisdom and the book of Proverbs* (New York 1986) 60-81; E. LIPIŃSKI, The goddess Aṯirat in ancient Arabia, in Babylon and in Ugarit, OLP 3 (1972) 101-119; W. A. MAIER, *ʾAšerah: Extrabiblical Evidence* (HSM 37; Atlanta 1986); B. MARGALIT, The meaning and significance of Asherah, *VT* 40 (1990) 264-297; S. M. OLYAN, *Asherah and the cult of Yahweh in Israel* (SBLMS 34; Atlanta 1988); R. PATAI, The goddess Asherah, *JNES* 24 (1965) 37-52; R. J. PETTEY, *Asherah, Goddess of Israel* (AUS VII 74; New York 1990); M. H. POPE, Atirat, *Wörterbuch der Mythologie* i (ed. H. W. Haussig; Stuttgart 1965) 246-249; J. B. PRITCHARD, *Palestinian Figurines in Relation to Certain Goddesses Known Through Literature* (AOS 24; New Haven 1943) 59-65, 89-90; W. L. REED, *The Asherah in the Old Testament* (Fort Worth 1949); S. SCHROER, Zur Deutung der Hand unter der Grabinschrift von Chirbet el Qôm, *UF* 15 (1983) 191-199; M. S. SMITH, *The early history of God* (San Francisco 1990); W. G. E.

WATSON, *Atṟt ym:* Yet Another Proposal, *UF* 25 (1993) 431-434; S. WIGGINS, The Myth of Asherah: Lion Lady and Serpent Goddess, *UF* 23 (1991) 384-394; WIGGINS, *A Reassessment of 'Asherah'. A Study According to the Textual Sources of the First Two Millennia B.C.E.* (AOAT 235; Kevelaer/Neukirchen-Vluyn 1993); N. WYATT, The theogony motif in Ugarit and the Bible, forthcoming in *Ugarit and the Bible* (eds. G. J. Brooke *et al,* AOAT; Neukirchen-Vluyn 1994).

N. WYATT

ASHḪUR → ISHḪARA

ASHIMA אשׁימא

I. Ashima was the god worshipped by the people of Hamath, who though deported to Samaria by the Assyrian king, continued to serve him in their new home (2 Kgs 17:30).

II. The name of the god, in its Biblical form, has been recovered only from the context of Arab tribes at Teima; in a dedicatory inscription from Teima, *ʾšymʾ* is invoked, along with the gods *ṣlm* and *šnglʾ* (See LIVINGSTONE 1983; BEYER & LIVINGSTONE 1987). This attestation is somewhat surprising if the primary association of Ashima is with the north Syrian Hamath (but cf. BECKING 1992:99, 102-104); trade contacts between the caravanning Arabs and the important centre of Hamath may explain the adoption of Ashima into the pantheon at Teima.

Prior to the discovery of the Teima inscription, Ashima was sought within the Canaanite/Phoenician cultural sphere, and was taken to be related to the god →Eshmun. But the name of this deity, attested in Phoenician and Punic inscriptions, as well as cuneiform texts, is always written with the final consonant *nun*, and so the identification with Ashima is questionable. See further s.v. Eshmun.

Some have claimed to have found the name Ashima at Elephantine in the compound divine name Eshem-Bethel (PORTEN & YARDENI 1993:234, 127) and as a theophoric element in over a half-dozen Aramaic personal names (GRELOT, LAPO 5 [1972] 464). The god's name may also be seen in a Greek transcription from Kafr Nebo, in the compound form Sumbetulos, i.e. Eshem-Bethel (LIDZBARSKI, *ESE* 2, 1908, 323-324). Therefore, a North Syrian Aramean locale as the home of the deity seems assured. The name Eshem may be the Aramaic form of the common Semitic noun for "name", and, according to ALBRIGHT (1969:168), its use is evidence for hypostatization, "the tendency to avoid the personal name of the deity and to replace it with more discrete expressions."

III. Many commentators find the name of the god Ashima in the threatening words of Amos 8:14 against those "who swear by the guilt (*ʾašmat*) of Samaria". While it is not impossible that this is an example of a prophetic play on words, *ʾašmat* = ʾAšîmāʾ (cf. Hosea 4:15, where the name Beth-aven "House of transgression" rather than Beth-el, alludes to the sin of idolatry at the site, cf. 13:1), the primary issue raised by Amos "is not an apostate invocation of some foreign deity ..., but rather the emphatic insistence on the deity's localization at a particular sanctuary ...Yahweh (had been) fragmented into several gods, conceived of as patron deities of territorial regions" (WOLFF 1975:332; contrast VAN DER TOORN 1992:91).

IV. *Bibliography*

W. F. ALBRIGHT, *Archaeology and the Religion of Israel* (5th ed.; Garden City 1969); B. BECKING, *The Fall of Samaria: an Historical and Archaeological Study* (Leiden 1992); K. BEYER & A. LIVINGSTONE, Die neuesten aramäischen Inschriften aus Taima, *ZDMG* 137 (1987) 285-296 esp. 286-288; A. LIVINGSTONE, B. SPAIE, M. IBRAHIM, M. KAMEL & S. TAIMANI, Taima: Recent Sounding and New Inscribed Material, *Atlal* 7 (Riyadh 1983), 102-116 + pls. 87-97 (esp. 108-111, pl. 96); B. PORTEN & A. YARDENI, *Textbook of Aramaic Documents from Ancient Egypt 3: Literature, Accounts, Lists* (Jerusalem 1993); K. VAN DER TOORN,

Anat-Yahu, Some Other Deities, and the Jews of Elephantine, *Numen* 39 (1992), 80-101; H. W. WOLFF, *Joel and Amos* (Hermeneia; Philadelphia 1975).

M. COGAN

ASHTORETH → ASTARTE

ASMODEUS Ἀσμοδαῖος

I. The etymology of this name is not beyond any doubt but Asmodeus is most probably derived from the Avestan words *aēšma-* and *daēuua* or their Middle Persian (Pahlavi) compound cognate *xēšm-dēw*, both meaning 'demon of wrath'. As Talmudic texts sometimes give the form אשמדאי or אשמדיי for Asmodeus, his name has been connected with Hebrew שמד (to destroy, exterminate), but this seems to be folk etymology. Asmodeus does not occur as a demonic name in the Hebrew Bible, but the apocrypha twice give the Greek Ἀσμοδαῖος (Tob 3:8.17).

II. The earliest occurrences of the Avestan demon *aēšma-* are the Gathic texts Yasna 29:2 and 30:6; those who choose the way of evil go the way of Aēshma and thus bring harm to the world, while otherwise the followers of Ahura Mazda's teachings become expellers of him (Yasna 48:12). With the help of Aēshma the evil powers of Zarathustra's dualistic cosmos can bring sickness and evil to mankind so that men behave like Angra Mainyu's creatures. It is also worth mentioning that Aēshma is the only demon who occurs in the Gathas. Outside the Old-Avestan corpus we find Aēshma in Yasna 57:10.25 (cf. Yasht 11:15), a hymn to Shraosha, who will smite and crush Aēshma and protect people from his deceptions. Yasht 10:97 tells us about Aēshma's fright of Mithra's mace which is the most victorious of all weapons (cf. →Mithras). As his standard epithet we find "of bloody club", so we can imagine him pictured as a savage ruffian. Of further interest is also Yasna 10:8 where we read that Aēshma brings drunkenness to men. The further development of Zoroastrianism brings a revival of the older Iranian gods and also the growth of the number of demons. Thus Aēshma occurs as a separate demonic being in the Pahlavi scriptures: Aēshma (*xēšm-dēw*) has now become one of the chief evil powers. He is equal to Ahreman and is the companion of Āz; the deities of Ohrmazd's (Ahura Mazda's) good creation are his antagonists, mostly Wahman and Shrosh. According to the Bundahishn (1:3), he is one of the seven *dēws* who were created by Ahreman; the Pahlavi Rivayat (56:13-15) gives the account of a conversation between Aēshma and Ahreman in which the former is enjoined to corrupt the good and efficient things of the creation. Aēshma is now the embodyment of →Wrath who in legends can bring all kind of (putatively) historical disturbance and uproar into the world. Thus Aēshma and the usurper Dahaka fight king Yima and kill him. In the Zādspram (9:1), Aēshma is one of the ancestors of five brothers who are the enemies of Zarathustra himself, while an account in the Dēnkard (Book 8) states that he incites Arjasp to wage war against Vištaspa, the protector of Zarathustra, and thus oppose the Iranian prophet.

These texts lead to the following conclusion: Aēshma (the personfied Wrath) has a separate existence and he is one of the powers of the evil sphere within Zoroastrian dualism. There he plays an important part in the struggle between good and evil and thus has a considerable influence upon history. In view of the spread of Zoroastrianism in the last centuries BCE from the Iranian areas to Mesopotamia and Anatolia it is possible to find traces of his influence in both Jewish and Christian literature.

III. The apocryphal book of Tobit probably shows some Iranian (Zoroastrian) influence (cf. BOYCE & GRENET 1991:414), namely the importance of generously dispensing alms (Tob 4:9-10; 14:2), the account of the little dog (Tob 6:1; 11:4) and the mentioning of the demon Asmodeus. In Tob 3:8 we read that in his jealousy he has already killed the seven successive husbands of Sara during their wedding-nights. Therefore →Raphael was sent to free Sara from this demon (Tob 3:17). The angel can tell Tobias a way to expel him by performing a purifying (?) ritual and banishing him to the Egyptian desert (Tob 6:8; 8:1-3). On the whole, Asmodeus does not figure prominently in the book of Tobit; but, once introduced into Jewish literature, he made his way into folklore. He is depicted as a malefactor bringing discord to husband and wife or hiding a wife's beauty from her husband (*T. Sol.* 2:3). Aggadic texts also say that Asmodeus is connected with drunkenness, mischief and licentiousness. In the Talmud there is a famous account (*Git.* 68a-b; cf. *Num. R.* 11:3) of Solomon's dealing with this demon: Asmodeus, the king of demons, was made drunk by Solomon and then led to the king whom he has to help by building the temple in Jerusalem. Then, however, the demon took the king's seal and seated himself down on the royal throne while the king must wander around as a beggar until God shows mercy on Solomon and restores his kingship. The whole legend does not depict Asmodeus as an evil-doer: his actions should open the king's eyes to the emptiness and vanity of wordly possessions. Such legends gave rise to the popular belief of Asmodeus as a beneficent demon and a friend of men—though he still remained king of the demons.

Another tradition remains closer to the malificent Asmodeus of the book of Tobit and to the Iranian concept of Aēshma as a demon of wrath. The Qumranic and Pauline scriptures (cf. BOYCE & GRENET 1991:446; PINES 1982:81) know a conception of Wrath as a nearly autonomous entity; so it is possible to see in that also the Iranian conception of *aēšma daēuua*, though there is no linguistic link. But we also have to take into account that this Qumranic and Pauline concept has one root in the OT's references of →Yahweh's wrath and is thus part of the divine sphere. This difference should not be ignored because Aēshma is the main auxiliary of the Iranian evil sphere. But nevertheless it cannot be ruled out that the apocryphal demon Asmodeus stemming from Iran is the other root of the hypostatized wrath as a destructive entity and for the creatures of wrath.

IV. *Bibliography*

M. BOYCE, *A History of Zoroastrianism. Vol. 1* (Leiden 1975) 87.201; M. BOYCE & F. GRENET, *A History of Zoroastrianism. Vol. 3* (Leiden 1991) 41, 425-426, 446; P. DESELAERS, *Das Buch Tobit. Studien zu seiner Entstehung, Komposition und Theologie* (OBO 43; Fribourg 1982) 87.98.147-148; S. PINES, Wrath and Creatures of Wrath in Pahlavi, Jewish and New Testament Sources, *Irano-Judaica. Studies Relating to Jewish Contacts with Persian Culture Throughout the Ages* (ed. S. Shaked; Jerusalem 1982) 76-82.

M. HUTTER

ASSUR אשור / אסר

I. Assur occurs in the OT as a person, the second son of →Shem in the table of nations (Gen 10:22), as a people or world power, and as the land of Assyria. While the concept of the power may have been sometimes subsumed in the concept of the deity certain attestation of the name of the deity can be found within the name of the king Esarhaddon (Isa 37:38 = 2 Kgs 19:37, Ezra 4:2).

II. Assur is the god of Assyria par excellence. His name is identical with that of the city of Assur, which with its temple, the *bīt Aššur,* later Ekur, was the main centre of his cult. The significance of the god in Assyrian royal ideology can be seen clearly in prayers associated with the coronation of the Assyrian king. It is worth quoting from these texts, because they epitomize from an Assyrian point of view the character of the national god, which is seen from the opposite point of view in the OT. A Middle Assyrian prayer belonging to the ritual includes the following lines: "Assur is king, Assur is king!" and, further on in the text, "May your (the king's) foot in Ekur and your hands (stretched) toward Assur, your god, be at ease! May your priesthood (*šangūtu*) and the priesthood of your sons be at ease in the service of Assur, your god! With your straight sceptre enlarge your land! May Assur grant you a commanding voice, obedience, agreement, justice and peace!" (MVAÄG 41 [1937] 9-13). Similar sentiments can be found in the Neo-Assyrian coronation hymn of Assurbanipal: "Assur is king—indeed Assur is king! Assurbanipal is the [...] of Assur, the creation of his hands. May the great gods establish his reign, may they protect the life [of Assurba]nipal, king of Assyria! May they give him a just sceptre to extend the land and his peoples! May his reign be renewed and may they consolidate his royal throne for ever!" (SAA III no. 11).

The coincidence of the name Assur as city and also as god appears from Old Assyrian documents from the trading colonies in Cappadocia to have been felt by ancient scribes: there is occasionally a lack of distinction between the two. Additionally, the term *ālum*, 'the city', is used in oaths along with the ruler in contexts where one would anticipate mention of the city god and the ruler. As noticed by LAMBERT (1983), the evidence shows that the god Assur is the deified city. While parallels from the original heartland of Mesopotamian civilization are rare, the deification or numinous character of geographical features is quite commonly attested in Northern Mesopotamia, especially in personal names. Analysis of the combined evidence led LAMBERT (1983) to the hypothesis that the site of the town Assur, which is an impressive natural hill, was a holy spot in prehistoric times. Having been settled as a place of strategic significance, its 'holiness' was exploited both practically—the growth of the town—and ideologically, leading to the dual character of city and god.

In the course of the history of Assyria, the god Assur, who was not originally a *deus persona* and thus did not originally have a family, was made to conform to the theology of southern Mesopotamia. Beginning in the second millennium Assur was given a theological personality by regarding him as the Assyrian Enlil, Enlil being the god of Nippur and one of the most important figures in the pantheon of Babylonia. This opened the way for the gradual adoption by Assur of everything originally pertaining to Enlil, from his wife Ninlil becoming the Assyrian →Mullisu, and later his sons Ninurta and Zababa, through various epithets down to items of furniture. This process of assimilation began in the time of Tukulti-Ninurta I (thirteenth century BCE) and continued into the Sargonid period (eighth to seventh centuries BCE). The only 'family member' of Assur's, not certainly of southern origin, is Šerū'a, and her exact standing is ambiguous.

In the Sargonid period it became a common scribal practice in Assyria to write the name of the god Assur with the signs AN.ŠÁR, originally used to designate a primeval deity in Babylonian theogonies. It seems that an ideological coup lies behind this innovation. In one Babylonian theogonic system, Anšar and Kišar—literally 'whole heaven' and 'whole earth'—precede the senior Babylonian gods Enlil and Ninlil, separated from them by Enurulla and Ninurulla ('Lord' and 'Lady' of the 'primeval city'). By this means the Assyrian Assur, who did not figure in the Babylonian pantheon at all, was made to appear at the head of it. This is explicitly stated in a learned Assyrian explanatory work: "It is said in *Enūma eliš*: When heaven and earth were not yet created, Assur (AN.ŠÁR) came into being" (SAA 3, no. 34:54).

After his sack of Babylon in 689 BCE, Sennacherib attempted to institute a number of religious reforms. These included an endeavour to replace the cult of →Marduk in Babylon by an analogous cult in Assyria with Assur playing the part of Marduk. It appears that, while Assyrian outposts outside Assyria would automatically represent areas where Assur was worshipped, worship of Assur replacing local cults was not required of conquered peoples. Rather, the opposite was the case in the sense that Assyrians ostensibly respected local deities, using them for propaganda purposes by declaring that they had abandoned their worshippers as the Assyrians victoriously advanced. In post-imperial Assyria Assur continues to be attested in personal names and in Aramaic votive inscriptions from the city itself.

III. In the OT *ʾaššûr*, 'Ashur; Assyria', occurs as a designation of the city (Gen 2:4), the country (e.g. Gen 9; Hos 7:11; Isa 7:8) or the people (e.g. Isa 10:5.12; Mic 5:4) of Ashur. The name of the deity occurs as theophoric element in the name of king *ʾēsar-ḥaddôn*, Esarhaddon (Isa 37:38 = 2 Kgs 19:37, Ezra 4:2; cf. the spelling *ʾsrḥʾdn*, Ahiqar:5). The /s/ reflects the Neo-Assyrian pronounciation of the alveolar (MILLARD 1976:9).

IV. *Bibliography*

B. AGGOULA, *Inscriptions et graffites araméens d'Assur* (Napoli 1985); M. COGAN, *Imperialism and Religion: Assyria, Judah and Israel in the Eighth and Seventh Centuries B.C.E.* (Missoula 1974); G. VAN DRIEL, *The Cult of Aššur* (Assen 1969); H. HIRSCH, *Untersuchungen zur altassyrischen Religion* (AfO Beiheft 13/14; Graz 1961); W. G. LAMBERT, The God Aššur, *Iraq* 45 (1983) 82-86; M. T. LARSEN, *The Old Assyrian State and its Colonies* (Copenhagen 1976); B. MENZEL, *Assyrische Tempel* (StPsm 10/I, II; Rome 1981); J. W. MCKAY, *Religion in Judah under the Assyrians, 732-609 B.C.* (London 1973); A. R. MILLARD, Assyrian Royal Names in Biblical Hebrew, *JSS* 21 (1976) 1-14; K. F. MÜLLER, Das assyrische Ritual, *Texte zum assyrischen Königsritual*, I (Leipzig 1937); K. TALLQVIST, *Der assyrische Gott* (StOr 4/3; Helsinki 1932).

A. LIVINGSTONE

ASTARTE עשׁתרת

I. This divine name is found in the following forms: Ugaritic *ʿṯtrt* ('Athtart[u]'); Phoen *ʿštrt* ('Ashtart'); Hebrew *ʿAštōret* (singular); *ʿAštārôt* (generally construed as plural); Egyptian variously *ʿsṯrt*, *ʿsṯrṯ*, *isṯrt*; Greek *Astartē*. It is the feminine form of the masculine *ʿṯtr* ('Athtar', 'Ashtar') and this in turn occurs, though as the name of a goddess, as Akkadian →Ishtar. The Akkadian *Aš-tar-*[*tum*?] is used of her (*AGE* 330). The etymology remains obscure. It is probably, in the masculine form, the name of the planet Venus, then extended to the feminine as well (cf. A. S. YAHUDA, *JRAS* 8 [1946] 174-178). It is unlikely that ROBERTSON SMITH's suggestion (*Religion of the Semites* [Edinburgh 1927³] 99 n. 2, esp. 310, 469-479), referring to Arabic *ʿāṯūr*, 'irrigated land', is of help; because it still leaves the *t*, which cannot be infixed, unexplained. Both god and goddess are probably, but not certainly, to be seen as the deified Venus (HEIMPEL 1982:13-14). This is indeed the case, since if the morning star is the male deity (cf. Isa 14:12), then the goddess would be the evening star: as she is in Greek tradition. (The two appearances of Venus are also probably to be seen as deified, cf. →Shahar and →Shalem.)

II. Ugarit. The goddess Ashtart is mentioned 46 times in the Ugaritic texts, but appears relatively rarely in the mythological texts. These appearances are as follows: in the Baal cycle (*KTU* 1.2 i 7-8) →Baal curses Yam (→sea), inviting →Horon (cf. →Horus!) and 'Ashtart-*šm*-Baal' (see below) to smash his skull—Keret uses the same curse on his son Yaṣib in *KTU* 1.16 vi 54-57, showing it to be formulaic language. When Baal loses control in the divine council at the appearance of Yam's ambassadors, →Anat and Ashtart restrain him forcibly (*KTU* 1.2 i 40). When Baal is about to kill Yam, Ashtart intervenes: either to taunt Baal(?), or more probably to urge him to deliver the *coup de grâce* (*KTU* 1.2 iv 28-30). In the Keret story, in addition to the curse noted above, Hurriya is compared in her beauty with Anat and Ashtart (*KTU* 1.14 iii:41-44 = vi:26-30). The fragmentary *KTU* 1.92 seems to have contained a myth concerning Ashtart (*PRU* 5, 3-5: §1; HERRMANN 1969:6-16). In *KTU* 1. 100, a series of spells against snake-bites, she is paired with Anat (in the order Anat and Ashtart) in ll. 19-24, in addition to further mentions alone, twice as a toponym (cf. *KTU* 1.108. 2). In the fragmentary *KTU* 1.107, another such text, Anat and Ashtart are invoked. The latter appears again as a toponym. In *KTU* 1.114 (the Marziḥu text), Ashtart and Anat (in that order) summon the dog-like Yarihu in order to throw him meat (ll. 9-11); and, when →El becomes drunk, Anat and Ashtart go off to find purgatives, returning as Ashtart and Anat (a chiastic arrangement, ll. 22-26).

The relation of Ashtart and Anat suggested by these occurrences is evidently close. It may represent an early stage in a process of syncretism of the two goddesses. It may be noted that their iconography is similar; because both appear armed and wearing the Egyptian Atef crown. This close relationship is also reflected in the Egyptian evidence. They are commonly understood to be consorts of Baal; but there is no direct evidence for this at Ugarit. The interpretation of various texts as describing sexual intercourse between Anat and Baal has recently been questioned (P. L. DAY, *The Bible and the Politics of Exegesis* [ed. D. Jobling; Cleveland 1991] 141-146, 329-333; id. *JNES* 51 [1992] 181-190), and no such relationship between Ashtart and Baal is mentioned. (The evidence cited could equally well be used to define her as Horon's consort.) The nearest the tradition comes even to associating them is in the title *ʿṯtrt šm bʿl*. This has been interpreted in two ways: as 'Ashtart-name-of-Baal', sc. as the reputation, honour, or even 'Shakti' of Baal (e.g. GINSBERG, *ANET* 130a), or as 'Ashtart-heavens-of-Baal' (DUSSAUD 1947:220-221, who cites Astarte's epithets Asteria, Astroarche, Astronoë and Ourania). The latter sense is to be preferred. This title also appears on Eshmunazar's sarcophagus (below). In addition to various mentions in minor texts, Ashtart appears in the pantheon lists (*KTU* 1.47. 25 = *KTU* 1.118. 24) as the equivalent of Ishtar in RS 20. 24. 24.

Egypt. Astarte is mentioned a number of times in texts from Egypt. In one instance, her name is written *ʿntrt*. Even if this is simply a misspelling, as LECLANT (1960:6 n. 2) suggests, it is still 'revealing' (but cf. *ANET* 201a n. 16). In the *Contendings of Horus and Seth* (iii 4), →Seth is given Anat and Astarte, the daughters of →Re, as wives. This is a mythologisation of the importing of Semitic deities into Egypt under the Hyksos and later, and the New Kingdom fashion for the goddesses in particular. Seth and Baal were identified. But this does not justify retrojecting Egyptian mythological relationships into the Ugaritic context. Anat and Astarte are described in a New Kingdom text (Harris magical papyrus iii 5 in: PRITCHARD [1943:79]) as "the two great goddesses who were pregnant but did not bear", on which basis ALBRIGHT (1956:75) concludes that they are "perennially fruitful without ever losing virginity". He also asserts that "sex was their primary function". Both assumptions are questionable, not to say mutually incompatible! As wives of Seth, who rapes rather than makes love to them, their fruitless conceptions are an extension of his symbolism as the god of disorder, rather than qualities of their own. In the fragmentary 'Astarte papyrus' (*ANET* 17-18; see HELCK 1983) the goddess is the daughter of →Ptah and is demanded by the →Sea in marriage. This myth may be related to a recension of the Ugaritic Baal myth: as well as to that of →Perseus and Andromeda. Astarte's primary characteristic in Egypt is as a war-goddess. An inscription at Medinet Habu (*ARE* iii 62, 105), for instance, says of Rameses III that Mont and Seth are with him in every fray, and Anat and Astarte are his shield. She frequently appears in New Kingdom art armed, wearing the Atef crown and riding a horse (LECLANT 1960). A Ptolemaic text (*ANET* 250 n. 16) calls her "Astarte, Mistress of Horses, Lady of the Chariot". The first part may echo *KTU* 1.86. 6, which appears to link Ashtart (and Anat?) with a horse (*PRU* 5, 189 [§158], WYATT, *UF* 16 [1984] 333-335). In the now lost Winchester stela (EDWARDS, *JNES* 14 [1955] 49) the goddess appears on a lion (a trait normally associated with Ishtar) and was apparently identified with Qadeshet and Anat.

Phoenicia. Though she was undoubtedly an important deity in Phoenicia throughout the first millennium, there is surprisingly little direct written evidence. *KAI* lists only 11 Phoenician examples: ranging from Ur and Egypt to Malta and Carthage. The most important items are the following. The sarcophagus of Tabnit from Sidon dates from the sixth century BCE (*KAI* 13, *ANET* 662a). Since the king is also priest of Ashtart, we may suppose she was an important goddess in the city: if not its patroness. This is in interesting tension with Athirat's apparently similar status in the Keret story (*KTU* 1.14 iv:34-36). The curse of the goddess is invoked against grave-robbers. The sarcophagus of his son Eshmunazar (*KAI* 14, *ANET* 662ab), from the beginning of the following century, states that his mother was priestess of Ashtart; and that the royal family sponsored (rebuilt?) a temple for Ashtart (in the form Ashtart-*šm*-Baal) in →Sidon, thus benefitting her cult in Byblos. A votive throne from south of Tyre, dating to the second century BCE (*KAI* 17), addresses the goddess as 'my Great Lady' (*rbty*); but perhaps without the old ideological overtones. The same expression is used of Ashtart and 'Tanit of the Lebanon' (this may denote a local feature at Carthage) on an inscribed slab, of uncertain date, from Carthage (*KAI* 81).

It will be apparent from the lack of biblical references to a living cult of Anat that the goddess must have undergone some transformation by about the beginning of the first millennium BCE. The constant juxtaposition of the goddesses in the Ugaritic and Egyptian records indicates what must have happened. They appear to have fused into the goddess →Atargatis; although we have just seen that Ashtart also retained her independence for centuries. The name Atargatis (Greek, Aramaic *'tr't'*) is generally agreed to be made up from the Aramaic development of Ashtart (*'štrt*) into Atar (*'tr'* note the weakening of the guttural) together with Anat (*'nt*) weakened by assimilation of the medial *n* into *'t(t)'*. Some see Asherah assimilated to Anat (see ASTOUR, *Hellenosemitica* [1967²] 206); but this is less likely. Occasional inscriptions to the goddess are found in Aramaic (*KAI* 239, 247, 248). Atargatis, in her form at Hierapolis in the second century CE, is the subject of Lucian's work *De Dea Syria*. Lucian writes of Astarte of Sidon, §4, whom he identifies as the →Moon. He also claims that the local priesthood identified her with Europa. He identifies the goddess of Byblos (probably another local Astarte) with →Aphrodite. The common identiate in the Cypriot cult (§6), the Astarte of a temple on the Lebanon mountain (sc. at Afqa), he says was founded by Kinyras (sc. Kinnor) (§9). The goddess (Atargatis) of Hierapolis, founded by Deucalion or Semiramis, he identifies with →Hera or Derceto (§§12, 14). Given the character of Atargatis, it is perhaps significant that Anat is called both 'mistress of dominion' and 'mistress of the high heavens' (*b'lt drkt b'lt šmm rmm*: the Ugaritic equivalents of Derceto and Semiramis) among other titles in *KTU* 1.108. 6-7. Much of Lucian's information seems to be a loose mixture of Greek and Syrian traditions, but still has some genuine echoes from the past. Another important source reflecting a Graeco-Semitic rationalising of tradition is Eusebius' *Praep. Ev.*, which has Astarte as a daughter of Ouranos (→Heaven) and sister to Rhea and Dione: all three become wives of Kronos. Astarte has seven daughters by Kronos. The latter appears to be the equivalent of →El. A direct quotation from Philo Byblius states that "Astarte, the great goddess, and Zeus Demarous, and Adodos king of gods, reigned over the country (sc. Phoenicia) with the consent of Kronos. And Astarte set the head of a bull upon her own head as a mark of royalty, and in traveling round the world she found a →star fallen from the sky, which she took up and consecrated in the holy island Tyre. And the Phoenicians say that Astarte is Aphrodite." (1.10:17-18, 21) The Greek goddess →Artemis may also preserve traits of Phoenician Ashtart (WEST, *UF* 23 [1991] 379-381).

III. The divine name Ashtart occurs nine times in MT, from which one should perhaps be subtracted (1 Sam 7:3) and to which a further instance should perhaps be added, i.e. Judg 3:7. This alteration, widely accepted, is based on the wording of Judg 2:13. It summarises the popular devotions of the pre-monarchical period as apostasy. This verse raises some interesting questions. MT reads *labbaʿal wĕlāʿaštārôt*, using the singular of *baʿal*, (supported by LXX) but, on most scholars' assessment, the plural form for the goddess (supported by LXX!). Thus RSV, REB, read respectively 'the Baals and the Ashtaroth' and 'the baalim and the ashtaroth'. Note, however, that *bĕʿālîm* does occur in the plural in 2:11. (Clearly there is some redundancy in vv 11-13.) RSV recognises the names, though plural. REB genericises them. JB, on the other hand reads 'Baal and Astarte'. The 'Baalim' are often referred to in the plural ('emphatic plural': BDB 127) and are so construed by many commentators. The Ashtaroth are, thus, understood as a class of goddesses. Whether or not *ʾăšērôt* should be corrected at Judg. 3:7, it is the same principle. But, given the phonology of the divine name, we should perhaps question the plural interpretation: even if it be allowed that it came to be understood in this way. The only vocalised forms of the name are, of course, the Hebrew and Greek. The other West Semitic forms are conventionally vocalised 'Ashtart' or 'Athtart'; but it is quite possible that the original vocalisation was **ʿat̲tarāt(u)*, which, with the southern shift of *ā* to *ô* (as in *Dāgān* > *Dāgôn*) would become *ʿaštārôt* in Hebrew. Conversely, the expected singular—if the form found were the plural—would be **ʿaštārâ*, with the final *-at* weakening to *â*. The toponyms mentioned below support this alternative explanation. Further, the three-vowel formation is supported by the other form occurring, viz. *ʿaštōret*. To argue that this formation is due to the adoption of the vowels of *bōšet* begs the question. There would have needed to be at least the vocal skeleton (that is, a word or in this case part of a word carrying two vowels) for the *bōšet* vowels to fit. The adoption of this vowel pattern (*bōšet*) is perhaps not in dispute, though the reason commonly given is arguably misconstrued. JASTROW's suggestion (1894) makes better sense, in offering a closer parallel to the revocalising of the tetragrammaton to carry the vowels of *ʾădōnay*. It is suggested, therefore, that 'Ashtaroth' is in fact a singular form, though it might well come to be interpreted in the plural, as an indication of the scribal tradition's view of the enormity of worshipping other deities, and thus representing all such cults as polytheistic. As for 'Ashtoreth' (*ʿaštōret*), this may well be explained as the singular carrying the vowels of *bōšet*; albeit on JASTROW's understanding of the usage (1894). It is, however, possible that another explanation of this form is the assumption of an early form **ʿaštārit*, in which case the conventional shift of *ā-i* to *ō-ē* (as in *šāpiṭ* > *šōpēṭ*) would occur. If this is so, we should look for dialectal variants of the name.

Judg 10:6, 1 Sam 7:4 and 12:10 all refer to 'the Baals and the Ashtaroth'. In the second instance, LXX has the curious reading *tas Baalim kai ta alsē Astarōth*, "and the (f.!) Baals and the (n. pl.!) groves-Ashtaroth", an impossible combination of Ashtart and Asherah elements, while in the third, LXX reads *tois Baalim kai tois alsesin*. In 1 Sam 7:3 the allusion looks like a secondary addition at the end of the sentence (*hāsîrû ʾet-ʾĕlōhê hannēkār mittôkĕkem wĕhāʿaštārôt*). LXX, however, reads *...kai ta alsē*, thus presupposing *hāʾăšērîm*. In 1 Sam 31:10, the armour of Saul is hung on the walls of 'the temple of Ashtart (*ʿaštārôt*)' (LXX *to Astarteion*, // 1 Chr 10:10: *bêt ʾĕlōhêhem*). Commentators usually change the pointing to *ʿaštōret* (thus SMITH, *The books of Samuel* [ICC Edinburgh 1899] 253) or regard the temple as dedicated to 'the Ashtaroth' (pl.: thus HERZBERG, *I and II Samuel* [London 1964] 233). On the basis of the argument that the form is singular, no change to MT is required.

The other three occurrences all point the name *ʿaštōret* and do not use the article. These passages overtly refer, however, not to an Israelite or Judahite goddess, but to 'Ashtoreth, goddess (*ʾĕlōhê*!) of the Sidonians' in 1 Kgs 11:5.33 as importations by

Solomon to please his wives; while in 2 Kgs 23:13, in the account of Josiah's destruction of Ashtart's shrine, she is referred to as *šiqqūṣ*, →'abomination'. It is probably Ashtart who was denoted by the title →'Queen of heaven', referred to in cults of the end of the monarchy (Jer 7:18; 44:17-19.25).

As well as serving as the divine name, the word appears in the expression *ʿaštĕrōt ṣōʾn* in Deut 7:13; 28:4.18.51. It means something like 'lamb-bearing flocks' or 'ewes of the flock'. This appears to be an application of the name of the goddess as a term for the reproductive capacity of ewes.

It also appears in a toponym, which goes back to the pre-settlement era. It denotes a city named after the goddess. Gen 14:5 mentions Ashtaroth Qarnaim, which ASTOUR (*ABD* 1 [1992] 491; contrast DAY, *ABD* 1 [1992] 492) takes to be Ashtaroth *near* Qarnaim, and identifies with the Ashtaroth associated with →Og king of →Bashan (Josh 9:10). In Josh 21:27, this appears as *bĕʿeštĕrâ*, (LXX *Bosoran* = Bosra!) which should, however, be harmonised with *ʿaštārôt* (LXX *Asērōth*) in 1 Chr 6:56 (71). In Jos 12:4; 13:12.31, this is linked with Edrei (the latter added to Josh 9:10 in LXX), and the two cities appear together as the seat of the chthonian god 'Rapiu' in *KTU* 1.108. 2-3 (most recently PARDEE, *RSO* IV [Textes paramythologiques; Paris 1988] 81, 94-97). It is probably also the city *Aštartu* mentioned in the Amarna letters (*EA* 197:10, 256:21). This pronunciation and obvious sense (as the name of a singular goddess) may be taken to confirm the singular interpretation of the biblical toponym and divine name. It and is supported by the reference to the Beth-Shean temple of the goddess in 1 Sam 31:10. 1 Chr 11:44 is the gentilic of the city.

The problem of pointing may be resolved thus: 'Ashtaroth' is the Hebrew and 'Ashtoreth' a Phoenician (Sidonian) form of the same name. The goddess is well-established as a war-goddess (by the Egyptian epigraphic and iconographic evidence, as well as the trophies offered at Beth Shean), while her 'sexual' role, conceived as primary by ALBRIGHT (1956), is scarcely hinted at by the evidence adduced. It appears, rather, to belong to a blanket judgment on Canaanite goddesses made by biblical scholars on the basis of meagre evidence such as Hosea's sexual allusions. It is better explained as a metaphor for apostasy (cf. B. MARGALIT, *VT* 40 [1990] 278-284). The Hebrew singular form *ʿaštārôt* has subsequently been read as a plural and incorporated into the reference to *bĕʿālîm wĕhāʿaštārôt*. In doing so, it has simply become, like a *bĕʿālîm*, a generic term. It is comparable to the Akkadian expression *ilānu u ištarātu*, 'gods and goddesses'.

IV. *Bibliography*

W. F. ALBRIGHT, *Archeology and the Religion of Israel* (Baltimore 1956[4]) 73-78; P. BORDREUIL, Ashtart de Mari et les dieux d'Ougarit, *MARI* 4 (1989) 545-547; D. J. A. CLINES, Mordecai, *ABD* 4 (1992) 902-904, esp. 902; A. COOPER, Divine names and epithets in the Ugaritic texts, *RSP* III §23, 403-406; J. DAY, Ashtoreth, *ABD* I (1992) 491-494; M. DELCOR, Le culte de la 'Reine du Ciel' selon Jer 7, 18; 44, 17-19, 25 et ses survivances, *Von Kanaan bis Kerala* (FS. Van der Ploeg, eds. W. L. Delsman *et al.*, AOAT 211; Neukirchen-Vluyn 1982) 101-122; R. DUSSAUD, Astarté, Pontos et Baal, *CRAIBL* (1947) 201-224; W. HELCK, Zur Herkunft der Erzählung des sog. "Astarte Papyrus", Fontes atque Pontes. FS. H. Brunner (ed. M. Görg; Wiesbaden 1983) 215-223; W. HEMPEL, A Catalog of Near Eastern Venus Deities, *SMS* 4 (1982) 9-22; W. HERRMANN, Aštart, *MIO* 15 (1969) 6-52; F. O. HVIDBERG-HANSON, La déesse TNT (Copenhagen 1979) i 106-112, ii 147-155; HVIDBERG-HANSON, Uni-Ashtart and Tanit-Iuno Caelestis, *Archaeology and Fertility Cult in the Ancient Mediterranean* (ed. A. Bonanno; Valetta 1986) 170-195; M. JASTROW, The element bošet in Hebrew proper names, *JBL* 13 (1894) 19-30; *J. LECLANT, Astarté à cheval d'après les représentations égyptiennes, *Syria* 37 (1960) 1-67; R. DU MESNIL DU BUISSON, ʿAštart et ʿAštar à Ras-Shamra, *JEOL* 3 (1946) 406; C. A. MOORE, Esther, Book of, *ABD* 2

(1992) 633-643, esp. 633; S. M. OLYAN, Some Observations Concerning the Identity of the Queen of Heaven, *UF* 19 (1987) 161-174; M. H. POPE, ʿAṯtart, ʿAštart, Astarte, WbMyth I/1, 250-252; *J. B. PRITCHARD, *Palestinian Figurines in Relation to Certain Goddesses Known through Literature* (AOS 24; New Haven 1943) 65-76, 90-95; M. WEINFELD, The worship of Molech and the Queen of Heaven and Its Background, *UF* 4 (1972) 133-154.

N. WYATT

ATARGATIS Ἀταργατῖς

I. The goddess Atargatis does not occur in the Bible, but her sanctuary, an Atargateion, is mentioned in 2 Macc 12:26. It was situated near Qarnaim, present day Sheich Saʿad 4 km north of Ashtarot—Qarnaim in the Hauran (cf. 1 Macc 5:42-44; 2 Macc 12:21-23; M. C. ASTOUR, Ashteroth-Karnaim, *ABD* 1 [1992] 49). Her name is a compound of Ashtarte (→Astarte) and ʿAnat (→Anat) and is spelled in various ways: in Aramaic *ʿtrʿth*, *ʿtrʿtʾ*, *ʾtrʿth*, *ʾtrʿtʾ*, *trʿt*, in Greek Ἀταργατῖς, Ἀτάργατις, Ἀτταγάθη, Ἀταράτη, Ἀταργάτη; the apocope form gave Derketo. Her main sanctuary was in Hierapolis/Mabbug in northern Syria, where she was venerated together with →Hadad (→Zeus), the Syrian god of →heaven, rain and fertility. From there her cult spread throughout Syria, northern Mesopotamia and into the West, where she is known as the Dea Syria.

II. The cult of Atargatis in Syria and Mesopotamia is known from a wide variety of literary sources, inscriptions, coins, sculptures and terracottas, which display a range of local variants as well as a general pattern. The earliest phase is represented by a bewildering variety of late 4th and early 3rd cent. BCE coins from Hierapolis. Her name occurs on them as *ʿth* and as *ʿtrʿth*. The original name of the goddess is certainly *ʿth*, whereas the element *ʿtr*, derived from *ʿštr*, has the meaning of goddess, so that the full name *ʿtrʿth* means "the goddess ʿAteh", ʿAteh being the goddess par excellence. The name *ʿth* is the Aramaic form of Anat and frequently occurs as a theophoric element in proper names in Syria and northern Mesopotamia (DRIJVERS 1980:88). The goddess is represented on these coins with a turreted tiara, with a lion or riding on a lion, between two sphinxes or enthroned, with a variety of objects in her right hand, a branch or a cup, and sometimes leaning on a sceptre. This iconographical repertoire represents a mother goddess, a protecting *potnia thērōn*, with life-giving and protective aspects. It is partly related to the iconography of →Cybele, the Magna Mater. Coins from Hierapolis from the 2nd and 3rd cent. CE usually picture an enthroned Atargatis between two lions with different attributes in her hand, tympanum, ears of corn, staff or spindle, mirror, sceptre, semeion, or a leaf, and with different jewellery and headdress, sometimes with fishes or →doves. Another type is Atargatis with a mural crown. As such she functions as the →Tyche of Hierapolis and other Syrian and Mesopotamian towns like Edessa, Harran, Nisibis, Resh Aina and Palmyra. Other iconographical types are an enthroned Atargatis accompanied by one lion, without lions, or in a standing position. This variety is partly caused by the spread of the dominant cult of Hierapolis throughout the Syrian and Mesopotamian area and the subsequent adaption of local cults of mother goddesses modelled on that of Hierapolis. The wide range of variants in the iconography as well as in the epigraphic repertoire of Atargatis demonstrates this process of religious assimilation which made Atargatis of Hierapolis into the Dea Syria venerated throughout the Roman empire. Lucian of Samosata wrote his *De Syria Dea* in the second century CE on the goddess of Hierapolis, her sanctuary and her cult in which he relates her to a range of other goddesses such as →Hera, →Athena, →Aphrodite, →Artemis, Nemesis and the Moirai, in order to explain her real character. She displays therefore aspects which are represented by other goddesses in hellenistic culture. This process often makes it difficult to decide whether the cult of Atargatis at a certain place is actually a branch of the sanctuary of Hierapolis or a local cult of a mother goddess adapted to the practice of Hierapolis/Mabbug.

At Hierapolis Atargatis' sanctuary functioned as an asylum, where it was strictly forbidden to kill an animal or a human being, in accordance with the goddess' life-giving and protective character. Emasculation was practised in her cult, a custom later widely observed in Christian Syria. A large pond with fish, usually carps, was part of her sanctuary at Hierapolis and at other places, e.g. at Edessa and on the island of Delos, and symbolised Atargatis' life-giving and fertility aspects. Purification rites were certainly part of her cult as well as a taboo on certain food.

III. The sanctuary of Atargatis near Qarnaim (2 Macc 12:26) has not been found by archaeologists. An altar from Tell el-Ashʿari near ancient Qarnaim is dedicated to *Artemidi tēi kurāi*, the mistress Artemis (IGR III, 1163; see D. SOURDEL, *Les cultes du Hauran à l'époque romaine* [Paris 1952] 42). Since Artemis is equivalent to Atargatis in various inscriptions from Syria, Artemis is here just another name of Atargatis, which highlights her character of protectress of animal and human life in the semi-nomad culture of the mainly Nabatean and Arab population of hellenistic Hauran. In such a society a sanctuary of Atargatis functioned as an asylum. The text of 2 Macc 12:21-26 suggests that Judas Maccabaeus' enemies took refuge inside the temenos of Atargatis, where Judas killed them (see E. KAUTZSCH, *Apokryphen und Pseudepigraphen des Alten Testaments* I [Tübingen 1900] 111, note c.). F. BAETHGEN (*Beiträge zur semitischen Religionsgeschichte* [Berlin 1988] 68; cf. e.g. J. A. MONTGOMERY & H. S. GEHMAN, *Kings* [ICC; Edinburgh 1951] 474; J. GRAY, *I & II Kings* [London ^{3}1977] 654) equated the enigmatic deity →Tartak, venerated by the settlers coming from Avvah (2 Kgs 17:31) with Atargatis. Since this identification is very unlikely from an etymological point of view, this interpretation is now abandoned (cf. L. K. HANDY, Tartak, *ABD* 6 [1992] 334-335).

IV. *Bibliography*

H. J. W. DRIJVERS, *Cults and Beliefs at Edessa* (EPRO 72; Leiden 1980) 76-121; DRIJVERS, Sanctuaries and Social Safety, *Visible Religion. Annual for Religious Iconography* 1 (1982) 65-75; DRIJVERS, Dea Syria, *LIMC* III, 355-358; N. GLUECK, *Deities and Dolphins. The Story of the Nabataeans* (London 1965) 359-392; M. HÖRIG, *Dea Syria. Studien zur religiösen Tradition der Fruchtbarkeitsgöttin in Vorderasien* (AOAT 208; Neukirchen-Vluyn 1979); HÖRIG, *Dea Syria—Atargatis*, ANRW II, 17,3 (1983) 1536-1581; R. MOUTERDE, Dea Syria en Syrie, *MUSJ* 23 (1942-43) 137-142; R. A. ODEN, *Studies in Lucian's De Syria Dea* (HSM 15; Missoula 1977); H. SEYRIG, Les dieux de Hiérapolis, *Syria* 37 (1960) 233-252; SEYRIG, Le monnayage de Hiérapolis de Syrie à l'époque d'Alexandre, *Revue numismatique* (1971) 11-12; P.-L. VAN BERG, *Corpus Cultus Deae Syriae* 1. *Les sources littéraires*, 2 vols. (EPRO 28; Leiden 1972); F. R. WALTON, Atargatis, *RAC* 1 (1950) 854-860.

H. J. W. DRIJVERS

ATHENA Ἀθηναία, Ἀθήνη

I. Athena is the main polis divinity in Greek religion. The Romans identified her with Minerva (etrusc. Menrva); the Greeks themselves found numerous homologues in the Ancient Near east, e.g. the Egyptian Neith of Saïs (MORA 1985:95) and the Ugaritic-Syrian →Anat (*CIS* 1,95). The affiliation between the armed Greek goddess and Near Eastern armed goddesses like Anat or →Ishtar (COLBOW 1991) is controversial, but Oriental influence is plausible. In the Bible, Athena occurs only as the root element in the toponym Athens (Acts 17:15) and in the anthroponym Athenobius (1 Macc 15:28).

II. An early form of her name, *Atana potinija*, is attested in a Bronze Age Linear B tablet from Knossos (GÉRARD-ROUSSEAU 1968:44-45). The meaning is disputed; presumably, it is "Mistress of (a place called) At(h)ana". The debate about the priority of Athenai (Athens) or Athena now favours the place name; the Homeric and later forms of her name, 'Αθηναία - 'Αθηναίη, are most easily understood as adjectives, "She from Athana(i)", "The Lady of Athens"; the Homeric epithet *Alalkemeneis* connects her with another town, the small Boeotian Alalakomenai.

A fundamental function of Athena is the protection of cities; as such, she bears the epithet Polias or Poliouchos. This function is already present in Homer. In time of crisis, the women of Troy offer a *peplos* to her enthroned image and pray for her protection (*Iliad* 6,302-303). Athens especially is defined through her cult and mythology (*Iliad* 2,549-550). In later texts, one of her main epithets is Polias or Poliouchos, and her temple is attested on many acropoleis throughout the Greek world; only Apollo is as often attested as owner of a main polis sanctuary.

After the Minoan and Mycenaean Bronze Age culture had been discovered as the possible precursors of Greek culture, scholars tried to derive Athena's paramount function and character from the role of a Mycenaean palace goddess which in turn would go back to a Minoan house goddess (NILSSON 1950:488-501). The main argument for the first thesis was that in Mycenae and presumably in Athens a temple of Athena in the first millennium preserved the location of a Mycenaean palace; other arguments—her relationship to the snake which had been understood as the guardian of the house, with the so-called Shield Goddess of Mycenae, known from iconographical sources—seemed to point in the same direction; the Minoan roots were seen in her association with snake and bird. The derivation remains hypothetical at best; especially the thesis of a Minoan origin seems to read diachronically what could also be viewed functionally.

Her protection takes two forms, that of a talismanic statuette of an armed goddess whose possession guarantees the safety of a town (the palladium, which Herodotus 4,189 defines as a "statue of (Pallas) Athena"), and that of her being the goddess of war or rather of warriors. According to myth, Troy would survive as long as the palladium was inside; the town fell, after Odysseus and Diomedes had stolen it. Other towns claimed to possess it afterwards, chiefly Athens (Pausanias 1,28,9) and Rome (Livy 5,52,7 etc.); in all cases, the story fits a pattern of myth and ritual which need not be connected with Athena.

Like the Palladion, Athena usually bears weapons, helmet, lance, and shield. As a warrior goddess, Athena is differentiated from →Ares, the god of war, though the two are often paired together as divinities of war and battle (e.g. Homer, *Iliad* 5,430). Ares represents the fierce forces of fighting and killing without relationship to polis life where he has no important festivals; as a foreigner to the polis, myth makes him come from Thrace (Homer, *Iliad* 13,301). Athena, on the other hand, is the warlike protectress of the polis against enemy attacks; as such, she protects the warriors. This role is reflected in the protection of mythical heroes, especially young ones like Achilles (*Iliad*) and Jason, but also Odysseus (*Odyssey*). This has been taken to mirror her role in initiation rituals of young warriors (BREMMER 1978); in fact, her connection with rituals which derive from this fundamental institution is somewhat tenuous: in the Athenian Aglaurion, she received the ephebic oath as Athena Areia, together with Ares, Enyo, Enyalios and other local divinities (M. N. TODD, *A selection of Greek Historical Inscriptions* II [Oxford 1948] no. 204), and she was the main divinity in the Attic-Ionian festival of the Apatouria (besides →Zeus) whose function—the integration of young members into the phratry—reflects similar concerns.

She is more prominent as a divinity presiding over the ritual passage of young girls into society, especially but not exclusively in Athens. The Athenian Arrhephoroi, two girls from noble families, had to serve a year on the acropolis. Their ritual obligations associate them with female adult life, their main duty being to start weaving the *peplos* for the goddess, their cultic roles bringing them together also with the cult of →Aphrodite; their aetiological myth, the story of Erichthonios and the daughters of

Cecrops, focuses rather on the themes of sexuality and its dangers (BURKERT 1966). Similar rituals lie behind, e.g. the ritual of the Locrian Maidens who were annually sent to Athena Ilias (GRAF 1978).

Compared to →Artemis, who is more prominent as a protectress of young women but whose main concern is with their biological function, Athena's domain is the correct social behaviour of women; from this stems her function as Ergane, in which she presides over the female work. But the role of Athena Ergane was more global: together with Hephaestus, she protected also the artisans over whose skills she watched; she had found out how to harness a horse, had taught how to build ships (her first construction was Jason's Argo) and had cultivated the olive tree. The common denominator of these functions, as DETIENNE & VERNANT (1974) pointed out, is Athena's role as purveyor of practical intelligence and cleverness as a fundamental ingredient of civilization; the myth of her contest with →Poseidon over the possession of Athens which was decided by the respective gifts, a salty spring from Poseidon, the cultivated olive tree from Athena, confront and evaluate miraculous nature which is socially useless as opposed to socially very useful nature, which has been transformed and civilized.

Athena's main Athenian festivals give ritual expression to these themes; they cluster around the beginning of Athenian year in the month Hekatombaion (July-August) (DEUBNER 1932:9-39; BURKERT 1977:347-354). The cycle begins towards the end of the last month but one, Thargelion (May-June): on its 25th day, the Plynteria ("Cleansing Festival"), the old wooden image of Athena on the acropolis was ritually cleansed: its garments and ornaments were taken off, the image was carried to the sea, bathed, and brought back towards night onto the acropolis, where it was clad with a new *peplos*. The ritual depicts, in an easily understandable and widely diffused symbolism, the periodical renewal of the city's religious centre. Early in the following month (MIKALSON 1975:167), during the Arrhephoria, the Arrhephoroi ended their year of service on the acropolis by a secret ritual which brought them from the realm of Athena to the one of Aphrodite (Pausanias 1,27,3), thus designating the passage to female adulthood; city and demes celebrated the day with sacrifices, i.e. to the polis protectors Athena Polias and Zeus Polieus, and to Kourotrophos, the protectress of human offspring.

The first month of the year saw two state festivals of Athena which both dramatized the polis itself. On Hecatombaion 16, the Synoikia recalled the (mythical) constitution of the polis from independent villages by Theseus; the goddess received a sacrifice on the acropolis. After the ritual refounding of Athens, the Panathenaia of Hecatombaion 28 presented the polis in all its splendour. Its main event was an impressive procession, idealized in Pheidias' frieze of the Parthenon; it moved from the margin of the city to its heart, the acropolis, and exhibited all constituent parts of the polis, from its officials at the head to its young warriors at the end; in the centre, it carried the new *peplos* for the goddess, which had been begun by the Arrhephoroi and was finished by representatives of all Athenian women. The presentation of this new garment links this final festival to the beginning of the cycle, the Plynteria. It also connects the Panathenaia with a further Athenian festival outside the New Year cycle, the Chalkeia of Pyanopsion 30 (October-November), in which the artisans, especially the metalworkers, led a sacrificial procession to Athena Ergane and Hephaistos.

Though her main festivals seem to express an understandable and easy symbolism, her mythology is not without paradoxes—she is not only a virgin and a female warrior, but also the mother of Erichthonios, sprung from the head of her father, fully armed; she is closely connected with the snake and the owl, animals of earth and night. Evolutionary models dissolved the tensions into a historical fusion of heterogeneous elements (synthesis NILSSON 1963:

433-444); KERÉNYI (1952) tried to dissolve some of the paradoxes with the help of analytical psychology; contemporary scholarship seems reluctant to follow and prefers functional analyses.

Athena's powers are ambivalent. Her warlike qualities protect the town but also make use of the horrors of war: her main symbol, often used as a deadly weapon, is the aegis; it contains the Gorgon's head surrounded by snakes whose looks turned all on-lookers to stone. Besides, she shares this ambivalence with the young warriors themselves who are positioned outside polis society. Her practical intelligence also is ambivalent because it is open to abuse; her mother Metis, "Crafty Intelligence", could have offspring which threatened Zeus' powers, therefore, the god swallowed the pregnant goddess and gave birth to Athena from his head (Hesiod, *Theog.*886-900. 924-926). The myth is comparable to the one of the ambivalent →Dionysos; similar to possible Near Eastern narrative models (KIRK 1970:215-217), the story evaluates civilizing intelligence as having a Zeus-like power, but lying outside the norms of nature; Hephaestos, the divine blacksmith and artisan, shares some of these ambivalences.

III. The Bible never mentions Athena, although Athens and the Athenians occur several times in NT (Acts 17:15-16; 17:21-22; 18:1; 1 Thess 3:1). Paul's discourse on the Areopagus (Acts 17:22) stresses the religious zeal of the Athenians without giving any details except the altar of the →Unknown God.

IV. *Bibliography*

J. BREMMER, Heroes, Rituals and the Trojan War, *Studi storico-religiosi* 2 (1978) 5-38; W. BURKERT, Kekropidensage und Arrhephoria. Vom Initiationsritus zum Panathenäenfest, *Hermes* 94 (1966) 1-25; BURKERT, *Griechische Religion der archaischen und klassischen Epoche* (RdM 15; Stuttgart 1977); G. COLBOW, *Die kriegerische Ištar. Zu den Erscheinungsformen bewaffneter Gottheiten zwischen der Mitte des 3. und der Mitte des 2. Jahrtausends* (Münchener Vorderasiatische Studien 12; Munich 1991); M. DETIENNE & J. P. VERNANT, *Les ruses de l'intelligence. La mètis des grecs* (Paris 1974); L. DEUBNER, *Attische Feste* (Berlin 1932); M. GÉRARD-ROUSSEAU, *Les mentions religieuses dans les tablettes mycéniennes* (Incunabula Graeca 29; Rome 1968); F. GRAF, Die lokrischen Mädchen, *Studi storico-religiosi* 2 (1978) 61-79; C. J. HERINGTON, *Athena Parthenos and Athena Polias* (Manchester 1955); K. KERÉNYI, *Die Jungfrau und Mutter der griechischen Religion. Eine Studie über Pallas Athene* (Albae Vigiliae, N.S. 12; Zürich 1952); G. S. KIRK, *Myth. Its Meaning and Function in Ancient and Other Culture* (Sather Classical Lectures 40, Berkeley 1970); J. D. MIKALSON, *The Sacred and Civil Calendar of the Athenian Year* (Princeton 1975); F. MORA, *Religione e religioni nelle storie di Erodoto* (Milan 1985); M. P. NILSSON, *Minoan-Mycenaean Religion and its Survival in Greek Religion,* 2nd edition (Lund 1950); NILSSON, *Geschichte der griechischen Religion. Erster Band: Die Religion Griechenlands bis auf die griechische Weltherrschaft*, 3rd edition (*HAW* V/2.1; Munich 1965).

F. GRAF

ATUM

I. Atum, sun god and eldest of the Ennead of Heliopolis, occurs in the Bible in the place-name Pithom (Exod 1:11), Gk Πατουμος, Eg *Pr-Itm* 'House of Atum'. Recently, it has been suggested to explain the place-name Etam (Exod 13:20; Num 33:6-8), the etymology of which H. CAZELLES was unable to determine with certainty (CAZELLES, Les localisations de l'Exode et la critique littéraire, *RB* 62 [1955] 321-364, 357-359) as an abbreviated spelling *(Pr)-Itm* '(House) of Atum' (M. GÖRG, Etam und Pitom, *BN* 51 [1990] 9-10). K. MYŚLIWIEC (*Zur Ikonographie des Gottes ῞ΗΡΩΝ* [StAeg 3; 1977] 89-97) connects the Greek name with ῞Ηρων (Heron), a god who is related to Atum (Heron-Atum). It is highly probable that Pithom/Heroopolis can be identified with Tell el-Maskhutah at the east end of the Wadi Tumilat, where a temple of Atum has been found (A. B. LLOYD, *Herodotus Book II, Commentary 99-182* [EPRO 43; Leiden 1988] 154-155). According to BLEIBERG (1983) the evidence for identifying Pithom with Heroopolis is inconclusive.

The name Atum is generally interpreted as a derivation from the Egyptian stem *tm* which can mean 'not to be' as well as 'to be complete' (BERGMAN 1970:51-54; MYŚLIWIEC 1979:78-83). In religious language, the different aspects of a god are often reflected in his name. Using theological puns, the Egyptians associated the name Atum with the complicated divine nature of the god who created the world by developing the potencies of his primordial unity into the plurality of the well-ordered cosmos. Though in the Hebrew Bible the god Atum occurs only as an element in toponyms, his role as a creator god bears some remarkable similarities with that of →Yahweh in biblical thought.

II. Atum was a highly speculative god (BARTA 1973:80-81), whose divine being was elaborated by the theologians in a cosmogonical doctrine. In the beginning there was, according to this doctrine, the Nun, a lightless and limitless abyss. The Nun represented the undifferentiated unity of the precreation state which the Egyptians conceived of as non-being. The Nun was the primary substance, the sum of virtualities, from which all life emerged. Nun is termed the Eldest One and the father of the gods (*CT* VI 343.j-344.g). Still Atum was not a younger and thus secondary god. He was coexistent and consubstantial with the →Chaos (J. ASSMANN, *Zeit und Ewigkeit im alten Ägypten. Ein Beitrag zur Geschichte der Ewigkeit* [AHAW 1; Heidelberg 1975] 21). Atum was a god who had no father and no mother. He was mysterious of birth, because he was unbegotten and came into being by spontaneous self-generation (DE BUCK 1947; cf. the self-produced [αὐτόγονος] and unbegotten [ἀγέννητος] god of the *Corpus Hermeticum*: F. DAUMAS, Le fonds égyptien de l'hermétisme, *Gnosticisme et monde hellénistique. Actes du Colloque de Louvain-la-Neuve 11-14 mai 1980* [Louvain-la-Neuve 1982] 3-25, esp. 19-20). The god owed his powerful creative force to nothing outside himself. He was the *causa sui.* Paradoxically, Atum and Nun were both absolute gods and they both could claim the priority which is a characteristic of a creator god (J. ZANDEE, De Hymnen aan Amon van papyrus Leiden I 350, *OMRO* 28 [1947] 66-75, 112-120).

Before creation, Atum was entirely alone in the Nun. According to Egyptian conceptions, the solitude of a god points to his primacy as a creator god (ASSMANN 1979:23-24). Atum was the primordial god who was regarded as already existing when nothing as yet existed (GRAPOW 1931:34-38). The urge, however, to create was inherent to Atum's nature. Being a creator god, Atum was in fact the creative will, the *causa efficiens*, which performed the transition from pre-existence to existence. In the older Heliopolitan version (S. SAUNERON & J. YOYOTTE, La naissance du monde selon l'Egypte ancienne, *La naissance du monde* [SO 1; Paris 1959] 17-91, esp. 46), the actual creative act is explained in terms of sexual appetite as the inclination towards Being (ASSMANN 1969:203-204, with references; cf. the Orphic cosmogonical Eros and →Zeus, who turned into Eros when about to create). Being alone in the Nun, the god had no female partner with whom to produce offspring. As characteristic of a creator god, Atum was a unity embracing both masculine and feminine elements (S. SAUNERON, Remarques de philologie et d'étymologie (en marge des textes d'Esna), *Mélanges Mariette* [IFAO 32; Cairo 1961] 229-249 § "Le Créateur androgyne"). Plurality is immanent in the primordial nature of Atum. In the same manner, creator goddesses like →Isis and →Neith were masculine for 2/3 in their nature and feminine for 1/3 (*ibid.* 244). Atum was man-woman, 'He-She' (Eg *pn tn*: *CT* II 161.a; cf. the dichotomic creator god in Gnosticism and the Neo-Platonic *Corpus Hermeticum*: P. LABIB, Egyptian Survivals in the Nag Hammadi

Library, *Nag Hammadi and Gnosis. Papers read at the First International Congress of Coptology, Cairo, December 1976* [NHS 14; Leiden 1978] 149-151; W. SCOTT, *Hermetica* III [Boston 1985] 135; Gen 1:1: Elohim created the world without a consort). The *actus purus* then is described as an act of masturbation. The god masturbated, swallowed his seed and gave birth to his son Shu by spitting him out and to his daughter Tefnut by vomiting her forth (*Pyr.* 1248.a-d; *CT* I 345.c, II 18.a-b; cf. *NHC* V 81.17-18; Philo of Alexandria, *Ebr.* 30: the creation of the visible world is the result of an act of begetting). In the Books of the Underworld (HORNUNG 1984:372, 438), ithyphallic creatures are often depicted as creative forces. →Apis, bull-god of fertility, is associated with Atum. Atum was the great masturbator (Eg *iw.s ꜥꜣ.s*) of Heliopolis who begot by using his fist and brought forth by his mouth which functioned as a womb (J. ZANDEE, Sargtexte, Spruch 77 (*CT* II, 18), *ZÄS* 100 [1973] 71-72). In texts dating to the Ptolemaic period, the goddess →Hathor had been introduced as the hypostasis of the god's sexual desire, whereas Jusaas (Eg *iw.s ꜥꜣ.s*, 'as she comes she grows (?)', a pun) had become the hypostasis of the acting hand (DERCHAIN 1972). It has been suggested that the Heliopolitan conception of creation resulting from masturbation found expression in the ithyphallic demiurge →Bes Pantheos and in the name Adoil *ydwʾl*, 'His-hand-is-god', in *2 Enoch* (*Religions en Egypte hellénistique et romaine. Colloque de Strasbourg 16-18 mai 1967* [Paris 1969] 31-34). It has also been supposed to be reflected in the rays of Aton ending in small hands reaching out to the King and the Queen in their role of Shu and Tefnut (K. MYŚLIWIEC, Amon, Atum and Aton: The Evolution of Heliopolitan Influences in Thebes, *L'Egyptologie en 1979. Axes prioritaires de recherches* [Colloques internationaux du C.N.R.S. 595; Paris 1982] 285-289). Tefnut was regarded as the hand of god (H. BRUNNER, *LdÄ* 3 [1980] 217-218).

Atum performed the creation on the Primordial Hill, a cosmic place, which was identified with the god (BARTA 1973:82) and later to be surmounted by the temple of Heliopolis. The god alighted at dawn on the Hill in the shape of the Bennu, a bird whose name could be a play upon the name *bnbn* of the Primordial Hill, on *wbn* 'to rise (of the sun)' and perhaps on *bnn* 'to beget' (ASSMANN 1969:203). It has been pointed out, that the Bennu is often depicted on a standard (V. NOTTER, *Biblischer Schöpfungsbericht* [SBS 68; Stuttgart 1974] 47) which was symbolic of victory over Chaos (ASSMANN 1969:195-196). The hierophany of the god drove off Chaos and called the well-ordered Cosmos into being. Atum was also said to have ascended from the chaos-waters with the appearance of a snake, the animal renewing itself every morning (BD 87). Chaos, however, was considered to be still immanent in the Cosmos (DERCHAIN 1962:177-178; H. HORNUNG, Chaotische Bereiche in der geordneten Welt, *ZÄS* 81 [1956] 28-32). At the creation, Atum reversed his nature of non-being and for this reason Chaos and Cosmos differred, not in contents, but in their organization. Creation is organised Chaos (DERCHAIN 1962:183). In the famous eschatological text BD 175 (J. ASSMANN, *Zeit und Ewigkeit* [AHAW; 1975] 24-26, with references to similar texts), which was still current in the Graeco-Roman period (E. OTTO, Zwei Paralleltexte zu TB 175, *CdE* 37 [1962] 249-256), Atum tells of his decision to annihilate the world he created, restoring it to its original state of Chaos (S. SCHOTT, Altägyptische Vorstellungen vom Weltende, *Studia biblica et orientalia*, III: *Oriens antiquus* [AnBib 12; Roma 1959] 319-330). Atum was the god of pre-existence and post-existence (ASSMANN 1979:23). The demiurge, who encompassed being and non-being as *coincidentia oppositorum*, causes both creation and annihilation (cf. Deut 32:39: "I destroy and I heal"). Only →Osiris was to remain as the Lord of Eternity together with Atum after the god had turned himself into his primordial form of a snake, symbol of time and eternity (L. KÁKOSY, Osiris - Aion, *OrAnt* 3 [1964] 15-25, 20-21, with references). In the Book of the Underworld *Amduat* (5th hour; see HORNUNG 1984:102-103, bottom register), the eschatological snake seems to be depicted in the cave of Sokaris containing the Chaotic powers of the Underworld. In the 11th hour of *Amduat* (HORNUNG 1984:174-175, upper register), Atum has taken on his human shape after the Chaotic powers had been defeated. To gain immortality, the deceased (= Osiris) is equated with Atum (BERGMAN 1970:53-54). A bronze statuette of Atum shows the god with the attributes of Osiris (J. BAINES, A bronze statuette of Atum, *JEA* 56 [1970] 135-140). In BD 87, the deceased wishes to turn into the shape of the snake Sato (Eg *sꜣ tꜣ,* 'son of the →earth'), the embodiment of Atum (M.-T. DERCHAIN-URTEL, *Die Schlange des "Schiffbrüchigen"* [SAK 1; 1974] 83-104, 90-92). Atum represents life after death (*CT* V.291.k). Atum and Osiris are often paired on stelae (K. MYŚLIWIEC, Beziehungen zwischen Atum und Osiris nach dem Mittleren Reich, *MDAIK* 35 [1979] 195-213) and at the Judgment of the →Dead Atum acts in favour of the deceased (R. GRIESHAMMER, *Das Jenseitsgericht in den Sargtexten* [ÄA 20; Wiesbaden 1970] 76-77).

Atum did not create from a primary substance but the god emanated, thus producing Shu, the air-god and his twin sister Tefnut (moisture?). Creation begins with the transition from unity to duality (B. STRICKER, Tijd, *OMRO* Supplement 64 [1983] 42-82, 64 n. 222; BERGMAN 1970:59-61). Shu and Tefnut became the parents of Geb, the earth, and his sister and wife Nut, the sky. Creation was a theogony and a cosmogony at the same time. The theologians incorporated the gods Isis, Osiris, →Seth and Nephthys, who reflected the social and political *conditio humana*, into the cosmogony. The gods constituted the Great Ennead of Heliopolis, i.e. the epiphany or Pleroma of Atum, who was called the creator of the gods (MYŚLIWIEC 1979:171-172) and the Great Bull of the Ennead, referring to his priority as a creator god. Atum is the god of many descendants (RYHINER 1977:132 n. 39). The Ennead was in fact the genealogical tree of the Pharaoh (BARTA 1973:41-48), headed by Atum and at the bottom →Horus, the god connected with historical times (ASSMANN 1984:144-148). Pharaoh was of cosmic dimensions and of primeval birth (L. KÁKOSY, *The primordial birth of the king* [StAeg 3; Budapest 1977] 67-73). He was crowned by Atum (*ARE* 2 [1906] 89-90, 92), his father (BARTA 1973:162), who once ruled the earth but was said to be weary of his reign (*Book of the Divine Cow*: E. HORNUNG, *Der ägyptische Mythos von der Himmelskuh. Eine Ätiologie des Unvollkommenen* [OBO 46; Freiburg, Göttingen 1982]). In his human shape, Atum is depicted wearing a bull's tail and the double crown, symbols of royalty (MYŚLIWIEC 1979:197, 213-227). As the god's representative on earth (R. ANTHES, Der König als Atum in den Pyramidentexten, *ZÄS* 110 [1983] 1-9), Pharaoh mediates between gods and men, thus maintaining the cosmic harmony (ASSMANN 1979:21, with references).

According to the Shu-spells *CT* I 314-II 45 (R. FAULKNER, Some notes on the god Shu, *JEOL* 18 [1964] 266-270), Shu was not generated through an act of self-begetting but Atum created him in his mind and exhaled him through his nostrils together with his sister Tefnut. The god embraced his children, thus guaranteeing the continuity of divine life and of the cosmic harmony which resulted from the god's creative act (ASSMANN 1969:103-105; MYŚLIWIEC 1978: 17). The name Shu is derived from Eg *šwj* 'to be empty' and Eg *šw* 'air', 'light' (BERGMAN 1970:54-55, with references). The god separated the sky and the earth (H. TE VELDE, The theme of the separation of heaven and earth, StAeg 3 [1977] 161-170), thus creating the cosmic space to be filled with the god's divine *parousia*. In fact, Shu was a second creator god, who sustained the world with life-giving air. Shu was created from the breath of Atum (e.g. *CT* I.338b, 345.b-c, 372b-374b). At the creation, Atum appeared from the chaos-waters as the Bennu, a bird connected with air and for this reason often compared with the breath of Elohim moving on the waters (V. NOTTER,

Biblischer Schöpfungsbericht [SBS 68; Stuttgart 1974] 46-54). Atum initiated the creation but he remained outside the created world with which he was connected through his son Shu (ASSMANN 1979:24-25). His hypostases, Shu and Tefnut, were the cosmic principles of life itself rather than constellative gods dominating a specific department (ASSMANN 1984:209-215).

Shu and Tefnut had been with their father in a spiritual state (*CT* 80). They were of one being (ὁμοούσιος) with Atum, thus making a trinitarian unity (DE BUCK 1947; S. MORENZ, *Ägyptische Religion* [RdM 8; Stuttgart 1970] 272-273, with references to Christian views on Trinity). Conceptually, the world existed before the actual creation. Creation by means of the divine Spirit and Word is considered to be a genuine Heliopolitan conception by some scholars, but according to others it has been taken from the Memphite cosmogonical myth (J. ZANDEE, Hymnical Sayings addressed to the Sun god by the High-priest of Amun Nebwenenef, from his tomb in Thebes, *JEOL* 18 [1964] 253-265). D. MÜLLER (Die Zeugung durch das Herz, *Or* 35 [1966] 256-274) has shown that creation by means of masturbation is inseparably linked to the god's heart or creative Spirit. At the creation, Atum mentioned the names of the primordial gods (*CT* II 7c-8a). Hu, the creative Word, and Sia, Intelligence, are the first-born children of →Re-Atum (BD 17, *CT* IV 227b-230b). They assisted at the creation and made life possible (ASSMANN 1969: 145). Atum created the world with his heart and his tongue (= Spirit and Word, ZANDEE 1964); cf. the role of pre-existential →Wisdom (*sophia/ḥokmâ*) and Word (→*logos/ dābār*) in e.g. Gen 1:1, Ps 33:6, 4 Ezra 6:38, John 1:1, Sir 1:1-4, 24:1-9.

The unique and single creative act by means of the Divine Word is opposed to the principle of cyclic creation. In the solar cycle, Atum usually represents the aging sun god, the Old One, to whom the solar Night-Bark was assigned (MYŚLIWIEC 1979:163-164). Atum is also regarded as the →moon, the sun's substitute at night (P. DERCHAIN, Mythes et dieux lunaires en Egypte, *La lune, mythes et rites* [SO 5; Paris 1962] 17-68). A bronze statuette shows Atum having the features of an old man (J. BAINES, A bronze statuette of Atum, *JEA* 56 [1970] 135-140; BAINES, Further remarks on statuettes of Atum, *JEA* 58 [1972] 303-306). In trigrams representing the three phases of the sun god (Khepri-Re-Atum), the god is symbolised by the hieroglyph of an old man leaning on a staff (RYHINER 1977:125-137). In the binary solar cycle, Atum is opposed to Khepri, the young sun god, whose name is derived from Eg *ḫpr* 'to become' (J. ASSMANN, Chepre, *LdÄ* 1 [1975] 934-940). Khepri-Atum encompassed the sunrise and the sunset, thus reflecting the entire solar cycle. In the *Book of the Earth* (HORNUNG 1984:430, 444), Khepri and Atum represent the Beginning and the End. In the context of *PGM* VII 515-524, the *vox magica* AΩ 'the First One and the Last One' could be interpreted as the composite Khepri-Atum (J. BERGMAN, *Ancient Egyptian Theogony*, [Numen supplement 43; Leiden 1982] 36; cf. Rev 21:6: "I am AΩ, the Beginning and the End"). The sun-disc is often depicted containing Khepri and the ram-headed sun god (= Atum: MYŚLIWIEC 1978:39-68). At the sunset as well as during the journey through the Underworld, Atum is regarded as the Living One (ASSMANN 1969:142-143). The entrance of the god at night into the body of Nut is equated with sexual union. Atum becomes the *Kamutef* 'Bull of his Mother', begetter of his own mother (*CT* I 237b, II 60c; BARTA 1973:150), who at dawn gives birth to Atum as the young sun calf (MYŚLIWIEC 1978:38) or as a beautiful lad. The god is *Puer-Senex*, thus showing the features of the pantheistic sun god (RYHINER 1977:137; cf. E. JUNOD, Polymorphie du dieu sauveur, *Gnosticisme et monde hellénistique. Actes du Colloque de Louvain-la-Neuve 11-14 mai 1980* [Louvain-la-Neuve 1982] 38-46). At night the god received his own eye (= sun-disc), vehicle of the young sun god and agent of renewal, and protected it during the journey through the Underworld (ASSMANN 1969:50-51). The god defeated the enemies of the sun, thus restoring harmony and entering into the role of Horus (HORNUNG 1984:206, with n. 14). As destroyer of enemies Atum can take on the shape of an ichneumon (E. BRUNNER-TRAUT, Ichneumon, *LdÄ* 3 [1980] 122-123) or he is represented as an arrow-shooting monkey (E. BRUNNER-TRAUT, Atum als Bogenschütze, *MDAIK* 14 [1956] 20-28). Atum is the father of the two horizontal lions, Shu and Tefnut, who assisted as midwives (*Pyr.* 1443a) at the birth of Re-Harakhte, the sun god (MYŚLIWIEC 1978:69-74). Atum, Shu and Tefnut are also represented in the shape of a sphinx (G. FECHT, Amarna-Probleme, *ZÄS* 85 [1960] 83-118, 117; MYŚLIWIEC 1978:12-27).

III. *Bibliography*

J. ASSMANN, *Liturgische Lieder an den Sonnengott* (MÄS 19; Berlin 1969); ASSMANN, Primat und Transzendenz. Struktur und Genese der ägyptischen Vorstellung eines "Höchsten Wesens", *Aspekte der spätägyptischen Religion* (ed. W. Westendorf; GOF IV,9; Wiesbaden 1979) 7-42; ASSMANN, *Ägypten. Theologie und Frömmigkeit einer frühen Hochkultur* (Stuttgart, Berlin, Köln, Mainz 1984) 144-149, 209-215; W. BARTA, *Untersuchungen zum Götterkreis der Neunheit* (MÄS 28; 1973); J. BERGMAN, Mystische Anklänge in den altägyptischen Vorstellungen von Gott und Welt, *Mysticism. Based on Papers read at the Symposium on Mysticism held at Åbo on the 7th-9th September 1968* (eds. S. Hartman & C.-M. Erdsman; Stockholm 1970) 47-76; E. L. BLEIBERG, The Location of Pithom and Succoth, *The Ancient World, Egyptological Miscellanies*, vol. VI (1983) 21-27 nos. 1-4; H. BONNET, Atum, *RÄRG* 71-74; A. DE BUCK, *Plaats en betekenis van Sjoe in de Egyptische theologie* (Amsterdam 1947); P. DERCHAIN, L'être et le néant selon la philosophie égyptienne, *Dialoog. Tijdschrift voor wijsbegeerte* 2 (1962) 171-189; DERCHAIN, *Hathor Quadrifrons. Recherches sur la syntaxe d'un mythe égyptien* (Istanbul 1972); E. HORNUNG, *Ägyptische Unterweltsbücher, eingeleitet, übersetzt und erläutert* (Zürich, München 1984); L. KÁKOSY, Atum, *LdÄ* 1 (1975) 550-552; K. MYŚLIWIEC, Studien zum Gott Atum I, *Hildesheimer Ägyptologische Beiträge* 5 (1978); MYŚLIWIEC, Studien zum Gott Atum II, *Hildesheimer Ägyptologische Beiträge* 8 (1979); M.-L. RYHINER, A propos de trigrammes panthéistes, *REg* 29 (1977) 125-137; J. ZANDEE, Das Schöpferwort im alten Ägypten, *Verbum. Essays on Some Aspects of the Religious Function of Words Dedicated to Dr. H. W. Obbink* (Utrecht 1964) 33-66.

R. L. VOS

AUGUSTUS → RULER CULT

AUTHORITIES ἐξουσίαι

I. The plural 'authorities' (*exousiai*) functions, strictly speaking, not as a name but as a cultic epithet denoting celestial forces (see GLADIGOW 1981:1217-1221, 1226-1231). The term is derived from Gk ἐξουσία and corresponds to the verb ἔξεστιν ('have permission, possibility, authority'). The designation then refers to those who have been given authority, the bearers of authority. Characteristically, in the NT (e.g. Eph 3:10, 6:12; Col 1:16; 1 Pet 3:22) the plural form of the term always occurs together with similar notions in liturgical formulae.

II. There are no antecedents for the NT usage of *exousiai* in the LXX or other pre-Christian Hellenistic texts. However, its origin must be sought in apocalyptic (see *1 Enoch* 61:10; *2 Enoch* 20:1 (J); *Ass. Isa.* 1:4; *T. Levi* 3:8; cf. *1 Enoch* 9:5 (Gk); *T. Levi* 18:12; *Apoc. Bar.* (Gk) 12:3; *T. Abr.* 9:8; 13:11; *T. Sol.* 1:1; 15:11; 18:3; 22:15, 20; *titulus* B I [p. *98 ed. McCown]), in magic (see *PGM* I.215-216; IV.1193-1194; XII.147; XVII.a.5), and perhaps in Gnosticism (see *Corp. Herm.* I.13, 14, 15, 28, 32; XVI.14; Frg. XXIII [*Korē Kosmou*] 55, 58, 63). Thus, the linguistic evidence is ambiguous with regard to any specific origin of the usage. Precise Hebrew or Aramaic equivalents or antecedents are missing (cf. Str-B 3.581-3.584; MICHL 1965:79-80); in the Lat *potestas* is used in translations (Vg).

III. In the NT the epithet is always found

in christological formulae of a hymnic nature. 1 Cor 15:24 speaks of the eschatological destruction of all celestial entities (*archē*, *exousia*, *dynamis*) as part of the completion of the kingdom of God. These entities can also be categorized as 'the celestials' (*ta epourania*) located in the middle ranges of the cosmos (Phil 2:10; Eph 1:3. 20-21; 2:6; 3:10; 6:12). →Christ's victory over them implies that these forces were regarded as evil prior to their defeat and subjugation by Christ, in whose service they continue henceforth. This change is the reason for the hymnic praises in Col 1:16; 2:15; Eph 1:21; 3:10; 6:12. As the lists of celestial beings indicate, they are many in number and include →*archai*, *exousiai* (Authorities), *kosmokratores* (→World Rulers), *pneumatika tēs ponērias* (Evil Spirits; Eph 6:12). Presumably, they possess their authority from primordial times when the creator bestowed it upon them; but, since they became evil and demonic, the redeemer had to subdue them. This happened after his resurrection when Christ ascended into →heaven and took his place at the right side of God (1 Pet 3:22). Christ's enthronement may also be the reason why their names (*onomata*) were withheld. God so exalted Christ that he 'gave him the →name that is above every name' (Phil 1:9; cf. Eph 1:21: 'above every name that is named'). This implies that the demons' lost their names as well as the power that goes with them. As a result, they are no longer to be invoked and worshiped. Rather, they themselves worship Christ (Phil 2:10; Rev 5:11-14; etc.).

IV. Use of the designation continues in later Christian sources, especially in the Apocryphal Acts of the Apostles (*Acts Andr.* 6; *Acts John* 79; 98; 104; *Acts Phil.* 132; 144; *Acts Thom.* 10:86; 133), and in Gnosticism (see *Patristic Greek Lexicon*, *s.v.* ἐξουσία, sec. A.8-10; F; G; MICHL 1965: 97-98; 112-114; SIEGERT 1982: 243).

V. *Bibliography*

C. E. ARNOLD, *Ephesians: Power and Magic. The Concept of Power in Ephesians in Light of Its Historical Setting* (SNTSMS 63; Cambridge 1989) [& lit]; BAGD, *s.v.* ἐξουσία [& lit]; I. BROER, ἐξουσία, *EWNT* II (1981) 23-29 [& lit]; W. CARR, *Angels and Principalities: The Background, Meaning and Development of the Pauline Phrase hai archai kai hai exousiai* (SNTSMS 42; Cambridge 1974) [& lit]; C. COLPE, J. MAIER, J. TER VRUGT-LENTZ, E. SCHWEIZER, A. KALLIS, P. G. VAN DER NAT & C. D. G. MÜLLER, Geister (Dämonen), *RAC* 9 (1976) 546-796 [& lit]; W. FOERSTER, ἔξεστιν, ἐξουσία κτλ. especially sec. C.6, *TWNT* 2, 557-572; *TWNT* 10, 1080-1081 [& lit]; B. GLADIGOW, Gottesnamen (Gottesepitheta) I (allgemein), *RAC* 11 (1981) 1202-1238; W. GRUNDMANN, *Der Begriff der Kraft in der neutestamentlichen Gedankenwelt* (BWANT 4:8; Stuttgart 1932); J. MICHL, Engel I-IX, *RAC* 5 (1965) 53-258; F. SIEGERT, *Nag-Hammadi-Register: Wörterbuch zur Erfassung der Begriffe in den koptisch-gnostischen Schriften von Nag-Hammadi.* (WUNT 26; Tübingen 1982).

H. D. BETZ

AVENGER גמר

I. In Ps 57:3 the designation →El →Elyon occurs in parallel with "the god who avenges me". DAHOOD took the expression *ʾēl gōmēr* to be a reminiscence of a divine name Gomer El (1953). He translated the expression as 'the Avenger El' (1968: 49).

II. The root GMR is well attested in the Semitic languages (Ges[18] 223). From the basic denotation 'to come to an end, to bring to an end', it has developed the secondary senses 'to destroy' (Phoen *mgmr* means 'destruction') and 'to avenge' (in Ugaritic and Hebrew). Though the latter meaning is sometimes related to a separate root (GMR II) meaning 'render good, protect' (so M. TSEVAT, *A Study of the Language of the Biblical Psalms* [Philadelphia 1955] 80-81), it is not at odds with the notion of bringing to an end; compare the verb *šallēm* (piʿel), 'to pay (back)', from the root ŠLM, 'to be complete'.

Both in the Ugaritic and the Hebrew onomasticon the root GMR occurs in theophoric names. Ugaritic examples are the names Gamiraddu ('Adad is avenger') and

Gimraddu ('Addu is my revenge', for both names and similar ones see F. GRÖNDAHL, *Die Personennamen der Texte aus Ugarit* [StP 1; Rome 1967] 128). As Hebrew counterparts one might adduce Gemaryah (Isa 29:3) and Gemaryahu (Jer 36:10-12.25). Such names demonstrate that the participle *gāmiru* (the one who avenges, avenger) could be used as a divine epithet. It does not occur as an independent divine name, however. Nor is it attested in the Ugaritic literature in connection with El, so that Dahood's hypothetical manifestation of the god El known under the name *Gamir-El remains without textual basis.

III. The phrase "I call upon Elohim-elyon, upon the god who avenges me" (*'eqrā' lē'lōhîm 'elyôn lā'ēl gōmēr 'ālay*) in Ps 57:3 does not need to contain an echo of the hypothetical divine name Gomer-El in order to make good sense. The principal reason to posit El-gomer or Gomer-El as a traditional El manifestation is the parallel with Eḷohim-elyon (and more particularly so if the latter were to be corrected into El-elyon, Elyon). Yet the parallelism of the verse is not synonymous but synthetical (W. BÜHLMANN & K. SCHERER, *Stilfiguren der Bibel* [Fribourg 1973] 38): hence the article before *'ēl*, serving here as a *relativum.*

IV. *Bibliography*

A. COOPER, Divine Names and Epithets in the Ugaritic Texts, *RSP* III (AnOr 51; Rome 1981) 444-445; M. DAHOOD, The Root GMR in the Psalms, *Theological Studies* 14 (1953), 595-597; DAHOOD, *Psalms II: 51-100* (AB 17; Garden City 1968) 49-55.

K. VAN DER TOORN

AYA

I. Aya was the name of a syncretistic deity in Ugarit, equated with the Mesopotamian deities Aya and Ea. The name is of unknown etymology. ROBERTS (1972: 20-21) argued for a original spelling *'ay(y)a* deriving from an original root *ḤYY "to live" and related it to the adjective *ḥayy(um)* "alive" in Hebrew, Syriac and Arabic. In the OT Aya occurs several times (e. g. Gen 36:24; 2 Sam 3:7; 1 Chr 7:28) as a proper name, the latter is regarded by some authors as a hypocoristic form and connected with the Ugaritic deity.

II. Aya is mentioned in the trilingual Ugaritic god-list RS 20.123+ (J. NOUGAYROL, *Ug* 5 [1968] 248:32): ^{d}A-A: *e-ia-an: ku-šar-ru*. The logographic writing ^{d}A-A is used in Mesopotamia to denote the goddess Aya, the spouse of the sun-god Shamash (→Shemesh). She was worshipped together with him in Sippar, Larsa and perhaps also in Babylon. Like Shamash she was a deity of →light sharing several aspects with →Ishtar too. The Babylonians worshipped her as a young girl and called her *kallatu* "bride" and *ḫīrtu* "spouse". Aya is attested already in Presargonic personal names (BOTTÉRO 1953:32) and therefore one of the oldest Semitic deities known to us from Mesopotamia. Her equivalent in the Sumerian pantheon was named Shenirda or Sudaga (A. FALKENSTEIN, *ZA* 52 [1957] 305). An Edomite king by the name of *Aya-rammu* is mentioned in Sennacherib's annals (D. LUCKENBILL, *The Annals of Sennacherib* [OIP 2; Chicago 1924] 30: ii 57).

In the Ugaritic god-list Aya is preceeded by the Ugaritic Sun-Goddess Shapshu. This deity was female, and this change in gender might have been the reason for connecting the logographic writing of her companion (^{d}A-A) with the almost homophonic Hurrian name (Eyan) of Ea, the Akkadian god of sweetwater and wisdom, and with his Ugaritic equivalent Kushara (*kṯr*, →Koshar).

Ea too is known from Presargonic personal names and belongs to the oldest Semitic pantheon in Mesopotamia (ROBERTS 1972). In all probability he was originally a god of springs and wells, and was soon equated with Enki, the Sumerian god of →wisdom and skills, whose domain was the Abzu—the subterranean sweet-water ocean—and who was worshipped in the South-Mesopotamian city of Eridu (modern Abu-Shahrain, →Ends of the Earth). He combined knowledge and wisdom with the cleansing and restorative powers of freshwater. In Sumerian mythology, Enki is one of the creators and organizers of the universe. Especially the creation of man is ascribed to him. Within Akkadian epic tradition he increasingly assumed the role of a trickster, whose advice saved gods and humans alike from seemingly hopeless situations. He was revered for instance, for saving the human race from total destruction by the deluge. As a patron deity of erudition and scholarship on the one hand, and incantations and purification rituals on the other, Ea became one of the supreme gods in the Mesopotamian pantheon. During the first millennium BCE most of his functions had already been transferred to his son →Marduk, the city god of Babylon, but Ea remained the ultimate source of wisdom and deep insight throughout Mesopotamian history.

III. In the OT Aya is found several times as a personal name. In Gen 36:24 and 1 Chr 1:40 as name of the eldest son of Zibeon and in 2 Sam 3:7; 21:8.10 and 11 as name of the father of Rizpah. Twice Aya is mentioned as the name of a place in connection with →Bethel (1 Chr 7:28 and Neh 11:31). Several authors (GINSBERG & MAISLER, *JPOS* 14 [1934] 257; W. FEILER, *ZA* 45 [1939] 219-220; J. BLENKINSOPP, *Gibeon and Israel* [Cambridge 1972] 126 n. 46) connected these names as hypocoristic forms with the Hurrian deity Aya. Other scholars regarded Aya as an animal name ("hawk, kite") used as personal name (*IPN* 230) or as interrogative pronoun "where is…?" (W. F. ALBRIGHT, *JAOS* 74 [1954] 225-227). Most dictionaries distinguish between the personal names and the place name.

IV. *Bibliography*

J. BOTTÉRO, Les divinités sémitiques anciennes en Mésopotamie, *Le antiche divinità semitiche* (StSem 1; Rome 1953) 17-63, esp. 32-33 and 36-38; EBELING, A.A, *RLA* 1 (1928) 1-2; E. EBELING, Enki, *RLA* 2 (1933) 374-379; D. O. EDZARD, Aja; Enki, *WbMyth* I/1, 39, 56-57; H. D. GALTER, *Der Gott Ea/Enki in der akkadischen Überlieferung* (Graz 1983) [& lit.]; S. N. KRAMER & J. MAIER, *Myths of Enki, The Crafty God* (Oxford 1989) [& lit.]; E. LAROCHE, Le "panthéon" Hourrite de Ras Shamra, *Ug* 5 (1968) 518-527, esp. 525; J. J. M. ROBERTS, *The Earliest Semitic Pantheon. A Study of the Semitic deities Attested in Mesopotamia before Ur III* (Baltimore 1972) 19-21.

H. D. GALTER

AYISH → ALDEBARAN

AZABBIM עצבים 'Idols'

I. The plural noun *ʿăṣabbîm,* 'idols', is derived from the verb *ʿāṣab* I, 'form, fashion, shape', which is attested in Job 10:8: "Your hands fashioned and made me" (see also Jer 44:19). The verb should not be confused with *ʿāṣab* II 'to be sad, sorrowful'. The singular of the noun *ʿeṣeb* meaning '(clay) vessel, pot' is attested in Jer 22:28: "Is this man Coniah a wretched broken pot, a vessel (*kĕlî*) no one wants? Why are he and his offspring hurled out, and cast away in a land they knew not?"

II. Attested 17 times in the Hebrew Bible, the plural noun *ʿăṣabbîm* 'idols' is especially characteristic of Hosea (4:17; 8:4; 14:9), who uses this noun to refer to the golden calves at Dan and Bethel (13:2). In the view of Hosea as in that of the unnamed author of 1 Kgs 12:28-30 the veneration of these cultic appurtenances by the people of the Northern Kingdom (Samaria) was apostasy no less than the worship of other gods, who were commonly represented by anthropomorphic statues.

Micah, speaking in the name of the LORD, tells us that the *ʿăṣabbîm*, i.e., cultic appurtenances of Samaria, will be destroyed; not because of their inherent inappropriateness to the worship of Yahweh, but rather because of the moral depravity involved in their having been provided by the generous donations of prostitutes from the fees they received for services rendered (Mic 1:7; cf. Deut 23:19).

From Pss 115:4 and 135:15 and their respective contexts we learn of a time, perhaps early in the Second Temple period, when Israel's neighbours taunted her for worshipping an unseen god while Israel in return taunted her neighbours for worshipping anthropomorphic *ʿăṣabbîm*, 'idols' fashioned by human hands from silver and gold: "They have mouths, but they cannot speak. They have eyes, but they cannot see. They have ears, but they cannot hear. They have noses, but they cannot smell. They have hands but they cannot touch, feet, but they cannot walk. They cannot make a sound with their throats" (Ps 115:5-7; cf. Ps 135:15:17).

III. The priesthoods of the ancient Near East distinguished between the cult statue fashioned by human hands and the divinity, which, it was believed, could be made to reside within—but not only within—the cult statue (DIETRICH & LORETZ 1992:20-37). However, many of the common people with whom Israelites came into contact did not always distinguish between the divinity and the cult statue. It should not be surprising, therefore, that especially in the heat of religious polemic reflected in Pss 115 and 135 the Israelite polemicist should poke fun at this aspect of the popular religion of peoples of the ancient Near East. The master polemicist of ancient Israel, the so-called Deutero-Isaiah, relates that at the time of the capitulation of Babylon to Cyrus in the autumn of 539 BCE the images representing Bel (→Marduk) and Nebo (→Nabû) were piled as a burden upon tired beasts, who "cowered, they (like Bel and Nebo) bowed as well. They (i.e., the beasts) could not rescue the burden (viz., the *ʿăṣabbîm*), and they themselves went into captivity" (Isa 46:2). Apparently, Deutero-Isaiah bears witness here to the fulfillment of the prophecy in Jer 50:2: "Declare among the nations, and proclaim: Raise a standard, proclaim; Hide nothing! Say: Babylon is captured. Bel is shamed. Marduk is dismayed. Her *ʿăṣabbîm* are shamed, her →*gillûlîm* are dismayed". In the Jeremian context both terms for idols refer to the gods of Babylon while in Deutero-Isaiah the term *ʿăṣabbîm* retains its primary meaning and designates anthropomorphic statues of gods.

According to 2 Sam 5:21 the Philistine soldiers abandoned their *ʿăṣabbîm*, i.e., cult statues, when they were defeated in the battle of Baal-perazim. The MT of 1 Sam 31:9 refers to Philistine temples as "temples of their *ʿăṣabbîm*" although the LXX reads "among their idols". The parallel passage in 1 Chr 10:9, which speaks of "spreading the bad news to their *ʿăṣabbîm*," appears to reflect the Philistine point of view and uses *ʿăṣabbîm* to refer to the deities represented by or embodied in the statues (SCHROER 1987:317-320).

According to Ps 106:36.38 the Israelites learned from their Canaanite neighbours to worship and offer sacrifices to the Canaanite *ʿăṣabbîm*. According to 2 Chr 24:17 the death of the virtuous Judean high priest Jehoiada was followed by many of the Judean nobility's abandoning worship of the LORD in favor of the worship of *ʿăṣabbîm*. Zech. 13:2, however, looks forward to the eschatological time when "the very names of the *ʿăṣabbîm*" will be erased.

Isaiah son of Amoz, speaking in the name of the LORD, puts into the mouth of the Assyrian king (probably Sargon II) the rhetorical question: "Shall I not do to Jerusalem and her *ʿăṣabbîm* what I did to Samaria and her gods (*ʾĕlîlîm*)?" (Isa 10:11). Of course, Isaiah's audience is meant to understand that Jerusalem does not rely upon *ʿăṣabbîm* but upon God.

IV. *Bibliography*

M. DIETRICH & O. LORETZ, *"Jahwe und seine Aschera". Anthropomorphes Kultbild in Mesopotamien, Ugarit und Israel* (UBL 9; Münster 1992); A. GRAUPNER, *ʿāṣab, *TWAT* 6 (1987) 302-305 (& lit); S. Schroer, *In Israel gab es Bilder. Nachrichten von darstellender Kunst im Alten Testament* (OBO 74; Freiburg & Göttingen 1987).

M. I. GRUBER

AZAZEL עזאזל

I. Both the etymology and the meaning of the name *ʿazāʾzēl*, which appears in the Old Testament only in Lev 16:8.10 [twice].26, are not completely clear. Although the etymological hypothesis *ʿzʾzl* <

*ʿzzʾl < ʿzz ('to be strong') + ʾl ('god'), i.e. the result of a consonantal metathesis, appears to be the most likely explanation (JANOWSKI & WILHELM 1993:128 with n. 98, cf. the form *ʿzzʾl* in 4Q 180, 1:8; 11QTemple 26:13 etc., see TAWIL 1980:58-59), the meaning of the name *ʿzʾzl* remains controversial. In the main the following possibilities are under discussion (cf. also *HALAT* 762): 1) 'Azazel' is the name or epithet of a demon. 2) 'Azazel' is a geographical designation meaning 'precipitous place' or 'rugged cliff' (DRIVER 1956:97-98; cf. *Tg. Ps.-J.* Lev 16:10.22 etc.). 3) 'Azazel' is a combination of the terms *ʿēz* ('goat') + *ʾozēl* ('to go away, disappear', cf. Arabic *zl*) and means 'goat that goes (away)', cf. ἀποπομπαῖος (Lev 16:8.10a LXX), ἀποπομπη (v 10b LXX), ὁ διεσταλμένος εἰς ἄφεσιν (v 26) or *caper emissarius* (Lev 16:8.10a.26 Vg), English scapegoat, French bouc émissaire.

In order to define the word as the name or epithet of a demon one could refer primarily to the textual evidence: According to Lev 16:8.10 a he-goat is chosen by lot 'for Azazel' in order to send it into the desert (v 10.21) or into a remote region 'for Azazel'. Since *laʿăzāʾzēl* corresponds to *lĕYHWH* (v 8), 'Azazel' could also be understood as a personal name, behind which could be posited something such as a 'supernatural being' or a 'demonic personality'. However, one should be cautious of too hasty an ascription.

II. Various theses have been proposed in recent scholarly discussion concerning the identity of the figure of Azazel, as well as concerning the understanding of the Azazel rite (Lev 16:10.21-22). These can be classified as the *nomadic*, the *Egyptian* and the *South Anatolian-North Syrian* models.

The underlying assumption of the *nomadic* model is that the 'scapegoat' is not only chosen by lot 'for Azazel' (Lev 16:8.10, cf. *mYom* III:9-IV:2), but is also sent 'to him' into the desert or a remote region (Lev 16:10.21-22, cf. 11QTemple 26:11-13; *mYom* VI:2-6). The result of this combination was the positing of a 'desert demon' Azazel. In other words, it was assumed that Azazel lived in the desert and was none other than a demon. DUHM and others spoke of a 'Kakodämon der Wüste', who was to be appeased through the offering of a he-goat (*śāʿîr*) and rendered harmless (DUHM 1904:56, cf. *Ges.17* 576; *HALAT* 762). This thesis is, however, to be viewed skeptically, since the goat chosen 'for Azazel' (v 8, the second goat is chosen 'for YHWH') is not sent 'to' (*ʾel* [or something similar]) Azazel but *'for* Azazel *into* the desert' (*laʿăzāʾzēl hammidbārâ*). The central issue is the explanation of the expression 'for (*lĕ*) Azazel'; the solution should lie in the *original meaning* of the ritual.

Nevertheless the thesis of a 'desert demon' Azazel has found acceptance and has been advocated until the present day. Variations of this thesis have been proposed by L. Rost (Passover ritual in the spring and 'scapegoat' ritual in the autumn as corresponding early Israelite rituals) and recently by A. Strobel (the integration of a pre-Israelite [El-]ritual into the Palestinian calendar and into the celebration of the Day of Atonement). In addition the original demonic character was always underlined through reference to the connection between the goat (*śāʿîr*) chosen for Azazel with the **śĕʿîrîm* Isa 13:21; 34:14, cf. Lev 17:7; 2Chr 11:15, which naturally results in the image of a demon in goat form for the 'scapegoat'. Finally, since the time of Eissfeldt the ivory plaque from Megiddo (LOUD, *The Megiddo Ivories* [OIP 52; Chicago 1939] Pl.5,4.5) has been viewed as an iconographic proof of the demon hypothesis (for a critique see JANOWSKI & WILHELM 1993:119-123).

Recently an *Egyptian* explanation has been proposed, which bases itself on the Egyptian *ʿḏꜣ* 'injustice; evil-doer, culprit' and Egyptian *ḏr* 'to expel' or *dr* 'to keep at a distance, remove'. According to this theory an original ritual of elimination has been enriched through the addition of the concept of a 'scapegoat'-receiver in the form of a demon, who bears traits of the Egyptian god →Seth, the classic 'God of Confusion'. This relationship is expressed in his name. According to Görg the name *ʿzʾzl* < Eg.

ʿḏȝḏr/l (< *ʿḏȝ* + *ḏr/l*) means 'the expelled or removed culprit' and is an expression of the interpretative model 'the guilty one belongs there whence his guilt ultimately comes' (GÖRG 1986:13), namely from the (eastern) desert. This is where the Egyptian model comes into contact with the nomadic one. This thesis is, however, inacceptable, since it neither accords with the perspective of Lev 16 nor is it supported by the adduced Egyptian comparative material (JANOWSKI & WILHELM 1993:123-129).

The third model is the *South Anatolian-North Syrian* one. It appears to be the most plausible one, both conceptually and perhaps even philologically. It holds that the Azazel rite is a type of elimination rite (spatial removal [*eliminatio*] of a physically understood pollution through the agent of a living substitute), for which there are parallels both within (Lev 14:2b-8.48-53; Zech 5:5-11) and outside the OT. The extra-biblical parallels point to an origin in the area of south Anatolian-north Syrian ritual tradition, whence this rite spread on the one hand into the Palestinian-Israelite ('scapegoat' ritual, Lev 16) and on the other into the Ionian-Greek sphere (Pharmakos-rites in Kolophon, Abdera, Athens and Massalia/Marseille). Its home is to be found most probably in Southern Anatolia-Northern Syria, as has become increasingly evident in recent years. In support of this conjecture the relevant Hurrian material from Kizzuwatna as well as the Canaanite 'scapegoat' ritual (*KTU* 1.127:29-31), which may form a missing link between the south Anatolian-north Syrian and the Palestinian-Israelite ritual traditions, can be adduced. How this transfer of ritual proceeded has not yet been worked out in detail. Just as questionable is whether there are analogies for the name and person of Azazel in Ugarit; LORETZ (1985) postulates a 'lesser divinity' *ʿzzʾl* analogous to Ugaritic *ʿzbʿl* (*KTU* 1.102:27).

III. The decisive question in the interpretation of Lev 16:10.21-22 in the context (!) of Lev 16 is whether the figure of Azazel is original to the chapter or has 'developed' in connection with the composition/redaction of Lev 16. In order to answer this question, it is necessary to differentiate between the religious history of Lev 16:10.21-22 and the tradition/redaction history of Lev 16.

In its ritual-historical aspect the Azazel rite belongs to the oldest core of the ritual and represents a type of ritual (the elimination rite), which is at home in South Anatolia-North Syria and is also known in Mesopotamia (WRIGHT 1987:31-74). The 'motif of the scapegoat' in its various manifestations is well attested particularly in the Hittite-Hurrian rituals from Kizzuwatna in southeast Anatolia (KÜMMEL 1968; JANOWSKI & WILHELM 1993:134-158). Various animals, such as cattle, sheep, goats, donkeys or mice, can be the bearers of the pollution which is magically eliminated by means of a living substitute. The term *ʿzʾzl* could be interpreted against the background of these Hurrian ritual traditions. JANOWSKI & WILHELM have proposed tying the term in with the Hurrian *azus/zḫi*. The latter is known in the form *azas/zḫu(m)* already in the Akkadian language oath ritual from north Syrian Alalaḫ (*AlT* 126:17.24.28), and in the form *azus/zḫi* it appears frequently in the great *itkalzi*-ritual in connection with sacrificial terms with negative connotations (e.g. *arni* 'sin' [< Akk *arnu*] etc.). The root can be assumed to be *azaz-* or *azuz-*, for which, however, only a Semitic etymology (root *ʿ*zz < Akk *ʿezēzu* 'be angry', Heb *ʿāzaz* 'be strong', etc.) but no Hurrian one can be posited. Since the 'anger of the divinity' in this ritual tradition can be understood as an impurity which is ritually redeemable, the expression *lʿzʾzl* (< **lʿzzʾl*) could then be derived from an original definition of the elimination-rite, whose meaning one could then transcribe as 'for *ʿazāzʾēl* = for [the elimination of] divine anger'.

The question of the integration of the Anatolian-North Syrian material of the second millennum BCE and in particular of the expression **ʿzzʾl* (> *ʿzʾzl*) into the tradition of the Day of Atonement in Lev 16 cannot be simply resolved. The following development, however, would appear to be possible:

Azazel belongs to the oldest core of the

ritual tradition of Lev 16. It is a part of the religious-magical conceptual world of North Syria, as becomes evident in the ritual tradition borrowed from there (Alalaḫ) and brought to Anatolia (Kizzuwatna). The Ugaritic religion possibly played the role of mediator in this process (see esp. *KTU* 1.127:29-31). At an early date the term *azaz/azuz*, also borrowed in this connection, would have been misunderstood. In the attempt to understand the term, the pattern of El-names used to describe demonic beings may have been influential, and may have determined the interpretation in the sense of a 'desert demon'. The adaptive process took place in the context of the tradition formation of Lev 16, when one was able to view 'Azazel' as the name of a demon according to genuine Israelite interpretative presuppositions, i.e. from the perspective of post-exilic monotheism. The integration of the figure named 'Azazel' into the tradition of Lev 16 was occasioned by the motive of the 'desert/steppe' or the 'remote region' (v 10.21-22) into which the goat is sent to remove the impurity. The concept of the 'desert demon' Azazel was born together with the desert motif.

Characteristic of the final form of Lev 16 is the symmetry of the two goats, the one for →Yahweh and the one for Azazel (v 8-10). The rituals tied in with them (the atonement rites v 11-19 and the elimination rite v 10.21-22) are to be understood as complementary acts, which have given the complex construction of Lev 16 its unmistakable form.

IV. The Jewish and Christian history of interpretation of the figure of Azazel stands in no relationship to its laconic treatment in Lev 16. In the latter Azazel receives no sacrifices (the 'scapegoat' is no sacrificial animal), nor are any (demonic) actions ascribed to him. The eliminatory function of the Azazel-rite stands in the foreground.

The process of the demonization of Azazel was intensively pursued in early Judaism under the influence of dualistic tendencies (*1 Enoch* 8:1; 9:6; 10:4-8; 13:1; cf. 54:5-6; 55: 4; 69:2; *Apoc. Abr.* 13:6-14; 14:4-6 etc.; see HANSON 1977:220-223; NICKELSBURG 1977:357-404; GRABBE 1987: 153-155; JSHRZ V/6 [1984] 520-521). Azazel taught human beings the art of working metal (*1 Enoch* 8:1), enticed them to injustice and revealed to them the primordial divine secrets (*1 Enoch* 9:6; cf. 69:2). As an unclean bird he is the personification of ungodliness (*Apoc. Abr.* 13:7; 23:9) and the lord of the heathens (*Apoc. Abr.* 22:6). As a serpentine creature he tempted Adam and Eve in paradise (*Apoc. Abr.* 23:5.9); the Messiah will judge him with his cohorts (*1 Enoch* 55:4; cf. 54:5 and *RAC* 5 [1962] 206f). In rabbinic Judaism the name is only rarely to be found (*RAC* 9 [1976] 684).

V. *Bibliography*

G. R. DRIVER, Three Technical Terms in the Pentateuch, *JSS* 1 (1956) 97-105, esp. 97-100; H. DUHM, *Die bösen Geister im Alten Testament* (Tübingen & Leipzig 1904); *M. GÖRG, Beobachtungen zum sogenannten Azazel-Ritus, *BN* 33 (1986) 10-16; GÖRG, Asasel, *Neues Bibellexikon* 1 (1991) 181-182; L. L. GRABBE, The Scapegoat: A Study in Early Jewish Interpretation, *JSJ* 18 (1987) 152-167; P. D. HANSON, Rebellion in Heaven, Azazel, and Euhemeristic Heroes in 1 Enoch 6-11, *JBL* 96 (1977) 195-233; *B. JANOWSKI & G. WILHELM, Der Bock, der die Sünden hinausträgt. Zur Religionsgeschichte des Azazel-Ritus Lev 16,10.21f, *Religionsgeschichtliche Beziehungen zwischen Kleinasien, Nordsyrien und dem Alten Testament* (OBO 129; Fribourg & Göttingen 1993) 109-169 [& lit.]; H. M. KÜMMEL, Ersatzkönig und Sündenbock, *ZAW* 80 (1968) 289-318; *O. LORETZ, *Leberschau, Sündenbock, Asasel in Ugarit und Israel. Leberschau und Jahwestatue in Ps 27, Leberschau in Ps 74* (UBL 3; Altenberge 1985) 35-57; J. MILGROM, *Leviticus 1-16* (AB 3; New York etc. 1991) 1071-1079; G. W. E. NICKELSBURG, Apocalyptic and Myth in 1 Enoch 6-11, *JBL* 96 (1977) 383-405; S. M. OLYAN, *A Thousand Thousands Served Him. Exegesis and the Naming of Angels in Ancient Judaism* (TSAJ 36; Tübingen 1993); A. STROBEL, Das jerusalemische Sündenbock-Ritual. Topographische und landeskundliche Erwägungen zur Überlieferungsgeschichte von Lev 16,10.21f., *ZDPV* 103

(1987) 141-168; H. TAWIL, Azazel. The Prince of the Steppe: A Comparative Study, *ZAW* 92 (1980) 43-59; WRIGHT, *The Disposal of the Impurity: Elimination Rites in the Bible and in Hittite and Mesopotamian Literature* (SBLDS 101; Atlanta 1987) 15-74; *D. P. WRIGHT, Azazel, *ABD* 1 (1992) 536-537.

B. JANOWSKI

B

BAAL בעל

I. The name *baʿal* is a common Semitic noun meaning 'lord, owner'. Applied to a god it occurs about 90 times in the OT. The LXX transcribes Βααλ, Vulgate *Baal*, plural Βααλιμ and *Baalim*. Though normally an appellative, the name is used in Ugaritic religion as the proper name of a deity. Also in the Bible, the noun occurs as the name of a specific Canaanite god.

II. According to Pettinato the noun *baʿal* was originally used as a divine name. It is attested as such already in third millennium texts. The mention of ^{d}*ba*$_{4}$-*al*$_{x}$ in the list of deities from Abu Ṣalabikh (R. D. BIGGS, *Inscription from Abu Ṣalabikh* [OIP 99; Chicago 1974] no. 83 v 11 = no. 84 obv. iii 8') provides the oldest evidence of Baal's worship. Since the Abu Ṣalabikh god list mentions the god amidst a wealth of other deities, each of them referred to by its proper name, it is unlikely that *baʿal* should serve here as an adjective. The appellative 'lord', moreover, has a different spelling, viz. *be-lu* or *ba-aḫ-lu*. In texts from Ebla (ca. 2400 BCE) the name Baal occurs only as an element in personal names and toponyms.

PETTINATO (1980) makes a case for Baal being an originally Canaanite deity (so also DAHOOD 1958:94; POPE & RÖLLIG 1965: 253-254; VAN ZIJL 1972:325), and argues that he should be distinguished from →Hadad. Their identity is nevertheless often emphasized in modern studies. Many scholars hold that Hadad was the real name of the West Semitic weather god; later on he was simply referred to as 'Lord', just like Bel ('lord') came to be used as a designation for →Marduk (so e. g. O. EISSFELDT, Baal/Baalat, *RGG* 1 [1957^{3}] 805-806; DAHOOD 1958:93; GESE 1970:120; DE MOOR & MULDER 1973:710-712; A. CAQUOT & M. SZNYCEṘ, LAPO 7 [1974] 73). Yet the parallel occurrences of *bʿl* and *hd* (Haddu) in, e.g., *KTU* 1.4 vii:35-37; 1.5 i:22-23; 1.10 ii:4-5 do not necessarily support this assumption. It could also be argued, with KAPELRUD (1952:50-52), that the name of the Mesopotamian weather god Hadad/Adad, known in the West Semitic world through cultural contact, was applied secondarily to Baal. If Baal and Hadad refer back to the same deity, however, it must be admitted that, in the first millennium BCE, the two names came to stand for distinct deities: Hadad being a god of the Aramaeans, and Baal a god of the Phoenicians and the Canaanites (J. C. GREENFIELD, Aspects of Aramean Religion, *Ancient Israelite Religion* [FS. F. M. Cross; ed. P. D. Miller, Jr., et al.; Philadelphia 1987] 67-78, esp. 68).

In the texts from Ugarit (Ras Shamra) Baal is frequently characterized as *aliyn bʿl,* 'victorious Baal' (see e.g. *KTU* 1.4 v:59; 1.5 v:17; 1.6 v:10; 1.101:17-18); *aliy qrdm,* 'mightiest of the heroes' (*KTU* 1.3 iii:14; iv:7-8; 1.4 viii:34-35; 1.5 ii:10-11, 18; for a closer analysis see DIETRICH & LORETZ 1980: 392-393); *dmrn*, 'the powerful, excellent one' (*KTU* 1.4 vii:39; cf. *KTU* 1.92:30); or *bʿl ṣpn* (*KTU* 1.16 i:6-7; 1.39:10; 1.46:14; 1.47:5; 1.109:9, 29 →Zaphon, →Baal-Zaphon). The latter designation is also found, in syllabic writing and therefore vocalised, in the Treaty of Esarhaddon of Assyria with king Baal of Tyre (SAA 2 [1988] no. 5 iv 10': ^{d}*Ba-al-ṣa-pu-nu*). It also occurs in a Punic text from Marseilles (*KAI* 69:1) and a Phoenician text from Saqqara in Egypt (*KAI* 50:2-3). The Baal residing upon the divine mountain of Ṣapānu (the Jebel el-Aqraʿ, classical Mons Casius, cf. the name *Ḫazi* in texts from Anatolia) is sometimes referred to in Ugarit as *il ṣpn* (*KTU* 1.3 iii:29; iv:19; note, however, that the latter designation may also be used to refer to the collectivity of gods residing on Mount Zaphon). Apparently, in the popular imagination, Baal's palace was situated on Mount Zaphon (*KTU* 1.4 v:55; vii:6; cf. *ṣrrt ṣpn*, 'summit of the Ṣapānu', *KTU* 1.3 i:21-22; 1.6 vi:12-13, and *mrym ṣpn*, 'heights of the Ṣapānu', *KTU* 1.3 iv:1, 37-38; 1.4 v:23). In a cultic context Baal was invoked as the god of the city-state of Ugarit under the name *bʿl ugrt* (*KTU* 1.27:4; 1.46:16 [restored]; 1.65: 10-11; 1.105:19; 1.109:11, 16, 35-36).

Such genitival attributions as *bʿl ugrt* may be compared with those that are known from Phoenician and Aramaic inscriptions: *bʿl krntryš* (*KAI* 26 A II:19); *bʿl lbnn* ('Baal of the →Lebanon', *KAI* 31:1-2); *bʿl ṣdn* ('Baal of →Sidon', *KAI* 14:18); *bʿl ṣmd* (*KAI* 24:15); *bʿl šmyn* ('Baal of the Heavens', *KAI* 202 A 3); *bʿl šmm* (*KAI* 4:3, →Baal shamem); cf. also *bʿl ʾdr* (*KAI* 9 B 5); *bʿl ḥmn* (*KAI* 24:16; →Hermon); *bʿl mgnm* (*KAI* 78:3-4). For other special forms of Baal see the survey by POPE & RÖLLIG 1965:253-264. It is also to be noted, finally, that the Ugaritic Baal in his capacity as lord over the fertile land is said to be *bn dgn*, 'the son of →Dagan' (*KTU* 1.5 vi:23-24; 1.10 iii:12, 14; 1.14 ii:25; iv:7). Yet as a member of the pantheon, the other gods being his brothers and sisters, Baal is also the son of →El—since all gods are 'sons of El' (*KTU* 1.3 v:38-39; 1.4 iv:47-48; v:28-29; 1.17 vi:28-29; once Baal addresses El as 'my father', *KTU* 1.17 i:23). There is no particular tension between these two filiations; they should certainly not be taken as an indication to the effect that Baal was admitted into the Ugaritic pantheon at a later stage. On the contrary: the appellative *bn* expresses appurtenance to a certain sphere. Baal was judged to be a member of the Ugaritic pantheon, and as such he was a son of El. Inasmuch as his activity was concerned with the fertility of the fields he was a son of the grain god Dagan.

The excavations at Ras Shamra have supplied us with various figurative representations of the god Baal (A. CAQUOT & M. SZNYCER, *Ugaritic Religion* [Leiden 1980] pl. VIII c (?), IX a-d, X, XII). Such iconographic representations are known from other places in the Syro-Palestinian area too, though their interpretation is fraught with difficulties; an unambiguous identification with Baal is rarely possible (P. WELTEN, Götterbild, männliches, *BRL* [1977²] 99-111; cf. R. HACHMANN [ed.] *Frühe Phöniker im Libanon: 20 Jahre deutsche Ausgrabungen in Kāmid ʾel-Lōz* [Mainz am Rhein 1983] 165).

The worship of Baal demonstrably pervaded the entire area inhabited by the Canaanites. During the period of the Middle Kingdom, if not earlier, the cult was adopted by the Egyptians, along with the cult of other Canaanite gods (S. MORENZ, *Ägyptische Religion* [RdM 8; Stuttgart 1977²] 250-255). In the wake of the Phoenician colonization it eventually spread all over the Mediterranean region.

The domain or property of the god consists either of a natural area or one created by human hand; the relationship of the god to his territory is expressed with a genitival construction: Baal is the lord of a mountain, a city, and the like. The place may either coincide with a sanctuary, or contain one. Since the separate population groups within the Syrian-Palestine area each knew their own Baal, as the literary documents show, it may be assumed that people had a well circumscribed image of the god as a deity of fundamental significance for the human existence (cf. A. CAQUOT & M. SZNYCER, LAPO 7 [1974] 77). The conclusion is confirmed by the frequency of Baal as theophoric component in personal names (*IPN* 114, 116, 119-122; *KAI* III, 45-52; F. GRÖNDAHL, *Die Personennamen der Texte aus Ugarit* [Rome 1967] 114-117.131-133). Also in the Amarna letters there occur proper names compounded with the divine name Baal (if ᵈIM may be read as *baʿlu*, e.g. *EA* 256:2, 5; 257:3; 314:3; 330:3).

Since the information concerning Baal in the Bible is negatively biased, a characterization of the god and his attributes must be based in the first place on texts from the Syro-Canaanite world. The examination of the Iron Age inscriptional material, however, be it Phoenician, Punic, or Aramaic, is not especially productive. Though Baal or one of his manifestations is frequently mentioned, he usually appears in conjunction with other gods, his particular field of action being seldom defined. Only the Phoenician inscription of Karatepe (8th century BCE) yields information in this respect (*KAI* 26). It tells about Baal in a way that is reminiscent of the mythic tradition of Ras Shamra. King Azitawadda calls himself 'steward' (*brk*, cf. Akk *abarakku,* Ebla *a-ba-ra-gu*, see M. KREBERNIK, *WO* 15 [1984] 89-92) and 'servant' (*ʿbd*) of Baal (*KAI* 26 A I:1). He claims that the god appointed him in order that he (i.e. the king) might secure for his people prosperous conditions (*KAI* 26 A I:3, 8; II:6). A possible counterpart may be found in the Aramaic inscription of Afis (8th century BCE) where King Zakir (or Zakkur) of Hamat and Luʿash says that Baal-Shamin appointed him king over Hazrak (*KAI* 202 A 3-4) and promised him aid and rescue in distress (lines 12-13). On occasion, Baal is asked to grant life and welfare (*KAI* 26 A III:11; C III:16-20; IV:12; cf. 4:3; 18:1,7; 266:2). In the Karatepe inscription, as in the inscription from Afis (B 23), the heavenly Baal (Baal-shamem) is mentioned besides other gods as guarantor of the inviolability of the inscription (A III:18; cf. *KAI* 24:15-16); it is an open question whether he differs from the god Baal or whether he is really the same deity approached from a different angle. Some random data may be culled from the remaining texts. The Phoenician incantation of Arslan Tash (*KAI* 27), presumably dating from the 7th century BCE (unless it is a forgery, as argued by J. TEIXIDOR & P. AMIET, *AulOr* 1 [1983] 105-109), has been thought to mention the eight wives of Baal (l. 18); it is also possible, if not more likely, that the epithet *bʿl qdš* refers back to →Horon, whose 'seven concubines' are mentioned in line 17 (cf. *NESE* 2 [1974] 24). A Neo-Punic inscription from Tunesia refers to Baal-hamon and Baal-addir (*KAI* 162:1), apparently as gods that are able to grant pregnancy and offspring. These few testimonies give only a very general idea of Baal. The capacities in which he acts, as kingmaker and protector, benefactor and donator of offspring, do not distinguish him from other major gods.

Far more productive are the mythological texts from Ras Shamra ca. 1350 BCE, which contain over 500 references to Baal. They help us to delineate the particular province of the god. The myths tell how he obtained royal rule and reigns as king (*KTU* 1.2 iv:32; 1.4 vii:49-50). He is called sovereign ('judge', *ṯpṭ*, a title more frequently applied to the god Yammu) and king (*KTU* 1.3 v:32; 1.4 iv:43-44). Several times his kingdom, his royal throne and his sovereignty are mentioned (*KTU* 1.1 iv:24-25; 1.2 iv:10; 1.3 iv:2-3; 1.4 vii:44; 1.6 v:5-6; vi:34-35; 1.10: 13-14). His elevated position shows itself in his power over clouds, storm and lightning, and manifests itself in his thundering voice (*KTU* 1.4 v:8-9; vii:29, 31; 1.5 v:7; 1.101:3-4). As the god of wind and weather Baal dispenses dew, rain, and snow (*KTU* 1.3 ii: 39-41; 1.4 v:6-7; 1.5 v:8; 1.16 iii:5-7; 1.101: 7) and the attendant fertility of the soil (*KTU* 1.3 ii:39; 1.6 iii:6-7, 12-13 [note the metaphor of 'oil and honey', for which see also the Hebrew phrase 'a land flowing with milk and honey' in Exod 3:8.17; Lev 20:24; Deut 26:9; cf. Amos 9:13; Ps 65:12]; *KTU* 1.4 vii:50-51). Baal's rule guarantees the annual return of the vegetation; as the god disappears in the underworld and returns in the autumn, so the vegetation dies and resuscitates with him. Being the major one among the gods, or rather perceived as such, Baal was naturally a king to his Ugaritic devotees. Yet kingship is not Baal's sole characteristic; it is merely the way he is extolled. His nature is far more rich.

Baal is seen at work not just in the cyclical pattern of the seasons. He is also called upon to drive away the enemy that attacks the city (*KTU* 1.119:28-34), which shows that the god also interferes in the domain of human history. His involvement in matters of sex and procreation, though often mentioned in secondary studies, is not very explicit in the texts. A passage in the Epic of Aqhat narrates how Baal intercedes with El, that the latter might grant a son to Dan'el (*KTU* 1.17 i:16-34). Yet this is almost the only testimony concerning Baal's involvement in the province of human fertility. The other texts referred to in older studies are either misinterpreted or highly dubious. Thus *KTU* 1.82 is not an incantation asking Baal to grant fertility, but a text against snake bites (G. DEL OLMO LETE, *La religión cananea según la liturgia de Ugarit* [Barcelona 1992] 251-255). *KTU* 1.13 may indeed be an incantation against infertility, with Baal in the role of granter of offspring (J. C. DE MOOR, An Incantation Against Infertility, *UF* 12 [1980] 305-310), but other interpretations can also be defended with some plausibilty (see, e.g., LAPO 14 [1989] 19-27). On the whole it seems mistaken to infer from Baal's role as bestower of natural fertility that he fulfilled the same role in the domain of human fertility. Also, at Ugarit, there are other gods who might equally be called upon to bless a family with children.

A further theme in the myths is the antagonism between Baal and Yammu the god of the →sea (*KTU* 1.2). In addition to this tablet from the Baal Cycle, other texts allude to the theme; they speak of Baal's combat against the →River (Naharu) and the monsters *tnn* (Tunnanu, →Tannin), *bṯn ʿqltn* (the twisted serpent), *ltn bṯn brḥ* (Litānu, the fugitive serpent; →Leviathan), and *šlyṭ* (Šalyaṭu; *KTU* 1.3 iii:39-42; 1.5 i:1-3, 27-30)—all belonging to the realm of Yammu according to *KTU* 1.3 iii:38-39. It is interesting to compare these data with the account by Philo Byblius: "Then Ouranos [= El?] again went to battle, against Pontos [= Yammu]. Yet having turned back he allied himself with Demarous [= Baal]. And Demarous advanced against Pontos, but Pontos routed him. Demarous vowed to offer a sacrifice in return for his escape" (Eusebius, *Praep. Ev.* I.10.28; cf. H. W. ATTRIDGE & R. A. ODEN, Jr., *Philo of Byblos: The Phoenician History* [Washington 1981] 52-53, 190 nn. 119-120).

These reports might lead to the conclusion that Baal is revered as the god who protects against the forces of destruction. More particularly, however, his defeat of Yammu symbolizes the protection he can offer sailors and sea-faring merchants. Baal is a patron of sailors (C. GRAVE, The Etymology of Northwest Semitic *ṣapānu*, *UF* 12 [1980] 221-229 esp. 228; cf. M. BIETAK, Zur Herkunft des Seth von Avaris, *Ägypten und Levante* 1 [1990] 9-16). In the Baal temple of Ugarit a number of votive anchors have been found. Sailors could descry from afar the acropolis temple, so they knew where to turn to with their supplications for safekeeping and help (cf. M. YON, Ougarit et ses Dieux, *Resurrecting the Past: A Joint Tribute to Adnan Bounni* [ed. P. Matthiae, M. van Loon & H. Weiss; Istanbul/Leiden 1990] 325-343, esp. 336-337). This observation is confirmed by a reference in the treaty of Esarhaddon with king Baal of Tyre. It shows that Baal Zaphon had power to rescue at sea, since the curse speaks about the possibility of Baal Zaphon sinking the Tyrian ships by means of a sea-storm (SAA 2 no. 5 iv 10'-13').

Finally attention should be paid to a rather different aspect of the way believers thought Baal might intervene in their lives. It concerns Baal's connection with the netherworld, as it is expressed in the myth about Baal's fight with →Mot (personified death). Mythological fragments not belonging to the Baal Cycle have increased our knowledge of this side of the god. Baal is called with the epithet *rpu* (Rāpi'u), 'healer' (cf. Hebrew *rōpē'*). DIETRICH & LORETZ have shown that Baal is called *rpu* in his capacity as leader of the *rpum*, the →Rephaim (1980:171-182). They find the epithet in *KTU* 1.108:1-2 and guess *KTU* 1.113 belongs to the same category of texts. The Rāpi'ūma (Hebrew *rĕpā'îm*) are the ghosts of the deceased ancestors, more especially of the royal family. Baal is their lord in the realm of the dead, as shown by the circumlocation *zbl bʿl arṣ* ('prince, lord of the underworld'; DIETRICH & LORETZ 1980: 392). According to *KTU* 1.17 vi:30 Baal is able to vivify, which DIETRICH & LORETZ interpret to mean that he activated the deceased and thus played a major role in the ancestor cult. The expression *adn ilm rbm* (*KTU* 1.124:1-2) may also be understood as an epithet of Baal, designating him as 'lord of the great gods', i.e. of the deified ancestors (1980:289-290).

III. The biblical references in which בעל means 'husband' (e.g. Gen 20:3; Exod 21:3.22) fall outside the scope of this article. Only Hos 2:18 is ambiguous in this respect. Evidently the verse did not originate as a dictum of Hosea; it was written at a later time (so already W. W. Graf BAUDISSIN, *Kyrios als Gottesname im Judentum und seine Stelle in der Religionsgeschichte* [ed. O. Eissfeldt; Giessen 1929], Vol. 3, 89-90; recently J. JEREMIAS, *Der Prophet Hosea* [ATD 24/1; Göttingen 1983], ad locum). In the eschatological future, according to the prophet, the Israelites will call →Yahweh 'my man' and no longer 'my Baal'. Since otherwise Baal is never used as a designation of Yahweh, both 'my man' (*ʾîšî*) and 'my Baal' (*baʿălî*) are to be understood as 'my husband', even though the former is more common in this sense than the latter (Gen 2:23; 16:3; Lev 21:7; Num 5:27 and often). In the background, however, the verse is a polemic against the cult of Baal (thus also the LXX by the plural Βααλιμ).

The name Baal is used in the OT for the most part in the singular, and rarely in the plural; it is generally preceded by the article (Num 22:41 is no exception because it characterizes a cultic place). On the basis of this data, EISSFELDT has denied that there were a great number of Baals, distinguished from each other by reference to a locality or some other specification, such as a genitival attribute (→Baal-berith) or an apposition (Baal-zebul, thus to be read instead of →Baal-zebub; see O. EISSFELDT, Baʿal-šamem und Jahwe, *ZAW* 57 [1939] 1-31, esp. 15-17 = *KS* II [1963] 171-198, esp. 184-185). The many local Baals are rather to be understood as manifestations of the one Baal worshipped among the Canaanite population (thus DE MOOR & MULDER 1973:709-710, 719-720; but note the critical observations by KÜHLEWEIN 1971:331).

The frequent occurrences of the name Baal in the OT are instructive about the kind of relations that the Israelites entertained with the deity. During the early history of Israel the name was by no means applied to Yahweh, as is sometimes affirmed (*pace* KAPELRUD 1952:43-44). The proper name Bealiah (1 Chr 12:6[5]), meaning 'Yahweh is Baal/Lord', is insufficient evidence to prove that Baal was a customary epithet of Yahweh. The theophoric component 'Baal' in proper names reveals most bearers of these names to be worshippers of Baal, or to come from a family of Baal worshippers. All kinds of observations in the Bible document the fact that the Israelites addressed a cult to Baal. From a religio-historical point of view this comes hardly as a surprise. Also among the Ammonites Baal enjoyed a certain popularity (see Gen 36:38-39 for Baal as theophoric element in an Ammonite personal name; the god is possibly mentioned in the Amman theatre inscription, see K. P. JACKSON, *The Ammonite Language of the Iron Age* [HSM 27; Chico 1983] 45 and U. HÜBNER, *Die Ammoniter* [ADPV 16; Wiesbaden 1992] 21-23; *bʿl* occurs as a theophoric element in a personal name on a seal from Tell-el-ʿUmērī: *bʿlyšʿ*, HÜBNER 1992:86; B. BECKING, *JSS* 38 [1993] 15-24). In addition to the more general references in Judg 6:31-32; 1 Kgs 18:21.26; 2 Kgs 10:19-20.28, there are references to the temple of Baal (1 Kgs 16:32; 2 Kgs 10:21. 23.25-27; 11:18); his altar (Judg 6:25.28.30-32; 1 Kgs 16:32; 2 Kgs 21:3); his cultic pillar (2 Kgs 3:2; 10:27); his prophets (1 Kgs 18:19.22.25.40; 2 Kgs 10:19); and his priests (2 Kgs 11:18). It cannot be said that the cult of Baal flourished only in certain periods or in a number of restricted areas; nor was it limited to the Canaanite part of the population (assuming that Canaanites and Israelites were distinguishable entities). The general impact of his cult is proven, in the negative so to speak, by the reports about its suppression in Israel and Judah (1 Sam 7:4; 12:10; 2 Kgs 10:18-28; 11:18; 23:4-5; 2 Chr 23:17; 34:4), and by the references to the handful of faithful who had not bowed to Baal (1 Kgs 19:18; 2 Chr 17:3). Similarly the increasingly sharp polemics which came to dominate the Israelite literature (cf. KÜHLEWEIN 1971:331) attest to the fact that during the early Iron Age the god Baal played a large part in the belief of the Israelite population. F. E. EAKIN, Jr. (Yahwism and Baalism before the Exile, *JBL* 84 [1965] 407-414) correctly emphasizes that until Elijah, the worship of Yahweh and the cult of Baal coexisted without any problem. It should be remembered, moreover, that the cult of Baal did not cease to be practised, notwithstanding the notice in 2 Kgs 10:28 which says that "Jehu wiped out Baal from Israel".

The polemics gained prominence as the worship of Yahweh gained ground. Their typical means of expression is the accusation that the Israelites turned away from Yahweh at a very early stage in their history; they allegedly preferred to bring sacrifices to the Baalim or to Baal, and they continued to do so until the end of the existence of the independent states of Israel and Judah (see e.g. Judg 2:11-13; 1 Kgs 16:31-32; 2 Kgs 17:16; Hos 11:2; Zeph 1:4; Jer 9:13). In Judaism the substitution of the reading 'Baal' by *bōšet*, 'ignominy, disgrace, dishonour' became customary (→Bashtu); the Septuagint used the terms αἰσχύνη (1 Kgs 18:19.25; with Aquila and Theodotion Jer 11:13) and εἴδωλον (Jer 9:13; 2 Chr 17:3; 28:2). The few references suggest that the Greek pejorative names were seldom used. Yet it should be noted that Βααλ is often preceded by the feminine article, which fact must be interpreted as a reflection of a reading ἡ αἰσχύνη. The Vulgate throughout renders *Baal* and *Baalim* (for the historic development of that usage cf. DE MOOR & MULDER 1973:719).

The figure of Baal which the Bible presents as being worshipped by the Israelites must have resembled the Baal known from Syrian and Phoenician sources, most notably the Ugaritic tablets. As the biblical data are unyielding with information about the nature of Baal, however, the researcher is often reduced to guesses based on comparative evidence.

The first source to be dealt with is the cycle of Elijah narratives, as they are concerned with the competition between Baal and Yahweh—or rather the respective groups that claim loyalty to the one or the other. The central issue of the battle is the ability to produce rain, and hence to grant fertility to the fields (cf. 1 Kgs 17:1.7.14; 18:1.2.41-46). It is Yahweh's prophet who announces the withholding of the rain and its ultimate return. His message is that rain and fertility of the soil do not depend on Baal but on Yahweh (cf. Hos 2:10). Apparently 1 Kgs 18:38 ("Then the fire of Yahweh fell") is to be understood as a reference to lightning and thunder. It has often been noted that this implies a transference of certain qualities of Baal onto Yahweh. Elsewhere, too, Yahweh has assumed characteristics of Baal. He is associated with winds, clouds, rain, flashes, and thunder (Exod 19:9.16; Amos 4:7; Nah 1:3; Ps 18 [= 2 Sam 22]:14-15; 77: 18-19). It is Yahweh who gives the 'dew of heaven' and the 'fatness of the earth' (Gen 27:28)—something normally associated with Baal.

Baal's chthonic aspect should also be taken into consideration. It, too, has been transferred and projected upon Yahweh, thus widening his sphere of action. Yet a distinctive difference remains. Unlike Baal in the Ugaritic tradition, Yahweh is never said to be descending into the netherworld for a definite amount of time, in order to fortify the dead. Yet Yahweh was believed to possess the ability to perform acts of power within the realm of the dead inasmuch as he was able to resuscitate from the dead, or to interfere in matters of the underworld. The texts that say so (Amos 9:2; Hos 13:14; Isa 7:11) date from the 8th century BCE. They voice a conviction not formerly found; it was a prophetic innovation with far-reaching consequences. The ground for it had been prepared by the popular belief that Baal, as an important deity in human life, must equally have power over the realm of the dead. In the mind of the believer, there are no fixed limits to the power of the god.

The tradition of Baal as the slayer of the sea and its monsters was also known in

Palestine (→Leviathan). This is shown, for instance, by the fact that in later times Baal's victories have been ascribed to Yahweh. In passages which are almost literal echoes of certain Ugaritic texts and expressions, Yahweh is celebrated as the one who defeated Yammu and the sea dragons *tannîn, liwyātān, nāḥāš, bārîaḥ* respectively *nāḥāš ʿaqallātôn* (Isa 27:1; 51:9-10; Jer 5:22; Ps 74:13-14; 89:10-11). In addition there is the defeated monster →Rahab, so far absent from the mythology of Ras Shamra.

The Canaanite cult of Baal as described in the Bible, and practised by the Israelites, has certain traits that are not without parallels outside the Bible. The ecstatic behaviour of the Baal prophets described in 1 Kgs 18:26.28, the bowing to the image of the god (1 Kgs 19:18), and the kissing of his statue (Jer 2:8; 23:13) are hardly typically Israelite (cf. R. DE VAUX, Les prophètes de Baal sur le Mont Carmel, *Bible et Orient* [Paris 1967] 485-497).

Considering the data about Baal surveyed until now, it cannot be excluded that the Palestinian Canaanites called their god Baal with the title 'king' as well—in the same manner as the Ugaritic texts do. El too may have received the title. Such practices will undoubtedly have been an influence in the Israelite use of the epithet in relation to Yahweh (cf. SCHMIDT 1966). Yet we are not in a position to determine exactly when and how the transfer of the title came about.

Because of the similarity between the two gods, many of the traits ascribed to Yahweh inform us on the character of the Palestinian Baal. For lack of other data, it is impossible to say whether the resulting image is complete. Also, it cannot be excluded that the Palestinian cult of Baal, and its theology, differed at various points from that which is found in the Ugaritic texts. The case of Rahab, mentioned before, offers a telling illustration. Something, however, which can hardly be correct about the Palestinian Baal is the accusation that child sacrifice was an element in his cult (Jer 19:5; 32:35). The two texts that say so are late and evidently biased in their polemic; without confirmation from an unsuspected source their information should be dismissed. Similarly the idea of cultic prostitution as an ingredient of the Baal cult should not be taken for a fact. This too is an unproven assumption for which only Jer 2:23 and Hos 2:15 can be quoted in support; neither text is unambiguous (cf. DE MOOR & MULDER 1973: 717-718).

Baal held a unique position among the inhabitants of Palestine. People experienced the pattern of the seasons, and the regular return of fertility, as an act of Baal's power. Yahweh was initially a god acting mainly in the realm of history. Owing to his growing place in Israelite religion, his sphere of influence gradually widened to eventually include what had once been the domain of Baal as well. His rise in importance was only possible, in fact, through his incorporation of traits that had formerly been characteristic of Baal only.

IV. *Bibliography*

M. J. DAHOOD, Ancient Semitic Deities in Syria and Palestine, *Le antiche divinità semitiche* (ed. S. Moscati; Rome 1958) 65-94; M. DIETRICH & O. LORETZ, Baal *Rpu* in *KTU* 1.108; 1.113 und nach 1.17 VI 25-33, *UF* 12 (1980) 171-182; DIETRIECH & LORETZ,Vom Baal-Epitheton *adn* zu Adonis and Adonaj, *UF* 12 (1980) 287-292; DIETRIECH & LORETZ, Die Baʿal-Titel *bʿl arṣ* und *aliy qrdm*, *UF* 12 (1980) 391-393; DIETRIECH & LORETZ, Ugaritische Rituale und Beschwörungen. Texte aus der Umwelt des Alten Testaments, *TUAT* 2 (1986-89) 328-357; O. EISSFELDT, *Baal Zaphon, Zeus Kasios und der Durchzug der Israeliten durchs Meer* (Halle 1932); G. FOHRER, *Elia* (Zürich 1968²); H. GESE, *RAAM*, 119-134; R. HILLMANN, *Wasser und Berg. Kosmische Verbindungslinien zwischen dem kanaanäischen Wettergott und Jahwe* (Halle/Saale 1965); A. S. KAPELRUD, *Baal in the Ras Shamra Texts* (Oslo 1952); J. KÜHLEWEIN, בעל, *THAT* 1 (1971) 327-333; J. C. DE MOOR & M. J. MULDER, בַּעַל, *TWAT* 1 (1973) 706-727; M. J. MULDER, *Baʿal in het Oude Testament* (Kampen 1962); MULDER, *Kanaänitische Goden in het Oude Testament* (Kampen 1965) 25-36; G. PETTINATO, Pre-

Ugaritic Documentation of Baʿal. *The Bible World. Essays in Honor of Cyrus H. Gordon* (ed. G. Rendsburg *et al.*; New York 1980) 203-209; M. H. POPE & W. RÖLLIG, Syrien. Die Mythologie der Ugariter und Phönizier, *WbMyth* I/1 217-312; W. H. SCHMIDT, *Königtum Gottes in Ugarit und Israel* (BZAW 80; Berlin 1966^{2}); P. XELLA, Aspekte religiöser Vorstellungen in Syrien nach den Ebla- und Ugarit-Texten, *UF* 15 (1983) 279-290 (esp. 284-286); P. J. VAN ZIJL, *Baal. A Study of Texts in Connection with Baal in the Ugaritic Epics* (Neukirchen-Vluyn 1972).

W. HERRMANN

BAALAT בעלה

I. *Baʿalat*, 'mistress', 'lady', 'sovereign' (Heb *baʿălāt*; Phoen/Ug *bʿlt*; Akk *bēltu*), is attested as both a divine name and an epithet in the ancient Near East from the middle third millennium BCE. Though the term is attested in the MT as a place name (Josh 19:44; 1 Kgs 9:18; 2 Chr 8:6), it does not occur in the biblical text as the designation of a divinity.

II. In Akkadian, the epithet is applied to a number of goddesses, most often associated with fertility and birth, as ^{d}*bēlit ilī*. In addition to being a common designation of →Ishtar, this epithet is also associated with specific goddesses, their cities, or their functions.

At Ugarit, *bʿlt* occurs as both an epithet and a divine name. In several ritual texts, offerings are made to *bʿlt bhtm*, 'the mistress of the palaces', whose identification remains questioned. M. C. ASTOUR (*JNES* 27 [1968] 26) suggested a relation with Akk *bēlet ekallim*, 'the mistress of the palace' (see also PARDEE 1989-90:445). In a mythological text (*KTU* 1.108:6-8), however, *bʿlt* is a designation for the goddess →Anat, called *bʿlt mlk bʿlt drkt bʿlt šmm rmm [ʿ]⌈n⌉t kpṯ*, 'mistress of kingship, mistress of dominion, mistress of the high heavens, Anat of the headdress'. It is also attested in the personal name ^{m}*abdi-*^{d}*bēltu*, 'servant of Beltu', from Ugarit.

The majority of the attestations of *bʿlt* as a divine name are associated with the goddess Baʿalat of Byblos (*bʿlt gbl*), 'the Mistress/Sovereign of Byblos', to whom a sanctuary from the early second millennium BCE was dedicated. As ^{d}*bēltu ša* ^{uru}*Gubla*, this goddess is regularly referred to in the Amarna correspondence of Rib-Addi to the Pharaoh from the fourteenth century BCE. The inscriptional evidence from the first millennium BCE demonstrates that she was the leading dynastic deity of that city. In the tenth century BCE inscription of Yeḥimilk, *bʿlt gbl* is invoked alongside →Baal-shamem as part of a pair in parallel to 'the assembly of the holy gods of Byblos' (*mpḥrt ʾl gbl qdšm*; *KAI* 4:3-4). The entire inscription of Yeḥawmilk (*KAI* 10; fifth century BCE) is dedicated to Baʿalat, indicating the importance of this goddess to the ruling dynasty of the city.

The relief on the upper register of the latter inscription depicts the deity with the headdress commonly associated with the Egyptian →Hathor, an identification also made with the Baʿalat (*bʿlt*) of the Proto-Sinaitic inscriptions (fifteenth century BCE). With which of the major goddesses of Canaan the 'Mistress of Byblos' is to be equated remains debated. Though it is common to identify *bʿlt gbl* with →Astarte, based on the association of Astarte with →Aphrodite in later sources, there appears to be good reason to question the equation. While there is evidence from Ugarit suggesting that *bʿlt* was an epithet of Anat, there are also reasons to interpret *bʿlt* as a title of →Asherah, who was known in Egypt as Qudšu. While it is possible that *bʿlt gbl* is to be equated with the great Canaanite goddess Asherah, this deity could have been a syncretistic deity that combined some of the aspects of Asherah, Ashtarte, and Anath.

III. In the OT, *bʿlt* does not occur as a divine name or as an epithet of a deity. It is attested, however, in two place names. In Josh 19:44, *baʿălāt* occurs as the name of a town included in the territorial allotment to Dan. A town by the same name is also listed among those sites which were fortified by Solomon (1 Kgs 9:18; 2 Chr 8:6). Its location remains uncertain. In Josh 19:8, in the list of towns allotted to the tribe of Simeon, occurs the name *baʿălat bĕʾēr*, 'Mistress of the Well', which could well be identified with Bir Rakhmeh to the southwest of Beersheba. Apart from the possible references to a divinity 'Baʿalat' that may have been the basis for the etymology of these two place names, there exists no evidence for the worship of a goddess 'Baʿalat' in the biblical materials.

IV. *Bibliography*

W. F. Albright, *The Proto-Sinaitic Inscriptions and Their Decipherment* (Cambridge, Mass. 1969) 16-17, 27-28, 39; R. J. Clifford, Phoenician Religion, *BASOR* 279 (1990) 55-64; R. S. Hess, Divine Names in the Amarna Texts, *UF* 18 (186) 149-168; W. A. Maier III, *ʾAšerah: Extra biblical Evidence* (HSM 37; Atlanta 1986) 81-96; R. A. Oden, Jr., *Studies in Lucian's De Syria Dea* (HSM 15; Missoula Mont. 1977) 77-78; D. Pardee, *Les Textes Para-Mythologiques de la 24e Campagne (1961)* (RSOu IV; Paris 1988); Pardee, Ugaritic Proper Names, *AfO* 36-37 (1989-90) 390-513; K. L. Tallqvist, *AkkGE* 57-66.272-276.

E. T. Mullen, Jr.

BAAL TOPONYMS

I. The nine toponyms →Baal-gad, →Baal-hamon, →Baal-hazor, →Baal-hermon, →Baal-judah, →Baal-meon, →Baal-perazim, →Baal-shalisha, and →Baal-tamar include various descriptive combinations which are compounded with the divine name or appellative Baal. They are all located in the Canaanite hill country, save for Baal-meon which is located on the plain east of the Dead Sea.

There is a difference in the distribution of toponyms which are named by masculine (Baal-X) and feminine (Baalah, Bealoth, Baalath-X) forms. The former are attached to the highlands whereas the latter appear in the lowlands (Baalath; Mt Baalah) and the Negeb (Baalah; Baalath-beer/Bealoth). An exception is Kiriath-jearim which appears both in the masculine (Kiriath-baal, Baal-judah) and feminine (Baalah) forms. The difference in distribution may be due to the connection of Baal-toponyms to mountain and hilly peaks, the feminine forms being reserved for other topographical areas.

II. Baal is neither attested in pre-Israelite place names nor does it appear in Syrian second millennium BCE documents. Moreover, Syro-Palestinian toponyms compounded with Baal are attested only in Neo-Assyrian records of the first millennium BCE, namely Baʾli-ṣapuna (Jebel Aqraʿ), Baʾli-raʾsi (Mount Carmel), Baʾil-gazara and Baʾli. The hill country of Canaan is hardly ever mentioned in the Egyptian sources of the second millennium BCE and we still do not know whether any of the biblical Baal toponyms antedates the Iron Age. Since most of them are located in the hill country, which was quite empty in the Late Bronze Age and was settled only in the Iron Age, most (or even all) of these sites must have been founded and named only at that time.

Place names in the former areas of Canaan are not called by the names of the new national gods of the first millennium BCE (e.g., →Yahweh, →Milcom, →Chemosh, →Qôs, etc.). On the other hand, many places are called by the names of the older Canaanite deities, like →Baal, →El (Bethel, Eltolad), →Dagan (Beth-dagon), Shamash (Beth-shemesh, see →Shemesh), →Horon (Beth-horon), Ashtoreth (Ashtaroth, see →Astarte) and →Anat (Beth-anath, Anathoth). Some of these names may be regarded as survivals of pre-Israelite names, others were apparently new settlements of the Iron Age I-II.

III. Names of individual gods can also be titles. Baal (like El) can be both the name of the god Baal or a title, 'lord', referring to another deity. Each Baal toponym must be analyzed in order to ascertain which of the two alternative interpretations is preferable.

IV. *Bibliography*

W. Borée, *Die alten Ortsnamen Palästinas* (Hildesheim 1968[2]) 95-97; B. S. J. Isserlin, Israelite and Pre-Israelite Place-Names in Palestine: A Historical and Geographical Sketch, *PEQ* 89 (1957) 133-144.

N. Naʾaman

BAAL-BERITH, בעל ברית, אל ברית

I. Baal-berith ('Baal of the Covenant'; Judg 8:33 and 9:4) and El-berith ('El of the Covenant; Judg 9:46) occur only in the Book of Judges as specifications of the

Canaanite fertility gods →Baal and →El of Shechem, an ancient Canaanite city in the hill country between Mount Gerizim and Mount Ebal. Also in Ugaritic texts *brt* ('covenant') is found in connection with Baal.

II. In the OT Shechem is often mentioned. Already in Gen 12:6-7 we are told that Abram went as far in Canaan as the sanctuary at Shechem, and the terebinth tree of Moreh, and that he built there an altar "to the LORD who had appeared to him". This suggests that already in 'patriarchal' times the Shechem area was a religious centre (see e.g. Gen 33:18-20; 35:4; Josh 24:32). In Josh 24 it is told that Joshua concluded a covenant at Shechem, resulting in a confederacy of twelve Israelite tribes. Josh 24:25-26 informs us that "Joshua drew up a statute and an ordinance" (cf. Deut 11:26-32) for this confederacy in Shechem, and that he took "a great stone and set it up under the terebinth in the sanctuary of the LORD". Many older scholars even suggested that Shechem was the original home of the Hebrew covenant as against Sinai-Horeb or Kadesh and that the city was the amphictyonic sanctuary of the tribal confederacy of Israel (ROWLEY 1950:125).

In this city the dramatic story of Abimelech, son of Jerubbaal (Gideon) by his Shechemite concubine (Judg 8:31) took place, as told in Judg 9. We are informed that in this time the gods of the city were the Canaanite gods Baal-berith and El-berith. So Shechem was a Canaanite enclave at the time of Abimelech, and the "citizens of Shechem" might not have been Israelites, but Canaanite inhabitants (FOWLER 1983: 52). A shrine of Baal-berith should have been in the city (9:4). But his cult must also have been popular among those Israelites who lived in the neighbourhood of Shechem (8:33). In 9:46, on the other hand, a crypt—be it a subterreanean cave or a hidden dark room or vault—of a temple of El-berith in Migdal-Shechem ('Tower of Shechem') is mentioned. Is this a reference to the temple of Baal-berith as that of El-berith, 'the covenant god', and is the substitution of 'El' for 'Baal' due to "scribal orthodoxy" (GRAY 1962)? Or have we to do with two different temples? In the opinion of SIMONS (1943; 1959) and other scholars Migdal-Shechem (Judg 9:46-49) is to be distinguished from the city of Shechem. It must have been situated in the neighbourhood of that city as its advanced defensive bulwark (Mount Zalmon, Judg 9:48, identical with 'Beth-Millo' in Judg 9:6.20). But in Abimelech's time this stronghold must have developed into a small settlement, depending on the mother-city of Shechem, symbolized by the surviving original name as well as by the cult of a common deity Baal-berith/El-berith. NIELSEN (1955) identified Migdal-Shechem and Beth-Millo (Judg 9:6.20) with the main building on the acropolis of Tell Balatah.

The questions to be dealt with here are primarily archaeological. The mound (Tell Balatah) of—presumably—biblical Shechem has been excavated by various expeditions since 1913 (Sellin and Welter between 1913 and 1934; G. E. Wright led eight campaigns between 1956 and 1969). According to Wright, a massive structure, with walls seventeen feet thick, had replaced the courtyard temples of Shechem at about 1650 BCE. According to CAMPBELL (1962), it is quite likely that all the structures mentioned in Judg 9:4.6 and 9:46 are part of the complex in Shechem's sacred precinct.

Other buildings which could be interpreted as sanctuaries, have been found within and nearby the city too (WRIGHT 1968). The existence of these sanctuaries outside the sacred precinct, and even outside Shechem, can throw indirect light on the traditions of sacred places in the Shechem pass. But at the same time it complicates the issue of whether there was only one temple for one deity called now Baal-berith now El-berith, or there were actually two shrines one for Baal-berith and one for El-berith. The latter possibility is accepted on good grounds by many modern scholars (SOGGIN 1967; 1988; DE MOOR 1990). There is also an identification of an excavated building on Mount Ebal with the El-berith temple of

Judg 9. It was Zertal who surveyed Mount Ebal during five campaigns (starting in 1982), and found there a "temenos wall" enclosing a large central courtyard. An artifact was discovered, which has been subjected to different interpretations: a great altar (ZERTAL 1985; 1986), a watchtower (SOGGIN 1988), or even an old farmhouse (KEMPINSKI 1986). Zertal saw it at first as a cultic site for the tribal Israelite confederacy which he associated with the biblical tradition (Deut 27:4; Josh 8:30-35). But Soggin is of the opinion that it could be the Migdal-Shechem, a small fortified settlement, with a holy place and an altar for El-berith. It ought to be said that the identification of the building within Shechem, excavated by Wright, as the temple of El-berith is also seriously disputed (FOWLER 1983).

As is known, El and Baal were important deities in the Ugaritic and Canaanite pantheon, and it is not unlikely that they could both have had a shrine in Shechem (MULDER 1962; SOGGIN 1967). In Ugarit too, El and Baal both had a temple (J. C. DE MOOR, *The Seasonal Pattern in the Ugaritic Myth of Baʿlu* [Kevelaer 1971] 111). Besides, in *KTU* 1.3 i:28, *brt* 'covenant' may have been used in connection with Baal. According to CROSS (1973) the name *il brt* is also used in a Hurrian hymn for El. SCHMITT (1964) argued that this god was originally identical with the Indian-Iranian god Mitra ('agreement' in Semitic form), for in the second millennium BCE the Indo-Iranians were widely scattered throughout the Near East.

III. It is not easy to determine which was the special character of Baal-berith and of El-berith in Judg 9. There is in the first place the question of the age and the composition of the traditions in Judg 9. JAROŠ (1976:76-77) takes Judg 9:8-15.26-40.46-54 as an old tradition; Judg 9:1-7.16a.19b-21.23-24.41-45.56-57 as a later one; Judg 16b-19a.22.55 were added by a later hand. The fact that both deities are mentioned in one and the same area only in this composite story (Shechem) could be an indication that there was a close connection between the two deities in the Shechemite pantheon, analogous to the connection between Baal and El in the Ugaritic pantheon. It may even be that the passage in which El Berith is mentioned is the older tradition. Baal Berith, however, is pictured as a Canaanite god who was worshipped by many Israelites too (Judg 9:33).

Of the old versions LXX offers two different translations of the book of Judges, one represented by codex B (Vaticanus), the other by codex A (Alexandrinus). LXX[A] tries to translate terms like Baal-berith (Βααλ διαθήκης), whereas LXX[B] often simply transcribes the Hebrew expression with Greek letters (v 4: Βααλβεριθ; v 46: Βαιθηλβεριθ; NIELSEN 1955:142). The Peshitta and the Targum translate the Hebrew text as *bĕʿal qĕyām*[*āʾ*] (Baal of the covenant). In v 46 the Targum paraphrases the difficulties in this way: "...to the gathering place of the house of God to cut a covenant". In the same way the Vulgate paraphrases the second part of v 46: "...they went into the shrine of their god Berith, where they had concluded a covenant with him, and therefore that very fortified place had got its name" (... *ingressi sunt fanum dei sui Berith ubi foedus cum eo pepigerant et ex eo locus nomen acceperat qui erat valde munitus*). In Judg 8:33 Vulg. translates as *Baal foedus*, but in 9:4 the Hebrew expression is oddly transcribed: *Baalberith*.

There are scholars who believe that Israel drew its belief in a divine covenant with Yahweh from an analogous cult of Baal-berith in Shechem, or even that *baʿal* was only an epithet for Yahweh in the stories of Judges (KAUFMANN 1961:138-139). The view that Baal-berith officiated as supervisor and guardian of a political treaty between Shechem and some other city-states or the local Israelite population is accepted by many scholars. Hence the explanation of his name as Baal-berith. But that there had been a profound influence from this Baal upon Israel is unprovable. Israel's tradition of the Sinai covenant was not moulded upon the pattern of the Shechem covenant of Baal-berith (CLEMENTS 1968). On the other hand the story in Judg 9 presupposes some normal relations between Shechemites and Israelites (NIELSEN 1955:171). But this does not mean that Yahweh was worshipped in Shechem with the name Baal-berith, as GRESSMANN (1929:163-164) suggested.

Another view regarding the nature of Baal-berith is that he was one of the parties of a covenant to which his worshippers formed the corresponding party, so that a religious, or cultic, covenant was involved. Clements points out that a part of the population of Shechem is described as "men of Hamor" (in Gen 34 the name Hamor means 'ass'), and that the ritual for the affirmation of a covenant by the slaughtering of an ass is testified in the ancient Near East. Those who were bound under covenant having participated in this ritual became "sons of Hamor" ("sons of the ass"). The covenant of Hamor "was almost certainly related to Baal-Berith, who was the chief god of the city" (CLEMENTS 1968:29; see also ALBRIGHT 1953:113, who was of the opinion that Baal-berith was an appellation of the god →Horon). This suggests a divine covenant between the local Baal and certain citizens of Shechem rather than a covenant in which Baal acted as the guardian of a local political treaty (CLEMENTS 1968:31).

In Judg 9 it is shown, however, that this god was also a god of fertility and vegetation (v 27)—so was Baal in the Canaanite pantheon: the men of Shechem went out into the field, gathered the grapes from the vineyards, trod them and held festival, coming "into the house of their god". The identity of this god goes unsaid, but it must be either El or Baal—and most likely the latter one. Much of the later Israelite ethos was opposed to the tradition of the Canaanite Baal. So it is very unlikely that the covenant tradition is derived from the covenant tradition of Baal-berith of Shechem. The name 'Berith', however, may refer to his function among the Shechemites "as the witness or guarantor of the covenant between two peoples" (LEWIS 1992).

IV. *Bibliography*

W. F. ALBRIGHT, *Archaeology and the Religion of Israel* (Baltimore 1953) 113; T. A. BUSINK, *Der Tempel von Jerusalem von Salomo bis Herodes I* (Leiden 1970) 388-394.595-597; E. F. CAMPBELL, Shechem (City), *IDBS* (1962) 821-822; R. E. CLEMENTS, Baal-Berith of Shechem, *JSS* 13 (1968) 21-32; F. M. CROSS, *Canaanite Myth and Hebrew Epic* (Cambridge, Mass. 1973); I. FINKELSTEIN, *The Archaeology of the Israelite Settlement* (Jerusalem 1988), esp. 81-85; M. D. FOWLER, A Closer Look at the "Temple of El-Berith" at Shechem, *PEQ* 115 (1983) 49-53; J. GRAY, Baal-Berith, *IDB* 1 (1962) 331; H. GRESSMANN, *Die Anfänge Israels* (Göttingen 1929, 2nd ed.); K. JAROŠ, *Sichem; Eine archäologische und religionsgeschichtliche Studie* (OBO 11; Freiburg & Göttingen 1976); Y. KAUFMANN, *The Religion of Israel*, transl. and abridged by M. Greenberg (London 1961); A. KEMPINSKI, Joshua's Altar—An Iron Age I Watch-tower?, *BAR* 12 (1986) 44-49; T. J. LEWIS, Baal-Berith, *ABD* 1(1992) 550-551; E. LIPIŃSKI, El-Berit, *Syria* 50 (1973) 50-51; M. J. MULDER, *Baʿal in het Oude Testament* ('s-Gravenhage 1962), esp. 134-139; J. C. DE MOOR, *The Rise of Yahwism. The Roots of Israelite Monotheism* (BETL 91; Leuven 1990); E. NIELSEN, *Shechem; A Traditio-Historical Investigation* (Copenhagen 1955, 2nd ed.); H. H. ROWLEY, *From Joseph to Joshua; Biblical Traditions in the Light of Archaeology* (London 1950), esp. 125-129; G. SCHMITT, El Berit - Mitra, *ZAW* 76 (1964) 325-327); J. A. SOGGIN, Bemerkungen zur alttestamentlichen Topographie Sichems mit besonderem Bezug auf Jdc. 9, *ZDPV* 83 (1967) 183-198; SOGGIN, The Migdal Temple, Migdal Šᵉkem Judg 9 and the Artifact on Mount Ebal, *'Wünschet Jerusalem Frieden'. IOSOT Congress Jerusalem 1986* (ed. M. Augustin & K.-D. Schunck; Frankfurt am Main 1988) 115-119; G. R. H. WRIGHT, Temples at Shechem, *ZAW* 80 (1968) 1-35; A. ZERTAL, Has Joshua's Altar Been Found on Mt. Ebal?, *BAR* 11 (1985) 26-43; A. ZERTAL, How Can Kempinski Be So Wrong!, *BAR* 12 (1986) 43,49-53.

M. J. MULDER

BAAL-GAD בעל גד

I. A location on the northern border of the allotments of the twelve tribes (Josh 11:17; 12:7; 13:5). Perhaps Baal should be taken as the name of the god and *gad* as an appellative ('Baal is fortune') rather than the other way round ('Lord Gad'). Gad is known both from place names (Migdal-gad) and personal names (Gaddi, Gaddiel, Gaddiyau) and is best understood as an appellative, i.e., 'fortune'. →Gad as a divine name is attested only in the post-exilic period (Isa 65:11) and since that time appears as a theophoric element in names (*TWAT* 1 [1973] 920-921).

II. Baal-gad appears in juxtaposition to Lebo-hamath (Josh 13:7), the northern border of the Land of Canaan. It is described as being situated "in the valley of Lebanon" (Josh 12:17), "below mount →Hermon" (Josh 13:5), and "in the valley of →Lebanon under mount Hermon" (Josh 11:17). The valley of →Lebanon is identified with the Beqaʿ of Lebanon and the Hermon is identical with Jebel esh-Sheikh, the southern peak of the Anti-Lebanon. The apparent discrepancy between the two descriptions ("in the valley of Lebanon" and "below Mount Hermon") may be accounted for assuming that the author of the descriptions treated the Liṭani river as part of the valley of Lebanon. For him, Lebo-hamath marked the northern end of the valley and Baal-gad its southern end. Baal-gad must be sought north or east of the land of Mizpeh (the Marj-ʿAyyun valley) (Josh 11:3), along the south-western foot of Mount Hermon. It is best located at the headwaters of the Ḥaṣbani river, near the modern town of Ḥaṣbaya.

Baal-gad appears as the opposite extremity of Mount Halak (Josh 11:17; 12:7), the south-eastern border of the tribal allotment, and marks the northern border of the tribal allotments. It must have been a prominent place, situated in a fertile watery region, and may well have been a cult place for a local Baal. Its location is about 17 km north of Dan, the main cult centre of →Yahweh in the north Israelite areas. The relationship of the two cult centres remains unknown (see also →Baal toponyms).

III. *Bibliography*

P. W. SKEHAN, Joab's Census: How far North (2 Sm 24,6)?, *CBQ* 31 (1969) 47-48; N. NA'AMAN, *Borders and Districts in Biblical Historiography* (Jerusalem 1986) 41-43.

N. NAʾAMAN

BAAL-HAMON בעל המון

I. A location of a plantation of Solomon which he granted to keepers and made highly profitable (Cant 8:11). Its name may be homonymous with the place Balamon mentioned in Jdt 8:3, but they are two different sites. The latter is probably located in the vicinity of Dothan (possibly Ibleam, today Kh. Belʿameh). The name Baal-hamon is not attested elsewhere in the OT and its position remains unknown.

II. Literally, Baal-hamon means either '→Baal of a multitude' or 'possessor of wealth'. The first interpretation may ostensibly be compared with the well known divine title "LORD of hosts" (→Yahweh Zebaoth). However, the literary character of the Song points strongly toward the second interpretation. Baal-hamon may well have been an actual site, but it was selected by the author due to its connotation of richness and abundance (see also →Baal toponyms).

III. *Bibliography*

A. ROBERT, Les appendices du Cantique des Cantiques (viii 8-14), *RB* 55 (1948) 171-174; M. H. POPE, *Song of Songs* (AB 7C; Garden City 1977) 686-688.

N. NAʾAMAN

BAAL-HAZOR בעל חצור

I. A location near the town of Ophrah/ʿEphraim (possibly modern eṭ-Ṭaibiyeh) where Absalom kept his sheep-shearers and where he assassinated his half-brother Amnon (2 Sam 13:23). It seems that →Baal should be construed as the name of god, i.e., 'Baal of Hazor'. It is generally identified with Jebel el-ʿAṣûr, the highest mountain of Mount Ephraim (1016 m. above sea level), 7 km. north-east of →Bethel. The site is not attested elsewhere in the OT and has nothing to do with the Hazor mentioned in Neh 11:33.

ABEL (1924) suggested to read 1 Macc 9:15 as *heōs Azōrou óros* (in place of *heōs Azōtou órous*), "as far as mount Hazor", identifying it with Baal-hazor. It is preferable, however, to assume that already in the Hebrew original text a mistake occurred, and to read *ʾšdwt* ('mountain-slopes').

The place where God appeared to Abraham after his separation from Lot (Gen 13:14) is called in the *Genesis Apocryphon* by the name Ramath-hazor (1QGenAp XXI:8). This town must have been in the vicinity of Bethel. The identification of Ramath-hazor with Baal-hazor is appealing in the light of the well known tendency to replace names of negative connotation by more neutral appellations. Also, according to the Genesis narratives, Abraham stayed near Bethel after his separation from Lot.

II. It is not clear whether Baal-hazor was a place of worship for Baal. Defining its location by the neighbouring town of Ophrah/ʿEphraim may indicate that the place was of secondary importance. Nor is the origin of its name clear. Was it called by the name of →Hadad or Baal of Hazor, the major Canaanite city of the second millennium BCE, by people who migrated thence after its destruction and settled in the hill country of Ephraim? In that case, no place by the name Hazor should be sought in the vicinity of the mount (see also →Baal toponyms).

III. *Bibliography*

F. M. ABEL, Topographie des campagnes Maccabéennes, *RB* 33 (1924) 385-387; W. F. ALBRIGHT, Ophrah and Ephraim, *AASOR* 4 (1924) 124-133; N. AVIGAD & Y. YADIN, *A Genesis Apocryphon: A Scroll from the Wilderness of Judaea* (Jerusalem 1956) 28.

N. NAʾAMAN

BAAL-HERMON בעל חרמון

I. A location on the northern border of the allotments of the twelve tribes (Judg 3:3; 1 Chr 5:23). It seems that →Baal should be construed as the name of a god, i.e., 'Baal of →Hermon'. Hermon is identical with Jebel esh-Sheikh, the southern peak of the Anti-Lebanon (Deut 3:8; 4:48; Josh 12:1, 5; Judg 3:3; 1 Chr 5:23). The place to which the toponym refers must be sought somewhere on its slopes.

II. In the list of people Yahweh left within the territory of Canaan appear "the Hivites who dwelt on Mount Lebanon, from Mount Baal-hermon as far as Lebo-hamath" (Judg 3:3). The same borders are defined in Josh 13:5 ("from →Baal-gad below Mount Hermon to Lebo-hamath") and Baal-hermon is seemingly identical to Baal-gad, a place located on the south-western side of Hermon. However, 1 Chr 5:23 describes the confines of the eastern half of Manasseh's dwelling places thus: "from →Bashan to Baal-hermon, Senir and Mount Hermon". Baal-hermon must accordingly be sought on the eastern side of Hermon and is possibly one of its south-eastern peaks.

How could we account for the discrepancy? Some scholars suggest that the text of Judg 3:3 is corrupted and should not be taken into account. Others suggest that 1 Chr 5:23 is a conglomerate of elements borrowed from various biblical sources (Deut 3:9; Josh 12:5; Judg 3:3) and is not a reliable source for topographical research. The first seems to be better founded. Baal-hermon was probably a cult place for a local Baal, at least in the time of the Chronicler. It was located on one of the peaks on the eastern slopes of Hermon and was deliberately selected by the Chronicler to define the border of Manasseh, the northernmost Transjordanian tribe, in analogy to Baal-gad which in the older sources defined the border of the tribal allotments on the western side of Hermon (see also →Baal toponyms).

III. *Bibliography*

B. MAISLER, *Untersuchungen zur alten Geschichte und Ethnographie Syriens und Palästinas* (Giessen 1930) 61-62, n. 7; W. RUDOLPH, *Chronikbücher* (Tübingen 1955) 49-50; M. WÜST, *Untersuchungen zu den siedlungsgeographischen Texten des Alten Testaments. I. Ostjordanland* (Wiesbaden 1975) 30 n. 100; 39.

N. NAʾAMAN

BAAL-JUDAH *בעל יהודה

I. Baal-judah is an appellation of the town of Kiriath-jearim, the element 'Judah' distinguishes it from other localities called by the name Baal (compare *byt lḥm yhwdh*). It was identified at Deir el-ʿAzhar, a tell near modern Abu-ghosh, about 12 km west-northwest of Jerusalem.

II. The place appears only once, in a corrupted form, in the introduction to the story of the transfer of the Ark to Jerusalem (2 Sam 6:2). MT has *mbʿly yhwdh* ("from the citizens of Judah"). However, not only does the sending of "all the people, who were with him, from the citizens of Judah" makes poor sense, but the subsequent *miššām* ("from there") is without antecedent. Most versions reflect *mbʿly yhwdh* thus indicating that the corruption in MT is very old. LXX^B adds afterwards *en anabasei* and LXX^L adds *en te anabasei tou bounou* ("in the ascent [*mʿlh*] of the hill"). Syr *wʾzl lgbʿ* agrees with the LXX^L.

1 Chr 13:6 reads *bʿlth ʾl qryt yʿrym ʾšr lyhwdh* ("to Baalah, that is, to Kiriath-jearim which belongs to Judah"). $4QSam^a$ and Josephus agree. It is clear however that the shorter unglossed reading of 2 Sam 6:2 in MT and LXX is superior to this version.

The original text must have read *mbʿl yhwdh* and the versions indicate that the *m* is original (PISANO 1984:102-103). On the basis of the LXX and Syr one may further suggest that the word *bmʿlh* originally followed (note the threefold play of words *mbʿl, bmʿlh, lhʿlwt*) and was dropped due to haplography. The ascent of the hill makes good literary sense since it plays a central role in the episode of the return of the ark and Uzza's death (vv 6-7). The text of v 2 may be reconstructed as follows: "And David arose and went with all the people who were with him from Baal-judah in the ascent, to bring up from there the ark of →God".

III. The city of Kiriath-jearim is referred to as Kiriath-baal in Josh 15:60 and 18:14 and as Baalah in Josh 15:9-10 and 1 Chr 13:6. The narrative about the stay of the ark at Kiriath-jearim indicates that a cult place of →Yahweh was located on the hill near the city (1Sam 7:1; 2 Sam 6:1-4). One may suggest that the theophoric element 'Baal' in the city's name is a honorific title of Yahweh, Lord of the city. Baal-judah is probably an appellation meaning 'Lord (of the land) of Judah' and Kiriath-baal means 'city of the Lord'. The designation 'Baalah' is either a hypocoristic form or a variant name meaning 'the Lady'. The city was apparently a pre-monarchial centre of the cult of Yahweh and lost its importance when David transferred its most sacred cult object, the ark, to Jerusalem.

LXX for both 2 Sam 6:2 and 1 Chr 13:6 has avoided the proper name Baal(ah) (PISANO 1984:103-104). This is part of a general tendency and is indicated in other toponyms that have the element →Baal (see also →Baal toponyms).

IV. *Bibliography*

R. A. CARLSON, *David, the Chosen King* (Stockholm 1964) 62-63; J. BLENKINSOPP, Kiriath-jearim and the Ark, *JBL* 88 (1969) 143-156; S. PISANO, *Additions and Omissions in the Books of Samuel* (Freiburg & Göttingen 1984) 101-104; P. K. MCCARTER, *II Samuel* (AB 8; Garden City 1984) 162-163, 168.

N. NAʾAMAN

BAAL-MEON בעל מעון

I. A place in the land of Moab listed among the towns of Reuben (Num 32:34; Josh 13:17; 1 Chr 5:8; Mesha's inscription). It is also known as Beth-baal-meon (Josh 13:17) and Beth-meon (Jer 48:23). It is generally identified with Khirbet Maʿin, about 8 km southwest of Madaba. However, no Iron Age remains were found in the course of excavations there. Baal-meon's exact location has yet to be found.

II. Baal-meon was an Israelite town which was conquered by Mesha, king of Moab, in the third quarter of the ninth century BCE. Mesha rebuilt the town and made a reservoir there (lines 9, 30 of his inscription). From that time and until its destruction Baal-meon was a Moabite town

(Jer 48:23; Ezek 25:9).

The name Beth-baal-meon indicates that the town has a temple dedicated to "the Lord/Baal of Meon". Who was 'the Lord' of the town? In the light of the analogy to Beth-peor (Deut 3:29; 4:46; 34:6; Josh 13:20), where the local manifestation of the Baal, →Baal of Peor, was worshipped, we may assume that Baal-meon was likewise the cult place of a local →Baal, who gave his name to the town (see also →Baal toponyms).

III. *Bibliography*

M. PICCIRILLO, Le antichità bizantine di Ma'in e dintorni, *Liber Annuus Studii Biblici Franciscani* 35 (1985) 339-364 (esp. 339-340); A. DEARMAN (ed.), *Studies in the Mesha Inscription and Moab* (Atlanta 1989) 175-176, 225-226; K. A. D. SMELIK, *Converting the Past* (OTS 28; Leiden 1992) 63, 66, 72.

N. NA'AMAN

BAAL OF PEOR בעל פעור

I. This local god, mentioned only in the OT, is associated with the mountain Peor in the land of Moab (Num 23:28) and the place Beth-Peor (Deut 3:29; 4:46; 34:6; Josh 13:20). He probably represents there the chthonic aspect of the Canaanite god of fertility, →Baal (SPRONK 1986:231-233). The name Peor is related to Heb P'R, 'open wide', which in Isa 5:14 is said of the 'mouth' of the netherworld (XELLA 1982: 664-666). According to Num 25 the Israelites participated in the Moabite cult honouring this god. This incident is recalled in Num 31:16; Deut 4:3; Josh 22:17; Hos 9:10; and Ps 106:28.

II. A connection may be assumed with the Canaanite deity Baal as known in Ugaritic mythology. In the cycle of Baal (*KTU* 1.1-6) it is told that in the struggle for dominion Baal is temporarily defeated by →Mot, the god of death. Baal has to descend into the netherworld to reside with the →dead. In *KTU* 1.5 v:4 this is described as Baal going down into the mouth of Mot (*bph yrd*). It was believed that this coincided with the yearly withering of nature in autumn and winter. In the ritual text *KTU* 1.109 we see that this had its repercussions on the cultic activities. In the offering list Baal is mentioned among gods who were supposed to be in the netherworld and who received their offerings through a hole in the ground (l. 19-23) (SPRONK 1986:147-148; *TUAT* II/3 316-317).

III. Num 25 describes the cult of the Baal of Peor as a licentious feast to which the men of Israel were seduced by Moabite women. In Ps 106:28 attachment to the Baal of Peor is specified as 'eating sacrifices of the dead' (LEWIS 1989:167). In later Jewish tradition the cult of the Baal of Peor is related to the Marzeah (*Sifre Num* 131 and the sixth century CE mosaic map of Palestine at Madeba). In the OT Heb *marzēaḥ* is attested in connection with mourning (Jer 16:5-7) and excessive feasting (Amos 6:4-7). So it unites the different elements of Num 25 and Ps 106:28. This is even more clear in the ancient Ugaritic texts about the Marzeah, though its connection with the cult of the dead remains a matter of dispute (MCLAUGHLIN 1991:281).

The sexual rites connected with the cult of the Baal of Peor have to do with the aspect of fertility. As this cult is addressed to Baal, who is the god of nature, it is hoped to contribute to his bringing new life out of death. It can be related to the myth of Baal describing how (the bull) Baal during his stay in the netherworld makes love to a heifer, mounting her up to eighty eight times (*KTU* 1.5 v:18-21).

The name of Peor in itself already points to a relation with the cult of the dead, especially when it is observed that it shares this association with other place names in this region east of the Dead Sea (SPRONK 1986:228-229): Obot (Num 21:10-11; 33: 43-44), which can be translated as '→spirits of the dead', Abarim (Num 21:11; 27:12; 33:44-48; Deut 32:49: Jer 22:20), 'those who have crossed (the river of death)' (cf. →Travellers), and Raphan (1 Macc 5:37), which can be related to the →Rephaim. It is also interesting in this connection to note that, according to Deut 34:6, →Moses was buried in the valley opposite Bet-Peor. It is added that no one knows the precise place of his grave. This has been interpreted in midrashic tradition as a "precaution, lest his sepulchre became a shrine of idolatrous worship" (GOLDIN 1987:223). Indeed, within this region this would not have been unlikely.

In Num 25:18; 31:16; and Josh 22:17 the Baal of Peor is indicated with the name Peor only. This may suggest reluctance to use the name of a pagan deity. On the other hand, the name Peor with its clear association to (the mouth of) the netherworld already indicates the nature of this cult as a way to seek contact with divine powers residing there.

IV. *Bibliography*

J. GOLDIN, The Death of Moses: An Exercise in Midrashic Transposition, *Love & Death in the Ancient Near East.* (FS Marvin H. Pope; ed. J. H. Marks & R. M. Good; Guildford 1987) 219-225; T. J. LEWIS, *Cults of the Dead in Ancient Israel and Ugarit* (HSM 39; Atlanta 1989); J. L. MCLAUGHLIN, The *marzēaḥ* at Ugarit: A Textual and Contextual Study, *UF* 23 (1991) 265-281; M. J. MULDER, *bāʿal*, *TWAT* 1 (1973) 719-720; K. SPRONK, *Beatific Afterlife in Ancient Israel and in the Ancient Near East* (AOAT 219; Neukirchen-Vluyn 1986); P. XELLA, Il culto dei morti nell'Antico Testamento: tra teologia a storia della religione, *Religioni e civiltà. Scritti in memoria di Angelo Brelich* (Bari 1982) 645-666.

K. SPRONK

BAAL-PERAZIM בעל-פרצים

I. A location south of Jerusalem, on the way to Bethlehem, where David won his first victory over the Philistines (2 Sam 5:18-20; 1 Chr 14:9-11). In the story the naming of the place is assigned to David and explained thus: "Yahweh broke (*pāraṣ*) through my enemies before me, like a bursting flood (*pereṣ māyim*)" (v 20). Since the name Baal-perazim is directly combined with the divine help of →Yahweh, it is clear that the element 'Baal' was understood by the author as a honorific title of Yahweh (compare Hos 2:18). Whether the site had a cult place for Yahweh is not clear. Its name should best be translated 'Lord of breaches' or even 'Lord of (divine) outburst'.

II. The Philistine onslaught apparently antedated the conquest of Jerusalem by David and was conducted from north to south, penetrating via the Valley of Rephaim to Bethlehem, David's ancestral town (2 Sam 23:13-17). Baal-perazim must be sought on the way to Bethlehem, and might be identified with the Iron Age I site excavated near modern Giloh. The site is located on the summit of a prominent ridge overlooking the Valley of →Rephaim and is a reasonable candidate for Baal-perazim.

III. Baal-perazim is called mount Perazim (*har pĕrāṣîm*) in Isa 28:21: "For the LORD will rise up as on Mount Perazim, he will be wroth as in the valley of Gibeon". The prophet alludes to David's two victorious battles against the Philistines related in 2 Sam 5:17-25 and 1 Chr 14:8-16: the one waged at Mount/Baal Perazim and the second waged in the valley near Gibeon. By interchanging the nouns, the author deliberately avoids the combination of Yahweh with a place whose name has the element Baal (see also →Baal toponyms).

IV. *Bibliography*

G. DALMAN, *Orte und Wege Jesu* (Gütersloh 1924) 20-21; A. MAZAR, Giloh: An Early Israelite Settlement Site near Jerusalem, *IEJ* 31 (1981) 1-36 (esp. 31-32); N. NA'AMAN, The 'Conquest of Canaan' in Joshua and in History, *From Nomadism to Monarchy, Archaeological and Historical Aspects of Early Israel* (ed. N. Na'aman & I. Finkelstein; Jerusalem 1994) 251-254.

N. NA'AMAN

BAAL-SHALISHA בעל שׁלשׁה

I. A town from which a man came to Elisha bringing "bread of the first fruits, twenty loaves of barley, and fresh ears of grain" (2 Kgs 4:42; compare Lev 2:11-12. 14-16). Elisha stayed then at Gilgal, near Jericho. According to Rabbi Meir, there was no other Palestinian place where fruits so easily come to fruition as in Baal-shalisha (*Tosefta Sanh.* 2,9; *bSanh.* 12a). Thus, Baal-shalisha must be sought either in the Jordan Valley or on the slopes overlooking Gilgal.

II. An important clue for the location of Baal-shalisha is the land of Shalisha, one of the four lands traversed by Saul while searching for his father's lost asses (1 Sam 9:4-5). Unfortunately, the description is unclear and no identification has gained scholarly acceptance. Since the land of Shaalim is doubtless located near modern eṭ-Ṭaiyibeh, the land of Shalisha may be located to its east, on the eastern slopes of the hill country. It is impossible to suggest a definite location for Baal-shalisha, but its identification with Kh. Marjameh (KALLAI 1971:191-196) is unlikely since it is situated too far north.

III. LXX rendered the name *Baithsar(e)isa.* This is part of the tendency of the LXX to avoid the element Baal. Eusebius likewise rendered it Baithsarisa and located it fifteen miles north of Diospolis (Lydda). It is clear that he was misled by the Greek rendering. Thus, all suggested identifications for Baal-shalisha in the area of Lydda (e.g., Kh. Sirisya, Kafr Thilth) must be abandoned (see also →Baal toponyms).

IV. *Bibliography*

W. F. ALBRIGHT, Ramah of Samuel, AASOR 4 (1924) 115-117; Z. KALLAI, Baal Shalisha and Ephraim, *Bible and Jewish History. Jacob Liver Memorial Volume* (ed. B. Uffenheimer; Tel Aviv 1971) 191-196 (Hebrew); D. EDELMAN, Saul's Journey through Mt. Ephraim and Samuel's Ramah (1 Sam. 9:4-5; 10:2-5), *ZDPV* 104 (1988) 44-58.

N. NA'AMAN

BAAL-SHAMEM בעל־שמין, בעל־שמם

I. The title 'Lord of Heavens', used for the various supreme gods in Syro-Palestine, Anatolia and Mesopotamia during the 2nd millennium BCE, later became the name of a specific deity venerated throughout the Semitic world from the 1st millennium BCE until the first four centuries of the Christian era. St. Augustin (*Quaest. Hept.* VII 16) refers to him as *dominus coeli.*

II. The earliest *Phoenician* attestation of Baal-Shamem comes from the building-inscription from the 10th century BCE of king Yeḥīmilk in Byblos (*KAI* 4). Here Baal-Shamem is named before the 'Lady of Byblos' and 'the assembly of the gods of Byblos'; by implication he represents the summit of the local pantheon. This is also true for the Karatepe-inscription dating from the last decades of the 8th century BCE (*KAI* 26 A III 18), where he heads a sequence of gods, being named before →'El, Creator of the Earth'. In the Luwian version of this bilingual inscription, the 'Weather-god of Heaven' corresponds to Baal-Shamem. In the treaty between Baal I of Tyre and the Assyrian king Esarhaddon from 675/4 BCE ^{d}*Ba-al-sa-me-me* is also in the first position, before Baal-malage and Baal-ṣapūnu (SAA 2,5 IV:10). Later, in the Hellenistic period, a temple at Umm el-Amed is dedicated to Baal-Shamem (*KAI* 18). In Greek inscriptions from this region he is called *Zeus hypsistos,* 'Highest →Zeus', *Zeus megistos keraunios,* 'Magnific lightning Zeus' (*CIS* II 3912) or *Theos hagios ouranios* 'Holy heavenly god' (name of a temple in the Phoenician town Qedeš/Kadasa). In Cyprus a Phoenician inscription mentions a priest of Baal-Shamem (*RES* 1519b); in Carthage, the cult of the god Baal-Shamem existed (*CIS* I 464; 4874): a votive-inscription (*CIS* I 3778 = KAI 78,2) mentions his name first and foremost, even before the prominent gods Tinnit and Baal-Ḥamōn; cf. also *CIS* I 139 = *KAI* 64,1 from Sardinia. In one of the minor phrases in Punic speech in Plautus' *Poenulus* (vers 1027) *bal samen* is mentioned in an uncertain context (M. SZNYCER, *Les Passages puniques en transcription latine dans le "Poenulus" de Plaute* [Paris 1967] 144).

The cosmogony and theogony of Sanchuniaton, transmitted to us by Philo of Byblos (through Eusebius of Caesarea), mentions that previous generations in times of extreme drought entreated the sun for help, "whom they take for the single god, the lord of the heaven named Beelsamen. This is the Lord of the Heaven among the Phoinikes, Zeus among the Greeks" (Eusebius, *Praep. Evang.* I 10,7 = *FGH* III C 790, F 2,7). This late source, dating from Hellenistic times, points to the character of the god Baal-Shamem, showing him to be the supreme god with solar features—who, when invoked because of drought, took on aspects of a weathergod, too.

Baal-Shamem was particulary venerated in the *Aramaic* kingdom Hamath in Northern Syria, and later on in many places throughout Aramaic-speaking regions. The inscription of Zakkur, king of Hamath, written around 800 BCE, is the earliest reference and depicts *bʿlšmyn* (this being the Aramaic orthography) as the deity of the state of Hamath and the personal god of the king (*KAI* 202 A 3.11.13. B 23). Again, he is mentioned at the top of the pantheon, the gods Iluwer, Šamš and Šaḥr being listed after him, which demonstrates that his character is not restricted to a specific function as weathergod or sungod in this period.

The next source, in which Baal-Shamem is referred to, is the famous Adon-letter from ca. 600 BCE (*KAI* 266), where he is called upon in the greeting-formula after the '(Lord[?]) of the heavens and the earth'. The boundary-inscription of Gözne (*KAI* 259), dated in the 5th-4th century BCE, invokes him before the Sun and the →Moon in the curse-formula.

In the Aramaic texts from Egypt of the Achaemenid period Baal-Shamem is not mentioned in the archives from Elephantine. But Proverb 13 in Ahiqar, transmitted on papyri from this colony, makes an allusion to this god as the Holy Lord who established the →wisdom for the people (J. M. LINDENBERGER, *The Aramaic Proverbs of Ahiqar* [Baltimore/London 1983] 68-70; LINDENBERGER, The Gods of Ahiqar, *UF* 14 [1982] 114-116).

In inscriptions the *Nabataeans* invoked Baal-Shamem as the 'Lord of the World' (*mrʾ ʿlmʾ*), to deter grave-robbers from Madain Ṣaleḥ. The Nabatean-speaking tribes in Hauran possessed a well-established cult of Baal-Shamem, concentrated mainly at the holy complex of Sīʾa, southeast of Kanatha, a pilgrims' sanctuary consisting of three temples and some other buildings; this cultic centre was erected between 33/32 and 2/1 BCE and, according to the latest inscription, was still in use in 41/54 CE. Here Baal-Shamem was worshipped along with the highest Nabataean god Dusares who possessed a temple on a lower terrace in the same holy precinct (H. C. BUTLER, Publ. Princeton Arch. Expedition to Syria, II A 6: Sīʿ [Seeia] [1916]).

In *Palmyra,* Baal-Shamem is one of the prominent gods along with Bel. He resided in a temple built in Corinthian style at the southern part of the main *stoa* of the city, which was constructed in 131 CE; along with Aglibol, the moongod, and Malakbel, the sungod, he formed a celestial triad and bore the epithet of a 'Lord of the world' (*māre ʿalmāʾ*).

At *Hatra,* in Northern Mesopotamia, Baal-Shamem (various spellings *bʿlšmyn, bʿšmyn* and *bʿšmn*) had his own sanctuary (the little 'Hofhaustempel' III, building inscription F. VATTIONI, *Le iscrizioni di Hatra* [1981] No. 49) and therefore his own cult in the 2nd/3rd century CE. He is sometimes named in inscriptions with the title *mlkʾ* 'king' or *qnh dy rʿh* 'Creator of the Earth' (Hatra 23 = *KAI* 244:3) but is always followed by the local triad Māran, Mārtan and Bārmarēn; cf. the personal name *brbʿlšmyn* Hatra 291,1; 314. In Hatra Baal-Shamem did not play as prominent a role as in the pantheon of Palmyra. According to Isaak Antiochenus, Baal-Shamem was venerated as 'chief of the gods' in a cultic procession at Nisibis/Nuseybin during the 4th century CE (P. BEDJAN, *Homiliae WS. Isaaci Syri Antiocheni* I [1903] 589, 16ff.). Besides this evidence, personal names exist such as *brbʿšm(y)n* in Syriac inscriptions (F. VATTIONI, *Aug* 13 (1973) 279ff., No. 51, 2.11.20; 69,8), in Latin *Barbaesomen, Barbaessamen* (*Dura Europos* V/1 [1959] 100, III-Vf.3; 100, XXXII,32) and in Greek *barbesamēn* (F. CUMONT, *Fouilles de Doura-Europos* [1926] 48).

A statue of Baal-Shamem (Baršamin) was transported by the king Tigranes of Armenia (first half of the 1st century BCE) from Northern Mesopotamia and carried to the temple of Tʿordan in Ekeleac in Upper Armenia (today Eastern Anatolia; Moses von Chorene II 14) during a military campaign.

Also the Manichaean tradition has a representation of a sort of sungod named *Balsamos* (i.e., Baal-Shamem), who bears the epithet *ho megistos angelos tou phōtos* 'the greatest angel of light' (Kölner Mani-Kodex 49,3-5, cf. A. HENRICHS & L. KOENEN, *ZPE* 19 [1975] 48-49), this being the last mention of the formerly highly esteemed supreme god.

From this survey of the history of Baal-Shamem's worship by Semitic peoples it is obvious that both his character and appearance have been subject to change. In the beginning he is a sort of high-ranked weather-god, therefore a god of farmers and city-dwellers alike. Later on, he develops many more solar features in accordance with a general kind of 'solarisation' in Hellenistic Syria, and his cult is also carried to 'caravan-cities' such as Palmyra and Hatra.

III. Since Baal-Shamem appears relatively late in the vicinity of Palestine, it is no surprise that there are no references to him in the classical books of the OT. Mere allusions such as Ps 104:1-4 or Hosea 6:3 to a kind of weather-god cannot prove any argument regarding this god. But in the conflict following the Seleucid policy against Juda, some passages in the book of Daniel may be interpreted as allusions to the Baal-Shamem, e.g. *happešaʿ šōmēm* (Dan 8:13); *šiqqûṣîm mĕšōmēm* and *šiqqûṣ šōmēm* (9:27 cf. 11:31; 12:11). In these references the term *šōmēm* could refer to the god, occasionally with a maledicant epithet bearing on the →*Zeus Ouranios* of Antiochos IV; but all these allusions are debated and far from being evident.

IV. *Bibliography*

J. BREMMER, Marginalia Manichaica, *ZPE* 39 (1980) 29-30; H. J. W. DRIJVERS, *Baal Shamem, de heer van de hemel* (Assen 1971); R. DU MESNIL DU BUISSON, *MUSJ* 38 (1962) 143-160; O. EISSFELDT, Ba'alsamem und Jahwe, *ZAW* 57 (1939) 1-31 (= *KS* 2 [1963] 171-198); G. GARBINI, Gune Bel Balsamen, *Studi magrebini* 12 (1980) 89-92; K. ISHKOL-KEROVPIAN, Barsamin, *WbMyth* 4, 104-105; H. NIEHR, JHWH in die Rolle des Baalšamem, *Ein Gott Allein* (eds. W. Dietrich & M. A. Klopfenstein; Freiburg/Göttingen 1994) 307-326; R. A. ODEN, Ba'al Samem and El, *CBQ* 39 (1977) 457-473; E. OLAVARRI, Altar de Zeus - Ba'alshamin, procedente de Amman, *Memorias de Historia Antigua* 4 (Oviedo 1980) 197-210; H. SEYRIG, Le culte de Bêl et de Ba'lshamem, *Syria* 14 (1933) 238-282; J. STARCKY, Le sanctuaire de Baal à Palmyre d'après les inscriptions, *RArch* (1974) 83-90; J. TUBACH, *Im Schatten des Sonnengottes* (Wiesbaden 1986) 43-45 [& lit] and passim; F. VATTIONI, Aspetti del culto del Signore dei Cieli, *Aug* 12 (1972) 479-515; 13 (1973) 37-73.

W. RÖLLIG

BAAL-TAMAR בעל תמר

I. A location north of Gibeah (Tell el-Fûl) where the Israelite troops stood firm against the pursuing Benjaminites after distancing them from their home town (Judg 20:33). Eusebius states that in his day there still existed a Beth-tamar near Gibeah, but does not specify its location. Since the second Israelite force which encamped west of Geba (modern Jebaʿ) conquered Gibeah through a surprise attack, it is clear that Baal-tamar must be sought north of the Geba road which starts near Ramah (modern er-Ram). Its exact location remains unknown.

II. The 'date palm' (*tāmār*) is a common element in biblical toponymy, particularly in the Judean desert and the Arabah (e.g., Tamar, Hazazon-tamar, and the descriptive name 'the city of palm trees' for Jericho and Tamar). In addition to Baal-tamar, a second hill country toponym with the element 'palm' is known, i.e., 'the palm (*tōmer*) of Deborah' (Judg 4:5). It must be sought in the vicinity of →Bethel, in the hill country of Ephraim. A prominent date palm must have stood at both sites and, like similar remarkable trees in ancient Palestine, was regarded as sacred and attracted cult. Whether Baal-tamar was sacred to →Yahweh or to →Baal cannot be established (see also →Baal toponyms).

III. *Bibliography*

M. ASTOUR, Place Names, *RSP* II, 335; H. RÖSEL, Studien zur Topographie der Kriege in den Büchern Josua und Richter, *ZDPV* 92 (1976) 31-46 (esp. 43-44); S. ELAN, Der Heilige Baum - ein Hinweis auf das Bild ursprünglicher Landschaft in Palästina, *MDOG* 111 (1979) 89-98.

N. NA'AMAN

BAAL-ZAPHON בעל צפון

I. Baal-zaphon literally means the 'lord of (mount) →Zaphon' and it is a designation of the Ugaritic god →Baal. Due to mount Zaphon's image as the cosmic mountain *par excellence* in Northwest-Semitic religions, the name 'Baal-zaphon' was transferred to further Baal-sanctuaries outside Ugarit. In the OT Baal-zaphon is a place name in northern Egypt where Israel rested during the exodus (Exod 14:2, 9; Num 33:7).

II. In Ugarit the divine name Baal-zaphon only occurs in ritual texts (*KTU* 1.39:10; 1.41:33 [rest.]; 1.46:12 [rest.].14; 1.47:5; 1.65:10; 1.87:36 [rest.]; 1.109:5 [rest.].9.29.32-33; 1.112:22-23; 1.118:4; 1.130:22; 1.148:2 [rest.].10.27; RIH 78/4:5 [*Syria* 57 (1980) 353-354, 370]), in letters (e.g. *KTU* 2.23:19; 2.44:10) and in Akkadian texts from Ugarit (references in RÖLLIG 1972-75:242). On the other hand mythological texts never speak of Baal-zaphon. By using this divine name the lists of the gods and offering texts make a distinction between Baal-zaphon and several other gods called Baal who were also entitled to receive offerings (*KTU* 1.47:5-11; 1.118:4-10; 1.148: 2-4; cf. RS 20.24,4-10 [*Ug* 5 (1968) 44-45, 379]). In several ritual texts Baal-zaphon and Zaphon stand in parallelism to Baal of Ugarit (e.g. *KTU* 1.41:33-35, 42; 1.65:10-11; 1.87:36-38; 1.109:9-11; 1.112:22-23; 1.130:22-25), thus indicating distinct manifestations of the god Baal. The Akkadian equivalent of Baal-zaphon is ᵈIM *be-el* ḪUR.SAG *Ḫa-zi* (RS 20.24:4 [e.g. *Ug* 5 (1968) 44-45, 379]), the Hurrian equivalent is *tšb ḫlbğ* (e.g. *KTU* 1.42:10; cf. E. LAROCHE, *Ug* 5 [1968] 520).

The oldest representation of Baal-zaphon in smiting posture and standing on two mountains is preserved on an Syrian seal of the 18th cent. BCE from Tell el-Daba'a in Egypt (BIETAK 1990; DIJKSTRA 1991). An illustration of Baal-zaphon is given by a votive stela found in the Baal-temple of Ugarit (*ANEP* 485; YON 1991:328 fig. 8a). This stela is dedicated to Baal-zaphon by an Egyptian officer, Mami, and it shows the dedicator venerating Baal-zaphon. The god is represented standing before a cult stand, wearing a crown and holding a sceptre in his left hand. An additional Egyptian inscription identifies the donator and the god. The stela was brought from Egypt to Ugarit, perhaps as the fulfillment of a vow made by an Egyptian officer, to the temple of Baal-zaphon in Ugarit; because Baal-zaphon was regarded as the protector of navigation. Baal's protection of navigation is also alluded to in Pap. Sallier IV vs 1,5-6 (*ANET* 249-250). This aspect of Baal-zaphon is also indicated by some stone anchors found in the precinct of the Baal-temple as votive-offerings to Baal-zaphon. An Egyptian stela from the time of Ramses II and perhaps devoted to Baal-zaphon was found in the Hauran (*RSO* 40 [1965] 197-200). In a 14th century letter (*KTU* 2.23) sent by the king of Ugarit to the Pharaoh, Baal-zaphon figures as the tutelary deity of the kingdom and king of Ugarit, whereas, according to this letter, →Amun fulfills this role for Egypt.

Outside the Northwest-Semitic realm Baal-zaphon was venerated under the name →Zeus Kasios. The second element of this Greek divine name is derived from Hurrian Mount Hazzi. Sanctuaries of Zeus Kasios are attested in Egypt, Athens, Epidauros, Delos, Corfu, Sicily and Spain. The last mention of Zeus Kasios, on a Latin-Greek bilingual text of the 3rd cent. CE found in Germany, was perhaps written by a Syrian soldier serving in the Roman army (*CIL* XIII 2,1 no. 7330).

In the first millenium BCE, Baal-zaphon is mentioned in three Assyrian texts. The annals of Tiglathpilesar III (*ARAB* I:274-275) and of Sargon II (*ARAB* II:13) speak of a mountain Baal-zaphon situated on the mediterranean coast. In the treaty of Asarhaddon with King Baal of Tyre, Baal-zaphon ranks behind the gods →Baal shamem and Baal malage. These three gods have power over the storm and the sea (*SAA* 2 no. 5 iv:10').

The veneration of Baal-zaphon in Tyre is also demonstrated by a Phoenician amulet from the region of Tyre which invokes the blessing of Baal-hamon and Baal-zaphon, thus reflecting the Hurrian parallelism of mount Amanus (?) and mount Zaphon (BORDREUIL 1986). The offering tariff of Marseille (*KAI* 69) mentions in its first line the "temple of Baal-zaphon". As the text stems from Carthage this is an indication that there was a temple of Baal-zaphon in Carthage. There is another reference to Baal-zaphon in a 6th cent. BCE papyrus of Tahpanes (*KAI* 50:2-3), according to which Baal-zaphon is the supreme god of the Phoenician colony of Tahpanes. In papyrus Amherst 8:3 and 13:15-16 Baal is mentioned together with mount Zaphon.

III. The appearance of the place name Baal-zaphon in the context of the exodus narratives (Exod 14:2, 9; Num 33:7) caused EISSFELDT (1932) to argue that it was originally Baal-zaphon who had saved Israel from Egypt. Only secondarily was this victory ascribed to Yahweh. This argument however has nearly always been rejected because Baal-zaphon in Exod 14:2, 9 and Num 33:7 is only a topographical indication without religio-historical relevance. It is only found in the Priestly Code where it is to be judged as part of a learned construction of the exodus itinerary.

IV. *Bibliography*

A. ADLER, Kasios 2, *PW* 10 (1919) 2265-2267; W. F. ALBRIGHT, Baal-Zephon, *FS A. Bertholet* (Tübingen 1950) 1-14; M. BIETAK, Zur Herkunft des Seth von Avaris, *Ägypten und Levante* 1 (1990) 9-16; *C. BONNET, Typhon et Baal Ṣaphon, *Studia Phoenicia* 5 (OLA 22; Leuven 1987) 101-143; BONNET, Baal Saphon *Dictionnaire de la Civilisation Phénicienne et Punique* (Turnhout 1992) 60-61; P. BORDREUIL, Attestations inédites de Melqart, Baal Ḥamon et Baal Ṣaphon à Tyr, *Studia Phoenicia 4* (Namur 1986) 77-86; P. CHUVIN & J. YOYOTTE, Documents relatifs au culte pélusien de Zeus Casios, *RArch* (1986) 41-63; A. B. COOK, *Zeus. A Study in Ancient Religion* II/2 (Cambridge 1925) 981, 984-986; M. DIJKSTRA, The Weather-God on Two Mountains, *UF* 23 (1991) 127-140; J. EBACH, Kasion, *LdÄ* 3 (1980) 354; O. EISSFELDT, *Baal Zaphon, Zeus Kasios und der Durchzug der Israeliten durchs Meer* (BRA 1; Halle 1932); EISSFELDT, Ba'al Ṣaphon von Ugarit und Amon von Ägypten, *FF* 36 (1962) 338-340 = *KS* 4 (Tübingen 1968) 53-57; W. FAUTH, Das Kasion-Gebirge und Zeus Kasios, *UF* 22 (1990) 105-118; H. GESE, Die Religionen Altsyriens, *RAAM* (Stuttgart 1970) 119-133; M. GÖRG, Baal-Zefon, *NBL* 1 (1991) 225-226; *R. HILLMANN, *Wasser und Berg* (diss. Halle 1965) 22-35, 76-87; A. KAPELRUD, *Baal in the Ras Shamra Texts* (Copenhagen 1952) 57-58; T. KLAUSER, Baal-Kasios, *RAC* 1 (1950) 1076-1077; K. KOCH, Ḫazzi-Ṣafôn-Kasion. Die Geschichte eines Berges und seiner Gottheiten, *Religionsgeschichtliche Beziehungen zwischen Kleinasien, Nordsyrien und dem Alten Testament* (ed. B. Janowski, K. Koch & G. Wilhelm; OBO 129; Fribourg-Göttingen 1993) 171-223; E. LIPIŃSKI, צָפוֹן ṣāpôn *TWAT* 6 (1987-89) 1093-1102; S. I. L. NORIN, *Er spaltete das Meer* (ConB 9; Lund 1977) 21-40, 46-51; M. H. POPE, Baal Ṣapān, *WbMyth* I/1 (1983^2) 257-258; W. RÖLLIG, Ḫazzi, *RLA* 4 (1972-75) 241-242; A. SALAC, Ζεὺς Κάσιος, *BCH* 46 (1922) 160-189; R. STADELMANN, *Syrisch-palästinensische Gottheiten in Ägypten* (Leiden 1967) 27-47; STADELMANN Baal, *LdÄ* 1 (1975) 590-591; P. VAN ZIJL, *Baal* (AOAT 10; Kevelaer-

Neukirchen Vluyn 1972) 332-336; M. YON, Stèles en pierre, *Arts et industries de la pierre* (ed. M. Yon; RSOu 6; Paris 1991) 284-288.

H. NIEHR

BAAL ZEBUB בעל זבוב

I. The name Baal Zebub occurs only four times in the OT (2 Kgs 1:2.3.6.16). In 2 Kgs 1 an accident of Ahaziah, the king of Israel, and his consulting the oracle of the god Baal Zebub of Ekron is described. For etymological reasons, Baal Zebub must be considered a Semitic god; he is taken over by the Philistine Ekronites and incorporated into their local cult. Zebub is the collective noun for 'flies', also attested in Ugaritic (W. H. VAN SOLDT, *UF* 21 [1989] 369-373: *dbb*), Akkadian (*zubbu*), post-biblical Hebrew, Jewish Aramaic (דיבבא), Syriac (*debbaba*) and in other Semitic languages.

II. On the basis *zebub*, 'flies', the name of the god was interpreted as 'Lord of the flies'; it was assumed that he was a god who could cause or cure diseases. F. BAETHGEN (*Beiträge zur semitischen Religionsgeschichte* [1888] 25) expressed the view that the flies related to →Baal were seen as a symbol of the solar heat; they were sacred animals. In early Israel, flies were considered a source of nuisance (Isa 7:18; Qoh 10:1). TÅNGBERG (1992) interpreted the name Baal-zebub as "Baal (statue) with the flies (ornamented)" analogous to the Mesopotamian 'Nintu with the flies'. This can be compared with the fact that the Greeks called →Zeus as healer ἀπόμυιος (Clemens Alexandrinus, *Protrepticus* II,38,4; Pausanias, *Graeciae Descriptio* V 14,1) and that they knew a ἥρως μυίαγρος (Pausanias, VIII 26,7: mainly concerning the driving away of the flies with sacrifices).

The LXX implies by its rendering Βααλ μυῖα (Baal the fly) the same wording as the MT (cf. Josephus, *Antiquitates* IX,2,1: Ἀκκάρων θεὸς Μυῖα, Vg: Beelzebub). In contradistinction the translation of Symmachus as well as the NT manuscripts have the forms Βεεζεβουλ respectively Βεελζεβουλ (Matt 10:25; 12:24.27; Mark 3:22; Luke 11:15.18-19). This rendering of the divine name might rely on a different textform or be based on oral tradition. Besides, Matt 12:24; Mark 3:22; Luke 11:15 use the apposition ἄρχων τῶν δαιμονίων 'head of the →demons'. The epithet Zabulus (*Ass. Mos.* 10:1) has no connection with Βεελζεβουλ. Greek δια- is frequently replaced by Latin za-, therefore Zabulus can be interpreted as a rendition of Διαβολος. Where one meets in the NT versions the wording Beelzebub, undoubtedly a later correction according to the canonical text of the OT (LXX) exists (so already BAUDISSIN 1897; further L. GASTON, *ThZ* 18 [1962] 251).

The view that Βεελζεβουλ is the original form of the name of the deity in 2 Kgs 1 is further suggested by the titles *zbl bʿl* and more frequently *zbl bʿl ʾarṣ* appearing in Ugaritic texts. Even before the excavations at Ras Shamra, MOVERS (1841:260) and GUYARD (1878) guessed Baal Zebul to be the name's original form. They explained the notion *zĕbûl*, however, after its occurrence in the OT (Deut 26:15; Isa 63:15; Ps 68:6) or otherwise by referring to the Akk **zabal*, 'residence' or 'lofty house' (though, in fact, there is no such word in Akkadian). CHEYNE (1899) asserted that the name Baalzebub most likely was "...a contemptuous uneuphonic Jewish modification of the true name, which was probably Baal-zebul, 'lord of the high house' [cf. 1 Kgs 8:13]". Similarly GASTON (*ThZ* 18 [1962] 251) understood the notion as referring to [heavenly and earthly] residence.

Reviving another explication, FENSHAM (1967:361-364) tried to interpret the Hebrew noun זבוב as derived from Ugaritic *ḏbb* which he understood as 'flame' (cf. Heb *šābîb*). He rendered בעל זבוב by 'Baal the →Flame' adducing the fire motif in the →Elijah tales as corroborating evidence. Yet his explanation fails to convince; the Ugaritic noun *ḏbb* is not clearly explained, and it is questionable whether there are religio-historical parallels. The NT, moreover, shows that the root is *zbl*, not *zbb*. Equally unconvincing is Mulder's proposal to explain זבול on the basis of Ug *zbl* 'illness' (*Baʿal in het*

Oude Testament [1962] 142-144); the Ugaritic word for illness is *zbln*. Above all it reckons, despite the statement in the NT, with the consonantal stock *zbb*. The same doubts are to be raised against MULDER's explanation of *bʿl zbl* by referring to Ug *zbl*, 'illness' particularly because this noun runs *zbln*.

Relatively soon after the findings at Ras Shamra, ALBRIGHT (1936) construed Ug *zbl* as passive participle *zabûl*. He derived the form from the verbal root ZBL—known in Akkadian and Arabic—and surmised the nominal meaning 'prince' or 'the elevated one'. The meaning fits with the frequent occurrence of *zbl* as a title for gods. This interpretation is widely accepted ('prince', 'princely state' or 'princeship') and it was included in *HALAT* (250).

Modifications and new readings have been proposed since. J. C. DE MOOR (*UF* 1 [1969] 188) rejected ALBRIGHT's explanation (1936) of the verbal form as passive participle **zabulu* and read **ziblu*, 'his Highness'. W. VON SODEN (*UF* 4 [1972] 159) vocalized the noun *zubūl*[*um*] referring to *zubultum* which is perhaps the title of the Ugaritic 'princess' as witnessed in two Akkadian documents from Mari. DIETRICH & LORETZ (1980) proved that the epithet *zbl bʿl arṣ* has the meaning 'prince, lord of the underworld'. They confirmed *baʿal zěbûb* to be an intentional misspelling of *bʿl zbl* 'Baal the prince', a chthonic god able to help in cases of illness. It may be added that this fact confirms Ugaritic incantations in which Baal is invoked to drive away the demon of disease (RIH I,16, 1-3; cf. *TUAT* 2 [1986-89] 335 and *ARTU* 183; perhaps also *KTU* 1.82:38; cf. *TUAT* 2, 339 [DIETRICH & LORETZ 1980]). The NT obviously preserved the correct form of the name (DIETRICH & LORETZ 1980:392). Likewise A. S. KAPELRUD (*Baal in the Ras Shamra Texts* [1952] 60); E. JENNI (*BHH* 1 [1962] 175-178.) and H. GESE (*RAAM* 122) recognize in *bʿl zbb* an intentional deformation of the original *bʿl zbl*. L K. HANDY (*UF* 20 [1988] 59) finally proposes to translate the noun as 'ruler', because *zbl* designates a person who is governing or ruling.

Consequently Masoretic *bʿl zbwb* of 2 Kgs 1:2-3.6.16 is to be emended to *bʿl zbwl* which is to be rendered 'Baal the Prince'. Most probably, the meaning of this god in the Syrian-Palestine area did not essentially differ from what can be deduced from the Ras Shamra texts though for a more accurate conception the data do not suffice.

III. *Bibliography*

W. F. ALBRIGHT, Zabûl Yam and Thâpiṭ Nahar in the Combat between Baal and the Sea, *JPOS* 16 (1936) 17-20; W. W. Graf BAUDISSIN, Beelzebub (Beelzebul), *RE* 2 (1897) 514-516; T. K. CHEYNE, Baalzebub, *EncBibl* I (1899) 407-408.; M. DIETRICH & O. LORETZ, Die Baʿal-Titel *bʿl arṣ* und *aliy qrdm*, *UF* 12 (1980) 391-393; F. C. FENSHAM, A possible Explanation of the Name Baal-Zebub of Ekron, *ZAW* 79 (1967) 361-364; S. GUYARD, Remarques sur le mot assyrien *zabal* et sur l'expression biblique *bet zeboul*, *JA* 7ème Série (1878) 220-225; F. C. MOVERS, *Die Phönizier* I (Bonn 1841); A. TÅNGBERG, A Note on Baʿal-Zěbub in 2 Kgs 1,2,3,6,16, *SJOT* 6 (1992) 293-296.

W. HERRMANN

BACCHUS Βάκχος

I. Bacchus is the form the Greek →Dionysus took in Rome. The name derives from the Greek epithet Βάκχος which denoted both the ecstatic Dionysus and his follower (fem. βάκχη). The epiclesis denoted a fundamental cultic aspect of the Greek god which had become prominent in Roman cult also, as had been the case in other neighbouring cultures: the Etruscans assimilated it as an epiclesis of their god Fufluns, the indigenous equivalent to Dionysus (Fufluns Paxies) (CRISTOFANI & MARTELLI 1978), the Lydians, like the Romans, transformed it into the name of the god (Bakis) (GRAF 1985:285-291). In the Bible Bacchus occurs only as a theophoric element in the personal name Bacchides (20 times in 1 Macc).

II. Roman religion had its own god Liber (paired with a goddess Libera) with whom Greek Dionysus was identified at an early age. The nature of Liber before the assimilation is difficult to grasp, besides the assumption of a general similarity in form and function; to judge from Italic rituals, the cult of Liber had sexual, even obscene features (DUMÉZIL 1977:382-383). At the time of our documentation, Liber and Bacchus are fully identified and understood as the Roman equivalents of Dionysus.

Two properties characterised Roman Bacchus, wine and ecstasy. Greek Dionysus was connected with wine and viticulture in the larger contexts of ecstasy and anti-structure; with Roman Bacchus (Liber), the connection with wine and viticulture had much more emphasis and paralleled the importance of cereals and agriculture of Roman Ceres. Cult and literature, however, are distinct in this sphere: Bacchus is the god of wine mainly in literature, while the cult kept to the traditional Latin name Liber.

Much more prominent is Bacchus in ecstatic and mystery rituals. The ecstatic cult was introduced in late 3d or early 2nd cent. BCE as a private cult, brought to Rome from Etruria by an itinerant priest and strictly confined to women. Somewhat later, a priestess from Campania opened the cult group to both genders; it quickly developed into a conspicuous though still private cult association whose ritual, the Bacchanalia, was well known to contemporaries (see Plautus, *Aulularia* 408, *Casina* 979-980). Roman political authorities were always wary of too independent private cults, and when, in 186 BCE, a citizen accused the officials of the Bacchanalia of sexual assault and ritual murder, the senate quickly intervened and reduced the cult to very small ritual congregations—without being able or willing to forbid it altogether (see Livy 39,8-18; DESSAU, *Inscriptiones Latinae Selectae* 18; PAILLER 1988). Private Bacchanalia continued to be celebrated in Rome and gained ground again during the first century BCE; by the time of the emperor Claudius, Messalina's licentiousness connected the cult with another scandal (Tacitus, *Annals* 11,31; HENRICHS 1978). Nevertheless, at the beginning of the imperial age Bacchic mysteries were an affair also of the upper classes, as is shown by the archaeological and epigraphical documents, esp. the reliefs from the Roman Villa Farnesina (dated early in the reign of Augustus), the imposing fresco in the Pompeian Villa dei Misteri (MATZ 1963), and the Bacchic inscription from Torre Nova (mid-second cent. CE SCHEID 1986). These monuments show that the Roman mysteries of Bacchus formed part of the mainstream Dionysiac movement in the late Hellenistic and Imperial periods; at the same time, they give a precious insight into particular aspects of the initiatory ritual and the structure and ideology of a larger cultic association (Dionysus).

In Latin literature, Bacchus is the god who provides poetic ecstasy and inspiration (Horace, *Carm.* 2,19 and 3,25; Properce 3,7; Ovid, *Trist.* 5,3). This is a Roman innovation: although already Democritus and Plato had developed a theory of ecstatic poetical inspiration, the inspirator remained Apollo. From Roman literature, the concept was taken over into later European poetology (MAHÉ 1988).

III. *Bibliography*

A. BRUHL, *Liber Pater. Origine et expansion du culte dionysiaque à Rome et dans le monde romain* (Paris 1953); M. CRISTOFANI & M. MARTELLI, Fufluns Pachies. Sugli aspetti del culto di Bacco in Etruria, *Studi Etruschi* 46 (1978) 119-133; G. DUMÉZIL, *La religion romaine archaïque, suivi d'un appendice sur la religion des Étrusques*, 2nd edition (Paris 1974); F. GRAF, *Nordionische Kulte. Religionsgeschichtliche und epigraphische Untersuchungen zu den Kulten von Chios, Erythrai, Klazomenai und Phokai* (Bibliotheca Helvetia Romana 21; Rome 1985); A. HENRICHS, Greek Menadism from Olympias to Messalina, *HSCP* 82 (1978) 121-160; N. MAHÉ, *Le mythe de Bacchus dans la poesie lyrique de 1549 à 1600* (Frankfurt, Bern etc. 1988); F. MATZ, *Διονυσιακὴ Τελετή. Archäologische Untersuchungen zum Dionysoskult in hellenistischer und römischer Zeit* (Abh. Mainz 1963:15; Wiesbaden 1963); J.-M. PAILLER, *Bacchanalia. La répression de 186 av. J.-C. à Rome et en Italie. Vestiges, images, traditions* (Rome and Paris 1988); J. SCHEID, Le thiase du Metropolitan Museum (*IGUR*

1,160), *Les associations dionysiaques dans les sociétés anciennes* (ed. O. de Cazanove; Rome 1986) 275-290.

F. GRAF

BAETYL Βαίτυλος

I. According to the classical texts, Baitylos (Greek *τ* for *θ*: see EISSFELDT 1962:228 n. 1; HEMMERDINGER 1970:60) is a 'Stone-god'. According to Semitic etymology the divine name could be interpreted as 'House of God/El', →Bethel. Some scholars therefore identify Baitylos with the deity Bethel. The divine name Bethel is known from Gen 31:13, 35:7, Amos 5:5 and elsewhere; it may be intended in Jer 48:13; as a theophoric element in a Babylonian personal name it occurs in Zech 7:2. The issue of the origin of the divine name Baitylos, of its occurrence in the OT, and of its possible Semitic roots are unsolved questions. There are three aspects of the problem: the cult of a god Baitylos/Bethel, the presence of many deities compounded with this name, and the baetyls as cultic objects.

II. In the Phoenician theogony of Philo Byblius (quoted by Eusebius, *P. E.* I 10, 16) the god Baitylos is a son of Ouranos ('Sky') and his wife-sister Gē (→Earth), with the brothers →El/Kronos, →Dagon and Atlas. This divine name seems unrelated to the baetyls (Gk *baitylia*), the 'stones endowed with life' invented by Ouranos, which Philo mentions a few lines further (Eusebius, *P. E.* I 10, 23), but the names are similar and the possibilities for confusion numerous. In the ancient Near East, the earliest certain occurrence of this god is from the 7th century BCE. In the treaty between Esarhaddon, king of Assyria, and Baal, king of Tyre, ^{d}*ba-a-a-ti*-DINGIR.MEŠ(*īlī*) = Bayt-el, is coupled with ^{d}*a-na-ti-ba-a-*[*a-ti*-DINGI]R.MEŠ(*īlī*) = Anat-Bayt-el (*ANET*, 534; *SAA* 2, 5 iv:6'). The same pair occurs in the list of divine witnesses invoked in the Succession Treaty of Esarhaddon (*VTE* 467 [reconstruction]; VAN DER TOORN 1992:83, 99 n. 18). In the 6th century BCE, the name of the god begins to occur as theophoric element in several West-Semitic personal names from Mesopotamia (HYATT 1939:82-84). Then, in the 5th century, his cult appears among the Egyptian-Jewish community at Elephantine. The Aramaic papyri from this colony attest the deity in composite names; the name of the deity is related to Eshem (*'šmbyt'l*, 'Name of Baitylos'), perhaps with Herem (*ḥrmbyt'l*, 'Sacredness[?] of Baitylos'; *pace* VAN DER TOORN 1986) and certainly with →Anat (*'ntbyt'l*, 'Providence, Sign, or Active Presence of Baitylos'). These composite names are to be explained as referring to separate deities, or as hypostatized aspects of the same god, Bethel. Finally, in the 3rd century CE, this deity is attested in three Greek inscriptions from Syria: at Doura Europos *Zeus Betylos* is mentioned as '(god) of the dwellers along the Orontes' (SEYRIG 1933:78); *IGLS* 376, from Kafr Nabo (near Aleppo), contains a dedication to the 'paternal gods' *Seimios*, *Symbetylos* ('Name of Betylos', see Eshem-Bayt-el at Elephantine) and to the Lion; *IGLS* 383 from Qal'at Kâlôta (the same region) attests the name of [*Zeus B*]*aitylos*.

Thus the question of the god's origin and of his functions remains enigmatic. The deity does not occur at Ugarit or in any other text from the second millennium BCE. VAN DER TOORN observes that the cult of this deity seems to be confined to North Syria, brought into Egypt in the 5th century by Northern Syrian Aramaeans (1992:85). He argues that Bethel and Anat-Bethel are a pair of late Aramaean deities. Note, however, the opposing views of J. P. Hyatt, M. L. Barré and J. T. Milik. The first suggests that Bethel became a deity as deification of the temple of El (or god), inhabitant of the sanctuary (HYATT 1939). The second scholar regards Bethel as a 'hypostasis or circumlocution of El' and argues that he was one of the supreme gods of the Tyrian pantheon (BARRÉ 1983:46-49). MILIK, finally, thinks of one 'Betyl' above all, morphologically distinguished from other *baitylia*, and judges Bethel and Anat-Bethel a pair of 'transfluvial' deities, not necessary Tyrians; in his view the cult of Bethel is of Sidonian origin

(1967:570, 576). Nevertheless, as for the name, in Akkadian documents there is no doubt that it should be explained on the basis of the Aramaic language rather than Phoenician; about the names compounded with Bayt-el, one may also bear in mind that 'binominal-gods' are known both in the Ugaritic pantheon and in first millennium BCE Phoenician and Punic inscriptions, e.g. →Eshmun-Melqart, Ṣid-Tanit and Ṣid-Melqart. As for the character, we have various and discordant pieces of information: the Succession Treaty of Esarhaddon affirms that Bayt-el and Anat-Bayt-el will punish the treaty breaker by sending hungry lions; Philo of Byblos, on the other hand, limits his observations to the divine (heavenly) genealogy of Baitylos and apparently does not link this god with the stones (*baitylia*) that Kronos endowed with vital force. Yet this kind of relationship is attested by several other documents. The Greek substantive *baitylos* and its diminutive *baitylion* occur only in late authors, none of whom seems to be earlier than Philo Byblius. Yet the worship of →stones as symbols of various deities is well attested in the Syrian religions, from the second millennium BCE documents (as *sikkanum* 'betyl'; DIETRICH, LORETZ & MAYER 1989; HUTTER 1993:88-91) up to Roman times (coins of Tyre, Sidon and Byblos); the Punic population of North Africa worshipped stones of the same kind apparently (e.g. *CIL* VIII 23283: vow of a *baetilum* to Saturnus; see ROSSIGNOLI 1992). More particularly, late Greek and Latin commentators, mythographers and lexicographers establish a special equivalence between what the Greeks called *Baitylos* and the Semitic cult of holy stones. It seems also possible that for the ancient writers the baetyl (Gk *baitylion*, Lat *baetulus*) denotes a particular kind of sacred stone, generally small and portable, of heavenly origin (real or supposed) and having magic qualities. Thus the baetyl was normally a meteoric stone endowed with divining faculties (UGOLINI 1981); Damascius (*Vita Isid.* 94 and 203, ed. Zintzen, 138 and 274-278) calls the stones that had fallen from heaven in the area of Mount →Lebanon *baityla* or *baitylia*; they were used for private oracles. In mythological records the baetyl occurs as well; the stone that Kronos swallowed, taking it for →Zeus, is called a baetyl. Hesiod tells (*Theog.* 485-490) that the goddess Rhea, who was delivered of Zeus, wrapped a stone in swaddling-clothes and gave it to Kronos to devour, which he did without noticing the substitution. As an adult, Zeus made Kronos vomit up all the children he had devoured. This stone/*Baitylos*, in some sources, has also the name *Abaddir*, a word attested epigraphically as theonym in Roman North-Africa (RIBICHINI 1985). Like the baetyls of Philo Byblius and of Damascius, Abaddir was an animated stone, which, vomited up by Kronos, 'had the shape of a human and was animated' (e.g. *Myth. Vat.* III 15, ed. Bode). Abaddir, moreover, is known both as a divine name and as a divine appellative (Augustine, *Ep.* XVII 2). These sources show, in the fusion of classical and Punic traditions, how an originally Semitic cult object came to be endowed with a personality and was credited with the ability to perform prodigies, to get excited and to give responses (see Josepp. Christ., *Libell. mem. in Vet. et Nov. Test.* 143, *PG* 106, 161 D).

III. According to Jer 48:13, the house of Israel put its trust in Bethel, as Moab did in →Chemosh. The parallelism with Chemosh makes it plausible that Bethel refers here to the god of that name, rather than to a topographical element. This fact is surprising, because the Northern Syrian deity is otherwise unconnected with Israel. Yet it must be assumed that some time before 600 BCE the cult of Bethel was introduced into Israel; it is hardly likely that the god Bethel is related to the biblical town Bethel (VAN DER TOORN 1992:90-91,99 n. 26; *pace* EISSFELDT 1930 = 1962).

It has been suggested that the god Bethel is mentioned in other biblical passages, e.g. Gen 31 and 35, Amos 3:14, 5:5. On the other hand, one may also postulate that the stone of Gen 28:10-22 (a *maṣṣēbâ*) on which Jacob slept and which he had anointed, must be connected to the cult of baetyls, as 'houses of God' and related with his vision, though the word *baetylia* does not appear in Greek OT.

IV. *Bibliography*

M. L. BARRÉ, *The God-List in the Treaty between Hannibal and Philip V of Macedonia: A Study in Light of the Ancient Near Eastern Treaty Tradition* (Baltimore 1983); A. I. BAUMGARTEN, *The* Phoenician History *of Philo of Byblos. A Commentary* (EPRO 89; Leiden 1981) 190, 202-203; E. R. DALGLISH, Bethel (Deity), *ABD* 1 (1992) 706-710; M. DIETRICH, O. LORETZ & W. MAYER, *Sikkanum* 'Betyle', *UF* 21 (1989) 133-139; O. EISSFELDT, Der Gott Bethel, *ARW* 28 (1930) 1-30 = *KS* 1 (Tübingen 1962) 206-233; B. HEMMERDINGER, De la méconnaissance de quelques étymologies, *Glotta* 48 (1970) 59-60; M. HUTTER, Kultstelen und Baityloi, *Religionsgeschichtliche Beziehungen zwischen Kleinasien, Nordsyrien und dem Alten Testament* (eds. B. Janowski, K. Koch & G. Wilhelm eds.; OBO 129; Freiburg & Göttingen 1993) 87-108; J. P. HYATT, The Deity Bethel in the Old Testament, *JAOS* 59 (1939) 81-98; J. T. MILIK, Les papyrus araméens d'Hermoupolis et les cultes syro-phéniciens (2. Dieu Béthel), *Bib* 48 (1967) 565-577; S. RIBICHINI, *Poenus Advena. Gli dèi fenici e l'interpretazione classica* (Roma 1985) 113-125; C. ROSSIGNOLI, Persistenza del culto betilico nell'Africa romana: un'iscrizione da Thala (Tunisia), *L'Africa romana. Atti del IX Convegno di studio, Nuoro, 13-15 dicembre 1991*, I (ed. A. Mastino; Sassari 1992) 73-96; H. SEYRIG, Altar Dedicated to Zeus Betylos, *Excavations at Dura-Europos, Preliminary Reports of Fourth Season*, (eds P. V. C. Baur, M. I. Rostovtzeff & A. R. Bellinger; New Haven 1933) 68-71; M. H. SILVERMAN, *Religious Values in the Jewish Proper Names at Elephantine* (AOAT 217; Neukirchen-Vluyn 1985) 221-229; M. UGOLINI, Il dio (di) pietra, *Sandalion* 4 (1981) 7-29; K. VAN DER TOORN, Herem-Bethel and Elephantine Oath Procedure, *ZAW* 98 (1986) 282-285; VAN DER TOORN, Anat-Yahu, Some Other Deities, and the Jews of Elephantine, *Numen* 39 (1992) 80-101; G. ZUNTZ, Baitylos and Bethel, *Classica et Medievalia* 8 (1946) 169-219.

S. RIBICHINI

BAGA

I. The personal name *Bagoas* to be found in Judith 12:11 is undoubtedly an Iranian name, although quite difficult to interpret. The second term *oas* cannot be explained with any certainty, as was acknowledged by EILERS (1954-56) after a strictly formal attempt and, more recently, by HUYSE with even stronger scepticism (1990). The first term *baga* raises problems of another kind. It is a common dialectal singularity of Iranian languages that they gave the old Indo-European word **deiuó* (Sanskrit *deva*, Lat *deus*) a negative value and substituted *baga-* for the former meaning of **daiua-*, which had come to mean 'evil spirit' (BURROW 1973; KELLENS 1976; SIMS-WILLIAMS 1989; according to the second author, *yazata-*, common in the Avesta, is not a general term concurring with *baga-*, but a specific title only for the deities close to →Mithra).

II. The whole question is to know whether *baga* is always the divine title *par excellence* or whether it may be the personal name of a Mazdaean god. It has been thought, albeit inconclusively, that the word might refer to Mithra (since MARQUART 1896) or be the Iranian name for Indian →Varuna (BOYCE 1981). HENNING (1965), relying on the Sogdian word for wedding, *bγʾny-pš-ktʾkw*, and GIGNOUX (1977; 1979), referring to onomastic data from epigraphic Middle-Persian, believe there is an Iranian god Baga corresponding to the minor Vedic deity Bhaga, who is the allegory of sharing or the agent *par excellence* of divine bounty. The inconclusiveness of their arguments was easily demonstrated by DIETZ (1978) for the former and by ZIMMER (1984) for the latter. SIMS-WILLIAMS (1989) advocates an intermediary position which sounds fairly reasonable: "It is probable that *baga-* 'god' sometimes designates a specific deity as 'the god' *par excellence* (...) but no basis has ever been stated for the assumption that *baga-* 'the god' (...) must refer to the same divinity at all periods and in all parts of the Iranian world".

III. *Bibliography*

M. BOYCE, Varuna the Baga, *Monumentum Georg Morgenstierne*, Vol 1 (Tehran-Liège 1981) 59-73; T. BURROW, The Proto-Indo-Aryans, *JRAS* (1973) 130; A. DIETZ, Baga and Miϑra in Sogdiana, *Etudes Mithriaques* (Tehran-Liège 1978) 111-114; W. EILERS, Neue aramäische Urkunden aus Ägypten, *AfO* 17 (1954-56) 327-328 n. 19; P. GIGNOUX, Le dieu Baga en Iran, *Acta Antiqua Hungarica* 25 (1977 [1980]) 119-127; GIGNOUX, Les noms propres en moyen-perse épigraphique, *Pad nām-i yazdān* (Paris 1979 [1980]) 88-90; W. B. HENNING, A Sogdian God, *BSOAS* 28 (1965) 242-254; P. HUYSE, Bagoas, *Iranisches Personennamenbuch,* Vol V 6a (Wien 1990) 39-40; J. KELLENS, Trois réflexions sur la religion des Achéménides, *Studien zur Indologie und Iranistik* 2 (1976) 121-126; J. MARQUART [MARKWART], *Untersuchungen zur Geschichte von Iran* I (Göttingen 1896) 63-65; N. SIMS-WILLIAMS, Baga, *Encyclopaedia Iranica*, Vol 3 (London-New York 1989) 403-405; S. ZIMMER, Iran. *baga* - ein Gottesname?, *Münchener Studien zur Sprachwissenschaft* 43 (1984) 187-215.

J. KELLENS

BARAD ברד

I. As used in two passages of the OT, Heb ברד, vocalized as *bārād*, has been interpreted as the name of an ancient deity of the Canaanite pantheon. In some texts from Tell Mardikh-Ebla of the third millennium BCE *dBaradu (madu)* occurs as a divine name. Etymologically, both biblical *bārād* and Eblaitic *Baradu (madu)* are to be related to the Semitic root *BRD and to be explained as "(big) Chill".

II. The Eblaitic god *Baradu madu* has been explained by G. PETTINATO as a divinized form of the →Euphrates (*Ebla: un impero inciso nell' argilla* [Milan 1979] 268). Since the name of this river occurs in the texts from Ebla under its 'classical' name Purattu (TM.75.G.2192 IV 1-2 = ARET 5 [1984], no. 3 iv 2-3: A *bù-la-na-tim* = **māwī Puran(a)tum*), Pettinato's interpretation cannot be upheld. It is very likely that Baradu is a personification of the hail (cf. ARET 5 [1984] no. 4 v 4-5 NA_4 *ba-ra-du*, "hail-stones", cf. Aram *[ʾbny b]rd* in Sefire I A 25), a minor deity of the local pantheon or a specific manifestation of the Storm-God Adda (→Hadad). The Eblaitic texts attest that Baradu received some sacrificial offerings like precious metals and sheep (TM.75.G.1376 = MEE 2 no. 48 r. vi 4 [*dba-ra-du ma-ad*]; TM.75.G.1541 = ARET 2 no. 8 ix 4; TM.75.G.2075 iv 29 = *OrAnt* 18 [1979] 149). The same god occurs perhaps as a theophoric element in the Ugaritic personal name *brdd* ('Haddu is Hail'[?]).

III. In the OT *Bārād* occurs in Ps 78:48, in a passage which concerns the seventh plague of Egypt, where Barad occurs in parallel with 'the Reshephs' (pl.): *wayyasgēr labbārād bĕʿîrām ûmiqnêhem lārĕšāpîm*, "He (= Yahweh) gave up their cattle to Barad, and their herds to the Reshefs." In Isa 28:2 *Bārād* is paralleled with a demon in the service of Yahweh, →Qeṭeb ('Destruction'). We have a very interesting antithesis between the chill and the stifling heat caused by the hot wind: *hinneh ḥāzāq wĕʾammiṣ laʾdōnāy kĕzerem bārād śaʿar qāṭeb*, "Behold, the Lord has a mighty and strong one, like a tempest of Barad, like a storm of Qeṭeb."

III. *Bibliography*

A. CAQUOT, Sur quelques démons de l'Ancien Testament, *Sem* 6 (1956) 53-68; P. XELLA, 'Le Grand Froid': Le dieu *Baradu madu* à Ebla, *UF 18* (1986) 437-444.

P. XELLA

BARAQ → LIGHTNING

BASHAN בשן

I. Hebrew *bāšān* I 'fertile, stoneless piece of ground' (*HALAT*, 158), should be distinguished from Heb *bāšān* II 'serpent', which is etymologically cognate with Ug *bṯn* 'serpent' (Akk *bašmu*; Ar *baṯan*; DAY 1985:113-119; see also Heb *peten*: cf. *HALAT* 930). A relation between *bāšān* I and II was proposed by Albright (*BASOR* 110 [1948] 17, n. 53; *HUCA* 23 [1950-1951] 27-28; cf. FENSHAM, *JNES* 19 [1960] 292-293; DAHOOD 1981:145-146). He interpreted Bashan, 'Serpent', as a nickname of the Canaanite god Yammu, the chaotic serpentine monster, given its apparent parallelism with *yām* in Ps 68:23, usually understood as a merism (KRAUS 1966:465; CARNITI 1985:95; TATE 1990; but cf. DE MOOR 1990:122). *bāšān* I occurs: a) As a geographical name, with article *habbāšān*, mainly in the dtr tradition (Deut 3:1-14; Josh 12:4-5; and approximately 40 times more) and in some historical hymns (Pss 135:11; 136:20), of a region of northern Transjordan conquered by the Israelites, formerly inhabited by the →Rephaim, whose king was the mythical →Og, and where afterwards a part of the tribe of Manasseh established itself (e.g. Deut 4:43; Josh 20:8; 21:6). This region also served as a delimiting point of the Israelite boundaries (e.g. Josh 12:5; 13:11, 30; 2 Kgs 10:33). b) As a literary and metaphorical reference, without article generally *bāšān*, given its proverbial fertility; in this connexion some prophetic traditions refer to its 'cows', 'bulls', 'rams', 'fatlings' and 'lions' (Amos 4:1; Mic 7:14; Ezek 39: 18; Ps 22:13; Deut 32;14), while others quote its 'oaks', as famous as →Lebanon's cedars (Isa 2:13; Jer 22:20; Ezek 27:6; Zech 11:1-2), and praise in general its fertility, comparing it with the →Carmel because of its rich pastures and proposing both of them as the recovered eschatological resting place, now destroyed and desolate (Jer 50:19; Mic 7:14; Isa 33:9; Nah 1:4). The geographical indication Bashan functions as the depiction of the divine abode in Ps 68:16 and Deut 33:22, also without article, related possibly to Canaanite mythology which places here the heavenly/infernal dwelling place of its deified dead kings, echoed in the Biblical geographical tradition mentioned in *bāšān* I a) and probably in b).

II. Biblical geographical tradition agrees with the mythological and cultic data of the Ugaritic texts. According to *KTU* 1.108:1-3, the abode of the *mlk ʿlm*, the dead and deified king (DEL OLMO LETE 1987:49-53), and his place of enthronement as *rpu* was in *ʿštrt-hdrʿy*, in amazing correspondence with the Biblical tradition about the seat of king Og of Bashan, "one of the survivors of the Rephaim, who lived in Ashtarot and Edrei" (Josh 12:4 [NEB]). This place *ʿštrt* is also treated in *KTU* 1.100:41; 1.107:17: and RS 86.2235:17 as the abode of the god *mlk*, the eponym of the *mlkm*, the deified kings, synonym of the *rpum*. For the 'Canaanites' of Ugarit, the Bashan region, or a part of it, clearly represented 'Hell', the celestial and infernal abode of their deified dead kings, →Olympus and →Hades at the same time. It is possible that this localization of the Canaanite Hell is linked to the ancient tradition of the place as the ancestral home of their dynasty, the *rpum*. The Biblical text also recalls that "all Bashan used to be called the land/earth of the Rephaim" (Deut 3:13 [NEB]), an ambiguous wording that could equally be translated as "the 'hell' of the Rephaim". In any case, the link between Bashan and the *rpum*/Rephaim in both traditions speaks in favour of a very old use of the two meanings of this last denomination: ancient dwellers of Northern Transjordan / inhabitants of 'Hell'.

III. Precisely this double semantic level referring to the dwellers also appears in connexion with the place, Bashan, namely, an empirical and mytho-theological denomination in the Biblical tradition as well. This mytho-theological resonance can be appreciated mainly in Ps 68:16 where it is plainly asserted that Bashan is a *har ʾĕlōhîm*, the same expression used in the Bible to designate →Yahweh's abode. But it is clear that such a denomination does not belong to the Israelite tradition about the dwelling place of their national God. According to the same Ps 68:9, 19 Yahweh has his original abode in Sinai whence He will move to 'the mount of his election'. Mount Bashan is rather set against Sinai in a conflict of

Olympi, aiming to defend its preeminence. This is to say, such a designation reproduces the Canaanite tradition that located the divine abode in the region of Bashan-Salmon (CURTIS 1986:89-95; 1987, 39-47). According to DE MOOR (1990:124-127) it is Yahweh-El who takes posession of this divine mountain as his own ancient abode. It is curious, nevertheless, that in connexion with this conflict the corresponding Canaanite deity who opposes Yahweh is not mentioned. In his place the *malkê ṣĕbāʾôt* (v 13), the *mĕlākîm* (v 15; cf v 30), usually interpreted as chiefs of either the enemy's or Israel's armies, are adduced; namely, the opponents of Yahweh are precisely, according to Ps 68, the same divine dwellers of Bashan whom the Ugaritic tradition records: the *mlkm/mĕlākîm* (*rpum*/Rephaim). The syntagma *har/hārîm gabnunnîm*, most commonly construed as a metaphor for 'high mountains', could also be considered a parallel designation of these deities (DEL OLMO LETE 1988:54-55), taking into account the parallelism *har ʾĕlohîm har bāšān har gabnunnîm har bāšān* (v. 16) and the tauromorphic appearance of →Baal and other deities in Canaan (*KTU* 1.12 I 30-33). In any case we are not dealing here simply with ordinary animals; the expression has mythological overtones that JACOBS (*JBL* 104 [1985] 109-110) also assumes in Amos 4:1: "cows of Bashan" as a title of Samaria's women in their role of 'Baal's wives' in the cult of the fertility god shaped as a bull.

Furthermore, Bashan, the divine mountain, is simultaneously the 'infernal' sphere from which the God of Israel promises to make his faithful return (v 23). This coincidence of the 'celestial' and 'infernal' levels is congruent with the Canaanite mythology that locates here the abode of its deified dead kings, the *mlk(m)/rpu(m)* that dwell(s) in *ʿštrt/hdrʿy*. Again the parallelism clarifies the issue, making plain the infernal character of Bashan through its being equated with *mĕṣûlôt yām,* these two lexemes being designations of Hell in the Hebrew Bible (TROMP 1969:56-64), not to be understood either as a simple literary merism indicating the cosmic sphere of Yahweh's activity or as a mythological designation of the god Yam. Perhaps this is a similar case to that offered by the Mesopotamian town of Kutha, center of the cult to →Nergal, that afterwards became a name for 'hell' (HUTTER 1985:55-56), as was also the case with the Hebrew toponym *gê(ʾ) hinnōm*, 'Gehenna'.

According to this interpretation, midway between a purely metaphorical sense (KRAUS, TATE, CARNITI) and an overall mythological reading (ALBRIGHT, FENSHAM, DAHOOD, TROMP, DE MOOR), the Hebrew Bible conflates Canaanite traditions that located their Heaven-Hell in the region of Bashan within a wider framework of mythical geography that included at least Mount →Hermon as →El's abode and the Hule marsh as the scene of Baal's hunting and death. The Hebrew Bible integrated these traditions when giving form to its epics of the Conquest of Canaan and the exaltation of its God as vanquisher and liberator from its 'demons'.

IV. *Bibliography*

L. R. BAILEY, The Gehenna: the Topography of Hell, *BA* 49 (1986) 187-191; C. CARNITI, *Il salmo 68. Studio letterario* (Rome 1985); J. B. CURTIS, *Har-bašan*, 'the Mountain of God' (Ps. 68: 16 [15]), *Proceedings of the Eastern Great Lakes and Midwest Biblical Societies* 6 (1986) 85-95; CURTIS, The Celebrated Victory at Zalmon (Ps 68:14-15), *Proceedings of the Eastern Great Lakes and Midwest Biblical Societies* 7 (1987) 39-47; M. DAHOOD, *Psalms II. 51-100* (AB 17; Garden City 1981[3]) 130-152; J. DAY, *God's Conflict with the Dragon and the Sea* (Cambridge 1985) 113-119; G. DEL OLMO LETE, Basán o el 'infierno' cananeo, *SEL* 5 (1988) 51-60; DEL OLMO LETE, Los nombres divinos de los reyes de Ugarit, *AulOr* 5 (1987) 39-66, esp. 50; J. C. DE MOOR, *The Rise of Yahwism* (BETL 91; Leuven 1990) 118-128; DE MOOR, East of Eden, *ZAW* 100 (1988) 105-111; M. DIETRICH & O. LORETZ, Rāpiʾu und Milku aus Ugarit. Neuere historisch-geographische Thesen zu *rpu mlk ʿlm* (KTU 1.108:1) und *mt rpi* (KTU 1.17 I 1), *UF* 21 (1989) 124-

130, esp. 123-127; H.-J. KRAUS, *Psalmen I. Teilband* (BKAT, XV/1; Neukirchen-Vluyn 1966[3]) 464; M. HUTTER, *Altorientalische Vorstellungen von der Unterwelt* (OBO 63; Freiburg/Göttingen 1985); M. E. TATE, *Psalms 51-100* (WBC 20; Dallas 1990) 159-186; N. J. TROMP, *Primitive Conceptions of Death and the Nether World in the Old Testament* (Rome 1969); G. WANKE, *Die Ziontheologie der Korachiten* (BZAW 97; Berlin 1966).

G. DEL OLMO LETE

BASHTU בשׁת

I. Akk *baštu* (in later texts *baltu*, Sum **tes**[2]) "dignity, pride, decorum" is sometimes characterized as a protective spirit in Mesopotamia. Heb *bōšet* occurs in personal names in the OT (2 Sam 2:8 and 4:4) as a substitute for the theophoric element. The Akkadian noun derived from the verb *ba'āšu* "to come to shame", which is of common Semitic origin (e.g. Ug *bṯ*, Aram *behet*, Heb *bōš*). VON SODEN (1964) tried to show that *baštu* had an original meaning "sexual power" and that it was part of a more complex concept for "life force", expressed by four words: *lamassu* "efficiency power", *šēdu* "vital power", *baštu* and *dūtu* "generative power". This interpretation is rejected in the *CAD*. As a positive quality *baštu* is used to describe deities, humans, cities and buildings (for evidence see *CAD* B 142-144 and *AHW* 112). Sometimes it is associated with garments or adornments. From Old Babylonian hymns to →Ishtar we know that the Babylonians regarded *baštu* as a divine gift.

II. In rituals and prayers from first millennium Mesopotamia, *baštu* is mentioned several times in connection with the protective spirits Shedu and Lamassu (for references see *CAD* B, 142-143 sub 1 a and 2 a), and in a late lexical list (MSL 14 [1979] 367:310 and 389:306) it is preceded by the divine determinative, again between Shedu and Lamassu. Therefore it is possible that like them *baštu* was regarded as a protective spirit at least during the first millennium BCE. In a late god-list (5 *R* 43: ii 38) ^{d}*Baltu* is equated with ^{d}*Nabû ili balti* "Nabû (as) god of dignity" and there also is evidence for a star named ^{mul}*Baltu* (5 *R* 46: 45).

From Old Akkadian times onwards *baštu* occurs in personal names like *Ilī-baštī* "My-God-Is-My-Bashtu", *Ina-īn-bašti* "In-the-Eye-of-Bashtu" or *Libūr-baštī* "My-Bashtu-May-Endure" (see *CAD* B, 143 sub 2 b and c). Although it is never written with the divine determinative, it can be interpreted as a theophoric element. In Mesopotamian belief there often was no distinction between a phenomenon and its personification as god or demon.

III. In the OT Hebrew *bōšet* denotes "shame": shame because of sins (e.g. 2 Sam 20:30; Jer 2:26; Ezek 7:18), shame because of violence (e.g. Obad 1:10) or after a defeat (e.g. Mic 7:10; Ps 89:46). In the two personal names Ishbosheth (2 Sam 2:8) and Mephibosheth (2 Sam 4:4 and 21:8) it is used instead of a theophoric element. This does not imply, however, that the reference is to a Hebraized form of the Akk Baštu (*pace* TSEVAT 1975). In these two variant forms of the names of Saul's son and grandson *bōšet* substitutes the original divine name →Baal (compare 1 Chr 8:33-34). As it seems, the scribe wanted to avoid the name of the rival Canaanite deity and replaced it with an expression with obvious pejorative connotations. The name Jerubbesheth (2 Sam 11:21) is another attestation of this phenomenon (compare Judg 6:32).

IV. *Bibliography*

E. EBELING, Baštum, *RLA* 1 (1928) 431; W. VON SODEN, Die Schutzgottheiten Lamassu und Schedu in der babylonisch-assyrischen Literatur, *BagM* 3 (1964) 148-156; J. STAMM, *Die akkadische Namengebung* (Leipzig 1939) 126 n. 2, 159-160, 311, 355 and passim; M. TSEVAT, Ishbosheth and Congeners: The names and Their Study, *HUCA* 34 (1975) 71-87.

H. D. GALTER

BASTET

I. The name of the Egyptian goddess

Bastet occurs in the Bible in Ezek 30:17 as part of the name Pibeseth, (פִּי־בֶסֶת) an Egyptian town in the Delta near the modern Zagazig. The place of the ancient town is called nowadays Tell Basta. The Greek name was Boubastis and the Hebrew rendering Pî-beset. The ancient Egyptian name of the town was *pr-bꜣstt* (lit. House of Bastet).

II. The Greek historian Herodotus (2:138) who travelled in Egypt in the 5th cent. BCE gives a description of the temple of the goddess Bastet which he calls Artemis and writes: "Other temples may be larger or have cost more to build, but none is a greater pleasure to look at". From his description and from Egyptian texts it may be deduced that the temple was surrounded on three sides by water which formed a lake or *isheru* like the lake which still surrounds the temple of Mut in Karnak on three sides.

Egyptian temples surrounded on three of the four sides by a so-called *isheru* were devoted to leonine goddesses e.g. Tefnut, →Hathor, →Mut, Sakhmet and Bastet who were called daughter of the Sun-god →Re or Eye of Re. These goddesses were considered to be representations of the original, first feminine being and to have a dual nature in which fiery anarchic and destructive characteristics coexisted with pacific and creative elements. These goddesses had to be pacified with specific rituals. According to a mythical story the original furious and fiery lioness changed into a peaceful cat and settled down in her temple. The lake around the temple was meant to cool off her burning wrath.

In older times since the third millennium BCE, Bastet was represented as a lion or lion-headed woman, but in the first mill. BCE when the cat had been domesticated and had reached the status of pet animal in Egypt, she was more and more represented as a cat-headed woman and became the typical cat-goddess of Egypt. The many cat-bronzes and cat-mummies were originally dedicatory offerings of pilgrims, though now found in Egyptian collections all over the world. They may come for a considerable part from the temple site of Tell Basta.

Herodotus (2:60) describes not only the temple but also a festival of Bastet in Bubastis: Men and women came by ship to the city in great numbers, up to 700.000 persons, singing, dancing and making music with flutes and castanets. Elaborate sacrifices were made and more wine was consumed than during all the rest of the year. This fits in with Egyptian sources according to which leonine goddesses had to be pacified with "the feast of drunkenness". Bastet was certainly a very popular and beloved goddess. One could characterize an Egyptian goddess by saying that she was raging like Sakhmet (the lion-goddess) and friendly like Bastet (the cat-goddess).

The writing and pronunciation of the name of the goddess as Bastet is a generally accepted convention in Egyptological literature, but is no more than a modern reconstruction. The second *t* in the word *bꜣstt* denotes the feminine ending and was usually not pronounced. It seems that the aleph (*ꜣ*) which is found in traditional Egyptian writing changed place and became a *Vortonsilbe bast(t) >ubesti* (J. OSING, *Die Nominalbildung des Ägyptischen* [Mainz 1976] 855-856 n. 1319 and 376 n. 55). An Aramaic writing of the name of the goddess was *ꜣbst* (*Wb* I, 423). The Egyptian pronunciation of the name of the goddess was more like 'obast' or 'ubesti' than 'bastet' in the 1st millennium BCE. It remains remarkable, however, that in the Hebrew rendering of the place-name the '*Vortonsilbe*' is not indicated: Pibeset. The difference in the Hebrew version with the Greek rendering Boubastis might be the work of the Masoretes, so that the pronunciation of the place-name might have been 'Bubast' or 'Bubeset'. The meaning of the name of the goddess is uncertain. The older, problematic explanation was "She of Bubastis" (*Wb* I, 423); a more recent explanation is "She of the ointment-jar" (S. QUIRKE, *Ancient Egyptian Religion* [London 1992] 31). Her name was indeed written with the hieroglyph ointment-jar (*bꜣs*) and she was among other things goddess of protective ointments. Bubastis or Pibeset was still one of the most important cities of Egypt in the time of Ezekiel. It had even been capital of Egypt during dynasties 22 and 23 (945-730 BCE).

III. The mentioning of the placename *pî-beset* in Ezek 30:17 has no religio-historical implications. A deity Bastet was not venerated by Ezekiel's Israelite contemporaries.

IV. *Bibliography*

E. OTTO, Bastet, *LdÄ* I, 628-630; J. QUAEGEBEUR, Le culte de Boubastis - Bastet en Egypte gréco-romaine, *Les divins chats d'Egypte* (ed. L. Delvaux & E. Warmenbol; Leuven 1991) 117-127.

H. TE VELDE

BEELZEBUL → BAAL-ZEBUB

BEHEMOTH בהמות

I. Despite frequent claims that Behemoth refers to one or another animal of the natural world, the Behemoth depicted in Job 40:15-24 (10-19) is best understood as a mythological creature possessing supernatural characteristics. By form *běhēmôt* is the intensive (feminine) plural of *běhēmâ* ('beast, ox'; collective: 'beasts, cattle'; see BOTTERWECK 1975:6-17); nevertheless, in Job 40:15-24 the grammatical forms pertaining to Behemoth are all masculine singular. The figure suggested is a singular being of awesome dimensions, a 'super ox' of mythic proportions and possessing supernatural characteristics, hence the 'Beast' par excellence. Whether Behemoth is attested in the Bible outside of Job 40:15-24 is disputed since the Hebrew vocable *běhēmôt* by form is ambiguous; in most instances it is the simple feminine plural of *běhēmâ*, i.e. 'cattle' or 'beasts.' Other biblical passages which may refer to Behemoth are Deut 32: 24; Isa 30:6; Job 12:7; Ps 73:22.

II. Although ancient Near Eastern precedents for biblical Behemoth have been suggested, there are no certain extrabiblical references to this figure apart from later Jewish and Christian literature and these are clearly derivative from the biblical tradition.

The only biblical reference to Behemoth is Job 40:15 (10), with its attendant description in vv 15-24 (10-19). But even in this case there is no consensus about the nature or even the existence of this being. Behemoth is clearly no ordinary beast: an awesome ox-like being that eats grass but is equally at home in the water as on land, with bones of metal and a tail (or penis?) comparable to a mighty cedar tree. This 'first of the works of →God' fears neither human nor beast; only the deity is capable of capturing him. Behemoth is paired with the mythic fire-breathing monster →Leviathan, whose description immediately follows in Job 40:25-41:26(41:1-34). Both Behemoth and Leviathan function in the second speech of →Yahweh in Job 40-41 to demonstrate the futility of Job in questioning the ways of the Almighty.

The interpretation of Behemoth is so highly controverted that any discussion of Behemoth must include a history of that interpretation. From numerous references to Behemoth in postbiblical Jewish and Christian literature it is clear that the earliest understanding of Behemoth was as some sort of unruly mythic creature akin to Leviathan, which in the end only God can subdue. Here only pseudepigraphic texts will be mentioned. (For the further development of the Behemoth tradition in posttannaitic midrashim, see GINZBERG V [1925, 1953] 41-46, esp. nn. 118, 127.) According to *1 Enoch* 60:7-9 Leviathan is a female monster dwelling in the watery Abyss (compare Mesopotamian →Tiamat), while Behemoth is a male monster dwelling in a hidden desert of Dundayin, east of Eden. *4 Esdr* 6:49-52 says that Leviathan and Behemoth were both created on the fifth day but then separated, with Leviathan being given a watery domain and Behemoth a home on land, until such time as God uses them as food for those designated. *2 Bar.* 29:4 adds the detail that it will be in the messianic age that Leviathan and Behemoth come forth from their respective places to serve as food for the pious remnant. It is obvious that this motif is in part derived from the account of the end of →Gog of →Magog (Ezek 39:17-20). Although Behemoth is not mentioned in the NT, Rev 13 patently is informed by the Leviathan-Behemoth tradition. In this pericope two kindred beasts rise up in united opposition to the righteous, the one beast 'from the →sea' (13:1) and 'another beast which rose out of the →earth' (13:11).

In modern times some commentators have attempted to reinforce the mythological character of Behemoth, while others have attributed to Behemoth a more naturalistic origin. Broadly speaking, modern interpretations may be grouped into three categories: (a) Behemoth is an animal of the natural world; (b) there was no Behemoth; (c) Behemoth is a distinct mythic being.

(a) Behemoth as a natural animal: Since the seventeenth century the theory has been advanced frequently that Behemoth represents the hippopotamus. This theory, first proposed by S. BOCHART (*Hierozoicon* 2 [1663] cols. 753-69) remains popular with scholars. Proponents even proposed an etymology for Behemoth as an Egyptian loanword: **p'-iḥ-hw*, 'the ox of the water'. Although it is now conceded that no such term existed in Egyptian or Coptic, the identification of Behemoth with the hippopotamus has persisted, though now often with a mythic overlay. KEEL (1978) adduces Egyptian iconographic evidence which portrays the Egyptian king as the incarnation of the god →Horus in the act of subjugating his divine foe →Seth, the latter depicted in the form of the red hippopotamus. Strengths of this theory are the amphibious nature of both the hippopotamus and Behemoth, and the analogous methods of capture in each case (Job 40:24). RUPRECHT (1971) and KUBINA (1979) also build upon this theory.

Occasionally an identification of Behemoth with an animal other than the hippopotamus has been proposed. Bochart himself had rejected an identification of Behemoth as the elephant. G. R. DRIVER (1956) claims that Behemoth is the crocodile (an opinion reflected in the NEB translation of Job 40). DRIVER's theory necessitates the creation of a hapax legomenon in Hebrew by emending MT *'ăšer 'āśîtî 'immāk* to *'imśāk*, by analogy to supposed cognates in other Semitic languages, Egyptian, Coptic, and Greek; Driver further emends 'he eats grass like cattle' to 'he eats cattle like grass'. COUROYER (1975) proposed that Behemoth was the water buffalo.

(b) There was no Behemoth: A second group of scholars argue that there was no such being as Behemoth, though their lines of argument diverge radically. N. H. HABEL (*The Book of Job* [OTL; Philadelphia 1985] 559) concludes that Behemoth is a creation of the Joban poet, a symbol to Job that he may constitute a threat to →God similar to chaotic forces which God created at the beginning and which need to be kept subjugated. WOLFERS (1990) also understands Behemoth as only a symbol, but of the errant people of Judah reaching out to Assyria in the eighth century BCE. N. H. TUR-SINAI (*The Book of Job* [rev. ed., Jerusalem 1967] 556-559) dismissed the entire notion of Behemoth as nothing more than a misreading of Job. He claims that the whole of Job 40:15-41:26 is a description of Leviathan, with certain verses perhaps out of order. He treats *bĕhēmôt* in 40:15 as a simple plural, as elsewhere in MT, and translates: "Behold, here are the beasts which I made with thee [Leviathan], (all) that eateth grass as cattle". TUR-SINAI assumes this to be a literary quotation from an ancient creation story and addressed to Leviathan as 'the first of God's ways'. The implication is that all the animals, herbivores, are food for Leviathan who thought to displace God and to rule in God's place.

KINNIER WILSON (1975) argues that the Behemoth pericope is a parody on what would happen if God were to follow Job's advice on how to run the cosmos: "(So) behold now 'Behemoth' which I have made with thy help". Behemoth is an invented name for the resulting incongruent, ridiculous 'ox-like' creature, so afraid of being ridiculed by the other creatures that it hides in the undergrowth around the →Jordan. The same point is made with Leviathan; just as Job cannot presume to play the creator, so neither can he act the part of the Hero-god who subdues the fire-breathing monster

Leviathan. The one idea is as ridiculous as the other.

Another group of scholars understand the whole of the Behemoth-Leviathan pericope as referring to a single being. Building upon the Seth-hippopotamus theory of KEEL (1978), RUPRECHT (1971) claims that the Joban poet has built a threefold meaning into to figure of Behemoth-Leviathan: the naturalistic (hippopotamus); the mythic (primeval evil in the form of the god Seth, the enemy of the creator); and the historical (political enemies, historical powers). The poet uses the hippopotamus, termed first Behemoth and then Leviathan, as his basic symbol for historical forces whom Yahweh controls and subdues, as elsewhere in the Bible. FUCHS (1993) posits that Job 40:15-41 contains a bipartite description of the well-known →chaos monster, named first as Behemoth and then as Leviathan. Part One of this description (Job 40:15-32) depicts a powerful, hippopotamus-like, gigantic beast with a passive, almost domestic character akin to Mother Earth. The hippopotamus in Egyptian tradition is symbolic of both the mother goddess and the chaos beast and corresponds to the two poles of the mother earth concept: the protective and the devouring. Part Two (41:5-26), in a heightening of imagery, is a deliberate distancing from any known animal in favour of the →dragon-like, fire-belching chaos monster.

(c) Behemoth as a distinct mythic figure: Given the obvious pairing of Behemoth with Leviathan in the second speech of Yahweh, a number of modern scholars see in Behemoth an independent mythic beast along the lines of Leviathan, but distinct from the latter—much like in early Jewish and Christian interpretations. At the end of the nineteenth century the mythological interpretation received renewed impetus from the studies of GUNKEL (1895) and others, who demonstrated points in common between biblical figures and ancient Near Eastern mythology. Perhaps most influential of all with regard to Behemoth specifically have been the studies of POPE, especially his AB commentary on Job (1973:320-322). On the basis of Ugaritic comparative evidence, POPE posited the existence of a prototype of Behemoth, as a companion to *ltn* (Lotan = Leviathan) already in Canaanite mythology. He called attention in the Ugaritic Baal myth to the obscure bovine creature called *ʿgl il ʿtk*, which he translated as 'the furious bullock of El' but which more likely should be translated as 'El's calf Atik'. Further, POPE compared Behemoth to 'the bull of heaven' slain by Gilgamesh and Enkidu in Mesopotamian myth (*ANET* 83-85). WAKEMAN (1972), too, posited a connection between Behemoth and 'El's calf Atik', also known as Arshu (*arš*). She seems to exceed the meagre biblical and Canaanite evidence, however, in positing that this second chaos monster was specifically an earth monster (Ugaritic *arṣ;* Hebrew *ʾereṣ*), which she claims is named in texts such as Exod 15:12; Num 16:32; Ps 46:7; 114:7. J. DAY (1985:80-84) seems to be more on target. As in Job 40-41 where the ox-like Behemoth is paired with the sea-dragon Leviathan, so at Ugarit El's calf Atik/Arshu is paired with seven-headed sea-dragon, both of whom →Anat claims to have defeated: "Surely I lifted up the dragon, I...(and) smote the crooked serpent, the tyrant with the seven heads. I smote Ar[shu] beloved of El, I put an end to El's calf Atik" (*KTU* 1.3 iii:43-44). Nevertheless, at Ugarit both of these creatures seem to be more at home in the sea than on land: "In the sea are Arshu and the dragon, May Kothar-and-Hasis drive (them) away, May Kothar-and-Hasis cut (them) off" (*KTU* 1.6 vi:51-53). This difference should not be overemphasized, however, since the basic character of Ugaritic Arshu seems to be bovine and Behemoth seems as much at home in the water (Job 40:21-23) as on land (Job 40:15.20). Given both such Ugaritic precedents and the weight of the mythological interpretations of Behemoth in early postbiblical Jewish and Christian traditions, it seems impossible to avoid the conclusion that Behemoth of Job 40 is a distinct mythic being possessing supernatural characteristics. Behemoth's character and function, however, remain obscure.

Whether Behemoth is attested elsewhere in the Bible is unclear. The two best candidates are Isa 30:6, "oracle against the Behemoth/Beast of the Negeb" (i.e. against Judah courting Egypt); and Ps 73:22, "I have been a Behemoth/Beast with you" (i.e. a deprecating self-characterization; see WOLFERS 1990:478-479). Other, less convincing proposals include Deut 32:34 (R. GORDIS, The Asseverative *Kaph* in Ugaritic and Hebrew, *JAOS* 63 [1943] 176-78: among the punishments threatened by God is 'the teeth of Behemoth' as parallel with →Resheph and other alleged demons); and Job 12:7 (so W. L. MICHEL, *Job in the Light of Northwest Semitic*, [BibOr 42; Rome 1987] 279-280).

IV. *Bibliography*

G. J. BOTTERWECK, בְּהֵמָה *behēmāh*; בְּהֵמוֹת *behēmôth*, *TDOT* 2 (1975) 6-20; B. COUROYER, Qui est Béhémoth?, *RB* 82 (1975) 418-443; J. DAY, *God's Conflict with the Dragon and the Sea: Echoes of a Canaanite Myth in the Old Testament* (Cambridge 1985) 62-87; G. R. DRIVER, Mythical Monsters in the Old Testament, *Studi Orientalistici in onore de Giorgio Levi della Vida,* vol 1 (Rome 1956) 234-249; G. FUCHS, *Mythos und Hiobdichtung: Aufnahme und Umdeutung altorientalischer Vorstellungen* (Stuttgart 1993) 225-264; L. GINZBERG, *The Legends of the Jews* I (Philadelphia 1909, 1937) 27-30; V (1925, 1953) 41-49, esp. nn. 118, 119, 127, 141; H. GUNKEL, *Schöpfung und Chaos in Urzeit und Endzeit* (Göttingen 1895) 48-67; J. GUTTMANN, Leviathan, Behemoth, and Ziz: Jewish Messianic Symbols in Art, *HUCA* 39 (1968) 219-230; O. KEEL, *Jahwes Entgegnung an Ijob: Eine Deutung von Ijob 38-41 vor dem Hintergrund der zeitgenössischen Bildkunst* (FRLANT 121; Göttingen 1978); J. V. KINNIER WILSON, A Return to the Problems of Behemoth and Leviathan, *VT* 25 (1975) 1-14; V. KUBINA, *Die Gottesreden im Buche Hiob* (Freiburg 1979) 68-75; M. POPE, *Job* (AB 15; 3rd ed.; Garden City 1973) 320-329; E. RUPRECHT, Das Nilpferd im Hiobbuch: Beobachtungen zu der sogenannten zweiten Gottesrede, *VT* 21 (1971) 209-231; M. K. WAKEMAN, *God's Battle with the Monster* (Leiden 1972) 106-117; D. WOLFERS, The Lord's Second Speech in the Book of Job, *VT* 40 (1990) 474-499.

B. F. BATTO

BEL → **MARDUK**

BELIAL בליעל 'wickedness'

I. In the manner of other ancient peoples, the Hebrews regularly personified physical forces and abstract concepts: sometimes describing them mythically as divinities. This holds for some OT depictions of בליעל. In 2 Sam 22:5 *naḥălê bĕliyyaʿal* 'torrents of Belial' in the sense of 'treacherous waters', are parallel to *mišbĕrê māwet* 'Breakers of Death': i.e., 'deadly waves'. The personification of death (with *môt* cf. Ugaritic →Mot, god of death) indicates here a similar personification of wickedness, treachery, or the like, as Belial. In the Psalms recension of the same text (Ps 18:5), *ḥeblê māwet* 'bonds of Death', stands in parallelism with *nahălê bĕliyyaʿal* 'torrents of Belial'. These same torrents are referred to later in the poem (2 Sam 22:17 = Ps 18:17) as 'mighty waters' (*mayyîm rabbîm*): a term with mythic associations (MAY 1955). The Hebrew tradition of personification is widened in the Vulgate, which transliterates, rather than translates, Belial in eight Hebrew passages (Deut 13:13; Judg 19:22; 1 Sam 1:16; 2:12; 10:27; 25:17; 2 Sam 16:7; Nah 1:15 (2:1). In 1 Kgs 21:13 Vulgate reads *diabolus* (GASTER 1962:377).

II. In most of its OT attestations, *bĕliyyaʿal* functions as an emotive term to describe individuals or groups who commit the most heinous crimes against the Israelite religious or social order, as well as their acts (MAAG 1965; ROSENBERG 1982:35-40). Such crimes include: inciting one's fellows to worship foreign gods (Deut 13:14); perjury (1 Kgs 21:10, 13; Prov 19:28); breach of hospitality (Judg 19:22; 1 Sam 25:17); lese-majesty (1 Sam 10:27); usurpation (2 Sam 16:7-8; 20:1); abuse of →Yahweh's sanctuary by female drunkenness (1 Sam 1:13-17); and the cultic misappropriation and sexual harassment of women by priests (1 Sam 2:12-22). Refusal to lend money on the eve of the Sabbatical year (Deut 15:9) falls into the category of heinous deeds because it indicates lack of faith in the divine ability to provide.

Grammatically, the term reveals some though not all features of personification. On the one hand, in its twenty-seven occurrences, (none in the tetrateuch) *bĕliyyaʿal*, like the proper names of individuals, is never attested in the plural. On the other hand, unlike true proper names of persons, the vocable takes the definite article in the construct chains *ʾîš habbĕliyyaʿal* 'scoundrel, worthless individual', (1 Sam 25:25; 2 Sam 16:7) and its plural *ʾanšê habbĕliyyaʿal* 'scoundrels' (1 Kgs 21:13).

Recent studies on Belial (*HALAT* 128; LEWIS 1992:654-656) show that there is no unanimity with regard to its etymology. The rabbis of late antiquity explained *bĕnê bĕliyyaʿal* punningly as *bĕnê bĕlî ʿōl* 'children without the yoke'; that is: those who had thrown off the yoke of heaven (*b. Sanh.* 111b). The medieval Jewish poet and philosopher Judah Halevi explained the term etymologically as a compound of the negation *bĕlî* and the third-person imperfect jussive of ʿLH 'ascend'; and semantically as a wish or prayer that malevolence should not prosper (WEISER 1976:258). Modern scholarship has added several other suggestions. One suggestion is a modification of Halevi's thesis: i.e. the wicked are those who do not ascend from the underworld (CROSS & FREEDMAN 1953:22) This explanation is effectively refuted by EMERTON (1987: 214-217) who cautions that in OT conceptions even the righteous do not ascend from the underworld. (Ps 30:4 does not refer to actual death, but to recovery from illness. The same holds for Ps 107:18, cf. v 21). Another interpretation connects the term with the verb BLʿ 'swallow', followed by afformative *lamed* (MANDELKERN 1896:202). Although this suggestion has the merit of calling attention to the fact that the wicked are sometimes depicted as 'swallowers' of the righteous (Isa 49:19; Hab 1:13; Prov 1:12; Lam 2:16; Cf. Ps 124:3), it must be recalled that God is likewise depicted as a 'swallower' (Ps 55:10; Job 2:3).

It has also been claimed that the term actually consists of two homonyms with different etymologies: *bĕliyyaʿal* I 'underworld', composed (as above) of *bl* and *ʿlh*, that is, the place from which none ascend; *bĕliyyaʿal* II 'wickedness': composed of the negation followed by a cognate of Arabic *waʿala* 'honour', 'lineage' (TUR-SINAI 1954: 134.) This ingenious solution does not carry conviction because there is no need to isolate 'death' semantically from 'malevolence'. Note the pairing of *hammāwet* and *hārāʿ*, death and evil, in Deut 30:15. Also, the fact that none of the Arabic speaking medieval Jewish commentators such as Qimhi, ibn Ezra or Saadia suggested a connection with *waʿala* (which is not the common Arabic word for 'honour') counsels caution. Alternatively the word has been linked with Arabic *balaġa* 'denounce', followed by afformative lamed (DRIVER 1934:52-53). This last suggestion is most unlikely (LEWIS 1992:655).

The most likely explanation of the term derives it from the negation *bĕlî* followed by a noun **yaʿal*, related to the root YʿL 'to be worthy, to be of value' (see e.g. PEDERSEN 1926:413; GASTER 1973). It will be recalled that Biblical Hebrew and Ugaritic provide structural parallels in words in which the first element is a negation and the second a noun. Note for example, Ugaritic *blmt* 'immortality', literally, 'without death', or *bilîmâ* 'nothingness' (GASTER 1973; cf. analogously, *ʾal-māwet* 'deathlessness'. [Prov 12:28]). The objection sometimes raised (TUR-SINAI 1954; ROSENBERG 198:235) that 'useless, worthless', is not a strong enough term to characterize *bĕnê bĕliyyaʿal* is contradicted by internal biblical evidence. Thus *bal-yôʿîlû*, 'they are ineffectual', is applied to idols (Isa 44:9; cf. *lĕbiltî hôʿîl* in 44:10 ibid). In addition, forms of the verb YʿL preceded by the negation *lōʾ* synonymous with *bal*, are used regularly to characterize foreign gods (1 Sam 12:21; Isa 44:9; Jer 2:8.11; 16:19) as well as idol manufacturers

(Isa 44:10. cf. Hab 2:18) and false prophets (Jer 23:32). The same construction is applied to →'lies' (Jer 7:8); and to ineffectual military allies (Isa 30:5-6). Thus *běnê běliyyaʿal* are 'worthless men' and a *bat běliyyaʿal* (1 Sam 1:16) is a 'worthless woman'. These worthless characters are apparently not different from *běnê-ʿawlâ* 'the wicked' (2 Sam 7:10; 3:34; 1 Chr 17:9). In fact, the Peshitta often translates *běliyya-ʿal* by *ʿwlʾ* 'wickedness' (Judg 19:22; 20:13; 1 Sam 30:22; 2 Sam 16:7; 22:5; 23:6; Pss 18:5; 30:22; 41:9; 101:3).

Further confirmation of this philological analysis may be adduced from Palestinian Jewish Aramaic in which worthy individuals are termed *bnwy dhnyyh,* that is 'beneficient ones', 'useful people', while their opposite numbers are קוקופרגמוניא, an Aramaic loanword from Greek κακοπράγμονες 'evil doers' (LIEBERMANN & ROSENTHAL 1983: xxxiv).

III. In pseudepigraphic literature, Belial is especially well-attested (LEWIS 1992:655) as the proper name of the →Devil, the powerful opponent of God, who accuses people and causes them to sin. This dualism is rooted in Zoroastrianism, the religion of the succesive Iranian empires within whose borders vast numbers of Jews lived for a millennium, in which *Drug* 'falsehood', 'wickedness', (personified already in the inscriptions of Darius the Great [522-486 BCE]) is opposed to *Aša* 'righteousness', 'justice', likewise personified, one of the bounteous immortals (GASTER 1973:429; BOYCE 1982:120). The regular form in the Pseudepigrapha, Beliar, and once, (*Testament of Levi* 18:4) Belior, may be a punning explanation of the Devil's name as 'lightness' (*bělî ʾôr*) because, in opposition to God's way, Belial's is the way of darkness (*T. Levi* 19:1). It may be observed that, according the Zoroastrian creation account, the Bundahishn, Ohrmezd (Ahura Mazda) dwells in endless light (*asar rošnīh*) while Ahreman (Angra Mainyu) dwells in endless darkness (*asar tārīgīh*).

Belial is very well attested in Hebrew texts from Qumran: especially in the War Scroll (1QM) and the Thankgiving Scroll (1QH). They describe an ongoing struggle between good and evil. On the human plane, the Teacher of Righteousness represents the forces of →light and the good; while his opponent, the wicked priest, represents the forces of darkness and evil. This same struggle is depicted mythically as a battle on high between the angel →Michael and Belial (SCHIFFMAN 1989:50). The present age is the time of Belial's rule (*mmšlt blyʿl*). He is the leader of 'people of the lot of Belial' *ʾnšy gwrl blyʿl* who are opposed to *ʾnšy gwrl ʾl* 'the people of the lot of God' (1QS 1:16-2:8). In this literature too, Belial leads the forces of darkness and malevolence (LEWIS 1992:655). According to one Qumran text (CD 4:12-15), the coming of Belial would not be permanent. After a momentous struggle, God would eventually bring about the permanent annihilation (*klt ʿwlmym*) of Belial and all of the forces of evil, both human and angelic (1QM 1:4-5, 13-16).

The association of Belial with darkness is found in Belial's single attestation in the New Testament (2 Cor 6:14-15): "What partnership can righteousness have with wickedness? Can light associate with darkness? What harmony (*symphonēsis*) has →Christ with Beliar or a believer with an unbeliever?"

In Sybilline Oracles 3:63-64, a text roughly comtemporary with 2 Corinthians, it is prophesied that Beliar will come *ek Sebastēnōn*. Inasmuch as Latin 'Augustus' was rendered in Greek by 'Sebastos', the verse has been construed as reference to the diabolical character of Nero, descendent of Augustus (COLLINS 1983:360, 363).

IV. *Bibliography*

M. BOYCE, *A History of Zoroastrianism* 1-2 (Leiden 1975, 1982); J. J. COLLINS in J. H. Charlesworth (ed.), *The Old Testament Pseudepigraphy* I (Garden City 1983); F. M. CROSS & D. N. FREEDMAN, A Royal Psalm of Thanksgiving: II Samuel 22 = Psalm 18, *JBL* 72 (1953) 15-34; G. R. DRIVER, Hebrew Notes, *ZAW* 52 (1934) 51-66; J. A. EMERTON, Sheol and the Sons of Belial, *EncJud* 4 (Jerusalem 1973) 428-429;

H. KOSMALA, The Three Nets of Belial, *ASTI* 4 (1965) 91-113; T. LEWIS, Belial, *ABD* 1 (1992) 654-656; S. LIEBERMAN & E. S. ROSENTHAL, *Yerushalmi Neziqin* (Jerusalem 1983); V. MAAG, Belīja‘al im Alten Testament, *TZ* 21 (1965) 287-299; S. MANDELKERN, *Hekal Haqqodesh* (Leipzig 1896); H. MAY, Some Cosmic Connotations of *Mayim Rabbīm,* 'Many Waters', *JBL* 74 (1955) 9-21; J. PEDERSEN, *Israel, its Life and Culture* (London 1926); R. ROSENBERG, The Concept of Biblical 'Belial', *Proceedings of the Eight World Congress of Jewish Studies* 1 (Jerusalem 1982) 35-40; L. SCHIFFMAN, *The Eschatological Community of Qumran* (Atlanta 1989); N. H. TUR-SINAI, בליעל, *EncMiqr* 2 (Jerusalem 1954) 132-133; A. WEISER, *Ibn Ezra Perushe Hattorah le-Rabbenu Avraham ibn Ezra* 3 (Jerusalem 1976).

S. D. SPERLING

BELTU *בלתי

I. The name of the Babylonian goddess Beltu (var. Belit, Belti) is the feminine form of Bel ('Lord'), and means 'Lady'. She is identified either with →Ishtar or Ṣarpanitu. Her mention in the Hebrew Bible is conjectural; P. DE LAGARDE (*Symmicta* [Göttingen 1877] 105) was the first to emendate *biltî* in Isa 10:4 into *bēltî*, 'my Lady'. The proposal cannot be seen in isolation from the emendation, in the same verse, of *ʾassîr* ('prisoner') into *ʾōsîr* (→Osiris).

II. Since the name Beltu is not really a name but an epithet ('Lady'), the identification with a specific deity is beset with problems. Used in genetival constructions such as Belet-Akkadî or Belet-ekallim, the epithet 'Lady' is an element in the name (or epithet) of numerous Babylonian and Assyrian (then Belat) goddesses (*CAD* B 189-190). The goddess to have been designated most frequently by this epithet, both in Sumerian (**nin**, Emesal **gašan**) and Akkadian (*bēltu*), is no doubt Ishtar (WILCKE 1976-80; cf. *AkkGE* 333-334). Many formerly independent goddesses, such as Bēlet-ilī and Bēlet-māti, were later increasingly identified with Ishtar as well (WILCKE 1976-80:77a).

Since 'Bel' came to acquire the status of a second name of →Marduk, it could be argued that the absolute use of Beltu should be taken to refer to Marduk's consort, i.e. Ṣarpanitu ('the silver-shining one'). In various texts, indeed, since the time of the Sargonids and notably in some younger New Year rituals, Ṣarpanitu is referred to simply as Bēlti, 'My Lady' (ZIMMERN 1926). Yet though Ṣarpanitu is at times referred to as Beltu (or as Bēlet-Bābili, 'Lady of Babylon', *AkkGE* 452), the identification is not universally valid. If Beltu were indeed mentioned in the Hebrew Bible, the current Western Mesopotamian association with Ishtar would be more natural. In Palmyra, the goddess Belti seems indeed to have been associated primarily with →Tammuz; in later times too, then, she was identified with Ishtar—presumably also when associated with Bel (HOFTIJZER 1968:46 n. 134; J. TEIXIDOR, *The Pantheon of Palmyra* [EPRO 79; Leiden 1979] 88).

The West-Semitic form of Beltu is →Baalat (*bʿlt*), grammatically the feminine counterpart of →Baal. At Palmyra, she was worshipped under the name Baaltak (*bʿltk*, 'Your Ladyship') and identified as *ʾštrʾ*, 'the goddess', literally 'the Ishtar'. She is indeed the equivalent of the Mesopotamian Ishtar, the female deity of heaven (TEIXIDOR, *The Pantheon of Palmyra*, 60-61). At Emar, the population knew a goddess ^{d}NIN-KUR(-RA), pronounced Baʿalta-mātim (AEM 1/1 no. 256:16), an Amorite deity regarded as the consort of →Dagan (J.-M. DURAND, La cité-état d'Imâr à l'époque des rois de Mari, *MARI* 6 [1990] 39-92, esp. 89-90). It should be noted, moreover, especially in view of the—conjectural—conjunction of Belti and Osiris in Isa 10:4, that Baalat as well as Baalat-Gebal, 'Lady-of-Byblos', were both identified with the Egyptian goddess →Hathor (PUECH 1986-87; J. G. GRIFFITHS, *Apuleius of Madauros. The Isis-Book* [EPRO 39; Leiden 1975] 38).

III. According to the emendation by DE LAGARDE (*Symmicta* [Göttingen 1877] 105), accepted by way of a proposal in the apparatus criticus of the BHS, Isa 10:4 should be rendered "Belti is writhing, Osiris is in panic" (*Bēltî kōra'at ḥat 'Ōsîr*; DE LAGARDE translated "Belthis is sinking, Osiris has been broken"). Though none of the versions supports the emendation, it is not impossible orthographically. Yet it does not fit the context (see K. BUDDE, Zu Jesaja 1-5, *ZAW* 50 [1932] 38-72, esp. 69-70). Assuming that v 4 takes up the rhetorical question of v 3 ("To whom will you flee for help, and where will you leave your wealth?"), Belti and Osiris either are or stand for the powers from which help is expected. Since the pairing of these deities is unusual, also if Belti should stand for Hathor, and there is no trace of their cult elsewhere in the Hebrew Bible, a literal interpretation of the emendated verse is not very possible. To say that the hypothetical Belti stands here for →Isis is at odds with the identifications current at the time (*pace* e.g. K. MARTI, *Das Buch Jesaja* [Tübingen 1900] 100; B. DUHM, *Das Buch Jesaja* [Göttingen 1968, 5th ed.] 97). A symbolical interpretation cannot be ruled out, however: Belti could stand for Assyria, and Osiris for Egypt. Yet this interpretation also, though possible, is unlikely: the customary symbols for Assyria and Egypt would be →Assur and →Rahab, respectively. The reading of the MT as it stands makes better sense: "(they have no option) but to crouch among the prisoners of war, or fall among the slain". The parallel use of *taḥat* is a serious argument not to separate the first תחת into ת en חת. DE LAGARDE's proposal, then, is on the whole more ingenious than convincing (for a fuller discussion see H. WILDBERGER, *Jesaja*, Vol. 1 [BKAT X/1; Neukirchen-Vluyn 1972] 179-180).

IV. *Bibliography*

J. HOFTIJZER, *Religio aramaica* (Leiden 1968) 46-47; E. PUECH, The Canaanite Inscriptions of Lachish and their Religious Background, *Tel Aviv* 13-14 (1986-87) 13-25; C. WILCKE, Inanna/Ištar, *RLA* 5 (1976-80) 74-87; H. ZIMMERN, Bēlti (Bēltija, Bēletja), eine, zunächst sprachliche, Studie zur Vorgeschichte des Madonnakults, *Oriental Studies dedicated to Paul Haupt* (ed. C. Adler & A. Embler; Baltimore/Leipzig 1926) 281-292.

K. VAN DER TOORN

BES

I. The name of the Egyptian god or demon Bes (Copt BHC; Gk βησας) occurs in the personal name *bēsāy* in Ezra 2:49, cf. Neh 7:52. In Egypt this divine name was also often used as a personal name.

II. The god or demon Bes was represented as a bandy legged deformed dwarf or more precisely as a lion-man (ROMANO 1980). His ugly human face, his animal hair or manes, ears and tail are indeed more likely those of a lion than of a human dwarf. He dances, plays musical instruments such as harp, flute and tambourine, or brandishes knife and sword to avert evil and to protect the pregnant and birth-giving mother. He sometimes shows an enormous phallus and may make dirty jokes (MALAISE 1990). Often a plurality of Bes-gods is represented, figuring in an erotic context. These erotic representations were supposed to bring about pregnancy and childbirth. L'amour pour l'amour, as well as l'art pour l'art, was largely unknown or unacceptable as a cultural expression in an ancient culture such as Egypt, although contraceptives were not unknown or forbidden (DERCHAIN 1981).

Several explanations of the name Bes have been given (MALAISE 1990:691-692). His name has been connected with verbs meaning "to initiate", "to emerge" and "to protect". Very recently, arguments have been brought forward that a Bes means a prematurely born child or foetus, which was enveloped in a lion's skin and kept in a basket of reeds or rushes (MEEKS 1992; BULTÉ 1991:102.108-109). So it seems possible that the dancing, jesting and sometimes aggressive gnome or lion-man Bes was a personification of a prematurely born child or foetus, who protects mother and child. It may be that the personal name Bes was considered to be a fitting name for prematurely born children.

III. Except for the PN *bēsay*, Bes is not attested in the OT. In epigraphical Hebrew, Bes occurs twice as a theophoric element in a PN: *q[.]bš* (Samaria Ostracon 1:5; Probably Egyptian 'Bes created', A. LEMAIRE, *Inscriptions Hébraïques* I [LAPO 9; Paris

1977] 54); *bsy* (R. HESTRIN & M. DAYAGI-MENDELS, *Inscribed Seals* [Jerusalem 1979] No. 54). On Pithos A from Kuntillet ʿAjrud two figurines occur which can be interpreted as Bes-depictions probably a male with a bisexual feminized variant (KEEL & UEHLINGER 1992:244-248). Bes-amulets from the Iron-Age have been excavated at e.g. Lachish, Tell-Jemme and Gezer (KEEL & UEHLINGER 1992:248-251). The archaeological evidence suggests that Bes was known in Palestine in the Iron Age as an apotropaic demon esp. in times of pregnancy and birth.

IV. *Bibliography*

J. BULTÉ, *Talismans égyptiens d'heureuse maternité* (Paris 1991); P. DERCHAIN, Observations sur les erotica, *The Sacred Animal Necropolis at North Saqqara* (ed. G. T. Martin; London 1981) 166-170; O. KEEL & C. UEHLINGER, *Göttinnen, Götter und Gottessymbole* (Freibourg, Basel & Wien 1992) 244-255; M. MALAISE, Bes et les croyances solaires, *Studies in Egyptology Presented to M. Lichtheim* (Jerusalem 1990) II 690-729 [& lit]; D. MEEKS, Le nom du dieu Bes et ses implications mythologiques, *The Intellectual Heritage of Egypt. Studies Presented to L. Kákosy* = StAeg 14 (Budapest 1992) 423-436; J. F. ROMANO, The Origin of the Bes-Image, *Bulletin of the Egyptological Seminar* 2 (1980) 39-56.

H. TE VELDE

BETHEL בית(י)אל

I. The name of this deity must be explained in accordance with Heb *bēt-ʾēl*, i.e. 'house/temple of god/El' (→God, El), cf. also the name of the town Bethel in central Palestine (former *Lûz*, see Judg 1:23). The name Bethel is a shortened version of the designation '(El of the) House of El', a kind of tautology or hypostasis not unfamiliar in Semitic god-names. This name originally did not point to the town of Bethel, but may have referred to open cult-places, as the aetiology of Bethel in the OT suggests (Gen 28:10-19). The god is known from the 7th century BCE, mostly in an Aramaic context—he replaces the ancient Semitic god El who from this time onwards is absent in personal names. Bethel is unknown in Ugarit.

II. Together with Anat-Bethel, i.e. 'Anat (the consort) of Bethel', Bethel is mentioned for the first time in 675/4 BCE among the oath-gods in the treaty between Baal I of Tyre and the Assyrian king Esarhaddon: ^{d}*Ba-a-a-ti*-DINGIR^{meš} ^{d}*A-na-ti-ba-a-*[*a-ti*-DING]IR^{meš} (SAA 2, 5 iv:6'. The orthography of the text suggests an Aramaic uncontracted name-form; the writing DINGIR^{meš} for *ʾil/ʾel* follows normal Assyrian scribal convention). Therefore there is doubt that Bethel was a specific Phoenician god, in spite of the fact that the name É.DINGIR-*a-di-ir* was that of a Phoenician (cf. R. ZADOK, *BASOR* 230 [1978] 61). The list of the oath-gods in the treaty continues with the "gods of Assyria and the gods of Akkad", i.e. with the Mesopotamian deities, but this does not mean that Bethel is of Mesopotamian origin. Rather it may have been a deity venerated by the Aramaeans. Therefore it is not surprising that several Aramaic personal names of the Neo-Babylonian and Achaemenid period in Babylonia and in Egypt are composed with this name of a deity: ^{d}É.DINGIR-ZALAG$_2$', 'Bethel is my light' (BE 9, 75:5; cf. *bytʾl-nwry*, I. N. VINNIKOV, *Palestinskij Sbornik* 67 [1959] 208); É.DINGIR^{meš}-*da-la-ʾ* PBS 2/1 222,11, cf. *bytʾldlny*, 'Bethel saved me' *KAI* 227 r.4 etc. (cf. R. ZADOK, *On West Semites in Babylonia* [Jerusalem 1978] 60-61; M. D. COOGAN, *West Semitic Personal Names* [HSM 2; Missoula 1976] 48-49; M. MARAQTEN, *Die semitischen Personennamen in den alt- und reichsaramäischen Inschriften* [Hildesheim/ Zürich/ New York 1988] 137-139; W. KORNFELD, *Onomastica aramaica aus Ägypten* [Wien 1978] 43).

The Aramaeans in contact with the Jewish community at Syene/Elephantine in Egypt worshipped this deity in a temple which is mentioned in a letter (found at Hermopolis) together with the temple of the →Queen of Heaven (BRESCIANI & KAMIL 1966:no. 4; A. JARDENI & B. PORTEN,

Textbook of Aramaic Documents from Ancient Egypt 1 [Jerusalem 1986] A2.1,1). The god Bethel is further on invoked as →saviour in a lengthy prayer of an Aramaic community in Egypt which is partly preserved on Papyrus Amherst 63 in Demotic script but Aramaic language (J. W. WESSELIUS & W. C. DELSMAN, *TUAT* II [1986/91] 930-932 [& lit]). The god is further to be found—worshipped besides →Yahweh by the Jews of Elephantine—as Ešem-Bethel 'Name of Bethel' and Anat-Bethel (A. COWLY, *Aramaic Papyri of the fifth Century B.C.* [Oxford 1923] 22 VII 122-124), probably a kind of triad with Anat-Bethel as the mother and Ešem-Bethel as the son. A judicial declaration (COWLY [1923] 7; A. JARDENI & B. PORTEN, *Textbook of Aramaic Documents from Ancient Egypt* 1 [Jerusalem 1986] B7.2,7-8) refers to a certain Ḥerem-Bethel which may have been another hypostasis of the Aramaic god. But besides these references the god's name is present as theophoric element in personal names only (see B. PORTEN, *Archives from Elephantine* [Los Angeles 1968] 328-331).

The theogony of Philo of Byblos, transmitted to us by Eusebius (*Praep. Evang.* I 9,16 = *FGH* III C 2,790, F 2,16), acknowledges four sons of Ouranos (→Heaven; →Varuna) and Ge: Elos (or Kronos), Baitylos, →Dagon (or Siton) and Atlas. The second is Bethel, but nothing relevant is told about him. But some paragraphs later (9,23 = *FGH* III C 2,790 F 2,23) it is reported that Ouranos contrived *baitylia*, namely 'animated stones'. Here the author connects the god Bethel with the well known *baityloi* (→Baetyl), the stone monuments broadly used for cultic purposes in the Semitic world. But this reference is no proof for a connection between these monuments and the god Bethel—Baitylos.

The latest reference to a "Zeus Betylos, (god) of the dwellers along the Orontes" can be found in a 3rd cent. CE inscription from Dura Europos (H. SEYRIG, *Excavations at Dura-Europos IV* [New Haven 1933] 68 no. 168) and it may refer, too, to a hypostasis of Bethel in an inscription from Kafr Nābo in the Antiochene named *sumbetyl* in a Greek inscription (*IGLS* II 215-216 no. 376).

III. Whether the Israelites in their homeland also worshipped the god Bethel is disputed, but Jer 48:13 (in the prophecy against Moab) "And Moab shall be betrayed by Chemosh, as Israel was betrayed by Bethel, a god in whom he trusted" points in this direction. It should be noted that the comparison with the highest Moabite god Kamoš (→Chemosh) suggests that Bethel played a prominent role in Israel. Further evidence for this cult may be found in prophetic sayings e.g. Amos 3:14; 5:5; Hos 4:15 (with the nick-name Bet-Aven) and 10:15, although here the place-name Bethel may be meant.

IV. *Bibliography*

M. L. BARRÉ, *The God-List in the Treaty between Hannibal and Philip V of Macedonia* (Baltimore/London 1983) 43-50; R. BORGER, Anat-Bethel, *VT* 7 (1957) 102-104; *Dictionnaire encyclopédique de la Bible* (Turnhout 1987) 205 [& lit]; E. BRESCIANI & M. KAMIL, *Le lettere aramaiche di Hermopoli* (Roma 1966); O. EISSFELDT, Der Gott Bethel, *ARW* 28 (1930) 1-30 (= *KS* 1 [1963] 206-233) [& lit]; J. P. HYATT, The Deity Bethel in the Old Testament, *JAOS* 59 (1939) 81-98; J. T. MILIK, Les papyrus araméens d'Hermoupolis et les cultes syro-phéniciens. 2. Dieu Béthel, *Bib* 48 (1967) 565-577; N. NA'AMAN, Beth-aven, Bethel and early Israelite sanctuaries, *ZDPV* 103 (1987) 13-21; A. VINCENT, *La réligion des Judéo-araméens d'Eléphantine* (Paris 1937) 562-677; S. P. VLEEMING & J. W. WESSELIUS, Bethel the Saviour, *JEOL* 28 (1983/4) 110-140.

W. RÖLLIG

BOAZ בעז

I. Boaz is the name given to one of the pillars flanking the entrance to the temple of Solomon. The name has been interpreted as a corruption of the name →Baal (H. GRESSMANN, Dolmen, Masseben und Napflöcher, *ZAW* 29 [1909] 122; for other examples see SCOTT 1939:145-146) or, alternatively, as an epithet of Baal (BRUSTON 1924).

II. The only proposal that takes Boaz as an independent surname or epithet of a deity has been made by BRUSTON (1924). He based himself on a Neo-Punic inscription from Tunesia, in which he read a reference to "Anat [אנת, sic] the daughter of Boaz". Bruston concluded that the epithet Boaz ('In him there is power') belonged to Baal, which deity he also found mentioned elsewhere in the text. More recent editions of the text (J.-G. FÉVRIER, *Sem* 4 [1951-52] 19-24; *KAI* 160) have shown hat Bruston's reading is erroneous. Instead of אנת בת ("Anat daughter of") one has to read the word אכתרת (which means 'capital', 'sum of money'), whereas בעז is in fact the beginning of the expression בעים = *bḥym*, 'at the (life-)time of' (see DONNER & RÖLLIG, *KAI* II, Literaturnachträge und Ergänzungen, pp. 340-341).

III. The various proposals to take the name Boaz as a reference to a known deity (usually Baal), either as a corruption of the latter's name or as an epithet, are based on the assumption that the name Boaz as it stands makes poor sense. If such were the case, however, the rule *lectio difficilior probabilior* would advise against texual emendation. Moreover, the name of the other pillar, Jachin, does not favour the hypothesis that Boaz is a divine name; Jachin rather looks like the beginning of a solemn wish ('May he render firm ...'). In the versions, there is no real support for a correction of בעז into בעל. Also the more fanciful variations on this solution (such as the suggestion that Boaz is an abbreviation of Baʿal-ʿaz, 'Baal is strong' [MONTGOMERY 1951] or a corruption of Baal-zebul, or even of →Tammuz [see SCOTT 1939:145-146]) reflect a scepticism about the reliability of the Masoretic text that seems unfounded—at least, in this case.

Though the cultic nature of the pillars Jachin and Boaz is beyond doubt, there is no reason to believe that they represented deities. Their symbolic significance is generally acknowledged (MEYERS 1992). The massive stone stelae probably had phallic associations and were—pre-Solomonic?—symbols of fertility and offspring. Originally, the name Boaz may well have been vocalized differently: *bĕʿōz* NN, 'By the strength (or potency) of NN'. It could have been the opening of a traditional formula pronounced at the occasion of royal rituals performed at the entrance of the temple (e.g. SCOTT 1939). As it stands now, the name means 'In him there is strength' (MULDER 1986).

IV. *Bibliography*

C. BRUSTON, L'inscription des deux colonnes du temple de Salomon, *ZAW* 42 (1924) 153-154; C. MEYERS, Jachin and Boaz, *ABD* 3 (1992) 597-598; J. A. MONTGOMERY, *The Books of Kings* (ICC; Edinburgh 1951) 170-171; M. J. MULDER, Die Bedeutung von Jachin und Boaz in 1 Kön. 7:21 (2 Chr. 3:17), *Tradition and Re-Interpretation in Jewish and Early Christian Literature. Essays in Honour of Jürgen C. H. Lebram* (ed. J. W. van Henten *et al.*; Leiden 1986) 19-26; R. B. Y. SCOTT, The Pillars Jachin and Boaz, *JBL* 58 (1939) 143-149.

K. VAN DER TOORN

BOSHET → BASHTU

BREASTS AND WOMB שׁדים ורחם

I. The expression *šādayim wārāḥam*, 'Breasts and Womb', (Gen 49:25) has been interpreted as an epithet echoing Ugaritic titles of the goddesses →Anat and →Asherah (VAWTER 1955; M. O' CONNOR, *Hebrew Verse Structure* [Winona Lake 1980] 178; SMITH 1990:17).

II. In a para-mythological text from Ugarit, it is said that the deities →Shahar and →Shalim are to be seen as those 'sucking the nipple (*ap*; lit. 'nose') of the breast (*ḏd*//*zd*) of Athiratu' (*KTU* 1.23:24.59.61). In the epic of Keret, Ilu promises Keret that his future son will 'suck the breast (*ṯd*) of Virgin Anat' (*KTU* 1.15 ii:27). In a comparable text, Anat is twice called the 'Breast (*ṯd*) of the Nations' (*KTU* 1.13:19-22); she is cast in the role of a Dea Nutrix of deities and nations. In the epic of Keret, Anat is depicted as the 'wet-nurse of the gods', *mšnqt ilm*, (*KTU* 1.15 ii:28). In different texts, Anat is called *rḥm*, 'Womb, Mamsel', (*KTU* 1.6 ii:5,27; 1.15 ii:6; 1.23:13.16; KORPEL 1990).

The imagery of the goddess as a wet-nurse occurs also in Neo-Assyrian prophetical texts. →Ishtar of Arbela is presented several times as the 'good wet-nurse (*mušēniqtu dēqtu*) of king Ashurbanipal'. In the text K 1285:32-34 (J. A. CRAIG, *Assyrian and Babylonian Religious Texts I* [Leipzig 1895] No. 5) she is presented as having four breasts to feed and still the king (WEIPPERT 1985:61-64). Here too, 'breasts' have no erotic connotation but symbolize the caring character of the goddess.

Archaeological findings from Iron Age I in Israel have brought to light a great number of plaque figurines showing a nude female figure with her arms sometimes pointing at her breasts and sometimes at her womb (see e.g. WINTER 1983:96-134). These figurines should be interpreted as referring to a goddess worshipped by families on account of her care for pregnant women and young mothers (WINTER 1983:127-134; KEEL & UEHLINGER 1992:110-122; *pace* TADMOR 1982). It should be noted that in Iron Age II, the monarchic period in Israel, these figurines are almost absent, but that in the 8th century BCE comparable artefacts, the so-called pillar-figurines occur quite frequently.

III. In the 'blessing of →Jacob' four pairs of divine epithets are present: (1) 'Bull of Jacob'—→'Shepherd'; (2) →'El'—→'Shadday'; (3) →'Heaven above'—'Deep crouching below' and (4) 'Breasts and Womb'—'Your Father' (VAWTER 1955:16-17). 'Your →Father', an epithet for El, stands in conjunction with an epithet for a female deity identified by SMITH (1990:18) as Asherah, the consort of El. Gen 49:25 would originally reflect an early non-monotheistic phase in the history of Israelite religion. In its present context, the phrase uses mythological terminology to refer to →Yahweh's power of benediction in the realm of birth and nutrition. The deity ultimately lurking behind the imagery of Gen 49:25 might be identical with the caring and suckling goddess known from Ugaritic texts and Israelite iconography.

A late relic of this imagery is present in Luke 11:27. After →Jesus drove out an unclean spirit, a woman in the crowd raised her voice and said to him and about him: "Blessed is the womb that bore you, and the breasts that you sucked!" thereby identifying →Mary with the type of goddess discussed above (J. A. FITZMYER, *The Gospel according to Luke (X-XXIV)* [AB 28A; Garden City 1985] 927-928).

IV. *Bibliography*

O. KEEL & C. UEHLINGER, *Göttinnen, Götter und Gottessymbole* (Freiburg/Basel/Wien 1992) 110-122,378-381; M. C. A. KORPEL, *A Rift in the Clouds* (UBL 8; Münster 1990) 123-125; M. SMITH, *The Early History of God* (San Fransisco 1990) 16-19; M. TADMOR, Female Cult Figurines in Late Canaan and Early Israel, *Studies in the Period of David and Solomon and Other Essays* (ed. T. Ishida; Winona Lake 1982) 139-173; B. VAWTER, The Canaanite background of Genesis 49, *CBQ* 17 (1955) 12-17; M. WEIPPERT, Die Bildsprache der neuassyrischen Prophetie, *Beiträge zur prophetischen Bildsprache in Israel und Assyrien* (ed. H. Weippert, K. Seybold & M. Weippert; OBO 64; Freiburg/Göttingen 1985) 55-93; U. WINTER, *Frau und Göttin* (OBO 53; Freiburg/Göttingen 1983).

B. BECKING

BROTHER אח

I. Heb *ʾāḥ*, 'brother', represents a primitive Semitic noun, of unknown etymology. The term refers to a biological brother or half-brother, a male member of comparable standing in a kinship group, or a male member of a larger community, such as Israel. In the ancient Near East, 'brother' also occurs as a theophoric element in personal names (FOWLER 1988:46-48, 280-281, 301-302).

II. Although the terms →'father' and →'mother' are common divine epithets in the biblical world with reference to the human community, the term 'brother' is not so used in literary or religious texts (*AkkGE*) nor, apparently, in private letters. With the semi-divine Sumerian kings of the Ur-III dynasty, there are exceptions. In addition to the special case of the deified Gilgamesh, a putative king of Uruk, cited by kings as 'his beloved brother', or as 'his/my brother (and) friend', Shulgi also cites the 'hero, Utu', the sun god, as 'my brother (and) friend', a relationship not established in the divine genealogies (A. FALKENSTEIN, *ZA* 50 [1952] 73-77; KLEIN 1981:82, 112, 198). In Sumerian personal names 'brother' is well-attested as a divine epithet (for the personal god), much more so than in Akkadian names (DI VITO 1993:89-93, 254-256, 264-265). In ancient Semitic personal names the epithet 'brother'—rarely 'sister'—may at times refer to a deity (ZOBEL 1932:35-42; STAMM 1939:53-57, 209, 222, 241; *AHW* 18b), as is especially clear in Akkadian names such as *Sin-aḫi-wēdi*, 'Sin is a Brother for the Only Child' (STAMM 1939:241; →Sîn). The names reflect the important role that brothers play within a patriarchal family system, especially—in the absence of the father—for sisters and younger brothers. For example, if the father is no longer living, brothers may have an important role in a sister's marriage. In the Laws of Hammurabi, under certain circumstances the brothers must present an unmarried sister with a dowry (§ 184, *ANET* 174), and in the Middle Assyrian laws the potential marriage assignment (by a creditor) of a debtor's daughter (in debt service) presupposes that her father consents or, if the father is no longer living, that her brothers decline the right of redemption (A§ 48, *ANET* 184). The special role of elder brothers and elder sisters is also illustrated in the Shurpu incantations which mention oaths "by the protecting deity of elder brother and elder sister" (*Šurpu* II 89), and oaths (of cursing) or other negative action toward an elder brother or elder sister (*Šurpu* IV 58; VIII 59; cf. II 35-36; V-VI 46-47), in contexts with reference to persons or powers of higher status. Striking also is the reference in the 9th cent. BCE Northwest Semitic inscription of Kilamuwa, from northwest Syria, in which the king says, concerning some subjects: "As for me, to some I was a father, and to some I was a mother, and to some I was a brother. ... They responded (to me) as the fatherless toward (its) mother" (*KAI* 24:10-11, 13). These important family relationships provide a basis for the expression of family or popular piety in personal names, unlike the conventions of 'official' religion (DI VITO 1993:92-93).

III. In Hebrew theophoric personal names known from the Bible and from inscriptions (ZADOK 1988:178-187), the most common elements, apart from *ʾēl*, 'god' (→El, →God), and variations of *yhwh* (→Yahweh), are *ʾāb*, 'father' (more than 30), *ʾāḥ*, 'brother' (more than 25), and *ʿamm-*, 'paternal uncle/kinsman' (more than 12). Note names such as Ahijah, 'Yah(u) is My (divine) Brother' (8 men, one woman?; STAMM 1980:111), Ahinadab 'My (divine) Brother is Generous' (one man), and Ahisamach, 'My (divine) Brother Has Helped' (one man), as well as Ahinoam, 'My (divine?) Brother is Gracious' (one man [Samaria ostraca], two women; STAMM 1980:113). Probable substitution names, such as Ahitub, 'My Brother is Goodness' (two men), also occur (STAMM 1939:279, 295; 1980:67, 69). In societies that rely heavily on the extended patriarchal family, as illustrated especially by the Books of Genesis and Ruth in the case of Israel, a brother or an uncle is commonly a primary authority figure, one whose protection is essential. (Though the precise relationship between Ruth and Boaz is not indicated, he is a male relative second in line; Ruth 4:3-6.) With reference to brothers, note the role of →Laban in the marriage of his sister, Rebecca (Gen 24:50-51), the role of Absalom in defence of his sister, Tamar (2 Sam 13), and the role of a brother, uncle (*dôd*, →Dod), or uncle's son (*ben dôd*) in redemption from debt slavery (Lev 25:48-49). As such the epithet 'brother' can be used of a deity, even if only in the popular or family piety reflected in personal names (ALBERTZ 1978).

IV. *Bibliography*

R. ALBERTZ, *Persönliche Frömmigkeit und offizielle Religion* (Stuttgart 1978); R. A. DI VITO, *Studies in Third Millennium Sumerian and Akkadian Personal Names. The Designation and Conception of the Personal God* (StPsm 16; Rome 1993); J. D. FOWLER, *Theophoric Personal Names in Ancient Hebrew: A Comparative Study* (JSOTSup 49; Sheffield 1988); J. KLEIN, *Three Šulgi Hymns* (Ramat-Gan 1981); H. RINGGREN, אח ʾāch, אחות ʾāchôth, *TDOT* 1 (1977) 188-193; J. J. STAMM, *Die akkadische Namengebung* (MVAÄG 44; Leipzig 1939); STAMM, *Beiträge zur hebräischen und altorientalischen Namenkunde* (OBO 30; Freiburg 1980); R. ZADOK, *The Pre-hellenistic Israelite Anthroponomy and Prosopography* (Louvain 1988); J. ZOBEL, *Das bildliche Gebrauch der Verwandtschaftsnamen im Hebräischen mit Berücksichtigung der übrigen semitischen Sprachen* (Halle 1932).

H. B. HUFFMON

C

CAIN קין

I. In Gen 4:1 the name of the first son of Adam and Eve, Cain, is related in a popular etymology to the Hebrew verb QNH 'to acquire'. More probably the name should be related to either the Ugaritic *qn* 'reed; shaft' and Heb *qayin* 'javelin' or to Syrian and Semitic words for 'smith'; e.g. Syr *qajnājā* '(gold)smith'; Thamudic *qjn*; *qn* and *qnt*, 'smith' (*HALAT* 1025; HESS 1993). His name might be related to a Thamudic deity *qayn*. Besides, the story on Cain and →Abel has been interpreted mythologically, Cain representing the deified sun (GOLDZIHER 1876:129-139).

II. In Thamudic inscriptions the personal name *'abd-qayn* is attested once (VAN DEN BRANDEN 1950:10). Qayn has been interpreted by Van den Branden as a Sabaean lunar deity. HÖFNER (*WbMyth* 1/I, 461-462; *RAAM,* 277) doubted the divine status of Qayn in view of the well attested Thamudic personal name Qayn and the noun *qayn* 'smith'. The construction *'abd*-NN leaves open the possibility that Qayn was a Thamudic deity or a deified ancestor, however. In view of the etymology of the name, Qayn may well have been a patron deity for the metal-workers. A relation with the South-Arabian deity Qaynān (→Kenan) is uncertain.

III. A tale about the rivalry of two brothers at the dawn of civilization has more than one religio-historical parallel: →Osiris and →Seth, Romulus and Remus, Eteokles and Polyneikes are just the more familiar ones (WESTERMANN 1974:428-430). In such stories the 'two brothers' can be seen as heroic figures. GOLDZIHER (1876:129-139) goes one step further in interpreting these tales as survivals of myths in which the ancestors of a culture are presented as divine beings. Cain is supposed to represent, originally, the solar deity in combat with the transient powers of darkness: Abel. In the current version of Gen 4 no traces of such a mythology are visible, however.

In the OT Cain occurs only in the story of Gen 4 where he is the cultural and moral opposite of Abel. Cain represents the realm of settled agricultural life. In the Epistle to the Hebrews, Cain is mentioned as the opposite of his brother Abel (Heb 11:4): "By faith Abel offered unto God a more excellent sacrifice than Cain". The author of this letter refers to the unanswerable question why Cain's sacrifice was rejected and Abel's accepted. This problem is discussed in some Hellenistic Jewish and Rabbinic sources too (→Abel). In the Letter of Jude, Cain is presented as the model for the evildoers from Sodom and Gomorrah who "went in the way of Cain" (Jude 11).

IV. *Bibliography*

A. VAN DEN BRANDEN, *Les Inscriptions Thamoudéennes* (Louvain 1950); I. GOLDZIHER, *Der Mythus bei den Hebräern und seine geschichtliche Entwicklung* (Leipzig 1876); R. S. HESS, *Studies in the Personal Names of Genesis 1-11* (AOAT 234; Neukirchen-Vluyn 1993) 24-27,37-39; M. HÖFNER, *WbMyth* 1/I, 461-462; C. WESTERMANN, *Genesis 1-11* (BKAT I/1; Neukirchen-Vluyn 1974).

B. BECKING

CALF עגל

I. Hebrew *'ēgel*, Ugaritic *'gl*, Aramaic *'îgla'*, the common word for 'calf' (sc. a young bull), is used of images worshipped by the Israelites in texts written from the deuteronomistic perspective.

II. The bull as a symbol of physical strength and sexual potency, together with all the economic benefits arising from herding, has an ancient pedigree in the religions of the Ancient Near East. From at least the time of Neolithic Çatal Hüyük in Anatolia, images have been prominent in glyptic art, sculpture and reliefs, and the animal has been prominent in iconography and theology. The use of cattle as sacrificial animals is common throughout the region. Bull-gods are widely evident. In Egypt the Mnevis bull of Heliopolis was regarded as a theriomorphic incarnation of →Re, while the Buchis bull of Hermonthis was one of Mont, and the →Apis bull of Memphis was one of →Ptah, later in the dyadic form →Osiris-Ptah. In Mesopotamia, Gugalanna, the 'Great Bull of Heaven', the husband of Ereshkigal, goddess of the underworld, was identified or associated with An, and was slain by Gilgamesh (tablet VI). The *Šedu*, *Lamassu* or *Karibu* colossi were the guardians of temples (cf. the →Cherub in Gen 3:24). In Ugaritic religion, →El was known as 'the Bull El' (*ṯr il*). This usage may belong in part to the convention of giving animal names as terms of rank to military personnel, as evidenced in *KTU* 1.15 iv 6-7: "Call my seventy bulls, my eighty gazelles", and suggests at least a popular etymological link between *ṯr* (Hebrew *šôr*, Akkadian *šaru*), 'bull' and Hebrew *śar*, Akkadian *šarru*, 'ruler', 'king'. (There is no formal link.) Near Eastern weather-gods are conventionally shown standing on a bull as vehicle, while →Baal is described in *KTU* 1.5 v 18-22 as copulating with a heifer, which suggests that he too could be regarded as a bull. Cult-images of bulls have been recovered from such sites as Ugarit, Tyre and Hazor.

III. A number of terms for cattle are used in the Bible as epithets of divine power. The title *Šôr ʾēl* ('Bull El') has been discerned (TUR-SINAI 1950) in the impossible **kî miyyisrāʾēl* ('for from Israel') of MT in Hos 8:6: read rather *kî mî šôr ʾēl* ('for who is Bull El?'), which fits well in the context. With this may be compared →Jacob's title in Deut 33:17 as *běkôr šôr* (MT *šôrô*), 'the first-born of the Bull'. In Gen 49:24; Ps 132:2, 5; Isa 49:26; 60:16 *ʾăbîr yaʿăqōb* probably has the sense of 'Bull of Jacob' (cf. Ugaritic *ibr*), while the divine title *ʾăbîr yisrāʾēl* of Isa 1:24 is comparable. The term *rěʾēm* (Akkadian *rêmu*) is generally thought to denote the aurochs (its semantic range is established by Deut 33:17 // *šôr*, and Ps 29:6 // *ʿēgel*), and appears as an epithet of El (sc. →Yahweh, though perhaps originally independent) in Num 23:22 = 24:8. This is important evidence for the tradition that El as a bull-god was the deliverer in the exodus tradition (see below).

The episodes of the Golden Calf and the Calves of Jeroboam, respectively in Exod 32 and 1 Kgs 12:26-33, appear to be unconnected. But their literary relationship is close, as established by ABERBACH & SMOLAR (1967). It may be argued that, historically speaking, the event under Jeroboam is the historical source of the Golden Calf episode as a midrash on the theme of apostasy and its punishment by exile. It is scarcely credible that a historical episode as described in Exod 32 actually predated the settlement in Palestine, as it presupposes a monotheism which could hardly predate Josiah at the earliest. A comparison of the wording of 1 Kgs 12:28, Exod 32:4.8 and of Neh 9:18 (WYATT 1992:78-79) allows us to conclude that the formula in 1 Kgs 12:28 is primary, and that the others have both developed from it, and transformed a soteriological statement (as surely intended by Jeroboam) into a declaration of apostasy. Contrary to the evident meaning of Exod 32:4, 8, which apparently attempts to construct two or more gods out of one calf(!), it is clear from the narrative in Kgs that one god was understood by the 'calf' image, and that Jeroboam's 'calves' were different images of the same god.

As to the identity of the god, suggestions have ranged from Yahweh (PATON 1894, OBBINK 1929 *et al.*), through Baal (ÖSTBORN 1955, DUS 1968), 'polytheism' (MONTGOMERY, *Kings* [ICC; Edinburgh 1951] 255), →Hathor (OESTERLY, *The legacy of Egypt* [1942[1]] 239) →Moses (SASSON 1968), and →Sîn (LEWY 1945-1946) to El (SCHAEFFER 1966, WYATT 1992).

The present writer has proposed (WYATT 1992:79) that the MT at Exod 32:4.8 has preserved an older strand of tradition, still formally dependant on Jeroboam's formula, but preserving the old notion (which was presumably the intention of Jeroboam's words) that one deity was to be identified by the formula, which read originally *ʾēl ʾĕlōhekā yisrāʾēl ʾăšer heʿelkā mēʾereṣ miṣrayim*, expressing the kerygma "El is your god, Israel, who brought you up out of the land of Egypt!" This has been deliberately perverted in transmission into "These are your gods…" by the simple expedient of adding matres lectionis which require a plural interpretation of the demonstrative, *ʾĕlōhêkā*, and the verb. The old consonantal text is capable of singular or plural interpretation.

A kerygma of El as the saviour from Egypt has left traces elsewhere, notably at Num 23:22; 24:8 noted above, Ps 106:19-22, Hos 7:16, where *laʿgām* (sic), 'their derision', is either to be corrected to *ʿaglām*, 'their calf', or more probably recognised as a vicious lampoon on a reference which is already a parody, by ridiculing the bull-god as a mere calf. This is congruent with the attack on bull-worship in Hos 8:1-6. The use of *ʾēl//ʾĕlōhê ʾābî* in Exod 15:2 may also be significant in view of the *Vorlage* of the latter formula (WYATT, *ZAW* 90 [1978] 101-104). This has important implications for the exegesis of Exod 3 (WYATT, *ZAW* 91 [1979] 437-442).

IV. *Bibliography*

M. ABERBACH & L. SMOLAR, Aaron, Jeroboam and the Golden Calves, *JBL* 86 (1967) 129-140; L. R. BAILEY, The Golden Calf, *HUCA* 42 (1971) 97-115; M. BIČ, Bet'el - le sanctuaire du roi, *ArOr* 17 (1949) 49-63; H. C. BRICHTO, The Worship of the Golden Calf: a literary analysis of a fable on idolatry, *HUCA* 54 (1983) 1-44; E. DANIELUS, The sins of Jeroboam ben-Nebat, *JQR* 58 (1967) 95-114, 204-233; J. DEBUS, *Die Sünde Jeroboams* (FRLANT 93; Göttingen 1967); H. DONNER, 'Hier sind deine Götter, Israel!', *Wort und Geschichte* (ed. H. Gese & H. P. Rüger, AOAT 18; Neukirchen-Vluyn 1973) 45-50; T. B. DOZEMAN, Moses: Divine Servant and Israelite Hero, *HAR* 8 (1984) 45-61; J. DUS, Die Stierbilder von Bethel und Dan und das Problem der 'Moseschar', *AION* 18 (1968) 105-137; O. EISSFELDT, Lade und Stierbild, *ZAW* 58 (1940-1) 190-215; J. LEWY, The Late Assyro-Babylonian Cult of the Moon and Its Culmination in the Time of Nabonidus, *HUCA* 19 (1945-46) 405-489; H. MOTZKI, Ein Beitrag zum Problem des Stierkultes in der Religionsgeschichte Israels, *VT* 25 (1975) 470-485; W. OBBINK, Jahwebilder, *ZAW* 47 (1929) 264-274; G. ÖSBORN, Yahweh and Baal, *LUÅ* 51.6 (1955); L. B. PATON, Did Amos Approve the Calf-Worship at Bethel?, *JBL* 13 (1894) 80-90; J. M. SASSON, The Bovine Symbolism in Exodus, *VT* 18 (1968) 380-387; J. M. SASSON, The Worship of the Golden Calf, *Orient and Occident* (ed. H. A. Hoffner, AOAT 22; Neukirchen-Vluyn 1971) 151-159; C-F. A. SCHAEFFER, Nouveaux témoignages du culte de El et de Baal à Ras Shamra et ailleurs en Syrie-Palestine, *Syria* 43 (1966) 16; H. TUR-SINAI, אֲבִיר אביר, *EncMigr* 1 (Jerusalem 1950) cols. 31-33; R. DE VAUX, Le schisme religieux de Jeroboam, *Angelicum* 20 (1943) 77-91; J. VERMEYLEN, L'affaire du veau d'or (Ex. 32-34), *ZAW* 97 (1985) 1-23; M. WEIPPERT, Gott und Stier, *ZDPV* 77 (1961) 93-117; N. WYATT, Of Calves and Kings: the Canaanite Dimension in the Religion of Israel, *SJOT* 6 (1992) 68-91.

N. WYATT

CARMEL כרמל

I. Carmel (Jebel Kurmul) is a promontory on the Mediterran Coast of Israel near Haifa which since ancient times was considered as 'holy'. A deity was worshipped there whose name occurs outside the Bible as "god of the Carmel". In the OT Mount Carmel is known especially as scene of a trial of strength between the prophets of →Baal and →Elijah, or rather, between Baal and →Yahweh (1 Kgs 18).

II. The 'holiness' of the Carmel may already have been mentioned in the listing of countries and cities of the conquering Pharaoh Thutmoses III in the second millennium (about 1490-1436 BCE) by the name 'Rash-Qadesh' ('Holy Head', *ANET* 243), although this identification is still uncertain. According to the Annals of Shalmaneser III, Mount Carmel appears as "the mountain of Baʿli-ra'ši", where the Assyrian king received tribute from Jehu of Israel (ASTOUR 1962). Based on this evidence Astour is of the opinion that this "testifies to the sacral character of Mount Carmel". In the fifth or fourth century BCE Pseudo-Scylax described Mount Carmel as "the holy mountain of →Zeus" (ὄρος ἱερὸν Διός; *Periplus* 104). Tacitus (*Hist.* II, 78) mentions the deity and the mountain Carmelus on account of the favourable promises to Vespasian in 69 CE: "Between Iudea and Syria lies the Carmel. Thus they called the mountain and the divinity. The god has no image or temple—according to the ancestral tradition—, but only an altar and a cult". Also Suetonius records about the same Vespasian (*De vita Vesp* VIII,6): "When he (i.e. Vespasian) was consulting the oracle of the god of Carmel in Iudaea, the lots were very encouraging, promising that whatever he planned or wished, however great it might be, would come to pass ...". In 1952 AVI-YONAH published a late second- or early third-century CE inscription on a big marble votive foot, found in the monastery of Elijah (on the north-west side of mount Carmel), with a dedication to the "Heliopolitan Zeus of the Carmel": ΔΙΙ ΗΛΙΟΠΟΛΕΙΤΗ ΚΑΡΜΗΛΩ. The statements of Tacitus and Suetonius, and also of this inscription, that Carmel(us) can be the name of the god may have been derived from the translation of the North-west-Semitic בעל כרמל. Iamblichus informs us at the beginning of the fourth century CE about the sojourn of a meditating Pythagoras on Mount Carmel (*De vita Pythagorica* III, 15) after he was brought by Egyptian sailors to this mountain to be alone in this holy place. In this connection he spoke about "the highest peak of the Carmel, which they considered as the holiest and for many people not to be trodden mountain". Iamblichus does not mention a deity, he speaks only about "a holy place". It is possible that this is the same place which Orosius calls an "oracle" (*Historia adv. paganos* VII, 9).

From these extra-biblical data one can infer (1) that the mountain was considered 'holy' since ancient times; (2) that there has probably never been a temple on Mount Carmel; (3) that the deity of the Carmel had a more than local meaning; and (4) that, especially in later times, there was a connection between Zeus Heliopolitanus and the deity of the Carmel.

The Heliopolis here mentioned is a town in Libanon/Syria in the Beqaʿ near the source of the Orontes, now called Baalbek. Its Greek name since the Seleucid period was "city of the sun" (Helio-polis), possibly because Baal was identified with 'the god of the sun'. The most ancient temple of Baalbek was originally dedicated to the Semitic stormgod →Hadad, and since Hellenistic times to Jupiter/Zeus. The sky-god →Baalshamem also merged with Jupiter. By the beginning of the Christian Era, the cult of the god of Heliopolis had even found its way as far as the Italian coast. A Latin inscription has been found in Puteoli (near Naples) which mentions *cultores Jovis Heliopolitani* (worshippers of the Heliopolitan Jupiter). In the time of Emperor Septimius Severus, Baalbek became an independent colony with an Italian legal system and games in honour of Heliopolitanus. Mount Carmel belonged to Acco/Ptolemais, where coins were found representing Jupiter Heliopolitanus flanked by bulls. A coin was also found with a picture of a →giant's foot. Above this picture can be seen the lightning of Zeus, beside it the *caduceus* (i.e. herald's staff), and under it an axe. The similarity of the picture on this coin with the marble votive foot, mentioned above, is most striking.

The great deity of Heliopolis/Baalbek could only be compared with the centuries older 'god of the Carmel', if one could find in this god something of the nature of Zeus. Zeus Heliopolitanus is perhaps a fusion of a Semitic weather, sky and fertility-god like

Hadad or Baalshamem, and the sun-god →Helios (EISSFELDT 1953; DAY 1992). He is a comparatively young member in a long list of Semitic gods of this type.

But who was the (Canaanite) god whose 'contest' with Yahweh on Mount Carmel in the time of Ahab is told in 1 Kgs 18? In the course of time many different answers have been given to this question. There are scholars who see in this Baal a local numen, others are of the opinion that he was the Baal *par excellence* or Baalshamem, the sky-god. Most scholars, however, see in this deity the Tyrian Baal who was identified with →Melqart (Greek →Heracles). A comparison of some data in 1 Kgs 18 with data known from the worship of the Tyrian Melqart seems to support this conjecture. Yet no consensus has been reached. ALT asserted that Yahweh on Mount Carmel did not have a contest with a Tyrian god, but with the old deity of mount Carmel itself. EISSFELDT was of the opinion that the Baal of mount Carmel was the same as the universal Baalshamem. DUSSAUD took the name of this Baal to be Hadad. Indeed, there is no need whatsoever to replace the name 'Melqart' for the Baal of this tale. Besides, it must be said that 'Melqart' is not a proper name but rather a title (BRONNER 1968; BONNET 1986); moreover, the Tyrian god was equated with Heracles rather than with Zeus.

One's view regarding the historicity of the tales of 1 Kgs 18 is essential for the solution of the problem of the 'real name' of the deity. Those who regard the stories on Mount Carmel as historically true are inclined to see in Baal the 'Tyrian Melqart' (thus e.g. DE VAUX 1941); those who regard these stories as novellas of a later time, which function as *haggadoth*, are inclined to see in the Baal of Mount Carmel only an indication of the old Baal *par excellence* (thus e.g. MULDER 1979). It is very difficult to demonstrate that 1 Kgs 18:26-29, an old reproduction of a—local?—Baal cult, could only fit a Tyrian sacrificial ceremony. Many details could have been found in other Baal ceremonies too, judging by what we know about the Ugaritic religion. Moreover, it is not until a second century BCE inscription from Malta that we find Melqart referred to as "Baal of Tyre" (*KAI* 47:1; DAY 1992: 548). One should always realize that the author of 1 Kgs 18, just like the other authors of the OT, did not intend to give some valuable information about a god who in his eyes was merely an idol (*interpretatio israelitica*). The identity, character and role of the deity of Mount Carmel—as described in 1 Kings 18—are those of a fertility and vegetation god. This fits precisely with the image of Baal obtained from the Ugaritic and other extra-biblical texts.

III. The nature of the biblical Baal of the Carmel and his worship emerges in 1 Kgs 18:26-28, where it is told that the 'prophets' of Baal offered a bull and invoked Baal by name, crying: "Baal, answer us". Meanwhile the prophets danced wildly beside the altar they had set up. After Elijah mocked them with the words: "Call louder for he is a →god, perhaps he is deep in thought, or otherwise engaged, or on a journey, or has gone to sleep and must be woken up", they cried louder still and gashed themselves, as was their custom, with swords and spears until blood ran.

This characterization of Baal is not peculiar to Melqart. In the Ugaritic texts we find a cult-cry: "Where is mightiest Baal, where is the prince lord of earth" (*KTU* 1.6 iv:4-5.; *CML* 78). The ecstacy of these prophets is reminiscent of the prophetic ecstasy reported in the tale of Wen-Amon (*ANET* 25-29); there are other extra-biblical parallels, too (GASTER 1969:504-510). Of the self-mutilation of the ecstatic Baal-worshippers, "as was their custom", we also have parallels in the Ugaritic texts: "he harrowed his collarbone, he ploughed his chest like a garden, he harrowed his waist like a valley" (*KTU* 1.5 vi:20-22; *CML* 73). The somewhat enigmatic words of the mocking Elijah: "he is deep in thought, or he is otherwise engaged", do not reveal anything specific about Baal. The absence, the journey, the sleeping and awakening of Baal are all in line with the idea of Baal as god of vegetation and fertility. This god is precisely the god who in later times was called "the god of the Carmel" or "the god Carmel".

It should be noted that it is told that Elijah "repaired the altar of Yahweh which had been torn down" (18:30). This confirms the older statement that there was already an altar on Mount Carmel before the time of the 'contest' of the gods, but not a temple. From 2 Kgs 2:25 and 4:23-25, we may infer that Mount Carmel was a place of pilgrimage for Israelite and Canaanite people, and a spiritual retreat for Elisha and other charismatic prophets too (THOMPSON 1992). The special circumstances for these festivals were new moon festivals and sabbaths. The authors of the biblical stories nevertheless deny any form of identification of Yahweh and "the god of the Carmel".

IV. *Bibliography*

A. ALT, Das Gottesurteil auf dem Karmel, *FS. G. Beer* (1935) 1-18 = *KS* 2, 135-149; M. C. ASTOUR, Carmel, Mount, *IBDS* (1962) 141; M. AVI-YONAH, Mount Carmel and the God of Baalbek, *IEJ* 2 (1952) 118-124; C. BONNET, Le culte de Melqart à Carthage. Un cas de conservatisme religieux, *Studia Phoenicia IV* (C. Bonnet, E. Lipiński & P. Marchetti eds.; Namur 1986); L. BRONNER, *The stories of Elijah and Elisha* (Leiden 1968); J. DAY, Baal, *ABD* 1 (1992) 545-549; R. DUSSAUD, *Les découvertes de Ras Shamra et l'Ancient Testament* (Paris 1941²); O. EISSFELDT, *Der Gott Karmel* (SDAW 1; 1953); K. GALLING, Der Gott Karmel und die Ächtung der fremden Götter, *Geschichte und Altes Testament, FS A. Alt* (1953) 105-125; T. H. GASTER, *Myth, Legend, and Custom in the Old Testament* (New York/Evanston 1969) 504-511; M. J. MULDER, *Baal in het Oude Testament* (The Hague 1962) 30-44; MULDER, *De naam van de afwezige god op de Karmel. Onderzoek naar de naam van de Baäl van de Karmel in 1 Koningen 18* (Leiden 1979); MULDER, כרמל, *TWAT* 4 (1984) 340-351; H. D. PREUSS, *Verspottung fremder Religionen im Alten Testament* (Stuttgart/Berlin 1971) 80-100; H. O. THOMPSON, Carmel, Mount, *ABD* 1 (1992) 874-875; S. TIMM, *Die Dynastie Omri. Quellen und Untersuchungen zur Geschichte Israels im 9. Jahrhundert vor Christus* (FRLANT 124; Göttingen 1982) 87-101; R. DE VAUX, Les prophètes de Baal sur le Mont Carmel, *Bulletin du Musée de Beyrouth* 5 (1941) 7-20 = *Bible et Orient* (Paris 1967) 485-497; E. WÜRTHWEIN, Die Erzählung vom Gottesurteil auf dem Karmel, *ZTK* 59 (1962) 131-144.

M. J. MULDER

CASTOR → DIOSKOUROI

CHAOS Χάος

I. The Greek word χάος (related to χάσκω or χαίνω, 'gape, yawn') literally means 'chasm' or 'yawning space'. There were various conceptions of it in Greco-Roman antiquity, because in various mythical cosmogonies Chaos played very different roles. The word occurs only twice in the Greek Bible, in Mic 1:6 and Zech 14:4, each time as a translation of the Hebrew *gy*ʾ, 'valley'; and 2 times in the Greek fragments of *1 Enoch* (10:13) and *Jubilees* (2:2), where it seems to be used for the abyss where the evil angels have been incarcerated forever. The modern sense of the word, i.e. 'disorder', developed only slowly and is not attested before the later Imperial Period.

II. Hesiod was the first to assign Chaos a position at the head of a cosmological genealogy. In *Theog.* 116-122 Chaos is either the personified murky and gloomy space below the →earth (thus WEST 1966: 192-3) or the vast gap between earth and →sky (thus KIRK, RAVEN & SCHOFIELD 1983:34-41); its children are Erebos (the realm of darkness associated with →Hades) and Nyx (→Night); cf. for this primary position also Acusilaos *ap.* Philodemus, *De pietate* 137,5 and Aristophanes, *Aves* 693. In various post-Hesiodic cosmogonical systems, Chaos receives different positions: e.g. in Orphic accounts it comes second, after Chronos (FAUTH 1975:1129; KIRK, RAVEN & SCHOFIELD 1983:26-28; further details in SCHWABL 1962:1467-84). In later authors Chaos develops the various notions of primordial matter (e.g. Ovid, *Met.* I 5-20), primordial water (e.g. Pherecydes 7B1a; Zeno, SVF I 103 [etymological derivation ἀπὸ τοῦ χέεσθαι]), primordial time (e.g. PGM IV 2535f.), the air between heaven and earth (e.g. Aristophanes, *Aves* 1218; Bacchylides 5,27), and the (whole or part of the) netherworld (e.g. Ps-Plato, *Axiochus* 371e; CUMONT 1942:51 and TERNUS 1954: 1032-1034 for further references). In various Gnostic systems Chaos plays a negative role in connection with the bad Demiurge (Hippolytus, *Refutatio* V 10,2; 14,1) or as the place of 'outer darkness', the 'abyss' (*NHC* I 5, 89; II 1, 30) or as designation of the cosmos (*BG* 8502, 118-121; see further *The Nag Hammadi Library in English* [San Francisco-Leiden 1977] 480 s.v.; SIEGERT 1982:323).

III. Chaos as a cosmogonic factor or principle does not occur in the Bible, although the statement in Gen 1:2 that the earth was *tohu wabohu* (LXX: ἀόρατος και ἀκατασκεύαστος) and that darkness covered the deep (→*tiamat*, LXX ἄβυσσος) shows some resemblance to the Hesiodic concept. In this connection it is interesting that Philo of Byblos, in his rendering of Sanchuniathon's Phoenician cosmogonical lore, says that "he posits as the ἀρχή of the universe a dark and windy air, or a stream of dark air, and turbid (or watery), gloomy chaos (χάος θολερὸν ἐρεβῶδες)", *ap.* Eusebius, *Praep. Evang.* I 10,1. However much this formulation may be due to an *interpretatio graeca*, it makes clear that the author apparently saw a close analogy between these Greek and Semitic protologies (BAUMGARTEN 1981: 106-108 *ad loc.* rightly refers to Gen 1:2). In an apocalyptic context, Chaos sometimes functions as an element in the eschatological cosmic upheaval (GUNKEL 1895), as may be seen e.g. in *4 Ezra* 5:8, where it is said that in the endtime in many places an abyss or chasm (the Latin here retains the Greek word *chaos*) will open up from which subterrestrial fire will break out. This may explain why the LXX translators twice chose the word χάος to render passages with an eschatological tone: in Mic 1:6 the LORD will destroy Samaria and hurl her stones into the *chaos*, and in Zech 14:4 the feet of the LORD will stand on the Mount of Olives and the mount will be cleft in two by an immense *chaos* stretching from east to west. The eschatological *chaos* as a place of eternal torment in *1 Enoch* 10:13 (see above) is paralleled in 2 Pet 2:4, where it is said that →God did not spare the angels who sinned, but consigned them to the dark pits of Tartarus.

IV. *Bibliography*

A. I. BAUMGARTEN, *The* Phoenician History *of Philo of Byblos* (Leiden 1981); F. CUMONT, *Recherches sur le symbolisme funéraire des Romains* (New York 1975 = Paris 1942); O. EISSFELDT, Das Chaos in der biblischen und in der phönizischen Kosmogonie, *KS* II (Tübingen 1963) 258-262; W. FAUTH, Chaos, *KP* I (1975) 1129-30; H. GUNKEL, *Schöpfung und Chaos in Urzeit und Endzeit* (Göttingen 1895); *G. S. KIRK, J. E. RAVEN & M. SCHOFIELD, *The Presocratic Philosophers* (Cambridge 1983[2]), index s.v.; H. SCHWABL, Weltschöpfung, *PWSup* 9 (1962) 1433-1582; F. SIEGERT, *Nag-Hammadi-Register* (Tübingen 1982); *J. TERNUS, Chaos, *RAC* 2 (1954) 1031-40; M. L. WEST, *Hesiod. Theogony* (Oxford 1966).

P. W. VAN DER HORST

CHEMOSH כמוש

I. The divine name Chemosh has the phonological forms '*kam(m)iṯ*' and '*kam(m)uṯ*'—the first one being attested in Eblaitic ^{d}*Ka-mi/mí-iš*, in the geographical name Karkamiš 'quay of Kamiš', and in כמיש Jer 48:7 (MÜLLER 1980), the other one in a couple of Semitic languages like Neo-Assyrian, Moabite, and perhaps in Ugaritic. The duplication of consonants would neither be indicated in Eblaitic cuneiform script nor in Ugaritic and Moabite. Both forms, *qattil* (*parris*) as a substantival participle of B-stem (*GAG* § 55:20aII) and *qattul* (*parrus*) as a verbal adjective of D-stem, may mean 'conqueror, subduer' as shown by Akkadian *kanāšu, kamāš/su* 'to submit to an overlord, a deity', D-stem: 'to bend down, to bow down' (*CAD* K 144-148; compare Old South-Arabic *hkms* 'to humiliate, crush'). The same is true in respect to Hebrew **kāmôš* < *'kam(m)âš'*, a *qattāl*-formation, as it is very often used for nomina agentis; in Ugarit, we find the personal name *(bin-)ka-ma-si* (GRÖNDAHL 1967), in Moab the royal name ^{m}*Ka-ma-aš-ḫal-ta-a*, both with *'a'* in the second syllable (WEIPPERT, *RLA* 5 [1976-1980] 328). Masoretic *kĕmôš* is voweled according to *bĕʾôš* 'stench' or the like and so deliberately misleading, since the correct vocalization is attested by χαμώς of the LXX and Chamos of the Vg, where the duplicated middle consonant is wanting for some reason or other. There is no etymological connexion to Middle Hebrew *kāmaš* 'to wrinkle, wither' nor to the rare Arabic *kamasa* 'to be/get harsh, sour, acid'. Nevertheless, a non-Semitic origin of the name cannot be rejected absolutely.

II. The great importance of the god Kamiš in the private as well as in the official religion of Ebla is to be seen from the use of this theonym as a theophoric element in personal names, from the bulk of sheep offering presented to him (TM.75. G.2075 obv. VII:6; rev. IV:4; VI:3, 13, 18; PETTINATO 1979: 147-159) and not least by the fact that the name of the 12th month is **itu nidba**$_{x}$ (MÙŠxKUR$_{6}$ or MÙŠ.KUR$_{6}$) ^{d}*Kà-mi-iš* 'month of the festival for Kamiš'; an **é** ^{d}*Kà-mi-iš* 'temple of Kamiš' is equally attested (PETTINATO 1974-1977; 1976, but also E. SOLLBERGER, *StEb* IV/9-10 [1980] 136; MÜLLER 1980; POMPONIO 1983:145, 156).

In Ugarit, the veneration of a binomial deity *ẓẓ.w kmṯ* or *ṯẓ.w kmṯ*, though not in a prominent place, can be deduced from the occurence in *KTU* 1.100:36; 107:16; 123:5. *ẓẓ* or *ṯẓ* means 'mud, clay' as a comparison with Akkadian *ṭīṭu* and Hebrew *ṭîṭ*, both of the same meaning, shows (XELLA 1981:219-220) and may account for the chthonic character of *kmṯ*, since the *wāw* in *ẓẓ.w kmṯ* is perhaps to be interpreted as a *wāw* explicationis in the sense of 'namely'. As all three attestations are in stereotyped contexts, the role of *ẓ/ṯẓ.w kmṯ* is easily exchangeable with an equal role played by other binomial deities. *KTU* 1.123 is virtually a god list.

According to the expression *ẓẓ.w kmṯ.ḥryth* in *KTU* 1.100:36, the city *ḥryth*, identifiable as *Ḫu-ur-ri-ya*^{ki} in Northern Mesopotamia (ARM VIII 100:19), or as ${}^{(uru)}$*Ḫu-ri-ja*^{ki} in the kingdom of Alalaḫ (*AlT* 201:15; cf. ASTOUR 1968), if not—less probably—as *Ḫa-ri-e-ta* near Qadeš on the Orontes (A. CAQUOT, Syria 46 [1969] 246), was the main cult place of *ẓẓ.w kmṯ*.

The Neo-Assyrian Chicago syllabary 136 gives the equations GUD = *Ka-mu-uš* = ^{d}*Ka-mu-uš* GUD (cf. *ŠL* II/2,515 [no. 13e]) for which we remember that GUD can be the word-sign for →*eṭemmu* 'spirit of a dead one', perhaps another hint to the chthonic character of Chemosh. For the same reason, ^{d}*Ka-am-muš* is identified with →Nergal in CT 24, 36:66 (*AkkGE* 339; W. G. LAMBERT, *RLA* 5 [1976-1980] 335).

As for the Moabite evidence, Chemosh is attested both in native inscriptions on the one hand and in royal names transmitted in cuneiform texts on the other hand; in the latter, however, Neo-Assyrian influence on spelling and even unconscious interpretation cannot be excluded. The well known Mesha stone *KAI* 181 names Chemosh 10 times, and once more in the binomial form *ʿštr.kmš* in line 17, and as a theophoric element in the king's father's name *Kmš[jt]* (line1) that we find again in a recently discovered second Mesha inscription. Mesha's stela no. 1 is a votive text erected on occasion of the building of the *bāmâ,* 'sacred high-place', mentioned in line 3. Because lines 1-21 and 31-33 report battles against Israel won by Mesha in honour of his god Chemosh and of himself, we can suppose from lines 3-4 that the *bāmâ* and the inscribed stela were constructed at the same time to celebrate these victories as mighty acts of the god Chemosh and king Mesha whose name means not without reason 'the Saviour'. Lines 21-31 glorify various efforts of Mesha as city founder or restorer and are noteworthily free from religious motifs. The main text (lines

1-21a, 31-33) refers to a holy war which seems to be performed like a ritual and is brought to an end by the ban (→Taboo) i.e. the execution of the subdued population, 'as a spectacle (*ryt*) for Chemosh and for Moab' (line 12); the technical term hiph'il *ḥrm* 'to ban' which is well known from the Old Testament is used in line 17. In a kind of functional monolatry, Chemosh is the only subduer of his enemies, just as →Yahweh in Israel, who is nevertheless overthrown in this case, so that Yahweh's holy implements (lines 17-18) as well as the *'r'l*, perhaps 'altar', of Israel's *dwd* (= Yahweh?) according to lines 12-13 are brought 'before Chemosh'. Altogether, following holy war ideology, Israel must have perished for ever (line 7; cf: Judg 5:31), whereas formerly, in his wrath, Chemosh had humbled Moab so that Israel had come to be victorious (line 5-6). The binomial signification *'štr.kmš* identifies Chemosh with the male god Ashtar who already plays a merely ridiculous role as a defunct deity in the Ugaritic Cycle of Baal (*KTU* 1.6 i:44-67), but may have remained still more vigourous in marginal regions like Moab. Once, he could have been martial like his female counterparts Ishtar and Astarte; his epithet *'rẓ* 'aweful' *KTU* 1.6 I:54-56, 61, 63 is at the same time atavistic and ironical (MÜLLER, *TWAT* 6, 454-456). Therefore the identification of Ashtar and Chemosh may have served to secure the functional monolatry of the latter in war affairs. A second Mesha inscription mentions the name of the king's father [*k*]*mšjt* 'Chemosh has given' again, and a [*b*]*t.kmš* 'house (temple) of Chemosh' into the bargain (*TSSI* 1, 83-84), the latter occurring as *bt k*[*mš*] in a third stela fragment found in 1951 (MURPHY 1952).

Moabite royal names in Neo-Assyrian cuneiforms are [I]*Ka-am/Kam-mu-su-nad-bi* 'Chemosh is generous to me' (cf. *kmšjt*); (Sennacherib, TIMM 1989:346-359); [I]*Ka-mu-šu-i-lu* 'Chemosh is god'; [d]*Ka-mu-šú-šar-uṣur* 'Chemosh, protect the king' (cf. *šwššr'ṣr* 'Šamaš, protect the king' on an Aramaic seal; TIGAY 1987:183 n. 28, 168-171) in which Babylonian influence is obvious (VAN ZYL 1960:183) and the above mentioned [I]*Ka-am-aš-ḫal-ta-a* of uncertain meaning (Assurbanipal, RÖLLIG; WEIPPERT, *RLA* 5 [1976-1980] 328, 335-336; TIMM 1989:374-388). *Kmš* occurs as theophoric element in personal names *kmš* (TIMM 1989:180-181); *kmšyḥy* (idem 162-165); *kmšm'š* (166-167); *kmš'm* (*bn*) *kmš'l* (168-170); *kmšṣdq* (171-173); *kmšdn* (178-179); *kmšntn* (182-183) on seals.

Papyrus fragments from Egyptian Saggara contain personal names such as *kmšjḥj* 'Chemosh may live', *kmsṣdq* 'Chemosh is righteous' and *kmšplṭ* 'Chemosh has saved' (AIMÉ-GIRON 1931; VAN ZYL 1960:40, 182). Whether a material figure between torches represented on Moabite coins is Chemosh is a moot point. In Hellenistic time, Chemosh has been identified with →Ares; therefore the name of the capital Diban is now changed to 'Areopolis' (GESE 1970:181).

Without any historical value is the information of the Suda, a Byzantine dictionary from the 10th century CE, that Chemosh was the god of Tyre and the Amorites.

Whether or not the figure on the left side of the famous Balu'ah monument (*ANEP*, no. 488) is Chemosh cannot be decided on the basis of the available evidence.

III. Biblical evidence on Chemosh is scarce and merely incidental. In announcements of disaster, Moab is called 'the people of Chemosh' in Num 21:29; Jer 48:46. The connexion between a single god and an ethnic community which the god seems to have chosen looks like a generalization of the functional monolatry we found in the Mesha inscription: the first millennium BCE is a time of national kingdoms in Syria and Palestine; the god of the nation represents its solidarity. Judg 11:12.24 takes Chemosh to be the god of the Ammonites, which conforms to the same scheme of thinking, but makes the wrong association.

That Solomon should have introduced, east of Jerusalem, the cult of Chemosh, →Astarte, and →Milcom (read *lĕmilkôm* 1 Kgs 11:7 instead of *lĕmôlek* according to LXX[L] and vv 5, 33 MT; cf. 2 Kgs 23:13) for the convenience of his distinguished foreign concubines is suspected to be a Deuteronomistic slander, in reality reflecting the idolatrous conditions of the exilic time. In v 7, Chemosh is called *šiqqûṣ mô'āb* 'the abomination of Moab' which, along with the formula *'āz yibneh* 'then ... built', may reflect earlier terminology (M. NOTH, BKAT IX/1, 246). Verse 33 speaks in clearly Deuteronomistic style about *kĕmôš 'ĕlōhê mô'āb* 'Chemosh the god of Moab', and that in a pretended announcement of disaster by Ahijah of Shilo. Deuteronomistic, too, is the reference in 2 Kgs 23:13, according to which Josiah had purified the mountains east of Jerusalem from the *bāmôt*, 'sacred high-places', of Astarte, Chemosh and Milcom. Here we find an exact localization that is missing in 1 Kgs 11:5 LXX and has been secondarily inserted in 1 Kgs 11:7. In my opinion, 2 Kgs 23:13 reflects an ideal of cultic purification cherished in pious exilic circles (MÜLLER, *TWAT* 6, 459-460).

Of particular interest is the remark in 2 Kgs 3:27 that Mesha, in a critical situation of battle, offered his son on the wall of his city, the consequence of which was that the wrath of Chemosh began to destroy Israel instantly; nowhere else is the mighty activity of a foreign god conceded in such an unrestrained manner. Unfortunately, we cannot reconcile this particular record with the largely ideological statements of the first Mesha inscription.

Jer 48:7 announces the exile of the god Chemosh (*kmjš* !), together with his priests and princes (*śārîm*). According to v 13, 'Moab shall be ashamed of Beth-El, their confidence'. The context of both passages confirms the martial character of Chemosh, which agrees with the first Mesha-inscription and with 2 Kgs 3:27, thus confirming its authenticity.

IV. *Bibliography*

M. N. AIMÉ-GIRON, *Textes araméens de l'Égypte* (Cairo 1931) 13; M. C. ASTOUR, Some New Divine Names from Ugarit, *JAOS* 86 (1966) 277-284, esp. 277-278; ASTOUR, Two Ugaritic Serpent Charms, *JNES* 27 (1968) 13-36, esp. 20; H. GESE, Die Religionen Altsyriens, (*RAAM* Stuttgart 1970) 3-232, esp. 140-141; F. GRÖNDAHL, *Die Personennamen der Texte aus Ugarit* (Rome 1967) 150; H.-P. MÜLLER, Religionsgeschichtliche Beobachtungen zu den Texten von Ebla, *ZDPV* 96 (1980) 1-19, esp. 10-11 [& lit]; MÜLLER, Die Inschrift des Königs Mesa von Moab, *TUAT* I/6 (ed. O. Kaiser; Gütersloh 1985) 646-650; R. E. MURPHY, A Fragment of an Early Moabite Inscription from Dibon, *BASOR* 125 (1952) 20-23; G. PETTINATO, Il calendario di Ebla al tempo del re Ibbi-Sipiš sulla base di TM.75.G.427, *AfO* 25 (1974-77) 28-36; PETTINATO, Carchemiš - Kār-Kamiš. Le prime attestazioni del III millennio, *OrAnt* 15 (1976) 11-15; PETTINATO, Culto ufficiale ad Ebla durante il regno di Ibbi-Sipiš, *OrAnt* 18 (1979) 85-215; F. POMPONIO, I nomi divini nei testi di Ebla, *UF* 15 (1983) 141-156; W. RÖLLIG, Kamoš, *WbMyth* I/1 (1965) 292; J. H. TIGAY, Israelite Religion: The Onomastic and Epigraphic Evidence, *Ancient Israelite Religion. Essays in Honor of F. M. Cross* (ed. P. D. Miller jr. *et alii*; Philadelphia 1987) 157-194; S. TIMM, *Die Dynastie Omri* (FRLANT 124; Göttingen 1982) 158-180; TIMM, *Moab zwischen den Mächten* (Wiesbaden 1989); P. XELLA, *I testi rituali di Ugarit* I (Rome 1981) 216-250 [& lit]; A. H. VAN ZYL, *The Moabites* (POS 3; Leiden 1960) esp. 180-183, 195-198.

H.-P. MÜLLER

CHERUBIM כרובים

I. The term 'cherubim' occurs 91 times in the Hebrew Bible. It denotes the Israelite counterpart of the sphinx known from the pictorial art of the ancient Near East. In the Bible the cherubim occur essentially in two functions: as guardians of a sacred tree or as guardians and carriers of a throne.

There is no consensus on the etymology of the term. While there are difficulties connected with the various suggestions that have been made (survey in FREEDMAN & O'CONNOR 1983) the most probable is that the Heb term is connected with Akk *kāribu*, *kurību*, both used with reference to genii in Mesopotamian mythology and art (see RINALDI 1967). But even so, this provides little help in understanding the Israelite cherubim.

II. The study of ancient Near Eastern iconography has been instrumental in the interpretation of the biblical cherubim and here interest has focussed on the sphinx, i.e. the winged lion with a human head (ALBRIGHT 1938; thorough documentation in DE VAUX 1967; METZGER 1985a: 259-83 and figs 1181-1222; GUBEL 1987: 37-84). The basic confirmation of this interpretation is found in the fact that sphinxes and biblical cherubim occur in precisely the same above-mentioned functions.

While the sphinx is known both in Mesopotamia and Egypt, the sphinx throne with the sphinxes as an integral element of the throne itself (thus not only flanking the throne) is a Syrian innovation from the time of the 19th Egyptian dynasty. While the Egyptian lion-paws throne never carried a →god, the Syrian sphinx throne was used for both gods and kings.

The classical examples of the sphinx throne are the ivory plaque from Megiddo stratum VIIA (Iron I), the small throne model from the same site, and the relief on the sarcophagus of Ahiram (late 2nd millennium). SEYRIG called attention to a group of small, mostly empty votive thrones from the Syro-Lebanese coastal area, dating from the 7th century BCE to Hellenistic times (METZGER 1985a: figs 1191-1199). Of these, one had a steeply leaning seat incapable of receiving an object (METZGER 1985a: fig. 1201), thus being empty from the beginning, without a cultic image, one had a spherical, aniconic object on the seat, and one had two sculptured stelae leaning towards the back. This may have implications for the understanding of the aniconism of the Solomonic temple, which was built by Tyrian architects. Sphinx thrones bearing a deity are known from Mediterranean scarabs from the 7th-6th centuries (METZGER 1985a: figs 1184-1188) and later Punic stelae and terracottae (METZGER 1985a: figs 1203-1217).

The deity on these thrones is either a male (→Baal Hammon) or a female one (→Astarte). The lion-paws throne from which the sphinx throne developed occurs as the throne of →El on the Ugaritic El stela (*ANEP* no. 493). The male deity on the sphinx throne, Baal Hammon (P. XELLA, *Baal Hammon* [Rome 1991] 106-140), is generally considered as something of an El figure (XELLA: 100-105, 233).

III. While the biblical cherubim sometimes appear as guardians of the sacred tree (1 Kgs 6:29-35; Ezek 41:18-25) or of the garden of Eden (Gen 3:24; Ezek 28:14,16), the most important function is that of bearers of →Yahweh's throne, cf. Ezek 10:20 and the divine epithet *yōšēb hakkĕrûbîm*, "he who is enthroned on the cherubim", applied to Yahweh already at Shilo (1 Sam 4:4; cf. 2 Sam 6:2; Isa 37:16 etc.). In this function the cherubim express the royal majesty of →Yahweh Zebaoth (METZGER 1985b), his holiness (cf. the cherubim as guardians), and his presence (METTINGER 1982; JANOWSKI 1991). In the early monarchy, this theology, which may be termed Zion-Zebaoth theology, focussed on the presence of Yahweh Zebaoth. In Ezekiel and P we encounter a Kabod theology of divine presence (→Glory); in the Deuteronomistic →Name theology the cherubim throne lost its importance (METTINGER 1982).

In discussing the cherubim, the iconography of the Solomonic temple and that of the Priestly tabernacle must be properly distinguished. The Solomonic cherubim are ten cubits high (1 Kgs 6:23) and stand parallel to each other in the adyton, facing the nave (2 Chron 3:13). Their inner wings meet each other and are conjoined (1 Kgs 6:27; 2 Chron 3:12) forming the throne seat of the invisible deity (HARAN 1959:35-36; KEEL 1977:24; contrast DE VAUX 1967:233-234). The ark is placed underneath the conjoined inner wings as the footstool of the LORD (1 Kgs 8:6-8; 1 Chr 28:2). The usual assumption is that the cherubim stand on all four legs, just as the sphinxes known from the plastic arts. METZGER (1985a: 309-51) has advanced a different interpretation: The cherubim stand on their back legs and do not form a throne. This interpretation is supported by a reference to the composition on the facade of a Hittite sanctuary at Eflatun Pinar (METZGER 1985a: fig. no. 1235). Various difficulties are connected with this interpretation (METTINGER 1986). It dissolves the connection between the cherubim formula and the iconography of the temple and it builds on more remote analogies than the established interpretation. That there is no explicit reference in 1-2 Kgs to the throne of the LORD is due to the Deuteronomistic name theology from the exilic period which relocated God from the temple to heaven (METTINGER 1982:46-52).

Ezekiel chaps 1 and 8-11 represent a visionary development of the iconography of the first temple; while chap 1 is more profoundly marked by Mesopotamian pictorial tradition with four creatures as carriers of heaven, chaps 8-11 still speak of cherubim (thorough analysis in KEEL 1977). In Ezekiel the cherubim throne has developed into the throne chariot. This is probably due to the importance of the theophany tradition in Ezekiel, since the theophany tradition has the notion of the mobile, coming God (Ps 18:10-11). In this verse the verb *rākab* should not be translated as "to ride" but as "dahinfahren" (*HALAT* 1149); Yahweh is not depicted as "riding" on a cherub but descending in his cherubim chariot (cf. Ps 77:19).

In the Priestly tabernacle the cherubim have undergone a mutation. They no longer stand parallel but face one another and are considerably smaller than the Solomonic cherubim since they stand on and are of one piece with the lid of the ark, the *kappōret* (Exod 25:19-20) which is only 2.5 by 1.5 cubits (Exod 25:17). Here the cherubim are no longer throne bearers but serve as guardians of the mercy seat from which the Kabod, the divine Glory, speaks to Israel. The iconography of P may thus have a different, Egyptian background (GÖRG 1977).

While there is now a fair amount of agreement about the iconographical background of the cherubim, there is still disagreement on the religio-historical implications. Since the cherubim serve both as Yahweh's throne and as his vehicle, the chariot (Ps 18:11; cf. Ps 104:3), it may be that the El traditions of the enthroned deity and the →Baal notions of the "Driver of the Clouds" have merged (METTINGER 1982: 35-36). Whether or not one should then presuppose an influence from the lion dragon of the weather god (thus METZGER 1985a: 315-323) is a different matter.

The empty cherubim throne in the Solomonic temple is an expression of Israelite aniconism. It is possible that Tyre and Sidon already had such empty thrones as the seat of an invisible deity. But even if this is so, Israelite aniconism is not as such a Phoenician import; it antedates the Solomonic temple by several centuries. It is originally related to the worship of standing stones, *maṣṣēbôt*. Moreover, the ark also expresses an aniconic theology of divine presence. Thus, the combination of the empty throne and the ark in the temple would seem to combine two varieties of aniconism. It should be noted that both the cherubim iconography of Jerusalem and the bull iconography of Bethel (with the invisible deity standing on the back of the bull) are in principle aniconic.

IV. The biblical notion of Yahweh's throne chariot (Ezek 1; 1 Chr 28:18) plays an important part in Jewish Merkabah mysticism (MAIER 1964; GRUENWALD 1980; esp. HALPERIN 1988). Early Jewish references to the (cherubim) chariot that are of interest in this connection are found in Sir 49:8, LXX Ezek 43:3; *Apoc. Mos.* 33; *Apoc. Abr.* 18:12; *Eth. Enoch* 61:10; 71:7. Also, the Sabbath Songs from Qumran contain noteworthy material (NEWSOM 1985:44-45). Thus, 4Q405 20-21-22:8 understands the throne as a heavenly secret: "The image of the chariot throne do they bless..." Other instances in these texts speak of the cherubim as animate beings offering praise to the godhead.

V. *Bibliography*

W. F. ALBRIGHT, What Were the Cherubim?, *BA* 1,1 (1938) 1-3; C. M. COCHE-ZIVIE, Sphinx, *LdÄ* 5 (1984) 1139-1147; A. DESSENNE, *Le sphinx. Étude iconographique* (Bibliothèque des écoles françaises d'Athènes et de Rome 186, Paris 1957); D.N. FREEDMAN & M. O'CONNOR, כרוב *kĕrûb, TWAT* 4 (1983) 322-334 [& lit]; M. GÖRG, Keruben in Jerusalem, *BN* 4 (1977) 13-24; I. GRUENWALD, *Apocalyptic and Merkavah Mysticism* (AGJU 14; Leiden 1980); E. GUBEL, *Phoenician Furniture* (Studia Phoenicia 7; Leuven 1987) 37-84; B. HALPERIN, *The Faces of the Chariot. Early Jewish Responses to Ezekiel's Vision* (TSAJ 18; Tübingen 1988); M. HARAN, The Ark and the Cherubim, *IEJ* 9 (1959) 30-38, 89-94; W. HELCK, Der liegende und geflügelte weibliche Sphinx des Neuen Reiches, *MIO* 3,1 (1955) 1-10; B. JANOWSKI, "Ich will in eurer Mitte wohnen". Struktur und Eigenart der exilischen *Schekina*-Theologie, *Jahrbuch für biblische Theologie* 2 (1987) 165-193; JANOWSKI, Keruben und Zion, *Ernten was man sät. Festschrift für Klaus Koch zu seinem 65. Geburtstag* (ed. D. R. Daniels *et alii*; Neukirchen 1991) 231-264; *O. KEEL, *Jahwe-Visionen und Siegelkunst* (SBS 84-85; Stuttgart 1977); J. MAIER, *Vom Kultus zur Gnosis. Bundeslade, Gottesthron und Märkābāh* (Kairos. Religionswissenschaftliche Studien 1; Salzburg 1964); T. METTINGER, *The Dethronement of Sabaoth. Studies in the Shem and Kabod Theologies* (ConB OTS 18, Lund 1982); METTINGER, Review of M. Metzger 1985a, *Svensk Teologisk Kvartalskrift* 62 (1986) 174-177; *M. METZGER, *Königsthron und Gottesthron* (AOAT 15:1-2; Neukirchen-Vluyn 1985) = 1985a; METZGER, Der Thron als Manifestation der Herrschermacht in der Ikonographie des Vorderen Orients und im Alten Testament, *Charisma und Institution* (ed. T. Rendtorff; Tübingen 1985) = 1985b; C. NEWSOM, *Songs of the Sabbath Sacrifice. A Critical Edition* (HSS 27; Atlanta 1985); G. RINALDI, Nota, *BeO* 9 (1967) 211-212; H. SEYRIG, Divinités de Sidon, *Syria* 36 (1959) 48-56 [Antiquités syriennes no. 70]; *R. DE VAUX, Les chérubins et l'arche d'alliance, les sphinx gardiens et les trônes divins dans l'ancient Orient, *Bible et Orient* (Paris 1967) 231-259 [originally publ. in *MUSJ* 37 (1960-61) 91-124].

T. N. D. METTINGER

CHRIST χριστός

I. The masculine form of the adjective χριστός is only found in the LXX, in a few early Jewish documents and in the writings of the NT. In the LXX the term is used in connection with kings, priests and prophets (the Hebrew equivalent is *māšîaḥ),* in *Pss. Sol.* 17:32; 18 superscr., 18:5.7 particularly in connection with the expected ideal king of the future. In the writings of the NT *christos* is used of the coming anointed one of Jewish expectation, or of →Jesus, believed to be this 'Messiah'—see John 1:41 "We have found the Messiah (transliterated in Greek *messian*) which is translated Christ (*christos)*"; cf. John 4:25.

The word occurs 531 times in the NT. It is often found in the combinations 'Jesus Christ' and 'Christ Jesus' and (as is usual in the case of *nomina sacra*) there is a great deal of variety in the manuscript tradition. In many cases, the word *christos* seems to function as a second name and cannot be demonstrated to carry the meaning 'Messiah'. Of the 531 instances just mentioned, 270 are found in the Letters of Paul, and another 113 in the Deutero-Paulines. It occurs 35 times in the Synoptics (but only 7 times in Mark, and never in Q, the common source of Matthew and Luke, as far as we can see) and 26 times in Acts, as well as 30 times in the Gospel and Letters of John. It is relatively frequent in 1 Peter (22x). The very high frequency of the word in Christian sources, and its function as central designation for Jesus, require an explanation.

II. The corresponding Greek verb *chriein* means 'to rub, anoint with scented unguents or →oil' or 'to wash with colour, to coat'. Anointing had its place in bodily hygiene, in athletic contests, at joyous and festive occasions, in medicine (and magic) and in burial rites; also in a cultic setting (anointing of statues of gods, of offerings and also of partakers in ceremonies). In the LXX we find it used of Saul's shield (2 Sam 1:21), and in connection with feminine make-up (Ezek 16:9; Jdt 10:3), and with preparations for a feast (Amos 6:6; Isa 25:6) as well as in a cultic setting. We hear of the anointing of the tabernacle, the ark of the covenant, the altar and other cultic objects (Exod 30:22-29; Lev 8:10; Num 7:1) and a few times the word is used in connection with unleavened cakes which are offered (Exod 29:2; Num 6:15). In Dan 9:24 Theod. 'to anoint a most holy place' refers to the (re)dedication of the temple (see also KARRER 1991:172-209). The neuter term *christon* occurs, however, very seldom; in Aeschylus, *Prometheus vinctus* 480, Euripides, *Hippolytus* 516, Ps.-Galenus, *De remediis parabilibus* 14,548,11 (cf. Theocritus 11,2) it is used of a medicine that 'has to be rubbed on'. In Josephus *Ant. Jud.* 8 §137 it means 'painted'. Interestingly Theophilus, *Ad Autolycum* 1,12, connects *christon* with a ship ('caulked'), a tower and a house ('whitewashed'), and the verb *chriein* with athletes and ornaments—to end with Christians who are 'anointed with the oil of God'. In Lev 21:10.12 LXX *to elaion to christon* ('anointing oil') is used during the consecration of the high priest; in Dan 9:26 LXX that speaks of the future destruction of the city and the holy place *meta tou christou*, the latter may mean 'with what was anointed' rather than 'with the anointed one' (Theod. 'with the coming leader'). As was already remarked, it is only in the Bible and in early Jewish and Christian sources that the adjective *christos* is used in connection with persons. In order to understand the use of *christos* for Jesus in the writings of the NT we shall, therefore, have to examine the instances in the OT (LXX) and the occurrences of the Greek word, and its counterparts in other languages, in early Jewish sources.

In the OT category 'anointed ones' may be priests, kings and prophets.The expression 'the anointed priest' is found in Lev 4:3.5.16 (LXX *christos*) and in 6:15 (LXX participle *kechrismenos*). The high priest is meant, just as in Lev 21:10.12 'the priest… on whose head the anointing oil has been poured…' (cf. Num 35:25). At God's command, Moses anoints Aaron together with his sons (Exod 29; 40:12-15; Lev 8:12-13, also Sir 45:15, cf. Exod 28:41; 30:30; Lev 6:13). Num 3:3 speaks of 'the anointed priests' in the plural (LXX *ēleimmenoi*), cf. 2 Macc 1:10 which mentions a certain Aristobulus 'who is of the family of the anointed priests' (LXX *christōn*). Anointing in this context means appointment and consecration, as is indicated by the parallel expressions used here. In fact it is the LORD himself who may be said to have anointed the priests (Lev 7:36). The priesthood of Aaron and his successors is meant to be eternal (Exod 40:15; Lev 6:15; 16:32-34, also Sir 45:7.15).

As to prophets: In Ps 105:5 (1 Chr 16:22) 'my anointed ones' occurs parallel with 'my prophets' in a context that speaks of the patriarchs. In 1 Kgs 16:16 (cf. Sir 48:8) →Elijah is told (among other things) to anoint Elisha to be his successor. In 1 Kgs 19:19-21, however, which describes Elisha's call, no anointing takes place: Elijah casts his mantle upon him. In 2 Kgs 2:1-14, at Elijah's departure to heaven, his successor is said to receive a double share of Elijah's spirit and to take up his mantle. We may compare Isa 61:1 where the prophetic author declares that the Spirit of God is upon him because the LORD has anointed him. In the case of prophets, the emphasis is clearly not on the rite of anointing, but on the gift of the Spirit of God.

Numerous instances refer to the anointing of kings. The emphasis on divine initiative in these cases is reflected in the popularity of the expression 'the LORD's anointed' (LXX *christos kuriou*) and the corresponding expression 'my, your, his anointed'. It is used in connection with Saul (1 Sam 12:3.5; 21:7.11; 26:9.11.16.23; 2 Sam 1:14.16, cf. Sir 46:19) and David (1 Sam 16:6; 2 Sam 19:22; cf. 2 Sam 23:3). In the case of these two kings, Samuel is God's agent (1 Sam 10:1-8; 16:1-13; cf. 2 Sam 12:7, and also Sir 46:13; Ps 151:4 LXX); in both cases there is an emphasis on the gift of the Spirit (1 Sam 10:6; 16:13, cf. 1 Sam 16:14, 2 Sam 23:2). The (Davidic) king is called 'anointed of the LORD' several times in the Book of Psalms (2:2; 18:51 [2 Sam 22:51]; 20:7; 28:8;

84:10; 89:39.52; 132:10 [2 Chr 6:42].17 [cf. 1 Sam 2:10.35]); compare also Hab 3:13, Lam 4:20. In these texts, the LORD's anointing denotes an exclusive relationship between the God of Israel and the king who reigns in his name and is, therefore, assisted and protected by him. Quite exceptional is the application of the term to the Persian king Cyrus in Isa 45:1 "Thus says the LORD to his anointed, to Cyrus" (cf. Hazael in 1 Kgs 19:15-17). This gentile king, who does not know or acknowledge the God of Israel, receives a commission and the power to secure peace and freedom for God's chosen people (Isa 45:1-7). He is God's shepherd (44:28) where Davidic kings have failed.

In the Royal Psalms (besides Pss 2; 18; 20; 89; 132 also 21; 45; 72; 101; 110; 144), the psalmists, referring to God's promises and instructions to David and his dynasty, make far-reaching assertions about the Davidic king and his family. They do not yet envisage a future ideal son of David. In later times, however, elements in these psalms have played a role in the expectations regarding a future Davidic anointed of the LORD. Strikingly, none of the passages in the Prophets announcing a decisive and lasting change in the plight of Israel, in which a descendant of David figures as an ideal king in the name of the LORD, uses the designation 'anointed of the LORD' (Isa 9:1-6; 11:1-9; Mic 5:1-3; Jer 23:5-6; 33:14-16; Ezek 17:22-24; 34:23-24; 37:24-25). These passages, too, have influenced later expectations.

After the return from the exile in Babylon, Zerubbabel, a descendant of David, is hailed by Haggai; but, in Zechariah, we note a juxtaposition of him and the high priest Joshua (Zech 3:8; 6:9-14 and especially 4:14 "they are the two 'sons of oil' who stand by the Lord of the whole earth"). A similar juxtaposition of the house of David and the levitical priests, said to last for ever, is found in Jer 33:17-26 (cf. 1 Sam 2:35; 1 Chr 29:22). Sir 49:11-12 praises Zerubbabel and Joshua jointly for rebuilding the temple. In a Hebrew addition to Sir 51:12 we find the house of David and the priests (called 'the sons of Zadok') again mentioned side by side. On the whole, however, Sirach's 'Praise of the Fathers' (chaps. 44-50) pays more attention to God's covenant with the priests—see the eulogy of Aaron (45:6-22), of Phinehas (45:23-26) and of Simon (ch. 50) over against the praise of David (47:1-11) and the long section on his descendants who receive praise and blame (47:12-49:4). The book's attention centres here around the temple and the priesthood. This is also the case in Dan 9:24-27 where in v. 25 'until the time of an anointed one, a prince' and in v. 26 'an anointed one will be cut off' refer to high priests, Joshua and Onias (in the time before Antiochus's capture of Jerusalem) respectively. One should note that here the word *māšîaḥ* is used twice absolutely, but without an article).

In early Jewish documents, the expectation of a 'messiah', i.e. a person said to be 'anointed', functioning as God's agent in his definitive intervention in the world's affairs in the (near) future, does not occur very often. The hope of divine intervention is important and even central in many writings; but God need not engage human (or angelic) agents of deliverance and these need not be called 'messiah'.

In a number of sources, the juxtaposition of kings and priest(s) receives attention. In *Jubilees,* Isaac's blessing of Levi and Judah is recorded in 31:13-17 and 31:18-20 respectively, but the emphasis is on the functions to be exercised by the two sons of Jacob and their descendants—although in v 18 we read "a prince shall you be, you *and one of your sons*" (David? a future Davidic king?). Also in the *Testaments of the Twelve Patriarchs* Levi and Judah occupy an important place; but the interpretation of this document is difficult because of an intensive Christian redaction (if not more), particularly noticeable in the eschatological passages. This is the case in *T. Levi* 18 which deals with the advent of a new priest and *T. Judah* 24 describing the coming of an ideal king, and the passages announcing a future →saviour/salvation connected with (one of) these tribes (*T. Sim.* 7:1-2; *T. Napht.* 8:2-3;

T. Gad 8:1; *T. Jos.* 19:6(11), cf. *T. Levi* 2:11; *T. Judah* 22:2; *T. Dan* 5:10). Twice, *in T. Levi* 17:2-3, the participle *chriomenos* is used for persons anointed for the priesthood. The word *christos* is found in *T. Reub.* 6:8 that limits Levi's priestly activities to the period 'until the consummation of times (the times) of the anointed high priest, of whom the Lord spoke'. In view of *T. Levi* 4:4; 5:2 and chaps 10; 14-15 and 16 this passage must be regarded as Christian.

The *Dead Sea Scrolls* mention anointing in connection with high priests, kings and prophets. The interpretation of this Qumran material is difficult because of the fragmentary nature of much of the evidence. Part of it may have originated after the group was formed under the leadership of the 'Teacher of righteousness'; part of it may date from an earlier period.

In a number of cases the prophets of the OT are called 'anointed'—see CD 5:21-6:1, 1 QM 11:7-8 and esp. CD 2:12 'the anointed ones of his →Holy Spirit' (cf. now 4Q286-287 MS B fr. 3,13). In 11QMelch 18 the term 'the anointed of the Spirit' is used for the 'one who brings good tidings' of Isa 52:7 (cf. Isa 61:1!). He announces God's intervention through →Melchizedek, conceived as an angelic figure. It may be that the same prophetic figure is meant in 4Q521 fr. 2 ii+4, beginning with "...the heavens and earth will listen to his anointed one" and describing what the Lord will accomplish for his righteous and pious servants at the end of times (here, however, the plural 'his anointed ones' is also possible).

Another future prophet is mentioned in 1 QS 9:11 "... until there shall come the prophet and the anointed ones of Aaron and Israel" (perhaps referring to Deut. 18:18-19, a text mentioned in 4QTestim alongside Num 24:15-17 and Deut 33:8-11). The term 'anointed one of Israel' returns in 1QSa 2:14.20, a description of an eschatological banquet where he and the high priest and their subordinates are present (whether in 2:11-12 'the anointed one' (*hammāšîaḥ*) is used absolutely, and then for the royal figure, is disputed). It is clear that the high priest is the leading figure: as in 1QM where he gives the directives for the eschatological war (1QM 2:1; 15:4; 16:13; 18:5; 19:11) and the 'prince of the congregation' is mentioned only in passing (1QM 5:1). Also in other texts where a royal and a (high) priestly figure(s) are mentioned together the latter is/are clearly the most important, as interpreter(s) of the Law (CD 7:18-21; 4QFlor 11; 11QTemple 56:20-21; 57:11-15; 58:18-21; 4Q161,8-10). In 4Q376 fr. 1 i we meet the expression 'the anointed priest', clearly to be identified with 'the anointed priest, upon whose head has been poured the oil of anointing' in 4Q375 fr. 1 i,9 (cf. Lev 21:10.12 and 1QM 9:8). The royal figure expected for the future is mostly called 'the prince of (all) the congregation' or 'Branch of David'; but, in 4QPatrBless 3, we find the expression 'the righteous anointed one' (lit. 'the anointed one of righteousness') and in 4Q458 fr.2,5 the term 'anointed with the oil of the kingship' occurs.

The meaning of the expression 'anointed one of Aaron and Israel' in CD 12:23-13:1; 14:19; 19:10-11 (cf. 20:1) is still disputed. The term 'anointed' is found here in the singular, but many have argued that the expression nevertheless admits of a plural interpretation. It is also possible that at some stage the prerogatives of the 'anointed one of Israel' were absorbed into the concept of the anointed Aaronic priest.

The texts preserved at Qumran show a great variety in images and concepts, as well as applications of texts from the Scriptures. One looks forward to the time when the Law will be fully understood and when the will of God will be obeyed completely. Then a duly appointed high priest and a Davidic prince—whose anointed status is sometimes mentioned—will discharge their functions in a proper way.

In the *Psalms of Solomon*, a group of pious Jews look out for God's deliverance in the time of the last Hasmoneans and Pompey. In *Pss. Sol.* 17 and 18 God is expected to act through a Davidic king who will rule as a representative of God who himself is king of Israel for ever (17:1.46).

In 17:21-45 the king's rule is described at great length, with many references to the OT psalms and prophecies mentioned above. The king will free Israel from its enemies and he will serve the Lord as an ideal righteous and wise man in the midst of a God-fearing people. In 17:32 and 18:5.7 (plus the superscription of that psalm) the king is called 'anointed'. In view of 'his anointed one' (18:5), the *christou kyriou* in 18:7 and 18 superscr. is to be translated 'of the anointed of the Lord'. This suggests that the expression *christos kyrios* ('an anointed lord' or 'anointed, a lord') found in 17:32 is the result of careless or deliberate alteration from the genitive to a nominative by a later Christian scribe. The most likely translation of the verse is, therefore: "And he (will be) a righteous king over them, instructed by God, and there is no unrighteousness among them in his days, for all are holy and their king an anointed of the Lord". In 17:32 the expression is still used as a qualification of the expected son of David; in Psalm 18 it has become a title.

In the *Parables of Enoch*, chaps 37-71 of the composite document known as *1 Enoch,* we find two instances of the term 'his anointed' (48:4; 52:4). The dating of this part of *1 Enoch* is still disputed; but most scholars assume a final redaction some time during the first century CE. The term is one of the designations of a heavenly redeemer figure who is thought to have been with God from the beginning (48:3.6) and who remains in God's presence as a champion of the righteous. He is often called 'that (the) →Son of man' (cf. Dan 7:9-14 referred to in *1 Enoch* 46:1-3), the Chosen One (cf. Isa 42:1, see e.g. *1 Enoch* 39:6; 40:5, cf. 46:3) or the Righteous One (38:2, cf. 46:3). 48:8-10 speaks about the defeat of the kings of the earth by God's elect because 'they have denied the Lord of Spirits and his anointed'. The reference to Ps 2:2 is obvious: it may have led to the use of 'his anointed' in this passage. In chap 52, the visionary sees mountains of various metals and is told by an accompanying →angel that "these will serve the dominion of his anointed that he may be potent and mighty on the earth" (52:4). In v 6 this is explained as their melting as wax before the fire in the presence of the Chosen one.

The next apocalypses to be discussed, the *Syriac Apocalypse of Baruch* and *4 Ezra,* reflect on the destruction of the temple in 70 CE and must therefore be dated some time after that event. In *2 Apoc. Bar.* 39:7; 40:1; 72:2 we find the expression 'my anointed', in 70:9 'my servant, the anointed one' and twice, in 29:3; 30:1, the absolute 'the anointed'. In all cases a royal figure is envisaged. He reigns for a limited period introducing a time of bliss and incorruptibility (see 30:2; 70:3 and esp. 40:3 "His kingdom will stand for ever, until this world of corruption comes to an end and the times appointed are fulfilled"). The anointed one/messiah judges and destroys Israel's final enemies (39:7-40:2; 70:9) and brings a period of peace and abundance (29:2-30:1; 40:2-3; 71:1). He is said 'to be revealed' (29:3; 39:7; cf. 73:1) and is clearly thought to have been with God before his appearance on earth. In 30:1 he is predicted to return in glory (cf. again 73:1) and a general resurrection follows.

In *4 Ezra* a future redeemer is mentioned in 7:26-29; 11:37-12:3 and 12:31-34; 13:3-13 and 25-52) and (in passing) in 14:9. There are considerable differences between these passages. In two instances the term 'anointed one' occurs. The first is 7:26-29 which describes how 'my anointed one' (or: 'my son/servant, the anointed one', see vv 28-29) will be revealed with his companions at the time the still invisible city and the still concealed land will become visible. The redeemer does not seem to have a function in realizing this turn in events. He is said to bring four hundred years of happiness to all who remain. After that period, everyone, including the anointed one, will die (v. 29). For seven days the world will return to primeval silence; after which a new age of incorruptibility will begin, bringing resurrection and judgment (vv 30-44). In the interpretation of the vision of the Eagle and the Lion (11:1-12:3), the lion is identified as 'the anointed one whom the Most High has kept until the end of days, who will arise from the seed of David' (12:32, cf. Gen. 49:9). The absolute form of the term is used (Lat. *unctus*) and the Davidic descent of the redeemer receives emphasis. In the vision (11:36-46) as well as in the interpretation (12:31-34) he charges his counterpart (the Roman empire) with his crimes. He will convict and destroy him, and give joy to the survivors in the land until the day of judgment comes. It should be noted that the messiah is already with God before he appears (cf. 7:28, and *2 Apoc. Bar.* and *1 Enoch*).

The term 'anointed one' is not found in any of the other early Jewish documents. It is never used by Flavius Josephus in his descriptions of royal and prophetic figures who were active as leaders of groups of people during the century before the fall of Jerusalem. A number of early writings collected in the NT, however, pay considerable attention to expectations concerning the messiah in contemporary Judaism—even more than the Jewish sources at our disposal would lead us to expect. This has to be explained by the conviction of the followers of Jesus that he was the long-expected messiah, and by discussions between them and other Jews precisely about this belief. In Acts e.g. Paul is portrayed as trying to convince members of diaspora synagogues that Jesus is the Messiah/Christ (9:22; 17:3; 18:5, cf. 18:28 of Apollos). In Mark 12:35, Jesus questions the—clearly common—conception of the scribes that 'the Christ is the son of David': and, in Mark 15:32, the chief priests and scribes speak of 'the Christ, the king of Israel'—in the context it is made clear that Jesus' mission has no political overtones. Mark 13:21-22 speaks about false messiahs and false prophets: clearly addressing the situation in the period before, during and after the Jewish war against Rome (→Roma). Also in the discussions between Jesus and 'the Jews' in the Fourth Gospel (although intended to bring out the essential points of Johannine Christology) we find a number of Jewish tenets concerning the messiah. For instance, it is said that the messiah will be a descendant of David and a native of Bethlehem (John 7:42). In 12:34 the Christ is expected 'to remain for ever' (cf. Ps 89:36-37). In 7:27 the statement 'when the Christ appears no one will know where he comes from' may be connected with the concept of the revealing of the messiah found in Jewish apocalyptic texts. In all these cases, the term 'the messiah'/'the Christ' is used without any further addition.

III. In the oldest Christian writings, the letters of Paul, the term *christos* occurs 270 times (out of a total of 531 for the entire NT!). It was clearly the central designation for Jesus in early Christian circles; but it received its content not through a previously-fixed concept of messiahship, but rather from the person and the work of Jesus—with special reference to his death and resurrection, the salvation effected by him and the intimate bond between him and his followers. In many instances the word functions as a (second) name, although Paul, of course, knew that it carried a special meaning, and his readers, in so far as they were familiar with the OT and Jewish tradition, must have realized this too. In a list of God's privileges for Israel Paul writes "of their race, according to the flesh, is *ho christos*" (Rom 9:5). The titular use of the term may also be, at least partly, intended in a number of other passages (Rom 15:7; 1 Cor 1:23; 10:4; 15:22-28; 2 Cor 5:10; 11:2-3; Gal 3:16; Phil 1:15.17; 3:7). But Paul clearly speaks about the one Christ, Jesus, and even in Rom 9:4 his point is equally valid for those readers who do not realize that he is using a 'technical' term. In 2 Cor 1:21 there is a play on words between 'Christ' and 'anointing' but the verb is not used for Jesus but for those united with him in baptism. In 1 Cor 1:23; Gal 5:11 and Gal 3:13 Paul argues that a crucified messiah was unacceptable for his fellow-Jews (this may have biographical overtones). Yet he regards it as unnecessary to argue that Jesus is the messiah expected by Israel; because both he and his readers are convinced that he is.

This is also evident in earlier formulae used in Paul's letters and clearly familiar to his readers: e.g. 'Christ died for us/you' found (with variations) in Rom 5:6.8; 14:15; 1 Cor 8:11; 2 Cor 5:14-15; 1 Thess 5:9-10. 'Christ' is also used in formulae speaking about death and resurrection (1 Cor 15:3-5; 2 Cor 5:15; Rom 8:34; 14:9). The term occurs repeatedly in connection with faith (e.g. Gal 2:16), preaching (e.g. 1 Cor 15:11-14) and especially with 'gospel' (Gal 1:7; 1 Thess 3:2). Next, Paul uses it where he stresses the close link between Christ and his followers: as in the expressions 'of Christ' (e.g. 1 Cor 1:12; 3:23; 15:23) and 'in Christ' (Rom 8:1; 12:5). This corporate language presupposes baptism (cf. Gal 3:26-28 ['baptized into Christ'], Rom 6:3-11).

At the time the oldest gospel, that of Mark, was written, it was clearly necessary to remind readers how the confession 'Jesus is the Christ' had to be understood. Outsiders regard Jesus, the herald of the kingdom of God (Mark 1:14), as a John the Baptist redivivus, or →Elijah, or one of the prophets (8:28, cf. 6:14-16). Peter, on behalf of the disciples, confesses: "You are the Messiah/Christ" (8:29). Jesus, however, tells his disciples to keep silent about him (8:30) and announces his suffering, death and resurrection (8:31, cf. 9:31; 10:32-34). In Mark 12:35-37, the scribes are portrayed as saying that 'the Christ is the son of David' (cf. 15:32 'the Christ, the king of Israel'). Jesus, twice addressed as 'son of David' by Bartimaeus (10:47-48) and associated with 'the coming kingdom of our father David' (11:9-10), refers to Ps 110:1. This passage is clearly hinted at in 14:61-62 where Jesus, standing before the Sanhedrin, acknowledges that he is "the Christ, the son of the Blessed One", but adds "you will see the Son of man seated at the right hand of the Power and coming with the clouds of heaven (Ps 110:1; Dan 7:13)". Jesus will reign as Son of man/Son of David—Messiah/Son of God when God's rule will fully be established on earth (cf. also 8:38-9:1; 13:26). The immediately following story of the trial before Pilate in chap. 15 makes clear that Jesus is not a 'king of the Jews' in the political sense of that term, or an insurgent like Barabbas. Only at the parousia, when God's kingdom will become full reality, will the royal rule of the crucified messiah be shown to be triumphant. Mark 15, as Mark 13 which speaks about false messiahs and false prophets (vv. 21-22), reflects the tensions connected with the war between the Jews and the Romans culminating in the destruction of the temple in 70 CE.

All in all, Mark uses *christos* rather sparingly. In Q—the sayings source behind Matthew and Luke—the term is not found at all. Matthew essentially underlines what is found in Mark, using the term more often than his predecessor. He emphasizes that Jesus is son of David (1:1-17.20; 21:9, cf. 22:41-42). In 2:1-6 he makes clear that 'Christ' denotes the Messiah, Son of David, king of Israel. The designation 'son of David' is especially used in stories about Jesus' healings (9:27-31; 12:22-23; 15:21-28; 20:29-34; 21:14-17).

In Luke-Acts we find the terms 'the anointed of the Lord' (Luke 2:26; Acts 4:26) and 'the anointed of God' (Luke 9:20; 23:35). It is specified that God anointed Jesus with the Spirit—so in Luke 4:18, quoting Isa 61:1, Acts 10:38 and also 4:27. 'Christ' and 'Lord' are found as parallels in Luke 2:12 and Acts 2:36. Another typical feature of the Lukan use of *christos* is found in a variant of the double formula about Jesus' death and resurrection, of which the first part speaks of the suffering of '(the) Christ' (Luke 24:26.46; Acts 17:3; 26:23, cf. 3:18; 25:19). In Acts, it becomes clear that this is a special debating point between Jews and Christians (cf. 9:22; 18:5.28 mentioned above). Finally it should be noted that in Acts 11:26 (cf. 26:28; 1 Pet 4:16) the designation 'Christians' is first used for the followers of Jesus in Antioch.

As already noted, the Gospel of John describes Jesus in an ongoing debate with Jewish opponents, in which interesting features emerge of Jewish expectations concerning the messiah. For the gospel itself, faith in Jesus as the Son of God (11:27; 20:31), living in a unique unity with the Father, is of primary importance. In the Johannine communities, this received so much emphasis that the author(s) of 1 and 2 John felt obliged to remind their readers that Jesus Christ had 'come in the flesh' (1 John 4:2-3; 2 John 7; cf. 1 John 5:6).

Among the other NT writings, Hebrews repeatedly calls Jesus 'high priest'. It makes clear that this has to be construed in the light of Ps 110:4 "you are a priest for ever according to the order of →Melchizedek" (e.g. 5:6; 7:17). In 7:4-14 it states explicitly that Melchizedek was superior to →Abraham who paid him tithes, and that, therefore, priests according to the order of Melchizedek are superior to those according to Aaron, descendant of Levi, great-grandson of Abraham. Jesus, descended from →Judah, belonged to the first category, and hence the salvation brought about by him is vastly superior to anything effected by those officiating according to the rules of the OT cult: particularly as this new high priest "offered himself without blemish to God" (9:14).

In Revelation the titular meaning of *christos* is evident in 11:15; 12:10 and 20:4.6. The announcement in 11:15 "The kingdom of the world has become the kingdom of the Lord and his anointed" is clearly influenced by Ps. 2:2 (cf. 11:18, reminiscent of Ps 2:1-2:5.12 and Ps 99:1). The emphasis is on God's sovereignty, as vv 17-18 show. In 12:10 the same theme is repeated: "now the salvation and the power and the kingdom of our God and the authority of his anointed have come". In 20:4-6 we find a description of the reign of the faithful who have given their lives for their testimony to Jesus and the word of God. They will come to life and will reign with the Anointed/ Christ for a thousand years. In chap. 5 the seer hears the announcement 'the Lion of the tribe of Judah, the Root of David has conquered' (v 5, cf. 3:7; 22:16). He sees a →Lamb standing near God's →throne 'as though it had been slain' (v 6, cf. 7:9-10.17; 13:8). This lamb is the Lion of Judah (cf. vv 12-13). In 17:14 the victorious Lamb is called 'the Lord of lords and King of kings': and the same name is inscribed on the robe and the thigh of the rider on the white horse in 19:11-16. During the persecution and the distress at the end of the first century CE, Christians in Asia Minor are (still) very much aware of the 'messianic overtones' in the designation 'Christ' which is used for Jesus.

It is not easy to explain how the term *christos,* found in relatively few passages in contemporary Jewish literature, became a central designation for Jesus that could very soon receive a specific Jesus-centered meaning.

The idea of an anointed high priest, important in the Dead Sea Scrolls, is not found in early Christian writings—the concept found in Hebrews is entirely different. The notion of a prophet 'anointed with the Spirit' found in Luke-Acts suits the picture of Jesus found in the Synoptic Gospels very well. Unfortunately we cannot prove that this interpretation of the use of *christos* is older than Luke. The related Q-passage Luke 7:18-23 par. Matt 11:2-6 does not use *christos.*

In most instances where 'messianic' connotations are evident in the Christian use of the term, we find emphasis on royal elements. In a number of cases Jesus' Davidic descent is mentioned, see e.g. Mark 12:35-37; 14:61-62 and (already) the pre-Pauline formula Rom 1:3-4 (cf. 2 Tim 2:8). The royal dominion of this son of David may have been believed to become evident at the parousia. Yet the Synoptics and John seem to prefer the term 'Son of man' in connection with this future event, whilst Paul prefers →*kyrios*. Only in Phil 1:6.10; 2:16; 1 Cor 15:23-28 do we find 'Christ' in connection with eschatological rule (cf. Acts 2:36, 3:20-21 and Revelation).

The story of Jesus' activities in Galilea and Judea reveals hardly any royal-messianic features. Were they connected with Jesus by over-ardent followers who regarded him as the expected messiah? Or was he falsely accused of being a royal pretender by his opponents who wanted to get rid of a dangerous person? It is often argued that this must have been the case and that, because Jesus was crucified as 'king of the Jews', his first followers took up the royal designation 'Christ' as an honorific and used it particularly in connection with his death and resurrection. It is difficult to verify this hypothesis. An unsatisfactory aspect of it is that it assigns a final role to Jesus' opponents in the choice of the term characterizing his public appearance.

Another hypothesis is that already during his lifetime, Jesus' disciples came to regard him as a special son of David/Messiah. Mark 8:29 makes Peter confess him as Messiah on the strength of Jesus' activity as (unique) preacher, teacher, healer and exorcist. Interestingly, contemporary Jewish sources portray David not only as king but also as prophet. Josephus, *Ant. Jud.* 6 §166-168, following 1 Sam 16:13-23, explains how after the divine Spirit had moved to David, the latter began to prophesy and to exorcise the →demons which troubled Saul (cf. Ps. Philo, *L.A.B.* 59-60). 11QDav Comp attributes 3600 psalms to David as well as 450 songs, four of which were 'songs for making music over the stricken' (lines 9-10). It is stressed that David spoke all these things through prophecy. We may compare here 2 Sam 23:1-2 (as well as Isa 11:1-5) and the statement 'David was a prophet' in Acts 2:30 (cf. 1:16; 4:25).

In view of these traditions, Jesus could be called a true son of David, and 'anointed of the Lord': not only in view of his future role when God's kingdom would reveal itself fully, but also in the present while he displayed God's power as prophet-teacher and exorcist. It is possible that Jesus himself used 'Christ'/'Messiah' as self-designation, creatively but modestly (see Jesus' reticence in Mark and the absence of the term in the sayings source Q): perhaps trying to avoid misunderstanding.

IV. *Bibliography*

J. H. CHARLESWORTH (ed.), *The Messiah. Developments in Earliest Judaism and Christianity* (Minneapolis 1992); F. GARCÍA MARTÍNEZ, Messianische Erwartungen in den Qumranschriften, *Jahrbuch für Biblische Theologie* 8 (1993) 171-208; M. HENGEL, Erwägungen zum Sprachgebrauch von Χριστός bei Paulus und in der 'vorpaulinischen' Überlieferung, *Paul and Paulinism. Essays in honour of C. K. Barrett* (ed. M. Hooker & S. G. Wilson; London 1982) 135-158; M. HENGEL, Jesus der Messias. Zum Streit über das 'messianische Sendungsbewusstsein' Jesu, *Messiah and Christos. Studies in the Jewish Origins of Christianity* (FS. D. Flusser, ed. I. Gruenwald *et al.*; TSAJ 32; Tübingen 1992) 155-172; M. DE JONGE, *Christology in Context. The Earliest Christian Response to Jesus* (Philadelphia 1988); DE JONGE, *Jewish Eschatology, Early Christian Christology and the Testaments of the Twelve Patriarchs. Collected Essays* (NovTSup 63; Leiden 1991) Chaps. 1-8, 12; M. KARRER, *Der Gesalbte. Die Grundlage des Christustitels* (FRLANT 151; Göttingen 1991).

M. DE JONGE

CLAUDIUS → RULER CULT

CLAY טיט

I. In the Ugaritic texts a binomial deity: *ẓẓ wkmṯ* (*KTU* 1.100:36; 1.107:16) is attested. VIROLLEAUD read the first name as *ṭṭ*. He and other scholars connected the word with Heb *ṭîṭ*; Akk *ṭidu(m), ṭiṭu, ṭiṭṭ/ddu*; Aram *ṭyn/ṭînā* (*DISO* 110); Ar *ṭîn* 'clay', 'mud'. It is the substance from which man was made (*Atra-Ḫasis* I.210-260). As such it is not mentioned in the OT, but here the word appears parallel to *ḥomer* (Isa 41:25; Nah 3:14, cf. Isa 45:9; 64:9; Job 10:9; 33:6). Otherwise it is a usual word for dirt, silt or any slimy deposit (Jer 38:6; Ps 18:43; Mic 7:10). Sometimes a more mythic connotation is implied when it refers to living conditions in the netherworld (Ps 40:3; 69:15; Job 41:22 KAPELRUD, *TWAT* 3, 343-344). Jewish exegetical tradition considers *ṭîṭ hayyāwen* (Ps 40:3) to be one of the designations of hell (ISRAEL 1991-92:61-62). The second name *kmṯ* has been taken as an attestation of the Moabite god, →Chemosh (VIROLLEAUD; ASTOUR 1966; MÜLLER 1980). Because this Moabite god—equated with Babylonian →Nergal—is seen as a god of infernal and chthonic nature, the binomen *ẓẓ* understood as *ṭîṭ* is sometimes adduced as evidence for the chthonic character of the deity (ISRAEL 1991-92; MATTINGLY 1989: 217). In the OT *ṭîṭ* has no divine status.

II. The Ugaritic binomial god is attested in three incantations and a text which looks like a god-list, but might have been a kind of litany or benediction (*KTU* 1.123; DE MOOR 1970). Twice the spelling *ẓẓ wkmṯ* is found (*KTU* 1.100:36; 1.107:16) and once *ẓẓ.wkmṯ/ḏ ilm[ ]* (*KTU* 1.82:42-43). The latter text confirms that the rendering ought to be *ẓẓ* and not *ṭṭ*. *KTU* 1.123 has *ṯẓ wkmṯ*, which is either a mistake or an alternative spelling for *ẓẓ wkmṯ*. In the incantation *KTU* 1.100 the cultplace of *ẓẓ* is *ḥryt*, perhaps identical with *Ḫûna* in Northern Syrian or Mesopotamia (*ARM* 8, 100:19; *AlT* 201:15; ASTOUR 1968). In *KTU* 1.82:41-42 the binomial deity appears as servant of the god →Horon, who is pre-emimently a god of spells and curses at Ugarit. That is virtually all that is known about their character. Presumably, the second divine name occurs in the Ug name DUMU(*bin*)-*ka-mi-ši* (*PRU* 3, 195 = RS 15.09: A.2) as it does in Ebla (MÜLLER 1980), but if alphabetic cuneiform *bn gmš* (*KTU* 4.611:18; 4.713:2) is the same name and person, the equation *kmṯ* = *Kamiši* becomes questionable (WATSON 1990:118).

III. The relationship between Ug *ẓẓ* and Heb *ṭîṭ* is rather problematic. KAPELRUD does not mention the Ugaritic evidence at all. If DE MOOR's analysis (1970) of Ug *ṭṭm* in *KTU* 1.1 iv:8 is correct, two or even three distinct words for 'clay','dirt' would already exist in Ugaritic like in Arabic (*ṯit; rṭ; ṭṭ[m]*; RENFROE 1992). The initial *ṭēt* is attested in all cognates, suggesting an original root *ṬYN. From a phonetic point of view the proposed derivation of *ẓẓ* is hard to maintain. DIETRICH & LORETZ think of a god of Hurrian origin, which would account for the diverse spellings (*TUAT* II/3, 348), but Hurrian-Hittite sources do not mention them. A god Kamish was definitely known in Ebla in the 3rd millenium (MÜLLER 1980; PETTINATO 1981; ISRAEL 1991-92) and he could be identical to Ug *kmṯ*, but even then the connection between *kmṯ* and Chemosh remains very tenuous. Most probably the divine name *ẓẓ* had nothing to do with *ṭîṭ*.

IV. *Bibliography*

M. C. ASTOUR, Some New Divine Names from Ugarit, *JAOS* 86 (1966) 277-284; ASTOUR, Two Ugaritic Serpent Charms, *JNES* 27 (1968) 13-36, esp. 20; F. ISRAEL, ṬṬ WKMṮ: Les avatars de l'enigmatique dieu ṬṬ, *Sem* 41/42 (1991-92) 59-62; A. KAPELRUD, ṭyṭ, *TWAT* 3 (1982) 343-344; G. L. MATTINGLY, Moabite Religion and the Meshaʿ Inscription, *Studies in the Mesha Inscription and Moab* (ed. A. Dearman; Archeology and Biblical Studies 2; Atlanta 1989) 211-238; H. P. MÜLLER, Religionsgeschichtliche Beobachtungen in den Texten von Ebla, *ZDPV* 96 (1980) 10-11; J. C. DE MOOR, Studies in the New Alphabetic Texts From Ras Shamra II, *UF* 2 (1970) 312-316, esp. 314; G. PETTINATO, *The Archives of Ebla. An Empire Inscribed in Clay* (New York 1981) 150-152, 245; F. RENFROE, *Arabic-Ugaritic Lexical Studies* (ALASP 5; Münster 1992) 67-68; C. VIROLLEAUD, *Ugaritica* V (1968) no. 7 (RS 24.244); no. 8 (24.251); no. 10 (RS 24.271); W. G. E. WATSON, Ugaritic Onomastics (1), *AulOr* 8 (1990) 113-127.

M. DIJKSTRA

CONSTELLATIONS מזלות

I. The Hebrew term *mazzālôt* (sing. *mazzāl*) occurs once in the Bible in 2 Kgs 23:5. Many authors hold that a second occurence may be found in Job 28:32 in the slight phonetic variant of *mazzārôt*. The context in Job is clearly astronomic, while mention is made in 2 Kgs 23 of astral cults which were prohibited by Josiah.

Mzl derives from the Akk *manzaztu* >*manzaltu*, 'abode' or 'station'. Perhaps they were originally the celestial abodes of the great gods represented by the →stars

(MOWINCKEL 1928:24). In the Babylonian Creation epic, →Marduk is represented as setting the heavenly bodies in order. He allotted their stations to the great gods, dividing the constellations of the zodiac and the months of the year among them (MAUNDER 1909[3]:244). Intended in a technically astronomical sense, they indicate the stations on the sidereal orbit of the →moon and those on the ecliptic of the sun (the ecliptic being the apparent annual celestial path of the sun [→Helios, →Shemesh] relative to the fixed stars). Thus they strictly indicated the constellations of the zodiac and, even more precisely, the term stood to indicate the zodiacal signs after the division of the ecliptic into twelve equal parts, each part being called after the constellation to which it most closely corresponded at the time (about 700 BCE in Mesopotamia). Zodiacal constellations or signs is the meaning that the Heb *mazzālôt* has in the Bible.

The term occurs in Phoen as *mzl*, 'fortune'; in MHeb as *mzl*, 'sign of the zodiac', 'planet' or 'luck'; in Jew Aram as *mzlʾ*, 'star of fortune' or 'planet'; in Syr as *mauzaltā*, 'zodiac'. There is also in Mandaean *mʾnzʾlʾtʾ*, 'signs of the zodiac' (borrowed directly from Akkadian) and *mandaltā*, Ar *manzil*, 'mansion of the moon'.

II. Typical of astrology in ancient Mesopotamia was the *omina* system which studied celestial phenomena as signs or indicators of future terrestrial events. However, the study of the *influence* of the heavenly bodies over the course of events on earth originated in the Hellenistic sphere (ROCHBERG-HALTON 1992:504). It is not clear just when the Greeks adopted the zodiac—and the notion of the ecliptic. These concepts are particularly important in the elaboration of genethlialogical or horoscopic astrology. Babylonian precedents, in existence before the Greek horoscopes (from ca. 400 BCE), recorded computed positions of the moon, the sun and the five planets—Jupiter, Venus, Mercury, Saturn and Mars—on the date of a birth (ROCHBERG-HALTON 1992:I 506). The Babylonians considered the sun, the moon and the five planets as their seven great divinities. The zodiacal constellations were closely connected to them and they themselves became objects of a religious cult.

III. A syncretistic cult of Assyrian influence is attributed to the biblical *mazzālôt* and they are mentioned in 2 Kgs 23:5 along with important astral divinities such as the sun, the moon and the →host of heaven, as well as the Syro-Canaanite →Baal. The listing of Baal, the sun and the moon is typically Syrian. We have here, therefore, constellations of the ecliptic, even though, if we reflect on the meaning which the term 'planets' has taken on in Jewish Aramaic and Middle Hebrew, we cannot exclude that this semantic value was already present in the biblical term (what is more, the "abodes" are also dwelling places for the planets). One must also consider that the passage under perusal in 2 Kgs is a later addition to the account of Josiah's cultic reform (GRAY 1977:732; MONTGOMERY & GEHMAN 1986:546). One could even compare it to parallel passages in Deut 17:3 (where the *mazzālôt* that became so popular in Israel in the late post-exilic and post-biblical periods are not even mentioned) or in Deut 4:19 (where "stars" are cited in general terms on the list of forbidden deities, perhaps meaning just special groupings of stars or else important planets as distinguished from the "host of heaven" in general). The moon's "abode" is mentioned in Hab 3:11 under the term *zbl*.

The interpretation of *mazzārôt* in Job 38:32 is problematic, because the feminine plural of the noun does not agree with the singular pronominal suffix of *bʿtw*: "Canst thou bring forth *mazzārôt* in its season?". In this context the stars are not deified. Indeed, the LORD →God reigns supreme in the universe which is disposed by Him. Not all authors support the "constellation" interpretation (still connected with the zodiac). MOWINCKEL (1928:27-36) cautiously proposes to interpret the term as Booetus. SCHIAPARELLI (1903:95-111) perceives both *mazzālôt* and *mazzārôt* as Venus in her twofold aspect of evening and morning star.

Regarding other specific constellations, the Bible provides very few plain facts. We may consider the names which appear in Job 9:9; 26:13; 37:9; 38:31-32 and Amos 5:8. There is a certain amount of consensus in interpreting *kîmâ* as the →Pleiades and *kĕsîl* as →Orion; *ʿayīš* or *ʿāš* could be →Aldebaran with the Hyades; *mĕzārîm* is interpreted as the two winnowing-fans, i.e. the Great Bear and the Little Bear (SCHIAPARELLI 1903:86-92) or Antares (MOWINCKEL 1926:16-23); *ḥadrê tēmān* are mostly considered as the Southern Cross, Canopus and Centauri, stars of the southern hemisphere which, in biblical times, were visible in the sky over Israel, though no longer so today because of the precession of the equinoxes—Canopus excepted. Also to be remembered is *nāḥaš*, usually understood to be Draco (→Dragon, →Serpent).

IV. The Targum translates *mazzālôt* as *mzlt*ʾ and *mazzārôt* as *šṭry mzly*ʾ which should indicate the signs of the zodiac; the LXX transcribes *mazourōth* without translating in either case; the Vg translates these terms as the twelve signs in 2 Kgs and Lucifer in Job. St. John Chrysostom adopted *zōidia*, the signs of the zodiac, noting however that many of his contemporaries interpreted *mazourōth* as Sirius. *Mzl* became of frequent use in the Talmud and in rabbinical literature, generally holding the meaning of 'planet' and 'zodiacal sign'. It also increasingly appeared with the meaning of 'luck'. It is not by coincidence that in a later period in the history of the Hebrew language this term was endowed with the meaning of 'luck', through a semantic loan already present in another Semitic language, Phoenician. A bilingual Greek-Phoenician inscription from the 4th century BCE which was discovered at Cyprus (KAI 42:5) has the term *mzl* corresponding to the Gk *tychē*, 'fortune' (→Tyche).

Once the threat of idolatry had faded away, the constellations (particularly those of the zodiac) enjoyed widespread propagation within the Hebrew culture. Philo of Alexandria (*De Vita Mosis* II 122-126) and Josephus Flavius (*Ant.* III 181-187) had already established, in the 1st cent. CE, allegorical links between some biblical concepts and the zodiacal signs. Abstracted from Hellenistic culture, the zodiac found itself perfectly set into the background of rabbinical literature. This was also due to the number twelve, which represented the number of tribes, that of the stones on the Ephod (Exod 28: 17-20), that of the oxen forming the base of the copper basin in the courtyard of the Temple (1 Kgs 7:23-26) and so on.

In *Pirqe de Rabbi Eliezer*, chaps. 6-8 are dedicated to the sun, the planets, the signs of the zodiac and the seasons. The twelve signs have a position of great importance in sacred poetry. In Eleazar ha-Kallir's famous Prayer for Rain (ca. 5th cent. CE) the signs of the zodiac appear in combination with those of the months (SARFATTI 1978:180-195). There is also a learned literary composition called *Barayta de-Mazzalot* of the 11th century, which deals with the signs of the zodiac and the planets. Finally, it is worth mentioning the artistic beauty and refined symbolism of the zodiac symbols which are portrayed on the mosaic floors of several synagogues in Israel of the Roman and Byzantine periods. The zodiac surrounding Helios (and the symbols of the months and seasons which are represented therein) rises to become a cosmic value and states that the sun is just the image of the triumphant →glory of the LORD God, and that God governs the cosmos and by Himself firmly holds the reins of the stars which the changing of the times and seasons depends on. This latter reality is fundamental for the life of men on earth.

V. *Bibliography*

A. BEER, Astronomy, *EncJud* 3 (Jerusalem 1974) cols. 795-807; E. BISCHOFF, *Babylonisch-Astrales im Weltbilde des Thalmud und Midrasch* (Leipzig 1907); G. R. DRIVER, Two Astronomical Passages in the Old Testament, *JTS* 4 (1953) 208-212; *JTS* 7 (1956) 1-11; S. R. DRIVER & G. B. GRAY, *The Book of Job* (Edinburgh 1977) 308-309; G. FOERSTER, The Zodiac in Ancient Synagogues and its Place in Jewish Thought and Literature *ErIsr* 19 (1987) 225-234

(Heb); J. GRAY, *I & II Kings* (London 1977) 730-733; E. W. MAUNDER, *The Astronomy of the Bible* (London 1909³) 243-257; J. A. MONTGOMERY & H. S. GEHMAN, *The Book of Kings* (Edinburgh 1986) 529-539, 546-548; S. MOWINCKEL, *Die Sternnamen im Alten Testament* (Oslo 1928) 16-36; P. PRIGENT, *Le Judaïsme et l'image* (Tübingen 1990) 157-173; F. ROCHBERG-HALTON, Astrology in the Ancient Near East, *ABD* 1 (1992) 504-507; G. SARFATTI, An introduction to "Barayta de-mazzalot", *Shnaton Bar-Ilan* 3 (1965) 56-82 (Heb); SARFATTI, Note di semantica, *Scritti sull'ebraismo in memoria di Guido Bedarida* (Firenze 1966) 206-209; SARFATTI, I segni dello zodiaco nell'iconografia ebraica, *Scritti in onore di Umberto Nahon* (ed. R. Bonfil *et al.*; Jerusalem 1978) 180-195; G. SCHIAPARELLI, *L'astronomia nell'Antico Testamento* (Milano 1903) 67-111; B. SULER, Astronomie. In der Bibel, *EncJud* 3 (Berlin 1929) cols. 591-595; I. ZATELLI, Astrology and the Worship of the Stars in the Bible, *ZAW* 103 (1991) 86-99.

I. ZATELLI

COUNCIL סוד

I. The noun *sôd* is found 23 times in the Hebrew Bible: twice in personal names, otherwise in poetry (though Ezek 13:9 may be termed high prose). Its semantic range includes 'council, assembly; counsel, deliberation, plan(s), will; company, fellowship, friendship'—each of which may be applied to both the human and divine spheres. It refers specifically to the divine court in four passages, implies its existence in two others, and could possibly refer to it in an additional two. *Sôd* is probably a primary noun. In Qumran Literature it appears beside the variant *yswd*, meaning both 'council' and 'counsel'—as it does in Mishnaic Hebrew. A cognate may be attested in a broken passage in Ugaritic:]*b*(.)*kqrb.sd*/[(*KTU* 1.20 i 4; for the reading see now W. PITARD, *BASOR* 285 [1992] figs. 1-6 and pp. 44-45). In Old South Ar *mśwd* is used of the 'assembly, council' of the heads of clans. Cognates in Aramaic and Arabic mean '(confidential) conversation, speech'.

A root SWD has been proposed and seen in the idiom *ysd* [Nif] *yaḥad ʿal* "conspire together against" (Ps 2:2; 31:14). Others propose for these two passages a root YSD II. The first certain appearance of the verb *swd* is in Sir (Qal 7:14 'chatter'; Hitpa 8:17; 9:14 'consult with'; 9:4; 42:12 'consort with'). Cognates are attested later in Syriac (Pa and Etpa) and Arabic (III), both meaning 'talk, converse'. Thus the verb has a narrower range of meaning than the noun, appears in only (but not all) those dialects in which the noun is attested and only in meanings derivable from the noun. It is therefore probably denominative.

It is now clear from the Mari correspondence that *pirištum* there served as a near synonym of *sôd*, meaning both 'secret' and 'council'—only a human council, however; see ARM 26 no. 101:26 and n. b; no. 307:3 and n. a.

Thus the use of *sôd* for the divine council (and counsel) seems to be original with the Israelites (the one possible instance of a Ugaritic cognate being of unknown referent). The contemporary and antecedent Semitic cultures all have the concept, but use a variety of other expressions: e.g. Akk *puḫur ilāni* and Ug *pḫr (bn) ilm* 'assembly of the gods', *pḫr mʿd* 'assembly of the meeting', *mpḫrt bn il* 'assembly of the gods', and *ʿdt ilm* 'meeting of the gods', Phoen (10th cent. Byblos) *mpḥrt ʾl gbl qdšm* 'the assembly of the holy gods of Byblos'. The gods (*šdyn*) also come together in a *mʿd* in the Balaam text from Deir ʿAlla. Ug *dr (bn) il* 'circle of the gods' and Phoen (8th cent. Karatepe) *kl dr bn ʾlm* 'the whole circle of the gods' are references to the collectivity of the gods, but do not necessarily imply their assembly in a formal council (cf. the simpler *kl ʾl X* 'all the gods of X'). The OT also uses other terms, including cognates of three of the preceding *-môʿēd, ʿēdâ* and *dôr*—beside *sôd* and *qĕhal qĕdôšîm* (Ps 89:6; →Saints).

II. While there is no clear case of the term *sôd* being used of the divine council outside Israel, there is abundant evidence of such a council and its functioning in the neighbouring literatures (→Angels, →Sons of (the) Gods, →Host of Heaven, etc.), especially those of Mesopotamia and Ugarit. The essential business of the council is discussion leading to a decision, but the actual process is highly variable. The great narratives of the Mesopotamian literary tradition are especially revealing. Enkidu gives an account of deliberations in the divine council that he witnessed in a dream: the high god Anu sets the terms of the debate; Ellil makes a proposal; Shamash objects but is discredited by Ellil (*Gilgamesh Epic* VII i [from the Hittite version]). In *Atrahasis* I Enlil calls a meeting of the great gods and informs them of a crisis (a rebellion of the lesser gods). Enlil and Anu make successive proposals which are carried out; but Anu's final solution refers the matter to Nintu, who in turn requires that Enki cooperate with her. In such literary texts the great gods appear free to make proposals, raise objections or state terms without any strict protocol, and the high god seems to exercise rather loose control over the proceedings.

In *Anzu* Anu calls for a god who can defeat Anzu. The gods summon various specific deities, all of whom decline. Finally, as the gods despair, Enki/Ea addresses Anu and offers to find one who will conquer Anzu. The gods agree. Here Anu is thoroughly passive after his initial appeal. It is the rest of the gods who make proposals or endorse those of others. A particular form of consultation emerges here that reappears at Ugarit and in the Bible: the high god calls for some god to volunteer to resolve a crisis; different members of the council may be proposed and prove inadequate; finally, when all appears lost, a winning proposal is made and accepted, and the saviour is commissioned. This is used in particular to depict the elevation of a deity to supremacy in the council. Thus in *Enūma eliš*, after Anshar has unsuccessfully approached a couple of possible champions, the gods silently despair of finding one who will conquer →Tiamat. Finally, prompted by Ea, →Marduk volunteers. Anshar gives him his blessing, but Marduk bargains for supreme authority. Accordingly Anshar convenes a special meeting of the council—the narrative details the gods' gathering, greetings, banqueting and drinking (II 129-138)—and they transfer all authority to Marduk.

In general it was in the supreme council that the destinies of individual gods (e.g. Marduk) and people (e.g. Enkidu), of cities (*Lament over Ur* 137-169) and indeed all of humanity (flood story) were decided.

In Ugaritic literature →El presides over the council. In the →Baal cycle the gods seem to speak and act with great freedom, and El exercises minimal control. In *KTU* 1.2 I the gods are banqueting when they see messengers coming from Yam (→Sea) and are cowed. Baal rebukes them and promises to come up with a response. On their arrival the messengers demand that Baal be handed over to Yam. El immediately gives his assent, but Baal attacks them furiously and has to be restrained by two goddesses. In *Kirta*, on the other hand, the traditional form of the appeal for a volunteer to resolve a crisis is used to show all the gods speechless and helpless in the face of Kirta's illness. Repeated appeals by El yield no response, so that finally he must propose and execute the solution himself (*KTU* 1.16 v 9-27). The mythology is actually more complicated. For example, in the course of the Baal cycle, El's council declares Baal their king (*KTU* 1.4. iv 43-44), and in the sacrificial text *KTU* 1.39:7, there is reference to a *pḫr bʿl* 'assembly of Baal'.

III. While the OT passages using the word *sôd* to refer to the divine council give little information about its operation, other biblical passages confirm that the ancient Near Eastern institution was well known in Israelite thought. Thus Micaiah's account of his vision (1 Kgs 22:19b-22) has →Yahweh seated on his throne with his court around him. He asks who will undertake a certain task. Various suggestions are made by members of the assembly. Finally one individual makes a proposal which Yahweh accepts. Yahweh commissions the proposer accordingly. Despite the terms 'host of heaven' for the court and 'spirits' for the individual members, the functioning of the old divine council is obvious. The setting is more ambivalent, but the traditional function is clear again in the vision report of Isa 6:1-11, in which the prophet is present as the volunteer. (With the first person plural of v 8, Yahweh speaks for the divine court as a whole; so also in the divine resolutions of Gen 1:26; 3:22; 11:7.)

Other references follow a less standard course, but equally clearly involve a dialogue between the supreme deity and members of his council, leading to a decision and the authorizing or commissioning of one of those present. In Job 1:6-12; 2:1-7a, scenes in heaven modelled on the epic tradition, Yahweh addresses a certain member of the divine council and introduces a particular topic. The individual proposes a particular course of action, and Yahweh authorizes it. Zech 3:1-7 is another vision report with a *mal'āk* 'envoy' representing Yahweh, and a priest present in the council as the object of interest. Yahweh rebukes one of the council who is maligning the priest, directs others to dress the latter in the regalia appropriate to a high priest, and then gives him a charge. Thus the divine council is not just an amorphous mass in Israelite literature: individual members appear as actors in these scenes. However, there is never any doubt of Yahweh's effective authority over the council.

Ps 82:1-7 recounts a unique procedure and judgement in the council, which is here called *'ădat 'ēl* 'meeting of El' (v 1): one deity (Yahweh) addresses all the other gods, announcing their demise as a consequence of their misrule of the world. His own assumption of world rule in their place is then acclaimed by the psalmist (i.e. congregation? v 8).

The opening verses of Second Isaiah (Isa 40:1-8) imply the same setting. They presuppose that a decision has been made. God now orders the council (plural imperatives) to act upon it. In particular, the prophet-author, conceived to be present in an audition (if not vision), is himself addressed by a member of the council ('a voice'): "Proclaim (singular imperative)!" and responds with a request for the message he is to deliver. (Cf. above on Isa 6.)

These, as well as the larger ancient Near Eastern tradition, provide the background for references to the *sôd yhwh*. As noted, *sôd* may refer to a council or assembly or other group, or to one of two more abstract concepts: the counsel or plan that such a group might devise, and the company or friendship that it might imply. All three meanings are found on the divine as well as the human plane.

In Ps 89:8 Yahweh's fearsomeness is expressed by reference to the rest of the divine court: *bĕsôd qĕdôšîm* "in the council of the holy ones" parallel to "over all those around him". The same group is referred to in the same context as "(the children of) the gods" (v 7) and *qĕhal qĕdôšîm* "the convocation of the holy ones" (v 6). There is no place here for reference to any particular members of the council, which is mentioned solely to emphasize the absoluteness of Yahweh's supremacy in it (cf. the function of the divine assembly scene in *KTU* 1.16 v).

Outside this psalm God's council is referred to only as the setting in which special mortals may have access to divine intentions and knowledge. Thus it is invoked as the source of true prophecy and of wisdom. It is in his council that Yahweh gives the message to and commissions the prophet. Only those who have stood in Yahweh's council (*'md bĕsôd-*) and heard his words can convey those words to his people (Jer 23:18, 21-22; cf. Isa 6). Eliphaz questions whether Job has got some special wisdom by listening *bĕsôd 'ĕlôah* "in the council of →Eloah" (Job 15:8).

Since the prepositional phrase *bĕsôd* always refers to a group (besides the preceding examples see those concerning a human group: Gen 49:6; Jer 15:17; Ezek 13:9; Ps 111:1), the personal name *Bĕsôdyâ* (Neh 3:6; cf. the hypocoristicon *Sôdî* in Num 13:10) must mean "In the council of Yah" (contrast M. Noth, *IPN*, 152-153). This might refer to the bearer's access to the council (as above) or to the divine origins of the decision to grant (to his parents) the conception of the bearer.

It is in his divine council (*sôd*) that God deliberates and decides on a plan (*sôd*). This is what lies behind the claim that Yahweh does nothing without first revealing his plan (*sôd*) to his servants, the prophets (Amos 3:7). This is probably the meaning also in Ps 25:14 which states that "those who fear Yahweh have his *sôd*, his *bĕrît* (covenant) to inform them".

In two other passages the abstract 'companionship, friendship' is perhaps more likely: "When God's *sôd* was beside my tent, when Shadday was with me" (Job 29:4-5; many emend to *sōk*); "for the devious are an abomination to Yahweh, but his *sôd* is with the righteous" (Prov 3:32). (However, a reference to the divine council here remains a possibility; cf. *KTU* 1.15 ii 1-iii 19, where, for El's blessing of Kirta on the occasion of his marriage, the gods gather around Kirta in a "meeting of the gods" *ʿdt ilm*).

In the NT the full portrayal of the divine council reappears elaborated in the dress of a Christian apocalypse (Rev 4-5): the writer has a vision of God, seated on his throne holding a sealed scroll and surrounded by twenty-four →elders also seated on →thrones. An angel appeals for a volunteer to break the seals and open the scroll. The writer reports that there is none in the entire universe able to perform this act. Finally, his attention is drawn to the →Lamb, who, acclaimed by the elders and myriads of angels, proceeds to open the seals. In the setting, the course of action, and even some of the wording the pattern laid down in ancient Mesopotamia remains visible, as does the purpose of the episode: the recognition of a new divine hero who will accomplish what none other can.

IV. *Bibliography*

G. Couturier, La vision du conseil divin: étude d'une forme commune au prophétisme et à l'apocalyptique, *Science et Esprit* 36 (1984) 5-43, esp. 14-35; F. M. Cross, The Council of Yahwe in Second Isaiah, *JNES* 12 (1952) 274-278; H. J. Fabry, סוד. Der Himmlische Thronrat als Ekklesiologisches Modell, *Bausteine Biblischer Theologie* (BBB 50; ed. H. J. Fabry; Köln & Bonn, 1977) 99-126; Fabry, סוד *sôd*, *TWAT* 5 (1986) 775-782; A. R. Hulst, Over de Betekenis van het Woord *sod, Vruchten van de Uithof: Studies opgedragen aan Dr. H. A. Brongers* (Utrecht 1974) 37-48, esp. 40-45; T. Jacobsen, Primitive Democracy in Ancient Mesopotamia, *JNES* 2 (1943) 159-172, esp. 167-172; A. Malamat, The Secret Council and Prophetic Involvement in Mari and Israel, *Prophetie und geschichtliche Wirklichkeit im alten Israel* (ed. R. Liwak & S. Wagner; Stuttgart, Berlin & Köln 1991) 231-236; E. T. Mullen, *The Assembly of the Gods* (HSM 24; Chico 1980); H.-P. Müller, Die himmlische Ratsversammlung, *ZNW* 54 (1963) 254-267; H. W. Robinson, The Council of Yahweh, *JTS* 45 (1944) 151-157; M. Saebo, סוד *sōd* Geheimnis, *THAT* II (1976) 144-148; R. N. Whybray, *The Heavenly Counsellor in Isaiah xl, 13-14* (Cambridge 1971); I. Willi-Plein, Das Geheimnis der Apokalyptik, *VT* 27 (1977) 62-81.

S. B. Parker

CURSE אלה

I. Some scholars have contended that in ancient Israel 'curse' (*ʾālâ*) was conceived of as a kind of demonic force that could invade the land or take over a person's being. Although curse could on occasion be personified, there is little evidence from the Bible that curse was thought to be a self-acting force. This is true not only for the root ʾLH but also for vocables from other roots used to express curses in the OT (notably ʾRR, QLL, QBB, and ŠBʿ). Etymologically the root ʾLH is cognate with Ar ʾLW (IV), 'to swear', 'to curse', and *ʾallu*, 'oath', 'curse'. In the OT the root is attested as a verb in the Qal (Judg 17:2; Hos 4:2; 10:4) and in the Hiphil (1 Sam 14:24; 1 Kgs 8:31 = 2 Chr 6:22); the noun *ʾālâ* occurs 36 times. In addition, the noun *taʾălâ* (Lam 3:65) is probably to be derived from this root. Despite the occasional personification of curses both in Israel and elsewhere in the ancient Near East, curses were thought to derive their effectiveness not so much from any inherent demonic force or magical power as from the agency of the cooperating deity invoked in such illocutionary or performative utterances.

II. There are no certain attestations of *ʾālâ* 'curse' in ancient Near Eastern literature outside the Hebrew Bible. In the alleged eighth-century BCE Phoenician inscription from Arslan Tash the word *ʾlt*—which occurs four or five times, depending upon one's interpretation—has been read variously as 'goddess', 'bond', or 'curse'. However, there is a growing conviction among scholars that the Arslan Tash inscription is in fact a forgery made in the 1930s and so will not be considered here (see J. TEIXIDOR, Les tablettes d' Arslan Tash au Musée d'Alep, *AulOr* 1 [1983] 105-108; P. AMIET, Observations sur les "Tablettes magiques" d'Arslan Tash, *AulOr* 1 [1983] 109). *ʾālâ* has also been read in line 2 of the Panammu II (*KAI* 215), an eighth-century BCE Aramaic inscription from Zinjirli. The word in question occurs in a broken and difficult context; it is usually read as *ʾzh*, i.e. a relative pronoun. However, CRAWFORD (1992:102-103), following GIBSON (*TSSI* 2.78-79) reads *ʾlh*, 'curse', and translates, "because of his father's righteousness the gods of Y'DY delivered him from destruction. There was a curse on his father's house, but the god →Hadad stood with him, and [...]." If correctly read as 'curse', then *ʾlh* here can be compared to the sanctions attached to a breach of ancient Near Eastern treaties (e.g. Sefire I.A.14-42; I.B.21-45; I.C.17-25) or to covenants (cf. Deut 30:7; Jer 23:10).

Although not cognates, Heb *ʾālâ* is often correctly compared to Akkadian *māmītu*, the semantic range of which extends from 'oath' (sworn by the king and the gods) and 'sworn agreement' to 'curse' (consequences of a broken oath attacking a person who took it, also as demonic power) (*CAD* M/1, s.v.). Both *ʾālâ* and *māmītu* have as their primary meaning 'oath', as in treaties and in promises of fidelity. Likewise, both terms are used by metonymy to refer to disasters and maladies considered to be sanctions for breaking an oath. Such disasters and maladies were thought to be inflicted by divine beings (→Sons of (the) Gods) explicitly or implicitly invoked to enforce the oath. Accordingly in Akkadian literature the disasters and maladies associated with *māmītu* were themselves on occasion demonized or deified (*CAD* M/1, *māmītu* 2c).

In the targums *ʾālâ*, like *šĕbûʿâ* (another word for 'oath'), is normally translated by Aram *mōmātā*, a cognate to Akk *māmītu*. In cases where *ʾālâ* and *šĕbûʿâ* occur together, *ʾālâ* is translated by Aram *līṭa* or *lĕwāṭā* ('curse').

III. The notion of *ʾālâ*, 'curse', as some kind of self-acting malevolent force has first been proposed by PEDERSEN (1926:437-443). Although Pedersen used the label *ʾālâ*, it is clear from the examples he used that 'curse' also includes vocables derived from other roots, notably ʾRR and QLL. PEDERSEN's conception of curse is intimately linked with his understanding of the soul in Israelite psychology. "Man, in his total essence, is a soul" (1926:99). In other words, were one to substitute 'person' for 'soul', one would have a more accurate understanding of what the Israelites meant by soul. The soul is a coherent whole characterized by volition realized in action. That is, human persons are by nature oriented toward accomplishment of what they conceive in thought. Moreover, this ancient psychology assigned a magical quality to language: words effect what they symbolize. Curses—like their opposites, blessings—operate by a power inherent in the words themselves and thus take on a life of their own once uttered. Blessing is the vital power that no living being can live without; it is the strength of life, a creative power manifested primarily in fertility but also in bringing about wealth. Great-souled persons possess greater blessing and the full life that goes with it. The act of blessing transfers this soul power to another person. The blessing is a self-fulfilling power that cannot be revoked, but it can be made more effective by joining human power with divine power.

Curse is just the opposite of blessing. Curse, like its counterpart, →sin, causes dissolution of the soul, diminishment of vitality, and destruction of the community. But unlike sin, the curse can be put into the soul from without. Like the blessing, the curse can be put into the soul by someone else uttering the curse. The power of the curse lies not in the wish or the words but in the mysterious power of souls to react upon each other. One whose soul creates something evil puts that evil into the soul of his neighbour, where it exercises its influence. Persons of stronger souls speak stronger curses than ordinary people (2 Kgs 2:24; cf. 6:16); persons like Balaam had special gifts for that kind of utterance (Num 22-24). Also, the strength of the word could be increased by uttering it in a holy place such as before the altar (1 Kgs 8:31).

Pedersen's views about curse as a self-operating power were adopted and developed in different ways by others. MOWINCKEL (1924) sought to ground curse, like blessing, in the cult. Although originally the power of blessings and curses may have been thought to arise from within the blesser or the curser and to be transmitted by means of the effectual word, in Israel blessing and cursing increasingly took the form of a wish or a prayer to →Yahweh to bless one's community or friends and to curse one's enemies or malefactors. In Mowinckel's theory, the magical quality of the word was not so much abandoned as transformed into a 'sacramental element' through which the deity's power could actually be strengthened. HEMPEL (1925) posited an even greater evolutionary development in the notions of blessing and cursing in Israel. In the folk religion stage, blessings and curses were magical and self-fulfilling. In the cultic stage, blessings and curses still required ceremonies and oral formulas to prompt the deity to bless or curse. In the ethical monotheism stage, blessings and curses lost their magical quality altogether; blessings and curses were now believed to come from the deity in accordance with the ethical values proclaimed by the prophets. That the genre of curse in ancient Israel underwent such evolutionary development, however, may be doubted. SCHARBERT (1958) is closer to the OT evidence in concluding that, although word-magic may still be present in a number of OT passages involving curses, the magical element was largely neutralized by faith in Yahweh. That is, the curse became more of a prayer to Yahweh to bring about the calamity on the evildoer and thus call the evildoer to account. But even this reconstruction depends too heavily upon a hypothesis of word-magic as the norm in the ancient Near East.

CRAWFORD (1992) has shown that none of the blessing and curse formulations in Syro-Palestinian inscriptions roughly contemporary with the monarchical period in Israel (ca. 1000-586 BCE) should be interpreted as vague magical imprecations; rather in every case they are dependent for their fulfillment upon the power of deities invoked either explicitly or implicitly. A closer analysis of OT curse formulations yields similar results (see BRICHTO 1963). The notion that words have power is based upon a modern misconception about the ancients' inability to distinguish between 'word' and 'thing'. With THISELTON (1974), blessing and curse are best understood as illocutionary or performative utterances. That is to say, the congruence between word and thing derives from the fact that they are uttered by an acceptable person at an acceptable time and in an acceptable manner. A divorce formula, for example, derives its force not from mere utterance but from being pronounced by the proper person(s) in a forum acknowledged by that society for that purpose.

Curse (*'ālâ*) in the OT was operative in two basic contexts: (1) As part of an oath, such as in the making of covenants or contracts. In this usage the curse is essentially an imprecation. That is, curses attached to covenant-making functioned as sanctions invoked upon oneself for breach of contract. Just as blessings motivated covenant fidelity through promise of a full life and prosperity, so curses militated against covenant infidelity through threat of loss of life and diminishment of community or wealth. The close connection between *ʾālâ* and covenant is particularly evident in Deut 29:9-20: "You are assembled today, all of you, before Yahweh your God [...] to enter into the covenant of Yahweh your God and into its curse" (vv 9-11, cf. vv 13, 20). A covenant context for *ʾālâ* is also explicit or implicit in passages such as Deut 30:7; Isa 24:4-6; Jer 23:10; Ezek 16:59; 17:11-19; 2 Chr 34:24; Neh 10:30; Dan 9:11; and perhaps also in the obscure passage Hos 10:4. Because of the close connection between curse and covenant, *ʾālâ* can by metonymy, specifically by synecdoche of the part for the whole, stand for the covenant itself (e.g. Deut 29:18, 19). Within a covenant context, it is obvious that the curses are not self-acting but rather are carried out by the deity or deities invoked to guarantee the integrity of the covenant. (2) As adjurations against another person (in grammatical 2nd or 3rd person formulations) (a) for the purpose of motivating witnesses or malefactors to come forward (e.g. Lev 5:1); (b) for the purpose of evoking a desired action or precluding an undesired action (e.g. Gen 24:41; Josh 6:22; 1 Sam 14:24, 28); or (c) as a conditional imprecation (or prayer) addressed to the deity to punish a malefactor whose guilt cannot be proved (e.g. Judg 17:2; Num 5:11-31; 1 Kgs 8:31-32=2 Chr 6:22-23). It was a breach of the moral code to evoke the deity frivolously or under false pretenses (Job 31:29-30; Hos 4:1-2; Ps 59:13).

In no passage does the curse operate independently of the agency of the deity, even in passages which have the most semblance of magic. An example is the frequently-cited case of a woman suspected of adultery who must endure a trial by ordeal wherein the woman is forced to drink water containing a curse (Num 5:11-31). Here the placing of the trial in the sanctuary (vv 15-16, 18, 30) and the explicit invocation of the deity to effect the curse (v 21, cf. v 25) make it clear that the words and the actions of the ritual have at most a sacramental quality; that is, they are merely material forms through which divine action is manifested. Even in cases where the actual words of the curse are not recorded, such as in Judg 17:2 where a distraught woman curses the unknown thief who stole her money, it is likely that the deity was invoked. For when the woman learned that the thief was her own son, in an attempt to counteract the curse, she immediately invoked Yahweh to bless her son. The logic here seems to be that, since her son was patently guilty, the imposition of the curse by the just divine judge could not be averted. However, the effects of the curse could be softened through blessing from the same deity.

Examination of other cases yields a similar conclusion. The curse in ancient Israel—whether expressed by *ʾālâ* or some other vocable—was not believed to be a magical, self-acting force. Rather, a valid curse was always conditional (a) upon the speaker having legitimate reason to utter the curse, (b) upon the object person being deserving of punishment, and most importantly, (c) upon the complicity of the deity in effecting the curse.

IV. *Bibliography*

S. BLANK, The Curse, Blasphemy, the Spell and the Oath, *HUCA* 23 (1950-51) 73-95; *H. C. BRICHTO, *The Problem of the 'Curse' in the Hebrew Bible* (Philadelphia 1963) esp. 22-71; T. G. CRAWFORD, *Blessings and Curse in Syro-Palestinian Inscriptions of the Iron Age* (American University Studies: Ser. 7, Theology and Religion 120; New York 1992); J. HEMPEL, Die israelitische Anschauungen von Segen und Fluch im Lichte altorientalischer Parallelen, *ZDMG* 79 (1925) 20-110 (Reprinted in BZAW 81 [1961] 30-113); S. MOWINCKEL, *Segen und Fluch in Israels Kult und Psalmendichtung. Psalmenstudien V* (Oslo 1924; reprinted Amsterdam 1961); MOWINCKEL, *The Psalms in Israel's Worship* (Oxford 1962) II, 44-52; J. PEDERSEN, *Der Eid bei den Semiten* (Strassburg 1914); PEDERSEN, *Israel: its Life and Culture* I-II (Copenhagen 1926) 437-443 (First published in Danish,

1920); J. SCHARBERT, "Fluchen" und "Segnen" im AT, *Bib* 39 (1958) 1-26; SCHARBERT, אלה 'ālāh, ארר 'rr, *TDOT* 1 (1974, rev. 1977) 261-266, 405-418; W. SCHOTTROFF, *Der altisraelitische Fluchspruch* (WMANT 30; Neukirchen-Vluyn 1969); A. C. THISELTON, The Supposed Power of Words in the Biblical Writings, *JTS* 25 (1974) 283-299.

B. F. BATTO

CYBELE

I. According to HOMMEL (1929), the field of Machpelah (Gen 23:9.17.19; 25:9; 49:30; 50:13) was named after the goddess Ma-Cybele.

II. Cybele (Κυβέλη) or Cybebe (Κυβήβη) is a goddess of the fertile earth originating from Asia Minor, where she was known in the second millennium BCE as Kubaba. Having made her way into the Greek world, the deity was identified with a number of other 'mother goddesses' such as Rhea, Agdistis, Ma, and Bellona. Her cult had orgiastic traits. The latter were accentuated in the course of time as the god Attis (in some respects comparable with →Adonis) was associated with Cybele. The goddess and her male consort were quite popular in the Hellenistic and Roman world (TURCAN 1989).

III. The connection made between Machpelah and Ma-Cybele is based purely on phonetic similarity. In fact, the construct Ma-Cybele is extremely rare; the conjunction Ma-Bellona is more frequent. The cult of Cybele would not have been known (certainly not under that name) in Palestine before Alexander the Great—which would mean that the Machpelah tradition is much younger than commonly accepted. Also, the word *makpēlâ* is a perfectly proper Hebrew *maqtēl* formation based on the root KPL, 'to be double' (cf. BAUER & LEANDER, *Historische Grammatik*, 492).

IV. *Bibliography*

H. HOMMEL, Das religionsgeschichtliche Problem des 139. Psalms, *ZAW* 47 (1929) 110-124, esp. 117 n.1; R. TURCAN, *Les cultes orientaux dans le monde romain* (Paris 1989) 35-75.

K. VAN DER TOORN

D

DAGON דגון

I. Dagon is the Hebrew form of the name of the god Dagan, who was an important Mesopotamian and West Semitic deity. Dagon occurs as a Philistine deity in the Hebrew Bible, specifically as the god of Ashdod (1 Sam 5:1-7 and 1 Macc 10:83-84; Judg 16:23 [Gaza]; 1 Chr 10:10 [Beth-Shan?]). The LXX also reads the name Δαγων instead of Nebo (→Nabû) in Isa 46:1.

The etymology of the name Dagan is uncertain. Etymologies based on *dāg*, 'fish', *dāgān*, 'grain', and on a root meaning 'be cloudy' (Arabic *dajj* or *dajana*) are all equally dubious and there is no contextual evidence from the Hebrew Bible or from Mesopotamian/West Semitic sources to give much support to these speculations. It is wiser to restrict oneself to what can be known from the evidence, principally that Dagan was a deity of major significance in the Mari region in the Old Babylonian period and that his worship appears to have spread widely in later times. He was thus adopted, no doubt in some syncretistic form, perhaps as a corn-god, by the Philistines.

II. Dagan is one of the most persistent deities of the world of Semitic religion. His worship is well attested from the third millennium BCE in the Ebla texts and he appears in Sargonic personal names, but neither source gives any hint of the precise nature of this deity. In Ebla, though important in cult, he is rarely named, but called by various titles including ^{d}BE (*bēlu*, 'Lord') and ^{d}LUGAL-*du-du-lu*^{ki} ('Lord of Tuttul'). Temples, festivals and even a section of the city were dedicated to Dagan.

Sargon attributed his conquest of Upper/Western Mesopotamia to Dagan and worshipped him in Tuttul. This confirms Dagan's regional authority, leaving southern Mesopotamia to other deities, including Enlil. He is well attested in the Mari texts as one of the principal deities of the Amorites of Old Babylonian Upper Mesopotamia and he is specifically linked with Mari, his great cult-centres being at Terqa and especially Tuttul. It may be noted that Dagan is often connected in the Mari texts with the activities of ecstatics/prophets who received messages from the god in his temple, which were then transmitted to the king.

In southern Mesopotamia Dagan was sometimes identified with the god Enlil. This may suggest some 'storm-god' aspect (supporting the etymology linking the name with the possible Arabic cognate noted above), though the significance of the equation may not be this aspect and the Arabic cognate is extremely remote.

The westward 'migration' of Dagan is already evident in the Ugaritic texts. He has a rather minor role in Ugaritic mythology, playing a very small and obscure part in the Nikkal poem. The context here is fragmentary, but it is possible that Dagan is mentioned as the father of the lunar deity Yarikh (→Moon) (*KTU* 1.24:14). He has no active role in the main myths and legends and is merely mentioned as the father of →Baʿal (called *bn dgn*, *ḥtk dgn*). His paternity of Baʿal might be interpreted as implying characteristics similar to Baʿal's. Be this as it may, Dagan's importance in Ugaritic religion is confirmed by his relative popularity in offering-lists and similar texts. From the fact that he is the recipient of offerings recorded on two stelae found in the precinct of a major temple (*KTU* 6.13 and 6.14) it appears that one of the two principal temples at Ugarit was dedicated to Dagan, though the evidence is not completely conclusive. The other temple was that of Baʿal. Ugaritic 'theology' (as opposed to the different world of Ugaritic mythology) may be reflected in the local pantheon lists and the main one of these, extant in several versions, puts Dagan in third place, after →El and →Ilib but before Baʿal (see *KTU* 1.47; 1.118 and Akkadian RS 20.24=*Ugaritica V* i, 18).

It is noteworthy that in the Ugaritic texts Dagan is twice called *dgn ttl*, 'Dagan of Tuttul' (*KTU* 1.100:15; 1.24:14 [*tt(l)*]), a title which shows the continuity of the Ugaritic Dagan tradition with that of Mari.

The fact of Dagan's having no active part in the main Baʿal myths may reflect the relative lateness of his arrival on the Syrian coast. References to Baʿal as 'son of Dagan' also present considerable problems, since he is clearly also the son of El. Some have sought to resolve this by assuming that Dagan is to be identified with El, but this idea is hard to maintain in view of the fact that the two were separately worshipped. Others suggest the title 'son of Dagan' reflects an awareness of Baʿal's foreignness and secondariness within the history of the Ugaritic pantheon. It may well be that the confusion arises from a lack of fixity in the genealogy of the Ugaritic gods.

Biblical evidence of Philistine worship of Dagan (below)—the form of the name recorded for this is Dagon, reflecting a shift of *ā* to *ō*—is uninformative in detail, but clearly implies that the deity was taken over by the Philistines as a national god. We must assume his worship had been widespread throughout the coastal (corn-producing?) area which the Philistines came to call their own. The adoption of pre-existing cults, no doubt still popular among the Semitic population, can be regarded as normal. It may be noted, however, that there is only one possible direct Phoenician allusion to Dagan/Dagon, in the phrase *ʾrṣt dgn hʾdrt*, 'the rich lands of Dagon', in the fifth century BCE Eshmunazar inscription (*KAI* 14:19). Dagon does, however, have a prominent role in Philo of Byblos' speculative account of Phoenician religion (below).

ROBERTS (1972:18-19) argued for Dagan having had an underworld role. His argument is largely based on the underworld aspect of Enlil, with whom Dagan was identified, though he also cites a Mari text in which Dagan is called *bēl pagrê,* which Roberts takes to mean 'lord of the sacrifices for the dead'. This translation is dubious: 'lord of sacrificial victims' may be more likely. There is, however, some slight evidence pointing in the direction of the funerary cult in that an inscription of Shamshi-Adad I seems to connect the *bīt kispi* ('temple of the funerary ritual') in Terqa with the temple of Dagan there.

We cannot resolve the question of the etymology of the name Dagan/Dagon. It could be pre-Semitic. The connection with 'fish' (cf. Biblical evidence as interpreted by Wellhausen [below], Jerome and later Jewish tradition [Rashi, Kimchi]) is entirely secondary, being based on a folk etymology. The name Dagan appears to have been a 'given' which needed explanation and the explanation arrived at would, conveniently, help to make sense of certain difficulties in one of the Biblical texts (see below). This made the 'fish' connection the more attractive, but it has little intrinsic merit. As an interpretation it is only loosely supported by the Philistine association with the sea and analogies with the goddess Derketo at a later date.

As for 'grain', this suggestion has a venerable ancestry in that this is the significance of Dagan in Philo of Byblos, where Dagon is identical with Siton and is regarded as having discovered grain and the plough. This cannot, however, be regarded as settling the issue and it is now a widely held view that the word for 'grain' comes from the name of the god and not *vice versa*. Perhaps more simply we might suppose that the connection with 'grain' is secondary and based on the coincidence of the West Semitic word for grain (e.g. Hebrew and Ugaritic [one doubtful occurrence: *KTU* 1.16 iii:13]) and the Mesopotamian name of the god being homonyms. The grain-related meaning of the root *dgn* is distinctively West Semitic. It would not have been known to a Mesopotamian worshipper of the deity and cannot have been at all prominent in the understanding of his name.

Finally the Arabic *dajana*, 'to be gloomy, cloudy', not found elsewhere in Semitic, has been adopted by many recent scholars. As we have seen, connection with storms (since Dagan was Enlil-like and also the father of Baʿal) is possible though never explicit. The appeal to such a remote Semitic cognate for etymology smacks of desperation.

III. 1 Sam 5:1-7 contains the most important of the Biblical references to Dagan/Dagon. The passage concerns the bringing of the Ark of the Covenant by the Philistines into the temple of their god Dagon in Ashdod. The introduction of the captured Ark into a temple is meant to be a sign of submission to the god of the particular temple. According to the story in 1 Sam, however, the statue of Dagon fell down (in submission) before the Ark and was smashed. There is a difficulty in the text of the end of v.4: *raq dāgōn nišʾar ʿālā(y)w*, apparently "only Dagon was left upon him". BHK and BHS recognise the need for a construct noun before 'Dagon' and this is reflected in the ancient versions (LXX: η ῥάχις, backbone; Vg: *truncus,* body without limbs; Tg: *gwpyh*, his body, Syr: *gwšmh,* his body). Wellhausen would correct *dāgōn* to *dāgō*, 'his fish(-part)', and this is still favoured by BHK. This would give 'only his fish-part remained upon him', which would, if accepted, support the connecting of Dagan's name with *dāg*, 'fish', a tradition represented in Jerome (<*dag ʾōn*, 'fish of tribulation'!) and in the Talmud. It is notable, however, that while the ancient versions are aware of a problem with the text, this is not an interpretation they put upon it. The Wellhausen suggestion is now rightly abandoned by BHS.

Of the remaining Biblical references to Dagan/Dagon, note may be made of other passages which confirm the association of the god with the Philistines. In Judg 16:23 the Philistine chiefs assemble, presumably in the temple of Dagon, to offer sacrifice of thanksgiving to Dagon for their capture of Samson. Dagon is called 'their/our god' and he receives a *zebaḥ gādōl*, 'a great sacrifice'. Although it is not explicitly stated here that there was a Dagon temple at Gaza, no change of locale is implied and it seems likely that there was such a temple, since there appear to have been many temples of the god. Josh 15:41 and 19:27, where the placename Beth-Dagon occurs, imply there were such temples in Judah and in Asher. According to 1 Chr 10:10 the head of Saul was initially displayed by the Philistines as a trophy of war in a temple of Dagon. This appears to have been at Beth-Shan (1 Sam 31:10).

That the cult of Dagon persisted into the intertestamental period is clear from 1 Macc 10:83-84, according to which the High Priest Jonathan burned down the temple of Dagon in Azotus, i.e. Ashdod, which had become the place of refuge of the cavalry of Apollonius, governor of Coele-Syria.

In addition to these explicit biblical references to the god Dagon, note should be made of a number of biblical verses in which it has been argued that the occurrence of the word *dāgān*, 'grain', intends an allusion to the deity. Thus in Gen 27:28 and Hos 7:14 and 9:1 (e.g. ALBRIGHT 1946: 1046). The claimed allusion in Gen 27:28 is without foundation, since nothing in the context suggests anything to do with foreign gods and *dāgān* is satisfactorily translated as 'grain', one of the divine gifts in Isaac's blessing upon his son. Here and elsewhere 'grain' is associated with →'dew' (*ṭal*), 'fatness of the earth' and 'new wine' (*tîrôš*, →Tirash). The fact that *ṭal* and *ṭîrôš* may elsewhere have mythological overtones does not prove that *dāgān* has such overtones in Gen 27:28.

The case of the Hosea passages is different, since it is clear that it is one of Hosea's themes that it was Yahweh, not the foreign gods, who gave Israel "the grain, the wine and the oil" (2:10-11.24). In these cases there may be a faint echo of the divine name Dagan (though the fact that the definite article is used means that it is indeed faint). In Hos 7:14 the specific context is that of turning to other gods and "for *dāgān* and *ṭîrôš* (without definite articles) they gash themselves" may plausibly be interpreted as an allusion to illicit cult, though the allusion could be simply to a cult of lamentation for the failure of vegetation. Hos 9:1, "you have loved a prostitute's payment upon all the threshing-floors of *dāgān*", could again contain an allusion to the deity.

IV. *Bibliography*

W. F. ALBRIGHT, *Archaeology and the Religion of Israel* (Baltimore 1946[2]); A. CAQUOT & M. SZNYCER, *Textes Ougaritiques. Tome I: Mythes et Légendes* (Paris 1974); A. COOPER, Divine Names and Epithets in the Ugaritic Texts, *RSP* III (Rome 1981) 361-363; L. K. HANDY, Dagon, *ABD* 2 (1992) 1-2; J. F. HEALEY, The Underworld Character of the God Dagan, *JNSL* 5 (1977) 43-51; HEALEY, The "Pantheon" of Ugarit: Further Notes, *SEL* 5 (1988)103-112; F. J. MONTALBANO, Canaanite Dagon: Origin, Nature, *CBQ* 13 (1951) 381-397; M. J. MULDER, *Kanaänitische Goden in het Oude Testament* (The Hague 1965) 71-75; G. PETTINATO & H. WAETZOLDT, Dagān in Ebla und Mesopotamien nach den Texten aus dem 3. Jahrtausend, *Or* 54 (1985) 234-256; H. RINGGREN, Dagan, דגן, *TWAT* 2, 148-151 (*TDOT* 3; 139-142); J. J. M. ROBERTS, *The Earliest Semitic Pantheon* (Baltimore/London 1972); H. SCHMÖKEL, *Der Gott Dagon, Ursprung, Verbreitung und Wesen seines Kultes* (Leipzig 1928); S. A. WIGGINS, Old Testament Dagan in the Light of Ugarit, *VT* 43 (1993) 268-274.

J. F. HEALEY

DANIEL דניאל

I. The name Daniel occurs in three contexts in the Hebrew Bible: (1) It occurs twice in the Book of Ezekiel. Ezek 14:14 says that when a land sins, "even if these three →Noah, Daniel and Job were in it, they would deliver but their own lives by their righteousness". Again in Ezek 28:3 the prophet taunts the king of Tyre (→Melqart) by asking: "are you wiser than Daniel?" (In both instances, the name is spelled דנאל, without the plene *yod*) It seems clear from these references that Daniel was already the name of a legendary figure, famed for righteousness and wisdom, in the time of Ezekiel. (2) Ezra 8:2 mentions a priest named Daniel, son of Ithamar, who went up from Babylon to Jerusalem with Ezra. This figure has no supra-human qualities. (3) The hero of the book of Daniel is ostensibly a Jew in the Babylonian exile, who distinguishes himself by his ability to interpret dreams and mysterious writing, and by surviving a sojourn in the lions' den. He is then the recipient of apocalyptic visions in the second half of the book. It is the consensus of modern scholarship that this Daniel never existed. In any case, he is not presented as a deity or a demon. The name Daniel, however, is used for a heavenly figure in post-biblical traditions.

The name Daniel means 'my judge is El' (*pace* M. NOTH *IPN*, who proposed 'God has judged'). The motif of judgment is prominent in the story of Susanna, but not in the other extant Daniel literature.

II. Daniel occurs as the name of a traditional, legendary, figure in the Aqhat story in the Ugaritic literature (*KTU* 1.17-19; *ANET* 149-55). There we find a king named Daniel (*dn'il*) who is initially childless. He supplicates the gods and is given a son Aqhat. The divine craftsman, Kothar-wa-Khasis gives Aqhat a present of a bow. The goddess →Anat takes a fancy to the bow and offers Aqhat silver and gold in exchange for it. Aqhat declines. Anat then offers to make him immortal, but Aqhat refuses to believe her, since old age and death are the lot of humanity. Anat then plots vengeance against him, and kills him by sending her attendant Yatpan in the form of a vulture to strike him down. The bow, however, is broken and falls into the sea. Messengers from Baal relate to Daniel and his daughter late-born Pughat what has happened. Daniel beseeches Baal to break the wings of vultures, so that he can rip them open and see if Aqhat's flesh and bones are in them. Eventually he retrieves his son for burial, and laments him for seven years. His daughter Pughat puts on male attire with dagger and sword, with a woman's cloak over it. She then sets out to the tent of Yatpan, who boasts to her of having killed Aqhat. The tablets break off at this point.

III. The Daniel in *KTU* 1.17-19 is evidently a righteous man, who supplicates the gods and, as king, gives judgment for widows and orphans. He is not portrayed as exceptionally wise, and even his righteousness is incidental to the story. If this is indeed the same hero Ezekiel refers to, the prophet must have known other traditions about him. Nonetheless it seems gratuitous to suppose that there were two unrelated legendary figures by the name of Daniel.

The relevance of this figure to the hero of the Book of Daniel is very limited. Only the name is taken over. He is given an entirely new identity as a Jew in the Babylonian exile. There is no reason to suppose that the authors or tradents of the tales were at all aware of the Ugaritic legend. Most probably the name was taken from Ezekiel. Since Daniel was not so well known as Noah and Job in Jewish circles, the post-exilic author was free to attach the name to a figure who would illustrate righteousness and wisdom in a historical context.

IV. A few other occurrences of the name Daniel should be noted. It is the name of one of the →Watchers, or fallen angels, in *1 Enoch* 6:7. It also appears as the name of a good angel on an Aramaic incantation bowl (ISBELL 1975:102-3). Finally, *Jub* 4:20 reports that →Enoch took a wife whose name was Edni, "the daughter of Danel, his father's brother". This latter figure may well be a variant of the Ugaritic *Dn'il*, but his tradition history remains obscure. Only in *1 Enoch*, and in the much later incantation bowl, is Daniel clearly the name of a heavenly being.

V. *Bibliography*

J. J. COLLINS, *Daniel* (Hermeneia; Minneapolis 1993) 1-2; J. DAY, The Daniel of Ugarit and Ezekiel and the Hero of the Book of Daniel, *VT* 30 (1980) 174-84; H. H. P. DRESSLER, The Identification of the Ugaritic Dnil with the Daniel of Ezekiel, *VT* 29 (1979) 152-61; DRESSLER, Reading and Interpreting the Aqhat Text, *VT* 34 (1984) 78-82; C. D. ISBELL, *Corpus of the Aramaic Incantation Bowls* (SBLDS 17; Missoula: 1975); B. MARGALIT, Interpreting the Story of Aqhat. A Reply to H. H. P. Dressler, *VT* 30 (1980) 361-5; M. NOTH, Noah, Daniel und Hiob in Ez 14, *VT* 1 (1951) 251-60; *IPN*.

J. J. COLLINS

DAPHNE Δάφνη

I. Daphne, metamorphosed into Apollo's laurel tree (Gk: *Daphnē*) to escape his amorous intentions, gave her name to a suburb of Antioch (2 Macc 4:33). The name can also result from the spelling in Greek of Hebrew placenames—the fortress Tahpanhes in the LXX (e.g. Jer 2:16) and a source of a tributary of the Jordan (Jos., *Bell.* 4:3 and *Tg.Num.* 34:11).

II. Stories involving Daphne are variously sited, but seem to go back to a tale focussing on the River Peneios or its tributary the River Ladon on the fringes of Elis and north-western Arcadia. She is depicted at the moment of maidenhood, refusing the company of men and typically hunting in the wilds. But Leukippos, son of the King of Elis, loves her and, masquerading as a maiden, becomes her friend. Discovered, he is killed by her group. Though Apollo instigated the death of Leukippos in some poems (Pausanias 8:20), he really belongs to a different story altogether: in love with Daphne, he pursues her till she prays for release to her father, the river, and is transformed into a *daphnē* —which then, aetiologically, becomes a plant appropriate to Apolline cult (Ovid, *Met.* 1:452-567). In the last century and the beginning of the 20th century, she was viewed by M. Müller as the dawn destroyed by the rising sun, by MANNHARDT (1904-05: I 297) as a tree-soul and by ROHDE as a symbol of the defeat of chthonic goddesses by the new oracular cult of Apollo (1898, I 141; II 58 n. 2). More recently she has lost speculative interest and become a straightforward aetiological figure, though I have remarked upon initiatory elements in the stories (DOWDEN 1989:177-179).

Nine kilometres south of Antioch lies the suburb Daphne, famous for its shrine of Apollo Daphnaios and →Artemis, founded by Seleukos I, and its huge grove (15 km in circumference, Strabo 16, 2, 6) and many springs. One spring was named 'Castalia' (as at Delphi). This shrine re-sited Apollo's pursuit: the grove actually contained a River Ladon and the very laurel tree into which Daphne had been metamorphosed. It also had a cypress, resulting from a transformation of a youth Kyparittos (Philostratos, *Vit.Ap.* 1:16). This is the holy place where the high priest Onias took sanctuary (2 Macc 4:33-4).

Another Daphne (at Tell Defne), whose springs feed a tributary of the Jordan, is mentioned by Josephus (*Bell.* 4:3) and by *Tg.Num.* 34:11 (*dpny*); it is confused with the Antioch Daphne by Jerome (*In Ezek.* 14, 47, 18) and probably by *Tg.Num.* (LE DÉAUT 1979:323 n. 25).

The fortress Tahpanhes (a Hebrew rendering of the Egyptian 'Fortress of the Black Man', now Tell Tefenne on the eastern fringes of the Delta) appears at Jer 2:16; 44:1; 46:14; Ezek 30:13-18. It is usually rendered in the LXX as 'Taphnai', though 'Daphnai' is also found—by assimilation to the Greek lexicon rather than with any particular semantic force. But at 1 (3) Kgs 11:19-20 the LXX does not take the opportunity to render the Pharaoh's sister and wife of Hadad, Queen Tahpenes, as 'Daphne'; she is, instead, 'Thekemina'.

III. *Bibliography*

K. DOWDEN, *Death and the Maiden* (London 1989) 174-179; J. LASSUS, Antioch on the Orontes, *The Princeton Encyclopedia of Classical Sites* (ed. R. Stilwell; Princeton 1976) 63 [& lit]; R. LE DÉAUT, *Targum du Pentateuque*, vol.3, Nombres (Sources Chrétiennes 261; Paris 1979); W. MANNHARDT, *Wald- und Feldkulte*, 2 vols. (2nd ed.; Berlin 1904-1905); E. ROHDE, *Psyche: Seelencult und Unsterblichkeitsglaube der Griechen*, (2nd ed.; Freiburg/Leipzig/Tübingen 1898); O. WASER, Daphne (6), *PW* 4 (1901) 2138-2140.

K. DOWDEN

DATAN → DEDAN

DAY יום

I. The Hebrew noun *yôm*, 'day', frequently occurs in the OT (2304 times; the Aram cognate *yôm* occurs 16 times in Dan and Ezra). The noun has a common Semitic background and is not derived from a verb (VON SODEN, BERGMAN & SAEBØ 1982:561-562). At some instances in the OT 'day' is personified. This use of 'day' indicating a malevolent being construed as acting in history has some parallels in Mesopotamian texts. In Ugaritic, *ym*, to be distinguished from *ym*, 'Sea', is attested as a deity in the Baal-epic and occurs in a syllabic god-list. In the Old Aramaic Sefire-treaty *ywm* occurs as a deified witness.

II. In some Mesopotamian laments, 'day' occurs, not as an abstraction, but as "a malevolent being, a demonic power that wilfully caused the evil ..." (JACOBSEN & NIELSEN 1992:189). In a Sumerian penitential psalm related to the cult of Damu (→Tammuz) a mother cries on the death of her boy: "Woe! Day destroyed him; lost me a son" (ca. 2000 BCE; OECT VI 15 Rev 3'-10'). In the Lamentation over the destruction of Ur 'day' is also personified: "... the day of storm was called off from the country—the people mourn ... the country's blood filled all holes like copper in a mould ..." (S. N. KRAMER, *Lamentation over the Destruction of Ur* [AS 12; Chicago 1940] 38-40:208-218). In a passage in the Epic of Gilgamesh, Belit-ili bewails the day on which the flood was ordered by addressing herself to a personified day: "O, that you, Day, had turned to clay on which I ordered evil in the assembly of the gods!" (GE XI:117-119).

This poetic personification of the day (of birth) should be distinguished from the use of *ūmū* as designation of supernatural beings, or demons, who are manifesting themselves as weather phenomena (Šurpu viii:8; Enuma Elish IV:50; GE VI:12; WIGGERMANN 1986:284, 295, 323).

In a passage in the Baal-epic where the forces of →Mot are attacking and threatening →Baal, Baal says to his boys: "Look, Gupanu-and-Ugaru! The sons of darkness obscure *ym*, the sons of deep darkness (obscure) the Exalted Princess!" (*KTU* 1.4 vii:53-56; J. C. DE MOOR, *The Rise of Yahwism* [BETL 91; Leuven 1990] 84, interprets this line as a metaphorical depiction of the effect of the hot desert wind, the sirocco, on the agricultural areas). The last two sentences form a parallelism. Since 'Exalted Princess', *rmt prʿt*, might be interpreted as an epithet for the sun-goddess Shapshu, *ym* can be interpreted as a deity 'Day, Daylight' indicating the Sun. The existence of this deity in the Ugaritic pantheon is established by a trilingual syllabic god-list in which 'Day' appears as the equivalent of the Mesopotamian deity Shamash and the Hurrian god Tuenni: ^{d}[U]$_4$ // *tu-en-ni* // *ya-m*[*u*] (*Ug* V No. 137 IVa:17). In a para-mythological text from Ugarit, three times the sentence occurs: "Let me invoke the gracious gods, the voracious sons of *ym*" (*KTU* 1.23:23.58-59.61). These lines refer to →Shahar and Shalim (→Shalem), the deities of dawn and dusk. Since they are seen as the beginning and end of the day, their lineage is presented as related to *ym*, 'Day', which might be a metaphorical depiction of Ilu (→El; M. C. A. KORPEL, *A Rift in the Clouds* [UBL 8; Münster 1990] 566-567)

In the Aramaic treaty between Bar-Ga'yah of KTK and Matiel of Arpad *ywm*, 'Day', occurs in a list of deities acting as witnesses and guarantors to the treaty: *wqdm ywm wlylh šhdn kl ʾ*[*lhy ktk* ..., 'and before Day and Night; [let all the gods of Ktk and of Arpad be w]itness' (*KAI* 222 A:12; J.A. FITZMEYER, *The Aramaic Inscriptions of Sefire* [BeO 19; Roma 1967] 38-39).

ZADOK (1984) interprets *ywm* as a West Semitic deity. The occurrence of the deity in a Neo-Babylonian or Late-Babylonian list of offerings (A. UNGNAD, *VAS* 6 [1908] Nr. 213:15: IGI ^{d}U$_4$-*mu* DINGIR É-*ti* ^{d}*Mi-šar-rà u* ^{d}DI-KUD; cf. a Neo-Assyrian list *Tākultu*, Nr. 236: ^{d}*ú-mu*) is interpreted by him as a trait of Aramaic influence in Mesopotamia.

It is possible to interpret 'day' as well as 'night' as a relic of the concept of →Olden Gods who are often found in pairs. In the lists of deities in the Hurro-Hittite treaties after the twelve (or nine) 'olden gods' various pairs of elements from the natural order are listed: Mountains and Rivers, Springs and Great Sea, →Heaven and Earth (CROSS 1976). In the Aramaic treaty, a comparable pattern seems to have been followed: after eleven pairs of deities with proper names, three pairs of deified elements from the natural order are invoked: Heaven and Earth; Abyss and Springs; Day and Night.

In Greek religion, ἡμέρα, 'day', rarely occurs as deified or personified. An interesting exception is found in Hesiod, *Theogony* 123-124, where it is stated that →Night and Desert—seen as divine—are the parents of Aither and Hemera/Day. The sequence Night - Day might indicate progress (WEST 1966).

III. In the OT *yôm* generally is used as a common noun denoting a part of time. 'Day' can be used to refer to a period of 24 hours, from sunset to sunset, or to the period of daylight as well, from dawn to sunset. The noun occurs in different constructions each referring to a specific time or period: *hāyyôm*, 'today'; *ʿad hāyyôm hazzeh*, 'until this day' (e.g. S. J. DE VRIES, *Yesterday, Today and Tomorrow* [Grand Rapids 1975]). In the construction *yôm yhwh*, 'the day of the LORD', a forthcoming period of change and ordeal is indicated. In the creation story (Gen 1:5) the day is interpreted as a created element (VON SODEN, BERGMAN & SAEBØ 1982).

A personified 'day' is found at Ps 19:3; Jer 20:14 and Job 3. In the first textual unit of Ps 19 it reads "A day relates it to the (next) day; a night announces knowledge to the (next) night". Since Ps 19 might be interpreted as a polemic against the cult of the sun-god (HOUTMAN 1993), the mythological background of 'Day' and 'Night', who like 'Heaven' (v 2), play a part in the announcement of divine majesty, adds a touch of piquancy to the poem. In Jer 20:14 and Job 3:1-10 the birthday of a sorrowful man is lamented presenting the 'day' in a way similar to the poetic personification in the Mesopotamian texts discussed above (JACOBSEN & NIELSEN 1992:192-204).

IV. *Bibliography*

F. M. CROSS, The 'Olden Gods' in Ancient Near Eastern Creation Myths, *Magnalia Dei* (FS G. E. Wright; ed. F. M. Cross, W. E. Lemke & P. D. Miller; Garden City 1976) 329-338; C. HOUTMAN, *Der Himmel im Alten Testament* (OTS 30; Leiden 1993) 164-167; T. JACOBSEN & K. NIELSEN, Cursing the day, *SJOT* 6 (1992)187-204; W. VON SODEN, J. BERGMAN & M. SAEBØ, *jôm*, *TWAT* 5 (1982) 559-586; M. L. WEST, *Hesiod Theogony* (Oxford 1966) 197; F. A. M. WIGGERMANN, *Babylonian Prophylactic Figures* (Amsterdam 1986); R. ZADOK, On the historical Background of the Sefire Treaty, *AION* 44 (1984) 529-538.

B. BECKING

DAY STAR → HELEL

DEAD מת / מתים

I. The Hebrew Bible uses the word *mēt/mētîm* to refer to the dead as well as the related term *rĕpā'îm* →'Rephaim'. Several words (*nepeš mēt, nepeš 'ādām, peger, gĕwiyyâ, nĕbēlâ, mappēlâ, gûpâ*) are used to refer to the corpses of humans and/or animals. On occasions, the word *'ĕlōhîm*, literally 'gods', is used to denote the preternatural character of the dead (cf. 1 Sam 28:13; LEWIS 1989:115-116). Shades of the dead are referred to by such terms as *'ôb/'ōbôt* (→Spirit of the dead) and *yiddĕ'ōnî/ yiddĕ'ōnîm* ('knowing ones'?) (→Wizard). The exact etymologies of these two terms are unclear although the 'knowing' aspect of *yiddĕ'ōnîm* may suggest a special knowledge which the dead were presumed to have.

Ugaritic refers to the dead with the similar terms *mt, rpu* (cf. *KTU* 1.161; *KTU* 1.6 vi:45-49); and, on occasions *il* and *ilnym* (cf. *KTU* 1.113; *KTU* 1.6 vi:45-49). *ilib* is used in numerous pantheon lists and sacrificial lists to designate the paternal ghost (LEWIS 1989:56). In Akkadian, *mītu* refers to dead people as well as to the spirit/ghost of the dead (cf. *CAD* M1 140-142). More common, however, is the use of the term *eṭemmu* to refer to one's ghost (*CAD* E 397-401; →Etemmu). Akk also uses *ilu*, literally 'god', to designate the spirits of the dead (LEWIS 1989:49-51). A dead person is called *mt* in Egypt. The word *nṯr*, 'god', is also used to denote the deceased (usually a king) (E. HORNUNG, *Conceptions of God in Ancient Egypt* [Ithaca 1982] 58-59). Yet the primary terms for referring to the various aspects of the dead are *ka*, *ba*, and *aḫ*. The concepts underlying this terminology are difficult to recover. These terms also seem to have been used in various ways throughout Egyptian history.

II. Ancient Near Eastern literature and cultic implements attest a fascination with the mysteries of death. What happened to the life force which once inhabited the flesh? Is there an afterlife? Where do the dead reside; and do they have a patron deity in whose charge they are placed? Is their state one of weakness or vitality? Do the dead have knowledge and/or abilities beyond those of the living so that they may be petitioned for favors? Or are the dead malevolent creatures who have to be accorded the proper funerary rites lest they harm the living with all sorts of diseases?

The various ancient Near Eastern cultures came up with different answers to these questions. All of these societies held beliefs which were very complex and even pluralistic. It is typical to find treatments which, due to their brevity, describe these cultures as if they were all monolithic and uniform throughout time. It is more accurate to underscore the complex nature of these civilizations which were not static through time. One should also underscore our inability to succeed in giving anything more than a rudimentary account of an ancient Near Eastern comparative thanatology.

Egypt. Egyptian practices varied through time and social class. A complete understanding of the Egyptian view of the dead is hampered by the elusive nature of the concepts of the *ka*, the *ba*, and the *aḫ* which depict various modes or forms of existence in which the deceased continued to abide (cf. H. BRUNNER, *Grundzüge der altägyptischen Religion* [Darmstadt 1983] 143); ŽABKAR (1968:113) has argued that "though the ancient Egyptian was thought to live after death in a multiplicity of forms, each of these forms was the full man himself". In contrast to this emphasis on monism, other scholars maintain that some kind of pluralism remains in these three components which together made up the human personality after death (J. G. GRIFFITHS, *JEA* 56 [1970] 228).

The *ka*, which is portrayed by two raised arms, has been thought to represent the vitality of a person although it is also associated with protection and embracing. The *ka* is created alongside of a person at birth. In the early period, only the king had a *ka*. When one dies he 'goes to his *ka*' which survives the death of the body. In the tomb, it is the *ka* which receives the food and drink offerings through the false door of the mastaba tomb. The *ba* is represented as a human-headed bird (occasionally with arms and hands); thus symbolizing movement and perhaps the notion of human freedom: even after death. The term *ba* is used to describe the substance and vitality of the gods as well as a living force which animates inanimate images. Similarly, the *ba* of the dead in some way represents the manifestation of the power of the deceased (but not an external 'soul' as some have argued). It has been described as the personification of a person's vital forces or even, as Žabkar remarks, the personified 'alter ego of the deceased' (ŽABKAR 1968:113, 160). It functions primarily after death where it is seen going in and out of the tomb door in order to perform duties for the dead (e.g. bringing food and drink offerings). It can also leave the tomb to travel with the Sun God. In the Coffin Texts, the *ba* is seen as the agent of sexual activity after death, a motif which was used to depict a pleasant afterlife (ŽABKAR 1968:101). The *aḫ* has been described as representing the transfigured or effective spirit which came into being only in the next world. While one's *aḫ* is usually beneficial in nature, on occasion it can refer to evil spirits (see below). Compare also the 'Antef Song' which protests the efficacy of the mortuary cult by advising one to be an *aḫ* on earth. In other words, one should enjoy earthly pleasures in one's lifetime because tombs (and perhaps the dead?) crumble and become non-existent (M. V. FOX, *The Song of Songs and the Egyptian Love Songs* [Madison 1985] 346-347).

The Egyptian evidence presents an equally complex picture when it comes to viewing the existence of the dead in the next world. On the one hand, we have contracts hiring *ka*-priests to continue providing offerings because of the fear of hunger and thirst in the afterlife. On numerous occasions we read in the Book of the Dead of the fear of being reduced to eating and drinking one's own excrement. Prayers were offered (often to →Osiris and Nut) to ensure good cuisine in the afterlife. Spells were invoked to ward off suffering from lack of provisions. One could also compare the various amulets fashioned for apotropaic purposes. ZANDEE has illustrated other aspects of death which the Egyptians saw as quite frightening (1960).

On the other hand, we have numerous descriptions of death as an idyllic existence where food and drink were supplied in abundance in a utopian place called the Field of Offerings or Reeds. Royalty could even enjoy the prospects of joining the sun god as he sailed across the sky in his solar barque. Upon death royalty, and non-royalty as time passed, were identified with Osiris, who was the primary god of the netherworld (J. G. GRIFFITHS, *The Origins of Osiris and His Cult* [Leiden 1980]). Similarly, mummification, the extremely intricate (almost 'scientific') practice of preserving the body itself for the next world, was extended beyond royalty after the Old Kingdom. In short, the Egyptian view of the afterlife held both these optimistic and pessimistic views together. One could be optimistic about the afterlife: yet also realistic about the dangers of the hereafter (and hence one should plan accordingly).

Provisions were sometimes given to the dead in order to secure favors from them. In the 'letters to the dead' (written by the living) we read of people promising to deposit offerings (or pour out water) for a deceased relative if he/she will remove an infirmity from or fight on behalf of the living. In the Paheri mortuary text we read of the dead promising favors to the living in exchange for food: "The dead is a father to him who acts for him, he does not forget him who libates for him." The dead were not usually thought to have an evil disposition toward the living; although some letters refer to their malevolence. The term *aḫ* can refer to an evil spirit (cf. the Coptic cognate which refers to a 'demon'). The Bentresh stela mentions an ill woman who was 'in the condition of one under the Akhs' (ŽABKAR 1968:88).

Mesopotamia. To say the least, people living in ancient Mesopotamia were not very optimistic when it came to death. They were acutely aware that death is human destiny. A well known passage from the Gilgamesh Epic informs us that, at the time of creation, the gods allotted death to humans. Utnapishtim, the hero of the flood story who receives immortality, is an exception to the rule. The gods kept immortality for themselves (gods can be 'killed' of course by other deities; but, in theory, they are immortal and never die a human death). Elsewhere Gilgamesh acknowledges human mortality by quoting a well known proverb about how humans ('even the tallest') cannot scale heaven for their days are numbered (cf. J. TIGAY, *The Evolution of the Gilgamesh Epic* [Philadelphia 1982] 164-165).

Mesopotamian societies did not develop the elaborate funerary industry of Egypt complete with professionals skilled in all matters of interment including mummification. Nor did the ancient Mesopotamians develop the Egyptians' notion of an idyllic afterlife full of pleasures untold. Nonetheless, the ancient Mesopotamians were just as much preoccupied with death (cf. SPRONK 1986:96-124). They chose, however, to concentrate on the horrors and difficulties of death: such as the arduous and dangerous journey to 'the land-of-no-return'. This land (**ki**, *erṣetu*) was the domain of →Nergal and Ereshkigal, the king and queen of the netherworld, Shamash (on Shamash's role in the underworld, see LEWIS 1989:35-42), the Anunnaki, and Gilgamesh not to mention a host of minor deities and demons (See also Tammuz). The dead were depicted as living in darkness eating mud and filth and drinking foul water (cf. *Ishtar's Descent to the Netherworld*; BOTTÉRO 1992:276-277). In addition to providing the dead with proper burial rites, the living (primarily a caretaker called a *pāqidu* or *sāḫiru*) were also responsible for offering the proper *kispu* cult which followed the initial interment. This included providing food offerings (*kispa kasāpu*), pouring water (*mê naqû*), and invoking the name of the dead (*šuma zakāru*) (BAYLISS 1973:116). These meals underscored and reinforced family/clan solidarity among the living and their dead ancestors. It was also thought that by offering the proper death cult one could possibly receive favors from the dead. We read of kings providing *kispu* meals for their deceased ancestors with the plea that they will bless the current reign. On other occasions, we hear of the dead interceding for the living before the council of the Anunnaki. Necromancy also allowed one to obtain information about the future from the deceased which would not otherwise be known to the living (FINKEL 1983-1984:1-17). Yet, much more often we find that proper services were rendered to placate the dead so that they might not act malevolently.

The existence of malevolent ghosts (*eṭemmu*; Sum **gidim** →Etemmu) who haunt and harm the living is ubiquitous. The primary reasons for a ghost to be angry were a violent death, lack of burial, or the lack of funerary offerings. SCURLOCK (1988:93-94) has also documented numerous other reasons which cause ghosts to be malevolent: a strange ghost; a relative's ghost; a forgotten ghost; a ghost from the distant past; a ghost who was not invoked by name; a ghost who had to roam the steppe-lands; a ghost who died as a result of a sin against a god or an offence against the king. Often even an irregular death, not necessarily a violent death, could explain the presence of a malevolent ghost. Malevolent ghosts may be the result of people who died in water, in a river, in a well, from a chill, from being thrown in a ditch, from physical hunger, from thirst, etc. Sometimes exorcism was needed for ghosts of those who have simply died of natural causes.

Exorcistic rituals were developed to ward off the effects of malevolent ghosts. Sometimes these involved funerary (*kispu*) offerings to satisfy the hunger and thirst of the dead. Other rituals for expelling malevolent ghosts involved intricate incantations involving donkey urine, groat water, ditch water, ashes, camelthorn, and other such 'eye-of-newt' ingredients (SCURLOCK 1988:271-273). These are not offerings to the ghosts but rather spells to ward off their perceived evil (cf. *namburbi* apotropaic rituals). Other exorcistic texts describe throwing substitute ghost statues into a river, providing a proper burial, drawing magic circles, knotting red and white wool together, etc. All of this was a part of the cult of the dead aimed at controlling the dead so that they would return once again to the land-of-no-return (note the logical inconsistency).

Canaan. Understanding the Canaanite view of the dead is more difficult because of a paucity of evidence both literary and archaeological. The Ugaritic tablets have increased our knowledge considerably, yet even they give a window into just one of the civilizations associated with Canaanite religion. (For an introduction to the Phoenician view of death, see S. MOSCATI, *The Phoenicians* [Milan 1988] 123-124). In addition, due to the poor state of preservation of the texts, as well as the lack of vowel indicators, many alternative readings and reconstructions are possible. In short, when it comes to defining many crucial aspects of Ugaritic religion, differing opinions are commonplace.

Ugaritic refers to the dead with the terms *mt /mtm* ('the dead'), *rpu/rpum* (the 'Rapiʾuma') and, on occasions *il /ilm* and *ilnym*, two terms which may reflect the preternatural character of the deceased. *KTU* 1.6 vi:45-49 seems to present all four of these terms as roughly parallel (cf. also the expressions *ilm arṣ* and *rpu arṣ,* where *arṣ* most certainly refers to the netherworld, similar to Akk *erṣetu* and Heb *ʾereṣ*). *npš* may refer to the life force which departs at death like a gust of wind or a whiff of smoke (*KTU* 1.18 iv:25, 36; but cf. the invocation of the *nbš* in a death banquet in *KAI* 214). *ilib* is used in numerous Ugaritic pantheon lists and sacrificial lists to designate the paternal ghost (→Ilib).

One of the major concepts used in connection with the dead (*rpu/rpum*) is shrouded in debate. Scholars are of divided opinion when it comes to deciding to what degree the Ugaritic *rpum* are identical to the Hebrew →Rephaim. The majority of scholars would see the term referring to the dead or, more accurately, the the denizens of the underworld. Both the Phoenician *rpʾm* and the Hebrew *rĕpāʾîm* amply attest this usage in unambiguous contexts. Some would restrict the term to refer only to the privileged dead: primarily to deceased kings. Far less likely is the view of some scholars who would deny *any* connection to the dead preferring to see the *rpum* as either lower deities or simply heroic warriors (cf. B. B. SCHMIDT, *Israel's Beneficent Dead* [diss. Oxford 1991] 124-161). The Ugaritic texts describe the *rpum* with bird imagery, a notion which is found frequently throughout the ancient Near East (SPRONK 1986:167; VAN DER TOORN 1988:211).

The etymology of *rpum* has occasioned an equal amount of discussion. In the past it has been connected with the Hebrew root *rph*, 'to sink, relax', assuming that this was the condition of the dead (cf. Isa 14:10). Few scholars would embrace this etymology today (but cf. J. C. DE MOOR, *ZAW* 88 [1976] 340-341 who sees the biblical vocalization as a deliberate misreading) and, as will be seen below, the *rpum* are anything but inactive. More recently, some scholars have translated *rpum* as 'healers' (vocalizing *rāpi'ūma* as an active participle) while others translate 'heroes' (vocalizing *rapi'ūma* as a stative with the connotation hale, hearty, robust) similar to the usage of *hērōs* in Greek funeral games and the cult of heroes.

The publication of the so-called Ugaritic Funerary Text (*KTU* 1.161) gives us one of our clearest pictures of the Ugaritic *rpum*. If the term *rpum* refers to the dead (which seems likely), then this text describes a ritual in which a new king (Ammurapi) invokes (cf. the Mesopotamian death cult rite of invoking the name mentioned above) the presence of deceased royal ancestors (called PN, the *rp'*) in order to partake in the funerary ceremony of the recently deceased king (Niqmaddu III). After offering the proper sacrifices, the new ruler then beseeches these '*rpum* of old' (also called the '*rpum* of the underworld') to bless his current administration with well-being (*šlm*). In short, this text demonstrates that the dead were not simply cut off from the living. Rather, they continued to exist in the underworld and, with proper invocation, could be beseeched to grant favors to the living. To what degree this was a royal prerogative only remains to be understood.

The 'land' (*arṣ* = netherworld) in which the dead reside is described as an abode of ooze (*hmry*), decay (*mk*), and slime (*ḫḫ*). Yet, on occasions, it is also described as *dbr // šd šḥlmmt*. These terms are difficult to interpret, but they seem to refer to the desert steppe: thus illustrating the forces of death and drought. The underworld is ruled by the deity →Mot ('Death') who is described as having a voracious appetite which cannot be quenched. Elsewhere we have a description of Mot eating with both hands (LEWIS, *ABD* 4, 922-924). The insatiable appetite of Death reflects the Ugaritic notion that all humans must die. Even King Keret who is described as El's son must die. Mot/Death can be conquered by Baal and Anat; but the texts at our disposal fall far short of supporting Spronk's claim that there was a periodic revivification of the dead (VAN DER TOORN, 1991:40-66).

Occasionally the term *ilu*, 'god', is used to refer to the dead. We have evidence of a divine determinative (*il*) used with royal names in the so-called Ugaritic King List (*KTU* 1.113) [cf. the usage of *ilu* in Akkadian to refer to the dead]. The term *ilm* 'gods' also seems to occur parallel to *mtm* 'the dead' in *KTU* 1.6 vi:48-49. This so-called 'deification of the dead' may have been due to Egyptian influence. Yet Ugaritic beliefs did not ascribe immortality to their dead (cf. Keret) such as was the case with the Egyptian pharaoh. By choosing the term *ilu* 'god' to describe the dead, the Ugaritians were probably trying to describe some type of transcendent character, perhaps what we would call preternatural (cf. the use of *'ĕlōhîm* in the Hebrew Bible below).

Additional deities intimately connected to the dead include Shapshu; a deity called *rpu mlk 'lm* probably referring to Milku; and *ilib*, a term used to refer to the paternal ghost.

Ugaritic contains the idioms 'to reach the sunset' and 'to enter the host of the sun' to signify death. Underlying these idioms was the assumption that the goddess Shapshu was intimately connected to the deceased (as was her male counterpart Shamash in the Mesopotamian sphere). Shapshu figures prominently in the Ugaritic Funerary Text (*KTU* 1.161). Her exact role is somewhat debated, however. Some have her burning brightly while others have her escorting the dead king or the ghost throne of the king down to the netherworld. The latter is congruent with the notion that the sun deity descends into the underworld each night and thus is the proper deity to escort the dead to their final abode. The end of the Baal cycle (*KTU* 1.6 vi:45-49) describes Shapshu as presiding over (some scholars would translate 'ruling' or 'judging') the dead.

Another chthonic deity goes by the name *rpu mlk 'lm*, (*KTU* 1.108). This deity would seem to be the eponymous patron deity of the *rpum*; but, once again, scholars are of differing opinion when it comes to his identity. Suggestions range from an independent god named Rapiu to →El, →Baal, →Mot,

→Resheph, and Milku (cf. →Molech; see PARDEE, *Textes para-mythologiques* [Paris 1988] 85-90). The Rephaim texts (*KTU* 1.20-22) are extremely relevant for our reconstruction of the Ugaritic dead, yet their poor state of preservation prevents us from drawing many conclusions with any certainty. If we are talking about references to the dead and not human warriors as some would assert, then the dead are described as quite active. The Ugaritic *rpum* hitch up horses, gallop on stallions, and ride for three days. They also sit down to a banquet set for them presumably by the god El (cf. *KTU* 1.114). Some scholars (POPE 1981:176) have argued that this banquet (*mrzʿ/mrzḥ*) was 'a feast for and with the departed ancestors, corresponding to the Mesopotamian kispu'. Others (e.g. LEWIS 1989:80-94; *ABD* 1, 581-582) have argued that the *mrzḥ* was primarily a drinking club which was only secondarily associated with funerary customs.

Attention must also be given to the deity *ilib* who occurs frequently in the Ugaritic epic texts, sacrificial and offering lists, and pantheon lists. The latter categorize deities in order of importance and it is quite remarkable that *ilib* is consistently ranked at the top. Though this deity has also been the subject of much speculation (especially because of its supposed relation to the biblical 'god of the fathers'), it seems most reasonable to suppose that *ilib* refers to the spirit of the dead ancestor (see →Ilib). This is supported both on etymological as well as comparative grounds (cf. the Hurrian equivalent *en atn*).

Finally, a word should be said about the use of archaeology to understand the treatment of the Ugaritic dead. Ever since C. Schaeffer's archaeological reports, various Ugaritic funerary installations (notably ceramic pipes and gutters, so-called 'libation pits', and windows and holes in ceilings) have been used to support the notion that an essential part of the Ugaritic cult of the dead, like the Mesopotamian practices mentioned above, was the duty to provide the dead with libations. New analyses of the archaeological material has overturned these conclusions. PITARD (fc.) has recently shown how Schaeffer misinterpreted the data (mistaking the harbor town for a necropolis) and that the archaeological installations are of the mundane variety (e.g. water gutters, latrines). Pitard concludes that there is simply no archaeological evidence for a regular, ongoing ritual of providing food and libations for the deceased at Ugarit.

III. The two main words used in the Hebrew Bible for the dead are *mēt/mētîm* and *rĕpā'îm*. These two terms occur parallel to each other in Ps 88:11 ('Do you work wonders for the dead, do the shades rise to praise you?') and Isa 26:14 ('The dead do not live, the shades do not rise'; cf. 26:19). The meaning of *mēt/mētîm* is not in doubt and refers to the dead regardless of the manner of death. Thus it can refer to a person who dies by the sword or famine (Jer 11:22) or even a stillborn (Num 12:12). When *mēt* refers to the corpse, the masculine form may be used for both genders (Gen 23:3-4).

In contrast to *mēt/mētîm*, the exact connotations of *rĕpā'îm* remain in doubt. A full treatment will be presented elsewhere (→Rephaim). It should be noted, meanwhile, that the term *rĕpā'îm* is used to represent the dead (Ps 88:11; Prov 2:18; 21:16; Isa 26:14; Job 26:5) as well as an ancient people sometimes referred to as →giants (Gen 14:5; cf. Deut 2:10; Num 13:33). Scholars have long debated the degree to which these two classifications are related. Perhaps the oldest substratum of the term referred to an ancient people, especially the royal heroes of old (cf. Isa 14:9 and the Ugaritic cognate [*rapi'ūma*] referring to the royal dead). As time went on, the term perhaps became democratized to refer to the dead in general.

The abode of the dead (→Sheol) is described with pervasive, negative imagery as a place of dust and silence with imprisoning bars and gates (LEWIS, *ABD* 2 101-105). Sheol is also personified as the chthonic power behind death (parallel to the power of Mot). Even the etymology of Sheol seems to underscore that it was viewed as anything but idyllic. Rather, it was a place of interrogation, judgment, and punishment. Another poetic name for the underworld, →Abaddon, means '(place of) Destruction'. Thus it is most difficult to equate the Israelite conception of the underworld with the Egyptian Field of Offerings. The comment in Job 7:9 that 'he who goes down to Sheol does not come up' (*yôrēd šĕʾôl lōʾ yaʿăleh*) echoes the Mesopotamian description of the netherworld as, 'the land of no return' (*māt la târi*) more than anything Egyptian.

Even though the Hebrew Bible uses *ʾādām* and *nepeš* as rough synonyms referring to a person of either sex (J. MILGROM, *Leviticus 1-16* [AB; New York 1991] 178-179), it also speaks of a person (*ʾādām*) being animated by a life force which is termed either a *nĕšāmâ* (cf. *nišmat ḥayyîm* in Gen 2:7) or a *rûaḥ* (cf. *rûaḥ ḥayyîm* in Gen 6:17; *nišmat rûaḥ ḥayyîm* in Gen 7:22). This life force comes from God and, upon death, returns back to God (Job 34:14; Eccl 12:7). Upon animation, an *ʾādām* becomes a living creature (*nepeš ḥayyâ*; cf. Gen 2:7). The departure of the life force (= biological death) is described as the 'going out' of the *nepeš* or *rûaḥ* (Gen 35:18; Ps 146:4). Once this life force departs, one is a *nepeš mēt* ('dead person'), an expression which refers to the corpse itself (Lev 21:11; Num 6:6; cf. M. SELIGSON, *The Meaning of nepeš mēt in the Old Testament* [Helsinki 1951]) as does *nepeš ʾādām* (Num 9:6.7; Ezek 44:25). Sometimes *nepeš* alone is used to designate the dead (e.g. the characteristic usage by the Holiness Code and P: Lev 19:28; 21:1; Num 5:2; 6:11; 9:10). Both *peger* and *gĕwiyyâ* can refer either to a living or a dead body (a carcass or corpse; cf. also *ḥālāl* 'slain' and *nāpal* 'to fall (= to die)'; cf. *nĕpîlîm*, '→Nephilim' (= fallen heroic dead?) which are equated with the Rephaim in Deut 2:11 (cf. R. HENDEL, *JBL* 106 [1987] 21-22; cf. *mappēlâ* 'carcass' only in Judg 14:8). Twice *peger* is modified by the word *mētîm* (2 Kgs 19:35; Isa 37:36). *peger* refers exclusively to the human corpse except for Gen 15:11. *gĕwiyyâ* (cf. *gûpâ* 1 Chr 10:12 // 1 Sam 31:12) can refer to a human corpse (Saul in 1 Sam 31:10.12) or an animal corpse (Judg 14:8-9). *nĕbēlâ* can also refer to the corpse of either an animal or a person, yet it is never used for a living body. In the Hebrew Bible, bones are known for their defiling property (cf. Num 19:16.18; 2 Kgs 23:20). 2 Kgs 13:20-21 shows that bones (at least Elisha's) were not viewed merely as skeletal remains, but rather could have healing powers. In this pericope, a corpse is revived when it comes into contact with Elisha's bones which still possess the healing powers that the prophet exhibited in his lifetime.

Ancient Israel possessed a strong notion of clan solidarity which is reflected in the description of the dead joining their ancestors in the underworld. According to P's characteristic vocabulary, when one dies he is said to 'be gathered to his kin' *neʾĕsap ʾel ʿammāyw* (Gen 25:8.17; 35:29; 49:29.33; Num 20:24.26; 27:13; 31:2). A variant of this formula stemming from the Deuteronomistic tradition is 'to be gathered to one's *fathers*' (Judg 2:10; 2 Kgs 22:20 = 2 Chr 34:28). The Deuteronomistic tradition also has its own distinctive vocabulary of 'resting with one's fathers' *šākab ʿim ʾăbôtāyw* (LEWIS 1989:164 n.11).

Shades of the dead are denoted by the terms *ʾôb/ʾōbôt* (→Spirit of the dead) and *yiddĕʿōnî/yiddĕʿōnîm* ('knowing ones'?) (Wizard). The exact etymologies of these words are unclear; though the 'knowing' aspect may suggest a special knowledge which the dead were perceived to have. The two terms are most often found together and may have functioned as a hendiadys. Both of these words can be used elliptically to refer to necromancers. In one instance (Isa 19:3), ghosts are referred to by the term *ʾiṭṭîm* which, although *hapax legomenon* in Hebrew, is certainly to be equated with the Akk *eṭemmu* 'spirit of the dead' (see above) despite the double *ṭ*. The biblical material is more like the Egyptian than the Mesopotamian in its general silence about the malevolent dead. The presence of amulets for apotropaic purposes at various burial sites (cf. BLOCH-SMITH 1992:83-85) suggests that we are not getting the whole story (but see below on the wisdom tradition).

Was there a cult of the dead in ancient Israel? The Deuteronomistic legal material in the Hebrew Bible reveals restrictions against consulting the dead (Deut 18:9-11): presumably presenting offerings to the dead (Deut 26:14), and engaging in certain practices associated with death rituals such as self-laceration (Deut 14:1; but cf. Jer 16:6; 41:5) which seem to have been typical of Canaanite death cult practice. The Holiness Code also contains categorical prohibitions against people who turn to necromancy and demands the death penalty for any mediums or necromancers (Lev 20:6, 27). From such laws we may safely infer that cults of the dead existed and flourished in ancient Palestine to the extent that they were considered a threat to what eventually emerged as normative Yahwism. This seems to be supported by references to Manasseh's necromancy (2 Kgs 21:6) and Josiah's eradication of it (2 Kgs 23:24) however the Deuteronomist may be using stereotypical lists (or catalogues) of sins and reforms. Lastly, specific death cult vocabulary seems to underlie Absalom's erection of a funerary monument as well as Jezebel's burial (LEWIS 1989:118-122).

Two passages in the Hebrew Bible confirm the existence of the well known *marzēaḥ* banquet (see above). In Amos 6:7, the *marzēaḥ* banquet is described as revelry without any ties to death cult practices. Yet in Jer 16:5 the *marzēaḥ* has clear funerary connections. The context is one of mourning and bereavement. As with the Ugaritic *mrzḥ*, some scholars see the *raison d'être* for the *marzēaḥ* to be a banquet with the dead. Other scholars describe its primary function to be that of a drinking banquet which could, on occasions, be associated with funerary feasts. Another subject of debate is whether post-interment funerary offerings were presented to the dead in ancient Israel. Most scholars see hints of long term offerings of some kind behind such passages as Deut 26:14 ('I have not offered any of it [i.e. sacred food] to the dead'); Ps 106:28 ('they ate the sacrifices of the dead') and Isa 57:6-8 ('Even to them [the dead] have you poured out libations and brought offerings'). Funerary offerings of food and libations are well attested in the archaeological data (BLOCH-SMITH 1992:25-62, 106-108) yet it is difficult to determine whether this was solely at the time of interment or whether such a practice was on-going as a part of a regular cult of the dead.

Due to the Deuteronomistic polemic against death cult practices, it is surprising that we have an account of a necromantic ritual preserved in the Deuteronomistic History. In 1 Sam 28 king Saul uses a necromancer at En-Dor to conjure up the dead Samuel from the netherworld whose preternatural character is described as an *ʾĕlōhîm* (literally 'god'; see above). Even the efficacy of the conjuring is left intact by the editor. Unlike Mesopotamian texts which describe necromantic procedures in detail (cf. FINKEL 1983-1984:1-17), the En-Dor episode is remarkably brief about describing for us what was entailed in such an episode. Nonetheless, the narrative in 1 Sam 28 shows us that necromancy was well known in ancient Israelite religion despite efforts by Deuteronomists and those of like mind to eradicate the practice.

Necromancy was also criticized by certain biblical prophets. Isa 8:19 mocks the practice by comparing it to chirping and muttering (cf. Isa 29:4). Necromantic practices are similarly ridiculed in Isa 19:3 which describes the Egyptians' resorting to necromancy because of their lack of any capacity to reason. This is ironic due to the virtual lack of necromancy attested in ancient Egypt. VAN DER TOORN (1988:199-218) has also elucidated how communication with the dead lies behind Isa 28:7-22, a passage replete with death cult vocabulary (e.g. those making 'a covenant with Death ... a pact with Sheol'). In short, contrary to 1 Sam 28, no efficacy is ascribed to necromancy by these texts. The amount of literature against the practice of necromancy shows that many people in ancient Israelite society (including priestly and prophetic elements) felt that it was a legitimate form of divining the will of Yahweh. Other prophetic denunciations of death cult practices may be found in Ezek 43:7-9; Isa 45:18-19; 57:6; 65:4.

The traditions reflected in the wisdom literature expand the Deuteronomistic and prophetic polemic against necromancy to a new level. In Job 14:21 the dead are described as having no knowledge about the affairs of humans. Likewise, Eccl 9:4-6.10 says quite bluntly that the dead know nothing, for 'there is no work or reason or knowledge in Sheol'. Both of these views are strikingly different from the one in 1 Sam 28 in their appraisal of the ability of the deceased. A similar polemic against ascribing any power to the dead may be found in Ps 88:11 'Do the shades rise up to praise you?' Whereas the Ugaritic Rapi'uma are very active (see above), we have very few descriptions of the Israelite denizens of the underworld in an active role. The most activity is found in Isa 14:9 where the Rephaim are roused to greet the king of Babylon. For the most part, the biblical Rephaim are stripped of any power, malevolent or benevolent (cf. Isa 26:14).

IV. *Bibliography*

M. C. ASTOUR, The Netherworld and Its Denizens at Ugarit, *Death in Mesopotamia* (ed. B. Alster; Mesopotamia 8; Copenhagen 1980) 227-238; L. R. BAILEY, *Biblical Perspectives on Death* (Philadelphia 1979); M. BAYLISS, The Cult of Dead Kin in Assyria and Babylonia, *Iraq* 35 (1973) 115-125; E. BLOCH-SMITH, *Judahite Burial Practices and Beliefs about the Dead* (JSOTSup 123; Sheffield 1992); J. BOTTÉRO, The Mythology of Death, *Mesopotamia: Writing, Reasoning, and the Gods* (Chicago 1992) 268-286; I. L. FINKEL, Necromancy in Ancient Mesopotamia, *AfO* 29-30 (1983-1984) 1-17; T. J. LEWIS, *Cults of the Dead in Ancient Israel and Ugarit* (HSM 39; Atlanta 1989); W. T. PITARD, The 'Libation Installations' of the Tombs at Ugarit, *BA* (forthcoming); M. H. POPE, The Cult of the Dead at Ugarit, *Ugarit in Retrospect* (ed. G. D. Young; Winona Lake 1981) 159-179; J. A. SCURLOCK, *Magical Means of Dealing with Ghosts in Ancient Mesopotamia* (diss. Chicago 1988); K. SPRONK, *Beatific Afterlife in Ancient Israel and in the Ancient Near East* (AOAT 219; Neukirchen-Vluyn 1986); K. VAN DER TOORN, Echoes of Judaean Necromancy in Isaiah 28, 7-22, *ZAW* 100 (1988) 199-218; VAN DER TOORN, Funerary Rituals and Beatific Afterlife in Ugaritic Texts and in the Bible, *BiOr* 48 (1991) 40-66; L. V. ŽABKAR, *A Study of the Ba Concept in Ancient Egyptian Texts* (Chicago 1968); J. ZANDEE, *Death as an Enemy according to Ancient Egyptian Conceptions* (Leiden 1960).

T. J. LEWIS

DEATH → MOT; THANATOS

DEBER דבר

I. The accepted meaning 'pestilence' may be a specific Hebrew development with scarce support from other Semitic languages (cf. Ug *dbr* 'pestilence' [?], Ar *dabr* 'death', *dabara* 'ulcer'); Akk *dibiru* 'misfortune, calamity' is probably a Sumerian word, having no connexion with Hebr *deber* (*CAD D* 134-135). Deber is one of the three proverbial causes of death on a wide scale. It is attested some 50 times in the Bible along with war (sword, blood) and famine (mainly in Jer and Ez). Besides this empirical meaning, it seems to be used a number of times in a personified sense as a demon or evil deity (Hab 3:5; Ps 91:3, 6; cf. Hos 13:14).

II. In Mesopotamia the representation of illnesses as demons is very common (E. EBELING *RlA* 2 [1938] 112; EDZARD *WbMyth* I 47), as well as among the Hittites (VON SCHULER *WbMyth* I 161). In this connexion the Ugaritic text *KTU* 1.5 vi:6 & par. can offer some support. It speaks in a parallelistic way of the *arṣ dbr//šd šḫlmmt.* But the personification can only be assumed here if *šḫlmmt* is construed as 'the lion of *Mamētu*' (*WUS*, no 2589), which is rather unlikely. The empirical meanings 'pestilence' or 'steppe' are more suitable (cf. VAN ZIJL 1972:172-175; DE MOOR 1971:186 for the various interpretations).

III. More cogent is the parallelism with

→Resheph in Hab 3:14, given the presence of this deity in the Ugaritic texts as a god of destruction (*KTU* 1.14 I 18-19; 1.82:3; DE MOOR & SPRONK 1984:239). The eschatological hymn in Hab 3 presents Deber and Resheph marching at →Yahweh's side as His helpers. This follows the ancient Mesopotamian tradition according to which 'plague' and 'pestilence' are present in the entourage of the great god →Marduk (DE MOOR 1990:134). On the other hand, in Ps 91:6 it is Yahweh who liberates his faithful from the fear of this nocturnal demon Deber, in parallel this time with →Qeteb, another awesome destructive demon. Echoes of this representation can also be heard in Hos 13:14 (ANDERSEN & FREEDMAN 1980: 640).

IV. *Bibliography*

F. I. ANDERSEN & D. N. FREEDMAN, *Hosea. A New Translation with Introduction and Commentary* (AB 24; Garden City, New York 1980); J. C. DE MOOR, *The Seasonal Pattern in the Ugaritic Myth of Baʿalu* (AOAT 16; Kevelaer/Neukirchen-Vluyn 1971); DE MOOR, *The Rise of Yahwism. The Roots of Israelite Monotheism* (BETL 91; Leuven 1990), 128-136; J. C. DE MOOR & K. SPRONK, More on Demons in Ugarit, *UF* 16 (1984), 237-240; P. J. VAN ZIJL, *Baal. A Study of Texts in Connexion with Baal in the Ugaritic Epics* (AOAT 10; Kevelaer/Neukirchen-Vluyn 1972).

G. DEL OLMO LETE

DEDAN דדן

I. Dedan is one of the ancestors of the royal families of Ugarit and Assyria. According to Ugaritic texts he was deified. In both Ugaritic and Akkadian texts he is also named Datan or Ditan. This name can be related to Akk *ditānu*, *didānu*, 'bison' (*AHW* 173) or to Akk *datnu*, 'warlike'. It also appears as a personal name in the OT, viz. *dātān* (Num 16; Deut 11:6; Ps 106:17).

II. Didanu, Ditanu, or also Tidanu, is the name of a tribe living in the western part of ancient Mesopotamia first mentioned at the end of the third millennium BCE. The name Ditanu appears as a component in personal names in the second millennium BCE; cf. the names of two kings of the First Dynasty of Babylon: Ammiditana, 'headman of Ditanu' and Samsuditana, 'sun of Ditanu'. Here it seems to indicate the tribe of that name. It is also mentioned as the name of one of the royal ancestors in the list of the Amorite dynasty of Hammurabi and with the spelling Didanu in the Assyrian King list (FINKELSTEIN 1966:98). Apparently this name was now regarded as an eponym, the name of the tribe having been derived from the king's name. It is not certain whether a king with this name actually existed. If so, he links the dynasties of Babylon, Assur, and Ugarit (KITCHEN 1977:142). This status, be it historical or mythical, accords well with the prominent place he takes in some Ugaritic ritual texts related to the cult of the dead. In *KTU* 1.161 the spirits of the royal ancestors ('the Rephaim of the earth') are called 'the assembly of Dedan'. The parallelism between 'Rephaim of the earth (i.e., the netherworld)' and 'the assembly of Dedan' indicates that Dedan was regarded as the first of the deified royal ancestors. In this text the names of the deceased kings are called one by one to receive sacrifices. In return they are asked to hail the living king and his city. This assembly also occurs in the Ugaritic legend of Keret. Here it is called 'assembly of Ditan' (*KTU* 1.15.III:2-4.13-15). King Keret is said to have been exalted to this assembly after he received the promise of being blessed with the offspring he had been longing for. According to *KTU* 1.124 Ditan could be called upon to help a sick child. His 'judgement' consists of precise indications for the medicines to be used.

III. *Bibliography*

J. J. FINKELSTEIN, The Genealogy of the Hammurapi Dynasty, *JCS* 20 (1966) 95-118; K. A. KITCHEN, The King List of Ugarit, *UF* 9 (1977) 131-142; B. A. LEVINE & J. - M. DE TARRAGON, Dead Kings and Rephaim: The Patrons of the Ugaritic Dynasty, *JAOS* 104 (1984) 649-659; E. LIPIŃSKI, DITANU, *Studies in Bible and the Ancient*

Near East Presented to S.E. Loewenstamm (ed. Y. Avishur & J. Blau; Jerusalem 1978) 91-110.

K. SPRONK

DEMETER Δημήτηρ

I. Demeter is the Greek deity known and worshipped for her power over grain and thus the fertility of the earth, the food supply for human beings, and mystery rites that provide a happy afterlife. Acts 19:24,38 refers to a man named after her, Demetrius, a craftsman who made shrines of →Artemis; another Demetrius is mentioned in 3 John 1:12 as a reliable Christian.

II. Daughter of Kronos and Rhea, sister of →Zeus, and mother of Kore-Persephone, Demeter was often called the Corn Goddess. Through her close relation to Persephone, Demeter has strong connections with the underworld; the two are frequently mentioned simply as the Two Goddesses. Kore-Persephone was the young daughter of Demeter as well as the wife of Aidoneus or →Hades, and thus the queen of the dead.

The myth of Demeter is related in the well-known *Homeric Hymn to Demeter*, a poem of 495 lines and dating to the seventh century BCE. It was not the only version known to the ancient Greeks, however. An early reference to Persephone's abduction by Aidoneus in Hesiod that suggests the myth was known already in the eighth century (*Theogony* 913-14). Pausanias mentions a hymn by Pamphos that he considers pre-Homeric as well as a version he traced to Sicily (7.21.9, 8.37.9; 9.31.9), and Apollodorus provides a summary of the myth by drawing upon several versions (1.5). A number of poets were reputed to have written hymns to Demeter, including Archilochus, Lasus, Bacchylides, Pindar, and Aeschylus, although little is known for certain about the poems. The Parian Chronicle refers to an Orphic version of the myth of Demeter (KERN 1922: test. 221), and Pausanias mentions that Musaeus wrote about characters who figure in the myth (1.14.3), but most likely these versions reflect the Eleusinian account. In any case, the variants demonstrate that the myth of Demeter was widely known in ancient Greece, and vase paintings also testify to its popularity. Two other legends were related about Demeter. In the first, she loved Iasion and made love with him in a field that had lain fallow but was ploughed three times; the offspring of this union was Plutos, or rich harvests as the wealth of the earth (Homer, *Odyssey* 5.125-128; Hesiod, *Theogony* 969-975; Apollodorus 3.138). According to the second, a Thessalian named Erysichthon cut down the trees of a grove sacred to Demeter in order to build a palace. Although Demeter herself took the form of her priestess to urge him not to commit such impiety, he would not listen. She indicated that he would need a large hall for banquets, but he became so hungry that although he continually ate, he could not satisfy his hunger; eventually he was reduced to begging (Callimachos, *Hymn* 6. 24-119; Ovid, *Metam.* 8.738-878).

Of all the versions, the *Homeric Hymn to Demeter* is the most complete. It tells how Persephone was taken away by Aidoneus or Hades when she was picking flowers with her friends: as the young woman reached down to pluck a flower, the earth opened up and, with the consent of his brother Zeus, Hades carried her off to his underground realm. A crisis ensued. Demeter heard her abducted daughter crying for help and forsook the company of her fellow Olympians to search the cosmos for her daughter. In her grief and anger, and disguised as an old woman, Demeter went to Eleusis. At the well of the city she offered her services as nurse or housekeeper to the daughters of King Celeus; they informed their mother, Metaneira, whose new son, Demophon, needed looking after. On entering the palace, Demeter was charmed from her depression by Iambe's jesting and Metaneira's cup of red wine, water, meal, and mint. As nurse to the young Demophon, Demeter was beyond comparison, for she anointed him with ambrosia and placed him in the fire to make him immortal. When interrupted by Metaneira, however, Demeter rebuked her for the foolishness that prevented Demophon from being immortalized. Demeter also revealed herself as the deity she was, whereupon the Eleusinians built her a temple and an altar. Rather than return to →Olympus, Demeter secluded herself within her temple and caused a famine which threatened human existence and would eventually deprive the gods of the honor rendered to them by sacrifices. Zeus sent Iris and other gods to persuade Demeter to relent, but only when →Hermes was dispatched to Hades to reclaim Persephone would Demeter acquiesce. Promising his wife honors, rights, and gifts among the gods and in the underworld as well, Hades gave her a pomegranate seed, which meant that she would spend part of each year in the earth. The reunion between mother and daughter was joyful, and Demeter accepted the terms Zeus established, with Persephone to spend one-third of the year in Hades and two-thirds on Olympus with her mother. Before departing from Eleusis for Olympus, Demeter taught humans her rites and mysteries which gave happiness to initiates, both while alive and after death.

The cosmology of this myth displays a world in crisis. The tensions are many. One consists of the conflicts that divide the gods: Demeter insists that her daughter is returned to her, no matter what the cost; Hades must retain his bride, even if deceiving her is the price; Zeus will continue to govern the cosmos, even if compromising with his sister Demeter and his brother Hades is necessary. Another is seen in the way humans depend on the gods for life and livelihood as distinct from the way gods command honor and worship, although the absence of worship comes perilously close to threatening the existence of the gods. Demeter conceals herself, too, from humans at the same time that she acts in a most motherly fashion to Demophon, her 'second child', but then reveals herself to be one of the august deities whose power over the food supply renders gods and humans vulnerable to her unless her motherly demands for her daughter are met. In both the human and the divine realms, the power of males is assumed and females are identified by their relation to male values, for as kings and their sons rule, females nurse and serve; in the divine world, the parallel to the gender division is the male privilege of marriage, as seen in Hades' abduction of Persephone which provoked the crisis, and Demeter's demands which prepared the way for resolution while restricting her identity to that of mother. The resolution of the crisis returned the cosmos to order, although the new order recognized the increased power of Demeter and Persephone and gave humans a new hope in an afterlife through the mystery rites of Demeter.

The celebration of the mystery rites of Demeter took place at many locations in Greece. Pausanias, who travelled in Greece around 150 CE, reported that more than 50 cities had temples of Demeter, demonstrating that both the cult and the myth of Demeter were widespread in ancient Greece. It was also kept secret, although architectural and iconographic as well as literary materials afford sufficient evidence to allow a general picture of the events as well as their meaning. Offerings of food and the sacrifice of pigs, and fasting and feasting, processions and bathing, sacred chests and torches at night were all part of the ceremonies. The many local variations could emphasize one or another of the aspects of the worship of Demeter. Some cultic practices excluded men but others made room for them, and some focused on clan membership but others on initiation; an interest in the life of women, in seed and the food supply and in an afterlife are general traits. In Hellenistic and Roman times, the mysteries, particularly those of Eleusis, gained in prestige as people came from many places to be initiated. In 395 CE the sanctuary was destroyed by the Goths.

The festivals—the Thesmophoria and Stenia in the fall, the Skira at the time of cutting and threshing grain, and the famous Mysteria of Athens and Eleusis—linked the fertility of humans and particularly women to the fertility of the earth. By linking the mother-daughter relationship together with its anguish over separation and joy upon reunion with the divine world of conflict and resolution, the human needs and emotions connected with marriage, food, birth, and death were brought together. (→Tammuz)

III. *Bibliography*

W. BURKERT, *Ancient Mystery Cults* (Cambridge, Mass. 1987); L. R. FARNELL, *The Cults of the Greek States*, vol. 3 (Oxford 1907) 1-279; O. KERN, *Orphicorum Fragmenta* (Berlin 1922); G. E. MYLONAS, *Eleusis and the Eleusinian Mysteries* (Princeton 1961); H. W. PARKE, *Festivals of the Athenians* (Ithaca NY 1977), esp. 55-72, 95-103, 156-169; N. J. RICHARDSON, *The Homeric Hymn to Demeter* (Oxford 1974).

L. J. ALDERINK

DEMON Δαίμων, Δαιμόνιον

I. The term 'demon' is the rendering of the cognate Greek words δαίμων and its substantivized neuter adjective δαιμόνιον; post-classical Latin borrowed the words in the forms *daemon* and *daemonium*. The original meaning of the term δαίμων from the time of Homer onward was 'divinity', denoting either an individual god or goddess (of →Aphrodite in *Il.* 3.420), or the Deity as an unspecified unity (*Od.* 3.27 "the Deity will put it in your mind"). Δεισιδαιμονία means 'reverence for the Divinity', or simply 'religion' (Acts 25:19; cf. 17:22). Plato derived the word from the near homonym δαήμων, meaning 'knowing' (*Crat.* 398b, from the root *δάω, 'to know'); Eusebius rejected this conjecture and instead derived the term from δειμαίνειν, 'to fear' (*Praep. Ev.* 4.5.142). The etymology more likely stems from the root δαίω,'to divide (destinies)'. Thus the word could designate one's 'fate' or 'destiny', or the spirit controlling one's fate, one's 'genius'. Commonly the word designated the class of lesser divinities arranged below the Olympian gods, the *daimones*. Hesiod describes them as the souls of those who lived in the Golden Age, who now invisibly watch over human affairs (*Erga* 122-124).

As nearly all deities in the classical period were morally ambiguous, the *daimones* could be described as either good or evil, and the same *daimon* could bring both good or ill according to one's piety or fate. Not until post-Exilic times in intertestamental literature, with the rise of dualism and the concept of the →Devil, did the word begin to display the meaning 'evil demon in league with the Devil' and take on an entirely negative connotation (e. g. 1 Cor 10:20; cf. LXX Ps 105:37). Christian writers use it almost exclusively in this later sense. The related term δαιμόνιον in the classical period meant similarly 'the divine power' or 'the Divinity' (Plato, *Rep.* 382e; cf. Acts 17:18). It could also mean the class of lower divine beings 'between gods and mortals' who mediated between the human and divine spheres (Plato, *Sym.* 202e). So it designated the famous *daimonion* of Socrates (Plato, *Apol.* 24b, 40a). Again after the Exile and the rise of dualism it came to be used for 'Satanic demons', especially among Jewish and Christian writers and in non-Christian magical texts.

Two verbs from this root are important in Biblical and related literature: δαιμονάω and δαιμονίζομαι. Both originally meant 'to be under the power of a god or *daimon*', which condition was often a blessing, producing prophetic utterance or heroic behavior; it could also be a curse, and the words could mean 'to be insane'. In later authors, especially Jewish and Christian, they came to mean 'to be possessed by a demon' which caused bodily infirmity or insanity; in the sense 'to be insane' it was used pejoratively of the 'ravings' (= 'doctrines') of heretics (Eusebius, *Hist. eccl.* 7.31.1 of Mani). Δαιμονίζομαι is found once in the New Testament as a verb in the phrase "cruelly tormented by a demon" (Matt 15:22); all other of the dozen further occurrences are of the participle meaning 'one who is demonized', 'a demoniac' (e. g., Mark 1:32).

II. The word and concept 'demon' underwent fundamental change in antiquity caused by the rise of dualism in the essentially monistic cultures of the Near East.

These monistic cultures viewed the universe as a unified system in which each member, divine and human, had its proper domain and function above, upon, or below the earth. There was (as yet) no arch-enemy Devil, nor a rival camp of Satanic demons tempting and deceiving humans into sin and blasphemy, eventually to be cast into eternal hell at the final end of the present age. Humans also had their function in this diverse but unified system: to serve the gods and obey their dictates, their Law, for which they received their rewards while alive. After death all humans descended into the underworld from which there was no return; there was no Last Judgment, and no hope of resurrection.

Every occurrence in the world of the ancients had a spiritual as well as physical cause, determined by the gods. To enforce divine Law, to regulate the balance of blessing and curse in the human realm, and to ensure human mortality, the gods employed, among other means, the *daimones* (cf. Hesiod, *Erga* 252-255). Just as εὐδαιμονία meant 'prosperity, good fortune, happiness', and depended on the activity of a benevolent spirit, so κακοδαιμονία, 'ill fortune', was caused by some dark but legitimate power. The latter were the spirits of calamity and death who performed the will of the greater gods. In 1 Sam 16:14, for example, an →Evil Spirit from the LORD torments Saul; in 1 Kgs 22:19-23 Yahweh sends a lying spirit of false prophecy to Ahab; in Ex 12:23, to kill the firstborn of Egypt, Yahweh sends the →Destroyer, an agent of the Lord mentioned again in 1 Cor 10:10 and perhaps as →Abaddon / Apollyon in Rev 8:11 (cf. the Erinyes, Greek spirits of retribution, in *Il.* 9.571). The Mesopotamian story of Atrahasis shows that the demon Pashittu, a baby snatcher, was created by the gods to keep down human population (*Atr.* III vii 3-4). Sir 39:28-29 speaks of spirits created by the LORD for vengeance: fire, hail, famine and pestilence. Such spirits were often the offspring of the greater gods themselves (JACOBSEN 1976:13).

These spirits occupied the dangerous places: the desert, the lonely wastes, the deserted by-ways. →Rabiṣu, for example, the Croucher of horrible aspect, lay in wait in dark corners and alleys (cf. Gen 4:7). The scapegoat was sent to →Azazel, a desert demon, on the day of Atonement (Lev 16:8-28). They held power during dangerous situations and times: chiefly at night, during sleep, during a wind storm or an eclipse or the heat of mid-day, and especially in childbirth. →Lilith, a lascivious female demon, haunted a man in his dreams. The desert storm winds were thought to bring calamity and disease (cf. the Babylonian Pazuzu, king of the wind demons). The seven evil gods (cf. Deut 28:22) attacked the moon and caused the eclipse, after which "they swept over the land like a hurricane" (SAGGS 1962:291). The →Midday demon attacked the unwary with various ills at the height of the sun. Lamashtu, a terrifying spectre, threatened women and newborns during childbirth and stole suckling infants (cf. the *Lamia* and *Gello* in Greece). She was later identified with Lilith, who was the child-stealer in later Jewish folklore. They were often personifications of dire situations, especially plague (cf. in Greece Ἄτη, *Delusion*, and Νέμεσις, *Divine Retribution*). Namtar (*Fate*), the plague demon, was henchman of →Nergal the king of the Mesopotamian Underworld. →Resheph ('Flame', the Canaanite plague demon) and Deber ('Pestilence) accompany Yahweh as attendants as he descends in wrath against the earth (Hab 3:5). One of their main activities was to bring death (JACOBSEN 1976:13).

In contrast to the gods of the upper world, these spirits were often not in human form. The *shedu*'s of Babylon and Assyria (cf. Deut 32:17; Ps 106:37) were depicted as winged bulls. In Isa 34:14 Lilith as a carrion bird finds a nest in the desert wastes, and is joined by wild desert animals, owls and kites. Resheph is also conceived as a carrion bird (cf. LXX Deut 32:24). The →Devil, ruler of the demons, is called the →Serpent and →Dragon (e. g., Rev 12:9), recalling the serpent in the Garden (Gen 3:1) and the Dragon in the Sea (→Leviathan; Isa 27:1).

→Jesus gave his disciples "authority to tread on snakes and scorpions" (Luke 10:19), referring to demons. The book of Revelation describes three demons as "unclean spirits like frogs" (Rev 16:13). They were often envisioned as composite beings, made up of the frightening aspects of animals, sometimes including human faces or bodies. *T. Sol.* 18.1-2 speaks of demons "with heads like formless dogs, ... [others] in the form of humans or of bulls or of dragons with faces like birds or beasts or the sphinx". Pazuzu, the wind demon of Mesopotamia, was a horrifying winged creature with human-like face (cf. the Sirens of Greece). Revelation also describes the (demonic) 'locusts' from the abyss, armed as battle-horses, with human faces (Rev 9:7). Demons could not only attack but also indwell humans and cause many types of ills: epilepsy, insanity, disability. Against them one protected oneself by prayer, incantation and magic. A magician was called in for exorcism, to diagnose the problem and recite the appropriate incantation. Incantations often took the form of an invocation to the higher gods and a verbal command to exhort evil forces to go away, and might be accompanied by magical aids or acts. Josephus tells of a magic root which drove out demons when applied to the sufferer (*Bel. Jud.* 7.185). Solomon, in Jewish, Christian and Muslim lore, is said to have had "the skill against the demons for help and healing" (Josephus, *Ant.* 8.45), and composed incantations and rituals of exorcism: in Josephus' own day, exorcism was performed in Solomon's name with a ring containing a magic root (*Ant.* 8.47). They could be exorcised by providing a substitute host body, usually an animal, but also a figurine or even a reed of the same size as the human sufferer (SAGGS 1962:300). That a demon needed a host is an idea found also in the New Testament: demons cast out of the Gerasene demoniac ask to enter a herd of swine lest, apparently, they be left homeless (Mark 5:12; cf. Matt 12:43-45).

III. In the Bible, old meanings and associations of the terms *daimon* and *daimonion* survived alongside the post-Exilic revaluation. The original neutral sense of 'divinity' is found in Acts 17:18, where Paul is described by pagan Athenians as a preacher of 'foreign deities' (*daimonia*). The Septuagint uses *daimonion* several times in the ancient Near Eastern sense of the spirits of the desert: it translates the Hebrew *śe'îrîm* (wild goats, →satyrs, goat demons; Isa 13:21), and *siyyim* (desert dwelling wild beasts; Isa 34:14), where desert spirits are said to inhabit cities laid waste (cf. also Bar 4:35). The book of Revelation describes the (future) fallen city of "Babylon" (= Rome) as "a dwelling place of demons and a haunt of every unclean spirit and a haunt of every unclean and hateful bird" (18:2), recalling the oracle of desert waste in Isa 13 against Mesopotamian Babylon. One of the major functions of such spirits was to bring fatal calamity: so *daimon* is used to designate a spirit of "famine and disease" (*Sib. Or.* 3.331). This inheritance explains the apparent anomaly that the main activity of demons in the New Testament ministry of Jesus is not to tempt to sin but to cause disability, disease and insanity: even though they are clearly associated with the activity of the Devil.

During the intertestamental period and the rise of Jewish literature in Greek, the terms *daimon* and *daimonion* began to assume among Jews the negative connotation of 'demon in league with the Devil'. The inspiration for this shift in meaning was the encounter during the Exile and later with Zoroastrian dualism. This cosmology postulated two warring spiritual camps controlled by their leaders, the Zoroastrian God and Devil, and commanded by archangels and archdemons and their descending ranks of lesser spirits. They fought over the loyalty of humans, loyalty expressed in righteous or unrighteous behavior and eventuating in eternal life or fiery destruction. The old gods of the nations and their servant divinities, the lesser spirits of nature and cosmos, were 'demonized', demoted to the class of wicked spirits, tempting humans to sin and enticing them from the true faith by the false doctrines of other religions. Eventually, however, there would be an End, a victory by God, a savior to bring the opposing powers to destruction, a Last Judgment, and a New Age. Circles within Judaism used this framework to revalue older myths and produced after the Exile the dualistic strains of Judaism visible in post-exilic and intertestamental literature and in Christianity.

As the gods of the nations were demonized, so 'demon' in the dualistic sense is found in the Septuagint (LXX) as a designation of pagan deities and spirits: in LXX Ps 95:5 the national deities of other peoples, said to be idols (*'elilim*) in Hebrew, become "demons" ("All the gods of the nations are demons"); in LXX Deut 32:17, the foreign divinities whom Israel worshipped, properly described in the Hebrew text as *šēdîm* (tutelary spirits), are again called "demons" ("They sacrificed to demons and not to God"; cf. LXX Ps 105:37; Bar. 4:7); in LXX Isa 65:11 *daimon* renders the Hebrew name of the pagan god of Fortune (→Gad), where the Israelites are said to have been "preparing a table for the demon". This conception of table fellowship with pagan gods who are in reality demons carries over into the New Testament: Paul warns the Corinthian Church that they may not eat sacrificial meals in pagan temples, for "that which the Gentiles sacrifice, they sacrifice to demons", meaning, for Corinth, the Greek gods Asklepios, Sarapis, and especially →Demeter. So Paul sets in opposition "the table of the Lord and the table of demons" (1 Cor 10:20-21). Likewise, the author of Revelation identifies the worship of idols with the worship of demons (Rev 9:20). In the intertestamental literature one finds "the evil demon →Asmodeus" (Tob 3:8, 17; the name may be derived from the Persian *aeshma daeva*, 'demon of wrath'). Demons become tempters who lead one into—and are even the personifications of—various sins: one finds the Seven Spirits of deceit (*T. Reub.* 2.1; 3.2ff.) which are named after and cause various sins; "demons of deceit" and "spirit of error" (*T. Jud.* 23.1; 20.1; cf. the "spirit of falsehood" in 1 QS 4.9ff.) connected with licentiousness, idolatry, and witchcraft; the "spirit of anger" (*T. Dan* 1-2) and "spirit of envy" (*T. Sim.* 4.7).

One ancient theory of the origin of the demons was that they were the souls of the dead who, having been unjustly treated or killed, sought retribution (as perhaps were the Erinyes; cf. the Biblical →Rephaim; also Tertullian, *De Anima* 57). Another conception was that they were the ghosts of the wicked dead (Josephus, *Bel. Jud.* 7.185: "demons [are] the spirits of wicked people who enter and kill the living"). Origen tells us that the Church had no clearly defined teaching on their genesis; his view was that the Devil, after becoming apostate, induced many of the angels to fall away with him; these fallen angels were the demons (*De Princ.* pref. 6; Tatian, *Adv. Gr.* 20; cf. Rev 12:4). The most popular myth, however, is found in the Bible, intertestamental literature, the rabbis and the Church fathers: demons are the souls of the offspring of angels who cohabited with humans. According to this story, a group of angels descended from heaven and mated with human women, producing as offspring a race of wicked →giants who conquered and defiled the earth with violence and bloodshed. To destroy them, God caused the Flood. The spirits of the drowned giants, neither angelic nor human, were trapped in the regions of the air which they haunt as demons, seeking host bodies to inhabit (cf. "the power of the air" Eph 2:2; and Eusebius, *Praep. Ev.* 4.5.142: [Greek theologians] assigned "the atmosphere to demons"). According to Justin Martyr, "the angels ... were captivated by love of women and engendered children who are called demons" (*2 Apol.* 5; cf. Gen 6:1-4; 1 Enoch 6-21; *Jub.* 4:22; 5:1ff.; Jude 6).

In the New Testament the word *daimon* occurs but once (Matt 8:31). The parallel passage in Luke 8:27 uses *daimonion*, a word found more than fifty times (but for Acts 17:18) for a wicked demonic spirit. Mark 5 describes the Gerasene demoniac as having an "unclean spirit" (πνεῦμα ἀκάθαρτον). The phrase is found twenty times in the NT (cf. also LXX Zech 13:2, of the spirit of false prophecy; *T. Ben.* 5.2). "Evil spirit" (πνεῦμα πονηρόν) is used for *daimonion* in Luke 8:2. From these passages one learns the nature and function of demons in the New Testament era: to defile and bring to evil their human subjects and hosts, in both physical and spiritual ways.

Demons sought to indwell humans and were able to do so in large numbers: the Gerasene demoniac was indwelt, as he said, by "→Legion, for we are many" (Mark 5:9). Mary Magdalene was said to have been healed of seven demons (Luke 8:2; cf. 11:24-26). This indwelling is described by the Biblical writers with the phrase "to have a demon" (ἔχειν δαιμόνιον) or "to be demonized" (δαιμονίζεσθαι). The indwelling spirit seems nevertheless to 'possess' the host, speaking through and casting the sufferer about as though animating a puppet from inside (Mark 1:24; 9:26). The main effect of demons on the host in the Synoptic writers was to cause physical and mental suffering, and anti-social behavior: the violent Gerasene demoniac lives in tombs and deserted places, is periodically bound and chained, continually crying out and gashing himself with stones (Mark 5:2-6). While demonization was often differentiated from debility and disease (Matt 4:24, Mark 1:32), demons also caused dumbness (Matt 9:32), blindness (Matt 12:22), deafness (Mark 9:17-29), epilepsy (Matt 17:18; lit. "being moonstruck"), and apparently fever and other diseases (Luke 4:39; 8:2). Its chief manifestation, however, was insanity: the Gerasene demoniac, when healed, is said to "be in his right mind" (Mark 5:15). So common was this idea that it was a popular calumny to claim that one with whom one disagreed was 'insane': so John the Baptist was slandered as demonized (= 'insane'; Luke 7:33), as was Jesus (John 8:48; cf. 10:20 "he has a demon and is insane").

Jesus, according to the New Testament, cast demons out (ἐκβάλλειν) with a word of command (Matt 8:16; in 8:32 the word is ὑπάγετε, "Go away!"). He gave his disciples authority to cast out demons in his name, which they did with remarkable success for centuries (Luke 10:17; Tertullian, *Apol.* 23.15-18; however, cf. Mark 9:18-19). The point of exorcism in the ministry of Jesus and the early Church was not only the relief of suffering, but the clash of the Kingdom of God and the Kingdom of the Devil. This evil kingdom was conceptualized as an army organized under the Devil with ranks of officers of various levels (cf. Luke 11:18, 26; Eph 6:12). When Jesus was accused of casting out demons by their ruler Beelzebul (a name for the Devil; Baal-zebub), he replied that his mission was to "enter the strong man's house and carry off his property" (Mark 3:27), to enter the kingdom of the Devil and rescue those who were oppressed; this he did by "binding the strong man", which was exorcism of demons by the Spirit of God (Matt 12:28). The demons apparently recognized Jesus on sight, often shouting, "I know who you are, the holy one of God" (Mark 1:24; cf. 1:34). They seemed terrified (cf. Jas 2:19), knowing of their coming judgment and that Jesus would bring their demise; so they cried out "Have you come to destroy us?" (Mark 1:24), or, "Have you come to torment us before the time?" (Matt 8:29; cf. Matt 25:41 "the eternal fire which has been prepared for the Devil and his angels"). In Luke 8:31, the Gerasene demons entreated Jesus not to send them into the abyss, which may refer to the desert prison of the fallen angels (cf. the "pits of darkness" to which the angels are assigned in 2 Pet 2:4; also cf. Rev 9:1-11).

For Paul and the Pauline school, the battle of the two kingdoms was more clearly a battle between cosmic powers and religious loyalties. The competing gods of the Greeks are *demons* (1 Cor 10:20-21; cf 1 Cor 12:2), and Christians were once under the spiritual powers of the "elements" (= the stars and signs of the Zodiac; Gal 4:3, 8-9; Col 2:8, 20; cf. *T. Sol.* 18.3: "the heavenly bodies, the world rulers of the darkness of this age"). Maybe they include the demonic "rulers of this age" who crucified Jesus in their ignorance (1 Cor 2:8). Nevertheless God disarmed the demonic rulers and authorities through →Christ (Col 2:15), and Christ at his resurrection was given mastery over all angelic and demonic "rule and authority and power and dominion" (Eph 1:21; cf 1 Cor 15:24-25); so Christians one day will sit in judgment over the (evil) angels (1 Cor 6:3). The demonic forces attack the Church: such →angels, principalities (→Archai), and powers try, but will fail, to separate believers from God's love (Rom 8:38); false Christian apostles, servants of Satan, attempted to deceive the Corinthians with false doctrines (2 Cor 11:13-15); an angel of Satan even torments Paul (2 Cor 12:7); the writer of the Pastoral epistles predicts that in the last days the unwary would follow "deceitful spirits" and "doctrines of demons", which included food taboos and the forbidding of marriage (1 Tim 4:1-3).

IV. *Bibliography*

G. A. BARTON, The Origin of the Names of Angels and Demons in the Extra-Canonical Apocalyptic Literature to 100 A. D., *JBL* 31 (1912) 156-167; W. CARR, *Angels and Principalities: The Background, Meaning and Development of the Pauline Phrase* hai archai kai hai exousiai (Cambridge 1981); S. EITREM, *Some Notes on the Demonology of the New Testament* (Uppsala 1966); N. FORSYTH, *The Old Enemy: Satan and the Combat Myth* (Princeton 1987); *T. H. GASTER, Demon, Demonology, *IDB* 1 (1962) 817-824; T. JACOBSEN, *The Treasures of Darkness: A History of Mesopotamian Religion* (New Haven 1976); H. A. KELLY, *Towards the Death of Satan: The Growth and Decline of Christian Demonology* (London 1968); H. B. KUHN, The Angelology of the Non-Canonical Jewish Apocalypses, *JBL* 67 (1948) 217-232; *E. LANGTON, *Essentials of Demonology: A Study of Jewish and Christian Doctrine, Its Origin and Development* (London 1949); J. Y. LEE, Interpreting the Demonic Powers in Pauline Thought, *NT* 12 (1970) 54-69; *E. C. E. OWEN, Δαίμων and Cognate Words, *JTS* 32 (1931) 133-53; H. W. F. SAGGS, *The Greatness That Was Babylon* (New York 1962) 288-314.

G. J. RILEY

DEREK → **WAY**

DESTROYER מַשְׁחִית

I. 'Destroyer' is the designation of a supernatural envoy from →God assigned the task of annihilating large numbers of people, typically by means of a plague. The noun is a *hiphil* participle of the root ŠḤT which is not attested in the OT in the *qal*. When the root appears in the *hiphil*, *hophal*, *piel*, and *niphal* stems, it describes the deterioration, marring, disfiguring, damaging and destruction of people and things, such as textiles (Jer 13:7), pots (Jer 18:4), vineyards (Jer 12:10), trees (Deut 20:19), cities (Gen 13:10) and buildings (Lam 2:6). It represents the kind of activity performed by plundering thieves (Jer 49:9). Deities in other ancient Near Eastern cultures who annihilate populations are identified by personal names that may reflect their function or devastating character (e.g. Namtar, 'Fate', →Resheph, 'Flame', 'lightning bolt').

II. The Destroyer must be distinguished from those supernatural figures who, in their capacity as angels/messengers of death, visit all men and terminate the lives of single individuals. In the Bible, the Destroyer does not kill all humans, nor is he dispatched by God to kill isolated individuals. Furthermore, unlike the angels of death who bring death of any sort (both natural and premature), the Destroyer brings specifically a premature and agonizing death.

It is true that in neighbouring cultures, almost any deity could conceivably decimate large populations: the god who afflicts is characteristically the same god who brings relief. But there were nevertheless certain deities whose specific expertise lay in their ability to exterminate humans *en masse*. The Erra Epic depicts Erra as a ruthless killer in an irrational and uncontrollable lust for war, death and destruction, ultimately calmed only by his aid Ishum. Erra was "everywhere a god of destruction" (LAMBERT 1973:356) and became identified with →Nergal, a god of war and sudden death, and the ruler of the realm of the dead (cf. his epithets "Great King of the Abyss"

lugal-gal-abzu and "King of the Dreadful Sword" **lugal-gír-ùr-ra**; *AkkGE* 390). When Enlil, in council with the other gods in *Atraḫasis*, wishes to thin the world's population with a plague, it is Namtar, the god of plague, who goes to work. The north-west semitic deity Resheph reflects the same profile, and he was indeed identified by the ancients with Nergal (*Ugaritica V* [1968] 45).

It is a feature of these deities that they do not discriminate between the innocent and the guilty, and that extreme measures are required to stop them before complete annihilation occurs. Erra's fury is calmed only by his assistant Ishum ("you killed the upright, you killed the one who is not upright", Erra IV 104-105), and after his rampage, Erra acknowledges that "like one who plunders a land, I do not discriminate between the upright and the wicked" (Erra V.10). Namtar stopped his plague only because the people's cultic attentions toward him shamed him into backing down (*Atr.* I viii).

III. The Hebrew word *mašḥît*, explicitly describing a supernatural creature commissioned by God to exterminate large groups of people, appears in only two contexts in the Bible (Exod 12:23; 2 Sam 24:16 // 1 Chr 21:15). The activity of such a creature can be further detected in at least four other passages, even though it is not there explicitly identified as a *mašḥît* (Num 17:11-15[16:46-50]; 2 Kgs 19:35 // Isa 37:36; Ezek 9; Rev 9:11).

The death of the firstborn in Egypt, in concert with all of the other plagues, is primarily attributed to the activity of Yahweh throughout the Bible: "I will kill (*ʾānōkî hōrēg*) your first-born" (Exod 4:23; cf. 11:4-5; 12:12-13.23a.27.29; Ps 78:51; 105:36). Nevertheless, Yahweh's involvement is further qualified in one passage: "Yahweh will pass through to strike down the Egyptians; when he sees the blood on the lintel and on the two doorposts, Yahweh will pass over the door and will not allow the destroyer (*hammašḥît)* to enter your houses to strike you down" (Exod 12:23).

The relationship between Yahweh and the Destroyer in this passage is hardly extraordinary in the context of the ancient Near East. One is to picture Yahweh, accompanied by a retinue of assistants, going against his enemies in judgment (MILLER 1973). Both Yahweh and his entourage can be depicted as active in the same conflict, and if Yahweh decides to restrain his weapons, he must also give orders to desist to the supernatural warriors that accompany him. In Exodus 12, therefore, Yahweh and at least one supernatural assistant are responsible for the deaths of the Egyptian first-born (cf. Ps 78:49); when Yahweh sees lamb's blood on door-posts, not only does he not kill, but he gives orders to the accompanying Destroyer to exercise similar restraint (biblical and later sources affirm that a number of plague and destroying angels do God's work; cf. Ps 78:49; *1 Enoch* 53:3; 56:1; 66:1; 1QS 4.12).

The means by which the Destroyer slew the Egyptian first-born is not immediately obvious, although the Hebrew term and its translation in the early versions point to a violent or painful death (Vg *percussorem*; LXX *ton olothreuonta*; Syriac and Targums employ the root *ḥbl*). This is confirmed by the statement that the Destroyer must be restrained from "smiting", *lingōp* (Exod 12:23), a verb whose root is identical to the root for the word 'plague' or 'pestilence' (*negep* Num 17:11-12[16:46-47]; Josh 22:17; *maggēpâ* Num 17:13-15[16:48-50]; 25:8-9.18-19; 1 Sam 6:4; Zech 14:12.18). The word translated 'plague', *negep*, is used in connection with the death of the first-born (Exod 12:13), as *maggēpâ* describes the other 'plagues' (Exod 9:14). There can be little question, therefore, that the Destroyer in Exod 12:23 belongs to the class of plague deities broadly attested in the ancient Near East.

The plague associations with the Destroyer are even more pronounced in 2 Samuel 24 (paralleled in a slightly different and more expansive version in 1 Chronicles 21) where Yahweh sends →'Deber' (Pestilence) at David's request (vv 13.15; cf. *maggēpâ* vv 21.25). In contrast to Exodus

12, the Destroyer, here called "the Destroying Angel" (*lammal'āk hammašḥît*, v 16; 1 Chr 21:15 [20 Syriac]; cf. *Pal. Tgs.* Exod 12:23), is depicted in considerable detail: he is of gigantic proportions (1 Chr 21:16) and visible to humans (v 17; cf. 1 Chr 21:16.20), with a hand (2 Sam 24:16; 1 Chr 21:15) holding a sword (1 Chr 21: 16.30; cf. "sword of Yahweh" v 12) which he replaces in its sheath when he is done with his destructive task (1 Chr 21:27). The Destroying Angel in this passage is also described as an →"angel of Yahweh" (2 Sam 24:16; 1 Chr 21:16.30), the "smiting angel" (*hammal'āk hammakkeh*, 2 Sam 24:17), and a "destroying angel of Yahweh" (*mal'ak YHWH mašḥît;* 1 Chr 21:12). As in Exodus 12, he takes orders from Yahweh who once again bids the Destroying Angel not to destroy all the people (1 Chr 21:15.27). Unlike Exodus 12, Yahweh is not described as participating in the slaughter, for he sends the Destroyer in his place (1 Chr 21:15).

The more expansive passage in Chronicles presents one peculiarity that is not characteristic of the Destroyer (and indeed is not found in the parallel passage in 2 Samuel). According to 2 Sam 24:18-19, Gad received from Yahweh directions for David to obey. 1 Chr 21:18-19 specifies that it is the Destroyer, called here the "angel of Yahweh", who gives this information to Gad. The syntax, vocabulary, and use of indirect discourse in the Chronicles passage point to a later formulation that could not have been in the Samuel text in this form. The Destroyer is otherwise a creature who specializes in mass slaughter (not verbal communication) and who does not act independently but only at the specific command of Yahweh. The present verse compromises both of these characteristics, and probably represents the later breakdown of the archaic perception of the Destroyer in the face of the developing angelology of the Second Temple period.

It has been common to seek an origin for the Destroyer in early or pre-Israelite cult traditions, but the association of Yahweh with plague and destruction is pervasive in the Bible, making the theory unnecessary. The imagery of a god destroying populations with a retinue of divine assistants (or envoys dispatched in the god's place) is so common in the Bible and the Near East as to moot the question of cultural or cultic borrowing.

Although these two passages (one of which appears in two parallel accounts) are the only places in the Bible where the Hebrew *mašḥît*, "Destroyer", is explicitly applied to a supernatural being, there is good cause to see such a figure at work elsewhere in the Bible. In Numbers 17 God's wrath against the Israelites in the wilderness once again prompts a plague (*negep*, Num 17:11.12[16:46.47]; *maggēpâ*, Num 17:13.14.15 [16:48.49.50]). This plague, described as "restrained" (vv 13.15) and as "wrath gone forth from Yahweh" (v 11), may be a personification (cf. *Tg. Ps.-J.* v 12). Like the preceding two stories (cf. also Namtar in *Atr.*), this destruction can be checked by a cultic act (blood on the door-posts, building an altar, offering incense). Also like the other two accounts, the destruction is indiscriminate in the annihilation of wicked and upright alike unless they are somehow formally distinguished (blood on door-posts, physical separation [Num 17:10(16:45)]).

In any case, the earliest traditions available to us interpret the story in Numbers 17 as the work of the Destroyer. The same term used to translate *mašḥît* in the LXX of Exodus 12 and 1 Chronicles 21 resurfaces in the NT and the Apocrypha to describe the creature who brings this plague in Numbers 17: "they were destroyed by the Destroyer" (*apōlonto hypo tou olethreutou*, 1 Cor 10:10), "the Destroyer" (*ho olethreuōn*, Wis 18:25). Targum Pseudo-Jonathan inserts the same Aramaic term in Num 17:11[16:36] ("Destroyer", *mḥbl'*) that was used to translate Hebrew *mašḥît* elsewhere. Although different terms appear in 4 Macc 7:11, once again a divine emissary—"the fiery angel", *ton empyristēn ... aggelon*—is pictured as bringing the plague in Numbers 17.

The term "Destroyer" does not appear in 2 Kgs 19:35 (// Isa 37:36) when the "angel of the Lord went out and struck 185,000 in the Assyrian camp" by night. However, early interpretations of this destruction describe it as a plague: *maggēpâ* in Sir 48: 21(24) appears in Vg LXX as "his angel"; Josephus sees a plague in *Ant.* X.21 but "an angel of the Lord" in *B.J.* V.388; Ramael is the angel who "burned their bodies within" in *2 Bar* 63:6-8 (cf. Herodotus II.141). Since one of the tasks of God's angels in general can be destruction, one cannot be confident that the specific angel in view here is the Destroyer, even though the early interpretative tradition moved in that direction.

None of the angelic figures who slaughter Jerusalemites in Ezekiel 9 are called "Destroyer", even though the word does appear as part of their commission (*lĕmašḥît,* v 6). Nevertheless, the imagery is suggestive of the Destroyer's activity elsewhere, for those who destroy do not act independently but must follow God's orders (vv 4.11), and the destruction is indiscriminate, arrested only if one has an external sign ("a mark on the foreheads", v 4).

In the NT, at least two texts reflect the influence of OT and ancient Near Eastern imagery associated with the Destroyer. Rev 9:11 gives the name "Destroyer" (*Apollyōn*) to the "angel of the abyss" (→Abaddon; cf. the epithet of →Nergal). Like the Destroyer in the OT, affliction is indiscriminate and overtakes all who are not distinguished in some external fashion ("seal of God on their foreheads", Rev 9:4), and the affliction is bodily pain (Rev 9:5.10). It is therefore possible that the imagery of Rev 19:11-15 also reflects features of the Destroyer.

IV. Without the imagery of the Near Eastern deity in conflict, the relationship between Yahweh and the Destroyer in Exod 12 can be problematic, for a less poetic analysis of the passage may insist that it cannot be both Yahweh and the Destroyer who together slay the Egyptian first-born (as source critical analysis has affirmed, FOSSUM 1985:225-226), or that the Destroyer is identical to Yahweh (GRAY 1899). When the NT with precision employs the same word found in the LXX of Exod 12:23 to refer to the Destroyer, it refrains from clarifying whether the Destroyer is God or an angel (*ho olethreuôn*; Heb 11:28); presumably the latter is intended, but the former is possible. Some interpreters simply ignore the presence of the Destroyer (Josephus *Ant.* II.313). Early rabbinic sources move in this direction, insisting that God himself was directly involved in the slaying of the firstborn, but later literature affirms that it was performed by an angel (GOLDIN 1968; GINZBERG, *Legends* V 433-434). Among those sources that distance God from the actual slaying, the Wisdom of Solomon expansively describes the Destroyer as God's personified Logos (cf. the *Memra* of Yahweh in *Tg. Ps.-J.* Exod 12:29) that came as a gigantic warrior from God's throne, holding God's "unambiguous decree as a sharp sword" (18:15-16). *Jub.* 49:2-4 goes further in multiplying the number of destroyers so that, following God's directions, "all of the powers of →Mastemah" (the chief demonic figure) pass over the Israelites and kill the Egyptian first-born (cf. "10,000 destroying angels" in *Pal. Tgs.* Exod 12:12). Ezekiel the Tragedian speaks of "the fearsome angel" (159) and "death" (187) that passed by. Maimonides nuances the passage so that God does the killing in the Egyptian community, while the Destroyer is the one who passes through the Israelite community.

It was emphasized above that there was originally a distinction between the angel of death who comes to an individual at the time appointed for him to die and the Destroyer who massacres entire populations with premature and violent deaths. Later traditions, however, fuse the two conceptions. Thus, "Destroying Angel" in 2 Samuel 24 is translated in Syriac as the "Angel of Death", an equation also made in later Judaism. In the Hebrew text of Exod 4:24-25 where it is Yahweh who tries to kill Moses, the *Pal. Tgs.* preserve traditions to the effect that it is the "Destroying Angel" or the "Angel of Death".

V. *Bibliography*
J. E. FOSSUM, *The Name of God and the Angel of the Lord. Samaritan and Jewish Concepts of Intermediation and the Origin of Gnosticism* (WUNT 36; Tübingen 1985); J. GOLDIN, Not By Means of an Angel and Not By Means of a Messenger, *Religions in Antiquity: Essays in Memory of Erwin Ramsdell Goodenough* (ed. J. Neusner; Leiden 1968) 412-24; G. B. GRAY, Destroyer, *Encyclopaedia Biblica* I (ed. T. K. Cheyne & J. S. Black; New York 1899) 1078; W. G. LAMBERT, Studies in Nergal, *BiOr* 30 (1973) 355-363; P. D. MILLER, *The Divine Warrior in Early Israel* (Cambridge 1973).

S. A. MEIER

DESTRUCTION → **QETEB**

DEVIL Διάβολος

I. The term 'devil' is a rendering of the Greek word διάβολος, used as a loan word by Latin Christian writers as *diabolus*. As a proper noun in intertestamental Jewish texts and Christian writers the word denotes the great Adversary of God and righteousness, the Devil. It is so used in the Septuagint as a translation for the Hebrew *śāṭān* (→Satan) (e. g. Job 1 and 2; 1 Chr 21:1), and appears often with this meaning in the New Testament (e.g. Matt 4:1). In ancient Greek usage, however, διάβολος was an adjective generally denoting something or someone 'slanderous' and 'defamatory'. So Aristophanes speaks of a 'most slanderous slave' (διαβολότατος *Eq.* 45), and Plutarch views the word as one function of the 'whisperer' (ψίθυρος *Mor.* 727d) and 'flatterer' (κόλαξ *Mor.* 61c). The Pastoral Epistles admonish women not to be 'evil gossips' (διαβόλους 1 Tim 3:11; Tit 2:3; cf. 2 Tim 3:3). Socrates describes the reason for his condemnation at his trial as the 'slanders' (διαβολαί) which had for long years been spoken against him (Plato, *Apol.* 37b). This noun (διαβολή) could also mean 'enmity' or 'quarrel', and the verb διαβάλλω (meaning literally 'to throw across' or 'to cross over') could mean 'to be at variance', 'to attack', and 'to accuse' (cf. Luke 16:1), as well as 'to slander'. So the Septuagint used the verb (ἐν)διαβάλλειν of the →Angel of the LORD who 'opposed' Balaam (LXX Num 22:22), and the noun διάβολος to mean 'enemy' (for the Hebrew *ṣorēr* in LXX Est 8:1) and 'adversary' (for *śāṭān* LXX Ps 108:6). It is in this sense that the Septuagint used the word διάβολος to render the Hebrew *śāṭān*, the super-human Adversary of God.

II. The Biblical idea that God and the righteous angels confronted the opposition of a great spiritual enemy, the Devil backed by the army of the demons, had a long history and development in the ancient world. Very old stories of conflict among the gods are found in each of the cultures which influenced the Biblical tradition, and these stories (known among scholars as the Combat Myth), coupled with dualism encountered during and after the Exile, contributed to the concept of the Devil. To cite but two examples, in the Babylonian story *Enuma Elish*, →Marduk combats the forces of →Chaos in →Tiamat, the great primeval sea, conceived of as a monstrous sea serpent or dragon. Tiamat is defeated, and out of her body Marduk creates the cosmos. In similar though not identical fashion, the Canaanite storm god →Baal, son and agent of the highest god →El, facing opposition in the council of the gods, is forced to battle Yam (the Sea). He defeats Yam (and also Lotan [→Leviathan], the dragon in the sea), and obtains a palace from which he thunders forth against his enemies in the council and on earth. Next he faces →Mot (Death), the ruler of the Underworld, a monster with a huge mouth and appetite who swallows the dead, swallowing even Baal for a time. He is nevertheless rescued from Mot and gains supremacy. The stories of Yahweh in pre-exilic Israel draw upon these and other myths (cf. the battles of →Zeus) to describe the conflicts against his enemies, both divine and human, and his gaining of sovereignty over the other gods of the nations in the council (Yahweh and the council: Deut 32:8-9; Pss 29:1; 82:1; 89:5-8; his mountain palace: Pss 18:6-15; 68; 29; 48:1-2; Yahweh and the Sea: Ps 74:13-17; Isa 51:9-10; cf. especially CROSS 1973 and SMITH 1990). The great enemies of the gods had been defeated in the mythic past and the human present was at (relative) peace. The world was conceived as a unified whole, with each member, divine and human, fulfilling a proper function. There was as yet no Devil, and the lesser spirits fulfilled their appointed roles. →'Demons' were terrifying but legitimate spirits of calamity, disease, and death, who served the will of the greater gods.

During and after the Babylonian Exile, however, Israel was influenced by the cosmological dualism of Persian Zoroastrianism. This system posited two warring camps of spiritual beings headed by twin but opposing siblings, the Zoroastrian God and Devil, who fought for the loyalty of humans in deadly combat. To assist in the battle the two had produced armies of lesser spirits, the angels and the demons. In one important text, 'the Evil One' declares to God: "I shall destroy you and your creatures forever and ever. And I shall persuade all your creatures to hate you and to love me" (BOYCE 1990:46). Creation was their battlefield and the present age was the time of spiritual warfare. At the end of this age of conflict, there would be a final battle in which the Devil and his hosts would be defeated and destroyed in a fiery Hell, and a new creation and new age would begin in righteousness. The value of this complex dualism and eschatology for some factions of post-exilic Judaism was that it provided an explanation for the sufferings of the Exile among a people who saw themselves as (relatively) righteous and undeserving of their plight (cf. Ps 44:17; Jer 31:29-30; Ezek 18:25): it was the Devil who persecuted the innocent and brought disaster as a trial of faith and character, attempting to turn them from God and goodness.

Such ideas were developed in differing ways in post-Exilic texts and intertestamental literature. Two types of Zoroastrianism of the period had postulated different myths of origin for the great Spirits of Light and Darkness: the first held that the two were co-eternal twins without source, essentially two opposite gods; the second claimed that Time (Zervan) as source had generated the two in eternity past as opposing aspects of the original and ambiguous →One. The latter concept of an original One melded most favorably with developing ideas of monotheism and the sovereignty of the God in Israel. The eternal dualism of the former view is explicitly rejected by Second Isaiah (Isa 45:5 "I am the Lord and there is no other; besides me there is no God"), and the God of Israel is seen as was Zervan, the source of both opposites: "I form light and I create darkness; I make wholeness and I create evil" (Isa 45:7). This idea that God created two divine spirits, good and evil, is clearly expressed in texts from Qumran (cf. 1QS 3:25 "[God] created the spirits of Light and Darkness").

That God should be the source of evil, however, or was in competition with another power, was difficult given the old view of God as sovereign and righteous (cf. Deut 32:4; 1 John 1:5). Other creative thinkers produced an alternate view which melded dualism with old traditions of the Combat Myth and Yahweh as →El, head of a heavenly council. In all versions of the Combat Myth and Zoroastrian doctrine, the upper world forces of Light ultimately defeat the forces of Darkness; the Enemies, though formidable, were weaker and lesser beings. Thus the one God, the God of Israel, could stand as the sovereign God of Light, presiding over the lesser divine beings of the heavenly council (the angels), some of whom were righteous, and others of whom (as Baal's enemies in El's council) by their own choice were the sources of evil. This allowed the origin of evil in heaven to be removed one stage from God: evil was the result of some failing in the lesser divine beings. These were led by a great opponent similar to the great enemies in the Combat Myth, the Devil, viewed as a rebellious angel followed by his hosts of demons, who assumed characteristics of the great mythic opponents of the heavenly gods, destined for defeat. He could be opposed by a great champion of righteousness, the →Angel of the LORD (cf. Zech 3:1; *Jub.* 17:15-18:16), or →Michael the archangel (cf. Jude 9), or in later Christian thought, by →Jesus.

III. More than one account of the origin of the Devil and fall of the angels is found in post-Exilic and subsequent literature. A very old and popular story was that certain of the →'sons of God' (angels) descended from heaven and mated with human women, giving birth to a race of →giants which was drowned by the flood (*1 Enoch* 6-16; Gen 6:1-4; Jude 6; 2 Pet 2:4); their disembodied souls became the demons. The leader of this band of fallen angels, →Azazel, although a messenger of Satan in *1 Enoch* 54:6, was identified as the Devil (*Jub.* 10:1-11) and as the serpent who deceived Adam and →Eve (*Apoc. Abr.* 23). He is also called →Baalzebub, the Prince of the demons, who was formerly 'the highest ranking angel in heaven' (*T. Sol.* 6:1-2). Two other stories relate the Devil to Adam: Adam was made in the image of God, and "through the Devil's envy, death entered the world" (Wis 2:24). Again, when God created Adam on the earth, the angels were commanded to reverence him as being the image of God; the angel who was to become the Devil refused on the grounds that he was both greater and older than Adam, and he was followed in his rebellion by the angels in his charge (*Adam and Eve* 13-15; Tertullian, *De Patientia* 5; *Qur'an* 15:26-35). Another account was inspired by the oracles against the king of Babylon (Isa 14:4-20) and the king of Tyre (Ezek 28:11-19): on the second day of creation, one of the archangels, in fact the highest archangel of all, had through pride attempted to set himself up to be worshipped as an equal to God (*2 Enoch* 29.4-5; cf. 1 John 3:8). The Latin translation of Isa 14:12 names this individual "Lucifer".

Intertestamental and later Jewish texts ascribe to the Devil a variety of names and activities. In *Jubilees* 'the chief of the [evil] spirits' is →Mastemah ('Hateful One', Heb משׂטמה, lit. 'animosity') and Satan, who accuses Israel before God, ensnares and corrupts them that they be destroyed (1:20). In the *Martyrdom of Isaiah*, the leader of the hosts of evil is called Sammael ('Blind god' 1:8, 11; 2:1; 5:15), Melkira (= 'King of Evil'; 1:8), Satan (2:2, 7; 5:16), and especially Beliar (a by-form of →'Belial' = 'Useless'; 1:8; 2:4; 3:11). He is 'the Angel of Iniquity who rules this world' and causes apostasy, sin, magic, and the persecution of the righteous, 'dwelling in the hearts' of the rulers of Israel (2:4-11); in the last days the children of Israel will abandon the Lord and ally themselves with him (*T. Iss.* 6). He rules the soul of the one perturbed by anger and falsehood, but flees from one who avoids wrath and hates lying (*T. Dan* 4:7-5:1). Beliar causes the righteous to stumble by promiscuity (*T. Reub.* 4:7-11), and sexual sin is also a failing of the Devil himself: the role of progenitor of →Cain was assigned to him, which later authors thought he accomplished by union with Eve in the garden (cf. *4 Macc.* 18:8 "the seducing and defiling serpent"; *Tg. Ps.-J.* Gen 4:1; *Pirke de R. El.* 21; Epiphanius, *Adv. Haer.* 40.5.3). The 'Prince of Error' blinded Simeon's mind so as to sell →Joseph into slavery (*T. Sim.* 2:7), and caused Judah to go astray by love of money (*T. Jud.* 19:4). The 'Prince of the Demons' is Beelzebul, who causes wars, tyranny, demon worship, violence and lust, and resides in the evening star (*T. Sol.* 6:1-7). The Devil "inhabits as his own instrument" one who does evil (*T. Naph.* 8:6). The 'wild old Lion' is the father of the Egyptian gods and persecutes Aseneth for turning away from him to God and destroying her family idols (*Jos. et As.* 12:9; 10:12). This enmity for escaping and attacking the Devil's power is the basis for the plot of the *Testament of Job*: Job destroys an idol temple and brings on himself the retributive wrath of the Devil (*T. Job* 4:4). Whatever the activity of the Devil, however, it is performed by permission of God and according to divine plan to test the righteous and demonstrate which among humanity are evil (*Jub.* 10:8-12; *T. Job* 8:2-3; 20:1-3; Rev 13:5, 7; cf. 1 Cor 11:19).

IV. In the Hebrew Bible, one finds the concept of the 'adversary' (Heb. *śāṭān*) in two senses: that of any (usually human) opponent, and that of Satan, the Devil, the opponent of the righteous. In the first sense, Hadad the Edomite acts as a *śāṭān* to Solomon (1 Kgs 11:14; cf. also 11:23, 25; 1 Sam 29:4); Haman is the 'enemy' of the Jews (Est 8:1); and even the Angel of the LORD acts as a *śāṭān* to Balaam (Num 22: 22). In each of these cases, the *śāṭān* is an 'opponent' in such public activities as politics, war, etc. In texts composed after the Exile, however, the concept manifests the growing changes brought about by influence of dualism: the *śāṭān* becomes the Devil (rendered by *diabolos* in LXX), the archenemy of God at war over the loyalty of humanity: the Devil attacks the bond between humanity and God, leading them to sin (cf. 1 Chr 21:1) and blasphemy in an attempt to destroy their allegiance to God. So the Devil in Job (lit. 'the *śāṭān*' or better 'the Adversary') is a divine figure, classed with the 'sons of the gods', who slanders and attacks Job in an attempt to cause him to 'curse' God 'to his face' (Job 1:11; 2:5). This is not the action of a mere heavenly prosecutor in the divine council, appointed by God to accuse the defendant of sin (cf. Zech 3:1-2); no prosecutor destroys the property of the defendant, then kills his children and destroys his health, in order to bring about hatred for the Judge. God and the Devil in Job are competing for Job's loyalty, which the Adversary calls into question. To settle the issue, God delivers Job over into the power of Satan for testing, "leading him into temptation" and "delivering him over to the Evil One" as God would later do with Jesus and his followers according to the New Testament (cf. Matt 6:13).

The Devil in the New Testament is wholly the enemy of God and righteousness. He is called by several different names, reflecting the several traditions which were melded to construct the concept of the Devil in the intertestamental period. In one remarkable passage we find "the great Dragon, ... the Serpent of old who is called the Devil and Satan" (Rev 12:9). The names 'Devil' and 'Satan' are used interchangeably without apparent difference in meaning (cf. Luke 8:12 and Mark 4:15). The →Dragon clearly recalls Leviathan, the great "dragon that is in the sea" (Isa 27:1; cf. Tiamat and Yamm), while the Serpent is also the "serpent [who] deceived Eve by his craftiness" (2 Cor 11:3; cf. Gen 3:1-15). Here, as in the intertestamental literature, images and names of the great opponents of the gods of heaven in the Combat Myth are used of the Devil. While Death (→Mot) is an enemy separate from the Devil in some texts (1 Cor 15:26; Rev 20:14), it is the Devil who has the power of death in Heb 2:14. The antithesis of Christ is Belial (2 Cor 6:15), and the spirit which he combats is Beelzebul (Mark 3:22). The Devil is the Tempter (ὁ πειράζων Mt 4:3), the Evil One (Matt 6:13), the Enemy (Matt 13:39), the Accuser (Rev 12:10), and the Ruler of this world (John 12:31).

The single most important function of the Devil in the New Testament is to rule the Kingdom of Darkness which opposes the Kingdom of God. The Devil is the chief of a host of wicked spirits (Luke 11:18) ranging from lesser indwelling demons who cause disease, disability, and insanity by 'possession' (e.g. Mark 1:34; 3:22; 5:1-20), to the great "world powers of this darkness" and "spiritual forces of wickedness in the heavens" (Eph 6:12; 1:21; Col 2:15). The latter are the angelic astral forces, 'the Devil and his angels' (cf. Matt 25:41; Rev 12:7, 9), who rule the stars and astral 'elements' (Gal 4:3, 9), and have access into the very heaven of God (Rev 12:10; Luke 10:18). The hosts occupy not only the heavens, but especially the air, and thus the Devil is the "ruler of the power of the air" (Eph 2:2), for in the air are trapped the lesser demonic spirits of the drowned giants from the Flood, offspring of the fallen angels and humans (cf. *Jub.* 10:4-11; *1 Enoch* 6-10; Eusebius, *Praep. Ev.* 4.5.142: [Greek theologians] assigned "the atmosphere to demons"). The Kingdom of Darkness includes the entire 'world', the very cosmos itself and apparently everything in it: "the whole world lies in [the power of] the Evil One" (1 John 5:19;

cf. Luke 4:6). So the Devil is the "ruler of this world" (John 12:31; 14:30; 16:11), and the "god of this world" (2 Cor 4:4). As inhabitants of this Kingdom, all humans before encountering the true God are also under the "dominion of Satan" (Acts 26:18) and "authority of Darkness" (Col 1:13), living "according to the spirit which works in the children of disobedience" (Eph 2:1-2). He blinds their minds to the light of the gospel (2 Cor 4:4), for the Devil "deceives the whole world" (Rev 12:9). To do so he even "disguises himself as an angel of light" (2 Cor 11:14, which he had done when tempting Eve: *Adam and Eve* 9; cf. 2 Cor 11:3).

This Kingdom of Darkness was invaded by Jesus as champion of the Kingdom of God. In fact, "the Son of God appeared for this purpose, that he might destroy the works of the Devil" (1 John 3:8). He was led into the desert to be tested by the Devil (Mark 1:9-13; Matt 4:1-11; Luke 4:1-13); soon he began casting out demons (Mark 1:21-28). This he describes as attacking and overpowering the Strong Man, "entering the Strong Man's house and carrying off his property" (Matt 12:28-29; Luke 11:20-22). The Strong Man is the Devil and the property which is plundered are the humans formerly subjected to demonic oppression. So when his disciples also begin casting out demons in his name, he watches "Satan fall from heaven like lightning" (Luke 10:17-18), and predicts that "the ruler of this world shall be cast out" (John 12:31). Jesus is the Sower who sows the word of the Kingdom, while Satan steals away the seed from the hearts of the unreceptive lest they be saved (Luke 8:12). Jesus is the Sower of Good Seed, who sows the seed of the children of the Kingdom in the field of the world, while the Devil sows tares, the children of the Evil One (Matt 13:36-40). The devil is able to influence the minds or indwell individuals whom he uses as his instruments: he so uses Peter (Mark 8:33), the opposing Jewish authorities (John 8:44), and finally Judas Iscariot (John 6:70; 13:2, 27) to accomplish the crucifixion of Jesus (Luke 22:53). Nevertheless, it is through this death, which the evil powers had brought about in ignorance (1 Cor 2:8), that the Devil would be "rendered powerless" (Heb 2:14).

After the ascension of Jesus, the disciples are left behind in the world, which is arrayed against them as it was against Jesus (John 15:18-19). He prayed that they be kept from the Evil One (John 17:15), and taught them to pray that God does not "lead them into temptation" as he had their Master, but "deliver them from the Evil One" (Matt 6:13). Satan nevertheless demanded that he "sift" Jesus' disciples "like wheat", which caused them to abandon him in his last hour; yet he prayed for Peter that his faith should not fail (Luke 22:31-32). It is their loyalty (Greek πίστις, 'faith') which is tested by persecution and temptation to sin. So it is that by "the shield of faith" that one extinguishes "the flaming missiles of the Evil One" (Eph 6:16). The Devil accuses the righteous "night and day" before God for their sins, attempting to prove that they belong to him (Rev 12:10; cf. Zech 3:1-5; Jude 9); yet they have an Advocate, a defense attorney, in Jesus (1 John 2:1).

During the present age the Devil uses many stratagems against the Church. He "prowls around like a roaring lion, seeking someone to devour"; they are to "resist him, firm in their faith" (1 Pet 5:8-9), for if they "resist the devil, he will flee" (Jam 4:7). He raises enemies from without, as Elymas the magician who contradicts the preaching of Paul (Acts 13:10). He prevents Paul from visiting the Thessalonians (using Roman officials?, 1 Thess 2:10). He instigates persecutions and imprisonments that they "may be tested" (Rev 2:10), and apparently is enthroned in the Roman government (Rev 2:13; 17:9). He also attacks individual Christians, leading them to lie (Acts 5:3), using sexual temptation to lead into sin (1 Cor 7:5; 1 Tim 5:15 ?), slander to destroy one's reputation (1 Tim 3:7), and physical disease to harm and humble the sufferer (cf. Paul's thorn in the flesh: 2 Cor 12:7). So authorities in the Church may "deliver" the unruly "over to Satan", which bodily suffering, it is hoped, will produce repentance (1

Cor 5:5; 1 Tim 1:20). Far more insidious, however, are the Devil's agents within the Church: he inspires false apostles who travel to Paul's churches and contradict his message (2 Cor 11:13-15), and heretical teachers are said to be in "the snare of the Devil, held captive to do his will" (2 Tim 2:26; cf. Rom 16:17-20). The final stratagem of the Devil at the end of the age will be to raise up the →Anti-Christ, who in competition with God will claim the religious loyalty of all on the earth (2 Thess 2:3-4; Rev 13). Nevertheless both the Devil and his hosts will be defeated at the *parousia* of the LORD in a great battle (2 Thess 2:8). According to Revelation, he will be bound for a thousand years and then released for one final combat, finally to be thrown into the lake of fire (Rev 20:7-10; cf. Matt 25:41).

V. *Bibliography*

W. BOUSSET, *The Antichrist Legend* (New York 1896); M. BOYCE, *Textual Sources for the Study of Zoroastrianism* (Chicago 1990); F. M. CROSS, *Canaanite Myth and Hebrew Epic* (Cambridge MA 1973); B. DE JESUS-MARIE, *Satan* (New York 1952); S. EITREM, *Some Notes on the Demonology of the New Testament* (Uppsala 1966); N. FORSYTH, *The Old Enemy: Satan and the Combat Myth* (Princeton 1987); L. JUNG, *Fallen Angels in Jewish, Christian and Mohammedan Literature* (New York 1974); J. KALLAS, *Jesus and the Power of Satan* (Philadelphia 1968); *E. LANGTON, *Essentials of Demonology: A Study of Jewish and Christian Doctrine, Its Origin and Development* (London 1949); R. SCHÄRF, *Die Gestalt des Satans im Alten Testament* (Zürich 1948); M. SMITH, *The Early History of God* (San Francisco 1990).

G. J. RILEY

DEW טל

I. 'Dew' (which, for the ancients, included very fine rain and mist and even exudations on leaves and was caused by the stars; cf. *ARTU* 7-8, note 38; Isa 26:19) has a special significance as a prerequisite of fertility in areas of the Middle East where rain is limited and there is no possibility of river-irrigation. It is especially important in the summer on the Palestinian coastal plain and nearby sea-facing slopes. Some specific crops depend on it. The withdrawal of rain and dew leads to drought (cf. e.g. 1 Kgs 17: 1; Hag 1:10).

The normal Hebrew word for 'dew' is *ṭal*. This has cognates in other Semitic languages, including Ugaritic, where *ṭl* is regarded as 'dew of the heavens' (*ṭl šmm*) and commonly associated with rain (*KTU* 1.19 i:41, 44; 1.3 ii:39, 40 etc.). There is a corresponding denominative verb in Ugaritic and in post-biblical Hebrew. More importantly from a mythological point of view, Ugaritic *ṭl* has generated a derivative epithet, a feminine noun-formation, *ṭly* (Ṭallay), meaning 'Dewy One', which is the title of one of →Baal's daughters.

II. Ugaritic Ṭallay is always described as *bt rb*, 'the girl of fine rain' or 'mist' (*ARTU* 4; cf. Hebrew *rĕbîbîm*) and she appears alongside Baʿal's other daughters, Pidray and Arṣay (*KTU* 1.3 i:24, iii:7; iv:51; v:42; 1.4 i:17; iv:56; vi:11; 1.5 v:6-11; v 7: 23[rest.]). Pidray and Arṣay appear in the Ugaritic 'pantheon' list (*KTU* 1.47 etc.), but Ṭallay does not. She may be subsumed under the name of some other goddess. In *KTU* 1.101:5 she appears to play a more independent role, grooming (delousing?) her father, Baʿal. That the three are daughters of Baʿal rather than his wives (*ARTU* 4, note 18; *pace*, e.g., U. CASSUTO, *The Goddess Anath* [(Jerusalem 1971] 113) is clear from the reference to Pidray as daughter of Baʿal in *KTU* 1.24:26-27.

In Ugaritic tradition dew and rain come from the god Baʿal (see especially *KTU* 1.19 i:38-46) and the daughters of Baʿal seem to represent types of mist or dew. GORDON (1965:406-407), in rejecting the seasonal interpretation of the Baʿal mythology, notes that dew is a year-round phenomenon. DE MOOR (1971:188), on the other hand, argues that Arṣay, unlike her sisters, is specifically the summer dew which does not disappear when Baʿal disappears to the underworld in accordance with the seasonal pattern of the

Ba'al mythology. This is suggested by *KTU* 1.5 v:10-11. Ṭallay may have been worshipped at *ybrd(m)* (*ARTU* on *KTU* 1.24:29). She also appears in the personal name [f]*Ṭá-la-ia* (RS 16.156:8, 17—*PRU* III, 61).

III. This deity does not appear in any Biblical source, though *ṭal* is frequently treated as a special gift of God (e.g. Prov 3: 20; Zech 9:12) and is sometimes associated with other common nouns which may have mythological overtones. Thus in Gen 27:28 (cf. also 39) we find in Isaac's blessing on Jacob: "May God give you the dew of heaven, and of the oil [= rain] of the earth, and plenty of grain and wine". Here 'grain' is *dāgān* (→Dagon) and '→wine' is *tîrôš* both of which *might* have mythological overtones, while the parallel phrases *ṭal haššāmayim* and *šěmannē hā'āreṣ* are also found in Ugaritic literature (*ṭl šmm* //*šmn arṣ*: *KTU* 1.3 ii:39-40; iv:43). The association of dew with the heavens is found in a number of Biblical Hebrew texts (e.g. Zech 9:12; Hag 1:10).

In Job 38:28 the denial that rain and dew have a father might have polemical force in the context of Ba'al's paternity of the dew and rain. Other texts which may have dew in some sort of magical or mythological role include Isa 18:4; 26:19 (both rather obscure and unconvincing) and Ps 110:3 (perhaps "like Dew I have begotten you", though the text is very difficult; cf. especially OTZEN 1982:349-350). Otherwise dew and rain appear together frequently (Deut 32:2; 2 Sam 1:21), with *ṭal* parallel to *māṭār*, 'rain', *rěbîbîm*, 'showers, fine rain', etc. It is possible that the feminine personal name Abital (*'ăbîṭal*: 2 Sam 3:4; 1 Chr 3:3) means 'my father is dew' and there is also the feminine name *ḥămûṭal* (2 Kgs 23:31; Jer 52:1), which is of unclear meaning, but both are often taken to be Aramaized forms related to *ṣēl* 'shadow'.

IV. *Bibliography*

A. CAQUOT, *Textes Ougaritiques I. Mythes et légendes* (Paris 1974); F. S. FRICK, *ABD* 5 (1992) 124-125; C. H. GORDON, *Ugaritic Textbook* (AnBib 38; Rome 1965) 406-407; P. HUMBERT, La rosée tombe en Israël, *ThZ* 13 (1957) 487-493; O. LORETZ, "Wasser- und Tauschöpfen" als Bezeichnung für Regenmagie in KTU 1.19 II 1-3A, *UF* 17 (1986) 95-98; LORETZ, *Ugarit und die Bibel* (Darmstadt 1990) 161-166; J. C. DE MOOR, *The Seasonal Pattern in the Ugaritic Myth of Ba'lu* (AOAT 16; Neukrichen-Vluyn 1971) 188; B. OTZEN, טל, *TWAT* 3 (1982) 344-352.

J. F. HEALEY

DIABOLOS → DEVIL

DIKE Δίκη

I. *Dikē* (originally 'customary behaviour', later 'justice') is the Greek deity of justice and occurs as a divine name in the Bible in Acts 28:4 and as a metaphor for a heavenly being in Wis 1:8-9 and 11:20. The personification of abstract concepts in the form of deities occurs in Greek literature as early as the second half of the eighth century BCE. Personifications appear first in poetry, then move into the visual arts (see e.g. Pausanias 5, 18, 2; further HAMDORF 1964:52-53, 110 et passim), and finally find their way into the realm of the cult.

II. The didactic poet Hesiod was the first to personify Dikē (Homer, *Iliad* 16: 387-8, is a dubious instance and probably an interpolation based upon Hesiod's *Erga*). Hesiod transforms Dikē into a daughter of →Zeus and →Themis (Themis is the personification of everything that is right and proper in nature and society) and a sister of Eunomia and Eirene (the three of them are the Hōrai). Highly respected by the gods of Olympus, she immediately reports to Zeus all the unrighteous deeds of mankind so that people will have to pay for their crimes. Whenever they injure her, their lives will end up in disaster (*Theog.* 901-3, *Op.* 213-285). This image of Dikē as the favourite daughter of Zeus, even as the one who shares his throne and is his assessor or adviser (*parhedros*), recurs very frequently in Greek authors from Hesiod until the end of antiquity (especially in the great tragedians; see the large collection of quotations in

Stobaeus' chapter on Dikē in his *Eclogae* I 3). Aeschylus, Sophocles, Euripides, Pindar, Bakchylides, Solon, Parmenides, Heraclitus, [Orpheus] *Hymn* 62, Plato, Aratus, Plutarch, Aulus Gellius, Athenaeus, Julian, Libanius, and many others (also Latin writers like Ovid and Virgil) give testimony to this (numerous references in HIRZEL 1907, WASER 1905, and HAMDORF 1964). Some authors identify her with Parthenos, i.e. the constellation Virgo (see esp. Aratus, *Phaenomena* 96-136, and Virgil, *Georgica* IV).

In the course of the centuries, Dikē, having originally only the positive characteristics of a goddess who watches over justice, gradually assumed the more negative aspects of the Erinyes, goddesses of punishment and revenge, as well (e.g. Sophocles, *Ajax* 1390). The original distinction between Dikē and such demonic deities became more and more blurred as Dikē progressively changed from an accuser or plaintiff into a mighty and relentless deity who wrathfully wielded the weapons of revenge. This entailed that her natural habitat also moved away gradually from the lofty Olympus to the netherworld (where the Erinyes had their residence as well), a process which was facilitated by the change in the image of Hades from a place of mere vengeance and torment to a place of pure administration of justice. The development of a belief in judgement after death among the Greeks played an important role in this process. Thus Dikē became a goddess of the netherworld with power over life and death (e.g. Sophocles, *Electra* 528, *Antigone* 450-1). Pythagoreans even developed an idea of tripartite justice: Themis wielded the scepter of justice in heaven, →Nomos on earth, and Dikē in the netherworld (Iamblichus, *De vita Pyth.* 46). So, in the course of time, Dikē ultimately became a goddess of death, a development in her character which was never shared by her mother Themis.

The existence of a cult of Dikē is not strongly attested—something which Dikē shares with the Erinyes. Athenaeus explicitly states that it is only from a few people that Dikē received sacrifices and worship (*Deipnosophistae* 12:546b). Although some literary sources refer to altars (Aeschylus, *Agam.* 383-4, *Eum.* 539; Demosthenes, *Contra Aristog.* 35) and temples (Pausanias 2, 20, 5) dedicated to Dikē, little unambiguous archaeological evidence for the existence of such cultic sites has been found (FARNELL 1909:475 n. 227). But, from the Roman period, statues and altars for *Iustitia* have been preserved, and Augustus erected a temple in her honour, probably after Greek models. In art, Dikē is often represented as bearing a sword or some other weapon.

III. In the Bible, Dikē, as belonging to a polytheistic system, inevitably plays only a very limited role (in spite of possible Oriental antecedents in the form of a personified Righteousness, →Zedeq; see ROSENBERG 1965 and BAUMGARTEN 1979). The author of the Wisdom of Solomon mentions a more or less personified Justice without, however, implying that she was a deity. When he says that Justice the accuser will not pass by anyone who celebrates injustice because a report of his words will come before the LORD (1:8-9, and cf. 11:20), he only uses a metaphor, also employed by his two contemporary coreligionists and compatriots, Philo (*Conf.* 118: God's minister Justice will punish men for their audacity; *Mut.* 194: the name Dinah is by interpretation Justice, the assessor [*parhedros*] of God; *Jos.* 48: even if no one denounces us, we should have fear or respect for Justice, the assessor of God, she who surveys all our doings; cf. *Jos.* 170; *Decal.* 95; *Spec. leg.* 4:201; *Prob.* 89) and Pseudo-Phocylides (77: leave vengeance to Justice). By this formulation the author of the Wisdom of Solomon does not want to deify Justice, although his concept of Wisdom as a *parhedros* of God (9:4) may have facilitated for him the notion of a female heavenly power separate from God. (Compare the way in which the author of 4 Macc speaks about the anger of divine justice [or Justice?, he always uses the formula *hē theia dikē*], 4:21, or about the eternal torment inflicted by divine justice, 9:9 and 12:12; at the end of the book, at 18:22, he has divine justice pursue the accursed tyrant;

also Josephus' use of *dikē/Dikē* is heavily influenced by his classical models: see *Bell.* 7:34; *Ant.* 6:305).

In Acts 28:4 we have quite a different case. Here the pagan inhabitants of Melitē (Malta or Kephallenia?), after the shipwreck and rescue of Paul and his fellow travellers, react to Paul's being bitten by a venomous snake by saying: "No doubt this man is a murderer. Though he has escaped from the sea, Dikē has not allowed him to live" (RSV). Here we can clearly perceive the later Greek concept of Dikē as the goddess who pursues the wrongdoer and takes revenge for crimes that have gone undetected and unpunished by human judges. The people described by Luke as *barbaroi* (28:2) evidently draw from the fact that Paul was attacked by a deadly poisonous reptile the conclusion that the goddess of justice has finally caught up with him. Luke again turns out to be well informed about pagan concepts and beliefs of his time (cf. Acts 14:8-13; 17:22-23; 19:23-41; etc.).

IV. *Bibliography*

J. M. BAUMGARTEN, The Heavenly Tribunal and the Personification of Ṣedeq in Jewish Apocalyptic, *ANRW* II 19,1 (Berlin-New York 1979) 219-239; W. BURKERT, *Greek Religion* (Cambridge, Mass. 1985) 184-186, 249; V. EHRENBERG, *Die Rechtsidee im frühen Griechentum* (Leipzig 1921) 54-102; L. R. FARNELL, *The Cults of the Greek States* 5 (Oxford 1909) 443-447, 475; H. VON GEISAU, Dike, *KP* 2 (1975) 24-26; W. K. C. GUTHRIE, *The Greeks and Their Gods* (London 1950) 123-127; *F. W. HAMDORF, *Griechische Kultpersonifikationen der vorhellenistischen Zeit* (Mainz 1964) 51-53, 110; *R. HIRZEL, *Themis, Dike und Verwandtes* (Leipzig 1907) esp. 138-158; K. LATTE, *Römische Religionsgeschichte* (München 1960) 300; M. P. NILSSON, *Geschichte der griechischen Religion*, 2 vols. (München 1955-1961) s.v.; L. PETERSEN, *Zur Geschichte der Personifikation in griechischer Dichtung und bildender Kunst* (diss. Würzburg 1939); R. A. ROSENBERG, The God Ṣedeq, *HUCA* 36 (1965) 161-177; G. QUELL & G. SCHRENK, *TWNT* 2 (1935) 180-183; C. SPICQ, *Notes de lexicographie néotestamentaire. Supplément* (OBO 22,3; Fribourg 1982) 120-122; *O. WASER, Dike, *PW* 5 (1905) 574-578.

P. W. VAN DER HORST

DIONYSUS Διόνυσος

I. Dionysos, the Greek god of ecstasy, bears a name of uncertain etymology, although resembling the usual Greek types of anthroponyms (e.g. Dio-doros, "gift from Zeus"). Accordingly, ancient authors agree to see the name of Zeus (gen. Διός) in the first half; some understood -νυσος as a foreign word for son ("Son of Zeus"), others derived it from the mythical place of his upbringing, Nysa ("Zeus from Nysa"). These etymologies are linguistically valueless, but reflect the god's status with regard to Zeus, whom mythology makes his father.

At the same time, Greek myth regularly tells of Dionysos' arrival from abroad, especially from those foreign places, where Nysa was located (Stephanus Byz. gives a list of ten places, from Asia Minor to Ethiopia and India). By reading these myths historically, insisting on Dionysos' non-Gk characteristics, and pointing out his absence from Homer, modern historians of religion, from N. Fréret and E. Rohde to M. P. Nilsson theorized that Dyonysos was a god of foreign origin and had arrived from Thrace or Phrygia (or from both) during the Archaic age (see MCGINTY 1978); others protested, notably MEULI (1975), OTTO (1933) and KERÉNYI (1976). The dispute has been settled by the decipherment of the Mycenaean (so called Linear B) documents: like other later Olympians, Dionysos is present in the pantheon of Mycenaean Greece, and a recent text from Mycenaean Chania in Crete is witness to a cult together with Zeus (HALLAGER 1992).

Dionysos was equated with several gods of surrounding civilizations—with the Thracian Sabazios, the Etruscan Fufluns, the Roman Liber (for both see →Bacchus), but also with the Egyptian →Osiris (Herodotus, 72, 42) and the Jewish →Yahweh (see below III).

In the Bible, Dionysos is mentioned in 2

Macc 6:7; 14:33 and 3 Macc 2:29 in the context of anti-Jewish undertakings of the kings Antiochos IV, Demetrios I and Ptolemy IV.

II. Dominant among the traits of Dionysos is his anti-structural character. In cult, he is associated with rituals and festivals of reversal; myths tell of his foreign origin and surround him with his own crowd of menads and satyrs, ecstatic women and ithyphallic, sexually aroused and frequently drunk animal-like males, free from the bonds of ordinary behaviour of the genders in Greek society; already in late Archaic times, he had become the divinity of mystery cults who in turn break away from the *polis* order (BURKERT 1987).

Dionysiac festivals usually take place in winter or early spring; they reenact the periodical disruption of order through the intrusion of the god and his forces. The two main types are the nearly Panhellenic Agrionia and the Athenian and Ionian Anthesteria. Both are widespread on both sides of the Aegean which points to their pre-migration, i.e. Bronze Age origin.

The Agrionia festival lent its name to several local month names. It was celebrated in a wide variety of local rituals (BURKERT 1972:189-200). It seems common to split society into its two gender halves which sometimes clash in a potentially violent way. In Boeotian Orchomenos, Plutarch (*Quaest. Graec.* 38) tells of two groups, black-clad men and white-clad women; the priest of Dionysos chased the women with a sword and had originally had the freedom to kill them. In other places, the disruption of elementary social life was enacted more peacefully: in Chaeroneia, the women went to seek the baby Dionysos, dined together, and gave themselves to ritual joking (Plutarch, *Quaest. symp.* 717 A). Aetiological myths explain the ritual by stories of how the women resisted Dionysos on his first arrival and were struck with madness from the god; they ran wild, killed their children, and left town for the wilderness (MEULI 1975:1018-1021).

An even more violent expression of Dionysiac otherness lies behind rituals whose origins go back to human sacrifice. They mostly belong to a closely circumscribed area of North Eastern Aegaeis and to a Dionysos, whose epithets are *Omadios* ("Raw, i.e. Wild one", on the island of Chios), *Omēstēs* ("Raw-Eater", on neighbouring Lesbos) or *Anthrōporrhaistēs* ("Ripper of Humans", on the island of Tenedos). Presumably, they preserve older forms of an Agrionia festival (GRAF 1985:74-80).

The Anthesteria are well known only from Athens (DEUBNER 1932:93-123; HAMILTON 1992); the Ionian cults are important as pointing to a Bronze Age origin of the festival. The Athenian festival, celebrated in the month Anthesterion (February-March), consisted of three days, Pithoigia ("Opening of the Barrel"), Choes ("Jugs"), and Chytroi ("Pots"). The main event of the first day was the opening of the barrels with the new wine; it was ritually done in the Limnaion, a sanctuary of the god "In the Swamps". Wine is not harmless; Dionysos' first arrival with the wine, according to an Attic myth, brought death to his host, Ikarios, and his daughter Mestra, and only after men had learned how to mix it with water, did it lose some of its dangers (FLÜCKIGER-GUGGENHEIM 1984). The second day saw the arrival of the god in his ship cart, followed by the satyrs; the paradox of a ship on land, attested also for the Anthesteria of Ionia, depicts the anomaly of Dionysos' festival; the implication is that the god arrived from beyond the sea, from the outer margins of the world. The main event of the day was a drinking competition among the Athenian men which inverted ordinary symposiastic rules: every man drank in isolation, in utter silence, and not from a common mixing bowl but from his own jug (which gave the day its designation). A sacred marriage between the god and the "Queen", the wife of the main sacred official, *archōn basileus*, on the evening of the day led back to community and felicity. On the third day, pots (*chutroi*) with a primeval meal were offered to Hermes as a commemoration of the Flood, and the Kares (barbarian Carians, said also to be former inhabitants of Attica) or Keres (souls of the dead, according to some, but see BREMMER 1983:113-118), those uncanny powers whose presence had marked the festival, were chased away; characteristically, the arrival of Dionysos went together not only with the arrival of the new wine, but also of uncanny powers.

The Athenian Anthesteria were part of a wider cycle of Dionysiac festivals which extended from the Rural Dionysia in Posideon (December-January) via Lenaia (in Gamelion, January-February) and Anthesteria to the City Dionysia in Elaphebolion (March-April). Every festival projected its own image of Dionysiac epiphany. The Rural Dionysia were characterized by male sexuality; its main rite being a phallic procession. Aristophanes reenacts the rite in his *Acharnenses*; the choral song to Phales, the deified phallos (263-279), indicates that the phallic ritual was associated with male sexual pleasure and violence, not with fertility. The Lenaia (Dionysia on the Lenaion) are but imperfectly known; they featured Dionysiac dancing, the Lenaion being a dancing floor on the Agora (SHAPIRO 1989:85-87). The City Dionysia, the most recent festival, again displayed a phallic procession; but their main event, from the early 5th century onward, was the staging of tragedies on the three successive days of the festival, as comedies were staged at the Lenaia. Already ancient authors noted the absence of Dionysian subjects in tragedy (BIERL 1991). The relationship between god and tragedy lies on another level. On the one hand, Dionysiac ritual with its masks, dancing and singing had formed a nucleus from which dramatic representations grew; on the other hand, the atmosphere of Dionysian otherness and ambiguity provided the background for the sort of self-reflexion about the *polis* Athens, its values and its traditions which is fundamental to Athenian drama. By the Hellenistic age, dramatic performances had emancipated from Athens and from its citizen choirs, but not from Dionysos; the association of Dionysian *technitai*, a "trade union" of the performers of drama which organized itself around the cult of Dionysos, had become important: one of their foremost centres was the sanctuary of Dionysos in Teos (PICKARD-CAMBRIDGE 1968:279-321).

Hellenistic Dionysia (and, to a certain degree, those of the Imperial epoch) thus were characterized by the splendour of theatrical performances: a really Greek town has to have a theatre, and very often the Dionysia are used also for the display of civic honours. Besides the theatre, Dionysiac processions were another occasion for display; their fantastic and picturesque elements (ship cart, satyrs and menads, phalloi) caught the imagination of Hellenistic rulers. We still have the description of such a procession in Alexandria under Ptolemy II, written by Kallixeinos of Rhodes (*FGH* 627 F 1).

The god's most conspicuous worshippers are the ecstatic women, the maenads (connected with the Gk *mania*, "madness", and *mainesthai*, "to be mad") (HENRICHS 1978). As the satyrs are a mythical image of the male human worshipers of Dionysos, the maenads are an image of the ecstatic women; but while mythical satyrs are clearly differentiated from real men by their pointed animal ears and horse tails (HEDREEN 1992), there exists no comparable differentiation between mythical and historical maenads. The prominence of women in Dionysos' cult is another sign of his otherness, as is ecstasy; both enact the radical disruption of societal borders—for which Euripides' *Bacchai* are the most powerful literary expression; besides this symbolic value, the rituals of purely feminine groups, leaving their usual confinement in house and town, may have a socio-psychological function as well (JEANMAIRE 1951; KRAEMER 1979). Dionysos' connection with women does not necessarily include ecstasy; in a rite from Elis, a group of women calls the god from the sea in the shape of a bull (Plutarch, *Quaest. graec.* 36), and the Athenian sacred marriage is the affair of another ritual group of women (AVAGIANOU 1991:177-197). On the other hand, male ecstatic followers of Dionysos are attested as early as the beginning of the

5th cent BCE (Herodotus 2,79), and a prominent epiclesis of Dionysos, *Bakchos*, also designates his male ecstatic follower, the male equivalent of a *Bakchē* or maenad. Maenads, however, are known already to the poet of the *Iliad* (who is otherwise reticent as regards Dionysos, for poetological, not historical reasons); from the late 6th cent. onwards, they are attested in different Greek cities as regular part of the city's cultic activities (see e.g. the epigram for a Milesian priestess (HENRICHS 1969) or the inscription from Magnesia-on-the-Meander recording the institution of three local thiasoi after a miracle had occurred, (*Inschriften von Magnesia* no. 215). Maenadic ritual comprises the leaving of the town in order to go into forest or mountain (*oreibasia*—meaning real physical exertion e.g. when the Athenian maenads walked to and climbed Mt. Kithairon near Delphi), where the women (or, at least in later times, mixed private thiasoi as well) danced and performed sacrifices; the myths talk also about the killing of live animals and of eating their raw flesh (*ōmophagia*); there are no indications as to the corresponding ritual behaviour.

The ritual of private *thiasoi*, which had grown very numerous by Hellenistic times, shades into Bacchic mystery cults. Ecstatic groups which perform openly in the streets but which are confined to initiated members are first attested in Olbia at the Northern shore of the Black Sea at the beginning of the 5th cent. BCE (Herodotus 4,72); later in the century, in the same town, enigmatic inscriptions connect Dionysos with Orpheus or Orphica (WEST 1982), and the same Herodotus equates eschatological believes of Bacchic and Orphic mystery cults with Pythagorean and Egyptian ritual (2,81). At the turn of the fifth to the fourth century, there are the first of a series of hexametrical texts on gold leaves; they all come from graves and hold out eschatological promises to the buried; their Bacchic context has become clear from more recent finds (GRAF 1993). Their distribution in time and space demonstrate the importance of Dionysiac mystery cults; the dates range from late 5th cent. BCE to the imperial Age, with a peak in the 4th and 3d cent. BCE; they were found especially in the margins of the Greek world, Northern Greece (where two late 4th cent. graves of Derveni contained a papyrus book with verses of Orpheus and a crater with Dionysiac scenes), Crete and Southern Italy; in Italian Cumae, an inscription from the mid-fifth century BCE delimits a graveyard for a closed group of *bakchoi* (TURCAN 1986). From Southern Italy, Dionysiac mysteries entered Rome at the outset of the 2nd cent. BCE (BOTTINI 1992).

It would be wrong to expect a closed system of beliefs in all these mystery groups; the popularity of Dionysiac associations in the Hellenistic and Imperial epoch was based not on theology but on the fact that they offered security and religious identity in an open and rapidly changing society. But even in the more open groups, some vestiges of the disruptive character of the god could be preserved; the cult place often was an (artificial) grotto (LAVAGNE 1976), female participants donned the costume of the menads (with its association of wilderness), male ones could be called *boukoloi*, shepherds (with similar associations); use of the drug alcohol and heightened sexual tensions must have been present. When introduced into Rome, these features were enough to trigger, in 186 BCE, the Bacchanalia scandal which led to severe restrictions in the freedom of cult (→Bacchus); in Ptolemaic Egypt, Ptolemy IV controlled the sacred books of the Bacchic mysteries which must have contained both myths and ritual regulations (*SB* 7266). Such sacred books existed more widely, and they provided a very loose doctrinal coherence at least among the mystery groups.

This also explains why, despite wide variations, some features were very widespread. Many mystery groups, at least those of the gold leaves, believed in a blessed existence after death as a consequence of the initiation; to some, this went together with the belief in an original divine nature of the soul (or the entire person); metempsychosis, however, belongs only to a smaller group.

An impressive series of iconographical documents from late Hellenistic-early Imperial times (Villa Farnese in Rome, Villa dei Misteri in Pompeii, MATZ 1963) gives insight into ideology and initiation rituals. Prominent among the rituals and often represented is the confrontation with male sexuality, ritualized as an encounter with the phallos (BURKERT 1987:95-96); the Pompeian fresco also confirms the key role of sacred books well attested in Greek Dionysiac (Orphic) ritual and features a unique flagellation scene which might be read literally or symbolically.

These features of his cult reflect themselves not only in local aetiological myths, but also in the greater Panhellenic ones. Already Hesiod tells of Dionysos' birth from the union of Zeus and the mortal princess Semele (*Theog.* 942); by the 5th cent. BCE, the rest of this myth is well attested—how Semele died when seeing Zeus as lightning, how the god saved the yet unborn and carried it in his thigh till its birth; a first birth from a dead woman, a second one from a man underscore Dionysos' position between categories, as does the deification of someone born from a mortal woman. Late archaic and classical ages were more interested in his ecstatic qualities as shown by the myth of how he fetched back Hephaestos to Olympus, a myth very often depicted on Attic vases. When the Greek world opened to the East, the arrival of Dionysos from the fabulous margins of the world became prominent; like a prefiguration of Alexander, Dionysos conquered the East with his forces and brought the wine before, finally, coming back to Greece and introducing there his cult and his gifts.

III. In the Bible, Dionysos plays no direct role, besides the occurrence of the very common theophoric names Dionysius (Areopagita) in Acts 17:34 and Bakchides in 1 Macc 7:8-19 and three references to the god in 2 and 3 Macc, two in relation to Jerusalem, one to the Jews of Egypt. According to 2 Macc 6, in 168 BCE Antiochos IV Epiphanes pressed the Hellenization of Jerusalem by dedicating the Temple to Zeus (Olympios), replacing sabbath by the monthly birthday of the king and compelling the Jews to celebrate the Dionysia with a procession of ivy (2 Macc 6:7). When, after his victory over Antiochos' son Antiochos V, Demetrios I Soter wished the extradition of Judas Maccabee, his governor threatened to destroy the Temple and to build a sanctuary of Dionysos in its place (2 Macc 14:33). As to the Egyptian Jews, Ptolemy IV threatened to stigmatise them with the brandmark of "the ivy-leaf sign of Dionysos" (3 Macc 2:29).

In all cases, Dionysos could simply represent one of most popular Greek gods whose public cult offered Hellenistic kings an occasion for the display of luxury, and Ptolemy IV had anyway a peculiar interest in Dionysos. But at least 2 Macc 14:33 and 3 Macc 2:29 point to a closer connection between Dionysos and Yahweh. Greek and Roman authors currently identified the two; the arguments are collected in Plutarch (*Quaest. conv.* 4,6) and Tacitus (*Hist.* 5,5) (FAUTH & HEUBNER 1982:87-90). Both base the identification on details of Jewish cult; Plutarch insists on the Dionysiac character of the Feast of Tabernacles and of Hannukah, and on a series of Dionysiac features in the Temple cult, but also on the association of sabbath with Sabazios and *sabos,* which in turn had been identified with the ecstatic Dionysos and his followers; Claudius Iolaus (*FGH* 788 F 4) then derived the *Ioudaioi* from *Oudaios*, a follower of Dionysos. At least in these writers, it seems a learned way to classify Jewish religion according to the rules of *interpretatio Graeca*. But the identification contains polemical potentialities, given the contrast between Dionysiac licence and Jewish morality which was exploited by Tacitus and which could have been used already by the Hellenistic kings.

IV. Under the influence both of neoplatonic spiritualisation of Orphic writings and perhaps of Christian soteriology, in later antiquity Dionysos could develop into a saviour figure whose reign, following the one of Zeus (Orpheus, frg.101 KERN, from Proclus, but already Orph. frg. 14, Plato,

*Phlb.*66 C), would bring back a new age of happiness. The best expression of these hopes are images like the mosaics from a villa in Nea Paphos on Cyprus from the first half of the 4th cent. CE (DASZEWSKI 1985); but the importance of the god is shown also in the huge poem *Dionysiaka* by the Christian Nonnos of Panopolis, written in the 5th cent. CE (for the relationship between Nonnos' Christian faith and the poem on a pagan subject see WILLERS 1992).

V. *Bibliography*

A. AVAGIANOU, *Sacred Marriage in the Rituals of Greek Religion* (Bern 1991); J. N. BREMMER, *The Early Greek Concept of the Soul* (Princeton 1983); A. F. H. BIERL, *Dionysos und die griechische Tragödie* (Classica Monacensia 1; Tübingen 1991); A. BOTTINI, *Archeologia della salvezza. L'escatologia greca nelle testimonianze archeologiche* (Milan 1992); W. BURKERT, *Homo Necans. Interpretationen altgriechischer Opferriten und Mythen* (RGVV 32; Berlin and New York 1972); BURKERT, *Ancient Mystery Cults* (Cambridge, Mass. 1987); W. A. DASZEWSKI, *Dionysos der Erlöser* (Mainz 1985); L. DEUBNER, *Attische Feste* (Berlin 1932); W. FAUTH & H. HEUBNER, *P. Cornelius Tacitus. Die Historien. Kommentar,* vol. 5 (Heidelberg 1982); D. FLÜCKIGER-GUGGENHEIM, *Göttliche Gäste. Die Einkehr von Göttern und Heroen in der griechischen Mythologie* (Bern 1984); F. GRAF, *Nordionische Kulte. Religionsgeschichtliche und epigraphische Untersuchungen zu den Kulten von Chios, Erythrai, Klazomenai und Phokaia* (Rome 1985); GRAF, Dionysian and Orphic Eschatology. New Texts and Old Questions, *Masks of Dionysos* (eds. T. Carpenter & C. A. Faraone; Ithaca N.Y. 1993) 239-258; E. HALLAGER et al., New Linear B Tablets from Khania, *Kadmos* 31 (1992) 61-87; R. HAMILTON, *Choes and Anthesteria. Athenian Iconography and Ritual* (Ann Arbor 1992); G. M. HEDREEN, *Silens in Attic Black-Figure Vase-Painting. Myth and Performance* (Ann Arbor 1992); A. HENRICHS, Die Mänaden von Milet, *ZPE* 4 (1969) 223-341; A. HENRICHS, Greek Menadism from Olympias to Messalina, *HSCP* 82 (Cambridge Mass. 1978) 121-160; H. JEANMAIRE, *Dionysos. Histoire du culte de Bacchus* (Paris 1951); C. KERÉNYI, *Dionysos. Archetypal Image of Indestructible Life* (Bollingen series LXV: 2, Princeton 1976); R. S. KRAEMER, Ecstasy and Possession. The Attraction of Women to the Cult of Dionysos, *HTR* 72 (1979) 55-80; H. LAVAGNE, *Operosa antra. Recherches sur la grotte à Rome de Sylla à Hadrien* (Rome/Paris 1976); P. MCGINTY, *Interpretation and Dionysos. Method in the Study of a God* (Den Haag 1978); F. MATZ, *Διονυσιακὴ Τελετή. Archäologische Untersuchungen zum Dionysoskult in hellenistischer und römischer Zeit* (Abh. Mainz 1963:15, Wiesbaden 1963); K. MEULI, *Gesammelte Schriften* (ed. T. Gelzer; Basel 1975); M. P. NILSSON, *The Dionysiac Mysteries of the Hellenistic and Roman Age* (Lund 1957); W. F. OTTO, *Dionysos. Mythos und Kultus* (Frankfurt 1933); A. PICKARD-CAMBRIDGE, *The Dramatic Festivals of Athens,* 2nd edition (Oxford 1968); E. ROHDE, *Psyche. Seelencult und Unsterblichkeitsglaube der Griechen*, 2nd ed. (Freiburg i.B./Leipzig/Tübingen 1898); H. A. SHAPIRO, *Art and Cult under the Tyrants in Athens* (Mainz 1989); R. TURCAN, Bacchoi ou bacchants? De la dissidence des vivants à la ségrégation des morts, *L'association dionysiaque dans les sociétés anciennes* (ed. O. De Cazanove; Rome 1986) 227-246; M. L. WEST, The Orphics of Olbia, *ZPE* 45 (1982) 17-29; D. WILLERS, Dionysos und Christus - ein archäologisches Zeugnis zur 'Konfessionsangehörigkeit' des Nonnos, *MusHelv* 49 (1992) 141-151.

F. GRAF

DIOSKOUROI Διόσκουροι

I. The Dioskouroi, twin heroes and brothers of Helen, occur as the mascot or ensign of the ship in which Paul and his fellow-travellers reach Syracuse after their shipwreck on Malta (Acts 28:11). They presumably also lend their name to the month Dioskoros at 2 Macc 11:21.

II. 'Dios-kouroi' ('youths of →Zeus') in

mythology is the title of the Tyndarids (sons of Tyndareus) at Sparta, namely Kastor and Polydeukes (in Latin, via Etruscan, Castor and Pollux). The Greeks inherited these horsemen twins from Indo-European times, as congeners in Sanskrit (the Aśvins) and Latvian show (WARD 1968: ch. ii). In mythology they rescue their sister Helen (from Theseus or from a Spartan called Enarsphoros) who in the Indo-European myth (cf. →Menelaos) had surely been their wife too. Wife-snatching in Greek mythology is transferred to their 'Rape of the Leukippides', the daughters of Leukippos, →Phoebe and Hilaeira—themselves worshipped in Sparta with (nubile?) maidens as priestesses (Pausanias 3, 16, 1). The end comes when the mortal twin Kastor is killed as they rustle cattle from the two sons of Aphareus, Idas and keen-sighted Lynkeus; but Polydeukes strikes a deal and they live alternate days (Apollodoros 3, 11, 2), whether in rotation or together.

In Greece, they are associated with Sparta (and its double kingship), where they receive some cult (WIDE 1893:315), and with warriors, particularly lending their assistance in battle; such assistance, in a cavalry battle of 499 BCE, led to their adoption in Rome too, clearly in the wake of considerable popularity in the Greek towns of Italy (Livy 2, 20, 12 and e.g. BURKERT 1985:213). But the Dioskouroi did not just rescue cavalry or soldiers: they also specialised in the rescue of sailors in distress, appearing as St Elmo's fire—electricity discharged from the masthead, hence their appearance as the ensign of Paul's ship.

Such rescue took on a metaphorical, metaphysical dimension, as they were initiated at the Mysteries at Eleusis (a model to humanity seeking a pagan solution to the problem of death) and were immortalised as stars. They had, after all, overcome their own deaths and symbolised in perpetuity the contrast between mortality and immortality: "ils passent tour à tour des ténèbres subterrestres à la gloire de l'empyrée, à laquelle ne cessent plus de participer, avec eux, les deux filles de Leucippe qu'ils ont épousées: Phoïbè, brillante comme le soleil, et Hilaeira, dont le nom garde, en grec, la caresse d'un rayon de lune" (CARCOPINO 1927:111). This resonance may be a factor in the author of Acts choosing to mention the ensign (it was not just the name of the ship, as the *Revised English Bible* might lead one to believe). It also explains the depiction of the Dioskouroi on the main vault of the mystic 'Pythagorean' basilica at the Porta Maggiore in Rome (ca. 50 CE), and on sarcophagi (NILSSON 1974: II 495)—where CARCOPINO (1927: 111) and CUMONT (1942) thought of the two hemispheres, of subterranean darkness and of life, a Dioscuric symbolism going back, it seems, to the Pythagoreans and a commonplace in later mysticism (e.g. Sextus Emp., *Adv. Math.* 9:37, CUMONT 1942:68-69). Their abduction of the Leukippides too could represent the raising of the human soul to the heavens (CUMONT 1942:99-103).

The conceptual space of the Dioskouroi was enhanced by their progressive association with other plural and obscure gods—the Anak(t)tes ('Lords'), the Great Gods, the Kabeiroi (maybe Phoenician in origin), Kouretes and Korybantes (NILSSON 1974: I 406-7; BURKERT 1985:212).

III. The two young men who appear to Heliodoros in the Temple at 2 Macc 3:26 were interpreted by HARRIS (1906:156-157) as 'Dioscuric', but the term so used has scant cash value (cf. idem 1906: 34: "we cannot so easily affirm →Cain and →Abel to be Dioscuri, though there are some things that look that way").

IV. *Bibliography*

E. BETHE, Dioskuren, *PW* 5 (1905) 1087-1123; W. BURKERT, *Greek Religion, Archaic and Classical*, ET (Oxford 1985) 212-213; J. CARCOPINO, *La basilique pythagoricienne de la porte majeure* (Paris 1927, repr. 1943); F. CUMONT, *Recherches sur le symbolisme funéraire des romains* (Paris 1942) ch. 1 [though N.B. in general the caution expressed by R. TURCAN, Les sarcophages romains et le problème du symbolisme funéraire, *ANRW* II 16, 2 (1978) 1700-35]; J. R. HARRIS, *The Cult of the Heavenly Twins* (Cambridge 1906); G.

KOCH & H. SICHTERMANN, *Römische Sarkophage* (München 1982) 144; M. P. NILSSON, *Geschichte der griechischen Religion*, 2 vols. (3rd ed., München 1974) i, 406-11. ii, 495; D. J. WARD, *The Divine Twins: an Indo-European myth in Germanic tradition* (Berkeley & Los Angeles 1968); M. L. WEST, *Immortal Helen* (London 1975) 8-9; S. WIDE, *Lakonische Kulte* (Leipzig 1893) 304-325.

K. DOWDEN

DIVINE BEINGS → SONS OF (THE) GOD(S)

DOD דוד

I. In the Hebrew Bible the word *dwd* means 'Beloved', 'Love', 'Uncle' (father's brother). The etymology of the word is problematic (SANMARTIN-ASCASO 1977:153; *HALAT* 206). The connection to the name David has become rickety (STAMM 1960: 166-169). It has been assumed that Dod serves in the Hebrew Bible as an epithet for →Yahweh (e.g. VAN ZIJL 1960:190).

II. In Akkadian one finds the word *dādu(m)*, 'Beloved', 'Darling', used of family members, kings, and deities (*CAD* D 149). A distinction should be made between the assumed Mesopotamian deities Dada, Dadu, Dadudu, on the one hand, and the kinship term **dād* (paternal uncle) used as a theophoric element in personal names (HUFFMON 1965:181-182; GELB 1980: 17.574). The names of the former group can probably all be related to the god Adad or →Hadad (cf. EBELING 1938). The use of Dadu as theophoric element in anthroponyms, on the other hand, is a case in point of the deification of dead kin, also evidenced by the use of →Father and →Brother as theophoric elements.

Deities by the names of Dad and Dadat, reconstructed from onomastic evidence, are known from pre-classical North Arabic inscriptions from around the middle of the last millennium BCE (HÖFNER *WbMyth* 1/1 432; *RAAM* 369.371). The element *dd* also appears in epigraphic Aramaic (HERR 1978:16 no. 13), and Palmyrene onomastics (STARK 1971:14.83). In Ugaritic we do not find *dd* as an element in theophoric names (GRÖNDAHL 1967:122). However, divine appellatives constructed with forms from the root YDD are known, e.g. *mddbʿl*, 'Beloved of Baal' (GRÖNDAHL 1967:143).

In the discussion of *dwd* in the Hebrew Bible some weight has been put on the expression *ʾrʾl dwdh* occurring in the Mesha-inscription (*KAI* 181:12). It has been assumed that the word must have something to do with a deity (*KAI* II p. 175); it has even been speculated that the word served as an epithet for Yahweh (VAN ZIJL 1960: 190). It is important to be aware of the fact that this understanding is based purely on guesswork, and it has been claimed recently that "after one hundred years of study directed at the MI [= Mesha Inscription], it is safe to say that an exact understanding of these words is still a mystery" (JACKSON 1989:112). Since several words in the context clearly have not been properly understood, it seems advisable to conclude that *dwdh* in the Mesha-inscription is best left untranslated.

On the whole, the ancient Near Eastern material apparently raises more problems than it solves. When should *dd* in these texts be rendered with 'Beloved' and when with (paternal) 'Uncle'? What is the semantic (and etymological?) relationship between names constructed with *wdd/ydd* and those constructed with *dd/dwd*? We note that in addition to the *dd*-names in ancient Arabic mentioned above, pre-Islamic central Arabia also knew a major deity by the name of Wadd ('Love'). In ancient South Arabian religion Wadd was the official name for the popular moon god (HÖFNER *WbMyth* 1/1 476-477, 549-550). Altogether, the ambiguity of the extra-biblical evidence complicates its usefulness in relation to Hebrew *dwd* (SANMARTIN-ASCASO 1977:154-156).

E. A. KNAUF, A. DE PURY & T. RÖMER suggested to interpret *bytdwd* in line 9 of the fragmentary Aramaic inscription from Tel Dan as **baytDōd*, 'temple of Dôd' (**Bayt-Dawīd* ou **BaytDōd*? Une relecture de la nouvelle inscription de Tel Dan, *BN* 72 [1994] 60-69; *pace* the editors of the inscription: A. BIRAN & J. NAVEH, *IEJ* 43 [1993] 95-96) suggesting that Dod was worshipped by the Aramaic inhabitants of Dan in the ninth century BCE, whereas F. H. CRYER (On the recently discovered "House of David" inscription, *SJOT* 8 [1994] 3-19) believes that we here find a reference to a toponym or to the eponymous ancestor of the lineage that ruled Judah. Future discussions on a possible deity Dod will have to take also this new evidence, if it is, into consideration.

III. Given all the uncertainty concerning the very existence of a deity *dd/dwd* in the cultures surrounding ancient Israel, it is understandable that the former view that a deity *dwd* was also worshipped in ancient Israel has been dwindling among scholars over recent years. Today, the assumption that a deity *dwd* is explicitly referred to in the Bible, a view going back to the last century, and based on the belief that a deity *dwd* was widespread in the Semitic world, in particular in Mesopotamia (BJÖRNDALEN 1986:258-259; AHLSTRÖM 1959:164-165), has been replaced by a new consensus where it is claimed that *dwd* is not a divine name at all, hardly in the biblical *Umwelt* and most certainly not in the Bible itself. Rather, what we are dealing with in the Hebrew Bible are occurrences of the word *dwd* being used as a divine epithet for Yahweh (SANMARTIN-ASCASO 1977; BJÖRNDALEN 1986; OLYAN 1991).

The most important biblical texts adduced to show that Yahweh might be referred to as *dôd* are Isa 5, Am 8:14, Song of Songs, as well as biblical names. The occurrence of *dwd* in Song of Songs is unproblematic. Whereas it was earlier assumed by some scholars (AHLSTRÖM 1959:163-173) that the references to *dwd* in Song of Songs were to a vegetation and fertility god, consensus today quite correctly regards these texts as erotic poetry. The word *dwd* is used in this text to refer to the darling lover *par excellence*. This usage is close to Ugaritic *dd*, and no mythology should be read into this text. The term does not refer to Yahweh or any other god.

Other references to *dwd* as a divine epithet for YHWH are hardly more convincing. Thus, the well-known emendation from *drk* to *ddk* in Am 8:14 was created in a time with a different mentality, and today there is as little need to change the text to find a deity Dod ('your Dod') in Am 8:14. Today we should not only be aware of the difficulties with a deity Dod, but also of the fact that the *drk* of Am 8:14 may be explained otherwise (→Way). The reference to Isa 5 in support of the claim that *dwd* may sometimes be used an an epithet of Yahweh is equally mistaken. The use of *dwd* in this piece of poetry is strictly metaphorical and not epithetical. The textual basis for a deity or a divine epithet *dwd* in ancient Israel is very meagre indeed. It seems to have been based more on the widespread belief in an ancient Near Eastern deity *dwd*, rather than on a careful study of the Hebrew texts themselves.

The only valid evidence for the claim that *dwd* may be used as an epithet for Yahweh in ancient Israel appears to be onomastic. Yet names in the Bible which may be composed with *dwd* as one of the elements (SANMARTIN-ASCASO 1977:160) are problematic. In 2 Chr 20:37 there appears the name *ddwhw*. In commentaries the reading *dwdyhw* has become common (mostly following NOTH *IPN* 240). That this reading is not so simple may be seen from the complex text history of this name, where such different forms as *dwdwyhw, dwdwhw, dwdyhw, ddwhw, dwdhw, ddyhw, drwhw, dwryhw, dwydwhw* are witnessed (NORIN 1986:182 n. 61). We are hardly able to say anything about the meaning of this name at all.

A seal in the Israel museum, of unknown provenance, has been thought to contain the name *ddyhw* (DAVIES 1991:330). Also this reading is uncertain and most probably the name should be read *ʿdyhw*, i.e. the popular personal name Adayahu found in the Bible and also on a seal from Beth-Shemesh and on an Arad ostracon (HESTRIN & DAYAGI-MENDELS 1979 no. 56).

Of interest, also, is the epigraphic Hebrew name *ddymš,* which actually goes against a divine understanding of the element *dd*. But this name, too, may be read differently and can hardly be used decisively in any way (LAYTON 1990:178).

Yet even if *dwd* should appear in theophoric names which might be read as 'Friend/Beloved of Yahweh', or 'Yahweh is a friend', or anything similar, this does not imply that the word necessarily must function as a divine epithet. It is methodologically unsound to classify all word elements appearing in 'theophoric' names as epithets of deities. Since names are constructed as sentences, different 'ordinary' words may be used in theophoric names. Not all predicates are automatically 'epithets'.

From the above we may conclude that even if the occurrence of *dwd/dd* in names appears to have been widespread in the ancient Near East, there is little evidence to support the existence of a deity Dod. Also, there is no evidence in the Hebrew Bible supporting the existence or worship of a deity *dwd*. The word *dwd* may have been used as an appellative or epithet of deities in ancient Israel, including Yahweh, but the evidence is far from conclusive.

IV. *Bibliography*

G. W. AHLSTRÖM, *Psalm 89. Eine Liturgie aus dem Ritual des leidenden Königs* (Lund 1959); A. J. BJÖRNDALEN, *Untersuchungen zur allegorischen Rede der Propheten Amos und Jesaja* (BZAW 165; Berlin 1986); G. I. DAVIES, *Ancient Hebrew Inscriptions. Corpus and Concordance* (Cambridge 1991); E. EBELING, Dada, Dadu, Dâdudu, *RLA* 2 (1938) 97.98; J. D. FOWLER, *Theophoric Personal Names in Ancient Hebrew. A Comparative Study* (JSOT SuppSer 49; Sheffield 1988); I. J. GELB, *Computer-Aided Analysis of Amorite* (AS 21; Chicago 1980); F. GRÖNDAHL, *Die Personennamen der Texte aus Ugarit* (StP 1; Rome 1967); L. G. HERR, *The Scripts of Ancient Northwest Semitic Inscriptions* (HSM 18; Missoula 1978); R. HESTRIN & M. DAYAGI-MENDELS, *Inscribed Seals. First Temple Period Hebrew, Ammonite, Moabite Phoenician and Aramaic* (Jerusalem 1979); M. HÖFNER, *RAAM* Stuttgart 1970) 233-402; H. B. HUFFMON, *Amorite Personal Names in the Mari Texts. A Structural and Lexical Study* (Baltimore 1965); K. P. JACKSON, The Language of the Mesha Inscription, *Studies in the Mesha Inscription and Moab* (ed. A. Dearman; Atlanta 1989) 96-130; S. C. LAYTON, *Archaic Features of Canaanite Personal Names in the Hebrew Bible* (HSM 47; Atlanta 1990); S. NORIN, *Sein Name allein ist hoch. Das Jhw-haltige Suffix althebräischer Personennamen untersucht mit besonderer Berücksichtigung der alttestamentlichen Redaktionsgeschichte* (ConB OTS 24; Malmö 1986); *S. M. OLYAN, The Oaths in Amos 8,14, *Priesthood and Cult in Ancient Israel* (ed. G. A. Anderson & S. M. Olyan; JSOT SupplSer 125; Sheffield 1991) 121-149; *J. SANMARTIN-ASCASO, דּוֹד, *TWAT* 2 (1977) 152-167 [& lit]; J. J. STAMM, Der Name des Königs David, *Congress Volume Oxford 1959* (VTSup 7; Leiden 1960) 165-183; J. J. STARK, *Personal Names in Palmyrene Inscriptions* (Oxford 1971); A. VAN ZIJL, *The Moabites* (Leiden 1960).

H. M. BARSTAD

DOMINION κυριότης

I. The word κυριότης occurs 4 times in the NT (not in the LXX), twice referring to Jesus' power or position as Lord (κύριος) and twice referring to members of a class of angels (Eph 1:21; Col 1:16).

II. In extrabiblical literature, κυριότης occurs only very rarely. When it does, it has the meanings of 'lordship, rule' and 'special meaning'. It is only in writings influenced by the NT that the term is used to refer to a class of angels; see the many references in LAMPE's *PGL* 788b. When in a fragment of the originally Jewish *Apocalypse of Zephaniah* the author is said to have been brought up into the fifth heaven where he saw "angels who are called lords" (ἀγγέλους καλουμένους κυρίους, quoted by Clement of Alexandria, *Strom.* V 11,77,2), we may have here a kind of Jewish precursor of the Christian usage of κυριότης, but the origin of this passage remains debated (contrast the opinion of BIETENHARD 1951:105 n.2 with O. WINTERMUTE in *OTP* I 508 n.*b*), although Acts 10:4 (κύριε said to an angel) would seem to corroborate its Jewish character. The same uncertainty attaches to the 'dominions' mentioned as a class of angels in the longer recension of *2 Enoch* 20:1, handed down only in an Old Church Slavonic version, and to the 'angels of dominions' in *1 Enoch* 61:10, preserved only in a (Christian) Ethiopic translation (W. FOERSTER, *TWNT* 2 568). If these passages could be proved to be of Jewish origin, the NT authors would reflect Jewish usage here, as is also the case with the other designations of angelic classes (BIETENHARD 1951:105; for the use of abstract instead of concrete nouns see FOERSTER in *TWNT* 3 1096). That these (evil?) angels were originally regarded as powerful 'Lords' is apparent from this designation (SCHROEGER 1981:821).

III. In Eph 1:21 κυριότης is part of an enumeration of supernatural powers. The author says that God has raised →Jesus →Christ from the dead and seated him at his right hand in the heavenly places "far above all rule and authority and power and dominion and every name that is named" (ὑπεράνω πάσης ἀρχῆς καὶ ἐξουσίας καὶ δυνάμεως καὶ κυριότητος καὶ παντὸς ὀνόματος ὀνομαζομένου, Principalities [→Archai], →Authorities, Power [→Dynamis], →Name). Col 1:16 states that in Jesus Christ "all things in heaven and on earth were created, things visible and invisible, whether thrones or dominions or rulers or powers" (εἴτε θρόνοι εἴτε κυριότητες εἴτε ἀρχαὶ εἴτε ἐξουσίαι). In both instances the conviction is clearly stated that all angelic (and demonic) powers are completely subordinated to Christ; being his own creatures, they are his servants and hence no longer a threat to be feared by God's children (see R. SCHNACKENBURG, *Der Brief an die Epheser* [Neukirchen-Vluyn 1982] 77).

IV. *Bibliography*

H. BIETENHARD, *Die himmlische Welt im Urchristentum und Spätjudentum* (Tübingen 1951) 104-106; H. SCHLIER, *Mächte und Gewalten im Neuen Testament* (Freiburg 1958); F. SCHROEGER, κυριότης, *EWNT* II (1981) 820-821; Str-B III 581-584.

P. W. VAN DER HORST

DOVE περιστερά

I. Although the derivation of the Greek word from the (unattested) Semitic *peraḥ-Istar*, 'bird of →Ishtar', is probably mistaken, there can be no doubt that the dove in the Eastern Mediterranean world was the bird of the mother- and love goddess (→Aphrodite) in various forms. That the dove also was regarded as soul-bird is shown by dove-grottos in burial grounds (GREEVEN 1968:65) and funerary inscriptions, Jewish as well as Gentile (GREEVEN 1968:67). In Israel, turtledoves and pigeons were the only birds offered for sacrifice (Lev 1:14). Before the Mandean death-mass (*masiqta*), a dove named *ba*, the Egyptian name of the soul-bird, is sacrificed as a symbol of the soul attaining eternal life (E. S. DROWER, *The Secret Adam* [Oxford 1960] 8, 32).

In the NT versions of the baptism of Jesus, the dove plays an important part (Mark 1:10; Matt 3:16; Luke 3:22; John 1:32). Mark, Matthew and John state that the spirit descended "as/like a dove". Behind the former phrase we may be right in seeing the Aram *b-dmuthā d*, which—although it literally means 'in the form of'—may be translated 'as' or 'like'. *Gos. Eb.*, which is not simply based on the NT gospels, actually reads that the spirit descended "in the form of a dove" (*en eidei peristeras* [*apud* Epiphanius, *Panarion* 3:13:7]). Justin Martyr, *Dialogue* 88:3, and the different versions of the Diatessaron, which draws upon a Jewish Christian gospel tradition, also read "in the form of a dove". In any case, it is improbable that "as/like a dove" refers to the mode of descent rather than the spirit (GUNKEL 1987:158; BULTMANN 1957:262; GREEVEN 1968:68). The dove is the form of manifestation of God's spirit descending 'into' (? [*eis*] Mark) or 'upon' ([*epi*]

Matthew, Luke, John) Jesus when he was baptized.

II. Evidence for a dove goddess in the Minoan-Mycenaean culture takes us back to the second millennium BCE. The Cypriote Aphrodite is shown as a dove goddess on many coins. In the West, the origin of the cult of the dove goddess was acknowledged to be Oriental (GREEVEN 1968:64-65). The dove was the sacred bird of a goddess (perhaps →Astarte, i.e. ʿAthtart) worshipped at Beisān. Lucian, *De Dea Syria* 33, reports that Semiramis, the daughter of →Atargatis (i.e. ʿAttar-ʿatteh, the first part being the Aramaic counterpart of ʿAthtar[t], the second part perhaps a variant form of →Anat), had the dove as her symbol. Semiramis on one occasion even had turned herself into a dove; thus the inhabitants of Hierapolis (i.e. Bambyke on the Upper Euphrates) regarded doves as holy (ibid. 14). Diodorus Siculus says that Semiramis upon passing away "turned into a dove", and that "the Assyrians therefore worship the dove as a goddess, thus deifying Semiramis" (*Bibliotheca Historica* 2:20:2). In another place, Diodorus says that all the inhabitants of Syria honour doves as deities, because the name of Semiramis is similar to the word for 'doves' (ibid. 2:4:6). The name of Semiramis would seem to reflect the Semitic divine name →Ashima (in Greek sources, Sēmea, Sima, Simē) and the root idea of *rwm*, 'high' (Ass: *Sammu-rāmat*, etc.); folk etymology would have no difficulty in connecting the divine name with the Assyrian word *summatu* (*simmatu*), 'dove'.

The Jewish allegation that the Samaritans worshipped a dove image on Mt. Gerizim appears to be a misunderstanding or deliberate distortion of the Samaritan cult of *Šemâ*, 'the Name', i.e. Yahweh. The implication of the Jewish allegation would seem to be that the Samaritans worshipped the goddess Ashima, whose cult is said to have been brought into the vanquished Northern Kingdom of Israel by the Assyrian colonists (2 Kgs 17:29-30).

III. In the version of the baptism of Jesus in *Gos. Heb.*, the Spirit is represented as Jesus' mother, and it is she who speaks the words addressed to Jesus (*apud* Jerome, *Comm. in Is.* 4, *ad* 11:2; cf. Origen, *Comm. in Ioann.* 2:12). But *Gos. Heb.* does not portray the Spirit in the form of a dove (in *Acts of Thomas* 50, however, the Spirit is called "holy dove, who engendered the twin-boys" [Jesus and Judas Thomas]); there is in fact no evidence for a myth in which the mother- and love-goddess chooses an aspirant to kingship to be her son or lover.

On the other hand, an OT-Jewish background is not sufficient in order to explain the figure of the dove as a form of manifestation of the divine Spirit. The cooing of doves in the temple could be seen as a reminiscence of the *bath qol*, 'daughter of the voice', a substitute for the prophetic Spirit (*b.Ber.* 3a). In *Tg.* Cant 2:12, the 'voice of the turtle-dove' is said to be 'voice of the Spirit of deliverance', other interpretations being the voice of the Messiah or the voice of Moses. A saying ascribed to a rabbi of the second century CE compares the Spirit hovering over the primordial waters (Gen 1:2) to a dove hovering over her young (*b.Hag.* 15a [in other variants the bird is an eagle]). Philo can take the dove as a symbol of Sophia (→Wisdom) (*Quis rer. div. her.* 127). In other Philonic texts, the dove appears as a symbol of *logos* or *nous* (GREEVEN 1968:66). In all these texts, the dove is only compared to God's Spirit, or used allegorically; it is not represented as a form of manifestation of the Spirit.

That the new king is designated by a bird is a widespread folktale motive. A Jewish development of this motive appears to be found in the *Zohar*, where it is related that the dove that did not return to Noah (Gen 8:10) one day will come back with a golden crown in the beak and put it on the head of the Messiah (*Bammidbar* 68:3-4). Influence from the same folktale theme seems to be found also in *Tg.* Esth II, where the throne of Solomon is described as being decorated with golden doves; thus, a dove was seen bringing the king the Law, while another dove with a hawk in its beak was regarded as a symbol of the future deliverance of the gentiles into the hands of the Messiah (GERO 1976:21-22 [n. 7]). *Esther R.* 1:2, in a description of the throne of the Iranian ruler, says that a golden dove above the throne had a crown in its beak; when the king would wait to sit down, the crown would "touch and not yet touch" him. The dove election motif may possibly be seen also in the tradition that the dove was one of the symbols of Israel (Ps 74:19; 2 Esdr 5:26; many rabbinic texts, especially in *Cant R.*).

The folktale motif of the election of the new king by a dove also appears in some of the versions of the baptism of Jesus. The *Heliand*, an old Saxon poem on the life of Jesus, says that the the Spirit "came in the form of a lovely bird, and landed on the shoulder of our Lord" (BULTMANN 1957: 256 n. 1). *Odes Sol.* 24:1-2 reads: "The dove fluttered over the head of [our Lord] the Messiah, because he was her head. She sang over him, and her voice was heard." In this version, the Spirit is not even mentioned. The *Heliand* would seem to have combined the canonical description with an old folkloristic version. The old folktale theme is discernable already in John, where the Baptist says that he received a revelation imparting that the Son of God would come to him incognito, and would have to be recognized by "the Spirit descending from heaven as a dove" and "remaining on him" (1:32-33). Here the folktale motif of the election of the king by a bird has been welded with the Israelite idea of the union of the Spirit with the Messiah (1 Sam 16:13; Isa 11:2; 61:1). In the Synoptics, the former is not clearly present.

IV. *Bibliography*

R. BULTMANN, *Die Geschichte der synoptischen Tradition* (FRLANT N. F. 12; 3rd ed.; Götttingen 1957) 263-267; J. FOSSUM, Samaritan Demiurgical Traditions and the Alleged Dove Cult of the Samaritans, *Studies in Gnosticism and Hellenistic Religions* (EPRO 91; eds. R. van den Broek & M. J. Vermaseren; Leiden 1981) 143-160; S. GERO, The Spirit as a Dove at the Baptism of Jesus, *NovT* 18 (1976) 17-35; H. GREEVEN, περιστερά *TDNT* 6 (1968) 63-72; H. GUNKEL, *The Folktale in the Old Testament* (trans. M. D. Rutter; Sheffield 1987) 158-159 and 196-197 (notes).

J. FOSSUM

DOXA → GLORY

DRAGON Δράκων

I. *Drakōn* is the Greek word (Latin *draco*) which is used in LXX (33 occurrences), NT and Pseudepigrapha for a large monster which often appears as opponent of God or his people. It is often related to the sea and can be identified or associated with a snake (→Serpent). In the NT the word only appears in Revelation (13 occurrences).

II. In ancient mythology the dragon could be depicted as a real animal like a snake or crocodile or as a large imaginary monster living in the sea or on land. Certain types of these monsters can be discerned in mythological writings. Some share with Chimaera a lionlike front, the central part of a he-goat and the hind-quarters of a snake. →Python and →Typhon are also characterized as a dragon. However, *drakōn* can also be synonomous with *ophis* or other words for snakes (MERKELBACH 1959:226). The word was connected in antiquity with δέρκομαι/δρακεῖν, hence the meaning "seeing clearly", which matches one of the functions of dragons as watchers of a sanctuary. The dragon has often a fiery appearance, behaves in an aggressive, insolent and lecherous way and often represents the powers of chaos, especially in primordial times (e.g. Tiamat, →Giants, Typhon). The dragon is sometimes connected with (unusual) natural phenomena like storm, flood or drought (MERKELBACH 1959:227; FONTENROSE 1980:348, 581). The partly subterranean river Orontes in Asia Minor is also called *Drakōn*, which is connected to traditions concerning the conflict between →Zeus and Typhon, which offer an explanation of the typical bed of the river (Strabo 16.2.7). Also one of the northern constellations was called *Drakōn*/Draco.

Mesopotamian, Hittite, Canaanite, Egyptian, Iranian and Greek myths describe battles between a figure representing chaos and causing rebellion and a (still young) supreme god who restores the order of the gods by overcoming the monster: →Marduk versus Tiamat, the Weather God versus Illuyankas, →Baal versus Yam (→Sea), →Horus versus →Seth, Indra versus Vritra, →Apollo versus Python and Zeus versus Typhon; see for a survey of these and related conflict myths WAKEMAN (1973) and FONTENROSE (1980). The conflict usually takes place in primaeval ages, but is sometimes transposed to the world of human history and reenacted on special occasions like a military victory or an accession ceremony, whereby the king appears as the god who triumphs over the dragon (e.g. Purulli and Akitu festivals, see Marduk, Typhon). The execution of rebels and other enemies seems sometimes to have been inspired by the killing of the dragon in mythological traditions (MERKELBACH 1959:234-235). Mithridates gave orders to execute Manius Aquilius, a Roman governor of Asia Minor, by pouring liquid gold into his pharynx (Appianus, *Hist. rom.* 12.21; Pliny, *Nat. hist.* 33.48; cf. Bel et Draco 23-42, see below; see also Typhon).

III. In LXX *drakōn* may be the translation of several Hebrew nouns which are connected with existing animals or monsters living in the sea: young lion (*kĕpîr*, Job 4:8[10 LXX], 38:39), he-goat (*'attûd*, Jer 50:8[27:8 LXX]), asp (*peten*, Job 20:16), jackal (*tan*, Mic 1:8; Jer 9:11[10 LXX]; Lam 4:3), snake (*nāḥāš*, Amos 9:3; Job 26:13; cf. Isa 27:1), →Leviathan (Job 40:20[25 LXX], Ps 74[73 LXX]:14; Ps 104[103 LXX]:26; Isa 27:1) and →Tannin/Tannim (Exod 7:9, 10, 12; Deut 32:33; Job 7:12; Ps 74[73 LXX]:13; 91[90 LXX]:13; Isa 27:1; Jer 51[28 LXX]:34). Leviathan (Lotan) and Tannin/m appear in the Hebrew Bible in their earlier (Ugaritic) shape as chaos monsters living in the sea (e.g. Job 7:12; Ps 74:13-14; cf. also →Rahab, Job 26:12-13), but are also connected with real animals like the snake and the crocodile (e.g. Ps 91:13; Ezek 32:2). The incorporation of pagan traditions belonging to conflict myths in the Bible seems to serve the purpose of discrediting the foreign nations which oppress Israel (Egypt, Assyria, Babylon) and to announce their ruin (Ezek 29; 32; cf. Isa 14; 30:7 and Jer 51). Nah 1:8 contains a hint of God's triumph over the chaos monster. The connection between the lion and the dragon (cf. Job 4:10; 38:39; Ps 91:13; also Sir 25:16) may be inspired by Persian conceptions. A relief of the palace of Darius at Persepolis depicts the king fighting against a lion-dragon (MERKELBACH 1959:234).

Drakōn appears also in the Apocrypha (8 times) and in Greek texts of the Pseudepigrapha (about 17 times). The identification of *drakōn* with snake appears from Wis 16:10, where the venom-spraying snakes seem to be inspired by the combination of Exod 10:1-20 and Num 21:4-9 (see *ophis*, Wis 16:5; cf. also *Bel et Draco* 23-42; *1 Enoch* 20:7; *T. Abr.* rec. long. 17:14; *Sib. Or.* 3:794). In the LXX version of Esther the story of the rescue of Israel is placed in an apocalyptic setting (Fragments A1-11 and F1-10; Ed. Rahlfs 1:1a-l and 10:3a-k, see EHRLICH 1955), in which the protagonists Haman and Mordecai are depicted as dragons fighting each other (A5/1:1e; F4/10:3d). This battle could be a reminiscence of the conflict between the Babylonian supreme god Marduk and Tiamat (the primordial goddess of salt water) in Mesopotamian myths, all the more since Mordecai is a theophorous name containing the name of Marduk (see already ZIMMERN 1891, who, however, incorrectly traces back the Purim feast and the Hebrew word *pûr* to Akkadian *puḫru* "meeting"; i.e. the meeting of the gods which determined the lots and was reenacted during the Akitu feast; *pûr* may derive from Akkadian *pûru*, the lot that one casts, cf. Esth 3:7 and 9:24; HALLO 1983). Part of the same myth may be the basis of the second part of the story of *Bel et Draco* (vv. 23-42; see for textual criticism and commentary KOCH 1987), one of the Greek additions to Daniel. Daniel unmasks the fraud of the Babylonians with the divine giant snake (*drakōn*), by brewing a concoction of pitch, fat and hair and feeding it to the snake. The snake bursts open and dies because of the food. Daniel has to suffer for this performance and is thrown in a lions' den, receives food from Habakkuk in a miraculous way during his sixth day in the pit (see →Angel) and leaves it, unharmed and in a healthy condition on the seventh day, thereby proving the existence of the God of Israel. GUNKEL assumed that the story is a Jewish adaptation of a passage of the Babylonian creation epic Enuma Elish (1895:320-323, see esp. Tablet IV ll. 93-104, *ANET* p. 67). Other scholars refuted this hypothesis by pointing out that the connection with Tiamat is far-fetched, that she is never described as a snake and that the Babylonians did not revere living snakes (DAVIES 1913:653-654; MOORE 1977:123-124; 143; KOCH 1987:I 184). *T. Asher* 7:3 alludes to Ps 74 (73 LXX):13-14, *T. Job* 43: 8 probably to Job 20:16 LXX.

The dragon of Rev (12:3-4.7.9.16-17; 13:2.4.11; 16:13 and 20:2) is a combination of several traditional figures, as appears from Rev 12:9. The dragon is identified with the old snake of Gen 3 (cf. Rev 12:15-16) and the one who is called →Devil (Seducer) and →Satan (cf. 12:10: "the Accuser"). Like in Isa 27 the context of the appearance of the dragon is transposed from primordial time or even the creation (see e.g. Ps 74) to the final period of history (cf. *Sib. Or.* 8:88). It is common opinion that John the Prophet incorporated pagan traditions connected with dragon myths into his vision of the two heavenly signs. Traditions concerning a pursuit of a pregnant goddess by a dragonlike god were combined with another myth about the fallen angels (cf. *1 Enoch* 6-11, see Angel and Giants), which might also go back to a pagan myth, possibly the myth of Athtar who tries to take over the kingship of Baal (YARBRO COLLINS 1975:79-83). There is a considerable structural similarity between the content of Rev 12 and the pattern of myths concerning the conflict of a dragonlike monster (respectively a god who appears as enemy of other gods) and a god associated with creation and/or order (see further FONTENROSE 1980:9-11, 267-273; YARBRO COLLINS 1975). The pattern of combat myths shows at the same time that the original residence of the dragon in heaven (which is probably bound up with the constellation Draco, also mentioned in *Sib. Or.* 5:522, or Hydra, see BOLL 1914; BERGMEIER 1982) and the fact that he has more than one opponent (→Michael, →Jesus and finally →God) are pecularities of Revelation. Several scholars assume that Rev 12 is partly dependent on a specific pagan myth (see Python and Typhon). The search for pagan mythological analogies to the dragon of Rev should not be restricted to chap. 12 but also concern chap. 13 and 19:19-21; 20:1-3.7-10. This appears from the common terminology in these passages, compositional factors and the fact that the slaying of the dragon is depicted in Rev 20:7-10. The allies of the dragon are the two beasts of Rev 13 representing the Roman emperors and their cult (13:2.4.11; 16:13; →Ruler Cult), which can be partly understood against the background of the dragon as a symbol for the wicked foreign king, see already Ezek 29:3; 32:2 (Pharaoh), Jer 51(28 LXX), Est 1; *Pss. Sol.* 2:25; *Sib. Or.* 8:88 (DAY 1985:88-140; see also Typhon). The connection of a dragon with a (turbulent) river is analogous to mythological traditions (Typhon) and occurs besides Rev 12:15-16 in *T. Abr.* rec. long. 17:16; 19:5.

IV. *Bibliography*

R. BERGMEIER, Altes und Neues zur "Sonnenfrau am Himmel (Apk 12)", *ZNW* 73 (1982) 97-109, esp. 100-101; F. BOLL, Aus der Offenbarung Johannis, *Stoicheia* 1 (Leipzig/Berlin 1914) 98-124; W. DAVIES, Bel and the Dragon, *APOT* I (Oxford 1913) 652-664; E. L. EHRLICH, Der Traum des Mordechai, *ZRGG* 7 (1955) 69-74; W. FOERSTER, δράκων, *TDNT* II (Grand Rapids 1964) 281-283; J. FONTENROSE, *Python. A Study of Delphic Myth and its Origins* (Berkeley/Los Angeles 1959; 1980[2]); H. GUNKEL, *Schöpfung und Chaos in Urzeit und Endzeit. Eine religionsgeschichtliche Untersuchung über Gen 1 und Ap Joh 12*

(Göttingen 1895); W. W. HALLO, The First Purim, *BA* 46 (1983) 19-26; C. KLOOS, *Yhwh's Combat with the Sea. A Canaanite Tradition in the Religion of Ancient Israel* (Amsterdam/Leiden 1986); K. KOCH, *Deuterokanonische Zusätze zum Danielbuch. Entstehung und Textgeschichte* I-II, (AOAT 38; Kevelaer/Neukirchen-Vluyn 1987) I 159-187; II 154-205; J. DAY, *God's Conflict with the Dragon and the Sea. Echoes of a Canaanite Myth in the Old Testament* (Cambridge 1985); W. K. HEDRICK, *The Sources and Use of Imagery in Apocalypse 12* (Diss. Berkeley 1970); R. MERKELBACH, Drache, *RAC* IV (Stuttgart 1959) 226-250; C. A. MOORE, *Daniel, Esther and Jeremiah. The Additions. A New Translation with Introduction and Commentary* (AB 44; Garden City 1977) 117-149; M. SCHLÜTER, *Derāqôn und Götzendienst: Studien, ausgehend von mAZ III 3* (Frankfurt am Main/Bern 1982); M. K. WAKEMAN, *God's Battle with the Monster. A Study in Biblical Imagery* (Leiden 1973); N. WALTER, δράκων, *EWNT* I (Stuttgart 1980) 853-855; A. YARBRO COLLINS, *The Combat Myth in the Book of Revelation* (Missoula [Mont.] 1975); H. ZIMMERN, Zur Frage nach dem Ursprung des Purimfestes, *ZAW* 11 (1891) 157-169.

J. W. VAN HENTEN

DYNAMIS δύναμις

I. Before becoming a divine name or epithet, 'power' (*dynamis*) has had a long and diversified history. As name or epithet, 'power' can be used in many different ways in biblical and post-biblical literature. This usage must be distinguished from more general notions of divine power. All of antiquity assumed that deities have power, dispense power, and interfere in human life with their power. The degree of power deities were believed to control determined their status and place in hierarchies as well as the kind of cultic worship they received from human beings. Cultic worship of deities was not only motivated by such power, but was itself a way of participating in it.

Attributed to the highest deities, the epithet 'power' indicates total sovereignty and control, while lesser deities, angels, demons, elemental forces, and even human 'divine men' are agents of the former, having been endowed or charged by them. Beings endowed with divine power then function as administrators or representatives of those who are in control. In a Hellenistic environment the Greek epithet *dynamis* could develop into a hypostasis of its own and even become a name, as in the case of →Simon Magus who, according to Acts 8:10 was called 'the power of God that is called great' (*hē dynamis tou theou hē kaloumenē megalē*). In most biblical instances, however, 'power' is regarded as an attribute either of God who is in control of all powers, or of subservient divine agents acting on his behalf through delegated powers. In the biblical and post-biblical literature these powers include →angels, →demons, →stars, →Stoicheia, and the →Holy Spirit; in the NT, in addition, →Christ is integrated in the hierarchy.

II. By way of development, the biblical and post-biblical occurrences must be seen in their respective religious and cultural environment.

In the OT, the language and imagery describing divine power is extensive and cannot be fully surveyed at this point. It is an important fact that this language and imagery is taken from the spheres of divine warfare and kingship. It is God's mighty arm that shatters the enemies (Exod 15:6; Ps 89:10.13; Isa 40:10; 48:14; etc.). He is the strong warrior: 'The LORD goes forth like a soldier, like a warrior he stirs up his fury; he cries out, he shouts aloud, he shows himself mighty against his foes' (Isa 42:13). Frequently, he is called 'the LORD of hosts' (1 Sam 1:3.11; 4:4; 15:2; 17:45; →Host of Heavens, Yahweh Zebaoth). The epithet of *ṣĕbā'ôt* which occurs more than two hundred times in the Hebrew Bible is frequently translated by the LXX by Hellenistic epithets such as *kyrios pantokratōr* (see →Almighty) or →*kyrios (ho theos) tōn dynameōn*, but it can also appear as a new name Sabaoth. While *ṣābā'* means 'army',

Greek translators transposed it into Greek cosmological concepts. This development was preceded by the universal character of post-Exilic theology, for which the Lord of hosts is 'the God of the whole earth' (Isa 54:5). His 'army' even includes all powers of heaven and earth (Isa 40:12-26; Pss 93; 95-99; 147:4-6; 148:1-4; 1 Chr 29:11; 2 Chr 20:6; LXX Dan 3:52-90; etc.). Thus, Hellenistic Judaism of the LXX reinterprets the old warrior god in terms of a cosmic deity in control of all natural and supernatural forces. For further discussion see H. EISING, *TWAT* 2, 902-911, *s.v. ḥayil* especially sec. VI-VII; H. RINGGREN, *TWAT* 4, 130-137, *s.v. kōaḥ*; RINGGREN, *TWAT* 6, 871-876, *s.v. ṣābā';* H.-J. ZOBEL, *TWAT* 6, 876-892, *s.v. ṣĕbā'ōt*.

In Greek theology, the concept of divine power is understood cosmologically (see GRUNDMANN, *TDNT* 2, section A). The Pythagorean Ecphantus may have been the first to conceive of divine power as among the primordial realities of the cosmos which to him was by nature divine (Hippolytus, *Ref.* 1.15; DIELS-KRANZ 51.1 [I, 442, 12-14]; GUTHRIE 1962:324-1.327). Since Anaximander took the *apeiron*, 'the Boundless' that encompasses everything, to be divine (Aristotle, *Phys.* 203b6; DIELS-KRANZ 12 A 15 [I, 85, 20]; GUTHRIE 1962: 87-89), it was not too great a step to interpret the gods as forces of nature. When and by whom this step was first taken is not altogether clear (see GUTHRIE 1965:478-483; BALTES 1988:60-68), but for the physician Eryximachos in Plato's *Symp.* 186e it is self-evident that the god Eros governs the cosmos through 'the mightiest power of all' (ibid., 188d). In *Crat.* 438c Plato reports the view that the names (*onomata*) were first given by a superhuman power (*dynamis*), whether that name-giver was some sort of spirit (*daimōn*) or god (*theos*). Aristotle concurs (*Met.* 4,12, p. 1019a26) that *daimones* are called 'powers' (*dynameis*). These suggestions are then fully developed into an all-encompassing system by the Stoics, foremost by Posidonius (see NILSSON 1974: 263-264, 534-539). Accordingly, the divine universe is held together by a primordial *autokinētos dynamis* (Sextus, *Adv. math.* 9.75 [*SVF* 2.112-113]), and the traditional gods can now be identified as specialized agents of the universal divine power: "The deity, say they, is a living being, immortal, rational, perfect or intelligent in happiness, admitting nothing evil (into him), taking providential care of the world and all that therein is, but he is not of human shape. He is, however, the artificer of the universe, and, as it were, the father of all, both in general and in the particular part of him which is all-pervading, and which is called many names according to its various powers (*dynameis*)". What follows is a list of Olympian gods and the powers represented by them (Diogenes Laertius 7.147, trans. R. D. Hicks, LCL edition; see also *SVF* 2.305-2.321: *De natura deorum*). These ideas made it possible to interpret the popular pantheon with all its gods and demons in a philosophical manner, a possibility that profoundly changed all ancient theology (see especially Ps.-Aristotle, *De mundo* 6, 396b 29, 397a16, 397b19-398a6, 398b8, 20-25, 399b19-28; Cornutus, *Theologiae Graecae Compendium* [ed. C. Lang 1881] 4.12; 13. 11; 45.4 etc.).

In the Hellenistic era, *dynamis* was an established divine epithet, so much so that for some philosophers the names of the gods became superfluous (see Cleanthes, *Hymn* [Stobaeus, *Ecl.* 1, 1, 12, p. 25,3; *SVF* 1. 121]; Epictetus, *Ench.* 53; Seneca, *Epist.* 107.10). Plutarch (*De Is. et Os.* 67, 377F-378A) represents what can be taken as the opinion of many at his time: "... we have regarded as gods the beings who use the products of nature and bestow them upon us, providing us with them constantly and sufficiently, nor do we regard the gods as different among different peoples nor as barbarian and Greek and as southern and northern. But just as the sun and the moon, heaven, earth and sea are common to all, though they are given various names by the varying peoples, so it is with the one reason (*logos*) which orders these things and the one providence which has charge of them, and the assistant powers (*dynameis*) which are assigned to everything; they are given different honours and modes of address among different peoples according to custom ..." (trans. GRIFFITHS 1970:223-225). For popular religion, however, the concepts of divine power provided an enormous boost. Gods and demons could be understood as conduits of divine power (*dynamis*, *energeia*) in all its applications. The epithet *dynamis tou theou* became more important than the names which could be exchanged or accumulated or fused with each other. A new practice in magic arose by which the names of gods were bundled and merged so as to increase divine power (see NILSSON 1974:2.534-2.539).

Hellenistic Judaism reflects these developments. The powers of the universe were easily identified with the angels and demons which multiplied into ever greater numbers (*Jub.* 2:2-3; *1 Enoch* 40:9; 61:10; 82:8; *4 Esra* 6:6; etc.). Later Jewish magic and mysticism (Hekhalot literature) is preoccupied with constantly expanding systems of angels, demons, elemental spirits, personifications and hypostatic entities, with which the universe is filled. As especially Philo of Alexandria shows, these doctrines of divine powers allowed, on the one hand, to maintain God's sovereignty over all the powers, while, on the other hand, incorporating the complexities of the universe (see GRUNDMANN, *TDNT* 2, sec. C.1-2; DILLON 1977: 161-174; DILLON 1983; SEGAL 1977:159-181; SIEGERT 1980, 1988, 1992 [indices]; MACH 1992:85-86, 93).

III. In the NT the traditions outlined continue with some important changes. For Christian theology God is in essence power (Rom 1:20; 9:17 [Exod 9:16]; Matt 6:13 *var. lect.* [doxology]) who dispenses it through the traditional intermediaries to whom is now added Christ (1 Cor 5:4; 2 Cor 12:9; 13:4; 2 Pet 1:3) and his apostles (Acts 4:33; 6:8; etc.), the Holy Spirit (Luke 1:34; 4:14; Acts 1:8, and often in Luke and Acts; Rom 15:13.19; Eph 3:16) and the gospel (Rom 1:16; 1 Cor 1:18.24). Part of Christ's victory is to subjugate 'the powers of heaven' (Mark 13:25-26 par.; 1 Cor 15: 24; 2 Thess 1:7). Interpreting Ps 110:1 (Mark 12:36 par.), the coming of the →Son of Man (Mark 14:62 par.) means seeing him 'sitting at the right side of the power', with 'power' substituting God himself. In lists of celestial beings, 'powers' have their place and they are associated with angels (Rom 8:38; 1 Cor 15:24; Eph 1:21; 1 Pet 3:22; cf. 2 Thess 1:7; 2 Pet 2:11; Rev 1:16).

IV. In the post-apostolic and patristic literature these lines of tradition continue and expand. There are new developments as well. While the NT speaks of the *dynamis* of the devil (Luke 10:19; Rev 13:2) and 'the devil and his angels' (Matt 25:41; cf. Rev. 12:7.9; 2 Pet 2:4; Jude 6), Ignatius prefers the plural 'the dynameis of Satan (*Ign. Eph.* 13:1), an indication of the growing gnostic dualism. Also Acts 8:10 is special in that its report of Simon Magus being regarded as 'the power of God that is called great' points to gnostic developments related to the cult of Simon Magus and beyond (see for passages *Patristic Greek Lexicon*, *s.v.* δύναμις, sec. VI.B and VII; FASCHER, *RAC* 4, 441-451; SIEGERT 1982:235-236).

V. *Bibliography*

C. E. ARNOLD, *Ephesians: Power and Magic: The Concept of Power in Ephesians in Light of Its Historical Setting* (SNTSMS 63; Cambridge 1989); BAGD, *s.v.* δύναμις; M. BALTES, Zur Theologie des Xenokrates, *Knowledge of God in the Graeco-Roman World* (ed. R. van den Broek, T. Baarda & J. Mansfeld; EPRO 112; Leiden 1988) 43-68; G. B. CAIRD, *Principalities and Powers: A Study in Pauline Theology* (Oxford 1956); W. CARR, *Angels and Principalities: The Background, Meaning and Development of the Pauline Phrase hai archai kai hai exousiai* (SNTSMS 42; Cambridge 1974); J. DILLON, Philo's Doctrine of Angels, *Two Treatises of Philo of Alexandria: A Commentary on De Gigantibus and Quod Deus Sit Immutabilis* (ed. J. Dillon & D. Winston; BJS 25; Chico 1983) 197-205; DILLON, *The Middle Platonists: A Study of Platonism 80 B.C. to A.D. 220* (London 1977); E. FASCHER, 'Dynamis', *RAC* 4 (1959) 415-

458; G. FRIEDRICH, *EWNT* (*EDNT*) 1, *s.v.* δύναμις; J. G. GRIFFITHS, *Plutarch's De Iside et Osiride* (Cambridge 1970); W. GRUNDMANN, *TDNT* 2, *s.v.* δύναμαι κτλ., esp. sections C.1.b, D.2.a-b; GRUNDMANN, *Der Begriff der Kraft in der neutestamentlichen Gedankenwelt* (BWANT 4:8; Stuttgart 1932); W. K. C. GUTHRIE, *A History of Greek Philosophy*, vols. 1-2 (Cambridge 1962, 1965); M. MACH, *Entwicklungsstadien des jüdischen Engelglaubens in vorrabbinischer Zeit* (TSAJ 34; Tübingen 1992); M. P. NILSSON, *Geschichte der griechischen Religion* (3rd ed.; 2 vols.; Munich 1967, 1974); A. D. NOCK, Divine Power, *Essays on Religion and the Ancient World* (Cambridge 1972) 34-45; F. PREISIGKE, *Die Gotteskraft in der frühchristlichen Zeit* (Leipzig/Berlin 1922); J. RÖHR, *Der okkulte Kraftbegriff im Altertum* (Philol. Suppl. 17; Leipzig 1923); A. F. SEGAL, *Two Powers in Heaven: Early Rabbinic Reports about Christianity and Gnosticism* (SJLA 25; Leiden 1977); F. SIEGERT, *Nag-Hammadi-Register: Wörterbuch zur Erfassung der Begriffe in den koptisch-gnostischen Schriften von Nag-Hammadi* (WUNT 26; Tübingen 1982); SIEGERT, *Philon von Alexandrien, Über die Gottesbezeichnung 'wohltätig verzehrendes Feuer' (De Deo)* (WUNT 46; Tübingen 1988); SIEGERT, *Drei hellenistisch-jüdische Predigten* (2 vols.; WUNT 20 & 61; Tübingen 1980, 1992); H. S. VERSNEL (ed.), *Faith Hope and Worship: Aspects of Religious Mentality in the Ancient World* (Leiden 1981).

H. D. BETZ

E

EA → AYA

EARTH ארץ

I. Earth (ארץ) is one of the most common words in the OT with more than 2500 occurrences. The word—and its etymological cognates—is widely attested in other Semitic languages, e. g. *arṣ* in Ugaritic and Phoenician, *ʾrḍ* in Arabic, *ʾrq* or *ʾrʿ* in Aramaic and *erṣetu* in Akkadian. The Sumerian equivalent is **ki** or **uraš**; a corresponding Hittite word can be seen in *daganzipa*, while in Greek we find γῆ or γαῖα.

II. As is also the case with →Heaven, references to Earth as a separate goddess receiving an elaborate cult, are rather limited. The main occurrences of a goddess Earth can be found in cosmogonical passages. Thus we know from the Sumerian Harab myth (JACOBSEN 1984) that Harab (Plough) and Ki (Earth) were the first parents who cultivated the land and begot Shakkan, the cattle-god. Earth desired her son and together they killed Harab so that Shakkan could marry Earth. Then Earth is also slain by Shakkan's sister →Tiamat. Another Sumerian tradition states that the goddess Nammu was the mother of heaven and earth; afterwards she gave birth to the first generation of the gods, beginning with Enlil. A reflection of this cosmogonical myth can be found in the Enuma Elish (I 1-15) where the first divine pair Apsu (→Ends of the Earth) and Tiamat begot →Lahmu and Lahamu; They gave birth to Anshar (Lord Heaven) and Kishar (Lady Earth) who became Anu's parents. Other—and unharmonized—traditions about cosmogony and theogony begin with the pair Enki and Ninki, namely Lord Earth and Lady Earth, leading down through various generations to the birth of Enlil. Such Mesopotamian lists (LAMBERT 1975:52-53) show how the elements were deified in the beginning but such (primeval) 'gods' very seldom had any cultic and further theological importance. In these cosmological traditions we also encounter the myth of the separation of heaven and earth or the mythological reference to the birth of the →Pleiades who are considered children of Anu and Earth (*Erra* i 28-29). On the whole Mother Earth has no prominent role within the pantheons of Mesopotamia but some aspects of her can occasionally be found in connection with other goddesses whose dominion is the realm of life and/or death, such as →Ishtar, Nintu or Ereshkigal.

From the Syrian and Anatolian area we get the following impression: Based on etymology we find an earth-goddess in Ugarit, namely Baal's daughter Arṣayu (*KTU* 1.3 iii 7; 1.4 i 18; etc.). As the Akkadian pantheon list from Ugarit equates her with the Babylonian goddess Allatu (RS 20.24; cf. *KTU* 1.118:22), we can deduce that she was also considered a goddess of the netherworld. According to the list *KTU* 1.106:32 the offerings to her follow those to the gods of the netherworld. A similar connection with the netherworld can be seen in the case of the Hittite deity Daganzipa, literally the 'genius of the earth', we read that the dark Daganzipa shall take away every illness with her hand (KUB XVII 8 iv 8). But Daganzipa can also receive offerings (KUB X 89 ii 27) or she can be supplicated together with heaven to hear the prayers (KUB VI 45 i 35-36). This reference clearly points towards →Heaven-and-Earth as cosmic entities who are witnesses in treaties. Occasionally Daganzipa can be called the daughter of the →Sun (KBo III 38:3), she is called Mother Earth (*annaš daganzipaš*: KUB XLIII 30 iii 5), or she appears together with the stormgod (KBo XI 32:31-32). Thus we can deduce that Daganzipa was a minor goddess in Hittite religion (cf. OTTEN 1973: 37) although most Hittite texts refer to earth only with physical or geographical connotations.

The theogonical aspect of earth is also known from Greek texts where Gē impregnated by Ouranos brings forth the →Titans and →Giants (Hes., *Theog.* 117ff.). In Homeric texts she is seen as a goddess who is a witness to oaths (*Il.* 3,104; 19,259); maybe she was also concerned with oracles. But on the whole Gē is more a cosmic aspect than a personified deity. Thus she is only venerated later with very limited cults while →Demeter has become the goddess who brings life and growth to the earth.

In conclusion: earth does not feature as a great goddess in the surrounding cultures of the OT. As a cosmic entity she could be connected with theogonical and cosmogonical speculations; she is also referred to as a divine witness. On the other hand she is connected with gods of the netherworld or with goddesses who bring life. But earth herself did never gain the importance of these personal deities.

III. A comparable picture emerges from the Hebrew Bible. In the many occurrences of the word, *ʾereṣ*, 'earth' is a cosmic entity (TSUMURA 1988:264-268), either as a complement to heaven (cf. e. g. Gen 1:1; 14:19, 21; Amos 9:6) or within a tripartite cosmos together with heaven and the sea (cf. Exod 20:4.11; Deut 5:8; Pss 24:2; 82:5; 104:5-6; 136:6). But *ʾereṣ* also refers to the ground (cf. Gen 7:14; Exod 8:12-13; 2 Sam 12:17. 29; Ezek 26:15; Job 2:13) or to geographical and political units (cf. Exod 6:4; Deut 4:46-47; Judg 10:8; 1 Sam 13:19; 1 Kgs 9:19; Jer 30:10; 46:27; 51:28 etc.). As the earth is the "land of the living" (cf. Isa 38:11) it is the opposite of the realm of death which can be termed the "land below" (cf. Ezek 31:14. 16.18; 32:18.24; Isa 44:23; Ps 139:15). Some occurrences of *ʾereṣ* refer exclusively to →Sheol (cf. Exod 15:12; Jer 17:13; Jonah 2:7; Pss 22:30; 71:20).

The divine character of earth is rather restricted: Maybe some oaths and curses where Heaven-and-Earth are mentioned (cf. Deut 4:26; 30:19; 31:28; 32:1; Isa 1:2; Mic 6:2; Ps 50:4) may reflect the well-known idea from the ancient Near East that both entities can be called to witness in such circumstances. A further allusion to a certain mythological background of *ʾereṣ* is 'Mother Earth'. Thus earth is called the "mother of all living beings"; they have come from her and will return to her (cf. Job 1:21; Ps 139: 15; Sir 40:1). One can see further a faint allusion to the notion of mother earth in Deut 12:24 where it is said that the blood of the offerings should be poured out upon the earth like water; maybe this commandment reflects the idea of feeding the earth. But besides such allusions to earth's divinity the OT always stresses that it is God who has made it (cf. Gen 2:4; Exod 20:11; Isa 40:28; Jer 10:12; Zech 12:1; Ps 24:2 etc); thus she cannot have divine power and greatness.

IV. *Bibliography*

T. JACOBSEN, *The Harab Myth* (SANE 2/3; Malibu 1984); W. G. LAMBERT, Sumer and Babylon, *Ancient Cosmologies* (C. Blacker and M. Loewe ed.; London 1975) 42-65; LAMBERT, Kosmogonie, *RlA* 6 (1980/83) 218-222; H. OTTEN, *Eine althethitische Erzählung um die Stadt Zalpa* (Wiesbaden 1973) 37; M. OTTOSON, ארץ ʾæræṣ, *TWAT* 1 (1970-1973) 421-436; G. RYCKMANS, Heaven and Earth in the South Arabic Inscriptions, *JSS* 3 (1958) 225-236; D. T. TSUMURA, A "Hyponymous" Word Pair: *ʾrṣ* and *thm*(*t*) in Hebrew and Ugaritic, *Bib* 69 (1988) 258-269.

M. HUTTER

EBEN → STONE

ED → WITNESS

EDOM אדם

I. As a deity, Edom is possibly attested in the Egyptian Leiden Magical Papyrus 343+345 V 7, otherwise only in personal names. ʿObed Edom (LXX *Abdedom*) 2 Sam 6:10-12 (//1 Chr 13:13-14; 15:25) is a citizen of Philistine Gath—and the owner of an estate between Baalath-Jehudah and Jerusalem—who accommodated the ark for three months. In Chronicles, he is transformed into a Levite (1 Chr 15:18.21.24; 16:5.38) and the ancestor of a Levitical clan (1 Chr 26:4.8.15). In Punic, *ʾdm* is attested in the personal names *mlkʾdm* and *ʿbdʾdm* (BENZ 1972: 260).

II. The deity Edom could be identical with, or derived from, the country of Edom (cf. *HALAT* 12). As a toponym, Edom (<**ʾudum*), 'reddishness' refers to the colour of that country's soil. If the god and the country are to be connected, Obed-Edom would stand for **ʿbd qws ʾl(h)/bʿl ʾdm*, 'Servant of Qaus, the god/lord of Edom' (cf. similar ancient South Arabian names, e.g. Sabaic *ʿbdʾwm* for *ʿbd ʾlmqh bʿl ʾwm*, 'Servant of Ilmaqhâ, the lord of (the sanctuary of) ʾAwwām', or Nabataean *ʿbdʾlgy*, i.e. 'Servant of the god Gaia'; cf. KNAUF 1988: 46-47). The name would then presuppose the establishment of Edomite statehood, which did not exist before the 8th century BCE (→Qôs). A Philistine named after the Edomite god is conceivable for the 7th or 6th centuries, when the southern Palestinian cities were linked to Edom by profitable trade (cf. Amos 1:6). Whereas the ark narrative may well be dated into that period, there is hardly a connection between the country of Edom and the Phoenician colonies in North Africa. The 'Edomite/Arabian connection' may, however, help to elucidate the unusual vocalisation *ʿobed* in the Masoretic tradition, which might allude to Arabic *ʿābid* 'worshipper'.

Alternatively, **ʾUdum*, "Redness", may be seen as a Canaanite lesser deity, mentioned as the wife of →Resheph in the Leiden Magical Papyrus 343+345 V 7 (cf. DAHOOD 1963:292, who equates her with Arṣay). This theory is not wholly satisfactory either. Egyptian *itwm* could also relate to Canaanite *yātōm*, 'orphan' (which would match Resheph's image more appropriately). On the other hand, GÖRG (1987) identified a deity *ḥmrq*, "→Amalek" in the same papyrus (obv. III, 9 XXIII 3), which lends support to the geographical pertinence of that source's Edom (cf. for a possible connection between Resheph and the country of Edom Isa 63:1-6; Hab 3). In spite of some additional evidence, it is still not possible to advance the interpretation of a putative deity Edom beyond F. BUHL (1893: 42; cf. also BARTLETT 1989:196).

III. *Bibliography*

J. R. BARTLETT, *Edom and the Edomites* (JSOTSup 77; Sheffield 1989); F. L. BENZ, *Personal Names in the Phoenician and Punic Inscriptions* (StP 8; Rome 1972); F. BUHL, *Geschichte der Edomiter* (Leipzig 1893); M. DAHOOD, Hebrew-Ugaritic Lexicography I, *Bib* 44 (1963) 289-303; M. GÖRG, Ein Gott Amalek? *BN* 40 (1987) 14-15; E. A. KNAUF, *Midian. Untersuchungen zur Geschichte Palästinas und Nordarabiens am Ende des 2. Jahrtausends v. Chr.* (Abhandlungen des Deutschen Palästina-Vereins; Wiesbaden 1988).

E. A. KNAUF

EHAD → ONE

EL אל

I. The name El, *ʾēl, il(u)*, is, with the exception of Ethiopic, common Semitic and originally means →God. Etymologically the origin of the appellative cannot be determined with certainty. Most likely, the noun can be derived from the verb ʾWL (the root ʾLH has also been suggested) 'to be strong' also 'to be in front, dominate' (DAHOOD 1958:74). The substantive (formed as a stative participle or adjective; POPE & RÖLLIG, *WbMyth* I:217-312) denotes 'strength, force, power, might, mana'. Related to a personal god, the noun has as meaning 'the strong one; mighty one; head, chief, leader'. Other scholars, however, construe *ʾil* as an original Semitic noun, not derived from a verb, meaning 'chief, god' (STARCKY 1949:383-386).

The noun *ʾēl* occurs some 230 times in the OT (except the problematic testimonies Num 12:13; Ps 52:3; Job 41:17). In the LXX it is mostly rendered by Θεός. Exceptions are ἰσχυρός (2 Sam 22 [= Ps 18]:31-

33. 48; 23:5; Ps 7:12; several times in Job; Neh 1:5; 9:31), ὑψηλός (Lam 3:41), ἄγγελος (Isa 9:5; Job 20:15), μάρτυς (Isa 43:12), κύριος (e.g. Isa 40:18; Ps 15 [16]:1; Job 5:8). Job 20:29 reads ἐπίσκοπος; Isa 7:14 construes Ἐμμανουήλ, Isa 8:8,10 however μεθ' ἡμῶν ὁ θεός. The *kôkĕbê ʾēl* of Isa 14:13 are rendered in Greek as ἄστρα τοῦ οὐρανοῦ. Vg normally reads *deus* for *ʾēl*. Some exceptions can be noted: 'fortis' (Exod 15:11; Jer 51:56; Ps 94 [95]:3); 'fortissimus' (Jer 32:18); 'dominus' (Ps 15 [16]: 1; Ps 35 [36]:7; Ps 150:1; Lam 3:41). Further peculiarities are 'filii Israhel' (Deut 32:8—like MT) and the translation of *ʾēlîm* (Ps 28 [29]:1) by 'arietes' (derived from *ʾayil*). The Samaritan Targum often renders *ʾēl* by Aram *ḥêlâ* 'the Power' (→Dynamis).

II. In Ancient Mesopotamia *ilu* is attested as an appellative for deities, though a deity *Il* is not attested. It has been suggested that *Ilu* as a deity was attested at Emar (D. ARNAUD, *Recherches au Pays d'Aštata. Emar VI/3* [Paris 1986] No. 282:16-18: ^{d}*Ilu*). This suggestion is, however, based on an incorrect reading of the text (J. M. DURAND, *RA* 84 [1990] 80): ^{d}GAŠAN*$^{!}$-*kà-si*, 'Nin-kasi'. The position held by El e.g. in the Ugaritic pantheon can be compared to the position of Ea (→Aya) in Mesopotamia though in god-lists Ea is equated with Kothar (W. G. LAMBERT, The Pantheon of Mari, *MARI* 4 [1985] 525-539; E. LIPIŃSKI, Éa, Kothar et El, *UF* 20 [1988] 137-143).

The Ugaritic texts from Ras Shamra supply more than five hundred references to El. The noun *il* in the Ugaritic texts frequently has the appellative meaning too, especially in the epistolary literature, but partially also in the mythological, cultic, and epic texts. In about half of the occurrences, El denotes a distinct deity who, residing on the sacred mountain, occupies within the myths the position of master of the Ugaritic pantheon. He bears the title *mlk* 'king' (*KTU* 1.1 iii:23 [restored]; 1.2 iii:5, 1.3; v:8. 36; 1.4 i:5; iv:24. 38. 48; 1.5 vi:2 [restored]; 1.6 i:36; 1.17 vi:49; 1.117:2-3; cf. 1.14 i:41) and possesses ultimate authority. In these cases *il* is therefore likewise to be understood as a proper name.

In the literature El is depicted as *qdš* 'holy' (*KTU* 1.16 i:11. 22) and appears as an aged deity (→Ancient of Days); the grey hair of his beard (*šbt dqn*) is referred to (*KTU* 1.3 v:2. 25; 1.4 v:4; 1.18 i:12 [restored]). The frequently employed epithet *ltpn il dpid* 'the benevolent, good-natured El' (e.g. *KTU* 1.4 iv:58; 1.6 iii:4. 10. 14; 1. 16 v:23; see for the etymology LORETZ 1990:66) characterizes the deity even better. Sometimes one of the two nouns (*lṭpn/dpid*) occurs without the other or in another connection. It might be presumed that this epithet characterizes the attitude and the experience of mankind in its relation to El. The heavenly gods guaranteed and promoted human life. To El was attributed the kind of wisdom that made him judge everything rightly (*KTU* 1.3 v:30; 1.4 iv:41; v:3-4; 1.16 iv:1-2). On the other hand, El is known as the one who is able to cure diseases (*KTU* 1.16 v:23-50; 1.100; 1.107; possibly also *KTU* 1.114; cf. 1.108 and *ARTU* 191-203). Further, El is designated as *ṯr* 'bull'. This metaphor expresses his strength and divine dignity (e.g. *KTU* 1.2 i:33. 36; 1.3 v:35; 1.14 i:41).

The problem concerning El as creator is not easily solved. It is suggested by the epithet *ṯr* and, more clearly, by formulaic language to be discussed. In the mythological texts, El is often depicted as father of the other gods. Moreover, he is called in the Keret epic *ab adam*, 'father of mankind', obviously because he is the creator of humanity. The construction *bny bnwt* occurs several times in the myths and once in the Aqhat epic. The expression allegedly refers to El's creative activity. Traditionally *bny* has been understood as the participle of the G-stem and *bnwt* as a noun derived from the same root. Thus the construction is translated 'creator of creatures'. However, since RS 24.244 and RS 24.251 have become known, this interpretation is no longer uncontested, as *bnwt* occurs unconnected in those documents (*KTU* 1.100:62; 1.107:41, if correctly restored). These texts gave new life to the interpretation of VIROLLEAUD (*Ug.* V [1968] 571. 580) who rendered the noun 'virilité, force créatrice'. This rendering was supported by M. DIETRICH, O. LORETZ & J. SANMARTÍN (Bemerkungen zur Schlangenbeschwörung RS 24.244 = UG. 5, S. 564FF. NR. 7, *UF* 7 [1975] 124: 'Kraft, Zeugungskraft') and S. SEGERT (*A Basic Grammar of the Ugaritic Language* [Berkeley 1984] 181: 'engendering power, virility'). However, the interpretation of *bnwt* is still undetermined. DE MOOR (1990: 69) continues to interpret the words as referring to El as creator. In relation to mankind, it is only said that El blesses Keret and Dan'il in order to give them descendants (*KTU* 1.15 ii:16-28; 1.17 i:25. 42). The mythical procreation of gods, on the contrary, might have been recognized at Ugarit though the textual basis is small (*KTU* 1.10 iii:5; 1.23; M. DIETRICH & O. LORETZ, *TUAT* II [1986-89] 350-357; *ARTU* 117-128). In *KTU* 1.3 v:36; 1.4 iv:48 and 1.10 iii:6 El is depicted as the one who appointed →Baal as king. The verb used here to describe the action, *kn* [*kwn*], however, does not mean 'to create'. The usual Ugaritic verb signifying 'to create' is *qny*. It is used in relation to gods in *KTU* 1.10 iii:5. The meaning of the verb is obscure in *KTU* 1.19 iv:58 (it describes the relation of El to a locality; possibly to be explained either 'to own' or 'to produce, create'). The Phoenician inscriptions attest only once *qny*, 'to create', and that with regard to the earth (*KAI* 26 A III:18). It is doubtful whether El was conceived of as →'El creator of the earth' at Ugarit since there is no reference to the concept (POPE 1987:219-230; RENDTORFF 1966:287; contrast DE MOOR 1980; 1990: 69). As regards the creative activity of El the Ugaritic conception differed from that in the remaining Syrian-Palestinian area.

It has been suggested that El was deprived of his authority in the course of history and relegated to a lower position in the Ugaritic pantheon. Several observations were intended to support this supposition (esp. POPE 1955:90-104; 1987:227-229; OLDENBURG 1969). One view holds that Baal was promoted to the position of El. It has been examined by C. E. L'HEUREUX (*Rank among the Canaanite Gods. El, Ba'al, and the Repha'im* [Missoula 1979]), who concluded that this view can no longer be maintained as it rested on too many conjectures. On the contrary, El kept his authority unceasingly according to the belief of the Ugaritic population. The myths do not refer to any discord between El and Baal (SCHMIDT 1966:64-67; H. GESE, *RAAM* 1-232; esp. 112; P. J. VAN ZIJL, *Baal. A Study of Texts in Connection with Baal in the Ugaritic Epics* [AOAT 10; Neukirchen-Vluyn 1972]; S. E. LOEWENSTAMM, Zur Götterlehre des Epos von Keret, *UF* 11 [1979] 505-514; M. YON, Ougarit et ses Dieux, *Resurrecting the Past* [FS A.-Bounni; P. Matthiae, M. van Loon & H. Weiss eds.; Istanbul 1990] 325-343, esp. 337). It is inadmissible to posit a major religio-historical development on the basis of the position held by El in the Ugaritic documents to that of *'l* in the Phoenician and Aramaic inscriptions. The religious conceptions of the various areas and periods need not have been congruent.

Views diverge about the significance of the epithet *ab šnm* (B. MARGALIT, *UF* 15 [1983] 90-93). The interpretation of the text *KTU* 1.65 by M. DIETRICH; O. LORETZ & J. SANMARTÍN (*UF* 7 [1975] 523-524) is not entirely convincing. P. D. MILLER (El the Warrior, *HTR* 60 [1967] 411-431) mentions the possibility that Philo Byblius knew El as a bellicose deity, based on his interpretation of the epithet under consideration. This is unfounded. The expression *ab šnm* presumably characterizes El as the oldest among the gods (*ARTU* 16 n. 83).

Finally, it should be observed that El was iconographically represented by his worshippers. Unfortunately, it is seldom possible to identify him among the images preserved. The material is collected by A. CAQUOT & M. SZNYCER (*Ugaritic Religion* [Leiden 1980] pl. VII, assumedly VIII a); by M. YON & J. GACHET (Une statuette du dieu El à Ugarit, *Syria* 66 [1989] 349) and by P. WELTEN (Götterbild, männliches, *BRL2*, 99-111; cf. the comments by N. WYATT, The Stela of the seated God from Ugarit, *UF* 15 [1983] 271-277).

In the Phoenician, Aramaic, Punic and Neo-Punic inscriptions the noun *'l* is generally used as appellative in the sense of 'god, godhead' or as adjective 'divine'. This use of the term is also known from the Ugaritic texts of Ras Shamra and from the OT. Yet, El was also used as proper name, e.g. when El is mentioned alongside other gods. This is the case in the Aramaic inscription of Panammuwa I king of Samʾal (*KAI* 214) dating from the middle of the eighth century BCE. The text mentions the gods →Hadad, El, →Resheph, →Rakib-el and Shamash (→Shemesh) as benefactors of Panammuwa, bestowing upon him the kingship and welfare of his state (*KAI* 214:1. 2. 11. 18). The gods Hadad, El, Rakib-el and Shamash are found also in the closing formula of the inscription on the statue of Panammuwa II. Moreover, the first stela of the Aramaic Sefire-inscription (eighth century BCE) containing the text of the treaty between the kings of KTK and Arpad (*KAI* 222) mentions El alongside *ʿlyn* (→Elyôn) and other gods (*KAI* 222A:11). In a Phoenician votive inscription from the Hellenistic era, discovered at Umm el-ʿAwāmīd, the name El is also used absolutively (M. LIDZBARSKI, *Ephemeris für semitische Epigraphik*, vol. II [1903-1907] 166 a. 1; cf. RÖLLIG, 1959:409). W. W. Graf BAUDISSIN (*Kyrios als Gottesname im Judentum und seine Stelle in der Religionsgeschichte* III [ed. O. Eissfeldt; Giessen 1929] 11) already noted the divine name *rkbʾl* (e.g. *KAI* 24:16) might contain the proper name El. This opinion is endorsed by RÖLLIG (1959:409). Finally, El is attested in the inscription of Deir ʿAllā, dating from about 700 BCE, (second combination II:6; see J. HOFTIJZER, *TUAT* II,1 [1986] 145; on *ʾēl* used as a proper name among the southern Arabians, see CROSS 1973:260-261). It is therefore not astonishing that El was still known as an independent deity to Philo Byblius who calls him ἦλος (Eusebius, *Praep. evang*. I,10:16. 20. 29. 44).

The Phoenician inscription of Karatepe dating from the late eighth century BCE quotes beside other gods *ʾl qn ʾrṣ* 'El-creator-of-the-Earth' (*KAI* 26 A III:18). The same epithet occurs in a second century CE Neo-Punic inscription (*KAI* 129:1). It qualifies El as creator of the earth. The name has ancient roots as witnessed by the divine name ^{d}*El-ku-ni-ir-ša* in a myth discovered at Boghazköy. It must be emphasized that nowhere in the Phoenician and Punic inscriptions is El mentioned as president of the other gods (RENDTORFF 1966).

P. BORDREUIL (Les noms propres Transjordaniens de l'Ostracon de Nimroud, *RHPR* 59 [1979] 313-317) has pointed out that in Ammonite personal names the theophoric element *ʾl* predominates. However, these names do not prove that El was worshipped in Ammon, since the theophoric element under consideration should presumably be interpreted as referring to the Ammonite national deity →Milcom (SMITH 1990:24; see also U. HÜBNER, *Die Ammoniter* [ADPV 16; Wiesbaden 1992] 256, for a more cautious view). El is not attested in the Ammonite inscriptions.

III. The population of Palestine in the first millennium BCE knew the deity El. Already F. C. MOVERS (*Die Phönizier* 1 [Bonn 1841] 389) held that the Israelites worshipped El as a god distinct from Yahweh (but cf. SCHMIDT 1971:146). As a result the OT contains texts where the Canaanite background of the name is still recognizable. In these few instances El refers to a deity other than Yahweh. The evidence will pass in review.

The expressions *ʾēl ʾĕlōhê yiśraʾēl*, 'El, the god of Israel' (Gen 33:20) and *hāʾēl ʾĕlōhê ʾābîkā*, 'El, the god of your father', (Gen 46:3) should be discussed first. The present context of both phrases relates them to the patriarch Jacob and his God in whom none other than Yahweh could be seen (SMITH 1990:11). Yet it is the Canaanite El who is depicted here as the God of Israel (contrast Josh 8:30). In all probability Gen 33:20 represents an old tradition. It shows that El was worshipped at least by some of the proto-Israelites (but cf. the interpretation of the Greek translation: καὶ ἐπεκαλέσατο τὸν θεὸν Ισραηλ). O. LORETZ (Die Epitheta *ʾl ʾlhj jśrʾl* (Gn 33,20) und *ʾl ʾlhj ʾbjk* (Gn 46,3), *UF* 7 [1975] 583) estimates *ʾĕlōhê* to be a later expansion of an original *ʾēl ʾābîkā*; cf. the explanation by C. WESTERMANN (*Genesis* [BK I/2; Neukirchen-Vluyn 1981] 644-646; [I/3; Neukirchen Vluyn 1982] 171). DE MOOR (1990:245) construes an original reading *ʾn yhʾl ʾlhy ʾbyk*, 'I am YH-El, the God of your father'. This seems to be highly speculative, however. The surmise that *ʾēl* in Gen 46:3 has been transformed from a proper noun into an appellative is supported by the fact that there are numerous cases where the proper name Yahweh is supplemented by a genitive employed in apposition: e.g. *yhwh ʾĕlōhê ʾăbōtêkem* (e.g. Exod 3:15-16; Deut 1:11. 21; 6:3; Josh 18:3). The same can be observed at Num 23:8. 19. 22-23; 24:4. 8. 16. 23; 2 Sam 23:5.

The view that El was worshipped among the Israelites is supported by Isa 14:4b-20, a lamentation about the downfall of a universal ruler. The text relates that the tyrant intended to ascend to heaven in order to set his throne above the *kôkĕbê ʾēl*, 'the stars of El', and thus settle himself upon the divine mountain in the outmost north (v 13). This was an attempt to exercise dominion over the universe, something traditionally reserved for El, the divine lord. The text alludes to Canaanite traditions. POPE interpreted a line in a Punic inscription from Italy—*KAI* 277:10-11—as follows: *km hkkbm ʾl*, 'like the stars of El' (apud CROSS 1973:272). This interpretation has been challenged by SPRONK (*Beatific Afterlife* [AOAT 219; Neukirchen-Vluyn 1986] 215n1) who apparently renders 'like these stars'. However, *ʾl* can be interpreted as a genitivus qualitatis: 'these divine stars'. The divine mountain (→Zaphon, →Baal Zaphon)was an important element in this Canaanite/ Ugaritic mythology.

Another trace of El-worship in ancient Israel is found in Ezek 28:2 (*pace* CROSS 1973:271). The king of Tyre regarded himself a god and thought that he possessed a divine residence in the midst of the sea (→Melqart). Here, the allusions to Canaanite mythology are unmistakable. The residence of El (*mṯb il*) is referred to in *KTU* 1.3 iv:48; v:39; 1.4 i:12; iv:52. El's mythic dwelling is situated at *mbk nhrm/ apq thmtm*, 'the fountainhead of the two rivers/ bedding of the two floods' (e.g. *KTU* 1.2 iii:4; 1.6 i:33-34).

Further hints to the worship of El are given by the names *ʾēl bĕrît* (→Baal Berith; Judg 9:46), *ʾēl ʿôlām* (→El-olam; Gen 21:33), *ʾēl ʿĕlyôn* (Most High →Elyon; Gen 14:18-22; Ps 78:35), *ʾēl roʾî* (God of seeing →El-roi; Gen 16:13), and *ʾēl šadday* (→Shadday; Gen 17:1; 28:3; 35:11; 43:14; 48:3; 49:25 [cj.]; Exod 6:3; Ezek 10:5) as well as by genitival constructions containing El: *bĕnê ʾēl* (Deut 32:8. 43; LXX: υἱοὶ θεοῦ; 4QDtn^{g} *bny ʾl[hym]*; P. W. SKEHAN, A fragment of the "song of Moses" (Deut. 32) from Qumran, *BASOR* 136 [1954] 12-15; O. LORETZ, Die Vorgeschichte von Deuteronomium 32,8f.43, *UF* 9 [1977] 355-357) respectively *bĕnê ʾēlîm* (Ps 29:1; 89:7), *môʿădê ʾēl* (Ps 74:8), and *ʿădat ʾēl* (Ps 82:1; H. NIEHR, Götter oder Menschen – eine falsche Alternative: Bemerkungen zu Ps 82, *ZAW* 99 [1988] 94-98).

Finally, Hebrew proper names with the theophoric element *ʾēl* known from the OT as well as from ancient Hebrew inscriptions should be taken into account. It is not clear whether the element *ʾēl* refers to a deity in general or to El in particular (for Ugarit see EISSFELDT 1951:46-52; F. GRÖNDAHL, *Die Personennamen der Texte aus Ugarit* [StP 1; Roma 1967] 94-97; for the other regions see M. NOTH, *IPN* 82-99; J. H. TIGAY, *You Shall Have No Other Gods* [HSM 31; Atlanta 1986] 12. 83-85). In the main, the noun *ʾēl* is used in the OT in a way comparable to the Ugaritic and Canaanite inscriptions, i.e. as an appellative meaning 'god'. This use survived alongside the divine designation *ʾĕlōhîm* (e.g. Exod 15:11; Isa 44:10. 15. 17; 46:6; Ezek 28:9; Ps 36:7; 80:11; 104:21[?]; Dan 11:36). There are cases where *ʾēl* refers to Yahweh. Apparently there was no restraint in ancient Israel in using the substantive since Yahweh—in spite of his incomparability—was also perceived as a deity comparable to the gods of the Canaanite world (e.g. Gen 35:1. 3; Exod 15:2; Deut

3:24; Isa 5:16; 7:14; 8:8. 10; 31:3; Jer 51:56; Hos 11:9; 12:1; Mic 7:18; Ps 63:2; SMITH 1990:7-12; DE MOOR 1990).

The identification of El with Yahweh opened the possibility of adopting ideas and concepts connected with the El religion. A problematic case is the designation *ʾēl qannāʾ (qannôʾ)*, 'a jealous god' for Yahweh (Exod 20:5; 34:14; Deut 4:24; 5:9; 6:15; Josh 24:19; Nah 1:2) since in the Ugaritic literature jealousy and violent behaviour is a characteristic not of El, but of the goddess →Anat (*KTU* 1.3 v:22-25; 1.17 vi:41-45; 1.18 i:9-12). It is easier to find the antecedent to the characterization of Yahweh as *ʾēl raḥḥûm wĕḥannûn ʾerek ʾappayim wĕrab ḥesed*, 'a merciful and gracious god, long-suffering and abundant in goodness' (Exod 34:6; Jonah 4:2; Joel 2:13; Ps 86:15; 103:8; 145:8; Neh 9:17; many other passages contain separate elements of this confession). This phrase is related to the epithet of El of Ugarit *ltpn il dpid* discussed above (SMITH 1990:10). Most probably, this trait of El was also known in the more southern Canaanite regions. The fact that it was taken over to characterize Yahweh underlines the continuation between the Ugaritic/Canaanite El religion and later Yahwism (DE MOOR 1990: 69-82. 234-260; KORPEL 1990; SMITH 1990: 7-12.21-26; LORETZ 1990:73. 182; pace e.g. L. KÖHLER, *Theologie des Alten Testaments* [Tübingen 1936 = [4]1966] 30). An important feature is the designation of Yahweh as 'king', though this title is not applied to El in the Ugaritic inscriptions but to Baal. Nonetheless, this metaphor hints at a Canaanite heritage. The moment of attribution of the epithet 'king' to Yahweh is a question of debate. The concept of Baal as king might have been of influence (SCHMIDT 1966; KORPEL 1990:281-286).

The Phoenician inscriptions from Karatepe reveal El as a creator-god. Therefore it is plausible that the Canaanite population of Palestine has taken over the view of El as a creator, which was only late applied to Yahweh. It should be noted however that it is not clear from the Ugaritic texts that El was seen as creator. The view that mankind was the creation of Yahweh is known from sources which are not earlier than the seventh century BCE (Gen 2:7. 22; Exod 4:11; Deut 4:32; 32:6. 15; Isa 29:16; Hos 8:14; Prov 14:31; 17:5; 22:2; 29:13 [cf. 20:12; Ps 139:13]), and the view of Yahweh as the creator of mankind cannot certainly be traced back to the concept of creation of the earth by Yahweh (Gen 2; 14:19. 22). However, it should also be taken into account that the idea of Yahweh as creator was borrowed by the Israelites from the Phoenician →Baal-shamem religion (H. NIEHR, *Der höchste Gott* [BZAW 190; Berlin New York 1990] 119-140).

The fact that Yahweh obtained, though relatively late, the title *ʾāb*, '→Father' (Isa 63:16; Jer 3:4; 31:9; Mal 1:6) probably also shows Canaanite influence though attestations that El was seen as 'father' are only known from Ugaritic sources (e.g. *KTU* 1.2 i:33; 1.3 v:35; 1.4 iv:47; 1.14 i:41; KORPEL 1990:235-239).

S. E. LOEWENSTAMM (*Comparative Studies in Biblical and Ancient Oriental Literatures* [AOAT 204; Neukirchen-Vluyn 1980] 157-159) connects Num 12:13 to the Canaanite concept of El as healer (→El-rophe) and 2 Sam 14:20, as well as Job 12:12, to El's wisdom. It should be remarked that the references applying the noun *ʾēl* to Yahweh increase from the Babylonian era onward (Isa 40:18; 42:5; 43:10, 12; 45:14, 15, 20-22; 46:9; Num 16:22; 1 Sam 2:3; Josh 22:22; Isa 12:2; Lam 3:41). They prove that El did not disappear from the religious sphere and should likewise be judged as an intentionally archaizing element. The name El is employed for Yahweh particularly often in the Psalter (e.g. 5:5; 7:12; 18 [= 2 Sam 22]:3. 31. 33. 48; 102:25).

IV. *Bibliography*

F. M. CROSS, *ʾēl*, *TWAT* 1 (1973) 259-279; M. J. DAHOOD, Ancient Semitic Deities in Syria and Palestine,. *Le antiche Divinità Semitiche* (J. Bottéro & S. Moscati eds.; Roma 1958) 65-94; O. EISSFELDT, El and Yahweh, *JSS* 1 (1956) 25-37 = *KS* III [1966] 386-397; EISSFELDT, *El im ugari-*

tischen Pantheon (Berlin 1951); E. JACOB, El, *BHH* 1 (1962) 386-389; M. C. A. KORPEL, *A Rift in the Clouds* (UBL 8; Münster 1990); O. LORETZ, *Ugarit und die Bibel* (Darmstadt 1990) 66-73; J. C. DE MOOR, El, the Creator, *The Bible World. Essays in Honor of Cyrus H. Gordon* (ed. G. Rendsburg et al.; New York 1980) 171-187; DE MOOR, *The Rise of Yahwism* (BETL 91; Leuven 1990); M. J. MULDER, *Kanaänitische Goden in het Oude Testament* (Den Haag 1965) 13-24; U. OLDENBURG, *The Conflict between El and Baal in Canaanite Religion* (Leiden 1969); M. H. POPE, *El in the Ugaritic Texts* (VTSup 2; Leiden 1955); POPE, The Status of El at Ugarit, *UF* 19 (1987) 219-230; R. RENDTORFF, El, Ba'al und Jahwe. Erwägungen zum Verhältnis von kanaanäischer und israelitischer Religion, *ZAW* 78 (1966) 277-291; W. RÖLLIG, El als Gottesbezeichnung im Phönizischen, *Festschrift J. Friedrich zum 65. Geburtstag* (R. von Kiele et al.. eds.; Heidelberg 1959) 403-416; W. H. SCHMIDT, *ʾēl*, *THAT* 1 (1971) 142-149; SCHMIDT, *Königtum Gottes in Ugarit und Israel* (BZAW 80; Berlin ²1966); J. STARCKY, Le nom divin El, *ArOr* 17 (1949) 383-386.

W. HERRMANN

EL-BERITH → BAAL BERITH

EL-CREATOR-OF-THE-EARTH

I. The second element of the name of the deity *ʾl qn ʾrṣ* can etymologically be connected with the verbal-root QNY 'create, acquire (a property)', which is used for example, in Ps 139:13 (*ʾattā qānîtā kilyōtai* 'you created my kidneys'). The interpretation of the god as 'El-Creator-of-the-Earth' therefore seems highly justified. Contrast E. LIPIŃSKI (*TWAT* 7 [1990-1992] 68) who preferred a derivation from QNY 'to keep, to possess' and translated: 'El-the-Owner-of the Earth'. The God is mentioned in Gen 14:19.22.

II. The name of the deity first occurs outside the Bible in Phoenician in the Karatepe-Inscription (*ʾl qn ʾrṣ KAI* 26 A III 18 = *TSSI* III 15 A III 18, end of the eighth century BCE). The hieroglyphic-Luwian version mentions the Mesopotamian god of wisdom and sweet-water Ea in the writing ᴰ*a-ā-ś*. El-Creator-of-the-Earth is mentioned in the curse-formula between →Baʿal Šamēm, i.e. the Lord of Heaven, and Šamš ʿolam, i.e. the Sun-god of Eternity. Traces of the Canaanite god and his worship can be found much earlier. A mythological text from the Hittite archive of Ḫattuša tells the story of ᵈ*el-ku-né-er-ša*, the husband of ᵈ*a-še-er-tum* (→Ashera). He dwells in a tent at the sources of the river Mala i.e. the →Euphrates (*ANET*³ 519, cf. H. OTTEN, *MIO* 1 [1953] 125-150; *MDOG* 85 [1953] 27-38). The Weathergod, embarrassed by the sexual overtures of Ashertu, pays a visit to Elqoneh who advises him to injure the goddess. He complies by murdering 77 or 88 sons of Ashertu. The slaughter gives rise to great mourning. The myth breaks off here, but it is certain that it is Canaanite in origin. The god El-Creator-of-the-Earth who lives in a tent by the Euphrates, moreover, points to a nomadic cultural setting. In the writing ᵈ*ku-né-er-ša* (i.e. without the opening godname, if not to be found in the determinative) the god also occurs in a fragmentary Hittite ritual (KUB 36,38 rev.8) as one of the 'thousand gods of Ḫatti-land'. Centuries later, in the second cent. BCE, an exedra and a porticus were dedicated to *ʾl qn ʾrṣ* in Leptis Magna (Tripolitania) by a man named Candidus, son of Candidus, who gave notice of it by means of a NeoPunic inscription (*KAI* 129 = LEVI DELLA VIDA & AMADASI GUZZO 1987, No. 18). In the Aramaic world, we also know some *tesserae* from Palmyra, which mention *ʾl q(w)n ʾrʿ* (INGHOLT, SEYRIG & STARCKY, *Recueil* [1955] No. 220-223). From the same place there is even a bilingual dedication *[l]ʾl qwn ʾrʿ ʾlhʾ ṭbʾ* 'To El-Creator-of-the-Earth the good god', Greek *poseidōni theō* (J. CANTINEAU, *Syria* 19 [1938] 78:5). This divine figure may also be represented by the *bʿ[l]šmwn qnh dy rʿh*, 'Baal-shamen creator of the earth' in the Hatra-Inscription 23,3 (*KAI* 244) and the *Konnaros* of a Latin and a Greek inscription from Baalbek (*IGLS* VI No. 2743; 2841).

These widespread references show that El-qoneh was venerated for a very long time in the West-Semitic world. He is best regarded as a manifestation of the highest god →El: simply in his role as *creator mundi*. In Hatra Baal-shamen was accorded the highest rank among the gods; and therefore assumed El's power as creator.

III. In the late (but in its core early) Biblical midrash about the meeting between →Melchizedek and Abram (Gen 14), the latter is blessed by the High Priest of (Jeru)salem in the name of *ʾēl ʿelyōn qōnē šāmayim wāʾāreṣ* (v 19). He answers by swearing an oath in the name of the same god (v 22). It is to be noticed, that a contamination of *El* and *Elyōn* here took place, perhaps in a later Yahwistic tradition. The tradition epithet is extended: the creation comprises heaven and earth, a development which made H. GESE think of a divine *triad* consisting of an *ʾēl ʿElyōn*, *ʾēl qonē ʾāreṣ* and *ʾēl qonē šāmayim* (*RAAM* [1970] 114). It is interesting to note that 1 QGenApocr 22:16.21 uses the Aramaic title *mrh*, i.e. 'Lord (of Heaven and Earth)' in his translation instead of *qonē*. With this interpretation, the offensive contamination is rejected in favor of an interpretation of the unified name of the god *ʾēl ʿElyōn*. The reference to El Qoneh in Gen 14 shows that this Canaanite god was well known to the Israelites but did not find his place in any official (and private?) cult.

IV. *Bibliography*

H. A. HOFFNER, The Elkuniršа Myth Reconsidered, *RHA* 23 (1965) 5-16; G. LEVI DELLA VIDA & M. G. AMADASI GUZZO, *Iscrizioni puniche della Tripolitania (1927-1967)* (Roma 1987) 46; P. D. MILLER, El, the Creator of Earth, *BASOR* 239 (1980) 43-46; M. WEIPPERT, Elemente phönikischer und kilikischer Religion in den Inschriften von Karatepe, *ZDMG* Suppl.1/1 (1969) 203-204.

W. RÖLLIG

ELDERS πρεσβύτεροι

I. The noun *presbyteros*, usually meaning 'older', or in a technical sense 'elder' (Jewish) or 'presbyter' (Christian), occurs 12 times in Rev referring to beings in heaven. They are always identified as 'the twenty-four elders'.

II. Twenty-four elders appear for the first time in the vision of heaven in chap. 4 and are described as sitting on 24 thrones situated around the throne of God, dressed in white garments and with golden crowns on their heads (4:14). Also around the throne, probably in the area between the throne of God and the 24 thrones of the elders, four living creatures are positioned (4:6-8). Their task is to praise God without ceasing and their praise is supported by the 24 elders who prostrate themselves (lit. 'fall', *piptō*) before the throne of God and worship him (*proskyneō*).

The triad of the throne of God, the four living creatures and the 24 elders is subsequently used to describe the central place in heaven where specific events take place: the appearing of the →Lamb (5:6) and the worship of the Lamb by the →angels (5:11), the worship of God by the angels (7:11) and the singing of the new song (14:3). In these texts no actions of the elders are mentioned.

When they come into action it is to worship God together with the four living creatures. Their worship is described in the same way as in chap. 4. It occurs when the Lamb receives the scroll (5:8-10) and at the end of the same scene (5:14); when the seventh angel has blown his trumpet (11:16), and at the great Hallelujah in heaven (19:4). Twice one of the elders acts as an *angelus interpres*, viz. when the Lamb is announced (5:5) and when the countless multitude (7:9) is identified as those who have passed through the great ordeal (7:13-17). The thrones on which the elders are sitting are mentioned only in the introductory description in 4:4 and in 11:16 where they serve to identify the elders (if the article *hoi* is retained). Usually the throne is the throne of judgment (cf. 20:4; Matt 19:28; Luke 22:30; Dan 7:9-10; Ps 121:5 LXX), but the occupants of the throne in 20:4 are not the elders but the martyrs risen from death. The golden crowns on the heads of the elders are mentioned only in 4:4 and in 4:10 where they are laid before the throne of God as an act of submission.

To sum up, the 24 elders have their place in a circle around the throne of God and their sole function is to worship God, they are explicitly distinguished from the angels in 7:11 and implicitly in 5:11.

The idea of a divine household surrounding God is known in the OT (cf. 1 Kgs 22:19; Job 1:6; 2:1; →Council) and widespread in Jewish apocalyptic traditions but no mention is made of elders (except, possibly, Isa 24:23 LXX, if *enōpion tōn presbyterōn* refers to heavenly beings and not to the elders of the people as suggested in the Targum).

Since no clear connections with other traditions, Jewish or non-Jewish, can be established the following hypotheses to explain the 24 elders in heaven are proposed.

The elders may represent or reflect earthly institutions, such as the elders of the people of Israel (cf. Isa 24:23, quoted above; Exod 24:11), or the 24 priestly orders (2 Chr 24:1-19; cf. in the Mishnah 'the elders of the priesthood', *Yoma* 1,5), or the twelve patriarchs and the twelve apostles (mentioned together in Rev 21:12-14) representing together the people of God of the OT and the NT, or the presbyters of the Christian church. This last interpretation would also explain why the 24 elders carry the incense which represents the prayers of the saints (5:8). But nowhere in Rev are elders or presbyters referred to as church officers.

The idea of the 24 elders in heaven may go back to ideas from the *Umwelt*, such as the 24 Babylonian astral deities mentioned in Diodorus Siculus II 31,4 (quoted in BOUSSET 1906; CHARLES 1920) and called 'judges of the universe' (cf. *2 Enoch* A IV,1); or the 24 Iranian heavenly Yazatas (possibly referred to by Plutarch, *Isis et Osiris 47*, cf BOUSSET 1906; CHARLES 1920). But the 24 elders are neither rulers nor judges. Their only task is to worship God. It is true that the number of 24 has cosmic connotations but this is too general to be helpful. Non of these hypotheses can give a satisfactory explanation of the origin and background of the 24 elders in heaven. The parallels quoted or referred to may somehow have contributed to the idea but they are no more than analogies.

III. *Bibliography*

E. B. ALLO, *L'Apocalypse de Saint Jean* (Paris 1921) 54-56; W. BOUSSET, *Die Offenbarung Johannis* (Göttingen 1906) 245-247; G. BORNKAMM, πρέσβυς, *TWNT* 6 (1959) 668-670; R. H. CHARLES, *A Critical and Exegetical Commentary on the Revelation of St. John* (Edinburgh 1920) I 128-133; A. FEUILLET, Les vingt-quatre vieillards de l'Apocalypse, *RB* 65 (1958) 5-32; J. MICHL, *Die 24 Ältesten in der Apokalypse des heiligen Johannes* (München 1938).

J. REILING

ELEMENTAL SPIRITS OF THE UNIVERSE → STOICHEIA

ELIJAH אליהו, אליה, Ἠλ(ε)ίας

I. Elijah = "Yahweh is God" (cf. 1 Kgs 18:36,37) is the name (surname?) of an Israelite prophet (9th century BCE), and occurs 68 times in the OT (62x in 1 Kgs - 2Kgs 2), 29 times in the NT and further in 1 Macc 2:58; Sir 48:1,4,12. On account of his ascension (2 Kgs 2:11) he is considered to have been transferred to heavenly existence and accordingly his return could be expected (Mal 3:23,24).

II. Stories about men who have been transported bodily from the realm of humankind to a domain inaccessible to ordinary mortals (heaven, paradise or some other inaccessible place), are known from antiquity, especially from Greece and Rome (STRECKER 1962:461-476; LOHFINK 1971: 32-79), but also from Mesopotamia (SCHMITT 1973:4-23). In Rome the emperor's removal to heaven was a condition for his apotheosis and cult. In the NT →Jesus' ascension is described as a removal in Mark 16:19; Luke 9:51; Acts 1:2.9.11.22; 1 Tim 3:16.

The ascension traditions have a number of characteristic traits in common (cf. HOUTMAN 1978:301-303). With regard to the story of Elijah's translation, the following elements can be pointed out: they have the purpose of telling about a person's removal in the flesh to the divine world. Usually they are told from the perspective of the spectator(s). The circumstances and the place of the ascension are described rather fully (cf. 2 Kgs 2:1-18; Luke 24:36-53; Acts 1:4-11). No detailed information, however, is given about the journey, the route and the destination of the transported person (cf. 2 Kgs 2:11.12; Luke 24:51; Acts 1:2.11.22). He has vanished without a trace. Non of his mortal remains can be found on earth (cf. 2 Kgs 2:16-18; Luke 24:1-11.23.24). God or the gods are regarded as the agent(s) of the translation (2 Kgs 2:1 presents an interpretation of 2 Kgs 2:11; cf. Luke 24:52.53). Often fire (cf. Judg 13:20) and meteorological phenomena carry away the person concerned and/or conceal the event (cf. 2 Kgs 2:11.12; Acts 1:9; 1 Thess 4:17; Rev 11:12). By his assumption he is qualified as an exceptional being (cf. Judg 13:6.8.10-23). As a miracle the removal demands belief. Such belief can be elicited, for instance, as the result of an inquiry (cf. 2 Kgs 2:16-18) or by (a) witness(es) (cf. 2 Kgs 2:12.18; Acts 1:10.11; Rev 11:12), by the appearance of heavenly beings (cf. Acts 1:10.11) or by a voice from heaven (Rev 11:12). To be taken up is exceptional and a great honour. It happens only to extraordinary mortals. By ascension immortality and a divine status are acquired. Among the heavenly beings the person in question lives on. So he can be a helper for people on earth (cf. Matt 28:30; Rom 8:34). From his exalted position he can return to earth (cf. Mal 3:23.24; Acts 1:11; Rev 1:7; 14:14-16). Bodily translation does not always exclude dying, but in that case resurrection is supposed (cf. Luke 24:51; Acts 1:9; Rev 11:11.12 and see 1 Thess 4:16.17).

III. In the books of Kings, Elijah is depicted as a real man of God. Thanks to his intimate relation with the LORD he was in possession of supernatural powers and in a position to do miracles (1 Kgs 17:8-16; 18:37.38; 2 Kgs 2:8). He had at his disposal both life and death (1 Kgs 17:1, cf. Sir 48:3; Luke 4:25.26; Jas 5:17.18; Rev 11:6; 1 Kgs 17:17-24; 2 Kgs 1:10-14). He was a champion of justice (1 Kgs 21) and distinguished himself by his combat against →Baal-worship and by his zeal (cf. 1 Kgs 19:10.14) for the LORD (1 Kgs 18-19, cf. Rom 11:2-5; 2 Kgs 1; Sir 48:3b, cf. Luke 9:54; 2 Chron 21:12-15). To a certain extent Elijah has the traits of a new →Moses (cf. e.g. G. FOHRER 1968[2]:55-57). Great homage was paid to Elijah. By means of divine chariots (cf. Dan 7:13; Mark 13:26 par.; 14:62 par.) he was carried up to heaven (2 Kgs 2:1.11; Sir 48:9.11.12), according to 1 Macc 2:58 for being zealous and fervent for the law. Within the OT no other person's removal is narrated with such clarity as Elijah's. The translation of →Enoch is only suggested (the verb *lqḥ* in Gen 5:24 permits various interpretations). Clear evidence about the assumption of other prominent OT figures such as Moses, Baruch and Ezra belong to the traditions outside the OT. Already within the OT Elijah's return is announced and associated with the Messianic age (Mal 3:1. 23.24, cf. Sir 48:10).

The phrase "to heaven" in 2 Kgs 2:1.11 has been translated in the LXX in a remarkable way by *hōs eis ton ouranon*, "as if to heaven" (see also some MSS of 1 Macc 2:58). The reason for this dilution of the Heb text is not clear. Did the translator reject the miracle? (SCHMITT 1973:150). According to an interpretation which is mentioned in the Babylonian Talmud (*Sukkah* 5a), Elijah's ascension to heaven is excluded by Ps 115:16 (cf. Str-B 4 [1924] 765). The view that Elijah had not ascended to heaven is also ascribed to the Evangelist John (John 3:13, cf. John 8:52.53) (MARTYN 1976:181-219). In Samaritan tradition, Elijah is depicted as a rascal who on his flight for king Ahab drowned in the river Jordan (*The Samaritan Chronicle No. II*; ed. MACDONALD 1969:163, 164). Did the translator intend to eliminate the chronological problem of 2 Chron 21:12—a letter of Elijah reached Joram of Judah who lived after Elijah's ascension—by suggesting that Elijah had only been lifted up "as if to heaven" and had been brought to another place on earth (cf. 1 Kings 18:12; 2 Kgs 2:16; Acts 8:39.40)? Or did he hold a dissenting view on Elijah's destination, viz. that Elijah had been carried to paradise (cf. Jub 4:23), the place for the elect and righteous ones (*1 Enoch* 70)? An indication of Elijah's destination is lacking in LXX Sir 48:9 and in Josephus' description of Elijah's removal (*Ant.* 9.28) (cf. HOUTMAN 1978: 298-300). The rabbis (Str-B 4 [1924] 765-766) as well as the Fathers (e.g., Irenaeus, *Contra Haereses* 5.5.1; Gregory the Great, *Homilia XXIX*; PL 76 [1849] 1216) had no uniform view of Elijah's destination.

According to the NT some people believed Jesus to be Elijah (Matt 16:14; Mark 6:15; 8:28; Luke 9:8,19; see also Luke 22: 43, cf. 1 Kgs 19:5,7), but in conformity with his Messianic claim he himself designated John the Baptist as having been the precursor and herald of the →Messiah (Matt 11:14; cf. Matt 17:13; Luke 1:17; see on the contrary John 1:21.25). In the role of a precursor of Jesus, Elijah appeared together with Moses (cf. Mal 3:22-24) on the Mount of Transfiguration. There they talked with Jesus (Matt 17:1-13; Mark 9:2-13; Luke 9:28-36). By their coming the beginning of final age is announced (cf. also Rev 11:3-12). In extra-biblical literature Elijah, as a precursor of the Messiah, is accompanied by Enoch (e.g., *1 Enoch* 90:31; *4 Ezra* 6:26). In Rev 11:3-12 reference is made to Moses and Elijah (cf. Rev 11:6) as preachers of repentance in the last time. In their confrontation with the beast (cf. the description of Elijah's and Enoch's struggle with the →Antichrist in chap. 4 of the Elijah Apocalyse) they suffered death, but after their martyrdom they were raised from the dead and ascended to heaven (Rev 11:7-12). As appears from Matt 27:47.49; Mark 15:35.36, Elijah was considered the helper of the hopeless (cf. 1 Kgs 17:8-24) in popular Jewish belief.

IV. Ancient witnesses attest to the existence of several apocryphal works which are attributed to Elijah. Two complete Apocalypses of Elijah are known: a Coptic document and a Hebrew *Sefer Eliyahu* which is significantly different from the Coptic work (cf. DEHANDSCHUTTER 1988:59-68). In rabbinical literature Elijah plays a prominent role. The solution of halakhic problems is expected of him. Rabbis and pious men were considered to have been guided by him in their studies. He is a precursor and active partner of the Messiah. On account of his burning zeal for the LORD he is identified with Aaron's grandson Phinehas (cf. Num 25:7-13; Ps 106:30). In various guises he appears as the redeemer and the helper of the poor and the hopeless. In Jewish mysticism Elijah is regarded as a supernatural being not born of a woman. He is an angel descended from heaven for the purpose of being useful to humankind and a teacher of Kabbalah. In Jewish folklore Elijah is a favourite hero. He combats social injustice, helps the poor and turns against the proud and the oppressors. He also figures in humoristic stories and in religious customs ("the chair of Elijah" at the circumcision ceremony; "the cup of Elijah" at the Passover Seder). With the name Ilyaas, Elijah occurs in the Koran (Sura 6:85; 37:123-130) and in Islamic tradition (cf. *HIsl*, 204-206; A. J. WENSINCK, *EncIsl* 3 [1927] 470-471).

V. *Bibliography*

R. BAUCKHAM, The Martyrdom of Enoch and Elijah: Jewish or Christian?, *JBL* 95 (1976) 447-458; J. BOWMAN, Elijah and the Pauline Jesus Christ, *AbrN* 26 (1988) 1-18; B. DEHANDSCHUTTER, Les apocalypses d'Élie, *Élie le prophète: Bible, tradition, iconographie* (ed. G. F. Willems; Leuven 1988) 59-68; *Élie le prophète I: Selon les écritures et les traditions chrétiennes; II: Au Carmel, dans le Judaïsme et l'Islam*, (Bruges 1956); M. M. FAIERSTEIN, Why Do the Scribes Say that Elijah Must Come First, *JBL* 100 (1981) 75-86; G. FOHRER, *Elia* (Zürich 1968[2]); R. HAYWARD, Phinehas - the same is Elijah: The Origins of a Rabbinic Tradition, *JJS* 29 (1978) 22-34; C. HOUTMAN, Elia's hemelvaart, *NedTTs* 32

(1978) 283-304; *J. Jeremias, *TWNT* 2 (1935) 930-943; *TWNT* 10/2 (1979) 1098-1099; G. Lohfink, *Die Himmelfahrt Jesu* (StANT 26; München 1971) 32-79; J. L. Martyn, We have found Elijah, *Jews, Greeks and Christians: Essays in Honor of W. D. Davies* (ed. R. Hamerton-Kelly & R. Scroggs; Leiden 1976) 181-219; A. Schmitt, *Entrückung - Aufnahme - Himmelfahrt* (Stuttgart 1973); H. Schwarzbaum, *Studies in Jewish and World Folklore* (Berlin 1968) 522 [Index]; Schwarzbaum, Elias, *EdM* 3 (1981) 1342-1354; Schwarzbaum, *Biblical and Extra-Biblical Legends in Islamic Folk-Literature* (Walldorf-Hessen 1982) 219 [Index]; H. Seebass & N. Oswald, Elia, *TRE* 9 (1982) 498-504; A. F. Segal, Heavenly Ascent in Hellenistic Judaism, Early Christianity and their Environment, *ANRW* 2.23.2 (ed. W. Haase; Berlin 1980) 1333-1394; G. Strecker, Elijah *RAC* 5 (1962) 461-476; K. Wessel, Elias, *RAC* 4 (1959) 1141-1163; H. Wissmann & O. Betz, Entrückung, *TRE* 9 (1982) 680-690; O. S. Wintermute, Apocalypse of Elijah, *The Old Testament Pseudepigrapha* 1 (ed. J. H. Charlesworth; London 1983) 721-753.

C. Houtman

ELOAH אלה

I. The Hebrew word *ʾĕlōah* is derived from a base *ʾilāh-*, perhaps a secondary form of the Common Semitic word *ʾil-*, 'god'. Cognate terms are known from Ugaritic, Aramaic, and Arabic/Arabian. The relationship between the common noun and the divine name is complicated and it varies considerably from one language to another. In Aramaic and in the epigraphic Arabian dialects, it is primarily a common noun, while in Ugaritic, Hebrew, and Arabic (Allah < *al-ʾilāhu*, 'the god') the usage as a divine name is clearly attested. There can be no doubt that the more common biblical and Jewish designation of 'god' as Elohim represents an expansion of Eloah, though there is debate both as to the 'meaning' of Eloah and as to the origin of the expanded form (→God).

II. The earliest certain attestations of both the singular and plural forms are in Ugaritic (the existence of the word in Amorite is doubtful: F. M. Cross, *TWAT* 1 [1973] 260). There can be no doubt that both *ilh* and *ilhm* occur in Ugaritic ritual texts, though the precise analysis of the form and meaning of *ilhm* is not always perfectly clear. These divine names are attested to date in only two ritual texts, *KTU* 1.39 and 1.41 (the second text has a near duplicate, *KTU* 1.87, which permits fairly certain restoration of a basic text) and in one text with mixed characteristics (*KTU* 1.108:13). In the ritual texts, both *ilh* and *ilhm* are listed as recipients of sacrifices. The presence of the singular form *ilh* is established by parallel versions of a sequence of sacrifices (*KTU* 1.39:5 and 41:14, 30 *ilh* ... *ilhm* ... *ilhm*), while the form *ilhm* occurs in three distinct contexts: (1) the one just cited, where *ilhm* is repeated twice after *ilh* in a sequence of three sacrifices; (2) *ilhm bʿlm* (*KTU* 1.39:9 and 41:18); and (3) as an independent divine entity (*KTU* 1.39:3 and 41:6.12.28). In this third context, where *ilhm* is a discrete entity in an offering list, it appears in three different sequences of divinities: (1) *ilš*, *ilhm*, end of section (*KTU* 1.41:6); (2) beginning of section, *ilhm*, *ṯkmn w šnm* (*KTU* 1.39:3 and 41:12); (3) *inš ilm*, *ilhm*, *špš* (*KTU* 1.41:27-28). The existence of different sequences establishes the use of the form *ilhm* to fill the slot otherwise occupied by a divine name, and explanations of *ilhm* in the first two contexts that do not take this fact into consideration are thereby weakened. In particular, the interpretation of *ilhm* as an appellative in the phrase *ilhm bʿlm*, i.e. 'Baal-gods', is without parallel in the ritual texts. It is preferable, therefore, to recognize in it two distinct divine names, 'the *ʾIlāhūma* (and) the *Baʿalūma*'. The term expressing the simple notion of 'gods' in these texts is *ilm* which, as such, never fills the 'deity' slot in an offering list because it occurs only in composite divine names or in reference to a specific group of deities. It is always, therefore, to be translated 'gods' rather than 'God(s)'.

The one occurrence of *ilh* in a text containing mythological elements, i.e. *KTU* 1.108:13, is of little help in defining the character and function of the deity because the passage in question is badly broken (cf. D. PARDEE, *Les textes para-mythologiques de la 24e Campagne* (*1961*) [RSO IV; Paris 1988] chap. II). The text does not belong to the group of primary mythological texts. It also contains none of the elements on which scholars have based their proposals for the early dating of the major myths. The group of texts to which this one belongs occasionally show definite ritual elements. So this poem may have been intended primarily for cultic use. The fact that it ends with a benediction on behalf of the king and the city of Ugarit adds credence to this classification. The restoration of the form *ilhm* in another of the 'para-mythological' texts, *KTU* 1.107:11 (line 36' in PARDEE's new edition, *Les textes para-mythologiques*, chap. VIII) is hypothetical, though not impossible.

The distribution and the function of the feminine form *ilht* are quite different: that form appears only in mythological texts where it means 'goddesses'. It functions therefore as the plural of *ilt*, 'goddess'. The form clearly belongs to the old poetic language because it appears in all of the major cycles as well as in briefer texts (*KTU* 1.24 and 1.25). The distribution of forms is thus the following: *ilht*, meaning 'goddesses', occurs only in the mythological texts, where *ilm* is the standard plural of *il*, 'god'. On the other hand, *ilhm* appears alongside *ilm* in the ritual texts, though each has a different function: *ilm* is a common noun and it never fills the 'deity' slot in the offering lists except as part of a composite name (e.g. *pḫr ilm*, 'the assembly of the gods'), while *ilhm* does fill the 'deity' slot, both in the immediate environment of *ilh* and alone.

The presence of *ilht* in the mythological texts shows that the root ʾLH is quite old, while the absence of the singular form *ilh* in the major mythological texts, together with its presence in the ritual prose texts, may be taken as indicating, at least in the light of present data, that the plural form preceded the singular. One can thus posit that *ilhm*/*ilht* were originally expanded plurals (*ilh* is not, therefore, a broken plural!) of *il*/*ilt* and that *ilh* is a secondary formation. In the ritual texts, the fact that *ilhm* appears just before the deity *ṯkmn w šnm*, the youngest of →El's offspring, may indicate that the term has come to designate certain of El's descendants. The precise reason for the secondary creation of a deity *ilh* can only be a subject for speculation, though there is a parallel in Ugaritic religion if one accepts that the divinity *rpu* is a back-formation from the plural form *rpum*. (see PARDEE, *Les textes rituels* [RSO; Paris, f.c.], chap. I, on RS 1.001:3).

The word for 'god' in Aramaic, from Yaudic to Syriac, is *ʾlh*, and the word *ʾl* is basically absent from the various Aramaic dialects as a common noun (where *il* does occur, either it denotes the deity El, as is frequent in personal names, or else the text is of Jewish origin—see J. M. LINDENBERGER, *The Proverbs of Ahiqar* [Baltimore 1983] 93). Normally the plural denotes true plurality in Aramaic, though in Jewish texts the plural form is used in imitation of biblical and Jewish usage of Hebrew *ʾĕlōhîm* to designate Yahweh. Other than the identification in Jewish texts of *ʾĕlāh/ʾĕlāhîn* with the corresponding Hebrew deity, there is no evidence presently available for the existence of a divine name *ʾlh* in Aramaic. Because there are no second-millennium texts of a truly Aramaic character, we can only reconstruct hypothetically the pre-Yaudic history of the Aramaic word *ʾlh*. The essential absence of the common noun *ʾl* in the Aramaic dialects indicates that *ʾlh* displaced *ʾl* in that function at a very early date.

In the dialects of epigraphic Arabian, one finds both *ʾl* and *ʾlh* as common nouns meaning 'god' and occurring in various configurations (M. HÖFNER, *WbMyth* I, 420-422, on North and Central Arabian). In the South Arabian dialect of Qataban, for example, the form *ʾlh* exists as a singular common noun, but it also provides the plural of *ʾil* (S. D. RICKS, *Lexicon of Inscriptional Qatabanian* [StP 14; Rome 1989] 10-11).

The importance of a divine name in anthroponymy is of interest for determining the place of the divinity in a given society (PARDEE 1988, with previous bibliography). The case of Eloah is instructive because it is absent, both as a true theophoric element and as an appellative, from both Ugaritic and Biblical personal names, where the deity plays a minor role, though it does appear in Aramaic as well as in Arabian names (cf. M. MARAQTEN, *Die semitischen Personennamen in den alt- und reichsaramäischen Inschriften aus Vorderasien* [Hildesheim 1988] 45, 223; J. K. STARK, *Personal Names in Palmyrene Inscriptions* [Oxford 1971] 68; G. LANKESTER HARDING, *An Index and Concordance of Pre-Islamic Arabian Names and Inscriptions* [Toronto 1971] 71-72, 91, 118). One may draw the preliminary conclusion, which is supported by the other literary *genres*, that the divinity *ʾIlāhu* was a minor one in Ugaritic culture. The case of the Israelites is more complicated, for there Eloah is relatively unimportant while Elohim is very important but neither form appears in proper names (on the general absence in personal names of theophoric elements the form of which is plural or composite, see PARDEE 1988). On the other hand, the common noun *ʾilāh-* was used in personal names only in those cultures where the word was an important part of their vocabulary.

III. In the Hebrew Bible, *ʾĕlōah* appears fifty-seven times (as compared with nearly 100 occurrences of *ʾĕlāh* in the Aramaic sections, which constitute, of course, only a fraction of the total text). The plural form *ʾĕlōhîm* occurs some 2750 times, both as a common noun and as a divine name. That this form had the status of a divine name is proved, among other indicators, by the use of singular forms used to modify the formally plural form. In the case of the singular, that morpho-syntactic marker is not present and other criteria must be used to determine whether the function is that of a divine name or of a common noun. There can be no question of the word *ʾĕlōah* being of late Aramaean origin in biblical Hebrew because the word shows the characteristic Canaanite shift of /ā/ to /ō/. Any putative Aramaic origin must therefore predate that shift.

Eloah occurs as a divine name most frequently in the book of Job, where that term, →El, and →Shadday are the standard words for 'God' in the poetic sections (Eloah forty-one times, El fifty-five times, Shadday thirty-one times). The divine name Yahweh appears almost exclusively in the prose sections and in some transition indicators in dialogues. The other three terms are used much as Elohim or Yahweh are used in the rest of the Hebrew Bible (the plural form *ʾĕlōhîm* occurs only four times in the poetic sections of Job). Outside the book of Job, only in Ps 50:22, 139:19, and Prov 30:5 does the formulation clearly indicate that *ʾĕlōah* is being used as a divine name.

The appellative function is unmistakable in several passages: in Deut 32:17 there appears the expression *lōʾ ʾĕlōah*, 'no god', and in Ps 18:32 one finds the phrase "Who is *ʾĕlōah* but Yahweh?", parallelled in 2 Sam 22:32 by "Who is *ʾēl* but Yahweh" (cf. also Isa 44:8). Finally, in Dan 11:37-39 *ʾĕlōah* is used much like *ʾĕlāh* in the Aramaic chapters, while the appellative function is clear in Deut 32:15, Hab 1:11, Ps 114:7, Neh 9:17, and 2 Chr 32:15 as well.

In Hab 3:3, the function of the term is debatable: *ʾĕlōah mittêmān yābôʾ wĕqādôš mēhar-pāʾrān,* "Eloah has come from Teman, Qadosh from Mount Paran". Is the parallelism here 'God//(the) Holy One' or 'a god//a holy one'? In the context of Hab 3 one would not wish to doubt that the reference is monotheistic and to Yahweh; but does the expression make use of the common noun as an epithet of Yahweh or of a divine name equivalent to Yahweh?

Except in details of distribution, therefore, with the usage as a divine name being rare except in Job, the usage of Eloah is similar to that of Elohim. Lack of data precludes any conclusions about the possible relationship between the Ugaritic concepts of *ʾIlāhu/ʾIlāhūma* and the origin and development of Hebrew views of the same terms. The relationship between Eloah/Elohim and

Yahweh must be elucidated, to the extent that presently available data permit such decisions, in the broader context of the identification of Yahweh with other deities/-divine names (El, Eloah, Elohim, Yah, Elyon, and Shadday are the permitted ones, though the range of popular usage may have been more extensive—see PARDEE 1988, with previous bibliography).

IV. *Bibliography*

H. BAUER, Die Gottheiten von Ras Schamra, *ZAW* 51 (1933) 84-85; M. DIETRICH, O. LORETZ & J. SANMARTÍN, Die ugaritischen und hebräischen Gottesnamen, *UF* 7 (1975) 552-553; M. DIETRICH & O. LORETZ, Baal *RPU* in KTU 1.108, *UF* 12 (1980) 177; D. PARDEE, An Evaluation of the Proper Names from Ebla from a West Semitic Perspective: Pantheon Distribution According to Genre, *Eblaite Personal Names and Semitic Name-giving* (ARES I; Rome 1988) 119-151; PARDEE, *Les textes rituels* (RSO; Paris, f.c.), chap. I; *Ges.18* Vol. 1 (1987) 61-62.

D. PARDEE

ELOHIM → GOD I

EL-OLAM אל עולם

I. In the Old Testament, the divine name *ʾĒl ʿôlām* is attested in Gen 21:33, i.e. in the conclusion of the story of Abraham's encounter with the Philistine king Abimelek in Beersheba (Gen 21:20-34). After having attested—by the token of seven ewe lambs—that he himself has dug the well of Beersheba (vv 28-30) and after the conclusion of a covenant with Abimelek and the departure of his visitor (vv 22-24.27.32), Abraham plants a tamarisk (*ʾešel*) in Beersheba and invokes the name of *yhwh ʾēl ʿôlam*. The two vv 33-34 are often held to be an addition to an already composite narrative (stratum A: vv 22-24.27.32; stratum B: vv 25-26.28-30.31, see WESTERMANN 1981:423-428). Others think that these verses have been displaced from another context (see EISSFELDT 1966:393 n. 5).

In the context of his story, the author of Gen 21:33 clearly treats El-Olam as a divine epithet for →Yahweh, and not as a separate god. It is possible, of course, that *yhwh* is a secondary intrusion into the narrative: in vv 22 and 23, the divinity is designated as 'God' (*ʾĕlōhîm*), in the discourse of Abimelek, and that God is obviously considered as binding both Abraham and Abimelek. This is consistent with the outlook of the 'elohistic context' to which Gen 20-22 have traditionnally been attributed: even if one keeps in mind that a pre-exilic dating of these chapters has now become improbable (VAN SETERS 1975:227-240; BLUM 1984: 405-419).

II. Independent of the date of the redaction of the Genesis narrative, the question of the traditional background needs to be raised, and in that context the question of the 'identity' of the figure standing behind El-olam. Until the late seventies, it was common to assume (see WESTERMANN 1981: 116-138) that El-olam in Gen 21:33, as well as most of the other occurences of El-titles in the patriarchal narratives, were the relics of divinities belonging to a pre-Israelite or 'proto-Israelite'—or at the very least, pre-Yahwistic—stratum of the history of biblical religion. This perspective was suggested by ALT's (1929; 1953) 'discovery' of the 'god of the fathers', that type of nameless tutelary deity that supposedly belonged to the social and historical phase of the still purely nomadic clans that were to become Israel. ALT (1953:47-52) also suggested that the cult of the local *ʾēlîm* reflected a later, post-settlement stage, during which the proto-Israelite immigrants had become familiar with the various cults practiced by the autochthonous 'Canaanites' at local sanctuaries. In that context, El-olam would be the autochthonous god venerated at the shrine of Beersheba (ALT 1953:7). After the discovery of the texts of Ugarit, the *ʾēl* of the Genesis narratives ceased to be considered as a mere appellative and began to be identified with →El, the creator god of Ugarit. El-olam of Gen 21:33 could now be seen as one of the many local hypostases of the great Canaanite god, i.e. the god El of Beersheba, later identified with Yahweh (EISSFELDT, *KS* 3, 393-394; *KS* 4, 196-197; DE VAUX 1971: 262-263; WORSCHECH 1983:178; etc.). ALBERTZ (1992:57) doubts that the various *ʾēl*-deities of the patriarchal narratives have much in common with the great heavenly El of the Ugaritic pantheon, but the addition of *ʿôlām* suggests that the deity of Gen 21:33 was not considered as simply a local *numen*.

Some scholars (e.g. VAN DEN BRANDEN 1990:36) have tried to show that *ʿôlām* as applied to a deity could be used alone—i.e. without association with *ʾēl* or the like—so in Dt 33:27a, where the expression *zĕrōʾôt ʿôlām* would not mean 'the ancient/eternal arms' but 'the arms of (the god) olam', and they surmised the existence—or at least the 'survival' in Biblical tradition—of a god called Olam. Many of the occurrences of *ʿôlām* in the Psalms were interpreted by DAHOOD (1966; xxxvii and *ad loc.*) as divine names (Pss 24:7.9; 52:11; 66:7; 73:12; 75:10; 89:3), but all these passages are better explained by assuming the common meaning of *ʿôlām* in the Old Testament. As CROSS (1973:48 n.18) remarks: "Had he found fewer instances his case would appear stronger". In the pantheons of the ancient Near East, as will be shown below, *ʿôlām* often appears in conjunction with a divine name: but apparently does not occur as a divine name in itself. It is better, therefore, not to construe Olam as a divine name.

But how then is *ʾEl ʿôlām* to be translated? According to JENNI (1976:236), *ʾEl ʿôlām* should be construed as a construct: 'El/God of eternity', i.e. 'the eternal El/ God', rather than as a name preceded by an independent appellative: 'the god 'Olam', or 'El, the Ancient One', as CROSS (1955:236, 240) would have it, but CROSS (1973: 46-50, see 49) argues that the proper name El cannot be taken in a construct relationship to the noun *ʿôlām*. In his opinion, a liturgical formula of the type *ʾEl d̲u ʿôlam* ('El, the one (i.e.lord) of eternity') must underlie the name *ʾEl ʿôlām*. CROSS (1973:49 n. 23) further points to the possibility of compound divine names, like *Ilib* or *ʿštrtkmš*, implying that El and Olam could be two compounded divine names. But El-olam could also be the combination of a divine name and an epithet. In the Ugaritic texts, gods appear to be identified as *il malk* ('El, the king') or *ršp mlk* ('Resheph, the king'); or, in a much rarer combination, *ʾil hd* ('the god Haddu') (see CROSS 1973:50). Since Olam is not attested as an independent deity (see below), it still remains very likely that, in Gen 21:33, *ʿôlām* is used as an epithet: irrespective of whether *ʾēl* is construed an appellative or a divine name. In that case, El-olam should be rendered as 'El/God, the Eternal/ Everlasting/Ancient one'. This interpretation is corroborated by such texts as Isa 40:28 ("Yahweh is the God of Eternity" *ĕlōhê ʿôlām yhwh*) or Jer 10:10 ("Yahweh is God <and> is truth [i.e. is the true God], he is God <and> is life [i.e. is the living God] and the king of eternity [i.e. the eternal king]"). The suggestion by VAN DEN BRANDEN (1990:52) to vocalize, in the light of Isa 45:15, *ʾEl ʿôlām* and to understand that divine title as 'the God who hides himself' lacks support in the texts.

ALBRIGHT (1966:24; no. 358) and CROSS (1962:238-239) have read the name El-olam (*ʾil d̲ū ʿôlami*) in a proto-sinaitic inscription, presumably dating to the 15th cent. BCE. CROSS has used this evidence as a decisive argument for the characterization of primitive Yahwism as a form of El worship (in the same vein, see DE MOOR 1990:253). But DIJKSTRA (1987:249-250) has reexamined the reading of CROSS and shown that El-olam is absent from the inscription. Even though the title El-olam is not attested in Ugarit, a Ugaritic text gives us the first occurrence of *ʿlm* in conjunction with a divine name: the goddess Šapšu bears the epithet *špš ʿlm* ('Sun the everlasting') (*KTU* 2.42 [= *UT* 2008], 7). In the Aramaic inscription from Karatepe (8th cent. BCE), we find the god Šamaš ʿôlām (*šmš ʿlm*, 'Sun the everlasting') mentioned alongside →Baal-Shamen (*bʿl šmm*, «the lord of heaven») and 'El the Creator of Earth' (*ʾl qn ʾrṣ*) (*KAI* 26 III:19; cf. IV:2 *šm ʾztwd ykn lʿlm km šm šmš wyrḥ* 'may the name of ʿZTWD stand fast forever, like the name of the sun and the moon'; see also WEIPPERT 1969). The Phoenician incantation of Arslan Tash (7th cent. BCE) mentions a goddess *'lt 'lm* 'the goddess, the everlasting' (*KAI* 27: 9-10), though the expression could also be taken to mean 'everlasting oath'. It seems that the eptithet *'olām* is felt to be especially fit for solar deities: the sun being the everlasting god par excellence (see STÄHLI 1985:27). One could therefore ask the question, whether the mention of a deity named El-olam should be seen in the context of the 'solarization' of the system of religious symbols that KEEL & UEHLINGER (1992:282-321) have detected for Israel (9th-8th cent.) and Judah (8th-7th cent.), without however establishing a link with *'olām*.

III. There remains the fundamental question: Does the El-olam of Gen 21:33 go back to a deity effectively worshipped or at least so designated in a preliterary context, or is that name simply an *ad hoc* invention of the author of our Genesis passage? Obviously, Gen 21:33 does not constitute sufficient evidence for postulating the existence of a cult dedicated to a specific El-olam, presumably located in Beersheba. But, if one bears in mind that belief in El is attested for the 9th and 8th cent. BCE not only in Deir Alla (in a presumably non-Israelite context) but also in Kuntillet 'Ajrûd (see KEEL & UEHLINGER 1992:235-237, 277-278), it remains probable that the author of Gen 21:33—and perhaps the circles responsible for the Abraham traditions as a whole—wanted to connect their patriarch with a form of pre-Yahwistic or para-Yahwistic piety that, in his opinion—but perhaps rightly so—was prevalent in early times or in marginal zones. According to ALBERTZ (1978:77-91; 1992:47-53), that type of piety was rooted in private family-life (as opposed to the official state cult which was linked to the national and cosmic Yahweh). But another possibility should also be explored: perhaps 'patriarchal' religion is the form of national religion—another form of Yahwism—that was prevalent among the tribal elites of Israel down to the monarchic period; i.e. before the prophetic movement propagated the ideal of a non-tribal and non-genealogical Yahweh linked to the Exodus tradition? That seems to be the case at least in Northern Israel where the →Jacob legend functioned as a national legend of origin of its own (see DE PURY 1991:88-96). In that case, El-olam, even if rooted in the south and embedded in a late narrative context, might not have been picked entirely out of the blue.

IV. *Bibliography*

R. ALBERTZ, *Persönliche Frömmigkeit und offizielle Religion. Religionsinterner Pluralismus in Israel und Babylon* (CTM 9; Stuttgart 1978); ALBERTZ, *Religionsgeschichte Israels in alttestamentlicher Zeit* (ATD Ergänzungsreihe 8/1; Göttingen 1992); W. F. ALBRIGHT, *The Proto-Sinaitic Inscriptions and their Decipherment* (Cambridge, Mass. 1966); A. ALT, *Der Gott der Väter* (BWANT III,12; Stuttgart 1929) = *KS* 1 (1953) 1-78; E. BLUM, *Die Komposition der Vätergeschichte* (WMANT 57; Neukirchen 1984); A. VAN DEN BRANDEN, Les Dieux des Patriarches, *BeO* 162 (1990) 27-53; F. M. CROSS, Yahweh and the Gods of the Patriarchs, *HTR* 55 (1962) 225-259; CROSS, *Canaanite Myth and Hebrew Epic* (Cambridge, Mass. 1973) 44-75; M. DAHOOD, *Psalms* I, II, III (AB 16, 17, 17A; New York 1966, 1968, 1970); M. DIJKSTRA, El 'Olam in the Sinai?, *ZAW* 99 (1987) 249-250; O. EISSFELDT, El und Jahwe, *JSS* 1 (1956) 25-37 = *KS* 3 (1966) 386-397; EISSFELDT, 'Äh^{e}yäh '^{a}sär 'äh^{e}yäh und 'El 'ōlām (1965), *KS* 4 (1968) 193-198; E. JENNI, *Das Wort* 'ōlām *im Alten Testament* (Berlin 1953); JENNI, עוֹלָם 'ōlām Ewigkeit, *THAT* 2 (1976) 228-243; O. KEEL & C. UEHLINGER, *Göttinnen, Götter und Gottessymbole* (Quaestiones Disputatae 134; Freiburg-Basel-Wien 1992); M. KÖCKERT, *Vätergott und Väterverheissungen* (FRLANT 142; Göttingen 1988); J. C. DE MOOR, *The Rise of Yahwism. The Roots of Israelite Monotheism* (BETL 91; Leuven 1990); A. DE PURY, Le cycle de Jacob comme légende autonome des origines d'Israël, *Congress Volume Leuven* (VTSup 43; Leiden 1991) 78-96; H.-P. STÄHLI, *Solare Elemente im*

Jahweglauben des Alten Testaments (OBO 66; Fribourg/Göttingen 1985); J. van Seters, *Abraham in History and Tradition* (New Haven & London 1975); van Seters, The Religion of the Patriarchs in Genesis, *Bib* 61 (1980) 220-233; R. De Vaux, *Histoire ancienne d'Israël. Des origines à l'installation en Canaan* (Etudes Bibliques; Paris 1971); M. Weippert, Elemente phönikischer und kilikischer Religion in den Inschriften von Karatepe, *ZDMG* Suppl. I (1969) 204-205; J. Wellhausen, *Geschichte Israels* (Berlin 1878); C. Westermann, *Genesis* (BKAT I,2; Neukirchen 1981); U. Worschech, *Abraham. Eine sozialgeschichtliche Studie* (Europäische Hochschulschriften XXIII/225, Bern, Frankfurt/M. etc. 1983).

A. de Pury

EL-ROI אל ראי

I. The name *'Ēl ro'î* (El/god of seeing/vision) is attested only once in the OT, in Gen 16:13. It is best interpreted as a pseudo-archaic divine name inserted by a later redactor of Gen 16.

II. The name El-roi is given by Hagar, →Sarah's runaway and pregnant maid, after her flight into the desert and her encounter with a divine messenger. The messenger foretold the birth of a son whom she is instructed to name →Ishmael (v 12), a theophoric name of a common type constructed with →El and the imperfect of *šmʿ* ('may El hear'). Vv 13-14 introduce a new sequence which is not really warranted by the preceding verses. These two verses possibly represent an addition to the original story (Van Seters 1975:193), since they pursue a different purpose: in opposition to v 12b, where Ishmael's God was identified as →Yahweh ('for *Yahweh* has *heard* of your misery'), v 13 introduces the name El Roi. The apparent aim of the addition is to ensure that the non-Israelite Ishmaelites have no part in the worship of Yahweh. The etiology given in v 13 poses a number of difficulties of grammatical and syntactical nature. Even if the famous conjecture of Wellhausen (1878:329 n. 1: 'I have seen God and have stayed alive') is still very speculative (cf. Booij 1980; Koenen 1988), the MT seems to suppose that El Roi allowed himself to be seen by Hagar. After a very careful analysis, Koenen (1988:472) proposes the following translation of v 13: "And she called the name of (the) Yahweh who spoke to her: "You are the God who sees [i.e. saves] me"" [vocalizing *rō'î* – participle with suffix: 'seeing me', in accordance with LXX, Vg, *Tg. Onq.*– instead of MT *rā'î* infinitive construct with suffix: 'my seeing'], for she said: "Indeed, here I have seen the one [literally: the effects of the one] who sees [i.e. chooses/saves] me".

The name El-roi together with the other 'El deities mentioned in the Genesis narratives, has often been interpreted as a distant reminder of one of the manifestations of the great god El supposed to have been worshipped by the Patriarchs (Cross 1973:46-60; Albertz 1992:55). In this context, El-roi was seen as the particular form of El venerated by the clan of Abraham (Worschech 1983:172). Independently of all the other problems raised by this theory, one must note that *rō'î* as an epithet of El never appears in any document of the ancient Near East (Köckert 1988:75; Knauf 1989:48).

It is true that, in a Babylonian prayer of the Kassite period, we find an invocation of →Marduk as "my father, Great Lord Marduk, the one who sees me" (Albertz 1978: 124), but that last element is neither an epithet nor a name. An Egyptian document of the time of Merneptah (Papyrus Anastasi III), which records the border traffic, mentions a traveller designated probably as 'the slave (of) Baal-Roy': "There went up the servant of Baal Roy (*R'-y*), son of Zeper of Gaza" (*ARE* III, § 630; cf. *ANET*, 258). Although the numerous problems posed by the hieroglyphic transcription of Semitic names cannot be discussed fully here, this text does not prove that 'Roy' was ever the name of a Semitic deity (against van der Branden 1990:35). In the transliteration, the element -y derives more probably from a suffix pronoun of the 1st singular ('Baal sees me' or

'Baal is my shepherd'). One further possibility to find an attestation of a divine epithet with the root R'H has been suggested by KNAUF (1989:48). Speaking of the (proto-) Arabic imagery of Gen 16, he speculates about a possible divine epithet of Arabic origin: **ar-rā'iyu* - 'the one who sees'. But, even here, we have no direct attestation of that name or epithet, except for the fact that pre-islamic Arabic tradition seems to use the word *rā'i* in speaking of demons (PARET 1980:25). In the present state of our knowledge, we must conclude that the word *Ro'i* of Gen 16:13 is not a common—or even a sporadic—epithet of the god El.

The El-roi of Gen 16:13 could therefore be nothing more than an invention of the redactor of vv 13-14 (VAN SETERS 1975:193, 288; KÖCKERT 1988:76). His aim could have been to 'correct' both the identification of El and Yahweh and the privileged relation between Hagar and Yahweh, and to this end he may have thought of a pseudo-archaic divine name in the style of →El Olam and →El Shadday whom he probably knew from written or oral traditions about the Patriarchs. Why the name 'Roi'? This name could derive from an interpretation of *'Bĕ'ēr-laḥai-rō'î'* in v 14, or, even more simply, from the fact that 'seeing' (which also implies 'fulfilling' a prayer, or 'taking care of' somebody) is an activity commonly attributed to gods in the Semitic world: 'El who sees me (i.e. chooses/saves me)'. As we have seen, this is also the way the original text of Gen 16:13 was meant to be understood.

III. *Bibliography*

R. ALBERTZ, *Persönliche Frömmigkeit und offizielle Religion. Religionsinterner Pluralismus in Israel und Babylon* (CTM 9; Stuttgart 1978); ALBERTZ, *Religionsgeschichte Israels in alttestamentlicher Zeit* (ATD Ergänzungsreihe 8/1; Göttingen 1992); E. BLUM, *Die Komposition der Vätergeschichte* (WMANT 57; Neukirchen 1984); T. BOOIJ, Hagar's Words in Genesis XVI 13b, *VT* 30 (1980) 1-7; A. VAN DEN BRANDEN, Les dieux des patriarches, *BeO* 162 (1990) 27-53; F. M. CROSS, *Canaanite Myth and Hebrew Epic* (Cambridge, Mass. 1973) 44-75; E. A. KNAUF, *Ismael. Untersuchungen zur Geschichte Palästinas und Nordarabiens im 1. Jahrtausend v. Chr.* (ADPV, 2. Aufl. 1989); M. KÖCKERT, *Vätergott und Väterverheissungen* (FRLANT 142, Göttingen 1988); K. KOENEN, Wer sieht wen? Zur Textgeschichte von Genesis xvi 13, *VT* 38 (1988) 468-474; R. PARET, *Mohammed und der Islam* (Stuttgart etc. 1980[5]); J. VAN SETERS, *Abraham in History and Tradition* (New Haven/London 1975); VAN SETERS, The Religion of the Patriarchs in Genesis, *Bib* 61 (1980) 220-233; J. WELLHAUSEN, *Geschichte Israels* (Berlin 1878); U. WORSCHECH, *Abraham. Eine sozialgeschichtliche Studie* (Europäische Hochschulschriften XXIII/225; Bern, Frankfurt/M., etc. 1983).

A. DE PURY

EL ROPHE *אל רפא

I. The enigmatic line in Num 13:19 *'ēl nā' rĕpā' nā' lāh*, traditionally rendered as "O, God, do heal her", has been construed as containing originally the divine name *'ēl rōpē'*, 'El Rophe; Healing God' (ROUILLARD 1987). This divine name has been compared with the Ug epithet *rpu*, 'Saviour', occurring in the expression *rpu mlk 'lm* and *mt rpi*, and with the →Rephaim (ROUILLARD 1987:35-42).

II. The expression *rpu mlk 'lm* is generally translated as 'the Saviour, the eternal King' (e.g. DE MOOR, *ARTU* 187) and interpreted as an epithet either of →Baal seen as the head of the Rephaim (e.g. DE MOOR 1976:329) or of Ilu (→El; e.g. J. DAY, *VT* 30 [1980] 176). The expression occurs only four times in what might be called a liturgical address (*KTU* 1.108:1.19'-20'.21'.22'). Without the extension *mlk 'lm*, *r[p]i* occurs in the same text (23'-24') but as a clear reference to the Rephaim. B. MARGULIS (*Bibl* 51 [1970] 57; *JBL* 89 [1970] 293-294; cf. VAN DER TOORN 1991:57) has pointed to the fact that in *KTU* 1.108 it is said that *rpu mlk 'lm* is 'dwelling in Athtaroth' (l. 2) and 'judging in Edrei' (l. 3). This suggests that the deity *rpu mlk 'lm* is identical with

Milku/Maliku who is said to be in Athtarot (*KTU* 1.100:41; 1,107:17; RS 86.2235; cf. J. DAY, *Molech. A God of Human Sacrifice* [Oxford 1989] 46-50; VAN DER TOORN 1991:57; see also Deut 1:4; Josh 9:10; 12:44; 13:12.31 where →"Og the *mlk* of →Bashan, who dwells in Athtarot" is mentioned). This implies that the expression *rpu mlk ʿlm* is to be seen as a reference to a chthonic deity (VAN DER TOORN 1991:57-60). It is possible, though not necessary, that this is El.

The expression *mt rpi*, 'man of Rpi' (e.g. *KTU* 1.20 ii:8), has been interpreted as a reference to Dan'el's personal god: judging by his name, the identification with El is more likely than that with Baal (*pace* DE MOOR 1976:326-327).

In the Ugaritic texts various deities are depicted as healing gods. The Rephaim are known for their saving activities. *KTU* 1.82:6 relates that Baal has the force to drive out serpent-demons. In a para-mythological text, the goddesses Ahtartu and →Anat are said to be healers of their father Ilu, who had become sick from drinking too much wine (*KTU* 1.114:27-28; DE MOOR, *UF* 16 [1986] 356). The deity →Horon is said to be able to neutralize the effects of poison from serpents (*KTU* 1.100:61-69).

III. In the OT Yahweh is seen as—among other things—a healing God (NIEHR 1991). This becomes clear from several texts, e.g. Ex 15:26 where Yahweh is called a *rpʾ*, 'healer; saviour', and from personal names like *rĕpāʾēl*, →'Raphael' (e.g. 1 Chron 26:7; Tob 3:17); *rĕpāyâ*, 'Rephajah' (e.g. Neh 3:9; 1 Chron 3:21; 4:42; 7:2); *yrpyh*, 'Yirpeyah; Yahweh heals' (M. LIDZBARSKI, *Ephemeris für semitische Epigraphik* 3 [Giessen 1915] 22) and the hypocoristic *rpʾ*, 'Rapha' (Samaria Ostracon 24:2; 1 Chron 8:2; Num 13:19; cf. M. NOTH, *IPN* 179).

Rouillard's interpretation of the enigmatic line in Num 12:13, though ingenious, is not convincing. Her textual reconstruction is not supported by any of the ancient versions which all construe *rpʾ* as an imperative and not as a participle (see the outline in ROUILLARD 1987:20-21). Her reconstruction produces a sentence which contains only a vocative. That Moses' intercessory prayer on behalf of his sister would be limited to the words "O healing God!", seems to be an oddity from a narrative point of view. Besides, the divine epithet *ʾēl rōpēʾ* does not occur elsewhere in the OT.

IV. *Bibliography*

J. C. DE MOOR, Rapiʾuma - Rephaim, *ZAW* 88 (1976) 323-345; H. NIEHR, JHWH als Arzt, *BZ* 25 (1991) 3-17; H. ROUILLARD, *El Rofê* en Nombres 12,13, *Sem* 37 (1987) 17-46; K. VAN DER TOORN, Funerary Rituals and Beatific Afterlife in Ugaritic Texts and in the Bible, *BiOr* 48 (1991) 40-66.

B. BECKING

ELYON עליון

I. Derived from the Hebrew verb *ʿālâ*, meaning 'to ascend', *ʿelyôn* in the OT may be used either as an adjective, describing something that is spatially higher than something else ('upper', 'highest'), or as a substantive, used primarily in reference to the 'most high' deity. In Ps 89:27, however, it is used in reference to the king. As a divine name, ʿElyôn appears either on its own (e.g. Ps 9:3; Isa 14:14), in combination with other divine names (Yahweh, Elohim [→God], →El e.g., Pss 7:18; 57:3; 73:11) or in association with lesser divine elements (*bĕnê ʿelyôn*, Ps 82:6; cf. Aramaic references to *qaddîšê ʿelyônîn* in Dan 7:18, 22, 25, 27). An abbreviated form may also be attested in Hos 11:7 (על) and 1 Sam 2:10 (עלו/י). In the LXX, ʿElyôn is translated as *Hypsistos*.

In the present form of the biblical text, the term is understood to be an epithet for Yahweh, the God of Israel. It is possible, however, as some have argued, that the epithet may conceal a reference to a separate deity, possibly an older god with whom Yahweh came to be identified. This has been argued, for example, with reference to Gen 14:18, Num 24:16 and Deut 32:8. The matter cannot be resolved without considering occurrences of ʿElyôn in other texts from the ancient Near East. ʿElyôn is attested in a variety of extra-biblical literature such as Aramaic, Phoenician, Ugaritic and Greek. As a theophoric element, ʿElyôn may also be traced in South-Semitic personal names. These wide-spread Ancient Near Eastern attestations have led to numerous hypotheses regarding the nature of the more ambiguous references to ʿElyôn in the OT, discussed below. In addition to its attestation in the OT, ʿElyôn appears as →*Hypsistos* in the NT, as well as in the apocryphal and pseudepigraphic books. ʿElyôn is also attested in Qumran literature (see esp. 1QapGen).

II. In order to understand the character and role of ʿElyôn, it must first be determined whether or not the word refers to an independent deity or functions always as an epithet for another god. The clearest example of ʿElyôn functioning autonomously is found in the fragments of Sanchuniathon's 'Phoenician Theology' preserved by Eusebius (*Praep. evang.* 1.10.15-29) using Philo of Byblos as his source. According to Sanchuniathon, a certain Elioun, called 'Most High' (*Hypsistos*) dwelt in the neighbourhood of Byblos, along with his wife, Berouth. To them was born a son, Epigeius, or Autochthon—who was later called Ouranos (Heaven)—and a daughter, Ge (Earth). Sometime later, Elioun died in an encounter with wild beasts and was thereupon deified. His children also became deities, and through the union of Ouranos and Ge, the god Kronos was born. Later, a union of Ouranos and his favourite mistress produced →Zeus (Demarous). With certain exceptions, this cosmology is closely related to others in the ancient Near East. Texts such as the Hurro-Hittite 'Song of Kumarbi' (also known as 'Kingship in Heaven'), Hesiod's Theogony, and various Ugaritic myths about El and →Baal all display striking similarities to the ordering and functioning of gods in Sanchuniathon. Notably absent in the latter two sources, however, is any clear indication of a counterpart to Sanchuniathon's Elioun. Even the Hurro-Hittite Alalu, though sharing the same hierarchical relationship to other gods as Elioun, does not display much similarity in character (see "Song of Kumarbi" in HOFFNER 1990:40-43). Thus, although we find clear reference to ʿElyôn as an autonomous deity in Philo's Elioun, similar cosmologies in the ancient Near East do not appear to have shared this view. In fact, closer inspection of Philo's account betrays a conflation of traditions that may not be true to their earlier forms. For instance, the name Epigeius would suggest that the deity arose from Ge (cf. Hesiod). However, these gods are brother and sister according to Philo. It appears that contemporary cosmological conceptions have been absorbed into Philo's account of more ancient traditions. His understanding of Elioun as an independent deity may reflect first century influences.

A possible exception to this conclusion is found in the Sefîre I inscriptions (*KAI* 222 A) of the eighth century BCE, written in Aramaic. As a treaty between Bir-Gaʾyah, the king of *KTK* and Matîel, the king of Arpad, the inscription lists the major deities of each side as witnesses to the agreement. Listed between a series of divine names occurring in pairs and the great natural pairs of Heaven and Earth, Abyss and Streams, →Day and →Night, we find *ʾl wʿlyn*. This has been thought by many to confirm the existence of ʿElyôn as an independent deity (e.g. DELLA VIDA 1944; RENDTORFF 1967). However, several considerations mitigate against such a conclusion. First, El and ʿElyôn are not consorts, as are the preceding divine pairs. Secondly, the divine pairs are not followed immediately by El and ʿElyôn, but are interrupted by other clauses where there are references to non-paired deities. Finally, El and ʿElyôn may not be part of the pantheon of Bir-Ga'yah, which lists the divine consorts, but that of Matîel (LACK 1962:57; cf. SEOW 1989:52 n. 146). On the other hand, ʿElyôn may be understood as an epithet of El in this inscription. The conjunction may be a *waw* explicativum (DE VAUX 1961:310; SEOW 1989:52n), rendering, "El, that is, ʿElyôn". One notes this same phenomenon earlier in the list (line 9), where we find *šmš wnr* (L'HEUREUX

1979:46); →Shemesh; →Light. One notes as well the frequent occurrence of double divine names in the Ugaritic corpus where each is joined by a *waw* conjunction (e.g. *Kṯr-w-Ḫss*, *Mt-w-Šr*, *Qdš-w-ʾAmrr*). It is possible that the Sefîre inscription bears witness to this phenomenon, or that it betrays a separation of an early epithet of El that has split into a separate cult and deity (CROSS 1973:51). Whatever the case may be, it must be admitted that the treaty gives us no conclusive evidence for or against the existence of ʿElyôn as an independent deity.

In contrast to the mixed evidence to support the identification of ʿElyôn as autonomous, there is a wide range of evidence to suggest that ʿElyôn was a common epithet in the West Semitic region, applied at different times and in different cultures to any god thought to be supreme. One example of the fluidity of this epithet is in its application to the Canaanite deities El and Baal. Although El is nowhere referred to as ʿElyôn in the extant Ugaritic literature, numerous attestations, both biblical and extra-biblical, link the two closely. We have already seen, for instance, that, if nothing else, El and ʿElyôn are closely linked in the Sefîre I inscription. Similarly, in South Semitic inscriptions, one finds a shortened form of ʿElyôn, *ʿly* (and sometimes *ʿl*; →Al) applied to El (RYCKMANS 1934:243). In the OT, ʿElyôn appears several times with El, either in collocation (Gen 14:18-22; Ps 78:35), or in parallelism (Num 24:16; Pss 73:11; 107:11). Many scholars believe that the pre-Israelite cult at Jerusalem worshipped the god El-ʿElyôn. There is also evidence to suggest that Yahweh was originally worshipped as El-ʿElyôn at Shiloh before David's capture of Jerusalem (see below). These indicators all point to ʿElyôn being an early epithet of El. Yet, other texts link Baal with this same epithet in its abbreviated form. The clearest example is found in the Keret epic (*KTU* 1.16 iii:5-8) where *mṭr bʿl*, 'the rain of Baal', is twice parallelled by *mṭr ʿly*, 'the rain of the Most High'.

In the Bible, also, there exists a possible indication of Baal's designation as Most High. In the book of Hosea—a text well-known for its unrelenting polemic against Baalism—we find such an indication (although some would amend the shortened form *ʿl* to *bʿl*, lectio facilior): "My people are bent on turning away from me. To the Most High (*ʿl*) they call, but he does not raise them up at all" (Hos 11:7). Further, in Isa 14:13-14, we find a satire of the King of Babylon that may reflect the myth of the rise of Baal. In Canaanite lore, Baal is the god who ascends the clouds and sits on 'the heights of Zaphon'. Eventually he came to replace El as high god of the Canaanite pantheon. It is intriguing, then, to find in Isaiah: "You said in your heart, 'I will ascend to heaven; I will raise my throne above the stars of El; I will sit on the mount of assembly, on the heights of Zaphon; I will ascend to the tops of the clouds, I will make myself like ʿElyôn.'" Thus, if a Baal myth lies behind this text, then we would have not only another association of El and ʿElyôn, but a reflection of Baal's eventual surpassing of El, so that he himself became the 'Most High' god.

The fluidity of the epithet ʿElyôn is far from restricted to Canaanite tradition alone. The epithet became firmly associated with the Israelite god, Yahweh, for instance. This tradition carries over into later Jewish pseudepigraphic literature and inscriptions and is also found within the NT. The epithet is frequently attested in Greek culture in reference to Zeus as well. We know that the cult of 'Zeus Hypsistos' was recognized at Thebes, Iasos, Mylasa and Edessa. Further, in Lydia, some form of the Mother goddess was called 'Thea Hypsiste'. In Egypt, Hypsistes was an epithet for →Isis (TREBILCO 1989:52). Thus, the epithet ʿElyôn seems to have enjoyed a rich and widespread usage in the ancient West Semitic world. Not only was it associated with the 'high gods' of different cultures, but it could also be used within the same culture for different gods as one ascended in significance over the other to become the Most High God.

III. It is clear that Israel appropriated ʿElyôn as an epithet for its own High God,

Yahweh. This is evident in the numerous passages where ‘Elyôn appears either in conjunction with Yahweh (Pss 7:18; 47:3) or Elohim (Pss 57:3; 78:56) or is found in parallelism or close association with either of these (e.g. Pss 21:8; 46:5; 83:9; 50:14). In some passages, the title ‘Elyôn is applied to Yahweh as an explicit assertion of Yahweh's distinctiveness. In Ps 97:9, for instance, one finds: "For you, Yahweh, are ‘Elyôn over all the earth; You are greatly elevated above all gods." Similarly, in Ps 83:19 one finds: "And let them know that your name is Yahweh; You alone are ‘Elyôn over all the earth." One notes that in 1 Sam 2:10, Yahweh may be associated with ‘Elyôn, attested in an abbreviated form, if the MT's *‘lw* is understood as arising from common confusion of *w/y* (accepted by NEB, and now also by NRSV): "Yahweh, his adversaries are shattered; The Most High (*‘lw*) thunders in heaven." In a number of passages, ‘Elyôn is simply one of a number of appellations used for the God of Israel. In Ps 91:1-2, for instance, we find: "Let the one who sits in the shelter of ‘Elyôn, who spends the night in the shadow of →Shadday, say to Yahweh, 'My refuge and my fortress, my God (Elohim), in whom I trust.'"

In the few extant cases where ‘Elyôn stands independently of any reference to Yahweh, the title nevertheless remains closely tied to the God of Israel. Thus, although ‘Elyôn is unmodified in Ps 9:3, which reads, "I will be glad and exult in you; I will sing praise to your name, O ‘Elyôn," the title ‘Elyôn nevertheless refers to Yahweh, as is evident from the numerous references to Yahweh throughout the Psalm. ‘Elyôn is also found paired with El in the OT. Although El may refer either to 'God' (of Israel) or to Canaanite El, in most cases the context in which it occurs clearly indicates that the God of Israel is the intended referent. In Ps 78:35, for instance, we find El-‘Elyôn in parallelism with Elohim: "They remembered that Elohim was their →rock, El-‘Elyôn was their redeemer (→Goel)."

In Ps 57:3, we find a similar phenomenon, except this time ‘Elyôn is paired with Elohim, and these stand in parallelism with El: "I call to Elohim-‘Elyôn, to El, who fulfills his purpose for me."

In some cases, El and ‘Elyôn are paired without direct reference to Yahweh or Elohim. In Ps 107:11, the psalmist speaks of those who had "rebelled against the words of El, and spurned the counsel of ‘Elyon." Again, the context of the psalm dictates that the intended referent is Yahweh. Yet, in a few passages in the OT, the pairing of El with ‘Elyôn is more ambiguous. In these instances, some scholars find reflections of an earlier stage of tradition, where the title ‘Elyôn may have referred originally to a god other than Yahweh. The primary examples of such occurrences are Gen 14:18-22, Num 24:16 and Deut 32:8. With regard to the last passage, some scholars find an early reference to ‘Elyôn as a supreme god to which Yahweh is subordinate. ‘Elyôn divides the nations among the gods (LXX; 4QDeut) and grants Yahweh an allotment like the rest. Yet, contextual considerations suggest that the preposition *kî* in v 9 be translated as an asseverative particle, rendering, "*Indeed*, Yahweh's own portion was his people, Jacob was the territory of his possession." Thus, ‘Elyôn is more plausibly understood as functioning as an epithet for Yahweh.

In an oracle of Balaam, son of Beor, in Num 24:16, we find what may be the earliest reference to ‘Elyôn in the OT. Although its early date is not uncontested, many would locate the poem in the eleventh or tenth century BCE. Here Balaam describes himself as "one who hears the words of El, who knows the knowledge of ‘Elyôn, who sees the vision of *Šadday*." Although the context and content of the oracles dictate that Yahweh is the god to whom these titles refer, it is curious that Balaam, a prophet to a non-Israelite group, living along the Euphrates, who is summoned by the King of Moab to curse the Israelites, would be considered a prophet of Yahweh (22:8, 18; 23:5, 16; 24:1, 13). Given the association of the oracles with the 'words of El' it is possible that an earlier stage of the tradition knew Balaam as a prophet of El. This notion is supported by the Deir ʿAllā inscriptions where Balaam, son of Beor is attested. Although the inscriptions date to the eighth century BCE, Balaam the Seer was apparently part of a long-standing tradition, well-known by the people to whom the inscription was addressed (HACKETT 1984:124). He is described as a 'seer of the gods', who are also identified as Shaddayīn. The vision he reports is 'an utterance of El' (Combination I 1,2). The similarity between the Deir ʿAllā inscriptions and the biblical tradition of Balaam is striking and has been long noted by scholars. It would appear that the biblical material shares a common tradition with that of the Deir ʿAllā inscriptions. Given the occurrence of El and Shaddayīn in the inscriptions, it is likely that El was also known as Shadday (see HACKETT 1984:85-89). And given its close links with the biblical account—in terms of geography, the prophet's name, and the chief god El (//Shadday)—it is possible that El was also known as ʿElyôn in the tradition attested at Deir ʿAllā.

Perhaps the most difficult text to assess in terms of the history of tradition behind ʿElyôn is Gen 14:18-22. Here, a certain →Melchizedek, king of Salem and priest of El-ʿElyôn, blesses →Abraham in the name of "El-ʿElyôn, maker of heaven and earth" (*ʾl ʿlywn qnh šmym wʾrṣ*). Significantly, attestations of a shortened version of this title for El are widespread in ancient Near Eastern inscriptions. Examples are:
(1) The Hittite divine name Ilkuniršа, occurring in a Hittite translation of a West Semitic myth from Boghazköy prior to 1200 BCE, appears to be a reference to El (OTTEN 1953; see HOFFNER 1965). (2) *ʾl qnʾrṣ* in an eighth century BCE bilingual god list from Karatepe (*KAI* 26 A III.18). (3) [*ʾl*] *qnʾrṣ* is the probable restoration of a Hebrew inscription of the eighth-seventh century BCE from Jerusalem (AVIGAD 1972; see MILLER 1980). (4) *ʾlqwnrʿ* in a first century CE Aramaic inscription from Palmyra, which, with DELLA VIDA 1944, is to be read *ʾ lqn (ʾ)rʿ(ʾ))*. (5) *ʾlqnrʿ* in four tesserae from Palmyra (INGHOLT 1955). (6) *ʾl qn ʾrṣ* in a second century CE Neo-Punic inscription from Leptis Magna (*KAI* 129:1). Note that the long form of this title has been read by J. T. MILIK in an inscription from Palmyra (*Recherches d'épigraphie proche-orientale* [Paris 1955] 182): *ʾ[l gwnʾ ʾ]r[ʿ]ʾ w šm[y]ʾ*.

Owing to the attestation of El-ʿElyôn in Gen 14:18-22, along with the expanded El title *qnh šmym wʾrṣ*, Melchizedek would appear to be a representative of the cult of El-ʿElyôn, whom the biblical tradition associated with the city of Salem (note that the reference to Yahweh in v 22 is absent in LXX, Syr, 1QapGen; Sam attests *ʾl hʾlhym*). Most likely, Salem is a short form of Jerusalem. It only appears in one other place in the OT (Ps 76:3) where it stands in parallelism with →Zion. That Melchizedek's Salem was considered Jerusalem in Jewish tradition is evident in 1QapGen 22:13, which adds "that is, Jerusalem," to a reference to Salem, in *Tg. Onq.*, which renders it simply as 'Jerusalem', and in Josephus (*Ant.* 1:180). It is attested in the Amarna Letters as *ú-ru-sa-lim* (*EA* 290:15). Owing to the likely connection between Salem and Jerusalem, a number of scholars have supposed Melchizedek to be the representative of a dominant Jebusite cult of El-ʿElyôn from which Israel drew much of its theological inspiration after the city's capture by David (e.g. SCHMID 1955:168-197; CLEMENTS 1965:43-48).

Although this supposition is not without merit, Genesis 14 provides the only evidence to link the cult of El-ʿElyôn with Jerusalem. On the other hand, significant, though not decisive, evidence may be adduced that would render an easy association between El-ʿElyôn and the Jebusite cult open to question. One notes that the name Salem suggests links to the astral deity Šalim (→Shalem). Further, the names Melchizedek ('My king is Ṣedeq') and Adonizedek ('My Lord is Ṣedeq', Josh 10:1)—both identified as kings of Jerusalem—suggest links to the West Semitic deity Ṣedeq (→Righteousness), who may also be an astral deity (note also David's high priest Zadok). These deities, Shalim and Ṣedeq, are at least as likely to have been central to the pre-Israelite Jerusalem cult, as it is that the cult of El-ʿElyôn was the dominant religious institution (see fuller discussion in SEOW 1989:43-47). One notes that, even if the existence of a Jebusite cult of El-ʿElyôn is granted, it is unlikely that the Israelite identification of Yahweh as El-ʿElyôn derives its origin from this tradition. The presence of ʿElyôn in Deut 32 and Num 24, which may in some form be pre-monarchical, gravitates against such a hypothesis. Further, as SEOW has convincingly argued, Yahweh is likely to have been venerated as El-ʿElyôn at the sanctuary of Shiloh well before David's capture of Jerusalem (SEOW 1989:11-54, esp. 41-54).

As an epithet applied with a significant degree of fluidity throughout the West Semitic region, it is easy to understand how ʿElyôn may have made a relatively easy transition from El-veneration to Yahwistic cultic tradition in early Israelite religion. Curiously, the OT traditions rarely attest ʿElyôn standing alone, without modification. In the Aramaic sections of Daniel, however, references to Yahweh as ʿElyon (*ʿlyʾ/ʿlʾh*) often stand independently, without modification, although the intended referent is clearly Yahweh (Note that *qdyšy ʿlywnyn* is also attested). A similar phenomenon is evidenced in the frequent references to ʿElyôn (*hypsistos* [*altus* in 2 Esdr]) in the apocryphal books (1 and 2 Esdr, Tob, Jdt, Add Esth, Wis, Sir, Pr Man, 2 and 3 Macc). In Sir, it is the most common divine name after *kyrios*. The epithet also occurs in varous pseudepigraphical works, particularly in *T. 12 Patr.*

In the NT, *hypsistos* is a decidedly Lucan title for God (TREBILCO 1989:58). Used five times in the Gospel of Luke (1:32, 35, 76; 6:35; 8:28) and twice in Acts (7:48; 16:17), *hypsistos* is only attested in two non-Lucan contexts—once in Mark (5:7), and once in Hebrews (7:1, which is a quotation of Gen 14:18). In Luke's Gospel, the term is employed in the angel's announcement to →Mary that her child will be called 'Son of the Most High' (*huios hypsistou*; Luke 1:32) and that the 'power of the Most High' will come upon her (*dynamis hypsistou*; Luke 1:35). In 1:76, Zechariah predicts that his son will be called 'prophet of the Most High' (*prophētēs hypsistou*). Those who love their enemies are called 'children of the Most High' by →Jesus (*huioi hypsistou*; Luke 6:35), and the Gerasene demoniac identifies Jesus as 'son of the Most High God' (*huie theou tou hypsistou*; Luke 8:28 par. Mark 5:7; cf. Matt 8:29). In Acts, Stephan asserts that 'the Most High' (*ho hypsistos*; Acts 7:48) does not dwell in houses made with human hands, and a slave girl from Philippi declares that Paul and his group are 'servants of the Most High God' (*douloi tou theou tou hypsistou*; Acts 16:17). Although there is not enough evidence to make a firm case, it would appear as if Luke employs the term *hypsistos* or *ho hypsistos* in Jewish contexts, and *ho theos ho hypsistos* in Gentile ones. As TREBILCO (1989:58-59) suggests, this may be because Luke was aware of the non-specific nature of the term *hypsistos* in a Gentile setting and sought to avoid confusion by employing a superlative of more significance for Gentiles. [For a further discussion of the Greek data see →Hypsistos]

IV. *Bibliography*

N. AVIGAD, Excavations in the Jewish Quarter of the Old City of Jerusalem (1971; *IEJ* 22; 1972) 193-200; R. E. CLEMENTS, *God and Temple* (Philadelphia 1965) 40-62, esp. 43-48; F. M. CROSS, Yahweh and the God of the Patriarchs, *HTR* 55 (1962) 225-259; CROSS, *Canaanite Myth and Hebrew Epic* (Cambridge, MA 1973) 44-60; G. L. DELLA VIDA, El ʿElyon in Genesis 14:18-20, *JBL* 63 (1944) 1-9; O. EISSFELDT, El and Yahweh, *JSS* 1 (1956) 25-37; J. A. EMERTON, Some Problems in Genesis XIV, *Studies in the Pentateuch* (ed. J. A. Emerton; Leiden 1990) 73-102; L. R. FISHER, Abraham and His Priest-King, *JBL* 81 (1962) 264-270; J. A. Fitzmyer, *The Aramaic Inscriptions of Sefîre* (Rome 1967); J. HACKETT, *The Balaam Text From Deir ʿAllā* (HSM 31; Chico 1984); C. E. L'HEUREUX,

Rank Among the Canaanite Gods (HSM 21; Missoula 1979); H. A. HOFFNER, Jr., The Elkunirsa Myth Reconsidered, *RHA* 76 (1965) 5-16; HOFFNER, *Hittite Myths* (Atlanta 1990); H. INGHOLT et al, *Recueil des tessères de Palmyre* (Paris 1955); R. LACK, Les origines de Elyon, le Très-Haut, dans la tradition culturelle d'Israël, *CBQ* 24 (1962) 44-64; P. D. MILLER, 'Ēl, The Creator of Earth, *BASOR* 239 (1980) 43-46; E. T. MULLEN, Jr., *The Assembly of the Gods* (HSM 24; Chico 1986); H. NIEHR, *Der Höchste Gott* (Berlin 1990); R. A. ODEN, Ba'al Šamēm and 'Ēl, *CBQ* 39 (1977) 457-73; H. OTTEN, Ein kanaanäischer Mythus aus Boğazköy, *MIO* 1 (1953) 125-150; S. B. PARKER, *KTU* 1.16 III, the Myth of the Absent God and 1 Kings 18, *UF* 21 (1989) 283-296; M. H. POPE, *El in the Ugaritic Texts* (Leiden 1955) 55-58; R. RENDTORFF, The Background of the Title אל עליון in Gen XIV, *Fourth World Congress of Jewish Studies* vol. 1 (Jerusalem 1967) 167-170; J. J. M. ROBERTS, The Davidic Origin of the Zion Tradition, *JBL* 92 (1973) 329-344; G. RYCKMANS, *Les noms-propres sud-sémitiques,* Vol. 1 (Louvain 1934); H. SCHMID, Jahwe und die Kulttraditionen von Jerusalem, *ZAW* 67 (1955) 168-97; C. L. SEOW, *Myth, Drama, and the Politics of David's Dance* (HSM 46; Atlanta 1989); F. STOLZ, *Strukturen und Figuren im Kult von Jerusalem* (BZAW 119; Berlin 1969) esp. 134-137; P. R. TREBILCO, Paul and Silas—'Servants of the Most High God' (Acts 16:16-18), *JSNT* 36 (1989) 51-73; R. DE VAUX, *Ancient Israel* (London 1961) 289-311; H. ZOBEL, עליון, *TWAT* 6 (1987) 131-152.

E. E. ELNES & P. D. MILLER

EMIM → REPHAIM

EMMANUEL עמנו אל 'Εμμανουήλ

I. In Isa 7:14, the prophet Isaiah announced the birth of a child whose name will be *'Immānû'ēl* ('God with us'); its mother is designated as 'the young woman'. This birth will be a sign to the wavering King Ahaz of Judah at the time King Rezin of Syria and King Pekah of Israel had gone up to attack Jerusalem. The name returns in Isa 8:8, whereas in 8:10 the expression 'God with us' is used as an assurance of God's protection for Israel. Isa 7:14 reappears in Matt 1:23 as one of the formula quotations characteristic of this gospel. Isaiah's prophecy will be fulfilled in the birth of →Jesus from the virgin →Mary, after being conceived from the Holy Spirit. Matt 1:23 retrieves the term *hē parthenos* (the virgin) found in the LXX and uses the Greek transliteration *Emmanouēl*; and explains: "which means 'God is with us'".

II. The notion that God is with human beings, personally and collectively, is very prominent in the OT. It is found in divine promises, in wishes and promises uttered by human beings; and in solemn assertions that 'God is with him, you, me, us'. It is an expression of God's guidance and assistance of prominent Israelites like the patriarchs, Joseph, Gideon or David, and also of the people as a whole. Hence 'God with us' can be used as an affirmation of trust in Isa 8:10, just as the refrain "The LORD of hosts is with us, the God of Jacob is our refuge" in Ps 46 (see vv 8 and 12). The notion is found in all parts of the OT, as well as in Jdt 5:17; 3 Macc 6:15; in Qumran (1 QM 12:7-9; 19:1), and its use is continued in the NT (see e.g. Acts 7:9-10; 18:9-10; Rom 15:33; 2 Cor 13:11; Phil 4:9; 2 Thess 3:16). Whilst central to Israelite religion as reflected in the OT few direct parallels have been found in religious texts of surrounding peoples (see PREUSS 1968:161-171; 1973: 487).

III. The exact interpretation of Isaiah 7 and 8 is beset with difficulties. We do not know who is meant by 'the young woman' in Isa 7:14, but there is no indication that there will be anything abnormal or special about her pregnancy (present or immanent) or the birth of her child. The birth of the child (in the royal family of David?) and his name will be a sign from the LORD. Before the boy will know how to refuse the evil and to choose the good, the threat from the two enemy kings will be removed. In Judaism, Isa 7:14 is not used in connection with a future messianic saviour.

For Matthew's interpretation of the passage, it is essential that the young woman is a virgin whose pregnancy is due to divine intervention. And, whereas in Isa 7:14 it is the young mother who chooses the name of the child, Matt 1:23 stipulates that the name Emmanuel will be given by others: "they shall name him Emmanuel"—not by Mary, or Joseph (who, in v 21, receives the command to call Mary's son →Jesus, "for he will save his people from their sins"). Presumably the 'they' of v 22 are 'his people' of v 21. Many people of whom it is said that God was with them are portrayed as having been specially endowed with the Spirit (e.g. Joseph in Gen 41:38; Gideon in Judg 6:34; Saul in 1 Sam 10:6.7; David in 1 Sam 16:13). Hence Matthew may have seen the role of the →Holy Spirit in the birth of Jesus as a decisive factor for his life in an intimate relationship with God (Matt 3:16-17; 11:25-30; 12:17-21.28; 16:16; 17:5; 26:39). In this way, Jesus' activity represents God's presence among his people. The gospel ends with the assurance "I am with you always to the end of the age" (Matt. 28:20, cf. 17:17, 18:20, 26:29). Later Christians mention Emmanuel as the name of the Incarnate Word (→Logos) (LPGL 454).

IV. *Bibliography*

A. LAATTO, *Who is Immanuel? The Rise and Foundering of Isaiah's Messianic Expectations* (Åbo 1988); H. D. PREUSS, "...ich will mit dir sein!", *ZAW* 80 (1968) 139-173; H. D. PREUSS, *TWAT* 1 (1973) 485-500; W. C. VAN UNNIK, *Dominus Vobiscum.* The Background of a Liturgical Formula, *Sparsa Collecta* 3 (NovTSup 31; Leiden 1983) 362-391.

M. DE JONGE

ENDS OF THE EARTH אפסי ארץ

I. The expression *ʾapsê ʾereṣ*, 'The ends of the →Earth' occurs 16 times in the OT, mainly in poetic texts (e.g. Deut 33:17; Isa 45:22; 52:10; Mic 5:3; Zech 9:10; six times in the Pss). The first element of this construct chain, *ʾepes*, denotes the end or limit of space or time. The noun has cognates in Ug *ʾps*, 'upper edge', (*KTU* 1.6 i:61); Phoen *ʾps*, 'end', adverbially used as 'finally; even' in *KAI* 26 IV:1, and in the Canaanite noun *upsu*, 'extremity', (EA 287:70'; 289:50; 366:34; R. DEGEN, *WdO* 6 [1971-72] 60). Not convinced by a Semitic etymology for *ʾepes*, some authors have suggested a relation with Mesopotamian Apsu, the deified subterranean waters (WENSINCK 1918:21; POPE 1955:71-72). An improbable etymology has been offered by SCHUMAN (*BiOr* 33 [1976] 161) who construed a common etymology for Mesopotamian Apsu and the WSem noun *ʾps* in Proto-Semitic **ḳabas-*, 'surrounding fence or wall'.

II. The Akkadian noun *apsu* is a loanword from Sum **abzu**$_x$ (= ZU-AB) or **ab.zu**, 'subterranean waters'. The pronunciation with a /p/ is confirmed by its occurrence as Ἀπασών in Greek tradition (Damascius, *De principiis* § 125). In Mesopotamian mythology, Apsu was regarded as the abode of strange composite creatures of different kinds. They could be of benevolent or of malevolent character. In *Maqlû* VIII 38, the Apsu is the abode of the 'Wise Apkallū' (→Apkallu). The Apsu was the realm and the home of Enki/Ea, the god of wisdom. →Marduk, the son of Ea, was born and raised in the Apsu, according to *Enuma Elish* (*Ee* I 77-88; cf. R. BORGER, *Inschrifte Asarhaddons* [AfO Beiheft 9; Graz 1956] § 61:20; E. EBELING, *Stiftungen und Vorschriften für assyrische Tempel* [Berlin 1954] 4:8). The Apsu is not identical with the underworld which was located even further down. In some traditions a river, the →Hubur, had to be crossed in order to reach the underworld. This river is sometimes identified with or incorporated in the Apsu.

In *Enuma Elish* Apsu appears as a god acting in a primeval drama. He was the lover and husband of →Tiamat, the saltwater ocean. They engendered the first generation of deities: →Lahmu and Lahamu; Anshar and Kishar; Anu and Nudimmud/Ea (*Ee* I 9-18). These younger gods rebelled against Apsu and Tiamat. Against the will of Tiamat, Apsu plotted against the gods his offspring. Thereupon, Ea—by means of a magic spell—made Apsu sleep forever and took away from him his symbols of power: his crown and his cloak of fiery rays (*Ee* I 55-71; JACOBSEN 1976).

In ancient Greek mythological thought, the edges of the earth are seen as surrounded by an Ocean that could not be crossed by mankind, and near it there lived strange beings, such as the Hyperboreans and the *Kynokephaloi* (ROMM 1992). WEST (1963) has argued that in early Greek cosmologies the concept of Ocean as primordial water inhabited by monsters and →giants—to be overcome before the universe is properly ordered—has been borrowed from ancient Near Eastern myths.

III. In the OT 'the ends of the earths' do not have a mythological bias. In several texts they are mentioned to emphasize the worldwide character of the rule of →Yahweh (1 Sam 2:10; Isa 45:22; 52:10; Jer 16:19; Ps 22:28; 59:14; 67:8; Prov 30:14; Sir 36:22) or his earthly representative (Deut 33:17; Mic 5:3; Ps 2:8; 72:8; 98:3). In parallellism with other geographic designations 'ends of the earth' indicates in a merism 'the whole earth' (with →Sea and →River: Zech 9:10; Ps 72:8; Sir 44:21). A connection with Mesopotamian Apsu seems unlikely. Etymologically there is no necessity to relate *ʾepes* with *apsu*. In the OT other expressions for 'ends of the earth' are found (*qĕṣēh hāʾāreṣ* (e.g. Deut 13:8), *yarkĕtē ʾāreṣ* (e.g. Jer 6:22; 25:32); *kanpôt hāʾāreṣ*, 'hems/edges of the earth', Job 37:3; 38:13; Isa 11:12; Ezek 7:2). In the NT the expressions ἕως ἐσχάτου τῆς γῆς, 'to the end of the earth' (Acts 1:8; 13:47) and πειράτα τῆς γῆς (Matt 12:42; Luke 11:31) occur.

IV. *Bibliography*

V. HAMP, *ʾepes*, *TWAT* 1 (1971) 389-391; T. JACOBSEN, *The Treasures of Darkness* (New Haven/London 1976) 168-172; P. JENSEN, Apsû, *RLA* 1 (1928) 122-124; M. H. POPE, *El in the Ugaritic Texts* (VTSup 2; Leiden 1955) 71-72; J. S. ROMM, *The Edges of the Earth in Ancient Thought* (Princeton 1992); A. J. WENSINCK, *The Ocean in the Literature of the Western Semites* (Amsterdam 1918); M. L. WEST, Three Presocratic Cosmologies, *CQ* 13 (1963) 154-176.

B. BECKING

ENOCH חנוך

I. The enigmatic reference to Enoch in Genesis 5:24 has generated a welter of speculation about his person and a range of literature attributed to him which is found in a variety of forms. Our knowledge of its early form has been transformed by the discovery of the fragments from Cave 4 at Qumran, many of which correspond to what we know as *1 Enoch*. This apocalypse is extant in its complete version in Ethiopic and includes a variety of material from different periods (the chapters 37-71, which speak of the →Son of Man and Enoch's identification with this heavenly figure, appear not to have been known at Qumran).

II. The legend of Enoch's righteousness, his position in →heaven and his wisdom, provide opportunities for displaying a vast array of information in the apocalyptic mode concerning astronomy, eschatology and paraenesis. The reference in chapter 5 of Genesis already suggests that at the time of the redaction of this chapter, probably during the Exilic period, speculation about Enoch was well established. The allusion to the 365 days of the year in the length of life accorded to him hints at the calendrical wisdom which was to be such an important component of the ideas about him in later Jewish tradition (see the summary in *Pirke de Rabbi Eliezer* 9a).

The discovery of the Enoch fragments from Qumran have added weight to the view that there was a wide range of speculation about Enoch of which the brief mention in Genesis is by no means the only or even the earliest example. Possibly the earliest evidence for speculation outside the Bible is to be found in *1 Enoch* where, as a scribe, he is located in a privileged position (*1 Enoch* 12). Such a position gives him access to God with whom he intercedes on behalf of the

→Watchers (*1 Enoch* 12), the fallen angels of Gen 6:1-4. For this purpose Enoch ascends to heaven and, in a description reminiscent of the visions of Ezekiel and Isaiah and a prototype of later visions of God in apocalyptic literature and in the Jewish mystical (*Hekaloth*) tradition, he ascends through the palaces of heaven to receive a message of judgement from God on the Watchers (*1 Enoch* 14). Following the heavenly ascent Enoch wanders the earth and visits many places including the Paradise of Righteousness. His position as scribe is echoed in *Jub.* 4:17-21 (cf. *T.Abr.*, B 11), in which he is said to have been the first to have learnt writing and the signs of heaven. His final dwelling-place is in the Garden of Eden (see also *T. Benj.* 10.6 and Christian testimony to Enoch's place in the heavenly paradise in *Apoc. Paul* 20, *Clementine Recognitions* 1.52, *Acts of Pilate* 25 and the *Ascension of Isaiah* 9.6). Here he writes down the judgement and condemnation of the world and acts as a priest "burning the incense of the sanctuary, sweet spices, acceptable before the Lord on the mount" (*Jub.* 4:23-24). This priestly role is one that is reflected in several later sources (e.g. *Apostolic Constitutions* 8.5; the *Cave of Treasures* and the *Book of the Rolls*).

In the Hebrew of Sirach, at 44:16, Enoch's perfection is stressed and he is called a sign of knowledge (*'ôt daʿat*) for every generation (cf. *Jub.* 4:17). In the same book, at 49:14, his ascent to God is referred to allusively (*nilqaḥ pānîm*, evidently a technical term meaning something like "taken into the divine presence"). In the Greek of Sirach, at 44:16, Enoch heads the list of famous men, the text claiming for him that he "pleased the Lord, and was translated, being an example of repentance to all generations", a theme reflected in Philo's *Questions on Genesis* 1.82. At 49:14 his translation is again noted, and the great men named after him include →Joseph, →Shem and →Seth. He is said to have been unique ("none was created like him"), which is proved by his translation from the earth (*anelēmphthē*, cf. 2 Kgs 2:11). In the *Wisdom of Solomon* Enoch is seen as the example of the righteous man whose death is mistaken as judgement but in whom in reality the wisdom and righteousness of age reached fruition in youth. Here he is said to have been snatched away (*hērpagē*), a verb used in the New Testament as a technical term for the ascent to heaven (see 2 Cor 12:2-4; 1 Thess 4:15-17; Rev 12:5). His privileged position in heaven made him a resource which succeeding generations might hope to benefit from as the fragmentary *Genesis Apocryphon* 2 demonstrates (cf. *1 Enoch* 106:7). Enoch's opportunity to consult the heavenly tablets gave him a position of wisdom and insight (cf. *1 Enoch* 103). Josephus speaks of Enoch as returning to the divinity (exactly the same words he uses of the end of →Moses in *Antiq.* 1.85, cf. *Ant.* 4.326). In describing the end of →Elijah Josephus links him with Enoch and speaks of both as becoming invisible (*aphaneis*), since no one knew of their death. Philo's view of Enoch in part anticipates the line which will be found in the isolated references in the rabbinic midrash: Enoch becomes upright when he became a father, and Enoch's repentance led to constancy in uprightness for which he was rewarded.

The speculation about Enoch continued in the literature attributed to Enoch which emerged over a period of about four hundred years at the beginning of the Christian era. The earliest material, much of which has parallels in fragmentary form among the Aramaic fragments from Qumran Cave 4, is to be found in the Ethiopic Apocalypse of Enoch. This is a mixture of visions and paranaesis on subjects as diverse as eschatology and astronomy. In the Slavonic Apocalypse of Enoch (*2 Enoch*) Enoch ascends through seven heavens, in a heavenly journey in which the component parts of the heavenly world and their inhabitants are briefly described. His return to earth is the opportunity for a discourse of a testamentary kind. In the Hebrew Book of Enoch (also known as *3 Enoch*), a solitary example of the extravagant Enochic speculation preserved in the Jewish tradition, Enoch is transformed into the angel Metatron (an event with a parallel in *1 Enoch* 71 where Enoch seems to become the heavenly Son of Man referred to in earlier chapters). The transformation of the antediluvian hero into an exalted angel and a position on a throne like that of God is the highwater mark of the Enoch legend. Even in this work the dangers of such speculation are recognised and Enoch-Metatron is humiliated when he fails to stand in face of the confused early second century CE tanna Elisha ben Abuyah who, when he ascends to heaven, mistakes Enoch-Metatron for a second God and supposes that there are two powers in heaven (*3 Enoch* 16 and b. *Hagigah* 15a). Surprisingly Enoch makes little appearance in the Hekaloth tradition where the role as mystagogue is given to famous tannaitic figures like Rabbi Ishmael and Rabbi Akiba. The extravagant claims about Enoch are not echoed in other Jewish sources. In commenting on Gen 5:24, *Bereshith Rabbah* 25 demystifies Enoch completely by suggesting that his removal was the result of death. In the Targumim we have a variety of interpretations of Enoch's end. His death is emphasised by Onkelos in line with attempts to play down Enoch's role. In the Fragment Targum mention is made of Enoch's worship of God (identical in wording with Ps. Jonathan), but this targum seems to be agnostic about Enoch's end merely speaking of him being taken away. Neofiti is similar. As one might expect, Ps. Jonathan is much more extensive and reflects the more extravagant Enochic speculation. Like *Jub.* 4:23 it has Enoch taken from the dwellers on earth to become a heavenly scribe, but it also speaks of his being taken up to the firmament and his name being "Metatron the great scribe" (b. *Hagigah* 15a and *3 Enoch* 16; cf *1 Enoch* 12).

III. In the Christian tradition there is occasional interest in Enoch. He is cited as an example of faith manifest in the fact that he was pleasing to God (Hebrews 11:5-6). The Enochic literature is treated as prophecy in Jude 14 (the authority of Enochic literature often being supported in various pre-Nicene sources e.g. *Epistle of Barnabas* 4.16; Tertullian *de cultu feminarum* I.3; *Apostolic Constitutions* 6.16). There has been debate over the extent of the indebtedness to the figure of Enoch in the New Testament. It is likely that the Last Judgement scene in Matt. 25:31-46 is indebted to the son of man figure (subsequently identified with Enoch) in *1 Enoch* 37-71, especially 69:27, though in Matthew, of course, it is Jesus as heavenly son of man who so sits. John 3:13 has been taken as an indication of polemic against the contemporary claims made on behalf of figures like Enoch and Moses to have ascended into heaven by asserting the superiority of Jesus the Son of Man's ascent and descent (cf. the similar contrasts in Cyril of Jerusalem's *Catechetical Lectures* 14:25; Ambrose, *De fide* 4.1). In 1 Pet 3:16.18-22 Christ's proclamation to the imprisoned spirits may reflect Enoch's proclamation of judgement to the Watchers who had been imprisoned and sought Enoch's intercession (*1 Enoch* 12-16 cf. Hippolytus, *Antichrist* 45). Like Enoch →Christ passes through the heavens and attains a position of pre-eminence in the process (1 Pet 3:22). In the book of Revelation John of Patmos is appointed as a scribe to write to the angels of the seven churches in Asia, emulating the role of Enoch. In later interpretation of Rev. 11 the two witnesses mentioned there are identified with Enoch and Elijah. They are sent to convict the →Antichrist (Hippolytus *Antichrist* 43; *Historia Josephi* 25; John of Damascus, *Exposition of the Orthodox Faith* 4.26; Ethiopic *Apocalypse of Peter* 2; Ephraem, *Discourse on the Consummation* 11). In the Samaritan literature Enoch is said to have opened the storehouse of righteousness and fed his soul on the provisions of eternal life (*Tibat Markah* 4.9), and like Adam, worshipped at Mount Gerizim (*Markah* 2.10). In the Samaritan targum to Gen 5:24 Enoch is said to have been taken by an angel. In the Qur'an Enoch (= Idris) is called a man of truth who was raised to a lofty place for his steadfastness and patience.

IV. *Bibliography*

R. H. CHARLES, *The Book of Enoch* (Oxford 1912); J. DRUSIUS, *Henoch. Sive de patriarcha Henoch, eiusque raptu et libro quo Judas Apostolus testimonium profert: ubi de libris in scriptura memoratis, qui nunc interciderunt* (Franeker 1615); J. A. FABRICIUS, *Codex pseudepigraphicus veteris Testamenti, collectus, castigatus testimoniisque, censuris et animadversionibus illustratus* (Hamburg 1722-1741); P. GRELOT, La légende d'Hénoch dans les apocryphes et dans la Bible: origine et signification, *RSR* 46 (1958) 5-26; 181-210; E. G. HIRSCH, Enoch, *The Jewish Encyclopedia* 5 (New York 1903) 178-179; H. L. JANSEN, *Die Henochgestalt: Eine vergleichende religionsgeschichtliche Untersuchung* (Oslo 1939); J. T. MILIK, *Books of Enoch: Aramaic Fragments of Qumran Cave 4* (Oxford 1976); H. ODEBERG, Enoch, *TDNT* 2 (Grand Rapids 1964) 556-560; J. C. VANDERKAM, *Enoch and the Growth of the Apocalyptic Tradition* (Washington 1984).

C. ROWLAND

EQUITY → MISHARU

ESAU עשׂו

I. Esau, twin brother of →Jacob is known as the eponym of the *bĕnê ʿēsāw* (Gen 25:19-34; 36:1-43) and the father of →Edom (Gen 36:9.43; Akk *Udumu*; Ug *udm* (?); Eg *idm;* Gk *Idoumaia*). His name, sometimes connected to Ar *aʿṯa*, 'to be hairy' (Gen 25:25), is more likely explained as a hypocoristicon of ʿŚW or ʿŚY (*HALAT* 845; cf. epigraphic Hebr *ʿśw*; Nabataean *ʿsw*). Early critical scholarship surmised behind the saga of Jacob and Esau a mythological tale of twin rivalry (GOLDZIHER 1876; MEYER 1906). Frequent reference has also been made to the culture myth of *Samēmroumos* and *Ousōos* as narrated by Philo of Byblos (H. W. ATTRIDGE & R. A. ODEN, *Philo of Byblos: The Phoenician History. Introduction, Critical Text, Translation, Notes* [CBQ Monogr. Ser. 9; Washington 1981] 43-44). Esau was identified with this cultural hero Ousōos, hunter and inventor of cloths made of animal hides. Furthermore, his name has been connected with an Asiatic goddess **ʿšit* depicted as a hunting and horse-riding deity in New Kingdom texts and iconography (MEYER 1906:278-279 n.2).

II. A relation between Esau's name and the Asiatic goddess **ʿšit* does not exist. Her name ought to be read as *ʿšty* (presumably pronounced 'Ashtay), which originated as a scribal and phonetic variant of Semitic →Astarte (R. STADELMANN, *Syrisch-Palästinensische Gottheiten in Ägypten* [Leiden 1967] 99-101). The connection between Ousōos and Esau is highly questionable, too, notwithstanding some motives shared between myth and saga. Ousōos is more probably Greek for Uzu or Ushu, the ancient name of the mainland settlement opposite Tyre (*ANET*³ 287.300.477; M. NOTH, *Überlieferungsgeschichte des Pentateuchs* [Stuttgart 1948] 105-106), whereas Samēmroumos is reminiscent of *šmm rmm* 'Shamem romim', a temple quarter in or near Sidon (*KAI* 15; see also *šmm ʾdrm KAI* 14:16; O. EISSFELDT, Schamemrumim "Hoher Himmel", ein Stadtteil von Gross-Sidon, *FF* 14 [1938] 171-173 = *KS 2*, 123-126; GESE, *RAAM*, 147-148; ATTRIDGE & ODEN, *Philo of Byblos: The Phoenician History* 82-83 n.56).

III. Biblical tradition connects Esau, and thus also the *bĕnê ʿēsāw*, to the land of Edom and the mountains of Seir (Gen 36:1-8). There is a distant memory of blood-ties between Jacob and Esau (e.g. Gen 36:6; Deut 23:7; Amos 1:11; Ob 10), presumably dating back to their Transjordan symbiosis (Gen 32-33; MEYER 1906; NOTH, *Überlieferungsgeschichte,* 104-108). A kind of kinship continued to be felt even after Esau's migration to the south (Gen 36:6-8). Clans of the 'Edomite' tribe of Kenaz (Kenizzites) developed close ties with Judah in and around Hebron (Num 32:12; Josh 15:13-19; Judg 1:10-15; MEYER 1906:348-354; DE VAUX 1971:496-501). The mention of *yhwh tmn* ('Yahweh of Teman') in the texts from Kuntillet Ajrud (Horvat Teman, in the

Negev) also indicates ancient cultural and religious ties between Israel and Edom. No clear memories about Esau's tomb and ancestral cult have survived in the biblical accounts. There is a Jewish legend relating the death of Esau at Machpelah because of his infamous claim to the Cave (*bSotah* 13a; *Pirqe de Rabbi Eliezer* XXXIX). According to this story, his head was kept at Machpelah and his body sent back to Seir.

IV. *Bibliography*

I. GOLDZIHER, *Der Mythos bei den Hebräern und seine geschichtliche Entwicklung* (Leipzig 1876; reprint 1987); E. MEYER, *Die Israeliten und ihre Nachbarstämme* (Halle 1906).

M. DIJKSTRA

ESH → **FIRE**

ESHMUN Ἔσμουνος

I. The name of the Phoenician god of health, Eshmun (*ʾšmn*), has been used by some scholars to explain the *hap. leg.* of Isa 59:10 אשׁמנים as an abstract plural meaning 'health'. Eshmun has also been connected with →Ashima, the deity of the settlers from Hamath referred to in 2 Kgs 17:30.

II. From the 8th century BCE onward, the cult of the god Eshmun is attested in Syria, Palestine, Cyprus, Egypt, Carthage and other Punic cities. In a broken context, the Treaty of Ashurnerari V with Mati-ilu of Arpad mentions ^{d}*Ia-su-mu-na* in the list of divine witnesses next to →Melqart (SAA 2 no. 2 vi 22); so does the treaty between Esarhaddon of Assyria and Baal of Tyre (SAA 2 no. 5 iv 14'). The reading *ʾšmn* on an 8th century BCE fragment of pottery from Shiqmona is doubtful (B. DELAVAULT & A. LEMAIRE, Les inscriptions phéniciennes de Palestine, *RSF* 7 [1979] 17 no. 33a). The name Eshmun might be connected with a Semitic stem denoting fatness and health (ŠMN with prothetic aleph); the common Semitic word for 'oil' derives from the same root. Eshmun should thus be explained as 'healing god, healer' (XELLA 1991 and previously BAUDISSIN 1911; LIPIŃSKI 1973 and others). If this etymology is correct, the god may have ancient antecedents. Since the Eblaite onomasticon contains theophoric names compounded with Sum **ì-giš** ('oil') or Eblaite *sì/ziminu* ('oil'?), it could be argued that divine figures resembling Eshmun, if not identical with him, were already worshipped at Ebla. A forerunner of Eshmun was probably known, too, at Ugarit and Ibn Hani, where a god *šmn* is attested in some ritual texts (for lit. see D. PARDEE, Ugaritic Proper Nouns, *AfO* 37/37 [1989-90] 458 s.v. ŠMN).

In Graeco-Latin sources Eshmun is identified with Asclepius/Aesculapius, which confirms his character of superhuman healer, also attested by a 2nd century BCE trilingual inscription (Punic/Greek/Latin: *KAI* 66, from S. Nicolò Gerrei, Sardinia), which explicitly associates the god Eshmun/ Asclepius/Aesculapius *Merre*, with healing ("He heard his voice and healed him"). Some scholars identify Eshmun with the Greek hero Iolaos, who brought →Heracles to life by means of a quail. The ties of Eshmun with healing are perhaps implied already in the Esarhaddon Treaty: he is called upon to punish any violation of the treaty with deprivation of food, clothing and oil for ointment.

Already in antiquity, the name Eshmun received explanations other than those connected with 'oil' and healing. Philo Byblius (in his *Phoenician History* quoted by Euseb., *P.E.* I 10,25 and 38) adopts an interpretation of the name derived from the number eight (*šĕmōneh* in Hebrew); he makes Asclepius the eighth brother of the Cabiri, sons of Sydyk (the 'Just One'; →Zedeq). Also Damascius (*Vita Isid.* 302, ed. Zintzen, 307-308) who considers the *Esmounos*/ Asclepius in Beirut to be the eighth son of Sadykos, after the →Dioskouroi or Cabiri, is aware of this explanation of the god's name.

Despite his relatively late appearance in the Phoenician records, Eshmun appears to have had an important role. His cult is attested epigraphically in Syria-Palestine at Amrit (BORDREUIL 1985), in the 6th-5th century BCE; at Sarepta and Nebi-Yunis he seems to be mentioned as well (B. DELAVAULT & A. LEMAIRE, Une stèle "molk" de Palestine dédiée à Eshmoun? RES 367 reconsidéré, *RB* 83 [1976] 569-583) in the 3th-2nd century BCE. His cult enjoyed particular importance at Sidon, where Eshmun was the chief deity since about 500 BCE. He had a temple in the centre of town where he was worshipped together with →Astarte, and another sanctuary not very far from the city (at Bostan esh-Sheikh), near a spring (see *KAI* 14.15.16 and elsewhere). The inscriptions qualify Eshmun as the *šr qdš*, 'Holy Prince' according to current opinion (a reading *šd qdš*, 'holy spirit', might also be considered), and *bʿl ṣdn*, 'Lord of Sidon' (*KAI* 14:18). Eshmun occupied a special place also in the Phoenician colonies of the ancient Mediterranean world, whether alone or in the company of Melqart (e.g. *CIS* I 16, 23-28, 42-44, from Kition, Cyprus), or Astarte (e.g. *CIS* I 245, from Carthage).

The classical tradition ascribes to the Phoenician Asclepios a premature death and a marvellous revival: Damascius reports that Asclepios of Beirut was a young hunter beloved by the Phoenician goddess Astronoe (probably to be identified with Astarte), mother of the gods; in order to escape her amorous overtures, he emasculated himself with an axe. Our rash hero died, but Astronoe, greatly grieved, brought him back to life and made him into a god. The tale appears to be an etiology of Eshmun's divinization (for this story of a 'dying god' see S. RIBICHINI, *Poenus Advena. Gli dèi fenici e l'interpretazione classica* [Roma 1985] 43-73). Some see a relationship between Astronoe's quickening warmth and the reviving warmth associated with Eshmun (so LIPIŃSKI 1973:166).

III. In Isa 59:9-15 there is a description of the hopeless situation of the prophet's audience. In Isa 59:10 two conditions are contrasted with each other; the second is that of the dead (*baṣohŏrayim*), while the first is said to be *bāʾašmannîm*. In view of the context, this hapax legomenon seems to denote a condition of strength and vigour. 1QIsa[a] reads אשמונים, with a clear *waw* (M. BEEGLE, *BASOR* 123 [1951] 26-30), which recalls also the non-Phoenician transcriptions of the divine name *ʾšmn* (esp. in the personal names: cf. Akk *Sa-mu-na-ia-tu-ni*, Gk Εσμουνος, Εσυμσεληµ, Αβδυζμουνος, Lt *Asmunis*, *-ismunis*, *-usmyn*; see F. L. BENZ, *Personal Names in the Phoenician and Punic Inscriptions* [Rome 1972] 278-279). LXX interprets *bāʾašmannîm* as a verb (στενάξουσιν), and Vg renders *in caliginosis* (*quasi mortui*), "in mist, in obscurity". Gesenius would explain it as an elative of the adjective *šāmēn* 'fat'; modern scholars usually translate it as an adjective, 'stout' or 'lusty', and RSV renders "among those in full vigour we are like dead men". According to W. F. ALBRIGHT, the term *bāʾašmannîm* is very likely based on the name of the Phoenician god Eshmun; it means 'well-being, in good health'. ALBRIGHT compares the name of the Black Nightshade, ἀστιρσμουνίμ, '(herb of) good health', mentioned by Dioscurides, *De materia medica* IV 70 and already interpreted on the basis of the Hebrew by S. Bochart, as ἀσὶρ ἐσμουνί (ALBRIGHT 1946; see also LIPIŃSKI 1973:167). The common elements of the biblical and the Greek terms are obviously the plural form and the semantic evolution of **šmn*, from 'fat, oil' to 'healer'. In this connection it seems appropriate to note the etymological explanation of Eshmun by Damascius (*Vita Isid.* 302): "He was named Esmounos by the Phoenicians with reference to the warmth of life" (Ἔσμουνον ὑπὸ Φοινίκων ὠνομασμένον ἐπὶ τῇ θέρμῃ τῆς ζωῆς). Note that also Pausanias (VII 23, 7-8) quotes a Sidonian interpretation of the god Asclepios, associating the god with the ability 'to impart to the air its healthiness'. In the light of these facts E. LIPIŃSKI renders the biblical *hapax* as 'healers' ('among healers we are as dead men' 1973:179), and supports his rendering by referring to the expression cited by Dioscurides, which he translates 'healer's herb'. He also observes that "there is no reason to suppose that the Hebrew writer would have employed the name of the Phoenician deity as a poetic word for 'physician', even if

Eshmun were known at that time in Southern Palestine. The use of the plural form of the noun in the Punic name *ḥăṣīr ʾešmunîm* and the rather clear semantic evolution of *šmn*, 'oil' > 'anointer', i.e. 'healer', seem to show with sufficient evidence that *ʾešmun* was at first a common noun. It then became an epithet of the Sidonian god and finally a divine name of its own" (LIPIŃKSI 1973: 180).

The parallel with Ashima is a different and more hypothetic case. According to R. ZADOK (Geographical and Onomastic Notes, *JANES* 8 [1976] 118-119), the resemblance of the two divine names may be merely morphological, having no bearing upon their characters, powers or functions.

IV. *Bibliography*

W. F. ALBRIGHT, *Archaeology and the Religion of Israel* (2nd ed., Baltimore 1946) 196 n. 25; *W. W. BAUDISSIN, *Adonis und Esmun* (Leipzig 1911); A. I. BAUMGARTEN, *The* Phoenician History *of Philo of Byblos. A Commentary* (EPRO 89; Leiden 1981) 190, 228-231; P. BORDREUIL, Le dieu Echmoun dans la région d'Amrit, *Studia Phoenicia III. Phoenicia and its Neighbours* (Leuven 1985) 221-230; T. K. CHEYNE, A Dark Passage in Isaiah, *ZAW* 25 (1905) 172; E. J. & L. EDELSTEIN, *Asclepius. A Collection and Interpretation of the Testimonies*, I-II (Baltimore 1945); *E. LIPIŃSKI, Eshmun 'Healer', *AION* 33 (1973) 161-183; S. V. MCCASLAND, The Asklepios Cult in Palestine, *JBL* 58 (1939) 221-227; O. MASSON, Pélérins chypriotes en Phénicie (Sarepta et Sidon), *Sem* 32 (1982) 45-49; E. WILL, Eshmoun, *LIMC* IV 1, 23-24; P. XELLA, D'Ugarit à la Phénicie: Sur les traces de Rashap, Horon, Eshmun, *WO* 19 (1989) 45-64; *P. XELLA, Etimologie antiche del teonimo fenicio Eshmun, *Atti del Sodalizio Glottologico Milanese* 39 (1988[1991]) 145-151; XELLA, Eschmun von Sidon. Der phönizische Asklepios, *Mesopotamica – Ugaritica – Biblica* (M. Dietrich & O. Loretz eds.; FS Bergershof; AOAT 232; Neukirchen Vluyn 1993) 481-498.

S. RIBICHINI

ETEMMU אטים

I. *Eṭemmu* is the main term for 'ghost' in Akkadian. It is the primary Akkadian equivalent or translation of Sum **gidim**, from which word it may derive. The term *eṭemmu* seems to underlie the biblical *ʾiṭṭîm* in Isa 19:3, where however the final *mem* is treated as if it were the Hebrew marker of the masculine plural.

II. *Eṭemmu* is a spirit, more properly a ghost. Wind imagery is associated with ghosts (and demons)—note the use of **líl** for 'ghost' (→Lilith). Ghosts are heard, felt and especially seen, particularly in dreams. Ghosts are also designated by or associated with 'divinity'. Of particular significance is the etiology of *eṭemmu* found in the Old Babylonian *Atraḫasīs* epic I 206-230. There, mankind is created from a mixture of clay and the flesh and blood of a slain god. This god's name is *Wê-ilu,* and he is characterized as one who has *ṭēmu*, 'understanding, intelligence' or perhaps even 'psyche'. Note the similarity in sound and the punning between *awīlu* and *wê(-)ila* and between *we-e... ṭēma* and *eṭemmu.* Thus, when alive, mankind receives both its life and the name *awīlu*, 'man', from this god *(a)wê-ilu*. But also because of this god and man's divine origin, mankind survives after death in the form of a ghost, and this too is signalled by a name; for this text implicitly treats *eṭemmu*, 'ghost', as having been formed from the combination of the *Wê* of the god's name and his *ṭēmu*.

After death, what remains is the lifeless body and some form of intangible, but visible and audible 'spirit'. The body must be buried; otherwise, the ghost will have no rest and will not find its place in the community of the dead, usually associated with the netherworld. In addition, the dead are to be the recipients of ongoing mortuary rites, which include invocations of the name of the deceased, presentation of food and libation of water. In this way the dead are cared for and their memory is preserved. The dead may be remembered as individuals for up to several generations and then become part of the ancestral family (*eṭem kimti*). It needs always to be emphasized that Mesopotamian burial and mortuary rituals as well as beliefs about the dead are not simply an autonomous area of religious life; they also reflect social structure and psychological experience. In any case, care for the dead may provide an occasion for the maintenance of social bonds. The living and dead maintain a permanent relationship and form an ongoing community. Dead and living kin in Mesopotamia are dependent upon each other and therefore their relationship will naturally reflect or express both hostility and love.

Normally the dead body was buried and burial allowed for the preservation and maintenance of the deceased's identity after death and for his continued connection with both the living and dead members of the family. Burial is crucial, for if a corpse is left unburied and/or is destroyed by animals, fire, or the like, the dead person cannot be integrated into the structured community of the dead and thereby into the ongoing and continuous community of the living and the dead. He loses his human community and human identity. This is not only the fate of those who do not receive burial immediately after death. The same fate awaits the dead who are disinterred and whose skeletal remains are destroyed. In some cases, the remains are so totally transformed and disintegrated that the dead loses all vestiges of human identity.

The unburied or disinterred may become roaming and troublesome ghosts; more important, some texts suggest that they are relegated to the formless and chaotic world sometimes associated with steppe and winds, and may even become part of the demonic world that is neither human nor god, male nor female. Hence **gidim**/*eṭemmu* may become associated with the demonic class **udug**/*utukku* and even be so designated.

Lack of burial and/or destruction of the body will often occur accidentally and belongs psychologically together with the fear of premature death; such treatment of the body may also be imposed as a punishment for a crime. It is among the most dreadful sanctions of Mesopotamian society.

Information about the condition of the dead is found in a variety of sources. Particularly worthy of note are a) rituals, especially therapeutic ones, that deal with ghosts and their effects on humans, b) 'descents' to the netherworld, and c) curses that describe the various evils which may befall human beings.

a) Magical and medical texts that deal with ghosts usually focus on those ghosts who plague the living. The topos of a restless and troublesome ghost is particularly prevalent. Ghosts who plague the living may either belong to one's own family or be strangers who have attached themselves to the victim. These ghosts are often said to have not been provided with mortuary rites or, even worse, to have not received a proper burial in the first place. Mention must also be made of the dead who had led unfulfilled lives and are drawn back to the world of the living, either out of envy or malice, or out of the desire to complete 'unfinished business'. Various physical and psychological symptoms are attributed to ghostly seizures in therapeutic texts. Notable, in addition, is the frequent mention of visions of the dead, often in dreams. Some therapeutic texts prescribe material cures (e.g. potions, salves); others operate more in the magical and symbolic realms and try to rid the victim of the ghost either by providing the ghost with proper burial and/or mortuary treatment or by performing some other form of expulsion.

In other instances, ghosts—usually the family manes (*eṭem kimti*)—are invoked to help the living by taking one or another form of evil down to the netherworld. Of great interest, especially in view of the aforementioned biblical passage (and similar passages which mention the *ʾôb* and *yiddĕʿōnî* though not the *ʾiṭṭîm*), are attempts to raise the dead for purposes of necromancy. One designation of the necromancer is *mušēli eṭemmi.*

b) Among the 'descents', pride of place should perhaps go to the descent of Enkidu to the netherworld in the Sumerian *Gilgamesh, Enkidu, and the Netherworld*

(//Gilg. Tablet XII) and in the later Gilg. Tablet VII. In the former—which represents an early text—the state of the dead is described in terms of and related to the human support system (e.g. number of children), the manner of death and the treatment of the body. In the main, the dead are pale imitations of the living—they are human in form but seem to lack animation and energy. In later descriptions, by contrast, the vision of the dead is more horrific and shows us a netherworld inhabited by monsters and demons and dead who no longer look human. Here, mention should be made especially of *The Netherworld Vision of an Assyrian Prince* as a late text which exhibits this horrific vision of the netherworld (SAA 3 [1989] no. 32).

Equally illuminating historically as regards changes in the idea of the netherworld is the graphic description of the dead and of the netherworld in the opening lines of the *Descent of Ishtar*: To the dark house, dwelling of Erkalla's god / To the house which those who enter cannot leave / On the road where travelling is one-way only / To the house where those who enter are deprived of light / Where dust is their food, clay their bread / They see no light, they dwell in darkness / They are clothed like birds, with feathers / Over the door and the bolt, dust has settled. (S. DALLEY, *Myths from Mesopotamia* [Oxford/New York 1989] 155:4-11) Here I would make several historical observations. Firstly, it is significant that the older *Descent of Inanna* (from which the *Descent of Ishtar* derives) does not focus upon or even contain this type of description. Moreover, in the later text, the dead are described as birds and not humans. Furthermore, the description of the netherworld in the later text is itself a later image, one that has been superimposed upon the earlier vision of the netherworld as a city which is entered through gates and in which the dead are housed or even imprisoned. Its secondary nature is clear from the fact that the house of the dead is here described as one whose door and bolt are covered with dust, for the earlier image—an image which is even used of Ishtar's own descent later in the text—is that of gates through which the dead constantly go and which therefore would not be covered by dust. This image of the dusty netherworld and with it the image of the dead as birds would seem to derive from that of a tomb or even a ruin and/or a cave. More than the earlier texts, these later visions serve to draw a sharper line and a greater contrast between the living and the dead.

c) Often, texts whose purpose is to maintain or protect the 'status quo' (e.g. boundary stones, treaties, laws, building and tomb inscriptions, etc.) include sanctions in the form of curses. Notable among these curses are various threats associated with death: death itself, denial of burial, destruction of the corpse, deprivation of rites which provide care for the dead. Most powerful are those curses which seem to suggest that the transgressor will not only suffer death but will also be excluded, one way or another, from the organized community of the dead.

On occasion, it appears that the transgressor is punished whether he is dead or alive; he does not escape retribution. Thus, the living criminal is killed, his ghost made to wander, and even his remains destroyed. For his part, the criminal who had died before being punished is deprived of mortuary rites; moreover, his burial may be reversed by exhumation and, occasionally, his remains destroyed. His ghost, too, is thus excluded from the community of the dead and made to wander. (Passages such as CH rev. xxvii, 34-40 and *VTE* 476-477—"above, among the living, may he (Shamash)/ they (the great gods) uproot him/you; below, in the earth, may he/they deprive his/your ghost of water"—may stipulate not only two sequential punishments for the same person, but also two separate, parallel punishments for either eventuality). The *eṭemmu*, then, does not escape punishment and may even lose its human identity. In this construction, as I understand it, the criminal must not only be killed but must also be kept from being integrated or reintegrated into the netherworld. For the netherworld and the heavens form a connected structure or even continuum, and if the criminal were allowed to remain in the netherworld, he would find a place in the cosmic state.

This approach to sanction involves the exclusion of the transgressor from the organized cosmos of the divine, the living, and the dead. It forms one of the underlying principles of Sargonid treaty ideology and explains the 'vengeful' behaviour of Esarhaddon and Assurbanipal to the corpses and skeletons of those who violated their treaty obligations. It operates no less in the symbolic sphere as evidenced, for example, by the anti-witchcraft ceremony *Maqlû* ('Burning'). *Maqlû* took place at the time of the annual reappearance of ghosts in Abu. One of its central purposes was to ensure that all witches be expelled and kept outside the organized social and cosmic community. 'Live' witches were judged and destroyed; 'dead' witches were captured and expelled. Thus, all witches were to be prevented from having a proper burial. They were deprived of burial in order to prevent them from finding a place in the netherworld and consequently in the cosmic state.

III. In the Hebrew Bible the *ʾiṭṭîm* are mentioned only in Isa 19:3: in an oracle against Egypt it is stated that Yahweh will "frustrate the spirit of Egypt and destroy their plans". In a reaction to this prophecy of doom the Egyptians are expected to intensify their divinatory practices, among which are "the consulting of mediums and the asking of *ʾiṭṭîm* for advice".

IV. *Bibliography*

T. ABUSCH, Mesopotamian Anti-Witchcraft Literature: Texts and Studies. Part I: The Nature of *Maqlû*: Its Character, Divisions, and Calendrical Setting, *JNES* 33 (1974) 251-262, esp. 259-261; ABUSCH, Ishtar's Proposal and Gilgamesh's Refusal: An Interpretation of *The Gilgamesh Epic,* Tablet 6, Lines 1-79, *HR* 26 (1986) 143-187; ABUSCH, Observations on the Cosmology, Imagery, and Social Setting of *Maqlû*, unpublished paper (1990), to be included in my forthcoming *Towards an Understanding of Maqlû* (HSS); M. BAYLISS, The Cult of Dead Kin in Assyria and Babylonia, *Iraq* 35 (1973) 115-125; J. BOTTÉRO, La mythologie de la mort en Mésopotamie ancienne, *Death in Mesopotamia* (ed. B. Alster, Mesopotamia 8; Copenhagen 1980) 25-52; J. BOTTÉRO, La création de l'homme et son nature dans le poème d'*Atraḫasîs*, *Societies and Languages of the Ancient Near East, Studies in Honour of I. M. Diakonoff* (Warminster 1982) 24-32; J. BOTTÉRO, Les morts et l'audelà dans les rituels en akkadien contre l'action des 'revenants', *ZA* 73 (1983) 153-203; E. CASSIN, Le mort: valeur et représentation en Mésopotamie ancienne, *La mort, les morts dans les sociétés anciennes* (eds. G. Gnoli & J.-P. Vernant; Cambridge 1982) 355-372; H. R. COHEN, *Biblical Hapax Legomena in the Light of Akkadian and Ugaritic* (SBL DS 37; Missoula 1978) 42; I. L. FINKEL, Necromancy in Ancient Mesopotamia, *AfO* 29-30 (1983-1984) 1-17; S. A. GELLER, Some Sound and Word Plays in the First Tablet of the Old Babylonian *Atramhasīs* Epic, *The Frank Talmage Memorial Volume* I (ed. B. Walfish; Haifa 1993); B. GRONEBERG, Zu den mesopotamischen Unterweltsvorstellungen: Das Jenseits als Fortsetzung des Diesseits, *AoF* 17 (1990) 244-261; T. JACOBSEN, The lil$_2$ of ^{d}En-lil$_2$, *Dumu e2-dub-ba-a, Studies in Honor of Ake W. Sjöberg* (eds. H. Behrens *et al.*; Philadelphia 1989) 267-276, esp. 271-275; J. SCURLOCK, *Magical Means of Dealing with Ghosts in Ancient Mesopotamia* (unpublished dissertation, University of Chicago 1988); K. SPRONK, *Beatific Afterlife in Ancient Israel and in the Ancient Near East* (AOAT 219; Neukirchen-Vluyn 1986) 96-125; A. TSUKIMOTO, *Untersuchungen zur Totenpflege* (kispum) *im alten Mesopotamien* (AOAT 216; Neukirchen-Vluyn 1985).

T. ABUSCH

EUPHRATES פרת

I. The MT refers to the Euphrates as *Pĕrāt*, 'Euphrates', *nĕhar Pĕrāt*, 'River Euphrates', and as *(han)nāhār*, '(the) River'. The designation *hannāhār haggādôl*, 'the

Great River', was applied to the Euphrates (Gen 15:18; Deut 1:7; Josh 1:4) as well as to the Tigris (Dan 10:4). The two streams appear as a pair in the dual *nahărayim*, 'the two rivers', confined to the expression *ʾăram nahărayim*, '(Western) Mesopotamia'.

Hebr *Pĕrāt* (and its Qumran variant *Purat*, פורת, 1QapGen xxi 12.17.28; 1QM ii 11) derives from Akk *Purattu* <*Purantu*, cf. the forms *Purantum* in the Mari letters and *Puranatu(m)* in Ebla lists (**a** *bù-la-na-tim* = *māwī Puranatim*, *ARET* 5 [1984] no. 3 iv 2-3 & p. 23) and first millennium texts from Assur (*Atr.* 149). The Hurrian forms are *Puranti* and *Uruttu*, while the river occurs in Hittite texts as *Purana* (*RGTC* 6 [1978] 396-398). The Akkadian designation is likely to go back to a pre-Sumerian name. The female ending, characteristic of the Akkadian form but lacking in the Hittite variant *Purana*, shows that the Euphrates was conceived as a female entity. It should be noted that not all rivers are female, cf. →Hubur. The name Euphrates comes from Gk Εὐφράτης which, in its turn, is based on Old-Pers *Ufrâtu*.

The Euphrates occurs as a divine name outside the Bible in Mari and Babylonia.

II. Whereas in Akkadian texts from 2000 BCE onward the Euphrates is never preceded by the divine determinative (in contrast to the →Tigris), the river occurs as a deity in pre-Sargonic lists from Mari (written ^{d}**kib-nu-na**, *MARI* 5 [1987] 92). The evidence for the deification of the river is thus limited to the West, though this may be sheer coincidence. As a deity, the Euphrates appears in these early texts as a *numen loci*, comparable to →Assur, →Hubur, etc.

Judging by the epigraphical evidence of the second and first millennium BCE, the Euphrates lost its divine aura. In a greeting formula in a Middle Babylonian letter there is a reference to 'the gods of the Euphrates' (*BE* 17/1 [1908] no. 87:5). The expression is curious, but does not seem to imply that a divine nature was ascribed to the river, though an echo of its earlier deification can still be heard in some of the anthroponyms. In the Old Babylonian names Mar-Purattum, 'Son-of-Euphrates', and Purattum-ummī, 'Euphrates-is-my-mother' (*RGTC* 3 [1980] 305) and the North Syrian name Iš-Puratte [=*ʾiṯ-Purattu, 'The-Euphrates-is-present', cf. such names as ʾEt-Baʿal] (*Emar* no. 138: 34), the name of the river functions as a theophoric element, witness the comparison with analogous names. The fact that the name does not bear a divine determinative indicates that people were no longer aware of its original significance.

A mythological speculation found in *Enūma eliš* V 55 says that the Euphrates and the Tigris sprung from the eyes of →Tiamat, the divine antagonist of →Marduk. An esoteric commentary from the first millennium BCE specifies that "the Tigris is her right eye, the Euphrates is her left eye" (*SAA* 3 [1989], no. 39 r.3). Since both Tiamat and the Tigris are known as deities, such speculation may imply the same for the Euphrates. The gradual reduction of the Babylonian pantheon did not leave room for the Euphrates as an independent deity. But it retained a divine function, as is shown by a statement in a theological speculative text saying that it is the Euphrates "which served Shamash" (*RA* 60 [1966] 73:10). The justification for this view seems to have been the practice of the water ordeal (→River), an important judicial instrument and as such associated with the god of justice (→Sun).

The analysis of the place of the Euphrates in Mesopotamian mythology is complicated somewhat by the fact that the god Irḫan has been identified with the Euprates. Irḫan is both a river-god and a snake-god. In an Akkadian hymn to Nisaba, the grain-goddess, he is called 'father of all the gods', which shows that he is a form of the primeval River (*RLA* 6, 220). The lexical series Antagal identifies him with the Euphrates (*MSL* 17 [1985] 233 no. 24.2:6'); the series Erimḫuš with the Araḫtu, a branch of the Euphrates passing through Babylon (*MSL* 17 [1985] 82:48). Identification with the Euphrates suggests that Irḫan came to be regarded as female. In incantations, she is referred to as "river Irḫan with her banks" (CT 23 Pl. 1:7; 2:20; *BAM* no. 124 iv

7//127:7) and credited with powers of healing, since a drawing of Irḫan is used in therapeutic rituals (CT 23 Pl. 1:2.12). Rabbinical tradition on the beneficial effects of "bathing in the waters of the Euphrates" (*b. Ketub.* 77b) probably preserves the Babylonian view.

Despite occasional identification with the god Irḫan, the Euphrates cannot have been commonly regarded as divine in the second and first millennia BCE. In current usage, the name of the river never bears the divine determinative. Though originally belonging to the pre-Sargonic pantheon of Mari and Ebla, the river was only deified in later times inasfar as it was conceived as a manifestation of the god Nāru (→River) or Irḫan. The latter were forms of the primeval River. It had an important place in the cosmology of the ancients, being the frontier between the earth and the netherworld (cf. J. BOTTÉRO, CRRA 26 [1980] 31).

III. In the more than fifty passages where the Euphrates is mentioned in the Bible, the river is never ascribed divine status. It occurs mostly as a topographical point of reference. As such it marks the northern border, ideally, of the promised land (e.g., Gen 15:18). From the perspective of the Deuteronomists, it is the frontier between two distinct cultures (cf. Josh 24:2.3.14.15).

In a few instances, however, the Euphrates takes on mythological dimensions. In the Paradise Myth, the Euphrates is one of the four branches into which the stream springing from Eden divides (Gen 2:14). Eden, the "garden of God" (Ezek 28:13), equivalent to the "mountain of God" (Ezek 28:16), is to be located in the North (Isa 14:13), more specifically in the Northwest, the region of the Amanus and Antilebanon mountains (→Lebanon). According to a semi-mythical topography, the sources of the four life-giving waters of the universe, one of which was the Euphrates, are here. Together with the Pishon, the Gihon and the Tigris, the other Paradisiac streams, the Euphrates is mentioned in Sir 24:25-27 as an image of the overflow of Wisdom bestowed by the Law.

The Euphrates, being a branch of the primeval river, could be associated with an unknown land inhabited by people long since vanished. It is in this sense that the apocalyptic writings elaborated upon the Isaianic prophecy according to which the remnant of Israel in Assyria would return by way of the Euphrates, smitten into seven channels (Isa 11:15). In Rev 16:12, the dried-up bed of the Euphrates functions as a highway for "the kings from the east", perhaps a designation of the rulers of the nether world. In Rev 9:14, the river is the boundary between the world of the living and the realm of the dead: four death-dealing angels were kept in check on the Euphrates. According to 2 Esd 13:39-45, finally, the Israelites, whom Shalmaneser took captive, found refuge in Arzareth, "a region where no human being had ever lived", which they reached by the narrow passages of the Euphrates. This 'Other Land', as Arzareth can be rendered (Hebr *ʾereṣ ʾaḥeret*), stands for the nether world, from which the dispersed Israelites would return in the end of time. On their way back, "the Most High will stop the channels of the river again" (2 Esd 13:47), so that they might pass the river of death. This concept might be based on an interpretation of 2 Kgs 17:6 // 18:11 in which the Habur river near Gozan, to which the Israelite were exiled, is interpreted as the Hubur, river of death.

To some extent, then, the view of the later Biblical writings reflects Babylonian mythology. To the Mesopotamians of the first millennium BCE, the Euphrates is divine inasmuch as it is an aspect of the primeval river linking the earth with the underworld. Though the Euphrates never has divine status in the Biblical texts, it does have a mythological significance inasmuch as it is considered to be a branch of the Primeval River and marks the line of transition between the world of the living and the regions beyond: that is, the kingdom of the dead.

IV. *Bibliography*

T. S. FRYMER-KENSKY, *The Judicial Ordeal in the Ancient Near East* (Yale 1977) 583-

596; M. KREBERNIK, *Die Beschwörungen aus Fara und Ebla* (Hildesheim, Zürich & New York 1984) 298-300; G. MEIER, Eufrat, *RLA* 2 (1938) 483-484.

K. VAN DER TOORN

EVE חוה

I. Eve is mentioned by name four times in the Bible, twice in Genesis and twice in NT. It is after the 'fall' narrated in Gen 3:1-19 that the Man (*hāʾādām*) names his wife *Ḥawwâ* ('Eve', LXX *Zoē*); because 'she was the mother of all living things' (*kî hîʾ hāyĕtâ ʾēm kol-ḥay*). The tradition understands a significant link between name and function, suggesting that *ḥawwâ* is to be related etymologically to *ḥayâ*, 'live' (old ḥayin waw for later ḥayin yodh). Cf. Ugaritic *ḥyy/ḥwy* (*UT* §19. 856). WALLACE (1985:151) sees a Ugaritic noun *ḥwt*, meaning 'life', in such passages as *KTU* 2.27. 2, 15 etc. This may not be the scientific etymology, but is the theological link made by the author. She is 'born' from the Man's side, being formed from a rib (Gen 2:21-23). Within the confines of this story, Eve is the prototypical woman, and is wholly created. (The Man is also her 'mother' in a sense.) Many commentators have noted Aramaic *ḥewyaʾ* and variants, and Arabian *ḥayya*, meaning 'serpent'. WALLACE (1985:148) draws attention to *Gen. Rab.* 20, which gives a rabbinic assessment: 'the serpent is your (sc. Eve's) serpent and you are Adam's serpent'. The Theban 'Qadeshet' stelae have also been adduced as parallels. But WALLACE's attempt to link these to Ugaritic Athirat on the basis of the term *qdš*, (1985:155) is misconceived. The Egyptian form is *qdšt*.

II. It is evident, that despite Eve's present creaturely status, various fragments of mythological tradition are present in the story, and various scholars have concluded from these that a goddess lies behind Eve. Thus, the Sumerian divine name **nin.ti**, 'Lady of Life' (*AGE* 419), which is structurally similar to the aetiology for Eve offered above, and is itself ambiguous in meaning, having also the sense 'Lady of the Rib', is cited by GASTER (1969:21). KIKAWADA (1972:33) draws attention to the Akkadian formula *bēlet kala ili*, 'Mistress of all the gods', applied to the goddess Mami in *Atr.* I 246-248, and suggests that Mami underlies Eve, who is however supposedly demythologised (34-35). We may also add, from a nearer cultural milieu, the epithets of Ugaritic Athirat (→Asherah), *qnyt ilm* ('Progenitrix of the gods', *KTU* 1.4 i:22 etc.) and *um il[m]*, ('mother of the gods', *KTU* 2.31. 43). A goddess named *Ḥwt* appears in *KAI* 89. 1, in a votive stela from the Carthaginian necropolis, beginning with the invocation *rbt ḥwt ʾlt mlkt...*: 'Great Lady, Havvat, Goddess, Queen(?)!' HROZNY (1932: 121-122) proposed that *ḥwt* is related to the Hurrian divine name →Hebat. She was the consort of Teshub, the Hurrian storm-god.

III. The second OT reference to Eve (MT *Ḥawwâ*, LXX *Eua*) is in Gen 4:1, where on giving birth to →Cain, Eve cries in triumph "I have given birth to a man by Yahweh!" or "I have acquired a husband, Yahweh!" Both senses are possible, though hardly the usual meaning adduced, "I have acquired/ begotten a man *with the help of* Yahweh!" unless it be conceded that the implications of the phrase are not compatible with →Adam's paternity. Whether Yahweh is the father of the man she has begotten or the husband she has acquired, the implication is that Eve plays the role of, indeed is, a goddess. It is all the more remarkable that MT has preserved such clear echoes in contradiction of the opening phrase "the Man had intercourse with his wife Eve". Since Cain bears many features of a 'first Man', however, it is not unreasonable to see the generations preceding him—Man (*ʾĀdām*) born from the soil (*ʾădāmâ*), Woman (*ʾiššâ*) born from man (*ʾîš*)—as being originally divine generations in an old theogonic tradition, of which mere echoes survive. A further hint of this perspective is supplied if we enquire into the origins of Cain's wife who abruptly appears in 4:17; the simplest solution is to understand her to be his mother, so that human origins go back to an incest myth which is at the same time the epitome of the sacred marriage (WYATT 1986; cf. the story of Lot and his daughters in Gen 19:30-38). It is also of interest, in view of the different scenarios offered for the origins of Yahwism (with →Moses, Exod 3:13-15; 6:2-3; Abram, Gen 12:7; Cain or Enosh, Gen 4:26 [see LEWY, *VT* 6 [1956] 429-435), that Eve refers to the deity by name.

In much of this discussion, the symbolic elements emerging suggest a link of some kind between Eve and the goddess Asherah: wife of Yahweh, linked to a tree, the mother of a 'primal man' (sc. royal) figure, autochthonous (thus legitimizing territorial control) etc. Tantalising though this is, however, it is difficult to prove any links, not least because of the problematic status of Asherah in Israel and Judah.

The NT references to Eve, in 2 Cor 11:3 and 1 Tim 2:13, offer nothing in the present context, simply providing the classical Christian interpretation of the Eden narrative as the 'fall', with Eve (the prototype of all women) primarily culpable because she yielded to the serpent's seduction. In mediaeval hermeneutics much was made of →Mary's role as the antitype of Eve ('the second Eve'), and the old ideological symbols are reinforced (cf. O'REILLY 1992).

IV. *Bibliography*

T. H. GASTER, *Myth, Legend and Custom in the Old Testament* (London 1969) 21; H. GRESSMANN, Mythische Reste in der Paradieserzählung, *ARW* 10 (1907) 345-367; J. HELLER, Der Name Eva, *ArOr* 26 (1958) 636-656; B. HROZNY, Une inscription de Ras-Šamra en langue churrite, *ArOr* 4 (1932) 118-129; I. M. KIKAWADA, Two Notes on Eve, *JBL* 91 (1972) 33-37; J. O'REILLY, The Trees of Eden in Mediaeval Iconography, *A walk in the garden* (eds. P. Morris & D. Sawyer, JSOTSup 136; Sheffield 1992) 167-204; J. SKINNER, *Genesis* (ICC; Edinburgh 1910) 85-87; N. WALKER, Adam and Eve and Adon, *ZAW* 74 (1962) 66-68; H. N. WALLACE, *The Eden Narrative* (HSM 32; Atlanta 1985) 147-181; C. WESTERMANN, *Genesis 1-11* (London 1984) 268-269; A. J. WILLIAMS, The Relationship of Gen 3:20 to the Serpent, *ZAW* 89 (1977) 357-374; N. WYATT, Cain's Wife, *Folklore* 97 (1986) 88-95, 232.

N. WYATT

EVERLASTING GOD → EL-OLAM

EVIL SPIRIT OF GOD רוח אלהים רעה

I. There are references to 'an evil spirit' (*rûaḥ rāʿâ*) sent by God in Judg 9:23 and 1 Sam 16:23. In the latter case, the spirit which afflicts Saul is also called *rûaḥ ʾĕlōhîm rāʿâ,* 'an evil spirit of God' or 'evil divine spirit' (1 Sam 16:15.16; 18:10), *rûaḥ YHWH rāʿâ,* 'an evil spirit of Yahweh' (1 Sam 19:9), and, in its first occurrence, *rûaḥ rāʿâ mēʾēt YHWH,* 'an evil spirit *from* Yahweh' (1 Sam 16:14).

Rûaḥ, the Hebrew word commonly translated 'spirit', has primary meanings of both 'breath' and 'wind'. The notion of 'spirit' arose in part from an abstraction of the concept of breath as the animating force of a living being. Spirits retain the character of winds inasmuch as they move about invisibly.

II. Other ancient Near Eastern civilizations shared this understanding of spirits. Winds that affect human fortunes are described in Mesopotamian texts in terms of a contrast between the 'good wind' (*šāru ṭābu*) and the 'evil wind' (*šāru lemnu* or *šāru lā ṭābu*), the latter being exemplified especially by a group of seven evil spirits deemed responsible for a variety of human afflictions and miseries (see R. C. THOMPSON, *Devils and Evil Spirits of Babylonia* [New York 1976 repr.] 1: XLVII-XLVI). A proposal (RIESSLER 1911:118) to recover an allusion to this group in Mic 5:4 by revocalizing MT *šibʿâ rōʿîm,* 'seven shepherds', as *šibʿâ rāʿîm,* 'seven evil (spirits),' has received only limited acceptance (cf. SELLIN 1922:290; SARACINO 1983:265-266). Similarly, Egyptian texts associate diseases with wind-born evil spirits, agents of the lion-goddess Sekhmet, who surreptitiously introduce afflictions into the body via the left ear (cf. P. GHALIOUNGUI, *Magic and Medical Science in Ancient Egypt* [London 1963] 74-75).

III. The *rûaḥ*, 'spirit,' 'wind' or 'breath', of →Yahweh or God is often mentioned in the OT as a vehicle of divine intervention in human affairs (1 Kgs 18:12; 2 Kgs 2:16). The spirit of Yahweh enables individuals to assume roles of leadership (Num 11:17.24; Judg 3:10); the spirit of God inspires them to prophesy (Num 24:2) and may manifest itself in berserk or frenzied behaviour (Judg 14:19; 15:14-15). On a small number of occasions, God sends a spirit that is harmful or hostile, that is, 'an evil spirit' (*rûaḥ rāʿâ*). As stated explicitly in Judg 9:24.56-57, the purpose of the evil spirit that God places between Abimelech and the lords of Shechem (v 23) is to punish Abimelech for the assassination of his brothers (v 5) and the people of Shechem for their complicity in the fratricide. The evil spirit that afflicts Saul seems to come to him as a replacement for the spirit of God that entered him when he was chosen by Yahweh to lead Israel (1 Sam 11:6) and, at least initially, expressed itself in the form of prophetic frenzy (10:6.10; cf. 19:19-24). This spirit of God departed from Saul after Yahweh rejected him (1 Sam 16:14). So the evil spirit serves in the narrative as an objectification of Yahweh's abandonment of Saul; especially in contrast to David who has been chosen to supplant him. David is brought to court to alleviate Saul's suffering by playing the lyre (1 Sam 16:16), and at first the music causes the evil spirit to depart (v 23). Because of David's achievements on the battlefield, however, his popularity grows and Saul becomes increasingly jealous (1 Sam 18:6-9). When the evil spirit torments him again, he goes berserk and attempts to kill David while he is playing (1 Sam 18:10-11; cf. 19:8-10).

Neither the evil spirit in Judg 9 nor the evil spirit in 1 Sam 16-19 is personified. The former manifests itself in an attitude of hostility between Abimelech and the lords of Shechem; the latter in Saul's unstable psychological condition. On the other hand, "a certain spirit" (*hārûaḥ*) introduced in 1 Kgs 22:21, although never explicitly described as 'evil', might be cited as an example of an evil spirit that is personified and depicted as at least partly independent of Yahweh. In the vision of Micaiah, son of Yimlah (1 Kgs 22:19-22), this spirit steps forward before the throne of Yahweh in the heavenly courtroom and volunteers to entice Ahab to take part in the battle of Ramoth-gilead, where he will be slain (cf. 2 Kgs 19:7). The spirit does this by acting as 'a lying spirit (*rûaḥ šeqer*) in the mouth of all [Ahab's] prophets' (vv 22.23). Another *rûaḥ* that should be mentioned in this regard is the 'wind' that brushes the face of Eliphaz in his sleep, stops at his bedside and expounds on the subject of the impossibility of human perfection in light of the failings of angels (Job 4:12-21). This spirit, which seems to operate quite independently of God, has a discernible form (*tĕmûnâ,* v 17), so that what Eliphaz sees can be called an apparition, comparable to the appearance of the ghost or spirit of Samuel to Saul (1 Sam 28:8-19), though this is not characteristic of encounters with a spirit in the OT.

IV. *Bibliography*

R. ALBERTZ & C. WESTERMANN, *rwḥ THAT* II (1971) 726-753; C. DOHMEN, *rʿʿ TWAT* 7 (1990-1992) 582-611, esp. 600-601; H.-J. FABRY, *rwḥ TWAT* 7 (1990-1992) 385-425, esp. 411-12 [&lit]; F. LINDSTRÖM, *God and the Origin of Evil* (ConB, OT Series 21; Lund 1983); P. RIESSLER, *Die kleinen Propheten* (Rottenburg 1911); F. SARACINO, A State of Siege: Mi 5 4-5 and an Ugaritic Prayer, *ZAW* 95 (1983) 263-269; E. SELLIN, *Das Zwölfprophetenbuch* (KAT 12; Leipzig 1922).

P. K. MCCARTER

EXALTED ONES שׁנים

I. The expression *bĕqereb šānîm*, occurring twice in Hab 3:2 and traditionally rendered as 'within years; in the midst of the years' or the like (*HALAT* 1478), has been interpreted as referring to deities: 'when the Exalted Ones are approaching …' (REIDER 1954; WIEDER 1974) or as an epithet for →Yahweh 'The Exalted One' (HAAK 1992). This proposal is connected with the interpretation of a Ugaritic epithet for →El *ab šnm* which is then supposed to mean 'Father of the Exalted Ones'.

II. The translation 'father of the years' for *ab šnm* read as **abu šanima* being an epithet for El as the oldest among the Ugaritic gods (→Ancient of Days), is not unchallenged. Two different objections are made. 1) The plural of the Ugaritic noun for 'years' is normally construed in the feminine *šnt* and not with the masculine *šnm*. Therefore, scholars have been arguing for different interpretations of the noun (see D. PARDEE, *UF* 20 [1988] 196 n. 2 for the manifold proposals). 2) *šnm* occurs as the second element in the binomial deity *Ṯkmn-w-Šnm*, →Thukamuna; →Shunama. H. GESE (*RAAM* 97-98, 193-104); A. JIRKU (*Šnm* (Schunama), der Sohn des Gottes 'Il, *ZAW* 82 [1970] 278-279) and C. H. GORDON (El, Father of Šnm, *JNES* 35 [1976] 261-262) read the expression *ab šnm* as 'the father of Shunama'.

One of the alternative interpretations of *šnm* is to construe it as a noun meaning 'the Exalted Ones' (e.g. REIDER 1954; POPE 1955:33; J. GRAY, *The Legacy of Canaan* [VTSup 5; Leiden ²1965] 189. 205; WIEDER 1974). The interpretation implies a root III ŠNH 'to be exalted' which is attested in Hebrew (Prov 24:21. 22; Esth 2:9) but does not occur in Ugaritic (*pace* J. A. EMERTON, *VT* 24 [1974] 25-30; *šntk* in *KTU* 1.2 i:10; 1.16 vi:58 means 'your years'; cf. *ARTU* 30, 223). Moreover, two remarks should be made. 1) The epithet *ab šnm* occurs only in a formulaic sentence: "She/He/They appeared in the encampment of El and entered the camp of the King, the Father of Years" (Baal-epic: *KTU* 1.1 iii:23-34; 1.2 v:6; 1.3 v:7-8; 1.4 iv:23-24; 1.5 vi:1-2; 1.6 i:35-36; Aqhat: *KTU* 1.17 vi:48-49). 2) Although *šnm* is not the regular plural for the feminine noun 'year', it should be noted that other nouns have variant plural-forms; e.g. *riš*, 'head', is attested in the plural as *rišt* as well as *rišm*. These remarks imply that the interpretation 'Father of the Exalted Ones; Exalted Father' is less probable than the rendering 'Father of years'.

III. The expression in Hab 3:2 is best understood when reading *biqrob šānîm*, 'In the approaching of the years ...' (e.g. B. MARGULIS, *ZAW* 82 [1970] 413). An interpretation of *šānîm* as referring to a deity is not supported by the ancient versions (COPELAND 1992).

IV. *Bibliography*

P. E. COPELAND, The Midst of the Years, *Text as Pretext* (FS R. Davidson; R. P. Carroll ed.; JSOTSup 138; Sheffield 1992) 91-105; R. HAAK, *Habakkuk* (VTSup 44; Leiden 1992) 79-80; M. H. POPE, *El in the Ugaritic Literature* (VTSup 2; Leiden 1955) 33; J. REIDER, Etymological Studies in Biblical Hebrew, *VT* 4 (1954) 283-284; A. A. WIEDER, Three philological Notes, *Bulletin of the Institute of Jewish Studies* 2 (1974) 108-109.

B. BECKING

EXOUSIAI → AUTHORITIES

F

FACE פנים

I. In quite a number of biblical texts the *pānîm* of YHWH is YHWH's hypostatic Presence. Thus it serves the same function as *Šēm* →'Name' in Deuteronomistic theology, *Kābôd* →'Glory' in the Priestly tradition, and *Shekinah* in later Jewish writings. By recourse to such concepts, the ancient Israelites were able to speak of the deity's simultaneous transcendence and immanence.

II. Elsewhere in the ancient Near East, *pan* 'face' or 'presence' is also used in the sense of the persona or some representation of deity. So the goddess Tannit is frequently known in Punic inscriptions as *pn bʿl* (*KAI* 78:2; 79:1, 10-11; 85:1; 86:1; 87:2, 88:1; 137:1). The literal meaning of the epithet *pn bʿl* is 'the Face of →Baal' (i.e. *panē baʿl*), rather than 'the Pearl of Baal', as it is sometimes supposed. This is evident from the alternate spelling *pʿn bʿl* (*KAI* 94:1; 97:1; 102:1; 105:1) and from the Greek transcriptions of the name as *phanē bal* (*KAI* 175:2) and *phenē bal* (*KAI* 176:2-3). Some scholars have argued that *pn bʿl* is to be interpreted as a place name like *pĕnûʾēl* ('the Face of God') in the Bible, and they cite *Prosōpon Theou* ('the Face of God'), said to be the name of a promontory north of Byblos (HALEVY 1874). But coins from the Roman period depicting a warrior goddess have been found in Palestine stamped with the name *phanēbalos*, evidently the Greek form of Semitic *panē baʿl* (HILL 1914). Indeed, one of the coins bears both the name of the deity and a triangular symbol identified as 'the sign of Tannit' (DOTHAN 1974). Thus, *pn bʿl* is probably not a place-name, but an epithet. This designation of the deity as *pn bʿl* is very similar to the epithet of the goddess ʿAṯtart/ʿAštart *šm bʿl* "the Name of Baal" attested in the Eastern Mediterrannean coast (*KTU* 1.16 vi:56 [cf. 1.2 iv:28]; *KAI* 14:18). The similarity of the epithets of these goddesses is particularly intriguing in the light of the name *tntʿštrt* 'Tannit-ʿAštart' found in a Phoenician inscription from Sarepta (PRITCHARD 1978). Indeed, it is possible that the role of ʿAṯtart/ʿAštart in the Eastern Mediterranean world was replaced in North Africa by the goddess Tannit, a development evidenced in part by the dominance of Tannit in the texts along with the persistence of theophoric ʿAštart names (CROSS 1973). In any case, *pn bʿl* appears to be the equivalent of *šm bʿl* (cf. also the Hebrew proper names *pĕnûʾēl* and *šĕmûʾēl*).

One may surmise that 'name' and 'face' mean the same thing essentially, inasmuch as each is representative of its subject. Thus, as ʿAṯtart (→Astarte) in Ugaritic mythology represents Baal-Hadad, so one may assume that Tannit somehow represents →Baal-Hamon in North Africa. Furthermore, 'face' (presentation > appearance) may be semantically related to →'image' (representation > likeness). If so, one may also consider Akkadian personal names like [d]BE-*ṣal-mu*-DINGIR.MEŠ '(the god) Ea is the image (representative) of the gods' (see *CAD* Ṣ 85). Greek lexicographers identify a certain goddess known as *Salambas* (Etymologicum Magnum) or *Salambo* (Hesychius), names which are universally recognized by scholars as coming from Semitic *ṣlm bʿl* 'Image of Baal'. This deity is identified in the sources as the goddess →Aphrodite-Astarte. As is well attested in Akkadian literature, the *ṣalmu* 'image' represents or substitutes for the presence of kings and deities. So, too, Aphrodite-Astarte was recognized as representing Baal in some way. The epithet *ṣlm bʿl* is in fact analogous to Phoen *sml bʿl* 'statue/image of Baal', which appears in an inscription from the Roman period dedicated "to our lord and to the image of Ba'l" (*KAI* 12:3-4; cf. the personal name *Pnsmlt* 'presence of the image' in *KAI* 57). In sum, the expressions *pn*-DN, *šm*-DN, *ṣml*-DN, and *slm*-DN in each case refer to a representation or a representative of the deity in question.

III. As in many other languages, the Hebrew word for 'face' (*pānîm*) may be used in the broader sense of 'presence'. The word may also be a metonym for 'person'. Thus, in secular usage, 'bind their faces' (Job 40:13) means 'bind their persons', hence 'bind them' (// *ṭomnēm* 'hide them'). By the same token, Hushai's political counsel to Absalom was issued thus: "I advise that all Israel from Dan to Beersheba be gathered to you—as numerous as the sand by the sea—and that you personally (lit. 'your face/presence') go into battle" (2 Sam 17:11). A similar usage of the word may be discerned in Pss 42:6 (reading *yĕšû'ôt pānay wē'lōhay*), 12; 43:5; Prov 7:15. The Greek word *prosōpon* may, likewise, refer to the whole person (1 Thes 2:17; 2 Cor 5:12).

Since *pānîm* may mean personal presence, the idiom *pānîm 'el pānîm* "face to face" (also *pānîm bĕpānîm* in Deut 5:4) signifies the most direct and personal encounter, but, curiously, only of human beings with the numinous (Gen 32:30; Exod 33:11; Deut 34:10; Judg 6:22; Ezek 20:35; cf. Gk *prosōpon pros prosōpon* in 1 Cor 13:12). It is in this sense of a direct encounter that the Bible sometimes speaks of seeing the 'face' of the deity, despite the tradition asserting that no one can see face of the deity and live (Exod 33:10). The idiom is rooted in cultic language articulating the personal experience of divine presence, perhaps in a theophany or vision (Pss 11:7; 17:15; cf. 42:3). The related expression 'to seek the face' of the deity, similarly, means to seek divine presence, as the parallelism in Ps 105:3 suggests. In various Akkadian texts, too, the idiom *amāru pānī* 'to see the face of NN' means to visit someone personally and it is used of encounters with kings and deities (*CAD* A/II, 21-22). It is from the cultic use of the idiom that personal names of the types *Pān-DN-lūmur* "May I see the face of DN" and *Pān-DN-adaggal* "I will look upon the face of DN" are derived (STAMM 1969). The Akkadian idiom 'to see the face (of the deity)' probably had its origin in the confrontation of the cult image (*ṣalmu*) in the sanctuary; those who went to the temple literally 'saw' a representation of the deity. Israel's strong tradition of aniconism, of course, does not permit such a literal interpretation of the related Hebrew idioms. On the other hand, the technical term *lipnê YHWH* 'before →YHWH' (lit. 'at the face of YHWH') very often implies some kind of representation of YHWH's presence, notably the Ark, the functional equivalent of the cult image in ancient Israel. Thus, David danced "before YHWH" (2 Sam 6:5.14.16.21), Hezekiah prayed "before YHWH" who is said to be enthroned on the cherubim in the temple (Isa 37:14-20 = 2 Kgs 19:14-19), and the Israelites passed on "before YHWH" as they crossed the Jordan (Num 32:21.27.29; cf. "pass on before the Ark of YHWH" in Josh 4:5). Various ritual acts are said to be performed "before YHWH" (Lev 1:5; Josh 18:6; Judg 20:26). It has been argued, therefore, that *lipnê YHWH/'ĕlōhîm* in cultic contexts is virtually synonymous with 'before the Ark' (DAVIES 1963). Thus, all occurrences of "before YHWH" and "before →God" in the Enthronement Psalms are thought to allude to the presence of the Ark (Pss 95:6; 96:13; 97:5; 98:9), and the placing of cultic objects "before YHWH" is taken to mean that they were placed before the Ark (Exod 16:33, an anachronistic text; cf. v 34). Others consider the expression typically to imply the presence of a sanctuary, but that conclusion cannot be sustained (FOWLER 1987). One can only say that *pānîm* is closely associated with divine presence, which is at times symbolized by the presence of cultic objects. It is not amiss, in any case, to observe that the *leḥem (hap)pānîm* "bread of Presence" (Exod 25: 30; 35:13; 39:36; 1 Sam 21:7; 1 Kgs 7:48; 2 Chron 4:19) was placed in the tabernacle and its table was known as *šulḥan happānîm* "the table of Presence" (Num 4:7; cf. 2 Chr 29:18).

The usage of *pānîm* for divine presence is most evident in Exod 33:14-16, where it is said that the deity's *pānîm* will go with the people. There *pānîm* means divine Presence; the idiom *pānîm hōlĕkîm* in this context does not mean simply 'to go before' and hence 'to lead' (SPEISER 1967), for the deity is said to be 'with' the people, not 'before' them (vv 14-16). The LXX takes *pānîm* in this context to refer to God personally, translating the term as *autos su* 'you yourself'; but Targ. Onkelos takes it as a reference to the Shekinah, God's hypostatic Presence (so Rashi). It is not clear that *pānîm* here is a hypostasis; it may well be that the meaning is that YHWH will go with the people *personally* (cf. 2 Sam 17:11). Nevertheless, the text goes on quickly to ensure that the deity's transcendence is not forgotten; it makes clear that the accompanying Presence does not mean that mortals can literally see the deity's face (v 20). Moses asked only to see God's *Kābôd* →'Glory' (v 18), and the deity willed only that his *ṭûb* 'Goodness' should pass by and his *Šēm* →'Name' is proclaimed (v 19). Clearly, the passage speaks of the deity's immanence, but not at the expense of the notion of transcendence.

Other passages that mention the deity's *pānîm* likewise reflect this theological tension between transcendence and immanence. So →Jacob is said to have seen God "face to face" (Gen 32:30), but the account of his encounter at Jabbok speaks of the opponent only as *ʾîš* 'a person' and later traditions refers to the stranger as *malʾāk* 'an →angel' (Hos 12:5). In Deut 5:4, YHWH spoke to →Moses "face to face" but the words came out of the fire, and elsewhere it is emphasized that Moses heard only the voice out of the fire "but saw no form" (Deut 4:12.15). Moreover, in contrast to Exod 33:14-16, it is not the *pānîm* itself that goes with the people; rather, YHWH is said to have led the people out of Egypt *with* his *pānîm* (Deut 4:27). This is another attempt to preserve the notion of transcendence. The *pānîm* here represents the deity's presence; it is not literally the deity's *person*, but the divine *persona*, as it were.

Isa 63:9 is most suggestive in this regard, although the interpretations of the MT (supported by 1QIsa[a]) and LXX are at variance. The former suggests that it is the "angel of Presence" (*malʾak pānâyw*) that delivered Israel from Egypt. The latter, however, contrasts angels with YHWH's *pānîm*: "not an angel or a messenger; his Presence delivered them". Here the LXX interprets *pānîm* as *Autos* (the deity *himself*), as in Exod 33:14. In either case, *pānîm* refers in some sense to YHWH's presence to save (cf. *Odes Sol.* 25:4). Elsewhere, however, the deity's *pānîm* is also capable of destruction. Thus, in Lam 4:16 it is YHWH's *pānîm* that destroys people (cf. Ps 34:17), and people perish at the rebuke of YHWH's *pānîm* (Ps 80:17).

IV. The Hebrew Bible uses the term *pānîm* to speak of the presence of God, sometimes obliquely: the *pānîm* either *is*, or *represents*, the appearance of the deity. Later Jewish literature, however, goes beyond the idea of hypostatic Presence to designate a distinct celestial creature known as *malʾak pānîm* '(the) angel of Presence'. The concept appears to be a development of Isa 63:9, according to the tradition preserved in the MT and 1 QIsa[a], which attributes the deliverance of Israel to the 'angel of Presence'—probably a circumlocution for the deity's very presence. Later Jewish texts, however, speak not only of 'the angel of presence' in the singular (*Jub.* 1:27, 29; 2:1; 1QSb iv 25), but of several 'angels of presence' (*Jub.* 2:2, 18; 15:27; 31:14; *T. Judah* 25:2; *T. Levi* 3:5; 1 QH vi 13). The 'angels of Presence' minister to God in the heavenly abode and, as such, they are known as 'the ministers of Presence' or 'the ministers of the Glorious Presence' (4QSirSabb 40:24). In the angelic hierarchy, they and 'the angels of sanctification' are superior to all others (*Jub.* 2:18; 5:17). The literature even asserts that the elect will share a common lot with these 'angels of Presence' (1 QH vi

13) and become princes among them (*Jub.* 31:4; 1 QSb iv 25-26).

V. *Bibliography*

F. M. CROSS, *Canaanite Myth and Hebrew Epic* (Cambridge, Mass. 1973) 28-36; G. H. DAVIES, The Ark in the Psalms, *Promise and Fulfillment* (Edinburgh 1963) 60-61; *E. DHORME, L'emploi métaphorique des noms des parties du corps en hébreu et en akkadien. III. Le Visage, *RB* 30 (1921) 374-399; M. DOTHAN, A Sign of Tanit from Tel ʾAkko, *IEJ* 24 (1974) 44-49; M. D. FOWLER, The Meaning of *lipnê* YHWH in the Old Testament, *ZAW* 99 (1987) 384-390; J. HALÉVY, *Mélanges d'épigraphie et d'archéologie sémitiques* (Paris 1874) 42-48; G. F. HILL, *Catalogue of the Greek Coins of Palestine* (London 1914) 115-139; F. O. HVIDBERG-HANSEN, *La déesse TNT* (Copenhagen 1979) I, 15-18; F. NÖTSCHER, *"Das Angesicht Gottes schauen" nach biblischer und babylonischer Auffassung* (Würzburg 1969); J. B. PRITCHARD, *Recovering Sarepta, A Phoenician City* (Princeton 1978) 104-106; J. REINDL, *Das Angesicht Gottes im Sprachgebrauch des Alten Testaments* (Leipzig 1970); E. A. SPEISER, The Biblical Idiom *pānīm hōlekīm, The Seventy-Fifth Anniversary Volume of the Jewish Quarterly Review* (Philadelphia 1967) 515-517; J. J. STAMM, *Die akkadische Namengebung* (Darmstadt 1968) 195.203.

C. L. SEOW

FALSEHOOD שקר

I. The basic meaning of the verbal root *šqr*, attested inter alia in Hebrew, Old Aramaic, Jewish Aramaic, and Syriac is: 'to deceive, act perfidiously', with corresponding nominal derivations (cf. *HALAT* s.v. *šeqer*), not 'to lie', as has been established by KLOPFENSTEIN (1964; cf. KLOPFENSTEIN 1976:1010). In combination with the word *rûaḥ*, 'spirit', *šeqer* can personify the notion of falsehood in the Hebrew Bible. The Hebrew *qitl*-nominal-formation *šeqer* 'falsehood, deceit, perfidy' is often used in regard to false prophecy: the adversaries of Jeremiah 'prophesy falsehood' (*šeqer* Jer 14:14), or 'by (in the sense of: based on) falsehood' (*baššeqer* 5:31; 20:6, *bĕšeqer* 29:3), or 'for falsehood' (*laššeqer* 27:15); their divinations originate in 'fraudulent dreams' (*ḥălōmôt šeqer* 23:32; cf. οὖλος ὄνειρος below sub II) or in 'a fraudulent vision' (*ḥăzôn šeqer* 14:14). Isaiah speaks about 'prophets who teach falsehood' (Isa 9:14); according to Micah, a false prophet 'comes about with wind' (*hālak rûaḥ*) and 'lies falsehood' (*šeqer kizzēb*), preaching on beer and wine (2:11). For the holophrastic use of *šeqer* in the sense of 'that is not true' cf. 2 Kgs 9:12; Jer 37:14; 40:16. From phrases like that, we understand that the phenomenon of false salvation-prophecy is reflected as the outcome of *rûaḥ šeqer* 'a deceiving spirit' in 1 Kgs 22:19-23, an expression which is without any direct equivalent inside and outside the Bible; it is an ad hoc concept meant as a mythic means to come to terms with the perplexing way of God's economy. The same is true, on the other hand, when *ḥokmâ* 'wisdom' has the connotation of 'truth' as in Job 28; even *ḥokmôt* 'Lady →Wisdom' Prov 1:20; 9:1; 14:1 (*ḥkmh* Sir 24) need not be modelled after a consistent divine figure such as →Isis; it could be a personification of a common wisdom notion, a personification which later became conventional.

II. The only functional parallel to the *rûaḥ šeqer* of 1 Kgs 22 is the οὖλος ὄνειρος 'fraudulent dream' in Homer's *Iliad* II:6.9; cf. the *ḥălōmôt šeqer* Jer 23:32 mentioned above. By this misleading omen, Agamemnon is summoned to undertake a battle which destiny determines to be unsuccessful; this trick enables →Zeus to extract himself from an embarrassment in which he got involved because of the quarrel and distrust of the Olympians, especially on the part of the divine ladies. The motif is an attempt to overcome the ambivalent character of reality, disappointment at unforseeable and senseless misfortunes or at the nonfulfilment of oracles for instance—namely by its projection into the world of the gods.

The 'divine trickster' known from the phenomenology of religion is no parallel: this one is an inferior god or demon standing on the side of men to support them by deceiving the great gods or one of them—as does Prometheus, for example.

III. In 1 Kgs 22, we are told that the king of Israel, who, according to v 20, is to be identified with Ahab, has been seduced to enter into a hopeless battle by a band of false prophets; hopeless is the battle as Yahweh and his →council had doomed it to be so. The King of Israel is nevertheless guilty since he did not believe what the only authentic prophet of Yahweh, Micah ben Yimlah, was able to reveal about acts that really happened in the divine council; moreover, he ventured to outwit his destiny by manipulating his outward appearance (vv 30-37).

Yahweh himself sent one of the deities forming 'the →host of heaven' to become 'a deceiving spirit' in the mouth of the king's official prophets. The motif of a divine or human emissary sent out from a divine or human royal council is attested in Sumerian, Akkadian, Ugaritic as well as in Biblical texts (cf. Rev 5:1-5); its object is to introduce an unforeseen change of plot or fate, especially in an epical procedure (see A. B. LORD, *The Singer of Tales* [Cambridge Mass. 1960]; MÜLLER 1974; 1992). In 1 Kgs 22:19-23, it is the problem of theodicy which has to be solved in that way: why does God deceive his people by a seducing prophecy speaking of salvation where there is none? The answer: it was not Yahweh himself but one of his subordinate servants who did so. And above all: there was one right prophet who saw through the fraud of the *rûaḥ šeqer*, but nobody was prepared to hear him. The question remains: why was God able to admit and even cause all this?

The function of the *rûaḥ šeqer* of 1 Kgs 22 has a parallel in the role of Isaiah as it is seen in his vocation narrative (chap. 6). However, Isaiah must not seduce his people, rather he must make it stubborn, and that not by false salvation-prophecy, but by an ambivalent proposition both of salvation and disaster in his proclamations during the Syro-Ephraimite war (734 BCE), proclamations which we hear about in Isa 7:2-8:18. Again, it is the problem of theodicy which Isaiah confronts: why did Yahweh send a prophet to his people although he was not willing to make them listen to him? Why does he misuse his servant to increase his people's misfortune instead of preserving them from disobedience by means of his very words and deeds? The answer is that he *wanted* to do so; it is not his powerlessness that forced him. The question of his grace and righteousness, on the other hand, remains equally open since Yahweh caused a prophetic mission which, obviously, was not to be taken seriously.

IV. *Bibliography*

S. BEYERLE & K. GRÜNWALDT, Micha ben Jimla, *TRE* XXII 4/5 (1992) 704-707; M. A. KLOPFENSTEIN, *Die Lüge nach dem Alten Testament* (Zürich & Frankfurt M. 1964); M. A. KLOPFENSTEIN, שקר *šqr* täuschen, *THAT* II (ed. E. Jenni & C. Westermann; München 1976) 1010-1019; H.-P. MÜLLER, Glauben und Bleiben. Zur Denkschrift Jesajas Kapitel vi 1 - viii 18, *Studies on Prophecy* (ed. P. A. H. de Boer; VTSup 24; 1974) 25-54; MÜLLER, Sprachliche und religionsgeschichtliche Beobachtungen zu Jesaja 6, *ZAH* 5 (1992) 163-185, esp. 173-178 [& lit]; G. QUELL, *Wahre und falsche Propheten* (Beiträge zur Förderung christlicher Theologie 46/1; Gütersloh 1952) 71-85; J. J. M. ROBERTS, Does God lie? Divine deceit as a theological problem in Israelite prophetic literature, *Congress Volume Jerusalem 1986* (ed. J. A. Emerton; VTSup 40; 1988) 211-220; M. WAGNER, Beiträge zur Aramaismenfrage im alttestamentlichen Hebräisch, *Hebräische Wortforschung. Festschrift zum 80. Geburtstag von Walter Baumgartner,* (VTSup 16; Leiden 1967) 355-371, esp. 364-365.

H.-P. MÜLLER

FAMILIAR SPIRIT → WIZARD

FATHER אב

I. Heb *'āb*, 'father' (a primitive Semitic noun, with idiosyncratic plurals), is of unknown etymology but is widely taken to represent a child's early stammer. *ʾĀb* and its congeners refer to the biological or social father—ancestral figure, protector—and are used as an honorary title for men of importance, such as elders or the king, and for deities. In the Bible, 'father' occurs frequently as a divine epithet and as a theophoric element in personal names.

II. In religious conceptions worldwide, various divine powers, especially creator gods, are described as 'father'. In ancient Mesopotamia, e.g. 'father' occurs as a divine epithet expressing the divine-human relationship—e.g. 'father of the 'dark-headed' people'; 'father of the land/the (four) regions'—and as a simile—e.g. the deity is 'like a (merciful) father'—although it is much less commonly used than many other epithets (*AkkGE* 1-2). In the Ugaritic texts, one of the titles of →El is *ab adm*, 'father of humankind'. →Chemosh, the Moabite deity, is pictured as a father of the Moabites (Num 21:29). In Egypt as well, various deities have the title 'father (and mother) of humankind'. Moreover, 'father' occurs frequently as a theophoric element in personal names throughout the ancient Near Eastern world. Such usage is more reflective of popular piety than of the literary tradition.

III. 'Father' occurs throughout the Bible as an epithet of →God. In contrast to the biblical *Umwelt*, where the epithet 'father' occurs especially of creator gods with reference to other gods, in the Bible the epithet occurs with reference to people. The operative analogy is that of parental or parental-type authority, care, and protection. In ancient Israel the epithet does not occur as frequently in the texts as it does in personal names. Apart from *ʾēl*, 'god', and variations of →Yahweh, *ʾāb* is the most common theophoric element in personal names, occurring in more than thirty names in the Bible and in ancient Hebrew inscriptions (ZADOK 1988:178; STAMM 1965: 59-79). These names celebrate a deity as a gracious protector or provider (e.g. Abinadab, 'My [divine] Father has been Generous', 3 men; Abihail, 'My [divine] Father is Strength', 3 men; Abitub, 'My [divine] Father is Good'), or as involved in the creation of the child (e.g. Abiasaph, 'The [divine] Father has added [a Child]'; Abigail, 'My [divine] Father rejoices [at the Birth]', 2 women). ('Father' also occurs in names that designate a child as a substitute for a deceased [grand]father; e.g. Jeshebeab, 'The Father remains [Alive]', or 'He (God) has restored the Father').

In spite of the popularity of the epithet 'Father' in personal names, the epithet is not common in the texts. God can be addressed as 'My/Our Father' (Jer 3:4.19; Isa 63:16; 64:7[8]) and can be characterized as a father/creator, with Israel as his son/children (Exod 4:22; Deut 14:1; 32:6.18; Hos 2:1 [1:10]; 11:1; Isa 1:2; 45:10-12; Jer 31:9; Mal 1:6; 2:10; cf. Num 11:12; Ps 68:6[5]). Another illustration is Jeremiah's accusation that some people address a piece of wood with "You are my father", or a bit of →stone with "You gave birth to me" (Jer 2:27), using language that should be reserved for God only. In the texts, God is also identified as 'like a father' (Ps 103:13; Prov 3:12), and, in keeping with the parental model, even as a →mother (Isa 42:14; 45:10; 49:15; 66:13), but various other metaphors are more frequently used. As 'father', the emphasis is on God as protective and compassionate. Israel was reluctant to describe God as a physical father, except in an ultimate sense. In particular, God is described as father of the Davidic king (2 Sam 7:14; 1 Chr 28:6; Pss 2:7; 89:27-28[26-27]; Isa 9:5[6]), who in turn may have the title 'Eternal Father' (Isa 9:5[6]). The emphasis, however, is on sonship via adoption: "This day have I given birth to you" (Ps 2:7).

At least one scholar has viewed *ʾĀb*, 'Father', as an old Hebrew deity, citing the personal name Eliab (borne by several persons), interpreted as 'My God is Ab', rather than 'My God is a Father' (or 'El is a Father'), i.e. an epithet that becomes a divine name (BARTON 1894:26-27), but this is a rare and unconvincing opinion.

'Father' (Aram *abba*, Gk *patēr*) occurs as

a divine epithet in in the Apocrypha (Tob 13:4; Wis 14:3; Sir 23:1, 4; 51:10; STROTMANN 1991), in Philo and Josephus, but is especially noteworthy in the NT. The conception remains basically the same, but with well over 200 occurrences—more than 120 in the Johannine corpus alone—the epithet 'Father' virtually explodes in popularity. While remaining primarily an epithet, 'Father' is also used in direct address to God. The use of this title in the Aramaic-speaking circles of the early Christian community is retained in the double invocation "Abba, Father" in a Gethsemane prayer by →Jesus (Mark 14:36) and in the Spirit cry, cited by Paul (Rom 8:15; Gal 4:6). In John 8:39-47, we find an intriguing range of application: persons can use the title 'father' with reference to →Abraham (the biological or traditional father), God (the loving, redemptive father, especially connected with Jesus), or the →devil (the murderous, lying authority). Indeed, in John 8:44 the devil is described as "a liar and the father of it (lying)". The emphasis in the use of the metaphor 'Father' for God in the Bible, just as in the case of the use in personal names, seems to be the personalized relationship between God and the people.

IV. *Bibliography*

G. A. BARTON, Native Israelitish Deities, *Oriental Studies: a Selection of the Papers Read Before the Oriental Club of Philadelphia* (Boston 1894) 86-115; J. JEREMIAS, *The Prayers of Jesus* (London 1967); H. RINGGREN, אב, ʾāb, *TDOT* 1 (1977) 1-19; G. SCHRENK & G. QUELL, πατήρ, *TDNT* 5 (1967) 945-1014; J. J. STAMM, Hebräische Ersatznamen, *Studies in Honor of Benno Landsberger* (AS 16; Chicago 1965) 413-424 = *Beiträge zur hebräischen und altorientalischen Namenkunde* (OBO 30; Freiburg 1980) 59-79; A. STROTMANN, *"Mein Vater bist Du!" (Sir 51,10). Zur Bedeutung der Vaterschaft Gottes in kanonischen und nichtkanonischen frühjüdischen Schriften* (Frankfurter Theologische Studien 39; Frankfurt 1991); R. ZADOK, *The Pre-hellenistic Israelite Anthroponomy and Prosopography* (Louvain 1988).

H. B. HUFFMON

FATHER OF THE LIGHTS πατὴρ τῶν φώτων

I. James 1:17 is the only biblical text where →God is called the "Father of the Lights" (πατὴρ τῶν φώτων). Most scholars agree that the expression means "the creator of the celestial bodies", i.e. of the heavenly beings. In early Judaism there was a widespread belief that →stars were →angels (SCHRENK 1954:1015 n. 410; DIBELIUS-GREEVEN 1964:130-131). That God created the heavenly bodies is a commonly accepted belief in the OT and in ancient Judaism (e.g. Gen 1:14-18; Ps 136:7; Sir 43:1-12; see τὰ φῶτα αὐτοῦ in LXX Jer 4:23; Philo, *De Abrahamo* 156-159), but the expression of this idea by means of the term "Father of the lights" is very rare (although the idea that God himself is →Light is current; cf. Philo, *De somniis* I 75 ὁ θεὸς φῶς ἐστιν, with SPICQ 1982: 681-2). The only instance is in the Greek *Life of Adam and Eve* 36:3, where the sun and the →moon are said to look like two black Ethiopians (35:4) who "are not able to shine because of the light of the universe, the Father of the lights, and therefore their light has been hidden from them". The words "the Father of the lights" are omitted here in a number of mss (see D. BERTRAND, *La vie grecque d'Adam et Ève* [Paris 1987] 98, 139; in 38:1 the words are weakly attested as a variant), but they seem to belong to the original text (STROTMANN 1991:294-296). Here, too, 'father' has the connotation of 'creator', upon whom the luminaries are dependent. The same applies to *Testament of Abraham* rec. B 7:6, where the expression πατὴρ τοῦ φωτός is used of God in the sense of 'creator', although some take it to refer here to an angel or the archangel Michael (for this and the text-critical problem involved see STROTMANN 1991: 207-209; *ibid.* at 360-361 one finds a survey of various word-combinations in which 'father' means 'creator'; in CD 5:18 and 1QS 3:20 *śar ʾôrîm*, 'prince of lights', may refer to an →archangel or to God). This Jewish terminology is used in Jas 1:17, where the train of thought seems to be that, although God is the Father of the lights, he is nevertheless fundamentally different from these heavenly bodies, because they are constantly moving but God is unwaveringly the same: "there is no variation or shadow due to change with him" (1:17; cf. for a similar contrast Philo, *De posteritate Caini* 19).

II. *Bibliography*

M. DIBELIUS & H. GREEVEN, *Der Brief des Jakobus* (KEK 15; Göttingen 1964); R. P. MARTIN, *James* (WBC 49; Waco 1988); G. SCHRENK, πατήρ, *TWNT* (1954) 1015-1016; *C. SPICQ, *Notes de lexicographie néotestamentaire III: Supplément* (Fribourg-Göttingen 1982) 674-691; *A. STROTMANN, *Mein Vater bist Du (Sir 51,10). Zur Bedeutung der Vaterschaft Gottes in kanonischen und nichtkanonischen frühjüdischen Schriften* (Frankfurter Theologische Studien 39; Frankfurt 1991).

P. W. VAN DER HORST

FEAR OF ISAAC פחד יצחק

I. No definite interpretation can be given for the expression *paḥad yiṣḥāq*. It only occurs in Gen 31:42.53 (in the latter verse as *paḥad ʾābîw yiṣḥāq*). *Paḥad yiṣḥāq* was interpreted as a divine name by ALT (1929) because of its archaic impression (cf. *ʾăbîr yaʿăqōb*) and because of its apparent resemblance to divine names of the "God of X" type. This designation was used for the god of Isaac, which Alt thought belonged to the category of the God of the Fathers.

II. The interpretation of the expression as a divine name, as well as the definition of the role and character of the deity in question, depend upon the interpretation of the genitive and of *paḥad*.

The expression may be translated in terms of a *genitivus subiectivus* or *auctoris*, i.e. "Schrecken, der von Isaak ausgeht" (HOLZINGER 1898; STAERK 1899). The analogous phrase *paḥad yhwh* points in this direction; it clearly characterises the terror worked by →Yahweh in Isa 2:10.19.21; Ps 64:2 and 1 Sam 11:7; 2 Chr 14:13; 17:10 etc. In this case there would be no relation to the alleged God of the Fathers. LUTHER (1901) and MEYER (1906:255), however, thought Isaac (as the patriarchs in general) to have been an originally Canaanite local deity. This far-flung conclusion was dismissed for good by researchers starting with Alt. Alternatively, the expression can be understood in terms of a *genitivus obiectivus*: One was to interpret *paḥad yiṣḥāq* "als archaische Bezeichnung des Numens (...), dessen Erscheinung Isaak in Schrecken gesetzt und eben dadurch für immer an sich gebunden hat" (ALT 1953:26, so again ALBERTZ 1992:54 [without further information on how one is to conceive God in terms of numinous terror]). BECKER plays down the numinous, preferring to understand *paḥad* in terms of cultic "Ehrfurcht, Verehrung" (1965:178). Yet, there is only scanty and late evidence for this (G. WANKE, *TWNT* IX, 200, only cites 2 Chr 19:7; Ps 36:2). MÜLLER (1988:559-560) translates the phrase in terms of a *genitivus possesivus*, meaning Isaac to be "der Nutzniesser eines an Feinden wirksamen numinosen Schreckens". Since Alt's interpretation hardly fits in with the other characteristics of the Father Gods noted by him, ALBRIGHT traced *paḥad* back to the Palmyrene word *paḥdâ*, i.e. 'family, clan, tribe', to Ar *faḫiḏ*, 'a small branch of a tribe consisting of a man's nearest kin' and to Ug *pḫd* ('flock'). He suggested the rendering 'the kinsman of Isaac' (1946:327). This would square well with the personal names rooted in the same milieu, whose theophoric elements were formed in using terms of kinship (like *ʿam*, *ʾāb*, *ʾāḥ*, Kinsman [→Am], →Father, →Brother). Alt thought Albright's interpretation noteworthy; O. EISSFELDT (*KS* III [Tübingen 1966] 392), R. DE VAUX (*Histoire ancienne d'Israël* [Paris 1971] 256-261) and others agreed with it. Philologically speaking, however, this interpretation is not valid. Albright's explanation implies an irregular phonetic shift from Proto-Semitic *ḏ* to Hebrew *d* where one would expect *ẓ*. Ug *pḫd* does not have anything to do with *pḫd* in the sense of 'thigh, clan'. Finally, "in no Semitic language is there a *paḥad*, 'kinsman'. Only in Arabic, and in Palmyrene as a loan word, is there a *paḥad* meaning 'clan, tribe'" (HILLERS 1972:92; cf. PUECH 1984 and MÜLLER 1980, with detailed analysis of the philological problems).

Some exegetes work from an Aramaic root PḤD II (cf. Ar *faḫiḏ*) in the sense of 'thigh' (BRASLAVI 1962; KÖCKERT 1988; KOCH 1980 = 1988; MALUL 1985) which occurs in Job 40:17 (HILLERS 1972:91, also with reference to the Tg of Lev 21:20, which mentions *paḥdîn*, 'testicles'). Their reason for doing so is that *paḥad* cannot be linked to a positive experience of God coming close (KOCH 1980:207) and that there is no evidence supporting the translation of *paḥad* as 'kinsman'. Provided that it is correct to start from the Aramaic root PḤD II, one could read Gen 31:53 to the effect that Jacob is swearing "bei der Lende oder dem Zeugungsglied seines Vaters Isaak", whose procreative capacity "sich sogar in der Fruchtbarkeit und Zeugungskraft der zum Haus gehörenden Tiere auswirkt v. 42" (KOCH 1980:212). MALUL (1985:200), following BRASLAVI (1962) puts it slightly differently: "'The thigh of Isaac'... symbolizes the family and ancestral spirits of Isaac". They were invoked for the "protection of their descendants". He explains the use of the Aramaic loan-word with a reference to the Aramaic context of the scene. In this interpretation *paḥad yiṣḥāq* has got nothing to do with a term characterising an ancestral god in the sense of Alt; the oath by the *paḥad ʾābîw* may belong to the ancient fund of family religion, though. In Gen 31 the *paḥad* of the father is not linked to his corporal presence. This is why UTZSCHNEIDER (1991:81) interprets it in terms of a 'numinoses alter ego' of the *pater familias* who plays an important part in the protection of family and property. His parallel is the ancient Roman *Genius* representing the procreative capacity and personality of the master of the house and to whom the members of the household take the oath (1991:84 with reference to G. WISSOWA, *Religion und Kultus der Römer* [München 1902] 141-149).

Objections have been raised on philological and technical grounds against derivation from Aram *pḥd* ('thigh, procreative capacity'). The shift from Heb *z* (from Proto-Semitic *ḏ*) to Aram *d* is said to have occurred as late as the 7th century BCE (ALBERTZ 1992:54 n. 28, with reference to I. KOTTSIEPER, *Die Sprache der Aḥiqarsprüche* [Berlin & New York 1990]), whereas the composition Gen 25-32* dates back—according to E. BLUM (*Die Komposition der Vätergeschichte* [Neukirchen-Vluyn 1984] 202-203)—to the late 10th century BCE. MÜLLER (1988:561) says that one would rather expect →Laban to use an Aramaic loan-word, as is shown in v 47. The ceremonies of oath-taking that KOCH (1980=1988) and MALUL (1985; 1987) refer to for analogies (Gen 24:2.9 and 47:29) mention *yārēk* (not *paḥad*), whereas conversely, neither *yārēk* nor the phrase "put the hand under the thigh" can be found in Gen 31 (MÜLLER 1980). Obviously, they must be lacking because the father whose *paḥad* Jacob swears by is not corporally present in Gen 31.

It is doubtful whether *paḥad* itself can be understood in terms of a divine name. The personal and tribal name *ṣlpḥd* (Num 26:33; 27:1; 36:10; Josh 17:3) as vocalised by LXX provides too slim a basis. Besides, it is ambiguous (BECKER 1965:173; LEMAIRE 1978:323-327; MÜLLER 1980:120: "[schützender] Schatten des *Paḥad*"; cf. however PUECH 1984:360 n. 10: "La crainte divine est un refuge"). This is why it is doubtful whether *paḥad* might be justifiably compared to the god *Phobos* in Greek folk-religion. The latter is mentioned after →Zeus, though in advance of all other gods in a votive inscription at Selinunte dating back to the 5th century BCE. At Sparta, a temple proper is said to have been dedicated to him (PW XXI:309-318). In Hellenistic days, *Phobos* is reduced to a mere bogy as shown in IG XIV:2413,8 (on an amulet stone) (cf. *paḥad laylâ* in Ps 91:5 →Terror of the Night and Cant 3:8).

If, because of the philological problems, one does not want to interpret *paḥad* as 'thigh', it is advisable to start from *paḥad*'s original meaning 'terror' as attested in Hebrew and to interpret the phrase *paḥad ʾābîw* (which in terms of tradition history, is the more original one, KÖCKERT 1988:62) in the context of Gen 31 (H. GUNKEL, *Genesis* [1910, 3rd ed.] 349). In the narrative, the introduction of *paḥad ʾābîw* is prepared for by the nocturnal appearance of Jacob's family god in vv 24 and 29. In fact, this is about the fear with which the god threatens Laban to the advantage of (cf. *hyh lî* v 42) Jacob and his kin. In confirming the terms of contract with an oath to the *paḥad ʾābîw* (v 53), Jacob will draw the fear upon himself (in the context of the conditional curse uttered against oneself as implied by an oath) if he breaks the contract. We must leave it open, though, whether the fear worked by the deity watching over the contract, has "animatisiert" "zu einer eigenständigen Gestalt, dem 'Schrecklichen'" (MÜLLER 1988:560) or is "a principal attribute of the God of Isaac, whose protective power sows terror among all his enemies" (PUECH 1992:780).

III. *Bibliography*

R. ALBERTZ, *Religionsgeschichte Israels in alttestamentlicher Zeit I* (ATD Erg. Bd. 8/1; Göttingen 1992) 53-54; W. F. ALBRIGHT, *From the Stone Age to Christianity* (Baltimore 1946) 188-189; A. ALT, *Der Gott der Väter* (BWANT III/12; Stuttgart 1929 = *KS* I [München 1953] 1-77) 24-29; J. BECKER, *Gottesfurcht im Alten Testament* (AnBib 25; Rome 1965) 177-179; Y. BRASLAVI, *Pḥd yṣḥq* and the Blessing of Ephraim and Manasseh, *Beth Mikra* 14 (1962) 35-42; D. R. HILLERS, PAḤAD YIṢḤAQ, *JBL* 91 (1972) 90-94; H. HOLZINGER, *Genesis erklärt* (KHC I; Freiburg 1898) 206; M. KÖCKERT, *Vätergott und Väterverheissungen. Eine Auseinandersetzung mit A. Alt und seinen Erben* (FRLANT 142; Göttingen 1988); K. KOCH, *paḥad yiṣḥaq* - eine Gottesbezeichnung?, *Werden und Wirken des Alten Testaments* (ed. R. Albertz; FS C. Westermann; Göttingen 1980) 107-115 = KOCH, *Studien zur alttestamentlichen und altorientalischen Religionsgeschichte* (Göttingen 1988) 206-214; A. LEMAIRE, Les Benê Jacob, *RB* 85 (1978) 323-327; LEMAIRE, A propos de paḥad dans l'onomastique ouest-sémitique, *VT* 35 (1985) 500-501; B. LUTHER, Die israelitischen Stämme, *ZAW* 21 (1901) 1-76; M. MALUL, More on *paḥad yiṣḥaq* (Genesis xxxi 42, 53) and the Oath by the Thigh, *VT* 35 (1985) 192-200; MALUL, Touching the Sexual Organs as an Oath Ceremony in an Akkadian Letter, *VT* 37 (1987) 491-492; E. MEYER, *Die Israeliten und ihre Nachbarstämme* (Halle 1906) 253-259; H. P. MÜLLER, Gott und die Götter in den Anfängen der biblischen Religion. Zur Vorgeschichte des Monotheismus, *Monotheismus im Alten Israel und seiner Umwelt* (ed. O. Keel; Fribourg 1980) 99-142; MÜLLER, *paḥad*, *TWAT* VI (1988) 552-562; E. PUECH, "La crainte d'Isaac" en Genèse xxxi 42 et 53, *VT* 34 (1984) 356-361; PUECH, Fear of Isaac, *ABD* 2 (1992) 779-780; H. P. STÄHLI, *pḥd* beben, *THAT* II (München 1976) 411-413; W. STAERK, *Studien zur Religions- und Sprachgeschichte des Alten Testaments I* (Berlin 1899) 59-61; H. UTZSCHNEIDER, Patrilinearität im alten Israel—eine Studie zur Familie und ihrer Religion, *BN* 56 (1991) 60-97.

M. KÖCKERT

FIRE אש

I. The Hebrew word for 'fire', *ʾēš*, is common Semitic (with the exception of Arabic) but there is not a strong tradition of deified fire in the ancient Near East. Any echoes of this tradition in the Bible, therefore, are harder than usual to detect. In spite of an apparent similarity with the Semitic word for 'fire' and even some association with fire (ROBERTS 1972), the Babylonian god Išum was not a god of fire. However, dI-ša-*tú* does occur as a divine name in Ebla (PETTINATO, *OrAnt* 18 [1979] 105) and *išt* is a goddess in Ugaritic mythology.

II. The Ugaritic goddess *išt*, 'fire', glossed *klbt ilm*, 'Divine Bitch' (*KTU* 1.3 iii:45), is listed among the deities defeated by →Anat. Otherwise, she is unknown and has no role in Ugaritic religion. The Sumerian names for the fire-god are **gibil** or **girra** (Akk. *girru*), the son of the sky-god Anu; his mother, possibly Šala, is probably of Hurrian origin. Also associated with fire was the god Nusku (Old Aram *nsk*). Philo lists the three Phoenician gods Phos, →'Light', Pyr, 'Fire' and Phlox, →'Flame' (*Phoenician History* in Eusebius, *PE* I 10,9) and the second can perhaps be identified with Ug *išt*.

III. In Ps 104:4 fire and flame (if read *'š* <*w*> *lhṭ* for MT *'eš lōhēṭ*, where 'flaming' [m.] is in gender disagreement with 'fire' [f.],) are →Yahweh's ministers (*mšrt*; here pl.), perhaps demythologized minor deities, but more probably metaphors for lightning. More vivid is the phrase "Fire (*'ēš*) walks ahead of him and sets ablaze his enemies round about" (Ps 97:3). Joel 2:3 is less clear. Yahweh uses fire as a means of punishment (Gen 19:24; Num 11:1-3; Deut 32:22; Amos 1:4 etc.) or to consume sacrifice (Lev 9:24; Judg 6:21). In addition, Yahweh is portrayed as a →Humbaba-type figure, breathing smoke, flames and fire, in 2 Sam 22:9 (= Ps 18:9); Isa 30:27.33; 33:11; 65:5. He manifests himself in fire: as the "smoking fire pot and flaming torch" in the covenant rite (Gen 15:17), in the burning bush (Exod 3:2) and as the pillar of fire (e.g. Exod 13:21). In Deut 9:3, "Yahweh your god who crosses over [the Jordan] ahead of you is a consuming fire (*'š 'klh*)".

IV. *Bibliography*

A. I. BAUMGARTEN, *The* Phoenician History *of Philo of Byblos. A Commentary* [& lit] (Leiden 1981) 152-153; R. S. HENDEL, 'The Flame of the Whirling Sword': A Note on Genesis 3:24, *JBL* 104 (1985) 671-674; W. G. LAMBERT, Fire Incantations, *AfO* 23 (1970) 39-45; *P. D. MILLER, JR., Fire in the Mythology of Canaan and Israel, *CBQ* 27 (1965) 256-261; J. J. M. ROBERTS, *The Earliest Semitic Pantheon. A Study of Semitic Deities Attested in Mesopotamia before Ur III* (Baltimore/London 1972) 40-41.

W. G. E. WATSON

FIRST-BORN OF DEATH בכור מות

I. Though the deity →Mot ('Death') occurs frequently in Canaanite and Israelite lore, the expression *běkôr māwet* (translated either 'First Born of Death' or 'First Born Death') occurs only in Job 18:13 in a context having to do with death and disease.

The Hebrew term *běkôr* (fem *běkîrâ*) clearly refers to the first-born (human or animal) as does the majority of cognate terms (cf. Aram *bûkrā'*, Ar *bikr*, Eth *bakwr*, OSA *bkr*, Ug *bkr*). In contrast, the Akk cognates *bukru* ('son, child, offspring') and *bukurtu* ('daughter') refer primarily to deities (rarely to humans) and are not restricted to the first-born which is usually designated with the addition of the modifier *rēštû*, 'eldest' (*CAD* B, 309-310). Akk *bakru* (fem *bakartu*) is used in MB personal names to refer to the first-born.

II. In order to describe the ancient Near Eastern background for the expression 'First-born of Death' scholars have looked to the Ugaritic and Mesopotamian literature which mention various deities associated with death and disease. Three deities (Mot, →Resheph, and Namtar) have been promoted as particularly relevant to understanding the connotation of *běkôr māwet* in Job 18:13.

The Ugaritic texts are our single most important source for depicting the Canaanite deity Mot ('Death'). Yet even in these texts we are told little about Mot's immediate family or ancestry. He bears the epithets 'the son of →El' (*bn ilm*) and 'Beloved of El' (*ydd/mdd il*), yet no reference is made to whether he was the eldest child. We have no reference to any children of Mot first-born or otherwise (although we do have the curious Ugaritic personal name *bn mt* which P. WATSON (*Mot, The God of Death at Ugarit and in the Old Testament* [diss. Yale 1970] 155) translates 'son of Mot', cf. the Hebrew personal name *'ăḥîmôt* I Chron. 6:10). These data are congruent with what we know to be an absence of a cult of Mot at Ugarit. There is no mention of Mot in any of the pantheon lists. His name is absent from all the sacrificial and offering lists as well. It is thus not surprising that we have not found any sanctuary dedicated to him.

The cult of the Canaanite god Resheph is well attested throughout Syria-Palestine and far beyond (Egypt, Ugarit, Phoenicia, Cyprus, and Mesopotamia) usually in syncretism with other deities (see Y. YADIN, in

Biblical and Related Studies Presented to Samuel Iwry [ed. A. Kort & S. Morschauser; Winona Lake 1985] 259-274 [& lit]). Here, it is relevant to note that Resheph in Northwest Semitic mythology was a god of pestilence and, contrary to Mot, was thought to have children (to judge from Job 5:7).

A pantheon list from Ugarit identifies Resheph with →Nergal, the Mesopotamian deity of pestilence and the underworld. Resheph is also associated with 'arrows' at Ugarit (*KTU* 1.82:3) and in Cyprus (*KAI* 32:3-4) which some take to refer to his role in bringing plagues (although S. IVRY construed the arrows as a sign of luck because of the practice of belomancy; cf. W. J. FULCO, *The Canaanite God Rešep* [New Haven 1976] 49-51; J. C. DE MOOR, *UF* 16 [1984] 239). Resheph's connection with plagues and pestilence is also found in Hab 3:5 (cf. Deut 32:24) where he forms part of Yahweh's chthonian entourage along with →Deber ('Pestilence'). Most noteworthy for the present discussion is the reference to 'the sons of Resheph' in Job 5:7. Historians of Israelite religion use Job 5:7 (and similarly the *bĕkôr māwet* material [see below]) to form one of two conclusions. They argue that the expression 'the sons of Resheph' refers either to (a) the children of Resheph (= minor deities) who, like their father, bring disease or (b) a transformed biblical idiom (emasculating Canaanite myth) for various forms of illness. But these are not mutually exclusive positions. A vivid mythology can still underlie figurative language.

Namtar was a Mesopotamian deity associated with bringing plague and pestilence. He is best known as the *sukkallu*, vizier (minister or 'lieutenant') and *mār šipri*, messenger, of Ereshkigal, the queen of the underworld (cf. the Nergal and Ereshkigal myth). He also bore the titles *sukkal erṣeti* 'the vizier of the underworld' (*CAD* S, 359) and 'the offspring (*ilittu*) of Ereshkigal'. Namtar is not explicitly called the first-born of Ereshkigal. This has not prevented scholars from drawing such a conclusion (see below).

The Akk word *namtaru* (Sum **nam.tar**) can also refer to 'fate, destiny' as well as a group of demons who were harbingers of death (*CAD* N1, 247-248). Thus illnesses may be referred to in a personified form as 'the sons of Namtar' who as messengers leave the underworld and overcome humans (S. MEIER, *The Messenger in the Ancient Semitic World* [HSM 45; Atlanta 1988] 122).

III. Biblical scholars, depending on the degree to which they think Canaanite myth has penetrated the Bible, treat the expression *bĕkôr māwet* in one of three ways.

1) The phrase 'first-born of death' is an idiom for deadly disease. Even some scholars who recognize the Canaanite imagery of Mot behind this text conclude that the expression here is largely metaphorical. Thus M. H. POPE (*Job* [AB 15; Garden City 1973] 135) comments that "the view commonly held that the expression is a metaphor for a deadly disease, or for the specific malady that afflicts Job ... is probably correct". L. R. BAILEY (*Biblical Perspectives on Death* [Philadelphia 1979] 41), who views the phrase 'the first born of death consuming one's limbs' as a formalized idiom for the deterioration of the body, recognizes a vestigial usage behind Bildad's speech, yet concludes that Bildad "likely would not mean thereby what a Canaanite might mean, that the god Mot ('Death'), a demonic, autonomous power, had seized the person".

Further support for *bĕkôr māwet* being an idiom may be found in the expression *bĕkôrê dallîm* ('the first born of the poor') in Isa 14:30; but the meaning of this expression is equally difficult. *bĕkôrê dallîm* is taken by some scholars to designate the very poorest of society (parallel to *ʾebyônîm*, 'destitute'). Similarly, *bĕkôr māwet* could refer to the deadliest of diseases. *māwet* is also used idiomatically on its own (without *bĕkôr*) to represent superlatives with a negative sense (B. K. WALTKE & M. O'CONNOR, *An Introduction to Biblical Hebrew Syntax* [Winona Lake 1990] 269; D. W. THOMAS *VT* 3 [1953] 219-224; *VT* 18 [1968] 122-123).

The phrase *bĕkôr māwet* may find an analogue in the expression *ben māwet* (lit. 'a son of death') which refers to someone deserving death (1 Sam 20:31; 26:16; 2 Sam 12:5; cf. *TDOT* II 153). In these passages *ben māwet* certainly does not refer literally to a son of Mot. If P. K. McCarter's (*II Samuel* [AB 9; Garden City 1984] 299) translation of 'scoundrel, damnable fellow' would prove to be correct one could posit a derived meaning.

2) The phrase 'First-Born of Death' is a title referring to an offspring (representing a particular disease) of a deity representing or associated with death and/or diseases. This interpretation relies heavily on the cognate material from neighboring cultures mentioned above.

Namtar was a popular choice prior to the discovery of the Ugaritic texts. E. Dhorme (*A Commentary on the Book of Job* [Nashville 1984 from 1926 French original] 265), for example, argued that "as a general rule, the *sukallu* is the first born ... of the god who employs his services". Even after the Ugaritic discoveries, a few scholars have argued that a strong circumstantial case can be built that the author of Job was referring to Namtar. Most recently Burns (1987:363) notes that Namtar is Ereshkigal's offspring (*ilittu*). He also argues that "in Mesopotamian mythology the first-born, if male, was generally the vizier of his parent". Reasoning in reverse direction, if we know that Namtar was Ereshkigal's vizier, then he may have been her first-born too. Thus Burns concludes that Namtar is 'The First-Born of Death' in Mesopotamia and the likely deity behind Job 18:13.

The weakness of this view is the lack of attestation of Namtar bearing the explicit epithet 'first Born of Death'. If this epithet was so well known that the author of Job borrowed it, should not one expect to find at least a single example of the epithet in the extant Akkadian corpus? In addition, the data are hardly precise. First, Namtar is never called the 'first-born' of Ereshkigal and secondly, Ereshkigal, the queen of the netherworld, is not identical to a deity who personifies 'Death'.

The majority of biblical scholars have been influenced by the Ugaritic texts and their description of the activities of Mot, the god of Death. Such scholars reject Namtar as a likely candidate preferring to turn to cognate evidence from an adjacent Canaanite culture. U. Cassuto (*The Goddess Anat* [Jerusalem 1971 from 1951 Hebrew original] 63) was one of the first scholars to bring in the Ugaritic data for Job 18:13. He concluded that "*māwet* is a distinct personality that has a first-born son, and this son is, as it were, the embodiment of the diseases". Following Cassuto, Sarna (1963:316) equated the →King of Terrors in Job 18:14 with Mot whose first-born son (*bĕkôr māwet*) would "occupy the same position in Canaan as did Namtar, the ... son of Ereshkigal in Babylonian mythology".

The weakness of this view is the simple fact that Mot is nowhere described as having children. When the study of the Ugaritic texts was still in its infancy, some scholars (N. M. Sarna, *JBL* 76 [1957] 21 n. 54; but cf. Sarna 1963:316 n13) thought that *KTU* 1.6 vi:7-9 may have described seven sons of Mot, yet further studies have shown that the seven lads (*šbʿt ǵlmh*) mentioned in this text are most likely servants of Mot whom he consumes. Yet lack of any mention of Mot's offspring is not an insurmountable problem and may be due to our limited number of texts. Pope (*Job* [AB 15; Garden City 1973] 135) admits Mot's lack of children yet states that "it is understandable that any death-dealing force like disease or pestilence might be regarded as his offspring". Other scholars would disagree, with some (Burns 1987:363) suggesting that Resheph would be a more likely candidate for a Canaanite god of pestilence who has children.

3) Similar to the second view, the third views looks to the mythological cognate material (particularly the Ugaritic sources). Yet this alternative differs in treating *bĕkôr māwet* as an attributive genitive in which the two words stand in apposition to each other (cf. B. K. Waltke & M. O'Connor, *An Introduction to Biblical Hebrew Syntax* [Winona Lake 1990] 149-150). Thus they translate 'Firstborn Death' as a title of Mot who, they posit, was the first-born of →El.

Wyatt (1990:208) remarks that, by seeing Mot behind the term *běkôr māwet*, we are free from the 'wild goose chases' that have to look far afield to come up with a plausible offspring of a death deity. Furthermore he argues, death-like plagues are often personified by Resheph who is nowhere described as a child of Mot.

Though a circumstantial case can be built for Mot being the first-born of El (WYATT 1990:210-211), we have no *explicit* evidence that Mot was the first-born child of El. Ugaritic knows the concept of the first-born (cf. *KTU* 1.13:28; 1.14 iii:40; 1.14 vi:25; 1.15 iii:16) yet never uses the term *bkr* to refer to Mot, or for that matter, to any other deity. We are also not certain about the meaning of Mot's title 'the Beloved of El'. Rather than a term of endearment, some scholars (BURNS 1987:362) think this title is actually "a euphemism for a feared and repulsive divinity". WYATT (1990:211-212; *Bib* 66 [1985] 112-125) counters that *ydd/ mdd* is not an expression of affection or a euphemism, but rather a legitimation formula, which "lends weight to the idea that Mot (along with Yam) was understood in Ugarit to be El's first-born, even if the tradition did not actually say so".

Grammatical analysis may present another problem with this view. Attributive genitives are very common in biblical Hebrew, yet the noun which serves as the attributive genitive is usually an abstract noun of quality. Thus the use of the noun *māwet* as an abstract genitive in the expression *běkôr māwet* would correspond to the adjective 'dead'. In short, if *běkôr māwet* is an example of an abstract genitive, it would more likely mean 'a dead firstborn' rather than 'firstborn Mot'. Furthermore, *běkôr* is a relational term which seems to call for its source to be expressed in the genitive. It is hard to read *běkôr māwet* without asking the question 'the first-born of whom?'

In conclusion, it is safe to say that scholars will continue to analyze *běkôr māwet* in one of these three ways depending on the amount of Canaanite mythology they find in the entire chapter of Job 18 which contains other allusions to Mot such as the King of Terrors.

IV. *Bibliography*

J. B. BURNS, The Identity of Death's First-Born (Job xviii 13), *VT* 37 (1987) 362-364; N. M. SARNA, The Mythological Background of Job 18, *JBL* 82 (1963) 315-318; N. WYATT, The Expression *Bekôr Māwet* in Job xviii 13 and its Mythological Background, *VT* 40 (1990) 207-216.

T. J. LEWIS

FLAME להב

I. Three terms for 'flame' in Hebrew, *lāhāb*, *lěhābâ* and *šalhebet* are all derivations from the same root, LHB. Another root is LHṬ, 'to blaze up, flame'. 'Flame' has sometimes the traits of a deity in the Bible.

II. The only divine name for flame attested outside the Bible is ^{d}*Na-ab-lum* = **sukkal** ^{d}BIL.GI.**ke**$_{x}$(KID), 'Flame' = 'vizier of the Fire-god', in a Babylonian god-list (An = *Anum* II 342, cited CAD N/1, 26b). Less clear is the Babylonian god Erra (perhaps derived from **ḥrr*, 'to scorch, char' [J. J. M. ROBERTS, *JCS* 24 (1971) 11-12]) associated with Išum (→fire) in the Epic of Erra and Isum. The Ugaritic word *dbb*, usually taken to denote the deity 'Flame' because it occurs in parallelism with *išt*, 'fire' (*KTU* 1.3 iii:46), most probably means 'Fly' (W. VAN SOLDT, *UF* 21 [1989] 369-373). In Egyptian, words for 'flame', such as *nsrt* and *nbit* also occur as designations for goddesses like Sachmet.

III. There are some indications that 'flame' (like 'fire') was some sort of lesser deity subservient to →Yahweh, as in Joel 2:3: "fire devours in front of them (= the approaching enemy) and behind them a flame burns"; also Joel 2:19-20. Together with fire, flame was a messenger of Yahweh (Ps 104:4). In Gen 3:24, *lahaṭ haḥereb hammithappeket*, "the flame of the whirling sword" is stationed by Yahweh as a distinct minor divinity alongside the →cherubim at the entrance to the Garden of Eden. Although various minor deities carry swords, only the guardian god 'flame' has a whirling sword. This is as typical of the flame-god as the arrow is of →Reshep (HENDEL 1985).

Other passages which can be cited where flame is used by God are Judg 13:20

(Yahweh's →angel ascends in the flame); Isa 29:6; 30:30 and 66:15 (the flame of a devouring fire accompanies theophany); Ezek 20:47 (God threatens unquenchable flame); Ps 29:7 (Yahweh's voice flashes out flames of fire); Ps 106:18 (fire and flame consume the wicked), etc. Since there is no strong tradition of a deity associated with flame in the ancient Near East, it is not surprising that there are so few echoes in the Bible.

IV. *Bibliography*

*R. S. HENDEL, "The Flame of the Whirling Sword": A Note on Genesis 3:24, *JBL* 104 (1985) 671-674; P. D. MILLER, JR., Fire in the Mythology of Canaan and Israel, *CBQ* 27 (1965) 256-261.

W. G. E. WATSON

FLOOD → **ID**

FORTUNA

I. Fortuna is the Roman personification of good luck and success (from *fero*, 'to bring'; *fors*, 'chance', 'luck'), which is also expressed in the anthroponym Fortunatus, a popular Latin name, especially during the Hellenistic period. It occurs but once, however, in the Bible (I Cor 16:17).

II. Fortuna's character, despite her Latin name, may have originated with the well-known and well-developed Etruscan notion of fate (KAJANTO 1981:506-509). Her oldest cult site may have been Praeneste, where she was known as *Fortuna Primigenia* (*CIL* 14, pp. 295-296), under which name she later had a sanctuary on the Capitol in Rome (Plutarch, *Fest. Rom.* 322F). According to Roman tradition, her cult was introduced to the city during the period of Etruscan dominance by Servius Tullius, sixth king of Rome (578-535 BCE), to whom is attributed the construction of the temples of *Fors Fortuna* on the bank of the Tiber (Varro 200. 6.16; Dionysius Halic. 4.27.7; Ovid, *Fasti* 6.773-784; Plutarch, *Fort. Rom.* 5) and of *Fortuna* in the *Forum Boarium* (Ovid, *Fasti* 6.569-636; Dionysius Halic. 4.40.7; Valerius Maximus 1.8.11). Her temple in the *Forum Boarium* stood next to that of the *Mater Matuta*, a goddess of the Roman family (Ovid, *Fasti* 6.473-568; Plutarch, *Quaest. Rom.* 267D; Augustine, *De Civ. D.* 4.8) with whom Fortuna originally may have been associated as a deity of women: both temples were simultaneously rebuilt shortly following their destruction in the fire of 213 BCE (Livy 25.7.5; 24.47.15). Although there is also a (later) *Fortuna Virilis* (Ovid, *Fasti* 4.145-150), Fortuna nevertheless retained her status as primarily a goddess of luck.

Occasionally described in cult as a malevolent power to avoid, *Brevis*, for example (Plutarch, *Quaest. Rom.* 281D) or *Mala* (Cicero, *Nat. D.* 3.63, *Leg.* 2.28; Pliny, *HN* 2.16), Fortuna was almost always portrayed as a benevolent figure, the protector of a people and of their city or state: *Fortuna Populi Romani*, for example (KAJANTO 1981:514), who had a temple on the Quirinal (*CIL* 1.2, p. 319), and of their rulers who embodied these political entities: *Fortuna Caesar*, for example (Velleius Paterculus 2.51.2; Plutarch, *Caes.* 38.3), or especially *Fortuna Augusta* (KAJANTO 1981: 517-518). In addition to the fortune of people or place, numerous other titles for the Roman Fortuna have been identified in accordance with the Roman practice of specifying the nature of deities by attaching epithets to their names stipulating their varying manifestations, for example: *Aeterna*, *Armipotens*, *Bona*, *Dea*, *Domestica*, *Magna* (KAJANTO 1981:510-516). Fortuna was portrayed in cult with imagery taken over from Greek representations of →Tyche, the Greek personification of capricious luck, good or bad: the rudder, the cornucopia, and the globe; in addition, the wheel, an image of her transient nature, was a frequent literary attribute of Fortuna (e.g., Cicero, *Pis.* 22; Tacitus, *Dial.* 23; Ammianus 26.8.13).

In contrast to the beneficent Fortuna of popular cult, the Roman literary tradition increasingly emphasized the influence of *Tyche*, the Greek personification of capricious fortune. Consequently, Fortuna acquired such attributes as ambiguity and fickleness (e.g., Sallustius, *Cat.* 8.1; Curtius

Rufus 4.5.2; Seneca, *Benef.* 2.28.2; Tacitus, *Hist.* 4.47; Firmicus Maternus, *Math.* 1.7.42; Ammianus 14.11.29), and blindness (e.g., Pacuvius 41; Cicero, *Phil.* 13.10; Ovid, *Pont.* 3.1.125-126; Pliny, *HN* 2.22; Apuleius, *Met.* 7.2; Ammianus 31.8.8; Isidorus, *Orig.* 8.11.94). Tyche/Fortuna thus came to embody the Hellenistic perception of existence as fortuitous or transitory (e.g., Apuleius, *Met.* 1.6), and constituted, thereby, a dominant contextual or situational category of this culture. She was so comprehensive, albeit in an ambiguous way, that she was seen by many as a surrogate for god (Pliny, *HN* 2.5.22).

The cultic and literary traditions of Fortuna seem to merge in Apuleius' second-century CE novel, *Metamorphoses*, or *The Golden Ass*, in which the effects of a capricious Fortuna are overcome through initiation into the cult of →Isis, who undertook the role of a good Fortuna "that is not blind, but can see" (*Met.* 11.15). The philosophical tradition also, especially amongst the Stoics, opposed perceptions of the random play of fortune by emphasizing the human spirit and rationality: "the sage is unconquered and unsubdued and unharmed and unaffected by chance" (*Stoicorum Veterum Fragmenta*, ed. H. von Arnim [Leipzig 1903-1904]: 1.99.22; see also Seneca, *Ep.* 16.5-6, 98.2, *Prov.* 4.12), as did the Epicureans (Epicurus, *Ep. Men.* in Diogenes Laert. 10.133-135) and the Neo-Platonists (Plotinus, *Enn.* 3.1.10). The Church Fathers treated such notions as "providence and fate and necessity and fortune and free will" as pagan, and therefore as erroneous, explanations of what had been revealed to Christians as the supreme dialectic of power between "the Lord God and his adversary the →devil" (Tertullian, *De Anima* 20).

III. According to 1 Cor 16:15-17, a certain Fortunatus (*Phortounatos*) was a member of the Christian church in Corinth, the capital of the Roman Province of Achaia that included most of Greece and which was also the residence of its governing Proconsul (Acts 18:12). Fortunatus, together with his fellow-townsmen, Stephanas and Achaicus, constituted a delegation from the Corinthian church to Paul in Ephesus. As the known names of Christians from Corinth are mostly of Roman or servile origin, it is possible that Fortunatus and Achaicus (a freedman or client of the family of L. Mummius, who earned the name by his conquest of Achaia in 146 BCE(?): J. HASTINGS, *A Dictionary of the Bible* [New York 1898-1902] s.v. 'Achaicus') belonged to the *oikia* (household) of Stephanas and were "the first converts in Achaia" (1 Cor 16:15).

Although the name is otherwise unknown in the New Testament, a Fortunatus appears in the delegation sent by the Roman church to Corinth (*1 Clem.* 65.1); though it is highly unlikely that this common name refers to the same person. The name was especially popular among African Christians, especially as a martyr-name, and was the name of a Manichaean presbyter opposed by Augustine (*Acta contra Fortunatum*). Although theophoric names ideally indicated alliance with the deity from whom they were taken and something of their "power and honour" (Plutarch, *Def. Orac.* 421E), the uses of Fortunatus in the Christian context are undoubtedly simply in the popular sense of wishing good fortune.

IV. *Bibliography*

J. CHAMPEAUX, *Fortuna: recherches sur le culte de la fortune à Rome et dans le monde romain des origines à la mort César*: I. *Fortuna dans la religion archaïque*; II. *Les transformations de Fortuna sous la République* (Rome 1982, 1987) [& lit]; W. EISENHUT, Fortuna, *KP* 2 (1967) 597-600; W. W. FOWLER, Fortune (Roman), *ERE* 6 (1913) 98-104; G. HERZOG-HAUSER, Tyche und Fortuna, *Wiener Studien* 63 (1948) 156-163; I. KAJANTO, Fortuna, *ANRW* II 17, 1 (1981) 502-558 [& lit]; W. OTTO, Fortuna, *RE* 7.1 (1910) 12-42; H. R. PATCH, The Tradition of the Goddess Fortuna, *Smith College Studies in Modern Language* 3 (1922) 132-177; R. PETER-W. DREXLER, Fortuna, *ALGRM* 1.2 (1886-1890) 1503-1515.

L. H. MARTIN

G

GABNUNNIM גבננים

I. The expression *har gabnunnîm* in Ps 68:16, literally 'mountain of peaks' and usually translated as 'mighty mountain' (RSV), is interpreted by DEL OLMO LETE (1988:54-55) as 'mountain of the Gabnunnim', the latter being a designation of underworld deities.

II. The reasoning that lies behind del Olmo Lete's suggestion is based on the opposition in Ps 68 of Mt. Sinai versus Mt. Bashan, the one being the holy mountain of →Yahweh, the other the holy mountain of a group of Canaanite gods (vv 15-17). For his interpretation of →Bashan as a dwelling-place of gods, del Olmo Lete was able to adduce the expression *har-ʾĕlōhîm* in the first half of v 16. The gods in question must have been underworld deities, argues del Olmo Lete, as Mt. Bashan is in the region of Athtaroth and Edrei, the dwelling place of →Og, king of the →Rephaim. The 'kings' (*mĕlākîm*) scattered by Yahweh (v 15) are the deities that belong to the retinue of →Milcom, the Canaanite god of the nether world.

III. Though Mt. Basan has undoubtedly mythological overtones in Ps 68, the interpretation offered by del Olmo Lete is difficult to uphold. The root GBN (from which Heb **gabnôn* is derived) is known in several Semitic languages. It basically denotes a marked elevation of the surface (*Ges.*[18] 195; *HALAT* 167; J. HUEHNERGARD, *Ugaritic Vocabulary in Syllabic Transcription* [HSS 32; Atlanta 1987] 115-116); hence the translation 'peaks' for *gabnunnîm*. As the traditional translations make perfect sense, and since there is no further attestation of a group of gods called the Gabnunnim, del Olmo Lete's proposal must be rejected.

IV. *Bibliography*

G. DEL OLMO LETE, Bašan o el 'Infierno' Cananeo, *SEL* 5 (1988) 51-60.

K. VAN DER TOORN

GABRIEL גבריאל

I. Gabriel appears in the Book of Daniel as the →angel who explains the vision of the he-goat and the ram (8:16) and the prophecy of the seventy (weeks of) years (9:21). He is usually assumed to be also the revealing angel of Daniel 10. In the New Testament, he is the angel of the Annunciation (Luke 1:19,26) and is identified with 'the angel of the Lord'. The name is usually understood as 'man of God', but is better taken as 'God is my hero/warrior' (FITZMYER 1981: 328, who argues from the analogy of the first person plural suffix in the name [I]*Ré-i-na-*[d]*Adad*, "Adad is our shepherd", at Ebla). In Daniel he is explicitly said to have the appearance of a man (8:15) and is referred to as "the man Gabriel" (האיש גבריאל), probably because of the element גבר, man, in his name.

II. Gabriel and →Michael are the only angels mentioned by name in the Hebrew Bible (→Raphael is also mentioned in the Book of Tobit). Both Michael and Gabriel appear in the oldest extant list of four →archangels in *1 Enoch* 9:1 with Sariel and Raphael. While the composition of this list often varies in post-biblical Jewish writings, Michael, Gabriel and Raphael are constant members (1QM 9:14-16; *1 Enoch* 40:9; 54: 6; 71:8; *Life of Adam and Eve* 40:3; *Num. Rabbah* 2:10; *Pesiqta Rabbati* 46; *Pirqe de Rabbi Eliezer* 4; →Uriel and Phanuel often appear as the fourth archangel). Gabriel also appears in the list of seven archangels in *1 Enoch* 20, with Uriel, Raphael, Raguel,

Michael, Sariel and Remiel. He is one of "the glorious ones of the Lord" in *2 Enoch* 21:3.

The names of angels proliferated in the Hellenistic period. The names themselves, however, are typically archaic theophoric names, ending with the name of the Canaanite god →El, who was, of course, identified with Yahweh in the Hebrew Bible. There is no evidence, however, that these names are in fact older than the Hellenistic period.

III. The primary function of Gabriel is that of revealer. In the Book of Daniel he interprets mysterious visions and prophecies. In the Gospel of Luke he is a messenger from God, and takes over the role of the 'Angel of the LORD' of the Hebrew Bible, in announcing the birth of John the Baptist and Jesus. He comforts Zechariah (father of John) and Mary, and tells them not to be afraid. In *2 Enoch* 21, he has similar words of encouragement for Enoch, and then he carries him up, "like a leaf carried by the wind", into the presence of the LORD. In *1 Enoch* 9, Gabriel and the other archangels intercede for the earth, and ask the LORD to punish the →Watchers. In the following chapter, Gabriel is charged to "proceed against the bastards and the reprobates and against the children of adultery, and destroy the children of adultery and expel the children of the Watchers from among the people". The archangels have a similar role in punishing the wicked by casting them into a furnace on the day of judgment in *1 Enoch* 54:6. The militant role of the archangels is also in evidence in the Qumran War Scroll, where their names are inscribed on shields and towers in preparation for the final battle (1QM 9: 14-16). If the revealing angel in Daniel 10 is indeed Gabriel (as he is explicitly identified in the two preceding chapters), then he also has a militant role there, as he stands with Michael against the heavenly →'princes' of Persia and Greece. Gabriel's high rank is confirmed in *2 Enoch* 24:1, where he is seated on the left hand of God. In *1 Enoch* 20 he is in charge of Paradise, and in *1 Enoch* 40:9 he is set over all the powers.

An interesting function of Gabriel and other angels appears in the Aramaic incantation bowls, which come from Babylonia and are later than 600 CE. Here the names of Gabriel, Michael and other angels are invoked to put spells on people, and Gabriel is sometimes given precedence over Michael (MONTGOMERY 1913:96; ISBELL 1975:22, 25).

IV. The Targumim introduce Gabriel into narratives of a much earlier period, so that he leads →Joseph to his brothers (Gen 37:15), participates with Michael in the burial of →Moses (Deut 34:6) and is sent by the LORD to destroy the armies of Sennacherib (2 Chron 32:21).

V. *Bibliography*

J. A. FITZMYER, *The Gospel According to Luke I-IX* (AB 28; Garden City 1981); C. D. ISBELL, *Corpus of the Aramaic Incantation Bowls* (Missoula 1975); J. A. MONTGOMERY, *Aramaic Incantation Texts from Nippur* (Philadelphia 1913); Y. YADIN, *The Scroll of the War of the Sons of Light against the Sons of Darkness* (Oxford 1962).

J. J. COLLINS

GAD גד

I. Gad is the name of a deity of good luck, equivalent to the Greek →Tyche and Latin →Fortuna. Gad is mentioned together with →Meni in Isa 65:11 as being worshipped in post-exilic Judah. The god is also attested in personal names (e.g. *Gaddî*, Num 13:11; *Gaddî'ēl,* Num 13:10; *'Azgād*, Ezra 2:12) and place names (e.g. *Ba'al-gād*, Josh 11:17 etc.; *Migdal-gād*, Josh 15:37), most probably in the sense of an appellative meaning '(good) fortune' rather than as the name of a deity. As god of fortune, Gad is attested in texts from Canaan, Phoenicia (and the Punic world), Hauran and Arabia.

II. When it comes to the the earliest West-Semitic attestations of the god Gad, attention must be paid first to *gd* as an element of personal names in Ugaritic, Amorite, Phoenician and Punic (GRÖNDAHL 1967:126; HUFFMON 1965:179; BENZ 1972:

294-295); it is often difficult, however, to ascertain whether it should be taken as an appellative or as the name of a deity. In Phoenician and Punic names, the word *gd* occurs chiefly as the expression of a wish in names that are not necessarily theophoric. The frequency of feminine names compounded with *nʿm*, in the onomastics of Carthage, Constantine and Spain, moreover, suggests an association with childbirth (BENZ 1972:295), and reminds us of Gen 30:10-13, where →Leah, at the birth of the first son of Zilpah, exclaimed "Good fortune" and called his name Gad.

A 'proto-Canaanite' inscription from Tell ed-Duweir (Late Bronze Age) contains, perhaps, the earliest attestation of Gad as a divine name. According to G. W. AHLSTRÖM (1983), the fragmentary inscription *gdy*... could be translated "My Gad ..." (i.e. an incomplete personal name?). He tentatively suggests that it is possible to conclude that the deity was worshipped in Transjordan in pre-Israelite times, and that Tell ed-Duweir was one of the cult places of this god. In the Punic world, three inscriptions attest to the use of Gad as divine epithet. *RES* 1222 from Nora, Sardinia (4th-3rd century BCE) contains a dedication "for the Lady, for Tanit Face-of-Baal and Fortune" (*lrbt ltnt pn bʿl wgd*). *KAI* 72 from Ibiza, Spain (about 180 BCE) also uses the name next to Tanit, in the formula *lrbt ltnt ʾdrt whgd*, i.e. "For the Lady, for Mighty Tanit, and the Fortune". *KAI* 147:2, a neo-Punic inscription from Mactar (Tunisia), mentions *gd hšmm*, 'Gad of the heavens', which perhaps corresponds to the North-African deity *Caelestis* (see *CIL* VIII 6943: *Fortuna Caelestis sacrum*; but note that Latin *Caelestis* corresponds to the Punic deity Tanit). So it seems possible that Gad was a divine epithet of Tanit in her capacity as goddess of fate for the Punic cities. She, in turn, could be identified with the '*daimon* of the Carthaginians', mentioned by Polybius (VIII 9) among the gods of the Punic pantheon, and possibly the major patroness of Carthage and of Punic Africa (GARBINI 1965; GROTTANELLI 1982). Gad is also well known from Palmyrene inscriptions, which often mention gods to whom the Palmyrenes give the title *gd*, equated with Fortuna or Tyche. A bilingual inscription (*CIS* II 3927, ca. 140 CE) equates the Palmyrene Gad and the Greek Tyche. The word also occurs in a large number of personal names, in combination with several deities. It may be concluded that Gad personified the lot reserved by a god or a goddess for a believer, a group of individuals (tribes or families), a town (note the existence of Gad of Dura Europos, of Tadmor and of Palmyra) or a village, and even rivers or gardens. This Gad, then, stood for the theological concept of divine providence rather than for a particular and individual deity (TEIXIDOR 1979: 89.94-95). As an allomorph of classical Fortuna or Tyche, Gad was identified in Syria with the →Artemis of Gerasa, with the →Atargatis of Palmyra and with the god Yarhibol. In the Greco-Roman Near East, then, Gad serves as a generic title of city deities connected with prosperity and good luck, but without a definite personality.

III. It is generally admitted that Isa 65:11 (RSV: "But you who forsake the LORD, who forget my holy mountain, who set a table for Fortune [*gād*], and fill cups of mixed wine for Destiny [*mênî*]") refers to cultic meals (*lectisternia*) eaten in honour of two deities, Gad and Meni. The LXX renders Gad as δαίμων and Meni as Τύχη; Vg renders "Fortune" (*qui positis Fortunae mensam et libatis super eam*) and ignores Meni. The latter is to be interpreted as a god (or spirit) of fate, possibly identical (in spite of the masculine gender of the noun) with the pre-Islamic Arabic goddess Man(aw)at (→Meni); consequently also Gad seems to be used as a divine appellative.

There are other biblical references that might be connected with Gad. For the place names *Baʿal-gād* (Josh 11:17; 12:7; 13:5), and *Migdal-gād* (Josh 15:37) various explanations are conceivable. The first could be interpreted as 'Gad is Lord', or as 'Baal is fortune', or as 'Baal of (the clan of) Gad' (→Baal-Gad); the second could be translated as 'Tower of Gad' (see *Migdal-ʾēl* in Josh

19:38), or as 'Tower of fortune' (see esp. MAIER III *ABD* 2:863-864), or as 'Tower of (the clan of) Gad'. In personal names, Gad occurs over 40 times as a (theophoric?) element. The seventh son of Jacob was welcomed at his birth by Leah's cry "Good fortune" (Gen 30:11: *bāgād*, LXX ἐν τύχῃ), and therefore named *gād*; by this etiological explanation of the tribal name the author of the narrative clearly wishes to exclude any theophoric associations—though they may have initially been present. In the names *Gaddî*, *Gaddî'ēl*, and *'Azgād*, it is very doubtful as well that *gd* is a theophoric element. *Gaddî* means 'My fortune' rather than 'My Gad'; *Gaddî'ēl* (compare the extra-biblical *gdyhw*), probably means 'El/ God is fortune', or 'Blest of God' (though the presence of two theophoric elements is not excluded), while *'Azgād* contains apparently the name of the deity, plus the divine appellative 'Strength, Protection' ('Strong is Gad'?). Compare also the extra-biblical Hebrew names *gdyw*, *gdmlk* ('Gad is king' or 'the King is fortune'), and *'bgd* ('Gad is father' or 'the [divine] Father is fortune') (FOWLER 1988:67-68).

IV. Gad is attested in later Jewish literature, in which he was identified with the planet Jupiter. The name also acquired the general meaning of *numen* 'spirit' (see F. DELITZSCH, *Isaiah* [Grand Rapids 1980] 482-483).

V. *Bibliography*

G. W. AHLSTRÖM, Was Gad the God of Tell ed-Duweir?, *PEQ* 115 (1983) 47-48; M. L. BARRÉ, *The God-List in the Treaty between Hannibal and Philip V of Macedonia* (Baltimore 1983) 64-67; F. L. BENZ, *Personal Names in the Phoenician and Punic Inscriptions* (Rome 1972) 294-295; H. J. W. DRIJVERS, *The Religion of Palmyra* (Leiden 1976) 13.19; T. FAHD, *Le panthéon de l'Arabie centrale à la veille de l'Hégire* (Paris 1968) 78-80; J. D. FOWLER, *Theophoric Personal Names in Ancient Hebrew. A Comparative Study* (JSOTSup 49; Sheffield 1988) 67-68, 322, 340; G. GARBINI, Note di epigrafia punica-I, *RSO* 40 (1965) 212-213; F. GRÖNDAHL, *Die Personennamen der Texte aus Ugarit* (Rome 1967) 126-127; C. GROTTANELLI, Astarte-Matuta e Tinnit-Fortuna, *VO* 5 (1982) 103-116; H. B. HUFFMON, *Amorite Personal Names in the Mari Texts. A Structural and Lexical Study* (Baltimore 1965) 179; W. A. MAIER III, Gad (Deity), *ABD* 2 (1992) 863-864; D. SOURDEL, *Les cultes du Hauran à l'époque romaine* (Paris 1952) 49-52; J. TEIXIDOR, *The Pantheon of Palmyra* (EPRO 79; Leiden 1979) 88-100.

S. RIBICHINI

GAIUS → RULER CULT

GEPEN גפן

I. Gapnu, 'the vine', is well attested as a divine name in the Ugaritic mythological texts, always in the binomial *gpn w ugr*, 'vine(yard) and field' (*KTU* 1.3 iii 37; 1.4 vii 54; 1.4 viii 47; 1.5 i 12). In spite of some dissenting opinions, this interpretation of the names is widely accepted today (PARDEE 1989/1990). The Ugaritic name is etymologically connected with Heb *gepen*, 'vine'.

II. GINSBERG (1944) has established that, in spite of the lack of separate attestations of *gpn* and *ugr*, various accompanying forms in the texts show that the phrase *gpn w ugr* does not designate a single deity, but two. The primary function of these two deities was to serve as →Baal's messengers (see S. A. MEIER, *The Messenger in the Ancient Semitic World* [HSM 45; Atlanta 1988] 124-128). To date, neither of the deities is attested in the ritual texts, whilst no personal name attests unambiguously to the use of *gpn* as a theophoric element.

III. Though a deified *gepen* has not been identified in the Hebrew Bible, the word is on occasion used metaphorically. In Hos 10:1 and Ps 80 the people of Israel are likened to a vine. A similar usage of the term occurs in the New Testament in Jesus' claim (John 15:1) to be the true vine (*ampelos*) and his father the vinedresser (*geōrgos*). Such metaphorical use of the term does not indicate, however, that the vine was ever deified in ancient Israel.

IV. *Bibliography*

H. L. GINSBERG, Baal's Two Messengers, *BASOR* 95 (1944) 25-30; D. PARDEE, *AfO* 36/37 [1989/1990] 446.

D. PARDEE

GETHER גתר

I. Gatharu (*gṯr*) is attested as a divine name in several genres of Ugaritic texts (vocabulary texts, rituals, a letter) and in sacrificial lists from Emar. The name is also attested as a theophoric element at Mari. It is plausibly derived from a root GṮR. It denotes :'to be strong', provided that the relationship with the Akkadian adjective *gašru* be accepted, where the strength denoted is particularly fierce and war-like. The god Gatharu has been tentatively connected with the bibilical anthroponym Gether (Gen 10:23).

II. The deity is most clearly at home in Syria in the second millennium BCE, though the veneration of the deity in first-millennium Phoenicia is attested by the personal name *bdgšr* (P. Bordreuil *apud* PARDEE 1988:92 n. 56).

The divine determinative on the first element of the personal name ᵈ*Ga-aš-rum-ga-mil* (ARM 22: 13 ii 28) proves the existence of the deity by the eighteenth century, while multiple appearances in the Emar texts illustrate his relative popularity on the middle Euphrates in the fourteenth century (D. ARNAUD, *Emar* VI/3 [1986] 268, text 274:19' = Msk 74298a:7'; p. 354, text 373: 119' = Msk 74292a; p. 375, text 379:5 = Msk 74264). DE MOOR has suggested the presence of this deity behind the Sumerian divine name Ninurta in *EA* 74:31 (1990:244; see N. NA'AMAN, *UF* 22 [1990] 252-254, for the history of the discussion and another hypothesis).

The vocalization in Ugaritic as *ga-ša-ru* (= /gaṯaru/) is known from three entries in one of the polyglot vocabularies (J. NOUGAYROL, *Ug* V [MRS 16; Paris 1968] 248-249, text 137 IVa 15; IVb 11, 13). In this vocabulary, Gatharu is given each time as the equivalent of the Hurrian diety *mi-il-ku-un(-ni)*, apparently the Hurrianized form of the West Semitic deity Milku. On the other hand, the Sumero-Akkadian equivalent appears to vary, Tišpak being extant in the first entry (137 IVa 15), Ningirsu/Sakkud in all probability to be reconstructed in the others (137 IV b 11, 13; cf. NOUGAYROL, ibid., p. 248 n. 7, and W. W. HALLO & W. L. MORAN, *JCS* 31 [1979] 72 n. 23; W. L. MORAN, LAPO 13 [1987] 252 n. 10). These equivalences show that Gatharu was considered at Ugarit to have both chthonic and belligerent characteristics. The divine name occurs as the theophoric element in the proper name *ʿbdgṯr* (F. GRÖNDAHL, *Die Personennamen der Texte aus Ugarit* [StP 1; Rome 1967] 131).

Gatharu plays an important role in the ritual text *KTU* 1.43:11.14, while the existence of a statuette of this divinity is proven by a letter according to which 'the gods' Baʿlu and Gatharu are entrusted to two individuals (*KTU* 2.4). It is in the form of such a statuette that Gatharu would have participated in the 'rite of entry' prescribed in *KTU* 1.43:9-16. The existence of distinct statuettes of Baʿlu and Kotharu (→Koshar) proves that Gatharu was not identified with Baʿlu, as some scholars have held (M. DIETRICH & O. LORETZ, *UF* 12 [1980] 175; DE MOOR 1990:72 n. 174; cf. PARDEE 1988:91-92 n. 56). This datum is congruent with the data provided by the polyglot texts, where Gatharu is never identified with a weather deity.

The understanding of the divine name at Ugarit is complicated by the occurrence in the ritual texts of a form written *gṯrm* (*KTU* 1.43:9, 17, 19; 1.109:26; 1.112:18, 19, 20), interpreted by some as a dual, by others as a plural (for an overview of opinions, see PARDEE, *Textes rituels*, f.c., chap. IV). Because one of the sets of occurrences (*KTU* 1.43) of *gṯrm* is in immediate contiguity with *gṯr*, *špš* (the Ugaritic solar deity), and *yrḫ* (the principal Ugaritic lunar deity), one plausible interpretation is to see *gṯrm* as a plural, i.e. as a substantivized adjective referring to *gṯr*, *špš* and *yrḫ* (PARDEE 1993; idem, *Textes rituels*, f.c., chap. IV).

No evidence exists as yet for the identification of a royal figure in the Ugaritic dynastic lineage who would have borne the same name as the divinity (DIETRICH & LORETZ 1992:69, 73).

III. Though the name Gether in Gen 10:23 may indeed be derived from the same root as the deity *Gatharu* (as a 'son of Aram', the correspondence /ṯ/ : /t/ poses no problem), it is impossible to say whether the biblical name directly reflects the deity (DE MOOR 1990:244). The theonym is not yet attested in Aramaic sources.

IV. *Bibliography*

G. DEL OLMO LETE, Ritual procesional de Ugarit (KTU 1.43), *Sefarad* 46 (1986) 363-371; M. DIETRICH & O. LORETZ, *"Jahwe und seine Aschera". Anthropomorphes Kultbild in Mesopotamien, Ugarit und Israel. Das biblische Bilderverbot* (UBL 9; Münster 1992) 39-76; J. C. DE MOOR, *The Rise of Yahwism* (BETL 91; Leuven 1990); D. PARDEE, *Les textes para-mythologiques de la 24e Campagne (1961)* (RSO IV; Paris 1988) 83-94, 101-103; PARDEE, RS 1.005 and the Identification of the *gṯrm*, *Ritual and Sacrifice in the Ancient Near East* (OLA 55; ed. J. Quaegebeur; Leuven 1993) 301-318; PARDEE, *Les textes rituels* (RSO; Paris, f.c.); P. XELLA, *I Testi Rituali di Ugarit*. I. *Testi* (StSem 54; Rome 1981) 43-54, 86-90.

D. PARDEE

GHOST → **SPIRIT OF THE DEAD**

GIANTS γίγαντες

I. In the strict sense the Gigantes in Greek mythology were the serpent-footed giants who were born from the blood-drops of the castration of Uranus (→Heaven) that had fallen on →Earth (Hesiod *Theogony* 183-186). The term *gigantes* occurs about 40 times in the LXX and refers there respectively to: a) the giant offspring of 'the sons of God' and 'the daughters of mankind' (Gen 6:1-4; Bar 3:26-28; Sir 16:7); b) strong and mighty men, like →Nimrod (Gen 10:8-9); c) several pre-Israelite peoples of tall stature in Canaan and Transjordania. The etymology of the name, which may be pre-Greek, is unknown, but was in Antiquity thought to be γηγενής or 'born from earth'.

II. As Gaea-Earth was vexed with the sorry fate of the →Titans after their battle with the Olympian gods, she now stirred up her other sons, the Giants, against the Olympians. They endeavoured to storm heaven by building a tower (cf. Gen 11:4), that is by piling up the mountains Pelion, Ossa and →Olympus on top of one another (Homer, *Od.* 11,315-316). According to an oracle, the gods could not destroy the Giants unless they were helped by a mortal man. In the ensuing Gigantomachy it was →Heracles who assisted the gods, killing off the Giants with his arrows after they had already been wounded, mainly so by →Zeus' thunderbolts (Apollodorus, *Library* 1,6,1-2). Out of their blood-drops that fell on Earth such a new race of savage and bloodthirsty men was born that Jupiter destroyed them by the Flood (Ovid *Metam.* 1,151-162; 262-312). Not all of them were killed, however, though some were punished in the Nether World or Tartarus and were supposed to lie as prisoners under islands and volcanoes.

In Antiquity the story was sometimes believed literally, skeletons of whales or dinosaurs being explained as the bones of the Giants (Suetonius, *Augustus* 72,3), but sometimes it was dismissed as fiction (Plato, *Euth.* 6b-c; *Resp.* 2,378c). Between these two extremes there were various other opinions: Ephorus of Cyme considered the Giants to have been a historical tribe of barbarians in Chalcidice which had been defeated by Heracles (*FGH* 70F34); Proclus saw the Gigantomachy psychologically as the battle between reason and the lower passions (*In Plat. Parmenidem* 127c), Joannes Lydus as the victory of sunlight over winter (*De mensibus* 4,3), etc. As a literary motif it was often used in panegyrics in honour of rulers or generals who had defeated the tall Celts or Germans: Claudian makes the Visigoth Alaric as the 'Giant' the opponent of the god Eridanus, the river Po (*On the 6th Consulship of Honorius* 178-186).

III. In the LXX-translation the word γίγαντες correponds to four or five Hebrew words or expressions in the MT: (1) →*nĕpîlîm* = the offspring of the sons of God (Gen 6:1-4); rarely the same people as (2), in Num 13:33; (2) →*rĕpā'îm*, the tall, original inhabitants of the promised land; the word was also left untranslated as Rafaeim or Rafaein e. g. Gen 15:20; (3) 'sons of Râphâ(h)', the eponymous ancestor of the *rĕpā'îm* (2 Sam 21:22); (4) 'sons of *'ănāqîm*' (Deut 1:28), tall people living near Hebron (Num 13:22.33) and in Philistia (Jos 11:22); the remaining instances of Hebrew *'anāqîm* are matched in the LXX by Enakim, only in Deut 9:2 by Enak; the Hebrew name has nothing to do etymologically with τῶ Ἄνακε or οἱ Ἄνακες (as the →Dioscuri, who were otherwise gigantic of stature, could also be called) because the latter derives from an older Greek Ϝάνακε(ς); (5) *gibbôrîm*, strong, mighty men or heroes, such as Nimrod. In the MT a number of these Hebrew names occur side by side, as synonyms, (1) and (4) at Num 13:33, (1) and (5) at Gen 6:4, (2) and (3) at 1 Chr 20:4-8, and (2) and (4) at Deut 2:10-11. It is therefore quite understandable and expectable that all could apparently be rendered by the one Greek term γίγαντες, sometimes with the variant reading Τιτᾶνες.

A god whose sons marry mortal women on earth, could, of course, by opponents of Judaism easily be taken to refer to no one else than Cronus, whose sons Zeus and →Poseidon had a reputation for having fathered many earthlings, especially ancestors of royal dynasties, such as Heracles the son of Zeus from whom the Macedonian kings claimed descent (Plutarch, *Alexander* 2,1). Probably in order to prevent such interpretations, the expression 'the sons of God' was replaced by 'the angels of God' in a number of manuscripts of the LXX and also by Philo of Alexandria. He denies that Gen 6:1-4 is a piece of mythology and likewise makes 'the giants' sons of 'the angels of God' and of earthly women, while he explains their name as 'the earthborn' or those who indulge in the pleasures of the body (*On the Giants* 6 and 58-60; *Questions and Answers on Gen* 92; cf. also Josephus *Ant* 1,73). These →angels were sinners because they mixed with mortal women, and their sinful giant children were named Nephilim, since they caused the downfall of the world (so *Gen. Rabbah* 26, 7, deriving the name from נפל 'fall'). In *1 Enoch* 6,2 one finds the combination οἱ ἄγγελοι υἱοι τοῦ θεοῦ to refer to the giants' fathers, while Syncellus' version of this passage has οἱ ἐγρήγοροι or 'the →watchers' (so also in *T. Rub.* 5,6; cf. עירין or עירין in 4QEn a,1,1,5 etc.). It was they who taught people on earth all kinds of science and technology (*1 Enoch* 7,1), and astrology in particular (*ibid* 8,3). According to *Jub.* 8,3 Kâinâm, here the son of Arpachshad (contrary to Gen 5:9 and 10:24), even found rock inscriptions made by 'former' generations (Syncellus and Cedrenus: "of the giants"), which contained the very teaching of these Watchers, which is then further described as the observation of celestial omens (cf. *Gen. Rabbah* 26,5). Josephus, however, ascribed not only the inscriptions, but also the invention of astronomy itself to the sons of Seth (*Ant.* 1,70-71). Apart from these passages there existed a special, more detailed apocryphon about the Giants, of which only fragments have been preserved from Qumran (4 QEnGiants, in Aramaic) and from the Manichaean tradition (in Soghdian and Uigur). Here the various giants have received names, and of two of them, the brothers Ôhyâh and Hahyâh, it is related that they had prognostic dreams, which were then explained by →Enoch. The race of the giants was mostly supposed to have drowned in the Flood (3 Macc 2,4; Wis 14,5-6), numbering then 409.000 (*3 Apoc. Bar.* 4,10). Their souls lived on as evil spirits who caused harm to mankind (e. g. *1 Enoch* 15,8-16,1; *Jub.* 10,1-3; *Test. Sal.* 17,1). The *angels* who had sinned were "thrown down", according to 2 Pet 2:4 by God himself into "the Tartarus", to be kept there for the coming judgment. The author makes use here of the verb ταρταρόω, which is the typical expression for the punishment of the Titans, cf κατεταρτάρωσεν in Apollodorus, *Library* 1,2,3 and Sextus Empiricus *Pyrrh.* 3,210. The substantive Τάρταρος, however, is found more often, though not as frequently as →Hades, referring to the Hebrew →Sheol e.g. LXX Prov 24:51 (30:16); cf. 1 *Enoch* 20,2 where the angel →Uriel is the prince of the Kosmos and the Tartarus.

As to the fate of the Giants, the Samaritan anonymus (Ps-Eupolemus) relates that some of them were saved from the Flood and became the builders of the Tower of Babylon (*frg* 1 in Eusebius, *P. E.* 9,17,2). This may show the influence of the current story of those other giants, Otus and Ephialtes, who were no sons of Uranus and Gaea; they wanted to storm Heaven by means of piling up some mountains on top of Olympus (Homer, *Od.* 11,305-320). Ovid ascribed this to the Giants in the proper sense (see above).

The exegesis itself of 'the sons of God' as fallen angels at Gen 6:2 did not go unchallenged. Tryphon is reported to have considered the whole idea of sinning angels as such to be blasphemy (Justin Martyr, *Dial.* 79). Symmachus' translation of the passage had οἱ υἱοὶ τῶν δυναστευόντων or "the sons of those holding power" and similarly, *Gen. Rabbah* 26,5 has the tradition that they were to be seen as "sons of nobles". Julius Africanus simply wanted to explain them as the sons of the rightful Seth and the daughters of mankind as descendants of Cain (*Chron.* frg. 2), thus removing the slightest trace of mythology.

IV. *Bibliography*

H. VON GEISAU, Gigantes, *KP* 2 (1975) 797-798; J. T. MILIK (& M. BLACK), *The Books of Enoch. Aramaic Fragments of Qumrân Cave 4* (Oxford 1976) (298-339 for the Book of Giants); J. C. REEVES, *Jewish Lore in Manichaean Cosmogony. Studies in the* Book of Giants *Tradition* (Cincinnati 1992); W. SONTHEIMER, Gigantomachie, *KP* 2 (1975) 798; W. SPEYER, Gigant, *RAC* 10 (1978) 1247-1276; F. VIAN, *La guerre des géants. Le mythe avant l'époque hellénistique* (Paris 1952).

G. MUSSIES

GIBBORIM גבורים

I. The 'warriors that were of old' (*gibbôrîm 'ăšer mē'ôlām*) mentioned in Gen 6:4 and identified with a special class of superhuman beings (the →Nephilim) in the antediluvian period are clearly a race apart from David's champions *(gibbôrîm)* listed in 2 Sam 23:8-39 (= 2 Chr 11:10-47). The further definition *mē'ôlām* is important here because it locates the activities of the *gibbôrîm* in the primeval period and not in the recent historical past. The first named *gibbôr* on earth was →Nimrod and the meaning of this epithet, like the Akk *gabbāru* 'strong' and Ar *al-jabbār* 'the giant (i.e. →Orion)', identifies Nimrod's prowess notably as a mythical hunter, and lord of the kingdoms of Babel, Erech and Accad and founder of Nineveh, Rehobothir, Calah and Resen (Gen 10:8-12; VAN DER TOORN & VAN DER HORST 1990:1-2). His activities thus resemble the exploits of the Mesopotamian hero Gilgamesh recorded in the Old Babylonian tablet of that name (I, 3-28). KRAELING (1947) suggests that Ezekiel, in his fondness for dwelling on the primeval history, sheds—in his figurative description of the fate of Egypt (32:17-32)—more light on the ancient *gibbôrîm.* A special quarter is reserved in the depths of →Sheol for 'the *fallen warriors* of long ago' which will not be shared by the likes of Egypt, Assyria and Elam. The *gibbôrîm* lie, as it were, in state with their swords and shields intact. Alive, they had once been the terror of the land of the living, and now in Sheol they occupied a place of honour. Perhaps it was their quest for fame and glory in the manner of the tower builders in Gen 11 that led to their inevitable downfall; although, as the text stands in Gen 6:4, the redactor clearly associates these warriors with the Nephilim who were destroyed in the flood because they were the monstrous issue of 'the sons of God' and 'the daughters of humans'. The priestly view (elaborated in *1 Enoch* 9:1-2 and *Jub.* 2-3) that the flood was provoked because 'the earth was filled with violence' is consonant with this idea of the *gibbôrîm* and their legendary deeds, ('confident in their strength they rebelled' Sir 16:7).

II. *Bibliography*
E. G. KRAELING, The Significance and Origin of Gen 6.2-4, *JNES* 6 (1947) 193-208; J. SKINNER, *Genesis* (ICC; Edinburgh 1910); E. A. SPEISER, In Search of Nimrod, *Eretz Israel* 5 (1958) 32-45; K. VAN DER TOORN & P. W. VAN DER HORST, Nimrod before and after the Bible, *HTR* 83 (1990) 1-29; C. WESTERMANN, *Genesis 1-11* (Neukirchen-Vluyn 1974); W. ZIMMERLI, *Ezekiel 2*, II Teilband (Neukirchen-Vluyn 1969; English Translation Philadelphia 1983).

P. W. COXON

GILLULIM גלולים εἴδωλα

I. Within the context of OT anti-iconic polemics the designation of deities and/or their images as *gillûlîm* occurs 48 times (39 in Ezek). The etymology of the noun is a subject of discussion. Many scholars follow BAUDISSIN (1904) in deriving Biblical Heb *gillûlîm* from a hypothetical singular noun **galol* 'stela', whose vocalization has been deliberately modified by the Israelite prophets to correspond to the vowel pattern of the word *šiqqûṣîm* →'abominations'. This interpretation rests on an observation in the Aramaic-Greek bilingual Palmyrene inscription *CIS* 147, where Aramaic *gĕlālāʾ* corresponds to Greek στήλη 'stela', both of which correspond semantically to Biblical Heb *maṣṣēbâ*. Thus an originally neutral term for 'cult objects' became a dysphemism for deities other than the LORD, as well as for the cult statues, that represented those deities (PREUSS, *TWAT* 2, 1-2; *HALAT* 185 sub a). Medieval Hebrew exegetes and others regard *gillûlîm* as a dysphemism. They assume that the term is derived from *gĕlālîm* which means 'faeces' (e.g. Ezek 4:12, 15; 22:3; 30:13) and that the term *gillûlîm* was meant to make people abhor the worship of deities other than the LORD (*HALAT* 75 sub b; SCHROER 1987:418-419).

II. The majority of the biblical references to *gillûlîm* are found in the Book of Ezekiel, which, like the Book of Jeremiah, continually points to Judaeans' worshipping other gods during the last generation before the destruction of the Temple. It has been suggested that Ezekiel was the author of the term *gillûlîm* (SCHROER 1987:418). He might, however, have adopted the designation from the deuteronomistic writers. Most likely, the background of this emphasis on *gillûlîm* 'idols' during the period between Josiah's reform (622 BCE) and the destruction of the Temple (586 BCE) is the failure of that reform to provide a religious institutional infrastructure for worship of the LORD. As an outcome of the royal reading of the Torah Scroll found in the Temple (2 Kgs 22) all altars for worship of the LORD other than the one on Mount Moriah in Jerusalem must have been destroyed.

WEINFELD writes in his commentary on Deuteronomy (1991:80), "The destruction of the high places and the provincial sanctuaries created a vacuum, which was filled by the institution of the synagogue. After the reform, the people who, until this point, had entered into their religious experience in a sanctuary close to where they lived or in a high place situated in their town, needed to find a substitute. The aboliton of the high places without any provision of a replacement for them would have been tantamount to the destruction of daily religious experience, a thing that, unlike in our own times, would have been impossible in the ancient world. This substitute was found, therefore in prayer and reading of the book of the Torah, which comprised the worship of God in the synagogue." Weinfeld is correct in his argument that for many Judaeans, at least, a substitute had to be found and was found. However, the oldest extra-biblical evidence for the institution of the synagogue is from 3rd century BCE Egypt. However, it is not the argument from silence which challenges Weinfeld's suggestion that the synagogue was the substitute for the erstwhile "high places" but rather the clear voices of the Books of Jeremiah and Ezekiel. These books tell us that when the Josianic reform had successfully dismantled Yahwistic high places all over the Land of Israel, many Judeans found a substitute in what Ezekiel calls the 'idols': "You shall know that I am the LORD when your slain lie among the 'idols' round about their altars, on every high hill, on all the mountain tops, under every green tree, and under every leafy oak—wherever they presented pleasing odours to all their *gillûlîm* 'idols'" (Ezek 6:13).

The nine biblical references to *gillûlîm*, 'idols', outside the Book of Ezekiel consist of references to King Asa of Judah's attempt to eradicate the worship of gods other than the LORD (1 Kgs 15:1); Ahab's embracing the worship of →Baal (1 Kgs 21:26); the practice of idolatry in the Northern Kingdom (Samaria), which justified God's allowing the northern tribes to be exiled by Sargon II after 720 BCE (2 Kgs 17:12); King Manasseh's and King Amon's royal patronage of idolatrous cults (2 Kgs 21: 11, 21); King Josiah's attempt to remove idolatrous cults (2 Kgs 23:24); two references to the destruction of Israelites' idols in Pentateuchal imprecations calling for the punishments of the Israelites should they be disloyal to the LORD (Lev 26:30; Deut 29:16); and Jeremiah's reference to Babylonian cult statues as *ʿăṣabbêhā* and *gillûlêhā*, both meaning 'her idols, her cult statues' (Jer 50:2).

The LXX translates *gillûlîm* with εἴδωλα 'idols' (it occurs 91 times, but it should be noted that εἴδωλον is often a translation of *ʿaṣab*, *pesel*, and other terms). The derogatory sense is taken over in the NT, where εἴδωλον is used in a polemical context 11 times, of which 7 are by Paul (4 times in 1 Cor: 8:4.7; 10:19; 12:2). Paul regards εἴδωλα not as divine, but as demonic powers. They do exist, but they do not exist 'for us' (cf. 1 Cor 8:6; see HÜBNER 1980: 938-939).

III. *Bibliography*

W. W. BAUDISSIN, Die alttestamentliche Bezeichnung der Götzen mit gillūlim, *ZDMG* 58 (1904) 395-425; D. BODI, Les *gillûlîm* chez Ezéchiel et dans l'Ancien Testament, *RB* 100 (1993) 481-510; M. GREENBERG, *Ezekiel* (AB 22; Garden City 1983); C. R. NORTH, The Essence of Idolatry, *Von Ugarit nach Qumran* (ed. W. F. Albright; BZAW 77; Berlin 1958) 151-160; H. D. PREUSS, *gillûlîm*, *TWAT* 2 (1974) 1-5; H. HÜBNER, εἴδωλον κτλ., *EWNT* I (1980) 936-941; S. SCHROER, *In Israel gab es Bilder* (OBO 74; Freiburg & Göttingen 1987) 418-419; M. WEINFELD, *Deuteronomy 1-11* (AB 5; New York 1991).

M. I. GRUBER

GIRL נערה

I. The identity of 'the Girl' in the phrase "A man and his father go to the girl" (Amos 2:7) is most probably solved when interpreted as a depreciative designation of a female deity, perhaps →Ashima (ANDERSEN & FREEDMAN 1989:318-319) or →Ashera.

II. The identity of the deity being unknown, it is impossible to provide information about her. In the ancient Near East comparable words can be used when referring to the feminine deity: in Mesopotamian hymns related to marriage between →Ishtar and Dumuzi (→Tammuz) the goddess is presented as a young nubile woman (WILCKE 1976-80:84); in Ugaritic texts →Anat receives the epithet *btlt* 'virgin' (for instance in the Baal-cycle *KTU* 1.3 ii:32); from Ugarit the designation of a member of a despised class of female deities as *amt* 'handmaid' is known (*KTU* 1.4 iv:61).

III. Following the Old Greek translation ('A man and his father go to the *same* maid'), the phrase in Amos 2:7 has been interpreted as a designation of illicit sexual conduct (most recently REIMER 1992:39-42) or as a reference to a sacred marriage and/or prostitution (e.g. BIČ 1969:57-58). The wording of Amos 2:7, however, does not imply a kind of forbidden sexual behaviour (BARSTAD 1984:17-21). The institution of cultic prostitution in the ancient Near East is unprovable (RENGER 1972-75). Relating Amos 2:7 to 2:8, Barstad surmises that in these verses there is a polemic against the institution of the *marzeaḥ* (a guild-like gathering of upper class people, with slightly religious overtones; Amos 6:7; Jer 16:5; Ugarit: *KTU* 1.20-22; 1.114). He interprets the נערה 'maid' as a *marzeaḥ*-hostess

(BARSTAD 1984:33-36). The *parallellismus membrorum* with Amos 2:8 'in the house of their God' suggests the interpretation of נערה as a divine being (ANDERSEN & FREEDMAN 1989:318-319). The designation of this goddess with נערה —the term refers to a subordinate person—suggests, that נערה is a nick-name, indicating the religious evaluation of the deity by Amos. The use of the article in הנערה indicates that she was a deity well-known to the Samarians. Any identification with otherwise known deities remains hypothetical.

IV. *Bibliography*

F. I. ANDERSEN & D. N. FREEDMAN, *Amos* (AB 24A; New York 1989); *H. M. BARSTAD, *The Religious Polemics of Amos* (VTSup 34; Leiden 1984); M. BIČ, *Das Buch Amos* (Berlin 1969); H. REIMER, *Richtet auf das Recht! Studien zur Botschaft des Amos* (SBS 149; Stuttgart 1992); J. RENGER, Heilige Hochzeit, A. Philologisch, *RLA* 4 (1972-75), 251-259; C. WILCKE, Inanna/Ištar, *RLA* 5 (1976-80) 74-87.

B. BECKING

GLORY כבוד δόξα

I. *Kabôd* occurs 200 times in MT, but *doxa* 453 times in the LXX (since it is also used as a translation of more than 20 other Hebrew terms) and 166 times in the NT. The standard translation, 'glory', is inadequate, for it does not convey the specific connotations of these words. The LXX translators chose in *doxa* a term which in classical Greek means 'opinion' or 'reputation', especially good reputation, hence also 'honour'. It is not quite clear how *doxa* could be found suitable to render *kābôd* as the luminous phenomenon characteristic of theophanies or even as the name of the human-like form of God (NEWMAN 1992: 134-152).

II. The basic idea of the Heb *kābôd* is that of weightiness. People become 'weighty' through riches. "Abraham became very weighty in livestock, in silver, and in gold" (Gen 13:2). Through his cattlebreeding, Jacob became 'weighty'; long life and children have the same effect (Prov 3:16; Hos 2:11). The word *kābôd* was also used of the sentiments inspired by the concrete blessings. God gives Solomon "both riches and *kābôd*" (1 Kgs 3:13). "He who possesses righteousness and love, finds life, prosperity and *kābôd*" (Prov. 21:12). The restored →Zion will be given the "*kābôd* of →Lebanon" (Isa 35:2). The 'weighty' person is given more *kābôd* by gifts (Num 22:17.37; 24:11; Judg 13:17; 1 Sam 9:6-9). God is given *kābôd* by praises (Ps 22:24; 29:1-2.9; 96:7; Isa 24:15).

God's 'glory' is to be perceived in his works, i.e. the world, human beings, and historical events (Num 14:21-22; Ps 8:5; 57:6.12; Isa 6:3). In the age to come, it will be revealed so that all flesh will see it (Isa 40:5; Hab 2:14). This revelation of divine glory can be connected with the restoration of Israel (Isa 42:8; 43:6-7; 48:10-11; 58:8; 60:1-3) and/or God's judgement (Isa 59:19; Ezek 28:22; 39:13.21).

In some texts belonging to the Priestly Document (P), one of the sources of the Pentateuch, the Glory is associated with the Pillar of Cloud and fire, which according to older sources, encompassed →Yahweh leading the People through the desert and indicated God's presence at the Tabernacle: "... the Glory of Yahweh appeared in the Cloud" (Exod 16:10); "The Glory of Yahweh rested on Mount Sinai, and the cloud covered it ... the Glory of Yahweh looked ... like a devouring flame on the top of the mount" (Exod 24:16-17; cf. 40:38: at night, there was fire in the Cloud); "The Cloud covered it [the Tabernacle], and the Glory of Yahweh appeared" (Num 17:7; cf. Exod 24:43-44). While the description of the Glory in Exod 24:16-17 may reflect the memory that Mount Sinai was a volcano (NOTH 1960:131), other texts seem to suggest a cultic background for the concept of the Glory. When the Cloud covered the Tent, the Glory 'filled' it (Exod 40:34-35). The Glory 'filled' the Temple (1 Kgs 8:10-11). Lev 9:23-24 appears to connect the Glory with the altar fire consuming the sacrifice. In the light of 1 Sam 3:3 and 4:21, the Glory would rather seem to be some sort of lamp associated with the Ark (cf. Exod 27:20-21).

Some OT texts attribute a human-like form to God's Glory. In Exod 33:18-34:8, it is told that God arranged for Moses to see his Glory (MT Exod 33:19 actually reads 'Goodness', but LXX has 'Glory'; v 22 as well as v 18 reads 'Glory'). Due to a merger of different sources, however, it is related that Moses saw God himself, albeit only his back (33:23; 34:6). The picture emerging from this story is that of indistinguishability between the divine Glory and the anthropomorphous Deity. The relationship between God and his Glory is here thus comparable to that between God and the →Angel of Yahweh, the human-like Messenger of God.

In Ezek 1, the prophet recounts that he once had a vision of a throne-chariot in heaven. Seated upon the throne was a "likeness as the appearance of a man (*ʾādām*)" (v 26). Ezekiel describes the body of this figure: his torso was like gleaming metallic substance, and his lower body was like fire. The prophet concludes: "This was the appearance of the likeness of the Glory of Yahweh" (v 28). In 8:2, Ezekiel relates another vision of the Glory, again described as a "likeness as the appearance of a man" (emending *ʾēš*, 'fire', to *ʾîš*, 'man'; cf. LXX and the Old Latin, 'man'). The body of this figure is described similarly to that of the Glory in 1:27. In 8:2, however, the Glory appears without the throne-chariot. In the second appearance of the throne-chariot, this time in the Temple, the Glory moves from above the chariot and takes up a position in another part of the sanctuary (10:4). The Glory is thus not bound to the throne.

In Ezek. 9:3-4, Yahweh and the Glory even appear as interchangeable, as is the case with God and the Angel of Yahweh in Genesis, Exodus and Judges: "Now the Glory of the God of Israel had gone up from the cherubim on which He rested to the threshold of the house and called to the man in linen ... and Yahweh said to him ..." However, the Glory has a radiant body and is accompanied by phenomena similar to those associated with the Glory in the P source and the texts influenced by it: When the Glory rose from the →cherubim, the Temple was "filled with the Cloud, and the court was full of the brightness of the Glory of Yahweh" (9:4).

In Ezekiel, the Glory is also associated with the Temple. Because of the sins of Israel, the Glory leaves the Temple (11:22-23). When Israel is restored, the Glory will return (43:2). Seen as returning from the mountain east of the city, the Glory is assimilated to the sun god entering the temple each morning (43:1-5; cf. 11:23; 44:1-2; 47:1; Zech 14:4; *Sukkah* 5:4, citing Ezek 8:16; see METTINGER 1982).

III. Ezek 1:26-28 was the starting-point of a mystical tradition describing the vision of the divine Glory on the heavenly →throne. *1 Enoch* 14:18b-21 portrays the 'Great Glory' enrobed in a splendid white garment and seated upon a crystal-like chariot-throne whose wheels are like the sun. None of the angels can look upon him, but →Enoch, after having been transported to heaven, was granted a vision. *T. Levi* 3:4 contains a short reference to the vision of the 'Great Glory' dwelling in the Holy of Holies in the uppermost heaven (cf. 5:1). In the Similitudes of Enoch (*1 Enoch* chaps. 37-71), which may be somewhat younger than the rest of *1 Enoch*, God is known as the 'Lord of Glory' (40:3). Another divine name which is used is 'Glory of the Lord of the Spirits' (41:7; cf. 40:4-7.10, where 'Lord of the Spirits' is parallel to 'Lord of Glory'). God's throne is called the 'Throne of Glory' (9:4; 47:3; 60:2; cf. Jub 31:20). If 'Glory' does not qualify the 'Throne', but refers to its occupant, special heed must be given to the idea that God places his vicegerent, the 'Elect One' or 'Son of Man', upon the 'Throne of Glory' (45:3; 55:4; 61:8; 62:2 [reading, "has seated him", instead of, "has sat down"]; 69:29). The latter executes the eschatological judgement.

When the →Son of Man is introduced in *1 Enoch*, he is described as one "whose face was like the appearance of a man" (46:1). This is reminiscent of the representation of the Glory in Ezek 1:26 and the descriptions of an especially important angelic figure in Daniel. It is possible that the "one like a son of man" as well as the →Ancient of Days in Dan 7 goes back to the figure of the Glory in Ezekiel (PROCKSCH 1950:416-417; BALZ 1967:80-95). Moreover, the "one like a son of man" appears to be identical with the special angel who is described as having the "appearance of a man" (8:15; 10:18) or being in the "likeness of the son of men" ([variant, "son of man"] 10:16). The descriptions of this angel allude to the representation of the Glory as a "likeness as the appearance of a man" in Ezek 1:26 (FEUILLET 1953:183-202; BLACK 1975:97).

Influence from Ezekiel and Daniel can be seen in various descriptions of the principal angel of God (ROWLAND 1982:94-109). In *T. Abr.*, both Adam and →Abel are enthroned in heaven, the latter being the judge of the souls. With reference to Adam, who is sitting on a golden throne, it is said that "the appearance of the man was fearsome, like that of the Lord" (Rec. A, 11:4). In Rec. B, Adam's throne is said to be a "Throne of Great Glory" (8:5). Sitting upon a crystal throne which blazes like fire, Abel is "a wondrous man shining like the sun, like unto a son of God" (Rec. A, 12:5). *Joseph and Asenath* 14:3 describes the angel →Michael as a 'man' or '(one) similar to a man'. One manuscript reads 'man of light', apparently identifying Michael with the "great and unutterable light" which appeared when the heaven was torn apart (v 2; cf. *T. Abr.* Recension A, 7:3, where Michael, descending from the opened heaven, is a luminous man, shining more than seven suns). His heavenly enthronement is assumed, because he has a crown and a royal staff (v 9). *Sib. Or.* V:414 as well as *Joseph and Asenath* 14:3 (and *T. Abr.* Recension A, 7:3) testifies to the idea of the man-like figure who "comes from heaven" (cf. 1 Cor 15:47). In *Sib. Or.* V:415, he has a "sceptre in his hand which God has given him". In *Apoc. Abr.* 11:3, the angel Yahoel, who is said to be "in the likeness of a man", possesses a 'golden sceptre'.

In the *Exagoge* of Ezekiel Tragicus, →Moses has a vision of a noble 'man' seated upon an enormous throne on the summit of Mount Sinai (Eusebius, *Praep. Ev.* IX 28:2). The 'man' hands Moses his diadem and sceptre, and then leaves the throne to the prophet. Here we can detect influence from exegetical occupations with the vision of Moses and his companions as related in Exod 24:10, "And they saw the God of Israel, and there was under his feet as it were a pavement of sapphire stone, like the very heaven for clearness." *Tg. Onq.* and *Tg. Ps.-J.* take this to be a throne vision, the occupant of the throne being called the 'Glory (*yĕqārāʾ* [an Aram equivalent of *kābôd*]) of the God of Israel'. The Samaritan theologian Marqah takes the 'sapphire stone' to be the 'Throne of the Glory (*kābôd*)' (COWLEY 1909:25 line 15). The name 'Glory' in Marqah's work does not denote God, but is a designation of the Angel of Yahweh (FOSSUM 1985:224-225 [cf. *Tg. Ps.-J.*, which says that the '*yĕqārāʾ* of the God of Israel' is the 'Lord of the world', a title which could be referred to the principal angel as well as God (*b. Yeb.* 17b; *b. Hull.* 60a; *b. Sanh.* 94a; *Exod R.* 12:23; *3 Enoch* 30:1-2; 38:3; *Pirke de R. Eliezer* chap. 27)]). In a rabbinic tradition ascribed to R. Meir (2nd cent. CE), the 'sapphire stone' in Exod 24:10 is said to be the 'Throne of Glory', the proof-text being found in Ezek 1:26, which says that the throne of a man-like figure of the Glory was "in appearance like sapphire" (*b. Men.* 43b).

In the mystical Merkabah texts ([*maʿaseh*] *merkabah* being a later technical term for the throne-chariot in Ezek. 1 and even for the chapter itself), we find detailed descriptions of the *Shiʿur Qomah*, the 'Measure of the [divine] Body', upon the heavenly throne. Now these accounts clearly do not refer to "the 'dimensions' of the divinity, but to those of its corporeal appearance. ... Already the 'Lesser Hekhaloth' interpret the anthropomorphosis of the *Shiʿur Komah* as a representation of the 'hidden glory'" (SCHOLEM 1954:66; cf. FOSSUM 1989:198).

IV. The NT continues the usage of the LXX; *doxa* in the NT should often be seen as a technical term loaded with the Jewish understanding of "glory". *Doxa* is a phenomenon of light characteristic of angelophanies, theophanies, and Christophanies (Luke 2:9; 9:31-32; Acts 7:55; 2 Pet 1:17). The Son of Man will come in or with God's glory (Mark 8:38 [cf. 2 Thess 1:7]; 13:26; cf. 10:37; Matt 19:28).

The Gospel of John speaks of "seeing" the glory of God (11:40) or the glory of the Son (1:14; 12:41; 17:24; cf. 2:11). In 1:14 ("we saw his glory"), the background may be the vision of the Glory described in Exod 33:18-34:8 (HANSON 1977:90-100); it is thus possible that John regards the Son not only as the one who manifests the divine presence and power through his words and works, but as the personified Glory. It is noteworthy that the phrase "saw his glory" is repeated in 12:41: "he [Isaiah] saw his [Christ's] glory". Isa 6:1, however, reads "I saw the Lord seated upon a high and lofty throne... ." *Tg. Isa.* 6:1 reads, "*yĕqārā'* of the Lord", but *Tg. Isa.* 6:5 says that the prophet saw "the glory (*yĕqārā'*) of the Shekinah of the King of the Worlds". While *šĕkînâ* in the Targums is generally regarded as a buffer word meant to safeguard God from coming into too close contact with the world, the Merkabah mystics used it as an alternative term for the Kabod. Thus, *Ma'aseh Merkabah* contains the statement, "I gazed upon the Shekinah and saw everything that they do before his Throne of Glory (*kābôd*)" (SCHÄFER 1981:§592). When it is said that Isaiah saw the glory of →Christ, it is implied that the Son is the divine manifestation upon the heavenly throne, even the Glory.

There are other NT texts where →Jesus may be seen as the Glory. The conjunction *kai* ('and') in Acts 7:55 may be epexegetical: "... he saw the Glory of God, namely (*kai*) Jesus standing at the right hand of God" (MARTIN 1967:312). The idea of Jesus being seated at the right hand of the "Power" (Mark 14:62 [Luke 22:69: "Power of God"]), however, may be taken to imply that he was enthroned alongside the Glory, since the mystical texts use "Power" as a synonym of "Glory" (FOSSUM 1989:191-193).

The christological hymn in Phil 2 says that Christ was "existing in the form (*morphē*) of God" (v 6). This description corresponds to the subsequent incarnational phrases, "taking the form of a slave", "becoming in the likeness of men", and "being found in the fashion as a man" (vv 7-8). Given the OT evidence that God's visible form is the man-like form of the Glory, Phil 2:6 would seem to say that Christ is the divine Glory. The same idea is expressed by the title, "image of the invisible God", in the beginning of the hymn on Christ in Col 1:15-20 (FOSSUM 1989:185-190). In Biblical terminology, "image" (and "likeness"), "form", and "glory" are interchangeable (FOSSUM 1985:269-270.284).

In Eph 1:17, we find the phrase, "the God of our Lord Jesus Christ, the Father of the Glory". The parallelism suggests that "our Lord Jesus Christ" is "the Glory". Tit 2:13 may be translated, "the Glory of our great God and Saviour, Christ Jesus". Here Christ Jesus may be the Glory of "our great God and Saviour". Jas 2:1, a notoriously difficult verse to translate, may in effect say, "our Lord Jesus Christ, the Glory". 1 Pet 4:14 says, "... the Spirit of the Glory and of God rests upon you." Here, too, the Glory may be the Son.

Phil 3:21 speaks of Christ's "body of glory" to which the body of the believers will be conformed. The term may reflect that of *gûp hakkābôd* or *gûp haššĕkînâ* found in the Jewish mystical texts (SCHOLEM 1991:278 n. 19). The idea that one who ascended to heaven was transformed, often as a result of the vision of God (or his garment) or the divine Glory, is found in several texts (MORRAY-JONES 1992:11.14.22-26). In 2 Cor 3:18, Paul says that the Christians, "gazing with unveiled face on the Glory of God, are being transformed into the same image, from glory to glory." Here mystical terminology has been adapted to describe what goes on when the

Christians are reading the Scriptures. In contrast to the Jews (cf. vv 13-16; 4:4), the Christians see the Glory of God. Moreover, they are transformed into the "same image", obviously that which they behold. A few verses later, it is said that Christ is the "image of God" (4:4). The Glory obviously is Christ.

Rom 8:29-30 says that the elect will be "conformed to the image of His Son" and be "glorified" (cf. vv 17-18; Col 3:4; 1 John 3:2). The same eschatological adaptation of this thought is found in 1 Cor 15:49, "... we shall bear the image of the heavenly man." Paul can even say the the Christian male *is* the "image and glory of God" (1 Cor 11:7). The statement alludes to Gen 1:26 and presupposes that Christ is the heavenly Adam, the Glory, after whose image and likeness man was created (cf. 4Q504, frag. 8, "You have fashioned Adam, our Father, in the image of [Your] Glory").

There is some evidence from later times that also the Spirit of God could be seen as the Glory (FOSSUM 1983, 284 n. 94), but biblical foundations for this view are weak. In Ezek 8:3, the glory, whose body is described in the preceding verse, is referred to as the "Spirit". A Jewish amulet, which appears to allude to Ezekiel's description of the retreat and return of the Glory, calls the Glory *pneuma hagiōsynēs*, the "Spirit of Holiness" (PETERSON 1959:351-352). In Rom 1:4, it is said that Jesus was designated as the Son of God "*kata* the Spirit of Holiness by resurrection from the dead". The resurrection of Jesus may here be understood as being effected by the Spirit. In Rom 6:1, it is stated plainly that Jesus was resurrected by the Glory of God.

V. *Bibliography*

H. R. BALZ, *Methodische Probleme der neutestamentlichen Christologie* (WMANT 52; Neukirchen 1967); M. BLACK, Die Apotheose Israels: Eine neue Interpretation des danielischen "Menschensohns", *Jesus und der Menschensohn. A. Vögtle Festschrift* (eds. R. Pesch & R. Schnackenburg; Freiburg 1975) 92-99; A. E. COWLEY, *The Samaritan Liturgy* (Oxford 1909); A. FEUILLET, Le fils de l'homme et la tradition biblique, *RB* 60 (1953) 107-202, 321-346; J. E. FOSSUM, Jewish-Christian Christology and Jewish Mysticism, *VC* 37 (1983) 260-287; FOSSUM, *The Name of God and the Angel of the Lord* (WUNT 36; Tübingen 1985); FOSSUM, Colossians 1.15-18a in the Light of Jewish Mysticism and Gnosticism, *NTS* 35 (1989) 183-201; A. T. HANSON, John 1, 14-18 and Exodus 34, *NTS* 23 (1977) 90-100; R. P. MARTIN, *Carmen Christi* (SNTSMS 4; Cambridge 1967); T. N. D. METTINGER, *The Dethronement of Sabaoth. Studies in the Shem and Kabod Theologies* (ConB OT series 18; Lund 1982) 80-115; C. R. A. MORRAY-JONES, Transformational Mysticism in the Apocalyptic-Merkabah Tradition, *JJS* 43 (1992) 1-31; C. C. NEWMAN, *Paul's Glory Christology* (NovTSup 69; Leiden 1992); E. PETERSON, *Frühkirche, Judentum und Gnosis* (Rome 1959); O. PROCKSCH, *Theologie des Alten Testaments* (Gütersloh 1950); G. QUISPEL, Ezekiel 1:26 in Jewish Mysticism and Gnosis, *VC* 34 (1980) 1-13; C. ROWLAND, *The Open Heaven* (London 1982 and reprints); P. SCHÄFER, *Synopse zur Hekhalot-Literatur* (TSAJ 2; Tübingen 1981); G. SCHOLEM, *Major Trends in Jewish Mysticism* (3rd ed.; New York 1954); SCHOLEM, *On the Mystical Shape of the Godhead* (New York 1991).

J. E. FOSSUM

GOD (I) אלהים

I. The usual word for 'god' in the Hebrew Bible is *ʾĕlōhîm*, a plural formation of *ʾĕlōah*, the latter being an expanded form of the Common Semitic noun *ʾil* (→Eloah). The term *ʾĕlōhîm* occurs some 2570 times in the Hebrew Bible, with a variety of meanings. In such expressions as "all the gods of Egypt" (Exod 12:12) it refers to a plurality of deities—without there being a clear distinction between these gods and their →images. Far more frequent is the use of the plural with reference to a single being: →Chemosh is the *ʾĕlōhîm* of Moab (1 Kgs 11:33); the plural here is a plural of excellence or of majesty (Joüon/Muraoka § 136*d*). Though having the generic sense of 'god', the term is also used in an absolute sense ('*the* god', e.g. Gen 5:22) whence it developed the function of a proper name ('God'): when an Israelite suppliant says his soul thirsts for *ʾĕlōhîm* he is not referring to just any god but to →Yahweh the god of Israel (Ps 42:3). Since the Israelite concept of divinity included all praeternatural beings, also lower deities (in modern usage referred to as 'spirits', 'angels', 'demons', 'semi-gods', and the like) may be called *ʾĕlōhîm.* Thus the →teraphim (Gen 31: 30.32), anonymous heavenly beings (Ps 8:6; LXX ἄγγελοι), and the →spirits of the dead (1 Sam 28:13) are referred to as 'gods'. A metaphorical use of the term—metaphorical from our point of view—occurs when it is applied to living human beings, such as →Moses (Exod 4:16; 7:1) and the king (Ps 45:7).

Other Hebrew words for 'god' are *ʾēl* (→El) and *ʾĕlōah.* Though both are used as proper names ("El your father", Gen 49:25; "Can mortal man be righteous before Eloah?", Job 4:17), they can also have generic meaning; in the latter case they are more or less interchangeable with *ʾĕlōhîm* (RINGGREN 1970-73:291).

Gods can also be collectively referred to with the constructions *bĕnê ʾēlîm* (Ps 29:1; 89:7), *bĕnê ʾĕlōhîm* (Gen 6:2; Job 1:6; 2:1; 38:7; cf. Deut 32:8 4QDeut, see SKEHAN 1954), or *bĕnê ʿElyôn* (Ps 82:6). The latter expression ('the sons of →Elyon') suggests the possibility that the second element of the construction be understood as a proper name of a single deity, so that the expressions compare with Ug and Phoen *bn il(m)* 'the sons of El' (MULLEN 1980:117-119; *KAI* no. 26A iii 19, and commentary in *KAI* II, p. 43). In view of the Ugaritic formula, the plural *ʾēlîm* in Pss 29:1 and 89:7 may have to be interpreted as the proper name El followed by enclitic *mem.* The expression *ʿădat ʾēl* ('the council of El', Ps 82:1) might be taken in corroboration of that possibility (→Council).

II. The main cultures surrounding ancient Israel have each developed special vocables for the notion of deity. Though these words are currently rendered as 'god' by modern translators, it should not be assumed that the ancient Near Eastern conceptions of 'god' are in perfect correspondence with those of modern people. It is therefore essential not to stop short at the mere translation of the terms, but to probe their significance and connotations by a careful study of the way and the context in which they have been used.

In *Egypt* the customary word for god is *nṯr*. The word occurs as an element in the new name Pharaoh gave to →Joseph (Gen 41:45): Zaphenath-paneah, צפנתפענח, is interpreted by Egyptologists as *ḏd-pꜣ-nṯr-ỉw.f-ʿnḫ*, 'God has said: he will live' (H. RANKE, *Die ägyptischen Personennamen*, Vol. 2 [Glückstadt/Hamburg 1952] 334). *Nṯr* is conventionally pronounced as 'neṯer', though the Coptic *noyte* makes an original pronunciation 'naṯir' more likely (HORNUNG 1971:30). The etymology of the term is uncertain; so is the original significance of the hieroglyph for *nṯr*: speculation about the one or the other gives no assured indication as to the nature of the gods (contrast WESTENDORF 1985). It seems more relevant to note that the word is applied to gods, kings, and the dead. The same holds true of the adjective *nṯry*, 'divine' (TRAUNECKER 1992: 34-35), which may also be used with reference to animals and inanimate objects. All beings and objects that participate in the sphere of the sacred (*ḏsr*; for the distinction between profane and sacred, see ASSMANN 1984:9-10) are 'gods', and thus 'divine'. It has been suggested that in the Egyptian conception divinity is not an essential but an accidental quality: one becomes and remains 'god' or 'divine' only by means of certain rites (MEEK 1988). While this is perhaps put too boldly, it is certainly true that the dividing line between gods and humans is not absolute. Also, some gods are more 'divine' than others; thus →Isis is said to surpass the other gods when it comes to divinity (HORNUNG 1971:53).

Many of the characteristics of gods are

not exclusively theirs: gods are said to be 'great', 'powerful', 'strong', 'beautiful' (*nfr*), 'compassionate', 'exalted', and 'righteous'. A survey of this short list shows that the qualities of gods are basically those of humans; the former possess them merely in purer form than the latter. What actually raises the gods above ordinary mortals is primarily their power; a goddess can be more divine than her peers if she is more powerful. This power, however, was precarious; concentrated in the name of the god, it could be lost if the secret of the name were divulged (TRAUNECKER 1992:36-38).

Gods were believed to be recognizable by their smell and radiance: they had the penetrating smell of incense, stirring humans out of their sleep (HORNUNG 1971:122-123); their radiance is that of polished gold. Both elements are based on the reality of the temple cult, in which the brilliant images of the gods stood erect in a cloud of incense. Between these images and the gods they represented there was believed to be a close correspondence. The appearance of gods was believed to be accompanied, moreover, by such phenomena as storm, thunder, and earthquake—the traditional elements in theophany descriptions. In exceptional cases the appearance of humans (e.g. the king) was thought to produce similar effects.

In order to define the relation between divine essence and manifestation the Eyptian theologians have had recourse to a number of notions, the precise meaning of which is sometimes still obscure. An important aspect of the gods is their *ba*. The *ba* (*bꜣ*), often translated 'soul', is an hypostasis of the gods (or the dead) in their capacity to move from one realm (one reality, one plane of being) to another. Thus the dead are present among the living as *ba'u* (the plural of *ba*), iconographically rendered as birds. The *ba* of the god is his visible face to humans. Thus the night is the *ba* of Kek, the deified obscurity; water is the *ba* of Nun, the primeval ocean. Though the *ba* is distinguished from the god, the god is really present in his *ba*. The example shows that the Egyptians had by no means crude notions of the gods; on the contrary, they developed a sophisticated theology rich with distinctions no less subtle than the Deuteronomistic distinction between God and his →name or his →glory.

It should be stressed that the Egyptian gods are not eternal, not all-seeing and all-knowing, and not all-powerful. The gods are not eternal because they have a beginning and an end; gods are born and eventually die. The birth of →Horus is a well-known mythological theme; yet birth is an experience all gods have gone through. Similarly, the death of →Osiris is a constant theme in mythological material; yet decrepitude and death (which in the Egyptian conception is not the same as complete annihilation) await all gods. Gods are entangled in the cycle of life and death without which the world cannot subsist. Their death is also a form of regeneration and renewal. Likewise, gods possess neither unlimited faculties of perception nor absolute powers of action. Some are credited with many ears and many eyes; yet omniscience is out of their reach. The power of the gods is exalted, yet circumscribed: it is limited to a topographical area or a specific field of action. In their abilities and qualities gods are superior to humans, yet not infinitely superior.

Owing to the nature of the extant sources an outline of the development in the Egyptian notion of god is a hazardous endeavour. The once popular view that the anthropomorphic vision of the gods was preceded by a theriomorphic and a chrematomorphic stage (the thesis of the *Vermenschlichung der Mächte* championed by Kurt Sethe) is now either abandoned or radically modified. In the historically recoverable phases of the Egyptian vision of the gods, an anthropomorphic element has always been present. Yet it would be misleading to picture the Egyptian theology as a stagnant pool; there is change and movement, though often difficult to perceive because of the strongly conservative nature of the written sources. One development many researchers agree upon is the increasing transcendency ascribed to the gods. This aspect comes to the fore in statements about the invisibility and inscrutability of the gods, on the one hand, and the tendency towards an inclusive monotheism (all gods are aspects of the one god), on the other (ASSMANN 1979).

The preceding observation is a reminder of the fundamentally polytheistic nature of the Egyptian theology. Also in the later monotheistic tendencies, evidenced for instance in the figure of →Bes *pantheos*, the existence of a plurality of gods remains a postulated reality. Such polytheism was not particular to the Egyptians, of course. It was the rule in the ancient Near East. Except for the brief interlude of Echnaton (*ca.* 1365-1345), the king who preached that there was no god but Aton (cf. ASSMANN 1972), the Egyptian culture adhered to the notion of polytheism. Yet the monotheism of Echnaton is indicative of another aspect of the Egyptian theology, perhaps an undercurrent, which emphasizes the existence of one god transcending all others. Whether this all-embracing god is to be imagined as a person or an abstract (the one divine nature from which all gods draw their essence), remains often unclear. The tension between a latent (and incidentally patent) monotheism and the traditionally pluralistic view of the divine world might be considered a major force in the development of the Egyptian theology.

A factor that was both formative and conservative for the vision of the gods as a plurality is the cosmological aspect of many Egyptian deities. As individuals and collectively, the Egyptians felt inferior to and dependent upon the powers of nature. Awed by the world around them, the Egyptians conceived of its elements as gods; gods in the plural because the cosmos was experienced as a play in which many actors had a part. The world of the gods mirrored the phenomenal world. To reduce this richly variegated reality to a single divine being would have seemed an intolerable impoverishment. Faced with the choice between the one and the many, the Egyptians—like the Mesopotamians and the Greeks—opted for the many. Yet at the same time some kind of unity among the gods is never absent; they all partake of the same divine essence. Individual gods could have many names and epithets; yet the same names and epithets were sometimes applied to other gods. Though the divine plurality was always retained, the distinctive traits of the gods remained fluid; they frequently constituted syncretistic compounds (in addition to →Amun and →Re there is Amun-Re) and could eventually be viewed as aspects or manifestations of the one deity behind all gods (HORNUNG 1971).

Another factor that favoured the pluralist conception of deity was the phenomenon of the city gods. No country in the ancient Near East was as densely dotted with temples as Egypt. The gods dwelling in these earthly abodes were considered to be the lords and owners of the land. In this respect, they had a political and a topographical dimension. Human rulers owed their mandate to the gods; they exercised authority in lieu and by the grace of the gods. As the totality of the gods stood for the notion of 'Egypt', so the individual god stood a symbol for the city where he had his *pied-à-terre*. Each Egyptian city was the city of a god, a view that still transpires from some of the Hellenic place-names: Hermopolis, Heliopolis, and Panopolis are *interpretationes graecae* of a truly Egyptian concept. The citizen was expected to loyally serve the god or goddess of the city; thus a citizen of Hermopolis would have →Hermes (→Thoth) for a personal god (ASSMANN 1984:26-35). Political fragmentation and plurality, then, are reflected in the pantheon. It is perhaps even permitted to say that the tension between the one and the many in the Egyptian conception of god mirrors a comparable tension between political unity and local autonomy.

An arresting phenomenon in the religious literature is the occurrence of the word for god *nṯr* in contexts that do not specify which particular god is meant. Translators usually render 'the god'—a distinct possibility since Egyptian dispenses, as a rule, with the article, whether definite or indefinite (cf. A. GARDINER, *Egyptian Grammar* [Oxford[3] 1957] § 21). This absolute use of the word 'god' is particularly at home in the wisdom literature, both in such collections of precepts and counsels as the Teachings of Amenemope, and in theodicy texts such as the Admonitions of Ipuwer and the Instructions of Merikare. Though it has been suggested that the 'god' of the wisdom teachers is an anonymous *monotheos* (e.g. VERGOTE 1963), this can hardly be the case. The Counsels of Ani, for instance, advise the reader to observe the rites of 'the god', which shows that a definite god must be meant, since there was no cult of an anonymous high-god in Egypt (HORNUNG 1971: 41). The unspecified *nṯr* is rather to be understood as "the god with whom you have to reckon in the circumstances" (FRANKFORT 1948:67).

In the study of the *Mesopotamian* conception of the gods, it is not unusual to make a distinction between the Sumerian and the Akkadian side of the matter—Sumerian being the language spoken by the third millennium BCE inhabitants of the country, Akkadian being the language of the Assyrians and the Babylonians in the second and first millennia BCE. Though necessary from a linguistic point of view, the distinction is not self-evident in terms of culture. The Babylonians and Assyrians inherited the Sumerian culture; they adopted and developed it, but this by itself was nothing new: accretions and modifications did also occur before 2000 BCE. There is no clash between ethnic groups, and no revolutionary change of cultural or religious paradigm (cf. JACOBSEN 1970:187-192). The Sumerian and Akkadian material will therefore jointly be dealt with.

Though neither the Sumerian word **dingir** ('god') nor the Akkadian term *ilu* ('god') can illuminate the nature of the Mesopotamian conception of god, the cuneiform sign used for these words offers a first point of orientation. The oldest forms show that it is a schematic representation of a →star, which may be taken to mean that →heaven was seen as the proper domain of the gods. Yet Mesopotamian gods are not by definition celestial. Mythology knows in fact two locations of the gods: on high in heaven, and down below beneath the →earth. Since the latter realm is included in the word for 'earth' (Sum **ki**, Akk *erṣetu*), the standard reference to the pantheon as 'the gods of heaven and earth' should be understood to mean 'the gods of the heaven and the nether world'. An elaborate theology of the dwelling-places of the gods is found in *Enuma elish*: as →Marduk had defeated →Tiamat, he built the heavenly Esharra temple as a replica of the Apsu temple (→Ends of the earth) located in the waters beneath the earth (*Ee* IV 135-145); the earthly abodes of the gods are temporary homes, visited by them when the gods of below and on high meet for their annual assembly in the 'Gate of the gods', as Babylon was theologically etymologized (*Ee* V 113-130).

Many of the observations made about the Egyptian conception of the gods hold good as well for the Mesopotamian theology. The Mesopotamian gods, too, are closely associated with elements of the cosmos. In the earliest documents of Mesopotamian theology, the so-called god lists (cf. LAMBERT 1957-71; MANDER 1986), pride of place is given to such gods as An, Enlil, Inanna, Enki, Nanna, and Utu. They bear Sumerian names that can be translated as, respectively, 'Heaven', 'Lord Air', 'Mistress of Heaven' (i.e. the planet Venus, visible as the evening and the morning star), 'Lord Earth', →'Moon', and 'Sun'. With the exception of Inanna (→Ishtar), the compound names (Enlil and Enki) are not genitival constructions; the deities in question, therefore, are apparently identical with the cosmological phenomena with which they are associated. In the course of time it becomes clear, however, that the gods do not wholly coincide with 'their' phenomena. By means of the sign for 'god' (**dingir**, *ilu*) immediately preceding a term to mark it as a divine name, it was possible to distinguish between the sun as a natural phemenon and the Sun as a god (T. JACOBSEN, The Graven Image, *Ancient Israelite Religion* [ed. P. D. Miller, Jr, et al.; Philadelphia 1987] 15-32, esp. 18 and n. 7).

Most Mesopotamian gods, in addition to being associated with certain natural or cultural phenomena, were each linked with a city. Each community had its own temple, in which its particular god or goddess was worshipped. An (later Anu) was the god of Uruk, Enlil of Nippur, and Enki (→Ea) of Eridu. For reasons that are still elusive, nearly every city had a different patron deity; duplications are rare. This remarkable distribution of the gods over the various cities can hardly be accidental; it looks like the implementation of an early agreement and would thus seem to attest to the one time existence of a Sumerian league (for this 'Kengir League' see JACOBSEN 1970:139-141). The association of gods with cities gave Mesopotamian theology a political dimension: since a god's glory reflects on his city, city theologians endeavoured to promote their god to a superior position in the divine hierarchy. The career of Marduk, consolidated in *Enuma elish*, illustrates how gods could rise in rank as their cities rose in importance: listed as number 294 in a mid-third millennium catalogue of gods (MANDER 1986:29), Marduk had become 'king of the gods of heaven and earth' by the end of the second millennium (LAMBERT 1964; 1984).

In what has been described as the 'city theology' of the Mesopotamians, the observable monotheistic tendencies have a political flavour as well. As the one city-state extended its sphere of influence, turning others into its satellites, its god reduced those of the others to subordinate deities. The redefinition of their mutual relations could lead to the absorption of the lesser deity by the greater god: the former might live on as a name or an aspect of the latter. In this process, the god triumphant might add a number of new traits to his 'biography': thus Marduk of Babylon became the son of Ea (Sumerian Enki) by the identification with Asalluhi of Kuar subsequent to the entry of the latter village into the orbit of Babylon. The merging of deities sometimes took remarkable forms. The most arresting examples are, once more, from the Marduk theology. Thus a small god list, conceived in the style of the classical ones, interprets a number of important gods as facets of Marduk: Ninurta (→Nimrod) is "Marduk of the pickaxe", →Nergal is "Marduk of battle", Enlil is "Marduk of lordship and consultations", and Shamash is "Marduk of justice" (LAMBERT 1975). Is this monotheism? Considering the fact that similar statements were made about gods other than Marduk it was a local form of monotheism at best. Since, moreover, the existence of other gods was not denied, but rather integrated into a overarching design, this monotheism should be qualified as inclusive.

Because there is no Mesopotamian treatise on the nature of the gods, the characteristics that make gods stand apart from other beings, and mark them off as divine, must be culled from a variety of disparate sources. Fundamental for the Mesopotamian conception of the gods is their anthropomorphism: gods have human form, male or female, and are moved by reasons and sentiments similar to those of humans. Their divinity lies in the fact that they are in a sense superhuman. They surpass humans in size, beauty, knowledge, happiness, longevity—briefly: in all things that were positively valued. When a god appears in a dream, the sleeper typically sees "a young man of gigantic size, with splendid limbs, and clad in new garments" (*Ludlul* III 9-10). Size, beauty, power and vitality combine to constitute the *melammu* which the gods exude. This *melammu* is conceived of materially as an invisible raiment endowing the gods with a terrifying lustre. Every being endowed with *melammu* is a god or like a god (*Ee* I 138; II 24; III 28). Since humans might possess such splendour as well, though not with the same intensity, the *melammu* might be compared with the nimbus from Christian iconography.

Insouciance and a life of ease are other characteristics of gods. Unlike humans, they do not have to work for their daily bread. It was precisely for that purpose that they had created humankind, as the myths explain (most notably *Atrahasis*). The temple cult, performed by priests on behalf of the city, has been aptly characterized as "the care and feeding of the gods" (OPPENHEIM 1977:183-198). Since all humankind is ultimately in the service of the gods, the latter are able to spend their days in a condition of gentle slumber. Their sleep should not be mistaken for impotence, however. Enlil, for instance, is said to be sleeping a 'deceptive' (*sarru*) sleep: at any moment he may wake up and start to rage like a roaring lion. Besides the pleasures of a good meal and the attendant drowsiness, the gods also know the pleasures of the flesh. In cult and mythology, the gods engage in intercourse—though often in mysterious ways. In the event of conception, the period of pregnancy lasts only nine days after which the child is painlessly born (B. ALSTER, Enki and Ninhursag, *UF* 10 [1978] 15-27, esp. 17).

Of particular interest for the Mesopotamian ideas about the nature of the gods is the Epic of Gilgamesh. The subject of the Epic has often been characterized as the unsuccessful quest for immortality. It is more apt to say that it is conceived as a meditation upon the human condition; as the originally independent Gilgamesh stories, some of which are known from the Sumerian tradition, were transformed into a grandiose tale, they were impressed with a vision about humankind as being halfway between the animals, on the one hand, and the gods, on the other. Indirectly, then, the epic is instructive for the Mesopotamian view on the realm of the divine.

The hero of the epic, the legendary king Gilgamesh, is presented as being two-thirds divine and one-third human. His divinity is evident from his length: according to the Hittite version of the epic, Gilgamesh is 11 cubits (ca. 5 meter) tall (KUB VIII 57:8; see J. FRIEDRICH, Die hethitischen Bruchstücke des Gilgameš-Epos, *ZA* 39 (1930) 1-82, esp. 4-5). His gigantic proportions are clear, moreover, from the fact that during the march to the cedar forest Gilgamesh walks fifty leagues (*ca.* 500 km) a day (*Gilg.* IV i 1'-5'). Gilgamesh' special friend Enkidu is of similar stature: he can drink seven whole jars of beer without detrimental effects (*Gilg.* OB II 'Pennsylvania Tablet' iii 17-19)—a feat normally performed by gods only. Enkidu too, then, is "like a god", as the prostitute observes (*Gilg.* OB II 'Pennsylvania Tablet' ii 11).

In the Old Babylonian version of the epic, Enkidu is likened to a god on account of his size and beauty. In the Standard Babylonian version, almost a thousand years younger, the divinity of Enkidu consists not in his size and stature, but in his wisdom and experience. Enkidu has been transformed into a human being through the intercourse with a prostitute. The domestication of the savage is complete when the animals scatter at his sight: he is no longer one of them. Through the contact with the prostitute Enkidu has "extended his intellect" (*urappaš ḫasisa*, *Gilg.* SB I iv 29). As Enkidu realizes he no longer belongs among animals, the prostitute explains: "You have become wise ([*em*]-*qa-ta*), Enkidu, you have become like a god; why should you roam open country with wild beasts?" (*Gilg.* SB I iv 34-35). Wisdom obtained by experience is precisely what characterizes Gilgamesh, too, according to the SB prologue: "he experienced the whole and gained complete wisdom" (*Gilg.* SB I i 4). This wisdom, though possessed by humans, renders its owners divine in a way. Deities excel in wisdom and knowledge; humans who acquire these things become like gods (cf. Gen 3:22 "the man has become like one of us, knowing good and evil").

Yet Enkidu and Gilgamesh are only divine in part; they are not invulnerable: death they cannot escape. Human mortality *versus* divine immortality is indeed a major theme in the epic. When Enkidu is frightened by the prospect of the journey to the dangerous cedar forest, Gilgamesh reminds him of the human condition: "Who can go up to heaven, my friend? Only the gods are forever in the company of the Sun-god; as for humankind: its days are numbered" (*Gilg.* OB III 'Yale Tablet' iv 5-7). Human mortality is presented here as the distinctive difference: the lasting fame Gilgamesh hopes to achieve is only a substitute of eternity (*Gilg.* OB III 'Yale Tablet' iv 13). In contrast to humans and animals, then, gods have access to an abundance of vitality and life. "When the gods created humankind, they gave death to humankind; life they kept in their own hands" (*Gilg.* OB X 'Meissner Tablet' iii 3-5). Unlimited life is pictured as a divine prerogative. Gods are eternal, not because they live in a zone of timelessness, but because they constantly renew themselves, like stars (*CAD* E s.v. *eddešû*).

It is no mere accident that the two-thirds divine Gilgamesh is a king. Deification after death, especially of kings, is nothing unusual in the Mesopotamian conception. Yet the claim of divinity by, or its attribution to, rulers during their lifetime is restricted to certain periods of Mesopotamian history, most notably the late third millennium BCE (Cf. W. W. HALLO, *Early Mesopotamian Royal Titles* [New Haven 1957] 56-65). Thus, on his seal, Naram-Sin refers to himself as 'the god of Akkad'. It should be stressed, though, that the deification of the living king is exceptional. Kings, it is true, are in many ways like gods. In the third and second millennia BCE, people take an oath by the life of the king as they take one by the life of the gods; frequently, god and king are mentioned in one breath in the oath formula. The common characteristic here is the privileged access to information and the possession of power to punish. Power and authority, whether real or perceived as such, are also responsible for the comparison of the royal command with the word spoken by a god. Allies of the king may call him god out of a sense of dependence: similar in this to a god, the king can extend protection. Appurtenance to a venerable lineage, too, bestows a kind of divinity upon the king; it makes him the incarnation of an everlasting dynastic identity.

The fact that the analogy between god and king may earn the latter the title of 'god', used in both a literal and a figurative sense, is indicative of the relative nature of divinity. As in Egypt, there is no absolute chasm between human and divine. There has been a time when the gods were human, according to the famous opening line of the Old Babylonian Atraḫasis Myth (*inūma ilū awīlum*). When LAMBERT's restoration of the relevant passage is correct, the myth looks upon death as a postdiluvial institution (1980:57-58). The same suggestion is contained in the SB version of the Gilgamesh Epic: after the apotheosis of the flood hero (here Utanapishtim), the gods brought death into the world (LAMBERT 1980:54-57). The very point of difference between humans and gods, then, is accidental rather than essential; it was not there from the beginning. According to this view, the separation between the two realms has been a gradual process: there once was a Golden Age, before the Flood, when gods and humans moved in the same world. Under exceptional circumstances, humans may still cross the dividing line—especially after death.

In *Canaanite* religion (this term is commonly used to refer to Ugaritic religion as well) the usual word for 'god' is Ug *il*, plural *ilm*, corresponding with Phoen *ʾl* and *ʾlm*. The form *ilh* seems to be used only as a proper name (→Eloah), though there is a plural form *ilhm* usually translated as 'gods'; perhaps the term refers specifically to the gods of the netherworld (PARDEE 1988:111). A similar form may be attested at Emar, if *wābil i-la-i* should be interpreted as *wābil ilāhī*, 'bearer of the gods [=statues]' (so J. HUEHNERGARD apud D. E. FLEMING, *The Installation of the High Priestess at Emar* [HSS 42; Atlanta 1992] 85 n. 56). Morphologically, this is the equivalent of the Hebrew plural *ʾĕlōhîm*. Forms occurring only in the plural are Ug *ilnym* (cf. DEL OLMO LETE, Los nombres 'divinos' de los reyes de Ugarit, *Aula Orientalis* 5 [1987] 39-69, esp. 63-64) and *ilnm*; the latter is also attested in Phoenician. The Ugaritic word for goddess is *ilt*, plural *ilht*, dual *iltm*. Aramaic inscriptions have the form *ʾlh* and *ʾlht*.

Typically West-Semitic, though not exclusively so, is the use of the divine plural where a single entity is concerned. In texts that use the alphabetic script such plurals of excellence are not readily recognizable. Where the Akkadian writing system is used, combining a syllabic script with various logograms, plural forms are less ambiguous. A good illustration of the plural of divinity is found in the Amarna letters, where the Pharaoh is repeatedly addressed by his Canaanite vassals as DINGIR.MEŠ-*ia*, literally 'my gods', but plainly referring to one person only (JIRKU 1938; cf. N. NA'AMAN, DINGIR^{meš} in the Amarna Letters, *UF* 22 [1990] 255). F. M. T. BÖHL defines this plural as a *pluralis amplitudinis* (*Der Sprache der Amarnabriefe* [LSS V/2; Leipzig 1909] §23e). It also occurs as a designation of the personal god (*EA* 96:4; 97:3; 189 Rev. 13-14) in combination with a verb in the singular; this phenomenon parallels the Hebrew use of *'ĕlōhîm* (BÖHL, *Der Sprache*, §23f). A balanced assessment of the significance of these data should take into account, though, that the sign MEŠ is sometimes used as a logogram marker in peripheral Akkadian (W. H. VAN SOLDT, *Studies in the Akkadian of Ugarit* [AOAT 40; Kevelaer/Neukirchen-Vluyn 1991] 428-429). There are some rare examples of a *pluralis divinitatis* in Akkadian texts; most of them betray West-Semitic influence (cf. DALLEY 1989:164, 177 n. 11). Judging by the Babylonian *Theodicy* (*BWL* 63-91), however, it was not uncommon in Standard Babylonian to refer to the personal god with the plural form 'gods' (LAMBERT, *BWL*, 67).

Characteristically West-Semitic is the use of the term 'gods' to designate the spirits of the dead. The short hymn to Shapshu that closes the Baal Cycle uses *rpim* (→Rephaim) in parallelism with *ilnym*, and *ilm* in parallelism with *mtm* (*KTU*1.6 vi 45-49; cf. M. S. SMITH, *The Early History of God* [San Francisco 1990] 128). At Emar, the plural 'gods' occurs in a fixed hendiadys: the heirs are to invoke, to honour, and to care for 'the gods and the dead' of their forebears. The expression is best understood as a reference to the deified ancestors (K. VAN DER TOORN, Gods and Ancestors in Emar and Nuzi, *ZA* 84 [1994] 38-59). The Ugaritic figure of the *ilib* belongs to the same complex of ideas: the term does not stand for 'the god of the father', as has sometimes been said, but designates the 'deified father', i.e. the ancestral spirit (K. VAN DER TOORN, Ilib and the 'God of the Father', *UF* 25 [1993] 379-387).

The literary heritage of Canaanite religion is rarely explicit about the characteristics of divinity. A frequent epithet of the gods is *qdš*, 'holy'; the pantheon of Byblos, for instance, is referred to as 'the assembly of the holy gods of Byblos' (*mpḥrt 'l gbl qdšm*; *KAI* 4:4-5, 7). The adjective is so intimately associated with gods, that it is exceptionally used absolutively. Thus the Arslan Tash amulet mentions the *dr kl qdšn*, 'the Council of all the Holy Ones' (*NESE* 2 [1974] 22-23). It is against this background, perhaps, that Ps 16:3 is to be understood (M. DAHOOD, *Psalms I* [AB 16; Garden City 1965] 87-88). The precise meaning of 'holiness' is not specified in the texts. From a comparative study it would seem that the notion is the semantic equivalent of the Mesopotamian idea of the divine *melammu*: gods are holy in the sense that they exude radiance, splendour, and luminosity.

Canaanite religion, like the Mesopotamian, distinguishes between gods of heaven and gods of the underworld. The typical abode of the gods in mythology, however, is some place at the end of the horizon. Mount →Zaphon (modern Jebel el-Aqra, some 50 km North of Ugarit-Ras Shamra) is inhabited by →Baal and his entourage. El lives at 'the source of the two rivers'—presumably a reference to the mythical place from which both the ocean around and below the earth, and the ocean above the heavens, take their water. Both locations may be viewed as an attempt to situate the gods at the outer limits of the inhabited world: they are half-way between immanence and transcendence.

One characteristic which the Canaanite gods share with the Mesopotamian deities is the possession of life everlasting. Though it is doubtful whether this concept should be translated in terms of absolute eternity, the longevity of the gods represents a distinct difference from humans. Not unlike the Gilgamesh Epic in this respect, the Epic of Aqhat deals with the impossibility of humans attaining the life of the gods. A crucial episode in the Epic is the meeting between →Anat and Aqhat. The goddess wishes to obtain the bow of Aqhat and tries to make the hero part with it by holding out the promise of life: "Ask for life (*ḥym*), o hero Aqhat, ask for life and I will give it to you, immortality (*blmt*) and I will send it to you. I will let you count the years with Baal, with the sons of El (*bn il*) you will count the months" (*KTU* 1.17.vi.26-29). Aqhat rejects her proposal: "I shall die like all (humans) die; yea, I shall surely die" (*KTU* 1.17.vi. 38). Unlike humans, gods ('the sons of El') possess 'life' and 'immortality' (*blmt*, literally 'non-death').

III. The Israelite concept of God shares many traits with the beliefs of its neighbours. The most fundamental correspondence concerns the anthropomorphic nature ascribed to God. God's anthropomorphism is external (anthropomorphism in the strict sense of the term) as well as internal (also known as anthropopathism). God possesses hands, ears, a mouth, eyes, fingers, feet, and other bodily parts. Largely lacking in the Hebrew Bible are references to sexual characteristics of God. Internal anthropomorphism is at stake when God is said to be moved by desires, feelings, and passions closely resembling those of humans. Thus God is said to be capable of feelings of love, anger, jealousy, compassion, and the like.

An anthropomorphic vision of God underlies many of Israel's religious institutions. The temple cult, for instance, can be considered the Israelite version of 'the care and feeding of the gods', to use Oppenheim's term. The temple in which God is thought to reside may be viewed as his earthly palace, conceived as a replica of his royal mansion on high. Here he wishes to dwell protected from noise (Ps 65:2; cf. 1 Kgs 6:7) and sunlight (1 Kgs 8:12). The sacrifices that are brought were originally meant as God's food (*leḥem*, e.g. Lev 21: 21); the morning and the evening sacrifice of God (Exod 29:41; Ps 141:2) are modelled after the morning and the evening meal of humans. Meanwhile incense is burned; God is also anthropomorphic in this respect that he is sensitive to a pleasant smell (*rêaḥ nîḥôaḥ*, e.g. Exod 29:41). His servants have to be pleasing to the eye as well: no priest 'who has a blemish' is to appear before God (Lev 21:17).

Over against the anthropomorphism of God found in the Hebrew Bible, there are those texts that stress the difference between God's divinity and man's humanity. The opposition can assume different nuances. "God is not a man that he should lie, nor a son of man that he should repent" (Num 23:19). The expressions 'man' (*ʾîš*) and 'son of man' (*ben-ʾādām*) are used here adjectively; they could be translated as 'human'. The noun 'God' occurs likewise as an adjective, and may be so rendered, in such texts as Isa 31:3 "The Egyptians are human (*ʾādām*), and not divine (*ʾēl*), and their horses are flesh and not spirit." A closer look at these examples shows that the opposition does not invalidate the idea of divine anthropomorphism. God's qualities are human qualities, yet purified from imperfection and amplified to superhuman dimensions. Sincerity and reliability are human virtues—even if only God is wholly sincere and reliable. Strength, too, is not the exclusive prerogative of God; he is merely incomparably stronger than humans or animals.

In view of the passages dwelling upon the contrast between God and man, the thesis of God's anthropomorphism should be modified in this sense that God is more than human. Though man has been created in the image of God (a proposition the historian of religion might be tempted to reverse), there is a huge difference of degree—yet not of nature. In this respect the view found in the Hebrew Bible does not radically differ from the conviction concerning the similarity between gods and humans in the Babylonian Atraḫasis myth. God has human form, but not human size. In visions, God proves to be so high and exalted that the earthly temple can barely contain the fringes of his mantle (Isa 6:1). Gates have to lift their heads when God enters Jerusalem (Ps 24:7.9). In addition to his physical size (which transcends even the highest heaven, 1 Kgs 8:27), God surpasses humans in such aspects as wisdom (Job 32:13) and power (Ezek 28:9). His divine superiority also has a moral side: God excels in righteousness (Job 4:17; 9:2; 25:4), faithfulness (e.g. Deut 32:4), and other moral qualities.

The notion that gods are celestial beings, wide-spread in the ancient Near East, is also found in the Bible. It is often connected with the idea of God's extraordinary powers of vision and intervention. "Our God is in the heavens; he does whatever he pleases" (Ps 115:3). From his exalted abode he looks with an ever-watchful eye at the doings of humankind. When they revolt against the divinely appointed monarch, "He who sits in heaven laughs in derision" (Ps 2:4). Since heaven is a place to which humans have no access—at least not during their lifetime (cf. VAN DER TOORN 1988)—, the heavenly nature of God is another reason why he transcends humans. Especially in the later sections of the Hebrew Bible, God is typically 'the God of Heavens' (*'ĕlōhê haššāmayim*, e.g. Neh 1:4). The expression may have been influenced by Mazdaism, or by the worship of Baal as →Baal-shamem, but it is not at odds with earlier views.

A concept connected with God's celestial nature is his invisibility; this concept is emphatically present in later texts. Deuteronomy stresses that the Israelites did not see God's form at the Mountain, but merely heard his voice (Deut 4:12.15). Also God spoke from heaven, not from the mountain top (Deut 4:36). These statements bespeak a sense of divine transcendence more acute than in some of the Exodus accounts. The same tendency is manifest in other passages. Man-made idols are there for all to see; yet God is divine in that he is a God "who hides himself" (Isa 45:15). Humans cannot see God because he is in heaven and they are on earth (Ps 115:2-3.16). Under normal circumstances, humans cannot see God and remain alive (Exod 33:20). Even Moses, in one tradition, has his eyes covered by God's hand when God passes by; he catches a glimpse only of God's back (Exod 33:21-23).

God's invisibility might be interpreted as a radicalization of his →glory. The Mesopotamian concept of *melammu* has a counterpart in the Hebrew Bible in the notion of *kābôd*, 'glory'. This glory is a luminosity which both frightens and fascinates; it is, in terms of Rudolph Otto, truly numinous. Since radiance and splendour are part of the notion of God's glory, the association between God and →light (*'ôr*) does not come as a surprise. God can be said to 'shine forth' (*hôpîa'*, Deut 33:2), to 'flash up' (ZRḤ, Isa 60:2), and to 'shine' (NGH, 2 Sam 22:29; Isa 4:5), verbs usually connected with the sun. Like the sun, God is all-seeing and all-knowing; his eyes bring 'hidden sins' to the light (Ps 19:13). This solar imagery may have favoured the development of the concept of God's invisibility: just as no-one can look at the midday sun for a sustained period of time, so no-one can see God and not lose his sight. The light (*'ôr*) with which God is covered like a garment (Ps 104:2) is increasingly conceived of as 'an unapproachable light' (φῶς ἀπρόσιτον, 1 Tim 6:16).

The Hebrew has no proper word for 'goddess': in 1 Kgs 11:5 Ashtoreth (a dysphemic vocalisation for →Astarte) is called the *'ĕlōhîm* of the Sidonians (cf. Joüon/Muraoka § 134*d*) This lexicographical observation should not be interpreted to mean that the Israelites did not recognize any goddess alongside Yahweh. The inscriptions from Kuntillet 'Ajrud and Khirbet el-Qom show otherwise (→Asherah). It is mainly due to the theological bias of the editors of the Hebrew Bible—those who selected the texts, and who corrected them if need be—that many goddesses have been doomed to oblivion (cf. O. KEEL & C. UEHLINGER, *Göttinnen, Götter und Gottessymbole* [Freiburg/Basel/Wien 1992]).

The one great difference between the Israelite conception of God and the beliefs of its neighbours is usually considered to be the notion of monotheism. The belief that there is only one God, it is often suggested, overshadows all possible similarities and reduces them to superficial resemblances. This position is open to criticism. Whilst monotheism eventually became a distinctive trait of Israelite religion, it cannot be isolated from its historical milieu. It is no coincidence that the anonymous author of Isaiah 40-55, traditionally regarded as the champion of Israelite monotheism, is known as a vehement critic of Babylonian idol worship. His monotheism has an anti-Babylonian edge. Such monotheism—assuming it really is monotheism—should not be interpreted as the answer of a great mind to an intellectual problem. It is too closely tied up with political and cultural interests to be considered a dispassionate theological statement. There can be no question of true monotheism, in the philosophical sense of the word, as long as the belief in other heavenly beings (→'sons of God') is not eschewed. Only when the subordinate deities are degraded to →angels, created by the God they serve, can one speak of monotheism.

Since the demarcation lines between human and divine are not as clearly drawn in the ancient Near East as they are in many current religions, the word *ʾĕlōhîm* can be used in the sense of 'divine' or 'extraordinary'. It is doubtful, however, whether in these instances the word is used merely as a superlative. The *rûaḥ ʾĕlōhîm* of Gen 1:2 is perhaps not 'the spirit of God', but it is hardly to be rendered as 'a terrible storm' either. It is best translated as 'a divine wind'; similarly, the *ḥerdat ʾĕlōhîm* mentioned in 1 Sam 14:15 is indeed a 'divinely inspired panic'. Such use of the pural 'gods' in the meaning 'divine' is also known in Akkadian: the *šaturri* DINGIR.MEŠ mentioned in the Tukulti-Ninurta Epic is a 'divine womb' (W. G. LAMBERT, *AfO* 18 [19] 50 F col. Y 9).

Related to the adjectival use of *ʾĕlōhîm* for something out of the ordinary is the occurrence of the term for the →spirits of the dead. The one indubitable instance of this use is found in 1 Sam 28:13 where the ghost of Samuel is described as *ʾĕlōhîm* "coming up from the earth". Another text often adduced in example is Isa 8:19; though probably correct, the interpretation of *ʾĕlōhîm* as 'spirits of the dead' in this case is not obligatory. Perhaps the term *ʾĕlōhîm* in Mic 3:7 should be understood as 'spirits', too, since the passage deals with 'soothsayers' (*qōsĕmîm*), usually a term for necromancers (cf. VAN DER TOORN 1990: 213-214). A text seldom quoted in this connection is Exod 21:6 which says that the slave who waives his right of manumission and enters his master's household for good is to be brought 'to the gods' (Exod 21:6). A commentator has added that the man shall be brought 'to the door or to the doorpost,' perhaps the place where the 'gods' were thought to reside. These 'gods' are probably to be identified with the family ancestors (H. NIEHR, Ein unerkannter Text zur Nekromantie in Israel, *UF* 23 [1991] 301-306, esp. 304). Considering the fact that the expression 'inheritance of the gods' (*naḥălat ʾĕlōhîm*, 2 Sam 14:16) is a parallel to the 'inheritance of the fathers' (*naḥălat ʾābôt*), it may be that *ʾĕlōhîm* in 2 Sam 14:16, too, refers to the (deified) ancestors (T. J. LEWIS, The Ancestral Estate (*naḥălat ʾelōhîm*) in 2 Samuel 14:16, *JBL* 110 [1991] 597-612).

IV. *Bibliography*

J. ASSMANN, Die 'Häresie' des Echnaton von Amarna. Aspekte der Amarna-Religion, *Saeculum* 22 (1972) 109-126; ASSMANN, Primat und Transzendenz. Struktur und Genese der Ägyptischen Vorstellung eines "Höchsten Wesens", *Aspekte der spätägyptischen Religion* (ed. W. Westendorf; GOF 9; Wiesbaden 1979) 7-42; ASSMANN, *Ägypten. Theologie und Frömmigkeit einer frühen Hochkultur* (Stuttgart 1984); J. BLACK & A. GREEN, *Gods, Demons and Symbols of Ancient Mesopotamia* (London 1992); E. CASSIN, *La splendeur divine* (Paris/The Hague 1968); S. DALLEY, *Myths from Mesopotamia* (Oxford/New York 1989); H. FRANKFORT, *Ancient Egyptian Religion*

(Chicago 1948); E. HORNUNG, *Der Eine und die Vielen. Ägyptische Gottesvorstellungen* (Darmstadt 1971); T. JACOBSEN, *Towards the Image of Tammuz and Other Essays on Mesopotamian History and Culture* (ed. W. L. Moran; Cambridge, Mass. 1970); JACOBSEN, *The Treasures of Darkness. A History of Mesopotamian Religion* (New Haven/London 1976); A. JIRKU, Elohim als Bezeichnung einer Gottheit, *RLA* 2 (1938) 358; W. G. LAMBERT, The Reign of Nebuchadnezzar I: A Turning Point in the History of Ancient Mesopotamian Religion, *The Seed of Wisdom* (ed. W. S. McCullough; Toronto 1964) 3-13; LAMBERT, Götterlisten, *RLA* 3 (1957-71) 473-479; LAMBERT, The Historical Development of the Mesopotamian Pantheon: A Study in Sophisticated Polytheism, *Unity and Diversity. Essays in the History, Literature, and Religion of the Ancient Near East* (ed. H. Goedicke & J. J. M. Roberts; Baltimore/London 1975) 191-200; LAMBERT, The Theology of Death, *Death in Mesopotamia* (CRRA 26; ed. B. Alster; Copenhagen 1980) 53-66; LAMBERT, Studies in Marduk, *BSOAS* 47 (1984) 1-9; P. MANDER, *Il pantheon di Abu-Ṣālabīkh* (Napoli 1986); D. MEEK, Notion de 'dieu' et structure du panthéon dans l'Egypte ancienne, *RHR* 205 (1988) 425-446; E. T. MULLEN, Jr., *The Assembly of the Gods. The Divine Council in Canaanite and Early Hebrew Literature* (HSM 24; Chico 1980); A. L. OPPENHEIM, *Ancient Mesopotamia: Portait of a Dead Civilization* (Chicago/London 1977) 171-227; D. PARDEE, *Les textes para-mythologiques de la 24e campagne (1961)* (Paris 1988); H. RINGGREN, אלהים, *TWAT* 1 (1970-73) 285-305; P. W. SKEHAN, A Fragment of the 'Song of Moses' (Deut. 32) from Qumran, *BASOR* 136 (1954), 12-15; K. VAN DER TOORN, *"De mens kan niet ten hemel klimmen, noch afdalen naar het dodenrijk"* (Inaugural lecture; Utrecht 1988); VAN DER TOORN, The Nature of the Biblical Teraphim in the Light of the Cuneiform Sources, *CBQ* 52 (1990) 203-222; C. TRAUNECKER, *Les dieux d'Egypte* (Paris 1992); J. VERGOTE, La notion de Dieu dans les livres de sagesse égyptiens, *Les sagesses du Proche-Orient ancien* (J. Leclant et al.; Paris 1963), 153-190; W. WESTENDORF, *Das Aufkommen der Gottesvorstellung im Alten Ägypten* (Göttingen 1985).

K. VAN DER TOORN

GOD (II) Θεός

I. The word θεός occurs 5302 times in the Greek Bible: 3984 occurrences in the LXX and 1318 in the NT. In almost all of these instances the word refers to the God of Israel, →Yahweh (and of course in the plural to pagan gods); some exceptions will be discussed below. In Greek literature the terms θεός, ὁ θεός, θεοί, οἱ θεοί, and later also τὸ θεῖον, are often used without much difference in meaning (GIGON 1965:194). The word is of uncertain etymology. The only aspect to be dealt with in this entry is the use of the word θεός (and *deus*) in ancient literature and its difference from biblical usage (on the causes of the lack of a comprehensive theology among pagan Greeks and Romans [except in Neoplatonism] see DÖRRIE 1983).

II. In pagan Greek literature the use of the word θεός is markedly different from what we find in the Bible. The difference is not only that θεός is applied by the Greeks to a plurality of personal divine beings, but also that often the word is used for human beings and impersonal objects and even abstract concepts that would not readily be called θεός (or θεοί) in the monotheistic Judaeo-Christian tradition (cf. W. SCHOTTROFF, Gottmensch I, *RAC* 12 [1983] 210-211). The same applies to the use of *deus* in pagan Latin literature. Both terms are predominantly used as a predicate (WILAMOWITZ 1931:I 17), unlike in biblical usage (KLEINKNECHT 1938:68 remarks that an ancient Greek would never have said, "God is love" [I John 4:16], but "Love is god"; cf. VERDENIUS 1954:244: "Der griechische Gott ist nicht göttlich, weil er Gott ist, sondern er ist Gott, weil er etwas Göttliches ist"). From early times onwards the Greeks regarded certain individuals as more than human and could call them θεός, either unreservedly or with reference to themselves ('he is a god to me' [cf. here Exod 4:16 and 7:1, exceptional in the Bible!]). If one recognized in a person the essential characteristics of a particular god, one might call him by the name of that god, again either unreservedly or only with reference to oneself. "To the ancients the line of demarcation between god and man was not as constant and sharp, or the interval as wide, as we naturally think" (NOCK 1972:145). There were, however, no institutional controls and no uncontroversial criteria for the use of the word 'god' (PRICE 1984:81). Throughout Greek literature we find the use of θεός and θεοί to denote the incalculable non-human element in phenomena, and of θεός for anything out of the ordinary (cf. the statement in a 2nd cent. CE papyrus quoted by PRICE 1984:95: τί θεός; τὸ κρατοῦν, 'What is a god? The exercise of power'). Also the abstract τὸ θεῖον becomes finally an expression for the irrational in human life, that which cannot be explained by natural causes, or for anything seemingly exempt from decay and other human limitations. For instance, exceptional physical beauty could be sufficient reason to bestow the predicate θεός upon a person (Charax, *FGH* 103F13; cf. Diogenes Laertius X 5). Cicero calls the consul Lentulus *parens, deus, salus nostrae vitae* (*Post reditum ad populum* 11; cf. *Pro Sexto* 144), and he calls Plato *deus ille noster* (*Ad Atticum* IV 16,3; cf. *De natura deorum* II 12, 32; *Leges* III 1; and the remarks on this usage by Augustine, *Contra Julianum Pelag.* IV 76). Terence, *Adelphi* 535, has one of his characters say: *facio te apud illum deum; virtutes narro*. Aristotle, *Politica* III 13 (1284a7-12), remarks that, if a person has really superior qualities, injustice will be done to him if he is reckoned only as the equal of those who are far inferior to him in excellence and in capacity: "Such a man may truly be deemed a god among men". It is for that reason that in the writings of the Neoplatonists their great Plato is so frequently designated as θεός or θεῖος (see the excellent note in PEASE 1968:619-620). The Platonist Arcesilaos calls the philosophers Crates and Polemon θεοί τινες (Diogenes Laertius IV 22). In Heliodorus, *Aethiopica* IV 7,8, a successful doctor is called σωτὴρ καὶ θεός (for more instances see BAUER-ALAND 727). It is striking to find still a clear instance of this usage even in a second century Christian document, the *Epistle to Diognetus,* when it states: "Whoever takes upon himself his neighbour's burden, whoever wishes to benefit another who is worse off in something in which he himself is better off, whoever provides to those in need things that he has received from God, and thus becomes a god to those who receive them, this one is an imitator of God" (10:6). For the application of this usage of θεός in the hero- and ruler cult, see →Heros and →Rulercult (with DÖRRIE 1983:95-98, 139-141, and PRICE 1984).

Also non-personal concepts and events (among the Pythagoreans even numbers) could be designated θεός. Already Hesiod says, after having pictured the power of φήμη (rumour), that it is a θεός (*Erga* 764). Aeschylus, *Choephoroi* 59-60, has the chorus say that for some men good luck is a god or even more than a god (τὸ δ' εὐτυχεῖν, τόδ' ἐν βροτοῖς θεός τε καὶ θεοῦ πλέον). Sophocles, fragm. 922 Radt, says that φρόνησις ἀγαθή is a great god. Euripides has Helen, when in a critical situation she recognizes her husband Menelaus, say to him in her joy that recognizing friends is 'god' (ὦ θεοί, θεὸς γὰρ καὶ τὸ γιγνώσκειν φίλους, *Helena* 560). In Euripides' *Orestes* 399 a great grief is called a terrible goddess (δεινὴ θεός), and in his satyrplay, *Cyclops* 316, the protagonist says that for wise men wealth is a god. The tragedian Hippothoon (fragm. 2) calls envy a most wicked god. "Prädiziert wird immer eine dem Menschen überlegene Macht" (WILAMOWITZ 1931:I 18). Therefore, Menander says (fragm. 223 Körte-Thierfelder in Stobaeus, *Eclogae* III 32, 11, and Artemidorus, *Oneirocritica* II 36): everything that is powerful is regarded as a god (τὸ κρατοῦν γὰρ πᾶν [or: νῦν] νομίζεται θεός); cf. also the expression τὰ τοῦ θεοῦ for 'the weather' in Theophrastus' *Charakteres* 25:2, the identification of wine with the god →Dionysus (DÖRRIE 1983:109-110), and the expression οἱ κρείττονες, 'the stronger ones', for the gods. Finally an example from the Roman world, where Pliny the Elder presents us with the following definition: when a mortal helps a mortal, that is god (*deus est mortali iuvare mortalem*; *Naturalis Historia* II 18). It would seem that sometimes θεός (and *deus*) means little more than 'god-given'.

Although deification of personified abstractions does occur from Hesiod onwards, in general it can be said that during the archaic and classical period this phenomenon was relatively rare. But in the fourth century BCE and in the Hellenistic and Roman periods an unbridled growth of 'Kultpersonifikationen' can be witnessed (NILSSON 1952; HAMDORF 1964; cf. also NESTLE 1933:21-23; DÖRRIE 1983:117-118). PÖTSCHER (1959), however, has rightly pointed out that the term 'personification' should be used with caution, since in the ancient 'Person-Bereichdenken' the work of the god and the god who works are identical: his person and his 'domain' coincide and form a synthetic unity. It is for that reason that it is often very hard to decide whether in text-editions one has to print Ἄρης or ἄρης, Γῆ or γῆ, Δίκη or δίκη, Ἥλιος or ἥλιος. Moreover, it is often hard to establish whether the mention of a deified abstraction in an ancient source always implies a real cult or is just a metaphor. A very great number of deified abstractions is attested (see DEUBNER 1909), the following of which occur also in the Greek Bible, albeit almost never personified: Aidos (→Bashtu), Anaideia, →Ananke, Ara (→Curse), Arete, Asebeia, Asphaleia, Athanasia, Bia, Boule, Charis, Chronos (→Aion), Demos, Dikaiosyne (→Zedeq), →Dike, →Dynamis, Eirene (→Shalem), Eleos, Eleutheria, Elpis, Eniautos, Eris, Eulabeia, Euphrosyne, Euporia, Eusebeia, Gamos, Gelos, Geras, Gerousia, Hedone, Hegemonia, Homonoia, Hora, Horme, Hybris, Hygieia, Hypnos, Kairos, Lethe, Limos ('Hunger'), Mania, Metanoia, Mneia, →Nike, Ochlos, Paranomia, Peitho, Penia, Pheme, Philia, Phobos, Pistis, Ploutos, →Pronoia, Sophrosyne, Soteria, Techne, →Thanatos. (Only some of the most important deified abstractions have received a separate entry in this dictionary, because they do occur in personified form in the Bible, e.g. Dike, Thanatos). These θεοί, even though recognized as gods, probably did not often have temples or cultic sites of their own.

Of the greatest importance for the development of ancient Greek concepts of god is the rise of philosophical criticism of religious and mythological traditions in the late sixth and early fifth centuries BCE, in which Xenophanes of Colophon played a seminal and Plato a capital role (DECHARME 1904: 43-50, 181-219; GRANT 1986:76-77). This signalled the start of a long process of spiritualization (and depersonalization, DÖRRIE 1983:141-150) of the traditional notions of god, that culminated in the (Neo-)Platonic concept of a radically transcendent deity (in a henotheistic sense) that was intrinsically unknowable and could only be spoken about in terms of a *theologia negativa.* A key element in this development was the concept of (what the Stoics later termed) the θεοπρεπές, what is befitting God, *dignum deo* (DREYER 1970). The gradual purification of the concept of deity to the effect that all traces of anthropomorphism (human affections and behaviour) were removed from it had as a consequence, *inter alia*, that old mythological stories about the gods were either discarded or gave rise to allegorical interpretation, and that there was an ever widening gap between the image of the biblical God, who sympathizes with his children and experiences a wide range of emotions, on the one hand, and the increasingly dispassionate Greek conception of God on the other (FROHNHOFEN 1987). And, apart from the question of God's *apatheia*, the biblical God is a God who acts and speaks, whereas the Platonic god neither acts nor speaks (VERDENIUS 1954:256-258). It was the contribution of the Jewish philosopher Philo of Alexandria that he, in an impressive *tour de force*, tried to reconcile these strongly diverging images and to bridge the gap by a bold synthesis of biblical and Greek theology that had a lasting influence on Christian theology (DREYER 1970:68-145).

III. The Greek use of θεός (i.e. not for 'God') can be found in the Greek Bible only very rarely. Deification of personified abstractions is almost lacking. Deification of humans is rare (and strongly criticized, see e.g. Acts 12:22-23) and occurs actually only in connection with →Jesus in a relatively late stage of the development of christology in the first century. One passage in John would at first sight seem to suggest that in general human beings could also be called gods (10:34-35). The reference there to Ps 81:6 ("I said, you are gods") apparently implies that what Jesus said about himself in 10:30 ("I and the Father are one") and in 10:36 ("I am God's son") is to be interpreted in the sense that he shares in God's divine nature (discussion in G. R. BEASLEY-MURRAY, *John* [WBC 36; Waco 1987] 175-177). Yet Jesus is not explicitly and unambiguously called God here. That does happen, however, both earlier and later in the same Gospel: firstly in the very opening verse of the Gospel, where it is said that "the →Logos was God" (1:1, and cf. 1:18), and secondly at the very end of the Gospel, after Jesus' resurrection, when Thomas confesses that Jesus is "My Lord and my God" (20:28; also 1 John 5:20 probably has to be interpreted as referring to Jesus). From the same period (end of the first century) is Heb 1:8-9, where there can be little doubt that the words "o God" in the quote from Ps 45:7-8 are meant by the author to refer to Jesus. Tit 2:13 and 2 Pet 1:1, again passages from the late first or early second cent., clearly refer to Jesus as θεὸς καὶ σωτήρ. But earlier NT passages that have been claimed as calling Jesus God are more controversial (CULLMANN 1975:314-323; BOOBYER 1967/68). Both Rom 9:5 and 2 Thess 1:12 (middle of the first century) leave open the possibility that the θεός spoken about in the text is not Jesus Christ but God the Father, which seems more probable (see J. D. G. DUNN, *Romans 9-16* [WBC 38; Dallas 1988] 535-536, and F. F. BRUCE, *1 and 2 Thessalonians* [WBC 45; Waco 1982] 156-157). So in the NT it is only in a few late passages that Jesus begins to be called God and the boundaries of Jewish monotheism are broken (CASEY 1991; HARRIS 1992; cf. H. C. YOUTIE, *ZPE* 18 [1975] 151-152). But soon after, already in Ignatius of Antioch, we see the frequency of this usage increase strongly. Because neither in the NT nor in the Churchfathers did that usage imply *per se* an ontological equation of Jesus with God, the problem of the relation between these 'two gods' arose, which was later 'solved' by the trinitarian dogma. (Later Christian instances of the other 'Greek' uses of θεός and θεῖος for humans can be found in Lampe's *PGL* s.v. θεός K, 635b, and s.v. θεῖος B 11, 620a; also J. GROSS, *La divinisation du chrétien d'après les pères grecs* [Paris 1938]).

IV. *Bibliography*

G. H. BOOBYER, Jesus as Theos in the New Testament, *BJRL* 50 (1967/68) 247-261; W. BURKERT, *Greek Religion* (Cambridge MA 1985) 271-272; P. M. CASEY, *From Jewish Prophet to Gentile God. The Origins and Development of New Testament Christology* (Cambridge-Louisville 1991); O. CULLMANN, *Die Christologie des Neuen Testaments* (5th ed. Tübingen 1975); P. DECHARME, *La critique des traditions religieuses chez les grecs des origines au temps de Plutarque* (Paris 1904); L. DEUBNER, Personifikationen abstrakter Begriffe, *ALGRM* III (1909) 2068-2169; H. DÖRRIE, Gottesbegriff, *RAC* 11 (1981) 944-951; *DÖRRIE, Gottesvorstellung, *RAC* 12 (1983) 81-154; O. DREYER, *Untersuchungen zum Begriff des Gottgeziemenden in der Antike* (Hildesheim 1970); G. FRANÇOIS, *Le polythéisme et l'emploi au singulier des mots THEOS, DAIMON* (Paris 1957); H. FROHNHOFEN, *Apatheia tou Theou. Über die Affektlosigkeit Gottes in der griechischen Antike und bei den griechischsprachigen Kirchenvätern bis zu Gregorios Thaumaturgos* (Frankfurt etc.

1987); O. GIGON, Griechische Religion, *DTV Lexikon der Antike* (Religion, Mythologie) II (1965) 187-205, esp. 191-195 (Gottesvorstellung); R. GRANT, *Gods and the One God. Christian Theology in the Graeco-Roman World* (London 1986); F. W. HAMDORF, *Die griechische Kultpersonifikationen aus vorhellenistischer Zeit* (Mainz 1964); M. J. HARRIS, *Jesus as God. The New Testament Use of* Theos *in Reference to Jesus* (Grand Rapids 1992); *H. KLEINKNECHT, θεός, *TWNT* III (1938) 65-79; W. NESTLE, *Griechische Religiosität vom Zeitalter des Perikles bis auf Aristoteles* (Berlin & Leipzig 1933); M. P. NILSSON, Kultische Personifikationen, *Eranos* 50 (1952) 30-40; A. D. NOCK, *Essays on Religion and the Ancient World* (2 vols., Oxford 1972); A. S. PEASE, *M. Tulli Ciceronis de natura deorum libri III* (Darmstadt 1968 = 1955); W. PÖTSCHER, *Theos. Studien zur älteren griechischen Gottesvorstellung* (diss. Vienna 1953); PÖTSCHER, Das Person-Bereichdenken in der frühgriechischen Periode, *WS* 72 (1959) 5-25; S. R. F. PRICE, Gods and Emperors: The Greek Language of the Roman Imperial Cult, *JHS* 104 (1984) 79-95; R. SCHROEDER, Das griechische Gottesverständnis, *Theologische Versuche* 6 (1975) 79-88; W. SCHWERING, *Deus* und *divus:* eine semasiologische Studie, *Indogermanische Forschungen* 34 (1914/15) 1-44; W. J. VERDENIUS, Platons Gottesbegriff, *La notion du divin depuis Homère jusqu'à Platon* (ed. H. J. Rose; Entretiens de la Fondation Hardt 1; Vandoeuvres 1954) 241-293; U. VON WILAMOWITZ-MOELLENDORFF, *Der Glaube der Hellenen* I (Darmstadt 1955 = 1931) 17-21.

P. W. VAN DER HORST

GOD OF FORTRESSES אלה מעזים Θεὸς μαωζιν

I. As used in Dan 11:38, the 'god of fortresses' (אלה מעזים) has been treated in the Greek Theodotion and in the Vulgate translation of the book of Daniel as a divine name (θεὸς μαωζιν respectively *deus Maozim*). This name has ever since been equated with a variety of Semitic, Greek or Roman deities.

II. Jerome already mentions in his commentary on Dan (11:31; *GLAJJ* 2, 469) Porphyry, who "offered an absurd explanation" of the god Maozim. For the latter asserted that the generals of Antiochus IV 'Epiphanes', ruler of the Seleucid empire, set up a statue of Jupiter in the village of Modin, some miles NW of Jerusalem, from which came Mattathias and his sons (the Maccabees). Theodoretus explains the deity even as the →Antichrist, 'a god strong and powerful' (cf. the Peshitta-translation: 'the strong god'). Hugo Grotius, in the wake of Ephrem Syrus, considered the god as the Syrian deity Azizos, which was identified with Mars (or →Ares). Many scholars in modern times hesitate especially between Jupiter Capitolinus, for whom Antiochus began to build a temple in Antioch (Livy xli 20), or Jupiter (→Zeus) Olympius (2 Macc 6:2). The latter has also been identified with the *šiqquṣ šōmēm* (Dan 11:31; 12:11; cf. Dan 9:27; 1 Macc 1:54; Matt 24:15; Mark 13:14), 'the abomination of desolation', in which already E. NESTLE (*ZAW* 4 [1884] 248) saw a satirical pun on the name →Baal Šamêm, a high god of Semitic origin.

Yet there are also scholars who consider the title god of fortresses 'entirely obscure' (*e.g.* Montgomery). SANDERS (1962) is of the opinion that the title refers satirically to Antiochus himself in the context of Dan 11:36-39. BICKERMANN (1937) proposes as numen of the 'Akra' (= fortress, fortification (citadel) of the old 'city of David' in Jerusalem made by the Seleucids) 'Zeus'-Baalsamin, and HENGEL (1973) suggests that he should be 'the god of the Akra' (and not Jupiter Capitolinus; cf. an inscription found in Scythopolis, in which a dedication to 'Zeus Akraios', the god of the mountain top and of the fortresses [Akra], is mentioned). BUNGE (1973) opines that the title 'god of fortresses' does not refer to any known Semitic deity, but to a ciphered Greek god. Dan 11:36-39 has not to be considered as a report of historical occurences in Judaea or Jerusalem in the days of the religious persecutions of Antiochus, but as a mere reflection on the behaviour of that king himself. It is known, however, that Antiochus had a considerable predeliction for the Olympic Zeus.

III. In the context of Dan 11:38 it is said that "the king (=Antiochus) will exalt and magnify himself above every god...To no god will he pay heed but he will exalt himself above them all" (vv 36-37). GINSBERG (1948; followed by DILELLA 1978) has pointed out that in v 38a *yĕkabbēd*, 'he will honour' has to be taken as a variant of this word in v 38b, and that it has ousted the word that originally followed *māʿuzzîm*: 'he will defy', or 'insult'. The word מעזים (seven times in the singular and in the plural in this chapter) is an erroneous rendering of an Aramaic word meaning 'saints' (= the Jewish people; Dan 7; 8:24; cf. 12:7). 'On his stand' (= on his altar) has to be transposed from before the first (wrong) 'he will honour' to before the second. So v 38 has to be translated: "Even the God of the pious ones (= Jewish people) he will despise, and on that God's stand he will honour...a god whom his ancestors did not know" (DI LELLA 1978). In this context 'the God of the pious ones' is none other than →Yahweh, the God of Israel.

IV *Bibliography*

F.-M. ABEL, Antiochus Epiphanes, *RB* 50 (1941) 248; E. BICKERMANN, *Der Gott der Makkabäer* (Berlin 1937) 111-116; J. G. BUNGE, Der 'Gott der Festungen' und der 'Liebling der Frauen'. Zur Identifizierung der Götter in Dan. 11, 36-39, *JSJ* 4 (1973) 169-182 [& lit]; A. A. DILELLA, Introduction and Commentary on Chapters 10-12, *The Book of Daniel* (ed. L. F. Hartman, AB; Garden City 1978); H. L. GINSBERG, *Studies in Daniel* (New York 1948) esp. 42-49; H. L. GINSBERG, מעזים (אלה), *EncMiqr* 5 (1968) 190-191 [Hebrew]; M. HENGEL, *Judentum und Hellenismus* (Tübingen 1973²) 515-519 [& lit]; J. A. SANDERS, Fortress, *IDB* 2(1962) 321.

M. J. MULDER

GOD OF HEAVEN אלהי השמים

I. The conception of a god of heaven was developed in the Northwest Semitic religions of the 1st millennium BCE, where a new type of supreme god, →Baal shamem, arose. This god is first found in Phoenician inscriptions from the mid 10th cent. BCE onwards and taken over into the Aramaic and Judaeo-Israelite religion, where →Yahweh was equated with the god of heaven.

II. In the Israelite-Jewish religion the explicit designation of Yahweh as 'god of heaven' occurs independently in the 5th century Elephantine papyri and in several post-exilic books of the OT. The antecedents for this development lie in the pre-exilic period.

Originally Yahweh was a local weather-god of the Midianite-Edomite region. Also in later Judaeo-Israelite religion Yahweh was seen as a weather-god who was responsible for rain and fertility (e. g. 2 Sam 22:8-16 = Ps 18:8-16; Jer 10:13 = 51:16; 14:22; 31:12; Hos 2:10-11; Hag 1:2-11; 2:15-19; Joel 2:21-24; Ps 29; 65:10-14). Due to the rise of the monarchy in Judah and Israel, Yahweh abandoned his status as local weather-god and rose to the position of a supreme and universal weather-god, a position which according to the Phoenician expression, was reserved for the 'god of heaven'.

The political and religio-historical background for conceiving Yahweh as god of heaven is to be seen in the Phoenician supremacy over the kingdoms of Judah and Israel from the second half of the 10th century onward. The temple of Jerusalem was built under Phoenician influence (1 Kgs 5: 15-32; 7:13-51). In this national sanctuary of Judah, Yahweh was venerated as "enthroned upon the →cherubim" (1 Sam 4:4; 2 Sam 6:2 = 1 Chr 13:6; 2 Kgs 19:15 = Jes 37:16; Pss 80:2; 99:1). This theologoumenon is of Phoenician provenience and designates Yahweh as divine king. A direct relationship between Yahweh and Baal shamem cannot, however, be recognized in the temple of Solomon. At this stage of the religious history of Judah, Yahweh was venerated as the supreme god according to Phoenician standards.

A direct link between Yahweh and Baal shamem was established when the Omrides organized their kingdom in conformity with the Phoenician organization. In the temple Ahab had built in Samaria, Yahweh the state god, was venerated as Baal shamem (1 Kgs 16:32) in order to stress the ties between Omride Israel and Phoenicia.

Beyond the level of official religion as practised in the temples of Jerusalem and Samaria, a reception of the god Baal shamem on a popular level can also be observed. This reception is to be seen within the context of the 'astralization' of the Northwest Semitic religions during the first millenium BCE. Iconographical and textual evidence demonstrates a solarization of the Yahweh-religion from the 8th century onward (NIEHR 1990:147-163; →Shemesh). On the basis of this background, Yahweh became a 'god of heaven' in popular religion. Yahweh's status as 'god of heaven' is further demonstrated by his endowment with celestial powers. Thus he was surrounded by a 'host of heaven' (→Host of heaven) serving as his divine →council (1 Kgs 22:19). In this context, the worship of the 'queen of heaven' (→Queen of Heaven) must be mentioned. The 'queen of heaven', to be identified with Yahweh's →Asherah known from the inscriptions of Kuntillet Ajrud and Khirbet el-Qom, was Yahweh's paredra in the Jerusalem temple cult (Jer 7:18; 44:15-25). Her presence emphazised his status as 'god of heaven' (KOCH 1988:115-120).

The explicit reception of the title 'god of heaven' can be observed for the first time in the 5th century papyri of the Judaeo-Aramaic colony of Elephantine. In the correspondence directed to non-Jewish addressees, the inhabitants of Elephantine speak of Yahweh as "(Yahu), god of heaven" (*AP* 27:15 [rest.]; 30:2.27-28; 31:2.26-27 [rest.]; 32:3-4) or as "lord of heaven" (*AP* 30:15). But also, in intra-Jewish communication, Yahweh is called "god of heaven" (*AP* 38:2 [rest.] 3.5; 40:1 [rest.]).

Also in Palestine, from the same time onwards, Yahweh is designated as the "god of heaven" in Hebrew (Gen 24:3, 7; Jonah 1:9; Esr 1:2; Neh 1:4-5; 2:4, 20; 2 Chr 36: 23; Ps 136:26) and in Aramaic (Dan 2:18-19, 37, 44; Ezra 5:11-12; 6:9-10; 7:12, 21, 23); also "lord of heaven" (Dan 5:23) and "king of heaven" (Dan 4:34). The deuterocanonical books Judith and Tobit use Greek equivalents of this title (references in NIEHR 1990:49-50).

The fact that the two titles for Yahweh, 'god of heaven' and 'lord of heaven', are not exclusively used in communication with the Persian overlords, but also in intra-Jewish communication, is a decisive argument against the alleged Persian provenience of the title 'god of heaven' applied to Yahweh in post-exilic texts. The cult of Baal shamem, who had become the dominant god of the Phoenician and Aramaic religion, already exerted his influence both on the official and the popular level of the Judaeo-Israelite religion in the First Temple period. As the Elephantine papyri and the biblical books demonstrate, the influence of Baal shamem grew increasingly during exilic and post-exilic times.

Yahweh as 'god of heaven' was thus modelled after a Syro-Canaanite supreme god. This is evident from his characteristic traits: Yahweh is the highest of all gods who presides over the divine assembly (e.g. Deut 32:8; 1 Kgs 22:19; Isa 6; 14:13-14; Pss 82:6; 89:6-8; 95:3: 96:4: 135:5); he is enthroned on the divine mountain (e.g. Isa 14:13-14; Pss 46:5-8; 48:3; 68:16-17; 87:1b, 5b; 89:13; →Zaphon); he is the creator and fights the chaos (e. g. Gen 14: 19, 22; 2 Sam 22:14-18 = Pss 18:14-18; 74:13-17; 89:10-13; Isa 51:9-16) and is a solarized god (e.g. Ps 84:12; Mal 3:20, Shemesh).

The identification of Yahweh and Baal shamem is demonstrated by the installation of the cult of Baal shamem under his Hellenistic name of →Zeus Olympios in the temple of Jerusalem under Antiochus IV Epiphanes in 167 BCE, which was not a pagan measure but the result of an intra-Jewish prohellenistic development. Its goal was not to replace Yahweh by another god or to introduce a new god into the temple of Jerusalem. Yahweh himself was henceforth to be venerated as Baal shamem with the character of a universal god. The Jewish opposition against this measure can be seen in the polemics against the *šiqqûṣ (mĕ)šōmēm* ('devastating evil') in Dan 11: 31; 12:11 (cf. Dan 8:13; 9:27; 1 Macc 1:54). Even after the Maccabaean period, Yahweh could be designated as 'god of heaven' (references in NIEHR 1990:58-59).

III. *Bibliography*

D. K. ANDREWS, Yahweh the God of the Heavens, *The Seed of Wisdom.* FS T. J. Meek (ed. W. S. McCullough; Toronto 1964) 45-57; E. BICKERMANN, *Der Gott der Makkabäer* (Berlin 1937) esp. 90-116; O. EISSFELDT, Baalšamēm und Jahwe, *ZAW* 57 (1937) 1-31 = *KS* 2 (1963) 171-193; M. HENGEL, *Judentum und Hellenismus* (WUNT 10; Tübingen 1988[3]) 532-548; R. HILLMANN, *Wasser und Berg* (diss. Halle 1965); C. HOUTMAN, *Der Himmel im Alten Testament* (OTS 30; Leiden 1993) 98-107; B. JANOWSKI, Keruben und Zion, *"Ernten, was man sät".* FS K. Koch (ed. D. R. Daniels e.a.; Neukirchen 1991) 231-264; O. KEEL & C. UEHLINGER, *Göttinnen, Götter und Gottessymbole* (QD 134; Freiburg 1992) esp. 296-298, 302-321; K. KOCH, *Das Buch Daniel* (EdF 144; Darmstadt 1980) 136-140; KOCH, Aschera als Himmelskönigin in Jerusalem, *UF* 20 (1988) 97-120; E. NESTLE, Zu Daniel, *ZAW* 4 (1884) 247-250; H. NIEHR, *Der höchste Gott* (BZAW 190; Berlin-New York 1990); R. RENDTORFF, El, Baal und Jahwe, *ZAW* 78 (1966) 277-292; F. VATTIONI, Aspetti del culto del signore dei cieli (II), *Aug* 13 (1973) 37-74, esp. 41-52; A. VINCENT, *La religion des Judéo-Araméens d'Eléphantine* (Paris 1937) 92-143.

H. NIEHR

GOD OF SEEING → EL-ROI

GODDESS → TEREBINTH

GO'EL גאל

I. In ancient Israel, the *gō'ēl*, 'redeemer', acted within the social system as the protector and defender of the interests of the kinship group. Metaphorically *gō'ēl* occurs as an epithet for →Yahweh; besides, in Job 19:25, *gō'ēl* indicates an independent deity. On a societal level, several functions are attributed to the *gō'ēl* in the Hebrew texts: he acted as the next of kin to buy up or buy back property to prevent its being lost from the group (Lev 25:25); he could redeem, or pay off the debt, of a kinsperson who had fallen victim to debt slavery (Lev 25:47-49); he bore the responsibility of securing an heir to continue the name of a deceased head of family who had died without male offspring (Deut 25:5-10); and he was responsible for blood vengeance within the clan (Num 35:31-34; Deut 19:6-12). The order of kinship by which the *gō'ēl* was determined is given in Lev 25:48-49. Though similar social functionaries are attested in other tribal cultures, the terminology associated with the *gō'ēl* is almost exclusively Hebrew, and its basic meaning of 'redeem', 'buy back', 'recover' is derived from its use in family law and custom. In the Hebrew Bible, this terminology is frequently applied to the divine realm.

II. A verbal form of *gā'al* is applied to the activity of Yahweh some nineteen times, mainly in poetry, thus extending the metaphor of the kinship relationship to apply to Israel as Yahweh's inheritance or portion. In his role as 'redeemer', Yahweh acts on behalf of Israel to deliver it from bondage in Egypt (Exod 6:6; 15:13; Pss 74:2; 77:16; etc.) or in the exile (Isa 43:1; 44:22-23; 48:20). On an individual level, Yahweh ransoms the pious and the needy, most specifically the widow and orphan (Gen 48:16; Pss 69:19; 72:14; 103:4; 107:2; etc.).

The substantive *gō'ēl* is applied as an epithet to Yahweh some seventeen times in the Hebrew texts in a similar number of settings (e.g., Prov 23:11; Jer 50:34; Pss 19:15; 78:35). Ten of these applications occur in Deutero-Isaiah, where *gō'ēl* is applied to Yahweh with little or no explicit connection to any specific situation, indicating that it had become a stereotyped epithet for the deity. In these materials, Yahweh is called *gōʾēl* in parallel with such standard epithets as 'the Holy One of Israel' (*qĕdôš yiśrāʾēl*; Isa 41:14; 43:14; 47:4; 48:17; 54:5; cf. 49:7), 'the King of Israel' (*melek yiśrāʾēl*; 44:6), 'Yahweh of Hosts' (*yhwh ṣĕbāʾôt*; 44:6; 47:4; 54:5), and 'Deliverer' (*môšîaʿ*; 49:26). In the context of Deutero-Isaiah, the epithet conveys the image of Yahweh as redeemer of his people from the bondage of the exile.

In addition to its application to Yahweh, the term *gōʾēl* is applied to a heavenly figure in the enigmatic passage in Job 19:25. It is clear from the context of this passage that Job expresses the desire that his personal *gōʾēl* intervene on his behalf and vindicate his innocence and integrity. It is commonly accepted that this *gōʾēl* is to be equated with the figure of the heavenly →'witness' (*ʿēd*) and 'interpreter' (*mēlîṣ* →Mediator I) referred to in 16:19-22, and possibly with the 'arbiter' (*môkîaḥ*) noted in 9:33-35. The recognition of such an intercessor is further suggested in 33:23-24, where Elihu tells Job that unless he has an →'angel' (*malʾāk*), an 'interpreter' (*mēlîṣ*) to proclaim his justice and to ransom him from →Sheol, he is doomed.

Since Job's reference to the *gōʾēl* in 19:25 occurs in the context of a dispute with God in which he seems to have rejected the possibility of God's hearing his plea and acting in his behalf, it seems unlikely that the *gōʾēl* is to be identified with Yahweh. Rather, these references to a heavenly *gōʾēl* and *ʿēd* more probably reflect the ancient Near Eastern concept of either a personal deity who would intercede for an individual with the high god or a specialized role associated with one of the members of the heavenly assembly, who could also intercede with the head of the →council on behalf of a patron.

III. *Bibliography*

M. L. BARRÉ, A Note on Job xix 25, *VT* 29 (1979) 107-110; W. L. IRWIN, Job's Redeemer, *JBL* 81 (1962) 217-229; S. MOWINCKEL, Hiob's gōʾēl und Zeuge im Himmel, *Vom Alten Testament: Festschrift für Karl Marti*, (ed. K. Budde; Giessen 1925); 207-212; M. POPE, *Job* (AB 15; New York 1965) 146-147; H. RINGGREN, גָּאַל *gāʾal*; גֹּאֵל *gōʾēl*; גְּאֻלָּה *gĕʾullāh*, *TDOT*, Vol. II, 350-355; R. DE VAUX, *Ancient Israel*, Vol. 1 (New York 1965) 21-22.

E. T. MULLEN, JR.

GOG גוג

I. Gog (*gwg*) occurs as the name of a mysterious figure in Ezek 38-39. Its etymology is uncertain. A derivation from Sumerian **gug** ('black spot', 'cornelian', or 'shining', depending on the identification of the root) has been proposed (A. VAN HOONACKER, *ZA* 28 [1914] 336), but is highly implausible. The connection with a hypothetical deity 'Gaga', mentioned in *Ee* III 3 as the vizier of Anshar (→Assur), the father of the gods, must be abandoned as the name of the deity in question is to be pronounced Kaka (D. O. EDZARD, *RLA* 5 [1976-80] 288; see also *Šurpu* 59 ad VIII 30 on the reading ^{d}*Ga-a-gi*). No particular significance seems to have been attached to the literal meaning of the name—assuming that it was known to the author of Ezek 38-39.

II. In an attempt to identify Gog as a historical person, attention has been drawn to a city prince Gâgi mentioned in the annals of Ashurbanipal (Cylinder B iv 2), a powerful ruler of a belligerent mountain people not far to the north of Assyria (Delitzsch, Lenormant, Dürr, Streck, see GRONKOWSKI 1930:162). More freqently, though, Gog is identified with Gyges (Gûgu in the Rassam-Cylinder, II 95), king of Lydia (Delitzsch, see ZIMMERLI 1969:942). Note, however, that the Gog of Ezekiel has the Cimmerians or Gomer as his ally, whereas the same Cimmerians appear to have attacked and defeated Gyges of Lydia. Such data suggest that Gog can hardly be identified with Gyges. Alternatively, Gog has been said to be the name of a country, *Gaga* or *Gagaia,* allegedly mentioned in the El Amarna Letters (*EA* 1:38). It has become clear, however, that the writing *ištēn* ^{kur}*Ga-ga-ya* is erroneous for *ištēn* ^{kur}*Ga-<aš>ga-ya*, 'one Kashkaean' (E. VON SCHULER, *Die Kaskäer* [Berlin 1965] 81; cf. *EA* 31:25-27), so this identification must be abandoned as well.

Taking into account the 'prophetic' and 'apocalyptic' character of Ezek 38-39, many recognize in Gog the enemy of the final days. This implies that he is not a figure of the past but a person of the present or the future. Depending on the date of composition of Ezek 38-39, and the date of the eschaton as seen by Ezekiel or a later redactor, this enemy could be identified with an officer in the army of the younger Cyrus, with Alexander the Great, Antiochus IV, or many others in later periods.

Many are convinced that the name Gog is not related to a historical personage. The Septuagint manuscripts seem to confuse him with →Og, the mythological king of →Bashan (see also below). He is a cipher for the evil darkness of the north and personifies the powers hostile to the LORD (AHRONI 1977).

III. Many consider Ezek 38-39 to be a complex unity. There is no consensus about the history of its literary growth. Yet in recent literature most authors agree that 39: 1-5, combined with 39:17-20 and perhaps parts of 38:1-9, constitute the oldest layer.

In one of the later additions (38:17), a redactor notes that Gog, coming from the remotest parts of the north (38:15), is the one spoken of by the earlier prophets or claims to be that one (BARTHÉLEMY 1992: 306). The reference is to the fulfilment of the prophecies of Jeremiah (1:3-16; 4-6), and perhaps also of Joel (2:20), who announced the coming of the foe from the north. Most often this enemy is identified with the Babylonians or with the Scythians. In Ezekiel, the foe has mythological overtones. He is to come "after many days", "in the latter years" (38:8). In later tradition, these and similar expressions were used to denote the eschaton. Gog's army, including Meshech, Tubal, Kush, Put, Gomer, Togarmah (38:2-6), is constituted by the peoples listed in Gen 10 (DHORME 1951:170-171). This suggests that the final days will correspond to the first. In 38:18-23, the battle of these days has an apocalyptic dimension as can be seen in the earthquake terminology which often accompanies divine manifestations and interventions (see Am 9). The scene is completed by a description of an exuberant meal, combining aspects of the apocalyptic feast on the mountain described in Isa 25:6-7 with the fearsome characteristics of the sacrificial meal pictured in Jer 46:10. The conclusion must be that, in the final redaction of Ezek 38-39, Gog is portrayed as a mythological figure personifying the eschatological enemy and the darkness of the north where he is located.

IV. In the LXX, Gog appears more frequently. In the third oracle of Balaam in Num 24:7, it is prophesied that the kingdom of the →Anthropos (man) will be higher than that of Gog. In the MT there is no equivalent for 'man', and Gog replaces the historical king Agag, defeated by Saul (1 Sam 15). The LXX has given an eschatological twist to the oracle (see GERLEMAN 1947:132-146). In Amos' vision of the plague of locusts (7:1), the LXX translator read *gōg* for *gzy* (mowings?), focusing on Gog as the leader of a threatening army represented as a swarm of locusts. In Sir 48:17, Gog seems to stand for the Hebrew *mym*. The Greek text can be translated as follows: "Hezekiah fortified his city, and brought Gog in the midst of it. He dug into the hard rock with iron and made wells for water". In the LXX^{B} version of Deut 3:1.13; 4:47, Gog stands for Hebrew Og (king of Bashan). On the other hand, P 967 reads Og instead of Gog in Ez 38:2.

In the intertestamental texts and in Qumran, Gog is rarely mentioned (*Sib. Or.* 3,319-320). Rabbinic literature often mentions Gog and →Magog as leaders of the enemy destined to attack the faithful in the Messianic Age; e.g. *b.Ab.Zar.* 3b: "When they witness the war of Gog and Magog, he will say to them, 'Against whom have you come?' They will say, 'Against the LORD and against his Anointed'", compare *b.Ber.*

7b; *Tg. Neof.* Num 11:26: "Eldad and Medad prophesied that, in the end of the days, Gog and Magog will come up against Jerusalem with their army, and will fall by the hand of the king Messiah".

In early Christian times, Gog and Magog were often identified with the Romans and their emperor. Eusebius seems to have been the first Churchfather to suggest this identification. In his view, Gog is the prince of 'Ros', which stands for the Roman Imperium (*Dem. Ev.* 9,3.6). In later times, Gog was seen as the →Antichrist. Some identified him with Napoleon, others with Hitler. Fundamentalist Christian belief (*Scofield Reference Bible*; GESENIUS, *Thesaurus* 1835, 1253) holds that the prophet was speaking about the modern state of Russia. The basis for this belief is the LXX's reading of the Hebrew *ros* as the proper name "Ros" which could easily be interpreted as a code-name for "Russia".

V. *Bibliography*

J. G. AALDERS, *Gog en Magog* (Kampen 1951); R. AHRONI, The Gog Prophecy and the Book of Ezekiel, *HAR* 1 (1977) 1-27; R. H. ALEXANDER, A Fresh Look at Ezekiel 38 and 39, *JETS* 17 (1974) 157-169; M. C. ASTOUR, Ezekiel's Prophecy of Gog and the Cuthean Legend of Naram-Sin, *JBL* 95 (1976) 567-579; D. BARTHÉLEMY, *Critique textuelle de l'Ancien Testament*, Tome 3, *Ezéchiel, Daniel et les 12 Prophètes* (OBO 50/3; Fribourg, Göttingen 1992); D. I. BLOCK, Gog and the Pouring out of the Spirit, *VT* 37 (1987) 257-270; W. H. BROWNLEE, 'Son of Man Set Your Face,' Ezekiel the Refugee Prophet, *HUCA* 54 (1983) 45-110, esp. 107-108; E. DHORME, Les peuples issus de Japhet d'après le chapitre X de la Genèse, *Recueil E. Dhorme* (Paris 1951) 167-189 = *Syria* 13 (1932) 28-49; G. GERLEMAN, Ezekielsboken Gog, *SEÅ* 12 (1947) 132-146; W. GRONKOWSKI, *Le messianisme d'Ezéchiel* (Paris 1930) 129-173; F. HOSSFELD, *Untersuchungen zu Komposition und Theologie des Ezechielbuches* (FzB 20; Würzburg 1977) 402-509; E. LIPIŃSKI, Gygès et Lygdamis d'après les sources hébraiques et néo-assyrienes, *OLP* 24 (1993) 65-71; *B. OTZEN, Gog, *TWAT* 1 (1973) 958-965 [& lit]; H. L. STRACK & P. BILLERBECK, *Kommentar zum NT aus Talmud und Midrasch* III (München 1926) 831-840; W. ZIMMERLI, *Ezechiel* (BKAT XIII/2; Neukirchen 1969) 933-948.

J. LUST

GUSH גשׁ

I. Though the evidence for the worship of a deity *Gesh or *Gush is scant if not absent, the biblical names *Girgash (Girgashites; MAISLER 1930) and Goshen (JIRKU 1963) have been adduced to demonstrate that the forebears of the Israelites once worshipped a god *Gš*.

II. There is only a single instance where the name Gush appears in the capacity of a god. In the Ugaritic personal name Bin-Gushi, the element Gushi is preceded by the divine determinative (J. NOUGAYROL, PRU III [1955] 199:5 = RS 16.257+, Face A, 5': ^{I}DUMU-^{d}*Gu-ši*). Since there is otherwise no trace of a god Gush in the records from the ancient Near East, the element Gushi is probably to be interpreted as a shortened form of the divine name Kuṯar (→Kothar) or Kušuḫ (F. GRÖNDAHL, *Die Personennamen der Texte aus Ugarit* [Rome 1967] 305). Other occurrences of the element Gus/Guš are short for Agus(h): ביתגש stands for Bīt-Agūsi of the Assyrian records, a small Syrian state with Arpad as its capital. The Agusites (cf. the name ברגש, *KAI* 202 A 5) were the reigning dynsasty of Arpad (DONNER & RÖLLIG 1973; FITZMYER 1967). There is no indication that the name Gush or Agus is theophoric.

III. The very fact that a god Gush is only mentioned once if at all, and that a god Gesh is simply unattested, weakens the plausibility of the speculations about גשׁ (Gesh or Gush) being a theophoric element in Hebrew names. The name of the Girgashites (cf. Ug *grgš*, *bn grgš*, and *bn grgs*, GRÖNDAHL, *Die Personennamen der Texte aus Ugarit* [Rome 1967] 384) has received no satisfactory explanation. The toponym Goshen, the name of a locality in southern

Palestine (Josh 10:41; 11:16; 15:51) as well as a place in Egypt (several times in Gen 45-50; also in Exod 8:18; 9:26) could be convincingly related to a supposed god Gush (the final *nun* might represent an original ending *-ôn* not uncommon in toponyms, cf. *Ṣîdôn*, →Sidon, BAUER & LEANDER, *Historische Grammatik der hebräischen Sprache*, § 61 *qθ*) only if that deity were sufficiently attested to in the written sources.

IV. *Bibliography*

H. DONNER & W. RÖLLIG, *KAI* II (1973) 207, commentary to no. 202 A 5; J. A. FITZMYER, *The Aramaic Inscriptions of Sefîre* (Rome 1967) 40-41; A. JIRKU, Zu einigen Orts- und Eigennamen Palästina-Syriens, *ZAW* 75 (1963) 86-88; B. MAISLER, Zur Götterwelt des alten Palästina, *ZAW* 50 (1932) 86-87.

K. VAN DER TOORN

H

HABY חבי

I. In Isa 26:20 the term חבי (*ḥăbî*) is usually considered a Qal imperative (aramaizing: חבי = חבה) and translated 'hide thyself'. GORDON (1985 & 1986) has proposed to understand it as a divine name, Haby, and to interpret this character as the forerunner of the →Devil: *lēk ʿammî bōʾ baḥădārêkā ûsĕgōr dĕlātĕ(y)kā baʿădekā ḥăbî kimʿaṭ-regaʿ ʿad-yaʿăbo(w)r-zāʿam*, "Go, my people, enter into your chambers, and shut your door behind you, until Haby, the Wrath, in a little while will have passed". Haby would occur also in Hab 3:4, where חביון is considered by GORDON as a variant of the same name: *wĕnōgah kāʾôr tihyeh qarnayim miyyādô lô wĕśām ḥebyôn ʿuzzōh*, "And Brilliance shall be as the light; he has horns from his hand; and there is Hebyôn, his strength". The relation of its etymomlogy to the root *ḤBY 'to hide' is probable but not certain.

II. In the Ugaritic texts a divine name *ḥby* occurs in *KTU* 1.114:19-20 and this personage is described as *bʿl qrnm wḏnb*, "possessor/lord of horns and tail". This difficult text deals with the *marzēaḥ* of the god →El and with his drunkenness (see SPRONK 1986:198-200). The Father of the gods, full of wine, has an infernal vision and sees this *ḥby*, a divine or demonic entity, who perhaps soils him with his excrements and urine. El's condition is that of the dead in the Netherworld and this may suggest that *ḥby* is here a chthonic deity. It is not unlikely that this personage, who appears to El in an alcoholic trance during a feast related to the cult of the dead, is really an infernal god; horns and tail may allude to his bovine/taurine form.

It is doubtful whether the same deity occurs at Ebla, in a reduplicated form *ḫa-ba-ḫa-bi* (TM.75.G.1649 I 2: D. O. EDZARD, ARET V, p. 17, Nr. 1), as proposed by GORDON. In this context, a magic spell, it deals rather with a part of the door or a tool.

III. As regards the OT, the imagery of both biblical passages (Isa 26:20 and Hab 3:4) seems to continue the imagery of Ugarit, showing the character of Haby as a terrible entity (Haby, the Wrath) now at the service of YHWH ('His strength')(see e.g. R. D. HAAK, *Habakkuk* [VTSup 41; Leiden 1991] 90). From this perspective, the mention of the horns in Hab is also significant. It should not be excluded that we have here a transmission of a mythological element from Bronze Age Syria to the OT, even if it is perhaps too hazardous to speak of the forerunner of the Devil and the iconography of →Satan (see the sceptic remarks by SPRONK 1986:199 n. 4).

IV. *Bibliography*

*P. FRONZAROLI, Tre scongiuri eblaiti (ARET 5,1-3), *VO* 7 (1988) 11-23; C. H. GORDON, The Devil, ḥby, *Newsletter for Ugaritic Studies* 33 (1985) 15; *C. H. GORDON, ḤBY, Possessor of Horns and Tail, *UF* 18 (1986) 129-132; M. KREBERNIK, *Die Beschwörungen aus Fara und Ebla* (Hildesheim, Zürich & New York 1984) 134-135; K. SPRONK, *Beatific Afterlife* (AOAT 219; Neukirchen-Vluyn 1986); *P. XELLA, Un antecedente eblaita del "demone" ugaritico ḤBY ?, *SEL* 3 (1986) 17-25.

P. XELLA

HADAD הדד

I. Hadad is the name under which the ancient Near Eastern storm god was known among various groups in the Mesopotamian and Syrian world. The god is also mentioned in a number of biblical texts and names. In this article, the biblical material will be dealt with in conjunction with the epigraphic data from the Near East.

II. Hadad makes his first appearance as Adad in Old Akkadian texts, and in this guise he is important in the Mesopotamian world through the neo-Assyrian and neo-Babylonian periods. Hadad in all likelihood means 'thunderer' and as the storm-god he brings both fertility through abundant rains and destruction through fierce winds and storms. His voice (*rigmu*) can be a sign of both blessing and curse. He was associated with the Sumerian god Ishkur and ^{d}IM, the logogram for Ishkur, is used for writing Adad, and for other 'ethnic' versions of the storm-god such as Haddu/Baʿlu, Hurrian Teshup, and Hittite Tarhunza. In the Ebla texts from the Old Akkadian period the god Hadda (written ^{d}*à-da*) is found in the lists of the gods who receive monthly offerings from the king and others, and ^{d}*à-da* is a known theophoric element in personal names. Hadda (^{d}*à-da*) occurs together with the Sun-goddess (^{d}UTU) as guarantors at the end of the treaty between Ebla and Abarsal, a role similar to that which was to become traditional for these two deities in the course of Mesopotamian history. Adad functions as a god of oracles and judgement (*bēl terēte, bēl purussê*). The name Haddu, and its variants, is frequent in the onomastics of the Mari texts and other West Semitic ('Amorite') material from the 2nd millennium BCE onwards (H. B. HUFFMON, *Amorite Personal Names in the Mari Texts* [Baltimore 1965] 156-158, 'DD). Together with Dagan (→Dagon) and Itur-Mer, also storm-gods in all likelihood, he is listed among the major deities. In a 13th century letter from Mari to Ugarit (RS 34.142) the three deities appear together and are called 'great gods' *ilāni rabûtu.* During the Old Babylonian period the major sanctuary of Hadad was in the city of Aleppo (Yamḫad) and it is there that the 'weapon with which he smote the Sea', a reference to Hadad's battle with Yam (→Sea), was kept. Aleppo, therefore, had the status of an asylum city during this period and later. The prophets of Hadad took the credit for restoring Zimri-Lim to the throne of his father, demanded his loyalty and instructed the king to act in a righteous manner. The god Adad of Aleppo was assimilated to the Mesopotamian pantheon and appears later together with the *sibitti*, the →Pleiades, among the witnesses to treaties. In some areas his title *baʿlu* 'lord' essentially replaces his personal name, and the divine name Baʿlu exists alongside of Haddu/Hadad. Thus at Ugarit he is known primarily as Baʿlu, but Haddu is also found in the literary texts usually in parallelism with Baʿlu. A good example may be found in *KTU* 1.101:1-4 where Baʿlu/Haddu, who dwells on Mount Saphon, holds in his hands 'lightning and a bundle of thunder' (→Lightning). In a list of divine names Haddu is called the *bʿl* of Hazi, Mons Casius and in treaties ^{d}IM *bēl ḫuršan ḫazi.*

Neither the Akkadian texts dealing with Adad nor the later Aramaic inscriptions provide a developed mythology of Hadad. We must turn to the mythological and epic texts from Ugarit to learn about Baʿlu/Haddu and his role in the West Semitic pantheon. It is clear that he was considered a son of Dagan rather than →El, and that his rise to power came after his victory over both Yam and →Mot, who were El's favorites. A major theme in the Ugaritic myths is his striving for a grand palace of his own to be built on the heights of Mount Saphon (classical Mons Casius, modern Jebel el-Aqraʿ). When Baʿlu/Haddu is 'dead' for seven years the land suffers from lack of rain, the former prosperous state is restored only after he returned to life. In the inscription on the statue of Idrimi from Alalah, the seven years that he spent with the Habiru are refered to as 'the seven years of the storm-god', a possible reference to the seven years in which Baʿlu/Haddu is 'dead' (S. SMITH, *The Statue of Idrimi* [London 1949] 19:29-30). At Emar, where Dagan is still the high god, the storm god, written ^{d}IM, has a prominent role. The name Baʿlu is more frequent, but Haddu is also used, and both occur in personal names (F. M. FALES, Notes on the Royal Family of Emar, *Marchandes, diplomates et empereurs, Etudes offertes à P.*

Garelli [Paris 1991] 81-90, esp. 82 n. 8). In the Hittite sphere Tarhunza the storm-god of Aleppo, usually written with the ideogram dIM, plays a very important role. In Canaan during this period we find the use of both names widespread, as witnessed by Amarna onomastics, with such names as Rib-Hadda, Yapah-Hadda and Zimredda on the one side and Baʿlu-shipti, Baʿlu-mehir (= *bʿl mhr*), and Pu-Baʿla on the other. It is only from the later periods that two subsidiary Hadad deities are known, the first (H)adad-milki occurs as the theophoric element in names in the personal names from Gozan and surely stands behind the →Adrammelech of 2 Kgs 17:31. The second Apladda (apil-Adda), the 'son' of Hadad/Adad, worshipped in Suhi on the Middle →Euphrates is known to us both from personal names and from texts and is found on a cylinder seal discovered at Tel Beer Sheba. In the Roman period the god Aphlad, from the city of Anat also on the Euphrates, is known from a relief found at Dura-Europos (S. DOWNEY, *The Stone and Plaster Sculpture* [Dura Europos III i, 2; Los Angeles 1977] Pls. I, 3; XII, 46.

The iconography of the storm god is quite distinctive. In the Akkadian period Ishkur or Adad is portrayed with thunderbolt and mace on the back of a lion-dragon, but during the Old Babylonian period he is usually shown on cylinder seals standing on the back of a bull, brandishing a mace or an other weapon in his right hand and thunder in some form in the other. He is bearded and wears a conical head-dress. In the glyptic of northern Syria, as represented at Ebla at this period, Hadda may be seen brandishing a mace and holding the bridle of his bull in the other hand. At Ugarit, Baʿlu may be seen in the well-known stele of 'Baʿal with the thunder-bolt' brandishing a mace in his right hand and a spear touching the ground with the rays of thunder at its other end, and has a slightly curved dagger in the belt of his kilt. He is bearded, wears a horned head-dress, and according to a recent, plausible interpretation is treading on mountain tops at the feet of which there are waves.

It is in the 9th century when the Arameans are settled in the western marshes of the Assyrian empire, in Syria and in parts of Anatolia, that Hadad's dominant role can be documented. A clear bifurcation had taken place in the use of the names Baʿlu and Hadad. Baʿlu—biblical Baʿal—is now confined to the Canaanite god, worshipped in the Phoenician cities and their colonies, and mentioned often in the OT, while Hadad is the head of the Aramean pantheon. He is best known as the god of Damascus, and was also called by the epithet *Rammānu* 'the thunderer' (vocalised *Rimmôn* in 2 Kgs 5:18). The combined form Hadad-Rimmon is found in Zech 12:11 (see below). The name Bar-Hadad was frequently taken by Aramean kings and both Hadad/Hadda and Ramman are frequently used as the theophoric element in Aramaic names (note the Aramean ruler Tabrimmon). The temple of Hadad in Damascus (2 Kgs 5:18) is in all likelihood to be located in the precincts of the great Umayyad mosque; the site has previously served as the site of a temple to →Zeus in the Hellenistic era and as a church in the Byzantine period. Other temples of Hadad existed in Gozan-Sikanu, Sefire, Aleppo, Samʾal, Mabbug (Hierapolis) and elsewhere. The temple at Gozan-Sikanu is attested from the 9th to the 7th century. Hadad, in his role of divine supervisor of the celestial and terrestial water sources, was envisioned by his followers as the god who brought fertility and prosperity to the land (Tel Fekherye inscription, A. ABOU-ASSAF *et al.*, *La Statue de Tell Feherye* [Paris 1982]; J. C. GREENFIELD & A. SHAFFER, Notes on the Akkadian-Aramaic Bilingual Statue from Tell Fekherye, *Iraq* 45 [1983] 109-116; GREENFIELD & SHAFFER, Notes on the Curse Formulae of the Tel Fekherye Inscription, *RB* 92 [1985] 47-59). The title *raḥmān* 'merciful' was applied to him, but as a god of judgement (*bēl dīni*) he was also vengeful as the name Niqmaddu (Ugarit) and other names with the element *nqm* show. In the recently discovered Aramaic inscription from Tel Dan (line 5) "Hadad went before" the king (probably Hazael) and thus brought him victory (A. BIRAN & J. NAVEH, An Aramaic Stele fragment from Tel Dan, *IEJ* 43 [1993] 81-98). He also claimed that Hadad made him king. Booty taken by the victorious Hazael was considered a gift of Hadad as may be read on a horse's forehead ornament and a horse's blinker, both found in Greece. In the inscriptions from Zenjirli Hadad is listed at the head of the pantheon (*KAI* 214, 215), and is credited by Panamuwa I (*KAI* 214) together with the other gods for standing by him since his youth, and giving him rule over Y'dy/Sam'al, but Hadad is specificaly credited with giving him the 'sceptre of succession'. In gratitude he built a temple for Hadad, and set up the stele upon which a large statue of Hadad stood. The name Hadad/Haddu appears frequently in the onomastics of this period: *gbrd*, *br hdd*, *hddʿzr/hddʿdr*, *hdrqy*, *hddnwry*, *hddsmny*, *ypʿhd*, *mrʾhdd*, *ʿbdhd*, *mtʿhdd*, etc. In the Hellenistic period it is found in names such as: Adadiabos, Baradados, Zabidadados, Rageadados, etc.

Elements of cult and worship may be gleaned from the Biblical text and from epigraphic and other sources. Hadad was worshipped by prayer and prostration (2 Kgs 5:18), and *if* we may judge by the references to the altar copied from the Damascus temple in 2 Kgs 16:10-15, by blood sacrifices, as well as by the wide-spread burning of incense. The belief in the efficacy of prayer (lifting the hands) may be seen in the inscription set up by Zakkur, king of Hamat and Luʿash (*KAI* 213) where there is also a reference to the use of prophets and seers (*ʿddn* and *ḥzyn*) for oracles (J. C. GREENFIELD, The Zakir Inscription and the Danklied, *Proceedings of the Fifth World Congress of Jewish Studies* [Jerusalem 1969] vol. I [Jerusalem 1971] 174-191). Hadad is called by the ancient name Elwer (Akk Iluwer). The equation is found in Assyrian lexical texts, but this may represent the typical syncretistic tendency of the late period. He had the central role in the propitiary rite in memory of dead ancestors (*kispu*). Thus in the Tel Fekherye inscription (ll.16-18) whosoever will remove Hadad-yishi's name is cursed in that Hadad will not accept bread or water from him, while in the Panamuwa I inscription (*KAI* 214) we are told that the name of the deceased was to be invoked together with that of Hadad, while calling upon the soul of the deceased to eat and drink, and only then was the sacrifice acceptable as a gift to Hadad. From the Tel Fekherye inscription and the Zakkur inscription we learn that statues with the inscriptions were set up in the temples. From the Sefire inscriptions (*KAI* 223C) it is also clear that the treaty inscriptions were also set up in the temples. Aleppo's particular importance of as a place of asylum in the Mari period was noted above. Shalmaneser III sacrificed to Hadad there, and it follows from Sefire III (*KAI* 224) ll. 4-7 that Aleppo, no longer a city of political importance, remained a place of asylum in the 9th and 8th centuries BCE (J. C. GREENFIELD, Asylum at Aleppo: A Note on Sfire III, 4-7, *Ah Assyria: Studies in Assyrian History and Ancient Near Eastern Historiography Presented to Hayim Tadmor* [ScrHier 33; Jerusalem 1990] 272-278). During the Hellenistic and Roman periods this city flourished and was called Beroea; among the little known to us about it is that in the 4th century CE Julian, 'the apostate', sacrificed a white bull to →Zeus on the acropolis of the city.

The verse in Zech 12:11 states that in the future the mourning in Jerusalem will be as great "as the mourning for Hadad-Rimon in the plain of Jezreel" (RSV). It is now widely accepted that the reference is to a mourning rite celebrated in the agriculturally rich area of the 'plain of Megiddo' in which the death or disappearance of Baʿal/Hadad was mourned, and an attempt to revive him was made through prayers and rituals. The death and disappearance of Baʿal, the drought that followed, and Baʿal's return is known from the Ugaritic texts (*KTU* 5 and 6). In the light of these texts we may assume that the body was lacerated, the hair of the head and the beard was plucked out, sack-cloth was worn and ashes were strewn on the head, accompanied by calls of "Hadad-Ramman is dead". We may assume that these rites were widely known, and were not limited to the 'plain of Megiddo' (cf. Ezek 27:30-31). Baʿal/Hadad is both a fertility god, and one who has overcome the powers of Death.

The iconography of the storm-god, Hadad or Tarhunzas of Aleppo, in the first half of the first millennium BCE is known from stelae found in Syria and Anatolia. He is bearded, wearing a horned, high head-dress, either conical or flat. Some of the figures are standing on an ox and some are moving forward. They usually wear a kilt, and carry a sword in their belt. They usually hold a thunder-bolt in one hand and an axe or mace in the other. In one the god may be holding an ear of corn in his right hand (J. D. HAWKINS, What does the Hittite Storm god Hold?, *Natural Phenomena, Their Meaning, Depiction and Description in the Ancient Near East* [ed. D. J. W. Meijer; Amsterdam 1992] 53-82). Most of these stelae come from the northern Luvian area, but others show Assyrian influence. It may be assumed that stelae from the south would not have been very different.

An additional source of information for the worship of Hadad comes from coins minted at Mabbug/Hierapolis in North Syria in the 4th century BCE. He was the chief god of the city, and some coins have the legend *hdd mnbg*, i.e. Hadad of Mabbug. On a unique coin the reverse portrays ʿAbd-Hadad, priest of Mabbug (*kmr mnbg*), who stands before a *thymiatērion*, an incense altar, one hand raised perhaps in prayer, and the other extended towards the altar; he wears a long robe and has a conical pilos on his head. On the obverse there is the image of Hadad, horned and bearded, wearing a long Persian-style robe, with his hands raised in blessing, the inscription reads "who sings the praises of Hadad his lord". Two signs of the storm god accompany this image—the schematic head of a bull to his right and the double-axe to his left. This coin may be instructive as to the way the worshippers of Hadad envisioned their god (H. SEYRIG, Le monnayage de Hiérapolis de Syrie, à l'époque d'Alexandre, *Revue numismatique* VI/12 [1971] 11-21).

In the Babylonian tradition the consort of Adad was the goddess Shala, and she thus occurs in the neo-Assyrian version of the Tel Fekherye bilingual; in the Aramaic version she is called Sala. This is the only Aramaic inscription which mentions her. It is at Mabbug/Hierapolis, on coins roughly contemporary to those noted above, that we first find a reference to the goddess ʾAtarʿate (*ʾtrʿth*), called in Greek →Atargatis. She was particularly associated with this city and is called *ʾtrʿth mnbgyt*ʾ in a Nabatean text. In texts from the Hellenistic period, now primarily in Greek, Adados and Atargatis are frequently found together. In a 2nd century BCE inscription from Kafr Yassif, near Akko, an altar is dedicated to "Adados and Atargatis, the gods who listen to prayer". In pseudo-Lucian's work on the Syrian Goddess (2nd century CE), they have been hellenised and occur as Zeus and →Hera.

The worship of the pair was widespread, and even without inscriptions they are easily identified—the bearded god sits on a throne between two oxen and the goddess between two lions, the ancient symbol of →Ishtar. Atargatis had long since become the more prominent of the pair, and often has an independent existent of her own. On a stela from Dura-Europos they are seen seated together with the *sēmeion* between them, Atargatis is larger with lions on either side; Hadad with only a diminutive bull to his right, has a bunch of wheat in his right hand and perhaps holds a sceptre in his left one. However, on another stela from Dura-Europos, probably from the 1st century CE, Hadad is seated, with bulls on both sides; he is clearly identified by the incised thunderbolt to his left and the double-axe in his left hand; the right hand is broken off and we may only surmise that he held a bunch of grain or fruit, or a sceptre in it. This is his last solo appearance.

III. *Bibliography*

A. ABOU-ASSAF, Die Ikonographie des Altbabylonischen Wettergottes, *BagM* 14 (1983) 43-66; P. AMIET, Le dieu de l'orage dans l'iconographie des sceaux-cylindres d'Ugarit, *Natural Phenomena, Their Meaning, Depiction and Description in the Ancient Near East* (ed. D. J. W. Meijer; Amsterdam 1992) 5-18; M. AVI-YONAH, Syrian Gods at Ptolemais-Accho, *IEJ* 9 (1959) 1-12; P. BORDREUIL, *Une bibliothèque au sud de la ville* (RSOu VII; Paris 1991) text 47; BORDREUIL, Le répertoire iconographique des sceaux araméens inscrits, *Studies in the Iconography of Northwest Semitic Inscribed Seals* (Fribourg 1993) 74-100; D. CHARPIN & J. M. DURAND, "Fils de Sim'al": les origines tribales des rois de Mari, *RA* 80 (1986) 141-183, esp. 173-174; H. J. W. DRIJVERS, Dea syria, *LIMC* III/1 355-358; III/2 364-367; J. M. DURAND, Le combat entre le Dieu de l'orage et la Mer, *MARI* 7 (1993) 41-61; J. R. DUSSAUD, Le Temple de Jupitter Damascène, *Syria* 3 (1922) 219-250; I. EPHAL & J. NAVEH, Hazael's Booty Inscriptions, *IEJ* 39 (1989) 192-203; D. E. FLEMING, *The Installation of Baal's High Priestess at Emar* (Atlanta 1992) 214-219; M. GAWLIKOWSKI, Hadad, *LIMC* 1V/1 365-367; *LIMC* 1V/2 209-210; H. GENGE, *Nordsyrisch-südanatolische Reliefs* (Copenhagen 1979); J. C. GREENFIELD, Un rite religieux araméen et ses paralleles, *RB* 80 (1973) 46-52; GREENFIELD, The Aramaic God Ramman/Rimmon, *IEJ* 26 (1976) 195-198; GREENFIELD, Aspects of Aramaic Religion, *Ancient Israelite Religion, Essays in Honor of F. M. Cross* (Philadelphia 1987) 67-78; GREENFIELD, To Praise the Might of Hadad, *La vie de la Parole: de l'Ancien au Nouveau Testament. Etudes offertes à P. Grelot* (Paris 1987) 3-12; GREENFIELD, The Aramean God Hadad, *ErIsr* 24 (FS A. Malamat; Jerusalem 1993) 54-61; P. HOUWINK TEN CATE, The Hittite Storm God, his Role and his Rule According to Hittite Cuneiform Sources, *Natural Phenomena, Their Meaning, Depiction and Description in the Ancient Near East* (ed. D. J. W. Meijer; Amsterdam 1992) 83-148; H. KLENGEL, Der Wettergott von Halab, *JCS* 19 (1965) 87-95; K. KOCH, Ḫazzi-Ṣafôn-Kasion, *Religionsgeschichtliche Beziehungen zwischen Kleinasien, Nordsyrien und dem Alten Testament* (ed. B. Janowski *et al.*; OBO 129; Freiburg 1993) 172-223; M. KREBERNIK, *Die Personennamen der Ebla-Texten* (Berlin 1988) 74; B. LAFONT, Le roi de Mari et les prophètes du dieu Adad, *RA* 80 (1986) 7-8; W. G. LAMBERT, The Pantheon of Mari, *MARI* 4 (1985) 525- 539; M. LINDNER & J. ZANGENBERG, The Rediscovered *Baityl* of the Goddess Atargatis, *ZDPV* 109 (1993) 141-151; E. LIPIŃSKI, Apladad, *Or* 45 (1976) 53-74; LIPIŃSKI, Archives from the Gozan-Harran Area, *Biblical Archaeology Today* (ed. J. Amitai; Jerusalem 1985); J. J. M. ROBERTS, *The Earliest Semitic Pantheon* (Baltimore 1972) 13-14, n.18; E. SOLLBERGER, The So-Called Treaty Between Ebla and 'Ashur', *StEb* III, 9-10 (1980) 129-155; A. VANEL, *L'iconographie du dieu de l'orage dans le Proche-Orient ancien jusqu'au VIIe siècle avant J.C.* (Paris 1965).

J. C. GREENFIELD

HADES Ἅιδης

I. Hades is the Greek name for the underworld and its ruler, as is the case in the Bible. The spelling of the name sometimes varies (Aides/Hades, Aidoneus) and the etymology is debated. The most recent analysis sees a link with the root **a-wid-*, 'invisible' (RUIJGH 1991:575-576, but see also BURKERT 1985:196). Most likely, Hades first denoted a place name and was only later personified. Only the personification will be discussed here. Hades occurs 111 times in the LXX, most often as equivalent of Heb *šĕʾôl*, and 10 times in the NT.

II. Hades is a shadowy god in Greece who has few myths and even fewer cults; he does not even occur with certainty on the archaic vases (DALINGER 1988:389). His connection with the underworld makes him 'horrible' (*Il.* 8.368) and 'the most hated of all the gods' (*Il.* 9.158). Such a god can hardly receive a cult and in Greece only Elis seems to have worshipped him in a temple (Strabo 8.3.14; Pausanias 6.25.2).

Homer (*Il.* 15.187-93) mentions that he acquired the underworld through a lottery with his brothers →Zeus and →Poseidon; the passage possibly derives eventually from the Akkadian epic *Atrahasis* (BURKERT 1992: 90-91). Homer also represents him as the ruler of the underworld, but only post-Homeric times depict him as a judge of the dead (Aeschylus, *Eum.* 273). On late- and post-classical Apulian vases Hades is often connected with Orpheus—perhaps a sign of a changing role in South-Italian religious ideas (DALINGER 1988:394).

The most famous myth of Hades is his abduction of Persephone, which was localized at various spots in the Greek world (RICHARDSON 1973:74-78). As Persephone was associated with love and marriage (SOURVINOU-INWOOD 1991:147-188) and an abduction was part of Spartan wedding rites, the myth will originally have been a narrative representation of pre-nuptial girls' rites. Less clear is an allusion in the *Iliad* (5.395-7) that Hades was wounded by Heracles 'at Pylos among the dead'. This myth is probably part of Heracles' function as Master of Animals (BURKERT 1979:86) and suggests that the personification of Hades goes back into the Bronze Age.

III. In the Bible Hades usually occurs as the abode of the dead but a few passages employ the name of Hades as Death (→Thanatos) personified (1 Cor 15:55 v.l.; Rev 6:8, 20:13-14). This personification of Death probably derives from OT usage (→Mot) and the idea of the personal Greek god is hardly present in these cases.

IV. *Bibliography*

W. BURKERT, *Structure and History in Greek Mythology and Ritual* (Berkeley, Los Angeles & London 1979); BURKERT, *Greek Religion* (Oxford 1985); BURKERT, *The Orientalizing Revolution* (Cambridge, Mass. & London 1992); S.-F. DALINGER *et al.*, Hades, *LIMC* IV.1 (1988) 367-94; N. J. RICHARDSON, *The Homeric Hymn to Demeter* (Oxford 1973); C. J. RUIJGH, *Scripta minora* I (Amsterdam 1991); C. SOURVINOU-INWOOD, *'Reading' Greek Culture* (Oxford 1991).

J. N. BREMMER

HAIL → BARAD

HAM חם

I. Ham is the second son of →Noah, and the brother of →Shem and →Japheth. His name occurs 17 times in the Bible. He is sometimes said to originally represent a (semi) divine figure, either because his name is that of a supposed west-Semitic sun-god called Ḫammu (LEWY 1944), or because it is connected to Eg *ḥm*, '(divine) majesty' (GORDON 1988).

II. The evidence adduced by Lewy for a solar deity called Hammu is onomastic: the theophoric element Ḫammu or Ammu (as in Ḫammu-rabi, Aqba-ammu, and the like) would go back to the name *ḥammu*, 'hot one', a designation of the sun-god. It is clear, however, that Akk *(ḫ)ammu* corresponds to Heb *ʿam*, 'people, clan'. Its occurrence in theophoric names illustrates the deification of dead kin; it may be compared with the use of *ʾāb* (→father) and *ʾāḥ* (→brother) as theophoric elements (NOTH 1953:148).

On the face of it, the proposal to connect the name Ham with Eg *ḥm*, 'majesty', makes sense. In some of the biblical psalms, the name Ham is used in apposition to Egypt (Pss 78:51; 105:23.27; 106:22). An Egyptian etymology, though perhaps not likely, cannot be excluded. Yet if *ḥm*, majesty, were the correct etymology, this would not imply divine status for Ham. Although the Egyptian Pharoah in function is more than a mere mortal, the expression *ḥm* by itself does not convey the notion of divinity.

III. The speculations about the divine status of Ham are based on ill-founded interpretations of the extra-biblical material. In the biblical records there is no trace of a Ham's supposed divinity. No sure etymology of his name can be given (proposals include a connection with Akk *emmu*, 'father in law', and Eg *keme*, 'the black land').

IV. *Bibliography*

C. H. GORDON, Notes on Proper Names in the Ebla Tablets, *Eblaite Personal Names and Semitic Name-Giving* (ARES 1; ed. A.

Archi; Rome 1988) 154; J. LEWY, The Old West-Semitic Sun-God Ḥammu, *HUCA* 18 (1943-44) 429-488; M. NOTH, Mari und Israel: Eine Personennamenstudie, *Geschichte und Altes Testament. Aufsätze Albrecht Alt zum 70. Geburtstag* (Tübingen 1953) 127-152.

K. VAN DER TOORN

HAMARTIA → SIN

HAOMA

I. The personal name *Hammadatha* to be found in Esther 3:1 represents the Iranian name **Haumadata*, 'given by *hauma*' (or, in the Avestan form, '*haoma*'), which is common in Achaemenid territory (MAYRHOFER 1973). Iranian *haoma* is the equivalent of the Indian form *soma*, a name which simply means 'juice'. *Soma*, to which the 9th book of Rigveda is devoted, is a liquor extracted from a plant which is ground in a stone mortar, then filtered and lengthily clarified through a horsehair sieve. The drink, offered to the gods and also consumed by sacrificers, is particularly appreciated by the warrior god Indra, whom it enables to accomplish his extraordinary feats. *Soma/haoma* is not only a plant, but also a god. It is a sacerdotal god, being both a deity and an offering to the gods, and it has a complex and paradoxical relation to death: it is mortal, as pressing kills it, yet at the same time it is immortal in that its virtues are reproduced indefinitely and it secures immortality to those who drink it.

II. Whereas the offering of *soma* disappeared early from Indian practices, the main Iranian liturgy, the *yasna* service, consists even today in a ceremonious preparation of *haoma*. A precise description and subtle interpretation was given by BOYCE (1970). The plant-god grants remarkable descendants, ensures victory over evil spirits, provides a happy drunkenness resulting in enhanced mental power and is used by the dying as provisions for immortality. It receives a definite sacrificial ration: the tongue, cheeks and left eye of the victim.

It is generally admitted that the plant from which soma is derived is a species of ephedra, which is still used today in the surviving Mazdaean communities. For a number of years there has been a tendency to think that ephedra is a substitute and other solutions have been suggested: *amanita muscaria* or fly-agaric (WASSON 1968, ingeniously supported by GERSCHEVITCH 1974), ginseng (WINDFUHR 1985), harmal or African rue (FLATTERY & SCHWARTZ 1989). But the ephedra fragments in a mortar discovered recently on a Bactrian site seem to put a definite end to the controversy.

The offering of *haoma* was a common practice among Achaemenids; the Haumavarga Scythians probably owe their name to the fact that they did not press the plant but strewed it ritually (HOFFMANN 1975).

Many specialists believe that the offering of *haoma* was condemned by the prophet Zarathustra, but was restored after his death (most recently DUCHESNE-GUILLEMIN 1988). In fact, the ancient Avesta makes two possible references to *haoma*, which might both be abusive. The first (*Yasna* 32.14) criticizes an offering characterized as *dūraoša-* (an obscure word, probably meaning 'difficult to burn'), an epithet applying exclusively to *haoma* in the recent Avesta, but whose Indian equivalent *duróṣa(s)-* does not necessarily apply to *soma*. The second (*Yasna* 48.10) refers to an intoxicating liquor causing diarrhoea and a particular urine. It cannot be assessed with any certainty either that those allusive strophes effectively refer to *haoma*, or that they condemn it in the absolute. Some specialists have put forward the hypothesis that they were arguments concerning certain details of the preparation, such as a mixture with the victim's blood (HUMBACH 1960; HOFFMANN 1975).

III. *Bibliography*

M. BOYCE, Haoma Priest of the Sacrifice, *W. B. Henning Memorial Volume* (London 1970) 62-80; J. DUCHESNE-GUILLEMIN, Haoma proscrit et réadmis, *Mélanges Pierre Lévêque* (Paris 1988) 127-131; D. S. FLATTERY & M. SCHWARTZ, *Haoma and Harmaline* (Berkeley 1989); I. GERSHE-

VITCH, A Iranianist's view of the Soma controversy, *Memorial Jean de Menasce* (Louvain 1974) 45-75; K. HOFFMANN, *Aufsätze zur Indoiranistik*, Vol 2 (Wiesbaden 1975) 611-612 n. 6; H. HUMBACH, Der Iranische Mithra als daiva, *Festgabe für Herman Lommel* (Wiesbaden 1960) 78-79; M. MAYRHOFER, *Onomastica Persepolitana* (Wien 1973) 244; R. G. WASSON, *Soma Divine Mushroom of Immortality* (New York 1968); G. WINDFUHR, Haoma/Soma: the Plant, *Papers in Honour of Professor Mary Boyce*, Vol 2 (Leiden 1985) 699-726.

J. KELLENS

HARAN חרן

I. It has been speculated that the city of Haran (7 times in Genesis; see also 2 Kgs 19:12; Isa 37:12; Ezek 27:23) was named after a deity Haran (LEWY 1934). The available evidence does not support the contention.

II. The grounds on which a cult of a god Haran is postulated are not very firm. In an Old Assyrian letter (CCT 4 Pl. 35b:19-20), LEWY found a reference to a "priest of Ḫarranātum" (*ku-um-ra ša Ḫa-ra-na-tim*; the alleged goddess is also mentioned in CCT 4 Pl. 48b:20). LEWY concluded that Ḫarranātum must have been a goddess, and deemed it likely that she should have had a male counterpart presumably called Ḫarrān (1934). As it turns out, the very basis of the conjecture is wrong as the expression *ša ḫarrānātim* refers to a forwarding agent, or a carrier ('he in charge of the caravans', *AHW* 327 s.v. *ḫarrānu* IV; *CAD* Ḫ 113). Doubts about the interpretation of Ḫarranātum as a goddess were first expressed by I. J. GELB (*Inscriptions from Alishar and Vicinity* [OIP 27; Chicago 1935] 54 n. 1); Lewy's interpretation was definitvely refuted by HIRSCH, who also corrected the reading *ku-um-ra* into *Ku-ú-ra* ([2]1972).

The biblical place name Haran refers to the city known as Ḫarrān in cuneiform sources; it is situated about 100 miles north from the confluence of the Euphrates and the Balikh rivers. The name of the city is usually written with the Sumerogram KASKAL, which stands for 'way, road'. The Akkadian word *ḫarrānu* does indeed refer, amongst other things, to a highway, a road, or a path (*CAD* Ḫ 106-113). Though in some contexts the road may be deified as the numinous power by which an oath was sworn (*Šurpu* V-VI 191; *Maqlû* I 67; →Way), there is no trace in the cuneiform sources of a cult to a deity Haran.

III. *Bibliography*

H. HIRSCH, *Untersuchungen zur altassyrischen Religion* (AfO Beiheft 13/14; Osnabrück [2]1972) 29 n. 149; Y. KOBAYASHI, Haran, *ABD* 3 (1992) 58-59; J. LEWY, Les textes paléo-assyriens et l'Ancien Testament, *RHR* 110 (1934) 46-47.

K. VAN DER TOORN

HATHOR

I. Hathor ("Mansion of →Horus") is an Egyptian goddess. According to CLÉDAT (1919), Hathor occurs as the second element in the place-name *Pî haḥîrōt*, Exod 14:2.9; Num 33:7-8. The first part renders Eg *pr*, "House (of)", but was interpreted (KB) as Heb "Mouth (of the Canals)".

II. Hathor is often pictured as a woman in the prime of life. Sometimes, however, bovine ears, and frequently horns betray her original, non-antropomorphic shape. She is a cow from time immemorial. Hathor creates and sustains life in that capacity. The same applies to her as a tree goddess, the "Lady of the (Southern) Sycamore" (→Sycomore). She, the "Lady of the West", assists the revived dead as well. Both maternal and sexual love, merriment and festivals, singing and playing music, dancing and drinking are characteristic of her. She is strongly attached to women; the Greek identify her with →Aphrodite.

As the heavenly cow, Hathor gives birth to the sun; this possibly finds expression in her name. She is seen as the eye of this deity and one calls her "Gold" perhaps for that reason. The eye in turn is equated with the cobra (Uraeus). At the same time, the goddess is the spouse of the sun or light god: →Re in Heliopolis and Horus in Edfu. She is not always an attractive and amiable figure. As the grim avenger of an injury (a conspiracy against Re), she would become a ferocious →lioness. Hathor was worshipped throughout the country and even abroad. Her main sanctuaries are in Denderah and Deir el-Bahri. But she is also "Lady of Byblos", and "Lady of the Turquoise" on the Sinai peninsula.

This many-sided, complicated, and popular deity is not a unique personality. Egyptians distinguish eighteen forms of her. And there is a group of seven Hathors who proclaim the fate of a new-born child.

III. *Pî haḥîrōt* is situated on the route of the Exodus. It was, according to the Bible, the last halting-place before the crossing of the Sea of Rushes. The identification of CLÉDAT (1919) is open to question. It is not satisfactory from an etymological point of view. There has been a "House of Hathor" in the region. Its nature and location are still unknown, however (see GOMAÀ 1976).

IV. *Bibliography*

S. ALLAM, *Beiträge zum Hathorkult (bis zum Ende des Mittleren Reiches)* (MÄS 4; Berlin 1963); C. J. BLEEKER, *Hathor and Thoth* (SHR 26; Leiden 1973); H. BONNET, Hathor, *RÄRG* 277-282; J. ČERNÝ, *Ancient Egyptian Religion* (London 1952) 155; J. CLÉDAT, Notes sur l'isthme de Suez, *BIFAO* 16 (1919) 201-228, cf. 218-219; F. DAUMAS, Hathor, *LdÄ* II (1977) 1024-1033; F. GOMAÀ, Gebel Abu-Hassa, *LdÄ* II (1976) 432-433; E. HORNUNG, *Der Eine und die Vielen* (Darmstadt 1971) 274.

M. HEERMA VAN VOSS

HAYIN

I. The word *hyn* occurs a number of times in Ugaritic texts as an epithet of Kothar-wa-Hasis (→Kothar). It has been suggested that the same word is found in Hab 2:5 (ALBRIGHT 1943; 1968) and Job 41:4[12] (POPE 1965) as a divine title.

II. The word *hyn* occurs in *KTU* 1.3 vi:22-23; 1.4 i:23; 1.17 v:18, each time in a synonymous parallelism with Kothar-wa-Hasis. The interpretation of the term is based on comparative Semitic philology: Syr *hawnâ* means 'intelligence', hence Ug *hyn* is usually translated as 'intelligent', This meaning fits well with the name Kothar-wa-Hasis: 'Skilful-and-Wise' (for other suggestions see the literature mentioned by D. PARDEE, Ugaritic Proper Nouns, *AfO* 36-37 [1989-90] 449). There is no reason to believe that *hyn* is the proper name of the god; a connection with the Greek god Hephaestus is far-fetched (*pace* B. HARTMANN, *De herkomst van de goddelijke ambachtsman in Oegarit en Griekenland* [Leiden 1964]).

III. The attempts to find the epithet *hyn* (conventionally vocalized *Hayin) in the Hebrew Bible must be regarded as unsuccessful. The first proposal concerns Hab 2:5 (ALBRIGHT 1943). Though perhaps not "totally unconvincing" (DAY 1985), it has little to commend itself. The expression היין בוגד, literally "wine is treacherous", is suspect, since the notion of treason (BGD) implies volition. Moreover, the expected word הוי ('Woe') is missing; it may be concealed by היין (note that 1QpHab VIII 3 reads הון). Commentators have therefore proposed to emendate the text (for a survey see *HALAT* 391 s.v. יין). The interpretation of היין as Hayin (Hîyôn: "and though he be crafty as Hîyôn, a faithless man shall not succeed" ALBRIGHT 1943) is definitely one of the less likelier emendations (also modifications in the vocalisation of the MT must be regarded as textual emendations), see HAAK 1992:60-61.

The second passage, Job 41:4[12], is probably also textually corrupt. The correction into *hayin*, though orthographically possible, necessitates another minor correction. POPE translates "Did I not silence his boasting, by the powerful word Hayyin prepared?" (1965:335), which implies a reading בדבר for ודבר. The suggestion is ingenious, though not very probable. It is true that in the Ugaritic myths there are references to →Baal having slain →Leviathan, and since Leviathan is a sea-monster Baal may have done so with the help of the weapons Koshar made for him. Yet it seems strange that the rare epithet Hayin should be used for Koshar by an author addressing an audience that was hardly familar with the details of Ugaritic mythology. More probable textual solutions have been offered. They include the correction of *ḥîn* into *ḥêl*, 'strength' (DAY 1985: "I will not remain silent ... with regard to the might and strength of his frame"), or *ʾên ʿărōk*, 'unparalleled' (A. B. EHRLICH, *Randglossen zur hebräischen Bibel*, Vol. 6 [Leipzig 1918] 340).

IV. *Bibliography*

W. F. ALBRIGHT, The Furniture of El in Canaanite Mythology, *BASOR* 91 (1943) 40 n. 11; ALBRIGHT, *Yahweh and the Gods of Canaan* (London 1968) 221 n. 135; A. COOPER, *RSP* III (1981) 445; J. DAY, *God's Conflict with the Dragon and the Sea* (Cambridge 1985) 63 n. 8; R. HAAK, *Habakkuk* (VTSup 44; Leiden 1992) 60-61; M. H. POPE, *Job* (AB 15; Garden City 1965) 335.338-339 (on Job 41:4[12]).

K. VAN DER TOORN

HE-OF-THE-SINAI זה סיני

I. Occurring twice in the OT (Judg 5:5; Ps 68:8-9) *zēh sinai* 'He-of-the-Sinai' is to be understood according to the analogous Nabatean divine name 'Dushara' as the 'God (Lord) of the Sinai' (H. GRIMME, *ZDMG* 50 [1896]:573 n. 1).

II. The divine epithet 'He-of-the-Sinai' appears in Judg 5:5. Here 'He-of-the-Sinai' is a qualification of →Yahweh, and stands in parallelism to the epithet 'God of Israel'. Before becoming the god of Israel Yahweh was the lord of the Sinai who came from Seir/Edom to fight for Israel (Judg 5:4-5; cf. Deut 33:2; Hab 3:3).

The Hebrew construction *Yahweh zēh sinai* has an anology in the Nabatean designation Dushara 'He-of-the-Šara[-mountain]'. The original name of this deity has been completely superseded by the epithet *'dušara'*. Several authors want to delete 'He-of-the-Sinai' from Judg 5:5 as a gloss. Thus FISHBANE argues that it is an interpolation indicating that "this (refers to the event at) Mount Sinai" (1985:75). Considering the Nabatean analogy, this suggestion is open to debate.

The argument in favour is strengthened further by a second mentioning of 'He-of-the-Sinai' in the OT. Ps 68:8-9 is a quotation of Judg 5:4-5 which shows that the author of this psalm treated 'He-of-the-Sinai' in his Vorlage as a divine name. Furthermore, the author of Ps 68:9 replaced Yahweh on the basis of Judg 5:4-5 by *ʾēlohîm* thus creating a distich "before God the Lord of Sinai, before God, the God of Israel". (Note, however, that Fishbane reverses the chronological order of these hymns).

Judg 5:4-5 and Ps 68:8-9 show that there was a tradition of a god 'Yahweh-he-of-the-Sinai'. This was originally a specification of a god according to his cult-place. It can be understood in analogy to the Ugaritic divine name →'Baal Zaphon' by which a local manifestation of the Northern Syrian weather-god is differentiated from other Baal-deities also venerated in Ugarit. That further local Yahweh-manifestations were also known in Israel are shown by the inscriptions of Kuntillet Ajrud which know "Yahweh of Teman" and "Yahweh of Samaria" (G. I. DAVIES, *Ancient Hebrew Inscriptions* [Cambridge 1991] no. 8.016; 8.017).

III. *Bibliography*

M. Fishbane, *Biblical Interpretation in Ancient Israel* (Oxford 1985); J. JEREMIAS, *Theophanie* (WMANT 10; Neukirchen 1965) 8-9; E. A. KNAUF, *Midian* (ADPV; Wiesbaden 1988) 48-50 [& lit.]; T. F. MCDANIEL, *Deborah never Sang. A Philological Study on the Song of Deborah* [Judges Chapter V] (Jerusalem 1983) 173-174; P. MAIBERGER, *TWAT* 5 (1984-1986) 819-838, esp. 824-825 [& lit.].

H. NIEHR

HEALING GOD → EL-ROPHE

HEAVEN שמים οὐρανός (-νοί)

I. The Hebrew word שמים (*šāmayim*)

is plurale tantum and occurs 420 times in the OT; only a limited number of these occurrences refer to heaven as being divine. It has its cognates in other semitic languages (e. g. Akk *šamû* or *šamā'ū*, Ug *šmm*, Aram *šmayyā*, Ar *samā'*); the equivalent in Sumerian is **an**, in Hittite we find the word *nepiš* for 'heaven'. The etymology of the word is not completely certain; it is possible to derive it from Akk *ša mê* ("of water", CT 25,50:17), but this can also be popular etymology.

II. The Sumerian cuneiform sign **an** means heaven and it is also used for writing the name of the Sumerian god An, the god of heaven, and his Babylonian equivalent Anu. He can be considered as the personified heaven (and sky, as the Sumerians and Babylonians did not distinguish between heaven and sky). His antiquity is still open to debate but in the middle of the 3rd millennium BCE he is mentioned in the god-lists from Fara. At the time of Gudea of Lagash he is already at the head of the Sumerian pantheon; during the Ur III and Isin-Larsa periods his cult is also well documented by hymns and prayers. He maintained this position during the Old Babylonian period; together with Enlil and Ea (and sometimes a female deity like Nintu or →Ishtar) he was usually acknowledged as one of the senior deities of the pantheon. As the god of heaven he was not only considered the father of the gods (cf. *Atr* i 7) but sometimes also of the demons. His consort was either the goddess Antu (the 'feminine heaven') or the goddess **ki** or **uraš**, 'Earth', which clearly shows the cosmic relationship of →Heaven-and-Earth. Within the pantheon and also Babylonian theology he was in charge of the 'divine ordinances' (**me**) and he decreed—as the ultimate source of authority—the fates. After the rise of Nippur some of Anu's prerogatives were taken over by Enlil. Nevertheless Anu's cult was strong until the Late Babylonian period, where he still had his huge temple at Uruk; also rituals for him from the Seleucid era have been preserved there. There too he was connected with Ishtar, his consort.

Outside the Sumero-Babylonian world, heaven attained only a limited divine rank. In the texts from Ugarit we can see that the pair Heaven-and-Earth is deified and thus can also receive offerings (*KTU* 1.47:12; 1.118:11; 1.148:5.24); there is also a relation to those texts which refer to Heaven-and-Earth as witnesses to an oath in treaties (cf. RS 18.06+17.365, line 6). *KTU* 1.100 has an interesting beginning: an incantation against snake-bites. In lines 1-2 we find an allusion to a theogony which might be of Hittite-Hurrian origin (*ARTU*:146). At the head of this list we find the sun-goddess Shapshu who is the mother of Heaven and Flood, who gave birth to Spring and →Stone, the parents of the She-ass, who is the main figure of the incantation. On the other hand heaven does not figure prominently as a divine entity in the Ugaritic pantheon. Poetical texts suggest that heaven can speak (e.g. *KTU* 1.3 iii:24) but as a rule heaven is merely the abode of the (heavenly) gods. Worthy of special mention is →Baal shamem, the 'Lord of heaven', whose cult gained great importance among the Phoenicians and the Arameans in the first millennium. Texts from Anatolia give a similar picture: Heaven (*nepiš*) is invoked as witness in treaties (e.g. KUB 21.1 iv 26; KBo 8.35 ii 12), often together with Earth. As a rule, though, heaven is only the abode of gods; Hittite texts treat the (unspecified) gods of heaven (*nepišaš* DINGIR^{MEŠ}, DINGIR^{MEŠ} *ŠAMÊ*) as a category of their own or opposed to the gods of earth. The Sungod and the Stormgod can often get the epithet 'of heaven'. Some offering lists and festival texts also refer to heaven (and earth) in a quite parallel way as these texts refer to the other gods. Thus we can conclude that—as in Ugarit—heaven and earth as cosmic entities were sometimes considered divine; but their role is in no way comparable to Anu's position as a heavenly god and the personified heaven in Mesopotamia.

In Greek religion heaven (Ouranos) is an old but subordinate deity. According to Hesiod (*Theog.* 126-128) he was born from Gaia (→Earth) whose husband he subsequently became. He begets with her the →Titans and Cyclops. He is also incorporated in the theogonical myth where his son Kronos dethrones him; only to be dethroned himself by →Zeus later. This theogony was clearly influenced by myths from the ancient Near East. Outside mythology, Ouranos does not play a role of any importance. On occasion he features as a god connected with the taking of oaths (Homer, *Il.* 15:36; *Od.* 5:184).

III. Only a limited number of the 420 occurrences of 'heaven' in the OT refer to its divinity. Heaven is the term for the space above the earth where we can find the sun, the →moon and the →stars, but also water (Jer 10:13; Ps 148:4), rain (Gen 8:2, Deut 11:11), →dew (Gen 27:28; Deut 33:28) or snow (Isa 55:10). Since it is also the place for the birds (e.g. Deut 4:17; Jer 8:7; Ps 8:9; Lam 4:19), there is no real difference between heaven and sky. So it is no wonder that heaven (or sky) can be opposed to Earth thus forming the common Near Eastern pair of 'Heaven-and-Earth' as description of the whole cosmos. The word *rāqîaʿ*, 'firmament' can be used (cf. Gen 1:14-15.17.20; Ps 19:2; Ezek 1:23.25-26; 10:1; Dan 12:3) in parallelism with *šāmayim*. Some occurrences of *šĕḥāqîm*, 'clouds' (cf. Deut 33:26; Jer 51:9; Pss 36:6; 57:11; 78:23; 108:5; Job 35:5; 38:37) as parallel to *šāmayim* give the impression of heaven being first of all the space above the earth. Of further importance is the widely held view of the OT that heaven was created by →God and thus cannot obtain sanctity by itself (Isa 42:5; 45:18; Pss 8:4; 33:6; Prov 3:19; 8:27; Neh 9:6).

Another aspect of heaven is its role as the abode of God. God is in heaven where he dwells on his throne (cf. Ps 2:4; 11:4; 1 Kgs 8:30), surrounded by the →Host of heaven and all his →angels (Gen 28:12; 1 Kgs 22:19; 2 Chr 18:18; Pss 89:8-9; 103:21; Neh 9:6; Dan 7:10; cf. Job 1:6; 2:1). An ancient idea of God's being in heaven has been preserved in Deut 33:26 and Ps 68:34 where he is called the "rider upon the heavens" which can be compared to the idea of God being the "rider upon the clouds" (Ps 68:5; Isa 19:1), a term which can be used in a similar way in connection with Baal, the →Rider-upon-the-Clouds. As God is present in heaven, he also acts from there either speaking to men (Gen 21:17; 22:11,15; Exod 20:22; Deut 4:26; Ps 76:9; Neh 9:13) or closing up or opening heaven (e. g. Deut 11:17; 2 Sam 21:10; 1 Kgs 8:35; Ps 147:8). Thus there is a close connection between God and heaven—though God is always more than heaven (1 Kgs 8:27; 2 Chr 2:5; 6:18; Jer 23:24).

Though heaven was not originally considered a mythical being in the OT, we can find a kind of re-mythologization since the Persian era: At a first stage we find the divine title →"God of heaven" (Ps 136:26; Jonah 1:9; Ezra 1:2; 2 Chr 36:23; Neh 1:4-5, 2:4.20; Dan 2:18-19; Jdt 5:8; 6:19). Probably this is a revival of an older concept (cf. Gen 24:3.7), as a male "God of Heaven" is not unknown in the ancient Near East, which also corresponds to a female →Queen of Heaven. In the Persian era it is possible that this revival is due to Iranian influence on the biblical religion: We can find Ahura Mazda as a "god of heaven" who has created heaven and earth. In such late texts not only the God of Israel has become the God of heaven; it is also possible now to speak of heaven as a synonym for God himself. In the Book of Daniel King Nebuchadnezzar is humiliated to make him recognize "that Heaven rules" (Dan 4:26)—which means nothing other than to recognize God's rule. A similar manner of speaking can be found throughout the Books of Maccabees (1 Macc 3:18; 4:10.24.55; 12:15; 2 Macc 7:11): Heaven can save even a small number of the Maccabees from their enemies when they pray to heaven; the quotation from Ps 118:1 in 1 Macc 4:24 clearly shows that no difference is made between God and heaven. The idiom here is the same as that of the NT.

IV. In the NT (as in the LXX) the semitizing plural *ouranoi* (used in about one third of the instances) has the same meaning as the singular. Only in 2 Cor 12:2-4 where Paul relates that he was caught up to the third heaven (v 2), that is to Paradise (v 4), is the existence of more than one heaven assumed (for Jewish and later Christian parallels, see *RAC* 15, 190-192, 202-204). Also for early Christians God is the God of heaven (Rev 11:13; 16:11), the Lord of heaven and earth (Matt 11:25 par.; Luke 10:21; Acts 17:24). He may be called (my, our, your) Father in heaven (Mark 11:25-26; Matt 5:16.45; 6:1.9; 7:11.21; 10:32.33; 16: 17.19; 18:10.14.19). Heaven is called his throne (Matt 5:34; 23:23; Acts 7:49 [Isa 66:11]). In Mark 6:41 par. Matt. 14:18; Luke 9:16 Jesus looks up to heaven before blessing and breaking the bread. God speaks (and acts) 'from heaven' (Mark 1:10-11 par. Matt 3:17; Luke 3:22; John 12:28, cf. Mark 8:11 par. Matt 16:1; Luke 11:16 and Luke 17:29; Rom 1:18; see also Rev 10:4; 11:12; 20:9). Hence it is said that the New Jerusalem will come down from God and out of heaven (Rev 3:12; 21:2.10).

'In heaven' means 'with God (and/or his angels)'. One may have a 'reward in heaven' (Matt 5:12 par. Luke 6:23; cf. Matt 6:1) or 'a treasure in heaven' (Matt 6:20 par. Luke 12:33; Mark 10:21 par. Matt 19:21; Luke 18:22, cf. Col 1:5). In Luke 10:20 Jesus assures his disciples that their names are written down 'in heaven'. What Peter binds or looses on earth will be bound or loosed 'in heaven' (Matt. 16:19), and the same is promised to the disciples in Matt 18:18. Parallel to Luke 15:7 speaking about 'joy in heaven' over a repentant sinner, Luke 15:10 speaks about 'joy in the presence of the angels of God' (cf. Luke 12:8.9 'before the angels of God' in contrast to 'before my Father in heaven' in the parallel passage Matt 10:32.33).

In a relatively small number of cases 'heaven' is used as a metonym for God. This is the case in Mark 11:30-32 par. Matt 21:21-26; Luke 20:4-5, where in a discussion between Jesus and the Jewish leaders the question of the authority of John the Baptist (and Jesus) is raised. Here 'from heaven' stands in contrast to 'from men', i.e. 'of human origin'. The same usage is found frequently not only in 1 Macc but also in later Jewish sources (see Str-B I 862-865). We may compare the Johannine use of 'from heaven' (John 3:27.31, cf. 6:31-58) together with 'from above' (3:3.7.31; 8:23; 19:11, cf. Jas 1:17; 3:15.17) and 'from God' (6:46; 8:42.47; 9:33; 13:3). Next, the Prodigal Son declares: "Father I have sinned against heaven and before you" (Luke 15:18.21). Finally one should notice that Matthew, who shares the notion 'Kingdom of God' with the other Synoptics, prefers the use of the expression 'Kingdom of heaven' without a clear difference in meaning (the latter is used 32 times, in contrast to 'Kingdom of God' 4 times).

V. *Bibliography*

G. Dalman, Vorsichtige Redeweisen von Gott, *Die Worte Jesu* I (Leipzig 1930[2], repr. Darmstadt 1965) 167-191; C. Houtman, *Der Himmel im Alten Testament* (OTS 30; Leiden 1993); B. Lang & C. McDannell, *Heaven. A History* (London, New Haven 1988); G. Lohfink, "Ich habe gesündigt gegen den Himmel und gegen dich". Eine Exegese von Lk 15,18.21, *TQ* 155 (1975) 51-52; M. Metzger, Himmlische und irdische Wohnstatt Jahwes, *UF* 2 (1970) 139-158; G. Ryckmans, Heaven and Earth in South Arabic Inscriptions, *JSS* 3 (1958) 225-236; Str-B 1, 172-184, 862-865; H. Traub & G. von Rad, οὐρανός, *TWNT* 5 (1954) 496-543; A. Wohlstein, *The Sky-God An-Anu* (Jericho, N.Y. 1976).

M. Hutter (I-III) & M. de Jonge (IV)

HEAVEN-AND-EARTH שמים וארץ

I. In accordance with Mesopotamian, Anatolian and North Syrian evidence we find the word-pair 'heaven and earth' also in the OT scriptures, mainly in deuteronomistic and prophetic texts, where the cosmos is called upon as a witness. Besides these occurrences we find heaven and earth in parallelism to describe the whole cosmos.

II. Outside the Biblical world the pair heaven-and-earth has different degrees of divinity. First of all we can find certain gods who bear epithets (*AkkGE* 54.64.81-82.133-134.236-237. 39) such as "lord/king of heaven and earth" (*bēl/šarri šamê u erṣeti*), "judge" (*dayyānu*) or "light" (*nūru*) or "creator" (*bānû)* of heaven and earth. In addition gods can be referred to as the "gods of heaven and earth" (*ilāni ša šamê u erṣeti*). Such phrases refer to heaven-and-earth as a cosmic entity where certain gods can reside, but which has no divinity of its own. Of greater importance are those texts where heaven and earth are entreated—parallel to other personal gods (cf. the references given by MEISSNER 1925:215-217.222.230.233. 236)—to witness the conclusion of a treaty. Within the curse formulas we find different gods side by side with the divine pair heaven and earth. Thus we must conclude that, in such occurences we deal with a (semi-)divine name. This we can observe not only in Mesopotamian but also in Ugaritic and Hittite texts: In Hittite sources heaven and earth can appear among the divine witnesses in treaties (FRIEDRICH 1926: 24-25; 1930:80-81.112-113; KBo 8:35 ii 12; KUB 26:39 iv 24-25), a similar picture is provided by the Akkadian treaties from Hattusha (WEIDNER 1923:30-31.50-51.68-69.74-75). In Ugarit heaven and earth occur in offering lists and in the godlist (*KTU* 1.47:12; 1.118:11; 1.148:5.24; RS 20.41:11) as well as in treaty texts (RS 17.338 r. 4; 18. 06 +:6; cf. also the Sfire-Treaty *KAI* 222:11) which may be due to Hittite influence. In theogonic speculations there seems to be no place for the divine pair heaven-and-earth as the ancestors of the other gods but such a tradition is not totally unknown in Phoenicia because Philo of Byblos treats *ouranos* and *gē* as the parents of Kronos and thus indirectly of the other gods (BAUMGARTEN 1981:188-191.236-237).

III. The materials from the OT yield a picture which fits in neatly with the ancient Near Eastern background concerning the divinity of both cosmic entities. First of all we find the word-pair (or parallelism) heaven-and-earth as a fixed term for the whole cosmos which has been created by god (cf. Gen 1:1; 2:1.4; 14:19.22; Ps 148: 13; Prov 3:19; 8:27; Isa 42:5; 45:18; Amos 9:6; Neh 9:6); these references are an expression of the conception of 'God, creator of Heaven and Earth', an idea which is not unfamiliar in the Near Eastern cultures (cf. →El-Creator-of-the-Earth). Besides 'Heaven and Earth' having no divinity, they are also depicted as trembling before God (Joel 4:16). They even bring their praises to him (Ps 69:35). We find another aspect of heaven and earth in prophetic texts of judgement and in deuteronomistic curse formulae: Here again heaven and earth are god-like and thus godly witnesses against those who transgress the oaths or divine commandments (cf. Deut 4:26; 30:19; 31:28; 32:1). In other instances they are invoked to hear the prophetic and divine judgement against Israel (cf. Isa 1:2; Mic 6:2; Ps 50:4). Such references can scarcely be separated from the 'treaty-gods' of the surrounding cultures. But the OT also clearly shows that heaven and earth are always subordinate to the God of heaven and earth.

IV. *Bibliography*

A. I. BAUMGARTEN, *The Phoenician History of Philo of Byblos. A Commentary* (EPRO 89; Leiden 1981); J. FRIEDRICH, *Staatsverträge des Hatti-Reiches in hethitischer Sprache. Vol 1* (MVAÄG 31; Leipzig 1926); *Vol 2* (MVAÄG 34,1; Leipzig 1930); B. MEISSNER, *Babylonien und Assyrien.* Vol. 2 (Heidelberg 1925); E. WEIDNER, *Politische Dokumente aus Kleinasien* (BoSt 8-9; Leipzig 1923).

M. HUTTER

HEAVENLY BEINGS → SONS OF (THE) GOD(S)

HEBAT

I. Hebat (or Hepat) is an important goddess venerated by the Hurrians as well as the Hittites. Her name is found as a theophoric element in the biblical anthroponym Eliahba (2 Sam 23:32 = 1 Chr 11:33), written אליחבא, and originally pronounced *Elli-Heba, 'Elli of Hebat' (MAISLER 1930).

II. In the Hurrian pantheon, the goddess Hebat occupies a high rank: she is the wife of the weather-god Teshub and the mother of Sharruma (DANMANVILLE 1972-75:326). Her epithet 'Lady of heaven' or →'Queen of Heaven' underscores her celestial character. In the course of tradition, she has been assimilated to the sun-goddess of Arinna. Yet Hebat is not a solar deity. The theologians of Ugarit equated her with Pidraya, one of the daughters of →Baal (*Ug.* 5 [1968] 503.525). She may have been associated more particularly with Venus, as she corresponds rather closely to →Ishtar. In Nuzi, the spouse of Teshub is called Ishtar (R. F. S. STARR, *Nuzi*, Vol. 1 [Cambridge MA 1939] 529), and elsewhere Pidraya ([d]*Pi-id-di-r*[*i-ya*]) is assimilated to Ishtar (CT 25, Pl. 17 ii 12).

Though Hebat's role in the mythology known to us is restricted, her cult was important in the ancient Near East. Kizzuwatna was a major centre of her worship. Outside Anatolia het cult was known in Aleppo, Alalakh, and Ugarit (DANMANVILLE 1972-75:328). Whether Hurrian or pre-Hurrian (I. J. GELB, *Hurrians and Subarians* [SAOC 22; Chicago 1944] 106-107), Hebat was especially popular in the earliest times at Aleppo. It is significant that her name occurs most often in anthroponyms from Syria and Palestine. The Amarna letters show that the city of Jerusalem had a king called Abdi-Heba in the Late Bronze Period ([I]ÌR-[d]Ḫe-ba; EA 280:17.23.34; 285:2.14; 286:2.761; 287:2.65; 288:2; perhaps 119: 51).

III. Though the name Eliahba is traditionally analysed as consisting of *ʾēl* (God) plus HBʾ in the hiphil (to conceal, to protect), yielding a sense like 'God protects' (NOTH, *IPN* 197; *HALAT* 53-54; W. F. ALBRIGHT, *JPOS* 8 [1908] 234 n. 2), the alternative analysis defining it as a Hurrian name is attractive. The name Abdi-Heba attested for the king of Jerusalem shows that the pronounciation Ḫeba for Ḫebat, with deletion of the final -t, had gained ground in Palestine. Considering the spread of the cult of Hebat in Syria and Palestine, reflected in the distribution of the relevant theophoric anthroponyms, it does not come as a total surprise to find one of David's combatants (not necessarily an Israelite) carrying a name referring to the Hurrian goddess.

IV. *Bibliography*

J. DANMANVILLE, Ḫepat, Ḫebat, *RLA* 4 (1972-75) 326-329; W. FEILER, Ḫurritische Namen im Alten Testament, *ZA* 45 (1939) 216-229; B. MAISLER, *Untersuchungen zur alten Geschichte und Ethnographie Syriens und Palästinas* (Giessen 1930) 38.

K. VAN DER TOORN

HEBEL → ABEL

HELEL הילל

I. The astral being Hêlēl, occurs as a divine name only in Isa 14:12: "How you have fallen from heaven, Bright Morning Star (*hêlēl ben-šāḥar*), felled to the earth, sprawling helpless across the nations!" (NEB). However, translations of this verse vary. After the opening words, the RSV continues: "O Day Star, son of Dawn! How you are cut down to the ground, you who laid the nations low!" Alternatively, in view of Gilg. XI 6, where the hero is described as lying on his back doing nothing, the second half of the verse may be rendered "(How) you've been cut down to the ground, helpless on your back!" (VAN LEEUWEN 1980, rejected by SPRONK 1986:214 n. 4). The last three words of the v. remain difficult.

The Hebrew expression *hêlēl ben-šāḥar* means 'Shining one, son of dawn'. Heb *hêlēl* comes from the root HLL, 'to shine', and means 'the Shining, Brilliant One', here evidently an epithet of the Morning-star, Venus.

Etymologically, Heb *hêlēl* corresponds to Ugaritic *hll* which occurs in the following expressions: *bnt hll snnt*, 'daughters of Brightness, swallows (or perhaps 'Shining Ones')' and *bnt hll bʿl gml*, 'daughters of Brightness, Lord of the Crescent Moon' (*KTU* 1.24:41-42) used of the Kathirātu (Ug. *kṯrt*) who feature largely in the same text as handmaidens to Nikkal. Ug *hll* is not to be connected with (Thamudic) Arab *hilal*, 'new moon'. Shahar also occurs in Ugaritic mythology as the other half of the divine pair

→Shahar and →Shalim, 'Dawn' or 'Morning Star' and 'Dusk'.

II. The search for a comparable myth in neighbouring religions has led scholars to Babylonian, Ugaritic and Greek mythology. It would seem that Isa 14:12-15 reflects the episode in Ugaritic myth where Athtar failed to replace →Baal on the throne. Baal was dead, and after mourning, burial and sacrifice the goddess →Anat asked →El for a successor. He in turn asked Athirat (cf. →Asherah) for one of her sons and eventually they decided on Athtar. "Thereupon Athtar the Tyrant went up into the heights of Ṣaphon; he sat on the throne of Mightiest Baal. His feet did not reach the footstool, his head did not reach its top. And Athtar the Tyrant spoke: 'I cannot be king in the heights of Saphon'". Accordingly, he came down and became king over the whole earth or perhaps the netherworld (*KTU* 1.6 i). However, no mythological episode in Ugaritic connects either *hll* or *šḥr* with the presumption of rising to heaven and instead being thrust into the underworld (cf. →Sheol).

Hêlēl has been considered to represent an aspect of the →moon. However, this would involve repointing as *hêlal* and correcting *šḥr* to *śhr*. Helel has also been identified with the Babylonian underworld god →Nergal or with Jupiter. Yet another identification is with Phaethon, of Greek mythology. Phaethon was the son of Eos, the Dawn-goddess, and this is matched by Hêlēl's own parentage (*bn šḥr*) since there is strong evidence that in Hebrew, too, *šaḥar*, 'Dawn', was feminine.

It has also been suggested that the pair of gods *ngh w srr* (*KTU* 1.123:12), alleged to mean 'Brightness and Rebellion', is "the earliest occurrence of the magnificent mythological poem, Isaiah 14:12-15" (ASTOUR 1964;1966). However, *srr* means 'last night of the lunar month' (Arab) and both terms refer to the moon, not to Venus, so there is no connection with Isa 14.

III. In Isa 14:12-21, Hêlēl, son of Shahar is asserted to have said to himself: "I will go up to →heaven, above the →stars of God I will place my throne on high. I will sit on the Mount of Assembly in Saphon, I will rise above the heights of the clouds, I will make myself like the Most High". His presumption, instead, resulted in his translation to the very depths of the underworld, to be mocked as the erstwhile all-powerful tyrant. If there are mythological overtones, as is probable, it remains to be determined how the myth was transmitted to Isaiah and used by him.

One reconstruction of the transmission history of Isa 14:12-15 suggests that an original poem on the fall of a king, and based on Canaanite verse tradition, was transferred to the fate of a king of Babylon. His downfall was explained by means of the myth of Hêlēl, son of Dawn, in the light of current belief concerning good and evil spirits and angels. Babylon and its kings were represented as a manifestation of the rebellious fallen angels (LORETZ 1976).

Alternatively, in pre-Classical Greece there was already confusion between Phaethon and Heosphoros (or Venus as the morning star), both being sons of Eos by different fathers. When the Phaethon myth reached the Levant, Phaethon's attempt to scale the heights of heaven became confused with the episode of Athtar's failure to gain the throne in Ugaritic mythology. The Greek names were simply translated into Hebrew, but *šḥr*, as in Ugaritic, remained masculine (MCKAY 1970).

It is also possible to treat the whole of Isa 14 as a parody of the dirge and in particular of the lament in 2 Sam 19:1-27. In Isa 14:12-15 an ancient myth of Hêlēl was transmitted by the poet in the form of a dirge. "By embedding this dirge in the center of the overall lament, the poet assimilates the tyrant to this primordial figure, identifying the tyrant's rise and fall with that of Hêlēl, the Bright One. Thus, for the poet, the tyrant's transgression, his harsh oppression of the people, is ultimately traceable to his consummate arrogance in desiring to be like God. As Hêlēl climbed higher and higher only to fall deeper and deeper, so too is the tyrant's fate" (YEE 1988:577-579).

Etymologically, Heb *hêlēl* can be explained by Ug *hll* (see above), but at the level of myth the strongest affinity is between Isa 14 and the Athtar episode in the Ugaritic Cycle of Baal. This is strengthened by common terminology, in particular *hr mʿd*, 'mount of the assembly' and *yrkty ṣpwn*, 'heights of Ṣaphon' (v. 13) which correspond to Ug *pḫr mʿd*, 'plenary session' (*KTU* 1.2 i:14) and *mrym ṣpn*, 'heights of Ṣaphon' (*KTU* 1.3 iv:1) respectively. It has even been suggested that Athtar's epithet, *ʿrz*, means 'luminous' rather than 'tyrant'. This would lend further support to this identification (CRAIGIE 1973), but this is not the accepted opinion. In Isa 14, the King of Babylon is designated mockingly as Hêlēl in the guise of Athtar; but there is no evidence for the acknowledgement of Hêlēl's real existence or of his cult.

IV. *Bibliography*

M. C. ASTOUR, *Hellenosemitica* (Leiden 1964) 268-271, 394-395; ASTOUR, Some New Divine Names from Ugarit, *JAOS* 86 (1966) 277-284; P. C. CRAIGIE, Helel, Athtar and Phaeton (Jes 14:12-15), *ZAW* 85 (1973) 223-225; S. ERLANDSSON, *The Burden of Babylon. A Study of Isaiah 13:2-14:23* (Lund 1970); D. E. GOWAN, *When Man Becomes God: Humanism and Hybris in the Old Testament* (Pittsburgh Theological Monograph 6; Pittsburgh 1975) 45-67; P. GRELOT, Isaïe XIV et son arrière-plan mythologique, *RHR* 149 (1956) 18-48; GRELOT, Sur la vocalisation de הילל (Is. XIV,12), *VT* 6 (1956) 303-304; S. L. LANGDON, The Star Hêlēl, Jupiter?, *ExpTim* 42 (1930-1931) 173; R. C. VAN LEEUWEN, *Hôleš ʿal gwym* and Gilgamesh XI,6, *JBL* 99 (1980) 173-184; O. LORETZ, Der kanaanäische Mythos vom Sturz des Šaḫar-Sohnes Hêlēl (Jes. 14, 12-15), *UF* 8 (1976) 133-136 [& lit]; J. W. MCKAY, Helel and the Dawn-Goddess. A re-examination of the myth in Isaiah XIV 12-15, *VT* 20 (1970) 451-46; E. T. MULLEN, *The Assembly of the Gods in Canaanite and Early Hebrew Literature* (Chico 1980) 238-241; U. OLDENBURG, Above the Stars of El. El in Ancient South Arabic Religion, *ZAW* 82 (1970) 187-208; W. S. PRINSLOO, Isaiah 14:12-15-Humiliation, Hubris, Humiliation, *ZAW* 93 (1982) 432-438; K. SPRONK, *Beatific Afterlife in Ancient Israel and in the Ancient Near East* (AOAT 219; Kevelaer/Neukirchen-Vluyn 1986) 213-231; G. A. YEE, The Anatomy of Biblical Parody: The Dirge Form in 2 Samuel 1 and Isaiah 14, *CBQ* 50 (1988) 565-586, esp. 577-579.

W. G. E. WATSON

HELIOS Ἥλιος

I. The word ἥλιος, sun, like *šemeš* →Shemesh, is ambivalent between a true name and a common noun. Only the context can determine which aspect—stellar, religious, cosmic, political—is predominant in a given text. The standard etymology (H. FRISK, *Griechisches etymologisches Wörterbuch* [Heidelberg 1954] 1:631-632; P. CHANTRAINE, *Dictionnaire étymologique de la langue grecque* 2 [Paris 1970] 410-411) appeals to the psilotic epic form ἀέλιος and a Cretan (Hesych.) or Pamphylian (Heracleides of Miletus) form ἀβέλιος to postulate an original *σαϝέλιος, cognate with Sansc. *sūrya* : in each case an *-l* stem, **sāu̯el-*, **sūl-*, will have been given a suffix in *io-* to mark personification. *Helios* would thus be one of a well-known group of Indo-European words for the sun and cognate concepts (Lat. *sol*, Gaulish *sulis*, Lith. *sáulė*, Goth. *sauil*, OHG *sōl*, Slavic *sólnitse*; cf. OIr. *sūil*, 'eye') which has been used to posit the existence of an Indo-European sun-god or sun-goddess. But in historical times, Helios was weakly personified: sun worship was an individual rather than a civic matter. In the Graeco-Roman world, the religious value of Helios was exploited mainly within the context of changing cosmologies and the elective affinity between absolutism and solar imagery.

Helios occurs extremely frequently in the Bible (196 times in LXX, 32 times in NT). For OT senses, see →Shemesh. In early Judaism and the NT the meaning of the word draws primarily upon this heritage, connoting concretely day(-light), time of day, direction, or figuratively brightness, esp. in relation to divine *kābôd* or *doxa* (→Glory); in apocalyptic contexts, a typical image of the end of this world order is the abolition or reversal of the luminaries. The boldest of these figurative images is the *šemeš ṣĕdāqâ*, ἥλιος δικαιοσύνης, of Mal 3:20 (4:2), "in whose wings lies salvation", which must draw upon, while also contrasting with, Near Eastern imagery of the winged sun as bringer of justice (W. RUDOLPH, *Kommentar zum Alten Testament: Haggai ... Maleachi* [Gütersloh 1976] 289). Some Babylonian influence upon Jewish cosmology, esp. Enochian and Qumran 'astronomy', is probable, but its theological influence was negligible. Philo's debt to the Stoic/Middle Platonic view of the sun is meagre by comparison with the influence of later Judaic conceptions. The composite philosophic 'solar theology' of the later Principate had no perceptible influence upon early Christian thought and imagery, though some limited iconographic transfer took place.

II. Among the divinities sustained by the collective imagination in Archaic and Classical Greece the bodies of the visible heavens received scant attention: they were, as Preller put it, "Nebengötter". The political character of that religion, its variety across the spectrum of city-states and *ethnē*, gave priority to divine figures not implicated in natural rhythms, which could be given specific local character in myth and cult. The heavenly bodies were a common property: "to see the light" is a standard Homeric phrase for being alive (*Iliad* 18:61; *Od.* 4:540 etc.), frequently imitated by later poets, as in Pindar's apostrophe to light, "mother of eyes" (*Paean* 9:2 Snell); "to leave the sun's light" is a common periphrasis for "to die" (Hesiod *Op.* 155; Theognis 569). Helios shines alike on mortals and immortals (*Od.* 3: 1-3); he is "most prominent of all the gods" (Sophocles, *Oed. Rex* 660). This quality of belonging to the neutral "fabric of things" is expressed formally in the status of Helios, Eos (Dawn) and Selene as →Titans, belonging to the direct descent of Ouranos and Gaia, through Hyperion and his sister Theia (Hesiod, *Theog.* 371-374; cf. Apollodorus, *Bibl.* 1.2. 2). In Homer, Helios has virtually no identity separate from the solar disk: his commonest epithet is *phaethōn*, "radiant"; another Iliadic epithet is *akamas*, "tireless", which links the sun to its congener, →fire, itself *akamaton* (e.g. *Il.* 5:4); he can be forced by →Hera to set (*Il.* 18: 239-241), and is not even identified explicitly as a charioteer, though this detail appears already in the *Titanomachia* frg. 3 Allen and Hom. Hymn *Demeter* 88-89 (ca. 7th-6th century BCE). The comparative lack of individuality persists into the 4th century BCE: the poets failed to discover more than a paltry local narrative or two; his amours could scarcely be fewer or more perfunctory, consisting as they do mainly of alternative mothers of his ill-fated son Phaethon (JESSEN 1912:80-81); the 'Homeric' *Hymn to Helios* (no. 31; prob. late 4th century BCE) is a patchwork of pallid epic clichés. In the early iconography, c. 500-480 BCE, and frequently well into 5th century BCE, Helios is identified only by a disk bizarrely placed upon his head (e.g. YALOURIS 1990: nos. 2-4, 6-8, 10-12, 14; 105-108); on the 4th century BCE Apulian vases, his head, or even the entire figure with chariot, is depicted within a nimbus (ibid. 18-28; 77-82; 124-127). Moreover, the myth that accounted for Helios' role at Rhodes also noted the general absence of civic cult to the Sun in other Greek cities: at the original division of the earth between the Olympian gods, Helios was not present, and failed to obtain a lot; →Zeus would have insisted upon another allocation of fiefs, but Helios spied the island of Rhodes emerging from the depths, and claimed it as his own (Pindar, *Olymp.* 7: 54-76 with Scholiast; cf. Diod. Sic. 5.56.3-5). All in all, "seine Persönlichkeit ist ... wenig ausgeprägt und sein Kult gering" (M. P. NILSSON, *Griechische Feste* [Stuttgart 1906] 427).

Nevertheless, the two aspects of Helios which were later to be most productive are already present in the epic and sub-epic tradition: Helios as an eye, a tireless observer of the human world; and Helios as a sign or guarantor of (cosmic) order.

(1) Helios "observes everything, hears everything" (*Od.* 11.109), is "spy upon gods and men" (Hom. Hymn *Dem.* 62; cf. *Od.* 8:302), "looks down on all the earth and sea with [his] rays from the divine aither" (Hymn *Dem.* 69-70; cf. *Od.* 11:16). This view of Helios, frequent in the tragedians, e.g. Aeschylus, *Agam.* 632-633; [Aesch.], *Prom.* 91; Sophocles, *Trach.* 102) should be thought of as an implicit explanation of the fact that Helios was one of the elemental gods, including Gē and Zeus, invoked to sanction an oath: the exemplary instance occurs at *Iliad* 3:103-107, 268-313; cf. 19: 249-265; Euripides, *Medea* 746-747/753-754. This usage is not only parallel to Near Eastern oaths, but may well be based on Indo-European practice. In historical times, ordinary civic gods are perhaps most common, but appeal to Helios remained a major sanction in oaths (e.g. sympolity treaty between Teos and Kyrbisos, 3rd century BCE: *SEG* 26:1306.52) and it may be assumed that many of the rather limited numbers of altars and votives to Helios known from Greece outside Corinth, Macedonia and Rhodes, have some relation to oath-taking. At Troezene, for example, Pausanias noted (2. 31. 5) an altar to Helios *eleutherios*, which he believed to have been dedicated in gratitude after the Persian War of 490-489 BCE; if so, the choice may well have been routed through the practice of freeing slaves by fictitious dedication to Helios as god of oaths (cf. JESSEN 1912:59). The notion of Helios as a sanction of the oath thus passed imperceptibly into a view of Helios as witness, to unadmitted love, for example, as in a skolion on a black-figure vase by the Amasis painter found on Aigina (*SEG* 35:252, side A, ca. 540 BCE), but in particular of wrong-doing: the victim of an alleged injustice, or his friends, appealed to Helios as a witness of his maltreatment (Aeschylus, *Hiket.* 213; *Choeph.* 984-989; Sophocles, *Elect.* 824-825; Apollonius Rhod., *Argon.* 4:229-230) or of his innocence (Euripides, *Herakles* 858; cf. Soph. *Oed. Rex* 660-661). Though the motif seems already present in the Odyssean scene of Helios requiring Zeus to punish Odysseus and his companions for slaughtering his herds (*Od.* 12:374-388), its development was motivated by the institution in democratic Athens, and elsewhere, of public courts; it depended upon familiarity with legal procedure. Awareness of the importance of witnesses, and the ease with which false witness could be bought, gave rise to the notion of the Sun as an ideal, incorruptible witness of a subjective truth. Helios, having always been *hagnos* (Pindar, *Olymp.* 7:60, cf. Parmenides, 28 F10.2 Diels-Kranz), became *dikaios* too ("eye of justice, light of life" in *Hymn. Orph.* 8:18). As such, the notion might over time be indefinitely banalized, as on a boundary-marker from Esençiftliği in Bithynia, which routinely calls upon Helios *panepoptēs* to guarantee the integrity of the boundary (*SEG* 37. 1036.15-17, 2nd-3rd century CE). Moreover these two aspects of Helios were often fused in the Hellenistic and Roman periods: Helios, in his capacity as all-seeing witness (Κύριε Ἥλιε, ὥς δικαίως ἀνατέλλις, μὴ λάθοιτό σε... from Salamis in Cyprus, 3rd century BCE: *SEG* 6. 803, cf. *ZPE* 61 [1985] 212-213) is commonly invoked to avenge present or even anticipated wrongs unconnected with oaths, above all to avenge unsolved or alleged murder (D. M. PIPPIDI, Tibi commendo, *RivStorAnt* 6-7 [1976-1977] 37-44). Though CUMONT (1923) claimed that the origin of this belief was Syrian, the evidence for this role is widely spread in space and time; in Asia Minor at any rate there can be little doubt that indigenous notions of the sun's justice fused with Greek ones after Alexander's conquest (cf. G. BJÖRCK, *Der Fluch des Christen Sabinus* [Uppsala 1938] 72). It is this theme of the sun's justice that inspires not only the tradition of solar utopias, based on the "table of the Ethiopians" in Herodotus 3:17, cf. *Orph.* frg. 217 Kern, but also the oracular and apocalyptic motif of the "saviour from the sun" (*Sib. Or.* 13:151, cf. D. S. POTTER, *Prophecy and History in the Crisis*

of the Roman Empire [Oxford 1990] 326-327).

(2) Helios as an emblem and guarantor of cosmic order. The main stimulus to representing Helios as witness and →avenger of those unable to help themselves was the sun's light, evoked as a token of an ideal incorruptibility. But empirical familiarity with the astronomical sun raised obvious questions about its nature. In a word, the sun invited cosmological speculation. Though Homer is generally content to have Helios rise out of, and fall into, Oceanus, the *Odyssey* knows an island of Syria, where the "turnings of the sun"—presumably the summer solstices—take place (15:403-404), a crux that gave rise to considerable debate in Alexandrian Homer-scholarship; and soon after Homer the issue of what happens to Helios at night was tackled by Mimnermus (ca. second half of the 7th century BCE), who imagined him floating in a winged golden bowl from West to East along the Ocean (frg. 10 Diehl; cf. Stesichorus, frg. 8.1-4 Page). This became quite a favourite subject for vase-painters (J. DÖRIG & O. GIGON, *Der Kampf der Götter und Titanen* [Olten & Lausanne 1961] 56-59). The regularity of the sun's (mutable) course, its "tirelessness", always attracted attention: Helios's threat to "descend to →Hades and shine among the dead" (*Od.* 12:383) is the earliest in a long tradition of reversals represented in terms of solar aberration. The sun's elemental constancy inspired Zeus' sacrifice to Helios (and Ouranos and Gē) before the battle with the →Giants (Diod. Sic. 5.71.3). Observations of solstices (and of star-settings) were made all through the Archaic period (cf. Cleostratus, 6 F4 D-K); though Thales' prediction of the solar eclipse of 585 BC probably depended upon Babylonian records, it was grounded in Greek practical astronomy. In their different idioms, the Presocratics assumed that the sun's regular motions, daily and seasonal, had to be explained: Anaximander's image of the chariot-wheel (12 A11 D-K), Anaximenes' raised North (13 A7; 28 D-K), Parmenides' strange "garlands" (28 A37 D-K), Anaxagoras' rotation of the *aither* (59 A42 D-K) are all attempts to come to terms with the complex problems involved. By the 5th century BCE, drawing upon this speculation, the poets routinely think of the sun as fire ([Aesch.], *Prom.* 22; Eur. *Phoen.* 3; *Phaethon* 6 Diggle). A fragment from an unknown play by Sophocles, invoking Helios as "parent of gods and father of all" (frg. 752 Radt), confirms that the blending of this cosmological speculation with mythological tradition was well under way in the second half of the 5th century BCE.

Notwithstanding Parmenides', and Heraclitus' view of the sun as kept to its path by the Erinyes (22 F94 D-K), the decisive move towards combining cosmological speculation with a self-consciously elevated religiosity was made by the Pythagorean Philolaus, for whom the sun reflected to earth the cosmic fire (44 A19 D-K) within the context of a complex model of the divinely-ordained universe. The elaborate cosmologies of Plato's *Timaeus* (32a-40d) and *Epinomis*, drawing upon Philolaus, Parmenides and probably Eudoxus, invest the fixed and mobile →'stars' with divinity and soul. Zeno's view of them as "intelligent, rational and fiery" (SVF 1.120) is directly descended from Plato's cosmology; but in the early Stoic system the sun's fire plays a key role in the *ekpyrōsis*, since, as the guiding principle, it gradually absorbs the other stars and the rest of matter into itself until the entire universe is consumed (SVF 1.510). In some sense, at least, the Stoic sun is to be identified with Zeus, Soul and →Pronoia (Cleanthes); and as such, despite Panaetius' reconsideration of *ekpyrōsis*, is described by Cicero as *dux et princeps et moderator luminum reliquorum, mens mundi et temperatio* (*Rep.* 6:17, cf. *Tusc.* 1:68; *Div.* 2:89). In the same tradition, Seneca uses the sun's relation to the world as an image of the role and power of the World Soul (*Epist. Mor.* 41:5; cf. M. Aurelius, *Conf.* 12:30). A diffuse Stoic cosmology combined in the later Hellenistic period with the spread of astrological ideas (e.g. O. NEUGEBAUER & H. D. VAN HOESEN, *Greek Horoscopes*

[Philadelphia 1959] nos. 46.1; 81.48-51) to promote the role of Helios as lord of the ordered universe (*mundi totius animum ac planius mentem*: Pliny, *HN* 2: 12-13, cf. Diod. Sic. 2. 30-31; Menander, *Rhet. gr.* 3: 438.10-24 Spengel; CUMONT 1909 with NILSSON 1974). The finest poetic expression of this awareness of the sun as the most splendid of the heavenly bodies is Mesomedes' *Hymn* (Hadrianic) (HEITSCH 1960: 144-150). As such, the sun became one of the counters to be shuffled about by cosmological speculation quite unconstrained by empirical concerns: in Middle Platonism, Helios is the "heart" of the body of the cosmos (Plutarch, *de fac.* 928a-b), the embodiment or receptacle of cosmic reason (cf. *ibid.* 943a-e); in the Orphic *Rhapsodies*, he is set by the demiurge Phanes in command of all things (frg. 96 Kern); in one Hermetic cosmology, by extension of his traditional promotion of life, he becomes himself a demiurge vivifying matter by means of light (*Corp. Herm.* 16:3-12; KLEIN 1962:149-156); in the Mithraic mysteries, he has a complex relation, of identity and difference, with →Mithras himself, *sol invictus Mithras*; the Mnevis bull at Heliopolis in Egypt, descending from, and ascending to, the sun, provides the author of the gnostic *Origin of the World* with a "witness" to the redeeming work of Sabaoth (NHC II.5, 122:22-24). Porphyry, whether or not he wrote a book on 'Helios', played an important part in the genesis of Macrobius' solar syncretism in *Sat.* 1. 17-23 (FLAMANT 1977).

Helios was perfectly suited to fulfil the role of →mediator required by the geocentric cosmology that established itself—not merely among the educated—during the Hellenistic period, and for that reason was recruited under the Principate into all manner of philosophico-religious systems with tiny circulations. But the elective affinity between Helios and monarchic power undoubtedly also played a part in legitimating such speculation. Though this affinity was exploited above all during the 3rd century CE crisis of the Roman Empire (L'ORANGE 1935 with reservations; R. TURCAN, Le culte impérial au IIIe siècle, *ANRW* II, 16.2 [1978] 996-1084), it originates in the solar imagery used of Demetrius of Phalerum, Antigonus Gonatas and Demetrius Poliorcetes at the very beginning of Hellenistic monarchy. The discovery of Augustus' *solarium* at the Ara Pacis, centred on the solar obelisk (E. BUCHNER, *Die Sonnenuhr des Augustus* [Mainz 1982]), has reinforced the traditional view of the cosmic symbolism of the cuirass of the Augustus of Prima Porta (SCHAUENBURG 1955:38-39; contrast REBUFFAT). Moreover, since SEYRIG (1971) poured cold water on the traditional assumption that all Syrian city cults were solar, there has been markedly less enthusiasm for seeing imperial solar imagery even after Septimius Severus as due primarily to 'oriental influence' (cf. HIJMANS 1989, GAWLIKOWSKI 1990). Even Aurelian's cult of Sol Invictus, based on his vision at Emesa (*HA Aurel.* 23:3-6), was primarily a pulling together of traditional threads of imperial imagery, to serve as a focus of religious *loyalisme* at a period when the central authority was in virtual collapse. Constantine's deployment of Sol Invictus as *comes Augusti*, in the imagery of the Arch (completed 315), his coinage between 309-325 (BRUUN 1958; J. BLEICKEN, *Constantin der Große und die Christen* [München 1992] 34-38, 58-61), and on his statue on the porphyry column in the new Forum at Constantinople, is an analogous strategy in different circumstances. And, as the Calendar of Filocalus makes clear, the association between sun and imperial power continued well into the 4th century CE in the context of the games of 19-22 October and the birthday of Sol Invictus on 25 December.

III. Despite considerable continuity, especially in liturgical contexts, with OT conceptions of light and the luminaries, some differences in cosmology are perceptible in apocryphal and pseudepigraphic texts (AALEN 1951:97-102). The luminaries are conceived as prior to the cyclic changes of human significance: the sun brings morning and its setting brings nightfall; at creation, it decides between →light and darkness (*Jub.*

2:8). The sun that shows God's glory is an observed and observable sun, that daily rises to its zenith and declines to its nadir (Sir 43:1-5; cf. 26:16), just as what is worth remarking about the →moon is its regular phases (Sir 43:6-8). In some cases it is probable that the influence is from non-Jewish sources. The account of the sun in *1 Enoch* 72:6-35, designed to explain the observed variation in the length of the day over a year by appeal to a theory of 12 'portals', is probably ultimately Babylonian. Characterized by a "rigid schematism unrelated to reality" (M. BLACK, *The Book of Enoch* [Leiden 1985] 387), the description is a blend of religious imagination and disinterested speculation: the sun, like the moon and →stars, is controlled by the angel →Uriel (cf. also 75:3; 82:8); they are driven on their courses by heavenly wind (18:4; 72:5); the sun disappears in the west and is borne at →night round to the north (72:5). Still more flamboyant is the description in *3 Apoc. Bar.* 6:1-12, derived indirectly from Greek sources, of the sun's chariot drawn by 40 angels, and preceded by the →phoenix that prevents the sun from burning up the earth. Each evening four angels remove the sun's crown and bring it back up to heaven refurbished for the following day (8:3-4). In this account, there is a separate 'portal' for each day of the year (6:13).

But the sun is of most value in early Judaism, as in the OT, as an image of divine *kābôd.* At creation, God rides through the light like the sun (*2 Enoch* 24B:4). There is an essential continuity between the sun and heavenly light (Sir 42:17), even though divine *doxa* is much more brilliant: "the eyes of the Lord are 10,000 times brighter than the sun" (23:19, cf. *3 Enoch* 5:4). The angels' *doxa* is often compared to the sun's brilliance (*2 Enoch* 19A:1; *3 Enoch* 48 C 6 [p.168-169 Odeberg]). Indeed, some passages give the impression that *doxa* is imagined as itself a sort of luminary: "their eyes saw the majesty of his glory" (Sir 17:13); part of it was revealed to →Moses (45:3; cf. Exod 33:18); "I saw the eyes of the Lord shining like the rays of the sun" (*2 Enoch* 39A:4). Such imagery prompted Philo's analogies between →wisdom and the sun, which is "an imitation and likeness" of God's light (*Migr. Abr.* 40). The parallel between heavenly *doxa* and the empirical sun gives plausibility to the psychological slide that makes mystical experience normative (*Somn.* 1:72, cf. *Mut. nom.* 6). Philo, though, is anything but systematic: elsewhere, it is human *nous* which is analogous in the person to the sun in the cosmos; the one emits physical light (*phengos*), the other rays (*augai*). When reason sets, mystical vision is possible: when divine *phōs* shines, human reason is occluded (*Heres* 263-264).

The most sustained Philonic account of the analogy occurs at *Somn.* 1:77-91, where the sun is argued to have four allegorical meanings in exegesis of passages in Genesis: = *nous* (77-78); sense perception (79-84); the divine *logos*—the intelligible sun, the *paradeigma* of the natural sun (85-86); and, as lord of the cosmos, God, to whom all is as an open book (87-91; KLEIN 1962:24-31). From this and other passages, Philo's conception of light may be divided into two parallel pairs, structured upon the contrast invisible/visible. God is the archetypal exclusive light, parallel to the empirical sun in the visible world. The divine →*Logos*, which derives from God, is 'intelligible light', 'the intelligible sun', 'wisdom', *pneuma.* To it corresponds 'inauthentic light', the natural light of the world. Opposed to these parallel pairs is 'darkness', itself composed of two absences, of spiritual and natural light. The mediatory role of the sun in all this is obvious; it spans the disjunctures between physical and spiritual, visible and invisible, presence and absence. Philo's exegesis is nevertheless for the most part only a slight extension of religious metaphors already current in early Judaism: only the fourth, and inexplicit, allegory of *Somn.* 1:87-91 seems to be based on Stoic, or Middle Platonic, solar imagery.

The same is emphatically true of the role of the sun in the NT, which, ignoring Philo's allegorizing, remains faithful to the OT habit of taking natural phenomena as concrete images for spiritual truths. The empirical sun is never simply that, it always has a residual connotation, as the visible agent of God's impartial mercy (Matt 5:45, cf. the argument for God's justice by the gnostic Epiphanes, ap. Clement Alex., *Strom.* 3.2.6.1 p.198 Stählin), as a marker of time in the cycle of day/night established at creation (Mark 16:2, cf. Eph 4:26; Mark 1:32; cf. Luke 4:40 par), as the giver of the light that the living see, but neither the dead nor the blind (Acts 13:11; cf. Ps 58:8 etc). At Rev 7:2, 16:12, "from the rising of the sun" is not merely a direction but an allusion to the OT notion that the East denotes the quarter from which divine activity is to be expected (Ezek 43:1-2, cf. AALEN 1951: 82-86). The OT fusion of fire and (sun-)light as attributes of God stands behind the burning sun of the parable of the sower (Mark 4:6; cf. Matt 13:6; see also James 1:11, Rev 7:16; 16:8-9; cf. Ps 121:6; Isa 49:10). Other occurrences are directly related to Jewish imagery. Saul's vision on the road to Damascus, the light brighter than the sun (Acts 26:13), is a reprise of passages such as Sir 23:19. The Jewish hierarchy of *doxa*, from God's, through the angels' to that of the saints (cf. Dan 12:3; 4 Ezra 7:97; *1 Enoch* 38:4; *2 Enoch* 66:7 etc.), lies behind various other passages in which 'the sun' is an image for heavenly brightness: the faces of →Jesus at the Transfiguration (Matt 17:2) and the angel at Rev 1:16; the saints at Matt 13:43 (cf. Greg. Nyssa, *In psalm. inscr.* 2:6, PG 44, 611a). The hierarchy is evoked explicitly by Paul, 1 Cor 16:41. Finally, the sun plays a notable part in the imagery of NT apocalypse, drawing upon Isa 13:10, 34:4 and esp. 60:19, "the sun shall be no more your light by day" (cf. *Ass. Mos.* 10:5). Here again there is a contrast, implied or explicit, between the abolition of the luminaries at the end of time, and the *doxa* of God and of Israel, which will shine alone (Rev. 21:23, 22:5, more loosely, 8:12, 9:2). The light is sometimes itself seen as destructive of the wicked (e.g. QH VI.17-19 Dupont-Sommer). This contrast is carried over directly into the Christian vision by Mark 13:24 ~ Matt 24:29; the parallel phenomena in the "days of the sinners" (e.g. *Sib. Or.* 3:802-3) are alluded to by the Lucan eclipse at the crucifixion (Luke 23: 45; cf. 21:25). At Pentecost, Peter cites Joel 3:1-5 [2:28-32] (Acts 2:20, cf. Rev. 6:12).

Early Christian comparisons between God and the sun derive directly from this Judaic notion of divine *doxa* (*Odes Sol.* 11:13-4; Theophilus of Antioch, *Ad Autol.* 2:15; Min. Felix, *Octavius* 32:5-6, 8-9). Already in Hebr 1:3, Christ's relation to the Father is represented as the brightness (*apaugasma*) of divine *doxa* (cf. Wis 7:26; AALEN 1951: 201-202), and this image is common in 2nd-3rd century CE (Justin, *Dial. Tryph.* 128:3-4; Tertullian, *Apol.* 21:12-14), giving way in later 3rd century CE to the formula "light from light" (DÖLGER 1929:284-286). The transfer of the image of Mal 3:18-20 [4:2], the "sun of righteousness" (Jerome, *In Amos* 3, 6:12/15, CCSL LXXVI p.312), to Christ depends upon the apocalyptic side of the same tradition, in the context of the suffering of the righteous ("righteousness shall be revealed like a sun governing the world": 1Q27:1 tr. Vermes; cf. Wis 5:6; AALEN 1951:178-179). Both themes are already present in the Christian adoption, from the early 2nd century CE, of Sunday as the *status dies* (Justin, *1Apol* 67:8; Tertullian, *Apol.* 16:11), which is figuratively also the 'eighth day', the end of the world (*Barn.* 15: 8b-9 with PRIGENT ad loc.). Sun as *doxa* fuses with purging fire to produce the striking apocalyptic imagery of *Thomas the Contender* (*NHC* II.7, 144, probably from Edessa, 3rd century CE). The iconography of the three early cases (3rd century CE) of Helios representing Christ, on the other hand, derives from the model of imperial *Sol Invictus*, signifying Christ's majesty (HUSKINSON 1974:78-80).

IV. *Bibliography*

S. AALEN, *Die Begriffe 'Licht' und 'Finsternis' im AT, im Spätjudentum und im Rabbinismus* (Oslo 1951) 96-236; P. BRUUN, The disappearance of Sol from the coins of Constantine, *Arctos* 2 (1958) 15-37; F. CUMONT, La théologie solaire du paganisme romain,

Mémoires prés. par divers Savants 12, 2 (Paris 1909) 448-480; CUMONT, Il sole vindice dei delitti ed il simbolo delle mani alzate, *Memorie della Pontificia Accademia romana di Archeologia* 1 (1923) 65-80, with *Syria* 14 (1933) 392-393; F. J. DÖLGER, *Die Sonne der Gerechtigkeit und der Schwarze* (Münster [3]1971; ed. 1, 1918); DÖLGER , *Sol salutis: Gebet und Gesang im christlichen Altertum* (Münster [3]1972; ed. 1, 1920); DÖLGER, Sonne und Sonnenstrahl als Gleichnis in der Logostheologie des christlichen Altertums, *Antike und Christentum* 1 (1929) 271-290; J. FLAMANT, *Macrobe et le néoplatonisme latin à la fin du IVe siècle* (EPRO 58; Leiden 1977) 652-680; M. GAWLIKOWSKI, Helios (in peripheria orientali), *LIMC* 5 (1990) 1034-1038 (icon.); E. HEITSCH, Drei Helioshymnen, *Hermes* 88 (1960) 139-158; S. E. HIJMANS, *Sol Invictus, een iconografische studie* (Diss. Groningen 1989); J. HUSKINSON, Some pagan mythological figures and their significance in early Christian art, *Papers of the British School at Rome* 42 (1974) 68-97; O. JESSEN, Helios, *PW* 8 (1912) 58-93; F.-N. KLEIN, *Die Lichtterminologie bei Philon von Alexandrien und in den Hermetischen Schriften* (Leiden 1962); C. LETTO, Helios/Sol, *LIMC* 4 (1988) 592-625 (icon.); H. P. L'ORANGE, Sol Invictus Imperator. Ein Beitrag zur Apotheose, *Symbolae Osloenses* 14 (1935) 86-114, repr. in *Likeness and Icon* (Odense 1973) 325-344; M. P. NILSSON, *Geschichte der griechischen Religion* II (München 1974[3]) 507-519; L. PRELLER, *Griechische Mythologie* I.2 (rev. ed. C. Robert; Berlin 1894[4]) 429-437; R. REBUFFAT, Les divinités du jour naissant sur la cuirasse d'Auguste de Prima Porta, *MEFR(A)* 73 (1961) 161-228; K. SCHAUENBURG, *Helios: archäologisch-mythologische Studien über den antiken Sonnengott* (Berlin 1955); H. SEYRIG, Antiquités syriennes 95: Le culte du soleil en Syrie à l'époque romaine, *Syria* 48 (1971) 337-373; N. YALOURIS, Helios, *LIMC* 5 (1990) 1005-1034 (icon.).

R. L. GORDON

HERA Ἥρα

I. The name *Hēra* (the form of her name in Mycenaean Greek is Era), perhaps a feminine form of the Greek noun *hērōs* ('hero', meaning 'master'), or *hōra* ('season', see Pausanias 2.13.3), was genealogically linked with other Greek deities as the daughter of Kronos and Rhea (Hesiod, *Theog.* 454), and sister of →Zeus. While the name Hera itself does not occur in either the Bible or the Apocrypha, nevertheless the theophoric name Herakles (→Heracles) does occur in 2 Macc 2:19-20. This name is composed of two elements, 'Hera' and '-kles'. Though the -a- is problematic, since theophoric names based on 'Hera' normally use an -o-, as in Herodotus and Herodikos, nevertheless it is certain that the goddess Hera is part of the etymology of the name Herakles. Some have conjectured that the morpheme *-kles* was derived from the Gk term *kleos*, 'fame', and proposed that Herakles means 'fame of Hera', or 'one who became famous because of Hera'. Yet while Hera is prominent in the Herakles cycles of myth, she is usually cast in the role of his antagonist. The name Herakles is simply a common personal name formed in a way analogous to names such as Diocles, Athenocles, and Hermocles. The names Herod (Ἡρῴδης) and Herodias, however, are connected to the Greek *hērōs.*

II. One of the more important early centres of Hera's cult was a sanctuary between Argos and Mycenae in the Peloponnesus, while another was on Samos, an island off the west coast of Asia Minor. A number of the earliest and larger temples erected in the Greek world were dedicated to Hera, usually outside cities, including the Temple of Hera on Samos (ca. 800 BCE), and two large temples in Paestum (Italy) built in the sixth and fifth centuries respectively. In Olympia, a temple was dedicated to Hera earlier than the famous sanctuary dedicated to Zeus. In Greek myth and religion, Hera played two important roles, one as the queen of the gods, also called "the mother of the gods" (Pausanias 2.4.7), who sits on a golden throne (Pausanias 2.17.4; 5.17.1), the only legitimate wife of Zeus. Her other major role was as the goddess primarily responsible for overseeing the institution of marriage (Aristophanes, *Thesm.* 973; Pausanias 3.13.9) and many other important and risky aspects of the life of women (Pausanias 8.22.2), particularly childbirth (Homer, *Iliad* 11.270-271; Hesiod, *Theog.* 921-922). However, Hera was never invoked as a →mother, and is never depicted as a mother with a child. The marriage of Zeus and Hera was understood as a sacred marriage (*hieros gamos* or *theogamia*) in many city-states of the Greek world, serving as a prototype for human marriage. The ritual reenactment of the sacred marriage of Zeus and Hera was also performed to ensure fertility. In Athens, the month Gamelion (meaning 'marriage month') was dedicated to Hera, and sacrifices were made to her and Zeus Heraios. On the twenty-sixth of Gamelion the anniversary of the sacred marriage of Zeus and Hera was celebrated.

III. *Bibliography*

W. BURKERT, *Greek Religion* (Cambridge MA 1985) 131-135; C. DOWNING, *The Goddess: Mythological Images of the Feminine* (New York 1981); W. K. C. GUTHRIE, *The Greeks and their Gods* (Boston 1950); K. KERÉNYI, *Zeus and Hera* (Princeton 1975); C. R. LONG, *The Twelve Gods of Greece and Rome* (Leiden 1987); M. P. NILSSON, *The Mycenaean Origin of Greek Mythology* (Berkeley 1932) 189-192; H. W. PARKE, *Festivals of the Athenians* (London 1977) 104-106; W. PÖTSCHER, Der Name des Herakles, *Emerita* 39 (1971) 169-184; P. E. SLATER, *The Glory of Hera: Greek Mythology and the Greek Family* (Boston 1968).

D. E. AUNE

HERACLES Ἡρακλῆς

I. Heracles was undoubtedly the most popular mythical hero of ancient Greek mythology; he was also one of the most complex. Etymologically the name derives from Ἥρα (Hera) and κλέος (fame). Though he is explicitly mentioned only in 2 Macc 2:19-20, there is evidence to suggest that Heracles traditions were incorporated into the cycle of Samson legends found in the Old Testament and in certain aspects of the depiction of →Jesus in the Christology of Hebrews.

II. Ancient mythographers divided the exploits of Heracles into three groups: (1) The Twelve Labours (*athloi* or *erga*), or canonical adventures (performed for Eurystheus in order to purify himself for killing his wife Megara and his children). These included the almost impossible task of conquering a number of nearly invulnerable beasts including the Nemean Lion (which provided his characteristic lionskin cloak), the Lernaean Hydra, the Erymanthian Boar, the Ceryneian Hind, the Stymphalian Birds, the Cretan Bull, the Thracian mares, the cattle of Geryon and Cerberus the hound of →Hades, as well as such impossible tasks as cleaning the stables of Augeas, getting the Amazon Hippolyta's girdle, and retrieving the apples of Hesperides; (2) the Subsidiary Activities (*parerga*) or noncanonical adventures, considered incidental to the Twelve Labours; and (3) the Deeds (*praxeis*), a variety of exploits including military-type expeditions during which Heracles conquered and civilized much of the world. These three categories of heroic adventures were framed by accounts of Heracles' miraculous birth and death and apotheosis. The birth of Heracles was extraordinary, as one might expect of a demi-god. →Zeus had sexual relations with the mortal Alcmene, disguised as her husband Amphitryon (Hesiod, *Shield of Heracles* 35-56). Twins were born, though Iphicles was the real son of Amphitryon, but Heracles the son of Zeus. →Hera (the patron of Eurystheus) tried to destroy Heracles by sending a serpent to kill him, but the infant strangled it (Pindar, *Nem.* 1.50-70). At the end of his life, mortally wounded by a poisoned garment, Heracles died on a funeral pyre on Mount Oeta and was apotheosized joining the immortal gods on →Olympus (Apollodoros 2.7.7). The cycle of Heracles myths reflected in these major categories (with the exception of his apotheosis) were already well known in Homer, and can be traced back to the Mycenaean period (1550-1150 BCE), for the two places most closely associated with Heracles were Thebes and Tiryns, important Mycenaean centres. Heracles differed from other Greek heroes in several respects: (1) Though the worship of heroes characteristically centered at their tombs where their physical remains were thought to be buried, no specific tomb was associated with Heracles. (2) Heracles was worshipped at some locations as a deceased hero, i.e. a chthonic deity apotheosized through death, and at others as an Olympian god. While some ancients suggested that these two forms of worship indicated that there were originally two different figures named Heracles (Herodotus 2.43-44; Cleanthes in *Stoicorum Veterum Fragmenta* 1.115-16, frag. 514; Diodorus 1.24.1-8; 5.76.1-2), others were able to reconcile the apparent contradiction by supposing that while the phantom (*eidôlon*) of Heracles resided in Hades, Heracles himself dwells with the immortal gods on Olympus (*Odyssey* 11.602-4; a later interpolation; Hesiod, *Theog.* 950-55; *Ehoeae* or *Catalogue of Women* frag. 25, lines 20-28). Arrian took this speculation a step further and proposed three different figures named Heracles: the son of Alcmene, the Tyrian Heracles and the Egyptian Heracles (*Anabasis Alexandri* 2.16; see Diodorus 3.74.4-5), while Varro proposed that forty-three different figures bore the name Heracles (Augustine *Civ. Dei* 18.12).

Archaeological evidence from Mesopotamia suggests that the figure of Heracles is found as early as the middle of the third millennium BCE (SCHWEITZER 1922:133-141; BURKERT 1979:80-83). In the representations on Akkadian cylinder seals, a hero probably named Ninurta (the son of Enlil the storm god), is shown conquering lions, bulls, snakes, and even a seven-headed snake (→Nimrod). In Sumerian representations a hero is fitted out, like the later Greek Heracles, with a club, bow and lion-skin. Heracles' quest for the apples of Hesperides is similar to the quest for immortality in the popular epic of Gilgamesh. The various traits of this superhuman helper which became part of the folklore of the archaic Greeks centered around the Heracles figure (the name emerged long after the patterns were set), not as a warrior but as a master of animals (BURKERT 1979:94-98). In many of the exploits of Heracles, he transfers the mastery of animals (particularly the dangerous one and the one difficult to obtain or conquer), to people.

According to the lexicon of the *interpretatio Graeca* which prevailed from the fifth century BCE on, Heracles was identified with →Melqart, whose name means "king of the city", and who was called the 'Baal of Tyre' (*CIS* I.122), a west Semitic god who was the primary deity of the Phoenician city of Tyre, and later of its major colony at Carthage (Herodotus 2.44; Arrian 2.24.5-6; 3.6.1; Curtius 4.2.10; Diodorus 5.20.2; Strabo 16.2.23). The Carthaginian triad of deities consisting of →Baal Shamen, →Astarte and Melqart became known through their Hellenistic counterparts of Zeus, Asteria and Heracles (Athenaeus, *Deipn.* 392d). The Samaritans worshipped Melqart as Zeus Xenios on Mount Gerizim (2 Macc 6:2). Both Greeks (as early as the sixth century BCE) and later the Romans identified Melqart with Heracles (2 Macc 4:18-20; Josephus, *Ant.* 8.146; *Contra Ap.* 1.118-19; Eusebius, *Praep. evang.* 1.10 [38a]), and depicted him wearing a lion skin. Menander of Ephesus, quoted in Josephus, *Ant.* 8.146 and *Contra Ap.* 1.118-19, mentions that Hiram king of Tyre built new temples in honour of Heracles and Astarte. These two figures are associated in a tradition perhaps of Samaritan origin in Epiphanius *Haer.* 55.2.1, to the effect that the father and mother of the Biblical →Melchizedek were Heracles and Astarte. In Palmyra, Heracles was identified with →Nergal, an underworld deity in Mesopotamian mythology, and is depicted with both club and lion's skin along with other items of a more explicitly chthonic nature (SEYRIG 1945; TEIXIDOR 1977:145-146).

III. Several variations of the Heracles-figure occur in Israelite and early Jewish sources. The legendary Old Testament figure Samson belongs to the Levantine Heracles tradition, and Samson continued to be connected to Heracles by Christians in late antiquity (Augustine, *Civ. Dei* 18.19), and in the frescoes of the Via Latina catacomb Samson is depicted as Heracles (SIMON 1955; MALHERBE 1988:581-583). The name Samson means 'man of the sun', a legendary ancient Israelite hero endowed with supernatural strength and who performed many fantastic feats which have parallels in cycles associated with such mythical heroes in Greece and Mesopotamia as Heracles, Ninurta and Gilgamesh. MARGALITH (1987) has argued that the figure of Samson is linked to a variety of heroic adventures from the late Bronze Age cycle of Heracles stories. Such scenes as Samson having his hair cut in the rooms of Delilah resembles Heracles at the court of Queen Omphale (the motif of magic hair is a Greek, not a Near Eastern mythical theme). Samson's slaying of a lion bare-handed (Judg 14:6, as Heracles killed the Nemean lion) to win the favour of a maiden is a common motif in Greek legend.

Heracles is explicitly mentioned in the lost writings of a Semitic (possibly Jewish) author named Kleodemus Malchos, possibly a resident of Carthage. A single fragment of his work is found in Josephus (*Ant.* 1.240-41; see Eusebius, *Praep. evang.* 9.20; Jerome, *Quaest. in Gen.* 25.1-6), in a quotation of Alexander Polyhistor. In an expanded interpretation of Gen 25:1-6, using a *interpretatio Iudaica,* Kleodemos claims that Japhras and Apheras, sons of →Abraham and Keturah, joined Heracles in a campaign against Libya and the Libyan →giant Antaios (an exploit narrated in Diodorus Siculus 4.17.4-5; Apollodorus 2.5.11), and that he later married Abraham's granddaughter.

The enormous popularity of Heracles was due to several factors. While the gulf between mortality and immortality was rarely bridged in Greek religious tradition, the fact that Heracles achieved immortality at the end of his life provided hope for ordinary people. Further, the life of Heracles became a paradigm for Stoics and Cynics for the positive value which could be placed on suffering. The similarities between some of the important themes associated with the life of Heracles and the historical →Jesus in Hebrews suggests that the author of Hebrews modelled Jesus at least in part on Heracles as a Hellenistic saviour figure. According to Heb 12:3-4, Jesus is held up as one who endured despite abuse, hostility and suffering and received a heavenly reward. In the Hellenistic world, Heracles was similarly held up as an example of endurance in suffering (Aristides, *Or.* 40.22; Dio Chrysostom, *Or.* 8.36; 9.8). One distinctive feature of Hebrews is that Jesus is presented as having undergone a process of education or *paideia* through which he learned obedience and ultimately attained perfection (Heb 2:10; 5:8-9; see 12:7). This correlation between suffering and training was associated with Heracles (Dio Chrysostom, *Or.* 4.29-32; Epictetus 3.22.56-57). According to Heb 4:14-16, Jesus is a great high priest who has "passed through the heavens" and can therefore understand our weaknesses since he has experienced temptation as have Christians who can pray boldly for grace to help in times of need. One important function of Heracles was as a helper and giver of strength in the difficulties of life. There are numerous examples of prayers and references to prayers to Heracles to help in the trials of life (Pindar, *Nem.* 7.94-97; Homeric *Hymn to Heracles* 9; Julian, *Or.* 7.220a; Dio Chrysostom, *Or.* 8.28). The obedience of Christ to the will of the Father is emphasized in Heb 5:8-9 and 10:5-10. The exemplary obedience of Heracles to the will of Zeus is frequently mentioned in ancient sources (Diodorus 4.11.1; Epictetus 2.16.44; 3.22.57; Menander Rhetor 2.380). These are some of the more significant ways in which popular conceptions of Heracles contributed toward the rather distinctive presentation of the image of Jesus found in Hebrews.

IV. *Bibliography*
D. E. AUNE, Herakles and Christ: Herakles Imagery in the Christology of Early Christianity, *Greeks, Romans and Christians: Essays in Honor of Abraham J. Malherbe* (Minneapolis 1990) 3-19; C. BONNET, *Melqart: cultes et mythes de l'Héraclès tyrien en Méditerranée* (Studia Phoenicia VIII; Leuven 1988); W. BURKERT, *Griechische Religion der archaischen und klassischen Epoche* (Stuttgart 1977) 319-324; BURKERT, *Structure and History in Greek Mythology and Ritual* (Berkeley 1979) 78-98; A. J. MALHERBE, Herakles, *RAC* 14 (1988) 559-583; O. MARGALITH, Samson's Riddle and Samson's Magic Locks, *VT* 36 (1986) 225-234; MARGALITH, More Samson Legends, *VT* 36 (1986) 397-405; MARGALITH, The Legends of Samson/Heracles, *VT* 37 (1987) 63-70; M. P. NILSSON, *The Mycenaean Origin of Greek Mythology* (Berkeley 1932) 187-220; F. PFISTER, Herakles und Christus, *ARW* 34 (1937) 42-60; H. J. ROSE, Heracles and the Gospels, *HTR* 31 (1938) 113-142; B. SCHWEITZER, *Herakles* (Tübingen 1922); H. SEYRIG, Heracles-Nergal, *Syria* 24 (1945) 62-80; M. SIMON, *Hercule et le Christianisme* (Paris 1955); J. TEIXIDOR, *The Pagan God: Popular Religion in the Greco-Roman Near East* (Princeton 1977); A. VERBANCK-PIERARD, Le double culte d'Héraclès: légende ou réalité? *Entre hommes et dieux* (ed. A.-F. Laurens; Paris 1989) 43-65.

D. E. AUNE

HEREM → TABOO

HERMES Ἑρμῆς

I. Hermes was one of the most popular and frequently represented, if most complex, of the Greek Olympian deities. Identified by the Romans with Mercury, he was associated from the archaic through the Hellenistic periods with cunning and theft, music and eloquence, travel and commerce, and (especially as the Hellenistic Hermes Trismegistus) magic, alchemy and astrology. In the Bible, Hermes occurs as a divine name in Acts 14:12, and as the name of an otherwise unknown Roman Christian greeted by Paul in Rom 16:14.

II. The name, Hermes, is attested from three palace archives of the Late Bronze Age: Knossos, Pylos, and Thebes (SIEBERT 1990:285-286). The nature of the Greek Hermes is neither Minoan nor Mycenaean, however, but is associated with the *hermae*, ithyphallic stone pillars capped with a head or bust of Hermes that were employed throughout Greece as topographic markers. The oldest form by which Hermes was represented (Herodotus 2.51; Dio Chrysostom 78.19; Pausanias 1.24.3, 4.33.3), these ubiquitous herms stood upon the thresholds of private homes and estates, at the gateways of towns and cities, before temples and gymnasia, along the side of roadways and at crossroads, at the frontiers of territories and upon tombs, the portal between this and the underworld, to mark the boundaries of inhabited space and to protect its productive areas against incursions.

In Homeric myth, in which the character of Hermes is already fully developed, he is the son of →Zeus and the Arcadian nymph Maia (the daughter of Atlas), and the younger half-brother, therefore, of →Apollo (Homer, *Od.* 14.435; Hesiod, *Th.* 938; *H. Merc.* 1-4; Pindar, *Ol.* 6.80). Even as an infant, Hermes' *kratos*, 'strength' or 'might', is compared to that of his older brother (*H. Merc.* 406-407), and, emphasized by the Homeric tradition, becomes one of Hermes' epithets (*Il.* 16.181, 24.345; *Od.* 5.49; see also *H. Merc.* 101, 117; *H. Cer.* 346, 377).

On the evening of the day of his birth, Hermes stole fifty head of cattle from Apollo's sacred herd (*H. Merc.* 18-19, 68-74) to ensure, as one of the younger of the Olympian deities, that he might be honoured in the same way as Apollo and the other Olympians (*H. Merc.* 173) by instituting the equitable practise of sacrifice (*H. Merc.* 115-137; see *Od.* 14. 418-436). As 'lord of the animals', both domestic and wild (*H. Merc.* 564-571), Hermes is frequently represented in art as the *Kriophoros*, the 'ram-bearer' or 'good shepherd' (Pausanias 4.33.5, 5.27.5.

9.22.1), caring for and guarding his flocks against predators; because domesticated animals are not only required for all sacrifice, but are the basis of the 'riches and wealth' of the pastoral economy of ancient Greece over which Hermes, as 'keeper of the herd' (*H. Merc.* 488) and their increase, presides (Hesiod, *Th.* 444; Homer, *Il.* 14. 490-491; *H. Merc.* 491-494, 529; Pausanias 2.3.4). It is not surprising that some considered the Arcadian shepherd-god, Pan, to be Hermes' son (*H. Pan.* 1, 27-41), and the two are often invoked together (Aristophanes, *Th.* 977).

Wherever livestock represent the principal form of wealth, cattle-theft will be frequent (Homer, *Il.* 11.677-681; Hesiod, *Op.* 348; *Th.* 1.5.3), and Hermes is described as the very 'prince of thieves' (*H. Merc.* 175, 292), a 'thief at the gate' (*H. Merc.* 15), a cunning and crafty "watcher by night" (*H. Merc.* 15) and the ally of nocturnal activity (*H. Merc.* 97, 290). Throughout the night, the wily Hermes hastily drove his purloined cattle "through many shadowy mountains and echoing gorges and flowery plains" (*H. Merc.* 94-97), having them walk backwards so that their hoofprints gave an appearance of their joining Apollo's main herd rather than being stolen away. Walking normally himself, he relied on newly fabricated sandals to disguise the tracks of his own 'swift feet' (*H. Merc.* 75-86; 225). Hermes' extraordinary mobility, even as an infant, is thus emphasized by Homer who elsewhere portrays the divine traveler as flying "over the waters of the sea and over the boundless land", borne by immortal, golden sandals (*Od.* 5.44-46; *Il.* 24.340-342; see also *H. Cer.* 407; *H. Pan.* 29; Horace, *Carm.* 2.7.13; *Orph. Hymn* 28.4), an image that anticipates the common representation of Hermes (and his Roman counterpart Mercury) as having winged shoes or sandals (e.g., Philo, *Quod Omn. Prob.* 99; *PGM* 5.404, 7.672, 17b.5).

As quick of mind as swift of foot, the clever and cunning →shepherd provided an image for success not only for a pastoral economy, but also for cultural agonistics and urban commerce. Apollo's anger at the theft of his cattle had been assuaged by Hermes' singing to the accompaniment of the lyre which Hermes had invented on the day of his birth even before the cattle-theft (*H. Merc.* 17, 39-61), and which Apollo accepted as a payment that he conceded was worth the fifty cattle (*H. Merc.* 437-438). The association of the lyrical competition between Hermes and Apollo (Pausanias 9.30.1) was celebrated at the Pythian games from their beginnings where contests of musical performance were honoured alongside athletic prowess (Pindar, *Pyth.* 12). Established later at the Nemean and Isthmian games, music became part of Greek classical education in which proper styles of music were held to contribute to courage (Plato, *Resp.* 398C-399D; *Leg.* 653D-673A; 795A-812E) and to ethics (Aristotle, *Pol.* 1339A-1342B). The herm or statue of this 'leader of men' (Pausanias 8.31.7) came to stand, therefore, before the entrance to stadiums (Pausanias 1.17.2; 5.14.9; 8.32.3; 8.39.6), where he was honoured as the god of gymnastics and agonistics (Pindar, *Ol.* 6.79, *Pyth.* 2.10, *Isthm.* 1.60; Pausanias 1.2.5, 5.14.9; Horace, *Carm.* 1.10.3; Ovid, *Fast.* 5.667; Aristides, *Or.* 37.21, 26.105).

Plato intellectualized Hermes' creative talents as having to do with speech (*logos*): "he is an interpreter (*hermēneus*), and a messenger (*angelos* [Homer, *Od.* 5.29; *H. Cer.* 407; *H. Pan.* 29; see Philo, *Quod Omn. Prob.* 99]), wily and deceptive in speech, and is oratorical. All this activity is concerned with the power of speech" (Plato, *Crat.* 407E-408A; see *Phdr.* 264C). This abstracted and rationalized view of Hermes was continued by the philosophical tradition (Cornutus 16; Porphyry in Eusebius, *PE.* 3.114; Aristides, *Or.* 37.21) as well as in popular perception (*PGM* 5.403, 407; 7.670; 17b.3). As a figure of the word (*logos*), Hermes was reportedly equated with the →Saviour by the Naassenes, an early Christian-Gnostic group (Hippolytus, *Ref.* 5.2). As his associations with the lyre and music, together with poetry and oratory were one, the divine composer and poet became the deity of littérateurs, called by Horace "*Mercuriales viri*" (*Carm.* 2,17.29-30).

As the deity chartered by Zeus himself to preside over trade (*H. Merc.* 516-517), Hermes was invoked further as the "Hermes of the Market" (Pausanias 1.15.1, 2.9.8, 3.11.11, 7.22.2, 9.17.2), and deity of Merchandise and Sales (Aristides, *Or.* 37.21). Diodorus Siculus reports that Hermes invented "measures and weights and profits to be gained through merchandizing, and how also to appropriate the property of others all unbeknown to them" (5.75.2), an association between commerce and theft already explicit in the *Homeric Hymn* (*H. Merc.* 514-517). And, the Greek Magical Papyri preserve a spell in which a figure of Hermes, the "finder of thieves" (*PGM* 5.188), was used to promote good business (*PGM* 4.2359-2379). Even today, in parts of modern Greece, theft is equated with courage, ingenuity and entrepreneurship, an ethos of cunning deception that is still considered primarily a sporting contest in which a challenge with respect to status is communicated (STEWART 1991:73, 62).

As a good thief is clearly a brave and clever man, there is a correlation between good thieving and good marriage (STEWART 1991:69-73), a relationship that suggests the ancient association between Hermes and Hestia, goddess of the hearth. Although Plutarch reports that the ancients associated Hermes with →Aphrodite (*Coniug. praec.* 138D) with whom he fathered Hermaphroditus (Ovid, *Met.* 4.288-293), he was more often paired 'in friendship' with Hestia, first-born of Rhea and Kronos, in both literature (*H. Vest.* [29]) and in representation (Pausanias 5.11.8). Whereas Hestia represents the spatial principle of stability around a fixed centre of home or village that is inhabited and known, Hermes is the personification of the ambiguities and uncertainties of encounters with social others in a variegated external world of travel, trade and commerce that, while unpredictable, must necessarily be traversed (VERNANT 1983); it is in the *Homeric Hymn to Hermes* that the proverb is preserved: "It is better to be at home: harm may come out of doors" (*H. Merc.* 36-37).

Hestia's hearth is round whereas the herm is square (Thucydides 6.27), and Hermes is known as the *tetragōnos* (Heraclititus, *All.* 72.6; Pausanias 4.33.4; Babrius 48); in the *Greek Magical Papyri*, Hermes, as 'square', is contrasted with the circle (*PGM* 5.402, 8.670, 17b.3); and he was born on the fourth day of the month (*H. Merc.* 19; Aristophanes, *Pl.* 1126). The number four is, according to Plutarch, "particularly associated with Hermes" (*Q. Conviv.* 9.2). He surveys, in other words, the cardinal points of the terrestrial world (KERÉNYI 1986:67-68; VERNANT 1983:147), in addition to the chthonic world in which his herm is so firmly planted (Cicero, *Leg.* 2.26.65; Horace, *Sat.* 1.8; see *PGM* 4. 1444, 1464) and whose portals he guards (Aeschylus, *Ch.* 1, 620; *Pers.* 628-632; Sophocles, *El.* 110-111). As such, Hermes is the deity 'most friendly' to mortals (*Il.* 24.334-335; *Orph. Hymn* 28.4, 9), lending 'grace and glory to all [their] work' (*Od.* 15.319-320) as he guides them along the road of life (*Od.* 15.319; *Il.* 24.153, 182, 437-439, 461, 681; Aeschylus, *Eum.* 89-92), during the dark night also when, as the deity of sleep (Homer, *Il.* 24.343-344; *Od.* 5.47-48, 24.3-4), Hermes is the 'conductor of dreams' (*H. Merc.* 14). In perhaps his most well-known role, that of *psychopompos*, he continues his tutelage until the dangerous frontier of death is finally passed (*Il.* 24.334-338; *Od.* 24.1-18; Diodorus Sic. 1.96; Plutarch, *Amator.* 758B; and in iconography) —a frequent theme of the tragedians (e.g., Aeschylus, *Ch.* 124-126; Sophocles, *Aj.* 832, *OC.* 1540-1548; Euripides, *Alc.* 743-744) that was adopted by the Pythagoreans (Diogenes Laertius 8.1.31). It is in this comprehensive sense of the protective guide of humans in their quotidian activities that Hermes is *euangelos*, the 'bringer of glad tidings' (*IG* 12.5.235 [1st century BCE]; Hesychius *s.v.*), and implementer of Zeus' will, or that of the celestial Olympians collectively, among the inhabited world (*Il.* 24.169, 173; *Od.* 1.38, 84-86; 5.29; *H. Cer.* 407-408; *H. Pan.* 28-29; *H. Vest.* 8). In the summary of Plato, Hermes was dispatched by Zeus "to bring respect for others and justice among men, to the end that there might be order in the cities and a bond of friendship among them" (Plato, *Prot.* 322C). Thus was Hermes viewed as the divine figure in accordance with whom humans might discover their rightful place in the socio-political world, even as the ancient herms provided the markers for organizing their world topographically.

As 'Lord of the World' (*PGM* 5.400, 7.668, 17b.1), of its order and its Elements (*PGM* 17B.16-19), Hermes came to be associated with the central Hellenistic notion of →Tyche/→Fortuna, 'luck' or 'fortune' (*PGM* 8.52). Roman coins of the Imperial period depict Fortuna carrying the typical *caduceus* of Hermes (RIC 2, p. 16, no. 11 [69-71 CE]). The Greek word *hermaion*, 'gift of Hermes', has the sense of an unexpected, i.e., godsent, piece of luck, and one of Hermes' epithets is *Kerdōos*, 'the gainful' (Lucian, *Tim.* 41; Alciphron 3.47; see Plutarch, *De Tranq. An.* 12). In the Greek Magical Papyri, Hermes is equated with the 'thread of the *Moirai*', 'the fates' (*PGM* 7.675-676, 17b. 11). A third century BCE inscription identifies Hermes with *tychōn* (*Inschr. Magn.* 203; compare Clement of Alexandria, *Protr.* 10.81 and Hesych. in Theognost, *Can.* 33), who apparently was personified as a minor god of chance even as was *tychē* as the goddess (*LS*[7]). Related to the phallic character of the herms, Tychon was originally a priapic deity (Diodorus Sic. 4.6; Strabo 588) who may have originated in Cyprus (H. USENER, *Der heilige Tychon* [Leipzig/Berlin 1907]). The name, which carries a general sense of *tychē* or luck for its bearer (*ALGRM* 5: 1386), may have preserved this attribute of Hermes as a Christian homonym in the hagiography of St. Tychon, a fifth-century bishop of Amathus in Cyprus, (A. B. COOK, *Zeus. A Study in Ancient Religion* [Cambridge 1914-1940] I: 175-176, in addition, see II.1: 675; and II.2: 878 n. 11, 879 n. 17 and 1163 re: Zeus; K. PREISENDANZ, Tychon, *ALGRM* 5: 1381-1387).

Although one of the most well-known and often-mentioned deities of the Greco-Roman world, few temples were dedicated to Hermes and few festivals celebrated in his name, and these were predominantly in Arcadia, the likely region of his historical origins (*H. Merc.* 1-2; 18.1-2). Pausanias refers to a festival of Hermes in Tanagra in which a boy carries a lamb around the walls of the city on his shoulders in imitation of Hermes who allegedly had averted a plague by this same apotropaic practice (9.22.2); Athenaeus writes of the *Hermaia*, a Cretan festival characterized by the reversal of social roles (639B). Although he had been given a technique of divination by Apollo (*H. Merc.* 550-568), Hermes had little to do with such activity apart from a minor oracle at Pharae (Pausanias 7.22.2-3).

A late Hellenistic (second-fourth centuries CE) anthology of philosophico-religious writings, including also magical, alchemical and astrological texts, was collected under the name of Hermes Trismegistus or 'Hermes the thrice-great', the Hellenistic name for the Egyptian deity →Thoth (*PGM.* 4.886, 7.551-557), one of the most diverse and popular of the Egyptian deities. Survivals of a more extensive literature (see now, for example, Codex VI 6 from the Nag Hammadi library), the sometimes contradictory teachings of this *Corpus Hermeticum* have little in common but their claim to this common revelatory deity. And some have argued that Thoth, sometimes euhemerized in the Hermetic literature as an Egyptian sage, shares little or nothing with the Greek Hermes but his name. However, Thoth had already been identified with the Greek Hermes in the fifth century BCE by Herodotus (2.67, 2.138; see thereafter Diodorus Sic. 1.16, 5.75; Strabo 104, 816; Plutarch, *Q. Conviv.* 9.3, *Is. et Os.* 3, *De Gerr.* 2; Cicero, *De Nat. Deor.* 3.22.56; Horace, *Carm.* 1.10.3; Ovid, *Fasti* 5.668). Another tradition, attributed to the third century BCE Egyptian priest, Manetho, reports that the 'second Hermes', i.e., Hermes Trismegistus, had received his teachings from 'Thoth, the first Hermes' (Ps.-Manetho; Appendix I, *Manetho*, ed. W. G. WADDELL [Cambridge, Mass. 1964] 208-211).

Like the Greek Hermes, the Egyptian Thoth was a guide of souls who conducted the dead to the underworld, an inventive trickster and the messenger of the gods, the inventor of writing (see Pliny, *HN* 7.191) and the lord of wisdom (FOWDEN 1986:22-23; COPENHAVER 1992:xiii-xlv). Thoth's association with wisdom may be alluded to in the Bible in Job 38:36: "who has put wisdom into *ṭḥwt*" The Hebrew word *ṭḥwt*, otherwise unknown, corresponds closely to the consonantal orthography of the Egyptian form of 'Thoth' during the 18th Dynasty when the deity's popularity had spread to Phoenicia (M. POPE, *Job*, 3rd. ed. [Garden City 1973] 302). Further, Thoth was the god of language, magic, medicine, the heavenly bodies and their influence on individual destiny (FOWDEN 1986:22-23). Hermes had been associated specifically with language since Plato (see above), as had been Thoth (*Phdr.* 274D; *Phlb.* 18B); and with magic, or 'wonderous deeds', since Homer. The sandals which Hermes fabricated to help his escape with Apollo's cattle, for example, are described as "wonderful things, unthought of, unimagined" (*H. Merc.* 80-81). Further, Hermes is described as possessing a golden staff or wand (*rhabdos*) which, similar to Circe's own magic wand (Homer, *Od.* 10. 238, 319), enabled him to overpower human senses (Homer, *Il.* 24.343). Hermes' *rhabdos* is described as the gift of Apollo: "gold, with three branches...accomplishing every task, whether of words or deeds that are good, which [Apollo] claim[s] to know through the utterance of Zeus" (*H. Merc.* 529-532). *Chrysorrhapis*, 'of the golden wand' is, in fact, also one of Hermes' epithets (Homer, *Od.* 5.87, 10.277; *H. Merc.* 539). According to the *Odyssey*, Hermes showed Odysseus the uses of the herb 'Moly' (10.302-306), a *pharmakon* that protected him against Circe's own alchemical *pharmakon* (*Od.* 10.287-292). And, in the Hellenistic period, he was known as the 'inventor of drugs' (*PGM* 8.27) and one of the founders of the Hellenistic alchemical tradition (Zosimos, *On the Letter Omega* 5). Some considered Hermes also to be the inventor of astrology (Hyginus, *Poet. Astr.* 2.42.5) and the Christian-Gnostic Peratai cited Hermes Trismegistus in their astrological speculations (Hippolytus, *Ref.* 5.9). R. REITZENSTEIN has suggested that these Hermetic texts may constitute '*Lese-Mysterien*', 'literary mysteries', in which a reader experiences the effects of actual cultic initiation imaginatively (*Hellenistic Mystery-Religions* [1926], Eng. trans. J. E. Steely [Pittsburgh 1978] 51-52, 62). Whatever their social and cultic origins, one of the most interesting characteristics of these texts, the production of which was contemporary with those of the New Testament, is the influence of the Old Testament and intertestamental traditions upon both (DODD 1964).

III. The Greek Hermes played a continuing role in the religious environment of early Christianity (see e.g., Philo, *Decal.* 54; *Quod Omn. Prob.* 101; *Leg.* 93-102), as evinced by the recurring polemics of the Church Fathers against him (e.g., Justin, *1 Apol.* 21-22; Hippolytus, *Ref.* 5.2; Clement of Alex., *Protr.* 2.24, 4.44, 10.81; Origen, *C.Cels.* 1.25, 6.78; Lactantius, *Inst.* 1.10.7); and he is one of the few Greco-Roman deities mentioned in the New Testament by name. When Barnabas and Paul fled the hostile mobs that confronted them in Iconium, they went first to the city of Lystra in Lycaonia (Acts 14:5-6), a Roman colony established by Augustus as part of the defence of the Province Galatia, where, upon the healing of "a man cripple from birth" by Paul (Acts 14:8-10; compare the similar account in Acts 3:2-8 of a healing by Peter), the crowds acclaimed the apostles as "gods come down to us in the likeness of men". Whereas Paul was reputedly taken for a deity also by the inhabitants of Malta following his survival of a poisonous snake bite (Acts 28:6—in this case, however, a healing follows the acclamation), the deities with whom the apostles were identified in Lycaonia were specifically named by the Lystrans: "Barnabas they called Zeus, and Paul they called Hermes" (Acts 14:11-12). The two apostles were identified with deities by the Lystrans because of Paul's wonderous cure of the cripple (Acts 14:11), but Paul was identified specifically with Hermes "because he was the chief speaker" (*ho hēgoumenos tou logou*)—almost precisely the characterization of Hermes by the third-century neo-Platonist, Iamblichus, as the god "who is the leader in speaking" (Iamblichus, *Myst.* 1.1: *ho tōn logōn hēgemōn*). Inscriptions and statues associating these two deities are documented from this region, but only from the third century CE (H. SWOBODA, J. KEIL & F. KNOLL (eds.), *Denkmäler aus Lykaonien, Pamphylien und Isaurien* [Brno/Leipzig/Vienna 1935] no. 146). At the beginning of the first century, however, Ovid had told a story, set in nearby Phrygia, in which Jupiter (Zeus) and Mercury (Hermes) also appear together disguised as mortals (*Met.* 8.611-725).

The narrative point of the identification of Barnabas and Paul with Zeus and Hermes by the Lystrians and the dramatic rejection of this identification by the apostles (Acts 14:14) seems to be the establishment of a sharp contrast, in the context of the Lycaonian mission, between gentile deities and the Christians' "living God" (Acts 14:15), on the one hand, even as a distinction between the "unbelieving Jews" and the Christians is made in the previous and following passages (Acts 14:1-7, 19-23), on the other. Additionally, the warrant of Hermes and Zeus had been associated, since Plato, with the veracity of ambassadors and messengers (*Leg.* 941A; Diodorus Sic. 5.75.1; see Philo, *Quod Omn. Prob.* 99). Thus, the author of Acts is also indicating the legitimacy of the Christian foreign mission in the narrative context of Paul's and Barnabas' first entirely non-Jewish audience.

'Hermes' also appears in the New Testament as a personal name in the list of those to whom Paul sends greetings in Rome (Rom 16:14). Hermes was the most common theophoric name in the Roman empire, including Greece (J. BAUMGART, *Die römischen Sklavennamen* [diss. Breslau 1936] 47); even as Hermes was "essentially a god of simple people" (GUTHRIE 1955:91), his name was borne mostly by humble people and especially by gladiators (see, e.g., Martial 5.24 and the analysis by VERSNEL 1990:206-251). Theophoric names ideally indicated an alliance with the deities from whom they were taken and something of their 'power and honour' (Plutarch, *Def. Orac.* 421E); but despite the account in Acts of Barnabas' and Paul's rejection of any association with Zeus and Hermes, the elimination of pagan theophoric names was not so early and thorough as might have been expected. The frequency of the name Hermes in Christian circles, especially as a martyr-name, is a case in point (I. KAJANTO, *Onomastic Studies in the Early Christian Inscriptions of Rome and Carthage* [Helsinki 1963] 87, 97). Although nothing more is known with any certainty about the Hermes of Rome greeted by Paul, he was, according to Eastern (Greek) liturgical tradition, one of the 'seventy' disciples of Jesus (Lk 10:1) who succeeded Titus as Bishop of Dalmatia to become Bishop of Salona (Spalato) in Dalmatia before suffering martyrdom (the *Menaion* and the *Menologion* for November 4; see also the sixth-century Pseudo-Dorotheus and Pseudo-Hippolytus).

IV. *Bibliography*

W. BURKERT, *Greek Religion* (Cambridge, Mass. 1985) 156-159, 283-284; B. P. COPENHAVER, *Hermetica: the Greek Corpus Hermeticum and the Latin Asclepius in a new English translation, with notes and introduction* (Cambridge 1992); C. H. DODD, *The Bible and the Greeks* (London 1964); S. EITREM, L. BÜRCHNER & A. STEIN, Hermes, *PW* 8 (1913) 738-792 ; L. R. FARNELL, *The Cults of the Greek States*, vol. 5 (Oxford 1909) 1-31; B. C. FARNOUX, Mercure romain, les 'Mercuriales' et l'institution du culte impérial sous le Principat augustéen, *ANRW* II 17, 1 (1981) 457-501; W. FAUTH, Hermes, *KP* 2 (1967) 1069-1076; G. FOWDEN, *The Egyptian Hermes. A Historical Approach to the Late Pagan Mind* (Cambridge 1986) [& lit]; W. K. C. GUTHRIE, *The Greeks and their Gods* (Boston 1955) 87-94; K. KERÉNYI, *Hermes der Seelenführer* (Zürich 1944); Eng. trans., M. Stein (Dallas 1986); M. P. NILSSON,

Geschichte der griechischen Religion, 2 vols. (München 1955-1961) 1:501-510; W. F. OTTO, *The Homeric Gods*, trans. Moses Hadas (Boston 1964) 104-124; W. H. ROSCHER, W. DREXLER & C. SCHERER, Hermes, *ALGRM* 1, 2 (1886-1890) 2342-2432; *G. SIEBERT, Hermes, *LIMC* 5, 1 (1990) 285-387 [& lit]; C. STEWART, *Demons and the Devil* (Princeton 1991); P. STOCKMEIER, Hermes, *RAC* 14 (1988) 772-780; J. P. VERMANT, Hestia-Hermès: Sur l'expression religieuse de l'espace et du mouvement chez les Grecs, *Mythe et pensée chez les Grecs*, 3d ed. (Paris 1971), I:124-170; Eng. trans. (London 1983) 127-175; H. S. VERSNEL, *Ter Unus. Isis, Dionysus, Hermes. Three Studies in Henotheism* (Leiden 1990) 213-251; F. J. M. DE WAELE, *The Magic Staff or Rod in Greco-Italian Antiquity* (The Hague 1927).

L. H. MARTIN

HERMON חרמן

I. Mount Hermon is mentioned several times in the Hebrew Bible (e.g. Deut 3:8; Josh 11:3.17). The prominent mountain at the west-end of →Lebanon and Anti-Lebanon rises to a height of 2.814 m above sea-level. Its modern name is *Jebel eš-Šeḫ* "Mountain of the Hoar" or *Jebel et-talǧ* "Mountain of Snow", both designations pointing to the long-lasting snow-cap on its summit. The etymology of Hermon (heb *ḥermōn)* is disputed: a) The root ḤRM I Niph. means "to be split", cf. Ar *ḥarama* "perforate". This may describe the situation of the mountain massif separated from the Lebanon. b) ḤRM II Hiph./Hoph. only, means "consecrate (to annihilation)" and belongs to the same word-field as Ar *ḥaram*, the "consecrated, separated district" and may refer to the exalted position of the mountain and his holiness, too. The ending *-ōn* may be used in analogy to *lĕbānôn* as an denominative adjective. As an imposing mountain, Hermon has been endowed with divine traits in West Semitic traditions.

II. In early times the name of the Hermon is not known in extra-biblical sources, but according to Deut 3:9 "the Sidonians call him →Sirion, the Amorites Senir". This last designation, used also in Egyptian (*snr* Ramses III, see J. SIMONS, *Handbook for the Study of Egyptian Topographical Lists Relating to Western Asia* (Leiden 1937) list XXVII 117, ś-n-n-r) and the OT in Ezek 27:5; Cant 4:8; 1 Chr 5:23, is in the Assyrian annals of Shalmaneser III reported as the refugee of king Hazael of Damascus (kur*sa-ni-ru, WO* 1 [1947/1952] 265:6; 2 [1954/1959] 38:49; *Iraq* 24 [1962] 94:22). Later on the Assyrians in the time of Sennacherib, Esarhaddon and Ashurbanipal used the name kur*si-ra-ra* (references in S. PARPOLA, *Neo-Assyrian Toponyms* [AOAT 6; Kevelaer/Neukirchen-Vluyn 1970] 312) with the additional information that cedar-beams had been cut there. It is probable that not Hermon alone but the whole Anti-Lebanon is meant in this context. Therefore in a *lipšur*-litany (used as an incantation for purification) the kur*si-ra-ra (*Var.[*si-r*]*a-a)* besides the Lebanon is invoked.

According to the OT Hermon is inhabited by Hiwites (Josh 12:5; Judg 3:3), belongs to →Og from →Bashan (Josh 12:5) and forms, as the region belonging to the tribe of Manasseh, the northern frontier of the Eastern-Jordan country (Josh 11:17; Deut 3:8). These—historically incorrect—attributions show the significance of the landmark of this holy mountain, where →Baal Hermon (Judg 3:3; 1 Chr 5:23) was venerated. Therefore in Ps 89:13 Hermon and Mount →Tabor "sing forth Your (Yahweh's) name". Nevertheless no Iron Age sanctuary has yet been found on Hermon or in its surrounding valleys.

III. In Hellenistic-Roman times Hermon belonged to the kingdom of the Ituraeans. The ruins of various little temples of Hellenistic type may point to places where Ituraean cults were performed. At the top of the mountain at Qasr ʿAntar a sanctuary with an oval *temenos* has been identified (C. WARREN, *PEFQS* 1 [1869/1870] 210-215) and an inscription is dedicated *tou theou megistou k(ai) hagiou,* "to the greatest and holy god". He is adored by people who swore in his name. This brings to mind the tale in *1 Enoch* 6:4-6 about the 200 →angels who met on the top of Hermon, swearing an oath there before they came down to impregnate human wives. Another inscription from Qal'at Gandal, dated 282 CE, mentions a priest of "Zeus megistos", the Greek designation of the Baal Hermon. At the foot of the mountain another sanctuary has been identified with the cult of *Leukothea*, probable a local representation of →Astarte (*OGIS* 611). Not far from there a little sanctuary has been found at Senaim with an altar showing the relief of →*Helios*, so this sun-god may also have been venerated at Hermon. Bearing this in mind it is not surprising to hear that Eusebius in his *Onomasticon* (ed. Klostermann, Vol.III/1 [1904] 20) *sub Aermon* testifies that Hermon was still venerated as a holy mountain in his day.

IV. *Bibliography*

S. APPLEBAUM (ed.), *The Hermon and Its Foothills* (Tel Aviv 1978); C. CLERMONT-GANNEAU, Le Mont Hermon et son dieu d'après une inscription inédite, *Recueil d'archéologie orientale* 5 (1903) 346-366; S. DAR, The History of the Hermon Settlements, *PEQ* 120 (1988) 26-44; R. DUSSAUD, *Topographie historique de la Syrie antique et médiévale* (Paris 1927) 389-395; Y. IKEDA, Hermon, Sirion and Senir, *Annual of the Japanese Biblical Institute* 4 (1978) 32-44; E. LIPIŃSKI, El's Abode *OLP* 2 (1971) 13-69; P. MOUTERDE, Cultes antiques de la Coelésyrie et de l'Hermon, *MUSJ* 36 (1959) 51-87; A. DE NICOLA, L'Hermon, monte sacro, *BeO* 15 (1973) 239-251.

W. RÖLLIG

HEROS ἥρως

I. Heros (ἥρως) is a word of uncertain etymology, perhaps related to the name →Hera (Augustine, *CD* 10,2; ADAMS 1987). It has two main semantic fields: in Greek myth and epos, a heros is a human warrior of the heroic age; in religion, he is a (real or fictitious) dead person who remained powerful also in death, and who therefore received cult. Religious theorists defined heroes as intermediate beings between man and →god (ἡμίθεοι, half-gods). In the Bible Heros occurs only in the toponym 'City of the Heroes', which is the LXX rendering for Goshen in Gen 46:28-29.

II. Greek religion counted a theoretically limitless number of heroes who range from godlike figures like →Herakles to ordinary dead humans. Evolutionary historians of religion tried to categorize them along two main lines of development (BRELICH 1958:11-16): a Euhemeristic model understood all heroes as former mortals who had become objects of cult, and a rival theory defined them as decayed gods; combinations were tried as well (FARNELL 1921; BURKERT 1977:314).

In the course of Greek religious history, the concept of heros underwent some changes. It is uncertain whether heroes existed already in Mycenaean religion; the Linear B tablets seem to attest offerings to Trisheros (*Tiriseroe* in Pylos, GÉRARD-ROUSSEAU 1968:222-224). In the hexametrical poetry of the early archaic age (Homer and Hesiod), the *hērōes* were the human warriors of an earlier age: they had fought the wars of Thebes and Troy, they were sung in the epos, and they partly continued their existence on the Islands of the Blessed (Hesiod, *Erga* 156-173). Together with the rise of the *polis* in the 8th century BCE, many formerly unattended Mycenaean tombs began to receive cult as the presumed graves of heroes known through the epos, especially local ancestors, like Menelaus in Sparta or Agamemnon in Mycenae; often, their cult place was transferred onto the agora—they had become symbols of political identity (WHITLEY 1988; CALLIGAS 1988). Greek colonization introduced the cult of the founder hero (*oikistēs*), usually on the *agora* of the colony; it became one of the main cultic tokens for the colony's political identity. Hero cult continued this function; when political circumstances changed, a hero could be replaced by another one (e.g. Sikyon, 6th century BCE: Herodotus 5,67: Amphipolis, 422 BCE: Thucydides 5,11).

To the Greeks, heroes always were historical beings, often ancestors, despite their frequent origin from myth and epic. This opened up the possibility of heroization of deceased historical persons, even contemporaries. But at least in the archaic and classical ages, heroization always resulted from a particular status during life, or from an unusual death. Founding heroes (who could be purely mythical, like the Neleid founders of Ionian cities) and warriors had performed special deeds during their life; warriors still fitted into the epic definition of heroes. In other cases, symbolic value and future protection seem more important, as with the heroes of Kleisthenes' newly founded ten tribes (KRON 1976).

A second wave of heroic cults is attested in the 4th century BCE. It resulted from the new need for Greek self-definition best attested by Isocrates which lead to the restoration and intensification of traditional hero cults (ALCOCK 1991). During the Hellenistic age, ordinary humans, whose heroization had began in extraordinary cases during the archaic and classical age, were more and more honoured with heroic cult; only in very rare cases, was this honour extended to living contemporaries. Though modern interpreters tend to emphasize the indiscriminate use of the title *hērōs* which would made it virtually synonymous for "dead", the evidence proves that on the contrary *hērōes* still were humans whose life or death was in some way outstanding (GRAF 1985:123-137). Prominent among the new heroes are (1) the *ahōroi* (those who died young) and (2) the *euergetai*, the benefactors; both often received tomb and cult not among the ordinary dead outside the city walls, but inside the *polis* in the *gymnasium* or on the *agora*.

A hero makes himself felt by showing superhuman power after death—he is at least expected or dreaded to do so; this holds true for traditional heroes and for more recent ones. The epic heroes promoted to national powers are protectors of their polis; in order to increase such protection, a community could introduce a new heroic cult or reinforce an existing one like the Spartan cult of Orestes, whose bones were brought to Sparta and buried in the newly founded Oresteion during a calamitous war with Tegea in order to help them (Herodotus 1,67 Pausanias, 3,11,10; WIDE 1893:352). During the reconstruction after the Persian wars, Kimon brought the bones of Theseus into his earlier sanctuary on the *agora* (Plutarch, *Theseus* 36; for a list of Attic cults of Theseus, see KEARNS 1989:168-169); in this case and in that of all founder heroes, the hope of continued protection by the heros fits into his role as a national symbol (GARLAND 1992:82-98). Athletes had to show not only extraordinary prowess in order to receive cult, but also a special form of death, be it madness and miraculous disappearance (Cleomedes of Astypalaea, Pausanias, 6,9,7; FARNELL 1921:365-366) or less common features (Theagenes of Thasus whose statue killed an enemy, Paus.6,11,8; FARNELL 1921:365).

This continued with the heroicized mortals of the hellenistic epoch. The *euergētai* (benefactors) often were extraordinary men, and their cult as *hērōes euergētai* did not only commemorate their benefactions but also express the wish for continual benefit. In some cases mortals received heroic cult not with their individual name but with a designation of their heroic function, *hērōs ploutodotēs* ("Giver of Riches", GRAF 1985: 129-130), *hērōs eumenēs* ("Well-disposed", GRAF 1985:121-125); this is comparable to the old *hērōs Iatros* ("Physician") in Athens (KEARNS 1989:171-172). Those who had died young (*ahôroi*) were a dangerous category among the dead; they were not called for, they came back out of an unfulfilled desire for life and potential hate for those still living; the making of a hero was preceded by manifestations of their continued activity, like appearance in dreams (a young man, HERMANN & POLATKAN 1969:Nr. 1) or more dreadful signs (the heros of South Italian Temesa who was identified with Polites, a Homeric hero whom the Temesians had killed; he strangled the natives of Temesa until he was appeased by sacrifice and finally driven out, VON GEISAU 1975). Such malevolent heroes (*ahōroi, biaiothanatoi*) could play a role in magic, as mediators between the world of the living and the dead and helpers of the sorcerer (*PGM* IV 1390-1495, "heroes or gladiators or other victims of violence").

Heroic cult was never uniform. Though often containing elements of non-Olympian ritual, it does not altogether fit into the dichotomy of Olympian and chthonic (BURKERT 1977:306-312). The sanctuaries of heroes were not only tombs but exhibited different forms, from the enclosed tomb to the *temenos* with grove, well, temple and altar (KEARNS 1992). Only when divine and heroic cult are paired, does the dichotomy become relevant (e.g. in Olympia, where the nightly sacrifice of a black victim into a pit in the precinct of Pelops preceded the sacrifice at the altar of →Zeus Olympios). In other instances, a heroic cult may contain elements of Olympian ritual as well as those of funeral cult, including ritual lament. The one central feature of heroic cult, though, is the common meal at the *hêrôion* (NOCK 1944) as an expression of the importance which the hero has for the community gathered around his cult-place; from it, heroic iconography developes the meal scene as standard theme of heroic iconography (DENTZER 1982).

III. *Hērōs* appears in Gen 46:25 LXX (Jos. *Ant.*2,184) as the translation of Heb *Gešen*, Heroopolis in Egypt. Jewish writers could consider heroes as a typical Greek phenomenon (Philo, *plant.* 14; Josephus *Bell. Iud.* 2,156). Philo disputes the mythological concept of *hēmitheoi* as the offspring of divine and human on theological grounds (*vit. contempl.* 6,3; *decal.* 156); but he accepts the philosophical definition of heroes as the purest souls living close to the ether, and he identifies them with the *angeloi* of Mosaic tradition (*Plant.* 14; but see *Gig.* 6, where he considers the →angels of Gen 6:2 as *daimones*).

Christian writers first accepted the term and the concomitant belief in dangerous and demonic dead (Tertullian, *De an.* 49,2). Augustine, however, argued for a positive connotation of the term and a differentiation from the negative *daemones*: in the Christian sense, heroes were the martyrs (*CD* 10,21). This not only followed a use of the word already known in Christian poetry, but laid the theoretical foundation for the cult of the saints as the Christian hero cult (BROWN 1981).

IV. *Bibliography*

D. Q. ADAMS, Hêrôs and Hêrâ, *Glotta* 65 (1987) 171-178; S. E. ALCOCK, Tomb Cult and the Post-classical Polis, *AJA* 95 (1991) 447-467; P. BROWN, *The Cult of the Saints. Development and Function in Latin Christianity* (Chicago 1981); A. BRELICH, *Gli eroi greci. Un problema storico-religioso* (Rome 1958); W. BURKERT, *Griechische Religion der archaischen und klassischen Epoche* (Stuttgart 1977); P. C. CALLIGAS, Hero-Cult in Early Iron Age Greece, *Early Greek Cult Practice. Proceedings of the Fifth International Symposium at the Swedish Institute at Athens* (eds. R. Hägg & N. Marinatos & G. C. Nordquist; Stockholm and Göteborg 1988) 229-234; J.-M. DENTZER, *Le motif du banquet couché dans le Proche-Orient et le monde grec du VIIe au IVe siècle avant J.-C.* (Paris 1982); L. R. FARNELL, *Greek Hero Cults and Ideas of Immortality* (Oxford 1921); R. GARLAND, *Introducing New Gods. The Politics of Athenian Religion* (London 1992); H. VON GEISAU, Polites 2, *KP* 4 (1975) 978; M. GÉRARD-ROUSSEAU, *Les mentions religieuses dans les tablettes mycéniennes* (Rome 1968); F. GRAF, *Nordionische Kulte. Religionsgeschichtliche und epigraphische Untersuchungen zu den Kulten von Chios, Erythrai, Klazomenai und Phokaia* (Rome 1985); P. HERMANN & K. Z. POLATKAN, *Das Testament des Epikrates* (Sitzungsberichte Wien 265:1, 1969); E. KEARNS, *The Heroes of Attica* (BICS, Suppl. 57; London 1989); KEARNS, Between God and Man. Status and Functions of Heroes and Their Sanctuaries, *Le sanctuaire grec, Entretiens sur l'antiquité classique 37* (eds. O. Reverdin & B. Grange; Vandoeuvres/Genève 1992), 65-99; U. KRON, *Die zehn attischen Phylenheroen. Geschichte, Mythos, Kult und Dastellung* (Mitteil. Arch. Inst. Athen. Beih. 5; Berlin 1976); A. D. NOCK, The Cult of Heroes, *HTR* 37 (1944) 141-174 = *Essays on Religion and the Ancient World* (Oxford 1972), vol. 2, 575-602; J. WHITLEY, Early States and Hero Cults. A Reappraisal, *JHS* 108 (1988) 173-183; S. WIDE, *Lakonische Kulte* (Leipzig 1893).

F. GRAF

HOBAB → HUMBABA

HOKMAH → WISDOM

HOLY AND RIGHTEOUS → HOSIOS KAI DIKAIOS

HOLY SPIRIT רוח הקדש πνεῦμα ἅγιον

I. The expression 'holy spirit' occurs only three times in the OT (Ps 51:13; Isa 63:10.11) but is part of a large semantic field in which *rûaḥ*, referring to some form of divine action, is the central component (about 250 times in the OT). In the NT the expression occurs 84 times whereas *pneuma*, referring to the divine spirit (with or without attributes), occurs about 350 times. Within the Bible neither *rûaḥ* nor *pneuma* are used as a divine name. They are not worshipped as divine beings. The religious use of the words derives from general, non-religious usage. The basic meaning of both words is 'air in motion', either as 'wind' or as 'breath'. 'Wind' as an action beyond human control easily develops into a metaphor of divine or supernatural action. 'Breath' is inherent in every living creature and hence becomes an equivalent of 'life' and 'soul' as opposed to 'death' and →'dead'. It develops into the meaning 'spirit', i.e. that which distinguishes man from other creatures. In the realm of the divine it means 'spirit' as a quality or attribute of the deity as distinct from the earthly world.

II. In the OT, the two basic meanings of Heb *rûaḥ*, 'wind' and 'breath', converge when the word is connected with →Yahweh as his 'spirit' (23 times) or as the 'spirit of →God' (16 times), or with a possessive pronoun referring to the deity.

The most important areas of divine action in which the divine *rûa ḥ* is involved are (a) the charismatic leadership in the early period before kingship, and (b) ecstatic prophecy.

(a) *Charismatic leadership*: In times of distress and oppression Yahweh singles out leaders to liberate the oppressed people and empowers them through his *rûaḥ* to fulfil this task. Often the spirit enables them to perform miraculous acts of military or even physical strength. 1 Sam 11:6 shows that the spirit may also arouse anger. Usually these experiences are transitory. 1 Sam 16:13 tells that the spirit of God came upon David 'from that day onward' this marks the transition from an occasional action of the spirit to a frequent repetition of the same experience which leads to the idea of a permanent endowment. The connection between kingship and the spirit, so prominent in Saul and David, is not found in later texts. It returns in prophecies of an eschatological →saviour, king or prophet (Isa 11:2; 42:1; 61:1).

(b) *Ecstatic prophecy*: in 1 Sam 10:10 Saul meets a company of prophets (*ḥebel nĕbîʾîm*) who are in ecstasy (*hitnabbēʾ*) and Saul soon shares their experience when the spirit seizes him. Nothing is said about their prophesying activities, but in 10:6 Saul is told that they come with harp, tambourine, flute and lyre and that he, like them, will become another man. A similar story is told in 1 Sam 19:18-24: Saul's messengers meet a company of prophets (*lahăqat hannĕbîʾîm,* LXX *ekklēsia prophētōn*) in ecstasy (*nibbĕʾîm*, niphal), with Samuel standing at their head and soon they share this experience as the spirit of God comes upon them. This happens also to the second and the third group of messengers and finally even to Saul himself. These stories show that such companies of prophets operating under the influence of the spirit of God were no exception. Samuel's participation implies that such collective ecstasy was considered legitimate within Jahwistic religion.

Apart from Num 11:16-30, where the

moment of ecstatic behaviour serves to legitimate the administrative office of the elders, no outbursts of the spirit are recorded in pre-conquest traditions. Presumably collective ecstatic experiences as recorded in 1 Sam 10 and 19, though familiar in many cultures (cf. J. LINDBLOM 1962:58), originate in Canaanite religion (see RINGGREN 1982:195-196). This is confirmed by the story of 1 Kgs 18:20-40, where the prophets of →Baal are said to 'rave' (*yitnabbĕ'û*, as 1 Sam 10:5-13 and 19:20-24).

This type of collective prophecy developed into a more institutional form in the pre-exilic period. A classic example is 1 Kgs 22:5-28: the king of Israel assembles four hundred prophets to give him an oracle on his plans to attack Ramoth-Gilead. Apparently they belong to the royal court. Over against these institutional prophets there is the solitary prophet Micaiah, a representative of the type of prophets like →Elijah and Elisha. Both the royal prophets and the independent prophet claim to possess the spirit of Yahweh and the verb NB' is applied to both in the meaning 'to prophesy'. This is also the case in the prophetic writings, esp. in Jeremiah and Ezekiel.

It is significant that, apart from Mic 3:8, *rûaḥ* is never used to authorize the prophets who claim to speak the word of Yahweh. The reason for this is probably that the prophets whom they considered to be false prophets claimed to possess the spirit as in 1 Kgs 22:24 (see ALBERTZ 1979:748-749). In post-exilic prophetic texts prophecy and the spirit are again connected (cf. Isa 61:1, Zech 7:12, Ezek *passim*: the spirit not only falls upon him and makes him speak the word of Yahweh but also 'moves' him to various places where he receives messages to proclaim, cf. 3:12, 14; 8:3; 11:1, 24; 43:5), not as a real event but as a visionary experience, as stated explicitly in 11:24.

The idiom in connection with *rûaḥ* as 'wind' or 'breath' (as e.g. 'blowing' [NŠB, Isa 40:7] or 'bursting forth' [NS', Num 11:31]) is not transferred to the usage of *rûaḥ* as spirit. The spirit-idiom serves to express the way in which the spirit is experienced, either as moving towards people or as being in or with them.

A distinction can be drawn between animistic and dynamistic idiom. In animistic idiom the spirit is pictured as a more or less personal being who 'comes upon' people (HYH *'al*, Num 24:2, Judg 3:10; 11:29; 1 Sam 19:20, 23; 2 Chr 15:1; 20:14), or 'overpowers' them (ṢLḤ *'al*, lit. 'to be strong', mostly rendered as 'to take possession', Judg 14:6, 19; 15:4; 1 Sam 10:6, 10; 11:6; 16:13; 18:10), or 'falls upon' them (NPL *'al*, Ezek 11:5). The spirit 'moves' (P'M, Judg 13:25), 'carries away' (NŚ', 1 Kgs 18:12; 2:16; Ezek 3, 14; 8, 3; 11, 1; 43, 5). The spirit 'departs' from people (SWR, 1 Sam 16: 14) or 'passes' from one person to another ('BR, 1 Kgs 22:24; 2 Chr 18:23). In dynamistic idiom the spirit 'clothes' or 'surrounds' (LBŠ, mostly rendered 'takes possession', Judg 6:34; 1Chr 12:19; 2 Chr 24: 20). People may be 'filled with spirit' (ML', Exod 28:3; 31:3; 35:21.31). The spirit is 'poured out upon' all people collectively ('RH, Isa 32:15; ŠPK, Ezek 39:29; Joel 3:1-2; Zech 12:10; YṢQ Isa 44:3).

When the coming of the spirit is not experienced as a momentary event it results in enduring presence of the spirit. This state is expressed in a much simpler idiom in which the distinction between animistic and dynamistic is less prominent. The idiom consists of two different phrases: that of the spirit 'resting upon' people (NWḤ *'al*, Num 11:25-26; 2 Kgs 2:15; Isa 11:2, often without a verb as e.g. Num 11:17) which may have been understood originally as animistic, and that of the spirit 'being in or with' people (HYH *bĕ*, Gen 41:38; Num 27: 18; Isa 61:1) which may have been of dynamistic origin. They are, however, no longer connected with different concepts of the spirit.

In the OT the spirit is primarily an instrument of divine action upon individuals or on the community, not in a metaphorical way (like 'hand' or 'arm') but as belonging to God or even as a part of God. In Isa 30:1 and 40:13 the spirit is mentioned in juxtaposition to God himself, thus preparing the way to a concept of God as spirit (John 4:24). The OT does not represent the spirit as a divine being connected with, yet distinct from God. It is always functioning as an intermediary between God and mankind.

The phrase 'holy spirit', so prominent in the NT and subsequent Christian literature, appears in the OT only three times. In Ps 51:13 the psalmist prays that God will not drive him from his face, i.e. from his presence, and will not take away from him his holy spirit. The parallelism suggests that the divine spirit stands for the principle of life in the human person: the plea of the psalmist is that he stay alive. In Isa 63:10-11 there is a double reference to the spirit of God's holiness, representing his holy presence among his people. When they sin and rebel against God they grieve his representative in them, the holy spirit.

III. *Pneuma* occurs 379 times in the NT. In the singular it always means 'spirit', either divine or human (except in 2 Thess 2:8). The plural usually refers to →unclean spirits, →angels (Heb 1:7.14), or to multiple manifestations of the divine spirit (Rev 1:4; 3:1; 4:5; 5:6).

The word *Pneuma* occurs independently, though in nearly two-thirds of the cases characterized as *hagion*, 'holy'; less frequent are the occurences in genitival constructions with such terms as *theou, kyriou* (either God or →Christ), *Christou* or *Iēsou*. It also occurs with following qualifying genitive, as e.g. 'truth' (John 14:17; 15:26; 16:13), or as a hendiadys with qualifying nouns, as e.g. 'power' (1 Cor 2:4).

In the imagery used in connection with the spirit, two groups of related images can be distinguished. In the one the spirit is described in a personal way, either as subject or as object; in the other the spirit is described as a power, force or influence, either material or immaterial. The language used is partly derived from biblical idiom and partly from contemporary hellenistic material. The following a representative survey.

In the capacity of a person, the spirit is described as being sent by God (Gal 4:6 *exapesteilen*, in 4:4 used with reference to the →son of God, 1 Pet 2:12, the Paraclete-sayings in John 14:26; 15:26), or as coming upon people (Acts 1:8; 19:6; John 16:13), presumably to stay with them and to become active when called upon (like the *daimōn paredros,* see REILING 1973:88-90). In particular in Acts this personal idiom is used: the spirit speaks (8:29; 10:19; 11:12; 13:2; 20:23), sends (13:4), forbids (16:6) and appoints (20:28). Alternatively people can lie to (5:3), tempt (5:9), resist (7:51), grieve (Eph 4:30) or insult (Heb 10:29) the spirit. This usage paves the way to later doctrinal developments.

Otherwise, the spirit is described as being poured out like rain (Acts 2:17-18.33; 10:45, cf. Rom 5:5); people are filled with the spirit (Acts 2:4; 4:8.31; 9:17; 13:9) as a momentary experience, or are full of the spirit (Acts 6:3; 7:55; 11:24; 13:52; Eph 5:18) as a permanent endowment. The same imagery is found in hellenistic sources (see REILING 1973:114-121). Baptism in or with the spirit (Mark 1:8 and par.; John 1:33; cf. 1 Cor 12: 13) is a metaphor derived from immersion in water. Like the Delphian *enthousiasmos* the spirit can be quenched (cf. VAN UNNIK 1968). The idiom of the gift, or the giving of the spirit is also part of non-personal usage (Luke 11:13; John 3:34; Acts 8:18; 15:8; 1 Cor 12:7; 1 Thess 4:8; 1 John 3:24; 4:13). The general phrase 'to receive the spirit' (John 20:22; Acts 2:38; 8:15.17.19; 10:47; 19:2; Rom 8:15; 2 Cor 11:4; Gal 3:2, 14) is ambiguous.

In the gospel tradition →Jesus is pictured as a *pneumatikos*, a man full of the spirit and acting in the power of the spirit. The spirit was bestowed on him immediately after having been baptized by John. Mark 1:10 describes the descending of the spirit as a visionary experience of Jesus himself, Matt 3:16 and Luke 3:21-22 as a visible event. John refers to it as an event observed by John the Baptist. The symbol of the →dove (not mentioned in John) may refer to *bat qôl* because of the following proclamation from heaven (cf. H. GREEVEN, περιστερά, *TWNT* 6 [1959] 68, →Dove) or to the image of the so-called 'soul-bird' (*'Seelenvogel'*, see A. SCHIMMEL, Seelenvogel, *RGG* 5 [1961] 1637), but it plays no part in the symbolism of the holy spirit until much later. This common tradition identifies Jesus as the eschatological prophet of Isa 61:1, anointed with the spirit (cf. 11QMelch 18; Luke 4:18-21; Acts 10:38).

The first act of the spirit is to send Jesus into the wilderness to be tempted by the →devil. The words used by the evangelists are indicative of their respective ideas of the relationship between Jesus and the spirit. In Mark 1:12 the spirit drives him (*ekballei*, a technical term of exorcisms) more or less violently, in Matt 4:1 he is led by the spirit (*anēchthē hypo tou pneumatos*, a neutral phrase). In Luke 4:1 Jesus is the subject of the clause: he returns full of the spirit (*plērēs pneumatos hagiou*, in Acts 6:3.5.8; 7:55; 11:24 used to describe permanent endowment with the spirit) and he is led in, not into, the wilderness under the influence of the spirit (*en tōi pneumati*, a less explicit phrase than those of Mark and Matthew). This picture of a spirit-endowed prophet is also reflected in Luke: Jesus returns to Galilee endowed with the power of the spirit (*en dynamei pneumatos* 4:14) and in the synagogue of Nazareth he identifies himself as the spirit-anointed prophet of Isa 61:1.

In the synoptic report of Jesus' ministry the spirit is mentioned only twice: in the logion of the →sin against the holy spirit (Mark 3:29; Matt 12:31-32; Luke 12:10 but placed in a different context), and in the Q-logion of Matt 12:28 (Luke 11:20 has 'finger' instead of *pneuma*), inserted in the Marcan Beelzebul-controversy preceding the logion. The common element in these texts is that Jesus drives out →demons through the spirit and to ascribe this to Beelzebul is an unforgivable sin. The spirit both authorizes and empowers Jesus to drive out the demons (cf. Luke 4:36). Their overthrow is proof of the presence of the kingdom of God and, implicitly, of the power of the spirit through Jesus.

In Matthew and Luke the story of Jesus' public ministry is preceded by stories about his birth in which the spirit plays an important part. Matt 1:18-23 tells that before having had intercourse with Joseph →Mary was found to be pregnant of the holy spirit (*ek pneumatos hagiou*) and that this was confirmed to Joseph by an angel in a dream. In Luke the angel →Gabriel tells Mary that she will have a son and that the holy spirit will come upon her and that the power of the Most High will overshadow her. Therefore her son to be born will be called 'holy 'and 'son of God'. Matthew's statement is too short to admit of any interpretation of the role of the spirit. The Lucan version, however, is more explicit: the spirit comes upon Mary (*eperchomai*) as upon the disciples at Pentecost (Acts 1:8; the actual story has 'filled with the holy spirit', 2:4). The overshadowing (*episkiazein*) of Mary by the power of the Most High recalls the cloud which overshadows Jesus and those with him in the transfiguration story (Mark 9:7 and par.) and the cloud overshadowing the tent of meeting and the →glory of God filling the tent (Exod 40:35 LXX; Num 9:18; 10:34-36, cf. Deut 33:12 LXX; Isa 4:5). These parallels refer to the active presence of God in a general way but not to anything near the conception of a human or divine being as in Luke 1:34. The association of the spirit with conception cannot therefore be explained in terms of this usage, nor in terms of the divine spirit overshadowing and obscuring *nous* when entering a human person (Philo, *Somn* I 119, see LEISEGANG 1922:25-27). Whatever the origin and background of this image, the intention of both statements in Matt 1:18 and Luke 1:34 is to connect Jesus with the spirit from his conception on. Yet this does not keep the evangelists from recording the common tradition of the spirit descending upon Jesus at baptism. The fact that nowhere in the rest of the NT the so-called virginal conception is mentioned or alluded to suggests that it is a secondary tradition, not supported by the pre-gospel tradition nor by the primitive teaching as transparent from the Pauline letters. Despite its great impact on later doctrinal developments the notion of the virginal conception does not belong to the earliest picture of Jesus as the messenger of the kingdom of God, anointed with the holy spirit (for a theological interpretation of these texts see R. E. Brown, *The Birth of the Messiah* [New York 1993²]).

The experience of the spirit is one of the most characteristic features in the life of the earliest Christian communities. The promise of its coming, recorded in the gospel tradition (Mark 1:8 and par.; Luke 24:49; Acts 1:8; John 7:39; 20:22; see also the Paraclete-sayings in 14:26; 15:26; 16:7-11.13-15), reflect this experience. The Book of Acts reports its coming in the community of Jesus' followers in Jerusalem (2:1-4) and its reception when people accept the gospel (8:15; 10:44; 19:6, also referred to in the phrase *lambanein to pneuma* Gal 3:3; Rom 8:15-16; 2 Cor 11:4). Hence the spirit was believed to be permanently present in the communities and to influence the conduct of the believers towards one another (Gal 5:22; Rom 14:17), and to inspire them to lead a life *kata pneuma*, following the guidance of the spirit. Those who fail to meet this standard are not entitled to be called *pneumatikos* (1 Cor 3:1-4).

The spirit was experienced in more direct manifestations, either as a rekindling of a present gift or as a sudden outpouring. These manifestations relate to (1) revelation, (2) power, and (3) worship.

(1) Paul ranks apostles, prophets and teachers (in this order) at the top of an enumeration of gifts of the spirit (1 Cor 12:28) and claims that the wisdom which he preaches as an apostle, his gospel, was revealed to him by the spirit (1 Cor 2, 10) and this may also apply to prophecy and teaching. Of these two prophecy is the most prominent revelatory manifestation of the spirit. It is attested in three Pauline letters (1 Thess, 1 Cor, Rom), in Rev, 1 John, *Did.* 11 and Hermas, *Man.* 11.

The *Sitz im Leben* of primitive Christian prophecy is the gathered community, the 'gathering of righteous men who have faith in the divine spirit' (Hermas, *Man.* 11, 9), where the spirit is present and can become active when invoked. The presence of the spirit in the gathered community is a presupposition for prophecy to function. When prophets speak their messages the congregation has to judge whether or not they are inspired by the spirit of God. Discerning the spirits (*diakrisis pneumatōn)* is itself a gift (1 Cor 12:10; 14:29) and a case of the principle *similia similibus cognoscuntur*. Yet sometimes external criteria are mentioned, pertaining either to the moral (Matt 7:15-20; *Did.* 11, 8-12) or the doctrinal (1 Cor 12:3; 1 John 4:1-6) side of the phenomenon.

Prophecy is instant speech inspired by the spirit and spoken *hic et nunc* in the congregation. More than one prophet may speak but a certain order must be kept (1 Cor 14:29-33). Direct inspiration by the spirit does not cause a loss of consciousness as with the Montanist prophetesses (Eusebius, *Eccl. Hist.* V 17); the prophet is supposed to have control over his prophetic inspiration (1 Cor 14:32).

The content of prophetic speech is not clearly stated. The Book of Acts mentions prophetic predictions of events to come (11:28; 21:4) and Paul states that prophecy serves "for upbuilding, encouragement and consolation" (1 Cor 14:3). Presumably, prophecy, preaching and teaching overlap in the life of the community. The 'word of wisdom' and the 'word of knowledge' which Paul mentions in 1 Cor 12:8 are probably favourite terms in the church of the Corinthians since they are not mentioned elsewhere.

(2) The standard phrase to describe acts of power effected or inspired by the spirit is 'miracles and signs' *(terata kai sēmeia)*, probably to be understood as a hendiadys: miraculous acts which signal the power of the spirit, usually in support of the preaching of the gospel (Acts 2:43; 5:12; 14:3; 15:12; 2 Cor 12:12; Rom 15:19; Heb 2:3). The Greek expression reflects the Hebrew idiom *ʾōtôt ûmôpĕtîm*, 'signs and wonders' (see, e.g. Deut 4:34). The nature of the miracles is never specified. Sometimes the word 'power' (*dynamis*) is added as a qualification of the miracle (Acts 8:13; Rom 15:19, 2

Cor 12:12), sometimes 'acts of power' (*dynameis*) are mentioned as an equivalent (Acts 19:11; 1 Cor 2:4; 12:10, 28; 1 Thess 1:5). According to 1 Cor 12:9-10 they are to be distinguished from 'acts of healing' (*charismata iamatōn*). Such acts are reported in Acts, sometimes as a collective event (5:16; 8:7; 28:9), sometimes as an individual healing (3:6-8; 9:18; 16:18; 20: 10). Acts 19:12 shows that in Luke's understanding there is no clear distinction between acts of power and acts of healing.

(3) Prayer, too, is experienced as an act of the spirit. The *Abba*-invocation is described both as spoken by the believers under the inspiration of the spirit (Rom 8:15) and as an utterance of the spirit itself in the hearts of the believers (Gal 4:6). The same concept of the spirit-inspired prayer (*oratio infusa*, see HEILER 1920:224-227) underlies Rom 8:26. Whether the 'groans that cannot be spoken' (*stenagmoi alalētoi*) refer to glossolalia is not certain. Speaking in tongues, or languages, is mentioned in Mark 16:15, in Acts and in 1 Cor 12 and 14. In Mark 16:15 speaking in new tongues is one of the signs that will accompany the believers. In Acts 2:1-13 "speaking in other tongues" (*lalein heterais glōssais*) is speaking in foreign languages understood by the inhabitants of the countries where the languages are spoken; in 10:46 it is mentioned together with praising God and in 19:6 together with prophecy. Apparently the author of Acts does not know glossolalia from personal experience. In 1 Cor 12 and 14 Paul attempts to tone down an overestimation of the phenomenon by comparing it to prophecy: speaking in tongues is an individual experience of prayer in incomprehensible words. The words must be translated in order to be understood by the congregation. Whether or not such translations occurred is not indicated. 1 Cor 14:13-19 shows that speaking in tongues comes close to praying and singing.

(c) Notwithstanding the frequent occurrence of *pneuma* or *pneuma hagion* as an independent notion, in the NT the spirit is not envisaged as a divine being (hypostasis), but as an instrument of divine action or revelation.

The relationship between the spirit and the exalted Christ is described in various ways. Acts 2:33 sees the spirit as poured out by Christ and 16:7 refers to the spirit as *pneuma Iēsou* (cf. also Phil 1:19; 1 Pet 2:11). Rom 8:9-11 shows how easily the phrases *pneuma theou, pneuma Christou* and *Christos* can be used interchangeably.

IV. *Bibliography*

R. ALBERTZ & C. WESTERMANN, רוח *Rûaḥ*, *THAT* 2 (1979) 726-753; *D. E. AUNE, *Prophecy in Early Christianity* (Grand Rapids 1983); H. CROUZEL, Geist (Heiliger Geist), *RAC* 9 (1976) 490-545; G. DAUTZENBERG, Glossolalie, *RAC* 11 (1981) 225-246; DAUTZENBERG, *Urchristliche Prophetie* (Stuttgart 1975); J. D. G. DUNN, *Baptism in the Spirit* (London 1970); *DUNN, *Jesus and the Spirit* (London 1975); H. GUNKEL, *Die Wirkungen des heiligen Geistes nach der populären Anschauung der apostolischen Zeit und der Lehre des Apostels Paulus* (Göttingen 1888); F. HEILER, *Das Gebet* (München 1920); J. JEREMIAS, נביא *nābîʾ*, *THAT* 2 (1979) 7-26; *H. KLEINKNECHT *et al.*, Pneuma etc., *TWNT* 6 (1959) 330-453; H. LEISEGANG, *Pneuma Hagion; Der Ursprung des Geistbegriffs der synoptischen Evangelien aus der griechischen Mystik* (Leipzig 1922); J. LINDBLOM, *Prophecy in Ancient Israel* (Oxford 1962); D. LYS, *RUAH Le souffle dans l'Ancien Testament* (Paris 1962); W. E. MILLS, *Speaking in Tongues, A Guide to Research on Glossolalia* (Grand Rapids 1986) [& lit]; S. MORENZ *et al.*, Geist, *RGG* 2 (1962^3) 1268-1279; E. MOSIMAN, *Das Zungenreden geschichtlich und psychologisch untersucht* (Tübingen 1911); J. PANAGOPOULOS (ed.), *Prophetic Vocation in the New Testament and Today* (Leiden 1977); F. PFISTER, Ekstase, *RAC* 4 (1959) 944-987; J. REILING, *Hermas and Christian Prophecy* (Leiden 1973); H. RINGGREN, *Israelitische Religion* (Stuttgart 1982); H. SAAKE, *Pneuma*, PWSup XIV (1974) 387-412; H. SCHLÜNGEL-STRAUMANN, *Ruah bewegt die Welt* (Stuttgart 1992); *W. H.

SCHMIDT *et al.*, Geist/Heiliger Geist/Geistesgaben I, II, III, *TRE* 12 (1984) 170-196 [& lit]; W. C. VAN UNNIK, 'Den Geist löschet nicht aus' (1 Thessalonicher V 19), *NovT* 10 (1968) 255-269; VAN UNNIK, A Formula describing Prophecy, *Sparsa Collecta* 2 (Leiden 1980) 183-193; H. WEINEL, *Die Wirkungen des Geistes und der Geister im nachapostolischen Zeitalter bis auf Irenäus* (Freiburg 1899); R. R. WILSON, Prophecy and Ecstasy: A Reexamination, *JBL* 98 (1979) 321-337.

J. REILING

HOREPH חרף

I. The name 'Horeph' is a hapax in the OT. It occurs as a possible theophoric element in the personal name Elihoreph: one of Solomon's secretaries in 1 Kgs 4:3. It has been connected with the Egyptian god →Apis: and, alternatively, with the Kassite god *Ḫarpa/e*. In epigraphical Hebrew, the putative divine name Horeph is probably attested in the seal inscription *lʿzyhw bn ḥrp* (DIRINGER 1934:196 No 37; TIGAY 1986: 77). Besides, in Hebrew a noun *ḥōrep* occurs indicating the autumnal season (e.g. Gen 8:22; Zech 14:8; Ps 74:17). It is unclear whether this noun and the possibly theophoric element are identical or homonyms.

II. According to a proposal by MARQUARDT (1896), Horeph is a misspelling of the Egyptian deity Apis. The name Elihoreph is to be read *ʾrḥp*, 'Apis is my light', or *ʾlyḥp*, 'Apis is my god'. Additional arguments have been adduced by DE VAUX (1939) and METTINGER (1971). In this connection, Phoenician personal names with the theophoric element Apis are cited by DE VAUX: *bnḥp* and *ytnḥp*. The LXX reads Ελιαφ (B), or Ελιαβ (LucRev). This supports the interpretation of DE VAUX and METTINGER. The vocalisation of the MT is explained by METTINGER as follows: "For religious reasons (Apis as sacred bull and god of fertility), this *mixtum compositum* with the name of a foreign god was intentionally distorted to form a pejorative by the insertion of a *resh*. This insertion associated the name with the Hebrew root connected with shame, disgrace, blasphemy. The pointing could represent a revocalisation with the vowels of בֹּשֶׁת shame" (1971:30). The Egyptian etymology corresponds to the Egyptian background of the Solomonic state offices proposed by DE VAUX and METTINGER. This background is contested by MAZAR, who supposes a Canaanite origin. Accordingly, Horeph is interpreted in a different way: "I propose that the second component of the name is the god *Ḫarpa/e*. This deity was worshipped by the Kassites in Babylonia, and identified by them with Enlil, the lord of the Gods. He was also worshipped by the Hurrians, and his name appears as a component in personal names from Nuzi" (MAZAR 1986:137-138; for the equation EN.LÍL = *Ḫarbē* see K. BALKAN, *Kassitenstudien I* [AOS 37; New Haven 1954] 106-107). The deity Harbe allegedly occurs as a theophoric element in a personal name known from the El Amarna correspondence: *ka-da-aš-ma-an*-EN.LÍL, 'Kadashman-Harbe, king of Babylon ' (EA 1:1; 2:2; 3:3; 5:2; R. S. HESS, *Amarna Personal Names* [Winona Lake 1993] 156). Against Mazar, TIGAY (1986:77) argues that the Kassite deity Ḫarpa/e is not mentioned in inscriptions from the first millennium BCE. He then suggests a relation between *ḥrp* and the personal name *ḥārîp* in Neh 7:24; 10:20.

III. The evidence of the LXX led MONTGOMERY & GEHMAN (1951:115) to a completely different emendation. The Greek addition in 1 Kgs 2:46 reads "over the plinthion". "The plinthion was the quadrans (...), which was not only a sun-dial but also an instrument for determining the seasons by the the lengths of the sun's shadow, the instrument being adjusted to the latitude." Thus the putative name is emended to a title: *ʿl hḥrp* 'Over-the-Year' (compare BHS): "The office was parallel to that of the Assyrian *līmu*, after the years of which functionaries all official documents were dated." (MONTGOMERY & GEHMAN 1951:115). This construal is perhaps misleading; see REHM, who argues for a different interpretation of plinth(e)ion and a military function of the office (1972:98). Such proposals are interesting but remain doubtful. So the question of the origin of 'Horeph' is still left open in the new Hebrew dictionaries (*HALAT* 54; *Ges.*[18] 64).

IV. *Bibliography*

D. DIRINGER, *Le iscrizioni antico-ebraiche palestinesi* (Firenze 1934); J. MARQUARDT, *Fundamente israelitischer und jüdischer Geschichte* (Göttingen 1896); B. MAZAR, *The Early Biblical Period. Historical Studies* (S. Aḥituv & B. A. Levine, eds.; Jerusalem 1986) 126-138; T. N. D. METTINGER, *Solomonic State Officials* (ConB OT Series 5; Lund 1971); J. A. MONTGOMERY & H. S. GEHMAN, *A Critical and Exegetical Commentary on the Books of Kings* (Edinburgh 1951); M. REHM, Die Beamtenliste der Septuaginta in 1 Kön 2,46h, *Wort, Lied und Gottesspruch.* FS J. Ziegler (J. Schreiner ed.; Würzburg 1972) 95-101; J. H. TIGAY, *You Shall Have No Other Gods* (HSM 31; Atlanta 1986); R. DE VAUX, Titres et fonctionnaires égyptiens à la cour de David et de Salomon, *RB* 48 (1939) 394-405.

U. RÜTERSWÖRDEN

HORON חרן

I. In the OT, Horon is a divine element in the place-name Beth-Horon (House of Horon; *Ges.*[18] 146). Two cities were known as Beth-Horon, the one Lower Beth-Horon (*bēt 'ūr el-fōqa*; 16 km nw of Jerusalem) and the other Upper Beth-Horon (*bēt 'ūr et-taḥta*; 18 km nw of Jerusalem). The toponym is known from a topographical list of the pharao Shoshenk at Karnak (VAN DIJK 1989:60) and from a Hebrew ostracon from *Tell el-Qasīle* (*TSSI* I 4 B). Perhaps Horonaim in Moab (Isa 15:5, Jer 48:3) is also related to the god Horon (*KAI* II, 179). The name of the deity may be connected with arabic *ḥaur* 'bottom (of a well), (broad) depression'. "It is not impossible that the name of the god is a similar adjectival expression, meaning primarily the 'deep one, the one inhabiting the underworld.'" (ALBRIGHT 1936:9).

II. Horon is mentioned as an element in personal names from Mari (H. HUFFMON, *Amorite Personal Names in the Mari Texts* [Baltimore 1965] 32,192) and from the Egyptian execration texts (VAN DIJK 1989: 59). In Ugarit, some of his character traits can be recognized, though he does not play a prominent role in the pantheon (DE MOOR, *UF* 2 [1970], 222). Horon does not appear in Ugaritic proper names (NA'AMAN, *UF* 22 [1990], 253 n. 28); there is only one *'bdḥwrn* on a Phoenician seal (XELLA 1988: 57).

In the Ugaritic myths and epics, Horon is invoked in curses, in *KTU* 1.16 VI 54-58. Kirtu says to his son: "O son, Horonu break, Horonu break your head, (and) 'Athtartu, consort of Ba'lu, your skull! May you fall down at the height of your years, in the prime of your strength, and yet be humbled!" (*ARTU* 222-223) The same formulation is used in Yammu's speech adressed to →Baal (*KTU* 1.2 i: 7-9 reconstructed).

In Ugaritic incantations, Horon is invoked against snakes. One of these incantations, perhaps the best preserved Ugaritic text (*KTU* 1.100), is difficult to understand. According to KOTTSIEPER (1984:109), the sun goddess is sent by her daughter from east to west to ask several gods and goddesses to provide her with snake charms. Finally, Horon agrees. The text shows that his dominion lies in the netherworld, referred to as *mṣd* 'fortress' (Translation: *ARTU* 146-156; DIETRICH & LORETZ, *TUAT* II, 345-350). In the incantation *KTU* 1.82, the 'creatures of Horon' (Ugarit *bnt ḥ[rn]*) are (evil) ancestral spirits from the netherworld (*ARTU* 177; DE MOOR & SPRONK, *UF* 16 [1984] 242-243). In this ritual, Horon occurs several times. He is viewed in a negative sense, as the chief of harmful →demons. In this role, Horon is ambivalent; he can also be invoked against demons (RIH 78/20; *ARTU* 185; DIETRICH & LORETZ, *TUAT* II, 333-336). This is also evident in *KTU* 1.107 (CAQUOT, LAPO 14, 95-100): →El and Horon shall take away the poison of a snake. It is interesting to see that Horon is placed here at the top of a list of deities.

The wives of Horon are mentioned in the first Phoenician incantation on an amulet from Arslan Tash (7th century). The passage reads: "with an alliance of Horon whose command is perfect and of his seven concubines, yea, the eight wives of the holy Lord." (*KAI* 27:15-18; DE MOOR 1983:108).

This positive aspect of Horon as a helper against demons is also found in the Egyptian Papyrus Harris. In a passage referring to magical means of rendering a wolf harmless it is stated: "Horon makes thy fangs impotent, thy foreleg is cut off by Arsaphes, after →Anat has cut thee down." (ALBRIGHT 1936:3; perhaps →Resheph is mentioned [instead of 'Arsaphes']; VAN DIJK 1989:63). Another passage reads: "O Horon, drive (the beasts) from the (harvest) field; O Horus, let none enter!" (ALBRIGHT 1936:4). In this context Horon is called a →'shepherd'.

During the first millenium BCE the cult of Horon spread throughout the Meditteranean World. He is mentioned in a Punic inscription from Antas (SZNYCER 1969-1970); here he is connected with Ṣid (→Sidon). In a Greek inscription from Delos, Horon is mentioned together with →Heracles as a god venerated by the people of Jamnia (in Palestine). The final note is interesting: "Everything may be sacrificed except goat" (ALBRIGHT 1936:4-5).

Horon was also venerated in Egypt since the time of Amenhotep II (STADELMANN 1967:81; HELCK 1971:454). In texts from the Theban West Bank, he was identified with Shed. Horon is depicted as a falcon clutching snakes in its talons; the reason lies in the identification with →Horus (VAN DIJK 1989:62-63). In the delta Horon was worshipped as a desert-god, protecting against the enemies coming from the desert. In Giza, Horon was identified with Harmakhis, the Great Sphinx (VAN DIJK 1989:65-68).

III. *Bibliography*

W. F. ALBRIGHT, The Canaanite God Ḥaurôn (Ḥôrôn), *AJSL* 53 (1936) 1-12; A. CAQUOT, Horon: revue critique et données nouvelles, *AAAS* 29-30 (1979/80) 173-180; J. VAN DIJK, The Canaanite God Ḥauron and his Cult in Egypt, *GM* 107 (1989) 59-68 [& lit]; J. GRAY, The Canaanite God Horon, *JNES* 8 (1949) 27-34; W. HELCK, *Die Beziehungen Ägyptens zu Vorderasien im 3. und 2. Jahrtausend v. Chr.* (Wiesbaden 1971[2]); I. KOTTSIEPER, *KTU* 1.100 - Versuch einer Deutung, *UF* 16 (1984) 97-110; J. C. DE MOOR, Demons in Canaan, *JEOL* 27 (1983) 106-119; R. STADELMANN, *Syrisch-palästinische Gottheiten in Ägypten* (Leiden 1967); M. SZNYCER, Note sur le dieu Ṣid et le dieu Ḥoron d'après les nouvelles inscriptions puniques d'Antas (Sardaigne), *Karthago* 15 (1969-1970) 69-74; P. XELLA, Per una riconsiderazione della morfologia del dio Horon, *AION* 32 (1972) 271-286 [& lit]; XELLA, D'Ugarit à la Phénicie: Sur les traces de Rashap, Horon, Eshmun, *WO* 19 (1988) 45-64.

U. RÜTERSWÖRDEN

HORUS חור, *חר

I. Hor, Gk *Horos* (Horus) is the name of a number of Egyptian gods. It has been suggested that it occurs, as a (theophoric element in) biblical personal name(s). It is found in *Šîḥôr,* Josh 13:3; Isa 23:3; Jer 2:18; 1 Chr 13:5; cf. Josh 19:26. This toponym renders Eg "Lake of Horus" (on the n.-e. Egyptian border), in spite of the Hebrew interpretation as "The Black One" (BIETAK 1983:625).

II. Two are very prominent among the Horuses. The sky-god (A), and the son of →Osiris and →Isis (B). A is also called "Horus the Elder" (Haroëris) or "Horus the Eldest", B "Horus the son of Isis " (Harsiëse) and "Horus the Child" (Harpokrates). A is depicted as a falcon or falcon-headed human. "Distant One"—possibly the right translation of his name—is a suitable description of the high-flying bird of prey. B is a boy, reared and sheltered by his mother. As a young man, he becomes Osiris' vindicator and successor to the throne. He is the prototype of the "Beloved Son" who takes care of his father after his death. Harpokrates was very popular in the Graeco-Roman period.

A and B have some characteristics in

common so that amalgamations become understandable. They are both confronted with →Seth as an antagonist. Fighting with his rival (and brother), A was wounded in the eye, the source of light. Assignment of a territory to each of them ended the struggle. The eye was made "healthy" *(udjat)* again. A later version of this myth looks upon Seth not as an equal opponent, but as a criminal. B takes Seth, his uncle, for an evil god from the beginning, because he murdered Osiris. The latter conflict resulted in the villain's condemnation. A is a royal deity right from the start of Egypt's history. He protects the earthly ruler who is identified with him. Taking over office from Osiris, B is the predecessor of the Pharaohs. He also looks after the deceased king. The august sky-god was "He of Behdet (Edfu)" where he enjoyed his main cult. Influence from Heliopolis, the solar centre, during the Old Kingdom generated "Horus of the Horizon" (Horakhty). Syncretized with the sun-god →Re, he became Re-Horakhty. The disk is his typical head-gear, and, provided with wings, his conspicuous manifestation.

III. The biblical anthroponyms in which the name Horus allegedly occurs are *ʾašḥûr* (1 Chr 2:24; 4:5); *Ḥûr* (Ex 17:10.12; 24:14); *Ḥûrî* (1 Chr 5:14); *Ḥûray* (1Chr 11:32); *Ḥûrām* (1 Chr 8:5); *Ḥarneper* (1 Chr 7:36); *ʿammîḥûr* (2 Sam 13:37), and *Pašḥûr* (Jer 20:1 etc.; 21:1; 38:1; Ezra 2:38; 10:22; Neh 7:41; 10:4; 11:12; 1 Chr 9:12). Some identifications are, however, disputed, others are at the very least uncertain; cf. KB and *HALAT* s.v. The one instance which gives the impression of being positively Egyptian is *Ḥarneper*, though that name may contain Eg *ḥr*, "face".

IV. *Bibliography*

M. Bietak, Schi-Hor, *LdÄ* V (1983) 623-626; H. Bonnet, Horus, *RÄRG* 307-314; and cf. entries p. 306, 314-318; J. Černý, *Ancient Egyptian Religion* (London 1952) 155; E. Hornung, *Der Eine und die Vielen* (Darmstadt 1971) 274; W. Schenkel, Horus, *LdÄ* III (1977) 14-25; and cf. entries p. 13, 25-64.

M. Heerma van Voss

HOSIOS KAI DIKAIOS Ὅσιος καὶ Δίκαιος

I. Both ὅσιος ('pious, holy') and δίκαιος ('just, righteous') occur countless times in the Greek Bible as epithets of both humans and →God. Also the combination of both words occurs, e.g. Deut 32:4; Tit 1:8; Rev 16:5; cf. Eph. 4:24, as is very often the case in pagan Greek literature. As the name of an →angel or a pair of angels Ὅσιος καὶ Δίκαιος occurs, almost always in this combination, on several dozen inscriptions, mostly from third century CE Phrygia and Lydia in Asia Minor, which were discovered during the last decades (many of them were published in MAMA IX and *TAM* V 1; see also Drew-Bear 1978: 38-40).

II. Divine angels played an important role in the pagan world of the second and third centuries CE (Mitchell 1993:46-47). The inscriptions inform us about the existence of a cult of an *angelos* or *angeloi* in central and western Asia Minor, sometimes organized in the form of an 'Association of Friends of the Angel(s)' (φιλαγγέλων συμβίωσις), viz., *Hosios kai Dikaios*. In a number of inscriptions the double names only refer to one supernatural being, in other ones, however, to a pair (e.g. Θεοῖς Ὁσίῳ καὶ Δικαίῳ); sometimes Hosios is the only deity mentioned (e.g. Drew-Bear 1978:39 n. 5; *ibid.* 40 n. 29 further examples). There is some debate about whether this *angelos* or those *angeloi* are just (a) messenger(s) of the gods or rather a particular type of supernatural being(s). The latter is suggested by the fact that some of the inscriptions are dedicated to →'Zeus Most High and the Divine Angel'; in such cases Θεῖος Ἄγγελος seems to be a separate deity (references in Kearsley 1992:207). But on some of the reliefs below or above these inscriptions the representation of a Hermes-like male figure bearing a winged herald's staff suggests, rather, that we have to do with (a) messenger(s) between the divine and human world, although this is far from conclusive. Some scholars believe that the rather uncommon term *angelos* was borrowed from Graeco-Jewish communities in the area, especially because the terms ὅσιος and δίκαιος are standard epithets of God in the LXX (SHEPPARD 1980/81). These are not persuasive arguments, but Jewish influence certainly cannot be ruled out altogether. The nature of the cult of *Hosios kai Dikaios* remains still largely unknown to us. Their female counterpart Hosia is less frequently attested (MITCHELL 1993:25-26).

III. Although dating from the post-NT period, these inscriptions may shed some light on the question of angel-worship in Asia Minor (SHEPPARD 1980-81), much discussed in connection with Col. 2:18 where Paul (?) warns his readers against the adherents of angel-worship (θρησκεία τῶν ἀγγέλων), which apparently played a role in Colossian 'philosophy' (Col. 2:8). This syncretistic movement was profoundly influenced by Jewish ideas and customs or may even have been of Jewish origin (but see SCHWEIZER 1976:100-104 and POKORNÝ 1987:95-101).

IV. *Bibliography*

T. DREW-BEAR, *Nouvelles inscriptions de Phrygie* (Zutphen 1978); *R. A. KEARSLEY, Angels in Asia Minor: The Cult of Hosios and Dikaios, *New Docs* 6 (1992), 206-209; S. MITCHELL, *Anatolia: Land, Men, and Gods in Asia Minor*, vol. 2 (Oxford 1993); P. POKORNÝ, *Der Brief des Paulus an die Kolosser* (Berlin 1987); M. RICL, Hosios kai Dikaios, *Epigraphica Anatolica* 18 (1991) 1-53; 19 (1992) 71-102; E. SCHWEIZER, *Der Brief an die Kolosser* (Neukirchen 1976); A. A. R. SHEPPARD, Pagan Cults of Angels in Roman Asia Minor, *Talanta* 12-13 (1980-81) 77-101.

P. W. VAN DER HORST

HOST OF HEAVEN צבא השמים

I. At the origin of the conception of a 'host of heaven' stands the metaphor of →Yahweh as warrior. When waging his wars, Yahweh was helped by warriors and an army (e.g. 2 Kgs 6:17; 7:6; Isa 13:4-5; Joel 4:11; Hab 3:8; Ps 68:18). Only a few examples of this military background of the host of heaven have been preserved in the OT (Dan 8:10-11, cf. Josh 5:13-15). Due to a semantic shift, host of heaven also designates the divine assembly gathered around Yahweh, the heavenly king (1 Kgs 22:19 = 2 Chr 18:18). In the course of Israelite religious history this concept underwent several changes.

II. The clearest impression of the Israelite conception of host of heaven is given by an early prophetic narrative (1 Kgs 22:1-28). In a vision Micah ben Jimlah sees "the LORD seated on his throne, with all the host of heaven standing beside him on his right and on his left" (1 Kgs 22:19). This picture is borrowed from terrestrial realities: A king sitting on his →throne and his ministers and attendants surrounding him. Though not using the term 'host of heaven' this picture of the divine →council also underlies Isa 6, where Yahweh as king carries the title 'LORD of hosts' (Isa 6:3.5). In the course of time, the host of heaven was subject to an astralization in accordance with previous developments in Mesopotamian and Syro-Canaanite religions. This is shown by the texts which understand the host of heaven as sun, →moon and →stars (Deut 4:19; cf. Ps 148:2-3) or set host of heaven in parallelism to sun and moon, thus meaning the stars alone (Deut 17:3; 2 Kgs 23:5; Jer 8:2; cf. Dan 8:10). The veneration of the astralized 'host of heaven' took place on the roofs (Jer 19:13; Zeph 1:5). That this veneration was not confined to popular religion is shown by the fact that even kings were reproached for having practized this cult (2 Kgs 21:3, 5 = 2 Chr 33:3, 5; Jer 8:2; 19:13). Also in the temple of Jerusalem there were altars for the worship of the host of heaven (2 Kgs 21:5), which were removed during the cult-reform by Josiah (2 Kgs 23:4-5). Under the influence of the Assyrian domination of Judah, a tendency towards Yahweh monolatry arose, which implied a rejection of the astralized host of heaven in Deuteronomistic circles. That is why in Judaean texts of late pre-exilic and exilic times the worship of the host of heaven, often set in parallelism to the worship of foreign gods (Deut 17:3; 2 Kgs 17:16; 21:3; 23:4-5; Jer 19:13; Zeph

1:4-5), is strictly forbidden to the Judaeans. As a result of the rise of monotheism during the exilic and postexilic periods, Yahweh became a universal god. In spite of the Deuteronomistic rejection of the astralized host of heaven, theologians continued to use the model of host of heaven. In the texts mentioning Yahweh's domination over the host of heaven this term can mean everything in heaven. 'Host of heaven' is used in this sense in the creation story of the Priestly Code, where the end of Yahweh's creation work is described as "And heaven and earth were completed and all their host" (Gen 2:1). Here and in postexilic texts the meaning of 'host of heaven' remains vague. Perhaps stars or celestial beings are meant (Isa 24:21-23; 34:4; 40:26; 45:12: Jer 33:22 [cf. Gen 15:5]; Ps 33:6; Neh 9:6; cf. Aram Dan 4:32). In a series of other postexilic texts, 'host of heaven' has regained its ancient positive connotation of Yahweh's divine council. In most cases Yahweh's hosts and not the hosts of heaven are mentioned. In Ps 103:19-21 Yahweh is said to be enthroned in heaven. All his messengers, mighty ones, hosts and ministers are called upon to bless him. This is also the case in Ps 148:1-5, where Yahweh's messengers and hosts are called upon to praise Yahweh. Additionally in v 3 the parallelism of 'host of heaven' and sun, moon and stars has been preserved. According to Dan 8:9-13, Antiochus III is represented as a he-goat. His horn grew as great as the host of heaven and "it cast down to the earth some of the host and some of the stars and trod them underfoot". As in Ps 148:3, the parallel of 'host of heaven' and the stars is maintained.

In the NT *stratia tou ouranou* occurs twice. Here it can mean the assembly of angels praising god, thus reflecting the OT conception of the divine council (Luke 2:13). In Acts 7:42 the host of heaven is referred to in an OT allusion.

IV. *Bibliography*

L. K. HANDY, *Among the Host of Heaven. The Syro-Palestinian Pantheon as Bureaucracy* (Winona Lake 1993); C. HOUTMAN, *Der Himmel im Alten Testament* (OTS 30; Leiden 1993) 67-72, 194-207; O. KEEL & C. UEHLINGER, *Göttinnen, Götter und Gottessymbole* (QD 134; Freiburg 1992) 390-399; T. N. D. METTINGER, YHWH SABAOTH – The Heavenly King on the Cherubim Throne, *Studies in the Period of David and Solomon and other Essays* (ed. T. Ishida; Tokyo 1982) 109-138, esp. 123-128; E. T. MULLEN, *The Divine Council in Canaanite and Early Hebrew Literature* (HSM 24; Chico 1980) 111-280; H. NIEHR, *Der höchste Gott* (BZAW 190; Berlin 1990) 71-94; H. RINGGREN, צָבָא *ṣābā'*, *TWAT* 6 (1987-89) 871-876; H. SPIECKERMANN, *Juda unter Assur in der Sargonidenzeit* (FRLANT 129; Göttingen 1982) 221-225; A. S. VAN DER WOUDE, *THAT* 2 (1976) 498-507; M. WEINFELD, The Worship of Molech and of the Queen of Heaven and its Background, *UF* 4 (1972) 133-154, esp. 149-154; G. WESTPHAL, צבא השמים, *Orientalische Studien*. FS T. Noeldeke 2 (ed. C. Bezold; Giessen 1906) 719-728.

H. NIEHR

HUBAL הבל

I. As used in Deuteronomistic polemics, Hebrew הבל, vocalized *hebel*, has been interpreted as a divine name. Identified as a putative Canaanite fertility god *Hubal, he has been equated with the pre-Islamic central-Arabian deity Hubal (BARSTAD 1978).

II. Hubal was a central-Arabian deity. His cult has endured until today. A statue of Hubal is still standing near the Ka'ba in Mecca. He has been related to divination. An arrow oracle of Hubal has been famous (FAHD 1958:54-79; HÖFNER, *WbMyth* 1/I 447-448). In a Nabataean inscription a deity *hblw* occurs between Dusares and Manāt (CIS II 198; CANTINEAU 1932:25-27). This deity could be identical with Hubal.

III. *Hebel* occurs frequently in OT religious polemics (Deut 32:21; 1 Kgs 16:13. 26; 2 Kgs 17:15; 8 times in Jer; Zech 10:2; cf. Ps 31:7 and Jona 2:9; →Vanities). The word is construed as a deprecating reference to foreign deities. Barstad argues that *hebel* is not simply a derogatory term, but the distorted name of the presumed Canaanite fertility-god Hubal. Jer 8:9; 10:3.8.15; 14:22 and Zech 10:2 suggest (so Barstad) that *Hubal was associated with rain and expected to bring prosperity upon the fields and the country.

This proposed identification is open to serious objections: 1) A Canaanite deity *Hubal is not known from the sources. 2) The plural of *hebel* (*hăbālîm*) occurs several times, which is uncommon for the proper name of a god. The comparison with בעלים is not convincing because בעל (→Baal) can also function as a generic term. 3) The interpretation of Jer 10:3 "*Hubal is really only a piece of wood" seems to prove the existence of the name, but is based on a grammatically unsound understanding of the text. The words הבל הוא are part of the main nominal clause: "The institutions of the nations are empty/false/idle" (BECKING 1993).

Connections with the pre-Islamic deity Hubal are uncertain. There is too great a distance in time. The gap of nearly a millennium cannot be filled up with the single reference to a deity *hblw* in a Nabataean inscription from the first century CE and the unproven theory of a Moabite origin (BARSTAD 1978).

IV. *Bibliography*

H. M. BARSTAD, *HBL* als Bezeichnung der fremden Götter im Alten Testament und der Gott Hubal, *ST* 32 (1978) 57-65; B. BECKING, Does Jeremiah X 3 refer to a Canaanite Deity called Hubal?, *VT* 43 (1993) 555-557; J. CANTINEAU, *Le Nabatéen* II (Paris 1932); T. FAHD, Une pratique cléromantique à la Kaʿba préislamique, *Sem* 8 (1958) 54-79.

B. BECKING

HUBUR

I. According to Mesopotamian tradition the border of the netherworld was marked by a river called *Ḫubur* in Akkadian and **i$_7$-kur-ra** "river of the netherworld", **i$_7$-lu$_2$-ku$_2$-ku$_2$** "man-devouring river" or **i$_7$-lu$_2$-ru-gu$_2$** "river that runs against man" in Sumerian. Hubur, according to the dictionaries (*AHW* 352 and *CAD* H 219) a Sumerian loan-word, also occurs as a synomym for the whole of the netherworld (W. G. LAMBERT, *AfO* 17 [1954-56] 312:9; *BWL* 58:7) and as the name of the place of the river-ordeal (*CAD* H 219 [a]). It has been equated with the river *Ḥābōr* in the OT (e.g. 2 Kgs 17:6).

II. In Mesopotamia there was no homogeneous tradition about the river Hubur, as in general there were several views about the netherworld. The Hubur was believed to be located—either far to the west, or in the mountains of the east—in front of the gates of the netherworld. It had to be crossed by the dead before they reached their final destination. In the Babylonian theodicy we can read: *na-a*[*d*]*-nu-ma ab-bu-nu il-la-ku ú-ru-uḫ mu-ú-t*[*u*] *na-a-ri hu-bur ib-bi-ri qa-bu-ú ul-tu ul-la* "Our fathers in fact give up and go the way of death; it is an old saying that they cross the river Hubur" (*BWL* 70: 16-17). This transition from life to death by crossing a river is also illustrated by the fact that several boat models from bitumen were found in the royal graves of Ur (C. L. WOOLLEY *et al.*, *Ur Excavations II: The Royal Cemetry* [London 1934] pl. 20a, 86b). The Sumerian epic "Enlil and Ninlil" relates how Enlil, the supreme god of the Sumerian pantheon, once was banished to the netherworld and how Ninlil, his wife, followed him there. The epic also mentions the river **i$_7$-lu$_2$-ku$_2$-ku$_2$** and a boatman connected with it (H. BEHRENS, *Enlil und Ninlil* [StPsm 8; Rome 1978] 192-195, 199). In the Gilgamesh epic (Gilg. X iii and iv) the ferryman is called Urshanabi and according to the Neo-Assyrian "Vision of the Netherworld" (W. VON SODEN, *ZA* 43 [1936], 1-39: rev.5) the demon Ḫumuṭ-tabal, a four-handed creature with a face like the stormbird, took the dead to the other side of the river, where the city of the dead was located. Several Akkadian incantations were meant to chase demons to the netherworld, where they were held back by the river Hubur (for references see *AHW* 352 and *CAD* 219). In these incantation rituals boat models were used too.

The deified river ^{d}*Ḫubur* is mentioned in the brick inscription of Ilum-ishar of Mari (F. THUREAU-DANGIN, *RA* 33 [1936] 178), who set up a statue for him. In the great god-list An: *Anum* (*CT* 24, 36: 61) **^{d}lugal-ḫu-bur** "king Hubur" is one of the names of →Nergal and in the Enuma Elish (i 133, ii 19, iii 23, 81) →Tiamat is called "mother Hubur, who creates everything". Hubur is also attested in a Old Assyrian personal name (*Šu-Ḫubur;* H. HIRSCH, *AfO* Beiheft 13/14 [Graz 1961] 33), and the Assyrian calender used before the time of Tiglath-pileser I (1114-1076), contained a month-name Ḫibur/Ḫubur, probably for the 10th month (H. HIRSCH, *AfO* Beiheft 13/14 [Graz 1961] 54 and fn. 280; W. RÖLLIG, *RLA* 4 [1972-76] 469, 3).

There seems to be no connection between ^{d}*Ḫubur* and the divine couple ^{d}*Ḫabūr* and ^{d}*Ḫabūrtu* mentioned in the Assyrian "Götter-adressbuch" (*Tākultu* 124). They were probably associated either with the river Habur in Upper Mesopotamia, the place Ḫaburā (K. NASHEF, RGTC 4 [1991] 44) or the town Ḫaburatum east of the →Tigris (B. GRONEBERG, RGTC 3 [1980] 284) just like the goddess ^{d}*Ḫaburītum* mentioned in Ur III texts from Puzrish-Dagan (D. O. EDZARD & G. FARBER, RGTC 2 [1974] 266). The Habur-river occurs several times in personal names from the second millennium BCE (K. NASHEF, RGTC 4 [1991] 144 and RGTC 5[1982] 299), but is never written with a divine determinative. There is no evidence for an identification of the Habur with the river of the netherworld.

III. In the OT (2 Kgs 17:6; 18:11; 1 Chr 5:26) *Ḥābōr* is always used as a geographical designation—as the name of the river of Gosan (Akkadian Guzana, modern Tell Ḥalaf), where Sargon II deported the people from the kingdom of Israel (cf. BECKING 1992:84-89).

IV. *Bibliography*

B. BECKING, *The Fall of Samaria: An Historical and Archeological Study* (Leiden 1992); D. O. EDZARD, Ḫabūrā(tum), Ḫabūr, Ḫabūrtum, Ḫaburītūm, *RLA* 4 (1972-76) 29; EDZARD, Unterwelt, Unterweltsfluß, *WbMyth* I/1 (Stuttgart 1965) 130-132; S. N. KRAMER, Death and Netherworld according to the Sumerian Literary Texts, *Iraq* 22 (1960) 59-68; J. LEWY, The Assyrian Calendar, *ArOr* 11 (1939) 35-46, esp. 42-43; W. RÖLLIG, Ḫubur, *RLA* 4 (1972-76) 468-469 [& lit]; K. TALLQVIST, *Sumerisch-akkadische Namen der Totenwelt* (StOr 5/4; Helsingforsiae 1934) 24, 33-34.

H. D. GALTER

HUMBABA

I. In the Mesopotamian mythological tradition, Ḫumbaba is the superhuman guardian of the Cedar forest in the West (→Lebanon). He was killed at the hands of Gilgamesh and Enkidu (TIGAY 1982:6-7.32-33.93-94.112-114; and see index s.v.). His name has been connected with that of Hobab the Kenite, a relative of Moses (Num 10:29; Judg 4:11).

II. Ḫumbaba (Old Babylonian Ḫuwawa) occurs already in the Sumerian Tale known as Gilgamesh and the Land of the Living, one of the sources of the integrated Gilgamesh Epic that took shape in the Old Babylonian period (TIGAY 1982:32-33). Though the descriptions of his physiognomy vary, Ḫumbaba is consistently cast in the role of guardian of the cedar forest whom Gilgamesh and Enkidu have to beat in order to fetch cedars for a palace in Uruk. In the Babylonian Epic, the severed head of Ḫumbaba is fastened to the cedar door offered as a present to Enlil (WIGGERMANN 1992:146). The scene seems to be an aetiology of the apotropaic use of Ḫumbaba faces. Such Ḫumbaba faces are frequently seen on Old Babylonian clay plaques and seals, usually set high in the background as though they were hung on the wall. An actual example of a Ḫumbaba face, carved in stone, has been found at the entrance of the temple of Tell al-Rimaḫ (BLACK & GREEN 1992).

The figure of Ḫumbaba is often believed to go back to the Elamite god Ḫumban (for whom see H. KOCH, *Die religiösen Verhältnisse der Dareioszeit* [Wiesbaden 1977] 101-105). A Neo-Assyrian text portrays this god, together with the Elamite deities Yabnu and Naprushu, as guardian of the corpse of Sennacherib (SAA 3 no. 32 r. 25), which tallies with the role of Ḫumbaba as protective spirit. In later tradition, Ḫumbaba survives in the figure of Kombabos, a legendary hero whose exploits have been described by Lucian (?) in *De Dea Syria*.

III. The suggestion that Hobab the Kenite bears the name of Ḫumbaba, and should perhaps be identified with him (JEAN 1931), lacks all ground. Apart from the fact that there is no functional analogy whatsoever between the two figures, and that they are also geographically worlds apart, the proposal fails to explain the loss of the *-m-* (apparently a stable element in the name, as witnessed by Gk Κομβαβος). Such objections cannot be countered by the equation of Ḫumbaba with the Anatolian goddess Kubaba (→Cybele) proposed by LEWY (1934). For the etymology of the Hebrew name, a derivation from ḪBB (denoting cunning) or ḤBB (denoting kindness) is far more attractive (cf. *HALAT* 273).

IV. *Bibliography*

J. BLACK & A. GREEN, *Gods, Demons and Symbols of Ancient Mesopotamia* (London 1992) 106; C.-F. JEAN, *La religion sumérienne* (Paris 1931) 124 n. 8; J. LEWY, Les textes paléo-assyriens et l'Ancien Testament, *RHR* 110 (1934) 47-48 n. 44; J. H. TIGAY, *The Evolution of the Gilgamesh Epic* (Philadelphia 1982); F. A. M. WIGGERMANN, *Babylonian Protective Spirits* (Groningen 1992) 146, 150.

K. VAN DER TOORN

HUNGER → MERIRI

HYLE Ὕλη

I. The word ὕλη is relatively rare in the Greek Bible. When used, it is always in the neutral meaning of 'material, matter, wood' (e.g. Jas 3:5). In philosophical and religious literature of the early Roman Empire, however, one sees ὕλη, 'matter', evolve into a kind of demonic power.

II. Due to an increasingly negative assessment of the material world in later Platonic philosophy, one finds in the writings of some philosophical circles of the early Christian centuries a correspondingly negative use of the word ὕλη. Philo, the Jewish philosopher from Alexandria, already exhibits this tendency to a certain extent, but it is only in some Gnostic writings (e.g. *NHC* VI 3, 27, 28 and *NHC* VI 4, 47, 7; see further F. SIEGERT, *Nag-Hammadi-Register* [Tübingen 1982] 316) and especially in the late second century *Oracula Chaldaica* that the demonisation of Hyle becomes full-fledged (LEWY 1978:304-309, 375-394). As LEWY rightly remarks: "The Chaldaean views on matter conform to those of the later Platonists, but they are bound up with demonological and magical beliefs which changed the spirit of the Platonic doctrine" (304). These *Oracles* designate Matter as "the worker of evil" and the →demons as "offsprings of evil Matter". The 'hylic demons' (ὑλικοὶ δαίμονες) have the whole of matter as their sphere of activity. This virtual identity of the material and the demonic transformed Hyle into the diabolic principle *par excellence*, which was seen as an aggressive and destructive power (MAJERCIK 1989:175-6). The Chaldaean →Hades-Hyle connection underscores this change of Hyle from a cosmological principle to a personal demonic potency. Influence of this view may be discerned not only in later pagan Platonists but also in a Christian Platonist like Synesius of Cyrene, who speaks in his *Egyptian Myth* about Matter's sending her demonic offspring down to the earth (LEWY 1978:306).

III. *Bibliography*

H. LEWY, *Chaldaean Oracles and Theurgy*, nouvelle édition par M. Tardieu (Paris 1978); R. MAJERCIK, *The Chaldean Oracles. Text, Translation, and Commentary* (Leiden 1989); E. DES PLACES, *Oracles Chaldaïques* (Paris 1971), index *s.v.* (p. 238).

P. W. VAN DER HORST

HYMENAIOS Ὑμέναιος

I. Hymenaios is the name of the Greek

god of the wedding. The name is derived from the Greek word for wedding song, *hymenaios*, which in turn derives from a ritual cry during the wedding procession, *hymen o hymenai' o*. Its etymology is obscure (CHANTRAINE 1980). As a theophoric name, it occurs twice in the NT (1 Tim 1:20; 2 Tim 2:17).

II. Hymenaios is a relatively late creation. As a personification of the wedding song he occurs first in Pindar (fr. 128c Maehler) and Euripides (*Troades* 310, 314 etc.; see also J. DIGGLE on Euripides, *Phaeton* 233-234); in the innovative fourth-century choral lyric he seems to have been a favourite subject (HENRICHS 1984:56). However, in the available sources he is not invoked as the god of the legitimate wedding before the Roman poets Catullus (61) and Seneca (*Medea* 67). In analogy with Muses, satyrs and other divine groups, a graffito in Dura-Europos even mentions Hymenaioi (*SEG* 17.772).

The background of the wedding song is clear in the various genealogies proposed by various late sources. Most popularly, Hymenaios is represented as the son of a Muse, but, alternatively, he can also be the son of the musicians →Apollo or Magnes (sources: LINANT DE BELLEFONDS 1988: 583; add HENRICHS 1984:55). Interestingly, he is sometimes said to be the son of →Dionysos (Seneca, *Medea* 110; Servius on Virgil, *Aeneid* 4.127), the god who also in the *Anthologia Palatina* (9.524.21) receives the epithet *hymeneios*; indeed, in various late representations the god is pictured with Dionysiac colours (LINANT DE BELLEFONDS 1991). Apparently, the joyful sphere of the Dionysiac world provides the background to this genealogy.

We nowhere hear about a cult for Hymenaios, and his mythology is limited to only a few details. Servius (*Aeneid* 4.99) mentions the following adventure. One day an Athenian, Hymenaios, and a group of girls, who were travelling to Eleusis, were captured by pirates and taken aboard. Hymenaios, whose beauty had made him hardly distinguishable from a girl, killed the pirates and married the girl with whom he had fallen in love. Since this adventure the Athenians invoke the name of Hymenaios during their weddings. The defeating of the pirates and the girlish appearance of the god strongly suggest an influence of the *Homeric Hymn to Dionysos*: an additional testimony of the connection between Hymenaios and Dionysos in later antiquity.

The first-century author Cornelius Balbus (quoted by Servius, *Aeneid* 4.127) relates that Hymenaios died during the wedding of Dionysos and Althaea, where he was singing: apparently, the god of the wedding should not be older himself than the bridal couple. The myth of the god's death goes back at least to Hellenistic times because Apollodorus (*FGH* 244 F 139) mentions that according to the Orphics Hymenaios was resurrected by Asclepius (O. KERN, *Orphicorum fragmenta* [Berlin 1922] fragment 40).

III. Hymenaios occurs twice in the NT (1 Tim 1:20; 2 Tim 2:17) where he is mentioned by Paul (?) among those who claimed that the resurrection already had taken place. It fits in with the late appearance of Hymenaios as a god that the theophoric name Hymenaios is also relatively late (SOLIN 1982:I.522-523, III.1369).

IV. *Bibliography*

P. CHANTRAINE, *Dictionnaire étymologique de la langue grecque* (Paris 1968-80); A. HENRICHS, Ein neues Likymniosfragment bei Philodem, *ZPE* 57 (1984) 53-57; P. LINANT DE BELLEFONDS, Hymenaios, *LIMC* IV.1 (1988) 583-585; LINANT DE BELLEFONDS, Hyménaios: une iconographie contestée, *Mélanges de l'École française à Rome* 103 (1991) 197-212; H. SOLIN, *Die griechischen Personennamen in Rom* I-III (Berlin & New York 1982).

J. N. BREMMER

HYPSISTOS ὁ ὕψιστος

I. Ὕψιστος is a superlative form from the adverb ὕψι (there is no positive adj.) "most high, highest". With the article ὁ it serves as a noun, having the sense "the most high" or "the highest". In the Greek translations of the Hebrew Bible עליון (→Elyon) is always translated by (ὁ) ὕψιστος. In these instances, as in the Greek literature of Judaism of the Second Temple Period and in the literature of primitive Christianity, the expression ὁ ὕψιστος refers to the God of →Abraham, Isaac and →Jacob. In non-Jewish or non-Christian texts written in Greek, the expression occurs as a divine name for →Zeus, the supreme god.

II. The Greeks proclaimed Zeus as God of the mountain tops and worshipped him as "Zeus of the Mountain" or "of the Peak", "of the Point", "of/on the Summit", "of the Head". When called "the High" or "the Most High", these epithets originally had a literal rather than a metaphorical sense (cf. COOK 1925:876). Later however, these epithets designated Zeus as the highest God of the Greek →Olympus. In Hellenistic times the expression was used as a divine name for various local mountain gods, e.g. Zeus Bennos in Phrygia or →Baal in Syria. Inscriptions and archaeological data from a wide area demonstrate that Zeus *Hypsistos, Theos Hypsistos,* or *Hypsistos* was revered from Athens, through Asia Minor, Syria and in Egypt (cf. CUMONT 1914; COOK 1925: 876-890). Due to the influence of the LXX and because the Jews believed their God to be supreme, Jews in the Diaspora used (ὁ) ὕψιστος as a divine name for the God of their fathers. This can be seen from the literary and widespread epigraphical evidence.

III. In the Greek translations of the Hebrew Bible ὁ ὕψιστος translates *'Elyôn* (Ps 49[50]:14) and sometimes *mārôm* (eg. Job 25:2; Ps 148:1). Almost constantly the article is used to determine ὕψιστος, be it in the absolute form ὁ ὕψιστος, even if the Hebrew has merely עליון (cf. Deut 32:8; 2 Kgs 22:14; Tob 1:13; 4:11) or ὁ θεὸς ο ὕψιστος (e.g. Ps 56[57]:3; 77[78]:35, 56; cf. var. lect. Dan 5:1) or κύριος ὁ ὕψιστος (e.g. Ps 7:18; 12[13]:6; Dan 2:18-19). Except in the vocative or in genitive constructions (e.g. Lam 3:35.38), the undetermined form ὕψιστος is rare and ὁ ὕψιστος θεός κύριος is unusual. This tendency to determine the superlative is common in the literary and non-literary texts attributed to Diaspora Judaism and might provide reason to suspect a monotheistic sense, although the expression ὁ ὕψιστος itself does not exclude polytheism.

In Gen 14:18-20 אל עליון is translated by ὁ θεός ὁ ὕψιστος. In v 22 (יהוה אל עליון) the Tetragrammon (→Yahweh) is not translated, although some versions later added κύριον (→Kyrios) to τὸν θεὸν τὸν ὕψιστον, ὃς ἔκτισεν τὸν οὐρανὸν καὶ τὴν γῆν. According to the Greek translation of Gen 14:18-20, →God, "the Most High"—in the Greek tradition a divine name for Zeus—is none but Yahweh, the God of Abraham, the Creator of heaven and earth. May He be blessed (v 20: εὐλογητὸς ὁ θεὸς ὁ ὕψιστος). This text from the Greek translation of the Torah clearly influenced the post-biblical use of *hypsistos* amongst Jews of the Second Temple Period.

The expression ὁ ὕψιστος does not exclude polytheism. The translator of Hebrew Ps 83:19 thus read *lĕbaddekā* as part of v 19b and translated (cf. Ps 82(83):19b) almost monotheistically σὺ (sc. κύριος) μόνος ὕψιστος ἐπὶ πᾶσαν τὴν γῆν. Polytheistic characteristics are not generally barred from the translations. Following the Hebrew, Ps 96(97):9 states that "the LORD (Heb יהוה, Gk κύριος) is the Most High over the whole earth, he is very highly exalted above all Gods". The →God of Heaven (cf. Ezra 1:2 and 2 Esdr 1:2; Dan 2:18) is identified as "the most high Lord" in the interpretation of the Hebrew or Aramaic in 1 Esdr 2:2 and θ´ Dan 2:18. *Hypsistos* is thus used with a spatial connotation. The Most High is Lord over the Kingdom of man (θ´ Dan 4:14); he lives forever in the heights (Isa 57:15; cf. 14:13-14).

In Ps 17(18):14-15 (cf. the parallel 2 Kgs 22:14-15) the LORD, the Most High, is depicted in language reminiscent of Zeus. They both thunder (βροντᾶν) from heaven and scatter their arrows (βελή). As great king over all the earth, the LORD most high is Israel's Helper and Redeemer (e.g. Ps 56[57]:3; cf. 77[78]:35). In Greek tradition Zeus is helper of the weak, the →Saviour (cf. SCHWABL 1978:1026-1025, 1055-1057). In the Psalms there are epithets which are unfamiliar in connection with Zeus Hypsistos. In the Psalms the Most High is Israel's Refuge and Power; the tabernacle in the city of the Most High shall not be removed (Ps 45[46]:2,4-5). These functions of the Most High are taken up from the Greek translations by Jews in the Diaspora, as can be seen from epigraphical evidence (*RECAM* II no. 141; cf. *Jos. As.* 8:9; 11:9).

Ben Sira used (ὁ) ὕψιστος as the translation for Elyôn (Sir 41:4,8; 42:2,18; 44:20; 50:16) and →El (e.g. 7:15; 12:6). The Greek *Hypsistos,* which Ben Sira often uses like a proper name, replaces the abbreviation of the Tetragrammon (e.g. 12:2: The Hebrew text reads מיהוה, the LXX translates παρὰ ὑψίστου. Cf. 43:2; 48:5). Hellenistic terminology is transferred to the Most High. "The Most High" is often combined with παντοκράτωρ (e.g. Sir 50:14.17; →Almighty), he is the King of everything (παμβασιλεύς, Sir 50:15). The most high God is LORD, the God who created heaven and earth (Jdt 13:18). 1 Esdr 2:2-3 relates polemically that Cyrus, the king of the Persians, grasped the truth: The Lord of Israel, the most high LORD, appointed him as king of the whole world. In the Greek paraphrase of Neh 8:6 in 1 Esdr 9:46, the LORD is not only great (cf. the translation in 2 Esdr 18:6), he is the highest God, the God of Hosts, the *Pantokrator* (→Almighty; although this term is a common name for God in the LXX, παγκρατής is a common epithet for Zeus, cf. COOK 1925:15, 1940:931; SCHWABL 1972: 346; *SEG* 18 no. 153; 22 no. 274). He lives in the highest places (*Pss. Sol.* 18:10).

As can be expected, the documents from the LXX originally written in Greek also identify the Most High with the LORD, the God of Israel. The expressions *Kyrios* and *Hypsistos* are thus used in parallel constructions referring to the same divine being (Wis 5:15; 6:3). In 3 Macc 6:2 Eliazar addresses God as βασιλεῦ μεγαλοκράτωρ, ὕψιστε, παντοκράτωρ θεέ. The Most High is "the Ruler of all power" (3 Macc 7:9). The apocrypha thus document the tendency to use different names for the God of Israel. The focus seems to be on the Most High as the Almighty, Creator and Ruler over everything.

In the NT the absolute use of ὁ ὕψιστος is confined to Acts 7:48. In contrast to Jewish belief, the author of Luke-Acts does not subscribe to the view that the Most High has his temple in →Zion. According to the Lukan version of Q 6:35/5:45, those who love their enemies will be "Sons of the Most High" (the translator of Ps 81[82]:6 translated בני עליון with υἱοὶ τοῦ ὑψίστου and in Add Esth 8:12-13 the Jews are called the "sons of the most high, greatest living God"). For Luke, →Jesus is the Son of the Most High, because the power of the Most High overshadowed →Mary (Luke 1:32,35). Heb 7:1 follows LXX Gen 14:18: →Melchizedek is the priest of the most high God. Luke 1:76 calls John the Baptist a prophet of the Most High and Paul and his companions are called δοῦλοι τοῦ θεοῦ τοῦ ὑψίστου by the girl possessed by a spirit of divination (Acts 16:17). Similarly supernatural spirits recognise Jesus as υἱὸς του ὑψίστου (Mark 5:7). [For other NT data see also →Elyon, end]

IV. In the Jewish literature from the Second Temple Period written or transmitted in Greek, that was not included in the versions of the LXX, the expression ὁ ὕψιστος (cf. *Sib. Or.* 3:519, 574) refers to the God, who has his →throne in heaven (cf. *T. Abr.* A 9:1-3). The Most High is the Creator, the Life-giver of τὰ πάντα (Gk *Enoch* 9:5; *Sib. Or.* 3:704-709; *Jos. As.* 8:9). He is the Creator (→heaven and the →sea with all its moving water are works of the Most High [Gk *Enoch* 101:1.6]). →Enoch calls the Most High κύριος τῶν κυρίων καὶ θεὸς τῶν θεῶν και βασιλεὺς τῶν αἰώνων and states that the throne of his glory stands unto all the generations of the ages. His name is holy, great and blessed unto all the ages (Gk *Enoch* 9:4). The "Most High" is ο ἅγιος ὁ μέγας (Gk *Enoch* 10:1 in Georgius Syncellus), the most high Leader (ἄκτωρ ὕψιστος), who created Jerusalem as highly blessed seat of the great whole (Philo the epic poet 24:1 in Euseb., *Praep. Ev.* IX 24,1). In the tradition of Ps 45 (46):2.5.8.12 *Jos. As.* calls "the Most High" the →"Mighty One of Jacob". He is the God of heaven, the most high God of life (21:15). Abraham and Jacob are each called "friend of the most high God" (*T. Abr.* A 16:9; *Jos. As.* 23:10). Levi is a prophet of the Most High (22:13). →Joseph is called "begotten →son of God", but Aseneth is to become "daughter of the Most High" (cf. 21:4).

Terminology used for Zeus and in Hellenistic times for political leaders is transferred to the Most High and combined with divine attributes. Abraham addresses the Most High as κύριε παντοκράτωρ (*T. Abr.* A 15:12). He is not only ὁ δεσπότης (*T. Abr.* A 16:2. NB δεσπότης is also used for Zeus (SCHWABL 1972:297) τῆς κτίσεως ὁ ἀθάνατος (since Homer [*Iliad* 2:741] in connection with Zeus) βασιλεύς, but also ὁ ἀόρατος πατήρ, ὁ ἀόρατος θεός (*T. Abr.* A 16:2-3). Greek *Enoch* uses the expression "the highest" mainly in contexts, where the Most High acts as judge (93-94; 99:3). Till the day of judgement every unjust deed is recorded in the presence of the Most High (98:7). *Sib. Or.* calls the great eternal God (3:698), the Creator, the δικαιοκρίτης τε μόναρχος, the ἀθάνατος, ἅγιος (ἅγιος is also an epithet for Zeus, (cf. COOK 1925: 879; SCHWABL 1972:225-226), the great eternal king, ὁ ὕψιστος θεός (cf. 3:704, 709, 717, 719). The law of the Most High is mentioned, stressing that he is most righteous of all throughout the world (cf. 3: 720,580. δικαιόσυνος is also an epithet for Zeus—cf. COOK 1925:1092; 1940:951).

Philo uses the expression ὁ θεὸς ὁ ὕψιστος when citing LXX Gen 14:22 and ὁ ὕψιστος when citing LXX Deut 32:8 or Num 24:16. In the other instances, the expression is used in the set form ὁ ὕψιστος θεός and refers specifically to the God of the sacred temple in Jerusalem (*Leg. Gai.* 278; *Flacc.* 46), to whom even Caesar has ordered offerings to be made (*Leg. Gai.* 157,317). Philo leaves no door open to interpret the expression in a polytheistic manner. After citing LXX Gen 14:18 (where Melchizedek is called "priest of the Most High"), Philo excludes the possibility that there is any other Most High, ὁ γὰρ θεὸς εἷς ὢν (*Leg. All.* 3:82). An anonymous *Samaritan* author from the 2nd century BCE translated 'Αργαριζίν with ὄρος ὑψίστου (Eusebius, *Praep. Ev.* IX 17,5).

In dealing with non-literary evidence, it is extremely difficult to decide whether an inscription mentioning the most high God refers to the God of Israel. The mere occurrence of the expression ὕψιστος does not guarantee its Jewish origin (Cos, *ZPE* 21 [1976] 187 = TREBILCO 1991:134; Acmonia, *SEG* 26 nos. 1355-1356; cf. *NewDocs* 1 no. 5). In a late imperial inscription from Dierna in Dacia the plural θεοὶ ὑψ(ίστοι) is used (cf. *NewDocs* 2 no. 12). A Lydian inscription is dedicated to θεᾷ ὑψίστῃ (cf. COOK 1925:881).

Sometimes the influence of the LXX on the expression or phrases in an inscription (Delos = *CIJ* 1^2 no. 725a+b; Acmonia, *CIJ* 2 no. 769), or added epithets like παντοκράτωρ and εὐλογητός (*CIJ* 1^2 690^a [= *SEG* 32 no. 790]; similarly *CIJ* 1^2 no. 690; *CIJ* 1 no. 78*) or perhaps an effort in Thessalonica to transliterate the Tetragrammon (*CIJ* 1^2 no. 693d), might give some degree of certainty. Inscriptions that refer to or were found near a building that might be identified as a προσευχή, might be Jewish (Alexandria, *CIJ* 2 no. 1433 [= *CPJ* 3, pp. 134-5]; Athribis, *CIJ* 2 no. 1443 [= *CPJ* 3, p. 142]; Leontopolis, *SEG* 33 no. 1326]. In a building: Delos, *CIJ* 1^2 nos. 727-730).

Using this scant evidence some outlines of a picture might be drawn. For inhabitants of Delos ὁ θεὸς ὁ ὕψιστος is the Lord of the spirits and of all flesh. He oversees everything (*CIJ* 1^2 725a+b; cf. DEISSMANN, *Licht vom Osten* [Tübingen 1908] 305-316). Using metaphoric language of LXX Zech 5:1-5, Acmonian Jews attributed the function of judgment to the Most High (*CIJ* 2 no. 769). Along the Bosporus, the God most high is the blessed Almighty (θεῶι ὑψίστωι παντοκράτορι εὐλογητῶι; *CIJ* 1^2 690^a [Gorgippa = *SEG* 32 no. 790], similarly *CIJ* 1^2 no. 690, *CIJ* 1 no. 78*). Although παγκρατής is a common epithet for Zeus (cf. PW s.v.; *SEG* 18 no. 153; 22 no. 274), εὐλογητός most likely indicates that these inscriptions were erected by Jews (cf. LXX Gen 14:20-22; Jdt 13:18) in the first century CE and that they used both epithets, ὕψιστος and παντοκράτωρ, together. In Sibidunda in Pisidia the God most high is called "holy Refuge" (ἁγία καταφυγή - *SEG* 19 no. 852 = TREBILCO 1991:136). Although ἅγιος is a common epithet for Zeus in Syria and Palestine, this does not apply to καταφυγή. In the LXX this term is often used for God. It is not an epithet for Zeus or another deity. In the 3rd century CE he is called "the great God, the Most High, the Heavenly" by Jews near Ankara (*RECAM* 2 no. 209B). This last epithet (ἐπουράνιος) is, like μέγιστος and ὕψιστος, often used for Zeus (cf. SCHWABL 1972:308, 335). Such names were used when dedicating a marble column to the Most High and his προσκυνητῇ προσευχῇ.

Amongst early Christian writers, Clement of Rome illustrates the Christian dependence on the Jewish use of ὁ ὕψιστος (*1 Clem* 29:2 citing Deut 32:8-9; *1 Clem* 45:7 as reception of Dan 3:19-25) and addresses Him, whose name is the beginning of all creation, as "the only Highest in the Highest, the Holy One, resting amongst the holy" (*1 Clem* 59:3). Ignatius of Antioch combines Jewish and Christian tradition and speaks in the salutation of his letter to the Romans of "the most high →Father" (for the Apologists cf. BERTRAM 1969:619).

V. *Bibliography*

*G. BERTRAM, ὕψος, *TWNT* 8 (1969) 613-619; C. COLPE, Hypsistos, *KP* 2 (1975) 1291-1292; *A. B. COOK, *Zeus. A Study in Ancient Religion* II/2, III (London 1925, 1940); F. CUMONT, Ὕψιστος, PW 9 (1914) 444-450; *A. D. NOCK, C. ROBERTS & T. C. SKEAT, The Gild of Zeus Hypsistos, *HTR* 29 (1936) 39-88 (reprinted, omitting Introduction, Greek text, detailed commentary and plate in A. D. Nock, *Essays on Religion and the Ancient World* I [Oxford 1972]) 414-443; Greek text in *NewDocs* 1 no. 5); H. SCHWABL, Zeus I, PW 19 (1972) 253-376; H. SCHWABL, Zeus II, PWSup 15 (1978) 994-1481; M. SIMON, Theos Hypsistos, *Le Christianisme antique et son contexte religieux. Scripta Varia.* Volume II (WUNT 23,2; Tübingen 1981) 495-508; *P. TREBILCO, *Jewish Communities in Asia Minor* (SNTSMS 69; Cambridge 1991) 127-144.

C. BREYTENBACH

I

IBIS Ἶβις

I. The Ibis was considered to be the visible manifestation of the Egyptian god of →wisdom →Thoth. The ibis occurs in the Bible in the LXX versions of Deut 14:16 and Isa 34:11 as rendering of MT ינשׁוף, vocalised *yanšûp*, presumably a kind of long-eared owl (?). Whenever the opportunity presented itself, the LXX translators polemised against Egyptian cults (compare their polemics against the cult of →Apis in Jer 46:15). Here they equated the ibis with the owl which in Deut 14:16 and Lev 11:17 appears in lists of unclean birds (BECHER 1967:379-380; MORENZ 1964:253-254; GÖRG 1978:177-178).

The Egyptian name of the ibis is *tḫn* or, since the New Kingdom, *hb* (ZIVIE 1980: 116). The Gk ἶβις, instead of the expected ἷβις, has been understood as a case of psilosis, characteristic of the Ionian dialect (MUSSIES 1978:831).

II. The Ibis religiosa (*threskiornis aethiopica*) is a white shining bird except for the black head and tail-feathers. He was worshipped in the shape of a statue having a bronze head, tail and feet and a gilded or white painted body (SMELIK 1979:230, with n.21). The Ibis-worship has been attested since the second half of the New Kingdom (KÁKOSY 1981:43; SMELIK 1979:227, n.8). It was not limited to a particular cult-place, as with most other sacred animals (for instance Apis) but since the New Kingdom the number of cult-places spread rapidly throughout Egypt to reach its greatest profusion during the Late Period (from 700 BCE; SMELIK 1979:228-229 provides a comprehensive list of the cult-places).

The close relation between Thoth and the Ibis is apparent from the fact that Thoth is called the Ibis, the venerable Ibis or the Ibis-great-in-magic (BOYLAN 1922:191). According to Egyptian conceptions, the Ibis reveals the hidden nature of Thoth on earth (RAY 1976:137). The Egyptians associated Thoth, the oracle god "who hears", to his earthly counterpart the Ibis, who is called "The Face has spoken" (QUAEGEBEUR 1975). Thoth was the Lord of Laws and the founder of social order (BOYLAN 1922:88-89). Thus Thoth and the Ibis are invoked to deliver those who are in distress (SMELIK 1979:237-238). The Ibis also seems to have served in a private cult (KÁKOSY 1981:44, with n.36).

The Ibis revealed the lunar science of arithmetics (ZIVIE 1977:23-24). His snake-killing activities (KÁKOSY 1981:43) reflected Thoth's nature as a destroyer of enemies. Like Thoth the Ibis was a physician, who was said to have introduced the clyster (Plutarch, *de Iside et Osiride* 75). As the emanation of Thoth, the god of wisdom, the Ibis made up the first letter of the Egyptian alphabet (KÁKOSY 1981:42, n.7 with references). The Ibis was also associated with Imhotep, the archetypical scientist and physician (ZIVIE 1980:118, with n.46). Thoth was regarded as the father or tutor of →Isis (RAY 1976:158-159; KÁKOSY 1981:43, with n.14 and pertinent references) and ibises and baboons, both embodiments of Thoth, are depicted in temples of Isis in Italy (SMELIK 1979:241).

The Ibis reveals Thoth's creative powers. The step of the bird is said to measure one cubit (Aelian, *Nat. anim.* 10.29) and the spreading of the legs formed an equilateral triangle (Plutarch, *de Isid. et Osirid.* 381D, *Quaest. conviv.* 670C; compare the white triangle on Apis's brow). The cubit was sacred to Thoth and by means of it the god measured the cosmos and its counterpart Egypt, thus establishing the cosmic order (Eg *Maat*). Votive cubits, found in tombs, are often inscribed with the measurements and names of Egypt's provinces (ZIVIE 1977:33-34). Using a theological pun, the Egyptians associated the name of the Ibis (Eg *hb*) with the important role of Thoth as the heart (Eg *ib*), i.e. the creative Thought, of the demiurge, the sun god →Re (ZIVIE 1980:117, with n.36). Sometimes the Ibis is identified with the palette of Thoth (SCHOTT 1968:55) by means of which the god designed the world, the *pictura mundi* (DERCHAIN-URTEL 1988:1-26). In *PGM* I. 54, the sun god is said to assume the shape of the Ibis in the 9th hour.

The Egyptians associated the Ibis (= →moon) to his solar companion the Hawk (= sun; →Helios, →Shemesh). According to temple texts, the Ibis and the Hawk lay down the rules of the world's regiment and announce to the world the king's crowning (SCHOTT 1968). Clement of Alexandria, *Stromat.* V.7.43, 1-3 states that the golden statues of a Hawk and an Ibis are carried along in Egyptian processions. The cults of the Ibis and the Hawk are often combined (SMELIK 1979:240-241). At Saqqara, the Ibis- and Hawk-galleries are found in the same area and both cults are administered together (RAY 1976:137).

Relatively little is known about the Ibis cult itself. The king granted the temple and the land to provide the sustenance of the birds. The temple housed the cult statue which served in processions. A special building, called the birth chapel, was intended for the incubation of the eggs (RAY 1976:138).

Ibises were mummified after the example of →Osiris (*RÄRG* 321, with references). Large quantities of mummified eggs have also been found (RAY 1976:138). According to the cosmogony of Hermopolis, the chief centre of Thoth's cult, the world originated in a cosmic egg. Aelian, *Nat. animal.* 2.35, remarks that the hatching of ibis eggs takes 28 (lunar) days. The mummified ibises were provisionally stored away in the so-called houses of rest. The mass interment coupled with a procession was performed once yearly (RAY 1976:140).

III. In Deut 14:16 the *yanšûp*, 'long eared owl (?)', is mentioned in a list of unclean animals. This list has a duplicate in the P source (Lev 11:17). In an oracle against Edom (Isa 34) the forthcoming devastation of this country is depicted e.g. with the imagery that the country will be the abode of owls and →ravens (Isa 34:11; B. DICOU, *BN* 58 [1991] 30-45). In the MT the bird is not deified. In LXX Deut 14:16 and Isa 34:11 *yanšûp* is rendered with ἰβ(ε)ις. It is not clear whether the translators had a polemic against Egyptian cults in mind (MORENZ 1964) or were just identifying the bird referred to.

With P. DHORME (*Le livre de Job* [Etudes bibliques; Paris 1926] 541) the noun *ṭuḥôt* in Job 38:36 is generally construed as a reference to a bird, especially the ibis (e.g. O. KEEL, *Jahwes Entgegnung an Ijob* [Göttingen 1978] 60; A. DE WILDE, *Das Buch Hiob* [OTS 22; Leiden 1981] 369), though not deified.

IV. *Bibliography*

I. BECHER, Der heilige Ibisvogel der Ägypter in der Antike, *Acta Hungarica* 15 (1967) 377-385; H. BONNET, Ibis, *RÄRG* 320-321; P. BOYLAN, *Thoth. The Hermes of Egypt* (Oxford 1922); M.-T. DERCHAIN-URTEL, *Thot à travers ses épithètes dans les scènes d'offrandes des temples d'Epoque gréco-romaine* (Bruxelles 1981); M. GÖRG, Ptolemäische Theologie in der Septuaginta, *Das Ptolemäische Ägypten* (Akten des internationalen Symposions 27.-29. September 1976 in Berlin; Mainz 1978) 177-185; L. KÁKOSY, Problems of the Thot-cult in Roman Egypt, *Selected Papers (1956-73)* (StAeg 7; Budapest 1981) 41-46; S. MORENZ, Ägyptische Spuren in den Septuaginta, *JAC* Ergänzungsband 1 (1964) 250-258; G. MUSSIES, Some Notes on the Name of Sarapis, *Hommages à Maarten J. Vermaseren* (eds. M. den Boer *et al.*; EPRO 68/II; Leiden 1978) 821-832; J. QUAEGEBEUR, Teëphibis, dieu oraculaire?, *Enchoria* 5 (1975) 19-24; J. RAY, *The Archive of Ḥor* (London 1976); S. SCHOTT, Falke, Geier und Ibis als Krönungsboten, *ZÄS* 95 (1968) 54-65; K. A. D. SMELIK, *The cult of the Ibis in the Graeco-Roman Period, Studies in Hellenistic Religion* (ed. M. J. Vermaseren; EPRO 78; Leiden 1979) 225-243; A. P. ZIVIE, L'ibis, Thot et la coudée, *BSFE* 79 (1977) 22-41; ZIVIE, Ibis, *LdÄ* 3 (1980) 115-121.

R. L. VOS

ID אד

I. According to Gen 2:6, the primordial world was watered by a 'flood' (*ʾēd*) that arose from the earth prior to the advent of rainfall. It is probable that Hebr *ʾēd* was borrowed from Akk *id,* 'Id', which occurs in cuneiform sources (usually written dÍD) as a name for the →river as a deity, especially in connection with the river ordeal, a juridical process by which an accused person was tried by being thrown into the river (*CAD* I/J [1960] 8; *AHW* 364). Akkadian *id* was derived from the Sumerian name for the river god, who was believed to officiate over the ordeal. The common Akkadian noun corresponding to Sum **id** is *nārum,* 'river', which, though ordinarily feminine, occurs in Old Babylonian personal names as a masculine divine name, d*Nārum,* so that it is not always clear whether to read dÍD as *id* or *nārum* (LAMBERT 1985). Nevertheless it is certain from occasional syllabic spellings, such as d*I-id* (e.g, R. M. WHITING, *Old Babylonian Letters from Tell Asmar* [Chicago 1987], no. 21:5), that the river god was commonly called Id in Akkadian.

An alternative proposal (SPEISER 1955) is that *ʾēd* was borrowed from Akkadian *edû,* 'onrush of water, high water' (*CAD* E 35-36; *AHW* 187). It has been further suggested that Hebrew *ʾêd,* a noun meaning 'distress' or 'calamity' and customarily associated with an unattested Heb verb **ʾûd* (cf. Arabic *āda* [<*awada*], 'bend, burden, oppress') also derives from *id* (MCCARTER 1973).

II. The Mesopotamian god Id, the divine river, was a leading deity at Mari and elsewhere in the Old Babylonian period (ALBRIGHT 1967; LAMBERT 1985). He was associated with the dispensation of justice and in particular with the river ordeal, a procedure in which the guilt or innocence of the accused was determined by casting him into the waters. If the river god held him, he was believed to be guilty; if he escaped, he was deemed to be innocent. No comparable ordeal is known in the jurisprudence of Syria-Palestine, though Ugaritic *ṯpṭ nhr,* 'Judge River,' an epithet of Yamm, the →sea god, is suggestive (River). Even in the absence of an actual legal procedure in the Northwest Semitic region, it is nevertheless possible that a notion of judgment by ordeal in the cosmic waters at the entrance to the underworld existed as a religious concept expressed in a corresponding literary motif.

III. Whatever the background and derivation of the term, the 'flood' or primeval river of Gen 2:6 is not represented as a deity or a divine river. Nor does the noun *ʾêd,* in those biblical passages where it might mean '(river) ordeal' (Deut 32:35; 2 Sam 22:19 [=Ps 18:19]; Job 21:17.30; 31:23), refer directly or indirectly to a river god. Though the ordeal sometimes seems to take place in the cosmic waters at the entrance to the underworld (2 Sam 22:17 [=Ps 18:17]; cf. Jonah 2:4.6-7), it is depicted as an affliction or tribulation under Yahweh's control: and thus an instrument of his justice rather than an independent power with its own judicial authority (2 Sam 22:17-21 [=Ps 18:17-21]; cf. Ps 124:2-5).

IV. *Bibliography*

W. F. ALBRIGHT, *Yahweh and the Gods of Canaan* (Garden City, N.Y. 1968) 92, n. 99; E. DHORME, L'arbre de vérité et l'arbre de vie, *RB* 4 (1907) 274; W. G. LAMBERT, The Pantheon of Mari, *MARI* 4 (1985) 525-539, esp. 535-536; P. K. MCCARTER, The River Ordeal in Israelite Literature, *HTR* 66 (1973) 403-412; M. SÆBO, Die hebr. Nomina *ʿed* und *ʿēd, ST* 24 (1970) 130-141; E. A. SPEISER, *ʾed* in the Story of Creation, *BASOR* 140 (1955) 9-11.

P. K. MCCARTER

IDOLS → AZABBIM; GILLULIM

ILIB

I. The term *ilib* is found in Ugaritic texts both cultic and literary. In the former the *ilib* receives offerings and in the latter it is mentioned incidentally as the object of a particular family cult. There is very slight evidence for the *ilib* otherwise in Israelite literary and epigraphic sources.

There are various explanations of the form, the most obvious and widely accepted being that it is a modification of *ʾil* + *ʾab*, 'god' + 'father'. Ilib would, on this argument, be the 'divine ancestor' par excellence. Others, however, have sought explanations in Hittite *a-a-bi* (also the deity ^{d}*A-a-bi*), referring to a sacrificial/necromantic pit, thus linking the word with Hebrew *ʾōb*, 'ghost, necromancer, etc.' (cf. Lev 20:27; Isa 29:4 →Soothsaying Spirit) (see especially HOFFNER 1970-1973) or in the Arabic root *laʾaba*, 'set up', a derivation which might imply 'stele, standing stone'.

II. The Ugaritic appears only a few times in the texts but in quite unexpected contexts and in ways which are not easy to reconcile. On the one hand *ilib* appears at the head of god-lists. Indeed, in the 'pantheon' list *ilib* appears in the first place, above →El and →Baʿal (*KTU* 1.47:2; 1.118: 1). *ilib* also has a prominent role in rituals, often in receipt of offerings (*KTU* 1.41:35; 46:17[rest.]; 56:3, 5; 87:38; 91:5; 109:12, 15, 19, 35; 148:10, 23). On the other hand, in *KTU* 1.17 i 26 (and parallels 17 i 44; ii 16) *ilib* appears to refer to the dead ancestors, to whom, in fulfilment of a family duty, a stele or stelae are to be erected. (There are disagreements about details, though not really affecting the question of the meaning of *ilib*). From the context it appears that the cult of the *ilib* was a duty incumbent upon the eldest son in the family. If the person responsible is indisposed, his son must carry out this duty for him. It is noteworthy that the *ilib* can be referred to with pronoun suffixes as 'my/his *ilib*', as if *ilib* were a common noun. It is closely parallel to *ʿm*, 'clan, kinsman, ancestor'.

We thus appear at first to have two different significances for the term and some have in consequence sought to separate them completely from each other, seeking to identify *ilib* with a specific deity. The only plausible direct identification with another deity, taking *ilib* to be a specific divine name, is suggested by LAMBERT (1981), who has drawn attention to a Mesopotamian parallel, Ilaba, attested from the period of the dynasty of Akkad and down to ca 1600 BCE. This *ilib* would be quite distinct from the *ilib* of *KTU* 1.17. The separation of the two manifestations of *ilib* is not, however, necessary.

Our best clue to *ilib* is provided by the so-called Ugaritic 'pantheon' list. While the accuracy of the equations implied in this series of texts cannot be relied upon without reserve, the parallel versions in Akkadian (syllabic cuneiform DINGIR *a-bi* = *ilabi*) and the Hurrian equivalent (*in atn*: *KTU* 1.42:1) argue strongly for understanding the form to be a combination of *il* and *ab*, rather than based on any other roots. The slightly strange vocalisation (*a* > *i*) is not a serious obstacle, being paralleled by other such shifts (cf. Ugaritic *iḫ* for *aḫ*: *KTU* 2.41:18). Vowel harmonisation may be at work. Precise interpretation, however, still remains difficult.

The vocalisation of the syllabic version suggests the meaning 'El/God of the father(s)' or possibly 'El is my father'. The former would evoke echoes of the patriarchal 'God of the Fathers'. The syllabic spelling may, however, be an approximation rather than an exact rendering and the Hurrian suggests something more like 'divine father'. This meaning or 'divine (divinised) ancestor' is the most commonly adopted translation. The term might be a general one for such deified persons (SPRONK 1986). Such an interpretation, combined with the high position assigned to this figure in the lists and his general importance in the cult, suggests that he is an ancestral deity of the royal family and was highly revered. That such a royal ancestor cult was important in ancient Ugarit (and elsewhere in ancient Syria) is clear from abundant evidence, especially the evidence of the *rpum* (→Rephaim), and it is not surprising to find *ilib* in this sense at the head of pantheon lists, though this should not be taken to imply a *deity* more important than El, Dagan and Baʿal.

This interpretation is also compatible with

the other group of texts (e.g. *KTU* 1.17 i:26) in which Dan'il's ancestor-cult has to be carried on, since *ilib* would in both groups of texts be a common noun, which could apply to the domestic context of family shrines or to the national royal cult. In this context it may be noted that SPRONK (1986) would identify the *ilib* cult and the *rpum* cult, which is better known. Indeed it is not impossible that *ilib* is in fact a plural, 'the divine ancestors', and it is so interpreted by several scholars.

III. The evidence for ancestor cult in ancient Israel is widespread, but the Israelite epigraphic evidence for *ilib* is limited to a single seal bearing the Hebrew personal name *'bd'l'b* (cf. G. A. COOKE, *Textbook of North-Semitic Inscriptions* [Oxford 1903], no. 150:6, pl. xi, 6: the reading is not entirely certain). This implies that a divine *'l'b* was known in later times. This evidence is extremely slender.

One allusion to *ilib* has been detected in Hebrew literature—by ALBRIGHT in relation to Isa 14:19, where he would emend *yōrĕdê 'el 'abnê bôr*, "you who go down to the stones of the Pit", to *yûrĕdû 'el'ĕbê bôr*, "let them be brought down (to Sheol), O ghosts of the Nether World". In view of the acute difficulties in this verse it seems unwise to invent a *hapax legomenon* to solve them! We may note also the personal name Eliab (אליאב) in the Hebrew Bible (1 Sam 16:6, etc.), though it is doubtful that this is relevant.

Finally and for completeness mention should be made again of Hebrew *'ōb*, 'necromancer' (e.g. Lev 19:31), 'ghost' (e.g. Isa 29:4) and, according to HOFFNER, 'necromantic pit' (1 Sam 28:8), the origin of which has been explained in a variety of ways, though HOFFNER (1970-73) would relate it to *ilib*.

IV. *Bibliography*

W. F. ALBRIGHT, *Yahweh and the Gods of Canaan* (London 1968) 122-124; A. COOPER, Divine Names and Epithets in the Ugaritic Texts, *RSP III* (ed. S. Rummel; Rome 1981) 342-343; J.-M. DE TARRAGON, *Le culte à Ugarit* (Paris 1980) 151-156; M. DIETRICH, O. LORETZ & J. SANMARTÍN, Ugaritisch *ilib* und Hebräisch *'(w)b* "Totengeist", *UF* 6 (1974) 450-451; J. F. HEALEY, The *Pietas* of and Ideal Son in Ugarit, *UF* 11 (1979) 353-356; HEALEY, The Akkadian 'Pantheon' List from Ugarit, *SEL* 2 (1985) 115-125; H. A. HOFFNER, אוֹב *TWAT* I, (1970-73) 141-145 (*TDOT* I, 130-134); W. G. LAMBERT, Old Akkadian Ilaba = Ugaritic ilib?, *UF* 13 (1981) 299-301; K. SPRONK, *Beatific Afterlife in Ancient Israel and in the Ancient Near East* (AOAT 218; Kevelaer/Neukirchen-Vluyn 1986) 146-149.

J. F. HEALEY

IMAGE צלם

I. The Babylonian word *ṣalmu* is used as the equivalent of Sum **alam**, **dùl** and **nu**. It refers both to statues and other symbols of gods and humans. Though occasionally preceded by the divine determinative (**dingir**), the image (*ṣalmu*) was not viewed as a god itself. A cult of a deity 'Image' (**Ṣulmu*), however, is attested for the city of Taima in north-west Arabia. The closest analogy in the Hebrew Bible is the cult of erected stones (*maṣṣēbôt*), whose anointment with oil reflects a kind of worship.

II. Images played an important role in Babylonian religion. Both images in the sense of statues in the round and a variety of different types of symbol could represent deities. Objects or symbols pertaining to a particular deity could be used in swearing oaths. While a deity was normally regarded as being present in his statue or symbol, he could withdraw of his own free will, or be forced to withdraw, for example by desecration of the physical object. In this case complicated rituals were required to bring the material artefact back into religious life (such as *pīt pî* and *mīs pî* rituals, literally 'opening-of-the-mouth' and 'washing-of-the-mouth'). A worshipper could sometimes be regarded as represented by a votive statuette placed in a temple. The worshipper would normally avoid referring to the statue as such, but simply make reference to the deity by name.

However, there is direct evidence in the *tākultu* texts involving use of the word *lamassu*: "the pictorial representations of cities, the statues of fallen gods" (*Tākultu*, 5 i 30). Moreover Aššurnaṣirpal II (883-859 BCE) refers to a *lamassu* ('representation') of '(Ninurta's) great godhead' (E. A. W. BUDGE & L. W. KING, *The Annals of the Kings of Assyria* [London 1902] 210, 19; 345, ii 133). This contrasts with *lamassatu* in reference to →Ishtar (BUDGE & KING, *The Annals of the Kings of Assyria,* 164, 25). The arguments of SPYCKET (1968), questioning actual representation of deities for the third millenium BCE, are mainly arguments from silence. While it is often uncertain whether a statue or symbol is involved, there are of course references from the later period (second millennium BCE and later) which point unambiguously to an anthropomorphic representation. An example is an omen text based on the appearance of →Marduk as he leaves his temple Esagil in Babylon for the New Year's festival. This includes direct references to his eyes, mouth and facial expression (*SBTU* 2 no. 35).

Mesopotamian *ṣalmu* could refer not only to statues or symbols (such as *šurinnu*), but also to stelae with representations in relief, what is meant usually being apparent from the context. A Neo-Assyrian letter illustrates the closeness of symbol and deity: "The *kizertu* is set up in the temple; they say about it 'It is →Nabû'" (*LAS* 318: 6-7). In the Mesopotamian cultural context caution should be exercised with regard to the Babylonian word *ṣalmu*, 'statue', 'image', or 'likeness'. This is a functioning word within the language and its particular nuance depends on the specific context. Thus, even if the word is equipped with the divine determinative, it need not refer to the same thing or deity in different contexts. In the hyperbole of Neo-Assyrian letters the king can be said to be the image of Šamaš, as well as of other deities. This is best seen as belonging to the imagery of mytho-poetic diction.

There existed in Taima in north-west Arabia a cult or cults of *ṣlm* known from several Imperial Aramaic (ca. 400 BCE) inscriptions. The god *ṣlm*, known in Latin inscriptions as *Sulmus*, Gk Σολμος, was the chief deity of Taima. Since he had the winged sun-disk as his symbol (DALLEY 1986), it is possible that the god Ṣulmu (assuming that such was the pronunciation) is originally the hypostatized image of the sun god (cf. J. C. L. GIBSON, *TSSI*, Vol. 2 [1975] 150 ad line 2). Its closest parallels are the gods →Bethel and Sikkanu (attested, e.g. in the name Sanchuniathon = סכניתן), both deified cult →stones. The cult of Ṣulmu in Taima may have been brought there by people from Hamath, whose presence at Taima is attested by the cult of →Ashima (B. AGGOULA, Studia aramaica II, *Syria* 62 [1985] 61-76, esp. 70-71). Interpretational difficulties within the Arabian material preclude at present making any connection with Mesopotamian religion.

III. Etymologically corresponding to Akk *ṣalmu* is Heb *ṣelem*. Like its Akkadian (and Aramaic) counterpart, it can be used to designate the image of a deity. Thus Num 33:52 demands the destruction of all *ṣalmê massēkôt*, cast (i.e. metal) images (of idols). Such images were to be found in temples like the Baal temple in Jerusalem (2 Kgs 11:18//2 Chr 23:17). Also Judaeans were known to worship such idols (Ezek 7:20; 16:17). According to the difficult text of Amos 5:26, the Israelites engaged in the worship of →Kaiwan their 'image' (*Kiyyûn ṣalmêkem*). It is generally believed that the polemics against the worship of 'images' is exilic or post-exilic. The term *ṣelem* is not the technical term for the representation of an idol; *pesel* and *massēkâ* are more frequent (F. J. STENDEBACH, צלם, *TWAT* 6 [1989] 1046-1055, esp. 1051). 'Image' (*ṣelem*) as an hypostatized or even deified object is not attested in the Hebrew Bible; what comes closest to the worship of a god Ṣulmu among the early Israelites is the anointment of erected stones (e.g. Gen 28:18). The terms *ʾeben* and *maṣṣēbâ* used in this connection indicate that the parallel, if parallel there be, is not etymological but material (for further discussion →Bethel).

IV. *Bibliography*
K. BEYER & A. LIVINGSTONE, Die neuesten aramäischen Inschriften aus Taima, *ZDMG* 137 (1987) 285-296; BEYER & LIVINGSTONE, Eine neue reichsaramäische Inschrift aus Taima, *ZDMG* 140 (1990) 1-2; S. DALLEY, The God Ṣalmu and the Winged Disk, *Iraq* 48 (1986) 85-101; A. L. OPPENHEIM, The Golden Garments of the Gods, *JNES* 8 (1949) 172-193; J. RENGER & U. SEIDL, Kultbild, *RLA* 6 (1980-83) 307-318; A. SPYCKET, *Les statues de culte dans les textes mésopotamiens des origines à la 1re dynastie de Babylone* (Paris 1968); C. B. F. WALKER, *Material for a Reconstruction of the mīs pî Ritual* (Thesis, B.Phil.; Oxford 1966).

A. LIVINGSTONE

INANNA → ISHTAR

ISHḪARA

I. The personal name *ʾašḥûr*, Ashhur (1 Chron 2:24; 4:5)—traditionally construed as a derivation from the root ŠḤR, 'to be black' (*HALAT* 91)—has been interpreted by CASSUTO (1947:472) as "belonging to *Išḫara*". Išḫara is known as a Babylonian goddess.

II. Išhara, ᵈ*Iš-ḫa-ra*, also written *Aš-ḫa-ra* and *Eš-ḫa-ra*, is one of the names for Inanna/→Ishtar. In *Atr* I 301-304 and Gilg. II ii 35-50 mention is made of a 'bed laid for Išhara'. From this it can be inferred that Ishtar was called Išhara during the marriage rites. Therefore, she can be depicted as a goddess of love and/or a mother goddess (D. O. EDZARD, *WbMyth* 1, 90; LAMBERT 1976-80:176-177). Her astrological constellation was the scorpion (DOUGLAS VAN BUREN 1937-39). In the Hurrian pantheon a goddess with the same name appears. The South-Anatolian deity, however, is related with the underworld (FRANTZ-SZABÓ 1976-80). The goddess is also found in texts from Ugarit.

III. The traditional etymology of the name Ašhur is to be preferred to the fanciful interpretation offered by Cassuto. Derived from the root ŠḤR, 'to be black' with a preformative *ʾaleph*, the name probably refers to the colour of the skin. In two genealogical lists in Chronicles, Ašhur is presented as the father of Tekoa (1 Chron 2:24; 4:5). The Old Greek version, however, sees him as the father of Caleb (Lo 1992). From the Iron Age, the name is attested epigraphically in the seal inscription *ʾšḥr b*[*n*] *ʿśyhw*, 'Ašhur the so[n] of Asajah' (G. I. DAVIES, *Ancient Hebrew Inscriptions* [Cambridge 1991] no. 100.532) and in an ostracon from Samaria (*ʾšḥr*, 13:3-4; LEMAIRE 1977:31.49-50). Alternatively, the name can also be construed as containing the theophoric element →Horus (e.g. LEMAIRE 1977:49-50; J. H. TIGAY, *You Shall Have No Other Gods* [HSS 31; Atlanta 1986] 66).

IV. *Bibliography*
U. CASSUTO, Le tre alef dell'alfabeto ugaritico, *Or* 16 (1947) 466-476; E. DOUGLAS VAN BUREN, The Scorpion in Mesopotamian Art and Religion, *AfO* 12 (1937-39) 1-28; G. FRANTZ-SZABÓ, Išḫara, *RLA* 5 (1976-80) 177-178; W. G. LAMBERT, Išḫara, *RLA* 5 (1976-80) 176-177; A. LEMAIRE, *Inscriptions Hébraïques* I (LAPO 9; Paris 1977); H. C. LO, Ashhur, *ABD* 1 (1992) 487.

B. BECKING

ISHMAEL ישמעאל

I. Ishmael is the eponym of the Ishmaelite tribes who traced their ancestry back to →Abraham/Abram and visited his tomb at Hebron (Machpelah, Gen 25:9). The name as such is common Semitic and is attested from the earliest times onward (KNAUF 1985:38 n.170; ARCHI 1988:51). His name is explained in Gen 16:11 (J) and 21:17 (E) as a wish for answer, an explanation which tallies with the traditional understanding of this name (NOTH, *IPN*, 198). The name is not only found in early Mesopotamia (3rd millennium), but also in Middle Bronze Hazor *Iš-me-ìl*(DINGIR) (HOROWITZ & SHAFFER 1992) and perhaps Late Bronze Sinai (*CPSI* no. 34). From Old Babylonian Larsa a toponym *Iš-me-ìl*(DINGIR) is known (YOS 8 no. 173:11, cf. RGTC 3, 119) and from Mari a tribe *Iš-nu-lu-um*

(ARM V, 33:6). Toponyms and tribal names are sometimes derived from clans and their locally revered ancestors (MEYER 1906:297).

II. According to biblical genealogy Ishmael is the son of Abraham and →Sarah's slave-girl Hagar, given in marriage to the patriarch in order to achieve a natural heir and to create a heir by adoption for Sarah (Gen 16:2; 30:3). In this way Israelite tradition acknowledges the 'Abrahamite' origin of the Ishmaelite confederation (Gen 17:20; 25:12-18). The name Ishmael is also known as a divine name: ᵈ*Iš-me-la-(a)*/ ᵈ*Ša!-me-la-a* (*Tākultu*, 94:92; WEIPPERT, *RLA* 5 [1976-80] 251), one of the ten divine Judges of the temple of Assur in Nineveh. In the form ᵈ*Iš-me-lúm* this god is already known in an Old Assyrian inscription of Erishum I (*ARI* 1, 12). In Sabaean sources a similar divine name *Samāʿ* appears, probably an epithet of the Moongod (HÖFNER, *WbMyth* I/1, 467.528; *RAAM* 247-248). Other divine names of this type are attested in Mari and elsewhere, like, for instance ᵈYakrub-El/ ᵈIkrub-El (EDZARD, *RLA* 5, 254). An original connection between this god and the Ishmaelite eponym is, however, unprovable. Most probably they were not related, because the Ishmaelites appear as the *Šumuʾil* in the Assyrian sources (KNAUF 1985). This identification with the *Šumuʾil* has been challenged (EPH'AL 1982), but the equation is linguistically possible when it may be assumed that the Assyrian name is a standardized corruption of the early Western South-Semitic name (cf. also ᵏᵘʳ*Sir-ʾi-la-a-a* = Israel; ᵈ*Iš-me-la-a* = ᵈ*Ša-me-la-a*, etc.). From an historical and geographical point of view the identification is very plausible. It is uncertain whether the Ishmaelites originated from North-Sinai in the second millennium BCE (Gen 16 [J] and 21 [E], MEYER 1906: 322-328; differently KNAUF 1985, Nachwort), but early in the first millennium BCE they become historically manifest as a tribal confederation opposite the Palestinian monarchies in an area stretching "from Havilah to Shur near the border of Egypt" (Gen 25:18), i.e. from the isthmus of Suez to Duma (Dūmat al-Jandal) and Nefūd in the Arabian desert. Since the 8th century BCE the members of the confederation of *Šumuʾil* = Ishmael headed by the Qedar-tribe, are known as *Aribi, Arabu, Arabaia* in the Assyrian sources. In contemporary biblical texts *ʿrb(y)* 'Arab(i)' also started to replace 'Ishmaelite' (Isa 13:20; 21:13; Ezek 27:21 etc.).

An original ethnic connection between "the mother of Ishmael", Hagar and the biblical *hagriʾîm* (1 Chron 5:10.18-22) is not likely (MEYER 1906; NOTH 1948; KNAUF 1985), though 1 Chron 5:19-20 (also Ps 83:7) suggests an alliance between Hagarites and Ishmaelites. This however, reflects a much later historical state of affairs (perhaps Persian times, KNAUF 1985: 52).

III. There is a possibility that ᵈ*Išme-ilu* was an early Semitic deified ancestor-king or tribal saint of the kind listed among the ten ancestor-kings in the Assyrian Kinglist (*ANET*³, 564) and also the first ten deified kings of Ebla (ARCHI 1986; on deified ancestors see also M. STOL, Old Babylon Personal Names, *SEL* 8 [1991] 191-212, esp. 203-205). Personalities with a similar kind of name were venerated like deities in Ugarit (cf. *ydbil* and *yaršil* in *KTU* 1.106:3-4). However, it is impossible to prove that this ancestral divinity was identical to the eponym of Ishmael = *Šumuʾil.* Biblical traditions about Ishmael's burial, the whereabouts of his tomb and indications of his veneration are unknown. Only his death is mentioned by P (Gen 25:17). Scholars supposed a central Ishmaelite sanctuary at Beer →Lahai-roi (Gen 16:14) in the Negev or North-Sinai (MEYER 1906; NOTH 1948), but in this case one has to assume that Isaac's connection to this place is secondary (Gen 24:62; 25:11). There is no way to check the reliability of this tradition; nor is the place of Beer Lahai-roi established geographically. It is only Muslim tradition which tells us more about Ishmael's life and death, in particular how he and his mother settled near the well Zamzam between the hills al-Safa and al-Marwa in the neighbourhood of Mekka and how they were adopted by the

Jurhum tribe. Quran and Hadith provide a complete *hieros logos* for the Abrahamite origin of the Holy House in Mekka, and besides that, also traditions about the tombs of Ishmael and his mother Hagar, which are exhibited in the *hiğr* of the Haram of the Ka'aba at Mekka (PARET 1972).

IV. *Bibliography*

A. ARCHI, Die ersten zehn Könige von Ebla, *ZA* 76 (1986) 213-217; G. I. DAVIES, Hagar, El-Heğra and the Location of Mount Sinai, *VT* 22 (1972) 152-163; I. EHP'AL, *The Ancient Arabs. Nomads on the Borders of the fertile Crescent 9th-5th Centuries BC* (Jerusalem/Leiden 1982); R. FRANKENA, *Tākultu. De sacrale maaltijd in het Assyrische ritueel met een overzicht over de in Assur vereerde goden* (Leiden 1954); W. HOROWITZ & A. SHAFFER, An Administrative Tablet from Hazor. A preliminary Edition, *IEJ* 42 (1992) 17-33; E. A. KNAUF, *Ismael. Untersuchungen zur Geschichte Palästinas und Nordarabiens im 1.Jahrtausend v. Chr* (ADPV; Wiesbaden 1985; 1989 2nd enlarged ed.); E. MEYER, *Die Israeliten und ihre Nachbarstämme* (Halle 1906); M. NOTH, *Überlieferungsgeschichte der Pentateuch* (Stuttgart 1948); R. PARET, Ismā'īl, *The Encyclopaedia of Islam*, Vol 2 (Leiden 1972) 184-185.

M. DIJKSTRA

ISHTAR

I. The major Mesopotamian goddess of love, war, and the planet Venus is known primarily by the Sumerian name Inanna and the Akkadian name Ishtar. Although the name Inanna is usually translated as 'Lady of Heaven' (**nin.an.ak**), the alternative translation 'Lady of the date clusters' (**nin.ana.ak**), suggested by JACOBSEN (1976: 36), seems preferable. The name Ishtar is Semitic and earlier was pronounced Eshtar. Ishtar is not simply a Semitic name brought in and applied without further change to a pre-existing Sumerian goddess, but rather represents an independent Semitic deity who helped shape the personality of the Mesopotamian goddess. Ishtar derives from common Semitic *'aṯtar*. (A masculine god with this name appears in Southern Arabia and Ugarit [*'aṯtar*], though a feminine form [→Astarte] is also attested in Canaanite literature and in the Bible.) In the course of time, Ishtar became the generic name for goddess and *ištarātu*, a plural form of her name, the term for goddesses. Sometimes the name is superimposed upon other goddesses without, however, necessarily changing the separate identity of the underlying god (e.g. the use of the name Ishtar for the mother-goddess in the *Epic of Gilgamesh*, Tablet XI).

There are a few oblique references to Ishtar in the Bible.

II. Though she has other filiations, Inanna is best known as the daughter of the moon god Nanna/Sîn and his wife Ningal and as the sister of Utu/Shamash, the sun god. In the Sumerian literary traditions reflecting fertility rituals, especially those rooted in Uruk, the goddess is depicted as the wife of various Dumuzi/→Tammuz figures, fertility gods who are the power for new life and growth. She is also the wife of An, the god of the sky. This latter association may be a late development, but it seems more likely that here is preserved an older tradition in which Inanna/Ishtar represents a variant of the earth: Ki ('earth'), the wife of An, or Ereshkigal ('mistress of the great earth'), the goddess of the netherworld who was the wife of An in his bull form, Gugalanna.

The goddess Inanna/Ishtar seems to exhibit a greater variety of (perhaps inconsistent) traits and qualities than most other deities and plays a wide variety of roles. She is a goddess of sexual love and possesses strong powers of sexual attraction. In the fertility cult, she receives foodstuffs and appears to be the numen of the communal storehouse. In addition, Inanna/Ishtar is a rain-goddess who, like other storm gods, is also a war goddess and personifies the battle-line. She is also the patroness of prostitutes and other independent women as well as the goddess of the morning and evening star (Venus). The character of the goddess is arresting: "love and sensuality alongside battle and victory. On the one hand, therefore, Ištar was depicted as hierodule (naked goddess) and on the other as heroine and queen" (RÖMER 1969:132).

The goddess is the spouse and lover of the king with whom she participates in the ritual of the sacred marriage. She provides the king with economic blessings as well as power and victory in war. Inanna/Ishtar is associated with the cults of many cities; she is particularly prominent in Uruk, Akkad, Kish, Nineveh, and Arbela. In Uruk, but particularly in Akkad and Assyria, she is a goddess of war and victory.

In Mesopotamian literary texts, Inanna/Ishtar has a coherent and believable, if complex, personality. Inanna/Ishtar is a young, independent, and wilful woman of the upper class. She is a product of an urban world and is closely associated with cities more than with cosmic functions. She seems to be constantly on the move, perhaps because of her association with heavenly bodies and unencumbered women; in any case, her movement expresses and enhances a quality of discontent and restlessness that characterizes her. Inanna/Ishtar often appears as a sexually attractive being, but she remains unsatisfied and is constantly 'injured', striving, and contentious. She tends toward anger and rage and 'troubles heaven and earth'. (One is tempted to talk of early 'psychic wounds'.) Her roles (as wife, mother, etc.) are not fully realized; she behaves as if she were incomplete. Yet there is also sometimes real loss; thus, for example, her husband dies prematurely. But while the death of Tammuz reflects the cycle of fertility and is understandably emphasized in her cult and related myths, this loss remains determinative in the formation of her personality even when her personality and story are freed from the fertility context. Ishtar reminds us of Gilgamesh, a powerful individual with great energy who always remains dissatisfied with the allotted role or portion and is constantly driven to go beyond. They seem to be male and female counterparts.

The figure who appears under the name of Inanna or Ishtar possesses a number of sharply delineated characteristics. The goddess seems even to exhibit contradictory or conflicting traits. She seems to encompass polar opposites: she is death and life, male and female, she is a female who does not nurture nor have a permanent partner, a sexual woman who is warlike and glories in aggression and destruction, etc. She is glorified but frightening, exalted but also intimidating. Moreover, a number of possibly separate goddesses appear under the name Ishtar of a particular place (e.g. Ishtar of Nineveh). In view of her diversity, several questions about the goddess should be asked. In simplified form, these questions are: 1) Is the Inanna/Ishtar of Mesopotamia a single goddess, a conflation of several goddesses, or separate goddesses under a single name? 2) As a single goddess or a conflation of several, did she possess a coherent personality? Recent attempts to understand the nature of Inanna/Ishtar have emphasized either the continued existence of separate goddesses of love and of war, or the existence of a single goddess whose nature is in fact expressed by or related to the very quality of variety or even contradiction.

1) It is likely that Inanna-Ishtar is an amalgam of several different Sumerian, or southern Mesopotamian, goddesses as well as a fusion of this amalgam with a Semitic goddess, Ishtar. Inanna and Ishtar seem already to be identified early in Mesopotamian history. But although the goddess has evolved from different figures, she nevertheless seems to possess a believable, even coherent personality. While it is tempting to believe that this persona constituted a new entity, formed by the merger of separate goddesses, it is equally possible, perhaps more reasonable, to suppose that it was the similarities between goddesses that led to the original merger. While different traits or configurations of traits may originally have been associated, respectively, with the Semitic and the Sumerian goddesses, it is likely that the two were identified because they, in fact, resembled each other and contained

features associated both with sexual love as well as with military (Semitic) or social (Sumerian) conflict.

2) Various explanations for the occurrence in one persona of the aforementioned contradictory traits have been offered. Thus, for example, it has been suggested that the goddess is the embodiment of qualities or lifestyles that seem contradictory and paradoxical and call into question the categories or values of the society and thus confirm their existence; an embodiment, that is, of figures who are marginal (e.g. a prostitute), bi-sexual, or anomalous (e.g. a woman of the respectable upper class who, however, is powerful, free and undomesticated). Alternatively, it has been suggested that she is the embodiment of strife.

Without wishing to suggest that these issues are anything but complex, I shall offer a somewhat subjective and simplifying hypothetical construction. I would suggest that under the figure of the goddess Inanna/Ishtar there originally existed a unitary power that encompassed an extensive range of continuous, if diverse, qualities and activities, and that later the goddess drew to herself different characteristics and roles that were then perceived as conflicting.

This original power was, in effect, an earth goddess who partook of and generated both death and life. To use an evocative, if hackneyed phrase, the goddess was both womb and tomb. Her nature and behaviour are characteristic of a type of early earth goddess who was both the source of fertility and life as well as the cause of death. She is the receiver of the dead and the mother of the living. Ishtar gives and takes life-force and power. She embodies the female principle. But as with other primitive earth or mother goddesses, she did not need a male and contained within herself all forms and stages of life and death. She projects or personifies both the fear of death and sexual interest and arousal.

For our purposes here, it suffices simply to note several indications of Inanna/Ishtar's association with death/life and the chthonic realm in the myth(s) known as *The Descent of Inanna/Ishtar*. They are: her very descent to the netherworld; her threat to bring up the dead to eat the living; her own death there; with her death, the absence of human and animal fertility as a consequence of the loss of sexual attraction, drive, and activity; even as the dead goddess is brought back to life, it is at the price of another's death as her substitute. Inanna/Ishtar is thus also the cause of death to others as well as the one who brings back fertility and sexual interest when she returns to this world.

The figure of Ereshkigal, the mistress of the netherworld and Inanna's elder sister, is informative here, for Ereshkigal represents death, but yet gives birth to young who die before their time; she is a mother, but also a virgin. (It is only the later mythological tradition that cannot understand the virgin mother and thus represents her as a girl who, before the appearance of Nergal, had yet to enjoy a male and needs one.) Similarly, Ishtar spends most of her life without a husband or children, for her husbands change their nature almost immediately after consummation or die before their time. Everything is premature, aborted, embryonic.

Inanna/Ishtar is a goddess of life and death; but unlike Ereshkigal, she is not rooted in a single realm or cut off from the living world. She is peripheral and moves between the dead and the living. She is concurrently central and marginal to the living community. Moreover, she is not static; in fact, she is the principle of movement and dynamism that is used to explain the interchange of death and life. Where Ereshkigal is static, Inanna/Ishtar is the dynamic principle of change. She is movement and change, hence also insatiability and discontent. Most of all, she represents transformation and unpredictability. Hence, also, her power of attraction and repulsion, even aggression.

Her underlying power acts in the life-death and dynamic fashion descibed above in many of the natural and social forms associated with the goddess. This is especially true of the numen of the underground storehouse, for in it is found food that has been buried in the earth and that could either spoil or provide life-giving sustenance. (The underground house is similar to, or perhaps identical with, a place of burial.) In fact, the location of this storehouse (and of burials) further contributes to the formation of the character of Inanna/Ishtar, for as an underground place of death and life, it is central (to the community), yet set apart (from its living or social space). Like the goddess, it is both marginal and unpredictable.

In the course of societal development, perhaps already in the late fourth millennium, the type of earth goddess that stood behind the historical Inanna/Ishtar became less understandable and acceptable. Qualities that were a natural part of one unified power began to fragment, for they seemed disparate, even mutually exclusive. The goddess was seen to possess unrelated features, for how could one goddess be a power for both life and death? When it was felt that one character could no longer contain all these features, a re-conceptualization of the older form occurred; the goddess was now re-defined in terms of sets of characteristics that were seen as culturally connected, if opposite, to each other and could therefore be imposed on the older form. Thus, on the original death-life continuum were imposed new polar opposites: love/death; sex/war; male/female; upper class establishment/social fringe, opponent of convention. The new sets of opposing characteristics were now united in a newly-formed character whose opposing sides were construed as a meaningful construction of opposites. Accordingly, the fragmentation of the original goddess led to the attraction of qualities of a bi-polar nature and the creation of what seems to be a conflicted personality, a personality of contraries. As part of this process of re-constitution, other gods were introduced and identified with the original goddess. Hence, Inanna/Ishtar grows out of an earlier goddess and is formed by a concomitant re-definition of that goddess and syncretism with various other Sumerian goddesses and a Semitic god of war and of the planet Venus.

III. As a deity, Ishtar is not mentioned in the Bible. Commonly, the name *ʾestēr*, Esther, has been interpreted as derived from Ishtar (NOTH, *IPN* 11; *HALAT* 73), although other interpretations have been proposed: J. SHEFTELOWITZ (*Arisches im Alten Testament* [1901] 39) suggested a derivation from Old Indian *strī*, 'young woman', the Rabbis connected the name with the Persian noun *stāreh*, 'star' (*HALAT* 73), while A. S. YAHUDA (*JRAS* 8 [1946] 174-178) proposed a relation with an alleged Old Median noun **astra*, 'mirtle-tree'.

M. DELCOR (Allusions à la déesse Ištar en Nahum 2,8?, *Bib* 58 [1977] 73-83) vocalized the enigmatic *huṣab* in Nah 2:8 as *haṣṣĕbi*, 'ornament; glory' interpreting the noun as an epithet for Ishtar.

It is possible that the →Queen of Heaven mentioned in Jer 7:18 and 44:17-19.25 refers to Ishtar.

IV. *Bibliography*

T. ABUSCH, Ishtar's Proposal and Gilgamesh's Refusal: An Interpretation of *The Gilgamesh Epic,* Tablet 6, Lines 1-79, *HR* 26 (1986) 143-187; T. FRYMER-KENSKY, *In the Wake of the Goddesses* (New York 1992) 25-31, 45-69, 222; B. GRONEBERG, Die sumerisch-akkadische Inanna/Ištar: Hermaphroditos?, *WO* 17 (1986) 25-46; R. HARRIS, Inanna-Ishtar as Paradox and a Coincidence of Opposites, *HR* 31 (1991) 261-278; W. HEIMPEL, A Catalog of Near Eastern Venus Deities, *SMS* 4 (1982) 59-72; T. JACOBSEN, *The Treasures of Darkness* (New Haven & London 1976) 25-73, 135-143; JACOBSEN, Mesopotamian Religions, *ER* 9 (New York 1987) 458-461; W. G. LAMBERT, The Cult of Ištar of Babylon, *Le Temple et le Culte* (CRRA 20; Istanbul 1975) 104-106; J. J. M. ROBERTS, *The Earliest Semitic Pantheon* (Baltimore & London 1972) 37-40; W. H. P. RÖMER, Religion of Ancient Mesopotamia, *Historia Religionum: Handbook for the History of Religion*, vol. 1 (ed. C. J. Bleeker & G. Widengren; Leiden 1969) 115-194, esp. 132-133; H. L. J. VANSTIPHOUT, Inanna/Ishtar as a Figure of Controversy, *Struggles of Gods* (ed. H. G. Kippenberg et al., Religion and Reason 31; Berlin 1984) 225-238; C. WILCKE, Inanna/Ištar, *RLA* 5 (1976) 74-87.

T. ABUSCH

ISIS

I. Isis (*ꜣst*, Gk Εἶσις, Ἶσις, Copt *ēce*, *ici*), perhaps a theophoric element in the personal name Ἰαμβρες, *Iambres* (2 Tim 3:8-9, var. Mambres); the identification seems very doubtful. Like →Osiris, Isis does not belong to the early attested deities but makes her first appearance only in the Pyramid texts where she plays, however, a very prominent role (end of the 5th dynasty, over 70 occurrences). The etymology of her name is not clear. Her symbol which she often wears as a headdress is the seat or throne *s.t* which also serves in writing her name, but this writing has to be regarded as defective because her name must be transcribed as *ꜣst*. (OSING, *MDAIK* 30 [1974] 94-102).

II. Until the Late Period, the nature of Isis remains purely 'constellative', i.e. showing no autonomous identity outside her roles in the Osiris-Isis-Horus myth. Within this cycle, however, she shows an unusual variety of aspects. The myth or cycle of myths can be arranged in five major episodes:

1. the murder of Osiris by →Seth and the quest of Isis for the scattered limbs of the corpse; 2. the ritual lamentations and glorifications (or 'transfigurations', e.g. *sꜣḫw*) of the dead Osiris by Isis and Nephthys, the temporary reanimation of the dead body and the conception of →Horus by Isis; 3. the bringing up of Horus by Isis in the Delta swamps and his protection against all kinds of dangers and persecution; 4. the combat of Horus and Seth; 5. the triumph of Horus and his initiation, by Isis, into his kingdom.

Isis appears not only as a protagonist in almost all of these episodes but she plays very different roles in them. In 1 and 2 she appears as the ideal sister-wife and widow, in 3 and 5 as the ideal mother. In 4 she experiences a loyalty crisis, because she cannot completely forget that Seth is her brother. In 5 she appears as the mother of the reigning king. Moreover, the different episodes of the myth form the basis of different discourses: 1 and 2 are treated in funerary texts, 3 in medico-magical texts, 4 in funerary, magical and literary texts and 5 in royal inscriptions. Only Plutarch and Diodorus give a coherent narration of the whole cycle. This multiplicity of mythical roles and aspects may to a certain extent explain the enormous and ever increasing importance of Isis in Egyptian society. 1 and 2 connect her with the realm of the dead and the funerary rites, 3 with the sphere of medicine and domestic magic, 3, 4 and 5 with royal ideology (MÜNSTER 1968).

The only cult of Isis outside the Osirian context is Koptos where Isis is worshipped as both wife and mother of →Min. Min, the ancient god of Koptos, has been identified with Horus and enters with Isis into a 'Kamutef'-constellation. (The Egyptian expression means "bull of his mother" and denotes a god who by marrying his mother as father begets himself in his son-form. It is the usual epithet of Min.)

In the New Kingdom the nature of Isis extends even beyond the different spheres that find expression in the mythical cycle of Osiris. The reason of this expansion lies in her identification with other goddesses and above all with →Hathor. Originally, Isis and Hathor denote a contrast within the overarching concept of femininity. Isis is the goddess of family and motherhood, Hathor the goddess of love and beauty. Hathor has strong cosmic associations: she is the goddess of heaven and, like Nut, the heavenly cow. By identification with Tefnut, the →lioness and daughter of the sun god →Re and "solar eye" whom he placed at his front as Uraeus serpent and symbol of rulership, Hathor-Tefnut is the companion of the sun god and the personification of the celestial light, both in its life-giving and agressive aspects. Isis owes her cosmic aspect to her early identification with Sothis (= Sirius), the star announcing the annual inundation. She is thus associated with the year and the →Nile. Isis-Hathor becomes an all-including deity: the mistress of heaven, the solar eye;

the lady of the year and the inundation; the mistress of erotic love and of husbandry, motherhood and female fertility; the personification of pharaonic kingship who elects and initiates the legitimite heir; the chief magician who overcomes all dangers that menace the solar course, the life of the patient (especially the child), and even the fatal blows of death. A further step in this process of expansion is reached in the Late Period, when Isis and →Neith merge. Isis then transcends even the border of sex and assumes the character of a male-female primaeval deity beyond creation and differentiation. Until then, the cosmogonic dimension was missing in her theology. In her newly acquired identity of Neith, she inherits the characteristics of the "cosmic god" of Ramesside theology: a god who is One and All, hidden and manifest, transcendent and immanent, who created the world by transforming him/herself into the world and who preserves the world and each individual being by his/her will, planning and order. Another decisive factor in the singular career of Isis was "the victory of Osiris" which characterised late Egyptian religiosity. The festivals of Osiris: the Khoiak rites consisting both in public processions by land and by water and in mysteries performed in secluded parts of the temple such as the fabrication of a corn mummy, the performance of the "hourly vigil" (*Stundenwachen*), the lamentations by Isis and Nephthys etc. were celebrated in all the religious centres of Egypt. Osiris and Isis became the quintessential representatives of Egyptian religion (cf. Plutarch, *De Iside*).

Egyptian texts in Graeco-Roman temples identify Isis with all Egyptian goddesses (see, e.g., DAUMAS, *Les dieux de l'Égypte* [Paris 1965] 98). Greek texts extend these identifications beyond the borders of Egypt and include all known goddesses from Greece to Anatolia, Babylonia and Abessinia (POxy 1380, see B. P. GRENFELL & A. S. HUNT, *The Oxyrhynchus Papyri* XI [London 1915] 196-202 Nr. 1380; B. A. VAN GRONINGEN, *De papyro Oxyrhynchita 1380* [Groningen 1921]; hymns of Isidorus at Medinet Madi, see M. TOTTI, *Ausgewählte Texte der Isis-Serapis-Religion* [Subsidia Epigrapha XII; Hildesheim 1985] 76-82 [& lit.]; Apuleius, Met. XI, see J. G. GRIFFITHS, *Apuleius of Madauros: The Isis-Book (Metamorphoses, Book XI)* [EPRO 39; Leiden 1975] 70-71, 114-123). She is praised as 'polymorphos' and 'polyonyma' or 'myrionyma', the One and All, *una qui es omnia* (L. VIDMAN, *Sylloge inscriptionum religionis Isiacae et Sarapidae* [Berlin 1969] Nr. 502.), *mounē su ei hapasai* (Medinet Madi, F. DUNAND, Le syncrétisme isiaque à la fin de l'époque hellénistique, *Les syncrétismes dans les religions grecque et romaine*, Colloque de Strasbourg, Bibliothèque des Centres d'Études supérieures spécialisés [eds. F. Dunand, P. Levêque; Paris 1973] 79-93).

Her main cult centre was Philae at the first cataract, a temple founded only in the Late Period and rebuilt and enlarged in magnificent fashion by Ptolemaic rulers and Roman emperors. In antiquity it became a famous centre for pilgrimage from all parts of the world. It was the last Egyptian temple to be closed in Byzantine times and was active until 537 CE. Cult centres and communities of Isis spread all over the Mediterranean world in the Hellenistic and Roman eras. These cults seem to be rather different from Egyptian religion and to belong rather to Hellenistic mystery cults (but see JUNGE 1979 [& lit]). The syncretistic Graeco-Egyptian Isis-religion finds its literary expression in 'aretalogies', hymns in the 1st ps.sg. in Greek language but following Egyptian modes of thought and expression (D. MÜLLER, *Ägypten und die griechischen Isis-Aretalogien* [Berlin 1961]; J. BERGMAN, *Ich bin Isis. Studien zum ägyptischen Hintergrund der griechischen Isis-Aretalogien* [Uppsala 1968]; *LdÄ* I:425-434 [& lit].)

III. The name of the Ammonite King Baalis (*baʿălîs*; Jer 40:14) has been interpreted as a misspelling of an original name Baʿal-Isis (F. ZAYADINE, Die Zeit der Königreiche Edom, Moab and Ammon, *Der Königsweg. 9000 Jahre Kunst und Kultur in Jordanien und Palestina* [Köln 1987] 120).

In view of the recently found Ammonite seal-inscription *lmlkmʾr ʿbd bʿlyšʿ* 'to Milkom-Or, the servant of Baalisha' (ed. L. G. Herr, *BA* 48 [1985] 169-172) the name of the Ammonite king should be construed as a derivation from *baʿălîšāʿ* "My lord helps; My lord is noble' (B. BECKING, *JSS* 38 [1993] 15-26), however.

The question of whether or not the element *-es* in the name Jambres (one of the two Egyptian magicians Jannes and Jambres who opposed →Moses according to 2 Tim 3:8) derives from the name Isis is hard to decide, although nowadays a derivation from the Hebrew root MRH (to be rebellious, contentious) is most often assumed. On the various Jewish, Christian, and Pagan traditions concerning these two persons and the origin of their names, see A. PIETERSMA, *The Apocryphon of Jannes and Jambres the Magicians* (Leiden 1994).

IV. *Bibliography*

J. BERGMAN, Isis, *LdÄ* III:186-203 [& lit]; F. DUNAND, *Le culte d'Isis dans le bassin oriental de la Méditerranée*, 3 vols. (EPRO 26; Leiden 1973); F. JUNGE, Isis und die ägyptischen Mysterien, *Aspekte der spätägyptischen Religion* (ed. W. Westendorf; Göttingen 1979) 93-115; M. MÜNSTER, *Untersuchungen zur Göttin Isis vom Alten Reich bis zum Ende des Neuen Reichs* (MÄS 11; Berlin 1968).

J. ASSMANN

J

JACKALS איים

I. The noun *ʾiyyîm*, the plural of I אִי*, is attested in Isa 13:22; 34:14 (IQIsa[a] *ʾyyʾmym* [?]) and Jer 50:39. It is generally derived either from Eg *jw* or *jwjw* 'dog' (cf. Arab. *ibn ʾāwā* 'jackal') or from III אִי* (< אִיי*) '(ghostly) islander, beach demon, goblin' (*HALAT* 37; *Ges.*[18] 44). The ancient versions (LXX ὀνοκένταυροι, Vg *sirenes, onocentauri, fauni*) imagine a tailless ape, or in a derived sense an impure →demon. Even if the meaning of the word *ʾiyyîm* is controversial, nothing speaks against the assumption that a zoologically definable species can *also* be meant by it.

II. If the derivation from Eg *jw* or *jwjw* is correct, then the *ʾiyyîm* would belong to the family of (wild) canines, and their name could perhaps be explained onomatopoeically ('howler'). The distinction to the 'jackal' (Heb *tan*, Canis aurea) cannot be exactly determined. The *tannîm* (jackals, wolves?) possibly represent a subspecies distinct from the *ʾiyyîm*.

III. It is possible that the *ʾiyyîm* ('jackals') of Isa 13:22; 34:14 and Jer 50:39 are zoologically definable animals, i.e. nocturnal consumers of carrion, who appear in pairs or in packs. However, this cannot be conclusively proven. The uncertainty of the identification is made clear by the following considerations.

In Isa 13:22 the *ʾiyyîm* stand in parallel to the *tannîm* (jackals, wolves?); therefore these *ʾiyyîm* could be referring to animals. Both of these species 'hide themselves' or 'howl' in their chosen abodes. In Isa 34:14 the **ṣiyyîm* ('wild beasts') meet with the *ʾiyyîm*; the **śĕʿîrîm* (→'satyrs') also join them. Consequently the context is demonic. Jer 50:39 reports a similarly uncanny assembly: devastated Babylon is populated by *ṣiyyîm*, *ʾiyyîm*, and *bĕnôt yaʿănâ* (ostriches). It therefore appears that the ambivalence of zoologically definable species and demonic beings is intentional even in the case of the *ʾiyyîm*. Their association with theriomorphic demons such as the *ṣiyyîm*, the *śĕʾîrîm*, and the demon →Lilith, is intended to place the aspect of the counter-human world in the foreground (cf. e.g. the topic of 'Sodom and Gomorrah' in Jer 49:18).

IV. *Bibliography*

F. S. BODENHEIMER, *Animal and Man in Bible Lands* (Leiden 1960) Index s.v. *canis aurea*; E. FIRMAGE, Zoology, *ABD* 6 (1992) 1109-1167, esp. 1151-1159; H. G. FISCHER, Hunde, *LdÄ* 3 (1980) 77-81; M. GÖRG, 'Dämonen' statt 'Eulen' in Jes 13,21, *BN* 62 (1992) 16-17; O. KEEL, M. KÜCHLER & C. UEHLINGER, *Orte und Landschaften der Bibel 1: Geographisch-geschichtliche Landeskunde* (Zürich/Einsiedeln/Köln/Göttingen 1984) 147; P. MAIBERGER, Hyäne, *NBL* 7 (1992) 206; G. WANKE, Dämonen II, *TRE* 8 (1981) 275-277 [& lit.].

B. JANOWSKI

JACOB יעק(ו)ב

I. Jacob son of Isaac is the eponym of the *bĕnê yaʿăqôb* (Gen 34:7.13; 35:5; Ps 77:16), more frequently called *bêt yaʿăqôb*. He became the most colourful and revered ancestor of the early Israelite confederation. The name Jacob is most probably a hypocoristicon of Jacob-El frequently found in Mesopotamia from the early second millennium BCE onwards (FREEDMAN 1963:125-126; DE VAUX 1971:192-193) and also carried by a 16th dynasty Hyksos-ruler (DE VAUX 1971:193 and n. 85, see however on the theophoric element *-hr*, not to be equated with *il*, WARD 1976). In the New Kingdom topographical lists, a locality situated in Palestine called Yaʿqubʾilu is mentioned (AḤITUV 1984:200). The name appears also in other hypocoristic forms in Hebrew (1 Chron 4:36), in Ugarit and elsewhere. The element *Yaqubu could even become a divine epithet in the Ugaritic PN *Abdi*(ÌR)-*ya-qub-bu* (for similar Amorite names, compare *Ḫabdi-Tarim* ARM XVI/1, 267; *A-ḫi-i-ku-ba* and *Ši-me-ta-gu-ub* KIENAST 1978).

In the astro-mythological interpretation popular by the end of the 19th century, Jacob is said to represent the nocturnal sky, catching the heel *(ʿāqēb)* of his predecessor, the Sun. In his capacity as the nightly sky, Jacob has to engage in a vigourous fight against →Esau, the Red and →Laban, the White. They are manifestations of the Sun in the morning and in the evening (GOLDZIHER 1876). MEYER thought that these sagas of rivalry between twin brothers reflected ancient mythology, adducing the myth of *Samēmroumos* (*Hypsouranios*) and *Ousōos* in support of this view (1906:278; ATTRIDGE & ODEN 1981:43). Israelite tradition however transformed the mythological figures into genealogical heroes. In his opinion this hero (or deity) Jacob would have been at home in Transjordan; he was presumably the local numen worshipped in Jacob-El (MEYER 1906:281).

II. Genealogical tradition concerning Jacob is extremely complicated, especially because of his identification with the other ancestor Israel (Gen 32:28; 2 Kgs 17:34). The connection between both ancestral personalities is still a much debated and unsolved problem. Israel is not a topographical name originally, but an ancient tribal designation, which as early as the song of Deborah (11th century BCE) is attested as the name of a confederation of tribes. Outside biblical sources it is not only a common Semitic personal name from the earliest times onwards (Ebla *Iš-ra-ìl*(DINGIR) = Ug *yšril*), but in Merenptah's stela of the 5th year (ca. 1208 BCE) it is also a demographic entity in Middle Canaan of unfortunately unclarified ramifications. As a topographical name it does not seem to be attested before the Divided Monarchy and then only restricted to the Kingdom of Israel (also in the Mesha-stela and the stela of Tel Dan, ca. 850 BCE).

The historical existence of a tribal forefather (and a tribe) called Israel originally distinct from Jacob can be neither excluded nor confirmed. Judging from his name and saga Jacob was neither a personified mythic concept nor a deity. Jacob was, even more than the elusive ancestor Israel, a genuine tribal ancestor, presumably of Amorite (Proto-Aramean?, Deut 26:5) or Transjordanian provenance. Later tradition connected him closely with Bethel, perhaps because of his identification with the Cisjordanian ancestor Israel. In any case, in early prophecy Jacob son of Isaac is firmly rooted in northern Israelite tradition (Amos 3:13; 6:8; 7:2; 8:7; Hos 10:11; 12:3-6).

III. In Gen 50:12-13 (P) Jacob's burial and tomb in Hebron (Machpelah, Harim al-Khalil; JEREMIAS 1958:90-94) are reported, but critical scholarship supposed that an early Israelite tradition of Jacob's own sepulchre in an otherwise unknown Goren Haʿatad ('the threshing floor of Atad') in Transjordan (Gen 47:29-30; 50:1-11) was converted into this Judean Hebron tradition (MEYER 1906:280-281; NOTH 1948:97; slightly differently WESTERMANN 1982:227-228). It is impossible to say whether this original place of Jacob's tomb was in turn identical to Jacob-el. If so, this early location was forgotten in the course of tradition. Other tribal and topographical names of the same type →Ishmael, Jerahmeel, Iphtah-el, Jabneel, Jekabzeel, Yibleam and perhaps also Asriel = Israel (LEMAIRE 1973) testify to the fact that ancestors of quite a number of clans lived on in places called after them, most probably because their veneration played a role in the community's tradition.

The Samaritan tradition presents no real alternative to Jacob's tomb at Hebron, which seems to imply that it simply no longer existed in post-exilic times, when the originally Judean cult of the saints at Hebron was shared by Jews and Idumeans alike, to be eventually crowned with the magnificant mausoleum ascribed to Herod (JEREMIAS 1958:90-94). The Samaritan tomb of the sons of Jacob at Shechem (Nablus) is not so much an echo of Jacob = Israel's original home, but rather an extension of the Joseph connection (Acts 7:15-16; Jerome, *Ep.* 108: 13; JEREMIAS 1958:36-38). Early Jewish, Samaritan and Christian literature reveals extensive knowledge of the cult of the biblical saints, in particular the intercession of Abraham, Isaac and Jacob at the Machpelah Cave in Hebron (Mark 12:27; JEREMIAS 1958:133-138).

IV. *Bibliography*

S. AḤITUV, *Canaanite Toponyms in Ancient Egyptian Documents* (Jerusalem 1984); D. N. FREEDMAN, The Original Name of Jacob, *IEJ* 13 (1963) 125-126; I. GOLDZIHER, *Der Mythos bei den Hebräern und seine geschichtliche Entwicklung* (Leipzig 1876; reprint 1987); J. JEREMIAS, *Heiligengräber in Jesu Umwelt* (Göttingen 1958); B. KIENAST, *Die altbabylonische Briefe und Urkunden aus Kisurra* (Wiesbaden 1978); A. LEMAIRE, Asriel, Šr'l, Israël et l'origine de la confédération israélite, *VT* 23 (1973) 239-243; E. MEYER, *Die Israeliten und ihre Nachbarstämme* (Halle 1906); M. NOTH, *Überlieferungsgeschichte des Pentateuchs* (Stuttgart 1948); R. DE VAUX, *Histoire ancienne d'Israël* (Paris 1971); W. A. WARD, Some Personal Names of the Hyksos Period Rulers and Notes on the Epigraphy of their Scarabs, *UF* 8 (1976) 358-359; C. WESTERMANN, *Genesis 37-50* (BKAT I/3; Neukirchen-Vluyn 1982).

M. DIJKSTRA

JAEL יעל

I. Jael at whose hands →Sisera met his death (Judg 4-5) has been interpreted as a demythologized incarnation of the goddess →Amaltheia (GARBINI 1978).

II. The principal motive for speculations about the mythological background of Jael is the conjectural connection between the name Sisera (סיסרא) and the name *(j)a-sas-sa-ra* in a votive text written in Minoan 'Linear A'. The latter corresponds with Gk ΣΑΙΣΑΡΑ and belongs to →Zeus Krētogenēs, the god born on the isle of Crete (G. PUGLIESE CARRATELLI, ΣΑΙΣΑΡΑ, *La parola del passato* 31 [1976] 123-128). GARBINI argues that if the figure of Sisera goes back to Zeus, then Jael must go back to a figure of mythology as well. Since Jael means 'ibex' or 'wild goat' (*HALAT* 402), GARBINI believes that the biblical heroine is a reflection of Amaltheia who is said to have had the shape of a goat. Jael's offering of milk to the thirsty Sisera would be patterned upon Amaltheia's feeding of the infant Zeus (1978:27-28).

This fanciful interpretation has failed to carry conviction. Though Sisera's name is often said not to be Semitic (cf. *HALAT* 710), the possibility that it is should not be ruled out (cf. T. SCHNEIDER, *Asiatische Personennamen in ägyptischen Quellen des Neuen Reiches* [OBO 114; Freiburg/Göttingen 1992] 192, 260). A meaning 'Sun beams' (see H. BAUER, Die Gottheiten von Ras Schamra, *ZAW* 51 [1933] 81-101, esp. 83-84 n. 4, on the basis of Ar *šariya*, 'to be resplendent, to shine') is conceivable. Jael, at any rate, is a perfectly Hebrew name. It was not uncommon for Israelite women to receive animal names (compare e.g. Rachel, Deborah; J. J. STAMM, Hebräische Frauennamen, *Beiträge zur hebräischen und altorientalischen Namenkunde* [OBO 30; Freiburg/Göttingen 1980] 125-126). Speculations about the mythological prototype of Jael rest entirely upon the hypothetical identification of Sisera with Zeus. As the latter identification is doubtful at best, and since the biblical story makes good sense without assuming Greek deities in the background, Jael is best regarded as the human character which the biblical records convey she was.

III. *Bibliography*

G. GARBINI, Il cantico di Debora, *La Parola del passato* 33 (1978) 5-31.

K. VAN DER TOORN

JAGHUT

I. The Edomite personal name *Yĕʿûš*

(Gen 36:5.14.18; 1 Chr 1:35; 7:10; 8:39; 23:10.11; 2 Chr 11:19) has been interpreted as a theophoric name comparable with the Arabian lion god *Yaǧūṯ*,'the protector', and the Nabataean deity *yʿwt* (ROBERTSON SMITH 1912).

II. Islamic traditions refer to the worship of a deity called *Yaǧūṯ* among the pre-islamic tribe of the Maḏḥiǧ and in the area of Ǧuraš in Yemen. Qur'an Sura 71:20-25 and Ibn al-Kalbi's Book of Idols (ed. KLINKE-ROSENBERGER 1942:34-35) interpret this deity as one of the idols of the contemporaries of →Noah. The meaning of the name of this deity 'he helps' can be an indication that *Yaǧūṯ* was a nick-name (*WbMyth* I/1, 478).

In Nabataean personal names, a deity *yʿwt* occurs as a theophoric element. From Thamudic personal names the deity is known as *yʿwṯ*. He is especially present in Southern Thamudic inscriptions from the area around Ǧuraš.

III. In the Old Testament, Jeush is considered only as a human being (BARTLETT 1989:196). The name is borne by four persons, only one of them of explicit Edomite lineage. Besides, a *yʿš* occurs in Samaria Ostracon 48:3. The name can be interpreted as a hypocoristicon for '(God) helps' (NOTH *IPN*, 196) or for '(God) does' (LEMAIRE 1977:53). An identification with *Yaǧūt* is improbable.

IV. *Bibliography*

J. R. BARTLETT, *Edom and the Edomites* (JSOTSup 77; Sheffield 1989); R. KLINKE-ROSENBERGER, *Das Götzenbuch* (Winterthur 1942); A. LEMAIRE, *Inscriptions Hébraïques. I Les ostraca* (LAPO 9; Paris 1977); W. ROBERTSON SMITH, *Lectures and Essays* (London 1912).

B. BECKING

JALAM יעלם

I. The Edomite personal name Jalam/*Yaʿlām* (Gen 36:5.14.18; 1 Chr 1:35) has been considered a theophoric containing the presumed Arabic animal-deity *Jaʿlam* 'Ibex'. (ROBERTSON SMITH 1912).

II. Unlike the other animal-deities proposed by Robertson Smith (→Jaghuṯ; →Yaʿûq), Jalam is not attested in pre-Islamic Arabic sources.

III. In the light of the evidence available, it is impossible to decide whether the name Jalam is theophoric or not. The name can be interpreted alternatively as a hypocoristic sentence name: 'He is hidden' (from *ʿlm* I) or 'He is dark' (from *ʿlm* II; cf. *HALAT* 402). In the Old Testament, Jalam occurs only as a human being. The general theory behind the proposal—names of animals used in anthroponyms are reminiscent of animal worship or totemism—has encountered serious criticism. Jalam does not refer to an Edomite or Arabian deity (BARTLETT 1989: 196).

IV. *Bibliography*

W. ROBERTSON SMITH, *Lectures and Essays* (London 1912); *J. R. BARTLETT, *Edom and the Edomites* (JSOT Suppl 77; Sheffield 1989).

B. BECKING

JAPHETH יפת

I. The personal name *Yepet*/Japheth (Gen 5:32; 6:10; 7:13; 9:18-27; 10:1.2.21; 1 Chron 1:4.5; Jdt 2:25 refers to a place name Japheth), does not have a clear Semitic etymology, except for the popular interpretation found in Gen 9:27: *yapt ʾĕlōhîm lĕyepet*, "May God enlarge Japheth", suggesting a connection between the name and I PTH 'to enlarge' (*HALAT* 405-406; LAYTON 1990: 90). A relation with II PTH 'to be youthful' or with YPH, 'to be beautiful', is also possible, though (ISAAC 1992:641). Japheth has been compared with the Greek Titan Japetos.

II. In Greek literature Ἰαπετός is known as the Titan (→Titans) father of Prometheus and the progenitor of humanity (Homer, *Ilias* 8:479; Hesiod, *Theogony* 134. 507-525; Apollodorus, *Library*, I 2:3; NEIMAN 1986: 126; HESS 1993). WEST (1966:202-203) lists four similarities between Japheth and Japetos: (1) The name itself. In the LXX Japheth is rendered as Ἰαπετός [this is, however, incorrect]; (2) Japetos' brother castrates his father. West interprets Gen 9:21-22 as Japheth's brother Ham doing the same to →Noah. This text, however, only relates that Ham saw his father's nakedness; (3) both characters are indirectly related to a deluge: Japheth through Noah, Japetos through his grandson Deucalion; (4) both are related genealogically to Asia Minor. There exist two different views to explain the relation between Japhet and Japetos. On the one hand, it has been suggested that Japetos is a Greek interpretation of a Hebrew Japheth (West 1966:203; Hess 1993). Alternatively, Neiman (1986) proposed that in the 11th century BCE the Sea Peoples acted as intermediary between Hellenes and Israelites. Through them the Israelites knew the figure of Japetos, whom they construed to be the ancestor of Hellenic and Anatolian peoples. In view of historical probability, the first interpretation mentioned should be preferred.

III. In the Bible Japheth is not cast in a heroic role. He is the youngest of the three sons of Noah (Gen 5:32; 6:10). Together with his brothers →Shem and Ham and their respective wives he entered the ark and was saved from the flood. In genealogical lists it is recorded that Japheth had seven sons: Gomer, →Magog, Madai, Javan, Tubal, Meshech and Tirash (Gen 10:2-5; 1 Chron 1:5-7). Japheth is thus depicted as the ancestor of peoples and tribes inhabiting lands north of Canaan (Isaac 1992). This observation is underscored by the topographical remarks in Jdt 2:25 and *Jub* 8:29; 9:7-13. In Jewish traditions, Japheth occurs only in genealogical contexts (e.g. *2 Enoch* 73:5; *Apoc Adam* 4:1; *T. Sim* 6:5; PsPhilo, *LAB* 1:22; 4:1-5).

IV. *Bibliography*

R. S. Hess, *Studies in the Personal Names of Genesis 1-11* (AOAT 234; Neukirchen-Vluyn 1993) 31-32; E. Isaac, Japheth, *ABD* 3 (1992) 641-642; S. C. Layton, *Archaic Features of Canaanite Personal Names in the Hebrew Bible* (HSM 47; Atlanta 1990); D. Neiman, The Date and Circumstances of the Cursing of Canaan, *Biblical Motifs. Origins and Transformations* (A. Altman ed.; Cambridge 1966) 113-134; M. L. West, *Hesiod. Theogony* (Oxford 1966).

B. Becking

JASON Ἰάσων

I. The name of Jason, the hero who led the Argonauts in their quest for the Golden Fleece, is borne by several persons in 2 Macc and in the NT.

II. The name 'Iason' appears to refer to 'healing' (ἰάομαι), something for which one might naturally turn in cult to a hero. Correspondingly, Pindar referred to a myth that the centaur Cheiron taught Jason medicine (*Pyth.* 4:119 and scholiast). Yet one cannot help suspecting that this is folk-etymology, given his father 'Aison' and a possible tribal name and eponym 'Iasos' (speculatively, Dowden 1989:122). He receives cult at Abdera, Cyzicus, Colchis and inland in Asia Minor, presumably in the wake of Argo (Farnell 1921:336).

Jason comes from Iolkos and presumably belongs to an Iolkan tradition of epic poetry (West 1985:137). The story of Jason, and of the Argonauts, supports the view that Iolkan poetry had been to our eyes the closest to folk-tale (West 1985:138). In the 6th century BCE (West 1985:164), Ps.-Hesiod's *Catalogue of Women* (fr. 40) presents Jason as the son of Aison and has him educated (like Achilles) by the centaur Cheiron on Mt Pelion. He comes in from the wild into the city of Iolkos, but is signalled by his single sandal (in fact an aetiology of a custom found also amongst Aitolian warriors, Aristotle fr. 74) as a threat to King Pelias. Pelias sends him, like →Perseus or →Herakles, on a dangerous mission—the voyage of Argo (often seen as the first ship) to recover the Golden Fleece. The story was well known at an early date, for instance by Homer, and in surviving literature is told by Pindar (elliptically, *Pythian* 4) and notably by Apollonios of Rhodes in Greek and Valerius Flaccus in Latin. The sense of achievement is rather undermined by the figure of Medea, daughter of Aietes King of

Colchis. A barbarian who helps Jason by betraying her home and family, who butchers her brother and causes the daughters of Pelias to mince their father, she is eventually abandoned by Jason at Corinth in preference for a Greek wife. This is the scene for Euripides' *Medea*, where she even kills her (Jason's) children, though in local cult the Corinthians annually atoned for their own murder of the children. In any case, Jason has no offspring and exists for his achievements, not his genealogy. His tale "highlights the crises of transition from one stage of life to another" (SEGAL 1986: 56, based on insights of VIDAL-NAQUET), bringing together kingship, sexuality, family relationships, mastery of earth-born warriors and leadership of seafaring heroes, as well as religion and magic. In interpretation his story has rewarded those interested in folktale, shamanism, psychoanalysis, initiation (and other) rituals, and historical colonisation.

III. Greeks chose names because of their associations. This resonance in turn might result from the meaning of the constituent elements of the name (e.g. Kleo-menes, 'Fame-might') or from previous bearers of the name. The name might echo one's father's, be the same as one's grandfather's, or even be that of a hero from the legendary past. Heroic names, unusual before the mid-5th century BCE (FICK-BECHTEL 1894:314), became commoner in the Hellenistic age as the classical authors and culture became canonical in response to a world grown larger, more varied and more multi-cultural. This process reached a peak in the second century CE (BOWIE 1974:199-200).

For the Hellenising Jews at the time of the Maccabaean revolt, the adoption of resonant Greek names was a way of expressing adhesion to Hellenic culture—as much as building a gymnasium (1 Macc 1:14) at the foot of a Temple Mount now perceived as an acropolis. Thus the Jason who had supplanted his brother Onias in the high priesthood in 175 BCE (2 Macc 4:7-10) had, according to Josephus (*Ant.* 12:239), assumed this name in place of his own name Jesus (Joshua) (cf. HENGEL 1974: I 64). This is the man who "made his fellow-Jews conform to the Greek way of life" (2 Macc 4:10). Plainly the phonetic shape of the name Jason assisted its adoption in a Semitic culture and this may explain its special frequency. Elsewhere in the Bible we find: (a) Jason of Cyrene, the author of the (presumably Greek) 5-book predecessor of 2 Macc (2:22) and maybe a contemporary of the events; (b) Jason son of Eleazar, emissary sent to Rome by Judas Maccabaeus (1 Macc 8:17, also Jos., *Ant.* 12:415, 419, 13: 169); (c) a 'kinsman' of Paul sending greetings through him at Rom 16:21, presumably the same as the Christian sympathiser at Thessalonica, the host of Paul and Silas (Acts 17:5-9).

The name is extremely common in the Eastern Mediterranean and its associations may be correspondingly vague. FRASER-MATTHEWS (1987) list 183 occurrences, a great many dating from the last centuries BCE and the first century CE—and many of these in Cyrenaica where there was a substantial Jewish population.

IV. *Bibliography*

E. BOWIE, Greeks and their Past in the Second Sophistic, *Studies in Ancient Society* (ed. M. I. Finley; London 1974) 166-209; B. K. BRASWELL, *A Commentary on the Fourth Pythian Ode of Pindar* (Berlin 1988) esp. 6-23 [& Lit]; K. DOWDEN, *Death and the Maiden* (London 1989); L. R. FARNELL, *Greek Hero Cults and Ideas of Immortality* (Oxford 1921); A. FICK & F. BECHTEL, *Die griechischen Personennamen nach ihrer Bildung erklärt und systematisch geordnet* (2nd ed.; Göttingen 1894); E. FRAENKEL, Namenwesen, *PW* 16 (1935) 1611-70; P. M. FRASER & E. MATTHEWS (eds.), *A Lexicon of Greek Personal Names*, vol. I: The Aegean Islands, Cyprus, Cyrenaica (Oxford 1987); M. HENGEL, *Judaism and Hellenism: Studies in their Encounter in Palestine during the Early Hellenistic period*, Eng. tr. (London 1974); K. MEULI, *Odyssee und Argonautika* (Berlin 1921); C. SEGAL, *Pindar's Mythmaking: The Fourth Pythian Ode* (Princeton 1986); P. VIDAL-NAQUET, *Le chasseur noir* (Paris 1981); M. L. WEST, *The Hesiodic Catalogue of Women* (Oxford 1985).

K. DOWDEN

JEPHTHAH'S DAUGHTER

I. The story of the unnamed daughter of Jephthah is told in Judges 11. Jephthah vows that, if →Yahweh will give him victory over the Ammonites, he will offer up to Yahweh the one who first comes out to meet him when he returns home (v 31). This turns out to be his unnamed daughter. Jephthah's daughter accepts the consequences of her father's vow, but asks that she and her female companions be permitted to go into the mountains so that they can lament. Her father grants this request and, at the end of two months, she returns home and her father offers her up as a holocaust sacrifice (*ʿōlâ*) to Yahweh. Thereafter, for four days every year, it became customary for "the daughters of Israel" to commemorate her (v 40). Because the story of the sacrifice of Jephthah's daughter explicitly functions as the foundation legend for the annual four-day rite, it can be argued that Jephthah's daughter has attained the more-than-mere-mortal status of a culture heroine.

Because she is referred to in the biblical text simply as "Jephthah's daughter", it is not possible to discuss the etymology or the meaning of her name. It can be noted, however, that in Christian and Jewish tradition she has been given various meaningful names (see, for instance, Pseudo-Philo's *LAB* 40).

II. The precise story of Jephthah's daughter does not appear outside the Hebrew Bible in the literature of any contemporary culture. However, numerous scholars have observed similarities between Jephthah's daughter and various Greek mythological heroines, most frequently Iphigeneia and Kore/Persephone. DAY (1989) offers the most sustained discussion in favour of seeing meaningful parallels among the stories of Jephthah's daughter, Iphigeneia and Kore. The viability of the parallels she suggests is dependent on her interpretation of the nature of the annual rite mentioned in the biblical text (see below). MARCUS (1986) presents the most sustained argument against seeing meaningful parallels among the stories. A few scholars have proposed connecting Jephthah's daughter's lamenting in the mountains with mourning the death of male deities, for example →Baal (GRAY 1957:53), →Adonis (ROBERTSON 1982:339-340) and →Eshmun (PECKHAM 1987:84). Given that the biblical text states that the lament is related to the fact that Jephthah's daughter is a *bĕtûlâ* (see below) and not to the death of a god, the proposals connecting the lament with mourning the death of a male deity are unsubstantiated and hence unconvincing.

III. It is clear from the biblical text that the story of the sacrifice of Jephthah's daughter functioned as the foundation legend for an annual women's rite. Hence an understanding of the role that Jephthah's daughter played in Israelite tradition is contingent upon determining the nature of the commemorative rite. BOSTRÖM (1935:115-20) interpreted this rite as a survival in Israelite tradition of a religious practice commonly referred to in the scholarly literature as "sacred prostitution' or 'cultic sex'. More recently, however, serious doubts have been raised about whether sacred prostitution ever existed in the ancient Near East (ODEN 1987:131-153; BIRD 1989:75-94), and the burden of proof has shifted onto those who would continue to argue for its existence. To date, no convincing arguments have been forthcoming; hence, Boström's interpretation must be discarded. The only other sustained hypothesis is that put forward by BAL (1988:46-52.65-68) and DAY (1989), who independently argue that the story recounts the alleged origin of a rite that marked a transition from one stage to another in the life-cycle of Israelite females. Both base their arguments on understanding the term *bĕtûlîm* (vv 37 and 38) as referring to an age group/social status rather than meaning 'virginity', as it is typically translated in English Bibles. Also, both assume that the activities comprising the rite bear some direct relationship to the activities described in the story. So if the story is about a life-cycle lament, then the rite centres on this same activity. Following this interpretation, Jephthah's daughter can be understood as a culture heroine. Her story is the foundation legend for an annual rite in ancient Israel that socially acknowledged a young woman's nubility and hence her marriageability.

IV. *Bibliography*

M. BAL, *Death and Dissymmetry: The Politics of Coherence in the Book of Judges* (Chicago 1988); BAL, *Anti-Covenant: Counter-Reading Women's Lives in the Hebrew Bible* (Sheffield 1989); P. BIRD, 'To Play the Harlot': An Inquiry into an Old Testament Metaphor, *Gender and Difference in Ancient Israel* (ed. P. L. Day; Minneapolis 1989) 75-94; G. BOSTRÖM, *Proverbiastudien* (Lund 1935); A. BRELICH, Symbol of a Symbol, *Myths and Symbols* (ed. J. M. Kitagawa & C. H. Long; Chicago 1969) 195-207; C. A. BROWN, *No Longer Be Silent: First Century Jewish Portraits of Biblical Women* (Louisville 1992); P. L. DAY, From the Child Is Born the Woman: The Story of Jephthah's Daughter [& lit], *Gender and Difference in Ancient Israel* (ed. P. L. Day; Minneapolis 1989) 58-74; J. C. EXUM, Murder They Wrote: Ideology and the Manipulation of Female Presence in Biblical Narrative, *USQR* 43 (1989) 19-39 [reprinted in *The Pleasure of Her Text* (ed. A. Bach; Philadelphia 1990) 45-67]; EXUM, The Tragic Vision and Biblical Narrative: The Case of Jephthah, *Signs and Wonders* (ed. J. C. Exum; Atlanta 1989) 59-84; E. FUCHS, Marginalization, Ambiguity, Silencing: The Story of Jephthah's Daughter, *Journal of Feminist Studies in Religion* 5 (1989) 35-45; T. H. GASTER, *Myth, Legend and Custom in the Old Testament* (New York 1969); J. GRAY, *The Legacy of Canaan* (Leiden 1957); A. HENRICHS, Human Sacrifice in Greek Religion: Three Case Studies, *Le sacrifice dans l'antiquité. Entretiens sur l'antiquité classique*, vol. 27 (Geneva 1980) 195-242; K. KEUKENS, Richter 11, 37-38: Rite de Passage und Übersetzungsprobleme, *BN* 19 (1982) 41-42; D. MARCUS, *Jephthah and His Vow* (Lubbock, TX. 1986); R. A. ODEN Jr., Religious Identity and the Sacred Prostitution Accusation, *The Bible without Theology* (San Francisco 1987) 131-153; B. PECKHAM, Phoenicia and the Religion of Israel: The Epigraphic Evidence, *Ancient Israelite Religion: Essays in Honor of Frank Moore Cross* (ed. P. D. Miller *et al*; Philadelphia 1987) 79-99; N. ROBERTSON, The Ritual Background of the Dying God in Cyprus and Syro-Palestine, *HTR* 75 (1985) 313-359; W. RUDOLPH, Präparierte Jungfrauen? *ZAW* 34 (1963) 65-73; W. O. SYPHERD, *Jephthah and His Daughter: A Study in Comparative Literature* (Newark, Del. 1948); P. TRIBLE, *Texts of Terror* (Philadelphia 1984) 93-116; G. J. WENHAM, *bĕtûlāh* 'A Girl of Marriageable Age', *VT* 22 (1972) 326-348.

P. L. DAY

JEREMIEL ירמיאל

I. An angel bearing this name is attested in this form only in 4 Ezra (4:36), i.e. in a work that belongs only to a part of the Vg-tradition. The name probably derives from the Hebrew root *rûm*, 'to be high, exalted'. Since the '-el' ending already includes the theophoric element, one should see in the beginning 'ye-' part of the conjugation of a Hebrew verb in the Hifil-clause. The meaning, then, would be 'God will/may exalt me'.

In 4 Ezra the angel is mentioned as the one who answers the questions of the dead concerning their future, i.e. the day of the last judgment and their final exaltation; thus Jeremiel expresses by his very name the hope for the future exaltation of the dead righteous ones.

II. The Syriac version reads at this point 'Ramael' instead of Jeremiel. In that form the (Syriac!) *2 Bar* knows Ramael as the angel appointed over true visions (55:3; 63:6 cp. 56:1; that might be the same angel as the one in *3 Bar* 11:7), which shows that the name of this angel has considerably changed in the course of the translations. This may explain the fact that Ramiel, Remiel, Rumiel, and Eremiel, are often variants of one and the same angel (cf. MICHL 1962:no. 179, 182, 187). The *Apoc. Zeph.* describes Eremiel as the angel presiding over →Hades (6:11-15, *OTP* I 497-515; cf. Rev. 1:13-15; Dan 10:5-6). An angel Ramiel is one of the four archangels in a group of manuscripts in *Sib. Or.* 2:215-217, there again connected with the last judgment. In this military context Ramael is identified as the anonymous angel mentioned in 2 Kgs 19:35 and Isa 37:36.

Though the different names seem to point to the same angel, it is not necessary to identify him with Jerachmeel as variously suggested. On the other hand, the quite similar names of the fallen angels according to *1 Enoch* 6:7 (Ramʾel); 69:2 (Rumiel) and the archangel (one out of seven) according to *1 Enoch* 20:8 (Remiel, only in the Greek) warn not to take all these names as one. The different names are attested in later literature, so in the Coptic magical papyri (Jeremiel: KROPP 1930/1931:XLVII 2, 12; cf. Rumiel: MÜLLER 1959:230, 303, 315), in the *Sefer Ha-Razim* (MARGALIOTH 1966:I, 211), a Jewish amulet (NAVEH & SHAKED 1985 4,3) and in the *hekhaloth* texts (SCHÄFER 1981:§§ 212. 230. 233 and more often); for astrological parallels cf. PETERSON 1926:no. 91.

III. *Bibliography*

A. M. KROPP, *Ausgewählte koptische Zaubertexte* 1-3 (Bruxelles 1930/1931); J. MICHL, Engel V (Katalog der Engelnamen) *RAC* 5 (1962) 200-239; C. D. G. MÜLLER, *Die Engellehre der koptischen Kirche* (Wiesbaden 1959); J. NAVEH & S. SHAKED, *Amulets and Magic Bowls. Aramaic Incantations of Late Antiquity* (Jerusalem/Leiden 1985); E. PETERSON, Engel- und Dämonennamen. Nomina barbara, *RhMus* 75 (1926), 392-421, no. 51 and 91; P. SCHÄFER, *Synopse zur Hekhalot-Literatur* in Zusammenarbeit mit M. Schlüter und H. G. von Mutius hrsg. (Tübingen 1981); M. MARGALIOTH, *Sepher Ha-Razim.* A Newly Recovered Book of Magic from the Talmudic Period. Collected from Genizah Fragments and other Sources (Jerusalem 1966) [Heb].

M. MACH

JESUS Ἰησοῦς

I. *Iēsous* is the Greek form of the Hebrew personal name *yĕhôšûʿa* stamped after its postexilic variant *yēšûʿa*. The *votive* name means "Yahweh is help (salvation)" as rightly interpreted by Philo, *Mut.* 121. It is derived from the root YŠʿ, frequent in other Hebrew and Semitic personal names, too (*TWAT* 3 1037-1038). In its postexilic form the theophoric element is no longer clearly recognizable. The etymologies in Sir 46:1 and Matt 1:21 only perceive the verb *yšʿ* "to save". In the OT the most famous and most often mentioned bearer of the name is the successor of Moses, Joshua, the son of Nun. Extrabiblical documents (*Ep.Arist.,* Jos., ossuaries, papyri) attest its popularity until the beginning of the 2nd century CE in both its Aramaic and Greek form.

The NT has *Iēsous* twice for the OT hero, 3 or 4 times for other persons, and 913 times for "Jesus of Nazareth". This distinctive apposition occurs 19 times in the Gospels and Acts; it was necessary because of the frequency of the name and was perhaps already used in Jesus' lifetime. Anarthrous *Iēsous* (with or without the article) prevails in the Gospels and in Rev (574 out of 600 examples), while in the NT letters the name usually is combined with titles like →Christos, →Kyrios (*EWNT* 2 444). The fact indicates that the name in itself designates the historical man; it became a divine name only in the development of post-Easter faith.

II. It is notoriously difficult to reconstruct a coherent view of Jesus' rather short activity, because in the Gospels we have only heterogeneous fragments of tradition transmitted in different layers and often formed and supplemented by the post-Easter experience. Nevertheless, we shall make such an attempt. Generally, it is agreed that Jesus' fundamental prophetic mission was to announce that the Reign of God was drawing close. Its explicit formulation is only preserved in a redactional summary (Mark 1:15) and echoed in the commission of Jesus' messengers (Matt 10:7b//Luke 10:9b), but it constitutes the background of Jesus' promises—notably the original beatitudes Luke 6:20-21—and of his parabolic warnings to exploit the last opportunity (e.g. Luke 16:1-7). This implies that God's Reign, when overtaking the unprepared, will turn into judgement. Here, Jesus is at one with John the Baptist, only he does not offer a sacramental rite to avoid the doom, but proclaims a general amnesty for every member of Israel, the outcast included. This is reflected in the parables dealing with God's mercy on the lost (e.g. Luke 15). Whether Jesus himself forgave sins individually—in the name of God or even with the same authority as God (Mark 2:5b; cf. Luke 7:48 probably dependent on this passage)—cannot be established with certainty. God's initiative of forgiveness is supposed to be followed on the side of man by repentance (Mark 1:15; Matt 11:21-22/Luke 10:13-14; Matt 12:41//Luke 11:32; Luke 13:1-5). In this respect too, Jesus resumes the appeal of the Baptist. Exhortations such as contained in the Sermon on the Mount illustrate the change of mind Jesus wished to see come about. Such ethical teaching is sapiential in style and motivation. Thus, it does not point to the imminent Reign of God as, for example, the so-called "entrance-logia" (e.g. Mark 10:25). Yet the presupposed eschatological frame adds urgency to the moral demands. More radical still—and sometimes opposed to the legal custom (cf. Matt 8:21-22//Luke 9:59-60)—are the conditions for those who want to follow Jesus directly. The disciples form a kind of eschatological sign (esp. the Twelve) foreshadowing the people of God under His rule. Another prophetic action was Jesus' participation in banquets with public sinners. Demonstrating God's joyful acceptance of the lost, he in some way acts on behalf of the loving Father. But in doing so he does not yet realize the Kingdom of God. This happens only in his miraculous healings which demonstrate God's salvation and his victory over the demons (cf. Mark 3:23-27 and the prophetic vision Luke 10:18). In a probably secondary argument Jesus' exorcisms are interpreted as the arrival of the Reign of God (Matt 12:28//Luke 11:20). In this sense the eschatological fulfilment can already be verified in Jesus' words and deeds (Matt 13:16-17//Luke 10:23-24; cf. Luke 16:16 and Jesus' answer to John the Baptist Matt 11:2-6//Luke 7:18-23, which, however, seems a later scriptural elaboration). To bring God's saving power to everybody, Jesus sometimes disregarded the rules of purity and the Sabbath. But his position on the Law remains ambiguous. On the one hand he sets aside ceremonial law (Mark 7:15), on the other he sharpens the Halakah; note the strict prohibition of divorce (Luke 16:18) or the primary antitheses (Matt 5:21.22; 5:27-28). The will of God is concentrated and intensified to facilitate and direct the new life requested in view of the coming Kingdom. The action in the temple court in his last days aims at a renovation of the cult in this eschatological moment. This, as well as an oracle of doom against the existing temple, may have motivated the clergy to react against Jesus so as to put him to death.

Most of these actions and utterances can be subsumed under prophetic categories, though Jesus does not legitimize himself with the messenger-formula. But he also integrates in his discourse popular wisdom and rabbinical disputation. Yet, unlike the rabbis, he does not appeal to tradition in explaining God's will. He rather sometimes puts his authority in opposition to the Mosaic law. He appears to speak out of a certain intimacy with God parallelled by few contemporary Jewish charismatics (VERMES 1973). This special relationship may be indicated by the address *ʾabbā*, though it is better attested as an acclamation of Christian pneumatics and only in an unhistorical context in Jesus' mouth (Mark 14:36). Jesus cannot be said to have revealed God as →father to his disciples because as Israelites they were already acquainted with Him and were used to call him 'father' in their prayers (two examples of *ʾābî* as divine address recently came to light in Qumran). But he certainly actualized this tradition drawing on his personal relationship with God. His words and acts betray a unity with God transcending traditional labels. The observation is typical that he puts God in the centre and not explicitly himself as →mediator between God and men (Luke 12:8-9 seems to belong to a situation after Easter). The qualification of his person is due to the eschatological relevance of his work and speech. If God's last envoy is refused, he does not need a personal vindication; his vindication is the arrival of God's judgement. Possibly he announced it in the traditional figure of the coming →Son of Man without directly identifying himself with him (cf. Luke 12:39-40; 17:23-24.26-27).

Can the phenomenon of Jesus be called 'Messianic'? Teaching and healing are not specific for the Messiah. Maybe some traits in the Jewish picture of David and Solomon could prefigure an exorcising Messiah, but normally he has other tasks (→Christ). Thus, a confession like Mark 8:29 betrays anachronisms. Yet, there could arise Messianic expectations among Jesus' followers and the people, especially when he moved to Jerusalem, the place where the Kingdom of God was supposed to appear. That the idea of God's Kingship does not preclude a human representative is evident from *Ps.Sol.* 17. Jesus' spectacular entrance in Jerusalem may have aroused the hope of the restoration of David's Kingdom in some pilgrims and the fear of political disorder in the Jewish dignitaries. They delivered Jesus to the Romans as a pretender to kingship as it is formulated in the inscription on the cross. This can hardly be explained as a theological construction. Such suspicion is more appropriate in the case of Jesus' self-definition in front of the Sanhedrin (Mark 14:61-62), because the claim to be the Messiah could not provoke a Jewish sentence of death.

One of the last words of Jesus generally accepted as authentic is Mark 14:25. Here he envisages his death, but in the same time he is confident about his eating and drinking in the Reign of God. In this perspective Jesus' message was not invalidated by the demise of the messenger. But in fact, his humiliating execution on the cross caused a heavy crisis with the disciples. It could (although not necessarily) be interpreted in the light of Deut 21:23 as God's cursing; anyway it did not fit in with the picture of a possible Messiah at all. Nevertheless, only a few weeks after the crucifixion we find the Twelve (plus the mother and the brothers of Jesus) back again in Jerusalem, preaching on the basis of appearances that God had raised Jesus from the dead. In this proclamation *Iēsous* means the crucified teacher from Nazareth (Mark 16:6). One can also conjecture that *Iēsous* was the object in an early resurrection-formula that we can still grasp in later sources (Rom 8:11; Acts 5:30; postponed in 1 Thess 1:10; cf. also *Iēsous* as subject in 1 Thess 4:14).

Originally, there may have existed different representations of the Easter-event leading to different christological conceptions. In 'Q' there is only a hint of Jesus' rejection in Jerusalem, his disappearing and coming again as the Son of Man (Matt 23:37-39// Luke 13:34-35; perhaps Luke 11:29-30). He is announced as the future judge who will condemn those not believing in his mission. The identification of Jesus with the coming Son of Man must have been made on the basis of the Easter-event. It serves to re-evaluate the past, but is oriented primarily to the future. Another set of traditions concerns the present state of Jesus. Since resurrection does not mean return to this life, one concludes that Jesus is in the glory of God, enthroned at his right hand (cf. Rom 8:34; Acts 2:33-36). Thus, he is vindicated as Messiah, as mighty representative of God, but on a very different level. In heaven he is installed in power as God's Son (→Son of God) (Rom 1:4) and thus realizes the promises given by Nathan (2 Sam 7:12-14). This understanding could throw light back onto Jesus' passion. He also was the Christ in his vicarious suffering for our sins (1 Cor 15:3). Here probably the image of the suffering servant (Isa 52:13-53:12) is fused with that of the 'Messiah'. The heavenly enthronement of Jesus also seems to be presupposed when he is invoked "our Lord - come" (→*Kyrios*). This means prayer, recognition of his sovereignty, but not yet adoration. Through his resurrection and installation at the side of God, Jesus could continue to be effective on earth: His missionaries and charismatic miracle-workers prophesied and exorcised "in his name". That does not necessarily mean: by using the name *Iēsous* as a magic formula, but in his authority, enlarging in this way his terrestrial dominion. In the *māranā'-tā'* we hear the voice of the Aramaic first community. It cannot be proved with certainty that also the explicit "christology of exaltation" making use of Ps 110:1 and the conception of an atoning death of Christ can be assigned to this community. Many scholars relocate this idea to the Jewish Christian 'Hellenists'. But one should not forget that they originally lived in neighborhoods close to the 'Hebrews' (HENGEL 1972).

In a Hellenistic environment *Iēsous* did not suggest a mythical deity, but the concreteness of a historical person with a singular destiny. This Jesus was acclaimed *Kyrios* with a formula of the Greek speaking community. In the name of Jesus the crucified every knee now has to bow (Phil 2:10). In the allegedly pre-Pauline hymn Phil 2:5b-11 Christ's preexistence in a godlike fashion preludes the pattern self-humiliation - exaltation. This should help to estimate the depth of self-abasement described with the pagan vocabulary of divine metamorphosis. For the godlike existence a title is lacking, but one may surmise that *Son of God*—now in a new interpretation—would be appropriate. At least it is the stereotype in the formula "God sent his Son" common to Pauline and Johannine tradition (Rom 8:3-4; Gal 4:4-5; John 3:17; 1 John 4:9.10.14). This means that God himself engaged in the work of salvation, the Son remaining subordinate to him. In Gal 4:4 it seems plausible that a heavenly existence preceded his being born of a woman. Thus, in the Hellenistic community, the idea of the incarnation of a divine being was added to the exaltation-model. Besides the hymn of Phil 2 one might also compare the Johannine prologue (John 1:1-18). Here one normally sees the impact of Wisdom-Christology as for example in 2 Cor 4:4; Col 1:15; Heb 1:2c. 3a, too (Christ, the image and radiance of God). Yet though OT wisdom writings are familiar with the concepts of a personified wisdom from before the creation, it is never said that Wisdom becomes an actual man. Here one should not overlook the pagan parallels (ZELLER 1988, MÜLLER 1989) where the motif of a theophany in a human form is sometimes transferred to 'divine men'.

Paul does not add much to the received christology. He underlines Christ's mediating function; so the reign of the risen one is limited and serves the glorification of the Father (cf. 1 Cor 15:20-28). Though the final realization of God's Rule coincides with the parousia of the Lord Jesus Christ, in the end he will hand over the Kingdom to God the Father. On the other side, final judgement is committed to Christ (2 Cor 5:10). Furthermore, Paul explains the incarnation as salutary exchange (2 Cor 5:21; 8: 9; Gal 3:13; 4:4-5; Rom 8:3-4) and recalls that it is the crucified who now, through God's powerful act, has become the source of eschatological life. To participate in that life the apostle has to assimilate himself to the crucified. It is probably not by chance that Paul in this context speaks of "Jesus' death" (2 Cor 4:10) or "Jesus' marks" (Gal 6:17) he is bearing in his body. In a similar way the Epistle to the Hebrews uses an anarthrous *Iēsous* in connection with Christ's suffering (2:9; 10:19; 13:12). But in other Pauline contexts *Iēsous* seems interchangable with Christ. Together with this former title it forms a kind of double name. The Gospels demonstrate the identity of the Christ, the Son of God, as the early Church confessed him to be, with Jesus in his earthly existence. This is already shown by the superscription of the first representative of this genre (Mark 1:1). The manifestation of

Jesus' true dignity marks its beginning (baptism 1:11), middle (Peter's confession 8:29; Jesus' transfiguration 9:2-8) and end (Jesus' self-revelation Mark 14:61-62; the centurion's avowal 15:39). In the first part, Jesus' teaching with authority and his miracles finally lead to Peter's acknowledgment of his being the Messiah. Until then this was known to the →demons (cf. "Son of God" resp. "Son of the →most High" Mark 3:11; 5:7), but hidden to the people. In the second part, the disciples have to learn that this Messiah will be the suffering and risen Son of Man. In the Gospels of Matthew and Luke the revelation of Jesus' divine and royal majesty is anticipated in the stories of Jesus' childhood. There his human name is foreordained by the angel (Matt 1:21a; Luke 1:31); Matt 1:21b moreover explains it by his saving activity (also cited by Justin, *Apol.* I 33:7-8). As in other birth-oracles of extraordinary men in the Bible and the Jewish Haggada (but also in the Roman-Hellenistic world)—the name appears as imposed by divine providence. The later Gospels amplify the godlike image of Jesus. Thus Matthew multiplies the prostrations before Jesus reserved to God according to Matt 4:10; this could reflect the practice of worship in his Church. In the Fourth Gospel the Logos is said to be God, certainly distinguished from "*the* God", but in close union with him (John 1:1-2.18). Traditional miracle stories are interpreted by speeches of Jesus, so that they become transparent for his life-giving mission out of God's eternity. God's sending of his Son gets a circular structure, because the Son returns to heaven. 'John' joins the christology of exaltation to the christology of mission; but paradoxically the faithful can already see the exalted one on the cross. The narrative culminates in the confession of Thomas before the risen one "my Lord and my God" (20:28). Such an enhancement of Jesus' divinity always remains integrated in a conception of divine sonship, where the Son does not make himself God, as the opponents pretend (John 10:33), but has the origin of his divinity in the Father. The first epistle of John already struggles against the gnostic dissolution of Christ into a temporary, human element and into a divine one, the latter the sole one to be important. Here *Iēsous* becomes an identity marker. To "confess Jesus" is an abbreviation for the belief that "Jesus Christ came in the flesh" (cf. 1 John 4:2-3). In Rev Christians distinguish themselves from the hostile synagogues by sticking to the "testimony of Jesus" (5 times). Thus, confrontation with adversaries within and outside the communities constrains the theologians to maintain in Jesus the starting point of the Christian religion. On the other hand one can observe in later writings a certain confusion between Jesus and God, especially in liturgical language. While in the original Pauline letters *ho theos* is never applied to Jesus Christ (Rom 9:5b refers to the author of the Jewish salvation history), this happens in the citation of Ps 47:7 LXX in Heb 1:8-9, in the affirmation 1 John 5:20 and possibly in some disputed cases where Christ is subsumed under one article with "God" (2 Thess 1:12; Titus 2:13; 2 Petr 1:1 →God [II]). From the beginning there was prayer to Jesus who together with the Father in the Pauline writings is supposed to be gracious and to fulfill the supplications of his believers. Only, the fragments of hymns discernible in the letters are not directed to him, but narrate the great feats of God achieved with him. Later on, Christians sing to their Lord (Eph 5:19), and Plinius, *Ep.* 10,96:7 rightly understands this as worship to Christ as god. It is significant too, that doxologies which in Jewish and early Christian texts are exclusively directed to God are now addressed to Christ (2 Tim 4:18; 2 Petr 3:18; Rev 1:5-6). But to all appearances even Jewish-Christians did not feel any contradiction to their monotheistic faith. They conceived of Jesus as taking part in God's glory; after describing the majesty of God and the investiture of the Lamb as his plenipotentiary, the author of Rev 5:13 can speak of every creature offering praise to both, the →One seated on the throne and the Lamb.

III. The tendency to call Jesus simply

God continues in the Church Fathers from the prescript of Ign., *Eph* onwards; in 18:2 of the same letter Ignatius can speak of "our God Jesus, the Christ" who was borne in the womb of →Mary in conformity with the economy of God; he does this obviously without any fear of ditheism. The Acts of Peter, Paul, John, and Thomas celebrate Jesus even as "unique God". Critics from outside also manifest their impression that Christians worship Jesus as God besides the one God (cf. Origen, *Cels.* 8:12.14.15; Lucian, *Per.* 13). *Iēsous* in the magical papyri is a powerful name of a god (e.g. *PGM* 12:192), sometimes identified with the OT Yahweh (*PGM* 4:3019-3020 "the God of the Hebrews, Jesus"). On the other hand in a theological framework *Iēsous* may signal the true humanity of Christ; thus, Justin considers it the name of the man and saviour, while 'Christ' can already designate a function of the Logos (*apol.* II 6:3-4). The typology Joshua-Jesus is exploited (Justin, *Dial.* 75:1-2; 113:1-4; *Barn.* 12:8-10; Irenaeus, *Epid.* 27). The *Gospel of Philip* seems to be conscious of the contingency of *Iēsous*. It is a 'hidden name', not translatable into other languages, in opposition to the revealed name Christ (*NHC* II 3,56, 3.5.6). But gnostic writings can speak without differentiation of "our god Jesus", too (*NHC* VIII 2,133,8). It is not until the first Ecumenical Councils that it is clarified in what sense Jesus can be called God. There the incarnation model triumphs.

IV. *Bibliography*

R. BAUCKHAM, Worship of Jesus (Christ), *ABD* 3 (1992) 812-820; G. BORNKAMM, *Jesus von Nazareth* (Urban Bücher 19; Stuttgart 1956; ET New York 1960); H. BRAUN, *Jesus* (Themen der Theologie 1; Stuttgart/Berlin 1969, enlarged 1984); C. BURCHARD, Jesus von Nazareth, *Die Anfänge des Christentums* (J. Becker u.a.; Stuttgart 1987) 12-58; B. CHILTON & C.A. EVANS (eds.) *Studying the Historical Jesus* (NTTS 19; Leiden 1994); H. CONZELMANN, Jesus Christus, *RGG* III (1959) 619-653; H. CONZELMANN, *Jesus Christus in Historie und Theologie* (ed. G. Strecker; Tübingen 1975); N. A. DAHL, *Jesus the Christ* (ed. D. H. Juel; Minneapolis MN 1991); J. DUPONT (ed.), *Jésus aux origines de la christologie* (BETL 90; Louvain/Gembloux [2]1989); J. D. G. DUNN, *Christology in the Making* (Philadelphia 1980); DUNN, Christology (NT), *ABD* 1 (1992) 979-992; C. A. EVANS, *Life of Jesus Research. An Annotated Bibliography* (NTTS 13; Leiden 1989); W. FOERSTER, Ἰησοῦς, *TWNT* III (1938) 284-294; X 2 (1979) 1118-1120 [& lit.]; R. H. FULLER & P. PERKINS, *Who is this Christ?* (Philadelphia 1983); J. GNILKA, *Jesus von Nazaret* (HTKNTSup 3; Freiburg/Basel/Wien 1990); F. HAHN, *Anfänge des Christentums* (eds. C. Breytenbach & H. Paulsen; Göttingen 1991); M. HENGEL, Christologie und neutestamentliche Chronologie, *Neues Testament und Geschichte* (ed. H. Baltensweiler & B. Reicke; Zürich/Tübingen 1972) 43-67; A. J. HULTGREN, *New Testament Christology. A Critical Assessment and Annotated Bibliography* (New York 1988); L. W. HURTADO, *One God, One Lord* (Philadelphia 1988); J. JEREMIAS, *Neutestamentliche Theologie I. Die Verkündigung Jesu* (Gütersloh 1971); M. DE JONGE, *Christology in Context* (Philadelphia 1988); L. E. KECK, *The Future of Christology* (ed. A. J. Malherbe & W. A. Meeks; Philadelphia 1993); K. KERTELGE (ed.), *Rückfrage nach Jesus* (QD 63; Freiburg/Basel/Wien 1974); W. KRAMER, *Christos Kyrios Gottessohn* (ATANT 44; Zürich/Stuttgart 1963) esp. 37-38 & 199-202; H. LEROY, *Jesus* (Erträge der Forschung 95; Darmstadt 1978); J. P. MEIER, *A Marginal Jew. Rethinking the Historical Jesus* (New York I 1991, II 1994); B. F. MEYER, Jesus (Christ), *ABD* 3 (1992) 773-795; U. B. MÜLLER, *Die Menschwerdung des Gottessohnes* (SBS 140; Stuttgart 1989); C. PERROT, *Jésus et l'histoire* (Paris 1980); W. PESCH (ed.), *Jesus in den Evangelien* (SBS 45; Stuttgart 1970); E. P. SANDERS, *Jesus and Judaism* (London 1985); L. SCHENKE, *Die Urgemeinde* (Stuttgart 1990), esp. 116-156; H. SCHUERMANN, *Jesus. Gestalt und Geheimnis* (Paderborn 1994); R. SCHNACKENBURG, Christologie des Neuen Testamentes, *Mysterium Salutis* III 1 (ed. J.

Feiner & M. Löhrer; Einsiedeln/Zürich/Köln 1970) 227-383; SCHNACKENBURG, *Die Person Jesu im Spiegel der vier Evangelien* (HTKNTSup 4; Freiburg/Basel/Wien 1993); G. SCHNEIDER, Ἰησοῦς, *EWNT* II (1981) 440-452; E. SCHWEIZER, *Jesus Christus im vielfältigen Zeugnis des Neuen Testaments* (Siebenstern-Taschenbuch 126; München/ Hamburg 1968); G. N. STANTON, *Jesus of Nazareth in New Testament Preaching* (SNTSMS 27; Cambridge 1974); G. VERMES, *Jesus the Jew* (London 1973); A. VÖGTLE, Der verkündigende und verkündigte Jesus 'Christus', *Wer ist Jesus Christus*? (ed. J. Sauer; Freiburg 1977) 27-91; VOEGTLE, Jesus Christus, *Bibeltheologischer Wörterbuch* (Graz ^{2}1994) 333-345; K. WENGST, *Christologische Formeln und Lieder des Urchristentums* (StNT 7; Gütersloh 1972); D. ZELLER, Die Menschwerdung des Sohnes Gottes im Neuen Testament und die antike Religionsgeschichte, *Menschwerdung Gottes - Vergöttlichung von Menschen* (ed. D. Zeller; NTOA 7; Fribourg & Göttingen 1988) 141-176.

D. ZELLER

JEUSH → **JAGHUT**

JEZEBEL איזבל

I. Daughter of Eth-Baal, king of Sidon, and wife of Ahab, king of Northern Israel.

She was an active propagator of the →Baal cult (1 Kgs 16:29-33; 18:19; 19:1-2; 21:25; 2 Kgs 9:30-37), who persecuted the →Yahweh prophets (1 Kgs 18:4). The meaning of her Phoenician name is disputed; mostly interpreted as 'where is the →Prince', →'Prince' being an epithet of Baal (Heb *ʾîzebel*, pause form *ʾîzābel*; LXX-NT: Ιεζαβελ; Josephus: Ιεζαβελη, variant reading Ιεζαβηλα).

II. In the NT Jezebel occurs in Rev 2:18-29, in the Letter to the Church at Thyatira (Lydia), as the derogatory nickname of a self-styled prophetess in the Jewish or Christian community there. She taught her fellow church members to fornicate (μοιχεύω) and eat food sacrificed to idols. In the parallel Letter to Pergamum such teaching is ascribed to 'Balaam' and 'the Nicolaitans' (Rev 2:14-15; cf. 2:6). Possibly, "to fornicate" (2:20 πορνεῦσαι) and "committing adultery with her" (2:22 μοιχεύοντας) are in this context synonymous with "eating food sacrificed to idols" (2:20). Compare Jer 3:6-10 LXX, where these two verbs are unmistakably used as metaphors for idolatry. Queen Jezebel herself was also explicitly accused of fornication (πορνεῖαι) and sorcery (φάρμακα) in LXX 4 Kgdms 9:22 (= MT 2 Kgs 9:22).

III. In 1892 E. SCHÜRER first advocated the hypothesis that this NT Jezebel was not a synagogue or church member, but the priestess of a local cult of the Oriental Sibyl named Sambêthê (Σαμβήθη). The sanctuary of this Sibyl would be the σαμβαθεῖον which is mentioned in an inscription from Thyatira, *CIJ* 752 (= *CIG* 2,3509 = *IGR* 4,1281). Schürer was well aware, though, that this word could also refer to a synagogue, like the σαββαθεῖον (*varia lectio* σαββατεῖον) in Josephus, *Ant.* 16,164, which was in the province of Asia, too. The difference between μβ and ββ would be no hindrance, since fluctuation of the two is well attested, especially in σάββατον (Hebrew *šabbāt*) and derived words, compare also Latin 'sabbata' (Suetonius, *Aug.* 76,2) alongside 'sambatha' (*P. Ryl.* 4,613). The main argument for not interpreting the word as 'synagogue' in this inscription is the mention of a sarcophagus being placed in an open space (ἐπὶ τόπου καθαροῦ, cf. LSJ s. v. καθαρός I 3a) near this sambatheion, in 'the precinct (περίβολος) of the Chaldaean', along the public road. The vicinity of a tomb would have made, it was argued, a synagogue ritually unclean. The argument is, however, not compelling, because a corpse was considered to defile only within a distance of at most four yards with regard to the Shemaʿ, so that it was allowed to be recited only beyond that distance (*b.Berakhoth* 18a; *b.Sotah* 43b; 44a, according to Beth Shammai). This makes it very doubtful that a graveyard as such could defile a synagogue building. Moreover, the location of the tomb is not presented as disputed in any respect.

The Sibyl, to whom we have assigned the comprehensive name of 'Oriental', figures in a number of interdependent testimonies, in which she is considered to have been both a blood relation and the daughter-in-law of →Noah (*Sib. Or.* prol. and 3,827). She is therefore referred to as 'Jewish', 'Hebrew', 'Persian' and 'Chaldaean' at the same time (*FGH* 146,1). Only Pausanias speaks about a Palestinian-Babylonian-Egyptian Sibyl named Sabbê, a name which is evidently a hypocoristic of Sambêthê (*Description of Greece* 10,12,9). A third variant of her name may have been preserved on a 3rd-4th cent. CE ostracon from Karanis (Fayûm), apparently a list of divine names and a writing exercise of some kind (*O. Mich.* 657 = *CPJ* 496). Here she probably appears as Σαμβαθίς, unless the name is to be read as Σαμβάθι(ο)ς, showing the well-attested Koine Greek shortening of words ending in -ιος or -ιον. In the latter case, the name could refer to 'the god of the Shabbath', the god of the Jews. Unlike the other Sibyls listed by the ancients, the Oriental Sibyl is not connected with a specific town or place. SCHÜRER also assumed that "the precinct of the Chaldaean" mentioned in the inscription, was named after a 'Chaldaean' or soothsayer who used to make statements in the name of this Chaldaean-Jewish Sambêthê. Jezebel would then have performed the same function as this 'Chaldaean' towards the end of the first century CE. This theory (a combination of three unprovable assumptions) has not found wide acceptance. It seems certain, at least, that consultants of such an oracle did not constitute a regular congregation as implied by Rev 2:18-29. Nor would Jezebel, if she were an outsider, have been allowed to 'teach' in the local Christian community (cf. 1 Cor 8). It is much more likely that she was a church member in the ordinary sense, given the fact that she was allowed some time 'to repent', that is to revoke her heresy (2,21). The σύνοδος σαμβαθική figuring in a I CE inscription from Naucratis (Egypt) (*SB* 12; reign of Augustus?), refers, therefore, not so much to a group of Sambêthê-adherents as to an assembly of Sabbatists or Godfearers, if not to an ordinary synagogue meeting.

IV. *Bibliography*

E. SCHÜRER, *The History of the Jewish People in the Age of Jesus Christ (175 B. C. - A. D. 135),* [Revised Edition by G. Vermes, F. Millar & M. Goodman] (Edinburgh 1986) III 1, 19; 622-626; V. A. TCHERIKOVER, A. FUKS & M. STERN, *Corpus Papyrorum Judaicarum* (Cambridge 1964) III 43-87; H. C. YOUTIE, Sambathis, *Scriptiunculae* I (Amsterdam 1973) 467-477; C. BURCHARD, Sambethe, *KP* 4 (1972) 1531.

G. MUSSIES

JORDAN ירדן Ἰορδάνης

I. The name of the river of Jordan, (*hay*)*yardēn*, occurs 177 times in the OT. In the NT Ἰορδάνης is attested 15 times. The etymology of the name is debated. A derivation from the root YRD, 'to descend', implying an interpretation 'the river that comes down' (e.g. Philo, *Leg. All.* II:89; b*Bech* 55a; BDB 432-434) probably rests on popular etymology. Generally, the name is interpreted as non-Semitic in origin. One proposal connects the element *dan* with Indo-Aryan *don*, 'river' (cf. e.g. Danube; Djnepr) and interprets *yar-* as related to Indo-european 'year'. The name then would mean 'perennial river' (e.g. KÖHLER 1939; COHEN, *IDB* 2, 973-978). In favour of this approach it must be observed that in Greece two rivers are called Ἰάρδανος, one in Elis (e.g. Homer, *Iliad* 7:135; Strabo 8,3:20) and one in Crete (e.g. Homer, *Odyssey*, 3:292; Pausanias 6,21:6). HOMMEL construes both the Canaanite river name and the Greek rivers as derived from Hittite and compares the name with the Armenian and Persian noun *ward*, 'rose' (1927:170; see also J. R. HARRIS, Crete, the Jordan and the Rhone, *ExpTim* 21 [1909-10] 303-306; J. HEMPEL, *PJB* 23 [1927] 64; W. VON SODEN, *ZAW* 57 [1939] 153-154) On the other hand, the element *yar-* has been construed as related to Hurrian *iar*, 'water', while *den* was interpreted either as referring to the tribe of Dan or as a derivation of DYN, 'to judge'. The name of the river then has as meaning 'the water of Dan/of the ordeal' (ALDEN 1975). The occurrence at Emar of the noun *yardu* (*Emar* 363:2), supports a Semitic origin of the name Jordan, if the word should indeed mean 'river' (see Arnaud).

II. Outside the Bible, the Jordan is first mentioned in records from the nineteenth Egyptian dynasty: *yrdn* (J. SIMONS, *Handbook of Egyptian Topographical Lists* [Leiden 1937] 201; *ANET* 242.255.477). The name here occurs as an indication of a geographical entity that can be crossed. The name is also attested in the list depicting the campaign of Pharaoh Sheshonq in the tenth century BCE (SIMONS, *Handbook*, 180, No. 150 *jrdn*).

In texts from Emar, mention is made of an offering to a deity ^{d}EN *ya-ar-da-ni* 'the lord of the flowing rivers' (*Emar* 378:23). Besides, the name of a gate: KA_2 *ša* ^{d}*wa-ar-da-na-ti*, 'the gate of the river goddesses' (*Emar* 137:1), occurs. They do not refer to the Jordan river as such, but can be interpreted as an early attestation of →river-deities.

III. The River Jordan runs from Mount →Hermon to the Dead Sea in the south. In a rather speculative article, HOMMEL compares the Jordan with the mystic and mythic river Eridanos, known from Greek sources. He then surmises that ancient, pre-Israelite myths were brought—by the intermediary of Phoenicians—to Greece where they were reformulated as the Phaeton-legends. In Palestine, the Jordan kept its religious significance as a river of ordeal (1927).

In the OT the river has a religious significance (HULST 1965), though it is never treated as a god. In the Book of Joshua the Jordan is the border-river to be crossed to enter the promised land. Traditions concerning the event of the 'conquest under Joshua' are connected to a commemorative feast (E. OTTO, *Das Mazzotfest in Gilgal* [BWANT 107; Stuttgart 1975]). Furthermore, the Jordan is ascribed mysterious and magical powers: The Ascension into heaven of →Elijah took place on the other side of the Jordan. In the story of Elisha and Naaman, the water of the Jordan has a healing force (2 Kgs 5:13-14). DAHOOD (1966:258; cf., however, GÖRG 1982:903) construes *ʾereṣ yardēn* in Ps 42:7 as 'the land of descent' interpreting it as an expression for the netherworld. He compares the expression with a line from the →Baal-epic *tspr byrdm arṣ*, 'You will be counted among those who went down into the earth' (*KTU* 1.4 viii:8-9).

In early Judaism, the Jordan has no specific significance. In *Life of Adam and Eve* 6-8 it is told that →Adam, as penitance for his →sin, spent 40 days fasting and praying in the Jordan while →Eve did the same for 37 days in the →Tigris.

In the NT the Jordan is the place where →Jesus and many others were baptized by John (Mark 1:1-11//). Hebr 3:17-19 might be interpreted as implying a metaphorical Jordan, as a symbol of crossing from life to death (THOMPSON 1992:957)

IV. On the architrave of the triumphal arch of Titus, the part facing the Colosseum, three Romans are depicted bearing the Jordan river. He is presented as a river deity in the form of an old man. The scene resembles the way in which elsewhere rivers as personifications of conquered provinces were represented in the procession of the victor (RENGSTORFF 1968:613; PFANNER 1983).

From the sixth century CE onward, in Christian mosaics depicting the baptism of Jesus, a figure is present which can be interpreted as a deified Jordan river. The iconography of the scene and the figure indicates that the Jordan-character was modelled after a pagan, Graeco-Roman river deity (JENSEN 1993; *pace* RENGSTORFF 1968:613). In the light of the OT roots of a deification of the Jordan a revival of popular belief can be assumed too.

V. *Bibliography*

R. ALDEN, Jordan, *Zondervan Pictorial Encyclopedia of the Bible* 3 (Grand Rapids 1975) 684-692; M. J. DAHOOD, *Psalms* I (AB 16; Garden City 1966) 258; M. GÖRG,

Jarden, *TWAT* 3 (1982) 901-909; E. HOMMEL, Der Name und die Sagen des Jordan in altkanaanänischer Zeit, *Journal of the Society of Oriental Research* 11 (1927) 169-194; A. R. HULST, Der Jordan in den alttestamentlichen Überlieferungen, *OTS* 14 (1965) 162-188; R. JENSEN, What are Pagan River Gods doing in Scenes of Jesus's Baptism?, *Bible Review* 9 (1993) 34-41; L. KÖHLER, Lexikologisch-geographisches. 1. Der Jordan, *ZDPV* 62 (1939) 115-120; M. PFANNER, *Der Titusbogen* (Mainz 1983); K. H. RENGSTORFF, Ποταμός, ποταμοφόρητος, Ἰορδάνης, *TDNT* 6 (1968) 595-623; H. O. THOMPSON, Jordan River, *ABD* 2 (1992) 953-958.

B. BECKING

JOSEPH יוסף

I. In biblical genealogical tradition Joseph is the son of →Jacob and →Rachel (Gen 30:22-24). His name is a hypocoristicon, presumably of **yôsîp-ʾēl*/DN like *yôsîpyāh* (Ezra 8:10). Tradition preserves two explanations of his name, the one linking it to the root ʾSP (Gen 30:23 E?), the other to YSP (Gen 30:24 J?); the latter interpretation is probably correct. The name expresses the classical wish for a quiver full of children (Ps 115:14; NOTH, *IPN*, 212; DE VAUX 1971; ANDRÉ, *TWAT* 3 [1977-82] 685). The form *yĕhôsēp* (Ps 81:6), frequently found in later Hebrew, is perhaps a case of hypercorrection. In 19th century research the story of Joseph was often interpreted in terms of a fertility myth, in particular the seasonal contest between rain and drought (WESTERMANN 1975:56-64). He is identified with the fertilizing rain, being a child of Rachel and Jacob, who are identified with respectively the clouds and the nightly sky (GOLDZIHER 1876:191-194). Others hold that Joseph, an ancient Canaanite numen of Joseph-El, was turned into an Israelite eponym by the tribes of Ephraim (MEYER 1906).

II. The story of Joseph (Gen 37:39-47:50; Ps 105:16-22; Sir 49:15), does not tell us much about the origins of the tribe or 'house' of Joseph. The story supposes knowledge of the patriarchal sagas, in particular the ancient tradition that "Jacob and his sons went down to Egypt" (Josh 24:4; NOTH 1948; WESTERMANN 1982). Joseph's story in its present form, whether taken as a didactic narrative from the wisdom school, or as a specimen of a diaspora story (MEINHOLD 1975), is the tale of a young Hebrew far from his home-country rising to power under Yahweh's guidance. It gives interesting insights into the Hebrew soul and to a lesser extent into Egyptian society, but hardly preserves a reminiscence of a Middle Palestinian tribe by the name of Joseph. The story may share some episodes and motifs with the Egyptian 'Tale of the Two Brothers'. The fact that the latter tale is about the gods Anubis and Bata, Bata being a pastoral god, taking either the form of a ram or a bull, does not imply that Joseph was a mythological hero in Israelite tradition, even when, according to an alternative interpretation, he is compared to a young bull (*bn prt* Gen 49:22; Deut 33:17; SALO 1968). The background of Joseph's career may be found in the genres of the *Königsnovelle*, the success story of the wise Courtier (Gen 41) and similar stories of Asiatics who carved their way high up into a foreign administration (→Moses, Biya, →Daniel. etc.; DE VAUX 1971). Attempts to find the precise historical setting of the story in the Hyksos period are highly questionable.

III. Joseph is the eponym of a tribe Joseph (Num 13:11) or a group of tribes, known as the *bĕnê Yôsēp* (Num 1:10; 34:23; Josh 16:1; 17:14) or the *bêt Yôsēp* (Josh 17:14-18; Judg 1:22-23; 2 Sam 19:21; 1 Kgs 11:29; Amos 5:6). The last expression is attested outside the Hexateuch as opposite to the house of Judah (Judg 1:22-23.35; 2 Sam 2:8-11; 19:20; 1 Kgs 11:28; Amos 5:6). This seems to be a rather ancient usage though the exact geographic and demographic ramifications remain unclear. In later tradition Joseph's ancestorship is limited to the tribes of Ephraim and Manasseh, but whether they became Joseph's house together, or split up in separate tribes is still a disputed question. In a number of cases Joseph is a synonym for →Jacob/Israel (Ps 77:16; 81:6; Ezek 37:16.19; Amos 5:15; 6:6; Obad 18), either meaning the northern kingdom or the people of Israel. Apart from the Joseph story itself, sources about the patriarch Joseph are rather poor. Except for traditions about Joseph's name and the tradition of his tomb near →Shechem; →Thukamuna (Josh 24:32), some obscure allusions are found in the tribal sayings (Gen 49:22-26; Deut 33:13-16) and topographical texts (Josh 17:14-18). Later Jewish tradition tells about Joseph's sarcophagus sunk into the Nile (Mek.Exod 13:19; Str.-B. II 674), referring to the →Osiris-myth (JEREMIAS 1958:131), but the story of Joseph is neither a myth, nor the usual kind of patriarchal saga. There is no reason to suppose that Joseph was originally a hero or a city-god. The alleged toponym Joseph-El does not exist (*pace* MEYER 1906:292; cf. DE VAUX 1971:297 n. 87). The name is characteristic of the Amorite onomasticon in the early second millennium BCE, so in this respect he might indeed have been one of the early Israelite ancestors, remembered and perhaps even venerated at a place somewhat east of Shechem on the border between the later tribes of Ephraim and Manasse (Gen 33:18-19; Josh 17:7; John 4:5; Acts 7:16; JEREMIAS 1958:31-36). According to a fragmentary tradition in Gen 48:22 Shechem was given to Joseph by Jacob, but the relation to 33:18-19 remains unclear (DE VAUX 1971:584-587; WESTERMANN 1982:217-218; *pace* NOTH 1948:90-91). According to later tradition Joseph, not Jacob, was the 'owner' of the plot of land at Shechem, and subsequently believed to be buried there amidst the clans that traced their origins back to him. In connection with the sons of Joseph, viz. Ephraim and Manasseh, similar wishes for progeny are expressed as with Rachel and →Leah (Gen 41:52; 48:13-20). Joseph was known not to be buried in Machpelah—which confirms the strong tradition of his own sepulchre and veneration, notwithstanding medieval Jewish and Muslim tradition.

IV. *Bibliography*

J. JEREMIAS, *Heiligengräber in Jesu Umwelt* (Göttingen 1958) 31-36.130-131; M. MEINHOLD, Die Gattung der Josephgeschichte und des Estherbuches: Diasporanovelle II, *ZAW* 88 (1976) 72-93; E. MEYER, *Die Israeliten und ihre Nachbarstämme* (Halle 1906); M. NOTH, *Überlieferungsgeschichte des Pentateuchs* (Stuttgart 1948) 90-91; V. SALO, Joseph, Sohn der Färse, *BZ* 12 (1968) 94-95; R. DE VAUX, *Histoire Ancienne I* (Paris 1971) 277-303; J. VERGOTE, *Joseph en Egypte. Genèse 37-50 à la lumiere des études égyptologiques récentes* (Louvain 1959); C. WESTERMANN, *Genesis 12-50* (EdF 48; Darmstadt 1975); WESTERMANN, *Genesis 37-50* (BKAT I/3; Neukirchen-Vluyn 1982).

M. DIJKSTRA

JUDAH → YEHUD

K

KABOD → GLORY

KAIWAN כיון

I. Kaiwan occurs under the form *Kiyyûn* in Amos 5:26, after *Sikkût* (→Sakkuth). The Masoretic vocalisation is that for idols →Abominations. The real pronunciation must have been *Kaiwān*, cf. Syr. *Keywân* (and variants), the name of the planet Saturn. Both go back to the Babylonian name for Saturn, *Kajjamānu*, "The Steady One". The Hebrew text used by LXX was already corrupted in having an initial *r* instead of *k* resulting in *Rayphan* (and variants); in Acts 7:43 *Rompha*. CD VII 15 mistook the name as a word meaning "base", cf. Heb *kēn* (BORGER 1988:78-9).

II. In Assyrian / Babylonian religion, *Kajjamānu*/Saturn was not of great importance. The name of the star mainly occurs in astronomical texts (e.g. in *SAA* 8). That *Kajjamānu*/Saturn was seen as a divine entity can be inferred from the fact that the name is preceded by the determinative for deities. In Mesopotamia, Saturn is the only star not related to one of the major deities (BARSTAD 1984:123).

III. In the OT, the name is attested only in Amos 5:26, together with the equally unique Sakkuth. Both are foreign idols made by the Israelites. Sakkuth is qualified as "your king", Kaiwan as "your images" (plural); after a pause (*atnāḥ*) follows: "the star, your god which you made for yourselves". One tends to reverse the order of these qualifications, as LXX already did: "the star of your god Rayphan, their images which you made for yourselves"; see also BORGER (1988:79 n. 5). It should be noted that *Ṣalmu*, lit. "image", was a god in Assyria and in Arabian Taima; (→Image; S. DALLEY, *Iraq* 48 [1986] 85-101, E. A. KNAUF, *Ismael*, 2. Auflage [Wiesbaden 1989] 78-79, 150-151; KNAUF, *Transeuphratène* 2 [1990] 212).

A. KUENEN (*De godsdienst van Israël* [Haarlem 1869] 260) suggested that the Israelites worshipped Saturn, having adopted his cult from the Kenites. It is more probable, however, that the Israelites had borrowed the worship of this planet from the Assyrians. In this case there are two options. (1) The Israelites took over the worship before the fall of Samaria. Then Amos 5:26 can be interpreted as a prophetic accusation for not having served →Yahweh (e.g. BARSTAD 1984). (2) Amos 5:26 refers to one of the deities mentioned in 2 Kgs 17:28-30 who were brought to the Samaritan area by Assyrian settlers. This view implies that the text is a later insertion by a (deuteronomistic) redactor who confused the situation before and after the conquest of the capital (H. W. WOLFF, *Dodekapropheton 2. Joel und Amos* [BKAT XIV/2; Neukirchen-Vluyn 1969] 310-311).

III. *Bibliography*

H. M. BARSTAD, *The Religious Polemics of Amos* (VTSup 34; Leiden 1984) 118-126; P. R. BERGER, Imaginäre Astrologie in spätbabylonischer Propaganda, *Die Rolle der Astronomie in den Kulturen Mesopotamiens* (ed. H. D. Galter; Graz 1993) 275-289; esp. 277 n. 2; *R. BORGER, Amos 5,26, Apostelgeschichte 7,43 und Šurpu II, 180, *ZAW* 100 (1988) 70-81; O. LORETZ, Die babylonischen Gottesnamen Sukkut und Kajjamānu in Amos 5, 26, *ZAW* 101 (1989) 286-289.

M. STOL

KELTI

I. In the Amarna letters the name of the Judean town of Keila (Josh 15:44; 1 Sam 23; 1 Chr 4:29; Neh 3:17-18) is written [uru]*Qi-il-te/tu*, probably to be pronounced

/Qiʿiltu/ (*EA* 279:12; 280:11.17; 287:11; 289:28; 290:10.18). JIRKU related the name to a god whose name he read as ^{d}*Ki-el-ti* (1930).

II. The text in which Jirku found the god Kelti mentioned is *KUB* 17 no. 20 ii, part of a ritual for the →'olden gods' (for a transcription and translation see H. T. BOSSERT, *MIO* 4 [1956] 202-203). Line 7 of column ii mentions ^{D}*Ki-el-ti* DUMU ^{D}A.A as one of the recipients of the offerings. Kelti the son of the goddess →Ayya, the spouse of the Babylonian sun-god Shamash, is the deified personification of the forest (cf. E. VON SCHULER, *WbMyth* I/1, 189-190). His name is the Hurrianized form of Akk *qištu*, 'wood, forest' (H. EHELOLF, *Kleinasiatische Forschungen* 1 [1930] 143 n.2; C.-G. VON BRANDENSTEIN, Ein arisches und ein semitisches Lehnwort im Churrischen, *AfO* 13 [1939-40] 58 and n.2), which also occurs in the by-form *qiltu* (*CAD* Q 272). In spite of the Akkadian origin of the name, there is no unambiguous evidence of the deification of woods and forests in Mesopotamian religion: the rare occurrences of ^{d}**tir** (**tir** is Sumerian for 'forest') should be understood as ^{d}**še.tir**, i.e. the grain-god Ashnan (P. MANDER, Brevi considerazioni sul testo "lessicale" SF 23 = SF 24, *OA* 19 [1980] 191).

III. Though the god Kelti is definitely known in the ancient Near East, it is extremely unlikely that he is in some way connected with the place-name Keila. The presence of the *ʿayin* in the biblical toponym can simply not be explained on the basis of Kelti < Akk *qiltu*. Also, there is no need to search for an Anatolian deity in order to explain the toponym *Qĕʿilâ*. More than thirty years after his first etymology, JIRKU himself came up with the far more plausible suggestion that Keila is related to the Ugaritic word *qʿl* (1963:87). This term is to be explained as 'hill' or 'mountain ridge' (NEIMAN 1971:65-66). The city of Keila would owe its name, then, to a distinctive feature of the landscape in which it was situated (cf. LIPIŃSKI 1973).

IV. *Bibliography*

A. JIRKU, Der Ursprung des Namens der südpalästinensischen Stadt Ḳeʿīla, *ZAW* 48 (1930) 228-229; JIRKU, Zu einigen Orts- und Eigennamen Palästina-Syriens, *ZAW* 75 (1963) 86-88; E. LIPIŃSKI, Recherches ugaritiques, *Syria* 50 (1973) 36-37; D. NEIMAN, *ʿBR.IHT.NPŠMM* (*ʿNT*:VI:8-9): A Proposed Translation, *JNES* 30 (1971) 64-68.

K. VAN DER TOORN

KENAN קינן

I. In genealogical lists of the antediluvian heroes, the son of Enosh is called *qênān*/Kenan (Gen 5:9-14; 1 Chr 1:2; cf. Luke 3:37 *Kainam*). Etymologically the name can be interpreted as derived from the noun or name *qayin* →Cain with a diminutive ending *-ān*. The name can mean either 'smith; javelin' (*HALAT* 1026) or 'little Cain' (HESS 1993). The name has been compared to a Southarabian deity *Qaynān* (ROBERTSON SMITH 1894:43 n. 4; WESTERMANN 1974:483).

II. From Himyaritic inscriptions a Sabaean deity *Qaynān* is known (CIH 2, 232). He was especially worshipped by the tribe of the *ḥsʾm* (RÉS 3974, 4648, 4649). In view of the etymological relation with the Arabic noun *qayn* 'smith' it stands to reason that *Qaynān* has been a patron deity of smiths and metalworkers (HÖFNER, *WbMyth* 1/I, 524).

III. In the OT only genealogical information on Kenan is given (HESS 1993). He lived for 910 years (Gen 5:14) and begot Mahalalel when he was 70 years old. The identity of his name with the Sabaean deity is probably sheer coincidence.

IV. *Bibliography*

R. S. HESS, *Studies in the Personal Names of Genesis 1-11* (AOAT 234; Neukirchen-Vluyn 1993) 67-68; M. HÖFNER, *WbMyth* 1/I, 524; W. ROBERTSON SMITH, *The Religion of the Semites* (London 1894); C. WESTERMANN, *Genesis 1-11* (BKATI/1; Neukirchen-Vluyn 1974).

B. BECKING

KESIL → ORION

KHONSU

I. The name of the Egyptian god Khonsu occurs once in the Apocrypha of the Old Testament (3 Macc 6:38) as part of the Egyptian name of the ninth month of the year and first month of the summer season: Pachôn, i.e. 'He of Khonsu'.

II. The god Khonsu was mostly represented in the form of a mummy with the head of a child wearing the sidelock of youth or with the head of a hawk. In both cases he usually wears the sign of the moon on his head. He was a moongod. His name might be explained as the "wanderer" or "he who comes and goes". He was the divine child of →Amun and Mut in the divine triad of Karnak. He had a beautiful temple in the precinct of Amun at Karnak. The famous Bentresh-stela which extols Khonsu as a healing god was found in another temple of Khonsu in Karnak. Besides in Karnak or Thebes, Khonsu was venerated together with Amun and Mut in many places and temples in Egypt.

III. This ninth month of the Egyptian calendar received its name after the festival of the god Khonsu (BRUNNER, *LdÄ* I, 962; ALTENMÜLLER, *LdÄ* II, 174). The name Pakhôn/Pashons is still retained as the name of a month in the Christian-Coptic calendar (April 26 - May 25).

IV. *Bibliography*

J. VON BECKERATH, Kalender, *LdÄ* III 297-299; H. BRUNNER, Chons, *LdÄ* I 960-963; G. POSENER, Recherches sur le dieu Khonsu, *Annuaire du College de France* 65 (1965-1966) 342-343; 66 (1966-1967) 339-342; 67 (1967-1968) 345-349; 68 (1968-1969), 401-407; 69 (1969-1970) 375-379; 70 (1970-1971) 391-396.

H. TE VELDE

KHVARENAH

I. The Iranian divinity Khvarenah (Avestan *Xvarenah*), Glory, is once found in the Bible as an element of a personal name. In Num 34:25 mention is made of *Parnāk* (LXX *Pharnach*), which resembles Old Iranian **farnāka*, comparable to other hypocoristic theophoric names attested in the Persepolis Fortification Texts, such as **Mazdāka*, **Mithraka* and **Bagaka*. This resemblance can only be a coincidence in the context of Moses, but the adversary of Judith in the book named after her is called by the truly Iranian name *Holophernēs*, probably borrowed from the historical Cappadocian prince *Orophernēs*. The etymology of this name is a matter of dispute, but it probably derives from **varufarnah*, meaning "having wide Glory". (For all these names, M. MAYRHOFER, *Onomastica Persepolitana* [Wien 1973]; for **varufarnah,* R. SCHMITT, Einige iranische Namen auf Inschriften oder Papyri, *ZPE* 17 [1975] 15-24).

II. Although the Zoroastrian divinity Glory is mainly known by his Avestan name Khvarenah, the noun meaning "glory" is attested in almost every Iranian language with initial *f.* Thus we have Old Pers **farnah* (abundantly attested in personal names), Soghdian *prn*, Khotanese *phārra-*, Bactrian *farr.* It occurs in Armenian as a loanword, *pʿarkʿ*, and is also attested in the isolated north-eastern Iranian languages, Scythian **farna*, Ossetic *farn*, although in these languages it may be a West Iranian loanword. The occurrence of the word in all Iranian languages indicates that the idea of a divine glory has a common Iranian background and cannot be attributed exclusively to the Zoroastrian tradition. In view of the general lack of information concerning non-Zoroastrian Iranian religions, however, the evidence we have for the divinity can only be grasped from the Zoroastrian sources. The etymology of the word *xvarenah/farnah* is a matter of debate. BAILEY suggested that it derives from a root **hvar*, to acquire, and hence means "the good things of life" (1971: XXIII-XXIV). DUCHESNE-GUILLEMIN however took up the old suggestion that it derives from Old Iranian **hvar*, "sun", and that it means "solar fluid", the essence which causes life to prosper (1963). The use of the rare suffix *-nah*, which is only used after verbal roots, seemed to secure BAILEY's etymology, but by now DUCHESNE-GUILLEMIN's etymology is commonly adopted.

Khvarenah occurs in the Avesta both as a noun, meaning "glory" and as a personified abstract divinity "Glory". It is a frequent element in personal names both in Avestan and in all other Iranian languages. Therefore, it is to be considered a very important religious distinction in the Iranian tradition. Khvarenah in the Avesta is in the first place a quality possessed by the gods. Ahura Mazda calls himself the "glorious" and the "most glorious" (Yt. 1.12), Verethraghna, the god of Victory introduces himself with the words "I am the most glorious in glory" (Yt. 14.3) and the important river-goddess Anāhitā is said to possess "as much glory as the whole of the waters" (Yt. 5.96).

In the hymn to the sun (Yt. 6) and the hymn to the moon (Yt. 7) Glory is described as something the gods give to the earth: "(The spiritual yazatas) gather that Glory, they pour down that Glory, they give (it) unto the Ahura-created world, to increase the worlds of Righteousness, to increase the creatures of Righteousness" (Yt. 6.1). In this respect Khvarenah belongs to a sphere of ancient divine concepts of fertility and seemingly amoral elements of fortune, sharing important characteristics with the goddess Aṣ̌i (fortune) and the above-mentioned Verethraghna (KREYENBROEK 1991:137-138). Khvarenah withdraws itself, it flees from those who possess it, when they lie, but also when they are faced with oppression and hardship.

Khvarenah has two important and obvious connections in the Avesta, with sovereignty and with the Iranians. For both these connections it has special epithets, i.e. *kaoiia* (kingly), *uγra* (strong), *airiiana* (Iranian) and *axᵛareta* (a word of unknown meaning, either "unseizable" or "lightless"). There are two hymns in the Avesta devoted to Khvarenah and to those who possessed it, Yt. 18 and Yt. 19. The short Yt. 18 (inscribed to the goddess of Justice, *Arštāt*) is devoted to Glory of the Aryans, a special aspect of Khvarenah as the protector and upholder of the well-being of the Iranians. Of more theological interest is the much longer Yt. 19 (inscribed to the goddess of the earth, *Zam*), which is an elaborate description of Khvarenah and of the different persons who possessed Glory or who tried to seize it, but failed. Despite its obvious connection with fire and warmth, Khvarenah is often said to hide in Lake *Vourukaša*, where it is safely kept by the water-god *Apąm Napāt*. All important heroes of Iranian mythical history are represented as possessors of the kingly Glory, when they performed their miraculous works. The most important of these is *Yima*, who possessed Glory until it left him because he lied (Yt. 19.31-34). The Glory leaving *Yima* is embodied in the shape of a bird. There is a detailed description of *Frangrasyan,* one of the most hated enemies of the Iranians, who undresses himself and swims in Lake *Vourukaša* to get hold of the Khvarenah, but never succeeds (although in Yt. 19.93 he actually possesses Glory for a very short while). The glory that *Frangrasyan* tries to steal from Lake *Vourukaša* is described as "the Glory that belongs to the Aryan nations, born and unborn, and to the holy Zarathustra" (Yt. 19.64), and the fact that Zarathustra actually possessed Glory is a consistent element in the Avesta and in the later Zoroastrian tradition, culminating in the story of the journey made by Glory before it came to Zarathustra's mother as described in *Dēnkard* VII. After Zarathustra the Khvarenah is passed on to *Vištāspa,* his patron and it is said to come to the future Saviours at the end of time.

Apart from the information provided by the Avesta and by the occurrence of *farnah* in personal names, a wealth of iconographical material, from the Achaemenid era onwards, provides an important insight into the practical and political meaning of Glory. It has by now been accepted by most scholars that the famous "figure in the winged disk", that can be found in very many specimens of Achaemenid art, is a representation of the kingly Glory, a divine symbol of the orthodoxy and sovereignty of the king of kings. The interpretation of the "figure in the winged disk" as Glory was convincingly given by SHAHBAZI (1974-1980; BOYCE 1982:100-105). It appears on some of the majestic Achaemenid reliefs, where it carefully mirrors the gesture and appearance of the king, it appears in the presence of the sacred fire and it appears as an ornamental symbol in solitary works of art. The identification of this symbol with the kingly Glory is not completely unproblematic (LECOQ 1984), but the fact that it often appears as the exact similitude of the king makes an identification with Ahura Mazda (as upheld by LECOQ) unlikely. The omnipresence of the symbol, and the combined evidence of classical authors, who frequently mention the khvarenah, translating it with *tychē*, (→Tyche) *daimōn* (→Demon) or *doxa*, indicate that under the Achaemenids the concept of Khvarenah clearly had both a religious and a political meaning, even though it is conspicuously absent from their inscriptions. The Achaemenid kings professed their religious affiliation by endlessly invoking Ahura Mazda as the god who gave them their sovereignty, who made them king, who appointed them as his chosen ones. The external evidence for this special position was the appearance of the divine Glory, carefully fostered in art and in ceremony. The idea of a divine glory with special links with the sovereign continued to play an important part in the following Iranian dynasties, and can be found in Parthian, Sasanian and early Islamic literature and art. The divinity Glory, apart from being praised in two hymns, is also worshipped in several prayers and rites of personal devotion.

III. *Bibliography*

H. W. BAILEY, *Zoroastrian Problems in the Ninth Century Books* (Oxford 1971, repr.); M. BOYCE, *A History of Zoroastrianism II: Under the Achaemenians* (HdO VIII.1.2. 2.2A; Leiden 1982); J. DUCHESNE-GUILLEMIN, Le X^{v}arenah, *AION, Sezione Linguistica*, 5 (1963) 19-31; J. DUCHESNE-GUILLEMIN, La royauté iranienne et le x^{v}arenah, *Iranica* (ed. G. Gnoli & A. V. Rossi; Napoli 1979) 375-386; G. GNOLI, Note sullo "X^{v}arenah-", *Acta Iranica* 23 (1984) 207-218; B. JACOBS, *Das Chvarnah - Zum Stand der Forschung*, *MDOG* 119 (1987) 215-248 [& lit]; P. G. KREYENBROEK, On the Shaping of Zoroastrian Theology, *Histoire et cultes de l'Asie centrale préislamique* (ed. P. Bernard & F. Grenet; Paris 1991) 137-145; P. LECOQ, Un problème de religion Achéménide: Ahura Mazda ou Xvarnah?, *Acta Iranica* 23 (1984) 301-326; A. S. SHAHBAZI, An Achaemenid Symbol I. A Farewell to "Fravahr and Ahuramazda", *AMI* 7 (1974) 135-144; A. S. SHAHBAZI, An Achaemenid Symbol II. Farnah "(God given) Fortune" Symbolised, *AMI* 13 (1980) 119-147.

A. F. DE JONG

KIMAH → PLEIADES

KING OF TERRORS מלך בלהות

I. The Designation 'King of Terrors' (*mlk blhwt*) occurs only once in the OT, in Job 18:14. Some commentators describe the term 'King of Terrors' as a metaphorical expression with some mythological background that was common in the ancient world; compare *rex tremendus* in Virgil, *Georgics* 4.469 (FOHRER 1988:304).

II. Attempts at identifying the 'King of Terrors' with ancient Near Eastern deities of the underworld remain doubtful. According to IRWIN, Job 18:14 is an allusion to the rule of Ereshkigal, queen of the 'Land of no Return' (1962:222). The argument could be based on the feminine verbal form *wtṣ'dhw* (compare v. 15), but the form is not quite clear (leaving aside conjectures). SARNA proposed a t-preformative for the 3.m.s. (1963:318; compare Job 20:9; *EA* 143:27-28; 323:22). This proposal is discussed by CLINES (1989:406).

Some interpretations relate the 'King of Terrors' to the *bkwr mwt* in v13 (→First-Born of Death), but the identification of this term is controversial. The crucial point is the question whether there is a Mesopotamian or Canaanite background for *bkwr mwt*.

BURNS (1987; 1993) argues strongly for the Mesopotamian option: "There, Namtar is the god of plague and pestilence. He is described as *sukallu* (sic) *irṣiti*, the 'vizier of the underworld'. He is also the *ilitti* ^d^*Ereškigal* the 'offspring of Ereshkigal', who was queen of the netherworld. In Mesopotamian mythology the first-born, if male, was generally the vizier of his parent." (BURNS 1987:363; *AGE* 387-388; compare already DHORME 1926:240). The 'King of Terrors' may be identified with Nergal, the husband of Ereshkigal. BURNS cites a passage from a vision of the realm of death: "The netherworld was filled with terror; before the prince lay utter *sti[ll]ness*... With a fierce [c]ry he shrieked at me wrathfully like a fu[rio]us storm; the scepter, which befits his divinity, one which is full of terror, like a viper." (*ANET* 110, Col. I; the relevant Akkadian terms are *puluḫtu* and *šiššu*; VON SODEN, *ZA* 43 [1936] 17, 53; see also SAA 3 [1989] no.32 r.13-15). BURNS comments on this passage: "The image conveyed is quite clear. The 'First-Born of Death', Namtar, god of pestilence, lays hold on the wicked man, devours his skin with burning fevers, consumes his shrivelled limbs and drags him before Nergal, king of the underworld and husband to Ereshkigal the mother of Namtar." (1987:364) The difficulty with BURNS' approach lies in the fact that Namtar's status as the firstborn son of Ereshkigal is not explicitly expressed in the texts; it is only a matter of reconstruction.

A Canaanite background was emphasized by SARNA: in v. 13 *mwt* is a designation for the well-known deity of death and the netherworld (→Mot). The 'King of Terrors' may be identified with this deity. The problem with SARNA's view is apparent in the designation *bkwr mwt.* Mot's firstborn would "occupy the same position in Canaan as did Namtar, the messenger (...) and son of Ereshkigal in Babylonian mythology. He would be a demon of evil fate, the grim herald of Mot, assigned the function of driving the souls into →Sheol" (1963:316). But, as SARNA clearly states, in Canaanite mythology no mention of Mot's sons has yet turned up (1963:316 n. 13).

The identification of the 'King of Terrors' with Mot is adopted by WYATT (1990:215). Trying to avoid the problems concerning Mot's sons, he suggests that *bkwr* in *bkwr mwt* be taken as an apposition, translating 'Firstborn Death'. According to his reconstruction 'firstborn' should be a designation for Mot as a son of →El; but this designation is not found in the Ugaritic texts. It seems doubtful that *bkwr* should be understood as a title; *bkwr* is a relational term, which simply emphasizes that the figure in question is the firstborn of another. This indication would be missing in WYATT's proposition.

III. The noun *ballāhâ* derives from the root BLH which is etymologically related to BLH. The meaning of *ballāhâ* is 'terror', especially in the plural form which is characteristic of the book of Job (18:11,14; 24:17; 27:20; 30:15; so BDB 117). As SARNA has pointed out, every usage of *ballāhâ* in Job is associated with a figure of destruction. The term describes an objective disaster rather than a subjective experience (CLINES 1989:419). The association with *ṣlmwt* in Job 24:17 (cf. 10:21; 38:17) demonstrates that *ballāhâ* is a designation for the netherworld (SARNA 1963:315). In Job 18:14 the LXX and Vg differ from the MT (DHORME 1926:240). The identification of the 'King of Terrors' with Nergal seems to be the most appropriate option (T. H. GASTER, *IDB* I, 820-821; his textual evidence is problematic though; instead of EBELING, *TuL* 35, see VAN DIJK, *SKIZ* 4). The terrifying luminosity (German 'Schreckensglanz') of this god is described in various Sumerian and Akkadian terms; as VON WEIHER has pointed out, this refers to Nergal as a luminous deity (1971:73-75). The mention of Nergal's kingdom and of his terror is found in a Sumerian hymn (*SGI* II, 1,7-9. 55). The deity is well attested in the West (*KAI* 222 A 9) and once in the OT (2 Kgs 17:30 as the deity of Babylonian colonists after the Fall of Samaria); the cult continues up to the second century CE (VON WEIHER 1971:105-106).

IV. *Bibliography*
J. B. BURNS, The Identity of Death's First-Born (Job xvii 13) *VT* 37 (1987) 362-364; BURNS, Namtaru and Nergal – down but not out: a Reply to Nicolas Wyatt, *VT* 43 (1993) 1-9; D. J. A. CLINES, *Job 1-20* (WBC 17; Dallas, Texas 1989) 403-425; P. DHORME, *Le Livre de Job* (Paris 1926²) 233-244; G. FOHRER, *Das Buch Hiob* (KAT 16; Gütersloh 1988²) 296-306; W. A. IRWIN, Job's Redeemer, *JBL* 81 (1962) 217-229; N. S. SARNA, The Mythological Background of Job 18, *JBL* 82 (1963) 315-318; E. VON WEIHER, *Der babylonische Gott Nergal* (AOAT 11; Kevelaer, Neukirchen-Vluyn 1971); N. WYATT, The Expression *bekôr māwet* in Job xviii 13 and its Mythological Background, *VT* 40 (1990) 207-216.

U. RÜTERSWÖRDEN

KING OF TYRE → MELQART

KINNARU כנור

I. The word *kinnôr* ('lyre') occurs some 42 times in MT. Stringed instruments used in the cult, such as the lyre, were at times deified in the cultures surrounding Israel.

II. The term *knr* appears 6 times in the Ugaritic texts, both as a stringed instrument (e.g. *KTU* 1.19 i:8; 1.108:4), and as a divine name in the Ugaritic pantheon lists *KTU* 1.47:32 = 1.118:31, in the Akkadian list RS 20.24:31 (d.giš*ki-na-rum*), and in the sacrificial list *KTU* 1.148:9.38, where the god receives one sheep. In view of the close relationship between cult, religious language and music, it is not surprising to find the instrument to whose sounds hymns were sung, deified, the instrument's 'song' being the voice of the god. The identity of the instrument—'harp' or 'lyre'—is disputed. Gk *kinyras* is commonly derived from West Semitic (e. g. ALBRIGHT 1968:125 n. 91, 128; but cf. M. H. POPE, *El in the Ugaritic Texts* [VTSup 2; Leiden 1955] 53-54).

III. In most cases where the lyre is mentioned in the Hebrew Bible it is simply a matter of the use of the instrument in popular (Job 21:12) or cultic (2 Sam 6:5) context, often in association with other instruments. In no instance can it be understood as a divine name as in Ugaritic, but the following passages may faintly echo the old theology, albeit long reinterpreted. Ps 49:5[4] explicitly refers to the cultic use of the instrument: *ʾaṭṭeh lĕmāšāl ʾoznî* "I incline my ear to the proverb", *ʾeptaḥ bĕkinnôr ḥîdātî* "I expound my enigma to the accompaniment of the lyre". This may well be stereotyped language, meaning no more than that the singing is accompanied. But the form of words points to an older situation in which the instrument contributed (as a conscious participant?) to the process, as a divine mouthpiece. In Ps 57:9[8] = 108:3[2] the lyre is invoked along with another stringed instrument, the *nebel*. In the context this may be no more than poetic apostrophe (cf. e.g. Ps 24:7.9; 148 passim), but again it echoes an older usage when minor gods of the pantheon were called upon to glorify their overlord (*KTU* 1.108:4 cited above may echo the same motif).

In 1 Sam 10:9-13 Saul joins a band of ecstatic prophets following his election as king; their spirit-possession is certainly enhanced, if not caused by, the playing of the instruments listed, lute, drum, pipe and lyre (v 5). And in 2 Kgs 3:15 Elisha summons a minstrel, and is possessed when the man plays. The instrument is not specified, but in view of the single use of the instrument by David to placate Saul's evil spirit (1 Sam 16: 14-23), it is possible that the same is used here. So the instrument appears to be credited in the tradition with the ability to enable communication between the spiritual and natural worlds. There is however no direct biblical evidence for the survival of the deified instrument in Israel or Judah.

The hypothesis which sees in the biblical toponym Chinnereth (cf. V. FRITZ, Chinnereth, *ABD* 1 [1992] 909-910) a reflection of a goddess Kinnartu, the counterpart of Kinnaru, has no foundation in the texts whatsoever (contra JIRKU 1960; CF. ALBRIGHT 1968:125 n. 91).

IV. *Bibliography*
W. F. ALBRIGHT, *Yahweh and the Gods of Canaan* (London 1968) 125, 128; A. COOPER, Divine Names and Epithets in the Ugaritic Texts, *RSP* 3 (1981) 384-385; A. JIRKU, Gab es eine palästinisch-syrische Gottheit Kinneret?, *ZAW* 72 (1960) 69; J. NOUGAYROL, *Ug V* (1968) 59.

N. WYATT

KOKABIM → STARS

KOSHAR כשר

I. The deity Kotharu (/kôṯaru/ < /kawṯaru/) appears in Ugaritic as an independent deity, and as part of the binominal *kṯr w ḫss*, 'skillful and cunning', of which the regular parallel is *hyn d ḥrš ydm* (lit. 'the deft one who is a worker with his hands'). The meanings of the name and the associated epithets are in keeping with Kotharu's function as craftsman deity. It has been proposed that this deity, under the form of Koshar, is alluded to in Ezek 3:32 and Prov 31:19. His name may occur, moreover, as an element in the name Cushan-Rishathaim (Judg 3:8.10).

II. In the Ugaritic 'pantheon' texts, as well as in the polyglot vocabularies, *kṯr/ku-šar-ru* is identified with the Mesopotamian craftsman deity Ea/Aya (J. NOUGAYROL, *Ugaritica V* [Paris 1968] 45, 51 [text 18:15]; 248 [text 137 iva 19]). The plausible interpretation of several mythological passages as indicating that Kotharu was at home in both Egypt and Crete implies the view that the arts and industries were particularly associated with these ancient centres of civilization (on the history of discussion regarding the identification of *ḥkpt/ḥqkpt* and *kptr*, see SMITH 1985:101-104).

The vocalization of the first syllable as /kô/ < /kaw/ is established by analogy to the feminine form (→Kosharoth); because that form appears to have been vocalized /kawšuratum/ in the Old Babylonian period (J.-M. DURAND, *MARI* 4 [1985] 161-164).

In the Ugaritic mythological texts, Kotharu is the craftsman deity *par excellence*. He plays the roles of architect (in the Baʿlu cycle), artisan (in the Baʿlu and ʾAqhatu cycles), and musician/diviner (in *KTU* 1.108 and *KTU* 1.6 vi 42-53). A detailed presentation of these various roles and an analysis of the relevant texts can be found in SMITH 1985; cf. the bibliography in D. PARDEE, *AfO* 36/37 (1989/1990) 454-455.

The deity was important in the religious life of Ugarit; because, in addition to his presence in a broad spectrum of mythological texts, he is fairly frequently named as the recipient of sacrifices in the ritual texts (P. XELLA, *I testi rituali di Ugarit*. I. *Testi* [StSem 54; Rome 1981] 389). He also appears as the theophoric element in several personal names (F. GRÖNDAHL, *Die Personennamen der Texte aus Ugarit* [StP 1; Rome 1967] 152).

Veneration of Kotharu continued in Phoenician society, as is indicated by the theophoric element *k(y)šr* in Punic and Neo-Punic personal names (F. L. BENZ, *Personal Names in the Phoenician and Punic Inscriptions* [StP 8; Rome 1972] 336) and by the reference to the deity Chousor in Phylo Byblius' *Phoenician History* (H. W. ATTRIDGE & R. A. ODEN, JR., *Phylo of Byblos. The Phoenician History* [CBQ Monograph Series 9; Washington, D.C. 1981] 45, 84; SMITH 1985:473-476) and in Mochos' *Phoenician Mythology* (ATTRIDGE & ODEN, *ibid.*, p. 102-104).

A relic of the divine name may be preserved in the Quranic reference to al-Kawthar (Sura 108; cf. COOPER 1981:386).

III. There is no certain reference to Koshar in the Hebrew Bible, and one can doubt even the presence of allusions to the deity in Prov 31:19 and Ezek 33:32 (see COOPER 1981:386). In Prov 31:19, there is no need to emend *kîšôr*; the translation 'distaff' is quite satisfactory. So is the understanding of *šîr ʿăgābîm* as 'love songs' in Ezek 33:32. Finally, the presence of *reš* in the second element of the personal name *kûšan rišʿātayim* (Judg 3:8, 10) allows one to doubt that the renditions *Chousarsathōm / Chousarsathaim* in LXX and *Chousarthos* in Josephus represent a tradition according to which the first element of the name would have been *kūšar*. HOFFMANN (1896) mentions the forms without accepting the identification with *Chousor*.

IV. *Bibliography*

A. COOPER, Divine Names and Epithets in the Ugaritic Texts, *RSP*, vol. III (AnOr 51; Rome 1981) 333-469; G. HOFFMANN, Aramäische Inschriften aus Nêrab bei Aleppo: Neue und alte Götter, *ZA* 11 [1896] 207-292, esp. 255; M. S. SMITH, *Kothar wa-Hasis, the Ugaritic Craftsman God* (diss. Yale 1985).

D. PARDEE

KOSHAROTH כשרות

I. The *kôṯarātu*, apparently 'the (female) skillful ones', appear in Ugaritic mythological texts in passages dealing with human conception and in the 'pantheon' texts as the equivalent of Mesopotamian mother-goddesses. A biblical reference to these goddesses has been proposed in Ps 68:7 (e.g. W. F. ALBRIGHT, *Yahweh and the Gods of Canaan* [London 1968] 119).

II. The plural form *kṯrt* appears in the Aqhat legend (*KTU* 1.17) and in the Marriage of Nikkal text (*KTU* 1.24) in contexts associated with marriage and conception: and in poetic parallelism with *bnt hll snnt*. From the first fact it is clear that the *kôṯarātu* are not 'midwives' as such, because their intervention precedes pregnancy. The interpretation of *hll snnt* has been disputed, some scholars construing the phrase as denoting 'song', others as denoting 'brightness, purity' (for bibliography see SMITH 1985:467-468; D. PARDEE, *AfO* 36/37 [1989/1990] 455-456). The regular parallelism with *bnt*, an unambiguously plural form, as well as the verbal form *ʿrb* in *KTU* 1.17 ii 26, show that *kṯrt* in these texts is plural.

The other primary set of data from Ugarit is provided by the 'pantheon' texts, where one finds two variants in the syllabic entries corresponding to *kṯrt* in the Ugaritic versions: ^{d}**nin maḫ** (RS 26.142:16', RS 1992.2004:4) and ^{d}*sa-sú-ra-tu*$_4$ (RS 20.24:12). When publishing RS 20.24, J. NOUGAYROL first interpreted the Akkadian entry as a singular, then as a plural (*Ugaritica* V [MRS 16; Paris 1968] 50, 63). From his comments on RS 26.142 (*ibid*., 322), it is clear that he did not realize the identification of ^{d}**nin maḫ** with ^{d}*sa-sú-ra-tu*$_4$, an identification which became clear only from the comparison of this 'pantheon' text with the Ugaritic ritual text *KTU* 1.148 *verso*. This identification was pointed out by M. C. ASTOUR, who interpreted ^{d}*sa-sú-ra-tu*$_4$ as a singular on the basis of the logographic entry (*Studies on the Civilization and Culture of Nuzi and the Hurrians* 2 [Winona Lake 1987] 56 n. 405. On Ninmah as mother-goddess and creatrix, see D. O. EDZARD, *WbMyth* I 105).

The plural form **dingir meš** *ka-ša-ra-ti* appears in a list of divine names from Emar (D. ARNAUD, *Emar* VI/3 [1986] 372, text 378 ii 18).

Because ^{d}**nin maḫ** can be used to designate a plurality (E. LAROCHE, *RHA* 34 [1976] 111), and because the form *s/šassūrātu* is only a plural in Akkadian, it appears best to understand all references in the Ugaritic texts as designating a plurality, rather than positing the presence of a singular in the 'pantheon' and ritual texts and a plural in the mythological texts. If the element *kṯrt* in the personal name *bn kṯrt* (F. GRÖNDAHL, *Die Personennamen der Texte aus Ugarit* [StP 1; Rome 1967] 152) is theophoric, that element may be singular. The presumed occurrences of the Kosharoth in a cuneiform tablet from Beth-shemesh (W. F. ALBRIGHT, *BASOR* 173 [1964] 51-53) are based on an erroneous reading (see M. DIETRICH & O. LORETZ, Die Alphabettafel aus Bet-Šemeš und die ursprüngliche Heimat der Ugariter, *Ad bene et fideliter seminandum. Festgabe für K. Deller* [AOAT 220; ed. G. Mauer & U. Magen; Kevelaer/Neukirchen-Vluyn 1988] 61-85).

In the mythological texts the *kôṯarātu* bless marriages and foster conception. The epithet *bnt hll* in these texts may denote either an abstract quality (as has generally been held) or a filiation (cf. the deity *Hulēlu* at Emar: ARNAUD, *Emar* VI/3 [1986] 328, text 369:73; cf. idem, *SEL* 8 [1991] 38). In sequence with *hll*, the second epithet, *snnt*, is better derived from a root denoting 'brightness, purity' (A. VAN SELMS, *Marriage and Family Life in Ugaritic Literature* [London 1954] 86 n. 24) than construed as 'swallows (i.e. the birds)' (for bibliography on the latter interpretation, see SMITH 1985). The phrase would mean 'the daughters of purity/Hulel, the pure ones'. Whether these goddesses were also lunar goddesses, as VAN SELMS thought, still remains to be proved.

No Ugaritic text attests to the perception of a relationship between Kotharu and the Kotharatu; so such a connection can therefore only be envisaged on the basis of etymology (both names show the root KṮR) and function (Kotharu as 'maker' of things, the Kotharatu as responsible for human conception). See SMITH 1985:469.

III. Following Albright, various authors have argued that Ps 68:7 must be interpreted as an allusion to the Kosharoth. J. C. DE MOOR translates "Elohim ... leads out the prisoners among the Kosharoth" (1990:119; cf. COOPER 1981:387-388). This interpretation has been refuted by LICHTENSTEIN (1972). Since Ps 68 contains no hint of childbirth, a reference to goddesses of conception and birth is indeed unlikely. It is therefore preferable to translate *bĕkôšārôt* as either 'in prosperity, in good health, unscathed' (cf. A. EMBER, *AJSL* 21 [1904-1905] 229) or 'deftly'.

IV. *Bibliography*

A. COOPER, Divine Names and Epithets in the Ugaritic Texts, *RSP*, III 333-469; M. H. LICHTENSTEIN, Psalm 68:7 Revisited, *JANES* 4 (1972) 97-112; J. C. DE MOOR, *The Rise of Yahwism* (Leuven 1990) 119, 124, 170; M. S. SMITH, *Kothar wa-Hasis, the Ugaritic Craftsman God* (diss. Yale 1985).

D. PARDEE

KUBABA → CYBELE

KYRIOS κύριος

I. Kyrios (fem. *kyria*) is a substantivated adjective probably deriving from a thematic form **kyros* (Sanskrit *sūra* 'strong', 'hero'). In Greek profane life it means a man of superior status, who has authority and can dispose of things and persons under his control. As a religious title it betrays the respect of a deity's 'servant' and can function as a proper name.

II. Though Pindar, *Isthm.* 5:53 (first half of the 5th century BCE), praises →Zeus, who destines everything, as *ho pantōn kyrios* (Lord of all things), usually there are other titles expressing the sovereignty of the traditional Greek gods: *potnia, anax, medeōn* in epics, *basileus, despotēs* in poetry, *despoina* for goddesses connected with nature. A recently reconstructed hymn from Epidauros (*SEG* 36,350) invokes the →Father of the gods as *kyrios*. Otherwise, for Zeus we only have examples in Roman provinces north of Greece or in Syria. There, some local deity may hide behind him as is the case in *kyrios tyrannos Zeus Masphaletēnos* (*CIG* 3438, Lydia, beginning of 2nd century CE). This indicates that the designation *kyrios* for gods is mainly a non-Greek, oriental phenomenon from Hellenistic and Roman times. The tragedian Sosiphanes (4th century BCE) who calls Hades *kyrios* (*TGF* I 92 fr. 3) may be an exception. It is hardly a cultic title for the god of the underworld (DREXLER 1890-94: 1762, no. 23 [Pluton] stems from Thracia).

In Egypt, hundreds of testimonies of personal piety in inscriptions or on papyrus (*proskynēma*-formulas, entreaties and thanksgiving votive gifts, acclamations, requests for oracles) add *kyrios* or *kyria* to the name of the individual deity. They concentrate on *kyria Isis* (Philae from the second half of the 2nd century BCE onwards, RONCHI (III 1975:601-611) has 85 instances, for the Mediterranean areas. SIRIS 261.332.334. 491, for *domina* s. Index p. 344) and *kyrios Sarapis* (cf. RONCHI III 1975:627-635 with 87 instances, SIRIS 26.172.306.498), esp. in invitations to sacred meals (listed in *ZPE* 2 [1968] 121-126; add *SB* 11049; *NewDocs* I 1). Several other Egyptian (esp. Mandulis,

Amenothes, →Bes, Ammon, see RONCHI III 1975:614-616.618-619.622-625) and Syrian deities (for the Semitic origin see →Lord) are called *kyria* or *kyrios*, as occasionally Men (besides *tyrannos*) in Asia Minor and Sabazios in Thracia. The title is favoured for the Ephesian →Artemis, Thracian gods and heroes, esp. for Asklepios (127 times) in Moesia and Thracia assimilated to a Thracian horseman (*SEG* 30, 717-783). Only in Thracia is it attested for →Hera (25 times), →Herakles (9 times), the Nymphs (17 times). →Mithras, too, is titled *dominus* (CIMRM 333[2].764.1483; cf Porph., *antr Nymph.* 24: γενέσεως δεσπότης). If the names of Greek deities, e.g. →Apollon, in Egyptian or Thracian documents are adorned with *kyrios* or *kyria*, they often represent non-Greek gods or goddesses. Thus →Hermes (12 cases in RONCHI III 1975:619-620.) may be →Thoth. Phylacteries or tablets of imprecation appeal to anonymous *kyrioi theoi* (R. WÜNSCH, Deisidaimoniaka, *ARW* 12 [1909] 1-45 esp. 38-39; *BullEpigr* 1952,13; *SEG* 38, 1926; cf. *PGM* IV 687, VII 368-369, 707). In the magical papyri (3rd-4th cent. CE) the address *kyrie* or *kyria*, sometimes composed with the name, is current for Egyptian as for Greek gods as well. In the predication "he is the lord of the gods, he is the lord of the ecumene" (*PGM* V 135-136) the influence of Jewish prayer language is sensible.

A genitive connected with the term circumscribes the domain. Such an addition is traditional with hieroglyphic *neb*. In her aretalogies →Isis predicates herself as mistress ruling over the elements of the sea, over fertility, and warfare (TOTTI 1:31.41-42, 49, 54; 20:122-123, 194-195, 236-240; Apuleius, *Met.* 11:5 *elementorum omnium domina*). She is not only the lady of all the land, but of the whole world (TOTTI 20:23.121 *anassa*; 1:3 *tyrannos*; Apuleius, *Met.* 11:7; Plutarch, *Mor.* 367a; *CIG* II 3724 *anassa*). In the same manner territories are assigned to Greek gods in more literary texts, too (Dio Chrys. 37:11; Plutarch, *Mor.* 365a.675f: →Helios, Lord of the fire; →Poseidon, Lord of the water, the latter element belonging to →Dionysos, too; 413c Apollon, Lord of the sun). Philo of Byblos interprets Baalshamen as *monos ouranou kyrios* (Eusebius, *Praep. Ev.* 1:10,7). The →Sun is named 'Lord of heaven and earth' (*PGM* IV 640). The title 'Lord of all things' (see above Pindar on Zeus, allusions in Demosthenes 60:21 and Plutarch, *Mor.* 426a; cf. Diodorus Sic. 3:61,4 *kyrion ... tōn holōn* for the God of the Jews) is applied to →Osiris in Plutarch, *Mor.* 355e (cf. 353b.354f Lord and King), to the Sun in *PGM* I 212, to Iao in *PGM* XIII 201-202 and to God in general in Iamblichus, *Vita Pyth.* 137 (cf. Plutarch, *Numa* 9: plural).

The appellative *kyrios* is also used for kings and the Roman emperor. In Egypt, the political sense is evident in the formulas *kyrios basileiōn* (Ptol. V) or *kyrios basileus*. The combination *theos kai kyrios* is customary with the last Lagides and twice attested for Augustus. Absolute *ho kyrios* dominates from Nero onwards. Even in the phrase "the Lord of all the world", applied to Nero *Syll.* 814, 30-31, the title in itself does not imply deification, but probably the association of *dominus et deus* introduced by Domitian does so (*dominus* corresponding to Gk *despotēs*, which suggested oriental tyranny and therefore was refused by the first *principes* as *primi inter pares*). It is only in the context of emperor worship that Christian martyrs are confronted with the alternative: *kyrios Kaisar* or acknowledgment of their own *kyrios* (cf. *Mart. Pol.* 8:2; *Acta Mart. Scill.*; CERFAUX 1954:56-57). Tert., *Apol.* 34:1 would not refuse to call the emperor Lord, if he is not constrained to do this instead of thus honouring God. See →Ruler cult.

III. In the LXX *kyrios* replaces the divine name →Yahweh (6156 times according to QUELL, *TWNT* 3 [1938] 1057; VON DOBSCHÜTZ 1931: 6742 times). In old mss. (cf. list in HOWARD 1977) the tetragram in Hebrew or Aramaic letters is left (this may in part be due to archaizing revisions: PIETERSMA 1984), but probably it was pronounced *kyrios* (cf. Origenes, *in ps.* 2,2). Less often the title corresponds to Hebrew appellatives for 'God' (279 times [QUELL]). Ca. 375 times (VON DOBSCHÜTZ [1931) it is translated from the Heb *ʾād\O(ô)n, ʾădōnī, ʾădōnāy* though in many cases the Hebrew or the Greek text is not ascertained. The custom of reading *ʾădōnāy* instead of the tetragram in Palestinian Judaism, now attested in 1QIsa^{a}, may have induced an analogous procedure in the Diaspora synagogue. Pagan influence, assumed by VON BAUDISSIN (1929) and others, can—especially in Egypt—not be excluded; but neither can it be proved. In biblical writings not contained in MT, *kyrios* as a designation for God occurs ca. 640 times. By comparison, the term *despotēs* is relatively rare for God. Sometimes it renders *ʾādôn* in the double expression *ʾadōn(āy) Yhwh* to avoid a *kyrios kyrios* otherwise current.

Regarding the semantics of the term in LXX when used as predicate, the correlation between 'Lord' and 'servant' is still perceptible (e.g. Mal 1:6). The formula *kyrios tōn kyriōn* exalts God above all other heavenly Lords (Deut 10:17; Ps 135:3) and earthly rulers (Dan 4:37; cf. 2:47; 1 Tim 6: 15; *1 Enoch* 9:4; 63:2). The universal dominion of the 'Lord of all the earth' (Josh 3:11.13; Mic 4:13; Zech 4:14; 6:5; Ps 96:5; Exod 8:22 only LXX; Josh 4:7 only LXX), the 'Lord of heaven' (Dan 2:37) resp. the 'Lord of heaven and earth' (Tob 7:17; Jdt 9:12 *despotēs*; cf. Luke 10:21; Acts 17:24) or the 'Lord of all things' (Add Esth 4:17c; *ho kyrieuōn hapantōn theos*, *Ep. Arist.* 18: 45; frequently *pantokratōr* is combined with *kyrios*; this also happens 7 times in Rev; cf. the addition in LXX Jer 39:19) is founded in his acts as creator (cf. Jer 39:17-19; 1 Esdr 6:12; Add Esth 4:17; Acts 17: 24); the claim is underlined against pagan concurrents (Dan 3:17.45; 1 Esdr 8:25; 2 Esdr 19:6; Add Esth 4:17l; Josephus, *Ant.* 20:90).

For Philo *kyrios* represents one of the main powers of God (in contradistinction to *theos*, the creator and father) and signifies his ruling activity. *Kyrios* does not per se connote divine monarchy; as in daily life, it can be used in a religious context as respectful address, thus for example for angels (e.g. the *angelus interpres* in Zech and Dan; cf. BERGER [1970/71] 417 n. 3). As a name for angels it is late (ib. 418 n. 1). In magic texts they are addressed as *kyrioi (theoi) aggeloi* (*PGM* 36:44.246; *BullEpigr* 1952, 13).

Kyrios for God occurs in the NT ca. 181 times (including 70 citations of the OT); more often it is used as a title for →Jesus →Christ (ca. 468 times, 11 OT quotations being related to him). In the Synoptics and in John people seeking miracles, but also disciples or potential followers, address Jesus as *kyrie* (cf. *ʾădōnî*, for Elijah, Elisha in 1-2 Kgs). The usage goes back to Q, could even be authentic and corresponds to Aram. *mārî*, attested as a form of address of persons in a position of authority. Its significance does not differ much from *rabbî*, (Gk *didaskale*) that sometimes (Matt 9:28; 20:33; Luke 18:41) is the Markan base of Matthean or Lukan *kyrie* (cf. the parallelism in the parabolic saying Matt 10:24 and in John 13:13). Matthew adds redactional *kyrie*; so does Luke who, however, prefers *epistata*. In the context of a plea for salvation (Matt 8:25; 14:30; 17:15)—often connected with a *proskynēsis*—it presupposes a divine faculty of the one addressed (cf. Epiktet, *diss.* II 7,12). In John 13 Jesus accepts the title 'master', but paradoxically behaves like a servant. As predicate *kyrios* in Mark 2:28 refers to the sovereignty of the →Son of Man over the →Sabbath. In Mark it is employed absolutely only in a reference by the disciples to 'the master', who can require the property of other people like a king (11:3).

More often Luke and John reflect the absolute usage of the Early Church, which probably spoke of 'Our Lord' in analogy to Aramaic-Semitic titling of kings (CERFAUX). The reason for this is not only the personal loyalty of the disciples to Jesus in his earthly ministry, but also his royal position on account of his resurrection. Otherwise, he could scarcely be invoked at all. So it is the risen one that the Jewish-Christian community addresses with Aram. *māranāʾ-tāʾ* (1 Cor 16:22, rendered Rev 22:20 'come, Lord Jesus', cf. *Did.* 10:6). Because he is now enthroned at the right hand of God, he is expected to realize his reign at his coming in glory (cf. the address of the king and judge Matt 25:37.44 *kyrie*).

It seems that this heavenly exaltation is expressed relatively early with Ps 110:1, though the argumentation Acts 2:34-36 (Jesus thus constituted by God *kyrios*) relies on the Greek text. Against BOUSSET (1921) the cultic appeal to the Lord is to be ascribed not only to the Greek speaking community. It is improbable that it is modelled after Hellenistic-Oriental cults. There is a certain continuity between the address *kyrie* directed to Jesus during his public life and to the risen one (so in Acts in the context of visions). But now He has a divine quality; therefore Thomas recognizes his Lord at the same time as his God (John 20:28) applying to him the language of the Psalms. The object of Easter visions is indicated by *kyrios* (1 Cor 9:1; Luke 24:34; John 20:18. 20.25; Acts 9:27). Yet this transition to the absolute use can be grasped only in the Greek phase of tradition. Especially in the letters of Paul we find fixed formulae whose pre-Pauline origin can be demonstrated. Thus, the stereotyped expression 'the brothers of the Lord' refers to the historical Jesus as does Paul when introducing authoritative sayings of the Lord. The Hellenistic communities took up the liturgical 'our Lord' affixing it to the double name 'Jesus Christ' with *kyrios*. In their worship they acclaimed Jesus, the risen one, as *kyrios* (1 Cor 12:3; Rom 10:9). He is the Lord not only of his believers, but of all mankind (Rom 10:12; 14:9; Acts 10:36), an affirmation that stimulated the mission to the gentiles. The exalted one dominates also the spiritual powers of the three zones of the world. God remains the cosmocrator, but in the pre-Pauline hymn Phil 2:6-11 he bestows an incomparable dignity ('name') on Jesus whom all have to acknowledge by the *kyrios*-acclamation. Sometimes the suggestion is made that this 'name' is the divine name as in Jewish tradition angels can be named after Yahweh, their king (*3 Enoch* 10:20; 12:20-23; cf. FOSSUM 1985:292-301). Yet it is not certain that *kyrios* (v 11) is meant as a translation of Yahweh, because the whole action aims at the glorification of God the Father. But as vv 10-11 allude to Jes 45:23 (a prophecy of the universal adoration offered to Yahweh) the way is open to apply to Jesus OT *kyrios*-passages in pre-Pauline tradition as well as in the NT itself. Thus, already before Paul, the Christians called themselves 'those invoking the name of the Lord', actualizing Joel 3:5 (1 Cor 1:2; cf. Rom 10:12-13; Acts 2:21; 9:14.21; 2 Tim 2:22). The 'day of the Lord' (cf. Joel 3:4) now was understood as the parousia of Christ. In general, eschatological utterances are often connected with *kyrios*. Paul in several places adduces OT texts where *kyrios* now must signify Jesus. Due to its use in the LXX, the title now points not only to Jesus' assuming divine functions, but also to his godlike status.

If we except Rom 10:9, where the confession *kyrios Iēsous* is the outward expression of the faith in his resurrection, and Acts 16:31, the title does not appear to have been part of the creed. Other titles like 'Christ' and 'Son of God' prevail. *Kyrios* primarily defines the relation of Christ to the believer resp. his 'servant', the apostle (cf. 2 Cor 4:5; *douleuein* Rom 12:11; Col 3:24; Acts 20:19). In a polemical context the title can become exclusive. So in 1 Cor 8:4-6: some Corinthians participated in sacral dinners—possibly in one of the Egyptian temples within reach. The *trapeza kyriou* (10:21)—though attested in the OT for the altar of God—may even form a contrast to the *klinē* of the *kyrios Sarapis* in the well-known invitations. That some Christians did not refuse to eat meat sacrified to pagan deities, constituted a problem for the community. Paul answers with the Jewish monotheistic belief, but in view of so many *kyrioi*, like the oriental gods, he adds a parallel christological statement analogous to pagan acclamations like *heis Zeus Sarapis:* 'and there is only one Lord, Jesus Christ, through whom all things (came into existence) and we (will be saved) through him' (8:6). It is unlikely that Paul here deliberately split the formula from Deut 6:4, as it is sometimes assumed. The soteriological role of Christ is affirmed against the competing oriental deities, whose importance for the individual had increased so much. It is anchored in the instrumental role of the preexistent one in God's creation, a function assigned in Judaism to →Wisdom (cf. Ps 101:26-28 in Heb 1:10-12, now addressed with *kyrie* to the Son). This is the unique passage where Jesus' being Lord is confronted explicitly with pagan competition. It scarcely gives a hint as to the origin of the concept (*pace* BOUSSET 1921), but rather develops his relevance in a world of different henotheistic movements. It is not certain whether human rulers—who could be in view v 5a ('Gods on earth')—are attacked, too. Only in Revelation the christological predications 'Lord of the lords and king of the kings' (17:14; 19:16—in the OT these titles are attributed to God) are pointed against arrogant worldly potentates. Eph 4:5 repeats the *heis kyrios* as foundation for the unity of the Church.

IV. *Bibliography*

W. W. GRAF BAUDISSIN, *Kyrios als Gottesname im Judentum und seine Stelle in der Religionsgeschichte*, 4 vols. (Giessen 1929); K. BERGER, Zum traditionsgeschichtlichen Hintergrund christologischer Hoheitstitel, *NTS* 17 (1971) 413-422; W. BOUSSET, *Kyrios Christos* (FRLANT 21; Göttingen [2]1921); F. F. BRUCE, 'Jesus is Lord', *Soli Deo Gloria* (ed. J. M. Richards; Richmond 1968) 23-36; L. CERFAUX, Le titre Kyrios et la dignité royale de Jésus (1922/23), *Recueil Lucien Cerfaux* (BETL 6/7; Gembloux 1954) 3-63; CERFAUX, Le nom divin 'Kyrios' dans la Bible grecque, *ib.* 113-136; CERFAUX, 'Adonai' et 'Kyrios' (1931), *ib.* 137-172; CERFAUX, 'Kyrios' dans les citations pauliniennes de l'Ancien Testament (1943), *ib.* 173-188; D. CUSS, *Imperial Cult and Honorary Terms in the New Testament* (Paradosis 23; Fribourg 1974) 53-63; A. DEISSMANN, *Licht vom Osten* (Tübingen [4]1923) 298-311; D. R. DELACEY, 'One Lord' in Pauline Christology, *Christ the Lord* (ed. H. H. Rowdon; Leicester 1982) 191-203; E. VON DOBSCHÜTZ, ΚΥΡΙΟΣ ΙΗΣΟΥΣ, *ZNW* 30 (1931) 97-121; W. DREXLER, Kyria und Kyrios, *LGRM* 2, 1 (1890-1894) 1755-1769; W. FAUTH, Kyrios bzw. Kyria, *KP* 3 (1975) 413-417; J. A. FITZMYER, The Semitic Background of the New Testament *Kyrios*-Title (1975), *A Wandering Aramean* (SBL MS 25; Chico 1979) 115-142; FITZMYER, κύριος, *EWNT* 2 (1981) 811-820; W. FOERSTER, κύριος, *TWNT* 3 (1938) 1038-1056.1081-1094; 10.2, (1979) 1152; J. E. FOSSUM, *The Name of God and the Angel of the Lord* (WUNT 36; Tübingen 1985); D. HAGENDORN & K. A. WORP, Von ΚΥΡΙΟΣ zu ΔΕΣΠΟΤΗΣ. Eine Bemerkung zur Kaisertitulatur im 3./4. Jh., *ZPE* 39 (1980) 165-177; F. HAHN, *Christologische Hoheitstitel* (FRLANT 83, Göttingen 1983) 67-125; A. HENRICHS, Despoina Kybele: Ein Beitrag zur religiösen Namenkunde, *HSCP* 80 (1976) 253-286; G. HOWARD, The Tetragram and the New Testament, *JBL* 96 (1977) 63-83; D. L. JONES, The title *kyrios* in Luke-Acts, *SBL Seminar Papers* 110,2 (1974) 85-101; J. D. KINGSBURY, The title 'Kyrios' in Matthew's Gospel, *JBL* 94 (1975) 246-255; W. KRAMER, *Christos Kyrios Gottessohn* (ATANT 44; Zürich/Stuttgart 1963) 61-103, 149-191, 215-222; P.-É. LANGEVIN, *Jésus Seigneur et l'eschatologie* (Studia 21; Bruges/Paris 1967); P. MAIBERGER & K. WOSCHITZ, Herr, *NBL* 2 (1991) 126-129; A. D. NOCK, *Essays on Religion and the Ancient World* (Oxford 1972) I 47.74-77; A. PIETERSMA, Kyrios or Tetragram, *De Septuaginta* (ed. A. Pietersma & C. Cox; Mississauga 1984) 85-101; H. W. PLEKET, Religious History as the History of Mentality: the 'Believer' as Servant of the Deity in the Greek World, *Faith, Hope and Worship* (ed. H. S. Versnel; Leiden 1981) 152-192, esp. 171-178; J. R. ROYSE, Philo, Κύριος, and the Tetragrammaton, *SPhA* 3 (1991) 167-183; G. RONCHI, Lexicon theonymon rerumque sacrarum et divinarum ad Aegyptum pertinentium quae in papyris ostracis titulis graecis latinisque in aegypto repertis laudantur III (Milan 1975); L. SCHENKE, *Die Urgemeinde* (Stuttgart 1990) 98-99, 342-347; G. SCHNEIDER, Gott und Christus als KYRIOS nach der Apostelgeschichte (1980), *Lukas, Theologe der Heilsgeschichte* (BBB 59; Bonn 1985) 213-226; S. SCHULZ, Maranatha und Kyrios Jesus, *ZNW* 53 (1962) 125-144; C. SPICQ, *Lexique théologique du Nouveau Testament* (Fribourg 1991) 859-872; H. STEGEMANN, Religionsgeschichtliche Erwägungen zu den Gottesbezeichnungen in den Qumrantexten, *Qumrân* (BETL 46; ed. M. Delcor; Paris/Gembloux/Leuven 1978) 195-217, esp. 204-207; M. TAČEVA-HITOVA, Über die Götterepitheta in den griechischen Inschriften aus Moesia inferior und Thracia, *Bulgarian Historical Review* 6 (1978) 52-65; G. VERMES, *Jesus the Jew* (New York 1973) 103-128; P. VIELHAUER, Ein Weg zur neutestamentlichen Christologie?, *Aufsätze zum Neuen Testament* (TB 31; München 1965) 141-198, esp. 147-167.

D. ZELLER

L

LABAN לבן

I. On the assumption that he was originally a semi-divine hero or a god (MEYER 1906), Laban, the son of Bethuel (Gen 28:5) and father of →Leah and →Rachel (Gen 29:16) has been connected with the Old Assyrian god Laba(n) (E. SCHRADER, *Die Keilinschriften und das Alte Testament* [Berlin 1903; 3rd ed. by H. Winckler & H. Zimmern] 363). The name of the latter deity has been interpreted as a shortened form of *Labnān*, which would mean that Laban was "originally an ancient West-Semitic deity venerated in the Lebanon" (LEWY 1934:45).

II. Laban occurs already in Old Assyrian personal names as the designation of a deity (HIRSCH 1972:33) and was still worshipped in Neo-Assyrian times (*Tākultu* 100). The character of the god remains uncertain. Though there can be no doubt about the veneration of the Lebanon, not only as the dwelling-place of the gods but as a deity in its own right (WEIPPERT 1980-83:648-649, esp. § 5.2; see also →Lebanon), it is not certain that Laban can be equated with Lebanon. Mt Lebanon is known in cuneiform sources as Labnān or Lablān (for these and other forms see WEIPPERT 1980-83:641-642), and it is difficult to see how a variant Laban or Laba could originate. The two names are now generally distinguished as belonging each to a separate deity.

III. The connection between the biblical figure Laban and the Assyrian god Laban (or Lebanon) rests on a number of unverified assumptions. Few modern scholars would be ready to accept that the majority of characters of the patriarchal narratives are demythologized deities, as was once widely believed. If there is no reason, *a priori*, for the assumption that Laban has a mythological background, however, there is no need to have recourse to a poorly known deity in order to explain Laban's name. The root LBN (to be white) is unproblematic in Hebrew; there is nothing unusual, moreover, in naming babies by the colour of their skin (cf. NOTH, *IPN* 225).

IV. *Bibliography*

H. HIRSCH, *Untersuchungen zur altassyrischen Religion* (AfO Beiheft 13/14; Osnabrück ²1972); J. LEWY, Les textes paléo-assyriens et l'Ancien Testament, *RHR* 110 (1934) 29-65, esp. 44-45; E. MEYER, *Die Israeliten und ihre Nachbarstämme* (Halle 1906) 245 n. 2; M. WEIPPERT, Libanon, *RLA* 6 [1980-83] 641-650.

K. VAN DER TOORN

LADY → ADAT; BELTU

LAGAMAL → LAGAMAR

LAGAMAR

I. The name *kĕdār-lāʿomer*, 'Chedorlaomer' king of Elam (Gen 14:1.4.5.9.17; 1QGenAp 21:23), is to be interpreted as a combination of the noun *kudur* (Akk) or *kutir/kut.e.r* (Elamite), 'protector' (see R. ZADOK, *The Elamite Onomasticon* [AION Sup 40; Napoli 1984] 25 for names containing this noun), with the name of the Elamite underworld deity Lagamal/Lagamar (BÖHL 1916:67; ASTOUR 1966:78; WEIPPERT 1976-1980; ASTOUR 1992:893). The name Lagamal means "No mercy" (LAMBERT 1980-83:418).

II. The name of the deity is written *La-ga-ma-al/mal* or *La-ga-ma-ru*. The /r/ occurs in Neo-Assyrian inscriptions only. The earliest attestation of the divine name is in an Old Akkadian seal inscription (PBS 14:138). By the Babylonians, Lagamal was interpreted as the son of Urash, the wife of An (An = Anum V:43; cf. J. A. CRAIG,

Assyrian and Babylonian Religious Texts I [Leipzig 1895] No. 58:21). In a letter from Mari, it is related that he, or his image, went from Mari to Terqa (*ARM* XIII 111:5-9). Lagamal is worshipped throughout the Neo-Elamite period (1000-539 BCE). His name occurs as a theophoric element in personal names and he had a temple at Susa (F. W. KÖNIG, *Die elamischen Königsinschriften* [AfO Beiheft 16; Graz 1965] 200). When Ashurbanipal conquered Susa he took away a statue of the deity as booty (M. STRECK, *Assurbanipal und die letzten Könige bis zum Untergang Nineveh's* [VAB VII; Leipzig 1916] 52:33; *ARAB* II § 810).

T. G. PINCHES (Certain Inscriptions and Records referring to Babylonia and Elam and their Rulers, and other Matters, *Journal of the Transactions of the Victoria Institute* 29 [1897] 43-89) published a small collection of Late-Babylonian texts from the Parthian period. The inscriptions are known as the Chedarlaomer or Spartoli texts. The texts—which give the impression of being copies of seventh to sixth century BCE originals—mention four kings who have as a common trait that they all sacked or oppressed Babylon and its holy shrine Esagila and that they were either murdered by their sons or died in the sea. The names of these four kings are written as cryptograms. The name of one of them, ^{p}KU.KU.KU.MAL or ^{p}KU.KU.KU.KU.MAL, has correctly been interpreted as ^{p}*Ku-dúr-náḫ-ḫúd* or ^{p}*Ku-dúr-náḫ-ḫun-tú* (e.g. ASTOUR 1966:91.93-94). An Elamite king Kudur-Nahhunte (II) is known who actually took part in a conquest of Babylon in the twelfth century BCE. This event is still recalled by Ashurbanipal (IIIR 38:12; *ARAB* II § 923; ASTOUR 1966:91). Gen 14 has been interpreted as the *interpretatio Israelitica* of an original seventh to sixth century BCE version of the Chedarlaomer-texts. Kudur-Nahhunte would have been a model for Chedarlaomer (ASTOUR 1992:894). In that case, the name element *lāʿomer* would refer to the Elamite deity Nahhunte, a sun god and a god of justice (cf. Elamite *naḫute*, 'sun').

III In Gen 14, Chedarlaomer is presented as king of Elam and as leader of a coalition of four kings who battled with →Abraham after having defeated a group of Canaanite tribes and having plundered Sodom and Gomorrah. From a linguistic point of view, a connection between *lāʿomer* and an Elamite deity Nahhunte is problematical. Firstly, an original form in Hebrew **lāʿomer* must be read with an interchange of /d/ to /r/. Secondly, it must be assumed that the consonant /n/ changed into /l/. Such a change is not attested in Elamite phonology. Thirdly, Heb /ʿ/ must be construed as a derivation via /ǵ/ from Elamite /ḫḫ/. Elamite /ḫ/, however, cannot be compared with a velar-sound, but should be connected to a weak pharyngal spirant, such as German /h/. A connection with Sem /ǵ/ and Hebr /ʿ/ is very unplausible (O. RÖSSLER, apud M. WEIPPERT, *Die Landnahme der israelitischen Stämme in der neueren wissenschaftlichen Diskussion* [FRLANT 92; Göttingen 1967] 96-97 n. 5; WEIPPERT 1976-80). This observation makes the alleged relation between Gen 14 and the Chedorlaomer texts less probable. Therefore, a connection between Laomer and Lagamal is more plausible. Assuming that the Elamite name was pronounced **laǵamar*, Heb *lāʿomer* can be understood on the basis of the similarity of /ǵ/ and /ʿ/ (WEIPPERT, *Landnahme* 96 n. 5). An Elamite king Kudur-Lagamal/r is not known from the sources.

IV. *Bibliography*

M. C. ASTOUR, Political and Cosmic Symbolism in Genesis 14 and in its Babylonian Sources, *Biblical Motifs* (A. Altman ed.; Cambridge 1966) 65-112; ASTOUR, Chedorlaomer, *ABD* 1 (1992) 893-895; F. M. T. (DE LIAGRE) BÖHL, Die Könige von Genesis 14, *ZAW* 36 (1916) 65-73; W. G. LAMBERT, Lāgamāl, *RLA* 6 (1980-83) 418-419; M. WEIPPERT, Kedorlaomer, *RLA* 5 (1976-80) 543-544.

B. BECKING

LAH לה

I. The element *laḥ* has been interpreted as a divine name in certain Hebrew proper names. These are the place names Beer-Lahai-roi (Gen 16:14; 24:62; 25:11), Ramath-lehi (Judg 15:17; 2 Sam 23:11) and Bethlehem, and in particular, the Hebrew personal name Methu-selah (Gen 5:21.22. 25.26.27; 1 Chr 1:3).

It has been suggested that the personal name Methu-selah is not to be analysed as *mt*, 'man' + *šlḥ*, '(the god) →Shelah', but rather as *mĕtu*, 'man' + *še*, 'of' + *laḥ*, '(the god) Laḥ'. Similarly, *lḥy* has been interpreted as a theophoric element in the name *b'r-lḥy-r'y*. Again, *lḥ* has been interpreted as a divine name in *btlḥm*; provided it is analysed as *bt*, 'house/temple of' + *lḥ* 'the god Lah' + enclitic *m*. The word *leaḥ* occurs in Hebrew with the meaning 'moist' (e.g. Gen 30:27) and the root *lḥḥ* in several Semitic languages means 'to be moist'. The god Lah would, then, be "an ancient Canaanite god of vital sap and vigour" (VAN SELMS 1966). Further evidence is provided by the Moabite place-name Luhith (*lwḥyt* Isa 15:5; Jer 48:5 qere: *hlḥyt*; ketib: *hlḥwt*), in the neighbourhood of Medeba. It is said to be derived from the name of a goddess (*lḥyt*) related to *laḥ*. Finally, the noun *ylḥn*, derived from *lḥ*, occurs in Ugaritic (*KTU* 1.5 ii:21; 1.6 i:48) and in *KTU* 4.35 i 8 as a personal name (*bn ylḥn*) with the meaning 'vital power' (VAN SELMS 1966).

II. Nevertheless, the following objections can be raised against the proposed identification:

(1) there is absolutely no evidence, even outside the Bible, for the existence of a god called Laḥ; (2) even though another name with the form *mt* ('man') + *š* ('of') + divine name is known in Hebrew (*mtš'l* = *mt* + *š* + *'l*) it is generally accepted that *mtšlḥ* means 'Man of (the god) Shelah' (i.e. *mt* + *šlḥ*) (TSEVAT 1954); (3) the place name *b'r-lḥy-r'y* means 'Well of the Living One who sees me' (the place-name *lḥy* probably means 'Jawbone'; cf. *lĕḥî*, 'jaw, cheek'): in neither does the alleged deity *lḥ* occur; (4) the place name *btlḥm* means 'House/Temple of the god *lḥm*' (→Lahmu); (5) the Ugaritic evidence is uncertain. the verb *lḥn* may be related to *lḥ(ḥ)* and mean 'to moisten', or it may have other meanings (DEGEN 1979; TROPPER 1990) but it provides no proof that a god *laḥ* existed; (6) the Moabite place-name may originate from the name of a goddess; but this is simply conjecture.

In short, the purported existence of the god *laḥ* is pure speculation. It is based on very vague evidence; proposed by but a single scholar (VAN SELMS 1966); and accepted by no-one.

III. *Bibliography*

R. DEGEN, Bemerkungen zu *lḥn* im Nordwestsemitischen, apud M. ULLMANN, *Waḥairu l-ḥadīṯi mā kāna laḥnar* (München 1979) 25-32; O. LORETZ, Der Gott *šlḥ*, He. *šlḥ* I und *šlḥ* II, *UF* 7 (1975) 584-585; *A. VAN SELMS, A Forgotten God: *Laḥ*, *Studia Biblica et Semitica Theodoro Christiano Vriezen dedicata* (Wageningen 1966) 318-326; J. TROPPER, *Der ugaritische Kausativstamm und die Kausativbildungen des Semitischen* (Münster 1990) 138-139; M. TSEVAT, The Canaanite God Šälaḥ, *VT* 4 (1954) 41-49.

W. G. E. WATSON

LAHAB → **FLAME**

LAHAI-ROI לחי ראי

I. The name *Laḥay Rō'î* appears only three times in the Hebrew Bible: always in the combination of the toponym *Bĕ'ēr Laḥay Rō'î*: Gen 16:14; 24:62; 25:11. In Gen 16:14, Lahai-roi (or Hai-roi) could be construed as a divine name in accordance with the versions. Yet the interpretation is speculative and not supported by extrabiblical evidence.

II. In the three biblical occurrences, *Bĕ'ēr Laḥay Rō'î* designates a well or a locality somewhere in the Negeb (24:62). Its localization is unknown. Gen 16:14 locates it "between Kadesh and Bered". It certainly confirms a southern location; but it is not very helpful because the location of Bered is equally unknown (KNAUF 1989:46 n. 211).

Gen 24:62 and 25:11 indicate that the environs of *Bĕ'ēr Laḥay Rō'î* are the current abode of Isaac; but they do not give any hint about the nature of that place or a clue to the meaning of its name. Moreover, both of these texts are considered to belong to the very latest strata of the →Abraham stories. Gen 24 is attributed by BLUM (1984:384-387, 390-391) to the postexilic D-composition; whilst Gen 25:1-11 is commonly regarded as P. Even in these late contexts, moreover, the two verses could be 'redactional additions' (see KNAUF 1989:26-27 nn. 113-116; 46 n. 210) influenced by Gen 16:14. We are thus left with Gen 16:14 as the only starting point for further investigation. One problem, however, remains: In Gen 24:62 and 25:11, the place is linked to Isaac, whereas in Gen 16:14 its naming is attributed to Hagar and connected with →Ishmael. How could an 'Ishmaelite' place have been connected with Isaac? Often, *Bĕ'ēr Laḥay Rō'î* has been considered as the place of origin (*'Haftpunkt'*) of the Isaac tradition; i.e. because Ishmael and Isaac were originally related groups (NOTH 1960:118-119, and for discussion, BLUM 1984:494-495; ALBERTZ 1987:295; SCHMID 1991:25-28, 30-31, 65, 73); but this already speculative hypothesis raises two further problems: first, in what sense could a watering place or a way station in the desert function as the *'Haftpunkt'* of a patriarchal tradition; and, second, what is then the meaning of the 'northern' associations of Isaac (Am 7:9.16; Gen 28:13; 31:42.53; 35:8)?

In Gen 16:14, *Bĕ'ēr Laḥay Rō'î* is connected with the theophany of →El-roi to Hagar. If this verse is read in the light of v 13, it functions as a succinct cult legend of the sanctuary of El-roi: a legend that has been integrated into the ethnological legend of the origin of the Ishmaelites (RENDTORFF 1983:101). Because it is possible that the name Lahai-roi has given rise to the name El-roi, the original value and meaning of Lahai-roi is not necessarily linked to the semantic context suggested by v 13. In the present context of the story, *Laḥay*—or, perhaps more probably, *ḥay—Rō'î* is presented as the equivalent of El-roi. It could therefore be construed as a divine name. This is actually the way in which early Jewish and Christian tradition has understood the passage. (LXX: *phrear hou enōpion eidon*, "well of the one before whom I have seen"; Vulgate: *Puteum Viventis Videntis me*, "well of the Living one who sees me"; rabbinical interpretations also go in that direction, Targum and Rashi paraphrasing: "The well at which the everlasting →Angel appeared to me"). Inspired by this traditional view, DE MOOR (1990:253) has suggested that Gen 16:14 is best understood as an allusion to the 'living' Yahweh-El, as polemically opposed to →Baal and his annual death. This interpretation is speculative, however, and not supported by any other observation. Since elsewhere in the region there is no divine name or epithet attested with the component *lḥy* there is little possibility that *(la)ḥay Rō'î* refers to an existing deity.

Unfortunately, we are also reduced to conjectures about the possible etymology of *Laḥay*. WELLHAUSEN (1878:329 n. 1) supposed that the toponym derived from **lḥy* 'jawbone', *r'y* coming from a defigurated animal name—in analogy to *lḥy* (*ḥmwr*) of Judg 15:18-19. Even if this proposal remains uncertain, it is indeed probable that *Bĕ'ēr Laḥay Rō'î* is a place name derived from a personal or a tribal name. KNAUF (1989:47-48) lists several instances from the pre-Islamic Arab world where hypocoristical names are composed with *lḥy* + a divine name (e.g. **lḥy 'ṯtr*) or a parental name (e.g. **lḥy'm/'mlḥy*). *lḥy* can also be the theophorical element in names such as *lḥyml's* or *šlmlḥy*. *Laḥay Rō'î* could then be a place name derived from a personal or tribal name composed with a divine name + epitheton; but that would hardly suffice to transform *Bĕ'ēr Laḥay Rō'î* into a cult place: and *(La)ḥay Rō'î* into a deity. The available documents are still far too scanty to permit firm conclusions.

III. *Bibliography*

R. ALBERTZ, Isaak I, *TRE* XVI (1987) 292-296; E. BLUM, *Die Komposition der Vätergeschichte* (WMANT 57; Neukirchen 1984); E. A. KNAUF, *Ismael. Untersuchungen zur Geschichte Palästinas und Nordarabiens im 1. Jahrtausend v. Chr.* (ADPV; Wiesbaden,

2. Aufl. 1989); J. C. DE MOOR, *The Rise of Yahwism. The Roots of Israelite Monotheism* (BETL 91; Leuven 1990); M. NOTH, *Überlieferungsgeschichte des Pentateuch* (Stuttgart 1948 = Darmstadt 1960); R. RENDTORFF, *Das Alte Testament. Eine Einführung* (Neukirchen 1983); H. SCHMID, *Die Gestalt des Isaak. Ihr Verhältnis zur Abraham- und Jakobtradition* (EdF 274; Darmstadt 1991); J. WELLHAUSEN, *Geschichte Israels I* (Berlin 1878).

A. DE PURY

LAHMU לחם

I. Laḫmu has been proposed as a divine name or theophoric element in the OT in certain especially old texts and names, particularly the Song of Deborah (Judg 5:8) and the place name Bethlehem.

II. Laḫmu is clearly (albeit rarely) attested in Sumerian and in the Akkadian literature of the Old Akkadian, Standard Babylonian and Neo-Assyrian periods and at Mari. As a divine name Laḫmu appears paired with Laḫamu in the theogony of *Enuma Elish*, begotten by →Apsu (→Ends of the earth) and →Tiamat (the waters) and begetting Anšar (sky) and Kišar (earth). Later in the same work, as well as in other texts, the term or its plural, *laḫmū*, appears as a name or description of one or more sea monsters in the great deep (allied with Tiamat in *Enuma Elish*). In Sumerian and later texts the plural also occurs with reference either to "apotropaic figures at the gates" (*CAD* L 42) or as "pillars of the earth", symbolized by the doorposts (LAMBERT 1985:199).

The etymology of Laḫmu as used in these contexts is the subject of debate. Some (such as T. Jacobsen) argue from the context of the *Enuma Elish* and from cognate derivatives of *lḫm* for a basic meaning "muddy", while others (LAMBERT 1985) prefer "hairy", based on both iconographic and textual data.

III. While some distant, historical connection between a deity Laḫmu (or *laḫmū*-monsters) and OT occurrences of *lḥm* cannot be apodictically denied, anything approaching the identification of a divine name or description in the OT is rendered highly suspect in the light of the following considerations: 1) The comparative evidence is relatively remote, being confined to Sumerian and Akkadian (East Semitic), with Mari the nearest location of an undisputed attestation. 2) There is no OT occurrence of a verbal form or noun of the root *lḥm* which cannot be satisfactorily explained as related to *lḥm*-I (fight) or *lḥm*-II (eat), including *lāḥem* in Judg 5:8 (most likely "war" or "fighting"). 3) The relation of the place name Bethlehem to Laḫmu was proposed by E. HONIGMANN (Bît-Laḫamu, *RLA* 2 [1933] 47), on the basis of one reference in the El Amarna letters. However, there is uncertainty as to the rendering of the ideogram, so that even the identity of the reference with Bethlehem is questionable. Even granted the reading "Bethlehem", moreover, an etymological connection with one of the established Hebrew uses of *lḥm*, as "house of bread" (or perhaps "house of fighting"), seems a more reasonable construing of the admittedly scanty evidence. (In this connection the conjecture of H. CAZELLES may be noted: a derivation from "house of Lahai"; cf. Gen 16:14; 24:62; *ABD* 1 [1992] 712).

IV. *Bibliography*

H. CAZELLES, Bethlehem, *ABD*, 1 (1992) 712-715; W. G. LAMBERT, The Pair Laḫmu-Laḫamu in Cosmology, *Or* 54 (1985) 189-202.

G. C. HEIDER

LAMB ἀμνός, ἀρνίον

I. In the NT →Christ is designated 31 times as a lamb. In John 1:29, 36 he is called the lamb (ἀμνός) of →God; in the Revelation of John (5:6, 8 et passim [29x]) he is depicted as a heavenly lamb (ἀρνίον) that receives honour and worship as if it is God himself.

II. There is much uncertainty and debate about the religio-historical background of the image of Christ as a lamb. There seems to be partly an OT background to this imagery, if one regards Isa 53:6-7 as the source of the remark in John's Gospel that →Jesus is the lamb of God that takes away the sins of the world (1:29; cf. Acts 8:32 and 1 Pet 1:19), which apparently links the Paschal sacrificial lamb of Exod 12 (cf. 1 Cor 5:7) with the lamb-like Suffering Servant (KRAFT 1974:109; MILES 1992:133), a thesis that certainly cannot be ruled out (*contra* DAUTZENBERG 1980:169-170). The fact that in Revelation the lamb is presented as slain (5:6; 13:8; etc.) also underscores the connection with the Paschal and Servant motive. But on the other hand there are many traits in the lamb-imagery of Revelation that certainly do not derive from this background. It is in keeping with the fact that *arnion*, the word always used in Revelation, originally meant 'ram', that several belligerent and judgemental (i.e. messianic) activities are attributed to this 'lamb'. For instance, it is said to be wrathful (6:16), to conquer its enemies (17:14), to carry seven horns as a symbol of its power (5:6), to be worthy to open the seals of the eschatological scroll (5:9), to be worthy "to receive power, wealth, wisdom, might, honour, glory, and blessing" (5:12), to be →"Lord of lords and King of kings" (17:14), to be "the Lion of Judah" (5:5), and to share God's glorious throne in rule over his people (22:1, 3; for a detailed analysis of all these and other passages see HOHNJEC 1980:34-149). "The association of these ideas of violence and power with the figure of a lamb is at first sight paradoxical" (DODD 1953:231). Yet it would seem that antecedents of this imagery are to be found in Jewish apocalypticism, although there are only two sources to support this hypothesis (one should note that the much discussed passage in *T. Jos.* 19:6 [the lamb that came forth from a virgin] is Christian and based upon Revelation; so rightly JEREMIAS 1966 *contra* KOCH 1966). Firstly, in the second part of the Enochic Book of Dreams (chaps. 83-90), the so-called Animal Apocalypse (chaps. 85-90), of *1 Enoch,* in chaps. 89-90, we find a survey of history covering the period from →Noah to the last judgement (written in the middle of the second century BCE; for an extensive commentary see TILLER 1993: esp. 269-382). The author makes use of many pastoral symbols, the most striking of which is the presentation of the great leaders of God's people as lambs/sheep/rams (the various versions have different designations here, cf. Isa 14:9), for instance David in 89: 45-46 and Judas Maccabaeus in 90:9, where this lamb is said to grow horns (!, as in Rev 5:6, probably due to a fusing of ram and lamb; on much later stories about →Moses as lamb see BURCHARD 1966). As →messiah-like figures these 'lambs' lead their flock towards victory over the enemies of God's children. Secondly, in the Tosephta-Targum on 1 Sam 17:43 and Targum Jonathan on 2 Sam 23:8, we find an old Aramaic song in which Goliath is called a bear and a lion but David a lamb. This song has clearly eschatological overtones in that David as the victorious lamb is presented as a messianic figure (with a throne) that will conquer all powers of evil in the end (VAN STAALDUINE-SULMAN 1993). It is very likely that this Jewish apocalyptic imagery forms the prototype of many lamb passages in Revelation. A most significant difference, however, is that, whereas the lambs in *1 Enoch* and the Targumic passages remain human beings, the author of Revelation has Christ as messianic Lamb almost united with God: in Rev 5:8-13 worship of the Lamb leads to the worship of God and the Lamb together, and the Lamb's throne is God's throne (5:6; 7:17; 22:1, 3; BAUCKHAM 1993:60). Yet this same lamb is identified with the sacrificial passover lamb that stands 'as slain' (5:6).

III. *Bibliography*

C. K. BARRETT, The Lamb of God, *NTS* 1 (1954/55) 210-218; R. BAUCKHAM, *The Theology of the Book of Revelation* (Cambridge 1993) 54-65; R. E. BROWN, *The Gospel according to John I-XII* (AB; Garden City 1966) 58-63; C. BURCHARD, Das Lamm in der Waagschale. Herkunft und Hintergrund eines haggadischen Midraschs zu Ex 1:15-22, *ZNW* 57 (1966) 219-228; G.

DAUTZENBERG, ἀμνός, ἀρήν, ἀρνίον, *EWNT* I (1980) 168-172; C. H. DODD, *The Interpretation of the Fourth Gospel* (Cambridge 1953) 230-238; N. HOHNJEC, *'Das Lamm – to arnion' in der Offenbarung des Johannes* (Rome 1980); J. JEREMIAS, Das Lamm, das aus der Jungfrau hervorging (Test. Jos. 19,8), *ZNW* 57 (1966) 216-219; K. KOCH, Das Lamm, das Ägypten vernichtet. Ein Fragment aus Jannes und Jambres und sein geschichtlicher Hintergrund, *ZNW* 57 (1966) 79-93; H. KRAFT, *Die Offenbarung des Johannes* (HNT 16a; Tübingen 1974) 107-110; J. R. MILES, Lamb, *ABD* 4 (1992) 132-134; E. VAN STAALDUINE-SULMAN, The Aramaic Song of the Lamb, *Verse in Ancient Near Eastern Prose* (ed. J. C. de Moor & W. G. E. Watson; Neukirchen-Vluyn 1993) 265-292; P. A. TILLER, *A Commentary on the Animal Apocalypse of* 1 Enoch (Atlanta 1993).

P. W. VAN DER HORST

LAMIA → LILITH

LAMP נר ניר,

I. The Hebrew noun *nîr* or *nēr*, denotes a light-giving body and is never used as a divine name, but it may occur as a surname of a deity or as the name of a being participating in the devine sphere, such as an →angel. Its Akkadian equivalent *nūru*, as well as Ugaritic *nrt* and *nyr*, are used metaphorically as epithets of the →Sun-deity called "the lamp of the gods" or "the lamp of heavens and earth" *(AHW* 805b; *CAD* N, 348-349; *KTU* 1.2.iii:15;1.3.v:17; etc.). Similar epithets are attributed also to other gods, even to →Yahweh in 2 Sam 22:29, where the poet addresses the LORD: "Thou, Yahweh, art my lamp", and he adds: "Yahweh will lighten my darkness". This image occurs also in proper names with a deity, the king, the father or the brother as subject of the nominal sentence constituting the proper name. Names of this type occur in Amorite (GELB 1980:331), Akkadian (*AHW* 805b; *CAD* N, 349a), Ugaritic (GRÖNDAHL 1967:165-166), Aramaic (ZADOK 1978: 100), Palmyrene (STARK 1971:39, 46, 75, 99, 108), North- and South-Arabian (LANKESTER HARDING 1971:585, 603), Phoenician (BENZ 1972:363), and Hebrew, with Abner, 'My father is a lamp', and Neriah/ Neraiah, 'My lamp is Yahweh' (ZADOK 1988:397-398, 438), paralleled in Aramaic by Yehonur in the Samaria Papyri. The Aramaized form of the latter name, Νωρία, was given later to the wife of →Noah and explained as 'Fire of God' by Epiphanius, *Haer.* XXVI,1.3. It is uncertain, however, whether Abner's patronymic Ner is a real Hebrew shortened name or a scribal creation based on the meaning of Abner's own name, viz. 'My father is *nēr*', i.e. 'a lamp'. The same name Nir was given in *2 Enoch* 22 to the second son of Lamech.

II. The Akkadian noun *nūru* is used sometimes with the determinative of divine names to designate the sacred lamp, which was the symbol of the god Nusku. It is depicted on boundary-stones (so-called *kudurru*'s), once even with the subscription 'Nusku' (*MDP* I, fig. 379). Some ritual prayers to Nusku had to be recited "before the lamp", *ana pān nūri* (OPPENHEIM, 1956, 340, Fragment III:1). The lamp (*nūru*) could be addressed as 'divine lamp' (^{d}**zalag**$_{2}^{!}$), 'king of the night, spreading light through the darkness' (*LKA* 132:19//*KAR* II 58:39). The 'divine lamp' (^{d}**izi-gar**) is also quoted in the incantations series *Šurpu* III 16-17.145. The Assyrian *Tākultu* ritual (108: 176, *BiOr* 18 [1961] 200: II 45) mentions a 'divine lamp-figure, ^{d}*Nu-ru-*^{d}*salmu*', standing in the temple of Adad (→Hadad). Being present in the temple, such lamps participated in the divine sphere.

In the Aramaic Sefire treaty, Aya, the consort of the Assyro-Babylonian Sun-god, is called *Nr* (*KAI* 222 A 9). It is even possible that the traditional cuneiform logogram ^{d}A.A of her name should be read *Nūr* in contemporaneous Assyrian texts as well (*SAA* 2, no. 2 vi 9; no. 3: 7. r. 2). Since many of the same pairs of gods are listed in the Sefire treaty and in the treaty of Aššurnirāri V with Mati'el, king of Arpad, comparison leaves little doubt that *Nūr* was a surname of Aya in that period. In any case, there is no reason to think that there was a distinct goddess *Nr* in that time. In the Ugaritic myth in which is narrated how the →moon-god Yariḫu obtained his bride Nikkal, the Ugaritic moon-god is called 'the luminary of heaven' (*nyr šmm*; *KTU* 1.24: 4.16).

III. The symbolic meaning of the 'lamp' in relation to God gave rise in the Jewish tradition to an angel named in Aramaic *Nūrî'el*, 'Fire of God', and called also *Nahrî'el*. In several passages of the Zohar →Uriel and Nuriel are the same angel, seen under different aspects. He is called Uriel when he appears as a merciful being, but Nuriel when the aspect of rigor and severity is to be stressed. This corresponds to his description in the text of an Aramaic incantation bowl from Late Antiquity: "Nuriel, the great Nuriel is his name. He is clad with fire and is covered with fire; a flame of fire comes out of his mouth" (NAVEH & SHAKED 1985:202-203:18). In the inscription of another bowl he is mentioned among seven supernatural beings, the first of which is *Šēdā'* (C. D. ISBELL, *Corpus of the Aramaic Incantation Bowls* [Missoula 1975] 110:1). The variant form of his name, *Nhry'l*, is attested by an amulet found at Ḥorvat Kanaf, on the Golan, where he is listed among angels (NAVEH & SHAKED 1985:50-51:9), without any specified function.

IV. *Bibliography*

F. L. BENZ, *Personal Names in the Phoenician and Punic Inscriptions* (StP 8; Roma 1972] 363); H. DONNER, Zur Inschrift von Sūdschīn Aa 9, *AfO* 18 (1957-58) 390-392; I. J. GELB, *Computer-Aided Analysis of Amorite* (Chicago 1980); F. GRÖNDAHL, *Die Personennamen der Texte aus Ugarit* (StP 1; Roma 1967); D. KELLERMANN, *nēr, nîr*, *TWAT* V (1986) 616-626 [& lit]; G. LANKESTER HARDING, *An Index and Concordance of Pre-Islamic Arabian Names and Inscriptions* (Toronto 1971); J. NAVEH & S. SHAKED, *Amulets and Magic Bowls* (Jerusalem 1985); M. NOTH, *IPN* 167-169; A. L. OPPENHEIM, *The Interpretation of Dreams in the Ancient Near East* (Philadelphia 1956) 298, 340; U. SEIDL, *Die babylonischen Kudurru-Reliefs* (Freiburg/Göttingen 1989) 128-130, XV; J. K. STARK, *Personal Names in Palmyrene Inscriptions* (Oxford 1971); R. ZADOK, *On West Semites in Babylonia* (Jerusalem 1978[2]); ZADOK, *The Pre-Hellenistic Israelite Anthroponomy and Prosopography* (Leuven 1988).

E. LIPIŃSKI

LAW → NOMOS; TORAH

LEAH לאה

I. Leah, the name of →Jacob's first wife is traditionally explained as '*defatigata*, weak' (WETZSTEIN 1876). STADE (1881) connected her name to Ar *lā'ā* 'Wildkuh' (a kind of antilope) and NÖLDEKE (1886), HAUPT (1909) and others to Akk *littu* 'cow' (*AHW* 557-558). Along these lines, the name *lē'â* came to be understood as a reminiscence of a goddess, or a tribal totem (GRAY 1896; SMITH 1894). Recently, her name has been quoted as the female counterpart of an epithet given to YHWH: *lē'* 'victor' (→Aliyan).

II. In ancient Near Eastern religions goddesses often received the epithet 'Cow' by virtue of their role as Magna Mater (LURKER 1985; e.g. →Hathor, Ninlil [*littu rabītu CAD* L 217], →Anat (*arḫ b'l KTU* 1.13:9-10), the *ilht arḫt* (*KTU* 1.4 vi 50) and also →Ba'alat (*CPSI* nos. 9,36). Tauromorphism is a well-known aspect of the iconography of these goddesses. In analogy to West Semitic names like *'bd-b'l, bn-b'l, bn-'nt,* and *'bd-lbit,* the second element in the Ugaritic name *bn-liy* (cf. the Phoenician and Punic names *'bd-l'yt, 'bd-l'(y),* and *'bdl(')t* (?) [= Akk. *Abdi-li'ti*, I R pl. 37 col. ii 49], and the Hebrew name *'mt-l'y* [*bBaba Bathra* 91a]) could refer to a deity (SZNYCER 1963). This element might be taken either as an epithet meaning 'strong, able, vigorous' (cf. Akk *lē'û, CAD* L 151-156) or as an animal name (cf. Ar *lā'ā;* Akk *lû(m)* and *littu AHW* 557-558.560; *CAD* L 217). However, this kind of surname given to gods is sometimes also given to human beings. It is impossible to decide whether names such as Akk [I]*La-i-um*, [f]*Le-i-i-tu*$_4$, Ug *bn.liy*, Heb *lē'â* and Ar *Lu'i*, *Lā'ā* imply more than a physical or moral quality. Animal names given to humans may simply express a wish or a pun; they do not necessarily imply totemistic concepts (NOTH, *IPN* 229). An emblematic understanding of the name (HAUPT 1909) can hardly be maintained: Israelite clans were never differentiated in such categories as peasants, herdsmen, and the like.

III. Very little is known about a cult of Leah as an ancestral saint. Her burial in the tomb of Machpelah (harim al-Khalil = Hebron) is only mentioned in passing in a very late P-addition to the Joseph story (Gen 49:32), which may imply that after the exile her cenotaph was shown in Hebron. Gen 29:30-35; 30:14-24; Ruth 4:11 mention her together with →Rachel, both her rival and the second mother of Israel. This may indicate that she was venerated together with Rachel in earlier Judean tradition, presumably at Rachel's tomb, in whose neigbourhood also Bilhah, Zilpah and Dinah were buried (*Jub* 34:15-16; *T.Jos* 20:3; JEREMIAS 1958:76-77).

IV. *Bibliography*

P. HAUPT, Lea und Rachel, *ZAW* 29 (1909) 281-286; J. JEREMIAS, *Heiligengräber in Jesu Umwelt* (Göttingen 1958); W. R. SMITH, *Lectures on the Religion of the Semites* (London 1927[3] repr.1969), 288-311; B. STADE, Lea und Rachel, *ZAW* 1 (1881) 112-116; M. SZNYCER, A propos du nom propre punique 'bdl'y, *Sem* 13(1963) 21-30; G. WETZSTEIN, in F. Delitzsch, *Das Buch Hiob* (Leipzig 1876) 507.

M. DIJKSTRA

LEBANON לבנון

I. Lebanon is the name of a mountain range in Syria (Ar *Ǧebel al-Lubnān*), which stretches ca. 170 km from the North (*Nahr al-Kabīr*) to the South (*Nahr al-Qāsimīya*), and rises from the Mediterranean Coast reaching a height (at *Qenāt al-Saudā*) of 3083 m; breaking off to the East it joins the long Biqā'-Valley. Opposite, to the East, we find the lower mountains of the Anti-Lebanon. This prominent range is mentioned in cuneiform documents from Old-Babylonian times on, often written *Lab-ni-ni* (cf. RGTC 5, 175), but also *La-ab-a-an*[ki] (RIMA 1, A.O.39.1, 84), *La-ab-la-na/ni* (cf. RGTC 6/1, 244) and—seldom—*Lib-na-nu* (*LKU* 39 I 4, collated text) or *Ni-ib-la-ni* (RGTC 6/1, 285). In Hebrew its name is *lĕbānôn*, Gk *libanos*. This corresponds to the Eg *r-mn-n* or *(p-)r-bꜣ-(r-)n-ꜣ* with uncertain vocalization. It is etymologically derived from *lbn* + *ān/ôn* 'the white (mountain)' with reference to its long-lasting snow-cap (cf. Jer 18:18). The Lebanon was famous for its wealth of wood, especially the aromatic 'cedars of the Lebanon' which were used for roofing temples and palaces. In some Hittite treaties the mountain Lebanon is deified.

II. The Lebanon is referred to in Ugaritic texts as an area producing trees. The building of the palace of →Baal is executed with beams from the Lebanon and the →Sirion, i.e. the Anti-Lebanon (*KTU* 1.4 vi:18-21). The bow of Aqhat is constructed by Kothar-wa-Ḫasīs with *ṯqb*-wood of the Lebanon together with sinews of buffalos, horn of an ibex etc., i.e. the best raw-material (*KTU* 1.17 vi:21). The abundance of the mountains with respect to fruits and water is cited in the →Rephaim-text *KTU* 1.22 i:20, 25; the reference in *KTU* 4.65,4 is doubtful. There are no traces of a deified Lebanon in Ugaritic.

In Old-Babylonian times, the Babylonian tradition of the Gilgamesh-Epic situates the 'cedar-forest', well guarded by the demon Ḫuwawa, in Lebanon (and Saria/→Hermon); it is called 'the hidden dwelling place of the Anunnaki', i.e. the gods of the upper world (S. GREENGUS, *Old Babylonian Tablets from Ishchali* (Istanbul/Leiden 1979) 277 r.13-20). By Middle-Babylonian times the 'forest of the cedars' is only mentioned as the place where the →demon Ḫuwawa lives without any exact localization (e.g. the MB Fragment from Megiddo, S. LEVY & A. GOETZE, *Atiqot* 2 [1959] *122 obv.7').

Hittite treaties concluded with princes in

Syria invoke the Lebanon and the Šaryana among the gods and various deified mountains; they are qualified as deities by their determinatives. Cf. KBo I 4 IV 36 (Šuppiluliuma I and Tette of Nuḫḫašše); V 9 IV 11 (Muršili II and Duppi-Tešup of Amurru); KUB III 7 + ... RS 3 (Šuppiluliuma I and Aziru of Amurru); KUB VIII 82 + ... RS 18 (Tutḫaliya IV and Šaušgamuwa). The mountain Lebanon is also invoked in Hurrian rituals such as KUB 27,14,7; KUB 17,27 RS III 22 (= *Corpus hurrit. Sprachdenkmäler* 5 [1988] 195), which demonstrates his prominent place among the mountain-deities in Ancient Syria.

In Phoenicia a *bʿl lbnn* 'Baal of the Lebanon' is known through the inscriptions on two bronze-bowls dedicated by a Tyrian governor of Qart-Ḥadašt (in Cyprus) which came to light in the last century in Limassol/Cyprus (*CIS* I 5 = *KAI* 31). Therefore a Baal of this mountain may have been venerated sometime in the middle of the 8th century BCE. Of controversial interpretation is a certain *tnt blbnn* 'Tinnit in Lbnn' in a Carthaginian inscription of the 2nd cent. BCE (*CIS* I 3914 = *KAI* 81), which commemorates the founding of new sanctuaries in a mountain. This cultic place, may be situated either on a white chalk hillside or it may be a place somewhere in Phoenicia. It must be stressed, however, that high-places and their sanctuaries were generally dedicated to male, not female, deities. That it was not just during the 2nd half of the 2nd millennium BCE, but also during the 1st millennium that the mountains of the Lebanon were venerated, is supported by Philo of Byblos (transmitted through Eusebius, *Praep. Evang.* I 10,9 = *FGH* III C 790, F 2,9) knowing of a generation of heroes with the names of mountains, *inter alia* Lebanon and Anti-Lebanon.

III. The Lebanon is mentioned about 65 times in the OT. The mountain-ridge is said to be famous for its cedar-wood (Cant 4:11). Like Sharon, →Bashan and →Carmel the Lebanon is mentioned as a relatively fertile region (Isa 33:9; Nah 1:4). Nowhere in the OT a divine status of the Lebanon is implied.

IV. *Bibliography*

O. EISSFELDT, *Der Gott Tabor* (Halle 1934) 35-36 = *KS* 2 (1951) 49; J. EBACH, *Weltentstehung und Kulturentwicklung bei Philo von Byblos* (BWANT 108; Stuttgart/Berlin/Köln/Mainz 1979) 132-148; R. H. SMITH, Lebanon, *ABD* 4 (1992) 269-270; M. WEIPPERT, Libanon, *RLA* 6 (1980-83) 641-650 [& lit].

W. RÖLLIG

LEGION λεγιών

I. Legion as a name of a →demon occurs only in Mark 5:9.15 and the parallel in Luke 8:30. The meaning is explained in the context, when the demon replies: 'Legion is my name, for we are many' (Mark 5:9). A somewhat different explanation occurs in Luke 8:30: 'Legion, for many demons entered into him' (sc. the Gerasene demoniac). The form of the name may also vary in the manuscripts, but *legiōn* seems more original, while *legeōn* is mostly the result of correction. The name is derived from the Latin *legio*, the designation of the largest unit in the Roman army (between 4,200 and 6,000 men, and a small contingent of cavalry). In Latin, the term was used also figuratively, e.g. to refer to a large 'army' of supporters (Plautus, *Cas.* 50; *Mos.* 1047; Pliny, *Nat. Hist.* 33.26). In Matt 26:53 Jesus applies the metaphor to →angels ('more than twelve legions of angels'), comparable to the apocalyptic 'myriads' of angels (Dan 7:10; Heb 12:22; Jude 14; Rev 5:11; 9:16; see also *PGM* I.208-209; IV.1203-1204; furthermore BAGD, *s.v.* μυρίας, 2).

II. While 'legions of angels' is also attested in later rabbinical literature (see for the passages Str-B 1.682[e], 997; 2.9), Legion as a name for a demon occurs only in the NT exorcism of the Gerasene demoniac (Mark 5:1-20 par.; Matthew has omitted the name in his version, Matt 8:28-34). The exorcism story apparently came from a pre-Marcan source; its anti-pagan (anti-Roman) tendency should be obvious (v 13 has Legion's cohorts destroyed by drowning together with 2,000 pigs).

III. While the Latin *legio* is feminine, Mark vacillates between the masculine name for the demon and the neuter *pneuma akatharton* describing his nature (Mark 5:2.8.13); Luke (8:27.29.30.33.35.38) prefers to speak of the plural *daimonia* (see on this also BDR § 38 [3]). Later occurrences of Legion as a demon's name are found in texts based on the story of the Gerasene demoniac. *Epist. Apost.* 5 (16) explicitly mentions the story and the name (see HENNECKE-SCHNEEMELCHER-WILSON, *Apoc* 1.193; SCHNEEMELCHER, *Apok* 1.208-1.209). An interesting development of the story is found in *T. Sol.* 11 (pp. 39*-41*, ed. McCown; trans. D. C. DULING, *OTP* 1.972-1.973, with the corrections by JACKSON 1985:50-51). In this development the dialogue takes place between king Solomon, a prominent figure in magic, and the demon. When questioned, the demon reveals that he and his company can be thwarted only 'in the name of the one who has submitted to suffer a long time hence many things (at the hand) of men, whose name is →Emmanuel, but who even now has bound us and will come to torture us (by driving us) into the water at the cliff' (*T. Sol.* 11:6). *T. Sol.* 11 also provides a demonological explanation for an ambiguity in the gospel narrative: Does the name belong to one demon or to a collective of demons? The question is answered by saying that Legion is not the demon's real name but a description of his activity (11:3; cf. Mark 3:22-27 par.): 'I assault (men) with the legions of demons subject to me... The name for all demons which are under me is legion'. What then is the real name of the demon? He replies: 'The Lion-Shaped Demon, an Arab by descent'. This description takes a pagan ('Arab') deity and demonizes it (see on this point BLAU 1898:65; MÜLLER, *RAC* IX 765-769), making it into a satanic figure (cf. 1 Pet 5:8 [Ps 21:14]; Rev 4:7; 9:8.17; 10:3; 13:2). This lion-shaped demon could then be identified with various other names (see *T. Sol.* 22:1-25:9; recension D 6:1-7:6, ed. McCown; also *PGM* I.144; III.510; IV.1667, 2112, 2132, 2302; XXXVIII.22; etc.; and JACKSON 1985, 1985b). For later interpretations of the story see McCown's edition, pp. 76-77. The suggestion by EITREM (1966:71) that the name Legion expresses hatred of the Roman military may find support in *PGM* XXII.b.35; XXXV.15.

IV. *Bibliography*

BAGD, *s.v.* λεγιών [& lit]; O. BAUERNFEIND, *Die Worte der Dämonen im Markusevangelium* (BWANT 44; Stuttgart 1927) 26-27, 34-56; L. BLAU, *Das altjüdische Zauberwesen* (Budapest 1898); C. COLPE, J. MAIER, J. TER VRUGT-LENTZ, E. SCHWEIZER, A. KALLIS, P. G. VAN DER NAT & C. D. G. MÜLLER, 'Geister (Dämonen)', *RAC* 9 (1976) 546-796 [& lit]; D. C. DULING, Testament of Solomon, *OTP* 1.935-1.959 [& lit]; S. EITREM, *Some Notes on Demonology in the New Testament* (Symbolae Osloenses, Suppl. 20; 2nd ed.; Oslo 1966) 70-72; H. M. JACKSON, *The Lion Becomes Man: The Gnostic Leontomorphic Creator and the Platonic Tradition* (SBLDS 11; Atlanta 1985) [& lit]; JACKSON, The Meaning and Function of the Leontocephaline in Roman Mithraism, *Numen* 32 (1985) 17-45; JACKSON, Notes on the Testament of Solomon, *JSJ* 19 (1988) 19-60; D. LÜHRMANN, *Das Markusevangelium* (HNT 3; Tübingen 1987) 93-101; C. C. MCCOWN, *The Testament of Solomon* (Leipzig 1922); R. PESCH, *Der Besessene von Gerasa: Entstehung und Überlieferung einer Wundergeschichte* (SBS 56; Stuttgart 1972); R. PESCH, *Das Markusevangelium*, I. Teil (HTKNT II:1; Freiburg 1976) 277-295 [& lit]; H. PREISKER, λεγιών *TDNT* 4 (1977) 68-69.

H. D. BETZ

LEL לל

I. The identification of a deity Lel in the West Semitic world is a very difficult subject for the historian of religions. The existence of the deity as such has been questioned and the meaning and etymology of the name are a matter of debate.

The deity has been related to *lyl* - *lylh* 'night' (hence the conventional pronunciation 'Lēl') (DIETRICH & LORETZ 1980:

403), but also to the Akkadian *lil(lu)* known in Old and Standard Babylonian as a god and as a →demon, meaning 'fool, simple' (THUREAU-DANGIN 1922, but cf. KREBERNIK 1987:20). The god has to be distinguished from *lilû*, fem. *lilîtu* (from Sum **lîl**, related to 'wind, breath';→Lilith). Recently, the name has been found in pantheon lists of Mari (TALON 1980:T 186:10,12-17, ^{d}*le-el-[lum]*), but the identification of this god has been debated by KREBERNIK (1987:20a), who interprets this theonym as *l-ʾl*, 'to →El' (but see RÖLLIG 1987 who refers to an offering list from Mari mentioning the god ^{d}*Li-lum*). Worshipped as a deity at Mari, Ugarit, and in Canaan, Lel survives only as a demythologized entity in the Hebrew Bible.

II. What about Lel in the Ugaritic texts, if it is not possible to identify *ll* either with *lilû* as A. HERDNER suggested (*Ug.* 7 [1978] 30 and n. 94) or with *lil(lum)* (KREBERNIK 1987:20)? DIETRICH & LORETZ (1980:403) have tried to prove that Ugaritic *ll* is not to be interpreted as a deity, but that it must simply be understood as 'night'. J. C. DE MOOR (The Semitic Pantheon of Ugarit, *UF* 2 [1970] 187-228, esp. 194) put *ll* in his list of deities with a question mark.

It must be admitted that the meaning of the two passages of *KTU* 1.132:16-17 *lpn / ll* and 25 *pn ll* is not entirely clear. The editor (HERDNER, *Ug.* 7 [1978] 42-44), followed with some hesitation by P. XELLA (*I testi rituali di Ugarit* [Roma 1981] 305-309) and DIETRICH & LORETZ (1980:403), has understood *(l)pn ll* as a temporal indication; she translates 'before the night'. J.-M. DE TARRAGON (*Le culte à Ugarit* [Paris 1980] 25, 118-119, 166), however, understood it as the name of a deity. The choice between the two options must be based on a close reading of the text. It seems clear that lines 2-3 have a corresponding section in lines 25-28: "the bed of Pidraya is prepared *bšt mlk*" (maybe to be rendered as "while the king is laying down" instead of the usual translation "with covers of the king"). The bed is then "undone" (*tnṯr* or *tnʿr*), and "at sunset, the king is desacralized". In such a context, *pn ll* (line 25) is best understood as a temporal construction "before the night"; the same meaning would fit also in lines 16-17. Such a solution is consonant with the fact that the text mentions Hurrian deities, *Pdry* being the rendering of →Hebat (lines 5, 14, 20); a deity with a Semitic name *ll* would be out of place.

The interpretation of *KTU* 1.106:27-28 (*wlll tʿr[k] ksu*) is not easy. Editor and commentators generally choose the translation "at night the throne is prepared ...", except J. M. DE TARRAGON (*Le culte à Ugarit* [Paris 1980] 24-25) who understands "for *Ll* the throne is prepared ..." The expression follows an indication of a ritual purification of the king on the 25th day (lines 25-27); the king is desacralized at the end after the answer is given (lines 32-33). This (second) ritual follows a previous one on the 8th day of the month, which finishes with lines 23-24: the answer is given and the king is desacralized. Lines 1 and 6 mention →Resheph (Resheph-*ḥgb* and Resheph-*mh[bn]*) as the main deity of this first ritual; corresponding to Resheph in the second ritual (starting at line 25) is *ll* (line 27). Here, *ll* is best understood as a deity (note that "the throne", *ksu* [in the expression *lk]su.ilt* 'for the th]rone of Elat; line 28] in the second ritual may correspond with the "couches" [line 15] in the first). A comparable succession of Resheph and Lel is found in *KTU* 1.90:2 *(ršp.ḥgb)* and 6 (*w.š ll[l.al]p*, see also line 20: *ršp.š.*).

In the list of offerings described in *KTU* 1.39, a number of Semitic gods and goddesses receive sacrificial offerings. Among them, Resheph is listed a prominent position; he is mentioned in line 4 after El (line 2) and in the company of →Anat (lines 7, 17). In line 12, Lel is mentioned; the sequence *wlll.špš pgr.w...* could well be understood as "and to Lel (and) Shapshu-*pgr* and ..." (cf. line 17 *[rš]p ʿnt.ḥbly dbḥm š[p]š pgr.*), and not as "at night, Shapshu-*pgr* and ..." (A. CAQUOT & J. M. DE TARRAGON, *Textes ougaritiques* II [LAPO 14; Paris 1989] 38 note 20). The same sequence is found in RIH 77/4(+11):1 [...].*ršp.wlll*[...],

"[...] Resheph and to Lel[...]"; 2 [...]*wršp.gn.y ṣ'n*[...], "[god X] and Resheph of the precinct will go out [...]". Two other broken tablets confirm our interpretation. In *KTU* 1.49, the sequence *lll.pr*[...] "to Lel a bull[...]" (line 9) follows *li[l]*, 'to El', (line 2), [...]*lpdr[...]*, 'to Pidar', (line 4), *lʿṯtrt*[], 'to Athtart (→Astarte)', (line 6). In *KTU* 1.50, the sequence *w.lll.ʿṣrm.w*[..], "and to Lel (two?) birds and[...]" (line 7) follows *lk*]*su.ilt*[, 'for the th]rone of Elat[(line 2), *lʿṯtrt*[..., 'for Athtart', (line 3), [*w.*]*lilt.š lcṯt*[*rt*, 'and for Elat [→Terebinth], a sheep, for Astarte', (line 4) and *lpdr.ṯṯ.ṣ*[*in*, 'for Pidar six pieces of small stock', (line 5).

All these examples, except *KTU* 1.132, reveal a consistent pattern: Lel is mentioned alongside Resheph and/or Pidraya (or Pidar). This is a strong argument in favour of an interpretation of Lel as a deity. The existence of a god Lel seems to be confirmed at Ugarit by a hypocoristic anthroponym *bn ll* among a list of anthroponyms on a tablet found at Ras Ibn Hani in 1983 (*CRAIBL* 1984:425).

The last Ugaritic instance of Lel occurs in the mythological text, *KTU* 1.2 i:[14], 20, in the expression *tk.ǵr.ll.ʿm.pḫr.mʿd,* "(in) the midst of the mountain of *ll* toward the meeting of the assembly" under the presidency of El. Now that the existence of the deity Lel seems to be proved, it is not necessary anymore to correct *ǵr.ll* to *ǵr.il* as some commentators have done (e.g. R. J. CLIFFORD, *The Cosmic Mountain in Canaan and the Old Testament* [Cambridge Mass. 1972] 42; DIETRICH & LORETZ 1980:403). But a difficulty remains. How do we have to understand the name of the mountain *ǵr ll*? Certain authors understand it as that of a divine mountain: "the mount Luli" (M. POPE, *El in the Ugaritic Texts* [VTSup 2; Leiden 1955] 68-72; A. CAQUOT, M. SZNYCER & A. HERDNER, *Textes ougaritiques*, I [LAPO 7; Paris 1974] 128-130 (note l.), 65; DE TARRAGON, *Le culte à Ugarit* [Paris 1980] 166); others as "the mountain of →Night" (C. H. GORDON, *Ugaritic Textbook* [AnOr 38; Rome 1965] 428 no. 1379 [mythological place]; E. LIPIŃSKI, El's Abode. Mythological Traditions Related to Mount Hermon and to the Mountains of Armenia, *OLP* 2 [1971] 13-69, esp. 41-43 [parallel to the Hebrew "mountains of darkness"]). It seems better to keep the reading *ll* (not *il*) and to understand it as a deity, 'Night' - *Lēl* (see the vocalisation *lēl* in a Canaanite gloss of *EA* 243:13) or even *Lilu* (see *ARTU* 31).

A Canaanite occurrence of Lel is to be read on a bowl sherd found in the Late Bronze Fosse temple at Lachish, where [...]*1 šyʿbrlll*|[...] is to be understood either as:...] 1(?) *š yʿbr lll*[..., '...] one(?) sheep he offers to Lel[...', or as: ...].*šy ʿbr lll*[..., '...]an offering [he had] offered to Lel[...'. Both readings are to be preferred above *llly(?)[t]*, "to Lili[th]" (PUECH 1986:15-17, 22).

The identity, character and role of Lel are difficult to assess because of the nature of the data. Is the Akkadian deity *lil(lu)* to be read in some of the Ugaritic texts as homograph of *ll* "night", or are all the Ugaritic passages to be understood as referring to "Night/Lel - night"? Compare *il*, which can mean either 'god' or be the proper name El, and *ršp* which may mean 'plague' or be the proper name Resheph. Because Lel is in some way connected to Resheph, a chthonic god who brings plague and sudden death (*KTU* 1.106; 1.39; 1.90; RIH 77/4[+ 11]); once associated to Nikkal, the wife of →Sin/ Yarikh; to the chthonic gods *ilm ar[ṣ]* (*KTU* 1.106:14, 30-32); and once associated to Shapshu-*pgr* (like Anath to Resheph; *KTU* 1.39), a goddess who knows the Manes-Rephaim during their nightly travel in the underworld and guides Anat looking for →Baal, it seems that Lel ('Night') is at least in some passages a lesser deity related to the underworld; and or as a god of the night he may also bring plague or disease.

Resheph is sometimes described as the gate-keeper of the →sun goddess (*KTU* 1.78:2-4, see *ršp ḥgb*, *KTU* 1.106:1 and 1.90:2). Further, the connection between Resheph and Lel might reflect the association of *ʾrq(/ṣ)ršp* of the Panamuwa inscription (*KAI* 214), for the god Arṣu at Palmyra or the Goddess Ruḍa of the Arabs is identified with the Evening star, Venus, who is brother of Shapshu and son of Yarikh and Nikkal. The gate-keeper of the sun goddess, who welcomes her to the underworld at the end of the day, is naturally related to the god of the night, the latter being himself related to the mountain (*ǵr ll*) behind which the sun is hiding at the sunset. As the sun sets, the world is plunged into darkness; Resheph and Lel, associated with a god of evening, spread plague, disease and death by the terror of the night. It is to be remembered in this connection that the Akkadian god Lilu is a son of Ninḫursag, "the great Lady of the Mountain" (THUREAU-DANGIN 1922). The observations made above concerning the nature of the Ugaritic deity Lel are supported by the still unique Canaanite text of Lachish, in which city the god Resheph was also known (PUECH 1986-87:15, 16).

A divinity of the Night is to be expected as a counterpart of *Yawm*, 'Daylight' (→Day; DE MOOR, The Semitic Pantheon of Ugarit, *UF* 2 [1970] 187-228, esp. 202). The existence of such a divinity is confirmed by the Aramaic treaties of Sefire from the 8th century BCE (*KAI* 222 A 12: "in the presence of Day and Night [*lylh*]"), where the natural phenomena possessing a numinous character were invoked as gods; they were witnesses to the treaties, and as such supposed to bring maledictions over transgressors, maybe under some Hittite-Hurrian influences (cf. the Assyrian *tākultu* ritual, W. L. MORAN, Some Remarks on the Songs of Moses, *Bib* 43 [1962] 317-327, esp. 319-320). Lel could be compared to νύξ, a goddess of the night in Greek mythology.

III. There is no example of Lel in the Bible, except maybe in a conjectural reading of a corrupt verse, Deut 32:10, to be understood "He found him in a land of wilderness and in a waste of (and) the night of a desert" (*yll* > *lyl* by metathesis, or *wll* by confusion of *waw/yod* after a *waw*) (see *llh* on the Mesha stela, *KAI* 181:15). In any case, there is no mention of a deity and the word is to be related to *lyl* (7 times) / *lylh* (225 times) "night". Elsewhere known as numinous forces, 'Day' and 'Night' have been demythologized by the Bible; only the phrase 'Heaven and Earth' retains mythological overtones at times (e.g. Isa 1:2; Mic 6:1-2, Ps 50:4, Deut 4:26; →Olden gods).

IV. *Bibliography*

M. DIETRICH & O. LORETZ, Kennen die Ugaritischen Texte den Babylonischen Gottesnamen LILLU(M)?, *UF* 12 (1980) 403; M. KREBERNIK, Lil, *RLA* 7 (1987) 19-20; E. PUECH, The Canaanite Inscriptions of Lachish and their Religious Background, *Tel Aviv* 13-14 (1986-87) 13-25; W. RÖLLIG, Lilum, *RLA* 7 (1987) 25; P. TALON, Un nouveau panthéon de Mari, *Akkadica* 20 (1980), 12-17 [lit.]; F. THUREAU-DANGIN, La passion du dieu Lillu, *RA* 19 (1922) 175-185.

E. PUECH

LEVIATHAN לויתן

I. *Liwyātān* is the Heb name of a mythical monster associated with the →Sea (or Yam). First attested in a Ugaritic text (*KTU* 1.5 i:1 ‖ 27) where it occurs as *ltn* (to be vocalized *lītānu*, as convincingly argued by EMERTON 1982), the name is related to a root LWY. Etymologically it might be interpreted either as 'the twisting one' (cf. Arab *lawiyā*) or 'the wreath-like', 'the circular' (cf. Heb *liwyâ*), both possibilities pointing to an original concept of Leviathan as a snake-like being. The second alternative should not, however, lead to the opinion that Leviathan were always imagined as the primeval sea-serpent thought to surround the earth (J. C. DE MOOR, *ARTU* 69, n. 323; cf. *BiOr* 31 [1974] 5a; for a late Kassite *kudurru*-relief showing such a being, see U. SEIDL, *Die babylonischen Kudurru-Reliefs* [OBO 87; Fribourg & Göttingen 1989] no. 40). Both Ugaritic and Biblical texts use *lītānu/liwyātān* as a proper name; consequently, the imagined physical appearance of Leviathan cannot be deduced from etymology alone, and as a matter of fact, the texts do not give a single, homogeneous portrait (see below).

The concept of Leviathan is closely related to →Rahab, insofar as the latter seems to be a late exilic adaption of the former, possibly supplemented from Babylonian →Marduk theology (U. RÜTERSWÖRDEN, *TWAT* 7 [1993] esp. 376). Both Leviathan and Rahab belong to the realm of →dragon-like monsters (→Tannin), both may be termed 'fugitive →serpent' (cf. Isa 27:1 with Job 26:13) and thus may sometimes have been confounded, although the book of Job clearly distinguishes between them (see 3:8, 40:25-41:26 on Leviathan and 9:13; 26:12 on Rahab, still 7:12 on Tannin).

Appearing in only one pre-Biblical text and mentioned six times in the Bible, Leviathan could seem to be a figure of minor importance. However, as a paradigmatic monster and enemy of considerable mythological attire, he outweighs other representatives of chaos and evil. The so-called 'Chaoskampf' constellation or 'combat myth' in which Leviathan plays the role of a threatening, but vanquished enemy, has been functionalized in politics and propaganda from the early 2nd mill. BCE until today, with T. Hobbes' *Leviathan* (a treatise on the modern state first published 1651) being only one peak in a tremendous 'Wirkungsgeschichte'. The study of this monster thus exemplifies how an ancient Near Eastern mythological concept could travel from one culture to another or adapt itself, within one given culture, to changing historical trends. It illuminates the fluidity in the development of ancient Near Eastern mythological imagination.

II. First of all, 'Leviathan' is a name and as such identifies an individual being. In *KTU* 1.5 i:1 ‖ 27, it designates a 'fugitive serpent' (*bṯn brḥ*, cf. Heb *nāḥāš bārîaḥ* in Isa 27:1 and Job 26:3) smitten by the victorious weather-god Baʿalu (→Baal). Two closely related epithets, 'wriggling serpent' (*bṯn ʿqltn*, cf. Heb *nāḥāš ʿăqallātôn* in Isa 27:1) and 'Mighty one(?) with the seven heads' (*šlyṭ d.šbʿt rašm*), are usually understood to refer to Leviathan, too, and the former is certainly used in this sense in Isa 27:1. Originally, however, they may well have referred to at least one other monster, mentioned again in *KTU* 1.3 iii:41-42 together with the god Yammu (→Sea), a →dragon (Tannin) and four other opponents. Clearly, Yammu had a number of helpers at his disposal—as did Mesopotamian representatives of chaos like Asakku, Anzû, →Tiamat (→Tehom) or the like—and Leviathan was but one of them. A seven-headed serpent (**muš-sağ-imin**) partly overcome by an anthropomorphic hero or god is attested as early as the third mill. BCE in Mesopotamian iconography (H. FRANKFORT, *Stratified Cylinder Seals from the Diyala Region* [OIP 72, Chicago 1955] 37, pl. 47:497) and texts (*Lugal-e* 133; *Angimdimma* 39, 62; cf. →Nimrod), but later survives in the textual records only, until he reappears in the Greek Hydra tradition from the 6th century on (BISI 1964-65; cf. *LIMC* V/1 [1990] 34-43). Consequently, when looking for Bronze Age pictorial representations of Leviathan, one should first consider his undisputed serpent nature. In contrast, the seven heads cannot be necessary prerequisites since they may well have belonged to some other monster and are at best secondary elements. Old Syrian seals (18th-16th century BCE) showing the weather-god killing a serpent, often in front of a goddess, are so numerous that there can be no doubt about their figuring the prototype of the Ugaritic Yammu/Leviathan conflict (see WILLIAMS-FORTE 1983; W. G. LAMBERT, *BSOAS* 48 [1985] 442-444; with KEEL 1992:212-215 for further material and interpretation). Although the weather-god was called at that time Haddu and his enemy *têmtum* (J.-M. DURAND, *MARI* 7 [1993] 41-61; the *roles* of the conflict between the weather-god and the Sea were then fixed for centuries to come. Interpreters of the Ugaritic texts discuss whether it was Baal who killed the dragon or Anat, since the latter claims the victory in *KTU* 1.3 iii:38-46 and may be invoked to trample on 'the Fugitive' (*brḥ*, see above) in the incantation *KTU* 1.82:38 (BINGER 1992; N. H. WALLS, *The Goddess Anat in Ugaritic Myth* [SBLDS 135; Atlanta 1992] 175-177). From the point of view of iconography, Haddu/Baʿalu has clear priority as the *serpent* slayer, and it may be more than mere coincidence if the Leviathan is not mentioned among Anat's victims in *KTU* 1.3; as a matter of fact, dozens of pictures testify that *this* victory, at least, was thought to be Baal's.

Some assimilation of Egyptian religious traditions and the Leviathan concept seems to have occurred in Southern Palestine and Northern Egypt already during the Hyksos period. It is documented by scarab seals showing a falcon-headed god mastering a crocodile. The falcon-headed Egyptian (sun-)god (→Horus) was identified in Middle Bronze Age Palestine with the Syrian weather-god, and the scene with the crocodile probably understood, in an *interpretatio semitica*, as the Egyptianizing version of the combat between the weather-god and the Sea (see O. KEEL, *Studien zu den Stempelsiegeln aus Palästina/Israel* II [OBO 88; Fribourg & Göttingen 1989] esp. 268-275). Clearly, we have here a precedent for the association made later of Leviathan with the crocodile (Job 40:25-41:26, and cf. Ezek 29:3 and 32:2 which call the crocodile a 'dragon' [Tannin]!). In general, however, the tradition representing Yammu or Leviathan as a serpent prevailed in Syria and Palestine. Later scarabs of the Late Bronze and early Iron age show the Syrian Baal, now identified with the Egyptian god →Seth, fighting with a lance against a horned serpent (O. KEEL & C. UEHLINGER, *Göttinen, Götter und Gottessymbole* [QD 134; Freiburg i. Br. 1993^2] § 45; KEEL 1992:209-212). The latter represents Yammu or Leviathan who may now have been assimilated to Apophis, a huge serpent who during the night tries to hinder the sun-god's travel through the netherworld (cf. *LdÄ* 1 [1975] 350-352). That Leviathan originated as a concept borrowed from Egypt, as suggested by S. I. L. NORIN (*Er spaltete das Meer* [ConB OT 9; Lund 1977] 67-70), is most improbable, since Apophis has no relationship to the Sea, which in turn is essential for Leviathan.

Whether the Ugaritic and other Syro-Palestinian 'combat myth' traditions should be interpreted as 'Chaoskampf', within the concept of 'creation', has been disputed by generations of scholars; it is largely a matter of definition (cf. PODELLA 1993). The Biblical texts clearly consider →Yahweh's mastering of Leviathan as an aspect of creational order, although neither necessarily in terms of a *creatio prima* or cosmogony nor in terms of combat.

III. In the Bible, Leviathan is mentioned exclusively in poetic texts, some of which are deliberately archaizing. Ps 74, a communal lament weeping over the profanation of Yahweh's sanctuary by enemies, contains a section which functions as a confessional reminder for the distressed (vv 12-17): Yahweh is king "from of old" (*miqqedem*, i.e. since primeval times), and his kingship specifically implies helpful dominion over the earth (v 12). This is illustrated by a reference to the 'traditional' victories of Yahweh over the sea (*yām*), the dragons (Pl.) and Leviathan (vv 13-14). As in Ugarit, Leviathan and the dragons are considered as Yam's associates of monstrous appearance (note *rāʾšîm*, mentioned twice, albeit with unspecified number); together, the three entities represent the maritime chaos which once had endangered the earth but was then overwhelmed by the creator-god and given as food to wild beasts (or possibly sharks). Yahweh's victory was a necessary prelude to his subsequent organization of the cosmos: the opening of springs and the division of time in day and night, summer and winter (vv 15-17). While this text alludes to a primeval battle appealed to in times of distress, an apocalyptic rejoinder in Isa 27:1 announces such a battle for the future: On the day when Yahweh will bring his wrath over a corrupt creation, sparing only his faithful people, he shall again draw his sword against Leviathan and kill "the dragon which is in midst of the sea"—an example of the analogy often drawn between *Urzeit* und *Endzeit*, the latter being conceived as a new, eventually better creation. Leviathan's disaster will coincide with the restoration of the vineyard Israel (v 2), which implies that

'Leviathan' here works as a metaphor for an historical-political entity, too, unnamed but identified with mere chaos. While the sequence 'fugitive serpent'—'wriggling serpent'—'dragon' is the same as in *KTU* 1.5 i:1-3 || 27-29, the name *liwyātān* is mentioned twice in Isa 27:1, and it is not altogether clear whether Leviathan and dragon are conceived as two different monsters or whether 'dragon' is simply used as a variant term to qualify Leviathan. In either case, it is notable that the biblical texts have developed little speculative knowledge of and terminology for monsters when compared to the much more detailed descriptions displayed by Mesopotamian, Ugaritic and Egyptian literature.

The two texts just mentioned are characterized by their blending together of the spheres of history and mythology, the conflict on one level mirroring a conflict on the other; consequently, Leviathan is considered a dangerous enemy and his monstrous force underlined, since this may serve to magnify the power of victorious Yahweh. In striking contrast, some sapiential texts rather dedramatize the mythical power of Leviathan. Amos 9:3 speaks of a mere snake on the bottom of the sea, and Ps 104:26 even considers Leviathan to be a harmless player therein. In the latter verse, the final *bô* is syntactically ambiguous: Yahweh has fashioned Leviathan, but was it that he might himself play 'with him' (according to Rabbinic tradition, during the last three hours of the day [*b.Ab.Zar* 3b]), or that Leviathan might simply play 'in it', i.e. the sea? Both readings are possible, and both imply that the Psalmist did not consider Leviathan dangerous any more. Consequently, Leviathan does not appear in Ps 104:6-9, where discrete conflict metaphors are used as a reminiscence of more dualistic creation theology; he is only mentioned in v 26b as a fitting example to demonstrate the somewhat playful nature of Yahweh's creation.

That such a detached, almost 'naturalistic' approach was not considered altogether realistic by other sages is shown by the book of Job. Job 3:8 mentions people "skilled in rousing up Leviathan." Apparently they practised some magical technique such as attested by much later Jewish-Aramaic incantation bowls (C. D. ISBELL, *Corpus of the Aramaic Incantation Bowls* [SBLDS 17; Missoula 1975] no. 2, 6, 7). Job 40:25-41:26, the second part of Yahweh's second answer to Job is entirely devoted to Leviathan. While the rhetorical questions of the first section (40:25-41:1) insist on Job's (as any human's) inability to capture him, the second (41:2-26) gives a panegyric description imbued with numinous fear. No doubt this text describes features of a crocodile, as recognized in 1663 by S. Bochart in his *Hierozoicon*. But the crocodile-Leviathan, 'king of all beasts(?)' (41:26), is not simply considered as a zoological species. In Egyptian iconography, the crocodile appears as an enemy of the sun-god and is subdued by the god Horus or the Pharaoh; early Iron age stamp seals from Palestine show a 'master of crocodiles' holding two of these beasts under his control (KEEL 1978:144-154; KEEL & UEHLINGER, *Göttinnen, Götter und Gottessymbole* [QD 134; Freiburg i. Br. 1993^2] §67). Obviously the author of Job 41 had access to some animal mythological literature relating to the Egyptian tradition. However, in contrast to this and to the Syrian tradition taken over by apocalypticists, he does not present his issue in terms of a mythological combat: Yahweh's own words are full of respect for the crocodile-Leviathan; the latter, just as →Behemoth, represents a symbolic residue, within reality, of evil and chaos which even the creator cannot expel beyond the boundaries of his creation. O. EISSFELDT (*Baal Zaphon, Zeus Kasios und der Durchzug der Israeliten durchs Meer* [Halle 1932] 25-50) compared the 'fourth beast' in Dan 7 with the Ugaritic *lôtān*. This comparison has been refuted by DAY (1985:152, 177).

IV. The post-biblical career of Leviathan developed in two directions: one, which may be termed naturalistic and de-mythologizing, identified him with a whale (*kētos*, as LXX Job 3:8); the other, apocalyptic and more influential, continued to consider him a dragon (Heb *tnyn*, Aram *tnyn'* or Gk *drakōn*, as LXX Job 40:25). According to *1 Enoch* 60:7-9, 24 Leviathan is a female dragon located at the bottom of the sea above(!) the sources, while Behemoth is a male dragon living in the desert; both will be prepared for the meal of the righteous at the eschatological banquet, an opinion shared by *2 Apoc. Bar.* 29:4 and the Rabbis (cf. also 4 Ezra 6:49-52). The fact that 'Leviathan' is a name identifying an individual being facilitated the relative continuity of the mythological imagination, attested by the incantatory tradition, in *Apoc. Abr.* 21:4 where Leviathan still appears as a monster having the sea as his domain and aiming to destroy the earth, right up to modern times.

V. *Bibliography*

T. BINGER, Fighting the Dragon. Another Look at the Theme in the Ugaritic Texts *SJOT* 6 (1992) 139-149; A. M. BISI, L'idra. Antecedenti figurativi orientali di un mito greco, *Cahiers de Byrsa* 10 (1964-65) 21-42; A. CAQUOT, Le Léviathan de Job 40,25–41,26, *RB* 99 (1992) 40-69; *J. DAY, *God's Conflict with the Dragon and the Sea* (UCOP 35; Cambridge 1985); J. EBACH, *Leviathan und Behemoth* (Philosophische Positionen 2, Paderborn 1984); J. A. EMERTON, Leviathan and Ltn: The Vocalization of the Ugaritic Word for Dragon, *VT* 32 (1982) 327-331; G. FUCHS, *Mythos und Hiobdichtung. Aufnahme und Umdeutung altorientalischer Vorstellungen* (Stuttgart/Berlin/Köln 1993); C. H. GORDON, Leviathan: Symbol of Evil, *Biblical Motifs. Origins and Transformations* (ed. A. Altmann; Cambridge MA 1966) 1-9; *O. KEEL, *Jahwes Entgegnung an Ijob* (FRLANT 121; Göttingen 1978) esp. 141-156; *KEEL, *Das Recht der Bilder, gesehen zu werden* (OBO 122; Fribourg/Göttingen 1992) esp. 209-222; *E. LIPIŃSKI, לִוְיָתָן liwjāṯān, *TWAT* 4 (1983) 521-527; T. PODELLA, Der 'Chaoskampfmythos' im Alten Testament. Eine Problemanzeige, *Mesopotamica–Ugaritica–Biblica* (FS K. Bergerhof; Kevelaer & Neukirchen-Vluyn 1993) 283-329; C. UEHLINGER, Leviathan und die Schiffe in Ps 104,25-26, *Bib* 71 (1990) 499-526; M. K. WAKEMAN, *God's Battle with the Monster* (Leiden 1973) esp. 62-68; E. WILLIAMS-FORTE, The Snake and the Tree in the Iconography and Texts of Syria during the Bronze Age, *Ancient Seals and the Bible* (Malibu, CA 1983) 18-43.

C. UEHLINGER

LIBRA מאזנים

I. The Hebrew word for the sign Libra is *mō'zĕnayim* and the Aram is *mō'znayā'*. They derive from an original root WDN/WZN; Ar *wazana* 'to ponder', Ug *mzn* 'weight', *mznm* 'scales', Ar *mīzān* 'scales' (*Ges.*[18] 1, 30). The term has a secondary derivation from Heb *'ōzen*, 'ear', which KB, 25 considers mistaken; it is also associated with Heb *'āzēn*, 'tool'. The Jewish Aramaic forms מודנא, מוזניא and מוזנון which mean 'scales' are also found.

The Hebrew term occurs 15 times in the Bible, especially in poetic and prophetic language, and the Aramaic term occurs once in Dan 5:27. They mean scales (with the two pans). מאזנים also appears in Sir 42:4 and מ(ו)זנים in 1QIsa[a] 40:12 still meaning scales. The biblical contexts in which the terms appear place considerable emphasis on divine and human justice and they stress the ethical value of proper conduct (e.g. Job 31:6). The image of the soul weighed on the scales appears in apocryphal literature: e.g. *1 Enoch* 41:1; 61:8; *2 Enoch* 49:2 (see NORTH 1984: cols. 614-616).

As a constellation of the zodiac, Libra has been involved in a process of deification in ancient Mesopotamian literature. In the Hebrew traditions, however, there are no evident traces of a specific divine status.

II. *Mō'zĕnayim* means Libra (the Latin word for scales), the sign of the zodiac, only in post-biblical literature, though the zodiac was in all likelihood already known to the Israelites in biblical times. The Hebrew names for the signs of the zodiac are in any case a translation of the parallel Greek terms. The word Libra has a calendaric origin as it alludes to the equilibrium between night and day (equinox; BOLL, BEZOLD & GUNDEL 1966[5]:52). It was included in the zodiac in Babylonian times, by the Mesopotamians, but there are many indications in later times that it was described as 'the claws' of the great Scorpio: Ptolemy was the most prominent person to have used this denomination.

The notion of the zodiac spread rapidly in the Jewish cultural tradition owing to Hellenism. Moreover, this is one of the motifs that appeared most frequently in the iconography of synagogues in Israel of the early centuries CE (4th-7th). In their mosaic floors and elsewhere, such as the Palmyra ceiling, Libra is always depicted as a person holding the scales in his right hand. In Greece and Egypt too the scales are sometimes held by a male or female figure. (In some cases in the synagogues in Israel the word is written מוזנים and not מאזנים.) The names of the signs of the zodiac have found their way into literature of the mystical currents, in rabbinical writings and particularly in the Piyyut, the liturgical poetry.

In Hekhalot literature the sign of Libra is mentioned in a Geniza fragment of *3 Enoch* (SCHÄFER 1988:15/ב2 G 12 [Geniza, fr. 12, 2b, 15. T.-S. K 21.95.L.]). In the *Sefer Yeṣira*, chap. V, we read "He made the letter Lamed reign, He intertwined it with a crown and formed מאזנים in the universe, Tishri in the year and the liver in living creatures". Libra is therefore associated with the letter Lamed, the North-West corner, action, the month of Tishri (September-October), the liver (in other mss. the colon). *Leviticus Rabba* 29:8 (comment on Lev 17:29-30 with Ps 62:10: "When they go up on the scales"): "In fact they are pardoned during Libra (that is to say) the month in which the constellation is Libra. Which month has Libra as its constellation? It is the month of Tishri, which means: You can dissolve (*tišre*), pardon and remit our sins. In fact (this happens) on Rosh Hashana, in the seventh month, on the first day of the month". *Pesiqta Rabbati* 40:7 (comment on the sound of the Shofar "in the seventh month"): "This is what is written (in Ps 62:10), "Oh how trifling men are, human beings are a falsehood. When they go up on the scales, together they are less than dust". What is "How trifling"? It means that (all) trifles and (all) lies that Israel has pronounced on all the days of the year will be charged to them "when they go up on the scales", in the seventh month under the sign of the zodiac Libra, מאזנים. (What does Tishri mean?) According to R. (Ḥiyya) ben Marya (who quotes R. Levi, it means): You dissolve (*tišre*) and pardon our sins (as though they were lighter than a breath). When? Just in the seventh month".

According to the *Yalqut Šimʿoni* (Exod 418) the standards of the 12 tribes correspond to the signs of the zodiac: in the west are stationed Ephraim, Manasseh and Benjamin with Libra, Scorpio and Sagittarius. (For a further list of references, see BEN YEHUDA 1960: IV 2759-2760.)

The rabbinical interpretation that connects the instrument of the scales with the constellation is based principally on Ps 62:10, and in particular on the term לעלות ('to go up'). Libra can not be said to have ever been a real deity in its own right in the Hebrew tradition (if we exclude the deification process that has involved the →stars in general and the presumable sanctification of the zodiacal constellations in particular during a certain period). Some allegorical links have been established between biblical concepts and this sign of the zodiac (as with other signs). In this particular case the symbol of justice is exalted.

III. *Bibliography*

E. BEN YEHUDA, *Thesaurus totius Hebraitatis*, 4 (New York/London 1960) 2759-2760; F. BOLL, C. BEZOLD & W. GUNDEL, *Sternglaube und Sterndeutung. Die Geschichte und das Wesen der Astrologie* (Stuttgart 1966^5) 7, 51-52; L. IDELER, *Untersuchungen über den Ursprung und die Bedeutung der Sternnamen* (Berlin 1809) 174-178; IDELER, *Über den Ursprung des Thierkreises* (Berlin 1838) 10-11; R. NORTH, מֹאזְנַיִם, *TWAT* 4 (1984) 614-616; G. SARFATTI, I segni dello zodiaco nell'iconografia ebraica, *Scritti in onore di Umberto Nahon* (ed. R. Bonfil *et al.*; Jerusalem 1978) 180-195; P. SCHÄFER, *Konkordanz zur Hekhalot-Literatur*, 2 (Tübingen 1988) 390.

I. ZATELLI

LIERS IN WAIT מארבים

I. In 2 Chr 22, Ammonites, Moabites and people of Mount Seir who have invaded Judah, are routed when the LORD sets 'liers in wait' (מארבים) against them. The 'liers in wait' are clearly not Judahites, and there is no reason to posit a third human party in the conflict. Most commentators have recognized that the reference is to a heavenly force (see RUDOLPH 1955:261; WILLIAMSON 1982:300).

II. "Liers in wait" is not the name of a group of →angels, but simply indicates a function of a batallion of the heavenly host. For the intervention of the heavenly host in time of battle compare Josh 1:13-15 (the prince of the army of the LORD); 2 Sam 5:24 (a sound of marching in the tops of the trees); 2 Kgs 6:16 (the mountainside filled with horses and fiery chariots around Elisha); 2 Kgs 7:5-7 (a sound of chariots and horses); 2 Kgs 19:35 (the angel of the LORD in the Assyrian camp).

III. *Bibliography*

E. L. CURTIS & A. L. MADSEN, *The Book of Chronicles* (New York, 1910) 409; R. B. DILLARD, *2 Chronicles* (WBC 15; Waco, Texas, 1987) 15; W. RUDOLPH, *Chronikbücher* (HAT 21; Tübingen, 1955) 261; H. G. WILLIAMSON, *1 & 2 Chronicles* (New Century Bible; Grand Rapids, 1982) 300.

J. J. COLLINS

LIES כזבים

I. The plural noun *kĕzābîm* 'lies' without any pronominal suffix is attested 10 times in the Hebrew Bible independent of any association with gods, demons or idolatry. It is widely held, however, that the form *kizbêhem* ('their lies' with third person plural pronominal suffix) in Amos 2:4, is employed there as a dysphemism referring to gods. According to this interpretation, which goes back to LXX, it is alleged there that in the middle of the 8th century BCE Judaeans abandoned the →LORD and His Teaching and reverted to the worship of other gods: "Their lies (i.e., false gods) whom their ancestors followed have led them astray".

Should this interpretation of Amos 2:4 be correct, the prophet reflects here the tradition expressed in Joshua's farewell prophecy in Josh 24:2: "In olden times your ancestors ... lived beyond the →Euphrates and worshipped other gods", namely, that worship of "other gods" had characterized Israel's ancestors before their arrival in Canaan.

The idea expressed by Amos' use of the term *kĕzābîm* 'lies' to refer to gods other than the LORD is similar to that expressed in Jer 2:13: "For My people have done a twofold wrong: They have forsaken Me, the Fount of living waters, and they have hewed out cisterns, broken cisterns, which cannot even hold water".

In Isa 28:15 the opponents of the prophet are introduced as saying " ... for we made Lie (*kāzāb*) our refuge and we take shelter in Deceit". VAN DER TOORN (1988:201-205) rightly interpreted *kāzāb* as a reference to a non-Judaean god associated with the underworld.

II. A minority of modern scholars (see HAYES 1988:101-104) maintain that the term *kĕzābîm* 'lies' in Amos 2:13 as in Isa 28:15-17; Hos 7:13; 12:1 refers not to apostasy but to foolish political alliances with foreign powers entered into by the King of Judah.

III. *Bibliography*

J. H. HAYES, *Amos* (Nashville 1988) 101-104; R. MOSIS, *kzb, TWAT* 4 (1982) 111-130; S. M. PAUL, *Amos* (Minneapolis 1991) 75; K. VAN DER TOORN, Echoes of Judaean Necromancy in Isaiah 28,7-22, *ZAW* 100 (1988) 199-217; M. WEISS, *The Book of Amos* (2 vols.; Jerusalem 1992), vol. 1, 46-47 (in Hebrew).

M. I. GRUBER

LIGHT אור

I. The Hebrew noun אור, traditionally vocalized *ʾûr* when it means 'fire', and *ʾôr* when it refers to the 'light' provided by fire, is never used as a divine name in the Bible. It occurs as a divine predicate, though, and was personified in the post-biblical period. The theophoric element אור of proper names mentioned in Aramaic inscriptions from the Persian period (L. DELAPORTE, *Epigraphes* *araméens* [Paris 1912], nos. 48-50) is a transcription of →Amurru (R. ZADOK, *On West Semites in Babylonia* [Jerusalem 1978²] 76), since in Neo-Babylonian /m/ in medial position changed to /w/, as in Shamash written *šwš* in Aramaic (I. J. GELB, *BiOr* 12 [1955] 101b). This theophoric element was reduced to *-wr* when it was in second position, as in *Prwr* (*KAI* 233:1), but *-wr* can also render Mēr, the name of the divine eponym of Mari (G. DOSSIN, *Syria* 21 [1940] 155), as in *ʾlwr* (*TSSI* II, 5, A, l), the Ilumer of the Assyro-Babylonian AN = *Anum* god list (*CT* XXIX, pl. 45:24; cf. pl. 20:7).

II. 'Light' is often used in the Bible as a divine predicate, when God is called Israel's 'light' or 'the light' of his devotee (2 Sam 22:19; Isa 10:17; 60:1; Mic 7:8; Ps 27:1). The same predicate occurs in proper names despite the vocalization *ʾûr* instead of *ʾôr*, which reveals the artificial character of this distinction. Thus, we know →Uriel, 'My light is →El', Urijah(u), 'My light is Yahweh', and the hypocoristic name Uri. The same names are also attested in epigraphical and papyrological sources (R. ZADOK, *The Pre-Hellenistic Israelite Anthroponomy and Prosopography* [Leuven 1988] 399), and they are paralleled by Amorite (I. J. GELB, *Computer-Aided Analysis of Amorite* [Chicago 1980] 208) and Phoenician personal names (F. L. BENZ, *Personal Names in the Phoenician and Punic Inscriptions* [Rome 1972] 274): *ú-ri-A-du*, 'My light is Haddu', *ú-ri-E-ra-aḫ*, 'My light is the →Moon-god', *èl-ú-ri*, 'El is my light', *ʾrbʿl*, 'My light is →Baal', *ʾr(y)mlk*, 'My light is Milku/the King'. See also the name of the servant of an alleged Ammonite king Baalisha: *mlkmʾwr* (ed. L. G. HERR, *BA* 48 [1985] 169-172). Such names and the divine predicate 'light' used in poetry are metaphors expressing the beneficial and salvific function of the deity in opposition to darkness, which symbolizes negative and destructive forces of the universe. This terminology is also used in Qumran texts. It constitutes the basis for the distinction between 'the Sons of the Light' and 'the Sons of the Darkness'. Although this division of humankind implies an ethical and theological dualism, the terms 'light' and 'darkness' can by no means be considered here as substitutes for two supernatural principles, such as Spenta Mainyu ('the Bounteous Spirit') and Angra Mainyu ('the Evil Spirit') in Zoroastrianism.

III. The divine predicate 'light' was personified in the late Persian or Hellenistic period as Uriel, 'Light of God', one of seven archangels. Perhaps Ps 104:2, describing the LORD "wrapped in a robe of light", had an influence on this evolution of Jewish thought concerning God's 'light'.

IV. *Bibliography*

S. AALEN, ʾôr, *TWAT* 1 (1973) 160-182 (bibl.); C. L. BLEEKER, Some Remarks on the Religious Significance of Light, *JANES* 5 (1973) 23-34; A. P. B. BREYTENBACH, The Connection between the Concepts of Darkness and Drought as well as Light and Vegetation, *De fructu oris sui. Essays in Honour of Adrianus van Selms* (ed. I. H. Eybers *et al.*; Leiden 1971) 1-5; J. CHMIEL, Quelques remarques sur la signification symbolique de la lumière dans la littérature de l'ancien Proche-Orient, *Folia Orientalia* 21 (1980) 221-224; J. H. EATON, Some Misunderstood Hebrew Words for God's Self-Revelation, *The Bible Translator* (1974) 331-338; B. LANGER, *Gott als "Licht" in Israel und Mesopotamien* (Klosterneuburg 1989).

E. LIPIŃSKI

LIGHTNING ברק

I. The root BRQ is common to the Semitic languages, where the nominal form refers to the meteorological phenomenon of lightning; the corresponding verb means 'to flash lightning' and is probably derived from the noun. The root occurs in the onomastica of numerous Semitic languages. As for Hebrew proper names, *Bārāq* was the Israelite commander immortalized in the Song of Deborah (Judg 5:2-31; see v 12). Josh 19:45 mentions *bĕnê bĕraq* (lit., 'sons of Beraq', apparently a geographical designation) in connexion with the territory allotted to the tribe of Dan. *Brqʾl* occurs in 6QEnGiants frg. 1:4 and *Barqāy* (with the gentilic suffix) is known from the Talmud. The root is not attested, however, in names in pre-exilic Hebr inscriptions (LAWTON:1984). As for other Semitic languages, *brq* appears in proper names in Ugaritic, Amorite, Phoenician-Punic, Palmyrene, Old South Arabic, and Akkadian. In the Neo- and Late Babylonian periods it functions as a theophorous element: *Ab-di-*dGÍR(*birqu*) (MARAQTEN 1988:146).

II. There is evidence that lightning was deified in ancient Mesopotamia, though he is never portrayed as independent of the storm-god. In the Babylonian god-list An = *Anum*, *Birqu* is called the vizier of the storm-god Adad. He is listed in the Neo-Assyrian 'Address-book of the Gods', where his name is juxtaposed to that of Adad (*Tākultu* 5 ii 17, 7 vii 8) as well as to that of Girra, god of fire (ibid., 6 ii 9, 7 vii 10). Elsewhere in this region, lightning, though not deified, was associated with the storm-god as his symbol and/or his weapon. A stylised lightning-bolt with two or three forks functioned as such a symbol in Mesopotamia (KRECHER 1971:485-486) as well as Anatolia, and north-central Arabia (HAUSSIG *WbMyth*:1:137, 209, 443). Upon conquering the Qumanians, Tiglath-Pileser I set up bronze lightning-bolts within their capital city, undoubtedly an emblem or weapon of Adad (*ARAB* §243). This recalls Adad's epithet *bēl birqi*, 'lord of the lightning-bolt' (*AfO* 14, 146, 121). A well known bas-relief of the god →Baal from Ugarit shows him holding a lightning-spear in one hand and a war-mace in the other (*ANEP* 168 No. 490; and see Baal-cycle *KTU* 1.3 iii:2).

III. In the OT lightning is never deified nor does it appear as a demonic force. Rather, it is associated with the God of Israel in a 'depersonalised' form under two aspects: (a) as a weapon in the divine arsenal and (b) as a standard feature of the theophany.

As in the case of Adad and Baal, lightning functions as a weapon of →Yahweh in his role as warrior/storm-god. In poetic texts in which storm language is present, Yahweh's 'arrows' refer to the lightning-shafts he hurls at his enemies: "He sent forth (his) *arrows* and routed them // (his) *lightning* and panicked them" (2 Sam 22:15 = Ps 18:15; cf. Pss 7:14; 77:18; 144:6; Zech 9:14). In Hab 3:11 his lightning-bolt is called a 'spear'. Lightning also appears as an instrument of divine judgement in Job 36:32-33; Sir 43:13. In other OT texts lightning is associated with God as one of the phenomena of the theophany, often together with thunder, cloud, and earthquake. Perhaps the *locus classicus* of lightning in a theophanic context is Exod 19:16-20:18. Exod 19:16a (J) (cf. 20:18 [E]) describes "thunders and lightnings and a thick cloud upon the mountain" preparatory to Yahweh's address to Israel. Ezekiel's description of Yahweh's presence signalled by the four 'living creatures' includes the detail of lightning (Ezek 1:13), a description echoed in Rev 4:5. For Elihu lightning and thunder serve to manifest God's power in the cosmos (Job 36:29-37:5); yet even here a theophanic underlayer shines through. The cosmic dimension is also evident in Ps 97:4: "Your lightnings light up the [whole] world". The theophanic aspect of lightning persists into the NT (see Rev 4:5).

Despite the disclaimer of JEREMIAS (1965:108), the military and theophanic uses of lightning are probably related (KUNTZ 1967:171 n.3). The two appear to be integrated, for example, in Ps 77:19. The immediate context (vv 16-20) envisions a battle with primordial, watery chaos ('arrows' in v 18); but other details ('thunder', 'whirlwind', 'the earth trembled') point to a theophany.

In a yet more demythologised usage lightning describes the brightness of beings from the heavenly world in late OT books and in the NT (Ezek 1:14; Dan 10:6; Matt 28:3). The description is most likely derived from the language of theophany, but in this case the meteorological term does not function to designate the divine presence. Rather, the focus is primarily on the element of brightness itself, with the implication of an other-worldly origin.

IV. *Bibliography*
J. JEREMIAS, *Theophanie: Die Geschichte einer alttestamentlichen Gattung* (WMANT 10; Neukirchen-Vluyn 1965); J. KRECHER, Göttersymbole und -Attribute, *RLA* (1971) 483-498; J. K. KUNTZ, *The Self-Revelation of God* (Philadelphia 1967); R. LAWTON, Israelite Personal Names in Pre-exilic Hebrew Inscriptions, *Bib* 65 (1984) 332-346; M. MARAQTEN, *Die semitischen Personennamen in den alt- und reichsaramäischen Inschriften aus Vorderasien* (Texte und Studien zur Orientalistik 5; Zurich/New York 1988).

M. L. BARRÉ

LILITH לילית

I. The Heb term *lîlît* as a →demon in Isa 34:14 is connected by popular etymology with the word *laylâ* 'night'. But it is certainly to be considered a loan from Akk *lilītu*, which is ultimately derived from Sum **líl**.

II. The Mesopotamian evidence for this demon reaches back to the 3rd millennium BCE as we can see from the Sumerian epic 'Gilgamesh, Enkidu and the Netherworld'. Here we find Inanna (→Ishtar) who plants a tree later hoping to cut from its wood a throne and a bed for herself. But as the tree grows, a snake makes its nest at its roots, Anzu settled in the top and in the trunk the demon **ki-sikil-líl-lá** makes her lair. Gilgamesh has to slay the snake, Anzu and the demon flee so that he can cut down the tree and give the timber to Inanna.

From the term **líl** we can see that these demons are related to stormy winds. In Akk texts *lilû, lilītu* and *(w)ardat lilî* often occur together as three closely related demons whose dominion are the stormy winds. Thus *lilû* can also be seen as the southwest wind, *lilītu* can flee from a house through the window like the wind or people imagine that she is able to fly like a bird.

Of greater importance, however, is the sexual aspect of the—mainly—female demons *lilītu* and *(w)ardat lilî*. Thus the texts refer to them as the ones who have no husband, or as the ones who stroll about searching for men in order to ensnare them or to enter the house of a man through the window (see the references given by FAUTH 1982:60-61; LACKENBACHER 1971; HUTTER 1988:224-226). But their sexuality is not a normal kind of sexuality because *(w)ardat lilî* is a girl with whom a man does not sleep in the same way as with his wife, as the texts tell us. In this aspect we can compare these demons with Ishtar who stands at the window looking for a man in order to seduce him, love him and kill him. The fact that Lilith's sexuality is not a regular kind of sexuality is also illustrated by references which show that she cannot bear children and that she has no milk but only poison when she gives her breast as a deceitful wet-nurse to the baby. In all these aspects Lilith has a character similar to that of Lamashtu. Thus, since the Middle Babylonian period Lilith and Lamashtu have been assimilated to each other. This also led to the spreading of Lilith from the Mesopotamian to the Syrian area. The traditional reading of Arslan Tash amulet I (*ANET* 658) suggests that she was revered in Phoenicia. A reconsideration of the original, however, forces a reading *ll wym* 'night and day' instead of *lly*[... 'Lili[th ... (BUTTERWECK *TUAT* II/3:437). Aramaic magical texts and the scriptures of the Mandaeans in southern Mesopotamia have clear allusions to the demon (FAUTH 1986). In conclusion we can say that the female demon—*lilītu, (w)ardat lilî*)—can be considered a young girl who has not reached maturity and thus has to stroll about ceaselessly in search of a male companion. Sexually unfulfilled, she is the perpetual seductress of men.

III. The only reference to this demon in the OT occurs in Isa 34:14. The whole chapter describes the prophetic judgement on →Edom which will become waste land. Then all kinds of demons will dwell there: among them hyenas, tawny owls, vultures and also Lilith. The different versions and ancient translations of the OT are of some interest in this case as we can see how they interpreted 'Lilith'. The LXX gives the translation ὀνοκένταυρος (cf. also LXX Isa 13:22; 34:11), Aquila's version has the transliteration Λιλιθ, while Symmachos' version gives the name of the Greek demon Λαμία, which corresponds to Jerome's Vulgate (also *Lamia*). In his commentary Jerome says: "Lamia, who is called Lilith in Hebrew. (...) And some of the Hebrews believe her to be an Ἔριννυς, i. e. fury". Still, these translations and interpretations of Lilith show her ancient connection to Lamashtu. The *onokentauros* of the LXX reminds us of those amulets where Lamashtu is standing upon a donkey. The Greek name Lamia might ultimately derive from Akkadian Lamashtu.

Although Isa 34 contains the only biblical reference to Lilith, she occurs fairly often in Jewish and Christian scriptures (KREBS 1975; BRIL 1984). In the Talmud she is a demon with long hair and wings (*Erub.* 100b; *Nid.* 24b), and *Shab.* 151b warns all men not to sleep alone in a house lest Lilith will overcome them. *B. Bat.* 73a makes her the daughter of Ahreman, the opponent of Ohrmizd in the Zoroastrian religion. Well known is also the legend of Lilith who was →Adam's first wife but flew away from him after a quarrel; since then she has been danger to little children and people have to protect themselves against her by means of amulets. Solomon in his great wisdom also possessed might over demons and the Liliths; in later Jewish legends one of the two wives from 1 Kgs 3:16-28 was identified with Lilith; so was the Queen of Sheba (1 Kgs 10).

Such legends spread until the Middle Ages. In popular belief Lilith became not only the grandmother of the →devil or the devil himself, but also the arch-mother of witchcraft and witches.

IV. *Bibliography*

J. BRIL, *Lilith ou la Mère obscure* (Paris 1984); W. FARBER, (W)ardat-lilî(m), *ZA* 79 (1989) 14-35; W. FAUTH, Lilītu und die Eulen von Pylos, *Serta Indogermanica. Festschrift für Günter Neumann* (ed. J. Tischler; Innsbruck 1982) 53-64; FAUTH, Lilits und Astarten in aramäischen, mandäischen und syrischen Zaubertexten, *WO* 17 (1986) 66-94; M. HUTTER, Dämonen und Zauberzungen. Aspekte der Magie im Alten Vorderasien, *Grenzgebiete der Wissenschaft* 37 (1988) 215-230; W. KREBS, Lilith - Adams erste Frau, *ZRGG* 27 (1975) 141-152; S. LACKENBACHER, Note sur l'*ardat lilî*, *RA* 65 (1971) 119-154; P. P. VÉRTESALJI, "La déesse nue élamite" und der Kreis der babylonischen "*Lilû*"-Dämonen, *Iranica Antiqua* 26 (1991) 101-148.

M. HUTTER

LIM

I. *Lim* occurs as a theophoric element in numerous personal names, primarily from northern Syria in the second millennium BCE. Attestations of Lim as a divine name in the Bible, though suggested, are highly dubious.

II. Among the bearers of Lim-names are *Ti-ša/šè-Li-im*, who is identified in an Eblaite text as "the queen of Emar" (MEE 2, 351), *I-bi-iṭ-Li-im*, an Eblaite king (*MAIS* [1967-1968], ll. 2.9.26), *ni-ši-Li-im*, an Ensi from Tuttul in the Ur III-period (*AfO* 19 [1959-60] 120:18), and several individuals of the Lim-Dynasty at Mari (GELB 1980). Despite the presence of Hurrian elements in a few examples and a twice-attested name from the Neo-Assyrian period containing an Akkadian element (see KREBERNIK 1990), it seems clear that the bearers of Lim-names belonged to the ethnic-cultural group known as the "Amorites".

The names appear almost exclusively in syllabic-logographic cuneiform texts. Significantly, *Lim* is ordinarily written without the determinative for divinity, the only exceptions being *ya-ku-un-*^{d}*Lim* (*OBTR*, 259), GUR*(itūr)-*^{d}*Lim* (*PRU* IV, RS 17. 394:3), and *zi-im-ri-*^{d}*Lim* (*PRU* IV, RS 17.110:2.4.7.11). The only certain example of a Lim-name written in alphabetic cuneiform is *yrgb lim* mentioned in an Ugaritic text (*KTU* 1.102:22). Among the Egyptian Execration texts, the identification of the personal name *mꜣkꜣm* as *mlklm* = **malki-Lim* seems plausible (NOTH 1942), but not the explanation of the place-name *ꜣwšꜣmm* as *rwš-lmm* "the hill of Lim"—with mimation! (JIRKU 1964).

The etymology of *Lim* is controverted. The best explanation relates it to Akk *līmu/limmu*, which may stand for *līm ilāni* "the thousand gods" (DHORME 1951). As such, the word is cognate to Hebrew *lĕʾōm* and Ugaritic *lim* "people, nation". The *līm ilāni* "thousand gods" are frequently invoked as witnesses in Syro-Hittite treaties and they are mentioned in an epistolary formula at-tested at Ugarit (NAKATA 1974). Thus, the deity *Lim* is thought to have been a personification of the entire assembly of the gods. Other scholars have suggested, however, that since Akk *līmu/limmu* is used as a title for an Assyrian high official, and since Heb *lʾmym* is sometimes rendered in the LXX as *archontes*, *lim* may have meant "Prince", and the word is to be related to the root Lʾʏ "to be strong" (GRAY 1965, 1979). The derivation of *Lim* from a III-Weak root Lʾʏ, as well as the relevance of the relatively late and unique Assyrian institution of the *līmu*, are highly questionable, however. To be rejected, too, is the explanation of *Lim* as an Amorite translation of Sumerian Dagan (→Dagon) by DOSSIN (1950)—an unlikely proposition, since Dagan is a West-Semitic word and the deity is foreign to the Sumerian pantheon. The explanation of *Lim* as a representation of the totality of the gods remains the most attractive. The root is Lʾᴍ, which is attested in classical Arabic with the meaning "fit together, assemble". It is probable that *Lim* was considered a personal god, an appropriate representative from among the gods. *Lim* may have had the same connotations as Arabic *liʾm* "fitting one, companion". This explains the name *Li-mi-*ᵈIŠKUR "My *Lim* (personal god) is Hadad".

Scholars have attempted to identify *Lim* variously with Dagan, →Baal-Hadad, →Shamash, and →Anat. Most of the arguments are extrapolations made on the basis of the traits of *Lim* suggested by the onomastica. The evidence hardly allows one to be so specific, however. Some names, like *Yabruq-Lim* may suggest a storm god (although *brq* is used of a lunar deity in Old South Arabic inscriptions; →Lightning), but others, like *Šamši-Lim* may point to a solar deity. Moreover, *Lim* occurs in kinship names like *ʾAbī-lim* and *ʾAḫī-lim*. Indeed, the majority of the traits may be appropriate for many, if not most, deities. The absence of the determinative for divinity indicates that the element *Lim* was originally a title, rather than a proper name. The appellative use of *Lim* is evident, too, where it occurs with specific divine names: *Li-ma-*ᵈ*Da-gan* (ARET 3, 290); ᵈ*Dagan-li-im* (ARET 1, 238), *Li-mi-*ᵈIŠKUR (ARM XVI/1, 146), *Li-ma-a-du* (Alt 322:7). In each case, the meaning of the name is simply, "DN is (my) *Lim*". Thus, *Lim* may not have been the same deity in every constituency and for every individual.

Apart from the personal names, there are no indisputable attestations of *Lim* as a divine appellation. Scholars have called attention to Anat's epithet, *ybmt limm* (esp. *KTU* 1.13:20), which has been taken by some to mean "the *ybmt*, Lim"—on the analogy with *btlt ʿnt* "the Virgin, Anat"—and by others to mean "the *ybmt* of Lim". This designation of Anat, however, occurs at least ten times in Ugaritic, always with *limm*, instead of *lim*—as in the only indisputable occurrence of that divine appellation in Ugaritic (*yrgb lim* in *KTU* 102.22). One should probably take *ybmt limm* to mean "the *ybmt* of the Nations" or, better yet, "the *ybmt* of the thousand (gods)"—even as Baal, Anat's male counterpart, is said to be *ybm lilm* "the *ybm* of the gods" in *KTU* 1.6 i:31 (WALLS 1992).

III. It has been suggested that if the problematic occurrence of *lmw* in Deut 33:2 (vocalized as *lāmô* in the MT) were emended to *lm*, and the word is then interpreted as *Lim*, a designation for →YHWH, we would have an instance of the appellation in the Bible (LIPIŃSKI 1967). The emendation has failed to convince, however. One should expect the form *lʾm* instead of *lm*. Likewise, the proposal that *lĕmûʾēl* in Prov 31:1 (cf. the variant *lĕmôʾēl* in v 4) is a

Lim-name cannot be sustained (JIRKU 1954). There are no clear attestations of Lim as a divine appellation in the Bible.

IV. *Bibliography*

*E. DHORME, Les Amorrhéens, *Recueil Édouard Dhorme: Études bibliques et orientales* (Paris 1951) 405-487; G. DOSSIN, Le panthéon de Mari, *Studia Mariana* (Leiden 1950) 49-50; DOSSIN, A propos du dieu Lim, *Syria* 55 (1978) 327-332; I. J. GELB, *Computer-Aided Analysis of Amorite* (AS 21; Chicago 1980) 313; J. GRAY, *The Legacy of Canaan* (Leiden 1965) 40; GRAY, The Bloodbath of the Goddess Anat, *UF* 11 (1979) 315-324; H. B. HUFFMON, *Amorite Personal Names in the Mari Texts* (Baltimore 1964) 226-227; A. JIRKU, Bemerkungen zu einigen syrisch-palästinischen Namen in ägyptischer Schrift, *ArOr* 32 (1964) 354-357; JIRKU, Das n. pr. Lemuel (Prov 31:1) und der Gott Lim, *ZAW* 66 (1954) 151; *M. KREBERNIK, Lim, *RLA* 7 (1990) 25-27; E. LIPIŃSKI, Le dieu Lim. *La civilisation de Mari* (CRRA 15; ed. J.-R. Kupper; Paris 1967) 151-160; M. NOTH, Die syrisch-palästinische Bevölkerung des Zweiten Jahrtausends v. Chr. im Lichte neuer Quellen, *ZDPV* 65 (1942) 9-67; I. NAKATA, *Deities in the Mari Texts* (diss. Columbia 1974) 344-353; W. RÖLLIG, Der Gott Lim im amoritischen Pantheon, *BZ* 12 (1968) 123-127; N. H. WALLS, *The Goddess Anat in Ugaritic Myth* (Atlanta 1992) 94-107.

C. L. SEOW

LINOS Λίνος

I. Linos is a minor Greek hero who is the personification of a cry in laments, *ailinon*, itself probably of oriental origin (CHANTRAINE 1980). As a theophorous name, it occurs only once in the NT (2 Tim 4:21).

II. The personification of the ritual cry *ailinon* is already found in Hesiod (fr. 305-306), where Linos is called the son of the Muse Urania; other genealogies mention the Muses Calliope, Terpsichore and Euterpe (HENRICHS 1975:14; 1984:55). Hesiod also connects him with singers and players of the *kithara* and we find this connection in various myths, which vary considerably because the absence of a specific cultplace prevented the birth of one authoritative myth. The mythological traditions seem to have focused on Argos and Thebes. In Argos, where the song is set, Linos was considered to have been the son of →Apollo and the local princess Psamathe. Here the women and maidens yearly lamented his death as a young boy, as he had been torn apart by the hounds of his grandfather, during a special, if rather obscure (BURKERT 1983:107-108), festival (VON WILAMOWITZ 1937; add Callimachus fr. 26-31a). It was also in the Argive funeral games for Pelias that Linos gained the first prize in singing (Hyginus 273.10-11).

The connection with music we find in Thebes, which evidently had claimed Linos as its native hero. The oldest tradition made Linos the music teacher of →Heracles who in a fit of anger killed him, after he had been smacked by his teacher. The scene was very popular on Attic red-figure vases of the earlier fifth century (BOARDMAN 1992) and also the subject of various comedies (Alexis fr. 140; Anaxandrides fr. 16) and a satyr play (Achaeus *TGrF* 20 F 26). A later Theban tradition told about his *agon* with Apollo, who defeated and killed him (WEILER 1974:63-66). The myth is clearly modelled on other myths about musicians challenging the gods, such as Marsyas and Apollo or Thamyris and the Muses (WEILER 1974:37-100).

Before the end of the third century BC Linos was listed as a sage and a cosmogonical poem was ascribed to him, which has only fragmentarily survived (WEST 1983:56-67). Later sources continuously expanded his role in music by making him the inventor of music intruments, rhythm, song and, eventually, of music (KROLL 1927:716). Linos now could even become the father of Eros (*SEG* 26.486). Linos did not have a permanent cult, but he received a prelimi-nary sacrifice on Mount Helikon, where Pausanias (9.29.5-6) saw his cult relief, before the one to the Muses, with whom he was so closely connected (above; add *SEG* 33.303).

III. In the Bible the name Linos occurs only once (2 Tim 4:21). The name is rare before the Roman period and may point to artistic pretentions of Linos' father.

IV. *Bibliography*

J. BOARDMAN, Linos, *LIMC* VI.1 (1992) 290; W. BURKERT, *Homo Necans* (Berkeley/Los Angeles/London 1983); P. CHANTRAINE, *Dictionnaire étymologique de la langue grecque* (Paris 1968-80); H. GREVE, Linos, *ALGRM* 2.2 (ed. W. H. Roscher; Leipzig 1894-1897) 2053-2063; A. HENRICHS, Philodems "De Pietate" als mythographische Quelle, *Cronache Ercolanesi* 5 (1975) 5-38; HENRICHS, Ein neues Likymniosfragment bei Philodem, *ZPE* 57 (1984) 53-57; W. KROLL, Linos, PW 13 (1927) 715-717; I. WEILER, *Der Agon im Mythos* (Darmstadt 1974); M. L. WEST, *The Orphic Poems* (Oxford 1983); U. VON WILAMOWITZ-MOELLENDORFF, *KS* V 2 (Berlin 1937) 108-113.

J. N. BREMMER

LIONESS לבאת

I. *Lb't* (fem. of *lb'*) occurs as a divine name or as a theophoric element in Canaanite personal names outside the Bible in the 2nd half of the 2nd millennium. The name of the deity, as part of a theophoric name *'bdlb't*, is engraved on five arrowheads found at el-Khadr, north-west of Bethlehem, and dated around 1100 BCE, but two occurrences are wrongly engraved: *'bdlbt* (II) and *'bdl't* (IV). It is found also on cuneiform tablets of the LB II strata at Ugarit, *'bdlbit* (see GORDON 1965:n° 321 III 38, p. 209 = *KTU* 4.63). The cult of the lioness deity is also attested in south-west Canaan for the same period by a biblical toponym mentioned in Josh 15:32 and 19:6 as *(byt) lb'wt*, but with a secondary late Hebrew pluralisation in the Bible against the accurate and original Canaanite orthography and spelling. The deity occurs also in Babylonian and Assyrian personal names and in cuneiform texts in Old Akkadian, Old Babylonian, and Standard Babylonian: *Labbatu*.

II. Given the evidence at present, it appears that the lioness goddess is attested in the West Semitic area mainly during the 2nd half of the 2nd millennium BCE in theophoric names at Ugarit and el-Khadr; the origin of the biblical toponym is much more difficult to establish. The editors of the el-Khadr engraved arrow-heads have already noticed some parallel anthroponyms on el-Khadr and Ruweiseh javelins and in the lists of military men at Ugarit (*'bdlbit, bn 'nt, 'ky*), and suggested the existence of a mercenary body of soldiers, mainly of bowmen, in Syria-Palestine during the LB II - early Iron I Periods. Thus, despite the migrations and changes of ruling classes, the profession survived because it was hereditary among certain families (see also the toponym *byt 'nwt* [wrongly spelled with plural fem.] south of Bethlehem).

This evidence tells us something about the identity, character and role of the deity among the West Semites, although the lioness could have been the animal of three chief Canaanite goddesses: →Asherah, →Astarte and →Anat. Under the epithet *Qudšu*, Asherah is represented standing on a lion on numerous Egyptian stelae dedicated to her, together with →Min and →Resheph. But Asherah is first of all a fertility goddess and for the anthroponyms of bowmen families a war deity is rather to be expected. Both goddesses Anat and Ashtoreth are usually characterized as war goddesses in the Canaanite and Egyptian texts and representations. They are the patronesses of chariot-warriors; the interest of Anat in the composite bow is well depicted in the Aqhat epic. In later times in Egypt, Ištart is frequently represented as a lioness-headed figure, or in the form of a sphinx. She is assimilated to the goddess Sekhmet and considered as a healing deity (see DE WIT 1951:368 and notes).

In Mesopotamia, the association of the goddess Ishtar with a lion(ess) is well documented by texts (e.g Nabonid, Stamboul Stela III) as well as by representations like the rocky reliefs of Maltaia (F. THUREAU-DANGIN, *RA* 21 [1924] 187,194-195), the stele of Tell Aḥmar (F. THUREAU-DANGIN & M. DUNAND, *Til Barsip* [Paris 1936] Pl XIV 1) and by a number of cylinder-seals.

The goddess is sometimes qualified as, or named, a lioness, for instance in the Old Babylonian hymn of Agušaya: *la-ba-tu Ištar* (V. SCHEIL, *RA* 15 [1918] 181, viii:24), or designated in a hymnic passage as *la-ab-bat* ^{d}*I-gi-gi*, "the lioness among the Igigi". Some vocabularies from Nineveh mention a lioness goddess (^{d}*La-ba-tu*) identified with Ishtar (CT XXIV 41:83; XXV 17 ii:22, see THUREAU-DANGIN 1940:105). But in Akkadian, *Labbatu* is attested only as epithet of Ishtar (*CAD*, L [1973] 23). This must help for the attribution of the animal to Astarte also in the West Semitic area, a war deity as well as the goddess of love. The lion(ess) symbolizes the military character of the goddess Ishtar.

In conclusion, the cult of this epithet of the Goddess seems to be fairly well documented in the Near East and peculiarly in the West Semitic area in the second part of the second millennium BCE, despite the lack of abundant textual documentation.

III. The deity had a Canaanite cultic place in the south-west of Judah, *(byt) lb'wt*, Josh 15:32 and 19:6.

IV. *Bibliography*

F. M. CROSS, Newly Found Inscriptions in Old Canaanite and Early Phoenician Scripts, *BASOR* 238 (1980) 1-20; C. DE WIT, *Le rôle et le sens du lion dans l'Egypte ancienne* (Leiden 1951); C. H. GORDON, *Ugaritic Textbook* (AnBib 38; Rome 1965); J. T. MILIK & F. M. CROSS, Inscribed Javelin-Heads from the Period of the Judges: A Recent Discovery in Palestine, *BASOR* 134 (1954) 5-15; E. PUECH, Origine de l'alphabet, *RB* 93 (1986) 161-213, esp. 163-167; F. THUREAU-DANGIN, Une tablette bilingue de Ras Shamra, *RA* 37 (1940) 97-118.

E. PUECH

LOGOS Λόγος

I. Logos (usually translated 'Word', sometimes also 'Reason') plays a central role in Greek thought, and is frequently associated with divinity. In the LXX the phrase the 'logos of →God' or the 'logos of the LORD' occurs frequently, mainly in the prophetic books. In Hellenistic-Jewish thought there is much theological speculation on the nature of God's Logos, whereby it is often associated with →Wisdom. In the NT the Logos makes a dramatic appearance in the Prologue to John's Gospel, where it is once called *theos* (1:1). Both Judaeo-Hellenistic and Johannine Logos theology is further developed in early Christian thought.

In order to come to terms with the wide range of meaning associated with the personified or theologized Logos (on which the treatment in this article concentrates), it is necessary to look more closely at the word itself. The Greek word is derived from the root *leg-*, meaning (1) to 'gather' or 'count' and (2) to 'speak'. From the former the noun comes to mean: ratio, proportion, order; from the latter a wider spectrum of meaning results: moving from concrete to abstract we may mention: word, saying, account, oracle, speech, conversation, dialogue, definition, argument, theory, reason or rationality (see W. K. C. GUTHRIE, *A History of Greek Philosophy* [Cambridge 1962–81] 1.419–424, STEAD 1991:§1). The meanings of the word most relevant to the divine are 'reason' (i.e. divine thought), 'speech' (divine revelation), and 'order' (divine activity).

II. In the enigmatic fragments of Heraclitus (ca. 500 BCE) *logos* means in the first place the account or explanation of the philosopher (fr. 1–2, 50 Diels-Kranz). It is claimed, however, that the account has a universal validity: all is one in a dynamic unity of opposites. The *logos* thus corresponds to the order or structure of the world of experience. The unity of opposites is predicated of a supreme deity: fr. 67, 'the god: day night summer winter war peace satiety famine—all opposites...—and it takes on various forms, such as fire'. It is but a short step to regarding this world-embracing immanent deity as the Logos. Whether Heraclitus actually took this step is debated, but the identification was certainly made by later ancient interpreters (cf. KIRK, RAVEN & SCHOFIELD 1983:187–200). In Stoic thought *logos* is one of the most important terms used to describe the active principle, also known as →Zeus, Reason, →Pronoia, Fate etc. (cf. Diogenes Laertius 7.134, 136). God as the Logos is the creative principle that pervades the entire universe and is responsible for its rational structure and ordered purposeful development (PÉPIN 1987; TODD 1978). In physical terms it is identified with a special kind of fire or later with *pneuma* (mixture of fire and air). The creative principle is also described as being present in the form of *spermatikoi logoi* (seed or sperm principles) in matter. The Logos is thus present at various levels in the universe, including most importantly the human soul. All these levels form a unity in the active principle. In the most famous extant text of Stoic piety, Cleanthes' *Hymn to Zeus*, the Logos is twice referred to (SVF 1.537): "with your thunderbolt you direct the common reason (*logos*) which passes through all things" (12–13); "you have welded all things together so thoroughly into one, the good with the bad, that they have all become one universal everlasting reason (*logos*)" (20-21). The Logos thus represents the cosmic activity of the all-pervading deity identified with Zeus.

Earlier the concept of *logos* played an important role in the philosophy of Plato and Aristotle in the meaning of human or divine reason, but was not used there as a name or a description of a cosmological principle. When outlining the reasoning activity of the World-soul, Plato describes it as 'true *logos*' (*Tim.* 37b), but the World-soul as such is not so called. In the Platonic revival which begins at the turn of the era, there is a ten-dency to describe the activity of the cosmic soul in terms that are highly reminiscent of Stoic doctrine, with the important difference that Soul, though spatially distended, never has a material composition. For example, Atticus "identifies Providence, Nature and the World Soul, and, although the Logos is not directly mentioned, it is that in fact that is the unifying concept" (DILLON 1977:252 on fr. 8). Characteristic of Middle Platonism is a two-level theology. The highest god is *Nous* (mind), fully transcendent and engaged in pure (i.e. intuitive) thought. At a lower level is the World-soul, whose intelligence is directed towards Nous, so that it can effortlessly order and administer the cosmos. This is the level of *logos*, i.e. discursive reasoning. The Neopythagorean philosopher Numenius (ca. 150 CE) explicitly distinguished between a first god and a second god. In Plutarch Platonist ideas are used to expound the Egyptian →Isis and →Osiris myth. Oriris as masculine ordering principle is equated with the Logos (*Mor.* 371B, 373B, but in the latter text somewhat confusingly →Hermes is also aligned with the Logos). Isis the female receptive principle yearns for him (372E–F). The soul of Osiris is said to remain eternal, whereas his body is torn to pieces by →Typhon (373A). The Logos here has a transcendent aspect (reason focused on the transcendent realm) as well as an immanent aspect (reason as ordering principle in the material world). The most systematic use of the concept of Logos by a Platonist philosopher is found in Plotinus. He denies that it is an independent hypostasis like Nous or Soul, but uses it as a metaphysical principle to describe the activity or productivity of an hypostasis at a lower level, and especially of Soul operating as Nature in the material realm (cf. R. T. WALLIS, *Neoplatonism* [London 1972] 68). Middle Platonist 'Logos theology', though not well developed, was important for early Christian thinkers, who were able to exploit it in their reflections on the cosmic role of →Christ the Logos (cf. LILLA 1971; DILLON 1989).

A number of gods in Greek and Hellenistic religion are associated with *logos* (LEISEGANG 1926:1061–69). Chief among them is Hermes, of whom Cornutus in his first century CE theological handbook says (§16): "Hermes represents the Logos, whom the gods sent down to us from heaven, when they made man alone of all living beings on earth a rational creature, a characteristic which they themselves regard as superior to all others." Hermes' allegorical association with *logos* is also encouraged by the fact that he is the messenger of the gods (*logos* also means 'speech'). In Egypt, Hermes was identified with the god →Thoth. In the *Corpus Hermeticum* philosophical speculation on the Logos is combined in a remarkable way with Greek and Egyptian religious doctrines. The Logos is both a creative principle that proceeds forth in matter from the highest principle Mind (Nous) and also an instrument of revelation (cf. KROLL 1914: 55–62, KLEINKNECHT 1967:88). In the *Poimandres* (*CH* 1) the Logos is also called 'son of God'. It is possible that this treatise is influenced by Jewish Logos speculation (C. H. DODD, *The Bible and the Greeks* [London 1954^2]).

Although the Logos has a rich history in Greek thought as a philosophical principle and is often associated with the divine (whether in general or with specific deities), it is not personified as an *independent* deity, and is not the object of cultic worship in the form of statues or altars (in contrast to personified gods such as →Dikē, Moira, →Tychē, Heimarmenē, →Pronoia). The reason for this may be the generality and abstract nature of Logos as rational or creative principle. In the meaning of word or speech it can be less abstract, e.g. in the revelation of a mystery (cf. examples in KLEINKNECHT 86), but in this case it is always associated with a particular deity or religious tradition.

III. In the biblical tradition *logos* first occurs in the LXX, where it is frequently (but not exclusively) used to translate *dābār* in the Hebrew Bible (more details in TOBIN 1992:349). The expression 'word of God' (*logos tou theou*) is comparatively rare (7x), but the phrase 'word of the Lord' (*logos tou kyriou*) is very frequent (179x). Both are almost always used in a prophetic context, where *logos* receives a more dynamic connotation than is customary in Greek thought (e.g. Isa 2:3 "And the Word of the Lord shall go forth from Jerusalem…"). An isolated but significant text is found at Ps 32:4–6 [MT 33:4–6]: "For the *logos* of the Lord is straight, and all his works are done in faithfulness… By the *logos* of the Lord the heavens were established, and all their power is in the breath of his mouth." Here there seems to be a direct reference to the repeated use of 'and God said' in the creation account of Genesis 1. God's *logos* is associated with action rather than rationality (cf. also Ps 147:4,7 [MT 15,18]), and is in no way yet regarded as in any way independent from God himself.

The theme is continued in the Wisdom literature. In a number of texts Sirach associates God's *logos* with the creation and maintainance of the creational order (39:17, 31; 43:10, 26). *Logos* is linked with the more prominent theme of Wisdom (Sophia), who is regarded as God's instrument in creation (Prov 8:22–31, Sir 24). In Wisdom theology a clear separation is made between God and His Wisdom: Prov 8:22 "God established me as beginning (*archē*) of his ways to brings about his works;" 8:30 "I was beside him bringing things together, and I was the one in whom he delighted" (translation of LXX text). Wisdom thus becomes an *hypostasis* (a self-subsistent entity), independent of God, but remaining very closely associated with Him (cf. PÉPIN 1987:10–11).

In the intertestamental period God's Logos becomes a central theme in Hellenistic Judaism. Unfortunately most of this literature is lost, so that it is difficult to follow its development. Aristobulus (2nd century BCE) affirms that according to Moses the entire genesis of the cosmos represents the words (*logoi*) of God because he writes in each case "and God said, and it came to pass" (Gen 1 *passim*). In the Wisdom of Solomon (first century BCE) creation of the world and of man is attributed mainly to God's wisdom but also to God's *logos* (esp. 9:1–2). But the concept of the divine Logos achieves the greatest prominence in the writings of Philo of Alexandria (ca. 15 BCE – 50 CE). Because he is well versed in Greek thought, Philo is able to exploit the various philosophical connotations of the concept in his exegesis of Mosaic scripture (WEISS 1966; WINSTON 1985; RUNIA 1986). It is clear, however, that he also makes use of earlier Alexandrian exegetical traditions, which make it difficult to distil a systematic and consistent Logos doctrine from his works (cf. TOBIN 1983:57–77). The following main characteristics of the divine Logos can be listed (important texts in WINSTON 1981:87–102). (1) The Logos contains or is the divine intelligible plan of the cosmos (cf. *Opif.* 16–25). (2) The Logos represents God's activity in the cosmos and embraces God's two chief powers of goodness and justice (cf. *Cher.* 27–30). (3) The Logos is God's instrument in creation (cf. *Leg. All.* 3.96; at *Her.* 134, 140 described as the Logos-cutter). (4) The Logos is the bond of the universe, providentially maintaining its order (*Plant.* 8–10). (5) Through his reason man is related to God as the image of God's Logos (*Opif.* 25, 69, *Her.* 231, exegesis of Gen. 1:26–27), and on account of this relationship can attain to the knowledge and vision of God (though not of His essence). It cannot be denied that Philo personifies the Logos when talking about him, but it remains difficult to interpret the extent to which he accords him separate existence. In many texts the Logos represents God's presence or activity in the world, so that the distinction between God and Logos is more conceptual than real. There are other texts, however, in which the Logos is presented as an *hypostasis* separate from and ontologically inferior to God Himself. The Logos is God's chief messenger (→*archangelos*), standing on the borderline between creator and creation, himself neither created nor uncreated but intermediate (*Her.* 205–6). In other texts he is called 'first-born →son of God' (*Conf.* 146, *Somn.* 1.215) or →'Man of God' (*Conf.* 41, 63, 146) or 'second to God' (*Leg. All.* 2.86). These texts were avidly seized upon by later Christian readers (RUNIA 1993). It is significant, however, that Philo generally refrains from describing the Logos as a 'second God' (exception at *QG* 2.62), thus avoiding a hierarchical theology such as was developed in Middle Platonism. Although personified to a greater extent than in Greek thought, the Logos remains primarily a conceptual and theological construct.

In the NT the term *logos* is very frequent in the sense of 'word' or 'revelation' of God as made manifest in the words and deeds of →Jesus Christ (e.g. Luke 1:2). For Paul this *logos* becomes the '*logos* of the cross' which for those who are saved is the power (→*dynamis*) of God (1 Cor 1:18). At Col 1:25 he describes his task as 'to make known the *logos* of God, the mystery hidden from ages and generations, but now revealed to the saints'. But in the personalized or hypostasized sense the Logos is found only in the Prologue to John's Gospel (1:1–18), to which reference is made in two subsequent writings of the Johannine community (1 John 1:1; Rev 19:13). The opening sentence of the Prologue (1:1) reads: "In the beginning was the Logos, and the Logos was with (the) God, and the Logos was God." The first phrase very clearly recollects both the opening words of the Torah (Gen 1:1) and the description of the pre-existent Wisdom of Prov 8:22. The second phrase emphasizes the intimacy of the Logos' relation to God (cf. Prov 8:31, also John 1:18 "in the bosom of the →Father"). The third phrase is climactic. "John intends that the whole of his gospel shall be read in the light of this verse. The deeds and words of Jesus are the deeds and words of God" (C. K. BARRETT, *The Gospel according to St. John* [London 1978²] 156). The predicative use of *theos* without the article is striking. "The Johannine hymn is bordering on the usage of "God" for the →Son, but by omitting the article it avoids any suggestion of personal identifcation of the Word with the Father. And for Gentile readers the line also avoids any suggestion that the Word was a second God in any Hellenistic sense" (R. E. BROWN, *The Gospel according to John*, [New York 1966–70] 1.24). In v 3, "all things were made through him", the cosmological aspect of Logos theology is made explicit (already implied in v 1). In v 14 the incarnation of the Logos is stated: "and the Logos became flesh and dwelt among us, and we observed his glory, glory as from the only-begotten of the Father." In v 17 follows the final identification with Jesus Christ. In v 18 the text is disputed: either 'the only-begotten Son' (*huios*) or 'the only-begotten God' (*theos*) has made the Father known. In the case of the latter reading (preferred by Nestle-Aland), there is a second reference to the deity of Christ the Logos.

There has been much debate on the background to the Evangelist's Logos doctrine. Attempts to demonstrate a Targumic or a Gnostic origin do not convince. The background is clearly to be located in Hellenistic Jewish Wisdom and Logos speculation (survey in TOBIN 1992:352–355, see also DODD 1965). A direct relation to Philo is unlikely (*pace* WOLFSON), because John's conception is theologically profound but lacks philosophical resonance. Identified with a man who 'dwelt among us' (1:14), the Logos becomes personalized beyond what had been developed in Jewish tradition. The mediatory role of the Logos, already present in Philo, is developed further. As the Son of God, the Logos has revealed God's glory (1:14) and made manifest the way to eternal life with the Father (cf. 1 John 1:2).

IV. In the Christian literature of the first two centuries, John's Gospel plays at most a minor role (STEAD 1991:§6–8). The Apologist Justin Martyr (110–165 CE) is the first Christian thinker to draw on Platonist and Philonic conceptions in his Logos theology. For Justin God is wholly transcendent. It is the Logos, the pre-existent Christ, who speaks whenever God appears in a theophany in the Old Testament. Thus the words "I am He who is, the God of Abraham, Isaac and Jacob" (Exod 3:14) are spoken by the Logos, not the Father (*Apol.* 1.63.11-14). Remarkably Justin argues that hitherto the Logos was present among Greek philosophers as seed of the Logos (*spermata tou logou*), but after the coming of Christ the Logos has appeared in the fullness of truth (*Apol.* 2.8) (see further CHADWICK 1967; OSBORN 1973; WASZINK 1964). In Christian Gnosticism the Logos is also prominent, esp. in the Valentinian school (LAYTON 1987:225, 256, 301). The decisive intervention which results in a fully developed Logos doctrine occurs in the Alexandrian theology of Clement and Origen, beginning with the lyrical description of the Logos as the 'new song' in Clement's *Protrepticus* (1–10). In the Christological struggles of the fourth century the earlier subordinationist theology influenced by Middle Platonism is gradually rejected in favour of a trinitarian understanding of the Logos (GRILLMEIER 1975; WILLIAMS 1987). In his *Confessions* Augustine famously declares that in the 'books of the Platonists' he found that 'in the beginning was the Word', but not that 'the Word became flesh' (7.9.13–14). As man Christ is mediator, but as Word he is not midway (*medius*), for the Word is 'equal to God' (Phil 2:6), 'God with God' (John 1:1), and at the same time there is only →One God (10.43.68). Fully personalized, the Logos is incorporated in Christian orthodoxy as the second Person of the Trinity, and as such is the object of devotion and veneration. There remains, however, plenty of scope for theological debate, as the long history of Christian dogma will show.

V. *Bibliography*

A. AALL, *Geschichte der Logosidee in der griechischen Philosophie*, 2 vols. (Leipzig 1896–99); *K. BORMANN, *Die Ideen- und Logoslehre Philons von Alexandrien: eine Auseinandersetzung mit H. A. Wolfson* (inaug. diss. Köln 1955); H. CHADWICK, Philo and the Beginnings of Christian Thought, *The Cambridge History of Later Greek and Early Medieval Philosophy* (ed. A. H. Armstrong; Cambridge 1967) 158–166; J. DILLON, *The Middle Platonists: a Study of Platonism 80 B.C. to A.D. 220* (London 1977); *J. M. DILLON, Logos and Trinity: Patterns of Platonist influence on Early Christianity, *The Philosophy in Christianity* (ed. G. Vesey; Cambridge 1989) 1–13; C. H. DODD, *The Interpretation of the Fourth Gospel* (Cambridge 1965^2) 263–285; *H. DÖRRIE, Logos-Religion? oder Nous-Theologie?: die Hauptaspekte des kaiserzeitlichen Platonismus, *Kephalaion: Studies in Greek Philosophy and its Continuation offered to Prof. C. J. de Vogel* (ed. J. Mansfeld & L. M. de Rijk; Assen 1975) 115-136; *F. G. DOWNING, Ontological Asymmetry in Philo and Christological Realism in Paul,

Hebrews and John, *JTS* 41 (1990) 423-440; *J. D. G. DUNN, *Christology in the Making* (London 1980) 213–251; A. GRILLMEIER, *Christ in Christian Tradition, vol. 1 From the Apostolic Age to Chalcedon (451)* (ET London/Oxford 1975[2]); *H. HEGERMANN, *Die Vorstellung vom Schöpfungsmittler im hellenistischen Judentum und Urchristentum* (TU 82; Berlin 1961); M. HEINZE, *Die Lehre vom Logos in der griechischen Philosophie* (Oldenburg 1872); *P. HOFRICHTER, *In Anfang war der "Johannes-Prolog": das urchristliche Logosbekenntnis – die Basis neutestamentlicher und gnostischer Theologie* (Biblische Untersuchungen 17; Regensburg 1986); W. KELBER, *Die Logoslehre von Heraklit bis Origenes* (Stuttgart 1976[2]); G. S. KIRK, J. E. RAVEN & M. SCHOFIELD, *The Presocratic Philosophers: a Critical History with a Selection of Texts* (Cambridge 1983[2]); H. M. KLEINKNECHT, G. KITTEL et al., λέγω, λόγος κτλ., *TDNT* 4 (1967) 69–143; J. KROLL, *Die Lehren des Hermes Trismegistos* (Münster 1914) 55–71; H. J. KRÄMER, *Der Ursprung der Geistmetaphysik: Untersuchungen zur Geschichte des Platonismus zwischen Platon und Plotin* (Amsterdam 1964) 264–292; E. KURTZ, *Interpretation zu den Logos-Fragmenten Heraklits* (Spoudasmata 17; Hildesheim 1971); B. LAYTON, *The Gnostic Scriptures* (Garden City N.Y. 1987); H. LEISEGANG, *Logos*, PW xiii.1 (1926) 1035–1081; S. R. C. LILLA, *Clement of Alexandria: a Study in Christian Platonism and Gnosticism* (Oxford 1971) 199–212; E. F. OSBORN, *Justin Martyr* (Beiträge zur historischen Theologie 47; Tübingen 1973) 28–43; J. PÉPIN, Logos, *ER* 9 (1987) 9–15 [& lit.]; D. T. RUNIA, *Philo of Alexandria and the* Timaeus *of Plato* (Philosophia Antiqua 44; Leiden 1986) 204–208, 446–451; RUNIA, *Philo in Early Christian Literature: a Survey* (CRINT 3.3; Assen/Minneapolis 1993); G. SELLIN, Gotteserkentniss und Gotteserfahrung bei Philo von Alexandrien, *Monotheismus und Christologie: zur Gottesfrage im hellenistischen Judentum und im Urchristentum* (ed. H. J. Klauck; Freiburg 1992) 12-40; G. C. STEAD, Logos, *TRE* 21 (1991) 432–444 [& lit.]; *M. THEOBALD, Gott, Logos und Pneuma: Trinitarische Rede von Gott im Johannesevangelium, *Monotheismus und Christologie: zur Gottesfrage im hellenistischen Judentum und im Urchristentum* (ed. H. J. Klauck; Freiburg 1992) 41–87; T. H. TOBIN, *The Creation of Man: Philo and the History of Interpretation* (CBQ Monograph Series 14: Washington 1983); *TOBIN, The Prologue of John and Hellenistic Jewish Speculation, *CBQ* 52 (1990) 252-269; TOBIN, Logos, *ABD* 4 (1992) 348–356 [& lit.]; R. B. TODD, Monism and Immanence, *The Stoics* (ed. J. M. Rist; Berkeley 1978) 137-160; J. H. WASZINK, Bemerkungen zu Justins Lehre vom Logos Spermatikos, *Mullus: Festschrift für Theodor Klauser* (Münster 1964) 380-390; reprinted in his *Opuscula Selecta* (Leiden 1979) 317-327; H. F. WEISS, *Untersuchungen zur Kosmologie des hellenistischen und palästinischen Judentums* (TU 97; Berlin 1966) 216–282; R. WILLIAMS, *Arius: Heresy and Tradition* (London 1987); D. WINSTON, *Philo of Alexandria: The Contemplative Life, The Giants and Selections* (The Classics of Western Spirituality; New York/Toronto 1981); WINSTON, *Logos and Mystical Theology in Philo of Alexandria* (Cincinatti 1985); H. A. WOLFSON, *The Philosophy of the Church Fathers: Faith, Trinity, Incarnation* (Cambridge Mass. 1970[3]) 177–286; WOLFSON, *Philo: Foundations of Religious Philosophy in Judaism, Christianity and Islam* (Cambridge, Mass. 1968[4]) 1.226–294.

D. T. RUNIA

LORD אדון, אדני, מרא

I. The title *ʾādôn*, Aramaic *maraʾ*, 'lord', is used of men and of gods and denotes one's authority (not: ownership; this notion is more attributed to the word →Baal). Usually it concerns the relation between a lord and his subordinates. Its etymology is uncertain (see for a survey of the many options JENNI 1971:31). Most likely seems to be a connection with Ugaritic *ad*, 'father' (EISSFELDT 1973:63).

Heb *ʾădōnāy* exclusively denotes the god of Israel. It is attested about 450 times in the OT, especially in Ezekiel (more than 200 times), usually with the name →Yahweh (see for exact figures JENNI 1971:32). *ʾădōnāy* is usually translated as 'my Lord', assuming a plural form (pluralis majestatis) of *ʾādôn*, but with a different vocalisation of the last syllable (*qāmēṣ* in stead of *pataḥ*), as in Gen 19:2. The use in the context of a prayer in the first person plural in Ps 44:23-24 suggests that at least here the poet no longer had this suggested original meaning in mind. The same phenomenon is attested in the use of *ʾădōnî* addressed to human beings (Gen 44:7, Num 32:25, 2 Kgs 2:19). We have to assume that the word *ʾădōnāy* received its special form to distinguish it from the secular use of *ʾādôn*. With the rise of monotheism this epithet of the god of Israel as a mode of address became more and more a name in itself. In Judaism (presumably from the third century BCE onwards) it replaced the holy name Yahweh. Being used as a name its original meaning must have receded into the background.

It is difficult to trace precisely this development from the use of *ʾădōnāy* as a title to its use as a name, because it cannot be excluded that the Hebrew text of the OT was edited according to new theological and liturgical insights. In the transmission of the text the final form of this name may have been used to replace older forms.

According to EISSFELDT it is also possible to regard the ending of *ʾădōnāy* as a postpositive element which is also attested in Ugaritic writing (1973:72) and which was problably meant to give emphasis. But his examples of this phenomenon in Ugaritic suggesting in his opinion a relation to Heb *ʾădōnāy* are open to debate. The first is taken from a part of the myth of Baal describing the struggle between →Yam and Baal: *larṣ ypl ulny wl ʿpr ʿzmny* (*KTU* 1.2 iv:5), "The strength of the two of us fell to the earth, the power of the two of us to the dust". EISSFELDT translates *ulny* with 'Vollmächtige' and *ʿzmny* with 'Vollstarke'. But it seems more appropriate to assume a dual suffix pertaining to Baal and his helper (probably this is the goddess →Athtart, who is mentioned in line 28; *ARTU* 39).

The letter *KTU* 2.11 offers a better example of the use of the ending *-(n)y: hnny ʿmny (...) ṯmny ʿm adtny* (10-15), 'here with us (...) there with our mistress'. LORETZ (1980:291) adds to these examples the word *nʿmy*, 'happiness', consisting of *nʿm* and *y* as used in *KTU* 1.5 vi:6 and 1.6 ii:19. Instead of interpreting it as a 'Kosewort für Baal', however, it is more likely to be one the euphemisms for the dreaded world of the dead (*ARTU* 79).

II. The title 'lord' for a god can be found in most religions. The word *ʾādôn*, however, is only known in the Canaanite languages. The most relevant parallels to the god of Israel being called *ʾādôn* are found in the literature of Ugarit. It appears that very few gods receive this title. →El is called *adn ilm*, 'lord of the gods' (*KTU* 1.3 v:9; *ARTU* 16) and it is addressed to Yam, when he is at the height of his power: *at adn tpʿr*, "you are proclaimed lord (of the gods)" (*KTU* 1.1 iv:17). Clearly the title *adn* is ascribed to them to denote their exceptional, superior place among the other gods. This can be compared to what is said to →Marduk in the Mesopotamian creation epic *Enūma eliš*. He is said to be 'the most honoured of the great gods' and the other gods say to him: "Lord, thy decree is first among gods" (iv 21).

In *KTU* 1.16 i:44 and 1.124:1-2 the title *adn* seems to have been ascribed to Baal. This is a matter of dispute; because Baal is not explicitly mentioned in these passages. The interpretation of *adn ilm rbm*, 'lord of the great gods' in *KTU* 1.124:1-2 decides the question. For a survey of the many different proposed identifications of the *adn* see DIETRICH & LORETZ (1990:207-216). They have retracted their earlier opinion that it was a title of Baal and now translate as 'der Meister über die 'Großen Göttlichen'', assuming that this was a human being performing the necromancy. VAN DER TOORN, again, states that this *adn ilm rbm* having to make a journey to the netherworld is hardly a human functionary. He argues that the most likely candidates are the chthonic deities Milku, Yarikh, Yaqar, and possibly also El (1991:60-61).

In the background of this discussion there is the question of the relation between Ugaritic *adn* and the god →Adonis. Because *adn* in *KTU* 1.16 i:44 and 1.124:1-2 is used absolutely, it can be interpreted as a first step towards using this word as the name of some deity. Moreover, it is tempting to relate Adonis to Baal as we know him from Ugaritic mythology, their stories and cults having so much in common (EISSFELDT 1973:64; LORETZ 1980:292; *ARTU* 89-90).

Finally, it should be noted that it was not unusual in the ancient Near East to refer to a god by a title only and that this title eventually replaced the original name. The best known examples of this are the Mesopotamian Bel for Marduk and the Canaanite Baal for →Hadad.

III. The use in the Old Testament of *ʾādôn* to denote the god of Israel resembles the use of *adn* in Ugaritic literature as outlined above. It means that this one god is singled out and is superior to the other gods. There is no need to assume here some kind of dependance, because the use of this title is so widespread. But texts like Deut 10:17 "Yahweh your God, is the God of gods and the Lord of lords", indicate that the writer had these other religions in mind (cf. also Pss 135:5 and 136:2-3). And a name like Adoniah, 'Yahweh is lord' or 'my lord is Yahweh', is a confession of faith over against others ascribing this title to El, Yam, or possibly Baal.

When Yahweh is called *ʾādôn* it emphasizes his power over the whole earth (Josh 3:13; Mic 4:13; Zech 4:14; 6:5; Pss 97:5; 114:7; cf. also Isa 10:33) and over all people (Exod 34:23-24; Isa 1:24; 3:1; and 19:4).

It is quite normal for the Israelite believer to address his god as '(my) lord'. The reason why this is written *ʾădōnāy* instead of the normal *ʾādôn*, *ʾādōnî*, or *ʾădōnay* may have been to distinguish Yahweh from other gods and from human lords. Whether this special title was formed by simply changing the vocalisation of the word *ʾădōnay* or by using some kind of archaic ending, cannot be decided with certainty, nor when it was used for the first time. The attempt by EISSFELDT to prove the early origin of this word is not convincing. We have to reckon with the possibility mentioned above of editors changing the original text, e.g. its vocals, according to later principles. EISSFELDT points to the fact that *ʾădōnāy* and Yahweh are used separately in parallel poetic lines (cf. Exod 15:17; Isa 3:17). He compares this to the phenomenon attested in Ugaritic texts that the double name of some deities could be split likewise (1973:73-74). He fails to notice, however, that in Ugaritic these double names are always connected by the conjunctive *w*. And with none of these double names does the first part show signs of having first been the title of a deity.

It seems logical to assume that *ʾădōnāy* developed from a title used to address Yahweh to a name gradually replacing the holy tetragram. This development must have been furthered by the fact that it fitted Yahwism very well, as it is symbolic for a belief accepting no other lords, be they divine or human, than Yahweh.

IV. *Bibliography*

M. DIETRICH & O. LORETZ, *Mantik in Ugarit. Keilaphabetische Texte der Opferschau – Omensammlungen – Nekromantie* (ALASP 3; Münster 1990); O. EISSFELDT, *ʾādôn, TWAT* 1 (1973) 62-78 [& lit]; E. JENNI, *THAT* 1 (1971) 31-38; O. LORETZ, Vom Baal-Epitheton *ADN* zu Adonis und Adonaj, *UF* 12 (1980) 287-292; LORETZ, *ADN* come epiteto di Baal e i suoi rapporti con Adonis e Adonai, *Adonis: Relazione del Colloquio di Roma, Maggio 1981* (Roma 1983) 25-33; K. VAN DER TOORN, Funerary Rituals and Beatific Afterlife in Ugaritic Texts and in the Bible, *BiOr* 48 (1991) 40-66.

K. SPRONK

LORDSHIP → DOMINION

LYRE → KINNARU

M

MA → CYBELE

MAGOG מגוג

I. Magog (*māgôg*) is known from the Bible only (Gen 10:2; Ezek 38-39; 1 Chr 1:5). Together with →Gog, Magog came to be used in traditions harking back to Ezek 38-39 as a symbol of the superhuman adversaries of God and his people at the end of time.

II. The etymology of Magog is uncertain. The word is almost certainly related to, and maybe derived from, Gog. The *ma* at the beginning of the word may be understood as representing the Assyrian determinative *mat* (*status constructus* of *matu*, 'country'), indicating that the following word is a country, e.g. *^{mat}*Gaga* (usually transliterated as *^{kur}*Gaga*) or it may be seen as an abbreviation of Heb *mīn* ('from'), or as a *mem-locale*, indicating a land. The interpretation of Magog is intimately connected with that of Gog, then.

A derivation of Gog from Sumerian **gug** ('black spot', 'cornelian', or 'shining', depending on the identification of the root) has been proposed (A. VAN HOONACKER, Eléments sumériens dans le livre d'Ezéchiel?, *ZA* 28 [1914] 333-336, esp. 336), but is highly implausible. The connection with a hypothetical deity 'Gaga', mentioned in *Ee* III 3 as the vizier of Anshar (→Assur), the father of the gods, must be abandoned since the name of the deity in question is to be pronounced Kaka (D. O. EDZARD, *RLA* 5 [1976-80] 288; see also E. REINER, *Šurpu*, 59 ad VIII 30 on the reading ^{d}*Ga-a-gi*). No particular significance seems to have been attached to the literal meaning of the name Gog; the same would hold for Magog, if the latter is derived from the former. If Gog were a Hebrew calque on the name of the Lydian king Gyges (Akk *Gugu*), then Magog might mean 'Land of Gyges'.

Alternatively, Gog may be a derivation of Magog. The latter may refer to the Magi living in the neighborhood of Cappadocia and Media, or it may refer to Babylon: *Mgg* could be a cryptogram for Babel. Writing מגג backwards (גגמ) and substituting for each letter the one preceding it in the Hebrew alphabet, one obtains בבל, i.e. Babylon. Compare Jer 25:26; 51:41 where the enigmatic Sheshach (שׁשׁך) can be read as Babel (בבל) by means of *ʾatbaš*, a process whereby the alphabet is folded in the middle as it were, so that the first letter coincides with the last, and the others are similarly matched (BROWNLEE 1983:107). The major problem with this interpretation is that it overlooks the vocal *w* in *mgwg*. For a full survey of a large variety of interpretations see AALDERS (1951:10-49). AALDERS' own views, unfortunately, are heavily influenced by his dogmatic convictions.

III. Magog is mentioned in the table of nations in Gen 10:2, and in 1 Chr 1:5, as one of the seven sons of →Japheth. Three of these sons occur in Ezekiel's Gog section as three countries or nations over which Gog is lording (Gomer, Tubal, Meshech: 38:3.6; 39:1). In Gen 10:3, Togarmah is listed as a son of Gomer. His name returns in Ezek 38:6 as Beth-togarmah alongside with Gomer. In Ezek 38:5 three other nations are said to be with Gog: Persia, Cush, and Put. The latter two occur in Gen 10:6 as sons of Ham. Only Persia (*pāras*) is absent from the list in Genesis.

In cuneiform texts the inhabitants of Gomer are known as the Gimirray, and in classical Greek literature as the Cimmerians. Originally they lived north of the Black Sea (Krim; see Homer, *Od.* 11:14). Later they defeated Gyges of Lydia and settled in Cappadocia, which is called Gamir by the Armenians. Tubal and Meshech are also in

Asia Minor, in or around Cappadocia. Cush is the land south of Egypt, i.e. Ethiopia, whilst Put is Lybia, west of Egypt. Since Josephus (*Ant.* I,6,1) Magog is usually identified with the Scythians who lived north of the Black Sea.

In Ezek 38:2 (cf. 39:6) the land of Gog is called Magog, or, perhaps more accurately, Gog is identified with the land of the Magog. In 38:2 'Gog' is loosely followed by 'land of the Magog'. It is probably a note of an editor who wished to identify Gog with Magog as one and the same nation, or as a person symbolizing that nation. This may be confirmed by the LXX, in which the use of the particle *epi* suggests that both Gog and Magog were understood as a country. The Greek rendering paved the way for the later view, according to which Gog and Magog were the names of *two* persons (see Rev 20:8). The LXX rendering of Ezek 39:6 has Gog for MT's Magog. This also seems to confirm that the names Gog and Magog were interchangeable.

IV. *Bibliography*

J. G. AALDERS, *Gog en Magog* (Kampen 1951); R. AHRONI, The Gog Prophecy and the Book of Ezekiel, *HAR* 1 (1977) 1-27; R. H. ALEXANDER, A Fresh Look at Ezekiel 38 and 39, *JETS* 17 (1974) 157-169; M. C. ASTOUR, Ezekiel's Prophecy of Gog and the Cuthean Legend of Naram-Sin, *JBL* 95 (1976) 567-579; D. I. BLOCK, Gog and the Pouring out of the Spirit, *VT* 37 (1987) 257-270; A. VAN DEN BORN, Etude sur quelques toponymes bibliques. Le pays du Magog, *OTS* 10 (1954) 197-201; J. W. H. BROWNLEE, 'Son of Man Set Your Face,' Ezekiel the Refugee Prophet, *HUCA* 54 (1983) 45-110, esp. 107-108; E. DHORME, Les peuples issus de Japhet d'après le chapitre X de la Genèse, *Syria* 13 (1932) 28-49 = *Etudes bibliques et orientales* (Paris 1951) 167-189; G. GERLEMAN, Ezekielsboken Gog, *SEÅ* 12 (1947) 132-146; W. GRONKOWSKI, *Le messianisme d'Ezéchiel* (Paris 1930) 129-173; F. HOSSFELD, *Untersuchungen zu Komposition und Theologie des Ezechielbuches* (Würzburg 1977) 402-509; *B. OTZEN, Gog, *TWAT* 1 (1973) 958-965 [& lit]; H. L. STRACK & P. BILLERBECK, *Kommentar zum NT aus Talmud und Midrasch* 3 (München 1926) 831-840; W. ZIMMERLI, *Ezechiel* (BKAT XIII/2; Neukirchen 1969) 933-948.

J. LUST

MAKEDON Μακεδών

I. Makedon ('Macedonian') is the eponymous hero of the inhabitants of Macedonia in northern Greece. Macedonia and Macedonians figure in both Apocrypha and NT.

II. Macedonians particularly need an eponym (→Thessalos), as Macedonia had only marginal claims to Greek status before the conquests of Philip II (359-336) and Alexander the Great (336-323). Their speech seems to have been intermediate in status between a dialect of Greek and a closely related language (Indo-European **bh* gives *b* not *ph*: hence the names *Berenike* and *Bilippos* not *Pherenike* and *Philippos*).

Makedon first appears in the Hesiodic *Catalogue of Women* (fr. 7 MERKELBACH & WEST, perhaps around 625 BCE), a work of systematic genealogy. His epithet, 'rejoicing in horses', though banal, reflects well the interests of Macedonian aristocrats. His parents are →Zeus (a regular source of kingship) and 'Thyia', a daughter of Deukalion —who re-established humanity after the flood (implications: DOWDEN 1992:142), therefore making a good grandfather for the eponym of the current culture (in Thucydides 1 3,2, he is the father of Hellen 'Greek'). The term 'Thyia' otherwise looks more like an eponym for the Thyiads—Maenads in the ecstatic cult of →Dionysos (certainly practised in Macedonia)—and this rare name is later corrupted from *kai Thyia* ('and Thyia') to *kai Aithria* and *kai Aithyia* (Scholiasts on Homer, *Iliad* 14, 226). His brother Magnes is the eponym of Magnesia (the eastern coast of Thessaly and peninsula adjacent to Macedonia)—appropriately if the name of the tribe *Magnetes* is a pre-Greek ethnic name in some way related to *Makedones*. Usually, however, *Makedon* is taken as an ablaut variant of *makednos*, a word meaning 'tall, slender' associated with the Greek *makros* ('long') and with words in other languages meaning 'thin' (Latin *macer*, Old High German *magar*, Dutch *mager*).

Elsewhere, Makedon is 'earth-born' (Ps-Skymnos, *Periegesis* 620 of c. 110 BCE—like Deukalion's sown men), or a son of Lykaon (Aelian, *de Natura Animalium* 10, 48; Apollodoros, 3 8,1, calling him 'Makednos'), another figure who lives in the interim period just before our society. Lykaon is son of Pelasgos, eponym of the Pelasgians, the mythical predecessors of Greek civilisation (DOWDEN 1992:75, 80-85, 110-112). Otherwise, Makedon is enrolled into the Aeolian division of the Greeks (contrasting with the Ionian and the Dorian), becoming one of the 10 sons of Aiolos (Hellanikos, *FGH* 4F74 Jacoby).

Makedon's myth is to give the name 'Macedonia' to the former 'Emathia' ('Sandy'-land), a real enough label for lower, coastal Macedonia found in Homer (*Iliad* 14,226) and in several (archaizing?) authors. His sons account for a random selection from the landscape and its settlements, suggesting that later geographers improvised in areas left untouched by early genealogists with no interest in the detail of marginal Macedonia. Atintan exists to claim Atintania (an area of N.W. Epeiros which later came under Macedonian control), Europos to name Europos (a fortified city in Emathia on the River Axios). The strategic and agricultural centre Beroia (in Emathia) is explained by Beroia daughter of the son Beres, who also accounts for an alleged 'city in Thrace' (though we only know another Beroia there, not a Beres). All this is enshrined from antiquity in Stephanus of Byzantium's *Ethnika* (a 6th century CE, or later, compilation), which adds a city Oropos with homonymous founder, by confusion with Europos. Makednos' son Pindos names the river (Aelian l.c., an alternative name of the upper Peneios), and Homer's mention of Pieria (around Mt Olympus) and 'lovely Emathia' may be explained (Scholiast bT to Homer, *Iliad* 14, 226) by 'Amathos' (reimposing the name the father was invented to displace!) and 'Pieros', who also serves the convenience of Pausanias (9, 29,3) by introducing the cult of the nine (Pierian) Muses at Thespiai in Boiotia. It is a sign of the marginality of this area that Pausanias' *Periegesis of Greece* does not bother with Thessaly or Macedonia.

Another Makedon is a companion of →Osiris in his conquest of Europe (Diodoros 1,18, 20), a curious instance of the reversal of the polarity of Alexander's conquest of Egypt (also visible in the *Alexander-Romance*, where Alexander is a son of the exiled Egyptian king Nektanebos, not of Philip). In this incarnation, Makedon dresses as a wolf, whilst his other companion Anubis is dressed as a dog. This oddity reflects (BURTON 1972:83, 254) the Greek perception of the recumbent jackal Anubis as a dog and the standing jackal Wepwawet as a wolf (as worshipped at Siut, the Greek Lykopolis).

III. The name Makedon is uncommon, with only 7 bearers in FRASER-MATTHEWS (1987) (Thessalos=29, Jason=183). Use as an ethnic label, with no reference to the mythology, seems sufficient to account for this (contrast Thessalos). The Greek kingdom of Macedonia and the Macedonians appear at Add Esth 16:10.14; 1 Macc 1:1; 6:2; 8:5; 2 Macc 8:20. In Acts and the NT Epistles the reference is usually to the Roman province of Macedonia (coupled, e.g. with Achaea at 1 Th 1:7), though occasionally 'Macedonian' is used of ethnic origin.

IV. *Bibliography*

A. BURTON, *Diodorus Siculus: Book 1: A Commentary* (EPRO 29; Leiden 1972); K. DOWDEN, *The Uses of Greek Mythology* (London 1992); P. M. FRASER & E. MATTHEWS (eds.), The Aegean Islands, Cyprus, Cyrenaica, *A Lexicon of Greek Personal Names* I (Oxford 1987); H. W. STOLL, Makedon, *ALGRM* ii (1890-1897) 2291-2292; S. EITREM, PW 14.1 (1928) 636-637.

K. DOWDEN

MAL'AK MELIṢ →MEDIATOR I

MAL'AK YAHWEH → ANGEL OF YAHWEH

MALIK מלך →Milcom, →Molech

I. The divine name Malik, once probably the absolute state of Mal(i)kum, must originally have been an epithet meaning 'prince, king' or 'advisor, counsellor', signifying an aspect of another god, perhaps →Dagan, the chief god of Ebla and of the old North-Semites. Consequently, we find it in cuneiform script with and without determinative, the latter especially when it is a theophoric element of a personal name. Since Old Babylonian times, Malik and Malku(m) were used with case endings and in the plural forms *Mālikū* and *Malkū*. The character of the formation as an absolute state has been forgotten or superseded by a new consciousness of its appellative meaning which is now connected with his/their funeral or underworld character. Muluk, which occurs in the local name *Ilum-Muluk* (ARM XVI/1,17) beside *I-lu-ma-li-ka-wi*^{ki} (G. DOSSIN, *RA* 35 [1938] 178 n.1) and in the personal name *I-tar-mu-luk* (CT 33, 29:15), may be a mere phonetic variant of '*Malik*'. In Ugaritic, we find *mlk*, with *-mil-ku*, -$^{(d)}$*ma-lik*, and *-mu-lik* as theophoric elements in personal names, and the plural *mlkm*. In Phoenician, there are the theophoric elements *mlk-* resp. ^{m}*mil-ki-* or *-mil-ki*, *μιλκ-* or *μαλκ-*, and *Milc(h)-* or *Malc(h)-* in personal names and the divine names *mlkʿštrt* and *mlqrt* (→Melqart). In Hebrew, we find the theophoric element *malk(î)-* and *-melek* in several personal names, but perhaps in the merely appellative meaning of 'king' as an epithet of Yahweh and other theonyms, not as divine name in a proper sense. The Hebrew personal name *mallûk* (cf. Palmyrene *mlwk'*), however, is obviously a *qattūl* intensive formation used as a predicate ('royal, kingly') from which the theophoric element has been dropped; compare Akkadian *Ba-(ʾ-)al-ma-lu-ku* and Phoenician *bʿlmlk*. Outside personal names, the theonym Malik is to be supposed only behind Masorretic *melek* in Isa 57:9. Instead of *lammelek* in Isa 30:33, *lmlk* 'as a sacrifice' should be read; but this phrase *gam-hûʾ lmlk* may be a gloss (cf. *BHS*).

No divine name underlies Masoretic *lĕmōlek*, *lammōlek* and *hammōlek*; because *(l)mlk* is, rather, a Canaanite term for a sacrifice (EISSFELDT 1935). Masoretic *lĕmōlek*, instead of *lĕmôlēk* < *la-mawlik*, for which (Phoenician and) Punic *mlk(t)/mlʾk* resp. the Latin transliteration *molc(h)* in the Ngaus inscriptions for child-sacrifices can be compared, is a causative nominal formation according to *maqtil(at)* from the root *jlk* (< *wlk*) 'to go' well known from Phoenician as well as Punic. Since a causative (hiphʿil/jiphʿil) of *(j)lk* (= *hlk*) means 'to present, offer', the noun '*(le-)môlēk*' resp. *mlk(t)/molc(h)* is best translated by '(as a) presentation, offering', while *lmlk* signifies 'as a sacrifice (scil. for Yahweh [cf. Judg 11:30-40])', the expression as being used in *lĕʿôlâ* 'as a burnt-offering' Gen 22:2 or *lĕʿāšām* 'as a guilt-offering' Lev 5:18. The misinterpretation of Hebrew *mlk* as a divine name which, in view of the story in Gen 22, is meant to liberate YHWH from the odium of requiring child-sacrifices, occurs in the phrase *zānâ ʾaḥărê hammōlek* 'to commit whoredom with the Molech' Lev 20:5. Which is possibly a gloss [M. NOTH, ATD 6 (1962) 128-129] or part of a later stratum [K. ELLIGER, HAT I 4, 269]. The misinterpretation is also implied in the Masoretic determinated form *lammōlek* Lev 18:21; 20:2-4: 2 Kgs 23:10; Jer 32:35, both styled according to *habbōšet* 'the shame'; already *lĕmōlek* is really not in ample agreement with a supposed original pronunciation like '*lĕ-môlēk*'. In earlier parts of the LXX like Lev 18:21; 20:2-5; 1 Kgs 11:7, *mlk* has been interpreted as the appellative noun 'king'. The formations *hammōlek* and *lammōlek* are followed by *ὁ Μολοχ* in later parts of the LXX (2 Kgs 23:10; Jer 32:35, cf. Am 5:26), in Aquila, Symmachus and Theodotion, by *Μολωχ* in the Suda, a Byzantine dictionary from the 10th century CE, and by Moloch in the Vg. For details and particularly for the abundant (Phoenician and) Punic evidence see MÜLLER (1984 [& lit]; thereafter ISRAEL 1990).

An identification of a *Mōlek* with *Mālik* is rejected by EISSFELDT 1935 and many others (see MÜLLER 1984 [& lit]; ISRAEL 1990); but it is accepted by HEIDER (1985) and DAY (1989). EDELMAN (1987) adopts an intermediate position.

II. In Ebla, Malik—spelled $^{(d)}$*Ma-lik*, with the variant *Ma-li-gú*—is often found as a theophoric element in personal names; and, moreover, in the geographic name *ù-ma-li-gú*^{ki}. But family religion as the source of name-giving is far from the specifications allotted to divine figures by the official cult. The frequency of names formed with Malik may prove the high age of the god, family religion being always of a conservative character. As for Akkadian, a god Malik may already occur in the Presargonic onomasticon where the noun can still figure as an adjective, e.g. *Ilšumālik* 'his God is king/advisor' (cf. ROBERTS 1972:105 n.338); but we do not know in what sense a predicate 'king/advisor' is used, whether euphemistically or in earnest. In the Drehem texts from the later Ur III period, offerings $^{(d)}$*Ma-al-ku-um/kum* ŠÈ 'for Malkum' are mentioned. From the Old-Babylonian period we know the—euphemistic (?)—expression ^{d}*Ma-lik u* ^{d}A.MÀ *liballiṭūka* 'Malik and A.MÀ may give you life' (*CAD* s.v. *Malku* B b]2'). The singular Malik is quite often found in personal names from Mari (ARM XVI/1, 265; cf. HUFFMON 1965). According to EBELING 1931, p. 12:20, ^{d}*Mālik* is a mythic 'King of Mari' (*šarru ša Ma-ri*^{ki}). In economic and administrative texts from Mari, the plural *Mālikū* is attested for numinous figures who receive cereal-offerings, among other materials such as oil which can be found in connexion with gifts in the cult of dead kings. In other Mari texts such as ARM IX 89:7-12, we hear about an 'offering for (the) dead kings' (*kispum ša šarrāni*^{meš}) consisting of victuals and oil together with small quantities of the same material *ana Mālikī* 'for the Maliku' (for the *kispum* ceremony cf. TSUKIMOTO 1985). Are these Maliku dead princes or kings resp. counsellors, or are we to think of particular deities of an underworld character?

In the omen CT 3, 3:41 'the hand (might) of the Maliku and of a spirit' is mentioned. Obviously the Maliku are to be distinguished from the spirit, though they belong to the same sphere. From a literary text, we may quote an uttering such as: "I gave presents to the Maliku, the Anunnaku and to the gods living in the earth" (EBELING 1931, p. 58 I:19-21), showing that the Maliku belong to deities, not to dead people. The difference between both will not have been clear-cut; because underworld deities and dead men are nourished by the same offering materials. In ceremonies of purification performed with refined oil (cf. ARM VII 8:1-9), people want, as far as we know, to cleanse themselves from contact with both the dead and the underworld gods. Are the Malikū the product of a theomorphic sublimation of the deceased? Has an older god Malik been multiplied to that end?

Another argument in favour of the subterranean character of Malik is the fact that he is identified with →Nergal in several Assyrian texts (*Tākultu* 102 [no.135]; E. EBELING, *Or* NS 24 [1955] 11). Has the appellative notion 'prince, king; counsellor' remained euphemistic until now? But perhaps the meaningful consistency of an Oriental god wandering from age to age and from one culture to another who, moreover, is named by an appellative noun of a somewhat common meaning at least in Northwest-Semitic languages, is easily overestimated. The title of →'prince, king' or suchlike is claimed by many Semitic deities and, of course, by humans.

Ugaritic *mlk* appears in compounds such as *mlk ʿṯtrt* RS 1986.2235:17, *mlk.ʿṯtrh KTU* 1.100:41 and *mlk.bʿṯtrt KTU* 1.107:17. In *ʿṯtrh* and *bʿṯtrt*, the *-h* and *b-* have a locative function ('Mlk in *ʿṯtrt*') which also seems to be the case in *mlk ʿṯtrt* RS 1986.2235:17. *mlk ʿṯtrt* is paralleled by Phoenician *mlkʿštrt*, this name, however, being comparable with *ʾšmn ʿštrt* where an interpretation of *ʿštrt* as a locative element may not be convincing. The locạlization here has become rather an identification: the local name being changed into the feminine theonym from which it was once derived. In *KTU* 1.108:1 1-3, *rpu* for a netherworld god or ghost is connected with the apposition *mlk ʿlm* 'eternal king' and combined with the epithet *[il] °g̱tr* 'strong god'. It is uncertain whether this 'Eternal King' is the same as Malik.

In *KTU* 1.47:33 = 118:32, as in two almost identical lists of Ugaritic divine names, we find the plural *mlkm* with which Akkadian *Mālikū* may be compared, while, in the following line, we recognize, in contrast to the sequence in *KTU* 1.100 and 1.107, the divine name *šlm*. To *mlkm* // *šlm* the Akkadian-Ugaritic equations ^{d}*ma-lik*^{meš}: *mlkm* // ^{d}*sa-li-mu*: *šlm* in the two corresponding lists of divine names RS 20.24: RS 1929, no.17 (*Ug* V, 45:32-33) can be compared. (For connexions with *-mlk-*, -^{d}*ma-lik*, *-mu-lik* and similar personal names cf. GRÖNDAHL 1967:79, 157-158; *Ug* V, 60.) The uncertain meaning of *qdš mlk* ('sanctuary of the king'?) in KTU 1.123:20 is not really relevant here.

The Phoenician divine name *mlqrt CIS* I 122:1 (Melqart) for the chief god of Tyre, i.e. ^{d}*Mi-il-qar-tu* in Asarhaddon's treaty with King Baal of Tyre, has been derived from an epithet ('King of the city') for another god, probably →Baal of Tyre. The worship of Melqart was known all over the Mediterranian countries, perhaps because of his identification with the young Herakles by Greeks (Herodotus II 44) and Romans (cf. BONNET 1988).

The above-mentioned Phoenician divine name *mlkʿštrt*—a combination of a male and a female theonym for a god who, according to *lʾdn* 'to the Lord' and *lʿbd-m* 'to his servants' *KAI* 71:1,2-3, was of male gender—is often attested in *Umm al-ʿAwāmīd* near Tyre during the 3rd and 2nd centuries BCE (MAGNANINI 1973:16-22). It is also attested in Carthage (*CIS* I 250:5), Leptis Magna (*KAI* 119) and Cádiz (*KAI* 71)—*CIS* I 8:1 (MAGNANINI 1973:16-17) and other passages show that *mlkʿštrt* is 'the god of Hammon' (= *Umm al-ʿAwāmīd*?; cf. Josh 19:28) (cf. *KAI* 19:4) and as such probably the predecessor of →Baal Hammon of Samʾal (*KAI* 24:16), Malta (*KAI* 61:3-4), Carthage and Africa, if the latter is not to be identified with the Hurrian ^{d}*Ha-ma-ni* Bo.8328:3 or *ḥmn* is not yet merely a sacred object (XELLA 1991). The character of *mlkʿštrt* still remains obscure. That the Ugaritic *mlk ʿṯtrt(h)* RS 1986.2235:17; *KTU* 1.100:41 resp. *mlk b ʿṯtrt KTU* 1.107:17-18 should be localized in Transjordan because of *KTU* 1.108:1-3 (M. DIETRICH & O. LORETZ, *UF* 22 [1990] 55-56) is hardly consistent with the Phoenician evidence on *mlkʿštrt.*

III. There is only one uncontested attestation of a god *Mlk* (Masoretic *melek*) in the Hebrew Bible, i.e. Isa 57:9. According to this verse, oil and spices are offered *lmlk* 'for *Mlk*'. The mythical conception associated with these sacrifices is that messengers from the worshipping congregation have to descend far down into the underworld. Oil offerings and their netherworld character remind us of the Maliku from Mari. It is well known that the community which Trito-Isaiah is addressing had a strong tendency to religious atavisms and in particular to funeral cults (cf. 65:4). —That 'the treaty with death' of Isa 28:15.18 or the reference to a →'King of terrors' in Job 18: 14 had *Mlk* in mind (DAY 1989:55, 58-64), cannot be proved.

For *malk(î)-* and *-melek* in personal names, see above (**I.**) and J. D. FOWLER, (*Theophoric Names in Ancient Hebrew* [JSOT, Suppl.Ser. 49; Sheffield 1988] 50-53 [& lit]). The professional name Ebed-Melech, 'servant of king' (Jer 38:7-12; 39:16) can be compared with cuneiform *Abdi-mil-ki* (K. L. TALLQUIST, *Assyrian Personal Names* [Helsingfors 1914] 3), which is obviously Canaanite (cf. Ug *ʿbdmlk* and Phoen *ʿbdmlkt*).

Canaanite '*milk*', as we find it in the theophoric element '*Milk*' of Phoenician personal names, together with either *-âm* > *-ôm* (as in Heb *Ḥîrâm* resp. Phoen *ʾAḥîrôm*) or with *-um* may be the origin of the Masoretic divine name *Milkôm* resp. *Milkōm* as the god of the Ammonites (1 Kgs 11:5.33; 2 Kgs 23:13). In 1 Kgs 11:7, we should read

Milkôm instead of Masoretic *mōlek* (according to LXX LucRec and v 5.33 MT; cf. emendations to 2 Sam 12:30; Jer 49:1.3; Zeph 1:5). It is not impossible that the theonym →Adrammelech in 2 Kgs 17:31 (cf. the same lexeme as anthroponym in 2 Kgs 19:37; Isa 37:38) is connected with the Phoenician personal name Μαλκανδρος, Plutarch, de Iside 15, in the sense of '*Malk-ʾaddir*' 'Mal(i)k is mighty/magnificent' (J. EBACH & U. RÜTERSWÖRDEN, *UF* 11 [1979] 219-226). The formation →Anammelech, following Adrammelech in 2 Kgs 17:31, may then mean →'Anath of *Mlk*' (cf. 'Yahweh and *his* →Ashera' from *Kuntillet ʿAǧrūd* and *Ḫirbat al-Qōm).*

Postbiblical evidence for Malik is Thamudic and Nabatean *mlk* together with Palmyrene *mlkʾ*; cf. HÖFNER. In Sure 43:77/8 of the Qurʾan, an →angel of hell is adressed as *ja-Māliku.*

IV. *Bibliography*

C. BONNET, *Melqart. Cultes et mythes de l'Héraclès tyrien en méditerranée* (Studia Phoenicia VII; Leuven & Namur 1988); P. BORDREUIL, À propos de Milcou, Milqart et Milkʿashtart, *Maarav* 5/6 (1990) 11-21; A. CAQUOT, Le dieu Milkʿashtart et les inscriptions de Umm el ʿAmed, *Sem* 15 (1965) 29-33; J. DAY, *Molech. A God of Human Sacrifice in the Old Testament* (UCOP 41; Cambridge 1989); E. EBELING, *Tod und Leben nach den Vorstellungen der Babylonier* I (Berlin - Leipzig 1931); D. EDELMAN, Biblical *Molek* reassessed, *JAOS* 107 (1987) 727-731; O. EISSFELDT, *Molk als Opferbegriff im Punischen und Hebräischen und das Ende des Gottes Moloch* (Beiträge zur Religionsgeschichte des Altertums 3; Halle 1935); F. GRÖNDAHL, *Die Personennamen der Texte aus Ugarit* (Rome 1967) 79, 157-158; G. C. HEIDER, *The Cult of Molek. A Reassessment* (JSOT Suppl.Ser. 43; Sheffield 1985); M. HÖFNER, Malik, Malka, *WbMyth* 1/I 453; H. B. HUFFMON, *Amorite Personal Names in the Mari Texts* (Baltimore 1965) 230-231; F. ISRAEL, Materiali per "Moloch", *RSF* 18 (1990) 151-155; P. MAGNANINI, *Le iscrizioni fenicie dell'oriente* (Rome 1973); H.-P. MÜLLER, Religionsgeschichtliche Beobachtungen zu den Texten von Ebla, *ZDPV* 96 (1980) 1-19, esp 11-14; H.-P. MÜLLER, מֹלֶךְ *molæḵ*, *TWAT* 4 8/9 (1984) 957-968 [& lit]; S. RIBICHINI & P. XELLA, Milkʿaštart, Mlk(m) e la tradizione siropalestinese sui refaim, *RSF* 7 (1979) 145-158; J. J. M. ROBERTS, *The Earliest Semitic Pantheon. A Study of the Semitic Deities Attested in Mesopotamia before Ur III* (Baltimore & London 1972); A. TSUKIMOTO, *Untersuchungen zur Totenpflege* (kispum) *im alten Mesopotamien* (AOAT 216; Neukirchen-Vluyn 1985) 65-69; P. XELLA, *I testi rituali di Ugarit* I (Rome 1981) 224-250; XELLA, *Baal Hammon* (Collezione di studi fenici 32; Rome 1991).

H.-P. MÜLLER

MAMMON μαμωνᾶς

I. Mammon (Aram. status emphaticus *mamōnāʾ*), the etymology of which is not completely certain, probably is a maqtāl form of the root *ʾmn* with the meaning of 'that in which one puts trust', with 'money, riches' as a derivative meaning (J. A. FITZMYER, *The Gospel according to Luke* II [New York 1985] 1109; for other etymologies see HAUCK 1942:390 n. 2 and RÜGER 1973:127-131; on problems of spelling see MASTIN 1984). It occurs in both Hebrew and Aramaic texts of the post-biblical period (HAUCK 1942:391; BAGD s.v.; BALZ 1981: 942; SOKOLOFF 1990:311; its occurrence in a 7th cent. BCE Aramaic inscription is very uncertain, see LIPIŃSKI 1975); in Greek transcription (μαμωνᾶς = *mamōnāʾ*) it is found only in four synoptic passages (Lk 16:9.11.13//Mt 6:24). Although a neutral term in itself, in later Jewish usage (esp. the Targumim) the word develops a predominantly negative meaning with connotations of the improper, the dishonest, the sinful aspect of wealth (HAUCK 1942: 391).

II. In the NT the word occurs only on the lips of →Jesus. In the Q saying Lk 16:13 // Mt 6:24 he seems to regard Mammon as an enslaving force or even as a god that one can serve: "No slave can serve two masters;

for a slave will either hate the one and love the other, or be devoted to the one and despise the other. You cannot serve God and Mammon". Here Mammon is personified as an evil and superhuman power that stands in competition to →God and by possessing people can even keep them from being devoted to God and make them hate Him. The two other texts, Lk 6:9.11 (also from the pericope immediately following upon the parable of the unjust steward) speak about 'unrighteous wealth' (ὁ μαμωνᾶς τῆς ἀδικίας and ὁ ἄδικος μαμωνᾶς, the second expression being the graecized form of the semitizing original that reflects Aramaic ממון דשקר) and they imply that believers may learn from the unjust steward to use wealth (in the sense of 'dispose of it') in the service of love for others, i.e. in the service of God (SCHMIDT 1987: 153-155). If the etymology suggested above is correct, there may be a wordplay with the root *ʾmn* in Lk 16:11: "If you have not been faithful (πιστοί) in the unrighteous *mamon*, who will entrust (πιστεύσει) to you the true (ἀληθινόν) riches?" (four words perhaps deriving from that root). That wealth can exercise an overwhelming power over people and enslaving them is an insight well-known also among Greeks and Romans as is evident from the much-quoted sentence that love of money is the root of all evil (1 Tim 6:10; cf. for its variants P. W. van der HORST, *The Sentences of Pseudo-Phocylides* [Leiden 1978] 142-143; K. S. FRANK, Habsucht, *RAC* XIII [1986] 226-247). In some later Christian sources Mamonas is depicted as a demon, 'wealth' being personified apparently on the basis of the fact that Luke 16:13 opposes *mamonas* to God and calls both God and Mammon →*kyrioi* (see E. PETERSON, Engel- und Personennamen, *RhMus* NF 75 [1926] 406-69).

III. *Bibliography*

H. BALZ, μαμωνᾶς, *EWNT* II (1981) 941-942; J. M. BASSLER, *God and Mammon. Asking for Money in the NT* (Nashville 1991); F. HAUCK, μαμωνᾶς, *TWNT* IV (1942) 390-392; E. LIPIŃSKI, An Assyrian Decree Law in Aramaic, *Studies in Aramaic Inscriptions and Onomastics* (Louvain 1975) 77-82; B. A. MASTIN, Latin Mam(m)ona and the Semitic Languages: A False Trail and a Suggestion, *Bib* 65 (1984) 87-90; H. P. RÜGER, μαμωνᾶς, *ZNW* 64 (1973) 127-131; T. E. SCHMIDT, *Hostility to Wealth in the Synoptic Gospels* (JSNTSS 15; Sheffield 1987); M. SOKOLOFF, *A Dictionary of Jewish Palestinian Aramaic of the Byzantine Period,* Ramat Gan 1990.

P. W. VAN DER HORST

MAN → ANTHROPOS

MARDUK מרדך

I. Marduk was the god of Babylon and the supreme ruler of the Mesopotamian universe. Normally, the name Marduk is written ^{d}AMAR.UD. The name has been treated by some as pre-Sumerian and the writing understood as a folk-etymology, whereby an unintelligible name is rendered understandable in Sumerian. It seems better, however, to treat the name as an original Sumerian name: **amar.uda.ak**. This agrees with the fact that the name possesses a long form: *(A)marut/duk* (= MT: *Mĕrōdāk*, LXX: *Marōdak*) in addition to its short form Marduk. While the name is usually interpreted as 'calf/son of the sun', the interpretation 'calf of the storm' is to be preferred, especially since Marduk is not a solar deity. There are other ancient interpretations of the name (e.g. *Enūma Elish* I 101-102).

With his exaltation, Marduk assumed the name →*Bēl* (= →'Lord', from the title *bēlu*; cf. Canaanite →*Baʿal* as well as Heb *ʾĂdōnāy* = Gk →*Kurios*) as his proper name.

II. Marduk's earliest beginnings seem to be as the local god and patron of Babylon. Already in the Old Babylonian period, he was incorporated into the Mesopotamian pantheon and considered to be the son of Enki/Ea and a member of the Eridu circle. It has been argued that Marduk became the son of →Ea because both he and Asalluḫe were gods of exorcism. Especially since Asalluḫe seems originally to have been the messenger of Ea and not a god of exorcism as such, it is more reasonable to assume that the connection with Ea arose from the desire to link Babylon and Marduk with Eridu, its traditions, and its god Ea. Continuing the tradition of the kings of Isin-Larsa who also had a special relationship to Eridu, the priests of Babylon were thus able to link Marduk to a major god other than Enlil and a venerable tradition other than Nippur. The subsequent identification of Marduk with Asalluḫe came about because both Marduk and Asalluḫe were associated with rain clouds and water and, as sons of Ea, both functioned as his messengers, agents, and executors. Eventually, Asalluḫe/Marduk indeed became an exorcist, perhaps because the human *āšipu*, who was the messenger of Ea and identified with Asalluḫe, preferred to assume an identification with a divine exorcist rather than remaining only a messenger, thus enhancing his power. (This development was part of the expanding role and status of this class of exorcists.)

As Babylon developed and grew in significance, Marduk's natural features were overlaid by characteristics and roles he assumed as the god of the city, and he himself incorporated features and identities of other gods (e.g. Tutu of Borsippa). Marduk is often treated as if he were a political construct lacking in natural features. This approach is understandable, given that, on the one hand, we have no early mythic materials which present him as a natural force or as a developed personality, and that, on the other hand, texts that provide a detailed picture seem to reflect a time when as the supreme god he had taken over many roles and identities. Still, it seems preferable to follow JACOBSEN's assessment and to treat Marduk as a god who was originally associated with thunderstorms and brought natural abundance by means of water. Accordingly, we should not explain all of Marduk's associations with water and vegetation as simply having been taken over from Ea and his circle. Note, especially, the identification of Marduk with Enbilulu in *Enūma Elish* VII and the emphasis in hymns and prayers upon Marduk's power to bring water and nourishment in abundance (sometimes in conjunction with the rendering of decisions and determination of destinies at the New Year). See, for example, A. LIVINGSTONE, SAA 3 (1989) 7-8; 21-23 and *BMS*, no. 12 (and dupls.):24-31. Also suited to (or derived from) his natural character are some of the storm-like (and hence war-like) features and deeds attributed to him in his fight against →Tiamat in *Enūma Elish* and the use there of →Ninurta traditions. In texts from the first millennium, Marduk's astral identification is especially with Jupiter.

The history of the god is of importance for an understanding of Mesopotamian religion and thought. We turn now, therefore, to that topic. Marduk has a more textured personality than simply that of the god of the expanded Babylon, and his full character and deeds should not be seen only as a projection of political developments. Still, his ascension to the head of the pantheon and the expansion of his powers are surely related to the gradual elevation of Babylon to pre-eminence.

Although mentioned as early as the Early Dynastic period (perhaps even ED II), it is only during the Old Babylonian period under Hammurapi—who for the first time made Babylon an important city and the capital of an extended state—that Marduk emerges as a significant god and a member of the Sumero-Akkadian pantheon. Thus the Code of Hammurapi begins: "When lofty →Anum, king of the Anunnaki, (and) Enlil, lord of heaven and earth, the determiner of the destinies of the land, determined for Marduk, the first-born of Enki, the Enlil functions over all mankind, made him great among the Igigi, called Babylon by its exalted name, made it supreme in the world, established for him in its midst an enduring kingship, whose foundations are as firm as →heaven and earth—" (Codex Hammurapi I 1-21 [*ANET*³]). Even here, Marduk's election is still the continuation of an older Mesopotamian tradition. In that tradition, the god of the politically dominant city ruled the land, but the central meeting place or assembly of the gods remains Nippur and ultimate power resides with the divine assembly and its leaders. One difference, however, from some earlier formulations seems to be the treatment of Marduk's kingship in Babylon as eternal. All the same, Marduk in the Old Babylonian period seems to be no more than a junior member of the pantheon; he is a local god but he is now a permanent member of the pantheon and god of a city that has become a permanent part of the ideological landscape.

As Babylon developed, so did the god. Beginning as the local god and patron of Babylon, Marduk became the god and master of the Babylonian national state and the supreme god and absolute ruler of the universe. However, during most of the second millennium, Marduk seems neither to have replaced the high gods of Babylonia nor to have ascended to the head of the pantheon. Only late in the second millennium does he take on many of Enlil's roles and become not only lord of the land but also king of the gods.

While there are indications that Marduk was emerging as supreme ruler already during the Kassite period (cf. e.g. the events associated with Adad-shuma-uṣur in A. K. GRAYSON, *Babylonian Historical-Literary Texts* [Toronto 1975] 56-77 [but note that this text contains anachronisms and was probably composed well after that reign]) and early in the second Isin period, his elevation seems to have been first publicly articulated only during the reign of Nebuchadnezzar I (1125-1104). This king defeated the Elamites and restored the plundered statue of Marduk to Babylon. Now, in addition to Marduk's rule over the city of Babylon, there was an open claim for Marduk's dominion over the gods and over the whole land. He takes on some of the roles of Enlil and occasionally even replaces him. Generally speaking, however, the other major gods are not replaced or made simply subservient to Marduk (especially in texts from cities other than Babylon). Rather, Marduk, no longer a junior, is now ranked with the supreme gods of the pantheon.

By the end of the second millennium, a Babylonian nation-state seems to have been created with the city Babylon as its centre and Marduk as its god. As mentioned above, Marduk is now even referred to occasionally as king of the gods, but it is only during the first millennium, culminating in the Neo-Babylonian empire, that we find this idea systematically carried through to its logical conclusion. This is evident from first-millennium documents describing the Akitu-New Year festival; for at that season, the gods all assembled in Babylon, where Marduk was declared king and where destinies for the New Year were determined. Certainly, during the Neo-Babylonian empire, Marduk was the supreme god of a universal empire ruled from Babylon.

The date of the elevation of Marduk has occasioned a variety of scholarly opinions. The problem is a knotty one and requires a nuanced approach. It is likely that the perception of Marduk as head of the pantheon was already developing even before the time of Nebuchadnezzar I. Already in the Kassite period, Babylonia became a national state with Babylon as its capital. But the conception of Marduk as king of the gods in the form known to us, for example, from *Enūma Elish*, could not be fully articulated until at least two conditions were met: 1) Babylon had to replace Nippur as the divine locus of power upon which the world, the nation, and the monarchy were based, and 2) a new model of world organization had to be available.

1) Nippur/Babylon: Even though the Kassite kings ruled the country from Babylon, they followed the older Nippur-Anu-Enlil construction of government and, in addition to being kings of Babylon, were kings of Sumer and Akkad. The nation, in accordance with the traditional cosmology, was imagined as being governed by the divine assembly in Nippur under Enlil. The nation/country of Babylonia and the city of Babylon were kept conceptually separate, with the kingdom of 'Sumer and Akkad'—not the royal capital—being perceived as the primary unit of government and source of power. Marduk was god of the city of Baby-

lon, the capital, and god of the royal family, but Enlil remained lord of the land.

Naturally, as the god of Babylon and of the royal family, Marduk's position continued to evolve. For residents of Babylon, for its priests and theologians, and even for the kings in their role of rulers of Babylon, Marduk might have been perceived as king of the gods even before Nebuchadnezzar I. However, as long as the Nippurian conception of governance of the Mesopotamian cosmos and territory remained operative, the concept of the nation and the role of Enlil would remain the same, and developments in Babylon would not initially have affected them. Thus, until the replacement of the political framework that had Nippur as its centre by a different framework centering on Babylon, Marduk's supremacy would not be expressed in political documents. Official recognition of Babylon as the permanent capital and source of legitimacy was a precondition to the public, official exaltation of Marduk as the supreme god.

2) World organization: But more was required than just the replacement of Nippur with Babylon to bring about such a change in the conception of Marduk. The recognition of Marduk as the supreme god was a new religious idea that depended upon a radical shift in thinking about the state. What was required was not only a different centre, but also a new conception of the cosmic and political world as a world-empire revolving around one central city. In this divine empire, everything revolves around the god of the central city; at home in their own cities, the other gods pay homage to the supreme god and also journey to the centre to do obeisance; their relationship to the supreme god defines the character of the divine world and their role within it. Such a conception depends not only on the existence of absolute kingship, but even more upon an imperial form of government. It is for this reason that Marduk's elevation to full divine supremacy could only take place in the first millennium at a time of world empire. (Compare, perhaps, Marduk's replacement of the divine assembly with developments in Egypt under Akhnaton.)

But regardless of how one assesses the evidence from/about the latter half of the second millennium and what one concludes regarding the date of Marduk's elevation, it is clear that in the first millennium the new image of Marduk as world ruler dominated Babylonian thinking. Marduk and Babylon have become the primordial god and city; the *Erra* poem can present Marduk as the god who ruled before the Flood and whose temporary absence brought about the Flood, and in this new antediluvian tradition, Marduk replaces the older gods Enlil and Ea. Nevertheless, despite the new supremacy of Marduk and the apparent existence of henotheistic tendencies, Mesopotamia remained polytheistic, with its several cities maintaining the cults of their gods.

Marduk's cult spread to Assyria before the Sargonids, but it was especially in the 8-7th centuries, when Assyria attempted to control Babylon, that interesting developments and conflicts surrounding Marduk and Babylon arose. The Assyrians had difficulty assimilating the Marduk cult or even defining an efficacious and stable relationship with Marduk and his city. An extreme form of the conflict is attested during the reign of Sennacherib when, alternatively, →Ashshur was cast in the role of Marduk and assumed his deeds or Marduk was made to function at the behest of Ashshur/Anshar.

During the late 7th and first half of the 6th century, under the Neo-Babylonian kings, Marduk was regarded as the principal god of the empire. Apparent threats to the prerogatives of the Marduk cult led the priests of Babylon to welcome and justify Cyrus's conquest.

Apparently, the events of the reign of Nebuchadnezzar I —especially the return of the statue of Marduk—occasioned the composition of literary works revolving around Marduk, his experiences and deeds, and his new exalted position of power and rank. In such texts as the Marduk *šuilla BMS* 9 obv. (and dupls.), Marduk is shown outgrowing the role of son of Enki and young prince of Eridu (a role in which he was comparable to Ninurta as son of Enlil and young prince in Nippur) and assuming the role of master of

Babylon and of the whole land. While recognizing that Babylon is the centre of the world, this text does not focus only on the city. Rather, it uses Babylon as a stepping-off point to the rest of the world. *BMS* 9 obv. is to be dated, I believe, to the aforementioned reign.

A somewhat different situation obtains, however, in *Enūma Elish*, for in addition to describing Marduk's ascendancy to the kingship of the gods, it focuses narrowly on Babylon, on its creation as the first city and designation as the centre of the world of the gods, and thus also displays an inward turning. For other reasons as well, *Enūma Elish* should perhaps not be dated to the time of Nebuchadnezzar I. We should now, therefore, discuss this document.

Enūma Elish ('When On High'), a seven tablet work, is certainly the most important document defining Marduk's elevation. It describes his rise to permanent and absolute kingship over the gods. His ascendancy is expressed not only by the recognition of his kingship over the gods but also by the naming of his fifty names, for by this naming many gods are identified with Marduk or are made aspects of him. In this work, the idea of an assembly ruled by Marduk from the Esagila in Babylon is clearly envisaged and worked out, and the earlier structure of a national assembly of the gods in Nippur (led by Enlil and Anu) is, by implication, replaced.

While various documents composed under Nebuchadnezzar I reflected the ascendancy of Marduk, it may be a mistake to include *Enūma Elish* among them. The date of composition of *Enūma Elish* is not without historical significance; moreover, the date has a bearing on the interpretation of the work and its relationship to other literatures. In the course of the last 60-70 years, various dates have been suggested for *Enūma Elish*. In the first flush of rediscovery of the Old Babylonian period and the Code of Hammurapi, the composition of *Enūma Elish* was dated to that period. (Such passages as the above-quoted passage from the prologue to Codex Hammurapi were used to support this notion.) More recently, dates in the latter half of the second millennium have been proposed. While W. von Soden suggests a date of composition around 1400, LAMBERT (1964) argues for the composition of *Enūma Elish* during the reign of Nebuchadnezzar I as a work celebrating Marduk's official elevation to leadership of the pantheon. JACOBSEN (1976), on the other hand, introduces a number of subtle distinctions and argues that the work dealt with issues surrounding Babylonia's re-conquest of the Sealand and national unification and should be dated subsequent to that event (after Ulamburiash) in the early part of the second half of the second millennium.

Previous attempts at dating and interpretation have assumed that the work reflects a period of ascendancy of the city Babylon and the Babylonian kingdom. If this were the case, we would expect our text to evidence characteristics of a work written either by temple circles or by palace circles and to support the interests of one or the other. Rather, it exhibits a mixed set of features with regard to temple and palace. This mixture can be explained if we assume that *Enūma Elish* was written not at a time of ascendancy, but rather at a time when the interests of temple and palace had coalesced because the seat of power had shifted elsewhere and it had become necessary to reassert the central importance of the god, his temple, and his city. Thus, rather than viewing *Enūma Elish* as a work composed during a period of Babylonian political ascendancy and as a reflection of the city's attainment of increasing power, I would suggest that we instead view *Enūma Elish* as having been composed at a time when it was necessary to preserve the memory of Babylon's ascendancy and to assert its claim to be a world capital on the grounds that it had been so since the beginning of time. It was composed some time during the early first millennium in a period of weakness of the city Babylon and served to bolster the city's claim to cultural prestige and privilege at a time when it was coping with the loss of political power and centrality. While supporting political aspirations, the work reflects even more the needs of a major temple organization to preserve its religious and cultural significance and may well have been composed in temple circles.

Thus, while *BMS* 9 obv. (and dupls.) is a more natural example of increasing strength, *Enūma Elish* is a conservative attempt to preserve something that was threatened with loss. The emphases and approach of *Enūma Elish* would agree with composition in the first millennium at a point when Babylon's ascendancy was threatened either by the Aramaeans or the Assyrians. Certainly, *Enūma Elish* exhibits a pronounced baroque style characteristic of late periods.

Moreover, while the universalistic world-view implicit in *Enūma Elish* is not consonant with the second millennium when the concept of world-empire had not yet become part of the Mesopotamian political and religious imagination, it does fit with the thought and experiences of the first millennium. *Enūma Elish* is rooted in the notion of Marduk as king of the gods; while the earlier period may have already articulated this idea, the vision of *Enūma Elish* reflects a radical extension of it, perhaps in reaction to the Assyrians and under the influence of the model provided by the Assyrian world-empire. It reflects the cultural needs of first millennium Babylon. For the time being, then, *Enūma Elish* should not be called upon to give testimony to the ascendancy of Marduk at the end of the second millennium.

Marduk's main sanctuary was located in the centre of Babylon and comprised a group of buildings, most notably the low temple Esagila and the temple tower (ziggurat) Etemenanki. Between these two complexes ran the main processional street. Esagila contained the major shrines of Marduk and his wife Ṣarpanītu as well as a number of chapels dedicated to other gods. On the top of the ziggurat, which was located within an enclosure, stood the high temple of Marduk, with rooms of worship for other gods. Among the gods who had chapels in these complexes special mention should be made of Marduk's son →Nabû, the scribe of the gods and god of Borsippa. Nabû, too, eventually attains high eminence among the gods alongside his father Marduk.

The New Year's festival in Babylon (usually referred to as the Akitu festival) was based in Marduk's temple complex and centered on his cult. Comprising several separate strands which were joined together over time, the rites of the festival, which took place in the spring during the first twelve days of the first month (Nisannu), centre upon the god, city, and king of Babylon. But although the Akitu festival had several originally independent dimensions (natural, cosmological, and political), it nevertheless remains true that *Enūma Elish* gives expression to some of the same basic issues and narrative themes as the late festival and corresponds to several of its major ritual enactments. *Enūma Elish* (probably our text, but possibly some other version or re-telling of the story) was recited before Marduk on the fourth day of the month (it may well have been recited in other months as well). Principal among the ritual events that should be mentioned here are: prayers for Babylon; divesting and re-investing the king before Marduk; ingathering of the gods from various cities to Babylon; gathering of the gods in assembly on two separate occasions in the shrine of destinies of the Nabû sanctuary for the purpose of determining destinies (parallel to the two assemblies in *Enūma Elish*, before and after the battle respectively); procession of Marduk and the other gods (with the king taking Marduk's hand) by way of the processional way and →Ishtar's gate, and travel on the river to the Akitu house, where a banquet takes place. Sitting down in the Akitu house has been taken as representing the victorious battle over →Tiamat, though this battle may be equally or better represented by the sailing on the river to the Akitu house. Thus, evidently battle, enthronement, and determining destinies are among the many acts that are celebrated during the Akitu festival.

III. *Merodach* is mentioned in Jer 50:2, where he is the god of Babylon and is referred to also under the name Bel. As Bel he occurs also in Jer 51:44 and Is 46:1; in the latter passage he appears together with his son Nebo = Nabû. For Bel in the OT Apocrypha, see Letter of Jeremiah (= Baruch 6):40 and Bel and the →Dragon (= addition to the Greek Daniel, Ch. 14): 3-22. All biblical references allude to the Marduk cult of the Neo-Babylonian period. Several Babylonian names with Marduk as the theophoric element appear in the Bible: Evil-merodach, Merodach-baladan, and perhaps Mordechai. (D. J. A. CLINES, Mordechai, *ABD* 4 [1992] 902-904, esp. 902; C. A. MOORE, Esther, Book of, *ABD* 2 [1992] 633-643, esp. 633).

IV. *Bibliography*

T. ABUSCH, The Form and Meaning of a Babylonian Prayer to Marduk, *JAOS* 103 (1983) 3-15; J. A. BLACK, The New Year Ceremonies in Ancient Babylon: 'Taking Bel by the Hand' and a Cultic Picnic, *Religion* 11 (1981) 39-59; M. J. GELLER, *Forerunners to* UDUG-ḪUL (FAOS 12; Stuttgart 1985) 12-15; T. JACOBSEN, Babylonia and Assyria, Part V. Religion, *Encylopedia Britannica* (1963) 2, 972-978, esp. 977 = Mesopotamian Gods and Pantheons, *Toward the Image of Tammuz* (ed. W. L. Moran; HSS 21; Cambridge Mass. 1970) 16-38, esp. 35-36; JACOBSEN, The Battle between Marduk and Tiamat, *JAOS* 88 (1968) 104-108; JACOBSEN, Religious Drama in Ancient Mesopotamia, *Unity and Diversity* (ed. H. Goedicke & J. J. M. Roberts; Baltimore/ London 1975) 65-97, esp. 72-76; JACOBSEN, *The Treasures of Darkness* (New Haven/ London 1976) 167-191; W. G. LAMBERT, The Great Battle of the Mesopotamian Religious Year: The Conflict in the Akītu House, *Iraq* 25 (1963) 189-190; LAMBERT, The Reign of Nebuchadnezzar I: A Turning Point in the History of Ancient Mesopotamian Religion, *The Seed of Wisdom: Essays...T. J. Meek* (ed. W. S. McCullough; Toronto 1964) 3-13; LAMBERT, Studies in Marduk, *BSOAS* 47 (1984) 1-9; LAMBERT, Ninurta Mythology in the Babylonian Epic of Creation, *Keilinschriftliche Literaturen* (ed. K. Hecker & W. Sommerfeld BBVO 6; Berlin 1986) 55-60; J. J. M. ROBERTS, Nebuchadnezzar I's Elamite Crisis in Theological Perspective, *Essays on the Ancient Near East in Memory of Jacob Joel Finkelstein* (ed. M. de J. Ellis; Hamden, Conn. 1977) 183-187; J. Z. SMITH, *Imagining Religion: From Babylon to Jonestown* (Chicago & London 1982) 90-96; W. SOMMERFELD, *Der Aufstieg Marduks* (AOAT 213; Neukirchen-Vluyn 1982); W. SOMMERFELD, Marduk, *RLA* 7, 5/6 (1989) 360-370.

T. ABUSCH

MARY

I. Mary, the mother of →Jesus, is mentioned by name only in the four Gospels and once in the Acts of the Apostles. The name, which occurs as *Maria* or *Mariam* in the Greek NT, and as *Mariamme* in Josephus, *Ant.* 3,54, corresponds with the Heb name *Miriam* (cf. Exod 15:20; Num 26:59). Because of Mary's symbolic role in the ascetic, dogmatic (especially christological) and ecclesiological reflection of the Church, mariology was developed in patristic times, which in its turn prepared the way for further developments in the Middle Ages and afterwards.

II. The earliest NT author, Paul, does not mention Mary, although he does refer to the birth of Jesus in Rom 1:3-4; Gal 4:4, 29 and Phil 2:6-7. The earliest references to Mary are Mark 3:31-35 and 6:1-6. In Mark 3, the mother and the brothers and sisters of Jesus, his physical family, are said to have no advantage in relationship to him; only those who do the will of →God are truly "his family." In 3:21-35, the suggestion is that what counts is the 'eschatological' family alone (BROWN *et alii* 1978:52-58). Mark 6:3 (par. Matt 13:55) lists Mary (this is the first time she is mentioned by name) and four brothers of Jesus. Some scholars also identify the Mary of Mark 15:40 (par. Matt 27:56), 15:47 (par. Matt 27:61) and 16:1 (par. Matt 28:1) with Mary the mother of Jesus. In view of the later doctrine of the perpetual virginity of Mary, which cannot be found in the NT, other scholars hold the brothers and sisters of Jesus to be more distant relatives, or sons of Joseph from an earlier marriage (cf. Hilary of Poitiers, *Comm.Matt.* I,4).

Matthew mentions Mary in the narrative of the birth of Jesus in chaps. 1 and 2. In the genealogy (1:1-17), we have the unusual appearance of five women of which Mary is the last. All five are marked by real (or apparent) irregularities in their marital unions, yet they, and last but not least Mary herself, were vehicles of God's messianic design (BROWN *et alii* 1978:81-83). The conception narrative (1:18-25) reinforces and specifies the exceptional nature of Mary's pregnancy: what appeared like adultery was in fact the work of the →Holy Spirit and part of God's plan to save his people. Matt 1:22-23 interprets this plan as announced in Isa 7:14. Matt 12:46-50 parallels Mark 3, but the suggestion is not, as in Mark, that the eschatological family has replaced the physical family. The same goes for Matt 13:53-58 which parallels Mark 6 (BROWN *et alii* 1978:98 etc.).

Of all NT writers, Luke has most to say about Mary. The infancy narrative serves the christological purpose to retroject the belief of the Church concerning Jesus' ministry and resurrection to his conception, birth and early youth (cf. Luke 1:35 with Rom 1:3-4; BROWN *et alii* 1978: 118-119). Only before the conception is Mary's virginity explicitly attested (cf. 1:27 with 1:31). As such, the birth from the Holy Spirit need not imply the absence of a human father, witness the "overshadowing" of men in 9:34 and Paul's reference to Isaac as "born according to the Spirit" in Gal 4:29; cf. Rom 9:8). Nevertheless, Luke may have intended to describe a virginal conception. Even more positive than Matthew's is Luke's attitude towards Jesus' physical family. His mother, who is praised in 1:38.42.45; 2:19.51 and 11:27-28 firmly remains 'his own'. In Acts 1:14, Mary is mentioned once more to show that she was part of those who waited for the outpouring of the Holy Spirit (BROWN *et alii* 1978:119-177).

The Gospel of John features Mary as the "mother of Jesus" or refers to her implicitly. The dominant motif of the story of the wedding at Cana (2:1-11) is christological, but the mother of Jesus does have an important role in the events leading up to the sign (BROWN *et alii* 1978:187). Though this scene seems to suggest imperfect belief on Mary's part, her faith as implied in 19:25-27 can be contrasted to the lack of it on the part of Jesus' brothers in 7:1-10: the natural family disqualifies itself but Jesus' natural mother and the beloved disciple are taken up into the eschatological family because of their faith (BROWN *et alii* 1978:213).

In Rev 12 a woman "clothed with the sun" appears. The description echoes various OT passages referring to messianic persons and their work. The woman symbolizes the people of God, Israel, the Church. Thus Rev 12 does not intend to refer to Mary, but aims to assure its readers of ultimate victory in times of persecution (BROWN *et alii* 1978:230-231). Yet from the fourth century onwards the woman was often taken to stand for Mary, since the description was interpreted as concerning the mother of the →Messiah.

III. After the NT, biblical themes are taken up, or reinterpreted to refer to Mary and new elements appear. Ignatius calls the virginity of Mary and her giving birth "mysteries worth shouting out" (*Eph.*19,1). Justin still knows people who do acknowledge Jesus as the Messiah, but also believe he was conceived naturally. He and most Christians, however, believe in the virginal conception (*Dial.* 48,4). For Irenaeus, the "sign of the →virgin," based on the LXX text of Isa 7:14, stands over against the—in his opinion—false translations of the term *'almâ* as "young woman" by Theodotion and Aquila, who were followed by the Ebionites in their conviction that Joseph was Jesus' father (*Adv. Haer.* III,21,1). Like Justin and Irenaeus, Tertullian adduces the virgin birth as a real birth worthy of God, as a proof of the true humanity of Jesus, over against gnostic docetism (*De carne Christi*).

After the demise of gnosticism, patristic interest in Mary is rekindled by the rise of asceticism. Clement of Alexandria (*Strom.* VII,16) paraphrases, and Origen (*In Matt* X,17) mentions, the *Protevangelium of James*, the first writing to express belief in Mary's perpetual virginity. In the fourth century, this motif came to be hotly debated during the Arian struggle. The word *aeiparthenos*, first attested as an epithet of Mary early in the fourth century in Peter of Alexandria, is used against the Arians by Athanasius, is found in Epiphanius, Didymus and others (LAMPE 1961) and then becomes most common in Greek theological and liturgical usage. At the level of ecumenical councils, Mary's virginity was confessed at Constantinople in 381 and her perpetual virginity in 553. In the Syrian East, Ephrem's *Hymni De Nativitate Domini* and others show Marian devotion; the probably spurious *Hymni de Beata Maria Virgine* are more explicit on issues like Mary's perpetual virginity.

In the West, Mary's virginity is first emphatically defended by Hilary of Poitiers (*Comm.Matt.* I,3) and after the adoption of the monastic ideal of virginity from the East, upheld against opponents of that ideal by Jerome (*Adversus Helvidium*, *Adversus Jovinianum*) and especially Ambrose, who has an exceptional interest in Mary as a person (*De virginibus, De virginitate, De institutione virginis*). Augustine has little specific interest in Mary herself, but insists on her perpetual virginity for christological reasons, adopting Zeno of Verona's phrase (I 54, II.5): *virgo concepit, virgo peperit, virgo permansit* on many occasions (e.g. *Sermons* 51, 170, 196, 231 etc.). The same Zeno (I 3, X.19) also introduced the idea of the conception through Mary's ear; this idea became popular in the Middle Ages (JONES 1951).

The clauses concerning the Virgin Birth in the Old Roman ('Apostolic') and the Nicaeno-Constantinopolitan Creed have a purely christological intention. That the main scope of Marian devotion in patristic times was in fact a christological one, becomes quite clear through the debate on the use of the word *theotokos* ('God-bearing'), first attested probably not in Hippolytus, but in the works of Alexandrians like Origen, Alexander and Athanasius, then in Epiphanius. It is insisted upon by the Cappadocians (Gregory of Nazianzus in *Epistula* 101: "If someone does not accept holy Mary as God-bearing, he is outside the Godhead"), and became a subject of controversy in the fifth century christological debate between Cyril of Alexandria and Nestorius. The latter proposed the term *christotokos* ('Christ-bearing') as a compromise between *theotokos* and *anthrōpotokos* ('man-bearing', a fourth century Antiochene term) but the term *theotokos* won, first at the council of Ephesus (431) and then at Chalcedon (451) (LAMPE 1961; BENKO 1993:250).

Latin theology put forward the thesis that Jesus had to be conceived by a virgin because the transmission of original sin was related to the sexual nature of human propagation. Thus, the virginal conception almost becomes a theologoumenon of Jesus' sinlessness. The idea appears in a fragment on Ps 22(23) ascribed to Hippolytus by Theodoret (*Eranistes* Florilegium I, 88; BROWN 1973:41) but is not developed until Ambrose (e.g. *Exp. Luc.* II 56 and in his commentary on Isaiah, known through quotations by Augustine, *Contra duas epistulas Pelagianorum* IV 29) and Augustine (especially in the Pelagian controversy, e.g. *De nuptiis et concupiscentia* II 15; *Opus imperfectum contra Julianum* IV 88). As a sequence to this theologoumenon, that of Mary's own immaculate conception arose. In the East, it was advocated from Photius onwards; in the West it was not articulated theologically until Paschasius Radbertus and Anselm of Canterbury (SÖLL 1978:137, 150, 165). The typology →Eve-Mary, first found in Justin Martyr (*Dial.* 4-5) and Irenaeus (e.g. *Adv.Haer.* III, 22, 4), contrasts the disobedience of Eve with Mary's obedience. Irenaeus calls Mary Eve's advocate (*Adv.Haer.* V, 19, 1). It stimulated the conviction that Mary was free from original sin. In the works of Ephrem the Syrian, this typology acquired ecclesiological significance (MURRAY 1971). Further thoughts on the connection between Mary and the Church were developed by fathers such as Cyprian, Augustine and others (SEYBOLD 1985:89, BENKO 1993:229).

Further Marian typologies were developed in the West on the basis of several OT passages, leading to many more epithets for Mary as found e.g. in the *Carmen in laudem sanctae Mariae* ascribed to Venantius Fortunatus. Generally speaking, it was the allegorical or 'spiritual' interpretation of Biblical texts, rather than the literal, which provided opportunities to lay a Biblical basis for mariological developments (SEYBOLD 1985:48). While the first Christian examples of the use of this exegetical method are to be found in the synoptic Gospels, it was first extensively developed by Origen and the School of Alexandria and eventually also made fruitful for the elaboration of mariology. Finally, Mary devotion in the West took a new turn at the end of the patristic period with fathers such as Leander and Isidore of Sevilla and Ildephonse of Toledo; the latter desire to serve Mary with a view to serving Christ *(De virginitate beatae Mariae* XII, 167, 10-19).

In the first five centuries of the Christian era, there is no absolutely clear and explicit testimony which gives support to the Roman Catholic dogma of Mary's assumption, formulated in 1950 (JUGIE 1945:101); the first hints come in 377 in Epiphanius, *Pan.* 78. 10,11,23 (BENKO 1993:241). In the fifth and sixth centuries, apocryphal *Transitus Mariae* are written which survive in different ancient languages. Here Mary's death, funeral and bodily assumption into Paradise are described. This, and the conviction that the immaculacy of the Virgin required a bodily assumption into heaven, is the basis for the elaboration of more details concerning the circumstances of Mary's passing away in later tradition.

Parallels between Mary and pre-Christian goddesses impose themselves but cannot be traced historically. Thus it is striking that several goddesses like Mary are called →'queen of heaven' (BENKO 1993:15, 21, 51, 112, 217; the argument however hinges on a mariological interpretation of Rev 12), and since 323 Mary has been identified with Virgil's virgin (Fourth Eclogue, cf. BENKO 1993:114). Iconographic parallels between the picture of →Isis and →Horus with that of Mary and the child Jesus have also been suggested (BENKO 1993:52), but all these parallels are more phenomenological than historically verifiable.

IV. *Bibliography*

S. ALVAREZ CAMPOS, *Corpus Marianum Patristicum*, I-VI (Burgos 1970-1981); S. BENKO, *The Virgin Goddess. Studies in the Pagan and Christian Roots of Mariology* (Leiden 1993); R. E. BROWN, *The Virginal Conception & Bodily Resurrection of Jesus* (London/Dublin 1973); R. E. BROWN, K. P. DONFRIED, J. A. FITZMYER & J. REUMANN (ed.), *Mary in the New Testament* (Philadelphia/New York/Ramsey/Toronto 1978; H. F. VON CAMPENHAUSEN, *Die Jungfrauengeburt in der Theologie der alten Kirche* (Heidelberg 1962); W. DELIUS, *Texte zur Geschichte der Marienverehrung und Marienverkündigung in der alten Kirche* (Kleine Texte für Vorlesungen und Übungen 178; Berlin 1956); D. GASAGRANDE, *Enchiridion Patristicum Biblicum Marianum* (Rome 1974); P. GRELOT, D. FERNANDEZ, T. KOEHLER, S. DE FIORES & R. LAURENTIN, Marie (Vierge) I-VI, *Dictionnaire de Spiritualité* 10 (Paris 1980) col. 409-440; E. JONES, The Madonna's Conception Through the Ear, *Essays in Applied Psychoanalysis* 2 (London 1951) 266-357; M. JUGIE, *La mort et l'assomption de la Sainte Vierge. Etude historico-doctrinale* (Studi e Testi 114; Citta del Vaticano 1945); G. W. H. LAMPE, *A Patristic Greek Lexicon,* s.v. *aeipartheneuō, aeiparthenia, aeiparthenos, anthrōpotokos, christotokos, theotokos* (Oxford 1961); E. LA VERDIERE, Mary, *Encyclopedia of Early Christianity* (ed. E. Ferguson; New York/London 1990) 583-587; F. A. VON LEHNER, *Die Marienverehrung in den ersten drei Jahrhunderten* (Stuttgart 1881); R. MURRAY, Mary the Second Eve in the Early Syriac Fathers, *Eastern Churches Review* 3 (1971) 372-384; MURRAY, *Symbols of Church and Kingdom.*

A Study in Early Syriac Tradition (Cambridge 1975) 144-150, 329-335; M. O'CARROLL, *Theotokos. A Theological Encyclopedia of the Blessed Virgin Mary* (Wilmington 1983); H. RÄISÄNEN, H. GROTE, R. FRIELING, F. COURTH & C. NAUERTH, Maria/Marienfrömmigkeit I-VI, *TRE* (Berlin/New York 1992) 115-161; M. SEYBOLD (ed.), *Maria im Glauben der Kirche* (Eichstätt/Wien 1985); G. SÖLL, *Handbuch der Dogmengeschichte III,4: Mariologie* (Freiburg/Basel/Wien 1978); G. SÖLL, E. PERETTO & M. MARINONE, Mary, *Encyclopedia of the Early Church* (eds. A. di Berardino & W. H. C. Frend; Cambridge 1992) 537-540; A. WENGER, *L'assomption de la S.Vierge dans la tradition byzantine du VIe au Xe siècle* (Archives de l'Orient Chrétien 2; Paris 1955).

M. F. G. PARMENTIER

MASHḪIT → DESTROYER

MASTEMAH משׂטמה

I. Mastemah appears as a noun meaning 'hostility' in OT (Hos 9:7-8) and Qumran writings. In Qumran literature the word is mostly connected with an evil angel (→Belial) and in *Jub.* Mastemah is always a proper name for the leader of the evil angels.

II. *Maśṭēmâ* originates from the Hebrew root ŚṬM, a by-form of ŚṬN (WANKE 1976: 821-822; [→Satan] cf. the noun שׂטמה in 1QM 14:9), and occurs also in Ethiopic. It is probable that the semantic evolution of Mastemah is like that of *'Abaddôn*: a noun for a certain concept is first connected with an →angel whose role is linked up with the concept and afterwards becomes the proper name for this angel (→Abaddon). The Qumran writings form the intermediary stage between OT and *Jub.* where the proper name occurs frequently. According to MACH (1992:81, 96) *Maśṭēmâ* as the prince of the demons developed from the →Angel of Yahweh who had to execute the punishment of the Lord (cf. Masorah and ancient versions of Exod 4:24 and *Jub.* 49:2). He assumes that changing views of theodicy led to the independence and demonization of this angel. A similar reasoning may account for the group of the Angels of Hostilities which appears in 4Q 385-389 4-6 line 13 and 4Q 390 1 1:11; 2 1:7.

III. In the only two instances in the OT, Hos 9:7-8, the word means 'hostility'. In Qumran literature *maśṭēmâ* occurs ten times, sometimes in connection to Belial. In 1QS 3:23 and 4Q 286 10 2:2 the word has a pronominal suffix and cannot be a proper name (KOBELSKI 1981:45). In the dualistic columns of 1QS an antithesis is described between the →Prince of Light and the Angel of Darkness (= Belial, VON DER OSTEN-SACKEN 1969:116, 198), who rules all children of falsehood, leads all children of righteousness astray and causes their unlawful deeds (3:20-25; cf. 1QM 13:10-12). 4Q 286 10 2:2 belongs to a passage with curses against Belial and his associates. 1QM 13:4 contains an almost verbal parallel to 4Q 286 10 2:2. In these three passages *maśṭēmâ* indicates the hostile scheming and activities of Belial against the children of light in the present (cf. 1QM 14:9/4QM^{a} 7 in the context of the eschatological war). In CD 16:5 and 1QM 13:11 the phrase *Mal'āk (ham-) maśṭēmâ* ('[the] Angel of Hostility' occurs; KOBELSKI 1981:45 and BERGER 1981:379 suggest 'Angel Mastemah' as an alternative translation in 1QM). In 1QM 13 the phrase is clearly a designation for Belial, who is created by the Lord to bring destruction. In 4Q 385-389 4-6 line 13 and 4Q 390 1 1:11; 2 1:7 the plural *Mal'ākê hammaśṭēmôt* occurs and these angels also seem to act destructively during a period when the Lord hides his face from his disobedient people (EISENMAN & WISE 1993:54-55, 60, 62). CD 16:5 is preceded by a reference to *Jub.* according to several scholars (CD 16:2-4a), but VON DER OSTEN-SACKEN (1969:198-199) considers CD 16:2-4a an interpolation and claims that CD 16:5 must be earlier than *Jub.*, where a more elaborate picture of Mastemah appears. In any case the tenor of the tradition in CD 16:4b-6 is similar to *Jub.* 15:32f.: every Israelite who obeys the Law of →Moses and is circumcised will not suffer from the Angel of Hostility (*Jub.* the evil angels). Finally the small fragment of 6Q18 9 (DJD III p. 135) contains hardly more than the word *maśṭēmâ*, which allows for the translation 'hostility' as well as '(Angel) Mastemah' (cf. also *hammaśṭēmâ* in 4Q 525 4 5:4).

In *Jub.* Mastemah is the Prince of the evil spirits who menace mankind. He is identified with Satan (cf. 10:8f. with 10:11; also *Acta Philippi* 18; BOUSSET & GRESSMANN 1926:333; BERGER 1981:379). He saves a tenth of the demons from being bound underground in the place of judgment, in order to exercise his authority among mankind. His evil spirits led the sons of →Noah astray so that they committed sin, pollution and idolatry (*Jub.* 11:3-7; cf. 19:28). Mastemah also urged the Lord to put →Abraham to the test and sacrifice Isaac (*Jub.* 17:16) and helped the Egyptians in trying to destroy Moses and his people (*Jub.* 48). Concerning Mastemah in the magical papyri see BERGER (1981:379-380).

IV. *Bibliography*

W. BAUMGARTNER, review of P. Wernberg-Møller, *The Manual of Discipline* (Leiden 1957) *JSS* 4 (1959) 398-399; K. BERGER, *Das Buch der Jubiläen* (JSHRZ II:3; Gütersloh 1981) 273-575; W. BOUSSET & H. GRESSMANN, *Die Religion des Judentums im späthellenistischen Zeitalter* HNT 27; Tübingen 1926) 332-334; R. H. EISENMAN & M. WISE, *The Dead Sea Scrolls Uncovered. The First Complete Translation and Interpretation of 50 Key Documents Withheld for Over 35 Years* (New York 1993); P. J. KOBELSKI, *Melchizedek and Melchirešaʿ* (CBQMS 10; Washington 1981); M. MACH, *Entwicklungsstadien des jüdischen Engelglaubens in vorrabbinischer Zeit* (TSAJ 34; Tübingen 1992); J. T. MILIK, Milkî-ṣedeq et Milkî-rešaʿ dans les anciens écrits juifs et chrétiens, *JJS* 23 (1972) 130-135; P. VON DER OSTEN-SACKEN, *Gott und Belial. Traditionsgeschichtliche Untersuchungen zum Dualismus in den Texten aus Qumran* (SUNT 6; Göttingen 1969); G. WANKE, שָׂטָן *śāṭān* Widersacher, *THAT* II 1/821-823.

J. W. VAN HENTEN

MATTER → HYLE

MAZZALOTH → CONSTELLATIONS

MEDIATOR I מלאך מליץ

I. The two Hebrew words appearing together only in Job 33:23 are not in a construct or genitive relationship (as is true of *mal'ak yhwh*, →Angel of Yahweh), for they are either in apposition, function as poetic parallels, or the first noun is modified by the second adjectival participle. *Mal'āk* means simply messenger or →angel. On the other hand, considerable difficulty has hindered the reconciliation of the negative connotations of the root LWṢ/LYṢ ('scoff, scorn, mock'; cf. Ps 119:51; Prov 3:34; 9:12) with the positive interpretations of the five biblical appearances of the *hiphil* participle ('interpreter', Gen 42:23; 'ambassador' 2 Chr 32:31; 'spokesman' Isa 43:27; 'mediator' Job 33:23; Job 16:20 continues to be interpreted either positively or negatively). Two different roots may be present, but if one accepts a general significance of 'talk freely, talk at length', it is possible that a single root has developed these quite distinct meanings. Apart from Phoenician, which depends upon Hebrew for its interpretation in this case with its even less helpful evidence (cf. *KAI* 26 I.8; 49.17; *CIS* I 44.12), no other semitic language preserves the root (*pace HALAT* 503 and *AHW* 539, *lâṣu* is not a loanword in Akkadian; see *CAD* Š/1 370 *šanāṣu*). The term designates some type of civil office in Phoenician and Sir 10:2 (in the latter it is subordinate to a city's 'judge', *šwpṭ*). 1QH records several occasions where the noun is in a construct expression (variously translated as 'interpreter of, spokesman of, preacher of, babbler of') with words such as →'falsehood' (2.31; 4.9), 'error' (2.14), 'knowledge' (2.6,13), and 'deception' (4.7,10). Because of the poor cognate data and the few and quite diverse contexts in which the noun appears, focusing its meaning must be admitted to be an unresolved problem.

II. If this creature's primary duty is to show solicitous concern for a particular human being and to intervene between a human and →God, Sumerian and Akkadian sources (textual and iconographic) abundantly document the central role of each human's personal god in this capacity. However, the Mesopotamian personal god is not an altogether comfortable counterpart to the figure in Job 33:23 where not every person can be expected to encounter this figure ("if there is..."), who here functions as the apparent last hope of an individual *in extremis*, and who takes some initiative in communicating with humans. The personal god in Mesopotamia, on the other hand, is frequently the first god presumed to be petulantly angry and frustrated into silence with an individual's behaviour and one to whom the worshipper must send other placating deities of higher rank.

If the words of intercession in Job 33:24 are to be attributed to the *mal'āk mēlîṣ* of v 23, it may reflect the common appearance of lower ranking—but still quite respectable (often a god's spouse or vizier)—Akkadian deities, who approach higher ranking gods to speak on behalf of a human ('to intercede', *abbūta ṣabātu*, *CAD* Ṣ 24-25; A/2 50). But unlike these Akkadian intercessory deities who are typically invoked by the human petitioner because of their particularly intimate relationship with the high god in question, in Job 33:23-24 the initiative is entirely in the divine realm (the afflicted man does not ask for help) and the relationship of the *mal'āk mēlîṣ* to God is undefined. More appropriate to the Job context, therefore, might be those deities who on their own initiative intercede for humans, e.g. Ishum, 'the intercessor' (*mukīl abbutti*), petitions the king of the underworld not to kill a man (SAA 3 [1989] no. 32 r. 16).

However, the closest counterpart in the ancient Near East to the activities of the *mal'āk mēlîṣ* in Job 33:23 occurs in *Ludlul Bēl Nēmeqi*, a text whose genre shows some overlap with the book of Job. There, the person whom →Marduk has afflicted (cf. Job 33:19-22 with *Ludlul* II 88-96) sees four dreams (cf. Job 33:15). In these dreams, gods (among them Marduk) and individuals otherwise unidentifiable send priests and perhaps supernatural beings (→Sons of God) to speak to the sufferer of his impending recovery (*Ludlul* III 9-45). As in Job 33:26-28, the afflicted one recovers and before men praises the god who healed him.

III. Angelic intercession for man before God is extremely rare in the OT (Job 5:1; Zech 1:12), a situation that dramatically contrasts with its frequency in later Jewish and Christian literature (e.g. Rev 8:3-4; Tob 12:15; *1 Enoch* 15:2; 39:5; 40:6; *T. Levi* 3:5; *T. Dan* 6:2). The infrequency of angelic intercession in the OT, where God and humans usually converse directly with each other, is a crucial contrast between Israelite and Mesopotamian religion (where appeals to interceding deities are frequent), encouraging caution in drawing parallels with the personal god in the latter.

The unique appearance of the combination *mal'āk mēlîṣ* in Job 33:23 is made even more problematic by its presence in a context where there is no agreement upon how the various characters relate to one another. What is beyond dispute about this figure in the text as it now stands can be briefly summarized. 1) Because the words *mal'āk mēlîṣ* have no definite article, they refer to an unspecified figure ('a *mal'āk*, a *mēlîṣ*') whose role here could be filled by a number of candidates; 2) Not every human encounters such a *mal'āk mēlîṣ*, for a conditional clause introduces his presence: "*If* he has a *mal'āk mēlîṣ*..."; 3) The task of a *mal'āk mēlîṣ* at minimum encompasses the conveyance of information about proper conduct to humans ("to tell his uprightness to mankind/a man", v 23). Because of these central facts, many comparisons commonly made between this figure and characters mentioned elsewhere in Job who are not so characterized (5:1; 16:19-22; 19:25-27) must be acknowledged to be tenuous.

Because the pronominal referents are imprecise in this passage, it must be underscored that God is the primary actor in 33:13-30 (see v 29) who deals with humans on the brink of death ('the pit', *šaḥat*; vv 18, 22, 24, 28, 30): God with great forbearance wants to preserve the individual whose recalcitrance is jeopardizing his own life. For this reason, any comparisons are inappropriate that identify either ancient Near Eastern deities who placate and intercede with a wrathful high god for humanity's sake (e.g. Ishum in the *Erra Epic*), or the numerous deities who plead on behalf of other deities held against their will or incapacitated in the underworld (IRWIN 1962). No interceding figure is needed in this passage to shield man from God's anger, for God is not depicted as angry.

This text may contain as many as five different clusters of participants: God, the afflicted man, a *mal'āk mēlîṣ*, →angels of death (*mĕmitîm* v 22), and a group of a thousand individuals from whom the *mal'āk mēlîṣ* emerges (v 23). The thousand may reflect a common allusion to the numerous gods in 2nd millennium BCE texts in the Hittite sphere (GEVIRTZ 1990); here of course, they would be creatures subordinated to God. There is no way of resolving whether or not one is to imply the difficulty of finding a *mal'āk mēlîṣ* (i.e. only one out of a thousand appears; cf. *Tg. Jonathan*; *b.Shab.* 32a) or the ease in finding a *mal'āk mēlîṣ* (i.e. only one is needed and there are so many from which to choose). The closest parallel to the passage yet identified (*Ludlul* noted above) presents both humans and divine beings in the role of a messenger sent to an afflicted man, an ambiguity also inherent in the Heb *mal'āk*. Indeed, Elihu is implicitly presenting himself as just such a messenger from God enlightening Job.

The major problem in defining the role of the *mal'āk mēlîṣ* is that the speaker and the addressee of v 24 cannot be determined with confidence. Is it the *mal'āk mēlîṣ* (as the most recently identified actor, v 23) or God (as the primary actor throughout the passage) who says, "Deliver him from going down into the Pit; I have found a ransom" (v 24; NRSV)? And who is spoken to as the one who should 'deliver him': God? the *mal'āk mēlîṣ*? one of the angels of death (v 22)? Most scholars would like to see these words spoken by the *mal'āk mēlîṣ*, in spite of the fact that such an address to God requires a complete reversal of the envoy's responsibility directed toward man depicted in v 23. Regardless of whether or not the term *mal'āk* preserves its significance of 'messenger' or is a generic term for supernatural beings, in v 23 it can only be an envoy from God to man, not man to God, further undermining any significant parallel between this figure and the personal god of Mesopotamia. In addition, it is irrelevant whether a *mal'āk*-envoy is gracious or not toward a human, for an envoy is obligated to behave and carry out his commission as his sender (God) has ordered. Consequently, the first word of v 24 ("he is gracious")—the key to identifying the speaker of the verse—most comfortably applies to God, the initiating agent throughout this passage.

It is often claimed that this figure "interprets suffering" (e.g. ROSS 1975:42). However, nowhere does this creature interpret anything (it informs) and any association of *mēlîṣ* with the notions 'interpret' or 'translate' should be avoided. Translation from one language to another is broadly and from great antiquity attested in the Semitic languages by the quadriliteral root TRGM (GELB 1968).

IV. Although some rely upon the *Tg. Jonathan* to define *mēlîṣ* (*TDNT* 5, 809), the Targum's rendering of *mēlîṣ* by *prqlyṭ'* (from Gk *paraklētos*, 'advocate in court, one pleading another's case') introduces later notions into the text that are not demonstrably there. The fact that a foreign, non-Semitic word is used to translate the Hebrew should alert one to the possibility that the *prqlyṭ'* is an institution foreign to the OT. The Johannine description of the →Holy Spirit (John 16:7-11) and →Jesus (1 John 2:1) each as such a *paraklētos* may reflect an interpretation of Job 33:23 along these lines, but the quite different Hellenistic cultural milieu of the NT appears several centuries too late to assist in defining what the text of Job originally meant.

V. *Bibliography*

M. A. CANNEY, The Hebrew מליץ, *AJSL* 40 (1923-24) 135-137; R. DI VITO, *Studies in Third Millennium Sumerian and Akkadian Onomastics: The Designation and Conception of the Personal God* (Harvard 1986);

I. J. Gelb, The Word for Dragoman in the Ancient Near East, *Glossa* 2 (1968) 93-104; S. Gevirtz, Phoenician *wšbrt mlṣm* and Job 33:23, *Maarav* 5-6 (1990) 145-158; W. A. Irwin, Job's Redeemer, *JBL* 81 (1962) 217-229; H. N. Richardson, Some Notes on ליץ and its Derivatives, *VT* 5 (1955) 163-179; Richardson, Two Addenda to "Some Notes on ליץ and its Derivatives", *VT* 5 (1955) 434-436; J. F. Ross, Job 33:14-30: The Phenomenology of Lament, *JBL* 94 (1975) 38-46; H. Vorländer, *Mein Gott. Die Vorstellungen vom persönlichen Gott im Alten Orient und im Alten Testament* (AOAT 23; Neukirchen-Vluyn 1975).

S. A. Meier

MEDIATOR II μεσίτης

I. The term *mesitēs* originates from Hellenistic legal terminology and was usually a technical term for a mediator or intermediary between two or more parties, such as the peace negotiator, the arbitrator between two legal parties, the witnesses in a legal transaction, the neutral party with whom a disputed object could be deposited, or the guarantor (see Schultess 1931 and Oepke 1942). Especially in the Hellenistic-Jewish sphere *mesitēs* is also used figuratively for the mediator between people (cf. Josephus, *Ant* 16,24), and between mankind and →God.

In the NT *mesitēs* occurs 6 times, twice (Gal 3:19-20) in reference to →Moses as a mediator of the law, and four times to →Christ as mediator between mankind and God (1 Tim 2:5) or as mediator of the new or better covenant (Heb 8:6; 9:15; 12:24).

II. 'Mediators' occur in various religious contexts. In the Ancient Near Eastern context of Israel, both the sacral kingdom and the priesthood were mediators between the divine world and mankind. If we are primarily concerned here with the connection between mankind and gods, then the subdivine mediating powers such as →demons, gods of the →heavens and →stars, and other lower gods also frequently have an ordering function in the cosmos.

The significance of mediators is above all reflected explicitly where the great distance—or even the contrast—between the mortal world and the divine sphere makes it seem necessary to bridge the gap. In this respect, the demonic in Plato's *Symp* 203a, for example, is just such a necessary mediating being (*metaxy esti*) between gods and mankind, since God and man had no direct contact (*theos de anthrōpōi ou meignytai*). The *daimonion* conveys to the gods the prayers and sacrifices of mankind and in turn passes on to mankind the gods' commands and the benefits they give in return for the sacrifices "so that the universe is bound together" (*Symp.* 202e). Plato particularly stresses that there are many such intermediary demons. The idea of only one specific mediator does not occur until very late in classical antiquity, and then relatively rarely. Its prerequisite is probably the 'spätantike Drang zum Monotheismus' (Nilsson 1974:577), advocated by philosophy and, at least equally strongly, by the political entity of the imperial monarch. The →one God, increasingly regarded as transcendent, became inaccessible for the everyday problems of mankind; correspondingly, the need grew for a mediator to be the side of godhood that was accessible to the world. Pagan references to such a divine mediator can be found, for example, in inscriptions in Asia Minor, in which the highest god was assigned a second god as *theios*, *theios* →*angelos* or *theios angelikos* (see Nilsson 1963).

Significantly, however, the term *mesitēs* has hardly come down to us at all in this context. The earliest example is to be found in Plutarch's *Is et Os* 46 (369e), where the Persian →Mithras is called *mesitēs*. Plutarch explains this as meaning that Mithras stands between the good god Ahura Mazda and the evil god Ahriman (*meson d' amphoin*). This probably is a reference to the celestial god's cosmic role as mediator between the opposing powers. Further details, however, about Mithras teaching mankind the appropriate way to deal with these gods, suggest that, at least in Plutarch, Mithras is seen also as a mediator between the mortal and the divine spheres. At the same time, Mithras is the god of amicable ties among mankind, as indeed his name implies ('contract'). This last, almost legal sense is applied to the (love) god in Ps-Lucian, *Amor* 47, as *mesitēs*, i.e. as guarantor and covenanter of the mutual passion felt by Pylades and Orestes. It is even more clearly applicable in Diodorus Siculus 4,54,7, where, after the murder of her children, Medea encumbers →Heracles with being the guarantor of a contract (*mesitēs tōn homologiōn*). In this respect, in early Judaism, too, God can be called *mesitēs*, as a guarantor and covenanter of an oath or a contract (Josephus, *Ant.* 4,133; cf. also Philo, *SpecLeg.* 4,31).

III. In the OT, too, there are figures who function as mediators. In addition to a king such as David, chosen by God, or a prophet such as Jeremiah, there is of course →Moses, who conveys God's will to the Israelites and, in turn, appears before →Yahweh on behalf of the people, and intercedes for them (cf. Exod 20:19; Num 21:7; Deut 18:16).

But even though Moses' role as mediator is repeatedly emphasised, the term 'mediator' is, significantly, not applied to him or to any other figure in the OT. The only time that the word *mesitēs* occurs in the LXX is Job 9:33, and there it is to lament the very lack of a *mesitēs* as an arbitrator (*môkîaḥ*) between God and mankind.

Since the idea of a specific mediator between the mortal and the divine world suggests itself primarily in connection with the concept of a monotheistic, transcendent God, it is not surprising that the term *mesitēs* occurs in this sense in the Hellenistic-Jewish sphere, where Israelite monotheism combines with Greek metaphysics. Here, there is reference to a *mesitēs* in the sense of a religious mediator, although also relatively rarely. This designation is primarily conferred on Moses. In *Vit Mos* 2,166, Philo refers to him directly as mediator and reconciler (*mesitēs kai diallaktēs*) or as protector and intercessor (*kēdemōn kai paraitētēs*), when, on the mountain, he hears of the apostasy of the people and thereupon intercedes on this people's behalf before God. In *Rer Div Her* 205-206 the Alexandrian religious philosopher, calls God's →Logos his chief messenger and →archangel (*archangelos*) who stands on the border and separates the creature from the Creator. Thus standing ontologically and physically between God and mankind, he is guarantor for both with both, almost becoming the guarantor of the cosmic order: he "is neither uncreated as God, nor created as you, but midway between the two extremes (*mesos tōn akrōn*), a surety to both sides; to the parent, pledging the creature that it should never altogether rebel against the rein and choose disorder rather than order; to the child, warranting his hopes that the merciful God will never forget His own work. For I am the harbinger of peace to creation from that God whose will is to bring wars to an end, who is ever the guardian of peace" (*Rer Div Her* 206). Philo is not alone in his deification of Moses: in a Greek fragment of *Ass.Mos.* 1:14, Moses says of himself that even before the creation of the world he was ordained by God to be the mediator of his covenant. In Rabbinic literature, too, Moses is repeatedly referred to as *sarsôr* (= *mesitēs*), although here the mediating function is largely restricted to the handing down of the →Torah (see Str-B 3,556).

It is chiefly in Hellenistic Judaism that Moses as a mediator can become a superhuman, semi-godlike figure of salvation. This position is also granted to →angels (as, indeed, when Philo once calls Moses *archangelos*). In *Somn* 1,142-143 Philo twice uses the term *mesitēs* to refer to angels as functionally mediating and ontologically intermediate beings, needed by mankind because it could not endure the direct confrontation with God. The parallel use of *logoi* to refer to these angels and the comment that the other philosophers call these angels demons (*Somn* 1,41) show that the chief influence on Philo here is Plato. Probably of greater significance for the early Jewish concept of an angel as mediator is

TDan 6:2 (*T.12 Patr.*). The closing exhortation of this testament calls for a turning (*eggizein*) towards God 'and towards his angel'. Here, then, is a second figure besides God, characterised as a mediator between God and mankind (*mesitēs theou kai anthrōpōn*). This mediating function expresses itself in two ways: on the one hand this angel intercedes with God for Israel, and on the other he fights for the 'peace of Israel' against the 'realm of the enemy' and strengthens God's people in times of crisis (*TDan* 6:2-6). Here, too, it is a single, unique mediator, standing between God and mankind as the 'angel of peace' (*TDan* 6:5) and, by means of mediation, bringing about *shalom*. It is particularly remarkable that this mediator becomes the object of religious worship alongside God.

By adopting the idea of a mediator, Christianity is following in the footsteps of Judaism. As far as Gal 3:19-20 is concerned, by saying that Moses was a mediator for the law, Paul was giving expression to a view widely held at that time in Judaism. The only new aspect is that Paul does not use this idea of a mediator (or the involvement of the angels) to increase the value of the Torah, but instead to relativise it inasmuch as the Torah thereby lacks the directness of the promises made to →Abraham by God himself. The meaning of the ensuing sentence (v 20) is a subject of dispute: "A mediator, however, is not needed for one; but God is one". The most likely explanation of this sentence sees *mesitēs* here as a representative of the (many) angels who, according to 3:19, ordained the Torah. This again underlines that the Torah does not have its direct origin in God, because he is →one and therefore does not need a mediator.

By contrast, there is a positive, christological application of the mediator concept in 1 Tim 2:5-6 and Hebr 8:6; 9:15; 12:24. In 1 Tim 2:5-6, a liturgical piece, it says: "For there is one God, and one mediator between God and men, the man →Jesus →Christ, who gave himself as a ransom for all". This clearly takes up the early Jewish speculation about mediators described above, speculation which claimed that it was precisely the relationship produced by the mediator between God and mankind that bestowed salvation. What is new is the reason for this position as mediator: the atoning death of Jesus, who despite his role as the bringer of universal salvation (*hyper pantōn*) is here pointedly called a 'man'.

Half of all the New Testament references to *mesitēs* are to be found in the Letter to the Hebrews (Hebr 8:6; 9:15; 12:24), and they are all in conjunction with *diathēkē* in the objective genitive. Just as the qualification of this covenant emphasises that it is a 'better' (8:6 cf. 7:22) or 'new' covenant (9:15; 12:24), all three references antithetically underline the superiority of the covenant conveyed by the *mesitēs* Jesus Christ over the hitherto covenant. The corresponding phrase in Heb 7:22, that Jesus is a 'surety (*eggyos*) of a better covenant', suggests that the term *mesitēs* in Heb should also be assigned its original juridicial meaning of 'guarantor' (cf. also Josephus *Ant* 4,133): the new covenant is at the same time guaranteed by Jesus as the true high priest. This interpretation of *mesitēs* is also corroborated by the verb *mesiteuō* (as a NT hapax legomenon) in Heb 6:17, where it says that God "confirmed the immutability of his counsel by an oath".

Irenaeus also takes up the Hellenistic-Jewish idea of the mediator when in *Adv. Haer.* 3, 18, 7 he makes the point that a mediator between God and mankind is required in order to make God known. According to Clement of Alexandrina *Paed* 3,1, the *logos* is 'mediator' to both God and mankind—as son and servant to God, and as →saviour and teacher to mankind. On the whole, however, it is noticeable that the concept of mediator which had became so important in later dogmatic theology is relatively rarely used even in early Christianity. Perhaps this is connected with the original juridical character of the concept. But presumably the obvious association of a semi-divine, ontologically intermediate being with regard to Christ was also felt to be somewhat problematic.

IV. *Bibliography*

K. GOLDAMMER & K. H. RENGSTORF, *RGG*³ 4 1063-1065; R. MERKELBACH, *Mithras* (Königstein/Ts. 1984) esp. 27; M. P. NILSSON, *Geschichte der griechischen Religion* 2 (München 1974³) 576-578; M. P. NILSSON, The High God and the Mediator, *HTR* 56 (1963) 101-120; A. OEPKE, *TWNT* 4 (1942) 602-629; D. SÄNGER, *EWNT* 2 (1981) 1010-1012; J. SCHARBERT, *Heilsmittler im AT und im Alten Orient* (Freiburg 1964) 82-92, 242-244; F. J. SCHIERSE, Mittler, *Handbuch theologischer Grundbegriffe* 2 169-172; SCHULTESS, Mesites, PW 15/1 (1931) 1097-1099; C. SPICQ, *Notes de Lexicographie Néotestamentaire* 2 (OBO 22,2; Fribourg/Götttingen 1978) 549-552.

R. FELDMEIER

MELCHIZEDEK מלכיצדק Μελχιζεδεκ

I. The name of Melchizedek appears twice in the OT, viz. Gen 14:18 and Ps 110:4, and eight times in the NT, viz. Hebrews (where Ps 110:4 is quoted or alluded to five times). The meaning of the name is either 'my king is righteousness' or 'my king is →Zedek'; probably 'king' refers to a deity and 'righteousness' is a divine attribute or 'Zedek' is the name of the deity (cf. *malkî'ēl*, Gen 46:17; Num 26:45; 1 Chr 7:31; and *malkîyâ*, e.g. Jer 21:1). It is a theophoric name. Outside the Bible the name of Melchizedek plays an important part in Jewish and Christian sources depending on the biblical data. The so-called Melchizedekians regarded him as a divine figure.

II. In Gen 14:8-20 the brief narrative of →Abraham's meeting with Melchizedek is inserted in another story, viz. the meeting of Abraham and the king of Sodom, and probably placed here in order to give a parallel to that story. Melchizedek is introduced as king of Salem, probably Jerusalem (cf. Ps 76:3; Josephus, *Ant.* I 180) and as priest of the god →Most High (*'ēl 'elyôn*, probably a Canaanite deity), the creator of →heaven and earth (also a Canaanite epithet, see WESTERMANN 1979:243). The combination of kingship and priesthood is not unknown in the ancient Near East. In a Phoenician inscription (*KAI* 13) both Tabnit and Eshmuneser are presented as royal priests: "priest of →Ashtarte and king of the Sidonians". Melchizedek supported Abraham with food and wine and conferred the blessing of his god upon him. Abraham in his turn gave Melchizedek a tithe of the booty. The story reflects the encounter of the nomadic religion of the patriarchs with the established cultic religion of the town and the recognition of the precedence of the latter. In the present context the god Most High is identified with →Yahweh (cf. Gen 14:22) and the story is understood as a sign of divine support and encouragement for Abraham.

Another occurence of Melchizedek is found in Ps 110:4. The psalm is a song for the enthronement of a ruler, probably a king (though the word 'king' is not used), in Jerusalem (cf. 'Zion' in v 2). The text abounds in textual and exegetical problems (cf. KRAUS 1960:752-764; HORTON 1976: 23-34). Recent scholarship locates the psalm in the time of the early Israelite kingship (M. GILBERT & S. PISANO, *Bib* 61 [1980] 356). It contains two oracles in which the king-to-be is directly addressed, probably by a prophet, viz. in v 1 and v 4. The former is the enthronement-formula which guarantees divine support for the new king, the latter, introduced by a divine oath, declares him to be priest for ever as well. His priesthood is defined as 'in' or 'after the manner of Melchizedek' (*'al dibrātî malkî-ṣedeq*). The exact meaning of this phrase is hard to establish. It may mean 'in the line of Melchizedek', i.e. inheriting the priesthood of Melchizedek, 'like Melchizedek', or 'on account of Melchizedek'. The common translation 'order' is due to the LXX where *'al dibrātî* is rendered *kata tēn taxin*. Probably the formula shows that the kings of Israel, beginning with David, inherited the tradition of the priest-king of pre-Israelite Jerusalem. This connection between kingship and priesthood apparently did not last very long since no king of Judah was called priest and allusions to priestly conduct are limited to

David and Solomon (cf. 2 Sam 6:14.18; 24:17; 1 Kgs 8:14.56; KRAUS 1960:760; BERNHARDT 1992:416). The title 'priest forever' is not found again until 1 Macc 14:41.

The only other reference to Melchizedek in the Bible is in Heb 7. The very special interpretation of Gen 14 and Ps 110 presented there cannot be understood without taking into account contemporaneous Melchizedek interpretations in Jewish sources, viz. (a) Josephus, (b) Philo, and (c) Qumran. Together with (d) Hebrews they present a very composite picture of Melchizedek.

In Josephus, *War* VI 438 Melchizedek is mentioned as a Canaanite chief (*dynastēs*). His Hebrew name is not mentioned but translated into Greek as 'righteous king' and this shows that Melchizedek is meant. According to Josephus, Melchizedek was the first one to build the temple and to act as priest of →God. In *Ant.* I 179-181 the story of Gen 14:18-20 is told with some minor embellishments. The name of Melchizedek is mentioned and again translated as 'righteous king'. Josephus adds that by common consent this was what he was and that for that reason Melchizedek was made priest of God. In both places Melchizedek is described as king and priest, i.e. as an historical person.

Philo mentions Melchizedek in three places: *De Abr.* 235, *De Congr.* 99, and *Leg. All.* III 79-82. In *De Abr.* 235 the story of Gen 14:18-20 is retold and embellished. Melchizedek is called 'the great priest of the Most High God': thinking that Abraham's success was due to divine wisdom and help, he stretched his hands to heaven and honoured him with prayers and offered sacrifices on his behalf and entertained him and his men lavishly. In the subsequent allegorical interpretation of the story of Abraham's warfare (Gen 14:1-24) Melchizedek is not mentioned again: he acts as an historical person only. In *De Congr.* 99 Melchizedek is mentioned in an excursus on the number ten (89-120) with reference to the fact that Abraham gave him one tenth of everything (Gen 14:20). This is interpreted metaphorically: 'everything' comprises the things of sense, speech and thought. Melchizedek is identified as the man who obtained the self-learned and self-taught priesthood, probably because no priest is mentioned before him in the Bible and later priesthood is not derived from him. In *Leg. All.* III 79-82 Melchizedek is presented as an example of people who are honoured by God without having done beforehand something to please Him. He was made king by God and he was the first to be worthy to be his priest. Philo contrasts this king with a despot (*tyrannos*) who is identified as 'mind' (*nous*) and decrees things that cause hurt, pain, wickedness and indulgence of passions. The king does not decree but persuades and exhorts people to let themselves be governed by the king as the good pilot who is the 'right reason' (*orthos logos*), at the same time a moral principle and the principle of divine wisdom. Melchizedek as the 'righteous king' is the incorporation of the 'right reason'. He is the prince of peace and brings bread and wine as food for the souls. The wine serves to make them participants of divine intoxication, more sober than sobriety itself. The king-priest who is *logos* (→Logos), viz. *ho orthos logos*, has God as his 'lot' (*klēros*) and thinks highly and sublimely of Him and calls up a 'picture' or 'image' (*emphasis*) of the Most High. In Philo's perspective Melchizedek as a king and priest does not cease to be an historical person but at the same time serves as the embodiment of the divine *orthos logos* and transcends history.

In the Qumran texts Melchizedek is mentioned twice. In 1QapGen 22 the story of Gen 14:18-20 is translated more or less literally with some minor additions. Melchizedek is represented as an historical person without comment or interpretation of his name. Far more important and intriguing is 11QMelch consisting of 13 fragments. In it Melchizedek plays a central role. The many lacunae make a conclusive interpretation virtually impossible. The text has the form of an eschatological midrash in which the liberation prophesied in Isa 61:1-7 is described in terms of the restoration of property during the year of Jubilee (Lev 25:13). The deliverer is Melchizedek. The 'year of the LORD's favour' (Isa 61:2) is called 'the year of the favour of (or: for) Melchizedek'. This liberation implies the judgment of the nations according to Pss 7:8 and 82:1. In the *pesher* of Ps 82:1 the opening word *ʾĕlōhîm* is interpreted as referring to Melchizedek (l. 10) since the preceding *ʿālāyw* clearly refers to him. *ʾĕlōhîm* is not understood as God but as a divine being. Whether the second *ʾĕlōhîm* in Ps 82:2 is interpreted as referring to divine beings who belong to the court of Melchizedek or to →demonic beings who are judged by him is not certain. The former seems preferable. The 'inheritance of Melchizedek' (l. 5) and 'the men of the lot of Melchizedek' (l. 8) probably refer to the captives who will be liberated by Melchizedek. This divine liberation is expected to take place at the end of the tenth Jubilee (l. 7) on the Day of Atonement. The verb KPR occurs in l. 8 and possibly also in l. 6 but in neither place is it clear whether Melchizedek is the priestly agent of atonement. In l. 15-16 Isa 52:7 (// Nah 2:2) is quoted and 'he who brings good news' (*mbśr)* is interpreted as 'the anointed by the Spirit' (*mšyḥ rûaḥ*). This may be understood as an allusion to the 'anointed prince' of Dan 9:25 or to the prophet upon whom the spirit of the LORD God is (Isa 61:1), probably the former. Whether this 'anointed one' is identical with Melchizedek is doubtful.

The early Christians made use of Psalm 110 for christological reasons. The hymn was seen as the scriptural proof for the exaltation of →Christ (cf. e.g. Mark 14:62 parr; Acts 2:34-35; 1 Cor 15:25) but only in Hebrews the reference to Melchizedek and his priesthood are used as part of the argument concerning the highpriesthood of Christ. Basically Melchizedek plays a hermeneutical role in Hebrews in order to establish the supremacy of that high priesthood over the priesthood of the tabernacle.

The description of Melchizedek in 7:1-3 consists of the following four sections: (1) A summary of Gen 14:18-20 (v 1-2a): relevant to the argument are the blessing of Abraham by Melchizedek and the giving of one tenth of everything to Melchizedek by Abraham, since they show that Melchizedek was superior to Abraham and, implicitly, to his descendants Levi and the Levite priesthood. Because of the relationship of Melchizedek and the →Son of God this superiority also applies to Christ; (2) An interpretation of the name as 'king of righteousness' and 'king of peace' (v 2b): this resembles the interpretation of Philo and Josephus and suggests a common exegetical tradition but plays no part in the argument. (3) A series of qualifications in the negative (v 3a): "without father, without mother, without genealogy, having neither beginning of days nor end of life". They are not mentioned in Gen 14 or Ps 110 nor in Philo, Josephus and or 11QMelch. Since nothing of this is transparent in Gen 14 these qualifications may have been deducted *e silentio,* according to the rule *quod non in Thora non in mundo*. In Greek sources *apatōr* and *amētōr* are often used with reference to the non-human origin of gods (G. SCHRENK, *TWNT* 5 [1954] 1021-1022; WILLIAMSON 1970:20-23). In the argument the qualifications serve to establish the permanent nature of Melchizedek's priesthood (v 3c). Apart from that they presuppose Melchizedek to be some sort of a divine being. (4) A description of the relationship between Melchizedek and the Son of God by the participle *aphōmoiōmenos* (v 3b): the introductory particle *de* suggests that this statement serves to qualify the preceding picture of Melchizedek. He is not a divine being in his own right but he is "made to be like the Son of God" as described in 1:1-14. The Son of God is the type and Melchizedek is the antitype. He appears on the one hand as a human and historical king and on the other hand as a more-than-human being resembling, and in a sense representing, the eternal Son of God. Over-all the author of the Epistle to the Hebrews combines the biblical traditions concerning Melchizedek with a tradition of Melchizedek as a divine being (perhaps similar to 11QMelch) to serve his hermeneutical and theological purpose.

The traditions concerning Melchizedek described so far have given rise to various speculations both in Jewish and Christian sources which testify to his deification. The evidence for these Melchizedekian sects is collected and interpreted in ATTRIDGE (1989:194-195) and HORTON (1976:87-147).

III. *Bibliography*

H. W. ATTRIDGE, *The Epistle to the Hebrews* (Philadelphia 1989) 186-197; K. H. BERNHARDT, T. WILLI & H. BALZ, Melchisedek, *TRE* 22 (1992) 414-423 [& lit]; *F. L. HORTON, *The Melchizedek Tradition* (Cambridge 1976); M. DE JONGE & A. S. VAN DER WOUDE, 11Q Melchizedek and the New Testament, *NTS* 12 (1972) 301-326; *P. J. KOBELSKI, *Melchizedek and Melchireša'* (Washington 1981); H. J. KRAUS, *Psalmen* (BKAT XV/2; Neukirchen-Vluyn 1960) 752-764; O. MICHEL, Melchisedek, *TWNT* 4 (1942) 573-575; J. T. MILIK, Milqi-Sedeq et Milki-Resa dans les anciens écrits juifs et chrétiens (I), *JJS* 23 (1972) 95-144; H. F. WEISS, *Der Brief an die Hebräer* (Göttingen 1991) 371-387; C. WESTERMANN, *Genesis* (BKAT I/2; Neukirchen-Vluyn 1977) 213-246; R. WILLIAMSON, *Philo and the Epistle to the Hebrews* (Leiden 1970); A. S. VAN DER WOUDE, Melchisedek als himmlische Erlösergestalt in den neugefundenen eschatologischen Midraschim aus Qumran Höhle XI, *OTS* 14 (1965) 354-373.

J. REILING

MELQART מלך צר 'King of Tyre'

I. The meaning of the name Melqart is generally acknowledged to be 'King of the City'. Since Melqart appears as the city god of 1st millennium BCE Tyre, the 'City', *qrt*, in question is mostly identified as a designation of Tyre. However, in view of the chtonic character of Melqart (the deity is equated with →Nergal, cf. *RAAM* 194-195), the 'City' could also be interpreted as a euphemism of the underworld, called "the great city", **iri.gal**, Akk *Irkallu*, in the Mesopotamian tradition.

Melqart is usually identified with the Greek (or Roman) →Heracles (Hercules). His character is that of a city god; his myths portray him as a *hērōs*. The identification of this god with the 'king of Tyre' mentioned in Ezekiel's prophecy against Tyre (Ezek 28:1-19) makes good sense. According to some scholars, the →Baal worshipped on the Mount →Carmel and mocked by →Elijah (1 Kgs 18:20-40) should be identified as the Tyrian Melqart. References to the 'Tyrian Heracles', finally, are found in 2 Macc 4:18-20.

Melqart occurs several times outside the Bible, in Semitic epigraphy, both as a divine name and as theophoric element in personal names. Besides, he is quoted by his title 'Baal of Tyre'; it is from Greek and Latin sources, however, that we derive the major part of our knowledge concerning his cult and his mythical stories.

II. The god of Tyre, Melqart is mentioned for the first time in an Aramaic inscription upon a stele from the ninth/eighth century BCE found North of Aleppo (*KAI* 201). On this stele dedicated by Bir Hadad, king of Aram, Melqart has the insignia of a warrior god. As ^{d}*Mi-il-qa-ar-tu* he is attested in the seventh century BCE treaty between Esarhaddon, king of Assyria, and Baal, king of Tyre, as one of the divine guarantors, together with the chief deity of Sidon, →Eshmun. These two deities will punish the treaty breaker by destroying his land, enslaving his people, and depriving him of food, clothing and oil (SAA 2, 5 iv:14; *ANET*, 534). A ninth century BCE treaty between Ashur-Nerari V and Matiel of Arpad might be restored on the basis of this Esarhaddon treaty as: 'Ditto by M[elqart and Esh]mun' (SAA 2, 2 vi:22); if this restoration is correct, the text would contain the oldest evidence of Melqart. In Phoenicia he is attested as *mlqrt bṣr*, 'Melqart in Tyre' (BORDREUIL 1990:19). A bilingual inscription from Malta (*KAI* 47; second century BCE), shows that Melqart/Heracles was specifically considered the *b'l ṣr*, 'Baal of Tyre', or, as the Greek has it, its ἀρχηγέτης, 'tutelary hero; eponymous ancestor', of his own city. Epigraphical, archaeological and classical records prove also that Melqart had a remarkable role in the religious ideology of the commercial expansion of Tyrians westward throughout the Mediterranean world, and that his cult was very popular in all Phoenician colonies, from Cyprus to Malta, from Carthage to the whole of North Africa, from Sardinia to Iberia (Cadiz esp.).

According to Cicero (*Nat. deor.* III 42) and Philo Byblius (in Eusebius, *P.E.* I 10, 27), Melqart is a descendant of Uranus, son of →Zeus Demarous and Asteria (the Phoenician →Astarte). Nonnos of Panopolis (*Dionys.* XL 311-580) links him with the foundation of Tyre, while Herodotus (II 44) says that his sanctuary was founded at the same time as the city. This historian gives also some precious data on the cult of the Tyrian Heracles (esp. about rites and the two pillars in his temple), a personage to whom, Herodotus says, the Tyrian people paid homage as if to a hero, i.e. as if to one who had died, one who was originally mortal. An important passage of Menander Ephesius (quoted by Josephus, *Ant. Jud.* VIII 146) informs us that Hiram, the king of Tyre contemporary with Solomon, pulled down the ancient temples and erected new ones to Heracles and Astarte; the same king was the first to celebrate the 'awakening' (Gk ἔγερσις) of Heracles, in the month of Peritios (February-March). Other references in classical literature inform us about this annual festival, which from many points of view recalls analogous cultic situations in honour of other dying and rising gods (cf. →Adonis and Eshmun). It was probably the greatest festival of Melqart: the god, burnt with fire, as the Greek hero, was brought to life by means of a hierogamic rite with his divine partner Astarte, through the participation of a particular celebrant, the *mqm ʾlm*, 'awakener of deity' (cf. perhaps the ἐγερσείτης of the Greek inscriptions). The myth runs parallel to this rite, describing the god's disappearance and return (Athenaeus IX 392 D and Zenobius, *Cent.* V 56). According to these traditions Heracles/Melqart was slain by the Libyan →Typhon and recalled to life by his friend Iolaos, who caused him to smell a roasted quail. In this connection one can also recall the gold lamina from the fifth century BCE, found at Santa Severa (Pyrgi, Southern Etruria) in a sanctuary of the Etruscan goddess Uni; it was dedicated to the Phoenician Astarte. The inscription mentions "the day of the burial of (an unnamed) deity", *ym qbr ʾlm*, i.e. perhaps, a ceremony of mourning for Melqart (*KAI* 277:8-9).

The evidence suggests that Melqart was originally at home in the traditions about deified kings and royal ancestors known from Bronze Age Syria (→Malik), gradually evolving towards the figure of a divine founder of towns and culture hero, then becoming a cosmic Lord, who grants prosperity (BONNET 1988).

III. It is generally admitted that the figure of Melqart and the forms of his cult are reflected in Ezekiel's oracle against the king of Tyre (Ezek 28:1-19). This passage consists of two different sections (vv 1-10 and 11-19), both referring to the same personage. The 'prince of Tyre' is a self-styled god who claims superior wisdom. The prophet compares the situation of the Tyrian king to that of the first man in the garden of Eden, and his fall to the fall of →Adam. The king deserved his punishment because he had aspirations to become the equal of God. In the mythical context of Ezek 28, it is quite legitimate to look for allusions to Melqart, the divine 'King of the city'. The prince lives in a garden, being "clothed with all kind of precious stones" (v 12): this reminds one of the clothes of the Tyrian god, "brightly decorated with the stars", according to Nonnos of Panopolis (*Dionys.* XL 367-369.408-423.578-579). The prince is said to owe his riches to trade, which appears to allude to Melqart's importance in the Tyrian maritime trade and colonization. The stones of fire in the midst of which he walked (v 14), and the fire which →Yahweh brought forth from the midst of the prince, to consume him (v 18), are perhaps an allusion to the burial-service of the Phoenician god, whom the Pseudo-Clementine *Recognitiones* X 24 calls "burned and buried in Tyre".

Most scholars agree that the 'Baal'

honoured by Queen Jezebel, the Phoenician wife of Ahab, and introduced into Israel by her (see 1 Kgs 16-18 and Josephus, *Ant. Jud.* VIII 317), was in fact Melqart. On the basis of this identification the cult of Baal on Mt. Carmel, celebrated by his four hundred and fifty prophets (1 Kgs 18:20-40), is interpreted as a cult of Melqart. DE VAUX (1971:238-251) interprets the rites and the performances of the prophets in this narrative, and even Elijah's closing words of v 27 ("Perhaps he [= Baal] is asleep and must be awakened"), as elements of and allusions to the practice of the 'awakening' of Melqart. But the question is still subject of debate (BRIQUEL-CHATONNET 1992), and other scholars prefer to see here the ceremonies for the god of Mt. Carmel, a local form of a Storm-God or Sky-God, identified as Zeus of Heliopolis/Baalbek by a Greek second century CE inscription from this site (→Carmel).

A trace of Melqart's worship at Tyre may also be found in 2 Macc 4:18-20, which tells that during the second century BCE, every five years games were celebrated in Tyre in honour of the local Heracles, i.e. Melqart. Most probably the king was present at these games and the rulers or heads of neighbouring states, peoples and provinces sent representatives bearing rich gifts; sacrifices were also offered to Heracles (MORGENSTERN 1960:162-163; BONNET 1988:57-58).

IV. *Bibliography*

*C. BONNET, *Melqart. Cultes et mythes de l'Héraclès tyrien en Méditerranée* (Studia Phoenicia 8; Namur/Leuven 1988) [& lit]; P. BORDREUIL, A propos de Milkou, Milqart et Milk'ashtart, *Maarav* 5-6 (1990) 11-21; F. BRIQUEL-CHATONNET, *Les relations entre les cités de la côte phénicienne et les royaumes d'Israël et de Juda* (Studia Phoenicia 12; Leuven 1992) 303-313 [& lit]; R. DE VAUX, *The Bible and the Ancient Near East* (Garden City, 1971) 238-251; J. DUS, Melek Ṣōr-Melqart? (Zur Interpretation von Ez 28,11-19), *ArOr* 26 (1958) 179-185; H. J. KATZENSTEIN, Phoenician Deities Worshipped in Israel and Judah During the Time of the First Temple, *Studia Phoenicia XI. Phoenicia and the Bible* (ed. E. Lipiński; Leuven 1991) 187-191; J. MORGENSTERN, The King-God among the Western Semites and the Meaning of Epiphanes, *VT* 10 (1960) 138-197; H. H. ROWLEY, *Men of God. Studies in Old Testament History and Prophecy* (London-Edinburgh 1963) 37-65.

S. RIBICHINI

MENELAOS Μενέλαος

I. The name of Menelaos, the husband of Helen, is borne by the emissary of the hellenising high priest →Jason at 2 Macc 4:23 who supplanted him ca. 172/1 BCE. He precariously maintained a successful relationship with Antiochos IV Epiphanes and subsequently Antiochos V Eupator until finally, around 163 BCE, the latter had him executed (2 Macc 13:3-8). Menelaos' name is of a common Greek type: he who puts 'might' (μένος) into the 'army' (λαός).

II. The story of Menelaos centres on the Trojan War. He exists in order to have Helen stolen from him by Paris and, together with his brother Agamemnon, to recover her having wreaked awful vengeance upon the Trojans. The recovery of a maiden by her twin brothers/husbands appears to be an Indo-European myth for which there are Sanskrit and Latvian parallels, though this myth is more closely instantiated in stories of the twin →Dioskouroi recovering Helen from e.g. Theseus (WARD 1968: ch. ii; PUHVEL 1987:141-143; WEST 1975:8-12).

Around this kernel, the picture of his life is elaborated as follows. When Thyestes kills their father Atreus and takes his kingdom, Menelaos and Agamemnon are restored by Tyndareus (Apollodoros, *Epitome* 2:15). He was the succesful wooer of Tyndareus' daughter Helen (as was Agamemnon of Helen's sister Clytaemestra). All the suitors took an oath to protect Helen and her husband from wrongdoing—standing on pieces of a sacrificed horse, commemorated in 'Horse Tomb' on the way from Sparta to Arcadia (Pausanias 3, 20, 9). When the Dioskouroi become gods, Tyndareus hands

Menelaos his kingdom, the kingdom of Sparta (Apollodoros 3, 11, 2). Not unnaturally, Menelaos has a part in several embassies to encourage participation in the Trojan War and to seek restoration of Helen (Apollodoros, *Epitome* 3:9; 3:28). In Homer's *Iliad* he fights the duel with Paris that one might have expected at the beginning of the war (*Iliad* 3:15-382). Paris is in fact slaughtered by Philoktetes, according to Lesches' *Little Iliad*, which also told how Menelaos mutilated his corpse (he mutilates that of Paris' successor, Deiphobos, according to Virgil, *Aeneid* 6:494-529). The curious story that only a phantom of Helen went to Troy and that Menelaos recovered the real Helen from Egypt at the end of seven years' wandering is owed to Stesichoros: in his *Palinode* he built this elaboration on the prophecy to Menelaos that he must go to Egypt before reaching home (*Odyssey* 4:475-84). This Egyptian scene is the setting for Euripides' *Helen*. Euripides (*Orestes*) also makes rather an unpleasant character of Menelaos' daughter, Hermione, whose main function in myth is apparently to bear Teisamenos to Orestes (the king driven out by the 'returning' Sons of →Herakles). At the end of his travels, reunited with Helen (whom Homer shows us as the ideal hostess in *Odyssey* 4), he will live until he is finally transported "to the Elysian plain and the →ends of the earth ... because you have Helen and are the son-in-law of →Zeus" (*Odyssey* 4:563. 569), an exceptional fate as ROHDE (1898: I 80) stressed long ago.

His tomb and Helen's were said to be in his temple at Therapne in Spartan territory (Pausanias 3, 19, 9, and other evidence in WIDE 1893:340-6). It is hard to trace his mythology to cult, if Helen is rightly understood as originally a tree-goddess (WIDE 1893:343) and if the myth to which he owes his existence goes back to Indo-European antiquity.

III. The extreme hostility of 2 Macc to the high priest Menelaos is due partly to his procuring the execution of the former high priest Onias (4:34) and partly to his close relationship with the régime of Antiochos IV in particular, who notably attempted to install hellenic paganism by force, for instance by re-dedicating the Temple at Jerusalem to Olympian Zeus (6:2). This hellenising trait is reflected by the name 'Menelaos' itself (cf. Jason), which Josephus alleges, in a confused passage, was a name he assumed instead of 'Onias' (*Ant.* 12:239, cf. KLETZEL 1924:783). FRASER-MATTHEWS list 30 examples of the name (Jason=183, Aeneas=35); it occurs also as the name of an Egyptian Greek in the mid-second century CE novel of Achilles Tatius (2:33)—just as 'Agamemnon' had in the *Satyricon* of Petronius (§1 - ca. 60 CE).

IV. *Bibliography*

P. M. FRASER & E. MATTHEWS (eds.), *A Lexicon of Greek Personal Names*, vol. I, The Aegean Islands, Cyprus, Cyrenaica (Oxford 1987); W. KLETZEL, Jason (1a), PWSup 4 (1924) 783-4; J. PUHVEL, *Comparative Mythology* (Baltimore 1987); E. ROHDE, *Psyche: Seelencult und Unsterblichkeitsglaube der Griechen* (2nd ed.; Freiburg, Leipzig & Tübingen 1898); D. J. WARD, *The Divine Twins: An Indo-European myth in Germanic tradition* (Berkeley/Los Angeles 1968); M. L. WEST, *Immortal Helen* (London 1975); S. WIDE, *Lakonische Kulte* (Leipzig 1893) 304-325.

K. DOWDEN

MENI מני 'Fortune'

I. While many Near Eastern gods of antiquity were credited with the ability to determine destiny (*AkkGE* 222-223; *WbMyth* 1/I 592; SPERLING 1981:16-17), some were specifically assigned that function. Two such gods are collocated in Isa 65:11. The Hebrew reads: *w'tm ʿzby yhwh hškḥym ʾt hr qdšy hʿrkym lgd šlḥn whmmlʾym lmny*, "But you who forsake Yahweh, who ignore my holy mountain, who set a table for Luck (→Gad), and fill the drink (cf. the same parallelism between 'drink' and 'wine' in Prov 23:30) for Fortune (Meni)". The wording of the verse makes clear that divine rivals to →Yahweh are involved. Thus, the verb עזב, here translated 'forsake', is regularly employed in contexts where Israel leaves Yahweh for other gods (Judg 2:12, 13; 10:6; 1 Sam 8:8); as is the verb שכח here translated 'ignore' (Deut 8:14; Jer 13: 25; Hos 2:15). The setting of a table and the preparation of a beverage are elsewhere in the Bible (Ps 23:5; Prov 9:2) associated with a banquet. Accordingly, we are concerned here with a lavish cultic meal prepared for the divinities. The passage is found in a context which contrasts the lot of Yahweh's chosen ones and servants (v 9), with those who fail to support his temple cult but instead treat Gad and Meni sumptuously. Their appropriate punishment will be to experience hunger and thirst while the faithful eat and drink (v 13).

II. Medieval Jewish commentaries (Rashi, Kimchi, Ibn Ezra) speculated that some astral divinity was involved and derived its name from מנה, meaning 'count', 'apportion', 'assign', in Hebrew and Aramaic. This speculation is confirmed by the Akkadian verb *manû* having the same meaning. Thus, Isa 65:11 puns on the connection between the verb and the name of the divinity in the phrase, ומניתי אתכם לחרב "I will assign you to the sword." (Kimchi; Cf. *u nīšīya imnû ana karaši* "and assigned my people to destruction" [Gilg XI 169]) Assuming a Semitic etymology for Meni, the medieval explanation of the name of the divinity accords well with the LXX identification of Meni with →Tyche. In biblical Hebrew one's 'portion' in life was a *mānâ* (Jer 13: 25 [*//gôrāl*]; Ps 11:6; of Menāt in 16:5 [an Aramaism in hendiadys with *ḥeleq*]), while the Arabic cognate *manīya* means 'fate' or 'destiny', and especially 'death (as one's ultimate destiny)' (KRAMER & WENSINCK 1941:418). There are close analogies in Akk *isqu* 'lot', 'destiny', related to *ussuqu* ,'to apportion' (*CAD* I 202) and in Greek *moira* 'fate', which is connected to *meros* 'portion' (GASTER 1985: 585).

From the single biblical attestation we cannot determine whether Meni was male or female. In addition, no outside witnesses to Meni contemporary with Isaiah 65 (sixth century BCE) have been attested. Nonetheless, both earlier and later sources have been interpreted as an indication of a long tradition behind the worship of this Semitic deity of fortune. It has been suggested (FAHD 1991:373) to relate Meni to Menītum, an epithet of →Ishtar found in a Mesopotamian god-list *AkkGE* 373). It must be cautioned however, that even if Menītum is related to the Akkadian verb *manû*, the connection with 'fortune' or 'destiny' would still be tenuous because the word, although well-attested in the sense of 'assign', is not employed in the specific sense of assigning one's lot or destiny (*CAD* M 221-227). Caution likewise must be exercised with regard to an Egyptian list of Asiatic gods (Papyrus Salier IV, verso, i 5-6) which is adduced as an attestation of Meni (FAHD 1991:373) because the reading is uncertain (*ANET* 250). More relevant data come from Nabataean sources. One inscription from El-Ḥejra (COOKE 1903:79:5-6; INGHOLT 1967:No 10: 5-6) from the first century BCE or CE reads in part: *wl'nw dwšr' wmnwt w qyšh kl mn dy yzbn kpr' dnh* "And may Dushara and Manutu and Qaishah curse anyone who sells this tomb". A similar inscription (COOKE 1903:80:3-4; INGHOLT 1967:11:3-4) adds Throne (?; *Mwtbh*) and Allat to the list, while yet another, dated 26 CE, (COOKE 1903:86:8) calls on Dushara and Manūtu to curse anyone who might alter the inscription. Manūtu is likewise found as a theophoric element in the Nabatean personal names *Whbmnwtw*, *Zydmnwtw*, *'bdmnwtw*, *'bdmnwty*, and *Tymmnwty* (NEGEV 1991:nos. 341, 386, 656, 809, 810). There can be little doubt that Nabatean Manūtu is identical to the classical Arabic goddess Manāt mentioned in the Qur'an (Surah 53:20): "What do you think of Allat, and Al-Uzzah and Manāt that other third goddess?". It appears that in the pre-Islamic period Manāt had been worshipped throughout Arabia. Originally represented by a simple rock, Manāt ultimately was sculpted with the face of the Asiatic Venus, i. e. →Fortune, who according to Pausanias was worshipped by the

Syrians on the banks of the →Euphrates. (FAHD 1991:374) The Qur'anic passage mentioned above seems to imply that Mohammed at first was willing to mitigate his somewhat dour monotheism and recognize Manāt as one of the three 'exalted ladies' who might intercede for the faithful, but then relented (GASTER 1985:585). Theophoric names compounded with the element Manāt are attested in medieval Arabic sources (WELLHAUSEN 1887:25-29).

In Greco-Roman sources, Manāt is identified with the Fortunae. In a mosaic from Palmyra she is seated with a sceptre in her hand in the manner of Nemesis, goddess of destiny (FAHD 1991:373). The body of evidence makes probable the extension of the equation of Manāt and Manūtu to include Meni.

III. No Talmudic sources comment on Meni. The Peshitta does not take Meni as a proper name, but includes both deities in the plural *gaddē*, 'gods of fortune'. The Vulgate—*qui ponitis Fortunae mensam et libatis super eam*—interprets *gad* as a personal name rendering it as Fortuna, 'luck; fortune', but does not treat Meni as a proper name. The so-called Targum Jonathan translates Gad by 'false gods' (טעון) and Meni by דחלתהון 'their (illicit) objects of worship'. Alone among the ancient versions, LXX (which translates Gad by the general term *daimonion* rather than as a proper name) identifies Meni with →Tyche, the Greek goddess of fortune, which, in keeping with the synonymous parallelism of the verse, would be matched nicely with Gad, god of luck.

IV. *Bibliography*

A. COOKE, *A Text-Book of North Semitic Inscriptions* (Oxford 1903); S. BROCK, *The Old Testament in Syriac According to the Peshitta Version* (Leiden 1987); T. FAHD, Manāt, *Encylopaedia of Islam New Edition* (Leiden 1991) 373-374; T. H. GASTER, *Myth, Legend, and Custom in the Old Testament* (New York/Evanston 1985); H. INGHOLT, Palmyrene-Hatran-Nabatean, in F. ROSENTHAL, *An Aramaic Handbook Vol I/i* (Wiesbaden 1967) 40-50; J. H. KRAMER & A. WENSINCK, Manāt, *Handwörterbuch der Islam* (Leiden 1941); A. NEGEV, *Personal Names in the Nabatean Realm* (Jerusalem 1991); A. SPERBER, *The Bible in Aramaic Vol 3: The Latter Prophets According to the Targum Jonathan* (Leiden 1962); S. D. SPERLING, A *šu-īl-lā* to *Ištar, WO* 12 (1981) 8-20; J. WELLHAUSEN, *Reste arabischen Heidentums* (Berlin 1887).

S. D. SPERLING

MERIRI מרירי

I. On the basis of the alleged parallelism of *mĕrîrî* with →Resheph and →Behemoth in Deut 32:24, GORDIS has urged that "it seems highly reasonable to assume that Meriri is also a mythological term, probably representing a type of →demon" (1943:178). Others make a similar suggestion (cf. *HALAT* 601 s.v. מרירי); it is without solid foundation, though.

II. Since a supposed demon Meriri is not attested in extrabiblical texts from the ancient Near East, the proof rests entirely on Deut 32:24. It cannot be denied that this verse lists a number of demons known from the Ugaritic texts or elsewhere. The fact is somewhat obscured in the RSV which renders: "They shall be wasted with hunger, and devoured with burning heat and poisonous pestilence; and I will send the teeth of beasts against them, with venom of crawling things of the dust." The Hebrew terms for 'burning heat', 'pestilence', and 'beasts', however, are, respectively, *rešep* (→Resheph), *qeṭeb* (→Qeteb), and *bĕhēmôt* (→Behemoth), all terms originally denoting deities. Because 'hunger' (*rāʿāb*) occurs in the same list, it has been speculated that this term, too, stands for a demon (J. C. DE MOOR, *The Rise of Yahwism* [Leuven 1990] 157). Even if it is assumed that the identification of three (or four) deities (or demons) is correct, the position of *mĕrîrî* is quite different. It is found in apposition to *qeṭeb*, and the usual translation 'bitter' (cf. *mĕrîrût*, 'bitterness', Ezek 2:11) makes excellent sense. It is conceivable to take *qeṭeb mĕrîrî* as a genetival construction, rendering 'the terror of Meriri', but that would mean creating an obscure demon at the expense of a—far less obscure—other one. The textual variant קטף מררים (Samaritan Pentateuch) means 'plucked-off bitter herbs'.

Though *mĕrîrî* is a hapax legomenon, the form מרירי is found one more time in the MT, viz. in Job 3:5. Referring to Rashi's commentary on this verse, GORDIS translates מרירי יום as 'the demon of the day' (1943: 178). The expression occurs in a difficult verse; a comparison with v 8 (where the *ʾōrĕrê yôm* are 'those who curse the day') could be made in favour of an emendation of מרירי into מארדי, also from the root ʾRR, 'to curse'. If the Masoretic text is left as it stands, the most plausible translation would be 'the bitterness of the day'. In neither case it is necessary to introduce a demon into the text.

III. *Bibliography*

R. GORDIS, The Asseverative Kaph in Ugaritic and Hebrew, *JAOS* 63 (1943) 176-178, esp. 177-178 ad Job 5:3.

K. VAN DER TOORN

MESITES → MEDIATOR II

MESSENGER → ANGEL I

MESSIAH → CHRIST

MICHAEL מיכאל

I. The name Michael appears as a personal name in the Bible: Num 13:13; Ezra 8:8; 7 times in 1 Chr and 2 Chr 21:2. It is commonly interpreted as 'who is like God?' The guardian of Israel referred to in Dan 10:13. 21; 12:1 is without doubt a heavenly figure.

II. Given the prominence of this →angel in ancient Judaism, it has been supposed that the origins of his name and functions should be seen in the Canaanite deity Mikal, explaining the name as deriving from the root *yk'l*, to be able etc. The 'aleph' would then be a later addition in order to bring this name into conformity with other angelic names which often end with '-el' (for references see M. HENGEL, *Judentum und Hellenismus* [2nd ed. Tübingen 1973] 344-345 and note 507). However, this explanation seems to be unwarranted since the personal name is quite frequent in the OT, and in this early stage of Jewish angelology there is hardly a need to make angelic names conform to one single pattern. Another attempt has been made to parallel Michael with the Persian Vohumanô (A. KOHUT, *Ueber die jüdische Angelologie und Daemonologie in ihrer Abhängigkeit vom Parsismus* [Leipzig 1866] 23-27).

The few biblical occurrences of the angel Michael belong to broader streams of traditions, mostly reflected in the extra-canonical writings of the Second Temple period, and must, therefore, be discussed with these together. Given the early date of parts of *1 Enoch,* it seems that the first biblical references to Michael in the Book of Daniel are already part of a second stage of development. However, it is generally difficult to point out the traditions connected with Michael, since this specific angel became much more prominent than any other angel. Consequently, he was likely to be identified with almost any unnamed biblical angel (see F. I. ANDERSEN, *OTP* I 136 note *e*). Modern scholarship should therefore try to differentiate between unnamed traditions that became part of the characteristics of Michael and more original Michael-traditions and not vice versa (contrast e.g. LÜCKEN 1898). The trend of the ancient authors to identify almost every angel with Michael goes on in our days. To illustrate the problem: Michael is quite often granted the title of an ἀρχιστράτηγος. Yet, this title occurs also in connection with →Rafael (*Gk Apoc. Ezra* 1:4; cp. *OTP* I, 566. 571). Does this mean that the unnamed 'chief of the →hosts' in *Jos. As.* 14 is Michael?

Dan 10 and 12 refer to Michael as one of the primary angels helping the angel speaking to Daniel against the angels of other nations (10:13: Persia; 10:20: Greece). The scene has, however, an eschatological undertone since the unnamed angel reveals what will happen "in the last days" (10:14). Michael's eschatological role is also apparent from Dan 12:1.

All these particular notions are prominent in the extra-canonical literature of the time: Michael is variously called ἀρχιστράτηγος (*T. Abr.* A 1:4; 2:16; 19:5 and passim; *T. Isaac* 14:7; *2 Enoch* 22:6f; 33:10f; 72:5 and passim; *Gk Apoc. Ezra* 4:24 [cf. M. E. STONE, *OTP* I, 566]; *3 Baruch* 11:4 [Greek version]; 11:6. 8; *PGM* XIII 925 and see DIETERICH 1905:202,1). It seems natural to assume that this title translates the 'chief of the LORD's hosts' from Jos 5:14, though the precise Greek term is not used in the LXX. One can hardly ascribe all these references to a Christian redaction of Jewish apocalyptic material in later times (*pace* ROHLAND 1977:22-24). One might add to this list the →'prince of the army' in Dan 8:11, although Michael is not mentioned there by name. He is 'chief of the angels' (*1 Enoch* 24:6; *T. Isaac* 1:6; *Mart. Isa.* 3:15-6; *3 Enoch* 17:3; *Hebr. T. Naph.* 8-9; cf. 1QM 17,7). In *3 Baruch* 11-15 he functions as the only →mediator between God and the guardian angels of men, i.e. he is the leading angelic figure here, too. Accordingly he is often mentioned as the only angelic mediator as in 1QM 17,6-8.

The 'prince of Israel' or its guardian angel is a problematic designation inasmuch as it contradicts the idea that only the nations are under an angelic guard whereas Israel has direct connection with God (apparently as early as in Deut 4:19-20). Yet, the designation is well known (e.g. *1 Enoch* 40:8-10; *2 Enoch* 18:9; *3 Baruch* 37:1; 44:10; *Pirke de Rabbi Eliezer* 4; see also TgPs 137:7). Along with the gradual transformation of the name 'Israel' into a more universalistic conception of the righteous in general, Michael becomes the angel of humankind (*Apoc. Mos.* 32:2-3; *Adam and Eve* 41:1; this might be the reason for some of the differences between the Greek and the Ethiopian versions of *1 Enoch* 20:5).

Michael's military functions are not specific to this angel. They are often attributed to the group of four (sometimes seven) archangels as in 1QM 9, 15-16; *1 Enoch* 20:5; 40; 54; 71: 8-9. 13; *3 Baruch* 4:7; *Apoc. Mos.* 40; *Sib. Or.* 2:214-237 (cf. 4Q285, 6, 8-9: J. T. MILIK, Milkî-ṣedek et Milkî-resaʿ dans les anciens écrits juives et chrétiens, *JJS* 23 [1972], 95-144, esp. 143). The judgment over the 'fallen angels' is conveyed to the group of the four (including generally Michael, →Gabriel, →Raphael and either →Uriel or Sariel, sometimes Suriel; see Y. YADIN, *The Scroll of the War of the Sons of Light against the Sons of Darkness* [Jerusalem 1957] 216; in magical literature this group is not as consistent, e.g.: S. EITREM, *Papyri Osloenses* I [Oslo 1925] 171, 309-310; E. R. GOODENOUGH, *Jewish Symbols in the Greco-Roman Period* II [New York 1953] 229 232, and frequently in *PGM*).

Inasmuch as military help is supposed to be part of the eschatological salvation, Michael is often associated with this specific notion: The punishment of the fallen angels in general has an eschatological connotation. Michael (and three other angels, Gabriel, Raphael and Uriel) punish the fallen angels: *1 Enoch* 10; 54 etc. Yet, only in connection with Michael *1 Enoch* 10 turns to a description of the future that should be understood in messianic terms (*1 Enoch* 10:11-16). Therefore, it is Michael who shows the seer the tree, the fruit of which will be eaten by the righteous in the future (*1 Enoch* 25). The messianic functions of Michael might still be seen in later texts (cf. S. AGOURIDES, *OTP* I 606). It is congruent with the idea that it is Michael who announces the final judgment, *1 Enoch* 68 (cf. Dan 8:13-14 without angelic names).

Once Michael's help is understood in these terms and the future salvation is construed as liberation from the fallen angels and/or →Satan, Michael is easily characterized as the opponent of Satan. The fight against Satan, the →dragon in Rev. 12:7-9, belongs to this tradition as well as to the literary context of Jude 9. The Life of →Adam (*Vita Adae*) reflects for the first time the opposition of Michael and Satan regarding God's command to worship Adam

(*Vita* 13-14; cf. *1 Enoch* 69). The angelic warrior on behalf of Israel, i.e. for the righteous ones, in the last days is later understood as one who assists in other means of salvation, too. So he receives the prayers of the virtuous ones (*3 Baruch* 11-15; cf. *b. Hag.* 12b; *2 Enoch* 33:10) and serves as the keeper of the keys for the highest of heavens (cf. also *Par. Jer.* 9:5). Michael's priestly role, decisively so only in later literature, might be based upon sources like *T. Abr.* B 4:4 (Michael as the first among the adoring angels, but cf. *Ass. Mos.* 10:2, where it is not clear whether or not this figure is to be identified with Michael). The connection with Metatron seems to be later than the NT writings (cf. P. S. ALEXANDER, *OTP* I 243-244).

III. Another corpus of traditions is alluded to in Jude 9, where Michael and Satan argue about the soul of →Moses. This particular item belongs to the broader stream of traditions characterizing Michael as a *psychopompos* who carries the soul of the seer as such (even for an apocalyptic journey) and serves as *angelus interpres*. Most naturally, the bulk of revelations received that way are concerned with the last day, the judgment of the deceased and such related matters. So Michael comes to take the souls of the fathers (*T. Abr.* A 7-8; *T. Isaac* 2:1; *T. Jacob* 1:6), of Ezra (*Visio Ezrae* line 59-59, cf. *Gk Apoc. Ezrae* 4:7 [journey to →Hades]) and the soul of Adam (cf. *Vita* 43:1-3; *Apoc. Mos.* 13:2-6). He is actually involved in burying-rites (*T. Abr.* A 20:10; *T. Isaac* 14; *T. Jacob* 5:13; *Vita* 46: 3; *Apoc. Mos.* 37:5-6; *Vita* 41:1, 47:2-3; 48:1-3; *Apoc. Mos.* 43:1; 40; see further: *1 Enoch* 71:3-5 inasmuch as Enoch's transformation marks his death; *2 Enoch* 22:8-9; *Mart. Isa.* 3:15-6; cf. S. E. LOEWENSTAMM, The Death of Moses, *Studies on the Testament of Abraham*, ed. G. W. E. Nickelsburg [Missoula 1976] 185-217, esp. 208-209). *Mart. Isa.* 3:15-6 expresses the inner correlation of the *psychopompos* and the revealer of eschatological secrets: "the angel of the →Holy Spirit and Michael, the chief of the holy angels, will open his (scil.: Jesus) grave on the third day", i.e., the one who is concerned with the care for the dead is also the one who will free him from his tomb (see *Par. Jer.* 9:5, cf. 8:12). A Qumran apocryphon ascribed to Michael ("The words of the book that Michael spoke to the angels") is still unpublished (see J. T. MILIK, *The Books of Enoch. Aramaic Fragments of Qumrân Cave 4* [Oxford 1976] 91 for literature and further suggestions). But the (apparently late) heading of *Apoc. Mos.* ascribes this book to him, too. Jude 9 combines, then, the idea of individual salvation with the concept of a struggle between two angels as in Zach 3:1-5 (cf. $4QAmr^b$ and see K. BERGER, Der Streit des guten und des bösen Engels um die Seele. Beobachtungen zu $4QAmr^b$ und Judas 9, *JSJ* 4 [1973], 1-18).

The angel set over the dead and their future salvation raises apocalypticists to heaven, so →Abraham in a chariot of →Cherubs (*T. Abr.* 10-15), Adam (*Vita* 25:2-3, for announcing his punishment! Cf. also *T. Job* 52:6-10, apparently concerning God and not Michael), →Eve (*Apoc. Mos.* 43:1-2), Ezra (*Visio Ezrae*, line 56-60. 79), →Enoch (*2 Enoch* 22:1-6) and →Melchizedek (*2 Enoch* 71:28; 72:3.5.8-9 [interestingly enough, this angel is Gabriel in the shorter version]; *1 Enoch* 71:3-5). The angel Jaoel refers to Michael's help: *Apoc. Abr.* 10:17. Michael functions as God's messenger to humankind (*Apoc. Mos.* 2:1; 3:2; 49:2; *1 Enoch* 25; 60:4-5) and is called "angel of truth and justice" (*Par. Ier.* 9:5; cp. 1QM 13, 10).

Michael has a specific connection to trees and medicine. Thus he teaches agriculture in *Vita* 22:2; reveals the fruits of the tree to be eaten in the future by the righteous in *1 Enoch* 25, and is one of the four who plant the trees in paradise in *3 Baruch* 4:7; he helps Eve (together with other angels) to give birth to →Cain (*Vita* 21:2 etc; *1 Enoch* 67:1-11 does not really belong to this body of tradition, but see ROHLAND 1977:26-27). His name therefore often occurs in magical texts (M. NAVEH & S. SHAKED, *Amulets and Magic Bowls. Aramaic Incantations of*

Late Antiquity [Jerusalem/Leiden 1985] Amulet 2, line 14; A. KROPP, *Der Lobpreis des Erzengels Michael* [Brussel 1966] 12-18.20-21, cf. EITREM and GOODENOUGH above). In *PGM* he is referred to either in a group or alone as the highest angel and his name serves as a magical sign. Perhaps Jewish Christians maintained specific traditions about Michael (see W. MICHAELIS, *Zur Engelchristologie im Urchristentum* [Basel 1942] 145-158); for later developments which treat Michael as a physician and as a military leader see esp. ROHLAND 1977.

Perhaps the archangel in 1 Thess 4:16 is originally connected with Michael who is portrayed as blowing the trumpet to call to judgment (*Apoc. Mos.* 22:1). The "angel of peace" (*T. Dan* 6:1-5; *T. Asher* 6:5; *T. Ben.* 6:1) identifies the four faces with the four archangels (*1 Enoch* 40:8), i.e., he himself is not to be confused with Michael. The "interceding angel" (*1 Enoch* 89:76; 90:14; *T. Levi* 5:6) could well be Michael, but he is not called so, although there are some resemblances: e.g. in *T. Asher* 6:5, entering into eternal life, or the dualism with Beliar (→Belial) in *T. Ben.* 6:1.

IV. *Bibliography*

A. DIETERICH, *Abraxas. Studien zur Religionsgeschichte des späteren Altertums* (Leipzig 1905 = Aalen 1979) 117-126; T. HOPFNER, *Griechisch-ägyptischer Offenbarungszauber* I (Leipzig 1921 = Amsterdam 1974) §§ 151-154; *W. LÜCKEN, *Michael. Eine Darstellung und Vergleichung der jüdischen und morgenländisch-christlichen Tradition vom Erzengel Michael* (Göttingen 1898) [1-61 = *Der Erzengel Michael in der Überlieferung des Judentums,* Diss. Marburg 1898]; M. MACH, *Entwicklungsstadien des jüdischen Engelglaubens in vorrabbinischer Zeit.* (TSAJ 34; Tübingen 1992), index s.v. Engel-Namen.; *J. MICHL, Engel VII (Michael) *RAC* V (1962) 243-251.; C. D. G. MÜLLER, *Die Bücher der Einsetzung der Erzengel Michael und Gabriel* I-II (CSCO 225-226; Louvain 1962); *J. P. ROHLAND, *Der Erzengel Michael. Arzt und Feldherr. Zwei Aspekte des vor- und frühbyzantinischen Michaelskultes* (BZRGG 19; Leiden 1977).

M. MACH

MIDDAY DEMON Δαιμόνιον Μεσημβρινόν

I. The Midday Demon is found in the Septuagint version of Ps 91:6 (LXX 90:6). In Ps 91:5-6, the Hebrew psalmist declares that the one who takes refuge in the →Almighty will not fear: "The →Terror of the night nor the Arrow that flies by day, nor the Pestilence (→*Deber*) that stalks in darkness nor the →Destruction (→*Qeṭeb*) that wastes at noonday".

The parallelism of the verses twice balances a night and a daytime →Evil, each of which was understood by rabbinic interpreters to refer to a demonic spirit: the daytime *Qeteb* is balanced by the →night →demon, Pestilence, *Deber*. In Deut 32:24 the 'poisonous *Qeteb*' is parallel to →Resheph, the well-known Canaanite demon of plague. Thus the *Qeteb* is the personified destruction or disease, riding the hot desert wind (cf. Isa 28:2 and the wind demons of Mesopotamia). In Ps 91:6b (Heb. קטב ישוד צהרים), the Septuagint translators confronted a different Hebrew text (with Aquila and Symmachus), reading ושד for ישוד, meaning 'Destruction and the demon (*shed*) of noontime', which the LXX rendered as "Misfortune and the Midday demon" (συμπτώματος καὶ δαιμονίου μεσημβρινοῦ). This variant violated the parallelism of the original, and added a fifth Evil (שד צהרים), the Midday demon.

II. The noon-day heat and the critical time at the sun's zenith was a common concern in the ancient Near East, and spirits of calamity were held responsible for sunstroke (GASTER 1969:770), feverish diseases, and other maladies (CAILLOIS 1937). The Latin of Jerome renders the verse as *morsus insanientis meridie*, "the bite of insanity at midday".

III. The Midrash *Tehillim* understood *Qeteb* here to refer to a terrifying demon: "the poisonous *Qeteb* is covered with scales and with hair, and sees only out of one eye, the other is in the middle of his heart" (LANGTON 1949:50). The indifference and listlessness (ἀκηδία *ennui*) which sometimes plagued Christian monks was attributed to this source. So Athanasius writes: "The Midday demon is said to be (the demon) of *ennui*" (*Exp. Ps 90:6*). Evagrius Ponticus writes: "The demon of *ennui*, which is the Midday demon, is more burdensome than all the demons. It besets the monk about ten o'clock, and encircles his soul until two o'clock" (*Vit. Cog.* 7); and again: "The other demons at the rising or setting of the sun seem to take hold of some one part of the soul, but the Midday demon is wont to surround the entire soul and suffocate the mind" (*Cap. Pract.* A 25).

IV. *Bibliography*

*R. CAILLOIS, Les démons de midi, *RHR* 115 (1937) 142-173; T. H. GASTER, Demon, Demonology, *IDB* 1 (1962) 820; GASTER, *Myth, Legend, and Custom in the Old Testament* (New York 1969); *S. LANDERSDORFER, Das *daemonium meridianum*, *BZ* 18 (1929) 294-300; E. LANGTON, *Essentials of Demonology: A Study of Jewish and Christian Doctrine, Its Origin and Development* (London 1949).

G. J. RILEY

MIGHTY ONE OF JACOB אביר יעקב

I. 'The mighty one of Jacob' was interpreted as a divine name by ALT (1929). He classified it as a designation of one of the anonymous gods 'of the father'. The only place where it may occur as a proper name is Gen 49:24; elsewhere it is always an epithet of →Yahweh (Isa 49:26; 60:16; Ps 132:2-5; cf. Sir 51:12; see also *ʾăbîr yiśrāʾēl* as a parallel to *ʾădōn* and *yhwh ṣĕbāʾōt* in Isa 1:24). It is doubtful whether *ʾăbîr Yaʿăqōb* may be translated as "Bull of Jacob" (CROSS 1973:4). The only possible evidence for this could be found in Ugaritic texts.

II. In *KTU* 1.12 ii:55 *ibr* is used to designate a strong animal (bull or wild bull) caught in a trap or something similar, while *KTU* 1.10 iii:35-37 and the personal name *ibrd* ("Haddu is a bull", or, if the name had a Hurrian background, "Haddu is lord", since Hurr *iwr* means "lord", see *WUS* No. 34; for *d* as 'Haddu' see *KTU* 4.33:26; 4.628:5) provide evidence for the use of *ibr* as an epithet for the storm-god. El is never referred to as *ibr*. Akk *abāru* means 'power, force' (*CAD* A s.v.) and is used without specific reference to the bull.

III. In the OT *ʾabbîr* is used as an attribute of strong men; it characterizes rulers, heroes and leaders (1 Sam 21:8; Isa 10:13; Job 24:22; 34:20; Lam 1:15; perhaps Jer 46:15 [the Pharaoh]). When used in combination with *lēb*, it means 'brave' (Ps 76:6; Isa 46:12). TORCZYNER wishes to assign a comparable meaning to the word in a military context, and translates "officers" where others usually render "stallions" (Judg 5:22; Jer 8:16; 47:3; TORCZYNER 1921:298). Yet in Jer 8 :16 there is the parallel of *sûs* and ṢHL, 'to neigh', and in 47:3 the one of *ʾabbîrîm* and *rekeb*. In Isa 34:7; Jer 50:11; Ps 22:13 and 50:13 the term refers to animals; in Isa 34:7, a distinction is made between wild bulls, bulls and *abbîrîm*. In Hebrew, as in Akkadian, the original meaning of *ʾabbîr* must have been 'strong, powerful'. Where *ʾăbbîr* was applied Yahweh, the Masoretes punctuated the word to read ʾabîr so as to prevent any association of *ʾăbîr Yaʾăqōb* with the bull (and the statue at Bethel).

ALT called the expression an "archaic term" used to characterize the ancestral god of the Jacob clan (1929:26). He said the phrase had not the form but the function of a proper name (1929:24). He dated it back to a preliterary tradition, because he judged the use of *ʾăbîr* to qualify God foreign to the theological views of later times; as a matter of consequence, the epithet could not be explained as a later invention projected back onto earlier traditions (1929:25). Alt has had great influence with this view: it was elaborated (MAAG 1959); adopted (e.g., FOHRER 1969, "Kämpfer, Verteidiger Jakobs"); or modified (MÜLLER 1980:125-128). Occasionally, attempts have been made to relate the epithet to the traditions of Shechem (cf. Gen 33:20; SEEBASS 1984) or Bethel (Gen 28:18.22). This was done by interpreting the parallel expression in Gen 49:24, viz. *rōʿeh ʾeben Yiśrāʾēl* (→Rock; →Shepherd), as meaning "Sheperd (or Ruler) at the Rock of Israel", the "rock" being a stela. By virtue of the assumption this stela was in Bethel (erected by Jacob, according to the cult legend), the →"Mighty One of Jacob" would then be a designation of the bull figures erected by Jerobeam I (cf. DUMMERMUTH, *ZAW* 70 [1985] 85-86).

A number of objections can be raised against the early date proposed for the expression *ʾabīr yaʿăqōb*. It occurs almost solely in late texts (Isa 49:26; 60:16; for Ps 132 cf. the bibliography given by B. JANOWSKI in *Ernten, was man sät* [Festschrift K. Koch; Neukirchen-Vluyn 1992] 245-246); the only possible exception is Gen 49:24, because its date of origin is subject to debate. Moreover, the expression does not occur in a patriarchal narrative properly speaking, but in a secondary supplement to a tribal saying on →Joseph (so C. H. J. DE GEUS, *The Tribes of Israel* [Assen 1976] 90-92; *pace* SEEBASS 1984:334-339). The earlier simile (v 22), as well as its later supplement (cf. the narrative forms in vv 23-24), are imbued by the atmosphere of a sedentary civilization, including its religiosity (KÖCKERT 1988:66-67); the same applies to the benediction in vv 24b-26, which derive from Deut 33:13-16.

According to v 25, the blessing is to come "from (*min*) the El of your father, together with (*wʾt*) →Shadday". Verse 24b calls El proleptically the "Mighty one of Jacob" from whose hands the blessing springs, and it puts the emphasis on the location (*miššām*) which he is specifically linked with as a 'shepherd' (*rōʿeh*). The text is complicated, though, and the question remains whether we are to interpret the "Rock of Israel" as a topographical indication or as a divine name (→Stone). However that may be, the "Mighty one of Jacob" must be identified with El in Gen 49 (MÜLLER 1980:117). Should the expression be connected with Gen 33:20 (Shechem) or 28:18.22 (Bethel), it will have to be understood as an epithet of El (cf. O. EISSFELDT, *KS* III [Tübingen 1966] 393, n. 2), secondarily applied to Yahweh. This hypothesis finds no support in the Ugaritic texts, though, because there the epithet of the bull for El is *ṯr* (*WUS* no. 2932). There is, in conclusion, insufficient evidence of a numen *ʾăbîr yaʿăqōb*, because the phrase "represents probably an epithet, and is not a proper name" (SEEBASS 1966:51).

IV. *Bibliography*

A. ALT, *Der Gott der Väter* (BWANT III/12; Stuttgart 1929 = *KS* I; München 1953:1-77) 24-29; F. M. CROSS, *Canaanite Myth and Hebrew Epic. Essays in the History of the Religion of Israel* (Cambridge, Mass. 1973) 3-12; G. FOHRER, *Geschichte der israelitischen Religion* (Berlin 1969) 20-27; A. S. KAPELRUD, *ʾăbīr*, *TWAT* 1 (1970) 43-46; M. KÖCKERT, *Vätergott und Väterverheißungen. Eine Auseinandersetzung mit A. Alt und seine Erben* (FRLANT 142, Göttingen 1988); V. MAAG, Der Hirte Israels. Eine Skizze von Wesen und Bedeutung der Väterreligion, *Schweizerische Theologische Umschau* 28 (1958) 2-28; repr. in *Kultur, Kulturkontakt und Religion* (Göttingen 1980) 111-144; H. P. MÜLLER, Gott und die Götter in den Anfängen der biblischen Religion. Zur Vorgeschichte des Monotheismus, *Monotheismus im Alten Israel und seiner Umwelt* (ed. O. Keel; Fribourg 1980) 99-142; H. H. SCHMID, *ʾabbīr* stark, *THAT* 1 (München 1971) 25-27; H. SEEBASS, *Der Erzvater Israel und die Einführung der Jahweverehrung in Kanaan* (BZAW 98; Berlin 1966); SEEBASS, Die Stämmesprüche in Gen 49, 3-27, *ZAW* 96 (1984) 333-350; H. TORCZYNER, *ʾābīr* kein Stierbild, *ZAW* 39 (1921) 296-300; H. J. ZOBEL, *Stammesspruch und Geschichte* (BZAW 95; Berlin 1965).

M. KÖCKERT

MIGHTY ONES → GIBBORIM

MILCOM מלכם

I. The deity of the Ammonites, Milcom, occurs three times in the MT: 1 Kgs 11:5.33; 2 Kgs 23:13. The Greek translators of the Septuagint or/and other Greek recensions and versions (Syrian, Latin) have read Milcom (Μελχομ, Μελχολ, Μολχομ, Μολχολ, possible confusion of M and Λ in uncial writing) in seven other instances: 2 Sam 12:30; 1 Chr 20:2; Amos 1:15; Jer 49(=30):1.3; Zeph 1:5; 1 Kgs 11:7. In a number of cases, the Greek translations show how difficult the reading of the Hebrew prototype *mlkm* was; it could be vocalised and understood as Milcom or as "their king" (*malkām*), or both as in 2 Sam 12:30 (dittography?).

To these 10 attestations, it is now possible to add some more instances found among the Ammonite archaeological data: as the divine name on the Amman citadel inscription, line 1 (end of 9th c.) and on a seal (7th c.) *brk lmlkm* (two other examples are modern forgeries), or as a theophoric element in Ammonite anthroponyms: on the Tell el-Mazar ostracon VII,1 (5th c.) *mlkmyt*, and on seals or bullae: *mlkm'wr* (ca 600), *bdmlkm*, *mlkmgd* and *mlkm'z* (6th c.) (HÜBNER 1992:252-253).

A divine name *Malkum* was already known by the tablets of Drehem and a god →*Malik* is documented by texts from Nineveh as well as a theophoric element in proper names on the Ebla and Mari Tablets (CAZELLES 1957:cols 1343-1344). Alphabetic and syllabic lists of deities' names found at Ugarit (*KTU* 1.47; 1.22; 1.118, HERDNER 1978:1-3, NOUGAYROL 1968:45, 60; see also *KTU* 1.119 = RS 24.266 but cf. HERDNER 1978:34-35) mention a god *mlkm* at the penultimate position, just before *šlm* - d*sa-li-mu*, which is rendered dMA.LIK.MEŠ (NOUGAYROL 1968:45, 60). Thus, it appears that the divine name is based on the root *mlk* "to rule" or "to counsel", and that hesitation between *muluk* and *malik* is no longer permitted, even though the element *mulug/k* is attested by some Amorite proper names and toponyms (HUFFMON 1965:230-231). Could then be the *mulug/k* form preferably be parallel to the spelling of Molok (→Molech)?

II. The relationship between *malik* and *mlkm* in the Ugaritic lists is not easy to define; a similar difficulty presents itself with the biblical occurrences of Molech and Milcom. What appears more secure is the secondary role occupied by the god(s?) *Malik - Mlkm* (*plurale tantum* ?) in the lists of the temple of Assur as well as in the pantheon lists at Ugarit.

Malik and/or *mlkm* are/is assimilated to →Nergal, god of the underworld and of fire, or counted among those deities whose infernal characters are well known, and who are associated with the funerary offerings (*kispum*). They appear in connection with the *Igigi* and *Anunnaki* as chthonic beings involved in the cult of the dead ancestors (HEALEY 1975). HEALEY (1978) has tried to prove a close connection between *rpum* and *mlkm*, supposing that *rpum* (→Rephaim) is simply a special epithet of *Mlkm*, although the two are not identical in meaning. Hence, since both refer to the same reality, shades of the dead or underworld deities, there was no need to include both in the pantheon list, but *mlkm* was presumably preferred. In any case, both would be secondary deities, or divinized ghosts involved in the cult of the dead, preferably the last dead kings of the dynasty, and more probably beneficial deities than demons (DIETRICH & LORETZ 1981). But a relationship to Milcom is not at all ascertained.

The Ammonite epigraphical evidence throws some light on the veneration of the Ammonite deity and his cultic place from the ninth to the fifth century BCE, contemporary with the biblical evidence (HÜBNER 1992).

III. Even if dMA.LIK.MEŠ should be an attempt to find a Mesopotamian equivalent to Ugaritic *mlkm*, it does not prove that biblical Molech and Milcom have to be identified as a single Ammonite national deity. In the biblical passages, they are separately worshipped and have a separate cult place in Jerusalem (1 Kgs 11:5.7 [Molech -MT but Milcom -Greek]33; 2 Kgs 23:10.13: a sanctuary south of the mount of Olives, east of Jerusalem, and a *tophet* in the valley of (Ben) Hinnom, south of Jerusalem). In 1 Kgs 11:33 Milcom is called "the god of the Ammonites" as →Chemosh was the god of Moabites and Athtart (→Astarte) the Goddess of the Sidonians or Yahweh the

God of the Israelites (cf. 1 Kgs 11:5 "Milcom the →abomination [*šqṣ*] of the Ammonites"; 2 Kgs 23:13 Milcom the horror [*tw'bt*] of the Ammonites); but in 1 Kgs 11:7, it is Molech who is described as "the abomination of the Ammonites".

The Hebrew text of the Bible and the oral tradition at the origin of the Greek translations or revisions, as well as the other versions (e.g. Syrian, Latin) show clearly that in many more passages the morpheme (*ketîb*) *mlkm* was read and rightly understood as "Milcom" and not as "their king" (*malkām, qerē*) (MT *et passim*). Surely, the national god Milcom was "king" of the Ammonites as Yahweh was king of the Judaeans, but this is not the specific meaning of these verses. The biblical prophetic oracle against Ammon in Amos 1:15, known and taken up again *verbatim* by Jer 49(= 30):3, is surely to be understood: "And Milcom will go into exile, *his priests* and his princes altogether, says Yahweh".

The mention of "his priests" in this kind of oracle (compare Jer 48:7 and 49:3) is another proof in favour of the reading Milcom (PUECH 1977). Further, it is possible to compare the iconographic representations of the divine statues going into exile after the capture of a capital by the Assyrian armies; this is the background for these prophecies. Whereas the reading is almost certain in Zeph 3:5, it is also probable in 2 Sam 12:30 // 1 Chr 20:2.

Whether or not Milcom was related to *Malik* - *mlkm* is impossible to establish. The Ammonite national god occupies a more preeminent place in the biblical texts and in the inscription of the citadel than as a theophoric element in the Ammonite onomasticon, where El, the chief god of the Canaanite pantheon, is much more frequent. Contrary to a common opinion (R. DE VAUX, *Les institutions de l'Ancien Testament*, II [Paris ²1967] 333), there is no proof (biblical or Ammonite) that Milcom is another form of the god *Molek* / *Malik*. Nowhere are sacrifices of children offered to Milcom; but, the references are always to Molech.

IV. *Bibliography*

W. E. AUFRECHT, *A Corpus of Ammonite Inscriptions* (Ancient Near Eastern Texts and Studies 4; Lewiston 1989); H. CAZELLES, Molok, *DBSup*. V (Paris 1957-) cols 1337-1346 [& lit]; M. DIETRIECH & O. LORETZ, Neue Studien zu den Ritualtexten aus Ugarit (I), *UF* 13 (1981) 63-100, pp. 69-74; F. GRÖNDAHL, *Die Personennamen der Texte aus Ugarit* (Roma 1967) 157-158; J. F. HEALEY, Malkū : Mlkm : Anunnaki, *UF* 7 (1975) 235- 238; HEALEY, Mlkm / Rp'um and the Kispum, *UF* 10 (1987) 89-91; A. HERDNER, Nouveaux textes alphabétiques de Ras Shamra - XXIVe campagne 1961, *Ugaritica* VII (Paris 1978) 1-74; U. HÜBNER, *Die Ammoniter* (ADPV 16; Wiesbaden 1992); H. B. HUFFMON, *Amorite Personal Names in the Mari Texts. A Structural and Lexical Study* (Baltimore 1965); J. NOUGAYROL, Textes suméro-accadiens des archives et bibliothèques privées d'Ugarit, *Ugaritica* V (Paris 1968) no. 18= RS 20.24 ("Panthéon d'Ugarit") 42-64; E. PUECH, Milkom, le dieu ammonite, en Amos I 15, *VT* 27 (1977) 117-125.

E. PUECH

MIN

I. Min is an Egyptian god of procreation and creation. It has been speculated that his name occurs in the place name Thakemeina (1 Kgs 11:19-20 LXX; MT Tahpenes), which ALBRIGHT analyses as **Tȝ-kȝi-(n.t)-mn*, "The Female Attendant (or the like) of Min" (1955:32), presumably the name of an Egyptian queen. The suggestion is implausible, however.

II. Min is the Greek form of Eg *mnw* or *mn*, the local god of Akhmin and later Coptos. In the iconography Min is represented anthropomorphically as an ithyphallic figure carrying two feathers as his headgear. The god personifies male potency and fertility; since the latter could be subsumed under the general notion of creativity, Min has come to be regarded as the creator god *par excellence*. Presumably because of the location of Coptos at the beginning of the caravan routes, Min was venerated as the lord of the eastern desert as well. Both in Akhmin and Coptos Min was equated with →Horus, Isis being regarded as his mother. In later syncretistic theology, Min has also been identified with →Amun of Thebes.

III. The mention of Min in the Hebrew Bible is extremely dubious. Against Albright and other exegetes, it must be maintained that Tahpenes is probably not a proper name, but rather the Hebrew transcription of *tꜣ-ḥm.t-pꜣ-nsw(.t)*, with the LXX rendering Thakemeina being derived from *tꜣ-ḥm.t-nsw(.t)*, both of which mean "the wife of the king" (BARTLETT 1976:211 nn. 17-18 [& lit]; but note the remarks on this name →Isis). This etymology invalidates the interpretation by Albright and makes clear that Min does not occur in the OT. The author of the Hebrew text apparently took a title for a name. The fact that the Egyptian is followed by "the queen" does not make it a proper name. In all probability, SCHULMAN is correct in suggesting that "the queen" following Tahpenes (LXX Thakemeina) "is nothing more than a Hebrew gloss on the transliterated Egyptian title" (1986:127 n. 18).

IV. *Bibliography*

W. F. ALBRIGHT, New Light on Early Recensions of the Hebrew Bible, *BASOR* 140 (1955) 27-33; J. R. BARTLETT, An Adversary against Solomon, Hadad the Edomite, *ZAW* 88 (1976) 205-226; *R. GUNDLACH, Min, *RdÄ* 4 (1982) 136-140 [& lit.]; A. R. SCHULMAN, The Curious Case of Hadad the Edomite, *Egyptological Studies in Honor of Richard A. Parker* (ed. L. H. Lesko; Hanover/London 1986) 122-135.

K. VAN DER TOORN

MIRE → CLAY

MISHARU מישור

I. Like Hebrew *mîšôr*, Ugaritic *mšr* derives from *yšr*, 'to be upright'; similarly, Akkadian *mīšaru* is a derivative of *ešēru*, 'to straighten up'. Evidence for *mîšôr* as a deity in Hebrew tradition is only indirect.

II. The name of the Babylonian male deity *mīšaru* occurs together with *kittu*, 'Justice', and either or both have the epithets *āšib maḫri Šamaš*, 'seated in front of Shamash' or *sukkallu ša imitti*, 'vizier of the right hand' (for references to ^{d}*Mīšaru* see *CAD M/2*, 118-119). The alphabetic and syllabic texts from Ugarit show that *mšr* did occur there as a divine name. In a catalogue of divine names *ṣdq mšr* is listed (*KTU* 1.123:14): whilst the god ^{d}*mišarum* is included in the god list 'Anu' (RS 20.121:166; *Ugaritica V* [Paris 1968] 220). The Ugaritic personal name *mšrn* (*KTU* 4.342:2), spelled syllabically *me-ši/ša-ra-nu* (*Ugaritica VI* [Paris 1969] 141), probably uses this divine name as well. Another occurrence is in an offering list in Ugaritic (*KTU* 1.148:39; less certain is *l.mš*[*r*(?)] in *KTU* 1.81 4); but, in *KTU* 1.40, the meaning of *mšr* is still uncertain (DE MOOR & SANDERS 1991).

Ugaritic *ṣdq mšr* corresponds exactly to Phoenician Misor and Suduk as known from Philo of Byblos (*Phoenician History* in Eusebius, *PE* I 10,13). These two Phoenician gods are said to have discovered the use of salt: presumably in connection with treaties (e.g. as in Num 18:19), because they are gods of justice. Misor's son was Taautos, the Egyptian god →Thoth, credited with the invention of writing (BAUMGARTEN 1991: 65-72).

III. Although there is no explicit reference to a deity called *mîšor* in the Hebrew Bible, a few passages suggest there was some belief in a (demythologized) god subordinate to →Yahweh. They are Ps 45:7: "A sceptre of Equity (*mîšôr)* is the sceptre of your rule"; Isa 11:4: "But he shall judge the poor with Righteousness (*ṣedeq*), and defend the humble in the land with Equity (*mêšārîm*)"; Ps 9:9: "He (Yahweh) judges the world with Righteousness, he adjudicates the peoples with Equity (*mêšārîm*)" and Isa 45:19 "I am Yahweh, speaking Righteousness, announcing Equity (again, plur.). See also Mal 2:6; Ps 67:5. Ancient Near Eastern texts indicate the existence of the god Equity; but there are scarcely any traces of this deity left in the Hebrew Bible.

IV. *Bibliography*
A. L. BAUMGARTEN, *The* Phoenician History *of Philo of Byblos. A Commentary* (Leiden 1981) esp. 175-177; *H. CAZELLES, De l'idéologie royale, *JANES* 5 (1973) 59-73; M. LIVERANI, Συδυκ e Μισωρ, *Studi in onore di E. Volterra*, VI (Rome 1969) 55-74; S. E. LOEWENSTAMM, Notes on the History of Biblical Phraseology, *Comparative Studies in Biblical and Oriental Literatures* (AOAT 204; Neukirchen-Vluyn 1980) 210-221, esp. 211-214 (originally published in the *Publications of the Israel Society for Biblical Research* 17(1965) 180-187 [Heb]); J. C. DE MOOR & P. SANDERS, An Ugaritic Expiation Ritual and its Old Testament Parallels, *UF* 23 (1991) 283-300 esp 288-290 [& lit]; G. DEL OLMO LETE, Ug. *mšr* (KTU 1.40:1) y el edicto *mîšarum*, *AuOr* 8 (1990) 130-133; DEL OLMO LETE, El sacrificio de expiación nacional en Ugarit (*KTU* 1.40 y par.), *La paraula al servei dels homes. XXV jornades de biblistes catalans (1963-1985)* (Barcelona 1989) 46-56; R. A. ROSENBERG, The God Sedeq, *HUCA* 36 (1965) 161-177.

W. G. E. WATSON

MISTRESS → ADAT; BELTU

MITHRAS

I. The name of the Indo-Iranian deity Mithra occurs as a theophoric element in the Iranian proper name Mithredath, Heb מתרדת, Ezra 1:8; 4:7, Gk Μιθριδάτης, 1 Esdr 2:8 and Μιθραδάτης, 1 Esdr 2:12. The different orthography points to two different persons. The first one was treasurer of the Achaemenid king Cyrus II (559-530 BCE), who ordered the rebuilding of the temple in Jerusalem. The second was a high functionary (a satrap?) in the Persian administration in Juda during the reign of king Arthaxerxes I (465-424 BCE), when the temple was actually rebuilt. The name means 'gift of Mithra' and refers to the Iranian religion in Achaemenid times.

II. The oldest attestation of Mitra can be found in the list of gods in the treaty and the counter-treaty between the Hittite king Shupiluliuma I and the Mitanni-Hurrian king Kurtiwazza. Here some deities occur which have been construed as Aryan: Mitra, →Varuṇa, Indra and the two *Nāsatyā* (*KBo* I 1 Rev:55; KUB III 1b Rev:21'; *KBo* I 3+ Rev:41; A. KAMMENHUBER, *Die Arier im Vorderen Orient* [Heidelberg 1968] 142-151; I. M. DIAKONOFF, Die Arier im Vorderen Orient: Ende eines Mythos, *Or* 41 [1972] 91-120). The relation of this deity to later Vedic and Avestan Mithras is unclear.

The god Mitra occurs in the Rigveda, esp. in the hymn Rigveda III.59, where he functions as the personified sacred concept 'Contract'. All the other deities together with whom Mitra is invoked are sacred concepts too, like Aryaman 'Hospitality' and in particular Varuna 'True Speech'. When *mitra* occurs as a common noun in the Rigveda it has the meaning 'friend acquired by contract', an 'ally'. In the Avesta, Hymn 10, Mihr-Yasht, dedicated to the god Mithra, the god also embodies sacred 'Contract, Treaty' and all his other functions derive from this central concept. Vedic Mitra as well as Avestan Mithra go back to the reconstructed Proto-Aryan **mitra* = 'contract'.

Mithra therefore supervises the inviolability of all sorts of contracts (*mithra*) and treaties between men. He protects those who keep their contractual word and punishes those who break it. He gives peace and prosperity, rain, vegetation and health to those who are loyal (Yasht 10.61). In particular contracts between kings representing their countries are sacred to Mithra. He bestows blessings on the country of the king who is faithful to a treaty; then the rain falls and plants grow. In this context a common epithet of Mithra in Yasht 10 "of wide cattle pastures" finds its explanation. Already in the Rigveda, Mitra and Varuna are connected with cattle pasture and fertility (Rigveda III.62.16). Wide cattle pastures, where cattle can freely graze, only occur in times of peace, the result of strictly keeping contracts and treaties (Yasht 10.29; 10.60). Mithra also punishes men who break their contracts and lames them (Yasht 10.23). He fights them standing in his chariot accompanied by Verethragna, 'god Victory' (Yasht 10.67; 124-127). The contracts Mithra guards in the Avesta are exclusively contracts between men or concluded by men. Later Mithraic communities therefore consist only of men and must be called 'Männerbünde'.

As a guardian of contracts Mithra obtains a middle position between the two parties involved. This also is clear from Mithra's position in the Iranian calendar. He is the eponymous deity of the 16th day of the month and of the 7th month of the year. Mithra consequently develops into the mediator (Plutarch, *Is. et Osir.* 46s 369D, *mesitēs*; →Mediator II) between light and darkness. In the Avesta Mithra is "watchful" (Yasht 10.97), he is the "observer" and "guardian" of the whole of creation (Yasht 10.54, 103), he overlooks "all that is between heaven and earth" (Yasht 10.95). In complete accordance with these aspects Mithra later develops into a solar deity.

III. That there is a link between the Iranian divinity Mithra and the eponymous god of the Mithraic mysteries Mithras is clear, but the exact nature of this link between the Iranian and the Roman Mithra(s)-cults is a passionately debated question. The situation in the arena of Mithraic studies has changed dramatically over the past three decades. The brilliant Belgian historian Franz Cumont is rightly called the founding father of Mithraic studies, for he not only provided the learned world with a collection of texts and monuments (CUMONT 1896-1899), but he also created an interpretive context, based on the identification of Mithraic gods with Zoroastrian divinities. His interpretation was universally followed for the greater part of this century (CUMONT 1903), even after the replacement of the collection of monuments by VERMASEREN (1956-1960). Cumont's reconstruction suffered a mortal blow at the first conference of Mithraic studies, held in Manchester in 1971 (GORDON 1975), and has not been revived since. The past twenty-five years have instead given rise to many—mutually exclusive—theories on the origin and nature of the Mithraic mysteries, which virtually all share a stress on the absence of links between Zoroastrianism and Mithraism. Apart from one attempt to interpret Mithraism as a mixture of Iranian beliefs and Middle Platonism (TURCAN 1975), the stress has either been on the creation of a Neoplatonic salvation mystery (MERKELBACH 1984), or—most prominently—on Mithraism as an astrological cult, by interpreting the central icon of the faith, the tauroctony (Mithras slaying the bull) as a star map (BECK 1984; 1988; ULANSEY 1989). More recently a new chapter has been opened in the study of Mithraism by the heightened interest in the practices and beliefs of two Kurdish sects, the Yezīdīs and the Ahl-e ḥaqq, who seem to have retained traces of a pre-Zoroastrian Iranian cosmogony in which Mithra slays a bull and who also appear to share several ritual and architectural characteristics with those known from Roman Mithraism (KREYENBROEK 1994).

Mithraism, though described in some detail by several classical authors (GEDEN 1990), is mainly known from a great number of cult-places, *Mithraea*, generally constructed in the likeness of a cave, with side-benches and a small apsis with a representation of the tauroctony. Mithraea have been found throughout the ancient world, from Britain to Syria, but with a particular density in those areas where Roman garrisons were prominent. The spread of Mithraism, being a cult where only men were admitted, is therefore often connected with the spread of the Roman army, to which it is suspected to have attracted many adherents.

Mithraism is one of the mystery religions of the ancient world and as such is centered around (personal) salvation, through successive grades of inititation (BURKERT 1987). In the absence of reliable texts, the exact contents of Mithraic mythology must be pieced together by comparing the many artistic representations of the accomplishments of Mithras. Mithras is born from the rock (Lat *saxigenus*, Gk *petrogenēs*, the

→rock itself is called *petra genetrix* and is equally the object of cultic reverence) and establishes himself as creator and lord of genesis (Porphyrius, *De Antro Nympharum* 24). Various episodes of his life are depicted on the more elaborate cult reliefs and some frescoes, such as the water miracle (where Mithras releases the secluded waters by shooting an arrow) and the hunt. Two scenes from his life are most prominent, the (catching and) killing of the bull and the meal with the →Sun (→Helios; →Shemesh). The central icon of the Mithraic cult shows Mithras—dressed in a cape and a "Phrygian" cap—killing the bull by plunging a knife in the animal's side, while pulling his head upwards by the nostrils. From the tail of the dying animal ears of corn sprout (sometimes also from the wound itself, VERMASEREN 1956, no. 593-594), a snake and a dog come towards the wound to lick the blood and a scorpion seizes the genitals. Though the exact interpretation of this most famous deed of Mithras is hotly debated, it is beyond doubt that it represents a creative act, cherished in the cult as an act of delivery. It is presumably this act of delivery that is referred to in the famous maxim from the Mithraeum under the Sta. Prisca in Rome *et nos servasti eternali* (?) *sanguine fuso*, "You have saved us as well, having shed the eternal (reading uncertain) blood" (VERMASEREN & VAN ESSEN 1965:217-221). In the act of killing, Mithras is often accompanied by two divinities, who are represented as smaller replicas of the god himself, called Cautes and Cautopates, the former carrying an uplifted torch, the latter carrying a torch bent downwards, symbolising coming into existence and passing away. Though being frequently invoked as the sun himself, Mithras is distinct from the Sun, with whom he shares a meal that is also frequently depicted. This meal of Mithras with the Sun was, so it seems, ritually re-enacted in the gatherings of the Mithraic communities. The holding of the communal meal was at the heart of the Mithraic rituals and was severely criticized by several Church fathers as a diabolic transvesty of the Christian eucharist. Other rituals of the Mithraic communities were also seen as imitations of Christian rituals, which makes it difficult to reconstruct Mithraic cultic activity (Justin Martyr, *Apologia* I 66.4; *Dialogus cum Tryphone* 70.1; 78.6). Mithraism knew a sevenfold initiation, represented as seven steps on a ladder (Origenes, *Contra Celsum* 6.22), with the grades of *corax* (raven), *nymphus* (bride), *miles* (soldier), *leo* (lion), *Perses* (Persian), *heliodromus* (sun-walker) and *pater* (father). The *pater* of a community was also its leader. It is within this sevenfold initiation, though imperfectly understood, that astrological symbolism is of great prominence. Having attracted a considerable following in the second and third centuries CE, the prominence of Mithraism waned rapidly, to disappear fully after the Theodosian legislations of the late fourth century.

IV. In the Bible Mithra is only indirectly attested in the proper name Mithredath, one of the most common Iranian names of male persons (SCHMITT 1978:398).

N. WYATT (The Story of Dinah and Shechem, *UF* 22 [1990] 433-458) has argued unconvincingly that there would have been a connection between an alleged Aryan Mithras/contract and the Israelite conception of *bĕrît*, 'covenant'.

V. *Bibliography*

*R. BECK, Mithraism since Franz Cumont, *ANRW* II.17.4 (1984) 2002-2115; BECK, *Planetary Gods and Planetary Orders in the Mysteries of Mithras* (EPRO 109; Leiden 1988); E. BENVENISTE, Mithra aux vastes pâturages, *JA* 248 (1960) 421-429; U. BIANCHI (ed.), *Mysteria Mithrae* (EPRO 80; Leiden 1979); M. BOYCE, On Mithra's Part in Zoroastrianism, *BSOAS* 33 (1969) 10-34; W. BURKERT, *Ancient Mystery Cults* (Cambridge, Mass. 1987); M. CLAUSS, *Mithras. Kult und Mysterien* (München 1990); F. CUMONT, *Textes et monuments figurés relatifs aux mystères de Mithra* (2 vols.; Bruxelles 1896-1899); CUMONT, *The Mysteries of Mithra* (London 1903); J. DUCHESNE-GUILLEMIN (ed.), *Etudes Mithriaques* (Acta Iranica 17; Leiden/Teheran 1978); A. S.

GEDEN, *Mithraic Sources in English* (Hastings 1990); I. GERSHEVITCH, *The Avestan Hymn to Mithra* (London 1959); *R. GORDON, Franz Cumont and the Doctrines of Mithraism, *Mithraic Studies* (ed. J. R. Hinnells; Manchester 1975) 215-248; P. G. KREYENBROEK, Mithra and Ahreman, Binyāmīn and Malak Ṭāwūs. Traces of an Ancient Myth in the Cosmogonies of two Modern Sects, *Recurrent Patterns in Iranian Religions. From Mazdaism to Sufism* (ed. P. Gignoux; Paris 1992) 57-79; KREYENBROEK, Mithra and Ahreman in Iranian Cosmogonies, *Studies in Mithraism. Proceedings of the Rome Conference 1990* (ed. J. R. Hinnells; Roma 1994) 173-182; A. MEILLET, Le dieu indo-iranien Mitra, *JA* X 10 (1907) 143-159; R. MERKELBACH, *Mithras* (Königstein 1984); H. P. SCHMIDT, Indo-Iranian Mithra Studies: The State of the Central Problem, *Etudes mithriaques* (Acta Iranica 17; Leiden/Teheran 1978) 345-393; R. SCHMITT, Die theophoren Eigennamen mit Altiranisch Mithra, *Etudes mithriaques* (Acta Iranica 17; Leiden/Teheran 1978) 395-455; P. THIEME, Mitra and Aryaman, *Transactions of the Connecticut Academy of Arts and Sciences* 41 (1957) 1-96; THIEME, The Concept of Mitra in Aryan Belief, *Mithraic Studies* I (ed. J. R. Hinnells; Manchester 1975) 21-39; THIEME, Mithra in the Avesta, *Etudes mithriaques* (Acta Iranica I,4; Leiden/Teheran 1978) 501-510; R. TURCAN, *Mithras Platonicus* (EPRO 47; Leiden 1975); D. ULANSEY, *The Origins of the Mithraic Mysteries. Cosmology and Salvation in the Ancient World* (New York etc. 1989); M. J. VERMASEREN, *Corpus Inscriptionum et Monumentorum Religionis Mithriacae* (The Hague 1956-1960); VERMASEREN, *Mithras, the Secret God* (London 1963); M. J. VERMASEREN & C. C. VAN ESSEN, *The Excavations in the Mithraeum of the Church of Santa Prisca in Rome* (Leiden 1965); G. WIDENGREN, *Die Religionen Irans* (Stuttgart 1965) 13-20; 117-121.

H. J. W. DRIJVERS (I, II, IV)
& A. F. DE JONG (III)

MOLECH מלך

I. Molech occurs as a divine name in the MT eight times: five times in Leviticus (18:21; 20:2-5); twice in Kings (1 Kgs 11:7, where it is probably confused with →Milcom of the Ammonites; and 2 Kgs 23:10); and once in Jeremiah (32:35). The LXX renders the name both as a common noun (*archōn,* "ruler", in Leviticus; *basileus,* "king", in 3 Kgdms 11:5 [MT 1 Kgs 11:7]) and as a proper name (*Moloch* in 2 Kgs 23:10 and Jer 39:35 [MT 32:35]). In addition, the LXX has *Moloch* for MT *malkĕkem* ("your king") in Amos 5:26; the LXX reading is quoted in the one NT occurrence of the name, Acts 7:43.

The etymology of the name is uncertain. Most scholars relate it in some way to the (West) Semitic root *mlk,* "to rule, to be king", either as a Masoretic distortion of *melek* ("king") using the vowels of *bōšet* ("shame"), or as a Qal participle, or as an otherwise-inexplicable 'segolate' noun form (given especially the variations of vowels in the comparative evidence, see discussions in HEIDER 1985:223-228, DAY 1989:56-58).

Contrary to the entire thesis of Molech as a divine name is the proposal of EISSFELDT (1935), that OT Molech is to be related to Punic *molk/mulk,* a technical term used in a cult of child sacrifice, and known from inscribed stelae in burial grounds at Carthage and elsewhere. According to his hypothesis, all occurrences of MT *mōlek* can be explained as a cognate common noun, so that the stereotypical phrase (as in 2 Kgs 23:10) *lĕhaʿăbîr ʾet-bĕnô wĕʾet-bittô bāʾēš lammōlek* is to be rendered "to cause one's son or one's daughter to pass through the fire as a *molk*-sacrifice". (Even given this understanding, the etymology remains problematic; the most widely accepted view is that of W. VON SODEN, who suggested a **maqṭil*-form of the root *h/ylk,* comparable to *môpēt* and *ʿôlâ* [Review of Eissfeldt, *Molk, TLZ* 61 (1936) 46].)

II. Eissfeldt's proposal has been widely persuasive, as it is founded on a rare combination of comparative literary, inscriptional and archaeological evidence. Both classical and patristic writers testify to a cult of child sacrifice, particularly in times of military emergency, in Phoenicia and at Carthage (translations are conveniently provided by DAY 1989:86-91). The aforementioned stelae, whose inscriptions appear variously in Punic, Neo-Punic and Latin transcription (as *molch*), regularly compound the *mlk*-element with another word, such as *ʾmr*. Eissfeldt read these latter elements as the second member of construct chains, specifying what sort of *molk*-sacrifice was commemorated by the stela (so that *mlkʾmr* was the sacrifice of a sheep [cf. Hebrew *ʾimmēr*], presumably as a substitute for a child, while *mlkʾdm* was a human sacrifice [cf. Hebrew *ʾādām*]). Finally, "sacrificial precincts" (or "tophets", borrowing the Biblical term for the locus of the Molech cult) have been excavated at Punic colonial sites in Sicily, Sardinia and North Africa, all containing the remains of children, as well as small animals.

Each of these categories of evidence has generated a considerable body of scholarly literature. For now, we may note a couple of points at which the case advanced by Eissfeldt and his supporters may not be as strong as at first appears. Most significantly, despite the classical and patristic citations, there is no sure archaeological evidence of the practice of a cult of child sacrifice in Phoenicia, leaving a crucial 'missing link' between Israel and the Punic colonies (and provoking the suspicion that the citations are polemical, directed chiefly at defaming the motherland of the Carthaginians). Secondly, compounding the problem of the 'missing link' is the relatively late date at which inscribed stelae begin to appear in the Punic cemeteries (7th-6th centuries BCE), as well as the discovery of stelae inscribed with *mlk* in places (such as Malta) where no cemetery has yet been found, raising the possibility that the sacrificial sense of *mlk* is an intra-Punic development. Thirdly, despite Eissfeldt's assertion that formulae such as *mlkʾmr* indicate an increase in the practice of animal substitution over time, the preliminary analysis of remains found at Carthage suggests that child sacrifice increased in frequency (relative to animal substitution), at least through the 4th-3rd centuries BCE (STAGER 1982). Finally, it should be noted that an increasingly vocal body of European scholars is challenging the interpretation of the Punic remains as indicating any cult of child sacrifice at all (D. PARDEE, Review of Heider, Cult of Molek, *JNES* 49 [1990] 372).

Recent research into comparative evidence has focused on deities named M-l-k (variously vocalized) in places closer to Israel, especially Mesopotamia and Syria-Palestine. A divine name →Malik is well-attested as a theophoric element at Ebla (third millennium BCE), although little can be determined of his nature or cult there. Amorite personal names from second-millennium Mari include the element Malik, as well as Milku/i, Malki and Muluk (each sometimes with the divine determinative and sometimes without, so that the common noun, "king", may in some cases be present, rather than a divine name). Of equal or greater interest at Mari are references to beings called *maliku* as recipients of funerary offerings, although it is not clear whether they are the shades of the dead or chthonic deities. Nevertheless, the underworld context regularly recurs in the other comparative evidence. Akkadian god lists from the Old Babylonian period onwards include a deity named Malik equated with →Nergal, and other Akkadian texts mention *mal(i)kū*-beings with the Igigi and Anunnaki, all in connection with the cult of the dead ancestors. (We may also note a god Milkunni attested in Hurrian.) But most significant of all, so far as the study of OT Molech is concerned, is the presence of a deity Mlk at Ugarit. In addition to its inclusion in personal names (vocalized as Malik, Milku and Mulik in syllabic texts), Mlk appears in two divine directories (actually, snake charms), as resident at *ʿṯtrt* (*KTU* 1.100:41; 1.107:17), the same location which is elsewhere assigned to the netherworld deity *Rpu* (*KTU* 1.108:2-3; but see DAY 1989:49-50, for a contrary view). While this collocation does not necessarily imply the identity of the deities, it is suggestive of some close relationship, as is the attestation of beings called *mlkm* in connection with the royal cult of the dead, along with the better-known *rpum* (OT →Rephaim), who appear to be the shades of dead royalty at Ugarit (or of all the dead in the OT; cf. Ps 88:11). Finally, we may note the similar divine names →Melqart of Phoenicia and Milcom of Ammon. While the equation of either deity with Molech is unlikely, it is at least intriguing that Melqart (literally, "King of the City") may also have connections with the underworld (particularly if one follows W. F. Albright in understanding "the City" as the netherworld), and equally of interest that the Ugaritic 'address' for Mlk, *ʿṯtrt*, is likely to be identified with the city Ashtaroth in →Bashan, just north of Ammon. In sum, the Semitic comparative evidence yields the portrait of an ancient god of the netherworld, involved in the cult of the dead ancestors (and perhaps their king, given the meaning of the root *mlk*, at least in West Semitic).

III. We turn, then, to a consideration of the Biblical evidence, focusing on the seven instances (less 1 Kgs 11:7) of *mōlek* in the MT, together with related material (especially other references to cultic child sacrifice).

The preponderance of occurrences are in the Holiness Code in Leviticus: once in 18:21; and four times in 20:2-5. The former verse speaks of "giving of your seed (*mizzarʿăkā*) to cause to pass over to Molech". As noted especially by WEINFELD (1972) the context (forbidden sexual relations) led some of the rabbis to propose that the cult of Molech entailed not sacrifice, but intercourse with Gentile women. WEINFELD builds on this point and others to propose a non-sacrificial interpretation of the cult, such that "to cause to pass through the fire to Molech" meant dedication to the deity, but not sacrifice; most scholars, however, remain persuaded that actual sacrifice by fire was involved, especially given Num 31:23, where *heʿĕbîr bāʾēš* clearly entails burning.

The four instances of Molek in Lev 20:2-5 move the discussion forward. First, the reference to the cult in v 5 as "playing the harlot after Molech" (*liznôt ʾaḥărê hammōlek*) presents a significant obstacle to the Eissfeldt hypothesis, that Molech is not a divine name in the OT. The presence of the article in *hammōlek* is problematic for his assertion that, based on the LXX evidence, the article should be eliminated from *lammōlek* elsewhere, thus preserving a parallel with phrases like *lĕʿōlâ* ("as a burnt offering"). More seriously, the object of the phrase "to play the harlot after" is uniformly a deity or supernatural object (such as Gideon's ephod in Judg 8:27), with the one possible exception of Num 15:39. Turning, then, to the constructive task, we note that the following context in v 6 repeats the "play the harlot" phraseology, only now with reference to doing so after "ghosts and familiar spirits" (*hāʾōbōt wĕhayyiddĕʿōnîm*). Again, we seem to be in the realm of the shades (→Spirit of the Dead; →Wizard).

That this linkage is not limited to this one passage is shown by Deut 18:9-14 which, although it does not contain the term Molech, includes at the head of a roster of "abominable practices of those nations" (i.e. the Canaanites) "one who makes his son or his daughter pass through the fire" (*maʿăbîr bĕnô-ûbittô bāʾēš*). There follows then a list of (other) illicit practitioners of contact with the spirit world: diviners, soothsayers, augurs, sorcerers, charmers, mediums, wizards, necromancers.

That the OT sees the cult of Molech as essentially a Canaanite practice (indeed, as the archetypical Canaanite abomination) is indicated both in Deuteronomy (12:31) and in the Deuteronomistic summary of the fall of the Northern Kingdom (2 Kgs 17:17). However, with the exception of the latter verse, its practice in Israel appears to have been restricted to the environs of Jerusalem. Both Ahaz (2 Kgs 16:3) and Manasseh (2 Kgs 21:6) are explicitly accused of participation, while Josiah is credited with having "defiled the Topheth, which is in the valley of the sons of Hinnom, that no one might cause his son or his daughter to pass through the fire to Molech" (2 Kgs 23:10). In fact, while the evidence is all too scanty, it appears to be within the realm of possibility that the cult was practised by the Jerusalem establishment prior to Josiah, presumably subsumed within the cult of Yahweh (e.g. Isaiah uses the imagery of the cult in describing what Yahweh would do to the Assyrian king [30:33]—one can hardly imagine Isaiah approving of the cult, but his words were intended to communicate, using known imagery). Its fate after Josiah is even harder to describe with certainty. Both Jeremiah (7:31-32; 19:5-6.11; 32:35; cf. 2:23; 3:24) and Ezekiel (16:20-21; 20:25-26.30-31; 23:36-39) condemn their contemporaries (presumably in Jerusalem, also for Ezekiel) for the practice. Even following the exile, Isa 57:5.9 suggests the continuation of the practice for at least a brief time (particularly if one reads *mōlek* for MT *melek* in v 9), at least in isolated locales ("the clefts of the rocks", v 5).

Among the many questions surrounding Molech and the related cult, none is so perplexing as the god's relationship to other deities (as has been seen already in the examination of the comparative evidence). The Biblical evidence suggests a distinction from Milcom of the Ammonites by specifying that Josiah destroyed distinct holy places for the two (2 Kgs 23:10-13) and by stressing that Molech's origins were Canaanite. On the other hand, many have read Jeremiah as indicating an equation with →Baal: "They built the high places of the Baal which are in the valley of the son of Hinnom to cause their sons and their daughters to pass over to Molech, something which I did not command them, nor did it enter my mind ..." (32:35; cf. 19:5, "they built the high places of the Baal to burn their sons in the fire as offerings to the Baal"). At most, however, this may reflect a popular confusion of the two (or their cults) since elsewhere they are spoken of distinctly (e.g. 2 Kgs 23:5.10). (See HEIDER 1985: 291-293, and DAY 1989:29-71 for discussion of other proposed divine equations, especially WEINFELD's proposal of Adad[milki] [1972].)

Also much discussed, in view of the comparative evidence and of other OT references to human sacrifice, is whether the cult of Molech was restricted to times of military emergency (cf. the classical and patristic references to the Carthaginian practice and the child sacrifices of Jephthah [Judg 11] and King Mesha [2 Kgs 3:27]) or to the firstborn (cf. the "Law of the Firstborn" in Exod 13:2.11-15; 22:28b-29 [ET 29b-30]; 34:19-20; and the *Akedah* [Gen 22]). Neither appears likely. First, the presence of "his daughter" in the standard formula describing the cult of Molech makes a connection with the sacrifice of firstborn *sons* unlikely. Second, because the few OT references to sacrifice in time of military emergency do seem to restrict the practice to firstborn and/or only children, the cult of Molech does not appear to have been practised for this reason, either. In this connection, it is of interest that STAGER has concluded that the Carthaginian cult was probably not one of military emergency, *pace* the classical/patristic testimonies, or of the firstborn (Child Sacrifice at Carthage—Religious Rite or Population Control?, *BARev* 10 [1984] 44; cf. STAGER 1982:161-162).

With so much uncertainty, it is no surprise that scholars have combed the OT for additional references and allusions to Molech or his cult, particularly where the MT has *melek* in a provocative context. With the exception of Isa 57:9 (discussed above), such attempts have commanded little assent. (A recent proposal, involving a passage without an alleged concealed occurrence of Molech, is that of DAY [1989:58-64] regarding Isa 28:15.18.)

In conclusion, the presence of a deity Molech and of his cult in ancient Israel seems established, although the details of either remain difficult to draw with precision. Based on the comparative evidence, the relatively few explicit Biblical references, and those additional passages which may be defended as relevant, Molech emerges as a netherworld deity to whom children were offered by fire for some divinatory purpose. Less certain, though suggestive, are connections with the cult of the dead ancestors.

IV. What is certain is the profound (one hesitates to say 'fiery') impact of those few Biblical references on the imagination of later writers. In addition to those rabbis who sought to interpret the cult of Molech as non-sacrificial (discussed with Lev 18:21 in III above), others described in great detail the deity's idol and cult, in terms borrowed from the classical/patristic writers on the Carthaginian practice (G. F. MOORE, Biblical notes. 3. The image of Molech, *JBL* 16 [1897] 161-165). The Quran (Sura 43:77) depicts Malik as an archangel who governs the damned on behalf of Allah: "'Malek', they will call out, 'let your Lord make an end of us!' But he will answer: 'Here you shall remain'" (trans. N. J. ONWOOD; Penguin classics; 3d ed. [Baltimore 1968] 150). Later writers built on the biblical, rabbinic and classical sources, including J. MILTON (*Paradise Lost*), C. DICKENS (*The Haunted Man*), G. FLAUBERT (*Salammbô*) and J. MICHENER (*The Source*), each by turns fascinated and horrified by the deity whom Milton termed "that horrid king besmeared with blood" (I. 392).

V. *Bibliography*

*J. DAY, *Molech: A God of Human Sacrifice in the Old Testament* (UCOP 41; Cambridge 1989) [& lit]; O. EISSFELDT, *Molk als Opferbegriff im Punischen und Hebräischen und das Ende des Gottes Moloch* (Beiträge zur Religionsgeschichte des Altertums 3; Halle 1935); *G. C. HEIDER, *The Cult of Molek: A Reassessment* (JSOTSup 43; Sheffield 1985) [& lit]; P. G. MOSCA, *Child Sacrifice in Canaanite and Israelite Religion: A Study in Mulk and mlk* (diss. Harvard 1975); L. STAGER, Carthage: A View from the Tophet, *Phönizier im Westen* (ed. H. G. Niemeyer; Madrider Beiträge 8; Mainz am Rhein 1982) 159-160; M. WEINFELD, The Worship of Molech and of the Queen of Heaven and its Background, *UF* 4 (1972) 133-154.

G. C. HEIDER

MOON ירח, כסא, לבנה, חדש

I. By far the most common biblical Hebrew word for 'moon' or 'Moon-god' is *yārēaḥ*, which appears 27 or 28 times in the OT. In 24 instances and in several Jewish pseudepigraphic and apocryphal works, *yārēaḥ* repeatedly appears in combination with *šemeš*, 'sun' or 'Sun-god' (→Shemesh). Its derivative *yeraḥ* occurs with the calendrical meaning 'month' and is also attested in early inscriptional Hebrew (cf. the Gezer calendar and Arad ostracon 20). The only biblical text where the reading *yārēaḥ* has been contested is Deut 33:14. In this passage, the phrase "the produce of the *yĕrāḥîm* (moons or months?)" forms the second half of a parallel bicolon alongside "the choicest fruits of the *šemeš*". *Yārēaḥ* is also often found grouped with terms designating the lesser astral bodies such as the →stars (*kôkābîm*), the →constellations (*mazzālôt*), or the →hosts of heaven (*ṣĕbāʾ haššāmayim*). The last, the hosts of →heaven, also functions in biblical Hebrew as a class inclusive of all the luminaries (including the moon).

Hebrew synonyms of *yārēaḥ* include the twice occurring *keseʾ*, 'full moon' (Ps 81:4 parallel with *ḥōdeš*; Prov 7:20; perhaps Job 26:9), and the feminine noun *lĕbānâ*, 'moon' or 'white lady', which appears in poetic texts and always in connection with the sun or *ḥammâ*, 'heat' (Eccl 6:10; Isa 24:23; 30:26). The noun *ḥōdeš*, 'new moon', appears some 280 times, but this term never refers to the moon as a luminous heavenly body. Rather, its customary meaning is month and so it more closely corresponds to the derivative *yeraḥ*. As for the etymology of YRḤ, it has been related to the Hebrew verb ʾRḤ, 'to travel', while semitic Y/WRḤ has been equivocally associated with Eg *ꜣʿḥ* or 'moon'. Cognates of *yārēaḥ* are well documented in the semitic languages. Akk *arḫu* can designate the moon, the new moon day, or the month (cf. Bab *arḫu*, Ass *urḫu*), but the Akkadian only rarely denotes the moon as the majority of occurrences refer to a calendar month. Moreover, the meaning 'new moon day' more closely corresponds to Heb *ḥōdeš*. Ug *yrḫ* can denote the calendrial month, the moon, or the moon-god Yarikh. Other cognates include Phoen *yrḥ* (moon, Moon-god [?], or month), Aram *yrḥ* (moon or month), Eth *wrḥ* (moon or month) and Ar *wrḥ* (month).

II. Any treatment of the ancient lunar cult traditions of the Levant demands that some account be given of the Mesopotamian traditions, for the latter significantly impacted the formulation of both religious belief and rite as associated with the moon in the contemporary cultures of the eastern Mediterranean. The Moon-god was known by at least three names in Mesopotamian tradition: Nanna, Suen, and Ashimbabbar. Scribes sometimes combined the Nanna or Suen elements to make Nanna-Suen. By the Old Babylonian period, Suen was also written as →Sîn and Sîn's wife was named Ningal. Their children were the →sun-god Utu and the goddess Inanna. The name Nanna dominates the sources reflective of southern Mesopotamia and the city of Ur, while Suen is attested early on in such far away sites as Ebla and Ugarit in western Syria. The different names possibly indicate two originally distinct lunar traditions that were subsequently conflated in early antiquity. The Nanna traditions emphasized the Moon-god's relation to his spouse, Ningal, and were decidedly sexual or erotic in nature, while the Suen or Sîn traditions described the Moon-god primarily in relation to his divine parents.

Whereas the sun, having overpowered the lesser celestial bodies, ruled the ancient Mesopotamian skies in solitude, the moon governed a vast and visible celestial assembly. The night luminaries moved across the skies with great regularity, they made manifest not only the power that controlled the heavens, but also an alien world possessed of a measure of stability that intensely enchanted those living a terrestrial existence. Accordingly, the moon's perceived position of pre-eminence in the night skies was awarded special place in Mesopotamian myth and ritual, for the Mesopotamian Moon-god was identified as both the immediate offspring of the great gods, Enlil and Ninlil, and as descendent of An, the great sky god. Not only had the Moon-god been created before the Sun-god, but he was portrayed as having given birth to that younger luminary of lesser status. Such traditions illustrate both the Moon-god's celestial status and his high ranking in the Mesopotamian pantheon.

Although for the ancient inhabitants of Mesopotamia, the moon's growth, disappearance and re-emergence in a never-ending cycle personified change, it was a change viewed from within the larger parameters of continuity. In fact, of all the nocturnal luminaries, the changes in shape and position of the moon were the most readily accessible to observe and chart. Its waxing and waning might symbolize both finite time and eternity, light transforming into darkness, and life into death and back again. Thus, lunar motion came to represent both the natural and cultural life cycle of birth, growth, decay, and death. The moon's periodic movements also functioned as the determining factor in the measurement of the year, the month and ultimately the entire cultic calendar. Major time periods and holidays were set to the phases of the moon—the new, the quarter and the full moons. Their importance was such that the king typically participated in the associated festivals along with the priests and the general population. The disappearance of the moon could also signify the displeasure of the gods and so the practices of offering prayers and lamentations to the divine assembly were enacted in order to appease the gods. The Moon-god might act as judge of fates during his disappearance from the night sky and subsequent sojourn in the netherworld, but once his work as judge was completed, he would reappear in the skies accompanied by the prayers and libations of the Anunnaki or underworld gods. Furthermore, the Mesopotamian Moon-god's monthly disappearance together with his return from the netherworld were linked with cycles of fecundity, and his rebirth into the world of light was thought to bring about renewed fertility. Accordingly, the lunar deity bestowed his rejuvenating powers upon the produce, livestock and human population as he possessed the restorative powers to keep herb, herd and humanity fertile and prolific. Epithets like 'the pure long horn of heaven' served to highlight these powers of the Moon-god, for it expressed the twofold image of the Moon-god as the crescent moon or boat of heaven that sailed the life giving waters, and as the raging bull empowered with the vigour to insure the longevity of the herds, the authority of the earthly king, and the security of the people. His role as fertility god was given further expression in his description as father of the people and in his frequent appearance in the guise of a bull or →calf. In sum, the Moon-god enjoyed widespread popularity in the history of ancient Mesopotamian religions. The continuous influence which these traditions exerted upon ancient Levantine cultures provides the needed socio-historical context within which to pursue the topic of lunar religion in ancient Israel.

The moon-god likewise enjoyed an elevated status in early Syriac traditions. In addition to Suen's attestation at late third millennium Ebla, the west Asiatic name for the moon-god, Yarikh, has been identified at that site. Furthermore, early second millennium Mari personal names like Abdu-Erakh, 'the servant of the Moon-god', Zimri-Erakh, 'the protection of the Moon-god', Yantin-Erakh, 'the Moon-god has given' and Uri-Eraḳh, 'the light of the Moon-god', probably reflect the Moon-god's important role in the religious life of that city. At late second millennium Emar, the Moon-god Sîn played a major role as one of the palace deities in the festivals and appears in theophoric names fourth in frequency only to the gods →Dagon, →Baal, and →Resheph. Shaggar (Sheger), perhaps a west Asiatic lunar deity, has also been identified at Emar. At the contemporary site of Ugarit, the moon-god Yarikh is mentioned a number of times and in various contexts such as legends (*KTU* 1.18 iv:9, 1.19 iv:2), incantations (*KTU* 1.100:26; 1.107:15), ritual texts (as the recipient of offerings, e.g. 1.148:5,29), god lists (cf. *yrḫ* of *KTU* 1.118:13 = ^{d}*sîn* of RS 20.24:13) and as a theophoric element in proper names (e.g. the name *ʿbdyrḫ*, 'the servant of the Moon-god'). A short hymn commonly thought to be a translation from an original Hurrian, *KTU* 1.24, celebrates the marital union of Yarikh and the moon-goddess Nikkal (= Ningal) whose cult developed independently in Syria lasting well into the common era. This cultic hymn gives expression to the aspiration to secure those blessings of fertility which the lunar deities could bestow upon their suitors.

On the basis of an Ugaritic text recounting →El's banquet (Ug *mrzḥ* = Heb *marzēaḥ*), Yarikh has been characterized as fulfilling the roles of judge and gatekeeper of the netherworld (*KTU* 1.114:4-8). Yet, it is more likely the case that this passage mocks the Moon-god's claim to pre-eminence (1.114:4-8): "Yarikh gets ready his (= El's) drinking vessel / like a dog, he fills up under the tables / The god who knows him (= Yarikh) / offers him food / The one who does not / beats him with a stick under the table." This disparaging of the Moon-god's role is further verified by the more prominent role uniquely attributed to the solar goddess at Ugarit. Shapash's regular receipt of offerings and sacrifices, her prominent role in serpent incantations, her association with the heroic →Rephaim/*rpʾ* traditions, her invocation as eternal sun (*špš ʿlm*) in royal correspondence second in position only behind Baal (2.42:6-7), the mention of her temple or *bt špš*, her epithet 'luminary of the gods' or *nrt ilm*, and her appearance as a theophoric element in proper names illustrate the solar deity's major role at Ugarit. Her position as judge over matters of life and death in the Baal-→Mot myth likewise affirms her exalted status. This reversal of station at Ugarit *vis-à-vis* the Moon-god and Sun-goddess clearly stands as an exception to the rule in early Levantine lunar traditions.

Turning to the relevant first millennium data from the Levant, a wide range of artefactual evidence—jewelry, glyptic, stelae and onomastica with lunar related theophoric names—testifies to the continuance of lunar religion in the region (see e.g. SCHROER 1987; WEIPPPERT 1988; KEEL & UEHLINGER 1992). In addition to the notoriety achieved by the cult of the Moon-god attested at the ancient Syrian city of Harran, two 7th cent. BCE Aramaic stele inscriptions preserve the names of a pair of priests in the service of the moon-god Sehr at ancient Nerab. In fact their names, Sinzeribni and Si'gabbar, consist of a theophoric element derivative of the Moon-god Sîn (the Si'-element in the latter instance being a shortening of that name).

While inscriptional Hebrew names containing a lunar element are presently lacking (but cf. *ks'* from Beth Shemesh), other regional first millennium onomastica such as the Phoenician names *'bdyrḥ*, 'the servant of the Moon-god', *'bdks'*, 'the servant of the Full Moon', and the Ammonite *yrḥ 'zr*, 'Moon is my Helper', confirm the existence of local lunar religions. In view of the Moon-god's occasionally attested dominance over the Sun-god in the early religious traditions of the Levant, several 8th to 6th cent. BCE →Yahweh names in inscriptional Hebrew might point to the definitive role which lunar imagery played in ancient Israel's formulation of Yahweh symbolism. Names like *yhwzrḥ*, 'the shining forth of Yahweh' (ZRḤ 'rise, shine forth'), *nryhw* 'the lamp of Yahweh' (cf. *nēr* →'lamp') or *'ryhw* 'the light of Yahweh' ('WR 'to be bright') might refer to the illumination or light originally thought to emanate from the Moon-god (rather than the Sun-god).

The identification of the specific sources underlying the Yahwistic lunar symbolism is extremely problematic, for the admixture of Mesopotamian and west Asiatic lunar traditions throughout the Levant is well documented and spans several centuries. For example, the second millennium evidence from Ugarit documents the presence of the Mesopotamian lunar couple Sîn and Ningal (= Nikkal) in early western Syria. Furthermore, the Neo-Assyrian kings from Shalmaneser III to Assurbanipal not only vigorously supported, but also exported the cult of the Harranian Moon-god to the farthest western reaches of their empire and Shalmaneser III is credited with having rebuilt the temple of Sîn at Harran. The king of Samal, Bar-Rakkab, an Aramaean vassal of Tiglath-pileser III, paid due recognition to the Moon-god of Harran by referring to that god as his 'Lord' in a stele inscription (*KAI* 218). Also relevant in this regard is the provenance of the inscription as it surrounds a lunar standard stele with pendant tassals on either side, a stereotypic emblem of the contemporary Moon-god cult.

The Moon-god's central role in royal ideology is made explicit in a letter addressed to Assurbanipal by a diviner who describes his father Esarhaddon's pilgrimage to the temple of Sîn at Harran. In this letter, the god Sîn is portrayed as a king leaning on a staff with two crowns on his head. Esarhaddon is commanded to take one of those crowns and place it on his head and to go forth and to conquer those lands that had yet to submit to Sîn. Some years later, the Babylonian king Nabonidus was moved by a dream to rebuild the great temple of Sîn at Harran following its destruction by the Medes and Babylonians in 610 BCE. His mother, Adad-guppi, was a priestess of the moon-god who in one text extolled Sîn for appointing her son to kingship. She proclaimed that Sîn was 'the king of all gods' and 'the lord of heaven and netherworld'. Nabonidus echoes these words of his mother in a stele inscription indicating his preference for Sîn over →Marduk as head of the Babylonian pantheon. Nabonidus also appointed one of his daughters as high priestess of Sîn at Ur thereby continuing the two thousand year tradition of lunar religion in that city. Furthermore, when Nabonidus took a ten year leave of absence from the political turmoil that gripped his capital city Babylon, he settled in Taima in north Arabia, a centre for lunar religion as suggested by a 5th cent. BCE Aramaic stele recovered from that site.

As for the encounter between east and west Asiatic lunar traditions in first millennium Israel-Judah, an Assyrian crescent shaped bronze standard was discovered in the 7th cent. Assyrian military fort at Tell esh-Shari^ca (Ziklag?; WEIPPERT 1988:627-628, fig. 4.66.6). A seal impression on a cuneiform tablet found at Gezer and dated to 649 BCE· depicts an Assyrian style lunar crescent standard with tassels mounted on a socle. Of particular importance is the fact that the name of the owner of this standard, one Natan-Yahu, a resident of Gezer, contains a Yahwistic theophoric element (WEIPPERT 1988:627-628, fig. 4.66.3). A considerable amount of biblical data likewise assumes that lunar cults once played significant roles in early Israelite religion. Proper names related to *yārēaḥ*, like Jerah (Gen 10:26; 1 Chr 1:20 pausal form only) and Jaroah (1 Chr 5:14 'devoted to Yerah'?), as well as a name like Hodesh or *ḥōdeš* (1 Chr 8:9) might attest to an ancient form of Israelite lunar worship. Likewise, the names of various sites such as Jericho (*yĕrîḥô*) mentioned in the Hebrew Bible and Beth-Jerah (*bēt yeraḥ* = Khirbet Kerak) known from the Talmud (*b.Bik.* 55a; *Ber. Rab.* 98:18) might testify to ancient lunar cults in the region.

Cults dedicated to the Moon-god are clearly presumed in several biblical passages wherein the Moon-god's powers are transferred to Yahweh and the moon is polemically portrayed as an object created and controlled by Yahweh. Moreover, a handful of legal prohibitions point to the religious nature of the rituals performed in deference to the moon. Violators are often depicted as having rendered 'service to' (ʿBD) or having 'bowed down to' (ŠḤH) the Moon-god. Lunar worship is also condemned in nonlegal texts like Job 31:26-28. These biblical prohibitions against lunar worship reinforce the likelihood that other biblical passages extolling Yahweh's pre-eminence over the moon are specifically aimed at disparaging lunar religion. The argument in Job 25:5 that →God does not regard the moon as very bright (read *yhl*?) probably rests on the prior assumption that the moon's brightness was held in some sectors of Israelite society to be supernaturally empowered for, as Job 31:26-27 intimates, the Moon-god's brightness apparently played a significant role in some forms of Yahwistic religion. Sir 43:6-8 similarly affirms the moon's brightness wherein it is depicted as a beacon or marvelous light shining in the vault of the heavens and 2 Esdr 5:4 notes that the moon will shine during the day in the eschaton.

The significant role of the Moon-god in various forms of Yahwistic divination and astrology is underscored in other biblical passages. As Ps 121:6 suggests, in certain Yahwistic circles the Moon-god was held to be an oracular god whose brightness could wreak havoc on its victims, rendering an individual a 'lunatic'. The psalmist on the other hand, claims that Yahweh possesses the power to restrain such ominous lunar forces. Isa 47:13 refers to the making of astrological prognostications at the time of the new moons (*ḥŏdāšîm*). According to the mantic wisdom reflected in Prov 7:20, the moon's waning was considered an unpropitious time for the conducting of business. In Jer 2:24, the appearance of the new moon is intimately connected with menstruation. The new moon also appears together with the →sabbath as sacred times requiring restricted trade (Amos 8:5), special sacrifice (Isa 1:13) or as a time especially conducive to the consultation of a prophet (2 Kgs 4:23). In fact, should those religious practices deemed unacceptable by some Yahwistic prophetic circles become attached to the new moon festivals, certain prophets did not hesitate to condemn them (Amos 8:5; Hos 2:11; Isa 1:13).

The data just discussed provide the immediate context for interpreting other biblical passages making mention of the moon. The new moon is coupled with the appointed feasts (*môʿădîm*) or with both the sabbath and the appointed feasts as times of celebration (Hos 2:13[11]) and of special religious observance (1 Chr 23:31; 2 Chr 2:3[4]; 8:13; 31:3; Ezra 3:5; Neh 10:34[33]; Ezek 45:17; 46:1-16). At these times the king's courtiers were required to dine with him (1 Sam 20:18-29) and the trumpet was blown in the temple signalling their commencement (Ps 81:4[3]). Interpreters have also surmised that the Passover feast has lunar cult associations owing to its initiation following the blowing of the trumpet at the new and full moons.

The moon is depicted as the lesser light that dominates the night in Gen 1:14-19 where it is superseded only by the sun.

While this passage maintains a clear status distinction between Yahweh and the moon, it nevertheless upholds a significant degree of continuity between Yahweh and the astral bodies as to their functions and powers. Another passage, Ps 104:19, evinces extensive familiarity with ancient Near Eastern astral worship (perhaps Egyptian Atenism?). While it is clearly polemical in tone, this psalm demonstrates that the astral imaging of Yahweh was at home in certain versions of the cult. It would appear that the astral bodies were simply emptied of their divine powers which were then transferred to the domain of Yahweh. Isa 24:23 presupposes this transformation, for this passage predicts the overthrow of the Moon-god (*lĕbānâ*) in an eschatological battle between Yahweh and the astral bodies—here referred to as the →host of heaven. To be sure, any simplistic equation of Yahweh and the moon and the other astral bodies or their corresponding forms is unequivocally spurned in the biblical traditions, but echoes of the above mentioned archaic transformations can nevertheless be discerned as underlying those traditions.

Furthermore, if the broader Levantine lunar traditions as well as the biblical prohibitions are any indication of the lunar cult's pervasiveness, a number of related themes in biblical tradition might contain veiled polemics against the lunar cult or against the moon in its natural unmediated state as a once dominant iconographic symbol of Yahweh. These themes include Yahweh's creation of and control over the moon (Gen 1:14; Ps 8:4; 104:19; 136:7, 9; Sir 43:6-8), the moon's resultant praise of Yahweh (Ps 148:3; cf. Gen 37:9) and Yahweh's manipulation of the moon, that is, his darkening of it, his turning it red, or its shining by day (for the last, cf. 2 Esdr 5:4) whether as a sign of Yahweh's power to bless (Deut 33:14; Isa 60:19-20; Jer 31:35) or to judge (Josh 10:12-13; Isa 13:10; Joel 2:10; 3:4; 4:15; Ezek 32:7-8; Hab 3:11; Job 25:5). All of these themes point to the persistence of an Israelite lunar religion against which they are aimed.

As for the biblical prohibitions, the worship of the Moon-god Yareah is prohibited in three deuteronomistic texts and in one prophetic text of deuteronomistic orientation: Deut 4:19; 17:3; 2 Kgs 23:5; Jer 8:2 (cf. also Wis 13:2). All four of these texts originate in the late pre-exilic period or thereafter. As mentioned previously, the illicit character of the lunar cult in Yahwistic religion is also dealt with in the post-exilic passage Job 31:26. What developments created the need to address the specific issue of astral worship in deuteronomistic circles? It might have been the case that an inner-Israelite struggle ensued over the continued role of the two major luminaries in Yahwistic religion. Outside deuteronomistic circles, the solar cult had overtaken that of the Moon-god as evidenced by the sun's elevated role in the Ugaritic text *KTU* 1.24 and in the Genesis creation account. Within deuteronomistic circles, the divine pantheon had been reduced to Yahweh and his servile *mal'ākîm* (→Messenger, →Angels) and so the worship of the moon and sun was outlawed. Nevertheless, aspects of the lunar cult had already made their way into the Yahwistic cult and symbolism by the time the prohibitions had arisen, therefore these elements had to be reinterpreted or rejected.

For example, Deut 4:15-20 underscores the point that the people should not attempt to make an image of Yahweh. The wholesale denial of any material image of Yahweh, whether man-made or naturally occurring is not at issue. In other words, the deuteronomistic circles merely endorsed a different iconographic symbol than those representative of the astral deities. Rather, this passage addresses the nation's ignorance of or disregard for Yahweh's proper symbolism according to deuteronomistic standards. As 4:11 reiterates, when the Sinai theophany took place, the people did not see Yahweh's form, for they stood only at the foot of the mountain. Only Moses saw Yahweh's form or *tĕmûnâ*, face to face, as traditions like Num 12:8 and Deut 34:10 make clear. (An alternative tradition in Exod 33:16-23 notes that Moses is allowed to see only Yahweh's glory and his back, but not his →face.) Similarly, a passage like 2 Kgs 18:4 might reiterate the deuteronomistic judgement that the nation continually misrepresented Yahweh in the cult. According to our author, Moses' bronze serpent (→Nehushtan) was removed from the Solomonic temple only several centuries after its introduction by king Hezekiah, who was otherwise considered a reformer in deuteronomistic circles. Perhaps this cryptic account reflects a once influential tradition that preserves a memory of a form of Yahweh's image distinct from that endorsed in later deuteronomistic ideology.

The assumption underlying these verses is that the astral bodies could and did represent a deity and that long ago Yahweh (identified in some instances with El) appointed them as gods to rule the other nations. The depiction of Yahweh in 1 Kgs 22:19 as seated on his throne with the host of heaven standing at both his right and left side confirms the independent, but subordinate, status of the celestial bodies and the elevation of the astral bodies to the status of major deities in the pantheon preceded Yahweh's rise to prominence as made evident in the textual traditions pertaining to Deut 32:8-9. According to the relevant LXX and Qumran readings of Deut 32:8-9, this passage describes how the →Most High or El (cf. Gen 14:18-22) had allotted to each of the nations one of the 'sons of El' (*bĕnê ʾēl*) or members of his pantheon. As the language shared by Deut 4:19 and 32:8-9 indicates, the underlings of El included the moon and the sun and the host of heaven. Therefore, it should come as no surprise that Deut 32:9 reveals that Yahweh was likewise included as an independent, but subordinate, deity who was assigned to →Jacob/Israel.

In sum, Deut 4:16-18 concerns the issue of making the wrong image of Yahweh. Deut 4:19-20 outlaws the adoption of the sun, moon, or host of heaven as phenomenological manifestations of Yahweh in contradistinction to widely accepted convention in non-deuteronomistic circles of Yahwism. Of further interest in this regard is the fact that non-astral inanimate objects are not singled out for censure. The same applies in the case of so-called mixed forms (Deut 4:16-17 only pertains to unmixed anthropomorphic and zoomorphic forms). Aside from such deliberate omissions one might speculate regarding the nature of the legitimate symbol of Yahweh on the basis of archaeological data. Perhaps Yahweh's image as viewed within deuteronomistic circles was a cultic object like the ark or a half animal/half man figure as attested at Kuntillet Ajrud.

2 Kgs 23:5 preserves a tradition in which priests burned incense not only to Baal, but also to the moon, the sun, and the →constellations, that is, to all the hosts of heaven throughout Judah and the Jerusalem environs. This passage also recounts how king Josiah of Judah purged these priests from the region. In 2 Kgs 21:3-5, king Manasseh is accused of worshipping the hosts of heaven and building altars to them in the two temple courts. In the light of 23:5, the hosts of heaven in 21:3-5 most likely include the moon along with the sun and →stars or constellations. In any case, 23:12 claims that Josiah tore down the altars in the temple courts that Manasseh had built, but notes that he also pulled down the roof-top altars on the upper chamber of Ahaz that had been built, not by Manasseh, but by 'the kings of Judah'. This may be an echo of the lunar cult's longstanding pervasiveness in ancient Judahite religion.

Exilic and post-exilic passages like Jer 19:13 and Zeph 1:5 likewise presuppose that the roof-top altars were erected for the worship of astral deities and specifically for the hosts of heaven. This practice had earlier Yahwistic antecedents, that is, if passages like 1 Kgs 22:19 are any indication of what constituted Yahwistic cosmology in former days: "... I saw Yahweh seated upon his throne with all the host of heaven standing in attendance to the right and to the left of him". If so, 1 Kgs 22:19 would indict king Hezekiah, the 'reformer', as a perpetrator of the cult associated with the roof-top altars. The ambivalence of the deuteronomistic ideology as to the extent of Hezekiah's reform also points in this direction. While Hezekiah is praised for his general reforming efforts in the deuteronomistic traditions, he nevertheless appears in those same traditions as a Judahite king tolerant of the astral religion of his forefathers. 23:12 suggests that as one of those 'kings of Judah' that preceded Manasseh, he allowed the offering of incense to the hosts of heaven and the rituals at the roof-top altars to continue unabated. If this tradition has any correspondence with the socio-historical realities of the late pre-exilic period, then it confirms the claim that astral religion, and especially the lunar cult, were very much a part of Yahwistic religion of the seventh century BCE and following. Such factors would also explain the vacillation evident in the deuteronomistic tradition's treatment of king Hezekiah.

A passage like Jer 8:2 further verifies not only the lunar cult's extent of influence in ancient Israelite religion and tradition, but also the continued threat which it posed as a alternative form of Yahwism being advanced by deuteronomistic circles. With a touch of the ironic, Jer 8:2 describes the exposure of corpses to the luminaries, as if to suggest the efficacy of the act. This practice is also attested in Assyrian texts wherein the victorious king would punish defeated enemies by desecrating their royal graves and exposing their contents to the sun and the moon. It should be recalled that as deities, the sun and the moon were judges of the netherworld and such exposure of the bodies meant that the Moon-god and Sun-god had determined that such ghosts could not be properly cared for and therefore would never rest in peace.

Although forms of lunar religion clearly have ancient roots in Canaan, some biblical traditions more likely concern themselves with the threat posed by later non-indigenous versions of lunar religion. If one assumes that the relevant biblical traditions are in many cases the productions of the exilic or post-exilic period, then one should not be surprised to find that the lunar cults, disparaged in the Hebrew Bible, have their origins in contemporary Syrian or Mesopotamian traditions. Assyrian style lunar cult reliefs, bronze lunar standard tops, and standard glyptics recovered from first millennium Levantine sites testify to the persistence of contemporary forms of Mesopotamian lunar religion in the region. The biblical characterization of these lunar cults as ancient and Canaanite would then reflect the ideological rhetoric of ancient writers who employed veiled polemics in their disparaging of competing cults. This in turn might suggest that eastern lunar influence on the Israelite-Judahite cultic traditions was more extensive than the mere borrowing of month names from the lunar festival calendar of Babylonian tradition as evidenced in the biblical tradition's portrayal of the new moon festival.

The image of the new moon festival as displayed in biblical traditions might have been informed by lunar traditions like those attached to the akitu festival observed in honour of the Moon-god at Harran. The Harranian lunar cult and akitu festival were revived, adapted and fervently sanctioned by the Assyrian and Babylonian royalty during the mid-first millennium. Therefore, one should not be surprised to find significant influence from Mesopotamian and Syrian lunar traditions on the biblical sketches of the new moon festival or, for that matter, on the late Judahite cults expressive of the social realities underlying those literary sketches. One's view on this and the broader question of Mesopotamian influence on mid-first millennium Israelite and Judahite religion are bound up with the questions of the dating and character of the biblical texts in question and with the nature of the relevant archaeological evidence, but any resolution of these issues lies well beyond the boundaries of the present essay.

V. *Bibliography*

M. E. COHEN, *The Cultic Calendars of the Ancient Near East* (Bethesda 1993); T. GREEN, *The City of the Moon-god: Religious Traditions of Harran* (RGRW 114; Leiden 1992); J. C. GREENFIELD & M. SOKOLOFF, Astrological and Related Omen

Texts in Jewish Palestinian Aramaic, *JNES* 48 (1989) 201-214; M. G. HALL, *A Study of the Sumerian Moon-God, Nanna/Suen* (Diss.; Philadelphia 1985); J. S. HOLLADAY Jr., The Day(s) the Moon Stood Still, *JBL* 87 (1968) 166-178; A. JIRKU, Der Kult des Mondgottes im altorientalischen Palästina-Syrien, *ZDMG* 100 (1950) 202-220; O. KEEL & C. UEHLINGER, *Göttinnen, Götter und Gottessymbole* (Freiburg/Basel/Wien 1992); J. LEWY, The Late Assyro-Babylonian Cult of the Moon and Its Culmination at the Time of Nabonidus, *HUCA* 19 (1943) 453-473; J. W. MCKAY, *Religion in Judah under the Assyrians* (London 1973) 50-53; G. DEL OLMO LETE, Yarḫu y Nikkalu: La mitología lunar sumeria en Ugarit, *AulOr* 9 (1991) 67-75; D. PARDEE, *Les textes paramythologiques de la 24e campagne* (RSOu 4; Paris 1988) 35-48, 60-62; M. PROVERA, Il culto lunare nella tradizione biblica e profana, *BeO* 33 (1991) 65-68; F. ROCHBERG-HALTON, *Aspects of Babylonian Celestial Divination: The Lunar Eclipse Tablets of Enūma-Anu-Enlil* (AfO Beih. 22; Horn 1988); S. SCHROER, *In Israel gab es Bilder: Nachrichten von darstellender Kunst im Alten Testament* (OBO 74; Fribourg 1987) 261-266; A. SJÖBERG, *Der Mondgott Nanna-Suen der sumerischen Überlieferung* (Stockholm 1960); A. SPYCKET, Le culte du Dieu-Lune à Tell Keisan, *RB* 80 (1973) 384-395; J. G. TAYLOR, *Yahweh and the Sun: Biblical and Archaeological Evidence for Sun Worship in Ancient Israel* (JSOTSup 111; Sheffield 1993); H. WEIPPERT, *Palästina in vorhellenistischer Zeit* (München 1988).

B. B. SCHMIDT

MOSES מֹשֶׁה Μωυσῆς

I. In the Bible Moses is the human →mediator of revelation par excellence. His name occurs ca. 765 times in the OT (especially in Exod [290x] - Josh) and ca. 80 times in the NT (more frequently than the name of any other OT person, especially in reference to Moses as lawgiver and author of the Pentateuch) and is borne by no other biblical figure. The name *mōšeh* is explained in Exod 2:10 by means of a wordplay with the root *mšh*, 'to draw': "I drew him out of the water". Probably, however, the name also contains an allusion to the destiny of its bearer: 'one that draws out, viz. his people from the waters of the sea and the bondage of Egypt' (Exod 12-15). Josephus (*Ant.* 2:228; *Contra Apionem* 1:286) and Philo of Alexandria (*Vita Mosis* I 17) explained the name with the aid of Egyptian/Coptic: 'the (one) rescued from the water'. This explanation probably forms the basis for the Greek version of the name Μωυσῆς [= *mō/mou* "water" + *esēs* "saved"]. The conception which is currently almost universally accepted is that the name should be explained with the aid of the Egyptian word *mśj* "produce", "bring forth", and that it is an abbreviated form of a theophoric name (e.g. Ptah-mose, "Ptah has been born/has engendered", cf. GRIFFITHS 1953:225-231). As appears from Matt 17:13 par. and Rev 11:3-12 Moses was considered to have been transferred like →Elijah to heavenly existence, at least according to some Jewish and Christian circles. Accordingly his return could be expected.

II. According to the OT and especially the pentateuchal traditions, Moses had a unique status among men (cf. Deut 34:10-12; Sir 44:23-45:5). He was the servant of the LORD (Exod 14:31; Num 12:7.8; Deut. 34:5, etc.), God's confidant, a prophet (Deut 18:15.18; 34:10; Hos 12:14) and priest (Ps 99:6; cf. Judg 18:30). Moses was the LORD's representative to Israel (Exod 3:15.16; 11:2; 12:3, etc.) and to Pharaoh, the king of Egypt (Exod 3:18; 5:1; 6:29; 7:10, etc.). He was the redeemer and leader of Israel (Josh 24:5; 1 Sam 12:8; Isa 63:11; Hos 12:14; Mic 6:4; Pss 77:21; 105:26); the initiator of its administration (Exod 18:13-26; Num 1-2; 26; Deut 1:9-18) and the founder of its cult (Exod 3:15; 12-13; 16:21-30; 40:17-33; Lev 8-9, etc.); the zealous champion of the true Yahweh-religion and the fighter against apostasy (Exod 32; Num 25). Moses interceded on Israel's behalf (Exod 32:7-14.30-32; 33:12-23; 34:9; Num

11:2; 12:13; 14:13-19; 16:22; 21:7; Jer 15:1; Ps 106:23); he had to suffer the enmity and lack of confidence of his people (Exod 2:14; 5:21; 14:10-12; 15:24; 16:2.3; 17:2-4, etc.). Though also condemned for lack of faith (Num 20:7-13; Deut 32:51; Ps 106:32-33), he was a real 'man of God' (Deut 33:1; Josh 14:6; Ps 90:1, etc.) who wrought impressive miracles and wonders (Exod 7:10-12:30; 14:15-15:27; 17:1-16, etc.). He was a poet (Exod 15; Deut 32-33; Ps 90) and a law-giver (Exod 24:3-4.7.8; 34:27.28; Deut. 31:9.24-26; Josh 1:7; 8:31.32; 22:5; 1 Kgs 2:3, etc.).

In their picture of Moses the NT passages again and again go beyond the information provided by the OT (e.g. Heb 11:22-28). Sometimes they present traces of the extra-biblical Moses' legends (e.g., Acts 7:22; 1 Cor 10:4; 2 Tim 3:8; Jude 9). In conformity with the OT, Moses often appears in the NT as Israel's lawgiver (Matt 8:4; 19:7.8; 23:2; Mark 7:10; 10:3.4; 12:9; Luke 2:22; John 7:19.22.23; 8:5; Acts 6:11.14; 13:39, etc.). He is also considered to be the author of the Pentateuch (Matt 22:24; Mark 12:26; Luke 16:29.31; John 1:17; Rom 10:5.19; Heb 7:14, etc.) and as such he is regarded as the announcer and prophet of →Jesus, the →Messiah (Luke 24:27.44; John 1:45; 5:45.46; Acts 26:22; 28:23), who can be described in the NT as a second Moses (Acts 3:22; 7:37), misunderstood and rejected like the first Moses (Acts 7:17-44). In various ways several OT traditions about Moses are used in the NT within the context of typological exegesis (e.g., John 3:14; 6:32-58; 1 Cor 10:1-13; 2 Cor 3:7-18; Heb 3:1-6; 9:16-28; 12:18-24; Rev 15:3).

In the OT as well as in the NT Moses is above all the mediator of revelation. Several times his most intimate relation with the LORD is emphasized (e.g., Exod 19:9.19; 20:18-21; 24:18; 33:11.18-23; Num 12:7-8; Deut 5:20-28; Ps 103:7; Sir 45:5; cf. John 9:29; Acts 7:38; Heb 8:5), evidently to emphasize that Moses' words and prescriptions really are the words and rules of the LORD himself. In connection with his role as a mediator of revelation, Moses is portrayed with superhuman traits (cf. also Deut 34:5; Sir 45:2). According to Exod 34:29-35 the skin of Moses' face radiated after his meeting with the Lord on Mount Sinai (Exod 34:29.30.35), i.e. his face was enveloped in a divine aura. By his nimbus Moses was legitimated as the true representative of the LORD (cf. Matt 17:2; Acts 6:15). The same fear which seized man at the theophany (e.g., Exod 20:18.21; 33:20), was according to Exod 34:30 evoked by the LORD's representative, the man who thanks to his long and rigorous fasting (Exod 34:28; cf. Exod 24:18; Deut 9:9.18) had reached the highest state of purity and holiness—with eating and drinking impurity may enter the body (cf. Matt 15:11)—and so had been transferred to heavenly existence (*2 Enoch* 56:2; cf. *2 Enoch* 22). Thus he was in a position to communicate with the Lord and so his face was transfigured (HOUTMAN 1989:7). Although he was a mortal, Moses had received the appearance of a divine being. The idea that God can be known to humankind only in and through Moses, is also expressed in extra-biblical literature, for instance in Ezekiel the Tragedian's *Exagoge*. He tells about a dream-vision in which Moses saw the following scene: God gave him the sceptre and the royal diadem. He himself descended from the throne and seated Moses upon it (Eusebius, *Praep. Evang.* 9.29.5). This daring concept is not found elsewhere. The view that Moses ascended to heaven (cf. Exod 20:21; 24:12-18; 34:2.4.27-29) and became God's viceregent or plenipotentiary by receiving divine and royal dignity, is attested, however, in Philo of Alexandria and in rabbinic and Samaritan literature (MEEKS 1968:354-371).

According to the OT Moses did die (Deut 34:5). His death occurred, however, under striking and mysterious circumstances. Moses was not worn with age. Despite his age, his sight was not dimmed, nor had his vigour failed (Deut 34:7). He died at the command of the LORD (cf. Deut 32:50; 34:5), at the moment he finished his duty (cf. Deut 32:48-52; 34:4). But how? No indication is given of the way he died. His burial is reported: *wayyiqbōr ʾōtô* "and he buried him" (Deut 34:6). Who performed this act is not mentioned explicitly, however. Notwithstanding the rather detailed information in the text about the location of Moses' burial-place, it is said to be unknown (Deut 34:6).

Various traditions on Moses' death are known from outside the Bible. They all express the uniqueness of Moses. In Pseudo-Philo (*LAB* 19; 20:8) and the Samaritan *Memar Marqah* V (ed. MACDONALD 1963) his death is even described as his glorification. According to rabbinic literature, Moses' life was not taken away by the →Angel of Death, but by the kiss of the LORD—*ʿal-pî yhwh* in Deut 34:5 is understood literally—(e.g., *Tg. Ps.-J.*; *MidrR. Deut.* 11:10; *MidrR. Cant.* I.2:5), the easiest form of death (*b. Ber.* 8a). In Rabbinic literature various views are found with regard to the agent of Moses' burial. According to a current interpretation Moses was buried by the LORD. This view is also attested in, for instance, Pseudo-Philo (*LAB* 19:16) and in *Memar Marqah* V § 4. According to another interpretation Moses has to be considered the agent of his own burial (e.g. *MidrR. Num.* 10:17). In the rabbinic elucidation of Moses' burial, →angels often play a role as supernumeraries (e.g. *Tg. Ps.-J*; *MidrR. Deut.* 11:10). Outside rabbinic literature the view is attested that Moses was buried by an angel (→Michael) or a number of angels (cf. the use of the plural "they buried him" in the LXX-version of Deut 34:6, in *Tg. Neof.*, and in some MSS of the Samaritan Pentateuch). Sometimes this depiction of the event is connected with a report of the dispute between Michael and the Angel of Death/the →Devil about Moses' body (cf. Jude 9). The concept of (an) angel(s) as the agent(s) of Moses' burial is found in Christian literature (HOUTMAN 1978:76-77), but is also known to Islam (WEIL 1845:186-191) and to the Falashas (ULLENDORFF 1961:419-443).

The predominant view in the tradition is that Moses did die and was buried. Also another view occurs, viz. that Moses has been taken up to heaven. This view is alluded to, for instance, in Josephus' version of Deut 34 (*Ant.* 4:323-326), in which no mention is made of Moses' burial place: yet communing with Eleazar and Joshua, who followed Moses to the place of his passing away, a cloud suddenly descended upon Moses (cf. 2 Kgs 2:11; Acts 1:9) and he disappeared in a ravine. Josephus adds that Moses had written in the sacred books that he died, lest they should venture to say that by reason of his surpassing virtue he had gone back to the deity, i.e. that he had been taken away bodily from the realm of humankind to God (cf. *Ant.* 1:85; 3:96). Josephus' description of the end of Moses' life is ambiguous. By using for Moses' disappearance a technical term for assumption (*aphanizomai*)—in *Ant.* 9:28 it is used in connection with Elijah's ascension—he suggests that Moses was taken up ino heaven, but by the determination of the place of Moses' disappearance ("in a ravine", cf. Deut 34:6) and his remark on Moses' authorship of his own death-report, he seems to deny such a suggestion. However that may be, Josephus was acquainted with the view that Moses had not died, but had been taken up in the flesh to heaven. That view is also attested in Philo of Alexandria (*Quaest. et sol. in Gen.* 1:86). In his *De vita Mosis* 2:288.291, however, he narrates Moses' pilgrimage from earth to heaven (the ascension of his soul), Moses thus leaving mortal life for immortality (cf. *De virt.* 76; *Sac.* 8-10), but also about his burial by immortal powers (for the concept of Moses' having a twofold demise cf. e.g. Clement of Alexandria, *Stromata* 6:15). In Deut 34 there are some points of contact for the concept of Moses' removal: in stories from antiquity about assumption (cf LOHFINK 1971: 32-79) the place of the removal of a person is often a mountain (cf. Deut 34:1; Acts 1:12; *2 Apoc. Bar.* 76); because he was translated bodily, the person in question has no burial-place (cf. Deut 34:6; Luke 24:1-11.23.24, and Josephus, *Ant.* 9:28 on →Enoch and →Elijah). Possibly the concept of Moses' removal has come into being under the influence of the tradition concerning Elijah's translation to heaven (2 Kgs 2:11; HOUTMAN 1978:79-80).

In Matt 17:1-13; Mark 9:2-13; Luke 9:28-36 Moses is mentioned together with Elijah (cf. also Rev 11:6), whose ascension was widely accepted. So it is likely that in these passages it is presumed that Moses enjoyed the same heavenly existence as Elijah. The concept of Matt 17:1-13 par. and Rev 11:3-12—the two witnesses of v 6 are to be identified with Moses and Elijah—must be distinguished from the concept of Moses' return after the resurrection of the dead (e.g., *MidrR. Deut.* 9:9) and the concept of the ascension of Moses' soul, about which the lost ending of the so-called *Assumption of Moses* (also known as *Testament of Moses*) may have reported. In Matt 17:1-13 par. Moses and Elijah appear from heaven in the role of precursors of Jesus, the →Messiah. By their coming the beginning of the final age is announced (cf. Mal 3:22-24). In Rev 11:3-12 they appear as preachers of repentance. In their confrontation with the beast (the →Antichrist) they suffered death, but after their martyrdom they were raised from death and so they were in the position to return bodily to heaven (Rev 11:11.12). The concept of Moses' removal to heaven is attested also in Rabbinic literature (e.g., *Sifre Deut.* § 357; *b. Sota* 13b; *Midr. ha-Gadol* [ed. S. SCHECHTER; Cambridge 1902: 213]), in *The Samaritan Chronicle or the Book of Joshua the Son of Nun* (ed. CRANE 1890: 31), in Christian pseudepigrapha (*Acts Pil.* 16:5.6) and in patristic literature (e.g., Jerome, *In Amos* IX 6).

III. By Hellenistic Jewish authors such as Eupolemus, Artapanus, Philo of Alexandria, and Josephus, the biblical narrative concerning Moses has been elaborated and expanded with many legends. They glorify Moses as an inventor, civilizer, lawgiver, philosopher, king, and prophet. Their ideal picture of Moses as a unique personality, a Divine Man, partly has its origin in their apologetic attitude in view of the strong anti-Semitic attacks on Moses by Hellenistic authors (Manetho, Chaeremon, Lysimachus, Apollonius Molon, Nicharchus).

In rabbinic literature, too, Moses' life and work are surrounded with legends. According to rabbinic tradition Moses was not only given the written law, but also the oral law. Several extra-biblical writings are ascribed to Moses (so, e.g., a Greek *Apocalypse of Moses* [*Adam and Eve*] and the *Assumption of Moses*). The book of Jubilees is presented as deriving from revelation given to Moses on Mount Sinai (1:1-7.26.27; 23:22). The same is the case with the Temple Scroll of Qumran (cf. WISE 1990). In Samaritan tradition Moses is the only prophet, God's highest and most direct means of revelation. In Samaritan eschatology Moses-typology plays an important role (cf. Deut 18:15.18). With the name Mūsā, Moses occupies a prominent place in the Koran and in Islamic tradition (cf. *HIsl*, 546-548).

In modern Moses interpretation S. FREUD's (1939) view of Moses as an Egyptian champion of monotheism, who was murdered by the Israelites, has drawn wide attention (STEMBERGER 1974). Such a tarnishing interpretation of Moses' demise had been suggested, however, already ca. 1775 by J. W. Goethe (BUDDE 1932). Of all biblical figures Moses has the most prominent place in literature, art and music. The picture of the horned Moses is widely known (cf. MELLINKOFF 1970).

IV. *Bibliography*

C. BEGG, Josephus' Portrayal of the Disappearances of Enoch, Elijah, and Moses: Some Observations, *JBL* 109 (1990) 691-693; K. BERGER, Der Streit des guten und des bösen Engels um die Seele. Beobachtungen zu 4QAmr[b] und Judas 9, *JSJ* 4 (1973) 1-18; S. BROCK, Some Syriac Legends concerning Moses, *JJS* 33 (1982) 237-255; K. BUDDE, Goethe zu Mose's Tod, *ZAW* 50 (1932) 300-303; H. CAZELLES, Moïse, *DBSup* 5 (1957) 1308-1337; *CAZELLES, *TWAT* 5 (1986) 28-46; G. W. COATS, Legendary Motifs in the Moses Death Reports, *CBQ* 39 (1977) 34-44; O. T. CRANE, *The Samarian Chronicle or the Book of Joshua the Son of Nun* (New York

1890); F. DEXINGER, Samaritan Eschatology, *The Samaritans* (ed. A. D. Crown; Tübingen 1989) 266-292; E. L. FLYNN, Moses in the Visual Arts, *Int* 44 (1990) 265-276; J. FOSSUM, Sects and Movements, *The Samaritans* (ed. A. D. Crown; Tübingen 1989) 293-389, esp. 321-324, 338-342, 380-382, 386-389; *Fragments from Hellenistic Jewish Authors* (ed. C. R. Holladay; Vol I Chico, California 1983; Vol II Atlanta, Georgia 1989); *Greek and Latin Authors on Jews and Judaism* (ed. M. Stern; Jerusalem 1974-1984) III 137-138 [Index]; J. GOLDIN, The Death of Moses: An Exercise in Midrashic Transposition, *Love and Death in the Ancient Near East. Essays in Honor of M. H. Pope* (ed. J. H. Marks & R. M. Good; Guildford, Conn. 1987) 219-225; J. G. GRIFFITHS, The Egyptian Derivation of the Name Moses, *JNES* 12 (1953) 225-231; K. HAACKER & P. SCHÄFER, Nachbiblische Traditionen vom Tode des Moses, *Josephus-Studien. Untersuchungen zu Josephus, dem antiken Judentum und dem Neuen Testament. Otto Michel zum 70. Geburtstag gewidmet* (ed. O. Betz et al.; Göttingen 1974) 147-174; P. W. VAN DER HORST, Moses' Throne Vision in Ezekiel the Dramatist, *JSS* 34 (1983) 21-29; C. HOUTMAN, De dood van Mozes, de knecht des Heren. Notities over en naar aanleiding van Deuteronomium 34:1-8, *De Knecht. Studies rondom Deuterojesaja aangeboden aan Prof. Dr. J. L. Koole* (Kampen 1978) 72-82; HOUTMAN, Het verheerlijkte gezicht van Mozes, *NedTTs* 43 (1989) 1-10; *J. JEREMIAS, *TWNT* 4 (1942) 852-878; *TWNT* 10/2 (1979) 1184-1185; G. LOHFINK, *Die Himmelfahrt Jesu* (StANT 26; München 1971) 32-79; J. MacDONALD, *The Theology of the Samaritans* (London 1964) 147-222, 420-446; W. A. MEEKS, Moses as God and King, *Religions in Antiquity. Essays in Memory of E. R. Goodenough* (ed. J. Neusner; Leiden 1968) 354-371; R. MARTIN-ACHARD et al., *La figure de Moïse* (Genève 1978); *Moïse l'homme de l'alliance* (Paris etc. 1955); R. MELLINKOFF, *The Horned Moses in Medieval Art and Thought* (Berkeley etc. 1970); J. PRIEST, Testament of Moses, *The Old Testament Pseudepigrapha* 1 (ed. J. H. Charlesworth; London 1983) 919-934; W. H. PROPP, The Skin of Moses' Face - Transfigured or Disfigured?, *CBQ* 49 (1987) 375-386; J. D. PURVIS, Samaritan Traditions on the Death of Mosis, *Studies on the Testament of Moses* (ed. G. W. E. Nickelsburg; Cambridge 1973) 93-117; A. SCHALIT, *Untersuchungen zur Assumptio Mosis* (ALGHJ 17; Leiden 1989); SCHWARZBAUM, *Studies in Jewish and World Folklore* (Berlin 1968) 563 [Index]; SCHWARZBAUM, *Biblical and Extra-Biblical Legends in Islamic Folk-Literature* (Walldorf-Hessen 1982) 228 [Index]; H. SPEYER, *Die biblischen Erzählungen im Qoran* (Gräfenhainchen 1931) 225-363; G. STEMBERGER, 'Der Mann Moses' in Freuds Gesamtwerk, *Kairos* 16 (1974) 161-215; J. D. TABOR, "Returning to the Divinity": Josephus's Portrayal of the Disappearances of Enoch, Elijah, and Moses, *JBL* 108 (1989) 225-238; E. ULLENDORFF, The 'Death of Moses' in the Literature of the Falashas, *BSOAS* 24 (1961) 419-443; M. WADSWORTH, The Death of Moses and the Riddle of the End Time in Pseudo-Philo, *JJS* 28 (1977) 12-19; G. WEIL, *Biblische Legenden der Muselmänner* (Frankfurt a. M. 1845) 186-191; M. O. WISE, *A Critical Study of the Temple Scroll from Qumran Cave 11* (Chicago 1990)

C. HOUTMAN

MOST HIGH → ELYON; HYPSISTOS

MOT מות

I. *māwet/mōt* is the Hebrew word for 'death'. It is also, however, the name of a specific Canaanite deity or →demon, Mot (more precisely Mōtu), known especially from the Ugaritic literature. Attempts to explain his name as connected with Akkadian *mutu*, 'warrior', and not with 'death', are to be discounted. In OT poetry Death is often personified (e.g. Hos 13:14), so that there is frequently the possibility that there may be mythological overtones in texts which could, however, be read in a totally demythologised way. Plausible cases of Hebrew passages referring to Death with mythological overtones may number about a dozen.

II. Although there is plenty of evidence of underworld deities and demons in ancient Mesopotamia, there is only limited evidence of the personification of Death (cf. *CAD* M/II, 317-318). So far as mythologisation of Death is concerned we may note ^{d}*mu-tu*, who appears as a Death deity in a seventh century BCE Assyrian text describing an underworld vision (W. VON SODEN, Unterweltsvision eines Assyrischen Prinzen, *ZA* 43 [1936] 16).

Our main evidence in this matter comes from the Ugaritic mythological texts. Before proceeding to a detailed discussion of these, it may be worth noting that the only other evidence in western sources for this deity or demon, apart from possible occurrence of the divine name Mutu in Emarite and Eblaite personal names (SMITH 1990), is again in a mythical context, i.e. in the account of Phoenician mythology presented in Philo of Byblos, where Μώτ/Μούθ plays a small role. Μούθ was regarded as a son of Kronos and the text states that "the Phoenicians call him Death and Pluto" (apud Eusebius, *Praeparatio Evangelica* 1.10.34). Even without further evidence this would establish Mot as an underworld deity. By contrast, as we shall see, the Ugaritic cultic texts and the Ugaritic onomastica are totally ignorant of Mot and if we were to rely solely on such texts we could hardly discern his existence, let alone his mythological importance.

Mot's absence from the Ugaritic cult and personal names suggests that he was not a deity worshipped like others in the pantheon. In fact there are a few personal names containing the element *mt*, but this is probably the noun *mt* meaning 'man, warrior'. Mot is absent from the local 'pantheon' and offering lists. Although we cannot completely rule out the possibility that he is represented by some surrogate also connected with death and the underworld, it seems much more likely that Mot was not regarded as a deity to be worshipped like others. Some take the view that Mot is in Ugaritic simply the personification of death. He is more than that, as his role in the mythology shows, but he is not a deity in the full sense.

In Ugaritic mythology Mot is one of the main enemies of →Baal (alongside →Yam, the sea-god, who, unlike Mot, *was* the object of cultic veneration to some extent). He overcomes Baal and the latter has to descend into Mot's underworld domain. Baal is reported dead (*KTU* 1.5 v-vi), but the goddess →Anat hunts for him and attacks Mot (*KTU* 1.6 ii), who is vanquished. Baal revives and the two protagonists fight (*KTU* 1.6 vi:16-35). Eventually Mot is forced to concede, at least temporarily. The details are, of course, far from certain.

Mot is the enemy of Baal in so far as he is the representative of all that is contrary to Baal's nature. Baal represents principally the life-giving fertility associated with essential autumnal rainfall. Mot represents the death-dealing sterility associated, at least in part, with the summer heat and drought. This may be the specific significance of one of his titles, *ṣḥr mt*, perhaps 'heat of Mot' (*KTU* 1.6 v:4, though the reading is extremely uncertain). The same theme is reflected in the repeated circumstance that the →sun-goddess, Shapshu burns very hotly as a result of Mot's ascendancy (*KTU* 1.6 ii:24, e.g.).

Mot is called 'the beloved of El, the Warrior' (*ydd il: ǵzr:* e.g., *KTU* 1.4 vii:46-47), a slightly odd title given his negative role. It may be a conventional euphemism. He is also called *bn ilm* (see, e.g. *KTU* 1.6 ii:13; vi:24), literally 'son of El' or 'son of the god(s)'. This title is taken by some (e.g. GIBSON 1979) to mean nothing more than 'divine', but Mot's sonship of →El is quite explicit in *KTU* 1.6 vi:26-27, where the sun-goddess, Shapshu, in speaking to Mot, refers to 'the →bull El, your father' (*ṯr il abk*). It may be noted, however, that King Keret too is called 'son of El' (*KTU* 1.16 i:10, etc.) and the title need not imply real sonship on the mythic level. As for Mot's other notional family relationships, we may note the appearance of his brothers and other kin in *KTU* 1.5 i:22-25, while in *KTU* 1.6 vi Baal tricks him into eating his own brothers.

The main characteristic of Mot is that he is a voracious consumer of gods and men. He has an enormous mouth and an appetite to match. His gullet and appetite are frequently mentioned. At one point he defends himself against Anat thus: "My appetite lacked humans, my appetite lacked the multitudes of the earth" (*KTU* 1.6 ii:17-19). *KTU* 1.5 ii:2-4 pictures his mouth: "A lip to the earth, a lip to the heavens, ...a tongue to the stars! Baal must enter his stomach, Go down into his mouth." It is dangerous to get too near to him, "lest he make you like a lamb in his mouth, and like a kid you be crushed in the crushing of his jaws" (*KTU* 1.4 viii:17-20).

In this voraciousness Mot is closely associated with the underworld. Mot dwells in the underworld, which is an unpleasant (muddy) place of decay and destruction. This is most explicit in *KTU* 1.4 viii, in which Baal despatches messengers to Mot in his subterranean realm, a city which is reached through an entrance at the base of the mountains and of which Mot is king (see *KTU* 1.6 vi:27-29). Descent into the gullet of Mot is the equivalent of descent into the underworld.

Scholars are, however, uncertain about whether Mot should be seen in a specifically agricultural role. This may be implied by his opposition to Baal and his association with the destruction of life, but it is is not certain whether it is specifically implied in an important text which has often formed the basis for this kind of agricultural understanding of Mot. The text in question is *KTU* 1.6 ii:30-35 (cf. also v 11-16), in which Anat is described as attacking Mot: "She seized divine Mot, With a sword she split him, With a sieve she winnowed him, With fire she burned him, With mill-stones she ground him, In the field she scattered him."

That agricultural imagery is prominent here is clear enough and even the burning *might* have agricultural significance (see HEALEY 1984). However, it is very difficult to see how we can conclude that Mot is treated as grain in the sense of being the representative of the positive product of agriculture. He is not. Rather the imagery is based on the *destructive* treatment of grain: like the grain in at least some of the images employed, he is destroyed, scattered in the fields. Indeed the text goes on to say that his limbs are eaten by the birds (35-37). There are similar cases from the Hebrew Bible in which destruction is expressed in such terms. Apart from the commonplace threshing-chaff imagery, we should note the treatment of the Golden →Calf in Exod 32:20, where the same sequence of actions appears. It too is ground up like corn and consumed (by the Israelites). The meaning is simply destructive (see WATSON 1972). For the destructive scattering of limbs to the birds, we may compare 1 Sam 17:44 and the treatment of Apophis in Egyptian myth.

The only way that Mot could be understood as being involved here in some kind of agrarian ritual might be on the assumption of a ritual like that of the first sheaf (cf. Lev 2:14): i.e. the ritual destruction of the first of the crop, perhaps designed to drive the evil from the crop. This would have been part of the annual New Year festival celebrating the renewal of Baal's power.

The role of Mot as a demonic force to be held in check is well illustrated by *KTU* 1.23, which describes among other things the birth of Shaḥar and Shalim. The ritual destruction of Mot in sympathetic magic plays a part in this. Under the double epithet *mt wšr*, perhaps 'Death and Dissolution,' and described as carrying 'the sceptre of bereavement' and 'the sceptre of widowhood', he is pruned like a vine, i.e. attacked, in an apotropaic ritual to protect the deities who are to be born. According to J. C. DE MOOR (*The Seasonal Pattern in the Ugaritic Myth of Baʿlu* [AOAT 16; Kevelaer/Neukirchen-Vluyn 1971] 213, n. 10) Mot is attacked here and in *KTU* 1.6 ii as an act of destruction of the ugly and evil god. Mot's sceptre appears also in *KTU* 1.6 vi:29 and although there is no certain iconographic representation of Mot, such suggestions as have been made involve images of a god or demon carrying a sceptre or sceptres (see POPE 1961, TSUMURA 1974).

Mot is not a deity in the normal sense. He is never the object of worship and he has no role in Ugaritic personal name formation. He does not appear in the otherwise more or less complete 'pantheon' list of local gods. He is, rather, to be regarded as a demonic figure, wholly evil and without redeeming features. In at least one Ugaritic text, ritual *KTU* 1.127:29 (a liver omen text), Mot appears to be a simple demon of the kind that can attack the people of a city. This is probably also the implication of the ritual text *KTU* 1.119:26-36. It would be meaningless to ask Mot for help or blessing and to name a child after Mot might be regarded as witchcraft. He is, therefore, not a part of the Ugaritic pantheon, despite his role in myth.

We may note in this connection the attempts by several scholars to identify Mot with another deity within the Ugaritic pantheon. This is tempting in the absence of Mot from offering texts and from the 'pantheon' lists. In the grain context, one candidate has been Dagan (→Dagon). Others include Yam (also an enemy of Baal) and →Resheph (in his clearer role of underworld deity). There is little plausibility in and no clear evidence for these suggestions.

Returning to the overall theme of the Baal versus Mot conflict, it is clear that Mot is in the ascendant when Baal appears to be dead and *vice versa*. This alone is sufficient to make us conclude that Mot's role is somehow connected with the agricultural cycle. Several authors have noted, however, that the mythological texts suggest a seven-year cycle, not an annual cycle. Despite this, there can be little doubt that the Mot (and Yam) texts played a role in an annual renewal of Baal's authority in the cult. Ultimately, although he is strong (both in his fight with Baal: "Mot was strong, Baal was strong" [*KTU* 1.6 vi:17] and as the demonic menace to men in *KTU* 1.119:26-36), Mot cannot win his battle with Baal, since the latter must be renewed every year.

The general absence of any Death-deity in Mesopotamian mythology is remarkable and SMITH (1990) has tentatively suggested that the Mesopotamian theme of the hero who descends to the underworld, is sought and lamented by a spouse and returns to the earth, has been replaced in West Semitic tradition by a conflict between the hero-figure and personified death. The new form of the narrative may have been formed on the pattern of the Baal-Yam conflict.

III. It is not always possible to be certain that there is a mythological element in OT passages in which Mot or simply 'death' plays a part. Personification is easier to detect, but it need not always imply a prior demythologisation (as is clear from the personification of death in the European cultural tradition, which is no more than a figure of poetry).

Death appears, for example, in a personified guise in Hos 13:14: "Shall I ransom them (Ephraim) from the power of →Sheol? Shall I redeem them from Death? Death, where are your plagues? Sheol, where is your destruction?" Here the personification is very clear, but there is no need to assume a mythological overtone or to rule it out. TROMP (1969) regards Death/Sheol as a person, plague(s) and destruction (*dbr/qṭb*) as his servants. In the following verse the scourge of the east wind is threatened and SMITH (1990) would associate this with Mot.

In other texts there is mention of specific characteristics of Death which have some sort of parallel in the picture of Mot painted by the Ugaritic texts. Thus in Hab 2:5 the insatiability of personified Death is mentioned ("whose greed is as wide as Sheol, and like Death he is never satisfied") and this may echo the background cultural tradition of Mot, but the comparison is with the insatiability of the arrogant man and does not directly touch on matters religious. The same idea, though applied to a personified Sheol, is found in Isa 5:14 ("Therefore Sheol has enlarged its appetite, and opened its mouth beyond measure": and cf. Prov 1:12; 27:20; 30:15-16; Ps 141:7). It is difficult to be sure whether these texts reflect awareness of the Baal-Mot conflict, since the voracity of Death may well have been an idea which existed independently of the myth.

In Job 18:13-14 the personification is taken a step further in that Death's firstborn son, disease, is mentioned, but there is no evidence of Ugaritic Mot having offspring. Isa 25:8 on the other hand has →Yahweh swallowing up Death and this indicates more clearly a parallel with Canaanite mythology: normally it was Mot who did the swallowing, but in this case Yahweh makes nonsense of the law of Canaanite myth by himself swallowing the swallower. This seems to imply awareness of the Canaanite Mot. There may be a similar play on tradition in Hos 13:1, perhaps to be translated "he incurred guilt with regard to Baal and died (i.e. came under Mot)."

Similar cases of implicit treatment of Death/Mot as a deity who is a theoretical rival to Yahweh are found in the texts which speak of the Israelites making a 'covenant with Death/Sheol' (Isa 28:15.18). Here we go beyond mere personification to the point of regarding Mot as a 'divine' being, but as in the case of Mot's firstborn we are dealing with an aspect of the deity (covenant-making) which is not known in the Ugaritic sources. It could be that the application of the covenant to Mot is secondary, an invention of the originator of the Hebrew text.

Another case in which there is a close parallel with the Ugaritic texts is Ps 49:15, which says of the over-confident: "Like sheep they are appointed for Sheol; Death shall be their shepherd; straight to the grave they descend." Here we have Death leading people into Sheol and this reflects the way the Ugaritic texts convey the idea that it is necessary to beware of Mot, since he can entrap the innocent and is specifically mentioned as consuming sheep (*KTU* 1.4 viii: 17-20). He is not, however, a shepherd in Ugaritic.

In Cant 8:6 the strength of Mot is proverbial and compared with the power of love: *ʿazzâ kammāwet ʾahăbâ.* Mot's strength may be seen also in his fight with Baal: "Mot was strong, Baal was strong" (*mt ʿz bʿl ʿz*: *KTU* 1.6 vi:17). However, CASSUTO (1962) misinterpreted a phrase in a Ugaritic letter, *KTU* 2.10:11-13, as providing a parallel with Cant 8:6. Mot is there described as strong (*ʿz*) and may be personified, but there is no reference to love, since *yd ilm* is a disease (see PARDEE 1987).

In many cases it is far from clear whether the Canaanite Mot is being alluded to in biblical passages (Pss 18:5-6; 33:19; 68:21; 116:3; 118:18; Prov 13:14; 16:14).

A much-vaunted, but doubtful case of an echo of Canaanite myth appearing in the Hebrew Bible is found in Jer 9:20, which alludes to Death entering by means of windows. CASSUTO (1962), MULDER (1965) and others have made comparison with the Ugaritic episode of Baal's reluctance to have windows incorporated into his palace because of fear of attack (*KTU* 1.4:vi-vii). It has been noted, however, that the attack on Baal was to come from Yam (*KTU* 1.4:vi 12), not Mot (SMITH 1987). The window-attack theme may be of interest in terms of Hebrew-Ugaritic parallels, but it has no direct bearing on Mot. In Jer 9:20 Death is an attacking demon, as in *KTU* 1.127:29 (and implicitly in ritual text *KTU* 1.119:26-36). PAUL (1968) makes a comparison with the Mesopotamian *lamaštu* demon.

COOPER (1981) notes extensively other possible biblical appearances of Mot. Some rely on conjectural emendation of texts. Thus in Hab 3:13 ALBRIGHT read *mwt* for MT *mbyt* (after LXX θάνατον) a reading which gives the meaning "You struck the head of wicked Mot." This, if correct, would give very explicit evidence of a battle-like conflict between Yahweh and Mot. The emendation has not been accepted by all scholars. In Hab 1:12 TROMP (1969) emended *lʾ nmwt* to *lʾn mwt*, supposedly "the Victor over Death". Note also Ps 55:16, emended by some to give "Let Death come upon them." A text which is usually emended, Ps 48:15, can in fact be read as referring to Yahweh's leading his people 'against Mot'. In fact this phrase, *ʿal-mūt*, is usually corrected to *ʿōlāmôt* and often read as the title of Ps 49. All four of these 'Yahweh versus Mot' passages are, therefore, problematic.

Finally mention must be made of the possible appearance of the divine name Mot in the much-discussed Hebrew word *ṣlmwt* (e.g. Isa 9:1), as argued by TROMP (1969), among others. This is not the place for a detailed discussion of this word. Suffice it to note that the *-mwt* element *may* originally have been the word 'death' and perhaps even the name of the deity. In this context *māwet/môt* might have indicated the grammatical superlative ('shadow of death, extreme darkness'), inviting contrast with the use of *ʾēl/ʾĕlôhîm* in superlative expressions (WINTON THOMAS 1962). Note also *šdm(w)t* in e.g. Isa 16:8, in this context (LEHMANN 1953).

There are a few Hebrew personal names (e.g. *ʾḥymwt* ['Death is my brother'?]: 1 Chron 6:10; *ʿzmwt* ['Death is strong'?] 2 Sam 23:31, etc.) and geographical names (*ḥṣrmwt*: Gen 10:26) which *might* contain the name Mot and suggest some continued interest in the Canaanite deity, but all are very uncertain (→Thanatos).

IV. *Bibliography*

W. F. ALBRIGHT, The Psalm of Habakkuk, *Studies in Old Testament Prophecy* (ed. H. H. Rowley; Edinburgh 1950) 1-18; H. W. ATTRIDGE & R. A. ODEN, *Philo of Byblos: The Phoenician History* (Washington 1981); U. CASSUTO, Baal and Mot in the Ugaritic Texts, *IEJ* 12 (1962) 77-86; A. COOPER, Divine Names and Epithets in the Ugaritic Texts, *RSP III* 392-400 [& lit]; M. DIETRICH & O. LORETZ, *mt* "Môt, Tod" und *mt* "Krieger, Held" im Ugaritischen, *UF* 22 (1990) 57-65; J. C. L. GIBSON, The Last Enemy, *Scottish Journal of Theology* 32 (1979) 151-169; J. F. HEALEY, Burning the Corn: New Light on the Killing of Mōtu, *Or* 53 (1984) 245-254; M. R. LEHMANN, A New Interpretation of the Term שדמות, *VT* 3 (1953) 361-371; T. J. LEWIS, Mot, *ABD* 4, 922-924; M. J. MULDER, *Kanaänitische Goden in het Oude Testament* (The Hague 1965) 65-70; D. PARDEE, As Strong as Death, *Love and Death in the Ancient Near East* (eds. J. H. Marks & R. M. Good; Guilford, CT 1987) 65-69; S. M. PAUL, Cuneiform Light on Jer 9, 20, *Bib* 49 (1968) 373-376; M. H. POPE, Mot, *WbMyth* I/1, 300-302; M. S. SMITH, Death in Jeremiah, ix, 20, *UF* 19 (1987) 289-293; SMITH, *The Early History of God* (San Francisco 1990) 53, 72-73; N. J. TROMP, *Primitive Conceptions of Death and the Nether World in the Old Testament* (Rome 1969); D. TSUMURA, A Ugaritic God, *Mt-w-šr*, and His Two Weapons (UT 52:8-11), *UF* 6 (1974) 407-413; P. L. WATSON, The Death of 'Death' in the Ugaritic Texts, *JAOS* 92 (1972) 60-64; D. WINTON THOMAS, *Ṣalmāwet* in the Old Testament, *JSS* 7 (1962) 191-200.

J. F. HEALEY

MOTHER אם

I. The mother-goddess is the most common and pluriform deity of the religions of the ancient Near East. Because the Canaanite →Asherah, worshipped also as the →Queen of Heaven, is not unknown to OT tradition, scholars have found references to her mythical role and imagery, particularly in the person of →Eve, the mother of all the living (Gen 3:20). Many scholars suppose that the title *ʾēm kol ḥay* originally referred either to Mother Earth (see also Sir 40:1) or the primeval mother-goddess (VRIEZEN 1937:192-193; WESTERMANN 1974:365; KAPELRUD 1977:795).

II. The Sumerian mother-goddess is simply called **ama/amma,** 'Mother'. She has no specific name, but her many titles and epithets like Ningal, Ninma, Nintu 'the lady who gave birth', Ninḫursag 'mistress of the mountains' etc., testify to an immense spread and variety of her cults. In Akkadian context the mother-goddess is pre-eminently known by the name and title Bēlit-ilī ('Mistress of the gods', in Atra-Ḫasis also called Mami, Mama, Nintu). Also other goddesses as Gula, →Ishtar, Nikkal are called *ummu*, 'mother', and assume aspects of the mother-goddess (*AkkGE* 21-23). As such they receive for instance the title *ummu šiknāt napišti*, 'mother of the living creatures'. In Egypt besides a number of primeval mothers (Nut, Mut etc.), particularly →Hathor—in her bovine form representing the Cow of Heaven—is the outstanding *magna mater* and *mšt nṯrw*, 'creatress of the gods' before she merged with →Isis, *mwt nṯr*, 'the mother of god' (= →Horus; ASSMANN 1982:267-268). Also outside the Mesopotamian sphere Semitic **'immu/ 'ummu* is attested from ancient times as the name and title of numerous mother-goddesses. In the context of Ugaritic myth *um* refers to the divine mother (*KTU* 1.6 vi:11, 15), presumably Asherah because the texts call the gods exclusively "the (seventy) sons of Asherah/Qudshu" (*KTU* 1.4 vi:46), whereas she receives frequently the epithet *qnyt ilm*, 'creatress of the gods' (e.g. *KTU* 1.4 i:23). Less clear is *um ilm**, 'divine mother', in the broken context of *KTU* 2.31:45, though it is usually taken as a reference to Asherah (GESE, *RAAM*, 149; *UT* § 19.225). There exist many Assyrian, Canaanite and South Semitic names of the type of DN-*ummi/um/'m* and *ummi/um/'m*-DN, e.g. in Mari: *Ummi-Ḫanat, Ummi-*^{d}*Išḫara; Ummi-*^{d}UD-*ši; Ummi-ili* etc. (ARM 16/1, 208-209); in Ugarit: *[f]Um-mi-a-da-te* (*PRU* VI, 107:7); *'ttrum* (*KTU* 4.410:31; 4.426:1; 4.504:2); *f*AMA-*Na-na* (*PRU* III, 168:1); *fAnati-ummi* (RS 14.16:7) etc.; Phoen *'m'štrt* (I/Umm-Astarte *KAI* 14:14; 89:2 passim) and *'m(')šmn* (I/Umm-Eshmun). The latter is comparable with *'ttrum* and Neo-Punic *b'l'my* (*KAI* 155) and South Semitic *'m'trsm* (Umm-Atarsam). In Sabaean and Thamudic a goddess *'mm'ṯt(r)* ('Ummi'aṯtar), 'mother of Astar' is known. It is here perhaps an epithet of the →Sun-goddess.

III. An interesting feature of some of the afore-mentioned names is that male gods receive the epithet 'mother'. In these names it is used as a metaphor, sometimes also attested in biblical context for man and →Yahweh (Num 11:12; Isa 49:14; 66:13). Another question is whether, apart from the mother metaphor for the divine, the word *'ēm*, 'mother' in biblical tradition may refer to a female deity or ideas derived from female mythic imagery. There is no example in which *'ēm* refers to a female deity. The only text which could be taken in consideration is Hos 4:5: *wĕdāmîtî 'immekā*, "So I will destroy your mother". One could here think either of the 'mother of Israel' meaning the capital Samaria (cf. also this form of speech in 2 Sam 20:19, Jerusalem Isa 50:1, Babel Jer 50:12) or the priest (cf. Jer 22:26). In the first case, an echo of mythical imagery in the personification of the (genius of the) city may have been preserved.

The idea of a mother-goddess as primeval creatress does not seem to be completely absent in OT tradition. Ezek 8:3-5 may contain a distorted reference to the cult-place and statue of Asherah, called *haqqin'â hammaqneh*, "who creates the livestock", recalling Ugaritic *qnyt ilm*. In Gen 3:20, 4:1 we may find a faint echo of a theogonic, genealogical myth describing the marriage of the →Earth (*'ădām*) and the Netherworld as source of life (*Ḥawwâ*) bringing forth a 'creature' (*qayin*, WESTERMANN 1974:394; →Cain) called man. Particularly, because in Eve's words: *qānîtî 'îš 'et YHWH*, "I created (a) man with the help of Yahweh"—an utterance which originally intended to express more than the birth of a male child—a mythical concept is implied. The connection between *Ḥawwâ* = *'ēm kol ḥay* and the mother-goddess giving birth to mankind has often been made. Such a mythical concept underlying the present narrative is not improbable, even if in the biblical tradition Yahweh acts as an associate in this act of creation of man (WESTERMANN 1974: 396-397; VAN WOLDE 1991:26-27).

IV. *Bibliography:*

J. ASSMANN, Muttergottheit, *LdÄ* 4 (1982) 266-271; A. S. KAPELRUD, *ḥawwâ*, *TWAT* 2, 794-798; W. VON SODEN, Muttergottheiten, *RGG* IV, 1228-1229; T. C. VRIEZEN, *Onderzoek naar de Paradijsvoorstelling bij de Oude Semitische Volken* (Wageningen 1937); C. WESTERMANN, *Genesis 1-11* (BKAT 1/1; Neukirchen-Vluyn 1974); E. VAN WOLDE, The Story of Cain and Abel: A Narrative Study, *JSOT* 52 (1991) 25-41.

M. DIJKSTRA

MOUNTAINS-AND-VALLEYS ההרים והעמקים

I. Broken up, the word pair 'mountains and valleys' occurs in Mic 1:4 in the context of a theophany: "and the mountains will melt under him, and the valleys will be cleft". Until recently, the pair was thought to reflect the Ugaritic binominal deity *Mountains-and-Valleys (**ǵrm wʿmqt*, *[d]ḪUR.SAG.-MEŠ *u a-mu-tu*[*m*]).

II. The alleged Ugaritic divine pair *Mountains-and-Valleys, frequently compared with a similar pair →Heaven-and-Earth (*arṣ wšmm*, [d]IDIM *ù* IDIM, *šamû-erṣetum*; see R. BORGER, *RA* 63 [1969] 171), is based on a misreading of the texts. The pantheon list *Ug*. 5 no. 18:18, read as [d]ḪUR.SAG.MEŠ *ù a-mu-tu*[*m*] by J. Nougayrol, should in fact be read as [d]ḪUR.SAG.MEŠ *ù* A-*mu-ú*, the last word meaning 'waters' and not 'valleys'. A duplicate text found in 1992 has [d]ḪUR.SAG.MEŠ *ù* [d]A.MEŠ (RS 1992.2004:29, courtesy D. Arnaud), which confirms that the corrected reading of *Ug*. 5 no. 18:18. RS 1992.2004 is a deity list corresponding to RS 26.142 (= *Ug*. 5 no. 170), which, as is now clear, corresponds to RS 24.643 Rev. (= C. VIROLLEAUD, Les nouveaux textes mythologiques et liturgiques de Ras Shamra, *Ug*. 5 [1969] no. 9). The entry there corresponding to RS 1992.2004:29 is [*ǵr*]*m wthmt*, 'mountains and deep waters' (no. 9:41). This means that the entry *ǵrm w*[----] in the first part of RS 24.643 is to be read *ǵrm w*[*thmt*] (line 6). These data mean that there is no divine pair Mountains-and-Valleys in the Ugaritic pantheon texts, nor in the corresponding rituals. What we do find, however, is another divine pair: Mountains-and-Deep-Waters.

III. In the Hebrew Bible, both mountains and the subterranean waters are often connected to specific theological concepts, in the background of which the divine status of these elements (known from various traditions in the ancient Near East, particularly Anatolia and Syria) is still visible. Mountains (*hārîm*) have a quite positive value in the biblical tradition (see e.g. 1 Kgs 20:28: Yahweh is god of the mountains; cf. Gen 31:54; Hab 3:10), in contrast to the valleys, which are cradles of urban and agricultural civilizations that are denigrated by several biblical writers. The valleys are related to →Sheol and the →Rephaim (Job 11:8; 12: 22; Prov 9:18; Josh 15:8; 18:6; 2 Sam 5:18.22//1 Chr 14:9-13; 2 Sam 23:13//1 Chr 11:15; Isa 17:5) and the Last Judgement (Joel 4:2.12). The Bible contains a tradition of the Mountain as a holy place (see the terminology of the Holy Mountain for Jerusalem and Mt Zion) and the seat of hierophanies. Mountains are often considered more ancient than creation itself (Job 15:7; Prov. 8:25); they will exist forever (Gen 49:26; Hab 3:6). Their sacrality and holiness can be explained on the basis of a widespread symbolism, also known outside the borders of the ancient Near Eastern religious traditions.

In addition to the fact that Tehom (cf. Akk →Tiamat) has retained traces of a deity at some places in the Hebrew Bible (→Tehom), it is connected with 'mountains' as a divine pair at Hab 3:10. In response to the cosmic upheaval brought about by God's epiphany, "the Mountains (*hārîm*) saw you and agonized ... and the Deep (*tĕhôm*) started to scream". Since the Psalm of Habakkuk features several pairs of Canaanite deities, such as Pestilence (→Deber) and Plague (→Resheph; Hab 3:5), →River and →Sea (Hab 3:8), and →Sun and →Moon (Hab 3:11), it is conceivable that 'the Mountains and the Deep' is originally another such pair.

IV. *Bibliography.*

*J. CLIFFORD, *The Cosmic Mountain in Canaan and in the Old Testament* (Cambridge, Mass. 1972); P. S. CRAIGIE, A Note on "Fixed Pairs" in Ugaritic and Early Hebrew Poetry, *JTS* 22 (1971) 140-143; L. KRINETZKI, "Tal" und "Ebene" im Alten Testament, *BZ* N.F. 5 (1961) 204-220; M. METZGER, Himmlische und irdische Wohnstatt Jahwes, *UF* 2 (1970) 139-158; *A. SCHWARZENBACH, *Die geographische Terminologie im Hebräischen des Alten Testamentes* (Leiden 1954).

D. PARDEE & P. XELLA

MOUTH פה

I. The mouth or utterance of a god—the two notions are often expressed with the same word (Sum **ka**, Akk *pû*)—is sometimes made into an independent deity in Mesopotamia. The etymological equivalent in Hebrew (*peh*) does not seem to have enjoyed a comparable divine status.

II. In third millennium texts the Akkadian word *pûm*, 'mouth, word', occurs repeatedly as a theophoric element in personal names; its divinity is marked by the divine determinative (GELB 1992:126-127). First found as a deified entity in Middle Babylonian (Kassite) seal inscriptions, the deity Pû(-u)-lišānu, 'Mouth(-and)-tongue' (^{d}KA-EME, *Tākultu* no. 181) is mentioned in a limited number of Assyrian texts of the first millennium BCE. The expression refers to both a physical object of worship to which prayers were addressed, and to a supernatural phenomenon acting as an intercessor with various gods on behalf of private supplicants (OPPENHEIM 1965:261). The object presumably had the form of a speaking mouth and served as a kind of 'communication device' (OPPENHEIM 1965:263). The possibility of a Hurrian background to this instrument has not been substantiated (cf. B. MENZEL, *Assyrische Tempel, II* [StP s.m. 10/II; Rome 1981] 108* n. 1489).

III. According to the anthropomorphic vision of divinity found in the Hebrew Bible, →Yahweh also possesses a mouth (GARCÍA LÓPEZ 1987-89:530-531). Yet even though the 'mouth of Yahweh' (*pî yhwh*) is frequently hypostatized, it is never spoken of as a separate manifestation of the deity. Also in the Qumran texts, where God's mouth is said to be 'glorious' (1QH 6,14) and 'true' (1QH 11,7), a deification of the mouth is not found. It must therefore be concluded that the Mesopotamian deities Pûm and Pû-lišānu have no analogues in the Bible.

IV. *Bibliography*

F. GARCÍA LÓPEZ, פה *pæh*, *TWAT* 6 (1987-89) 522-538; I. J. GELB, Mari and the Kish Civilization, *Mari in Retrospect* (ed. G. D. Young; Winona Lake 1992) 121-202; A. L. OPPENHEIM, Analysis of an Assyrian Ritual (KAR 139), *HR* 5 (1965) 250-265.

K. VAN DER TOORN

MULISSU

I. Assyrian divine name, attested as theophoric element in the name of one of the sons of Sennacherib who murdered him, Arad-Mulissu. Adrammelech (*'adrammelek*) in 2 Kgs 19:37, par. Isa 37:38, is a corrupted form of this Assyrian name. Greek traditions assign him the names Adramelos and Ardumuzan (M. STRECK, VAB VII/1 [1916] CCXXXIX-CCXL; PARPOLA 1980:176 notes 4-5). Parpola demonstrated that these names are corruptions of Arad-Mulissu. This human being Adrammelech = Arad-Mulissu in 2 Kgs 19:37 and Isa 37:38 should not be confused with the deity →Adrammelech, one of the gods worshipped by the Sefarvites who repopulated the Samarian territory conquered by the Assyrians (2 Kgs 17:31).

II. Mulissu is the reconstructed Assyrian name of the spouse of the god →Assur. The Assyrians identified Assur with the Sumerian god Enlil. There is evidence that the name of the spouse of Enlil, written ^{d}NIN.LIL$_{2}$, was pronounced as Mulliltum, in view of the the occurrence of a name Mulliltum in an Old Babylonian list of gods, and of optional writings ^{d}nin.lil$_{2}$-*tum/-tim* in earlier periods (PARPOLA 1980:177, a-c; D. R. FRAYNE, *BiOr* 48 [1991] 406; ARCHI & POMPONIO 1990). Only in recent years could it be decisively demonstrated that Babylonian *Mulissu* or *Mullissu* is the reading of the Sumerogram ^{d}NIN.LIL$_{2}$, only seemingly 'Ninlil'. The reconstructed form Mulissu is based on *Mu-li-si,* once written in Assyrian context; in the geographic name KAR-*Mu-li-si.* The Aramaic treaties from Sefire call her *mlš* (*KAI* 222 A 8) and Herodotus records for the Babylonian →'Aphrodite' the name Mylitta (I 131, 199; DALLEY 1979).

Enlil was originally the main god of the Sumerian pantheon; he and his spouse Ninlil resided in Nippur. In the second millennium, the Assyrians identified Enlil with Assur (R. BORGER, *Einleitung in die assyrischen*

Königsinschriften I [Leiden 1964] 66 [& lit]). Later, Mulissu (always written 'Ninlil') replaced Sheru'a as Assur's spouse and Sennacherib stated that Sheru'a was his 'sister' (MENZEL 1981, with II 63* n 782).

III. *Bibliography*

A. ARCHI & F. POMPONIO, *Testi cuneiformi neo-sumerici da Drehem N. 0001-0412* (Milan 1990) 51, on no. 35; *S. DALLEY, dNIN.LÍL = *mul(l)is(s)u,* the Treaty of Barga'yah and Herodotus' Mylitta, *RA* 73 (1979) 177-178; B. MENZEL, *Assyrische Tempel* I (StPsm 10; Rome 1981) 63-65; *S. PARPOLA, The Murderer of Sennacherib, *Death in Mesopotamia* (ed. B. Alster; CRRA 26; Mesopotamia 8; Copenhagen 1980) 171-182.

M. STOL

N

NABÛ נבו

I. Nabû is the Babylonian god of writing, occurring in Isa 46:1 with his father →Marduk, and as a theophoric element in Babylonian personal names rendered into biblical Hebrew such as Nebuchadrezzar and Nebuzaradan.

II. Nabû appears in Akk sources from early in the second millennium BCE as *Na-bi-um*, a form which suggests his name comes from the base NB', 'to call', and may mean 'herald' (see *AHW* 697-698). There is no trace of Nabû in the texts from Ebla, or in Old Akkadian. In the latter part of the Old Babylonian period, Nabû's name becomes a regular component in the human onomasticon, although the terminology of the names reveals no special attributes for him, most of the forms occurring with names of other deities also. Occurrence of Nabium-šar-ilī, 'Nabû is king of the gods' in one text (YOS 13 [1972] no. 304.14) simply reveals a parent's devotion. Letter-writers of the period occasionally invoked the blessing of Nabû, coupled with Marduk or →Amurru. Old Babylonian cylinder seals add information: some proclaim their owners 'servant of Nabû', although far more acknowledge Adad (→Hadad), →Sîn and Shamash (→Sun), but a few reveal Nabû's status as 'scribe of Esagila', that is, Marduk's temple in Babylon, as 'chief priest of rites' and as 'lord of wisdom'. Lists of gods place Nabû with deities of Eridu as son of Marduk, son of Enki (Ea, →Aya) and include him with Nisaba and Haya, goddess and god of writing. Hammurabi named his sixteenth year after the creation of a throne for Nabû (ca. 1776 BCE) and Samsuiluna his seventeenth after the introduction of a statue of Nabû into Esagila (ca. 1732 BCE). Nabû shared a festival with Marduk and also had a shrine at Sippar.

Lack of sources obscures the history of Nabû thereafter until late in the second millennium. The fourteenth to eleventh centuries BCE saw his worship growing. Boundary stones (*kudurru*) from Babylonia hail him as 'scribe of Esagila', one 'who fixes destinies' and associate him especially with Borsippa where, as 'king of Ezida' (the temple), his cult begins to replace Marduk's. The *kudurrus* often depict the symbol of Nabû, usually a stylus or wedge, sometimes a tablet or writing board. His cult spread with cuneiform writing at this time, scribes at Ugarit seeking the favour of Nabû and Nisaba and a Hittite scribe invoking him in Amarna Letter 32.

The rise of the Neo-Assyrian power from ca. 925 BCE carried Nabû worship to its peak. By the seventh century BCE Nabû was the most common divine element in personal names, Marduk and Nabû far outnumber all other deities in epistolary greetings and Nabû stands with →Assur, Sîn, Shamash, Adad and →Ishtar as one of the principal gods of Assyria. Temples dedicated to him stood in the chief cities and at Sargon II's new capital, Dur-Sharruken (now Khorsabad) the main shrine in the citadel was his temple. Best known are the twin temples at Kalakh (modern Nimrud) within a large sacred precinct on the citadel, rebuilt by Adad-nirari III about 800 BCE for Nabû and his wife Tashmetu, then repaired by several of his successors. Devotion to Nabû is seen at its deepest in the words engraved on statues of attendant gods erected there by the local governor, 'Trust in Nabû; do not trust in any other god.' In the seventh century BCE Ashurbanipal claimed to have been trained under Nabû's aegis, expressed in a dialogue, and his skill in reading was undoubtedly part of that education.

The situation in Babylonia mirrored

Assyria's love for the god. His name is next most frequent to Bel-Marduk's in personal names, notably royal names (e.g. Nabunaṣir, Nabonidus) where it is not found in Assyria, with Bel he is common in letter greetings and the two head lists of deities in royal inscriptions. The Ezida at Borsippa was subject to splendid refurbishments by Nebuchadrezzar and was still functioning when Antiochus Soter restored it in the third century BCE (see *ANET* 317).

Hymns to Nabû, prayers and incantations seeking his aid survive from the early first millennium BCE. They use phrases found in poems for other gods, such as 'lover of justice', 'light of the gods', 'the one who formed human and animal features and acted as shepherd', but also display the special attributes of Nabû and often apply to him terms which had primary application to Marduk and Ninurta. These include some of the Fifty Names of Marduk presented in the creation poem *Enuma elish*, in which Nabû has no place, seeming to imply a transfer of Marduk's position to his son (see SEUX 1976:124-128), and the killing of the evil Anzû-bird, an exploit of Ninurta, son of the former chief god Enlil, whom Marduk replaced (LAMBERT 1971:337). However, no myths describing Nabû's activities have come to light, nor does his name replace that of any other god in a copy of any myth. One hymn identifies various minor deities as aspects of his character (SEUX 1976:134-136).

As scribe of the gods, 'holder of the reed stylus,' Nabû reflected the powerful position of human scribes and they viewed him as their patron and protector. Colophons at the end of tablets from Ashurbanipal's library at Nineveh, and on tablets from Assur and Sultantepe, appropriately ask his protection for the texts and his curse on anyone who steals them. At Kalakh and at Nineveh, the temples of Nabû had their own libraries, with very varied contents, some of them recovered through excavation. Ashurbanipal augmented his collection at Nineveh with tablets from Nabû's Ezida temples in other towns of his realm. As scribe, Nabû had access to secrets that others could not read, and so could control religious rites and was regarded as especially wise, although the title 'lord of wisdom' was more usually applied to Ea and Marduk. He wrote down the decisions of the gods and was the one who kept accounts, reckoning credit and debit, titled Nabû 'of accounts' as a manifestation of Marduk. An Assyrian letter of the seventh century BCE prays that Nabû may enter the account of the king and his sons on his 'tablet of life' for all time (*ABL* 545, see *CAD* N/2 [1980] 228a). The turn of the year was the time for inspecting past accounts and planning the next session. While this is not specifically mentioned, it was possibly part of the Babylonian New Year Festival when Nabû left the Ezida in Borsippa, travelled to Babylon partly by boat, then along the street called 'Nabû is the judge of his people' to meet his father Marduk. The gods left Esagila in procession for the House of the New Year's Festival (*bit akiti*) outside the city. Near the end of the celebrations, on the eleventh day of Nisan, Marduk and Nabû settled the fate of the land for the ensuing year, and Nabû inscribed it on his tablet.

Nabû's tablet of destinies has similarities to the book in which →God was believed to record the names of those he favoured, or who pleased him (Exod 32:32-33; Pss 69:28; 139:16). The concept continued in later times, notably in Revelation where there are the 'book of life' (Rev 3:5; 20:12, 15; 21:27), books recording the deeds of mankind (Rev 12, 13) and the sealed book containing the final fate of the world (Rev 5 etc.).

In Assyria Nabû's spouse is Tashmetu, her temple being the twin of Nabû's at Kalakh. A detailed ritual prescribes the celebration of their marriage early in the month of Iyyar. In Babylonia Tashmetum occurs beside Nabû in some texts from early in the second millennium BCE, but Nanaya also appears as his spouse there, according to one poetic composition concerning their union (MATSUSHIMA 1987). A hymn honouring Abi-eshuh of Babylon (ca. 1711-

1684 BCE) relates an amatory dialogue between Nanaya and the god Muati. As he is clearly reckoned to be the same as Nabû in later times, it is possible that he was in Abi-eshuh's reign, making this an early example of Nabû's marital affairs. At present the reason why Nabû's spouse is sometimes Nanaya and sometimes Tashmetu is obscure.

The Assyrian imperial policy of uprooting and replacing rebellious conquered peoples helped some aspects of Assyrian and Babylonian culture to spread, among them the worship of Nabû. The Aramaic treaty texts from Sefire list Nabû (*nb'*) and, probably, Tashmet after Marduk and Sarpanit as divine witnesses (*KAI* 222:8), but until the identity of *Br-g'yh,* the senior party in the treaty, is clear, the home of these deities is uncertain. Nabû's cult is especially well-attested among the Aramaic-speaking communities of north Syria, with Sî' (Sîn) and Nasukh (Nusku). Nabû is frequent in the onomastica, combined with local, Aramaic elements from the seventh century BCE on into Persian times (e.g. Nabû-sagib, Nabû-zabad, see Zadok 1977:par. 111221). Aramaic personal names composed with Nabû are more numerous than those composed with the name of any other pagan divinity in the Aramaic papyri from Elephantine and Hermopolis, and they and another document mention a temple of Nabû (*byt nbw*) which stood at Elephantine (Syene). His name was invoked in greetings and in the sanctions on parties who broke an agreement (see Porten 1968:164-167, 157, 159). In the Parthian era the cult of Nabû continued in northern Mesopotamia as demonstrated by dedications and personal names at Hatra and Assur (see Vattioni 1981 no. 340 and Index of names; Aggoula 1985 nos. 10, 14 and Index of names). At Palmyra Nabû and Nanay were worshipped beside Bel, →Nergal and local gods, the temple of Nabû occupying a prime site near the temple of Bel. A *marzeaḥ*-feast was held there in his name, and many men bore names compounded with it. In other cities, notably Dura-Europos and Edessa, people honoured the god, some writing his name in Greek as Ναβου, others equating him with →Apollo. Still the types of personal name do not hint at the particular role of Nabû. In Babylonia, magic bowls and Mandaean texts of the first millennium CE mark the final stage of the cult, the Mandaeans recalling his role as god of wisdom and writing but decrying him as a false →Messiah.

III. Isa 46:1 depicts Bel and Nabû led in procession, no longer in the splendour of the New Year Festival on chariots or the shoulders of their devotees, but on animals stumbling along the path to captivity, the once revered statues reduced to objects of booty. In the Bible Nabû is of no importance, the powerless representative of "Babylon, fairest of kingdoms ... overthrown by God" (Isa 13:19).

Although a village named Kefar Nabu existed in Syria and Jebel Siman was once known as Jebel Nabu (Porten 1968:167, 172-173), there is no compelling reason, apart from the identical spelling, to associate the places in Judah (Ezra 2;29; Neh 7:34) and Moab (Num 32:3 etc.; Moabite Stone 14, written *nbh*), or the mountain in Moab where Moses died (Num 33:47; Deut 32:49; 34:1), with the Akkadian god (as do BDB and *HALAT*), for Nabû is not known to have had devotees in those regions.

In Babylon, Daniel's companion Azariah was given the name Abed-nego (עבד־נגו, Dan 1:7) when the other three youths received Babylonian names. That name is usually explained as a corruption of Ebed-Nebo, 'servant of Nabû', (BDB; *HALAT*). However, the second element may be better understood as 'the shining one', from the base NGH, found in Aramaic personal names from Assyrian times onwards (Zadok 1977: par. 112111128), referring, perhaps, to Nabû by reference to his planet, Mercury.

IV. *Bibliography*

B. Aggoula, *Inscriptions et graffites araméens d'Assour* (AION Supp. 43; Naples 1985); W. G. Lambert, The Converse Tablet: A Litany with Musical Instructions, *Near Eastern Studies in Honor of William Foxwell Albright* (ed. H. Goedicke; Baltimore 1971) 335-353; E. MATSUSHIMA, Le rituel hiérogamique de Nabû, *Acta Sumerologica* 9 (1987) 131-175; *F. POMPONIO, *Nabû. Il culto e la figura di un dio del Pantheon babilonese ed assiro* (StSem 51; Rome 1978); B. PORTEN, *Archives from Elephantine. The Life of an Ancient Jewish Military Colony* (Berkeley 1968); M.-J. SEUX, *Hymnes et prières aux dieux de Babylonie et d'Assyrie* (LAPO 8; Paris 1976); F. VATTIONI, *Le iscrizioni di Hatra* (AION Supp. 28; Naples 1981); R. ZADOK, *On West Semites in Babylonia during the Chaldean and Achaemenian Periods* (Jerusalem 1977).

A. R. MILLARD

NAHAR → RIVER

NAHASH → SERPENT

NAHHUNTE → LAGAMAR

NAHOR

I. It has been speculated that the city of Nahor (Gen 24:10) was named after a deity Nahor. Nahor the grandfather of →Abraham (Gen 11:22-25; Josh 24:2) and Nahor the brother of Abraham (Gen 11:26-29; 22:20-24; 24:15.24.47; 29:5; 31:53) would have been named after the city of Nahor, and thus, indirectly, after the god of that name (LEWY 1934).

II. There is no extra-biblical evidence whatsoever attesting to the cult of a god Nahor. Lewy's argument is based on circular reasoning. He writes: "In view of the evidence that the cities of Ḫarrān, Naḫur, and Sarūg bear the names of ancient deities ... it is permitted to conclude that the parents of the patriarchs in Western Mesopotamia are, at least in part, ancient West-Semitic deities that have later been invested with a human nature" (LEWY 1934 [tr. KvdT]). The evidence he refers to is non-existent. Also, the theory seems to be indebted more to the once popular view of Genesis as a euhemeristic account of ancient Semitic religion, than to a dispassionate study of the texts.

III. It is possible that the personal name Nahor comes from the cityname Naḫur, known from the Mari archives, and situated in the vicinity of Haran (C. WESTERMANN, *Genesis 1-11* [BKAT I/1; Neukirchen-Vluyn 1974] 748). Other suggestions have also been made, though (HESS 1992). None of the possible explanations of Nahor's name can be used as evidence of a god Nahor.

IV. *Bibliography*

R. S. HESS, Nahor, *ABD* 4 (1992) 996-997; J. LEWY, Les textes paléo-assyriens et l'Ancien Testament, *RHR* 110 (1934) 47-48.

K. VAN DER TOORN

NAME שם

I. Name (Heb *šēm*, representing a common Semitic noun) refers to a designation of a person, an animal, a plant or a thing. It also refers to reputation, progeny (as continuation, remembrance), and posthumous fame. The name of a person or deity is especially closely associated with that person or deity, so that knowledge of the name is connected with access to and influence with—even magical control of—the named. In particular, God's name, which in some traditions is specifically revealed, can become a separate aspect of →God, in such a way as to represent God as a virtual hypostasis. It is not as developed a hypostasis in the OT as is God's word or God's wisdom (→Wisdom) or even God's spirit (RINGGREN 1947), but it is more significant than the role of God's arm (e.g. Isa 51:9).

II. Certain deities in the Ancient Near East are celebrated for the multiplicity of their names or titles, e.g. the 50 names of →Marduk in *Enuma Elish*, the 74 names of →Re in the tomb of Thutmosis III and the 100-142 names of →Osiris in Spell 142 of the Book of the Dead. The deities may also have hidden or secret names, so as to emphasize their otherness and to guard against improper invocation by devotees. (Note the story about how →Isis persuaded Re to divulge his secret name, thereby lending great power to her magic; *ANET* 12-14.) In addition, we frequently find aspects or epithets of particular deities becoming separate divine entities with separate cults, as also happens in the case of deities who become differentiated by reference to different localities or cult centres (e.g. →Baal-zaphon and →Ishtar of Nineveh as independent deities). The separability of aspects is illustrated by the Egyptian hymn to →Amun in which "his ba is in the sky [for illumination], his body is [resting] in the West (underworld), (and) his image is in Hermonthis", serving as the sign of his presence among men (BARUCQ & DAUMAS 1980:224). More pertinently, as one text says of the deceased, "Your ba lives in the sky with Re; your ka has a place in the presence of the gods, your name endures on earth with Geb". Indeed, in the New Kingdom kings could be as portrayed offering their name to a deity (*RÄRG* 503).

III. In Israel, God's name is not secret but public, with specific accounts of the revelation of the name (Exod 3:13-14; 6:2-3). In spite of scholarly uncertainty as to the etymology of God's special name, →Yahweh, to the early Israelites presumably God's name was not obscure in meaning. But even with no secret name to be invoked by the initiate, the name is so closely related to God that misuse of the name is prohibited (Exod 20:7; note Lev 24:10-15). Eventually God's particular name could be uttered only by the priest in the temple (*m. Sot* 7:6, *Sanh* 10:1, *Tam* 3:8), even though it might still be written—often in archaic script in the Qumran texts—and a substitute title, such as *ʾădōnāy*, →'Lord', was otherwise pronounced.

The separation out of God's name as an independent aspect of God occurs in several forms. First, there is the occurrence of phrase- doublets such as "Praise the LORD" (quite common) and "Praise the name of the LORD" (Pss 113:1; 135:1; cf. 148:5, 13; 149:3; Joel 2:26); "Sing praises to the LORD" (Isa 12:5; Pss 9:12; 30:5; 98:5), "Sing praises to His Name" (Pss 68:5; 135:3) and "Sing praises to the glory of His Name" (Ps 66:2); "To give thanks to the LORD" (Ps 92:2; 1 Chr 16:7; 2 Chr 5:13; 7:6), "To give thanks to the name of the LORD" (Ps 122:4; cf. Pss 54:8; 138:2; 140:14; 142:8), "To give thanks to His holy name" (Ps 106:47; 1 Chr 16:35) and "Let them give thanks (to) your great and terrible name, for it is holy" (Ps 99:3); "They will fear the LORD" (2 Kgs 17:28; cf. Ps 33:8) and "(They) will fear the name of the LORD" (Isa 59:19; Ps 102:16); "Trust in the LORD" (Isa 26:4; Pss 4:6; 115:11), "Let him trust in the name of the LORD" (Isa 50:10; cf. Zeph 3:12) and "We trust in His holy name" (Ps 33:21); "To love the LORD your God" (Deut 11:13, 22; 19:9; 30:6, 16, 20; Josh 22:5; 23:11) and "To love the name of the LORD" (Isa 56:6).

Secondly, there are references such as "You (O LORD) are great, and your name is great in might" (Jer 10:6) and "Glorify the LORD ..., (even) the name of the LORD" (Isa 24:15). Prov 18:10 says "the name of the LORD is a strong tower". In the light of these references, we find God's name acquires mobility. In Exod 23:21, God advises obedience to the messenger/→angel, "for my name is in him"; Ps 75:2 describes God's name as 'near'; and Isa 30:27, following the traditional text, says "the name of the LORD comes from far off".

The most important separation of God's name occurs in the apparent Deuteronomic innovation that although God cannot, in a seemingly crude, polytheistic fashion, specifically inhabit the tent/temple and certainly cannot be present in the form of a traditional Near Eastern cult statue (wherein, contrary to the biblical polemic, the deity is symbolically and graciously manifest or made concrete), God's name can 'tabernacle' in the temple (VON RAD 1953; a parallel is the Priestly notion that God's *kābôd*, →'glory', can be present in the temple). From another perspective, the presence of God's name, invisible and without props, provided a means to respond to "the plundering and destruction of the Temple" in the early 6th cent. BCE (METTINGER 1982:79). God's presence is disconnected from the physical status of the temple building. In either perspective God's name has become virtually an independent entity, separate from God, i.e. a hypostasis. Yet the name does not become a fully separate entity, as the cult is offered "in the presence of (*lipnê*) the LORD", not "in the presence of the name of the LORD" (VAN DER WOUDE 1979:954). Nevertheless, through the presence of the name as a virtual entity, God is separate from the natural order and "superior to all his creation" (CLEMENTS 1965:95). The Deuteronomic tradition is consistent with this, emphasizing that the temple is built not as God's house, but as a place for God's name (2 Sam 7:13; cf. Isa 18:7), a place where God's name is invoked (Exod 20: 21[24]), as with Shiloh, where God formerly allowed his name to tabernacle (Jer 7:12). The temple is built "to/for the name of the LORD" (e.g. 1 Kgs 3:2; 5:17[3].19[5]; 8:16-20). There in the temple God has placed his name (Deut 12:5, 21; 14:24; 1 Kgs 9:3; 11: 36; 14:21; 2 Kgs 21:4.7); there, using the more distinctive phrase, God's name 'tabernacles' (ŠKN; Deut 12:11; 14:23; 16:2.6.11; 26:2; Jer 7:12; Neh 1:9); it is present, not merely pronounced (cf. VAN DER WOUDE 1979:954-955). Thus God's name takes the role of the cultic symbols such as the ark or a cult statue, having "a constant and *almost* material presence ... at the shrine" (VON RAD 1953:38; italics added). On postbiblical Jewish speculations on the hypostatized name see FOSSUM (1985).

IV. *Bibliography*

A. BARUCQ & F. DAUMAS, *Hymnes et prières de l'Egypte ancienne* (Paris 1980); R. E. CLEMENTS, *God and Temple. The Idea of the Divine Presence in Ancient Israel* (Oxford 1965); J. E. FOSSUM, *The Name of God and the Angel of the Lord* (Tübingen 1985); O. GRETHER, *Name und Wort Gottes im Alten Testament* (BZAW 64; Giessen 1934); T. N. D. METTINGER, *The Dethronement of Sabaoth. Studies in the Shem and Kabod Theologies* (ConB, OTS 18; Lund 1982); G. VON RAD, *Studies in Deuteronomy* (SBT 9; London 1953) 37-44; H. RINGGREN, *Word and Wisdom. Studies in the Hypostatization of Divine Qualities and Functions in the Ancient Near East* (Lund 1947); A. S. VAN DER WOUDE, שׁם šēm Name, *THAT* 2 (1979) 935-963, esp. 953-962.

H. B. HUFFMON

NANEA Ναναία

I. Nanēa is the goddess in whose temple Antiochus IV Epiphanes was killed by the priests according to one tradition about his obscure death, the letter to Aristobulus, 2 Macc 1:13 (the fullest discussion remains M. HOLLEAUX, *REA* 18 (1916) 77-102; cf B. Z. WACHOLDER, *HUCA* 49 [1978] 89-133; criticisms: J. M. GOLDSTEIN, *II Maccabees* [AB 41A; New York 1983] 163). Her name is only mentioned here; her temple had the name Naneion (v 15). This happened in 164 BCE in 'Persis', actually Elymaïs, as is clear from other sources, like 1 Macc 6:1-4. Pretending to perform a sacred marriage (*sunoikein*) with the goddess, Antiochus' real intent was to plunder the treasures, says the text.

II. Nanēa or Nanaea (Nanâ in earlier lit., now often Nanay or Nanaya) enjoyed an increasing popularity in the Near East, starting in Mesopotamia and expanding over the Persian empire (AZARPAY 1976). She was the goddess of erotic love. She was originally (and always remained) a goddess of Uruk, often mentioned together with An (→Anum) and Inanna (→Ishtar), also residing in Uruk. In Sumerian her name is invariably written **dNa-na-a** and this remained the standard writing. Several times we find in Akkadian context—notably of the Old Babylonian period and then particularly in personal names—the form *dNa-na-a-a*, probably to be pronounced as Nanay. This is confirmed by later renderings in other languages, as in Aramaic (*nny* or *nn'*; cf. M. HELTZER, *PEQ* 110 [1978] 8-9 [& lit]) and Greek (*Nanaia, Nanai*).

Ur III texts refer to Nanay of Uruk alone (HEIMPEL 1982); Old Babylonian texts speak of a triad of feminine gods, An-Inanna, Nanay, Kanisurra, attested in Uruk (and temporarily in Kish). The triad survived until the Hellenistic period, as →Ishtar-of-Uruk, Nanay, Uṣur-amassa (according to CHARPIN 1986:411-413). Numerous texts from late first millennium Uruk, especially on prebends, mention her together with other gods (O. SCHROEDER, SPAW 49 [1916] 1184-1186; P.-A. BEAULIEU, *ASJ* 14

[1992] 53-60: she is the twelfth god). Her temple in Uruk was named **É.ḫi.li.an.na** 'House of the Allurement of Heaven' (A. FALKENSTEIN, *Topographie von Uruk* [Leipzig 1941] 41) and she is described in hymns and epithets as a symbol of sexual attraction (Sum. **ḫi.li**, Akkadian *kuzbu*; cf. the epithet **nin ḫi.li** in inscriptions of Kudur-mabuk and Sin-kashid, RIME 4 [1990] 275, 451). She is closely associated with the goddess of love, Ishtar (R. D. BIGGS, TCS 2 [1967] 31, 44). The few Old Babylonian hymns addressed to Nanay include a prayer for a king (W. W. HALLO, *BiOr* 23 [1966] 242-244; K. HECKER, TUAT II/5 [1989] 724-726, 741-743). Hymns of the Assyrian kings Sargon II and Assurbanipal are also known (SAA 3 [1989] nos. 4, 5). The best known hymn to Nanay is self-laudatory and syncretistic (REINER 1974).

During the first millennium BCE Nanay came to be associated with the god of Borsippa, →Nabû (F. POMPONIO, *Nabû* [Rome 1978] 43, 50, 66-67, 102, 239; A. R. GEORGE, *SAAB* 1 [1987] 38). A prelude to this is the sacred marriage between her and the god Muati, later identified with Nabû (Old Babylonian; LAMBERT 1966). In the first millennium Nabû was to take a second place after →Marduk of Babylon; his consort always remained Tashmētu. An inscription of Merodach-Baladan I (1173-1161) already reflects his association with both goddesses in mentioning together "Nabû, Nanay and Tashmētu" in a curse formula (S. PAGE, *Sumer* 23 [1967] 66 III 21; cf. also *Šurpu* II 155-6); this triad occurs in stock phrases in late Sumerian litanies. Elsewhere we find just "Nabû and Nanay" (*RA* 16 [1919] 130 IV 2; POMPONIO, *Nabû*, 67). Other texts call her explicitly "spouse of Nabû" (VAS 1 36 I 5, with *RA* 16 [1919] 141; R. BORGER, *AfO* Beiheft 9 [1956] 77 § 49). The elevated status of Nanay in Borsippa is clear from a late sacred marriage ritual performed in Babylon(!) by Nabû and Nanay in the second month (*SBH* VIII col. II, with E. MATSUSHIMA, *ASJ* 9 [1987] 158-161). It could be that Tashmētu retained her status in Assyria as Nabû's consort, while in Babylonia Nanay assumed this position (thus MATSUSHIMA 1980:143-144). Even in the Aramaic/Demotic Papyrus Amherst 63 we find "Nabû of Borsippa" and "Nanay of the Ajakku (*j'k'*)" together (R. A. BOWMAN, *JNES* 3 [1944] 227).

Nanay became increasingly important in the Persian, Hellenistic, Parthian and Sassanian world. The Persians identified her with Anahita, a cult promoted by Artaxerxes II, according to Berossus (*FGH* 3 C 1 [1958] 680 F 11; S. M. Burstein, *The Babyloniaca of Berossus* [Malibu 1978] 29 [= 171]; cf WIKANDER 1946). The Eastern Iranians identified her with Ārmaiti (AZARPAY 1976). The Arameans adopted her in their pantheons where she survived into the fifth-sixth century CE (CUMONT 1926; Jacob of Sarug in his *Homily on the Fall of the Idols*; see B. VAN DEN HOFF, *OrChr* NS 5 [1915] 247-249; S. LANDESDORFER, MVAÄG 21 [1916] 110-111, 114). Her cult is known in Assur (AGGOULA 1985), Palmyra (Comte DU MESNIL DU BUISSON 1962; HOFTIJZER 1968; M. GAWLIKOWSKI, ANRW II/18.4 [1990] 2645-46), Dura-Europos (CUMONT 1926), Susa (WIKANDER 1946; LE RIDER 1965). To the Greeks, she was →Artemis, and Nabû was →Apollo; Strabo wrote: "Borsippa is the holy city of Artemis and Apollo" (16.1.7). A Greek hymn by Isidorus celebrating Isis informs us "The Syrians call thee →Astarte-Artemis-Nanaya"; another hymn names Isis "the Nania in Susa" (M. TOTTI, *Ausgewählte Texte der Isis- und Serapis-Religion* [Hildesheim/Zürich/New York 1985] 77 no. 21:18; 68 no. 20:105-6). The name Isis can be followed by 'Nanay' (G. RONCHI, *Lexicon Theonymon rerumque sacrarum* IV [Milan 1976] 736). 'Nanaîon', the name of Nanay's temple in "Persis" (= Susa) according to 2 Macc 1:15, is also known from Egyptian papyri where this sanctuary is mentioned as a depository for official documents (RONCHI, *Lexicon Theonymon*, 812-3).

III. Without advocating the historicity of the passage in 2 Macc, we can adduce a few elements suggesting some reality in its setting. Nanay was indeed an important goddess venerated in Susa (LE RIDER 1965). Her sanctuary was the Nanaîon, a name also known from Egypt where Isis was identified with Nanaya. A sacred marriage ritual involving Nanay is known for Babylon but her consort is the god Nabû, not the king, and it is performed in the second month. The pretended sacred marriage by Antiochus IV Epiphanes followed by his death took place in the ninth month, Kislev, according to 2 Macc, and he did indeed die in this month according to the List of Hellenistic Kings (*RLA* VI/1-2 [1980] 99-100, rev. 14). Assurbanipal restored and inaugurated the temple of Nanay in Uruk on the first of the ninth month which could imply a regular festival in Kislev (M. STRECK, VAB VII/2 [1916] 58 Rassam Cyl. VI 107-124).

IV. *Bibliography*

B. AGGOULA, *Inscriptions et graffites araméens d'Assour* (AION Suppl. 43) (Naples 1985) 18-22; *G. AZARPAY, Nanâ, the Sumero-Akkadian goddess of Transoxiana, *JAOS* 96 (1976) 536-542; D. CHARPIN, *Le clergé d'Ur au siècle d'Hammurabi* (Genève/Paris 1986) 254.404.410-413; *F. CUMONT, *Fouilles de Doura-Europos* (1922-1923) (BAH IX; Paris 1926) 195-198; A. DEIMEL, *Pantheon Babylonicum* (Rome 1914) 187-188 no. 2264; *W. HEIMPEL, A Catalog of Near Eastern Venus Deities, *Syro-Mesopotamian Studies* 4/3 (December 1982) 9-22 [= 59-72], esp. 3. Nanay, 15-17 [= 65-67]; J. HOFTIJZER *Religio Aramaica* (Leiden 1968) 45-46; W. G. LAMBERT, Divine Love Lyrics from the Reign of Abieshuḫ, *MIO* 12 (1966) 41-56, esp. 43-45; *Comte DU MESNIL DU BUISSON, *Les tessères et les monnaies de Palmyre* (Paris 1962) 381-385; *E. MATSUSHIMA, Problèmes des déesses Tashmētum et Nanaia, *Orient* (Tokyo 1980) 133-148; *E. REINER, A Sumero-Akkadian Hymn of Nanâ, *JNES* 33 (1974) 221-236; *G. LE RIDER, *Suse sous les Séleucides et les Parthes* (MAI = MDP 38) (1965) 292-296; *K. TALLQVIST, *AGE* 385-386; J. TUBACH, *Im Schatten des Sonnengottes* (Wiesbaden 1986) 277-279. 387; S. WIKANDER, *Feuerpriester in Kleinasien und Iran* (Lund 1946) 70-75.

M. STOL

NARCISSUS Νάρκισσος

I. Narcissus is a Greek hero, whose name is carried once in the Bible by a Roman (Rom 16:11). The etymology of his name is probably pre-Hellenic (CHANTRAINE 1980), as of so many plants.

II. The aetiological myth of Narcissus is only attested in relatively late sources and is hardly older than Hellenistic times. The mythographer Conon (*FGH* 26 F 1.26), who lived under Augustus but had access to many local myths, relates the fate of a handsome youth from Boeotian Thespiae who rejected all male advances, even of Eros himself. When his admirer Ameinias committed suicide in front of his door in order to avenge his unrequited love, Narcissus fell in love with himself when contemplating his own reflection in a spring. In the end he also committed suicide and Thespiae, which had a well-known cult of Eros (SCHACHTER 1981:216-219), decided to pay even more honour to the god Eros. The Thespians thought that the Narcissus flower first grew in that place where Narcissus spilt his own blood. Ovid (*Met.* 3. 339-510) embellished the story with many details, amongst which was Narcissus' encounter with the nymph Echo, which became extremely popular in Late Antiquity; Plotinus even seems to have used the myth as a vehicle for his philosophy (HADOT 1973).

The myth is most likely to be connected with the cult of Eros, who also was the god of homosexual love. The refusal by Narcissus of a lover meant in Greek terms the refusal of the transition to adulthood because a homosexual relationship was an indispensable part of growing up for the upper-class Greek adolescents (BREMMER 1991). The fatal consequence of Narcissus' refusal is the falling in love with himself, that is the refusal of any meaningful relationship.

III. Narcissus does not occur in the Bible but his name occurs as one of the Romans greeted by Paul (Rom 16:11). Among the names carried by Greeks in Rome Narcissus was one of the most popular (SOLIN 1982: 1100-1103) and often given to slaves and freedmen. Paul's acquaintance, then, may also have belonged to one of these categories.

IV. *Bibliography*
J. BREMMER, Greek Pederasty and Modern Homosexuality, *From Sappho to De Sade. Moments in the History of Sexuality* (ed. J. Bremmer; London 1991²) 1-14; P. CHANTRAINE, *Dictionnaire étymologique de la langue grecque* (Paris 1968-80); S. EITREM, Narkissos, PW 16.2 (1935) 1721-1733; P. HADOT, Le mythe de Narcisse et son interprétation par Plotin, *Nouvelle revue de psychoanalyse* 7 (1973) 27-48; H. & R. KAHANE, The Hidden Narcissus in the Byzantine Romance of Belthandros and Chrysantza, *Jahrb. Österr. Byzant.* 33 (1982) 199-219; B. MANUWALD, Narcissus bei Konon und Ovid, *Hermes* 103 (1975) 349-372; E. PELLIZER, Reflections, Echoes and Amorous Reciprocity: On Reading the Narcissus Story, *Interpretations of Greek Mythology* (ed. J. Bremmer; London 1988²) 107-120; B. RAFN, Narkissos, *LIMC* VI.1 (1992) 703-711; A. SCHACHTER, *Cults of Boiotia* I (London 1981); H. SOLIN, *Die griechischen Personennamen in Rom* II (Berlin/New York 1982).

J. N. BREMMER

NARU → RIVER

NECESSITY → ANANKE

NEHUSHTAN נחשתן

I. The word *nĕḥuštān* occurs once in MT, in 2 Kgs 18:4, where it is the name of the bronze (or copper) serpent (*nĕḥaš hannĕḥōšet*) that →Moses had made in the wilderness (as related in Num 21:8-9) and that King Hezekiah destroyed. The word is a compound of **nuḥušt* (Hebrew *nĕḥōšet*), 'bronze, copper', plus the **-ān* affix (preserved as *-ā-* in Hebrew by dissimilation from the *-o-* type vowel in the previous syllable). The word *nĕḥuštān* literally means 'the (specific) thing of bronze/copper' (cf. the similar morphology of *liwyātān*, →Leviathan). Implicit in this name is a verbal play on *nāḥāš*, 'snake', of which *nĕḥuštān* is an image. Nehushtan appears to have been a ritual symbol which effected the cure of venomous snake bites, and which was the object of veneration (the burning of incense) by Israelites in the Jerusalem Temple courtyard.

II. The use of snake images to effect the cure of venomous snake bites is consistent with the ritual symbolism of snakes in the ancient Near East (→Serpent). In Egypt snake amulets could be worn by the living or the dead to ward off venomous snakes. The Uraeus serpent protected gods and kings from danger; and because of his snake-nature the king was immune to snake venom and could cure others. Protective snake figurines are also found in Mesopotamia, including reliefs and amulets of two snakes entwined, a symbol later inherited in Greek culture as the healing symbol of Asclepius. In Canaanite culture snake images also seem to have had some ritual use; numerous examples of bronze snake figurines have been excavated, including Late Bronze Age figurines from Hazor, Gezer, Megiddo, and Shechem. The most remarkable instance is a gold-plated bronze snake found at the Iron I Midianite shrine at Timna (ROTHENBERG 1988). Also of interest are two Phoenician engravings of snakes resting on top of poles (BARNETT 1967; SCHROER 1987): one is a winged Uraeus serpent engraved on a bronze bowl found at the eighth century Assyrian royal palace at Nimrud, and the other is a wingless snake carved on a stone bowl from the fourth or third century. These Phoenician emblems are also likely related to Nehushtan.

III. In the Bible the bronze/copper serpent is evaluated quite differently in its two occurrences in Num 21 and 2 Kgs 18. In the former, the snake image is mandated by →Yahweh as a cure for the venomous bites of the *śārāp* (lit. 'burning') snakes, while in the latter the image is conceived as a non-Yahwistic or idolatrous religious object, which Hezekiah rightly destroys. In the clash between these two texts we find contested claims about the ritual figurine. It is plausible that the cause of this clash was the prophetic critique of ritual symbols, in which a number of traditional Yahwistic concepts and symbols came to be reinterpreted as idolatrous or 'Canaanite', including the 'high places' (*bāmôt*), the 'standing stones' (*maṣṣēbôt*), and the 'sacred posts' (*'ăšērâ, 'ăšērîm*), which are also destroyed by Hezekiah in 2 Kgs 18:4. This reevaluation of traditional symbols, evidenced in the eighth century prophets and in Deuteronomy, may be the motivation for Hezekiah's destruction of Nehushtan. The statement in 2 Kgs 18:4 that the Israelites had burned incense to the statue suggests that the Israelites worshipped it as a god, but the polemical thrust of this remark may be a revisionist gloss on ordinary Yahwistic cultic piety. The bronze snake probably belonged to the traditional repertoire of Yahwistic symbols, this emblem signifying Yahweh's power to heal (so Numbers 21). Its destruction seems to have occurred in the wake of a wide-ranging reconception of religious practice and symbolism.

IV. *Bibliography*

R. D. BARNETT, *Layard's Nimrud Bronzes and their Inscriptions*, (ErIsr 8; 1967) 3* and fig. 2; BARNETT, *Ezekiel and Tyre*, (ErIsr 9; 1969) 8* and pl. 4; H.-J. FABRY, *nĕḥōšet*, *TWAT* 5 (1986) 397-408; B. HALPERN, 'Brisker Pipes than Poetry': The Development of Israelite Monotheism, *Judaic Perspectives on Ancient Israel* (eds. J. Neusner, et al.; Philadelphia 1987) 77-115; K. JAROŠ, *Die Stellung des Elohisten zur kanaanäischen Religion* (OBO 4; Freiburg 1982) 151-165; K. R. JOINES, *Serpent Symbolism in the Old Testament* (Haddonfield 1974) 61-96; B. ROTHENBERG, *The Egyptian Mining Temple at Timna* (London 1988) 66 and pls. 11-12; S. SCHROER, *In Israel Gab Es Bilder: Nachrichten von darstellender Kunst im Alten Testament* (OBO 74; Freiburg 1987) 104-115; L. STÖRK, Schlange, *LdÄ* 5 (1984) 644-652.

R. S. HENDEL

NEITH

I. Neith (*N.t*, *Nj.t*, Gk Νηιθ) occurs as a theophoric element in the name אסנת, Asnath, Gk Ασεννέθ, the daughter of Potiphera, a priest in Heliopolis, and wife of Joseph (Gen 41:45, see EL SAYED 1982 II:400-401 doc. 446). The etymology of the name is not clear, but associations point in two entirely different directions: 1. both the name of the goddess and the name of the crown of Lower Egypt (*N.t*) might go back to a fuller form *Nr.t*, meaning 'the terrible one'. This meaning connects well with the typical attribute of Neith: a shield with two crossed arrows; 2. In its form, *N.t* the name resembles the usual word for 'flood, inundation'. This association corresponds to the central theological aspect of Neith as a goddess of 'watery preexistence'.

II. Neith belongs to the few Egyptian divinities whose attestation goes back to protodynastic times. She plays an important role in archaic documents (EL SAYED 1982 II:docs. 1-117) and must have been the leading goddess of Lower Egypt. Her role is less dominant in the Middle and New Kingdoms—though she continues to rank among the great deities—but becomes prominent again with the rise of the Saite dynasty in the 7th century BCE. The Greeks identified her with →Athena, an interpretation that can be based on several common traits: both goddesses are associated with arms and weapons; both are patronesses of crafts, especially weaving (Neith is the goddess of weaving, Athena invented the loom) and sciences (Neith is associated with magic and medicine); both are chiefs of cities that were (or considered themselves to be) closely related.

In the theology of Neith her bellicose and royal nature as displayed in her iconography plays a comparatively subordinate role (but see EL-SAYED 1982 I:72-76). Much more important is her attribute as a cosmogonic deity. She probably underwent a process of reinterpretation. Originally, Neith must have been the personification of a kind of Lower Egyptian political identity as symbolized by the red crown and the royal title *bjt* 'bee' or 'who belongs to the bee'. She often bears the title "Opener of ways" (EL-SAYED 1982 I:67-69), which shows that she formed a Lower Egyptian counterpart to the Upper Egyptian god Upuaut (Ophois) and acted like him as a leader of the king on his processions and military or hunting campaigns. But already in the Old Kingdom she appears in connection with Sobek (Souchos), the crocodile god of water (*Pyr.* 510; R. EL-SAYED 1982 II:doc. 197), and with *Mḥt-wrt* (Methyer), the cow-shaped goddess of preexistence and cosmogony (*Pyr.* 507-509; EL SAYED 1982 II:doc. 196). Both associations might of course be much earlier than their first attestations in the Pyramid Texts.

In the funerary context, Neith appears as one of the four tutelary goddesses who protect the corpse of →Osiris and the coffin of the dead, her partners being →Isis, Nephthys and Serqet. Neith and Serqet are goddesses of protective magic and medicine. As a goddess of weaving, Neith is also responsible for the mummy wraps and other tissues in the context of mummification (EL SAYED 1982 I:76-80). But there is one important document which shows the funerary role of Neith in a different light: the inscription on the sarcophagus lid of king Merenptah (see J. ASSMANN, *MDAIK* 28 [1972] 47-73, 115-139). In this long text Neith appears as the heavenly cow, mother of →Re and mistress of all the other gods whom she appoints to serve the king in his afterlife. She thus plays the role of an omnipotent and all-encompassing super-goddess.

This role corresponds to her cosmogonic attribute as *Mḥt-wrt*, 'the great swimming (cow)', a deity who like →Atum and →Amun personified both preexistence and creation. Methyer is said to have created the universe by means of her seven *ṯzw*, a word meaning originally 'nod' but also 'spell', 'utterance'. Perhaps already in the Coffin Texts (EL-SAYED 1974), but certainly since the New Kingdom texts this term is understood in its linguistic meaning and thus expresses the concept of 'creation by speech'. The seven cosmogonic utterances of Neith-Methyer acquire a personality of their own, with a hawk's body, a proper name and a function in the protection of the deceased (EL-SAYED 1974). As a personification of preexistence, Neith is described as beyond sexuality or bisexual ("two thirds masculine and one third feminine", see SAUNERON 1962:110, 113(a); S. SAUNERON, Le créateur androgyne, *Mélanges Mariette* [1962] 240-242; *Corpus Hermeticum* I, 9, 20; *Horapollon* §12: *arsenothelys*; see EL-SAYED 1982 II:674 doc. 1115). The hymns in the temple of Esna (first centuries CE, see SAUNERON 1962) praise Neith as creator of the world, who transformed herself into the celestial vault, who gave birth to the sun, who appeared in the shape of the serpent, the symbol of pharaonic rule, order and justice (Ma'at) in front of the sun god, and who extended the universe in the form of water, thus forming the netherworld, the →Nile, the inundation and the vegetation. Her last cosmogonic manifestations concern the pharaonic state: as the mistress of combat who drives away the enemies of Pharaoh and as the lady of the palace who elects and protects the king. Neith appears as universal goddess encompassing both the cosmic and the socio-political spheres. All traditions consent in ascribing to Neith primordial antiquity and universal power.

Plutarch writes that Neith-Athena has been identified by the theologians of Sais with Isis and that her seated statue bore the inscription "I am all that has been and is and will be; and no mortal has ever lifted my mantle" (*De Is.*). Proclus, in his commentary on the *Timaeus*, gives a longer version of this same inscription, adding: "the fruit of my womb is the sun". These quotations might go back to a Greek inscription in the form of the Greek 'aretalogies'. But it is also possible that they translate an Egyptian original which can be reconstructed as follows: *jnk nbt* (or: *qmꜣt*) *ntt jwtt / nn kjj wp-ḥr.j / jnk jht msjt Rʿw.* A correct rendering would be: "I am the mistress (or: the creator) of all that exists and that does not exist; there is no other (god) except myself (the Egyptian idiom can also mean: "there is no other who has opened [= unveiled] my face"); I am the cow that bore Re".

III. The only occurrence of the goddess Neith in the Bible is in the name אסנת, Asenath, Gk Ἀσεννέθ, the daughter of Potiphera, a priest in Heliopolis (On), and wife of Joseph (Gen 41:45). It is a common

Egyptian type of name and means 'She belongs to Neith'. Since Neith is celebrated as the mother of Re, her cultic presence in Heliopolis is not unnatural. The author of Gen 41 merely notes that Joseph came to marry the daughter of an Egyptian priest. Later Jewish tradition, ill at ease with a pagan priest as the father-in-law of the patriarch, came up with various explanations (APTOWITZER 1924). Asenath became the female protagonist of the anomymous Jewish-Greek work *Joseph and Aseneth*, written between the 1st cent. BCE and the 2nd cent. CE. She is presented as a daughter of Pentephres, satrap of Pharaoh, who preferred her idols to her suitors. Having seen Joseph she falls in love; in spite of her beauty, though, Joseph rejects her. Only after she has converted to the God of the Hebrews does the pious patriarch take her as his legal wife.

IV. *Bibliography*

V. APTOWITZER, Asenath, the Wife of Joseph, *HUCA* 1 (1924) 239-306; H. BONNET, Neith, *RÄRG* (Berlin 1952), 512-517; D. MALLET, *Le culte de Neit à Sais* (Paris 1888); S. SAUNERON, *Les fêtes religieuses d'Esna aux derniers siècles du paganisme* (Esna V; Cairo 1962); R. EL-SAYED, *REg* 26 (1974) 73-82; EL-SAYED, *Documents relatifs à Sais et ses divinités* (Cairo 1975); EL-SAYED, *La déesse Neith de Sais*, 2 vols. (Cairo 1982).

J. ASSMANN

NEPHILIM נפילים

I. The bald allusion to the Nephilim (lit. fallen ones) in Gen 6:3 ('The Nephilim were on the earth in those days ... ') fits uneasily into a context that has always presented a challenge to exegetes. Although designated an 'antiquarian gloss' (SKINNER 1910:147) the sentence in which it appears does bind it to the theological scene which depicts a fresh threat to the God-given distinction between divine beings and humans. It raises again the worst fears expressed at the close of Gen 3 ('the man has become like one of us ... and now he might ... eat, and live forever') but in the new shape of gross physical contact between the sons of God and the beautiful daughters of humans. On the face of it, the human race could now be immune from mortality. The Nephilim were the mythical semi-divine beings spawned by these illicit liaisons. WESTERMANN (1974:494-497) indicates in detail that there are insufficient grounds for disturbing the sequence of 6:1-4 as it stands: 6:1-2 describe the upsetting of the boundaries that divide divine beings and humans; 6:3 God's judgement stops short of annihilating the evil-doers (just as it did in the Fall and the First Murder incidents) but curtails the human life-span; 6:4 prodigies were the offspring of divine-human marriages. The resulting prodigies of the action in 4b —'the sons of God went in to the daughters of humans'—are referred to in 4a (the Nephilim) and again much more clearly in 4b (→'heroes of old ... warriors of renown'). Outrageous activity of this kind which resulted in violence and corruption on the earth provoked God's judgement in the form of the Flood. The monstrous Nephilim were swept away by it and humans would not live forever.

II. The Nephilim are found once more in the Hebrew Bible in Num 13:33 when Moses' spies exaggerate the strength of the pre-settlement occupants of Canaan by reporting the sight of the gigantic Nephilim before whom they felt like grasshoppers (cp. the Amorites 'whose height was like the height of cedars' Am 2:9). Allowing for the awe felt by nomads for settled folk and its resultant hyperbole, the postdiluvian designation does refer to an ancient race of great stature but without the mythological overtones of the semi-divine beings or demigods characteristic of the primeval period. The Nephilim have been 'historicised' and transferred to the still distant heroic period of pre-settlement Canaan. However, something of the flavour of the older sense of the term might be preserved in Ezek 32:27 where the warrior nations 'fall' (*npl*) down into →Sheol but are not privileged to lie with the *gibbôrîm nĕpilîm*, 'the fallen warriors', or as KRAELING (1947) and ZIMMERLI (1969) would have it, the Nephilim (*nĕpilîm*) warriors, mythical semi-divine beings in the manner of Babylonian and Greek myths. Certainly *npl* is a keyword in Ezek 32 and exploits the etymological significance of Nephilim.

GUNKEL (1910:58-59) thought that the term Nephilim in Gen 6:4a, obsolete at the time of the writer, was explained and at the same time given a historical dimension in 6:4c: 'these were the heroes ... of remote antiquity'. The Versions emphasise the heroic qualities of the Nephilim, calling them →'giants' (LXX and Vg *gigantes*). The Aram. cognate *npyl'* 'giant' occurs several times in the Dead Sea Scrolls: in the Targum of Job 38:31 it translates the name of the constellation →Orion (Heb *kĕsîl*) which was regarded as early as Homer (Od. 5.121) as the image of a gigantic hunter. Appropriately the Enochic *Book of the Giants* attests the Nephilim several times; once they are called 'the Nephilim of the earth' or the 'earthly Nephilim' (*npyly 'r'*; *4QEnGi^b^* 3:8) possibly drawing attention to the restricted arena of their activities i.e. the earth, despite their heavenly origin. *Tg. Onq.* has *gbry'* 'mighty ones' in agreement with *Gen. Rab.* XXXI 7 (*gbrym*) and *Tg. Neof.* ABERBACH points out that this official Targum conspicuously avoids the 'fallen →angels' tradition which exploited the plain etymology of the word, from *npl* 'to fall'. Others connect it with *nēpel* 'miscarriage' and so meaning dead persons and thence ghosts or spirits of miscarriage, or even (spirits of) children born dead, miscarriages or the like regarded as ill-omened (SCHWALLY, *ZAW* 18 (1898) 142-148; KB 624). *Tg. Ps.-J.* has no such qualms and actually names the angels who fell from heaven (Shamhazai and Azael). In *1 Enoch,* the parallel account to Gen. 6:1-4, 'the angels, the sons of heaven' saw and desired the daughters of men. Semyaza (= *Tg. Ps.-J.* Shamhazai) appears as their leader; they all, two hundred of them, 'came down' (6:6) and acted promiscuously with earthly women (7:1), polluting the earth with their monstrous progeny, the Nephilim (9:9; 10:9). The ambivalent nature of the mysterious Nephilim stems from the far from clear identification of their parents in the Genesis pericope, the 'sons of the gods (or of God)'. Were these superhuman creatures, demigods, like Gilgamesh who was said to be two-thirds god and one-third human, or can they be regarded as completely human, stemming from the aristocratic line of →Seth? Or are they rulers in the manner of Keret, king of Ugarit, or David, king of Israel, whose traditional epithets derived from sacral kingship? Most modern exegetes recognise the validity of the first interpretation which is supported by a consistent picture of God's heavenly court and →council in the Hebrew Bible (Pss 29:1; 82:6; 89:6; Job 1-2; 1 Kgs 22:19-22; Isa 6:1-8). The NT notion of the fallen angels who like →Satan (Luke 10:18) plummeted to earth because they failed to recognise their position in the divine hierarchy (2 Pet 2:4; Jude 6) has clear allusions to the Nephilim. The antipathy of the translator in Targum Onqelos towards the proliferation of angelic powers and in particular, the angels who fell from grace, espoused in the Palestinian Targums and in the Enochic traditions might be due partly to the popularity of this kind of material in the early Judaeo-Christian community. Certainly the view that the 'sons of God' were angels was replaced in second century CE mainstream Judaism by the theory that they were righteous men. Etymologically, the basis of Nephilim is transparent. This explains the wealth of allusions which exploits the *fall* from heaven or the *fall* from Edenic bliss.

III. Mythological analogies from the ancient world have been drawn on as background to the original Hebrew. From classical mythology, e.g. the incident in which →Zeus, with the help of thunder and lightning, hurled Cronos and the other →Titans from heaven, has been noted, and KRAELING (1947) drew attention to the Mesopotamian Atrahasis legend in which the decision to destroy humans by means of a flood follows a population explosion on earth which threatened the equilibrium that existed between gods and men. Ezek 32 with its use of the keyword *npl* delineating the fate of fallen warriors who go down to Sheol with their weapons of war suggests that the Nephilim were the Fallen, i.e. their status as extinct during the period when the events are recorded. As such they are associated with the massed community of the dead, the →Rephaim (Deut. 2:11; Ps 88:11; Isa 14:9). DRAFFKORN KILMER has argued that the Nephilim are to be identified with the primeval *apkallu* 'sages, experts' of Mesopotamian tradition whose responsibility it was to maintain cosmic order. According to Berossus they brought to mankind the divine power of wisdom and all the benefits associated with civilized life; *Berossus* Book II 1:1-11 (BURSTEIN 1978:18-19).

WESTERMANN (1974:511-512) points out that in Gen 6:4 the Nephilim were identified with the 'heroes that were of old, warriors of renown' and that there was nothing mythical here. But the Nephilim of 4a, in the light of Ezek 32:27, are clearly mythical. He concludes that two narrative conclusions were blended in 6:4, one following the mythical line, the other simply the etiological line. The thrust of the mythical line was the telling of the story of the transgression of the divine order which ensured the separation of gods and men in accordance with the theme of similar stories in the primeval narrative (cp. Gen 3 and 11). Later traditions 'historicized' the Nephilim and transformed them either into the legendary precursors of the Israelites in Canaan or elaborated the tradition of fallen angelic beings who were actively engaged in stirring mankind into rebellion against divine authority.

IV. *Bibliography*

M. ABERBACH & B. GROSSFELD, *Targum Onkelos to Genesis* (Denver 1982); P. S. ALEXANDER, The Targumim and Early Exegesis of 'Sons of God' in Genesis 6, *JJS* 23 (1972) 60-71; S. M. BURSTEIN, *The Babyloniaca of Berossus* (SANE 1,5; Malibu 1978); U. CASSUTO, The Episode of the Sons of God and the Daughters of Man, *Bible and Oriental Studies*, Vol I. Trans I. Abrahams (Jerusalem 1973) 17-38; A. DRAFFKORN KILMER, The Mesopotamian Counterparts of the Biblical Nephilim, in: *Essays and Poems in Honor of F.I. Andersen's Sixtieth Birthday*. July 28, 1985 (Winona Lake 1987) 39-43; H. GUNKEL, *Genesis* (Göttingen 1910); E. G. KRAELING, The Significance and Origin of Gen. 6:1-4, *JNES* 6 (1947) 193-208; J. T. MILIK, *The Books of Enoch. Aramaic Fragments of Qumran Cave 4* (Oxford 1976); J. SKINNER, *Genesis* (ICC; Edinburgh 1910); C. WESTERMANN, *Genesis 1-11* (Neukirchen-Vluyn 1974; ET London 1984); W. ZIMMERLI *Ezekiel 2, II Teilband* (Neukirchen-Vluyn 1969; ET Philadelphia 1983).

P. W. COXON

NEREUS Νηρεύς

I. Nereus is a minor Greek god, whose name may be connected with Lithuanian *nérti* 'to dive' (CHANTRAINE 1980). As a theophoric name, it occurs once in the Bible (Rom 16:15). It is also the name of Job's brother in *Test. Job* 51:1. It remains unclear why the author of this Jewish pseudepigraph chose precisely this name.

II. Nereus has only a shadowy role in Greek mythology. He is a typical 'Old Man of the Sea', a category which is usually anonymous in Homer (*Il.* 1.358, 18.141 etc.), who also uses it for other sea-deities like Proteus (*Od.* 4.365) and Phorkys (*Od.* 13.96). These deities, and comparable ones like Glaucus, Thetis and Triton, have the gift of prophecy and the ability to change shapes. In the background is the belief in a Master of the Animals, a protector of all animals or those of one species (BREMMER 1983:129), but the feature of prophecy is a typical Greek development, which the Greeks themselves seem to have connected with the god's knowledge of the 'depths of the whole sea' (*Od.* 4.385). In Peloponnesian and Athenian iconography Nereus is indeed represented as an old man, but the earliest certain appearance in Greek art shows him fish-tailed (PIPILI 1992:835-837). Nereus' main qualities are his fight against

→Heracles and his fatherhood of the Nereids. Nereus' fight with Heracles was a favourite theme of archaic Greek art (PIPILI 1992). It is a 'double' of Heracles' fight with another shape-changing deity, Periclymenus. The theme of the fight against a Master of Animals goes back to the earliest Indo-European mythology and, eventually, finds its origin in shamanistic myths and rituals concerning the quest for food (BURKERT 1979:95-96).

The Nereids were the nymphs of the sea, who also possessed the gift of prophecy and shared an oracle with Glaucus on Delos (Aristotle fr. 490). The way they are mentioned both by Homer, who does not mention Nereus himself, and Hesiod, strongly suggests that they already existed before Homer (EDWARDS 1991:147-149; WACHTER 1990). The Nereids received sacrifices from the Persians (Herodotus 7.191) and Alexander the Great (Arrian, *Anabasis* 1.11.6), and Pausanias (2.1.8) observes that they had altars at various places in Greece. On the other hand, a cult of Nereus is hardly attested. Ovid (*Metamorphoses* 11.359-61) is the only source to mention a temple for Nereus and the Nereids. Pausanias (3.21.9) identified a cult for an 'Old Man' in Gytheion with Nereus, but that is clearly his personal interpretation. Yet in the second century people apparently still dreamt of him (Artemidorus 2.38). Given Nereus' shadowy existence, one may well wonder whether Hesiod did not invent him as a father for the pre-existing Nereids.

III. In the Bible Nereus occurs as one of the members of the Roman congregation, who is greeted by Paul (Rom 16:15). In Rome Nereus is quite a popular name among the Greek population (SOLIN 1982: 394-395) and often carried by slaves and freedmen, as 'Nereus and his sister' may well have been.

IV. *Bibliography*

J. BREMMER, *The Early Greek Concept of the Soul* (Princeton 1983); W. BURKERT, *Structure and History in Greek Mythology and Ritual* (Berkeley/Los Angeles/London 1979); P. CHANTRAINE, *Dictionnaire étymologique de la langue grecque* (Paris 1968-80); M. W. EDWARDS, *The Iliad: A Commentary* V (Cambridge 1991); M. PIPILI, Nereus, *LIMC* VI.1 (1992) 824-837; H. SOLIN, *Die griechischen Personennamen in Rom* I (Berlin/New York 1982); R. WACHTER, Nereiden und Neoanalyse: Ein Blick hinter die Ilias, *Würzburger Jahrbücher für die Altertumswissenschaft* NF 16 (1990) 19-31.

J. N. BREMMER

NERGAL נרגל

I. Nergal with his city Cutha is mentioned in 2 Kgs 17:30 within the description of the cults of the foreign settlers in Samaria. The particular relevance of Nergal in this context is to be explained by the fact that inhabitants of Cutha had been settled in Samaria while Samarians had been deported to Assyria (H. WINCKLER, *Die Keilschrifttexte Sargons* [Leipzig 1889] 100:23-24; C. J. GADD, *Iraq* 16 [1954] 179-180 iv:25-41; BECKING 1992:25-31.97). The deity also occurs as theophoric element in the personal name Nergal-sharezer (Jer 39:3,13).

II. An early attestation of Nergal and Cutha, a northern Babylonian city some 20 miles north-east of Babylon, is in Narām-Sîn's Bāṣetki inscription (*Sumer* 32 [1976], pl. facing p. 59). A further Narām-Sîn inscription (LAMBERT 1973:357-363) must also be mentioned since it concerns building operations for Erra (= Nergal, see below) with his spouse Lāz in his temple Emeslam in Cutha. The much later Epic of Erra also indicates the interchangeability of the names Erra and Nergal. In addition to other evidence to be inferred from the Epic, there is the fact that the two names occur in apposition (V 39-41). Nergal was understood by ancient scribes as 'Lord of the netherworld' (*EN-ERI$_{11}$-GAL). This is shown clearly by the Emesal ^{d}**umun.urugal**, which demonstrates that this opinion existed in ancient times, irrespective of the actual origin, etymology or even language of the name. Whatever the etymology of the name Erra (see ROBERTS 1972:11-16: 'parched earth'), it appears that a Semitic deity associated with plague, pestilence, war and sudden death has been merged with a Sumerian deity with broadly similar characteristics. A Babylonian etiological myth, Nergal and Ereshkigal, explains how Nergal became spouse of Ereshkigal, already the lady of the underworld.

In the Ur III period Nergal's name or aspects included Meslamtaea, a name he bore in direct relation to his temple of Emeslam in Cutha, the name meaning 'the one who comes out of Emeslam'. In the wider context of Sumerian mythology Nergal was regarded as the son of Enlil of Nippur. In this respect he took on the epithet 'avenger of his father, Enlil', an epithet which he shares with Ninurta, a deity which could along with Zababa, already be identified with Nergal in the Old Babylonian period. In the Old Babylonian period the cult of Nergal is widely attested, e.g. in Dilbat, Isin, Larsa, Nippur, Sippar, Ur, Uruk. An aspect of Nergal as god of war appears in Old Babylonian texts in which the deity is asked to break the weapons of the enemy. Already at this time the cult of Nergal had spread to Mari and Elam. Nergal and the theology of his cult was taken up and expounded in the learned works of the Babylonian scribes.

The character of the deity can be encapsulated from the point of view of the syncretistic Babylonian theology of the later period. In a hymn to →Marduk (*KAR* 25, II 3-10) Nergal is explained as the 'might' of Marduk, while in a syncretistic list Nergal is 'Marduk of battle' (CT 24, 50b obv. 4). The worship of Nergal was an important part of official Assyrian cult in Neo-Assyrian times. In the later period Nergal is attested in a 3rd century BCE, Phoenician-Greek bilingual from Piraeus (*KAI* 59), at Palmyra, and appears in Hatra in inscriptions dating from the first and second centuries CE.

III. Since Cutha is nowhere mentioned in the inscriptions of Sargon II, it is unlikely that the deportation of its inhabitants was conducted by this king. A conquest of Cutha accompanied by deportations is known from the reign of Sennacherib 703 BCE (L. D. LEVINE, *JCS* 34 [1982] 29-40; BECKING 1992:97) which would imply a relatively late date for the repopulation of the Samarian area by Cuthaeans. From the scarce information of 2 Kgs 17:30 it can be inferred that the settlers from Cutha erected an image of Nergal implying that they were allowed to continue their traditional religion. The deity also occurs as a theophoric element in the personal name *Nērgal šar-eṣer*, Nergal-sharezer, 'May Nergal protect the King' (Jer 39:3, 13), thought by some to be Neriglissar, king of Babylon, 560-556 BCE (*HALAT* 683; W. L. HOLLADAY, *Jeremiah*, vol. 2 [Minneapolis 1989] 291). A witness Nergal-shar-uṣur, PU.GUR.20.PAP, is mentioned in a Neo-Assyrian contract for the selling of a parcel of land excavated at Gezer (649 BCE; BECKING 1992:117-118)

IV. *Bibliography*

B. BECKING, *The Fall of Samaria* (SHANE 2; Leiden 1992); E. DHORME, *Les religions de Babylone et d'Assyrie* (Paris 1945) 38-44, 51-52; W. G. LAMBERT, Studies in Nergal, *BiOr* 30 (1973) 355-363; LAMBERT, The Name of Nergal Again, *ZA* 80 (1990) 40-52; J. J. M. ROBERTS, Erra - Scorched Earth, *JCS* 24 (1972) 11-16; ROBERTS, *The Earliest Semitic Pantheon* (Baltimore 1972); P. STEINKELLER, The Name of Nergal, *ZA* 77 (1987) 161-168; E. VON WEIHER, *Der babylonische Gott Nergal* (AOAT 11; Neukirchen Vluyn 1971).

A. LIVINGSTONE

NIBHAZ נבחז

I. Nibhaz is a deity who, like →Tartak, was 'made' by the men of Awwah (var. Ivvah, 2 Kgs 19:13) when the Assyrians settled them in Samaria, 2 Kgs 17:31.

II. Identification of Awwah with a place written in cuneiform as Ama or Awa is strengthened by the occurrence beside it of Amatu in texts of Sargon II, probably the Hamath of 2 Kgs 17:30 (H. WINCKLER, *Die Keilschrifttexte Sargons* [Leipzig 1889] 46:273-277; cf. BECKING 1992:98-99), a collocation observed by DRIVER (1958:18) and developed by ZADOK (1976:117-123). These towns lay in Babylonia, east of the Tigris, in the area occupied by the Chaldaean Bit Dakkuri tribe, with other places called by West Semitic names. By the end of the eighth century BCE the whole of Babylonia had a very mixed population of village dwelling tribesmen, the result of earlier migrations and of Assyrian deportations. Sargon II warred against Merodach-Baladan in that region, so transportation of some of the populace from there to another conquered territory, Samaria, would be normal. This eastern location for Awwah links neatly with the comparison between Nibhaz and the divine name Ibnahaz found in a list of Elamite gods equated with the Babylonian Ea (→Aya), god of fresh water and wisdom (L. W. KING, CT 25 [1909] pl. 24), observed by F. HOMMEL (*OLZ* 15 [1920] 18). A name which has been taken as the origin of Tartak follows in the same list.

Between the Tigris and the Zagros in Babylonia there had long been a mingling of peoples and languages, so the presence of West Semitic speakers who took up the worship of local, Elamite deities is not surprising. Regrettably, nothing is known about Ibnahaza. This explanation is preferable to the strained attempt to derive Nibhaz from *mizbeaḥ*, 'altar', by a series of phonological shifts, influenced by the occurrence of Greek Μαδβαχῳ (J. A. MONTGOMERY & H. S. GEHMAN, *Kings* [ICC; Edinburgh 1951] 474; J. T. MILIK, *Bib* 48 [1967] 578, 606). The Masoretes noted their uncertainty about the strange name by writing the last letter larger than the others, thus probably giving rise to the rabbinic reading *Nibḥan*, explained as a barking dog, from the root NBḤ (*b.Sanhedrin* 63b). The LXX *eblazer* should be treated as no more than a blundered rendering of a name incomprehensible to the translators.

III. From the use of the verb *'śh*, 'to make', it can be inferred that an image of Nibhaz was erected by the people from Awwah in Samaria. The fact that they were apparently allowed to erect such an image could hint at a liberal attitude of the Assyrians regarding religious symbols of exiled people (M. COGAN, *Imperialism and Religion* [Missoula 1974]).

IV. *Bibliography*

B. BECKING, *The Fall of Samaria. An Historical and Archaeological Study* (SHANE 2; Leiden 1992) 98; G. R. DRIVER, Geographical Problems, *ErIsr* 5 (1958) 16-20; W. J. FULCO, Nibhaz, *ABD* 4 (1992) 1104; F. HOMMEL, *Ethnographie und Geographie des Alten Orients* (München 1926) 987; R. ZADOK, Geographical and Onomastic Notes, *JANES* 8 (1976) 114-126.

A. R. MILLARD

NIGHT לילה Νύξ

I. Heb *laylâ* is based on a common Semitic vocable for 'night'; cf. Ug *ll*, Old South Ar *ll*, Canaanite *l[el]a* (EA 243:13), Ar *lail(at)*, Akk *liliātu* ('evening'). The term is not used in the formation of personal names in East or West Semitic onomastica. Outside the Hebrew Bible, 'night' is sometimes ascribed divine status.

II. 'Night' was deified in some areas of the ancient Near East and the Mediterranean world. It was occasionally venerated as a god in Hatti (^{d}*Išpant-*), just like 'good [i.e. lucky] day' (GOETZE 1951:473). In the Aramaic Sefîre treaties *lylh* is paired with *ywm*—→'Day and Night'—in a list of gods and other quasi-divine 'natural elements' before whom the treaty is sworn by the contracting parties, similar to elements listed in Hittite treaties (*KAI* 222 IA:12; FITZMYER 1967:38-39); however, night does not appear as a divine witness in treaties from Hatti. It was not deified in Mesopotamia (Sum **ge**$_6$, Akk *mūšu/mušītu*), although it was occasionally personified (e.g. *Maqlû* I 2). According to Greek mythology (Hesiod, *Theog.* 123-124) the goddess Νύξ was born of Chaos and gave birth to such evils as Ἔρις ('Strife') and Νέμεσις ('Retribution'). In the later Orphic cosmogony 'night' played an even more important role, although its place in the genealogy of the early gods varies in the sources (VON GEISAU 1972:220).

III. There is no convincing evidence for

a deification/demonisation of 'night' in the Biblical books. M. DAHOOD had posited such a meaning in Job 27:20 (*laylâ gĕnabtô sûpâ*, "Night kidnaps him like the whirlwind" [TROMP 1969:96 n.76]), but his view has won no support (the subject is *sûpâ*, not *laylâ*). In contrast to 'darkness', which belongs to the chaotic elements that characterize the period before creation (Gen 1:2), night is part of the ordered cosmos, especially when paired with 'day' (Gen 1:4; 8:22; Ps 74:16). On the other hand, it never completely loses overtones of chaos and the sinister, particularly as the setting for the operation of forces hostile to mankind. According to Ps 91:5 →Yahweh protects the psalmist from the →'terror of the night' (*paḥad lāylâ*), an expression that may allude to demonic forces. Similarly it is at night that →Jacob is accosted by a supernatural being with whom he wrestles till daybreak (Gen 32:22-24). A night-time setting is implied for Yahweh's 'demonic' attack upon →Moses (Exod 4:24; note *bammālôn*, 'at the lodging-place'). According to the gospels →Jesus is arrested at night, whose connection with the forces of evil is signalled by Luke's reference to "the power of darkness" (22:53). After noting that →Satan entered into Judas Iscariot at the Last Supper (13:27), John adds suggestively, "Now it was night" (13:30).

Night is also the time par excellence when the wicked do their lawless deeds, especially thieves (Job 24:14; Jer 49:9; Obad 1:5; Matt 24:43; 1 Thess 5:2). It is no coincidence that the wily woman of Proverbs 7, the antitype of Lady →Wisdom, also plies her trade at night (v 9). In Rom 13:13 Paul contrasts upright conduct symbolised by daytime ("Let us conduct ourselves becomingly as in the day") with immoral behaviours associated with night (reveling, drunkenness, debauchery, etc.).

It was undoubtedly these negative, 'chaotic' associations of night that motivated the author of Revelation to declare that with God's final victory night—like the →sea, the primary symbol of chaos (21:1)—shall be no more (22:5; cf. 21:25). (See also →Lilith.)

IV. *Bibliography*

J. A. FITZMYER, *The Aramaic Inscriptions of Sefîre* (BibOr 19; Rome 1967); H. VON GEISAU, Nyx, *KP* 4 (1972) 219-220; A. GOETZE, On the Hittite Words for 'Year' and the Seasons and for 'Night' and 'Day', *Language* 27 (1951) 467-476; N. J. TROMP, *Primitive Conceptions of Death and the Nether World in the Old Testament* (BibOr 21; Rome 1969).

M. L. BARRÉ

NIKE Νίκη

I. Nike was the Greek deity of victory whose popularity grew rapidly in the mid-sixth century BCE Greek world. Lacking any extended myths and rarely worshipped, she was hardly an independent deity in her own right; she was a feature or attribute of →Athena: and thus esteemed and revered as the giver and rewarder of victory. Several names in the New Testament reveal etymological connections with *nikē*: e.g. Nikanor and Nikolaos in Acts 6:5; Nikodemos in John 3:1-9; 7:50 and 19:39, as well as a group of people, called Nikolaitans in Rev 2:6 and 15. In addition, the concepts of conquering, winning, and victory are found throughout the New Testament: as in the discussions of the whole armor of God in Eph 6:10-17 and in running the race in Phil 2:16, put in the context of faith.

II. The earliest mythical reference to Nike is in Hesiod, *Theogony* 375-404, where she is the daughter of the →Titans Styx (daughter of Okeanos) and Pallas. Having helped →Zeus fight the war against the Titans, she and her parents and siblings, Kratos or Strength and Bia or Force, dwelt on →Olympus with Zeus. Herodotus 8.77 reports that according to an oracle of Bacis, Zeus and Nike would bring about the day when Greece would be free from the Persians. Later literary references are numerous. The chorus in Sophocles' *Antigone* 147-148 attributed the Theban victory over the seven warriors from Argos to Nike's response to the Theban call. In his conflict with Philoctetes, Odysseus requested guidance from →Hermes and asked Nike Athena Polias to preserve him (according to Sophocles, *Philoctetes* 133-134).

Euripides referred twice to Athena Nike on the subject of conflict. In the context of the tension between Athens and Delphi, the chorus in the *Ion* 457 appealed to Athena Nike to leave Olympus and come to Delphi in order to establish that Creusa's lover and thus Ion's father was →Apollo: thus providing the Athenians with support for their praise of Apollo for fathering the Athenian people. Later, in 1528-1529, Creusa herself swears by Athena Nike to her son Ion that Apollo was his father, the very Apollo who fought with Zeus against the race of →Giants and who reared Ion. In such passages, Athena Nike was treated as a deity who brought victory in social or military conflict. Nike appears in comedy as well as tragedy. The chorus in Aristophanes' *Knights* 589-591 prays to Pallas Athena Nike for victory as well as an omen as a sign of victory: i.e. as the guardian of Athens, a land most noble in war and art.

In addition to giving victory in military and social conflict, Nike gave and rewarded victory in civic contests. Pindar's *Nemean* 5.75-76 and *Isthmian* 2.26 depicted a victorious athlete as taken into her arms or falling upon her knees. Bacchylides wrote about an aspect of Nike that is familiar from vase painting, a figure crowning those who compete successfully in poetic as in athletic contests (10.15-18), standing beside Zeus to assess the courage of human beings (11.1-2), and accompanying victorious horses at Olympia (3.5-7). Similarly, Euripides ended *Phoenician Women*, *Orestes*, and *Iphigenia in Tauris* with prayers for the protection and crown of Nike.

Artistic representations of Nike in Greek temples are numerous. Pausanias mentions temples to Athena Nike in Megara (1.42.4) and Olympia (5.26.6) as well as to Athens (1.22.4). Images were placed on the roofs of many temples and treasuries; 31 examples of such sculptures have been found in Greece, dating from the late sixth and fifth centuries, with most found in Delphi, Athens, Corinth, and Olympia. A winged form shows her pouring a libation, crowning an athlete, or leading animals to an altar to be sacrificed as an offering for victory. A wingless form is also known: with the right arm and knee raised and the torso slightly turned as in a running pose. A Nike, located on the Athenian Acropolis, commemorated Kallimachos for his victories in the games; and for his victories as a general in the battle of Marathon (BOARDMAN 1991a:86-87, fig. 167). Another came from Olympia. It celebrated a military victory and is signed by the sculptor, a certain Paionios of Mende (BOARDMAN 1991b:176, fig. 139). The famous Nike of Samothrace alighting on the prow of a ship commemorates a victory at sea (BOARDMAN 1964: illus. 197).

A temple of Athena Nike, built on the bastion of the Athenian Acropolis late in the fifth century BCE, was incorporated into the Panathenaic festival, instituted in the mid-sixth century. This festival, which combined religious rites and athletic contests, glorified Athens and Athena. To judge from the temple balustrade and the friezes emphasizing war, worship, and victory, Athena was remembered for the help she provided Zeus in the battle of the gods against the →giants. On the Acropolis, statues of Athena were devoted to several of her aspects: Athena of the city (*polias*); the virgin (*parthenos*); the worker (*ergane*); the war-like (*promachos*); of health (*hygieia*); and victory (*nike*). The image of Athena in the Athena Nike temple was wingless: and was thus more likely to have been a votive than a victory statue.

The literary, artistic, and archaeological materials lead to the conclusion that Athena Nike provided help in two types of contest: military conflict and civic competition. We can notice a distinction between Nike and Athena, because Nike appears independently in Hesiod. She is, however, neither worshipped nor a subject of mythology according to our best evidence, while Athena is widely worshipped and is a rich subject of myths. Where Athena is worshipped, her image is wingless. We may also observe, however, a close association of Nike and Athena, for Athena conferred victory on many occasions and thus would be presented as a winged figure leading in conquest and alighting upon the victors.

III. *Bibliography*

J. BOARDMAN, *Greek Art* (London 1964); BOARDMAN, *Greek Sculpture: The Archaic Period* (London 1991[a]); BOARDMAN, *Greek Sculpture: The Classical Period* (London 1991[b]); L. R. FARNELL, *The Cults of the Greek States* 1 (Oxford 1896) esp. 258-376; M. Y. GOLDBERG, Archaic Greek Akroteria, *AJA* 86 (1982) 193-213; J. NEILS, Goddess and Polis: The Panathenaic Festival in Ancient Athens (Princeton 1992); K. SHEEDY, The Delian Nike and the Search for Chian Sculpture, *AJA* 89 (1985) 619-626.

L. J. ALDERINK

NILE יאור

I. The name of the Egyptian river Nile is attested many times in the Bible e.g. Gen 41:1-3.17-18; Ex 1:22; 2:3; 7:15-25; 8:3. 9.11; Jes 19:5-9; Jer 46:8; Ez 30:12; Amos 8:8. *Yĕ'ōr*, the Hebrew name of the Nile is a loanword; it is a derivation from the Egyptian word *itrw*: the river, i.e. the Nile. This word has dropped its *t* at an unknown date in the course of the history of Egyptian language, probably much earlier than the new Kingdom when the first variant in writing is found without *t* (*Wb* I, 146; DE BUCK 1948: 1). The Coptic phonetic writing *eioor* confirms a pronunciation of the word in Egypt corresponding with the Hebrew *Yĕ'ōr*.

The Greek name *Neilos* is also a loanword derived from *itrw*. The *n* presents the definite article *nꜣ* regularly used in Late Egyptian and onwards. Egyptian postvocalic *r* was weak. The Fayumic Coptic dialect writes the root in the form *iaal*. Whether the final *o* of *Neilos* should represent the plural ending *w* of *itrw* rather than the plural adjective *ꜥꜣw* "great" is debatable (SMITH 1979:163; LUFT 1992:403-411).

II. The Egyptian word for river or Nile *itrw* contains the word *tr* meaning season or time. The name of the Nile then, would mean something like the 'Seasonal One', the 'Recurrent One' or the 'Periodic One' (KADISH 1988:194). This name refers to the recurrent, periodic or annual flooding of the Nile or inundation called Hapy. The difference between the minimum and the maximum waterlevels could be ca. 7 metres in Assuan. The rising of the Nile began in June, the maximum height was reached in September-October. The Nile valley and Delta were turned into an enormous lake for 6-10 weeks. Only the sandy higher places and settlements on tells remained dry as the desert did. The retreat of the floodwaters began in November and the Nile reached its lowest point in April. The rising and falling of the Nile was well-known in Israel (Amos 8:8; Jer 46:7, Ez 30:12 etc.). The Greek saying that Egypt is a gift of the Nile (Herodotus II 5) is famous. The river itself, however, was not venerated as a god. The term Nile god found in modern publications refers to Hapy, the Inundation of the Nile. He is the personification of the fertility inherent in the Nile. He was depicted as an obese human figure with a clumb of papyrus on his head and with a huge paunch and pendant breasts, the image of welfare and prosperity. He was often called father of the gods. He was honoured with offerings, hymns and festivals.

III. *Bibliography*

J. BAINES, *Fecundity Figures* (Warminster 1985); A. DE BUCK, On the Meaning of the Name Ḥꜥpy, *Orientalia Neerlandica* (Leiden 1948) 1-22; K. W. BUTZER, Nil, *LdÄ* IV 481-483; G. E. KADISH, Seasonality and the Name of the Nile, *JARCE* 25 (1988) 185-194; D. KURTH, Nilgott, *LdÄ* IV 485-489; U. LUFT, Neilos. Eine Anmerkung zur Kulturellen Begegnung zwischen Griechen und Ägyptern, *The Intellectual Heritage of Egypt. Studies Presented to L. Kakosy = Studia Aegyptiaca* 14 (Budapest 1992) 403-410; H. S. SMITH, Varia Ptolemaica, *Glimpses of Ancient Egypt. Studies in Honour of H.W. Fairman* (Warminster 1979) 163-164.

H. TE VELDE

NIMROD נמרוד

I. In the Hebrew Bible, Nimrod is the name of a Mesopotamian →hero known to have been a famous hunter as well as the founder of major Mesopotamian cities and of the first state in (post-diluvian) primaeval times. The name Nimrod might be interpreted as a 1st pl. qal of the root MRD ('to rebel', i.e. 'we shall rebel') and has indeed been understood in this sense by Jewish tradition, which considered Nimrod to be a paradigm of god-offending hybris. This distorting negative valuation, underscored by an artificial etymology, is not yet found in the biblical texts, however. The name Nimrod most probably derives from that of a major Mesopotamian deity, i.e. Ninurta (Sum **dNin-urta** 'Lord of arable →Earth', Akk *Ninurta*, *Inurta*, *Nurti*, *Urti* etc.). This etymological derivation alone could support an identification of the Biblical hero either with the Mesopotamian god or with a king such as the Assyrian Tukultī-Ninurta I (ca. 1243–1207 BCE, as suggested by SPEISER 1958, but see below). Still, the precise development from the Sumerian prototype to its Hebrew affiliate remains unclear as potential intermediates (e.g. for a shift from **nwrt* > **nmrt* > *nmrd*) are still lacking while attested variants (such as *ʾnšt* on Aramaic dockets or *ʾnrt* in Aramaean and Ammonite inscriptions of the 7th century BCE: Sefire I A 38, *KAI* no. 55; cf. H. TADMOR, *IEJ* 15 [1966] 233-234) represent separate developments.

For the time being, the ultimate identification of Nimrod with Ninurta seems the most reasonable one. However, it does not rest upon linguistic reasoning, but represents a majority view based on circumstantial arguments such as the comparison of the Mesopotamian god's image and functions with those of the biblical hero. Among alternative proposals, obsolete historical identifications such as Nazimaruttaš (a Kassite king of ca. 1300 BCE), Amenophis III (*Nb-mꜣʿt-rʿ* called Nibmu'areya in the Amarna correspondence) may be disposed of, but one should note an ingenious hypothesis linking Nimrod to the Babylonian god →Marduk (LIPIŃSKI 1966). Impossible on strictly philological grounds, it postulates a deliberate scribal manipulation (*tiqqûn sôpherîm*: deletion of the final *kaph*, addition of a prefixed *nun*) but does not explain why the scribes should have left unchanged the name of Marduk, e.g. in Jer 50:2.

II. Ninurta is thought to have been a god of fertility, responsible for growth in field and herd and even among the fish. Son of Enlil, the lord of the gods, he belongs to the cultic tradition of Nippur. Another god called Ningirsu, whose main centre was the town of Girsu/*Tallô* near Lagash shares the same functions as Ninurta, and the two seem to have been basically identical, although a god-list may consider them to be brothers. Their virtual identity has found different interpretations: while most authors hold Ningirsu to be a local variant or specification of Ninurta, VAN DIJK (1983) has argued that the latter was originally a warrior god who progressively took over Ningirsu's prerogatives, thus entering late into the domain of agriculture. At any rate, Ninurta is then called 'ploughman of Enlil' in Sumerian hymns and gives advice on the cultivation of crops in the so-called 'Sumerian Georgica'. But he also acts as a champion warrior against various kinds of inimical monsters who try to impede the institution of irrigation, agriculture and civilization in general. One major myth about Ninurta, going back to the 3rd millenium, is a composition called *Lugal-e* 'King, a storm whose radiance is princely...' (VAN DIJK 1983; cf. BOTTÉRO & KRAMER 1989, no. 20): it relates several battles of Ninurta against the 'Slain Heroes', the Asakku monster who is vanquished by a deluge, and other adversaries killed 'in the mountain' such as the seven-headed serpent, the six-headed ram, the lion, the bison, the buffalo etc. (→Dragon, →Tannin and cf. *ANEP* 671). Just as with Ninurta's other combat against the Anzû bird-monster (BOTTÉRO & KRAMER 1989, no. 22), the whole issue not only mirrors contradictory forces of nature, but also the political and cultural antagonism between Mesopotamia and the north-eastern mountain regions, the so-called 'rebel lands', claiming divine protection and superiority for the Mesopotamian civilization. As a result of Ninurta's victory, irrigation and agriculture are instituted in *Lugal-e,* while in the Anzû myth, Ninurta is granted kingship by the other gods (cf. H. W. F. SAGGS, *AfO* 33 [1986] 1-29), a promotion also told in independent compositions such as 'The Return of Ninurta to Nippur' (or *Angimdimma*: J. S. COOPER, *The Return of Ninurta to Nippur* [AnOr 52, Rome 1978]; cf. BOTTÉRO & KRAMER 1989, no. 21).

Not surprisingly, Ninurta who has *qardu* 'fierce', 'heroic' and *qarrādu* 'warrior', 'hero' among his standard epithets (note S. MAUL, "wenn der Held (zum Kampfe) auszieht...". Ein Ninurta-Eršemma *Or.* n.s. 60 [1991] 312-334), is attested as a patron god of royal war and hunt from Middle Assyrian times on. In the 9th century BCE, at the time of Assurnasirpal II, Ninurta became the main deity of the capital city Kalah. Astronomers of the 8th-7th century added further connotations, identifying Ninurta (or Pabilsag) with Sagittarius or, alternatively, associating Ninurta with the planet Sirius (called *šukūdu* 'arrow'), the major star of Canis maior (Akk *qaštu* 'bow'). Numerous Neo-Assyrian and Neo-Babylonian cylinder seals show a divine hero drawing his bow against various kinds of monsters, some of them clearly identical with the Anzû on a famous monumental relief from the Ninurta temple at Kalah. It is probable that some of them are related to Ninurta's combats, and as such seals have found their way to Palestine (O. KEEL & C. UEHLINGER, *Göttinnen, Götter und Gottessymbole* [QD 134, Freiburg i.Br. 1993[2]] §§ 169-170), pictorial sources may well have contributed to Ninurta/ Nimrod's heroic hunter image. Similarly, the Labours of →Heracles contain clear reminiscences of the Mesopotamian Ninurta tradition.

III. As they stand, the biblical texts mentioning Nimrod show no awareness of his ultimately divine identity. The *god* Ninurta is probably meant in 2 Kgs 19:37 par Isa 37:38 relating the murdering of Sennacherib 'in the temple of his god →Nisroch', since Nisroch is best understood as a textual corruption from Nimrod (graphically מ > ס, ד > ך). But wherever the texts retain the name Nimrod, they have in mind a *human* hero of (post-diluvian) primaeval times.

The main biblical reference is Gen 10:8-12, a secondary addition to the so-called Table of Nations. As it stands, the text considers Nimrod to be a son of Kush (v 8a) and grand-son of →Ham, the father of the African branch of humanity. However, this presentation does not fit Nimrod's otherwise clearly Mesopotamian location and image, a problem which is not solved by an emendation of Kush to Put (as suggested by NAOR 1984). The confusion simply results from a blending of two independent traditions: the Table of Nations where Kush stands for Nubia, and the Nimrod passage from another source mentioning another(!) Kush, probably the eponym of the Kassites (Akk *kaššu*, Nuzi *kuššu*). V 8b considers Nimrod to have been the first 'hero' on earth (*gibbôr*, →Mighty Ones)—clearly an echo of Ninurta's epithet. V 9 speaks about his proverbial prowess in hunting (*gibbôr-ṣayid*) 'before →Yahweh'. Later tradition inferred an opposition of Nimrod against Yahweh interpreting *lipnê* 'before' as 'over against', but the text definitely does not support this interpretation; it rather sees a positive relationship between the (major) god and the hero, mirroring the Enlil – Ninurta relationship of much earlier Mesopotamian sources. The only facets of the biblical portrait which are not directly rooted in the Ninurta tradition are his kingship in Babel, Uruk and Akkad (Gen 10:10) as well as the building account concerning Assyrian cities such as Nineveh and Kalah (vv 11-12). Together with heroism in war and hunting, these underline the royal characteristics of Nimrod (note *mamlaktô* in v 10). While they are undisputably of Mesopotamian origin, too, it is not possible to identify either the ultimate source (a lost chronicle of the 7th century?) or to identify Nimrod with one single monarch of Mesopotamian history. Similarly, neither do we know the intermediaries (Phoenician?, cf. the hellenistic Ninos) by which the whole tradition reached a post-exilic Judaean historiographer, nor can we ascertain whether the telescoping of various aspects of Mesopotamian religious and royal fame into one legendary founder hero was realized by the biblical author or already prepared by the latter's sources. Mic 5:5 (post-exilic?) offers interesting complementary information insofar as it considers Nimrod to be the heroic founder of Assyrian military strength. In contrast, 1 Chr 1:10 merely represents a short excerpt from Gen 10:8-9.

IV. Nimrod is a quite prominent figure in Jewish (later Christian and Islamic) tradition (cf. VAN DER HORST 1990; UEHLINGER 1990). Following Gen 10, he was regarded as the first post-diluvian king, founder of state and city builder, but his positive biblical image was radically altered. The LXX of Gen 10:8-9 considered Nimrod to have been a giant and translates 'before Yahweh' by *enantion kyriou tou theou*, which Philo (*Quaest. in Gen* 2, 82) and subsequent tradition interpreted as 'in opposition *against* God'. One may note a general influence of Greek tradition about the →giants' revolt against the →Olympian gods (Philo, *Quaest. in Gen* 2, 82; *Conf.* 4-5; cf. the anonymous author cited in *Praep. Ev.* 9, 17, 2-3; *Sib. Or.* 1, 307-318). This and etymological elaboration on Nimrod's name (Philo, *Gig.* 66; *Tg. Ps.-J.* on Gen 10:8-9; *b.Erub.* 53a) made him appear as the prototype of tyrannical *hybris* (cf. explicitly Josephus in *Ant* 1, 113-114). Early midrash further associated Nimrod with idolatry and made him the instigator of the building of the Tower of Babel (already Philo, *Quaest in Gen* 2, 82; on *Praep. Ev.* 9, 18, 2, see UEHLINGER 1990: 91-92 n. 225), who persecuted →Abraham because the latter refused to join his project (Ps-Philo, *LAB* 6; *Tg. Ps.-J.* on Gen 11:28; cf. Wis 10:5; 4 Ezra 3:12). As a result, the valiant Mesopotamian hero defending arable land against dreadful monsters of chaos was finally turned himself into "a deceiver, oppressor and destroyer of earth-born creatures" (Augustine, *Civ. D.* 16, 4). As such he has remained famous in literature and art through the ages. Islamic legend and toponymy—partly based on local traditions of Babylonian Jews which may be traced back to the 3rd century CE—maintained the memory of the famous builder at various places such as, e.g. *Birs Nimrūd* (ancient Borsippa) and *Tall Nimrūd* (ancient Kalah).

V. *Bibliography*

S. ABRAMSKI, Nimrod and the Land of Nimrod, *Beth Mikra* 25/82-83 (1980/1) 237-255, 321-340 [Heb]; J. BOTTÉRO & S. N. KRAMER, *Lorsque les dieux faisaient l'homme* (Paris 1989) 338-429; *J. VAN DIJK, *LUGAL UD ME-LÁM-bi NIR-ĞÁL* (Leiden 1983); D. O. EDZARD, Ninurta, *WbMyth* I/1 (1965) 114-115; E. LIPIŃSKI, Nimrod et Aššur, *RB* 73 (1966) 77-93; P. MACHINIST, Nimrod, *ABD* 4 (1992) 1116-1118; M. NAOR, And Cush Begot Nimrod (Gen 10:8), *Beth Mikra* 30/100 (1984) 41-47 [Heb]; E. A. SPEISER, In Search of Nimrod, *ErIsr* 5 (1958) 32*-36*; SPEISER, *Oriental and Biblical Studies* (Philadelphia 1967) 41-52; *K. VAN DER TOORN & P. W. VAN DER HORST, Nimrod before and after the Bible, *HTR* 83 (1990) 1-29 [& lit] (the second part, with minor changes, also in P. W. VAN DER HORST, Nimrod after the Bible, *Essays on the Jewish World of Early Christianity* [NTOA 14; Fribourg/Göttingen 1990] 220-232); C. UEHLINGER, *Weltreich und «eine Rede»* (OBO 101; Fribourg/Göttingen 1990) [index s.v. & lit]; UEHLINGER, Nimrod, *NBL* Lfg. 11 (1995[2]) [fc.].

C. UEHLINGER

NINURTA → NIMROD; NISROCH

NISROCH נסרך

I. The name Nisroch appears in 2 Kgs 19:37 (// Isa 37:38) where it apparently designates an Assyrian deity, since king Sennacherib is said to have been assassinated "when he was praying (in) the temple of Nisroch, his god".

II. The identity of this deity has been a subject of much scholarly debate, since the sources relating to the Assyrian pantheon do not attest a god of such a name. On the other hand, it seems improbable that the biblical author simply invented an Assyrian divine name. Therefore, many scholars have tried to equate Nisroch with one of the known Assyrian gods. Among the suggested candidates, Enlil/Mullil, whom Neo-Assyrian state religion identified with the national god →Assur, could probably have been considered as 'Sennacherib's god' by a Judaean author, but the equation with Nisroch is impossible on philological grounds. In contrast, the name of Nusku could lie behind Nisroch—the latter being the result of a scribal error at some point in the chain of transmission; yet his identification with Nisroch is improbable for religio-historical reasons: although of some importance in Neo-Assyrian religion (where he was considered the vizir of →Sîn, see D. O. EDZARD, *WbMyth* I/1 116–117; B. MENZEL, *Assyrische Tempel* [StP 10; Rome 1981], I 80, 88, 110), Nusku, the Assyrian god of light, was not a major god of the state pantheon and apparently did not have a temple of his own; moreover, why should he be called 'Sennacherib's god' when he is mentioned only most sporadically in inscriptions of that king? →Marduk is out of the question, since the policies of Sennacherib are known to have been directed against this major god of rival Babylon. The hypothesis which interprets the name Nisroch as a conflation of Assur and Marduk is to be rejected as pure speculation. Though the god Assur took over epithets and functions of Marduk after Sennacherib's conquest and flooding of Babylon, and even if the statue of Marduk was put in the Assur temple until early in the reign of Ashurbanipal, the god Assur never usurped Marduk's name and a dyad Assur-Marduk is not attested in the sources. Finally, a recent suggestion to understand *nisrok* simply as 'idol' (*nesek* or *nisôk*, with an enclitic *r* functioning as 'signal letter' pointing to the god Assur [VERA CHAMAZA 1992:248–249]) is philologically untenable. These considerations leave Ninurta as the most serious candidate for the identification with Nisroch.

All the proposals surveyed so far concur in that they consider Nisroch to be the name of a deity. According to a recent ingenious interpretation offered by LIPIŃSKI (1987), however, *bêt-nisrok* would be an intentional correction of original *byt-srkn* or *byt-srk*, considered by LIPIŃSKI to be a toponym which he equates with Assyrian BÀD-*Šarrukīn*. The latter is a transcription of *Dūr-Šarrukīn*, i.e. the name of Sargon II's famous capital identified with modern *Ḥorṣabad*. A Judaean scribe would have misunderstood *srk(n)*, i.e. the name of Sargon, as a divine name and changed it to *nisrok* by adding a *ni*-prefix, a procedure also applied, according to LIPIŃSKI, in the case of the divine names →Nimrod and →Nibhaz (2 Kgs 17:31). Finally, one correction calling for another, LIPIŃSKI suggests that Sennacherib might not have been 'in prostration' (*mištaḥaweh*) in front of a god but simply engaged in a 'banquet' (*mišteh*) when he was murdered.

Too much speculation cannot create history, and LIPIŃSKI's proposal has to be rejected for several reasons: First, BÀD is merely a logogram for Akk *dūru* and was read /*dūr*/, so that there is no link with Heb *byt* at all. Second, we know from Isa 20:1 that in Hebrew the name of Sargon was transcribed *srgn* (A. R. MILLARD, *JSS* 21 [1976] 8). Third, at the time of Sennacherib's death in 681 BCE, Dur-Sharrukin had already lost much of its prestige. After the death in battle of its illustrious but somewhat improvident founder, it was relegated to the rank of a minor provincial town, if not almost abandoned. Why should Sennacherib, who had ostentatiously chosen Nineveh as his new capital, have gone banqueting to such a lost place? As a matter of fact, the murder of Sennacherib is partly elucidated by a nearly contemporary document from Nineveh (*ABL* 1091, see S. PARPOLA, The Murderer of Sennacherib, *Death in Mesopotamia* [Mesopotamia 8; Copenhagen 1980] 171–182; and see S. ZAWADZKI, Oriental and Greek Tradition about the Death of Sennacherib, *SAAB* 4 [1990] 69–72) mentioning a conspiracy against the king's life fostered by his son Arda-Mulišši, the Biblical Adrammelek. The assassination took place either at Niniveh, if we follow an implicit reference by Sennacherib's grandson Ashurbanipal (VAB VII/2 38 iv 70–73), or at Kalḫu if biblical *bêt-nisrok* should refer to the latter town's famous Ninurta temple (see von Soden 1990).

III. With reasonable certitude, the Assyrian deity who hides behind the name Nisroch may be identified with Ninurta. The spelling נסרך is probably best understood as a textual corruption from נמרד (graphically מ > ס, ד > ך), philological speculations thus being dispensable. נמרד ultimately relates to Ninurta (→Nimrod). A major patron of war affairs in the Assyrian pantheon and known otherwise in Palestine, Ninurta does not occupy a favourite position in Sennacherib's cultic policy but could nevertheless be called 'Sennacherib's god' by the biblical author. A letter from Ninurta addressed to an unnamed Assyrian king (SAA III no. 47 obv.) may relate to the growing tension against Sennacherib towards the end of his reign; in this letter, the god informs the king that he is angry and distressed in his temple and seems to complain about some disregard. Unfortunately very fragmentary, this letter apparently was considered a useful reference text to be kept in the archives, as the actual tablet which preserves the only extant copy dates to the reign of Ashurbanipal. While von Soden (1990) thinks that the letter was written after the murder and was originally sent to Esarhaddon, it may well antedate the crime and express a warning for the king, if it is not actually a trap and part of the conspiracy against Sennacherib.

With regard to the biblical account, at any rate our most explicit source, one should note that 2 Kgs 19:37 represents the author's closing remarks of his report about Sennacherib's campaign against Judah. The Rabshakeh's speeches and Sennacherib's letter to Hezekiah tend to drive a wedge between the Jerusalemites and their king, and between Hezekiah and →Yahweh, "your god in whom you trust" (2 Kgs 19:10), pressing the Judaeans to choose between Yahweh and the great king of Assyria. The latter are thus designed as the real antagonists of the story, and its end makes clear to whom the victory belongs: not only does Yahweh overpower the Assyrian army, but Sennacherib who attempted to challenge the one universal god (2 Kgs 19:15.19) is personally punished. Murdered by his own sons while praying to 'his god' who cannot help him, he meets a destiny which was decided and announced by Yahweh (2 Kgs 19:7). Sennacherib's forlorn trust in a powerless god marks a final counterpoint to Israel's trust in the one true god. Note that an alternative theological interpretation, attested by a stela of Nabonidus from Babylon (VAB 4, 272 i 35-41), gave Marduk the ultimate credit for the conspiracy against Sennacherib.

Originally the result of a scribal accident, the name Nisroch, once fixed, allowed eloquent second thoughts. Since Aramaic S/ŚRK denotes 'appendage', 'burdock', 'catch' etc., it could be understood as a 1st pl. verbal form meaning 'we shall catch up', 'we shall trap'.

IV. *Bibliography*

A. K. Grayson, Nisroch, *ABD* 4 (1992) 1122; E. G. Kraeling, The Death of Sennacherib, *JAOS* 53 (1933) 335–346; C. F. Lehmann-Haupt, Zur Ermordung Sanheribs, *OLZ* 21 (1918) 273–276; J. P. Lettinga, A note on 2 Kings xix 37, *VT* 7 (1957) 105–106; E. Lipiński, Bet-Sarruk(in), *Dictionnaire Encyclopédique de la Bible* (Maredsous 1987) 208–209; A. Ungnad, Die Ermordung Sanheribs, *OLZ* 20 (1917) 358–359; G. W. Vera Chamaza, Sanheribs letzte Ruhestätte, *BZ* 36 (1992) 241–249; W. von Soden, Gibt es Hinweise auf die Ermordung Sanheribs im Ninurta-Tempel (wohl) in Kalaḫ in Texten aus Assyrien?, *NABU* 1990, no. 22.

C. Uehlinger

NOAH נח Νῶε

I. The etymology of the name Noah has never been satisfactorily explained. It is usually connected with the verb root NWḤ 'rest, settle down' (of the ark Gen 8:4), 'repose, be quiet' (after labour Exod 20:11) and so Noah may mean 'rest' possibly in association with the resting of the ark on the mountains of Ararat after the flood. The root appears in Akk *nâḫu* to rest, as in *inūḫ tâmtu ... abūbu ikla* 'the sea *subsided* ... the flood ceased' in the Babylonian account of the flood (*Gilg.* xi, 131) and NOTH (1951: 254-257) has identified *Naḫ* as a theophoric element in personal names as early as the 19th-18th centuries BCE.

II. Noah appears as the tenth and last name in the great primordial genealogy of Gen 5 and is unique in the list in having a name explanation: "Out of the ground that the LORD has cursed this one shall create relief (*yĕnaḥămēnû*) from our work and from the toil of our hands" (Gen 5:29). The explanation closely resembles the reason given for the creation of mankind in *Enuma Elish* when Ea "imposes [on men] the services of the gods to set the gods free" (VI, 34). In the biblical story, Noah is cast as a pioneer figure in the cultivation of the hitherto stultified earth. The folk definition from NḤM in the MT, however, is unsound etymologically: hence the LXX reading *dianapausei hēmas* which makes better sense and presupposes the Hebrew *yĕnîḥēnû* 'he will give us rest'. Relief from the worst effects of divinely cursed earth (Gen 3:17-19) is held in abeyance until the flood has cleansed it of the progeny of the →Sons of God and the daughters of men. When this has been effected, Noah is blessed in the manner of the first man ('Be fruitful and multiply, and fill the earth' Gen 9:1) and as a man of the soil becomes the first to plant a vineyard (Gen 9:20). WESTERMANN (1974: 487-488) supports the idea that the relief brought to Noah in Gen 5 is the science of viticulture which would act as a refreshing antidote to the cursing of the earth and the punitive burden of physical labour imposed on mankind in 3:19. Other contexts in the Hebrew Bible refer to wine as the symbol of comfort and joy (Judg 9:13, Ps 104:15, Prov 31:6-7 and Jer 16:7). The beneficial evolution to viticulture is not negated by the incident of Noah's drunkenness in 9:21. The only culpability here attaches to →Ham's filial failure to cover his father when he saw him lying naked in his tent. In the Ugaritic legend of *Aqhat* it is the dutiful son who 'takes him (i.e. his father) by the hand when he is drunk, [and] carries him when he is satiated with wine' (e.g. *KTU* 1.17 i:30-32; ii:20-22; cf. 1.114:15-19).

Noah in his role as flood survivor has illustrious counterparts in ancient Mesopotamian literature. In the Sumerian Flood myth, the main text of which dates from the OB period, Ziusudra, a humble and pious king, is secretly forewarned of the gods' decision to send a flood, is saved and granted eternal life. A fuller account is given in the Akkadian Myth of Atraḫasis which survives in several fragments from the Old and Neo-Babylonian period and also in Neo-Assyrian tablets. The 'exceedingly wise' Atraḫasis is informed in a dream by the god Enki of the coming deluge and survives by building himself a boat. As with Ziusudra, eternal life is bestowed on him and he is granted a place 'among the gods'. The best-known version of the Flood-myth which contains numerous analogies to the biblical acount is contained in the eleventh tablet of the Epic of Gilgamesh. The hero Gilgamesh, in his quest for immortality, seeks out Utnapishtim, Noah's counterpart, who in the first person tells him the story of the universal flood and how he survived it.

III. In contrast to the universal degeneracy of contemporary society, Noah is described in Gen 4 as 'a righteous man, blameless in his generation', who like →Enoch before him, 'walked with God' (6:9; cp. 5:24). Early Jewish sources revelled in the exploits of these primordial →heroes and though Enoch was the prime target of their speculation, his great grandson Noah, the father of →Shem, Ham and →Japheth whose offspring were to people the new world after the flood, was also of special interest. Among the Dead Sea Scrolls *1QapGen* (col. I-V) used Gen 5:28-29 as the basis for haggadic expansions on the birth of Noah. The Aramaic text consists of a description of

Lamech's uneasiness that Noah's conception was 'due to the →Watchers, or ... to the Holy Ones, or to the →Nephilim' (II, i). Bitenosh his wife thereupon pleaded her innocence stating that no Watcher or 'any one of the sons of heaven' (II, 16) had implanted seed in her. At length Enoch, the great sage of primordial Jewish history, assuaged his fears.

1 Enoch contains a variant tradition of the commotion occasioned by Noah's birth which depicted his body as 'white like snow and red like the flower of a rose ... the hair of his head white like wool and his eyes like the rays of the sun' (106:2.5.10). Enoch reassured Lamech, Noah's father, that these amazing physical characteristics were not due to angelic interference but did mark Noah out as an extraordinary individual 'through whom the Lord will do new things on the earth' (106:13). The allusion here is to the fresh start Noah and his three sons will inaugurate on the earth after the flood has swept away the old corrupt generations of humanity.

In the NT the eschaton will recapture the sense of urgency of the days of Noah (Matt 24:36-39). As the Flood marked an end of the old order and the start of the new, so the eschatological appearance of the →Son of Man will be cataclysmic. Like Noah of old, the end will be swift and sudden and precipitate universal judgement on the wicked. In a puzzling passage in 1 Pet the apostle has →Christ go and make a proclamation to the spirits in prison who 'in former times did not obey, when God waited patiently in the days of Noah, during the building of the ark' (3:19-20). Here the Flood is made analogous to Christian baptism imaging salvation by means of water. Noah, who in Ezek 14:14.20 is listed with →Daniel and Job as paragons of righteousness, is held up as a 'herald of righteousness' (*dikaiosunēs kēruka*) in 2 Pet 2:5. The latter expression has been compared with the "teacher of righteousness" known from the Qumran sources (VERMES 1950:73)

IV. *Bibliography*

J. A. FITZMYER, *The Genesis Apocryphon of Qumran Cave I. A Commentary* (Rome 1966); W. G. LAMBERT & A. R. MILLARD, *Atra-ḫasis: The Babylonian Story of the Flood* (London 1969); G. LEICK, *A Dictionary of Ancient Near Eastern Mythology* (London 1991); M. NOTH, Noah, Daniel and Hiob in Ezechiel xiv, *VT* 1 (1951) 251-260; G. VERMES, La communauté de la Nouvelle Alliance d'après ses écrits récemment découverts, *ETL* 21 (1950) 70-80; C. WESTERMANN, *Genesis 1-11* (Neukirchen-Vluyn 1974; English Translation: London 1984).

P. W. COXON

NOBLE ONES אדירים

I. In the OT the adjective *ʾaddîr* is used in describing →Yahweh (Exod 15:11; 1 Sam 4:8; Pss 8:2.10; 76:5) and also of persons or things of more than normal stature or strength, like the sea (Ps 93:4), the mighty cedars of the Libanon (Ezek 17:27), mighty people (Ezek 32:18), or kings (Ps 136:18). In Ps 16:3 it seems to denote pagan deities (TOURNAY 1988:335).

II. In the ancient Ugaritic legend of Aqhat the *ʾadrm* are mentioned together with the king fulfilling his usual duties (*KTU* 1.17 v:7). They reside on the threshing-floor. According to *KTU* 1.20-22 this is also the terminus of the invoked spirits of the deified royal ancestors called *rpum* (cf. →Rephaim). In a Phoenician inscription on a sarcophagus from the Persian period (Byblos 13:2) the adjective *ʾdr* is used for →Og, who is known from Josh 12:4 as 'the last of the Rephaim'. In this Phoenician inscription he appears to be worshipped as a chthonic deity (RÖLLIG 1974:5-6, SPRONK 1986:210-211).

III. This chthonic aspect is also present in Ps 16 referring to 'the →saints who are in the →earth (i.e., the netherworld)'. This expression stands in poetic parallelism with 'the noble ones who only have delight in themselves'. So these Noble Ones are probably to be sought in the netherworld as well (SPRONK 1986:334). With regard to the interpretation of the Hebrew text of this verse there are still many unsolved problems, but we can safely assume that trust in Yahweh is contrasted here with the hope for the help of powers from the netherworld.

Ezek 32:18-32 can also be read against this background. It describes the descent of the mighty (*'addîrîm*) peoples into the netherworld. The only thing that can be said of them now, is that they are slain, fallen by the sword. Contrary to what was believed in Canaanite religion, nothing good can be expected from them anymore.

IV. *Bibliography*

G. W. AHLSTRÖM, אַדִּיר *TWAT* I (1973) 78-81; W. RÖLLIG, Eine neue phoenizische Inschrift aus Byblos, *NESE* 2 (Wiesbaden 1974) 1-6; K. SPRONK, *Beatific Afterlife in Israel and in the Ancient Near East* (AOAT 219; Neukirchen-Vluyn 1986); R. TOURNAY, Le Psaume 16 1-3, *RB* 95 (1988) 332-336.

K. SPRONK

NOMOS νόμος

I. Usually, in the Greek Bible the word *nomos,* law, is used to refer to the OT and Jewish →Torah as a set of rules for life. (For a general treatment of the role of the law in Jewish writings of the Second Temple Period see the overview of SANDERS 1992; the NT material is dealt with by HÜBNER 1981.) In the letters of Paul and in the Jewish apocalypse *4 Ezra,* however, the word sometimes seems to designate a supernatural power or agent.

II. The word *nomos* is not often used as a personification (cf. LSJ *s.v.*). For Pindar (cf. Frag. 169—also quoted by Plato, *Gorg.* 484b) the Law is the king of all, both mortals and immortals (cf. also Euripides, *Hecuba* 800). In the *Crito,* Plato presents the personified law in dialogue with Socrates (50a), in the letters he can even call it *theos* (*Ep.* VIII 354e). Dio of Prusa (*Or.* 1:75), when describing the female deities Royalty, Justice and Peace, writes: "But he who stands near Royalty, just beside the scepter and somewhat in front of it, grey-haired and proud, has the name of Law; but he has also been called Right Reason, Counselor, Coadjutor, without whom these women are not permitted to take any action or even to purpose one" (transl. LCL).

In Jewish literature from the Second Temple Period the identification of Law and →Wisdom (*sophia*) is made by Sir (cf. 24:1-6, 23) and presupposed in some of the Pseudepigrapha (cf. *Pss. Sol.* 4:10-11; *4 Ezra* 8:12; 13:54-55; *Syr. Bar.* 38:2-4; 48:24; 51:4; 77:16). Like Wisdom, the Law is sometimes depicted as an acting subject: "The Law does not perish but remains in its glory" (*4 Ezra* 9:37). In the final judgement the law is like fire, an instrument to destroy the sinners (13:38). It will then demand its right (*Syr. Bar.* 5:2; 48:27). Although the divine origin of the law is generally presupposed (cf. *Syr. Bar.* 4:1; *4 Ezra* 3:19; 5:27; 7:81; 9:36; *Jub.* 2:33; 6:14; *Sib. Or.* 3:719-20, 757; Josephus, *Ant.* 3:286; 20:44; Philo, *Decal.* 18), 'the Law' is not a god, nor do Jewish texts use *nomos* as a divine name.

III. In the NT *nomos* can refer to the Jewish religion (cf. Acts 18:15; 23:29). Christian authors, however, used the expression *nomos* to refer to aspects of their own faith. In order to do this, *nomos* is qualified by Paul. He thus can refer to the love commandment—which is the fulfillment of the law as law of →Christ (Gal 6:2; this should not be confused with those instances where *nomos* refers to a basic principle as governing power: the 'law' that causes faith [Rom 3:27], the 'law' of the Spirit that causes life in Christ [Rom 8:2]).

The apostle Paul uses the expression *ho nomos* to refer to the Torah, the 'law of →Moses' (1 Cor 9:9). The reference is not restricted to the books of Moses, however. In Rom 3:19 *nomos* designates all of the holy scriptures of Judaism. In this utterance Paul assigns *ho nomos* an active role: it 'speaks' (cf. also 1 Cor 9:8). The law and the prophets testify to the *dikaiosynē theou* (Rom 3:21). The active role of the law is also expressed by the phrase 'by the law' *(dia nomou).* Taking into account Rom 4:15 ("The law causes →wrath"), the law not only is the means by which God will judge sinners (Rom 2:12) and by which →sin is known (Rom 3:20; 7:7), the law is also the agent through which mankind is drawn into God's judgement. Paul thus can say the law killed him (Gal 2:19). In 1 Cor 9:20 and Gal 4:21, *hypo nomon* has no negative connotations; it simply designates the Jews or those who want to live like Jews. In Gal 5:18 and Rom 6:14-16, though, *hypo nomon* is opposed to being led by the Spirit or to be in the realm of God's grace *(hypo charin)*. Like →sin, the *nomos* reigns over those human beings (Rom 7:1) who are not in the realm of God's grace in Christ. They are *hypo nomon* (cf. also Gal 3:23; 4:4-5) or *hypo hamartian* (e.g. Gal 3:22). The law is a transsubjective active power that enslaves mankind (Gal 4:4-5). Humans are detained by the law (Rom 7:6); it makes them prisoners of war (Rom 7:23); scripture locks them up (Gal 3:22); the law keeps watch over them (Gal 3:23). Although the law has the characteristics of a ruling power in Paul's letters, it is neither a deity nor a →demon. According to Romans, it is rather the holy law of God (Rom 7:12) that is in the power of sin (Rom 7:13; cf. 8:3). Through Christ's death the believer is freed from the bondage of the law (Gal 2:19-20; Rom 7:4, 6).

IV. Amongst the Apostolic Fathers the expression 'the new Law of our Lord →Jesus Christ' is in use (*Barn.* 2:6; cf. Ignatius, *Magn.* 2). Hermas goes further and identifies the Law, which was given unto the whole world, with the →'Son of God', who is preached unto the end of the earth (*Sim.* 8:3 [= 69:2]). The identification of Christ with the Law (cf. *Kerygma Petrou* in Clement of Alexandria, *Strom.* I 182:3; II 68:2; VII 16:5) has a different background, be it Jewish (e.g. Justin, *Dial* 11:2; 43:1) or Stoic (e.g. *Acta Johannis* 112). In Patristic texts, the law is understood to be divine (cf. G. W. H. LAMPE, *A Patristic Greek Lexicon* [Oxford 1961] 921).

V. *Bibliography*

H. HÜBNER, νόμος, *EWNT* 2 (1981) 1158-1172 [& lit]; *H. KLEINKNECHT & W. GUTBROD, νόμος, *TWNT* 4 (1942) 1016-1029, 1040-1084; E. P. SANDERS, Law in Judaism of the NT Period, *ABD* 4 (1992) 254-265; N. WAGNER, Nomos (νόμος), *ALGRM* III/1 (1897-1903) 455.

C. BREYTENBACH

NYMPH Νύμφη

I. *Nymphai* are minor Greek gods, who appear once in the NT as a theophoric element (Col 4:15). Greek *nymphē* means 'young girl', 'bride' and 'clitoris' (WINKLER 1988:181-184), but its etymology is obscure (CHANTRAINE 1980).

II. In the *Iliad* (6.420 etc.) the Nymphs are the daughters of →Zeus, the divine father *par excellence*, and this is the most common genealogy, although their connection with water (below) led to many →rivers also being seen as their father (HERTER & HEICHELHEIM 1936:1529-1530). It fits in with Zeus' fatherhood that the Nymphs are called 'goddesses' (*Il.* 24.615-6), but later times also considered them mortal or only 'long-living' (Sophocles, *Oed. R.* 1099). They are young and beautiful (*Od.* 6.108); their number could vary greatly, from two to the inflated numbers of Roman times (1000: Virgil, *Aeneid* 1.499-500). The confusing multitude of Nymphs was systematized in Hellenistic times and various categories were distinguished, such as Naiades, Oreades and Dryades (HERTER & HEICHELHEIM 1936:1582-1583).

The collectivity of the Nymphs may be best seen as the reflection of young girls on the eve of adulthood (CALAME 1977:70-74). In the Archaic period the goddess most frequently associated with the initiation of girls was →Artemis, whose initiatory sanctuaries were preferably situated in the country in marshy or watery surroundings. The images of Nymphs dancing on meadows or Artemis wandering through the woods and valleys in the company of Nymphs (*Od.* 6.105-109), as in the myth of Callisto (HENRICHS 1987: 258-267) thus reflect the initiatory dances, the situation outside civilisation and the aristocratic leadership of female initiates. The connection with initiation made the Nymphs suitable as educators of divine and human children (HERTER & HEICHELHEIM 1936:

1550) and they were invoked during the wedding ritual (GRAF 1985:105); indeed, many children were seen as a gift of the Nymphs, witness the frequent name Nymphodorus. Rather strikingly, as the Greeks normally did not give humans names of divinities, girls could receive the name Nymphe: striking confirmation of the connection between Nymphs and girls.

The connection of the Nymphs with water led to their association with →sources, rivers, the Acheloos (GRAF 1985:105) and lakes (HERTER & HEICHELHEIM 1936:1535-1538). As water was seen by the Greeks as having a prophetic quality, prophetic gifts could be interpreted as the result of a seizure by the Nymphs. In fact, nympholepsy was a common way of interpreting various forms of possession (CONNOR 1988). Moreover, as the Greeks also associated running water and healing, the Nymphs were often worshipped together with Asclepius and Hygieia, and invoked in times of distress (VAN STRATEN 1976).

On the ritual level, the Nymphs were regularly worshipped in gardens, the reflection of their mythical favourite place (Ibycus fr. 286), which might well include trees and flowers; these gardens of the Nymphs could even become amorous places like in Longus' *Daphnis and Chloe* (1.4). In this case, the Nymphs had a cave as well, which also was a favourite place to worship them, often in company with Pan (BORGEAUD 1979:75-76; AMANDRY 1985); they did not have proper temples. As the Nymphs were especially associated with coming of age, a period of marginality in Greece, they often did not receive the normal offerings but non-animal sacrifices and wine-less libations (HERTER & HEICHELHEIM 1936:1556-1557).

III. In the Bible the Nymphs appear only once in the name of a woman, Nympha, in Laodicea (Col 4:15). The majority text reads here "Nymphās", a man's name.

IV. *Bibliography*

P. AMANDRY, Le culte des Nymphes et de Pan, *L'Antre Corycien* II = *BCH* Suppl. IX (1985) 395-425; P. BORGEAUD, *Recherches sur le dieu Pan* (Rome 1979); C. CALAME, *Les choeurs de jeunes filles* I (Rome 1977); P. CHANTRAINE, *Dictionnaire étymologique de la langue grecque* (Paris 1968-80); W. R. CONNOR, Seized by the Nymphs: Nympholepsy and Symbolic Expression in Classical Greece, *Classical Antiquity* 7 (1988) 155-189; F. GLASER, Nymphen und Heroen, *Jahresh. Österr. Arch. Inst.* 53 (1981-1982) Beiblatt 1-12; F. GRAF, *Nordionische Kulte* (Rome 1985); A. HENRICHS, Three Approaches to Greek Mythography, *Interpretations of Greek Mythology* (ed. J. Bremmer; London 1988[2]) 242-277; H. HERTER & F. HEICHELHEIM, Nymphai, *PW* 17 (1936) 1527-1599; F. MUTHMANN, *Mutter und Quelle* (Basel 1975); F. T. VAN STRATEN, Daikrates' Dream, *Bulletin Antieke Beschaving* 51 (1976) 1-38; J. J. WINKLER, *The Constraints of Desire* (New York & London 1988).

J. N. BREMMER

O

OAK אלון

I. According to ALBRIGHT (1968:165) both the oak, Quercus coccifera, Quercus aegilops, אלון, *ʾēlôn* or *ʾallôn*, and the →terebinth, *אלה, were deified in the Mediterranean area.

The common view is that אלון, like אלה and אל, is connected with the root *אול II, 'to be first' or 'to be strong'. POPE claims that the etymology of אל remains obscure and he simply refuses to decide whether אל, אלה, and אלון should be derived from ʾW/YL or from some other root (1955:16-19). In his review of Pope's monograph ALBRIGHT states that אלון and Aram *ʾillān* come from ʾLL (1956:161, but cf. ALBRIGHT 1968:165-166). Uncertainty about its etymology suggests it may be more rewarding to analyze the semantic field of the word.

II. In the Near Eastern world, pictures of holy trees are often found on seals or as decoration in temples (GALLING 1977:34-36). The close relationship between goddesses such as →Asherah (in Ugaritic texts the consort of →El) and the tree shows that trees connote fertility. For further information on holy trees in the Near East (Ugarit, Egypt, Mesopotamia) see JAROŠ 1974:214-217.

ALBRIGHT points out that in Greek tradition the dryas (from drys, 'oak') and hamadryas both refer to minor divinities (→nymphs). It may be, he adds, that the Ugaritic *ilnym,* which stands in parallelism with *ilm*, 'gods', refers to minor divinities of the same type, though we cannot be sure that these particular minor divinities were attached to oak trees as such. Albright suggests that *ʾēlôn* (often meaning 'sacred tree'), might be a back-formation from the plural *ʾĕlônîm* (gods) (1968:165-166). Even if Albright is right in suggesting this etymology for the word אלון, it does not necessarily imply that users of the word considered the oak as a deity.

III. The oak is mentioned several times in the OT in connection with holy places and cultic activities. It was obviously considered a holy tree. In Gen 12:6 the holy place at Shechem is also the place of the oak of Moreh, i.e. the Diviners' oak (Judg 9:37); in Gen 35:8 Rebekah's nurse is buried under an oak below Bethel; in 1 Sam 10:3 three men of God go to meet Saul at the oak of →Tabor. Isa 6:13 also presupposes the idea of the holy tree.

In the OT the attitude towards the oak is ambivalent. On the one hand the oak, like the terebinth, signals the holy. The name of the oak in Gen 12:6, Deut 11:30 and Judg 9:37, the Diviners' Oak, shows the connection between trees and oracle activity. JAROŠ combines this with the Ugaritic text *KTU* 1.1 iii: (to be restored on the basis of *KTU* 1.3 iii:23; iv:15), where the trees are said to talk, and an Arabic example of a tree oracle (1974:217-218). The traditions about →Abraham locate the patriarch by the oaks of Mamre, where he built an altar to →Yahweh, Gen 13:18. In Gen 35:8 Rebekah's nurse is buried under an oak below Bethel. The oak is called 'oak of weeping'. This may indicate burial rites taking place under the tree. The meeting in 1 Sam 10:3 between the three men of God and Saul, who had just been anointed king by Samuel, will take place at the oak of Tabor. The whole setting connotes cultic activity and makes it natural to understand this oak as a holy tree. In Judg 9:6 Abimelech is made king at the oak of the pillar. According to ALBRIGHT the word *ʾēlôn* here refers to a dead tree or even a post replacing an original tree (1968:166). Isa 6:13 too presupposes the idea of the holy tree. The oak must fall, but its stump is holy seed, the prophet says. The oak is certainly a holy tree, although it is not identified with a deity. The oak is used metaphorically to announce the coming king (see further NIELSEN 1989:149-153).

There is also a polemic against the cult of oaks (Hos 4:13). The cult must have been some kind of fertility cult. This might indicate a special relationship between the oak and a goddess (ALBRIGHT 1968:165). In Isa 2:13 the prophet proclaims that Yahweh of hosts has a day against all that is proud and lofty, among which the oaks of →Bashan are mentioned as a parallel to the cedars of →Lebanon. The oaks are metaphors for those who consider themselves strong and can be interpreted here as metaphors for those who worship foreign gods (cf. the oracle in Isa 1:30-31 about the withering terebinth; NIELSEN 1989:201-215). The polemic against idolatry can also be found in Isa 44:14-15, where the making of an idol is described: The carpenter chooses an oak, he takes part of it to warm himself and bake bread, and part of it he uses to make himself a god to worship.

The oak was evidently regarded a holy tree in Israel. Nevertheless, it is never seen as a representation of Yahweh. Now and then the oak is connected with idolatry in a way that suggests a certain relationship between the oak and a foreign deity, but in these cases the attitude is always polemical.

IV. *Bibliography*

W. F. ALBRIGHT, Review of Marvin H. Pope: El in the Ugaritic Texts, in: *JBL* 75 (1956) 255-257; ALBRIGHT, *Yahweh and the Gods of Canaan. A Historical Analysis of Two Contrasting Faiths* (London 1968); G. DALMAN, *Arbeit und Sitte in Palästina I,1-2* (Gütersloh 1928); K. JAROŠ, *Die Stellung des Elohisten zur kanaanäischen Religion* (Göttingen 1974); K. NIELSEN, *There is Hope for a Tree. The Tree as Metaphor in Isaiah* (Sheffield 1989); M. H. POPE, *El in the Ugaritic Texts* (Leiden 1955); P. WELTEN, Baum, sakraler, *BRL*², 34-35; M. ZOHARY, *Pflanzen der Bibel. Vollständiges Handbuch* (Stuttgart 1982).

K. NIELSEN

OB → SPIRIT OF THE DEAD

OBERIM → TRAVELLERS

OG עוג

I. Of unknown etymology, although some connexion with Osa *ğaig* (?), Soqotri *ʿaig*, Hatraean *ʿgʾ* 'man' could be established (RABIN *ErIsr* 8 [1967] 251-154; cf. also Ug PN *bn ʿgy*, *KTU* 4.611:19), Og is attested 22 times in the Bible as the king of →Bashan, along with the Amorite king Sihon, both of them vanquished by the Israelite newcomers. More specifically it is said of him that he was "one of the survivors of the →Rephaim" (Deut 3:11; Josh 12:4; 13:12 [NEB]) and was huge in stature, as fitted this race of →giants; this could be verified by the dimensions of his iron bed, preserved in Rabbat Ammon in the days of the redactor (?) (Deut 3:11) and usually still taken as a reference to a Dolmen tomb (?) (MILLARD 1988:484-485). In this way the tradition moves between the 'historical' and the 'mythological', as happens also with the other biblical references to the Rephaim. It is also said of this king (Ug *mlk*) and Rephaite (Ug *rpu*) that he "lived (*hayyôšēb*) in Ashtarot and Edrei" (Josh 12:4; 13:12 [NEB]), obviously the capital cities of his kingdom Bashan, a region of northern Transjordan according also to these sources. Egyptian documents and two Amarna letters mention rulers of Ashtarot in the fourteenth century BCE (BARTLETT 1970:266-268).

II. Well known are the echoes and agreements of these data in the Ugaritic mythology and cult. Leaving aside the cultic myth of the *Rpu/im* (*KTU* 1.20-22) and the characterization as such of the legendary kings Keret and Aqhat (*KTU* 1.15 iii:14; 1.17 i:17) and of empirical kings, ancient and contemporary, like Ammishtamru and Niqmaddu (*KTU* 1.161:2-12), text *KTU* 1:108:1-3 reports that the *mlk ʿlm*, the dead and deified king, "the eternal king", when enthroned as *rpu, yšb bʿštrt špṭ bhdry*, "sits enthroned in Ashtarot, judges in Hedrei", in amazing correspondence with the biblical tradition of Og, king of Bashan, which in this way appears as a kind of Canaanite Hell, or more exactly, Elysian Fields. The city of *ʿštrt* Ashtarot is also mentioned as the dwelling place of the god *mlk* in *KTU* 1.100:41, 1.107:17 and RS 86.2235:17 place. Now, the equivalence of Ug *rpu(m)* and *mlk(m)* is reasonably clear (DEL OLMO LETE 1985:58-62), while at the same time biblical tradition also asserts that Og was 'king' (*mlk*) and one of the Rephaim (*rpu*) (FORD 1992:84-87). Phoenician tradition also seems to record the existence of a deity *ʿg*, protector of tombs (POPE 1977:171; MÜLLER *ZA* 65 [1975] 122), thus in a funerary context consequently.

III. Given all these data, it is not easy to clarify the identity of the biblical Og, king of Bashan, in connexion with the Ugaritic mythological and cultic tradition (PARDEE 1988:86-87). Evidently this does not refer directly to this 'late' Amorite king of Transjordan, assuming that he were a historical character (BARTLETT 1970:266-268), nor does he play any role in it. Nevertheless, later Phoenician tradition treats him as a mythical divine entity (*hʿg ... hʾdr*, RÖLLIG 1974:2). So we have a three stage development: the mythical ideological framework in Ugarit; the 'historical' record in the Hebrew Bible; the mythological transformation in Phoenicia. In this way, Og, now turned into *mlk(m)/rpu(m)*, can be assumed to have been a historical (but cf. DE VAUX 1971:524) Amorite/Canaanite king of the region which, according to the Ugaritic tradition, was the place where its dead deified kings dwelled. Thus he was himself "a survivor of the Rephaim", a *rpu*, like any other king in this ideology. According to later 'Phoenician' religion he may have become a poliadic deity of Rabbat Ammon, where his cult was celebrated, as the presence of his ceremonial 'bed' certifies (DE MOOR 1976:338), or just a demonic genius; it is not necessary to resort to a hypothetical and misinterpreted inscription to explain this tradition. The apparent difficulty that being king of Bashan involves, "living in Ashtarot and Edrei", and to have the 'bed' in Rabbat Ammon could be due to a more general misunderstanding of Canaanite ideology in ancient Hebrew tradition. Og, maybe an Ammonite King, could be said "to 'sit' in Ashtarot and Edrei", once dead, *hayyôšēb bĕʿaštārôt ûbĕʾedreʿî* being a sacral mythological technical expression exactly corresponding, even morphosyntactically (participle), to Ug *yšb bʿštrt ... bhdrʿy*. It was treated afterwards as the record of a 'historical' fact: thus causing the whole story to be founded on Bashan and its conquest by the Israelites. On the other hand, starting from the same mythological royal ideology, the cult of a famous, already deified, king of Bashan, Og by name, could have been normal in Ammon. Even its identification with →Milcom, the traditional god of the Ammonites, presents no special difficulty, this name also being a transformation of *mlk(m)*, i.e. the eponym of the deified kings. Anyone of them could in principle be Milcom (DEL OLMO LETE, *SEL* 5 [1988] 52; VAN DER TOORN 1991:58; but cf. DIETRICH & LORETZ 1991:87-88). Furthermore, were the proposed etymology accepted (cf. *supra* I.), Og could be another of the substantivated divine titles that Canaanite kings bore (DEL OLMO LETE 1987:57-66): 'man' (*par excellence*). Such a use is amply testtified in the Northwest Semitic tradition (*ʾîš, amēlu, mt*) in relation mostly to military activity, the most striking case being *mt rpi*, applied to king Aqhat (MARGALIT 1989:300). The title would finally have turned into an eponymic divine name, like others. Either proposal is valid.

VAN DER TOORN (1992:93) suggests reading the name of the enigmatic deity Anammelek of the Sepahrvites in 2 Kgs 17:31 as *ʿgmlk* *Og-Melech underscoring the chtonic character of the deity Og.

IV. *Bibliography*

J. R. BARTLETT, Sihon and Og, Kings of the Amorites, *VT* 20 (1970) 257-277; M. DIETRICH & O. LORETZ, Zur Debatte über "Funerary Rituals and Beatific Afterlife in Ugaritic Texts and in the Bible", *UF* 23 (1991) 85-90; J. N. FORD, The "Living Rephaim" of Ugarit: Quick or Defunct?, *UF* 24 (1992) 73-101; B. MARGALIT, A Ugaritic Psalm (RS 24.252), *JBL* 89 (1970) 292-304;

A. R. MILLARD, King Og's Bed and Other Ancient Ironmongery, *Ascribe to the Lord. Biblical and other studies in memory of Peter C. Craigie* (ed. L. Eslinger & G. Taylor; JSOTSup 67; Sheffield 1988) 481-492; J. C. DE MOOR, Rāpi'ūma - Rephaim, *ZAW* 88 (1976) 324-345; G. DEL OLMO LETE, Los nombres 'divinos' de los reyes de Ugarit, *AulOr* 5 (1987) 39-66.; D. PARDEE, *Les textes para-mythologiques de la 24e campagne (1961)* (RSOu IV; Paris 1988); M. H. POPE, Notes on the Rephaim Texts from Ugarit, *Ancient Near East Studies in Memory of J. J. Finkelstein* (ed. M. de J. Ellis; Hamden 1977); W. RÖLLIG, Eine neue phönizische Inschrift aus Byblos, *NESE* 2 (1974) 1-15; K. VAN DER TOORN, Funerary Rituals and Beatific Afterlife in Ugaritic Texts and in the Bible, *BiOr* 48 (1991) 40-66; VAN DER TOORN, Anat-Yahu and the Jews of Elephantine, *Numen* 39 (1992) 80-101; R. DE VAUX, *Histoire ancienne d'Israël. Des origines à l'instalation en Canaan* (Paris 1971).

G. DEL OLMO LETE

OIL יצהר

I. The term *yiṣhar* describes the quality of oil as 'shining', and denotes oil freshly-pressed. This term for oil is used almost exclusively in OT in variations of the formula 'corn, new wine and oil' 22 times, sometimes within a longer list of commodities. The usage is always distinctive, falling into the following categories: i) as tithe, to be eaten by faithful at central shrine (Deut 12:17) or by priests alone (Num 18:12); ii) as sign of original blessings of election (Hos 2:8; Joel 1:10) or restoration (Hos 2:22; Joel 2:19 etc.); iii) as plunder by enemies (Deut 28:51).

The oil in these passages, the type of which is not usually identified with certainty, but is no doubt olive oil (see Zech 4:14 below), is not to be distinguished from the other commodities occurring in various lists. Together with them, it represents the essentially concrete form in which 'blessing' was conceptualised in Hebrew thought (cf. Deut 28:1-14). It may be seen that such reifications of divine pleasure could be seen as actual manifestations of divine activity, and therefore as minor gods. That is why ALBRIGHT asserted that *yisḥar* is "almost certainly the name of an old god of olive oil" (*Yahweh and the Gods of Canaan* [London 1968] 162).There is, however, no specific clue to this effect in the contexts.

II. The term for oil used in the cult was usually *šemen*, as in Exod 25:6, where it is used of the oil both for the Menorah and for ritual anointing purposes. But in Zech 4:14 the two pipes through which the Menorah oil pours, or the two olive trees to the left and the right of the Menorah (cf. overloaded text) are identified as 'sons of the oil' (*bĕnê yiṣhar*), 'anointed ones' (RSV, JB), 'consecrated ones' (REB). *yiṣhar* is thus established as having the same reference as *šemen*. The oil is here metaphorically the father of those who by virtue of anointing become the two →Messiahs (sc. anointed ones) to come. The two in question are Joshua the high priest and Zerubbabel, a royal descendant of Jehoiakin so far as Zechariah is concerned. The oil, as the fuel, is also of course a metonymy of the Menorah itself, which symbolised both the divine presence, and that of Yahweh's subordinate assistants in the temple. The king was one of these (BARKER 1987:224, 229-230) and the oil, used for anointing purposes, was therefore the medium that conferred the power and status (sc. quasi-divine rank) of kingship. There is however no clear indication of the deification of oil (either under this designation or as *šemen*) in biblical usage.

III. *Bibliography*

M. BARKER, *The Older Testament* (London 1987) 224-230; C. L. MEYER & E. M. MEYER, *Haggai, Zechariah 1-8* (AB 25b; New York 1987) 258-259; H. G. MITCHELL, J. M. P. SMITH & J. A. BEWER, *Haggai, Zechariah, Malachi and Jonah* (ICC; Edinburgh 1912) 164-166.

N. WYATT

OLDEN GODS

I. As a distinct category of deities, 'olden gods' manifest themselves in a variety of ways in the literature of ancient Near Eastern cultures. Their histories are recounted in theogonies where they take centre stage, and in cosmogonies, where younger gods fight against them in battles over succession. As a class, they are identified in Hittite literature by the technical term *karuileš šiuneš*, 'olden gods', in Akk translation as *ilānū ša dārūti* or *ilānū ša dārātim*, 'primeval gods', and in Egypt as *nṯr.w pꜣw.ty.w*, 'primeval gods'. Residual notions of the 'olden gods' have been found in the Bible.

II. 'Olden gods' are generally understood to have been active in the earliest, most chaotic times, generating various elemental deities through sexual (often incestuous) procreation. Thus, for instance, in Hesiod's *Theogony*, →Heaven (Ouranos) unites with his mother, →Earth (Gaia), who gives birth to such gods as Great →River (Oceanus), Law (→Themis) and Memory (Mnemosyne). Frequently, 'olden gods' are found in pairs consisting of male and female deities, often with rhyming or etymologically related names. Great variation exists among theogonies in the number of generations that separate the primordial order from the contemporary pantheon, as well as in the names of the gods. Nevertheless, a feature common to many is that the 'olden gods' are either killed or banished to the netherworld by a younger generation of deities. As a result, 'olden gods' were ordinarily understood as no longer serving a major role in the divine economy. With the exception of the funerary cult of the Egyptian Ogdoad, they were not normally chief deities in temples or cults. They did not often receive sacrifices or prayers. Though their realm was in the netherworld, 'olden gods' were not generally considered 'dead' in the sense of altogether ceasing to function in the cosmic order. Frequently they are attested alongside active gods in treaty texts where they are listed in pairs and invoked to serve as witnesses to the mutual oaths. To judge by their titles (WILHELM 1989:56), some Hurro-Hittite 'olden gods' may have served some function in taking oracles, interpreting dreams, and mediating judgment. In Hittite rituals, various 'olden gods' are occasionally called upon to judge and lure all adversity into the netherworld (ARCHI 1990:116).

Despite rich variation, much of the lore concerning 'olden gods' in the ancient Near East shares strikingly similar characteristics. Although precise lines of origin and transmission are impossible to draw, it is believed by many scholars that Greek, Phoenician, Hurro-Hittite, and Mesopotamian theogonies and cosmogonies concerning the 'olden gods' are related to some degree. The extent of their relationship has been vigorously debated for some time.

In his well-known *Theogony*, Hesiod recounts the history of the principal Greek gods whose lineage is traced back to Gaia (Earth). Gaia produces Ouranos (Sky) through generation rather than sexual union. After subsequently lying incestuously with Ouranos, Gaia produces eighteen children (including the →Titans). These offspring are kept penned-up by Ouranos within Gaia's bowels, apparently by continuing intercourse with her (WEST 1966:19). Feeling the strain within, Gaia groans in anguish and urges her children to take vengeance upon their father using an adamantine sickle. Kronos rises to the challenge and, when next Ouranos approaches Gaia with amorous intent, he cuts off his father's genitals and throws them into the →sea. In the process, blood from Ouranos' wound drips on Gaia impregnating her with various sub-divine beings. Floating in the sea, Ouranos' severed member forms a white foam from which →Aphrodite is born. Having apparently assumed the throne, Kronos has six children by Rhea and proceeds to act just as unjustly as his father. Afraid of a prediction that he would be overcome by one of his children, Kronos swallows each as they are born, giving Rhea no rest from grief. Upon the birth of →Zeus, however, Rhea conspires with Gaia and Ouranos to hide the child in the bowels of the earth. A rock wrapped in blankets is handed over to Kronos who, thinking it his son, swallows it. As predicted, Zeus eventually usurps the kingship from Kronos. Later Kronos vomits the children he had swallowed along with the rock which Zeus then places under the slopes of Parnassus to be a sign and wonder to humankind. Zeus also frees his uncles who had been bound by Ouranos. In gratitude, they give him thunder, lightning-bolt and flash which become his principle weapons.

The *Theogony* of Hesiod has long been thought to have influenced Philo's history of the gods. In his eight (Porphyry *abst.* 2.56) or nine (Eusebius, *Praep. evang.* I.9.23) books dedicated to the subject, Philo of Byblos (ca. 70-160 CE) claims to render an accurate translation of the *Phoenician History* of Sanchuniathon, who is said to have lived before the Trojan War. Fragments of Philo's work are preserved primarily by Eusebius in his *Praeparatio evangelica* in which he quotes Philo extensively. In one section of the *Phoenician History*, Philo gives an account of a certain Elioun, called 'Most High' (→*Hypsistos*) who, through his wife Berouth has a son, Epigeius, or Autochthon—later called Ouranos (Heaven) —and a daughter, Gē (Earth). Through an incestuous union between Ouranos and his sister Gē, four sons are born: →El (also called Kronos), Baithylos (→Baetyl), →Dagon (also called Siton) and Atlas. Ouranos also takes other wives, making Gē jealous in the process and causing their separation. This does not prevent Ouranos from raping Gē several times and attempting to destroy their children. In response to his father's frequently violent behaviour towards his mother, El-Kronos repels Ouranos using an iron sickle and spear and usurps the kingship. In the battle, a pregnant mistress of Ouranos is taken. She later gives birth to Zeus-Demarous. The subsequent rule of Kronos is more violent than that of his father who later rises up and makes war on him. In the thirty-second year of his reign, El-Kronos ambushes Ouranos and cuts off his genitals. As Ouranos breathes his last breath, his blood drips into springs and rivers. Later, →Astarte, Zeus-Demarous, and Adodos, king of the gods, reign with the consent of Kronos.

The possibility of Philo's work representing a Late Bronze/Early Iron Age source has long been open to question. Earlier scholarship tended to view it as strongly indebted to the *Theogony* of Hesiod. However, with the publication of Ugaritic and Hittite texts which in some instances parallel Philo over against Hesiod, this understanding underwent certain modification (L'HEUREUX 1979: 32-34; WEST 1966:24-28). While there is no longer significant doubt that Philo presented Phoenician traditions as he claimed, recent scholarship has tended to view Philo as constructing contemporary versions of Phoenician myths, influenced by Hesiod, and modified to fit his own Hellenistic-Roman perspective (BAUMGARTEN 1992:342-343).

Many scholars believe that the traditions represented by Philo and Hesiod share a common ancestry in older Hurro-Hittite and Mesopotamian lore transmitted through Phoenicia (see references in L'HEUREUX 1979:33). While the precise route of transmission is difficult to discern, their mutual relationship, at least in broad outlines, is much clearer. In Hurro-Hittite lore, the 'Song of Kumarbi' (*CTH* 344; also called 'Kingship in Heaven'; see translation in HOFFNER 1990:40-43) recounts the history of the gods. In the proem, the 'olden gods' (*karuileš šiuneš*) are addressed by name and exhorted to listen. Among those listed in the extant portions of the text are: Nara, Napsara, Minki, Ammunki, Ammezzadu, Enlil and Ninlil. In this song, Alalu exercises kingship in heaven during the early primeval years. After nine years of rule, however, his cup-bearer Anu—the "foremost of the gods"—rises up against Alalu, who then flees into the Dark Earth. In the ninth year of his reign, Anu's cup-bearer, Kumarbi—an offspring of Alalu—seizes the throne, driving Anu off to the sky. As Anu flees, however, Kumarbi bites off his genitals, causing Anu's 'manhood' to unite with Kumarbi's bowels. Before hiding himself in the heavens, Anu turns and admonishes Kumarbi to stop rejoicing, for his genitals have impregnated him with the Storm God (Tešub), the →Tigris River, and Tasmisu. In response, Kumarbi spits Anu's semen from his mouth which apparently becomes a source of further generation where it falls. Kumarbi then goes to the city of Nippur where he takes up his kingship. At one point, in an attempt to kill Tešub, Kumarbi eats a stone which does nothing but injure his teeth. Although there is a lacuna in the text after Tešub comes forth from Kumarbi's bowels, Tešub eventually supersedes Kumarbi as king in heaven, as is clear from a sequel to this song—the 'Song of Ullikummi' (*CTH* 345; see HOFFNER 1990:52-61). Here, Kumarbi plots vengeance against Tešub for supplanting him by having intercourse with an enormous rock. The rock gives birth to a stone child, named Ullikummi, who is hidden in the sea for fifteen days until he is large enough to reach into the heavens. After various failed attempts to do battle with Ullikummi, Ea speaks to the 'olden gods', asking them to "open again the old, fatherly, grandfatherly storehouses" and "bring forth the primeval copper cutting tool with which they cut apart heaven and earth." With it, says Ea, "We will cut off Ullikummi, the Basalt, under his feet, him whom Kumarbi raised against the gods as a supplanter (of Tešub)." This effort apparently succeeds.

Aside from their appearance in Hurro-Hittite mythological texts, the 'olden gods' also appear frequently in lists and ritual materials. In Hurro-Hittite texts (treaties and the magic of Kizzuwatna), certain 'olden gods' appear regularly, in more or less canonical order. This is particularly true in Hittite treaties. Falling under the command of Ereshkigal, goddess of the underworld, whom the Hittites called either 'Sun of the Earth' or 'Lelwani', these gods are related to the Sumerian Anunnaki (note the parallels in OTTEN 1961: text III.32-34; IV.46, 52, and nn. 258 and 262). In nearly every extant treaty text, twelve deities are listed (an exception is *CTH* 76 which lists only nine). Although there is minor variation in the twelve gods who appear in the texts, generally one finds two series of deities, six of which are of uncertain origin, six of which have Mesopotamian roots. Of uncertain origin are: Naras, Napsaras (or Namsaras), Minki, Ammunki, Tuhusi and Ammizadu. Those of Mesopotamian origin are: Alalu, Anu, Antu, Apantu, Enlil and Ninlil (CROSS 1976:331). After the 'olden gods', various pairs of elements from the natural order are frequently listed: Mountains and Rivers, →Springs and Great Sea, →Heaven and Earth, Winds and Clouds. Although their nature is less transparent, these elements call to mind the deified elements attested in Phoenician and Greek mythologies as well as those in Mesopotamia.

Two Mesopotamian texts are particularly relevant to the topic of 'olden gods'. These are the creation myth, *Enūma eliš* (English translation in *ANET*, 60-72), and the so-called Harab Myth (CT 46.43; English translation in *ANET*, 517-518; cf. translations and treatment in LAMBERT & WALCOT 1965; JACOBSEN 1984; MILLER 1985; L'HEUREUX 1979). The first twenty lines of *Enūma eliš* recount the primordial era beginning with the time when heaven and firm ground "had not been named." At that time, →Apsu and →Tiamat (i.e. Fresh Water and Salt Water) commingled producing →Lahmu and Lahamu (Note that these monsters are understood to exist beyond primordial time), and Anshar and Kishar (Sky Horizon and Earth Horizon). These latter gods brought forth Anu (Heaven) who begot Nudimmud (i.e. Ea, the earth- and water-god). After this brief history, *Enūma eliš* moves on to describe the conflict arising between Apsu and Tiamat and the succeeding generations of gods. These latter gods eventually overcame the former ones and their allies which led to the creation of the cosmos, the installation of →Marduk as king of the gods, and the founding of Babylon. In relation to the other ancient Near Eastern texts described above, *Enūma eliš* is quite different. However, general lines of similarity between the 'olden gods' in *Enūma eliš* and the other myths do exist. The cosmogonic character of the 'olden gods', their pairing, and their conflict over kingship all display points of contact with the other myths. A text bearing even greater similarities—especially to Hesiod's *Theogony*—is the so-called 'Harab Myth'.

The Harab myth is set within a linear or sequential movement beginning with Harab (?) ploughing Earth (Erṣetu). This results in the creation of →Sea and Sumuqan. Next, they build the city of Dunnu and Harab is established as its lord. Subsequently, Sumuqan kills his father, thereby taking over lordship, and unites incestuously with his mother, Earth. Sumuqan then takes his older sister, Sea, for a wife. However, Sumuqan's son, Gaiu, rises up and kills him, taking over the lordship and kingship. His mother, Sea, marries Sumuqan and kills her own mother, Earth. This cycle of incest and parricide continues for three more generations until Haharnum is simply imprisoned, not killed, by his son Haiašum (who, nevertheless, marries his own sister). There follows a series of lacunae. If JACOBSEN's interpretation of the remaining fragments is correct (1984), it would appear that the successive ruling generations lead down to Enlil, who peacefully hands over power to his son Ninurta by assent of the gods. This may reflect the perspective of the existing world order of the writer (JACOBSEN 1984 posits the period of Isin-Larsa).

Worthy of brief mention is the concept of 'olden gods' in Egypt and Ugarit. While there exist no theogonies in the extant Ugaritic texts, the god →Ilib may bear some resemblance to the olden gods of other cultures. In a Hurrian god-list found at Ras-Shamra, when compared with a Ugaritic god-list, the following correspondences can be observed: ilib = in atn, 'Ancestral Spirit' / il = il, El / dgn = kmrb, Dagan/Kumarbi / bʿl = tšb, →Baal/Tešub.

What is particularly interesting about this list is the similarity it bears to the 'olden gods' in the 'Song of Kumarbi' (Alalu, Anu, Kumarbi, Tešub) and Philo (Elioun, Ouranos, El-Kronos, Zeus-Demarous). If Ilib does, in fact, correspond in some way to Alalu, then Ilib may represent a primeval god who long ago ceased activity and dwells in the netherworld. As an Ancestral Spirit, the gods may have honoured him as humans honoured their deceased ancestors (VAN DER TOORN 1993 [1994]; XELLA 1983). It is possible that Ilib is the product of theological speculation, like Enmesharra ('Lord World Order') in Sumerian religion (SAGGS 1978:102). As such he may represent a number of forgotten 'olden gods' now dwelling in the netherworld.

Finally, we may note that the concept of 'olden gods' was not lost on Egyptian religion. The Ogdoad of Hermopolis, for instance, was comprised of four symmetrical, theogonic pairs of gods. Referred to as *nṯr.w pꜣw.ty.w*, 'primeval gods' these deities were ancestors of the creator god and regularly received funerary offerings. Their abstract names attest to their origins in theological speculation (CROSS 1976:332): 'Inertness' (Nun), 'Unbounded' (Huh), 'Primeval Darkness' (Kuk), 'Invisibility' (→Amun), 'Nothingness' (*Nyꜣ.w*).

III. In the Bible, various scholars have identified what they believe to be residual notions of 'olden gods' in various texts. While many of these identifications are highly dubious and speculative (viz. biblical →Japheth thought to be the equivalent of the Titan Iapetos in Hesiod; see WEST 1966: 202-203), two of these deserve special notice. The first is associated with Israel's understanding of the covenant lawsuit. As discussed above, 'olden gods' frequently occur in pairs in the ancient theogonies and often represent elements of the natural order. In texts of diverse origins in the ancient world, these pairs of deities are invoked to serve as witnesses to treaties and covenants. We find analogous petitions made in OT covenant lawsuit formulas used by the prophets. Isaiah (Isa 1:2) invokes the Heavens and the Earth to act as witnesses against Israel for breaking the covenant with →Yahweh. The prophet Micah makes a similar appeal (Mic 6:2; cf. Jer 2:12). While these elements were by no means considered divine by the prophets, their use in covenant lawsuit formulas indicates a common rhetorical form whose origins may be traced back to originally mythological conceptions. As has been recognized for a number of years, the creation account in Gen 1 takes the form of a theogonic history. The ancient gods, however, have been thoroughly 'demythologized', possibly with polemic intent against polytheistic notions of creation. Pairs such as →light and darkness, earth and sea, →day and →night, are no longer understood as ancient deities, but as mere creations within the natural order governed by →God. It has been suggested that the great Babylonian sea →dragon, →Tiamat, appears as a lifeless shadow of her former self in Gen 1, where darkness is said to have covered the face of the deep (Hebrew *tĕhōm* = Babylonian *Ti'āmat*; cf. Egyptian *Nūn*). CROSS (1976:335) has proposed identifying the "chaos and disorder" of Gen 1:2 (*tōhû wā-bōhû*) with Sanchuniathon's *Baau* and Hesiod's *Chaos* (both 'olden gods' appearing in sections other than those discussed above) and the divine wind soaring over the surface of the deep with the primordial wind found in Sanchuniathon and Anaximenes.

IV. *Bibliography*

R. ANTHES, Egyptian Theology in the Third Millennium B.C., *JNES* 18 (1959) 160-212; A. ARCHI, The Names of the Primeval Gods, *Or* 59 (1990) 114-129; A. I. BAUMGARTEN, Philo of Byblos, *ABD* 5 (New York 1992) 342-344; *F. M. CROSS, The 'Olden Gods' in Ancient Near Eastern Creation Myths, *Magnalia Dei, The Mighty Acts of God: Essays on the Bible and Archaeology in Memory of G. Ernest Wright* (ed. F. M. Cross, W. E. Lemke & P. D. Miller; Garden City 1976) 329-338; A. GOETZE, *Kulturgeschichte Kleinasiens* (München 1957); O. R. GURNEY, *Some Aspects of Hittite Religion* (Oxford 1977); H. G. GÜTERBOCK, Hittite Mythology, *Mythologies of the Ancient World* (ed. S. N. Kramer; Garden City 1961) 139-179; C. E. L'HEUREUX, *Rank Among the Canaanite Gods* (HSM 21; Missoula 1979); H. A. HOFFNER, Jr., *Hittite Myths* (SBLWAW 2; Atlanta 1990); T. JACOBSEN, *The Harab Myth* (SANE 2; Malibu 1984); W. G. LAMBERT & P. WALCOT, A New Babylonian Theogony and Hesiod, *Kadmos* 4 (1965) 64-72; E. LAROCHE, Les Dénominations des dieux 'antiques' dans les textes hittites, *Anatolian Studies Presented to Hans Gustav Güterbock on the Occasion of His 65th Birthday* (ed. K. Bittel, P. H. J. Houwink Ten Cate & E. Reiner; Istanbul 1974) 175-185; LAROCHE, Hurrian Borrowings from the Babylonian System, *Mythologies* (ed. Y. Bonnefoy & W. Doniger; Chicago 1991) 225-227; P. D. MILLER, Eridu, Dunnu, and Babel: A Study in Comparative Mythology, *HAR* 9 (1985) 227-251; H. VON OTTEN, Eine Beschwörung der Unterirdischen aus Boğazköy, *ZA* 54 (1961) 114-157; H. W. F. SAGGS, *The Encounter with the Divine in Mesopotamia and Israel* (London 1978); K. VAN DER TOORN, Ilib and the "God of the Father", *UF* 25 (1993 [1994]) 379-387; M. L. WEST, *Hesiod: Theogony* (Oxford 1966); G. WILHELM, *The Hurrians* (Warminster 1989) [& lit.]; P. XELLA, Aspekte religiöser Vorstellungen in Syrien nach den Ebla- und Ugarit-texten, *UF* 15 (1983) 279-290, esp. 286.

E. E. ELNES & P. D. MILLER

OLYMPUS Ὄλυμπος

I. Mount Olympus is the holy, mostly snow-capped mountain of the ancient Greeks, lying on the borders of Thessaly and Macedonia. It was considered the dwelling place of the third generation of the gods, who are for that reason called 'the Olympians'. The name occurs in 2 Macc 6:2 in 'Zeus Olympius', and in Rom 16:15 in the personal name Ὀλυμπᾶς, with the textual variants Ὀλυμπίδα (F,G), and 'Olympiadem' (Latin versions). All three are hypocoristics, respectively in -ᾶς (masculine) and -ίς, -ιάς (both feminine), formed on the basis of full names composed either with Ὀλυμπο- like Ὀλυμπογένης, or with Ὀλυμπιο- like Ὀλυμπιόδωρος, Ὀλυμπιοδώρα. Only in the former case would there be a connection with Mt. Olympus, while the second are properly speaking derivations of the epithet 'Olympius'. In the plural the latter could refer to all the gods together (e. g. *Iliad* 1,399), in the singular especially to →Zeus, even without mentioning his name (e. g. *Iliad* 18,79; Hesiod, *Op.* 474). What the full name of the person mentioned in Rom 16:15 was, is now untraceable. In the later tradition this Roman Christian was made one of the seventy apostles, his festal day being fixed on the 10th of November.

II. In Greece and Asia Minor there were in Antiquity some fifteen mountains that bore the name of 'Olympus' varying in hight from that of a hill to over 9500 ft. Since the name has no Indo-European etymology, it is most probably to be explained as a pre-Greek word that had the meaning 'mountain' or 'height' as such, and not as a specific characteristic because it was apparently applied to a variety of mountains. Apart from the famous one in Thessaly, there was an Olympus, for instance, in Crete, Lesbos, Cyprus, Mysia, Lycia, Galatia, and according to Strabo 8,3,31, also one in Elis which may have given its name to the town of Olympia. Only the Thessalian mountain had religious importance. Although Homer calls it 'snowy' on several occasions (e. g. *Iliad* 1,420), the actual abode of the gods there is pictured as free of snow, rain and wind, and always bathing in bright light (*Odyss.* 6,41-47). Together with the earth the Olympus belongs to that part of the kosmos that has not been allotted to either Zeus, →Poseidon or →Hades, being common to all gods (*Iliad* 15,193). The entrance to both Olympus and to →Heaven, the proper domain of Zeus, are the gates, which are opened and closed by the Horae or season-goddesses with a loud noise, but these gates are at the same time described as a thick cloud or mist (*Iliad* 5,749-751). The god Hephaestus is reported to have built there a palace for each of the gods (*Iliad* 1,607-608).

In the course of time 'Olympus' became more or less equivalent with 'Heaven' in the sense of 'Zeus' or 'the gods'. Both occur also in asseverations, "by the Olympus" in e.g. Sophocles, *Ant.* 758, and "by Heaven" in e. g. Aristophanes, *Plutus* 267.

In Greek mythology Olympus was also the name of several male persons, some of whom may have been mountain spirits in origin. The best known is the traditional Phrygian inventor of music and father of Marsyas the flautist. He is mentioned by Tatian (*Against the Greeks* 1,1) in order to demonstrate that the Greeks had hardly invented anything themselves.

III. Mt. Olympus is not mentioned in OT or NT. The 'mountain of meeting (or: assembly) far in the North', which figures in a prophecy of Isaiah directed against the king of Babel (14,13), is modelled upon Mt. →Zaphon, the traditional abode of the Canaanite gods, not on Mt. Olympus of the Greeks. Only the pseudepigraphical *Testament of Solomon,* a magical work dating from the (early?) Imperial period, refers to it. The seven evil female demons who pass before Solomon (cf. Matt 12:42-45), tell him that they live alternatively in Lydia, on Mt. Olympus, and on the High Mountain (8:4). In this Jewish context Mt. Olympus is the equivalent of 'Hell' rather than of 'Heaven'.

IV. *Bibliography*

E. OBERHUMMER & J. SCHMIDT, Olympus (1), *PW* XVIII (1939) 258-310 (mountain and religion); M. WEGNER, Olympus (26), *PW* XVIII (1939) 321-324 (persons).

G. MUSSIES

ONE אחד

I. In Deut 6:4 it is asserted that "the LORD is our (i.e. the Israelites') God, the LORD is One (*'eḥād*)". Though the epithet can also mean 'first', it is usually understood to mean '(only) one'. In both Akkadian and Ugaritic texts, the equivalent epithet (Akk *ištēn*, Ug *aḥd*) can be used in connection with gods. It has sometimes been assumed that Heb אחד in Isa 66:17 conceals the name of a foreign god or goddess (STENHOUSE 1913:298).

II. The use of 'One' as a divine name or epithet of God is not confined to the Bible. In ancient Mesopotamia, both humans and gods may be called *ištēn*, 'unique, outstanding', literally 'one' or 'first' (*CAD* I/J [1960] 278). An example may be taken from an Old Assyrian letter in which a human being is flattered in the following terms: *ištēn atta ilī tukultī u bāštī*, "you are unique, my god, my trust and my glory" (J. LEWY, *KTS* no. 15:41-42). The epithet is also applied to Lamashtu and to →Ishtar. Note also that Anu, the primordial sky-god, is designated by the sign for 'one'. Yet, though referred to as *ilu rēštû* "first, foremost deity", he is never designated *ištēn*, 'One'. The Akkadian terminology is foreshadowed, so to speak, in the Sumerian. Thus Enlil, one of the major Mesopotamian deities, is once referred to in a Sumerian hymn as "the only king" (**lugal diš-àm**).

In the Ugaritic Baal Epic, →Baal says "I alone (*aḥdy*) am the one who can be king over the gods" (*CTA* 4.vii:49-50 = *KTU* 1.4. vii:49-50). This phrase "implies a definite pretension to be the Only One on whom all other deities are dependent" (J. C. DE MOOR, *The Rise of Yahwism* [Leuven 1990] 77). In Egyptian texts, the designation "One" is applied to Atum, →Re, →Amun, →Ptah, Aton, →Thoth, Geb, →Horus, Haroëris, Khnum, →Khonsu, and →Isis.

III. The epithet *ʾeḥād* in Deut 6:4, one of the key texts of the Hebrew Bible, is usually interpreted as 'one' or 'the only one'. It could either mean that the LORD is the only God the Israelites are to worship, or that there is only one Yahweh. The latter interpretation is the more plausible one, in view of the mono-Yahwistic tendency of Deuteronomy. In Mal 2:10 the rhetorical question, "Has not one God (Heb *ʾēl ʾeḥād*) created us?" takes it for granted that Israel's God is the creator of all humankind. The same idea is taken for granted also in Job's rhetorical question in Job 31:15: "Did not he that made me in the womb, make him (i.e., my manservant or my maidservant)? and did not One (Heb. *ʾeḥād*) fashion us in the womb?" God appears to be referred to as *ʾeḥād* 'One' also in Eccl 12:11, which asserts that "the sayings of the wise ... were given by One →Shepherd".

Zechariah, the penultimate Hebrew prophet, tells us that in the time to come "the LORD shall be king over all the earth; in that day the LORD will be 'One', and His Name will be 'One'" (Zech 14:9). This verse is often taken to mean that in the time to come peoples of diverse nations who had already perceived and worshipped the LORD under a variety of names (cf. Mal 1:11; Acts 17:23) will recognize God by His true Name 'Yahweh'. GORDON (1970), however, argues that the true meaning of Zech 14:9 is not that God will have only one name but that in the *eschaton* the official name of God will be *ʾeḥād* 'One'. Notwithstanding the possible use in antiquity of this numeral to designate other deities, such an official Name of God would, according to this exegesis, remind people that there is only one Yahweh and that He alone is to be worshipped as God.

The assumption that the term אחד conceals a non-Israelite divine name in Isa 66:17 (STENHOUSE 1913:298) is no longer adopted by modern scholars.

IV. The hope for a universal veneration of Yahweh is expressed in the Jewish liturgy in the daily prayer (*Aleynu*) for a speedy end to the worship of other deities and the fulfilment of the prophecy of Zech 14:9. Gordon's interpretation of Zech 14:9 (for which see above) is foreshadowed in the Jewish liturgy for Sabbath Afternoon. There it is stated, "You are One and Your Name is One, and Who is like Your people Israel, One Nation in the World?" Here are juxtaposed the interpretation of Zech 14:9 as meaning "God's name is *ʾeḥād* 'One'" and the understanding of 2 Sam 7:23 (=1 Chr 17:21) as a mirror image of Zech 14:9. The understanding of these respective assertions concerning God and Israel as mirror images is reflected also in the Rabbinic tradition according to which just as Jews wear *tefillin* in which are inscribed "Hear, O Israel: the LORD is our God, the LORD is 'One'", so are there heavenly *tefillin* in which are inscribed, "Who is like Your people Israel, One Nation upon earth?" Rabbinic exegesis sees in Gen 1:8, which refers to the first of the days of Creation as *yôm 'eḥād*, literally "day of One", a reference to God, who had not yet created the ministering angels.

Because Jews have long perceived *'eḥād* as a Name of God, the number thirteen, the sum of the numerical values of the letters of this name, is commonly regarded by Jews as especially auspicious.

V. *Bibliography*

E. B. BOROWITZ (ed.), *Ehad: The Many Meanings of God is One* (New York 1988); C. H. GORDON, His Name is 'One', *JNES* 29 (1970) 198-199; F. PERLES, Was bedeutet יהוה אחד? *OLZ* 2 (1899) 517-518; N. LOHFINK & J. BERGMAN, אחד, *TWAT*, vol. 1 (1970-73) 210-218; T. STENHOUSE, Baal and Belial, *ZAW* 33 (1913) 295-305.

M. I. GRUBER

OPHANNIM → ANGELS

ORION כסיל

I. The Heb word כסיל, vocalized *kĕsîl*, is the name of a →constellation or individual →star mentioned three times in the OT (Amos 5:8; Job 9:9; 38:31), in each instance in connection with *kîmâ* (→Pleiades), and once in a plural form at Isa 13:10. It is usually identified with Orion, though the evidence of the ancient versions and later sources is ambiguous. The plural should be understood in a general sense as 'constellations'. As a common noun, *kĕsîl* has the sense 'fool', 'stupid fellow'.

A widespread view holds that the mention of *kĕsîl* at Job 38:31 contains a reference to some lost legend of a →giant or primeval →hero who, having rebelled against God, was subdued, bound, and placed in the sky. TUR-SINAI (1967) goes even further and understands all appearances of *kĕsîl* and *kîmâ* in the OT as mythological (rather than purely astronomical) references. Others have seen in the use of these words in Amos 5:8 a veiled polemic against astral worship.

II. The ancient versions are not consistent in their translations of *kĕsîl*. In Amos 5:8 the LXX does not recognize the names of astronomical bodies; Symmachus translates *astra*, 'stars'; Theodotion renders 'Hesperus' (the evening star); and Aquila and the Vg translate 'Orion'. In Job 9:9 the LXX translates 'Hesperus', while the Vg translates 'Orion'; in Job 38:31, on the other hand, the LXX translates 'Orion', but the Vg translates 'Arcturus'. In Isa 13:10 the LXX translates 'Orion'; Aquila and Theodotion transliterate; and the Vg gives *splendor earum*, 'their brilliance'. The Targum translates Amos 5:8 by the cognate *ksyl'* and renders *kĕsîl* by *npl'* (11QTgJob 38:31 *npyl'*), 'giant', in the passages in Job and *kĕsîlêhem* by *npylyhwn* in Isa 13:10. The Peshitta translates *'ywt'* (a star or constellation of uncertain identity, either Aldebaran or Capella or, perhaps, Leo) in Amos 5:8; *gbr'*, 'giant', 'hero', in Job 9:9 and 38:31; and 'their hosts' in Isa 13:10.

Several medieval Jewish scholars (Saadya, Ibn Janâḥ, Ibn Bal'am, and Bar Ḥiyya) identify *kĕsîl* with Canopus (*al-suhayl*), the second brightest star (after Sirius) in the sky; Ibn Ezra, on the other hand, takes it to be Antares ('the heart of Scorpio'). However, with the exception of DALMAN (who accepts the equation *kĕsîl = al suhayl* but takes the latter to be Sirius, DALMAN 1928), modern opinion is virtually unanimous in identifying *kĕsîl* with Orion.

Orion and the Pleiades are mentioned together in a number of Mesopotamian texts (*ŠL* IV/2 nos. 279 IV B12, 348 III B4; *CAD* Z, s.v. *zappu*), as well as in Homer (*Iliad* 18:486-489; *Odyssey* 5:272-274) and Hesiod (*Works and Days* 615, 619). In Mesopotamian religion, stars are considered either gods or symbols of gods (→constellations, →God, →Stars). GASTER (1961) has claimed a connection between the Ugaritic story of Aqhat and the myth of Orion, arguing that both are seasonal myths of the 'disappearing god' type, tied to astral phenomena. Despite the impressive amount of comparative material he adduces from Mesopotamia, Egypt, Greece, and elsewhere, his attempt at a synthesis of the data remains, at best, highly conjectural.

III. A plausible case can be made for the view that the Hebrews saw in *kĕsîl* a constellation representing a giant or hero. The translation of *kěsîl* in the Tg and Peshitta by words (*nĕpīlā', gabbārā*) having these meanings (cf. Gen 6:4, where the *nĕpīlîm* are explicitly called 'primeval heroes') as well as the Akkadian name of the constellation, *šitaddalu*, 'the broad man, giant' (*ŠL* IV/2 nos. 348 I, 393), point in this direction. So, too, the Arabic name for Orion is *al-jabbâr*, 'the giant', though this apparently reflects Greek influence (HESS 1932:97). In Greek mythology, Orion was seen as a figure of gigantic stature (*Odyssey* 11:309-310, 572). For traditions identifying Orion with →Nimrod see K. PREISENDANZ, PW 17 [1936] 625.

The claim that behind the reference to *kěsîl* at Job 38:31 lurks some ancient myth of "a giant who, confiding foolishly in his strength, and defying the →Almighty, was, as a punishment for his arrogance, bound for ever in the sky" (DRIVER & GRAY 1921:86) is less secure. This claim is based in part on etymological considerations. Thus it is argued (DHORME 1967:132; GASTER 1961: 32, 328) that the Hebrew root KSL, 'to be thick, stout', develops the sense of 'to be coarse, clumsy', leading to such meanings for *kěsîl* as 'impious rogue' on the one hand and 'oaf', 'gawk' on the other; development of the same root in a different direction leads to *kesel, kislâ*, 'confidence', whence 'foolish confidence'. However, the only meaning for the common noun *kěsîl* actually attested in the OT is 'fool', 'stupid one', the sense of 'impious', 'rogue' being reserved for such partial synonyms as *nābāl* and *lēṣ* (Prov 1:22; 17:21; 19:29). The notion of the 'binding' of *kěsîl* is founded largely on the translation "Canst thou ... loose the bands of Orion?" (KJV) of Job 38:31. Unfortunately, the word *mōšěkôt* translated 'bands' (or 'bonds'), is a hapax legomenon, whose exact nuance remains elusive; and equally acceptable translations (JPSV: "Can you ... undo the reins of Orion?" NEB: "Can you ... loose Orion's belt?") avoid any reference to bonds or fetters. On balance, the judgement (DRIVER & GRAY 1921:334) that "with the ambiguity of the nouns ... and our imperfect knowledge of the Hebrew mythology or stories of the constellations, it is impossible to get beyond very uncertain conjectures as to the exact meaning or the exact nature of any of the myths which may be alluded to" remains as valid today as when it was first stated.

The Talmud (*b. Ber.* 58b) records a tradition that should a comet pass through *kislā'*, the world would be destroyed. It also connects *kěsîl* with heat (and *kîmâ* with cold): "Were it not for the heat of *kěsîl*, the world could not endure the cold of *kîmâ*; were it not for the cold of *kîmâ*, the world could not endure the heat of *kěsîl*."

IV. *Bibliography*

G. DALMAN, *Arbeit und Sitte in Palästina* I (Gütersloh 1928) 39, 485-501; E. DHORME, *A Commentary on the Book of Job* (Nashville 1967); G. R. DRIVER, Two Astronomical Passages in the Old Testament, *JTS* N.S. 7 (1956) 1-11; S. R. DRIVER & G. B. GRAY, *The Book of Job* (ICC; Edinburgh 1921); T. H. GASTER, *Thespis* (New York 1961²) 320-329; J. J. HESS, Die Sternbilder in Hiob 9_9 und 38_{31} f., *Festschrift Georg Jacob* (ed. T. Menzel; Leipzig 1932) 94-99; S. MOWINCKEL, *Die Sternnamen im Alten Testament* (Oslo 1928) = *NorTT* 29 (1928) 5-75, esp. 36-45; G. SCHIAPARELLI, *Astronomy in the Old Testament* (Oxford 1905) 60-61; N. H. TUR-SINAI, *The Book of Job* (Jerusalem 1967) 159-161, 531.

L. ZALCMAN

OSIRIS *אסיר

I. Osiris is a prominent Egyptian god. P. DE LAGARDE (*Symmicta* [Göttingen 1877] 105) proposed to replace *'assîr*, 'prisoner', in Isa 10:4 by *'ōsîr*. He thus obtained a reading similar to the Phoenician and Aramaic renderings of the name of the Egyptian god Osiris. Another reflection of the cult of Osiris might be found in the personal name אסיר, if indeed it stands for Osiris (Exod 6:24; 1 Chr 6:7.8.22; NOTH, *IPN* 63 n. 2).

II. Osiris' anthropomorphic body is always represented wrapped up like a mummy or a statue (except for the head). As a statue, he is usually depicted wearing a specific crown, a crook and a 'whip'. These attributes symbolize his kingship, first on earth and later on in the realm of the dead. The meaning of the deity's name, Usir, is uncertain; Osiris is the Greek rendering. "Foremost of the Westerners (= the deceased)" is prominent among his epithets. It was the name of the god of Abydos in Upper Egypt originally. Osiris' cult spread from Busiris in the Delta to the South during the Old Kingdom. Abydos became his main cult centre, and he took over his local predecessor's designation. Myths inform us that the earthly sovereign was murdered by his brother and rival →Seth. The latter disposed of his victim by means of the river →Nile. But →Isis, the widow and sister, went in search of the body and recovered it. Her husband fathered →Horus on her posthumously, and was brought back to (complete) life. Later on Horus saw justice done to Osiris, who became ruler of the →dead and was succeeded by his son on the throne of Egypt.

The god's kingly character is very ancient. His connections with natural phenomena, however, are in all probability not more recent. He is identified with various forms of vegetation (trees and corn), with the field, with the overflowing of the Nile, and with the →moon. These various aspects have the idea of rebirth in common. Dying and revival were reenacted in rites and mystery-plays. In an old dramatic performance, threshing barley meant killing Osiris, and sowing the fields at the ceremony of "hacking the earth" stood for his burial. Beds showing the god's contours were planted with corn seeds; the sprouting realized his resurrection. Greeks and Romans witnessed the pouring of water by priests (interpreted as the "finding of Osiris" recorded in the myth), and their modelling of a crescent-shaped image. Both practices were designed to grant the god new life.

Other rites are not particularly concerned with vegetation. In the mysteries at Abydos mock fights took place. Osiris was slain by Seth and his followers, mourned and carried to his tomb. But the defeat of his attackers and his own resuscitation and triumph followed. Litanies came into vogue too. Priestesses impersonating Isis and her sister Nephthys had a momentous role in the songs, lamentations, and hour-watches. All of them should bring about the continuation of the god's existence.

Osiris' vicissitudes were essential to the welfare of the individual Egyptians. They hoped to return to life as he had done, and to get a verdict in the judgement of the dead at which the god presided. Having been declared "true of voice" (like Osiris in his conflict with Seth), their prospects in the hereafter were excellent. It was their ideal to be like him, even to be him. Identification with the god became a royal privilege in the course of the Old Kingdom. After that, the names of deceased private persons began to be preceded in the same way by "Osiris".

The dead had not only Osiris as their prototype. →Re, the sun going down and rising again, was also a great example worth following for everybody wishing to continue his life. Efforts to bring together the two otherwise quite dissimilar deities started in the Old Kingdom. The culmination point was reached with the tendency to syncretize them. Another—late—fusion was that of Osiris and the sacred bull →Apis: Osorapis. Ptolemy I introduced the general worship of this god, called now Sarapis. Isis was made his wife, and both reached an immense popularity throughout the Greek and Roman empires.

III. According to the emendation by DE LAGARDE (*Symmicta* [Göttingen 1877] 105), accepted by way of a proposal in the apparatus criticus of the *BHS*, Isa 10:4 should be rendered "Belti is writhing, Osiris is in panic" (*Bēltî kōraʿat ḥat ʾŌsîr*; DE LAGARDE translated "Belthis is sinking, Osiris has been broken"). Though none of the versions supports the emendation, it is not impossible orthographically. Yet it does not fit the context well (as already shown by K. BUDDE, Zu Jesaja 1-5, *ZAW* 50 [1932] 38-72, esp. 69-70). Assuming that v 4 takes up the rhetorical question of v 3 ("To whom will you flee for help, and where will you leave your wealth?"), Belti and Osiris either are or stand for the powers from which help is expected. Since the pairing of these deities is unusual, also if Belti should stand for →Hathor, and there is hardly a trace of their cult elsewhere in the Hebrew Bible, a literal interpretation of the emended verse is not really possible. To say that the hypothetical Belti stands here for →Isis is at odds with the identifications current at the time (*pace* e.g. K. MARTI, *Das Buch Jesaja* [Tübingen 1900] 100; B. DUHM, *Das Buch Jesaja* [Göttingen 1968, 5th ed.] 97). A symbolical interpretation cannot be ruled out, however: Belti could stand for Assyria, and Osiris for Egypt. Yet this interpretation also, though possible, is unlikely: the customary symbols for Assyria and Egypt would be →Assur and →Rahab, respectively. The reading of the MT as it stands makes better sense: "(they have no option) but to crouch among the prisoners of war, or fall among the slain". The parallel use of *taḥat* is a serious argument not to split the first תחת into ת and חת. DE LAGARDE's proposal, then, is on the whole more ingenious than convincing (for a fuller discussion see H. WILDBERGER, *Jesaja*, Vol. 1 [BKAT X/1; Neukirchen-Vluyn 1972] 179-180).

The possible reference to fertility gardens (so-called 'beds' of →Adonis) in Isa 17:10-11 can only indirectly be connected with Osiris.

IV. *Bibliography*

H. BONNET, Osiris, *RÄRG* 568-576, cf. entries p. 567-568, 576-577; J. ČERNÝ, *Ancient Egyptian Religion* (London 1952) 157; J. G. GRIFFITHS, *The Origins of Osiris and his Cult* (Leiden 1980); GRIFFITHS, Osiris, *LdÄ* IV (1981) 623-633; E. HORNUNG, *Der Eine und die Vielen* (Darmstadt 1971) 277.

M. HEERMA VAN VOSS

OURANOS → HEAVEN; VARUNA

P

PAHAD LAYLAH → TERROR OF THE NIGHT

PANTOKRATOR → ALMIGHTY

PATROKLOS Πάτροκλος

I. The name of Patroklos, the close companion of Achilles in the Trojan War, is given to the father of Nikanor, the high-ranking Greek commander of a force of 20,000 men with instructions to put down the revolt of Judas Maccabaeus (2 Macc 8:12).

II. From the perspective of Trojan War mythology, Patroklos would appear to be a figure developed by Homer in his *Iliad* to anticipate the death of Achilles' close friend Antilochos and Achilles' own death—a later part of the story of Troy which Homer does not himself tell. If this is so, it would explain the lack of mythological depth surrounding Patroklos himself, whether he was invented by Homer (VON SCHELIHA 1943: 391 [& lit]; SCHADEWALDT 1944:178-81), or simply brought from obscurity to play a fuller role (KULLMANN 1960:44-45.193-194)—his slaughter of the Paionian leader Pyraichmes could be a traditional combat for a real Thessalian →hero (*Iliad* 16:287, cf. ROBERT 1920:83).

Patroklos was brought when still a child to the house of Achilles' father Peleus by his own father Menoitios: he had accidentally killed a playmate—or so his ghost tells Achilles (*Iliad* 23:85-8). Patroklos and Achilles, raised together by Peleus, are inseparable friends in the *Iliad* and become, through the influence of this poem, a byword for friendship—even if Greeks themselves were uncertain whether to detect a sexual element (DOWDEN 1992:157). Indeed the plot of the *Iliad* shows an Achilles who, alienated by the Greek leader Agamemnon, can only be motivated to return to the fight against the Trojans by the bitter emotional need to avenge the death of the friend that had taken his place.

III. The name Patroklos (variant Patrokles) is a perfectly good Greek name, irrespective of its heroic associations: he who perpetuates the 'fame' (κλέος) of his 'fathers' (πατέρες). "So lässt sich nicht beweisen, dass die Πατροκλῆς und Πάτροκλος guter Zeit nur in Hinblick auf den Freund Achills benannt seien" (FICHT-BECHTEL 1894:307). It is, however, not common: Patroklos is absent from FRASER & MATTHEWS, and PAPE-BENSELER list only one instance (in addition to an elephant so named); Patrokles is modestly popular, though not many are attested after the second century BCE.

IV. *Bibliography*

K. DOWDEN, *The Uses of Greek Mythology* (London 1992); A. FICK & F. BECHTEL, *Die Griechischen Personennamen nach ihrer Bildung erklärt und systematisch geordnet* (2nd ed.; Göttingen 1894); P. M. FRASER & E. MATTHEWS (eds.), *A Lexicon of Greek Personal Names*, vol. I: The Aegean Islands, Cyprus, Cyrenaica (Oxford 1987); W. KULLMANN, *Die Quellen der Ilias* (Hermes Einzelschrift 14; Wiesbaden 1960); W. PAPE, revised by G.E. BENSELER, *Wörterbuch der griechischen Eigennamen* (Braunschweig 1884); C. ROBERT, *Die griechische Heldensage* (4th ed.; Berlin 1920); W. SCHADEWALDT, *Von Homers Welt und Werk* (2nd ed.; Stuttgart 1951); R. VON SCHELIHA, *Patroklos* (Basel 1943).

K. DOWDEN

PEOPLE → AM

PERSEUS Περσεύς

I. Perseus, the name of the slayer of the

Gorgon Medousa and the rescuer of Andromeda, is also the name of the elder son and heir of Philip V of Macedon (ruled 179-168 BCE). His defeat by the Romans at Pydna, which ended the Third Macedonian War (171-68 BCE), is referred to at 1 Macc 8:5 ("Perseus king of the Kittieis").

II. The more memorable stories of Perseus are woven into a single narrative of birth by →Zeus to Danaë (despite her imprisonment), of being cast adrift in a chest (λάρναξ) with his mother, of conflict at adolescence with a hostile king (Akrisios), of the gaining of the flying horse Pegasos and of overpowering the three hags (*Graiai*) to obtain directions, of slaying the Gorgon Medousa with the help of →Athena, of wreaking vengeance on his enemies, defeating a sea-monster, and winning as his bride Andromeda. Special equipment, too, characterises his story—not just the horse, but the scimitar (ἅρπη), wallet (κίβισις), winged sandals and a Greek Tarnhelm ("Αϊδος κυνῆ). This tale has an international flavour: Danaë starts in Argos, the chest lands in Seriphos, scenes with the Graiai and Medousa play in the distant West, and Andromeda in the Near East (see below). Another feat, however, is closer to home: he chases →Dionysos into the swamp of Lerna (killing him, for it was an entrance to the Underworld) and Pausanias (2, 20, 4) knew the tomb of Choreia ('Dance'), one of many maenads killed by Perseus, in the agora at Argos. But Mycenae appears to be his real home: legend has him take on the kingship of Tiryns and Mycenae in lieu of Argos; the name 'Mycenae' is allegedly derived from his scabbard (μύκης) and his only significant cult-site, other than at Seriphos and, oddly, Athens (Pausanias 2, 18, 1), was near Mycenae—as well as a spring Persea which may now have been found (JAMESON 1990: 213-5).

The Perseus mythology has proved both attractive and susceptible of greatly varying approaches. It can be seen as a part of Greek mythology especially close to folktale (cf. KIRK 1970:41; 1974:149), or as a sequence of Freudian codes concerning the boy, his absent father, present mother, impotence and sexuality (SLATER 1968:31-32.313). The slaying of the Gorgon was once viewed as an obvious nature myth (with Medousa as Mother Earth and Pegasos the primal horse, ROBERT 1920:222-227) but recently attention has switched to masked dances and initiation of boys into puberty (JAMESON 1990). There does, however, seem to be some possibility of bringing together a psycho-sexual interpretation with one focussing on the rituals marking the progress of boys towards adulthood.

The story of Perseus is particularly connected with the Near East (BURKERT 1984: 82-83; FONTENROSE 1959). His rescue of Andromeda takes place in "Aithiopia" (Apollodoros 2, 4, 3), or more specifically at Joppa (Jaffa), and his name, coincidentally similar to that of the 'Persians', is made to account for them: Perses, son of Perseus and Andromeda, is the eponymous ancestor of the Persian kings (Herodotos 7, 61, 3. 150, 2; Apollodoros 2, 4, 5).

III. Perseus (or its variant Perses) is not a common Greek name, though the name is borne by (1) a painter of the school of Apelles around 300 BCE; (2) a 2nd century BCE mathematician (both: PW s.v.); and (3) more relevantly, a Macedonian general active in 211 BCE (WALBANK 1940:86)—around the time the king was born. The choice by Philip V of this name for his first son may be significant, like the naming of a town Perseis in his honour in 183 BCE (Livy 39, 53, 16). The name has a heroic ring to it (πέρθω, 'sack' cities, like Odysseus πτολίπορθος), but in the context of the Macedonian ruling dynasty is more likely to recall Alexander's almost mythic defeat of the Persians, which made him a world-ruler in the imagination of posterity. The name 'Perseus' achieves this through the mythology, which asserts by genealogy Greek primacy over the Persian race—in the words which Herodotos (7, 150, 2) attributes to Xerxes, "In this way we would then be your offspring". "In short, Perseus became the hero of integration between East and West" and even, as a result, appeared on the coins of various cities of Asia Minor in the wake of Alexander's conquest (LANE FOX 1973: 201).

IV. *Bibliography*

W. BURKERT, *Die orientalisierende Epoche in der griechischen Religion und Literatur* (Heidelberg 1984) 82-84; K. DOWDEN, *The Uses of Greek Mythology* (London 1992) 142-144; J. FONTENROSE, *Python: A Study of Delphic Myth and its Origins* (Berkeley, Los Angeles & London 1959) ch. xi; M. H. JAMESON, Perseus, the Hero of Mykenai, *Celebrations of Death and Divinity in the Bronze Age Argolid* (ed. R. Hägg & G. C. Nordquist; Stockholm 1990) 213-222 [& lit]; G. S. KIRK, *Myth, Its Meanings and Functions in Ancient and Other Cultures* (Cambridge 1970); KIRK, *The Nature of Greek Myths* (Harmondsworth 1974); R. LANE FOX, *Alexander the Great* (London 1973) 200-201; C. ROBERT, *Die griechische Heldensage* (4th ed.; Berlin 1920); F. W. WALBANK, *Philip V of Macedon* (Cambridge 1940); P. E. SLATER, *The Glory of Hera: Greek Mythology and the Greek Family* (Boston 1968).

K. DOWDEN

PHOEBUS → APOLLO

PHOENIX Φοῖνιξ חול

I. The phoenix is a Greek mythical bird which under this name is not found in the Greek Bible (the name of the city Phoenix, Acts 27:12, has nothing to do with this bird; it may derive from a grove of date palms, *phoenices* [BILLIGMEIER 1977:2-3]), but according to early rabbis and several modern scholars it is referred to in the MT of Job 29:18 under the name *ḥôl*.

II. The origin and early development of the classical Phoenix myth is almost completely unknown. Most probably, its origin lies in the widespread oriental idea of the bird of the sun (→Shemesh, →Helios), which seems to have entered the Greek world from Phoenicia. In Linear B texts the word *po-ni-ke*, φοῖνιξ, seems to have indicated the griffin; it most probably means 'the Phoenician bird' (this derivation seems far more likely than that from the Eg *benu*, 'heron', supposedly pronounced as *boin* or *boine*) The homonymy of the phoenix' name and the word for palm (Gk *phoinix*, Lat *phoenix*), led several Latin authors to assume a relationship between bird and tree (Lactantius, *De ave phoen.*, 69-70; Isidore of Sevilla, *Etymol.*, XVII.7:1). Tertullian, *De resurr. mort.*, XIII:3, read in Ps 91:13 [LXX]: "The righteous shall flourish like the phoenix" (also in Pseudo-Ambrose, *De trin.*, 34 [PL 17, 545A]; *On the Origin of the World, NHC* II 122:28-29; *Byzantine Physiologus*, 10).

In Greek literature, the phoenix first occurs in Hesiod, frg. 304 (Merkelbach-West = Plutarch, *De def. orac.* 11 [415c]), who puts its lifespan at 972 generations. Later reports on the phoenix' age vary considerably, though the opinion that it lived 500 years was most widely accepted, as was already observed by Tacitus, *Ann.* VI:28. From the beginning the phoenix myth implied the bird's long life, renewing itself according to a fixed cycle (which made it a popular symbol of the beginning of a new era), and its close association with the sun. The various stories on the phoenix, as we know them from Greek and Latin authors, must have developed on Greek soil; there is no evidence of similar traditions in the Egyptian or Semitic world.

With only a few exceptions, the many references to the phoenix in Classical and early Christian literature can be reduced to one of two main versions. According to the less common version, the phoenix dies on its nest of aromatic herbs, and decomposes; from its decaying body the new phoenix is generated, usually starting as a worm. The young bird carries the remains of its predecessor to Heliopolis in Egypt and puts them on the altar of the sun. The first author to tell this story of the phoenix' rejuvenation is Manilius (1st cent. CE; in Pliny, *Hist. Nat.* X:4), who, however, locates the altar of the sun in Panchaia, not in Heliopolis. This version of the rebirth of the phoenix might already have been presupposed by Herodotus (*Hist.* II:73), who only speaks of the bird's external appearance, the flight to Egypt and the events that happened there. According to the other, more widespread version, the old phoenix burns itself on its nest of aromatic herbs, which event is often said to take place on the altar of the sun at Heliopolis; from its ashes the new phoenix arises. This version is first mentioned by Latin authors of the 1st cent. CE, without any doubt by Martial, *Epigram.* V.7:1-4, and Statius, *Silvae*, II.4:33-37; III.2:114. Their short references to the bird's cremation prove that this version was already so generally known that an allusion to it could suffice. We may assume that both main versions had been in existence long before their first attestation in the 1st cent. CE, but there is no evidence to prove that with any certainty. It is this state of affairs which gives the exegesis of Job 29:18 a broader interest than the correct explanation of this biblical text only; if the phoenix is really mentioned there it would be the first text to attest the bird's cremation.

III. Job 29:18 literally reads: "I shall die with my nest (*qinnî*) and I shall multiply my days like the *ḥôl*". Wherever the word *ḥôl* occurs in the OT it means 'sand'. Used as an image, it indicates a large quantity and so it seems appropriate to suggest here the idea of a long life: "I shall multiply my days like sand". It was taken in this sense by the *Targum on Job* and the Syriac version and by several modern commentators. On the basis of the reading of the LXX (*hōsper stelechos phoinikos*) and Vg *(sicut palma)*, other scholars emendated *kaḥôl* into *kannaḥal* "like the palm tree" (see DE WILDE 1981: 289-291). Taken in itself, the second part of the verse does not seem to contain any reference to a bird whatsoever. As a matter of fact, the only word which suggests that Job 29:18 might deal with a bird is the word *qēn*, 'nest' in the first part of the verse. The *parallelismus membrorum* suggests that both parts of the text express the expectation of a long life. However, this idea is not immediately visible in the first part of the verse. The words "die with my nest" evoke the idea of a bird that perishes together with its nest, but they do not say anything about a long life. Therefore, several commentators interpreted the word 'nest' as meaning 'children, posterity' (cf. Deut 32:11; Isa 16: 2): "I shall die with my children" would then express the expectation of a long life. Other scholars, led by the reading of the LXX (*hē hēlikia mou gērasei*), emendated *qny*, 'my nest' into *zqny*, 'my old age'.

However, some commentators of Job 29: 18 are convinced that the word *ḥôl* in this particular context indicates a bird ("where there's nest, there must be a bird!", DAHOOD 1974:86) and refers to the phoenix. It has been argued that this *ḥôl*/phoenix already occurs in Ugaritic texts (DAHOOD). In that interpretation, the words "I shall die with my nest" presuppose the cremation version of the phoenix myth. But the simple fact remains that this version is not attested before the first century of our era and that it is only known from the Graeco-Roman world. Therefore, the interpretation by DE WILDE (1981) and others who translate 'palm', is more favourable. Besides, DE WILDE (1981:290) recalls the fact, that Job certainly did not belief in immortality. The hellenistic Jewish writer Ezekiel the Tragedian, who most probably lived in Alexandria in the 2nd cent. BCE, is the first Jew known to have introduced the phoenix into his work. In his *Exagoge*, 254-269 (preserved in Eusebius, *Praep. Evang.* IX.29:16; ed. H. Jacobson [Cambridge 1983] 66-67), he described the external appearance of the bird and its manifestation to Israel in the desert, but without mentioning its name nor saying anything about its death. It is in the Midrash on Genesis (*Bereshit Rabbah*, XIX, 5) that the *ḥôl* of Job 29:18 was identified with the classical phoenix for the first time. From Gen 3:6 ('she *also* gave her husband') it is derived that Eve had offered the forbidden fruit to all the animals too. Only the bird *ḥôl* refused to eat it, "as it is written: "Then I said: I shall die with my nest and I shall multiply my days as the *ḥôl*"". The text continues by saying that there was a difference concerning its death between the

School of R. Jannai and that of R. Judan ben R. Simeon. R. Jannai (ca. 225 CE) holds that the bird was burned with its nest after a 1000 years, R. Judan (ca. 320 CE) that its body decomposed and its wings dropped off. In both cases only an egg was left, from which the *ḥôl* came to new life again. These two traditions reflect so clearly the two main versions of the classical myth of the phoenix (which, again, are unknown from Semitic or Egyptian sources) that there cannot be any doubt that the rabbis, like many modern commentators, concluded from the difficult word 'nest' in Job 29:18 and the longevity mentioned there that the phoenix was meant by the word *ḥôl* (according to KIMCHI, *Sefer-ha-Shorashim*, s.v. *ḥwl*, the rabbis at Nehardea pronounced the name as *chûl*). It is rather hazardous to assume that the identification of the Graeco-Roman phoenix with the *ḥôl* of Job 29:18, as made by rabbis of the 3rd and 4th cent. CE, was already known to the author of Job, who is usually thought to have lived between the 5th and 3rd cent. BCE. We need not assume that the rabbis came to their exegesis under the influence of the LXX reading and the double meaning of the Gk *phoinix*, nor that the reading of the LXX developed out of an original reading *phoinix*, meaning the bird.

IV. *Bibliography*

J.-C. BILLIGMEIER, Origin of the Greek Word Phoinix, *TAΛANTA: Proceedings of the Dutch Archaeological and Historical Society* 8-9 (1977) 1-4; R. VAN DEN BROEK, *The Myth of the Phoenix according to Classical and Early Christian Traditions* (EPRO 24; Leiden 1972); M. DAHOOD, Nest and Phoenix in Job 29,18, *Bib* 48 (1967) 542-544; DAHOOD, Ḥôl 'Phoenix' in Job 29:18 and in Ugaritic, *CBQ* 36 (1974) 85-88; J. HUBAUX & M. LEROY, *Le mythe du phénix dans les littératures grecque et latine* (Liège/Paris 1939); A. RUSCH, Phoinix, PW 20/1 (1941) 414-423; A. TAMMISTO, PHOENIX.FELIX.ET.TU: Remarks on the Representation of the Phoenix in Roman Art, *Arctos. Acta philologica fennica* 20 (1986) 171-225; A. DE WILDE, *Das Buch Hiob* (OTS 22; Leiden 1981) 281, 289-291.

R. VAN DEN BROEK

PLEIADES כימה

I. The Hebrew noun כימה, vocalized *kîmâ*, is the name of a →constellation or individual →star mentioned three times in the OT (Amos 5:8; Job 9:9; 38:31), in each instance in connection with *kĕsîl* (→Orion). It is usually identified with the Pleiades, although the evidence of the ancient versions is highly equivocal. This identification is confirmed by Geez, Tigre *kema* = Pleiades and by the appearance (LAMBERT 1984:396-397) of *kà-ma-tù* in a lexical list at Ebla as the equivalent of Sumerian **mul-mul**, 'Pleiades', lit. 'the stars' (*ŠL* IV/2 no. 279; HOROWITZ f.c., chap. 7 table 1). The etymologies proposed relate *kîmâ* to Ar *kûm*, 'herd (of camels)', and *kûmah*, 'heap', and to Akk *kimtu*, *kīmu*, 'family'. Thus the basic sense is that of group or aggregate. A fanciful etymology proposed in the Talmud (*b. Ber.* 58b) suggests that the constellation is called *kîmâ* because it consists of 'about a hundred' (Aram *kim'â*) stars.

The mention of *kîmâ* in Amos has sometimes been taken as a veiled polemic against astral worship. TUR-SINAI (1967) sees in all three biblical passages an echo of an ancient myth concerning a rebellion of primeval heroes against God.

II. The Pleiades and Orion are mentioned together in both Homer (*Iliad* 18: 486-489; *Odyssey* 5:272-4) and Hesiod (*Works and Days* 615, 619), as well as in a number of Mesopotamian texts (*ŠL* IV/2 nos. 279 IV B12, 348 III B4; *CAD* Z, s.v. *zappu*).

III. The passages in the OT in which *kîmâ* (and *kĕsîl*) appear all describe the tremendous power of God as Lord of Nature. Generally, they have been taken to refer to the regular progression of the seasons; but they have also been interpreted as an implicit polemic against the worship of heavenly bodies, which are themselves creations of the Deity, lacking any divine status. TUR-SINAI (1967) argues that *kîmâ* and *kĕsîl* were primeval →heroes in some lost legend who, having rebelled against divine authority, were subdued, chained, and installed in the sky as constellations. So far as *kîmâ* is concerned, the only evidence for this is the difficult first colon of Job 38:31, which may be translated "Have you bound the chains of *kîmâ*?" Since other translations are equally possible (JPSV: "Can you tie cords to Pleiades?" NEB: "Can you bind the cluster of the Pleiades?"), this is too slender a thread from which to hang such a theory, which must be judged as purely speculative. For the 'sweet influences of Pleiades' of the KJV, see DRIVER & GRAY 1921:306-307.

The ancient versions show no consistency in their translations of *kîmâ*. In Amos 5:8 the LXX does not recognize the names of astronomical bodies; Symmachus and Theodotion translate 'Pleiades' and 'Pleiad' (the singular form), respectively; and Aquila and the Vg give 'Arcturus'. In Job 9:9 the LXX translates 'Arcturus' (or, though this requires reordering the text, 'Pleiad') and the Vg 'Hyades'. In Job 38:31 the LXX and Symmachus translate 'Pleiad' and the Vg 'Pleiades'. Cognate forms are used to translate *kîmâ* in the Tg (*kymh*, *kym'*, *kymt'*) and the Peshitta (*kym'*).

Among medieval Jewish scholars, opinions as to the proper identification of *kîmâ* varied. Saadya translates it as *al-ṯurayyâ*, 'the Pleiades', while Ibn Janâḥ gives the same translation in his *Kitâb al-Uṣûl* but translates *al-farqadân* (= the stars β, γ in Ursa Minor) in the *Kitâb al-Luma'*. In his biblical commentaries, Ibn Ezra cites the 'opinion of the ancients' that *kîmâ* = Pleiades but rejects it in favour of Aldebaran ('the left eye of Taurus'); however, in *Kĕlî hanNĕḥōšet*, his treatise on the astrolabe, he identifies *kîmâ* with Capella. Identifications proposed over the past century and a half include Scorpio, Sirius, Canis Major, and Draco. However, the balance of evidence strongly favours the identity *kîmâ* = Pleiades (MOWINCKEL 1928:45-51); and the remarkable persistence of this equation from ancient Ebla to contemporary Ethiopia renders this identification virtually certain.

In the Talmud, *kîmâ* is mentioned in connection with the Deluge: "[God] took two stars from *kîmâ* and brought a flood on the world" (*b. Ber.* 59a, *b. RH* 11b-12a). It is also associated with cold (as *kĕsîl* is with heat): "Were it not for the heat of *kĕsîl*, the world could not endure the cold of *kîmâ*; were it not for the cold of *kîmâ*, the world could not endure the heat of *kesîl*" (*b. Ber.* 58b).

IV. *Bibliography*

G. DALMAN, *Arbeit und Sitte in Palästina* I (Gütersloh 1928) 39, 485-501; G. R. DRIVER, Two Astronomical Passages in the Old Testament, *JTS* N.S. 7 (1956) 1-11; S. R. DRIVER & G. B. GRAY, *The Book of Job* (ICC; Edinburgh 1921); J. J. HESS, Die Sternbilder in Hiob 9_9 und 38_{31} f., *Festschrift Georg Jacob* (ed. T. Menzel; Leipzig 1932) 94-99; W. HOROWITZ, *Mesopotamian Cosmic Geography* (Winona Lake f.c.); W. G. LAMBERT, The Section AN, *Il bilinguismo a Ebla* (ed. L. Cagni; Naples 1984) 393-401; S. MOWINCKEL, *Die Sternnamen im Alten Testament* (Oslo 1928) = *NorTT* 29 (1928) 5-75; G. SCHIAPARELLI, *Astronomy in the Old Testament* (Oxford 1905) 62-63, 163-167; N. H. TUR-SINAI, *The Book of Job* (Jerusalem 1967) 159-161, 531.

L. ZALCMAN

POLLUX → DIOSKOUROI

POSEIDON Ποσειδῶν

I. Poseidon, the Greek god of the →sea, occurs in the Bible only in the Apocrypha, as a theophoric name (Poseidonios: 2 Macc 14:19). Numerous dialectal forms occur in inscriptions, the main division being between the ποσ- and ποτ- (western dialects, Corinth, Crete, Rhodes) forms. The dominant form occurs in a number of Linear B tablets from Pylos and once at Knossos (nom. po-se-da-o, also po-si-). But the 'original' form was probably *Ποτ(σ)ειδάẖ-ων. No etymology so far proposed (a selection in BURKERT 1985:402 n. 2) is without serious difficulties: the weakness of the assumptions that underlie the most commonly accepted, (FICK and) P. KRETSCHMER'S "Lord/husband of earth" (*Glotta* 1 [1909] 27-28), has been exposed by CHADWICK (1983) among others. The intervocalic aspirate of the 'original' form suggests a prehellenic (viz. 'Pelasgian') rather than a Greek Indo-European source (RUIJGH 1967), so that it may well be pointless to look for a Greek etymology.

II. Throughout the historical period, Poseidon was overwhelmingly considered a marine divinity, the god *par excellence* of the (eastern) Mediterranean Sea. This facet of his personality is dominant from the Archaic period. Homer describes how, in his passage across the sea in his chariot, the creatures of the deep come to the surface and gambol about him, "and did not ignore their lord" (*Iliad* 13:20-31). Though he appears on →Olympus, his own palace, golden, eternal, lies beneath the waters off the coast at Aegae, which in antiquity was identified with the place of the same name in the Corinthian Gulf (*Il.* 13.21; *Odyssey* 5:381). With his trident he whips up storms by churning the open sea (*Od.* 5:291-292) and wrecks ships on reefs (4:506-507). It is this aspect which appears in the earliest iconography, the quantities of late-Corinthian *pinakes* from the grove of Poseidon found in 1879 at Pente Skouphia near Acrocorinth (A. FURTWÄNGLER, *Beschreibung der Vasensammlung des Antiquarium* 1 (Berlin 1885) nos. 347-540, 787-846; cf. *IG* IV. 1, 210-294) and the black-figure vase by Sophilos in the British Museum depicting the marriage of Peleus and Thetis (BM 1971.11 - 1.1, 580-570 BCE). Poseidon appears alone carrying the trident or with Amphitrite, the nurse of the creatures of the deep (*Od.* 5.421-422; 12.96-97). As the god of the sea, he is paired, and contrasted, with his brother →Zeus, god of Olympus, as on a black-figure fragment by Kleitias (ca.570 BCE) found at Cyrene (M. B. MOORE, *The Extramural Sanctuary of Demeter and Persephone at Cyrene* [ed. D. White; Philadelphia 1987] 389, no. 257). In Homer, Poseidon is represented as the younger brother obliged to reluctant deference by Zeus' superior wisdom (*Il.* 13:351-357), but this is probably epic local colour: the painting by Cleanthes of Corinth (6th century BCE) of the birth of →Athena in the sanctuary of →Artemis Alpheionia in Elis showed him bringing a tunny to his brother during the pains of birth (Athenaeus, *Deipn.* 8.36:346bc).

Although the Aegean and the Ionian seas were generally safe between April and October, the variable Etesian winds during high summer, and the great numbers of local micro-climates, made sea journeys at best unpredictable. This uncertainty is reflected in the very high rates of interest payable on bottomry loans. Marine Poseidon is lord of this risk, associated particularly with the raising of sudden squalls, such as that which destroyed the Persian fleet off Cape Sepias in 480 BCE: this was caused by a dawn North-Eastern wind familiar enough to the local inhabitants to be given a name, 'a Hellespontian', but quite unpredictable to strangers (Herodotus, *Hist.* 7.188.2). The wind was acknowledged as the ultimate cause, but the Greeks offered libations to Poseidon *sōtēr* as the power that destroyed the ships. Aside from the famous temples of Poseidon at Onchestus (cf. *SEG* 36:434, 436-437; possibly the origin of *Poseidōn Helikonios*), Helice (cf. Pausanias, *Gr. descr.* 7.24.5-6), the Isthmus of Corinth (cf. Pausanias, 2.1.6-9; *SEG* 35: 257 [6th century BCE]), Sounion, Taenarum (Pausanias, 3.25.4; *IG* V. 1, 1226-1236), Tenos (*IG* XII. 5, 812 etc.), and Mykale (Herodotus, 1.148), there were relatively few institutionalized cults in the Greek world. The worship of marine Poseidon was primarily a matter of votive religion.

In some ways Poseidon is closely associated with Pontos, the spirit of the open sea (*Poseidōn pelagios, mesopontios, pontomēdōn* etc). Since human beings are creatures of the land, Pontos expresses one important form of the Other in Greek culture (DETIENNE 1974:208-215). Whereas the land is (notionally) stable, the sea is in ceaseless movement; the land provides food ('barley-eating mortals'), the sea is 'sterile'; the land is criss-crossed by fixed paths, the sea is a trackless waste. The land, in a word, is prescriptive 'home', the sea 'strange'—only the magical ships of the Phaeacians can traverse it without helmsman or steering-oar (*Od.* 8: 558-559). This quality of the sea makes it an ideal place of transformation and marvel, as in Mikon's painting in the Theseum at

Athens of Theseus diving down to collect Minos' ring and surfacing a hero certified by Amphitrite's gift of a golden wreath (Pausanias, 1.17.3) or the tales of dolphins carrying persons—Arion, Phalanthos, Enalos and others—to safety. Poseidon is lord of this world, and therefore of the ships that trespass upon it: on their return, the Argonauts dedicated the first ship to Poseidon at the Isthmus of Corinth (Apollodorus, *Bibl.* 1.9.27). But his specific form of assistance is not to guide ship-construction nor aid navigation nor appear to distressed mariners, but essentially negative: Poseidon is 'saver of ships' insofar as he neglects to raise storms at sea (*Poseidon asphaleios*), cf. *Hom. Hymn.* 22:7. As such, he is associated with mercantile gain (there was an association of Poseidoniastai among the Roman citizens on Delos, in Latin Neptunales: IDélos 1751 etc.; cf. Heliodorus, *Aethiop.* 6. 7.1); with harbour works (cf. the famous Balıktash at Cyzicus, commemorating the canals and harbours built at the expense of Antonia Tryphaena, mother of Rhoemetalces and Polemon, in 37/38 CE: L. ROBERT, *Hellenica* 10 [1955] §24); with success in fishing (Hesiod, *Theog.* 441-442; Lucian, *Pisc.* 47; Pausanias, 10.9.3-4); and with naval victory (the Greeks dedicated a bronze colossus of Poseidon at the Isthmus after the Persian Wars: Herodotus 9.81.1; cf. Timoleon's dedication after the battle of Krimisos in 341 BCE [*Corinth* 8, 3; no. 23]). In all these forms of votive religion, it is Poseidon's acquiescence in human endeavour that is emphasized: the disquieting otherness of the sea is temporarily veiled.

These aspects of Poseidon's activity self-evidently cohere: it is the others which have excited most modern discussion. In the Homeric poems his most frequent epithets are ἐνοσίχθων, γαιήοχος, ἐννοσίγαιος, 'earth-shaking/holding'. They are apparently unintegrated into the main picture, and point to a god of earthquakes, or at any rate of the foundations of the earth. ROBERT (PRELLER 1894) thought that this feature could be reconciled with the marine divinity by postulating a folk-representation of the land encircled by sea, i.e. 'held' by it. Such a notion might explain why Poseidon is also so intimately associated with isthmuses, and why he is a god of fresh water and springs (*Poseidōn epilimnios*; Aeschylus, *Sept.* 304-311; Pindar, *Olymp.* 6:58; *IG* XII. 2, 95 = *SEG* 28:690 [Mytilene, 4th century BCE]; 32:1273 [Phrygia, 2nd-3rd century CE], etc.), indeed of fertility, *Poseidon phytalmios* (e.g. *SIG*³ 1030, Lindos). A more radical tack was taken by VON WILAMOWITZ (1931-32; followed by WÜST 1953), who sought to show that Poseidon was originally not a marine god at all, but had once been a high god, later pushed out by →Zeus. The crucial evidence comes from Arcadia and indicates that he was a god of the depths of the earth in the shape of a horse. SCHACHERMEYR (1950) picked up this last theory, urging that Poseidon must have developed in a creative encounter between Mycenaean Greeks arriving with the horse, an emblem of fertility and the underworld, and the prehellenic population, who had a mother-goddess. He emphasized esp. Poseidon's cult-title *Hippios* (cf. Diod. Sic. 5.69.4; Pausanias 7.21.8; 8.14.5; Schol. Pindar, *Pyth.* 4:246a), cult-myths relating Poseidon to →Demeter at Onkion (Thelphusa), Phigaleia and Lykosoura, and a myth recounting how Rhea pretended to Kronos that her baby Poseidon was a foal, which she gave him to eat (Pausanias 8.8.2). But at least the association between the Mycenaeans and the introduction of the horse must be wrong: on the one hand, the entry of the Indo-Europeans, complete with horse, must be dated ca. 2000 BCE; on the other, the horse-burial at Marathon is intrusive (Sub-mycenaean). Nevertheless PALMER (1983), basing himself on Kretschmer's etymology, has recently argued that there are parallels between this postulated Mycenaean Poseidon and the Canaanite divinity →Aliyan, Lord (of the) Earth, and used the Ugaritic myth of →Horon and the Mare to suggest the origin of the Arcadian association between Poseidon and the Despoinai (Demeter and Persephone). There are good general reasons for rejecting this notion; moreover, it wrongly assumes that the Arcadian material is primitive and uncontaminated (cf. BREGLIA-PULCI DORIA 1986). CHADWICK (1985) has emphasized that the tablets from Pylos provide no information about the nature of Poseidon there, except that he had a female counterpart Po-si-da-e-ja; DIETRICH (1965:118-138) had already shown that there is no need to look beyond the Minoan-Mycenaean world to explain the complex.

It has seemed to many that what is needed is a plausible explanation of how Poseidon's three main realms relate to one another. But it remains elusive. NILSSON (1967), while accepting that Poseidon originally had the form of a horse, was convinced that he was an Indo-European god of the waters, salt and fresh, brought with them by the Greeks: the land-locked Arcadians developed one aspect, that of earthquakes, horses and fertility; the Ionians another, the god of the open sea. The case of Italic Neptunus, originally a god of fresh waters, might support this. W. PÖTSCHER once suggested (*Gymnasium* 66 [1959] 359) that the essence of Poseidon, as of Zeus, lay in sheer might, expressed in natural phenomena conceived as the product of quasi-human emotion: the analogy between the raging of the sea and the trembling of the earth cannot be overlooked (cf. *Hom. Hymn.* 22:2). Perhaps the most promising avenue is the contrastive 'Dumézilian' approach advocated by DETIENNE, who showed how Poseidon's relation to the horse gains point and meaning through comparison with Athena *Hippia* (1974:176-200). Given the almost complete absence of reliable dating, there is much to be said for renouncing pseudo-history in favour of structure.

III. Despite the extensive evidence for votive dedications to Poseidon from 6th century BCE, personal names calqued on the god's name occur only intermittently in the inscriptions of mainland Greece, and are absent from the epigraphy of Syria collected in *IGLS*, though the Stoic philosopher Posidonius (ca.135-51/0 BCE), the most famous bearer of such a name, came from Apamea on the Orontes (Kala'at el-Medik), a Poseidonios of Sidon competed at the Panathenaic Games at Athens in 191 or 182/181 BCE (*IG* II^2, 2:2314.21), and the marine →Baal of Berytus was hellenized as Poseidon (cf. *BMC Phoenicia* pl. VII. 1-5, 12; IDélos 1520). Such names, of which Poseidonios and Poseidippos are by far the most common, occur with some frequency only in the Aegean islands and Cyrene. The Poseidonios of the Macc. passage (directly from Jason of Cyrene), who acted as a negotiator between Nicanor, general of Demetrius I, and Judas Maccabaeus in the discussions leading up the short-lived truce prior to Nicanor's death at the battle of Adasa (13 Adar, 161 BCE), is otherwise unknown.

In post-biblical literature, Poseidon occurs in two pseudepigraphic contexts, in the *Sibylline Oracles.* The first passage (3:142) occurs in the reworking of the story of Kronos and Rhea based indirectly on the *Sacred History* of Euhemerus of Messene (cf. Ennius' paraphrase, JACOBY: *FGH* 63 F 14), and directly on a Stoic commentary on the mythology of Jupiter of the type also used by Lactantius in *Inst. Div.* 1:11. In this version, Rhea only has to smuggle away her male children, Zeus, Poseidon and Pluto. The reference to Poseidon is unfortunately brief; the most elaborate surviving allegorical account of the god in this general vein is L. Annaeus Cornutus, *Theol. graec. comp.* 22 (first century CE) (cf. G. W. MOST, *ANRW* 36, 3 [1989] 2014-2065). The second passage (5:157) is unintelligible in its context (see GEFFCKEN *ad loc.*), and must have been displaced from elsewhere. But in itself, it draws both on the common metonymy by which Poseidon or Neptune stands for the sea (e.g. Aeschylus *Pers.* 749-750; Horace, *Epod.* 7:3-4) and on the familiar institution of propitiatory sacrifice to Poseidon before a sea-journey to avoid a storm (Homer, *Od.* 3:178-179; Appian, *Bell. civ.* 5:98).

IV. *Bibliography*

L. BREGLIA-PULCI DORIA, Demeter Erinys Tilphussaia tra Poseidon e Ares, *Les Grandes Figures religieuses: Colloque Besançon 1984* (Ann. litt. Besançon, 329; Paris 1986) 107-126; W. BURKERT, *Greek Re-*

ligion (Cambridge, Mass. and Oxford 1985) 136-139; J. CHADWICK, Intervention after L. R. Palmer's paper, in *Res Mycenaeae: Akten des VII int. mykenologischen Colloquiums (Nürnberg 1981)* (eds. A. Heubeck & G. Neumann; Göttingen 1983) 363-365; CHADWICK, What do we know about Mycenaean religion?, *Linear B: A 1984 Survey: Proceedings of the Mycenaean Colloquium (Dublin 1984)* (eds. A. Morpurgo-Davies & Y. Duhoux; Bibl. Inst. Ling. Louvain 26; Louvain-la-Neuve 1985) 191-202; M. DETIENNE, Le Mors éveillé, and La Corneille de mer, *Les ruses de l'intelligence: la mètis des grecs* (M. Detienne & J.-P. Vernant; Paris 1974) 176-200, 201-241; B. C. DIETRICH, *Death, Fate and the Gods* (London 1965) 118-135; M. P. NILSSON, *Geschichte der griechischen Religion* I (München 1967[3]) 444-452; L. R. PALMER, Mycenaean Religion. Methodological Choices, *Res Mycenaeae: Akten des VII int. mykenologischen Colloquiums (Nürnberg 1981)* (eds. A. Heubeck & G. Neumann; Göttingen 1983) 338-362; L. PRELLER, *Griechische Mythologie* I.2 (rev. ed. C. Robert; Berlin 1894[4]) 566-596; C. J. RUIJGH, Sur le nom de Poséidon et sur les noms en -a-ϝον, -ῑ-ϝον-, *REG* 80 (1967) 6-16; F. SCHACHERMEYR, *Poseidon und die Entstehung des griechischen Götterglaubens* (Bern/München 1950) (with Nilsson's review, *AJP* 74 [1953] 161-168); U. VON WILAMOWITZ-MÖLLENDORFF, *Der Glaube der Hellenen* I (Berlin 1931-1932, repr. Basel 1956) 211-216; E. WÜST, Poseidon, PW 22 (1953) 446-557.

R. L. GORDON

POWER → DYNAMIS

PRESBYTEROI → ELDERS

PRINCE שׂר

I. In Dan 10:13, the angelic interpreter tells →Daniel that he has been sent in response to the visionary's prayer, but he has been delayed because "the prince of the kingdom of Persia opposed me twenty-one days, so Michael, one of the chief princes, came to help me". He adds that when he is through with this first prince, "the prince of Greece will come" (10:20). He also refers to →Michael as "your prince" (10:21) and as "the great prince, the protector of your people" (12:1). By analogy with Michael it is clear that the "princes" of Greece and Persia are the patron angels of these nations.

II. The notion that different nations were allotted to different gods or heavenly beings was widespread in the ancient world. In Deut 32:8-9 we read that "When the Most High gave to the nations their inheritance, when he separated the sons of men, he fixed the bounds of the peoples according to the number of the sons of God" (The MT reads "sons of Israel" but the LXX reading ἀγγέλων θεοῦ is now supported by a Hebrew fragment from Qumran Cave 4 [4QDeut^{j}] which reads בני אלהים; DIETRICH & LORETZ 1992:153-157).

The origin of this idea is to be sought in the ancient Near Eastern concept of the Divine →Council. The existence of national deities is assumed in the Rabshakeh's taunt: "Who among all the gods of the countries have delivered their countries out of my hand that the LORD should deliver Jerusalem out of my hand?" (2 Kgs 18:35 = Isa 36:20). Closer to the time of Daniel, Sirach reaffirms Deuteronomy 32: "He appointed a ruler over every nation, but Israel is the LORD's own portion" (Sir 17:17; cf. Jub 15:31-32). In the *Animal Apocalypse* (*1 Enoch* 89:59) the →angels or gods of the nations are represented by seventy →shepherds, to whom Israel is handed over. It should be noted that in the Hebrew Bible prior to Daniel, the LORD serves as ruler of Israel, a role given to Michael here.

The title 'prince' might seem to imply a demotion for the old national gods, but this is not necessarily so. In Dan 8:11 we read that the "little horn" acted arrogantly against the "prince of the host", and took away his burnt offering and overthrew the sanctuary. The prince of the host here can be none other than the God of Israel (cf. Dan 11:36, where the king speaks horrendous things against the God of gods).

A precedent for the title 'prince' applied to an angel can be found in the שׂר צבא יהוה, the prince of the army of the LORD, who appears in Josh 5:14. Before the siege of Jericho, Joshua encounters a man standing before him with a drawn sword in his hand. Joshua asks whether he is "one of us or one of our adversaries". The man then identifies himself as "the prince of the army of the LORD". The implication is that Joshua will be aided by an angelic army in his assault on Jericho. The prince, in this case, is not further identified. His function is that of a military commander.

III. The reference to an angelic 'prince' in the Book of Joshua is an isolated occurrence in the Hebrew Bible. In the Hellenistic period, however, 'principal angels' became the subject of considerable speculation. In the dualistic world of the Dead Sea Scrolls, 'princes' of →light and darkness hold sovereignty under God. "All the children of righteousness are ruled by the Prince of Lights, and walk in the ways of light, but all the children of →falsehood are ruled by the Angel of Darkness and walk in the ways of darkness" (1QS 3:20; compare CD 5:18, where →Moses and Aaron arose by the hand of the Prince of Lights, while →Belial raised up Jannes and Jambres). According to 1QM 13:10, God appointed the Prince of light to protect the faithful, while he made Belial to corrupt. In 1QM 17:5-6, Belial is the "prince of the dominion of wickedness". The dominion of these rival princes is called משׂרה, a term derived from שׂר. So we read of the guilty authority (משׂרה אשמתו) of Belial (1QM 13:4) and the dominion of →Michael (משׂרה מכאל) among the gods (אלים), which parallels the rule of Israel among all flesh (1QM 17:7). Not all Jews welcomed the new prominence of these angelic princes. The Book of Jubilees still insists, in the spirit of Deuteronomy 32, that over Israel God appointed no angel or spirit, for he alone is their ruler (Jub 15:32).

We also find a more generic use of 'princes' in the Dead Sea Scrolls. In the Songs of Sabbath Sacrifice we read of 'princes of holiness' (שׂרי קדשׁ), and another word for prince, נשׂיא, is often used for angels (NEWSOM 1985: 26-28).

IV. *Bibliography*

W. BOUSSET, *Die Religion des Judentums* (Berlin 1903) 324 [Tübingen 1966[4]]; M. DIETRICH & O. LORETZ, *"Jahwe und seine Aschera". Anthropomorphes Kultbild in Mesopotamien, Ugarit und Israel* (UBL 9; Münster 1992); M. MACH, *Entwicklungsstadien des jüdischen Engelsglauben in vorrabbinischer Zeit* (Tübingen 1992) 257-262; A. MONTGOMERY, *Daniel* (New York 1927) 419-20; C. NEWSOM, *Songs of the Sabbath Sacrifice: A Critical Edition* (Atlanta 1985); Y. YADIN, *The Scroll of the War of the Sons of Light against the Sons of Darkness* (Oxford 1962).

J. J. COLLINS

PRINCE (NT) → ARCHON

PRINCE OF THE ARMY OF YAHWEH → PRINCE

PRINCIPALITIES → ARCHAI

PRONOIA Πρόνοια

I. Pronoia, Latin Providentia, means in Homer anticipation or foreknowledge, but already by the 5th century BCE often expressed intention, especially in a legal sense, and care, for one's family and in military planning. An analogous care was ascribed to the gods; the early Stoa built on this traditional sense in developing its notion of providence, the divine governance of the world, equivalent of →Zeus and →Logos. This sense, more or less indebted to Stoic theory and always qualified by 'divine' or the like, is to be found in some Hellenistic biblical texts (Wis 14:3; 17:2; 3 Macc 4:21; 5:30; 4 Macc 9:24; 13:19; 17:22) and elsewhere, especially in Philo, an extensive fragment of whose Stoicizing *On Providence* survives in Greek.

II. The concept of divine providence is intimately linked with the process of rationalizing traditional Greek religious belief. At the same time, it formalizes a notion of divine purposiveness which in some guise or other is essential to any religious view of the world, and certainly present in Greek religious thinking: the Homeric scenario of divine debate on →Olympus is both a narrative framing device and an assertion that beneath the apparent confusion of events there lies a purposive order; Hesiodic Zeus safeguards his power by swallowing Metis and marrying Themis (*Theog.* 886, 901). Alcman (say 650-600 BCE) calls →*Tyche* daughter of *Promathēa* (frg.64 Page, *PMG*). Standard religious reinterpretation of 'coincidence' (Euripides, *Phoen.* 637; Sophocles, *Oed. Col.* 1180), the separation of civic and religious spheres (*Antig.* 282-283) and the issue of divine foreknowledge institutionalized in public and private oracles (*Trach.* 823; *Oed.Rex* 978; Xenophon, *Mem.* 4:3, 12) provided nodes around which speculation buzzed. Anaxagoras's cosmogonic *Nous*, the idea of divine intentionality as a primal cause (59 B11-14 DIELS & KRANZ, fl. 470-460 BCE), is thus based indirectly on traditional concepts. A more specific view of divine providence, drawing upon Anaxagoras and Heraclitus, was developed by one of the last Presocratics, Diogenes of Apollonia (fl. 440-430 BCE). His *On Nature* urged a providential view of the ordering of the seasons and weather-patterns, and apparently all other natural phenomena, including anatomical and physiological details, by sentient, all-knowing soul-air (64 A4, B3, 5, 8 D-K). Some early texts that explicitly adduce divine providence do so in connection with puzzles taken from the natural world, the difference in reproductive energy between predators and their prey (Hdt 3: 108, 1), and the exquisite organization of the body (Xenophon *Mem.* 1:4, 5-6); it has been plausibly urged that they are at least inspired by Diogenes (THEILER 1924). On the other hand, an argument standard among Stoic justifications for providence, that animals exist in order to be exploited by mankind, which is also adduced by the Xenophontic Socrates (*Mem.* 4:3, 10), probably derives from another late 5th century BCE source. The context of this later 5th century BCE speculation about divine providence was a vigorous interest in human provision for the future (e.g. Thucydides 2:89, 9; Xen., *Mem.* 2:10, 3) and ability to anticipate (e.g. Thucydides. 2:62, 5; 3:38, 6; Xenophon *Cyrop.* 8:1, 13). Both are taken as typical expressions of human rationality; once rationality came to be an essential predicate of divinity, providence was sure to become an explicit theme.

Plato's arguments for the providentialism of the world order, from the purpose of the senses (*Tim.* 46c-48c), and the demonstrations of the intelligence of the world (*Tim.* 29d-30b) and of the gods' *epimeleia* (*Laws* 10:897c-903a), thus emerge from earlier debate. It was this position that Epicurus denied: the world is evidently imperfect, and cannot therefore have been divinely ordered (Lucretius, *Rer. nat.* 5:156-194). The Stoic defence of divine providence, which draws upon Plato either through Polemon the third head of the Academy or through Theophrastus, was specifically aimed at Epicurus. *Pronoia* became central to Stoic theology, as the lists of equations indicate (= *heimarmenē*, *physis*: *SVF* 1:176; = Zeus, *logos, dikē*: *SVF* 2:937). For Zeno (say 333/332-262 BCE), god is unique, immortal, rational, self-sufficient in blessedness, impervious to evil, προνοητικὸν κόσμου τε καὶ τῶν ἐν κόσμῳ (*SVF* 2:1021). The traditional gods of the Greek pantheon are merely 'powers' or aspects of the one god. The cosmos is itself rational and vital (ἔμψυχος) (LONG & SEDLEY 1987:§ 54F, G). In Cleanthes' (after 330-232/231 BCE) *Hymn to Zeus*, this view of providence is expressed in traditional terms: "Nothing supervenes, Lord, on earth, in the divine vault of heaven or in the sea, without you" (*SVF* 1:537, 15-16). For Chrysippus (say 281/277-208/204 BCE), who wrote a book *On Providence* in at least four volumes, god is not merely immortal and blessed but also beneficent, provident and succouring (SVF 2:1126). The cosmos is rational and sentient (Cicero, *Nat. Deor.* 2: 38): the existence of providence is demonstrated by the ordering of its constituent parts (Cic., *Nat. Deor.* 2:75-76; cf. 90-153).

Zeno's view of Pronoia is intimately linked to his reflections on Plato's and Aristotle's cosmology (MANSFELD 1979:161-169). Analogously, Chrysippus argued that Zeus and the ordered universe resemble the composite human being: Pronoia, equivalent of the World-Soul, is to the universe what the soul is to man (Plutarch, *Comm. not.* 36, 1077e with Cherniss, LCL). At *ekpyrosis*, Zeus "retires into Pronoia" and together they become *Aither*, the ruling part of the cosmos (SVF 2:1064).

The implications of this view of Providence were followed up rigorously by the early Stoa. The cosmos has a purpose, it exists for the sake of its reasonable beings, gods and mankind (Cic., *Nat.Deor.* 2:133). 'Nature' is both a descriptive and a normative notion: man was formed by the gods to live a virtuous life. Teleology was pushed to absurdity in Chrysippus' argument that bedbugs have been created in order to make sure we wake up betimes, and that flies ensure that we do not lay things down carelessly (SVF 2:1163); or that pigs exist in order to be sacrificed (LONG & SEDLEY 1987:§ 54P). And the further the arguments from design were pressed, the more tricky became the issue of evil. Chrysippus had two main theses here: moral failings, and their consequences in action, are the necessary corollary of moral virtues (there must be evil if there is good); and evil, esp. disease and infirmity, is an unintended but necessary consequence (κατὰ παρακολούθησιν) of the beneficial design of the world (SVF 2:1169-1170). Moreover, particular evils do not affect the economy of the cosmos as a whole, and can only function within that economy (SVF 2:937; 1181) (LONG 1968). It was in relation to this issue that Cleanthes already differentiated between Fate and Providence (SVF 2:933), and on which the sceptic Carneades (ca. 214-129 BCE) later roundly attacked the very notion of Providence (Cic., *Nat. Deor.* 3:79-85). In the face of this, contemporary Stoics, notably Panaetius, preferred to muffle the cosmic role of Pronoia and save the freedom of the individual to live in keeping with his rational nature. Posidonius (ca. 135-51/50 BCE) succeeded in producing a theory that reaffirmed Pronoia's identity with god as 'artisan of destiny', while making each individual responsible for his own rational development. Later Stoics were mostly content to resume this position (DRAGONA-MONACHOU 1994). Stoic *Pronoia* thus tended to lose its distinctive cast, and merge with the traditional view of the gods' beneficence (e.g. *IKyme* 13:90, 106 [after 130 BCE]; *SEG* 32: 1385.8-9 [after 62 BCE]). Mediated through Cicero as *Providentia deorum*, this weak sense became a significant prop of imperial ideology (MARTIN 1982). With Antiochus of Ascalon (first century BCE), providence came to play a role in the cosmology and anthropology of the Academy, embroiling Middle Platonists in a tricky tension between determinism and free will (cf. Plutarch, *de facie* 927a-e): Philo's *On Providence* 2 (largely preserved in Greek in Eusebius, *PE* 8.14: 386-399, cf. Colson in LCL 9:458-506) provides a good example of the tone of first century CE school debate (cf. *Confus. Ling* 114-5). The latest significant deployment of the concept in a political sense is Synesius' integration of *pronoia* into the neoplatonic hierarchy of existence in *De providentia* 1 (July 400 CE) (CAMERON & LONG 1993).

III. The providential plan of God for his people is a fundamental theme of the OT, expressed in devotional contexts in terms of the individual being in God's hands (BEHM 1940:1008). In wisdom and apocalyptic literature one conventional expression of this providence is the schematization of world history, another, the notion that history has a goal, the establishment of God's kingdom. Individual wisdom writers, such as Ben Sira (J. MARBÖCK, *Weisheit im Wandel* [Bonn 1971] 88-94, 143-145) and Aristobulus and the translator of the LXX version of Prov. 8:22-31, associate cosmic →wisdom (*ḥokmâ*), as a regulative principle in the world created by →God, with the history of Israel both collective and individual (HENGEL 1973[2]). The spread of Hellenistic rhetorical and philosophical education within the Jewish élite both in Palestine and the Diaspora encouraged the emergence of a 'providential koine' from the 2nd century BCE into the 2nd century CE: the congruence between Hellenistic Jewish wisdom and Stoic *Pronoia* is expressly marked by 'Menedemus' in *Ep. Arist* 201 (MARTIN's redating to ca. 210-190 BCE [1982:24 n.135] is quite unfounded). This blending is apparent in Wisdom and 3-4 Maccabees, where Pronoia is a natural force (4 Macc 13:19), a synonym for God's saving intervention at decisive junctures (Wis 6:7; 14:3; 3 Macc 4:21; 5:30) but also his long-term plan for his people (Wis 17:2; 4 Macc 9:24; 17:22). In Philo, with his formal knowledge of Greek philosophy, we can observe a modulation between Poseidonian themes, including the role of divination (*De Ios.* 116, 161; *Vit. Mos.* 2:16; *Virt.* 215), and wisdom theology. Several arguments seem to allude to Poseidonian themes: those who assert that the world is eternal and uncreated 'occlude Providence'—the creator necessarily cares for his creation just as parents for their children (*Opif. Mundi* 9-10; cf. *Praem.* 42; *Ebr.* 199; *Spec. Leg.* 2:310, 318); our bodies have a physical existence over time thanks to God's Pronoia (*Quis rer. div.* 58); this same Pronoia makes the world eternal (*Decal.* 58; *Aetern.* 47) and is indeed its Soul (*Aetern.* 49-51). Others are drawn from wisdom themes: →Joseph's story is an exemplification of God's Pronoia (*Ios.* 236); the burning bush represents God's care for his people (*Vit. Mos.* 1:67); the prophets take cognizance of God's Pronoia (*Mut. nom.* 25). By contrast, the usage in Josephus is flattened and banalized: he draws much more upon the conventional invocation of divine beneficence (*BJ* 4:219; 7:82, 318, 453; *AJ* 4:157, 239; 5:107; 6:159 etc.); much the same applies to the usage in *Sib. Or.* 5: 227, 323. The occasional deployment of *Pronoia* in Gnostic cosmologies (e.g. *Apocryphon of John* 5:16; 6:5, 22, 30, etc. [*NGH* II.1]; *Origin* 108:11, 15; 111:18, 32 [II.5]; *Expos.Valent.* 37:21 [XI.2]) presumably draws upon the Hellenistic-Jewish 'koine'.

Though the NT takes over and adapts much Hellenistic wisdom thinking, it ignores *Pronoia* in this sense, employing only traditional non-philosophical denotations of the term: the scrupulous execution of his supervisory duties by a middle-ranking official (Acts 24:2, cf. MARTIN 1982:11-12); "care" or "thought for" (Rom 13:14, in a standard phrase, e.g. Dan 6:18 LXX; Philo, *Ebr.* 87). Providentialism is nevertheless diffused, in the notion of God's fatherhood, protection of creation, and working out of his purpose within individuals (Phil 2:13). It is in this soteriological perspective that God's Pronoia is invoked in the apostolic writings, in the context of the argument for resurrection from the crop-cycle in *1 Clem.* 24:5, and in a hendiadys with *sophia* at Hermas *Vis.* 1:3, 4. The apologists tend to revive the philosophical perspective; the most systematic patristic exploitation of divine Pronoia is by Clement of Alexandria, who develops its activity at three levels, the natural world, human communities (esp. the Jews), the individual (*Str.* 7:6, 1), materially, spiritually and intellectually (FLOYD 1971).

IV. *Bibliography*

J. BEHM, Προνοέω κτλ., *TWNT* 4 (1940) 1004-1011; A. CAMERON & J. LONG, *Barbarians and Politics at the Court of Arcadius* (Berkeley & Los Angeles 1993) 253-336; M. DRAGONA-MONACHOU, Providence and Fate in Stoicism and Prae-neoplatonism: Calcidius as an authority on Cleanthes' theodicy, *Philosophia* 3 (Athens 1973) 262-306; DRAGONA-MONACHOU, *The Stoic Arguments for the Existence and Providence of the Gods* (Athens 1976); DRAGONA-MONACHOU, Divine Providence in the Philosophy of the Empire, *ANRW* II 36.7 (1994) 4417-4490; W. E. G. FLOYD, *Clement of Alexandria's Treatment of the Problem of Evil* (London 1971) 34-40, 92-97; M. HENGEL, *Judentum und Hellenismus* (Tübingen 1973[2]); A. A. LONG, The Problem of Evil in Stoicism, *PhilQuart* 18 (1968) 329-343; A. A. LONG & D. N. SEDLEY, *The Hellenistic Philosophers* 2 (Cambridge 1987) §54; J. MANSFELD, Providence and the Destruction of the Universe in early

Stoic Thought, *Studies in Hellenistic Religions* (ed. M. J. Vermaseren; EPRO 78; Leiden 1979) 129-188; J.-P. MARTIN, *Providentia Deorum: Aspects religieux du pouvoir romain* (Coll. École fr. de Rome 61; Rome 1982); M. POHLENZ, *Die Stoa. Geschichte einer geistigen Bewegung* 2 (Göttingen 1959) 1: 98-101, 2: 55-58; W. THEILER, *Zur Geschichte der teleologischen Naturbetrachtung bis auf Aristoteles* (Diss. Zürich 1924) 6-36.

R. L. GORDON

PROTECTORS

I. The common semitic verb ŠMR/III ZMR/ḎMR 'to protect; to watch' can be used with a religious connotation, as becomes clear from personal names like Zimri-Lim, '→Lim is my Protection'. At Ugarit, the ancestral gods (→Ilib) are probably once depicted as *ḏmr ʾṯrh*, 'Protector(s) of his place'. In the OT Yahweh is seen as the 'protector' of his people (e.g. Exod 15:2; Ps 121). At Nah 2:3 *zĕmōrêhem šiḥētû* might be rendered as 'slaughtered their protectors'.

II. In the epic of Aqhat a list of filial duties is given. One of these duties is that a son is supposed to be the "one who sets up the stelae of his ancestral gods, in the sanctuary the marjoram of his clan, one who makes his smoke come out from the earth, from the dust *ḏmr ʾṯrh*" (*KTU* 1.17 i:26-28). The final words of this unit have been interpreted as 'the Protector(s) of his place' (O. LORETZ, *BN* 8 [1979] 14-17; DE MOOR 1986; MARGALIT 1989; DE MOOR 1990). This interpretation implies that the ancestral deities were seen as protective spirits comparable to the →Rephaim. This interpretation is, however, not unchallenged. Others have construed *ḏmr* as a perfect tense and translate the phrase with " ... and from the dust protect his place" (e.g. A. CAQUOT, M. SZNYCER & A. HERDNER, *Textes Ougaritiques* I [LAPO 7; Paris 1974] 422; K. VAN DER TOORN, Funerary Rituals and Beatific Afterlife in Ugaritic Texts and in the Bible, *BiOr* 48 [1991] 45-46). The interpretation of Y. AVISHUR (*UF* 17 [1985] 52-53) who translates *ḏmr ʾṯrh*" by 'the perfumes of his place' is to be dismissed since it rests on an obsolete etymology.

III. In Biblical Hebrew the Semitic root ḎMR is generally developed into the verb ŠMR 'to protect'. Metaphorically, Yahweh is seen as the *šōmēr*, 'protector', of Israel (Num 6:24; Ps 121; 146:6; M. KORPEL, *JSOT* 45 [1989] 3-13). In some dialects of Hebrew the verb III ZMR, 'to watch, to protect' is attested. In Ex 15:2—a text quoted at Isa 12:2 and Ps 118:14—the formula *ʿozzî wĕzimrātî yhwh* should be rendered 'my strength and my protection is Yahweh'. DE MOOR (1990) compares this formula with a line from an Ugaritic incantation—recited at the banquet on the New Year festival as de Moor surmises—in which the Ugaritic king prays to the founder-fathers of his dynasty, the ancestral gods Yaqaru and Gathru, for *ʿz*, 'strength', and *ḏmr*, 'protection', (*KTU* 1. 108:21-24; J. N. FORD, *UF* 24 [1992] 76-80). DE MOOR interprets this comparison in the framework of an originally ancestral character of Yahweh (1990).

The enigmatic text Nah 2:1-3 has been clarified by VAN DER WOUDE (1977:115-120). The traditional rendition of the word *zĕmōrêhem*, 'their shoots; vines', should be abandoned since it is a masculine plural to a female noun *zĕmōrâ*, 'shoot'. Therefore, the noun can better be related to Ugar *ḏmr*, 'to protect; protection' and Heb *zimrâ*, 'protection'. VAN DER WOUDE (1977:119) renders **zōmĕrêhem* with 'their soldiers'. The word, however, can better be translated with 'their protectors'. Nah 2:3b depicts the fate of Nineveh, the city that held captive the exiles from Israel. But now "plunderers shall plunder them and slaughter their protectors", i.e. Nineveh will stand without defense in days of disaster to come. The protectors probably refer to military aid but might contain a reminiscence of ancestral deities.

IV. *Bibliography*

B. MARGALIT, *The Ugaritic Poem of AQHT* (BZAW 182; Berlin/New York 1989) 118, 144, 273; J. C. DE MOOR, The Ancestral Cult in KTU 1.17:I.26-28, *UF* 17 (1986)

407-409; DE MOOR, *The Rise of Yahwism* (BETL 91; Leuven 1990) 247-248; A. S. VAN DER WOUDE, The Book of Nahum: a Letter written in Exile, *Instruction and Interpretation* (OTS 20; Leiden 1977) 108-126.

B. BECKING

PTAH

I. Josh 15:9 and 18:15 mention the "(Spring of the) Water of *Neptôaḥ* ". This is, however, a secondary interpretation of the "(Spring of) Merenptah". This Merenptah is Pharaoh Merenptah (ca. 1224-1214 BCE) whose name (*Mr.n Ptḥ*) means "Beloved by (the god) Ptah". Other occurrences of the Egyptian god Ptah have been found in the expression *baṭṭuḥôt* (Job 38:36; GÖRG 1980) and in the Hebrew word Topheth (GÖRG 1988).

II. Ptah is anthromorphic. His close-fitting garment covers his feet and legs, which are not apart, and arms hardly showing. He usually has a staff in his hands and wears a cap. Ptah was the main deity of Memphis, the Egyptian capital and royal residence until the end of the Old Kingdom, and a very influential centre ever since. This explains Ptah's high national position, independent and unweakened throughout Egyptian history. The link between him, "King of the two lands (= Egypt)", and the Pharaohs remained very strong. They were enthroned in his local temple.

The god is creative, a master craftsman, identified as Hephaistos in the *interpretatio graeca*. His high-priest is the "greatest of those who direct crafts". His cap, and perhaps his name, point in the same direction. His productive activities cover a wider field. Being the demiurge, he is self-begotten, as well as the creator of the cosmos. Gods originated from his body, and men were made by him. He created all that exists, ever feeding his creatures.

The most comprehensive and impressive document in this respect is the "Memphite theology". This is a highly intellectual treatise. Though its antiquity is in dispute, it certainly contains some very ancient ideas. It tells how Ptah allotted life to all gods and every other being. He conceived of his creation by thinking and realized it by speaking. His tongue repeated what his heart devised; his mouth pronounced the names of all things. Food and offerings are also due to his utterance. At his command, the righteous are rewarded with life, while the wrongdoers have to face death. Being a source of creativity, the god passed on his power to his creatures. Their activities emanate from his thought and word in an uninterrupted flow.

The "Memphite theology" mentions a number of deities as forms or as parts of Ptah. Among them, the chthonic Tatenen is often syncretized with him in other texts, whereas Nefertem became his son by a marriage arranged with the →lioness Sekhmet. Relations with the local necropolis god Sokar, also a craftsman, became so close that they resulted in the union Ptah-Sokar. The Memphite bull →Apis too is on the record as a son. Ptah, by rewarding and punishing is a deity of destiny and "Lord of Truth". He is quite popular in personal devotion and piety as the one "who listens to prayer".

III. Though the occurrence of Ptah as a theophoric element in the toponym Nephtoah is uncontested (for the location of the spring see KRAUSS 1980:74 n. 13), the other biblical references to Ptah are very dubious. The interpretation of Topheth (*tōpet*) as a simplified Egyptianism going back to *tꜣ (st n) Ptḥ*, 'the place of Ptah' (Ptah being defined as a god of fire), may be simply dismissed as a far-fetched speculation (*pace* GÖRG 1988). The suggestion that the expression *baṭṭuḥôt* (Job 38:36) conceals in fact a reference to Ptah deserves more serious consideration (GÖRG 1980). The relevant verse speaks about →wisdom, a characteristic attribute of Ptah. Yet in view of the occurrence of *ṭuḥôt* in Ps 51:8 and Job 12:6, an emendation of Job 38:36 does not commend itself. A meaning 'hidden recesses (of the earth)' makes good sense (cf. Y. TIRQEL, *Beth Mikra* 26 [1981] 353-357 [Hebrew]).

IV. *Bibliography*
H. BONNET, Ptah, *RÄRG* 614-619; J. ČERNÝ, *Ancient Egyptian Religion* (London 1952) 158; M. GÖRG, Ijob aus dem Lande *'Uṣ*: Ein Beitrag zur 'theologischen Geographie', *BN* 12 (1980) 7-12; GÖRG, Topaet (Tofet): Die (Stätte) des Feuergottes?, *BN* 43 (1988) 12-13; E. HORNUNG, *Der Eine und die Vielen* (Darmstadt 1971) 277; R. KRAUSS, Merenptah, *LdÄ* IV (1980) 71-76; G. RENDSBURG, Merneptah in Canaan, *JSSEA* 11 (1981) 171-172; M. SANDMAN-HOLMBERG, *The God Ptah* (Lund 1946); H. TE VELDE, Ptah, *LdÄ* IV (1982) 1177-1180.

M. HEERMA VAN VOSS

PYTHON Πυθών

I. *Pythōn* occurs just once in NT and indicates the oracular spirit of a slave-girl (Acts 16:16). There are two further occurrences in the *Sibylline Oracles* (5:182; 11: 315). *Sib. Or.* 11:315 is possibly connected with the dragon Python. Traditions concerning Python may be incorporated in Rev 12.

II. Python is the →Dragon (*drakōn* Euripides, *Iph. Taur.* 1245; Pausanias 10.6.6; Lucian, *De Astr.* 23; *draco ingens* Hyginus, *Fab.* 140; δράκαινα *Hom. Hymn to Apollo* 300) or →Serpent (FONTENROSE 1980:55) that protected the sanctuary of Delphi near Mount Parnassus (see e.g. Strabo 9.3.12) before the arrival of →Apollo. His link with Delphi may, however, be secondary, since many places besides Delphi claimed Apollo's triumph over the dragon as their local legend (OTTO 1962:107-108; cf. FONTENROSE 1980:46-69). Ephorus (fourth century BCE) seems to have been the first author who used the name Python for this Delphic 'dragon' in a rationalistic version of the myth (*FGH* 70 Fragm. 31; Strabo 9.3.12). Python is usually considered a son of Ge. According to *Hom. Hymn to Apollo* the dragon is female, see e.g. vv 300-306. The name is related to the site of Delphi (*Pythō*) and is associated with the rotting of the dead body of the dragon (*Hom. Hymn to Apollo* 356-374; Pausanias 10.6.5; *pythō* = 'become rotten'). Python was defeated by Apollo, who took over the oracle and became the patron deity of the sanctuary of Delphi. This struggle for rulership over the sanctuary (see e.g. Euripides, *Iph. Taur.* 1245-1258) can be considered as a conflict between a chthonic god and a god of a different kind (VON GEISAU 1972). Mythographers describe how Python pursued the pregnant Leto in order to prevent the birth of Apollo and →Artemis. Apollo killed him, however, as a newborn babe (Euripides, *Iph. Taur.* 1249; Hyginus, *Fab.* 140). According to some texts Python was sent on his deathly mission by →Hera who was jealous because of the favours of →Zeus to Leto.

From several (late) sources there appears a semantic development from the specific Delphic dragon to an oracular spirit in general. According to the Suda, sub voce *Pythōnos,* Python was a *daimonion mantikos*. This development is probably connected with the figure of the *Pythia*, the prophetic priestess of Apollo at Delphi, who was called a *mantis* (Aeschylus, *Eum.* 29) or a *promantis* (Herodotus 6.66). Hyginus, *Fab.* 140, considers Python himself a prophet and suggests that he revealed the oracular sayings before the time of Apollo. His mortal remains were said to have been buried under the tripod of the Pythia or to be preserved in this tripod (Hyginus, *Fab.* 140). Some sources suggest that the odour of Python's dead body inspired the Pythia (FOERSTER 1978:919).

III. Acts 16:16 refers to a slave-girl who was possessed by an oracular spirit. *Pythōn* occurs as apposition to *pneuma*. The passage can be interpreted against the background of the semantic development of *Pythōn*. The Delphic dragon himself became a mantic animal (cf. Hyginus, *Fab.* 140; Lucian, *De Astr.* 23) and lent his name to predicting →demons. In Philo, *Prob.* 19; 160, the word *pythochrēstos* is used with the general meaning 'oracular saying'. According to FOERSTER (1978:918-920) *pythōn* can only mean a ventriloquist in the first century CE (synonym of *eggastrimythos*; see e.g. Plutarch, *De def. orac.* 9 = *Mor.* 414E), which is possibly connected with the strange sounds of the Pythia. Ventriloquism was, however, usually thought to be inspired by a god or a demon (Origen, *Princ.* 3.3.5). Therefore, Acts 16:16 should not be necessarily understood as a reference to a female ventriloquist. The passage may refer in a more general sense to a predicting demon (cf. Pseudo-Clement, *Hom.* 9.16.3; also Vg Lev 20:27 *pythonicus spiritus*; FOERSTER 1978: 919).

Traditions concerning Python are probably incorporated into the passages on the Dragon in Revelation, although the name Python is not used (YARBRO COLLINS 1975: 57-100; 245-252 building upon DIETERICH 1891). The pattern of the Leto-Apollo-Python myth, especially in the version of Hyginus, *Fab.* 140, is closely related to the war of the Dragon in Rev 12 (and 20), and this myth was widely known in Asia Minor. Nevertheless, there are also some dissimilarities (Python pursues Leto *before* the birth of Apollo and Artemis, the rescue of Leto by Boreas and →Poseidon does not match the rescue of the woman in Rev 12 and the dragon in Revelation is originally located in heaven and has several opponents). Moreover, there are also striking correspondences with combat myths concerning →Typhon, which implies that John may have incorporated traditions concerning Typhon as well.

In *Sib. Or.* 5:182 *Pythōn* is a corruption of the name Pithom for an Egyptian city, but in *Sib. Or.* 11:315 *Pythōn* probably refers to the area or city of Pytho which was connected with Delphi, as appears from the second name in this passage Panopeia (= Panopeus), which indicates a city in the neighbourhood of Delphi. This seems to imply that the Sibyl presents herself at the end of book 11 as the chanter of oracles of Apollo (vv 315-324; cf. Pausanias 10.12.6), although this is denied explicitly in *Sib. Or.* 4:4-5.

IV. *Bibliography*

A. DIETERICH, *Abraxas: Studien zur Religionsgeschichte des späteren Altertums* (Leipzig 1891) 111-126; W. FOERSTER, πύθων, *TDNT* VI (Grand Rapids 1978) 917-920; J. FONTENROSE, *Python. A Study of Delphic Myth and its Origins* (Berkeley & Los Angeles 1959; 1980²); H. VON GEISAU, Python, PW 24 (Stuttgart 1963) 606-610; H. VON GEISAU, Python, *KP* 4 (1972) 1280; K. KERÉNYI, *Die Mythologie der Griechen. Die Götter- und Menschheitsgeschichten* (Zürich 1951) 128-136; O. KERN, *Die Religion der Griechen* (Berlin 1935) II 96-97, 102-110; W. F. OTTO, Mythos von Leto, dem Drachen und der Geburt, *Das Wort der Antike* (Stuttgart 1962) 90-128; H. D. SAFFREY, Relire l'Apocalypse à Patmos, *RB* 82 (1975) 416-417; G. TÜRK, Python, *ALGRM* III.2 (Leipzig 1902-1909) 3400-3412; A. YARBRO COLLINS, *The Combat Myth in the Book of Revelation* (Missoula 1975).

J. W. VAN HENTEN

Q

QATAR

I. The name *qēdār*, Qedar, carried by a tribe of the Ishmaelites as well as by its eponymous ancestor (Gen 25:13; 1 Chron 1:29; Isa 21:16.17; 42:11; 60:7; Jer 2:10; 49:28; Ezek 27:21; Ps 120:5; Cant 1:5), has been related to the alleged Amorite deity Qudur or Qadar (LEWY 1934:48). The suggestion lacks sufficient ground.

II. According to LEWY (1934:48 n. 48), the name of an Amorite deity Qudur/Qudar/Qadar is attested as theophoric element in four Mesopotamian names: *qù-du-ur-ì-li* (AO 9356:1); *qú-da-ri-li* (BIN IV 25:34); *qá-dá-ar*-AN (BAUER 1926:17) and *ya-ṣi-qa-dar* (BAUER 1926:30). The interpretation of these names by Lewy is problematical, however, because he fails to separate the element Qudur/Kudur from the name Qatar/Qaṭar. *Qudur/Kudur* may be interpreted as the Akkadian form of Elamite *kutur*, 'protector', used to qualify gods and kings (ZADOK 1984). With BAUER (1926:91) it must be distinguished from the theonym Qatar (Bauer reads *Ga-ta-ar*-AN and *Ia-ṣi-qa-tar*) or Qaṭar (GELB 1980). Since this allegedly Amorite deity is otherwise not attested, its character cannot be determined. Etymologically the name Qatar may be connected to the Semitic root QṬR/QTR 'to make smoke, to make incense' (cf. *HALAT* 1002).

The Qedarites were one of the most prominent tribes of the Ishmaelites. The earliest attestation of their land is to be found in an inscription from Tiglath Pileser III from 738 BCE containing a list of tributaries (L. D. LEVINE, *Two Neo-Assyrian Stelae from Iran* [Toronto 1972] 18, II:2; cf. M. WEIPPERT, *ZDPV* 89 [1973] 26-53); here Qedar is mentioned alongside Arabia. Since 'Zabibi, the queen of the Arabs' is the only Arab mentioned in the list, it may be assumed that she is the first known ruler of the Qedarites (KNAUF 1985:4 n.17). Qedar and the Qedarites are further known from Assyrian, Persian and Hellenistic sources up to Pliny (*Nat. Hist.* V 11 [12] 65: *Cedrei*; KNAUF 1985:66.96-108).

III. In the OT, the Qedarites are mentioned in oracles against the nations (Isa 21:16.17; Jer 49:28) and in poetic texts as inhabiting the →ends of the earth (Isa 42:11; Jer 2:10; Ps 120:5). They are depicted as sea-faring traders (Isa 60:7; Ezek 27:21). Their tent-dwellings were famous for their beauty (Cant 1:5). All these occurrences reflect Judahite knowledge of the Bedouin tribe in late pre-exilic, exilic and early post-exilic times. The Priestly author of Gen 25:13 has used this knowledge in his reconstruction of the earliest history of the Israelites in relation to neighbouring groups and nations (KNAUF 1985:56-65). Most probably, Qedar was not an historical figure from the second millennium BCE, but a retrojection of a people living in post-exilic times into times immemorial. Qedar can hardly be interpreted as a god or a semi-god; a relation with the Amorite deity Qatar is implausible.

IV. *Bibliography*

T. BAUER, *Die Ostkanaanäer* (Leipzig 1926); I. J. GELB, *Computer-aided Analysis of Amorite* (AS 21; Chicago 1980) 173; E. A. KNAUF, *Ismael* (ADPV 1; Wiesbaden 1985); J. LEWY, Les textes paléo-assyriens et l'Ancient Testament, *RHR* 110 (1934) 29-65; R. ZADOK, *The Elamite Onomasticon* (Suppl. AION 40; Napels 1984) 24-25.

B. BECKING & K. VAN DER TOORN

QEDAR → **QATAR**

QEDOSHIM → **SAINTS**

QETEB קטב

I. The term *Qeṭeb* appears four times in the OT. Its basic significance is 'destruction', (perhaps etymologically 'that which is cut off') though the contexts suggest that other nuances are present. Various scholars have translated it as 'plague' or 'pestilence' in the context of its parallel use with *rešep*, *deber*. The term has overtones of a divine name.

II. *qẓb* occurs once in Ugaritic (*KTU* 1.5 ii:24) and may be a kinsman of →Mot (J. C. DE MOOR, 'O Death, Where is Thy Sting', *Ascribe to the Lord: Biblical and Other Studies in Memory of P. C. Craigie* [ed. L. Eslinger & G. Taylor; JSOTSup 67; Sheffield 1988] 100-107), but the text is broken. DEL OLMO LETE links this word with *qṣb*, 'cut' (*Mitos y leyendas de Canaan* [Madrid 1981] 617). In the treaty between Esarhaddon and Baal of Tyre R. DUSSAUD (*Les religions des Hittites et des Hourrites, des Phéniciens et des Syriens* [Mana 2; Paris 1945] 361) detected a deity Qatiba ('entité incertaine'), but failed to give a specific reference; the suggestion is apparently based on a misreading of iv 6 (DINGIR-*a Qa-ti-ba* x°-[xxx]x instead of ᵈ*A-na-ti-Ba-a*°[-*a-ti* DINGI] R.MEŠ).

III. With so few biblical references to work from, each must be treated exhaustively to glean what information such scant evidence may provide. The most useful information comes from Deut 32:24, where the following tricolon occurs in →Yahweh's curse of apostate →Jacob: *mězê rāʿāb* 'sucked dry by Hunger*', *ûlĕḥumê rešep* 'and devoured* by Pestilence*' *wĕqeṭeb mĕrîrî* 'and bitter* Destruction*'. Several words here (marked *) are ambiguous, giving rise to rich nuances. Thus 'Hunger' is probably an epithet of Mot (Heb *Māwet*), god of death; *lĕḥumê*, 'devoured', can also be construed as 'fought against', cf. the arrow metaphor of v 23; 'Pestilence' is personified as →Resheph, the plague-god, who in Ugaritic is represented as an archer (*KTU* 1.82:3); *Qeṭeb* appears to be a divine name, in accordance with the other two, while *mĕrîrî*, 'bitter', may also have the sense of 'strong' (M. J. DAHOOD, Qoheleth and Recent Discoveries, *Bib* 39 [1958] 302-318, esp. 309-310) or even 'eclipse' (M. H. POPE, *Job* [AB 15: New York 1973] 29); cf. →Meriri. There is no compelling reason not to accept the clearly mythological sense of this passage, which appears therefore to list a triad of demonic figures, all associated with death (R. GORDIS, The Asseverative *kaph* in Ugaritic and Hebrew, *JAOS* 63 [1943] 176-178, esp. 178). Since however both Mot and Resheph are identified with Babylonian →Nergal, whose cult was attested in Palestine as late as hellenistic times (J. B. CURTIS, An Investigation of the Mount of Olives in the Judaeo-Christian Tradition, *HUCA* 28 [1957] 137-180), it is as plausible to see all three terms above as relating to the one figure. 'Destruction' would thus represent the full implementation of Death's powers.

Ps 91:5-6 lists enemies from whom Yahweh will rescue the faithful. They appear, following v 3 with its references to the Fowler (TROMP 1969:175) and Pestilence (*Deber*), to be confederates or aspects of Death. The tetracolon of vv 5-6 is complex, and needs to be analysed as a whole: *lōʾ tîrāʾ mippaḥad laylâ* 'You will not fear the →Terror of the night,' *mēḥēṣ yāʿûp yômām* 'nor the arrow flying by day'; *middeber bāʾōpel yahălōk* 'nor Pestilence that stalks the gloom', *miqqeṭeb yāšûd ṣohŏrāyim* 'nor Destruction that devastates at noon'. *Qeṭeb* occurs in v 6 in parallel to *Deber*: in some sense, therefore, it complements it. But its diurnal danger, in contrast to *Deber*'s nocturnal threat, also balances the diurnal arrow of v 5, which in turn contrasts with the 'Terror by night'. The arrow provides the clue, being a metaphor for the fevers sent by Resheph the plague-god. Since *Deber* seems here to be his double, the two gods operating by day and by night respectively, we arrive at the following equation: the Terror is *Deber*, while the arrow (of Resheph) is *Qeṭeb*, the personification of the destruction the god wreaks. This seems to corroborate our findings in Deut 32:24 above. But there may also be a chiasmus over the whole tetracolon, giving rise to the equations Terror = Destruction (a and d) and Arrow (of Resheph) = *Deber* (b and c). The demonic powers are of protean form and character.

At Hos 13:14, in the two bicola of the verse, →Sheol and Death are found twice in parallel, indicating that Sheol is here another name for the god of death, by metonymy. In the second bicolon, *Deber* and *Qeṭeb* (or rather Qoṭeb, see H. BAUER & P. LEANDER, *Historische Grammatik der hebräischen Sprache* [Halle 1922] 582) are again parallel terms, and are clearly the agents of Death's purposes: *miyyad šĕʾôl ʾepdēm* 'Shall I ransom them from the hand of Sheol', *mimmāwet ʾegʾālēm* 'shall I redeem them from Mot?', *ʾehî dĕbārêkā māwet* 'Where are your Pestilences, Mot?', *ʾehî qoṭobkā šĕʾôl* 'Where is your Destruction, Sheol?' The LXX of the second bicolon is paraphrased (as a hymnic excerpt?) at 1 Cor 15:55 (→Thanatos).

Isa 28:2 is part of a taunt against Ephraim, alluding to the agent of Yahweh's destructive visitation which is imminent: *hinneh ḥāzāq wĕʾammîṣ laʾdōnāy* 'Lo, the Lord has someone Bold and Powerful', *kĕzerem bārād śaʿar qāṭeb* 'like a storm of hail (→Barad), a tempest of Destruction', *kĕzerem mayim kabbîrîm šōṭĕpîm* 'like a storm of mighty flooding waters.' As in the first passage, many of the words used here are susceptible of a mythological interpretation, in particular *Bārād* and *Mayim. Qeṭeb* appears to operate here through the tempest, and here too there is the possibility of deliberate ambiguity, where *śaʿar* suggests the arch-demonic form of a →satyr, *śāʿîr*. The tempest metaphor, continuing that of Hail, is probably to be taken to combine the two figures of overwhelming flood-waters, and the dart-like effects of hail and heavy rain, evoking the arrows of the plague-god. Both are metaphors for Death and its powers.

Our four passages are allusive rather than strictly informative, but suggest that *Qeṭeb* is more than a literary figure, living as a spiritual, and highly dangerous, reality in the minds of poets and readers. We can see a slow process of reinterpretation taking place in the treatment of the four passages in LXX, where in each instance it is translated by a different term. These are respectively *opisthotonos* 'vengeance' (lit. 'bending backwards' or 'drawn', as of a bow), *symptōma,* 'occurrence, accident', *kentron*, 'goad, sting', and *ouk ... skepē*, 'no ... shelter'. It may be coincidence that in discussing 'the destruction that ravageth at noon' in Ps 91, GASTER (1969:770) explains *Qeṭeb* as sunstroke, and notes that Theocritus identifies 'this demon' with Pan (cf. the 'satyr' suggestion at Isa 28:2).

IV. *Bibliography*

A. CAQUOT, Sur quelques démons de l'Ancien Testament: Reshep, Qeteb, Deber, *Sem 6* (1956) 53-68; T. H. GASTER, *Myth, Legend and Custom in the Old Testament* (London 1969) 321, 770; W. O. E. OESTERLY & T. H. ROBINSON, *Hebrew Religion, its Origin and Development* (London 1930) 70-75; N. J. TROMP, *Primitive Conceptions of Death and the Netherworld in the Old Testament* (BibOr 21; Rome 1969) 107-108, 163.

N. WYATT

QÔS קוש

I. Qôs is the national deity of →Edom. He is attested only once in the Hebrew Bible as an element in the personal name Barqos, "Qôs gleamed forth" (cf. Lihyanite *qwsbr*; BARTLETT 1989: no. 34; South Safaitic *brqs*, BARTLETT 1989: no. 36), indicating the 'father' of an exiled clan of *nĕtînîm* returning from Babylon (Ezra 2:53 = Neh 7:55). This clan or family must have been of Edomite or Idumaean origin. (The name Kushaiah, 1 Chr 15:17, cannot be connected with Qôs [*pace* BARTLETT 1989:200-201]: according to 1 Chr 6:29, Etan's father was also called Kishi, and Qôs is never spelled with [*š*] in Canaanite and Aramaic texts).

II. Well before the emergence of an Edomite state and an Edomite nation (8th century BCE; cf. BARTLETT 1989; KNAUF 1992), Qôs was already present in or near his later domain. Egyptian listings (SIMONS 1937:XXIII 7; 9; 13; 21) of what must have been the names of Shasu clans from the 13th century BCE (ODED 1971; KNAUF 1984) mention *qśrʿ* ("Qôs is [my] shepherd" or "Qôs is [my] friend"), *qśśpt*, *qśsnrm* ("Qôs is verily exalted", Egyptian /n/ stands for Semitic /l/), and *qśrbn* ("Qôs is brilliant, radiant"; here, Egyptian /r/ stands for Semitic /l/).

As Edom's national deity, Qôs is attested in the names of the Edomite kings Qaus-malak (BARTLETT 1989: no. 1), contemporary with Tiglath-Pileser III, and Qaus-gabar, who ruled under Esarhaddon and Ashurbanipal (BARTLETT 1989: nos. 2 and 8). His official status is also attested by the Ḥorvat ʿUza ostracon, a piece of Edomite administrative correspondence from the first half of the 6th century: *hbrktk l-qws* "I bless you (in the name) of Qôs" (KNAUF 1988a:78-79; BARTLETT 1989:221-222). Qôs may have been the owner of an estate at (or the recipient of revenues from) Aroer in the Negeb (BARTLETT 1989:213 no. 4). He is also mentioned, in a broken context, however, at the Edomite capital Bozrah (BARTLETT 1989: 223 no. 3). Qôs is further attested in the non-royal Edomite names *qwsʿnl* (BARTLETT 1989: no. 9; BARTLETT 1989:214 no. 6; cf. Idumaean *Kōsanélou* BARTLETT 1989: no. 51), *bdqws* (BARTLETT 1989: no. 10), *pqʿqws* (BARTLETT 1989: no. 11), *qwsb[nh]* (BARTLETT 1989: no. 12, cf. *Kosbanou* BARTLETT 1989: no. 52), and *qwsny* (BARTLETT 1989: no. 13; BARTLETT 1989: 219-220 no. 7) from Tell el-Kheleifeh/ancient Elath, and *qwsʿ* from Aroer in the Negeb (BARTLETT 1989: no. 14). A building complex from the seventh/sixth century BCE excavated at Ḥorvat Qiṭmiṭ—10 km south of Arad—has been interpreted as an Edomite santuary (BEIT-ARIEH 1985:201-202). Archaeological findings indicate that Qôs had been worshipped there together with an unnamed female consort. An abundance of ostriches among the votive gifts characterize him as a desert god, and as another god fulfilling the role of the 'lord of the beasts' (see →Shadday; cf. KEEL & UEHLINGER 1992: 440-444).

Most references to Qôs derive from the period after the decline of the Edomite state (552 BCE) and testify to an uninterrupted continuity of population in southern Palestine and the Transjordan in the second half of the first millennium BCE.

The majority of the references to Qôs is Idumaean. Although Idumaea was not organized as a distinct administrative district before the early 4th century BCE, the Edomites of the post-state period can conveniently be called Idumaeans. A cuneiform contract found at Tawilan and dated to the accession year of (most probably) Darius I contains two Qôs-names: Qôs-šamaʿ and Qôs-yadaʿ (BARTLETT 1989: nos. 3 and 4). Edomites/Idumaeans exiled to Babylonia are attested under Artaxerxes I (Qôs-yadaʿ and Qôs-yahab from Nippur, BARTLETT 1989: nos. 5 and 6). The Aramaic ostraca from Tell es-Sebaʿ (ca. 400 BCE) contain 14 Qôs-names (BARTLETT 1989: nos. 15-28). Whereas *qwsynqm* (33.3), *qwsbrk* (33.4, cf. *Kosbarakos* BARTLETT 1989: no. 53), *qwsml[k]* (33.4, cf. *Kosmalachos* BARTLETT 1989: no. 55), *qwsgbr* (37.4) and *qwsḥnn* [sic! *ed. princeps* reads *-ḥbn*] (41.6) continue Edomite/Canaanite name types, some of the Idumaean names are Arabic: *qwsnhr* (28.2; with Arabic *nahār* replacing Canaanite *nūr*), *qwsʿwt* (34.1; *-ǵauṯ*) and *qwswhb* (36.1); *qwsʿdr* (34.6; cf. *Kosadaros* BARTLETT 1989: no. 49) could be Aramaic as well as Canaanite.

Most Qôs-names in Greek inscriptions and papyri (mostly from Egypt) should have belonged to Idumaeans (some may refer to Nabataeans or Hijâzians, see below). In addition to those already mentioned, these include *Abdokōs/ʿbdqws* (BARTLETT 1989: no. 48), *Kosadou/qwsʿdh* (from Marissa, BARTLETT 1989: no. 50), *Kosgērou/qwsgr* (BARTLETT 1989: no. 54), *Kosnatanos* (Marissa; BARTLETT 1989: no. 56) and *Kousnatanos/qwsntn* (BARTLETT 1989: no. 59; from Zenon's archive, 259 B.C.E.), *Kosramos/qwsrm* (BARTLETT 1989: no. 57), *Kostobaros/qwsgbr* (or *-br*? BARTLETT 1989: no. 58; Jos. *Ant.* XV 8,9) and *Pakeidokōsōi/pqydqws* (BARTLETT 1989: no. 60, from Delos). A bilingual ostracon from Khirbet el-Qôm, dated to 277 BCE (GERATY 1975), contains the Idumaean name *qwsydʿ/Kosidē* (line 2).

In the course of the first half of the 6th century BCE, Edom established a colony at Dedan, a North Arabian caravan town (Isa 21:13; Jer 49:8; Ezek 25:13; Thr 4:21). Hence, some Qôs-names are attested in local inscriptions (fifth - third century BCE), e.g. *qwsmlk* (BARTLETT 1989: nos. 32-33) and *qwsbr* (334; BARTLETT 1989: no. 34; names ending in *-qs* may refer to the North Arabian deity Qais, and North Minaean *slmtqs* [BARTLETT 1989: no. 35] is better disregarded in the present context, as Minaean transliterates foreign /s/ by [*t*]).

The southern part of what had been Edom became the cultic centre of the Nabataean realm (in Arabic, *aš-Šarā*, culminating in the environs of Petra). The Nabataean national deity Dushara (*Ḏū-Šarā*) 'The One of the Sharâ-Mountains' can hardly refer to any deity other than Qôs (KNAUF 1989: 110-111; 158-159; KNAUF 1991). Under his proper name, Qôs is mentioned in the Nabataean inscriptions of Jebel et-Tannūr, where his consort is a goddess belonging to the →Atargatis-type. Here, Qôs is called the "god of Ḥaurā" (*ḥwrwʾ*, presently el-Ḥumaimah, in the Ḥismā district of Southern Jordan; KNAUF 1988b:89-90) by a certain *qsmlk* (BARTLETT 1989: no. 47). After the decline of the Nabataean state, Qôs still receives the dedication of an eagle at Bosra (IGLS XIII 9003; 2nd-3rd centuries CE; BARTLETT 1989: no. 44). From roughly the same period stem the graffiti in the Nabataean script in southern Sinai, whose authors mostly came from the northern Hejâz (MORITZ 1916); here, another *qwsʿdr* (*CIS* II 923.2; BARTLETT 1989: no. 45) is attested; from Hegra (Madāʾin Ṣāliḥ, the Nabataean successor of Dedan el-ʿUlā) came a *qsntn* (*CIS* II 209; BARTLETT 1989: no. 46). Furthermore, Edomite emigration is attested by the occurrence of the personal names *qwśnhr* and *qwśdkr* in the Samaria-papyri excavated at Wadi ed-Daliyeh.

As a deity, *qws* is once mentioned in a Thamudic inscription from the vicinity of Jerash (KNAUF 1981, roughly contemporary with the Nabataean references to Qôs). Several Safaitic and Thamudic persons were called *qs*, which is better interpreted as *Qais, a frequent Arabic name (BARTLETT 1989: nos. 37-42), and two Safaites named *qsl* (BARTLETT 1989: nos. 42-43) may have been called either **Qōsīl*, "Qôs is (my) god", or, more likely, **Qēsīl*.

It is generally accepted that the etymon of Qôs is Arabic *qaus* "bow" (BARTLETT 1989: 200-204). The Semitic word for "bow" belongs to the few words with biradical roots: *qs_1 became triradical by suffixation of a *-t* in Akkadian, Ethiopic, Canaanite and Aramaic (Heb *qešet*, pl. *qĕšātôt*), and by infigation of an *-u-* in Arabic (*qaus*, pl. *qusiyy* and *qisiyy*). The orthography of the divine name in Edomite and Aramaic poses, however, a problem which is widely disregarded: Proto-Semitic /s_1/ corresponds to /š/ in 1st millennium BCE Canaanite, whereas Qôs is consistently spelled with <s> (representing Proto-Semitic /s_3/). An historic solution of this problem assumes that /qaus$_1$/ is a loan-word in Canaanite Edomite from a language that had not yet participated in the Canaanite shift /s_1/: [s] > [š]; /s_3/: [ts] > [s] (KNAUF 1988b:73-76), i.e. Qôs was at home in one of the Proto-Arabian languages of the Shasu-bedouins in southern Edom at the end of the 2nd millennium BCE (with Egyptian /s/ for /s_1/) and was borrowed into the Canaanite Edomite of the incipient Edomite state (originating in northern Edom; KNAUF 1992) during or shortly before the 8th century (KNAUF 1984b).

Meaning "bow", Qôs is the deified weapon of the weathergod (cf. Gen 9:13) or a war-god (hardly an alternative in the barely specialized pantheon of a simple farmer-herder society at the fringe of the agricultural area); deified divine weapons or tools are also known from Ugarit (*ygrš KTU* 1.2 iv:12). Although the inventory of the Qiṭmīt sanctuary is rather late, it presents Qôs in the role of the 'lord of the animals' (a role also played by a close relative of Qôs, the Israelite →Yahweh; see below), a connection that may help to elucidate Esau's 'ritual hunt' in Genesis 27 (cf. esp. 27:27-29). The worship of Qôs seems to originate in Southern Edom, i.e. south of Wādī-l-Ghuweir or even south of Rās en-Naqb, in the Ḥismā area of southern Jordan and Northwest Arabia. Close to the present Saudi-Jordanian border, a Jabal al-Qaus is recorded (MUSIL 1926:41). According to his attestations, Qôs entered the Edomite pantheon not long before, probably with the foundation of the Edomite state in the 8th century BCE. He was supremely *en vogue* among the Idumaeans under Persian rule, when loyalty to the national deity probably compensated for the loss of national independence (a process that may find a parallel in the history of Yahweh). The presence of Qôs in North Arabia and among ancient Arabs can be explained as a cultural loan from the Edomites (and their successors). The inscriptions from Khirbet et-Tannūr, still link him though to the Ḥismā.

III. His area of origin and his nature as an aspect of the Syrian weathergod present Qôs as closely related to Yahweh. Could the two have originally been identical? At Kuntillet Ajrud around 800 BCE, a "Yahweh of Teman" is attested besides "Yahweh of Samaria". Teman was another designation for northern Edom (cf. Amos 1:12; Jer 49: 7.20; Ezek 25:13), but could also refer to any area south of Samaria in this context. In addition, Yahweh arrives from Seir to fight for his people in the archaic song of Deborah (Judg 5:5; Ps 68:9). One may further note that Qôs is not mentioned in the Hebrew Bible (nor is there any 'national deity' for Edom mentioned), whereas the Ammonite →Milcom and the Moabite →Chemosh are (BARTLETT 1989:197-200). Yahweh, Qôs and Dushara are primarily epithets that were used instead of the god's real name, →Haddu/Hadad (another of his epithets was, of course, →Baal). From an historical point of view, one may claim the five deities mentioned as differentiations of a single deity; his different names indicate, however, that various groups of believers stressed various aspects of that generic 'Syrian weathergod'. What they thought about the identity or non-identity of their respective gods is, for the lack of unambiguously phrased source material, presently beyond our insight (cf. KNAUF 1991).

IV. *Bibliography*

I. BEITH-ARIEH, Ḥorvat Qiṭmiṭ, *IEJ* 35 (1985) 201-202; J. R. BARTLETT, *Edom and the Edomites* (JSOTSup 77; Sheffield 1989); L. T. GERATY, The Khirbet el-Kôm bilingual ostracon, *BASOR* 220 (1975) 57-61; O. KEEL & C. UEHLINGER, *Göttinnen, Götter und Gottessymbole* (Freiburg-Basel-Wien 1992); E. A. KNAUF, Zwei thamudische Inschriften aus der Gegend von Ǧeraš, *ZDPV* 97 1981) 188-192; KNAUF, Qaus in Ägypten, *GM* 73 (1984a) 33-36; KNAUF, Qaus, *UF* 16 (1984b) 93-95; KNAUF, Supplementa Ismaelitica 13: Edom und Arabien, *BN* 45 (1988a) 62-81; KNAUF, *Midian. Untersuchungen zur Geschichte Palästinas und Nordarabiens am Ende des 2. Jahrtausends v. Chr.* (ADPV; Wiesbaden 1988b); KNAUF, *Ismael. Untersuchungen zur Geschichte Palästinas und Nordarabiens im l. Jahrtausend v. Chr.* (ADPV 7, Wiesbaden ^{2}1989); KNAUF, Dushara and Shai' al-Qaum. Yhwh und Baal. Dieu, in: *Lectio difficilior probabilior? L'exégèse comme expérience de décloisonnement. Mélanges offerts à Françoise Smyth-Florentin* (ed. Th. Römer; DBAT Beih 12; Heidelberg 1991), 19-29; KNAUF, The cultural impact of secondary state formation: the cases of the Edomites and Moabites, *Early Edom and Moab: The Beginning of the Iron Age in Southern Jordan* (ed. P. Bienkowski; Sheffield 1992); B. MORITZ, *Der Sinaikult in heidnischer Zeit* (Berlin 1916); A. MUSIL, *The Northern Ḥeǧāz* (New York 1926); B. ODED, Egyptian References to the Edomite Deity Qaus, *AUSS* 9 (1971) 47-50; J. SIMONS, *Handbook for the Study of Egyptian Topographical Lists relating to Western Asia* (Leiden 1937).

E. A. KNAUF

QUEEN OF HEAVEN מלכת השמים

I. As a designation of a goddess, **malkat haššāmayim* occurs in Jer 7:18; 44:17-19.25 as well as in Hermopolis Letter 4.1

from South Egypt (5th century BCE; BRESCIANI & KAMIL 1966). In the MT *mlkt* (a number of MSS have *mlk't*) *hšmym* has been vocalized as *mĕleket* (= *mĕle'ket*) *haššāmayim*, "the work of heaven" which, as appears from a comparison of Gen 2:1 with Gen 2:2, apparently has to be interpreted as *ṣĕba' haššāmayim*, "the host of heaven" (cf. LXX Jer 7:18, *hē stratiā tou ouranou*, "the →host of heaven"). So it is likely that the punctuators of the Hebrew text wanted to suggest that Jer 7:18; 44:17-25 deal with the worship of the heavenly bodies. It is now commonly agreed that the original vocalization of *mlkt hšmym* was *malkat haššāmayim*, "the Queen of Heaven" (cf. LXX Jer 51 [44]:17-25, *hē basilissa tou ouranou*). Evidently the Masoretic vocalization was an intentional variation which was focused on the removal of any suggestion that the people of Judah had engaged in the worship of the Queen of Heaven.

II. The designation "Queen of Heaven" qualifies its bearer as a mighty, universal and leading goddess. In the ancient Near East similar designations were borne by prominent divinities such as the Babylonian-Assyrian goddess →Ishtar and the West Semitic goddesses →Anat and →Astarte. They have several traits of character in common and are generally regarded as fertility goddesses. It is doubtful whether they are characterized by their title as astral divinities. With regard to Ishtar and Astarte such an interpretation is possible—they are equated with Venus—, but with regard to Anat, for instance, the identification with a heavenly body is not likely.

Ishtar is called *malkat šamāmi*, "Queen of Heaven," *šarrat šamāmi u kakkabê*, "Sovereign of Heaven and Stars", *šarrat šamê*, "Sovereign of Heaven", *belit šamê*, "Lady of Heaven", etc. (*AkkGE* 39, 64, 129, 186, 239, 240). In numerous inscriptions from New Kingdom Egypt the epithet *nb.t p.t*, 'Lady of Heaven', is used for Anat, Astarte, Ishtar and also for Qudshu, "the Holy One" (STADELMANN 1967:88-123). The identity of Qudshu is disputed. Her equation with Canaanite →Asherah is defended (e.g., OLYAN 1987: 163). In the Ugaritic literature Anat is called *b'lt šmm rmm*, "Lady of the Exalted Heaven", (*KTU* 1.108:7). According to a current but uncertain interpretation (cf. CHR. BUTTERWECK, *TUAT* 2 [1988] 592) *šmm 'drm* in the Phoenician Esmun'azar inscription (*KAI* 14:16) must be construed as a title of Astarte, "*Lady* of the Highest Heaven". Oriental →Aphrodite (= Astarte), whose cult is attested in the latter half of the first millennium and was spread throughout the Mediterranean world, was designated by the title *Ourania*, 'The Heavenly One' (cf. DELCOR 1982: 115-119; HÖRIG 1979: 41, 125, 158-159).

III. In the book of Jeremiah only the goddess' title is mentioned. Her proper name is concealed. Because all of the great goddesses of the ancient Near East could be denoted by epithets such as Lady of Heaven, it is not surprising that various suggestions are made with regard to the identity of the Judaean Queen of Heaven. Ishtar, Anat, Astarte, Asherah and even the Ug sun-goddess Shapshu (DAHOOD 1960:166-168) are presented as candidates. Evidently, the Queen of Heaven was a Canaanite fertility goddess, a mother goddess, whose cult was known and practised in Israel and Judah long before Jeremiah. It is possible that Manasseh as a vassal of Assur introduced the cult of Ishtar in Jerusalem, but in practice his concern would certainly be a stimulus for the people to worship a Canaanite counterpart of the Mesopotamian goddess. As a matter of course the time-honoured connections of Canaan with Mesopotamia can have resulted in the adoption of some foreign traits in the Canaanite/Israelite cult. In this connection it is worth mentioning that *kawwānîm*, the term for the cakes which were used in the cult of the Queen of Heaven (Jer 7:18; 44:19), is cognate to Akk *kamānu*, which is used among others in connection with offerings to Ishtar (*CAD* 8 [1971] 110-111). As for the identity of the Queen of Heaven, it is difficult to make a choice between Anat—Anatyahû and Anatbayt'il of the fifth century BCE Elephantine papyri (B. PORTEN 1968: 171, 177, 179)—,

Asherah (2 Kgs 21:7; 23:4.7) and the West Semitic Astarte (e.g., OLYAN 1987:166-174).

The question of her identity appears, however, not to be of considerable importance. In the syncretistic world of the first millennium BCE Near East, the title Queen of Heaven was evidently a designation for the universal mother goddess, who according to the time and the place of her worship could have a different character. The use of the goddess' title without mentioning her proper name may be considered as a symptom of a religious atmosphere in which the qualities of a deity are held to be of more importance than her name (cf. DELCOR 1982: 115-119).

The cult of the Queen of Heaven, as depicted in the book of Jeremiah, was practised in Jerusalem and the cities of Judah (Jer 7:17) as well as among the Judaean emigrants in Egypt (Jer 44:15). The people of Judah, but also their kings and princes, were devoted to her worship (Jer 44:17). Her cult was a task of the whole family, but the leading role in it was played by the women (Jer 7:18; 44:15.19). In honour of the Queen of Heaven sacrifices were burned and drink-offerings were poured out (Jer 44:17-19). By the women cakes were made, either in the shape of the (naked?) goddess or of a star, her emblem, or marked with her image or her emblem (Jer 7:18; 44:19). Prosperity and protection against calamities were regarded as the consequences of paying homage to her (Jer 44:8.17).

In the Bible no sanctuary is mentioned in connection with the cult of the Queen of Heaven (cf. Jer 7:17; 44:17). It goes too far, however, to conclude that her cult was only of a private nature (cf. 2 Kgs 21:7; 23:4.7). In the Hermopolis letter 4:1, which is of non-Jewish origin, mention is made of a temple to the Queen of Heaven (*byt mlkt šmyn*) in Syene, in that part of Egypt where Judaean emigrants had established themselves (cf. Jer 44:1.15).

IV. The cult of the Queen of Heaven maintained its position long into the Christian Era. Epiphanius (4th century) criticizes certain women in Thracia, Scythia, and Arabia, on account of their habit of adoring the Virgin →Mary as a goddess and offering to her a certain kind of cake (*kollyrida tina*), whence he calls them "Collyridians" (*Adv. Haereses* LXXIX; PG 42 [1863] 741, 752). Isaac of Antioch (5th century) equates the Queen of Heaven of the book of Jeremiah with the Syr goddess Kaukabta, "the Star" (= Venus). He also identifies the Arab goddess Al-Uzza with the Queen of Heaven (*Opera omnia* I, ed. G. BICKEL [Giessen 1873] 210, 244-247). Some traits in the cult of Al-Uzza have been borrowed from her cult (J. WELLHAUSEN 1897:34-45). Acquaintance with the cult of the Queen of Heaven may be present in *Tg. Jer.* 7:18; 44:17-19.25. *mlkt hšmym* has been translated with *kwkbt šmy'*, 'the →stars of heaven' (cf. MT) or more likely 'the Star of Heaven' (= Venus). In the worship of the Blessed Virgin Mary (*Regina Coeli*) the cult of the Queen of Heaven is continued up to the present (OLYAN 1987:169; LORETZ 1990: 88).

V. *Bibliography*

S. ACKERMANN, "And the Women Knead Dough": The Worship of the Queen of Heaven in Sixth-Century Judah, *Gender and Difference in Ancient Israel* (ed. P. L. Day; Minneapolis 1989) 109-124; E. BRESCIANI & M. KAMIL, *Le Lettre aramaiche di Hermopoli* (Rome 1966); M. DAHOOD, La Regina del Cielo in Geremia, *RivBib* 8 (1960) 166-168; *M. DELCOR, Le culte de la "Reine du Ciel" selon Jer 7,18; 44,1-19,25 et ses survivances, *Von Kanaan bis Kerala. Festschrift für Prof. Mag. Dr. J. P. M. van der Ploeg O.P.* (ed. W. C. Delsman et al.; Kevelaer/Neukirchen-Vluyn 1982) 101-122; M. HÖRIG, *Dea Syria* (AOAT 208; Kevelaer/Neukirchen-Vluyn 1979); *C. HOUTMAN, *Der Himmel im Alten Testament* (OTS 30; Leiden 1993); K. KOCH, Aschera als Himmelskönigin in Jerusalem, *UF* 20 (1988) 97-120; O. LORETZ, *Ugarit und die Bibel* (Darmstadt 1990); R. DU MESNIL DU BUISSON, *Études sur les dieux phéniciens hérités par l'empire romain* (Leiden 1970) 119, 126-127; J. T. MILIK, Les papyrus araméens d'Hermoupolis et les cultes syro-phéniciens en Egypte perse, *Bib* 48 (1967) 556-564; *M. OLYAN, Some Observations concerning the Identity of the Queen of Heaven, *UF* 19 (1987) 161-174; B. PORTEN, *Archives from Elephantine* (Berkeley/Los Angeles 1968); W. E. RAST, Cakes for the Queen of Heaven, *Scripture in History and Theology. Essays in Honor of J. Coert Rylaarsdam* (ed. A. L. Merrill & T. W. Overholt; Pittsburgh 1974) 167-180; S. SCHROER, *In Israel gab es Bilder* (OBO 74; Freiburg/Göttingen 1987) 273-281; R. STADELMANN, *Syrisch-Palästinensische Gottheiten in Ägypten* (Leiden 1967); J. WELLHAUSEN, *Reste arabischen Heidentums* (Berlin 1897) 34-45; U. WINTER, *Frau und Göttin* (OBO 53; Freiburg/Göttingen 1983) 561-576.

C. HOUTMAN

QUIRINUS

I. Quirinus, a Roman god progressively identified with Romulus, occurs as a theophoric element in the name of P. Sulpicius Quirinius at Luke 2:2.

II. It is difficult to obtain any accurate understanding of archaic Roman religion (say, before 509 BCE) and Quirinus is even by these standards unclear. His festival is obviously the Quirinalia on 17th February, but what happened there is known neither to us nor, apparently, to Ovid. For some reason his name links with the title of the Roman citizens in assembly, the 'Quirites'. The Quirinal Hill at Rome is evidently named after him and his temple there is "one of the oldest shrines" in Rome (Pliny, *HN* 15:200). But his name, an adjective in formation, has suggested that he was the god of a forgotten area *Quirium, perhaps the home of the original Quirites (WISSOWA 1912:153, an idea which largely goes back to B. G. NIEBUHR, cf. KRETSCHMER 1920:147). Others, since antiquity, have considered the possibility that he is a peaceful form of Mars, Mars Quirinus, Mars of the Quirites (PALMER 1970:167, but cf. SCHOLZ 1970: 18-20 and RADKE 1981:140-141). He certainly has features in common with Mars. Both have a *flamen*, the archaic Roman priesthood perhaps cognate with the Sanskrit *brahman*: the three major *flamines* are, in order, the *flamen Dialis* (of Jupiter), the *flamen Martialis* and the *flamen Quirinalis*. Like Mars, he has a set of *Salii*, 'Leaping' priests whose duties notably included dances in armour during March (the month of Mars); and like Mars he had his own weapons and armour (Festus p. 238 Lindsay, cf. PALMER 1970:162). One reading of the evidence associates him with the structuring of early Roman society into *curiae* (voting divisions; >**co-uiriae*) and with the assembled Roman citizenry (Quirites), making him very much the god of the Roman 'Männerbund' (e.g. KRETSCHMER 1920:150; DUMÉZIL 1966; but cf. RADKE 1981:144-147). Whatever his origins, the deified Romulus came gradually to be identified with him during the last centuries BCE and this at least gave him an identity for Romans in the time of →Christ.

III. Quirinus, with his awkward Latin *Qui-* (pronounced *Kwi-*), is Κυρῖνος in Greek (e.g. Dion.Hal., *Ant.Rom.* 2, 63, 3) and Quirinius is Κυρήνιος in Luke; in turn this is rendered back into Latin as *Cyrinus* in Vg. It seems, therefore, unlikely that Jerome (or even Luke) was particularly aware of the theophoric nature of this name. Publius Sulpicius Quirinius was a man of relatively undistinguished origins whose military skills had won him a consulate in 12 BCE. He displayed consistent loyalty to the future emperor Tiberius (Tac., *Annals* 3:48) which won him influence and ultimately (21 CE) a public funeral. He was governor of Syria in 6 CE (Jos., *Ant.* 18:26), which poses chronological difficulties for his mention at Luke 2:2 in connection with the contentious census. PW lists seven Quirini, mostly from the Greek eastern Mediterranean and also a Quirinius, but Luke's is the only Sulpicius Quirinius known to us.

IV. *Bibliography*

A. BRELICH, Quirinus. Una divinità romana alla luce della comparazione storica, *SMSR* 31 (1960) 63-119; G. DUMÉZIL, *La religion* *romaine archaïque* (Paris 1966) ch. v; C. KOCH, Quirinus, PW 24 (1963) 1306-22; P. KRETSCHMER, Lat. Quirites und quiritare, *Glotta* 10 (1920) 147-57; K. LATTE, *Römische Religionsgeschichte* (München 1960) 133-134; R. E. A. PALMER, *The Archaic Community of the Romans* (Cambridge 1970) 160-172; G. RADKE, *Zur Entwicklung der Gottesvorstellung und der Gottesverehrung in Rom* (Darmstadt 1987) 138-156; *RADKE, Quirinus. Eine kritische Überprüfung der Überlieferung und ein Versuch, *ANRW* II.17.1 (1981) 276-299 [& lit]; U. W. SCHOLZ, *Studien zum altitalischen und altrömischen Marskult und Marsmythos* (Heidelberg 1970); R. SYME, *The Augustan Aristocracy* (Oxford 1986) 55. 338-340; G. WISSOWA, *Religion und Kultus der Römer* (2nd ed., München 1912) 153-156; G. WISSOWA, Quirinus, *ALGRM* iv (1909-15) 10-18.

K. DOWDEN

R

RABIṢU רבץ

I. *Rābiṣu* (Sum **maškim**) is formally an Akkadian participle from *rabāṣu*, 'to crouch, lie in wait'. Evidence from Arabic suggests that Proto-Semitic contained two different roots: RBḎ and RBṢ. In Arabic the former is used with reference to small cattle and denotes their 'crouching' or 'lying down' (cf. OSA *mrbḏn*, 'sheepfold'), though it can also mean 'to lurk'. The latter has the second (negative) meaning only. The root is not used as a divine element in Semitic onomastica.

In Akkadian texts, the title *rābiṣu* is also applied to certain deities. In Gen 4:7, the Hebrew word *rōbēṣ* is often considered a loan of Akk *rābiṣu*: sin is 'crouching' at Cain's door like a demon.

II. The root meaning of Akk *rābiṣu* seems to be 'one who lies in wait'. Yet the term was not always employed in a negative sense. Its usage may be divided into two categories: (a) referring to human officials and (b) referring to deities or demons.

Rābiṣu was the name of a high official in Mesopotamia (the title is often translated 'commissary', 'bailiff', *Sachwalter*, etc.). The office included a judicial aspect. It is well attested in the Ur III period, where the *rābiṣu* was the most important official after the judge and was responsible for the preliminary examination at trials. A '*rābiṣu* of the judge' (*rābiṣ dayyānim*) is attested at Sippar from the time of Sabium until that of Samsi-iluna of Babylon.

No mention of the *rābiṣu* is found in Mesopotamian legal and administrative texts after the Old Babylonian period (OPPENHEIM 1968:178); yet the title continued in use in the West. In the Amarna correspondence *rābiṣu* designated a high Pharaonic official to whom the local ruler was answerable. In *EA* 256:9 (cf. 362:69) LÚ.MEŠ.MAŠKIM is glossed by *sú-ki-ni* (probably Canaanite **sōkinu*—cf. Phoen *skn*, 'ruler, governor') and in 131:21 by *ma-lik*.MEŠ, 'counsellors'. At Ugarit the *rābiṣu* (LÚ.MAŠKIM) appears as a contracting party or a witness in documents. In RS 16.145:25-26 he is listed as the last witness, and is described as "he who brings forth the royal seal".

The title is applied to certain deities (chiefly male) in a positive sense, designating them as heavenly counterparts of the human *rābiṣu.* Underlying this conception may be his judicial role: in the event of certain transgressions such deities could be expected to bring guilty parties to judgment. Moreover, gods could be invoked in curses to act as a *rābiṣu* against the offending party. The drafters of these curses may have had the demonic aspect of the *rābiṣu* in mind. One also finds certain unnamed deities or →demons bearing the title *rābiṣ X*, usually with respect to a certain city (e.g. Mari: ARM 10 no. 9 rev 23'-26') or temple (*Tākultu* III rev 66). Here belongs also *rābiṣ šulmim*, '*rābiṣu* of well-being' (YOS 10, 53: 30), whose opposite is the *rābiṣ lemuttim* ('*rābiṣu* of evil').

Late in the Old Babylonian period the *rābiṣu* developed the character of a malevolent demon, often qualified as *lemnu*, 'evil'. This development may have arisen from the aspect of the human official as a powerful and fearsome figure (OPPENHEIM 1968:178-79), someone not to be trifled with (EDZARD & WIGGERMANN 1989:450). Such demons are typically named in the context of other evil spirits and are considered responsible for various evils. In medical omen texts one finds the diagnosis, "a *rābiṣu* has seized him" (*TDP* 158:12) and "he has walked in the path of a *rābiṣu*" (*TPD* 34:23). Such texts also mention specific types of *rābiṣu*, who were thought to ambush their victims in various places:

rābiṣ ūri, "the *rābiṣu* of the roof" (*TPD* 214:11); *rābiṣ musâti*, "the *rābiṣu* of the lavatory" (*TPD* 188: 13); *rābiṣ nāri*, "the *rābiṣu* of the river/canal" (*TPD* 190:24-25); *rābiṣ ḫarbati*, "the *rābiṣu* of the wasteland" (*STT* 91:84); *rābiṣ urḫi*, "the *rābiṣu* of the road" (*TPD* 182:40).

III. It is commonly held among OT commentators that Akk *rābiṣu* appears as a loanword in Gen 4:7 (Hebr *rōbēṣ*). Unfortunately this hypothesis is complicated by the extremely problematic nature of this passage; no satisfactory solution to its difficulties has yet been reached. The verse in question is situated in a context in which →Yahweh is addressing →Cain, who was depressed and angry ("his face fell"—4:5) because an offering from his harvest was not pleasing to God. The reason for the divine disapproval is not stated.

The import of God's words to Cain in v 7 is far from clear. Specifically, *wĕʾim lōʾ têṭîb lappetaḥ ḥaṭṭāʾt rōbēṣ* is usually understood to mean, "But if you do not do well/do your best, sin is a croucher-demon at the door". This interpretation has the advantage of providing the masculine antecedent presupposed in the subsequent clause (*tĕšûqātô ... bô*; the same idiom occurs in Gen 3:16). But there are problems. For example, one would expect the antecedent to be the subject (*ḥaṭṭāʾt*, 'sin') rather than the predicate nominative (*rōbēṣ*). Also, the position of *lappetaḥ* is odd if in fact it means 'at the door/opening [of a tent]'. On this interpretation it should most likely come after *ḥaṭṭāʾt rōbēṣ*.

Nevertheless, if one accepts the MT reading, the *hapax legomenon rōbēṣ* could refer to a *rābiṣu* demon, instigating Cain to commit murder. The fact that this demon is said to lurk "at the (tent?)-opening" fits with the character of the *rābiṣu*, namely to lurk in ordinary places to spring his ambush. On the other hand, the Akkadian sources portray the *rābiṣu* as a being that attacks its victims, not as one that tempts them to commit sin.

IV. *Bibliography*

*D. O. EDZARD & F. A. M. WIGGERMANN, maškim (*rābiṣu*) 'Kommissar, Anwalt, Sachwalter', *RLA* 7 (1989) 449-455 [& lit]; A. L. OPPENHEIM, The Eyes of the Lord, *JAOS* 88 (1968) 173-180; *C. WESTERMANN, *Genesis 1-11* (2d ed.; BKAT 1/1; Neukirchen-Vluyn, 1976) 406-410 [& lit].

M. L. BARRÉ

RACHEL רחל

I. Rachel is in biblical tradition →Jacob's favourite wife and mother of →Joseph and Benjamin (Gen 30:23-24; 35:16-20). Outside the Pentateuch she is mentioned in 1 Sam 10:2; Ruth 4:11 and Jer 31:15. Rachel was originally an animal name. The noun *rāḥēl*, 'ewe', is attested in Hebrew (Gen 31:38; Isa 53:7), Aramaic (also the Deir Alla inscription I,11) and classical Arabic. STADE (1881), HAUPT (1909), O. PROCKSCH (*Die Genesis* [KAT 1; Leipzig 1913] 334-335), and M. NOTH (*Das System der Zwölf Stämme Israels* [Stuttgart 1930] 83) believed her name, as well as →Leah's, was originally an emblem of different tribal groups of cattle-breeders. In these animal names other scholars discovered evidence of animal worship and totemism in early Israel (SMITH 1894; GRAY 1896; MEYER 1906:274); some even saw in Rachel a mythological personification of the rain-clouds ('Wolkenkuh', GOLDZIHER 1876).

II. The Akkadian word *laḫru* (ewe) is often quoted as a cognate to *rāḥēl* (*CAD* L 42-44; *AHW* 528; *HALAT* 1134), but this linguistic connection is not certain. Laḫar ([UDU].U$_8$) is a Babylonian cattle-god, presumably of Sumerian origin, usually mentioned together with the grain-god Ashnan (W. G. LAMBERT, Laḫar, *RLA* 6 [1980-83] 431). Even if a connection exists, the Babylonian cattle-god and biblical Rachel hardly share more than a common etymology. Rachel was neither a totem nor a local numen, whose sanctuary was turned into a sepulchre (MEYER 1906:274), let alone a fertility-goddess, though she was certainly venerated in Israel as an ancestral saint.

III. The location of the tomb of Rachel on the border of Benjamin and Ephraim near Ramah (Gen 30:16,18; 48:7; 1 Sam 10:2;

Jer 31:15; cf. Jer 40:1, presumably at present *er-Rām* at the head of W. Fāra, cf. *HALAT* 908; J. J. SIMONS, *The Geographical and Topographical Texts of the OT* [Leiden 1959] § 327.I.8), confirms Rachel's connection to the early Israelite tribes of Joseph and Benjamin. The location south of Ramat Rachel near Bethlehem—where a mediaeval *qubbet Rāḥīl* is still shown—may reflect a secondary Judaean location (JEREMIAS 1958:75-76, *pace* SIMONS, *The Geographical and Topographical Texts of the OT* §§ 383, 666-668), which gained prominence in later Jewish and Christian tradition (Matt 2:16-18). Two explicit references from the monarchic period (1 Sam 10:2; Jer 31:15) and the ancient blessing, preserved in Ruth 4:11, present limited but clear evidence of a living ancestral cult around Rachel's tomb in OT times (TSEVAT 1962). It is not surprising to find evidence for more than one tomb. Also in modern times Muslim and Christian saints sometimes have more than one *maqaam* with a shrine or a cenotaph (E. W. LANE, *Manners and Customs of the Modern Egyptians* [London 1836; repr. 1978]). The existence of a younger rival tradition near Bethlehem cannot be excluded (examples in JEREMIAS 1958:114-117). The bold personification of mother Rachel in Jer 31:15-16 is more than prophetic imagination or figurative speech. Even if the historial reference is to the Exile of 587 BCE, the underlying tradition is that of the barren Rachel crying for children she cannot conceive (Gen 30:1-2; 1 Sam 1:7-8). It is only in the interpretation of the prophet and in the midrash of Matt 2:18 that the barren Rachel also becomes the bereft mother of Israel (cf. the role of Ephraim in 1 Chr 7:22). Her cry may refer to a ritual performed by women at her tomb, venerating her as the ancestral mother. These women, having experienced barrenness and bereavement, may have honoured her as their patroness, and may have asked for her intercession (Gen 35:16-20; Ruth 4:11; Jer 31:16). Part of the folklore was also the application of Mandragora as an aphrodiasic stimulating sexual desire and fertility (Gen 30:14-15; Cant 7:14; J. G. FRAZER, *Folklore in the Old Testament*, Vol 2 [London 1918] 372-397; G. DALMAN, *Arbeit und Sitte*, Vol. I [Gütersloh 1928] 250-251), a phenomenon which is quite well attested in other ancient fertility and modern saint cults.

IV. *Bibliography*

I. GOLDZIHER, *Der Mythos bei den Hebräern und seine geschichtliche Entwicklung* (Leipzig 1876; repr. 1987) 187-191; G. B. GRAY, *Studies in Hebrew Proper Names* (London 1896) 86; P. HAUPT, Lea und Rachel, *ZAW* 29 (1909) 281-286; J. JEREMIAS, *Heiligengräber in Jesu Umwelt* (Göttingen 1958); E. MEYER, *Die Israeliten und ihre Nachbarstämme* (Halle 1906); W. ROBERTSON SMITH, *Lectures on the Religion of the Semites* (London 1927[3]; repr. 1969) 288-311; B. STADE, Lea und Rachel, *ZAW* 1 (1881) 112-116; M. TSEVAT, Saul at Rachel's Tomb, *HUCA* 33 (1962) 107-118.

M. DIJKSTRA

RAHAB רהב

I. Rahab is one of the names in the OT of the chaos monster(s) (cf. also →Leviathan, →Tannin, Tehom, and Yam). Although there are in the neighbouring cultures many parallels to this phenomenon of chaos monsters, the name Rahab seems to have no cognates. The only exception is in an Akkadian text about a chaos monster usually called Labbu. The first syllable in this name is written with the sign KAL which can be read as *lab* as well as *reb*; so the reading Rebbu (<**reb-bu*) is possible too (LAMBERT 1986:55 n.1). The Hebrew name is probably related to Heb RHB, 'assail', 'press', and Akk *ra'ābu(m)*, 'tremble (with fear or rage)' and especially with its derivate *rūbu*, 'overflow', because this is not only said of rage but also of water, whereas Rahab is usually related to the →sea. It occurs as a divine name in Isa 51:9; Ps 89:11; Job 9:13; 26:12; and Sir 43:25; and as a reference to Egypt in Isa 30:7 and Ps 87:4. The plural *rĕhābîm* in Ps 40:5 can be interpreted as a reference to related →demons.

II. The reference to Rahab in the OT

should be read against the background of ancient Near Eastern mythology describing creation as based on victory over the powers of chaos, viz. the primordial oceans. These powers are represented as monsters. The best known example is the Babylonian myth *Enūma eliš* describing →Marduk's creation of the kosmos by defeating the chaos monster →Tiamat with her helpers. In the Ugaritic myth of →Baal there are references to a primordial battle between Baal or his consort Anat against the god of the Sea Yam and other chaos monsters (*KTU* 1.2 iv; 1.3 iii; 1.5 i). The same myth tells us that this battle did not stop with the creation of the world: the powers of chaos remain a threat which has to be confronted again and again. A ritual text (*KTU* 1.82) describes how these forces can afflict human life and how they can be exorcized.

A clear picture of such a watery chaos monster can be found on an Assyrian cylinder seal (KEEL 1977:43, pl.48) which shows a →dragon with a body of waves. The dragon is attacked by a warrior with two helpers. On a Hittite cylinder seal (*ANEP* 670 and KEEL 1977:44, pl.50) we see two gods fighting a dragon pictured as waves curling over.

III. In the OT texts relating Rahab to the sea its original character of chaos monster is preserved. They also point to a conception of a battle between →Yahweh and →chaos preceding the creation of →heaven and →earth. Job 26 describes the steadfast order of the universe preserved by God after having struck down Rahab (cf. also Ps 89:7-13). Job 9:13 mentions Rahab's helpers. This has a parallel in the army of monsters siding with Tiamat according to *Enūma eliš* I 125ff and also in 'the Big Ones', monsters supporting the sea god Yam, the adversary of Baal and Anat in *KTU* 1.3 iii:38ff. And the ritual text *KTU* 1.109:21 mentions helper-gods among a number of gods residing in the netherworld (*TUAT* II/3, 317).

In Isa 51:9-10 the reference to Yahweh as victor in the battle 'in the days of old' against the monsters of chaos is used, just as in the Ugaritic myth of Baal, as a reason for hope in the present situation: this victory can be repeated in new situations of distress. The prophet has associated the creation of heaven and earth out of the oceans of chaos with the deliverance of the people of Israel out of Egypt through the waters of the Reed Sea. The god of Israel is called upon to repeat such an act of salvation on behalf of the people of Judah living in exile by the rivers of Babylon. The prophet appears to have been inspired by the prophecy in Isa 30:7 against Egypt. To the people looking for help against Assyria, Egypt is described as a worthless ally. This is expressed in what must have been intended to be a nickname: *rahab hēm šābet*, 'You are Rahab? Inaction!' Because of its uncommon syntax this is usually emended to *rahab hammošbāt*, 'Rahab who is brought to a standstill'. The problem of the best text can be left aside here, because the prophet's message is clear: Egypt is like one of the monsters of chaos, but lacks their power. When we take into account the above etymology of the name of Rahab proposed above, the words of this text are in fact a *contradictio in terminis*. This can be compared to the mocking song on the king of Babylon in Isa 14, celebrating his downfall into the realm of death. Isa 14:4 also speaks of him being stopped (Heb *šbt*) and he seems to be denoted by a word derived from the stem *rhb* as well. Unfortunately, the Hebrew text is uncertain here too.

Ps 87:4 shows that this nickname for Egypt became more or less common, because it is used here without further comment. This may have been favoured by the fact that travelling from Israel to Egypt has always been called 'going down', using the same verb that denotes the journey from the land of the living to the world of the →dead, which is surrounded by the watery powers of chaos.

The plural *rĕhābîm* in Ps 40:5 can be interpreted as referring to demonic forces related to Rahab. In this psalm they are opposed to Yahweh: 'Blessed is the one who trusts in Yahweh, who turns not to *rĕhābîm* and becomes entangled in →falsehood'. This last word (Heb *kāzāb*) is used in Isa 28:15 to describe a 'covenant with death' and in Amos 2:4 it denotes the false gods. All this makes it likely that Ps 40:5 refers, as was earlier suggested by GUNKEL and others, to the forbidden attempt to obtain help from divine forces in the netherworld. The OT leaves us in no doubt that this was incompatible with the worship of Yahweh as the one god, just as in Ps 40:5 the *rěhābîm* are oppossed to Yahweh. The attestation of *rěhābîm* next to Rahab can be compared to the relation between *rpum* (→Rephaim) and the god Rapi'u in the religion of Ugarit. There may also be a connection with the 'helpers of Rahab' mentioned in Job 9:13. From Ugaritic ritual texts we learn that not only benign powers from the netherworld were invoked; evil forces were also called upon. In an incantation recited 'to cast out the flying demons which possess a young man' (RIH 78/20), the god →Horon, master of black magic, is called a friend. Apparently one hoped to persuade this dreadful god to use his powers in a favourable way. In this way a 'covenant with death' (Isa 28:15) could benefit the living. The same conception seems to be hinted at in Matt 12:25, "driving out the evil spirits by Beelzebul, the lord of the spirits".

IV. *Bibliography*

J. DAY, *God's Conflict with the Dragon and the Sea* (Cambridge 1985); J. DAY, Rahab, *ABD* 5 (New York 1992) 610-611; G. R. DRIVER, Mythical Monsters in the Old Testament, *Studi orientalistici in onore di Georgio Levi della Vida*, I (Roma 1956) 234-249; O. KEEL, *Die Welt der altorientalistischen Bildsymbolik und das Alte Testament am Beispiel der Psalmen* (Neukirchen-Vluyn 2. Auflage 1977); W. G. LAMBERT, Ninurta Mythology in the Babylonian Epic of Creation, *Keilschriftliche Literaturen: Ausgewählte Vorträge der X. Rencontre Assyriologique Internationale* (ed. K. Hecker & W. Sommerfeld; Berlin 1986) 55-60; U. RÜTERSWÖRDEN, Rahab, *TWAT* 7 (Stuttgart 1990) 372-378 [& lit].

K. SPRONK

RAKIB-EL

I. Rakib-El is known to have been the god of the kings of Sam'al, a Neo-Hittite dynasty in South-East Anatolia. It has been suggested that the Rechabites, a religious minority group in ancient Israel, were originally named after Rakib-El (RAMEY 1968). A variant proposal connects the name with the god *Rkb*, presumably short for Rakib-El or the epithet *rkb ʿrpt*, 'Rider of the clouds' (BLENKINSOPP 1972)

II. Rakib-El is a poorly known deity whose name occurs a number of times in Phoenician and Aramaic inscriptions from Zinjirli (*KAI* 24:16; 25:4.6; 214:2.3.11.18; 215:22; 216:5). He was worshipped by King Kilamuwa and his family as their divine patron (*bʿl bt*, 'Lord of the Dynasty'). The character of Rakib-El has not been established beyond doubt. If LANDSBERGER is correct in his understanding of the name as 'Charioteer of →El' (1948), it is quite possible that Rakib-El has to be associated with the storm-god →Hadad. In Ugaritic texts Hadad (better known as →Baal) bears the epithet →'Rider of the clouds' (*rkb ʿrpt*); Rakib-El could be another epithet of the same deity. Others have suggested that Rakib-El was a moon-god identical to the Ugaritic god Yarih, adducing in support of this identification the parallelism between Rakib-El and Baal Haran ('the lord of Haran'), an epithet of the moon-god →Sîn, and because of the lunar symbolism on the Zinjirli stela (e.g. F. M. CROSS, *Canaanite Myth and Hebrew Epic* [Cambridge 1973] 10 n. 32; more cautiously LANDSBERGER 1948; DONNER & RÖLLIG 1964:237). The arguments in support of the lunar character of Rakib-El are not entirely convincing, however. The mere fact that 'the Lord of Haran' is also referred to as 'my lord' (*mrʾy*) by Bar-Rakib (*KAI* 218) need not imply an identity for him and Rakib-El, since we cannot be sure that the title was used for one god exclusively. And even if the two were—secondarily?—identified, it is conceivable that Baal-Haran is not Sîn but 'the Baal of Haran'. In the latter case, the connection between Rakib-El and Baal (Hadad) would be reinforced.

III. Irrespective of the specific nature of Rakib-El, the hypothesis which links him with the Rechabites appears to be far-fetched. In the biblical tradition the Rechabites figure as staunch defenders of an austerely Yahwistic religion, in which there is no place for the recognition of other gods. Moreover, it should be remembered that the title 'Rider' or 'Charioteer' is not attested independently as a divine epithet; should the name Rechab (from whom the Rechabites descended) be connected with Rakib-El, the form of the anthroponym would have to be longer. An independent "Semitic storm-deity *rkb*" is simply a phantom (*pace* BLENKINSOPP 1972).

IV. *Bibliography*

R. D. BARNETT, The Gods of Zinjirli, *Compte-rendu de l'onzième Rencontre Assyriologique Internationale* (Leiden 1964) 59-87; J. BLENKINSOPP, *Gibeon and Israel* (Cambridge 1972) 24; H. DONNER & W. RÖLLIG, *KAI* II (1964) 34; B. LANDSBERGER, *Sam'al: Studien zur Entdeckung der Ruinenstätte Karatepe* (Ankara 1948) 45-46; G. G. RAMEY, *The Horse and the Chariot in Israelite Religion* (unpub. Ph.D. diss. Southern Baptist Theological Seminary 1968), see *ZAW* 81 (1969) 253.

K. VAN DER TOORN

RAM

I. Ram has been speculated to be the name of a deity on the basis of the name Abram, interpreted theophorically as 'Ram is father' (LEWY 1934).

II. The only extra-biblical evidence in support of an alleged deity Ram is the Assyrian anthroponym Shu-Rama, 'He of Rama' (LEWY 1934:59 n. 72). There can be no doubt about the correctness of Lewy's reading. In addition to the two references given by Lewy (CCT 1 Pl. 46a:20; Pl. 46b: 14), the name also occurs in *AKT* 1.72:2.3.6; KBo 9.6:2; KBo 28.159:2; 167:3. Though the element *Ra-ma* is never preceded by the divine determinative DINGIR, the form of the name does suggest that it is the name of a god (cf. e.g. Shu-Nunu, Shu-Laban). Yet HIRSCH does not mention Rama in his survey of theophoric elements in Old Assyrian names (1972:31-34), and the theophoric interpretation is far from assured. It could be a geographical reference.

III. As the traditional interpretation of the name Abram as 'the (divine) Father is Exalted' is perfectly satisfactory (NOTH, *IPN*, 52), there is no need to have recourse to an obscure divine name in order to explain the biblical name. Lewy's suggestion should therefore be regarded as mistaken.

IV. *Bibliography*

H. HIRSCH, *Untersuchungen zur altassyrischen Religion* (AfO Beiheft 13/14; Osnabrück 1972[2]); J. LEWY, Les textes paléo-assyriens et l'Ancien Testament, *RHR* 110 (1934) 58-59.

K. VAN DER TOORN

RAPHA רפה

I. In 2 Sam 21:16.18.20.22 (// 1 Chron 20:4.6.8) mention is made of *rāpâ*, 'Rapha', the ancestor of various warriors who battled with David. Rapha has been connected to the →Rephaim and interpreted as a deity whose cult centre was in Gath (L'HEUREUX 1974; MCCARTER 1983:449-450; *HALAT* 1191).

II. 1 Sam 21:15-22 relates quarrels between David and a group of Philistine warriors: Jisni-Benob; Saph and an anonymous →giant with six fingers on each hand. They are presented as *yělîdê hārāpâ*, 'descendants of Rapha'. WILLESON (1958) interpreted *hārāpâ* as the rendition of a Greek word ἀρπή, 'scimitar', supposing that the Philistines were via the Sea Peoples related to the Greek world. The expression then would refer to a distinguished guild of Philistine soldiers. With L'HEUREUX and MCCARTER the word *hārāpâ* can better be seen as a variant to Heb *hārāpā'*, lit. 'the Healer', connecting the ancestor of this group of soldiers with the Rephaim. Rapha would then refer to a Canaanite underworld deity.

III. *Bibliography*

C. L'HEUREUX, The Ugaritic and Biblical Rephaim, *HTR* 67 (1974) 265-274; P. K. MCCARTER, *II Samuel* (AB; Garden City

1983) 449-450; F. WILLESON, The Philistine Corps of the Scimitar from Gath, *JSS* 3 (1958) 327-335.

B. BECKING

RAPHAEL רפאל

I. This name is based upon the Hebrew root RP', to heal, hence *rōpē'*, physician etc. Raphael, then, might be translated 'God healed'. The relation of this name to the →Rephaim has not yet been studied.

II. The angel Raphael occurs in biblical literature for the first time in the book Tobit. He is apparently one of the four highest →angels, known as the →archangels in most of the old lists (four in most manuscripts of *1 Enoch* 9. 10. 40:9; 54:6; 71:8-9. 13; 1QM 9, 15; *Apoc. Mos.* 40; seven *1 Enoch* 20). Most revealing is his short speech, Tob 12: 11-15, which shows that Raphael is one of the seven angels who are allowed to enter before the →glory of God. According to Tob 3:16, 12:12, Raphael listens to the prayers of the righteous ones. He accompanies Tobit's son, Tobias, and acts according to his secret knowledge as healer: i.e. as a physician as well as a binder of demons. He knows how to use the power inherent in some parts of an extraordinary fish (6:1-9), only a part of which is used to heal a disease of Tobit's eyes, the others help to expel the demon →Asmodaeus who is bound by Raphael (8:3). It is in accordance with this that Raphael's task in *1 Enoch* is described as healing the earth from all the deeds of the fallen angels, including the binding of →Azazel (10:1-11; cf. 54:6). He is 'set over all disease and every wound of the children of the people' (*1 Enoch* 40:9). Raphael also knows other details which have been told in his absence (Tob 6:16). Only seldom is Raphael connected with the future fate of souls as in *1 Enoch* 22:3; *Gk Apoc. Ezra* 6:1-2 or with the divine judgment: *Sib. Or.* 2:215. Sometimes he functions as angelus interpres e.g. *1 Enoch* 22:2; 32:6. He is called ἀρχιστράτηγος in *Gk Apoc. Ezra* 1:4.

III. His healing activity is mentioned later in rabbinic writings (e.g. *b.Yoma* 37a) as well as in numerous magical texts: In *T. Sol.* he stands over against the sixth demon (5:9; 13:6; 18:8; 23P). Jewish magical texts as well as prayers address him (STÜBE 1895: 28, line 55; PRADEL 1907:55-56; NAVEH & SHAKED 1985:Amulet 3:9; 7:2), as do Christian ones: KROPP 1930/1931:XLVIII 38-40. 117; LXXVI 79-122; XLVII 2, 5; *PGM* XXXV 3; XXXVI 170 (cf. A. TRAVERSA, Dai papiri inediti della raccolta milanese: 25 Frammento di papiro magico, *Aegyptus* 33 [1953], 57-62; ET: H.-D. BETZ, *The Greek Magical Papyri in Translation including the Demotic Spells* Vol. 1: Texts. Chicago/London 1986, 302 [text no. XC]) and F. MALTOMINI, I Papiri Greci, *Studi Classici e Orientali* 29 (1979), 55-124, here papyrus 1, line 59, ET: BETZ ibid. no. CXXIIIa; cf. also MONTGOMERY, Text 15, 9 and 96-97.

IV. *Bibliography*

A. M. KROPP, *Ausgewählte koptische Zaubertexte* 1-3 (Bruxelles 1930/1931); *J. MICHL, Engel VIII (Raphael), *RAC* 5, 252-254; J. A. MONTGOMERY, *Aramaic Incantation Texts from Nippur* (Philadelphia 1913); J. NAVEH & S. SHAKED, *Amulets and Magic Bowls. Aramaic Incantations of Late Antiquity* (Jerusalem/Leiden 1985); F. PRADEL, *Griechische und süditalienische Gebete, Beschwörungen und Rezepte des Mittelalters* (Giessen 1907); R. STÜBE, *Jüdisch-Babylonische Zaubertexte* (Halle 1895).

M. MACH

RAVEN ערב

I. The raven, known in the Old Testament as a messenger bird (Gen 8:7), has been associated with the divine in Mesopotamia (NASH 1990:75) and Ugarit.

II. In the Neo-Assyrian 'God description text', the parts of the body of a deity are mystically compared with elements, metals, animals, foods, trees, fruits etc. known from the physical world. The 'mole' of the deity is metaphorically seen as a 'raven': Ú.NAGA. MUŠEN (*āribu*) *ki-pil-šú* 'his mole is a raven' (LIVINGSTONE 1986:94 I:9 = SAA 3, 39:9). In the Neo-Assyrian incantation cycle

Utukkū lemnūtu, a passage occurs in which the incantation priest has two birds in his hands. Both the raven and the hawk function as animals in which antidemonic divine powers are present (*Utukkū lemnūtu* I, 129-135; NASH 1990:75). From Neo-Assyrian astrological reports a →star (or →constellation?) MUL.UGA*ú-ga* 'Raven' is known (SAA 8, 74 Rev:1; 82:5; 414 Rev:1). Although stars are seen as divine in Mesopotamia, the name of the Raven-star is never preceded by the determinative for a deity.

In Ugarit, birds were seen as divine messengers of the deities (KORPEL 1990:544-549). In a passage from the Legend of Keret, it is stated that the divine beings Ilišu (*ilš*) and his wife were heralds of →El. The wording of this function (*ngr*/*ngrt*; meaning 'raven' in the first place; KORPEL 1990:292) indicates that they were seen as ravens (*KTU* 1.16 [Keret III] iv:10-16).

III. In the ancient Near East the raven is only associated with the divine and not identified as such. In the Old Testament stories of →Noah and →Elijah, the raven is only interpreted as instrumental, either to give orientation after the flood (Gen 8:7; KEEL 1977:79-91) or to feed an isolated prophet (1 Kgs 17:2-6).

IV. *Bibliography*

O. KEEL, *Vögel als Boten* (OBO 14; Freiburg/Göttingen 1977); M. C. A. KORPEL, *A Rift in the Clouds. Ugaritic and Hebrew Descriptions of the Divine* (UBL 8; Münster 1990); A. LIVINGSTONE, *Mystical and Mythological Explanatory Works of Assyrian and Babylonian Scholars* (Oxford 1986); T. NASH, Devils, Demons and Disease. Folklore in Ancient Near Eastern Rites of Atonement, *The Bible in the Light of Cuneiform Literature. Scripture in Context III* (eds. W. W. Hallo, B. W. Jones & G. L. Mattingly; Lewiston 1990) 57-88.

B. BECKING

RE רע

I. Re (*Rꜥw*, Akk. *Riꜥa*, Heb *Raꜥ*) occurs as a theophoric element in Potiphera (פוטיפרע = *PꜣdjpꜣRꜥw*, name of the father of Asenath Gen 41:45), a short form of Potiphar (פוטיפר) the name of Joseph's Egyptian employer, Gen 37:36; 39:1) and Hophra (חפרע), Jer 44:30 (*ḥꜥꜥjbRꜥw*, Gk Apries, name of Pharao *WꜣḥjbRꜥw*).

Re is the Egyptian god of creation, the sun and the state, for he symbolizes the cosmogonic energies and qualities that rule the universe and that find their terrestrial incarnation in Pharaoh. Re is the chief of the gods and the father of the king. →Amun achieves this same position only via syncretistic identification with Re. The traditional centre of Re-worship is Jwnw, Heb און (Ezek 30:17) אן (Gen 41:45), the Greek Heliopolis.

II. The Egyptians divided the day into three periods which correspond to three phases of the solar journey, the apparent course of the sun around the earth, which the Egyptians depicted as a journey in two boats, one for the day (*Mꜥnḏt*) and one for the night (*Msktt*). These periods are morning, midday and evening, or sunrise, crossing and sunset. The night usually belongs to the third phase. The three phases of the solar circuit are expressed in a triad of gods: Chepre (morning), Re (midday) and →Atum (evening and night). But these three gods can also be seen as mere aspects of one single god who is called either Re or Re-Harakhte. Later theological speculation develops a doctrine of 12 or 24 forms of Re, one for every hour. The 'litany of Re', a text belonging to the 'books of the netherworld', praises Re in 75 different forms (HORNUNG 1975). Each of the three major forms of Re has a special religious significance. Chepre symbolizes the cosmogonic energies; he is the god who "emerged by himself" (*ḫpr ḏs.f*, Gk *autogenēs.*) Re symbolizes the rulership of the creator, his justice, executive power and omniscience; Atum symbolizes the virtuality of preexistence into which the creator relapses during the night in order to start creation again the following morning (ASSMANN 1969).

The traditional cult of Re addresses not only the god but rather the 'solar circuit', which is considered the central life process of the universe and a drama in which virtually the whole pantheon cooperates. The cult supports this drama by incessant ritual performances, mostly in the form of hourly recitations of hymns ('hourly ritual', ASSMANN 1975a:1-12), but also fumigations, libations, offerings and the like. The popular sun hymns reflect the 3-phase structure of the solar circuit: they usually contain three stanzas, each of them devoted to a specific phase of the journey. The topic of these hymns is not the theology of the sun god, but the drama of the solar journey (ASSMANN 1969; 1983 chap. 2).

The Heliopolitan concept of cosmogony does not know of any closure of the creative process but conceives of creation as the 'first time' (*zp tpj*) of an endless cycle of decay and regeneration (E. HORNUNG, Verfall und Regeneration der Schöpfung, *Eranos* 46 [1977] 411-449). But unlike the 'first time' when light and life were disclosed without meeting any resistance, the daily circuit has continuously to combat a cosmic enemy, the personification of chaos, darkness, dissolution and evil who in the form of a huge →serpent threatens to swallow up the celestial ocean and to bring the solar course to a standstill. This enemy has constantly to be overthrown, he can never be definitely annihilated but remains omnipresent as a kind of gravitation towards →chaos or 'virtual apocalypse' which must be averted by incessant effort in order to keep the world going. The cult is the terrestrial part of this effort of cosmic maintenance. It is the task of the king whom Re "has installed on the earth of the living for ever and ever, judging men and satisfying gods, realising Maʿat (truth/justice/order) and annihilating Isfet (disorder)" (Text ed. ASSMANN 1971; cf. ASSMANN 1990:205-212). There exists a close parallelism between the dominance of the creator which he exerts in the sky in order to maintain creation against the rebellious resistance of chaos, and the governance of Pharaoh on earth and his struggle against political enemies, a parallelism which reveals much of the "solar language" that can be found in Biblical texts (M. SMITH, *The Early History of God* [San Francisco 1990] 115-144; B. JANOWSKI, *Rettungsgewißheit und Epiphanie des Heils. Das Motiv der Hilfe Gottes «am Morgen» im Alten Orient und im Alten Testament. Band I: Alter Orient* [WMANT 59; Neukirchen-Vluyn 1989])

But the solar journey reflects or imparts not only the political conceptions about justice, rulership and political welfare, but also the anthropological conceptions about death, rebirth and immortality. The individual hopes to enter the cosmic cycle after death and to be reborn in the hereafter to join the retinue of the solar boat (the "bark of millions"). The nocturnal phase of the solar journey is depicted in the form of a *descensus ad inferos* (HORNUNG 1984). The god who himself undergoes death and resurrection/rebirth during this journey, visits the corpses in the depth of the earth and reanimates them temporarily by his radiance and his life-giving words. At midnight, in the extreme depth of the netherworld, the sun god unites with →Osiris, the 'Ba'-soul with his corpse. This union links 'yesterday' and 'tomorrow', 'Neheh'-time in form of endless repetition and 'Djet'-time in form of inalterable duration, father (Osiris) and son (Re = →Horus) and thus produces continuity. Between one cycle and another, there is the mystery of renewal which for a moment dives into the outworldly depths of preexistence. A late text describes this union as a most dangerous secret: "Whoever gives this away will die of a violent death, for this is a very great secret. It is Re and it is Osiris" (Pap. Salt 825, xviii.1-2; P. DERCHAIN, *Le Papyrus Salt 825 (B.M. 10051), rituel pour la conservation de la vie en Égypte* [Brussels 1965]). This same mysterious union forms the basis also for the individual's hope for renewal and immortality. The cosmic drama is interpreted, by 'analogical imagination', in a way that reflects the fundamentals of human life: social justice and harmony, political order and authority, and individual hopes for health, prosperity and—above all—life after death. It is this relationship of mutual illumination of cosmic, sociopolitical and individual essentials that conveys to this world-view and interpretation of reality the character of truth and of natural evidence.

During the New Kingdom, a new concept of the solar journey arises according to which the sun god performs his course in complete solitude. The traditional imagery of the living god—reliving and rejuvenating his daily life within the constellations of the divine world—is now transformed into the concept of the life-giving god who is not included and embedded in divine interaction but confronts the world from high above and sends from there his life-giving rays into the world (For the vertical division of the world into upper and lower, heaven and earth see ASSMANN 1969:302-306). The transformation can be described as one from constellational intransitivity to confrontational transitivity. Instead of a reciprocal relationship between heavenly and earthly, cosmic and political action, we have the direct transitive subject-object relation between god and earth. God and world, creator and creation, are confronted in a huge distance to each other. The world, however, still includes the traditional deities and is still divine. But the monotheistic revolution of Akhenaten does away even with this last remnant of traditional polytheism. But this is a radicalization which did not affect the new world view. After Amarna, the development resumed. The great discovery of Akhenaten which lay behind his monotheistic revolution consisted in the observation that the sun not only generated the →light but also time, time in the double sense of divine cosmic energy *and* individual lifetime. Cosmic time and the lifetime of all living creatures are created by the motion of the sun as the light is created by its radiation.

After Amarna, this concept of the constant divine creation or 'emission' of lifetime develops into a concept of divine will and human fate. Re not only generates time but also its content, i.e. fate and destiny, history and biography, life with all its vicissitudes on the individual, social and political planes emanate from the will of Re who creates time (ASSMANN 1975[b]). The rule of Re over time implies a concept of omniscience. In two hymns this idea is expressed in terms strongly reminiscent of Ps 90:4: "eternity is in your eyes as yesterday when it has passed" (ASSMANN 1975[a]:Nr.127B, 82; Nr.144A, 27). But this concept of time and fate as emanations of divine planning remains not restricted to solar theology but develops into a general 'theology of will' that changes the structure and essence of Egyptian religion.

In hymns of the Ramesside and later periods, the 'non-constellative' view of the solar journey as the action of a solitary god animating, ruling and preserving his creation strangely coexists with the 'constellative' one that views the same journey as a drama where many gods cooperate and where the sun god plays not only the active roles of ruler, judge and saviour, but also the passive ones of a child that is born and raised, a king who is crowned and adored, an old man who is guided and helped, a dead man who is 'transfigured', rejuvenated and reborn.

In the Late Period, Re and Osiris, who according to the traditional conception 'unite' during midnight, fuse into a syncretistic deity.

III. Potiphera, the Egyptian name of the father of Asenath (Gen 41:45), means 'the one given by Re' (*KAI* II, p. 280; cf. Potiphar in Gen 37:36; 39:1). The noun in the name of the Egyptian king Hophra (Jer 44:30; cf. 37:5) means 'Happy-hearted is Re' (D. B. REDFORD, Hophra, *ABD* 3 [1992] 286). The suggestion according to which the Hebrew expression RʿH *rāʿâ* / *bĕrāʿ* in Exod 5:19; 10:10 etc. contains a reference to Re should be rejected as fanciful and unfounded (*pace* RENDSBURG 1988).

IV. *Bibliography*

J. ASSMANN, *Liturgische Lieder an den Sonnengott. Untersuchungen zur altägyptischen Hymnik I* (Berlin 1969); J. ASSMANN, *Der König als Sonnenpriester. Ein kosmographischer Begleittext zur kultischen Sonnenhymnik in thebanischen*

Tempeln und Gräbern (Glückstadt 1970); ASSMANN, *Ägyptische Hymnen und Gebete* (Zürich 1975[a]); ASSMANN, *Zeit und Ewigkeit im alten Ägypten. Ein Beitrag zur Geschichte der Ewigkeit.* (Heidelberg 1975[b]); ASSMANN, *Re und Amun. Die Krise des polytheistischen Weltbilds im Ägypten der 18.-20. Dynastie* (OBO 51; Fribourg/Göttingen 1983[a]); ASSMANN, *Sonnenhymnen in thebanischen Gräbern (Theben I)* (Mainz 1983[b]); ASSMANN, *Ägypten—Theologie und Frömmigkeit einer frühen Hochkultur* (Stuttgart 1984); ASSMANN, *Maʿat. Gerechtigkeit und Unsterblichkeit im alten Ägypten (*München 1990); E. HORNUNG, *Das Amduat. Die Schrift des Verborgenen Raumes,* 3 vols. (Wiesbaden 1963/67); HORNUNG, *Das Buch der Anbetung des Re im Westen (Sonnenlitanei),* 2 vols. (Geneva 1975); HORNUNG, *Ägyptische Unterweltsbücher* (Zürich [2]1984); G. A. RENDSBURG, The Egyptian Sun-God Ra in the Pentateuch, *Henoch* 10 (1988) 3-15.

J. ASSMANN

REPHAIM רפאים

I. The term *rĕpāʾîm* occurs 25 times in the Hebrew Bible, most notably in the poetical and the so-called 'historical' books. Designating the spirits of the dead, the Hebrew term is related to Ug *rpum*, a name for the deified royal ancestors. In several places in the Hebrew Bible, the Rephaim designate the ancient inhabitants of Palestine, characterized by gigantic size. The most probable etymology of the term connects it with the root RPʾ, 'to heal'.

II. The Rephaim, commonly vocalized as an active participle *rāpiʾūma*, from RPʾ, 'to heal', occur frequently in texts from Ugarit. In *KTU* 1.6 vi:45-46, a fragment from a hymn to Shapshu, the *rpum* occur in parallelism with the *ilnym*, 'divine ones'. Both groups are said to be 'under' (*tḥt*) the sun goddess, i.e. submitted to her. The location corresponds with their place in the netherworld, an idea also familiar from the biblical writings. Lines 47-48 of the same text mentions the *ilm* (gods) and the *mtm* →(dead) as denizens of the same abode. Close to them lives Kothar-wa-Khasis (→Koshar), who navigates and travels like them (*KTU* 1.108:6).

The so-called Rephaim text, *KTU* 1.20-22, consists of three fragmentary tablets that share as a kind of chorus line an invitation addressed to the *rpum.* According to DEL OLMO LETE (1981:405-424) and SPRONK (1986), it is Danʾilu who invites the *rpum* to his palace. VAN DER TOORN (1991:54) construes the series of invitations as being formulated by different speakers. Among the more limpid parts of this obscure text, there is a reference to a three-day journey by chariot leading to the 'threshing floors' and the 'orchards' where a seven-day banquet is celebrated. The *rpum* leave the city to participate in the revelry—no doubt a metaphor for their ascent from the underworld. According to SPRONK (1986:276), Hos 6:1-3 is to be interpreted in the light of this text: it is a polemical allusion to the Ugaritic conceptions of the afterworld, and more particularly to the three-day journey of *KTU* 1.20 i:24-25. The swiftness required of the *rpum* (*KTU* 1.20 ii:1-7; 21 ii:1-13; 22 ii:1-25) accentuates the urgency of the convocation, to be situated perhaps in the interval between the death of a king and his burial.

If the rendering of *KTU* 1.20 i:3, *k mt mtm*, as "when the men are dead" is accepted (so A. CAQUOT & M. SZNYCER, *Textes ougaritiques*, Vol. 1 [LAPO 7; Paris 1974] 477; M. DIJKSTRA & J. C. DE MOOR, Problematical Passages in the Legend of Aqhâtu, *UF* 7 [1975] 171-215, esp. 214), the link between the *rpum* and the dead is explicit from the outset. In *KTU* 1.22 i:8-10, two *rpum* are mention, viz., "Thamaqu, the *rpu* of Baʿlu (→Baal), warrior of Baʿlu, warrior of →Anat", and "Yahipanu, the champion, the everlasting royal prince". The anthroponym Thamaqu is also known from *KTU* 4.93 iv:3. An alternative translation for *rpu bʿl* ('the *rpu* of Baʿlu') is 'the Rephaite, the lord'. The expression *dnil* [*mt.rpi*] in *KTU* 1.20 ii:8 might be understood as "Danʾilu, the man of healing", that is, the man bound to be delivered from his suffering—a suffering caused by his childlessness after Aqhat's death. Alternatively, one could opt for the translation 'the man of *rpu*", the *rpu* being "the title of a god known under another name, or a particular deity" (CAQUOT 1985:351). The latter interpretation might explain the frequency of the expression in the cycle of Dan'ilu (*KTU* 1.17 i:1.17.34.37.42; ii:28; v:5.14.34; vi:52; *KTU* 1.19 i:20.36-39; ii:41; iv:13.17.36). C. VIROLLEAUD rendered it as "Mot guérisseur" (→'Mot the healer'), and drew a comparison with Shadrapha, 'Shed the healer' (*La légende phénicienne de Danel* [Paris 1936] 87). The correspondences reveal the affinity—recognized by Virolleaud—between the cycle of Dan'ilu and Aqhat, on the one hand, and the 'Rephaim text', on the other. It is possible that the conditions of the murder of Aqhat were recreated by means of a ritual that sought to undo the consequences of his death (*KTU* 1.22 i:11) with the help of an intervention by the *rpum* (CAQUOT 1985:346). The beneficial action of the latter would consist of their restoring the lost fertility, not so much that of the country (in spite of the mention of the 'threshing floors' and 'orchards'), both a reflection and a result of the death of Aqhat (J. GRAY, The Rephaim, *PEQ* 81 [1948-49] 127-139), but rather that of the king they were bound to bless with offspring (*KTU* 1.22 i:1-5). According to SPRONK (1986: 160-161), the 'Rephaim text' is a witness to the belief in the ability of Ilu (→El) and/or Baʿlu to revivify the dead. Their return among the living would take place during the autumn festival (SPRONK 1986:164). For TROPPER (1989:141) and VAN DER TOORN (1991:52), *KTU* 1.22 i:1-4 is a dynastic oracle. TROPPER does not regard the autumn festival as the setting for a return to life of some of the dead, but for necromantic practices. VAN DER TOORN argues that the relations between Dan'ilu and the *rpum* do not prove that there was an annual meeting between the living and the death, whether provoked by a *marzahu* or by necromancy.

The Kirtu legend contains two allusions to the *rpum*. Toward the end of a benediction, the god Ilu expresses the wish that Kirtu be glorified "among the *rpim* of the earth, in the assembly of the clan of Ditanu" (*btk rpi arṣ bpḫr qbṣ dtn*, *KTU* 1.15 iii:3-4.14-15). The blessing introduces the annunciation to Kirtu of the birth of six daughters. Initially the *rpum* were believed to designate the original inhabitants of the country. J. GRAY (*Dtn* and *rp'um* in Ancient Ugarit, *PEQ* 84 [1952] 39-41) showed that these 'healers' or 'dispensers of fertility' of the earth were the kings of yore; his demonstration carried general conviction (cf. for this concept in the Greek world Hesiod, *Works and Days*, 121-123). M. HELTZER has voiced dissent (The *rabba'um* in Mari and the *rpi(m)* in Ugarit, *OLP* 9 [1978] 5-20, esp. 15). He urges that the *rpum* must be clan members, analogous to the *rabba'um* of Mari, since Kirtu appears to be one of them. The seeming contradiction is resolved by CAQUOT (1985:353), who suggests that the poetic blessing is posterior to the rest of the poem and is to be situated after the death of Kirtu. Though *dtn* has been interpreted as 'kingdom' (Ginsberg, Driver), and 'men in command' (so Jirku, arguing on the basis of the equivalence made in Akkadian between *datnu* and *qarradu*, cf. *AHW* 165), it is now generally regarded as a personal name.

KTU 1.161, either the libretto of a funerary service for a king who recently died, or a ritual in commemoration of his death, completes the information yielded by *KTU* 1.20-22. The king in question could be Niqmaddu III, predecessor of Ammurapi and last king of Ugarit (A. CAQUOT, *Textes Ougaritiques*, Vol. 2 [LAPO 14; Paris 1989] 104). The sacrifice lasts seven days, just like the banquet offered to the *rpum* in *KTU* 1.22 i:22-25. The *rpum* are also called *ẓlm*: meaning 'shadows' rather than 'images' (M. DIETRICH & O. LORETZ, Neue Studien zu den Ritualtexten aus Ugarit (II)—nr. 6—Epigrafische und inhaltliche Probleme in KTU 1.161, *UF* 15 [1983] 17-24). The expression brings to mind the biblical Rephaim. Like the Rephaim, too, the *rpum* act as a group, viz. as the company of Ditanu (*KTU* 1.161:3 and 10, cf. Prov 21:6). This *dtn*, to be identified with the *dtn* mentioned in *KTU* 1.15 iii:3-4 and 14-15, is most likely one of their leaders, if not their leader in command. The role of Shapshu as *psychopompos* in ll. 18-19 conforms with her function in the cycle of Baʿlu, where she assists Anat in her quest for the dead god (*KTU* 1.6 i:8-9.13-15; iii:24; iv:1-22). T. H. GASTER compares the role of Shapshu (known as 'the lamp of the gods') to that of →Helios in the myth of →Demeter and Kore, and to that of the sun god in the myth of Telepinu (*Thespis* [New York 1950, 1961^2] 162-184, resp. 172-200). Also the expression *'ṯr bʿlk*, 'after your lord' (*KTU* 1.161:20) is reminiscent of the descent of Baʿlu (the 'Lord') among the dead—unless the *bʿl* in question be Didanu or *rpu* (also known as *bʿl* in *KTU* 1.22 i:8). The journey to the underworld and the descent into the dust agree with what is known about the biblical Rephaim. Lines 31-32 of the text express the purpose of the ritual: peace to the king and the citizens of Ugarit.

KTU 1.108 is a ritual for the royal dead. The obverse of the broken tablet describes a banquet for the *rpum* presided at by one *rpu*. D. PARDEE (*Les textes paramythologiques* [Paris 1988] 118; so too C. E. L'HEUREUX, *Rank Among the Canaanite Gods* [HSM 21; Missoula 1979] 186) feels that the mythological elements predominate over the ritual traits. The presence of Anat at this feast of the dead (ll. 6-10) is hardly surprising, considering her complex role in the poem of Aqhat and her endeavours to save Baʿlu from the death. The banquet of the dead in company with the god *rpu* is reminiscent of the food enjoyed by the 'soul' of Panammu in the company of →Hadad, mentioned in *KAI* 214:21-22 (CAQUOT, LAPO 14 [1989] 111). The Ugaritic text closes with a blessing by the *rpu* of—presumably—the king 'in the middle of Ugarit (*btk ugrt*)', which confirms the dynastic and political bias of the ritual. The *rpu* who presides over the banquet is also referred to as *mlk ʿlm*. The latter expression has been rendered as 'king of the world' (Virolleaud), 'king everlasting' (see also the majority of scholars), and—recently—as 'king of yore' (PARKER 1970: 249; CAQUOT 1976:299). This *mlk ʿlm* can be identified neither with Baʿlu (*pace* J. DE MOOR, Studies in the new Alphabetic Texts from Ras Shamra, I, *UF* 1 [1969] 167-188, esp. 176; DE MOOR 1976:329; A. F. RAINEY, The Ugaritic Texts in Ugaritica 5, *JAOS* 94 [1974] 184-194, esp. 188) nor with Ilu (*pace* J. BLAU & J. C. GREENFIELD, Ugaritic Glosses, *BASOR* 200 [1970] 11-17, esp. 12; GESE *RAAM*: 92; A. S. KAPELRUD, The Ugaritic Text RS 24.252 and King David, *JNSL* 3 [1974] 35-39, esp. 35; L'HEUREUX 1974:268; J. DAY, The Daniel of Ugarit and Ezekiel and the Hero of the Book of Daniel, *VT* 30 [1980] 174-184, esp. 176). The *mt rpi* (*KTU* 1.20 ii:8), then, is 'the man of *rpu*' (B. MARGULIS, A Ugaritic Psalm (RŠ 24.252), *JBL* 89 [1970] 292-303, esp. 301; PARKER 1970:249; CAQUOT 1976:299), that is, the man of the *mlk ʿlm*. Gatharu and Yaqaru, instead of being alternative designations of the *rpu*, are rather members of the group of the *rpum*. In ll. 2-3 the names *ʿṯtrt* and *hdrʿi* refer to the two dwelling-places of →Og king of →Bashan, the remnant of the Rephaim (Deut 1:4; 3:11; MARGULIS 1970:301); their interpretation as theonyms (→Astarte and 'Haddu the shepherd') is best abandoned.

According to SPRONK (1986:184), *KTU* 1.108 is to be situated in the context of the New Year festival during which Baʿlu returned to life. He identifies *rpu mlk ʿlm* (line 1) and *ʿnt gṯr* (line 6) with Baʿlu (so too TROPPER) and "Anat (the spouse) of Gatharu", respectively. Anat occurs here as the tutelary goddess of the king. VAN DER TOORN (1991:57) understands *rpu* (to be vocalised as *rapiʾu* or *rapʾu*), in the expression *rpu mlk ʿlm*, as an adjective with the meaning 'pure', rather than an active participle meaning 'healer' (so DE MOOR 1976:329) or a stative meaning 'hale' (F. M. CROSS, *Canaanite Myth and Hebrew Epic* [Cambridge, Mass. 1973] 263; L'HEUREUX 1974:269-270; E. T. MULLEN, *The Divine Council* [HSM 24; Chico 1980] 262; LEWIS 1989:14). *Rpu mlk ʿlm* can be equated with Milku, who can be equated in turn with Og (van der Toorn 1991:57-58, against Pardee 1988:85-90, who rejects the identification with Og). It is because Milku reigns over the kings in the netherworld, whom he represents, that he is in the forefront of the liturgy (van der Toorn 1991:59).

The *rpum* revel amid music and dance (ll. 3-4). Their characterization as *ḥbr kṯr ṭbm*, "the happy companions of Kothar" (Caquot 1989:115), underlines that, on the one hand, the *rpum*, just like the biblical Rephaim, constitute a homogeneous group, and that, on the other, Kothar, who accompanied Shapshu during her descent to the netherworld, is still going to and fro in the realm of the dead. The liturgy closes with an extended blessing (ll. 19-27) addressed first to the *rpum* of the underworld, then to the actual king, and finally to the citizens of Ugarit for ever more.

KTU 1.124 is another 'paramythological' text yet, the mythology being put to the service of a ritual. Ditanu, the protagonist of the text, intervenes in the world of the living in order to lift the blight of infertility. His ability to do so is based upon the power of the *rpum* to grant offspring to the royal family. The first two lines mention one *adn ilm rbm*, 'master of the many gods': is this Ilu (Caquot 1989:119)? Pardee (1988: 185) believes Yaqaru is this master, the 'great gods' being the more recent members of the *rpum*. Spronk opts for Baʿlu (1986:193), whereas Tropper takes it as a designation of the necromancer in charge of the royal cult of the *rpum* (1989:154). Van der Toorn (1991), finally, considers various infernal deities as possible candidates: Milku, Yarikhu, and Yaqaru. The 'decision concerning the child' (*mṯpt yld*) could imply that the child is ill; yet the term *ḫlh* might also refer to problems caused by infertility or a painful delivery (Caquot, LAPO 14 [1989] 119-123).

According to van der Toorn (1991:62), *KTU* 1.124 cannot be adduced as a witness to the belief in a regular return to life of Baʿlu and the dead, nor as proof of the existence of necromancy at Ugarit; it merely illustrates the conviction that some exceptional dead such as Ditanu had therapeutic knowledge which they could communicate to the living by means of a divine intermediary. The relations between the living and the dead were limited to mortuary offerings (1991:65). To say that the biblical authors were convinced of God's power to vivify the dead, but that they refrained from explicitly expressing this idea for fear of Baalism, is based on preconceived ideas. There is no reason to dismiss the widespread opinion that the extension of God's power over the realm of the dead is a later development in Israelite religion (1991:64).

In addition to the occurences of the *rpum* in the Ugaritic text, the extra-biblical evidence about the Rephaim includes three attestations from the first millennium BCE. Two funerary inscriptions from the kings Tabnit and Eshunazar from Sidon (*KAI* 13 and 14), from the 6th and 5th centuries, warn anyone contemplating violating the royal tomb that, should he execute his plans, there will be no resting-place for him with the *rpʾm* (cf. Isa 14:18-20). The Neo-Punic/Latin bilingual of Al-Amruni (*KAI* 117) has the Latin *D(is) M(anibus)* as the equivalent of לעל[נ]א ראפאמ, "to the gods of the Rephaim" or לעל[נמ] אראפמ, "to the gods [i.e.] the Rephaim" (J. Friedrich, Kleine Bemerkungen zu Texten aus Ras Schamra und zu phönizischen Inschriften, *AfO* 10 [1935-1936] 80-83, esp. 83).

III. The treatment of the biblical material concerning the Rephaim should distinguish between the occurrences in the poetic texts, and those in the so-called historical texts. A key text in the books of the prophets is Isa 14:9. Here the Rephaim are mentioned in parallelism with "all the leaders (literally: goats) of the earth" (*kol-ʿattûdê ʾāreṣ*) and "all the kings of the nations" (*kōl malkê gôyim*). Their royal character is evident. The text in question is part of a funerary complaint (a so-called *qînâ*) addressed to the king of Babylonia in view of his imminent death. The song describes the prospective upheaval among the defunct monarchs come to meet his royal highness, now become one of them—and even their inferior because he has died without burial, name or offspring. The Rephaim all belong to "the netherworld below" (v 9, *šĕʾôl mittaḥat*), deep down in the Pit (v 15, *yarkĕtê-bôr*). They constitute a somnolent community, waking up only to greet and speak with a new arrival (vv 9-10). Like him, they were leaders and kings in life (v 9), yet realize they are now without force ("You too have become as weak as we", v 10). The text establishes a link between the Rephaim and the deceased kings; every dead monarch is one of them, whether his end be glorious or ignominious, and whether he rest in a grave or on 'a bed of maggots' (v 11). Transcending the boundaries of time, space, and morality, the community of the Rephaim embraces all the royal dead. If the 'mountain of the divine assembly', the 'far north (*ṣāpôn*; →Zaphon)', and the highest heaven which the deceased hoped to reach do not correspond with the usual topographic notions of a Babylonian king, they faithfully reflect the mythical geography of Ugarit. It is presumably because the very notion of the Rephaim originates from northern Syria that the biblical passage mentions Mt Zaphon, the Jebel el-ʿAqra, as the divine abode.

Isaiah 26, part of the Apocalypse of Isaiah (Isa 24-27), is a kind of psalm in which the Rephaim occur twice. At v 14, they appear in a synonymous parallelism with the dead: "The dead will not live, the Rephaim will not rise". Using the same imagery as Isa 14:9 (QWM), the passage affirms the impossibility of a resurrection. Also in this text there are Canaanite traits. Those who who have 'ruled over' (BʿL) the Israelites, "other lords besides thee" (*ʾădōnîm zûlāteka*), are the Baals worshipped by the people; their name and remembrance is wiped out by Yahweh (vv 13-14). This polemical allusion to Baʿlu seems to be based on the association (or analogy) between the Ugaritic *rpum*—the deified royal ancestors—and the god Baʿlu, believed to die annually at the period of drought and to return to life at the onset of the rainy season (cf. Hos 6:2). Isa 26:19 also mentions the Rephaim, but in a rather different context; the text strikes a note of optimism at the conclusion of a rather grim oracle. The author has used nouns (dead, corpses, dust, earth) and verbs (to live, to rise, to awaken, to arouse) which belong to the semantic field of death and the afterlife. Whereas the dead and the Rephaim of v 14 are to be identified with the Baals mentioned in v 13, the resurrected dead of v 19 are contrasted with the infertility of the inhabitants of the land in v 18 (note that the last part of v 19, "and Earth will make the Rephaim fall", means that the underworld will reject the dead). The expression "your dead" in v 19 (*mētêkā*) refers to all the Israelite dead who will participate in a national restoration of the kind described in Ezek 37:1-14. The Peshitta of v 19 reads "You will make the land of the →giants perish", thus establishing a link between the texts presenting the Rephaim as the inhabitants of →Sheol, on the one hand, and those presenting them as the original inhabitants of Syria and Transjordania, on the other.

The notion of the Rephaim as denizens of the netherworld is also found in the Books of Job and Psalms. According to Job 26:5, the Rephaim are situated "below the waters and their inhabitants". Canaanite imagery is present in v 7 with such terms as as 'Zaphon' (*ṣāpôn*, north), 'void' (*tōhû*), '(under)world' (*ʾereṣ*) and 'nothing' (*bĕlîmāh*). Not too far removed from the Job passage is Ps 88, an individual complaint arguing that only the living can experience God's goodness: "Do you work wonders for the dead? Will the Rephaim rise up to praise you?" (v 11[10]). The syllogism is based on the premise that the dead and the Rephaim are identical; for neither of them there is hope, like in Isa 14. According to SPRONK (1986:272), the verse is a polemic against the Canaanite belief in the revivification of the dead: the dead are unable to rise (QWM). Also belonging to the semantic field of the Rephaim and the dead are such expressions as *yōrĕdê-bôr*, 'those who go down to the Pit' (v 5[4]), *geber ʾên-ʾĕyāl*, 'man without strength' (v 5[4]), *ḥălālîm šōkĕbê qeber*, 'the slain that lie in the grave' (v 6[5]), *ʾăšer lōʾ zĕkartām ʿôd*, 'those whom you remember no more' (v 6[5]), *bôr taḥtiyyôt*, 'the depths of the Pit' (v 7[6]), *maḥăšakkîm*, 'dark places' (v 7[6], cf. 13[12] and 19[18]), *mĕṣōlôt*, 'deep regions' (v 7[6]), *qeber*, 'tomb' (v 12[11]), *ʾăbaddôn*, 'the place of destruction' (v 12[11], →Abaddon), and *ʾereṣ nĕšiyyâ*, 'land of forgetfulness' (v 13[12]). The affinities between Ps 88 and Job 26:5-14 do not diminish the resemblances with Isa 14. In contrast to Isa 14, however, Isa 26:19, Job 26:5 and Ps 88: 11[10] do not speak of the royal dead.

At the three places where the Rephaim are mentioned in the Book of Proverbs they symbolize death. Death is the destiny of those who follow the strange woman, Lady Folly, the counterpart of Lady →Wisdom: "her house sinks down to death, and her paths to the Rephaim" (Prov 2:18). From this realm of the dead there is no way back (Prov 2:19). It is the place where the wicked are gathered, according to the moralist view of the sapiential writers. The context of Prov 9:18 is similar. Those who yield to the invitations of Lady Folly ignore the fact that "the Rephaim are there (i.e. in her house)" and that "her guests are in the depths of Sheol". The verse qualifies for a comparison with the description of the sojourn of Baal in the world below (*KTU* 1.5 vi:4-7 = 27-30). The expression 'guests' (literally 'her invited ones', *qĕrūʾêhā*) is reminiscent of *KTU* 1.161, notably lines 2, 9-10 (*qritm*), 4-7, 11-12 (*qra*), and 8 (*qru*). The message is the same in Prov 21:16, a text belonging to an ancient collection of wisdom counsels: "A man who wanders from the way of understanding will rest in the assembly of the Rephaim". The verse is situated in a series of oppositions between the wicked and the righteous: the former will meet with anxiety and death, whereas the latter will be rewarded with life and prosperity—in conformity with the doctrine of retribution. The company (*qĕhal*) of the Rephaim, condemned to rest (NWḤ), belong to the realm of fear and death.

In the 'historical' books (i.e. the Hexateuch and the Books of Samuel) different aspects are stressed. According to Deut 3:11, "Og, king of Bashan, was the only remnant of the last Rephaim". Og is connected with a region North-East of Israel, and South of Syro-Phoenicia. He is a king of giants, dwelling in the ever-terrifying North (Jer 46:20.24; 47:2). Deut 3:10-11 specifies that Og, whose large iron bedstead was still to be seen at Rabbat Ammon, reigned at Salecah and Edrei in Bashan. The dimensions given for his bedstead bring to mind the legends surrounding the dolmens from Brittany, and allow one to grasp how an historical kernel (a king imprisoned in his capital) could develop into a fanciful tale.

Also the early inhabitants of Moab, known as the *ʾēmîm*, were considered to have been Rephaim, just like the Anakim (cf. G. L. MATTINGLY, Anak, *ABD* 1 [1992] 222), whom they resembled in size and number (*ʾēmîm* seems to have been the Moabite designation of the Anakim). The Rephaim were believed to have occupied almost all Transjordania, since they also inhabited—under the name of Zamzummim—the land of the Ammonites before the latter disinherited them (Deut 2:20). Thus, the term Rephaim, like Anakim, seems to have served as a general designation of the mythical inhabitants of southern Syria and Transjordania, before the settlement of the Ammonites and the Moabites. Deut 3:13 limits their expansion to the northern part of Gilead and to Bashan, the kingdom of Og: "All the region of Argob, with all of Bashan, is called the land of the Rephaim". Og also occurs in Josh 12:4. In an enumeration of the Transjordanian territories conquered by the Israelites, various kings are listed, beginning with Sihon the Amorite, who dominated the land from southern Gilead to the Arabah. The second one is Og, king of Bashan "one of the remnant of the Rephaim, who dwelt at Ashtaroth [Tel Ashtara, about 20 km NW of Deraʿa] and at Edrei [modern Deraʿa, at the Syro-Jordanian border]." The relation with the Ugaritic *mlk ʿlm* reigning at *ʿṯtrt* and *hdrʿy* (*KTU*1.108:2-3) is clear. The Rephaim are also mentioned as a group of original inhabitants of the Transjordan in Josh 17:15.

Gen 14:5 describes the victory of Chedorlaomer over the Rephaim at Ashtaroth-karnaim, south of Damascus, the Zuzim at Ham (presumably to be identified with the Zamzummim of Ammon mentioned in Deut 2:20), and the Emim in Shaveh-kiriathaim in Moab (modern el-Qureyat or el-Qaryatein, cf. also Deut 2:20). The chapter apparently contains mixed traditions, since the coalition of the kings, after its victory over the Syro-Transjordanian populations, descends again towards the southern tip of the Dead Sea (where they had initially come together) to subdue all the country of the Amalekites around Kadesh and Hazazon-tamar (cf. 2 Sam 21:15-22).

Another occurrence of the Rephaim is found in the list of the inhabitants of the land between the →Nile and the →Euphrates—the land that Yahweh will give to Abram's seed (Gen 15:19-21). They are mentioned after the Kenites, Kenizzites, Kadmonites (South-West of Palestine), Hittites and Perizzites (Central-West and North-Central-East), and before the Amorites, Canaanites, Girgashites and the Jebusites (Central-West). The verses are a gloss describing the situation of Palestine before the settlement of the Israelites. Both passages from Genesis are probably Deuteronomistic; they conform with the location of the Rephaim as found in the Book of Deuteronomy.

In spite of the Deuteronomic topography, most scholars believe that the Transjordanian location of the Rephaim is secondary (e.g. CAQUOT 1985:345-346). Indeed, several early texts (Josh 15:8; 18:16; 2 Sam 5:18-25 [1 Chr 14:8-16]; 2 Sam 23:13 [1 Chr 11:15]) speak about a 'Valley of the Rephaim' (*ʿēmeq rĕpāʾîm*) close to Jerusalem. Though different identifications have been proposed, there is agreement that the valley must have been in the immediate vicinity of the city (Josephus, *Ant.Jud.* vii 312; Eusebius, *Onomasticon* 288, 22; H. VINCENT, *Jérusalem. Recherches de topographie, d'archéologie et d'histoire*, vol. 1 [Paris 1912] 123; J. SIMONS, *The Geographical and Topographical Texts of the Old Testament* [Leiden 1959] 79). Other occurrences of the Rephaim do not fit the Deuteronomistic location, either. At Isa 17:5 there is mention of the Valley of the Rephaim in an oracle addressed against Ephraim, yet replete with Judaean images. Since the text seems to conjure up the spectre of infertility, the Valley of the Rephaim in this passage is generally taken to have been a fertile area in the country. The text of 2 Sam 21:15-22 (cf. 1 Chr 20:4-8) does not fit the Deuteronomistic location, either. During his battle against the Philistines, David and his men defeat four champions presented as "descendants of the →Rapha" (*yĕlîdê hārāpâ*). The LXX interprets הרפה as the singular of *rĕpāʾîm*, plus the article (vv 16.18 ἐν τοῖς ἐκγόνοις τοῦ Ῥάφα; v 20 ἐτέχθη τῷ Ῥάφα). The Lucianic recension of vv 15-16 has "Dadou, son of Ioas, who was of the descendants of the giants". Also the Targum ("of the Giant") and the Peshitta ("David, Joab, and Abishai were terrified by a giant") witness to the antiquity of the interpretation of רפה as רפא. The same is true of the LXX in 2 Sam 21:22, where there is a textual conflation: "These four descended as offspring from the Giants in Gath, the house of Rapha". This ancient notice situating the Rephaim in Philistia reflects a pre-Deuteronomistic tradition.

The Rephaim are presented as a conglomerate consisting of various pseudo-ethnic groups, each with its own characteristics (Gen 14:5; Deut 2:10.11.20; Josh 17:15). Thus, e.g. the Anakim ('descendants of Anak'), builders of fortified cities in southern Judah (Num 13:22; Josh 11:21; 15:13; Judg 1:20), are Rephaim bearing a nickname alluding to their size. The Rephaim were traditionally associated with giants, as the description of the *yĕlîdê hārāpâ* still shows (Caquot 1985:346-347).

The ancient versions of the Hebrew Bible have linked the *rĕpāʾîm* designating the early inhabitants of Palestine and the *rĕpāʾîm* designating the spirits of the dead. The LXX sometimes offers a mere transcription (e.g. Deut 3:11 *Raphain*), as does the Vulgate (*Rafaim*, Gen 14:5; 15:20; Josh 12:4; 13:12; 17:5; 2 Sam 21:18.22; 1 Chr 11:15; 14:9.13), yet usually renders as *gigantes* (→Giants). Also the other versions generally opt for 'giants', except Aquila (who usually gives a transcription in Greek characters). The basis for this interpretation has been elucidated by CAQUOT (1985:348); it is the fable reflected in *Bereshit Rabbah* 26:7; 31:12 and *Pirqe de R. Eliezer* 34 according to which *rĕpā'îm* was one of the names of the →Nephilim, creatures born from the union between the sons of El with the daughters of mankind (Gen 6:1-4). The elaboration upon this episode in *I Enoch* 6-14 relates that their giant offspring had been cast into the netherworld, which explains why they could be called *rĕpā'îm*. The chthonic nature of these creatures, and the analogy with the →Titans, suggests the renderings *titanes* (LXX^{L} 2 Sam 21:13), *theomachoi* (Sym Prov 9:18) and *gēgeneis* (LXX Prov 2:18; 11:18).

The discovery of the *rpum* in the texts from Ugarit has put the question of the biblical *rĕpā'îm* in a new perspective. What is the etymology? Arguing that *rpum/ rĕpā'îm* are collective designations, H. L. GINSBERG (*The Legend of King Keret* [New Haven 1946] 41) proposes a connection with Ar *rafa'a*, 'to sew'. J. AISTLEITNER prefers a derivation from *RBB/RBH, on the basis of an alleged correspondence with Akk *rabû/rubû*, 'prince' (*Untersuchungen zur Grammatik des Ugaritischen* [Leipzig 1954] 12, 37). Most scholars, however, choose between the alternative roots RPH, 'to become weak, to relax', and RP', 'to heal'. Are the Rephaim 'healers' (or 'hale ones', if the form is interpreted as intransitive) or 'impotent ones'? A number of authors feel that the term *rĕpā'îm*, due to its very ambivalence, possesses both senses. According to J. D. Michaelis (as quoted by *Ges.*[17] 1302), both giants and deceased inhabit the underworld. The explanation of Rephaim by the root RPH assumes that the weakness of the shades of the dead is constitutive for their name (so *b.Ket* 111b; *Bereshit Rabbah* 26, 7 and many modern authors).

Various authors have tried to account for the co-existence of two opposite meanings by assuming a development in the significance of the term. Thus F. SCHWALLY (*Das Leben nach dem Tode* [Giessen 1892] 64 n. 1) suggests that the name Rephaim was applied first to the powerless but disquieting spirits of the dead, and secondarily to the ancient inhabitants of Palestine, the heroes of many a terrifying legend. A. CAQUOT constructs a development going from the ancient traditions about the Rephaim to the men whom God cast in the underworld, and who now haunt the living as revenants (*DBSup* X, 1985, 350).

The connection between the Rephaim and the root RP', 'to heal', is already found in the LXX of Isa 26:14 and Ps 88:11: "The healers (*iatroi*) will not rise up". The same exegesis is found for Deut 2:20 and 3:13 in the Samaritan Targum. Among modern authors, this ancient interpretation was adopted by M. J. LAGRANGE (*Etudes sur les religions sémitiques* [Paris 1905[2]] 318), who argued that the Rephaim were, by virtue of their connections with the netherworld, the healers *par excellence*. Today there is a nearly complete agreement that the Ug *rpum* were believed to watch over the dynastic continuity, granting offspring when needed. These royal dead were thus in a sense 'healers'.

Well before the discovery of the Ug *rpum* led to a better understanding of the biblical Rephaim, the latter were linked with the →teraphim, 'ancestor statuettes' (VAN DER TOORN 1990:220), on the basis of te root RP' (F. SCHWALLY, *Das Leben nach dem Tode nach der Vorstellungen des alten Israel und des Judentum* [Giessen 1892] 36 n. 1). The noun *tĕrāpîm* was analyzed as a *nomen agentis*, formed with a preformative *ta-* and having lost the *aleph* (TROPPER 1989:335 n. 64). Such an etymology, however, is invalidated by the inexplicable loss of the *aleph*, as well as by the absence of West Semitic parallels for a nominal form with prefixed *t-*. According to O. LORETZ (Die Teraphim als "Ahnen-Götter-Figur(in)nen" im Lichte der Texte aus Nuzi, Emar und Ugarit, *UF* 24 [1992] 133-178, esp. 149-152), neither the Ugaritic nor the biblical data warrant the hypothesis that in Hebrew the Canaanite form *rpu(m)* could have developed in a form *trp(ʾ)ym.* Though Phoenician and Punic sources know a form *rpʾym*, there is no single attestation of a supposed form **trpʾ(ym).* If the →teraphim are to be understood in connection with the Rephaim, it is not for philological or etymological reasons. The theological circles that wished to interpret the Rephaim on the basis of the root RPH, pejoratively vocalizing the word in analogy with *rĕšāʿîm*, 'wicked' (LIWAK 1990:629; cf. DE MOOR 1976:341 n. 107), are also responsible for deforming the term Rephaim into teraphim. Inimical against a cult of ancestors with its attendant apparel of images and offerings, they invented the term Teraphim on the basis of the pejorative root TRP, the vocalisation being the same as for Rephaim (LORETZ 1992:149-152).

According to 2 Chr 16:12, king Asa, "even in his disease, did not seek Yahweh, but sought help from physicians (*rōpĕʾîm*)". The observation (absent in 1 Kgs 15:23) implies the healing powers of Yahweh; yet Asa preferred to seek help from the *rōpĕʾîm*. The latter are not physicians in the usual sense of the term, however, but the Rephaim in their capacity as 'healers' (LIWAK 1990: 629). The text is at home in a polemic tradition criticizing the use of necromancy (cf. Deut 18:11; Isa 8:19; 19:3; 1 Chr 10:13). The vocalisation of רפאים in 2 Chr 16:12 betrays the kind of systematic correction which led to the fifteen occurrrences of the word teraphim. In a number of places the teraphim occur in a parallelism with *ʾĕlōhîm*, 'gods' (Gen 31:30; Judg 18:24), a term also used for the ancestors or their images (Exod 21:6; 1 Sam 28:13; 2 Sam 12:16; Isa 8:19). The equivalence between teraphim and Elohim, then, is based upon the equivalence between Rephaim and Elohim—which reflects the Ugaritic correspondences between *rpum*, *ilnym*, *ilm* and *mtm* (*KTU* 1.6:46-48).

IV. *Bibliography*

A. CAQUOT, Les Rephaïm ougaritiques, *Syria* 37 (1960) 79-90; CAQUOT, La tablette RS 24.252 et la question des Rephaïm ougaritiques, *Syria* 53 (1976) 296-304; CAQUOT, Rephaim, *DBSup* 10 (1985) 344-357; T. J. LEWIS, *Cults of the Dead in Ancient Israel und Ugarit* (HSM 39; Atlanta 1989); C. E. L'HEUREUX, The Ugaritic and the Biblical Rephaim, *HTR* 67 (1974) 265-274; R. LIWAK, רפאים, *TWAT* 7/3-5 (1990) 625-636; O. LORETZ, Die Teraphim als 'Ahnen-Götter-Figur(in)en' im Lichte der Texte aus Nuzi, Emar und Ugarit, *UF* 24 (1992) 133-178; J. C. DE MOOR, Rapiʾuma - Rephaim, *ZAW* 88 (1976) 323-345; G. DEL OLMO LETE, *Mitos y leyendas de Canaan segun la tradicion de Ugarit* (Valencia/Madrid 1981); DEL OLMO LETE, *La religión cananea segun la litúrgia de Ugarit. Estudio textual* (AuOrSup 3; Barcelona 1992); D. PARDEE, *Les textes para-mythologiques* (RSOu 4; Paris 1988) 75-118, 179-192; S. B. PARKER, The Feast of Rāpiʾu, *UF* 2 (1970) 243-249; H. ROUILLARD, El Rofé en Nombres 12,13, *Sem* 37 (1987) 17-46; H. ROUILLARD & J. TROPPER, *trpym*, rituels de guérison et culte des ancêtres d'après 1 Samuël XIX11-17 et les textes parallèles d'Assur et de Nuzi, *VT* 37 (1987) 340-361; K. SPRONK, *Beatific Afterlife in Ancient Israel and in the Ancient Near East* (AOAT 219; Kevelaer/Neukirchen-Vluyn 1986); K. VAN DER TOORN, The Nature of the Biblical Teraphim in the Light of the Cuneiform Evidence, *CBQ* 52 (1990) 203-222; VAN DER TOORN, Funerary Rituals and Beatific Afterlife in Ugaritic Texts and in the Bible, *BiOr* 48 (1991) 40-66; J. TROPPER, *Nekromantie und Totenbefragung im Alten Orient und im Alten Testament* (AOAT 223; Kevelaer/Neukirchen-Vluyn 1989); A. TSUKIMOTO, *Untersuchungen zur Totenpflege* (kispum) *im alten Mesopotamien* (AOAT 216; Neukirchen-Vluyn 1985).

H. ROUILLARD

REPHAN → KAIWAN

RESHEPH רשף

I. Reseph occurs as *ršp* in Ugaritic, Phoenician, and Aramaic, as *rešep* in Hebrew (8 times), as *ra-sa-ap* at Ebla and in Akkadian, and as *r-š-p(-w)* in Egyptian. It is the name of one of the most popular West-

Semitic gods, venerated in Syria, Palestine and Egypt. The etymology of the name is still very uncertain. It is often assumed that it is related to a root *RŠP (?) with the basic meaning "to light, to set on fire" or "to burn" (cf. e.g. Jud.-Aram *rišpâʾ* "flames, lightning"). Yet also a derivation from roots such as *ŚRP, *ŠRB (metathesis?), or even *RṢP can be considered, as well as a possible connection to Akk *rašābu(m)* I and *rašbu(m)*. The name was probably pronounced Rašapu or Rašpu (cf. the Amorite form Rušpan). Heb *rešep* is a segolate form, a fact which confirms the original triliteral structure of the name. The meaning generally assumed is "He who is burning" (referring to →fire, lightning or even to plague in a metaphorical sense). Though it fits the personality of the god Resheph, the etymological foundation of the interpretation is problematic. In fact, all the proposed etymologies are based on what we actually know about the character of this god; therefore, there is a serious risk of circular argument.

II. Resheph is attested at Tell Mardikh-Ebla in the 3rd Millennium BCE, where he seems to have been a very popular deity. He may have been related to the royal necropolis as a chthonic god. Priests of Resheph are also attested to. The god had a consort named Adamma. His name occurs as theophoric element in personal names from Ur III, Mari, Terqa and Ḫana, but it is especially at Ugarit and Ras Ibn Hani during the Late Bronze Age, and later in the Phoenician-Punic world, that we are given information about the god's personality. Identified with →Nergal and attested as a plague-god in the Keret poem (*KTU* 1.14 i: 18-19; 1.15 ii:6), Resheph is very frequently mentioned in the Ugaritic ritual texts in the capacity of a chthonic deity, gatekeeper of the Netherworld. He is the lord of battle and of diseases, which he spreads through his bow and arrows. These aspects of Resheph's personality are confirmed by the Amarna letters (see e.g. *EA* 35). His fierce nature apparently did not affect his popularity both in private devotion (as reflected by the theophoric personal names) and in the official cult. In fact, the epithets he receives show that he is an ambivalent god, dangerous as well as benevolent; he can hurt but also heal.

In Egypt from the New Kingdom onwards the cult of Resheph gained prominence under the influence of immigrated Asiatic people. The god was officially adopted at the court of Amenophis II; the Pharaoh regarded this deity as his special protector during military enterprises. In the Ramesside period, Resheph's veneration also spread among the common people: textual and iconographical data testify both to his worship at the highest levels of the society and to the devotion of the general population. The iconography of Resheph is relatively well known. It confirms the double character of Resheph: benevolent, on the one hand, dangerous, on the other. In some stelae of the New Kingdom Resheph is also depicted in the attitude of the Pharaoh striking his enemies, an element which suggests that the so-called "Smiting God" of the Syrian iconographical tradition is a representation of our deity. Traces of the cult of Re-sheph are also found in Hittite Anatolia. At Zenjirli, in the 8th century BCE, the local king Panamuwa mentions the god (together with *ʾrqršp*) as his dynastic deity (*KAI* 214: 2.3.11).

In the Phoenician-Punic world, the earliest evidence of the god is to be found at Byblos. If there is no proof in favour of a relation of Resheph with Herisheph the god of the "Obelisk Temple", it is nonetheless quite probable that our god was identified at a very early stage with said Egyptian deity, mentioned in the "Pyramid Texts" (§§ 242, 423, 518) and on the so-called "Cylindre Montet" (but note the cautionary remarks of FULCO 1976:55). The first direct evidence of the cult of Resheph in Phoenician texts, however, is found in the Karatepe portal inscription (*KAI* 26, 8th century BCE); here Azitawada mentions →Baal and Resheph-*ṣprm* as dynastic deities. The epithet *ṣprm* can mean "(Resheph) of the goats" or "(Resheph) of the birds", if it is not a Cilician place-name. Later, in 5th century Sidon, the inscriptions of the local king Bodashtart reveal that there was a whole quarter in the town named "Land of the Reshephs" (*'rṣ ršpm*: *KAI* 15). Yet the textual occurrences of this god are chiefly concentrated in Cyprus. Here we find traces of the ancient Ugaritic tradition of the Archer-God, which merged with the figure of an archaic local →Apollo (see also the Homeric tradition of Apollo's arrows, *Iliad* I 43-67). Especially important among the various documents is the dedication to Resheph written on the base of a statue (Palaeo-kastro, 7th century BCE, see A. CAQUOT & O. MASSON, Deux inscriptions phéniciennes de Chypre, *Syria* 45 [1968] 295-321, esp. 295-300). This text is perhaps to be related to a Kition inscription of the 4th century BCE mentioning the dedication of two lion-heads (*'rwm*) to the same god by a priest of "Resheph of the arrow" (*ršp hṣ*, *KAI* 32; M. G. AMADASI GUZZO & V. KARAGEORGHIS, *Fouilles de Kition – III. Inscriptions phéniciennes* [Nicosia 1977] III A 2). The epigraphic documentation from Cyprus attests moreover to some local manifestations of Resheph, always identified with Apollo: *Ršp-(b)mkl*, "Resheph-Amyklos" at Idalion (*KAI* 38-40 and CAQUOT & MASSON, Deux inscriptions phéniciennes de Chypre, *Syria* 45 [1968] 295-321, esp. 302-313; cf. *a-mu-ko-lo-i*, dative, in syllabic Cyprian), *Ršp-'lhyts*, "Resheph-Alasiotas" at Tamassos (*RES* 1213; cf. *a-la-si-o-ta-i*, dative, in syllabic Cyprian), and *Ršp-'lyyt*, "Resheph-Eleitas" also in Tamassos (*RES* 1212; cf. *e-le-ta-i*, dative, in syllabic Cyprian). Finally, it must be added that the god *bʿl ʿz*, "The Lord of the power", attested in a recently published Phoenician royal inscription from Kition (M. YON & M. SZNYCER, Une inscription phénicienne royale de Kition (Chypre), *CRAIBL* 1991, 791-823), was probably a particular manifestation of Resheph-*mkl*, a god especially venerated at Idalion.

From an historical point of view, these testimonies show that the personality of Resheph at Cyprus retained the general features which characterize the god in Syria-Palestina during the Bronze and the Iron Ages. Some changes in his cult are nevertheless perceptible. For example, it is noteworthy that we know very few personal names of this period which contain the name of Resheph. This could be explained as an indication of the god's loss of prominence in popular devotion, in contradistinction to his role and importance at a more official level. This process culminates perhaps at Carthage, where we have only one personal name with Resheph as theophoric element (*ʿbdršp: CIS* I 2628,6). Yet in the Punic metropolis, too, it is certain that the god enjoyed a certain popularity, because he had at least one temple in the very centre of the town with cultic personnel devoted to him (*CIS* I 251). Some classical authors (Valerius Maximus I 1,18; Appian, *Lyb.* 127) inform us that there was a golden statue of the god, as well as an altar of gold. It is probable that the Phoenician Apollo—whom Pausanias (VII 23,7-8) identifies as the father of →Eshmun—was none other than Resheph—a tradition perhaps confirmed by Cicero (cf. *Arsippus* in Cicero, *Nat. deor.* III 22,57). If the Apollo mentioned in the treaty between Hannibal and Philip of Macedonia (Polybius VII 9,2-3) is to be identified with Resheph, it would confirm the leading role of the god in the Carthaginian pantheon, as the text mentions him in the first divine triad together with →Zeus and →Hera. In Phoenicia, a late trace of the god is finally found in the name of the ancient Apollonia, a town which is called Arsūf in Arabic.

III. The original divine nature of Resheph is detectable in the OT. Like various other ancient Semitic deities, he is generally considered as a sort of decayed →demon at the service of →Yahweh. 1 Chr 7:25 presents Resheph as one of the Ephraim's sons, but the text is corrupted and a different reading has been proposed for this passage. The tradition of Resheph as a god of pestilence is attested in Deut 32:24 and Ps 78:48. The first text, a passage of the Song of Moses, deals with those who provoked God to anger and were unfaithful: they are punished with hunger and destroyed by Resheph and →Qeteb ("I will heap (?) evils upon them, my arrows I will spend on them; wasted with hunger, devoured by Resheph and Qeteb the poisonous one", Deut 32:23-24a). There is no doubt that we have to do here with two ancient Canaanite gods (perhaps conceived as flying demons), personifications of the scourges that they spread. In Ps 78:48 we have an allusion to the seventh plague of Egypt: God has given up the cattle to →Barad (Hail) and the herds to the Reshephs (pl.: *wayyasgēr labbārād bĕʿîrām ûmiqnêhem lārĕšāpîm*). Here too, the poet deals with decayed deities, Barad//Resheph(s), depicted as malevolent spirits which accompany God in his destructive action.

In Hab 3:5 we have the description of a theophany and the attendant natural phenomena. God is described as a divine warrior, Lord of light; before Him goes →Deber (master of epidemics, cf. Exod 9:3 and Jer 21:6), while Resheph (Pestilence) follows on God's heels (*lĕpānāyw yēlek dāber wĕyēṣēʾ rešep lĕraglāyw*). Deber and Resheph must be seen, here too, as two personalized natural powers, submitted to Yahweh. Ps 76:4 mentions the *ršpy qšt*, an expression which could be interpreted as "the Reshephs of the bow" and be related to the imagery of the god armed with bow and arrows ("[In Zion, God] shattered the *ršpy qšt*, the shield, the sword, the weapons of war"). Job 5:7 is a very difficult text, inserted in a passage dealing with the need for man of absolute trust in God. Here 'the sons of Resheph' (*bĕnê rešep*) are mentioned ("and the sons of Resheph fly high"); they seem to be winged demons, particularly if we think of Ps 91:5, where the expression *ḥēṣ yāʿûp* "the arrow that flies" could be an allusion to Resheph. The plurals, here and elsewhere, remind us of the *ršpm* attested both in Ugaritic and in Phoenician texts. This passage is perhaps to be related to Sir 43:17, where Resheph is a bird of prey flying in the sky (reading *kršp* with the Masada scroll, see F. Vattioni, *Ecclesiastico. Testo ebraico con apparato critico* [Napels 1968] 233). In Cant 8:6 we have another echo of the "fiery" character of Resheph. The 'flames' (*rešep*, plural) of love are characterized as a 'fire of Yahweh' in a context dealing with love, death, and the Netherworld.

To sum up, in the OT Resheph is a demonized version of an ancient Canaanite god, now submitted to Yahweh. He appears as a cosmic force, whose powers are great and terrible: he is particularly conceived of as bringing epidemics and death. The Hebrew Bible shows different levels of demythologization: sometimes it describes Resheph as a personalized figure, more or less faded, sometimes the name is used as a pure metaphor. At any rate it is possible to perceive aspects of the personality of an ancient chthonic god, whichs fits the image of Resheph found in the other Semitic cultures.

IV. *Bibliography.*

M. G. Amadasi Guzzo & V. Karageorghis, *Fouilles de Kition – III. Inscriptions phéniciennes* (Nicosia 1977); *A. Caquot, Sur quelques démons de l'Ancien Testament: Reshef, Qeteb, Deber, *Sem* 6 (1956) 53-68; *W. J. Fulco, *The Canaanite God Rešep* (New Haven 1976); G. Garbini, *ršp ṣprm*, *RSF* 20 (1992) 93-94; *E. Lipiński, Resheph Amyklos, *Studia Phoenicia* 5 (Leuven 1987) 87-99; F. Pomponio, Adamma paredra di Rašap, *SEL* 10 (1993) 3-7; *P. Xella, Le dieu Rashap à Ugarit, *AAAS* 29-30 (1979-80) 145-162; Xella, D'Ugarit à la Phénicie: sur les traces de Rashap, Horon, Eshmun, *WO* 19 (1988) 45-64; Xella, Le dieu BʿL ʿZ dans une nouvelle inscription phénicienne de Kition (Chypre), *SEL* 10 (1993) 61-70.

P. Xella

RIDER UPON THE CLOUDS רכב בערבות

I. In Ps 68:5[4] Yahweh is referred to as the *rōkēb bāʿărābôt*. Though often translated as 'rider through the steppe' (based on the meaning 'steppe' of Hebr *ʿărābâ*), the expression is thought to reflect the Ugaritic epithet *rkb ʿrpt*, 'Rider upon the clouds', traditionally given to →Baal.

II. In the mythological texts of Ras Shamra the god Baal repeatedly gets the epithet *rkb ʿrpt.* It is rendered with slight nuances as 'Rider of the Clouds', 'Rider on the Clouds', 'Who mounts the Clouds'. Epithets based on the root RKB, 'to ride', occur quite frequently in connection with gods. The name →Rakib-el is a good example, demonstrating that the epithet could eventually turn into a proper name (cf. *KAI*, II 34, commentary at no. 24:16).

The epithet *rkb ʿrpt* refers to Baal as driving his chariot of clouds (cf. LORETZ 1979-80; G. DEL OLMO LETE, 'auriga de las nubes' [*Mitos y Leyendas de Canaan* (Barcelona 1981), see Glosario s. v. *rkb*]). This explanation agrees with the one advanced by J. C. DE MOOR: Baal rides upon the clouds as the driver in a chariot; he goes out to distribute rain (*The Seasonal Pattern in the Ugaritic Myth of Baʿlu* [Neukirchen-Vluyn 1971] 98; cf. DIETRICH-LORETZ, *UF* 21 [1989] 116). At the same time, it casts Baal in the role of warrior-god (Miller 1973).

III. Normally, the Hebrew term *ʿărābâ* has the meaning 'steppe' or 'desert'. Consequently the expression in Ps 68:5[4] is usually understood as 'the one passing through the steppes'. Yet because Yahweh is celebrated in v 34[33] as the 'Rider in the heavens, the heavens of old' (*rōkēb bišmê šĕmê-qedem*), it has been surmised that *ʿărābôt* in v 5[4] is in fact a word for 'clouds' (cf. Akk *urpatu, erpetu* 'cloud', plural *urpātu, urpētu, erpētu*: *CAD* E [1958] 302-304; *AHW* 243, 1432). If *ʿărābôt* stands indeed for clouds, a shift *p* → *b* may be assumed (so S. MOSCATI et al., *An Introduction to the Comparative Grammar of the Semitic Languages*, [Wiesbaden 1980²] 25-26; but contrast L. L. GRABBE, Hebrew *pāʿal* / Ugaritic *bʿl* and the supposed *b/p* Interchange in Semitic, *UF* 11 [1979] 307-314). Alternatively the text might be emended to read בעבות, 'in/upon the clouds' (see already P. HAUPT, *ExpTim* 22 [1910-11] 375). The correction finds some support in other passages where Yahweh is said to be a 'rider in the heavens' (Deut 33:26), or even a 'rider upon a swift cloud' (Isa 19:1; cf. 2 Sam 22:11 = Ps 18:11). Another reference still could be made to Isa 5:30, where the noun **ʿărîpîm* could possibly signify 'clouds'.

In order to explain the Hebrew collocation, ULLENDORFF (1956) drew a comparison with the epithet νεφεληγερέτης, 'Cloudgatherer', attributed to →Zeus, because the root RKB originally denotes 'to compose, put together, collect'; the meaning 'to ride (on a horse)' is a late development based on RKB in the meaning 'to harness'. Though Ullendorff was followed by S. BROCK (*VT* 18 [1968] 395-397), his interpretation is hardly correct. K. J. CATHCART (*TRKB QMḤ* in the Arad Ostracon and Biblical Hebrew *REKEB,* "Upper Millstone", *VT* 19 [1969] 121-123, esp. 121-122) has shown Ullendorff's interpretation of the verb RKB to be incorrect; as a matter of consequence, the comparison of νεφεληγερέτης and *rkb ʿrpt* is without factual basis (M. WEINFELD, 'Rider of the Clouds' and 'Gatherer of the Clouds', *JANES* 5 [1973] 421-426).

GALLING has convincingly demonstrated that *rōkēb* denotes 'rider' or 'charioteer' (1956:132). A combination of this fact with the information of Hab 3:8, where Yahweh is said to drive a horse-drawn chariot (cf. M. HARAN, The Ark and the Cherubim, *IEJ* 9 [1959] 30-94), an image reminiscent of that of the storm-god setting out for battle (MILLER 1973:41), suggests that the clouds in Ps 68:5[4] are God's mythological chariot (MOWINCKEL 1962:298-299; cf. W. L. MORAN, *Bib* 43 [1962] 323-325). The particle *bĕ* ('in, upon') shows that God is the driver of the nubilous vehicle (S. E. LOEWENSTAMM, Grenzgebiete ugaritischer Sprach- und Stilvergleichung, *UF* 3 [1971] 93-100, esp. 99-100).

Yet the rendering in the LXX (Ps 67:5) does not favour the explication of the Hebrew phrase in analogy with the Ugaritic epithet of Baal, since it has understood *ʿărābôt* as δυσμαί, 'sunset'. The Hebrew word *ʿărābôt* was apparently associated with *ʿereb*, 'evening, sunset' (the same interpretation is found in the Peshitta: *lĕdrākib lĕma ʿarbā*). The Old Latin translation followed its own course and translated *coelos coelorum*, presumably on the basis of v 34[33]. Another translation of the Hebrew is provided by the Psalterium iuxta Hebraeos with its *per deserta,* which is supported by Symmachus ἐν τῇ ἀοικήτῳ (F. FIELD, *Origenis Hexaplorum quae supersunt*, II [Oxford, 1875] at Ps 67:5).

In the context of Ps 68, the word *ʿărābôt* makes good sense when translated as 'steppe, desert'. Verses 8-10[7-9] refer to the Exodus, using the word *yĕšîmôn* as a designation of the wilderness in v 8[7]. Though the fact remains that the Israelites imagined Yahweh as being capable of moving about in a nubilous chariot (see in addition to the texts already mentioned Ps 104:3), this by itself is not enough to maintain that *ʿărābôt* needs to be understood as 'clouds'. The choice of the word *ʿărābôt* should rather be explained as a deliberate attempt to differentiate Yahweh from Baal; the Baal epithet was adopted yet modified in such a way that it came to signify something entirely different (cf. H. GESE, *RAAM*, 122-123; W. B. BARRICK & H. RINGGREN, *TWAT* 7/3-5 [1990] 511; A. COOPER & M. H. POPE, *RSP* III [Rome 1981] 458-460; cf. O. LORETZ, *UF* 10 [1978] 480). A similar modification is evident in v 8 [7] of the Psalm, where a quotation from Judg 5:4 has been adapted. "When thou didst go forth from Seir" (Judg 5:4a) became "When thou didst go forth before thy people" (Ps 68:8a [7a]); "When thou didst march from the Field of Edom" (Judg 5:4b) was changed into "When thou didst march through the wilderness" (Ps 68:8b [7b]). The change of Ug *ʿrpt* into Heb *ʿărābôt* fits this pattern of modification.

IV. *Bibliography*

K. GALLING, Der Ehrenname Elisas und die Entrückung Elias, *ZTK* 53 (1956) 129-148; O. LORETZ, Baal, le Chevaucheur des Nuées, *AAAS* 29-30 (1979-80) 185-188; LORETZ, Der ugaritische Topos *bʿl rkb* und die "Sprache Kanaans" in Jes 19:1-25, *UF* 19 (1987) 101-112; P. D. MILLER Jr., *The Divine Warrior in Early Israel* (Cambridge Mass. 1973) 41; S. MOWINCKEL, Drive and/or Ride in the Old Testament, *VT* 12 (1962) 278-299; E. ULLENDORFF, The Contribution of South Semitics to Hebrew Lexicography, *VT* 6 (1956) 190-198; ULLENDORFF, Ugaritic Studies within their Semitic and Eastern Mediterranean Setting, *BJRL* 46 (1963-64) 236-249.

W. HERRMANN

RIGHTEOUSNESS → ZEDEQ

RIVER נהר

I. Rivers, as sources of water, are of great importance for agricultural life: especially in regions with large streams and irrigation culture. In such areas, rivers provide the possibility of shipping, but they can become threatening when there is serious flooding. They are a means of economical and cultural exchange. At the same time, however, rivers demarcate frontiers whose crossing is dangerous. Water currents in the desert are especially unpredictable. As a rule, wadis are dry; but, if there is intense rain, they soon become dangerous torrents. In Hebrew, a permanently flowing river is called *nāhār*: in contrast to the *naḥal.*

II. The cultural significance of the river is represented in religious symbolism. The great streams of Mesopotamia and Egypt are interpreted anthropomorphically. The god of the →Nile, Hapi (male, but with full breasts, occasionally conceptualized as a dyad of gods, corresponding to Upper and Lower Egypt) is called 'father of the gods'. Sometimes he is linked with the primeval ocean, Nun, and with other deities: e.g. Chnum, Satis and Anukis. He represents the fertility of the river which is active in the annual inundation. The Nile god is not a subject of myth or ritual; but he does appear in the iconography (holding two vases).

In Mesopotamia, rivers in general are represented by the divinity ÍD (= *nāru*?, →Flood) occurring in lists of gods and in the Theogony of Dunnu (as daughter of Earth and Gaju, possibly Laḫar, see W. G.

LAMBERT, Laḫar, *RLA* 6 [1980-83] 413). The →Euphrates and the →Tigris are the most prominent divine rivers. The earliest mythological elaboration of the river theme is preserved in the Sumerian myth Lugal-e: Subdued by the power of the mountain-demon Azag, the rivers cannot flow but are frozen into stone. After the victory of Ninurta (→Nimrod), the rivers begin to flow and fertilize the land; the cultural work of irrigation can start (cf. the Indian tradition of Indra's victory over Vṛtra). According to a later tradition, the Euphrates and the Tigris were created immediately after →Marduk's victory over →Tiamat: The body of the smitten goddess is covered with →earth, and the perforation of her eyes brings forth the springs of the great streams. Finally, Enki, the god of the subterranean ocean, is connected with the waters of irrigation. The rivers, though related to different mythological contexts, always have their origin in a 'marginal', chaotic area; but they transform the water into a form which can be used by human culture. Furthermore, the Euphrates and the Tigris are important as deities responsible for the water ordeal.

The Mesopotamian river deities are known well beyond their area of origin. They are worshipped in Anatolia where they even play a role in mythology (which is not the case in Mesopotamia). Here, Tigris and Euphrates are, to a greater degree than in Mesopotamia, seen anthropomorphically (and theriomorphically, e.g., the Tigris assumes the form of an eagle and takes part in a meal). Not only Mesopotamian, but also domestic rivers are important. A ritual text shows that pestilence was explained as a consequence of the omission to bring offerings to the river Mala.

In the Syro-Palestinian area, rivers are closely related to the sea. The God Yam (→sea) is often called *zbl ym ṭpṭ nhr,* 'prince Sea, ruler River'. He seems to be the deity of every kind of water. According to Strabo (16, 750-751), Typhon, a Greek parallel to the chaotical enemy of →Baal, is identified with the Orontes: one of the prominent rivers of Syria. Furthermore, Okeanos possesses the spring of the Tyrian cult. As a river deity, Yam seems to represent the destructive power of water: e.g. in flash floods.

Although there is no precise conception of the netherworld, there are some ideas about a river →Hubur (identified with Tiamat) in that region. The myth of Enlil and Ninlil tells of this river: and a ferryman is charged with the traffic. Similarly, Gilgamesh has to cross the waters of death located beyond the cosmic mountain in order to reach Utnapishtim on the island of Dilmun (Bahrein!). Sea and river, the netherworld and the landscape at the end of this world, are not really differentiated. The western Semites seem to know such a river too (*KTU* 1.5 i 22). In any case, →Mot's dwelling place is mud: a mixture of water and earth.

III. The torrent, as an evil power, is also attested in the Psalms (Ps 124:4-5). Note the expression "mighty waters" (*mayim rabbîm/ 'addîrîm*), which is connected with the water of a torrent as well as with the primeval water—and the water of the Sea of Reeds (Ps 29:3; 32:6; 77:20; 93:4).

In biblical symbolism, however, rivers represent not only evil but also blessing. Descending from the spring, especially the sacred temple spring, there is a river fertilizing the land. This image is known for Jerusalem (Ps 65:10-14; 46:5-6), but it seems to belong to the common temple ideology. The river *(nāhār)* is related to the concept of *šālôm.* This type of river does not belong to the sphere of the god Yam, but rather to →Shalem. Shalem was probably worshipped in Jerusalem in pre-Israelite times and possibly later (identification with →Yahweh?). Hence the metaphorical use of the river image (Isa 48:18; 66:12). Likewise, the river of blessing becomes an eschatological theme: The stream rising from the temple fertilizes the whole land (Isa 33:21; Ezek 47; Zech 14:8; cf. Rev 22:1-2).

In the Bible, the experiences of danger intrinsic to river crossings are a subject of religious interpretation. Fords are threatened by →demons and protected by sanctuaries. The story of Gen 32:22-32 is such an etiological narrative with a Yahwistic interpretation. A similar tradition is known for the Jordan ford near Gilgal. In this case, the interpretation is linked to the Exodus tradition (Josh 3-4; Ps 114).

Rivers also have a cosmological quality. They are taken to be 'primeval deities', which, together with elements such as →sources, →heaven and →earth, are called as witnesses when treaties are concluded or oaths are sworn. This feature is also stressed in the conception of four cosmic streams which correspond to the four quarters of the heavens. In Mesopotamia, this idea is represented iconographically. The paradise story says (in a secondary passage) that the spring in the garden of Eden was divided into four rivers. Two of them can be located geographically (Euphrates and Tigris); the other two (Pishon and Gihon) cannot be thus identified. However, the temple spring of Jerusalem is called Gihon too. The temple of Jerusalem is, according to the cultic ideology, the centre of the world: so there could be a relation between the insignificant spring Gihon and the cosmic river Gihon.

In the Israelite area, only the →Jordan permanently carries water. In the OT, however there is no evidence for an anthropomorphic conception of a Jordan deity. However, the ark of Titus contains such a representation: and, in later Christian iconography, the Jordan river is frequently conceived as an anthropomorphic figure.

IV. *Bibliography*

H. G. MAY, Some Cosmic Connotations of *mayim rabbim,* 'Many Waters', *JBL* 74 (1955) 9-21; K. H. RENGSTORFF, potamos, *TWNT* 6 (1959) 595-607; P. REYMOND, *L'eau, sa vie et sa signification dans l'Ancien Testament* (VTSup 6; Leiden 1958); A. SCHWARZENBACH, *Die geographische Terminologie im Hebräischen des Alten Testaments* (Leiden 1954); E. VON SCHULER, Flußgottheiten, *WbMyth* I/1 (1965) 164; L. A. SNIJDERS, Nāhār, *TWAT* 5 (1986) 281-291; W. A. WARD, Notes on Some Semitic Loanwords and Personal Names in Late Egyptian, *Or* 32 (1963) 413-436; O. WASER, Flußgötter, PW VI/2 (1958) 2774-2815; WASER, Der Flußgott Jordan und andere Personifikationen, *Festgabe für A. Kaegi* (Frauenfeld 1919) 191-217.

F. STOLZ

ROCK צור, סלע

I. The name 'Rock' (*ṣwr*) is very common as a metaphor for God in the Hebrew Bible (e.g. 2 Sam 22:3 = Ps 18:3; a few times in Deut 32). Etymologically the original form of the word *ṣwr* will have been **ẓr*, as may be concluded on the basis of the cognates in other Semitic languages (*HALAT* 953). Like 'mountain' (→Mountains-and-Valleys; →Shadday) and →Stone the term was used in the Semitic world as a divine epithet, but in contrast to *ʾbn*, stone, it never became obsolete.

II. The Ugaritic texts mention *ǵrm*, in god lists, but although the word is etymologically related to Hebrew *ṣwr*, the Ugaritic noun denotes a mountain. For etymological reasons it is difficult to assume a connection with Ugaritic *ṣrrt*, a part of →Baal's holy mountain →Zaphon. It may well be that the normal Ugaritic word for 'rock' was *slʿ* which is attested in hypocoristic personal names like *slʿy*, *slʿn*. (cf. the relevant entries in F. GRÖNDAHL, *Die Personennamen der Texte aus Ugarit* [StP 1; Roma 1965]).

However, *ṣwr* 'rock' does occur in Amorite, Phoenician and Aramaic and possibly Proto-Sinaitic personal names. A few times the Ugaritic Mt. Ṣapanu is deified and the name of Ṣapanu could also be used to mask the name of Baal. It is said that by the hand of 'Ṣapanu' some are victorious and some are without triumph (*KTU* 1.19 ii:35). A personification of a rock as the parent of a god is known from Hittite Song of Ullikumi (→Olden Gods).

III. The name 'Rock' (*ṣwr*) is very common as a metaphor for God in the OT. With regard to the remarkable use of this metaphor in Deut 32:4.15.30.31 (cf. KNOWLES 1989) scholars differ in opinion: should this be attributed to old tradition, or is it a late innovation? In any case Hab 1:12 seems to allude to Deut 32. The prophet states that the 'Rock' God cannot wish the death of his people because he uses the enemy only to punish his people. Deut 32:18 speaks of the Rock who has begotten his people, the God who has borne them (cf. Ps 89:27). It cannot be doubted that figurative language is used here, but the imagery comes close to the theogony of the Ugaritic text in which the Stone was the male deity who begot the first animated creature (*KTU* 1.100). The image of the rock is here tied to the motif of creation (OLOFSSON 1990:38). But there is no reason to doubt the metaphorical intention of the author. In Isa 51:1-2 →Abraham and →Sarah seem to be the rocks who gave birth to the people of Israel. The same imagery recurs in the New Testament (Matt 3:9; Luk 3:8).

Nowhere else but in Deut 32:31.37 is the epithet 'Rock' applied to other gods, albeit in such a way that the author evidently took the view that other gods were called by this epithet illegitimately. In the Old Testament five personal names confirm the antiquity of the epithet *ṣwr*. All names containing the theophoric element Rock are premonarchical (FOWLER 1988:54). Unfortunately, this datum has not been confirmed by epigraphical findings until now.

In addition to *ṣwr* the OT uses its synonym *slʿ*. The supplicant calls God his *slʿ* (Pss 42:10; 71:3). 2 Sam 22:3 (= Ps 18:3) is helpful with regard to the interpretation of the metaphor. David regards →Yahweh as his rock, his fortress and his deliverer. In short, the tenor of the metaphor may be summarized as 'protection'. It is therefore a deliberate deviation from this traditional imagery when Isaiah (8:14) announces that Yahweh will become a Stone that causes men to stumble, and a rock (*ṣwr*) that makes them fall.

→Moses and Aaron are ordered to speak to the rock, so that it will yield water (Num 20:8). This would seem to imply that the rock could hear. However, because in this case a miracle is involved one should not put too much weight on the fact that it is a real stone which is addressed as an animate being. Later on the water-giving rock became a motive of blessing and the New Testament applies the imagery to →Christ in 1 Cor 10:4. The Greek equivalent πέτρα sometimes is used as epithet for Christ (Matt 21:42; Rom 9:32-33; 1 Pet 2:6), and the disciple Simon receives the epithet as a new name, Peter (Matt 16:18).

IV. *Bibliography*

D. EICHHORN, *Gott als Fels, Burg, Zuflucht* (Bern 1972); J. D. FOWLER, *Theophoric Personal Names in Ancient Hebrew* (JSOTSup 49; Sheffield 1988); M. P. KNOWLES, 'The Rock, his Work is Perfect': Unusual Imagery for God in Deuteronomy XXXII, *VT* 39 (1989) 307-322; S. OLOFSSON, *God is my Rock: A Study of Translation Technique and Theological Exegesis in the Septuagint* (Stockholm 1990) esp. 35-50.

M. C. A. KORPEL

ROMA Ῥώμη

I. Roma occurs only as toponym and as the name for the capital of the Roman Republic or Empire in Biblical and related literature. As a personification of the city and the republic, Roma attained divine status outside the Bible.

II. According to legends the toponym Roma originated from the foundation of the city to which Trojans were forced, after one of their women, Rhome, encouraged the destruction of their ships. In the Greek world Roma was considered to be the personification of the Roman people or state, analogous to the Demos of Athens. Such personifications were deified and honoured with cults and festivals. Their cult can be considered as a democratic counterpart of the Hellenistic →Ruler cult (MELLOR 1981: 956). In connection with Rome's manifestation in the eastern part of the Mediterranean world, cults of Roma appeared from the beginning of the second century BCE onwards, with temples, altars, priests and Rōmaia-festivals (Smyrna 195 BCE; Chalcis 194; Delphi and Lycia 189; Alabanda 170).

After the Roman victory at Pydna (168 BCE) the cults increased and most of the Greek cities created an altar or temple for Roma. These cults were inspired by similar motives to those which led to the foundation of local and provincial ruler cults (→Ruler cult). The cult at Smyrna, for instance, was a reward for the Roman help against Antiochus III. Roma's most common epitheta also remind one of the ruler cult (*euergetēs, sōtēr, epiphanēs and theos*).

→Zeus or Jupiter usually joined Roma, not so much as patron deity of Rome but as protector of oaths and treaties. After the emperor joined in cults with Roma he was often associated with Zeus/Jupiter, whose characteristics were transferred to the emperor. Shortly after the coming to power of Octavian, temples for Roma and Augustus were founded in several provinces of Asia Minor (Pergamum in Asia, Nicomedia in Bithynia and Ancyra in Galatia). The high priest of these cults was called *Archiereus Theas Rōmēs kai Autokratoros Kaisaros (Theou Hyiou Sebastou)*. Tacitus refers to the Asian cult as one for Augustus and the city of Rome (*Ann.* 4.37.3), but Greek inscriptions point out that the goddess Roma was worshipped. A coin depicts Augustus (Claudius) and a personified Roma in their temple of the provincial cult at Pergamum. Somewhat later similar cults were established in the western part of the empire. The cults with their annual festivals (Romaia Sebasta) were a central activity of the provincial conventions. Also local cults for Roma and the divine emperor came into being. Roma appears as goddess on coins a few times in the Republican period, but more often since the first century CE. Her portrayal changes from a symbol of military hegemony to a stately representation of the empire. She is depicted with a mural crown (cf. →Tyche), a crested helmet, or a *modius*, and sometimes bareheaded.

III. *Rōmē* occurs in 1 Macc as a toponym (1:10; 7:1; 8:19) and also as the name for the Roman Republic in the context of treaties of alliance between the Jews and Rome (8:17-32; 12:1-4; 14:24; 15:15-24; cf. 2 Macc 11:34-38; GRUEN [1984]). It is referred to eight times in the NT, twice as the place of residence of a Christian community (Rom 1:7, 15). Acts 18:2 refers to Claudius's decision that all Jews had to leave Rome. The other occurrences concern Paul's missionary activity at Rome and his staying there. Rome is hinted at in 1 Pet 5:13 and Rev 14:8; 16:19; 17:5 and 18:2, 10, 21 through the symbolic name Babylon (also *Sib. Or.* 5:143). Rome occurs frequently in the often anti-Roman Sibylline Oracles, e.g. in oracles which predict its downfall (3:350-380), or in connection with a return of Nero from the East (e.g. 5:137-154). It is not certain, whether there is any reference to the goddess Roma in *Sib. Or.* (MELLOR 1981: 971) or Revelation "... it is difficult to say whether her [i.e. Roma's] cult (as distinct from the general imperial cult) is actually alluded to in this book" (MELLOR 1975: 128). Herod the Great founded a temple for Augustus and Roma in Caesarea to prove his loyalty to Augustus (Josephus, *Bell.* 1.414; *Ant.* 15.339).

IV. *Bibliography*

H. BALZ, Ῥώμη, *EWNT* 3 (Stuttgart 1983) 519-520; E. S. GRUEN, *The Hellenistic World and the Coming of Rome* I-II (Berkeley 1984) 42-46, 745-751; R. MELLOR, *ΘΕΑ ΡΩΜΗ. The Worship of the Goddess Roma in the Greek World* (Hypomnemata 42; Göttingen 1975); MELLOR, The Goddess Roma, *ANRW* II 17/2 (Berlin/New York 1981) 950-1030 [& lit]; F. RICHTER, Roma, *ALGRM* 4 (Leipzig 1909-1915) 130-164.

J. W. VAN HENTEN

RULER CULT

I. A technical phrase for the phenomenon of the ruler cult does not appear in biblical literature. Nevertheless, ruler cult understood as specific institutions devoted to sacrificial or related activities for the worship of a ruler (Hellenistic rulers as well as Roman emperors) may form part of the background of some passages in the Bible and related literature (Dan 3 Gk, Rev and Martyria). Several terms which have been associated with the ruler cult appear in the NT (e.g. *euergetēs, sōtēr, kyrios, Asiarchēs*).

II. Although the Egyptians considered the pharaoh a divine being (→Horus), they only worshipped him as a god during limited periods. Ruler cult seems to be chiefly a Greek innovation, which is closely related to the religious ideas of the Greeks. Augustus took this over from them, but adapted the concept in line with the new situation in the Mediterranean world after the battle of Actium (FISHWICK 1987). The divine status of the figure who was worshipped by a community depended on his or her ability to confer special benefactions to it. So the cultic veneration by an individual, a city or a province of a ruler reciprocated his benefactions, which means that the ruler cult was part of a mutually advantageous relationship. This appears already from decrees concerning the establishment of a cult for the successors of Alexander the Great and remains valid for the imperial period. The dynastic cults, set up by the rulers themselves, legitimized their power as rulers. Both type of cults intensified the relationship between the ruler and the subjects of the state. The ruler cult was connected to politics and diplomacy, "the (imperial) cult was a major part of the web of power that formed the fabric of society ... The imperial cult, along with politics and diplomacy, constructed the reality of the Roman empire" (PRICE 1984:248).

A forerunner of the ruler cult was the cult of heroes (→Heros). A similar veneration as a lesser god could also be received by special human persons, who were the founders of a city or died on the battlefield or had accomplished another feat of importance. The hero cult, however, differs from the ruler cult because of its local character and the limited power of the hero, whose divine help could only be called in at a certain place and under certain circumstances. Founders or liberators of cities and other heroes were often only venerated after their death (see e.g. Plutarch, *Arat.* 53.3f. concerning Aratus of Sicyon), while rulers of states in the Hellenistic period and emperors were also worshipped during their lifetime. Only rarely were cults for emperors established after their death. The Spartan general Lysander (died 395 BCE) can be considered as an early example of a human person who was worshipped as a god during his life (according to Duris of Samos, *FGH* 76 F 71; FEARS 1988:1051-1052). Probably elements were incorporated into the ruler cult from divine as well as from hero cult (cf. PRICE 1984:32-36, 233, who argues that ruler cult was modelled on divine cult).

Shortly after Alexander the Great ruler cult became an important factor in the Hellenistic world. Alexander's successors established a posthumous cult for him. Out of the veneration of the deceased ruler, which was organized in Egypt from Ptolemy II onwards until the end of the reign of that dynasty, there arose cults for living rulers and their families. Besides, cities took the initiative in worshipping rulers. Antigonus and his son Demetrius Poliorcetes were venerated as *theoi sōtēres* at Athens and other Diadochi received the same honours from other cities (HABICHT 1956). The koinon of Asia decreed between 268 and 262 BCE a cult for Antiochus I with sacrifices to all the gods and goddesses, to Antiochus and his wife Stratonice and their son Antiochus II. An altar of the kings was part of the temenos (*OGIS* no. 222 lines 42-43; HABICHT 1956: 91-93). That the divine ruler was expected to bring benefactions to the cities can be seen from the direct connection in this inscription between the cult for the ruler and his protection of the rights of the cities (lines 14-18). In return for benefactions like the restoration of freedom Greek cities bestowed the same honours upon Roman individuals like governors and charismatic generals or venerated the Roman Demos or goddess →Roma in the second and first centuries BCE (FEARS 1988:1057).

In 42 BCE Caesar was declared Divus Julius which implied for Octavian a status as Divi filius. It is important to distinguish between the ruler cult from the perspective of the Roman state religion and that of the indigenous worshippers in the provinces. In the context of state religion the deification of the emperor after his death and his posthumous veneration were the standard. Only the *genius* or →Tyche and *numen* of the emperor were venerated during his lifetime. From the Flavian emperors onward it was usual to swear to the *genius* or *tychē* of the living emperor. The first provincial imperial cults were established for Octavian shortly after his triumph at Actium, in Asia at Pergamum (29 BCE) and in Bithynia at Nicomedia. From Dio Cassius 51.20.7 and Tacitus, *Ann.* 4.37, it appears that the initiative was taken by the provinces. The cult was dedicated to the ruler (Augustus) and to Roma. At the same time Octavian decreed that a cult for Roma and Divus Julius had to be set up in the provinces of Asia (Ephesus) and Bithynia (Nicaea). The cults requested by the provinces were for the indigenous worshippers and the ones for Rome and Divus Julius for the Romans present. The provincial cult at Pergamum still flourished in the time of Hadrian. Shortly after the incorporation of Galatia in the Roman Empire a temple for Roma and Augustus was built at Ancyra for the provincial cult of Galatia (probably around 25-20 BCE). In the Western part of the empire an emperor cult was established in 12 BCE, when the Gallic provinces dedicated an altar to Roma and Augustus at Lugdunum (FISHWICK 1987-1992; for early foundations of provincial imperial cults see DEININGER 1965:16-35).

None of Augustus's successors exceeded in principle the bounds set by him, although some emperors bore marks of divinity (Nero, Domitian, Trajan). After the successful prosecution of two Roman officials charged with maladministration, the cities of Asia decreed a temple for Tiberius, Livia and the Senate at Smyrna, which was ratified by the Senate in 26 CE. A third provincial cult of Asia at Miletus was dedicated to the emperor Gaius only and may have been instigated by Gaius himself. In an inscription concerning this cult the word *theos* is used in the name of Gaius (ROBERT 1949:206 line 2; →God II). In order to maintain good relations with Rome Miletus had to terminate the cult after Gaius's death. After Augustus the imperial cults tended to be directed to imperial authority in general rather than to the reverence for an individual emperor (PRICE 1984:57-59). The emperors became the only object of reverence and in this respect the cult for the Sebastoi at Ephesus (see below) was the trend setter. For the motives of the cities of Asia to establish these cults and the conditions that had to be fulfilled for a successful initiative see FRIESEN 1993:7-28.

Thirteen inscriptions from Ephesus with (originally) dedications from various cities in Asia are witness to another provincial cult of Asia for the Flavian imperial family and its temple at Ephesus. The inscriptions are connected with the inauguration of the temple in 89-90 CE. This temple in Ephesus is called common to Asia, and the city of Ephesus is described as *neōkoros*, i.e. caretaker, of the cult (cf. Acts 19:35). The cult was for the Emperors. Domitian was probably its central figure at first, but after his death his name was erased and changed into God Vespasian on all inscriptions but one. The motives for the dedications of the cities are usually their reverence (*eusebeia*) for the Sebastoi and their goodwill (*eunoia*) toward Ephesus (FRIESEN 1993: esp. 29-49). Connected with the provincial imperial cult at Ephesus were Olympic games, held at the complex of gymnasium, palaestra and baths of the Sebastoi (to a certain extent modelled on the gymnasium and palaestra buildings at Olympia), which was built during Domitian's rule. After the death of Domitian the games stopped, but they were reorganized from the emperorship of Hadrian onwards (FRIESEN 1993:117-141).

In the ruler cult the religious and the political world went hand in hand, which does not mean that the divinity of the ruler was not taken seriously. The emperor was worshipped as a god on public and private occasions (games, mysteries, processions, lamps, incense and libations, sacrifices with the consummation of the victim, hymns in honour of the emperor and banquets; FISHWICK 1991:475-590). Statues and other representations of the divine emperor were present everywhere in the Greek cities. PRICE (1984:146-156 and 210-233) dwells on the divine nature of the emperor and claims that he did not match the status of the traditional gods. He points among other things to the statues of emperors in the sanctuaries of other gods and to sacrificial practice. Sacrifices were often made to a deity on behalf of the emperor. This view is criticized by FRIESEN (1993:74-75, 119, 150-151 and 166; cf. also VERSNEL 1988:234-237): the temple of the Sebastoi at Ephesus towered above the other temples and the statues of emperors were depicted much larger than those of the gods; the emperor exercized godlike authority in the context of a specific hierarchical relationship and he deserved a divine status, because he accomplished the works of the gods in an unparalleled manner. One should not assume that there existed rivalry between the imperial cult and the worship of the other deities, the imperial cult united the other cultic systems and the peoples of the empire. The emperor's role was similar to that of →Zeus in the Olympian pantheon.

The imperial cult seems to have declined well before Constantine and disappeared in the fourth century. Cultic activities in the provinces and cities dropped to a minimum by the second half of the third century.

III. Several phrases in biblical and related literature can be connected to ruler cult, although there usually is not a close connection to a specific cult. References to the veneration of a ruler also have a general character.

Dan 3 LXX and Theod., Jdt, 2 Macc 6-7; 4 Macc contradict what we know about the general policy of religious tolerance of Hellenistic rulers towards the Jews, which raises the question of to what extent these texts reflect historical events. In all these texts Jews are forced to renounce their religion and participate in a pagan sacrificial ritual or the veneration of the ruler. According to Jdt 3:8 Nebuchadnezzar had decreed that all other gods be destroyed in order that he alone should be worshipped by every nation and invoked as a god (*epikalesōntai auton eis theon*) by men of every tribe and tongue. There is no evidence that Antiochus IV forced the Jews to venerate him personally as Zeus Olympios or another god. The surname Epiphanēs of Antiochus IV and other rulers from the Hellenistic period points to the appearance of a redeeming god (cf. 2 Macc 14:33) or the cultic acting of a divine ruler. The name occurs e.g. in 1 Macc 1:10; 10:1; 2 Macc 2:20; 4:7; 10:9, 13; 4 Macc 4:15 (cf. also Philo, *Leg.* 346: Caligula wanted to change the name of the Jerusalem temple into 'temple of Gaius, the new Zeus Epiphanes'). The fact that related expressions appear relatively frequently as attributes of the Lord in Jewish literature of the Maccabean period (e.g. 2 Macc 3:30; 15:34) may be understood as part of the refutation of a divine status for the Greek rulers. Also other phrases like *euergetēs*, *sōtēr* and *kyrios* may reflect the pagan use of these words (cf. Luke 22:25-26), which gradually took on a divine meaning and could be connected to ruler cult (see further DEISSMANN 1923:287-324; CUSS 1974:50-88), but also indicated the Lord respectively →Jesus →Christ as the sole benefactor, →saviour or Lord of the Jews or Christians (cf. Jude 4; →Kyrios). This usage implied at least a repudiation of the divinity of the ruler, which becomes explicit in some Early Christian martyr texts.

As in Jewish texts which hint at the veneration of a ruler, the possible references to the imperial cult in Rev 13 go hand in hand with a self-image which contrasts strongly with the picture of the world of the Roman ruler. Rev 13 contains several allusions to Dan 3, especially in connection with the worship of the first beast and its image. The second beast of Rev 13, also characterized as the false prophet (16:12; 19:20 and 20:10), is probably a symbol which can be connected with the high priesthood of the imperial cult (e.g. CUSS 1974: 20, 96-112). Maybe the blasphemous titles of the first beast hint also at the cults for the emperor. John presents the Roman government with the imagery of Rev 12-13

(→Dragon) and 17-18 in a completely unfavourable light. According to several scholars the imperial cult of Domitian at Ephesus was the immediate cause for the putting into writing of Revelation (STAUFFER 1955:147-191; PRICE 1984:197-198; SCHÜSSLER FIORENZA 1985:192-199; cf. PRIGENT 1974-1975). In any case the imperial cult was a source of conflict between Christian and Roman ideologies. The sacrifices, statues (cf. Rev 13:14-15; 14:9, 11; 16:2; 19:20; 20:4), prayers, games and other forms of worship connected with the imperial cult rendered the emperor divine honours and titles which belonged only to God and Jesus Christ (see e.g. 1 Cor 8:5-6). Even if Christians tried to be loyal to the Roman government as much as their belief allowed them to, when they were forced to acknowledge the emperor as Kyrios they had to refuse, because they could not bestow divine honours upon him. Martyr texts focus on this dilemma of loyalty (e.g. *Mart. Pol.* 8-11: Polycarp had to call the emperor Lord, to offer him incense, to swear to the *genius* of the emperor and to blaspheme Christ; in *Mart. Scil.* 3; 5; 14 the proconsul Saturninus offers the martyrs the opportunity to return to the way of life of the Romans [*ad Romanorum morem redeundi*] by swearing to the *genius* of the emperor). The ideological conflict comes to light in a most painful fashion in the execution of the martyrs, which often took place in the context of games linked with imperial festivals or organized by imperial priests (cf. FISHWICK 1991:577-579).

However, it was not especially the refusal to venerate the emperor that led to the persecutions of Christians, as appears from Pliny's famous letter to Trajan and the Rescript (*Ep.* 10.96-97) and Christian martyr texts. Until the reign of Decius the emperor did not take steps against the Christians on his own initiative, and only responded to questions from the provinces. Usually the refusal by arrested Christians to worship the gods in general (including the emperor) led to their execution (for a collection of the evidence see MILLAR 1973; cf. KERESZTES 1979; PRICE 1984:123-126, 220-222), although Pliny (*Ep.* 10.96) and some martyr texts refer to the obligation to venerate the emperor or to perform acts which belonged to the imperial cult (*Mart. Pol.* 8-9; *Mart. Pion.* 8; 18; Eusebius, *Hist. eccl.* 7.15.2; MILLAR 1973:150, 154-155; FISHWICK 1991: 527, 534, 577-579). Before the first state persecution by Decius (249-251 CE), however, persecutions of Christians were usually the result of successful pressure by city mobs (cf. Acts 17:6-7) and especially local actions, inspired by fear of unrest and triggered by epidemics, famine and other disasters (VERSNEL 1988:250-253).

The second beast of Revelation is often connected with the high priesthood of the emperor cult. According to DEININGER (1965:41-50) and many other scholars the offices of Asiarch (*Asiarchēs*) and provincial high priest were identical. FRIESEN (1993: 92-113), however, rejects a direct connection between the Asiarch and the imperial cults on good grounds and assumes that the Asiarchate was an office of the city implying various duties. This means that the Asiarchs who are together at the same time at Ephesus according to Acts 19:31 do not have to be understood as high priests or delegates of the provincial council which met at Ephesus. *Mart. Pol.* 21 mentions Philip of Tralles as the high priest at the date of Polycarp's Martyrdom. Several scholars consider chap. 21 a later interpolation, but a Gaius Julius Philippus is mentioned as Asiarch and also as the high priest of Asia in inscriptions (dates of attestation between 161-169 and 150-170 CE respectively; FRIESEN 1993:101; 179; 195), so that the Philip of the Martyrdom may very well be the Gaius Julius Philippus mentioned.

IV. *Bibliography*

D. CUSS, *Imperial Cult and Honorary Terms in the New Testament* (Paradosis 23; Fribourg 1974); J. DEININGER, *Die Provinziallandtage der römischen Kaiserzeit von Augustus bis zum Ende des dritten Jahrhunderts n. Chr.* (Vestigia 6; München 1965); A. DEISSMANN, *Licht vom Osten. Das Neue Testament und die neuentdeckten Texte der hellenistisch-römischen Welt* (Tübingen 1923); J. R. FEARS, Herrscherkult, *RAC* 14 (Stuttgart 1988) 1047-1093 [& lit]; D. FISHWICK, *The Imperial Cult in the Latin West. Studies in the Ruler Cult of the Western Provinces of the Roman Empire* I:1; I:2; II:1; II:2 (EPRO 108; Leiden 1987-1992); S. FRIESEN, *Twice Neokoros. Ephesus, Asia and the Cult of the Flavian Imperial Family* (Religions in the Graeco-Roman World 116; Leiden 1993); C. HABICHT, *Gottmenschentum und griechische Städte* (Zetemata 14; München 1956); D. L. JONES, Christianity and the Roman Imperial Cult, *ANRW* II 23,2 (Berlin/New York 1980) 1023-1054; P. KERESZTES, The Imperial Roman Government and the Christian Church, *ANRW* II 23,1 (Berlin/New York 1979) 247-315, 375-386; F. MILLAR, The Imperial Cult and the Persecutions, *Le culte des souverains dans l'Empire romain* (ed. W. den Boer; Entretiens Fondation Hardt 19; Vandoeuvres-Genève 1973) 143-165; S. R. F. PRICE, *Rituals and Power. The Roman Imperial Cult in Asia Minor* (Cambridge 1984); P. PRIGENT, Au temps de l'Apocalypse, *RHPR* 54 (1974) 455-483; 55 (1975) 215-235; 341-363; L. ROBERT, Le culte de Caligula à Milet et la province d'Asie, *Hellenica* 7 (1949) 206-238; S. SCHERRER, Signs and Wonders in the Imperial Cult, *JBL* 103 (1984) 594-610; E. SCHÜSSLER FIORENZA, *The Book of Revelation. Justice and Judgment* (Philadelphia 1985); E. STAUFFER, *Christ and the Caesars. Historical Sketches* (London 1955); H. S. VERSNEL, Geef de keizer wat des keizers is en Gode wat Gods is. Een essay over een utopisch conflict, *Lampas* 21 (1988) 233-256.

J. W. VAN HENTEN

S

SABBATH Σάββατον *Sabbatum*

I. A deity called Sabbath does not occur in the Bible. For the first time it seems to be found in Valentinian 'mythology'. It is quite probable that the creation of a deity with this name was based on the interpretation of a NT passage (Luke 6:5).

II. Tertullian (*Adv.Val.*20:1-2) describes the Valentinian view of creation: the Demiurge made this world and its hemisphere, then "completed the sevenfold stage of →heavens, with his →throne above it. That is why he is called *Sabbatum*, because of the hebdomad of his residence". In other descriptions (Irenaeus, Hippolytus) the deity himself is called *Hebdomas* or *Topos*, whereas his residence has the same names. In his commentary on Tertullian's treatise, J. C. FRÉDOUILLE, *Tertullianus, Quintus Septimius Florens: Contre les Valentiniens* [Paris 1980] *ad locum*) was puzzled by the name *Sabbatum*: 'ce nom du Démiurge n'apparaît ni dans nos sources patristiques..., ni, semble-t-il, dans les traités de Nag Hammadi'. This is not a correct observation. In the Gnostic 'Heavenly Dialogue' quoted by Celsus (Origen, *C.C.* VIII:15-16) the following passage is found: "If the Son is stronger than God, and (if) the →Son of Man is his Lord, and (if) some Other reigns over the mighty God, how does it come that many are around the well, and nobody in the well?" The text contrasts 'the Son', 'Son of Man', or 'some Other', that is, the Son of the true →God with another 'God', 'the mighty God', who is the Demiurge. Whereas the apodosis agrees with Logion 74 of the *Gospel of Thomas*, the hypothetical sentence is playing with motives from the Gospels. The phrase "(if) the Son of Man is his (*i.e.* God's) Lord" is hinting at Luke 6:5, "Lord of the Sabbath is the Son of Man". This implies that *sabbaton* is interpreted as a name of the Demiurge, which is in conformity with Tertullian's description. The Gnostic *Apocryphon of John* (*NHC* II.1, 11: 34-35; III:1, 18:7-8) describes the Created of the Demiurge Jaldabaoth, i.e. the sevenfold cosmic reality with the respective →Archons, in the following way: "This is the Hebdomas of the Sabbath". This phrase which is usually interpreted as 'This is the sevenness of the week', but in view of the Demiurge's name *Sabbatum*-Σάββατον one should interpret it as 'the seven stages of the Cosmos and their Archons created and ruled by Jaldabaoth'. *Sabbaton* is another name for the Demiurge Jaldabaoth. When in the same treatise the Demiurge is contrasted with the true God—denoted as 'Man' or 'Son of Man' (*NHC* II:1, 14:4-5; III:1, 21:17-18; cf. IV:1, 22:17-18)—who appears to be the supreme deity which reigns both over the visible and invisible realities, it is clear that here again the source of the name may be a Gnostic interpretation of Luke 6:5.

Logion 27 of the *Gospel of Thomas* presents us with this word of →Jesus: "If you do not fast with respect to the world, you will not find the Kingdom of God, if you do not sabbatize the Sabbath, you will not see the Father". Whatever the source and original meaning of this logion be, in the context of the *Gospel of Thomas* it must be interpreted in a gnostic way: the world, the created Cosmos, is contrasted with the realm of the true God; the true God, the →Father, is contrasted with the Sabbath. The latter may be taken to be the name of the Demiurge. The true Gnostic abstains from this world and its Creator, in order to find the true Kingdom and to see the true God, the Father. This Gnostic identification of *sabbaton* and the Demiurge found its point of departure in a specific interpretation of Luke 6:5. However, its origin may be a pagan identification of the Jewish God as Saturn (Heb *šbty*). 'The day of the Sabbath', the seventh day, was linked with the planet Saturn and called 'the day of Saturn' or 'the day of Kronos'. One might seriously consider the possibility that Juvenal's reference to people who had a father who revered the Sabbath (*metuentem sabbata*, 14:96), and consequently worshipped nothing but the clouds and the →God of heaven, implies that he thought of the worship of the God *Sabbata* (Aram *šbt'*).

III. *Bibliography*

T. BAARDA, 'If you do not sabbatize the Sabbath...', The Sabbath as God or World in Gnostic Understanding (Ev.Thom., Log. 27), *Knowledge of God in the Graeco-Roman World* (ed. R. van den Broek, T. Baarda & J. Mansfeld; EPRO 112; Leiden 1988) 178-201; R. GOLDENBERG, The Jewish Sabbath in the Roman World, *ANRW* II 19, 1 (Berlin 1979) 414-447; A. PELLETIER, Sabbata, Transcription grèque de l'Araméen, *VT* 22 (1972) 436-447; M. STERN, *Greek and Latin Authors on Jews and Judaism* II (Jerusalem 1980) esp. §§ 301, 406, 414.

T. BAARDA

SAINTS קדושים

I. 'Saints' or 'holy ones' translates the Hebrew *qĕdôšîm*: the masculine plural of the adjective *qādôš* 'holy'. *Qĕdôšîm* occurs thirteen times in the Bible. It is used variously of people, of divine beings, and of →Yahweh. The Aramaic cognate, *qaddîšîn*, is used in Daniel of people and of divine beings. The root does not appear in any Israelite personal name inside or outside the Bible.

QDŠ is a common Semitic root referring to the quality or property of holiness, sacredness, as opposed to what is profane. In adjectival form, it is sometimes found as an attribute of deities and occasionally as a title of a deity.

II. *Qĕdôšîm* refers to the gods as a collectivity that is widely attested throughout the ancient Near East under other names (→Sons of the gods, →council, etc.). As a title, however, 'the Holy Ones' is rarely used outside the Bible. A group of 'the holy gods' (*ilū qašdūtum*) is invoked in an Old Babylonian incantation (W. VON SODEN, review of H. H. Figulla, CT 42, *BiOr* 18 [1961] 71-73, esp 71:13). At Ugarit, the gods are referred to as *bn qdš* 'holy ones' or 'children of *Qdš*' (always parallel to *ilm* 'gods'; *KTU* 1.2 i:21, 38; 17 i:3, 8, 13, 22). *Qdš* 'the holy one' refers either to →Asherah or to →El in the epithet of King Kirta, *šph ltpn w qdš* 'Offspring of the Gracious One and the Holy One' (parallel to 'Kirta is son of El'). The word *qdš* also appears in *Qdš w Ammr* 'Holy and Powerful', the name of Asherah's personal assistant(s) in the story of the building of →Baal's palace (*KTU* 1.3 vi:10-11; 4.iv:1-17). This binomial recurs in a list of paired divine names in *KTU* 1.123:26. Outside the literary texts, Ugarit also knows a goddess, *Qdšt* (*KTU* 1.81:17; cf. the personal name *bn qdšt KTU* 4.69 v:11; 4.412 i:11; (*bin-*) *qadišti* (J. NOUGAYROL, Textes suméro-accadiens des archives et bibliothèques privées d'Ugarit, *Ug* 5 [1968] no. 7:14). The plural form *qdšm* is used only as the title of a class of temple officials.

However, *qdšm* is used attributively of the gods of tenth century Byblos: *'l Gbl qdšm* 'the holy gods of Byblos' (*KAI* 4 [=*TSSI* 6]:4-5, 7), and of the gods in general at fifth-century Sidon: *(h)'lnm hqdšm* 'the holy gods' (*KAI* 14 [=*TSSI* 28]:9, 22) in both cases alongside the named chief gods. The thirteenth of the sayings of Ahiqar (ll. 94-95) ends *bš[my]n šymh hy ky b'l qdšn nš'[h]* "She [Wisdom] has been placed in heaven, for the Lord of Holy Ones has elevated her" (i.e. to their company; cf. the parallelism of *[mn] šmyn* and *[mn] 'lhy* "[from] heaven ...[from] the gods" at the beginning of the saying).

III. The relative frequency of the term in the Bible (specifically in post-exilic literature) may be related to the even more frequent designation of Yahweh as 'the Holy One': especially in the epithet *Qĕdôš Yiśrā'ēl* 'Holy One of Israel'. It is not always easy to distinguish when 'holy ones' refers to divine beings and when it refers to Yahweh himself (as a 'plural of majesty') or to human 'saints'.

Qĕhal qĕdôšîm, 'the assembly of the Holy Ones', and *sôd qĕdôšîm,* 'the council of the Holy Ones', (→Council) are two of the several terms for the collectivity of divine beings which is contrasted with Yahweh's uniqueness in Ps 89:6-8 (5-7). A similar contrast appears in Exod 15:11, where, although MT reads the singular *qōdeš* 'holiness' (or 'sanctuary'), the LXX reads the plural: 'the holy ones' which parallels *ʾēlîm* 'gods' in v 11a. The moral inferiority of these 'saints' is stated sharply by Eliphaz in Job 15:15 (Kethib): God treats them (parallel: 'the heavens') as untrustworthy (cf. Sir 42:17, 21).

In Job 5:1, Eliphaz refers to the divine holy ones as the object of human appeals, hence, presumably, as intercessors with God. In Dan 4:14 (17), they appear in the ancient role of the divine council that issues decrees. The singular (parallel: *ʿîr* 'watcher') refers to a messenger from the divine court in Dan 4:10, 20 (13.23; →Watchers; →Saints of the Most High) and to two individual members of the court whom Daniel hears in conversation during his vision (Dan 8:13). However, the mythological background of the vision in Daniel 7 does not require that the 'holy ones' at war in vv 21.22 be construed as the →host of heaven. Rather, they are probably the faithful Jews: referred to as 'the people of the holy ones' in Dan 8:24. Yahweh's faithful are again clearly the referent in Num 16:3; Ps 34:10 (9).

'All the holy ones' accompany Yahweh when he comes to establish a new order in Zech 14:5. The text of Deut 33:2-3 is corrupt; but the same group may appear as 'myriads of holy ones' (cf. Syr) accompanying Yahweh in this theophany (v 2b). The identity of 'all the holy ones' of v 3a is still disputed. In Ps 16:3 'the holy ones who are in the land' is parallel to 'the →noble ones': both probably referring to gods rather than people; but the context is difficult.

In some passages, the divine court is so absorbed into and identified with Yahweh that the holy ones virtually become the Holy One, the grammatical form of the word remaining plural (cf. the use of the plural *ʾĕlōhîm* 'gods' for 'God'.) Thus Yahweh is *ʾĕlōhîm qĕdōšîm* 'a holy god' (Josh 24:19). Again, it may be difficult to determine whether the one deity or a plurality of heavenly beings is intended. In Prov 9:10 'knowledge of the Holy One/the holy ones' is parallel to 'the fear of Yahweh'. The same ambiguous expression appears parallel to 'the kingdom of God' in Wis 10:10. In Hos 12:1 (Eng 11:12), Judah is said to be faithful to *qĕdōšîm* (parallel to *ʾēl*). While the old divine name El suggests a reference to the 'holy ones' of the deity's court, both words may be titles of Yahweh: 'God the Holy One'. In the Sayings of Agur, wisdom is parallel to *daʿat qĕdōšîm* (Prov 30:3) 'knowledge of the holy ones/the Holy One'.

The word is used attributively of the gods (as in Phoenician) in Dan 4:5.6.15 (Eng 8. 9.18); 5:11 in the phrase 'spirit of the holy gods,' by which the Babylonian court here refers to a source of supernatural enlightenment.

According to Sir 45:2 LXX, God made →Moses equal in glory to the holy ones. The righteous are counted among the same body in Wis 5:5 (parallel: the children of God). In the NT, God's heavenly retinue may be envisaged in 1 Thess 3:13; 2 Thess 1:10; Col 1:12, though particularly in the last two cases good arguments have been made for a reference to human saints.

IV. *Bibliography*

C. H. W. Brekelmans, The Saints of the Most High and their Kingdom, OTS 14 (Leiden 1965) 305-329; L. Dequeker, Les qĕdôšîm du Ps. LXXIX à la lumière des croyances sémitiques, *ETL* 39 (1963) 469-484; P. Xella, QDŠ. Semantica del 'sacro' ad Ugarit, *Materiali Lessicali ed Epigrafici* 1 (1982) 9-17; C.-B. Costecalde, La racine *qdš* et ses dérivés en milieu ouest-sémitique et dans les cunéiformes, *DBSup* 10 (1985) 1346-1393, esp. 1380-1381.

S. B. Parker

SAINTS OF THE MOST HIGH קדישׁי עליונין

I. The 'Saints of the Most High' are introduced in chap. 7 of the Book of Daniel, in the →angel's explanation of →Daniel's dream. Daniel had seen four beasts come up out of the →sea, which were then condemned in a judgment scene, after which "one like a →son of man" approached the divine →throne and was given →dominion and →glory and kingdom. The angel explains that the four beasts were four kings who will arise on earth, but "the Saints of the Most High" will receive the kingdom (7:18). Later, in a more extended explanation, he adds that "the people of the Saints of the Most High" will receive the kingdom (7:27).

The traditional translation (Saints of the Most High) assumes that עליונין is used substantively, presumably to refer to God, who is called עליא in 7:25 and elsewhere in Daniel. The plural עליונין is then explained as a plural of majesty, on the analogy of Hebrew אלהים. The construct chain is definite because עליונין is considered a proper name. The Hebrew קדושי עליון (saints or holy ones of the Most High) in CD 20:8 may be cited as a parallel although it renders 'the Most High' by the singular. An alternative translation 'most high holy ones' or 'holy ones on high', has recently been defended by GOLDINGAY 1988, who explains the second term of the construct chain (עליונין) as epexegetical or adjectival. The plural of the second term, then, would correspond with the number of the first. The phrase would be indefinite and equivalent to קדישין עליונין. The Aramaic for highest, however, is עליא (plural). עליון is an epithet for the deity. The plural, then, should be taken as a plural of manifestations, and the traditional translation maintained.

II. Traditionally, the holy ones have been identified as human beings, the 'saints' by Christians, and the Jewish people by Jews. In recent times, however, the phrase has given rise to extensive debate. The stimulus to this discussion lies in the observation that 'holy ones' (קדושים) are usually heavenly beings in the Hebrew Bible and other West Semitic texts, and the realization that this understanding of the word is congenial to the world-view of Daniel.

While the adjective 'holy' is often applied to Israel and other human entities in the Hebrew Bible, the substantival use of the word is usually reserved for heavenly beings. There is only one clear exception in the Hebrew Bible, Ps 34:10, where "his holy ones", who are exhorted to fear the LORD, are evidently human. There are a few disputed cases, but the great majority of the references are clearly to celestial beings (e.g. Ps 89:6.8; Job 5:1; 15:15; Zech 14:5). This usage can be traced back to the divine *bn qdš* in the Ugaritic texts, who are "sons of the Holy One", probably →Asherah.

The Dead Sea Scrolls now provide numerous instances of the use of קדושים for heavenly beings. There are a number of disputed cases in the Scrolls and the issue is complicated by the idea that members of the Qumran community could mingle with the heavenly host in this life. So we read in 1QH 3:21-22: "and I know that there is hope for him whom you have created from the dust for the eternal assembly, and the perverse spirit you have cleansed from great transgression to be stationed with the host of the holy ones and to enter into fellowship with the congregation of the children of heaven". Again in 1QM 12:6: "the congregation of thy holy ones is among us for eternal alliance".

There is, then, a fluid boundary between the heavenly holy ones and the earthly community, at least in some of the Scrolls. Nonetheless, the predominant sense of קדושים in the Scrolls refers to heavenly beings.

The angelic sense also prevails in Pseudepigrapha originally composed in a Semitic language (see e.g. *1 Enoch* 1:9, where God comes with ten thousand holy ones, or 14:23, which speaks of Holy Ones in attendance on the divine throne). There is, however, a new development in the *Similitudes of Enoch*, which distinguish between the holy ones in heaven (*1 Enoch* 47:2, 4) and those on earth (48:4, 7 etc.). The idea here is that there is an affinity between the righteous and holy on earth and the angels in heaven, and this will be perfected at the resurrection, when "the chosen begin to live with the chosen". The use of "saints" for the early Christians (1 Cor 14:33; Phil 1:1, etc.) may have arisen in the same way, in anticipation of eschatological communion. In the writings of the Hellenistic Diaspora, composed in Greek, 'holy ones' is used both in the sense of angels (Wis 5:5; 10:10) and with reference to human beings (Wis 18:9 and 3 Macc 6:9).

The meaning of the phrase 'saints of the Most High' in Daniel 7 cannot be settled conclusively from the usage of 'holy ones' elsewhere. There was a precedent for using the term to refer to a human group in Psalm 34, and, since the adjective was commonly applied to people, it was not a great step to extend the substantival use. This step was certainly taken in the *Similitudes of Enoch* and in the New Testament. Nonetheless, the predominant usage of the Hebrew Bible and of Hebrew and Aramaic Jewish writings down to the second century BCE must influence the reader's expectations.

III. The reader's expectation is more immediately influenced by the usage in the Book of Daniel itself. The Aramaic קדישין is used of heavenly beings, parallel to →Watchers, in 4:14, and the singular is found in 4:10,20. In the Hebrew part of the book, Daniel hears one קדוש speaking to another in 8:13, and these are evidently members of the heavenly court. These are the only undisputed instances of holy ones in Daniel. The reference to עם קדש, the holy people, at 12:7, is relevant to the interpretation of the 'people of the saints' but it cannot determine the meaning of קדישין used substantivally.

In view of the clear use of 'holy ones' to refer to angels in the Book of Daniel itself, we must expect that it carries that reference in chap. 7 also. The 'people of the saints' in Dan 7:27 probably refers to the Jewish people (compare Dan 12:7 and the expression עם קדושי ברית, the people of the holy ones of the covenant, in 1QM 10:10), but this is compatible with the interpretation of holy ones as angels, if the genitive is understood as possessive (the people that belongs or pertains to the angels). Indeed the relation between the Jewish people and the angels is fundamental to the understanding of Daniel's vision.

The most basic objection to the angelic interpretation of the 'Saints' in Daniel 7 arises from the conviction of some modern scholars, expressed most straightforwardly by DiLella, that "Daniel 7 would then have virtually no meaning or relevance for the addressees of the book, viz. the disenfranchised Jews..." (Hartman-DiLella 1978:91). The inadequacy of this objection should be apparent from the parallel treatment of the Antiochan persecution in Daniel 10-12. There the author speaks unmistakably of angelic →'princes' who are engaged in warfare against the 'princes' of Persia and Greece. At the end of the conflict "→Michael will arise", the prince of Israel. His victory in the heavenly battle entails the victory of the persecuted Jews on earth. In the resurrection that follows, the wise will shine like the stars, which is an apocalyptic idiom for fellowship with the angels. There is, then, a synergism, or dynamic correspondence, between the faithful Israelites on earth and their angelic counterparts in heaven. When the Jews are in distress, the heavenly host is cast down (Dan 8:10). When Michael prevails, so do the Jews on earth. To the pious Jews of the Maccabean era who had a lively belief in supernatural beings, nothing could be more relevant than that their angelic patrons should "receive the kingdom".

One other correlation is crucial to the understanding of the 'Saints'. The 'Saints of the Most High' are said to receive the kingdom, which was given in the vision to the 'one like a son of man'. The interpretation of this figure too is disputed. Traditionally, he was identified as the Messiah (→Christ). In modern times, he has often been taken as a collective symbol for the Jewish people. In recent years, a strong case has been made that he should be identified as Michael, the 'prince' of Israel.

There is no doubt that both the "one like a son of man" and the "Saints of the Most High" represent the Jewish people in some way. It is unlikely, however, that they are 'mere' symbols. It is clear from Daniel 10-12 that the authors envisaged a world where the fate of human communities was dependent on the conflict between heavenly forces. The angelic interpretation of the "one like a son of man" and the "Saints of the Most High" does justice to the imaginative fullness of Daniel's symbolic world.

IV. The angelic interpretation of the holy ones also throws light on a peculiarity of some NT 'Son of Man' sayings. In Mark 8:38 the Son of Man is said to come "in the glory of his Father with the holy angels" (compare Matt 16:27; Luke 9:26). Also in Matt 25:31, "he comes in his glory, and all the angels with him". It would seem that the coming of the Son of Man in these passages is assimilated to traditional theophanies such as Deut 33:2 (OG) or *1 Enoch* 1:9: "he comes with ten thousand holy ones...". The assimilation is most easily explained if the holy ones in Daniel 7 were understood as angels, as in *1 Enoch*, and thought to accompany the "one like a human being".

The terminology of Daniel 7 is reflected some centuries later in *3 Enoch* 28:1,7, where the watchers and holy ones are said to be exalted מכל בני עליונים, above all the sons of the Most High, all of whom sit before the Holy One when he judges the world. They are also called שׂרי העליונים princes of the Most High. עליונים here seems roughly equivalent to אלהים and to refer to the Deity. The בני העליונים are clearly heavenly beings.

V. *Bibliography*

C. W. Brekelmans, The Saints of the Most High and their Kingdom, OTS 14 (Leiden 1965) 305-329; J. J. Collins, *Daniel* (Hermeneia; Minneapolis 1993) 313-317; L. Dequeker, The 'Saints of the Most High' in Qumran and Daniel, OTS 18 (Leiden 1973) 133-62; J. Goldingay, 'Holy Ones on High' in Daniel 7:18, *JBL* 107(1988) 497-99; L. F. Hartman & A. A. DiLella, *The Book of Daniel* (AB 23; Garden City 1978); M. Noth, The Holy Ones of the Most High, *The Laws in the Pentateuch and Other Essays* (Philadelphia 1967) 194-214.

J. J. Collins

SAKKUTH סכות

I. Sakkuth occurs under the form *Sikkût* in Amos 5:26, and is followed by *Kiyyûn*. The Masoretic vocalisation of both names is that for idols (→Abominations, →gillulim). The real pronounciation must have been *Sakkut*, if we may identify this name with the obscure Babylonian god Sakkud (or Sakkut). Already LXX and CD took the name to be a word with the basic meaning "hut" (*sukkat*): not "Sakkuth, your king", but "tent of the Moloch" (LXX; also Acts 7:43), or "tabernacle of your king" (CD VII 14). Some modern scholars are also of this opinion (Borger 1988:77-80; W. W. Hallo, *HUCA* 48 [1977] 15).

II. The parallelism between Sakkuth and →Kaiwan (*Kiyyûn*) suggests that Sakkuth is a divine name since Kaiwan goes back to Babylonian *Kajjamānu*, the planet Saturn, which was worshipped as a deity. The only god known to us having a similar sounding name is Babylonian Sakkut (*Sag-kud*). The alleged association of this god with Saturn in *Šurpu* II 180 ("Sakkut and Saturn") has been invalidated by Borger (1988:74-76): the originals do not offer SAG.UŠ ("Saturn") but UŠ (= Nita). Both Sakkut and Nita were identified with Ninurta. Sakkut was a "cupbearer" of the gods and was associated with the city Dēr, bordering on Elam. The name could be Elamite rather than Sumerian (thus Borger 1988:73); cf. the Elamite god *Šimut*. This fits the final *-t* in the Hebrew text. *Šurpu* II 180-181 now has the sequence AN.TI.BAL – Sakkut – Nita –Immerija (Wēr). The first (also named "Tibal") seems to be an astral god as it is elsewhere identified with "the position of Venus, the →star" (MSL 17 [1985] 86 Erimḫuš VI, 178; cf. W. G. Lambert, *Studies F. R. Kraus* [Leiden 1982] 215, to IV 3). Sakkut might have been a planet, or a star.

III. The problem of why the Israelites adopted an obscure god like Sakkut remains unsolved. The Israelites may have borrowed the worship of this planet from the Assyrians. In this case there are two options. (1) The Israelites took over the worship before the fall of Samaria. Then Amos 5:26 can be interpreted as a prophetic accusation for not having served →Yahweh (e.g. BARSTAD 1984). (2) Amos 5:26 refers to one of the deities mentioned in 2 Kgs 17:28-30 who were brought to the Samaritan area by Assyrian settlers. This view implies that the text is a later insertion by a (deuteronomistic) redactor who confused situations before and after the conquest of the capital (H. W. WOLFF, *Dodekapropheton 2. Joel und Amos* [BKAT XIV/2; Neukirchen-Vluyn 1969] 310-311).

IV. *Bibliography*

H. M. BARSTAD, *The Religious Polemics of Amos* (VTSup 34; Leiden 1984) 118-126; P.-R. BERGER, Imaginäre Astrologie in spätbabylonischer Propaganda, *Die Rolle der Astronomie in den Kulturen Mesopotamiens* (ed. H. D. Galter; Graz 1993) 275-289; esp. 277 n. 2.; *R. BORGER, Amos 5,26, Apostelgeschichte 7,43 und Šurpu II, 180, *ZAW* 100 (1988) 70-81; O. LORETZ, Die babylonischen Gottesnamen Sukkut und Kajjamānu in Amos 5, 26, *ZAW* 101 (1989) 286-289.

M. STOL

SAMSON → HERACLES

SAR → PRINCE

SARAH שׂרה//שׂרי

I. The name of the matriarch Sarah *śārâ* (Gen 12-15; 49:31; Isa 51:2), alternatively spelled *śāray* (Gen 11-17), is derived from a noun **śarr-* 'sovereign; prince', the name meaning 'princess' or the like (ZADOK 1988:148; pace *HALAT* 1262). The Book of Tobit relates about another Sarah, daughter of Raguel destined to become the wife of Tobias (Tob 2:8-9). Several proposals have been made to connect Sarah with a goddess.

II. Sarah has been interpreted as the goddess of Machpelah (→Cybele; MEYER 1906:270; GRESSMANN 1910:5). GUNKEL connected the names of the wives of →Abram and Nahor, Saraj and Milka, with Babylonian *Šarratu* and *Malkatu*, designations for the wife of the moon-god →Sîn and →Ishtar respectively (1910:163; WESTERMANN 1981:158). Connections with the moon-god would underscore a provenance of the Abraham-group from the Harran-area. According to MEYER (1906:268-269), Sarah should be related to an element in the name of the ancient Arabian and Nabataean deity Dushara: "He-of-Sharâ". This name being a construction parallel to →"He-of-the-Sinai", the element Sharâ in it refers to a locality or to a numen revered at that locality.

In the OT Sarah is presented as the wife of Abraham. She is the matriarch of Israel. The historicity of this character can neither be proven nor falsified. It is not impossible to suppose that Sarah originally was an ancestral goddess who was historized during the process of Judaean self-identification after the catastrophe of 587 BCE and from then onward was honoured as a mother of the people (LORETZ 1978).

In the NT Sarah is mentioned a few times. In Heb 11:11 she is honoured for her faith (for the interpretation of this verse see VAN DER HORST 1990).

III. *Bibliography*

H. GRESSMANN, Sage und Geschichte in den Patriarchenerzählungen, *ZAW* 30 (1910) 1-34; H. GUNKEL, *Genesis übersetzt und erklärt* (Göttingen 1910); P. W. VAN DER HORST, Sarah's Seminal Emission: Hebrew 11:11 in the Light of Ancient Embryology, *Greeks, Romans and Christians* (FS A. J. Malherbe; D. L. Balch, E. Ferguson, W. A. Meeks eds.; Minneapolis 1990) 287-302; O. LORETZ, Vom kanaanäischen Totenkult zur jüdischen Patriarchen- und Elternehrung, *Jahrbuch für Anthropologie und Religionsgeschichte* 3 (1978) 149-203; E. MEYER, *Die Israeliten und ihre Nachbarstamme* (Halle 1906); C. WESTERMANN, *Genesis. 2. Teilband: Genesis 12-26* (BKAT I/2; Neukirchen-Vluyn 1981); R. ZADOK, *The pre-hellenistic Israelite Anthroponomy and Prosopography* (OLA 28; Leuven 1988).

B. BECKING

SASAM סםס

I. Sasam is interpreted as a theophoric element in the personal name *sismāy* (1 Chr 2:40; *HALAT* 719; FOWLER 1988: 64). The deity is attested in Canaanite theophoric personal names and as a →demon in a Phoenician incantation.

II. Sasam appears in West semitic theophoric personal names (FAUTH 1970:229-233). West Semitic: *ša-aš-ma-a* (*ADD* 151: BE:1); Ugaritic: *ʿbdssm* (*UM* 73 Rev 6), *bn ssm* (*PRU* II 47:18); Phoenician: *ʿbdssm* (*KAI* 35:1; 40:3; 49:11.46.47; mainly from Cyprus); [*s*]*smy* // Σεσμαος (*KAI* 42:3; Cyprus) *ʿbdssm* // *A.pa.sa.so.mo.se* (= Αψασωμος; RES 1213; Cyprus); Aramaic: in the grafitto *lssm br pth* (MOOREY 1965: 33-41). An amulet from Syria is inscribed with the name of what is most probably a tutelary deity: *ssm* (*RES* 1505; FAUTH 1970: 229).

A demon Sasam is mentioned three times in a seventh century BCE Phoenician incantation on an amulet from Arslan Tash (CROSS & SALEY 1970: DE MOOR 1981-82: 108-110; pace *KAI* II No. 27; the arguments of J. TEIXIDOR & P. AMIET, *AulOr* 1 [1983] 105-109, against the authenticity of the amulet are not convincing). (1) In the opening lines, it is stated that the incantation is directed against 'the Flying One, the goddess; (against) Sasam the son of Padar (*ssm bn pdr*)'; and against 'She-who-strangles-the-sheep'' (*KAI* 27:1-5). Traditionally, the name of the demon is rendered 'Sasam, the son of Padrashasha (*bn pdršš*ʾ)' (e.g. FAUTH 1970). CAQUOT has shown that the first /š/ in *pdršš* is no more than a stroke and that the last two signs of the divine name should be construed as *ś*ʾ, an imperative of the verb NŚʾ, 'to raise (one's voice)' being the beginning of a new sentence: "Pronounce the conjuration ..." (1973:47). This implies that Sasam should be seen as the son of *pdr*. This deity probably can be related to Pidrayu, one of the three daughters of →Baal known from the Ugaritic texts (see e.g. FAUTH 1970:242-249; S. RIBICHINI & P. XELLA, *UF* 16 [1984] 271-272; this deity can be equated with Ḫebat). (2-3) The legend relating to the axe-wielding deity on the amulet should be read: *ssm ʾl ypth ly / wʾl yrd lmzzt / yṣʾ šmš lssm / tlp wlrd ʿp* 'Sasam, let (the door) not be opened for him. Let him not come down to the doorposts. The sun rises, O Sasam: disappear and fly away to descend!' (*KAI* 27:22-27). On the basis of this inscription, it becomes clear that Sasam is a threatening night-demon. The picture of the axe-wielding deity suggests that he was represented as more or less anthropomorphic. The background of Sasam is probably not Semitic (FAUTH 1970). It has been suggested that Sasam might have had a Hurrian origin (*KAI* II, 44; MOOREY 1965:40). In view of the evidence available this can neither be proved (GRÖNDAHL 1965:187; BENZ 1972: 368) nor disproved (FAUTH 1970), although the interpretation that Sasam was a son of Pidrayu who can be equated with Hurrian Ḫebat might support an Anatolian background.

Although a distinction between a deity and a demon is not always clear, it is remarkable that Sasam appears both as a deity—i.e. as a theophoric element—and as a demon. Most probably the numen was revered differently in different locations.

III. The personal name *Sismāy* is a hapax legomenon in the Old Testament (1 Chr 2: 40). It appears but once in a genealogical list of people of Israelite lineage. The worship of a Phoenician deity in Judah during the Persian period cannot be proved from the personal name *Sismāy* alone. Most probably the name was not understood as containing the name of a non-Israelite deity in the Persian period.

IV. *Bibliography*

F. L. BENZ, *Personal Names in the Phoenician and Punic Inscriptions* (StP 8; Roma 1972); *C. BUTTERWECK, Eine phönizische Beschwörung, *TUAT* II/3, 435-437; A. CAQUOT, Observations sur la première tablette magique d'Arslan Tash, *JANES* 5 (1974) 45-51; F. M. CROSS & R. J. SALEY, Phoenician Incantations on a Plaque of the Seventh Century B.C. from Arslan Tash in Upper Syria, *BASOR* 197 (1970) 42-49; *W.

FAUTH, SSM BN PDRŠŠ', *ZDMG* 120 (1970) 229-256; J. D. FOWLER, *Theophoric Personal Names in Ancient Hebrew* (JSOTSup 49; Sheffield 1988); F. GRÖNDAHL, *Die Personennamen der Texte aus Ugarit* (StP 1; Roma 1965); J. C. DE MOOR, Demons in Canaan, *JEOL* 27 (1981-82) 106-119; P. R. S. MOOREY, A Bronze 'Pazuzu' Statuette from Egypt, *Iraq* 27 (1965) 33-34.

B. BECKING

SATAN שׂטן Σατάν, Σατανᾶς

I. The proper name 'Satan' is an Anglicization of the Hebrew common noun *śāṭān*. The noun *śāṭān* has been related etymologically to a variety of geminate, third weak and hollow verbs in Hebrew and in the cognate languages. These proposals include verbs meaning 'to stray' (Ar ŠṬṬ, Heb ŚṬH, Eth ŠṬY, Akk *šâṭu* 1 and Syr SṬ'), 'to revolt/fall away' (Aram SWṬ, Mandaean SWṬ and Heb SWṬ), 'to be unjust' (Ar ŠṬṬ), 'to burn' (Syr SWṬ and Ar ŠYṬ) and 'to seduce' (Eth ŠṬY and Heb ŚṬH). These proposals require discounting the *nûn* of the noun *śāṭān* as part of the root, and attributing it to an *-*ān* suffix which has been appended to a nominal base. There are two reasons why it is unlikely that the *nûn* should be attributed to an *-*ān* suffix. Firstly, the *-*ān* suffix when appended to a nominal base normally results in an abstract noun, an adjective or a diminutive. The noun *śāṭān* fits none of these categories. Secondly, in Hebrew *-*ān* is typically realized as *-ôn*. There are exceptions, but among the standard conditions proposed to explain the atypical retention of *-*ān*, none apply to the noun *śāṭān*. Therefore it is preferable to regard the *nûn* as part of the root and analyze *śāṭān* as a noun of the common *qāṭāl* pattern. The fact that the geminate, third weak and hollow verbs listed above have meanings that are arguably appropriate to Satan should be viewed as resulting from interaction between popular etymological speculation and developing traditions about Satan.

The root *ŚṬN is not evidenced in any of the cognate languages in texts that are prior to or contemporary with its occurrences in the Hebrew Bible. KB (918) incorrectly cites an alleged Akk *šatānu*, but the forms to which KB refers are *Št* lexical participles of *etēmu/etēnu* (*AHW*, 260). Thus the meaning of the noun *śāṭān* must be determined solely on the basis of its occurrences in the Hebrew Bible, where it occurs in nine contexts. In five it refers to human beings and in four it refers to celestial beings. When it is used of human beings it is not a proper name, but rather a common noun meaning 'adversary' in either a political or military sense, or 'accuser' when it is used in a legal context. In the celestial realm there is only one context in which *śāṭān* might be a proper name. In the other three contexts it is a common noun, meaning 'adversary' or 'accuser'. [P.L.D.]

Σατάν and Σατανᾶς are transliterations of the Heb *śāṭān* (cf. 3 Kgdms 11:14.23; Sir 21:27) or Aram *sāṭānā'* and mean 'adversary'. In such instances 8ḤevXIIgr and the LXX translate the Hebrew expression with *Diabolos* →Devil, meaning 'the Slanderer'. *Ho Satanās* (rarely used without article) thus designates the opponent of →God. In the NT *Satanās* and *Diabolos* can refer to the same supernatural being (cf. Rev 20:2) and can thus be interchanged (cf. Mark 1:13 and Luke 4:2). This highest evil being can also be referred to as *ho ponēros* ('the evil one', cf. Matt 13:19) and *ho peirazōn* ('the tempter' – cf. Matt 4:3; 1 Thess 3:5). [C.B.]

II. Although the noun *śāṭān* has no cognates in texts that are prior to or contemporary with the biblical texts in which it occurs, there are in Akkadian three legal terms meaning 'accuser' that can have both terrestrial and celestial referents. These terms are *bēl dabābi*, *bēl dīni* and *ākil karṣi*. Each can refer either to a human legal opponent or to a deity acting as an accuser in a legal context, and thus each term functionally parallels the noun *śāṭān* even though there is no etymological relationship. For example, the deities Nanay and Mār-Bīti are charged to guarantee an agreement sworn in their names. Should anyone attempt to alter the agreement, these deities were to assume the role of legal adversaries (EN.MEŠ *di-ni-šu* [VAS 1 36 iii.4]). Standing behind this notion of deities playing legal roles with respect to earthly happenings is the well-known idea of the divine →council, acting as a judiciary body.

III. The noun *śāṭān* is used of a divine being in four contexts in the Hebrew Bible. In Numbers 22:22-35 Balaam, a non-Israelite seer, sets out on a journey, an act that incurs God's wrath. God responds by dispatching his celestial messenger, the *mal'āk yhwh*, described as a *śāṭān*, who stations himself on the road upon which Balaam is travelling. Balaam is ignorant of the sword-wielding messenger but his donkey sees the danger and twice avoids the messenger, for which Balaam beats the animal. The messenger then moves to a place in the road where circumvention is impossible. The donkey lays down, and is again beaten. At this point Yahweh gives the donkey the ability to speak, and she asks why Balaam has beaten her. A conversation ensues and then Yahweh uncovers Balaam's eyes so that he can see the sword-wielding messenger, and Balaam falls down to the ground. The messenger asks why Balaam struck his donkey and then asserts that he has come forth as a *śāṭān* because Balaam undertook his journey hastily. The messenger states that, had the donkey not seen him and avoided him, he would have killed Balaam. Balaam then admits his guilt, saying that he did not know that the messenger was standing on the road, and offers to turn back if the messenger judges the journey to be wrong. The messenger gives Balaam permission to continue, but adjures him to speak only as instructed.

Prior to the work of GROSS (1974) most scholars attributed the above passage to the J source, which would have made it the earliest context in which the noun *śāṭān* is applied to a celestial being. However, since Gross' study the tendency has been to date the passage to the sixth century BCE or later. With the exception of the above story, which obviously ridicules Balaam, he is characterized in an extremely positive way in Num 22-24. Outside those chapters, the first clear indications that he is being viewed negatively are attributable to P (Num 31:16) and Dtr^2 (Josh 13:22), both of which are typically dated to the sixth century. Thus the available evidence suggests that Balaam was viewed positively in earlier, epic tradition, but negatively in later sources. Given that the story under discussion views Balaam negatively, the story most likely stems from a later source.

As can be readily seen, the heavenly being who acts as a *śāṭān* in Numbers 22 has very little in common with later conceptualizations of Satan. He is Yahweh's messenger, not his archenemy, and he acts in accordance with Yahweh's will rather than opposing it. Indeed, Yahweh's messenger here, as elsewhere in the Hebrew Bible, is basically an hypostatization of the deity. Hence, as KLUGER (1967:75) has remarked, the 'real' *śāṭān*/adversary in Numbers 22 is none other than Yahweh himself.

The opening chapter of the book of Job describes a gathering of the →'sons of God', i.e. a meeting of the divine →council. Present at this gathering is a being called *haśśāṭān*: this is the common noun *śāṭān* preceded by the definite article. The definite article makes it virtually certain that *śāṭān* is not a proper name (contra B. WALTKE & M. O'CONNOR, *An Introduction to Biblical Hebrew Syntax* [Winona Lake 1990] 249). Most scholars translate *haśśāṭān* as 'the Accuser', which they understand to be a title that describes a specific role or office. However, it should be noted that no analogous office has been convincingly identified in the legal system of ancient Israel, nor do the divine councils of the surrounding cultures include a deity whose specific assignment is to be an accuser. Some scholars have argued that professional informers/accusers existed in the early Persian period, and that the *śāṭān* in Job 1 and 2 is modelled on these informers. The evidence for this is inconclusive. Given the uncertainty of the existence of adducible legal parallels, another possibility would be to understand the force of the definite article differently. For example, in Gen 14:13 a certain person who has escaped from a battle is referred to as *happālîṭ*. The precise identity of the character is not important to the story. What is important for the narrative is the character's current and temporary status of escapee. The force of the definite article is to deemphasize precise identity and focus on the status of the character as it is relevant to the narrative plot (cf. Ezek 24:26; 33:21 and P. Joüon, *Grammaire de l'Hébreu biblique* [Rome 1923] 137n). Attributing this force to the definite article of *haśśāṭān* in Job 1:6 would lead us to understand that a certain divine being whose precise identity is unimportant and who has the current and temporary status of accuser is being introduced into the narrative. The advantage of this interpretation is that it is consistent with known Israelite (and Mesopotamian) legal practice in that 'accuser' was a legal status that various people temporarily acquired in the appropriate circumstances, and not a post or office.

When Yahweh asks the *śāṭān* whether he has given any thought to the exemplary and indeed perfect piety of Job, the *śāṭān* links Job's piety with the prosperity he enjoys as a result. If the pious inevitably prosper, how do we know that their piety is not motivated by sheer greed? Given that God is responsible for the creation and maintainance of a world order in which the righteous reap reward, what the *śāṭān* is in fact challenging is God's blueprint for divine-human relations. In other words, the *śāṭān* is questioning the validity of a moral order in which the pious unfailingly prosper. The test of true righteousness would be worship without the promise of reward. Yahweh accepts the *śāṭān's* challenge: he permits the *śāṭān* to sever the link between righteousness and reward. Although Job is blameless, he is made to suffer, losing first his wealth and his children, and eventually his own good health. In the end, a suffering and impoverished Job nevertheless bends his knee to a god whose world order is devoid of retributive justice, thus proving the *śāṭān* wrong.

In Job, the *śāṭān* seems clearly to be a divine being, although most scholars would agree that *śāṭān* is not a proper name. Though he challenges God at a very profound level, he is nonetheless subject to God's power and, like Yahweh's messenger in Num 22, acts on Yahweh's instructions. He is certainly not an independent, inimical force.

The book of Job does not contain references to historical events, and hence dating it is problematic. Most modern scholars read it as a response to theological problems raised by the Babylonian exile and consequently date it to the latter half of the sixth century BCE.

In a vision of the prophet Zechariah (Zech 3), the high priest Joshua is portrayed as standing in the divine council, which is functioning as a tribunal. He stands in front of Yahweh's messenger, with *haśśāṭān* on his right-hand side to accuse him. The messenger rebukes the *śāṭān*, and orders that Joshua's filthy garments be removed and replaced with clean clothing. In the name of Yahweh the messenger promises Joshua continuing access to the divine council in return for obedience.

As in Job 1 and 2, the noun *śāṭān* appears with the definite article, and hence is not a proper name. The presence of the definite article also raises the same question as to whether it denotes an office of Accuser in the divine council. See the above section on Job 1 and 2 for a discussion of this problem. In order to understand Zechariah's vision and the *śāṭān's* role in it, it is necessary to address the historical context of the vision. While the vision cannot be dated exactly, the general context of Zechariah's prophecy was the Jerusalem community after the return from exile around the time of the rebuilding of the temple (ca. 520 BCE). Those scholars who see this community as basically unified view Joshua as a symbol of the community and interpret his change of clothes as symbolizing a change in the community's status from impure to pure, or sinful to forgiven, in the eyes of Yahweh. In this interpretation, the *śāṭān* is understood as objecting to the change in the community's status: Yahweh wishes to pardon his people, and the *śāṭān* is opposed. However, this interpretation overlooks evidence that the restoration community was deeply divided over cultic issues, including the issue of the priesthood (HANSON 1979:32-279). When this fact is taken into account it becomes unlikely that Joshua should be understood as a cypher for the whole community. Rather, the vision reflects a rift in the community over the issue of whether Joshua should become the high priest. Zechariah's vision supports Joshua, and implicitly claims that the matter has been decided in Joshua's favour in the divine council itself, with Yahweh taking Joshua's side. In this interpretation, the *śāṭān* can be described as a projection into the celestial realm of the objections raised by the losing side. If this interpretation is the correct one, then the noun *sāṭān* is here associated with a division that is internal to the community in question. This interpretation would add support to PAGELS' (1991) theory that the notion of Satan developed among Jews who wished to denounce other Jews whose opinions they did not share.

As in Num 22 and Job 1 and 2, *śāṭān* in Zech 3 is not a proper name. In Zech 3 the *śāṭān* is clearly not Yahweh's messenger; indeed, the *śāṭān* and Yahweh's messenger are on opposing sides of the issue of whether Joshua should become the high priest. Hence Num 22 and Zech 3 use the noun *śāṭān* to describe different divine beings. It is unclear whether the *śāṭān* of Job 1 and 2 is the same celestial being as the *śāṭān* of Zech 3. If *haśśāṭān* should be translated 'the Accuser' with the understanding that there is a post or office of Accuser in the divine council, then it is most likely that the same divine being is envisaged in both contexts. However, if the definite article carries the connotations outlined above, then it is quite possible that Job 1 and 2 and Zech 3 do not have the same divine being in view.

In 1 Chr 21:1 the noun *śāṭān* appears without the definite article. The majority of scholars therefore understand *śāṭān* to be the proper name Satan, though some maintain that the noun refers to a human adversary and others argue that it refers to an unnamed celestial adversary or accuser.

1 Chr 21:1-22:1 is paralleled in the Deuteronomistic History by 2 Sam 24. Both passages tell the story of a census taken during the reign of David, an ensuing plague, and an altar built on the threshing floor of Araunah/Ornan (→Varuna). In 2 Sam 24 the story begins, "and the anger of Yahweh again burned against Israel, and he provoked David against them, saying 'Go number Israel and Judah'". The corresponding verse in Chr reads, "And a *śāṭān*/Satan stood up against Israel and he provoked David to number Israel." In both versions the act of taking a census is adjudged sinful. Given that the Chronicler used the Deuteronomistic History as a source text, it is clear that the Chronicler has altered his source in such a way as to take the burden of responsibility for the sinful census away from Yahweh. Some scholars interpret this to mean that the Chronicler was striving to distance Yahweh from any causal relationship to sin, or to rid Yahweh of malevolent behaviour in general. However, this explanation cannot account for passages such as 2 Chr 10:15 and 18:18-22, where Yahweh is clearly portrayed as sanctioning lies and instigating behaviour that was designed to cause harm. Another explanation notes that, in comparison to the Deuteronomistic History, the Chronicler presents an idealized portrait of David's reign. In general, the Chronicler deletes accounts that cast David in a dubious light. Contrary to this general tendency, the Chronicler was obliged to retain the story of the census plague because it culminated in the erection of what the Chronicler understood to be the altar of the Solomonic Temple, and David's relationship to the Jerusalem Temple is another theme of crucial concern to the Chronicler. Given that the incident could not, therefore, be deleted, the Chronicler modified his source text so that the incident no longer compromised Yahweh's relationship with David, the ideal

king. The Chronicler also shifts blame for the sinfulness of the census from David to Joab by stating that the census was not sinful *per se*, but was sinful because Joab did not take a complete census (1 Chr 21:6-7; 27:24).

It is important to establish why the Chronicler changed his source text because his motivation has implications for how we understand *śāṭān* in this passage. If the Chronicler was trying to generally distance Yahweh from malevolent behaviour and accomplished this by attributing such behaviour to another divine being, then we can see in this passage the beginnings of a moral dichotomy in the celestial sphere. If Yahweh is no longer thought to be responsible for malevolent behaviour toward humankind, and another divine being capable of acting efficaciously, independent of Yahweh, is, then it would be quite appropriate to translate *śāṭān* with the proper name Satan. However, if the introduction of *śāṭān* into the census story has the more circumscribed objective of portraying the relationship between Yahweh and David favourably, and not of ridding Yahweh of malevolent intent more generally, then even if *śāṭān* in this passage is a proper name, the term is still a long way from connoting Satan, God's evil archenemy.

Although there is no consensus position regarding the dating of Chronicles, the most persuasive arguments favour dating the first edition of the Chronicler's history to ca. 520 BCE. If this is correct, then there are two additional reasons against translating *śāṭān* as a proper name. Firstly, Zechariah, a contemporary, does not use *śāṭān* as a proper name. Secondly, the earliest texts that indisputably contain the proper name Satan date to the second century BCE (*Ass. Mos.* 10:1; *Jub* 23:29; possibly Sir 21:27), which would mean that more than 300 years separate the Chroniclers text from the first certain references to Satan.

In summary, the four Hebrew Bible texts that mention a celestial *śāṭān* are most probably dateable to the sixth century BCE or later, and it is clear that the *śāṭān* envisaged in Zech 3 is not the same divine being who acts as a *śāṭān* in Num 22. Moreover, in none of the four texts is *śāṭān* indisputably used as a proper name. Given these data, it is difficult to maintain, as many scholars have, that we can see in the Hebrew Bible a developing notion of Satan. First of all, if Satan is not mentioned in the Hebrew Bible, then the statement that the Hebrew Bible evidences a developing notion of Satan is obviously anachronistic. Secondly, the statement is difficult to maintain because at least two of the texts clearly refer to different divine beings. And thirdly, if the texts are relatively closely clustered in terms of date, then there is less likelihood that they would evidence conceptual development.

IV. In Hebrew texts from the Second Temple Period the use of *ṣāṭān* is limited. The sinner seeks forgiveness from →Yahweh, who is asked to prevent the rule of Satan or an unclean spirit (cf. 11 QPs[a] *Plea* 19:15). Satan's power threatens human beings. Accordingly the time of salvation is marked by the absence of Satan and evil (4 QDibHam[a] 1-2,IV,12; cf. *Jub.* 23:29; 40:9; 46:2; 50:5). Satan is standing among the winds (3 *Enoch* 23:16). The council of the Qumran community had a curse in which they imprecated that satan with his hostile design and with his wicked spirits be damned (cf. 4 QBer[a,b]). In the LXX 'Satan' as a divine name possibly occurs in Sir 21:27: "When the ungodly curses Satan, he curses his own life."

Being a transliteration from the Hebrew or Aramaic and almost lacking in the LXX, the Greek form of the name "Satan" is rarely used in Jewish literature of the Second Temple Period (cf. *T. 12 Patr., T. Job* and *Life of Adam and Eve* 17:1). *Ho Diabolos* (Devil), preferred by *Life of Adam and Eve*, Philo and Josephus, is more common. "Satan" and →"Belial" are used to refer to the same superterrestrial being (cf. the Dead Sea Scrolls; *Mart. Isa.* 2:1.4.7 [= Gk 3:2; 3:11]) and "Satan" and "Devil" are synonymous in their reference (cf. *T. Job.* 3:3.6 and 16:2 + 27:1 with 17:1 + 26:6). The incidental use of *Satanās* in some Greek texts, such as the NT, is a clear Semitism.

According to the various NT authors Satan (in Q the Devil) rules over a Kingdom of darkness. Satan is thus depicted as major opponent of →Jesus and tries to deceive him (Mark 1:13). As the opposing force to God, the Synoptic Tradition identifies Satan with Beelzebul, the principal of the devils (Luke 11:15-19 // Matt 12:24-27 // Mark 3:22-23.26). Jesus defeats his power by exorcizing →demons and curing the ill and thus inaugurates the reign of God which ends Satans' rule (Matt 12:28 // Luke 11:20). For Luke, Jesus' ministry is the time of salvation and thus puts a temporary end to the reign of Satan (10:18). The conversion of the gentiles leads them from darkness to light, from the power of Satan to God (Acts 26:18). Apostates are handed back to Satan (1 Cor 5:5; 1 Tim 1:20 cf. 5:15). As principal of the God-opposing forces, Satan poses a threat to the Christian communities (e.g. Rom 16:20; 2 Cor 2:11). He can still influence the daily life and thwart human plans (1 Thess 2:18). Through demons he causes illness (e.g. Luke 13:16; 2 Cor 12:7); he deceives humans (1 Cor 7:5; Rev 20:3) and is even disguised as an angel of light (2 Cor 11:14). Grave errors of members of the community are ascribed to the influence of Satan. Peter is rebuked as "Satan" intending "the things of man" and thus opposing God (Mark 8:33; Luke 22:31). Judas' betrayal of Jesus (Luke 22:3; John 13:27) and Ananias' fraud (Acts 5:3) for instance, are understood to be caused by Satan. Opposing religiosity, such as the Jewish refusal to accept →Christ (cf. Rev 2:9; 3:9), heresy (cf. Rev 2:24) or cults which endanger the Christian communities in Asia (cf. Rev 2:13) are seen as threats coming from Satan. In Jewish apocalyptic tradition, the eschatological fall of Satan is expected (Rom 16:20; Rev 20:7-10).

In the *post-NT tradition* the →Antichrist is very closely associated with the Devil and Satan. False teaching originates with them (Pol. *Phil.* 7:1). The "angels of Satan" control the dark way of false teaching and authority, opposing the angels of God, who are guiding to the way of light (*Barn.* 18:1. On the Apostolic Fathers, Apologists and Gnostics, see RUSSEL 1981).

V. *Bibliography*

O. BÖCHER, *EWNT* 3 (1983) 558-559; BÖCHER, *Das NT und die dämonischen Mächte* (Stuttgart 1972); H. BOECKER, *Law and the Administration of Justice in the Old Testament and Ancient Near East* (Minneapolis 1980); A. BROCK-UNTE, "Der Feind": Die alttestamentliche Satansgestalt im Licht der sozialen Verhältnisse des nahen Orients, *Klio* 28 (1935) 219-227; F. M. CROSS, A Reconstruction of the Judean Restoration, *JBL* 94 (1975) 3-18 [& lit]; P. L. DAY, *An Adversary in Heaven: śāṭān in the Hebrew Bible* (Atlanta 1988) [& lit]; H. DUHM, *Die bösen Geister im Alten Testament* (Tübingen 1904); W. FOERSTER, *TWNT* 7 (1964) 151-164; N. FORSYTH, *The Old Enemy: Satan and the Combat Myth* (Princeton 1987); W. GROSS, *Bileam: Literar- und formkritische Untersuchung der Prosa in Num 22-24* (München 1974); V. P. HAMILTON, Satan, *ABD* 5 (1992) 985-998; P. HANSON, *The Dawn of Apocalyptic* (Philadelphia 1979); H. KAUPEL, *Die Dämonen im Alten Testament* (Augsberg 1930); R. S. KLUGER, *Satan in the Old Testament* (Evanston 1967; original German version: Zürich 1948); A. LODS, Les origines de la figure de satan, ses fonctions à la cour céleste, *Mélanges syriens offerts à Monsieur René Dussaud* vol. 2 (Paris 1939) 649-660; K. MARTI, Zwei Studien zu Sacharja: I. Der Ursprung des Satans, *TSK* 65 (1892) 207-245; E. T. MULLEN, *The Assembly of the Gods: The Divine Council in Canaanite and Early Hebrew Literature*, (HSM 24; Chico 1980); J. D. NEWSOME, Towards a New Understanding of the Chronicler and his Purpose, *JBL* 94 (1975) 201-217; L. OPPENHEIM, The Eyes of the Lord, *JAOS* 88 (1968) 173-180; E. PAGELS, The Social History of Satan, The 'Intimate Enemy': A Preliminary Sketch, *HTR* 84 (1991) 105-128; P. RICOEUR, *The Symbolism of Evil* (Boston 1967); G. ROSKOFF, *Geschichte des Teufels* (Leipzig 1869); J. S. RUSSEL, *The Devil. Perceptions from Antiquity to Primitive Christianity* (Ithaca 1977); RUSSEL, *Satan. The Early Christian Tradition* (Ithaca 1981).

C. BREYTENBACH (I, IV)
& P. L. DAY (I-III)

SATURN → KAIWAN

SATYRS שׂעירים

I. The word *śĕʿîrîm*, the plural of *śāʿîr* 'hairy' (Gen 27:11 and often), i.e. '(hairy) he-goat' (over 50 examples, in addition to its synonyms *ʿattûd* 'he-goat', *ṣāpîr* and *tayiš*), describes a group of creatures which are usually identified as 'hairy demons, satyrs' (Lev 17:7; Isa 13:21; 34:14; 2 Chr 11:15; *HALAT* 1250; for older translations see SNAITH 1975). The conjectured reading *śĕʿîrîm* for MT *šĕʿārîm* 'gates' in 2 Kgs 23:8 is old (*BHS*), but is to be rejected on the basis of current knowledge (SCHROER 1987: 133 with n. 292). On *śĕʿîrîm* in Deut 32:2 ('May my discourse come down as the rain, My speech distil as the dew, Like showers [*śeʿîrîm*] on young growth, Like droplets on the grass.') see *HALAT* 1250-1251, s.v. *śāʿîr* IV and M. DIETRICH & O. LORETZ, *UF* 21 (1989) 113-121, esp. 116-117.

II. KEEL's opinion that we do not know enough about →demons in the Syro-Palestinian region (1984) is to be reevaluated on the basis of more recent examinations. Nonetheless we do not possess clear iconographic witnesses to flesh out our conceptions of demonic 'desert beings', as the *śĕʿîrîm* must have been. The engraved scene on a Late Bronze Age ivory plaque from Megiddo (G. LOUD, *The Megiddo Ivories*, [OIP 52; Chicago 1939] Pl. 5:4.5), which has been discussed in this context (KEEL 1984:73 fig. 97), could hardly represent such a being (→Azazel). It belongs rather to the group of scenes of fighting animals, as they are known from Mesopotamia in Middle Assyrian glyptic art: a (male) sphinx in battle against a capride/bovide which he overcomes.

III. According to 2 Chr 11:15 a special cult was established for the *śĕʿîrîm* of Jeroboam I ('having appointed his own priests for the shrines, goat-demons [*śeʿîrîm*], and calves which he [Jeroboam] had made'), although their veneration had been expressly forbidden according to Lev 17:7: 'and that they [the Israelites] may offer their sacrifices no more to the goat-demons [*śĕʿîrîm*] after whom they stray'. In this case the demonic intermediate creatures are employed in an *ex post facto* critique of the worship of foreign deities. It is possible that behind 2 Chr 11:15 are pictorial representations of *śĕʿîrîm*

W. R. Smith, J. Wellhausen and others have compared the *śĕʿîrîm* with Arabic *ǧinn* (hairy demons in animal form, who can transform themselves into various shapes, including human form). On the other hand SNAITH considered the *śĕʿîrîm* of Lev 17:7; Deut 32:2 [*sic*!] and 2 Chr 11:15 storm demons ('the rain-gods, the fertility deities, the →Baals of the rain-storms' [1975:118]), while those of Isa 13:21 and 34:14 were simply animals ('he-goats') without any religious connotation (1975:115). Although this theory is not convincing in light of the inclusion of Deut 32:2, it is still difficult to say what manner of being the *śĕʿîrîm* were.

The following considerations are to be included in determining their function: The appearance of the *śĕʿîrîm* is nowhere described. Yet the image of a hairy (cf. *śāʿîr* 'hairy'), goat-like (cf. *śāʿîr* 'he-goat') creature is probably not far off the mark; the *śĕʿîrîm* appear in uninhabited and devastated surroundings (Isa 13:19-22; 34:9-15; cf. Lev 17:5 'in the open'), which they haunt; they appear in the company of other sinister creatures (Isa 13:21-22: *ṣiyyîm*, *ʾōḥîm* [owls, hyenas or demons?], *bĕnôt yaʿănâ* [ostriches], **ʾiyyîm*, *tannîm* [jackals, wolves?]; 34:13-15: *tannîm*, *bĕnôt yaʿānâ*, **ṣiyyîm*, **ʾiyyîm*, →*Lilith* [cf. Akkadian *lilītu*], *qippôz* [a type of bird?], *dayyôt* [vultures?]), with whom they 'meet' (Isa 34:14); there they hold a (hopping/stamping) dance (*rāqad* pi. Isa 13:21, M. J. MULDER, *TWAT* 7 [1992] 665-668, esp. 666-667); finally for their negative connotation it is significant that the *śĕʿîrîm* appear in oracles of doom against Babylon (Isa 13:19-22) and Edom (Isa 34:9-15).

Thus the enigmatic *śĕʿîrîm* could have been beings of mixed form (he-goat/demon), who according to Isa 13:21; 34:14 inhabitated and symbolize an inhospitable world of derelict habitations. They were—illicitly—venerated (Lev 17:7; 2 Chr 11:15). The prohibition to worship the *śĕʿîrîm* is an expression of post-exilic polemic against foreign gods.

Various factors, including the development of the Jewish religion and Persian and Egyptian influences, led to pronounced but variant demonic conceptions in early Judaism (*RAC* 9 [1976] 627-631, 636). Belief in demons is widely attested not only in the Midrashim, but especially in the Babylonian Talmud (names and taxonomy in *RAC* 9 [1976] 669-674, 679-680). As dwelling places they preferred devastated areas, graveyards, ruins and the like, but also trees such as the palm. They surround human beings in vast numbers, attack them at night and steal whatever is not fastened or sealed. In regard to the *śĕʿîrîm*, *SifreLev* 17:7 gives the following definition: '*śĕʿîrîm* 'the goat-like ones' (Lev 17:7) means nothing other than demons *šdym*, as it is written: And *śʿyrym* (= demons) shall dance there (Isa 13:21).' In a comparable way the Targums translate *śʿyrym* in Lev 17:7; Isa 13:21; 34:14 (*śʿyr*); 2 Chr 11:15 as *šdym* 'demons', cf. also *GenR* 65:10; *LevR* 22:5; b. *Ber.* 62b; b. *BabBat.* 25a; etc. (*RAC* 9 [1976] 670).

IV. *Bibliography*

M. GÖRG, Dämonen, *Neues Bibellexikon* 1 (1991) 375-377; B. JANOWSKI & U. NEUMANN-GORSOLKE, Das Tier als Exponent dämonischer Mächte, *Gefährten und Feinde des Menschen. Das Tier in der Lebenswelt des alten Israel* (ed. B. Janowski *et al.*; Neukirchen-Vluyn 1993) 278-282 [& lit.]; O. KEEL, *Die Welt der altorientalischen Bildsymbolik und das Alte Testament. Am Beispiel der Psalmen* (Zürich, Einsiedeln, Köln & Neukirchen-Vluyn ^{4}1984) 68-74; J. C. DE MOOR, Demons in Canaan, *JEOL* 27 (1981-1982) 106-119; *S. SCHROER, *In Israel gab es Bilder. Nachrichten von darstellender Kunst im Alten Testament* (OBO 74; Fribourg & Göttingen 1987) 133-135; N. H. SNAITH, The Meaning of שְׂעִירִם, *VT* 25 (1975) 115-118; T. STAUBLI, *Das Image der Nomaden im alten Israel und in der Ikonographie seiner seßhaften Nachbarn* (OBO 107; Fribourg [CH] & Göttingen 1991) 177-179, 259-268; G. STEMBERGER, Dämonen III, *TRE* 8 (1981) 277-279; *G. WANKE, Dämonen II, *TRE* 8 (1991) 275-277 [& lit.]; H. WILDBERGER, *Jesaja 13-27* (BKAT X/2; 1978) 523-524; H. WOHLSTEIN, Zur Tier-Dämonologie der Bibel, *ZDMG* 113 (1963) 483-492, esp. 487-489; D. P. WRIGHT, *The Disposal of Impurity: Elimination Rites in the Bible and in Hittite and Mesopotamian Literature* (SBLDS 101; Atlanta 1987) 22-23, 27-28.

B. JANOWSKI

SAVIOUR Σωτήρ

I. Σωτήρ is the nomen agentis of the stem σω-, which is also present in the verb σῴζω, and thus in essence denotes a person who saves or preserves (or has done so). It can be used about those who have saved a community or a group of persons or an individual from an undesirable condition. In a specifically religious sense it functions as an honorific title of several gods, e.g. →Zeus, Asklepios, Sarapis, or of men whose status has been raised to the divine sphere, e.g. kings and outstanding Roman →authorities, later mostly, though not exclusively, the Roman emperor. In the LXX almost all its occurrences concern →God (as the translation of various forms of the Hebrew stem YŠʿ); in the NT it is more often used about →Jesus →Christ (especially in the later epistles).

II. In a general reflection about Xerxes' expedition against Greece Herodotus 7.139.5 states that the Athenians might well be called "saviours of Hellas". In Aristophanes' *Equites* 149 a slave exhorts the sausage-seller to manifest himself to the city as its 'saviour'. Such a use of the term is, however, far less frequent than its occurrences in honour of gods, especially Zeus. The oldest extant case is Pindar, *Olymp.* 5.17: "O saviour Zeus, in the clouds on high". It can refer to a specific saving act, e.g. when gratitude was expressed to Zeus for having saved Delphi from an attack of Gauls in 279/8 (*SIG*^{3} 408). In their capacity of gods of sailors the →Dioscuri also were often honoured by the title. Leda is said to have borne sons who were "saviours of men living on the earth and their quick-going ships" (*Homeric hymn to the Diosc.* 6-7, see also *SB* 5795). The healing god Asklepios was very often called *sōtēr* (e.g. IG IV^2 1.127, *OGIS* 332.8) and it developed into his specific title, as can be witnessed in Aelius Aristides' *Sacred Tales.* "Die Bezeichnung *ho sōtēr* ist für Aristides so sehr ein Name des Asklepios geworden, daß er ihn gebraucht wie bei Herakles die Bezeichnung Kallinikos (und Alexikakos)" (DÖLGER 1950:262). Among the gods whose cult spread in Hellenistic and Roman times especially →Isis and Sarapis held the title (*OGIS* 87: *Sarapidi Isidi Sōtērsi*); for Isis the feminine *sōteira* was used (e.g. VIDMANN 1969: 247). Apuleius coined the neologism *sospitatrix* to render this into Latin (*Met.* 11.9.1, 11.15.4, 11.25.1). A list of all the gods who are called *sōtēr* or *sōteira* is provided by HÖFER 1909-1915.

The title is, however, also assigned to great politicians or generals for their achievements. The first reliable contemporary record of this is Thucydides 5.11.1 about the Spartan general Brasidas, who in defeating an Athenian army in 422 was himself mortally wounded. He received sacrifices as a *hēros*, was honoured as a *ktistēs* and regarded as a 'saviour'. Obviously *sōtēr* figures here within a religious context. The object of the honours has exceeded normal human bounds. Others were to follow and indeed to be honoured during their lifetime. In 302 BCE the Athenians greeted Demetrios Poliorketes and his son Antigonos as *theoi sōtēres* (Plutarch, *Dem.* 10.4, Diodorus Siculus 20.46.2, cf. IG II^2.3424.12 and HABICHT 1970:44-48). When the Romans intervened powerfully in Hellenic affairs, such treatment also fell to their share. Titus Quinctius Flamininus (229-174) is the first example (Plutarch, *Titus Flam.* 10). A contemporary inscription found in the Laconian seaport Gytheum testifies to this: *Titon Titou Koigktion, stratagon hypaton Rōmaiōn, ho damos ho Gytheatan ton autou sōtēra,* "Titus Quinctius, son of Titus, Roman consul, is honoured by the people of Gytheum as their saviour", (*SIG*^{3} 592 = *IGLS* 8766). In the first century BCE such honours befell Caesar (*SIG*^{3} 759, Athens) and Pompeius (*SIG*^{3} 749b, Samos). An Ephesian inscription in honour of Caesar emphasizes the religious context: ... *ton apo Areōs kai Aphrodeitēs theon epiphanē kai koinon tou anthrōpinou biou sōtēra,* "the manifest god, who is descended from →Ares and →Aphrodite, and the common saviour of human life", (*SIG*^{3} 760). This is not to deny that the assignment of the title could assume a stereotyped character. Thus Verres, who as a proconsul of Sicily in 73-71 was guilty of all the typical abuses of the Roman aristocratic administration of provinces, had also been honoured in such a way: *Itaque eum non solum patronum illius insulae, sed etiam sōtēra inscriptum vidi Syracusis,* "And thus at Syracuse I saw an inscription in which he was not only called protector of that island, but even its saviour", (Cicero *Ver.* 2.2.154). In explaining the importance of the title, Cicero adds that it cannot be rendered by one Latin word: *Is est nimirum sōtēr qui salutem dedit,* "He no doubt is a saviour who has provided salvation". Later, in the introductory part of his *State,* Cicero stressed its weight in an indirect way: *neque enim est ulla res in qua propius ad deorum numen virtus accedit humana quam civitates aut condere novas aut conservare iam conditas,* "Human virtue nowhere comes nearer to the majesty of the gods than in founding cities or saving those which were founded", (*Resp.* I 12). The title *ktistēs,* 'founder', is indeed more than once assigned in combination with *sōtēr,* e.g. to Pompeius at Mytilene (*SIG*^{3} 751). More often, however, *sōtēr* is combined with *euergetēs,* 'benefactor'.

Undoubtedly, such titles also occurred in a less exalted sphere, witness this Laconian inscription dating from the Augustan age: *ha polis kai hoi Rōmaioi Gaion Ioulion Euryklē Lacharous hyion ton autas sōtēra kai euergetan,* "the city and the (locally active) Romans honour Gaius Iulius Eurycles, son of Lachares, as their saviour and benefactor", (*SEG* XXIX 383). A more curious case is the freedman Milichus, who, having been rewarded for his part in the dismantling of the Pisonian conspiracy against the emperor Nero, *conservatoris sibi nomen Graeco eius rei vocabulo adsumpsit,* "he assumed the title 'saviour' in its Greek version", (Tacitus *Ann.* 15.71.1). Of course, the purist Roman historian was precluded from using the term *sōtēr*. NOCK (1972:727-730) mentions other cases in which "*sōtēr*, while most often used of Emperors, was at times formally applied to local dignitaries and to Imperial functionaries, in a manner which indicates that it was not felt to be excessive or invidious" (727). NOCK is in general reluctant to link the title prematurely to the divine sphere. Nevertheless, such a link is explicitly made in an edict of 19 CE by Germanicus, when he orders the Alexandrians to avoid certain acclamations, "which are for me invidious and which belong to the level of divinity, for they are suitable only for him who is really the *sōtēr* and *euergetēs* of the whole human race", i.e. Tiberius (*SB* 3924.35-40). NOCK stresses the cautiousness of Germanicus' words in regard to the official emperor. In this he is right, but *sōtēr* and *euergetēs* were obviously regarded as divine titles. Indeed, in answer to the proconsul Fabius Maximus' appeal in 9 BCE the Greek cities of the province Asia honoured Augustus as having been sent by Providence as a "saviour, who was to stop war and to establish peace" (*OGIS* 458 = EHRENBERG & JONES 1955:98.36-37).

In fact, such texts can be regarded as belonging to the domain of the →ruler cult. In this respect the title *sōtēr* was at first awarded for specific salutary achievements, as in the decree of the league of Aegean islands concerning Ptolemy I in 280/279 (*SIG*[3] 390.27; cf. also Pausanias 1.8.6 about the Rhodians and HABICHT 1970:158) or in Phylarchus' report on the way Seleucus I and his son Antiochos were honoured by the Athenians of Lemnos when they had been liberated from Lysimachos' administration (*FGH* 81 F 29; cf. HABICHT 1970:89-90). Gradually, however, it developed into a more general honour. See for this RONCHI (1977:1054-1064) about the successive Ptolemies. Antiochos IV was hailed as *sōtēr tēs Asias* (*OGIS* 253) and Caesar even as *sōtēr tēs oikoumenēs* (IG XII. 5.557), a title which is also attested for Nero (*OGIS* 668) and (with addition of *holēs*) for Marcus Aurelius (*SB* 176, 6674). One further step was possible, viz. to regard the emperor as a 'Weltheiland'. In an inscription of Halicarnassus Augustus is hailed as saviour *tou koinou tōn anthrōpōn genous* (G. HIRSCHFELD, *Collection of Ancient Greek Inscriptions in the British Museum* IV [1893] 894 = EHRENBERG & JONES 1955:98a.6-7), the context giving further testimony to his salutary influence on society and nature. Later Hadrian was indeed called *sōtēr tou (sympantos) kosmou* (T. B. MITFORD & I. K. NICOLAOU, *The Greek and Latin Inscriptions from Salamis* [Nicosia 1974] 13 and 94, *CIG* III 4335).

Generally speaking, the salvation provided in the cases dealt with above concerns material life in the present world. The title occurs far less in a spiritual domain. For Dio Chrysostom philosophers can heal psychical damage and thus are *sōtēres* (*Or* 32.18). This use of the term is, however, by no means widespread. Remarkably enough, the 'atheistic' Epicurus was celebrated as a *sōtēr* by his followers. This is implicit in Lucretius' eulogy in *De rerum natura* V 1-54 (Epicurus is called *deus* in v 8), but the title is explicitly used in Plotina's letter to the Athenian Epicureans of 121 CE (*SIG*[3] 834.21) and in *PHerc* 346 IV 26-27 (*hymnein ton sōtēra ton hēmeteron*). This stresses the 'soteriological' aspect of Epicureanism, which is so clearly expressed in the curious inscription at Oenoanda, the author of which, a certain Diogenes, states that he wanted *ta tēs sōtērias protheinai pharmaka*, viz. by an epigraphic survey of Epicurus' doctrine. See for further discussion of Epicurus as *sōtēr* CAPASSO (1982:112-115).

III. In the LXX *sōtēr* almost always is a title of God. Only in Judg 3:9, 15; 12:3 and Neh 9:27 the 'judges' are awarded the title. FOHRER (*TWNT* 7, 1013) notes that the →Messiah is never called *sōtēr* (but cf. Isa 49:6 and Zech 9:9). Philo of Alexandria often calls God *sōtēr*, a few times in combination with *euergetēs* (e.g. *Opif.* 169), once each with the addition *tou pantos* (*Deus* 156), *pantōn* (*Fug.* 162), *tou kosmou* (*Spec.* 2.198). Apart from this he uses the title *sōtēr kai euergetēs* for the emperor in *Flac.* 74 and *Gaius* 22.

There are 24 instances of *sōtēr* in the NT, of which eight concern God and 16 Jesus Christ. In the Pastoral Epistles the term occurs ten times, six of which about God; the five instanced in 2 Peter all concern Jesus Christ. It seems prudent to follow FOERSTER's strategy in *TWNT* 7, 1015-1017 in first dealing with the other cases.

Both in Luke 1:47 (the beginning of the *Magnificat*) and Jude 25 (doxology) God is called saviour in a manner reminiscent of the OT. In the Lucan texts Luke 2:11, Acts 5:31; 13:23 Jesus is announced as specifically the Saviour of Israel, but in John 4:42 and 1 John 4:14 he is called *sōtēr tou kosmou*. The two oldest occurrences are in the Pauline epistles. In an eschatological context Phil 3:20 gives vent to the Christian expectation that the Saviour, the →Lord Jesus Christ, will come from heaven to transform "our humble bodies". Wholly differently, Eph 5:23 states that Christ is the saviour of the body, which within the context of the Epistle means the Church. In five passages in the Pastoral Epistles (1 Tim 1:1; 2:3, Titus 1:3; 2:10; 3:4) God is called "our saviour"; 1 Tim 4:10 ("God is the saviour of all men") might be polemical against those who tended to narrow salvation to a small group. This could also apply to Titus 2:10, since v 11 adds that God's grace brings salvation to all men. Jesus Christ is called "our saviour" in Titus 1:4, where it is purely formulaic, and in 1 Tim 1:10, Titus 2:13; 3:6, where the title is elaborated in the context that follows. Such an elaboration is absent in 2 Pet 1:1.11; 2:20; 3:2.18. Among these texts 2 Pet 3:2 stands out as the only example of Christ being referred to as "Lord and Saviour" without mention of his name.

In rendering the title in Latin, Christian authors availed themselves of a variety of terms, e.g. *conservator, salutificator, sospitator*, but the Christian neologism *salvator*, a nomen agentis derived from *salvare*, itself a neologism, prevailed. It is used in (some branches of) the VL and became normal in the Vg.

IV. *Bibliography*

M. CAPASSO, *Trattato etico epicureo (PHerc 346)* (Naples 1982); F. J. DÖLGER, Der Heiland, *Antike und Christentum* 6 (Münster 1950) 257-263; F. DORNSEIFF, *Σωτήρ*, PW II 5 (1927) 1211-1221; V. EHRENBERG & A. H. M. JONES, *Documents Illustrating the Reigns of Augustus and Tiberius* (Oxford 1955); W. FOERSTER, Σωτήρ, *TWNT* 7, 1004-1022; C. HABICHT, *Gottmenschtum und griechische Städte* (München 1970[2]); O. HÖFER, Soteira; Soter, *ALGRM* 4 (1909-1915) 1236-1272; H. LIETZMANN, Der Weltheiland, *KS* I (Berlin 1958) 25-62; M. P. NILSSON, *Geschichte der Griechischen Religion* II, *Die Hellenistische und Römische Zeit* (München 1988[4]) 184-185, 389-391; A. D. NOCK, *Essays on Religion and the Ancient World* (ed. Z. Stewart, Oxford 1972) I 78-84, II 720-735; G. RONCHI, *Lexicon Theonymum rerumque sacrarum et divinarum ad Aegyptum pertinentium quae in papyris ostracis titulis Graecis Latinisque in Aegypto repertis laudantur*, Fasc. V (Milan 1977) 1048-1077; C. SPICQ, *Notes de lexicographie néotestamentaire. Supplément* (OBO 22,3; Fribourg 1982) 636-641; L. VIDMANN, *Sylloge inscriptionum religionis Isiacae et Sarapiacae*, (RGVV 28; Berlin 1969); P. WENDLAND, ΣΩΤΗΡ, *ZNW* 5 (1904) 335-353.

J. DEN BOEFT

SEA ים

I. As a geographical entity, the sea delimits both cultural and political areas. On the one hand, it provides connections: since the third millennium there has been shipping along the coast of the Persian Gulf (in the direction of Bahrein and India) and the Mediterranean region. The sea is a threatening power which annihilates life by drowning it. On the other hand, the sea is the inexhaustible reservoir of water, the source of life. These multiple and ambivalent relations are represented in the various symbolic systems. The relationship between the sea and other forms of water (→river, →source) is not consistent: not even within one and the same symbol system. There is never an absolute difference between these forms. Water is a particularly shapeless element. It is associated with the shapelessness of the →serpent, which participates in the ambivalence of both sea and water. The different cultural areas of the ancient Near East developed variations on similar themes which have mutually influenced each other. Just how these influences occured historically is not easy to discern.

II. In Egypt, the designation for the sea, 'the great green' or 'the great black', is more geographical, while that for the primeval sea, *Nun,* is more mythological. Nun surrounds the world. The rising of the sun god from Nun is therefore an everyday cosmological event. Another elementary manifestation of Nun is the annual inundation of the →Nile. The appearence of the fertile →earth (symbolically shaped as the 'primeval hill') is also an elementary cosmological event. Nun is occasionally conceived as a pair: Nun and Naunet; but the gender of the figure does not matter at all. The primeval water is associated with a serpent. A text from the Book of the Dead presents an image of the end of the universe which corresponds to its beginning: "Further, I shall destroy all I have made, and this land will return into Nun, into the floodwaters, as (in) its first state. I (alone) am a survivor together with →Osiris, when I have made my form in another state, serpents which men do not know and gods do not see" (*ANET* 9). In the Story of the Shipwrecked Sailor, a benevolent serpent deity is lord of the sea; and the paradise-like island where the shipwrecked mariner is saved is a product of water and returns to water. Sometimes the dangerous mythical power of the sea is stressed. Already the instructions of King Merikare (*ANET* 417) say: "Well directed are men, the cattle of the god. He made heaven and earth according to their desire, and he repelled the water-monster" (*snk n mw,* lit. 'submerger of the water', marked by the determinative of a crocodile, an animal which, according to the iconography, belongs to the chaotic powers). Later, →Seth is the typical overwhelmer of this enemy. One of Seth's roles consists in accompanying the sun god →Re in his daily fight against Apophis, a coiled serpent with destructive power. The sea, and the serpent correlated to it, have thus an ambivalent character. Since the time of the New Kingdom, there has been a distinct Canaanite influence, and Seth became identified with →Baal (the mythical opposition in the Astarte Papyrus—the sea on one side, Astarte and Seth-Baal on the other—is a Canaanite constellation).

An early Mesopotamian concept of the sea is found in the notion of **abzu**, the 'hidden', subterranean ocean (→Ends of the earth). Associated with the god Enki/Ea (→Aya), it appears as overflowing water fertilizing the dry land. The marshes in south Mesopotamia, abounding in fish, are another manifestation of abzu. Enki and his gifts are essential for life in general. Originally, the goddess Nammu might have been a female personification of the primeval water (the sign for her name is ENGUR, an expression for water). The texts call Nammu "Mother who gave birth to heaven and earth", who "bore all the gods". According to the Sumerian tradition, Nammu is the mother of Enki and the creatrix of men. In the Akkadian literature, Nammu is no longer important.

Later on, in a Semitic milieu, the abzu concept is differentiated. The beginning of *Enūma eliš* tells us that the waters of →Tiamat (salt water) and Apsu (fresh water) were originally mixed. The separation of the two types of water is the first cosmogonical stage. Ea's (= Enki's) victory over Apsu initiates the development of life. However, the difference between the two types of water is not absolute. When Tiamat is subdued by →Marduk, the eyes of this being become the springs of the rivers →Euphrates and →Tigris. Ea and Tiamat are surrounded by →Laḫmu, →dragons, serpents and different kinds of 'mixed beings' marking a state of 'primitive', undifferentiated being. These monsters are not only attested by textual evidence, there are also iconographical representations. The description of Gudea's temple shows that the conception of the primeval sea is essential for temple symbolism. There is an architectural representation of abzu and many monsters belonging to it. The temple, the link between →heaven and earth, has its roots in the primeval sea: and thus comprises the whole of the universe. The earth is not only based upon, but also surrounded by, the sea. This is confirmed, too, by a 'map' on which the earth, a circular shape, has a 'bitter stream' flowing around it. According to the Gilgamesh epic, the 'end' of the world is marked successively by the desert, a mountain range and the ocean of death's water. ('Paradise', the island of eternal life, lies paradoxically within this ocean.) The path of the sun-god starts in this area.

Cosmogonies make use of these concepts. A late text speaks of a time when "the Apsu had not been made, ... all the lands were sea" (HEIDEL 1951:62:8.10). The plot of *Enūma eliš*, the New Year myth of Babylon, has already been mentioned. Creation begins with the separation of the waters: it is completed by cutting Tiamat into two parts and making a space within the flood. The earth is erected on the lower part of Tiamat. Similar combat tales were told in places other than Babylon, and with other protagonists (e.g., the fight of Inanna against Ebiḫ). Chaotic power is not necessarily related to the sea, but the structural parallel is quite clear. Other cosmogonies combine the theme of the primeval water with the other model of Mesopotamian cosmogony: i.e. the separation of heaven and earth. The combat pattern is well represented in Mesopotamian iconography: especially on seals (representations of the battle, see, e.g., KEEL 1972: 39-47) and on boundary stones *(kudurru)*. The elements of cosmic order are based upon or framed by serpents (examples in *ANEP* 519-521).

Exorcisms sometimes entail this type of cosmogony: Evil is seen as a manifestation of Tiamat's chaotic power; whilst →demons connected with her are driven out by spells (one is supplied with a very instructive enumeration of *utukku*-demon types: *utukku*'s of the desert, of the mountains, and of the sea—all regions beyond the civilised world).

The power of the sea is not subdued forever; because the idea that it might increase again is the theme of the flood story. There is a badly preserved Sumerian version. In the Akkadian Atrahasis epic, the function of the flood is clear: i.e. to end the overpopulation of primeval humankind and balance it with excessive destruction. Thereafter, a more reasonable balancing mechanism takes over. The best-known version of this story belongs to the Gilgamesh epic, within the context of Gilgamesh's search for eternal life.

As to biblical traditions, the (fragmentary) Eridu Genesis is especially interesting. Its themes include the creation and humanization of human beings, the antediluvial kings (with extremely long lives) and the flood. The antediluvial →apkallu's are the subject of another tradition. They came from the sea in order to teach humankind cultural achievements such as the cuneiform script.

In Anatolia, there is above all Hittite evidence for religious conceptions of the sea; but mythologies of various origins (especially Hurrian) also strongly influenced these conceptions. The Hittites knew a male sea deity with decidedly anthropomorphic characteristics. The sea god is able to travel on the earth and in the netherworld: and he shows emotions like anger and pain. He does not belong to the primeval gods; but his mother was a healing goddess. In the conflict between the ruling weather god and the displaced king of the gods, Kumarbi, he belongs to the partisans of the latter. In the Ullikummi myth, the role of the sea is very significant. This tale tells how Kumarbi tried to recover his dominion over the universe. He created a monster called Ullikummi and placed it in the realm of the sea on a shoulder of an Atlas-like deity. Ullikummi has the form of a rock and grows steadily upwards toward heaven. The gods were not able to prevent this growth. The symbolism of this scene is clear: the separation of heaven and earth, the starting point of the cosmogony, is threatened. The two themes 'sea' and 'unification of heaven and earth' are associated in one and the same myth. The solution offered by Ea (the Babylonian deity!) is quite simple: the saw which once separated heaven and earth is borrowed from the primeval dieties and Ullikummi is cut away. The action takes place near the mountain Ḫazzi—the →Zaphon of the Ugaritians (known also in Israel and there identified with →Zion). This region is well represented in the mythology of the Syro-Canaanite traditions.

As to the Syro-Phoenician area, economical and cultural exchange with Mesopotamia, Egypt, Asia Minor and the Aegaeis is reflected in mythological and cultic data. The area surrounding the Mediterranean Sea is essential, and so the cult of a sea god protecting the sailors is obvious. A deity comparable to the Greek god →Poseidon is attested to archaeologically in various places.

The Ugaritic texts give the clearest view of the mythological organization of powers associated with the sea. The 'father of the gods', Il (→El), is situated "at the fountainhead of the two Rivers, in the middle of the bedding of the two Floods". This is a cosmological qualification; because Il's abode lies in a cosmic centre where the upper and lower waters come together. This centre is very remote; so the younger gods have to make a long journey in order to get to the high God. On the other hand, Il's residence is situated on a (cosmic) mountain. It seems that Shukamuna-wa-Shunama (→Shunama), probably an Atlas-like deity, is associated with Il (D. PARDEE, *Les textes para-mythologiques* [Paris 1988] 59-60). The two concepts cannot be harmonized—symbol systems do not strive after logical consistency. There are no mythical tales about Il's cosmological functions, but only short, formulaic descriptions.

In mythical contexts (*KTU* 1.1-6), the sea is represented by the anthropomorphically shaped Yam, the enemy of →Baal. Obviously Yam is not only the deity of the sea, but also of the rivers (he is often called *zbl ym ṯpṭ nhr,* 'prince Sea, ruler River'). In this context, the rivers are to be construed as destructive powers. Yam is closely connected with Il ('son of Il, beloved of Il'); but, whereas Il represents the cosmic aspect of the primeval water, Yam reflects its chaotic aspect (which parallels the situation in Anatolia where the sea god is correspondingly related to the old god Kumarbi). Various monsters occur together with Yam (and were possibly sometimes identified with him): Lotan (→Leviathan), a seven-headed serpent; Tunnanu (→Tannin); Arishu and 'Atiqu. The conflict between Yam and Baal is complex. A crucial question is which of the two should be allowed to have a 'house'. This might reflect a historical conflation of the cults of two different gods (Baal seems to be a newcomer in Ugarit), with Yam representing the ousted deity. Furthermore, Yam represents the power of chaos which appears in the sea and the rivers. To what extent Yam represented a seasonal phenomenon is controversial. However, this is not a primary aim of the Baal-Yam constellation, in contrast to the Baal-Mot constellation, which primarily represents the annual change of the wet and dry seasons. The destructive powers of Yam and →Mot are somehow connected. Both are called 'beloved of Il'. Baal's fight against Yam and Mot are also connected (cf. *KTU* 1.5—a very difficult text). Mot, though a representation of the summer heat, is located in subterranean mud which resembles the shapelessness of water.

Magical texts make use of the Baal-Yam constellation. In *KTU* 1.83, there is a spell which advises the destruction of Yam (depicted in the form of a →dragon with a fish tail) by binding him on the →Lebanon Mountains—obviously in order to dehydrate him. The difficult text *KTU* 1.82 contains a spell against Tunnan, serpents and associated beings. The threatening power of chaos appears thus in everyday experiences.

The Baal-Yam paradigm was popular in

the Late Bronze Age not only in the Syrian and Anatolian area, but also in Egypt. In the Astarte Papyrus, the goddess Astart and Seth (= Baal) fight against the sea-god. Baal Zaphon becomes the god of sailors and so succeeds previous deities of the sea. A famous sanctuary of Baal Zaphon is situated near the 'Bitter Lake' in Egypt.

III. The situation in Ancient Israel is in many respects comparable to that of Ugarit. Firstly, the sea is a cosmological element of the universe as a whole: along with other elements (a triadic concept consists of heaven, earth and sea [Ps 69:35; Exod 20: 11]. This structure is also recognizable in formulas such as "animals of the field, birds of the heaven, fishes of the sea" [Ps. 8:8-9]). The most detailed cosmogony (Gen 1, P) starts with the (uncreated) primeval sea (*tĕhôm*, associated with the desert, *tōhû).* Then the heaven is created in order to delimit the upper part of the ocean. Finally, the earth comes into being, providing the possibility of further creations. This process resembles the cosmogony of *Enūma eliš* and, if one takes into consideration the further context of the primeval story, the Eridu Genesis. However, the elements of combat have disappeared completely: the sea has become mere unstructured material to be brought into order. Other cosmogonical sketches of the beginning of the universe present less elaborated cosmogonies: The earth is founded upon the sea (Ps 24:2); it is determined by a limit (Jer 5:22; Job 38:1). Not only the earth in general, but in particular the sanctuary (of Jerusalem), is protected against the attack of the chaotic water (Ps 46:3).

In cultic literature, the cosmogony is clearly depicted as a fight between →Yahweh and the personified power of the sea. Yam (and *tĕhôm*—contrary to Ugarit but analogous to Mesopotamia, this term plays a role in the context of cosmological combat) are again associated with other monsters: e.g. →Tannin, →Leviathan and a female being named →Rahab. While Ugaritic mythology seems to know only male powers of chaos, within the context of destructive powers Israel recognizes both sexes. The enemy is represented as a serpent or as a seven-headed dragon. It is difficult to know whether at an early time the cosmological battle was conveyed in a tale (a myth in a restricted sense of the word) or whether it was even enacted in a cultic drama. In the tradition as preserved, the battle concept is only a complex of mythological elements within the context of hymns, prayers, etc. The most detailed accounts of the fight can be found in Ps 74:13-14; Ps 89:10; Ps 18: 16; Nah 1:4). Yahweh 'rebukes' the sea (possibly an anthropomorphic interpretation of the thunder emanating from the weather god); he smites the heads of the enemy; he delimits the realm of the sea or makes the water dry. Sometimes, the fighting god is depicted as one riding on a →Cherub or a chariot (Ps 18:11; 77:19). Very often, the battle against the sea consists of a mere allusion (Hab 3:8; Ps 46:3-4; Jer 31:35; Isa 51:15; Jer 5:22; Ps 29; the symbolism of Ezek 27:1-28:10 is characterized by the ambivalence of the sea theme). In theologically refined passages, the idea of the battle has nearly vanished (Ps 104:6-7; Job 38:8-10, and especially in the already mentioned cosmogony of P, Gen 1).

There is a strong association between the destructive power of the sea and other realms of destruction. The proximity of sea and desert has already been mentioned: the same can also be said about the sea and death (Ps 88:7). In Job 26:12-13, the fight against the serpent Rahab clears the heavens. The monster, normally located in the sea, seems to be associated with clouds: as is the case with the Egyptian serpent Apophis.

Temple symbolism (analogous to that of Mesopotamia) contains an iconic representation of the sea (the "brazen sea", 1 Kgs 7:23-26.44; 2 Chr 4:2-10; cf. KEEL 1972: 120-121), a round vessel with a diameter of about 4.5 m and a height of about 2.25 m. It was supported by twelve bulls (each of the four groups of three bulls corresponding to one of the four quarters of heaven), symbols of power and fertility. According to 2 Kgs

16:15-17, these bulls were, as a consequence of a cult reform, removed. The brazen serpent (→Nehushtan, originally an element of the temple in Jerusalem, 2 Kgs 18:4, then connected with the desert tradition, Num 21:9) belongs to the same symbolic context. Its prophylactic power against snakebites is congruent with the concept of sympathetic magic.

The cultic treatment of the power of chaos is present in a more private sphere as well. Black magic consists in "waking Leviathan" in order to cause evil on certain days (Job 3:8—the text must not be emended). On the other hand, there are apotropaic precautions taken against such activities of the evil powers (Job 7:12).

The Israelite versions of the flood story also found their place in the context of the cosmogony (Gen 6-8): The parallel between creation and destruction is obvious. The conclusion of both versions (J and P) emphasizes the uniqueness of the catastrophe (Gen 8:20-22; Gen 9:8-17) and the guarantee of an everlasting creation.

At a certain point in the tradition, the Exodus story was influenced by the motif of the battle against chaos (e.g., Ps 77:16-21; 66:5; 106:7-12; Exod 15:8-10). The reminiscence of a military catastrophe of the Egyptian enemy caused by sea or water in general (whatever may have been the exact circumstances) gave rise to such an interpretation. Those waters were now understood to be a manifestation of the primeval water: Israel was able to cross the realm of destruction, whereas the Egyptians were annihilated. The 'cleaving' of the water, an element of some Exodus versions (Exod 14:6; 15:8, P and related material), reflects the 'splitting' of the hostile monster. 'Natural', 'historical' and 'mythical' qualities are inseparably conflated.

Not only the Exodus theme is interpreted in such a manner, but also the motif of the crossing of the Jordan. The Jordan water was cleaved and made to dry up: just like the water of the Sea of Reeds (cf. Josh 3-4; Ps 114). Fords, as places of danger, are often associated with cults. In this case, the memory of such a local cult is attached to the traditional complexes of Exodus, Conquest and cosmogony.

In a late stage of Israelite history, the battle against the sea was projected into the future. The final victory of God against his enemy then becomes a matter of hope: and the significance of 'chaos' and 'cosmos' is reinterpreted. Which means that the powers dominating history are offsprings of the sea; but their end is determined and realized when the eschatological rule of God arrives. This projective interpretation (a typical element of crisis cults) occurred first in the time of the exile (Deutero-Isaiah: Isa 51:9; 43:16-21). Apocalyptic conceptions develop these images (Dan 7:1-14). Leviathan will be eventually exterminated (Isa 27:1). The sea will dry up at the precise moment when heaven and earth are reconstructed (Rev 21:1). Such conceptions are elements of apocalyptic speculation. They are combined with other mythological themes without forming a coherent conceptual whole.

The dualistic vision of apocalyptic texts is sometimes directly contradicted. In Job 40-41, the hippopotamus (→Behemoth) and the crocodile are characterized as creatures of God. Thus they are not chaotic beings—the creative power of God reaches even into the deep regions of the sea. The same conception occurs in the book of Jonah. The prophet tries to escape from Yahweh; but, even on the ship in the middle of the high seas, he was reached by God. Ultimately, it is the fish monster (servant of Yahweh!) who brings him back to land. This is congruent with the 'universalistic' view of the book as a whole.

IV. *Bibliography*

C. AUFFARTH, *Der drohende Untergang. "Schöpfung" in Mythos und Ritual im Alten Orient und Griechenland* (Berlin 1991); M. H. CARRE GATES, Casting Tiamat in another Sphere, *Levant* 18 (1986) 75-81; G. CASADIO, El and Cosmic Order: Is the Ugaritic Supreme God a deus otiosus?, *Studia Fennica* 32 (1987) 45-58; R. J. CLIFFORD, Cosmogonies in the Ugaritic Texts and the Bible, *Or* 53 (1984) 183-210; A. H. W.

CURTIS, The "Subjugation of the Waters" Motif in the Psalms: Imagery or Polemic?, *JSS* 23 (1978) 245-256; J. DAY, *God's Conflict with the Dragon and the Sea* (Cambridge 1985); M. DIETRICH & O. LORETZ, Baal vernichtet Jammu (*KTU* I.2.IV 23-30), *UF* 17 (1986) 117-121; G. R. DRIVER, Mythical Monsters in the OT, *Festschrift für G. Levi della Vida* I (Rome 1956) 234-249; O. EISSFELDT, Gott und das Meer in der Bibel, *KS* III (Tübingen 1966) 256-264; H. GESE, Die Religionen Altsyriens, *RAAM* (1970); J. H. GRØNBAEK, Baal's Battle with Yam - a Canaanite Creation Fight, *JSOT* 33 (1985) 27-44; H. GUNKEL, *Schöpfung und Chaos in Urzeit und Endzeit* (Göttingen 1895); A. HEIDEL, *The Babylonian Genesis* (Chicago [2]1951); T. JACOBSEN, The Eridu Genesis, *JBL* 100 (1982) 513-529; JACOBSEN, *The Harab-Myth* (SANE; Malibu 1984); O. KAISER, *Die mythische Bedeutung des Meeres in Ägypten, Ugarit und Israel* (BZAW 79; Berlin [2]1962); O. KEEL, *Die Welt der altorientalischen Bildsymbolik und das Alte Testament* (Einsiedeln & Neukirchen-Vluyn 1972); C. KLOOS, *Yhwh's Combat with the Sea* (Leiden 1986); S. E. LÖWENSTAMM, Die Wasser der biblischen Sintflut: Ihr Hereinbrechen und ihr Verschwinden, *VT* 34 (1984) 179-194; O. LORETZ, *Ugarit und die Bibel. Kanaanäische Götter und Religion im Alten Testament* (Darmstadt 1990); S. NORIN, *Er spaltete das Meer* (ConB, OT Series 9; Lund 1977); J. C. DE MOOR, *An Anthology of Religious Texts from Ugarit* (Leiden 1987); P. REYMOND, *L'eau, sa vie et sa signification dans l'Ancien Testament* (VTSup 6; Leiden 1958); H. RINGGREN, Yahvé et Rahab-Léviatan, *Mélanges bibliques et orientaux en l'honneur de M. Henri Cazelles* (ed. A. Caquot & M. Delcor; Kevelaer/Neukirchen-Vluyn 1981) 387-393; RINGGREN, *jam, TWAT* 3 (1982) 645-657; W. ROBERTSON SMITH, *Lectures on the Religion of the Semites. First Series. The Fundamental Institutions* (Edinburgh & New York 1889); F. STOLZ, *Strukturen und Figuren im Kult von Jerusalem* (BZAW 118; Berlin 1970); M. WAKEMAN, *God's Battle with the Monster* (Leiden 1973); W. A. WARD, Notes on Some Semitic Loanwords and Personal Names in Late Egyptian, *OrNS* 32 (1963) 413-436; A. J. WENSINCK, *The Ocean in the Literature of the Western Semites* (Amsterdam 1918, repr. 1968).

F. STOLZ

SEIRIM → SATYRS

SELA → ROCK

ṢELEM → IMAGE

SENEH → THORNBUSH

SERAPHIM שׂרפים

I. The word 'Seraphim' is the name given to the beings singing the trishagion to →Yahweh as king in Isa 6:2-3 and carrying out an act of purification in vv 6-7. The Seraphim are now generally conceived as winged →serpents with certain human attributes. The word *śārāp* has three ocurrences in the Pentateuch (Num 21:6.8; Deut 8:15) and four in Isa (6:2.6; 14:29; 30:6). It is generally taken as a derivative of the verb *śārap*, to "burn", "incinerate", "destroy". Since the verb is transitive, *śārāp* probably denotes an entity that annihilates by burning. While the etymological sense is thus "the one who burns (the enemies etc.)", the term refers several times to some serpentine being. According to some scholars the connection with the Heb verb *śārap* is only a secondary association, the original etymon being Eg *sfr* / **srf* (cf. *srrf*), "griffin" (JOINES 1974: 8 and 55 n. 15; GÖRG 1978).

II. The study of the ancient Near Eastern evidence, esp. iconographic representations, has been instrumental in the attempts to clarify the meaning and background of the seraphim. While some scholars have hinted that the seven thunders of →Baal and his lightning bolts or their iconography might provide illuminating parallels (cf. *ANEP* no. 655), there is now an emerging consensus that the Egyptian uraeus serpent is the original source of the seraphim motif

(JOINES 1974; DE SAVIGNAC 1972). This interpretation was worked out by KEEL (1977:70-124) who was able to adduce iconographic evidence showing that the uraeus motif was well known in Palestine from the Hyksos period through the end of the Iron Age (on scarabs and seals). During the 8th century BCE the two-winged and, in Judah especially the four-winged, uraeus is a well attested motif on seals, while six-winged uraei do not seem to occur. Friezes with uraei (without wings) are found in Egyptian and Phoenician chapels. The English term "uraeus" is a loan-word from Greek which was in turn taken from the Egyptian word for the cobra figure worn on the forehead of Egyptian gods and kings, whom the cobra protects by means of her "fire" (poison). Among the Egyptian designations for the uraeus one finds the word *ꜣḫt,* "flame". The pre-eminent cobra deity in Egypt was the crown god Uto.

III. Previous attempts to take the two occurrences in Isa 6:2.8 as more or less distinguished from the rest of the attestations (BDB 977) have now been generally abandoned. In the Pentateuch we find Yahweh sending *hannĕḥāšîm haśśĕrāpîm*, "the fiery serpents" (RSV), among the people (Num 21:6), commanding →Moses to make →Nehushtan, "fiery serpent" (Num 21:8). The desert is the place of "fiery serpents" (Deut 8:15), the abode of "the flying serpent" (*śārāp mĕʿôpēp,* Isa 30:6). In Isa 14:29 "the flying serpent" is used as a political metaphor for a new leader: "... for from the serpent's root will come forth an adder, and its fruit will be a flying serpent." That all five of the passages apart from Isa 6, understand *śārāp* to be a serpentine being is clear from the terminology used in the contexts in question, and two passages explicitly mention a winged serpent.

In Isa 6, the seraphim appear in connection with the enthroned heavenly king, →Yahweh Zebaoth. The following may be said about their position, form, number and function. Their position, *ʿōmĕdîm mimmaʿal lô,* "standing above" Yahweh (v 2), lends itself to comparison with the raised uraei on the chapel friezes, where the uraei are however without wings. Whether their shape is serpentine or more humanoid is a matter of dispute. As for number, there are probably two seraphim in Isa 6 (cf. v 3a). Concerning their function Isa 6 displays a noteworthy mutation of the uraeus motif (KEEL 1977: 113): instead of protecting Yahweh the seraphim need their wings to cover themselves from head to feet from Yahweh's consuming holiness; Yahweh does not need their protection. Isaiah thus uses the seraphim to underscore the supreme holiness of the God on the throne.

IV. The seraphim occur a number of times in the pseudepigrapha and later Jewish literature (see *OTP* 2, index sub seraphim and J. MICHEL, *RAC* 5, 60-97). The seraphim, →cherubim and ophanim are described as "the sleepless ones who guard the throne of his glory" (*1 Enoch* 71:7).

V. *Bibliography*

J. DAY, Echoes of Baal's Seven Thunders and Lightnings in Psalm XXIX and Habakkuk III 9 and the Identity of the Seraphim in Isaiah VI, *VT* 29 (1979) 143-151, esp. 149-151; E. EGGEBRECHT, Greif, *LdÄ* 2 (1977) 895-896; M. GÖRG, Die Funktion der Serafen bei Jesaja, *BN* 5 (1978) 28-39; K. JOINES, Winged Serpents in Isaiah's Inaugural Vision, *JBL* 86 (1967) 410-415; JOINES, The Bronze Serpent in the Israelite Cult, *JBL* 87 (1968) 245-256; JOINES, *Serpent Symbolism in the Old Testament* (Haddonfield 1974); *O. KEEL, *Jahwe-Visionen und Siegelkunst* (SBB 84-85; Stuttgart 1977), esp. 70-124; K. MARTIN, Uräus, *LdÄ* 6 (1986) 864-868; U. RÜTERSWÖRDEN, שָׂרָף *śārap*, forthcoming in *TWAT;* J. DE SAVIGNAC, Les "Seraphim", *VT* 22 (1972) 320-325; P. WELTEN, Mischwesen, *BRL*[2] (Tübingen 1977) 224-227.

T. N. D. METTINGER

SERPENT נחש

I. In MT the generic word for a venomous snake or serpent is *nāḥāš* (31 times). In Semitic the only certain cognate noun is Ugaritic *nḥš*, 'snake' (numerous times in *KTU* 1.100 and 1.107), with a possible cognate in Arabic *ḥanaš*, 'snake' (via metathesis and an altered sibilant). The origin of the word may be onomatopoeic, derived from the hissing sound of a snake. Other words for snakes in MT include *peten* (cf. Ug *bṯn*, Akk *bašmu* and *bšn* in Deut 33:22; →Bashan), *śārāp* (lit. 'burning one'), *ṣipônî*, *ʾepʿeh*, *ʿakšûb*, *qippōz*, *šĕpîpōn*, and *tannîn* (which can also mean 'dragon'). It is difficult to correlate these names with the numerous species of snakes native to the region. It is likely that all of these were regarded as venomous snakes, a common attribution in traditional cultures. The Hebrew noun *nāḥāš* also has the apparently related meanings of 'divination' (Num 23:23 and 24:1) and 'fortune, luck' (attested in numerous personal names). The denominative Piel verb *niḥēš* means 'to practice divination' (attested also in Aramaic). Occasionally *nāḥāš* and other words for snake can be applied to mythical dragons (→Dragon, →Leviathan).

The snake is commonly associated with selected deities and →demons and with magic and incantations in the ancient Near East. The latter association is found particularly in connection with the cure or avoidance of snake bites. The most common symbolic associations of the snake include protection, danger, healing, regeneration, and (less frequently) sexuality.

II. In Mesopotamian mythology and iconography the snake can be associated with a range of deities and demons. Depictions of a god whose lower body is a snake may represent the deity Niraḫ, chief minister to Ishtaran, the city-god of Der, on the border with Elam. The frequent reliefs of snakes on kudurru's (boundary-stones) may represent Niraḫ in the role of protective spirit. Perhaps related are the frequent Elamite images of a high god seated on a throne of coiled snakes. The symbol of the underworld deity Ningishzida is a venomous horned snake, which is depicted rising from his shoulders. Ningishzida is named in incantations as a guardian of underworld demons, and in the Adapa myth is a guardian of the gates of →heaven. The female demon Lamashtu is depicted grasping snakes in both hands, while the male demon Pazuzu can be depicted with his exposed phallus as a snake. In these divine representations the image of the snake suggests associations with fear, danger, and death or with a protective power, depending on whether the snake is the emblem of an adversary or a benefactor.

Another dimension in the Mesopotamian symbolism of the snake is found in the Gilgamesh epic; the animal steals away Gilgamesh's plant of rejuvenation (XI:279-289). This episode shows not only the futility of Gilgamesh's quest for immortality, but also explains in folkloric fashion why snakes shed their skin and rejuvenate. The knowledge of this plant is described as a 'secret of the gods'.

In Egyptian mythology and iconography the snake is a dominant and multivalent symbol. HORNUNG notes: "An schillernder Vieldeutigkeit übertrifft die Schlange jedes andere Tier der Ägyptischen Mythologie ... Im Bild der Schlange verkörpert sich ein Symbolgehalt, dessen Tiefe und dessen Vieldeutigkeit keine Grenzen kennen" (*LdÄ* 5 [1984] 648). The snake can appear in many roles: as an adversary or a protector, a deity or a demon, and can signify life and regeneration or death and nonexistence.

A venomous snake (the Uraeus serpent) protects kings and gods; the king has the snake as part of his being, and so is immune to snake bites and can heal others. Fierce snakes are guardians of the twelve gates of the underworld. The *ba*'s of all the gods live in snakes, and the →dead in the Netherworld become snakes. The sun-god in his nightly passage through the primeval waters of Nun is rejuvenated inside the body of a snake before his reappearance at dawn. The primeval gods at the beginning of time are embodied as snakes in the primeval waters, and time itself can be depicted as a snake. At the end of time →Atum and →Osiris return to snake-beings in the eternal waters. The deadly and the regenerative powers of the snake occur in varying proportions in these instances; hence the complexity of the snake symbol.

The semantic range of the snake in Egypt is well-illustrated by the contrast between two cosmic snakes: Apopis and Ouroboros. The Apopis serpent is the cosmic adversary of the sun god, each day attempting to consume the sun and to return the cosmos to primeval chaos and darkness. Apopis is destroyed each day by powerful magic, yet cannot be killed; it returns eternally as the force of chaos and non-existence, ever threatening to erase the order of being. The Ouroboros ('tail-swallower') is the world-encircling snake who marks the boundary between the ordered cosmos and the endless chaos around it. In the contrast of Apopis and Ouroboros the snake appears as both exponent of and limit on the powers of chaos and non-existence.

In Canaanite and Phoenician mythology and iconography the symbolism of the snake is less diverse than in Egypt or Mesopotamia. There are numerous images of snakes in various media, at times curled around the openings of vessels in a protective pose, but other meanings in other contexts remain obscure. In the so-called Qudšu iconography the snake is associated with a goddess, probably →Asherah, the mother of the gods in Ugaritic mythology. In this pose the goddess is depicted naked, standing on a lion, and holding snakes in one or both hands, sometimes also holding flowers in one hand. There are numerous examples of this image in Syro-Palestinian and Egyptian figurines and plaques from ca. 1700-1200 BCE. A goddess-epithet from the Proto-Sinaitic inscriptions, *ḏt bṯn* ('The One [fem.] of the Snake'), has also plausibly been associated with the goddess Asherah. Whether the snake in its association with Asherah connotes rejuvenation, rebirth, protection, sexuality or some other nuance or conjunction of meanings is unclear. In a Ugaritic mythological incantation against snakebites (*KTU* 1.100) the god →Horon is the chief dispeller of snake venom and at the end presents a brideprice of snakes (*nḥšm*) to a minor goddess. In Syro-Palestinian cylinder seals the snake is sometimes depicted as an enemy of the warrior-god, probably representing some of the various chaos-monsters of Canaanite mythology.

A Hellenistic period recapitulation of Phoenician mythology (from Philo of Byblos) presents our only direct commentary on snake symbolism from a non-biblical West Semitic source (including an admixture of Hellenistic influences): "Taautos himself regarded as divine the nature of the serpent and snakes... [it is] fiery and the most filled with breath of all crawling things... It is also exceedingly long-lived, and by nature not only does it slough off old age and become rejuvenated, but it also attains greater growth. When it fulfils its determined limit, it is consumed into itself, as Taautos himself similarly narrates in his sacred writings. Therefore, this animal is included in the rites and mysteries" (Eusebius, *Praep. ev.* 1.10.46-47; trans. ATTRIDGE & ODEN 1981).

III. In the Hebrew Bible the snake is associated with →Yahweh or with magic on several occasions. The most notable instances are the stories of the Garden of Eden (Gen 3), the Egyptian plagues (Exod 4 and 7), the bronze serpent (Num 21 and 2 Kgs 18), and possibly Isaiah's initiatory vision (Isa 6).

The snake symbolism in the stories of the Egyptian plagues and the bronze serpent is representative of traditional Near Eastern associations with the snake. In Exod 4:1-5 (JE) and 7:8-13 (P) as a sign of Yahweh's power, Moses' and Aaron's rod turn into venomous snakes (*nāḥāš* and *tannîn*, respectively). In the JE story the magical transformation serves to show the Israelites that Yahweh has indeed revealed himself to →Moses, while in the P story the transformation is a sign to Pharaoh of Yahweh's might. The common Near Eastern resonance of this scene is shown in the P story when the Egyptian magicians also transform their rods into snakes; Yahweh's greater might is demonstrated only in that his snake devours the Egyptian snakes. The association of venomous snakes with magic is part of the implicit sense of these passages, an association with which Israelite authors seem familiar (e.g. Ps 58:5-6). In the story of the bronze serpent in Num 21:4-9 (JE), Yahweh commands Moses to construct a snake statue mounted on a standard to cure the deadly bites of the *śĕrāpîm* (lit. 'burning') snakes. When the Israelites see the statue, their bites are healed. Here also is a traditional association of the snake in its symbolic use in healing rites for venomous snake bites. Yahweh is the deity responsible for healing through the symbolic instrument of the bronze snake (*nĕḥaš nĕḥōšet*—note the assonance in the ritual phrase). Due apparently to a reevaluation of the ritual objects associated with Yahweh, Hezekiah destroys the bronze serpent in 2 Kgs 18:4. In this passage the snake image is associated with idolatrous, non-Yahwistic worship, though it is more likely that the snake was a traditional sign of Yahweh's healing power (→Nehushtan).

In Isaiah's initiatory vision in Isaiah 6, the prophet sees *śĕrāpîm* (lit. 'burning ones') in Yahweh's heavenly temple. These creatures have faces, legs, and six wings; they fly and chant praises to Yahweh. It is possible that these are winged snake-beings, like the *śārāp*-snakes of other passages (note the 'flying' *śārāp*-snakes of Isa 14:29 and 30:6, and cf. Herodotus 2.75 on flying snakes in the Arabian desert). While depictions of the winged Uraeus serpent are common in seals of this period, it may be more likely that these 'burning ones' in Isaiah's vision are variants of the 'fiery' lesser deities found in other passages who are members of Yahweh's divine assembly (→Angel(s), Host of Heaven). The closest parallels are to other divine fiery beings such as 'his servants, →fire <and> →flame' (Ps 104:4), the creature *rešep* (lit. 'burning', cf →Resheph) who accompanies Yahweh, and the enigmatic 'flame of the whirling sword' who, with the →Cherubim, guards the way to the Garden of Eden (Gen 3:24). Also related may be Ezekiel's vision of fire moving among the heavenly Cherubim and God's fiery presence in Ezek 1. Since the 'burning ones' of Isaiah's vision are not overtly depicted as snakes (note that all the attestations of *śārāp*-snakes are explicitly marked by other words for snakes), and since the prophet remarks on other features of their bizarre appearance, it is perhaps more likely that they are fiery beings than snake-beings.

The most interesting biblical snake with mythological associations is the snake (*nāḥāš*) in the Garden of Eden (Gen 3). This snake is identified as belonging to the class of 'creatures of the field that Yahweh God had made', though it is distinguished from the other animals by his greater 'cleverness' (Gen 3:1). This clever animal plays the role of the trickster in the Eden story, skilfully deceiving the Woman into disobeying the divine command concerning the fruit of the Tree of Life. Cross-cultural studies have shown that trickster figures characteristically are ambiguous figures who cross or blur the accepted categories of existence. The snake in Eden is true to his trickster identity in crossing or blurring the boundaries between the categories of animal, human, and divine. While the snake is defined as an animal, he is also different from them with respect to his knowledge or cleverness. In addition, like a human, the snake has the power of speech (cf. Gen 2:19-20 in which the power of naming clearly differentiates human from animal), and he tricks the Woman through this characteristically human ability. Unlike the humans, but like God, the snake knows that the humans will not die upon eating the forbidden fruit, but will become 'like the gods, knowing good and evil' (Yahweh God acknowledges that this is the case in Gen 3:22). Hence the snake is an animal, but is like humans with respect to the power of language, and is like the gods with respect to secret knowledge. The snake's identity partakes and combines, in complex measure, characteristics of these three distinct categories of being. The effect of the snake's actions are correspondingly coloured by multiple meanings and ambiguity. While the human transgression is depicted as sinful, it also brings the human a greater, divine-like knowledge: their eyes are indeed 'opened' (though what is gained—knowledge of nakedness—seems ironic and obscure). Like tricksters of other traditions (cf. Prometheus and Epimetheus of Greek tradition), the boon of the trickster is both a benefit and a loss, for which humans pay the price. The choice of a venomous snake for this trickster figure seems predicated on traditional Near Eastern associations with the snake: associations with danger and death, with magic and secret knowledge, with rejuvenation and immortality, and with sexuality. It is also possible that the snake's association with the nude goddess in Canaanite iconography lies behind the scene of the snake and the naked woman (who is called in Gen 3:20 'Mother of all Life', seemingly a goddess epithet) in the divine garden.

IV. In post-biblical interpretive traditions the biblical snakes, particularly the bronze serpent and the snake in Eden, are commonly drawn into new frameworks of meaning. In the New Testament, the lifting up of the bronze serpent is a symbol of →Christ, the saviour lifted up on the cross who grants life (John 3:14-15). In Philo the bronze serpent is a symbol of the power of self-control, which wards off the temptation of sensual pleasure, represented by the snake in Eden (Philo, *Leg. Alleg.* 2.71-82). The snake in Eden also comes to be associated in both Jewish and Christian traditions with →Satan, through whose envy death came into the world (possibly Wis 2:24 and Rev 12:9; more clearly in *Apoc. Mos.* 16-19, Justin, *Dial.* 124, Origen, *Princ.* 3.2.1, and commonly in Rabbinic literature). In the antithetical exegesis of Gnostic traditions, the snake in Eden is viewed as a figure of →Christ, effecting spiritual liberation from the oppression of the earthly demiurge (*Testimony of Truth* 9.45-49), a view that irritated Irenaeus and other patristic authors (Irenaeus, *Haer.* 1.30.15).

V. *Bibliography*

H. W. ATTRIDGE & R. A. ODEN, *Philo of Byblos: The Phoenician History* (CBQMS 9; Washington DC 1981) 63-69; J. BLACK & A. GREEN, *Gods, Demons and Symbols of Ancient Mesopotamia* (Austin 1992) 166-168; H.-J. FABRY, *nāḥāš*, *TWAT* 5 (1986) 384-397; N. FORSYTH, *The Old Enemy: Satan and the Combat Myth* (Princeton 1987) 223-242, cf. (rev.) H. A. Kelly, *Journal of American Folklore* 103 (1990) 77-84; L. GINZBERG, *The Legends of the Jews* 5 (Philadelphia 1909-1938) 94-124; E. HORNUNG, *Conceptions of God in Ancient Egypt: The One and the Many* (Ithaca 1982) 160-179; K. R. JOINES, *Serpent Symbolism in the Old Testament* (Haddonfield 1974); O. KEEL, *Jahwe-Visionen und Siegelkunst* (SBS 84/85; Stuttgart 1977) 110-124; B. A. LEVINE & J.-M. DE TARRAGON, 'Shapshu Cries Out in Heaven': Dealing with Snake-Bites at Ugarit (*KTU* 1.100, 1.107), *RB* 95 (1988) 481-518; W. A. MAIER, *ʾAšerah: Extrabiblical Evidence* (HSM 37; Atlanta 1986) 81-191; P. DE MIROSCHEDJI, Le dieu élamite au serpent et aux jaillissantes, *IrAnt* 16 (1981) 1-25; W. H. PROPP, Eden Sketches, *The Hebrew Bible and Its Interpreters* (eds. W. H. Propp, B. Halpern & D. N. Freedman; Winona Lake 1990) 197-200; L. STÖRK, Schlange, *LdÄ* 5 (1984) 644-652; H. N. WALLACE, *The Eden Narrative* (HSM 32; Atlanta 1985) 147-181.

R. S. HENDEL

SERUG שׂרוג

I. It has been speculated that the biblical figure of Serug, a relative of the Israelite patriarchs (Gen 11:20-23), bears the name of the city Sarug known from first millennium cuneiform sources. The city, in turn, would have been named after a deity (LEWY 1934).

II. There is no extra-biblical evidence whatsoever attesting to the cult of a god Serug (or Sarug). Lewy's argument is based on circular reasoning. He writes: "In view of the evidence that the cities of Ḫarrān, Naḫur, and Sarūg bear the names of ancient deities ... it is permitted to conclude that the parents of the patriarchs in Western Mesopotamia are, at least in part, ancient West-Semitic deities that have later been invested with a human nature" (LEWY 1934 [tr. KvdT]). The evidence he refers to is non-existent. Also, the theory seems to be indebted more to the once popular view of Genesis as a euhemeristic account of ancient Semitic religion, than to a dispassionate study of the texts.

III. Though the connection between the anthroponym Serug and the cityname Sarug is attractive (compare the case of →Haran, both the name of a relative of Abraham and of a West-Mesopotamian city), it does not follow that Sarug is the name of a deity.

IV. *Bibliography*

R. S. HESS, Serug, *ABD* 5 (1992) 1117-1118; J. LEWY, Les textes paléo-assyriens et l'Ancien Testament, *RHR* 110 (1934) 47-48.

K. VAN DER TOORN

SETH

I. A number of oblique references to the Eyptian god Seth have been found in the description of the hippopotamus (→Behemoth) in the Book of Job.

II. Seth (Σηθ) is the Greek transcription of Eg *Sth̲*, son of Geb and Nut, and brother and rival of →Osiris. According to the Osiris mythology, known from allusions in Egyptian ritual texts and in its full-fledged form from the account of Plutarch (ca. 60-120 CE), Seth is responsible for the untimely death of Osiris. The son of Osiris, →Horus, avenges his father by slaying his murderer. Seth is in many ways the opposite of Horus: whereas Horus is the god of the clear skies, Seth is the god of storm and darkness. In that capacity he has been equated with →Baal at an early date. In addition to the struggle between Seth and Horus on account of Osiris, there are many references in the Egyptian tradition to various other contests of the two. A widely found motif has Horus robbed of his eyes by Seth, and Seth of his testes by Horus; the mythical motif has been interpreted as a homosexual assault by Seth on Horus (TE VELDE 1967). A cosmogonical interpretation is also possible, though.

In the Egyptian tradition, Seth is increasingly seen as the god of the foreign lands. Beside the identification with Baal, Seth has been identified as well with Teshub, the Hittite storm god. Because of his foreign associations, Seth came to be a symbol of the forces of chaos and evil. He was identified with →Typhon by the Greeks.

III. A number of authors have suggested that the confrontation between →Yahweh and Behemoth in Job 40:15-24[10-19] is patterned upon the battle of Horus (Yahweh) against Seth (Behemoth). The description of Behemoth, then, would reflect aspects of Seth (RUPRECHT 1971; KEEL 1978; KUBINA 1979). The basis for the alleged parallelism is the fact that in some Egyptian texts the red hippopotamus symbolizes Seth (RUPRECHT 1971:213). Other facets would corroborate the hypothesis. Thus the bones "like iron bars" which Behemoth is said to possess (Job 40:18) are reminiscent of the "bones of Seth" mentioned in the Pyramid texts and by Manetho (LANG 1980).

The tentative parallel between Behemoth and Seth has proved productive for the interpretation of the relevant passage, but remains hypothetical. In its defence it may be said that →Leviathan, too, is probably modelled on a divine figure—known from the Ugaritic texts, though, not the Egyptian. Also, in the poetic description of Behemoth there are a significant number of traits that cannot very well apply to a mere animal: Behemoth does have supernatural dimensions. Whether these considerations justify its identification with Seth is uncertain. On the whole, the association between Seth and the hippopotamus seems to have been a secondary aspect of the god's mythology.

IV. *Bibliography*

J. GWYN GRIFFITHS, *The Conflict of Horus and Seth* (Liverpool 1960); O. KEEL, *Jahwes Entgegnung an Ijob* (Göttingen 1978) 127-141; V. KUBINA, *Die Gottesreden im Buch Hiob* (Freiburg 1979) 68-76; B. LANG, Job XL 18 and the "Bones of Seth", *VT* 30 (1980) 360-361; E. RUPRECHT, Das Nilpferd im Hiobbuch, *VT* 21 (1971) 209-231; H. TE VELDE, *Seth, God of Confusion* (Leiden 1967).

K. VAN DER TOORN

SEVEN → APKALLU

SHA שׁע

I. Sha' has been construed as a theophoric element in the common West Semitic name Elisha. The identity of the deity is unclear. Albright related the name with the Aramean form of the moongod: *Si'* →Sîn (AVIGAD 1964:190).

II. An identification of Sha with the moongod *Si'* or *Sin* is unlikely; because the rendering of Sin in West Semitic alphabetic scripts is always *š'* with an *'āleph* and never *š'* (TIGAY 1986:81). A deity Sha' is not attested in cuneiform or West Semitic inscriptions. In the Hebrew personal names known from epigraphical material: *š'ybb* (AVIGAD 1964:190-191 + Pl 44 A), *š'np* (ed. HESTRIN & DAYAGI 1978:No. 85) and [...]*š'* (ed. AVIGAD 1986:No. 182) Sha' has been construed as a theophoric name (AVIGAD 1964:190). There is no compelling reason, however, to interpret *š'* as a theophoric element. The element can alternatively be construed as a noun meaning 'salvation' or as a verbal form derived from YŠ' or ŠW' II. The same must be said concerning the Ammonite personal name *b'lyš'* (ed. HERR 1985).

III. It would be strange if the name of the prophet Elisha were to contain a theophoric element referring to a non-Israelite deity. This, however, is not a convincing argument against the existence of the deity Sha'. The linguistic analysis of the name makes the assumption of Sha' as a theophoric element improbable. The name *'elišā'* should be construed either as 'my god helps', or as 'my god is noble' (BECKING 1993).

IV. *Bibliography*

N. AVIGAD, Seals and Sealings, *IEJ* 14 (1964) 190-194; AVIGAD, *Hebrew Bullae From the Time of Jeremiah* (Jerusalem 1986); B. BECKING, Elisha: "*Sha'* is my God"?, *ZAW* 106 (1994) 113-116; L. G. HERR, The Servant of Baalis, *BA* 48 (1985) 169-172; R. HESTRIN & M. DAYAGI-MENDELS, *Ḥôtāmôt mîmê Bayit Ri'šôn* (Jerusalem 1978); J. H. TIGAY, *You Shall Have No Other Gods. Israelite Religion in the Light of Hebrew Inscriptions* (HSS 31; Atlanta 1986).

B. BECKING

SHADDAY שׁדי

I. Shadday is an abbreviation for *'ēl šad(d)ay*, "God of the Wilderness". The name occurs 48 times in the OT; the occurrence in Job 19:29 is disputed. The longer form is attested 7 times: Gen 17:1; 28:3; 35:11; 43:14; 48:3; Exod 6:3; Ezek 10:5; *šadday* on its own occurs 41 times: Gen 49:25; Num 24:4.16; Ruth 1:20.21; Isa 13:6; Ezek 1:24; Ps 68:15; 91:1 and 31 times in Job. The deity is attested as a theophoric element in Egyptian, Ugaritic, Phoenician and Thamudic personal names from the Late Bronze Age onwards.

A convincing etymology has until now not been offered (a nearly complete list of various etymologies for El Shadday is given by WEIPPERT 1976; two additions are discussed by KNAUF 1985:97 n. 4; see now NIEHR & STEINS 1993:1080-1082). On the basis of the equation between Akk *šadû*, 'mountain', and Heb *šadday*—first proposed by F. DELITZSCH (*Assyrisches Handwörterbuch* [Leipzig 1896] 642-643)—and in view of the Akk noun *šaddā'u/šaddû'a*, 'inhabitant of the mountain', a rendering of *šadday* with 'He of the mountain' has been widely accepted (e.g. W. F. ALBRIGHT, *Yahweh and the Gods of Canaan* [London 1968] 94; F. M. CROSS, *Canaanite Myth and Hebrew Epic* [Cambridge 1973] 52-60). An Egyptian etymology—as offered by M. GÖRG (*BN* 16 [1981] 13-15)—yields too many phonetic problems (KNAUF 1985:97 n. 4; NIEHR & STEINS 1993:1082).

However, the theophoric element in the Thamudic personal name *'lšdy* presupposes an original *Śaday, the first consonant correctly to be rendered by /s/ in Late Egyptian, and by /š/ in Ugaritic, Phoenician and Israelite (KNAUF 1990). Both Akkadian *šadû*, 'the mountain wilderness (as seen from the cultivated alluvial land along the rivers →Tigris and →Euphrates)' and Biblical Hebrew *śādeh*, 'the (uncultivated) field', i.e. the area of hunting (cf. e.g. Gen 25:27; 27:3, and the opposition *bĕhēmâ – ḥayît haśśādeh*, e.g. Gen 2:20; 3:14) go back to the root ŠDY. Any El Shadday is, therefore, a 'god of the wilderness' and can be connected with the iconographical motive of the 'lord of the animals'. In Judaean (and hence, Biblical) Hebrew, El Shadday is a 'loan-word' from Israelite; otherwise, one would expect **śaday* (note that the initial *š* predates the Masoretic pointing system as evidenced by the puns in Gen 49:25; Isa 13:6; Joel 1:15).

II. Late Bronze Age attestations of this deity (or group of deities) include *šȝ-d-ï-ʿ-m-y* *Śadayʿammī "Shadday is my paternal relative" (SCHNEIDER 1992:195-196), a name still to be found in Achaemenid Egypt (*šdʿm*, KORNFELD 1978:72); in Ugaritic, possibly *bʿlšd* (*Baʿlušadā? GRÖNDAHL 1967:191-192); and *KTU* 1.108:12 *ʾilu šadī yaṣīdu*, "El Shadī is hunting" (LORETZ 1980; NIEHR & STEINS 1993:1080). The expression can also be read as: *ʾilu šadā yaṣīdu* "El, in the wilderness he is hunting", then too →El acts as an El Shadday.

Epigraphical references from the Iron Age include the *šdyn*-gods interceding with El on behalf of the people of Sukkoth in the presumably Israelite (KNAUF 1990) Tell Deir ʿAllā inscription (WEIPPERT & WEIPPERT 1982:88-92), and *ʾlšdy* in a Thamudic inscription from the vicinity of Taymāʾ (JS 255, 5th-3rd centuries BCE; KNAUF 1981). Prosopographic attestations are scarce: in addition to Egyptian Aramaic *šdʿm*, there are *ʿbdʾšdʾ* and *ʿbdšdʾ* in Punic (BENZ 1972: 414).

III. The biblical references to El Shadday or Shadday are, in their present form, exilic or, mostly, post-exilic. (El) Shadday is consistently used as an epithet for →Yahweh (with the sole exception of Job 19:29, where the **šadayīn* (Ketîb, same form as in epigraphical Israelite) may be mentioned as revenger gods. These references contribute little to a clarification of the nature of this group of gods prior to the second half of the first millennium BCE.

Of possibly Israelite origin are Gen 49:25 and Ps 68:15. In Jacob's blessing of Joseph, Gen 49:25, El Shadday (*txt. em.* for *ʾet šdy*) parallels "the god of your father" (the father being Jacob, 'god' refers presumably to Yahweh, the *ʾabbîr Yaʿăqôb*; →Mighty One of Jacob; cf. KÖCKERT 1988:63). If Yahweh is responsible for "the blessings from the skies above", El Shadday may be connected with "the blessings of the primordial waters that lie beneath". Gen 49:23-24 presupposes military encounters not earlier than the 9th/8th centuries BCE; the reference to the "blessings of →breasts and womb" (v 25) presupposes the elimination of the Goddess from Israelite/Judaean religion, and dates the present form of Jacob's blessing in the aftermath of Hosea and his followers (KNAUF 1981:23-24; KÖCKERT 1988:66-67). The "breasts" (Heb *šādayim*, root ṮDY; but note that Shadday does not mean 'breast(s)' *pace* P. DHORME, *RB* 31 [1922] 230-231) may have crept into the verse as an allusion to El Shadday; in this case, they testify to the re-etymologization of the god's name already in what may form its first biblical attestation. Jacob's, i.e. (northern) Israel's special connection with El Shadday may also be referred to in Gen 43:14, part of the Jerusalemite Joseph-novella of the late 8th or early 7th century BCE. Another possibly Israelite text in Judaean reception may be represented by Ps 68. In its present form, the hymn is post-exilic (cf. especially vv 2-8.10-11.17.29-36). The basic theme of Jerusalem-centered *gōlâ* theology, however, is embellished by quotations from ancient Israelite traditions as, e.g., the song of Deborah (vv 9.14.28). Ps 68:15—connecting Shadday with snow on mount Zalmon (*Jabal ad-Drūz*)—may allude to another possibly Israelite tradition.

In Judaean texts, El Shadday is predominantly defined by the use which P made of the name. P (6th-5th centuries BCE) formulates a theory about 'salvation history' according to which Yahweh revealed himself to →Abraham, Isaac and →Jacob, but not yet under his 'real' name (Gen 17:1; 28:3; 35:11; Exod 6:3). P takes into account that the God who revealed himself to Abraham must also have been known to Ishmael and →Esau (whose descendants in the 6th century BCE did not betray any signs of orthodox Yahwism). In this case, P may refer to the wide range of this god's spatial distribution (see above). The author of the book of Job (late 6th-5th centuries BCE) follows P's historical theory closely when he puts Shadday into the mouths of Job and his friends, given the Arabian locale and the patriarchal traits of his hero. Since the Pentateuch originated as a 'dialogue', if not compromise between conflicting traditions (BLUM 1990), P's 'El Shadday' refers also to the various 'El-gods' in the JE tradition (→El Roi, →El Olam). Whereas the JE tradition may have intended to facilitate the identification of gods also worshipped in post-exilic Palestine or its environs with Yahweh (cf. DE PURY 1989; KNAUF 1991: 25-26), P insists that the 'era of syncretism' is past, and that, →Moses having spoken, the allegiance of every Israelite is due to Yahweh alone.

In Ezek 10:5—hence Shadday in Ezek 1:24, missing in the LXX—El Shadday is a god whose voice is comparable to a considerable storm. In *kĕšōd miššadday yābô'* (referring to the day of Yahweh) Isa 13:6 = Joel 1:15 (6th-4th centuries BCE), Shadday is re-etymologized by the root ŠDD. This understanding of the name may also have influenced the use of Shadday (as the "violent/powerful" god) in Ruth 1:20-21 and Ps 91:1. For Num 24:4.16, Shadday is just another epithet for Yahweh like El or →Elyon (contrary to the widely held opinion of the archaic character of Balaam's oracles, TIMM 1989). In the biblical references, Shadday is a rather universal/cosmic god; not a single attestation refers to the level of 'family religion' (*pace* ALBERTZ 1992:56), or links him specifically with Abraham or his clan (*pace* KNAUF 1985).

In the fictitious list of the heads of Israelite clans in Num 1 (P^s), three names contain the element Shadday: Shede'ur, father of Elizur, from Reuben (v 5); Zurishaddai, father of Shelumi'el, from Shimeon (v 6); and Ammishadday, father of Ahiezer, from Dan. The list, transmitted within a post-exilic literary context, contains orthographically late features (like *pdhṣwr* v 10). Nothing corroborates the view that this late list contains ancient traditions (cf. already KELLERMANN 1970:155-159). The fact that all three Shadday-names appear in the generation preceding Moses' contemporaries suggests that the list was constructed in accordance with Exod 6:3 (P).

The biblical authors used an archaic deity (still worshipped, however, in Arabia at the time of their writing) according to their purposes; they do not testify to an ancient, or widespread, cult of that deity among tribal Israelites or Judaeans, and they contribute little to our knowledge of the nature of that deity before it entered the literary process. That much is clear from the erroneous etymologies involved in the puns employed by these authors: ṮDY in Gen 49:25, ŠDD in Isa 13:6; Joel 1:15. A third aberrant etymology may have led to the Massoretic form with lengthened /d/: **šad-day* "which is sufficient" (cf. *hikanos* as the 'translation' of Shadday in some instances in the LXX).

Although it is always difficult to identify divine characters from iconographic sources and to equate them with deities known from written material, an attempt will be made to connect some iconographically known figures with (El) Shadday. The effort is made under the assumption that with the emergence of the plough and incipient statehood, the 'Great Goddess' of the Neolithic period gave way to a male head of the pantheon (El) and his active son, the weather-god. The goddess was marginalized as 'mistress of the animals', a 'goddess of the wilderness' (*bēlet ṣēri*; in Ugarit, *'ṯtrt šd*, *KTU* 4.182:55; 1.91:10, cf. DAY 1992; for the iconography of the 'mistress of animals' in Palestine during the Middle and Late Bronze ages see KEEL & UEHLINGER 1992: 25, 53, 62). The (neolithic or even pre- neolithic) 'lord of the beasts/god of the wilderness' survived in marginal groups (cf. KEEL & UEHLINGER 1992:206 and see also above for the LB references to El Shadday) and made a powerful come-back in the 12th to the 8th centuries as 'lord of the scorpions' (KEEL & UEHLINGER 1992:132, 147), who developed into a 'lord of the ostriches' in Israel and Judah (KEEL & UEHLINGER 1992:157-158, 196-199, 205) and 'lord of Capridae' in Israel (KEEL & UEHLINGER

1992:206, 317). The desert god connected with the ostriches might be related to Yahweh, who, however, is just one of the 'lords of the beasts' seen in a wider context (not restricted to the kingdoms of Israel and Judah). Although the 'goddess of the wilderness' lost her prominence during the early Iron Age (but did not completely disappear), it is significant that at Tell Deir ʿAllā the Shadday-deities act as lesser gods within a pantheon that is dominated by two goddesses, Shagar and Ashtart. If the national deity Yahweh was present in the local pantheon of Sukkoth at all, he must have been included among the 'gods of the wilderness'.

In the Iron IIC and III periods, i.e. under Assyrian, Babylonian and Persian rule, the iconographic motive of the 'lord of the beasts' was swallowed up by imperial propaganda presenting the 'king of kings' as victor over the chaos of the wild (KEEL & UEHLINGER 1992:330-301.434.438). For the period in which the Bible was written, El Shadday (the 'lord of the beasts') was indeed a memory from a time that had passed, surviving only at the fringes of Palestine among, e.g. the Edomites (cf. KEEL & UEHLINGER 1992:444). El Shadday may thus serve as a prime example of the long way that a deity from ancient Canaan and early Israel had to go until it became an item of OT theology, and of the impossibility of drawing conclusions from this theology regarding the reality of religion in the late 2nd and early first millennium BCE—there were no contemporary inscriptions and pictures to elucidate the life and reality of what was only a faint memory, and a tradition only half understood, for the biblical authors.

In the LXX *šadday* has been rendered with various words and expressions. In the Old Greek version of Job, the rendition (ὁ) παντοκράτωρ, '(the) →Almighty', is predominant. This translation—to be interpreted against its contemporary Hellenistic religious and philosophical background—together with its Latin cognate, *omnipotens*, opened the way for theological speculations concerning omnipotence as a divine attribute.

IV. *Bibliography*

R. ALBERTZ, *Religionsgeschichte Israels in alttestamentlicher Zeit*, Vol. 1 (Göttingen 1992); F. L. BENZ, *Personal Names in the Phoenician and Punic Inscriptions* (StP 8; Rome 1972); E. BLUM, *Studien zur Komposition des Pentateuch* (BZAW 189; Berlin New York 1990); F. GRÖNDAHL, *Die Personennamen der Texte aus Ugarit* (StP 1; Rome 1967); P. L. DAY, Anat: Ugarit's "Mistress of Animals", *JNES* 51 (1992) 181-190; O. KEEL & C. UEHLINGER, *Göttinnen, Götter und Gottessymbole. Neue Erkenntnisse zur Religionsgeschichte Kanaans und Israels aufgrund bislang unerschlossener ikonographischer Quellen* (Freiburg/Basel/Wien 1992); D. KELLERMANN, *Die Priesterschrift von Numeri 1,1 bis 10,10 literarkritisch und traditionsgeschichtlich untersucht* (BZAW 120; Berlin 1970); E. A. KNAUF, El Šaddai, *BN* 16 (1981) 20-26; KNAUF, El Šaddai - der Gott Abrahams? *BZ* 29 (1985) 97-103; KNAUF, War Biblisch-Hebräisch eine Sprache? Empirische Gesichtspunkte zur Annäherung an die Sprache der althebräischen Literatur, *ZAH* 3 (1990) 11-23; KNAUF, Dushara and Shai' al-Qaum. Yhwh und Baal. Dieu, *Lectio difficilior probabilior? L'exégèse comme expérience de décloisonnement. Mélanges offerts à Françoise Smyth-Florentin* (ed. T. Römer; DBAT Beih. 12; Heidelberg 1991) 19-29; M. KÖCKERT, *Vätergott und Väterverheissungen* (FRLANT 142; Göttingen 1988); W. KORNFELD, *Onomastica Aramaica aus Ägypten* (Wien 1978); O. LORETZ, Der kanaanäische Ursprung des biblischen Gottesnamens *El Šaddaj*, *UF* 12 (1980) 420-421; H. NIEHR & G. STEINS, *šaddaj*, *TWAT* 7 (1993) 1078-1104; A. DE PURY, Le cycle de Jacob comme légende autonome des origines d'Israël, *Congress Volume Leuven* (SVT 43; Leiden 1989) 78-96; T. SCHNEIDER, *Asiatische Personennamen in ägyptischen Quellen des Neuen Reiches* (OBO 114; Fribourg/Göttingen 1992); S. TIMM, *Moab zwischen den Mächten. Studien zu historischen Denkmälern und Texten* (Wiesbaden 1989); H. WEIPPERT & M. WEIPPERT, Die "Bileam"-Inschrift von Tell Dēr ʿAllā,

ZDPV 98 (1982) 77-103; M. WEIPPERT, Šaddaj (Gottesname), *THAT* II (1976) 873-881.

E. A. KNAUF

SHAHAN

I. In the biblical toponym Beth-shean (בית־שׁאן or בית־שׁן, Josh 17:11.16; Judg 1:27; 1 Sam 31:10.12; 2 Sam 21:12; 1 Kgs 4:12; 1 Chr 7:29), JIRKU detected a reference to the Babylonian deity Šaḫan (1926:84).

II. In Old Babylonian texts the god Šaḫan occurs a number of times as theophoric element in personal names and place-names; it is always preceded by the divine determinative (references KREBERNIK 1984). So far, only one independent attestation of the deity is known. One Warad-Šaḫan refers to himself in the inscription on his cylinder seal as "servant of the god Šaḫan" (YOS 14 no. 68). Little is known about the deity. Though identified once with the god Irḫan (→Euphrates), the two are to be distinguished; confusion could arise because [d]*Ir-ḫa-an* has sometimes mistakenly been read as [d]*Sa-ḫa-an*.

III. A connection of Šaḫan with the element *šĕʾān* or *šan* in the place name Beth-shan is unlikely on more than one count. The element Shan could reflect the name of a god: Egyptian writings of the name (*btsir*, *Ges.*[18] 148) sometimes denote the last element as a foreign deity by including the 'inverted legs' sign (S. AḤITUV, *Canaanite Toponyms in Ancient Egyptian Documents* [Jerusalem 1984] 78-79). Such a qualification could also be explained, though, if the Egyptian rendering were to go back to Heb *bêt-šĕʾôl*, 'Necropolis', since the netherworld (→Sheol) and the →dead could both be ascribed divine status. The name Beth-shan ('House of rest') would then have to be considered as a euphemistic correction of the original toponym (SEEBASS 1979:170). Should Shan nevertheless refer to a god, the toponym would compare to such names as Beth-Dagon, Bethel, and Beth-Horon. Yet the god could hardly be identified with Šaḫan. Phonetically, it is difficult to conceive that a hard guttural such as the Akkadian ḫ should become a mere *aleph* in Hebrew, or be dropped altogether (note that the reference to [d]*Ša-an* quoted by JIRKU 1927 cannot be sustained; a reading *An-ša-an* is more likely). There is, however, a more satisfying solution to the etymology of Beth-shan. The root šʾN is well attested in the Semitic languages, and has the meaning 'to be peaceful, quiet'. Beth-shan is therefore most likely to be interpreted as 'House of rest' (*HALAT* 1280).

IV. *Bibliography*

A. JIRKU, Zur Götterwelt Palästina und Syriens, *Sellin-Festschrift. Beiträge zur Religionsgeschichte und Archäologie Palästinas* (ed. A. Jirku; Leipzig 1927) 83-86, esp. 83-84; M. KREBERNIK, *Die Beschwörungen aus Fara und Ebla* (Hildesheim 1984) 333-334 n. 185; H. SEEBASS, Der israelitische Name der Burcht von Bēsān und der Name Beth Schean, *ZDPV* 95 (1979) 166-172.

K. VAN DER TOORN

SHAHAR שׁחר

I. In the Hebrew Bible *šaḥar* "dawn" appears in a variety of prose and poetic texts (23 times), in three personal names, a place-name, and the superscription of a psalm. It is possible that a few of these were understood to allude to a deity. Cognates of *šaḥar* occur as a divine name at Ugarit (*Šḥr*), at Emar (*Šaḫru*, *Emar* nos. 369:24, 52; 371:10), and in Old South Arabic (*Sḥr*), and may be interpreted as referring to a deity in personal names in various Semitic languages.

The Akkadian cognate, *šēru*, may refer specifically to the morning star and as such occurs as a deity in several personal names, e.g. *Šērum-malik, Šērum-tukulti, Šērum-ili* (*AHW* 1219a). In West Semitic texts of the first millennium *šḥr* (the f. form, *šḥrt*, in Moabite) appears only as a common noun except in personal names, where its function is often ambiguous. It is clearly theophoric in such names as *ʿbdšḥr* (Punic).

II. The Ugaritic *šḥr*, used with the meanings "dawn" and "tomorrow", also sometimes refers to "the morning star" as a deity. In the god list *KTU* 1.123:11 *šḫr w šlm* (*Shaḫru wa Shalimu*, "Dawn and Dusk" or "Morning Star and Evening Star") appear among several divine pairs. They reappear with some of the same pairs in *KTU* 1.107:18, in which they join the Sun-goddess in collecting snake venom. In *KTU* 1.100:52, along with several of the same gods, they fail to dispose of the snake's venom. *KTU* 1.23:49-54 recounts their siring by →El, their birth, and their placement with the sun(-goddess) and →stars.

Their residence is also given as the heavens in *KTU* 1.100:52. It is moot whether the Shahru and Shalimu of *KTU* 1.23.49-54 are identical with the lovely and beautiful, but also cruel and voracious, gods who are the chief subject of the text. Like the sun, dawn/the morning star has links both with the heavens and the underworld. At Emar, *Šaḫru* appears alongside underworld deities as the object of offerings (*Emar* no. 369:24-25). The same Emar text also links *Šaḫru* with the storm god. The Hurrian (and eventually Hittite) deities, Sheri and Hurri (→Day and →Night), may share some features with *šḫr w šlm*. They are portrayed as the divine bulls that pull the storm god's chariot and intercede with him on behalf of supplicants. Old South Arabic *Šḥr* is often found in collocation with ʿAthtar and with a →dragon's head as associated symbol.

III. In prose and in one poetic passage (Hos 10:15) *šaḥar* appears in temporal references, but in several poetic passages in the Bible it has been claimed that *šaḥar* refers to a deity. Unfortunately, so little is known of the mythology of Shaḫru that such allusions cannot be demonstrated; and in most contexts it seems likely that the Israelite poets are using poetic expressions without assuming divine associations.

As a natural phenomenon *šaḥar* was created by God (Amos 4:13) who gave it its allotted place, as implied in the rhetorical question of Job 38:12. Despite the mythological allusions of the surrounding verses, the personification of dawn in Job 38:13, which speaks of it taking the edges of the earth as if it were a cloth and shaking off the wicked, is probably to be understood as a poetic portrayal of the disappearance of nocturnal miscreants at the break of day. Dawn is also personified in a single clause in Ps 57:9 = 108:3: "I will wake up dawn!" The context of both verses is an extended, enthusiastic announcement of praise to God, in which harp and lyre are also called upon to "wake up".

In four texts *šaḥar* is used in a simile. It is an image of a bride looking down (i.e. from a window; Cant 6:10; the parallel terms for "sun" and →"moon" avoid the nouns that are also used of deities); the crack of dawn is an image of the inauguration of a new era (Isa 58:8); the coming of dawn is an image of what is reliable (Hos 6:3; also 1QH 4,6); the spread of dawn across the hills is an image of an invading hoard (of locusts; Joel 2:2). An actual—rather than a deified—dawn serves as a perfect image in all these cases, with the possible exception of Cant 6:10; and there a goddess would fit better than a god.

Job prays that the day of his birth might not see the "eyelids of dawn" (some insist that *ʿpʿpym* means "eyes"; Job 3:9). This refers not to a detail of a divine image, but to opening eyelids as a poetic image of the first appearance of light on the horizon. The same expression appears as an image of →Leviathan's eyes (Job 41:10). Ps 139:9 refers to the *kanpê* ("wings" or "skirts") of dawn (opposed to the remotest sea)—i.e. the eastern (as opposed to the western) edge of the world. While the context refers to mythological cosmology, the parallelism does not suggest divine associations.

Finally, in Isa 14 former rulers now in the underworld greet the fall of the king of Babylon, recalling how he had said he would erect his →throne above the divine →stars (*kôkĕbê ʾēl*) on the mount of assembly in the far north and become like →Elyon (vv 13-14). The clearly mythological references in this passage suggest that the terms in which he is addressed—*Hêlēl ben šaḥar* "Day Star, son of Dawn" (v 12)—are also mythological. The divine Shahar may be the father of the Morning Star in an unknown myth, or the patronymic may be a poetic conceit—thus LXX naturalizes it: "which rises early" (similarly Vg).

The present context of each of these verses generally allows them clear and rich meaning without reference to the deity, and there is no observable connection between them and the few mythological data currently known concerning the extra-biblical *Šaḥru*. It remains possible, however, that one or more of these expressions were traditionally associated with the deity, and that such associations might be evoked in the minds of those who knew of the deity or his mythology.

Two late biblical names, *'ăḥîšāḥar* (1 Chr 7:10) and *Šĕḥaryâ* (1 Chr 8:26), probably reflect the common noun (cf. the comparison of Yahweh with the dawn in literary passages—e.g. Deut 33:2; Isa 60:1-2; Mal 3:20). The same is true of the several hypocoristica consisting only of the element *šḥr* found on inscriptions. The name *Šaḥărayim* (1 Chr 8:8), if genuine, probably reflects the time of the bearer's birth (M. NOTH, *IPN*, 223 n. 5).

The remaining references are less clear. In Isa 8:20 *šaḥar* may be either the common noun ("he shall have no dawn") or possibly a different word. A mythological reference to the womb of Shahar(!) has been seen in Ps 110:3, but the whole verse is obscure. While it is possible that the deity is referred to in the place name *Ṣeret haššaḥar* (Josh 13:19) and in the phrase *'ayyelet haššaḥar* "Hind of the Dawn" (in the superscription of Ps 22:1) the reference in both is too uncertain to warrant any commitment.

IV. *Bibliography*

G. DEL OLMO LETE, *Mitos y Leyendas de Canaan* (Madrid 1981) 427-448; H. GESE, M. HÖFNER & K. RUDOLPH, *RAAM* 80-82, 168-169, 253, 271-272, 317; A. JIRKU, 'Ajjelet haš-Šaḥar (Ps 22_1), *ZAW* 65 (1953) 85-86; J. W. MCKAY, Helel and the Dawn-Goddess. A re-examination of the myth in Isaiah XIV 12-15, *VT* 20 (1970) 451-464; S. A. MEIER, Shahar, *ABD* 5 (1992) 1150-1151; J. H. TIGAY, *You Shall Have No Other Gods: Israelite Religion in the Light of Hebrew Inscriptions* (HSS 31; Atlanta 1986) 79 n. 26, 80; H. WILDBERGER, *Jesaja* (BKAT X/2; Neukirchen 1978) 550-553.

S. B. PARKER

SHALEM שלם

I. Shalem (presumably the divine power symbolized by Venus as the Evening Star) occurs as a deity (*Šlm*/Salim) in the texts from Ugarit and may well occur as a divine name Šalim/Salim in personal names among the earliest known Semites of Mesopotamia and the later Amorites. Shalem is interpreted as a divine name in the place names Jerusalem (*yĕrûšālaim*) and Salem (*Šālēm*), and is also interpreted as a theophoric element in some personal names, notably those of David's sons Absalom (*'Abšālôm*) and Solomon (*Šĕlōmōh*).

II. The brief Ugaritic mythological text *KTU* 1.23, known as 'The Gracious and Beautiful Gods', is the most important source concerning the god Shalem. In this text, primarily a fertility ritual, Šalim (Evening Star) is linked with Šahar (Morning Star) as offspring of the head of the pantheon, →El, and two 'women' he encountered by the seashore. These two gods, aspects of Athtar/Venus, are nursed by 'the Lady', surely →Anat or Athirat (→Asherah), and have insatiable appetites—'(one) lip to the earth, (one) lip to the heavens', like →Mot. They symbolize the powerful new life associated with the sacred marriage. In other texts (*KTU* 1.100; 107) the two gods are associated with the sun goddess. In the texts from Ugarit, Shalem also occurs separately in the god lists (Ug *Šlm*; Akk *Salimu*). The occurrences of *šlm*/*šalim* in personal names at Ugarit may be taken as a divine name or as an epithet (*RSP* 3.487). Attempts to characterize Shalem beyond the evidence from Ugarit, e.g. as connected with child sacrifice (STOLZ 1970:205-209), reflect speculative reconstruction. The nature of Shalem remains little known (HANDY 1992).

The earliest possible attestations of

Šalim/Salim occur in Pre-Sargonic and Sargonic personal names (GELB 1957:273; ROBERTS 1972:51, 113). But in these names, like the Old Assyrian and Amorite names with Šalim/Salim, one cannot clearly distinguish a divine epithet from an unmarked divine name. (Many divine names, of course, derive from epithets.) In many of the personal names Šalim/Salim can be interpreted as a deity (as known from Ugarit)—although the element is not marked as a divine name—or as a divine/human epithet, '... the complete/healthy one'. In names with kinship terms that presumably denote the name-bearer as a substitute for a deceased family member, i.e. a substitution name, *šalim/salim* is an epithet of the child, 'the/my 'kin' is healthy' (STAMM 1939:294-295). The latest possible occurrences of the West Semitic deity Šalim, in Phoenician-Punic personal names (BENZ 1972:417-418), some of which are semantically equivalent to the much earlier Sargonic names, present the same problems in interpretation.

III. Shalem is not directly attested in the Bible, although there are various possible traces of this deity. Central to all reconstructions is the place name, Jerusalem (*Yĕrûšāla[y]im*, ketiv *Yĕrûšālēm*), commonly interpreted as 'Foundation of (the deity) Shalem'.

Actually, Jerusalem as the name of the city is attested already in the Egyptian Execration Texts (nineteenth century BCE), which mention *ʾwšʾmm*, representing *R(a)wuš()l-m-m* (HELCK 1962:52, 59), and Jerusalem occurs in the Amarna letters (mid-fourteenth century BCE) as Urusalim. This means that the connection of the city with Shalem—if the proposed etymology is correct—dates from at least the early second millennium BCE. Such a connection is further supported by the identification of →Melchizedek as king of Salem (*Šālēm*) in Gen 14:18, a place name usually interpreted as a variant of Jerusalem, as in Ps 76:3 and in much of the post-biblical Jewish tradition. The further identification of Melchizedek as a priest of El Elyon (→Most High)—El being the father of Šalim in Ugaritic mythology—is also quite significant. Surely El (Elyon) and other Canaanite—and non-Canaanite—gods were worshipped in Jerusalem prior to David's capture of the city in the early tenth century BCE. Since →Shahar, closely linked with Shalem at Ugarit, is mentioned in the Bible (Isa 14:12), a cult of Shalem is quite plausible. But the direct evidence for the continuing cult of Shalem in the city bearing the deity's name is rather questionable. The most widely cited evidence comes from the names of two of David's sons, namely, Absalom (*ʾAbšālôm*, LXX *Abessalom* = Heb **ʾAbîšālôm*) and Solomon (*Šĕlōmōh*). (The objection that Absalom is born in Hebron, prior to the capture of Jerusalem, is countered by the observation that Absalom's mother is the daughter of the king of Geshur, an Aramaean realm, and that she may have abetted the recognition of 'foreign' gods. Solomon, of course, was born in Jerusalem.) These two names, if revocalized as *šālēm* (which overlaps semantically with *šālôm*), could be viewed as recognition of the Canaanite god Shalem, and many scholars so argue (GRAY 1965: 185-186; STOLZ 1970:9, 204). However, in either vocalization the names most probably represent the large class of personal names that express the sense of substitution for a deceased relative. The name *ʾAb(î)šālôm*, 'My Father is at Peace', honours a deceased father or grandfather, whereas the name *Šĕlōmōh* indicates 'His (David's?) Peace', or, more probably, 'His (the deceased's) Healthiness' (STAMM 1980:45-57). The element *šlm* is also known in personal names in Hebrew inscriptions, with the same issues in interpretation (TIGAY 1986:67-69, 79-80). The altar that Gideon erected in Ophrah, called *Yhwh šālôm* (Judg 6:24), is alternatively interpreted as identification of →Yahweh with the deity Shalem or with the epithet 'ally', a bringer of peace (TIGAY 1986:69).

Rather more speculative are connections of Shalem with the supposed cult of the Venus star in Jerusalem and with the plausible cult of Ṣedeq (GRAY 1965:184-185;

STOLZ 1970)—Melchizedek and Adonizedek provide a connection with Jerusalem. Ṣedeq provides another example of the interplay between divine epithets and divine names. For Shalem, the 'evening star', connections have even been suggested with the Star of Bethlehem.

IV. *Bibliography*

F. L. BENZ, *Personal Names in the Phoenician and Punic Inscriptions* (Rome 1972); I. J. GELB, *Glossary of Old Akkadian* (MAD 3; Chicago 1957); J. GRAY, *The Legacy of Canaan* (VTSup 5; Leiden 1965); L. K. HANDY, Shalem, *ABD* 5 (1992) 1152-1153; W. HELCK, *Die Beziehungen Ägyptens zu Vorderasien im 3. und 2. Jahrtausend v. Chr.* (Wiesbaden 1962); F. B. KNUTSON, *RSP* 3 (1981) 471-500; J. J. M. ROBERTS, *The Earliest Semitic Pantheon* (Baltimore 1972); J. J. STAMM, *Die akkadische Namengebung* (MVAÄG 44; Leipzig 1939); STAMM, *Beiträge zur hebräischen und altorientalischen Namenkunde* (OBO 30; Freiburg 1980); F. STOLZ, *Strukturen und Figuren im Kult von Jerusalem* (BZAW 118; Berlin 1970) 181-218; J. H. TIGAY, *You Shall Have No Other Gods. Israelite Religion in the Light of Hebrew Inscriptions* (Atlanta 1986).

H. B. HUFFMON

SHALMAN

I. The name of king Solomon has, among other things (*HALAT* 1425), been interpreted as related to an Arabic deity *s/šlmn* (M. HÖFNER, *RAAM* 372; *WbMyth* I, 466-467). This deity can, probably, be equated with the West Semitic god Shalman /Shalaman.

II. The oldest attestation of the deity occurs as a theophoric element in the Middle-Assyrian personal name ^{d}*Sa-la-ma-an-mu-šab-ši* (C. SAPORETTI, *Onomastica medio-assira* [StP 6; Roma 1970] 387). In an Egyptian votive stela from the 20-21st dynasty a deity (*Ršp*)-*Šl/rmn* is attested (R. STADELMAN, *Syrisch-palästinensische Gottheiten in Ägypten* [Leiden 1967] 55). In Ugaritic personal names the (theophoric) element *šlmn* occurs (F. GRÖNDAHL, *Die Personennamen der Texte aus Ugarit* [StP 1; Roma 1967] 193. 414). The Egyptian and the Ugaritic attestations have been interpreted as referring to a deity →Shulman (e.g. W. F. ALBRIGHT, The Syro-Mesopotamian God Šulman-Ešmun and Related Figures, *AfO* 9 [1931-32] 164-169) as well as to Shalman (HELCK 1971). The element *Salaman* occurs in personal names from Neo-Assyrian deeds and documents without, however, the determinative for gods (TIMM 1989:317). In a Neo-Assyrian contract on the selling of a woman, ^{d}*Sal-ma-nu* is mentioned alongside Ashur (→Assur) and Shamash (→Shemesh) as one of the prosecutors for the buyer (ND 7091 = S. DALLEY & J. H. POSTGATE, *The Tablets from Fort Shalmaneser* [CTN 3; Oxford 1984] 47:24). The name of a Moabite king ^{p}*Sa-la-ma-nu* (Tiglath-Pileser III Display inscription from Nimrud:10'; *TUAT* I/4) and the Edomite personal name *šlmnʿbd* (Ostracon 6:1; J. R. BARTLETT, *Edom and the Edomites* [JSOTSup 77; Sheffield 1989] 219) have been interpreted as containing the theophoric element Shalman (TIMM 1989:315-318). In Hatra, Palmyra and in North and South Arabian texts the deity *s/šlmn* is attested. According to HÖFNER (*WbMyth* I, 466-467) Shalman must be interpreted as a horseman's deity. The god survived until Seleucid and Roman-Byzantine times (TIMM 1989:315n43).

III. The name of king Solomon can better related to the verb ŠLM and the noun *šālôm*, 'peace', than with a deity Shalman. The personal name *šalman* (Hos 10:14) cannot be regarded an OT attestation of Shalman. The text contains the memory of "the ravaging of Beth-arbel by Shalman on the day of battle" and may refer to an attack on the Israelite town by an Assyrian monarch Shalmaneser, perhaps Shalmaneser III in the mid-9th century BCE (ASTOUR 1971; TIMM 1989:319-320). The name of the Assyrian king Shalmaneser (2 Kgs 17:3; 18:9) contains the theophoric element →Shulman.

IV. *Bibliography*

M. C. ASTOUR, 841 BC, The First Assyrian

Invasion of Israel, *JAOS* 91 (1971) 383-389; W. HELCK, *Die Beziehungen Ägyptens zu Vorderasien im 3. und 2. Jahrtausend v. Chr.* (Wiesbaden 1971) 452; M. HÖFNER (& E. MERKEL), Salman (Salmān), *WbMyth* I, 466-467; S. TIMM, *Moab zwischen den Mächten* (ÄAT 17; Wiesbaden 1989) 311-320.

B. BECKING

SHAUSHKA

I. Shaushka can be treated as an important Hurrian goddess. Her name is written either in syllabic (e.g. *ᵈŠa-(u)-uš-ga*) or in ideographic form (e.g. *ᵈIŠTAR(-ka)*) in texts from Boghazköy, Nuzi or Alalakh; alphabetic texts from Ugarit spell her name *šušk* or *šwšk*. In Jer 25:26; 51:41 the name Sheshach has been erroneously interpreted as a reference to this goddess.

II. The ideographic spelling of the name suggests that Shaushka is connected with →Ishtar (of Niniveh) with whom she shares some characteristic features. The centre of her cult was southern Anatolia and northern Syria; but during the time of the Hittite Empire she enjoyed great popularity; thus Hattushili III made her his tutelary goddess. Her place within the family of the gods is not entirely certain: according to some texts Anu or →Sîn is her father; the weather-god Teshub (→Hadad) is her brother and husband in texts from the eastern Hurrian sphere and from Ugarit; Hittite texts say that Hebat is Teshub's wife, though. To Shaushka's circle belong some minor deities; most notably Ninatta and Kulitta who accompany her as musicians and hierodules.

The reliefs at Yazılıkaya near Boghazköy show the goddess twice: relief no. 56 presents her with the goddesses, relief no. 38 with the male gods; the fact that she has male and female characteristics is also evident from Hittite texts about Shaushka of Lawazantiya: She is clothed like a man and like a woman (KUB XXXI 69:5-6), and has male attributes such as an axe or weapons. Sometimes this has been taken as a sign of her bisexual (androgynous) character but this is not absolutely certain. Shaushka's male and female aspects can also be connected with her role as goddess of love and war. Her warlike traits may interfere with her role as patroness of love; though she is usually said to promote harmony and conjugal love, some texts say that her love (and sexuality) is unpredictable or even dangerous. A similar ambivalence surrounds Shaushka when it comes to magic and healing. In some Hurrian texts she is the goddess from whom the magicians, whether male or female, obtain their power; in this respect she resembles the Luwian goddess Kamrushepa; Shaushka's main preserve is sexual magic because she can change the sex of men and women; according to KUB XV 35 she is able to take manliness, virility and vitality away from men, further to take their weapons, bows and arrows and give them spindle and distaff instead and clothe them in female fashion; women she can rob of motherhood and love. In the so-called 'soldiers' oath' (KBo VI 34), garments of a woman, a distaff and a mirror are shown to the soldiers; these will be their proper assets if they break their soldiers' oath. A ritual text against impotence (KUB VII 5+) can be cited too: here the magician gives a bow and an arrow to the impotent man and says "I have taken womanliness away from you and given you back manliness. You have cast off the ways of a woman, now show the ways of a man". Bow and arrow, on the one hand, and distaff and mirror, on the other, are the typical symbols of the goddess of war and love. Her magic is able to heal as well as to destroy.

Being an important Hurrian goddess in Northern Syria and Anatolia, Shaushka is celebrated in various cults. In nearly all major festivals she receives offerings; her cult centre was located at Samukha, a town situated near the upper Halys or the upper Euphrates; other famous cult centres for her are Alalakh, Nuzi, as well as Ugarit.

III. There is no direct reference to this goddess in the OT. SARSOWSKY's (1914) proposal that Sheshach (Jer 25:26; 51:41) was an appellation of Assyria because

Shaushka was an Assyrian goddess cannot be maintained. Sheshach does not mean 'the land of the goddess Shaushka'; it is most probably to be interpreted as an *atbash* kind of cryptogram for Babylon (HOLLADAY 1986:675).

However, Shaushka may be relevant for the understanding of some other biblical passages. Phenomenologically we can find the idea of Shaushka's changing peoples' sexuality in Deut 22:5 where it is forbidden for a woman to dress like a man and for a man to dress like a woman (RÖMER 1982 relates this to the Mesopotamian Ishtar). Another point of Shaushka's biblical connections can be seen in relation to the →Queen of Heaven. Shaushka was not only the daughter of Anu. In northern Syria she was also assimilated to other goddesses such as →Anat. In the first millennium →Astarte or →Atargatis are reminiscent of Shaushka. As all these Syrian goddesses influence the OT's references to the Queen of Heaven, one might also be entitled to assume that Shaushka's character was not unknown in ancient Israel. Archaeological material seems to point to familiarity with her within the geographical area of the OT: she is depicted on the Hittite ivory from Megiddo (ALEXANDER 1991), though we do not know precisely how this ivory dated to the second half of the 2nd millennium BCE reached Megiddo.

IV. *Bibliography*

R. A. ALEXANDER, Šaušga and the Hittite Ivory from Megiddo, *JNES* 50 (1991) 161-182; W. L. HOLLADAY, *Jeremiah 1* (Hermeneia; Philadelphia 1986); W. H. P. RÖMER, Einige Überlegungen zur heiligen Hochzeit nach altorientalischen Texten, *Von Kanaan bis Kerala. FS van der Ploeg* (AOAT 211; Kevelaer & Neukirchen 1982) 411-428; A. SARSOWSKY, ששך and זמרי, *ZAW* 34 (1914) 64-68; I. WEGNER, *Gestalt und Kult der Ištar-Šawuška in Kleinasien* (AOAT 36; Kevelaer & Neukirchen-Vluyn 1981).

M. HUTTER

SHEAN → SHAHAN

SHEBEN שׁבן

I. The element *šbn*, Sheben, which occurs in various Hebrew personal names, may be theophoric. From the limited evidence available, it is likely that a divinity Sheben was known in Levantine culture. If so, all that is known of the god for the time being is its name.

II. A Neopunic inscription on a sepulchre from Sardina (*CIS* I, 152) lists as one donor *ʿbdmlqrt [b]n bdʾ [b]n ʾḥšbn*, 'Abd-Melqart, [s]on of Bodo, [s]on of Ahsheben'. It has been observed (S. HARRIS, *A Grammar of the Phoenician Language* [New Haven 1936] 66) that Phoenician contains a plethora of construct-state names expressing the relationship of the bearer to the deity and that such names are those meaning 'son', 'daughter', 'brother', 'sister', 'male-slave', and 'female-slave'. Such construct-phrase names are constructed on the pattern of a common noun followed by a divine name in which the common noun is nomen regens while the divine name is nomen rectum (BENZ 1972:225). In the above inscription *ʿbdmlqrt* surely means 'Slave-of Melqart'. As for *ʾḥšbn*, it may also be a construct-state name, meaning 'brother of Sheben'. Because Phoenician and Punic orthography do not distinguish a suffix ending from a construct singular (BENZ 1972:232), however, and because this inscription is not accompanied by a transcription into Greek or Latin, the name *ʾḥšbn* might equally reflect a pronunciation Aḥî-Šeben. This would have been understood as a nominal sentence 'My-brother-is-Sheben' (XELLA 1975:81). The construct-state pattern, though common in Phoenician, is rare in other Semitic languages (HARRIS 1936:66). The nominal interpretation would provide *ʾḥšbn* with numerous onomastic structural parallels (NOTH *IPN* 66-75). In either case, *-šbn* would appear to be the name of a god, but one whose sex would not be determinable on the construct-state interpretation.

Another possible attestion of this divinity

is in the name *ʿbdʾšbn* in which the *aleph* can be taken as a mater lectionis, as in the names *ḥnʾmlk*, and *mtnʾbʿl* (XELLA 1975:82). It cannot be discounted, however, that *ʿbnʾšbn* is a misspelling of the extremely common *ʿbdʾšmn* (BENZ 1972:150).

Possible early traces of this divinity may be adduced from Ugarit (XELLA 1975:82). In *UT* 10:24, *šbn* is a proper name. In *UT* 1052:5, it could either be a personal name or a toponym which is attested in the Akkadian texts of Ugarit: e.g. URU *šub-ba-ni.* (*UT* Glossary no. 2379; XELLA 1975:82). Ugaritic (*UT* 15:1) may provide the closest parallel to the Neopunic reference in *btšbn* (XELLA 1975:82).

III. Various Hebrew proper names, such as *šbnʾ*; *šbnyh*, *šbnyw*; and *šbnyhw* (*HALAT*), attested in the Bible and epigraphically, may shed some light on the problem. Yet the traditional explanation of these names, which takes the element *šbn* as a finite form of the verb *ŠBN (NOTH, *IPN*, no. 1303), is not seriously undermined by possible attestations of a deity Sheben. The combination with the divine name *yh* or *yhw* makes it unlikely that *šbn* in Hebrew anthroponyms serves as the name of a—pagan—god (cf. J. H. TIGAY, *You Shall Have No Other Gods* [HSM 31; Atlanta 1986] 61-62).

IV. *Bibliography*

F. L. BENZ, *Personal Names in the Phoenician and Punic Inscriptions* (Rome 1972); P. XELLA, Un dio punico šbn?, *RSF* 3 (1975) 81-83.

S. D. SPERLING

SHECHEM → THUKAMUNA

SHEGER שגר

I. The word *šeger* occurs six times in the Hebrew Bible, always in connection with the offspring of cattle. The stereotyped expression *šĕgar ʾălāpêkā*, forming a fixed pair with *ʿaštĕrôt ṣôʾnkā*, 'the offspring of your flock' (Deut 7:13; 28:4.18.51), refers to the increase of herds. Whereas the *peṭer-reḥem* designates the human firstborn (literally 'that which opens up the womb'), the *peṭer šeger bĕhēmâ* is the firstborn of cattle (Exod 13:12). In the Hebrew text of Sir 40:19 *šgr* is mentioned alongside *nṭʿ* ('orchard') in the meaning of '(young) cattle'; both blessings are inferior to a devoted wife (for a synopsis of the Hebrew, Greek, Latin, and Syriac texts see F. VATTIONI, *Ecclesiasticus* [Napoli 1968] 216-217). Outside the Hebrew Bible Sheger occurs as a deity in Ugaritic texts, a Punic personal name, and—perhaps—the Deir ʿAllā inscription.

II. In Ugaritic texts, the god *Šgr* is mentioned twice in a broken passage of the Baal cycle (*KTU* 1.5 iii:16, 17), and once in an offering list (*KTU* 1.148:31). In the latter text *Šgr* forms a binomial pair with the god *iṯm* (*šgr w iṯm*; →Asham). In RS 1992. 2004:14 (reading and interpretation courtesy D. Arnaud) the entry corresponding to *šgr w iṯm* is **ᵈḫar** *ù* **ᵈgir₃**, indicating that *iṯm* is the Ugaritic equivalent of the Mesopotamian deity Ishum (cf. →Fire), and that *šgr* is parallel to Mesopotamian Shaggar. The identification of Shaggar with a moon deity is explicit in Hieroglyphic Hittite correspondences to syllabically written personal names (ᵈ30 = sà-ga+ra/i; cf. E. LAROCHE, *Akkadica* 22 [1981] 11; H. GONNET, *apud* D. ARNAUD, *Textes syriens de l'âge du bronze récent* [AuOr Suppl 1; Barcelona 1991] 199.207). It appears thus that this deity not only had a connection with small cattle (as suggested by the biblical evidence) but also with the moon, and the pair *šgr w iṯm* therefore shows a certain similarity to the *ad hoc* pair *yrḫ w ršp* (*KTU* 1.107:15). Given the fact that Yarihu is the primary lunar deity at Ugarit and Rashap (→Resheph) the primary underworld deity, Shaggar and Yarihu would bear a functional resemblance to each other, Shaggar being perhaps the deity of the full moon. It is not without significance, in this connection, that in an Emar ritual the fifteenth day of the month is ascribed to Shaggar (*Emar* no. 373:42). This lunar god Shaggar is to be distinguished from ᵈḪAR/ᵈ*sag-gar* the deified Jebel Sinjar (STOL 1979). Note that the personal name which Arnaud read as ᴵ*Itti-Šagru* (short for *Iddin-^{d}Šagru*, 'Sheger-has-given') is rather to be analysed as ^{I}*Itti-ša-aqru* (J.-M. DURAND, review of *Emar*, *RA* 84 [1990] 62).

The occurrence of Sheger (alongside 'Ashtar) in the Deir 'Allā text (Combination I 14[16]) is not very revealing. It is unclear whether the terms are used as divine names ('full moon' and 'morning star') or merely as words for animal offspring (cf. J. A. HACKETT, *The Balaam Text from Deir 'Allā* [HSM 31; Chico 1984] 41; H.-P. MÜLLER, Einige alttestamentliche Probleme zur aramäischen Inschrift von *Dēr 'Allā*, *ZDPV* 94 [1978] 56-67, esp. 64-65; MÜLLER, Die aramäische Inschrift von Deir 'Allā und die älteren Bileamsprüche, *ZAW* 94 [1982] 214-244, esp. 230; H. & M. WEIPPERT, Die "Bileam"-Inschrift von Tell Dēr 'Allā, *ZDPV* 98 [1982] 77-103, esp. 100-101). That Shaggar was still known as a deity in the first millennium BCE is reflected by the theophoric name *'bdšgr* ('servant of Sheger') in a Punic inscription (F. L. BENZ, *Personal Names in the Phoenician and Punic Inscriptions* [Rome 1972] 163, 413).

Further information on Shaggar (Sheger) is provided by the biblical data. The combination with →Astarte (whether the plural form *'aštĕrôt* is a real plural or an artificial vocalisation based on a misunderstanding of the form *'štrt* is a delicate matter), suggests that Sheger is connected with fertility. Because in Exod 13:12 *šeger* as a symbol of animal fertility contrasts with the female womb as a symbol of human fertility, *šeger* has been interpreted as 'the womb of beasts' (FEIGIN 1926). Etymologically, however, the meaning 'offspring' is preferable (cf. *HALAT* 1315 s.v. *שֶׁגֶר). The connection between Shaggar as a deity of full moon and Shaggar (Sheger) as a deity of the fertility of cattle is not as far-fetched as it may seem; the influence of the moon on conception and birth was a widespread tenet in the ancient Near East (see e.g. P. DERCHAIN et al., *La lune: mythes et rites* [SO 5; Paris 1962] 33-35, 100).

III. The central issue in the discussion of the biblical occurrences of *šeger* is whether or not the word was originally the name of a deity (see, e.g. DELCOR 1974:14; LORETZ 1990). STAMM (1990) regards the development from a common noun to a proper divine name the most plausible reconstruction; this would mean that the biblical usage has retained the original non-hypostasized meaning. This explanation would have to hold for Astarte and →Dagon as well—which is quite unlikely. Originally, there was no clear distinction in the Near East between grain (Dagan), wine (→Tirosh), increase of cattle (Sheger), and the fecundity of the flocks ('Ashtaroth), on the one hand, and the deities responsible for these things, on the other. The occurrence of the foursome in Deut 7:13 (cf. M. WEINFELD, *Deuteronomy 1-11* [AB 5; New York 1991] 373) marks a point where the link between the phenomena and their gods has been severed; there is hardly a trace left of the mythological background of the concepts.

IV. *Bibliography*

M. ASTOUR, Some New Divine Names from Ugarit, *JAOS* 86 (1966) 277-284, esp. 281; M. DELCOR, Astarté et la fécondité des troupeaux en Deut. 7,13 et parallèles, *UF* 6 (1974) 7-14; S. FEIGIN, שגר, "Womb of Beasts", *AJSL* 43 (1926) 44-53; J. HOFTIJZER & G. VAN DER KOOIJ, *Aramaic Texts from Deir 'Alla* (Leiden 1976) 273-274; O. LORETZ, *Ugarit und die Bibel* (Darmstadt 1990) 87; J. J. STAMM *et al.*, *HALAT*, Vol. 4 (1990) 1316; M. STOL, *On Trees, Mountains, and Millstones in the Ancient Near East* (Leiden 1979) 75-77.

K. VAN DER TOORN

SHELAH שלח

I. Shelaḥ has been interpreted as a theophoric element in the personal names *Mĕtûšālaḥ* (Gen 5:21.22.25-27; 1 Chr 1:3) *Šālaḥ* (Gen 10:24; 11:14; 1 Chr 1:18) and *Šilḥî* (1 Kgs 22:42; 2 Chr 20:31). He has been interpreted as the god of the infernal river of the Canaanite population of Palestine and Phoenicia (TSEVAT 1954). In Ugarit *šlḥ* is one of the names of the river of death.

II. The deity occurs in the Phoenician

personal names אבשלח (HARRIS 1936:27; not attested in BENZ); שלח (RES 906:2); משלח (CIS 4207:5) and אשרשלח (CIS 65.1-2; BENZ 1972:416). This last name has been interpreted as an explanatory name: 'Osiris is *Šālaḥ*' (TSEVAT 1954:45). This identification would identify Shelah as a deity of the underworld, like →Osiris.

In the Baal-cycle from Ugarit, in a paradoxical passage on love and death, →Baal makes love with a young cow beside the river of death, the *šlḥ* (*KTU* 1.5 [Baal V] v 19). In the epic on Keret, *šlḥ* occurs as the deified river of death. In the description of the awful fate of the seven wives of Keret, it is stated that 'his seventh wife fell [sc: to death] by *šlḥ*' (*KTU* 1.14 [Keret I] i:20-21; LORETZ 1975; DIETRICH & LORETZ 1987: 204 n.67; contra VERREET 1990:331). This passage implies that Shelah should be identified as a deified form of the river of the death, comparable to *naharu* in Ugarit →River; →Hubur in Mesopotamia (TROMP 1969:147-151) and Styx in Greece.

III. Of the three personal names mentioned, only *Šilḥî* occurs in pre-exilic documents. However, this name of the grand mother of king Josafat should more probably be interpreted as 'my off-shoot' (*HALAT* 1406). It is possible to interpret the name of the antediluvian Methushelah as containing the theophoric element *Shelah*: 'man of Shelah'. Against Tsevat, however, it should be noted that the element *mtw-* should not necessarily be translated with 'adherent; worshipper' (HUFFMON 1965: 234). The genealogical list in Gen 5 being late (P), it is questionable whether the ancient Israelites regarded the name as theophoric. *Šālaḥ* occurs likewise only in lists with a post-exilic redaction. The interpretation of the name is uncertain. It might be a shortened form of *Šilḥî*.

The interpretation of *šlḥ* as the deified River of Death in the epic of Keret has implications for the reading of two passages in the Book of Job. In Job 33:18, Elihu is arguing that some kind of human conduct can save man from death: "to save his soul from the Pit and his life from crossing the *šlḥ*." In Job 36:12, Elihu is repeating his argument in parallel wording: "But if they do not obey, they will pass *šlḥ* and they shall die without knowledge". Traditionally, *šlḥ* has been construed as a javelin (FOHRER 1963:454). The parallelismus membrorum and the meaning of *šlḥ* in Ugaritic imply that *šlḥ* refers to the 'River of Death' in both passages. In Israel, however this river is not interpreted as a deity (TROMP 1969: 147-151; LORETZ 1975).

There are no relations between *šlḥ* 'River of Death' and *šillûḥîm* 'marriage gift' (1 Kgs 9:6) or *šelaḥ* 'off-shoot' (Cant 4:13; →Thillaḫuha). The interpretation of VAN SELMS (1966) who construes *šĕlaḥ* as the divine name →Laḥ coupled with the relative pronoun *š*, should be dismissed since no names with a parallel construction are known (HESS 1993).

IV. In Rabbinic sources an opposition is made between a סדה בית הבעל, a field irrigated by rain from above, and a סדה בית השלחין a field artificially irrigated with water from underneath the earth; see e.g. *Mo'ed Kaṭan* I,1. In this second designation an echo of *šlḥ* in its meaning as 'River of Death; Underworld River' is transmitted (TSEVAT 1954:45-46).

V. *Bibliography*

F. L. BENZ, *Personal Names in the Phoenician and Punic Inscriptions* (StP 8; Roma 1972); M. DIETRICH & O. LORETZ, Das Porträt einer Königin in KTU 1.14 I 12-15, *UF* 12 (1980), 199-204; G. FOHRER, *Das Buch Hiob* (KAT 16; Gütersloh 1963); Z. S. HARRIS, *A Grammar of the Phoenician Language* (AOS 8; New Haven 1936); R. S. HESS, *Studies in the Personal Names of Genesis 1-11* (AOAT 234; Neukirchen-Vluyn 1993) 70-71; H. B. HUFFMON, *Amorite Personal Names in the Mari Letters* (Baltimore 1965); O. LORETZ, Der Gott *šlḥ*, He. *šlḥ* I und *šlḥ* II, *UF* 7 (1975) 584-585; A. VAN SELMS, A forgotten God: LAḤ, *Studia Biblica et Semitica* (FS Th. C. Vriezen; ed. W. C. van Unnik & A. S. van der Woude; Wageningen 1966) 318-326; N. J. TROMP, *Primitive Conceptions of Death and the Netherworld in the Old Testament* (BeO 21;

Roma 1969); M. TSEVAT, The Canaanite God *Šälaḥ*, *VT* 4 (1954a) 41-49; TSEVAT, Additional remarks on 'The Canaanite God *Šälaḥ*', *VT* 4 (1954b) 322; E. VERREET, Der Keret Prolog, *UF* 19 (1987), 317-335.

B. BECKING

SHEM שֵׁם

I. The name of Shem, one of the three sons of →Noah, literally means 'name' (Gen 5:32; 6:10; 7:13; 9; 10; 1 Chron 1; Sir 49: 16; *HALAT* 1435). *šm* occurs as a theophoric element in personal names from Ebla (GORDON 1988:153-154). A deity Shem is probably present as theophoric element in names like *šĕmîdāʿ*, Shemida (Josh 17:2; 1 Chron 7:19), and *šĕmûʾēl*, Samuel (JIRKU 1927). The name of this deity should be distinguished from the use of the noun *šem* as an hypostatical indication of Yahweh; →Name.

II. In Mesopotamian personal names—mostly in Amorite ones—the element *s/ś/šumu*, 'name; progeny', occurs (H. B. HUFFMON, *Amorite Personal Names in the Mari Texts* [Baltimore 1965] 249-250; J. J. STAMM, *Die Akkadische Namensgebung* [Darmstadt [2]1968] 40-42. 236. 303-304. 366-367). Although the determinative for deities is not often placed before the element in these names, I. J. GELB (*Computer-aided Analysis of Amorite* [AS 21; Chicago 1980] 82) designates *šum* as a deity. In bilingual lexical texts from Ebla *šu-um* is equated with **dumuzi** (MEE IV 1 Rev vii':6'-7' 9-11 Rev xi:6-7; →Tammuz). For some scholars this equation definitively proved Shumu to be a deity (LUBETSKI 1987:2-5; GORDON 1988:153-154).

In Ugaritic and Phoenician inscriptions too the element *šm* occurs in personal names (F. GRÖNDAHL, *Die Personennamen der Texte aus Ugarit* [StP 1; Roma 1965] 31. 34. 117. 193-194. 355. 414; F. L. BENZ, *Personal Names in the Phoenician and Punic Inscriptions* [StP 8; Roma 1972] 419). A deity Shumu is not attested, however. In *KTU* 1.2 i:8 and 1.16 vi:56 mention is made of *ʿṯtrt šm bʿl*. This locution has been interpreted as a divine triad: →Astarte-Name-→Baal (LUBETSKI 1987:4). Since divine triads are otherwise unknown at Ugarit, the element *šm bʿl* can be better understood as an epithet, either 'name/emanation of Baal' (M. DIETRICH & O. LORETZ, *Jahwe und seine Aschera* [UBL 9; Münster 1992] 61) or 'consort of Baal' (J. C. DE MOOR, *ARTU*, 30. 222).

All these observations imply that the worship of a deity Shumu cannot be proved. The Eblaite equation can also be interpreted as an indication that the (theophoric) element *s/ś/šumu* functions as reference and substitution for another deity.

III. Shem is the eponymous ancestor of Semitic speaking peoples in the view of Genesis. He is not cast in a heroic or semi-divine role in the OT. Together with his father Noah, his brothers →Ham and →Japheth and their respective wives he entered the Ark and was saved from the flood (Gen 6:9; 7:1-13; 9:1-18). With his brothers he shared the divine blessing and covenant (Gen 9:1. 17). In the *Sibylline Oracles* the sons of Noah are given the names of Greek gods. Shem is there identified with Kronos. In some Rabbinic traditions, Shem is identified with →Melchizedek, king of Salem (*Gen. Rab.* 44:8; *Tanḥuma* Lech Lecha 19); in other traditions he is seen as the founder of the first school (*bMak* 23b; *Gen. Rab.* 36:8; *Tg. Ps.-J.* Gen 9:27).

In the OT, some names occur which—according to ZADOK (1988:182)—contain the theophoric element *šm*: (1) *šĕmîrāmôt*, 'Semiramoth' (1 Chron 15:18.20; 16:5; 2 Chron 17:8) construed by ZADOK (1988:48) as 'Shem-is-height'; (2) *šĕmîdāʿ*, 'Shemida' (eponymous ancestor of a tribe; Num 26:32; Josh 17:2; 1 Chron 7:19) probably a derivation of *šĕmyādāʿ*, 'Shem has acknowledged' (JIRKU 1927:84-85; ZADOK 1988:24); (3) *šĕmûʾēl*, 'Samuel', this name has preserved an old nominative ending *-u* after the subject and can be rendered as 'Shem is god' (*HALAT* 1438; ZADOK 1988:46). In view of the observations made above, it can be assumed that the element *šm* in these names does not refer to a deity Shem, but functions as a substitution for a godhead. Therefore, e.g. *sĕmû'ēl*, 'Samuel', can be interpreted as meaning 'Yahweh-is-god' (T. N. D. METTINGER, *The Dethronement of Sabaoth* [CB OTS 18; Gleerup 1982] 131).

LUBETSKI (1987) offers an unusual interpretation of Gen 11:4. In the story on the Tower of Babylon the phrase occurs "Let us make for ourselves a name (*šēm*)". In Rabbinic traditions this *šēm* has been interpreted as referring to an idol. LUBETSKI connects this view with the alleged worship of a deity Shem in the ancient Near East and comes to the conclusion that the Generation of Dispersion was punished for having constructed the image of a non-Yahwistic deity on top of the building at Babel (1987:6). His view has been dismissed by C. UEHLINGER (*Weltreich und "eine Rede": Eine neue Deutung der sogenannten Turmbauerzählung* [OBO 101; Freiburg/Göttingen 1990] 41-44. 380-396) who remarks that the phrase *'āśâ šēm*, 'to make a name', has nothing to do with cultic practices or idolatry but should be connected with Mesopotamian royal ideology: Assyrian kings tried to 'establish their name' in view of eternal remembrance.

IV. *Bibliography*

C. H. GORDON, Notes on Proper Names in the Ebla Tablets, *Eblaite Personal Names and Semitic Name-giving* (ARES I; A. Archi ed.; Roma 1988) 153-158; E. ISAAC, Shem (person), *ABD* 5 (1992) 1194-1195; A JIRKU, Zur Götterwelt Palästinas und Syriens, *Sellin-Festschrift* (ed. A. Jirku; Leipzig 1927) 83-86; M. LUBETSKI, *Šm* as a Deity, *Religion* 17 (1987) 1-14; R. ZADOK, *The pre-hellenistic Israelite Anthroponomy and Prosopography* (OLA 28; Leuven 1988).

B. BECKING

SHEMESH שמש

I. As used in the Bible, Hebrew שמש, vocalized *šemeš* in the MT, is never an actual divine name. Palestinian toponymy of biblical times reflects, nevertheless, the Canaanite cult of the Sun-god, as shown by the place names Beth-Shemesh (Josh 15:10; 21:16, etc.), En-Shemesh (Josh 15:7; 18:17), Ir-Shemesh (Josh 19:41). They preserve the memory of sanctuaries devoted to the solar deity, which is probably mentioned ca. 800 BCE in the Deir 'Allā plaster inscription (I,6). The *bêt Šemeš* in Jer 43:13 is, instead, the temple of the Egyptian Sun-god in Heliopolis (→Re). Surprisingly enough, Hebrew anthroponomy does not contain obvious traces of a solar cult, for Samson's name may simply mean 'little sun', as suggested by the diminutival suffix *-ōn* < *-ān*, while the Aramaic proper name Shimshai (Ezra 4:8-9, 17, 23) can just be 'sunny' or 'sunlit'. The same meaning can be attributed to Shashai (Ezra 10:40), that may originate from Šamšay, since *ss* transcribes Šamaš in the Tell Fekherye inscription (line 7).

II. The lack of evident traces of solar worship in Hebrew anthroponomy seems to indicate that the cult of the sun was not very popular in Syria-Palestine in the Iron Age, contrary to Egypt and to Mesopotamia. The Sun-god was a minor deity for the Phoenicians and the Aramaeans, despite the role the Ugaritic Sun-goddess Shapash plays in literary and ritual texts of the Late Bronze Age. The Deuteronomistic writer mentions worship of "the host of heavens", comprising "the sun, the moon, and the planets", only during the half a century of the reigns of Manasseh and Amon (2 Kgs 21:3; 23:5). Therefore, scholars generally suppose that this was an Assyrian astral cult which was imposed upon Judah as a symbol of subjection and vassalage. Its condemnation in Deut 4:19 and 17:3 reflects the views of the same Deuteronomistic school and does not imply any older practice.

The horses and of the chariot(s) of the sun (2 Kgs 23:11), as well as Ezekiel's vision of the men prostrating themselves before the rising sun (Ezek 8:16), are somewhat different. In fact, the horses and the chariot(s) were placed at the entrance to the Temple of →Yahweh and the men were practising their cult in the same Temple, facing eastwards, towards the gate by which Yahweh, the God of Israel, has entered the sanctuary (Ezek 43:2, 4; 44:2). These features indicate that the sun's chariot was Yahweh's vehicle and that the men seen by the prophet were not sun-worshippers, but devotees of Yahweh, just as the child-sacrifice performed in the Valley of Ben-Hinnom (2 Kgs 23:10; Jer 7:31) was intended to honour Yahweh himself (Mic 6:7).

The concept of a sun's chariot, born from the ancient idea that the sun is a wheel turning through the heavens, is already attested by the myth of the chariot of fire and the horses of fire which carried →Elijah up to heaven (2 Kgs 2:11-12; cf. 6:17; 13:14; Sir 48:9). This particular concept is probably implied also by the Aramaic inscriptions from Zinçirli, in the eighth century BCE, when the Sun-god is mentioned after →El and →Rakib-El, 'the Charioteer of El' (*KAI* 214:2.3.11.18; 215:22). The latter's name suggests that this was a divine triad conceived as a chariot's crew and, that the sun's chariot was in fact El's vehicle, driven by the Charioteer of El, who was actually the holy patron of the Aramaic dynasty of Zinçirli.

We can surmise that a similar conception existed also in Jerusalem, and even in North-Israel, as shown by the episode of the ascension of Elijah to heaven. Although king Josiah had abolished this particular form of Yahweh's cult and had destroyed the horses and the sun's chariot placed at the entrance of the Temple (2 Kgs 23:11), this conception underlines the symbolic vision of Ezek 1, as already understood by Sir 49:8 and the Mishna, *Ḥag.* 2:1, which actually uses the term *merkābâ* of 2 Kgs 23:11 to designate Yahweh's chariot as in Ezek 1. This term, which does not appear in Ezekiel—explained, perhaps, by the fact that the destruction of the *mirkebet haššemeš* 'the chariot of the sun' was still recent—is used instead in 1 Chr 28:18. It dates back to David "the model of the chariot", identified however by a glossator with "the →cherubim with their wings outspread to screen the Ark of the Covenant of Yahweh". The divine chariot also preoccupied the mind of the members of the Sadducean community of Qumran, whose Songs of the Sabbath Sacrifice mention 'the model of the throne of the chariot', *tabnît kissēʾ merkābâ* (4Q 403). According to their Ritual of the Daily Prayers (4Q 503), the morning service started "when the sun was coming out to shine over the earth", *bṣʾt hšmš lhʾyr ʿl hʾrṣ*. This confirms Flavius Josephus' statement about the Essenes, viz. that "their devotions to the divinity take a particular form: before the rising of the sun they utter no profane word, but recite some ancestral prayers facing the sun, as if they beseeched it to rise" (*Bell. Jud.* II,128). These "ancestral prayers" recall the men "with their faces to the east, prostrating themselves towards the rising sun", as Ezekiel saw them in the Temple (Ezek 8:16).

Relics of this ritual practice are found, perhaps, in the Blessing of the Sun, *Birkat haḥammâ*, a rabbinic prayer-service in which the sun is blessed in thanksgiving for its creation and its being set in motion in the firmament on the fourth day of the world (Gen 1:16-19). The ceremony is held once every 28 years, most recently on the 18th of March 1981. It takes place on the first Wednesday of the month of Nisan, after the morning prayer, when the sun is about 90° above the eastern horizon. The date of the *Birkat haḥammâ* is based on calculations by the Babylonian *amora* Abbaye (278-338 CE). The Blessing starts with Ps 84:12, where the psalmist states blandly that Yahweh is *šemeš ûmāgēn*, "sun and cover", an antithetic image that suggests the sunlight granted by the LORD and the protection he provides against heat. It contains Ps 19, that preserves a fragment of an old hymn to the sun (Ps 19:5c-7), and ends with Isa 30:26: "The light of the sun (*ʾôr haḥammâ*) shall be sevenfold, as the light of the seven days". There can be little doubt that the sun was conceived in biblical times as a vivid symbol of Yahweh's Glory (→Kabod). Yahweh's coming is decribed already in Deut 33:2 and Hab 3:3-4 as the rising of the sun, and his Glory comes from the East according to Isa 59:19 and Ezek 43:2, 4; 44:2, while Isa 60:19 announces that Yahweh's Glory will replace the sunlight when the new Jerusalem will arise. In Sir 42:16, the "rising sun" is paralleled by "Yahweh's Glory": *šmš zwrḥt ʿl kl nglth // wkbd yhwh ʿl kl mʿśyh*, "the rising sun shines on everything // and the Glory of Yahweh on all his works" (cf. Sir 43:2-5). According to the Book of Mysteries from Qumran, referring probably to the Day of Judgement, "justice will shine like the sun, the foundation of the Universe", *hṣdq yglh kšmš tkwn tbl* (lQ 27 I:6-7), and the author of lQH 7:25 addresses God as follows, "Thou art for me an eternal luminary" (*li mĕʾôr ʿôlām*). Similar accents can be heard in the *Odes Sol.*, whose author declares that the LORD "is my sun" (15:1-2) and that He is "like the sun upon the earth" (11:13). The importance of the sun is also underlined by Philo of Alexandria in *De somniis* I, 13.76-86, but Wis 7:29-30 stresses that →Wisdom is superior to the sun. It is uncertain whether the winged sun-disk represented on Judaean royal stamp-seal impressions (*ANEP* 809) is a Yahwistic symbol or rather a traditional royal emblem of the ancient Near East. Instead, the bearded male figure seated on a winged wheel, who appears on a fourth-century Judaean coin (*ANEP* 226), certainly expresses the conception of Yahweh's sun-throne iconographically. The wheel corresponds to the *glgl hšmš* (the wheel of the sun) of CD 10:15 and the *galgal ḥammâ* (the wheel of the sun) of the Babylonian Talmud, for instance *Yoma* 20b.

III. This solar symbolism might have represented a danger for the purity of Yahweh's worship, for the sun, the →moon, and the →stars are even somewhat personified in Joseph's dream (Gen 37:9). Job judges it necessary to profess that he never raised his hand in homage to the sun or the moon (Job 31:26-27). He even avoids using the word *šemeš* (sun) and replaces it by *ʾôr* (light), just as the priestly author of Gen 1:14-18, who stresses that God had created the sun. In a similar context, however, *šemeš* is used in Jer 31:35 and in Pss 74:16; 104:19; 136:8; 148:3-6. Whatever the original background of the ancient conjuration in Josh 10:12 was, the actual text of Josh 10:12-14 stresses Yahweh's authority over the sun and the moon (cf. Sir 46:4). A similar belief is reflected in Job 9:7 and Isa 38: 7-8 (cf. 2 Kgs 20:9-11; Sir 48:23), where the sun obeys a man of God.

It is difficult to ascertain whether the use of *ḥammâ* instead of *šemeš* in Isa 24:23; 30:26; Job 30:28; Cant 6:10 is intended to avoid some possible mythological connotations. In magical incantations from Late Antiquity one finds *ḥammâ* (J. NAVEH & S. SHAKED, *Amulets and Magic Bowls* [Jerusalem 1985] Amulet 4:20) as well as *šimšaʾ* (*ibid.*, Bowl 7,7), pronounced however in a way different from Shamesh (*šmyš, šʾmš*), the name of the Sun-deity inherited from the Babylonian tradition (*ibid.*, Bowl 13:11.21; C. C. ISBELL, *Corpus of the Aramaic Incantation Bowls* [Missoula 1975], nos. 38:2; 62:2). In later Jewish descriptions of the sun travelling in the firmament in his chariot one finds *šemeš* in the Midrash *Num. Rabba* 12: 4, but *ḥammâ* in *Pirqe de R. Eliezer* 6.

IV. In the Palestinian tradition, attested already by the oldest parts of the Books of Enoch, Aramaic manuscripts of which ($4QEn^a$ and $4QEn^b$) go back to the second half of the third century BCE, the fifteenth fallen angel was called Shamshi-El (*Šmšyʾl*), 'Sun of God' (*1 Enoch* 6:7; 8:3). He had taught men "the signs of the sun" (*nḥšy šmš*), i.e. astrology, and belonged therefore to the group of the ten angel-teachers. His name became Samsapeʾel or Simapiseʾel in the Ethiopic Book of Enoch and was shortened to Σαμιήλ or Σεμιήλ in the Greek fragments of the work. He appears under this name in *Sib. Or.* II, 215, an essentially Christian work, that mentions him among the angels intervening at the Last Judgment, but the first role is played there by →Uriel, who breaks open the door of →Hades and brings out its inhabitants (*Sib. Or.* II, 233-237).

V. *Bibliography*

A. CAQUOT, La divinité solaire ugaritique, *Syria* 36 (1959) 90-101; J. H. CHARLESWORTH, Les Odes de Salomon et les manuscrits de la Mer Morte, *RB* 77 (1970) 522-

549 (esp. 538-540); J. DUS, Gibeon—eine Kultstatte des *Šmš* und die Stadt des benjaminitischen Schicksals, *VT* 10 (1960) 353-374; H. VAN DYKE PARUNAK, Was Solomon's Temple aligned to the Sun?, *PEQ* 110 (1978) 29-33; J. D. EISENSTEIN, Sun, *Jewish Encyclopedia* XI (New York 1906) 589-591; R. EISLER, Jahves Hochzeit mit der Sonne, *FS F. Hommel* II (Leipzig 1918) 21-70; J. FERRON, Le caractère solaire du dieu de Carthage, *Africa* 1 (1966) 41-58; T. H. GASTER, *Thespis. Ritual, Myth, and Drama in the Ancient Near East* (Garden City 1961[2]) 66-67; J. F. HEALEY, The Sun Deity and the Underworld in Mesopotamia and Ugarit, *Death in Mesopotamia* (ed. B. Alster; Copenhagen 1980) 239-242; F. J. HOLLIS, The Sun Cult and the Temple at Jerusalem, *Myth and Ritual* (ed. S. H. Hooke; Oxford 1933) 87-110; HOLLIS, *The Archaeology of the Herod's Temple*, (London 1934) 125, 132-133; T. HARTMANN, שמש *šemeš* Sonne, *THAT* II, 987-999; E. LIPIŃSKI, Le culte du Soleil chez les Semites occidentaux du Ier millénaire av. J.-C., *OLP* 22 (1991) 57-72; LIPIŃSKI, Šaemaeš, *TWAT* 8 (1994) 306-315; J. MAIER, Die Sonne im religiösen Denken des antiken Judentums, *ANRW* II, 19/1 (Berlin/New York 1979) 346-412; P. MASER, Sonne und Mond. Exegetische Erwägungen zum Fortleben der spätantik-jüdischen Tradition in der frühchristlichen Kultur, *Kairos* 25 (1983) 41-67; H. G. MAY, Some Aspects of Solar Worship at Jerusalem, *ZAW* 55 (1937) 269-281; MAY, The Departure of the Glory of Yahweh, *JBL* 56 (1937) 309-321; J. W. MCKAY, *Religion in Judah under the Assyrians (732-609 B.C.)* (London 1973); MCKAY, Further Light on the Horses and Chariot of the Sun in the Jerusalem Temple, *PEQ* 105 (1973) 167-169; J. MORGENSTERN, The King-God among the Western Semites and the Meaning of Epiphanes, *VT* 10 (1960) 138-197 (esp. 159-161.179.182-189); MORGENSTERN, The Cultic Setting of the 'Enthronement Psalms', *HUCA* 35 (1964) 1-42; G. NAGEL, Le culte du Soleil dans l'ancienne Égypte, *ErJb* 10 (1943) 9-56; M. P. NILSSON, Sonnenkalender und Sonnenreligion, *ARW* 30 (1933) 141-173; W. O. E. OESTERLEY, Early Hebrew Festival Rituals, *Myth and Ritual* (ed. S. H. Hooke; London 1933) 111-146 (esp. 115-116, 133-135); G. PETTINATO, Is. 2,7 e il culto del sole in Giudea nel secolo VIII av. Cr., *OrAnt* 4 (1965) 1-30; A. RUBENS, Sun, *EncJud* 15 (Jerusalem 1971) 516-518; N. H. SNAITH, *The Jewish New Year Festival. Its Origin and Development* (London 1947) 90-93; H. P. STÄHLI, *Solare Elemente im Jahweglauben des Alten Testaments* (Freiburg/Göttingen 1985); K. VAN DER TOORN, Sun, *ABD* 6 (1992) 237-239; J. TUBACH, *Im Schatten des Sonnengottes. Der Sonnenkult in Edessa, Harran und Hatra am Vorabend der christlichen Mission* (Wiesbaden 1986); C. VIROLLEAUD, Le dieu Shamash dans l'ancienne Mésopotamie, *ErJb* 10 (1943) 57-79.

E. LIPIŃSKI

SHEOL שאול

I. Ideas of the underworld as the abode of the dead are known from ancient Israel, as well as from the surrounding cultures (MORALDI 1985; SPRONK 1986; XELLA 1987; LEWIS 1989; TROPPER 1989; BLOCH-SMITH 1992). In the Hebrew Bible *šě'ôl* is by far the most commonly used word for the netherworld, appearing altogether 65x (66x if the text in Isa 7:11 is emended). Also other words were used in ancient Israel to denote the realm of the dead (TROMP 1969: 23-128). The feminine noun Sheol appears only in Hebrew, and as a loanword in Syriac and Ethiopic (*HALAT* 1274). For some rare occurrences in Aramaic see *DISO* 286. A reference to Sheol in the Ebla-texts has been claimed, but remains to be further investigated (DAHOOD 1987:97). The etymology of Sheol has been widely discussed (GERLEMAN 1976:838, GÖRG 1982:26-33, WÄCHTER 1992:902-903, *HALAT* 1274, LEWIS 1992:101-102), but it is safe to conclude that despite a plethora of suggestions, no satisfactory solution has been reached in the matter.

There appears to be no textual support for

the claim that personifications of Sheol in the Hebrew Bible reflect mythological material.

II. In the Hebrew Bible we occasionally find descriptions of Sheol personified. These personifications have often been related to mythological descriptions found particularly in Ugaritic texts. Thought to be similar to representations of underworld deities elsewhere, these biblical portrayals have been felt to reflect not only the underworld itself, but also the personified chthonic power behind death, a demon or deity Sheol (GASTER 1962:788; PARKER 1976:224). Typically, it has been claimed that some of the descriptions of the insatiable appetite of Sheol in the Bible are "remarkably reminiscent of Mot's voracious appetite in CTA 5.1.19-20; 5.2.2-4" (LEWIS 1992:103). However, these and similar views are not shared by all scholars (PODELLA 1988:81; WÄCHTER 1992:907).

In Prov 1:12 the wicked highwaymen, tempting the young man to criminal behaviour, liken themselves to Sheol, swallowing their victims alive. Representing a broad scholarly consensus, it has been claimed that this metaphor "derives from a piece of Canaanite mythology" (MCKANE 1977:269). In a similar manner, in Prov 27:20, human greed is compared to the greed of Sheol and →Abaddon (another poetic name for the abode of the death. *Ketib* has here *w'bdh*). Behind this text, too, commentators have found a mythological delineation of the deity →Mot (MCKANE 1977:617-618). Also in Prov 30:16 the reference to the insatiability of Sheol has been interpreted as deriving from ancient Near Eastern mythology (MCKANE 1977:656). There is, however, no reason to read these texts in Prov against the background of 'Canaanite mythology'. All of these texts are typical wisdom texts, and there is nothing in them that goes beyond the wisdom observation that death claims a large toll, and that there apparently is no end to people dying. In particular Prov 30:15-16 indicates beyond doubt that this is how these expressions should be understood. The whole context concerns insatiability. As the leech (→Vampire) is insatiable in its greed for blood, Sheol is greedy for more human beings, the barren womb for offspring, the dry earth for water, and the fire for fuel. Apparently, there is no 'mythological background' for the metaphor of the two daughters of the leech, or the fire crying for more fuel. In a similar manner the inexorable greediness of death represents a piece of basic knowledge experienced by all men at all times. Rather than stemming from bits and pieces of Canaanite mythology it would seem that the personifications of Sheol derive from the daily experience that death has a great appetite for the living.

Similarly, in Hab 2:5, the personified Babylonian empire is compared to Sheol. In the same way as Sheol's appetite for dead is never satisfied the greed of the Babylonian empire for other nations is insatiable. The comparison, appearing in a word of doom against Babylon, probably reveals influence from wisdom traditions (cf. Hab 2:4). But again, the comparison is strictly metaphorical and poetical, and there is no reason whatsoever to see anything mythological in this text. In Isa 5:14, too, the metaphor of Sheol as a greedy monster, making his throat wide open in order to swallow the people, noble and common, is merely metaphorical (cf. also Hos 13:14, Isa 14:9, 11, 15; 28:15, 18; 38:18, Pss 6:6; 49:15).

Since the texts in which we find descriptions of Sheol personified in their present shape are purely poetical, any attempt to go beyond the texts and ask whether these texts ultimately go back to mythological descriptions is bound to end up as sheer speculations. Thus, when scholars have claimed that what we find in these personifications of Sheol does represent an act of demythologization, which may have a polemical tone, we shall have to characterize such statements as speculative (ALONSO SCHÖKEL 1988:125). Nor can we, on the basis of these texts say anything about what the writers who wrote them thought about such matters. Even if we should be dealing here with remnants of ancient theomachic conflicts, passages of this kind cannot be taken without further ado as evidence of Hebrew attitudes to life and death (BARR 1992:35). But it is doubtful whether in fact these and similar texts do reflect theomachic conflicts at all, or whether they may not merely be poetical expressions, utimately stemming from wisdom traditions.

The whole issue becomes even more vital when we know that no deity Sheol has ever been attested. In the discussion whether or not Sheol may appear as the name of a deity the personal name Methushael, occurring in Gen 4:18, has played a certain role (GASTER 1962:788; PARKER 1976:224; LEWIS 1992: 103). Quite commonly, the name Methushael has been interpreted as 'Man of [the god] Sheol'. However, most of the discussion of the name Methushael has been of a rather varying quality, and it is only through the important study by LAYTON that some progress towards a better understanding of this name seems to have been made (1990: 66-74). According to LAYTON, however, "The PN Metusha'el is probably nothing more (or less) than a corrupt form of the PN Metushelah. Whatever the case may be, no meaning can be assigned to the second element of the PN Metusha'el as pointed by the Massoretes" (1990:74). Even if LAYTON should not be correct in his particular claim, the difficulties in explaining the name Methushael as a derivation from an assumed deity Sheol are still too many to be overlooked, and the existence of a god Sheol can hardly be created on such a weak basis.

It is unfortunate that we still have no systematic and comprehensive study of the personifications of Sheol in the Hebrew Bible. The relatively lengthy treatment by TROMP, in particular working with Ugaritic texts, and attempting to demonstrate that many of the texts in question reflect a common ancient Near Eastern mythological language, altogether appears to be remarkably vague on the whole matter (TROMP 1969:22-23, 80, 102-107, 163, 186). Moreover, TROMP's study is methodologically weak as it avoids any discussion of personifications of Sheol and their relationship to 'demons', 'deities', 'hypostases' as opposed to mere 'metaphorical/poetical' descriptions in general.

Personification as a rhetorical/poetical device is very widespread in the Hebrew Bible (ALONSO SCHÖKEL 1988:123-125). Despite its enormous importance, the phenomenon has been little studied. Among the better known cases are Lady Wisdom (MURPHY 1990:133-149), and the personification of the city (GALAMBUSH 1992). In a similar manner personifications of 'death' and the 'netherworld' are known from most cultures. Thus, the personification of *māwet*—'death'—is also found in several texts in the Hebrew Bible, often appearing in word-pairs with Sheol. Obviously, it does not follow from this that in these texts we find references to a deity or demon 'Death' (cf. Jer 9:20, Ps 49:15, Job 28:22). That both 'death' and the 'realm of the dead' are personified in poetic texts is quite natural and one should not attempt to put anything more into it. This is shown also from the many texts where *māwet* and Sheol appear in word pairs (full survey in ILLMANN 1979:149-151). The personifications of *māwet*, too, are to be regarded purely as poetical/metaphorical (WÄCHTER 1992:908).

III. *Bibliography*

L. ALONSO SCHÖKEL, *A Manual of Hebrew Poetics* (Subsidia Biblica 11; Roma 1988); J. BARR, *The Garden of Eden and the Hope of Immortality* (London 1992); E. BLOCH-SMITH, *Judahite Burial Practices and Beliefs about the Dead* (JSOT/ASOR Monograph Series 7; Sheffield 1992); M. DAHOOD, Love and Death at Ebla and their Biblical Reflections, *Love & Death in the Ancient Near East. Essays in Honor of Marvin H. Pope* (Ed. J. H. Marks & R. M. Good; Guildford 1987) 93-99; J. GALAMBUSH, *Jerusalem in the Book of Ezekiel. The City as Yahweh's Wife* (SBL DS 130; Atlanta 1992); T. H. GASTER, Dead, Abode of the, *IDB* 1 (1962) 787-788; G. GERLEMAN, שְׁאוֹל, *THAT* II (1976) 837-841; M. GÖRG, 'Scheol' – Israels Unterweltsbegriff und seine Herkunft, *BN* 17 (1982) 26-33; K. -J. ILLMAN, *Old Testament Formulas about Death* (Publications of the Research Institute of the Åbo Akademi Foundation 48; Åbo 1979); S. C. LAYTON, *Archaic Features of Canaanite Personal Names in the Hebrew*

Bible (HSM 47; Atlanta 1990); T. J. LEWIS, *Cults of the Dead in Ancient Israel and Ugarit* (HSM 39; Atlanta 1989); LEWIS, Dead, Abode of the, *ABD* 2 (1992) 101-105; W. MCKANE, *Proverbs. A New Approach* (OTL; London 1977); L. MORALDI, *L'Aldilà dell'uomo nelle civiltà babilonese, egizia, greca, latina, ebraica, cristiana e musulmana* (Milano 1985); R. E. MURPHY, *The Tree of Life. An Exploration of Biblical Wisdom Literature* (New York 1990); S. B. PARKER, Deities, Underworld, *IDBS* (Abingdon 1976) 222-225; *T. PODELLA, Grundzüge alttestamentlicher Jenseitsvorstellungen שאול, *BN* 43 (1988) 70-89; K. SPRONK, *Beatific Afterlife in Ancient Israel and in the Ancient Near East* (AOAT 219; Neukirchen-Vluyn 1986); *Archeologia dell'inferno. L'Aldilà nel mondo antico, vicino-orientale e classico* (ed. P. Xella; Verona 1987); J. TROPPER, *Nekromantie: Totenbefragung im Alten Orient und im Alten Testament* (AOAT 223; Neukirchen-Vluyn 1989); N. J. TROMP, *Primitive Conceptions of Death and the Nether World in the Old Testament* (BibOr 21; Rome 1969); *L. WÄCHTER, שאול, *TWAT* VII/8 (1992) 901-910 [& lit].

H. M. BARSTAD

SHEPHERD רעה

I. On the basis of Gen 49:24, MAAG reconstructed the expression *Rōʿeh Yiśrāʾēl*, 'Shepherd of Israel' as the name of the personal god of Israel/Jacob, comparable in his view to the →'Fear of Isaac' and the →'Mighty One of Jacob' (1980:121). Since the name can only be obtained by textual emendation, Maag's proposal is hardly convincing (cf. KÖCKERT 1988:65-67). Though 'shepherd' is not unusual as an epithet for Near Eastern gods, it has nowhere attained the status of an independent divine name.

II. In antiquity the occupation of shepherd was regarded as a manly and noble one. It required courage, endurance, and a great amount of practical wisdom. The image of the shepherd offered an apt and much-used metaphor for human rulers and gods. Kings were like shepherds in the sense that they protected their subjects from harm and provided them with conditions in which they could thrive. In self-laudatory inscriptions of Mesopotamian and Egyptian kings, the comparison is quite frequent (VANCIL 1992:1188-1189). Some kings were not merely likened to shepherds, but credited with a career as one before they exercised kingship. According to the Sumerian King List, the famous kings Etana and Lugalbanda had both begun as shepherds (**sipa**; WAETZOLDT 1972-75:424). This biographical detail, that reminds one of David, may in fact have been a standard literary *motif*: shepherding constituted a kind of apprenticeship for kingship.

The parallel beween kings and gods need hardly be explained: the latter were simply more powerful. When the metaphor of shepherd is applied to gods, it is the notion of protection that predominates. Hence the regular occurrence of the epithet in theophoric personal names of the type Šamaš-reʾūa, 'Shamash is my shepherd' (see e.g. J. J. STAMM, *Die akkadische Namengebung* [Leipzig 1939] 214, 223). Yet also outside the realm of personal devotion to which these names attest we find the epithet 'shepherd' used for most of the major gods (*AkkGE* 164-165).

III. In the Bible the image of the shepherd is frequently—though not always explicitly—applied to God. He is represented as a sollicitous guardian of the herd, carrying the animals that cannot keep up, and not urging on those that have young (Isa 40:11). The image is not merely idyllic. God is also a powerful leader who drives out other nations to make room for his own flock (Ps 78:52-55.70-72). The classic elaboration of the shepherd metaphor is found in Ps 23: it describes the vindication of the suppliant before the eyes of his opponents during an ordeal ceremony (cf. K. VAN DER TOORN, Ordeal Procedures in the Psalms and the Passover Meal, *VT* 38 [1988] 427-445, esp. 441) as God's leading his devotee like a shepherd to green pastures.

The thesis put forth by Maag should be distinguished from the use of 'shepherd' as a metaphor for God. It implies that 'Shepherd' (or more precisely 'Shepherd-of-

Israel') was a name used for the 'God of the fathers' (cf. A. ALT, *Der Gott der Väter* [Stuttgart 1929]) whom Israel (or Jacob) worshipped. The thesis rests on the assumption that the word *ʾeben*, →'rock', now separating the words *rōʿeh* and *Yiśrāʾēl*, is a secondary interpolation. Admittedly, the present form of the text seems overloaded (H. GUNKEL, *Genesis* [HAT 1/1; Göttingen 1917] 486): one expects either 'the Shepherd of Israel' (cf. Ps 80:2; cf. 121:4 *šōmēr Yiśrāʾēl*) or 'the Rock of Israel' (cf. Isa 30:29 *ṣûr Yiśrāʾēl*). Yet neither expression seems particularly archaic; the supposition that either of them ever served as an independent designation of the personal or family god (the so-called 'god of the fathers' postulated by Alt) cannot be substantiated. Like the expression *ʾăbîr Yaʿăqôb*, 'Mighty One of Jacob', which also occurs elsewhere in the Hebrew Bible as an epithet of →Yahweh (Isa 49:26; 60:16; Ps 132:2.5; cf. Isa 1:24 *ʾăbîr Yiśrāʾēl*), both would seem to be poetic designations of Yahweh the God of Israel.

IV. *Bibliography*

M. KÖCKERT, *Vätergott und Väterverheissungen* (FRLANT 142; Göttingen 1988); V. MAAG, Der Hirte Israels. Eine Skizze von Wesen und Bedeutung der Väterreligion, *Kultur, Kulturkontakt und Religion. Gesammelte Studien zur allgemeinen und alttestamentlichen Religionsgeschichte* (ed. H. H. Schmid & O. H. Steck; Göttingen/Zürich 1980; originally published in the *Schweizerische Theologische Umschau* 28 [1958] 2-28) 111-144; M. SAEBØ, Divine Names and Epithets in Genesis 49:24b-25a, *Festschrift E. Nielsen* (VTSup 50; Leiden 1993) 126-127; J. W. VANCIL, Sheep, Shepherd, *ABD* 5 (1992) 1188-1190; H. WAETZOLDT, Hirt, *RLA* 4 (1972-75) 421-425.

K. VAN DER TOORN

SHEQER → FALSEHOOD

SHIELD OF ABRAHAM מגן אברהם

I. The phrase *māgēn ʾabrāhām*, 'Shield of Abraham', occurs only in Sir 51:12 [in the Hebrew text, not in LXX], the final song of thanksgiving in the context of a liturgical antiphony (cf. Ps 136). ALT (1929) and LESLIE (1936) assumed that *māgēn ʾabrāhām* was a special name of the god of Abraham, because God is described as presenting himself as "a shield for you" (*ʾānōkî māgēn lāk*, "I am a shield for you", Gen 15:1). The suggestion cannot be properly understood outside the context of Alt's hypothesis concerning the God of the Fathers.

II. ALT's reconstruction of the name "Shield of Abraham" presupposes that Genesis 15 goes back to a preliterary tradition (1929:48); this oral tradition would have preserved the ancient cult legend for the god of Abraham. In recent years well-founded objections have been raised against both presuppositions (for references see KÖCKERT 1988:204-247; BLUM 1984; WEIMAR 1989). One obvious criticism must be that *māgēn*, 'shield', though frequently occurring, especially in the psalter (13 passages), as an appellative of Yahweh, is never used in the form of "Shield of X" (Sir 51:12 derives from Gen 15:1b).

For a number of reasons, some exegetes question the vocalization *māgēn* and take the verbal root MGN for a starting-point instead. This root occurs in the *Piel* in Hos 11:8 (as a parallel to NTN) and Gen 14:20. The interpretation of מגן as a verbal form opens various possibilities. EHRLICH (1908: 58) and KESSLER (1964) adopt the reading *mōgēn*. KESSLER translates Gen 15:1 as "... I am about to give you your very great reward", because he thinks this fits in well with Abraham's question in v 2 (1964:496-497). Philologically speaking, this interpretation is not impossible, because one can indeed form an active voice participle analogous to *Qal* (cf. *dbr*) with verbs normally only used in *Piʿel*. All the same, *mgn Pi.* as used in Gen 14:20; Hos 11:8 and 1QM 18:13 means 'deliver up' and is used with the accusative of the person.

DAHOOD (1966) and CROSS (1973) adopt the reading *māgān*. They interpret this word in the light of of Ug *mgn* ('to bestow a favour' [CROSS 1973:4], 'beschenken' [*WUS* No. 1513]), as 'benefactor', 'suzerain' (DAHOOD 1966:414). Dahood supports his interpretation with a reference to Pun *māgōn*, Lat *imperator*, *dux* and Ps 84:12 (in this passage he translates *šemeš* in the light of Hittite contracts and El-Amarna letters as 'sovereign' and *māgēn* > *māgān* as 'suzerain' [1966-1970: 16]). He interprets Ps 47:10; 84:10; 89:19 in this sense as well, linking *ndyby 'mym*, *mšyḥ* or *mlk* with *mgn*. The evidence in support of the interpretation of *māgōn* as a Punic title for generals is doubtful, however (FREEDMAN & O'CONNOR 1984:658). There is no valid reason why one should read *māgēn* as *māgān* in the Book of Psalms (cf. the pertinent analysis in O. LORETZ 1974a:177-183).

DIETRICH, LORETZ & SANMARTÍN (1974: 32) distinguish between MGN I, 'Shield' (*KTU* 4.127:3); MGN II, 'Gift' (*KTU* 1.4 i:23; 1.8:1; 1.16 i:45); and MGN III, 'to bestow, to give' (*KTU* 1.4 iii:25, 28, 30, 33, 36). LORETZ sees Gen 15:1b as a "perfect bicolon according to the laws of Canaanite poetics". Because of the parallel of *mgn* and *śkr* he translates: "I (myself) am your gift / your generous reward!" (1974b:492). The question remains, though, whether such a spiritualized conception was really possible in the context of archaic oriental poetry.

The only possible interpretation of מגן in terms of a numen would be the one advanced by Dahood and Cross. By way of implication, however, this interpretation assumes the context of the oriental state ruled by a king; it does not fit in with the social reality of an existence on the fringes of nomadism. However, there is no need to change the textual basis for interpretation in Gen 15:1 in any of the modes suggested above. The various proposals are quite arbitrary when judged in the light of the evidence for 'shield' as a designation of God in cultic lyric poetry. In Gen 15:1 'shield' is an epithet of Yahweh. The use of a shield as a defensive weapon (cf. Deut 33:29) makes it possible to adopt that term as a metaphor of divine protection (cf. Deut 33:29; 2 Sam 22:3.31.36 and parallel passages; Ps 18:3.31. 36; Ps 3:4; 7:11; 28:7; 33:20; 59:12; 84:12; 115:9-11; 119:114; 144:2; Prov 2:7; 30:5, which may be compared with a Neo-Assyrian oracle to Esahaddon [see TUAT 2/1, p. 59 iv:18-19]: "Esarhaddon, in Arbela [I am] your effective shield"); the protection here is promised to the people represented by their ancestor. The one who makes the promise, however, and who needs to be identified in person with that protection, is Yahweh himself.

III. *Bibliography*

A. ALT, *Der Gott der Väter* (BWANT III/12; Stuttgart 1929 = *KS* I; München 1953:1-77) 24-29, 67 n. 4; E. BLUM, *Die Komposition der Vätergeschichte* (WMANT 57; Neukirchen-Vluyn 1984) 366-383; F. M. CROSS, *Canaanite Myth and Hebrew Epic. Essays in the History of the Religion of Israel* (Cambridge, Mass. 1973) 3-12; M. J. DAHOOD, Hebrew-Ugaritic Lexicography XI, *Bib* 47 (1966) 403-419; DAHOOD, *Psalms* (AB 16; New York 1966-1970) 16-17; DAHOOD, Hebrew-Ugaritic Lexicography XI, *Bib* 54 (1973) 361; M. DIETRICH, O. LORETZ & J. SANMARTIN, Zur ugaritischen Lexikographie XI, *UF* 6 (1974) 31-32; A. B. EHRLICH, *Randglossen zur hebräischen Bibel I* (Leipzig 1908) 57-58; D. N. FREEDMAN & M. P. O'CONNOR, *māgēn*, *TWAT* 4 (1984) 646-659; M. KESSLER, The "Shield" of Abraham?, *VT* 14 (1964) 494-497; M. KÖCKERT, *Vätergott und Väterverheißungen. Eine Auseinandersetzung mit A. Alt und seinen Erben* (FRLANT 142; Göttingen 1988); E. A. LESLIE, *Old Testament Religion in the Light of its Canaanite Background* (New York 1936) 37; O. LORETZ, Psalmenstudien III, *UF* 6 (1974a) 177-183; LORETZ, *mgn* – 'Geschenk' in Gen 15:1, *UF* 6 (1974b) 492; P. WEIMAR, Genesis 15. Ein redaktionskritischer Versuch. *Die Väter Israels. Beitrage zur Theologie der Patriarchenüberlieferungen im Alten Testament.* (FS J. Scharbert; ed. M. Görg; Stuttgart 1989) 361-411.

M. KÖCKERT

SHIMIGE

I. The biblical anthroponym Shamgar (Judg 3:31; 5:6) is most likely understood as a Hurrian name (*Šimig-ari*) meaning 'Shimige has given' (FEILER 1939). Shimige is the Hurrian sun-god (VON SCHULER 1983[2]).

II. In the religion of the Hittites a number of solar deities are worshipped, the main ones being the sun-goddess of Arinna, connected with the underworld, and the sun-god of the heavens, usually referred to in the texts as ᵈUTU. When it comes to the Hurrian sun-god, this Sumerogram has to be read as Shimige.

As regards his nature and function, Shimige has a lot in common with the Mesopotamian sun-god Shamash as well as with ancient Near Eastern solar deities in general (Sun; →Shemesh). Shimige is all-seeing, taking note of the acts of men, punishing the evil-doer and blessing the righteous. In his capacity as omniscient witness, he is often invoked in treaties. A divine judge, he announces the decisions of the council of the gods by signs on earth. Positive traits predominate in descriptions of the god: he is the shepherd of men, the upholder of justice, and the protector of the weak.

The cult of Shimige was not confined to Anatolia. Along the Phoenician coast also he had his worshippers. In the time covered by the Amarna letters, for instance, the ruler of Qatna honoured Shimige as his family god ("the god of my father", *EA* no. 55). The Ugaritic onomasticon, too, shows that Shimige was a familiar deity in Western Syria (cf. such names as *aršmg* and *ṯmgdl*, see F. GRÖNDAHL, *Die Personennamen der Texte aus Ugarit* [StP 1; Rome 1967] 253-254).

III. Though attempts have been made to find a Semitic etymology for the name Shamgar (VAN SELMS 1964:300-301), they have failed to carry conviction (DE VAUX 1973). Since the name Shimigar(i) is well attested in the Hurrian onomasticon, and considering the fact that the cult of Shimige was not unknown in the Syrian territory, Shamgar's name is best understood as Hurrian. The first to suggest a foreign origin was HAUPT (1914:199-200). Shamgar's patronym 'son of →Anat' (possibly an occupational designation) strengthens the hypothesis of the foreign origin of the man. There is no evidence of any awareness of the theophoric character of Samgar's name on the side of the biblical narrator.

IV. *Bibliography*

W. FEILER, Ḫurritische Namen im Alten Testament, *ZA* 45 (1939) 221-222; P. HAUPT, Die Schlacht von Taanach, *Studien zur semitischen Philologie und Religionsgeschichte Julius Wellhausen zum 70. Geburtstag* (ed, K. Marti; BZAW 27; Giessen 1914) 191-225; E. VON SCHULER, Sonnengottheiten, *WbMyth* I/1 (1983²) 196-201; A. VAN SELMS, Judge Shamgar, *VT* 14 (1964) 294-309; R. DE VAUX, *Histoire ancienne d'Israël*, Vol. 2 (Paris 1973) 127-128.

K. VAN DER TOORN

SHIQMAH → SYCOMORE

SHIQQUṢ → ABOMINATION

SHULMAN

I. A deity Shulman is known as a theophoric element in Mesopotamian personal names. The god's name has often been connnected with the noun *šulmu*, "welfare", suggesting that the god functioned as a divine healer (ALBRIGHT 1931-1932:167). Shulman occurs as a theophoric element in the name of the Assyrian king *šalmanʾeser*, 'Shalmaneser' (2 Kgs 17:3//18:9) and has been recovered in the personal names Solomon (B. MEISSNER, *Babylonien und Assyrien* II [Heidelberg 1925] 33, 40, 48; see however *HALAT* 1425) and Shalman (Hos 10:4).

II. The deity Shulman is attested only in theophoric elements of personal names, mostly from the final quarter of the 2nd millennium BCE (= Middle Assyrian period), e.g. ᴵᵈ*Šulmanu-ašared* (Shalmaneser), i.e. "(the god) Shulman is foremost, first-rank (among the gods)" (cf. TALLQVIST 1914). A form of the god Shulman seems to have survived in north Syria as late as the Hellenistic period and beyond (MILIK 1967a:578; 1967b:293-297).

In an Egyptian votive stela from the 20-21st dynasty a deity (*Ršp*)-*Šllrmne* is attested (R. STADELMAN, *Syrisch-palästinensische Gottheiten in Ägypten* [Leiden 1967] 55). In Ugaritic personal names the (theophoric) element *šlmn* occurs (F. GRÖNDAHL, *Die Personennamen der Texte aus Ugarit* [StP 1; Roma 1967] 193. 414). Though it is tempting to relate both deities to the Mesopotamian Shulman, they can better be interpreted as referring to a West-Semitic deity →Shalman.

III. In Hosea 10:4, the memory of "the ravaging of Beth-arbel by Shalman on the day of battle" may refer to an attack on the Israelite town by an Assyrian monarch Shalmaneser, perhaps Shalmaneser III in the mid-9th century BCE (ASTOUR 1971; S. TIMM, *Moab zwischen den Mächten* [ÄAT 17; Wiesbaden 1989] 319-320). The theophoric element Shalman is all that remains in this abbreviated name.

It has been conjectured that the god Shulman was known among the West Semites as →Shalem, the divinity whose name is thought to be a component of the name of the city Jerusalem, where a temple of the god was allegedly to be found (LEWY 1940).

IV. *Bibliography*

W. F. ALBRIGHT, The Syro-Mesopotamian God Šulman-Ešmun and Related Figures, *AfO* 9 (1931-32) 164-169; M. C. ASTOUR, 841 BC, The First Assyrian Invasion of Israel, *JAOS* 91 (1971) 383-389; J. LEWY, Les textes paléo-assyriens et l'Ancien Testament, *RHR* 110 (1934) 29-65 [62-64]; LEWY, The Šulmān Temple in Jerusalem, *JBL* 59 (1940) 519-522; J. T. MILIK, Les papyrus araméens d'Hermoupolis et les cultes syro-phéniciens, *Bib* 48 (1967) 546-584; MILIK, Inscriptions araméennes en caractères grecs de Doura-Europos et une dédicace grecque du Cordove, *Syria* 44 (1967) 289-306; K. L. TALLQVIST, *Assyrian Personal Names* (Helsingsfors 1914) 222-223.

M. COGAN

SHULMANITU

I. "The Shulammite" in Cant 7:1 is held by some scholars to be a reference to Shulmanitu, an Assyrian war goddess with underworld associations (ALBRIGHT 1963:5-6; 1969:134, 150, 187).

II. The name of the goddess is known from Middle Assyrian texts from the reign of Tukulti-Ninurta I (ca. 1243-1207 BCE), written dDI(SILIM)-*ni-tu* (cf. RIMA 1.259-263). The name also appears in the Tākultu ritual text (*KAR* 214, ii, 47) and the god list An = Anum (CT 24, 33, Obv. 16 dŠUL-MA-NI-TU = *Ištar*-URU-SILIM-MA). Albright explained the form of the name as being adjectival, i.e. the goddess →Ishtar, belonging to the god →Shulman; the ending *-itu* having both gentilic and adjectival meanings (ALBRIGHT 1931-1932:164-169). Later, he asserted: "The Hebrew form (in Cant 7:1) is presumably due to a conflation of (the goddess) *Šulmanit* with *Šunamit*, the Shunamite woman, appellation of the last consort of King David" (ALBRIGHT 1963:5). Yet the reading of the name of the goddess in the Tukulti-Ninurta inscription is far from certain and a number of scholars prefer *Dinitu*; (RIMA 1:259).

III. The word Shulammite appears only twice in the OT, both times in Cant 7:1. Commentators are far from unanimous as to its meaning; cf. the thorough survey of scholarly approaches in POPE 1977:596-600. If Canticles is interpreted as a text with roots in pagan fertility worship, the Hebrew Shulammite is seen as reflecting the name Shulmanitu, the feminine form of the divine name Shulman.

Yet the suggested cultic background of Canticles has not found much support in the work which is basically secular love poetry. Many take "the Shulammite" as an appellation, a form of "the Shunammite", (so ms. B of LXX), i.e. the woman from the town of Shunem. This woman is almost universally identified with Abishag, the maiden from Shunem who served as the elderly King David's bed companion (1 Kgs 1:3; cf., too, 2 Kgs 4:8). It is often noted that Eusebius identified Shunem with the village of Shulem near Mount Tabor (Onomasticon, No. 856); but this was with reference to Josh 19:18; a second Shunem, the one of Kings, was located in Samaria. One must also consider that if it is an appellative, then "the Shulammite" might be referring to an otherwise unknown "woman of Shalem", i.e. Jerusalem (cf. Gen 14:18; Ps. 76:3). Still others take Shulammite as a term of endearment; King Solomon's beloved is called "the Solomoness". A similar designation is used in the Ugaritic tale of Aqhat, in which the wife of Danel is called "Lady Dantay" (*ANET* 151a).

IV. *Bibliography*

W. F. ALBRIGHT, The Syro-Mesopotamian God Šulman-Ešmun and Related Figures, *AfO* 9 (1931-32) 164-169; ALBRIGHT, Archaic Survivals in the text of Canticles, *Hebrew and Semitic Studies Presented to G. R. Driver* (eds. D. W. Thomas & W. D. McHardy; Oxford 1963) 1-7, esp. 5-6; ALBRIGHT, *Yahweh and the Gods of Canaan* (Garden City 1969) 134, 150, 187; M. H. POPE, *Song of Songs* (AB 7C; Garden City 1977).

M. COGAN

SHUNAMA

I. The name of the city of Shunem, *šûnēm*, is attested in Josh 18:19; 1 Sam 28: 4; 2 Kgs 4:8 (see also the indication for inhabitants of that city **šûnammî*, 1 Kgs 1:3.15; 2:17.20-21; 2 Kgs 4:12.25.36). The etymology is unclear (*HALAT* 1339 offers no etymology), the name has been related to a Ugaritic deity Shunama occurring as an element in the binomial divine name *Ṯkmn-w-Šnm* (GINSBERG 1936:92; JIRKU 1980).

II. The binomial deity →Thakumanu-wa-Shunama is attested at Ugarit in literary-religious texts as well as in offering-lists. The two names appear together. In *KTU* 1.114, the description of a heavenly *marzeaḥ*, they are depicted as sons of →El and, probably, to be identified with the 'gate-keeper of the house of El' (D. PARDEE, *Les textes paramythologiques* [RSOu 4; Paris 1988] 59-60). Here, they perform the filial duty towards a drunken father referred to in the epic of Aqhat (*KTU* 1.17 i:30). In the ritual *KTU* 1.41:12.16 the offering of an ewe for the deity is prescribed for the ritual on the fifteenth day of the month 'First-of-the-Wine', besides which the offering of a ram is prescribed as an additional offering at the same event. On the third day of the festival an ewe must be offered to Thakumanu-wa-Shunama (*KTU* 1.41:31-32). In a list of deities in alphabetic script Thakumanu-wa-Shunama are presented as the sons of El (*KTU* 1.65:1-4).

The resemblance of Thukamuna with the Kassite deity *Šuqamuna* has induced scholars to identify Shunama with the consort of *Šuqamuna*, the mountain-goddess *Šulimaliya* (e.g. MIRONOV 1933:143; GRAY 1958:138; E. LIPIŃSKI, *OLP* 2 [1971] 66-67; WYATT 1990:447). It should be noted that Shunama is presented as the brother of Thukamuna and the son of El in the Ugaritic texts. These observations preclude an identification with an apparently feminine deity. Besides, the etymological relations between the names of the two deities are far from clear (PARDEE 1990:197-198).

The etymology of the name Shunama is still unclear in spite of many proposals (see the outline in PARDEE 1990:196 n. 2). The identification of Shunama with the second element in the epithet for El *ab šnm*, 'father of years' is proposed by JIRKU (1970:278-279) and C. H. GORDON (El, Father of Šnm, *JNES* 35 [1976] 261-262; see FERCH *JBL* 99 [1980] 82-83) who interpret the epithet as 'father of Shunama'. This proposal, however, is not convincing (→Ancient of Days).

Recently, Wyatt has proposed that the story in Gen 34 is an old Indo-European myth on sacred marriage brought to the region by the Hurrians (the Horites of the story; WYATT 1990). In his view the Ugaritic binomial deity contains an allusion to this myth. In Gen 34, Shanimu has been transformed into Dinah, daughter of →Jacob, by the adoption of the epithet *dnt* (cf. Hebrew *zōnâ*), 'harlot', 'whore', appropriate to a goddess engaged in sacred marriage myths and perhaps rituals. The ancient myth has been transformed into a moral tale. No hint of the ancient divine status of Shechem or Dinah survives. Wyatt's view rests on obsolete speculations regarding the presence of an influential

Aryan stratum in the ancient Near East in the second millennium BCE.

III. The toponym Shunem is also attested in the Amarna correspondence: *Šu-na-ma* (EA 250:43; 365:12.20) and in the list describing the ninth century BCE campaign of Pharaoh Sheshonk: *šá-na-m<a>* (15). The relation between the Ugaritic deity and the Canaanite/Israelite toponym is probably a case of homonymy. In the OT stories the name of the city of Shunem does not have a religious signification. The healing by a magic touch performed by Elisha in 2 Kgs 4 is not related to the city of Shunem as such.

IV. *Bibliography*

H. L. GINSBERG, *Kitve Ugarit* (Jerusalem 1936); J. GRAY, *The Legacy of Canaan* (VT Sup 5; Leiden 1958) 138; A. JIRKU, *Šnm* (Schunama), der Sohn des Gottes 'Il, *ZAW* 82 (1970) 278-279; N. D. MIRONOV, Aryan Vestiges in the Near East of the Second Millenium BC, *AcOr* 11 (1933) 140-217; *D. PARDEE, *Ṯukamuna wa Šunama, UF* 20 (1988) 195-199 (with lit.); N. WYATT, The story of Dinah and Shechem, *UF* 22 (1990) 433-458.

B. BECKING

SHUNEM שׁונם → **SHUNAMA**

SID → SIDON

SIDON צידן

I. The ancient Phoenician city of Sidon, situated 25 miles north of Tyre, plays a considerable role in biblical literature. It came to stand for Phoenicia in general (SCHMITZ 1992:17). LEWY has argued that the city bears the name of the demon Ṣīdānu known from the Myth of Nergal and Ereshkigal (1934).

II. In Assyrian records, the city of Sidon is written *ṣi-du-nu* (S. PARPOLA, *Neo-Assyrian Toponyms* [AOAT 6; Neukirchen-Vluyn 1970] 322-323). The name thus resembles the Akkadian word for vertigo (*ṣīdānu*), once treated as a demon in the Amarna fragment of the Myth of Nergal and Ereshkigal (^{d}*Ṣi-i-da-na*, *EA* 357:49). The phonological resemblance does not suffice, however, to posit that the one was named after the other. It would be highly unusual to find a city named after a demon—and a very minor one, at that.

Another possibility of linking the name of the city with the name of a god might be found in the god Ṣid whose cult was widespread along the Mediterranean coasts (TEIXIDOR 1977). Though the nature of the god is nowhere explicitly stated, his name is probably connected with fishing: in Hebrew the root ṢWD refers to both hunting and fishing. A connection with the god Agreus ('Hunter') mentioned by Philo of Byblos (quoted by Euseb., *Praep.Ev.* 1.10.11) is conceivable (H. W. ATTRIDGE & R. A. ODEN, *Philo of Byblos: The Phoenician History. Introduction, Critical Text, Translation, Notes* [Washinton DC 1981] 83-84). Yet though Sidon could be etymologically explained as 'belonging to the god Ṣid', the god Ṣid is never mentioned as the city god of Sidon; that position was for *bʿl ṣdn*, 'Baal of Sidon' (*KAI* 14:18). It is unlikely that this designation is an epithet of Ṣid who is never mentioned in texts from Sidon.

Though the city of Sidon is probably not named after the god Ṣid, it is very possible that the name of both the city and the god go back to the same root. This would mean that Sidon was named after one of its major sources of income: fishing (WESTERMANN 1974:695). In this respect, the toponym might be compared with Bethsaïda, 'house of fishing', a place at Lake Tiberias (Matt 11:21 and par.).

III. The denunciations of Sidon in the books of the major prophets indicate that the city was known as a centre of trade (Isa 23:2.4.12) and maritime supremacy (Ezek 27:8). Though the Deuteronomists refer polemically to 'the gods of Sidon' (Judg 10:6; 1 Kgs 11:5; 2 Kgs 23:13), there is no indication that Sidon was ever considered to have divine status or to have been named after a god.

IV. *Bibliography*

J. LEWY, Les textes paléo-assyriens et l'Ancien Testament, *RHR* 110 (1934) 48-49;

P. C. SCHMITZ, Sidon, *ABD* 6 (1992) 17-18; J. TEIXIDOR, *The Pagan God* (Princeton 1977) 41; C. WESTERMANN, *Genesis 1-11* (BK I/1; Neukirchen-Vluyn 1974) 695-696.

K. VAN DER TOORN

SILVANUS

I. Silvanus is used in Latin for the Greek name Silas (or vice-versa). This has the effect of remodelling the name into a theonym. The name is borne by a distinguished Christian in Acts and some of the letters.

II. *Silvanus* is an adjective ('of the woods'), which has led to speculation that this rustic god is a special form of some more substantive god, e.g. Faunus (WISSOWA 1912:213; cf. →Quirinus), and in any case there is a certain measure of confusion with the Greek 'Silenos' (WISSOWA 1912: 215 n. 11). A rustic god, he has no part in the state calendar or priestly apparatus, though inscriptions have revealed his altars and mini-temples (*aediculae*) even in Rome (WISSOWA 1912:213). In addition to his province of 'woods', he is viewed in relatively cultivated and cleared Italy (PETER 1915:843) as a "god of fields and flock" (Vergil, *Aeneid* 8, 600). Dolabella, a Roman surveyor, (*Gromatici latini* [ed. K. Lachmann; Berlin 1848] I 302) partitions his activity into (a) care of household goods (indeed inscriptions associate him with Lares and Penates); (b) care of flocks; (c) care of boundaries when a grove demarcates the boundaries of several properties. His cult typically took place in a small precinct with trees and mini-temple and had some organisational importance: women were excluded and men could be united into *collegia* through his cult, even when they were part of the imperial staff. Throughout the Western Empire (notably in Illyricum—the former Yugoslavia) there are substantial remains of his cult, because of the identification of local natural deities with a Silvanus who was evidently more popular on the ground than the writings of the Roman élite might lead us to believe. He is depicted bearded and rather long-haired, with a branch in his left hand and a pruning-hook in his right. In a sense he is a projection of the tree under which his statue may rest (cf. MANNHARDT 1905:121).

III. Silvanus is the Latin name in the Vulgate of the Greek Silas (itself representing an Aramaic name)—the leading Christian brother mentioned at Acts 15-18. Strikingly, even the Greek text names him as 'Silvanus' at 1 Thess 1:1 and 2 Thess 1:1 (and 1 Pet 5:12, unless that is a different Silvanus), suggesting the deliberate adoption of this Latin name by Silvanus himself (just as a Saul became Paul). It is possible, alternatively, that Silas is a contraction of Silvanus (cf. SCHMIEDEL 1903:4519). It is tempting to consider Silas-Silvanus welcoming association with a god close to the hearts of ordinary people and not especially regarded by the élite—or by books on Roman religion. The name is, however, not unparallelled: PW lists 6 examples, as do PAPE-BENSELER (including a philosopher mentioned by M. Aurelius 10:31) and there is the fascinating case of *POxy* 335 (c. 85 CE), where one Paulos sells a Nikaias Silvanos, "one of the Jews from Oxyrynchos", a sixth of a house (FRAME 1912: 68).

IV. *Bibliography*

P. F. DORCEY, *The Cult of Silvanus: A Study in Roman Folk Religion* (Leiden 1992); G. DUMÉZIL, *La religion romaine archaïque* (Paris 1966) 338-340; J. E. FRAME, *A Critical and Exegetical Commentary on the Epistles of St Paul to the Thessalonians* (Edinburgh 1912) 68; A. KLOTZ, Silvanus, *PW* 8A (1927) 117-125; W. MANNHARDT, *Wald- und Feldkulte* 2 (2nd ed.; Berlin 1905) 118-126; R. PETER, Silvanus, *ALGRM* iv (1909-15) 824-877; P. W. SCHMIEDEL, Silas, Silvanus, *Encyclopaedia Biblica* 4 (ed. T. K. Cheyne & J. S. Black; London 1903) 4514-4521; G. WISSOWA, *Religion und Kultus der Römer* (2nd ed.; München 1912) 213-216.

K. DOWDEN

SIMON MAGUS

I. The name *Simōn*, although Greek, was not uncommon among Jews and Samaritans. It was even substituted for *Symeōn*, the usual and indeclensionable form of the Semitic *Šimʿôn*; thus, the original name of Jesus' disciple, Peter, is mostly written *Simōn* (e.g. Mark 1:16), although the correct form, *Symeōn*, is also found (e.g. Acts 15:14). The sobriquet *magos* could be used to denote a Persian or Babylonian expert in astrology (cf. the *magoi* in Matt 2), but it was also the name for a magician (BAGD 486a). Simon was branded as a magician. When Philip came to "the city of Samaria" in order to preach the Gospel, he learnt "that a certain man by the name of Simon was already in the city practising magic (*mageuōn*) and astonishing the people of Samaria, saying to be someone great, to whom they all gave heed from small to great, saying, 'This man is the Power of God called the Great'" (Acts 8:9-10). Simon is said to have been converted along with the rest of the Samaritans. Later, he offered the apostles money for the gift of the →Holy Spirit and was therefore rebuked by Peter.

II. "The city of Samaria" must be Sychar (cf. John 4), the centre of the Samaritan community worshipping →Yahweh on Mt. Gerizim (FOSSUM 1985:163-164; FOSSUM 1989:363). The participle 'called' (*kaloumenē*) is an addition of the author of Luke-Acts, who often adds the present participle passive to a name or sobriquet of a person, place or thing (BAGD, 400a). Since Simon in later sources is known simply as 'the Great Power', the genitive 'of God' would also seem to be a Lukan addition (cf. below). Simon (by which name we do not have to think of the historical person) probably declared, "I am the Great Power" (which is the formula corresponding to the people's acclamation, "This one is the Great Power"). This was a genuinely Samaritan divine name. In the Samaritan Targum, the Hebrew *ʾēl*, →'God', is often represented by the Aramaic *ḥêlâ*, 'the Power'. In the earliest Samaritan hymns and the midrashic work, *Memar Marqah*, 'the Power' is often praised as being 'great' (*rab*). Even 'the Great Power' (*ḥêlâ rabbâ*) is found as a divine name and praised in the same way: "Great is the Great Power" (FOSSUM 1989: 364). Since the plural form *ḥêlîn* could be used about the →angels, another interpretation of 'the Great Power' may also be suggested: it denotes the principal angel. Paradoxically, the two interpretations are not mutually exclusive. In the Pentateuch and the Book of Judges, the so-called →'Angel of Yahweh (or, God)' frequently appears as indistinguishable from God himself. Thus, 'God' heard the cry of Hagar's son, but 'the Angel of Yahweh' addressed his mother (Gen 21:17); "the Angel of Yahweh appeared to him [i.e. Moses] in a flame of fire out of the bush", but "God called to him out of the bush" (Exod 3:2.4). Apparently, by introducing the figure of the Angel of the Lord, a later editor has tried to tone down the anthropomorphisms in the older source, where God himself appeared on earth and conversed with people.

In Exod 23:20-21 God even gives the Angel his own Name: "I am going to send an angel in front of you, to guard you on the way and to bring you to the place that I have prepared. Be attentive and listen to his voice; do not rebel against him, for he will not pardon your transgression; for My Name is in him." The Angel who is going to lead the Hebrews to the Promised Land is an extension of God's personality by virtue of sharing the divine Name, which in the ancient world denoted the nature or mode of being in its carrier. The Angel possessing the Name of God thus has the power to withold the absolution of sins, a divine prerogative.

Simon apparently was seen as the manifestation of God, 'the Great Power', in human form. The author of Acts has added the genitive in order to indicate that Simon was not regarded as the essential Godhead, but as the corporeal hypostasis of the deity (cf. Acts 3:2, "the gate of the temple called the Beautiful", which is the only phrase in Luke-Acts corresponding syntactically to that in Acts 8:10, "the Power of God called the Great": in the former phrase, the genitive is not apposite but possessive, implying that 'the Beautiful Gate' belongs to the temple [FOSSUM 1989:371]).

Luke asserts that Simon was a magician. Now in the world of religion, my miracle is your magic. Simon may have been a miracle worker. How is this function compatible with his title, 'the Great Power (of God)'?

In Samaritanism, →Moses is portrayed as the miracle worker *par excellence*. Around the beginning of our era, the Samaritans expected the coming of the Prophet like Moses, whose advent is prophesied in Deut 18:15.18. *Memar Marqah* III.1 warns against the false prophet who "states that he is like Moses in performing a wonder or a miracle." The arch-heretic in Samaritan sources, Dositheus, claimed to be the prophet like Moses. In Christian writings, Dositheus and Simon are associated, and in a Simonian tradition incorporated in the Pseudo-Clementine literature, they are even portrayed as rivals in a battle cast into the form of a miracle contest (*Homilies* II.24 [FOSSUM 1989:376-377]). Did Simon too claim to be the Prophet like Moses?

The Simonian legend in the Pseudo-Clementines relates that Simon beats Dositheus in a rivalry over the right to the title, 'the Standing One' (*ho hestōs*), which denotes imperishability. In Samaritan Aramaic texts, the participle *qā'ēm*, 'standing', which has the same significance, is used with reference to Moses as well as God and the angels (FOSSUM 1989:384-388). In Samaritanism, Moses shares the various divine names (FOSSUM 1985:87-92); he is thus assimilated to the Angel of the Lord (this is also seen from the fact that the Samaritan Targum to Exod 23:20 substitutes 'Apostle' (*šālîaḥ*) for 'Angel', because 'Apostle' was one of the favourite titles of Moses in Samaritanism [FOSSUM 1985:145-147]). In *Memar Marqah* IV.1, it is said: "Who can compete with Moses, whose name was made the Name of the Lord." In *Acts Pet.* 17, it is claimed that Simon's name is 'the Name of the Lord' (*cui nomen est autem nomen domini*). Thus, Simon's titles, 'the Great Power' and 'the Standing One', could designate him as the eschatological Prophet like Moses as well as the Angel of the Lord, the human manifestation of God.

Luke's account that Simon was converted by Philip cannot be true, for the only position allotted to Jesus in the Simonian system as reported by the heresiologists is that as a precursory incarnation of Simon himself. In fact, the figure of Jesus can be removed without any damage being done to the system as such. That Simon offered the apostles money for the gift of the Spirit is Christian polemics. Acts 8:14-25, which recounts the sanction of Philip's mission by the apostle and the affray between Peter and Simon, is a Lukan composition which does not have the same claim to authencity as the preceding verses.

III. The heresiologist Irenaeus (*ca.* 180 CE) makes Simon the author of Gnosticism. This report raises many questions. Does Irenaeus "mean to imply a genetic relationship, or merely that Simon was the first to take this line? How much of this report can be traced back to the historical Simon, and how much was fathered on him by later members of the sect? Was Simon himself a gnostic, and in what sense? Can we really identify Simon the heresiarch with the Simon of Acts, or has some development taken place in the interval between?" (WILSON 1979:486).

It is clear that we cannot derive each and every form of Gnosticism from Simon, but Simon could nevertheless have been "the first to take this line"—at least the first of whom the heresiologists had heard. It should be noted that the Simonian system is remarkably simple in comparison to the 2nd century Gnostic systems, to which it manifestly is related. Moreover, the teaching attributed to Simon lacks some of the Gnostic characteristics (e.g. the idea that matter is anti-divine and evil *per se*, and the doctrine that there is a divine spark in human beings which must be released from its imprisonment in the material body). Finally, Simon's system even contains some remarkably un-Gnostic features. Thus, the notion that God had to appear on earth as a human being in order to save his hypostasized Thought, who was incarnated in a prostitute, is highly original and runs counter to the docetic propensity of Gnosticism.

It would seem that the teachings ascribed to Simon amount to an early proto-Gnostic system. It is impossible to say how much derives from Simon himself, but we should at least allow for some kind of continuity between the teaching of Simon and that of his followers (WILSON 1979:490; FOSSUM 1989:359-361; but cf. HALL 1987:262-275).

IV. *Bibliography*

J. E. FOSSUM, *The Name of God and the Angel of the Lord* (WUNT 36; Tübingen 1985); FOSSUM, Sects and Movements, *The Samaritans* (ed. A. D. Crown; Tübingen 1989) 293-389; B. W. HALL, *Samaritan Religion from John Hyrcanus to Baba Rabba* (Sydney 1987) 262-275; G. LÜDEMANN, *Das frühe Christentum nach den Traditionen der Apostelgeschichte* (Göttingen 1987) 99-107; R. McL. WILSON, Simon and Gnostic Origins, *Les Actes des Apôtres* (BETL 48; ed. J. Kremer; Gembloux/Leuven 1979) 485-491; M. SMITH, The Account of Simon Magus in Acts 8, *H. A. Wolfson Jubilee Volumes* vol. 2 (Jerusalem 1965) 735-749.

J. FOSSUM

SIN ἁμαρτία

I. The most general word for sin, and the one most frequently used in the NT, is *hamartia*. It usually occurs in the plural; but it also occurs a number of times in the singular, referring to the totality of sin, or sinning as such—see John 1:29; 8:21.34; 9:41; 15:22; 16:8.9; 1 John 1:8; 3:4.8.9; Rom 8:2.3.10; 14:23; 2 Cor 5:21; Heb 10:18. There is a fluid transition between this use of the singular and the notion of sin as an active subject wielding power over human beings. This usage is found in several texts; but, in particular, in Paul's Epistle to the Romans chaps. 5-7. Personification is a figure of speech capable of referring to different sorts of 'being' and degrees of 'reality', ranging from little more than an image or a metaphor to condensation to gods or demons (see RÖHSER 1987). Hence, the personified use of *hamartia* has to be discussed here.

II. Sir 21:2 admonishes "Flee from sin as from a snake; for if you approach sin, it will bite you. Its teeth are lion's teeth, and can destroy human lives". Similarly, in Sir 27:10 sin is compared to a lion lying in wait for its prey. Jas 1:15 describes desire as giving birth to sin; and sin as giving birth to death; whilst Heb 3:13 warns people not to be hardened 'by the deceitfulness of sin'. John 8:34 seems to go one step further when it states that "everyone who commits sin is a slave to sin"—equated in v 44 with being 'from your father the devil' (cf. 1 John 3:8.10). John 8:34 links up with Paul's basic statement in Rom 3:9 that all Jews and Greeks are 'under sin': that is 'under the power of sin' (cf. Gal 3:22; Rom 11:32). As in John, this manifests itself in the fact that all, in fact, have sinned (Rom 3:23). Gal 2:17 emphasizes that →Christ could not possibly be 'a servant of sin'. On the contrary, God made him who knew no sin 'to be sin' (2 Cor 5:21); or, in other words, he sent 'his own Son in the likeness of sinful flesh' to condemn sin in the flesh (Rom 8:3; see below).

III. In Rom 5-7 Paul describes the all-pervading power and influence of sin. It came into the world through the transgression of one man, Adam, and through sin came death. "Death spread to all, because all have sinned" (Rom 5:12, a much discussed passage). Again, being under the power of sin and actual sinning are mentioned together. Sin exercised dominion in death (5:21)—but all this is mentioned because Paul wants to bring the good news of 'the abundance of grace and the free gift of righteousness' in Christ (5:17). Grace, in fact was meant 'to exercise dominion through righteousness, leading to eternal life through Jesus Christ our Lord'(5:21).

Those who are buried with Christ in baptism have died to sin and should therefore sin no more (6:1-11). Hence believers should 'not let sin exercise dominion' in their lives (6:12), not again become 'slaves to sin' (6:17.20). Notwithstanding their share in the life of Christ (6:4.5.7.11.22-23) and the fact that sin will have no dominion over them because they are 'not under the law but under grace' (6:14), those who live in communion with Christ clearly still have to be reminded of the ethical implications of the new life granted to them.

In chap. 7 Paul again describes the power of sin. Surprisingly, sin is aided by the law; "sin, seizing an opportunity in the commandment (i.e. "thou shalt not covet"), produced in me all kinds of covetousness. Apart from the law sin lies dead" (7:8, cf. the entire section vv 7-13). Law itself is spiritual, but human beings are 'of the flesh, sold (into slavery) under sin' (7:14). They are made captive to the law of sin that dwells in their members (7:23) and quite unable to obey the law of God. But God "sent his own Son in the likeness of sinful flesh; and, to deal with sin, he condemned sin in the flesh, so that the just requirement of the law might be fulfilled in us who walk not according to the flesh but according to the Spirit" (8:3-4). Those who live in communion with Christ may live a new life, not in the flesh but in the Spirit—still in the body and therefore subject to suffering, as well as to decay and to mortality, but in good faith expecting the redemption of their bodies, 'the freedom of the glory of the children of God' (8:12-25, esp. vv 20-24). At the final resurrection, at Christ's parousia, death will be annihilated as the last enemy (1 Cor 15:26, cf. vv 50-56).

A full discussion of Paul's understanding of sin would require a detailed analysis of his anthropology and soteriology. His daring personification of sin has produced a picture of an evil power bringing doom and death: thus thwarting human efforts to perform God's commandments in order to live in accordance with God's will. Yet always actual human sinning remains in the picture, and in that light we may also view Paul's picture of sin as the personifcation of the totality of human failure and resistance against God, rebounding on humanity—its fateful repercussions only to be undone by God's redemptive work in Christ, as described in Rom 8.

IV. *Bibliography*

G. RÖHSER, *Metaphorik und Personifikation der Sünde* (WUNT 2,25; Tübingen 1987); E. P. SANDERS, Sin, Sinners (NT), *ABD* 6 (1992) 40-47.

M. DE JONGE

SÎN -סן, -שׁן

I. Sîn is the name of the Babylonian moongod, attested as theophoric element in Assyrian and Babylonian personal names. In the Old Testament in the names Sanherib (*sanḥērîb*), Sanballat (*sanballaṭ*) and Shenazzar (*šen'aṣṣar*).

II. The name *Sîn* (earlier *Suen, Suin*) survived in the Aramaic speaking world as the name of the moongod residing in Harran (J. N. POSTGATE, *RLA* IV/2-3 [1973] 124-5; DRIJVERS 1980; TUBACH 1986; GREEN 1992). This cult, already attested at the beginning of the second millennium in Mari, was promoted by Nabonidus who gave Sîn epithets such as 'Lord/King of the Gods', or even 'God of Gods' (P.-A. BEAULIEU, *The Reign of Nabonidus, King of Babylon 556-539 B.C.* [New Haven and London 1989] 43-65). For this reason, the Aramaic name of the god *Mrlh'* (Marilahe, 'Lord of the Gods') has been identified with Sîn of Harran (GREEN 1992:67). Normally, the name of the moongod was *Šah(a)r* among the Aramaeans.

In Mesopotamia, the Sumerian and Babylonian moongod, Nanna/Sîn, was venerated everywhere, but Ur remained the centre of his cult. Nanna was born from an illicit union of the Sumerian gods Enlil and Ninlil. The name of the spouse of Sîn, written **^{d}Nin.gal**, was pronounced *Nikkal* (J.-M. DURAND, *NABU* 1987/14). This name was taken over as the name of the moongod's partner in the West-Semitic world: *nkl* in an Ugaritic myth (*KTU* 1.24), and in Aramaic inscriptions (*KAI* 225:9, 226:9; cf. 222 A I 9).

Sîn as element in Akkadian personal names written in an Aramaic context is rendered once as *Sn*, in the name *Sn'blṭ* (cf Biblical San-ballat), four times *Šn* (MARAQTEN 1988:244, 248). In Aramaic names, Sîn is attested as *Šn* once, *Š'* twice (MARAQTEN 1988:103, 101). In Akkadian syllabic writing the latter element appears as *Se*, *Se-e*, *Se-'* in Aramaic personal names (S. PARPOLA, *OLP* 16 [1985] 273 n 2 [& lit]).

It is striking that the name appears twice as *San-* in a Hebrew context, in Sanherib (Sennacherib) and Sanballat; in a Greek context *Sennachēribos* (LXX, Josephus), *Sanacharibos* (Herodotus); *Sanaballat* (LXX), *Sanaballetēs* (Josephus); see *HALAT* 718. The Aramaic Wisdom of Aḥiqar has both forms *S/Šn'ḥrjb*. The same development to *san-* can be observed in the Hebrew word for 'night-blindness', *sanwērīm*, to be derived from Akkadian *Sîn-lurmâ* (and variants) (M. STOL, *JNES* 45 [1986] 296-297). Some Assyrian names of men and women have the theophoric element ^{d}*Sa-a* (J. N. POSTGATE, *Iraq* 32 [1970] 139). Unrelated is perhaps the name of the moon ^{d}Sa-nu-ga-ru$_{12}$ (var. ITI) in the Ebla texts (ARET 5 [1984] 24 no. 4 III 6, var. no. 1 III 12). Once, we find in Hebrew context *Šen-*, in the name *Šen-'aṣṣar*, among the descendants of David, 1 Chr 3:18 (see *HALAT* 1475).

III. *Bibliography*

H. J. W. DRIJVERS, *Cults and Beliefs at Edessa* (Leiden 1980) 122-145; T. M. GREEN, *The City of the Moon God. Religious Traditions of Harran* (Leiden 1992); M. MARAQTEN, *Die semitischen Personennamen in den alt- und reichsaramäischen Inschriften aus Vorderasien* (Hildesheim/Zürich/New York 1988) 63-64; A. SJÖBERG, *Der Mondgott Nanna-Suen in der sumerischen Überlieferung* (Stockholm 1960); J. TUBACH, *Im Schatten des Sonnengottes. Der Sonnenkult in Edessa, Ḥarrān und Ḥaṭrā am Vorabend der christlichen Mission* (Wiesbaden 1986) 129-140.

M. STOL

SIRION שִׂרְיוֹן

I. According to some of our sources Mount Sirion/Siryon is part of the Hermon massif. Deut 3:9 gives it as the name of the mountain used by the Sidonians, but nevertheless the Amorite designation is Senir. This variant form of the name corresponds to the mountain *Saniru* being the refuge of Haza'el in the inscriptions of Shalmaneser III (E. MICHEL, *WO* 1 [1947/1952] 265:6). On the other hand the Hittite designation of the Anti-Lebanon is *Šariyana* and the same is true for Ug *šryn* and Eg *sꜣw-r-i-nꜣ*. According to the Baal-Myth (*KTU* 1.4 vi:19. 21) Sirion produced famous cedar-wood. Ezek 27:5 says that juniperwood from Sirion was used by the Tyrians for the planking of their ships. Therefore in Syriac *šarwajena* is the designation of *juniperus oxycedrus* (BROCKELMANN, *Lex. Syr.* 807).

Though deified in extra-biblical sources, Sirion is not mentioned as a deity in the Bible.

II. Among the gods listed in all treaties between Hittite kings and their Syrian vassals Mount Sirion is invoked in the spelling *Šarijana/i* or *Šariššija* as a deified mountain together with the →Lebanon (*Lablana)* and the unidentified mountain *Pišaiša*: the treaty between Šuppiluliuma I and Tette from *Nuḫḫašše* (E. WEIDNER, *Politische Dokumente aus Kleinasien* 68 [Leipzig 1923] 36-37) and his treaty with Aziru of Amurru (WEIDNER, ibid. 74 Rs.3-4; partly restored) and the treaty of Tudḫalija IV with Shaushgamuwa of Amurru (C. KÜHNE & H. OTTEN, *Der Šaušgamuwa-Vertrag* [StBoT 16; Wiesbaden 1971] 20:18). In this context the Anti-Lebanon is indicated and—like many Hittite mountain-gods—it has divine qualities. Beside this textual evidence there exist no further hints of a deification of the Anti-Lebanon (but cf. →Hermon), although the *sa-ri-a* beside the Lebanon in the Old Babylonian Gilgamesh fragment (T. BAUER, Ein Fragment des Gilgameš Epos, *JNES* 16 [1957] 256 r.13) is the home of the demon Ḫuwawa.

III. The Old Testament uses the name of this mountain in similes only: in Ps 29:6 the voice of the Lord makes "Lebanon and Sirjon skip like a steer"; in Cant 4:8 the bride shall "trip down from Amana's peak, from the peak of Senir and Hermon, from the dens of lions, from the hills of leopards". There are no traces of any cult of Sirion in OT sources.

IV. *Bibliography*

Y. IDEKA, Hermon, Sirion and Senir, *Annual of the Japanese Biblical Institute* 4 (1978) 32-44; I. SINGER, Emeq Saron or Emeq Siryon, *ZDPV* 104 (1988) 1-5.

W. RÖLLIG

SISERA סיסרא

I. The personal name סיסרא (Judg 4; 5; 1 Sam 12:9; Ps 83:10) has generally been interpreted as a non-Hebrew name (*IPN* 64). The name has been related to the Luwian personal name *zi-za-ru-wa* (*HALAT* 710; SOGGIN 1981:63). GARBINI related Sisera to the name of a Minoan deity *(j)a-sa-sa-ra* (1978:17-21).

II. The name *(j)a-sa-sa-ra* appears in some Minoan linear A inscriptions. It can be interpreted as a divine name. According to KTISTOPULOS (apud CARRATELLI 1976:125) this deity can be identified with Σαισάρα. He is known in the myth of Keleos to be a designation of →Zeus Kretogenes (NILSSON 1950:543.554).

III. An identification of this deity with the biblical Sisera suggests an interesting interpretation of the episode in Judg 4-5. It implies, however, that Sisera was the Philistine general of the Canaanite ruler Jabin. It underscores the tradition of the origin of the Philistines from Kaphtor or the Aegaean world. It also yields a construal of the Song of Deborah on two levels: the earthly combat between Israel and the Canaanites is parallel to a heavenly strife between →Yahweh and a Canaanite deity. The elements 'stars' and 'rain' could also be interpreted as survivals of the mythology of the weather-god Sisera. They are, however, now fighting against him (GARBINI 1978).

Against this interpretation it should be noted that recent onomastic research has shown that the name *Sîsĕra'* is Semitic (SCHNEIDER 1992:192.260). This implies that he can be interpreted as a Canaanite general. A hidden meaning in the story—if there is one—should more plausibly be sought in a conflict between the sexes than in a strife between male deities.

In the OT the name Sisera is also borne by an Israelite who returned from the Babylonian exile in Ezra 2:53; Neh 7:55.

IV. *Bibliography*

M. BAL, *Murder and Difference. Gender, Genre and Scholarship on Siserah's Death* (Bloomington 1988); G. P. CARRATELLI, ΣΑΙΣΑΡΑ, *La Parola del Passato* 31 (1976) 123-128; G. GARBINI, Il cantico di Debora, *La Parola del Passato* 33 (1978) 5-31; M. P. NILSSON, *The Minoan-Mycenaean Religion* (Lund 1950); T. SCHNEIDER, *Asiatische Personennamen in ägyptischen Quellen des Neuen Reiches* (OBO 114; Freiburg/Göttingen 1992); J. A. SOGGIN, *Judges. A Commentary* (London 1981).

B. BECKING

SKYTHES Σκύθης

I. Skythes ('Skythian') is the eponymous hero of the Skythians, an Indo-European people to the north of the Greek world. Skythians themselves have a mythic quality, occurring in 2-3-4 Macc and Col 3:11 as a byword for barbarism. Otherwise the name only occurs in the placename Skythopolis (1-2 Macc).

II. For the standard Greek use of eponymous heroes to account for the beginnings of a tribe, see →Thessalos. The Skythians are a rather different case, as they are a non-Greek tribe to whom Greeks credit the creation of an eponym on the Greek pattern. The Skythians in fact belonged to the Indo-Iranian branch of the Indo-Europeans and lived across a wide area from north of the Black Sea to the northerly parts of the Persian Empire, where they are generally known as *Sāka* in Persian and *Sakai* or *Skythai* in Greek (possibly *Ashkenaz* in Biblical Hebrew; see Gen 10:3, and *HALAT* 92). The Skythians may indeed have traced their national identity back to a single man (just as the Germans traced themselves back to 'Mannus' the first man, Tacitus, *Germania* 2:3): Herodotos (4:5-6) tells a Skythian story of a first man called Targitaos and his three sons Lipoxais, Harpoxais and Kolaxais.

A (Black Sea) Greek myth transposes this native story so as to deliver an eponym, Skythes, and is told in different versions by Herodotos 4:9 and Diodoros 2:43. In Herodotos, →Heracles (often a convenient transposition of a native hero) is passing through Skythia and lies with a snake-maiden in a cave in order to retrieve horses for which he is searching. Three children are begotten and on maturity are tested to see if they can handle Heracles' bow and wear his belt. Agathyrsos and Gelonos cannot and must migrate elsewhere, but the youngest, Skythes, succeeds. He is the ancestor of the Skythian kings and the Skythians henceforth wear this special sort of belt. In Diodoros' version, it is →'Zeus' not →'Heracles' who lies with the snake-maiden and only Skythes is born of the union. He now has two sons, Palos and Napes, the eponyms of the Paloi and Napoi tribes among the Skythians.

The Skythians were the remotest northerly people known to Greeks in classical times. Beyond them, according to Aristeas of Prokonnesos (ca. 675 BCE), a source still used by Herodotos (ca. 430/20 BCE), lay one-eyed Arimaspians who fought the griffins for their gold and beyond the Arimaspians only the blessed folk of →Apollo, the Hyperboreans. Skythians were where reality ran out and, whether truthfully or not, were viewed as prone to barbaric habits such as scalping enemies, drinking their blood, and using their skulls as tankards, not to mention cannabis sessions in wigwams (Herodotos 4:64. 75).

III. Skythian savagery became a commonplace of classical literature (Cicero, *2 Verr.* 5:150. *Pis.* §18; Pliny, *NH* 7:11) and so of Greek writers of biblical texts. At 2 Macc 4:47 even Skythians might have had more pity; an attempted lynching at 3 Macc 7:5 is what one might expect of savage Skythians; and an example of flaying alive at 4 Macc 10:7 is described as "Skythianing off the skin". At Col 3:11, they are an evocative proper name to figure next to 'barbarian' and 'slave'—they indeed often provided slaves for the civilised world (most notably the Athenian civil guard).

The town known at 1 Macc 5:52 as Baithsan (Bethsan) is referred to at 2 Macc 12:29-30 by its Greek name, Skythopolis ('city of the Skythians'). The origin of this new name for the city is still an unresolved issue.

IV. *Bibliography*

U. HÖFER, Scythes, *ALGRM* iv (1909-15) 1077-1080; F. HUMBORG, Skythes, *PW* 8A (1927) 693-694.

K. DOWDEN

SON OF GOD

I. The title 'Son of God', ascribed to Jesus in the NT, reflects a common ancient Near Eastern notion according to which the king could claim divine descent. The idea is also found in the OT. In relation to Jesus, the title eventually became associated with such concepts as divinity and preexistence.

II. In the entire Near East, the king could be called 'Son of God' or even 'God'. Pharaoh was the 'Good God' (MORET 1902: 296). The first of the five 'great names' which he received upon his enthronement was 'Horus', an old title designating him as the earthly manifestation of the falcon god →Horus, the ancient dynastic god of Egypt (GARDINER 1957:72). His incarnation was assumed: "He descended from heaven and was born in Heliopolis" (ERMAN 1923:340).

The Semitic rulers of Akkad (ca. 2350-2150 BCE) claimed divinity for themselves. Thus, Naram-Sin styled himself *ilu A-ga-de*, 'God of Akkad' (RADAU 1899:7). Following the example of the Akkadian rulers, the kings in the ensuing period of Sumerian renaissance had their names prefixed by the determinative for divinity (DHORME 1910: 170). They even enjoyed worship (RÖMER 1969:146). Bursin called himself 'the rightful God, the Sun of his country' (RADAU

1900:199, 201). The old titulary continued to apply to the later Semitic rulers. Thus, Hammurabi was the 'God' (*ilu*) and 'Sun' of his people (DHORME 1910:170), and his name was occasionally prefixed by the determinative for divinity (EDZARD 1965: 257-258).

The Syrian kings possibly claimed divinity for themselves. Ezek 28:2.9 mocks the king of Tyre (→Melqart) for claiming to be divine and occupying the throne of *'ĕlōhîm*, →'God(I)'. Virgil (*Aen.* 1:729 with Servius' note) and Silius Italicus (*Pun.* 1:86) state that the kings of Tyre traced their descent to →Baal. The later Seleucid rulers of Syria claimed to be *theos*, →'God(II)'. Josephus (*Ant.* 9.4.6) reports a worship of the deceased rulers of Damascus in his day.

Even more common than the designation 'God' for the King, was the title 'Son of God'. From the 1st dynasty (ca. 3000 BCE), the pharaohs were regarded as the 'sons of →Isis', and were represented as being suckled by her and sitting on her lap. The last of Pharaoh's royal names was 'Son of →Re', which he bore from the 4th dynasty (ca. 2500 BCE) onwards (GARDINER 1957: 74). The title indicated that he was the physical offspring of the sun god, as is shown in particular by the evidence from Deir el-Bahri, where →Amun-Re is represented as having united sexually with Pharaoh's mother (SETHE 1914:102-103).

In an inscription for Ramesses II, the god Amun-Re is introduced as saying: "I am your Father, who has engendered you as god in order that you be king of Upper and Lower Egypt on My throne" (ROEDER 1915: 158-159). Pharaoh ruled in the place of his divine father. He obviously had to answer for his father's possessions with which he had been entrusted.

Beginning with the Sumerian king Mesilim of Kish, the Mesopotamian ruler was seen as the 'son' or 'child' of his god or goddess (SJÖBERG 1972:87-112). The king is said expressly to have been 'born' of the deity, and we should obviously understand this sonship in physical terms. Abisare of Larsa is said to be the 'Pride of his physical Father' (**giri$_x$.zal.a.a.ugu.na**), the god Enlil (SJÖBERG 1972:96097). The male god could also be said to have implanted his seed into the womb of the king's mother, a goddess or a priestess representing her (SJÖBERG 1972:88, 93).

In the Ugaritic epic about Keret, the king is called the 'Son of El', and it is implied that, as one of the 'gods', he is supposed not to die. This is "a projection of cultic terminology" used to enhance the royal office and person (GRAY 1964:66-67).

The enthronement was the definitive act of begetting or deification in Egypt (PREISIGKE 1920:13-14). The technical term is *smen*, which corresponds to the verb in Ps 2:6, "I have set (*nāsaktî*) My king on →Zion, My holy hill". This is a parallel to the 'birth' in the next verse. Thutmosis III can say that he is God's "Son, whom He commanded that should be upon His throne ... and begat in uprightness of heart" (BREASTED 1906:59). The magico-religious birth occurs after the call to the throne.

In Mesopotamia, too, the divine birth of the king was celebrated on the day of his enthronement. In a description of the enthronement of Shulgi, it is said: "The En-priestess bore a good man, who had been placed in her womb, Enlil, the Mighty →Shepherd, made the youth stand forth, a son, who is well suited for kingship and the throne" (SJÖBERG 1972:104-105, with a slight change). A description of Shulgi being given the royal insignia follows. SJÖBERG (1972:107) also refers to a word of Gudea to the goddess Gatumdu: "My seed [i.e. the seed of my Father] You have received; in the sanctuary You have begotten me".

III. The Israelite king could also be called *'ĕlōhîm*, 'God' (Ps 45:6). Among the five names of the royal child who is to sit on David's throne, we find *'ēl gibbôr*, 'Mighty God' (Isa 9:6). It was more common to refer to the king in Israel-Judah as the 'Son of God'.

In the Nathan prophecy in 2 Sam 7, the relationship between God and the Israelite-Judaean king (David's 'seed') is described as a father-son relationship (v 14; cf. 1 Chr

17:13; 22:10; 28:6). In Ps 89:27-28, God is the 'Father' of the king, his 'firstborn'. The king was 'born' from God when he was installed, as is made clear by the declarations of →Yahweh in two Psalms which were used as liturgical texts at the enthronement ceremony: "You are My Son; this day I have begotten thee" (2:7); "In holy ornament out of the womb of Dawn, I have fathered thee as →Dew" (110:3; WIDENGREN 1976:186).

The Nathan prophecy guarantees the perpetuity of the Davidic dynasty (2 Sam 7:16). This promise gave rise to 'messianic' expectations (Isa 7:14-17 [a prophecy based on Egyptian and Canaanite oracles about the birth of the royal child from the queen, a representative of the goddess]; 9:6-7 [an oracle showing influence from the Egyptian royal titulary in the five names of the child who is to occupy the Davidic throne]).

Israel is also called God's 'Son' (Exod 4:22-23; Jer 31:20; Hos 11:1; see also Jer 31:9). All the individuals of the people are therefore God's 'sons' and 'daughters', or 'children' (Deut 14:1; 32:5, 19; Isa 30:1; 43:6; 45:11; Ezek 16:20-21; Hos 2:1). This usage of the name 'Son(s)' of God designates Israel as God's chosen and protected people. 'Sons of God' could also be used as a designation of the heavenly hosts.

IV. In the NT, the title 'Son of God', with the attendant implications, is found more especially in connection with →Jesus. Jesus spoke of God as 'Dad(dy)', using the diminutive form *ʾabbâ* (Mark 14:36 [Gal 4:6 and Rom 8:15 show that this memory was preserved]; cf. Luke 11:2). Matt 11:27 = Luke 10:22, where Jesus says that 'all things' (= 'all authority' [Matt 28:18]) have been delivered to him by his Father, the only one who knows him and who is known only by him and the ones to whom he chooses to reveal him, is a strongly literary passage and markedly different from other passages telling us anything about the self-consciousness of the historical Jesus. On the basis of this universal authority, Jesus can reveal the Father.

Mark 13:32 ("not even the angels, nor the Son, but only the Father" knows the last day) teaches the full subordination of the Son. But the intimate relationship between 'the Father' and 'the Son' is still present (the Son is closer to God than the angels). There is a tension between this absolute usage of 'the Father', which corresponds to that of 'the Son', and the words of Jesus about 'your Father'. Mark 13:32 as well as Matt 11:27 = Luke 10:22 is a clear Christological limitation of the Father name of God.

In Matt 28:18-20, the commission of the resurrected Jesus to the disciples to go and baptize people "in the name of the Father and the Son and the →Holy Spirit" follows upon the word about all authority having been given to the Son. The title 'the Son' has here found a new place in the baptismal liturgy, and the association of 'the Father' and 'the Son' has been expanded into a formula containing the names of all the three persons in the divine economy.

In his earliest letter, Paul speaks of the expectation of God's "Son from heaven, whom He [i.e. God] raised from the dead" (1 Thess 1:10). It has been suggested that this originally was a saying about the →Son of Man which Paul reinterpreted for his Hellenistic community (FRIEDRICH 1965:502-516). A merger of the messianic figure of the Son of God and the eschatological Son of Man is found in the account of the process against Jesus, where the high priest asks: "Are you the →Christ [= Messiah], the Son of the Blessed?" (Mark 14:61). Jesus' reply implies that he is the Son of Man who will be seen "seated at the right of the Power and coming with the clouds of heaven". The text takes 'the Son of the Blessed', a phrase which contains a circumlocution for the name of God, as a messianic designation and explains the function of the Messiah by reference to his enthronement by the side of God and return as the eschatological Son of Man.

Mark 14:62 describes Jesus as a heavenly being with reference to Ps 110:1 and Dan 7:13 (and Ps 80:17 [SEITZ 1973:481-485]?). In Peter's Pentecost sermon, Ps 110:1 is cited with reference to the ascension of Jesus (Acts 2:34-35). Being seated at the right of God, he was made "both Lord and Christ [= Messiah]" (v 36). During his lifetime, Jesus was only Messias designatus, "a man attested to you by God with mighty works and wonders and signs [...]" (v 22).

In Paul's speech in Pisidian Antioch, it is Ps 2:7, the other enthronement text in the OT, which is cited with reference to the resurrection of Jesus (Acts 13:33). In the beginning of Romans 1, Paul quotes an old confession formula saying that Jesus "was descended from David according to the Spirit of holiness by his resurrection from the dead [...]" (vv 3-4). During his life as a Davidide, Jesus was Messias designatus; it was first upon his ascension that he was made the messianic 'Son of God in power'.

The account of the transfiguration, according to which Jesus was identified by a heavenly voice as "My beloved Son" (Mark 9:7), may have been an original resurrection story (BULTMANN 1957:278). However, it may also be a text describing Jesus' installation as the eschatological king (RIESENFELD 1947:182-220, 223-225, 303-306) already during his human life. In either case, the idea of an ascent to heaven is implied, for the 'high mountain' (Mark 9:2) is a well-known image of heaven to which the king ascended and where he was enthroned (Isa 14:13-14; Ezek 28:2, 12-16).

Jesus' installation as the Son of God was also pushed back to the beginning of his earthly ministry in order to include this in the rule promised to David. Coming out of the waters of the →Jordan, the heavens were opened, the Spirit descended upon him in the form of a →dove, and a heavenly voice said: "You are My beloved Son, with thee I am well pleased" (Mark 1:11). Baptism or ritual washing was part of the royal installation. Upon his accession to the throne, Pharaoh was washed with waters out of which the sun god was born. When Pharaoh came forth begotten out of the water, the sun god had to recognize him as his son (BLACKMANN 1918:153-157). 1 Kgs 1:33-34 relates that Solomon was anointed king at the well of Gihon; perhaps he was washed as well as anointed. During his installation as the eschatological high priest(-king), Levi was washed with 'clean water' (*T. Levi* 8:5).

The unction, which belonged to the Semitic enthronement ritual, conveyed the Spirit of God (1 Sam 16:13). In Luke 4:18, Jesus cites the beginning of the royal hymn in Isa 61: "The Spirit of the LORD is upon me, for He has anointed me" (v 1). That this refers to the baptism of Jesus is seen from Peter's speech in Acts 10, where it is said that the word of God went forth "after the baptism which John preached: how God anointed Jesus of Nazareth with the Holy Spirit and power" (vv 37-38).

The words of the heavenly voice recite Isa 42:1 as well as Ps 2:7 (the latter text being quoted verbatim in the parallel in Luke 3:22 in Codex D [Bezae], some Itala manuscripts, and many Fathers). In the former text, the beginning of the first of the songs about the Suffering Servant of Yahweh, God says: "Behold My Servant, whom I uphold, My Chosen, in whom My soul delights; I have put my Spirit upon him". The Hebrew text reads *'ebed*, which means 'servant', while the LXX has *pais*, which means 'son' as well as 'servant'. Both the terms were royal titles (2 Sam 3:18; Ps 89:3; Ezek 34:23). In a text about Ashurbanipal, the two titles are used in parallelism (DHORME 1910:166-167). In the OT, they are closely associated (2 Sam 7:4, 8; Ps 89:21, 27-28). In the description of the righteous in Wis 2:12-20, divine sonship and service are associated. In *T. Levi* 4:2, it is said that the patriarch will become God's 'Son' (*hyios*), 'Servant' (*therapōn*), and 'Priest'. In 18:6, it is said that the heavens will be opened, and a 'fatherly voice' will sound when the Spirit is given to Levi (cf. *T. Judah* 24:2-3).

In quoting Isa 42:1, Matt 12:18 amplifies 'Chosen' with 'Beloved'. The latter as well as the former was a Near Eastern royal title for the former (DHORME 1910:150-152; 2 Sam 21:6; Ps 89:4). Mesilim of Kish was said to be the 'Beloved Son of Ninhursag' (**dumu.ki.ág.^{d}nin.ḫur.sag.a**; SJÖBERG 1972:

87 [for further Mesopotamian evidence, see DHORME 1910:164-166]). Pharaoh Thutmosis is the 'Beloved of →Hathor' (GARDINER 1957:72). Solomon the king is 'loved' by God (2 Sam 12;24; Neh 13:26). Targum Ps 2:7 reads: "Beloved as a son is to his father you are to Me".

The words that God is 'well pleased' with the Son also have parallels in royal ideology. At the installation of Hatshepsut, Re introduces her to the divine assembly and says: "Behold My daughter Hatshepsut; May she live; I love her; I am well pleased with her!" (SETHE 1914:113). The Targumic versions of Isa 42:1 and 43:10 read that God has found delight in the Messiah.

At an early stage, Jesus was even conceived of as the preexistent Son who had been sent by God into the world in order to bring salvation to humankind (Gal 4:4-5; Rom 8:3-4; cf. John 3:17; 1 John 4:9, 14). SCHWEIZER (*TDNT* 8 [1972] 375) has explained this notion against the background of Hellenistic Jewish ideas about God's personified word (→Logos) and wisdom. Now the divine Word is called God's 'Son' by Philo, but is not said to have been sent into the world, while Sophia (→Wisdom) in Wis 9 is said to have been sent (the sending of Sophia and the Spirit in vv 10 and 17 corresponds to that of the Son and the Spirit in Gal 4:4-6), but is not the 'Son' of God.

In a fragment of the *Prayer of Joseph*, we come across a representation of an angel by the name of Israel, who is said to be a 'ruling Spirit', the 'Firstborn of every living thing', the 'Archangel of the power of the Lord', the 'Chief Captain among the sons of God', and the 'First of those who serve before the Face of the Lord' (*Or. Jo.* 2:31). That the angel is said to be the 'Firstborn of every living thing' derives from an exegesis of Exod 4:22, where God says: "Israel is My firstborn son". This verse could be referred to the patriarch →Jacob, who was given the name Israel by God (*Jub.* 19:29; *Exod R.* 19:7; *3 Enoch* 44:10). In the *Prayer of Joseph*, the preexistent angel Israel, who is the chief 'among the sons of God', explicitly identifies himself as having become manifested in the patriarch: "I, Jacob, whom men call Jacob, but whose name is Israel".

Philo also furnishes evidence for the idea of the many-named intermediary in Hellenistic Judaism. In one passage, he heaps various epithets upon the intermediary: "God's Firstborn, the Word, who holds the eldership among the angels, their ruler as it were. And many names are his, for he is called 'Beginning', 'Name of God', His 'Word', 'Man after His image', and 'He that sees', i.e. 'Israel'" (*Conf.* 146). In another text, Wisdom (Sophia) is called 'Beginning', 'Image', and 'Vision of God' (*Leg. All.* I:43). The intermediary is also 'High Priest' (*Migr.* 102; *Fuga* 108-118; *Somn.* 1:215; 2:183). The many-named intermediary is also said to be God's 'Son': he is God's 'true Word and firstborn Son', who oversees the heavenly bodies whose courses regulate the life of the universe, "like a viceroy of a great king" (*Agr.* 51); "the incorporeal Man, who is no other than the divine Image, [is] His eldest Son, whom He elsewhere calls 'Firstborn' and the 'Begotten One'" (*Conf.* 62-63). Philo also calls the material world God's 'younger son', who can teach people about God (*Quod Deus* 31-32; *Ebr.* 30; *Cher.* 43-45). The 'eldest and firstborn Son' is the 'Word', which now is seen as the spiritual world of ideas. In this particular construal of the intermediary, a Platonic influence is seen at work, but there can be no doubt that one of the facets of the Philonic intermediary is an adaptation of a Jewish angelic figure with many names, one of which is 'Son of God'. That the Christians used the same model in representing the saviour is shown by the originally synagogal prayers which are embedded in the *Apostolic Constitutions*, Books VII-VIII, the works of Justin Martyr (cf. below), and Hermas, *Sim.* (FOSSUM 1992:131-132).

The idea of the preexistence of the Messiah could find some support in the OT. Mic 5:2 states that the origin of the Ruler to come is "from old, from ancient days" (LXX: "from the beginning, from the days of eternity"). Ps 89:28, which was applied to the Messiah by R. Nathan (ca. 160 CE [*Exod*

R. 19:7]) says that God calls the king his 'firstborn'. The LXX reads *prōtotokos*, which is similar to *prōtogonos*, an epithet which both Philo and the *Prayer of Joseph* bestow upon the preexistent intermediary (cf. Col 1:15, where the 'Son' of God is *prōtotokos*).

According to Paul, God sent his Son in order to set people free from slavery under the elemental spirits of the universe (→Stoicheia) and the Law (→Law) (Gal 4:3-5; Rom 8:2-4). People were thereby made sons of God by adoption and received the Spirit, through which they could cry: "Abba! Father!" (Gal 4:5-6; Rom 8:15). In the end, they would be "conformed to the image of His Son" (Rom 8:29). The specific act through which the Son effected the salvation was his death on the cross (Gal 2:20; Rom 8:3, 32 [see HENGEL 1976:7-15]).

The title 'Son of God' is a clue to the identity of Jesus in the gospel of Mark. It is found already in the first verse of the work (accepting the reading of Codex Sinaiticus[a], B, D, etc.), which is matched at the end of the Gospel by the exclamation of the Roman centurion at the cross (15:39). Jesus is solemnly declared to be the Son of God by a heavenly voice at two crucial points in his career, i.e. when he is installed as the Messiah (1:11) and right after the confession of Peter before the disciples that Jesus is the Messiah (9:7).

The exclamation of the demons that Jesus is the Son of God (3:11; 5:17) has another derivation, for the Messiah was not expected to expel demons. The appeal to the miracle-working 'divine men' in the Greco-Roman world would not seem to be of any avail, because the exact title 'Son of God' does not seem to have been applied to those people. Now in the mouth of the demons, the 'Holy One of God' appears to be a parallel title to that of the Son of God (1:24). In Ps 89:5-7, 'Holy Ones' and 'Sons of God' are parallel titles, designating the members of God's council. In Zech 14:5 (= *1 Enoch* 1:9; Jude 14) it is foretold that on the Day of the LORD, "God will come and all the Holy Ones with Him". Obviously, at the turn of our era, both 'Son(s) of God' and 'Holy One(s) of God' were regarded as angelic names.

Although the title of the Son of God reached Mark from different sources, it is clear that he attaches a unique significance to it. The demons are adjured to be silent; so are the disciples after the confession of Peter. It is only through his death that the deeper meaning of the divine sonship of Jesus can be grasped (cf. 15:39).

In Matthew, it is not the demons but only the disciples who proclaim that Jesus is the Son of God (14:33; 16:16). As is shown by Peter's confession, it is a title of the Messiah (cf. 26:63). The title implies service of God (3:17-4:10). Suffering is involved. The leaders of the Jews mockingly ask why God does not deliver Jesus from the cross, since he claims to be the Son of God (27:43). This reflects Wis 2:12-20, where the righteous, claiming to be the 'Son' and 'Servant' of God his 'Father', is oppressed, tortured and killed by the ungodly, who mock him for believing that he will be vindicated in the end by God. In the Sermon on the Mount, the believers demonstrating God's will and love are promised the status as God's 'sons' (5:10, 45 = Luke 6:35).

Luke does not assign any significant role to the title 'Son of God'. It is an equivalent to 'the Christ', the latter being preferred above the former, as can be seen when comparing Luke's text to the parallels in Mark and Matthew (Luke 9:20; 22:67-70; 23:47).

In the Annunciation, Jesus is identified as the Son of God and the heir to the throne of David (1:32-33, 35). Here Hellenistic 'divine man' and ruler ideology have been merged with messianism, for virgin birth was not predicated of the Messiah (in spite of the fact that Isa 7:14 LXX reads 'virgin' where the MT has 'young woman'). Now the 'divine men' and the imperial 'sons' of God were seen as the progeny of a god, either by direct engendering or by a woman, so there is no exact parallel to what is related by Luke. However, we should consider Plutarch's report that the Egyptians believed that the spirit of a god could work the beginnings of a new life in a woman (*Numa* 4).

John agrees with Paul that the purpose of

the sending of the preexistent Son of God was his death for the salvation of humankind (3:16-17; 10:11; 11:51-52; 13; 15; 1 John 4:10). Like Paul (Gal 3:26), John emphasizes faith as the condition for becoming God's son or child (1:12). Again like Paul, John holds that the Spirit is instrumental in this birth (3:5; 6:8).

In John, God is called 'Father' about 120 times. Jesus is '(the) Son'/'Son of God' 27 times. The correlation Father/Son suggests itself. The full title 'Son of God' is found primarily in confession-like formulas (1:34, 49; 20:31; also in 1 John 4:15; 5; 2 John 3). While 'Son of God' is associated with 'the Father' only twice (5:25; 10:36, 'the Son', which is found 18 times, is virtually always correlated with the idea of God as Father. The intimacy between the Father and the Son is thereby emphasized (1:18; 3:35-36; 5:19-26; 6:40; 8:35-36; 14:13; 17:10). The Son does only what the Father wants him to do; he is thus a true revelation of God.

The basic theme of Hebrews is the "representative atoning suffering of the Son" (HENGEL 1976:87), who is a preexistent divine being standing above the angels. Old notions about the Near Eastern priest-king are revived in order to explain his work. In contrast to the priest-king, however, Jesus sacrificed himself (9:12, 25; 10:10). He then took his seat at the right hand of God (1:2-3; 10:12-13). Denial of the Son of God by those who have been purged by his death is unforgivable (6:6; 10:29).

V. *Bibliography*

A. M. BLACKMANN, The House of the Morning, *JEA* 5 (1918) 148-165; J. A. BÜHNER, *Der Gesandte und sein Weg im 4. Evangelium* (WUNT 2, 2nd ser.; Tübingen 1977); R. BULTMANN, *Geschichte der synoptischen Tradition* (FRLANT 29; Göttingen 1957³); J. H. BREASTED, *Ancient Records of Egypt* 1 (Chicago 1906; reprinted New York 1962); C. COLPE, Gottessohn, *RAC* 12 (1983) 19-58; P. DHORME, *La religion assyro-babylonienne* (Paris 1910); J. DUPONT, L'arrière-fond biblique du récit des tentations de Jésus, *NTS* 3 (1956-1957) 287-304; D. O. EDZARD, *Primäre Zentren der Hochkultur*, (Saeculum Weltgeschichte 1; Stuttgart 1965); A. ERMAN, *Die Literatur der Aegypter* (Leipzig 1923); J. FOSSUM, Son of God, *ABD* 6 (1992) 128-137; G. FRIEDRICH, Ein Tauflied hellenistischer Judenchristen, *TZ* 21 (1965) 502-516; A. GARDINER, *Egyptian Grammar* (London 1957³); J. GRAY, *The Krt Text in the Literature of Ras Shamra* (Leiden 1964²); F. HAHN, *Christologische Hoheitstitel* (FRLANT 83; Göttingen 1964²); J. HARRIS, On the Name "Son of God" in Northern Syria, *ZNW* 15 (1914) 108-113; M. HENGEL, *The Son of God* (transl. J. Bowden; Philadelphia 1976); J. JEREMIAS, *Abba* (Göttingen 1966); W. VON MARTITZ, G. FOHRER, E. SCHWEIZER, E. LOHSE & W. SCHNEEMELCHER, υἱός, *TDNT* 8 (1972) 334-397; A. MORET, *Du caractère religieux de la royauté pharaonique* (Paris 1902); P. POKORNÝ, *Der Gottessohn*, (ThStud 109; Zürich 1971); F. PREISIGKE, *Vom göttlichen Fluidum nach ägyptischer Anschauung* (Heidelberg 1920); H. RADAU, *Early Babylonian History* (New York 1899); RADAU, *Early Babylonian History down to the End of the Fourth Dynasty of Ur* (New York/London 1900); H. RIESENFELD, *Jésus transfiguré* (ASNU 16; Uppsala 1947); G. ROEDER, *Urkunden zur Religion des alten Ägypten* (Religiöse Stimmen der Völker 4; Jena 1915); W. H. P. RÖMER, The Religion of Ancient Mesopotamia, *Historia Religionum* 1 (ed. C. J. Bleeker & G. Widengren; Leiden 1969) 115-194; A. F. J. SEITZ, The Future Coming of the Son of Man, *Studia Evangelica* 6 (Berlin 1973) 478-494; K. SETHE, *Urkunden der 18. Dynastie* 4,I (Leipzig 1914); Å. W. SJÖBERG, Die göttliche Abstammung der sumerisch-babylonischen Herrscher, *Orientalia Suecana* 72 (1972) 88-112; C. H. TALBERT, The Myth of a Descending-Ascending Redeemer in Mediterranean Antiquity, *NTS* 22 (1976) 418-439; G. WIDENGREN, *Religionsphänomenologie* (transl. R. Elgnowski; Berlin 1969); WIDENGREN, Psalm 110 und das sakrale Königtum in Israel, *Zur neueren Psalmenforschung* (ed. P. H. A. Neumann; Wege der Forschung 192; Darmstadt 1976) 185-216.

J. FOSSUM

SONS OF (THE) GOD(S)

בני עליון / אלים / (ה)אלהים

I. In several passages in the OT a group of heavenly beings other than Yahweh is referred to by the expressions *běnê ʿelyôn* "children of Elyon" (Ps 82:6) and *běnê ʾēlîm* (Ps 29:1; 89:7) or *běnê (hā) ʾĕlōhîm* (Gen 6:2.4; Job 1:6; 2:1; 38:7; and originally Deut 32:8) "children of God", "children of (the) gods" or "divine beings". The concept appears without the terminology in a few other passages in the OT. Corresponding Greek expressions appear in the NT to characterize the ultimate transformation of God's people into heavenly beings.

Of the cognate expressions referring to a plurality of divine beings at Ugarit *bn il* is more common than *bn ilm*. *Bn il* clearly refers to "the children of El"—at least, in one text El addresses the gods (*ilm*) as "my children" (*bny*) (1.16 v:24). *bn ilm* is found only once (*KTU* 1.4 iii:14). Here it is preceded by *pẖr* "assembly", which elsewhere is twice followed immediately by *ilm* (i.e. "assembly of the gods"—or possibly "assembly of El" [the divine name plus enclitic *m*]). The two expressions *bn il* "children of El" and *pẖr ilm* "assembly of the gods" have perhaps been conflated in the unique expression *pẖr bn ilm*. It remains uncertain, however, whether this is best rendered "assembly of the children of El", "assembly of the children of the gods", or "assembly of the divine beings". The simplest solution is to assume that *bn ilm* was understood as an idiomatic periphrasis for "the gods", i.e. "the divine beings". The one occurrence of *bn ʾlm* in a Phoenician text, *kl dr bn ʾlm* (*KAI* 26 A III 19) is probably to be understood similarly: "the whole circle of the divine beings".

In Hebrew it is arguable whether the plural form of the word for 'god' in the phrase *běnê (hā)ʾĕlōhîm* represents the plural concept, 'gods', or the singular 'God'. That upon reflection ancient Israelites might specify either a singular or a plural referent is suggested by the occasional substitution of *ʾēlîm* (plural) or *ʿElyôn* (singular) for the ambiguous *(hā)ʾĕlōhîm*. (However, some would see behind the MT *ʾēlîm* a singular reference to the more specific old divine name El with enclitic *m*).

If *ʾĕlōhîm* had singular reference, the expression *běnê ʾĕlōhîm* would correspond most closely to the Ugaritic expression *bn il*. The biblical identification of *ʾĕlōhîm* with →Yahweh would suggest that the *běnê (hā) ʾĕlōhîm* were not independent of, but essentially related to, Israel's god. This accords with Yahweh's occasional use of the first person plural (see below). Although this view is more appropriate to some contexts than to others, it clearly lies behind the LXX's consistent translation of both *(hā) ʾĕlōhîm* and *ʾēlîm* (!) in these phrases by *theou* (or *mou* in Job 38:7, where God is speaking). Other associations suggested by the term *běnê-* (descent from or participation in the nature of the following noun) might be problematic for people emphasizing Yahweh's uniqueness in the heavenly sphere, or understanding Yahweh's court to include the subjected gods of other nations. Such people would have favoured a plural reference for the second noun in *běnê (hā) ʾĕlōhîm* (which would then have been the formal equivalent of the Ugaritic *bn ilm*). This too would suit some contexts more than others. Probably, however, the expression was an idiomatic term for 'divine beings', as *běnê (hā) ʾādām* was for 'human beings'. Compare the parallelism of the two expressions in the original text of Deut 32:8 and the pairing of *běnê hā ʾĕlōhîm* and *běnôt hā ʾādām* in Gen 6:2 (see below; and note the similar suggestion in the case of Ugaritic *bn ilm* above). This being so, Israelites would not normally have stopped to think about the specific referent of the second term in the phrase.

II. At Ugarit the 'divine beings' appear in three of the traditional poems and in two religious texts (as well as one fragmentary context: *KTU* 1.62:7). They are cited for their immortality in the Tale of Aqhat, where they appear in parallelism with Baal: having offered Aqhat immortality, Anat promises he will have as many years//months in his life as Baal//"the divine beings" (*KTU*

1.17 vi:28-29). It is their ignorance that occasions their mention in one of the shorter Baal narratives—the incomplete line *KTU* 1.10 i:3 speaks of something "that the divine beings do not know". (The mention of Anat and Baal in the immediate [broken] context suggests that these two may share the knowledge denied to the *bn il*.) The following two lines preserve the expressions parallel to *bn il*: *pḫr k(b)kbm* and *dr dt šmm* "the assembly of the Stars" and "the circle of the heavenly ones (lit. those of the heavens)".

The gods are seen here as heavenly beings, associated or even identified with the stars. In the last passage the reference is apparently to all the gods except those named, and that would appear to be true in the first passage as well.

Collectives—such as *pḫr* and *dr*—are used with all the remaining cases of *bn il*, thus representing the gods as a collectivity. In *KTU* 1.4 iii:13-14 (in the main Baal cycle) Baal complains that he has been spat upon "in the assembly of the divine beings" (*btk pḫr bn ilm*). (In a god list [*KTU* 1.47: 29] and an offering list [*KTU* 1.148:9] the briefer phrase *pḫr ilm* "assembly of the gods" is used.)

In the first three lines of *KTU* 1.65 (a text of disputed genre, that focuses on El and a number of objects or attributes associated with him) *bn il* is used three times: *il bn il/dr bn il/mpḫrt bn il* "El, the divine beings/the circle of the divine beings/the totality of the divine beings". While widely regarded as a religious text, it has been argued that this tablet may have been used for a scribal exercise (M. DIETRICH, O. LORETZ & J. SANMARTÍN, RS 4.474 = *CTA* 30—Schreibübung oder religiöse Text?, *UF* 7 [1975] 523-524). But even if this is so, *KTU* 1.40 shows that the model for the phrases in question is a religious text. Similar expressions appear toward the end of each of the five sections of this ritual text. The full context reads: "May it (a sacrifice) be borne to the Father of the divine beings, may it be borne to the circle of the divine beings, to the totality of the divine beings". The use of the expression "the father of the divine beings" to refer to El tends to support the suggestion above that the phrase translated literally "the children of El" was already so idiomatic a term for the collectivity of the gods that it no longer conveyed the fatherhood of El, but was simply a periphrasis for "gods", i.e. "divine beings". This would explain how *bn il* might be interchanged with *bn ilm*, both in effect referring to the same collectivity. In any case, both texts explicitly associate this collectivity closely with El himself.

In literary texts from Ugarit then, the term refers to the generality of gods: they appear with Baal as a model of immortality, and in different contexts are differentiated from him by their insulting treatment of him and by their ignorance of something that he (apparently) knows. Religious texts present the *bn il* explicitly as a collectivity closely associated with El.

At Karatepe king Azatiwada curses anyone displacing his record, invoking "Baalshamem, El Creator of the Earth, the Everlasting Sun and the whole circle of divine beings". Here the same collective (*dr*) is used as in the religious texts from Ugarit, and the expression seems to be used to refer to all the gods beyond the three mentioned. (Contrast the more circumscribed group, *kl ʾln qrt* "all the gods of the city", mentioned a few lines earlier: *KAI* 26 A III 5.)

III. *Bĕnê hāʾĕlōhîm* appears in Gen 6:2.4; Job 1:6; 2:1; and without the article in Job 38:7. *Bĕnê ʾēlîm* appears in Pss 29:1 and 89:7. The LXX and Qumran Literature support the earlier reading *bĕnê ʾĕlōhîm* for MT's *bĕnê Yiśrāʾēl* in Deut 32:8. *Bĕnê ʿElyôn* is used only in Ps 82:6.

In Gen 6:2.4 the *bĕnê hā ʾĕlōhîm*, male deities (not—generically—"children of the gods") find *bĕnôt hāʾādām*, female humans, attractive and take in marriage whomever they choose. Yahweh is conspicuous by his absence from these mythical events. His speech in verse 3, while making clear that humans have no possibility of immortality through such divine connections, concerns humanity alone and ignores the *bĕnê hā ʾĕlōhîm*. It is clear that the author is summarizing traditional mythical material about divine-human unions as an illustration of the disorder that prevailed immediately before the flood. This is further linked by temporal references ("in those days", "of old") with traditions about the →Gibborim and the →Nephilim (v 4). The mythological character of these references leaves no doubt that the divine beings in question are the gods of traditional myth, known to us from various Near Eastern cultures. (For divine-human unions see e.g. *KTU* 1.23, the two versions of the Hattic myth of Illuyanka, and the references to the hero's parentage in the Epic of Gilgamesh, not to mention Greek myths.) This traditional mythology is granted a quasi-historical reality in the lapidary portrayal of the cosmic disorder that prevailed before the flood. But the reality conceded to the gods is not related to the reality of Yahweh. The gods have relations with humans, but not with God. Assigned to antediluvian times, they instantiate the disorder that motivated Yahweh's decision to punish the world with the Deluge.

In the earliest recoverable version of Deut 32:8 the old high god, here →Elyon, is portrayed as allotting their territories to all the peoples of the world: "When Elyon gave the nations their possessions, divided up humankind, he established the boundaries of the peoples according to the number of the divine beings" (reading *bny ʾlhym*, as reflected in the QL and LXX, for MT's *bĕnê Yiśrāʾēl* "Israelites"). According to this, the number of gods is the basis for the number of peoples and countries in the world. The final phrase implies not only that there was an identical number of gods, peoples and territories, but that each people received its god as well as its territory (or each god received his or her people and territory). As one of the divine beings, Yahweh received Israel at the hands of Elyon, as each of the other gods received his or her people and land from the same source. (Later the divine being in charge of a particular nation is called its *śar* "→prince, officer": Dan 10:13.20-21.) This is an appropriate myth to explain the contemporary situation as perceived by the composer: as the Israelites have one land and one god, so each other nation has its land and its god. Similar thinking appears in Judg 11:24, where Yahweh's gift of territory to Israel serves as an analogy for another nation's receipt of its land from its god.

In other contexts the matching of people and gods is even clearer, though at the same time Yahweh displaces Elyon as the distributor of benefices (see Deut 4:19; the gods are here "all the →Host of Heaven"; cf. further 29:25). The understanding of Elyon as an epithet of Yahweh leads to the interpretation of Deut 32:8 also as referring to Yahweh's distribution of lands to peoples.

By its substitution of *bĕnê yiśrāʾēl* for *bny ʾlhym* the MT later made the number of the descendants of Israel the model for Yahweh's distribution of peoples and lands and eliminated the divine beings altogether (cf. the substitution of *mišpĕḥôt ʿammîm* for *bĕnê ʾēlîm* in the tricolon Ps 96:7-8a as compared with Ps 29:1-2a—see below).

Ps 82 also envisages Yahweh as one of the gods, though only for the sake of making a radical distinction between him and them. Here the gods appear in assembly, and Yahweh now deals with them directly. In vv 6-7 he says: "I thought, 'You are gods (*ʾĕlōhîm*; →God[s]), children of Elyon, all of you'; but you will die like people, fall like any holder of high office". The "children of Elyon" appear in parallelism with *ʾĕlōhîm* "gods", and are addressed while gathered in the *ʿădat-ʾēl* "assembly of El, divine assembly"(v 1). The use of both El and Elyon and of the unique phrase *bĕnê ʿelyôn* in the one psalm indicates that the two older deities are here undifferentiated as the one high god from whom the other gods derive their identity as "divine beings".

The relationship of the divine beings to Yahweh is much more fully developed here than anywhere else. Yahweh charges them with mismanaging the world (v 2) and calls upon them to exercise just government (vv 3-4). They do not know the meaning of the term and proceed in ignorance, while the world in their charge begins to come apart.

Yahweh now rhetorically (ironically?) admits having thought that they were really gods, but proclaims his present recognition that they are mortal and doomed to fall from their positions of responsibility.

Thus the heavenly beings are here again the gods, generally believed to be the rulers of the world. The psalm's purpose is to expose their total failure as governors—more specifically, to have Yahweh expose that failure. For this purpose Yahweh is rhetorically portrayed as having formerly shared general beliefs about the gods. But Yahweh is also the one who exposes their true nature and announces their demise, and the one who in the last verse of the psalm is acclaimed as their successor, governor of the world and their heir to all the nations. Thus Ps 82 rhetorically acknowledges the gods' claims to be rulers of the nations, but does so only to demonstrate their failure and the justice of Yahweh's replacing them as ruler of the world.

Thus in Gen 6:1-4 the divine beings are portrayed in a reference to a traditional myth (or myths), which is given a place in events leading up to the deluge. Here they are radically differentiated and separated from Yahweh. In Deut 32:8-9 the divine beings appeared originally as Yahweh's peers, but the text is reread and eventually rewritten to make Yahweh the supreme, and then the only, deity. In Ps 82 Yahweh again appears as one of the divine beings, but only to expose his peers as total failures and to displace them as ruler of the world. In the remaining cases, the divine beings appear as Yahweh's court—his servants and worshippers.

Before a discussion of these, reference should be made to some other passages which, while not using the specific term, nevertheless seem to refer to these divine beings as Yahweh's peers. In Gen 3:22 Yahweh says: "The human has become like one of us". Only two kinds of being are envisaged here: divine and human. The human has acquired one of the divine characteristics (knowledge) and is threatening to acquire another (immortality v 22b; cf. 11:6-7). The phrase "one of us" clearly refers to any one of the group of divine beings, of whom Yahweh is *primus inter pares.* In the priestly text, Gen 1:26, God again uses the first person plural when proposing to make humanity "in our image, according to our likeness". In this case, human beings are modelled on the divine beings (among whom God is again by implication first among equals) and distinguished from the animal kingdom, which they are to rule. (Cf. Ps 8:6, in which *ʾĕlōhîm* should perhaps be translated "gods" rather than "God".) Another use of the first person plural by God in Isa 6:8 again suggests the presence of the divine beings, though more specifically convened as a →council and with Yahweh more explicitly in charge.

To turn now to other uses of the phrase "divine beings": in the two episodes in heaven in the prologue to the book of Job (Job 1:6-12; 2:1-7a) the *bĕnê hāʾĕlōhîm* present themselves to Yahweh, the →Satan among them. Yahweh initiates a topic of discussion, the *śāṭān* makes a proposal, and Yahweh authorizes an action, carefully delimited. It is clear from these passages that the divine beings in general customarily came together at certain times to report to Yahweh. This is modelled on the old divine Council convening to make decisions, with Yahweh here presiding as the high god. While the dialogues between Yahweh and the *śāṭān* reveal the character of the latter more than that of the group to which he belongs, they generally reflect the degree of initiative individual assembly members may take as well as the primacy of the interests and the final authority of the presiding officer. (Cf. the council's discussion in the vision report of Micaiah—1 Kgs 22:19b-22). Two passages refer to the divine beings as a heavenly group that recognizes and acknowledges Yahweh's greatness. In the first speech of Yahweh in the Job poem, Yahweh asks Job where he was at creation, at the time "when the morning stars rejoiced together and all the *bĕnê ʾĕlōhîm* shouted for joy" (Job 38:7). The parallelism of "stars" and *bĕnê ʾĕlōhîm* recalls the Ugaritic text

KTU 1.10 i:3-4 (*bn il//pḫr kkbm* "sons of god//assembly of stars"). The traditional understanding of such a juxtaposition certainly involved recognition of the identity of stars and gods, but the context gives no indication of how precisely they were conceived here, whether in the traditional way or in terms of the physical heavens with their stars (personified) and the mythological heavens with their messengers and hosts (→Messenger; →Host of heaven), as in Ps 148:1-3. In any case, Job 38:7 depicts both groups as present at the foundation of the earth (cf. Gen 1:26 above), rejoicing in Yahweh's great achievement. Like the divine assembly of the Babylonian *Enūma eliš*, their function is to give recognition and praise to the creator god.

Ps 29 begins by calling upon the *bĕnê ʾēlîm* to attribute honour and strength to Yahweh. Behind this lies the conception of Yahweh's court. V. 9b spells out that Yahweh is sitting in his heavenly palace/temple receiving honour (cf. v 10, where he is seated on the Flood as king forever). The divine beings are here, as in Job 38:7, an undifferentiated group whose function is simply to give due acknowledgement to Yahweh in recognition of his powers and accomplishments. Nevertheless, another psalmist is sufficiently uncomfortable with this expression to substitute *mišpĕḥôt ʿammîm* in the otherwise identical tricolon Ps 96:7-8a (cf. the history of Deut 32:8 above).

Ps 89:7 asks who is comparable with Yahweh among the *bĕnê ʾēlîm* (parallel to *baššaḥaq* "in the clouds"). The following verse further distinguishes Yahweh as a god feared in the Council of the Holy Ones (→Saints) and "among all those around him". Again the heavenly court is in view, and one of the terms by which its members are referred to is *bĕnê ʾēlîm*. The poet's use of this term to set off Yahweh's uniqueness is echoed in Exod 15:11, in which the term *bĕnê* is lacking: "Who is like you among the gods (*bāʾēlîm*), Yahweh?" The LXX has "holy ones" as the parallel term in the second colon (See also s.v. Saints). The comparison of the two verses shows the essential identity of function of the two terms and groups, namely to distinguish Yahweh from all other divine beings.

All except one of the passages reviewed so far have in view a group of divine beings to varying degrees associated with Yahweh and distinguished from humanity. The exception is Gen 6:1-4, where on the one hand the gods blur the line between divine and human by mating with women, and on the other the narrative does not acknowledge any relationship between them and Yahweh. By the last centuries BCE the dominant view of divine beings among Jews was that they were →angels, a lesser order of heavenly beings at the one God's beck and call. It was no longer necessary to assert God's superiority over them or difference from them, for they no longer partook of divinity. When Jews of this period read the passages commented on above they now understood them to refer, not to divine beings, but to angels. Thus beside the more literal *huioi theou* "sons of God" the LXX uses the word *angeloi* "angels".

There is a single reference in the OT to one of the divine beings, which illustrates this shift. In the story of the three Judeans cast into the furnace, Nebuchadnezzar, on looking into the furnace, sees four men, one of whom resembles *bar ʾĕlāhîn* "a divine being (lit. a son of gods)" (Dan 3:25). (This is the singular of the Aramaic equivalent of *bĕnê ʾĕlōhîm*.) In his own terms, Nebuchadnezzar might think of this as a god, but when he further expresses himself on the subject, he interprets the phenomenon in terms of the religion of the three Judeans—and of the Jewish teller and hearers of the story: after bringing the three out of the furnace, he blesses their god "who sent his messenger to save his servants ..." (3:28). This "divine being" is thus a manifestation of the traditional →"angel of Yahweh", a member of the divine court, here as elsewhere sent on an errand of mercy and deliverance. (The LXX already translates the expression in 3:25 by *angelos kyriou.*)

The apocrypha and pseudepigrapha conceive of the "children of God" as angels—though the term is also used of faithful Jews. These two uses are virtually conflated in the eschatological expectations of some texts, which see faithful Israel becoming heavenly beings in God's ultimate new order.

The NT adopts the idea and the term to embrace the newly defined community of God's people, and then also occasionally applies it to the quasi-angelic nature and status of the faithful in the final transformation. This eschatological sense of the terms "children of God" and "children of the Most High" appears in three passages in the gospels. According to the seventh beatitude in Matthew, peacemakers will be called *huioi theou* "children of God" (Matt 5:9). This is intended to suggest, not that the beneficiaries of the peacemakers will think of them as angels, but that God will ultimately call them his children, and therefore they will be such (cf. 1 John 3:1). In Luke's version of the Sermon on (or off) the Mount, those who love their enemies will receive a great reward and become "children of the Most High" (*huioi Hypsistou*; Luke 6:35). This is the only occurrence of this expression in the NT, as Ps 82:6 is the only occurrence in the OT. Here, as there, the reference is to the same group as the "children of God". The most precise definition of this eschatological reality appears in Luke 20:36, where Jesus says that those who experience resurrection will be *isangeloi* "the equivalent of angels" and *huioi theou* "children of God". This pair of expressions places the resurrected in the same order of being as angels, while distinguishing them from that group—they are not *angeloi* but *isangeloi* (cf. Mark 12:25 and Matt 22:30, which use only the expression *hōs angeloi* "like angels").

Another pertinent distinction is made in 1 John 3:2: those addressed are now *tekna theou* "children of God", i.e. angels, but will in the end be like God (*homoioi autōi*), i.e. divine beings. Here the traditional term ("children of God") is used to express the angelic nature presently enjoyed, while the traditional concept ("divine beings") is used to refer to the divine character ultimately to be assumed.

IV. *Bibliography*

B. BYRNE, *"Sons of God"—"Seed of Abraham". A Study of the Idea of Sonship of God of All Christians in Paul against the Jewish Background* (AnBib 83; Rome, 1979); G. COOKE, The Sons of (the) God(s), *ZAW* 76 (1964) 22-47; A. COOPER, Divine Names and Epithets in the Ugaritic Texts, *RSP* 3 (AnOr 51; ed. S. Rummel; Rome 1981) 371-500, esp. 431-441 [& lit]; J. L. CUNCHILLOS YLARRI, Los bene haʾelohîm en Gen. 6, 1-4, *Estudios Bíblicos* 28 (1969) 5-31; M. DIETRICH & O. LORETZ, *"Jahwe und seine Aschera"* (UBL 9; Münster 1992) 134-157 [& lit]; H. GESE, M. HÖFNER & K. RUDOLPH, *RAAM*, 100-102; W. HERRMANN, Die Göttersöhne, *ZRGG* 12 (1960) 242-251; E. T. MULLEN, *The Divine Council in Canaanite and Early Hebrew Literature* (HSM 24; Chico, 1980); A. OHLER, *Mythologische Elemente im Alten Testament* (Düsseldorf 1969) esp. 204-212; M. POPE, *El in the Ugaritic Texts* (VTSup 2; Leiden 1955) 48-49; W. SCHLISSKE, *Göttersöhne und Gottessohn im Alten Testament: Phasen der Entmythisierung im Alten Testament* (BWANT 97; Stuttgart 1973); H. WINDISCH, Friedensbringer—Gottessöhne, *ZNW* 24 (1925) 240-260.

S. B. PARKER

SON OF MAN בן אדם, בר אנשׁ, ὁ υἱὸς τοῦ ἀνθρώπου

I. Son of man is a typical Semitic expression ('son of...'= one of the species of) denoting an individual human being (Ps 8:4; Job 16:21). Paradoxically it comes to refer, in Jewish texts, to a heavenly figure who looks like a human being and, in New Testament texts, to →Jesus both in his humanity and in his identity as the heavenly figure described in the Jewish texts.

II. The earliest relevant text for the non-generic use of 'son of man' is Dan 7:13-14. The chapter purports to be a vision that →Daniel received while in exile in

Babylon. In fact it derives from the Hellenistic period, and its present form dates from the time of Antiochus Epiphanes' persecution of the Jews (167-164 BCE). The focus of the vision alternates between the earthly and heavenly realms. In the first half of the chapter Daniel describes his vision (vv 1-14). He sees four great beasts rising out of the sea. The tenth horn of the last and fiercest beast utters arrogant words. In heaven the aged deity ('the →ancient of days') convenes a court that condemns the beast, whose body is burned. At that point, 'one like a son of man' arrives on the clouds of heaven and is given everlasting 'sovereignty, glory, and kingly power'.

The second half of the chapter interprets the vision (vv 15-27). The four beasts represent four great kingdoms. The last of these is the Macedonian, and the tenth and last of its kings defies →God by making war on 'the holy ones of the Most High', the angelic patrons of Israel. The enthronement of 'one like a son of man' means that kingly power, sovereignty, the greatness of all the kingdoms under heaven will be given to the people of the holy ones of the →Most High, and this will last forever (v 27).

Not surprisingly, the origins of this vision and the precise meaning of many of its details are debated. The vision itself is widely recognized to have derived from ancient Near Eastern myth, although the precise provenance is debated. The closest parallel is in Canaanite combat myths that describe the triumph of →El over the forces of chaos, represented by Yamm (the →sea). The interaction between the ancient deity and the 'one like a son of man' also finds a counterpart in Canaanite myth, where El, depicted as an old man, is succeeded by →Baal, the rider of the cloud chariot.

In its present form, the chapter presents one of several visions in the Book of Daniel that see in the reign of Antiochus a supernatural clash between Israel's God, or God's →angels, and the demonic forces embodied in the Macedonian kingdom, and that anticipate the triumph of Israel and its God (chaps. 8 and 10-12; cf. chap. 2). The 'one like a son of man' is a high angel, perhaps to be identified with →Michael (cf. 10:13. 21; 12:1). His human-like appearance is traditional (cf. Dan 9:21, 'the man Gabriel', *hā'îš gabrî'ēl*), although it may be mentioned in 7:13 in order to contrast the figure with the beasts. The literary break between 7:12 and 7:13 indicates that the 'one like a son of man' appears on the scene only after judgment has been passed on the last beast. Thus, vv 13-14 do not ascribe judicial functions to the 'one like a son of man' (contrast 12:1) but describe his enthronement after the judgment, and the text emphasizes how he, the heavenly entourage in general, and Israel will exercise God's everlasting sovereignty over all the kingdoms on earth. A similar notion of dual, heavenly/earthly dominion (*miśrat/mmšlt*) appears in 1QM 17:6-8, which identifies Michael as 'the great angel' who helps Israel and holds dominion among the gods (*'lym*).

The second Jewish text to refer to a 'son of man' is the Parables or Similitudes of Enoch (*1 Enoch* 37-71), which date from around the turn of the era. Here the 'son of man' is a heavenly figure, whose origins predate creation but whose primary functions are related to the end time.

Enoch's portrait of the 'son of man' draws on three or four major strands of tradition. Chapter 46 introduces him in a scene that draws on Daniel 7:13 (cf. 46:1-3), and chap. 47 reflects Dan 7:9-10. Once the one "whose face was like the appearance of a man and full of graciousness like one of the holy angels" has been presented to God, who "had a head of days like white wool" (46:1), and to the reader, he is with some frequency referred to as 'this son of man', 'that son of man', or 'the son of man who…'. The term appears not to be a formal title, but a reference to a known human-like figure.

The Deutero-Isaianic servant poems are the second strand of tradition on which the Parables draw. Especially noteworthy is *1 Enoch* 48, where the naming of 'that son of man' is described in language taken from Isaiah 49. Similarly, the great judgment scene in *1 Enoch* 62-63 has been inspired by a traditional interpretation of Isaiah 52-53 which is also attested in Wis 5. The servant tradition is also evident throughout the Parables in the son of man's chief title, 'the Chosen One', whose Deutero-Isaianic origin is attested in *1 Enoch* 49:3-4 (cf. Isa 42:1), and quite possibly in the title 'Righteous One' (*1 Enoch* 38:2; cf. Isa 53:11).

The third major strand of tradition informing the Parable's portrait is found in the Davidic oracles of Isaiah and the royal psalms (cf. *1 Enoch* 48:8 ['kings of the earth'], 10 with Ps 2:2; *1 Enoch* 49:3-4a; 62:2-3 with Isa 11:1-5). The naming scene in *1 Enoch* 48 may indicate that Jewish speculation about the figure of Wisdom has also coloured the Enochic picture of this heavenly figure. In 48:3-5 the hiddenness of the 'son of man' is related to his existence before creation (contrast Isa 49:2 and see Prov 8:22-31 and Sir 24:1-6).

This remarkable conflation of traditions is not completely surprising when one considers the sources. Second Isaiah does not expect a restoration of the Davidic dynasty and invests the servant with qualities of the Davidic king, climaxing his references to the servant with a major scene of exaltation in the presence of the kings and the nations (52:12-15). Dan 7 describes the enthronement of one like a son of man, who receives 'sovereignty' (*šolṭān*) and 'kingly power' (*malkû*) 7:14. Nonetheless, the Enochic conflation significantly transforms the individual traditions. Expectations of a Davidic restoration have been replaced by belief in an enthroned heavenly deliverer who is identified with the servant and the Danielic one like a 'son of man'. The 'son of man', on the other hand, does not appear after the judgment, but is enthroned in order to execute divine judgment. The servant tradition is made focal, but the Chosen One is both pre-existent to creation and a major eschatological figure, with power to execute widesweeping judgment. The major objects of his judgment are the kings who, in Isa 52:13-15, are bystanders rather than the persecutors of the righteous. This last transformation is expressed in language drawn from Isaiah 14 (cf. *1 Enoch* 46:4-7), but corresponds to the opposition of the kings of the earth and the Lord's anointed one in Ps 2.

Thus the Parables feature a transcendent saviour figure, called 'son of man', 'the Chosen One' and 'the Righteous One'. Seated on God's throne of glory, he is invested with judicial functions and serves specifically as the eschatological champion and vindicator of the persecuted 'righteous ones' and 'chosen ones', gathering them into community with himself and condemning their enemies, 'the kings and the mighty' (chaps. 51, 62-63).

The Enochic conflation and transformation of traditions is attested, partly, in other Jewish texts, although the term 'son of man' occurs in none of them. Chief among these texts is 2 Esdr 11-13 and its descriptions of the anointed one and the man from the sea, which are clearly beholden to Daniel 7. Descriptions of a transcendental anointed one in *2 Bar* 29-30; 36-39; and 53-74 may also derive from this stream of tradition. Wis 2:4-5 is a special case. It features the traditional interpretation of Isa 52-53 found also in *1 Enoch* 62-63 and makes some use of Ps 2, though not identifying the central figure of that psalm as a son of David; however, it has no close connections with Dan 7. The significance of Wisdom of Solomon lies in the fact that the persecuted righteous one has no transcendent vindicator like the Chosen One in *1 Enoch* 62-63; rather, the tradition describes how, after death, the righteous one himself is exalted as judge of his enemies. The two options of interpreting Second Isaiah, in the Parables and Wisdom of Solomon, will reappear in the NT.

III. 'Son of man' is a major, though not widespread, NT title for Jesus. Its appearance is limited to the four gospels, one reference in Acts (7:56), and Rev 1:13, and it may be implied in Heb 2:6-9. Few topics in NT studies have generated as much literature and controversy as the gospel's use of 'son of man'. Some of the disputed points are the following: Do the gospels presuppose a Jewish tradition about a transcendent figure called '(the) son of man'? Do the gospels, which sometimes quote Dan 7, also know the tradition in the Parables of Enoch? Does 'son of man' sometimes mean humanity in general, or can it be a surrogate expression for 'me'? Did Jesus himself use the term? If so, was he referring to another, eschatological figure, or to himself? If the latter, did he mean 'this human' or did he imply his identity as the eschatological 'son of man'? Do certain Pauline passages reflect knowledge of 'son of man' traditions attested in the gospels? In addition, exegetes debate the meaning or function of the term in many passages. Consensus is notably lacking in all of these matters of interpretation. There is perhaps wide agreement that, on a purely descriptive level, one may classify 'son of man' sayings into three groups, which describe or refer to, respectively: the present, earthly activity of the son of man; the suffering, death, and resurrection of Jesus the son of man; the future, eschatological activity of the son of man. These are at least a helpful way into the texts, which can be treated here only briefly. Four preliminary remarks need to be made.

1) The evidence suggests that by the turn of the era, some Jewish apocalyptic circles envisioned the existence of a heavenly figure, sometimes referred to as 'son of man', but often not. The Parables of Enoch, 2 Esdr, and *2 Baruch* (and indirectly the Wisdom of Solomon) indicate that this figure was thought to have eschatological judicial functions, which indicates a significant change from the foundational text in Dan 7 brought about by conflation with other streams of Jewish tradition, notably Davidic royal oracles and Deutero-Isaianic servant texts. 2) The transformations in the tradition, both in the ascription of judicial functions not found in Dan 7 and in a consciousness of the royal and servant traditions, are evident in many NT passages. 3) For reasons that are not clear, 'son of man' becomes a dominant title, where it had not been in the Jewish tradition, and Dan 7 is quoted, even when the judicial interpretation in Enoch, with its transformation of Daniel, is present. 4) The absence of the title 'son of man' in the Pauline corpus should not prejudice our search for 'son of man' traditions that may be presented in connection with another 'christological' title.

The Gospel of Mark, the earliest extant Christian text with references to the son of man, plays on the ambiguities in the paradoxical use of the term mentioned above. Son of man denotes Jesus in his humanity and stands in contrast to 'son of God', the gospel's highest designation for him. At times, however, the expression is ambiguous and can also indicate the notion of a transcendent son of man. In 2:1-12, Jesus the man claims to have 'on earth' the 'sovereignty' (*exousia*) that Dan 7:14 (LXX) attributes to the eschatological cloud-borne 'one like a son of man', although forgiveness of sins suggests the judicial function not present in Daniel. Mark 14:61-62 exploits the ambiguity to the full. Asked if he is the →Messiah, the son of God, Jesus responds that Caiaphas, who is about to condemn him, will see to his detriment *the man* who stands before him, coming on the clouds of heaven as the eschatological *son of man*, seated at God's right hand as messiah and judge (Ps 110:1; but also *1 Enoch* 62:1). This juxtaposition of messiah and 'son of man' appears also in 8:29-31 and in 13:21-27, where he is the champion of the chosen as in the Parables of Enoch. Moreover, 8:29-31; 9:9; 9:31, and 10:33-34.45 refer to the suffering, death, and resurrection of the 'son of man', employing a pattern of persecution and vindication drawn from the interpretation of the servant poems attested also in Wis 5, where, different from *1 Enoch* 62-63, the central figure is the vindicated one rather than the vindicator. Thus, for Mark 'son of man' is a complex and ambiguous code word that denotes Jesus' humanity (the ordinary meaning of the expression), Jesus' identity as the eschatological son of man and messiah, and his fate in the role that Wisdom explicates for the servant and the central figure in Ps 2: the suffering and vindicated righteous one.

Q, the hypothetical document common to Matthew and Luke (alongside Mark), contained a number of sayings of Jesus regarding the judicial functions of the son of man. Especially noteworthy is Matt 24:26-27; 37-39 / Luke 17:22-37, where the epiphany of the 'son of man' is compared to the coming of the flood. In *1 Enoch*, the flood is the prototype of the final judgment. It is possible that this saying represents genuine Jesus tradition and that the 'son of man' is a figure other than Jesus. In Matt 10:32-33 / Luke 12:8-9 (cf. Mark 8:38), Jesus speaks of human confession or denial of him and its eschatological consequences. According to Luke and Mark, the eschatological judicial agent (whether judge or witness) is identified as 'the son of man', while Matthew explicitly identifies that figure as Jesus ('I'). If the original Q formulation was referring to the 'son of man' as a figure distinct from Jesus, then the Matthean and the Lukan/Markan options would parallel, respectively, the forms of the tradition in *1 Enoch* 62-63 and in Wis 5.

The Gospel of Matthew has a special interest in the *eschaton*, which is carried in part by Q 'son of man' traditions. However, Matthew's major addition to the corpus of 'son of man' texts is a description of the judgment (25:31-46), that closely parallels *1 Enoch* 62-63. The 'son of man' is called 'king', reflecting the royal stream of tradition. People are judged on the basis of their actions toward 'the least of these my brothers', which are, in fact, actions for or against Jesus. The solidarity between the heavenly one and his brothers and the criterion of judgment corresponds to *1 Enoch* 62:1, where the kings and the mighty are to recognize in the Chosen One the chosen ones whom they have persecuted.

Although Luke tends to dampen eschatological expectations, a text like 18:1-8 warns against complacency and indicates the son of man as the eschatological vindicator who can appear at any time. Taking a different tack, Luke 22:69 radicalizes eschatology by maintaining, as opposed to Mark 14:62, that the 'son of man's' enthronement is an accomplished fact (see also Acts 7:56 and cf. Matt 26:64).

Although the Fourth Gospel lacks many of the obvious apocalyptic traits of the synoptic gospels, it reflects notions of the 'son of man' that are at home in the synoptics and antecedent Jewish tradition. The author employs the term 'exalt' (*hypsoun*) only with reference to 'the son of man' and the parallel term 'glorify' mainly in connection with 'Jesus' and 'the son of man'. However, these terms, appropriate to the Jewish understanding of the eschatological son of man, do not refer to a future event, but express John's understanding of Jesus' death as synonymous with his exaltation. John 13:31-32 is remarkable because its language recalls Isa 53:12 and 49:3, thus reflecting the servant tradition that is paired with 'son of man' tradition in Jewish and synoptic texts. John 5:27-29 echoes the language of Daniel 7:14 and states explicitly that the 'son of man' has authority to execute judgment, as he does in *1 Enoch*.

Whether Paul knew synoptic 'son of man' traditions is a disputed point. A negative answer is supported by the complete absence of the term in the Pauline corpus. This absence is not surprising since the Semitic expression would have been meaningless to Paul's gentile audience. However, two passages in 1 Thess indicate remarkable verbal and conceptual parallels with synoptic 'son of man' traditions. In 4:15-17 Paul appeals to 'a word of the Lord' and then describes the parousia and resurrection in language reminiscent of Mark 13:26-27 and Matt 24:31. In 5:1-11 his discussion of the day of the Lord recalls the Q passage in Matt 24:43-44 // Luke 12:39-40, and some of his vocabulary parallels the Lukan ending to the synoptic apocalypse (Luke 21:34-36). Paul's discussion of the parousia and resurrection in 1 Cor 15:23-28 may also reflect 'son of man' tradition. Its combination of language found in Ps 110:1; Dan 7:14 and Ps 8:7 is reminiscent of the conflation of Ps 110:1 and Dan 7:13 in Mark 14:62 and the curious use of Ps 8:4-6 in Heb 2:6-9 with reference to Jesus' exaltation rather than humanity's dominion over creation. In summary, Paul's expectations about Jesus' parousia may well reflect tradition about Jesus as eschatological son of man. Moreover, his statements about Jesus' future function as judge (2 Cor 5:10; Rom 2:16) could also derive from that tradition. His use of the titles Lord and Son (of God) in such contexts can be explained as a mean of communicating to his non-Jewish audience.

The Book of Revelation, an apocalypse that parallels *1 Enoch* in many respects, attests knowledge of the conflated 'son of man', messianic, and (probably) servant tradition found in the Parables of Enoch and 4 Ezra, an apocalypse by a contemporary of John. Jesus is introduced in Rev 1:7 with imagery from Dan 7:14, and chapter 5 recasts Dan 7:13-14. After chap. 13 returns to the imagery of Dan 7, Jesus, the opponent of the great beast, is placed on Mount Zion with his entourage marked by the name of his 'father' (cf. Ps 2:6-7), and 19:11-21 reflects both Ps 2 and Isa 11, texts employed in the Parables. References to Jesus as →'lamb' recall Isa 53:7.11.

IV. *Bibliography*

J. J. COLLINS, *The Apocalyptic Vision of the Book of Daniel* (HSM 16; Missoula 1977); C. COLPE, Neue Untersuchungen zum Menschensohn-Problem, *TRev* 77 (1981) 354-371; J. R. DONAHUE, Recent Studies on the Origin of "Son of Man" in the Gospels, *CBQ* 48 (1986) 584-607 [& lit]; E. HAAG, Der Menschensohn und die Heiligen (des) Höchsten. Eine literar-, form- und traditionsgeschichtliche Studie zu Daniel 7, *The Book of Daniel in the Light of New Findings* (ed. A. S. van der Woude; BETL 106; Leuven 1993) 137-186; J. W. VAN HENTEN, Antiochus IV as a Typhonic Figure in Daniel 7, *The Book of Daniel in the Light of New Findings* (ed. A. S. van der Woude; BETL 106; Leuven 1993) 223-243; A. J. B. HIGGINS, *The Son of Man in the Teaching of Jesus* (SNTSMS 39, Cambridge 1980); H. S. KVANVIG, *Roots of Apocalyptic: The Mesopotamian Background of the Enoch Figure and of the Son of Man* (WMANT 61; Neukirchen 1987) [& lit]; B. LINDARS, *Jesus Son of Man* (London 1983); P. J. MOLONEY, *The Johannine Son of Man* (Biblioteca di scienze religiose 14, 2nd ed.; Rome 1978); U. B. MÜLLER, *Messias und Menschensohn in jüdischen Apokalypsen und in der Offenbarung des Johannes* (Studien zum Neuen Testament 6; Gütersloh 1972); G. W. E. NICKELSBURG, Son of Man, *ABD* 6 (1992) 137-150 [& lit]; J. THEISSOHN, *Der auserwählte Richter* (SUNT 12; Gottingen 1975); W. O. WALKER, Jr., The Son of Man: Some Recent Developments, *CBQ* 45 (1983) 584-607 [& lit].

G. W. E. NICKELSBURG

SOOTHSAYING SPIRIT → SPIRIT OF THE DEAD

SOPHIA → WISDOM

SOTER → SAVIOUR

SOURCE עין

I. Sources (Heb *ʿên*, *maʿăyān*) have great significance in the ancient Near East. Often essential as a water-supply in arid regions, sources could acquire the status of holy places. As such they were either identified as gods or as divine dwelling-places. Also in the Hebrew Bible, there are several traces of a cult of sources and source deities.

II. Sources are revered in most cultures, especially in arid regions. In the ancient Near East, the more distant they are from humid areas, the more important sources become. In the desert, rich sources can offer the possibility of oasis garden culture. Moreover, sources (and even cisterns) are traffic stations in the desert. Given their vital importance, sources are often places of cults. As such they receive offerings; cultic meals which are partaken near sources must be seen within this context. The equipment of the sacred place corresponds to that of other holy places (cf. 1 Kgs 1:9; Phoenician coins seem to represent both *maṣṣēbâ* and source together). Cultically important sources on the periphery of the settled areas are visited occasionally, either on the occasion of a migration or in order to perform a religious duty (visiting the spring Zamzam in Mekka still belongs to the *ḥaǧǧ* of the Muslims). According to later Arabic testimonies, such places are sometimes kept by priests.

Sources belong to the elementary forces of the universe (cf. Prov 8:34). Therefore, together with comparable elements, they are called as witnesses to treaties (Sefire: *KAI* 222). In a mythological text there is a goddess, who is the daughter of such elementary units ("daughter of Source and →Stone, daughter of →Heaven and Ocean" *KTU* 1.100:2). As an elementary force, sources have also cosmological significance. The Ugaritic god →El resides near the source 'of the two rivers', viz. the rivers of the upper and lower worlds which surround the earth. It is not known for certain whether this place was linked to a geographically identified cult. The possibility should not be excluded, though, for we know sanctuaries where the cosmological dimension of the source was represented, e.g. at Hierapolis. According to an ancient tradition (Lucian, *Dea syr.* 13.33.48), Hierapolis is the place where the waters of the →flood disappeared. The divine triad Zeus-Hadad, Hera-Atargatis, and 'Semeion' (a symbol correlated to Dionysos, Deukalion and Semiramis) are the gods of the place (→Zeus, →Hadad, →Hera, →Atargatis). This *semeion* is carried to the →sea in a procession. Water is drawn, carried back to Hierapolis, and poured into the cultically revered cleft. The symbolism is clear: flood and sea are representations of the waters of chaos; the ritual re-enacts the disappearance of the flood. The source emerging from the cleft reminds the onlookers of the fact that the primeval water is still present in a subterranean area (cf. also Ps 74:15, see EMERTON 1966). The 'Serpent's stone' in 1 Kgs 1:9 (*'eben hazzōḥelet*, translation uncertain!), possibly to be related to the 'Jackal's well' (*'ên hattannîn*) in Neh 2:13, could have received its name on account of a similar symbolism.

Very often the holiness of sources receives an anthropomorphical interpretation. The most prominent god of the oasis city Palmyra, Yarhibol, personifies the source and is represented in a *maṣṣebâ* (J. TEIXIDOR, *The Pantheon of Palmyra* [EPRO 79; Leiden 1979] 29-34). Mesopotamian iconography contains representations of gods holding vessels in their hands from which water streams flow to the left and the right (O. KEEL, *Die Welt der altorientalischen Bildsymbolik und das Alte Testament* [Einsiedeln/Neukirchen-Vluyn 1972] 166). Thus the human's drawing of water imitates the divine power of the spring as it provides the land with water. In cultic texts, the life-giving source becomes a common metaphor of the cultic language which transcends the range of concrete experience.

III. In the Hebrew Bible, too, there is unmistakable evidence of the religious significance of sources. Sources were originally seen as deities, or as the abode of deities (cf. the toponym Baalath-beer, 'Lady of the Source', Josh 19:8). That source deities may be identified with other divine figures is clearly seen from local names such as En-shemesh ('Source of the Sun[-god]', Josh 15:7; 18:17) or Beer-elim ('Source of the gods', Isa 15:8). Deities related to sources are often subjects of mythology. In the OT there are traditions from the nomadic milieu which tell about 'finding' a source (Kadesh: Exod 17:1-7; Num 20:8-13; Beersheba: Exod 21:30; 26:32-33; Beerlahairoi [→El roi; →Lahai-roi]); not localized: Gen 16; 21: 19; cf. also En-hakkore: Judg 15:18-19). Such events are linked with the wanderings of an ancestor who is considered to be the founder of the sanctuary. A typical feature of these stories is the role of the deity of the source, acting as a saviour when things are at their worst (Gen 16; Exod 17; Num 20; Judg 15:15-19). These narratives have eventually become specifically Israelite traditions (and the saviour god is now Yahweh).

Cults centering around sources are situated partly within the cultural centres, partly on the periphery. Many sanctuaries of cities and villages are located within close proximity to a spring, e.g. the temple of Jerusalem (spring Gihon on the flank of the south-eastern hill). Rituals which belong to such sources are almost completely unknown. We can assume, however, a rite of drawing water (cf. the allusion in Isa 12:3). Originally, this could have been a rite in case of drought (in 1 Sam 7:6 the drawing of water belongs to a ritual of fasting and lamenting). Also the Mishnah knows this rite (*Sukkah* 4:9-10).

The cosmological aspect of sources is expressed in various conceptions. In Gen 2 the beginning of creation is marked by a source (*ʾēd*, →Id) which flows in the desert—the model of an oasis (the connection with the four rivers is secondary). However, this oasis is without reality—it is very remote (both in time and space). It is reminiscent of the source of the two rivers in Ugaritic mythology, the abode of El. The 'paradise' is far away—with respect to time and space (*qedem*). It represents a world which in many regards is at the opposite of the real world. Another aspect of such an 'opposite reality' appears in eschatological texts. The temple source becomes a matter of expectation in Ezek 47; sometimes it is not possible to distinguish between the expression of concrete eschatological hope and the metaphorical use of the theme.

IV. *Bibliography*

T. CANAAN, Haunted Springs and Water Demons in Palestine, *JPOS* 1 (1920) 153-170; S. I. CURTISS, *Primitive Semitic Religion To-Day* (Chicago 1902) = *Ursemitische Religion im Volksleben des heutigen Orients* (Leipzig 1903); W. DAUM, *Ursemitische Religion* (Stuttgart 1985); J. A. EMERTON, "Spring and Torrent" in Psalm LXXIV 15, *Volume du Congrès, Genéve 1965* (VTSup 15; Leiden 1966) 122-133; P. REYMOND, *L'eau, sa vie et sa signification dans l'Ancien Testament* (VTSup 6; Leiden 1958); *J. SCHREINER, *ʿên/măʿjan*, *TWAT* 6 (1989) 48-56.

F. STOLZ

SPIRIT → HOLY SPIRIT

SPIRIT OF THE DEAD אוב

I. The term *ʾôb* is attested 17 times in the OT (one reference, Job 32:19, is dubious), for the most part followed by the term *yiddĕʿōnî*, (11 times). Though all scholars agree that the term relates to necromancy and to the conjuration and consultation of the spirits of the dead, its precise meaning and its etymology are still disputed.

II. The term *ʾôb* is interpreted in various ways. Consistent with the translations of the LXX (*engastrimythos*, 'one who speaks from the belly'), Vg (*magus,* 'magician') and Luther (*Warsager*, 'soothsayer'), the term *ʾôb* is generally rendered 'soothsayer' or 'magician' in modern translations. On the basis of Job 32:19, where *ʾôb*, to judge from the context, designates a wine-skin, and with an appeal to Ibn Ezra (Miqraot Gedolot: commentary on Lev 19:31), many scholars assume it designates some sort of tubular device with which the necromancer could produce the voice of the spirit. *ʾôb* is supposed by some to designate the point of contact between the present world and the realm of the dead, cf. Gk *bothros.* Some modern scholars (especially EBACH & RÜTERSWÖRDEN 1977 and 1980) have taken up this idea with further reference to Sum **ab**, Hurr/Hit *api* and Akk *apu*, all of which refer to an offering-pit into which offerings to the chthonic deities and to the dead themselves were placed. Heb *ʾôb* is often connected semantically and etymologically with these words (cf. Ges[18] 22 s.v.).

In recent research, *ʾôb* is increasingly interpreted as a designation of the spirits of the dead. The word might qualify the dead 'returning' (i.e. from the underworld), (French *revenant*) on the basis of Ar *ʾâba* 'return'; as 'hostile' (a derivation of the root *ʾyb* 'to be an enemy'); or as 'ancestral'. Advocates of the latter view (LUST 1974; TROPPER 1989) assume an etymological connection between *ʾôb* and *ʾāb* 'father, ancestor'.

The meaning 'ancestral spirit' for *ʾōb* is based on a number of considerations. In the ancient Orient, necromancy was part of the Cult of the Ancestors. This essentially involved the invocation and interrogation of the dead patriarch from whom a family could seek advice and assistance. Several times in the OT, the Heb term *ʾābôt* 'fathers', similar to *ʾōbôt*, designates dead ancestors (cf. the Lat expression *di parentes* 'divine ancestors').

The following list of parallel terms shows that *ʾôb* signifies persons rather than objects: *yiddĕʿōnî* 'knowing (one)' (occurs 11 times following *ʾôb*; →Wizard), *mētîm* →'the dead', *ʾiṭṭîm* 'ghosts' (Isa 19:3), →*tĕrāpîm* 'teraphim', →*ĕlōhîm* 'gods' (Isa 8:19), →*ʾelîlîm* 'false gods' (Isa 19:3), →*gillūlîm* 'idols' and *šiqqûṣîm* →'abominations' (2 Kings 23:24).

ʾôb is a genuine Hebrew term which, strictly speaking, occurs in this form only in the OT. There are expressions for the deified ancestral spirits among the other Semitic cultures of the ancient Orient which are comparable to *ʾôb* in both form and content. Among them, Eblaite **dingir**-*a-mu* (XELLA 1983), OAkk *ilaba* and Ug *ilib* (LAMBERT 1981), each of which is composed of the words for 'god' and 'father' and can best be rendered 'deified ancestor'. The role of the Ugaritic 'deity' *ilib*, about whom we are relatively well informed, is instructive when considering Heb *ʾôb*. We find *ilib* listed as the recipient of offerings in numerous ritual texts and sacrificial lists. He occurs mostly at the top of the list, before the great gods of Ugarit. We learn from the Aqhat epic (*KTU* 1.17 i:26, 44; 1.17 ii:16) that among a man's most important obligations is the cultic veneration of his departed father's spirit, i.e. his *ilib*. Thus, from the perspective of religious phenomenology, the identification of Ug *ilib* and Heb *ʾôb* is quite probable.

There is also a clearly observable semantic affinity between the Heb term *ʾôb* and the designations for the spirits of the dead in other languages and cultures, such as Ug *rpum* = Phoen *rpʾm* = Heb *rĕpāʾîm* (→Rephaim) and Akk *eṭemmu* = Heb *ʾiṭṭîm* (Isa 19:3). It is well known that both at Ugarit and in Mesopotamia the spirits of the dead were the object of cultic veneration. The texts show that the spirits could be summoned or sent back to the netherworld by means of magical incantation. Especially the text *KTU* 1.161 (invocation of the Rāpiūma-ancestors on the occasion of the death of king Niqmaddu III) is very informative about invocations of the dead at Ugarit. There existed in Mesopotamia an entire series of incantations called **gidim-ḫul** = *eṭemmū lemnūtu* (BOTTÉRO 1983), the object of which was the expulsion of malign spirits of the dead. There is a related series of specifically necromantic rituals to conjure up the spirits of the dead so that the people could 'see' them, could 'speak' with them and, with their help, could 'make a decision' in difficult situations. Three texts of this sort are already known (*AfO* 29/30, 8-10; *AfO* 29/30, 10-12; *SBTU* II nr. 20); they have been re-examined and interpreted by SCURLOCK (1988:103-124) and TROPPER (1989: 83-103). Unambiguous evidence of the interrogation of the *eṭemmu*-spirits is found outside these ritual texts in an Old-Assyrian (*TCL* 4,5) and in a Neo-Assyrian (*LAS* 132) letter.

III. The term *ʾôb* occurs 17 times in the OT. These attestations are found in various literary genres: 9 occurrences in narrative literature (1 Sam, 2 Kings, 1-2 Chron); 4 occurrences in legal contexts (Lev and Deut); 3 occurrences in Isa; 1 uncertain occurrence in Job.

The majority of the occurrences (9 in all) are in contexts which treat the cults of other gods and idols. The term *ʾôb* then generally occurs in the plural and is invariably followed by the parallel term *yiddĕʿōnî(m)*. It is accompanied by expressions such as *pānâ ʾel* 'to apply oneself to (cultically)' (Lev 19: 31; 20:6), *biqqēš ʾel* 'to seek out' (Lev 19: 31), *dāraš ʾel* 'to have recourse to in order to inquire of' (Isa 8:19; 19:3) and *zānâ ʾaḥar* 'to whore after' (Lev 20:6). Besides these there are usages which indicate an identification of the *ʾōbôt* with their physical cultic representations, things capable of being produced (*ʿāśāh* 2 Kings 21:6 // 2 Chron 33:6) and destroyed (*hēsîr* 1 Sam 28:3; *hikrît* 1 Sam 28:9; *biʿēr* 2 Kings 23:24). This vocabulary is characteristic of

OT pronouncements against idol worship, degrading the numinous *ʾôb* entities into mere products of human artifice and thus to lifeless material. The production of cultic images is equated with the introduction of cultic idolatry, the destruction of these images with the elimination of the idolatry. It is typical of the perspective of the Deuteronomic History that the 'good' kings, like the young Saul (1 Sam 28:3,9) and King Josiah (2 Kings 23:24), sought to eliminate the *ʾôb*-cult, whereas the 'evil' kings like Manasseh (2 Kings 21:6) promoted the *ʾôb*-cult. The equating of the ancestor cult and idol worship is a clear indication that the ancestors were the object of cultic veneration by their descendants. In accordance with the dictum in Lev 19:31, anyone who followed the practices of the ancestral cult was cultically unclean (*ṭāmēʾ*).

Five occurrences of the term imply necromancy and deal with the direct interrogation of the dead. The term *ʾôb* occurs consistently in the singular in these cases and is followed but once by the term *yiddĕʿōnî* (also singular). The verb *šāʾal* functions as a *terminus technicus* for directing inquiry to the ancestors (Deut 18:11; 1 Chron 10:13). 1 Sam 28:7 tells us that there were specialists who invoked the dead; and, in the specific case recorded in this passage, it was a woman, the *baʿălat-ʾôb,* 'mistress of the *ʾôb*'. This designation is analogous in form and content to the Sumero-Akkadian name for necromancers, the **lú gidim.ma** 'man/master of the spirit of the dead' and *ša eṭemmi* '(master) of the spirit of the dead' (MSL 12, 168:356; MSL 12, 226:148). The existence of such a profession shows that the invocation of a departed spirit was considered a dangerous undertaking, the success of which required a knowledge of certain rituals. According to 1 Sam 28:8, the necromancer was able to divine 'by the *ʾôb*' (*qāsam bāʾôb*). The statement is ambiguous and could be understood to mean that the *baʿălat-ʾôb* functioned as the medium of the ghost, so that the voice of the dead sounded through her.

Two occurrences of the term (*ʾôb* in the singular) suggest fortune-telling. It is doubtful that *ʾôb* in these passages (which reflect later conceptions) still signifies the spirit of a dead individual rather than some sort of unspecified soothsaying spirit. According to Lev 20:27, there are people who have an *ʾôb* in them and thus serve as the medium for the *ʾôb*. Such people were considered capital offenders in Israel and subject to death by stoning. Note also the voice of the *ʾôb* (Isa 29:4, cf. also Isa 8:19), described as 'softly whispering' (*ṣpp*) and 'murmuring' (*hgh*). Hence the assumption that the phenomenon of necromancy was transformed in the later Old Testament period into mere fortune-telling by means of a medium: and thus lost its connection with the ancestral cult. This cleared the way for the equating of *ʾôb*-divination with the divinatory activity of 'ventriloquizing', a phenomenon widespread in the Hellenistic cultural sphere. Thus the translators of the LXX usually render the Heb term *ʾôb* with the Gk word *engastrimythos* 'one who speaks from his belly'.

One final, albeit uncertain, occurrence of *ʾôb* is Job 32:19. *ʾôb* occurs here in a completely different context, namely in connection with new wine. Consequently, most OT lexicons isolate *ʾôb* Job 31:19 as a separate lexeme meaning 'skin' (e.g. Ges[17] and *HALAT* s.v.). The text is probably corrupt here and we are justified in asking whether the original reading was *nōʾdôt* 'skin' rather than *ʾōbôt.* The word *ʾôb* may have been a secondary insertion, influenced by the expression *rûaḥ biṭnî* 'the spirit of my belly' which occurs in the preceding verse. This would further confirm the contention that *ʾôb* was understood in the later OT period as the 'soothsaying spirit' (of one who speaks from his belly).

In conclusion it may be said that the term *ʾôb* in the OT primarily signified the deified spirit of the ancestors, and subsequently the cultic representation of the ancestor—the ancestral image. In the stereotypical expression *ʾōbôt wĕyiddĕʿōnîm* the term in question can metonymically designate the phenomenon of the ancestor cult as such as well as the necromantic practices it envolved.

Late attestations of the term show that *ʾôb* came to be understood as a divinatory or soothsaying spirit in general. Basically all of the attested occurrences of the term (except for Job 32:19) emphasize that the *ʾôb*-cult and *ʾôb*-divination were seen as incompatible with monotheistic Yahwism. Such activities were therefore considered 'foreign' in the sense of 'Canaanite' (Deut 18:9-12) and thus punishable by death (Lev 20:27).

IV. The treatment of the term in LXX and Vg indicates that the connection of the *ʾôb* with the ancestral cult was no longer known in the post-OT period. *ʾôb* was placed rather in the sphere of prohibited divinatory and magical practices. The term is no longer applied to the spirit in this period, but rather to the soothsayer or magician himself (LXX: *engastrimythos*, 'one who speaks from the belly'; Vg: *magus*, 'magician'; Luther: *Warsager,* 'soothsayer'). The expression *baʿălat ʾôb* (1 Sam 28:7) was consequently understood not as meaning 'necromancer' but rather 'magician' or 'witch' (at least since Luther and Calvin). The imposition of the death penalty on spirit-mediums in Lev 20:27 had particularly grave implications and was seen in the Middle Ages as a call for and legitimation of the persecution of individuals assumed to be witches (for the history of interpretation of *ʾôb* in the post-OT period, see ROUILLARD & TROPPER 1987).

V. *Bibliography*

J. BOTTÉRO, Les morts et l'au-delà dans le rituels en accadien contre l'action des 'revenants', *ZA* 73 (1983) 153-203; J. EBACH & U. RÜTERSWÖRDEN, Unterweltsbeschwörung im Alten Testament, *UF* 9 (1977) 57-70 and *UF* 12 (1980), 205-220; W. G. LAMBERT, Old Akkadian *ILABA* = Ug. *ILIB*?, *UF* 13 (1981) 299-301; J. LUST, On Wizards and Prophets, *Studies on Prophecy* (VTSup 26; Leiden 1974) 133-142; H. ROUILLARD & J. TROPPER, Vom kanaanäsichen Ahnenkult zur Zauberei, *UF* 19 (1987) 235-254; J. A. SCURLOCK, *Magical Means of Dealing with Ghosts in Ancient Mesopotamia* (Diss., Univ. of Chicago 1988); J. TROPPER, *Nekromantie. Totenbefragung im Alten Orient und im Alten Testament* (AOAT 223; Kevelaer & Neukirchen-Vluyn 1989); P. XELLA, Aspekte religiöser Vorstellungen in Syrien nach den Ebla- und Ugarit-Texte, *UF* 15 (1983) 279-290.

J. TROPPER

STARS כוכבים

I. The Hebrew term *kôkāb, kôkābîm* derives from the proto-Semitic root *KBKB, meaning 'star' in the great majority of the other Semitic languages (Ug *kbkb*; Akk *kakkabu*; Aram *kôkbāʾ*, *kôkabtāʾ* [specifically of Planet Venus]; Ar *kawkab*; Eth *kokab*). It is attested 37 times in the Bible. In the NT two Greek terms are used for 'star': ἀστήρ, attested 24 times, and ἄστρον, attested 4 times. Stars were widely regarded as gods.

II. The stars, as created by →God (Gen 1:16; Amos 5:8; Job 9:9; Ps 148:5; Wis 13:2), the work of his fingers (Ps 8:4), belong to the totality of the world of man and exercise their influence on it, in that they rule →day and →night (Gen 1:14-19; Jer 31:35; Ps 136:7-9).

Particularly evident is the admiration of man for the heavens and the multitude of stars, whose number, known only to God (Ps 147:4), is vast and uncountable: the descendancy of →Abraham and Isaac is numerous "as the stars in the heaven" (Gen 15:5; 22:17; 26:4; Exod 32:13); in Deut 1:10 the people of Israel itself becomes "numerous as the stars in the heaven"; see also Deut 10:22; 28:62; Jer 33:22; Nah 3:16; Dan 3:36; Neh 9:23; 1 Chr 27:23; cf. Heb 11:12. Their height above the →earth and their brightness are also impressive (Job 25:5; 31:26). The starry sky is wonderful (Ps 148: 3; Bar 3:34-35; Sir 43:9; Wis 7:29) and it is particularly splendid on a moonless night (Gen 1:15); on the contrary, the darkening of the stars is a sign of the approaching end of human life (Eccl 12:2) or of coming distress (Isa 13:10; 34:4; Ezek 32:7-8; Joel 2:10; 3:4; 4:15; Amos 8:9; Matt 24:29; Mark 13:25; Luke 21:25; Rev 8:12). Shulamit's beauty can be compared to the beauty of the →moon and the splendour of the sun (→Shemesh, →Helios; Cant 6:10). The High Priest Simon is also compared to the moon, the sun and the stars (Sir 50:6-7) and Daniel predicts that "the sages will shine as the splendour or the firmament; those who will cause many to righteousness will shine like stars for ever" (Dan 12:3; see also Matt 13:4). In Matt 17:2 the face of →Jesus during his transfiguration is compared to a shining sun, as the face of the →Son of man in John's vision (Rev 1:16).

Stars have individual names, given by God (Ps 147:4), and form a well-arranged army, in which every star has its place (Isa 40:26; Jer 33:22). In the creation the heavens form a hollow vault, a firmament above the earth, and, resting on the waters, describe a circle upon them (Job 26:10; 28:24; Prov 8:27; Sir 24:5). Therefore they could be spoken of as a veil or a tent spread out above the earth (Isa 40:22; Ps 19:6), across which stars move according to laws strictly fixed and determined by their Creator (Bar 3:34; Sir 43:10; Wis 7:19). Stars, as heavenly beings (→Sons of the Gods), are brighter than earthly beings, but even among them some are more brilliant than others, "for one star differs from another star in splendour" (1 Cor 15:40-41). The beauty of the firmament generated, even in the most faithful Jews, a strong temptation to worship the starry heavens, as typified by Job 31:26-28 (WELLHAUSEN 1961:209-210), but in spite of the admiration for the heavens, which according to Wis 13:2 was originally due to the ignorance of the true God, the religious cult of stars associated with specific deities seems to have almost totally disappeared from the present text of the Bible: the cosmic forces, originally capable of exerting powers on earth have been subjugated to God (Job 9: 7), their Creator (Job 9:9); the actual form of the constellations gives testimony to God's power (Job 38:31) and their brilliance (Wis 13:3) and regular movements find their origin in Him (Amos 5:8; Job 38:32-33); the stars are merely lamps (→lamp) of heaven, "obedient in the service for which they are sent" (Bar 6:59); compared to God even the stars lose their brilliance (Job 25:5); see also the praise rendered to God by all the cosmic forces (Ps 148:1-5) and the Song of the three Holy Children in Dan 3:62-63. Only God, having a universal knowledge of the rules of his creation, may use cosmic forces to control the succession of the seasons, of both time and weather and of man's day to day life (see Job 38:33; Sir 43:1-10). To stress God's power, his throne is imagined as being above the stars (Job 22:12), whereas the lower position of men is evidenced by the assumption that they cannot reach the stars (Obad 4). Only in this firmly monotheistic context is a personified →wisdom allowed to take part in the creational process of the firmament (Prov 8:27): wisdom, as a direct emanation of God, is therefore superior to any star or constellation (Wis 7: 29).

However, it is difficult to deny the existence of astrological references in the Bible, often hidden in the most ancient layers of the text, revealing deified aspects of cosmic phenomena as distinguished from mere physical/natural elements (ZATELLI 1991: 93). Jer 14:22 presents an interesting passage in which heaven is considered by his contemporaries as an astral deity instead of a physical/natural entity, completely dependent upon God's will. The prophet's condemnation of the heaven as a nullity reiterates the authentic divinity and the omnipotence of the God of Israel against the background of the idolatrous cults performed by the kings of Judah (→Yehud). In this context *šāmayim* corresponds to the syntagm *ṣĕbāʾ haššāmayim* = →Host of heaven, that appears 19 times in the Hebrew OT (and once in Sir 43:9, where *ṣābāʾ* alone occurs meaning *ṣĕbāʾ haššāmayim*): in Deut, in Kgs, in those prophets which immediately precede the exile, in DtIsa (Isa 40:26; 45:12 *ṣĕbāʾām* alone means *ṣĕbāʾ haššāmayim*), when idolatry is condemned, and in postexilic texts (Dan 8:10; Neh 9:6 [twice]; 2 Chr 18:18; 33:3-5 in the passages parallel to 1 Kgs 22:19 and 2 Kgs 21:3-5; ZATELLI 1991:90).

These occurrences would attest that the worship of the stars in Israel must have been strong during periods of pagan contacts, mostly under Mesopotamian political influence, already in the 8th century and later on in the 7th and 6th centuries BCE. Amos 5:26 deals with an idolatrous cult of →Sakkuth and →Kaiwan (in the LXX: Μολόχ καὶ [...] Ῥαιφάν), 'the stars of your God', where the two names are generally related to the planet Saturn. The whole passage is quoted in Stephen's speech in Acts 7:43 (here Ῥαιφάν appears in the variant reading Ῥομφά[ν]), where the adoration of the golden →calf (Exod 32:1-24) is evidently interpreted as well in connection with astral worship, according to an exegesis which has been developed in medieval Judaism.

Among the causes of the fall of the Northern Kingdom, according to 2 Kgs 17:16, are the cults offered by king Hoshea to "all the hosts of heaven". In the Kingdom of Judah, Manasseh would have been the first king to introduce idolatrous cults, by building altars to "all the hosts of heaven" in the two inner courts of the Temple (2 Kgs 21:5; 2 Chr 33:5). King Josiah fought against such practices: he burnt all the objects kept in the Temple and associated to astral cults, dismissed and killed the priests who had been appointed to offer sacrifices "to the sun, the moon, the constellations and all the heavenly hosts"; he also forbade ceremonial practices of sunworship instituted by the previous kings and destroyed the altars built by Manasseh (2 Kgs 23:4-5.11-12; but see 2 Chr 33:15; 34:4; cf. also Jer 8:2; 19:13).

However, astral cults were not entirely uprooted; they are often mentioned in prophetic texts. An example is Ezek 8:16, where the worship of the sun is said to be carried on in Jerusalem within the temple-court during the sixth year of the captivity of Jehoiachin (591 BCE). Particularly important as a private cult, and therefore not completely uprootable, was the worship of the →Queen of Heaven, probably →Ishtar venerated as a celestial goddess (a syncretistic deity incorporating West and East Semitic characters), once interpreted by scholars as a personification of the moon, more probably of the planet Venus. This cult, performed mainly by women (Jer 7:18; 44:17-26), after the Babylonian invasion and the destruction of the first Temple, persisted in Egypt among Judean refugees. Star worship was generally practised on house-tops, as in Mesopotamian custom (Jer 19:13; 32:29; Zeph 1:5).

Star worship is manifest even in superstitious forms of adoration: the symbolic act of the kissing of the hand (Job 31:26) is a clear reference to illicit practices of popular astral devotion, still common in a period in which astral cults should already have been forbidden. Traces of magic and divination associated with star cults, appearing to derive from Mesopotamian practices, are possibly present in Gen 37:9, where →Joseph has an astral dream, in Jos 10:12-13, which can be interpreted as an incantation prayer uttered in a context of astrological speculation (ZATELLI 1991:89, 94), possibly in 1 Chr 12:33, where the children of Issachar are spoken of as having "understanding of the times in order to know what Israel ought to do" and in Ps 121:6, where the negative powers of the stars will be kept afar by the presence of the LORD. An incantation formula seems to be alluded to also in Job 3:9 in which conjurors are invoked to turn a propitious day into an unpropitious one by darkening the stars of the twilight.

Prophets strongly condemn astral worship, the latter being condemned as one of the causes of the misfortunes of Israel: see Jer 10:2, where the author admonishes people not to be terrified by the *ʾōtôt haššāmayim*, a syntagmatic expression meaning 'celestial phenomena'; Zeph 1:5. In Isa 47:13 Babylonian astrology is even mocked: the *hōběrê šāmayim* (the masters of the heavenly course; LXX: ἀστρόλογοι) and the *ḥōzîm bakkôkābîm* (the star-gazers) are worthless. Star cults are condemned in Deut 4:19; 17:3. Exod 20:4 and Deut 5:8 forbid making and worshipping any image of "anything which is in heaven above", certainly implying also the stars. The generic prohibition to practice divination or magic in Lev 19:26 and Deut 18:10 was interpreted by later rabbis as related to astrology (see *B.Sanh.* 65b-66a).

The dominant attitude of Jewish religious thought is that the rules of the universe are a divine prerogative and cannot be interpreted by man, as shown in Job 38:33, where the hapax legomenon term *mišṭār* could be translated 'the power to decide the course of the stars', according to similar divine epithets attested in Ugaritic religious literature (ZATELLI 1991:97). The monotheistic principle of the religion of Israel was in any case an obstacle to the growth and the expansion of the 'Chaldean science' (on the word Chaldean as a synonym of astrologer, see Dan 2:2.4.5.10; 4:14; 5:7.11) and, in spite of the great number of *bĕʿalîm* (→Baal) never ceasing to exert influence in pre-exilic Israel, the original conception of →Yahweh as a storm and skygod probably prevented the worship of other star-gods (ZATELLI 1991:88); yet Yahwism and star worship long coexisted, especially in popular forms of veneration.

An interesting passage in Ps 89:6-9 shows the status of Yahweh among the sons of the gods: in this context the sky (in the sense of 'divinity') and the *qĕhal qĕdōšîm* ('the congregation of the saints', i.e. the gods of an originally polytheistic pantheon) praise the LORD, fear Him and are thankful for his extraordinary acts, his wonders: Yahweh is *ʾĕlōhê ṣĕbāʾôt* ('God of hosts'), the Almighty who rules over the skygods and is a *primus inter pares* in their assembly. Along the same lines another significant parallelism is to be found in Job 15:15, where Yahweh is again considered as a *primus inter pares* among *qĕdōšîm* and *šāmayim*, both of them to be interpreted as ancient divinities. In the poetic contexts of Judg 5:20 and Isa 14:12-13 we still find a conception of deified stars, very closely linked, particularly in the last case, to the originally pan-Semitic belief of a 'mount of congregation in the side of the north'. It seems that the Masoretic redactor of Deut 32:43 had deliberately avoided allusions to other divinities: if we read the verse "Rejoice, o nations, for his people" (according to the LXX: "Heaven(s), rejoice with him and may the sons of God adore him") we should evidently assume that the text underwent a radical change towards stronger monotheistic principles. A similar situation is to be found in Deut 32:8 where the MT reads "according to the number of the children of Israel" (*lĕmispar bĕnê yiśrāʾēl*), while in 4QDeut 32:8 we find: *lĕmispar bĕnê ʾēl*, and the LXX translates "according to the number of angels of God". Deut 32:8-9 could therefore be interpreted as a distinctive rule of the inferior gods over the nations, whereas Israel is reserved for Yahweh (ZATELLI 1991:91-92). From this verse and Deut 4:19-20 comes the belief, which is discussed in *B.Shab.* 156b and further on in the Middle Ages, that all the nations would be astrally determined, except for Israel. In the last instance of Deut 4:19 it is remarkable that the gods no longer possess the other nations, but the nations themselves, having adopted a deviant course, worship the stars. The God of Israel is no longer a *primus inter pares* accompanied by his entourage of skygods: He is the only God, the others are false and the people of Israel are warned lest they might erroneously worship the host of stars (or of angels) instead of the true Divinity, the actual Creator of the stars.

The identification of personified stars with angels of the heavenly hosts is well accepted within a totally monotheistic religious system: the stars stand in God's presence, to the right and the left of His throne (1 Kgs 22:19; 2 Chr 18:18); they serve Him (Ps 103:21; Neh 9:6); in Sir 43:8, 10 the identification of stars with soldiers of an army is particularly evident. See als Rev 1:20. At the head of the heavenly hosts stands a →'Prince of the army' (Josh 5:14-15; Dan 8:11), probably the highest star and the farthest from the earth, even if the actual leader is God, to whom the starry army belongs. From this conception derives the syntagm 'LORD/God of hosts' (*Yhwh/ʾĕlōhê ṣĕbā'ôt*) occurring in numerous biblical passages (→Yahweh Zebaoth).

The above mentioned passage of Job 25:5 is possibly to be compared to Job 15:15, where the stars appear as deities, along with the moon and the sky, all of them belonging to the entourage of the 'holy ones' of 'El'. Particular expressions denoting "the joy of the stars" in singing to or praising their Creator appear in Job 38:7 (in perfect parallelism with the syntagm *bĕnê 'ĕlōhîm*) and in Bar 3:34. In 11QTgJob 38:7, however, the original image looses any polytheistic meaning: "when the morning stars shone together and all the angels of God shouted together". Any allusion to star cults and to other deities is here avoided. Once the danger of idolatry has been removed, the relation between God and the stars is only that of the Creator with his creation (ZATELLI 1991:98).

In post-exilic religious thought, astral cults ceased to be performed in an official form, even if they were probably partially preserved as private traditional practices, and gave way to a form of non-religious observation of stars which, influenced by Hellenistic science, gradually became a form of astrological and astronomical speculation, which was later partly accepted by the rabbinic tradition (see e.g. the lengthy discussions in *B.Shab.* 156a-b) mostly connected with the determination of holy days (see e.g. *B.Suk.* 28a). Observation of the revolution of the heavenly bodies is regarded as a religious duty and such is the interpretation of Deut 4:6 according to *B.Shab.* 75a. Thus the observation and understanding of heavenly phenomena became a proper science, seen as a gift of God to the wise man: in Wis 7:18-19 Solomon prays to God in order to receive from Him "an unerring knowledge (...) of the beginning and end and middle of times, the alternations of solstices and the changes of seasons, the circuit of years and the positions of stars". Daniel, "whose light, understanding and wisdom was equal to the gods' wisdom" had been appointed chief of astrologers, Chaldeans and soothsayers by Nebuchadnezzar (Dan 5:11). This verse probably alludes to the fact that the study of Babylonian astral divination was common among Jews during and after the exile; however, Daniel himself claims the superiority of God's power over any astrologer or soothsayer in revealing mysteries (Dan 2:27), because God Himself is the giver of all knowledge (Dan 1:17; cf. Wis 7:15-21).

In the pseudepigraphic books we find contradictory views about astrology. *1 Enoch* 8:3; *Jub.* 12:16-18; *Sib. Or.* II 220-236 strongly condemn this discipline, praising men who, in the words of CHARLESWORTH (1987:933), "neither search the mystical meaning of the movements of the heavenly bodies nor are deceived by the predictions of Chaldean astrology", insisting on the necessity to worship only the true God. Yet some passages in the Pseudepigrapha show a relatively positive attitude towards astrology, betraying stronger Hellenistic influences (see e.g. *1 Enoch* 72:1-37; 75:3; *2 Enoch* 21:6; 30:3). Josephus Flavius writes that astrology was popular among Jews in his days and that misinterpretation of heavenly signs was partly responsible for the outbreak of the revolt against the Romans (*Bellum* VI 5,289). Misinterpretation of celestial phenomena is a subject frequently dealt with in haggadic and talmudic literature (see e.g. *Gen. Rabba* 85:2; 87:4; *Exod. Rabba* 1:18; *B.Sanh.* 101b): in these cases as well the authors want to stress the complete superiority of God's will and power over any astrological speculation.

The later conception that the celestial bodies are endowed with individual life, consciousness and intelligence is a further development of the observation of the movement of the stars across the heavens (see e.g. Pss 19:6-7; 104:19; Job 31:26; Eccl 1:5; Sir 43:2-12), supported by the ancient belief of the personification of stars (see e.g. the above mentioned passage of Judg 5:20) also related to Mesopotamian and Hellenistic astrological traditions. This view, "on the boundary line of mythology and astronomy" (*Legends* V:35, 40, n.112), is perceivable in the pseudepigraphic literature (see esp. *1 Enoch* 18:13-16; 41:5; cf. *1 Enoch* 72-82) and in haggadic traditions. However, in these cases too, the authors stress the dependence of the individual nature and will of the planets upon God's will (see Sir 43:5), Whose decisions and laws are unalterable: were these laws suddenly to be abrogated, then the whole creation would come to an end. Revolutions of the cosmic order mark the final phase of the created world in apocalyptic contexts (Isa 13:10; Jer 31:35-36; Ezek 32:7-8; Amos 8:9; Matt 24:29; Luke 21:25; Rev 6:13; 8:10.12; 9:1 [where the image of the fallen star is personified as →Satan; see Isa 14:12; Luke 10:18]; cf. also Acts 27:20).

As a prophetic symbol the stars are mentioned in Dan 8-10 as an allusion to the Jews who will succumb to Hellenistic paganism. In John's vision (Rev 1:16) seven stars appear as the symbol of the seven angels of the churches (Rev 1:20; 2:1; 3:1): the passage shows an example of the previously mentioned association of the stars with the angels which frequently occurs also in later pseudepigraphic literature. Astral symbolism is still to be found in Rev 12:1 and a mythological allusion may be seen in Rev 12:4.

In Num 24:17 we observe in the prophecy of Bileam an important clue to the symbolic-divine and regal value which the stars assume (ZATELLI 1991:93-94): messianic interpretations of the verse appear in *Tg. Onq.* and *Tg. Ps.-J.* and the name Bar Kochba (Aramaic: 'Son of the Star'), given to the famous leader of the rebellion against the Romans in the 2nd cent. CE, has to be understood in a messianic context (see *B.Sanh.* 97b). The star symbol reappears in Mat 2:1-10 where, however, the star is not identified with the Messiah (→Christ), being only an astrological phenomenon observed by heathen astrologers and associated with the birth of a great man. In Rev 22:16 Jesus uses the image of the star referring to Himself: "I am the root and the offspring of David, the bright and morning star" (see also Rev 2:28 and 2 Pet 1:19 where the Greek term φωσφόρος is used).

III. *Bibliography*

A. ALTMANN, Astrology, *EncJud* III, 788-795; E. BISCHOFF, *Babylonisches-Astrales im Weltbilde des Thalmud und Midrasch* (Leipzig 1907); G. H. BOX, Star, *A Dictionary of Christ and the Gospels* 2 (Edinburgh 1908) 674-676; C. F. BURNEY, Stars, *EncBibl* IV, 4779-4786; J. H. CHARLESWORTH, Jewish Interest in Astrology during the Hellenistic and Roman Period, *ANRW* II 20,2 (1987) 926-956; L. DEQUEKER, Les *qedôšîm* du Ps. LXXXIX, *ETL* 39 (1963) 469-484; M. J. DRESDEN, Science, *IDB*, 236-244, esp. 243; E. O. JAMES, *The Worship of the Sky-God* (London 1963); P. JENSEN, Astronomy, *The Jewish Encyclopedia* II (London 1903) 245-251; M. LEHMAN, New Light on Astrology in Qumran and the Talmud, *RQ* 32 (1975) 599-602; B. O. LONG, Astrology, *IDBS*, 76-78; L. LÖW, Die Astrologie in der biblischen, talmudischen und nachtalmudischen Zeit, *Ben Chanania* 6 (1863) 401-435; E. W. MAUNDER, *The Astrology of the Bible* (London 1909); A. ROFÉ, *The Belief in Angels in Israel in the First Temple Period in the light of Biblical Traditions* (Heb; Jerusalem 1969), English edition: *The Belief in Angels in the Bible and in Early Israel* (Jerusalem 1979); G. SCHIAPARELLI, *L'astronomia nell'Antico Testamento* (Milano 1903); M. SELIGSOHN, Star-Worship, *The Jewish Encyclopedia* XI (London 1905) 527-528; B. SULER, Astrologie, *EncJud* III 577-591; SULER, Astronomie, *EncJud* III 591-607; J. WELLHAUSEN, *Reste arabischen Heidentums* (Berlin 1961³); I. ZATELLI, Astrology and the Worship of the Stars in the Bible, *ZAW* 103 (1991) 86-99 [& lit].

F. LELLI

STOICHEIA στοιχεῖα τοῦ κόσμου

I. *Stoicheia tou kosmou* has several meanings. From the root *stich-*, meaning row or rank, the singular *stoicheion* designates the shadow cast by the pole of a sundial, a letter of the alphabet, the sound the human voice makes as a basic element of language, and an element as the fundamental constituent of an object or entity. Most likely derived from *stoichos*, the row or line in which soldiers stand, the plural with the addition 'of the world', *stoicheia tou kosmou* means the basic components of the world. The phrase is used three times in the New Testament, Gal 4:3, Col 2:8 and 2:20.

II. Plato distinguished fire, air, water, and earth as the components of particular physical objects and, indeed, of the kosmos. The combination and separation of the elements constitutes the process of change (*Timaeus* 48b and *Sophist* 252b). Plato thought and wrote in a tradition of cosmological interests. Before him, Heraclitus had conceptualized the coherence underlying all existing things as a →*logos* common to everything (Frs. 6 and 50). The cosmic arrangement is not simple, however, for it consists of a unity or even identity of opposites—such as disease and health, life and death, hunger and satiety, night and day—in which each pair of opposites forms both a unity and a plurality. Thus the opposition of hot and cold forms the single entity of temperature as well as the multiplicity of winter and summer (Frs. 204, 206, and 207). Change can be explained on the basis of tension or 'strife' (*eris*) between the opposites which maintains a balance of the elements in the universe. Heraclitus used *kosmos* to show the orderly arrangement of all the items in the world and fire (*pur*) to denote the interactions between them. For Heraclitus, then, the three terms *logos*, *kosmos*, and *eris* are central to a cosmological schema, with the *logos* not entirely distinct from deity, as the feature of the world which links the various parts of the world and directs change in an orderly and proportional fashion (Fr. 207).

The concepts and terminology which Heraclitus developed enabled him to construct an account of change which was philosophically and scientifically satisfying. Nevertheless, it was inadequate because it did not include a discussion of the things which undergo change. To this topic Empedocles devoted considerable attention. In his famous Fr. 6 he wrote about four roots (*rhizōmata*) of everything—bright →Zeus, life-bearing →Hera, Aidoneus, and Nestis who causes moisture—which are described in Fr. 17 as →Fire, →Earth, Air, and Water. These four roots have always existed and change is produced by their intermingling—mixing together and separating from each other—according to the two opposing forces, Love and Strife. The four roots are elemental in the sense of being the original substances; they are original in the sense that everything else in the world is derived from them as compounds of the primary elements.

The cosmological motifs of Empedocles were connected to his interest in moral and religious issues. His rejection of bloodshed, be it social as in warfare or religious as in sacrifice, was fundamentally moral, because the consequences of Strife or Hatred included harm done to animals as well as human beings and damage to the person caught in the net of Hatred. The transmigrations of the spirit stained with blood would endure for 30,000 years, including time spent as plant, human, bird, and fish (Fr. 117). Here, the cosmology of four primary elements also plays a role; because spirits are expelled from the Air to the Water, thence to the Earth and then to the Sun, which in turn pushes them to the Aither; all the elements receive such spirits but loathe having them (Fr. 115).

In the *Timaeus*, Plato uses the word *genē* for the four basic elements and *stoicheia* as a basic constituent to describe how one element can change into another, e.g. as when water hardens into earth or melts into air. Any object in the world or any substance is thus a compound of the four elements. Unlike Empedocles' theory, however, which cannot account for how one root or element can be transformed into another, Plato's theory can explain how water can be heated into air and condensed again into water. Yet like Empedocles' theory, movement across the elements is possible for the soul as it suffers the consequences of ignorance and bad deeds.

Aristotle as well as Plato stood in a long

line of cosmological speculation that focuses on the elemental constitution of the world. In Aristotle's view, stated in *De generatione et corruptione* 329b, all substances are considered to be compounds of the four basic elements, earth, water, air, and fire, and possibly a fifth, aither. In a spirit reminiscent of Heraclitus' effort to explain change with the concept of *eris*, Aristotle regarded each of the four elements as a combination of the four primary opposites: cold and hot; dry and wet. Hence, earth is cold and dry; water is wet and cold; air is wet and hot; and fire is dry and hot.

The Stoics, too, developed a complex cosmology in which the elements of the universe played a major function. According to Diogenes Laertius, 7:134-142, although the world as we know it consists of a mixture of the elements, the elements perish in the cosmic fire at the end of a world cycle. The kosmos has a history which begins in fire, changes to air, then to water, next into earth; and finally returns to fire in a cosmic conflagration. In this cosmology, the study of the universe was accompanied by an interest in the nature of human beings. According to Epictetus 3.13-15, for example, death, as a return to the elements, is not to be feared because it is a regular feature of elemental change in which the elements do not suffer; and Marcus Aurelius 4.32.3 describes death as a dissolution into the elements. According to Plutarch, *Fac. Lun.* 28, the various parts of the human body are correlated to various elements of the universe: the body comes from earth, the mind from the sun; and the soul from the moon. According to Diogenes Laertius, the philosopher Chrysippus thought the kosmos divine; the stars and the earth to be gods; and the mind to be the supreme god who inhabits the aither. Here, the stars and other planetary bodies were also associated with the elements of the kosmos. The Stoics combined natural philosophy with a system of morality in order to establish a way of life in which adjusting the human being to nature and its processes leads to happiness through harmony with nature.

Two writers of the first century BCE, Cicero and Ovid, also utilized the concept of 'elements of the universe' in ways that are consistent with the meanings assigned to the term by earlier Greek philosophers. Cicero thought that human beings are fashioned from earth, water, fire, and air, with the soul moving upward at death to the substance resembling itself, its natural home, there to remain forever (*Tusculan Disputations* 1. 17-19). Ovid considered the kosmos to be arranged according to an orderly structure of the four basic elements; but, should strife among them become too fierce, the universe would be destroyed (*Metamorphoses* 1.32-33 and 256-258). The orderly processes of change follow a sequence in which each element is derived from another: just as souls traverse the elements on their way to their home and reside in a number of bodies along the way. In both cases, a connection between the elements of the kosmos and the planetary bodies was established.

Jewish as well as Greek and Latin writers employed the concept of basic elements. In *4 Macc* 12:13, Antiochus IV Epiphanes is addressed as a man for whom the demands of justice has planned an eternal fire; because he had tortured and maltreated other humans "made of the same elements" as himself. Philo describes the constitution of the universe and the changes within it as well as the parallels between humans and the world by reference to the four basic elements. He also links them to the ascent of the soul to its ultimate destination in the aither (*Rer. Div. Her.* 280-83).

III. The three passages in which the phrase *ta stoicheia tou kosmou* is used in the New Testament have been the subject of vigorous debate. Several possibilities have emerged as the primary hermeneutical options. Behind Paul's argument in Galatians lays the distinction between pre-Christian slavery and the Christian freedom of his readers. In the argument, two forms of slavery are mentioned: the Jewish one consisting of living under the yoke of the Law; and the Gentile one of subjection to the elements of the kosmos. To the Gentile readers, Paul asserts that the desire to be subject to the Law in the form of observing the Jewish legal and ritual calendar is a return to their pagan situation when they revered the elements as deities. So they are now in bondage to beings that are not gods (4:8). And it can be argued that the "elements of the kosmos" are Jewish religious observances which the Galatians found alluring; although Paul's claim that mistaking the elements for gods is doubtful if the elements are only observances and regulations. Given the predeliction of many people in the Greco-Roman world for astral religious beliefs and practices, it could also be argued that the elements are planetary or other celestial bodies; or that the elements refer to spiritual beings: such as angels or demons who control earthly affairs and determine human destiny; although nothing in Paul's epistle requires either of these interpretations. A more likely interpretation is that Paul's use of the "elements of the kosmos" bears a meaning similar to its common meaning in the Greek philosophical tradition—the basic constituents of the universe in which the soul may be trapped in the elemental disharmony or the soul's misdeeds, and from which it can be freed through proper philosophical and religious knowledge. Thus, as Empedocles wrote about the power of the 'elements' and Philo described them as forces, so Paul could think of them as powers or, taken together, as the power the kosmos holds over people, even to the point of enslaving them to the world.

The phrase 'elements of the kosmos' is used twice in Col, at 2:8 and 2:20. It has evoked diverse interpretations similar to those given the passage in Galatians; although the context of the two passages is different and thus the meaning also varies. The author of Colossians distinguished philosophical traditions, characterized as empty and deceitful, from the truth of →Christ, portrayed as the first-born of creation and the fullness of God: as well as the unity and purpose of the kosmos. From this description, the author encouraged his readers to avoid captivity to the 'elements of the kosmos' that human philosophy entails. Instead, they should be mindful of their spiritual circumcision or baptism in Christ, which both forgives trespasses and raises believers from the dead. The consequence of dying to the elements with Christ he concluded, is two-fold. The first is that believers need not submit to regulations about food and drink and other forms of abstinence or observing festivals and rituals, thinking that such observances would enable their souls to rise with Christ or ascend to him after death. The second is that they should set their minds on Christ, who is at the right hand of God. He has returned to his divine origin, and has thus become the prototype for Christian believers.

The 'elements of the world' bears some relation to the teachings contained in the "philosophy according to human traditions" of 2:8. The phrase 'of the world' suggests that the issues at stake focus on the claims a particular philosophical tradition made, although the author's argument suggests that the content of the philosophy is the target of attack. One possible content for the claims would be that the 'elements of the kosmos' are the elemental spirits of the universe (1:16; 2:10.15) whom Colossian philosophers, following human thinking (1:18), identified as the powers and rulers who govern society or the angels (2:18). The identification of the elements with powers or angels as elemental spirits, however, may point to Colossians who wanted to die to the world and its rulers in order to achieve their aim of seeking things that are above where Christ is seated. The identification may equally well point to the four basic constituents of the kosmos (2:20) to which the Colossian Christians died with Christ: thus demonstrating that living without the world is as possible as living in the world.

IV. *Bibliography*

A. J. Bandstra, *The Law and the Elements of the World: an Exegetical Study in Aspects of Paul's Teaching* (Kampen 1964); F. F. Bruce, "Called to Freedom": A Study in Galatians, *The New Testament Age: Essays in Honor of Bo Reicke* (Macon, GA 1984) 61-71; W. BURKERT, ΣΤΟΙΧΕΙΑ: Eine semasiologische Studie, *Philol* 103 (1959) 167-197; B. REICKE, The Law and This World According to Paul: Some Thoughts Concerning Gal 4: 1-11, *JBL* 70 (1951) 259-276; D. RUSAM, Neue Belege zu den στοιχεῖα τοῦ κόσμου, *ZNW* 83 (1992) 119-125; E. SCHWEIZER, Slaves of the Elements and Worshippers of Angels: Gal 4:3, 9 and Col 2:8, 18, 20, *JBL* 107 (1988) 455-468; W. WINK, The "Elements of the Universe" in Biblical and Scientific Perspective, *Zygon* 13 (1978) 225-248.

L. J. ALDERINK

STONE אבן

I. The word *ʾbn* occurs in all Semitic languages, except Classical Arabic (COHEN 1970). It denotes natural stone. Veneration of stones occurs in all religions of the ancient world and is in fact attested in the Near East up to present times. According to the transmitted text of Gen 49:24 'Stone' (*ʾbn*) was an epithet of →El as the God of Israel. Also a toponym like Ebenezer suggests that Eben is an old divine name. The prophetic criticism against worship of stones stands in stark contrast to the erection of stones at holy sites by the patriarchs.

II. In the Ancient Near East veneration of stones was very common. Quarried stones played an important role in Egyptian religion and various magical properties were ascribed to different stones. In view of the influence of Amun-Re worship on Canaan during the New Kingdom it is interesting that Amun-Re was sometimes represented in aniconic form as a lump of stone (BISON DE LA ROQUE 1925:50-53; WAINWRIGHT 1980; METTINGER 1995:49-55). In Mesopotamia worship of stones is not attested, but magical properties were ascribed to several types of stone and in the Sumerian mythological poem Lugal-e the god Ninurta, assisted by certain animated 'good' stones, wages a battle against certain 'bad' stones (VAN DIJK 1983). The Hurrites too had their stone-demons (HAAS 1982:139-166), and they too ascribed mysterious powers to stones (HAAS 1982:167-183). In Ugarit some texts mention an announcement (*rgm*) and a whispering (*lḫšt*) of stones (*abnm*), paralleled by the speech of trees (*KTU* 1.3 iii:22-23; 1.82:43). Possibly this refers to oracles obtained from stones and trees. In any case the context excludes a metaphorical meaning and so here too stones are seen as animate beings. In *KTU* 1.100:1 a deified stone (*abn*) is the father of the first animated creature, the She-ass. Canaanite personal names suggest that *abnu* was a divine epithet: Amorite *Ḫa-ab-ni-Il* 'Il-is-my-Stone', *Ab-nu-ra-pí* 'A-Stone-is-Rapi', *Tu-tar-ab-nu* 'The-Stone-has-increased'. Ugaritic *bn abn* 'Son-of-the-Stone' (compare Jer 2:27), Phoenician *ʾbnšmš* 'The-Sun-is-a-Stone', Punic *ʾbnbʿl* 'Baal-is-a-Stone'. Compare also the god Abaddir (from **ʾbnʾdr*) mentioned in Latin texts from Punic North Africa (RIBICHINI 1985).

In Ugarit stone stelae were erected (*nṣb*) for the ancestors called *ilib* (→Ilib), 'Il-who-is-the-Father' because they were united with Il after their death (*KTU* 1.15 v:16-17). These stelae called *skn* are also attested in Emar and possibly in Am 5:26 (read *sknt* for *skwt*, KORPEL 1990:576). They are probably identical to the biblical *maṣṣēbôt* (from the root *nṣb*) and the rows of erected slabs of stone found at various sanctuaries (Ugarit, Gezer, Tell Mūsā, Hazor) which were probably connected with the cult of the ancestral gods. This would not run counter to the hypothesis that they represented local deities (WEIPPERT 1988:236; but see the discussion in METTINGER 1995:143-191). At least at Hazor an association of this type of ancestral cult with the cult of →El is likely.

Veneration of stones connected with saints continues up till present times. In Palestinian folklore many legends are connected with stones which in spite of Islam sometimes receive offerings or still have an oracular function (KRISS 1960-1962). Even in official Islam the Black and Lucky Stones at the east corner of the Kaʿba continue to have a religious function.

III. In Gen 49:24 →Yahweh is called an

ʾ*eben*. Scholars hesitate whether both this and the parallel epithet →'Shepherd' can be original (OLOFSSON 1990:94-95). Among those who maintain MT as the more difficult reading some propose a different interpretation ('son', 'sons', or 'our father'). In view of the comparative evidence this is unlikely. Comparable epithets like →Rock suggest that originally there existed no opposition whatsoever to this old Canaanite epithet. The toponym Ebenezer (*ʾbn hʿzr* 'Stone-of-the-Help,' 1 Sam 4:1; 5:1) is explained as applicable to Yahweh in 1 Sam 7:12. In any case the use in Gen 49:24 is clearly metaphorical, even if the accompanying 'Shepherd' is a gloss.

The epithet is not attested, however, among Hebrew personal names, neither in the OT, nor epigraphically. Whether or not this testifies to early opposition cannot be ascertained. Prophetic criticism against images of stone (Am 5:26 [KORPEL 1990: 576]; Isa 37:19; Jer 2:27; 3:9; Ezek 20:32) unmistakeably led to the disuse of the epithet. This in spite of the fact that the patriarchs were said to have erected and anointed stones at various holy sites where they had met El (Gen 28:18; 31:45-46; 35:14; see →Bethel). Also stones were supposed to be able to act as witnesses (Gen 31:46-47; Josh 24:27; 1 Sam 6:18 [read *ʾbn* instead of *ʾbl*]) and this function would seem to presuppose that they could speak.

The old epithet is reversed when it is said of Yahweh that he will become a stone that causes men to stumble, and a rock that makes them fall (Isa 8:14). According to Hab 2:11 a stone will cry from the wall to denounce injustice, but in 2:19 the idea that a dumb stone could be animate is critized. However, the crying stone is a metaphor; it may be compared with the statement of Eliphaz who says that the pious will have a covenant with the stones of the field, i.e. will live in harmony with nature (Job 5:23). In the New Testament the stone-epithet is applied to →Christ who is described as the stone which the builders rejected (Ps 118: 22, but the Hebrew meant the dejected supplicant), but who becomes a corner-stone (Matt 21:42, par.). In 1 Pet 2:7-8 this imagery is paralleled by Christ as the stone that makes the unbelievers stumble (cf. Isa 8:14).

IV. *Bibliography*

F. BISON DE LA ROCQUE, *Rapport sur les fouilles de Médamoud* (Cairo 1925) 50-53; G. BEER, *Steinverehrung bei den Israeliten* (Berlin 1921); D. COHEN, *Dictionnaire des racines sémitiques*, Fasc. 1 (Paris 1970) 4; J. VAN DIJK, *LUGAL UD ME-LÁM-bi NIR-GÁL*, 2 vols. (Leiden 1983); J. D. FOWLER, *Theophoric Personal Names in Ancient Hebrew* (JSOTSup 49; Sheffield 1988); V. HAAS, *Hethitische Berggötter und Hurritische Steindämonen* (Mainz 1982); A. S. KAPELRUD, *ʾbn*, *TWAT* 1 (1973) 50-53; M. C. A. KORPEL, *A Rift in the Clouds: Ugaritic and Hebrew Descriptions of the Divine* (UBL 8; Münster 1990) 578-587; R. KRISS & H. KRISS-HEINRICH, *Volksglauben im Bereich des Islam* (Wiesbaden 1960-1962); T. N. D. METTINGER, *No Graven Image?* (Stockholm 1995); S. OLOFSSON, *God is my Rock: A Study of Translation Technique and Theological Exegesis in the Septuagint* (Stockholm 1990); S. RIBICHINI, La pietra potente, *Poenus advena* (Rome1985) 113-125; G. A. WAINWRIGHT, The Aniconic Form of Amon in the New Kingdom, *ASAE* 28 (1980) 175-189; G. A. WAINWRIGHT, Some Aspects of Amun, *JEA* 20 (1934) 139-153; H. WEIPPERT, *Palästina in vorhellenistischer Zeit* (München 1988); P. XELLA, L'elemento ʾBN nell' onomastico fenico-punica, *UF* 20 (1988) 387-392.

M. C. A. KORPEL

STRONG DRINK שכר

I. *šēkār* occurs 23 times in the Bible, nearly always in conjunction with *yayin* 'wine', the two forming a kind of hendiadys which means 'an intoxicating wine' (similarly combined in Ugaritic, see *RSP* 1:209, no. 248). Only in two cases does *šēkār* occur alone: Num 28:7; Ps 69:13. The noun *šēkār* is derived from *šākar* 'to intoxicate, become intoxicated' (see, e.g., 1 Sam 1:13-14; Jer 25:27; 48:26; Prov 31:4-7).

šēkār denotes a strong and intoxicating

drink (thus also the LXX and Philo; and the *Tgs.* to Num 6:3; 28:7: "old wine"; to Lev 10:9: *mĕrawê* 'intoxicating drink'; others: 'mixed wine', 'beer') made probably of the fruits of the vine (→Gepen). Figs and pomegranates, however, were also used for manufacturing wine. Based on Akk *šik(ā)ru* 'beer' (brewed from barley; but also from dates), scholars (e.g. KELLERMANN 1977:48) have suggested that biblical *šēkār* be identified as beer too. There is, however, no clear evidence—archaeological (STERN 1976:678-679) or otherwise—that OT *šēkār* was brewed from barley (but see Kellermann's remarks).

ŠKR with the same basic meaning is a common Semitic root (BDB 1016a; *HALAT* 1390a). Note especially Akk *šik(ā)ru* 'beer' (*AHW* 1232f.), *šakāru* 'to become inebriated, drunk' (*CAD* Š/1 157b), *šākiru* 'habitual drinker', *šakartu* 'drunkenness', *šakkarû/ šakkurû* 'drunkard', etc. (*CAD s.v.*). An agricultural word, *šēkār* occurs in other languages as well, such as Greek σίκερα, Latin *sicera*, Italian *c/sidro*, Rumanian *thighir*, and even English *cider* (K. LOKOTSCH, *Etymologisches Wörterbuch der europäischen (germanischen, romanischen und slavischen) Wörter orientalischen Ursprungs* [Heidelberg 1927] no. 1787a).

As an alcoholic beverage, beer possessed semi-divine status in ancient Near Eastern conceptions (→Tirash). Strong Drink was purportedly used to elicit a divine oracle (compare DURAND 1982:43-50). In their banquets, gods were thought to enjoy large amounts of wine and beer.

There is no etymological connection between Heb *šēkar* and the Mesopotamian deity ^{d}*Šukurru*, the deified spear (see *CAD* 5/3, 234). Nor is there any evidence whatsoever suggesting that *šēkār* was ever considered as possessing divine status in the Hebrew Bible.

II. *šik(ā)ru* 'beer' in ancient Mesopotamia was a very widespread drink, known in all periods of history, and indulged in by all. Beer was given to gods, imbibed and poured in religious and magic rituals, used in medicine, and enjoyed on every possible occasion. Beer and bread were considered essential daily staples and were called "the life of the people/land" (*CAD* N/1 302f. 8). In the Gilgamesh Epic, these are called *simat balāṭim* 'that which fits life', and in another place beer is defined as *šīmti māti* 'the rule, custom of the land' (Gilg. P iii 14), something that every civilized human being is supposed to know and enjoy (addressed by the prostitute to the still-uncivilized brute, Enkidu).

III. In the Bible, *šēkār* occurs in various contexts, endowing it with both positive and negative connotations.

Positively, it was not only valued as one of the main ingredients for making a feast happy and lively (e.g. Deut 14:26; Isa 24:7-11; cf. Gen 43:34; Judg 9:13), but it was also one of the ingredients of the daily offering to God (Num 28:7; in Isa 65:11 strong drink [here *mimsāk*] is offered to foreign gods [→Gad and →Meni]). According to some texts, *šēkār* was one of the necessities of life, on the same level as bread, so that lacking it was something out of the ordinary (e.g., Isa 24:7-13 and especially Deut 29:4-5)

Taken in excess, however, *šēkār* could produce quite negative effects. The sage in Proverbs warns that the border-line between enjoying *šēkār* and succumbing to its bad effects is very thin (Prov 23:29-35, following 27-28; cf. Hab 2:5: wine is treacherous!). Such bad effects included inebriation, unconsciousness (note that awakening means becoming sober: Gen 9:24; cf. Ps 78:65), amnesia, the loss of ability to control oneself and (in the case of leaders) to govern properly (e.g. Isa 28:7; 29:9; Jer 51:57; Prov 31:4-9). Prov 20:1 sees a measure of stupidity in inebriation, and elsewhere a shameful scene of losing control of one's bodily functions (Isa 19:14; 28:7-8; Jer 25:27; 48:26; cf. *KTU* 1.114 describing drunken El—or someone else—wallowing in his own urine and filth) and placing oneself in embarassing situations is depicted (e.g., Gen 9:21; Lam 4:21; Hab 2:15-16).

An especially negative attitude toward alcohol is detected in Eli's strong rebuke of

Hannah whom he considered drunk (1 Sam 1:13-14; according to the LXX Eli's servant even asks Hannah to leave the sanctuary). Eli's rebuke may be understood against the background of the moral decline in the shrine of Shiloh, especially his sons' misdeeds and licentious behaviour with female worshipers (2:11-17.22-25). Hannah says in her defence that she drank neither *yayin* nor *šēkār* and asks that Eli not judge her to be a *bat bĕliyyaʿal* (→Belial).

Being a drunkard was thus tantamount to being a social misfit, comparable with other misfits such as idlers, belials, blasphemers, *rēqîm*, etc. As in the religious context where a dichotomy is evident between the inside sphere of cleanliness and the outside sphere of uncleanliness, so here a dichotomy is also evident between the inner and outer spheres of society respectively with social misfits and outcasts relegated to the latter. Being an habitual drinker of *šēkār* might cause one to be rejected from society and considered an outcast.

IV. *Bibliography*

J. M. DURAND, In Vino Veritas, *RA* 76 (1982) 43-50; L. F. HARTMAN & A. L. OPPENHEIM, *On Beer and Brewing Techniques in Ancient Mesopotamia* (JAOS Suppl. 10; Baltimore 1950); E. HUBER, Bier und Bierbereitung in Babylonien, *RLA* 2 (1938) 25-28; D. KELLERMANN, Bier, *BRL*² 48-49; E. STERN, *šēkār, Encyclopaedia Biblica* Vol. 7 (Jerusalem 1976) 677-680 (Heb).

M. MALUL

SUKKOTH-BENOTH סכות־בנות

I. Sukkoth-Benoth is a god said to have been worshipped by the Babylonians who were resettled in Samaria by an Assyrian king (2 Kgs 17:30). These new "Samarians" may have been transferred to the territory of the former Israelite state either by Sennacherib (*ARAB* 2.234, 339-341) or Ashurbanipal (*ARAB* 2.791-798), both of whom fought in southern Mesopotamia; cf. too, Ezra 4:9-10 (see BECKING 1992:95-97). Neither the double-name of the god nor its individual components is known from cuneiform sources.

II. Traditionally Benoth has been associated with the goddess Zarpanitu, the consort of Babylon's chief deity →Marduk; the consonants of the second element in the MT were assumed to be a corruption of that deity's name (STADE 1904:267; GRAY 1970: 653-654). As for the element Sukkoth, it has often been related to the word →Sakkuth which appears in a description of the transport of images (Amos 5:26); it is supposed, that the Hebrew transcribes the cuneiform ideogram ᵈSA.KUD, a Mesopotamian god with a similar-sounding name (e. g. DRIVER 1958:16*; WOLFF 1977:260-266). But the correct reading of the god's name is Madānu (cf. W. W. HALLO, *HUCA* 48 [1977] 15), and the meaning of Sakkuth within the context of the Amos passage is much disputed. Others prefer a connection of Sukkoth with Marduk, correcting MT and reconstructing the Babylonian divine pair, Marduk and Zarpanitu (STADE 1904:267; MONTGOMERY & GEHMAN 1951:474).

Assuming the integrity of the consonantal text, however, the MT may be interpreted as containing both a proper name and a common noun. The divine name Bānītu, "the creatress", (cf. *CAD* B 95a) is attested in both the Neo-Assyrian (TALLQVIST 1914:253a) and the Neo-Babylonian (TALLQVIST 1905: 232a/b) onomastica. The →Assur Temple in Nineveh housed a shrine to the goddess Bānītu (*STT* 88, III 6; cf. FRANKENA 1961: 207). As an epithet, Bānītu is applied to →Ishtar of Nineveh (*AkkGE* 70-71), and the name of the goddess Zarpanitu was popularly etymologized as *Zēr-bānītu*, "the creatress of seed/offspring" (*AHW* 1520a). Furthermore, a Neo-Assyrian literary text with ritual allusions seems to associate Bānītu with the god Ninurta (cf. DELLER 1983:142). Worship of Bānītu seems to have spread West and from there to Egypt; among the Aramaeans residing in Egypt during the Persian period, the goddess was worshipped at a temple in her honour in Syene (BRESCIANI & KAMIL 1966:No. 2:1,12; 3:1; cf. 1:7) and in several personal names her name appears as theophoric element, e.g. *Mkbnt*, *Bntsr* (BRESCIANI & KAMIL 1966:357-428; No.

4:8; 6:8). So far this goddess is unknown from texts before the first-millenium BCE, though earlier *bānītu* appears as an epithet of several goddesses; cf. e.g., the personal name *Amat-*[d]*Bānītu* on cylinder seal of the mid-2nd millenium BC from Jordan (R. TOURNAY, Un cylindre babylonien decouvert en Transjordanie, *RB* 74 (1967) 248-254, esp. 248). Perhaps, then, what was originally a popular epithet for the mother goddess was hypostasized (DELLER 1983: 142).

III. Banitu, therefore, is likely to be the divine name in 2 Kgs 17:30; note that major LXX traditions preserve a pronunciation of the name as *baineithei* (B), *benithei* (A). As to Sukkoth, unrelated as it is to any known divine name, it may be a common noun; perhaps meaning "aspect, image", from *skn/sknt*, attested in Ugaritic (LIPIŃSKI 1973: 202-204; M. KORPEL, *A Riff in the Clouds* [UBL 8; Münster 1990] 576). The proposed identification of Sukkoth-Benoth is, then, "the image of Banit(u)".

IV. *Bibliography*

B. BECKING, *The Fall of Samaria: an Historical and Archaeological Study* (Leiden 1992); E. BRESCIANI & M. KAMIL, *Le lettere aramaiche di Hermopoli* (Roma 1966); K. DELLER, STT 366: Deutungsversuch 1982, *Assur* 3/4 (1983) 139-148; G. R. DRIVER, Geographical Problems, *Archaeological, Historical and Geographical Studies dedicated to Professor Benjamin Mazar on his Fiftieth Birthday* (ErIsr 5; 1958) 16*-20*; R. FRANKENA, New Materials for the Takultu Ritual: Additions and Corrections, *BiOr* 18 (1961) 199-201; J. GRAY, *I & II Kings* (2nd ed.; Philadelphia 1970); E. LIPIŃSKI, SKN et SGN dans le sémitique occidental du nord, *UF* 5 (1973) 202-204; J. T. MILIK, Les papyrus araméens d'Hermoupolis et les cultes syro-phéniciens, *Bib* 48 (1967), 546-584; J. A. MONTGOMERY & H. S. GEHMAN, *The Books of Kings* (ICC; Edinburgh 1951); B. STADE, *The Books of Kings* (The Sacred Books of the Old Testament 9; Leipzig 1904); K. L. TALLQVIST, *Neubabylonisches Namenbuch zu den Geschäftsurkunden aus der Zeit des Samassumukin bis Xerxes* (Helsingfors 1905); TALLQVIST, *Assyrian Personal Names* (Helsingsfors 1914); H. W. WOLFF, *Joel and Amos* (Hermeneia; Philadelphia 1977).

M. COGAN

SUN → HELIOS; SHEMESH

SYCOMORE שקמה

I. According to ALBRIGHT (1968:165) the sycomore fig, Ficus sycomorus, was deified in Palestine, as in Egypt. There is no biblical evidence for such deification in Palestine.

II. The Egyptian name for sycomore is *Nht* (*LÄ* VI, 113-114). The goddess →Hathor in Memphis was worshipped as mistress of the sycomore tree. In private tombs from the 18th and 19th dynasty the sycomore is represented by the goddess Nut.

III. שִׁקְמָה, the sycomore, is a common tree in Palestine. The שקמה is a kind of fig tree. Its fruits resemble figs, but are not as palatable. According to 1 Kgs 10:27; 2 Chr 1:15; 9:27 Solomon made cedar as plentiful in Jerusalem as the sycomore of the Shephelah, and in his selfdescription Amos calls himself 'a dresser of sycomore trees' (Am 7:14). The sycomore tree is first of all appreciated as timber tree (ZOHARY 1982: 68). 1 Chr 27:28 tells us that one of David's men was over the olive and sycomore trees in the Shephelah. Compared with the cedar tree used for Solomon's palace and temple, the sycomore was less valuable, as is seen from the boast in Isa 9:9 "the sycomores have been cut down, but we will put cedars in their place" (NIELSEN 1989:75). Note finally that →Yahweh's signs in Egypt (Ps 78:47) include destruction of the vines and the sycomores with hail and frost, but nothing in the text suggests these trees should be regarded as holy trees or deities.

Unlike the →oak and the →terebinth, the sycomore is mentioned neither in connection with holy places nor in connection with any cultic activities in the OT. Albright's assertion can therefore only be based on Egyptian evidence.

IV. *Bibliography*

W. F. ALBRIGHT, *Yahweh and the Gods of Canaan. A Historical Analysis of Two Contrasting Faiths* (London 1968); G. DALMAN, *Arbeit und Sitte in Palästina I,* 1-2 (Gütersloh 1928); K. NIELSEN, *There is Hope for a Tree. The Tree as Metaphor in Isaiah* (Sheffield 1989); P. WELTEN, Baum, sakraler, *BRL*[2], 34-35; M. ZOHARY, *Pflanzen der Bibel. Vollständiges Handbuch* (Stuttgart 1982).

K. NIELSEN

T

TABOO חרם

I. *ḥērem* occurs 29 times in the OT (LOHFINK 1982:193-195, for distribution) and has been variously translated 'ban', 'excommunication', 'taboo', 'a consecrated or contaminated object/person'. It appears in Jewish Aramaic as *ḥirmāʾ,* in Syriac as *ḥermāʾ*, and in Arabic as *ḥaram*, meaning 'a consecrated and prohibited area'. (Note also Arab. *ḥarīm* 'wife', 'harem', Nabataean *mḥrmh* 'sanctuary', Sabaean *mḥrm* 'sanctuary, temple'.) Grammatically, BREKELMANS (1959:43-47) understood *ḥērem* to be a noun expressing a quality, like *qōdeš* and *ḥôl*. Others see it as a concrete noun or one expressing an action. However, idioms like *hāyâ/śîm/nātan leḥērem*, as well as the *Hiphîl* form *heḥĕrîm* 'to declare a person/object as *ḥērem*' (cf. *hiqdîš* 'to declare holy'; *hiṣdîq* 'to declare just', etc. *Ges.*[18] 53c), would tend to support Brekelmans' view: an object/person becomes a *ḥērem* by assuming the quality of the state of *ḥērem*.

ḥērem is derived from the root ḤRM (51 occurrences in the OT, LOHFINK 1982:193), a common Semitic root with the meaning 'separate', 'forbid', 'consecrate', and the like (LOHFINK 1982:201-202; note Akk *ḫarāmu* 'to separate', from which *ḫarimtu* 'prostitute', a woman set apart). Other suggested derivatives include the personal name Harim (e.g. Ezra 2:32, 39; Neh 3:11; 1 Chr 24:8); Mount →Hermon ('sacred/banned mountain'?); and the place name Hormah (Josh 12:14; Num 14:45; 21:3; etc.), which is based on a folk etymology.

Ḥerem occurs as a deity outside the Bible in theophoric names known from the Jewish colony at Elephantine (e.g. *Ḥrmntn*, see NOTH, *IPN* 129; BREKELMANS 1959:26). Contrary to accepted scholarly opinion, however, a god Herem-Bethel was never worshipped by the Elephantine Jews. In the relevant construction, *ḥrm* is not part of a compound divine name, but a designation of an inviolable piece of property such as temple treasure, on which occasionally an oath was sworn (cf. Matt 23:16-22; VAN DER TOORN 1986).

II. A usage of ḤRM similar to that in the OT occurs in the Mesha inscription where King Mesha reports having conquered Nebo and consecrated (*hḥrmth*) its inhabitants to the god Athtar-Cemosh (→Ashtoreth, →Chemosh) (*KAI* I 33:14-18; II 176-177; MATTINGLY 1989:233-237), which signifies total annihilation. Similar customs are attested in ancient Rome. The Celts, for example, would slay the defeated, pile up their goods and dedicate them to the deity. Any person daring to lay his hand on the spoil was put to death (Diodorus 5:32; Caesar, *De bello Gallico* 6:17; for other data see LOHFINK 1982:202-206, particularly his reference to the interesting institution of *devotio* at Rome, whereby executed criminals were consecrated to the gods of the underworld).

A Mesopotamian concept reflecting the basic characteristic of a taboo-object, something totally consecrated to the deity or priest and for the usufruct of no other, is that of *asakkum* (*CAD* A/2 326-327; Sum **kug-an**, interpreted by Landsberger to mean 'consecrated to the god'; see in general MALAMAT 1966). Violating the *asakkum* was expressed in Akkadian by means of the idiom *asakkam akālum* 'to eat the *asakkum*' (*CAD* A/2 327a b1'; note also the idioms *asakkam leqûm*, *šarāqum* 'to take/steal the *asakkum*', *ibid.* 2'). This idiom occurs, for example, in legal documents among the *Schlußklauseln*, the clauses which define the sanction awaiting the violator of the agreement signed in the contract. The party violating the agreement is considered to have "eaten the *asakkum* of the gods and/or the king". Similarly it is said in other contexts that a person who refuses to abide by the royal command or otherwise tries to evade it has thereby "eaten the *asakkum*" of the king: the crime is as serious as violating a sacred taboo (MALAMAT 1966). The sacred character of the *asakkum* is also reflected in the oath by the *asakkum* of a certain god or king, exactly as one would take an oath by the life of the god/king.

Asakkum occurs also in Mari texts from the 18th century BCE (MALAMAT 1966). In order to prevent pillaging, the booty was declared the *asakkum* of the god or king. Looters were considered to have eaten the *asakkum* and punished accordingly. According to the OT, the objects designated taboo were consecrated either to God or to the priests. At Mari, the *asakkum* could be consecrated not only to a god or a king, but also to high-ranking officials, and sometimes even to soldiers from the ranks. Anyone confiscating any consecrated objects is said to have eaten the *asakkum*.

III. In the OT, the concept of *ḥērem* has three applications: *ḥērem* of an entire community, *ḥērem* of an individual, and excommunication, ostracizing—all of them derived from the basic idea of separation and transfer to an outside sphere. The third usage (also called *niddûy* in the Talmud [H. H. COHN, *EncJud* Vol 8 (1971) 350-352], from the verb *niddâ*, attested also in the OT in the meaning 'to remove, expel' [Isa 66:5; Amos 6:3]) is believed to be a late development from the Second Temple period (Ezra 10:8) and is fully attested in rabbinical literature and later sources. In this usage the word seems to have lost the nuance of consecration. In earlier usages *ḥērem* denotes opposed values: it may pertain to the holy (Lev 27:28-29) or to the unholy, to impurity (Deut 7:26; Isa 43:28). Either might prohibit use or contact (cf. the familiar rabbinic statement "All Scripture defiles the hands" [*mYad.* 3e; *bShabb.* 14a], an ambivalent definition using a verb from the sphere of impurity [*ṭammēʾ*] with reference to the sanctity of Scripture)

The consecration of an inimical community to the deity signifies the extermination of the enemy, either following a vow made by the people (Num 21:1-3), or as a commandment imposed upon the people, esp. as regards the extermination of the seven peoples of Canaan, the Midianites and Amalekites (Deut 7:2; 20:16; 1 Sam 15:3-4; cf. also Num 31). Originally this seems to have meant the devotion of the enemy and his possessions to a deity (Josh 6-7), but, in the OT reconceptualization, 'devotion' becomes mere destruction of the enemy, while the possessions—esp. metal (gold and silver) utensils—were taken as booty (Deut 2:34-35; 3:6-7; Josh 8:2.26-27; 10:28-11:14). Sometimes virgins were spared and taken by the victors (Num 31:17-18).

Declaring booty as an *asakkum* in Mari was clearly an *ad hoc* measure taken by the high officials to prevent uncontrolled pillage, and it has been suggested that this is similar to the *ḥērem* in the OT in those contexts where it looks like an *ad hoc* commandment imposed for similar reasons (MALAMAT 1966:45-46; GREENBERG 1971: 347-348). Thus Joshua announces the *ḥērem* before the conquest of Jericho (Josh 6:16-18, as also in the case of the Ai, 8:2, 26-27), and Samuel issues a command regarding the *ḥērem* to be imposed on the Amalekites (1 Sam 15:3). In both cases, it was intended to prevent the people from laying hand on the booty. There is a difference, however, between the biblical *ḥērem* in the context of war and the Mari usages of *asakkum*. Whereas in the OT the *ḥērem* applies to the enemy himself, at Mari the practice applies only to the booty. One may accept LOHFINK's view (1982:205-206) that the concept of *ḥērem* in the OT is broader than that of the *asakkum* at Mari. Moabite usage and, further afield, that of the Celts, is closer.

Lev 27:28-29 introduces the *ḥērem* of the individual, which is similar in conception to that of the *ḥērem* of an entire community. A 'banned' person is devoted to the deity and put to death. His possessions are consecrated to God or given to the priest exactly as metal utensils were dedicated to God under the community *ḥērem* (Josh 6:19). Unlike objects designated by vow (Lev 27:1-27), nothing put under *ḥērem* may be sold, redeemed, or otherwise ransomed; it is "most holy unto God" (Lev 27:28, evidently the intention of Num 18:14 is the same).

The verb *ḥāram* and its cognate noun *ḥērem* occur in the OT as synonyms of the verb *qādaš* (usually in the *Hiphîl,* meaning 'to sanctify, consecrate'), as well as with verbs denoting destruction, annihilation and the like (*'bd, šmd, krt,* etc. LOHFINK 1982: 196-197). The two notions—consecration and destruction—coalesce in certain contexts such as Josh 6-7; Mic 4:13; cf. Num 21:2-3; Judg 21:5. (For the 'ambivalent' nature of the taboo in general, see M. DOUGLAS, *Purity and Danger. An Analysis of the Concepts of Pollution and Taboo* [New York/London 1966].) The very fact that the root ḤRM reflects two such apparently opposite notions leads one to the conclusion that it denotes something beyond mere destruction on the one hand, and consecration on the other. As regards destruction, the action and intention (removal of the destroyed object/person from the public sphere and the resultant prevention of contact with it and/or enjoyment of it) are adequately signalled by any verb of destruction. The root ḤRM, therefore, must introduce an additional nuance not covered by the other verbs. As regards consecration, one need only refer to Lev 27 where a clear gradation seems to be attested between mere consecration (vv 9-10.14-27) and placing under the *ḥērem* (vv 28-29). The latter is designated as *qodeš qodāšîm* 'exceedingly holy', which is to be understood as an attempt to address the particular nuance attaching to the root ḤRM.

On the basis of the available evidence, one may define ḤRM as denoting the idea of expulsion from the sphere of concern for human society. An object placed under *ḥērem* is destroyed in order to remove it from the social and legal classificatory sphere, that is, from the practical concern of a given community. A similar fate is shared by the spirit (→Etemmu) of a person deprived of due burial and cast as carrion to beasts of prey. Such a spirit is driven to the outside waste and lawless sphere where no rule of civilization applies. Physical death itself does not result in such a fate for the spirit. That fate is determined by the kind of death suffered and the deliberate prevention of appropriate burial rites. Similarly, ḤRM may be understood as denoting something more than physical destruction. It probably alluded to the manner of destruction and to the treatment of the physical remains of the enemy or criminal, as in the case of Achan (LOHFINK 1982:198-200; STERN 1989:419) By the same token, an object placed under *ḥērem* in the sense of being consecrated to a deity is also removed from the human sphere to the divine.

A human, therefore, may not enjoy the use of an object designated as *ḥērem*, for this would transgress the limits between his domain, with its protective socio-legal organization, and the outside non-classificatory domain and cause disequilibrium to encroach upon the former. Should such misuse occur, the perpetrator himself becomes contaminated by the object of the *ḥērem* and must be subjected to the same treatment as that object in order to ward off the consequent dangers to his community, as indeed in the case of Achan noted above (Josh 6-7). The notion of *ḥērem,* 'taboo', as outlined above, belongs to an extensive array of concepts pertaining to the general area of the impure, abhorrent, defiled, rejected and suchlike. Here, one may mention Heb. *tô'ēbâ* (related to *ḥērem* in Deut 7:26; 13:15-16; 20:17-18), *piggûl*, *tebel* and *nĕbālâ* (see →Abominations), and in Akkadian, besides *asakkum*, also *ikkibu* (commonly translated 'taboo', HALLO 1985; VAN DER TOORN 1985; KLEIN & SEFATI 1988; note, however, M. J. GELLER, Taboo in Mesopotamia, *JCS* 42 [1990] 218-220), *anzillum* (Sum **usug**), all of which may be objects of the verb *akālu* 'to eat' (see above); cf. OT "to eat the *qodeš*" (Lev 22:10.14.16). The semantic field of *ḥērem,* therefore, includes the above locutions, all denoting the general idea of something to be separated and removed from the life of the community.

ḥērem, however, seems to be neutral in terms of value, for it could signify (depending on context) both positive (consecration) and negative removal (destruction and defilement).

IV. *Bibliography*

C. H. W. BREKELMANS, *De ḥerem in het Oude Testament* (Nijmegen 1959); M. GREENBERG, Ḥerem, *EncJud* 8 (1971) 344-350; W. W. HALLO, Biblical Abominations and Sumerian Taboos, *JQR* 76 (1985) 21-40; J. KLEIN & Y. SEFATI, The Concept of 'Abomination' in Mesopotamian Literature and the Bible, *Beer-Sheva* 3 (1988), 131-148 (Hebrew); *N. LOHFINK, חָרַם *ḥāram;* חֵרֶם *ḥērem*, *TWAT* 3 (1982) 192-213 [& lit]; A. MALAMAT, The Ban in Mari and in the Bible, *Biblical Essays 1966* (De Ou Testamentiese Werkgemeenskap in Suid-Afrika; Bloemfontein 1966) 40-49; G. L. MATTINGLY, Moabite Religion, *Studies in the Mesha Inscription and Moab* (ed. A. Dearman; Atlanta 1989) 211-238; P. D. STERN, 1 Samuel 15. Towards an Ancient View of the War-Ḥerem, *UF* 21 (1989) 414-420; K. VAN DER TOORN, *Sin and Sanction in Israel and Mesopotamia* (Assen 1985) 41-44; VAN DER TOORN, Herem-Bethel and Elephantine Oath Procedure, *ZAW* 98 (1986) 282-285.

M. MALUL

TABOR תבור Θαβώρ, Ταβώρ, τὸ Ἰταβύριον

I. Tabor is the name of a mountain in Lower Galilee (1,700 ft above sea-level, 7km SE of Nazareth). It occurs three times in Josh 19, in the descriptions of the boundaries of respectively the tribes of Zebulon, Issachar and Naphthali, and is thus a point where the three tribal territories met (*vv.* 12; 22; 34). Moses' blessing of Zebulon and Issachar, which may date back to the heyday of Jeroboam II's reign, mentions "(the) mountain" to which they call the peoples to participate in rightful sacrifices (Deut 33: 18-19). In all likelihood, therefore, this is a reference to the mountain which they had in common and to a →Yahweh-cult. The prophet Hoseah, whose activity started in the last years of Jeroboam II, seems likewise to refer to a cult on the Tabor; but he does so in a rather negative way. He speaks of a "net" that had been spread there (5:1-3), which probably implies that, by his time, the cult had turned into idolatry, or had a non-Yahwistic competitor.

The meaning of the name Tabor is unknown. Jerome translates it in his onomastic writings by "*veniens lumen* " (*PL* 23,808) or "*veniat lux* " (*ibid.* 828), clearly assuming it, by popular etymology, to be the Hebrew phrase תבוא אור. As there was also an "Oak of Tabor" farther to the South, in the tribal area of Benjamin (1 Sam 10:3), a derivation from בור 'to lie waste' can be considered because it would fit a mountain as well as a place where a notable tree had been left to stand. If, however, the name was an abbreviation of an original Itabor as in the Greek Ἰταβύριον (Hos 5:1) and perhaps also in Γαιθβωρ (as in Jos 19:22 B, with γα- = גאה 'to rise up'?), this could indicate that the longer name was not understood: it may even have been non-Semitic.

II. Apart from these two rather vague OT allusions, nothing more is known about the role which the mountain may have played in religion. It has been supposed by COLPE (1975), however, that the cult there involved a Baʿal later known by the name of Ζεὺς Ἰταβύριος. This deity was venerated on Mt. Atabyrion (-ron; -ris) in Rhodes, and also on a homonymous mountain at Akragas in Sicily, which was a Rhodian colony. Polybius, who mentions both cults (9, 27), is also the only writer—apart from the much later compiler Stephanus of Byzantium—to refer to the Tabor in Galilee as τὸ Ἀταβύριον (5, 70) (with initial Ἀ- instead of Ἰ-). He probably did so on the analogy of the name of the Rhodian and Sicilian mountains; but this does not, of course, justify the conclusion that their specific Zeus was also worshipped on the Tabor. As nothing is known of or found in the mountain, LEWY's assumption that it was named after *ta-bu-ra*, 'metal worker', an epithet of Tammuz, is speculative (LEWY 1950-51).

III. In early Christianity, Mt. Tabor was

considered to have been the location of Christ's transfiguration, contrary to the Gospel of Mark, which places it in the neighbourhood of Caesarea Philippi (8:27-9:2). This tradition can be traced back to Cyril of Jerusalem (348 - *c.* 386 CE), who speaks of it in passing: "They (Moses and Elijah) were with Him when He was transfigurated on Mt. Thabor and told the disciples about the end which He was to fulfil in Jerusalem" (*Catech.* 12, 16). His contemporary Jerome (348 - 420 CE) likewise mentions it only casually when describing to Eustochium the journeys made in the Near East by her mother Paula: "She climbed Mt. Thabor on which the Lord was transfigurated" (*Epistle* 108, 13). Both authors create the impression that they are merely passing on what was a current opinion in their days. It may well date back to a much earlier time. It is difficult to decide whether the *Gospel according to the Hebrews* also refers to the transfiguration when it says: "Now my mother, the Holy Spirit, took me (Jesus) by one of my hairs and carried me to the great mountain Thabor" (*frg.* 3 HENNECKE). The translation to a high mountain reminds one of the story of Jesus' temptation (Matt 4:8; Luke 4:5). The detail of the hair seems to stem from Ezek 8:3 or from the story of Bel and the Dragon 33-39, where Ezekiel and Habakuk are said to have been translated in a similar way.

IV *Bibliography*

C. COLPE, Tabor, *KP* 5 (1975) 479-480; O. EISSFELDT, Der Gott des Tabor und seine Verbreitung, *ARW* 31 (1934) 14-41 = *KS* 2 (Tübingen 1963) 29-54; R. FRANKEL, Tabor, *ABD* 6 (1992) 304-305; J. LEWY, Tabor Tibar Atabyros, *HUCA* 23 (1950-51) 357-386.

G. MUSSIES

TAL → DEW

TAMMUZ תמוז

I. *Tammûz* is a deity of Mesopotamian origin whose cult, according to a vision reported in Ezek 8:14, was introduced into the temple in Jerusalem, where women are said to wail over the death of the god at the north gate of the temple.

Hebr *Tammûz* derives from Sum **ᵈDumuzi**. The Sumerian name means "the good son", or "the right son". In Akkadian the name is mostly written with the Sumerian ideogram and pronounced *Dumuzu*, or *Duwuzu*, Neo-Assyrian *Du'uzu* or *Dûzu*. The month named after him was rendered as *Du'uzu* (MSL 5, 25:225). The late Akkadian form is reflected in the Greek Daônos, to be amended to Daôzos, in Berossos (JACOBSEN 1939:73 n. 22).

II. In Sumerian mythology Dumuzi appears first of all as the shepherd and as a manifestation of all aspects of the life of the herdsmen, as opposed to that of the farmers. Contrary to what is often asserted, Dumuzi was no vegetation deity. It is only insofar as he borrowed certain features from amalgamation with Damu, originally an independent deity and a true vegetation deity, that Dumuzi can be said to have relations to the vegetation deities.

Although the god did not belong to the leading deities in any period of Mesopotamian history, Dumuzi has played a major role in discussions of ancient Near Eastern religion. This was a result of the ideas propounded by J. G. FRAZER in *Adonis, Attis, Osiris* (1905). According to him Tammûz was the prototype of the Dying God, whose annual death and resurrection from the dead personified the yearly decay and revival of life. He saw the god as fundamentally identical with the deities known as →Osiris in Egypt, as Adon or →Adonis among the Phoenicians and the Greeks, and as Attis in Phrygia, and their cult as a widespread phenomenon especially aimed at enacting the yearly cycle of vegetable life. He considered Adon or Adonis a mere title for the god whose real name was Tammuz. This identification was first suggested by Origen and is implied already in the Vg of Ezek 8:14.

LANGDON (1914) developed the idea that Tammuz was the son of Mother Earth, and that his cult was a popular mystery religion not related to the official cult of other deities. According to him, not only a large number of minor deities, but also →Marduk, Babylon's god himself, were aspects of the young dying god. The idea that Marduk was a dying and reviving deity later turned out to be based on a misunderstanding of an Assyrian text (VON SODEN, *ZA* 51 [1955]: 130-166). MOORTGAT, in a much criticized study (*Tammuz: der Unsterblichkeitsglaube in der altorientalischen Bildkunst* [Berlin 1949]), found the mystery cult, involving a belief in the immortality of the soul, reflected in a large number of objects of art. WITZEL (1935) considered Tammuz to be the very divine male principle in vegetation, while →Ishtar was the corresponding female counterpart, and according to him Tammuz was no less than the main god of the Babylonian pantheon.

In the studies mentioned above a number of deities who shared certain characteristics were uncritically thought to be 'aspects' or 'Erscheinungsformen' of the same deity. Already in 1909 ZIMMERN (*Der babylonische Gott Tamūz*) had warned against this lack of methodological stringency.

JACOBSEN's highly influential studies of Dumuzi are based on the fundamental assumption that the gods are "powers" in natural phenomena (esp. 1961). He distinguishes between four forms of Dumuzi and four corresponding manifestations in the external world. These are: (1) Ama-ushumgal-anna; (2) Dumuzi of the Grain; (3) Dumuzi the shepherd; and (4) Damu. He interprets these as (1) the power in storable dates; (2) the power in the Grain; (3), the power in milk; and (4) the sap that rises in trees and plants. JACOBSEN's concept of a separate aspect of Dumuzi as particularly related to Grain was inspired by agricultural myths of other cultures (in particular the rites of Ta'ūz at Harran in the tenth century CE), in which the grinding of the grain symbolizes the slaughter of the god of the Grain. The Mesopotamian evidence does not corroborate the assumption of the existence of a special aspect of Dumuzi connected with grain. Neither is there any need to see a special connection between Dumuzi or Ama-ushumgal-anna and products of the date-palm (see below). Dumuzi's true nature was always that of the shepherd, best illustrated in the contest between Dumuzi and Enkimdu, in which Dumuzi competes with his animal products against Enkimdu, the farmer, who brings his farm products, in the competition to win the goddess Inanna's favours as husband.

A totally different approach was introduced 1954 by FALKENSTEIN, who asserted that in origin Dumuzi was no god, but a human being who became deified. This idea accords with the Sumerian King List iii 14-20 (early second millennium BCE), which lists two rulers named Dumuzi. First, "Dumuzi, the shepherd", is said to have been king of the antediluvian dynasty of Badtibira, and, second, Dumuzi of Kuara, is listed as king of Uruk and successor to the well known legendary rulers Enmerkar and Lugalbanda, and predecessor of Gilgamesh. The latter is said to be a **šu-peš**, a term usually translated as "fisherman" (lit. "triple hand" or "thriving hand"), but the connotation of the term in this place is enigmatic—Dumuzi is not normally associated with fishing or hunting. Dumuzi is here placed in a sequence of rulers, among whom Lugalbanda and Gilgamesh were deified. This coincides with information provided by a historical inscription, according to which the divine Dumuzi/Ama-ushumgal-anna as well as Gilgamesh were divine protectors of Utuhegal of Uruk who defeated the Gutians (ca. 2300 BCE). Dumuzi as husband of Inanna exemplifies the pattern of a mortal ruler who became the husband of a goddess, like Enmerkar and Inanna, Lugalbanda and Ninsun. The idea was reflected in the Sumerian myth 'Dumuzi's Dream', line 206, where Dumuzi asks the sun god for special protection with the appeal "I am not a man, I am the husband of a goddess". A. FALKENSTEIN assumed that the historical person Dumuzi lived only a short time prior to the Early Dynastic period. He considered Ama-ushumgal-anna to be a predecessor to Dumuzi and the name of an actual ruler of Badtibira (CRRA 3, 43-44).

With our present state of knowledge it must be admitted that there is no way of reaching back to any historical facts relating to the alleged existence of a ruler Dumuzi in the first half of the third millennium BCE, and that the accuracy of the King List cannot be trusted for this early period. Neither is there any evidence that Dumuzi and Ama-ushumgal-anna were ever two distinct deities. In later texts the two names interchange at random. Archaeological evidence for the alleged even earlier existence of Dumuzi, such as attempts to interpret the so-called Uruk vase (ca. 3000 BCE) as a representation of the sacred marriage rite, in which a high priest is depicted as Dumuzi encountering Inanna (→Ishtar), cannot with certainty be said to belong to this set of ideas.

The name Dumuzi is first attested as a theophoric element in anthroponyms dating from the Fara period (ca. 2500 BCE). It does not appear in the earliest literary texts dating from the same period, but early forms of the name Ama-ushumgal-anna do occur, as Ama-Ushumgal in god lists, and as Ama-ushum, with the variant Ama-ushum-an, "Ama-ushum of Heaven", in a hymn from Abū Ṣalābīkh (OIP 99:278; duplicated in Ebla, ARET 5:20.21). In this text the designation "Enlil's friend" is used of Ama-ushum (OIP 99:278 III:11). This title recurs in the mythology of the second millennium BCE, and, although the precise implication is unknown, it suggests that specific sets of associations later related to Dumuzi's marriage do in fact reach back to the third millennium BCE.

The name Ama-ushumgal-anna itself has been variously interpreted. JACOBSEN assumed that in this case **an(-na)** means "date", and saw the name as referring to the nature of the god as a deity of dates, but **anna** is here doubtless used in its normal sense, "of heaven", and there is no need to see a special connection between this name and dates. FALKENSTEIN understood the name as "Die Mutter ist ein (oder der) (Himmels)drache", and according to him this was an anthroponym of a type characteristic of the archaic texts from Ur (ca. 2700 BCE). In the opinion of the present writer the name means approximately "The Lord (is a) Great Dragon of Heaven". **ama** is thus used, not in its normal sense, "mother", but as a unique archaic spelling convention rendering **en**, "lord", whose original form was **a(n)me(n)**, cf. the spelling **en-me-ušumgal-an-na** in a Seleucid text published by VAN DIJK (UVB 18 [1962] 43-52). The name recurs in litanies dating from the Old Babylonian period in enumerations of early rulers identified with Dumuzi, whose death was bewailed. A hint at the true connotation of the name can perhaps be found in a hymn (Old Babylonian period) that describes how Dumuzi/Ama-ushumgal-anna rises like the sunlight over the mountains and is reborn every month like the moon on the sky (CT 36, 33-34; cf. also CT 58, 14:48-51). The realm of the dead was generally thought to be the underworld, but there is some evidence of an alternative stream of tradition, according to which an apotheosis in heaven took place. In the Akkadian myth of Adapa, Dumuzi and Ningišzida appear as gatekeepers of heaven, contrary to the prevailing picture according to which the dead encountered Dumuzi in the netherworld.

From the Fara period (middle of the third millennium BCE) through the Old Babylonian period (first half of the second millennium BCE) only two major temples for Dumuzi, one in Badtibira and one in Girsu, are attested. The temple in Badtibira was built in the pre-Sargonic period (ca. 2400 BCE) by Enmetena of Lagash for Lugal-Emush, a local name for Dumuzi, and for the goddess Inanna. The temple is also attested in the Old Babylonian period. The Girsu temple is well documented in the Ur III period (ca. 2100 BCE). There is also some evidence of the cult of Dumuzi in Fara, Adab, Nippur, and Ur. There may have been a major cult centre for Dumuzi in Uruk, but practically no documents pertaining to its cult have been found. A local form of Dumuzi in the Lagash area was called Lugal-Urukar. A deity called Dumuzi-Abzu in the nearby Kinunirsha apparently became confused with Dumuzi, but was in fact a goddess in origin, and not identical with Dumuzi. With the exception of a cella in Assur, no Dumuzi temple later than the Old Babylonian period is known (cf. KUTSCHER 1990).

In the Ur III period a festival named "the festival of Dumuzi" was celebrated in Umma and the nearby Ki-dingir, in the twelfth month of the local calendar, that is, in spring (March), whereas in Lagash the Dumuzi festival took place in the sixth month (late summer). A single reference to "Dumuzi going to the priest(ess)", as well as two lists of expenditures for Dumuzi's wedding gifts have been interpreted as evidence for the celebration of the sacred marriage rite in Umma (JACOBSEN 1975:78 n. 6). A significant feature of the cult was the journey of the (statue of the) god visiting neighbouring cities. The local Dumuzi of Uruk is known to have visited Ki-dinger and Apisal. In the Lagash area, Dumuzi and two other deities journeyed by boat for three days and nights to visit local fields and orchards.

The few details known about the early cult of Dumuzi thus suggest that Dumuzi was related to the goddess Inanna at a very early time, and that the cult was usually a joyous spring festival in which his marriage with Inanna was celebrated. It is possible that the other aspect of Dumuzi's cult, the wailing over his death, also goes back to the third millennium BCE, but there is no direct evidence for this. Official documents pertaining to wailing rites for Dumuzi are first attested in Mari (Old Babylonian period), where a large quantity of grain for female mourners (ARM 9 no. 175) as well as the cleansing of the statues of Ishtar and Dumuzi are attested. The rite took place in the fourth month. This accords with evidence of the first millennium BCE, according to which the wailing for Dumuzi took place in the fourth (or fifth) month, that is, in mid summer (cf. KUTSCHER 1990:40). It is therefore likely that the festival that took place in Ur III Lagash in the sixth month of the local calender (summer) was also one of mourning rites, but this cannot be verified. The so-called **Edin-na ú-sag-gá** ritual, hitherto thought to be a spring ritual of fertility, is known by now to have been performed at the time of the harvest, and was connected with Dumuzi's disappearance or "seizure", a term often used for his death (CT 58, 15 no. 21). This does not necessarily mean that Dumuzi was a vegetation god. His disappearance rather symbolized the time when the hot season made the dry land completely barren, and coincided with the seasonal termination of the milk production of the sheepfold.

The largest group of literary texts pertaining to Dumuzi are Sumerian compositions dating from the Isin-Larsa or Old Babylonian periods (ca. 1800-1600 BCE). These form four groups. (1) Mythological texts, mainly referring to Dumuzi's death; (2) Pastoral poetry and love songs, mainly referring to Dumuzi's marriage to Inanna; (3) *Er-shemma* compositions, i.e., brief songs mainly lamenting Dumuzi's disappearance and death, with allusions to myths. A few *er-shemma*'s are joyous or humorous pastoral compositions; (4) Other lamentations, in particular Old Babylonian forerunners to the very repetitive so-called *balag* compositions (liturgical lamentations), of which a number relate to Dumuzi. These are mainly known from the first millennium BCE, and include a large corpus from the Seleucid period.

A relatively large number of the Sumerian literary compositions relating to Dumuzi are unique or nearly so, i.e., no or few duplicates have been found. Many are documented outside the literary standard repertoire of the Sumerian schools of Nippur and Ur. A relatively large proportion of the texts is written in the so-called *emesal* dialect, mainly spoken by women, and there are relatively many examples of syllabically written texts, such as transmit the sound pattern of texts that apparently were sung by people who no longer understood them fully. The literature and the cult connected with Dumuzi obviously developed under less restraint by official standardization, and had more popular appeal than that pertaining to the cult centres of the major gods. That the female point of view is strong accords well with the information given by the Bible, according to which Dumuzi was bewailed by women.

The relative instability of the tradition reflects the local character of the cult, which in many or most cases was performed with no relation to a specific temple. Academic compilation and standardization of the Dumuzi literature started in the late Old Babylonian period. In the lengthy *balag* compositions various types of literary tradition were compiled to form an apparent unity. The first millennium version of the **Edin-na ú-sag-gá** ritual is such a literary compilation, and one cannot rely on it as a source for the reconstruction of the full sequence of events of the original ritual. It is in these texts that Dumuzi borrowed features pertaining to vegetation deities, such as Damu and Ningishzida. Only in this specific context was Dumuzi's death connected with the disappearing and reviving vegetation. The burials of a number of rulers of the Ur III and first Isin dynasties are enumerated in the text. These rulers were apparently thought to be reincarnations of Dumuzi.

In Sumerian mythology, Dumuzi is the son of Duttur, the divine mother sheep. His sister, Geshtinanna, is always depicted as faithful and loyal to the point of self-denial. His father, Enki, plays no role in this capacity in the texts.

There is evidence that a few rulers of the Ur III and first Isin dynasties saw themselves as performing Dumuzi's role in celebrations of the sacred marriage rite with Inanna. According to a hymn of Iddindagan of Isin, this rite took place on New Year's day in Isin. However, the sacred aspect of the Sumerian love songs has been rather overrated. Some of the songs represent ordinary love songs and the wedding ceremonies of the upper social classes, in which the human roles of the bride and the bridegroom are assigned to Inanna and Dumuzi. Reading such songs as information pertaining directly to deities may lead to misinterpretation. The true reference is to human lovers, who, in this literary environment, were traditionally represented by Inanna and Dumuzi, the divine pair of young lovers par excellence. Other love songs clearly belong to the court, but even a well known love song of king Shusin is in reality no more than an ordinary love song, in which the name of the king could stand for the name of any lover (ALSTER 1985).

In the sacred wedding ceremonies the bridegroom was solemnly selected, sometimes during a verbal contest. Then the rhetorical question was raised, who was going to "plough" Inanna's vulva. The marriage was consummated when Inanna answered "the man of my heart", and the audience confirmed the choice with a song (ALSTER 1992). The sacred marriage rite was a rite with social implications: i.e. its emphasis was upon marriage relations and sexual productivity. The mention of sprouting grain and flax in such a context is a literary commonplace that points to the king as responsible for the well-being of the country in a general sense, rather than to a fertility rite relating to vegetable life. The performance of the sacred marriage rite ceased in the Old Babylonian period, when it started to provoke polemic attitudes. This trend culminated in the 6th tablet of the Ninevite Gilgamesh epic, where Ishtar is blamed for having instituted annual lamentation for Dumuzi. In the first millennium BCE the bewailing of Dumuzi's death became the climax of his cult. His journey to the netherworld became symbolic of exorcistic rituals aiming at the removal of everything evil.

How the two aspects of Dumuzi's cult, his joyous wedding to Inanna, and the bewailing of his untimely death, came to be combined in one person, is an interesting question. That the former tradition came from Uruk, and the latter from Badtibira (cf. FALKENSTEIN, CRRA 3:59; T. JACOBSEN, *JNES* 12 [1953] 162-163), is not really a fully-convincing explanation. Throughout the tradition, Dumuzi's death is described as the "seizure" by the gendarmes of the underworld. According to the Sumerian myth *Inanna's Descent*, Dumuzi was captured by gendarmes after Inanna had gone down to the netherworld, and was obliged to provide a substitute on her return to the world of the living. Dumuzi was chosen because, unlike two other deities in Inanna's entourage, he had sat on her throne and enjoyed himself with music instead of performing the mourning rites during her absence. The myth tells further that Dumuzi's sister, Geshtinanna, offered herself as a substitute every half year, so that Dumuzi and his sister could return one after the other in an eternal cycle. Dumuzi's unhappy fate is here used as a warning to those who did not participate in the mourning rites for Inanna. The theme was resumed later in the so-called Uruama-irabi-laments (VOLK 1989).

This explanation is to be seen as a later literary rationalization, and contradicts most of the literary tradition, according to which Inanna positively was depicted as innocent in Dumuzi's death, participated in the search for him, and begged Enlil to revive him. According to a hymn to Inanna-Ninegalla, the mourning rites took place when Inanna, as the descending →Venus star, met Dumuzi in the netherworld.

Another explanation, that Dumuzi, as the mortal husband of a goddess, had to die in order to restore the balance between the divine and the human, should be discarded as founded on a misinterpretation of a Sumerian hymn (SRT 31, see SEFATI 1990). Rather, the origin of this aspect of the Dumuzi cult seems to be a traditional mourning rite in which women could have expressed their sympathy for any young man who had disappeared or, like Adonis, died too young to have a family. As was the case with the love poetry, Dumuzi could be seen as the prototype of any sympathetic young man, whose lonely life in the desert was in fact constantly exposed to dangers. The mourning rites performed in sympathy with the deceased were accompanied by self-demolation of the body, tearing out hair, etc., but such extremes as self-castration as the culmination of a wild orgiastic feast, as known in the cult of Attis, is not attested in connection with Dumuzi (ALSTER 1983).

The question whether or not Dumuzi rose from the realms of the dead is perhaps best answered with the claim that since this was not celebrated in a cultic festival, it did not play any significant role in the literature. In the Akkadian myth *Ishtar's Descent to the Underworld*, it is clearly stated that Dumuzi "came up", but this does not refer to the resurrection of the god to the realms of the living. What is meant is Dumuzi's participation in a ritual, in which the spirits of the dead were invoked and manifested themselves for a short time.

In the Neo-Assyrian period the cult of Dumuzi culminated with the so-called "display" (*taklimtu*) of the dead body of the god, or perhaps rather of his grave goods (J. A. SCURLOCK, *NABU* 1991, 3). The term was copied in Greek *deiktērion*, found in a paryrus listing expenditures for an Adonis festival (STOL 1988:127).

III. The vision reported in Ezek 8:14 is followed by another, according to which the prophet saw men worshipping the sun (→Shemesh) at the entrance to the temple itself (Ezek 8:16). These are to be seen as extremely strong examples of Babylonian influence on the cult of Israel. There is no other evidence of the cult of Tammuz in the OT, but the type of cult may have been similar to the cult of →Hadad Rimmon referred to in Zech 12:11, a god for whom ritual laments were performed in the plain of Megiddo, and to the cult of *Ḥemdat našîm* 'the beloved of the women' (Dan 11:37).

IV. *Bibliography*

B. ALSTER, *Dumuzi's Dream* (Mesopotamia 1; Copenhagen 1972); ALSTER, The Mythology of Mourning, *ASJ* 5 (1983) 1-16; ALSTER, Sumerian love songs, *RA* 79 (1985) 127-159; ALSTER, The Manchester Tammuz, *ASJ* 14 (1992) 1-46; J. BOTTÉRO & S. N. KRAMER, *Lorsque les dieux faisaient l'homme* (Paris 1989); A. FALKENSTEIN, Tammūz, *CRRA* 3 (1954) 41-65; W. FARBER, *Beschwörungsrituale an Ištar und Dumuzi.* (Akademie der Wissenschaften und der Literatur; Wiesbaden 1977); O. R. GURNEY, Tammuz reconsidered: Some recent developments, *JSS* 7 (1962) 147-160;

T. JACOBSEN, *The Sumerian King List* (AS 11; Chicago 1939); JACOBSEN, Toward the image of Tammuz, *HR* 1 (1961) 189-213, repr. in: *Toward the Image of Tammuz and other essays on Mesopotamian History and Culture* (ed. W. L. Moran; Cambridge, Mass. 1970) 73-101; JACOBSEN, Religious drama in ancient Mesopotamia, *Unity and Diversity* (ed. H. Goedicke *et al.*; Baltimore 1975) 65-97; JACOBSEN, The name Dumuzi, *JQR* 76/1 (1985) 41-45; JACOBSEN, *The Harps that once ... Sumerian Poetry in Translation* (New Haven and London 1987) 1-84; S. N. KRAMER, *The Sacred Marriage Rite* (London 1969); R. KUTSCHER, The Cult of Dumuzi/Tammuz, in: *Bar-Ilan Studies in Assyriology dedicated to P. Artzi* (ed. J. Klein & A. Skaist; Ramat Gan 1990) 29-44; S. LANGDON, *Tammuz and Ishtar* (Oxford 1914); Y. SEFATI, An oath of chastity in a Sumerian love song (SRT 31)?, *Bar-Ilan Studies in Assyriology dedicated to P. Artzi* (ed. J. Klein & A. Skaist; Ramat Gan 1990) 45-63; M. STOL, Greek DEIKTHRION, *Funerary Symbols and Religion. Essays dedicated to Professor Heerma van Voss* (ed. J. H. Kamstra, H. Milde & K. Wagtendonk; Kampen 1988) 127-128; K. VOLK, *Die Balag-Komposition Uru Am-ma-ir-ra-bi.* (FAOS 18; Stuttgart 1989); M. WITZEL, *Tammuz-Liturgien und Verwandtes* (AnOr 10; Roma 1935).

B. ALSTER

TANNIN תנין

I. Tannin occurs in the OT in reference to a sea monster subdued or slain by →Yahweh (whether as a proper name or as a common noun meaning "sea monster" or "dragon" is unclear). The term is found also in the sense of "serpent" and (arguably) "crocodile"; further, it appears five times in the plural (*tannînîm*) with the meaning "sea monsters/dragons" or "snakes".

The etymology of Tannin is uncertain. BDB suggests a derivation from TNN-I, perhaps to be linked with TNH-II ("recount, rehearse") as "lament, i.e. howl", although this appears to work much better with *tan* ("jackal") than with *tannîn*. *HALAT* admits uncertainty in choosing between a primitive noun and a derivation from a root *tnn*, also a possible source for *tan*, but meaning "to stretch oneself" (which would be more clearly connected with animals of the sort *tannîn* describes, rather than "howl"), as suggested already by J. FÜRST (*Hebräisches und Chaldäisches Schul-Wörterbuch* [Leipzig 1842] 637). More recently, AARTUN (Neue Beitrage zum ugaritischen Lexikon [II], *UF* 17 [1986] 38-39) has revived the proposal of AISTLEITNER, that Tannin is derived from a geminate root TNN, "to smoke, ascension of smoke", leading to the Ugaritic "the dragon, (sea)monster, snake (stretching out/moving forward like smoke)". The suggestion of H. LEWY may be noted in passing, that *tannîn* may have found its way into Greek as *thunnos* ("tuna fish"; Dutch: *tonijn*) (*Semitische Fremdwörter im Griechischen* [Berlin 1895] 15).

Related to the issue of etymology is the question of the history of the form, *tannîn*. A Ugaritic polyglot text writes the word as *tu-un-na-nu* = /*tunnanu*/ or /*tunnānu*/ (*Ugaritica* V [1968] 137:I:8, pp. 240-241). J. HUEHNERGARD suggests that "the word is probably a D verbal adjective in origin, although the etymology remains obscure" (*Ugaritic Vocabulary in Syllabic Transcription* [HSS 32; Cambridge 1987] 72). The change in vocalization from Ugaritic *tunnanu* to Hebrew *tannîn* may be according to the development *quttal* > *qattil* known from Arabic, or it may have happened by analogy (or even confusion) with *tan* ("jackal"), as evidenced by the occurrence of *tannîn* in Lam 4:3 for *tannîm* ("jackals") and the reverse in Ezek 29:3 and 32:2 for "dragon" (or "crocodile") (so LOEWENSTAMM 1975: 22).

Tannin and cognate forms thereof also appear in the Qumran scrolls, Jewish and Egyptian Aramaic, Syriac, Arabic and Ethiopic, but all are late enough not to contribute independently to the foregoing discussion (and all except the Egyptian Aramaic appear to be dependent on the OT [so *HALAT*]).

II. In addition to the occurrence in the polyglot syllabary, noted above, *tnn* is found eight times in the Ugaritic corpus (R. E. WHITAKER, *A Concordance of the Ugaritic Literature* [Cambridge 1972] 619). Twice it is apparently part of a personal name (*KTU* 4.35:13 and 4.103:42). The other occurrences are in mythological texts. Three link Tunnanu with the great sea monster(s) defeated by →Anat (*KTU* 1.3 iii:40 and 1. 83:8) or, apparently, →Baal (*KTU* 1.82:1), while the remaining three are in fragmentary contexts (*KTU* 1.16 v:31,32, where *tnn* is apparently mentioned in connection with something created by →El to assist the ailing King Keret) or subject to disputed interpretation (*KTU* 1.6 vi:51, where J. C. L. GIBSON would read "In the sea are Arsh and *the dragon*" [*Canaanite Myths and Legends* (Edinburgh 1977) 81], while K. AARTUN has "On the day of the kindling and *the ascension of the smoke*" [*UF* 17 (1986) 38-39]). As for the monster's appearance, *KTU* 1.83:8 may suggest that Tunnanu had a double tail, while the syllabary text indicates an equation with the ideogram for "snake" (MUŠ = *ṣēru*).

Two issues concerning the Ugaritic evidence have generated some debate. The first is suggested by the reference to "sea monster(s)" in the preceding paragraph: are *tnn, ltn* and *ym* separate monsters or different names/epithets for the same being? COOPER (1981:424-425) summarizes the proposed alternatives, eventually leaning toward LOEWENSTAMM's suggestion "that at Ugarit, as in the OT, there are divergent adaptations of the battle tradition". Secondly, there has been some philological uncertainty regarding the verb which Anat uses to describe her subduing Tunnanu (*ištbm* in *KTU* 1.3 iii:40; *lšbm* in *KTU* 1.83:8). C. Virolleaud's proposal of "muzzle", based on Arabic *šabama* has been defended by S. LOEWENSTAMM and others, but attacked by J. Barr. In response, LOEWENSTAMM holds out for some manner of "tie, bind", but concedes that "the exact nature of the fettering device applied defies closer description".

III. The Biblical references to Tannin can be considered in four groups (building on the analysis of DAY 1985). First are those occurrences which link Tannin to creation. Most obviously this includes Gen 1:21, in which God creates the *tannînîm* on the fifth day. Ever since the pioneering work of GUNKEL (1921), scholarly opinion has commonly held that the OT's story of the creation was constructed in deliberate distinction from that of Mesopotamia (as represented by *Enuma Elish*), in which the creator god fashions the cosmos from the slain corpse of a sea monster (→Tiamat); by this reading Israel was saying that the great sea monsters were merely a part of the created order. More recently, DAY (1985) has proposed that Israel's story is set in contradistinction to a yet-unknown Canaanite creation myth, to which allusions may be seen in the Ugaritic references to the slaying of the sea monster(s) by Anat or Baal. Whatever the cultural foil, it is clear that the OT's reference in this instance is not to any cosmic, mythological enemy. (Similarly, Ps 148:7 calls upon the *tannînîm*, as part of the created order, to join in the praise of Yahweh.)

With other references to Tannin in the context of creation it is not so easy to determine whether we have to do with a mythical being or demythologized symbol (again, regardless of whether one reads Tannin as proper name or as common noun). Thus, both Job 7:12 and Ps 74:13 refer to Tannin (or its plural in the latter verse) together with (or perhaps in apposition to) the Sea and/or →Leviathan, as those whom God once subdued and now keeps in check (Job) or slew in the course of creation (Ps 74).

A second group of references reflects a linkage with some historical enemy of Israel, especially Egypt. Thus, while Isa 51: 9 might be categorized with the first group (linking Tannin with creation), were it taken out of context, the primary reference is shown by the following verse to be the deliverance at the Red Sea. (To say this is, of course, not to deny a secondary allusion to creation or Yahweh's victory over primordial chaos, however conceptualized.)

Three other references are unquestionably

to historical figures. Twice in his oracles against Egypt, Ezekiel addresses the pharaoh as Tannin (reading *tannîn* for MT *tannîm* with Gunkel and most subsequent commentators): 29:3 and 32:2. What has been debated in these verses is whether the prophet has in mind the supernatural sea monster/dragon of other references to Tannin (so GUNKEL 1921:71-77) or a natural (or supernatural) crocodile, as G. FOHRER and others argue, citing the presence of the crocodiles in the Nile, the simile of the pharaoh as "like a crocodile" in a hymn of Thutmoses III, and the alleged depiction of Leviathan as a crocodile in Job 40:25-41:26 (ET 41:1-34) (*Ezekiel* [HAT; Tübingen 1955] 166). Thirdly, Jeremiah compares Nebuchadnezzar of Babylon to Tannin, in having "swallowed me [Zion] like the *tannîn*" (51:34). Finally, we may note GUNKEL's proposal of yet another confusion in the MT of *tannîm* ('jackals') for *tannîn*: Ps 44:20 (1921:70-71). If he is correct, the reference is presumably to some historical oppressor nation; DAY proposes Babylon, Egypt and Assyria as candidates (1985:113).

A third category of references to Tannin is represented by Isa 27:1: Tannin as the eschatological enemy of God, to be slain "on that day". As in Isa 51:9 (where Tannin is juxtaposed with Rahab), this verse places the monster/dragon in parallel with Leviathan, so that one cannot be entirely sure how many figures are involved. Of greater moment is the attempt by O. EISSFELDT (*Baal Zaphon, Zeus Kasios und der Durchzug der Israeliten durch das Meer* [Halle 1932] 29-30) to see in this verse an eschatological extension of those passages which contained thinly veiled references to historical figures as monsters: in the case in point he sees Tannin as Egypt and Leviathan as Syria. As is so often true with apocalyptic (or proto-apocalyptic) writing, it is difficult to be certain about historical referents (if any); what seems far more sure is that Leviathan/Tannin in this passage (along with the serpent of Genesis 3 and the fourth beast of Daniel 7) supplied much of the background for the great dragon of Revelation 12-13 in the NT.

Fourthly, there are passages in which *tannîn(îm)* appears to refer to natural serpents: Exod 7:9-10.12; Deut 32:33; Ps 91:13. Even here, however, at least in the instance of the occurrences in Exodus and Psalms, WAKEMAN would see mythical overtones (1973: 77-79).

Finally, there is one passage which is difficult to place in the above schema: a place name for a spring near Jerusalem in Neh 2:13, *'ên hattannîn*.

What emerges from a review of the OT references is the portrait of a sea monster (or dragon) who served in various texts as a personification of chaos or those evil, historical forces opposed to Yahweh and his people. While the Tannin of the OT shares much in common with Tunnanu, as known from a handful of Ugaritic texts, we simply cannot be certain to what extent most uses of the Biblical term points to a demythologized symbol versus a "living myth". Certainly, as DAY suggests in his helpful discussion (1985:187-189), "even for some of those for whom it was living [myth] Israelite monotheism had transformed it out of all recognition."

IV. *Bibliography*

A. COOPER, Divine Names and Epithets in the Ugaritic Texts, *RSP* 3:425-428 [& lit]; *J. DAY, *God's Conflict with the Dragon and the Sea* (Cambridge Oriental Publications 35; Cambridge 1985) [& lit]; H. GUNKEL, *Schöpfung und Chaos in Urzeit und Endzeit* (Göttingen 1921); S. LOEWENSTAMM, Anat's Victory over the Tunnanu, *JSS* 20 (1975) 27; M. K. WAKEMAN, *God's Battle with the Monster: A Study in Biblical Imagery* (Leiden 1973).

G. C. HEIDER

TARTAK תרתק

I. Tartak is one of two gods (the other →Nibhaz) worshipped by the Avvites whom the Assyrians settled in Samaria, some time after the city's fall (2 Kgs 17:24.31). A god by this name is unknown in extra-biblical sources. In addition, the location of Avva is uncertain.

II. Two identifications of Tartak, both problematic, have been suggested. The first associates the Avvites with Elam. Avva is taken to be identical with the town Ama on the Uqnu River on the Babylonian-Elamite border, occupied by Aramean tribes (ZADOK 1976:120, BECKING 1992:98). The transfer of Avvites to Samaria might have occurred as early as the days of Sargon who fought and captured Ama in 710 BCE; or as late as Ashurbanipal, who defeated the Elamites in that same area in 646 BCE; compare the claim made by some of the Samarians, including those from Susa, of their arrival in Samaria during Ashurbanipal's reign (Ezra 4:9-10). In this case, Tartak would then be an Elamite deity. His name was found in the God list CT 25,24, where the Elamite gods ^d^*Ibnaḫaza* and ^d^*Dakdadra* seem to reflect the Biblical pair, Nibhaz and Tartak mentioned in 2 Kgs 17:31 (HOMMEL 1912); the transposed form of the name ^d^*Dakdadra* was read in the Naram-Sin treaty as ^d^*Dirtak* (HOMMEL 1926), which seemed even closer to the Hebrew transcription. But, though the name ^d^*Dirtak* is now apparently to be read ^d^*Siašum* (*dir* = *si* + *a*; *tak* = *šum*; cf. HINZ 1967:74), the Elamite provenance of the god is still favoured by some (e.g. DRIVER 1958: 19*).

A second possibility is the identification of Tartak with →Atargatis. If the town Avva is associated with the town of Hamath in northern Syria (cf. 2 Kgs 17:24), then the settlers in Samaria might have been Arameans; several sites in the region of Hamath are suggested for the town's location (cf. MONTGOMERY & GEHMAN 1951:472; GRAY 1970:651). The god name Tartak is taken to refer, then, to the Syrian fertility goddess, known from Greek texts as 'Atargate/ →'Atargatis; the Hebrew form *trtq* derives from a dissimilated and metathesized form of an Aramaic original (cf. ŠANDA 1912:2. 230-231; MONTGOMERY 1914:78; MONTGOMERY & GEHMAN 1951:474; GRAY 1970: 654), attested on coins and inscriptions as *'tr'tw/h; tr't'* (RONZEVALLE 1940:28-42). Besides these difficult linguistic transpositions, the supposed attestation of Atargatis among the Samarians would make this the earliest evidence for worship of the goddess, preceding the classical references by many centuries.

III. *Bibliography*

B. BECKING, *The Fall of Samaria* (SHANE 2; Leiden 1992); G. R. DRIVER, Geographical Problems, *Archaeological, Historical and Geographical Studies dedicated to Professor Benjamin Mazar on his Fiftieth Birthday* (ErIsr 5; 1958) 16*-20*; J. GRAY, *I & II Kings* (2nd ed.; Philadelphia 1970); W. HINZ, Elams Vertrag mit Narām-Sin von Akade, *ZA* 58 (1967) 66-96; F. HOMMEL, Die Gotter Nibhaz und Tartak. 2 Kon. 17.31, *OLZ* 15 (1912) 118; HOMMEL, Die Elamitische Götter-Siebenheit in CT 25,24, *Paul Haupt Anniversary Volume* (Baltimore & Leipzig 1926) 159-168; J. A. MONTGOMERY, Tartak, *JBL* 33 (1914) 78; J. A. MONTGOMERY & H. S. GEHMAN, *The Books of Kings* (ICC; Edinburgh 1951); S. RONZEVALLE, Les monnaies de la dynastie de 'Abd-Hadad et les cultes de Hierapolis-Bambycé, *Mélanges de l'Université Saint Joseph Beyrouth* 23 (1940) 28-42; A. ŠANDA, *Die Bücher der Könige* (Münster 1912); R. ZADOK, Geographical and Onomastic Notes, *JANES* 8 (1976) 113-126.

M. COGAN

TEHOM → TIAMAT

TERAH תרח

I. In biblical tradition, Terah is the son of Nahor and the father of Abram, Nahor, and Haran (Gen 11:24-27). Originally from Ur, where he worshipped gods other than Yahweh (Josh 24:2), Terah died in Haran where he had settled after his migration from Ur (Gen 11:31-32). Attempts have been made to connect Terah with a deity Trḫ supposedly mentioned in Ugaritic texts, and with the moon-god Teri or Ilteri; such identifications have now by and large been abandoned.

II. Soon after the discovery of the alphabetic texts of Ras Shamra, the figure of Terah was connected with a god whose name was read *itrḫ* or *trḫ* (C. VIROLLEAUD, La naissance des dieux gracieux et beaux, *Syria* 14 [1933] 149 and n. 1). Virolleaud's suggestion was accepted by a fair number of scholars (e.g. LEWY 1934; R. DUSSAUD, *Les découvertes de Ras Shamra et l'Ancien Testament* [Paris 1937] 81), until GORDON showed that *itrḫ* and *trḫ* were not personal names but finite forms of the verb *trḫ*, 'to pay the marriage price' (1938; see also ALBRIGHT 1938).

To be distinguished from the association with the phantom deity *trḫ* is the hypothesis of a connection between Terah and the moon-god Teri or Ilteri; this Aramaic god is known from theophoric personal names from the Persian period (B. LANDSBERGER & T. BAUER, Zu neuveröffentlichten Geschichtsquellen der Zeit von Assarhaddon bis Nabonid, *ZA* 37 [1927] 92 n. 4). He is once mentioned in the Verse Account of Nabonidus (Col. v 11) as the god who grants nightly visions (for the text see S. SMITH, *Babylonian Historical Texts* [London 1924] 27-97). Considering Nabonidus' devotion to the moon-god one would expect Ilteri to be a lunar deity; this he is indeed, as his name goes back to a combination of il + *Śahr > *Iltahri > Ilteri (R. ZADOK, *On West Semites in Babylonian During the Chaldean and Achaemenian Periods* [Jerusalem 1977] 42). On Śahar as the Aramaic equivalent of Babylonian →Sin see H. DONNER & W. RÖLLIG, *KAI* II (1964) 211 ad no. 202B 24.

III. For various reasons, attempts to find a Semitic god behind the figure of Terah are not much in favour today. The various deities proposed have either vanished on closer analysis of the texts, or are phonologically unrelated to Hebrew *teraḥ*. Teri (or Ilteri) cannot very well be linked with Terah, as this would imply a metathesis of the *ḥ*. Also, the search for a divine model for Terah is to be seen as part of the more general tendency among biblical scholars at the end of the 19th and the beginning of the 20th centuries to regard the Israelite patriarchs (as well as the wives of the patriarchs) as demythologized gods; Eduard Meyer, Bernhard Luther, and Julius Lewy are representative of this tendency. The current trend in interpretation is different. Patriarchal names are more fruitfully related to the Amorite onomasticon, and the human nature of their bearers is not in doubt. The name of Terah is perhaps to be connected with Akk *ṭurāḫu*, 'ibex, mountain goat' (*AHW* 1372; cf. JOÜON 1938).

IV. *Bibliography*

W. F. ALBRIGHT, Was the Patriarch Terah a Canaanite Moon-God?, *BASOR* 71 (1938) 35-40; C. H. GORDON, *TRḪ, ṮN* and *NKR* in the Ras Shamra tablets, *JBL* 57 (1938) 407-410; J. LEWY, Les textes paléo-assyriens et l'Ancien Testament, *RHR* 110 (1934) 45; P. JOÜON, Trois noms de personnages bibliques à la lumière des textes d'Ugarit (Ras Shamra): תרח, ישׂשכר, דנאל, *Bibl* 19 (1938) 280-281.

K. VAN DER TOORN

TERAPHIM תרפים

I. The word *tĕrāpîm* is found 15 times in the Hebrew Bible, occurring only in the plural even when it denotes one image (1 Sam 19:13, 16; cf. A. R. JOHNSON, *The Cultic Prophet in Ancient Israel* [Cardiff 1962] 32 n. 3, who suggests that some forms of the plural may be occurrences of the singular with mimation). For the most part the Septuagint translators chose to simply transliterate the term, yet on occasion they associated it with idols (*eidōlon*; →Gillulim) or a carved image (*glyptos*). There is even some attempt to connect it to healing (HOFFNER 1968:61 n. 2). The Targumic material usually renders *tĕrāpîm* by *ṣalmānayyā'*, 'images', or *dĕmā'în*, 'figures', although *Tanḥûma Wayyēṣē* 12 understands that the *tĕrāpîm* are so called "because they are works of *tôrēp* ('filth')".

Scholars have proposed numerous etymologies for *tĕrāpîm*, yet it is rare that any of them has met with widespread acceptance. The degree to which etymologies help us understand the true nature and function of the *tĕrāpîm* has also been questioned (VAN DER TOORN 1990:204; cf. LORETZ 1992:137-139).

Of the numerous etymologies suggested for *tĕrāpîm* the following are the most common. 1) *Tĕrāpîm* is to be understood as either a *taprīs-* or *taprās-* form of the root RP', 'to heal' (cf. DE WARD 1977:5-6; ROUILLARD & TROPPER 1987:357-361; TROPPER 1989:335). *Tĕrāpîm* then were associated with healing. 1 Sam 19, which has the *tĕrāpîm* (19:13.16) in the same narrative as sickness (19:14), is cited for support (but see below). The word →Rephaim, which some translate as 'healers', is also brought into the discussion despite its equally perplexing etymology. For example, ALBRIGHT at one point suggested that the Heb *tĕrāpîm* was a "contemptuous deformation (...) from the stem RP'" (W. F. ALBRIGHT, *Yahweh and the Gods of Canaan* [New York 1968] 168 n. 43; see LORETZ 1992:138-139; 141-142; 148-151; 167-168). For a critique of deriving *tĕrāpîm* from RP', see HOFFNER (1967:233-234; 1968:62). 2) *Tĕrāpîm* is to be derived from the root RPH, 'to sink, relax, be limp, sag', thus E. A. SPEISER (*Genesis* [Garden City 1964] 245) suggests 'inert things, idols' (cf. ALBRIGHT 1941:40 n. 8; N. SARNA, *The JPS Torah Commentary: Genesis* [Philadelphia 1989] 216). 3) *Tĕrāpîm* is cognate to Ug *trp* meaning 'to sag' (cf. again ALBRIGHT 1968[5]:206 n. 63 who says that the *tĕrāpîm* should be rendered 'old rags'; see also J. GRAY, *I & II Kings* [Philadelphia 1964] 745). 4) *Tĕrāpîm* is to be related to post-biblical *trp* (see above) and thus refers to 'vile things' (once again see ALBRIGHT, *From the Stone Age to Christianity* [Garden City 1957] 311; N. SARNA, *The JPS Torah Commentary: Genesis* [Philadelphia 1989] 216). 5) *Tĕrāpîm* is to be derived from an original *pĕtārîm*, 'interpreters (of dreams)', which was intentionally changed (by metathesis) at a later time by those interested in ridiculing these objects (so LABUSCHAGNE 1966:115-117, but see HOFFNER's critique (1967:232-233; 1968:61-62). 6) *Tĕrāpîm* is a loan word from Hit *tarpi(š)*, which "denotes a spirit which can on some occasions be regarded as protective and on others as malevolent" and which is parallel in lexical texts to Akk *šēdu*, 'spirit, demon' (HOFFNER 1967:230-238; 1968:61-68; *CAD* Š II, 256-259; SEYBOLD 1976:1057).

Of the above etymologies HOFFNER's would appear to be the most plausible although it too is not without its difficulties (see ROUILLARD & TROPPER 1987:360-361; F. JOSEPHSON, Anatolien TARPA/I-, etc., *Florilegium Anatolicum. Mélanges offerts à Emmanuel Laroche* [Paris 1979] 181).

II. Although the word *tĕrāpîm* is not attested anywhere outside of the Bible (unless it is in fact a loan from Hit *tarpi*), scholars have nonetheless frequently looked to extrabiblical sources to try to understand the function of the *tĕrāpîm* over against its ancient Near Eastern backdrop with particular attention being given to peripheral Akkadian texts (Nuzi and Emar). Ever since 1926, when the Nuzi text Gadd 51 was published (C. J. GADD, *RA* 23 [1926] 49-161, no. 51.10-17; see *ANET*, 219-220) and when S. SMITH (1932:33-36) drew a parallel between the *tĕrāpîm* and Nuzi *ilānu*, there has been a fascination with using the Nuzi texts not only to flesh out the phenomena of the *tĕrāpîm* specifically (especially the motive behind Rachel's theft of them), but also to reconstruct patriarchal practices of inheritance, property rights, adoption and the designation of family-headship (*pater familias*; e.g. E. A. SPEISER, *Genesis* [Garden City 1964] 250; C. H. GORDON, *BA* 3 [1940] 1-12; cf. the dissenting view of GREENBERG 1962:239-248). The greatest impact was left by DRAFFKORN-KILMER's *Ilāni/Elohim* article which argued that "the biblical *elohim/teraphim* correspond, in so far as Genesis 31 is concerned, with Nuzi *ilāni* in their intimate role in regard to family law" (DRAFFKORN 1957:222).

Most of the early studies using the Nuzi texts concluded that the *tĕrāpîm* were 'household gods' and this translation is reflected in most major translations of Gen 31:19, 34, 35 (cf. NRSV, NEB). This conclusion was seen to be definitive because the *tĕrāpîm* themselves are referred to as *'ĕlōhîm*, 'gods' (Gen 31:30; cf. Judg 18:24; →God I). Later studies have emphasized that three Nuzi texts (JEN 478:6-8; HSS 19, no. 27:11; YBC 5142:30) mention the *ilānu* in collocation with the →Eṭemmu, 'the spirits of the dead' (see CASSIN 1981:42-45; DELLER 1981:62, 73-74; ROUILLARD & TROPPER 1987:352-357; TSUKIMOTO 1989: 98-106; VAN DER TOORN 1990:219-221; LORETZ 1992:152-155). That the *tĕrāpîm* are to be equated with ancestor figurines is not a new proposal, yet previous studies were not based on such extensive comparative evidence which emphasizes that "the domestic cult at Nuzi included the care for the *eṭemmū* on the same footing as that for the *ilānu*" (VAN DER TOORN 1990:204 n. 8, 220). The Old Babylonian story of Etana, which contains the phrase "I honoured the gods, revered the spirits of the dead (*ilānī ukabbit eṭemmē aplaḫ*)," shows that the parallel *ilānu*//*eṭemmū* (and the ancestral cult to which it refers) was not restricted to the Nuzi peripheral material (see J. V. KINNIER WILSON, *The Legend of Etana: A New Edition* [Warminster, Wiltshire 1985] 100-101). A similar pairing of (household) gods (*ilānu*) and the deceased ancestors (*mētū*; →Dead) occurs in the recently published Emar texts. The four pertinent texts and their relevance to the *tĕrāpîm* have been discussed by VAN DER TOORN (1990:221; see also TSUKIMOTO 1989:9-11 and LORETZ 1992:166-167) who concludes that here too "we find the care for the ancestors linked with the worship of the family deities, both set within the context of the domestic cult". Particularly relevant in the Emar texts is the notion of *invoking* (unless we are to read *nubbû* as 'to wail, lament' [*nabû* D stem]) the gods//dead which is one of the most important essential services accorded to the dead (BAYLISS 1973:117).

Finally, scholars have also looked to the Assyrian as well as to the Ugaritic material to flesh out the ancient Near Eastern backdrop to the biblical *tĕrāpîm*. VAN DER TOORN (1990:217-219) points out the revering (*palāḫu*) and consulting (*ša'ālu*) of the *eṭemmū* mentioned in several Assyrian texts over a wide range of time (Old Assyrian to Neo-Assyrian). In particular he notes "the formal correspondence between Assyrian *eṭemmē ša'ālu* and Heb *šā'al battĕrāpîm*" which he calls an "intriguing parallelism between ancient Assyria and ancient Israel". The relevance of the Ugaritic material for understanding the biblical *tĕrāpîm* has been examined recently by LORETZ (1992:156-161, 164-166). In particular LORETZ suggests that the controversial *inš ilm* should be regarded as "eine Bezeichnung der Toten der königlichen Familie" which should be translated 'Götter der Sippe' or 'Sippengötter'. Nevertheless, the notorious difficulties of this material (as well as the other Ugaritic evidence LORETZ mentions such as the forms *ttrp* and *ilh/ilhm*) renders any conclusions (and comparisons with the *tĕrāpîm*) precarious.

III. The *tĕrāpîm* occur only fifteen times in the OT (Gen 31:19.34.35; Judg 17:5; 18:14.17.18.20; 1 Sam 15:23; 19:13.16; 2 Kgs 23:24; Ezek 21:26[21]; Hos 3:4; Zech 10:2), yet the number of conjectures regarding the identity and function of the *tĕrāpîm* surely would be tabulated in several multiples of fifteen. Faced with such *cruces interpretum* one could of course throw up one's hand in despair and assert that "what the Teraphim represented is anyone's guess" (B. B. SCHMIDT, *Israel's Beneficent Dead* [diss. Oxford 1991] 404 n. 4). Or, faced with what might be contradictory evidence, one could assert that the term *tĕrāpîm* may be a generic name or a single term used for various cultic items (cf. SEYBOLD 1976: 1057-1060; ACKROYD 1950-51:378-380). Most scholars try to reconcile all of the data (together with one's understanding of the etymology) in order to achieve a uniform interpretation. In addition to debates over the etymology of *tĕrāpîm* (see above), scholarly discussion of the *tĕrāpîm* usually concentrates on its form and function.

That the term *tĕrāpîm* referred to *objects* (or a singular object) of some sort can be easily inferred from the verbs associated with it which describe 'making' (Judg 17:5), 'finding' (Gen 31:35), 'removing' (2 Kgs 23:24), 'stealing' (Gen 31:19), 'taking, putting and covering' (1 Sam 19:13; Gen 31:

34) the *tĕrāpîm* image(s). As for the shape and size of the object(s), one must certainly caution against generalization. Our data are meagre and we have no way of knowing whether the form of the *tĕrāpîm* remained constant or whether it varied through time and/or from one locality to the next. The little evidence we do have suggests degrees of variation. We also have no information regarding the origin of the *tĕrāpîm* and our ignorance in this regard should keep us from making unsubstantiated assertions such as MAY's claim that Rachel's import of the *tĕrāpîm* "reflects the entrance of figurines into Palestine for the first time" (H. G. MAY, *Material Remains of the Megiddo Cult* [OIP 26; Chicago 1935] 27; cf. W. EICHRODT *Ezekiel* [Philadelphia 1970] 299; W. ZIMMERLI, *Ezekiel 1* [Philadelphia 1979] 444).

1 Sam 19:13-16 and Gen 31:34 are the only two biblical passages which give any hint regarding the actual form of the *tĕrāpîm*. 1 Sam 19:13, 16 suggests that a *tĕrāpîm* (note the plural used for a singular image) was an object approximating human form. The narrator tells us that Michal hides a *tĕrāpîm* in bed as a substitute for David whom Saul is trying to kill (cf. HOFFNER's [1967:233 n.19] attempt to equate the Hit *tarpiš* with substitute images). Many scholars (e.g. GORDON 1962:574) have assumed that the *tĕrāpîm* here was life-size and this certainly seems logical. Michal then puts goat's hair on its head and clothes it evidently to give it more of a human appearance (although *beged* may refer to a blanket as well as a garment and the goat's hair may also have been used to cloak the image rather than to represent a wig). Evidently Michal's *tĕrāpîm* was close enough to an anthropoid shape to fool Saul's messengers who depart without any further searching. (On the intricate details of this passage see ROUILLARD & TROPPER 1987 and VAN DER TOORN 1990.)

ALBRIGHT (1968:110) challenged this view on archaeological grounds stating that no life-size figurines "of comparable size have ever been found in Palestinian excavations". In concert with this we find quite a few scholars suggesting, based on 1 Sam 19:13-16 as well as the pottery masks from Hazor and Akhziv, that the word *tĕrāpîm* designated a cultic mask of some sort (HOFFMANN & GRESSMANN 1922:75-137; W. EICHRODT, *Ezekiel* [Philadelphia 1970] 299; G. VON RAD (& A. ALT), *Old Testament Theology* 1 [New York 1963] 216; G. FOHRER, *History of Israelite Religion* [Nashville 1972] 114; DE WARD 1977:5; A. REICHERT, Kultmaske, *BRL*², 195-196; W. ZIMMERLI, *Ezekiel 1* [Philadelphia 1979] 444, etc.). For superb pictures of the clay masks in question, see *Treasures of the Holy Land. Ancient Art from the Israel Museum* [New York 1986] catalogue nos. 6, 43, 86-87).

Nevertheless, this theory does not seem to be very likely. As VAN DER TOORN has noted, if we have a cultic mask here, the suffix on the expression *mĕraʾăšōtāyw* ('at its head') in 1 Sam 19:13 would be redundant. The covering of the *tĕrāpîm* with a *beged* also makes much more sense if we are talking about a life-size statue rather than simply a head mask. In short, VAN DER TOORN is certainly correct when he asserts that the *tĕrāpîm* here "had more to it than a sculptured head" (see VAN DER TOORN 1990:206, which also contains a critique of those using the clay masks found at Hazor and ez-Zib to support the cultic mask theory). If →Laban's *tĕrāpîm* referred to in Gen 31 were also anthropoid in shape, (especially if they were complete human figures and not masks) they would certainly have been much smaller in size in order to fit under the saddlebag on Rachel's camel. VAN DER TOORN (1990:205) even estimates that "their length will not have exceeded 30-35 cm".

Scholars have suggested numerous ways in which the *tĕrāpîm* may have functioned within ancient Israelite society and cult.

J. GRAY (*I & II Kings* [Philadelphia 1964] 745) associated the *tĕrāpîm* with "the many figurines with the features of Asherah and Astarte found at Palestinian sites" (→Asherah, →Astarte). These figurines, suggested GRAY, "rank as *tĕrāpîm*" and were used "in rites of imitative magic to promote fertility". GRAY here is certainly following ALBRIGHT who once made a similar claim (ALBRIGHT, *From the Stone Age to Christianity* [Garden City 1957] 311; cf. too H. G. MAY, *Material Remains of the Megiddo Cult* [OIP 26; Chicago 1935:27] who says that it is "extremely probable" that the term *tĕrāpîm* was used to designate mother-goddesses and other fertility figurines). There is no explicit evidence linking the *tĕrāpîm* to fertility rituals. ALBRIGHT asserted that later biblical writers (he did not state which ones) included fertility figurines under the general term *tĕrāpîm.* 2 Kgs 23:24 *associates* the *tĕrāpîm* with necromancy (*ʾōbôt*, →Spirit of the dead; *yiddĕʿōnîm*, →Wizard), idols (→Gillulim) and abominations (*šiqquṣîm*; →Abomination)—no explicit fertility nuance is specified—but does *not* suggest that any of these terms are subsumed under the heading *tĕrāpîm.* Similarly, Judg 18:14.17.18.20 lists the *tĕrāpîm* along with an ephod, a 'graven image' (*pesel*), and a 'molten image' (*massēkâ*), yet nowhere is *tĕrāpîm* used as a general heading for these terms. There is one text which uses *tĕrāpîm* as a general heading for idolatry (1 Sam 15:23) listing it in conjunction with iniquity (*ʾāwen*), yet there is no explicit mention of fertility in this passage. The only other passage of interest for this theory would be Rachel's comment in Gen 31:35 that she could not rise from her camel (in whose saddlebag the *tĕrāpîm* were hidden) because the 'way of women' was upon her. This passage can help us understand ancient Israelite taboos (→Taboo) concerning menstruation (see VAN DER TOORN, *From Her Cradle to Her Grave* [Sheffield 1994] 52-53), yet the jump from such a taboo to equating the *tĕrāpîm* with fertility (just because a woman is sitting on them) would be a large one.

DE WARD (1977:6), building on the work of A. Phillips and E. A. Speiser, suggested that the function of the *tĕrāpîm* may have been protective in nature similar to that of the Akk *pālilu*, 'protector', although at the same time he admits that "actually there is not very much evidence in the OT for belief in such personal protectors". Likewise C. WESTERMANN (*Genesis 12-36* [Minneapolis 1985] 493) takes the *tĕrāpîm* to be household gods which "as everywhere (...) confer protection and blessing". While a protective function is certainly in the realm of possibilities (especially if HOFFNER's [1967] suggested etymology would prove true), such a role is not explicitly attested in the 15 occurrences of the *tĕrāpîm* that we have mentioned in the OT. DE WARD (1977:6) stretches the evidence to include the reference to *ʾĕlōhîm* in 1 Sam 2:25 (already noticed by DRAFFKORN [1957:218] who emphasizes its divinatory character). But the fact that *tĕrāpîm* could be referred to as *ʾĕlōhîm* (see below) does not mean that an occurrence of *ʾĕlōhîm* must refer to the *tĕrāpîm.* (On other protective spirits see F. A. M. WIGGERMANN, *Mesopotamian Protective Spirits: The Ritual Texts* [Groningen 1992].)

Many of the scholars who look to the root RPʾ, 'to heal', for the etymology of *tĕrāpîm* infer that the *tĕrāpîm* must have had healing purposes (cf. ROUILLARD & TROPPER 1987:340-361). With a slightly different twist W. E. BARNES (*JTS* 30 [1928-29] 179) claims that the *tĕrāpîm* were used to "warn the would-be intruder that there is sickness about". If the etymology of *tĕrāpîm* is from RPʾ one could make some case for this position, yet this etymology is far from certain (see HOFFNER's critique mentioned above). Healing is never mentioned as the function of the *tĕrāpîm* in the 15 occurrences of *tĕrāpîm* in the Hebrew Bible. Only one occurrence (1 Sam 19:13-14) has any association with healing. Yet even here one simply cannot deduce from Michal's ruse about David being sick in bed that the *tĕrāpîm* were used for healing purposes. To argue that the mention of sickness in this one pericope denotes the use of *tĕrāpîm* for healing would be akin to stating that the sole mention of weapons of war in conjunction with the *tĕrāpîm* in Judg 18:16-17 denotes a military use of the *tĕrāpîm.*

As mentioned above, scholars have looked to the function of the *ilānu* in the

Nuzi texts to find a parallel to the function of the *tĕrāpîm* in the Hebrew Bible. In the words of one of the earliest proponents of this parallel, "the possessor of them [the *ilānu*/the *tĕrāpîm*] had a claim *de iure* to property if not *de facto*. (...) Laban's anxiety to recover his gods, like Rachel's desire to possess them, did not depend solely on their divinity or their value, but on the fact that the possessor of them was presumptive heir" (SMITH 1932:34-35). Until recently this suggested function for the *tĕrāpîm* has predominated biblical scholarship with some scholars preferring to emphasize property and inheritance rights while others emphasized the role of the *tĕrāpîm* for designating family-headship (*pater familias*; e.g. SPEISER, *Genesis* [Garden City 1964] 250; DRAFFKORN 1957:216-224). N. SARNA (*The JPS Torah Commentary: Genesis* [Philadelphia 1989] 216) has challenged the inheritance theory with respect to Jacob's case (→Jacob). "The *terafim*", he writes, "could not have assured inheritance rights since the patriarch claims nothing from Laban and, in any case, is leaving Mesopotamia for good" (see too DELLER 1981:48-57). With regard to family-headship, SPANIER (1992:405) has recently argued that Rachel's actions in Gen 31 were a part of her "continuing struggle for primacy within Jacob's household. (...) Rachel perceived that the teraphim would invest her own son →Joseph with a mantle of authority which would override all other considerations."

Finally, there are those who promote the divinatory function of the *tĕrāpîm*. Without a doubt, this function is the best attested among the occurrences of *tĕrāpîm* in the OT. In one way or another the word *tĕrāpîm* is associated with divinatory practices of some kind in all of the passages except for the episodes dealing with Rachel's theft of the *tĕrāpîm* in Gen 31 (but see below) and Michal's ruse hiding the *tĕrāpîm* in David's bed in 1 Sam 19.

The two examples which are the most explicit come from the late passages of Zech 10:2 and Ezek 21:26[21]. In Zech 10:2 the *tĕrāpîm* are portrayed as *oracular* devices which '*speak* iniquity' (*dibbĕrû ʾāwen*). They are condemned along with 'diviners' (*qôsĕmîm*) and false dream interpreters. Ezek 21:26 contains the famous passage about king Nebuchadrezzar using various types of divination to decide which fork in the road to take. Among the divinatory practices attributed to him are belomancy (use of arrows), the *tĕrāpîm*, and hepatoscopy (divination through examining livers). All three of these practices are summed up in Ezek 21:26 under the general heading of 'practicing divination' (*liqsom qāsem*). A third passage which also associates the *tĕrāpîm* with divination (*qesem*) is 1 Sam 15:23. Here too it is treated pejoratively and once again paired with 'iniquity' (*ʾāwen ûtĕrāpîm*). The *tĕrāpîm* are also found in collocation with the ephod (Judg 17:5; 18: 14.17.18.20; Hos 3:4). While the full picture of the ephod as a sacred vestment remains somewhat murky, its role in divination is beyond doubt (cf. 1 Sam 30:7-8 as well as the attachment of the Urim and Thummim to the breastpiece of the ephod).

Divination was a complex and highly specialized enterprise in the ancient Near East (especially in Mesopotamia but also in ancient Israel). Can we determine more precisely the type of divination with which the *tĕrāpîm* were associated? To judge from the passages just listed above, the word *tĕrāpîm* can be a generic term for tools of divination. Yet on one occasion (2 Kgs 23:24) the *tĕrāpîm* are listed alongside of the *ʾōbôt* and the *yiddĕʿōnîm*. These terms are clearly associated with necromancy and the shades of the dead (see →Dead, Spirit of the dead and Wizard). The collocation of these terms in 2 Kgs 23:24 may be sheer coincidence (or an editor's artificial attempt to make Josiah's reform look very thorough). On the other hand, the *tĕrāpîm* are also termed *ʾĕlōhîm* (Gen 31:30, 32; Judg 18:24) and this fact may provide a key to solving much of the mystery (as well as tying in the Mesopotamian material mentioned above). It is well documented that *ʾĕlōhîm*/*ilu* can refer to the dead (LEWIS 1989:49-51; *JBL* 110

[1991] 600-603; VAN DER TOORN 1990:210-211). Note the Mesopotamian material above which pairs the *ilānu* with the *eṭemmū* or *mētu*. In short, those scholars who have recently been suggesting that the Mesopotamian material underscores the use of the *tĕrāpîm* as ancestral figurines are certainly correct. It seems likely that the *tĕrāpîm* may have been ancestor figurines which functioned in necromantic practices in particular as well as divinatory practices in general (cf. HOFFNER 1968:68, who notes that both the Heb *tĕrāpîm* and the Hit *tarpi* have "a pronounced chthonic orientation"). If this is true, then Rachel's *tĕrāpîm* (which are referred to as *ʾĕlōhîm*) could also have been divinatory in nature and thus parallel to *all* of the other biblical passages (except for the ruse in 1 Sam 19) which mention the *tĕrāpîm* next to divination. In fact, as pointed out by GREENBERG (1962:239 n.2), there are many interpreters throughout history (*Tanḥûma Wayyēṣē*, *Tg. Ps.-J.*, Rashbam, Ibn Ezra, Qimhi; cf. N. SARNA *The JPS Torah Commentary: Genesis* [Philadelphia 1989] 216) who have asserted that Rachel's motive for stealing Laban's *tĕrāpîm* was to prevent him from using them in a divinatory fashion so as to detect Jacob's escape.

Lastly we may be able to tie in the form of the *tĕrāpîm* to this possible necromantic function. It is quite clear that necromantic rituals in Mesopotamia involved substitute figurines which often represented the ghost (*ṣalam* GIDIM) or the dead person (*ṣalam* LÚ.UG$_X$), among other things (cf. J. A. SCURLOCK, *Magical Means of Dealing with Ghosts in Ancient Mesopotamia* [diss. Chicago 1988] 53-64). In one instance, after mixing a concoction, one puts it on the figurine. As a result, "when you call upon him, he will answer you" (see I. J. FINKEL, *AfO* 29-30 [1983-84] 5, 9). This oracular aspect of the necromantic figurine fits well with the description of the *tĕrāpîm* 'speaking' in the divinatory context of Zech 10:2.

IV. *Bibliography*

P. ACKROYD, The Teraphim, *ExpTim* 62 (1950-51) 378-380; W. F. ALBRIGHT, *Archaeology and the Religion of Israel* (Garden City 1968[5]); ALBRIGHT, Are the Ephod and the Teraphim Mentioned in Ugaritic Literature?, *BASOR* 83 (1941) 39-42; M. BAYLISS, The Cult of Dead Kin in Assyria and Babylonia, *Iraq* 35 (1973) 115-125; E. CASSIN, Une querelle de famille, *Studies on the Civilization and Culture of Nuzi and the Hurrians in Honor of Ernest R. Lacheman* (ed. M. A. Morrison & D. I. Owen; Winona Lake 1981) 37-46; K. DELLER, Die Hausgötter der Familie Šukrija S. Ḫuja, *Studies on the Civilization and Culture of Nuzi and the Hurrians in Honor of Ernest R. Lacheman* (Winona Lake 1981) 47-76; A. E. DRAFFKORN, Ilāni/Elohim, *JBL* 76 (1957) 216-224; C. H. GORDON, Teraphim, *IDB* IV (1962) 574; M. GREENBERG, Another Look at Rachel's Theft of the Teraphim, *JBL* 81 (1962) 239-248; G. HOFFMANN & H. GRESSMANN, Teraphim. Masken und Winkorakel in Ägypten und Vorderasien, *ZAW* 40 (1922) 75-137; H. A. HOFFNER, The Linguistic Origins of Teraphim, *Bibliotheca Sacra* 124 (1967) 230-238; *HOFFNER, Hittite Tarpiš and Hebrew Terāphîm, *JNES* 27 (1968) 61-68; C. J. LABUSCHAGNE, Teraphim —A New Proposal for Its Etymology, *VT* 16 (1966) 115-117; T. J. LEWIS, *Cults of the Dead in Ancient Israel and Ugarit* (HSM 39; Atlanta 1989); *O. LORETZ, Die Teraphim als "Ahnen-Götter-Figur(in)en" im Lichte der Texte aus Nuzi, Emar und Ugarit, *UF* 24 (1992) 133-178 [& lit]; *H. ROUILLARD & J. TROPPER, TRPYM, rituels de guérison et culte des ancêtres d'après 1 Samuel XIX 11-17 et les textes parallèles d'Assur et de Nuzi, *VT* 37 (1987) 340-361; K. SEYBOLD, *tĕrāfîm* Idol(e), *THAT* 2 (1976) 1057-1060; S. SMITH, What Were the Teraphim?, *JTS* 33 (1932) 33-36; K. SPANIER, Rachel's Theft of the Teraphim: Her Struggle for Family Primacy, *VT* 42 (1992) 404-412; *K. VAN DER TOORN, The Nature of the Biblical Teraphim in the Light of the Cuneiform Evidence, *CBQ* 52 (1990) 203-222; J. TROPPER, *Nekromantie. Totenbefragung im Alten Orient und im Alten Testament* (AOAT 223; Neukirchen-Vluyn 1989); A. TSUKIMOTO, *Untersuchungen zur Totenpflege* (kispum) *im Alten Mesopotamien* (AOAT 216; Neukirchen-Vluyn 1985); E. F. DE WARD, Superstition and Judgment: Archaic Methods of Finding a Verdict, *ZAW* 89 (1977) 1-19.

T. J. LEWIS

TEREBINTH אלה

I. אלה I, Pistacia terebinthus, has been explained by W. F. ALBRIGHT as a Hebrew form of Canaanite *ʾēlat*, goddess, the feminine of *ʾēl*, which is also applied to →Asherah as →El's consort (ALBRIGHT 1968:165). The concept of the terebinth as a holy tree is well-known in the OT, but the terebinth is never seen as a representative of Yahweh. Sometimes the terebinth is connected with idolatry in a way that presupposes a relationship between the terebinth and a foreign deity, probably Asherah. In these cases, the attitude is clearly polemic. But whether the word אלה itself connoted the meaning 'goddess' is uncertain.

II. According to the common view, both אלה and אל derive from the Hebrew root *ʾWL II 'to be first' or 'to be strong'. POPE, however, claims that the etymology of אל remains obscure and sees no possible way to decide whether words like אל, אלה, and אלון should be connected with the middle weak root ʾWL/ʾYL or with some other root (1955:16-19). Uncertainty about the etymology suggests that in this case, as in many others, it may be more illuminating to analyze the semantic field of the word.

The conception of the tree as holy is well-known in the Near Eastern world, where pictures of holy trees are often found on seals or as decoration in temples (Cf. *BRL*² 34-36). The intimate relationship between goddesses like Asherah (in Ugaritic texts the consort of El, Athirat) and the tree (often the palm-tree) shows that trees connote fertility. For further information on holy trees in the Near East in general (Ugarit, Egypt, Mesopotamia) see JAROŠ 1974:214-217.

III. In the OT, the terebinth is frequently mentioned in connection with holy places like →Shechem (Gen 35:4), Ophrah (Judg 6:11.19) and Jabesh (1 Chr 10:12). In the book of Hosea the offerings under →oak, poplar, and terebinth are condemned as idolatry (Hos 4:13). In Isaiah, the terebinth is used as metaphor in ways which suggest that the terebinth was considered a holy tree by the prophet's audience.

More generally speaking, attitudes towards the terebinth are ambiguous. On the one hand, the terebinth, like the oak, suggests the sanctity of a given place. In Gen 35:4 Jacob hides the foreign gods under the terebinth that was near Shechem: an attitude that may reflect an old custom to hide valuable things at a sacred place. At any rate this text shows a respect for the foreign gods that is not found in the texts concerning the restoration of the cult, like 2 Kgs 23:4-25 (KEEL 1973:312-313, 331). Like wise it is preferable to bury one's dead under a tree. In 1 Chr 10:12 Saul and his sons are buried under a terebinth, and in Gen 35:8 Rebekkah's nurse is buried under an oak below Bethel. On some occasions, a holy person sits under a terebinth, in Judg 6:11 the →angel of Yahweh, in 1 Kgs 14:13 a man of God. The terebinth at Shechem is mentioned not only in Genesis, but also in Josh 24:26 (note the different spelling). Under the terebinth, in the sanctuary of Yahweh, Joshua sets up a great stone as a witness, after having made a covenant with the people. Isa 6:13, too, presupposes the idea of the holy tree, when it is said that the stump of the fallen terebinth (terebinth and oak are here used as parallels) is holy seed.

In these texts, the holiness of the terebinth seems to be taken for granted; but the tree itself is never identified with a deity. The covenant in Josh 24, for instance, is neither with the tree, nor with the stone, but between Yahweh and his people. Neither is the holy seed in Isa 6:13 identified with a deity: it is used metaphorically to announce the coming king (NIELSEN 1989:150-153).

In the polemics against the cult under every green tree, prophets like Hosea and Ezekiel condemn the cult under the terebinths (as in Hos 4:13; Ezek 6:13). The cult must have been some kind of fertility cult, and the reference to the terebinths may indicate a special relationship between this tree and a goddess (ALBRIGHT 1968:165). In Isa 1:30-31, the prophet uses tree imagery to spell out the doom of his audience. They shall be like a terebinth that withers, and they shall burn together with their strong ones, i.e. their idols. Possibly there is a play on words in v 29 between an implied אלים (gods) and אילים (the strong trees). This would make the oracle even more polemical (NIELSEN 1989:207).

IV. *Bibliography*

W. F. ALBRIGHT, *Yahweh and the Gods of Canaan. A Historical Analysis of Two Contrasting Faiths* (London 1968); G. DALMAN, *Arbeit und Sitte in Palästina I,1-2* (Gütersloh 1928); K. JAROŠ, *Die Stellung des Elohisten zur kanaanäischen Religion* (Göttingen 1974); O. KEEL, Das Vergraben der 'fremden Götter' in Genesis XXXV 4b, *VT* 23 (1973) 305-336; K. NIELSEN, *There is Hope for a Tree. The Tree as Metaphor in Isaiah* (Sheffield 1989); M. H. POPE, *El in the Ugaritic Texts* (Leiden 1955); P. WELTEN, Baum, sakraler, *BRL*^{2} 34-35; M. ZOHARY, *Pflanzen der Bibel. Vollständiges Handbuch* (Stuttgart 1982).

K. NIELSEN

TERROR OF THE NIGHT פחד לילה

I. *Paḥad laylâ* is *hap.leg.* in the OT, in Ps 91:5, where it appears in close conjunction with several terms referring to various demons (see below). Another combination of the word *paḥad*, lit. 'terror, dread', and *laylâ*, lit. 'night', occurs in Cant 3:8 where it also refers to a certain type of demon (see already the Targumîm and KRAUSS [1936] for references to other rabbinical sources). See also Deut 28:66.

The understanding of *paḥad* in Ps 91:5 as 'terror' is not the only one. M. DAHOOD has suggested e.g. the meaning 'pack (of dogs)' on the alleged basis of Ug *pḥd* (*Psalms II* [AB 17; Garden City 1979] 331). Dahood applied this meaning to other occurrences of *paḥad*, e.g. Cant 3:8; Prov 3:25; and more (see *RSP*, I 439 for a summary). There have been some attempts to relate *laylâ* etymologically to →Lilith (Is 34:14), Akk *(Ardat) lilî*, a night demon (DE FRAINE 1959:375). But this is no more than a folk etymology (*HALAT* 502b). Functionally, however, the demon *paḥad laylâ* reveals traits similar to those of the Mesopotamian *lilû* and *ardat lilî*, esp. in its occurrence in Cant 3:8 (see below).

paḥad denotes the object of fear rather than fear itself or its effects (psychological or physical) (MÜLLER 1989:554.556). The relationship between *paḥad* and *laylâ* does not necessarily need to be construed as an objective genitive, e.g., *paḥad 'ôyēb* (Ps 64:2, thus MÜLLER 1989:557), *laylâ* being the object of fear (*HALAT* 871, 1a), because it can also be treated as a *genitivus explicativus* (*Ges.* 128 k-q) denoting the time when such demons usually appear (cf. Deut 28: 66). Night and darkness are the normal context and cover of demons (thus clearly Cant 3:8).

II. Among the host of Mesopotamian demons, *Lilû* (Sum **lú.líl.lá** 'wind-man') and *Lilītu/Ardat lilî* most resemble the biblical *paḥad laylâ*. These demons seem to have been attached particularly to pregnant women and new-borns whom they harmed (FARBER, *RLA* 7 [1987-90] 23-24). A similar role is ascribed in cuneiform sources to the demon Lamashtu. In later texts, they are conceived as harmful to brides and grooms, whom they attack on their wedding night and prevent the consummation of the marriage (S. LACKENBACHER, *RA* 65 [1971] 119-154; M. MALUL, *JEOL* 32 [1991/1992: 78-85]). *Lilītu* survived a long time and occupies a central place in later Jewish demonology, whence she passed even into Arab demonology. Here, she seems to have retained her ancient character as a baby-killer, though she also appears (in Jewish *Qabbala*) as a stealer of men's semen (G. SCHOLEM, *EncJud* Vol 11, 245-249). As an attacker of brides and grooms she comes close to the *incubus* and *succubus* demons known all over the world.

III. A cursory look at the context in which *paḥad laylâ* occurs in Ps 91 reveals its demonic identity (OESTERLEY 1962:407-409). This psalm abounds with names of other demons, such as →*deber* (v 6, Pestilence), →*qeṭeb* (v 6, Destruction; the LXX reads here also καὶ δαιμονίου μεσηβρινοῦ = *wěšēd ṣohorāyim*, 'and a noon demon' instead of *yāšûd ṣohorāyim*, 'that wastes at noonday' [DE FRAINE 1959:377-379; cf. *Midr. Ps.* 91:3]; for *šēd* see also Ps 106:37 and Deut 32:17, OESTERLEY 1962:408-409; Shed), *peten* (v 13, →Serpent) and *tannîn* 'sea dragon' (v 13, perhaps meaning 'jackals', see also →Tannin), as well as *šaḥal* 'lion' and *kěpîr* 'young lion'—both perhaps denoting lion-headed demons (v 13, cf. Job 4:10-11). Also noteworthy are the verbs *hālak* 'to stalk', *šôd* 'to waste', *nāgaš* 'to draw near', and *qārab* 'to approach' (vv 6-7.10), all of which are commonly used in connection with activities of demons. All rabbinical sources, *Midrash* and *Targum,* identify here a host of *mazziqîm* and *šēdîm* (see in general OESTERLEY 1962; DE FRAINE 1959; KRAUSS 1936; note that *Gen. Rab.* 36:1 interprets *paḥad* in Job 21:9 also as meaning evil spirits—*mazziqîm*). In Jewish sources and liturgy the psalm is in fact called "a song for evil encounters" to be recited before sleep (*bSheb.* 15b; *Midr. Ps.* 91:1; cf. DE FRAINE 1959:374 n. 3; OESTERLEY 1962:407). It has been suggested that it refers here to various demons who have power over different phases of the day (morning, noon, evening and [mid]night; see DE FRAINE 1959; OESTERLEY 1962:407-411; and for the general belief in such demons throughout history see SPEYER 1984 [& lit]; for the Semitic world cf. W. H. WORRELL, *JAOS* 38 [1918] 160-166). The demon *paḥad laylâ* is then in charge of the night, the scene of his attacks (cf. the *mašḥît* →Destroyer in Ex 12:23, cf. 29 and 11:4-5; cf. *bPesaḥ.* 112b where one is counselled not to go out alone at night for fear of the haunting night demons). Note *Zohar* 11: 163b: 'dread in the nights' = 'Samael and his female', i.e. Lilith.

The name of this demon is clearly appellative, reflecting its most salient characteristics: Terror and night/darkness. These characteristics occur elsewhere in the OT in contexts which reveal other aspects of this demon only vaguely hinted at in Ps 91. Note especially Job 18:5-21 where an interesting combination is attested between the darkness falling on the wicked and the terror which ensnares him like a trap. The picture is of a person haunted by various evil spirits and demons (see →First-Born of Death, v 13; →King of Terrors v 14), who are said to catch their victims by nets and traps (vv 8-10, with various words for traps). Another colourful portrayal of intense (personified) night terror is in Job 4:12-16, where Eliphaz is terrified by an apparition (see the word *rûaḥ* 'ghost' in v 15) which appeared to him in the middle of the night (cf. Job 7:14; Isa 29:1-8). Saul is said to have been terrified (from *bāʿat,* for which see also Job 18:11 with *ballāhôt;* Ps 18:5 with *beliyyaʿal* →Belial; and Job 3:5 with *kimrîrê-yôm*) by the →Evil Spirit from God. For the trap used by these demons to ensnare their victims see especially the common combination *paḥad wāpaḥat wāpāḥ*, 'Terror and pit and trap', in Isa 24:17-18; Jer 48:43-44; cf. Lam 3:47.

The trap, which also occurs here in Ps 91:3, is only a metaphor for the element of suddenness, another characteristic of these demons (see the observations about *paḥad pitʾōm* below). They are said to lie in wait for their victim (cf. Gen 4:7 obliquely referring to the →Rābiṣu) and to fall upon him suddenly and unexpectedly. The terms used to denote this characteristic (*nāpal* 'to pounce upon', *petaʿ, pitʾōm* 'suddenly') are used also in the context of wars and in descriptions of attacks by enemies as well as by →wild beasts (for the relationship between demons and wild beasts see OESTERLEY 1962:410); see, e.g., Jer 6:22-26; Ps 64; and note the reference to the flying arrow in Ps 91:5.

A related significant expression is *paḥad pitʾōm* 'sudden terror' in Prov 3:25 (occurring also in Job 22:10), which the person is instructed not to fear (*ʾal tîrāʾ*, cf. *lōʾ tîrāʾ mippaḥad laylâ* 'You shall not fear Terror of the night!'). According to v 24 it is clear that this 'sudden terror' comes at night;

compare vv 23 and 26 with Ps 91:3.12. In view of the parallelism of *paḥad laylâ* and the 'flying arrow' in the second hemistich of v 5, the expression *ḥeṣ pitʾōm* 'a sudden arrow' (Ps 64:8; cf. Prov 7:22-23) suggests that the expression *paḥad pitʾōm* reflects a similar entity. Here it is interesting to note that according to Talmudic *Midrash*, a demon which shoots like an arrow is identified with Lilith. Furthermore, the meteorite was known in Jewish tradition as 'the arrow of Lilith' (OESTERLEY 1962:409; cf. also DE FRAINE 1959:375.376).

Other terms for terror, dread, such as *biʿût, ʾêmâ, pallāṣût, běhālâ* (for a collection of such terms see Exod 15:14-16; cf. also Is 21:2-5), evoke in their respective contexts a picture similar to that described above. See especially the use of *biʿût* in Ps 88:17-18, where *biʿût* occurs in parallelism with *ḥarôn* 'anger', and both are personified. Job 6:4 reads as follows: "For the arrows of the Almighty (→Shadday) are within me, my spirit drinks their poison (*ḥēmâ*), the terrors (*biʿûtê*) of God are arrayed against me." The *ḥārôn* 'anger' in Ps 88:17 parallels the *ḥēmâ* 'poison' in Job 6:4, and the latter is characteristic of the arrow! (Cf. Deut 32:23-25 where 'arrows', →Resheph, Qeteb, →Behemoth, "the venom [*ḥēmâ*] of serpents", and 'fear' [*ʾêmâh*]" occur together.) Also, the phrase about "the terrors of God" being "arrayed" (*ʿārak*) against their victim recalls the simile of the victim placed as a target for the arrows of the enemy in Lam 3:12 and Job 16:12 (cf. Ps 11:2). The word *ḥēmâ* 'poison, venom' (Akk *imtu*) is said to be a characteristic of the host of demons and monsters created by →Tiamat as an army in the war against →Marduk (*Ee* I 136-137 and cf. Deut 32:33; Ps 58:5; 140:4).

Another aspect of the demon Terror of the night is particularly relevant to Cant 3:8. On the theory that the Song of Solomon was a collection of wedding songs, it reflects the widespread belief in evil spirits and night demons lying in wait to harm the young couple, particularly whilst the marriage is being consummated: cf. the attendants carrying swords stationed in the bridal chamber to provide protection for the newly-wed couple (KRAUSS 1936:323-330; cf. L. KÖHLER, *ZAW* 34 [1914] 147-148 & lit; cf. M. MALUL, *JESHO* 32 [1989] 241-278, esp. 262-263.271). 'Terror of the night' was that particular demon fond of causing harm to the newly-weds on their wedding night, rather like the Mesopotamian demons Lilû and Ardat-lilî.

The polytheistic view reflected in Ps 91 should not be overlooked. On the one hand, there is a great god, but on the other a host of demons and evil spirits (cf. H. RINGGREN, *Israelite Religion* [Philadelphia 1963] 100-103). However, scholars have noted the polemical nature of the psalm, calling for a complete trust in →Yahweh as against the common resort to magic means for warding off evil spirits (e.g. DE FRAINE 1959; OESTERLEY 1962). Significant here is the verb *šāmar* 'to guard' in v 11 (Yahweh's angels shall 'guard' the believer against all demonic powers) which occurs also in Ex 12:42 *(lêl šimmurîm)* in connection with the protection against the nocturnal *mašḥît* (cf. KRAUSS 1936:329 [referring also to Num 6: 24].327). Also pointing in the same direction is the tendency towards demythologization reflected in the identification of these demons with human enemies and with the wicked (e.g. Ps 55; 64). Finally, in certain OT contexts those same demons and evil spirits can even become God's messengers and agents (e.g. Deut 32:23-25; Ps 78:49; cf. Ex 23:27-28).

IV. *Bibliography*

J. DE FRAINE, Le «Démon du midi» (Ps 91 [90], 6), *Bib* 40 (1959) 372-383 (& lit); S. KRAUSS, Der richtige Sinn von "Schrecken in der Nacht" HL III.8, *Occident and Orient. Gaster Anniversary Volume* (ed. B. Schindler & A. Marmorstein; London 1936) 323-330 (& lit); H.-P. MÜLLER, פַּחַד *pāhad, TWAT* 6 (1987-89) 552-562; W. O. E. OESTERLEY, *The Psalms* (London 1962); W. SPEYER, Mittag und Mitternacht als heilige Zeiten in Antike und Christentum, *Vivarium, Festschrift Theodor Klauser zum 90. Geburtstag* (ed. E. Dassmann; Münster 1984) 314-326.

M. MALUL

THANATOS Θάνατος Death

I. Thanatos is the Greek mythological personification of the power of death as a god or a demon. It occurs as the name of a demonic power in the NT (for OT see →Mot) in 9 passages (out of a total of 120 occurrences of the word *thanatos*) in Paul (e.g. 1 Cor 15:26, 54-56) and in Rev (e.g. 20:13-14).

II. Thanatos as a personification is not frequently found in Greek literature; and when it occurs, it is often doubtful whether the personified Thanatos is merely a poetic metaphor or a real figure of popular belief (KERN 1926:262-3; LESKY 1934:1245; VON GEISAU 1975:648-9; cf. also the remark in Hesychius s.v. θάνατος· ὅ τε θεὸς καὶ ὃ πάσχομεν, τέλος ὂν τοῦ βίου, "Thanatos: both the deity and what we suffer, namely the end of life"). The earliest occurrence of Thanatos personified is in Homer's *Iliad* XVI 667-675, where Zeus commands Apollo to take Sarpedon's dead body away from the battlefield and to put him in the hands of "the twin-brothers Sleep and Death" (Ὕπνῳ καὶ Θανάτῳ διδυμάοσιν, cf. XIV 231; other parallels in LESKY 1934:1251), who will quickly bring him to Lycia in order to bury him there. Hesiod mentions Thanatos and Hypnos (together with Doom and Fate) as the children of Night (*Theog.* 211-2, although Sophocles, *Oed. Col.* 1574-7 has Gē and Tartaros as parents of Thanatos); he portrays them as follows: "There the sons of gloomy Night have their dwelling, Sleep and Death, fearsome gods. (...) The one of them ranges the earth and the broad back of the sea gentle and mild towards men, but the other has a heart of iron and a pitiless spirit of bronze in his breast. That man is his whom he once catches, and he is hateful (ἐχθρός) even to the immortal gods" (*Theog.* 758-66, tr. M. L. WEST, *Hesiod, Theogony, Works and Days* [Oxford 1988] 25). The image of Thanatos as one who snatches away people out of life is fully developed by Euripides in the *Alcestis* (438 BCE), a play in which Thanatos is one of the characters. Here we find the widespread folktale about a man destined to die but whose wife consents to die instead of him; then a hero fights with Death to force him to release her. In the *Alcestis* Heracles besieges Thanatos and brings Alcestis back to her husband. In the opening scene, which is a dialogue between Apollo and Thanatos, the god clearly regards Thanatos as his adversary, whose mind Apollo, although a god, cannot change and whose decision is irrevocable (see esp. *Alc.* 49-62). The whole story of Heracles' victory over Thanatos is reminiscent of the tale of Sisyphus who outwitted Death and bound him so that nobody could die any longer (LESKY 1934:1246; KROLL 1932:373; *ibid.* 423-47 on Seneca's treatment of the theme in his Hercules dramas). In tomb inscriptions Thanatos is often called a jealous, hard, bitter, merciless etc. demon (δαίμων πικρός, ἄκριτος, λυπηρός, βαρύς, βάσκανος, κακός, πονηρός, references in WASER 1924:493). But sometimes Thanatos is regarded as a liberator from the evils of life; so e.g. in Sophocles, *Aiax* 854, where the tormented protagonist says, "O Thanatos, Thanatos, come now and look upon me", or *Philoctetes* 797-8, "O Thanatos, Thanatos, how can it be that I call on you always, day by day, and that you cannot come to me?"

In the classical and Hellenistic periods the functions of Thanatos seem gradually to have been taken over by →Hades and Charon (ROHDE 1898: II 199 n.3, 249 n.1; Charon is the only one of the three who has survived into modern Greek folk-belief). The fact that Thanatos was considered to be an inexorable deity may have contributed to this god's having no cult. An additional factor in this respect was certainly that in educated circles death was not regarded as a god or a demon but as a natural process; e.g. Carneades' scathing remarks about the deification of "Love, Guile, Fear, Toil, Envy, Fate, Old Age, *Death*, Darkness, Misery, Lamentation, Favour, Fraud, Obstinacy", etc., in Cicero, *De natura deorum* III 17, 44. The isolated reference in Pausanias III 18, 1 to the effect that there were cult-images of Sleep and Death in Sparta (cf. Plutarch, *Cleomedes* 9,1) are untrustworthy (LESKY 1934:1257-8). In art, mostly on vases, Thanatos is often represented as a winged demon (see the collection of pictures in WASER 1924:502-524; also the comments in LESKY 1934:1258-68). Hades and especially Charon seem to have played a much more prominent role in folk-belief than Thanatos, who became more and more a literary figure, even in the Orphic *Hymn to Thanatos*, no. 87 (see also the collection of statements about Death/death in Stobaeus' *Eclogae* IV 51).

III. In post-biblical Judaism we meet the personified Thanatos most clearly in the *Testament of Abraham* 15-20. Abraham refuses to follow →Michael to heaven, i.e., to die. Then God bids Michael to summon Death "who is called the (one of) abominable countenance and merciless look" (rec. A, 16:1) and who must take Abraham "with soft speech" (16:5). In spite of a beautiful disguise, he does not succeed. Only after long dialogues and negotiations does Abraham surrender: he kisses the right hand of Death and departs. Although there are some traces of personification of death in the OT (→Mot), Death as an acting and speaking figure in *Test. Abr.* is undoubtedly due to influence of Greek literature, especially the *Alcestis*.

IV. Although in the large majority of cases the use of the word *thanatos* in the NT does not show any tendency towards personification, there are some clear (and some less clear) examples of this phenomenon. In Rom 5:14 and 17 Paul writes that *thanatos* ruled as king (ἐβασίλευσεν) from Adam to →Moses because of the trespass of one man; and in 6:9 he adds that after →Christ's resurrection *thanatos* no longer exercises power over him. In 1 Cor 15:26 Paul says that the last enemy (ἐχθρός, as in Hesiod, *Theog.* 766) to be destroyed at the eschaton is *thanatos*; and in 15:54-55 he addresses *thanatos* with the defying words: "Where, O Death, is your victory? Where, O Death, is your sting?", because "Death has been swallowed up in victory". Although one cannot say on the basis of these few texts that death is in Paul's mind a full-fledged personal being, there can be little doubt that, just as in the case of →'sin' and →'law', Paul attributes to 'death' a superhuman and supernatural power that verges on personification (or rather demonification). The close connection between the powers of 'sin', 'death', and 'law' as co-operators in Paul's concept of 'anti-salvation-history' is a well-known feature of his theology (RÖHSER 1987).

In the Apocalypse of John the risen Christ says to the seer that he has "the keys of Death and of Hades" (Rev 1:18); in 6:8 the seer sees in a vision a pale green horse, and "its rider's name was Death, and Hades followed with him"; in 20:13-4 he sees how "Death and Hades gave up the dead that were in them" and how they "were thrown into the lake of fire"; and in 21:4 it is triumphantly said that "Death will be no more". Here we have in visionary language the same eschatological message as Paul's in 1 Cor 15:54-55, *mutatis multis mutandis*; the mythological imagery of Rev allows the author to develop the personification further than Paul did, especially in Rev 6:8.

V. In early Christian literature after the NT, one does not find many instances of personification of death, as was to be expected, but there are some notable cases, the most striking of which is found in the so-called *Book of the Resurrection of Christ by Bartholomew the Apostle*, which is extant only in a Coptic translation from the Greek original (ed. and tr. by E. A. WALLIS BUDGE, *Coptic Apocrypha in the Dialect of Upper Egypt* [London 1913]; see the summary by M. R. JAMES in his *The Apocryphal New Testament* [Oxford 1924] 181-186). In this work Thanatos asks after the death of Jesus why his soul has not gone down to Hades, whereupon he orders that Jesus be brought before him; thereafter follows a very colourful description of the confrontation between Thanatos and Christ, in which Christ is victorious (KROLL 1932:77-81). Possibly Christ is depicted here as greater than →Heracles (SIMON 1955:112-115). Another very vivid description of Christ's victory over Death is again found in an early Coptic writing, *The History of Joseph the Carpenter* (BRANDON 1960/61: 333-335).

VI. *Bibliography*
S. G. F. BRANDON, The Personification of Death in Some Ancient Religions, *BJRL* 43 (1960/61) 317-335; R. BULTMANN, θάνατος κτλ., *TWNT* 3 (1938) 7-25; J. C. EGER, *Le sommeil et la mort dans la Grèce antique* (Paris 1966); H. von GEISAU, Thanatos, *KP* V (1975) 648-9; O. KERN, *Die Religion der Griechen* I (Berlin 1926); J. KROLL, *Gott und Hölle. Der Mythos vom Descensus-kampfe* (Leipzig-Berlin 1932; repr. Darmstadt 1963); *A. LESKY, Thanatos, *RE* 5A (1934) 1245-68; G. RÖHSER, *Metaphorik und Personifikation der Sünde* (Tübingen 1987); E. ROHDE, *Psyche. Seelencult und Unsterblichkeitsglaube der Griechen* (Leipzig-Tübingen 1898; repr. Darmstadt 1961); M. SIMON, *Hercule et le christianisme* (Paris 1955); *O. WASER, Thanatos, *ALGRM* 5 (1924) 481-527.

P. W. VAN DER HORST

THEMIS Θέμις

I. Themis is the Greek goddess of what is just and lawful (θέμις = 'law', 'justice', 'custom', probably deriving from the stem θε-, 'to lay down, set, establish'; but see HIRZEL 1907: 53-56; EHRENBERG 1921: 41-43); she is the embodiment of the 'social imperative', the 'social conscience' (HARRISON 1927, 485-6). In the Bible *themis* does not occur as a goddess, but only twice in 2 Maccabees in the expression οὐ θέμις, 'it is not lawful'.

II. Themis is one of the many personified and deified abstract concepts (or rather a case of 'Person-Bereicheinheit', thus PÖTSCHER 1975:676) in Greek culture. The personification of all that is lawful and just, she is the daughter of Ouranos (→Heaven) and Gaia/Gē (Hesiod, *Theogony* 135; this perhaps indicates that the early Greeks saw justice and lawfulness as the foundation and basis of the human and divine order, thus HUNGER 1959, 397; but she is sometimes identified with Gaia (→Earth), e.g. Aeschylus, *Prometheus V.* 209-10; HARRISON 1927: 480-1). Themis is one of →Zeus' wives, and the mother of the Horai (→Dike [from whom she is often hardly distinguishable], Eirene, Eunomia; *Theog.* 901-2) and the Moirai. As a personification, Themis is found already in Homer, where she convenes the assembly of the gods (*Il.* 20:4-6; cf. 15:87-91 and *Od.* 2:68). According to later writers she took over from her mother the Delphic oracle and then gave it to →Apollo's grandmother, Phoibe (Aeschylus, *Eumenides*, prol.; Plutarch, *De defectu oraculorum* 21, 421C). Pausanias attests many altars and temples to her, although these cult centres seem to be limited to Central and Northern Greece (I 22, 1; II 27, 5; V 14, 10; IX 22, 1; IX 25, 4; X 5, 6; cf. also the inscriptions mentioned by LATTE 1934: 1628). In the imperial period, mysteries of Themis seem to have been created (see *Orphic Hymn* 79; Clemens Alex., *Protrepticus* II 19), although not much is known about them. For statutes of Themis see the pictures in WENIGER 1924: 578-581.

III. In the Bible the word *themis* is used only by the author of 2 Maccabees, in the very common expression that something is οὐ θέμις: 6:20, "... to refuse things that it is not *themis* to eat" (i.e., pork), and 12:14, about Judas' enemies who were "blaspheming and saying things which it is not *themis* to say". Here 'not *themis*' is used to indicate that certain types of food and certain forms of language are irreconcilable with obedience to God's will. Cf. the use of οὐ θεμιτόν in Tob 2:13.

IV. *Bibliography*
V. E. EHRENBERG, *Die Rechtsidee im frühen Griechentum* (Leipzig 1921) 3-52; *J. E. HARRISON, *Themis. A Study of the Social Origins of Greek Religion* (Cambridge 1927[2]; repr. London 1977) 480-535; *R. HIRZEL, *Themis, Dike und Verwandtes* (Leipzig 1907) 1-56; H. HUNGER, *Lexikon der griechischen und römischen Mythologie* (Wien 1959[6]) 397-398; K. LATTE, Themis, *RE* 5A (Stuttgart 1934) 1626-1630; W. PÖTSCHER, Themis, *KP* V (München 1975) 676; H. VOS, *ΘΕΜΙΣ* (diss. Utrecht 1956); *L. WENIGER, Themis, *ALGRM* V (1924) 570-606.

P. W. VAN DER HORST

THEOS → GOD II

THESSALOS Θεσσαλός

I. Thessalos ('Thessalian') is the eponymous hero of the Thessalians, the inhabitants of Thessaly in northern Greece. His name may be found in Thessalonike (modern Saloniki), the second city of modern Greece and already a place of importance by the time of Acts.

II. The Greeks often traced the beginnings of a tribe or a city to a significant person of mythic times (a 'hero'; →Heros) after whom that tribe or city was named (the 'eponymous' hero). The process is so old that some mythic eponyms survive whose tribes have been lost (DOWDEN 1992:75-76): Danaos (and his fifty daughters, the Danaids), the name of whose 'Danaoi' survives only for indiscriminate use in Homer to refer to 'Greeks'; and Pelops, the eponym of the Peloponnese, but surely also of a tribe of Pelopes. Surviving pairs of eponym and tribe include Arkas and the Arkades (Arcadians), but are more prevalent in northern Greece where tribes were often a more important focus of identity than cities: Aitolos and the Aitoloi (Aetolians), Phokos and the Phokeis (Phocians), Boiotos and the Boiotoi (Boeotians), →Makedon and the Makedones (Macedonians).

The Thessalians do not appear in the old epics, presumably because the tribes bearing that name had only arrived in Thessaly after the fall of the Mycenaean civilisation (the notional setting for the action of the epics), though the sons of 'Thessalos son of Heracles' make a brief bow in our texts of Homer's catalogue of ships (*Iliad* 2:679). A significant parent gave Thessalos such mythological depth as he could achieve, and descent from →Heracles is the standard mythological cover for tribes that entered Greece after the end of the Mycenaean age. Indirect descent from Heracles was achieved by making him a son of one Aiatos (Charax, *FGH* 103F6). Another tradition made him the son of Haimon, eponym of the Haimones, a tribe in Thessaly (Rhianos, *FGH* 265F30). Haimon was better rooted: he was a son either of Pelasgos, who often figures as a preliminary ruler in Greek landscapes, or of →Zeus himself. More colourfully, he might be a son of →Jason and Medea (Diodoros 4, 54, 1), thus allowing him to grow out of the age of heroes in which his tribe was too late to participate. His sole task in myth-history is to give his name to the Thessalians—though there were other, unspecified, accounts of how he got his name (Diodoros 4, 55, 2).

III. The name Thessalos is borne by 29 persons in FRASER-MATTHEWS (cf. Aeneas 35 times, Jason 183 times), especially in the 3rd/2nd centuries BCE, and by 11 in PAPE-BENSELER (cf. Aeneas 5 times, Jason 19 times), including Thessalos of Tralles who in Nero's reign founded or refounded the Methodical School of medicine and is the author of a work *De virtutibus herbarum.* It is a complication, however, that a recognisable name-type is derived from ethnic labels, without requiring an eponymous hero to mediate them—thus e.g. Attikos, Boiotos, Lokros and even Ioudaios ('Jew') (FICK-BECHTEL 1894: 332-337), although FICK-BECHTEL (1894: 309. 335) hold that in a Dorian context the name always summons up the son of Heracles so named. His name may be viewed as at best indirectly commemorated in the city of Thessalonike, founded around 316/5 BCE by Cassander (the ruler of Macedonia after the death of Alexander the Great). He in fact named it after a different eponym—his wife (though in later tradition its eponymy reverted to 'Thessalus son of Graecus', Isid. *Etym.* 15, 1, 48). This city brought together the inhabitants of around 25 smaller places, asserting a Thessalian identity which had been seeking cultural recognition for half a millennium. Thessalonike is mentioned at Acts 17:1.11.13; Phil 4:16; 2 Tim 4:10 and Thessalonians (Thessalonikeis) at Acts 20:4; 27:2; 1 Thess 1:1; 2 Thess 1:1.

IV. *Bibliography*

K. DOWDEN, *The Uses of Greek Mythology* (London 1992); A. FICK & F. BECHTEL, *Die Griechischen Personennamen nach ihrer Bildung erklärt und systematisch geordnet* (2nd ed.; Göttingen 1894); P. M. FRASER & E. MATTHEWS (eds.), *A Lexicon of Greek Personal Names*, vol. I: The Aegean Islands, Cyprus, Cyrenaica (Oxford 1987); U. HÖFER, Thessalus, *ALGRM* v (1916-24) 775-777; W. PAPE, revised by G. E. BENSELER, *Wörterbuch der griechischen Eigennamen* (Braunschweig 1884); F. SCHACHERMEYR, Thessalos, *PW* 6A (1936) 163-164.

K. DOWDEN

THILLAKHUHA

I. The Hebrew noun *šilluḥîm,* 'marriage gift' (1 Kgs 9:6), has been related etymologically with an alleged Ugaritic goddess Thillaḫuha. She is supposed to be one of the →Kosharoth (DE MOOR 1970:200).

II. The Ugaritic myth which relates how the moon-god Yariḫu obtained his bride Nikkal (*KTU* 1.24) is concluded by a hymn to the Kosharoth, the goddesses supervising delivery. This hymn is concluded by a list of seven words. This list is interpreted either as a list of seven nouns related to the process of marriage and parturition (CAQOUT et al. 1974:396-397) or as a list of seven deities (DE MOOR 1970:200; DEL OLMO LETE 1991:74-75). The latter interpretation is the more plausible. An argument for the interpretation as goddesses might be the fact that, like the seven Babylonian *šassurātu* (*Atr* S iii:9), there were seven Kosharoth. DEL OLMO LETE compared Thillaḫuha with the Sumerian deity **nin-ima**. This goddess is known from the myth 'Enki and Nin-mah' in which she occurs as an assistent to Nammu when creating mankind (1991:74-75). MARGULIT (1989:285) lists only five Kosharoth. He proposes an emendation for the first two nouns to *ṯlḫh* <n>.*wmlgh*<n> 'bridal gifts and trousseau' interpreted as given by the Kosharoth to the newly weds.

If *ṯlḫh* (Thillaḫuha) is a divine name, it should be construed as a derivation from a noun (*ṯlḫ*) with a suffix 3.f.s. As one construal 'her (i.e. the bride's) marriage gift' has been proposed (HERRMANN 1967:23.46-47; DE MOOR 1970:200). A relation with Heb *šelaḥ,* 'offshoot' is, however, more probable. Like the other Kosharoth, Thillaḫuha was considered to have the form of a swallow (*KTU* 1.17 [Aqhat] I ii:27; 1. 24:41).

III. In the Old Testament, *šillûḥîm* has the meaning 'marriage gift'. In 1 Kgs 9:6 the Israelite property of the city of Gezer is interpreted as a gift of the Egyptian Pharaoh to his new son-in-law Solomon. In Mic 1:14, the literary and religious context requires a translation as 'parting gift' (WOLFF 1982:10). The metaphors for mourning render a translation 'marriage gift' in this context less probable (*pace* DE MOOR 1970: 200). Although a 'marriage gift' had a social function in the religious and societal customs in Ancient Israel, there is only an etymological relation with the Ugaritic deity Thillaḫuha.

The noun *šelaḥ,* 'offshoot', occurs only once (Cant 4:13). In a hymn of the bridegroom to the beauty of the bride he compares her tenderness and sexual attraction metaphorically to the offshoot in a pleasure garden. This metaphor might have religious undertones. A relation of the goddess Thillaḫuha to *šelaḥ,* 'offshoot', seems more probable than a relation to *šilluḥîm,* 'marriage gift'. After all, the Ugaritic deity functions in the process of parturition and not in the ritual of marriage.

IV. *Bibliography*

A. CAQUOT, M. SZNYCER & A. HERDNER, *Textes Ougaritiques. Tome I* (LAPO 7; Paris 1974); W. HERRMANN, *Yariḫ und Nikkal und der Preis der Kuṯarāt-Göttinen* (BZAW 106; Berlin 1967); B. MARGULIT, *The Ugaritic Poem of AQHT* (BZAW 182; Berlin/ New York 1989); J. C. DE MOOR, The Semitic Pantheon of Ugarit, *UF* 2 (1970) 188-228; G. DEL OLMO LETE, *Yarḫu* y *Nikkalu.* La mitologia lunar sumeria en Ugarit, *AulOr* 9 (1991) 67-75; H. W. WOLFF, *Dodekapropheton 4. Micha* (BKAT XIV/4; Neukirchen-Vluyn 1982).

B. BECKING

THORNBUSH סנה, סבך, אטד

I. In Exod 3:1-6 →Yahweh appears in a burning bush (*sĕneh*). In Deut 33:16 Yahweh is called *šoknî sĕneh*, 'the Thornbush-dweller'. It has been suggested that the thornbush is used as a designation of Yahweh in Judg 9:14-15 (*'ṭd*) and Ps 58:10 (*'ṭd*). Outside the Bible the Egyptian national god Amun seems to be related to the *nbs*-tree, the Ziziphus spina Christi; a Ugaritic deity is called 'the god of the Ziziphus'; in Mesopotamia some deities have the 'thornbush' as their symbol.

II. In Egypt the *nbs*-tree which is the *Ziziphus spina Christi* was a holy tree (*LdÄ* 1 [1975] 659, 967). A reference to a so-called House of the *nbs*-tree is perhaps to be found on a fragmentary New Kingdom block at Tabo on which the name of Amun of Pnubs (*i.e.* Amun of the House of the *nbs*-tree) has been written. In Egypt the holy *nbs*-tree is the symbol of various deities: Amun-Re, Sopdu and →Hathor (SCHUMACHER 1988; *LdÄ* 4 [1982] 1067-1068.)

In a Ugaritic incantation a human being hopes to receive a favourable omen from the trees. In the trees winged spirits are perching. Among them is *il dʿrgzm*, 'the god of the Ziziphus' who is paralleled by 'the goddess who is on a twig' (*KTU* 1.20 i:8-9). The *ʿrgz* is member of the Ziziphus family, a thornbush. It is likely that the god of the jujube-trees does not refer to a tree-god, but to an ancestral god sitting on a branch of a tree with his female companion. However, there is no great difference between a deified tree and a tree in which a spirit is hiding. Tree-gods did occur in the ancient Near East. In Egypt many pictures have been found of tree-goddesses, mixed images of a tree and an anthropomorphic deity. These tree-goddesses were but metamorphoses of high goddesses like →Isis, Nuth, and Hathor.

In Mesopotamia *eddetu* 'boxthorn' is associated with certain deities in theological commentary texts (*CAD* E 23). The *amurdinnu* (bramble or rose) would be the emblem of a deity (*CAD* A/2, 91).

III. Probably the earliest designation of Yahweh as 'the Thornbush-dweller' (*šoknî sĕneh*) is found in Deut 33:16. The circumstance that this epithet was maintained in spite of the strong corrective tendency of later tradition might be interpreted as an argument in favour of its authenticity—*pace* W. H. SCHMIDT (*Exodus* [BKAT 2; Neukirchen Vluyn 1988] 116) who interprets *sĕneh* as a secondary addition to the Exod 3 account. The Yahwistic account of the appearance of the deity in a burning *sĕneh* in Exod 3:1-6 confirms the importance of this concept in early Israel. Because the *sĕneh* may probably be identified as *Ziziphus spina Christi*, this designation comes very close to the Ugaritic 'god of the Ziziphus (jujube-tree)'. The fact that already in the New Kingdom Egyptian gods—even the highest god Amun—may be described as dwelling in or sitting under the holy Ziziphus may be an extra argument for identifying the Hebrew *snh* with this Ziziphus.

It has long been observed that there may be a connection between the name of the Ziziphus-bush and the name of Sinai (DE MOOR 1990:194-195). In Judg 5:5 and Ps 68:18 God is called *zeh sînāy* →'He-of-the-Sinai' which may refer to an earlier 'He-of-the-Thornbush'. If the Ugaritic 'god of the Ziziphus' was an ancestral spirit, it may be that the Hebrew epithet 'Ziziphus-dweller' points to the earliest phase of Yahwism when Yahweh was still an ancestral manifestation of →El (DE MOOR 1990:232-234, 259-260). It is at least noteworthy that Yahweh was supposed to be able to make the sound (*qwl*) of marching steps (*ṣʿdh*) in the top of trees (2 Sam 5:24). To David this must be the sign that his God is marching against the Philistines. We may recall here that in Ugarit the bird-like ancestral spirits, the ghosts of great warriors who protected their offspring on earth, were even supposed to come rolling through the tops of the trees in their chariots.

In the Yahwistic account of Exod 3:1-6 the realistic nature of this imagery was mitigated, even if we assume that the angel of v 2 did not belong to the original account (cf. v 4). Yet the self-predication in v 6 would still seem to refer back to the ancestral cult. According to DE MOOR (1990:182-197) the tradition of the Thornbush-dweller found expression in two more texts, namely Judg 9:14-15 and Ps 58:10. Jotham's fable tells about a thornbush (*'ṭd*) who is asked by the other trees to rule over them. De Moor proposes to regard *'ṭd* as an alternative name of the Ziziphus and sees the original fable as a plea for polytheism in opposition to the early drive to make the Thornbush-dweller Yahweh king of the gods. (For other views see J. EBACH & U. RÜTERSWÖRDEN; Pointen der Jothamfabel, *BN* 31 [1986] 11-18).

In favour of this hypothesis one might point to the fact that in Egypt the holy *nbs*-tree is the symbol of various deities. The theory has attractive aspects because it solves a number of old puzzles with regard to the relation between the fable and the framework story. In DE MOOR's opinion this scornful epithet *'ṭd* was still known to the poet of Ps 58 who in his turn attacks the gods of Canaan (Ps 58:2). He translates Ps 58:10 as follows: "Before they understand—your thorns, O Thornbush! As soon as it is alive—let the blaze sweep it away!" (i.e. the untimely birth, cf. Ps 58:9). In this tradition the name of a thorny plant is accepted as an epithet for Yahweh, but the whole context shows that it was understood to be a metaphor, not a deification of the thornbush.

Perhaps the theophoric name *sbkyhw* occurs in Lachish ostracon no. 11:5. It might mean "Yahweh is a thorny bush" (cf. other theophoric names like *dltyhw*, 'Yahweh is a door', *hryhw*, 'Yahweh is a mountain').

IV. *Bibliography*

M. A. BEEK, Der Dornbusch als Wohnsitz Gottes (Deut XXXIII 16), *OTS* 14 (1965) 155-161; M. C. A. KORPEL, *A Rift in the Clouds: Ugaritic and Hebrew Descriptions of the Divine* (UBL 8; Münster 1990) 588-589, 591-593; J. C. DE MOOR, *The Rise of Yahwism: The Roots of Israelite Monotheism* (BETL 91; Leuven 1990) 182-197; I. W. SCHUMACHER, *Der Gott Sopdu: Der Herr der Fremdländer* (Göttingen 1988) 160-176, 178, 265.

M. C. A. KORPEL

THOTH

I. Despite many ingenious attempts scholars have failed to establish a plausible etymological explanation of the name of the Egyptian God Thoth (SPIES 1991:18-21 gives a convenient summary of current views). Aram *tḥwt* and *tḥwtmʿ* (= Gk *Thothomous*, 'Thoth is justified': SEGAL 1983: 47), Akk *tiḫut*, Lat *Theut* and Greek spellings (e.g. *Thōuth*, *Thōth* and *Thouth*: HOPFNER 1946:50-52) reflect Eg *Ḏḥwty*. Phoen *Taautos* (Eusebius, *Praep. evang.* I.29.24) has been suggested to refer to Thoth (J. EBACH, *Weltentstehung und Kulturentwicklung bei Philo von Byblus* [Stuttgart 1979] 60-67). It is extremely doubtful whether Thoth (Eg *Ḏḥwty*), the ibis-headed god of →wisdom and the Lord of Hermopolis, occurs in the Bible.

II. Thoth's cult seems to have had its origins in the Delta but already at an early date Hermopolis in Middle Egypt was his chief cult centre (ZIVIE 1973:ix-x). Thoth is a lunar deity who manifests himself as an →ibis or, since the Middle Kingdom (SPIES 1991:14), a baboon. The Egyptians associated the waning and reappearance of the →moon with the Eye of Horus which had been robbed or damaged by the wicked god →Seth. On the day of the full moon, Thoth retrieved or healed the Eye (Eg *wḏꜣ.t*, 'the Healthy Eye'). Thoth then mediates in restoring the harmony (Eg *Maat*) of the cosmos and thus of Egypt, its terrestrial counterpart (cf. the hieroglyph of the *wḏꜣ.t*-eye as designation of Egypt; *Wb.* I.425.18).

Thoth's role as a cosmic deity is attested since the Late Period. Thoth was regarded as the Thought (heart) of the sun god →Re (cf. Horapollo *Hierogl.* I.26) and as the creative Word (tongue) of →Ptah or →Atum (SAUNERON 1964:301-302). A Greek magical text calls Thoth the mind residing in the heart (A. DIETERICH, *Abraxas* [Leipzig 1891] 17, l.43). Thoth, the viceregency of Re, realises the plans of his Lord. He is the eldest child of Re (BOYLAN 1922:195) and a second god, without whose knowledge nothing comes into being. Re put Hu, the authoritative Utterance and motive force behind creation, in the mouth of Thoth (*Edfou* VI.298.7), the Lord of the divine words (BOYLAN 1922:92-97). At sunrise the loud cries of joy of the ithyphallic (= creative) baboon, the embodiment of Thoth, announced the appearance of the sun or the cosmic renewal (H. TE VELDE, Some Remarks on the Mysterious Language of the Baboons, *Funerary Symbols and Religion* [FS Heerma van Voss; Kampen 1988] 129-137). Thoth is equated with Sia, the divine Wisdom (DERCHAIN-URTEL 1981:206 n.63; SAUNERON 1964:302), and by means of his palette he designs the world, the *pictura mundi*, which existed already in the demiurge's mind. The palette of Thoth is called Seeing and Hearing, notions which are linked to the renewal of creation (DERCHAIN-URTEL 1981:88). Thoth, the *kosmokratōr*, organised the world (RUSCH 1936: 361). He is the Bull of the stars and designs the cosmic place of the temple. The building of a temple, which depended on fixed positions of the stars, was regarded as the earthly repetition of creation. Thoth fills the lunar eye, thus regulating the course of the stars and causing the cosmos to be renewed (DERCHAIN-URTEL 1981:34-35). He is found in the solar barque accompanied by Hu, Sia and Maat. As the substitute of Seth (OTTO 1938), he annihilates the foes of the sun and thus assists in restoring creation, symbolically expressed by the *wḏꜣ.t*-eye he offers to the sun god (J. ASSMANN, *Liturgische Lieder an den Sonnengott* [MÄS 19; Berlin 1969] 219, 308, with references). Thoth was associated with the inundation. According to Egyptian conceptions the full moon brought the inundation and fertility to the land (DERCHAIN 1962:34-35)

As Lord of Hermopolis (Eg *Ḫmnw*, 'City of the Eight') Thoth was regarded as a creator in his own right. Hermopolis was conceived as the primaeval Hill, where the Ogdoad came into existence. Thoth, the Eldest One and self-created god (BOYLAN 1922:193, 195; cf. Claudian, *Stilicho* II.434 and P. DERCHAIN, A propos de Claudien, *ZÄS* 81 [1956] 96) is sometimes represented as an ibis-headed nude man with the sidelock of youth, wearing dog-headed slippers. The creator god is young and old at the same time, thus guaranteeing the continuous renewal of the cosmos and of life itself. The dog-headed slippers associate the god with the Ogdoad who protect and assist the demiurge in creation (QUAEGEBEUR 1992).

The importance of Thoth as a funerary god is firmly rooted in religious literature (*Pyr.*, *CT* and BD) and seems to derive from his lunar nature (*RÄRG* 810). The deceased wishes to traverse the sky in the company of Thoth (*CT* VI.19.a) in order to be reborn after the example of the moon (W. HELCK, *LdÄ* IV [1982] 192). The fate of →Osiris, whose corpse was torn to pieces by Seth, is reflected in the moon's phases. Thoth reconstructs the corpse of Osiris (= the deceased: *Pyr.* 639.b, 830.a-b, *CT* VI.322.s). Sometimes Thoth and Shu, the air god, take care of the corpse of Osiris (J. VANDIER, Le Dieu Shou dans le Papyrus Jumilhac, *MDAIK* 15 [1957] 268-269). Thoth defends Osiris against his enemies and is asked to do for the deceased what he has done for Osiris (*CT* IV.91.b). He opens the mouth of the deceased and gives him the breath of life (SCHOTT 1972:23). The god functions as Psychopompos and together with Anubis he reconstructs the corpse of the deceased. In *PGM* IV 3131, Thoth seems to be associated with Hermanubis (cf. Eusebius *Praep. evang.* 3.11.43). Both Anubis and the Greek god →Hermes are often represented carrying the staff of the psychopompos. Thoth gives a letter to the deceased in order to enable him to pass by the doors of the Netherworld and to arrive at the Hall of Osiris (QUAEGEBEUR 1988). The god is present at the weighing of the heart of the deceased against *Maat* (P. DERCHAIN, L'Oeil, Gardien de la justice, *ZÄS* 83 [1958] 75-76) and he records the results (BD 125). Sometimes the god is represented as the scale of justice itself (*CT* I.181.c-d, IV.301.c-302.c). He is in charge of the funeral offerings which were due on fixed days of the lunar month (BOYLAN 1922:138; KURTH 1986:505). However, Thoth's nature has a dangerous side. He is called the Cutting One, whose knife is thought of as the crescent moon (KEES 1925). The god is often represented armed with a knife (ZIVIE 1977:30-31).

Thoth was regarded as the murderer of Osiris (*Pyr.* 329.a-e) because he was a bad protector of the moon's phases (DERCHAIN 1962:38). He appeared as hostile to the deceased (SPIES 1991:157) and to the gods (*Pyr.* 1963.b) who were afraid of his destructive powers (DERCHAIN-URTEL 1981: 164, with many references). Thoth had been born in an unnatural way from the head or the knee of Seth, the violent god par excellence (DERCHAIN 1962:22, with references). Indeed he was said to have no mother, although occasionally →Neith is mentioned as his parent (EL-SAYED 1969). To this may be added Thoth's bad reputation as a trickster who steals the offerings and mischievously diverts 1/4 of a day at the end of each month (SCHOTT 1970).

The moon is connected with the calendar, reckoning and science. Thoth, the lunar deity, is thought to reveal his nature especially in intellectual activities. The god develops this most famous aspect of his character especially since the New Kingdom. He is the reckoner of time and he distinguishes months and years (BOYLAN 1922: 183). The first month of the year is called after Thoth (Cicero, *Nat. deor.* III. 22). The god measures the fields (cf. Ampelius, *Liber Memor.* 9.5), calculates taxes (HELCK 1976), guarantees the accuracy of weights and measures (ZIVIE 1977). The cubit is sacred to Thoth and by means of it the god measures (= creates) the world (cf. the measuring of the world in Isa 40:12 and Job 38:5). Thoth, who defended →Horus (= the archetypical pharaoh) in the trial against Seth for the possession of Egypt, enthrones the pharaoh and gives him many jubilees. The god is associated with Meskhenet, the goddess of childbirth (BOYLAN 1922:84-86), and as inaugurator of time he is closely linked to fate and the Agathodaemon (*PGM* IV.655). Thoth is sometimes regarded as the father of Isis, the goddess of fate and mother of Horus (RAY 1976:158-159; KÁKOSY 1981:43, n.14 with many references). The ibis, the bird of Thoth, announces to the world the crowning of the pharaoh and the beginning of a new era (SCHOTT 1968). In the Late Period he was a god of oracles and dreams (RAY 1976:133; QUAEGEBEUR 1975). Thoth is the scribe of Re (SAUNERON 1962:287-289; cf. Eusebius, *Praep. ev.* I.10; Augustine *Civ. Dei* VIII.27). He is the patron god of scribes and bears titles of administrative dignitaries (SAUNERON 1963: 300). Thoth invented script and language (S. SAUNERON, La différenciation des langages d'après la tradition égyptienne, *BIFAO* 60 [1960] 31-41) and is the author of ritual books (SCHOTT 1963). Temples are founded and decorated according to Thoth's writings. The god's powerful creative word made him a great magician who was equated with Hike, the embodiment of Magic and the protector of Re against his foes (BOYLAN 1922: 124-135).

Thoth was also regarded as a great physician, because he cured the lunar eye (DERCHAIN 1962:26). Sometimes the god is represented holding the stick of Asclepius (KÁKOSY 1981:43).

III. In the beginning of this century, scholars often proceeded too uncritically in their eagerness to connect names of Egyptian gods with supposed equivalents in the Bible. More recently, however, KILIAN (1966) and NOTTER (1974) argued on good grounds that the Ogdoad of Hermopolis ("the souls of Thoth") is in the background of the Genesis creation myth. COUROYER (1987) seems to suggest an association between the biblical expression "the path of God" (cf. Gen 18:19) and its Egyptian counterpart "the path of Thoth". MOWINCKEL (1929), POPE (1965) and W. F. ALBRIGHT (*Yahweh and the Gods of Canaan* [London 1968] 212-214) state that the word טחות, vocalised *ṭuḥôt*, which in Job 38:36 appears in parallelism with *śekwî* 'cock', refers to Thoth. The meaning of *ṭuḥôt* has been disputed already in ancient times as can be inferred from varying translations in LXX, Vulg and Tg. Starting from *śekwî* 'cock', the majority of modern commentators on the book of Job (e.g. KEEL 1978:60) suppose that *ṭuḥôt* represents a bird and they take it to refer to the ibis, the bird sacred to Thoth (P. DHORME *Le livre de Job* [Etudes bibliques; Paris 1926] 541; KEEL 1978:60; A. DE WILDE, *Das Buch Hiob* [OTS 22; Leiden 1981] 369). HABEL (1985) and others reject any association with Thoth and the ibis.

The Christians associated Thoth with the Archangel →Michael (G. LANCZKOWSKI, Thoth and Michael, *MDAIK* 14 [1956] 117-127) and the Jews with →Moses (G. MUSSIES, The interpretatio judaica of Thoth-Hermes, *Studies in Egyptian Religion dedicated to Professor Jan Zandee* (M. Heerma van Voss *et al.*, eds.; Numen Supplement 43; Leiden 1982] 89-120). The Greeks recognised in Thoth many of the characteristics of the god Hermes. The Egyptian Hermes, known under the name of Trismegistos, was the reputed author of the *Corpus Hermeticum*, which was widely read by Gnostics and Christians.

IV. *Bibliography*

H. BONNET, Thoth, *RÄRG* 320-321; *P. BOYLAN, *Thoth, the Hermes of Egypt* (Oxford 1922); B. COUROYER, "Le dieu des Sages" en Egypte, *RB* 94 (1987) 574-603; P. DERCHAIN, Mythes et dieux lunaires en Egypte, *La lune, mythes et rites* (SO 5; Paris 1962) 17-68; *M.-T. DERCHAIN-URTEL, *Thot à travers ses épithètes dans les scènes d'offrandes des temples d'époque gréco-romaine* (Bruxelles 1981); N. C. HABEL, *The Book of Job. A commentary.* (London 1985); W. HELCK, *Der Name des Thoth* (SAK 4; 1976) 131-134; T. HOPFNER, Ägyptische theophore Personennamen, *ArOr* 15 (1946) 1-64; L. KÁKOSY, *Problems of the Thoth-cult in Roman Egypt* (StAeg VII; 1981) 41-46; O. KEEL, *Jahwes Entgegnung an Ijob* (Göttingen 1978); H. KEES, Zu den ägyptischen Mondsagen, *ZÄS* 60 (1925) 1-15; R. KILIAN, Gen I 2 und die Urgötter von Hermopolis, *VT* 16 (1966) 420-438; D. KURTH, Thoth, *LdÄ* 6 (1986) 497-523; S. MOWINCKEL, טחות und שׂכוי. Eine Studie zur Astrologie des Alten Testaments, *AcOr* 8 (1929) 1-44; V. NOTTER, *Biblischer Schöpfungsbericht und ägyptische Schöpfungsmythen* (Stuttgart 1974); E. OTTO, Thot als der Stellvertreter des Seth, *Or* 7 (1938) 69-79; M. H. POPE, *Job* (AB; Garden City 1965); J. QUAEGEBEUR, Teëphibis, dieu oraculaire?, *Enchoria* 5 (1975) 19-24; QUAEGEBEUR, Lettres de Thot et Décrets pour Osiris, *Funerary Symbols and Religion* (FS Heerma van Voss; Kampen 1988) 105-126; QUAEGEBEUR, Les pantouffles du dieu Thot, *Sesto Congresso Internazionale di Egittologia, Atti* Vol. 1 (Torino 1992) 521-527; J. RAY, *The archive of Ḥor* (London 1976); A. RUSCH, *Thoth*, PW XI (1936) 351-388; S. SAUNERON, Le dieu égyptien Thoth, *ACF* 62 (1962) 287-290; 63 (1963) 299-303; 64 (1964) 301-305; 65 (1965) 339-342; R. EL-SAYED, Thoth n'a-t-il vraiment pas de mère?, *REg* 21 (1969) 71-75; S. SCHOTT, Die Opferliste als Schrift des Thoth, *ZÄS* 90 (1963) 103-110; SCHOTT, Falke, Geier und Ibis als Krönungsboten, *ZÄS* 95 (1968) 54-65; SCHOTT, Thot le dieu qui vole, *CRAIBL* 1970 [Paris 1971] 547-556; SCHOTT, Thoth als Verfasser der heiligen Schriften, *ZÄS* 99 (1972) 20-25; B. SEGAL, *Aramaic Texts from North Saqqâra* (London 1983); H. SPIES, *Aufstieg eines Gottes* (Hamburg 1991); *A. P. ZIVIE, *Hermopolis et le nome de l'Ibis* (IFAO [Bibliothèque d'Etude] 66/1; Le Caire 1973); ZIVIE, L'ibis, Thot et la Coudée, *BSFE* 79 (1977) 22-41.

R. L. VOS

THRONES θρονοί

I. In a hymnic passage extolling Jesus Christ we read "for in (or: by) him all things in heaven and earth were created, things visible and invisible, whether thrones (*thronoi*) or dominions or rulers and powers—all things have been created through him and for him" (Col 1:16). Here the term 'thrones', like the other words, denotes heavenly beings. It occurs with this meaning only here in the Bible. The other words are found in similar lists (1 Cor 15:24; Eph 1:21; 3:10; 6:12; 1 Pet 3:22); whilst 'rulers' and 'powers' are mentioned together in Col 2:10.15.

II. A throne, the symbol of majesty and power to govern and to administer justice, is often mentioned in connection with kings and deities. This applies to the ancient Near

East (see FABRY 1984) and Greece (see HUG 1935), as well as to ancient Israel. In the OT the LORD's throne is connected with Sion (Isa 8:18; Jer 3:17; 14:21; 17:12; Ps 9:12) or said to be in heaven (Isa 66:1; Ps 2:4; 11:4; 123:1). Isaiah in a vision "saw the Lord sitting on a throne, high and lofty, and the hem of his robe filled the temple" (6:1). Ezekiel saw "something like a throne" and above it "something like a human form" (Ezek 1:26, cf. 10:1). This throne is situated above a chariot formed by winged creatures (elsewhere identified as cherubs [9:3; 10:1-22; 11:22, cf. Ps 18:11]). In Dan 7:9 'the →Ancient of Days', surrounded by a innumerable host and about to pronounce judgement, is situated on a similar throne; more thrones are set in place, clearly for those who are to sit in judgement with the Ancient One (v 10). We may compare here the visions in *1 Enoch* 14 (esp. vv 18.20) and *1 Enoch* 71 (esp. v 7) and those in Rev 4-7.

In the Similitudes of Enoch, not only God ('the Head of Days', 'the Lord of Spirits') will deliver judgement on his throne (47:3; 62:2.3), but also 'the Chosen One', 'the →Son of Man' will be seated on the throne of his glory (45:3; 51:3; 55:4; 61:8; 69: 27.29) to judge on God's behalf. Here we may compare the picture in Matt 25:31 of the Son of Man coming in glory with his angels and sitting on the throne of his glory, about to judge all the nations. In Matt 19:28 (par. Luke 22:30) he is accompanied by the twelve disciples, seated on twelve thrones and judging (the twelve tribes of) Israel. In Rev 4:4 (10) and 11:16 there are twenty-four thrones in heaven, before the throne of God, for heavenly beings called 'the twenty-four →elders', and in Rev 3:21; 22:1.3 the →Lamb shares the throne of God (cf. 7:17). In 20:4, clearly referring to Dan 7:9, the occupants of the thrones that are set up are not identified.

In Rev 3:21 'the one who conquers' will obtain a place with Christ on the throne which he shares with his Father. Compare *1 Enoch* 108:12 and 4Q521 (ed. É. PUECH, *RevQ* 15 [1992] 485) fragm. 2 ii+4, line 7, "the Lord will honour the pious ones on the throne of his eternal kingdom" (cf. *T. Job* 33, *Apoc. Elijah* [ed. Pietersma-Comstock] 2:3-6). In *Apoc. Zeph.* (acc. to Clem. Al., *Strom* 5,11.77.2) we meet angels called 'lords' occupying thrones in the fifth heaven, and in Wis 9:4 (cf. 9:10; 18:15) →Wisdom is said to sit by God's throne (here in Greek a plural of majesty is used, as often in Greek literature, cf. also Ezekiel's *Exagoge* 76 [next to the sing. in 73-75]).

It is difficult to find early parallels for the notion of 'thrones' as personified beings. It occurs in Christian sources, e.g. in Melito, *On Pascha* (ed. Hall) 603-607, "who fitted the stars in heaven, who lit up the luminaries, who made the angels in heaven, who established the thrones there", in Valentinian gnosis (acc. to Irenaeus, *Adv. Haer.* I 18 [ed. Harvey] and Clem. Al., *Exc. ex Theod.* 43.3) and in clearly Christian passages in *T. Adam* 4:8 and *Asc. Isa.* 7:21.27; 8:8; 11:25 (see also *Test. Sol.* MS D 8:6). Later Christian parallels are listed in *LPGL* 655, 2d. As to the OT pseudepigrapha, *T. Levi* 3:8 may also be mentioned, where in the fifth out of seven heavens 'thrones and →authorities' bear continuous praise to God. As the present Greek text of *T. Levi* has undergone Christian redaction (also in 3:6), we cannot be certain that this reference to 'thrones' is pre-Christian (the corresponding fragment of *Aramaic Levi* introduces a heavenly journey, but then breaks off). 'Thrones' are mentioned together with →angels, →archangels, →powers and →authorities in *T. Abraham* (ed. F. Schmidt), but only in the short recension represented by family EACDHI, not in that found in MSS BFG, or in the long recension. 'Thrones' are found in an enumeration of heavenly beings in the longer recension of *2 Enoch* 20:1, but not in the shorter one (nor in the list in *1 Enoch* 61: 10). Equally, 'thrones' as heavenly beings are mentioned in the Achmimic version of *Apoc. Elijah* (ed. Steindorff) 21:4.8.10, but not in the Sahidic parallel (ed. Pietersma-Comstock) 2:8-18. Much more work on these pseudepigrapha will have to be done before we are able to to decide where and when 'thrones' first appeared to denote a class of heavenly beings. In Jewish mystical literature from late antiquity, personification of God's throne is very often encountered (SCHÄFER 1991 passim).

How thrones could be personified may be illustrated by a passage in *Apoc. Mosis* (Greek *Life of Adam and Eve*) 23,2 where Eve confesses "I have sinned against you, I have sinned against your elect angels, I have sinned against the cherubs, I have sinned against your unshaken throne". The opinion found in the writings of a number of Christian writers (probably beginning with Clem. Al., *Eclogae* 57,1) that the cherubim were called 'thrones' because they supported the throne of God seems unlikely, however important Ezekiel's throne-vision has been in visions of heaven (e.g. *Apoc. Abraham* 18) and in Jewish mysticism.

III. The author of the Epistle to the Colossians is not interested in the exact function or hierarchy of the four heavenly beings mentioned in 1:16. He emphasizes that all of them are subordinate to the Creator and his Son, the firstborn of all creation, in whom they were created (cf. Col 2:10). They have definitely been subdued and rendered powerless at the death and exaltation of Christ (Col 2:15; 1 Pet 3:22); at the end of time 'every ruler, every authority and power' will be destroyed (1 Cor 15: 24). Human beings should worship God and his Son: not inferior angelic beings.

IV. *Bibliography*

H.-J. FABRY, *TWAT* 4 (1984) 247-272; A. HUG, PW II 6,1 (1935) 613-618; S. M. OLYAN, *A Thousand Thousands Served Him. Exegesis and the Naming of Angels in Ancient Judaism* (TSAJ 36; Tübingen 1993) 61-66; P. SCHÄFER, *Der verborgene und offenbare Gott. Hauptthemen der frühen jüdischen Mystik* (Tübingen 1991).

M. DE JONGE

THUKAMUNA

I. The name of the Ugaritic deity Thukamuna, occurring as element in the binomial divine name *Ṯkmn-w-Šnm*, has etymologically been related to the Hebrew noun *šekem* (GINSBERG 1936:92; WYATT 1990:446-449). *šĕkem* occurs in the OT as a noun meaning 'shoulder; back' (22 times; cf. Ug *škm*, 'shoulder' e.g. *KTU* 1.14 ii:11; iii:54; 1.22 i:5); as a toponym Shechem located in the highlands of Ephraim (e.g. Gen 12:6; 33:18; 35:4; 37:12. 14; Josh 17:7; 20:7; 21:21; 24:1. 25. 32; Judg 8:31; 9; 21: 19) and as a personal name borne by four different people in the OT (Gen 34:2; Num 26:31; Josh 17:2; 1 Chron 17:9).

II. The binomial deity Thukamuna-wa-→Shunama is attested at Ugarit in literary-religious texts as well as in offering-lists. The two names appear together. In *KTU* 1.114, the description of a heavenly *marzeaḥ*, they are depicted as sons of →El and, probably, to be identified with the 'gatekeeper of the house of El' (D. PARDEE, *Les textes paramythologiques* [RSOu 4; Paris 1988] 59-60). Here, they perform the filial duty towards a drunken father referred to in the epic of Aqhat (*KTU* 1.17 i:30). In the ritual *KTU* 1.41:12. 16 the offering of an ewe for the deity is prescribed for the ritual on the fifteenth day of the month 'First-of-the-Wine'; the offering of a ram is also prescribed as an additional offering at the same event. On the third day of the festival an ewe must be offered for Thukamuna-wa-Shunama (*KTU* 1.41:31-32). In a list of deities in alphabetic script Thukamuna-wa-Shunama are presented as the sons of El (*KTU* 1.65:1-4).

From J. W. JACK (*The Rash Shamra Tablets: Their Bearing on the Old Testament* [Edinburgh 1935] 22) onwards an etymological and formal relation between Thukamuna and the Cassite deity *Šuqamuna* is assumed (most recently WYATT 1990: 446). Within the Cassite pantheon *Šuqamuna* can be equated with the Mesopotamian →Nergal. The identification as well as the direction of influence, however, is open to debate. K. BALKAN (*Kassitenstudien I* [New Haven 1954] 117.121) seriously doubted the Cassite origin of the name *Šuqamuna*. Some scholars searched for an Indo-European etymology of the name (MIRONOV 1933:144;

WYATT 1990:446-447; Sanskrit: *śucamāna*, *śocamāna*, 'burning one; lamenting one; sorrowful one'); others prefer a Semitic derivation. The occurrence of the toponym *šu-ka-mu-na-tim* in a document from Mari (A. 4634; G. DOSSIN, *RA* 64 [1970] 43), the attestation of the noun *škm* in the Ugaritic language and the existence of the personal names *šu-ku-ma-na* and *šu-ka-ma-na* at Ugarit seem to favour the second possibility (E. LIPIŃSKI, El's Abode: Mythological Traditions Related to Mt. Hermon and to the Mountains of Armenia, *OLP* 2 [1971] 67; PARDEE 1988:199).

Recently, Wyatt has elaborated the view that the story in Gen 34 is an old Indo-European myth brought to the region by the Hurrians (the Horites of the story). The myth, which has been transformed into a quasi-historical legend, occurs in a number of Vedic recensions, and describes a sacred marriage followed by the sacrifice of the husband. At least one of the partners is divine. According to WYATT elements of the myth (and an accompanying ritual) are either alluded to, or narrated in full, in such passages as Ṛg Veda 10. 90 (Puruṣasūkta), Ṛg Veda 10. 95 – cf. Śatapatha Brahmaṇa 11. 5:1-10 (Pururavas and Urvaśī) and Aitareya Brāhmaṇa 7. 13-18 (Śunaḥśepa). The bride in the myth is the dawn-goddess Usha, the groom and victim a royal figure (1990). Two remarks should be made, however. Firstly, the Vedic material adduced to prove the view is open to discussion. Puruṣasūkta occurs in a creation myth in which the puruṣa (a primordial man seen as a cosmic figure) sacrifices himself in order to allow the universe to emerge. The happy-ending story of Pururavas and Urvaśī does not contain the element of sacrifice of the spouse. Secondly, it should be observed, moreover, that Wyatt's suggestion presumes the existence of a strong and influential Aryan upper-class in the ancient Near East in the second millennium BCE, who via the Mitanni-Hurrians transmitted religious ideas also known in the Vedic religion. This view has definitely been dismissed by KAMMENHUBER (1968) and DIAKONOFF (1972).

III. The city of Shechem has been a religious centre from of old. (e.g. G. E. WRIGHT, *Shechem. The Biography of a Biblical City* [London 1965]). Although Shechem is an enduring place for worship in Old Testament times and later by the Samaritans, the name of the city of Shechem as such is not an object of veneration. The personal name Shechem does not have a theophoric character (*HALAT* 1385-1386). The name Shechem should preferably be related to the noun *škm*, 'shoulder', indicating the geographical position of the city on the edge of a mountain. A relationship with the Ugaritic deity Thukamuna probably rests on homonymy.

IV. *Bibliography*

I. M. DIAKONOFF, Die Arier im Vorderen Orient: Ende eines Mythos, *OrNS* 41 (1972) 91-120; O. EISSFELDT, *Ṯkmn wšnm*, *ZDMG* 99 [NS 24] (1945-9 [1950]) 29-42; A. KAMMENHUBER, *Die Arier im Vorderen Orient* (Heidelberg 1968); N. D. MIRONOV, Aryan Vestiges in the Near East of the Second Millennium BC, *AcOr* 11 (1933) 140-217; *D. PARDEE, *Ṯukamuna wa Šunama*, *UF* 20 (1988) 195-199 (with lit.); B. THIEME, The 'Aryan' Gods of the Mitanni treaties, *JAOS* 80 (1960) 301-317; N. WYATT, The story of Dinah and Shechem, *UF* 22 (1990) 433-458.

B. BECKING

TIAMAT תהום

I. *Tĕhôm*, usually translated "the deep", occurs in Gen 1:2 as a designation of the primeval sea, and is frequently used in the OT to denote the cosmic →sea (Yam) on which the world rests, and from which all water comes, as well as any large body of water, including rivers, and the depth of the sea and the earth.

Heb *Tĕhôm* is etymologically related to Akk *Tiāmat*, which derives from an older Semitic root, *thm*, known in Ugaritic and other semitic languages as a designation of the sea. In Arabic *Tihāmat* denotes the coastal plain along the southwestern and southern shores of the Arabian peninsula. In Akkadian the root is known in the female form, *tiāmtu*, or *tâmtu*, 'sea'. The divine name Tiāmat, especially well-known from the Babylonian Creation Myth *Enūma eliš*, is the absolute state of the noun.

To the deification of Tiamat in Mesopotamian texts corresponds the deification of *thmt* in the divine pair *ǵrm wthmt* ('mountains and deep waters') in Ugaritic texts.

II. In the Babylonian creation epic *Enūma eliš*, Tiāmat (also called Mummu) is the personified primeval ocean that was defeated by →Marduk, whose supremacy over the Babylonian pantheon was established through battle. Marduk defeated Tiāmat in single combat, using the winds and a huge net as his weapons. The body of the dead Tiāmat was split like a fish to be dried into two halves, one of which became the sky. Having positioned the celestial bodies, Marduk used Tiāmat's spit for clouds, placed a mountain on her head, and made an outlet from her eyes for the waters of the →Euphrates and the →Tigris (*Enūma eliš* IV 93 - V 66).

The principle of creation that appears in the conversion of the carcass of the slain Tiāmat into a cosmic entity is paralleled twice in *Enūma eliš*. The first example is Apsu, Tiāmat's consort, who was killed by Ea. A sanctuary, in which Marduk was born, was established on his carcass. The third is Kingu, the leader responsible for organizing Tiāmat's battle to revenge Apsu. He was slaughtered, and mankind was created out of his blood by Ea.

Alongside with the violent principle of killing, sexual productivity appears in the poem as a means of creation. In the beginning Tiāmat and Apsu commingled their waters as a single body. Within them a generation of two pairs, first →Lahmu and Lahamu, then Anshar (the circumference of →Heaven) and Kishar (the circumference of →Earth), were produced. The latter became the parents of Anu (Heaven), who became the father of Ea (Nudimmud). Marduk was Ea's son.

In Assyriological literature Tiāmat is usually understood as the salt water ocean, in opposition to Apsu, which is supposed to represent the subterranean fresh water sources. However, the text itself makes no distinction between salt water and fresh water. *Enūma eliš*, V 52-66, considers Tiāmat to be the source of all fresh water, not only the Euphrates and the Tigris, but also other sources of water supply, as well as fog, mist, and snow. The place of these sources is clearly thought to be under the ground or a mountain, whereas older concept has it that Apsu represented the subterranean fresh water supply. Apsu, on the other hand, appears in *Enūma eliš* IV 144-145 to represent the lower part of the cosmos; the sky (here called Esharra) is established as a celestial counterpart to Apsu or the lower world. The significant opposition between Tiāmat and Apsu is thus that of feminine and masculine principles, rather than salt water versus fresh water.

Although *Enūma eliš* tends to play a dominating role in discussions of Mesopotamian religion, it should not be forgotten that, contrary to what is often assumed, there is no reason to believe that *Enūma eliš* goes back to the Old Babylonian or Cassite period, but in all probability was composed during the reign of Nebuchadnezzar I (1124-1103 BCE; but cf. →Marduk). The concept of a battle between the primordial cosmic sea and a leading god of the pantheon was an innovation in Babylonian religion introduced with *Enūma eliš*. The motif itself was probably inspired from the mythology of Western Asia, where it is represented by the Ugaritic myth of →Baal. After Yam had demanded Baal's surrender, Baal defeated Yam by means of two clubs given him by Kothar-wa-Hasis (*KTU* 1.2 iv:7-28). Unlike Tiāmat, Yam was apparently not completely destroyed, but only confined to his proper sphere. Originally Marduk was a rather vague mythological character, and in an attempt to give him his own identity by applying accounts of great mythological deeds to him, this may well have been a source of inspiration for *Enūma eliš*. Also the idea that the sky and the world below were formed out of the two parts of the body of a slain monster was new in Babylonian mythology, and so was the concept of Apsu as a personal mythological entity.

Sumerian and Akkadian texts reaching back to the third millennium BCE contain several accounts of the creation of the world. Mostly these occur as introductions to literary compositions and are focused on the particular subject of each poem. Though their pattern is not consistent and coherent, the following features are fairly common: After the separation of heaven and earth, the gods found their place in cosmos by distributing it in a peaceful way. A few allusions to the concept of a generation of gods preceding Enlil, the leader of the Sumerian pantheon, occur. The so-called *Theogony of Dunnu* is a unique text in which a detailed theogony appears. However, such conceptions do not belong to the main stream of Mesopotamian mythological thinking.

Since the discovery of a new spate of texts at Ugarit during the 1992 season, it has become clear that also in the Ugaritic sphere the watery deep, known in Hebrew as Tehom, has been deified. The pantheon list *Ug*. V no. 18:18, read as ^{d}ḪUR.SAG-MEŠ *ù a-mu-tu*[*m*] by Jean Nougayrol, should in fact be read as ^{d}ḪUR.SAG-MEŠ *ù* A.*mu-ú*, the last word meaning 'waters' and not 'valleys'. A duplicate text found in 1992 has ^{d}ḪUR.SAG-MEŠ *ù* ^{d}A-MEŠ (RS 1992.2004:29, courtesy Daniel Arnaud), which confirms the corrected reading of *Ug*. 5 no. 18:18. RS 1992. 2004 is a deity list corresponding to RS 26.142 (= *Ug*. 5 no. 170), which, as is now clear, corresponds to RS 24.643 verso (= C. VIROLLEAUD, Les nouveaux textes mythologiques et liturgiques de Ras Shamra, *Ug*. 5 [1969] no. 9). The entry there corresponding to RS 1992.2004:29 is [*ǵr*]*m wthmt*, 'mountains and deep waters' (no. 9:41). This means that the entry *ǵrm w*[----] in the first part of RS 24.643 is to be read *ǵrm w*[*thmt*] (line 6).

III. Tĕhôm occurs 35 times is the OT, both in the singular and in the plural. Like →Sheol, it is used as a semi-proper name without the definite article, except for the plural forms Ps 106:9 and Isa 63:13. In the OT *tĕhôm* never occurs as an personal deity. Although attempts have been made to find traces in the OT of a combat between →God and an alleged monster like Tiāmat (→Rahab and →Leviathan), there is no evidence that *tĕhôm* ever was such a personal mythological character. In the relevant passages, *tĕhôm* refers to the waters of the Reed Sea, and the separation of the waters refers to the Exodus rather than to the creation of the world. The scene is Israel's crossing the sea after God had separated its waters (Isa 27:1; 51:9-10; Ps 74:12-17; 89:9-12; Job 9:13-14; 26:12-13).

Another point of contact has been found in the concept according to which the splitting up of Tiāmat's body led to the isolation of the cosmic waters inside her, and that a crossbar and guards were established in order to check that the waters did not escape uncontrolled (*Enūma eliš* IV 139-140). This is corroborated by the Babylonian account of the Flood, where it is said that the Flood actually occurred when the posts were torn out (*Gilgameš epic* X 101). This is similar to Gen 1:6-7, where it is said that a firmament was erected "in the middle of the waters" in order to separate the waters below the firmament from the waters above it (cf. the hymnic paraphrase in Ps 104:6-10). This coincides with the idea that the flood occurred when the waters of the deep (i.e. *tĕhôm*, here the subterranean waters in opposition to the celestial waters) and the locks of the celestial waters were released (Gen 7:11). The idea is also echoed in Ps 148:4, "the waters above the heavens". This is reminiscent of the general idea promulgated in *Enūma eliš* V, that the celestial world is a replica of the lower world.

In this case the parallels are not sufficiently specific to warrant the conclusion that *Enūma eliš* was the source of the biblical account. Yet, the similarity of the ideas involved cannot simply be explained as reflections of universal concepts. A possible explanation would be that the ideas had spread and become commonly known in a larger area of the ancient Near East. Another possibility is that the Biblical account of the creation of the world, as expounded in Gen 1, was composed as a polemic response to the account of *Enūma eliš*. To what extent *Enūma eliš*, or at least the general outline of its plot, was known to the biblical authors and readers, is beyond the point of verification. Yet, the biblical account did not come into being in an intellectual vacuum, and the assumption would make it possible to see the organization of the biblical creation story as sophisticated transformation of mythology into theology. Summaries of *Enūma eliš* were given as late as the Hellenistic period by Berossos, and by the neo-Platonic Damascius (early sixth century CE).

IV. *Bibliography*

J. BOTTÉRO & S. N. KRAMER, *Lorsque les dieux faisaient l'homme* (Paris 1989) 602-679 (*Enūma eliš*), cf. 472-478 (*La Théogonie de Dunnu*); J. VAN DIJK, Existe-t-il un "Poème de la Création" Sumérien?, *AOAT* 25 (1976) 125-133; A. HEIDEL, *The Babylonian Genesis* (Chicago 1942) 96-114; T. JACOBSEN, The Battle Between Marduk and Tiamat, *JAOS* 88 (1968) 104-108; W. G. LAMBERT, Studies in Marduk, *BSOAS* 47 (1984) 1-9.

B. ALSTER

TIBERIUS → RULER CULT

TIGRIS חדקל

I. The OT refers to the Tigris as *Ḥiddeqel*. The designation *hannāhār haggādôl*, "the Great River" was applied to the Tigris in Dan 10:14, but otherwise refers to the →Euphrates. The two rivers appear as a pair in the expression *ʾaram naharayim*, "the Land of the Two Rivers", i.e. (Western) Mesopotamia.

Hebr *Ḥiddeqel* derives from an earlier Semitic form of the name which appears as *Idiqlat* in Akkadian, and **Idigna** in Sumerian. The female ending, characteristic of the Akkadian form, shows that the Tigris, like the Euphrates, was conceived as a female entity. The designation is likely to go back to a pre-Sumerian name. In later Akkadian and Aramaic the name became abbreviated to *Diqla(t)*. The name Tigris comes from Gk Τίγρις, which in its turn is based on Old-Pers *Tigrâ*. The name was not used in Hittite, where the Tigris was called Aranzi (RGTC 6 [1978] 524 and 530).

II. The name of the river bears the divine determinative in a Sumerian godlist dating from the first half of the second millennium BCE (TCL 15, 10:82), but in current usage the name of the river was never preceded by the divine determinative. Indications of the deification of the River can, however, be found in the Old Babylonian anthroponyms Ummī-Idiqlat, "The-Tigris-is-my-mother"; Idiqlat-ummī, "My-mother-is-the-Tigris" (RGTC 3 [1980] 287); Mār-Idiqlat; "Son-of-the-Tigris"; and especially in some Middle Assyrian names, Šēp-Idiqlat, "The-Foot-of-the-Tigris (scil. I seized)"; Arad-Idiqlat, "Servant-of-the-Tigris"; Idiqlat-rēmīni, "Tigris-be-merciful-to-me"; Idiglat-KAM, "He-of-the-Tigris"; Sīqi-Idiqlat, "Lap-of-the-Tigris"; Ṣillī-Idiqlat, "My-protection-is-the-Tigris"; Tašme-Idiqlat, "The-Tigris-listened"; and Kidin-Idiqlat, "(The-one-under-the-) Protection-of-the-Tigris" (RGTC 5 [1982] 301-302). Similar name forms, such as Kidin-Martu, "(The-one-under-the-) protection of Martu"; Kidin-Adad, etc., indicate that the name of the river here functions as a theophoric element. Yet, no evidence suggests that the Tigris was accorded divine status in the Mesopotamian mythology and cult of the third and early second Millennia BCE.

The assumption that the divine status assigned to the river in anthroponymns is an echo of the earlier deification of the river may not be the only way in which this occasional appearing of the river as a god can be explained. Three phenomena might have to be taken into account.

First, in ordinary theological thinking, natural forces, such as water, were regarded as means that could be used by the major gods of the pantheon in exorcistic and purifying rituals. During the performance of the incantation rituals these natural forces could themselves be regarded as divine powers. Owing to its cleansing and healing potential, this in particular applies to the water of the river.

Secondly, the Mesopotamian rivers played a role in the water ordeal (→River) which made it natural to regard the river not only as a means through which the divine will of the god of justice (→Sun) manifested itself, but also as an independent deity.

Thirdly, since the two rivers, the Euphrates and the Tigris, were the life-giving forces that made it possible to inhabit the alluvial plain, there was a tendency to regard the rivers as manifestations of the primeval river which, in mythological thinking, was said to be the creator of everything (*bānât kalama*) and to have spread fertility. The existence of the primeval river god Nāru can be inferred from anthroponyms from the Pre-Sargonic and Sargonic periods. The earliest reference to the primeval river in mythological context is the name **Id-maḫ**, "Mighty River" (written with the divine determinative) in a Sumerian myth (G. A. BARTON, *Miscellaneous Babylonian Inscriptions*, vol 1 [New Haven 1918] Barton Cylinder), dating from ca. 2300 BCE.

In the Sumerian mythology of the early second millennium BCE the Tigris does not appear as a personal deity. The Tigris and the Euphrates are said to have been filled with water when the god Enki erected his penis and ejaculated into the rivers (*Enki and the World Order* 251-254; BOTTÉRO & KRAMER 1989:173-174). In the mythological speculation of *Enūma eliš* V 55, the Euphrates and the Tigris are said to have sprung from the eyes of →Tiamat, the divine antagonist of →Marduk, and an esoteric commentary from the first millennium BCE specifies that "the Tigris is her right eye, the Euphrates is her left eye" (SAA 3 [1989], no. 39 r. 3). In ordinary Mesopotamian thinking the rivers were not regarded as divine, but the yearly flooding of the rivers, through which in particular the god Enki (Ea) bestowed his favours upon mankind, was a central feature of Mesopotamian religion. The precise location of the Tigris riverbed in southern Mesopotamia in antiquity is much debated, and it has been argued that only the Euphrates, and not the Tigris, played a role in the irrigation of the land. The textual evidence, however, clearly indicates that the two rivers were regarded as equally important for agriculture and transportation from the third millenium BCE onward.

III. In the Bible, the Tigris is never ascribed divine status. It occurs as a merely topographical point of reference in Dan 10:4, where the river bank is said to be the place where the prophet received his vision. The river does, however, take on mythological demensions in the Paradise Myth. The Tigris (*Ḥiddeqel*) is there said to be one of the four branches into which the stream springing from Eden divides (Gen 2:14), together with Pishon, Gihon, and the Euphrates. The information given there, that the Tigris flows east of →Assur, is topographically correct.

IV. *Bibliography*

J. BOTTÉRO, *Mythes et rites de Babylone* (Paris 1985) 290; J. BOTTÉRO & S. N. KRAMER, *Lorsque les dieux faisaient l'homme* (Paris 1989); W. HEIMPEL, Ein zweiter Schritt zur Rehabilitierung der Rolle des Tigris in Sumer, *ZA* 80 (1990) 204-219.

B. ALSTER

TIRASH תירושׁ תירשׁ

I. Heb *tîrôš* appears to be the term for 'new wine', i.e. wine which is incompletely fermented (though it should be noted that KÖHLER [1928] took the view that it simply meant 'wine' and was an archaic alternative to *yayin*: this question does not affect the present treatment). It occurs in Hebrew frequently in this plain meaning, often in the context of the formulaic phrase 'the grain, the new wine and the oil' (Deut 7:13; 11:14 etc.). There are analogous forms in Ugaritic (*trṯ: KTU* 1.114:4, 16 [//*yn*] and 1.17 vi:7 [with *yn*]) and Phoenician and Punic (*trš*: Karatepe *KAI* 26 A III 7, 9; C IV 7, 9; Carthage *CIS* I 5522:2). There appears also to be an etymological connection with Akk *siraš* (var. *siriš, širis*), both the word for beer and the name of the deity of beer and brewing (*CAD* S 306, cf. *AkkGE*, 448-449). The Hebrew word has been linked sometimes with a divine name attested both in Ugaritic and other sources and, less certainly, in the Hebrew Bible (Gen 27:28; Hos 7: 14; 9:2).

There is no clear etymology for the Ugaritic divine name, *trṯ*. It might be related to Hieroglyphic Hittite *tuwarsa* (RABIN 1963; C. H. GORDON, *Ugaritic Textbook* [AnOr 38; Rome 1965] 499). This would be unlikely if Ugaritic *mrṯ* (*KTU* 1.22 i:18, 20; 2. 34:32), which refers to a type of wine, is related to the same root as *trṯ*. RABIN, however, noting Jewish Aramaic *mēyrat* with a similar meaning (*Tg Deut* 29:5), separates *mrṯ* from *trṯ*, relating the former to Arabic *maraṯa*, 'steep fruit in water'. In any case others think the Hittite is borrowed from Semitic (e.g. AARTUN 1984). Comparison with Akk *siraš* suggests a root *ṮRŠ having something to do with the process of fermentation.

Older Hebrew dictionaries link the Hebrew to the root YRŠ. While it is difficult to find a suitable meaning in the common root YRŠ, 'take possession of', *tîrôš* in Mic 6:15 has been thought by some to present evidence of a second verb (YRŠ II). *Tîrôš* in this passage might be understood as an 'imperfect' meaning 'you will tread (grapes)' (P. HAUPT, Critical notes on Micah, *AJSL* 26 [1909-1910] 201-252, esp. 215, 223). Such a meaning would suit the common noun, providing the link with wine-making. The text is, however, by no means certain and the identification of YRŠ II here (and in Job 20:15, which is a less convincing case) has been rejected by other scholars (e.g. LORETZ 1971). Whether the existence of this verbal root is accepted or not, the divine name would still remain in doubt, since there is no contextual indication of a link between the divinity and wine.

II. The divine name is clearly attested in Ugaritic and in the El-Amarna personal name of a ruler of Hazor, ^{m}*Abdi-tir-ši* ('Servant of *Tiršu*': *EA* 228:3). As a deity, Ugaritic *trṯ* is found in *KTU* 1.39:16 and 102:9 in offering lists. Apart from the presumed association with wine, virtually nothing can be concluded about the nature of the deity. For ALBRIGHT (1968) and W. KUHNIGK (*Nordwestsemitische Studien zum Hoseabuch* [Rome 1974] 97, 112) Tirosh is a Canaanite →Bacchus; A. HERDNER (*Ug* 7 [1978] 5) suggests that we are dealing with a goddess of the new wine, drawing a parallel with the Mesopotamian deity Siraš (though even here the sex is uncertain). Even the association with wine is ambiguous, since it is possible (cf. the case of →Dagon) that the particular type of wine in question was named after the deity rather than *vice versa* (ALBRIGHT 1968).

III. This deity does not appear in the Hebrew Bible in any explicit narrative or unambiguous context, but the suggestion has been made that sometimes *tîrôš* 'new wine', contains an allusion to the Canaanite deity. In particular this kind of allusion is found by DAHOOD (e.g. 1974) and KUHNIGK (*Nordwestsemitische Studien zum Hoseabuch* [Rome 1974] 97, 112) in Gen 27:28; Hos 7:14 and Hos 9:2. In Gen 27:28, the suggestion of such an allusion is pure speculation. *Tîrôš* stands alongside *dāgān*, but nothing in the context suggests mythological overtones. *dāgān* is satisfactorily translated as 'grain', and 'plenty of grain and new wine' are simply divine gifts in Isaac's blessing upon his son.

On the other hand, it is one of Hosea's clear themes that it was →Yahweh, not the foreign gods, who gave Israel 'the grain, the new wine and the oil' (2:10-11.24). In Hos 7:14 the specific context is that of turning to other gods, and "for *dāgān* and *tîrôš* they gash themselves" may plausibly be interpreted as an allusion to illicit cult (though perhaps simply to a cult of lamentation for the failure of vegetation). Hos 9:2, "*tîrôš* shall fail them (corr.)", could well also be an allusion to the the deity. Caution is necessary even in the Hosea cases, however, since there is no contemporary evidence for the worship of such a deity in Palestine (though Dagon *is* so attested).

IV. *Bibliography*

K. AARTUN, Neue Beiträge zum ugaritischen Lexicon I, *UF*16 (1984) 1-52, esp. 35-36 no. 45, and 50 no. 64; W. F.

ALBRIGHT, *Yahweh and the Gods of Canaan* (London 1968) 186; A. COOPER, Divine Names and Epithets in the Ugaritic Texts, *RSP* III 428; M. DAHOOD, Hebrew-Ugaritic Lexicography XII, *Bib* 55 (1974) 381-393, esp. 387 s.v. תירוש [& lit]; L. KÖHLER, Eine archaistische Wortgruppe, *ZAW* 46 (1928) 218-220; O. LORETZ, Hebräisch *tyrwš* und *jrš* in Mi 6,15 und Hi 20,15, *UF* 9 (1977) 353-354; C. RABIN, Hittite Words in Hebrew, *Or* 32 (1963) 113-139, esp. 137-138 no. 20; H. H. SCHMID, ירשׁ *jrš* beerben, *THAT* I 778-781, esp. 780-781.

J. F. HEALEY

TITANS Τιτᾶνες

I. In the strict sense 'Titans' is the collective name of only six of the sons of Uranus-Sky and Gaea-Earth, whose six sisters and wives were called Titanesses (Τιτανίδες). The most important couple of these were Cronus and his sister-wife Rhea, who became the parents of →Zeus, →Hera and various other gods. The Greek name 'Titans' occurs in the geographical name "Valley of the Titans" in the LXX at 2 Sam 5:18.22; 23:13 (*Luc*); 1 Chr 11:15 (v. l. Hex), and as a synonym of →"giants" in Jdt 16:6. The name cannot be explained from Greek and is considered to be of pre-Hellenic provenance. According to the *Etymologicum Magnum* 760,53 there was a connection with τιτώ "day, sun" (cf. Τιθωνός, the husband of Eôs-Daybreak); Hesychius explains τιτήνη as βασιλίς "queen".

II. The other children of Uranus and Gaea were: the three Cyclops (personifications of lightning and thunder), and the three Hecatonchires (personifications of strength and power), who had been born before the Titans. After the Titans, according to Hesiod, the three Erinyes (goddesses of revenge), the various Giants, and the Melian →Nymphs were born. All this later offspring came into existence from the blood drops of Uranus' castration which fell on Gaea. As most of the Titans have no clear functions or names that can be explained from Greek, such as Cronus, Hera, Titan itself, it is usually assumed that they represent the pantheon of the original pre-Greek population. These gods were then largely superseded by the Olympians, the gods of the Greek invaders, especially Zeus, →Poseidon and →Hades. This fact would then be reflected in mythology by the "Titanomachy" or struggle between the second generation of the gods (Cronus and peers) and the third (Zeus and peers). Wars and conflicts, however, between successive generations of gods are not an uncommon phenomenon in the myths of other nations. In the Orphic variants of this myth mankind sprang from the ashes of the Titans, who were killed by Zeus' lightning because they had devoured his son →Dionysus. As a consequence, every man was considered in Orphism to contain both a Dionysiac or divine and a Titanic or rebellious element (cf. in Plato, *Leges* 3,701c Τιτανικὴ φύσις).

In a somewhat wider sense the name "Titans" was also applied to the offspring of the brothers and sisters of Cronus and Rhea, for instance, to Atlas and Prometheus, the sons of Iapetus (→Japheth), and to Helios, the son of Hyperiôn. And since most of the children of Uranus and Gaea were of gigantic stature, "Titans" in a still wider sense became more or less equivalent with "giants", and furthermore, with "evil powers", because they had been the opponents of Zeus both in the Titanomachy and in the Gigantomachy (cf. the Orphic view). It is only in these wider senses that "Titan(s)" is found in Hellenistic Jewish literature.

III. The LXX "Valley of the Titans" corresponds to the "Valley of the →Rephaim" in the MT, either without textual variation, or being itself a textual variant of "the Valley of the Ραφαιμ" or "γιγάντων" (2 Sam 23:13 *Luc* and 1 Chr 11:15 Hex; cf. Josephus, *Ant.* 7,71 v.l.). Since the Rephaim were considered to be the tall, original inhabitants of Canaan, "Titans" means here simply "giants". The same holds good of Jdt 16:6 where the two words occur in *parallelismus membrorum*: "neither did sons of Titans slay him (i. e. Holophernes), nor did tall giants attack him, but Judith ... put an end to him". They also occur side by side in

1 Enoch 6-7 and 9:9 where they refer to the giant offspring of "the sons of God" and "the daughters of mankind" of Gen 6:1-4 (LXX: γίγαντες only).

The name is not found as such in the writings of the NT, but may be hidden in "666" in Rev 13:18, the number of "the Beast" and also of a man. One of the solutions of this riddle that have been listed by Irenaeus, happens to be Τειταν (*Against Her.* 5,30,3), of which the numerical values 300+5+10+300+1+50 add up to 666. He comments that this solution is particularly convincing to himself, because it is not the name of an actually venerated god or a known king, but nevertheless a divine and kingly, even a tyrant's, name. A further NT link with the Greek Titans is the use of the verb ταρταρώσας in 2 Pet 2:4 by which the author describes how God cast down the fallen angels in Hell to keep them there for the final judgment. It is the typical word used for the punishment of the Titans after their defeat (e.g. Apollodorus, *Library* 1,2,3; Sextus Empiricus, *Pyrrh.* 3,210); the substantive "Tartarus", however, is found more often to refer to the Jewish Nether World, though by far not as frequently as "Hades"(→Giants).

The fact that Ezechiel Poeta makes the Egyptian messenger, who reports about the catastrophe of his country-men at the Red Sea, speak of "Titan Helios" rather than "Rê", when he has to say that the sun was setting (line 217) sheds some light on his Hellenism. More profound is the mythological Hellenization of Gen 10-11 which has been carried through in the *Sibylline Oracles*. Here we are told (3,105-158) that after the fall of the Tower and the confusion of languages, during the tenth generation of mankind since the Flood, three brothers ruled as kings simultaneously, each over a third part of the earth: Cronus, Titan, and Iapetus. Their father Uranus had made them swear to him that they would respect one another's realms. After his death, however, they began to fight, with the result that Cronus became sole king but had to promise Titan that he would not father any sons. When sons were born nevertheless, they were all swallowed by the Titans (plural), except for Zeus, Poseidon and Pluto, who had been sent to safe places by their mother Rhea. This became known and there arose a war between the seventy sons of Titan and the sons of Cronus, in which both parties perished in the end. After this war the Egyptian kingdom was established, next the kingdom of the Persians, etc. This story is a remarkable conflation of the Hesiodic myth, its Orphic variant (here the Titans, not Cronus, swallow newly born children), and elements from Genesis: the tripartition of mankind at a tenth generation (in Gen as reckoned from Adam, here since the Flood); according to Epiphanius, *Ancoratus* 114, it was →Noah who administered a similar oath to his sons as Uranus did, and in both cases there is a →Japheth/Iapetus among them. A different and much simpler version is found in *Sib. Or.* 1,283-323: the new generation born after the Flood is the Golden or sixth generation, who are ruled by three magnanimous kings, evidently Noah's sons; the next generation are the proud and rebellious Titans.

IV. *Bibliography.*

J. Dörig & O. Gigon, *Der Kampf der Götter und Titanen* (Olten 1961); H. von Geisau, Titanes, *KP* 5 (1975) 867-868; von Geisau, Titanomachie, *KP* 5 (1975) 868.

G. Mussies

TORAH תורה

I. The word Torah is usually connected with the root YRH, which means "to point, direct, teach" in the Hiphil conjugation. If so, the noun properly means "instruction, teaching, direction". Since Torah is used most frequently of specific cultic instructions, as well as the demands of the covenant, however, it is translated as *nomos* in Greek, hence Eng "law". Inasmuch as the word commonly refers to "the Torah of →Moses" and "the book of the Torah of Moses" (the Pentateuch), one may think of the Torah as "law" in the sense of the covenant community's "constitution". That is certainly the dominant meaning of the word in the Hebrew Bible. Along with that concept, however, was the understanding of the Torah not only as a body of rules, but as an embodiment of →wisdom (cf. Deut 4:1-8) which may be universally recognized for its effect on humanity (GREENBERG 1990). Indeed, the Torah may be understood collectively as the written and unwritten precepts that make up the regimen of a wholesome community. As such it was always central to the Israelites.

II. Heb *tôrâ* is often seen as the semantic equivalent of Akk *têrtu* "instruction, command". The equation is not without difficulties, however, for the Akkadian noun is derived from *wâru* (< *Wʾr), whereas one should expect a connection with *warû* (< *wrw), the Akkadian cognate to Heb yrh. It has been suggested that Heb *tôrâ* is, like Akk *têrtu*, derived from *wʾr and that the usage of yrh in the Hiphil is secondarily generated from the noun (ALBRIGHT 1927). The intriguing hypothesis remains problematic, however, in the light of the fact that the root *wʾr does not occur elsewhere in Hebrew. In any case, Akk *têrtu* has not became hypostatized. It is true that the legal notions of Kittu ('Right', →Zedeq) and →Mīšaru ('Equity') are deified in Akkadian literature, and these are to be identified with Misor and Sydyk mentioned in Sanchuniathon. But these are only broadly pertinent as analogies for the phenomenon of hypostases in general. The same may be said of the deification of *Ḥw* 'Authoritative Utterance, Ordinance' in Egyptian literature. Certainly no direct influence may be discerned as regards the personification of Torah in the Bible. Rather, the images and idioms pertaining to personified Torah are drawn from or otherwise inspired by older biblical sources, notably the portrayal of Wisdom and the *Kābôd* →'Glory'.

The centrality of the Torah led eventually to a pious devotion to it that borders on veneration. This is evident in Ps 119, where the poet uses language for the Torah and its precepts that is ordinarily reserved for the deity. Thus, instead of asking that God's →'face' should not be hidden, the supplicant implores: "Do not hide your commandments from me!" Here the Torah takes the place of God's 'Face' (*pānîm*), that is, God's Presence. The psalmist expresses trust (v 42) and speaks of lifting up the hands to the commandments (v 48). The author indulges in poetic licence, but since →God is addressed directly in this composition, one cannot yet speak of the Torah as hypostasis. It is even doubtful if one should think of the personification of the Torah here, although it has been observed that the word repeatedly used for the Torah as a 'delight' is the same one used of personified →Wisdom as God's 'delight' in Prov 8:30-31 (GREENBERG 1990).

It is not until the Wisdom of Ben Sira that one first encounters the explicit identification of the Torah with primordial Wisdom. Transparently dependent on Prov 8, the book begins by asserting that Wisdom was created before all things and was revealed to humanity (1:1-10). Then, at the climax of the book in chapter 24, the revelation of primordial Wisdom is audaciously identified with the revelation of the Torah on Mount Sinai (v 23). Personified Wisdom is plainly the Torah. She is said to have dwelled 'on high' with the pillar of cloud as her throne, but she was ordered to dwell (lit. 'tabernacle') among the Israelites. She was established on →Zion and ministered before the deity in the tabernacle. The theophanic symbolisms are obvious, and there can be no doubt that the Wisdom-Torah here is depicted in language reminiscent of YHWH's *Kābôd* →'Glory'. This identification of Torah with Wisdom persists in Bar 3:9-4:4, again with theophanic idioms. Wisdom-Torah is said to have "appeared upon earth and lived among human beings all who hold fast to her shall live and those who forsake her will die" (Bar 3:37-4:1).

III. In rabbinic literature, the Torah completely replaced Wisdom as hypostasis, although the portrayal of Wisdom remains foundational. Like Wisdom (Prov 8:22), the Torah is said to have been created before all things in the world (*Gen. Rabb.* 1:4; b. *Pes* 54a; b. *Ned* 39b). Of all the preexistent things, however, only the Torah and the →throne of Glory are said to have been created, while the others were only conceived, and of those, the Torah preceded the throne of Glory. Indeed, the opening word of Gen 1:1 is interpreted as referring to the Torah: Heb *bĕrē'šît* is taken not to mean "in the beginning", but "by the beginning", meaning the Torah (*Gen. Rabb.* 1:1). Support for this interpretation is found in Prov 8:22, "YHWH created me the beginning (*rē'šît*) of his way". The Torah is said to be the instrument through which the world was created (*Abot* 3:14; cf. *Sipre Deut* 48). God reportedly took counsel with the Torah before creation, and so the plural "us" in Gen 1:26 ("let us make humanity") is seen as a reference to God and the Torah (*Tanḥ. Pequde* 3; *Tanḥ. Berereshit* 1). Variously personified as daughter and bride, the Torah is depicted as reclining in God's bosom and joining angels in praising God (*Gen. Rabb.* 28:4). In some cases, the Torah is so closely associated with various manifestations of divine presence as to be virtually equated with them. Thus one reads: "The Holy One, blessed be He, says: 'If a person desecrates My daughter (i.e. the Torah), it is as if that one desecrates Me. If a person enters the synagogue and desecrates my Torah, it is as if that one rose and desecrated My Glory'" (*Tanḥ. Pequde* 4). Ultimately, among some Kabbalists, it was said that the Torah itself is the name of God and, indeed, that the Torah is God.

IV. *Bibliography*

W. F. ALBRIGHT, The Names "Israel" and "Judah", with an Excursus on the Etymology of *tôdah* and *tôrah*," *JBL* 46 (1927) 151-185; W. BOUSSET - H. GRESSMANN, *Die Religion des Judentums im späthellenistischen Zeitalter* (Tübingen 1926) 121, 347; L. DÜRR, *Die Wertung des göttlichen Wortes im Alten Testament und im antiken Orient* (Lepizig 1938) 122-157; M. GREENBERG, Three Conceptions of the Torah in Hebrew Scriptures, *Die Hebräische Bibel und ihre zweifache Nachgeschichte* (FS R. Rendtorff; Neukirchen-Vluyn 1990) 365-378; G. ÖSTBORN, *Tōrā in the Old Testament* (Lund 1945); H. RINGGREN, *Word and Wisdom: Studies in the Hypostatization of Divine Qualities and Functions in the Ancient Near East* (Lund 1947).

C. L. SEOW

TRAVELLERS עברים

I. The participle Qal plural *'ōbĕrîm* of the verb *'br*, 'to pass from one side to the other' received a special meaning in the context of the cult of the dead. Here it denotes the spirits of the dead crossing the border between the land of the living and the world of the dead. Its Ugaritic cognate is *'brm* in *KTU* 1.22 i:15. It occurs as a divine name in Ezek 39:11.14. This divine name is also preserved in the geographical name Abarim (Num 21:10-11; 27:12; 33:44-48; Deut 32:49; and Jer 22:20).

II. In the Ugaritic text *KTU* 1.22 describing a necromantic session, the king invokes the spirits of the dead (→Rephaim) and celebrates a feast, probably the New Year Festival, with them. It is told that they came over traveling by horse-drawn chariots. As they are taking part in the meal served for them they are explicitly called 'those who came over'.

In Job 33:18 the verb *'br* is used to denote the crossing of the river between life and death (FUHS 1986:1024). This represents the quite general ancient conception of a river or sea separating the world of the dead from the land of the living (cf. the Greek Styx and the Akkadian Hubur). In the Sumerian flood story Dilmun, the place of blissful afterlife, is called 'land of the crossing'(**kur-bal** *Atr* 144:260).

III. In Ezekiel the word *'ōbĕrîm* occurs several times, usually as an indication of spectators watching the misery of Israel being punished by →Yahweh (5:14; 36:34) or to indicate that it was made impossible to pass through the land (14:15; 29:11; 33:28). In chapter 39 the emphasis is on the action of men going through the land looking for the corpses of →Gog and his 'horde'. In v 14, however, the second occurrence indicates the dead. The solution to this *crux interpretum* is to relate *'ōbĕrîm*, here and in v 11, to the *'brm* mentioned in the Ugaritic text denoting the spirits of the dead. POPE translates all occurrences of *ʿōbĕrîm* in Ezek 39 with 'the Departed' (1977:173), but this leads to new problems for the interpretation of the text.

The valley of the *ʿōbĕrîm* is located 'east of the sea' (v 11), which is probably the Dead Sea. So it was part of Transjordan. This is a region which shows many traces of ancient cults of the dead, such as the megalithic monuments called dolmens and placenames referring to the dead and the netherworld, viz. Obot (→'Spirit-of-the-Dead'), Peor (cf →Baal of Peor), and Abarim (SPRONK 1986: 228-230).

According to the OT belief in Yahweh left no room for the veneration of the dead, but apparently such Canaanite practices were never eliminated completely. Ezek 39: 11-16 can be regarded as an attempt to eradicate such ancient beliefs: the powerful spirits of the dead who came over to the land of the living are defeated and buried for ever by ordinary people. The only 'crossing' that remains is their crossing over the land to search for those who have embarked upon the journey of no return.

IV. *Bibliography*

H. F. FUHS, *ʿābar*, *TWAT* 5 (Stuttgart 1986) 1015-1033 [& lit.]; M. H. POPE, Notes on the Rephaim Texts from Ugarit, *Ancient Near Eastern Studies in Memory of J. J. Finkelstein* (ed. M. de Jong Ellis; Hamden 1977) 163-182; S. RIBICHINI & P. XELLA, 'La valle dei passanti' (Ezechiele 39:11), *UF* 12 (1980) 434-437; K. SPRONK, *Beatific Afterlife in Ancient Israel and in the Ancient Near East* (AOAT 219; Neukirchen-Vluyn 1986).

K. SPRONK

TREES → OAK, SYCOMORE, TEREBINTH, THORNBUSH

TYCHE Τύχη

I. Tyche is the Greek personification of luck or success (from *tynchanō*, 'happen to one'), which is expressed also in the anthroponym Tychicus, an especially popular Greek name during the Hellenistic period that occurs five times in the New Testament.

II. *Tychē* means both 'good fortune' or 'success', or, 'luck' or 'chance', either good or bad as determined by context (Euripides, *Ion* 512-515). For the early Greeks, *tychē* could be considered, along with the *moirai* (the 'fates'), as an agent of human good and evil (Archilochus 8 *apud* Stobaus 1.6.3). As Archilochus conceded, however, that "all things are given by the gods" (Archilochus 58; see also D. 2.22) who are the masters of *tychē* (see E. *El.* 880-891), *tychē* came to be understood as the good obtained by their favour, as expressed in the common phrase *theiē tychē* (Herodotus 1.126, 3.139, 4.8, 5. 92) and, consequently, as the benevolent attribute of such deities as →Aphrodite, →Hermes, Rhea, or →Zeus (A. B. COOK, *Zeus, A Study in Ancient Religion* [Cambridge 1914-1940] I: 175-176; II. 1: 675; II. 2: 878 n. 11, 879 n. 17, 1163). First personified as one of the Oceanids, daughters of Oceanus and Tethys (Hes. *Th.* 360; *H. Cer.* 420), or as one of the *Moirai* (Pindar, *Frag.* 21), *tychē* became fully deified as a →'saviour': *Tychē Sōter* (Aeschylus, *Ag.* 664; Sophocles, *OC.* 80, 1080) or, as the daughter of Zeus, the Deliverer (Pindar, *Ol.* 12.2-12): *Tychē Sōteira* (12.3). Otherwise, no mythology developed around her in the classical period.

Pindar acknowledged Tyche as a goddess who "upholds the city" (Pindar, *Frag.* 39), a reference to the traditional association between *tychē* and certain cities (Thucydides 5.112). By the fourth century BCE, a public cult to ensure the good fortune of cities emerged in Thebes and, shortly thereafter, Agathe Tyche, or 'Good Fortune' began to receive sacrifice in Athens. In contrast to the traditional association of Greek deities with particular cities, Tyche could be associated with any city because of her comprehensiveness and by the third century, she possessed temples in nearly all large Greek cities; by imperial times, her worship had spread to many small towns as well. Finally, the Tyche of individual cities became transferred to the fortune of their collective ruler, the Hellenistic king or the Roman Emperor (*Mart. Pol.* 9.2; 10.1; Origen, *Mart.* 7; 40, *C.Cels.* 8.65, 67).

Because of her universal sovereignty (Pliny, *HN* 2.5.22; see already Euripides, *Cycl.* 606-607 and *Hec.* 488-492 where Tyche is described as more powerful than the gods), Tyche could be praised by early Hellenistic times as the "noblest of the gods" (Stobaeus 1.6.13), even while her unpredictability became increasingly emphasized (Pliny, *HN* 2.5.22; see already Euripides, *Alc.* 785-786). Her capricious nature, the embodiment of the perceived ambiguity of existence in the Hellenistic period (e.g., Apuleius, *Met.* 1.6), determined the character of the Roman goddess →*Fortuna* with whom Tyche became identified. During the Hellenistic period, however, a sympathetic Tyche with the sole qualifying attribute of *agathē* ('good') became differentiated from her recently emphasized ambivalent nature and associated with other benevolent goddesses of the period, especially Isis (V. F. VANDERLIP, *The Four Greek Hymns of Isidorus and the Cult of Isis* [Toronto, 1972] 31-32, 78, 94-96; Apuleius, *Met.* 11.15), or, as Tyche-Isis, in combination with other goddesses. There are, for example, statues of the Roman Fortuna with the attributes of Tyche-Isis (Brit. Mus. GR 1955.12-15.1), or of →Athena-Tyche-Isis (Brit. Mus. GR 1920. 2-18.1), as well as similar syncretistic representations on coins.

Tyche was most often depicted as a standing woman steering a course with a rudder in her right hand and holding a cornucopia in her left. According to Dio Chrysostomus, "the rudder indicates that Tyche directs the life of men; and the horn of →Amaltheia calls attention to the giving of good things and prosperity" (*Or.* 63.7). She is also associated with a globe, which may represent her universal rule, or, again according to Chrysostomus, her fickleness, "for the divine power is, in fact, ever in motion" (*Or.* 63.7). Chrysostomus' explanation is perhaps closer to the representation of Tyche, largely on coins, with a wheel—the image of her changeability.

Even as cities or rulers might have their own *tychē*, so individuals might have theirs (Demosthenes 18 [*De Cor.*]. 252-266). In this connection, personal names incorporating the word and indicating, thereby, the wish for good fortune are documented since Homer (*Il.* 7.220: Tychius), but became very common from the first century BCE on (e.g., Eutyches, Tychicus).

III. In the Bible, the name Tychicus appears in the deutero-Pauline literature of the New Testament as that of an associate of Paul. According to Acts 20:4, he is a native of the Roman Province of Asia who accompanied Paul on his third missionary journey from Corinth to Jerusalem (the Western text knows the name as 'Eutychus', the character in the following story, Acts 20:7-12). In Colossians and Ephesians, Tychicus is a "beloved brother and faithful minister in the Lord" who is to report to the recipients of the letter(s) about Paul and to encourage them (Col 4:7-8; Eph 6:21); according to Titus it is proposed to send him or Artemas to Titus in Crete (Tit 3:12); and according to 2 Tim, he is sent to Ephesus (2 Tim 4:12). In later Greek tradition, Tychicus was considered to be one of the 'seventy' disciples (Lk 10:1, see Pseudo-Dorotheus; Pseudo-Hippolytus) who either became the successor of Sosthenes as Bishop of Colophon (*Menalogion* for December 9), or was appointed Bishop of Chalcedon by the apostle Andrew (Pseudo-Epiphanius), or became Bishop of Neapolis in Cyprus, where the ninth-century Roman martyrologist, Ado, followed by Usuard, commemorates his feast at Paphos on April 29. Although theophoric names ideally indicated some alliance with the deities from whom they were taken and something of their "power and honour" (Plutarch, *Def. Orac.* 421E), the uses of the name, Tychicus, in the Christian context are in the popular sense of wishing good fortune.

IV. *Bibliography*

G. BUSCH, *Untersuchungen zum Wesen der* Τύχη *in den Tragödien des Euripides* (diss. Heidelberg 1937); H.-P. DRÖGEMÜLLER, Tyche, *KP* 5 (1975) 1016-1017; W. C. GREENE, *Moira. Fate, Good, and Evil in Greek Thought* (Cambridge, MA 1944) s.v.; F. W. HAMDORF, *Griechische Kultpersonifikationen der vorhellenistischen Zeit* (Mainz 1964) 37-39, 97-100; G. HERZOG-HAUSER,

Tyche und Fortuna, *Wiener Studien* 63 (1948) 156-163; HERZOG-HAUSER, Tyche, *RE* 7A [2. Reihe] (1939) 1643-1689; H. HERTER, Glück und Verhängnis. Über die altgriechische Tyche, *Hellas* 4 (1963) 1-10; M. P. NILSSON, *Geschichte der griechischen Religion*, 2 (München 1955) 200-210; L. B. RADFORD, *The Epistle to the Colossians and the Epistle to Philemon* (London 1946) 127-143, 324-326; N. ROBERTSON, Tyche, *OCD* (1970) 1100-1101; L. RUHL, Tyche, *ALGRM* 5 (1916-1924) 1309-1357; H. STROHM, *Tyche. Zur Schicksalsauffassung bei Pindar und den frühgriechischen Dichtern* (Stuttgart 1944).

L. H. MARTIN

TYPHON Τυφών

I. The adjective *typhōnikos* in Acts 27:14 indicates that the *Eurakylōn* was a stormy wind. The word derives from the noun *typhōn* which stands for a whirlwind in Philo, *Deus* 89. Both meanings can be connected with the monstrous figure *Typhōn* in Greek mythology. Josephus hints at a related god in *Ap.* 1.237.

II. Typhon appears in Greek myths as the opponent of →Zeus or even of all gods. He is the youngest son of Tartaros and Gaia and has several names (*Typhōeus*, *Typhōs*, *Typhaōn* and *Typhōn*), which were used interchangeably. In antiquity his name was derived from *typhoō* 'to be crazy' (e.g. Plutarch, *De Iside* 2, 351F) or *typhō* 'smoke', which is bound up with the idea that Typhon was the personification of vulcanism. The name resembles →Zaphon and there seem to have been connections between Typhon and →Baal-zaphon (EISSFELDT 1932; BONNET 1987). According to Apollodorus, *Bib.* 1.41, Typhon flees to Mount Kasios, the mountain of Baal-zaphon. The myths about Typhon may be influenced by oriental forerunners like Ullikummi in Hurrite texts (SEIPPEL 1939; VIAN 1960). Typhon is described as a primaeval monster which was defeated by Zeus, but lived on beneath the earth after his punishment (under vulcanos or in the Tartaros). He has gigantic proportions, often a lower part consisting of the bodies of snakes, further wings, a hundred arms, a hundred snakes' heads (according to Apollodorus, *Bib.* 1.39, there were a hundred *kephalai drakontōn* attached to his hands), and a human head as well. He spits fire and is called a →Dragon (e.g. Strabo 16.2.7). His terrible voice(s) and insolent behaviour are often emphasized (see for an extensive description SCHMIDT 1916-1924).

Hesiod describes the struggle between Zeus and Typhon for the rule over gods and men after the defeat of the →Titans. Zeus eliminates Typhon with his lightning and throws him into the Tartaros (*Theog.* 820-868). According to other texts Typhon ends up under the Etna (e.g. Aeschylus, *Prom.* 351-372) or the (volcanic) coast of Campania, from where he still causes volcanic eruptions. Typhon is related to several other sites. According to one version of the combat myth he brings Zeus after the seize of his sickle and sinews to his residence, the Corycian cave in Cilicia (e.g. Apollodorus, *Bib.* 1.42). He is also associated with the river Orontes (Syria). The partly underground bed of this river was explained by the elimination of Typhon, who fled from Zeus' thunderbolts and ploughed up the channel of the future river and disappeared into the ground and caused the fountain to break forth to the surface (Strabo 16.2.7; see for a related tradition FONTENROSE 1980:75, 277-278). Typhon's elimination is also linked with the sea. According to Nicander (see Antoninus Liberalis 28) Typhon tries to escape the lightning of Zeus and his burning by diving into the sea (cf. Valerius Flaccus, *Argon.* 2.25-29).

Typhon is connected with the Delphic Dragon Python (FONTENROSE 1980:77-93). According to *Hom. Hymn to Apollo* 305-355 →Hera produced Typhon because of her anger at Zeus over the birth of →Athena and asked the Delphic dragoness to raise him. Gradually Typhon became associated with the →Giants (Hyginus, *Fab.* 151; cf. Pindar, *Pyth.* 8.17-18). From the sixth or fifth century BCE onwards Typhon is identified with the Egyptian god →Seth (possibly already Pherecydes according to Origen, *Contra*

Cels. 6.42; Herodotus 2.144; 156; 3.5; Diodorus Siculus, *Bibl. hist.* 1.21-22; 88; passim in Plutarch, *De Iside*), who was initially a royal god but developed in the first millennium BCE into the prototype of evil and the god of the foreigners (TE VELDE 1977). The element of the flight of the gods before Typhon in several Greek and Latin texts (e.g. Nicander according to Antoninus Liberalis 28; Ovidius, *Metam.* 5.321-331; Hyginus, *Fab.* 196) is probably inspired by Egyptian traditions concerning Seth (GRIFFITHS 1960). The combat myth of Typhon has a different character in the texts where Seth and Typhon are identified. Typhon's opponents are in that case Osiris, →Isis and →Horus (→Apollo). Herodotus (3.5) mentions that Seth-Typhon ends up in the Serbonian Lake, at the coast near the eastern border of Egypt. The negative aspects of Seth matched well with the character of Typhon, who probably was the most prominent opponent of the Olympic gods (cf. Pindar, *Pyth.* 1.15 *theōn polemios*; Aeschylos, *Prom.* 358 *pasin theois antestē*; Hyginus, *Astr.* 2.28 *acerrimus gigas et maxime deorum hostis*; Nonnus, *Dion.* 2.571 *theēmachos*). This explains why Seth-Typhon came to be used as a kind of stereotype to characterize historical figures as the creators of chaos. Especially in texts from Ptolemaic Egypt there are several examples of a similar negative characterization of rebels or foreign enemies: Antiochus III in the Raphia decree, Harsiesis, the Greeks in the Oracle of the Potter; possibly also Antiochus IV (for references see VAN HENTEN 1993:224-225 and 239-243; cf. Apollonius Rhodius, *Argon.* 2.38). The opponent of the typhonic enemy is usually the king, who was associated with Horus. The mythic conflict between Seth-Typhon and Horus was part of the Ptolemaic royal ideology, which is evident from the coronation ceremony and other places (KOENEN 1983; VAN HENTEN 1993:224).

Typhon also appears as a demon of storms, whirlwinds (see already Hesiod, *Theog.* 846; 869-880; SCHMIDT 1916-1924: 1426; 1442-1445; FONTENROSE 1980: 126; 545-546, and Index A I s.v. motif 3G p. 581) and earthquakes and the originator of volcanic eruptions. Aristotle, *Met.* 1.1 339a, and Pliny, *Nat. hist.* 2.131-132 mention *typhōnes* as whirlwinds without a reference to Typhon.

III. The use of *typhōnikos* in Acts 27:14 is bound up with the meaning 'gale' of *typhōn* and Typhon as originator of storm winds. Because of the context it is unlikely that a whirlwind or waterspout was meant by Luke. Philo uses *typhōn* in the sense of whirlwind metaphorically in *Quod deus* 89 (cf. LXX Ps 148:8 v.l.).

Josephus *Ap.* 1.237 can be understood against the background of the identification of Seth and Typhon. Josephus transmits a passage of Manetho relating that the abandoned city of Avaris in the eastern delta of the Nile was given to the impure who laboured in the quarries nearby. The city is connected to Seth-Typhon in this passage by the adjective *Typhōnios*, which might have a historical basis in the foundation of the city by the Hyksos. The foreign god of the Hyksos was probably identified by the Egyptians with Seth, the Egyptian god of the foreigners (TE VELDE 1977:128). Because of Manetho's association of the impure with the Israelites, however, the import of the passage becomes strongly anti-Jewish: the Jews are presented as adherents of the now very evil god Seth-Typhon.

Although Typhon is not mentioned in Dan 7-12 or Revelation it is quite possible that the typhonic type which was taken from Greek and Egyptian mythology was incorporated into passages of these apocalyptic writings in order to emphasize the appearance of foreign rulers as the tyrannical eschatological adversary. The vision in Dan 7 shows not only correspondences with Canaanite mythology (→Baal, →Sea), but also with texts on Seth-Typhon (especially concerning the eleventh horn; VAN HENTEN 1993). The battle against heaven and the stars in Dan 8:10-12 and Rev 12:4; 7-9; 13: 6 of the little horn, the dragon and the first beast corresponds with the role of Typhon, who according to Apollodorus, *Bib.* 1.39-40, touches the stars with his head and attacks heaven (Claudian, *Carm.* 26.62-66; Nonnus, *Dion.* 1.291; 2.386-387). Valerius Flaccus (first century CE) even says that Typhon thought that he had captured the kingdom of heaven and the stars (*Argon.* 2.236-238).

According to several scholars also the pattern of Rev 12 shows strong similarities with a (Greco-Egyptian) version of myths concerning Seth-Typhon: the flight of Isis for Seth-Typhon; the birth and secret upbringing of Horus; and the revenge on Seth-Typhon by Horus for the killing of his father Osiris (sources: Herodotus 2.144; 156; 3.5; Plutarch, *De Iside*, esp. 12-21; Diodorus Siculus, *Bib.* 1.21-22; 88; BOUSSET 1906; VÖGTLE 1971; BERGMEIER 1982). This does not exclude similar correspondences with other dragon myths (Python, cf. YARBRO COLLINS 1975). Seth-Typhon shares, however, with the dragon of Revelation the fact that he fights against several opponents (Osiris, Isis and Horus) and pursues the woman after she has given birth to a son. The attempt to overwhelm the woman with a river (Rev 12:15) corresponds with the site of the conflict of Seth-Typhon, the delta of the Nile (cf. also Typhon's connection with the Orontes). If the author of Revelation actually has incorporated pagan material in chap. 12, he probably also has used traditions concerning Seth-Typhon, e.g. in addition to the traditions about the pursuit of Isis and Horus, also the attack on heaven and stars. Even the beginning of the vision with the two heavenly signs matches with traditions concerning Seth-Typhon. Isis and Seth-Typhon are connected with stars and constellations, Isis with the dogstar (Plutarch, *De Isid.* 21 = *Mor.* 359D) and Virgo, Seth-Typhon with pole stars and the Great Bear, according to some scholars also with Hydra (BERGMEIER 1982).

IV. *Bibliography*

R. BERGMEIER, Altes und Neues zur 'Sonnenfrau am Himmel (Apk 12)', *ZNW* 73 (1982) 97-109; C. BONNET, Typhon et Baal Saphon, *Phoenicia and the East Mediterranean in the First Millennium B.C.* (Orientalia Lovaniensia Analecta 22; ed. E. Lipiński; Louvain 1987) 101-143; W. BOUSSET, *Die Offenbarung Johannis* (Göttingen 1906) 351-356; O. EISSFELDT, *Baal Zaphon, Zeus Kasios und der Durchzug der Israeliten durchs Meer* (Halle 1932); J. FONTENROSE, *Python. A Study of Delphic Myth and its Origins* (Berkeley/Los Angeles 1959; 1980[2]); J. G. GRIFFITHS, The Flight of the Gods before Typhon: an Unrecognized Myth?, *Hermes* 88 (1960) 374-376; GRIFFITHS, *The Conflict of Horus and Seth from Egyptian and Classic Sources* (Liverpool 1960); J. W. VAN HENTEN, Antiochus IV as a Typhonic Figure in Daniel 7, *The Book of Daniel in the Light of New Findings* (ed. A. S. van der Woude; BETL 106; Louvain 1993) 223-243; L. KOENEN, Die Adaptation ägyptischer Königsideologie am Ptolemäerhof, *Egypt and the Hellenistic World* (Studia Hellenistica 27; eds. E. van 't Dack, P. van Dessel & W. van Gucht; Louvain 1983) 143-190; G. MICHAÏLIDÈS, Vestiges du culte solaire parmi les chrétiens d'Egypte, *Bulletin de la Société d'Archéologie Copte* 13 (1948-49) 37-110, esp. 84-100; J. SCHMIDT, Typhoeus, Typhon, *ALGRM* 5 (Leipzig 1916-1924) 1426-1445; G. SEIPPEL, *Der Typhonmythos* (Greifswalder Beiträge zur Literatur und Stilforschung 24; Greifswald 1939); H. TE VELDE, *Seth, God of Confusion. A Study of his Role in Egyptian Mythology and Religion* (Probleme der Ägyptologie 6; Leiden 1977[2]) [& lit]; F. VIAN, Le mythe de Typhée et le problème de ses origines orientales, *Éléments orientaux dans la religion grecque ancienne. Colloque de Strasbourg 22-24 mai 1958* (Paris 1960) 17-37; A. VÖGTLE, Mythos und Botschaft in Apokalypse 12, *Tradition und Glaube. Das frühe Christentum in seiner Umwelt, FS K.G. Kuhn* (eds. G. Jeremias, H.-W. Kuhn & H. Stegemann; Göttingen 1971) 395-415; A. YARBRO COLLINS, *The Combat Myth in the Book of Revelation* (Missoula 1975) 57-100.

J. W. VAN HENTEN

U

UNCLEAN SPIRITS πνεύματα ἀκάθαρτα

I. 'Unclean spirit' occurs only once in the OT (Zech 13:2 *rûaḥ haṭṭum'â,* lit. 'the spirit of impurity') and 21 times in the NT in both singular and plural. It is found only in the synoptic gospels and Acts and twice in Rev. The related phrase 'evil spirit' (*pneuma ponēron*) occurs in the OT (→Evil spirit of God) and eight times in the NT. Often the noun *daimonion* is used synonymously (see below and →Demon).

II. The belief in supernatural non-corporeal beings considered not to be gods and affecting the life of corporeal beings (men and animals) is widespread. Since they are invisible and yet present and active they are often called 'spirits'; this idiom is derived from the (invisible yet active) wind. They may appear as a group or band or as individual beings, often having a name and more or less personal ways of action.

These spirits are either benevolent and helpful or malevolent and harmful. In the latter case they are often called demons or ghosts. Often they take possession of human beings or animals and are identified with them. This belief is found in all religions of the ancient Near East and the Mediterranean. It appears to be intensified in Hellenistic and Roman times. It is well represented in the Jewish religion of these times, especially in apocalyptic writings.

III. The phrase 'unclean spirit' is part of the demonological idiom of Judaism (cf. e.g. *T. Benj.* V 2; *T. Sim.* IV 9; VI 6; *Jub.* 10,1; 11,4; 12,20; K. BERGER, *NTS* 20 [1973] 7 n. 28; Str-B IV,1 503-509). It is, however, not very common, probably because 'unclean' is a ritual concept. In the synoptic gospels it is synonymous with *daimonion* or circumscribed by a form of the verb *daimonizesthai* as is shown by the fact that both concepts occur in the same story (cf. e.g. Luke 9:37-43) or in parallel versions of the same story (cf. e.g. Mark 6:7; Matt 10:1 ['unclean spirit'] with Luke 8:33 [*daimonion*]; Mark 7:25 has 'unclean spirit', Matt 15:22 has *daimonizetai*). The description of the behaviour and actions of unclean spirits is identical with that of *daimonia*.

IV. *Bibliography*

*C. COLPE *et al.*, Geister (Dämonen), *RAC* 9 (1976) 546-797 [& lit]; F. HAUCK, Akathartos, *TWNT* 3 (1938) 430-432; G. LANCZKOWSKI, Geister, *TRE* 12 (1984) 254-259 [& lit]; Str-B, Zur altjüdischen Dämonologie, IV,1, 501-535.

J. REILING

UNKNOWN GOD Ἄγνωστος θεός

I. In the Book of Acts (17:23) Luke tells how Paul the apostle addresses the Athenians on the Areopagus and takes as his point of departure an inscription on an altar he saw in the city. This inscription, he says, ran as follows: "For an unknown god" (ἀγνώστῳ θεῷ).

II. All the other evidence for a cult of (an) unknown god(s) is later than Acts. In the 2nd cent. CE, Pausanias says that near the harbour of Phalerum (Athens) there were altars of gods named 'unknown ones' and of heroes (βωμοὶ δὲ θεῶν τε ὀνομαζομένων ἀγνώστων καὶ ἡρώων, I, 1, 4). In his description of the sanctuaries in Olympia he says that by the great altar of the Olympian →Zeus there is also an altar of unknown gods (ἀγνώστων θεῶν βωμός, V, 14, 8). In the early 3rd cent. CE, Diogenes Laertius tells that in the (probably) 6th cent. BCE the Athenians asked Epimenides from Cnossos to help them get rid of a plague: he brought sheep to the Areopagus and there he let them go wherever they wanted, and on each spot where a sheep lay down he had the

Athenians sacrifice to the deity concerned (τῷ προσήκοντι θεῷ), and he adds that even to his day altars may be found in various parts of Athens with no name inscribed upon them (βωμοὶ ἀνώνυμοι, I 110). His contemporary Philostratus, *Vita Apollonii* VI,3, has his hero praise Athens' prudence because there altars are set up in honour even of unknown gods (καὶ ἀγνώστων δαιμόνων βωμοὶ ἵδρυνται). This literary evidence seems to suggest that altars to unknown gods were inscribed either with a plural ἀγνώστοις θεοῖς (or ἀγνώστων θεῶν) or in the singular with an anonymous θεῷ (for extensive discussion and references to secondary literature see VAN DER HORST 1989:1428-1443). When one looks for epigraphical evidence to corroborate either of these hypotheses, it turns out that there is no unambiguous material. In 1910 a 2nd cent. CE altar inscription from Pergamon was published (HEPDING 1910) that reads: ΘΕΟΙΣ ΑΓ[.......] ΚΑΠΙΤ[..] ΔΑΔΟΥΧΟ[.], which could be restored as: θεοῖς ἁγιωτάτοις (or: ἀγνοτάτοις) Καπίτων δαδοῦχος (for other suggested restorations see VAN DER HORST 1989:1433), but HEPDING (1910: 455-456) proposed: θεοῖς ἀγνώστοις. In spite of objections to this proposal it still seems the most feasible one (see also WEINREICH 1915:30-32; NILSSON 1961:355; VAN DER HORST 1988:26). The same applies to another inscription from Dorylaeum (Phrygia), where θεοῖς ἀγνώστοις would seem to be the least problematic restoration (C. W. M. Cox, MAMA V [Manchester 1937] 56, with the discussion by VAN DER HORST 1989:1436-1437). So the scanty archaeological evidence clearly favours the hypothesis of a dedication in the plural. In addition to that, Churchfathers seem to imply that Luke's statement about an inscription in the singular is in need of correction. Tertullian perhaps makes already a tacit correction when he states that he knows of Athenian stupidity and idolatry with 'altars prostituted to unknown gods' (*Adv. Marc.* I 9; *Ad nationes* II 9,4), where one would expect him to use the phrase in the singular in view of the passage in Acts. But at the end of the 4th cent. CE Jerome is quite explicit: "The altar-inscription is not, as Paul asserted, 'To an unknown god', but as follows: 'To the gods of Asia, Europe, and Africa, to the unknown and foreign gods' (*diis Asiae et Europae et Africae, diis ignotis et peregrinis*). But since Paul did not need [or: could not use] a number of gods but only one unknown god, he used the word in the singular" (*Comm. in Ep. ad Titum* I 12 = PL 26:607). And later, in a letter of ca. 388 (*ep.* 70), he repeats that Paul "in his propaganda for Christ even skilfully rephrases (*torquet*) an inscription he came across by chance so as to turn it into an argument for faith" (a statement in which Jerome perhaps echoes Didymus of Alexandria; see the latter's comments on 2 Cor 10:5 in the catenae edited by K. STAAB, *Pauluskommentare aus der griechischen Kirche* [Münster 1933] 37). The opinion of these two (or three) Churchfathers that Paul (or Luke) changed the text of the inscription in order to get a suitable starting-point for his speech strengthens the impression that there may have been no such inscriptions in the singular at all, neither in Athens nor elsewhere, however much their testimonies do corroborate the pagan literary and epigraphical data to the effect that there were indeed cults of unknown gods in antiquity (for further testimonies from Churchfathers see LAKE 1933: 240-246; VAN DER HORST 1989:1440-1442).

The question as to what was the function of such cults is not easy to answer, since the expression ἄγνωστος θεός is not unequivocal. It may mean a god who is well-known to one people but not (yet) known to another (i.e. a foreign deity whose name and function are in principle knowable [for evidence that the god of the Jews may have been considered an 'unknown god' by pagans see VAN DER HORST 1989:1444-1446]); or a god whose name nobody knows, either because it has been forgotten (altar-inscriptions may have become unreadable) or since there is no way of knowing which god (maybe even which of the known gods) is the author of a calamity or of good fortune; or a god unknown to those who did not receive a special revelation or initiaton; or a god unknowable—ἄγνωστος can have this meaning as well!—because of the limitations of human knowledge, or in essence unknowable but partially knowable by inference from his/her works; etc. (see BIRT 1914; DODDS 1963; FESTUGIÈRE 1954). Probably the most frequent motive to raise altars for (an) unknown god(s) was uncertainty or doubt about the identity of the god who had caused a certain event. In ancient religions it was of the utmost importance to know the right name of the deity when invoking him/her or sacrificing to him/her. From Homer onwards one finds a variety of prayer formulas which aim to prevent the god invoked from being offended by an incorrect invocation, such as "Hear, Lord, whoever thou art" (Homer, *Od.* V 445; cf. Aeschylus, *Agam.* 160-161; Euripides, *Troad.* 884-887; Catullus 34:21-22; Apuleius, *Metam.* XI 2; Macrobius, *Sat.* III 9,10). The Romans even developed a specific formula that is often found not only in prayers but also in dedicatory formulas both in inscriptions and in literary texts, sc. *sive deus sive dea* (ALVAR 1985). Aulus Gellius reports: "The Romans of old (...), whenever they felt an earthquake or received a report of one, decreed a holy day on that account, but forbore to declare and specify in the decree, as is commonly done, the name of the god in whose honour the holy day was to be observed, for fear that by naming one god instead of another they might involve the people in false observance. If anyone had desecrated that festival, and expiation was therefore necessary, they used to offer a victim *si deo si deae* (...), since it was uncertain what force and which of the gods or goddesses had caused the earthquake" (*Noctes Atticae* II 28,2-3). Just as the Romans for fear or anxiety that by naming one god instead of another their acts of worship would not yield the results required, used the *sive deus sive dea* formula, so the Greeks, too, to keep on the safe side, could use the formula 'unknown god'. And this consideration makes it intrinsically probable that in such cases a Greek would use this expression in the singular, even in an altar-inscription (VAN DER HORST 1988:39-40). An additional motive in the cult of unknown gods certainly was the anxious concern not to run the risk that one did not know and hence did not worship the best divine helper and so failed to obtain the help one so badly needed. This danger could be warded off by a "möglichst vollständige Berücksichtigung der Gottheiten, also auch der unbekannten" (WACHSMUTH 1975:708). There is also some evidence that suggests that the term 'unknown gods' was used to designate the gods of the netherworld (χθόνιοι θεοί) or the Erinyes (called 'anonymous goddesses' by Euripides, *Iph. Taur.* 944; see KERN 1926:125-134), in order to avoid the naming of gods whom for safety's sake one preferred not to mention: Ovid, *Metam.* XIV 365-366; Statius, *Achill.* I 135-140; Pap. Chicago 1061 VI 26 (in J. U. POWELL, *Collectanea Alexandrina* [Oxford 1925] 85); for further passages see NORDEN 1923:115-124. On the different philosophical background (Platonic epistemology) of the unknown god in Gnosticism see FESTUGIÈRE 1954:1-140 and TURCAN 1987: 136-137.

III. By making Paul start his speech by referring to an inscription Luke makes use of a well-known literary device (cf. Ps-Heraclitus, *Ep.* 4; Ps-Diogenes, *Ep.* 36). There is a distinct possibility that Luke had his hero deliberately change the text of an inscription, for it would by no means be an isolated case. Before his days, the 2nd cent. BCE Jewish exegete Aristobulus quoted Aratus' *Phaenomena* but changed twice 'Zeus' into 'God' (he frankly adds: "We have given the true sense, as one must, by removing the name Zeus throughout the verses", *ap.* Eusebius, *Praep. Ev.* XIII 12,7). Philo also quotes Hesiod in a monotheistic form by changing θεοί into θεός (*De ebrietate* 150), and also later Christian writers, when quoting Plato or Plotinus or other pagan writers, adapt these texts to Christian usage by changing θεοί into θεός (e.g. Theodoret of Cyrrhus). But there is no absolute need to assume Luke did the same. The backgrounds of the cult of 'unknown gods' show that a dedication in the singular belonged to the possibilities and can never be ruled out, but the question must remain undecided. Whether or not there ever existed an altar for an unknown God (in the singular) in Athens, it is clear that Luke wants to present Paul as claiming that he is proclaiming to the Greeks the God of Israel whom they honour without knowing him, and that from now on they have no longer any excuse for their ignorance, since they have heard the message of this God's self-revelation in Jesus Christ.

IV. *Bibliography*

J. ALVAR, Materiaux pour l'étude de la formule sive deus sive dea, *Numen* 32 (1985) 236-273; T. BIRT, Ἄγνωστοι θεοί und die Areopagrede des Apostels Paulus, *RhMus* N.F. 69 (1914) 342-392; C. CLEMEN, *Religionsgeschichtliche Erklärung des Neuen Testaments* (2nd ed.; Gießen 1924) 290-304; E. R. DODDS, The Unknown God in Neoplatonism, *Proclus: The Elements of Theology* (Oxford 1963) 310-313; W. ELLIGER, *Paulus in Griechenland* (SBS 92/93; Stuttgart 1978) 193-199; A.-J. FESTUGIÈRE, *La révélation d'Hermès Trismégiste IV: Le dieu inconnu et la gnose* (Paris 1954) 1-140; H. HEPDING, Die Arbeiten zu Pergamon 1908-1909, II: Die Inschriften, *MDAI* (Abt. Athene) 35 (1910) 454-457; P. W. VAN DER HORST, The Unknown God (Acts 17:23), *Knowledge of God in the Graeco-Roman World* (eds. R. van den Broek, T. Baarda & J. Mansfeld; Leiden 1988) 19-42; *VAN DER HORST, The Altar of the 'Unknown God' in Athens (Acts 17:23) and the Cult of 'Unknown Gods' in the Hellenistic and Roman Periods, *ANRW* II 18, 2 (1989) 1426-1456; O. KERN, *Die Religion der Griechen* I (Berlin 1926) 125-134; K. LAKE, The Unknown God, *The Beginnings of Christianity* I, 5 (eds. F. J. Foakes Jackson & K. Lake; London 1933) 240-246; M. P. NILSSON, *Geschichte der griechischen Religion* II (2nd ed., München 1961); *E. NORDEN, *Agnostos Theos. Untersuchungen zur Formengeschichte religiöser Rede* (2nd ed., Leipzig 1923); R. TURCAN, Agnostos Theos, *ER* 1 (1987) 135-138; W. H. WACHOB, Unknown God, *ABD* 6 (1992) 753-755; D. WACHSMUTH, Theoi agnostoi, *KP* 5 (1975) 708; *O. WEINREICH, De dis ignotis observationes selectae, *ARW* 18 (1915) 1-52.

P. W. VAN DER HORST

URIEL אוריאל

I. The name appears in the OT as a personal name: 1 Chr 6:9; 15:5.11; 2 Chr 13:2. In *4 Ezra*, an angel of this name is mentioned as *angelus interpres*. The etymology depends upon the decision whether the root is Hebrew (light) or Aramaic (fire). *T. Abr.* A 13:11 knows an angel Purouel who has power over the fire (πύρ). It is tempting to identify him with Uriel.

II. Among the four archangels (e.g. *Gk Apoc. Ezra* 6:2; Mass. Hekalot, A. JELLINEK, *Bet ha-Midrasch* II [Leipzig 1853] 43-44) Uriel is replaced by Phanuel in the book of similitudes (*1 Enoch* 37-71), though in general he does appear in this group. *3 Baruch* 4:7 knows Uriel as the third of five archangels, other versions read here Phanuel. At other places Uriel interchanges with Sariel (J. Z. SMITH, *OTP* II, 709). It might be, too, that Vrevoil (*2 Enoch* 22:10, cp. F. I. ANDERSEN, *OTP* I, 140, note) is an original Uriel.

In accordance with his name Uriel seems to be connected mainly with astrology. *1 Enoch* 72-82 shows him as explorer of the stars and their ways in heaven (cp. 33:3-4). He is the guide of the heavenly luminaries (*1 Enoch* 72:1; 79:6; 82:7). *1 Enoch* explains the discrepancy between the Enochic calendar and astronomical reality already by the assumption that the stars err because of the sins of man. So the guidance of the stars, revealing their ways and their errors becomes tantamount to announcing the eschatological punishment of men and the stars, i.e. the fallen angels which are identified with stars in the Enochic corpus. It is nevertheless possible that the 'prince of light' is to be identified with Michael rather than with Uriel (cf. Y. YADIN, *The Scroll of the War of the Sons of Light against the Sons of Darkness* [Jerusalem 1957] 214-125).

Uriel knows and reveals the place of the future punishment and imprisonment of these stars (*1 Enoch* 18:14-19:2; 21:5-6.9). Accordingly he is depicted elsewhere as set over Tartarus (*1 Enoch* 20:2, Greek version) and even buries Adam together with Michael (*Vita Adae* 48:1). Accompanied by →Gabriel he serves as light for the resurrected (*Apoc. Eliah* 5:5). One group of manuscripts mentions Uriel among the four archangels who fulfil the eschatological judgment (*Sib. Or.* 2:215); Uriel alone breaks the gates of →Hades (ibid. 227-237, cp. *1 Enoch* 20:2) and leads the dead to their punishment.

III. In later times the tradition is mainly concerned with Uriel as revealing angel or *angelus interpres* as in *4 Ezra* 4:1; 10:28 and throughout. In this function Uriel is mentioned in rabbinic texts and remains a favourite in the magical texts (e.g. *T. Sol.* 2:4 [Q]; 2:7 [L]; 8:9 [P]; 17:7. 9 [H]; 18:7 [L]. 9.24 [H]. 27 [P], STÜBE, 22 l. 6; PRADEL, 55-56. 60; KROPP, XXVIII, 7, 47; XLV, *3*, 17; *4v*, 20; XLVI, *9v*, 15; LXXVI, 88; XLVII, *2*, 4 etc. Sefer Harazim I, 87; NAVEH & SHAKED, Amulet 11, l. 3; but only five times in *PGM*) as in early Jewish mysticism (SCHÄFER 1988:§§ 363. 372. 418. 493. 644). Fragments of the Hekhalot literature mention an angel Me'ori'el/מאורי׳אל. (P. SCHÄFER, *Geniza-Fragmente zur Hekhalot-Literatur* [Tübingen 1984], fragm. 13, p. 2b, line 10 and fragm. 16, p. 1b, line 12). This might be an original Uriel. The relations of Uriel to Suriel and Sariel need further study (cf. for the time: H. J. POLOTSKY, Suriel der Trompeter, *Le Muséon* 49 [1936], 231-243 = POLOTSKY, *Collected Papers* [Jerusalem 1971] 288-300; G. VERMES, The Archangel Sariel. A Targumic Parallel to the Dead Sea Scrolls, *Christianity, Judaism and Other Greco-Roman Cults* [Ed. J. Neusner; Leiden 1975] 159-166).

Uriel's fight against →Jacob/Israel does not really fit into these lines of tradition. It occurs in the relatively late *Prayer of Joseph*, fragm. A (J. Z. SMITH, *OTP* II).

IV. *Bibliography*

A. M. KROPP, *Ausgewählte koptische Zaubertexte* I-III (Bruxelles 1930/1931); M. MARGALIOTH, *Sepher Ha-Razim. A Newly Recovered Book of Magic from the Talmudic Period.* Collected from Genizah Fragments and other Sources; (Jerusalem 1966) [Heb]; *J. MICHL, Art. Engel IX (Uriel), *RAC* 5 (1962) 254-258; J. NAVEH & S. SHAKED, *Amulets and Magic Bowls. Aramaic Incantaions of Late Antiquity* (Jerusalem/Leiden 1985); *P. PERDRIZET, L'archange Ouriel, *Seminarium Kondakorianum* 2 (1928), 241-276; F. PRADEL, *Griechische und süditalienische Gebete, Beschwörungen und Rezepte des Mittelalters* (Giessen 1907); P. SCHÄFER, *Synopse zur Hekhalot-Literatur,* in Zusammenarb. m. M. Schlüter u. H. G. von Mutius (Tübingen 1981); R. STÜBE, *Jüdisch-Babylonische Zaubertexte* (Halle 1895).

M. MACH

V

VAMPIRE עלוקה

I. The noun *ʿălûqâ* occurs once in MT, in a proverbial expression in Prov 30:15. The word appears to be pan-Semitic, with cognates attested in Syriac (*ʿelaqtā*), Arabic (*ʿalaq*), Ethiopic (*ʿalaqt*), and Akkadian (*ilqu*). In each of these cognate languages the meaning is 'leech'. In Arabic there is a related word, *ʿawleq*, interpreted as referring to a kind of demon (CANAAN 1929:29). This latter sense has been conjectured for the word in MT (e.g. DE MOOR 1981-1982:111 n. 16).

II. The Arabic noun *ʿawleq* does occur meaning 'leech' or the like, but not specifically a demon. On the other hand, the second Phoenician amulet from Arslan Tash (ed. A. CAQUOT & R. DU MESNIL DU BUISSON, *Syria* 48 [1971] 391-398; cf. DE MOOR 1981-1982:110-112) contains an incantation against a demon which is most probably depicted on the plaque. According to the inscription on the plaque the demon is a personified 'Blood-sucker', *lḥšt lmzh* 'Incantation against the Blood-sucker'. The Phoenician *mzh* might be compared with Hebr *mzy rʿb*, 'the Suckers of Hunger' (Deut 32:24). Though the Phoenician demon is not identical with the Ar *ʿawleq*, the incantation makes clear that insects could be seen as demons.

III. The proverbial expression of Prov 30:15 reads (in MT): "The *ʿălûqâ* has two daughters (who say) 'Give, give!'" The common Semitic meaning, 'leech', would suit the context. Since the sayings in Proverbs often feature insects and other humble creatures (cf. the ants, locusts, and other animals in Proverbs 30), it may be unwise to posit here the unique occurrence of 'demon, vampire', based on an inner-Arabic semantic development.

The alternative etymology developed by GLUECK (1964) who connects *ʿălûqâ* with Ar *ʿalāqā*, 'copulation', and renders the Hebrew noun with 'erotic passion', has been criticised by NORTH (1965) in favour of the traditional rendering.

IV. *Bibliography*

T. CANAAN, *Dämonenglaube im Lande der Bibel* (1929) 29; J. J. GLUECK, Proverbs xxx 15a, *VT* 14 (1964) 367-370; J. C. DE MOOR, Demons in Canaan, *JEOL* 27 (1981-1982) 106-119; F. S. NORTH, The Four Insatiables, *VT* 15 (1965) 281-282; J. WELLHAUSEN, *Reste Arabischen Heidentums* (Berlin 1897) 148-159.

R. S. HENDEL

VANITIES הבלים

I. In Deuteronomistic religious polemics and related texts, 'vanities' (*hebelîm*) indicate images of non-Yahwistic deities. It is impossible to establish the identity of the deities involved (PREUSS 1971:160-164). Etymologically, *hebel* is related to words for 'breath; vapour and nullity'.

II. Since it is not clear to which deities the term *hebelîm* refers, their character cannot be described. It is characteristic of the orthodox form of the Yahwistic religion in ancient Israel to designate 'other deities' in a disparaging way. This has no counterpart in other ancient Near Eastern cultures. The Assyrians depict the deities of the people conquered as 'their deities' or 'the gods in which they trusted' (Sargon II; BECKING 1992:31). They consider them to be real deities and not mere idols.

III. The term 'Vanities' occurs frequently in OT religious polemics (Deut 32:21; 1 Kgs 16:13. 26; 2 Kgs 17:15; 8 times in Jer; Zech 10:2; cf. Ps 31:7 and Jona 2:9). By calling indigenous Canaanite and other deities 'vanities', their formal existence and practical efficacy is negated (EISSFELDT 1962: 271). This designation is comparable with the indication of the divine →Falsehood.

The etymology of the word *hebel* underscores this insight. The Hebrew word has no cognates in older Semitic languages. It can be considered as an onomatopoeic construction of the Hebrew language itself (SEYBOLD 1974:335-336) indicating human breath. Using *hebel*, the deities are compared by the deuteronomistic school to 'breath; vapour; transiency'. They stand in contrast to the everlasting character of Yahweh. This is apparent in a polemical passage from Jeremiah, where the non-Yahwistic divine is compared with 'breath'. The images of the artisan are classified as 'falsehood'; there is no life (*rûaḥ*) in them. They are "a nothing (*hebel*); a work of mockery" (Jer 10:14-15). In a similar context, Yahweh is introduced as speaking agent ridiculizing the carved images: "Why have they offended me with their idols, with alien nothings (*hablê nēkār*)?" (Jer 8:19). Here, the vanities refer to foreign deities, presumably introduced by the Assyrian or Babylonian overlords. In Postexilic hymns, the term 'vanities' is connected with the parallel noun *šāwʾ*, 'idle idols' (Ps 31:7; Jonah 2:9) indicating non-active deities in general.

The deuteronomistic concepts have been taken over by the authors of the NT. After the healing of a lame person in Lystra, Paul is identified by the Lycaonians as →Hermes and Barnabas as →Zeus. The inhabitants of Lystra believed the gods had come down as humans. Paul rejects this identification and summons the people to conversion *apo toutōn tōn mataiōn*, "from these vain idols", by which the Greek gods are meant (Acts 14:15). In 1 Pet 1:18, it is stated that the Gentile Christians have been redeemed from the idle conduct (*ek tēs mataias*) of their forefathers. The expression implies the reverence of idle idols (VAN UNNIK 1980:14-15).

A relation of *hebel* with the Central Arabian fertility god →Hubal is improbable.

IV. *Bibliography*

B. BECKING, *The Fall of Samaria* (SHANE 2; Leiden 1992); O. EISSFELDT, Gott und Götzen im Alten Testament, *KS* I (1962) 266-273; H.-D. PREUSS, *Die Verspottung fremder Religionen im Alten Testament* (BWANT 92; Stuttgart 1971); K. SEYBOLD, הֶבֶל *hæbæl*, *TWAT* 2 (1974) 334-343; W. C. VAN UNNIK, The redemption in I Peter i 18-19 and the problem of the First Epistle of Peter, *Sparsa Collecta Part Two* (NovTSup 30; Leiden 1980) 3-82.

B. BECKING

VARUNA

I. The name of the Jebusite Araunah, Heb *ʾărawnāʾ* (2 Sam 24:16.20-24; 1 Chr 21:15.18; 2 Chr 3:1), has etymologically been related to the Indian deity Varuṇa. In doing so, Araunah has been related to an alleged Aryan upper class in the ancient Near East (F. HOMMEL 1904:1011; H. HOMMEL 1929:117).

II. In the Vedas of ancient India Varuṇa played an important role. He often appears together with Mitra (→Mithras), both having an ethical character as guarantors of Ṛta. Varuṇa is related to the night. He rules over the invisible and is gifted with magic power: "I am King Varuṇa, these magic powers were first given to me" (Ṛg Veda 4,42:2. [181]). Varuṇa is seen as omnipresent and omniscient. He is revered as the creator and the wise sustainer of the world knowing and initiating the clockwork of creation. Since he also appears as God of →heaven, the etymological relation with *Ouranos* is plausible. In the so-called classical period reflected e.g. by the *Mahābhārata*, Varuṇa is still worshipped though in a less prominent role. He is relegated to the position of a god of death (DANIÉLOU 1964; DOWSON 1973; RENOU & FILLIOZAT 1985).

In the list of gods in the treaty and the countertreaty between the Hittite king Shupiluliuma I and the Mitanni-Hurrian king Kurtiwazza some deities occur which have been construed as Aryan: Mitra, Varuṇa, Indra and the two *Nāsatyā* (e.g. MIRONOV 1933; THIEME 1960). Although they occur in a minor position (Nos. 105-108 in the god-list) they have been interpreted as an indication of the presence of an Aryan upper-class in the ancient Near East. This interpretation as well as the identifications of Mitra and Varuṇa has now convincingly been challenged (KAMMENHUBER 1968; DIAKONOFF 1972). In the treaties *Varuṇa is written DINGIR.MEŠ *Ú-ru-wa-na-aš-ši-el* (*KBo* I 1 Rev:55; KUB III 1b Rev: 21') and DINGIR.MEŠ *A-ru-na-aš-ši-il* (*KBo* I 3+ Rev:41) respectively. Phonetic laws prohibit an identification with Varuṇa. The name should be interpreted as 'the gods of Urwan/the Urwanites they are' (DIAKONOFF 1972:106-107).

III. The name Araunah can be interpreted as Hurrian: the noun *eweri-* 'lord' with the extension *-ne* has the meaning 'feudal lord' (W. FEILER, Ḫurritische Namen im Alten Testament, *ZA* 45 [1939] 217-218.224-225; B. MAZAR, *The Early Biblical Period* [Jerusalem 1986] 41). N. WYATT ('Araunah the Jebusite' and the Throne of David, *StTheol* 39 [1985] 39-53) identified Araunah as Uriah the Hittite. A relation with Aryan groups in the ancient Near East is less plausible. Besides, the alleged relation rests on an obsolete and objectionable ideology.

IV. *Bibliography*

A. DANIÉLOU, *Hindu Polytheism* (London 1964) 118-121; I. M. DIAKONOFF, Die Arier im Vorderen Orient: Ende eines Mythos, *OrNS* 41 (1972) 91-120; J. DOWSON, *A Classical Dictionary of Hindu Mythology* (New Delhi 1973) 336-338; F. HOMMEL, *Grundriss zur Geographie und Geschichte des Alten Orients* (Leipzig 1904); H. HOMMEL, Das religionsgeschichtliche Problem des 139. Psalms, *ZAW* 47 (1929) 110-124; A. KAMMENHUBER, *Die Arier im Vorderen Orient* (Heidelberg 1968) 142-151; N. D. MIRONOV, Aryan Vestiges in the Near East of the Second Millennium BC, *AcOr* 11 (1933) 140-217; L. RENOU & J. FILLIOZAT, *L'Inde Classique* I (Paris [2]1985) 317-319; B. THIEME, The 'Aryan' gods of the Mitanni treaties, *JAOS* 80 (1960) 301-317.

B. BECKING

VINE → GEPEN

VIRGIN בתולה/עלמה παρθένος

I. In Hebrew two nouns occur which traditionally have been translated with 'virgin': *ʿalmâ* and *bĕtûlâ*. A convincing etymology of the noun *ʿalmâ* has not been given. The word has cognates in various Semitic languages; Ugar *ǵlmt*, 'girl'; Phoen *ʿlmt*; Aram *ʿljmt*. The exact meaning of these words, however, is not easily established. The proposal of DOHMEN (1987:172-173) who sees a relation—via Ugar *ǵlm*—between Heb *ʿalmâ* and Akk/Semitic *ṣlm*, '→image' and proposes a semantic field including 'image of' and 'image referring to', is unlikely. The noun *bĕtûlâ* is etymologically connected to Akk *batultu* and Ugar *btlt*. In both these languages the noun primarily refers to an age-group. With WENHAM (1972) it might be taken for granted that *bĕtûlâ*—and probably also *ʿalmâ*—refers to a 'girl of marriageable age' and not to a *virgo intacta*.

In the OT the nouns do not refer to a goddess; in Ugaritic texts they are both used as epithets for a deity. Early Christian theology identified the *ʿalmâ* of Isa 7:14 with the virgin →Mary.

II. In Mesopotamian hymns celebrating the love between →Ishtar and Dumuzi (→Tammuz) the goddess is presented as a young nubile woman (WILCKE 1976-80:84). In Egypt the epithets *ʿdd.t*, *rnn.t* and *ḥwn.t*, 'girl; young woman; virgin', are applied to many goddesses—e.g.→ Hathor and →Isis—who had not yet had sexual intercourse (BERGMAN, RINGGREN & TSEVAT 1972: 872-873).

In the Ugaritic myth in which it is narrated how the moon-god Yariḫu obtained his bride Nikkal, *ǵlmt* occurs as a designation for a goddess: *hl ǵlmt tld b(n)*, 'Look! The girl bears a son to him' (*KTU* 1.24:7). It is not clear whether *ǵlmt* is the name of a deity (W. HERRMANN, *Yariḫ und Nikkal und der Preis der Kuṯarāt-Göttinen* [BZAW 106; Berlin 1967] 7) or a reference to a goddess (KORPEL 1990:291). In the ritual text *KTU* 1.41:25, *ǵlmt* is used as an epithet for →Anat (*ARTU* 162). In *KTU* 1.4 vii:54 the expression *bn ǵlmt* should be rendered with 'sons of the darkness' (DOHMEN 1987:171; *ARTU* 65). The expression is an epithet for Gupanu-and-Ugaru and does not refer to the offspring of a female (or virgin) deity.

The Ugaritic goddess Anat is often called the *btlt* (e.g. *KTU* 1.3 ii:32-33; 1.3 iii:3; 1.4 ii:14; 1.6 iii:22-23). The epithet refers to her youth and not to her biological state since she had sexual intercourse more than once with her Baal (BERGMAN, RINGGREN & TSEVAT 1972:873-874; KORPEL 1990:322-323).

III. In the OT, both *ʿalmâ* and *bĕtûlâ* are used for human beings only and do not refer to deities. The noun *ʿalmâ* occurs 9 times in the OT. It refers to women in the royal harem (Cant 6:8); to a group of music making girls (Ps 68:26); to a musical indication (Ps 46:1); and to young women of marriageable age (Gen 24:43; Ex 2:8; 68:26; Isa 7:14; Prov 30:19; 1 Chron 15:20). Of great interest is the passage in Isa 7:14. Interpreting Isa 7 as a messianic prophecy and viewing the *ʿalmâ* as a virgin on the basis of the LXX rendering παρθένος, early Christians identified her with Mary and read the passage as the prediction of the virginal conception of →Emmanuel/→Jesus (Math 1:23).

The noun *bĕtûlâ* occurs 51 times in the OT. In three instances the noun might indicate a 'virgin' (Lev 21:13-14; Deut 22:19; Ezek 44:22). At Joel 1:8 it certainly does not refer to a virgin. The apposition "who had no intercourse" (Gen 24:16; Judg 21:12) should be interpreted as a modification to *bĕtûlâ* rather than the definition of a characteristic attribute (e.g. F. ZIMMERMANN, *JBL* 73 [1954] 98; BERGMAN, RINGGREN & TSEVAT 1972:875). In expressions like *bĕtûlat yiśrāʾēl*, *bĕtûlat bat ʿammî*, *bĕtûlat bat ṣiyyôn* that are to be interpreted as personifications of land, people or city, virginity is not implied (BERGMAN, RINGGREN & TSEVAT 1972:875).

IV. *Bibliography*

J. BERGMAN, H. RINGGREN & M. TSEVAT, *bĕtûlâ*, *TWAT* 1 (1972) 872-877; C. DOHMEN, *ʿalmāh, ʿælæm*, *TWAT* 5 (1987) 167-177; M. C. A. KORPEL, *A Rift in the Clouds* (UBL 8; Münster 1990); G. J. WENHAM, *Betûlāh*, 'a Girl of Marriageable Age', *VT* 22 (1972) 326-348; C. WILCKE, Inanna/Ištar, *RLA* 5 (1976-80) 74-87.

B. BECKING

WATCHER עיר

I. Daniel chap. 4 (vv 10, 14, 20) is the only passage in the Hebrew Bible where the noun עיר is commonly understood to refer to a heavenly being. Nebuchadnezzar reports that he saw in his dream "a watcher and holy one come down from heaven". The meaning of 'watcher' is assured by the juxtaposition with 'holy one' and the statement that he came down from heaven. The word is simply transliterated in Theodotion. The Old Greek uses the single word ἄγγελος (→Angel) in place of "watcher and holy one". Both Aquila and Symmachus read ἐγρήγορος, wakeful one or watcher, presumably from the Semitic root עור, wake up.

II. The 'Watchers' are widely attested in Jewish literature of the Hellenistic and early Roman periods. The most famous attestation is in the 'Book of the Watchers' (*1Enoch* 1-36) where the term is used for the fallen angels. The Enochic book is an elaboration of the story of the →'sons of God' of Gen 6, who took wives from the children of men. The episode in Genesis is elliptic, and is presented without clear judgment. The offspring of the 'sons of God' are presented in a positive light as "heroes of old, men of renown". In the Book of Enoch, however, the action of the Watchers is clearly rebellious. They swear an oath and bind each other with curses not to alter the plan. They conspire to take human wives, and two hundred of them come down on Mt. Hermon. They have intercourse with the women and beget →giants, who cause havoc on earth. The Watchers also impart illicit revelation, about astrology, roots and spells and the making of weapons. When the earth cries out to the LORD, the →archangels are sent to imprison the Watchers under the earth to await the final judgment. The Watchers subsequently appeal to →Enoch to intercede on their behalf, but he is instructed to tell them that they should intercede for men, not men for them (*1 Enoch* 15:2). The spirits of the giants are to remain on earth as evil spirits to disturb humanity (15:8 - 16:1).

A variant of this story in the Book of Jubilees has the Watchers come down to teach men to do what is just and right on earth (Jub 3:15). They are only subsequently corrupted when they see the daughters of men (Jub 5:1). In Jubilees, the evil spirits have a leader, →Mastema, who persuades God to let one tenth of the evil spirits remain with him on earth to corrupt humanity and lead it astray.

The term 'Watchers' occurs in Hebrew in CD 2:18, with reference to the fall of "the Watchers of heaven", a phrase used in *1 Enoch* 13:10 (in Aramaic); 12:4; 15:2 (Ethiopic). Further attestations with reference to the fallen angels are found in *T. Reuben* 5:6-7, and *T. Naphtali* 3:5 (Greek: ἐγρήγοροι). Such beings are not always referred to as 'Watchers'; cf. the 'Pesher on Azazel and the Angels' from Qumran (4Q180; MILIK 1976: 112) and the statement in 2 Peter 2:4 that "God did not spare the angels when they sinned".

The name "Watchers" is not confined to the fallen angels, however. Several passages in *1 Enoch* speak of angels "who watch" or "who sleep not": 20:1 (the four archangels); 39:12-13; 71:7. The Aramaic עירא is also found at *1 Enoch* 22:6 with reference to →Raphael, and again at 93:2 (plural) where the Greek and Ethiopic versions have "angel". In *2 Enoch* 18 (Slavonic Enoch) the "Grigori" (ἐγρήγοροι) are located in the fifth heaven. While "200 princes" of them have fallen, the remainder resume the heavenly liturgy. *2 Enoch* is usually dated to the late first century CE, but some scholars place it much later. The Hebrew *3 Enoch (Sefer Hekalot)* which dates from the fifth or sixth century discusses the "four great princes called Watchers and holy ones" in chap. 28, with specific reference to Daniel 4. Watchers and holy ones are frequently mentioned together, e.g., *1 Enoch* 12:2; 22:6; 93: 2 (Aramaic).

In 1QapGen the Watchers are associated with the holy ones and the Nephilim (2:1) and with the sons of heaven (2:16) in the context of the birth of Noah. The same context may underlie the references in the fragmentary 4QMessAr 2:16,18. The עירין are also mentioned in the fragmentary 4QEn-Giants, and 4QAmram.

III. The oldest non-biblical attestations are probably those in the Enochic 'Book of the Watchers' dating from sometime in the third century BCE. There are indications that the story as found in *1 Enoch* combines older sources, one of which names the leader Semihazah and focuses on the sin of illicit mingling with human women, while the other names him Asael or →Azazel and emphasizes the sin of illicit revelation (HANSON 1977). Contrary to the suggestion of MILIK (1976:31), however, no part of the story as found in *1 Enoch* is presupposed in Genesis, since the Genesis story does not even condemn the action of the 'sons of God' as sinful.

Attempts to identify the Watchers in earlier material are hitherto inconclusive. DAHOOD (1966: 55) proposed that Ps 9:7 וערים נחשת be translated "root out their gods" and derived ערים from Ugaritic *ǵyr* "to protect". He identified the same root and meaning in Mic 5:13; Jer 2:28; 19:15 and Dan 4 among other passages. Others (MURRAY 1984; BARKER 1987) have gone farther in suggesting that the Watchers were heavenly beings, venerated in the pre-exilic Jerusalem cult but deliberately suppressed in most of the Masoretic Bible. None of the proposed identifications of the noun עיר in the Hebrew Bible before Daniel is compelling, however. The idea of protecting deities or angels was widely known in the ancient world and re-appears in Daniel 10-12, but we do not have any reliable instance of the use of עיר in that context. Some biblical precedents for the notion of angelic beings as 'watchful ones', but with different terminology, have been proposed. The most noteworthy is Zech 4:10 which refers to seven "eyes of the LORD which range through the whole earth". The Watchers, however, never have this function in Daniel or the non-canonical literature. A more helpful biblical passage is found in Ps 121:4: "Behold, he neither slumbers nor sleeps, the guardian of Israel", with reference to →Yahweh himself (→Protectors). The "angels who keep watch" (*1 Enoch* 20:1) share this divine characteristic, and the class of heavenly beings known as Watchers may have been named in this way. Their function overlaps with that of the מלאך in so far as they can convey a divine message to earth, but they were apparently conceived as a distinct class of angelic beings.

IV. Interest in such intermediary beings was widespread in pagan as well as Jewish circles in the Persian and Hellenistic periods. According to Hesiod, *Works and Days*, 252-53: "Zeus has thrice ten thousand spirits, watchers of mortal men, and these keep watch on judgements and deeds of wrong as they roam, clothed in mist, all over the earth" (The word for watchers here, φύλακες, is not the same as that used in Daniel or *Enoch*). The most intriguing pagan parallel to the Watchers is found in the *Phoenician History* of Philo Byblios, which refers to the 'Zophasemin' (often corrected into Zophesamin = צפי שמין) or 'heavenly observers'. These creatures are mentioned in the context of a cosmogony and they are assigned no function which might be compared to the Jewish Watchers, but then Philo's Hellenized account hardly does justice to their role in Phoenician mythology. No conclusions can be based on such an enigmatic reference, however. Other (inconclusive) pagan parallels which have been suggested include "the many-eyed Amesha Spentas" of Zoroastrianism and the planetary gods of the Chaldeans in Diodorus Siculus 2.30.

V. *Bibliography*
M. BARKER, *The Older Testament. The Survival of Themes from the Ancient Royal Cult in Sectarian Judaism and Early Christianity* (London 1987) 114; M. BLACK, *The Book of Enoch or 1 Enoch* (SVTP 7; Leiden 1985) 106-107; M. DAHOOD, *Psalms I* (AB 16; Garden City 1966) 55; M. J. DAVIDSON, *Angels at Qumran. A Comparative Study of 1Enoch 1-36, 72-108 and Sectarian writings from Qumran* (JSP Sup 11; Sheffield 1992) 38-40; P. D. HANSON, Rebellion in Heaven, Azazel and Euhemeristic heroes in 1 Enoch 6-11, *JBL* 96 (1977) 195-233; M. MACH, *Entwicklungsstadien des jüdischen Engelglaubens in vorrabinischer Zeit* (Tübingen 1992) 34; L. D. MERINO, Los 'vigilantes' en la literatura intertestamentaria, *Simposio Biblico Espanol, Salamanca, 1982* (ed. N. Fernandez-Marcos; Madrid 1984) 575-609; J. T. MILIK, *The Books of Enoch* (Oxford 1976); R. MURRAY, The Origin of Aramaic *ʿir*, Angel, *Or* 53 (1984) 303-317.

J. J. COLLINS

WAY דרך

I. The swearing formula *ḥy drk bʾr šbʿ* ("As the way of Beersheba lives", RSV), occurring in Am 8:14, has caused problems to the interpreters ever since antiquity (BARSTAD 1984:191-201; OLYAN 1991:121-127). The main problem with this text concerns the rendering of *drk* with 'way', 'road'. Even if *drk* may be translated also with 'manner' or 'custom', both the use of the verb 'to swear' + *ḥy,* as well as the context, indicates strongly that we have a reference to some kind of deity in this text.

II. In the world of the Bible, roads—and more especially those used for pilgrimages—could acquire such status that they shared in the sphere of the gods. That is why many scholars still adhere to the view that in Am 8:14 the swearing is to the 'pilgrimage to Beer-sheba' (PAUL 1991:272). They sometimes compare the text with the Muslim practice of swearing by the pilgrimage route to Mecca. This custom, however, represents something quite different, and must be viewed within the broader context of Muslim swearing usage in general, where it is only attested in much later times. Also the occurrence of 'way' as a possible divine element in Akkadian (*Šurpu* V-VI:191: "the road, daughter of the great gods", *ḫar-ra-nu* DUMU.SAL DINGIR.MEŠ GAL.MEŠ) concerns a different matter and must be viewed within the broader context of deification of objects which we may sometimes find in Mesopotamian religion. Even if such a usage is also attested at Elephantine, it is hardly relevant in relation to Am 8:14 (OLYAN 1991:127 n. 4).

III. Scholarly discussion has come up with quite a number of different solutions to the problem of *drk* in Am 8:14. Since 'way', 'road', or 'manner' appear not to provide us with satisfactory readings of *drk* in Am 8:14, many scholars have emended the text to read another word. This, too, has turned out to be a problematic venture. One of the most common emendations has been to read *ddk* instead of *drk* (OLYAN 1991:121-135). Yet there seems to be no need for changing the text here (→Dod). The *crux* can hardly be solved on the basis of textual criticism. The context clearly demands that the reference is to some kind of deity. This was noted already by the Greek translator and is reflected in the *ho theós sou* of the LXX. Though the other deities mentioned in Am 8:14 cannot be discussed in depth here, it is important to stress that the goddess →Ashima is not so problematic as some scholars seem to believe (BARSTAD 1984: 157-181). A goddess Ashima is now also attested in an Aramaic text as a part of a *Göttertriade* (BEYER & LIVINGSTONE 1987: 287-88). There is sufficient evidence, then, to make the claim that Hebrew *drk* may be connected with some kind of a deity. It appears from a survey of the occurrences of *drk* in MT that we find also other texts where *drk* apparently cannot be translated with the traditional 'way', 'road', 'manner' (*HALAT* 223). Many scholars see a connection between these texts and the possibility that *drk* in Hebrew, as in Ugaritic, can also mean 'dominion', 'might', 'power'. Also in

Phoenician the word *drk* occurs in the meaning 'dominion' (CROSS 1979:43-44).

The appearance of our word in an Ugaritic divine epithet is interesting. In RS 24.252 (lines 6-7) Anat is called *bʿlt mlk bʿlt drkt bʿlt šmm rmm*, 'the Lady of Royalty, the Lady of Power, the Lady of Heavens on high' (PARDEE 1988:101). We should note, however, that there is no attestation of a deity *drkt* in Ugaritic, only the feminine noun meaning 'power', 'might'. We note with interest that in later Judaism words for 'power', 'might', and the like are often used as a substitute for the name of →Yahweh (URBACH 1979:80-96).

There is a possible connection between *drk* of Am 8:14 and the goddess Derceto (BARSTAD 1984:196-197). Several scholars have pointed to a connection between *bʿlt drkt* and *bʿlt šmm rmm* (for the latter expression, see also *KAI* 15) in the Ugaritic text and the much later Hellenistic legend of Derceto and her daughter Semiramis, in particular related to the city of Ashkelon (PARDEE 1988:103; GESE *RAAM* 214). Despite the great distance in time, the lexicographic similarities cannot be mere coincidences. The cult of the goddess Derceto is attested at several cities in the Hellenistic world. This may explain the presence of such a name or epithet also at Beersheba. Here, we must take into account the close contacts between the different regions of Syria/Palestine in antiquity. We know that there were contacts between Philistine cities, including Ashkelon, and Ugarit (DOTHAN 1989:60). Ashkelon and Beersheba are not very far from each other, and Philistine material remains have indeed been found at Beersheba (AHARONI 1975:151). Clearly, the cult at Beersheba must have been an important one (SCHOORS 1986:61-74).

Still it would be wrong simply to identify the *drk* of Beersheba mentioned in Amos with the Hellenistic deity Derceto. The relationship between Ugarit, Bersheba and Ashkelon may point to a possible diffusion of the cult of a deity referred to by the name or epithet *drk*, 'power', 'dominion'. This, however, does not help us much. The masculine/female forms *drk/drkt* may be comparable to e.g. *mlk/mlkt*, or *bʿl/bʿlt*, or *ʾdn/ʾdt* and be used 'originally' as generic or epithetical terms, appearing as a divine name only in later times. It is one thing to be able to say something about the origin and etymology of *drk* in Am 8:14, but it is quite another matter to identify the kind of deity we find behind this designation. Thus, the 'Power of Bersheba' *may* be a local →Baal, or a local Yahweh. The local character of monarchical Yahwism is now attested beyond doubt in extrabiblical sources (cf. 'Yahweh of Samaria' and 'Yahweh of Teman' at Kuntillet ʿAjrud). The fact that the ancient Near Eastern cults were basically local cults should not be underrated. Again and again we may witness how deities rising to fame and spreading over large areas were mixed with local cults, and sometimes totally absorbed. Thus, the 'same' name for different deities in different regions does not necessarily guarantee any stability or consistency in matters theological. Moreover, speculations about the etymology of divine names or epithets do not yield much information about the nature of the deity in question. For such reasons, we are hardly allowed to say anything very definite about the mysterious *drk* of Am 8:14.

III. *Bibliography*

Y. AHARONI, Excavations at Tel Beer-Sheba. Preliminary Report of the Fifth and Sixth Seasons 1973-1974, *Tel Aviv* 2 (1975) 146-168; *H. M. BARSTAD, *The Religious Polemics of Amos* (VTSup 34; Leiden 1984) [& lit]; K. BEYER & A. LIVINGSTONE, Die neuesten aramäischen Inschriften aus Taima, *ZDMG* 137 (1987) 285-296; F. M. CROSS, A Recently Published Phoenician Inscription of the Persian Period from Byblos, *IEJ* 29 (1979) 40-44; M. DOTHAN, Archaeological Evidence for Movements of the Early 'Sea Peoples' in Canaan, *Recent Excavations in Israel: Studies in Iron Age Archaeology* (ed. S. Gitin & W. G. Dever; AASOR 49; Winona Lake 1989) 59-70; *S. M. OLYAN, The Oaths in Amos 8,14, *Priesthood and Cult in Ancient Israel* (ed. G. A. Anderson & S. M. Olyan; JSOT SupplSer 125;

Sheffield 1991) 121-149 [& lit]; D. PARDEE, *Les textes para-mythologiques de la 24e campagne (1961)* (RSOu IV; Paris 1988); S. PAUL, *Amos. A Commentary on the Book of Amos* (Minneapolis 1991); A. SCHOORS, *Berseba. De opgraving van een bijbelse stad* (Kampen 1986); E. E. URBACH, *The Sages. Their Concepts and Beliefs* (Jerusalem 1979).

H. M. BARSTAD

WILD BEASTS צִיִּים

I. *ṣiyyîm*, sg. *ṣî* (< צִיִּי*), is a plural derivative from the feminine noun *ṣiyyâ*, which appears as an adjective to *ʾereṣ* 'land' with the meaning 'dry' and as a noun with the meaning 'dry land' (cf. *ṣāyôn* Isa 25:5; 32:2). The word is certainly attested only in Isa 13:21; 34:14; and Jer 50:39; it is possibly to be found in Pss 72:9; 74:14 (for its reflection in the ancient versions see MÜLLER 1989:990). In understanding the occurrence of *ṣiyyîm* in Isa 23:13 its homonyms *ṣiyyîm* I 'ships' (Num 24:24; Isa 33:21; Ezek 30:9; Dan 11:30) and *ṣiyyîm* II 'desert-dweller' are employed. The Qumran evidence for *ṣiyyîm* (4QShir[a] 1:5 [par. 4QShir[b] 10:2]) and for *ṣî* (4QWiles 3:4) does not contribute to the determination of the sense of the word.

II. In the conceptual world of the ancient Near East the 'steppe/desert' and 'ruins/ruined places' along with mountains and swamps were the habitations of the 'counter-human world'. Not only were definite 'desert animals' such as ostriches, gazelles and antilopes at home in the desert, but the desert also served as the habit of various fabulous creatures which did not belong to any definable species. These were rather exponents of the powers that were associated with this sterile and barren realm. In addition to the iconographic evidence (cf. the tomb paintings from Beni Hasan in Egypt in KEEL 1984:67 fig. 89), there are numerous texts which describe the negative qualities of desert and ruins. Thus for example in the Sefîre Treaty Inscription *KAI* 222A:32-33: "... Its (i.e. Arpad's) grass shall become desiccated, and Arpad shall become a desolate mound (cf. *yšmn*, Hebrew *yĕšimōn* Deut 32:10; Ps 68:8, etc.), [a habitation of wild animals], of gazelles, of jackals, of hares, of wild cats, of owls, of ... and of magpies!". In like manner Ashurbanipal once characterized the Syrian desert as "a place of thirst and hunger, where no bird of the heavens has ever flown, where no onager (or) gazelle has ever grazed" (Prism A III 87-90, cf. III 105-110 etc. [M. WEIPPERT, Die Kämpfe des assyrischen Königs Assurbanipal gegen die Araber, *WO* 7 (1973-1974) 39-85, esp. 43-44]).

III. The *ṣiyyîm* are evidently demonic beings (of the desert/dry land), whose exact definition is uncertain. *Ges.*[17] and *HALAT*, for example, arrange the evidence in the following manner: a type of desert animal (Isa 13:21; 23:13; 34:14; Jer 50:39; Ps 74:14; in Ps 72:9 to be read perhaps as *ṣārîm* [*Ges.*[17] 681]); desert animals (cf. the Arabic isogloss *ḏajūna* 'wild cats') or dwellers of the steppe/desert (Ps 72:9?) or demons (*HALAT* 956).

It is characteristic of *ṣiyyîm* that the lexeme is found in descriptive oracles of doom in Isa 13:21; 23:13(?); 34:14 and Jer 50:39, and in Pss 72:9(?); 74:14(?) in the context of descriptions of enemies/chaos monsters (fabulous sea creatures). The creatures listed in the oracles of doom against Babylon (Isa 13:19-22; Jer 50:33-40) and Edom (Isa 34:9-15) represent a counter-human world, which reaches out when people fall victim to God's judgement, and their places of habitation become desolate. The topos of the 'topsy-turvy/counter-human world' belongs to the ancient Near East in general (see e.g. the 'Balaam'-Inscription from Tell Deir ʿAlla, Combination I, sentences xxiv-xxx [according to the scheme of WEIPPERT 1991:159-160, 172-174]), and in this case it is present in the etymology and semantics of the word *ṣiyyîm* (= nisbe formation of *ṣiyyâ* 'dry land'). 'Desert' and 'dry land' are to a certain extent synonyms (e.g., Zeph 2:13 'arid as the desert' [*ṣiyyâ kammidbār*]. They are a favourite habitat of sinister creatures. Thus the sinister animals which, together with demons, are listed in Job 38:39-39:30 inhabit all manner of accursed and ruined cities and regions. The animals which appear together with the *ṣiyyîm* in Isa 13:21; 34:14 and Jer 50:39 possess the same sinister connotations: *bĕnôt yaʿănâ* (ostriches) and **iyyîm*, in addition to the *tannîm* ('jackals'?/'wolves'?) and *śĕʿîrîm* of Isa 13:21f; 34:13f. They are joined in Isa 34:14 by the demon →Lilith. These beings populate former human settlements, after they have been abandoned and returned to the desert whence they came (Isa 13:20; 34:13; Jer 50:39; cf. Jer 9:11; 51:37, and often).

Like Isa 23:13, Ps 72:9 and Ps 74:14 are controversial pieces of evidence in understanding the *ṣiyyîm*. It is possible that in both cases their embodiment of the chaotic or sinister forces is emphasized: In Ps 72:8-11 are to be found, among the beings/powers that must submit to the universal rule of the (Davidic) king (v 8), the *ṣiyyîm* (v 9, another reading: *ṣārîm* 'enemies' or *ṣārâw* 'his enemies', e.g., BHS; H.-J. KRAUS [*BKAT* XV/2 (1978) 656], and others), his 'enemies' (v 9), the 'kings of Tarshish', the 'islands' and the kings of South Arabia (v 10), indeed 'all kings' and 'all peoples' (v 11). If one does not want to stay with the interpretation of *ṣiyyîm* as '(sinister) desert beings', that give up their opposition to the rule of the reigning Davidic king, then the interpretations of LXX (Ἀιθίοπες) and Vg (*Aethiopes*), namely '(human) steppe-dweller' (also a nisbe form of *ṣiyyâ*) comes into consideration. In contrast, the phrase *lĕʿam lĕṣiyyîm* in Ps 74:14 is incomprehensible in the MT. If one were to read in its place *lĕʿamlĕse yām* 'to/for the sharks' or more probably (?) *lĕʿam ṣiyyîm* 'to/for the nation of desert beings', then the *ṣiyyîm* would receive the carcass of →Leviathan (v 14) as food. If this is the case, then there would exist in Ps 74:14 the opposition 'fabulous desert creatures :: fabulous sea creatures'.

Like the *śĕʿîrîm*, the *ṣiyyîm* are not a zoologically identifiable species. The term is rather a collective designation for demonic desert beings (perhaps 'those that belong to the dry land > desert beings', cf. the translation *bestiae* in Isa 13:21 Vg), who represent a 'counter-human world of devastated habitations' (MÜLLER 1989).

IV. *Bibliography*

G. FLEISCHER, צִיָּה, *TWAT* 6 (1989) 991-994; B. JANOWSKI & U. NEUMANN-GORSOLKE, Das Tier als Exponent dämonischer Mächte, *Gefährten und Feinde des Menschen. Das Tier in der Lebenswelt des alten Israel* (ed. B. Janowski et al.; Neukirchen-Vluyn 1993) 278-282 [& lit.]; *O. KEEL, *Jahwes Entgegnung an Ijob. Eine Deutung von Ijob 38-41 vor dem Hintergrund der zeitgenössischen Bildkunst* (FRLANT 121; Göttingen 1978) 63-81; KEEL, *Die Welt der altorientalischen Bildsymbolik und das Alte Testament. Am Beispiel der Psalmen* (Zürich/Einsiedeln/Köln/Neukirchen-Vluyn [4]1984) 53-67, esp. 66-67; *H.-P. MÜLLER, צִי, *TWAT* 6 (1989) 987-991; T. STAUBLI, *Das Image der Nomaden im Alten Israel und in der Ikonographie seiner seßhaften Nachbarn* (OBO 107; Fribourg/Göttingen 1991) 259-268; G. WANKE, Dämonen II, *TRE* 8 (1981) 275-277 [& lit.]; H. WEIPPERT, *Schöpfer des Himmels und der Erde. Ein Beitrag zur Theologie des Jeremiabuches* (SBS 102; Stuttgart 1981) 52-54; M. WEIPPERT, The Balaam Text from Deir ʿAlla and the Study of the Old Testament, *The Balaam Text from Deir ʿAllā Re-Evaluated* (eds. J. Hoftijzer & G. van der Kooij; Leiden 1991) 151-184.

B. JANOWSKI

WINE → TIRASH

WISDOM חכמה Σοφία

I. Wisdom, sometimes in scholarly literature referred to as 'Lady Wisdom' or 'Woman Wisdom', is the name of a biblical goddess. She figures prominently in one canonical book and several deuterocanonical writings of the OT: Prov 1-9, Sir, Bar, and Wis. Although modern interpreters have often treated her as a literary personification, it can be argued that what later came to be considered a mere figure of speech started its career as a 'real' deity. Wisdom, in Heb *ḥokmâ* (rarely *ḥokmôt* as sing. fem., Prov 1:20; 9:1) and in Gk *sophia*, is the goddess of knowledge, shrewdness (both implied in the semantic range of *ḥokmâ*), statecraft, and the scribal profession. The Heb and the Gk names are abstract nouns in the feminine gender, corresponding to German 'die Weisheit' or French 'la Sagesse'. Her name sums up what the goddess stands for and suggests that scribes and rulers must excel in intellectual qualities.

II. We cannot provide much evidence for the existence of a goddess by the name of Wisdom in the ancient Near East. The only possible evidence is in the Aramaic Ahiqar-story, found on papyrus leaves on the Nile island of Elephantine. From two fifth-century BCE papyrus leaves, the following fragmentary passage can be reconstructed tentatively: "From heaven the peoples are favoured; [Wisdom (*ḥkmh*) is of] the gods. Indeed, she is precious to the gods; her kingdom is eternal. She has been established by Shamayn (?); yes, the Holy Lord has exalted her" (Ahiqar 94-95 = LINDENBERGER 1983:68; *OTP* 2, 499). KOTTSIEPER translates somewhat differently: "... Among the gods, too, she is honored; [she shares with her lord] the rulership. In heaven is she established; yea, the lord of the holy ones has exalted her" (TUAT 3:335-336). The Assyrian provenance of the Ahiqar story and collection of sayings is clear from its references to seventh-century BCE Assyrian kings Sennacherib and Esarhaddon as well as to the Assyrian god Shamash. The exaltation of a deity, as referred to in the passage quoted, means his or her promotion to a higher rank and is quite characteristic of Mesopotamian mythology. Thus the goddess Inanna boasts in a hymn that she received lordship over heaven, earth, ocean, and war, for the god Enlil has "exalted" her (*ANET* 578-579). According to LINDENBERGER (1983), Wisdom, in the Ahiqar passage, would be "the special province of Baal Shamayn, one of the high gods of the Aramaeans". The reading of Shamayn as a divine name, however, is conjectural, and we may prefer Kottsieper's version which implies a co-rulership of Wisdom and the god El. Lindenberger suggests north Syria as the home of Ahiqar. Like the Ahiqar story as a whole, the home of this goddess called Wisdom must be 7th century BCE Mesopotamia or perhaps Syria. Possibly the Aramaic-speaking scribes shared the cult of Wisdom with their Hebrew-speaking colleagues. Unfortunately, the Ahiqar passage is too fragmentary to warrant further conjectures.

Elsewhere in the ancient East scribes also had their female patron deity. The Sumerians called her Nisaba, giving her the beautiful title of "Mistress of Science" (HAUSSIG 1965:115-116; SJÖBERG 1976:174-175), while the Egyptians referred to Seshat as "foremost in the library" or "she who directs the house of books" (*RÄRG* 699). Nisaba had a local cult, unlike Seshat.

Scholars have often referred to the Egyptian goddess, Maat, as an equivalent of, if not model for, Wisdom. However, the evidence produced by authors like KAYATZ (1966) and WINTER (1983:511-514) is not convincing. There is evidence, though, for the hellenistic goddess →Isis to be the Book of Wisdom's model for Sophia (KLOPPENBORG 1982). Isis, like Sophia, is both a savior involved with the endangered life of individuals, and a goddess associated with the king. "As many as are in prison, in the power of death ... and having called upon you to be present, are all saved", says a hymn to Isis (Isidorus 1:29.34 in TOTTI 1985:77); Sophia, in the same way, is with the prisoner (Wis 10:14). The triad God – Sophia – king Solomon (with Sophia being the spouse of both God and king: Wis 8:3.9) is probably patterned on the model of another triad: Re/Osiris – Isis – king of Egypt.

III. The chronology of the biblical and post-biblical writings, in which Lady Wisdom figures, is roughly as follows: (a) The earliest stratum of Prov 1-9—presumably 10th or 9th century BCE (much earlier than often suggested by scholars; the house with pillars [9:1] echoes pre-exilic domestic architecture); (b) Prov 1-9 in edited (canonical) form—date unknown (probably 5th century BCE ?); (c) Sir—early 2nd century BCE; (d) Aristoboulos—2nd century BCE; (e) Bar—1st century BCE; (f) Wis—1st century BCE or CE; (g) *1 Enoch*—1st century BCE.

The wide range of dates enables us to follow the career of an ancient Israelite deity from polytheistic, pre-canonical times to the monotheism, or qualified monotheism, of early Judaism.

Prov 1-9 is an ancient Israelite instruction manual composed of short discourses and poems used as texts for the training and education of scribes. An early-Jewish revision seems to have attenuated its original polytheistic orientation; however, the editor proceeded with much tact. He no doubt belonged to those circles which in post-exilic Israel developed their own, daring version of early-Jewish monotheism. Unlike Second Isaiah and the Deuteronomist (Isa 43:10; 44: 6; 45:5; Deut 4:35; 1 Sam 2:2), the editor did not espouse an absolute and uncompromising monotheism which declared all deities as simply inexistant. Rather, the editor must have held a view expressed in certain Psalms (Ps 95:3; 96:4-5; 97:7.9): Israel's god →Yahweh is not the only god, but he is the supreme one. As an absolute monarch, he rules over all the deities. For the editor, one of these deities is Lady Wisdom.

Prov 1-9 provides a fairly complete picture of Lady Wisdom: She is Yahweh's daughter and witnessed her father as he created the universe (Prov 8:22-30); she guides kings and their staff of state officials in their rule and administration (8:14-16); she teaches (no doubt, through human teachers) young men wisdom, a wisdom no doubt to be identified with the scribal art (1:20-33; 8:1-11.32-36; 9:1-6.11-12); she serves as the 'personal deity' of the student, for whom she acts as lover (4:6; 7:4), protector (3:23-25; v 26 may originally have referred to Wisdom rather than to Yahweh), and guide to success and wealth (3:16-17; 8:18). Abandoned by the personal goddess, the individual is lost (1:27-28). Although she may be angry with her protégé, she appears generally as a kindly, caring, assuring, motherly figure.

Prov 8 is one of the most developed mythological texts of the Bible, reminiscent of the kind of discourse characteristic of the Homeric Hymns. Unfortunately, this text, in some of its details, is not as clear as we would like. In 8:22-31, Lady Wisdom describes her career in three stages: she was *begotten* by Yahweh (22; not "created", as some translations have it); she witnessed her father's creative activity (vv 27-30); she established her relationship with humans (v 31). Only the middle one of these stages is fairly straightforward: witnessing how the world was created, Wisdom, as an infant (v 30; Hebr *ʾāmōn*; see LANG 1986:65-66), learned what constitutes the universe. She may also have acquired the (magical?) skills necessary to perform acts of creation. Accordingly, she is the wisest being one can imagine (cf. Wis 9:9). One aspect of the wisdom she acquires is no doubt the 'nature wisdom' elsewhere referred to in the biblical tradition and identified as knowledge about sky, earth, and sea, complete with beasts, birds, reptiles, fish (cf. king Solomon's wisdom in 1 Kgs 4:32-33; see also Wis 7:17-20). Thus, Lady Wisdom is uniquely qualified and authorized to teach. However, no precise idea is given about how the contact with the humans is established. The text as it stands now refers only to the playful frolicking of the wise infant who takes delight in "the sons of men" (v 31). Did Wisdom teach in a playful manner, instructing children in "nature wisdom" and presumably how to write their ABCs? Did the mythological text end here or was something omitted in the process of canonical editing? Leaving aside such issues, we may suggest that Prov 8 reflects the apprentice scribe's cosmic initiation: symbolically present at creation, the novice draws upon creation's fresh and inexhaustible powers; refreshed, empowered and instructed, he can now assume political and administrative responsibilities of cosmic dimensions.

Even more problems are involved in the birth of Lady Wisdom. The two verbs used to describe her origin are *qānānî*, "he has begotten me" (Prov 8:22), and *nĕsakkotî* (to be vocalized thus), "he fashioned me (in the womb)" (8:23). In the absence of a reference to a mother, are we to imagine a kind of male pregnancy known from the creation story in which →Eve comes out of Adam? Or was Wisdom born from the head (or mouth, cf. Sir 24:3) of her divine father just as →Athena, in Greek mythology, sprang from the head of →Zeus? And, moreover, who is her divine father? Since Yahweh seems to have become a creator god only late in his career, possibly not before the 6th century BCE (LANG 1983a:49; 1983b; W. HERMANN, *UF* 23 [1991] 165-180), the original, pre-canonical text may here have spoken of El or Elohim as her father. El(ohim) seems to have been the creator god of ancient Israelite polytheism, and we would expect Elohim, rather than Yahweh, to be the wise creator of Prov 3:19-20. In Ugaritic tradition, at any rate, El is the creator (*KTU* 1.16:V.26) and he is also called "wise" (*KTU* 1.3 v:30; 1.4 iv:41), possibly on account of his manual dexterity (and magical power?) to create. El is of course also the creator in a Phoenician inscription from Karatepe, dating from ca. 720 BCE (*ʾl qn ʾrṣ* "→El creator of the earth"; *KAI* 26 A:18; cf. P. D. MILLER, *BASOR* 239 [1980] 43-46). Prov 30:4 seems to imply that El(ohim) was Israel's creator god and Yahweh the creator's son (as in Deut 32:8-9, in the reading of Qumran and LXX). Thus in the pre-canonical view, Wisdom was Yahweh's sister!

Problematic, too, remains the precise meaning of Wisdom's speaking at the city gate and at the crossroads (Prov 1:20-21; 8:2-3). It has been suggested that she may have shrines there (BARKER 1992:61). At any rate, she seems to be connected with 'liminal' places. In Greece, the goddess Hekate presided over the entrances and crossroads where she had shrines; the Romans called her Trivia (JOHNSTON 1991): so Wisdom may be Hekate's Hebrew equivalent. Liminal places are conspicuous or even dangerous and need divine protection.

We do not know whether the cult of Lady Wisdom involved the existence of particular shrines. Nor do we know of any ritual activities, such as reciting prayers or giving offerings, by which some of the Israelites may have expressed their devotion to the goddess. The canonical re-interpretation of Lady Wisdom from a 'Yahweh-alone' perspective or from monotheism proper would certainly involve the destruction of shrines and the prohibition of any ritual forms related to the goddess. Understood as a deity strictly subordinated to Yahweh and having neither shrine nor receiving ritual respects, Lady Wisdom would not endanger monotheism.

Why did the Yahweh-alone editors revise, but not discard Prov 1-9 altogether? Retaining this semi-polytheistic piece of literature as a school text, they did not act differently from Christians in late antiquity. For many centuries, Christians never established their own curriculum for schools. Before the Middle Ages, Christians learned how to read and write on the basis of pagan literature such as the poetry of Homer or Virgil. Teachers were not known to be innovators; they relied on the received wisdom of their trade.

Prov 1-9, as a school text, remained a widely known piece of literature through many centuries, and we can find its echoes in several early Jewish writings. Ben Sira identifies Wisdom and →Torah: when the Law is read in the synagogue, it is Wisdom's voice that people can hear (Sir 24:2.23). Although Ben Sira may echo some features of the original mythology (Wisdom's birth out of the mouth of the creator?), he thinks of her as a poetic personification. In Bar 3-4, Lady Wisdom is a relatively pale figure, also understood as a poetic personification of the book of Law. Here Gunkel's intuition applies: "The sages had a kind of female patron deity of whom they sometimes spoke; Hebrew tradition calls her 'Wisdom'. For Israel's sages, this figure was perhaps a mere personification. Some of her features, however, betray her former divine nature" (GUNKEL 1903:26).

In Aristoboulos and the book of Wisdom, we find philosophical re-interpretations of the figure. Both the work of Aristoboulos and the book of Wisdom are in Greek; therefore they call Lady Wisdom by her Greek name, Sophia. They also re-cast Sophia in philosophical terms. Identified with *pneuma* (→spirit; Wis 7:22-26) and (intellectual) light (Aristoboulos, Fragment 5 = *OTP* 2, 841), Sophia is taken to be an impersonal power emanating from God and pervading his creation. She also resides in the souls of prophets and leaders, inspiring their divine utterances or guiding their deeds (Wis 7:27; 10:16).

Interestingly enough, the book of Wisdom retains the personal language and can portray Sophia as a goddess. Picturing Sophia as a goddess, the book of Wisdom draws upon both Prov 1-9 and the hellenistic favourite goddess, Isis. Like Lady Wisdom of the Book of Proverbs, Isis is a goddess related to kingship and nature. In the Old Greek version of Prov 8:30, Wisdom works as *harmozousa* at creation, which presumably means that she acts as a technician who 'arranges' or 'structures' things, putting them together in the appropriate manner (cf. Prov 9:1—Wisdom builds a house!). In the book of Wisdom, Sophia acts as an 'artisan' or 'master builder', possibly at creation and ever after (Wis 7:21[22]; 8:4; 14:2). She shares Yahweh's throne as his consort (9:4), and is also King Solomon's spouse (8:9).

The mixture of personal/mythological language with impersonal/philosophical notions makes the book of Wisdom a most attractive piece of literature. It allows for two interpretations of Sophia, a more philosophical one (for the elite, presumably) and a more mythological one (for others). In mythological terms, Sophia can be seen and appreciated as a deity strictly subordinated to Yahweh. Those ancient readers, to whom this reading appealed, adopted a 'monarchic monotheism'—one which considers Yahweh the king of all deities, thus permitting to retain a certain amount of polytheistic survivals. This kind of 'monotheism' also makes the Jewish religion not look too different from the polytheism of the hellenistic world. Concerning the other, philosophical reading, one can look beyond traditional mythology and give it a new, more abstract and sophisticated meaning. This side of the book of Wisdom reveals how Jewish philosophers began to play with their inherited mythology as well as the traditions of others. If these philosophers had lived at a later age, perhaps that of Plotinus in the 3rd century CE, they would have called Sophia an *hypostasis*: a being that emanates from a higher reality to which it owes its existence and force, but one which also enjoys a certain independence. Was not →Christ also such an emanated divine being, sent from a higher world? Here we can grasp one of the reasons why early Christians relied on Sophia, renamed →Logos ("speech, utterance"), for developing the Christology of the gospel of John (John 1). In a similar vein, Jewish Kabbalists perceived Torah as a hypostasis (HOLDREGE 1989).

The little Wisdom myth told in *1 Enoch* represents a special case. In a polemical piece the apocalyptic author relates how Wisdom, not finding a place to stay among humans, returns to her heavenly home: "Wisdom went out to dwell with the children of men, but she found no dwelling place. [So] Wisdom returned to her place and settled permanently among the angels. Then Iniquity went out of her rooms, and found whom she did not expect. And she [Iniquity] dwelt with them" (*1 Enoch* 42 = *OTP* 1, 33). While the idea of Wisdom searching for a home among mortals is indebted to Sir 24, the idea of return and the domination of Iniquity relies on pagan mythology. Greek mythology knows the story of the good goddess or goddesses who leave the country because of human iniquity. As they return to Mount Olympus, the land is dominated by crime and misfortune: and thus a new, less attractive era of human history begins, the Age of Iron. In Hesiod (*Op.* 197-201), the two goddesses forsaking the earth are Aidos (Shame) and Nemesis (Indignation); Theognis (*Elegiae* 1135-1142) calls them Pistis (Trust) and Sophrosyne

(Wisdom); in Aratos, it is only one goddess, →Dike (Justice). As injustice began to prevail on earth, "Dike, full of hatred for the human race, flew up to heaven, taking her abode at that place where, at night, she can still be seen by men" (Aratus, *Phaenomena* 133-135). Such is the Greek myth echoed in *1 Enoch*.

Perhaps the best way to sum up the career of the ancient Israelite Wisdom goddess is in terms of 'personification'. Originally, Wisdom was a mythological personification comparable to →Heaven and →Earth as deities in ancient Greek religion. Later, when Israel's religion came to be dominated by mono-Yahwism and eventually by monotheism, she was reduced to a merely poetic personification and thus lost much of her earlier, mythological vitality. Now, she represented God's Torah or his spirit, and her person-like appearance was designed to give vitality to an otherwise abstract concept. However, philosophers such as the author of the Book of Wisdom took great care not to lose the mythological connection which made for good literature and also attracted those who adopted a view of the divine world which retained its plurality while placing Israel's God at the top. The presence of the mythological material helped early Christians in their attempt to define the nature and function of Christ. Traces of a Sophia-Christology are already present in the NT writings: "this message is Christ, who is the power of God and the Wisdom of God" (1 Cor 1:24; cf. 1 Cor 2:7; Eph 1:17; Col 2:3; but also Mt 11:19 and Lk 7:35; see further CHRIST 1970). It was especially in the development of the idea of the pre-existence of Christ that Jewish Wisdom speculation made itself felt (see e.g. John 1:1-18; SCOTT 1992). As *bricoleurs*, the NT authors took elements of the old myth to construct a new one.

IV. *Bibliography*

W. F. ALBRIGHT, The Goddess of Life and Wisdom, *AJSL* 36 (1920) 258-294; *M. BARKER, *The Great Angel: A Study of Israel's Second God* (London 1992) 48-69; C. V. CAMP, *Wisdom and the Feminine in the Book of Proverbs* (Sheffield 1985); F. CHRIST, *Jesus Sophia. Die Sophia-Christologie bei den Synoptikern* (ATANT 57; Zürich 1970); M. DIETRICH & O. LORETZ, Die Weisheit des ugaritischen Gottes El im Kontext der altorientalischen Weisheit, *UF* 24 (1992) 31-38; H. GUNKEL, *Zum religionsgeschichtlichen Verständnis des Neuen Testaments* (Göttingen 1903); H. W. HAUSSIG (ed.), *WbMyth* 1/1 (Stuttgart 1965); B. A. HOLDREGE, The Bride of Israel: The Ontological Status of Scripture in the Rabbinic and Cabbalistic Traditions, *Rethinking Scripture* (ed. M. Levering; Albany 1989) 180-261; S. I. JOHNSTON, Crossroads, *ZPE* 88 (1991) 217-224; C. B. KAYATZ, *Studien zu Proverbien 1-9* (WMANT 22; Neukirchen-Vluyn 1966); *J. S. KLOPPENBORG, Isis and Sophia in the Book of Wisdom, *HTR* 75 (1982) 57-84; B. LANG, *Monotheism and the Prophetic Minority* (Sheffield 1983a); LANG, Ein babylonisches Motiv in Israels Schöpfungsmythologie, *BZ* 27 (1983b) 236-237; *LANG, *Wisdom and the Book of Proverbs: A Hebrew Goddess Redefined* (New York 1986); H. VON LIPS, *Weisheitliche Traditionen im Neuen Testament* (WMANT 64; Neukirchen-Vluyn 1990); J. M. LINDENBERGER, *The Aramaic Proverbs of Ahiqar* (Baltimore 1983); G. SCHIMANOWSKI, *Weisheit und Messias* (WUNT 2,17; Tübingen 1985); *M. SCOTT, *Sophia and the Johannine Jesus*, (JSNTSup 71; Sheffield 1992) 36-82; S. SCHROER, Die personifizierte Sophia im Buch der Weisheit, *Ein Gott Allein* (eds. W. Dietrich & M. A. Klopfenstein; Freiburg/Göttingen 1994) 543-558; A. W. SJÖBERG, The Old Babylonian Eduba, *Sumerological Studies in Honor of T. Jacobsen* (ed. S. J. Lieberman; Chicago 1976) 159-179; M. TOTTI, *Ausgewählte Texte der Isis- und Sarapis-Religion* (Hildesheim 1985); R. L. WILKEN (ed.), *Aspects of Wisdom in Judaism and Early Christianity* (Notre Dame 1975); U. WINTER, *Frau und Göttin. Exegetische und ikonographische Studien zum weiblichen Gottesbild* (OBO 53; Fribourg 1983).

B. LANG

WITNESS עד

I. As utilized in the biblical materials relating to the legal sphere, the 'witness' (*ʿēd*) was a person who had firsthand knowledge concerning an event or fact and who could provide either an affirmation or a refutation of testimony presented (i.e. Gen 31:45-52). The application of the role of 'witness' to members of the divine realm is especially relevant to the biblical metaphor of covenant. Ancient Near Eastern international treaty forms, from which the biblical ideal of covenant is derived, invoke extensive lists of deities or elements of the natural world, e.g. heaven and earth, who serve as witnesses to and as guarantors of the treaty agreement.

II. Note that in the ancient Near Eastern treaties the deities are not called or invoked as 'witnesses' as such. They play the role of witnesses. They should be compared, for instance, to the witnesses in Assyrian legal documents where it is stated that the transaction was made 'before *ina* IGI(*pān*) of X, X, ...'. In the vassal treaties of Esarhaddon it is stated that the treaty is concluded *ina* IGI(*pān*) of ᵈX ...' (SAA 2, 6 § 2). In these treaties the function of the deities is defined as follows: 'May these gods be our witnesses' (lit.: 'look for us'; DINGIR.MEŠ *an-nu-te lid-gu-lu*, SAA 2, 6 § 57:494). The Aramaic treaty between Bar-Gaʾyah and Matiel is concluded 'in front of (*qdm*) the deities' (*KAI* 222 A:7-12).

III. Because of the monotheistic tendencies of the Hebrew texts, such lists of deities are not found in the biblical accounts associated with covenants, either between human parties or between Israel and →Yahweh, though there are a number of instances where either deified elements of the natural world or other objects are invoked as 'witness' (*ʿēd*) to an agreement or contract. In Gen 31:45-52, a →stone pillar and a stone heap are invoked to witness a parity treaty between Jacob and Laban. A similar function is ascribed to an altar, guaranteeing an agreement among the tribes of Israel (Josh 22:26-27); to an inscription (Isa 31:8); and to a stela (Isa 19:19-22). In the context of the covenant between Israel and Yahweh, a stone is invoked as *ʿēd* in Josh 24:27 and, in Deut 31:19.21, the 'Song of Moses' stands as guarantor of the alliance.

As reflections of the '→olden gods', the natural pairs standing behind the active deities of the pantheon, '→Heaven and →Earth' are called by Yahweh to stand as witnesses (hiph. of *ʿûd*) to the covenant with Israel (Deut 4:26; 30:19; 31:29). Yahweh himself is invoked as a witness in a number of different contexts. The deity is invoked as *ʿēd* to the parity treaty in Gen 31:50 (cf. 1 Sam 20:23.42) and stands as witness between Samuel and the people in 1 Sam 12:5. In the prophetic materials, Yahweh is witness to oaths (Jer 29:23; 42:5) and stands as witness against those who violated the covenant (Mal 2:14; 3:5). Yahweh's role as witness is even extended beyond Israel in Zeph 3:8 (LXX) and Mic 1:2.

Despite the fact that Yahweh himself can be invoked as *ʿēd* in the Hebrew traditions, there are two instances where it is possible that the witness referred to in the texts is to be identified with a heavenly figure distinct from Yahweh. In Ps 89:38, the royal oracle (vv 20-38) concludes with a reference to a 'witness in the heavens' (*ʿēd baššaḥaq*), who might be identified with one of the members of Yahweh's heavenly court (*qĕdōšîm* // *bĕnê ʾēlîm;* vv 6-7; →Sons of [the] god[s]). While it is possible that he might be understood either as Yahweh himself or one of the members of his court, the Canaanite parallel of Baal as intercessor for the king before the high-god El in the assembly suggests the former (*KTU* 1.15.ii: 11-28; 1.17.i:16-27; 1.2.i:21).

That the biblical traditions were acquainted with the concept of a heavenly witness different from Yahweh, who could serve as interpreter and intercessor for a petitioner, is clear from Job 16:19-21. In this passage, Job appeals to a 'witness' (*ʿēd/śāhēd*) 'in heaven' // 'on high' (*baš-šāmayim* // *bammĕrômîm*; v 19) who would serve as an 'interpreter' (*mēlîṣ* →Mediator I) before God. As with the witness invoked in Ps 89:38, this *ʿēd* probably reflects either the concept of a personal deity or a specialized function of one of the members of the divine assembly. This figure is also commonly identified with the 'redeemer' (→*gō'ēl*) of Job 19:25 and the 'arbiter' (*môkîaḥ*) of 9:33-35, each of whom functions as a figure separate from, though subordinate to, Yahweh.

IV. *Bibliography*

F. M. CROSS, *Canaanite Myth and Hebrew Epic* (Cambridge, Mass. 1973) esp. 39-43; J. B. CURTIS, On Job's Witness in Heaven, *JBL* 102 (1983) 549-562; P. G. MOSCA, Once Again the Heavenly Witness of Psalm 89:38, *JBL* 105 (1986) 27-37; S. MOWINCKEL, Hiob's gō'ēl und Zeuge im Himmel, *Von Alten Testament: FS für Karl Marti* (ed. K. Budde; Giessen 1925) 207-212; E. T. MULLEN, JR., The Divine Witness and the Davidic Royal Grant: Ps 89:37-38, *JBL* 102 (1983) 207-218; T. VEIJOLA, The Witness in the Clouds: Ps 89:38, *JBL* 107 (1988) 413-417.

E. T. MULLEN, JR.

WIZARD ידעני

I. The term *yiddĕʿōnî* occurs 11 times in the OT, always in parallellism with *'ôb* 'ancestor, ancestral spirit, ghost' (Lev 19:31; 20:6.27; Deut 18:11; 1 Sam 28:3.9; 2 Kings 21:6 // 2 Chron 33:6; 2 Kings 23:24; Isa 8:19; 19:3; →Spirit of the dead). It is certain that the word is a nominal form (supplemented with the afformative *-ōn [< *-ān]* and the gentilic *-î*). The pattern is comparatively rare in Hebrew, though comparable forms exist in *qadmônî* 'east of, earlier', *'admônî* 'reddish', *ḥakmōni* 'knowledgeable', *naḥămānî* 'comforting' and *raḥămānî* 'merciful' (BAUER & LEANDER 1922:501 y). In contrast to the above-mentioned forms, the middle radical of the root is geminated in *yiddĕʿōnî*. This may be explained as a 'numinous doubling' (TROPPER 1989:318; other explanations in BAUER & LEANDER 1922:501 yθ), the emphatic pronunciation of words and names having great religious significance. This generally manifests itself in writing as the doubling of a consonant. As a consequence of the gemination, the vowel in the first syllable shifts from /a/ to /i/, (BAUER & LEANDER 1922:193 v). The precise semantic nuance of the adjectival formation *-ā/ōnî* is difficult to establish, given its scarce attestation in Hebrew. It is probable that adjectives of this type have a more intensive, emphatic signification than ordinary adjectives. Consequently *yiddĕʿōnî* would have meant 'extremely knowledgeable, all-knowing'. Given that this term always follows the term *'ôb*, it must originally have been an epithet of the deceased ancestors or a designation of the dead in general.

II. Throughout the ancient Orient, it was believed that the dead possessed occult powers inaccessible to the living. The knowledgeability of the dead was attributed on the one hand to experience gathered through a long life, on the other hand to the fact that, as numinous beings in the realm beyond, they now had available to them previously inaccessible sources of knowledge. On the basis of their comprehensive knowledge the dead, like the gods, functioned as dispensers of oracles in the ancient Orient.

III. Because the word *yiddĕʿōnî* '(all-) knowing' occurs exlusively as a parallel term to *'ôb*, no independent function for it can be ascertained. The significance and function of the Old Testament *'ōbôt*-ancestors applies equally to the *yiddĕʿōnî*. In the (older) passages in which *'ōbôt*-designated dead ancestors or the spirits of the dead in general (who were the object of cultic veneration, magical incantation and consultation in times of crisis) it may be said that *yiddĕʿōnî* also designated these ancestors and signified 'the all-knowing ones'. In Isa 19:3, for example, we read: "Then they (scil. the Egyptians) will turn (in their distress), consulting idols (*'elîlîm*), the shades (*'iṭṭîm*), the ancestors (*'ōbôt-*) and the 'knowing ones' (*yiddĕʿōnîm*)." As the meaning of the word *'ōb* subsequently changed to 'soothsaying spirit', the word *yiddĕʿōnî* began to function as an epithet of these soothsaying spirits as well which, according to Lev 20:27, served certain people as mediums: "Men or women in whom there is either an *'ōb*-spirit or a *yiddĕʿōnî*-spirit shall be put to death!" There is, however, no evidence that the term *yiddĕʿōnî* ever designated the medium used by such spirits (i.e. the soothsayers or magicians themselves) in the biblical period. As with *ʾôb*, the consultation of the *yiddĕʿōnî* was considered incompatible with monotheistic Yahwism and elicited the death penalty (Lev 20:27).

IV. Post-biblical tradition no longer understood *ʾōbôt* and *yiddĕʿōnîm* as soothsaying spirits, but rather as designations of the soothsayers and magicians who dealt with such spirits. The LXX, which generally translates *ʾôb* with *engastrimythos* 'ventriloquist', renders *yiddĕʿōnî* with *epaoidos* 'conjurer', *gnōstēs/gnōristēs* '(knowing) soothsayer', *teratoskopos* 'diviner' and *engastrimythos* 'one who speaks from the belly'. The Vulg. renders *yiddĕʿōnî* similarly: *harioli, incantores, divini, divinationes, haruspices.* These interpretations influenced all subsequent translations of the Bible, including the most recent of them.

V. *Bibliography*

H. BAUER & P. LEANDER, *Historische Grammatik der Hebräischen Sprache des Alten Testaments* (Halle 1922); H. ROUILLARD & J. TROPPER, Vom kanaanäischen Ahnenkult zur Zauberei, *UF* 19 (1987) 235-254; J. TROPPER, *Nekromantie. Totenbefragung im Alten Orient und im Alten Testament* (AOAT 223; Kevelaer & Neukirchen-Vluyn 1989).

J. TROPPER

WORLD RULERS κοσμοκράτορες

I. *Kosmokratōr*, 'lord of the world', 'world ruler', occurs in pagan literature as an epithet for gods, rulers, and heavenly bodies. The LXX does not use the term, and in the NT it occurs once, in Eph 6:12.

II. *Kosmokratōr* can occasionally be used to refer to earthly rulers (*CIG* 5892; *SB* 4275; Ptolemaeus, *Tetrabiblos* 175; Hephaestio Astrologus 1,1). In the *Historia Alexandri Magni* it is a common attribute for the Macedonian king. Likewise, a number of gods such as →Zeus, →Helios, →Hermes, and Serapis can be called *kosmokratōr* (see BAUER-ALAND 1988:905). In the Mithraeum under the thermae of Caracalla it occurs as an epithet for the Zeus—→Mithras (or Serapis; see CUMONT & CANET 1918)—Helios triad. The fact that heaven, too, is designated as *kosmokratōr* (*Orphic Hymn* 4,3) points to what is perhaps the most important area, astrology (sometimes combined with magic). The planets are called *kosmokratores* (cf. Vettius Valens 171,6; 360,7; cf. also 278,2; 314,16; Jamblichus, *de myst.* 2,3), not only because of their function as an organising principle in space, but chiefly because according to astrology they exercise a fateful influence over man. Magic promised release from this tyranny of the heavenly bodies. It is therefore no accident that the term *kosmokratōr* is included in the Magical Papyri, usually as an invocation of Helios (*PGM* III 135; IV,166.1599) but also of other deities such as Serapis (*PGM* XIII 619) and Hermes (*PGM* V, 400; XVII b1; see also IV 2198-2199).

III. In early Judaism the word hardly occurs at all: *kosmokratōr* is not to be found in the LXX, nor in Philo, Josephus, or in pseudepigraphic literature. The term occurs only once in the relatively late (1st - 3rd century CE) *T. Sol*, a haggadic-type folktale about Solomon's building of the Temple combined with ancient lore about magic, astrology, angelology, demonology, and primitive medicine. In this Jewish text reworked by Christians, which describes Solomon's power over the spirits, Solomon conjures up among other things 7 spirits, bound up together hand and foot. Asking them who they are, he receives the answer: "We are heavenly bodies, rulers of this world of darkness (*kosmokratores tou skotous*)" (*T. Sol* 8,1). They turn out to be planets (*T. Sol* 8,4). This is clearly linked to pagan demonology and astrology (cf. Jamblichus, *de myst.* 9,9), although the term is now used in a completely negative sense. Instrumental in this is not only the rejection of the cult of the heavenly bodies, but doubtlessly also the negative assessment of the *kosmos* (*ʿôlām*), which in some parts of early Judaism and early Christianity had become synonymous with a world alienated from God. Here, this is reflected in the qualification of this territory as 'darkness'.

The same concept and mode of expression are to be found in the (presumably older) Deutero-Pauline Epistle to the Ephesians. In the closing exhortation of the epistle, the Ephesians are called upon to take up the 'armour of God' in order to be able to resist 'the Devil's wily attacks' (Eph 6:10-11). The following verse (Eph 6:12) states the reason: "For we battle not against flesh and blood, but against powers, against forces, against the rulers of darkness in this world (*kosmokratores tou skotous toutou*), against the spirits of evil in the heavens". Here, the battle of the Christians has cosmic dimensions; *kosmokratores* refers to the demon world governed by the →Devil.

In Irenaeus, the term has developed into a direct reference to the Devil, "whom one also calls *kosmokratōr*" (*haer.* I,5,4). In Rabbinic literature (cf. *LevR* 18/118a) the Greek term occurs as a foreign word for the angel of death, who is identical to the Devil (see Str-B 2:552).

IV. *Bibliography*

W. BAUER, K. & B. ALAND, *Wörterbuch zum Neuen Testament* (Berlin, New York 1988[6]) 905; F. CUMONT & L. CANET, Mithra ou Serapis ΚΟΣΜΟΚΡΑΤΩΡ, *CRAIBL* 1918 [1919], 313-328; M. DIBELIUS, *Die Geisterwelt im Glauben des Paulus* (1909) 163-164, 230; W. MICHAELIS, κρατέω κτλ., *TWNT* 3 (1938) 913; LSJ 984; A. D. NOCK, Studies in the Graeco-Roman Beliefs of the Empire, *JHS* 45 (1925) 84-101; Str-B 2,552.

R. FELDMEIER

WRATH 'Οργή

I. A personified active principle of Wrath has been seen in two passages from the Pauline epistles. This supposed demon was interpreted in the light of the Zoroastrian demon *Aēšma,* one of the most important helpers of the Evil Spirit in Zoroastrian theology and possibly known to the Jews under the name →Asmodeus (PINES 1982; BOYCE & GRENET 1991:425-426, 446).

II. Although *Aēšma* was certainly perceived as a powerful demon by Zarathustra himself (his name has been attested several times in the Gāthās) and is very prominent in both Avestan and Pahlavi literature, the identification of *orgē* as used by Paul (Rom 9:22; Eph 2:3) with a concept derived from Zoroastrianism, seems to read more into the texts than there is to be read. In Iran, *Aēšma* (Pahlavi *Xēšm*) is represented as an evil being, holding a bloody club (Avestan *xruuī.dru-*), and as the special adversary of *Sraoša*, the god "Hearkening" (GRAY 1929: 185-187). In the texts he is presented as an evil-working demon and a destructive being, as indeed all the Daevas are. There are no passages whatsoever that indicate a special destructive quality for *Aēšma* (*pace* PINES 1982).

III. PINES has argued that the Zoroastrian demon *Aēšma* has influenced the concept of *orgē* (Wrath) in Rom 9:22; Eph 2:3 (PINES 1982). These two passages from the Pauline corpus are in fact dependent upon the OT usage of the word *ḥārôn*, 'wrath', although Paul seems to have created a new imagery of wrath. A decisive argument against seeing any influence of Zoroastrianism on the concept of wrath in Paul, is the fact that wrath occurs quite frequently in Romans in an eschatological context, in combination with justice (e.g. Rom 3:5; 9:22), as an essential element of the coming redemption, and hence is intimately connected with God. This is wholly alien to any Iranian system, where *Aēšma* is one of the main adversaries of Ahura Mazda and is in fact described as a demon who is chased away at the end of time (Yt. 19.95). There is no actively personified demon Wrath to be found in the Pauline corpus.

IV. *Bibliography*

M. BOYCE & F. GRENET, *A History of Zoroastrianism III: Zoroastrianism under Macedonian and Roman rule* (HdO VIII.1.2. 2.3; Leiden 1991); L. H. GRAY, The foundations of the Iranian religions, *Journal of the K.R. Cama Oriental Institute* 15 (1929) 1-228; S. PINES, Wrath and creatures of Wrath in Pahlavi, Jewish and New Testament sources, *Irano-Judaica: Studies relating to Jewish contacts with Persian culture throughout the ages* (ed. S. Shaked & A. Netzer; Jerusalem 1982) 76-82; G. STÄHLIN, orgē E, *TWNT* 5 (1954) 419-448.

A. F. DE JONG

Y

YAAQAN → YA'ÛQ

YAHWEH יהוה

I. Yahweh is the name of the official god of Israel, both in the northern kingdom and in Judah. Since the Achaemenid period, religious scruples led to the custom of not pronoucing the name of Yahweh; in the liturgy as well as in everyday life, such expressions as 'the →Lord' (*'ădōnāy*, lit. 'my Lord', LXX κύριος) or 'the →Name' were substituted for it. As a matter of consequence, the correct pronunciation of the tetragrammaton was gradually lost: the Masoretic form 'Jehovah' is in reality a combination of the consonants of the tetragrammaton with the vocals of *'ădōnāy*, the *ḥaṭēf pataḥ* of *'ădōnāy* becoming a mere *shewa* because of the yodh of *yhwh* (ALFRINK 1948). The transcription 'Yahweh' is a scholarly convention, based on such Greek transcriptions as Ιαουε/ Ιαουαι (Clement of Alexandria, *Stromata* 5, 6, 34, 5), Ιαβε/ Ιαβαι (Epiphanius of Salamis, *Adv. Haer.* 1, 3, 40, 5 and Theodoretus of Cyrrhus, *Quaest. in Ex. XV*; *Haer. fab. comp.* 5,3).

The form Yahweh (*yhwh*) has been established as primitive; abbreviations such as Yah, Yahû, Yô, and Yĕhô are secondary (CROSS 1973:61). The abbreviated (or hypocoristic) forms of the name betray regional predilections: thus *Yw* ('Yau' in Neo-Assyrian sources) is especially found in a North-Israelite context; the earliest instance is the personal name *ywḥnn* on an arrowhead dated 11th cent. BCE on the basis of its script (F. M. CROSS, An Inscribed Arrowhead of the Eleventh Century BCE in the Bible Lands Museum in Jerusalem, *ErIsr* 23 [1992] 21*-26*, esp. n. 3). *Yh*, on the other hand, is predominantly Judaean (cf. WEIPPERT 1980:247-248). The form *Yhw* is said to be originally Judaean (WEIPPERT 1980: 247), but its occurrence in the northern wayfarer's station of Kuntillet 'Ajrud shows that it was not unknown among Northern Israelites either. In the frequently attested Nabataean personal name *'bd'hyw* (variant *'bd'hy*), the element *'hyw* (*'hy*) has been interpreted as a spelling of the divine name Yahweh (M. LIDZBARSKI, *ESE* 3 [1915] 270 n. 1); it is not certain whether it is a theonym or an anthroponym, though, and a connection with the tetragrammaton is unproven (KNAUF 1984). It is unclear whether an allegedly northern Syrian deity Ιευώ (Porphyry, *Adv. Christ.* fr. 41, apud Eusebius, *Praep. Ev.* I, 9, 21; cf. Ιαώ in Theodoretus, *Graec. aff. cur.* II 44-45 and Macrobius, *Sat.* I 18-20) is related to the god Yahweh. In the Mishna, the divine name is usually written יי in combination with *šĕwā'* and *qāmeṣ* (WALKER 1951).

II. The cult of Yahweh is not originally at home in Palestine. Outside Israel, Yahweh was not worshipped in the West-Semitic world—despite affirmations to the contrary (*pace*, e.g. G. GARBINI, *History and Ideology in Ancient Israel* [London & New York 1988] 52-65). Before 1200 BCE, the name Yahweh is not found in any Semitic text. The stir caused by PETTINATO (e.g. Ebla and the Bible, *BA* 43 [1980] 203-216, esp. 203-205) who claimed to have found the shortened form of the name Yahweh ('Ya') as a divine element in theophoric names from Ebla (ca. 2400-2250 BCE) is unfounded. As the final element of personal names, *-ya* is often a hypocoristic ending, not a theonym (A. ARCHI, The Epigraphic Evidence from Ebla and the Old Testament, *Bib* 60 (1979) 556-566, esp. 556-560). MÜLLER argues that the sign NI, read *yà* by Pettinato, is conventionally short for NI-NI = *ì-lí*, 'my (personal) god'; it stands for *ilī* or *ilu* (MÜLLER 1980:83; 1981:306-307). This solution also explains the occurrence of the speculated element *ya at the beginning of personal names; thus ^d^*yà-ra-mu* should be read either as DINGIR-*lí-ra-mu* or as ^d^*ilix-ra-mu*, both readings yielding the name Iliramu, 'My god is exalted'. In no list of gods or offerings is the mysterious god *Ya ever mentioned; his cult at Ebla is a chimera.

Yahweh was not known at Ugarit either; the singular name *Yw* (vocalisation unknown) in a damaged passage of the Baal Cycle (*KTU* 1.1 iv:14) cannot convincingly be interpreted as an abbreviation for 'Yahweh' (*pace*, e.g., DE MOOR 1990:113-118). Also after 1200 BCE, Yahweh is seldom mentioned in non-Israelite texts. The assertion that "Yahweh was worshipped as a major god" in North Syria in the eighth century BCE (S. DALLEY, Yahweh in Hamath in the 8th century BC, *VT* 40 [1990] 21-32, quotation p. 29), cannot be maintained. The claim is based on the names Azriyau and Yaubi'di, attested as indigenous rulers from north Syrian states in the 8th cent. BCE. The explanation of these names offered by Dalley is highly dubious; more satisfactory interpretations are possible (VAN DER TOORN 1992:88-90).

The earliest West Semitic text mentioning Yahweh—excepting the biblical evidence—is the Victory Stela written by Mesha, the Moabite king from the 8th century BCE. The Moabite ruler recalls his military successes against Israel in the time of Ahab: "And →Chemosh said to me, 'Go, take Nebo from Israel!' So I went by night and I engaged in fight against her from the break of dawn until noon. And I took her and I killed her entire population: seven thousand men, boys, women, girls, and maid servants, for I devoted her to destruction (*hḥrmth*) for Ashtar-Chemosh. And I took from there the *ʾ[rʾ]ly* of Yahweh and I dragged them before Chemosh" (*KAI* 181:14-18). Evidently, Yahweh is not presented here as a Moabite deity. He is presented as the official god of the Israelites, worshipped throughout Samaria, as far as its outer borders since Nebo (נבה in the Mesha Stela, נבו in the Bible), situated in North-Western Moab, was a border town.

The absence of references to a Syrian or Palestinian cult of Yahweh outside Israel suggests that the god does not belong to the traditional circle of West Semitic deities. The origins of his veneration must be sought for elsewhere. A number of texts suggest that Yahweh was worshipped in southern Edom and Midian before his cult spread to Palestine. There are two Egyptian texts that mention Yahweh. In these texts from the 14th and 13th centuries BCE, Yahweh is neither connected with the Israelites, nor is his cult located in Palestine. The texts speak about "Yahu in the land of the Shosu-beduins" (*tꜣ šꜣśw jhwꜣ*; R. GIVEON, *Les bédouins Shosou des documents égyptiens* [Leiden 1971] no. 6a [pp. 26-28] and no. 16a [pp. 74-77]; note WEIPPERT 1974:427, 430 for the corrected reading). The one text is from the reign of Amenophis III (first part of the 14th cent. BCE; cf. HERMANN 1967) and the other from the reign of Ramses II (13th cent. BCE; cf. H. W. FAIRMAN, Preliminary Report on the Excavations at ʿAmārah West, Anglo-Egyptian Sudan, 1938-9, *JEA* 25 [1939] 139-144, esp. 141). In the Ramses II list, the name occurs in a context which also mentions Seir (assuming that *sʿrr* stands for Seir). It may be tentatively concluded that this "Yahu in the land of the Shosu-beduins" is to be situated in the area of Edom and Midian (WEIPPERT 1974: 271; AXELSSON 1987:60; *pace* WEINFELD 1987:304).

In these Egyptian texts *Yhw* is used as a toponym (KNAUF 1988:46-47). Yet a relationship with the deity by the same name is a reasonable assumption (*pace* M. WEIPPERT, "Heiliger Krieg" in Israel und Assyrien, *ZAW* 84 [1972] 460-493, esp. 491 n. 144); whether the god took his name from the region or vice versa remains undecided (note that R. GIVEON, "The Cities of Our God" (II Sam 10:12), *JBL* 83 [1964] 415-416, suggests that the name is short for *Beth-Yahweh, which would compare with the alternance between →Baal-meon and Beth-Baal-meon). By the 14th century BCE, before the cult of Yahweh had reached Israel, groups of Edomite and Midianite nomads worshipped Yahweh as their god. These data converge with a northern tradition, found in a number of ancient theophany texts, according to which Yahweh came from →Edom and Seir (Judg 5:4; note the correction in Ps 68:8[7]). According to the Blessing of Moses Yahweh came from Sinai, "dawned from" Seir, and "shone forth" from Mount Paran (Deut 33:2). Elsewhere he is said to have come from Teman and Mount Paran (Hab 3:3). The references to "Yahweh of Teman" in the Kuntillet ʿAjrud inscriptions are extra-biblical confirmation of the topographical connection (M. WEINFELD, Kuntillet ʿAjrud Inscriptions and Their Significance, *SEL* 1 [1984] 121-130, esp. 125, 126). All of these places—Seir, Mt Paran, Teman, and Sinai—are in or near Edom.

If Yahweh was at home in the south, then, how did he make his way to the north? According to a widely accepted theory, the Kenites were the mediators of the Yahwistic cult. One of the first to advance the Kenite hypothesis was the Dutch historian of religion Cornelis P. Tiele. In 1872 TIELE characterized Yahweh historically as "the god of the desert, worshipped by the Kenites and their close relatives before the Israelites" (*Vergelijkende geschiedenis van de Egyptische en Mesopotamische godsdiensten* [Amsterdam 1872] 559). The idea was adopted and elaborated by B. STADE (*Geschichte des Volkes Israels* [1887] 130-131), and it gained considerable support ever since, also among modern scholars (see, e.g., A. J. WENSINCK, De oorsprongen van het Jahwisme, *Semietische Studiën uit de nalatenschap van Prof. Dr. A. J. Wensinck* [Leiden 1941] 23-50; B. D. EERDMANS, *Religion of Israel* [Leiden 1947] 15-19; H. H. ROWLEY, *From Joseph to Joshua* [London 1950] 149-160; A. H. J. GUNNEWEG, Mose in Midian, *ZTK* 60 [1964] 1-9; W. H. SCHMIDT, *Exodus, Sinai, Wüste* (Darmstadt 1983) 110-118; WEINFELD 1987; METTINGER 1990:408-409). In its classical form the hypothesis assumes that the Israelites became acquainted with the cult of Yahweh through Moses. Moses' father-in-law—Hobab, according to an old tradition (Judg 1:16; 4:11; cf. Num 10:29)—was a Midianite priest (Exod 2:16; 3:1; 18:1) who worshipped Yahweh (see e.g. Exod 18:10-12). He belonged to the Kenites (Judg 1:16; 4:11), a branch of the Midianites (H. H. ROWLEY, *From Joseph to Joshua* [London 1950] 152-153). By way of Hobab and Moses, then, the Kenites were the mediators of the cult of Yahweh.

The strength of the Kenite hypothesis is the link it establishes between different but converging sets of data: The absence of Yahweh from West-Semitic epigraphy; Yahweh's topographical link with the area of Edom (which may be taken to include the territory of the Midianites); the 'Kenite' affiliation of Moses; and the positive evaluation of the Kenites in the Bible. A major flaw in the classical Kenite hypothesis, however, is its disregard for the 'Canaanite' origins of Israel. The view that, under the influence of Moses, the Israelites became Yahwists during their journey through the desert, and then brought their newly acquired religion to the Palestinian soil, neglects the fact that the majority of the Israelites were firmly rooted in Palestine. The historical role of Moses, moreover, is highly problematic. It seems more prudent not to put too much weight on the figure of Moses. It is only in later tradition that he came to be regarded as the legendary ancestor of the Levitical priests and a symbol of the 'Yahweh-alone' movement; his real importance remains uncertain.

If the Kenite hypothesis is to be maintained, then, it is only in a modified form. Though it is highly plausible that the Kenites (and the Midianites and the Rechabites may be mentioned in the same breath) introduced Israel to the worship of Yahweh, it is unlikely that they did so outside the borders of Palestine. Both Kenites and Rechabites are mentioned as dwelling in North Israel at an early stage; so are the Gibeonites, who are ethnically related to the Edomites (J. BLENKINSOPP, *Gibeon and Israel* [Cambridge 1972] 14-27). Some of these groups were not permanent residents of North Israel; they came there as traders. Already in Gen 37:28 Midianite traders are mentioned as being active between Palestine and Egypt (KNAUF 1988:27). If Yahwism did indeed originate with Midianites or Kenites—and the evidence seems to point in that direction—it may have been brought to Transjordan and Central Palestine by traders along the caravan routes from the south to the east (J. D. SCHLOEN, Caravans, Kenites, and *Casus belli*, *CBQ* 55 [1993] 18-38, esp. p. 36).

III. Explanations of the name Yahweh must assume that, except for the vocalisation, the traditional form is the correct one. The hypothesis which says that there were originally two divine names, viz. Yāhū and Yahweh, the former being the older one (MAYER 1958:34), is now generally abandoned in light of the epigraphic evidence (CROSS 1973:61; *pace* KLAWEK 1990:12). The significance of the name Yahweh has been the subject of a staggering amount of publications (for an impression see MAYER 1958). This "monumental witness to the industry and ingenuity of biblical scholars" (CROSS 1973:60) is hardly in proportion to the limited importance of the issue. Even if the meaning of the name could be established beyond reasonable doubt, it would contribute little to the understanding of the nature of the god. The caution against overestimating etymologies, voiced most eloquently by James Barr, holds good for divine names as well. From a perspective of the history of religion, it is much more important to know the characteristics which worshippers associated with their god, than the original meaning of the latter's name. Having said that, however, the question of the etymology of Yahweh cannot be simply dismissed. The following observations are in order.

In spite of isolated attempts to take *yhwh* as a pronominal form, meaning 'Yea He!' (from **ya huwa*, S. MOWINCKEL, *HUCA* 32 [1958] 121-133) or 'My One' (cf. Akk *ya'u*, H. CAZELLES, Der persönliche Gott Abrahams, *Der Weg zum Menschen, FS A. Deissler* [ed. R. Mosis & L. Ruppert; Freiburg 1989] 59-60), it is widely agreed that the name represents a verbal form. With the preformative *yod*, *yhwh* is a finite verbal form to be analysed as a 3rd masc. sing. imperfect. Analogous finite verbal forms used as theonyms are attested for the religion of pre-Islamic Arabs. Examples include the gods →Yaʿūq ('he protects', *WbMyth* I 479) and →Yaǵūṯ ('he helps', *WbMyth* I 478). Much earlier are the Akkadian and Amorite instances of verbal forms used as divine names: dIkšudum ('He has reached', ARM 13 no. 111:6) and Ešuḫ ('He has been victorious', H. B. HUFFMON, *Amorite Personal Names in the Mari Texts* [Baltimore 1965] 215) are just two examples (CROSS 1973: 67). Morphologically, then, the name Yahweh is not without parallels.

The interpretation of the theonym as a finite verb is already found in Exod 3:14. In reply to Moses' question of what he is to say to the Israelites when they ask him which god sent him, God says: "I AM WHO I AM", and he adds: "Say this to the people of Israel, 'I AM has sent me to you'". The explanation here offered is a sophisticated play based on association: the root HWH is understood as a by-form of HYH, 'to be' and the prefix of the third person is understood as a secondary objectivation of a first person: *yhwh* is thus interpreted as *'hyh*, 'I am'. Since the significance of such a name is elusive, the reconstructed name is itself the subject of a further interpretation in the phrase *'ehyeh 'ăšer 'ehyeh*, 'I am who I am'. Its meaning is debated. Should one understand it as a promise ('I will certainly be there') or as an allusion to the incomparability of Yahweh ('I am who I am', i.e. without peer)? Even in the revelation of his name, Yahweh does not surrender himself: He cannot be captured by means of either an image or a name. The Greek translation ὁ ὤν (LXX) has philosophical overtones: it is at the basis of a profound speculation on the eternity and immutability of God—both of them ideas originally unconnected with the name Yahweh.

Since the Israelite explanation is evidently a piece of theology rather than a reliable etymology, it cannot be accepted as the last word on the matter. Comparative material from Akkadian sources has been used to make a case for the thesis that **yahweh* is in fact an abbreviated sentence name. Among Amorite personal names, there are a number in which a finite form of the root HWY ('to be, to manifest oneself') is coupled with a theonym. Examples are Yaḫwi-ilum, Yaḫwi-Adad (ARM 23, 86:7), and Ya(ḫ)wium (= Iaḫwi-ilum, e.g. ARM 23, 448:13). These Amorite names are the semantic equivalent of the Akkadian name Ibašši-ilum ('God has manifested himself'). The objection that these are all anthroponyms, whereas Yahweh is a theonym, is not decisive. Cuneiform texts also recognize a number of gods whose names are in fact a finite verbal form with a deity as subject: ^{d}Ikrub-Il ('El has blessed') and ^{d}Išmêlum (= *Išme-ilum, 'God has heard') can be quoted in illustration. STOL has made a strong case for regarding these names as those of deified ancestors (M. STOL, Old Babylonian Personal Names, *SEL* 8 [1991] 191-212, esp. 203-205).

Some scholars believe that Yahweh, too, is the abbreviated name of a deified ancestor. Thus DE MOOR construes the original name of the deity as *Yahweh-El, 'May El be present (as helper)' (1990:237-239). In support of this speculated form he adduces the name Jacob (*Yaʿăqōb*), which is short for *Yʿqb-ʾl*, 'May El follow him closely' (cf. Yaḫqub-el, H. HUFFMON, *Amorite Personal Names in the Mari Texts* [Baltimore 1965] 203-204; S. AḤITUV, *Canaanite Toponyms in Ancient Egyptian Documents* [Jerusalem 1984] 200), and such names as Yaḫwi-Ilu in Mari texts. DE MOOR draws the conclusion that originally Yahweh was "probably the divine ancestor of one of the proto-Israelite tribes" (1990:244). Yet though theoretically possible, it is difficult to believe that the major Israelite deity, venerated in a cult that was imported into Palestine, was originally a deified ancestor. Though such gods are known, they are never found in a leading position in the pantheon. Their worship tends to remain local, as an ancestor is of necessity the ancestor of a restricted group.

There are admittedly ancient Near Eastern deities with a composite name who were never ancestors. Examples include *rkbʾl* (traditionally vocalized as →Rakib-el) from Samʾal (*KAI* 24:16), and Malakbel, ʿAglibol, and Yarhibol from Palmyra. Morphologically, however, these names do not compare with a speculated *yahweh-DN, since the first component of the name is a substantive. The names just mentioned are best interpreted as 'Charioteer of El' (cf. *TSSI* II 70), 'Messenger of Bel', 'Calf of Bol', and 'Moon of Bol' (cf. J. HOFTIJZER, *Religio aramaica* [Leiden 1968] 32-38), respectively. In addition to the morphological difference with a hypothetical *yahweh-DN, Rakib-el and his likes are names of subordinate deities; there is no example of such gods heading the pantheon. Another objection to the comparison is the fact that the Israelite cult does not seem to have known the complexity of that in the Syrian city-states from which the comparative material comes (cf. H.-P. MÜLLER, Religionsgeschichtliche Beobachtungen zu den Texten von Ebla, *ZDPV* 96 [1980] 1-19, pp. 18-19). Related to the thesis that **yahweh* is an abbreviated theonym is the suggestion that it is an abbreviation of a liturgical formula. The solution proposed by CROSS is an example. He speculates that the longer form of 'Yahweh' is extant in the title →Yahweh Zabaoth. The *ṣĕbāʾôt* (transcribed as Zabaoth in many English Bible translations) are the →host of heaven, i.e. the council of the gods. The name Yahweh Zabaoth is itself short for **Ḏu yahwī ṣabaʾōt*, 'He who creates the (heavenly) armies', according to CROSS (1973:70). Since in his view this is in fact a title of El, the full name might be reconstructed as **Il-ḏu-yahwī-ṣabaʾôt*. The analysis of Cross goes back to his teacher W. F. Albright (W. F. ALBRIGHT, review of B. N. Wambacq, *L'épithète divine Jahvé Sebaʾôt*, *JBL* 67 (1948) 377-381). D. N. FREEDMAN quotes from Albright's notes for an unpublished *History of the Religion of*

Israel listing a number of reconstructed cult names such as **'ēl yahweh yiśrā'ēl*, 'El-creates-Israel' (on the basis of Gen 33:20) and **'ēl yahweh rûḥôt*, 'El-creates-the-winds' (FREEDMAN *et al.* 1977-82:547). Instead of a reconstructed form **yahweh-'el*, then, Albright reckons with a form **'El-yahweh*—which could be complemented by various objects. DIJKSTRA, too, argues that the original form is El Yahweh, 'El who reveals himself'—a form still reflected in such texts as Ps 118:27 (M. DIJKSTRA, Yahweh-El or El-Yahweh?, short paper read at the IOSOT-congress, Paris July 1992, fc.).

Leaving aside for the moment the problem implied in the identification of Yahweh with El, the interpretation of Yahweh as an abbreviated sentence name (and possibly a liturgical formula) is not without difficulties. Since the idea that a human ancestor could rise to the position of national god flies in the face of the comparative evidence, a presumed El-Yahweh or Yahweh-El must of necessity be a divine name followed or preceded by a verbal form characterizing the deity. By implication, then, the proper name of the god has been replaced in the Israelite tradition by a verb denoting one of his characteristic activities. Such a process is unparalleled in ancient Near Eastern religions—unless one considers such Arab deities as Yaʿūq and Yaǵūṯ, epithets of another deity, which would suggest a South Semitic rather than a West Semitic background for Yahweh. Isolated verbal forms such as proper names, however, are not uncommon in the Semitic world, as witnessed by e.g. the name *Yagrušu of Baal's weapon. Solving the enigma of the tetragrammaton by positing another divine name is really a last option. A solution which explains the name in the form it has come down to us is to be preferred.

A problem hitherto unmentioned is the identification of the root lying at the basis of the form *yhwh*, and that of its meaning. Though some have suggested a link with the root ḤWY, resulting in the translation 'the Destroyer' (e.g. H. GRESSMANN, *Mose und seine Zeit* [Göttingen 1913] 37), it is generally held that the name should be connected with the Semitic root HWY. Also scholars who do not regard the tetragrammaton as an abbreviated theonym usually follow the Israelite interpretation insofar they interpret Yahweh as a form of the verb 'to be'; opinions diverge as to whether the form is basic or causative, i.e. a Qal or a Hiph'il. The one school interprets 'He is', i.e. 'He manifests himself as present', whereas the other argues in a favour of a causative meaning: 'He causes to be, calls into existence'. The first interpretation has an exponent in VON SODEN. Adducing comparative material from Akkadian sources, he urges that the verb should be taken in its stronger sense 'to prove oneself, to manifest oneself, to reveal oneself' (VON SODEN 1966). A representative of the second school is ALBRIGHT. He takes **yahweh* as a causative imperfect of the verb HWY, 'to be'. Yahweh, then, is a god who 'causes to be' or 'brings into being'. In this form, the verb is normally transitive (W. F. ALBRIGHT, *Yahweh and the Gods of Canaan* [London 1968] 147-149).

A major difficulty with the explanations of the name Yahweh on the basis of HWY interpreted as 'to be', however, is the fact that they explain the name of a South Semitic deity (originating from Edom, or even further south) with the help of a West-Semitic etymology (KNAUF 1984a:469). The form of the name has the closest analogues in the pre-Islamic Arab pantheon; it is natural, therefore, to look first at the possibility of an explanation on the basis of the Arabic etymology. The relevant root HWY has three meanings in Arabic: 1. to desire, be passionate; 2. to fall; 3. to blow. All three have been called upon for a satisfactory explanation of the name Yahweh. The derivation of the name Yahweh from the meaning 'to love, to be passionate', which resulted in the translation of Yahweh as 'the Passionate' (GOITEIN 1956) has made no impact on OT scholarship. Hardly more successful was the suggestion that Yahweh is 'the Speaker', also based on the link of the name with the root HWY (cf. Akk *awû, atmû*; BOWMAN 1944:4-5).

A greater degree of plausibility attaches to those interpretations of the name Yahweh which identify him as a storm god. Thus the name has been connected with the meaning 'to fall' (also attested in Syriac), in which case the verbal form is seen as a causative ('He who causes to fall', scil. rain, lightning, or the enemies by means of his lightning, see BDB 218a). Another suggestion is to link the name with the meaning 'to blow', said of the wind (cf. Syr *hawwē*, 'wind'). This leads to the translation "er fährt durch die Lüfte, er weht" (J. WELLHAUSEN, *Israelitische und jüdische Geschichte* [3rd ed.; Berlin 1897] 25 note 1; KNAUF 1984a:469; 1988:43-48). Especially the latter possibility merits serious consideration. In view of the south-eastern origins of the cult of Yahweh, an Arabic etymology has a certain likelihood. Also, his presumed character as a storm god contributes to explain why Yahweh could assume various of Baal's mythological exploits.

The interpretation of the name of Yahweh is not entirely devoid of meaning, then, when it comes to establishing his character. If *yhwh* does indeed mean 'He blows', Yahweh is originally a storm god. Since Baal (originally an epitheton of →Hadad) is of the same type, the relationship between Yahweh and Baal deserves to be analyzed more closely. In the Monarchic Era, Baal (i.e. the Baal cult) was a serious rival of Yahweh. The competition between the two gods (that is, between their respective priesthoods and prophets) was especially fierce since the promotion of the cult of the Tyrian Baal by the Omrides. Because there was no *entente* between Yahweh and Baal, Yahweh could hardly have inherited traits of a storm god from Baal. Inheritance is too peaceful a process. Yahweh's 'Baalistic' traits have a dual origin: some are his of old because he is himself a storm god, whereas others have been appropriated—or should we say confiscated—by him. Examples of the latter include the designation of Mount →Zion as 'the recesses of →Zaphon' (Ps 48:3), the motif of Yahweh's victory over Yam (→Sea; for a thorough study see J. DAY, *God's Conflict with the Dragon and the Sea: Echoes of A Canaanite myth in the Old Testament* [Cambridge 1985]) and →Mot (W. HERRMANN, Jahwes Triumph über Mot, *UF* 11 [1979] 371-377), and the Baal epithet of →'Rider upon the Clouds'.

Owing to the emphasis on the conflict between Yahweh and Baal, it is insufficiently realized that Yahweh himself, too, is "a deity who is originally conceived in the categories of the Hadad type" (METTINGER 1990:410). According to the theophany texts, the earth trembles, clouds drop water, and mountains quake at the appearance of Yahweh (Judg 5:4-5). Though such a response of the elements to Yahweh's manifestation need not imply that he is a storm-god, the latter hypothesis offers the most natural explanation. When Yahweh comes to the rescue of his beloved, he is hidden all around by darkness, thick clouds dark with water being his canopy (Ps 18:12[11]). As he lifts his voice the thunder resounds (Ps 18:14[13]). Like Baal, Yahweh is perceived as 'a god of the mountains' (1 Kgs 20:23), a characterization presumably triggered by the association of the weather-god with clouds hovering above the mountain tops.

Though few scholars would contest the fact that Yahweh has certain traits normally ascribed to Baal, it is often argued that originally he was much more like El than like Baal. In the patriarchal narratives of Genesis, El names such as →El Olam and →El Elyon are frequently used as epithets of Yahweh. Various scholars have drawn the conclusion that El and Yahweh were identified at a rather early stage. This identification is sometimes explained by assuming that Yahweh is originally an El figure (thus, e.g. H. NIEHR, *Der höchste Gott* [BZAW 190; Berlin/New York 1990] 4-5). CROSS has argued that Yahweh is originally a hypocoristicon of a liturgical title of El. Yahweh Zabaoth, allegedly meaning 'He who calls the heavenly armies into being', is not a name but an epithet. According to

CROSS, the god to whom it applies in the first place is El, since El is known in the Ugaritic texts as the father of the gods. The latter are conventionally referred to as 'the sons of El' (CROSS 1973). DE MOOR, who also holds that Yahweh is an abbreviated sentence name originally belonging to a human being, links Yahweh with El as well. Though *Yahweh-El was the name of an ancestor, the god at the same time was "an aspect of El" (DE MOOR 1990:244). In order to solve the apparent contradiction, DE MOOR explains that the deified kings of Ugarit, who 'joined' (*šrk*, *KTU* 1.15 v:17) El at their death, merged with the god (1990:242).

Speculations about the original identity of Yahweh with El need to be critically examined, however. There are problems concerning both the nature of the identification, and the divine type to which Yahweh belongs. It is insufficiently realised that, at the beginning of the Iron Age, El's role had become largely nominal. The process of El's retreat in favour of Dagan (the major god at Ebla in the late third millennium) and later Baal (the major god at Ugarit in the middle of the second millennium) had long been under way. By the beginning of the Iron Age, the cult of El survived in some border zones of the Near East. In most regions, however, including Palestine, El's career as a living god (i.e. as a cultic reality and an object of actual devotion) had ended; he survived in such expressions as *ʿdt-ʾl* ('the council of El') and *bny-ʾl* ('sons of El', i.e. gods), but this was a survival only in name. This fact explains why there are no traces of polemics against El in the Hebrew Bible. It can therefore be argued that the smooth identification of El as Yahweh was based, not on an identity of character, but on El's decay. His name was increasingly used either as a generic noun meaning 'god' or, more specifically, as a designation of the personal god. In both cases, Yahweh could be called *ʾēl*.

Along with the name, Yahweh inherited various traits of El. One of them is divine eternity. Ugaritic texts call El the 'father of years' (*ab šnm*) and depict him as a bearded patriarch; Yahweh, on the other hand, is called the →'Ancient of days', and also is wearing a beard (Dan 7:9-14.22). Like El, Yahweh presides over the →council of the gods. Compassion is another common trait: El is said to be compassionate (*dpid*), whereas Yahweh is called "merciful and gracious" (Exod 34:6; for these and other similarities see M. SMITH, *The Early History of God* [San Francisco 1990] 7-12). In some biblical passages, the parallels are consciously explored. Thus GREENFIELD has shown that Deut 32:6-7 applies to Yahweh various motifs and images originally associated with El. El (here Yahweh) is said to be Israel's 'father' and 'creator'; he is 'wise' and 'eternal' and has lived for 'the years of many generations' (J. C. GREENFIELD, The Hebrew Bible and Canaanite Literature, *The Literary Guide to the Bible* [ed. R. Alter & F. Kermode; Cambridge, Mass. 1987] 545-560, esp. 554).

An aspect of Yahweh that may be traced back to El, though only with great caution, is his solar appearance. Even though the theophany texts depict Yahweh primarily as a warrior storm-god, there are elements in their description which seem to assume that Yahweh is a solar deity. The Psalm of Habakkuk mentions God's 'splendour' (*hôd*), and possibly his 'shine' (*tĕhillâ*, v 3); God's appearance comes with brightness (*nōgah*) and rays of light (*qarnayim*, v 4). Likewise Deut 33:2 speaks about Yahweh 'shining forth' (ZRḤ) and lightning up (YPʿ, hiphil; for the terminology cf. F. SCHNUTENHAUS, Das Kommen und Erscheinen Gottes im Alten Testament, *ZAW* 76 [1964] 1-22, esp. 8-10). The closest extrabiblical parallel is found in a Hebrew text from Kuntillet ʿAjrud, in which the mountains are said to melt when El shines forth (*wbzrḥ ʾl* [...] *wymsn hrm*, "when El shines forth [...] the mountains melt"; M. WEINFELD, Kuntillet ʿAjrud Inscriptions and Their Significance, *SEL* 1 [1984] 121-130, esp. 126; S. AḤITUV, *Handbook of Ancient Hebrew Inscriptions* [Jerusalem 1992] 160-162). Also outside the theophany tradition there is evidence of Yahweh as a solar god. Thus the word *ʾôr*, →'light', is sometimes used as a divine title (Ps 139:11, cf. J. HOLMAN, Analysis of the Text of Ps 139, *BZ* 14 [1970] 37-71, esp. 56-58; for other solar language applied to Yahweh see M. SMITH, *The Early History of God* [San Francisco 1990] 115-124, Ch. 4: Yahweh and the Sun [but cf. the review by S. B. PARKER, *Hebrew Studies* 33 (1992) 158-162]; J. G. TAYLOR, *Yahweh and the Sun* [Sheffield 1993]).

A further link between El and Yahweh is the identity of their consort. Texts from Kuntillet ʿAjrud and Khirbet el-Qom refer to Yahweh 'and his →Asherah' (*wʾšrth*). Though several scholars argue that this 'Asherah' is merely a cult symbol or a designation for 'sanctuary' (cf. Akk *aširtu*), the interpretation of the word as a divine name is to be preferred (*pace* J. A. EMERTON, New Light on Israelite Religion: The Implications of the Inscriptions from Kuntillet ʿAjrud, *ZAW* 94 [1982] 2-20; see M. DIETRICH & O. LORETZ, *Jahweh und seine Aschera* [UBL 9; Neukirchen-Vluyn 1992] 82-103). In the light of these data, the suggestion to emendate אשדת in Deut 33:2e into אשרה ('and at his right hand Asherah'; H. S. NYBERG, Deuteronomium 33,2-3, *ZDMG* 92 [1938] 320-344, esp. 335; see also M. WEINFELD, *SEL* 1 [1984] 121-130, esp. 124) remains a distinct possibility. Since Asherah is traditionally the consort of El in the Ugaritic texts, the pairing of Yahweh and Asherah suggests that Yahweh had taken the place of El (cf. M. DIJKSTRA, El, YHWH, and their Asherah: On Continuity and Discontinuity in Canaanite and Ancient Israelite Religion, *Abhandlungen zur Literatur Alt-Syriens-Palästinas* [fc.], who finds here confirmation for the view that Yahweh is a particularized form of El).

Under northern influence, Yahweh came also to be paired with →Anat, possibly to be identified with the →Queen of Heaven mentioned in Jer 7:18; 44:17.18.19.25. Her link with Yahweh is evident from the name Anat-Yahu, attested in Aramaic texts from the Jewish colony at Elephantine (VAN DER TOORN 1992). Considering the fact that the only other male deities with whom Anat is paired are Baal and →Bethel (the deified baetylon, cf. also Sikkānu ['stone stela', Ug *skn*], a theonym surviving in the name Sanchunjathon = סכניתן), no influence from the cult or mythology of El is apparent here.

Though Yahweh was known and worshipped among the Israelites before 1000 BCE, he did not become the national god until the beginning of the monarchic era. Due to the religious politics of Saul, Yahweh became the patron deity of the Israelite state (VAN DER TOORN 1993:531-536). As David and Solomon inherited and enlarged Saul's kingdom, they acknowleged the position of Yahweh as national god. David brought the ark of Yahweh from Benjamin to Jerusalem (2 Sam 6); Solomon sought the blessing of Yahweh at the sanctuary of Gibeon, the national temple of the Saulide state (1 Kgs 3:4; VAN DER TOORN 1993:534-535). Evidence of the predominant role of Yahweh in the official cult during the Monarchic Era are the theophoric personal names, both the biblical and the epigrapical ones. The divine name Yahweh is by far the most common theophoric element (J. H. TIGAY, *You Shall Have No Other Gods: Israelite Religion in the Light of Hebrew Inscriptions* [Atlanta 1986]; S. I. L. NORIN, *Seine Name allein ist hoch. Das Jhw-haltige Suffix althebräischer Personennamen* [Malmö 1986]; J. D. FOWLER, *Theophoric Personal Names in Ancient Hebrew. A Comparative Study* [Sheffield 1988]).

The practical monolatry of Yahweh should not be taken for a strict monotheism. Not only did the Israelites continue to recognize the existence of deities besides Yahweh, they also knew more than one Yahweh. Though at the mythological level there is only one, the cultic reality reflected a plurality of Yahweh gods (MCCARTER 1987:139-143). Extrabiblical evidence from Kuntillet ʿAjrud mentions a 'Yahweh from Samaria' and a 'Yahweh of Teman'; it is possible that the two names designate one god, viz. the official god of the northern kingdom ('Samaria', after its capital). Yet the recognition of a northern Yahweh is mirrored by the the worship of a Yahweh of Hebron and a Yahweh of Zion. Though the constructions *bĕḥebrôn* and *bĕṣiyyôn* are normally translated 'in Hebron' and 'in Zion', a comparison of the name Milkashtart ('Milku of Ashtart') with the expression *mlk b'ṯtrt* ('Milku in Ashart') suggests that such expressions as *yhwh bĕṣiyyôn* (Ps 99:2) and *yhwh bĕḥebrôn* (2 Sam 15:7) should be understood as references to local forms of Yahweh (M. L. BARRÉ, *The God-List in the Treaty between Hannibal amd Philip V of Macedonia* [Baltimore/London 1983] 186 note 473; cf. 1 Sam 5:5 *Dāgôn bĕʾašdôd*, 'Dagan of Ashdod'). The religious situation in early Israel, therefore, was not merely one of polytheism, but also of poly-Yahwism. The Deuteronomic emphasis on the unity of Yahweh (→One) must be understood against this background.

IV. *Bibliography*

L. E. AXELSSON, *The Lord Rose up from Seir* (ConB OT 25; Lund 1987); B. ALFRINK, La prononciation 'Jehova' du Tétragramme, *OTS* 5 (1948) 43-62; R. A. BOWMAN, Yahweh the Speaker, *JNES* 3 (1944) 1-8; F. M. CROSS, *Canaanite Myth and Hebrew Epic* (Cambridge, Mass/London 1973) 44-75 [cf. pp. 60-61 n. 61 for lit.]; M. DAHOOD, The God Yā at Ebla?, *JBL* 100 (1981) 607-608; O. EISSFELDT, El and Yahweh, *JSS* 1 (1956) 25-37; D. N. FREEDMAN, M. P. O'CONNOR & H. RINGGREN, יהוה *jhwh*, *TWAT* 3 (1977-82) 533-554; S. D. GOITEIN, *YHWH* the Passionate, *VT* 6 (1956) 1-9; R. S. HESS, The Divine Name Yahweh in Late Bronze Age Sources?, *UF* 23 (1991[1992]) 181-188; A. KLAWEK, The Name Jahveh in the Light of Most Recent Discussion, *Folia Orientalia* 27 (1990) 11-12; E. A. KNAUF, Yahwe, *VT* 34 (1984a) 467-472; KNAUF, Eine nabatäische Parallele zum hebräischen Gottesnamen, *BN* 23 (1984b) 21-28; KNAUF, *Midian* (Wiesbaden 1988) 43-48; R. MAYER, Der Gottesname Jahwe im Lichte der neuesten Forschung, *BZ* n.s. 2 (1958) 26-53; P. K. MCCARTER, Jr., Aspects of the Religion of the Israelite Monarchy: Biblical and Epigraphic Data, *Ancient Israelite Religion* (FS F. M. Cross; ed. P. D. Miller, Jr., P. D. Hanson & S. D. McBride; Philadelphia 1987) 137-155; *T. N. D. METTINGER, The Elusive Essence: YHWH, El and Baal and the Distinctiveness of Israelite Faith, *Die Hebräische Bibel und ihre zweifache Nachgeschichte* (FS R. Rendtorff zum 65. Geburtstag; ed. E. Blum, C. Macholz & E. W. Stegemann; Neukirchen 1990) 393-417; J. C. DE MOOR, *The Rise of Yahwism* (Leuven 1990); H.-P. MÜLLER, Gab es in Ebla einen Gottesnamen Ja?, *ZA* 70 (1980) 70-92; MÜLLER, Der Jahwenamen und seine Bedeutung. Ex 3,14 im Licht der Textpublikationen aus Ebla, *Bib* 62 (1981) 305-327; A. MURTONEN, *The Appearance of the Name yhwh outside Israel* (StOr 16/3; Helsinki 1951); M. S. SMITH, Yahweh and other Deities in Ancient Israel: Observations on Problems and recent Trends, *Ein Gott Allein* (eds. W. Dietrich & M. A. Klopfenstein; Freiburg/Göttingen 1994) 197-234; W. VON SODEN, Jahwe, 'er ist, er erweist sich', *WO* 3/3 (1966) 177-187 [reprinted in *Bibel und Alter Orient* (ed. H.-P. Müller; BZAW 162; Berlin & New York 1985) 78-88]; K. VAN DER TOORN, Anat-Yahu, Some Other Deities, and the Jews of Elephantine, *Numen* 39 (1992) 80-101; VAN DER TOORN, Saul and the Rise of Israelite State Religion, *VT* 43 (1993) 519-542; N. WALKER, The Writing of the Divine Name in the Mishna, *VT* 1 (1951) 309-310; M. WEINFELD, The Tribal League at Sinai, *Ancient Israelite Religion* (FS F. M. Cross; ed. P. D. Miller Jr., P. D. Hanson & S. D. McBride; Philadelphia 1987) 303-314; M. WEIPPERT, Semitische Nomaden des zweiten Jahrtausends, *Bib* 55 [1974] 265-280, 427-433; *WEIPPERT, Jahwe, *RLA* 5 (1980) 246-253.

K. VAN DER TOORN

YAHWEH ZEBAOTH יהוה צבאות

I. "Yahweh Zebaoth" occurs 284 times as a divine name in the Heb Bible; 121 of these occurrences can be characterized as free, non-formulaic usage. This expression had a prominent function as a cultic name of Yahweh in Shiloh and Jerusalem. Serving as an important divine epithet in the Zion-

Zebaoth theology of the Jerusalemite temple, it is attested from the premonarchic period to postexilic times. The Zebaoth designation is an important signpost in the religious history of ancient Israel and has therefore been the subject of intensive scholarly discussion (surveys in SCHMITT 1972:145-159 and ZOBEL 1989:880-881).

Apart from an attempt to trace it to non-Semitic origins, assuming the Eg *ḏbꜣty* "the one of the throne-seat", as the etymon (GÖRG 1985), there is almost general agreement that the word *ṣĕbāʾôt* derives from the Semitic root ṢBʾ, found in e.g. Akk *ṣābum* (Mari *ṣābûm*), "people", pl. "soldiers", "workers" (*AHW* 1072) and Heb *ṣābāʾ*, "army; host". The Zebaoth designation is handled in three different ways in the LXX (OLOFSSON 1990:121-26). Often the translation is *pantokratōr*, the →"Almighty", a rendering which is also used for →Shadday. Especially in Isaiah, the LXX simply transcribes the Heb with Sabaoth. In a number of other cases we find *kyrios tōn dynameōn*, "the Lord of Powers". All of these translations describe →Yahweh as a deity of great power, the second taking the Zebaoth element as a personal name, the third as a plural of an appellative with the meaning "power".

The syntax of the Heb designation is a problem, since personal names in general are usually treated as determinate nouns. The occurrence of the proper name Yahweh in a construct relation stands out as exceptional. Hence attempts to understand the juxtaposition as a verbless clause ("Yahweh is Zebaoth"), as a verb plus its object ("He who creates armies"), or as two nouns in apposition, the Zebaoth element then being taken as a Heb counterpart of Akk abstract feminine nouns with *-ūtu*, denoting functions (*GAG* § 56 s.59a; CAZELLES 1985: 1125 "Yahweh, the warlike") or as an intensive abstract plural denoting "power", coming close to Almightiness (EISSFELDT 1950 = 1966). The traditional understanding, viz. as a construct relation, "Yahweh of *ṣĕbāʾôt*" seems the most probable solution and is made less problematical by the epigraphic attestation of analogues such as "Yahweh of Teman" and "Yahweh of Samaria" in Kuntillet Ajrud. But, even if this is the case, the construct relation itself allows for various interpretations of the Zebaoth element. Thus it has been suggested that the construct relation may bear an adjectival meaning: "Yahweh of Zebaothness", "Yahweh Militant". The argument that *sĕbāʾôt* is an abstract plural meets with an obstacle since it is well attested as a concrete plural, "hosts", "armies", a sense that is found already in one of the Canaanite glosses to the Amarna letters (*nērṣé-bá-at*, "600[hosts]", *EA* 154:21, courtesy of C. GRAVE). The referential meaning of such a concrete noun in the case of the Heb designation has been understood as alluding either to: (a) the armies of Israel (cf. 1 Sam 17:45); (b) the heavenly hosts, whether the hosts of stars or the heavenly council of Yahweh (cf. Ps 89:9); (c) the "domesticated" mythical forces of nature in Canaan; or (d) all creatures on earth and in the heavens (cf. Gen 2:1). The existence of two distinct plural forms of the noun, *ṣābāʾ*, both masculine and feminine, should not be made the starting point for semantic conclusions (cf. S. SEGERT, *A Grammar of Phoenician and Punic* [München 1976] § 52.15).

II. The use of the Zebaoth designation in Hebrew can be traced back as far as premonarchic Shiloh (1 Sam 1:3.11; 4:4). On the assumption that this was the cradle of the concept of Yahweh as Yahweh Zebaoth, certain cautious conclusions may be drawn as to the religio-historical background of the designation in question. There are increasing indications which show that there was cultic continuity at Shiloh from the Middle Bronze II period onward, including an isolated cultic site during the Late Bronze period when there was no real settlement at Shiloh (I. FINKELSTEIN, *The Archaeology of the Israelite Settlement* [Jerusalem 1988] 212-234). Given this early cultic activity, the temple (*hêkāl*) at Shiloh (1 Sam 1:9; 3:3) must be understood against a Canaanite background. The same may be true of the Zebaoth designation of the god worshipped there. While some scholars have attempted to trace the Canaanite parentage of Yahweh Zebaoth back to →Resheph (*ršp ṣbi*, *KTU* 1.91:15, "Resheph the Soldier" or "Resheph (the Lord) of the Army", LIVERANI 1967), or to →Baal (Ross 1967:89-90), the evidence points instead to the importance of the →El traditions (METTINGER 1982a:128-35; SEOW 1989). We thus find certain El features in the deity worshipped at Shiloh, who reveals himself in dreams (1 Sam 3), who is able to bestow children (1 Sam 1:11), who possesses the trappings of royalty (cf. the personal names at Shiloh such as Ahimelech and Ichabod), and who appears as *ʾēl* in certain personal names (1 Sam 1:1 with the app.). The iconography associated with Yahweh Zebaoth, the →cherubim throne (below), is congruent with this, since it draws its inspiration ultimately from the lion-paw throne of El. The fact that Yahweh has a chariot of clouds (Pss 18:10-11; 104:3; Isa 19:1) like Baal (cf. *rkb ʿrpt*, "the driver of the clouds") does not invalidate the conclusion that the winged cherubim throne has a background in the El traditions. Though no genuine Canaanite precursor to the Zebaoth designation has come to light, it is nevertheless most likely that it derives from the Canaanite milieu at Shiloh. The original form of the name may even have been *ʾel ṣĕbāʾôt*, in which case this and *ʾel ʿelyôn*, →"Most High", should be seen as twin designations of Yahweh as the supreme Lord of the divine host or assembly.

It may also be that the Zebaoth notion has an analogue or even its background in the notion of army gods such as "the Lulahhi gods" or "the Hapiri gods" (*ANET* 206; LIVERANI 1967). Note also that in Philo Byblius, El is a deity accompanied by his host, his "allies" or *symmachoi* (Euseb., *Praep. Ev.* 10.18 and 20), who assist him in battle. The allusion to the heavenly host (below) allows the Zebaoth designation to be used with both warlike and more peaceful connotations. Readily apparent instances of the former are to be found in texts which use the designation as part of a play on words with military overtones (1 Sam 17:45; Isa 13:4; 31:4). Indeed, the martial character of Yahweh Zebaoth is amply attested (1 Sam 4:4; Isa 10:23; 13:13; 14:24-27; 19:16; 22:5; 24:21-23; Jer 32:18; 50:25; Nah 2:14; 3:5; Pss 24:8.10; 46:8.12 and 59:6).

III. "Yahweh Zebaoth" occurs 284 times in the Heb Bible (not counting the Qere in 2 Kgs 19:31). The distribution is noteworthy (METTINGER 1982b:11-17). Jeremiah is a special case since the MT's more frequent attestation of the term (82 times) may have to be drastically reduced on the basis of the LXX (OLOFSSON 1990:122-24). It is worthy of note that attestations of the term are clustered in books representing a tradition linked to the theology fostered at the Jerusalem temple: Proto-Isaiah (56 times), Hag (14 times), Zech (53 times), Mal (24 times), Ps (15 times). The designation is completely absent from the Pentateuch and Ezek and occurs only sparsely in Sam - Kgs (11 times in 1-2 Sam; 4 times in 1-2 Kgs). The following contrast can be drawn: In Isa 1-39 (3 % of the text of OT) there are 56 occurrences (20 % of the total of 284), while in the Deuteronomistic Historical Work (28 % of the text of the OT) there are 15 occurrences (5 % of the total), and these are mainly found in the older source materials. From this it may be inferred that the designation was important in Jerusalem during the zenith of the temple theology, but was considerably less popular during the exile (no occurrences in Ezek and only 15 times in the D-work), though to be sure the term was in use during the exile (see below). The fifteen occurrences in eight different psalms are found in hymns (Pss 46; 48; 84; 89), psalms of lament (Pss 59; 69; 80) and entrance liturgies (Ps 24). Of the fifteen occurrences, ten are found in invocations, whether of lament or praise, a fact which reflects the cultic language of Jerusalem and Shiloh (cf. 1 Sam 1:11). Nevertheless the relatively low number of attestations of the formula in the Psalms is still a problem.

The strong linkage between the Zebaoth designation on the one hand and Zion and the temple, on the other, appears from a number of texts. Isaiah's temple vision is a case in point, where the Zebaoth designation occurs in a trishagion that probably comes from the temple liturgy (Isa 6:3; cf. v 5). Moreover, Yahweh Zebaoth is explicitly called "he who dwells (*haššōkēn*) on Mount Zion" (Isa 8:18; cf. Joel 4:17.21; Ps 135:21), and Jerusalem is called "the city of Yahweh Zebaoth" (Ps 48:9, cf. the designation of Zion as "the mountain of Yahweh Zebaoth" in Zech 8:3). Several attestations in the Psalms occur in the Zion hymns (Pss 46:8.12; 48:9; 84:2.4.9.13). The Isaiah Apocalypse relates how Yahweh Zebaoth established his royal reign over Zion (Isa 24:23) and follows with a description of the banquet he holds on this mountain (25:6). Connected with this latter notion is the portrayal of the nations as pilgrims of Yahweh Zebaoth streaming to Zion (Zech 14:16-17), bearing gifts (Isa 18:7).

The cherubim formula is especially important here, since the original, complete title would have been *Yhwh ṣĕbā'ôt yōšēb hakkĕrûbîm,* "Yahweh Zebaoth, who is enthroned on the cherubim" (1 Sam 4:4; 2 Sam 6:2; Isa 37:16). The few cases when the cherubim formula occurs alone hardly amount to proof that it was originally an independent designation. This early connection with the cherubim formula shows that Yahweh Zebaoth was conceived as enthroned in invisible majesty on the cherubim throne in the Solomonic temple, since comparison with Syro-Palestine pictorial art of the Late Bronze Age and Early Iron Age shows that the cherubim of the Solomonic temple (1 Kgs 6:23-28) formed an immense throne for the invisible deity (note the prohibition of images), while the ark served as the footstool of the cherubim throne (1 Chron 28:2; cf. Pss 99:5; 132:7). We are thus faced with a concept of deity that is at one and the same time aniconic (the throne is empty) and anthropomorphic (the deity is conceived of as an enthroned monarch; T. N. D. METTINGER, *No Graven Image?* [Stockholm 1995]). The cherubim throne forms the physical focal point of the symbolism of the Solomonic temple, and the invisible Yahweh Zebaoth occupies the conceptual centre of the theology linked with this sanctuary on Zion. Indeed, this theology is appropriately described as a Zion-Zebaoth theology (METTINGER 1982b:15, 24-37).

Two features of this concept of Yahweh in this Zion-Zebaoth theology are of special importance here: He is the one who is present in his temple and he is king. (a) The first-mentioned aspect is evidenced by the formulations listed above that testify to the connection between Yahweh Zebaoth and Zion and the temple. The notion of the LORD of the temple dwelling on his holy mountain and in his sanctuary is also articulated in a number of passages without the Zebaoth formula being used (Exod 15:17; 2 Sam 7:5; 1 Kgs 8:13; Jer 8:19; Pss 46:5-6; 48:1-3; 50:2; 68:17; 76:3; 132:13-14).

(b) The royal character of Yahweh Zebaoth is evidenced, to begin with, by its close connection with the cherubim throne (see above). Moreover, a number of texts explicitly express this royal connection. "Yahweh Zebaoth, he is the King of glory" (Ps 24:10). "Woe is me! ... For my eyes have seen the King, Yahweh Zebaoth! (Isa 6:5). The "city of Yahweh Zebaoth" (Ps 48:9) is "the city of the great King" (v 3). In Ps 89:9 the designation occurs in a context where Yahweh is described as a king, sitting on his throne (v 15), surrounded by his divine council (vv 6-8). The use of the Zebaoth designation in the prayer of Hezekiah at the Assyrian siege of Jerusalem (Isa 37:16) may be formulated to express a deliberate contrast between Yahweh Zebaoth and the great king of Assyria (cf. Isa 36:4.13). It is against the background of the notion of Yahweh Zebaoth as king that statements concerning his purposing and planning are to be understood. "Yahweh Zebaoth has purposed and who will annul it?" (Isa 14:27; cf. v 24). Isa 19:12 speaks of "what Yahweh Zebaoth has purposed against Egypt" (cf. v 17 and 23:9). In Isa 28:29 Yahweh Zebaoth is acclaimed as "wonderful in counsel and excellent in wisdom". These passages on the supreme decrees of Yahweh Zebaoth all use the terms *yāʿaṣ* / *ʿēṣâ,* verb and noun respectively, 'plan', 'purpose', a terminology that is also used in connection with the messianic king (Isa 9:5; 11:2). Thus, if the messianic king is to be called "Wonderful Counsellor" (Isa 9:5), this is even more true of the supreme king, Yahweh Zebaoth (Isa 28:29). Finally, the formulaic expression "says the King, whose name is Yahweh Zebaoth" (Jer 46:18; 48:15; 51:57) may be noted in this connection.

A further important aspect of the Zion-Zebaoth theology is the idea that the temple is the point of intersection between heaven and earth; the temple is the point at which the dimensions of space are transcended (M. METZGER, Himmlische und irdische Wohnstatt Jahwes, *UF* 2 [1970], 139-158; cf. O. KEEL, *Jahwe-Visionen und Siegelkunst* [SBS 84-85; Stuttgart 1977] 51-53). This mythical concept of space explains passages which in such apparent nonchalance locate God simultaneously on earth and in heaven e.g. Ps 11:4: "Yahweh is in his holy temple, Yahweh's throne is in heaven." In Ps 14 Yahweh looks down from Heaven (v 2) and sends his help from Zion (v 7); in Ps 76 he dwells on Zion (v 3) and utters his judgment from heaven (v 9). Similarly in two almost identical lines Yahweh is portrayed as roaring from Zion in one case (Am 1:2) and from heaven in the other (Jer 25:30; cf. Joel 4:16). By the same token, the Zion-Zebaoth theology was not characterized by a trivial and restrictive notion of divine immanence. Passages such as Isa 6:1 and Ps 24:7-10 speak of a God whose grandeur cannot be confined within the limits of the temple.

Against this background it should be noted that the root ṢBʾ appears in contexts which draw upon both its royal and its celestial connotations. Like terrestrial kings, the heavenly monarch has a court and council. Among the Heb terms for the divine council we find precisely *ṣābāʾ* (1 Kgs 22:19-23, Pss 103:19-22; 148:1-5; Dan 8:10-13). The fact that the Zebaoth designation occurs in passages in which the divine council plays a role corroborates this association. Ps 89:6-19 is an obvious case. Just as the Davidic king is the highest of the kings on earth (v 28), so Yahweh is the supreme monarch in the divine assembly (vv 6-9) and thus merits the designation Yahweh Zebaoth (v 9). Isa 6, with the Zebaoth designation in vv 3.5, is another example. Yahweh's question "who will go for *us*?" (v 8) contains an allusion to the deliberations of the divine council. The relative rarity of texts that use the root in connection with the heavenly host in a positive sense may have something to do with the syncretistic influences exerted by the astral cult during the eighth century BCE. In the OT texts that express criticism of these influences the phrase *ṣĕbāʾ haššāmayim* "the host of heaven" referring to the stars, is often used to refer to the object of worship of the illegitimate cult (Deut 4:19; 2 Kgs 23:4-5 etc.).

The Zebaoth designation also occurs in various formulaic expressions, notably "Yahweh Zebaoth is his name", which appears in Amos (4:13; 5:27), Isa 40-55 (47:4; 48:2; 51:15; 54:5) and Jeremiah (10:16; 31:35; 32:18; 46:18; 48:15; 50:34; 51:57). The motifs connected with this formula are judgment, creation and idolatry (CRENSHAW 1969; 1975). In the exilic community, the formula fulfilled a confessional function, referring to the power and majesty of God. This usage was probably derived from pre-exilic cultic usage.

While the designation was used in the way just mentioned during the exile, it is nevertheless strikingly rare in major works from this period, such as the Deuteronomistic Historical Work (15 times) and Ezekiel (0). The cognitive dissonance between the traditional faith of the Zion-Zebaoth theology and the harsh historical realities experienced by the nation including the downfall of the earthly abode of Yahweh Zebaoth, the Solomonic temple, provoked the development of new theological solutions: the Deuteronomistic →name theology and the Priestly theology of the divine →glory found in P and in Ezek (METTINGER 1982b). Nevertheless the Zebaoth designation again figures frequently in post-exilic writings such as Hag (14 times), Zech (53 times) and Mal (24 times).

IV. The designation does not occur at all in Ben Sira and only once in the Qumran texts. A notable part of its postbiblical history takes place on gnostic soil, where it represents part of a Jewish heritage. "Sabaoth" is thus used by the sects criticized by Ireneus and Epiphanius: the Sethites and the Ophites (WAMBACQ 1947:43-45). A Sabaoth conception plays an especially important role in two documents from the Nag Hammadi Corpus, viz. *The Nature of the Archons* and *On the Origin of the World*, where the enthronement of Sabaoth and the creation of his throne/chariot are prominent motifs (see FALLON 1978). In this gnostic system one finds three, rather than two gods, viz. the transcendent God, the evil god Ialdabaoth, and his repentant offspring the god Sabaoth. Whether another postbiblical development is made up by relations between Sabaoth and Sabazios is a moot point (JOHNSON 1978 and 1984).

V. *Bibliography*

*O. BORCHERT, Der Gottesname Jahwe Zebaoth, *TSK* 69 (1896) 619-642; H. CAZELLES, Sabaot, *DBSup* 10 (Paris 1985) 1123-1127 [& lit]; J. L. CRENSHAW, *YHWH ṣĕbāʾôt šĕmô*. A Form-Critical Analysis, *ZAW* 81 (1969) 156-175; CRENSHAW, *Hymnic Affirmation of Divine Justice: The Doxologies of Amos and Related Texts in the Old Testament* (SBL DS 24; Missoula 1975); S. DEMPSTER, The Lord is his Name. A Study of the Distribution of the Names and Titles of God in the Book of Amos, *RB* 98 (1991) 170-189; O. EISSFELDT, Jahwe Zebaoth, *Miscellanea Academica Berolinensia* II 2 (Berlin 1950) 128-150 = *KS* 3 (1966) 103-123; F. T. FALLON, *The Enthronement of Sabaoth. Jewish Elements in Gnostic Creation Myths* (NHS 10; Leiden 1978); J. GARCIA TRAPIELLO, El epíteto divino "Yahweh ṣabaot" en los libros históricos del AT, *28 Semana Bíblica Española* (Madrid 1971) 67-128; M. GÖRG, *ṣbʾwt* - ein Gottestitel, *BN* 30 (1985) 15-18; S. E. JOHNSON, Sabaoth/Sabazios. A Curiosity in Ancient Religion, *Lexington Theological Quarterly* 13 (1978) 97-103; JOHNSON, The present state of Sabazios research, *ANRW* II 17,3 (Berlin/New York 1984) 1584-1613; B. LAYTON, *The Gnostic Scriptures. A New Translation with Annotations and Introductions* (New York 1987), index under Sabaoth; M. LIVERANI, La preistoria dell'epiteto "Yahweh *ṣĕbāʾôt*", *AION* 17 (1967) 331-334; V. MAAG, Jahwäs Heerscharen, *Schweizerische Theologische Umschau* 20 (1950) 27-52 = IDEM, *Kultur, Kulturkontakt und Religion. Gesammelte Studien zur allgemeinen und alttestamentlichen Religionsgeschichte* (ed. H. H. Schmid & O. H. Steck; Göttingen 1980) 1-28; *T. N. D. METTINGER, YHWH SABAOTH - The Heavenly King on the Cherubim Throne, *Studies in the Period of David and Solomon and Other Essays* (ed. T. Ishida; Tokyo/Winona Lake 1982) 109-138 = 1982a; METTINGER, *The Dethronement of Sabaoth. Studies in the Shem and Kabod Theologies* (ConB OT Series 18; Lund 1982) = 1982b; METTINGER, *In Search of God. The Meaning and Message of the Everlasting Names* (Philadelphia 1988) 123-157; S. OLOFSSON, *God is My Rock. A Study of Translation Technique and Theological Exegesis in the Septuagint* (ConB OT Series 31; Uppsala 1990) 119-126; J. F. ROSS, Jahweh *ṣĕbāʾôt* in Samuel and Psalms, *VT* 17 (1967) 76-92; R. SCHMITT, *Zelt und Lade als Thema alttestamentlicher Wissenschaft* (Gütersloh 1972) 145-159; C. L. SEOW, *Myth, Drama, and the Politics of David's Dance* (HSM 44; Atlanta 1989) 11-54; B. N. WAMBACQ, *L'épithète divine Jahvé ṣĕbāʾôt* (Paris/Bruges 1947); A. S. VAN DER WOUDE, צָבָא *ṣābāʾ*, Heer, *THAT* 2 (1976) 498-507; H.-J. ZOBEL, צְבָאוֹת *ṣĕbāʾôt*, *TWAT* 6 (1989) 876-892 [& lit].

T. N. D. METTINGER

YAM → SEA

YAʿÛQ

I. A deity Yaʿûq was worshipped by pre-Islamic Arabs. The personal names *Yaʿăqān* (Num 33:31.32; Deut 10:6; 1 Chr

1:42) and *ʿăqān* (Gen 36:27) have been interpreted as containing a reference to an animal deity worshipped by the Edomites (ROBERSTON SMITH 1912:455-483).

II. Islamic traditions refer to the cult of a deity *Yaʿûq* among the pre-islamic tribe of the Hamdān. In the Yemenite village Ḫaiwān (North of Ṣanʿā), there was a cult-centre. The Qur'an Sure 71:20-25 and Ibn al-Kalbi's *Book of Idols* (KLINKE-ROSENBERGER 1942:35, 61) interpret the deity as one of the idols of the contemporaries of →Noah. The meaning of the name of this deity could be derived from Arab *ʿāqa* as 'he hinders', which indicates that *Yaʿûq* was probably the nick-name or an epithet of an otherwise unknown deity (M. HÖFNER *WbMyth* 1/1 479).

III. In the Old Testament Jaaqan, and Aqan are considered only as human beings. The general theory behind the proposal—animal-like personal names contain a reminiscence of animal or totemic worship—has encountered serious criticism. Besides, the tradition in Gen 36 links Aqan with the Hurrites. The names most probably do not refer to an Edomite or Arabian deity (BARTLETT 1989:196).

IV. *Bibliography*

J. R. BARTLETT, *Edom and the Edomites* (JSOT Supl 77; Sheffield 1989); R. KLINKE-ROSENBERGER, *Das Götzenbuch* (Winterthur 1942); W. ROBERTSON SMITH, *Lectures and Essays* (London 1912).

B. BECKING

YARIKH → MOON

YEHUD *יהוד

I. The name Judah, *yĕhûdâ*, occurs over 800 times in the OT and indicates (1) a person, e.g. the fourth son of →Jacob; (2) the tribe Judah; (3) the kingdom governed by the dynasty of David; (4) a province in the Persian empire. The etymology of the name is still unsettled. The name has been construed as containing a theophoric element: e.g. J. HEMPEL (*BHH* II, 898) interprets the name as a hypocoristicon of *yĕhûd-ʾēl*, 'Praised be →El'. A. ALT (Der Gott der Väter, *KS* I [München 1953] 5 n.1) suggested that Judah originally was a place name. The general tendency in OT studies, however, is to interpret Judah as originally a territorial or regional name which was later used as a name for the eponymous ancestor of the tribe living in that area (ZOBEL 1976-80:514-517; AHLSTRÖM 1986; DE GEUS 1992:1034). This tendency leaves undecided the problem from which root the name was derived. The OT itself suggests a derivation from YDH, 'to praise' (Gen 29:45; 49:8). E. LIPIŃSKI (*VT* 23 [1973] 380-381) surmised a *qātûl*-form connected with the Arab noun *wahda*, 'canyon'. A. R. MILLARD (The Meaning of the Name Judah, *ZAW* 86 [1974] 216-218) proposed to construe the name as a Hoph of YHD 'to praise'. Such proposals are hypothetical, though (ZOBEL 1976-80:516). NYBERG (1935) considered Judah to contain the name of a deity *Yhwd*.

II. NYBERG (1935) interpreted the name Judah on the basis of the view that the ending *-â* in place names is an indication that the city under consideration is a centre of worship from time immemorial: e.g. *baʿălâ*, 'Baalah', Josh 15:9, 'settlement of →Baal worshippers'; *rimmônâ*, 'Rimmonah', Josh 19:12, 'settlement of Rimmon worshippers'. Judah then would mean 'settlement of Yehud worshippers'. This interpretation of the ending *â* has not been taken over by other scholars. NYBERG's main argument for the existence of the divine name *Yhwd* is that it can be compared with names as Abihud, Ahihud and Ammihud (1935). These names, however, have their first part as a theophoric element (→Father; →Brother; →Kinsman) construed with the element *hûd*, 'highness; pomp; splendour' (NOTH, *IPN* 76-78, 148; *HALAT* 231).

Apart from the eponymous ancestor Judah, the personal name seems to occur only in postexilic texts. In Ezra and Neh the name is born by six different persons. Neither in the OT nor in later Jewish writings is Judah, the fourth son of Jacob cast in the role of a heroic figure.

III. *Bibliography*

G. W. AHLSTRÖM, *Who were the Israelites?* (Winona Lake 1986) 42-43; C. H. J. DE GEUS, Judah (Place), *ABD* 3 (1992) 1033-1035; H. S. NYBERG, *Studien zum Hoseabuche* (UUÅ 1935,6; Uppsala 1935) 76-78; H. J. ZOBEL, *Jehûḏāh*, *TWAT* 3 (1976-80) 511-533.

B. BECKING

YIDDEʿONI → WIZARD

YIZHAR → OIL

YOM → DAY

Z

ZAMZUMMIM זמזמים

I. Deut 2:20 presents the Zamzummites, *zamzummîm*, as the Ammonite designation of the former inhabitants of the Ammonite area. Since the Zamzummites are interpreted as a tribe of the →Rephaim related to the Enakites (→Giants), it can be assumed that the Zamzummites are enfeebled spirits of the dead (POPE 1981:170; HÜBNER 1992: 163-164). Their name is etymologically connected to ZMM, 'to contrive evil' (*HALAT* 262; HÜBNER 1992:212).

II. Unlike the Rephaim, the Zamzummites are not mentioned in texts outside the OT. The only information concerning their character can be inferred from the etymology of their name which might indicate that they were evil spirits. HÜBNER compares them to →Og, the →Molekh of →Bashan and interprets the Zamzummites as originally underworld spirits (1992:163-164).

In Deut 2:20-23, it is related that →Yahweh had driven out the Zamzummites in order to give their territory to the Ammonites as a parallel to the way He will give the territory of the Canaanites to the Israelites. Most probably, this notice—being drenched in deuteronomistic ideology—does not contain historically trustworthy information. The author has reshaped ancient religious traditions on the Zamzummites.

In 1QGenAp 21:29, the *zuzîm*, 'Zuzites', a Canaanite tribe mentioned in Gen 14:5, are indicated as *zmwzmyʾ*. Originally the author of 1QGenAp wrote *zmwzmyʾ*, but later a *mēm* was added above the line to give **zûmzammāyê*. Probably, the author of 1QGenAp could not identify the Zuzites and equated them with the Zamzummites of Deut 2:20.

III. *Bibliography*

U. HÜBNER, *Die Ammoniter* (ADPV 16; Wiesbaden 1992) 163-164, 212, 244; M. POPE, The Cult of the Dead at Ugarit, *Ugarit in Retrospect* (G. D. Young, ed.; Winona Lake 1981) 159-179.

B. BECKING

ZAPHON צפון

I. In the Northwest-Semitic languages, Zaphon is first attested in Ugaritic texts as a designation for Jebel al-Aqraʿ to the north of Ugarit. In the OT, Zaphon occurs in a general sense meaning 'north (-wind)' and in a special sense designating a divine mountain. In this latter sense Zaphon is used as a synonym for mount Zion (Ps 48:3). Etymologically, Zaphon can be derived from *ṣāpâ* 'to spy' (EISSFELDT 1932; BONNET 1987). Less likely are derivations from *ṣāpan* 'to hide' (DE SAVIGNAC) or from *ṣûp* 'to float' (LIPIŃSKI 1987-89).

II. 40 km to the north of Ugarit, Jebel al-Aqraʿ rises to the height of about 1770 meters. The identification of Jebel al-Aqraʿ with mount Zaphon in the Ugaritic texts, first proposed by EISSFELDT (1932), is unanimously accepted. Its peak being often shrouded with clouds, Mount Zaphon was regarded as a holy mountain in the mythological and ritual texts of Ugarit.

This holiness of Mount Zaphon is not an invention of Ugaritic mythology. In the earlier Hurrian and Hittite traditions of North-Syria, the mountains Hazzi (Zaphon) and Namni/Nanni (Amanus?) are mentioned in parallelism (RGTC 6 [1978] 106-107). Mount Hazzi is already venerated as a divine abode and also figures as a guarantor of Hittite treaties (RGTC 6 [1978] 106) and there are traces of a Hittite ritual adressed to mount Hazzi (*CTH* 785; AOATS 3 [1974] 260-263; RGTC 6 [1978] 106). In relief 42 of Yazılikaya, Hazzi and Nanni serve as a podest for the weathergod of heavens. This motif can also be found on seal impressions (VANEL 1965: nos. 34; 35; 52; 57; DIJKSTRA 1991: pl. 13).

In the god lists of Ugarit, Zaphon is regarded as a deity (*KTU* 1.47:15 [rest.]; 1.118:14; RS 20.24:14 [*Ug* 5, 1968, 44-45, 379]) and thus entitled to receive offerings, as the ritual texts show (*KTU* 1.27:11; 1.41:24 [rest.].34.42; 1.46:4.7.15 [rest.]; 1.87:27.37.46; 1.91:3; 1.105:7.10; 1.109:10. 34; 1.130:23.25; 1.148:6.29; RIH 78/4:6 [*Syr* 57 (1980) 353-354.370]; 78/11:8 [*Syr* 57 (1980) 354-355.370]).

The god list *KTU* 1.47:1 begins with *ʾl ṣpn.* This does not mean 'divine Zaphon' as in *KTU* 1.3 iii:29; iv:19; 1.101:2), but is to be understood as 'gods of Zaphon' (LIPIŃSKI 1971; BONNET 1987). It is also an indication that Mount Zaphon had become the place for the assembly of the gods who had, according to the older tradition, assembled on El's divine mountain. This new role of →Olympus taken over by mount Zaphon (cf. also *KTU* 1.4 vii:5-6) is further stressed by *dbḥ ṣpn* 'offering (for the gods) of Zaphon' (*KTU* 1.91:3; 1.148:1).

In the Ugaritic mythological tradition, Mount Zaphon receives its holiness from Baal's palace built on its peak (*KTU* 1.3-4). Nearly always in the mythological texts Mount Zaphon is mentioned together with Baal because mount Zaphon is his divine abode (*KTU* 1.3 I:21-22; iii:29.47-iv:1; iv: 19-20.37-38; 1.4 iv:19; v:23.55; 1.5 i:10-11; 1.6 vi:12-13; 1.10 iii:27-37), a fact already known from ritual (*KTU* 1.100:9) and religious (*KTU* 1.101:1-3) texts. From Mount Zaphon, Baal brings rain to the land of Ugarit (*KTU* 1.101:1-9). After his death, Baal was buried on mount Zaphon (*KTU* 1.6 i:15-18). The god Ashtar who tries to occupy Baal's throne on Zaphon after his death is not the right person to take Baal's place (*KTU* 1.6 i:56-67). Also Anat, Baal's paredra in the Ugaritic mythological tradition, is intimately linked to Mount Zaphon as it is shown by her epithet *ʿnt ṣpn* 'Anat from Zaphon'. This epithet, comparable to the divine name →Baal-Zaphon, occurs only in ritual texts (*KTU* 1.46:17; 1.109:13-14.17. 36; 1.130:13). In mythological texts Zaphon is qualified as Baal's mountain (*KTU* 1.3 iii: 29; iv:19 [rest.]; 1.16 i:6-7; ii:45; cf. 1.101: 2); his sanctuary (*KTU* 1.3 iii:30; iv:20 [rest.]); the mountain of Baal's heritage (*KTU* 1.3 iii:30; iv:20 [rest.]); a place of loveliness (*KTU* 1.3 iii:31; 1.10 iii:31); a hill of triumph (*KTU* 1.3 iii:31; 1.10 iii:28.31; cf. 1.101:3) and a bastion (*KTU* 1.16 i:7-8; ii:45-46).

The above-mentioned conception of Mount Zaphon as a deity is also indicated in the mythological traditon of Ugarit. In metaphorical language, mount Zaphon bewails the death of king Keret (*KTU* 1.16 i:6-11; ii:44-49). Zaphon can also be named instead of Baal because in the hands of Zaphon (= Baal) are victory and triumph (*KTU* 1.19 ii:34-36). Other mythological texts qualify Zaphon as a divine mountain (*KTU* 1.3 iii: 29; iv:19; cf. 1.101:2).

In the first millennium, Zaphon appears as a toponym in Neo-Assyrian texts (S PARPOLA, *Neo-Assyrian Toponyms* [AOAT 6; Neukirchen-Vluyn 1970] 304) and also in a hieroglyphic Ptolemaic name-list, where Zaphon means 'Syria' parallel to Phoenicia (M. GÖRG, *BN* 23 [1984] 14-17). In the Phoenician tradition, Zaphon is mentioned by Philo Byblios under its name Kassion, derived from Hurrian Ḫazzi (Eusebius, *Praep.Ev.* I 10, 9, 11), as a divine mountain. Furthermore Zaphon is a theophoric element in the Punic onomasticon of Carthage and in the Phoenician onomasticon of Egypt.

The aspect of the divine abode has also been preserved in the Aramaic tradition. In papyrus Amherst, a god is asked to bring help from Zaphon (Pap. Amherst 63:12, 13 [ed. I. KOTTSIEPER (UBL 6; Münster 1988) 55-75]). Zaphon stands here for the divine abode par excellence and it is not confined to Jebel al-Aqraʿ. This is shown by its parallel to the cave of Araš (perhaps Ras en-Naqura in southern Lebanon [*RB* 78 (1971) 84-92]). In 8:3 and 13:15-16 papyrus Amherst mentions Zaphon together with Baal.

In Greek texts, Zaphon lives on as →Typhon, who is now a dragon defeated by the weather-god (Apollodor I 6,3). Cultic activity on mount Zaphon in honour of →Zeus Kasios is attested until the time of Julian Apostata in 363 CE.

III. In the OT, Zaphon can also designate a divine abode. The king of Babylon wanted to sit "on the mountain of assembly on the summit of Zaphon" (Isa 14:13). In this context, Zaphon stands for the divine mountain *par excellence*, wherever it is located. According to Ps 89:13, Zaphon and Amanus (?), the ancient Hurrian-Hittite pair of divine mountains, is said to have been created by →Yahweh. The case is different in Ps 48:3 where "mount Zion is (on) the summit of Zaphon". Jerusalem's sacred mountain is called Zaphon because Yahweh, as supreme god of Israel, can only be enthroned on the divine mountain par excellence. This aspect also underlies Job 26:7 where Zaphon stands for 'heaven', meaning Yahweh's divine abode. Comparable is Job 37:22 with the description of Yahweh's epiphany from Zaphon (cf. Ezek 1:4).

IV. *Bibliography*

M. C. ASTOUR, *RSP* 2, 318-324 no. 89; *C. BONNET, Typhon et Baal Saphon, *Studia Phoenicia* 5 (OLA 22; Leuven 1987) 101-143; R. J. CLIFFORD, *The Cosmic Mountain in Canaan and the Old Testament* (HSM 4; Cambridge, Mass. 1972) 57-79, 131-160; A. COOPER & M. H. POPE, *RSP* 3, 410-413 no. 25; M. DIETRICH & O. LORETZ, Ugaritisch *ṣrt ṣpn, ṣrry* und Hebräisch *jrktj ṣpwn*, *UF* 22 (1990) 79-88; M. DIJKSTRA, The Weather-God on Two Mountains, *UF* 23 (1991) 127-140; J. EBACH, *Weltentstehung und Kulturentwicklung bei Philo von Byblos* (BWANT 108; Stuttgart 1979) 144-148; J. EBACH, Kasion, *LdÄ* 3 (1980) 354; O. EISSFELDT, *Baal Zaphon, Zeus Kasios und der Durchzug der Israeliten durchs Meer* (BRA 1; Halle 1932); W. FAUTH, Das Kasion-Gebirge und Zeus Kasios, *UF* 22 (1990) 105-118; H. GESE, *RAAM* 123-128; C. GRAVE, The Etymology of Northwest Semitic *ṣapānu*, *UF* 12 (1980) 221-229; V. HAAS, *Hethitische Berggötter und hurritische Steindämonen* (Mainz 1982) 115-124; R. HILLMANN, *Wasser und Berg* (diss. Halle 1965) 10-21, 24-30, 66-75, 158-194; A. LAUHA, *Zaphon. Der Norden und die Nordvölker im Alten Testament* (AASFB 49; Helsinki 1943); E. LIPIŃSKI, El's Abode, *OLP* 2 (1971) 13-68; LIPIŃSKI, *ṣāpôn*, *TWAT* 6 (1987-89) 1093-1102; E. LIPIŃSKI & C. Bonnet, *Dictionnaire de la Civilisation Phénicienne et Punique* (Turnhout 1992) 477; H. NIEHR, *Der höchste Gott* (BZAW 190; Berlin 1990) 95-117; H. PRIEBATSCH, Wanderungen und Wandelungen einer Sage, *UF* 16 (1984) 257-266; W. RÖLLIG, Ḫazzi, *RLA* 4 (1972-1975) 241-242; DE SAVIGNAC, Note sur le sens du terme Ṣâphôn dans quelques passages de la Bible, *VT* 3 (1953) 95-96; R. J. DE SAVIGNAC, Le sens du terme Ṣâphôn, *UF* 16 (1984) 273-278; W. H. SCHMIDT, *THAT* 2 (1976) 575-582; C. STEUERNAGEL & O. KEES, Kasion 2, *PW* 10 (1919) 2263-2264; E. VON SCHULER, Ḫazzi, *WbMyth* I (1983²) 171-172; A. VANEL, *L'iconographie du dieu de l'orage* (CRB 3; Paris 1965).

H. NIEHR

ZEDEQ צדק

I. The West Semitic deity Zedek, 'Righteousness', is found in the Bible only in the personal names →Melchizedek (Gen 14:18; cf. Ps 110:4; Heb 5:6; 6:20-7:17) and Adonizedek (Josh 10:1.3), both Canaanite kings of pre-Israelite Jerusalem. Zedek is probably to be identified with the deity known as Išar among the Amorites and Kittu in Babylonia, and thus a hypostasis or personification of the sun god Shamash's function (→Shemesh) as divine overseer of justice. The cult of Zedek appears to have been well established in pre-Israelite (Jebusite) Jerusalem. Some aspects of this cult apparently were translated into Yahwism; in a number of texts Righteousness appears either as a member of →Yahweh's court or as a personification of Yahweh's concern for justice. In the postbiblical period, the Righteousness tradition helped shape the thinking of the apocalyptic community of Qumran.

II. Evidence for the West Semitic deity

Zedek is mostly indirect but nonetheless compelling. Most decisive is a statement by Philo of Byblos that the Phoenicians had a god named Sydyk, i.e. Zedek. Philo, who claimed to get his information from the Phoenician writer Sanchuniaton, noted that the Phoenicians numbered among their gods "Misor and Sydyk, that is, 'Easy to loosen' and Righteous (*Misōr kai Sydyk, toutestin eulyton kai dikaion*); they invented the use of salt" (quoted by Eusebius, *Praeparatio Evangelica* i.10.13; instead of *Sydyk*, some manuscripts have *Sydek* or *Sedek*); the rendering εὔλυτος for Misor is apparently based on an erroneous etymology, deriving the name from the root ŠRH 'loosen, release'. The interpretation of *Sydyk* as an adjective rather than a substantive should be understood in the light of Philo's euhemerism. Philo goes on to say that Misor fathered Taautos (known to the Egyptians as →Thoth and to the Greeks as →Hermes), the inventor of writing, and that from Sydyk came various lesser divinities or heroes, namely, the Dioscouri (→Dioskouroi), the Cabeiri, the Corybantes, and the Samothracians. Patently, 'Misōr' and 'Sydyk' correspond to Heb *mîšôr*, 'justice', and *ṣedeq*, 'righteousness'. Zedek is not directly attested elsewhere as the name of a deity, but indirect evidence comes from two sources: the Amorite and Babylonian pantheons, and West Semitic personal names.

The West Semitic god Zedek seemingly corresponds to the deity known as Kittu in the Babylonian pantheon and as Išar in the Amorite pantheon. In Mesopotamia the preservation of truth and justice was considered to be the particular domain of the sun god Shamash. Truth or Right was personified and deified as the god Kittu ('Truth', 'Right'; from Akk root *kânu*, cf. Heb root KWN). Kittu was often invoked together with the god Misharu ('Justice') (see *CAD* K 471 s.v. *kittu* A 1b4; M/2 118 s.v. *mīšaru* A 2d; cf. Heb root YŠR). One or both of these deities were described as 'seated before Shamash', i.e. Shamash's attendant, or as 'the minister of (Shamash's) right hand'. While Misharu was always considered a male deity, Kittu was identified sometimes as the daughter of Shamash, sometimes as the son of Shamash. Meanwhile, at Mari offerings were made to the divine pair ᵈ*Išar u* ᵈ*Mešar* (ARM 24.210.24-25; cf. 263.5-6 where these same gods are listed separately but contiguously; see P. TALON, Un nouveau pantheon de Mari, *Akkadica* 20 [1980] 12-17). As a theophoric element Išar is common in both Akk and Amorite personal names (HUFFMON 1965:216). From the interchangeability of the names Kittu, Išar, and Ṣidqu/Zedek in the pairing with Mišar(u), it appears that the deity known as Kittu in Babylonia was known further to the West under the names Išar and Ṣidqu/Zedek—all three names having essentially the same meaning but operative in different linguistic communities. Additional support for the identification of Ṣidqu and Kittu comes from the Amorite royal name Ammiṣaduqa, which was translated in the Babylonian King List as Kimtum-kittum, showing an equivalence between the West Semitic root ṢDQ and Akk *kittu* (cf. BAUMGARTEN 1979:235).

The god Zedek is attested frequently in personal names. Admittedly, in numerous West Semitic personal names the root ṢDQ should be interpreted not as the name of a deity but, similar to biblical Yahwistic personal names, as a nominal formation (e.g. Zedekiah 'My righteousness is Yahweh') or as a verbal formation (e.g. Jehozadak/Jozadak, 'Yahweh is righteous'). This is the presumption with Israelite personal names, whether from the Bible or from Heb inscriptions (TIGAY 1986), despite the ambiguity of a name like *ʾlṣdq* which may be interpreted either as 'God/El/my god is righteous' or as 'God/El/my god is Zedek'. In non-Israelite contexts, however, the situation is less clear. West Semitic personal names containing the root ṢDQ are attested at many sites, including El Amarna, Ugarit, Rimah, and Mari (HUFFMON 1965; F. GRÖNDAHL, *Die Personennamen der Texte aus Ugarit* [Rome 1967] 187-188; S. DALLEY, C. B. F. WALKER & J. D. HAWKINS, *The Old Babylonian Tablets from Tell al Rimah* [British

School of Archaeology in Iraq; 1976] 262); the greatest concentration of such personal names occurs in texts from the Old Babylonian kingdom of Mari. Two forms are attested in syllabic cuneiform writing: *ṣidq-* and *ṣaduq* (besides the personal names listed by HUFFMON 1965, additional names are now attested from Mari: Ṣidqum-maṣi, Ṣidqu-Ištar, Ṣidqum-matar, Ṣidqiya, Abi-ṣaduq, Bahli-ṣaduq, Ṣaduqi-AN; and from nearby provincial Tell al Rimah [Karana]: Ṣaduq-dAšar, Ṣaduqqi). Although personal names are notoriously difficult to interpret, in some cases ṢDQ appears to be verbal or nominal: Ṣidqu-Ištar ('Righteousness-is-Ishtar' or 'Ishtar-is-righteous'), Ṣidqu-la-nasi ('Righteousness belongs to the prince'), Bahli-ṣaduq ('Baʿlu/Baal-is-righteous'; cf. Ug *ʿlṣdq*), Hammi-ṣaduq ('Hammu-is-righteous'), Ṣaduq-dAšar ('Ašar-is-righteous'; Rimah). But in other cases, based upon comparative onomastic evidence, it is difficult to avoid interpreting ṢDQ as a theophoric element: Ṣidqi-epuh ('Ṣidqu-is-brilliant'), Ṣidqum-matar ('Ṣidqum-is-outstanding'), Ili-Ṣidqum/Ṣidqi ('My god-is-Ṣidqu'); so also for Ug Pī-Ṣidqi ('Mouth/Command of Ṣidqu') and Amarna Rabi-Ṣidqi ('Ṣidqu-is-great', *EA* 170:37). More ambiguous are the personal names Ili-ṣidqum/ṣidqi, Ili-ṣaduq, and Ṣaduqi-AN (cf. Ugaritic alphabetic names *ilṣdq* and *ṣdqil*). On the one hand, Ili-ṣaduq and Ṣaduqi-AN perhaps mean 'El/My god-is-righteous' (against M. POPE, *El in the Ugaritic Texts* [Leiden 1955] 22, who interprets Ug *ṣdqil* as 'Zedek is [my?] god'). On the other hand, to judge from comparative evidence, Ili-Ṣidqum/ṣidqi almost certainly means 'My god-is-Ṣidqu'. Even the hypocoristic personal names Ṣidqan(a) and Ṣidqiya are probably theophoric. Ug *adnṣdq* ('Ṣidqu-is-[my?]-lord') and Amarna Rabi-ṣidqi ('Ṣidqu is great'; *EA* 170.37) witness to the continuing devotion to Zedek in the West through the end of the Late Bronze period.

Some scholars regard *ṣaduq* as a theophoric element (HUFFMON 1965:257), while other posit *ṣadoq* as an alternative for *Ṣidqu* or *Ṣedeq*, primarily on the translation of Ammi-ṣaduqa in the Babylonian King List as Kimtum-kittum (BAUMGARTEN 1979:235, following J. LEVY, The Old West-Semitic Sun-God Ḥammu, *HUCA* 18 [1944] 435). In the cases of Bahli-ṣaduq, (H)ammi-ṣaduq(a), and Ṣaduq-ašar, however, ṣaduq is likely only a divine epithet. By extension, the hypocoristic personal names Ṣaduqum, Ṣaduqqi, Ṣaduqan(a), Ṣaduqum (cf. Heb Zadok) also need not have reference to the cult of Zedek, though such is not excluded either.

III. In the Bible the god Zedek appears only in the personal names of two Canaanite kings of Jerusalem, Melchizedek (Gen 14:18) and Adonizedek (Josh 10:1.3), fueling speculation that Jerusalem was a cult centre for Zedek in pre-Israelite times. Melchizedek is identified not only as 'king of Salem' but also as 'priest of God →Most High' (*ʾēl ʿelyôn*, Gen 14:18), today usually understood to mean that Melchizedek was a devotee of the god El, head of the Canaanite pantheon. Others argue, however, that Melchizedek was priest of the god Zedek (see ROWLEY 1939:130, n. 50 for details). One hypothesis suggests that Zedek is to be identified with the god →Shalem, whose name is embodied in Jerusalem (H. WINCKLER, *Die Keilinschriften und das Alte Testament* [Berlin 31903] 224; cf. ROWLEY 1939:130-131, n. 50). Support for this hypothesis may come from the Ugaritic personal name *ṣdqšlm*, should this name mean 'Zedek-is-Shalem' rather than the more probable 'Shalem is righteous'. Shalem certainly has connections with a solar cult, aspects of which may have been incorporated into Israelite yahwistic religion. A long-standing cult of Zedek at Jerusalem could account at least partially for the fact that even during the Israelite period Jerusalem laid special claim to such titles as 'the city of Righteousness' (Isa 1:21, 26) and 'pasture of Righteousness' (Jer 31:23; cf. 33:16). Although evidence of a solar cult in the temple in Jerusalem has been exaggerated in the past by some scholars, nevertheless some form of a solar cult was practised in the temple in Jerusalem right up to the time when the temple was destroyed in the sixth century BCE (Ezek 8:16). It is unclear that this solar cult is traceable back to Jebusite times, however; it may be that Manasseh introduced this ritual only a century earlier under Assyrian influence. Josiah's reforms ca. 620 BCE, during which "the horses that the kings of Judah had dedicated to the sun, at the entrance to the house of the LORD" were removed and "the chariots of the sun" burned (2 Kgs 23:11; cf. Deut 4:19), were in part aimed at destroying the symbols of Assyrian hegemony over Judah.

Some have hypothesized that Zadok had been a priest in the Jebusite sanctuary at Jerusalem prior to his appointment by David as one of his two principal priests and that Zadok's name indicates an original connection with the cult of Zedek (see ROWLEY 1939). This hypothesis rests upon extremely tenuous evidence, as the discussion above concerning extrabiblical personal names indicates.

Aspects of the West Semitic god Zedek were absorbed into Yahwism (see MAY 1937 and ROSENBERG 1965). Rather than remaining as an independent deity, *Ṣedeq*, 'Righteousness', was translated as a quality of Yahweh. Thus, at times *Ṣedeq* and Yahweh are found in synonymous parallelism: "Harken to me, you who pursue Righteousness, you who seek Yahweh" (Isa 51:1); "They will be called the oaks of Righteousness, the planting of Yahweh" (Isa 61:3); "Sacrifice sacrifices of Righteousness and trust in Yahweh" (Ps 4:6). At other times Righteousness seems to be used as part of a compound name, "Yahweh-Righteousness" (Ps 17:1) or as substitute for Yahweh ("For unto Righteousness will judgment return"; Ps 94:15). In some instances Righteousness appears as a hypostasis of the divine sovereign's invincible right hand/arm by which he rules the world and protects his devotees: "Righteousness fills thy (Yahweh's) right hand" (Ps 48:11); "I (Yahweh) will support you with my right hand of Righteousness" Isa 41:10); "My (Yahweh's) Righteousness is near, my salvation has gone forth, and my arms will rule the peoples" (Isa 51:5). In Psalm 118 the two typologies are joined; after a reference to vindication through the "right hand of Yahweh" (vv 15-16), the psalmist prays (vv 19-20): "Open for me the gates of Righteousness; I will enter them, praising Yah." This is the gate to Yahweh, through which the righteous enter. Poetic parallelism here allows no doubt that the "gates of Righteousness" is the semantic equivalent of "the gate to Yahweh"; Yahweh is Zedek, the defender of righteous persons. Jer 33:16 also played upon this theme, declaring that in the endtime Jerusalem will be known by the name 'Yahweh-is-our-Righteousness'.

The original function of Righteousness as an aspect of the solar deity, who searches out and destroys injustice upon the face of the earth but vindicates the righteous, is only slightly veiled in Mal 3:19-20. The image concerns the dawning of the day of Yahweh, when the intense sun will consume the wicked like stubble, while for those who revere God "the sun of Righteousness (*ṣĕdāqâ*) shall rise with healing in its wings." Vestigial images of a solar deity of righteousness have been suggested also for Mic 7:9; Isa 45:8, 19; and Hos 10:12.

Zedek and Mišor as attendant deities of Shamash also have their reflexes in Yahwism as dual qualities of the God of Israel. Isa 11:4 says that the Spirit of Yahweh will possess the messianic king, with the result that "he will judge the weak with Righteousness, he will defend the poor of the earth with Justice" (cf. Ps 45:7-8). Other passages substitute the plural *mêšārîm* for *mîšôr* as the parallel word to *Ṣedeq*, but the concept is the same: "He judges the world with Righteousness; he judges the peoples with Justice" (Ps 9:9). Ps 58:2 contrasts the righteous rule of Yahweh with the chaotic rule of the false gods: "Do you truly, O gods, speak Righteousness; do you judge humans (with) Justice?" In Ps 98:9 even the normally rebellious waters of chaos acknowledge the kingship of Yahweh: "He will judge the world with Righteousness, and the peoples with Justice." In Isa 45:19 Yahweh derides the gods of other nations and proclaims that he alone is capable of salvation: "I am Yahweh who declares Righteousness, who announces Justice."

The reflex of Zedek as one of a pair of attendant deities is present in other passages as well. In Pss 89:15 and 97:7 Zedek and *mišpāṭ*—the latter an equivalent term for *mîšôr*—are said to be the foundation of Yahweh's throne. According to Isa 1:21 Zedek and *mišpāṭ* made Jerusalem their home (cf. also Isa 1:26). Ps 85:11-14 embellishes to its fullest the theme of attendant deities, understood very likely as personifications of Yahweh's qualities: "Steadfast Love and Faithfulness meet; Righteousness and Peace kiss; Truth springs up from the earth; and Righteousness looks down from the sky. Righteousness goes before him, blazing a path."

IV. The personification of Righteousness continued to develop along several lines in post-biblical Jewish literature (see BAUMGARTEN 1979); here mention can be made only of the particular personification of Righteousness in the apocalyptic literature of Qumran. According to the War Scroll, Zedek is a heavenly figure closely associated with →Michael in the struggle to overthrow the kingdom of wickedness; when the victory is finally achieved, God "will exalt the kingdom of Michael in the midst of the gods," while "Righteousness shall rejoice on high" (1QM 17:7-8). Moreover, the solar (or astral) connotations of Zedek were emphasized within the dualistic mythopoeic imagery of a battle between the forces of light and the forces of darkness. Righteousness is described in the imagery of the sun (alternatively, a morning star), at whose appearance darkness and wickedness retreat (e.g. 1QM 1:8; 1QMyst 5-6). Righteousness and light thus became symbols of theophany.

Melchizedek, too, acquired a new eschatological role. In 11QMelch Melchizedek is a heavenly figure—the archangel Michael in a different guise, according to the majority of scholars—one of two supreme figures created by God to overthrow →Belial and his wicked followers. Melchizedek will be assisted in this task by all gods of righteousness, a topos derived from a sectarian reading of Psalm 82 (ASTOUR 1992).

Members of the Qumran community attached particular significance to dawn as a time of prayer, and commonly referred to themselves as 'sons of Righteousness' (*bĕnê ṣedeq*) and 'sons of light' (*bĕnê 'ôr*). Perhaps the preference of the Qumran Zadokite priesthood for *bĕnê Ṣadoq* as an epithet reflected not so much a claim of superior pedigree as a commitment to specific ideals. Finally, the title of the enigmatic hero of the Qumran sect, 'the Teacher of Righteousness' (*môreh haṣṣedeq*), took on added meaning in light of the sect's dedication to personified Righteousness as a hypostasis of God. (See also →Dike.)

V. *Bibliography*

M. C. ASTOUR, Melchizedek (Person), *ABD* 4 (1992) 684-686; *J. M. BAUMGARTEN, The Heavenly Tribunal and the Personification of Ṣedeq in Jewish Apocalyptic, *ANRW* II 19 (1979) 219-239; C. F. BURNEY, *The Book of Judges* (London 1918; reprinted New York 1970) 41-43; R. FRANKENA, *Tākultu: De sacrale maaltijd in het assyrische ritueel* (Leiden 1954) 98, 104; H. B. HUFFMON, *Amorite Personal Names in the Mari Texts: A Structural and Lexical Study* (Baltimore 1965) 256-257; H. G. MAY, Some Aspects of Solar Worship at Jerusalem, *ZAW* 55 (1937) 269-281; *R. A. ROSENBERG, The God Ṣedeq, *HUCA* 36 (1965) 161-171; H. H. ROWLEY, Zadok and Nehushtan, *JBL* 58 (1939) 113-141; J. H. TIGAY, *You Shall Have No Other Gods: Israelite Religion in the Light of Hebrew Inscriptions* (HSS 31; Atlanta 1986) 79, 84.

B. F. BATTO

ZEH-SINAI → HE-OF-THE-SINAI

ZEUS Ζεύς

I. Zeus is the main divinity of the Greek pantheon. His name is of undisputed Indo-European origin, connected with Lat *Iu-piter*, Rigveda *Dyaus (pitar)* etc., derived from the root **diwu-*, "day (as opposed to night)" (Lat *dies*), "(clear) sky". He is identified with local weather gods of Asia Minor, with great sky gods (Zeus Beelsêmên, →Baalshamem) as well as local Baʿalim of Syria and Palestine, and with the Egyptian Amun/Ammon. In the Bible, he appears in 2 Macc 6:2 (the temple in Jerusalem and the sanctuary of Garizim are rededicated to Zeus) and in Acts 14:12-13 (the inhabitants of Lystra in Lycaonia call Barnabas Zeus, Paul →Hermes; the priest of Zeus prepares a sacrifice to them).

II. Zeus is the only major god of the Greek pantheon whose IE origin is undisputed. The Homeric and later epithet *patēr* is closely paralleled by Roman *Iu-piter* and Indian *Dyaus pitar*: his role as father must be already IE, not in a theogonical or anthropogonical sense (regardless of the frequent epic formula "Zeus, father of men and gods"), but as the Homeric variant Zeus *anax*, "Lord Zeus", proves, as having the power of a father in a patriarchal system. This role, which implies unrestricted power as well as its control by father-like benignity, continues as the fundamental role of Zeus in all antiquity and finds expression also in the standard iconography of a bearded but powerful man (SIMON 1985:14-34; ARAFAT 1990).

Accordingly, his cult is well attested in the Linear B tablets from Pylos and Knossos (GÉRARD-ROUSSEAU 1968:72-74; HILLER, in SCHWABL 1978:1001-1009), Thebes and Khania (HALLAGER 1992), though at least in Pylos he seems to share his prestige with Poseidon. The palaces of Pylos and Khania had a sanctuary of Zeus; a Knossian tablet attests a month name or, if already the Mycenaean names of months derive from festivals, a festival of Zeus; another one derives from the epiclesis Diktaios, Zeus of Mt. Dikte, which remained important in the first millennium. A Pylos text attests the common cult of Zeus, →Hera, and Drimios Son of Zeus: Drimios is unknown in the first millennium (though a tablet from Khania notes a common cult of Zeus and →Dionysos in the sanctuary of Zeus, and though a triad of Zeus, Hera and Dionysos is attested on Lesbos, Alcaeus frg. 129 L.-P., it would be rash to identify Drimios with Dionysos), but the connection of Zeus, Hera and a son of Zeus suggests Hera as consort of Zeus, as in later mythology.

The role of Zeus, the IE god of the bright sky, is transformed in Greece into the role of Zeus the weather god whose paramount place of worship is a mountain top; such a cult-place is specific to Zeus (see Herodotus 1,131,1). Among the many mountains connected with Zeus (list: COOK 1926:868-987), many are reflected only in an epithet which does not necessarily imply the existence of a peak sanctuary. Few such sanctuaries have been excavated (e.g. on Mt. Hymettos in Attica, LANGDON 1976); those attested in literature are mainly connected with rain rituals (Zeus Hyetios or Ombrios), though the sanctuary on the Arcadian Mt. Lykaion had an initiatory function as well (rain: Pausanias 8,38,4; initiations BURKERT 1972: 97-108). As Zeus "the Gatherer of Clouds" (*nephelêgeretês*, a common Homeric epithet), he was generally believed to cause rain, both in serious expressions ("Zeus rains") and in the comic parody of Aristophanes (*Nub.* 373). With the god of clouds comes the god of thunder (*hypsibremetês* "He Who Thunders High Up") and of lightning (*terpsikeraunos* "He Who Enjoys Lightning"); a spot struck by lightning is inaccessible (*abaton*) and often sacred to Zeus Kataibates ("He Who Comes Down"). As the Master of Tempest, he is supposed to give signs to the mortals through thunder and lightning and to strike evildoers, as he struck the →Giants and the monstrous →Typhon at the beginning of his reign.

This entire complex finds expression in the myth that Zeus lives on Mt. Olympos, together with all the gods of his household; from a real mountain, →Olympos was transformed into a mythical place already before Homeric poetry; the myth in turn provoked cult on the mountain (*Arch. Delt.* 22 [1967] 6-14). As Master of Lightning, he has the Cyclopes at his command, the divine blacksmiths who fabricate his main weapon.

The shift from Indo-European god of the

bright sky (according to the etymology) to the Greek Master of Sky and Storms makes Zeus a relative of the Weather Gods of Anatolia and Syria with whom he later was identified. This shift seems inconceivable without Near Eastern influence which is also tangible in the Hesiodic succession myth (see below).

Already for the early archaic Greeks, and conceivably the Mycenaeans (emphatically so KERÉNYI 1972:21-34), Zeus was a much more fundamental deity. According to the succession myth in the Hesiodic *Theogony*, Zeus deposed his father Kronos, who in turn had deposed and castrated his father Uranos; after his accession to power, Zeus fought the Giants and the monster Typhon who attacked his reign, and disposed the actual order of things by attributing to each divinity his or her respective sphere: to his brothers →Poseidon and →Hades-Pluton, he allotted two thirds of the cosmos, to the one the sea, to the other the netherworld; to his sisters Hera, his wife, and →Demeter, and to his many divine children their respective domains in the world of the humans; mankind had been preexistent to Zeus' reign. The main outline of this myth is known also in Homer (Zeus is the son of Kronos, *Kroniôn* or *Kronidês*, Rhea his mother *Il.* 15,188, the →Titans are sons of Uranos, *Il.* 5,898; the tripartite division of the world *Il.* 15,187; the deposition of Kronos and the Titans *Il.* 8,478. 14,200. 274. 15,225; the fight against Typhoeus *Il.* 2,780). The myth makes Zeus the ruler ("King", *anax* or, after Homer, *basileus*) both over the other gods (whom he overrules by sheer force, if necessary, e.g. *Il.* 8,18-27) and over the world of man: the order of things as they are now is the order of Zeus.

Closely related succession myths are attested from Hittite Anatolia and from Mesopotamia. In Hittite mythology, the succession passes through Anu, "Sky", who is deposed and castrated by Kumarbi, and finally to Teshub, the Storm God, who would correspond to Zeus; other myths narrate the attacks of Kumarbi and his followers on Teshub's reign (HOFFNER 1990). Myths from Mesopotamia present a similar, though more varied structure; the Babylonian *Enuma Elish* moves from a primeval pair Apsu and Tiamat to the reign of Marduk, the city god of Babylon and in many respects a Baʿal and Zeuslike figure; a later version of the Typhoeus myth (Apollodorus, *Bibl.*1,6,3) locates part of it on Syrian Mt. Kasion (Phoen. →Zaphon), seat of a peak cult of →Baʿal Zaphon (Zeus Kasios, SCHWABL 1972:320-321). The conception of Zeus the kingly ruler of the present world is as unthinkable without Oriental influence as is the figure of Zeus the Master of Storms.

But Zeus the king is no tyrant. One of his main domains is right and justice: he has ordered the world, and any transgression of this order is injustice, and Zeus watches over it; if necessary, he punishes transgressors (e.g. Salmoneus, who had made himself into an image of Zeus). Human kings are under his special protection, but they have to endorse the justice of Zeus (LLOYD-JONES 1971; →Dike). Zeus himself protects those outside ordinary social bonds, i.e. the strangers, supplicants (Homer, *Od.* 9,296-298) and beggars (*Od.* 6,207-208; 14, 57-60); the cult attests Zeus Xenios, "He of the Strangers" (SCHWABL 1972:341) and Zeus Hikesios, "He of the Supplicants" (SCHWABL 1972:317-318). In order to preserve the order he had set, he is himself subject to it; he has no right to change it out of personal whim—therefore, he feels himself liable to Fate (whom Homer can call "Fate of Zeus"; BIANCHI 1953).

In many instances, human affairs follow the plan of Zeus (the Trojan War, the return of Odysseus), despite apparent setbacks. He might hasten perfection, if asked in prayer to do so (Zeus Teleios, "He who Perfects", Aeschylus *Ag.* 973), and he might signal his will, either asked for or unasked, in dreams, augural signs, thunder and lightning (Homer *Il.* 2,353. 3,242), but also by provoking ominous human utterances (thunder and utterance, *phēmē*, combined in Hom. *Od.* 20,102-105). In cult, this function is expressed in rare epicleses like Phanter ("He Who Signals"), Terastios ("He of the

Omina"), Phemios ("Who gives Oracular Sayings") or Kledonios.

In these cases, Zeus' prophetic power is occasional and subordinated to his main role as guarantor of cosmic and social order. It becomes central in the only Greek oracle of Zeus, Dodona in Epirus (BOUCHÉ-LECLERCQ 2, 273-331; PARKE 1967: 1-163). The oracle is reputed to be the oldest Greek oracle; it was known already to Homer (*Il.*16,233-234; *Od.*14,327-328) and was active until late-Hellenistic times; though visited also by cities, its main clients were private people from North-western Greece. Zeus (surnamed Naios; he had a cult also on nearby Mt. Tomaros) is here paired with Dione, mother of →Aphrodite in ordinary Greek myth. Homer mentions the Selloi as prophets, "barefoot, sleeping on the earth" (*Il.* 16,234-235). They disappear without a trace; in the mid-fifth cent. BCE, Herodotus knows only of priestesses ("Doves", Peleiades), and later authors add that they prophecy in ecstasy, Aristides, *Or.* 45,11. Zeus manifested himself in the sounds of the holy →oak-tree (*Od.* 14,27-28, 19,296-297), in →doves, whose call from the holy oak-tree or whose flight are used as divine signs (Herodotus 2,55-58); other sources know also divination by lots (cleromancy), water vessels (hydromancy), and by the sounds of a gong.

Zeus has but few major polis festivals; and only a few month names attest to an important early festival of Zeus—the Bronze Age month Diwos (Knossos) to which correspond the Macedonian, Aetolian and Thessalian Dios, the Attic Maimakterion, which comes from the minor festival of a shadowy Zeus Maimaktes (a storm god?), the Cretan (V)elchanios which belongs to a typically Cretan (Zeus) Velchanos (an originally independent storm god? VERBRUGGEN 1981: 144). The relevant chapter in NILSSON (1908: 3-35) devotes much space to weather festivals, Lykaia and Buphonia. Of some interest were the Koan sacrifice of a bull of Zeus Polieus and the festival of Zeus Sosipolis in Magnesia on the Maeander, both attested by a Hellenistic law (Kos: SOKOLOWSKI 1969 no. 156; Magnesia: SOKOLOWSKI 1955 no. 32); they show the pomp with which Hellenistic poleis could celebrate the god whose cult expressed their identity and hope; both festivals emphasize the choice and importance of the victim.

Athenian festivals of Zeus (DEUBNER 1932:155-178) are less self-asserting. To the Koan and Magnesian festival, one might compare the Diisoteria with a sacrifice and a procession for Zeus Soter and Athena Soteira; again, it is a festival in the honour of Zeus Saviour of the Town. But as to calendar and to place, in Athens it was marginal: it was celebrated outside the town in Piraeus, although with the participation of the town. Closer to the centre were the Dipolieia and Diasia. The Dipolieia contained the strange and guilt-ridden sacrifice of an ox on the altar of Zeus Polieus on the acropolis (Buphonia: BURKERT 1972:153-161); they belong to the rituals around New Year. Aristophanes thought it rather old-fashioned (*Nub.*984): the ritual killing of the ox, the myth which makes all participants guilty, the ensuing prosecution of the killer with the formal condemnation of axe and knife enacts a crisis, not a bright festival.

The Diasia, "the greatest Athenian festival of Zeus" (Thucydides 1,126,6), had an even less auspicious character. The festival took place in honour of Zeus Meilichios who had the form of a huge snake. The cult place was outside the town, with animal sacrifice or bloodless cakes; the sacrificial animals were entirely burnt. This meant no common meal to release the tension of the sacrifice; instead, we hear of common meals in small family circles and of gifts to the children; the community passes through a phase of disintegration. The character fits the date, Anthesterion 23 (February/March); the main event of the month had been the Anthesteria which had a similar, but even more marked character of uncanny disintegration.

This apparent paucity of polis festivals is not out of tune with the general image of Zeus. Though he often is called Polieus, he has no major temple on an acropolis, unlike the Roman Iupiter Capitolinus, though he might be paired with Athena Polias. The polis has to be under the protection of her specific patron deity, Athena or Apollo. Zeus, the overall protector, cannot confine himself to one polis only – his protection adds itself to that of the respective deities.

On the other hand, he is prominent as a panhellenic deity from early times. Besides Dodona, whose founding hero Deukalion, father of Helen, discloses its panhellenic aspirations (BOUCHÉ-LECLERCQ 1879-82:2, 280), his main Greek festivals are the penteteric Olympia with the splendid sacrifice to Zeus Olympios and the ensuing panhellenic agon. Their introduction in 776 BCE, according to tradition, marked the end of the isolation of the Dark Age communities; the common festival took place at a spot outside a single polis and under the protection of a superior god. The analysis of the sacrifices points to an origin in initiation rituals of young warriors, related to the Lykaia (BURKERT 1972:108-119) which, however, had opened up itself at a time not too distant from the Homeric poems with their own universalist conception of Zeus.

Inside the polis, Zeus has his own specific province and cares for the smaller units whose lawful unification forms the polis. His own domain is the agora: as Zeus Agoraios, he presides over the just political dealings of the community (see the law from Erythrai, GRAF 1985:197-199); in this function, he can be counted among the main divinities of a city, Hestia Prytaneia and Athena Poliouchos or Polias (Crete: SCHWABL 1972:257-258). On the level of smaller units, he is one of the patrons of phratries (Zeus Phratrios or Zeus Patr(o)ios, sometimes together with Athena Phratria or Patr(o)ia, see Plato, *Euthyd.* 302 d) or clans (Zeus Patr(o)ios). In this function, he also protects the single households; as Zeus Herkeios ("He in the Yard"), he receives sacrifices on an altar in the courtyard (Homer *Il.*11,772-774, *Od.*22,334-336; every Athenian family had to have one, Aristotle, *Pol. Ath.*55, NILSSON 1965:403), as Zeus Ephestios ("He on the Hearth"), on the hearth of a house.

There are functions of Zeus on the level of the family which easily are extended both to individuals and to the polis. Since property is indispensable for the constitution of a household, Zeus is also the protector of property, Zeus Ktesios; as such, he receives cults from families (Thasos: Zeus Ktesios Patroios), from cities (Athens: a sacrifice by the prytaneis in 174/173 BCE) and from individuals (Stratonikeia: to Zeus Ktesios and Tyche) (SCHWABL I 326-327). In many places, Zeus Ktesios has the form of a snake (Athens, Thespiai): property is bound to the ground, at least in the still agrarian conception of ancient Greece, and its protectors belong to the earth (see Ploutos, "Richess" whose mother is Demeter, Hesiod, *Th.* 969, and Ploutôn, "The Rich One", one of the many names of the god of the Nether World). The same holds true for Zeus Meilichios, "The Gentle One". On the level of the individual, Xenophon attests his efficiency in providing funds (*anab.* 7,8), while in many communities, Zeus Meilichios protects families or clans; in Athens finally, he receives the polis festival of the Diasia; here and elsewhere, he also has the form of a snake (SCHWABL 1972: 335-337). And finally, one might add Zeus Philios, protector of friendship between individuals as among an entire polis (GRAF 1985:204-205).

As the most powerful god, he has a very general function which cuts across all groups and gains in importance in the course of time: Zeus is the →*Soter*, the "Saviour" par excellence. As such, he receives prayers and dedications from individuals, groups of every sort, and from entire towns (rarely specified as Sosipolis, see above; the evidence is too vast for a satisfactory collection, SCHWABL 1972:362-364); the dedications reflect all possible situations of crisis, from very private ones (where Zeus rivals with Asklepios Soter, see e.g. Zeus Soter Asklepios in Pergamon, *Altertümer von Pergamon* VIII:3 no. 63) to political troubles (Athens: *SEG* 26 no.106,7), natural catastrophes (earthquake *BCH* 102 [1978] 399) or military attacks (Delphi, Soteria after the attack by the Gauls, SCHWABL 1972:363,19).

The Zeus cults of Crete fit only partially into this picture (VERBRUGGEN 1981). Myth places both his birth and his grave in Crete: according to Hesiod, in order to save him from Kronos, Rhea gave birth to Zeus and entrusted the baby to Gaia who hid it in a cave near Lyktos, on Mt. Aigaion (*Theog.* 468-500). Later authors replace Gaia by the Kouretes, armed demons, whose noisy dance kept Kronos away, and name other mountains, usually Mt. Ida or Mt. Dikte. This complex of myths reflects cult in caves which partly go back to Minoan times (FAURE 1964) and armed dances by young Cretan warriors like those attested in the famous hymn to Zeus from Palaikastro (sanctuary of Zeus Diktaios) which belong to the context of initiatory rituals of young warriors (JEANMAIRE 1939:421-460); in the actual oaths of Cretan ephebes, Zeus plays an important role. In this function, Zeus can exceptionally be young—the Palaikastro hymn calls him κοῦρος, "youngster"; the statue in the sanctuary of Zeus Diktaios was beardless, and coins from Knossos show a beardless (Zeus) Velchanos. There certainly are Minoan (and presumably Mycenaean) elements present in the complex, but it would be wrong, as VERBRUGGEN (1981) rightly points out, to separate Cretan Zeus too radically from the rest of the Greek evidence; both the cults of Mt. Lykaios and of Olympia contain initiatory features.

Already in Homer (much more than in actual cult), Zeus had reached a nearly overpowering position. During the classical and hellenistic age, religious thinkers developed this into a sort of "Zeus monotheism". Already to Aeschylus, Zeus had begun to move away from simple human knowledge ("Zeus, whoever you are...", *Ag.* 160-161) to a nearly universal function ("Zeus is ether, Zeus is earth, Zeus is sky, Zeus is everything and more than that", frg. 105); and Sophocles sees his hand in all human affairs ("Nothing of this which would not be Zeus", *Trach.* 1278). Its main document is the hymn to Zeus by the Stoic philosopher Cleanthes (died 232/231 BCE) (text: *SVF* I 121 no. 537; translation LONG & SEDLEY 1987:1,326-327); Zeus, mythical image of the Stoic logos, becomes the commander over the entire cosmos ("no deed is done on earth ... without your office, nor in the divine ethereal vault of heaven, nor at sea") and its "universal law", and at the same time the guarantor of goodness and benign protector of man ("protect mankind from its pitiful incompetence"). This marks the high point of a development—other gods, though briefly mentioned, become insignificant besides universal Zeus

Neoplatonist speculation rather marks a regress: in the elaborate chains of divine beings, Zeus is never set at the very top—the neoplatonists allegorize the succession from Uranos over Kronos to Zeus and consequently assign him to a lower level.

III. 2 Macc 6 relates how, in 168 BCE, Antiochos IV Epiphanes sent an envoy to Jerusalem in order to press the Hellenization of Israel; foremost on his agenda was to rededicate the temple of Jerusalem to Zeus Olympios and the one on Mt. Garizim to Zeus Xenios. 2 Macc 6:4-5 describes the ensuing profanation of Temple and Altar, while 1 Macc 1:54 dates the building of *bdelygma erēmōseōs*, the altar (presumably) of Zeus, on the main Altar of the Temple; Judas Maccabee removed it in 165. From a political point of view, the identification of →Yahweh and Zeus, the main god of the Greek pantheon, imposes itself; when Hadrian rebuilt Jerusalem, he dedicated its main temple to Iupiter Capitolinus, the main god of the Roman pantheon. Besides, hellenized diaspora Jews identified their God with Zeus: they used Hypsistos (→Most High) as Greek name of their God, while it had been a poetic epithet of Zeus from the 5th cent. BCE onward and his cultic epiclesis first in Macedonia, then in the hellenized East (COLPE 1975); the syncretist magical papyri associate Iao (i.e. Yahweh) with Zeus, *PGM* I 300. V 471 (*Zeus Adōnai Iao*, cf. IV 2771). Finally, the cult of Zeus Olympios was widespread in Syria, Palestine and Phoenicia (SCHWABL 1972:343-344) as *interpretatio Graeca* of Ba'al Shamem (TEIXIDOR 1977:27; for Tyre Josephus, *Ant.* 8,145-147): seen from outside, this might legitimate the identification of Zeus and the Jewish supreme god (see the positive evaluation of Antiochos' programme in Tacitus, *Hist.* 5,8,2); seen from inside, it makes the Biblical protests all the more understandable. On Mt. Garizim near Shechem, the capital of Samaria, the Samaritans had built a temple to a nameless god (*megistos theos*) after their independence from Jerusalem in the 4th cent. BCE (Josephus *Ant.* 11, 322. 13,74-78); again, the hellenization of this Ba'al-like mountain god as Zeus is what one would expect. According to a anti-Samaritan tradition in Josephus *Ant.* 12, 262-263, the Samaritans had themselves hellenized the god as Zeus Hellenios in order to oblige Antiochos IV; this same anti-Samaritan point of view is manifest in the epiclesis transmitted in 2 Macc 6:2, Xenios, "He of the Foreigners", instead of Hellenios of Josephus.

The Lystra episode of Acts 14:12-13 fits into the context of the local religions of Asia Minor. After Paul and Barnabas had manifested superhuman powers by healing a lame man, the native Lystrans (speaking Lycaonian, their indigenous language) explained this with a well-known myth, the visit of gods in human disguise. The myth is widely attested (FLÜCKIGER-GUGGENHEIM 1984), but finds a very close parallel in the story of Philemon and Baucis who were visited by Zeus and Hermes in the shape of men (Ovid, *Metam.* 8, 618-724). This reflects local religious beliefs: in Ovid, who follows a local historian, Philemon and Baucis are Phrygians, and the common cult of Zeus and Hermes is well attested in the region (MALTEN 1940).

V. *Bibliography*

K. ARAFAT, *Classical Zeus. A Study in Art and Literature* (Oxford 1990); U. BIANCHI, *Dios Aisa. Destino, nomini e divinità nell'epos, nelle teogonie e nel culto dei Greci* (Rome 1953); A. BOUCHÉ-LECLERCQ, *Histoire de la divination dans l'antiquité*, 4 vols. (Paris 1879-1882); W. BURKERT, *Homo Necans. Interpretationen altgriechischer Opferriten und Mythen* (Berlin/New York 1972); C. COLPE, Hypsistos, *KP* 2 (1975) 1291-1292; A. B. COOK, *Zeus. A Study in Ancient Religion,* 3 vols. (Cambridge 1914, 1926, 1940); L. DEUBNER, *Attische Feste* (Berlin 1932); P. FAURE, *Fonctions des cavernes crétoises* (Paris 1964); D. FLÜCKIGER-GUGGENHEIM, *Göttliche Gäste. Die Einkehr von Göttern und Heroen in der griechischen Mythologie* (Bern/Frankfurt 1984); M. GÉRARD-ROUSSEAU, *Les mentions religieuses dans les tablettes mycéniennes* (Rome 1968); F. GRAF, *Nordionische Kulte. Religionsgeschichtliche und epigraphische Untersuchungen zu den Kulten von Chios, Erythrai, Klazomenai und Phokaia* (Rome 1985); E. HALLAGER et al., New Linear B Tablets from Khania, *Kadmos* 31 (1992) 61-87; H. A. HOFFNER Jr., *Hittite Myths* (ed. G. M. Beckman; Atlanta 1990); H. JEANMAIRE, *Couroi et Courètes. Essai sur l'éducation spartiate et sur les rites d'adolescence dans l'antiquité hellénique* (Lille 1939); K. KERÉNYI, *Zeus und Hera. Urbild des Vaters, des Gatten und der Frau* (Leiden 1972); M. K. LANGDON, *A Sanctuary of Zeus on Mount Hymettos* (Hesperia Suppl. 16; Princeton 1976); H. LLOYD-JONES, *The Justice of Zeus* (Berkeley/Los Angeles 1971, 1983); A. A. LONG & D. N. SEDLEY (eds.), *The Hellenistic Philosophers*, 2 vols. (Cambridge 1987); L. MALTEN, Motivgeschichtliche Untersuchungen zur Sagenforschung. I: Philemon und Baucis, *Hermes* 74 (1939) 176-206; 75 (1940) 168-176; M. P. NILSSON, *Griechische Feste von religiöser Bedeutung mit Ausschluss der attischen* (Leipzig 1907); NILSSON, *Geschichte der griechischen Religion* I: *Die Religion Griechenlands bis auf die griechische Weltherrschaft* (HAW V:2:1; München 1965^3); H. W. PARKE, *The Oracles of Zeus* (Oxford 1967); H. SCHWABL, Zeus. Teil I (Epiklesen), PW 10 A (1972) 253-376; SCHWABL, ZEUS, Teil II, PW Suppl. 15 (1978) 993-1411; E. SIMON, Zeus, Teil III, Archäologische Zeugnisse. Nachträge, PW Suppl. Bd. 15 (1978) 1411-1481; SIMON,

Die Götter der Griechen, (München 1985[3]); F. SOKOLOWSKI, *Lois sacrées de l'Asie mineure* (Paris 1955); SOKOLOWSKI, *Lois sacrées des cités grecques* (Paris 1969); J. TEIXIDOR, *The Pagan God. Popular Religion in the Greco-Roman Near East* (Princeton 1977); H. VERBRUGGEN, *Le Zeus crétois* (Paris 1981).

F. GRAF

ZION צִיּוֹן

I. Zion, a name for Jerusalem of uncertain etymology, referred originally to the fortified acropolis of the pre-Israelite city. The 'stronghold of Zion' (*mĕṣūdat ṣiyyôn,* 2 Sam 5:7 = 1 Chron 11:5; 1 Kgs 8:1 = 2 Chron 5:2) was located on top of the southeastern hill, overlooking the Valley of Kidron. David conquered it and renamed it for himself (2 Sam 5:9), and the meanings of both names—'Zion' and 'City of David'—were expanded as the city grew.

Zion does not occur as a divine name in the Bible, but it does designate a sacred place, and the personification of Jerusalem as *ṣiyyôn,* 'Zion', or *bat ṣiyyôn,* 'Daughter Zion', draws on language traditionally associated with the goddesses and female patron spirits of the cities of Syria-Palestine and Mesopotamia.

II. It was characteristic of the religious literature of Syria-Palestine to depict a city that served as the principal place of worship of a major deity as a sacral center with cosmic attributes, using language replete with national ideology and mythological embellishment. In Ugarit, for example, the seat of the worship of the →Baal-zaphon, is represented in the tablets from Ras Shamra as an impregnable fortress protected from invasion by Baal's presence in its midst.

Another common feature of Northwest Semitic religious thought was the feminine personification of a major city, which might be described as a mother (*metropolis*) of the people of the land: as is shown by the Phoenician example of *ṣr ʾm ṣdnym,* 'Tyre, mother of the Sidonians' (N. SLOUZSCH, *Thesaurus of Hebrew Inscriptions* [Hebrew; Tel Aviv 1942] 34). A city thus personified might be worshipped as a goddess who was thought of as the consort of the national or city god. The Hellenistic concept of the *tychē poleōs* ('luck of the city'; →Tyche), a goddess who was the benevolent patron spirit of a city, seems to have been derived in part from Semitic ideas.

In Mesopotamian religious literature, the chief goddess of a city is typically represented as intimately associated with its affairs and deeply concerned with the welfare of its people. This perspective is expressed most characteristically in the motif of the weeping goddess who grieves over the ruin of her city: as e.g. in the great Sumerian poem, 'Lamentation over the Destruction of Ur', which addresses the goddess Ningal as queen and mother of Ur and describes the fall of the city to the Elamites in terms of her grief and bereavement.

III. In the Bible, Zion refers to the City of David or Ophel; and, by extension, to the city as a whole. So 'Zion' and 'Jerusalem' become synonymous: frequently occurring as parallel terms in poetry. The name 'Zion' is commonly found in passages that refer to Jerusalem as a sacred city: especially as the city of →Yahweh and the place of his dwelling or cultic manifestation. Zion language, therefore, was an important part of the ideology of the Jerusalem Temple. In mythic terms, Zion could be described as a majestic mountain of unique stature and a perpetual source of life and prosperity. Because the Zion ideology included an eschatological component, this conceptualization held true even when the Temple lay in ruins and the city was abandoned. Thus, a preexilic oracle looked forward to the time when "the mountain of the house of Yahweh will be established at the head of the mountains" (Isa 2:2 = Mic 4:1); and a postexilic prophecy proclaimed that "all the land will turn into something like a plain...but Jerusalem will remain high on its site..." (Zech 14:10; cf. Ezek 40:2; Rev 21:10). From Mount Zion would flow the cosmic river of life (Ezek 47:1-12; Zech 14:8; cf. Joel 4:18), the source of purification, healing and nourishment for the people of Yahweh (Zech 13:1; cf. Rev 22:1-2).

Jerusalem is sometimes described as a mother to its people (cf. 4 Ezra 10:7; Gal 4:26), a concept associated with the name Zion in the Bible, where it first receives emphasis in Jeremiah 31 and Deutero-Isaiah (SCHMITT 1985:566). Thus, in Isa 49:14-18 Zion is portrayed as a mother whose children, having been taken from her (in the Babylonian exile), will be brought home; whilst in Isa 66:5-13 the vindication of Zion/Jerusalem is prophesied under the image of a woman who has laboured and given birth to children who will now be given to her to nurse and comfort.

Jerusalem is personified 26 times as *bat ṣiyyôn,* 'Daughter Zion,' or *bĕtûlat bat ṣiyyôn,* 'Virgin Daughter Zion' (2 Kgs 19:21 = Isa 37:22; Lam 2:13; →Virgin). They are titles which represent the city as divinely beloved and protected under the image of the inviolable bride of Yahweh, a concept drawn upon in prophetic literature when the city is threatened (Isa 1:8; 10:32; Jer 4:31; 6:2,23). The notion of the city's marriage to Yahweh is also used in a condemnatory way: e.g. when Daughter Zion is denounced as an adulteress because of Jerusalem's traffic with foreign powers and their gods. Under this image the destruction of the city is presented as condign punishment: and the grief of Daughter Zion is expressed in a way reminiscent of the weeping goddesses of Mesopotamian city lament. This is best exemplified by the Book of Lamentations where Daughter Zion is portrayed as a great lady whose majesty has departed (Lam 1:6): betrayed by her lovers and forsaken by her husband, she weeps in captivity over the loss of her children (Lam 4:2). The Bible also contains the promise of a time of salvation for 'Captive Daughter Zion' (Isa 52:2). When her fortunes are restored, she will rejoice (Zeph 3:14; Zech 9:9) and avenge those who abused her (Mic 4:6-13).

Though the personifications of Jerusalem as a mother to its people and as the aggrieved Daughter Zion are reminiscent of similar motifs in the writings of surrounding nations, there is no indication that they were regarded in Israel as anything other than literary devices or, in particular, that Zion was thought of as a goddess who might be honoured by her own cult.

IV. *Bibliography*

F. W. DOBBS-ALLSOPP, *Weep, O Daughter of Zion: A Study of the City-Lament Genre in the Hebrew Bible* (BeO 44; Rome 1993) esp. 75-90; A. FITZGERALD, The Mythological Background for the Presentation of Jerusalem as a Queen and False Worship as Adultery in the OT, *CBQ* 34 (1972) 403-416; A. FITZGERALD, *btwlt* and *bt* as Titles for Capital Cities, *CBQ* 37 (1975) 167-183; E. OTTO, *Ṣiyyôn, TWAT* 6 (1989) 994-1028 [& lit]; J. J. M. ROBERTS, The Davidic Origin of the Zion Tradition, *JBL* 92 (1973) 329-344 [& lit]; J. J. SCHMITT, The Motherhood of God and Zion as Mother, *RB* 92 (1985) 557-569.

P. K. MCCARTER

ZUR → ROCK

INDEX